S0-BTY-817

PRENTICE HALL

The Way
Into, Through & Beyond
the Finest Literature.

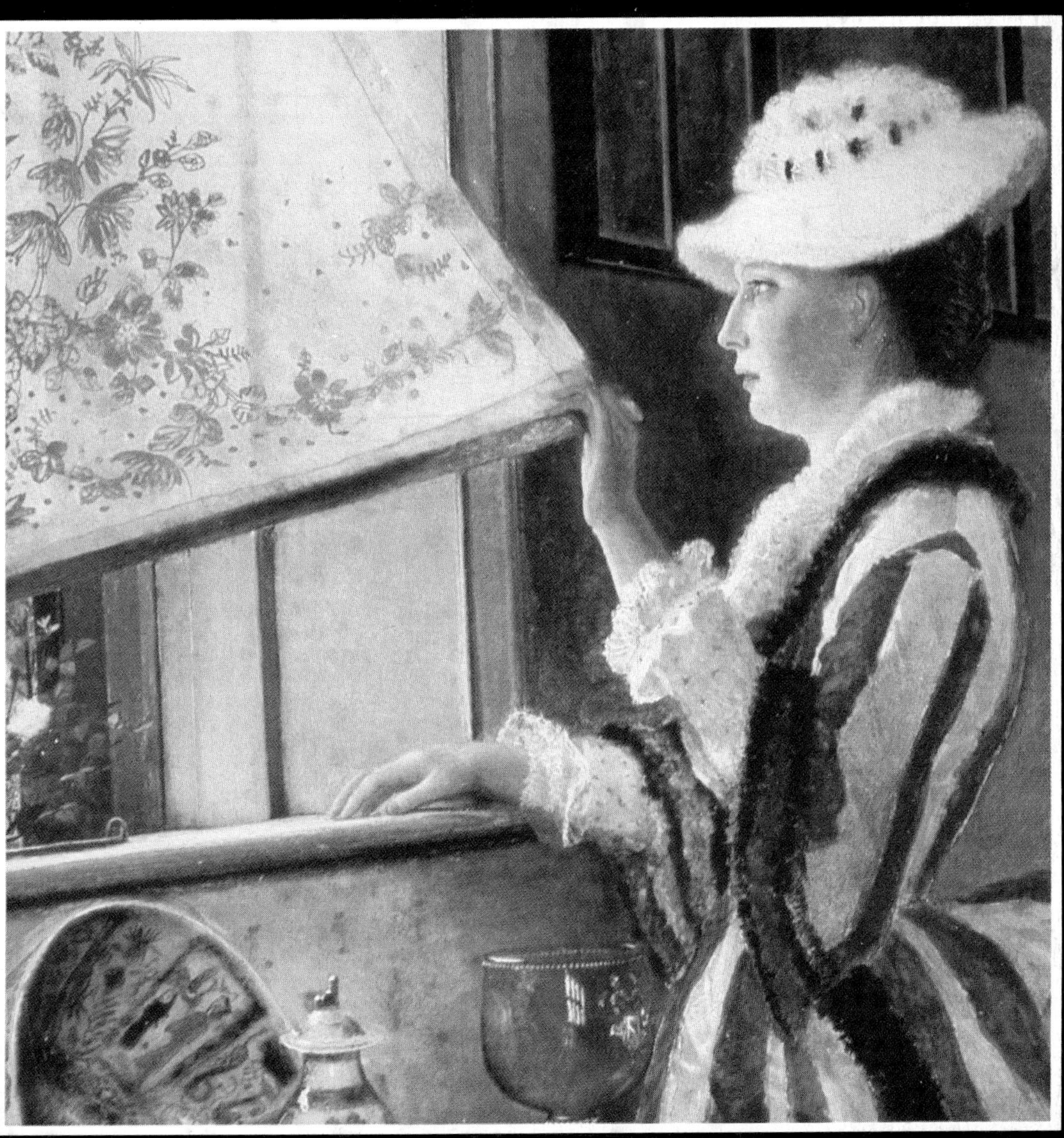

PRENTICE HALL
LITERATURE

Into,

. . . for grade 11 & 12 students

Before reading any selection in The American Experience or The English Tradition, your students:

Take an in-depth look at the author

WILLA CATHER

1873–1947

Willa Cather was born in a small town in western Virginia. When she was ten, her family moved to a farm near the frontier town of Red Cloud, Nebraska. Here, many of Cather's new neighbors were immigrants—Swedes, Germans, Slavs, and Russians—struggling to build a life for themselves in their new land and determined to preserve the culture of the land they left behind. Through her interaction with this diverse group of people, Cather developed an awareness of certain qualities shared not only by people of the frontier but by people from all over the world. She also gained a rich cultural background, studying foreign languages, history, and classical music and opera. She wrote of her childhood: "On Sundays we could drive to a Norwegian church and listen to a sermon in that language, or to a Danish or Swedish church. We could go to a French Catholic settlement or into the Bohemian township and hear one in Czech, or we could go to the church with the German Lutherans."

After graduating from the University of Nebraska, in 1895, Cather worked as an editor for a Pittsburgh newspaper, while writing poems and short stories in her spare time. Her first collection of stories, *The Troll Garden,* was published in 1905. The following year she moved to New York, where she worked as the managing editor for *McClure's Magazine.* In 1912, the year after she published her first novel, *Alexander's Bridge,* she left the magazine to devote all her energy to writing. During the next several years, she produced three novels: *O Pioneers!* (1913); *The Song of the Lark* (1915); and *My Antonia* (1918), which captured the flavor of life in the Midwestern prairies. In 1923 she won the Pulitzer Prize for her novel *One of Ours* (1922).

Cather shifted her attention from the Midwest to the Southwest in *Death Comes for the Archbishop* (1927) and to seventeenth-century Quebec in *Shadows on the Rock* (1931). She also published two collections of short stories: *Youth and the Bright Medusa* (1920) and *Obscure Destinies* (1932); and a collection of critical essays and recollections of earlier writers: *Not Under Forty.*

In her work Cather displayed her admiration for the courage and spirit of the immigrants and other settlers of the frontier while at the same time conveying an intense awareness of the loss felt by some of the pioneers as well as the loneliness and isolation from which they suffered. In "A Wagner Matinée" Cather captures this sense of loneliness and isolation by contrasting the stark realities of frontier life with the possibilities of life in a more cultured world.

550 *Short Stories*

No other literature textbook provides a head start on each selection!

GUIDE FOR READING

A Wagner Matinée

The Writer's Techniques

Characterization is the means by which a writer reveals a character's personality. Writers generally develop a character through one of the following methods: direct statements about the character, physical descriptions of the character, the character's thoughts and comments, or other characters' reactions to or comments about the character.

In the late 1800's and early 1900's, writers began turning to the first-person and third-person limited points of view. When a writer limits the point of view to one character, as Cather does in "A Wagner Matinée," you learn about all the characters primarily through the thoughts of the narrator.

Look For

Willa Cather asked for the following words from her novel *My Antonia* to be carved on her tombstone: ". . . that is happiness, to be dissolved into something complete and great." As you read "A Wagner Matinée," look for what the young man learns about his Aunt Georgiana. How does she give flesh and blood to Cather's epitaph?

Writing

Ralph Waldo Emerson has written, " [Music] takes us out of the actual and whispers to us dim secrets that startle us to wonder as to who we are, and for what, whence, and whereth." Discuss the meaning of this quotation. Think about the powerful effect music often has on people's memories and emotions. Recall a piece of music—one that has no lyrics—that can produce a strong effect on your memories and emotions. Then freewrite about it.

Vocabulary

Knowing the following words will help you as you read "A Wagner Matinée."

callow (kal′ ō) *adj.:* Immature; inexperienced (p. 552)
reverential (rev′ə ren′ shəl) *adj.:* Showing or caused by a feeling of deep respect, love, and awe (p. 554)
tremulously (trem′ yo͞o ləs lē) *adv.:* Fearfully; timidly (p. 554)
semi-somnambulant (sem′i säm nam′ byo͞o lənt) *adj.:* Half sleepwalking (p. 554)
trepidation (trep′ə dā′ shən) *n.:* Fearful anxiety; apprehension (p. 555)
inert (in urt′) *adj.:* Motionless (p. 555)
jocularity (jäk′ yə lar′ə tē) *n.:* Joking good humor (p. 558)

A Wagner Matinée 551

from The American Experience, grade 11

Prereading: What readers bring to the selection determines what they will take from the work.

Learn the literary technique

Focus their reading and thinking

Write as a motivation to read

Preview difficult vocabulary

The Guide for Reading enriches literature for your students.

Into,

. . . for the grade 11 & 12 teacher

The Annotated Teacher's Edition surrounds each student page with strategies for master teaching.

Background about the author adds to class discussion.

Critical quote brings a new dimension to the discussion.

Look at the teaching materials available for one selection—all are noted here.

More About the Author In 1944 Willa Cather received the Gold Medal of the National Institute of the American Academy of Arts and Letters in recognition of the entire body of her work. For a particular field, the medal is awarded only once a decade. In the 1910's it belonged to William Dean Howells, in the 1920's to Edith Wharton, and in the 1930's to Booth Tarkington.

Although Willa Cather is associated most strongly with Nebraska, she actually lived in New York City for the last forty years of her life. Ask students to discuss how a place can have such a hold on people that they turn to it often as a source of inspiration and material.

Quotation Willa Cather wrote, "Artistic growth is, more than it is anything else, a refining of the sense of truthfulness. The stupid believe that to be truthful is easy; only the artist, the great artist, knows how difficult it is." Ask students to discuss the meaning of the quotation. Why is it difficult to portray life truthfully? How do Cather's words highlight characteristics of the realistic movement?

WILLA CATHER

1873–1947

Willa Cather was born in a small town in western Virginia. When she was ten, her family moved to a farm near the frontier town of Red Cloud, Nebraska. Here, many of Cather's new neighbors were immigrants—Swedes, Germans, Slavs, and Russians—struggling to build a life for themselves in their new land and determined to preserve the culture of the land they left behind. Through her interaction with this diverse group of people, Cather developed an awareness of certain qualities shared not only by people of the frontier but by people from all over the world. She also gained a rich cultural background, studying foreign languages, history, and classical music and opera. She wrote of her childhood: "On Sundays we could drive to a Norwegian church and listen to a sermon in that language, or to a Danish or Swedish church. We could go to a French Catholic settlement or into the Bohemian township and hear one in Czech, or we could go to the church with the German Lutherans."

After graduating from the University of Nebraska, in 1895, Cather worked as an editor for a Pittsburgh newspaper, while writing poems and short stories in her spare time. Her first collection of stories, *The Troll Garden*, was published in 1905. The following year she moved to New York, where she worked as the managing editor for *McClure's Magazine*. In 1912, the year after she published her first novel, *Alexander's Bridge*, she left the magazine to devote all her energy to writing. During the next several years, she produced three novels: *O Pioneers!* (1913); *The Song of the Lark* (1915); and *My Antonia* (1918), which captured the flavor of life in the Midwestern prairies. In 1923 she won the Pulitzer Prize for her novel *One of Ours* (1922).

Cather shifted her attention from the Midwest to the Southwest in *Death Comes for the Archbishop* (1927) and to seventeenth-century Quebec in *Shadows on the Rock* (1931). She also published two collections of short stories: *Youth and the Bright Medusa* (1920) and *Obscure Destinies* (1932); and a collection of critical essays and recollections of earlier writers: *Not Under Forty*.

In her work Cather displayed her admiration for the courage and spirit of the immigrants and other settlers of the frontier while at the same time conveying an intense awareness of the loss felt by some of the pioneers as well as the loneliness and isolation from which they suffered. In "A Wagner Matinée" Cather captures this sense of loneliness and isolation by contrasting the stark realities of frontier life with the possibilities of life in a more cultured world.

550 Short Stories

Objectives

1. To understand methods of characterization
2. To make inferences about the effects of setting
3. To understand musical terms
4. To support an opinion

Teaching Portfolio: Support Material

Lesson Plan, pp. 55–58

Vocabulary Check, p. 59

Usage and Mechanics Worksheet, p. 60

Analyzing Literature: Understanding Characterization, p. 61

Critical Thinking and Reading: Making Inferences About the Effects of Setting, p. 62

Selection Test, p. 63

Art Transparency 2

550

Unprecedented teaching support—right on the page.

GUIDE FOR READING

A Wagner Matinée

The Writer's Techniques

Characterization is the means by which a writer reveals a character's personality. Writers generally develop a character through one of the following methods: direct statements about the character, physical descriptions of the character, the character's thoughts and comments, or other characters' reactions to or comments about the character.

In the late 1800's and early 1900's, writers began turning to the first-person and third-person limited points of view. When a writer limits the point of view to one character, as Cather does in "A Wagner Matinée," you learn about all the characters primarily through the thoughts of the narrator.

Look For

Willa Cather asked for the following words from her novel *My Antonia* to be carved on her tombstone: ". . . that is happiness, to be dissolved into something complete and great." As you read "A Wagner Matinée," look for what the young man learns about his Aunt Georgiana. How does she give flesh and blood to Cather's epitaph?

Writing

Ralph Waldo Emerson has written, " [Music] takes us out of the actual and whispers to us dim secrets that startle us to wonder as to who we are, and for what, whence, and whereth." Discuss the meaning of this quotation. Think about the powerful effect music often has on people's memories and emotions. Recall a piece of music—one that has no lyrics—that can produce a strong effect on your memories and emotions. Then freewrite about it.

Vocabulary

Knowing the following words will help you as you read "A Wagner Matinée."

callow (kal' ō) *adj.*: Immature; inexperienced (p. 552)
reverential (rev'ə ren' shəl) *adj.*: Showing or caused by a feeling of deep respect, love, and awe (p. 554)
tremulously (trem' yo͞o ləs lē) *adv.*: Fearfully; timidly (p. 554)
semi-somnambulant (sem'i säm nam' byo͞o lənt) *adj.*: Half sleepwalking (p. 554)
trepidation (trep'ə dā' shən) *n.*: Fearful anxiety; apprehension (p. 555)
inert (in urt') *adj.*: Motionless (p. 555)
jocularity (jäk' yə lar'ə tē) *n.*: Joking good humor (p. 558)

A Wagner Matinée 551

Student pages in the Annotated Teacher's Edition are slightly reduced in size.
The actual student page is 7½ inches by 9¼ inches.

Characterization Ask students to discuss whether one person can ever tell the whole truth about another person. Have them keep their responses in mind as they read the narrator's description of his Aunt Georgiana.

Look For Have students discuss the meaning of Cather's epitaph. Do they agree or disagree with it? Have them provide examples of people who have been "dissolved into something complete and great": for example, a doctor who dedicates her life to treating the poor and needy, or an artist who searches for beauty in his work.

Writing Explain to students that many writers have felt an affinity for music. Ask them to discuss why this might be so. What qualities do music and literature share? You might want to have your **more advanced** students discuss the following comparison by Lawrence Durrell: "As poetry is the harmony of words, so music is that of notes."

Vocabulary Have students provide sentences using each vocabulary word.

551

Probing questions clarify the author's technique.

Clear examples reinforce your points.

Writing prompts stimulate writing *before* reading.

A complete classroom lesson start is right in your hand.

The literature program developed by award-winning teachers.

Student pages in the Annotated Teacher's Edition are slightly reduced in size. The actual student page is 7½ by 9¼ inches.

But support doesn't st[...] the first page

Through,

. . . for the grade 11&12 teacher

Notes that capture the art of teaching:

Your comments elaborate and add interest

An award-winning teacher shares a good idea with you

Your questions ask students to think critically

You elevate vital ideas and extend meaning

You focus students' attention on the elements of literature

Motivation Have students discuss what makes life rich and fulfilling. In what way is the quality of life shaped by a person's environment? Can two people live in the same place and one be enriched by it and the other feel deprived? Why? Then ask students to think about the people who left the East in the second part of the 1800's to settle on the frontier. What would they have given up? What would they have gained?

Master Teacher Note Place Art Transparency 2, "Woman with Plant" by Grant Wood, on the overhead projector. It is a portrait of Grant Wood's mother, an Iowa pioneer. Have students discuss the strength and determination they see in the woman's face. What other qualities do they see there? Why do they think the artist shows her holding a plant? In what way does she represent frontier women?

Thematic Idea "A Wagner Matinée" presents a woman who has been wounded by life. Have students compare Aunt Georgiana with Granny in "The Jilting of Granny Weatherall," p. 748.

Purpose-setting Question Willa Cather wrote: "I like trees because they seem more resigned to the way they have to live than other things do." Is Aunt Georgiana truly resigned?

1 **Enrichment** Cather first published this story in *Everybody's Magazine*, in February 1904. She then included it with six others in her first short story collection, *The Troll Garden*. All the stories in the collection deal with art or artists. One of her long-held, deeply felt concerns was the conflict between the artist and the workaday world. She recognized that artists and the beauties that they cherish are sometimes vulnerable to the stronger demands of everyday life. In this story, this dichotomy is expressed between the love of music that could flourish in the more civilized, cultured East and the withering effects of the rude farming life of the pioneer West that allowed neither time nor energy for the pursuit of music.

2 **Literary Focus** In Aunt Georgiana the author has created a character who has literally layers of meaning. Peel back those layers. Create a chart that shows the type of person she is on the outside. As students read the story, have them fill in the chart, showing the layers of character until they have reached her inner being.

3 **Discussion** Why does Aunt Georgiana arouse these feelings in the narrator? What do these feelings reveal about him as well as about her?

552

A Wagner Matinée 1

Willa Cather

I received one morning a letter written in pale ink, on glassy, blue-lined notepaper, and bearing the postmark of a little Nebraska village. This communication, worn and rubbed, looking as though it had been carried for some days in a coat pocket that was none too clean, was from my Uncle Howard. It informed me that his wife had been left a small legacy by a bachelor relative who had recently died, and that it had become necessary for her to come to Boston to attend to the settling of the estate. He requested me to meet her at the station, and render her whatever services might prove necessary. On examining the date indicated as that of her arrival, I found it no later than tomorrow. He had characteristically delayed writing until, had I been away from home for a day, I must have missed the good woman altogether.

The name of my Aunt Georgiana called up not alone her own figure, at once pathetic and grotesque, but opened before my feet a gulf of recollections so wide and deep that, as the letter dropped from my hand, I felt suddenly a stranger to all the present conditions of my existence, wholly ill at ease and out of place amid the surroundings of my
2 study. I became, in short, the gangling farmer boy my aunt had known, scourged with chilblains and bashfulness, my hands cracked and raw from the corn husking. I felt the knuckles of my thumb tentatively, as though they were raw again. I sat again before her parlor organ, thumbing the scales with my stiff, red hands, while she beside me made canvas mittens for the huskers.

The next morning, after preparing my landlady somewhat, I set out for the station. When the train arrived I had some difficulty in finding my aunt. She was the last of the passengers to alight, and when I got her into the carriage she looked not unlike one of those charred, smoked bodies that firemen lift from the *débris* of a burned building. She had come all the way in a day coach; her linen duster[1] had become black with soot and her black bonnet gray with dust during the journey. When we arrived at my boardinghouse the landlady put her to bed at once, and I did not see her again until the next morning.

Whatever shock Mrs. Springer experienced at my aunt's appearance she considerately concealed. Myself, I saw my aunt's misshapen figure with that feeling of awe and respect with which we behold explorers 3
who have left their ears and fingers north of Franz Josef Land,[2] or their health somewhere along the upper Congo.[3] My Aunt Georgiana had been a music teacher at the Boston Conservatory, somewhere back in the latter sixties. One summer, which she had spent in the little village in the Green Mountains[4] where her ancestors had dwelt for generations, she had kindled the callow fancy of the most idle and shiftless of all the village lads, and had conceived for this Howard Carpenter one of those absurd and extravagant passions which a handsome

1. **duster,** *n.*: A short, loose smock worn to protect clothing from dust.
2. **Franz Josef Land:** A group of islands in the Arctic Ocean that are now part of the U.S.S.R.
3. **Congo:** River in central Africa.
4. **Green Mountains:** Mountains in Vermont.

552 *Short Stories*

Page-by-page notes provide:

- Motivation
- Discussion
- Ability Levels
- Literary Focus
- Enrichment
- Clarification
- Humanities
- Reading Strategy
- Setting the Purpose
- Thematic Idea
- Speaking and Listening
- Writing Across the Curriculum
- Challenge Questions
- Master Teaching Notes

Plus the *answers*—no flipping to another manual!

Over 2,000 teaching notes per Teacher's Edition.

FROM ARKANSAS, 1939
George Schrieber
Sheldon Swope Art Gallery

A Wagner Matinée 553

Humanities Note

George Schrieber (1904–1977) was born in Belgium and emigrated to the United States in the 1920's. Like so many American artists during the Depression, Schrieber turned his focus to the Great Midwestern farmland. In *From Arkansas*, he portrays the subject, an aproned woman, with stark realism. The hardships endured and the strength with which they were met are both reflected in the woman's countenance. A mood of loneliness and desolation is evoked by the distant shed and the bare tree branches. Although Schrieber was not a major figure in the Regionalist art movement, this painting demonstrated that he was caught up in recording the spirit of rural America during the Depression.

Ask students the following questions.

1. In what way does the woman in the painting seem like Aunt Georgiana?
2. What feelings can students infer from the way she holds her arms in front of her?

Fine arts background provides a literature-based humanities lesson.

553

19 **Teaching to Ability Levels** Point out Clark's condescending tone. Have your **more advanced** students find other examples of this tone. Ask them to discuss how it colors the picture they receive of Aunt Georgiana.

20 **Master Teacher Note** The *Ring* refers to *Der Ring des Nibelungen (The Ring of the Nibelung)*, which consists of four music dramas. It was first performed at Bayreuth, Germany, in 1876.

21 **Discussion** Have students discuss why she doesn't want to go. Do they think she will return home? Have them find evidence in the selection to support their answers.

16 kitchen. She had hovered about him until she had prevailed upon him to join the country church, though his sole fitness for this step, so far as I could gather, lay in his boyish face and his possession of this divine melody. Shortly afterward he had gone to town on the Fourth of July, lost his money at a faro[13] table, ridden a saddled Texas steer on a bet, and disappeared with a fractured collarbone.

17 "Well, we have come to better things than the old *Trovatore* at any rate, Aunt Georgie?" I queried, with well-meant jocularity.

18 Her lip quivered and she hastily put her handkerchief up to her mouth. From behind it she murmured, "And you've been hearing this ever since you left me, Clark?" Her question was the gentlest and saddest of reproaches.

19 "But do you get it, Aunt Georgiana, the astonishing structure of it all?" I persisted.

20 her, or past what happy islands, or under what skies. From the trembling of her face I could well believe that the *Siegfried* march, at least, carried her out where the myriad graves are, out into the gray, burying grounds of the sea; or into some world of death vaster yet, where, from the beginning of the world, hope has lain down with hope, and dream with dream and, renouncing, slept.

21 The concert was over; the people filed out of the hall chattering and laughing, glad to relax and find the living level again, but my kinswoman made no effort to rise. I spoke gently to her. She burst into tears and sobbed pleadingly, "I don't want to go, Clark, I don't want to go!"

I understood. For her, just outside the door of the concert hall, lay the black pond with the cattle-tracked bluffs, the tall, unpainted house, naked as a tower, with weather-curled boards; the crook-backed ash seedlings where the dishcloths hung to dry, the gaunt, moulting turkeys picking up refuse about the kitchen door.

12. Bayreuth (bī roit'): A city in Germany known for its annual Wagnerian music festivals.
13. faro (fer' ō): A gambling game in which players bet on the cards to be turned up from the top of the dealer's deck.

14. Siegfried (Sēg' frēd): A legendary hero in medieval German literature.

558 *Short Stories*

THINKING ABOUT THE SELECTION

Recalling

1. (a) Why is Clark's Aunt Georgiana coming to visit? (b) Explain his reaction to the news of her visit.
2. (a) Why does Clark take Aunt Georgiana to the Wagner matinée? (b) Why does he grow doubtful that she will enjoy it?
3. Describe three ways in which Aunt Georgiana indulged her love of music while living on the frontier.

Interpreting

4. (a) What impression is conveyed through the physical descriptions of Red Willow Creek? (b) Contrast the impression of life in Red Willow Creek with life in Boston.
5. (a) What does Aunt Georgiana mean when she comments, "Don't love it so well, Clark, or it may be taken from you"? (b) How does this reflect the theme, or main point, of the story?
6. (a) Why does the opera have such a powerful effect on Aunt Georgiana? (b) In what way does the effect of the music on Aunt Georgiana in turn awaken Clark?

Applying

7. In what way can environment shape character? In what way can people shape their environment?

ANALYZING LITERATURE

Characterization

Characterization is the means by which an author reveals a character's personality. Because of Cather's use of a first-person narrator, much of what we learn about Aunt Georgiana comes from Clark's thoughts and feelings regarding her.

1. What is revealed about Aunt Georgiana through descriptions of her physical appearance?
2. What does Aunt Georgiana's reaction to the opera reveal about her personality?
3. What is revealed about Clark's personality through his thoughts and feelings regarding his aunt?
4. How does the fact that much of what we learn about Aunt Georgiana is revealed through Clark's thoughts and feelings shape our impressions of her?

UNDERSTANDING LANGUAGE

Understanding Musical Terms

Musical terms often appear in works of literature and in everyday language. For example, the word *opera*, which refers to a type of drama in which all or most of the text is set to music, appears in "A Wagner Matinée." Use a dictionary to find the meaning of each of the following musical terms.

1. aria
2. solo
3. libretto
4. requiem
5. crescendo
6. raga
7. octave
8. dissonant

THINKING AND WRITING

Supporting an Opinion

Review the freewriting assignment you completed earlier. Do you think music is a valuable component of daily life? Write a short essay for your teacher discussing whether or not music adds to the quality of life. In your prewriting list evidence from daily life. Then, after organizing your evidence into an outline, write your essay using your evidence to support your argument. Use transitions to link your ideas, and vary your sentence structure. When you revise, make sure that you have included enough evidence to adequately support your argument.

A Wagner Matinée 559

(Answers begin on p. 558.)

In addition, people have been known to make paradises out of deserts. Even in a harsh environment, Aunt Georgiana manages to draw from the pool of human resources to pursue her love of music.

Challenge Usually we think of life as rich and fulfilling. What has life taken from Aunt Georgiana?

Challenge Would it have been better for Aunt Georgiana if she had *not* visited Boston? Why or why not?

ANSWERS TO ANALYZING LITERATURE

1. We see that she has been physically broken by life.
2. It reveals that her personality is rich and full.
3. Clark seems to be self-centered and condescending.
4. Since Clark does not understand his aunt until the end, her personality is slowly revealed to us, until we too see her take on tragic dimensions.

ANSWERS TO UNDERSTANDING LANGUAGE

1. an air or melody in an opera, especially one for a solo voice
2. a musical piece meant to be played or sung alone
3. the words or text of an opera
4. a musical setting for a Mass for the dead
5. gradual increase in loudness or intensity
6. a large number of traditional melody patterns
7. the eighth full note above a given tone
8. a chord that sounds incomplete

THINKING AND WRITING

Publishing Student Writing Have students read one another's essays and select the essay they consider the best. Offer it to the school literary magazine for publication.

Answers

ANSWERS TO THINKING ABOUT THE SELECTION

Recalling

1. (a) She has received a small legacy from a bachelor relative and is coming to Boston to settle the estate. (b) The news pulls him back to his childhood, making him feel again the "gangling farmer boy" his aunt had known.
2. (a) Because she loved music and had been a music teacher in Boston before her marriage, Clark thinks the concert will be a treat for her. He wants to thank her for her many kindnesses to him when he was a boy. (b) She seems so asleep, with her sensibilities dead, that he doubts she will enjoy it.
3. She played her little piano organ, which her husband had given her after fifteen years. She told stories of glorious performances she had seen of operas in her youth. She sang songs she remembered, and she sought the company of a farmboy who had sung in a chorus in Bayreuth. In addition, she attended church services.

Interpreting

4. (a) The impression of bleakness and desolation is created. (b) In contrast, life in Boston seems rich, varied, and fulfilling.
5. (a) Aunt Georgiana loves music intensely. She is probably referring to the pain she feels because music has been taken from her. (b) The theme of the story refers to the dichotomy where one can be asleep in life and alive in art. The isolation of the frontier has dulled Aunt Georgiana's sensibilities; however, in a way, it has been a saving grace. By being asleep, she can live; it is when she wakes up through music that she can no longer endure her life.
6. (a) The themes of the operas reflect her own life and awaken the passion within her. (b) It is through the music that Clark comes to understand his aunt.

Applying

7. Suggested Response: Environment can affect people for better or worse. Isolation and hardship can take a great toll on human beings. On the other hand, an environment that offers little challenge can weaken character.

558

559

You entice readers to question, respond, and express themselves.

Through,

. . . for grade 11 & 12 students

What shapes a work of literature? An annotated selection begins each unit with notes that explain the synergies of:

Historical context—
the events and realities of the time

Literary movements—
the prevalent thought and works of period writers

Writers' techniques—
a look at the writers' craft

READING CRITICALLY

The Literature of 1840–1855

During the years from 1840–1855, the United States continued to expand rapidly. A steady flow of American pioneers traveled westward, settling in the new frontier. At the same time, a group of writers in New England brought about a literary renaissance that earned the country a place among the world's great literary traditions.

Historical Context

The rapid growth and expansion of the United States helped bring about scientific advances that established the United States as one of the most technologically advanced nations in the world. New agricultural machines were invented, new roads, canals, and railroads were built, and telegraph lines were put into place. These developments brought about an overwhelming sense of optimism about the country's future.

Literary Movements

The sense of optimism that dominated many people's thoughts during this period was reflected in the ideas of the Transcendentalists, the members of one of the main intellectual and artistic movements of the period. Possessing a deep faith in human potential, the Transcendentalists believed that all forms of being are spiritually united through a shared universal soul. In contrast, two major writers who have come to be known as Anti-Transcendentalists espoused a much darker vision of the world, believing that the truths of existence tend to be elusive and disturbing. A third group of writers known as the Fireside Poets also made important contributions during this period. By creating poetry that was inspiring and easy to read, these poets helped to establish poetry as a popular literary form among the American public.

Writers' Techniques

Focusing on popular themes such as love and nature, the Fireside Poets wrote poetry using traditional poetic forms and techniques. Although Ralph Waldo Emerson, the founder of the Transcendentalists, also wrote poetry, the Transcendentalists are remembered mainly for their essays expressing their ideas and beliefs. The Anti-Transcendentalists, on the other hand, expressed their beliefs through the themes of their novels and short stories, often using symbols to convey their themes.

On the following pages is a selection by Henry Wadsworth Longfellow. The notes in the side column should draw your attention to Longfellow's literary techniques and help you to place the selection in its historical context.

258 New England Renaissance

Students grasp the interconnections of history and literature

Extra!
Blackline selections in the Teaching Portfolio provide fresh works for students to annotate themselves.

For American and English literature–the excitement of insight!

MODEL

The Skeleton in Armor

Henry Wadsworth Longfellow

Literary Movements: As much of the poetry of the Fireside Poets, this poem deals with a subject of interest to the common people.

This poem was written after a skeleton clothed in armor was unearthed near Fall River, Massachusetts.

"Speak! speak! thou fearful guest!
Who, with thy hollow breast
Still in rude armor drest,
Comest to daunt me!
Wrapt not in Eastern balms,
But with thy fleshless palms
Stretched, as if asking alms,
Why dost thou haunt me?"

Historical Context: The discovery of a skeleton in armor made it apparent that the Vikings had explored America long before the arrival of Columbus.

Then, from those cavernous eyes
Pale flashes seemed to rise,
As when the Northern skies
Gleam in December;
And, like the water's flow
Under December's snow,
Came a dull voice of woe
From the heart's chamber.

Writer's Technique: Notice the traditional poetic form. This poem is written in octaves, or eight-line stanzas, with an *aaabcccb* rhyme scheme.

"I was a Viking old!
My deeds, though manifold,
No Skald[1] in song has told,
No Saga taught thee!
Take heed, that in thy verse,
Thou dost the tale rehearse,[2]
Else dread a dead man's curse;
For this I sought thee.

Literary Movement: The poem's subject reflects the Fireside Poets' interest in capturing the American heritage.

"Far in the Northern Land,
By the wild Baltic's strand,

1. **Skald** (skôld): An ancient Scandinavian poet.
2. **rehearse** (ri hurs') v.: Narrate

Lay the groundwork with national background

THE ROMANTIC AGE

1798–1832

One impulse from a vernal wood
May teach you more of man,
Of moral evil and of good,
Than all the sages can.

Sweet is the lore which Nature brings;
Our meddling intellect
Misshapes the beauteous forms of things—
We murder to dissect.

Enough of Science and of Art;
Close up those barren leaves;
Come forth, and bring with you a heart
That watches and receives.

from "The Tables Turned"
William Wordsworth

BRITISH EVENTS

1819 Peterloo Massacre in Manchester.

Percy Bysshe Shelley publishes "Ode to the West Wind".

1820 King George III dies.

John Keats publishes "Ode on a Grecian Urn".

1821 *Manchester Guardian* begins publication.

John Constable paints *The Grove*

1823 **Charles Lamb** publishes *Essays of Elia*.

1824 First labor unions permitted.

1825 Horse-drawn buses begin operating in London.

John Nash completes rebuilding of Buckingham Palace.

1827 System for purifying London water installed.

1829 Catholic Emancipation Act passed.

Robert Peel establishes Metropolitan Police in London.

1830 Liverpool-Manchester railway opens.

1831 Michael Faraday demonstrates electromagnetic induction.

1832 First Reform Act extends voting rights.

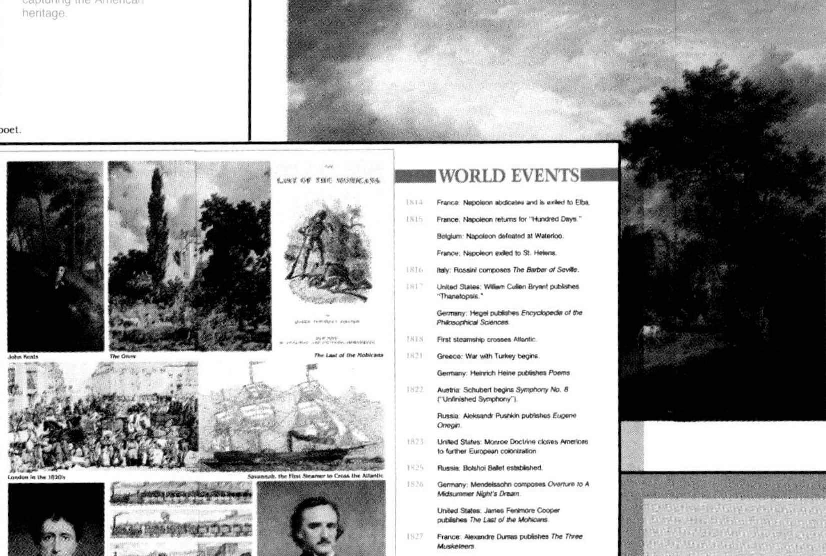

John Keats; The Grove; The Last of the Mohicans; London in the 1830's; Savannah, the First Steamer to Cross the Atlantic; Liverpool-Manchester Railway

WORLD EVENTS

1814 France: Napoleon abdicates and is exiled to Elba.

1815 France: Napoleon returns for "Hundred Days."

Belgium: Napoleon defeated at Waterloo.

France: Napoleon exiled to St. Helena.

1816 Italy: Rossini composes *The Barber of Seville*.

1817 United States: William Cullen Bryant publishes "Thanatopsis."

Germany: Hegel publishes *Encyclopedia of the Philosophical Sciences*.

1818 First steamship crosses Atlantic.

1821 Greece: War with Turkey begins.

Germany: Heinrich Heine publishes *Poems*

1822 Austria: Schubert begins *Symphony No. 8* ("Unfinished Symphony").

Russia: Aleksandr Pushkin publishes *Eugene Onegin*.

1823 United States: Monroe Doctrine closes Americas to further European colonization.

1825 Russia: Bolshoi Ballet established.

1826 Germany: Mendelssohn composes *Overture to A Midsummer Night's Dream*.

United States: James Fenimore Cooper publishes *The Last of the Mohicans*.

1827 France: Alexandre Dumas publishes *The Three Musketeers*.

1830 France: Stendhal publishes *The Red and the Black*.

1831 United States: Edgar Allan Poe publishes *Poems*.

France: Victor Hugo publishes *The Hunchback of Notre Dame*.

Give literary works a time and place with national and world timelines

Finally, a program puts together *all* the pieces.

& Beyond

. . . for the Classroom

For each selection you can count on:

Teacher Back-up

Including three additional writing activities per selection.

Vocabulary Check

Reinforce or test the words pretaught before the selection.

Usage and Mechanic Worksheet

Integrate grammar and editing skills with literature.

Name ______ Date ______

The Necklace Guy de Maupassant (text page 000)

Selection Test

A. Thinking About the Selection. In the space to the right, fill in the letter of the best answer to each question.

1. Madame Loisel is married to 1. ______
   a. an ambassador
   b. a minor civil servant
   c. a laborer
   d. an aristocrat
2. At first, Madame Loisel does not want to go to the ball because she 2. ______
   a. never enjoys herself at big parties
   b. feels she hasn't a thing to wear
   c. has no appropriate jewelry
   d. has lost her friend's necklace
3. When the Loisel's return the case to the jeweler whose name appears in it, they find that 3. ______
   a. the jeweler supplied the case but did not sell the necklace
   b. the necklace is a fake
   c. the necklace is exceedingly expensive
   d. the jeweler has gone out of business
4. The Loisels do all of the following to pay for the replacement of the necklace EXCEPT 4. ______
   a. borrow money
   b. use money Monsieur Loisel had inherited
   c. sign a promissory note offered by Madame Forestier
   d. take on extra jobs
5. When Madame Loisel tells Madame Forestier the truth about replacing the necklace, Madame Forestier 5. ______
   a. becomes angry
   b. offers to return the new necklace
   c. tells Madame Loisel that the original necklace was false
   d. calls the police

 The Necklace 5

Selection Test

More than just content, these tests gauge understanding of the literary element, critical reading skills and language skill.

The Teaching Portfolio– your literature-based language arts program.

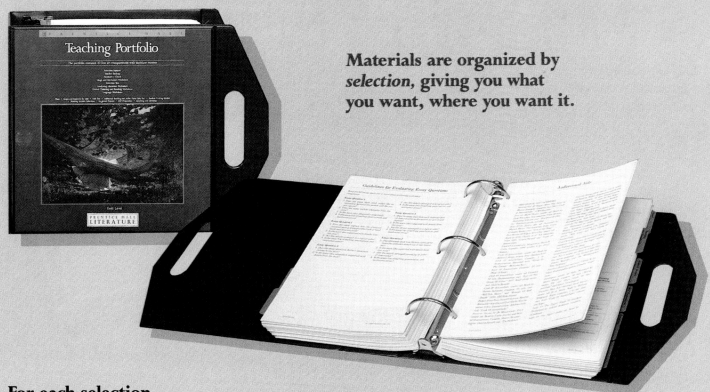

Materials are organized by *selection*, giving you what you want, where you want it.

For each selection, two of these are always available:

Analyzing Literature Worksheet
Extends understanding of the literary element.

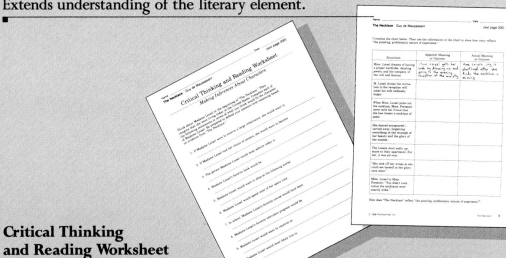

Language Worksheet
Beyond vocabulary to word origins, synonyms, dialects—and more.

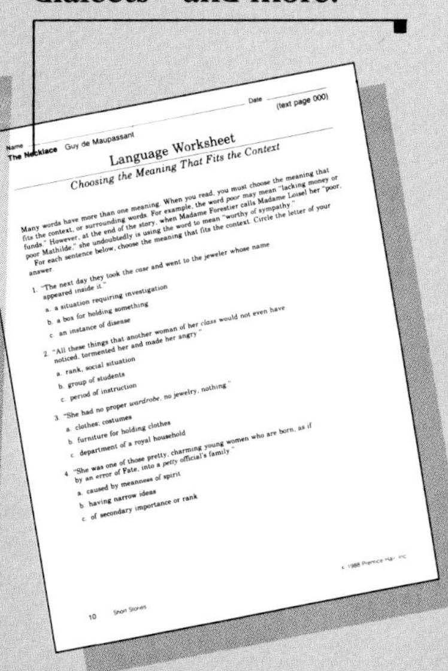

Name _______________ Date _______________

The Necklace Guy de Maupassant (text page 000)

Language Worksheet

Choosing the Meaning That Fits the Context

Many words have more than one meaning. When you read, you must choose the meaning that fits the context, or surrounding words. For example, the word *poor* may mean "lacking money or funds." However, at the end of the story, when Madame Forestier calls Madame Loisel her "poor, poor Mathilde," she undoubtedly is using the word to mean "worthy of sympathy."

For each sentence below, choose the meaning that fits the context. Circle the letter of your answer.

1. "The next day they took the *case* and went to the jeweler whose name appeared inside it."
   a. a situation requiring investigation
   b. a box for holding something
   c. an instance of disease
2. "All these things that another woman of her *class* would not even have noticed, tormented her and made her angry."
   a. rank, social situation
   b. group of students
   c. period of instruction
3. "She had no proper *wardrobe*, no jewelry, nothing."
   a. clothes; costumes
   b. furniture for holding clothes
   c. department of a royal household
4. "She was one of those pretty, charming young women who are born, as if by an error of Fate, into a *petty* official's family."
   a. caused by meanness of spirit
   b. having narrow ideas
   c. of secondary importance or rank

© 1988 Prentice-Hall, Inc.

10 Short Stories

Critical Thinking and Reading Worksheet
Promotes reading and reasoning.

& Beyond,

. . . for the classroom

Twenty full-color transparencies *Free* in the Teaching Portfolio.

Fine art transparencies provide a literature-related visual and stimulate student writing.

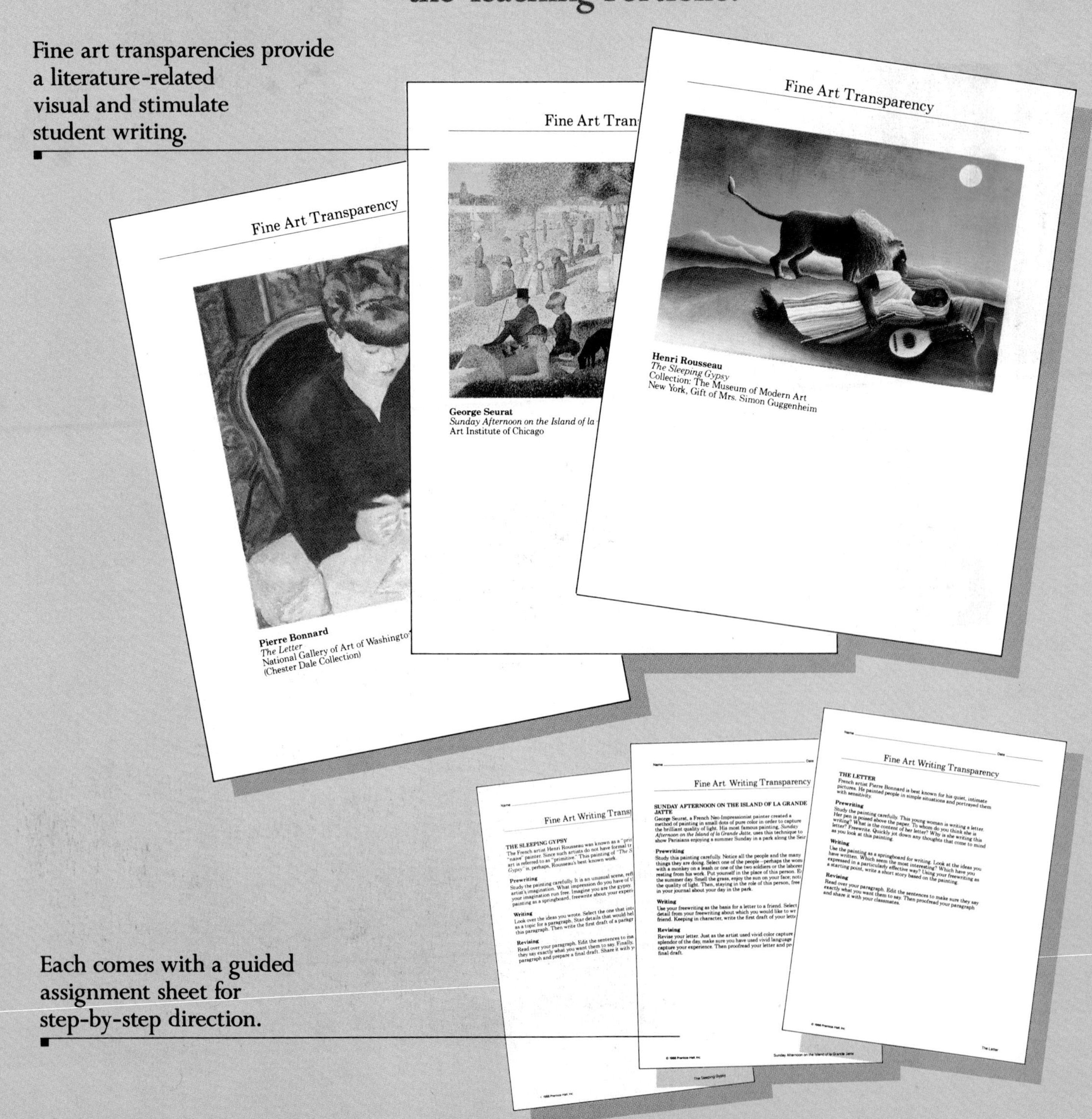

Each comes with a guided assignment sheet for step-by-step direction.

& still Beyond

Tailor the program to your own literature choices with Novel Study Guides.

What if your favorite novel or play is not in Prentice-Hall Literature? We still provide you with teaching support. Complete teaching guides for 26 novels and plays give you fresh insights to make the classics more interesting and relevant. Each guide contains:

- Author Background
- Synopses of Plot, Setting, Theme and more.
- Chapter-by-chapter Teaching Plans
- Writing Assignments
- Guidelines for Dealing with Provocative Themes
- Blackline Master Handouts and Test

Master Teacher Board

Roger Babusci
(Pennsylvania Teacher of the Year, 1983)
Schenley High School
Pittsburgh, Pennsylvania

Loutish Burns
(Houston Teacher of the Year, 1986)
Louie Welch Middle School
Houston, Texas

Guy Doud
(National Teacher of the Year, 1986)
Brainerd Senior High School
Brainerd, Minnesota

Terri Fields
(Arizona Teacher of the Year, 1986)
Sunnyslope High School
Phoenix, Arizona

Kermeen Fristrom
(1985 Distinguished Service Award of Merit, California)
San Diego City Schools
San Diego, California

Leroy Hay
(National Teacher of the Year, 1983)
Manchester High School
Manchester, Connecticut

Beth Johnson
(Florida Teacher of the Year, 1982)
Kathleen Senior High School
Lakeland, Florida

Evaline Kruse
(California Teacher of the Year, 1985)
Audubon Junior High School
Los Angeles, California

Jane McKee
(West Virginia Teacher of the Year, 1986)
Man High School
Man, West Virginia

Robert Seney
(Texas Curriculum Association's Exemplary Showcase Award for Literature)
Albright Middle School
Houston, Texas

Pat Weaver
(1986 National Outstanding Dissertation for Curriculum)
Arlington Independent School District
Arlington, Texas

Consultants

Joan Baron
University of Connecticut
Storrs, Connecticut

Charles Cooper
University of California
San Diego, California

Nancy Spivey
Carnegie-Mellon Institute
Pittsburgh, Pennsylvania

Contributing Writers

Frances Earle
Former English Teacher
Miralest High School
Palos Verdes, California

Sharon Glick
Formerly affiliated with Detroit Public Schools
Detroit, Michigan

Patricia McLaughlin
Former English Teacher
Our Lady of Lourdes High School
Poughkeepsie, New York

Howard Portnoy
Former English Teacher
Boston Latin School
Boston, Masaschusetts

Ruth Rose
Former English Teacher
Acton-Boxborough Regional High School
Acton, Massachusetts

Terry A. Sansom
Curriculum Director
Round Rock School District
Round Rock, Texas

Kathleen Scanlon
English Teacher
Cresskill High School
Cresskill, New Jersey

Richard West
Former English Teacher
Cherry Lawn School
Darien, Connecticut

Annotated Teacher's Edition

PRENTICE HALL LITERATURE

THE ENGLISH TRADITION

Cover
SUMMER
John Atkinson Grimshaw
Art Resource

PRENTICE HALL, Englewood Cliffs, New Jersey 07632

ISBN 0-13-693771-3

10 9 8 7 6 5 4 3 2 1

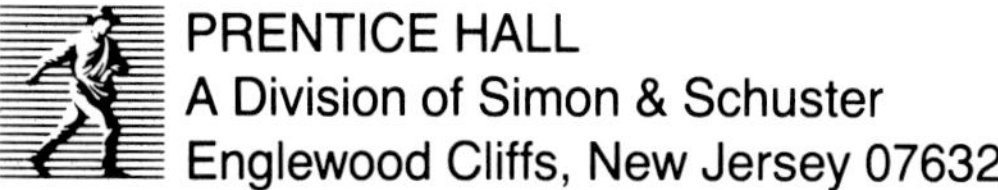

PRENTICE HALL
A Division of Simon & Schuster
Englewood Cliffs, New Jersey 07632

CONTENTS

The Prentice Hall Literature Program
OVERVIEW

THE STUDENT BOOK

The *Prentice Hall Literature Program* is a complete literature program, offering high-quality, appealing, traditional and contemporary literary selections, with study aids that will guide students into, through, and beyond the literature.

Organization

The selections on this level are organized chronologically to present the literature of the United States in a historical context. The following list shows the units and the sections within each unit into which the selections are organized.

The Anglo-Saxon Period
The Medieval Period
The English Renaissance
The Seventeenth Century: The Schools of Donne and Jonson, The Puritan Age
The Restoration and the Eighteenth Century: The Restoration, the Age of Pope and Swift, The Age of Johnson, Pre-Romantic Poetry
The Romantic Age: Poetry, Prose
The Victorian Age: Major Victorian Poets, Other Victorian Poets, Prose, The Victorian Novel
The Modern Period: Prose, Poetry, Drama
Contemporary Writers: Prose, Poetry

The number and variety of selections offers choice and flexibility in meeting curriculum requirements as well as student needs and interests.

Unique Features

Because the *Prentice Hall Literature Program* puts emphasis on the reading and appreciation of literature, it offers several unique features to help students become active readers.

Reading Critically Each unit begins with a feature called Reading Critically, which includes a summary of the historical context, the literary movements, and the writers' techniques of the period. This feature is followed by a Model for Reading Critically, which is annotated to demonstrate and explain to students how a good reader might apply this information to the analysis of a selection. This technique actively involves the reader in the text before reading and while reading. Such involvement and reaction are necessary if students are to learn. Students are encouraged to use this technique as they read other selections in the unit. This feature provides a method of scaffolding—giving students help and support while they acquire the skills to become successful readers of literature.

Guide for Reading All other selections begin with a Guide for Reading. This page contains useful prereading information. The Guide for Reading prepares students for successful reading in five ways:

- A biography of the author provides insight into how the author came to write the selection.
- A literary focus section introduces the literary concept that is taught with the selection.
- The Look For provides a specific goal—thematic, stylistic, or meaning-oriented—to guide the students' reading of the selection.
- A motivational writing activity puts students in an appropriate frame of mind.
- A vocabulary list presents, in glossary format, words from the selection that might present difficulty in reading.

This Guide for Reading provides the necessary background to enhance comprehension, motivates students to read, and gives them technical support to read successfully.

Each selection is self-contained and complete so that you can use them in any order that you like.

After Reading

Features at the end of the selection are designed to foster comprehension and encourage constructive response, either personal or literary. These features encourage the growth of skills needed by students to become independent readers. These features comprise five areas:

Thinking About the Selection: These study questions are built upon three levels of comprehension: the literal, the interpretive, and the applied. The questions are grouped by the levels of increasing complexity: recalling (literal), interpreting (inference, analysis), and applying (generalization extension, judgment). The different levels may be used as appropriate for different ability levels, or they may be used to take all students through different levels of thinking.

Analyzing Literature: This section develops and reinforces the literary concept or skill introduced on the Guide for Reading page and applies it to the selection. It helps students to understand literary concepts and appreciate writers' techniques, thereby enabling them to respond appropriately to literature.

Critical Thinking and Reading: This section introduces students to those critical thinking and critical reading skills that are necessary for understanding literature. It gives them an opportunity to apply these skills to the literary selections.

Understanding Language: Knowledge and appreciation of language are developed in this section, which contains activities on language prompted by the selection. The activities may be geared toward helping students appreciate writers' use of language, master skills needed to increase their vocabulary, or prepare for SATs.

Thinking and Writing: This is a composition assignment arising from the selection. This assignment, which may be creative or analytical, is process-oriented, suggesting steps for prewriting, drafting, and revising.

End of Unit

You the Writer, You the Critic At the end of each unit, there are six additional writing activities. Three of them, under You the Writer, are creative; three of them, under You the Critic, are analytical. Each activity is developed through the steps of the writing process.

End of Book

Three handbooks are provided at the end of *Prentice Hall Literature*: Handbook of Writing About Literature, Handbook of Critical Thinking and Reading Terms, and Handbook of Literary Terms and Techniques.

Handbook of Writing About Literature The Handbook of Writing About Literature is divided into five sections. The first section introduces the process of writing. The second requires students to analyze and interpret literature and teaches them how to write about the specific elements of literary works. The third requires students to interpret and synthesize literature while teaching how to write about the work as a whole. The fourth provides instruction in evaluating literary works. The fifth guides the students in the creation of their own literary works.

This Handbook may be used for direct instruction or as support for the individual writing assignments in *Prentice Hall Literature*.

Handbook of Critical Thinking and Reading Terms The Handbook of Critical Thinking and Reading Terms provides an alphabetical arrangement of the terms taught in the Critical Thinking and Reading activities at the end of selections. Each entry expands upon the original definition and provides one or more examples. This Handbook can be used to preteach terminology or to review information. It can also be used as an easy reference guide for students as they work on individual Critical Thinking and Reading assignments.

Handbook of Literary Terms and Techniques The Handbook of Literary Terms and Techniques provides an alphabetical guide to the literary terms introduced on the Guide for Reading page and taught in the Analyzing Literature activities at the end of selections. Each entry provides a full definition of the term or technique with one or more examples. The handbook is designed so that it can be used for preteaching, for review, or as a support for students as they work on individual Analyzing Literature activities.

TEACHING SUPPORT

THE ANNOTATED TEACHER'S EDITION

The annotated teacher's edition of *Prentice Hall Literature* is designed to be used both for planning and for actual in-class teaching. It offers planning aids and specific teaching suggestions for all selections. This planning and teaching material appears in the side columns next to the reduced student pages of each selection. These annotations, which correspond to the student material on that page, help you give your students positive and relevant experiences with literature by asking the right questions at the right time and by pointing out what is significant.

Preparing the Lesson

The annotations on the opening pages of the selection help you plan your presentation of the material. Each selection begins with notes that suggest ways to introduce or enhance the prereading instruction or activities presented in the students' Guide for Reading. These notes help you present the material or adapt if for less advanced or more advanced students. Objectives for each selection are keyed to the end-of-selection material. This page also includes a complete list of all other support material for this selection in the Teaching Portfolio. In the column next to the first page of the selection, you will find a motivation for reading suggestion and a purpose-setting question to prepare the students to read. Frequently, thematic ideas are given. These suggest other selections in this book that treat themes similar to those under discussion. You may want to use these selections together to integrate and reinforce universal concepts and themes. All of these annotations help you effectively prepare your lesson.

Teaching the Lesson

You may use the notes throughout the pages of the selection to direct your discussion of the selection in class. As you and your students read the selection, you will find additional notes. These notes will help you to increase your students' involvement in the work, enrich their reading of it, and enable them to deal with the particular genres. The following kinds of notes may direct your class discussions:

Master Teacher Notes These notes from master teachers give an approach, a strategy, or a very special bit of information that enlivens the selection or increases appreciation.

Humanities Notes For each piece of fine art in the student book, there is a humanities note giving information on the work of art and the artist. These notes generally point out features of the piece of art that relate it to the work of literature with which it is presented. Additionally, the humanities note concludes with questions that you may use if you wish to discuss the art as part of your discussion of the selection.

Enrichment Enrichment notes provide additional information on points of interest that arise in selections. You may use this information to enrich your students' knowledge of the background of a selection and appreciation of it.

Reading Strategies Strategies to promote student comprehension of the literary text reinforce the emphasis on enabling students to read literature.

Clarification Words, phrases, or ideas that might be obstacles to student understanding are clarified to ensure comprehension.

Discussion Throughout the selection, you will find additional questions and points for discussion. These help you proceed through the selection with students, eliciting their understanding and appreciation of significant passages and aspects of the selection.

Literary Focus To promote understanding of the writer's techniques, literary focus annotations direct attention to those aspects of the selection that reflect the literary concept presented with it.

Critical Thinking and Reading These notes reinforce the critical thinking and reading skills developed throughout the program.

There are probably more notes than you need for presenting any given selection. We emphasize the importance of selecting those annotations that are best suited to your classes and to your course of instruction.

Beyond the Lesson

Answers are provided for all questions in each feature following the selection. Where questions are open-ended, we present a suggested response or we suggest points that students should note in their answers.

The annotations after the selection also include the following:

Challenge These questions take students beyond those given with the instruction.

Publishing Student Writing For many selections, additional notes suggest ways to publishing the writing students have done in the Thinking and Writing feature.

Writing Across the Curriculum Where appropriate, you will see suggestions for additional assignments or suggestions for relating the Thinking and Writing assignment to students' work in another discipline.

In addition, you will find teaching suggestions for the special features in the student book—Reading Critically and You the Writer, You the Critic. You will also find annotations on the unit introductions, relating the information there to specific selections.

THE TEACHING PORTFOLIO

The Teaching Portfolio provides support for teaching and testing all of the selections and skills in *Prentice Hall Literature*.

Fine Art Transparencies

Twenty fine art transparencies with blackline masters are provided in the Teaching Portfolio. These can be used to introduce selections and motivate students to read, or they may be used as additional writing assignments in response to art. The fine art is keyed into the selections through Master Teacher Notes in the Annotated Teacher's Edition.

Beginning of Unit

Each unit begins with a list of objectives and a skills chart listing literary elements and skills covered in the unit.

The Selections

Full teaching support is provided for each selection. This support material is organized by selection for your convenience. The support for each selection consists of the following: Teacher Backup, Vocabulary Check, Usage and Mechanics Worksheet, Analyzing Literature Worksheet*, Critical Thinking and Reading Worksheet*, Language Worksheet* (there are always two of the starred three), and a Selection Test.

Teacher Backup Teacher Backup material is provided for each selection. This material consists of more information about the author, a critical quotation about the author, a summary of the selection, and a list of other works by the author. In addition, there is a Check Test that you can use to check if students have read the selection. Help in teaching and evaluating the writing assignment in the student text is provided as well as three alternative composition assignments for the students. One of these is less challenging than the assignment in the student text, one is more challenging, and one requires the student to write in response to literary criticism. Finally, answers to all worksheet activities and tests are provided.

Vocabulary Check The Vocabulary Check tests mastery of the vocabulary words listed on the Guide for Reading page before each selection. This blackline master can be used as a test or as an in-class or at-home assignment.

Usage and Mechanics The Usage and Mechanics Worksheet provides sentences dealing with the selection that contain errors in usage and mechanics. Such common problems as run-on sentences, sentence fragments, and subject-verb agreement are incorporated into these sentences as well as errors in spelling and punctuation. We suggest you have your students correct these sentences orally so that they can discuss each problem.

Worksheets The Analyzing Literature Worksheet, Critical Thinking and Reading Worksheet, and Language Worksheet support and expand upon the skills taught at the end of the selection in the student book. If no understanding Language assignment appears in the student book, one is provided in the Teaching Portfolio.

Selection Test A Selection Test is provided for each selection. This test provides for a check of comprehension as well as of mastery of the skills taught at the end of the selection.

Annotated Models For each selection that is annotated as a model in the student book, a selection is provided in the Teaching Portfolio for students to annotate themselves.

End of Unit

Each unit ends with a unit essay test, guidelines for evaluating student responses to the essay test questions, a list of suggested projects, a bibliography, and list of audio-visual aids.

End of Portfolio

The following resource material is provided at the end of the Teaching Portfolio: a brief guide to teaching with the handbooks, models of student writing, and a guide to evaluating student writing. In addition, there is a guide for taking the SATs and a guide for incorporating speaking and listening in your classroom.

NOVEL STUDY GUIDES

Novel Study Guides are available with *Prentice Hall Literature*. These guides will help you teach many of the novels of your choice as part of your total literature program.

Overview of the Novel

Each study guide provides an overview of the novel. This overview consists of information about the author, historical background, analysis of the characters, the plot, the setting, the theme, and other elements that make up the novel.

Chapter-by-Chapter Lessons

These lessons provide objectives and a list of difficult vocabulary. The guide for preteaching helps you direct your lesson toward the less advanced, average, or more advanced student. In addition, the lessons provide a summary of the chapter and commentaries on specific passages. At the end of each lesson are writing assignments and questions.

Essays and Imaginative Writing

Many writing assignments are provided for students. Each guide lists topics for short papers, topics for long papers, opportunities to respond to critical comments, and imaginative writing assignments. In addition, it provides guidelines for evaluating student writing.

Guidelines for Dealing With Provocative Themes

Novels may include themes that could cause problems in the classroom. This helpful guide provides tips for dealing with these themes.

Bibliography

A list of other works by the author is provided as well as a critical assessment of the author and the novel. In addition, suggestions for further reading are given.

Blackline Masters

Blackline masters are provided for your convenience. These offer skill worksheets and a test for the novel.

Composition Strand in Prentice Hall Literature

The following chart shows all composition activities and their location in the program. This chart is organized to show how these activities take students into, through, and beyond the literature.

Feature	In the Student Materials	In the Teacher Materials	Benefit
Into			
"Writing" activity *before* each selection	"Guide for Reading" page before each selection in student text	"Guide for Reading" teaching note in margin of Annotated Teacher's Edition	Current research reports that writing before reading is an ideal technique for getting students into literature.
Through			
"Thinking and Writing" composition activity after *each* selection	End of each selection in student text	In Teaching Portfolio: Teaching notes for activity labeled with writing process steps. Evaluation checklist for grading student writing In Annotated Teacher's Edition: Suggestions for publishing student writing	The writing activity that follows each selection in the textbook provides an immediate opportunity to respond in writing to the literary experience. The activity is worded in writing process format.
Three additional composition activities for *each* selection		Additional activities are in the Teaching Portfolio. These can be used as assignments, or as essay questions for selection tests	Three additional writing activities for *each* selection let you meet the needs of lower ability levels, or provide enrichment.
"Handbook of Writing About Literature," made up of two-page writing lessons	Handbook section at the end of each student text	Notes and support for using the handbook in the Teaching Portfolio	Guided lessons for writing about literature lead students step-by-step through case studies and activities.
"Unit Test" essay questions that address several selections in a unit		Test in Teaching Portfolio comes with evaluation checklists	Sharpen critical thinking and writing with thoughtful topics that compare and contrast thematic ideas, literary elements, and content from the unit.
"Setting Up a Reading Log" for informal writing about the selection		Motivation and instructions in the Teaching Portfolio	Encourage informal writing before, during and after reading to enrich each student's experience.
Beyond			
"You the Writer" creative writing activity with each unit	End of each unit in student text	Guidelines for evaluating student writing are in Annotated Teacher's Edition	Students try their hand at expressive writing aided by imaginative prompts and step-by-step encouragement.
"You the Critic" literary criticism activity with each unit	End of each unit in student text	Teaching notes in Annotated Teacher's Edition	Challenge analytical skills as your students respond to literary criticism.

(continued)

Composition Strand in Prentice Hall Literature

Feature	In the Student Materials	In the Teacher Materials	Benefit
"Writing Across the Curriculum" suggestions		Suggestions in Annotated Teacher's Edition	Broaden writing opportunities to other subject areas. Notes suggest assignments and ways of interacting with other departments.
"Fine Art Writing Activity" (from full color art transparency)	Handout sheet	Twenty fine art color transparencies with accompanying blackline masters in Teaching Portfolio	Use the dynamic combination of literature and writing for a humanities-based writing activity that stimulates first-rate student writing.

Skills Chart for Selections in Each Unit

The following chart shows the literary elements and skills covered with each selection. An asterisk (*) indicates that a worksheet appears in the Teaching Portfolio.

The Anglo-Saxon Period

Selection	Analyzing Literature	Critical Thinking and Reading	Understanding Language/ Speaking and Listening	Thinking and Writing
Reading Critically				
"The Seafarer, " p. 17	Understanding Anglo-Saxon poetry*	Comparing and contrasting attitudes	Appreciating Old English*	Writing about Anglo-Saxon beliefs
from *Beowulf,* p. 24	Understanding the Anglo-Saxon epic	Making inferences about beliefs* Making inferences about ideals	Using a glossary*	Writing about character traits
from *A History of the English Church and People,* Bede, p. 40	Understanding historical writing*	Making inferences about attitudes	Tracing word histories*	Writing a critical review

The Medieval Period

Selection	Analyzing Literature	Critical Thinking and Reading	Understanding Language/ Speaking and Listening	Thinking and Writing
Reading Critically				
from *Morte d'Arthur,* Sir Thomas Malory, p. 65	Understanding legends* Recognizing legends	Recognizing elements of fantasy*	Appreciating word origins	Writing about character
"Sir Patrick Spens," p. 78 "Get Up and Bar the Door," p. 82 "The Two Corbies," p. 84 "Barbara Allan," p. 85	Understanding the folk ballad*	Interpreting symbols in folk ballads	Appreciating language change* Recognizing language change Sharing folk ballads	Writing about a folk ballad
"The Prologue" from *The Canterbury Tales,* p. 91	Understanding characterization	Making inferences about characters*	Interpreting similes* Using similes	Writing a pilgrim's tale
"The Pardoner's Tale," Geoffrey Chaucer, p. 115	Understanding the anecdote (exemplum)*	Making inferences on the narrator's words* Making inferences	Reading Middle English aloud	Writing an analysis
from *Sir Gawain and the Green Knight,* page 124	Understanding medieval romances*	Making inferences about chivalric ideals* Making inferences about chivalry	Using abstract words	Evaluating the medieval romance
from *Everyman,* page 142	Understanding the morality play*	Interpreting names as symbols Using names as symbols*	Performing in a play	Discussing a morality play

The English Renaissance

Selection	Analyzing Literature	Critical Thinking and Reading	Understanding Language/ Speaking and Listening	Thinking and Writing
Reading Critically				
"Whoso List to Hunt," Sir Thomas Wyatt, p. 171	Understanding the Petrarchan sonnet*	Interpreting the figurative meaning*	Reading aloud classic British poems	Responding to criticism
Sonnet 31, Sir Philip Sidney, p. 176 Sonnet 39, Sir Philip Sidney, p. 178	Understanding poetic language Understanding a sonnet sequence*		Greek and Latin word parts*	Writing a letter of response
"The Passionate Shepherd to His Love," Christopher Marlowe, p. 182	Appreciating pastoral poems Appreciating lyric poetry	Inferring cultural attitudes*	Appreciating the multiple meanings of words*	Writing an invitation in verse
from *The Tragical History of the Life and Death of Dr. Faustus,* Christopher Marlowe, p. 185	Understanding historical context	Making inferences about characters*	Evaluating a dramatic reading*	
"The Nymph's Reply to the Shepherd," p. 190 "To His Son," p. 192	Identifying the speaker in a poem	Making inferences about tone* Making inferences about purpose	Understanding words based on Greek myths*	Writing your own reply
from *The Faerie Queene,* Edmund Spenser, p. 196 Sonnet 1, p. 197 Sonnet 26, p. 198 Sonnet 75, p. 199	Understanding the Spenserian stanza* Understanding the Spenserian sonnet		Interpreting personification* Choosing the denotation that fits the context	Comparing and contrasting sonnets
"A Litany in Time of Plague," p. 202	Understanding a litany	Generalizing from a set of assumptions*	Tracing word origins*	Writing about the concerns of a people
Sonnet 29, William Shakespeare, p. 207 Sonnet 73, p. 209 Sonnet 116, p. 210 Sonnet 130, p. 211	Understanding the Shakespearean sonnet* Understanding Shakespearean sonnets	Comparing and contrasting sonnet forms	Understanding prefixes and suffixes*	Comparing and contrasting sonnets

The English Renaissance (continued)

Selection	Analyzing Literature	Critical Thinking and Reading	Understanding Language/ Speaking and Listening	Thinking and Writing
"Tell Me Where is Fancy Bred?" p. 213 "It Was a Lover and His Lass," p. 214 "Fear No More the Heat o' the Sun," p. 216	Understanding Shake-spean's songs	Selecting details that develop mood* Finding details that develop mood Finding details that support purpose*		Writing about Shake-speare's songs
Macbeth, William Shakespeare, Act I, p.223	Understanding blank verse*	Making inferences about characters*	Reading blank verse aloud	Comparing and con-trasting characters
Macbeth, Act II, p. 243	Understanding atmosphere*	Interpreting symbols*	Choosing the meaning that fits the context	Writing about atmosphere
Macbeth, Act III, p. 257	Understanding irony*	Interpreting connotative meaning	Understanding figura-tive language*	Who is the third murderer
Macbeth, Act IV, p. 273	Understanding plot development*	Reading between the lines*		Writing about Macbeth's tragic flaw
Macbeth, Act V, p. 291	Understanding theme*	Analyzing cultural atti-tudes and customs	Understanding Shake-spearean English* Reading Shakespearen English	
The Tempest, William Shakespeare, Act I, p.307	Understanding exposi-tion and conflict*	Diagraming plot development*		Writing about conflict
The Tempest, Act II, p. 329	Understanding stock characters*	Recognizing themes	Recognizing diction as a character trait*	Writing about a charac-ter's function
The Tempest, Act III, p. 347	Understanding com-parison and contrast* Understanding characters	Recognizing plays on words	Choosing the meaning that fits the context* Finding meaning that fits the context	Writing about com-parisons and contrast
The Tempest, Act IV, p. 361	Understanding resolu-tion of plot*	Understanding cause and effect	Recognizing names from classical mythology*	Writing a resolution
The Tempest, Act V, p. 371	Analyzing Shake-spearean comedy and theme*		Distinguishing between comic and funny* Distinguishing between words	Recognizing themes
from *Novum Organum,* Idols of the Cave, Sir Francis Bacon, p. 383	Understanding aphorism*	Reasoning	Words from Latin roots Finding Latin roots*	Writing aphorisms
from the *King James Bible* Psalm 23, p. 388 The Parable of the Prodigal Son, p. 389 I Corinthians 13, p. 391	Recognizing a psalm	Analyzing the use of parallelism*		

The Seventeenth Century

Selection	Analyzing Literature	Critical Thinking and Reading	Understanding Language/ Speaking and Listening	Thinking and Writing
Reading Critically				
"To the Memory of My Beloved Master, William Shakespeare," Ben Jonson, p. 413	Understanding allusions*	Analyzing the effect of allusions	Tracing word origins*	Writing a letter
The Schools of Donne and Jonson				
"Song," John Donne, p. 420 Holy Sonnet 10, John Donne, p. 422 Holy Sonnet 14, John Donne, p. 424	Understanding paradox* Understanding metaphysical conceit*	Following an argument		Writing a philosophical argument
from "Meditation 17," John Donne, p. 427	Recognizing themes*	Arguing through analogy*		Writing about the theme of a work
"Virtue," George Herbert, p. 432 "Easter Wings," George Herbert, p. 434 "Man," George Herbert, p. 435	Understanding emblematic images*	Analyzing Herbert's style*	Recognizing differences among synonyms*	Writing about emblematic images
"To His Coy Mistress," Andrew Marvell, p. 440 "The Picture of Little T. C. in a Prospect of Flowers," Andrew Marvell, p. 442	Recognizing couplets and quatrains*		Recognizing syllables and pronunciations*	Comparing and contrasting styles
"On My First Son," Ben Jonson, p. 446 "Song: To Celia," p. 447 "Still to be Neat," p. 448	Understanding apostrophes*	Inferring the author's purpose*		Responding to criticism
"An Ode for Him (Ben Jonson)," Robert Herrick, p. 452	Understanding symbols*	Interpreting the difference among synonyms* Knowing differences among synonyms		Writing about thinking
"To the Virgins, to Make Much of Time," Robert Herrick, p. 454		Making inferences about the *carpe diem* trandition Understanding *carpe diem* tradition*		Writing a poetic response

The Seventeenth Century (continued)

Selection	Analyzing Literature	Critical Thinking and Reading	Understanding Language/ Speaking and Listening	Thinking and Writing
"The Constant Lover," Sir John Suckling, p. 458 "Song," Sir John Suckling, p. 459 "To Lucasta, on Going to the Wars," Richard Lovelace, p. 460 "To Althea, From Prison," Richard Lovelace, p. 461	Understanding tone*	Understanding the effect of connotative meaning*		Writing about tone Comparing and contrasting writers
The Puritan Age				
"When I Consider How My Light Is Spent," John Milton, p. 466 "On His Having Arrived at the Age of Twenty-Three," John Milton, p. 468	Understanding Italian sonnets*		Understanding the multiple meanings of words*	Comparing and contrasting the Italian and English sonnets
from *Paradise Lost,* John Milton, p. 470	Understanding epic poetry*			
from *The Pilgrim's Progress,* John Bunyan, p. 482	Recognizing allegory*	Interpreting the author's point of view*		Writing an allegory for today's world

The Restoration and the Eighteenth Century

Selection	Analyzing Literature	Critical Thinking and Reading	Understanding Language/ Speaking and Listening	Thinking and Writing
Reading Critically				
"Holy Thursday," William Blake, p. 507	Understanding paradox* Using sound devices	Analyzing the effect of sound devices	Finding antonyms*	Responding to criticism
The Restoration				
from "An Essay on Dramatic Poesy," John Dryden, p. 512	Understanding an essay	Charting an analysis Understanding analysis*	Appreciating specific words*	Writing an evaluation of an analysis
"A Song for St. Cecilia's Day," John Dryden, p. 517	Recognizing an ode*	Understanding the effect of sound	Appreciating rhythm*	Writing an ode
from *The Diary,* Samuel Pepys, p. 524	Understanding a diary	Finding main ideas and supporting details* Finding main ideas	Appreciating the language of the Restoration*	Using Pepys's diary as a model
from *A Journal of the Plague Year,* Daniel Defoe, p. 532	Recognizing first-person narrative	Comparing and contrasting writers*	Distinguishing between meanings*	
from *Gulliver's Travels,* Jonathan Swift, p. 538	Understanding satire*	Understanding generalizations*	Using words from literature	Writing a new adventure for Gulliver
from "Thoughts on Various Subjects," Jonathan Swift, p. 548	Understanding epigrams*		Completing word analogies*	Writing epigrams
"Country Manners," Joseph Addison and Richard Steele, p. 552	Informal essay	Recognizing characteristics of style*	Choosing the meaning that fits the context*	Writing an informal essay
"Thoughts in Westminster Abbey," Joseph Addison and Richard Steele, p. 555	Understanding the personal essay*	Understanding the cultural context*		Writing a précis
from *The Rape of the Lock,* Alexander Pope, p. 560	Understanding mock epic*	Inferring the author's purpose*		Writing about tone
from *An Essay on Man,* Alexander Pope, p. 573	Understanding a heroic couplet*	Generalizing Generalizing about emotion and intellect*		Responding to neoclassical criticism

The Restoration and the Eighteenth Century (continued)

Selection	Analyzing Literature	Critical Thinking and Reading	Understanding Language/ Speaking and Listening	Thinking and Writing
"Letter to Lord Chesterfield," Samuel Johnson, p. 578 from The Preface to *A Dictionary of the English Language,* Samuel Johnson, p. 580 from *A Dictionary of the English Language,* Samuel Johnson, p. 583	Analyzing diction and style	Making inferences about tone	Word building using root words*	Comparing and contrasting writing style Writing Johnsonian dictionary entries
from *The Life of Samuel Johnson,* James Boswell, p. 588	Understanding biography	Recognizing subjective information Recognizing subjective from objective information*	Understanding how words change in meaning*	Writing from Johnson's point of view
"Elegy Written in a Country Churchyard," Thomas Gray, p. 598	Understanding an elegy	Evaluating the effect of inverted sentences* Evaluating inverted sentences	Appreciating vivid verbs*	Writing an elegy
"Woman," Oliver Goldsmith, p. 605	Understanding poetic structure*		Completing word analogies*	
"To a Mouse," Robert Burns, p. 608 "To a Louse," Robert Burns, p. 611 "Afton Water," Robert Burns, p. 614 "John Anderson, My Jo," Robert Burns, p. 616	Recognizing dialect* Recognizing satire	Recognizing satire*		Comparing and contrasting two poems Writing about dialect
"The Lamb," William Blake, p. 620 "The Tiger," William Blake, p. 622 "The Human Abstract," William Blake, p. 624 "Infant Sorrow," William Blake, p. 625 "A Poison Tree," William Blake, p. 626	Recognizing symbolism Recognizing symbols*		Recognizing Latinate words*	Writing about symbolism

The Romantic Age

Selection	Analyzing Literature	Critical Thinking and Reading	Understanding Language/ Speaking and Listening	Thinking and Writing
Reading Critically				
"The Solitary Reaper," William Wordsworth, p. 649	Appreciating a writer's Diction	Appreciating sound devices* Understanding sound devices	Appreciating vivid verbs*	Writing a poem
Poetry				
"Lines Composed a Few Miles Above Tintern Abbey," William Wordsworth, p. 654 "My Heart Leaps Up When I Behold," William Wordsworth, p. 660	Understanding Romanticism*	Comparing and contrasting experiences* Interpreting a paradox		Writing about Romanticism Writing a nature poem
"Composed upon Westminister Bridge," William Wordsworth, p. 663 "It Is a Beauteous Evening, Calm and Free," William Wordsworth, p. 664 "London, 1802," William Wordsworth, p. 666 "The World Is Too Much with Us," William Wordsworth, p. 667	Recognizing a sonnet Recognizing a sonnet*		Completing word analogies*	
"The Rime of the Ancient Mariner," Samuel Taylor Coleridge, p. 670	Understanding sound devices*	Analyzing the effects of sound devices	Understanding archaic words and meanings* Using archaic words and meaning	Responding to a statement
"Kubla Khan," Samuel Taylor Coleridge, p. 695	Understanding Romanticism*		Understanding homophones*	
"She Walks in Beauty," George Gordon, Lord Byron, p. 700 "So We'll Go No More A-Roving," George Gordon, Lord Byron, p. 701	Understanding figurative language*		Understanding word origins*	

The Romantic Age (continued)

Selection	Analyzing Literature	Critical Thinking and Reading	Understanding Language/ Speaking and Listening	Thinking and Writing
from *Childe Harold's Pilgrimage,* "Apostrophe to the Ocean," George Gordon, Lord Byron, p. 702	Understanding figurative language			Evaluating a poem
from *Don Juan,* George Gordon, Lord Byron, p. 707	Understanding the mock-epic*	Analyzing technique in relation to meaning*		Writing about the Byronic hero
"Ozymandias," Percy Bysshe Shelley, p. 712	Understanding poetic structure*			
"Ode to the West Wind," Percy Bysshe Shelley, p. 714	Understanding the ode	Recognizing author's style*		Comparing and contrasting nature views
"To a Skylark," Percy Bysshe Shelley, p. 718				
"To—," Percy Bysshe Shelley, p. 722				
"A Dirge," Percy Bysshe Shelley, p. 723				
"On First Looking into Chapman's Homer," John Keats, p. 726	Understanding the sonnet*	Recognizing poetic forms*	Selecting music to accompany a poem	Comparing and contrasting sonnets
"Bright Star, Would I Were Steadfast as Thou Art," John Keats, p. 728				
"When I Have Fears That I May Cease to Be," John Keats, p. 729				Comparing and contrasting odes
"Ode to a Nightingale," John Keats, p. 731	Using imagery*	Comparing rhyme schemes*		
"Ode on a Grecian Urn," John Keats, p. 736				
"To Autumn," John Keats, p. 739				
Prose				
Introduction to *Frankenstein,* Mary Wollstonecraft Shelley, p. 744	Recognizing Gothic tradition*		Understanding Greek and Latin roots*	Writing in the Gothic tradition

The Romantic Age (continued)

Selection	Analyzing Literature	Critical Thinking and Reading	Understanding Language Speaking and Listening	Thinking and Writing
"Dream Children: A Reverie," Charles Lamb, p. 750	Understanding the familiar essay*	Inferring tone	Understanding the multiple meanings of words*	Analyzing a writer's attitudes
"Macbeth," William Hazlitt, p. 756	Understanding a critical essay*	Finding main ideas	Completing word analogies*	Evaluating literary criticism
from *Pride and Prejudice,* Jane Austen, p. 762	Understanding the novel	Viewing a novel as a mirror of society*	Using context clues*	Writing fiction

The Victorian Age

Selection	Analyzing Literature	Critical Thinking and Reading	Understanding Language/ Speaking and Listening	Thinking and Writing
Reading Critically				
"Ulysses," Alfred, Lord Tennyson, p. 791	Understanding dramatic monologues Understanding the speaker in poetry*	Understanding a character's motivation	Choosing the meaning that fits the context*	Writing a continuation of the poem
"The Lady of Shalott," Alfred, Lord Tennyson, p. 798 "Tears, Idle Tears," Alfred, Lord Tennyson, p. 804 "The Splendor Falls," Alfred, Lord Tennyson, p. 806	Recognizing meter and stanza structure*	Understanding the author's purpose*	Fitting the context	Describing the poet's style
from *In Memoriam, A.H.H.,* Alfred, Lord Tennyson, p. 809	Understanding an elegy	Making inferences about the subject Making inferences about the subject of an elegy*	Appreciation vivid verbs* Finding antonyms	Writing about symbols
"The Lotos-Eaters," Alfred, Lord Tennyson, p. 813	Recognizing symbols	Recognizing allusions		
"Crossing the Bar," Alfred, Lord Tennyson, p. 820		Comparing attitudes		

(This chart continues on page 1466.)

PRENTICE HALL
LITERATURE
THE ENGLISH TRADITION

PRENTICE HALL

LITERATURE

BRONZE

Annotated Teacher's Edition
Teaching Portfolio
Novel Study Guides

SILVER

Annotated Teacher's Edition
Teaching Portfolio
Novel Study Guides

GOLD

Annotated Teacher's Edition
Teaching Portfolio
Novel Study Guides

PLATINUM

Annotated Teacher's Edition
Teaching Portfolio
Novel Study Guides

THE AMERICAN EXPERIENCE

Annotated Teacher's Edition
Teaching Portfolio
Novel Study Guides

THE ENGLISH TRADITION

Annotated Teacher's Edition
Teaching Portfolio
Novel Study Guides

iii

Master Teacher Board

Roger Babusci
(Pennsylvania Teacher of the Year, 1983)
Schenley High School
Pittsburgh, Pennsylvania

Loutish Burns
(Houston Teacher of the Year, 1986)
Louie Welch Middle School
Houston, Texas

Guy Doud
(National Teacher of the Year, 1986)
Brainerd Senior High School
Brainerd, Minnesota

Terri Fields
(Arizona Teacher of the Year, 1986)
Sunnyside High School
Phoenix, Arizona

Kermeen Fristrom
(1985 Distinguished Service Award of Merit, California)
San Diego City Schools
San Diego, California

Leroy Hay
(National Teacher of the Year, 1983)
Manchester High School
Manchester, Connecticut

Beth Johnson
(Florida Teacher of the Year, 1982)
Kathleen Senior High School
Lakeland, Florida

Evaline Kruse
(California Teacher of the Year, 1985)
Audubon Junior High School
Los Angeles, California

Jane McKee
(West Virginia Teacher of the Year, 1986)
Man High School
Man, West Virginia

Robert Seney
(Texas Curriculum Association's Exemplary Showcase Award for Literature)
Albright Middle School
Houston, Texas

Pat Weaver
(1986 National Outstanding Dissertation for Curriculum)
Arlington Independent School District
Arlington, Texas

Consultants

Jack Armistead
University of Tennessee
Knoxville, Tennessee

Joan Baron
University of Connecticut
Storrs, Connecticut

Charles Cooper
University of California
San Diego, California

Wilfred Dvorak
University of Rhode Island
Kingston, Rhode Island

Nancy Spivey
Carnegie-Mellon Institute
Pittsburgh, Pennsylvania

Contributing Writers

Frances Earle
former English teacher
Miralest High School
Palos Verdes, California

Cosmo Ferraro
former English teacher
Riverdell High School
Oradell, New Jersey

Marcia Muth
former English teacher
Glendora High School
Glendora, California

Howard Portnoy
former English teacher
Boston Latin School
Boston, Massachusetts

Gerald Tomlinson
former English teacher
Horseheads Jr. High School
Horseheads, New York

iv

PRENTICE HALL

LITERATURE

THE ENGLISH TRADITION

 PRENTICE HALL, Englewood Cliffs, New Jersey 07632

ISBN 0-13-698648-0

10 9 8 7 6 5 4 3 2 1

Art credits begin on page 1460.

COVER AND TITLE PAGE: **SUMMER**, John Atkinson Grimshaw, Art Resource

PRENTICE HALL
A Division of Simon & Schuster
Englewood Cliffs, New Jersey 07632

ACKNOWLEDGMENTS

Grateful acknowledgment is made to the following for permission to reprint copyrighted material:

Edward Arnold (Publishers) Ltd.
"The Helping Hand" from *The Life to Come and Other Stories* by E. M. Forster. Copyright © 1972 The Trustees of the Late E. M. Forster.

Jonathan Cape Ltd. and the Estate of Henry Reed
"Naming of Parts" from *A Map of Verona* by Henry Reed, 1946.

Carcanet Press Ltd.
"November Sun" from *Selected Poems* by Elizabeth Daryush, 1972. Reprinted by permission of Carcanet Press Ltd.

Doubleday & Company, Inc.
"The Lagoon" from *Tales of Unrest* by Joseph Conrad, Doubleday, Page & Company.

Faber and Faber Ltd.
"Days" from *The Whitsum Weddings* by Philip Larkin. Copyright © 1960, 1961, 1962, 1964 by Philip Larkin. "Sunday Morning" and "The Sunlight on the Garden" from *The Collected Poems of Louis MacNeice* by Louis MacNeice. Copyright © the Estate of Louis MacNeice 1966. Reprinted by permission of Faber and Faber Ltd.

Farrar, Straus and Giroux, Inc. and Faber and Faber Ltd.
"Taylor Street" from *Selected Poems 1950–1975* by Thom Gunn. Copyright © 1957, 1958, 1961, 1967, 1971, 1973, 1974, 1975, 1976, 1979 by Thom Gunn. Published in London in *Touch* by Thom Gunn. "Follower" and "Shore Woman" from *Poems 1965–1975* by Seamus Heaney. Copyright © 1966, 1969, 1972, 1975, 1980 by Seamus Heaney. "Follower" published in London in *Death of a Naturalist* by Seamus Heaney, and "Shore Woman" published in London in *Wintering Out* by Seamus Heaney. "The Explosion" from *High Windows* by Philip Larkin. Copyright © 1974 by Philip Larkin. Reprinted by permission of the publishers.

Hamish Hamilton Ltd.
Lines from "In the Beck" from *The Collected Poems of Kathleen Raine*. Copyright © 1956 by Kathleen Raine. Reprinted by permission of Hamish Hamilton Ltd.

Harcourt Brace Jovanovich, Inc. and Faber and Faber Ltd.
"The Hollow Men," "Journey of the Magi," and "Preludes" from *Collected Poems 1909–1962* by T. S. Eliot, copyright 1935, 1936 by Harcourt Brace Jovanovich, Inc.; copyright © 1964 by T. S. Eliot. Reprinted by permission of the publishers.

Harcourt Brace Jovanovich, Inc., A. M. Heath & Company Ltd., the Estate of the Late Sonia Brownell Orwell, and Secker & Warburg Ltd.
"Shooting an Elephant" from *Shooting an Elephant and Other Essays* by George Orwell, copyright 1950 by Sonia Brownell Orwell; renewed 1978 by Sonia Pitt-Rivers. Reprinted by permission.

Harcourt Brace Jovanovich, Inc., The Hogarth Press Ltd., and the author's Estate
"The Lady in the Looking Glass: A Reflection" from *The Complete Shorter Fiction of Virginia Woolf* edited by Susan Dick, copyright © 1985 by Quentin Bell and Angelica Garnett. Reprinted by permission.

Harper & Row, Publishers, Inc.
"Woman" from *The Works of Oliver Goldsmith* edited by Peter Cunningham, Harper & Brothers. "The Horses" from *New Selected Poems* by Ted Hughes. Copyright © 1957 by Ted Hughes. Reprinted by permission of Harper & Row, Publishers, Inc.

(continued on page 1458)

vi

CONTENTS

THE ANGLO-SAXON PERIOD
449–1066

THE MEDIEVAL PERIOD
1066–1485

THE ENGLISH RENAISSANCE
1485–1625

THE SEVENTEENTH CENTURY
1625–1660

The Schools of Donne and Jonson

The Puritan Age

viii

THE RESTORATION AND THE EIGHTEENTH CENTURY
1660–1798

The Restoration

The Age of Pope and Swift

The Age of Johnson

Pre-Romantic Poetry

THE ROMANTIC AGE
1798–1832

THE VICTORIAN AGE
1833–1901

x

THE MODERN PERIOD
1901–1945

xi

Poetry

Drama

CONTEMPORARY WRITERS
1945–PRESENT

Prose

Poetry

xiii

PRENTICE HALL
LITERATURE
THE ENGLISH TRADITION

BAYEUX TAPESTRY: NORMAN CAVALRY CHARGE AT THE SHIELDWALL AT THE BATTLE OF HASTINGS
The Granger Collection

THE ANGLO-SAXON PERIOD
449–1066

When Angles and Saxons came hither from the east,
Sought Britain over the broad-spreading sea,
Haughty war-smiths overcame the Britons,
Valiant earls got for themselves a home.

from The Anglo-Saxon Chronicle

Humanities Note

Fine art, *The Bayeux Tapestry: The Norman cavalry charge at the shield-wall of the Battle of Hastings.* Made about 1080, the famous Bayeux Tapestry illustrates the story of the Norman Conquest of England. It is an embroidered wool on linen tapestry, 20 inches high and 230 feet long, which now hangs in the Town Hall at Bayeux, France. This segment of the tapestry portrays the charge of Norman horsemen at the Battle of Hastings. The Saxons are on foot, while the Normans hurl their lances from horseback. That the Normans were on horseback clearly gave them an advantage. As with all of the segments of this chronicle, this battle scene is illustrated with a wonderful liveliness. The designer has integrated narrative and ornament in telling the story of William the Conqueror's invasion of England. The Bayeux Tapestry is one of the best extant examples of the art of the Middle Ages.

1 **Enrichment** Because the Angles were the most numerous of the Germanic invaders, they gave their name to both the country and the language.

The passage on the previous page comes from a modern translation of *The Anglo-Saxon Chronicle,* an early record of English history. It tells of the attacks staged by warriors from Denmark and Germany on the rock-bound coast of Britain during the fifth century. Most of the fierce "war-smiths" identified themselves as Angles and Saxons, though some belonged to a smaller tribe, the Jutes. At first these pirates sailed their shallow boats across the "broad-spreading" North Sea to raid Britain's low-lying eastern coast. By A.D. 449, however, their raids had turned into a full-scale invasion.

The arrival of the Anglo-Saxons in Britain signaled the beginning of the English language. The "war-smiths" soon drove native Britons from the eastern, central, and southern portions of their island. Those areas became known as "Angles' land," or England. The
1 closely related Germanic languages spoken by the conquering tribes developed into a new language called "Angle-ish," or English. Although that language would change a great deal over the centuries, it was the ancestor of the English we speak today. As the language took shape, so did the literature of Britain, including that of Ireland, Scotland, and Wales.

To put these early times into historical perspective, we must first examine the people whom the Angles and Saxons conquered, the settlers of Britain before 449. As you read about this period, you may want to consult the map on page 000 to locate unfamiliar geographical details.

BRITAIN BEFORE THE ANGLO-SAXONS

British historian G. M. Trevelyan has compared his country's early history to a battle scene from Shakespeare's *Macbeth* (see page 223): "Prophecy hovers around. Horns are heard blowing in the mist, and a confused uproar of savage tumult and outrage. We catch glimpses of giant figures—mostly warriors at strife. But there are ploughmen, too, it seems, breaking the primeval clod, and we hear the sound of forests crashing to the axe. Around all is the lap of waves and the cry of seamen beaching their ships."

Who were these early warriors and ploughmen? The answer is not entirely clear, for some of them arrived in Britain in the dim recesses before recorded time. Among them were Iberians from present-day Spain and Portugal, who brought late Stone Age weapons to Britain's shores. The last, and by far the most important, of the early conquerors were the Celts, a people from southern Europe who had gradually migrated west. Between 800 and 600 B.C., two groups of Celts invaded the British Isles.

Arrival of the Celts

One group, who called themselves Brythons (now spelled "Britons"), settled on the largest island, Britain. The other, known as Gaels, settled on the second largest island, known to us as Ireland.

Gaels and Britons spoke different but related languages of the Celtic family. Celtic languages had nothing in common with the Germanic ones later associated with the Angles and Saxons. 2

The Celts were farmers and hunters. They organized themselves into tightly knit clans, each with a fearsome loyalty to its chieftain. When these clans fell into argument with one another, they often looked to a class of priests known as Druids to settle their disputes. Druids presided over religious rituals including sacrifices and prayers. They also had, as their duty, the memorizing and reciting of long, heroic poems that preserved the people's myths about the past. Some of the poems may have included fables about such leaders as Old King Cole of the nursery rhyme and King Lear of Shakespeare's tragic play.

RELIGIOUS CEREMONY OF THE DRUIDS
Forrest C. Crooks
Three Lions

Humanities Note

Fine art, *Religious Ceremony of the Druids,* by Forrest C. Crooks. Forrest C. Crooks (1893–1962) was an American illustrator, who lived in New York City and was active in the 1930's.

The Druids were the priestly, learned class of the ancient Celts. The subject of this illustration is a Druid ceremony. Elements of ritual are suggested by the darkness, the fire, and the bone. Especially prominent in the foreground of the scene are an oak tree and some mistletoe, which the Celts regarded as sacred.

2 **Enrichment** Although the Celtic and the Germanic languages were very different, both belong to the Indo-European language family; that is, there are some similarities in grammar, sound structure, and vocabulary.

BRITISH EVENTS

B.C.	
c. 8000	Celtics begin migrating to British Isles.
c. 2000	Stonehenge built.
55	Julius Ceasar invades Britain.
A.D.	
43	Britain made a Roman province.
407	Romans withdraw from Britain.
432	St. Patrick begins missionary work in Ireland.
449	Anglo-Saxon invasion.
537	Death of the legendary hero, King Arthur.
597	St. Augustine founds Christian monastery at Canterbury, Kent.
664	Synod of Whitbyu establishes Roman Church in England.
731	**Bede** completes *Ecclesiastical History of the English Church and People*.
c. 750	Surviving version of *Beowulf* composed.
792	Vikings attack Lindisfarne.
843	Scottish Ruler Kenneth MacAlprin unites Scots and Picts.
886	Truce with Danes establishes Saxon rule in south and Danish rule in east and north.
c. 930	Howel the Good unites kingdom of Wales.
c. 975	Saxon monks copy Old English poems into *Exeter Book*.
991	English defeated by Danes at Battle of Maldon.
1002	Brian Boru unites Kingdom of Ireland.
1034	Duncan I inherits Scottish throne.
1040	Macbeth murders Duncan I.
1042	Edward the Confessor becomes king of Saxons.
1066	Normans defeat Saxons; William the Conqueror becomes king of England.

Stonehenge

St. Augustine

Buddha Addressing

A Viking Sword

Danes Attacking a British Town

The Coronation of

A Roman Town After the Fall of the Empire

a Disciple

Charles Martel Battling the Moors

William the Conqueror

King Charlemagne

WORLD EVENTS

476 Western Europe: Fall of Western Roman Empire.

493 Italy: Thodoric the Great establishes Ostrogothic kingdom.

496 France: Clovis, King of Franks, converts to Christianity.

542 Eastern Europe: Plague kills half the population.

c. 550 Mexico: Toltecs defeat Mayas.

552 Japan: Buddhism introduced.

591 China: Beginning of book printing.

637 Middle East: Jerusalem conquered by Arabs.

641 Egypt: Library at Alexandria destroyed.

712 Spain: Seville conquered by Moors.

732 France: Charles Martel defeats Moors.

771 France: Charlemagne becomes king.

800 Peru: Incas build city of Machu Picchu.

c. 810 Persia: Algebra devised.

c. 821 France: Einhard writes *Life of Charlemagne*.

c. 855 Russia: Nation founded by Vikings.

861 North Atlantic: Vikings discover Iceland.

c. 900 Western Europe: Feudalism developed.

911 France: Normans establish Normandy.

982 Greenland: Eric the Red establishes first Viking colony.

c. 1000 North America: Viking explorer Leif Ericson explores Canadian coast.

1009 Middle East: Moslems destroy Holy Sepulchre in Jerusalem.

1045 Spain: Birth of El Cid, national hero who fought Moors.

1053 Italy: Normans conquer Sicily.

Humanities Note

Insignia of the Roman civil governor in charge of five British provinces. This illustration is from an early fifteenth-century copy of a page from the now-lost *Notitia Dignitatum Utriusque Imperii,* a fourth-century list of imperial magistrates, adorned with the symbols of their provinces. The design is roughly the shape of the island of Britain, with the symbols placed on the location of the provinces.

3 **Enrichment** These Roman camps, *castra,* gave their names to many English towns, in fact, all those whose names presently end in "caster," "cester," and "chester," such as Winchester and Lancaster.

4 **Historical Context** The Britons did not cede their country to the Germanic invaders without some struggle. The semi-legendary King Arthur organized a spirited resistance and presumably fought twelve successful battles against the Anglo-Saxons, the last of which occurred at Mount Badon, sometime between the years 490 and 503. An excerpt from Sir Thomas Malory's *Morte Darthur* appears in the next unit, on page 65.

INSIGNIA OF THE ROMAN CIVIL GOVERNOR IN CHARGE OF THE FIVE BRITISH PROVINCES
An Early 15th-Century Copy of a Page from the Now-Lost Notitia Dignitatum Utriusque Imperii, a 4th-Century List of Imperial Magistrates, Adorned with the Symbols of their Provinces
The Granger Collection

The Roman Conquest

The next conquerors of Britain were the far more sophisticated Romans. In 55 B.C. and again the next year, the Roman general Julius Caesar made hasty invasions. Although he barely penetrated the island, he quickly declared it conquered and returned to what is now France to work on his memoirs. The true conquest of Britain occurred nearly one hundred years later during the reign of the
3 Roman emperor Claudius. Disciplined Roman legions spread out over the island, establishing camps, which soon grew into towns.

The Romans transplanted many comforts of their urban, Mediterranean culture to the distant, rain-drenched north. In perhaps their greatest contribution, they constructed a system of well-paved roads through the woodland wilderness, highways that continued to link the island for centuries. The Romans also brought with them their skills in the art of warfare. Yet they apparently failed to teach the Britons much about self-defense.

The Roman rule of Britain lasted for more than 300 years. It ended only when northern European tribes invaded Italy and increased pressure on Rome itself. The last Roman legions departed from Britain to defend Rome in A.D. 407. By that time, some of
4 their towns were already falling to ruin, and the Britons were easy prey for a new set of invaders.

THE ANGLO-SAXON CONQUEST

As we have seen, the next invaders were the Anglo-Saxons. Who were these ancient people? Lacking authentic first-hand accounts from the period, historians simply have to guess. Some Anglo-Saxons appear to have been deep-sea fishermen, already accustomed to marauding coasts along the Baltic Sea. Others seem to have been farmers, perhaps seeking soil richer than the sandy or marshy land at home. Ferocious as the Angles and Saxons may have been, they did not perform their piracy merely for plunder—at least not for long. They sought and won territory, apparently by rowing their shallow boats up river into the British heartland and then building camps and waging war on the Britons. Gradually the newcomers gained the upper hand over the island's settlers and took over more and more of what today is England.

Early Anglo-Saxon Life

The first Angles, Saxons, and Jutes transferred to England their highly organized tribal units. Each tribe was ruled by a king, chosen by a *witan,* or council of elders. Each community had four distinct classes. The *earls* were a hereditary class of ruling warlords who owed their position to the king. The second class, *freemen,* were allowed to own land and engage in commerce. (This class included *thanes,* early barons, who were granted their status as a reward for

military service.) Lower on the social scale were *churls,* or serfs, 5
bonded servants who worked the land in return for military protection. Lowest of all were *thralls,* or slaves, usually military prisoners or people being punished.

Invading groups set up numerous small kingdoms, and at first the various kingdoms fought frequently. As time went on, however, many of these tribal differences faded. Anglo-Saxon kingdoms traded with one another. Men married women from different tribes. Kingdoms gradually absorbed one another until seven larger ones remained. As previously mentioned, all this intermingling produced a new language. We call it Anglo-Saxon or Old English to distinguish it from our modern form.

Anglo-Saxon Beliefs

The Anglo-Saxons brought to Britain their own pagan beliefs. In
the world of the sixth century, the ever-present dangers of death by 6
accident or warfare had led these people to take a rather grim view of life. In fact, the early Anglo-Saxons believed that every human life was in the hands of fate. Their attitude was sharply different from the

5 **Master Teacher Note** In anticipation of the study of Shakespeare's *Macbeth,* point out to students that the early barons or *thanes* are the chief characters in this play, written in Elizabethan England but set in Anglo-Saxon Scotland.

6 **Historical Context** The notion of the Anglo-Saxon as a crude, insular, and barbaric people was largely belied by the discovery in 1939 of a seventh-century royal burial site at Sutton Hoo in East Anglia. Artifacts found there suggest a heroic society rich in gold and craftsmanship with evidence of far-flung trading contacts. These artifacts are on display at the British Museum.

Humanities Note

Illumination, *Saxons, Jutes, and Angles arriving in Britain by sea.* Illumination was one of the earliest forms of book illustration. The illuminator, the "one who lightens up" a manuscript, refers to the artist who decorated the manuscripts that were produced in monasteries of the time. Many such illuminations are elaborate decorations of capital letters and marginal spaces, but others, like this one, illustrate scenes. This simple, stylized drawing represents the ships of the Anglo-Saxon invaders against whom the Britons were unable to defend themselves.

7 **Literary Movement** This fatalistic attitude characteristic of the Anglo-Saxons is evident both in *Beowulf* (page 24) with its frequent references to Wyrd and in "The Seafarer" (page 17).

8 **Master Teacher Note** To demonstrate the multi-cultural influences on our calendar, you might ask students to research the origins of the other days of the week.

9 **Historical Context** Columba, exiled from Ireland and remorseful because he had killed three thousand pagans in battle, settled with eleven followers on the first island from which he could no longer see his beloved native land. This island was Iona.

10 **Master Teacher Note** In anticipation of *Macbeth,* point out that Iona is the Columkille mentioned in the text, the burial place of Scottish kings.

SAXONS, JUTES, AND ANGLES ARRIVING IN BRITAIN BY SEA
English Manuscript Illumination
The Granger Collection

7 Christian belief in the freedom of an individual to determine his or her own path.

The early Anglo-Saxons worshiped ancient Germanic gods. They included Tiu, god of war and the sky; Woden, chief of the gods; and Fria, Woden's wife and goddess of the home. These gods were abandoned with the coming of Christianity. Even so, their names
8 survive in our words *Tuesday, Wednesday,* and *Friday.*

Dispersal of the Britons

In terror of the Anglo-Saxons, the Britons retreated to the edges of their island—and beyond. Some went to Cornwall on the southwestern tip of Britain, an area that remained Celtic long after the rest of the island was Anglo-Saxon. Others fled to Britain's hilly western region, an area that become known as Wales. Still other joined the Gaels of Ireland where they formed a splinter group named Scots (from *Scotia,* the Roman word for Ireland). This group then traveled back to Britain and settled in the northern part of the island, Scotland. In all these areas, people spoke Celtic languages—Cornish, Welsh, and Irish and Scottish Gaelic—until modern times. All but Cornish are still spoken today.

THE COMING OF CHRISTIANITY

During the fourth century, the Romans had accepted Christianity and introduced it to Britain. A century later, when the Celts fled the Anglo-Saxons, they took their Christian faith with them. During this period, the faith lived on in Wales. From there it spread to Ireland, assisted by the activities of the legendary St. Patrick.

After Rome fell to barbarian tribes in A.D. 476, communications weakened between Celtic and Roman Christians. While the Roman Church was recovering from political chaos, the Celtic Christian Church continued to thrive. In 563 a group of Irish monks set sail in tiny skiffs for the west coast of Scotland. Led by a soldier and abbot
9, 10 named Columba, they established a Christian monastery on the island of Iona. From this headquarters, Columba and his monks moved across northern Britain in the hope of winning additional souls for the faith. In their travels, they won ready acceptance among many Scots; then among some Saxons and Angles. Their conversions led, in turn, to the establishment of other monasteries in the north.

Resurgence of the Roman Church

Meanwhile, the Roman Church had reorganized itself and was beginning to send missionaries throughout Europe. In 597, the

Roman cleric Saint Augustine (not the famous scholar) arrived in southeast England and quickly converted King Ethelbert of Kent to Christianity. Augustine set up a monastery at Canterbury in Kent and began preaching his faith to other rulers in southern England. To win over a kingdom, Augustine and his followers needed only to convert the king, who would then make Christianity the religion of his realm. By the year 650, they had largely succeeded. Most of England was Christian in name, if not in fact.

The new religion had a profound effect on Anglo-Saxon civilization. It softened the ferocity of a warrior people and improved the conduct of the faithful. No longer could ruling warlords indulge themselves in the belief that they had descended from pagan gods. No longer could freemen think it permissible to treat their wives or children or slaves with cruelty. Christian clerics were now able to end old feuds by denouncing revenge and calling upon a higher law. By providing counsel to quarreling rulers, the church promoted peace and played a major role in unifying the English people.

Christianity and Literature

The church also brought to England two elements of civilization that had been missing since the departure of the Romans: education and written literature. Christian leaders established schools at Canterbury and York and supervised the preservation of learning in the island's monasteries. Within their secluded halls, monks often worked as scribes, recording and duplicating *manuscripts,* or books written by hand. At first they worked only in Latin, the language of church scholarship. Often several monks labored for years to complete a single manuscript. These volumes were elaborately painted and illuminated in gold and silver.

From such monastic training emerged a Northumbrian monk later considered the "father of English history." Today we know him as the Venerable Bede (673–735). Bede was a master of thorough research, tracking down information by studying earlier documents and interviewing people who had witnessed or taken part in past events. His most famous volume was *Ecclesiastical History of the English People,* a monumental work that offers the clearest account we have of early Anglo-Saxon times.

Although Christianity did indeed temper Anglo-Saxon civilization, it did not destroy the northerners' spirit. Glimpses of an earlier world lived on in the fragments of epics such as *Beowulf,* a long, narrative poem that depicted great battles between Anglo-Saxon warriors and superhuman monsters. The Anglo-Saxons remained a hardy group, fearless and loyal in their instincts even if less and less predatory in their habits. Now they were about to come face to face with a new peril from a people much like themselves— invasion by the Vikings.

AN ENGLISH MONK EXACTLY CONTEMPORARY WITH BEDE
Illumination from an early 8th-century Northumbrian Codex
The Granger Collection

Humanities Note

Illumination, *An English monk contemporary with Bede.* In the Dark Ages, classical learning and art were preserved in monasteries by monks, like the one pictured in this illumination, who copied manuscripts and illustrated them. This illumination, which is from an eighth-century Northumbrian Codex, or vellum manuscript, enables the viewer to envision Bede at work on his history.

Humanities Note

The ninth-century Oseberg Viking Ship. During the period from the 700's to the 1000's, the Vikings built the best ships in northern Europe. They are known for their long ships, of which this ship from Oseberg, Norway, is an example. These swift, light ships sailed well on rough seas or calm waters, enabling the Vikings to cross the North Atlantic to Greenland and North America, as well as to make their devastating raids on Britain. The prow of Viking warships curved gracefully upward and ended with a woodcarving of the head of a dragon or a snake. Possibly these heads were more than just decoration. There were laws among the Norwegian Vikings that required the captain of a ship to remove these figures before entering his home port, "so as not to frighten the spirits of the land."

THE FIRST DANISH INVASION

Between the eighth and twelfth centuries, a great restlessness overtook the region of northern Europe known as Scandinavia. Beset with a rising population and limited farmland, the people of Norway, the Norse, and of Denmark, the Danes, followed old traditions and took to the seas. In some of their most adventurous voyages, the Vikings (warriors) carried their piracy to the British Isles. The Norse set their sights on Northumbria, Scotland, Wales, and Ireland, whereas the Danes targeted eastern and southern England.

Viking Raids

Viking invaders sacked and plundered monasteries, destroyed manuscripts, and stole sacred religious objects. They burned entire communities and put villagers to the sword. Wherever the Vikings went, the sight of their square-sailed ships stirred specters of terror and destruction. One Anglo-Saxon prayer of the day reflected the fear that the Danish pirates inspired: "From the fury of the Northmen, O Lord, deliver us."

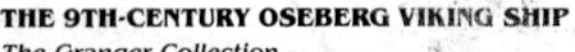

THE 9TH-CENTURY OSEBERG VIKING SHIP
The Granger Collection

Although the English fought back valiantly, the Danes made broad inroads. By the middle of the ninth century, most of northern, eastern, and central England had fallen to the invaders. They called their territory the Danelaw. Only the Saxon kingdom of Wessex managed to fight the Danes to a standstill.

Alfred the Great

In 871 a king ascended to the Wessex throne who would become the only ruler in England's history ever to be honored with the epithet "the Great." His name was Alfred, and he earned the title partly by resisting further Danish encroachment. Under a truce concluded in 886, England was formally divided: the Saxons acknowledged Danish rule in the east and north, but the Danes agreed to respect Saxon rule in the south. As the king of a much-expanded Wessex, Alfred the Great became a national hero.

Alfred's achievements went far beyond the field of battle, however. Not only was he instrumental in preserving the remnants of pre-Danish civilization in Britain, but he encouraged a rebirth of learning and education. To make literature and other documents more readily available, he himself translated Bede's *History* and other works from Latin into Anglo-Saxon, the everyday language of the people. In this way he fostered the growth of the English language and its literature. He also began to keep records of English history in *The Anglo-Saxon Chronicle,* today among our principal sources of information on early English life.

ALFRED THE GREAT ACKNOWLEDGED AS KING BY ALL MEN OF ENGLAND, 871 A.D.
Three Lions

PAGE FROM AN EARLY 12TH-CENTURY MANUSCRIPT OF THE *ANGLO-SAXON CHRONICLE* DESCRIBING THE NORMAN CONQUEST
The Granger Collection

Danish Contributions

Gradually the Danes became more peaceful, and old animosities subsided. A once war-obsessed people settled into the workaday world of farming, beer-brewing, and moving goods to market. Even before their arrival in England, many Danes had been accustomed to the merchant's trade, however crudely it may have existed in northern Europe at the time. Now they built their Danelaw communities not only as military fortresses but as trading centers, and one result was the growth of English towns.

Like the Anglo-Saxons, the Danes spoke a Germanic language, so they were able to communicate easily with the English. In fact,
11 many Norse words slowly crept into the English vocabulary. The word *law* is Danish, for example. Its use reflected the Danes' interest in legal procedures.

THE SECOND DANISH INVASION AND NORMAN CONQUEST

The peace and stability that began with Alfred's reign lasted more than a century. Immigration from Scandinavia dwindled, and

Humanities Note

Alfred the Great Acknowledged as King by All Men of England, 871 A.D. This anonymous print shows Alfred becoming king of the West Saxons. He later became known as "the Great" for his achievements. He resisted the attacks of the Danes, and in the treaty of Wedmore in 878, concluded an arrangement with Guthrum, the principal Danish leader, which effectively ended the Danish raids and brought peace to the island. Education had declined because the Danes had looted the monasteries and churches; therefore, Alfred brought learned men and teachers to Wessex from other parts of Britain and Europe. Alfred died in 899.

Humanities Note

Page from an early twelfth-century manuscript of the *Anglo-Saxon Chronicle.* One of Alfred the Great's achievements was the record he kept of current events, called the *Anglo-Saxon Chronicle.* After his death, the *Chronicle* was continued until 1154. This page, describing the Norman conquest, is typical in its illuminated decorations. The decoration of this secular work indicates that works other than religious ones were also being illustrated.

11 **Enrichment** Another Danish contribution is in the place-name suffix *by,* from the Old Norse *byr* for "town." The names of approximately six hundred towns in northern England still end this way.

Humanities Note

The Bayeux Tapestry: Edward the Confessor Speaks to Harold of Wessex. This segment of the famous Bayeux Tapestry shows Edward speaking to Harold, Earl of Wessex. When Edward died in 1066 without a direct heir to the throne, the English nobles chose Harold to succeed him. In the Norman invasion, Harold was killed and his forces defeated in the Battle of Hastings. Edward's gentle disposition and religious leanings are evident in this detail.

12 **Enrichment** The Normans were originally "Northmen," but their language was essentially Latin in origin rather than Germanic.

the descendants of Alfred the Great were able to regain much conquered territory. Toward the close of the tenth century, however, a new series of onslaughts began as more Danes from Europe attempted to recapture and widen the Danelaw. Once they had succeeded, they forced the Saxon witan to select a succession of Danish kings.

Edward the Confessor and the Normans

Then, in 1042, the line of succession returned to a descendant of Alfred the Great. This king, Edward, had gained the nickname "the Confessor" because he was a deeply religious Christian. He had spent many of his early years in Normandy, a region once
12 settled by Scandinavians and now a part of France. Norman on his
mother's side, Edward had developed a close friendship with his cousin William, Normandy's ruler. Once Edward took the English throne, his association with the Normans further weakened Saxon power. His death in 1066 led directly to a Norman conquest of England and brought the end of the Anglo-Saxon period of literature, as we shall see in the next unit.

ANGLO-SAXON LITERATURE

Scholars now believe that the literature of the British Isles began with Celtic Druids. These priests assumed the function of storytellers, memorizing and reciting long, heroic poems about Celtic leaders and their deeds. In the same way, Anglo-Saxon literature began not with books, but with spoken verse and incantations. Their purpose was to pass along tribal history and values to an audience that could not read.

To be sure, some Anglo-Saxons were familiar with the written word. In the third century in northern Europe, they had devised an alphabet of letters called runes. When they came to Britain, they brought this alphabet with them and used it until the Latin alphabet we have today superseded it. Yet they employed runes chiefly for inscriptions on important buildings, on statues, and the like. Few early Anglo-Saxons could read or write.

THE BAYEUX TAPESTRY: EDWARD THE CONFESSOR SPEAKS TO HAROLD OF WESSEX
The Granger Collection

Origins of Anglo-Saxon Poetry

The reciting of poems often occurred on ceremonial occasions such as the celebration of a military victory. A warrior's comrades would gather in his hall or castle, and the performance would begin. The performers were usually professional minstrels, known as *scops*, and their assistants, called *gleemen*. The scops and gleemen recited for hours and, in some instances, even for days.

Scholars now suppose that these recitations took place to the accompaniment of a harp. The poems followed a set formula of composition, which probably made them easier to memorize. A formal, rigid pattern of word stresses gave the lyrics a terse, sing-song effect. A mid-line pause, called a *caesura,* occurred in many lines. Another part of the pattern was *alliteration,* the repetition of sounds, especially initial consonant sounds.

Types of Anglo-Saxon Verse

Only about 30,000 lines of Anglo-Saxon verse still exist. Almost all of it is found in four works dating from about A.D. 975 to 1050. The early verse falls mainly into two categories. One is heroic poetry, which recounts the achievements of warriors involved in great battles. The other is elegiac poetry, sorrowful laments that mourn the deaths of loved ones and the loss of the past.

Copied many years after their probable composition, the poems have obviously undergone many changes. Later scops may have adapted them, and so may have monastic scribes. Nevertheless, pagan elements remain, particularly in the ever-present sense of an ominous fate, or *wyrd.* Consider, for example, these lines from one of the elegiac poems, "The Wanderer":

> He then, wise in soul, with weighty
> thought thinks deeply upon this dark-
> some life, this fallen fastness. . . .

The Beowulf Legend

Of the heroic poetry, the most important work is *Beowulf,* the story of a great pagan warrior renowned for his courage, strength, and dignity. *Beowulf* is an *epic,* a long heroic poem. Because it is the first such work to be composed in the English language, it is considered the national epic of England.

Like most Anglo-Saxon poets, the author of *Beowulf* is unknown. Although versions of the poem were probably recited as early as the sixth century, the text that we have today was composed in the eighth century and not written down until the eleventh. Thus, the poem includes many references to Christian ideas and Latin classics. Clearly evident in *Beowulf,* however, are the values of a warrior society, especially such values as dignity, bravery, and prowess in battle: 14

> And Beowulf was ready, firm with our
> Lord's
> High favor and his own bold courage and
> strength.

Emphasis on such values did not disappear in Christian times. It appeared in later Anglo-Saxon poems such as *The Battle of Maldon,* which commemorates a great military defeat to the Danes.

Poets of the Christian Era

Among the few known poets of the Christian era, two are worthy of mention—Caedmon and Cynewulf. Caedmon, who apparently

13 **Master Teacher Note** Besides these two characteristics of Anglo-Saxon poetry, you might cite other typical devices: the kenning, the four-beat line, the frequent reversal of word order. All these devices are evident in "The Seafarer," page 17, and in *Beowulf,* page 24.

14 **Historical Context** The dating of the present text has been narrowed down to the period between 680, the start of alliterative verse, and 835, the beginning of the Danish raids. After 835, such sympathetic treatment of the Danes would have been highly unlikely. The oldest extant copy, preserved in the British Museum, dates from the eleventh century.

Humanities Note

A page from the Caedmon manuscript, c. 1000. Caedmon was an English poet who lived in the late 600's. An uneducated herdsman, he entered the monastery at Whitby late in life. Bede reported in his *History* that Caedmon was commanded to sing the praises of God. He did so in what is now known as "Caedmon's Hymn." This beautifully illustrated page is from that manuscript.

15 **Enrichment** Caedmon, according to Bede, was a humble brother who tended the cows at Whitby Monastery and received divine inspiration for his poetry from a dream. He is generally regarded as the first English poet.

16 **Historical Context** Alfred's impact on English language and literature demonstrates only part of the effect this remarkable man had on ninth-century England. He dispatched diplomatic missions to fellow rulers, formulated a legal code, and established the first English "public schools."

A PAGE FROM THE CAEDMON MANUSCRIPT, c. 1000
The Granger Collection

lived in the seventh century, is mentioned in Bede's *History*. The poet's only authenticated verse consists of a few lines that Bede
15 recorded, called "Caedmon's Hymn." Nevertheless, the term *Caedmonian verse* is often used to identify other early Christian poetry in English. Scholars believe that Cynewulf lived around the turn of the ninth century. He is known because he "signed" his name, spelling it out in runes, on four poems that survive today.

Anglo-Saxon Prose

Before the reign of Alfred the Great, all important prose written in the British Isles was composed in Latin. The monks who transcribed these works regarded the vernacular, the language of the common people, as a "vulgar tongue." The greatest of England's Latin scholars was the Venerable Bede, as mentioned earlier. His *History* gives an account of England from the Roman invasion to his own time.

Bede's *History* concerns itself mostly with northern England, but it is not simply the story of Northumbria or the people who settled there. The monk couples his view of the Roman Church as a universal force with a distinctly nationalistic view of a unified English people. Although Bede wrote in Latin, his *History* may nevertheless be considered the first truly English prose work. From it we derive much of what we know about early Anglo-Saxon times.

Bede's successor as the leading English scholar was Alcuin (735–804), another monk who, like Bede, won fame throughout Europe. Trained at York, Alcuin traveled widely in Europe and eventually headed the palace school of the powerful European emperor Charlemagne. By the time of his death, Alcuin had produced many major works in philosophy, religion, and Latin grammar.

Alfred the Great and His Successors

Historians usually credit Alfred the Great with having changed
16 the course of British literature. The spur he gave to the English language was evident in its more widespread use among scholars after his death. Of these scholars, the foremost were Aelfric and Wulfstan, who lived in the second half of the tenth century. Aelfric, a monk of Wessex, wrote many works in the vernacular, including a series of *homilies,* or sermons, based on Bible stories. Though in prose, these sermons employ a great deal of the sort of alliteration more commonly associated with Anglo-Saxon poetry. Wulfstan, an archbishop of York, also wrote several sermons in Old English, including a famous speech on the devastation of the Danish raids.

After the Normans occupied England, they gradually transformed the English that the Anglo-Saxons spoke. Old English or Anglo-Saxon evolved into what we now call Middle English, whose literature we will explore in the next unit.

ENGLISH VOICES

Quotations by Prominent Figures of the Period

I sing of myself, a sorrowful woman.
Anonymous, "A Wife's Lament," translated by Kemp Malone

This tale is true, and mine. It tells
How the sea took me, swept me back
And forth, in sorrow and fear and pain.
Anonymous, "The Seafarer," translated by Burton Raffel

It is better never to begin a good work than, having begun it, to stop.
Bede, *Ecclesiastical History of the English People*

Out from the marsh, from the foot of misty
Hills and bogs, bearing God's hatred,
Grendel came.

Beowulf spoke, in spite of the swollen
Livid wound, knowing he'd unwound
His string of days on earth. . . .
My days
Have gone by as fate willed, waiting
For its word to be spoken.
Anonymous, *Beowulf*, translated by Burton Raffel

Light was first
Through the Lord's word
Named day:
Beauteous, bright creation!
Caedmon, *Creation. The First Day*, translated by Benjamin Thorpe

And those people should not be listened to who keep saying the voice of the people is the voice of God, since the riotousness of the crowd is always very close to madness.
Alcuin in a letter to Charlemagne

Alcuin was my name; learning I loved.
Alcuin in his own epitaph

Thought shall be the harder, heart the keener, courage the greater, as our might lessens.
Anonymous, *The Battle of Maldon*, translated by R. K. Gordon

Master Teacher Note You might show students Art Transparency 1, *Stonehenge*, by John Constable. 1776–1837. Constable is one of Britain's supreme landscape painters. This painting was produced around 1835. The arrangement of prehistoric monoliths that still stand on Salisbury Plain may be considered an enduring symbol of early England. What purpose the stones originally served has not yet been definitely established, though reasonable speculation includes religious rites and astronomical observations. You might ask your students to describe the mood the painting evokes. Ask them to tell what the monoliths may imply about the culture of prehistoric Britain.

Reading Critically The purpose of this feature is to help students place a work of literature in its historical context, understand the literary movements of the time, and appreciate the writers' techniques used to convey the ideas of the period.

Discuss the information on this page with your students. Explain that the selection that accompanies this page, "The Seafarer," is a model for reading critically the literature of this period. It contains in the side column notes that draw attention to elements that reflect the historical context, the influence of literary movements, and the writer's techniques in the poem. Ask students to pay attention to these notes as they read the poem. Also suggest that they make their own critical comments as they read the selection.

To give students further practice with the process of reading critically, use the selection in the Teaching Portfolio, page 000, "The Wife's Lament," following the Teacher Backup, which students can annotate themselves. Encourage students to use these strategies as they read the literature in this unit.

READING CRITICALLY

The Literature of 449–1066

When you read literature, it is important to know its historical context. Doing so will help you to understand the writer's ideas and techniques.

Historical Context

In 449 the island of Britain was invaded by warlike Germanic peoples known as Angles and Saxons. These invaders brought with them their pagan beliefs and traditions, which appear in Anglo-Saxon poetry and legends. They also brought with them a grim, fatalistic view of the world. These Germanic invaders were followed by Roman missionaries, who converted Britain to Christianity. During this time, different kinds of literature developed, including the oral poetry of the Anglo-Saxons and written historical and religious prose. The literature of the time shows both pagan and Christian influences.

Literary Movements

Very few people were able to read during this period. Therefore, an oral tradition flourished. The Anglo-Saxons were fond of poetry, which was developed and passed on by scops, or poet-singers. Eventually, some of this oral literature was written down by monks in monasteries, who are largely responsible for having preserved oral material.

Writers' Techniques

Because most literature was oral, it was composed in such a way that it was easily memorized. Lines of poetry with regular rhythms were easier to remember than was prose. Poets used alliteration for the same reason. In addition, Anglo-Saxon poets were fond of the kenning, a compound metaphorical name for something, such as "whale's home" for the sea. The Anglo-Saxon poetry that has been preserved illustrates these techniques.

On the following pages is an Anglo-Saxon poem, "The Seafarer." The notes in the side column point out features of the poem that show the historical context or the literary techniques of the period.

Objectives

1 To understand Anglo-Saxon lyric poetry
2 To compare and contrast the attitudes presented in the poem
3 To appreciate Old English
4 To write about Anglo-Saxon beliefs

Teaching Portfolio: Support Material

Teacher Backup, p. 000

Vocabulary Check, p. 00

Usage and Mechanics Worksheet, p. 00

Analyzing Literature Worksheet, Understanding Anglo-Saxon Lyric Poetry, p. 7

Critical Thinking and Reading Worksheet, p. 00

Language Worksheet, Appreciating Old English, p. 8

Selection Test, pp. 9-10

MODEL

The Seafarer

translated by Burton Raffel

This tale is true, and mine. It tells
How the sea took me, swept me back
And forth in sorrow and fear and pain,
Showed me suffering in a hundred ships,
In a thousand ports, and in me. It tells
Of smashing surf when I sweated in the cold
Of an anxious watch, perched in the bow
As it dashed under cliffs. My feet were cast
In icy bands, bound with frost,
With frozen chains, and hardship groaned
Around my heart. Hunger tore
At my sea-weary soul. No man sheltered
On the quiet fairness of earth can feel
How wretched I was, drifting through winter
On an ice-cold sea, whirled in sorrow,
Alone in a world blown clear of love,
Hung with icicles. The hailstorms flew.
The only sound was the roaring sea,
The freezing waves. The song of the swan
Might serve for pleasure, the cry of the sea-fowl,
The death-noise of birds instead of laughter,
The mewing of gulls instead of mead.
Storms beat on the rocky cliffs and were echoed
By icy-feathered terns and the eagle's screams;
No kinsman could offer comfort there,
To a soul left drowning in desolation.
    And who could believe, knowing but
The passion of cities, swelled proud with wine
And no taste of misfortune, how often, how wearily,
I put myself back on the paths of the sea.
Night would blacken; it would snow from the north;
Frost bound the earth and hail would fall,
The coldest seeds. And how my heart
Would begin to beat, knowing once more
The salt waves tossing and the towering sea!
The time for journeys would come and my soul
Called me eagerly out, sent me over
The horizon, seeking foreigners' homes.

Literary Movement: Because this poem was passed on in the oral tradition, different versions of it exist.

Historical Background: The poet's subject is the sea. The sea is a common subject because the British are an island people.

Writer's Technique: Anglo-Saxon poetry frequently uses a line divided by a caesura, a pause. Alliteration joins the two parts: an important word in the first part of the line has the same initial consonant sound as an important word in the second part of the line.

Writer's Technique: "coldest seeds" is a kenning, a metaphorical name, for "hail."

Motivation for Reading Read John Masefield's poem "Sea-Fever"—or another of his sea poems—and discuss the overwhelming power of the sea. Ask students if they feel that power? Are there modern occupations that might exercise this same drawing power?

Master Teacher Note Bring in pictures of Viking ships and maps of their sailing routes to introduce the subject and the period.

Thematic Idea Another selection that deals with the terrors of seafaring is "Rime of the Ancient Mariner," page 670.

Purpose-Setting Question What is the Christian message of the seafarer's story?

Enrichment Seafaring was a passion of the Anglo-Saxons' ancestors, who lived along the shores of the North Sea and from whom oral poetry like this was probably passed down.

Humanities Note

Fine art, illuminated manuscript, *The Whale.* The art of manuscript illumination underwent some changes after the Norman conquest because of the blending of the English and French cultures. The Franco-English school of illumination developed in the twelfth and thirteenth centuries. As a result, the monasteries employed more lay artists in their efforts toward higher artistic achievement.

The illumination *The Whale* is from a bestiary of that era. A bestiary is a secular collection of tales and fables about animals. In the illumination, three men in a boat are confronted by a gigantic fish. Although the whale seems content with its business of feeding, the men appear anxious and intent on navigating their craft out of the whale's reach. The sea is interpreted as an abstract shape with linear wave patterns. There is no perspective—the shapes of the boat and fish are placed flat on top of the water. The whale is fancifully depicted with an abundance of fins, hinting that the artist has never seen one first hand. It is a stylized, decorative portrayal of a fearsome marine encounter that borders on being humorous.

You might use the following questions for class discussion.

1. The seafarer speaks of his alienation and the severity of the sailing life. Does this illustration help you to visualize what he relates? Explain.
2. The poem expresses the speaker's feelings about the sea. Do the sailors in this illustration seem to share these feelings? Explain.

Enrichment Note the poet's ambivalence in lines 40–52. Some scholars think that the poem is a dialogue between an old, disillusioned sailor and a young sailor eager for adventure. Do you think the poem contains a single voice or two voices?

SHIPS WITH THREE MEN, FISH
Bodleian Library, Oxford

Historical Context: The Anglo-Saxons saw Fate as grim and overpowering.

But there isn't a man on earth so proud,
So born to greatness, so bold with his youth,
Grown so brave, or so graced by God,
That he feels no fear as the sails unfurl,
Wondering what Fate has willed and will do.
No harps ring in his heart, no rewards,
No passion for women, no worldly pleasures,
Nothing, only the ocean's heave;
But longing wraps itself around him.
Orchards blossom, the towns bloom,
Fields grow lovely as the world springs fresh,
And all these admonish that willing mind

Clarification "Givers of gold," in line 83, refers to the heroic kings of the Anglo-Saxons' ancestors, who rewarded their loyal thanes with booty.

Leaping to journeys, always set
In thoughts traveling on a quickening tide.
So summer's sentinel, the cuckoo, sings
In his murmuring voice, and our hearts mourn
As he urges. Who could understand,
In ignorant ease, what we others suffer
As the paths of exile stretch endlessly on?
And yet my heart wanders away,
My soul roams with the sea, the whales'
Home, wandering to the widest corners
Of the world, returning ravenous with desire,
Flying solitary, screaming, exciting me
To the open ocean, breaking oaths
On the curve of a wave.
Thus the joys of God
Are fervent with life, where life itself
Fades quickly into the earth. The wealth
Of the world neither reaches to Heaven nor remains.
No man has ever faced the dawn
Certain which of Fate's three threats
Would fall: illness, or age, or an enemy's
Sword, snatching the life from his soul.
The praise the living pour on the dead
Flowers from reputation: plant
An earthly life of profit reaped
Even from hatred and rancor, of bravery
Flung in the devil's face, and death
Can only bring you earthly praise
And a song to celebrate a place
With the angels, life eternally blessed
In the hosts of Heaven.
The days are gone
When the kingdoms of earth flourished in glory;
Now there are no rulers, no emperors,
No givers of gold, as once there were,
When wonderful things were worked among them
And they lived in lordly magnificence.
Those powers have vanished, those pleasures are dead.
The weakest survives and the world continues,
Kept spinning by toil. All glory is tarnished.
The world's honor ages and shrinks,
Bent like the men who mold it. Their faces
Blanch as time advances, their beards
Wither and they mourn the memory of friends.
The sons of princes, sown in the dust.

Historical Context: Fear of Fate was balanced with a firm reliance on God.

Critical Thinking and Reading
What Christian and pagan references exist side by side in the final thirty lines of the poem? What is implied about free will in lines 117–122?

The soul stripped of its flesh knows nothing
Of sweetness or sour, feels no pain,
Bends neither its hand nor its brain. A brother
Opens his palms and pours down gold
On his kinsman's grave, strewing his coffin
With treasures intended for Heaven, but nothing
Golden shakes the wrath of God
For a soul overflowing with sin, and nothing
Hidden on earth rises to Heaven.
          We all fear God. He turns the earth,
He set it swinging firmly in space,
Gave life to the world and light to the sky.
Death leaps at the fools who forget their God.
He who lives humbly has angels from Heaven
To carry him courage and strength and belief.
A man must conquer pride, not kill it,
Be firm with his fellows, chaste for himself,
Treat all the world as the world deserves,
With love or with hate but never with harm,
Though an enemy seek to scorch him in hell,
Or set the flames of a funeral pyre
Under his lord. Fate is stronger
And God mightier than any man's mind.
Our thoughts should turn to where our home is,
Consider the ways of coming there,
Then strive for sure permission for us
To rise to that eternal joy,
That life born in the love of God
And the hope of Heaven. Praise the Holy
Grace of Him who honored us,
Eternal, unchanging creator of earth. Amen.

Literary Movement: The prayerful ending may have been added by Christian monks in recording the oral poem.

"The Seafarer" was composed by an unknown poet, probably in the eighth century. It is one of relatively few poems that survive from the oral tradition in pre-Christian Britain. Preserved by Christian copyists in monasteries, it first appeared in the Exeter Book, a famous collection of Anglo-Saxon poems copied around 975 and donated to Exeter Cathedral, where it remains today.

Answers

ANSWERS TO THINKING ABOUT THE SELECTION

Recalling

1. The poet uses the image of the watch perched on the bow of a ship (lines 6–8), the image of the sea in winter, and the image of a storm beating against rocky cliffs to convey a sense of isolation.
2. Fate's three threats are illness, age, and an enemy's sword.
3. (a) "Fools who forget their God" will die;
(b) Those who "live humbly" will be given courage and strength and faith.

Interpreting

4. The poet loves the excitement of ocean travel and visiting foreign lands, but he also recognizes the danger and loneliness seafaring entails.

THINKING ABOUT THE SELECTION

Recalling

1. What are three images the poet uses in the first stanza to convey his sense of isolation?
2. The poet names "Fate's three threats." What are they?
3. (a) What happens to "fools who forget their God"? (b) What happens to those who "live humbly"?

Interpreting

5. How might you explain the mixed feelings about the sea that the poet seems to feel?
6. Pagans in Anglo-Saxon England—that is, non-Christians—felt themselves at the mercy of forces utterly beyond their control, while Christians put their trust in salvation and heaven. In what way do lines 39 through 43 show the influence of both beliefs?
7. Explain lines 66 and 67: "The wealth of the world neither reaches to Heaven nor remains."
8. "The Seafarer" is a poem of contrasts. What contrast is implied in lines 80 through 102?
9. What does the poet mean by the word *home* in line 117?

Applying

10. Explain how a person can dislike something as much as the sailor dislikes life at sea and yet keep going back to it.

ANALYZING LITERATURE

Understanding Anglo-Saxon Lyric Poetry

A **lyric poem** is one that expresses intense personal emotions. "The Seafarer" mixes pagan with Christian beliefs and expresses sorrow for something lost or past. At times the poet's feelings seem to border on despair.

1. What deep personal feelings does the poet express in the first part of "The Seafarer" that show this to be a lyric poem?
2. "The Seafarer" has two distinct parts, the second of which begins at line 64. What are some of the strong emotions expressed in the second part of the poem?

CRITICAL THINKING AND READING

Comparing and Contrasting Attitudes

To **compare** two ideas or attitudes is to point out similarities. To **contrast** them is to point out differences. Most people have mixed feelings on certain subjects.

Explain what accounts for the poet's state of mind at the beginning of the poem and at the end.

UNDERSTANDING LANGUAGE

Appreciating Old English

Old English is the English language as it existed from about 500 to about 1150. Our language has changed so much since then that Anglo-Saxon poems like "The Seafarer" must be translated, just as if they came from a foreign language, if modern readers are to appreciate them. Here are lines 42 and 43 from "The Seafarer" in Old English:

þæt he a his sæfore   sorge næbbe.
to hwon hine Dryhten   gedon wille.

A few Old English words still appear in dictionaries but are seldom used any more. Find the meanings of the following words.

1. churl
2. thane
3. tor
4. yare
5. yclept

THINKING AND WRITING

Writing About Anglo-Saxon Beliefs

"The Seafarer" is not an easy poem to understand. One critic has said that almost any theory can be made to explain its meaning. What is *your* theory? What main idea do you think the poet intends to convey? In your prewriting, list the various thoughts and feelings the poet expresses in the poem. Use these notes as the basis for a thesis statement in which you summarize what you think the main idea of the poem is. In writing a first draft, support your thesis statement with evidence from the poem. When you revise, be sure you have made clear the reasons for your conclusion.

(Answers begin on p. 20.)

5. Line 41 implies a belief that God bestows grace—and therefore protection, yet Line 43 indicates a belief in Fate and a lack of protection from Fate's whims.
6. Worldly possessions do not extend into the next life and do not endure even in this one.
7. In these lines the poet contrasts the world of his day and the world of an earlier, heroic time.
8. The poet is referring to heaven.

Applying

9. Suggested Response: Sometimes an attachment to something outweighs any fear of its negative aspects. Here, the sailor knows the hardships and perils of life at sea, but when the time for another journey arrives, he is overpowered by his attachment to seafaring. In addition, the Anglo-Saxons were very fatalistic, and so the poet accepts dangers and isolation simply as an unavoidable part of the life to which he is accustomed.

ANSWERS TO ANALYZING LITERATURE

1. The poet expresses feelings of sorrow, loneliness, fear, excitement, and anticipation.
2. The poet expresses a deep feeling that the trappings of this life are transient and a belief in the power of both Fate and God.

ANSWERS TO CRITICAL THINKING AND READING

1. At the beginning the poet is nearly in despair, and at the end he is praising God.
2. The poet meditates on the transience of everything on earth—its hardships as well as its riches—and begins to think of another life with God.

Challenge compare and contrast the poet's references to Fate and to God.

ANSWERS TO UNDERSTANDING LANGUAGE

1. A churl is "a rude, boorish person." (In Old English, *ceorl* meant "a free man of the lowest rank.")
2. A *thane* was in Anglo-Saxon England a freeman granted land by the king in return for military service."
3. A *tor* is "a high rock or pile of rocks on the top of a hill."
4. *Yare,* when applied to a vessel, means "manageable, maneuverable."
5. *Yclept* means "known as, named, or called."

THINKING AND WRITING

For help with this assignment, students can refer to Lesson 11, "Writing About Theme," in the Handbook of Writing About Literature.

Publishing Student Writing Ask for student volunteers to read their essays aloud. Have students in the audience record at least one noteworthy feature of each essay.

Challenge How might the first half of the poem be an allegory that is explained by the second half?

More About the Work *Beowulf* is the only surviving Old English heroic epic. It deals with a pagan world, yet is informed with Christian feelings and values. Nevertheless, the poem's celebration of human endurance is a world where nothing lasts for very long implies a deeply pagan view of life.

BEOWULF

700 [?]

Composed by an unknown poet who lived more than twelve hundred years ago, *Beowulf* marks the beginning of English literature. Minstrels called scops recited this poem to audiences in England for about three hundred years before it was first written down. Only one original manuscript of the complete 3128-line poem survives, but *Beowulf* is in no danger of becoming extinct. Not only does it have lasting historical importance as a record of the Angles, Saxons, and Jutes in England, but it also tells a hair-raising tale that has electrified readers and listeners through the centuries.

Beowulf, a Geat from a region that is today southern Sweden, sets sail from his homeland to try to free Danish King Hrothgar's great banquet hall, Herot, of a monster that has been ravaging it for twelve years. This monster, Grendel, is a terrifying swampland creature of enormous size whose eyes burn "with a gruesome light." The struggle between Beowulf, a young adventurer eager for fame, and Grendel, a fierce and bloodthirsty foe, is the first of three mortal battles in the long poem. The first battle is the one described in this book. The second struggle pits Beowulf against Grendel's "water-hag" mother, and the third, fifty years later, against a dragon.

Although the action takes place in sixth century Scandinavia, the poem is unmistakably English. Recited originally in Old English, *Beowulf* is based on legends and chronicles of the various Northern Europeans who migrated to England.

Objectives

1 To understand the characteristics of the Anglo-Saxon epic
2 To make inferences about ideals when reading an epic
3 To write a story illustrating character traits

Teaching Portfolio: Support Material

Teacher Backup, p. 000

Vocabulary Check, p. 00

Usage and Mechanics Worksheet, p. 00

Analyzing Literature Worksheet, p. 00

Critical Thinking and Reading Worksheet, Making Inferences About Beliefs, p. 17

Language Worksheet, Using A Glossary, p. 18

Selection Test, pp. 19-20

GUIDE FOR READING

from Beowulf

Literary Forms

Anglo-Saxon Epic Poetry. An epic is a long narrative poem, sometimes developed orally, that celebrates the deeds of a legendary or heroic figure. A few epics predate the Anglo-Saxon *Beowulf.* Well-known epics from earlier times include the Greek *Iliad* and *Odyssey* by Homer and the Roman *Aeneid* by Virgil. Typically, an epic, featuring a hero who is larger than life, concerns eternal human problems such as the struggle between good and evil. An epic is presented in a serious way, often through the use of elevated language. The hero of an epic represents widespread national, cultural, or religious values.

Beowulf is the oldest epic in any modern European language. Its hero, Beowulf, embodies the highest ideals of his time and place: loyalty, valor, unselfishness, and a sense of justice. He represents good, while Grendel represents evil. Throughout *Beowulf* there is a prevailing yet somewhat uneasy blend of Christian ethics and pagan morality. Against a backdrop of gloom that reflects the Anglo-Saxons' stoic acceptance of fate, the story applauds the highest virtues of human nature—courage, generosity, faithfulness. Despite its blood and horror, *Beowulf* is a deeply idealistic narrative.

Anglo-Saxon epic poetry, of which *Beowulf* is the great example, has certain distinctive features. One is the two-part line. Each line is separated by a pause, known as a caesura, and there are generally two strong beats per part. Another feature is the kenning, a colorful, indirect way of naming something: The sea is a *whale-path;* a battle is *spear play;* the sun is the *candle of the skies.*

Look For

As you read the poem, notice the character traits that show Beowulf to be an epic hero and Grendel to be a creature of pure evil.

Writing

At the time *Beowulf* was composed, the ideals of the Anglo-Saxons included loyalty, valor, unselfishness, and a sense of justice. Those are still highly regarded ideals, but they are not the only ones. List four other ideals that are important to Americans today.

Vocabulary

Knowing the following words will help you as you read the excerpt from *Beowulf.*

affliction (ə flik' shən) *n.*: State of pain or misery (l. 93)

solace (säl' is) *n.*: Comfort, relief (l. 100)

mail (māl) *n.*: Flexible body armor made of metal (l. 141)

mead-halls (mēd' hôlz) *n.*: Banquet halls; mead is a liquor made from fermented honey and water (l. 236)

Literary Focus You might bring in a Superman or He-Man comic book and have students compare it to this epic. *The Smithsonian Book of Comic-Book Comics,* Barrier and Williams, eds., (Smithsonian Press and Abrams, New York, 1981), includes the first Superman comic book.)

Look For You might want to remind your **less advanced** students that character traits are shown by what a person does, what a person says, and what others say about the person. A character's actions are the most important indicator, however, because words can sometimes be misleading.

Writing It might be helpful to discuss the differences between a celebrity and a hero, and the situations in which an individual can demonstrate heroism today.

Vocabulary Some of your **less advanced** students may not know these additional words: *spawned* (line 19), *sentinel* (line 217), and *shrouds* (line 280).

Teaching to Ability Levels You might ask some of your **more advanced** pupils to also read the later sections of *Beowulf* that describe Beowulf's battles with Grendel's mother and with a dragon. Students can then report to the class on these episodes.

Motivation for Reading Play a recording of "The Ballad of Davy Crockett" or another ballad as an example of how we still celebrate our heroes in song. Have students pick out Crockett's superhuman feats and keep them in mind as they read about Beowulf.

Master Teacher Note You might have students look at the picture of viking artifacts on pages 34 and 35. In addition, you might want to show pictures of other period artifacts, such as those of the Sutton Hoo archeological find in East Anglia in 1939. The British Library has Sutton Hoo slides and Anglo-Saxon postcards. For a catalog, write to British Library Publications, 46 Bloomsbury St., London WC1B3QQ, England.

In addition, the University of Toronto Media Center, 121 St. George St., Toronto, Ontario, Canada, makes available a video and a 16mm film on the Sutton Hoo archeological find.

Thematic Idea Another selection that concerns a hero going forth into danger is *Sir Gawain and the Green Knight,* page 124. You might have students compare and contrast Beowulf and Sir Gawain as heroes.

Purpose-Setting Question What are the roles of Fate and God in this epic?

1 **Discussion** What images does the poet use to contrast Grendel and the Danes?

2 **Enrichment** The king in heroic literature would build a hall for his thanes to reward them for their service to him. The name of this hall, Herot, means "hart."

3 **Discussion** What Christian and pagan references are used to describe Grendel? What is shown to be Grendel's motive for attacking Herot?

from Beowulf

translated by Burton Raffel

The selection opens during an evening of celebration at Herot, the banquet hall of the Danish king Hrothgar (hroth' gär). Outside in the darkness, however, lurks the monster Grendel, a murderous creature who poses a great danger to the people inside the banquet hall.

The Wrath of Grendel

A powerful monster, living down
In the darkness, growled in pain, impatient
1 As day after day the music rang
Loud in that hall,[1] the harp's rejoicing
Call and the poet's clear songs, sung
Of the ancient beginnings of us all, recalling
The Almighty making the earth, shaping
These beautiful plains marked off by oceans,
Then proudly setting the sun and moon
To glow across the land and light it;
The corners of the earth were made lovely with trees
And leaves, made quick with life, with each
Of the nations who now move on its face. And then
As now warriors sang of their pleasure:
2 So Hrothgar's men lived happy in his hall
Till the monster stirred, that demon, that fiend,
Grendel, who haunted the moors, the wild
Marshes, and made his home in a hell
Not hell but earth. He was spawned in that slime,
Conceived by a pair of those monsters born
Of Cain,[2] murderous creatures banished
By God, punished forever for the crime
Of Abel's death. The Almighty drove
3 Those demons out, and their exile was bitter,
Shut away from men; they split
Into a thousand forms of evil—spirits
And fiends, goblins, monsters, giants,
A brood forever opposing the Lord's
Will, and again and again defeated.

Then, when darkness had dropped, Grendel
Went up to Herot, wondering what the warriors
Would do in that hall when their drinking was done.

1. **hall:** Herot.

2. **Cain:** The oldest son of Adam and Eve, who murdered his brother Abel.

The instructional material with this selection covers the following essential elements:
Writing concepts and skills: 1A, E, F, G, H, I, J, K, L
Language concepts and skills: 2A, B, D
Literature concepts and skills: 3A, B, C, E, F, G
Reading concepts and skills: 4A, B, C, E, H, I

THE DRAGON FOR "THE HIGH KINGS"
George Sharp

Humanities Note

Fine art, *Monster,* 1983, by George Sharp. George Sharp is a contemporary British illustrator who began painting professionally in 1975. He studied art at the Nottingham School of Art in England. The painting *Monster* was done for the book *The High Kings,* by Joy Chant, published in 1983. Sharp was concerned with authenticity when creating the illustrations for this book. He spent many hours researching the myths and artifacts of ancient England. Sharp paints in a detailed illustrative style and uses transparent washes of color on a white ground. The monster he portrays is imaginative, and it is as fearsome-looking as the monsters portrayed in historic legends.

Call your students' attention to this painting, and ask whether the artist's image of this creature agrees with their concept of Grendel. Explain.

4 Discussion What had Herot represented in the land? When it stands empty, what does this mean about the king's power?

5 Enrichment Anglo-Saxon custom dictated that a person who killed someone, even accidentally, had to pay a "man-price," or *wergild,* to the dead person's kin or risk deadly retribution. A relative who didn't exact wergild from his kin's killer was humiliated. In this darkly cynical passage, the poet notes that the only payment Grendel makes is more murder.

6 Reading Strategy Summarize the situation of the Danes.

He found them sprawled in sleep, suspecting
Nothing, their dreams undisturbed. The monster's
Thoughts were as quick as his greed or his claws:
He slipped through the door and there in the silence
Snatched up thirty men, smashed them
Unknowing in their beds and ran out with their bodies,
The blood dripping behind him, back
To his lair, delighted with his night's slaughter.
At daybreak, with the sun's first light, they saw
How well he had worked, and in that gray morning
Broke their long feast with tears and laments
For the dead. Hrothgar, their lord, sat joyless
In Herot, a mighty prince mourning
The fate of his lost friends and companions,
Knowing by its tracks that some demon had torn
His followers apart. He wept, fearing
The beginning might not be the end. And that night
Grendel came again, so set
On murder that no crime could ever be enough,
No savage assault quench his lust
For evil. Then each warrior tried
To escape him, searched for rest in different
Beds, as far from Herot as they could find,
Seeing how Grendel hunted when they slept.
Distance was safety; the only survivors
Were those who fled him. Hate had triumphed.
So Grendel ruled, fought with the righteous,
4 One against many, and won; so Herot
Stood empty, and stayed deserted for years,
Twelve winters of grief for Hrothgar, king
Of the Danes, sorrow heaped at his door
By hell-forged hands. His misery leaped
The seas, was told and sung in all
Men's ears: how Grendel's hatred began,
How the monster relished his savage war
On the Danes, keeping the bloody feud
Alive, seeking no peace, offering
5 No truce, accepting no settlement, no price
In gold or land, and paying the living
For one crime only with another. No one
Waited for reparation from his plundering claws:
That shadow of death hunted in the darkness,
Stalked Hrothgar's warriors, old
And young, lying in waiting, hidden
6 In mist, invisibly following them from the edge
Of the marsh, always there, unseen.
So mankind's enemy continued his crimes,

Killing as often as he could, coming
Alone, bloodthirsty and horrible. Though he lived
In Herot, when the night hid him, he never
Dared to touch king Hrothgar's glorious
Throne, protected by God—God,
Whose love Grendel could not know. But Hrothgar's
Heart was bent. The best and most noble
Of his council debated remedies, sat
In secret sessions, talking of terror
And wondering what the bravest of warriors could do.
And sometimes they sacrificed to the old stone gods,
Made heathen vows, hoping for Hell's
Support, the Devil's guidance in driving
Their affliction off. That was their way,
And the heathen's only hope, Hell
Always in their hearts, knowing neither God 7
Nor His passing as He walks through our world, the Lord
Of Heaven and earth; their ears could not hear
His praise nor know His glory. Let them
Beware, those who are thrust into danger,
Clutched at by trouble, yet can carry no solace
In their hearts, cannot hope to be better! Hail 8
To those who will rise to God, drop off
Their dead bodies and seek our Father's peace!

The Coming of Beowulf

So the living sorrow of Healfdane's son[3]
Simmered, bitter and fresh, and no wisdom
Or strength could break it: that agony hung
On king and people alike, harsh
And unending, violent and cruel, and evil.
In his far-off home Beowulf, Higlac's[4]
Follower and the strongest of the Geats—greater
And stronger than anyone anywhere in this world—
Heard how Grendel filled nights with horror 9
And quickly commanded a boat fitted out,
Proclaiming that he'd go to that famous king,
Would sail across the sea to Hrothgar,
Now when help was needed. None
Of the wise ones regretted his going, much
As he was loved by the Geats: the omens were good, 10
And they urged the adventure on. So Beowulf
Chose the mightiest men he could find,
The bravest and best of the Geats, fourteen
In all, and led them down to their boat;
He knew the sea, would point the prow
Straight to that distant Danish shore.

3. **Healfdane's** (hā' alf den nəz) **son:** Hrothgar.

4. **Higlac's** (hig' laks): Higlac was the king of the Geats (gā' ats) and Beowulf's feudal lord and uncle.

7 **Clarification** This passage is confusing to scholars. Hrothgar and the Danes are spoken of as heathens here, even though at the beginning of the passage the scop is singing about God's creation, and later in the poem Hrothgar speaks as a Christian.

8 **Discussion** What is the Christian remedy and admonishment expressed here?

9 **Enrichment** Beowulf has chosen a heroic way of life, the goal of which is to attain glory, so he must go to fight Grendel.

10 **Discussion** Why did Beowulf's kinsmen urge him to go?

Humanities Note

Fine art, Illustration, 1983, by George Sharp. This painting by George Sharp of an ancient ship was done for Joy Chant's book *The High Kings,* published in 1983. Sharp's diligent research into ancient English myth and legend is reflected in the accurately detailed rigging of the ship. Executed in transparent color washes on canvas, this painting has a misty, dreamlike quality. It is as if the scene were painted on the shore by a witness in Beowulf's time.

You may wish to ask your students the following questions.

1. Do you feel that this contemporary painting technique properly illustrates this epic? Explain.
2. What mood does this painting create?

ARTHUR GOING TO AVALON FOR "THE HIGH KINGS"
George Sharp

Then they sailed, set their ship
Out on the waves, under the cliffs.
Ready for what came they wound through the currents,
The seas beating at the sand, and were borne 11
In the lap of their shining ship, lined
With gleaming armor, going safely
In that oak-hard boat to where their hearts took them.
The wind hurried them over the waves,
The ship foamed through the sea like a bird
Until, in the time they had known it would take,
Standing in the round-curled prow they could see
Sparkling hills, high and green,
Jutting up over the shore, and rejoicing
In those rock-steep cliffs they quietly ended
Their voyage. Jumping to the ground, the Geats
Pushed their boat to the sand and tied it
In place, mail shirts and armor rattling
As they swiftly moored their ship. And then
They gave thanks to God for their easy crossing.
High on a wall a Danish watcher
Patrolling along the cliffs saw
The travelers crossing to the shore, their shields
Raised and shining; he came riding down,
Hrothgar's lieutenant, spurring his horse,
Needing to know why they'd landed, these men
In armor. Shaking his heavy spear
In their faces he spoke:
"Whose soldiers are you,
You who've been carried in your deep-keeled ship
Across the sea-road to this country of mine?
Listen! I've stood on these cliffs longer
Than you know, keeping our coast free
Of pirates, raiders sneaking ashore
From their ships, seeking our lives and our gold.
None have ever come more openly—
And yet you've offered no password, no sign
From my prince, no permission from my people for your landing
Here. Nor have I ever seen,
Out of all the men on earth, one greater
Than has come with you; no commoner carries
Such weapons, unless his appearance, and his beauty, 12
Are both lies. You! Tell me your name,
And your father's; no spies go further onto Danish
Soil than you've come already. Strangers,
From wherever it was you sailed, tell it,
And tell it quickly, the quicker the better,
I say, for us all. Speak, say
Exactly who you are, and from where, and why."

11 **Discussion** What adjectives and descriptive phrases are used to describe the Geats' boat? Contrast these to the adjectives used to describe Grendel.

12 **Discussion** What heroic qualities does Beowulf's appearance suggest?

13 **Clarification** The Anglo-Saxons believed that the image of a boar on a helmet would protect the wearer in battle.

Their leader answered him, Beowulf unlocking
Words from deep in his breast:
"We are Geats,
Men who follow Higlac. My father
Was a famous soldier, known far and wide
As a leader of men. His name was Edgetho.
His life lasted many winters;
Wise men all over the earth surely
Remember him still. And we have come seeking
Your prince, Healfdane's son, protector
Of this people, only in friendship: instruct us,
Watchman, help us with your words! Our errand
Is a great one, our business with the glorious king
Of the Danes no secret; there's nothing dark
Or hidden in our coming. You know (if we've heard
The truth, and been told honestly) that your country
Is cursed with some strange, vicious creature
That hunts only at night and that no one
Has seen. It's said, watchman, that he has slaughtered
Your people, brought terror to the darkness. Perhaps
Hrothgar can hunt, here in my heart,
For some way to drive this devil out—
If anything will ever end the evils
Afflicting your wise and famous lord.
Here he can cool his burning sorrow.
Or else he may see his suffering go on
Forever, for as long as Herot towers
High on your hills."
The mounted officer
Answered him bluntly, the brave watchman:
"A soldier should know the difference between words
And deeds, and keep that knowledge clear
In his brain. I believe your words, I trust in
Your friendship. Go forward, weapons and armor
And all, on into Denmark. I'll guide you
Myself—and my men will guard your ship,
Keep it safe here on our shores,
Your fresh-tarred boat, watch it well,
Until that curving prow carries
Across the sea to Geatland a chosen
Warrior who bravely does battle with the creature
Haunting our people, who survives that horror
Unhurt, and goes home bearing our love."
Then they moved on. Their boat lay moored,
Tied tight to its anchor. Glittering at the top
13 Of their golden helmets wild boar heads gleamed,
Shining decorations, swinging as they marched,
Erect like guards, like sentinels, as though ready

To fight. They marched, Beowulf and his men
And their guide, until they could see the gables 14
Of Herot, covered with hammered gold
And glowing in the sun—that most famous of all dwellings,
Towering majestic, its glittering roofs
Visible far across the land.
Their guide reined in his horse, pointing
To that hall, built by Hrothgar for the best
And bravest of his men; the path was plain,
They could see their way . . .

Beowulf and his men arrive at Herot and are about to be escorted in to see King Hrothgar.

Beowulf arose, with his men
Around him, ordering a few to remain
With their weapons, leading the others quickly
Along under Herot's steep roof into Hrothgar's
Presence. Standing on that prince's own hearth,
Helmeted, the silvery metal of his mail shirt
Gleaming with a smith's high art, he greeted
The Danes' great lord:
"Hail, Hrothgar!
Higlac is my cousin[5] and my king; the days
Of my youth have been filled with glory. Now Grendel's
Name has echoed in our land: sailors
Have brought us stories of Herot, the best
Of all mead-halls, deserted and useless when the moon
Hangs in skies the sun had lit,
Light and life fleeing together.
My people have said, the wisest, most knowing
And best of them, that my duty was to go to the Danes'
Great king. They have seen my strength for themselves,
Have watched me rise from the darkness of war,
Dripping with my enemies' blood. I drove
Five great giants into chains, chased
All of that race from the earth. I swam
In the blackness of night, hunting monsters 15
Out of the ocean, and killing them one
By one; death was my errand and the fate
They had earned. Now Grendel and I are called
Together, and I've come. Grant me, then,
Lord and protector of this noble place,
A single request! I have come so far,
Oh shelterer of warriors and your people's loved friend,
That this one favor you should not refuse me—
That I, alone and with the help of my men, 16
May purge all evil from this hall. I have heard,
Too, that the monster's scorn of men

5. cousin: Here, used as a general term for relative.

14 **Discussion** What terms are used to describe Herot? How is Grendel's environment described elsewhere in the poem? Ask for a volunteer to give a dramatic reading of Beowulf's speech to Hrothgar.

15 **Enrichment** This boasting might offend some modern readers, but Beowulf is recalling his former courage as a way of making a vow of future courage.

16 **Discussion** Why might Beowulf want to fight Grendel alone, except for the help of his own men?

17 **Discussion** What heroic quality do these lines suggest? How would you characterize Beowulf?

18 **Discussion** Why wouldn't the Danes have to sew shrouds for the Geats if Grendel triumphs?

19 **Reading Strategy** Summarize what we have learned so far about Beowulf's character.

20 **Discussion** What do we know about Grendel's physical appearance? Why do you think the author is so vague about Grendel's specific features?

Is so great that he needs no weapons and fears none.
Nor will I. My lord Higlac
Might think less of me if I let my sword
17 Go where my feet were afraid to, if I hid
Behind some broad linden[6] shield: my hands
Alone shall fight for me, struggle for life
Against the monster. God must decide
Who will be given to death's cold grip.
Grendel's plan, I think, will be
What it has been before, to invade this hall
And gorge his belly with our bodies. If he can,
If he can. And I think, if my time will have come,
There'll be nothing to mourn over, no corpse to prepare
For its grave: Grendel will carry our bloody
Flesh to the moors, crunch on our bones
18 And smear torn scraps of our skin on the walls
Of his den. No, I expect no Danes
19 Will fret about sewing our shrouds, if he wins.
And if death does take me, send the hammered
Mail of my armor to Higlac, return
The inheritance I had from Hrethel, and he
From Wayland.[7] Fate will unwind as it must!"

6. **linden:** A very sturdy type of wood.

7. **Wayland:** From Germanic folklore, an invisible blacksmith.

The Battle with Grendel

That night Beowulf and his men take the places of Hrothgar and the Danes inside Herot. While his men sleep, Beowulf lies awake, eager to meet with Grendel.

Out from the marsh, from the foot of misty
Hills and bogs, bearing God's hatred,
Grendel came, hoping to kill
Anyone he could trap on this trip to high Herot.
He moved quickly through the cloudy night,
Up from his swampland, sliding silently
Toward that gold-shining hall. He had visited Hrothgar's
Home before, knew the way—
But never, before nor after that night,
20 Found Herot defended so firmly, his reception
So harsh. He journeyed, forever joyless,
Straight to the door, then snapped it open,
Tore its iron fasteners with a touch
And rushed angrily over the threshold.
He strode quickly across the inlaid
Floor, snarling and fierce: his eyes
Gleamed in the darkness, burned with a gruesome
Light. Then he stopped, seeing the hall
Crowded with sleeping warriors, stuffed
With rows of young soldiers resting together.

And his heart laughed, he relished the sight,
Intended to tear the life from those bodies
By morning; the monster's mind was hot
With the thought of food and the feasting his belly
Would soon know. But fate, that night, intended
Grendel to gnaw the broken bones 21
Of his last human supper. Human
Eyes were watching his evil steps,
Waiting to see his swift hard claws.
Grendel snatched at the first Geat
He came to, ripped him apart, cut
His body to bits with powerful jaws,
Drank the blood from his veins and bolted
Him down, hands and feet; death
And Grendel's great teeth came together,
Snapping life shut. Then he stepped to another
Still body, clutched at Beowulf with his claws,
Grasped at a strong-hearted wakeful sleeper 22
—And was instantly seized himself, claws
Bent back as Beowulf leaned up on one arm.
That shepherd of evil, guardian of crime,
Knew at once that nowhere on earth
Had he met a man whose hands were harder;
His mind was flooded with fear—but nothing
Could take his talons and himself from that tight
Hard grip. Grendel's one thought was to run
From Beowulf, flee back to his marsh and hide there:
This was a different Herot than the hall he had emptied. 23
But Higlac's follower remembered his final
Boast and, standing erect, stopped
The monster's flight, fastened those claws
In his fists till they cracked, clutched Grendel
Closer. The infamous killer fought
For his freedom, wanting no flesh but retreat,
Desiring nothing but escape; his claws
Had been caught, he was trapped. That trip to Herot
Was a miserable journey for the writhing monster!
The high hall rang, its roof boards swayed,
And Danes shook with terror. Down
The aisles the battle swept, angry
And wild. Herot trembled, wonderfully
Built to withstand the blows, the struggling
Great bodies beating at its beautiful walls;
Shaped and fastened with iron, inside
And out, artfully worked, the building
Stood firm. Its benches rattled, fell
To the floor, gold-covered boards grating
As Grendel and Beowulf battled across them.

21 **Enrichment** The poet uses foreshadowing here. He tells us ahead of time that Grendel will die, just as the Anglo-Saxons believed that their deaths were predetermined.

22 **Reading Strategy** How will Grendel's attack on Beowulf differ from his attack on the sleeping warrior?

23 **Literary Focus** Note the profusion of kennings in this battle passage—"shepherd of evil," "guardian of crime," "the Almighty's enemy," and "hell's captive." The primary purpose of kennings in the original Anglo-Saxon was to maintain the required alliteration. The first accented syllable after the caesura had to alliterate with at least one of the accented syllables in the first half of the line.

Hrothgar's wise men had fashioned Herot
To stand forever; only fire,
They had planned, could shatter what such skill had put
Together, swallow in hot flames such splendor
Of ivory and iron and wood. Suddenly
The sounds changed, the Danes started
In new terror, cowering in their beds as the terrible
Screams of the Almighty's enemy sang
In the darkness, the horrible shrieks of pain
And defeat, the tears torn out of Grendel's
Taut throat, hell's captive caught in the arms
Of him who of all the men on earth
Was the strongest.
That mighty protector of men
Meant to hold the monster till its life
Leaped out, knowing the fiend was no use
To anyone in Denmark. All of Beowulf's
Band had jumped from their beds, ancestral
24 Swords raised and ready, determined
To protect their prince if they could. Their courage
Was great but all wasted: they could hack at Grendel

THE SO-CALLED "SIGURD'S HELMET"
Statens Historiska Museet, Stockholm
Werner Forman Archive

COINS DEPICTING VIKING LONGSHIPS
Statens Historiska Muskeet, Stockholm
Werner Forman Archive

THE GOKSTAD SHIP
Viking Ships Museum, Bygdøy, Oslo
Werner Forman Archive

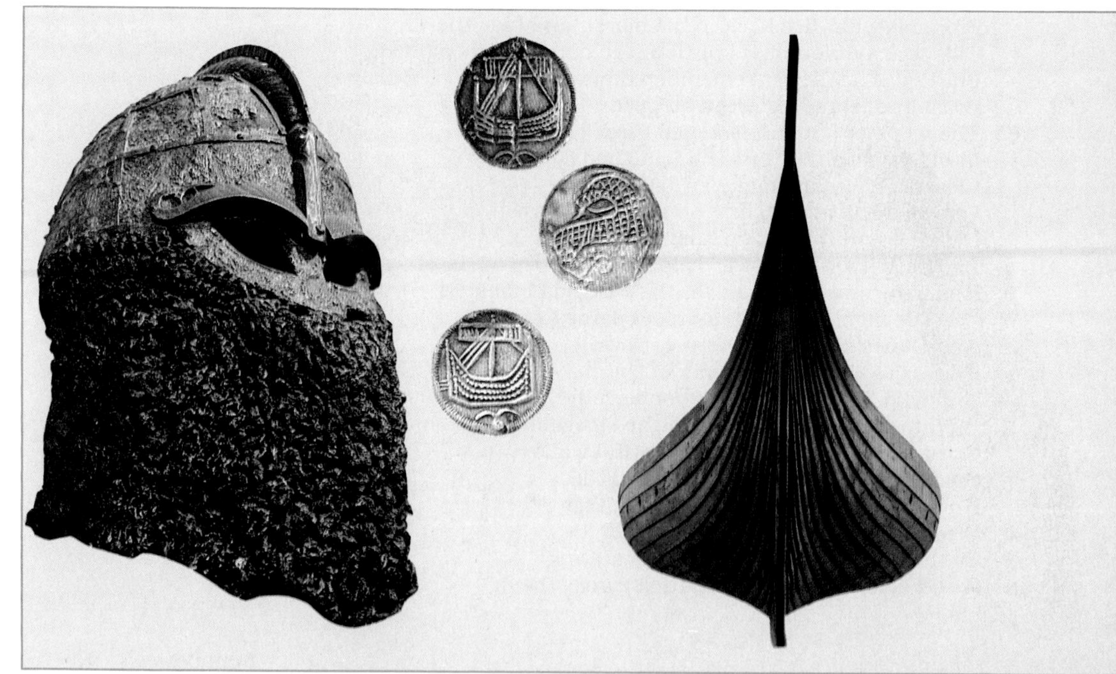

Humanities Note

Viking Artifacts

1. Sigurd's helmet from a pre-Viking grave in Vendel, Sweden. May have belonged to Sigurd the Volsung (d.575).
2. Viking silver coins, early ninth-century, probably struck in Hedeby, Denmark. This is an early form of coin that depended on the weight of the silver for its value. The design depicts Viking longships.
3. Prow of a restored tenth-century Viking longship, referred to as the Gokstad Ship. It was found in Norway in 1880. It is eighty feet long and built for sea and coastal maneuvers. Manned by a crew of thirty-two, it was a swift, silent raiding vessel.
4. The Oseberg Dragon, a wooden animal post head found among the furniture on the ninth-century Oseberg Ship, a royal barge used for the burial of a Norwegian queen. The post is covered with an intricate profusion of "gripping beasts," a classic Viking decorative pattern.
5. Vendel helmet, a seventh-century Swedish artifact. Composed of iron with a bronze crest and nose guard, it shows a Roman influence in the design.
6. Viking drinking horn. A cattle horn decoratively mounted with metal, it was used for drinking beer and mead. Its use required practice, as all of the liquid rushes out at once. The design prevented the horn from being put down until it was empty.

24 Master Teacher Note You might want to play a recording of *Beowulf* read in Old English at this point. Perhaps students can understand the drama of the battle scene as it was described by ancient scops. (Recording: *Beowulf*, Cadmon TC 4001)

From every side, trying to open
A path for his evil soul, but their points
Could not hurt him, the sharpest and hardest iron
Could not scratch at his skin, for that sin-stained demon 25
Had bewitched all men's weapons, laid spells
That blunted every mortal man's blade.
And yet his time had come, his days
Were over, his death near; down
To hell he would go, swept groaning and helpless 26
To the waiting hands of still worse fiends.
Now he discovered—once the afflictor
Of men, tormentor of their days—what it meant 27
To feud with Almighty God: Grendel
Saw that his strength was deserting him, his claws
Bound fast, Higlac's brave follower tearing at
His hands. The monster's hatred rose higher,
But his power had gone. He twisted in pain, 28
And the bleeding sinews deep in his shoulder
Snapped, muscle and bone split
And broke. The battle was over, Beowulf

HEAD OF CARVED POST FROM THE SHIP BURIAL AT OSEBERG
Werner Forman Archive

HELMET
Statens Historiska Museet, Stockholm
Werner Forman Archive

GOLDEN HORNS
National Museet Copenhagen

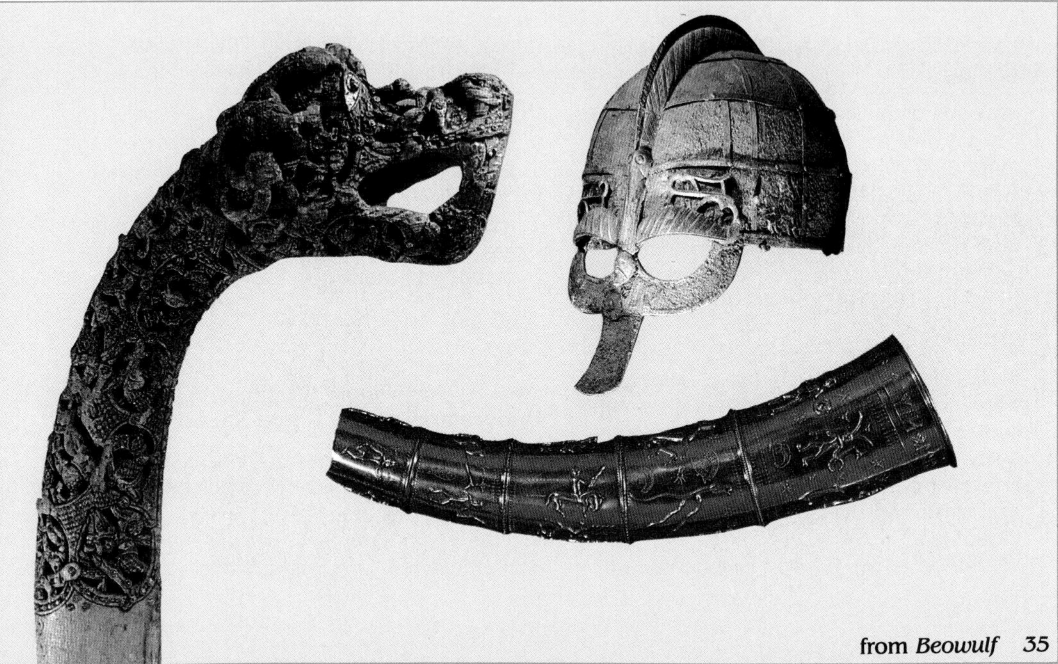

25 **Discussion** Why were Beowulf's men unable to help him kill Grendel?

26 **Enrichment** Note again the announcement of Grendel's death before it happens. After he has vividly described Grendel's murderous activities, the poet states simply—and rather anticlimatically—that Grendel will die at some future time.

27 **Discussion** Explain how the battle between Beowulf and Grendel takes on much greater significance at this point.

28 **Reading Strategy** Summarize the battle with Grendel and its outcome.

29 **Enrichment** The hanging of the monster's forequarters on the wall seems to reinforce the popular notion that the Anglo-Saxons were a barbaric, insular, and insensitive people. However, archaeological discoveries at Sutton Hoo in East Anglia in 1939 show that the seventh-century Anglo-Saxons had high artistic abilities and wide trading contacts. Also, while the epic was probably written in the mid-eighth century in England, it deals with an earlier time and place: fifth or sixth century Scandinavia.

Master Teacher Note You may want to have some of your **more advanced** pupils read John Gardner's novel *Grendel* or Richard Wilbur's poem "Beowulf" and compare or contrast these works with *Beowulf.*

Had been granted new glory: Grendel escaped,
But wounded as he was could flee to his den,
His miserable hole at the bottom of the marsh,
Only to die, to wait for the end
Of all his days. And after that bloody
Combat the Danes laughed with delight.
He who had come to them from across the sea,
Bold and strong-minded, had driven affliction
Off, purged Herot clean. He was happy,
Now, with that night's fierce work; the Danes
Had been served as he'd boasted he'd serve them; Beowulf,
A prince of the Geats, had killed Grendel,
Ended the grief, the sorrow, the suffering
Forced on Hrothgar's helpless people
By a bloodthirsty fiend. No Dane doubted
The victory, for the proof, hanging high
From the rafters where Beowulf had hung it, was the
29 monster's
Arm, claw and shoulder and all.

THINKING ABOUT THE SELECTION

Recalling

1. (a) When does Grendel first go to Herot? (b) Explain what the warriors are doing when he arrives. (c) What does he do to them?
2. Why is Grendel afraid of touching Hrothgar's throne?
3. (a) What is Beowulf's plan for fighting Grendel? (b) Why does he choose this plan?
4. How does Grendel die?

Interpreting

5. At the beginning of the poem, Hrothgar's warriors are happy, while Grendel is consumed by hatred. What causes these differences in attitude?
6. How does Beowulf's remark, "Fate will unwind as it must," reflect the Anglo-Saxons' attitude toward fate?
7. What traits of Beowulf and Grendel raise the fight between them to an epic struggle between two great opposing forces in the world?

Applying

8. Beowulf is thought to be a perfect hero for his times. (a) What qualities should a modern hero have? (b) In what situations might a modern hero demonstrate these heroic qualities? (c) Give examples of modern heroes or of heroic behavior.

ANALYZING LITERATURE

Understanding the Anglo-Saxon Epic

An **epic** is a long, narrative poem, presented in an elevated style, that celebrates episodes in a people's heroic tradition.

The Anglo-Saxon epic *Beowulf* has two distinctive features. One feature is the two-part line

Answers

ANSWERS TO THINKING ABOUT THE SELECTION

Recalling

1. (a) Grendel first goes to Herot one dark evening twelve years before Beowulf arrives.
   (b) King Hrothgar and his warriors are celebrating when Grendel arrives.
   (c) Grendel kills thirty warriors.
2. Grendel is afraid of touching Hrothgar's throne because it is protected by God.
3. (a) Beowulf's plan is to fight Grendel barehanded.
   (b) Answers may differ. Beowulf has heard that Grendel fears no weapons. Beowulf also thinks that his uncle might think less of him if he "hides behind" weapons or shields. Further more, Beowulf has a sense that Fate has brought him and Grendel together and that this battle will be the ultimate test for each of them.
4. Beowulf rips his arm off at the shoulder; Grendel escapes to his den to die.

Interpreting

5. Hrothgar's warriors are celebrating God's creation of the world; Grendel and his forebears have been exiled by God. Grendel's hate is fueled by hearing the happy war-

in which the two parts are separated by a caesura. Each part has two strong beats.

> Till the *mon*ster *stirred* / that *de*mon, that *fiend*

The kenning is another feature in *Beowulf.* A kenning is a colorful, roundabout way of naming something.

> That *shepherd of evil, guardian of crime*

1. What are the two parts and the four strong beats in each of the following lines?

   > As day after day the music rang
   > Loud in that hall, the harp's rejoicing

2. In addition to the example given, find another kenning in Beowulf.
3. Explain why you do or do not find the use of kenning effective.

CRITICAL THINKING AND READING

Making Inferences About Ideals

An **inference** is a conclusion you reach from stated information in literature. The hero in an epic embodies the highest ideals of the times. The Anglo-Saxon epic *Beowulf* reflects the values of the plundering Anglo-Saxon warriors. Beowulf himself is a fighting man, eager for challenging personal encounters in a good cause.

From Beowulf's description of his previous heroic feats (lines 247–254), you can infer that his listeners respected and admired the qualities that enabled Beowulf to accomplish such deeds. In addition, you can infer that they believed that such qualities enabled Beowulf to take on the evil Grendel.

1. In what specific way does Beowulf demonstrate loyalty to his lord and king?
2. In what specific ways does he demonstrate his valor?
3. In lines 378–380, Grendel realizes that he has been beaten:

   > "Now he discovered—once the afflictor
   > Of men, tormentor of their days—what it meant
   > To feud with Almighty God."

   What inference about Anglo-Saxon beliefs can you make from these lines?

UNDERSTANDING LANGUAGE

Using a Glossary

A **glossary** is a small, specialized dictionary designed to help you with unfamiliar words. Which of the following are included in the glossary entries in the back of this book?

1. pronunciation
2. part of speech
3. etymology
4. inflected forms
5. cross references
6. variant spellings

THINKING AND WRITING

Writing About Character Traits

Write a composition for your classmates in which you tell the incidents in *Beowulf* from Grendel's point of view. Begin by jotting down notes about Grendel's thoughts and feelings during his final, fatal visit to Hrothgar's hall. Then arrange these notes in a logical order to create a working outline. Next, write a draft, keeping in mind that you are giving Grendel's version of events, not your own or Beowulf's. Finally, revise your draft, improving your content and organization and correcting any errors you find in grammar or mechanics.

(Answers begin on p. 36.)

ANSWERS TO ANALYZING LITERATURE

1. "As *day* after *day* / the *mus*ic *rang* / *Loud* in that *hall,* / the *harp's* re*joic*ing"
2. Answers will differ but may include "That mighty protector of men" (line 365), "mankind's enemy" (line 79), and "the Almighty's enemy" (line 360).
3. Suggested response: The kenning adds colorful language to the poem and describes characters and things in ways that enlarge our understanding of them.

ANSWERS TO CRITICAL THINKING AND READING

1. Beowulf says that he wants to fight Grendel without weapons partly to make his king proud of him. If Beowulf is killed, he wants his armor sent to Higlac.
2. When Beowulf hears of Grendel's marauding, he quickly sets out to help the Danes. Beowulf puts himself in mortal danger by waiting in Herot for Grendel, and he fights Grendel to the death.
3. The Anglo-Saxons had been Christianized and believed that God would prevail over evil.

ANSWERS TO UNDERSTANDING LANGUAGE

Glossary entries in this book include a word's pronunciation and part of speech, as well as its meaning.

THINKING AND WRITING

For help with this assignment, students can refer to Lesson 9, "Writing About Character," in the Handbook of Writing About Literature.

Publishing Student Writing Have students work in groups of four to read each other's papers and to choose the one that they think is best to read to the class.

riors and by knowing that he must always be "shut away" from them.

6. Beowulf feels that he and Grendel have been brought together by Fate and that he will win or lose as Fate decrees; all has been predetermined.
7. Beowulf is the greatest of the Geats and of all men; he has previously rid the earth of giants and killed sea monsters. Grendel is part of a "brood forever opposing the Lord's Will"; he is described as the embodiment of Hate, as mankind's enemy, as the shepherd of evil, as the guardian of crime, and as the Almighty's enemy.

Applying

8. Answers may differ. Students may suggest that a modern hero is self-reliant, intelligent, committed to a cause, unflinching in the face of danger, and willing to take risks —that he or she is essentially larger than life. A modern hero might demonstrate these qualities by leading a cause or struggle, by taking great risks to help others, or by taking risks to expand the frontiers of knowledge. Some examples of modern heroes might be Martin Luther King, Steve Biko, John Glenn, Chuck Yaeger, and Mother Teresa.

Challenge Is it easier or more difficult to be a hero today? Why?

More About the Author The Venerable Bede wrote books on grammar and meter; Biblical commentary; scientific works on chronology, medicine, astronomy, and meteorology; the life stories of saints; and poems. He wrote mainly for students and other scholars. He spoke, wrote, and taught in Latin all his life, and he completed his ecclesiastical history in the last years of his life. What does this tell us about his qualifications as a historian? What does it suggest about his writing style?

BEDE

673–735

Much of what the world knows about England before A.D. 700 is based on a history written in Latin by a Benedictine monk, Bede, who is often called the father of English history. Bede was the most learned scholar of his day not only in England but in all of Western Europe. Although he wrote forty books on a variety of subjects, his reputation would be secure on the basis of a single book—his *Historia Ecclesiastica Gentis Anglorum,* or in English, *Ecclesiastical History of the English People.*

Bede was born in Wearmouth (now the city of Sunderland) on the northeast coast of England. As a child of seven, he entered the nearby monastic school of Jarrow on the river Tyne. A diligent student, he took full advantage of the library at Jarrow, in time becoming a priest, teacher, and scholar at the monastery. He remained at Jarrow for the rest of his life.

A contemporary of the unknown author of *Beowulf,* Bede was fascinated by a broad range of ideas. His writings summarize much of the thought and learning of his time. As the earliest important English prose writer, he concentrated on the Bible but did not neglect science and history. One of his innovations was putting into practice of dating events from the birth of Christ, a system that other scholars began to follow. It was through Bede's work that the Christian chronology in use today became common throughout Europe.

Bede had a deep love for his native island and its people, which led him to write *Ecclesiastical History of the English People.* In working on his history, Bede gathered information from many kinds of documents, interviewed knowledgeable monks, and, in general, proceeded very much like a modern historian, although he accepted as fact some miracles and supernatural events that a modern historian would not.

In the century after his death, King Alfred translated Bede's history from Latin into English. In the same century, the word *Venerable* was first applied to his name to honor his wisdom and achievements. The honor was well deserved. The Venerable Bede was largely responsible for what is sometimes called the Christian renaissance in eighth-century England.

Objectives

1 To understand the process of historical writing
2 To make inferences about attitudes in historical writing
3 To write a critical review of the excerpt from Bede's history

Teaching Portfolio: Support Material

Teacher Backup, p. 000

Vocabulary Check, p. 00

Usage and Mechanics Worksheet, p. 00

Analyzing Literature Worksheet, p. 00

Critical Thinking and Reading Worksheet, p. 00

Language Worksheet, p. 00

Selection Test, p. 00

GUIDE FOR READING

from Ecclesiastical History of the English People

Writer's Techniques

Historical Writing. A history is a factual narrative or record of past events. Unless a historian has actually observed the events being described, he or she must rely on outside sources. These sources include testimony from living witnesses, accounts in letters or memoirs, records from courts, businesses, churches, armies, or other groups. Today's historian has libraries of books, newspapers, films, and other items to consult, as well as unwritten records such as buildings, artworks, and various physical remains of bygone days. An enormous amount of historical material exists.

That was not the case in Bede's time. English monastic libraries had modest collections of documents that Bede read, cross-checked, and evaluated. He made excellent use of the limited sources of his time. Bede was an innovator among historical writers, and if he sometimes accepted unlikely tales as truth, he did so far less often than did most scholars of his era.

Look For

As you read the excerpt from Bede's history, notice how precisely the writer states his facts. At the same time, see if you can find at least one improbable tale that Bede accepted.

Writing

If you were writing a history of your community, you would have to find and use a number of different sources. List at least five specific sources that might be helpful.

Vocabulary

Knowing the following words will help you as you read the excerpt from *Ecclesiastical History of the English People.*

promontories (präm′ ən tôr ēz) *n*: High points of land extending into the sea (p. 40)

furlongs (fʉr′ lôŋz) *n.*: Units for measuring distance; a furlong is equal to one eighth of a mile (p. 40)

cockles (käk′ ′lz) *n.*: Edible shellfish with two heart-shaped shells (p. 40)

innumerable (i no͞o′ mər ə b′l) *adj.*: Too many to count (p. 40)

firth (fʉrth) *n.*: Narrow arm of the sea (p. 42)

Literary Focus Today, we tend to think of the monastic life as being isolating and out of the mainstream. Remind students that in Bede's day, most reading and writing was done in churches and monasteries. Therefore, Bede was in a good position to acquire a great deal of knowledge.

Look For Bede wrote this in the preface to his history: "I humbly entreat the reader, that if he shall . . . find anything not delivered according to the truth, he will not impute the same to me, who, as the true rule of history requires, have labored sincerely to commit to writing such things as I could gather from common report, for the instruction of posterity." What does this tell about Bede's attitude toward his material? How is the "true rule of history" different today?

Writing The historian Carlyle said, "In a certain sense, all men are historians. . . . Most men . . . . . . speak only to narrate." Discuss this statement with students in terms of what it hints about sources. Remind students that a source is not simply a location. Any written record is a source. When they go to a library, a museum, or a historical society, the materials that they find there are their sources.

Vocabulary Some of your **less advanced** students may not be familiar with these additional words: *corrupted* (page 40), *immunity,* (page 42), and *steeped* (page 42).

Teaching to Ability Levels You might have some of your **more advanced** students read one or more of the lives of saints which compose much of the rest of Bede's history.

Motivation for Reading Ask students what their favorite period of history is and whether they think history is a popular subject with students today. Tell them that Bede's work was immensely popular in Britain for longer than most modern historians can hope to stay in print. The history he wrote was still being copied by hand when the first printed edition came out in about 1475—seven hundred years after his death.

Master Teacher Note You might bring in prints of early maps of Britain to show students where Bede lived and where the "nations" he refers to settled. (A possible source: David Hill's *Atlas of Anglo-Saxon England.)*

Thematic Idea You might refer students to the excerpts from Samuel Pepys's diary that begin on page 524. Pepys did not intend his diary to be a history of contemporary events, yet it has helped historians understand more about the age in which Pepys lived.

Purpose-Setting Question What was Bede's attitude toward his subjects?

Literary Focus Bede's original text, written in Latin, was simple and direct in style with sincerity of purpose, no eccentricity of vocabulary, and no affectation of learning; this translation preserves these qualities.

1 **Discussion** How accurate is Bede's description of Britain? Have students check an almanac or atlas.

2 **Reading Strategy** Summarize the advantages of Britain as Bede knew it.

Ecclesiastical History of the English People

Bede translated by Leo Sherley-Price

The Situation of Britain and Ireland: Their Earliest Inhabitants

Britain, formerly known as Albion, is an island in the ocean, facing between north and west, and lying at a considerable distance from the coasts of Germany, Gaul, and Spain, which together form the greater part of Europe. It extends 800 miles northwards, and is 200 in breadth, except where a number
1 of promontories stretch farther, the coastline round which extends to 3675 miles. To the south lies Belgic Gaul,[1] from the nearest shore of which travelers can see the city known as Rutubi Portus, which the English have corrupted to Reptacestir.[2] The distance from there across the sea to Gessoriacum,[3] the nearest coast of the Morini, is 50 miles or, as some write it, 450 furlongs. On the opposite side of Britain, which lies open to the boundless ocean, lie the isles of the Orcades.[4] Britain is rich in grain and timber; it has good pasturage for cattle and draft animals,[5] and vines are cultivated in various localities. There are many land and sea birds of various species, and it is well known for its plentiful springs and rivers abounding in fish. There are salmon and eel fisheries, while seals, dolphins, and sometimes whales are caught. There are also many varieties of shellfish, such as mussels, in which are often found excellent pearls of several colors: red, purple, violet, and green, but mainly white. Cockles are abundant, and a beautiful scarlet dye is extracted from them which remains unfaded by sunshine or rain; indeed, the older the cloth, the more beautiful its color. The country has both salt and hot springs, and the waters flowing from them provide hot baths, in which the people bathe separately according to age and sex. As Saint Basil says: "Water receives its heat when it flows across certain metals, and becomes hot, and even scalding." The land has rich veins of many metals, including copper, iron, lead, and silver. There is also much black jet[6] of fine quality, which sparkles in firelight. When burned, it drives away snakes, and, like amber, when it is warmed by friction, it clings to whatever is applied to it. In old times, the country had twenty-eight noble cities, and innumerable castles, all of which were guarded by walls, 2
towers, and barred gates.

Since Britain lies far north toward the pole, the nights are short in summer, and at midnight it is hard to tell whether the evening twilight still lingers or whether dawn is approaching; for in these northern latitudes the sun does not remain long below the horizon at night. Consequently both sum-

1. **Belgic Gaul:** France.
2. **Reptacestir:** Richborough, part of the city of Sandwich.
3. **Gessoriacum:** Boulogne, France.
4. **Orcades:** The Orkney Isles.
5. **draft animals:** Animals used for pulling loads.
6. **jet** *n.*: A type of coal.

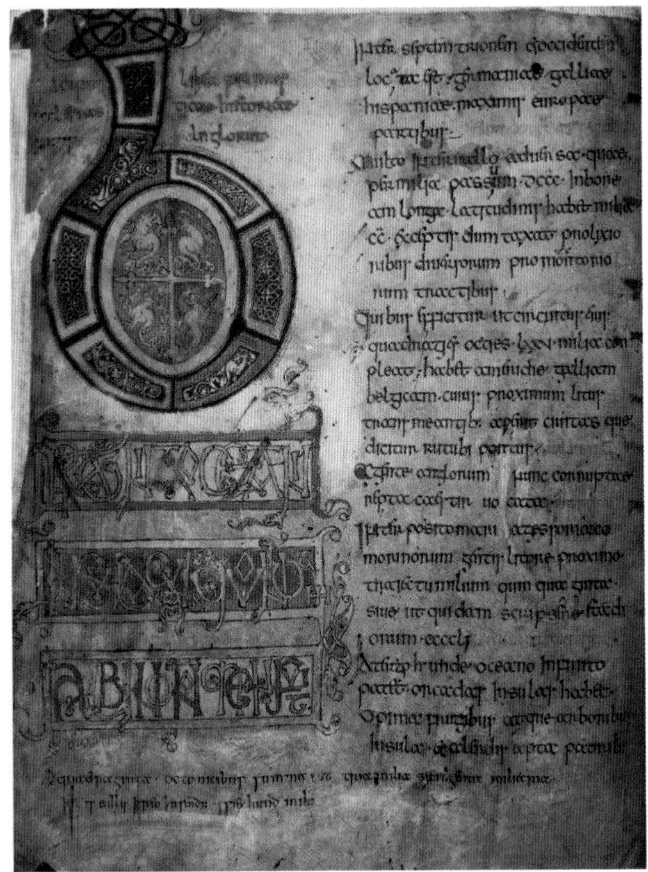

COTTON MS TIBERIUS C II FOLIO VERSO
Page of Bede's History
The British Library

3 mer days and winter nights are long, and when the sun withdraws southwards, the winter nights last eighteen hours. In Armenia,[7] Macedonia,[8] and Italy, and other countries of that latitude, the longest day lasts only fifteen hours and the shortest nine.

At the present time there are in Britain, in harmony with the five books of the divine law, five languages and four nations
4 —English, British, Scots, and Picts. Each of these have their own language, but all are united in their study of God's truth by the fifth, Latin, which has become a common medium through the study of the scriptures. The original inhabitants of the island were the Britons, from whom it takes its name, and who, according to tradition, crossed into Britain from Armorica,[9] and occupied the southern parts. When they had spread northwards and possessed the greater part of the islands, it is said that some Picts from Scythia[10] put to sea in a few long ships and were driven by storms around the coasts of Britain, arriving at length on the north

7. **Armenia:** Now part of the Soviet Union.
8. **Macedonia:** Now a region divided among Greece, Yugoslavia, and Bulgaria.

9. **Armorica:** Brittany, France.
10. **Scythia** (sith' ē ə): An ancient region in southeastern Europe.

Humanities Note

Fine art, a page of Bede's *History.* The word *illuminator,* one who "lightens up," appeared in the language in the twelfth century. It is descriptive of the artist who decorated the written vellum manuscripts that were being produced in monasteries at the time.

This decorative page is typical of the early, painstaking work done by these artists. The enlarged decorative capital letter is embellished with the sort of geometric design that is common to all barbaric art. The colorful lozenge shapes beneath it contain decorative words. Decorated pages such as this enhanced the reader's awe and enjoyment of the manuscript. They have left us with a record of the early art of painting that has had a lasting effect on the art of succeeding generations.

You might discuss the following with your class.

1. Try to imagine the labor that this artist went through to produce this image.
2. This artist not only had to grind his own paint and ink, he also had to make his paper, brushes, pens, and even the work table that he used. Did these difficulties detract from the beauty of what he produced here?

3 **Clarification** Bede understood the phenomenon of seasonal shifts in the earth's relation to the sun but believed that the sun, which was commonly believed to revolve around the earth, was doing the shifting.

4 **Clarification** "British" here refers to what we now call Welsh.

Humanities Note

Fine art, Illumination, *The Venerable Bede Writing His Book and Presenting It to the Bishop of Lindisfarne,* twelfth century. This illumination comes from a twelfth-century copy of Bede's *Life of St Cuthbert.*

1. Bede is an important historic figure. Does this illustration help in your appreciation of his work?
2. Are the people portrayed in this miniature that different in appearance from someone you might meet today?

5 **Enrichment** Most scholars think that this quotation is intended to enliven the text rather than report exact words.

6 **Enrichment** No one knows whether this story is true; Bede probably included it because it seemed to explain something that he did know, which was that the Pictish custom of succession was different from the one Bede knew.

7 **Discussion** What, then, did Bede think *Dalreudians* meant?

8 **Enrichment** Bede probably never went to Ireland, and he believed the geographical assumption of his day that the island extended far south of England.

9 **Critical Reading and Thinking** What does this passage show about Bede's attitude toward Ireland?

10 **Literary Focus** Love of truth is one of Bede's outstanding characteristics; when he relates a story on hearsay evidence, he carefully indicates this. Demonstrate in this and other passages.

11 **Clarification** This "extensive arm of the sea" is the Firth of Clyde.

MONKS
Bodleian Library, Oxford

coast of Ireland. Here they found the nation
of the Scots, from whom they asked permission to settle, but their request was refused.
Ireland is the largest island after Britain,
and lies to the west. It is shorter than Britain to the north, but extends far beyond it to
the south towards the northern coasts of
Spain, although a wide sea separates them.
These Pictish seafarers, as I have said,
asked for a grant of land to make a settlement. The Scots replied that there was not
room for them both, but said: "We can give
you good advice. There is another island not
5 far to the east, which we often see in the
distance on clear days. Go and settle there if
you wish; should you meet resistance, we
will come to your help." So the Picts crossed
into Britain, and began to settle in the north
of the island, since the Britons were in
possession of the south. Having no women
with them, these Picts asked wives of the
Scots, who consented on condition that,
when any dispute arose, they should choose 6
a king from the female royal line rather than
the male. This custom continues among the
Picts to this day. As time went on, Britain
received a third nation, that of the Scots,
who migrated from Ireland under their
chieftain Reuda, and by a combination of
force and treaty, obtained from the Picts the
settlements that they still hold. From the
name of this chieftain, they are still known
as Dalreudians, for in their tongue *dal* 7
means a division.

Ireland is broader than Britain, and its 8
mild and healthy climate is superior. Snow
rarely lies longer than three days, so that
there is no need to store hay in summer for
winter use or to build stables for beasts.
There are no reptiles, and no snake can
exist there, for although often brought over
from Britain, as soon as the ship nears land,
they breathe its scented air and die. In fact,
almost everything in this isle enjoys immunity to poison, and I have heard that folk
suffering from snakebite have drunk water
in which scrapings from the leaves of books
from Ireland had been steeped, and that this 9
remedy checked the spreading poison and
reduced the swelling. The island abounds in
milk and honey, and there is no lack of
vines, fish, and birds, while deer and goats 10
are widely hunted. It is the original home of
the Scots, who, as already mentioned, later
migrated and joined the Britons and Picts in
Britain. There is a very extensive arm of the 11
sea, which originally formed the boundary
between the Britons and the Picts. This
runs inland from the west for a great distance as far as the strongly fortified British
city of Alcuith.[11] It was to the northern
shores of this firth that the Scots came and
established their new homeland.

11. **Alcuith** (al kü′ əth): Dumbarton, Scotland.

Answers

ANSWERS TO THINKING ABOUT THE SELECTION
Recalling

1. Germany, Gaul (France), and Spain formed the greater part of Europe.
2. (a) The four nations in Britain were the English, the British, the Scots, and the Picts;
   (b) the Latin tongue, used in the study of the Scriptures, united the four nations.
3. Deer and goats were widely hunted in Ireland.

Interpreting

4. It implies that the people in Britain dyed their cloth and that they liked bright, rich colors.
5. Britain may have consisted of many separate political entities that did not necessarily get along with one another.
6. Bede reports that almost everything in Ireland is immune to poison.

Applying

7. Bede reports both fact and legend. You might consult a source that

THINKING ABOUT THE SELECTION

Recalling

1. What countries formed the greater part of Europe at the time of Bede's history?
2. (a) In Bede's time, what were the four nations in Britain. (b) What united them?
3. What animals does Bede say were widely hunted in Ireland?

Interpreting

4. What does the explanation about scarlet dye imply about the lifestyle of the people?
5. Bede states that Britain once "had twenty-eight noble cities . . . guarded by walls, towers, and barred gates." What does this statement suggest about the political situation at the time?
6. What is one unlikely tale that Bede includes in his history?

Applying

7. If you wanted to read a reliable history of early England, you would probably choose something other than Bede's work. Why? What kind of source might you choose?

ANALYZING LITERATURE

Understanding Historical Writing

A history provides factual information about the past. This information comes from a variety of sources, including books and other printed materials, public records, and, if possible, personal letters, memoirs, and interviews. A good historian like Bede does more than just list facts, however. Bede presents his facts as part of an understandable whole.

1. Accuracy is very important in historical writing. Read the quotation from the Scots on page 42. (a) Do you think the statement is an exact quotation? (b) If not, does it cast doubt on the accuracy of Bede's history? Explain.
2. Bede sometimes relies on people's oral statements for his information. On page 42 he makes a specific reference to such a source. What is it?

CRITICAL THINKING AND READING

Making Inferences About Attitudes

Bede's history reflects his own attitudes and those of the people he is writing about. Since these attitudes tend to be revealed indirectly, you must make inferences, or draw conclusions about them. For example, Bede states that the people of England are "united in their study of God's truth." From this statement you can infer that religion played an important role in the life of the people.

1. From Bede's comments on page 42, what do you think the general attitude was in Britain toward snakes?
2. Do you think the Picts and Scots got along well with each other? Cite the evidence on which you base your inference.

UNDERSTANDING LANGUAGE

Tracing Word Histories

An **etymology** explains the origin and history of a word. It usually appears in brackets in a dictionary entry.

amber *n.* [ME. *aumbre,* amber, ambergris <OFr. *ambre* < Ar. *'anbar,* ambergris]

The present English word *amber* is derived from the Middle English word *aumbre,* which came from Old French, and originally from Arabic.

Trace the history of the following words.

1. promontory
2. furlong
3. migrate
4. cockle

THINKING AND WRITING

Writing a Critical Review

Give your opinion of this excerpt from Bede's history. First, jot down your answers to the following questions: Does the history seem accurate? Is it clearly written? What do you find to be its most striking fact? Next, write a topic sentence that states your opinion clearly. Then write a draft, using examples to support your opinion. Finally, revise your draft, making sure that its sentences are in logical order.

(Answers begin on p. 42.)

2. The Picts and Scots probably did not get along. The Scots did not allow the Picts to settle in Ireland when the latter were blown ashore there. In addition, the Scots gave wives to the Picts but required the Picts to choose their rulers from the female, or Scots, lineage. Finally, the Scots eventually migrated from Ireland to the Picts's new home and displaced them "by force or treaty."

ANSWERS TO UNDERSTANDING LANGUAGE

1. *Promontory* is derived from the Medieval Latin word *promontorium,* an alteration of the Latin word *promunturium.*
2. *Furlong* is derived from the Middle English word *furlong,* which came from the Old English *furlang,* meaning "long furrow."
3. *Migrate* is derived from the inflected form *migrat-*of the Latin infinitive *migrare.*
4. *Cockle* is derived from the Middle English word *cokel,* which comes from the Old French word *coquille,* meaning "shell," which possibly came from the Vulgar Latin *conchillia,* which came from the Latin *conchylium,* which came from the Greek *konchylion,* the diminutive of *konchē,* which means "mussel."

THINKING AND WRITING

For help with this assignment, students can refer to Lesson 15, "Evaluating a Literary Work, in the Handbook of Writing About Literature.

Publishing Student Writing You might have students work in groups sharing their opinions. Perhaps each group could prepare a group opinion.

used not only Bede but also other surviving written records from the time, as well as archeological evidence.

ANSWERS TO ANALYZING LITERATURE

1. (a) The quotation could not be exact.
   (b) The modern reader might wonder what other quotations and "facts" have been fabricated. Students might also mention that this could be a stylistic device.
2. Bede says that he has heard that people have been cured of snakebite by drinking water in which scrapings from the pages of Irish books have been steeped.

Challenge The British historian H.A.L. Fisher (1865–1940) once wrote "There can be . . . only one safe rule for the historian: that he can recognize in the development of human destinies the play of the contingent and the unforeseen." Restate the quotation in your own words and explain why you think Bede would or would not have agreed with it.

ANSWERS TO CRITICAL THINKING AND READING

1. People undoubtedly hated and feared snakes.

The writing assignments on page 44 have students write creatively, while those on page 45 have them think about the selections and write critically.

YOU THE WRITER

Guidelines for Evaluating Assignment 1

1. Has the student written a narrative poem telling of the physical and mental hardships of the ocean voyage?
2. Has the student included sufficient details to describe each hardship?
3. Has the student written the narrative poem in chronological order?
4. Is the narrative poem free from grammar, usage, and mechanics errors?

Guidelines for Evaluating Assignment 2

1. Has the student presented a new view of a character or incident in Anglo-Saxon literature in a dialogue or narrative?
2. Does the paper contain sufficient detail?
3. Is the organization and structure sufficient?
4. Is the paper free from grammar, usage, and mechanics errors?

Guidelines for Evaluating Assignment 3

1. Does the article convey a clear, vivid picture of the student's day in the past?
2. Are the paragraphs fully developed and focused on a single impression or experience?
3. Does the structure and style add to the expressiveness?
4. Is the article free from grammar, usage, and mechanics errors?

YOU THE WRITER

Assignment

1. Imagine that you have been lost for many days in the north Atlantic Ocean in a small boat. At last you reach land. Write a narrative poem in which you describe the hardships, both physical and mental, that you endured. Use any verse form you feel is suitable.

Prewriting. First list several of the main sufferings you endured. Then make notes on the details of each. Think of ways to make your narrative as vivid and concrete as possible.

Writing. Write your first draft in chronological order, using description to expand on each of the basic hardships you are recounting.

Revising. When you revise, first see if you need to adjust the overall narrative structure of your poem. Then look to improve the details of each piece of description. Read your poem aloud. Can you improve its musical quality?

Assignment

2. Many notable works of literature are based on characters or incidents from earlier works. Select any character or incident from Anglo-Saxon literature and write a brief prose monologue or narrative based on the character or incident you have chosen.

Prewriting. First use your imagination to think up a new view of the character or incident. Then plan the structure and details of your monologue or narrative.

Writing. Your first draft should contain, in rough form, all the contents of your work—either your character's remarks or the details of the incident you are narrating.

Revising. When you revise, improve the organization and structure of your work. Then try to polish and perfect the details.

Assignment

3. Imagine that you have gone back in time to Anglo-Saxon England and, twenty-four hours later, have returned to the present. Write a brief magazine article whose purpose is to convey your discovery of the differences between the Anglo-Saxon world and the modern world.

Prewriting. List the details of what you saw, heard, and experienced. Then fit them into an outline that will enable you to convey a clear, vivid picture of your day in the past.

Writing. Following your outline, write fully developed paragraphs, each of which focuses on a single impression or experience. Conclude by summarizing the differences.

Revising. Can you replace one of the impressions or experiences with a better, more revealing one? Can you alter your structure or style for greater expressiveness? Revise according to these questions.

YOU THE CRITIC

Assignment

1. Write a critical evaluation of any one of the selections from the Anglo-Saxon period. The purpose of your evaluation should be to indicate what interest the work holds for a contemporary reader.

Prewriting. Answer these questions: What is my general opinion of this work? What specifically did I admire or dislike about it? What is the basic opinion I wish to share with readers who have not yet read the work?

Writing. Write an essay in which you first state in a topic sentence your critical judgment. Then offer your reasons. Refer to details of the work to clarify and support your argument.

Revising. Revise in the light of these questions: Is my opinion fair, objective, and clearly expressed? Can I make my argument more forceful and persuasive by citing other details or aspects of the work?

Assignment

2. Some readers suppose that the earliest literature of a people tends to be crude and primitive. Write a brief essay in which you point out the literary artistry—the imaginative power, sophisticated design, or stylistic appeal—of any one of the Anglo-Saxon selections you have read.

Prewriting. First decide what you liked about the work. Then analyze it to determine the methods the writer used to make it artistically effective.

Writing. First state or describe clearly the kind of literary excellence you see in the work. Then refer to specific aspects and details of the work to embody and clarify your view.

Revising. When you revise keep in mind the question, "Have I demonstrated and illustrated the artistic excellence I see in ———?" Make changes that help you show, not just talk about, the virtues of the literary work.

Assignment

3. Write an essay with the title "Anglo-Saxon Literature: Mirror of the Times." Show how the literature you have read reflects what you have learned about Anglo-Saxon history and life.

Prewriting. Review the introduction to the Anglo-Saxon period and any other information you have gathered about it. Which work that you have read comes to mind in the course of your review? What brings this work to mind?

Writing. Write a first draft based on this last question. Tell how Anglo-Saxon history or life reveals itself in the work you have selected. Your basic approach should be a descriptive comparison of the historical background and the literary expression of it.

Revising. Concentrate on increasing the clarity and precision of your description of the link between the literature and its historical setting.

YOU THE CRITIC

Guidelines for Evaluating Assignment 1

1. Does the critical evaluation begin with a topic sentence that states the student's critical judgment of a selection of Anglo-Saxon literature?
2. Is the opinion clearly stated, fair, and objective?
3. Is the argument made forceful by references to details of the work?
4. Is the essay free from grammar, usage, and mechanics errors?

Guidelines for Evaluating Assignment 2

1. Does the student explain clearly the kind of literary excellence he or she finds in the Anglo-Saxon selection?
2. Does the student refer to specific aspects and details of the work to support and clarify his or her opinion?
3. Does the student show, not just discuss, the virtues of the literary work?
4. Is the essay free from grammar, usage, and mechanics errors?

Guidelines for Evaluating Assignment 3

1. Does the essay demonstrate how Anglo-Saxon history or life is revealed in the literary work selected?
2. Has student used a descriptive comparison of the historical background and the literary expression of it as his or her approach to the essay?
3. Is there a clear, precise description of the link between the literature and the historical setting?
4. Is the essay free from grammar, usage, and mechanics errors?

Humanities Note

Detail of illuminated manuscript, *Pilgrims to Canterbury,* c. 1400. By 1400, illumination was a well-developed art, not limited only to religious works. This section from an English illuminated manuscript shows a group of Pilgrims on their way to Canterbury. Aspects of the time are reflected in the Pilgrims' dress and in the medieval structure in the background. Like Chaucer's pilgrims, these represent people from different walks of life, both clerical and lay.

PILGRIMS TO CANTERBURY: DETAIL OF AN ENGLISH ILLUMINATED MANUSCRIPT, c.1400
The Granger Collection

THE MEDIEVAL PERIOD

1066–1485

A Knyght ther was, and that a worthy man
That fro the tyme that he first bigan
To riden out, he loved chivalrie,
Trouthe and honour, fredom and curteisie

Geoffrey Chaucer

Humanities Note

The Bayeux Tapestry: Duke William encourages his men at Hastings. The Bayeux Tapestry, a wool-on-linen embroidery 20 inches high and 230 feet long, records the story of the Norman Conquest of England. Its many scenes depict different aspects of the invasion of England and the Battle of Hastings. In this detail, Duke William, later to be known as William the Conqueror, is shown encouraging his men at Hastings by raising his helmet.

1 **Historical Context** It is very likely that Edward had, in fact, promised the throne to his cousin William in 1051 but had revoked this promise under pressure from the Godwin family, Harold and his father.

2 **Master Teacher Note** In order for the students to visualize the events of the Norman Conquest, you might introduce pictures of the Bayeux Tapestry, an embroidered record supervised by William's wife, Matilda.

3 **Enrichment** The novel *The Golden Warrior* by Hope Muntz (Scribners, 1949) presents a beautifully written and historically accurate view of the invasion from the Saxon point of view.

RELIGIOUS CEREMONY OF THE DRUIDS
Forrest C. Crooks
Three Lions

The famous description on the preceding page comes from an English literary masterpiece, *The Canterbury Tales,* by Geoffrey Chaucer (1340?–1400). The passage reflects many of the ideas and attitudes held by Europeans during the fourteenth century. In these years knights lived by the code of chivalry, which stressed truth, honor, and courtesy off the battlefield and valor on it. The Roman Catholic Church had become the only force uniting most of Western Europe. Religion pervaded daily life, and to be a devout Christian —a worthy man—was important not only to knights but to all members of English society.

During these years the English language changed from its Anglo-Saxon form to one called Middle English, far more familiar to modern readers. Looking at Chaucer's words above, we can readily recognize their modern English counterparts—"knyght" is *knight,* "ther" is *there,* "fro" is *from,* "riden" is *ride,* "chivalrie" is *chivalry,* and so on. The change from Old English to Middle English took place gradually. Yet this change can be traced to one riveting event—the Norman invasion of 1066.

THE NORMAN CONQUEST

The Normans, or "north men," were descendants of Vikings who had invaded the coast of France in the ninth century. Over the years, these people had adopted many French ways. They had become devout Christians. They had accustomed themselves to speaking a dialect of the French language. They had also organized themselves according to the French political and economic system of the times—feudalism.

William, Duke of Normandy, had family ties to Edward the
Confessor, the English king. When Edward died in 1066, the Saxon
witan—the council of elders—chose Harold II as king. William of
Normandy, meanwhile, claimed that Edward had promised him the 1
throne. William thereupon led a few thousand Norman and French
troops across the English Channel to assert his claim by force.

He met King Harold at the Battle of Hastings near a seaside 2
village in southern England. Harold was killed, and William emerged
victorious. He then headed for London, brutally crushing all resist- 3
ance. At Westminster Abbey on Christmas Day, William "the Conqueror" took the throne of England as King William I.

Over the next five years, William consolidated his victory. He suppressed the Anglo-Saxon nobility and confiscated their lands. He saw to it that Normans controlled government at all levels. The Normans conducted their business in Norman French or Latin. They gradually remade England along feudal lines.

The Rise of Feudalism

Feudalism had taken root on the European continent at a time when no central government was strong enough to keep order.

Under the circumstances, nobles had to rely on their own warriors for help. The system they created was an exchange of property for personal service. The person who granted the property was the lord or overlord. The person who received it was the vassal. The vassal promised service to his lord in a ceremony called the act of homage. At the same time, the vassal usually pledged his faithfulness by taking the Christian vow of fealty.

4 In theory, all the land belonged to the ruler. The king kept some of it for his personal use, granted some to the church, and parceled out the rest among his powerful supporters. He gave these supporters noble titles—usually baron—and the special privileges that went with them. The parcels of land granted to the barons were known as fiefs.

As a vassal of his overlord, each baron was obliged to pay certain fees or taxes. He was also expected to supply a specified number of knights, or professional soldiers, should the king require them. In return for their services, knights usually received smaller parcels of land, called manors. The peasants who worked these manors were the lowest class in the feudal system, the serfs. Manors became the basic community of the feudal system. Most were self-sufficient, using their own craftsmen to provide nearly all their needs.

In the eleventh century, Europe had no nation-states with firm political boundaries. William and the Norman kings who followed him—William II, Henry I, and Stephen of Blois—held feudal domains in both England and France. Since they had two realms, Norman kings had far wider responsibilities than Saxon kings had faced. The situation also meant that English barons dissatisfied with their overlord could cross the English Channel and stir up trouble on the other side.

A BALIFF SUPERVISING THE HARVEST (THE MONTH OF AUGUST): MANUSCRIPT ILLUMINATION, ENGLISH, EARLY 14TH CENTURY
The Granger Collection

A Shifting Language

Like a great many of history's conquerors, the Normans thought themselves vastly superior to the people they had conquered. The invaders treated the Saxons and Danes as not quite human and sniffed at their language as unworthy of respect. The Normans substituted their dialect of French in the law courts as well as in the conduct of business in general. To this day, French words such as *bail* and *sergeant* remain embedded in the language of English law.

Traces of Norman discrimination against the Saxons have lingered for centuries. In his nineteenth-century novel *Ivanhoe,* Sir Walter Scott noted one aspect of Norman superiority. In the field, he wrote, a domestic animal is often referred to by its Saxon name—swine, sheep, or ox. When the same animal appears on a dinner table, however, it takes a French name—pork, mutton, or beef. In other words, the raising of farm animals was considered a Saxon activity, whereas the more elegant pursuit, dining, befitted the Normans.

Humanities Note

Illumination, A bailiff supervising the harvest (August). This early fourteenth-century illumination was probably from a book of days, a prayer book used by the nobility for daily prayer, with an illumination for each month. In such prayer books, a standard scene was used for each month. August, for example, would always be illustrated with a harvest scene.

This illumination shows the toil of the peasant on a manorial farm. The peasant's life was governed by the seasons, and late summer was the time for harvesting two major crops, wheat and rye.

4 **Historical Context** In order to obtain a record of these holdings, in 1086 William commissioned a census called the Domesday Book.

BRITISH EVENTS

1066 Saxons defeated at Hastings.

1073 Canterbury becomes England's religious center.

c. 1075 Construction on Tower of London begins.

1100 Henry I becomes king.

1110 First recorded miracle play performed at Dunstable.

c. 1130 Oxford becomes a center for learning.

c. 1136 Geoffrey of Monmouth writes *History Requm Britanniae*.

1151 Chess introduced to England.

1166 Thomas Becket, archbishop of Canterbury, murdered.

1171 Henry II conquers southeastern Ireland.

1176 First Eisteddfod, Welsh festival of poetry and music.

1180 Glass windows first used in private homes.

c. 1190 Beginning of legendary era of Robin Hood.

1215 King John forced to sign Magna Carta.

1218 First Newgate Prison built in London.

1233 First coal mined at Newcastle.

1258 First commoners allowed in Parliament.

c. 1265 Roger Bacon writes *Opus Majus*.

The Murder of Thomas Becket

King John Signs the Magna Carta

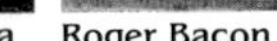

Roger Bacon

Pope Gregory IX

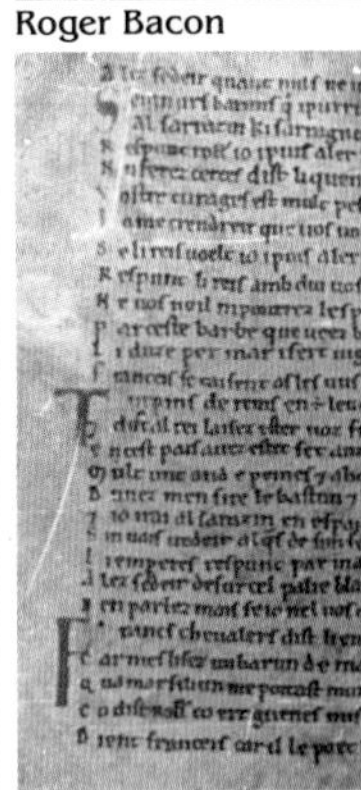

Manuscript of

The Siege of Jerusalem During the First Crusade

Genghis Khan

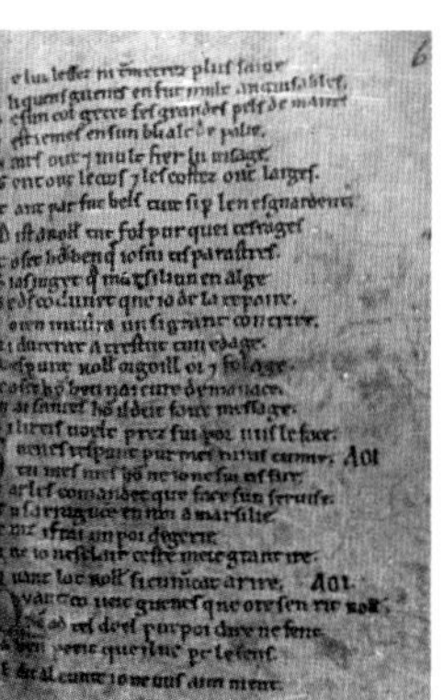

The Song of Roland

Twelfth-century Chess Piece

WORLD EVENTS

1096 Europe and Middle East: First Crusade begins.

c. 1100 France: *Song of Roland* written.

c. 1120 Portugal: Alfonso VII defeats Moors.

c. 1150 Spain: First paper manufactured.

Poem of El Cid written.

c. 1160 France: Troubadours glorify courtly love in poems and songs.

1174 Italy: Tower of Pisa built.

1189 Europe and Middle East: Third Crusade begins.

1192 Austria: Duke Leopold imprisons Richard I of England.

1194 Iceland: *Elder Edda*, a collection of Norse myths and legends, first appears.

1203 Germany: Wolfram von Eschenbach writes *Parzival*.

1214 China: Mongol leader Genghis Khan captures Peking.

1221 Italy: First known sonnet appears.

1233 Europe: Pope Gregory IX establishes Inquisition.

1241 Eastern Europe: Mongols withdraw from Poland and Hungary.

1266 Italy: Thomas Aquinas writes *Theologiae*.

BRITISH EVENTS

1272	Edward I becomes king.
c. 1281	Cambridge University founded.
1282	England conquers Wales.
c. 1285	The legendary Patrick Spens's ship wrecked off Aberdeen, Scotland.
1295	Edward I assembles Model Parliament.
1337	Beginning of Hundred Years' War with France.
1348	Black death begins sweeping through England.
1372	Bible first translated into English.
c. 1375	Surviving version of *Sir Gawain and the Green Knight* written.
1381	Peasants' Revolt.
1386	**Chaucer** begins writing *The Canterbury Tales*.
c. 1450	*The Second Shepherds' Play* first performed.
1455	Beginning of Wars of the Roses.
1460	Richard of York killed at Battle of Wakefield.
c. 1470	**Thomas Malory** writes *Morte D' Arthur*.
1476	William Caxton builds first English printing press.

François Villon

Joan of Arc

Printer's Device Used by Caxton

Black Death

Marco Polo

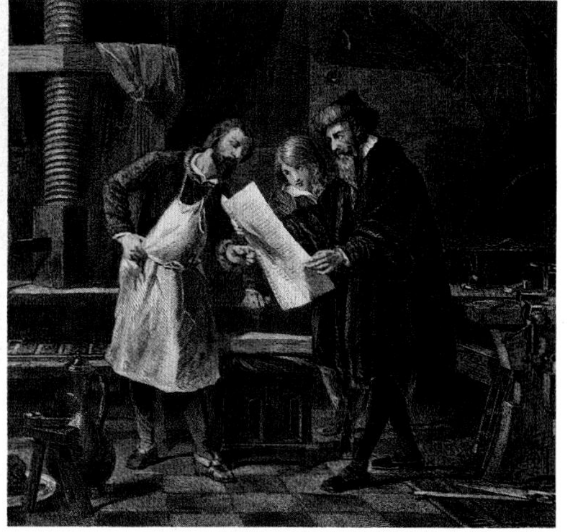
Johann Gutenburg Printing First Bible

Sweeps Through England

Canterbury Tales

Battle During the Hundred Years' War

WORLD EVENTS

1271 China: Marco Polo visits court of Kublai Khan.

1291 Europe and Middle East: End of Crusades.

1297 South Pacific: Moas, large flightless birds, become extinct.

1307 Italy: Dante begins writing *The Divine Comedy*.

1312 Africa: Mali Empire reaches its zenith.

1327 Mexico: Aztecs establish Mexico City.

1332 India: Bubonic plague begins.

1341 Italy: Petrarch crowned poet laureate in Rome.

1346 France: English defeat French at Crecy.

1348 Italy: Boccaccio publishes *Decameron*.

c. 1400 Italy: Beginning of Medici rule.

1416 Italy: Donatello sculpts *St. George*.

1428 France: Joan of Arc leads French in breaking Siege of Orleans.

1438 Peru: Inca Empire reaches its zenith.

c. 1450 North America: Iroquois nations unite.

1453 France: Hundred Years' War with England ends.

Germany: First Gutenberg Bible printed.

1461 France: François Villon publishes *Grand Testament*.

1483 Portugal: John II refuses to finance Columbus.

1484 Italy: Botticelli paints *Birth of Venus*.

5 **Historical Context** Henry II was, of course, a direct descendant of the Norman line through his mother, Maud, granddaughter of William the Conqueror.

6 **Enrichment** T. S. Eliot's play *Murder in the Cathedral* (Harcourt Brace Jovanovich, 1964) recreates this incident.

7 **Literary Movement** See the Prologue to the *Canterbury Tales* (page 91).

Reign of the Plantagenets

Although Norman influence continued for centuries, Norman rule ended in 1154 when Henry Plantagenet, Count of Anjou, came to the throne as Henry II. Henry founded the royal house of
5 Plantagenet, otherwise known as the Angevin (from Anjou) line of English monarchs. A strongly committed ruler, Henry established a record as one of England's ablest kings. He had an avid interest in government and a keen understanding of the law.

Henry II and the Church

Henry's concern with legal matters led him into direct conflict with the church. By the twelfth century, the church had grown ever more powerful, obtaining the authority to put clergymen on trial in church-run courts. Henry sought to curb some abuses connected with this privilege. When the archbishop's seat at Canterbury fell vacant, he appointed his friend Thomas Becket to the position, expecting Becket to go along with royal policy. Instead, Becket defied the king and appealed to the pope in Rome. The pope sided with Becket, provoking Henry to rage.

Some of Henry's knights misunderstood the royal wrath. In
6 1170, four of them went to Canterbury and murdered Becket in his cathedral. Henry quickly condemned the crime and tried to atone for it by making a holy journey, or pilgrimage, to Becket's tomb. Thereafter a pilgrimage to Becket's shrine at Canterbury became a
7 common English means of showing religious devotion. The characters in Chaucer's *The Canterbury Tales,* for example, make just such a pilgrimage.

Origins of Constitutional Government

The next king, Richard I, spent most of his reign staging military expeditions overseas. His activities proved costly, and his successor, King John, inherited the debts. John tried to raise money by ordering new taxes on the barons and saved money by curtailing services such as the sending of judges to local districts to settle quarrels. The barons resisted these measures, bringing England to the edge of civil war. To avert further trouble, King John at last agreed to certain of the barons' conditions by putting his seal to the Magna Carta (Latin for "Great Charter").

In this document, the king promised not to tax land without first meeting with the barons. He also said he would choose as his officers only those "who know the law of the realm and mean to observe it well." The Magna Carta produced no radical changes in government. Yet many historians believe that the document's restrictions on royal power marked the beginning of constitutional government in England.

Constitutional government continued to develop under subsequent kings. During the reign of Henry III, the Great Council of barons who advised the king came to be called Parliament. Henry's

KING JOHN SIGNING MAGNA CARTA AT RUNNYMEDE, 15TH JUNE 1215: COLORED ENGRAVING, 18TH CENTURY
The Granger Collection

successor, Edward I, became the first king to summon a Parliament partly elected by "free men"—a term that included some ordinary townspeople as well as barons. By the end of the thirteenth century, then, Parliament had already been established as a cornerstone of government in the British Isles.

The Growth of Towns

It was no accident that some members of Parliament now represented townspeople. In the thirteenth century, towns were becoming increasingly important in English life. The Crusades, a series of religious wars in the twelfth and thirteenth centuries, had stimulated trade between Europe and the Middle East. As trade expanded, so did Europe's trading centers. The largest of these centers in England was London, originally built by the Romans. Four times more populous than any other English community, London had already achieved status as a city.

In London and elsewhere, townspeople organized themselves into guilds, or associations, of various sorts. The two most significant types were merchant guilds and craft guilds. Merchant guilds were formed in an effort to promote business within a town, often at the expense of other towns nearby. As these guilds became more powerful, some of them virtually took over town governments. Craft guilds, like our modern labor unions, sought to protect the interests of workers such as weavers, carpenters, and tanners. They also tried to assure the quality of the work these craftspeople produced. Such organizations operated in a world in which advancement was tightly controlled. A young person typically entered a craft as an apprentice, or beginner, and worked his way up the ladder, sometimes reaching the highest rung as master craftsman.

The growth of towns meant that wealth was no longer restricted to land ownership, which remained a privilege of the nobility.

FOUR KINGS OF ENGLAND DEPICTED ON A PAGE OF A 13TH-CENTURY MANUSCRIPT
The Granger Collection

Humanities Note

Engraving, King John signing the Magna Carta at Runnymede. This eighteenth-century colored engraving depicts the historic signing of the Magna Carta on June 15, 1215, at Runnymede, a meadow on the banks of the Thames, about twenty miles from London. The Magna Carta was written in Latin on a parchment scroll. Later, copies were made and sent to cathedrals in all parts of England. Sheriffs were required to read it in the county courts four times yearly, bishops were allowed to denounce publicly those who did not observe it, and barons were encouraged to enforce it.

The unknown engraver of this picture plays up the significance of the event, as determined by history but probably not apparent to those present at the scene.

Humanities Note

Manuscript, Four Kings of England. This depiction of the kings on a thirteenth-century manuscript shows the first kings in the Platagenet line, clockwise from top left: Henry II, Richard I, Henry III, and John. Shown between Henry II and Richard I is the young Henry III. Henry II, became king in 1154. When he died in 1189, he was succeeded by his son Richard (1152–1199), known as the "Lion-Hearted." Killed during the seige of a French castle, Richard was succeeded by his brother John (1167–1216), signer of the Magna Carta. John was succeeded by his son, Henry III (1207–1272).

Humanities Note

Stained glass, Funeral of a plague victim. This funeral scene is depicted in a stained glass window in Trinity Chapel of Canterbury Cathedral. The bubonic plague —known as the Black Death— killed nearly a third of the population of Europe in the fourteenth century. This stained glass window commemorates that devastating event.

Stained glass was made by heating sand, salt, and ashes into a molten mass, and then coloring it with metallic oxides. To make a window, pieces of colored glass were inserted into the grooves of lead frames. The Gothic style of architecture in the twelfth and following centuries fostered the production of stained glass windows.

FUNERAL OF PLAGUE VICTIM IN HOUSE OF FITZEISULF TRINITY CAPEL WINDOW, CANTERBURY CATHEDRAL, 14TH CENTURY
The Granger Collection

Unfortunately, it also meant that people lived much closer together, often under conditions that were far from sanitary. When infectious diseases came to England, they spread havoc in the towns. The worst epidemic, a great plague called the Black Death, swept the island in 1348 and 1349, killing a third of the population.

THE LATER MIDDLE AGES

By the time of the Black Death, England had already passed into the period known as the Later Middle Ages. This period lasted from the beginning of the fourteenth century to the end of the fifteenth. During these years, the house of Lancaster replaced the Plantagenets on the throne, only to be replaced in turn by the house of York. The Lancastrian kings were Henry IV, Henry V, and Henry VI, all of whom later became central figures in the historical dramas of Shakespeare.

During the Later Middle Ages, the feudal system went into a steep decline. As new towns appeared, feudal notions of land tenure seemed more and more outdated. After the Black Death swept across England, a massive labor shortage increased the value of a peasant's work. More and more land owners began paying their farmers in cash, giving these workers a greater sense of freedom. Along with freedom went frustration, as peasants began complaining about discriminatory laws and onerous taxation. Finally, in 1381, peasants in southern England staged a revolt, demanding, among other things, an end to serfdom. Although the revolt was eventually crushed, many of its causes continued, and so did the peasants' discontent.

An Attack on the Church

At about the time of the peasants' revolt, other complaints were being directed at the church. They came from an outspoken scholar, John Wycliffe (c. 1320–84), who thought that religion had traveled far from its roots. Wycliffe opposed all forms of wealth among the clergy. He showed only scorn for monks, calling them men with "red and fat cheeks and great bellies." He believed that all religious authority sprang from the Bible, not from the church.

Wycliffe directed the translation of the Bible into English in the hope of making it more accessible to the people. He also helped to organize an order of "poor priests" known as Lollards. Eventually, the archbishop of Canterbury moved against the Lollards as heretics, people who attack church doctrine and undermine church authority. Yet the Lollards continued to spread Wycliffe's teachings for a number of years after the scholar's death.

Wars of the Roses

Just as the English Middle Ages had opened with a struggle for power, they closed with a similar conflict. This one began in 1453, when King Henry VI suffered the first of many bouts of madness. Parliament appointed his cousin Richard of York as temporary head of government. When Henry recovered briefly, Richard was forced from office, and Henry returned to the throne. Richard would not depart without a fight, however. The resulting civil war became known as the first War of the Roses, for it pitted the house of York, whose symbol was a white rose, against the house of Lancaster, whose symbol was a red rose.

In 1461, a Yorkist victory put Richard's son, Edward, on the throne. As Edward IV, he ruled England until his death in 1483, when his eldest son, still a boy, became Edward V. Soon afterward, Edward V and his brother died mysteriously in the Tower of London
8 while under the supposed protection of their uncle, Richard of Gloucester. Richard, accused by many people of these "Tower murders," then proclaimed himself King Richard III.

Two years later, Henry Tudor, a distant cousin and supporter of
9 the Lancastrian kings, led a rebellion against the unpopular King Richard and killed him. Tudor, crowned Henry VII, later married Richard's niece. By doing so, he united the houses of York and Lancaster and ended the Wars of the Roses. By the time Henry had established a new royal line, the house of Tudor, the English Middle Ages had ended.

CHIVALRY AND ROMANCE

Most societies have lived by a well-established set of ideals, and England of the Middle Ages was no exception. One set of standards by which people measured themselves during these years was the code of knightly behavior known as chivalry. The idea of chivalry first arose on the European continent at the time of the

KING HENRY VII OF ENGLAND
Panel, 1505, by Michiel Sittow
The Granger Collection

Humanities Note

Fine art, *King Henry VII of England,* 1505, by Michiel Sittow. Sittow (1469–1525) was a Spanish painter. This portrait, done in oil on a wood panel, captures Henry's cold, tough, and shrewd traits. During his reign, he instituted a number of practices that kept the nobles in fear and eliminated pretenders to the throne. To increase England's influence in Europe, Henry made important marriages for his children. Henry also showed an interest in the New World, sending John and Sebastian Cabot to explore North America in 1497.

8 **Enrichment** For a defense of Richard III, see Josephine Tey's *The Daughter of Time* (Bantam Books, 1985), an ingenious solution to a historic crime, presented in modern murder-mystery format.

9 **Historical Context** Henry Tudor was a direct descendant of the Duke of Lancaster, John of Gaunt, fourth son of Edward III.

Humanities Note

Fine art, *Sir Galahad,* 1864, by Dante Gabriel Rossetti. During the medieval period, the tales of King Arthur and his knights developed. Sir Galahad, one of Arthur's knights known for his purity and nobility of spirit, is an appropriate subject for Dante Gabriel Rossetti (1828–1882). Rossetti, a Victorian artist, was the leader of a group of friends known as the Pre-Raphaelite Brotherhood, whose desire was to paint in a simple, sincere way, true to nature. Their striving to show a simpler time is reflected in Rossetti's painting of Galahad, a pure and noble knight in an idealized world.

10 **Literary Movement** Three great bodies of narrative developed in the Middle Ages: the matter of Britain, which concentrated mainly on the Arthurian legend; the matter of France, which centered around Charlemagne; and the matter of Rome, which celebrated classical heroes.

Crusades. Although the Crusades often involved brutality and bloodshed, they encouraged warriors to search for higher rules of conduct.

At first the code dealt mainly with loyalty and valor, both on and off the battlefield. By the thirteenth century, however, chivalry had grown considerably more complex. Every knight was supposed to pledge his service to a lady. He might also be expected to joust for his lady's favor or to rescue maidens in distress.

French poets known as troubadours popularized this tradition in songs of gallant knights. Originally these songs were written in Romance, or Roman-influenced, languages rather than Latin, and so they were called romances. At the French court, it became important for knights to treat ladies with a respect that bordered on reverence. Gradually the same ideal took root in the English court.

The Legend of King Arthur

One example illustrating the development of chivalry originated with the Celts. For centuries after their defeat by the Anglo-Saxons, the Celts had told stories of a great hero, King Arthur. Inasmuch as historians cannot say for certain whether Arthur actually lived or not, tales about him are considered legends, a blend of fiction and fact. When the Normans were battling the Anglo-Saxons, they became interested in the old Celtic legends. In about 1136, a Welsh-born scholar, Geoffrey of Monmouth (c. 1100–54), drew upon his knowledge of Celtic legends and his readings of Bede to produce a *History of the Kings of Britain.* This fanciful history, though written in Latin, quickly popularized the early Celtic king.

10 Because of the Normans' French ties, the tales of Arthur spread not only in England but also in France. There they were influenced

SIR GALAHAD, 1864 (WATERCOLOR)
Dante Gabriel Rossetti
The Granger Collection

by other romances, often involving the French hero Charlemagne. New versions of the Arthur legend, though usually set in the past, began to depict Arthur as more modern in his practices. His Knights of the Round Table became paragons of chivalry, as adept in courtly love as they were in fighting battles. The legend also inspired *Sir Gawain and the Green Knight,* a fourteenth-century narrative poem by an anonymous author. In the poem an Arthurian knight, Sir Gawain, displays all the virtues of chivalry in his battles with the Green Knight, a supernatural figure.

Arthurian romance reached its height with *Le Morte d' Arthur (The Death of Arthur),* a fifteenth-century prose work by Sir Thomas Malory (d. 1471). Translating from French sources, Malory created the most complete Middle English compilation of the various legends involving Arthur and his court. *Le Morte d' Arthur* was printed in twenty-one volumes.

LEARNING AND LITERATURE

Although the Normans and French eventually had great influence on English letters, that development did not begin in 1066. To the contrary, the Norman invasion put a temporary halt to scholarship and literature in the British Isles. After the turbulence of conquest subsided, however, England experienced a "little renaissance," a small rebirth of learning, in the twelfth century. Although monasteries continued their scholastic traditions, new centers of learning emerged. Scholars flocked to the religious community at Oxford to hear lectures by noted visitors; then colleges were built to house the scholars, and the first English university was born. A second university at Cambridge followed some years later.

Probably the most famous scholar that Oxford produced in the Middle Ages was Roger Bacon (c. 1214–94), a scientist and mathematician now considered the father of English philosophy. A member of the Franciscan brotherhood, Bacon created his *Opus Majus* (Major Work), a Latin study of science, grammar, mathematics, and philosophy, at the request of the pope. Later, however, the church condemned Bacon as a heretic. The scholar died in obscurity, probably at Oxford, but his ideas were taken up a century later by another Franciscan, William Ockham (d. 1349). Like Bacon,
11 Ockham attempted to use a scientific approach in exploring the universe; he, too, was accused of heresy.

While Latin remained the language of church and university scholarship, Norman French was frequently used in government. Both languages contributed to what came to be called Middle English. Latin literature gradually gave way to literature written in the vernacular, or the language of the people. The use of the vernacular increased after 1372, when John Wycliffe began directing the English translation of the Bible. Wycliffe's work proved a major advance for literature, inasmuch as it encouraged more people to learn to read.

JOHANN GUTENBERG EXAMINING THE FIRST PROOF OF HIS PRINTED BIBLE FROM HIS PRESS AT MAINZ; AFTER THE PAINTING BY J. L. G. FERRIS
The Granger Collection

Humanities Note

Print, Johann Gutenberg examining the first proof of his printed Bible, after the painting by J. L. G. Ferris. Johannes Gutenberg, of Mainz, Germany, was the first to perfect the process of typography. The first book he printed was the Bible, now known as the Gutenberg Bible. This print from a later period shows the moment when Gutenberg sees his first proof of his Bible.

11 **Enrichment** Ockham is probably best remembered today for his law of parsimony, known as "Ockham's razor": an argument must be shaved down to its simplest terms.

Humanities Note

A page from the Lansdowne manuscript of Chaucer's *Canterbury Tales.* This page is from an early edition of *The Canterbury Tales.* Like other manuscripts of the period, the page is illuminated with decoration in the margin and of the capital *W.*

12 **Historical Context** Chaucer's connection with the English court was extensive. Not only did he serve as a page in the household of Lionel, Edward III's third son, but he also married Phillipa Swynford, sister of John of Gaunt's mistress, whose offspring were later legitimatized and whose descendants became the Tudor kings.

Another important invention of the period, printing from movable type, also encouraged literacy. In 1454 a German silversmith, Johann Gutenberg, devised a printing process with individual metal letters that could be used again and again. Printing spread rapidly from Germany to other parts of Europe, and further improvements were made. In 1476 a London merchant, William Caxton (c. 1422–91) set up the first movable-type press in England. This invention meant that English literature no longer needed to be hand copied by church scribes. Now it could be produced far more quickly and made available to a much wider circle of readers.

POETRY OF THE ENGLISH MIDDLE AGES

One of Caxton's first projects was the printing of *The Canterbury Tales*. His enthusiasm for this verse showed the importance that he and others placed on poetry in general. Two key poets of the period, William Langland and Geoffrey Chaucer, lived during the Later Middle Ages. Their writings marked the changes that were taking place in the English language and in society as a whole.

William Langland

Experts know very little about the poet they usually call William Langland. He appears to have come from western England and to have been a country boy. In his masterpiece, *Piers Plowman,* he followed a tradition of the Middle Ages by writing in the form of an allegory, a work in which most of the characters, settings, and plot events are arranged in a meaningful symbolical pattern. He also took a typically Anglo-Saxon delight in alliteration.

Like John Wycliffe, Langland was greatly concerned with the ways the wealthy oppress the poor. He left little doubt that his sympathies went out to those who had been treated harshly by the world. His most vivid writing concerned events he may have witnessed—tavern squabbles, for instance, or the misery of people suffering from the plague. Some scholars judge *Piers Plowman* one of the most deeply felt poems in all of English literature.

A PAGE FROM THE LANSDOWNE MS OF GEOFFREY CHAUCER'S CANTERBURY TALES
The Granger Collection

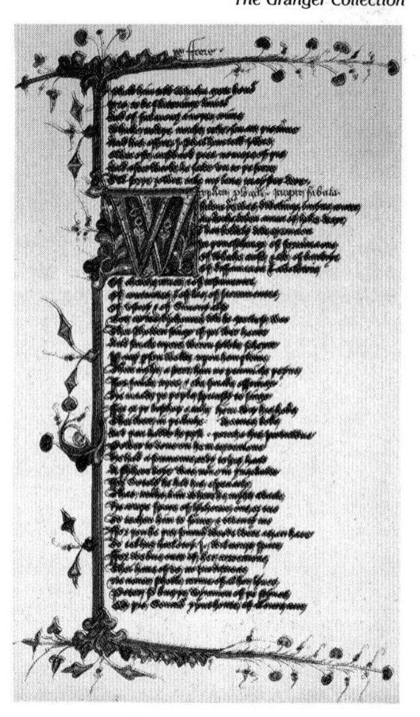

Geoffrey Chaucer

The towering figure of Middle English verse is Geoffrey Chaucer. In many estimates he ranks second only to Shakespeare as
England's greatest writer. Chaucer owed much of his early sophisti- 12
cation to his training as an attendant to King Edward III. The poet also traveled widely and familiarized himself with important Italian poets, including Dante and Petrarch.

Chaucer's major works include a number of narrative poems such as the verse romance *Troilus and Criseyde* (1372–86) and many short, allegorical poems. Yet his finest achievement was *The Canterbury Tales,* a series of verse stories told by different pilgrims on their way to the tomb of Thomas Becket. The pilgrims represent many walks of life—a knight, a squire, a clerk, a friar, a nun, a miller, a merchant, and so on. In Chaucer's deft hands, each storyteller emerges as a vivid personality in his or her own right. Some of the tales have religious themes; others are humorous or satiric. All in all, they provide a remarkable portrait of life in the Later Middle Ages.

Lyrics and Ballads

Europeans of the Middle Ages had a fondness for a harplike instrument called the lyre. In palaces and castles, poets often strummed lyres as they recited their verse. From this custom arose a tradition known as lyric poetry. Lyric poems came to be known as those expressing strong emotion.

Lyric poems of this period fall into two main categories, secular and religious. The usual topics of the secular poetry are love or nature; many of them celebrate the renewal of spring or the joys of summer:

Sumer is icumen in;
Lhude° sing cuccu! °Loudly

Religious lyrics might consist of a hymn praising God or a prayer beseeching Him, among other things. One of the most famous religious lyrics in Middle English celebrates the Virgin Mary:

I syng of myden
That is makeles;° °matchless
Kyng of alle kynges
To here son che ches. °she chose

Another includes the Latin line *Timor mortis conturbat me* ("The fear of death disturbs me") to teach the lesson that in the midst of life there is death:

In what state that ever I be,
Timor mortis conturbat me.

As I me walked in on° morning °one
I hard a birde both wepe and synge;
This was the tenor of her talkynge:
Timor mortis conturbat me.

13 Another popular poetic form was the ballad, a folk song that told a story. Experts find most surviving ballads impossible to date. Those from the Scottish border probably arose long after the Middle Ages, and those from before 1485 have most likely changed a good deal over the centuries.

One surviving series of ballads concerns Robin Hood, a legendary hero who may have existed around the turn of the thirteenth century. Robin, an outlaw, lives in the woods with his band of "merrye" men, robbing from the rich and helping the poor. He and his lady friend, Maid Marian, eventually became part of traditional

ROBIN HOOD
Richard Dodd
Center for British Art, Paul Mellon Collection

Humanities Note

Sketch of Robin Hood by Richard Dadd. Dadd (1817–1886), a British painter, studied at the Schools of the Royal Academy. He began his career as painter of genre scenes, or scenes of ordinary life. In 1842 he illustrated the ballad "Robin Goodfellow" for Hall's *Book of British Ballads*. This sketch of his is a nineteenth-century interpretation of the legend of Robin Hood (Robin Goodfellow). The lovely woodland scene and the dramatic clothing contribute to an idealized and romanticized picture of Robin Hood.

13 **Literary Movement** Ballads remained a totally oral form until the eighteenth century, when Bishop Percy began collecting and recording them.

14 **Enrichment** The chief moral lesson the morality plays taught was how a man could save his soul.

May Day festivities. These folk celebrations honoring the coming of spring took place each year on the first day of May.

DRAMA OF THE MIDDLE AGES

The theater of William Shakespeare had its roots in the dramas of the Middle Ages. During early Norman times, the church often sponsored plays as part of religious services. In time, these plays moved from the church to the churchyard and then to the marketplace. The earliest dramas were miracle plays, in England sometimes also called mystery plays. They retold stories from the Bible or dealt with some aspect of the lives of saints.

Over the years the theater gained in popularity among English townspeople. Several communities became famous for performing a particular series of plays, or cycle, which presented a Biblical history of humankind. York, the religious capital of northern England, had one of the largest cycles. Chester and Wakefield also staged multi-play productions. Clergymen usually wrote the plays, and actors performed them on wagons or fixed scaffolds. Each of the town's craft guilds would take turns producing one play.

During the turbulent years of the fifteenth century, a new kind of drama arose—the morality play. Morality plays depicted the life story of an ordinary person, sometimes from birth to death. Along the way the hero meets characters who symbolize abstract qualities
14 such as Vice or Virtue. The purpose of these allegorical dramas was to teach a moral lesson.

The most famous surviving morality play is *Everyman,* which had its origin in the Netherlands and was not adapted for English audiences until about 1500. By that time, Middle English was giving way to modern English, the form of the language we speak today. Even so, *Everyman* is usually studied as part of Middle English literature, for it is one of the most powerful examples of the kinds of morality plays performed in the Later Middle Ages.

Subsequent generations of writers owe a great debt to the literature of the English Middle Ages. In Chaucer, the era produced the first major writer in English to be known and respected for his craft. With works such as *Everyman,* the period produced the foundations of the great English dramatic tradition. In addition, the romantic adventures of King Arthur and his knights became a source to which future writers would turn again and again.

ENGLISH VOICES
Quotations by Prominent Figures of the Period

Manners maketh man.
William of Wykeham, Motto of two colleges at Oxford

It behooves us to place the foundations of knowledge in mathematics.
Roger Bacon, *Opus Majus*

Who pulleth out this sword of this stone and anvil, is rightwise king born of all England.
Sir Thomas Malory, *Morte d' Arthur*

In a somer seson whan soft was the sonne
Who will bell the cat?
William Langland, *Piers Plowman*

A foule may ek° a wys-man often gide.° °also °guide
Geoffrey Chaucer, *Troilus and Criseyde*

Looke who that is moost vertuous alway,
Pryvee° and apert, and most entendeth ay °private, secret
To do the gentil dedes that he kan;
Tak him for the grettest gentil man.
Geoffrey Chaucer, "The Wife of Bath's Tale," *The Canterbury Tales*

Pacience is an heigh vertu, certeyn.
Geoffrey Chaucer, "The Franklin's Tale," *The Canterbury Tales*

When captains couragious, whom death could not daunte
Did march to the seige of the city of Gaunt,
They mustered their soldiers by two and by three
And the foremost in battle was Mary Ambree.
Anonymous, "Mary Ambree"

Come listen to me, you gallants so free,
All you that loves mirth for to hear,
And I will you tell of a bold outlaw
That lived in Nottinghamshire.
Anonymous, "Robin Hood and Allen a Dale"

Reading Critically The feature on this page is designed to help students read critically the literature of the Medieval Period. The information given here helps students place a work of literature in its historical context, understand the literary movements of the time, and appreciate the writers' techniques used to convey the ideas of the period.

Discuss the information on this page with your students. Explain that the selection that accompanies this page, from *Morte D'arthur*, is a model for reading critically the literature of this period. It contains in the side column notes that draw attention to elements that reflect the historical context, the influence of literary movements, and the writer's techniques. Ask students to pay attention to these notes as they read the selection. Also suggest that they make their own critical comments as they read.

To give students further practice with the process of reading critically, use the selection in the Teaching Portfolio, "The Unquiet Grave," p. 000, following the Teacher Backup, which students can annotate themselves. Encourage students to use these strategies as they read the literature in this unit.

READING CRITICALLY

The Literature of 1066–1485

When you read literature, it is important to place it in its historical context. Doing so will help you to understand influences on the writer's ideas and techniques.

Historical Context

In 1066 the Normans conquered England by defeating the Anglo-Saxons at the Battle of Hastings. Although many Anglo-Saxon traditions and attitudes survived the invasion, the Normans dramatically changed English life by introducing a social, economic, and political system called feudalism. Under this system, land was divided among noble overlords. Controlling large, self-sufficient feudal manors, the overlords were served by knights, who provided protection, and serfs, who farmed the land and herded animals. Although it was an ideal that few of them may have actually attained, the knights tried to live according to the code of chivalry, which required them to be honorable, courteous, brave, and skillful. Toward the later part of this period, gunpower was replacing swords and the feudal order was being replaced by the aristocratic code.

Literary Movements

The concept of chivalry played an important role in shaping the literature of the Medieval Period. When chivalry was blended with such magical elements as giants, wizards, sorcerers, and dragons, the form of literature known as the romance was created. Filled with fantasy, adventure, and courtly love, romances were one of the most popular literary forms of the period. Apart from romantic literature, most of the literature of the period reflected the influence of religion. This influence is most noticeable in the two forms of drama that were popular during the period: mystery plays and morality plays.

Writers' Techniques

Although the first printing press was established toward the end of the Medieval Period, much of the literature of the period was composed orally. Folk ballads were sung or recited by common people and passed down from generation to generation. These ballads, along with most other medieval literature, were written in verse and told a story. Toward the end of the period, however, a number of writers began writing prose.

On the following pages is a selection by Thomas Malory, the writer responsible for recording the legend of King Arthur. The notes in the side column should help you to place the selection in its historical context.

Objectives

1 To analyze legends
2 To recognize elements of fantasy
3 To appreciate word origins
4 To write about character

Teaching Portfolio: Support Material

Teacher Backup, p. 000

Vocabulary Check, p. 00

Usage and Mechanics Worksheet, p. 00

Analyzing Literature Worksheet, p. 00

Critical Thinking and Reading Worksheet, p. 00

Language Worksheet, p. 00

Selection Test, p. 00

Art Transparency 2, *Morgan-le-Fay,* Frederick Sandys

MODEL

from Morte d'Arthur

Sir Thomas Malory

Historical Context: Malory's Morte d'Arthur was completed around 1470. The legend of a king who adheres to the principles of chivalry is a fitting subject for this period during which feudalism was dying. The legend itself may be based on the life of a Celtic Chieftain who lived during the sixth century.

This selection begins after King Arthur has traveled to France at the insistence of his nephew, Gawain, to besiege his former friend and knight, Lancelot, for his involvement with Queen Guenevere. However, the king's attempts to punish are halfhearted, and he is soon forced to abandon them altogether when he learns that his nephew, Mordred, has seized control of England. Arthur leads his forces back to England, and Mordred attacks them upon their landing. Gawain is killed in the fighting, but before he dies, he manages to send word to Lancelot that Arthur is in need of assistance.

Literary Movement: King Arthur was a common subject of medieval romances.

Literary Movement: Strange, unnatural beasts such as serpents are often depicted in medieval romances.

So upon Trinity Sunday at night King Arthur dreamed a wonderful dream, and in his dream him seemed[1] that he saw upon a chafflet[2] a chair, and the chair was fast to a wheel, and thereupon sat King Arthur in the richest cloth of gold that might be made. And the King thought there was under him, far from him, an hideous deep black water, and therein was all manner of serpents, and worms, and wild beasts, foul and horrible. And suddenly the King thought that the wheel turned upside down, and he fell among the serpents, and every beast took him by a limb. And then the King cried as he lay in his bed, "Help, help!"

And then knights, squires, and yeomen awaked the King, and then he was so amazed that he wist[3] not where he was. And then so he awaked until it was nigh day, and then he fell on slumbering again, not sleeping nor thoroughly waking. So the King seemed[4] verily that there came Sir Gawain unto him with a number of fair ladies with him. So when King Arthur saw him, he said, "Welcome, my sister's son. I weened ye had been dead. And now I see thee on-live, much am I beholden

1. **him seemed:** It seemed to him.
2. **chafflet:** Platform.
3. **wist:** Knew.
4. **the King seemed:** It seemed to the King.

Motivation for Reading Students are familiar with the Arthur legend and like it very much. Allow them to share with the class what they have learned from reading or from movies about Arthur and his kingdom. You can structure this in a variety of ways from speeches to skits to debates to informal discussions.

Thematic Idea Another selection that deals with the theme of chivalry is *"Sir Gawain and the Green Knight,"* page 124.

Purpose-Setting Question The code of chivalry demands a knight be loyal to his lord, fulfill his responsibilities to his vassals, respect the Christian faith, and be an example of courtly love. How well does Arthur fulfill the chivalric ideal? Which qualities are exhibited by Sir Gawain?

Master Teacher Note Medieval man tended to believe in the truth and prophetic power of dreams. It is interesting to note that a belief in the importance of dreams was revived in the nineteenth century with the investigations of Sigmund Freud into the human psyche. The study of dreams remains an essential element in contemporary psychoanalysis. In this story, does Arthur believe his dreams?

Clarification Sir Mordred is not only King Arthur's nephew, the half-brother of Gawain and the son of his half-sister Morgause, but he is also Arthur's son. Arthur, unaware of the blood relationship between them, had been seduced many years earlier by Morgause. It is because Mordred is his son that the treaty will give Mordred Cornwall and Kent during Arthur's lifetime and all of England upon Arthur's death. Mordred is portrayed by Malory as a disgruntled, vindictive and hate-filled young man.

unto Almighty Jesu. Ah, fair nephew and my sister's son, what been these ladies that hither be come with you?"

Literary Movement: In medieval romances chivalrous knights fought for and protected women.

"Sir," said Sir Gawain, "all these be ladies for whom I have foughten for when I was man living. And all these are those that I did battle for in righteous quarrels, and God hath given them that grace, at their great prayer, because I did battle for them for their right, that they should bring me hither unto you. Thus much hath given me leave God, for to warn you of your death. For and ye fight as tomorn[5] with Sir Mordred, as ye both have assigned, doubt ye not ye must be slain, and the most party of your people on both parties. And for the great grace and goodness that Almighty Jesu hath unto you, and for pity of you and many more other good men there shall be slain, God hath sent me to you of his special grace to give you warning that in no wise ye do battle as tomorn, but that ye take a treaty for a month from today. And proffer you largely,[6] so that tomorn ye put in a delay. For within a month shall come Sir Lancelot with all his noble knights and rescue you worshipfully and slay Sir Mordred and all that ever will hold with him."

Then Sir Gawain and all the ladies vanished. And anon the King called upon his knights, squires, and yeomen, and charged them wightly[7] to fetch his noble lords and wise bishops unto him. And when they were come the King told them of his avision,[8] that Sir Gawain had told him and warned him that, and he fought on the morn, he should be slain. Then the King commanded Sir Lucan the Butler and his brother Sir Bedivere the Bold, with two bishops with them, and charged them in any wise to take a treaty for a month from today with Sir Mordred. "And spare not: proffer him lands and goods as much as ye think reasonable."

So then they departed and came to Sir Mordred where he had a grim host of an hundred thousand, and there they entreated Sir Mordred long time. And at the last Sir Mordred was agreed for to have Cornwall and Kent by King Arthur's days, and after that, all England, after the days of King Arthur.

---

5. **and . . . tomorn:** If you fight tomorrow.
6. **proffer you largely:** Make generous offers.
7. **wightly:** Quickly.
8. **avision:** Dream.

Then were they condescended[9] that King Arthur and Sir Mordred should meet betwixt both their hosts, and each of them should bring fourteen persons. And so they came with this word unto Arthur. Then said he, "I am glad that this is done," and so he went into the field.

And when King Arthur should depart, he warned all his host that, and they see any sword drawn, "Look ye come on fiercely and slay that traitor Sir Mordred, for I in no wise trust him." In like wise Sir Mordred warned his host that "And ye see any manner of sword drawn, look that ye come on fiercely, and so slay all that ever before you standeth, for in no wise I will not trust for this treaty." And in the same wise said Sir Mordred unto his host, "For I know well my father will be avenged upon me."

And so they met as their pointment[10] was and were agreed and accorded thoroughly. And wine was fetched and they drank together. Right so came an adder out of a little heathbush, and it stung a knight in the foot. And so when the knight felt him so stung, he looked down and saw the adder. And anon he drew his sword to slay the adder, and thought none other harm. And when the host on both parties saw that sword drawn, then they blew beams,[11] trumpets, and horns, and shouted grimly. And so both hosts dressed them together. And King Arthur took his horse and said, "Alas, this unhappy day!" and so rode to his party, and Sir Mordred in like wise.

And never since was there never seen a more dolefuller battle in no Christian land, for there was but rushing and riding, lunging and striking; and many a grim word was there spoken of either to other, and many a deadly stroke. But ever King Arthur rode throughout the battle[12] of Sir Mordred many times and did full nobly, as a noble king should do, and at all times he fainted never. And Sir Modred did his devoir that day and put himself in great peril.

Historical Context: Bravery and skill in battle were important aspects of chivalry.

And thus they fought all the long day, and never stinted[13] till the noble knights were laid to the cold earth. And ever

9. condescended: Agreed.
10. pointment: Arrangement.
11. beams: A type of trumpet.
12. battle: Battalion.
13. stinted: Stopped.

Humanities Note

Fine art, Detail of *Arthur, The Nine Heroes Tapestry*. This Gothic tapestry, woven of vegetable-dyed wool, was probably made in France about 1385. There is no record of the maker, but it may be the work of the master weaver Nicholas Bataille. The tapestry was made for Jean, Duc de Berry, the third son of John III of France.

Tapestries were often commissioned by the nobility of the fourteenth century to use as covering and decoration for the cold stone walls of their fortified castles. Their portability made them especially useful to the ruling princes who took them along to beautify transient lodgings when traveling to do battle to collect tithes, or to oversee their lands.

The tapestry fragment, *Arthur*, from the *Nine Heroes Tapestry*, was originally part of a three-tapestry set. Each piece measured 21' x 16' and depicted a group of heroes from legend: three pagans, three Hebrews, and three Christians. Only the figure of Arthur remains on the Christian heres tapestry; the others have been lost over time. Arthur is identified by the three crowns on his tunic and banner representing England, Scotland, and Brittany. The field of the tapestry, divided by architectural motifs, is enlivened by various small figures. Although the once brilliant colors have faded with time, they are still a pleasing hue. The extreme skill of the weaver is evident in the delicate shading of the features and clothing of the king.

In discussing this work with your class you may wish to point out that the legend of King Arthur, alive in the fourteenth century, is still with us today, due in part to the unknown artisans who wove the Gothic tapestries.

THE NINE HEROES TAPESTRIES CHRISTIAN HEROES: ARTHUR WITH THREE CARDINALS
Probably Nicolas Bataille, Paris
The Metropolitan Museum of Art

Critical Thinking and Reading
Note the hyperbole in this battle description. In one day a hundred thousand men are slain. There are three left on Arthur's side, only Mordred on the other. What might be the purpose of such hyperbole in this romance?

they fought still till it was near night, and by then was there an hundred thousand laid dead upon the down. Then was King Arthur wood-wroth[14] out of measure when he saw his people so slain from him. And so he looked about him and could see no more of all his host, and good knights left no more on-live, but two knights: the t'one was Sir Lucan the Butler and the other his brother Sir Bedivere. And yet they were full sore wounded.

"Jesu, mercy," said the King, "where are all my noble knights become? Alas that ever I should see this doleful day! For now," said King Arthur, "I am come to mine end. But would to God," said he, "that I wist now where were that traitor Sir Mordred that has caused all this mischief."

Then King Arthur looked about and was ware where stood Sir Mordred leaning upon his sword among a great heap of dead men.

"Now give me my spear," said King Arthur unto Sir Lucan, "for yonder I have espied the traitor that all this woe hath wrought."

Writer's Technique: King Arthur is motivated by his love for his slain knights to confront Mordred.

"Sir, let him be," said Sir Lucan, "for he is unhappy. And if ye pass this unhappy day ye shall be right well revenged upon him. And, good lord, remember ye of your night's dream, and what the spirit of Sir Gawain told you tonight, and yet God of his great goodness hath preserved you hitherto. And for God's sake, my lord, leave off by this, for, blessed be God, ye have won the field: for yet we been here three on-live, and with Sir Mordred is not one on-live. And therefore if ye leave off now, this wicked day of destiny is past."

Historical Context: Sir Lucan demonstrates his loyalty to King Arthur. Loyalty to one's king or overlord was an important medieval virtue.

"Now, tide[15] me death, tide me life," said the King, "now I see him yonder alone, he shall never escape mine hands. For at a better avail shall I never have him."

"God speed you well!" said Sir Bedivere.

Then the King got his spear in both his hands and ran toward Sir Mordred, crying and saying, "Traitor, now is thy deathday come!"

And when Sir Mordred saw King Arthur he ran until him with his sword drawn in his hand, and there King Arthur smote Sir Mordred under the shield, with a thrust of his spear, throughout the body more than a fathom. And when

14. wood-wroth: Wild with rage.
15. tide: Befall.

Writer's Technique: Both Mordred and Arthur exhibit their skill in battle.

Sir Mordred felt that he had his death's wound, he thrust himself with the might that he had up to the burr[16] of King Arthur's spear, and right so he smote his father King Arthur with his sword holden in both his hands, upon the side of the head, that the sword pierced the helmet and the casing of the brain. And therewith Sir Mordred dashed down stark dead to the earth.

And noble King Arthur fell in a swough to the earth, and there he swooned oftentimes, and Sir Lucan and Sir Bedivere ofttimes heaved him up. And so, weakly betwixt them, they led him to a little chapel not far from the seaside, and when the King was there, him thought him reasonably eased. Then heard they people cry in the field. "Now go thou, Sir Lucan," said the King, "and do me to wit[17] what betokens that noise in the field."

So Sir Lucan departed, for he was grievously wounded in many places. And so as he walked he saw and harkened by the moonlight how that pillagers and robbers were come into the field to pill and to rob many a full noble knight of brooches and bracelets and of many a good ring and many a rich jewel. And who that were not dead all out there they slew them for their harness and their riches. When Sir Lucan understood this work, he came to the King as soon as he might and told him all what he had heard and seen. "Therefore by my read,"[18] said Sir Lucan, "it is best that we bring you to some town."

Writer's Technique: Arthur's dream foreshadows his death.

"I would it were so," said the King, "but I may not stand, my head works so. Ah, Sir Lancelot," said King Arthur, "this day have I sore missed thee. And alas that ever I was against thee, for now have I my death, whereof Sir Gawain me warned in my dream."

Then Sir Lucan took up the King the t'one party[19] and Sir Bedivere the other party; and in the lifting up the King swooned and in the lifting Sir Lucan fell in a swoon that part of his guts fell out of his body, and therewith the noble knight's heart burst. And when the King awoke he beheld Sir Lucan how he lay foaming at the mouth and part of his guts lay at his feet.

---

16. burr: Hand guard.
17. me to wit: Let me know.
18. read: Advice.
19. party: Side.

"Alas," said the King, "this is to me a full heavy sight to see this noble duke so die for my sake, for he would have helped me that had more need of help than I. Alas that he would not complain him for his heart was so set to help me. Now Jesu have mercy upon his soul."

Then Sir Bedivere wept for the death of his brother.

"Now leave this mourning and weeping, gentle knight," said the King, "for all this will not avail me. For wit thou well, and I might live myself, the death of Sir Lucan would grieve me evermore. But my time passeth on fast," said the King. "Therefore," said King Arthur unto Sir Bedivere, "take thou here Excalibur my good sword and go with it to yonder water's side; and when thou comest there I charge thee throw my sword in that water and come again and tell me what thou sawest there."

"My lord," said Sir Bedivere, "your commandment shall be done, and I shall lightly[20] bring you word again."

So Sir Bedivere departed. And by the way he beheld that noble sword, that the pommel and the haft[21] was all precious stones. And then he said to himself, "If I throw this rich sword in the water, thereof shall never come good, but harm and loss." And then Sir Bedivere hid Excalibur under a tree. And so, as soon as he might, he came again unto the King and said he had been at the water and had thrown the sword into the water.

"What saw thou there?" said the King.

"Sir," he said, "I saw nothing but waves and winds."

"That is untruly said of thee," said the King. "And therefore go thou lightly again and do my commandment; as thou art to me loved and dear, spare not, but throw it in."

Then Sir Bedivere returned again and took the sword in his hand. And yet him thought sin and shame to throw away that noble sword. And so eft[22] he hid the sword and returned again and told the King that he had been at the water and done his commandment.

"What sawest thou there?" said the King.

"Sir," he said, "I saw nothing but waters wap and waves wan."[23]

Writer's Technique: Notice the dilemma here. A knight's first duty is to obey his king, but Sir Bedivere sees the value of the sword and cannot bring himself to carry out King Arthur's command.

Enrichment Sir Bedivere's struggle to throw Excalibur into the lake—he fails twice to fulfill Arthur's command before he successfully hurls the sword on the third try—follows a typical pattern in legends: three tries at a task, with only the last successful. Ask students to give other examples of this pattern.

20. lightly: Quickly.
21. pommel . . . haft: Hilt and hand guard.
22. eft: Again.
23. waters . . . wan: Waters lap and waves grow dark.

"Ah, traitor unto me and untrue," said King Arthur, "now hast thou betrayed me twice. Who would have weened that thou that has been to me so loved and dear, and thou art named a noble knight, and would betray me for the riches of this sword. But now go again lightly, for thy long tarrying putteth me in great jeopardy of my life, for I have taken cold. And but if thou do now as I bid thee, if ever I may see thee I shall slay thee mine own hands, for thou wouldest for my rich sword see me dead."

Literary Movement: Magic was an important element of medieval romances.

Then Sir Bedivere departed and went to the sword and lightly took it up, and so he went to the water's side; and there he bound the girdle about the hilts, and threw the sword as far into the water as he might. And there came an arm and an hand above the water and took it and clutched it, and shook it thrice and brandished; and then vanished away the hand with the sword into the water. So Sir Bedivere came again to the King and told him what he saw.

"Alas," said the King, "help me hence, for I dread me I have tarried overlong."

Then Sir Bedivere took the King upon his back and so went with him to that water's side. And when they were at the water's side, even fast[24] by the bank floated a little barge with many fair ladies in it; and among them all was a queen; and all they had black hoods, and all they wept and shrieked when they saw King Arthur.

"Now put me into that barge," said the King; and so he did softly. And there received him three ladies with great mourning, and so they set them down. And in one of their laps King Arthur laid his head, and then the queen said, "Ah, my dear brother, why have ye tarried so long from me? Alas, this wound on your head hath caught overmuch cold." And anon they rowed fromward the land, and Sir Bedivere beheld all tho ladies go froward him.

Then Sir Bedivere cried and said, "Ah, my lord Arthur, what shall become of me, now ye go from me and leave me here alone among mine enemies?"

"Comfort thyself," said the King, "and do as well as thou mayest, for in me is no trust for to trust in. For I must into the vale of Avilion[25] to heal me of my grievous wound. And if thou hear nevermore of me, pray for my soul."

---

24. fast: Close.
25. Avilion: A legendary island.

72

But ever the queen and ladies wept and shrieked, that it was pity to hear. And as soon as Sir Bedivere had lost sight of the barge he wept and wailed, and so took the forest and went all that night.

And in the morning he was ware, betwixt two bare woods, of a chapel and an hermitage. Then was Sir Bedivere glad, and thither he went, and when he came into the chapel he saw where lay an hermit groveling on all fours, close thereby a tomb was new dug. When the hermit saw Sir Bedivere he knew him well, for he was but little tofore Bishop of Canterbury, that Sir Mordred put to flight.

"Sir," said Sir Bedivere, "what man is there here interred that you pray so fast for?"

"Fair son," said the hermit. "I wot not verily but by guessing. But this same night, at midnight, here came a number of ladies and brought here a dead corpse and prayed me to inter him. And here they offered an hundred tapers, and gave me a thousand gold coins."

"Alas," said Sir Bedivere, "that was my lord King Arthur, which lieth here buried in this chapel."

Then Sir Bedivere swooned, and when he awoke he prayed the hermit that he might abide with him still, there to live with fasting and prayers:

"For from hence will I never go," said Sir Bedivere, "by my will, but all the days of my life here to pray for my lord Arthur."

Writer's Technique: Sir Bedivere's request conveys his undying devotion to King Arthur.

"Sir, ye are welcome to me," said the hermit, "for I know you better than ye think that I do: for ye are Sir Bedivere the Bold, and the full noble duke Sir Lucan the Butler was your brother."

Then Sir Bedivere told the hermit all as you have heard tofore, and so he stayed with the hermit that was beforehand Bishop of Canterbury. And there Sir Bedivere put upon him poor clothes, and served the hermit full lowly in fasting and in prayers.

Thus of Arthur I find no more written in books that been authorized, neither more of the very certainty of his death heard I nor read, but thus was he led away in a ship wherein were three queens; that one was King Arthur's sister, Queen Morgan le Fay, the other was the Queen of North Galis, and the third was the Queen of the Waste Lands.

Writer's Technique: Malory's reference to the "books that been authorized" makes his account seem factual.

Now more of the death of King Arthur could I never find, but that these ladies brought him to his grave, and such one was interred there which the hermit bare witness that was

Master Teacher Note Place Art Transparency 2, *Morgan-le-Fay*, by Frederick Sandys, on the overhead projector. Point out that the woman represents the artist's idea of what Morgan-le-Fay might have looked like had she been a real person. Ask your students to describe what different, and maybe even conflicting, impressions they get of her. After they have read the selection from Malory, your students might return to the painting and discuss what they think of Sandys's conception of Morgan-le-Fay.

Master Teacher Note In the ruins of Glastonbury Abbey, identified as the original isle of Avalon, can be seen what is purported to be Arthur's grave. A marker on it reads:

SITE OF KING ARTHUR'S TOMB
In the year 1191 the bodies of King Arthur and his queen were said to have been found on the south side of the Lady Chapel.
On 19th April 1278 their remains were
removed in the presence of King Edward I and Queen Eleanor
To a black marble tomb on this site.
The tomb survived until the dissolution of the abbey in 1539.

Enrichment T. H. White's novel *The Once and Future King* takes its title from this epitaph and is a clever and charming modern version of Malory's work. As a matter of fact, Malory himself appears as a minor character at the end of White's story, charged with the responsibility for preserving Arthur's legend for posterity.

More About the Author Malory's violent behavior and misfortune—he was plagued by financial and political disasters—landed him in prison more than once. Malory wrote the *Morte Darthur* in prison and included in the manuscript notes asking the readers to pray for his release. "And I pray you all that readeth this tale to pray for him that this wrote, that God send him good deliverance soon and hastily. Amen." How could this years in confinement actually have helped him evolve his own eloquent and organized style of prose?

once Bishop of Canterbury. But yet the hermit knew not in certain that he was verily the body of King Arthur; for this tale Sir Bedivere, a knight of the Table Round, made it to be written.

Yet some men say in many parts of England that King Arthur is not dead, but carried by the will of our Lord Jesu into another place; and men say that he shall come again, and he shall win the Holy Cross. Yet I will not say that it shall be so, but rather I would say: here in this world he changed his life. And many men say that there is written upon the tomb this:

HIC IACET ARTHURUS, REX
QUONDAM, REXQUE FUTURUS[26]

---

26. *Hic . . . futurus:* Here lies Arthur, who was once king and king will be again.

Sir Thomas Malory 1405[?]–1471 spent most of his later years in prison, probably because he supported the Lancasters while the Yorkists ruled England during the War of Roses. While in prison, he wrote *Morte d'Arthur* by compiling and giving order to a collection of French, English, and Latin tales about King Arthur and the Knights of the Round Table. The work was first published in 1485 by William Caxton, after Caxton had established the first printing press in England.

Answers

ANSWERS TO THINKING ABOUT THE SELECTION

Recalling

1. Arthur is warned not to do battle with Mordred the next day or he will die.

THINKING ABOUT THE SELECTION

Recalling

1. What warning does King Arthur receive in his dream?
2. (a) What instruction does Arthur give his men before he leaves to meet Mordred? (b) What does Mordred tell his men?
3. (a) How does Arthur slay Mordred? (b) What does Mordred do just before he dies?
4. (a) What does Sir Lucan observe when Arthur sends him back to the battlefield? (b) How does Sir Lucan die?
5. (a) What does Sir Bedivere learn on the morning after the battle? (b) What does he decide to do as a result of his discovery?

Interpreting

6. (a) How would you characterize Arthur? (b) How would you characterize Mordred?
7. What do you think are Sir Lucan's reasons for twice failing to obey Arthur's request to throw Excalibur in the water?
8. What is ironic, or unexpected, about the way the battle begins?
9. How does the ending add to the mysterious, magical quality of the tale?

Applying

10. Why do you think the legend of King Arthur has retained its popularity for so long?

ANALYZING LITERATURE

Recognizing Legends

Legends are anonymous traditional stories popularly believed to be based on history. Generally, legends reflect the attitudes and values of the society that created them, and the heroes of legends usually possess qualities that the people of that society consider admirable. Legends also often involve evil characters who possess qualities considered undesirable.

1. What qualities does King Arthur possess that would have been considered admirable during medieval times?
2. What qualities does Mordred possess that would be considered undesirable?

CRITICAL THINKING AND READING

Recognizing Elements of Fantasy

Although legends are popularly believed to be based on history, they often involve characters with superhuman powers and contain fantastic events.

1. What incident occurs in this selection that is clearly an example of fantasy?
2. What makes the women who come for Arthur at the end of the selection seem magical and mysterious?

UNDERSTANDING LANGUAGE

Appreciating Word Origins

As a result of the Norman conquest, many French words were introduced into the English language. For example, Malory uses the word *quarrel,* which comes from the French word *querele,* meaning "complaint."

The words below are of French origin. Use your dictionary to find the French word and meaning from which each word comes.

1. vanish
2. preserve
3. rescue
4. depart

THINKING AND WRITING

Writing About Character

Write an essay in which you discuss what this excerpt reveals about King Arthur's character. Reread the selection, focusing on Arthur's comments and behavior. Also take note of how the other characters react to him. When you write your essay, use evidence from the selection to support your argument. When you finish writing, revise and proofread your essay.

(Answers begin on p. 74.)

2. (a) If a sword is drawn, attack Mordred. (b) If a sword is drawn, attack all the men in front of them.
3. (a) Arthur kills him with the thrust of a spear. (b) Mordred hits Arthur on the side of his head with his sword.
4. (a) Lucan sees pillagers and robbers stealing from the dead and killing the wounded for their valuables. (b) He dies trying to carry Arthur.
5. (a) Bedivere learns that three mysterious women have brought a body to the chapel for burial. (b) He decides to remain there at the chapel for the rest of his life, praying for Arthur.

Interpreting

6. (a) Arthur is a noble lord, the epitome of the chivalric king. (b) Mordred seems vindictive and insolent.
7. It seems a shame to waste such a beautiful sword. It seems almost sinful to him.
8. The battle begins by accident, when a knight tries to kill a snake that has bitten him. Neither side intentionally breaks the agreement, but neither waits for an explanation.
9. The implication that Arthur may return is a supernatural suggestion.

Applying

10. Answers will differ. Some possible answers might be that the desire for perfection, the loss of love, the idea that the righteous will triumph, and the element of mystery and magic are themes of timeless popularity.

ANSWERS TO ANALYZING LITERATURE

1. Arthur's admirable qualities would be willingness to do his duty, readiness to sacrifice, loyalty to his men, honor, a respect for truth, courteousness and gentleness, bravery in battle, and courage in death.
2. Lack of loyalty to his liege, lack of honor, and greed are some of Mordred's undesirable qualities.

ANSWERS TO CRITICAL THINKING AND READING

1. The incident involving throwing Excalibur into the lake and the summoning of the women of Avalon are fantasy.
2. The women arrive just at the minute Arthur is brought to the lake shore.

ANSWERS TO UNDERSTANDING LANGUAGE

1. *Vanquish* is from *veinquis.*
2. *Preserve* is from *preserver.*
3. *Rescue* is from *rescourre.*
4. *Depart* is from *departir.*

THINKING AND WRITING

For help with this assignment, students can refer to Lesson 9, "Writing About Character," in the Handbook of Writing About Literature.

Writing Across the Curriculum
After the students have written a draft of their essays, have them consult with the psychology teacher or counselor to check the validity of their observations. Schedules and time commitments permitting, invite a counselor, a psychology teacher, or the school psychologist into class to be interviewed about Arthur's character as revealed in his comments and behavior. After the interview, have the students revise their papers, adding insights from the discussion.

More About the Ballads Since ballads were part of an oral tradition, there is no evidence that even the earliest versions we have are, in fact, the original versions. Their composition flourished during the 14th and 15th centuries, then ceased. It was not, however, until the 1765 publication of Bishop Percy's *Reliques of Ancient Popular Poetry* that they were printed and widely circulated. You might wish to point out that Percy's book was based on an old manuscript he rescued at a friend's house in Shropshire from a housemaid who was about to light the fire with it. What kinds of changes do you think might have occurred during the intervening three hundred years?

GUIDE FOR READING

English And Scottish Folk Ballads

Long before most people in Britain could read or write, they were familiar with the stories told in ballads. A **ballad** is a narrative poem, usually brief, that is meant to be sung. When the writer is unknown, the ballad is called a **folk** ballad, or sometimes a **popular** or **traditional** ballad. Such ballads as "Barbara Allan" have been recited, chanted, or sung from their earliest appearance down to the present day.

No one knows when the first folk ballads appeared in Britain, but it was probably during the twelfth century. Since the ballads were unwritten, they were passed along orally for many centuries. Most of the earliest ballads we know about probably date from the fifteenth century. Even at that time, no one paid much attention to them as literature. Not until 1765, with the publication of Bishop Thomas Percy's *Reliques of Ancient English Poetry,* did ballads come to be recognized as a fascinating part of Britain's literary heritage.

Sir Walter Scott, the author of *Ivanhoe,* was one of a number of famous writers whose interest in old ballads was sparked by Percy's *Reliques.* Scott often traveled to the Scottish-English border region to collect material on the subject. His *Minstrelsy of the Scottish Border,* published in 1803, is a pioneer work of scholarship on the background and variations of Scottish ballads.

The four ballads in this unit originated in the wild, rugged border country between England and Scotland. Their language is the Scots dialect of English. As they were passed along from person to person, place to place, and generation to generation, these ballads often acquired new words and new verses. There is no such thing as a standard version of a folk ballad, because every balladeer feels free to make alterations. Literally hundreds of versions of "Barbara Allan" have appeared in print.

Folk ballads, with their familiar melodies, are truly songs of the people. Later writers, including Sir Walter Scott, produced literary ballads in imitation of the traditional ones. But few literary ballads have had the power of the old folk ballads to capture and hold the imagination.

Objectives

1 To analyze folk ballads
2 To understand language change

Teaching Resource Portfolio: Support Materials

Teacher Backup, p. 000

Vocabulary Check, p. 00

Usage and Mechanics Worksheet, p. 00

Analyzing Literature Worksheet, p. 00

Critical Thinking and Reading Worksheet, p. 00

Language Worksheet, p. 00

Selection Test, p. 00

Sir Patrick Spens; Get Up and Bar the Door; The Twa Corbies; Barbara Allan

Literary Forms

Folk Ballad. It is not surprising that folk ballads appeared on the rugged English-Scottish border. Folk ballads are typically found in areas where a formal, written literature has yet to develop, or where people's lives do not permit books and reading.

A folk ballad usually presents a single dramatic episode. It is told impersonally, through action and dialogue, with very little characterization, description, or motivation. The story seems to be simple and direct, yet because it often begins in the middle, lacks transitions, and skips over incidents without explanation, it can convey an air of mystery. Ballads deal with many subjects: adventure, love, jealousy, heroism, disaster, revenge. A few folk ballads are humorous.

Most ballads have quatrains, or four-line stanzas, in which the second and fourth lines rhyme. Often, but not always, there are eight syllables in the first and third lines and six syllables in the second and fourth lines. Ballads frequently have a refrain—a regularly repeated phrase or line at the end of a stanza, or sometimes a whole separate stanza. The general effect is musical, as you would expect in poems meant to be sung.

Look For

As you read the folk ballads that follow, think about some of the unanswered questions that the story in each ballad raises.

Writing

Most popular music has a brief life span. Songs from a few years ago tend to sound dated and sentimental to listeners today. Yet folk ballads have been sung for centuries and in some places are still performed for appreciative audiences. Why? What is it that can make a song so enduring? Freewrite about the qualities that you think make a song become a long-lasting popular classic.

Vocabulary

Knowing the following words will help you as you read the four folk ballads.

loath (lōth) *adj.*: Reluctant; unwilling (l. 29, p. 78)

fathoms (fath' əmz) *n.*: Units of measure for the depth of water; a fathom is six feet (l. 42, p. 78)

twa (twä) *n.*: Two *(Scot.)* (l. 13, p. 82)

gang (gaŋ) *v.*: To go or walk *(Scot.)* (l. 4, p. 84)

gowden (gou' d'n) *adj.*: Golden *(Scot.)* (l. 15, p. 84)

healths (helthz) *n.*: Wishes for happiness, as in drinking a series of toasts (l. 19, p. 85)

Literary Focus Although ballads were once considered to be communally produced songs, modern scholars have instead focused on individual authorship. The authors, all unknown, have left few individual marks on their work. Ballads, unlike lyric poetry, generally lack reflection and sentiment. They are impersonal in tone. They almost never employ a first-person point of view. They simply present the chief incidents of a story.

Look For As you read, remember that a ballad is essentially a story for a group of listeners. It demands immediate understanding, since it plunges the audience into the heart of the story. Why might some parts of the stories presented in the ballads have been left out?

Writing Ask the students what popular songs they think will become long-lasting. Write the titles on the board. Discuss what they have in common.

Vocabulary You might pronounce the words for the **less advanced** students and ask them to guess the meanings before they look at the words.

Sir Patrick Spens

This version of "Sir Patrick Spens" is in the original Middle English.

The king sits in Dumferling[1] toune,
Drinking the blude-reid wine:
"O whar will I get guid sailor,
To sail this schip of mine?"

Up and spak an eldern knicht,
Sat at the kings richt kne:
"Sir Patrick Spens is the best sailor,
That sails upon the se."

The king has written a braid letter,
And signd it wi his hand,
And sent it to Sir Patrick Spens,
Was walking on the sand.

The first line that Sir Patrick red,
A loud lauch lauchèd he;
The next line that Sir Patrick red,
The teir blinded his ee.

"O wha is this has don this deid,
This ill deid don to me,
To send me out this time o' the yeir,
To sail upon the se!

"Mak hast, mak hast, my mirry men all
Our guid schip sails the morne:"
"O say na sae, my master deir,
For I feir a deadlie storme.

"Late, late yestreen I saw the new moone,
Wi the auld moone in hir arme,
And I feir, I feir, my deir master,
That we will cum to harme."

O our Scots nobles wer richt laith
To weet their cork-heild schoone,
Bot lang owre a' the play wer playd,
Thair hats they swam aboone.

1. Dumferling: A town in Scotland near Edinburgh.

MEDIEVAL BARON DINING; FROM BREVIARIUM GRIMARI, 15TH CENTURY
The Bettmann Archive

Humanities Note

Fine Art, Illuminated manuscript: *Nobleman at Table,* 15th Century. The art of manuscript illumination flourished in the monasteries of England and Europe from the 11th to the 15th century. Beginning as decorative title pages and capital letters on handwritten vellum manuscripts, it evolved into a highly decorative art form. Miniature paintings in the margins were used to illustrate a point in the text or placed merely to suit the whim of the illuminator. The painter was given full rein to use his imagination and artistic skill. As a result, today we have a colorful historic record that is an invaluable aid in understanding medieval life. The miniature of the *Nobleman at Table* is from an illuminated manuscript. Rendered with stylized charm, it is typical of the efforts of a medieval manuscript illuminator.

1. What part of the ballad does this miniature most appropriately illustrate?
2. What impression of medieval life do you get from the miniature?

Sir Patrick Spens

This version of "Sir Patrick Spens" is in modern English.

The king sits in Dumferling town,
Drinking the blood-red wine: 1
"O where will I get a good sailor, 2
To sail this ship of mine?"

Up and spoke an ancient knight,
Sat at the king's right knee:
"Sir Patrick Spens is the best sailor,
That sails upon the sea."

The king has written a broad letter, 3
And signed it with his hand,
And sent it to Sir Patrick Spens,
Was walking on the sand.

The first line that Sir Patrick read,
A loud laugh laughed he; 4
The next line that Sir Patrick read,
The tear blinded his eye.

"O who is this has done this deed,
This ill deed done to me, 5
To send me out this time of the year,
To sail upon the sea!

"Make haste, make haste, my merry men all
Our good ship sails the morn:"
"O say not so, my master dear,
For I fear a deadly storm.

"Late, late yesterday evening I saw the new moon,
With the old moon in her arm,
And I fear, I fear, my dear master,
That we will come to harm."

O our Scots nobles were right loath
To wet their cork-heeled shoes,
But long before the play were played,
Their hats they swam above.

Motivation for Reading Play a recording of a modern ballad that is familiar to students. List characteristics of ballads that students observe in the song. Ask them to notice any similarities in the ballads they are about to read.

Master Teacher Note "Sir Patrick Spens" is one of the indisputably historical ballads. The hero was a warrior–mariner of the thirteenth century, beloved by all except a small faction of enemies.

Thematic Idea Sir Patrick's unquestioning obedience can be usefully compared and contrasted with Sir Bedivere's procrastinating obedience in the selection from Malory, page 000.

Purpose-Setting Question How does this ballad conform to the standards of a ballad? We often speak of a "no-win" situation. Is Sir Patrick Spens in one?

1 **Discussion** The subject matter of ballads is traditionally tragic. Does the description of wine as "blood-red" seem to be a foreshadowing?

2 **Enrichment** In one version the king explains that he must fetch his daughter home from "Noroway."

3 **Clarification** A "broad letter" is probably an official document.

4 **Critical Thinking and Reading** Another common ballad element is repetition. In this ballad it is incremental: repetition that advances the action. In what other lines does this same incremental repetition occur?

5 **Discussion** What does Sir Patrick's question here suggest? Does he believe he has enemies at court?

O lang, lang may their ladies sit,
Wi thair fans to their hand,
Or eir they se Sir Patrick Spens
Cum sailing to the land.

O lang, lang may the ladies stand,
Wi thair gold kems in their hair,
Waiting for thar ain deir lords,
For they'll se thame na mair.

Half owre, half owre to Aberdour,[1]
It's fiftie fadom deip,
And thair lies guid Sir Patrick Spens,
Wi the Scots lords at his feit.

---

1. **Aberdour:** A town near Edinburgh.

THINKING ABOUT THE SELECTION

Recalling

1. What problem does the king face at the beginning of the ballad?
2. From whom does the king get the idea of having Sir Patrick Spens sail for him?
3. How does Sir Patrick Spens react to the king's letter?

Interpreting

4. Why do you think the king's wine is described as "blood-red"?
5. Why does Sir Patrick Spens view the king's request as an "ill deed"?
6. In the seventh stanza, why does the sailor think the voyage is ill-fated?
7. (a) What happens to the Scots lords who dislike the idea of getting their "cork-heeled shoes" wet? (b) How do you know? (c) How is this outcome ironic?
8. In what way does Sir Patrick Spens seem to embody Medieval ideals of duty?

Applying

8. Sir Patrick Spens does his duty despite serious—and his well-founded—misgivings. What might he have done to avoid sailing? How wise would such a course of action have been?

ANALYZING LITERATURE

Understanding Folk Ballads

"Sir Patrick Spens," like most folk ballads, is short and deals with a single episode. Abrupt transitions and the absence of characterization and description force the audience to make assumptions about characters, places, and events. Dialogue moves the story along.

1. (a) How many characters are directly quoted in the poem? (b) Who are they?
2. What are some of the missing details in "Sir Patrick Spens" that, if included, would make the ballad easier to understand?

Answers

ANSWERS TO THINKING ABOUT THE SELECTION

Recalling

1. The king needs a good sailor to sail his ship.
2. An ancient knight suggests the king get Sir Patrick.
3. First Sir Patrick laughs and then he cries.

Interpreting

4. The wine is "blood-red" as a premonition of the ending.
5. It is an ill deed because the seas are treacherous that time of year.
6. The sailor notices that the moon looks strange.
7. They are drowned. (b) Line 32 states their hats swam above them. (c) More than their shoes get wet—they drown.
8. Sir Patrick obeys his king without hesitation.

Applying

9. Answers will differ but students should recognize Sir Patrick might have spoken directly with the king and tried to persuade him to change his mind. Such an attempt, however, might have been unwise, since to refuse the order could have brought disastrous results.

O long, long may their ladies sit,
With their fans into their hand,
Or ever they see Sir Patrick Spens
Come sailing to the land.

O long, long may the ladies stand,
With their gold combs in their hair,
Waiting for their own dear lords,
For they'll see them no more.

Halfway over, halfway over to Aberdour,
It's fifty fathoms deep
And there lies good Sir Patrick Spens,
With the Scots lords at his feet.

6

6 **Literary Focus** The climax in these concluding stanzas is considered by ballad scholars to be superb. Do you agree? Why?

Challenge Write the stanzas to fill in the holes in the poem that you mentioned in Analyzing Literature.

UNDERSTANDING LANGUAGE

Recognizing Language Change

A centuries-old ballad like "Sir Patrick Spens" looks different today from how it looked when it first appeared in print. Not only is the old Scots dialect unfamiliar to most modern readers, so is much of the spelling and vocabulary of the standard English of that day.

1. What are five words in the first stanza whose spellings have changed over the years?
2. In the fifth stanza, note that the *ei* spelling has changed in two different ways. What are the two ways?
3. How is each of the following words written in modern English?
   a. knicht
   b. lauch
   c. schoone
   d. owre
   e. kems

ANSWERS TO ANALYZING LITERATURE

1. (a) There are two characters quoted. (b) They are Spens and the sailor.
2. Answers will differ. Some possible responses would be why the ancient knight suggests Sir Patrick for the journey and why the king needs to send the ship out in a dangerous season.

ANSWERS TO UNDERSTANDING LANGUAGE

1. Five words spelled differently today are *town, blood, red, good,* and *ship.*
2. Two ways to spell the *ei* sound are *ee* and *ea.*
3. (1) knight, (2) laugh, (3) shoes, (4) before, (5) combs

Get Up and Bar the Door

1 It fell about the Martinmas[1] time,
And a gay time it was then,
2 When our goodwife got puddings to make,
She's boild them in the pan.

The wind sae cauld blew south and north.
And blew into the floor;
Quoth our goodman to our goodwife,
"Gae out and bar the door."

"My hand is in my hussyfskap,[2]
Goodman, as ye may see;
An it should nae be barrd this hundred year,
3 It's no be barrd for me."[3]

They made a paction[4] tween them twa.
They made it firm and sure.
That the first word whaeer shoud speak,
Shoud rise and bar the door.

Then by there came two gentlemen,
At twelve o'clock at night,
And they could neither see house nor hall,
4 Nor coal nor candlelight.

"Now whether is this a rich man's house,
Or whether it is a poor?"
But neer a word wad ane o' them[5] speak,
For barring of the door.

And first they[6] ate the white puddings,
And then they ate the black:
Tho muckle[7] thought the goodwife to hersel,
Yet neer a word she spake.

Then said the one unto the other,
"Here, man, take ye my knife;
Do ye tak aff the auld man's beard,
And I'll kiss the goodwife."

1. Martinmas time: November 11.

2. hussyfskap: Household duties.

3. "it should . . . me": It will not be barred in a hundred years if it has to be barred by me."

4. paction: Agreement.

5. them: The man and his wife.

6. they: The strangers.

7. muckle: Much.

Motivation for Reading Discuss the following ideas with your students. The "war" between men and women is the subject of movies, television series, novels, and poetry. Do you think it is real? Why or why not?

Master Teacher Note Many works of literature deal with the eternal question of male–female relationships. Why is this subject of timeless interest to writers?

Thematic Idea For a different poetic treatment of husband–wife relationships, see Robert Browning's "My Last Duchess," p. 824.

Purpose-Setting Question What does this poem imply about the war between men and women?

1 **Enrichment** In the Middle Ages holidays were literally holy days; consequently, seasonal references tended to be religious. *Martinmas* means *St. Martin's Mass,* or feast day, in the same way that *Christmas* means *Christ's Mass.*

2 **Enrichment** The "puddings" are not desserts here but dishes containing suet (animal fat) boiled in a bag. The black puddings mentioned in line 26 are probably blood sausages.

3 **Reading Strategy** Ask the students to predict the winner of the contest.

4 **Discussion** Why do you think the visitors could see neither coal nor candlelight?

"But there's nae water in the house,
And what shall we do than?" 5
"What ails ye at the pudding broo,[8]
That boils into[9] the pan?"

O up then started our goodman,
An angry man was he:
"Will ye kiss my wife before my een,
And scad[10] me wi pudding bree?"[11]

Then up and started our goodwife,
Gied three skips on the floor:
"Goodman, you've spoken the foremost word; 6
Get up and bar the door."

THINKING ABOUT THE SELECTION

Recalling

1. Why does the goodwife refuse to bar the door when her husband first asks?
2. What agreement do the husband and wife reach about barring the door?
3. To whom does the word *one* refer in line 29?
4. What do the two strangers plan to do to (a) the goodman? (b) the goodwife?
5. (a) Who wins the battle of wills between husband and wife? (b) How?

Interpreting

6. Why does the goodman want the door barred?
7. When do the goodman and his wife first become aware of the presence of the strangers?
8. In lines 25–29, the goodwife is thinking to herself. What might she be thinking?
9. What do you think the stranger means when he suggests taking "aff the auld man's beard"?
10. What serious point does this humorous ballad make?

Applying

11. Can people be hurt by stubbornness—their own or someone else's? Explain your answer.

5 **Discussion** Why does the visitor comment that there's no water in the house?

6 **Critical Thinking and Reading** Although most ballads are tragic in theme, "Get Up and Bar the Door" is an exception. It deals humorously with domestic argument. Why do you think the wife wins the argument?

Answers

ANSWERS TO THINKING ABOUT THE SELECTION

Recalling

1. The wife is busy with her housework.
2. Whichever speaks first must bar the door.
3. It refers to one of the gentlemen.
4. (a) One plans to scald his beard to scrape it off or worse. (b) The other will kiss the wife.
5. (a) The wife wins the contest. (b) She wins by remaining silent until her husband speaks first.

Interpreting

6. The cold wind is blowing in.
7. The couple become aware of the strangers when they enter and speak.
8. Answers will differ. A suggested response will reflect her anger about the fruits of her labor being consumed by the strangers.
9. He might be suggesting that a knife be held at the goodman's throat while the stranger kisses the wife.
10. The message is that stubbornness can have some serious consequences.

Applying

11. Answers will differ. Suggested response: Yes, stubbornness, by causing one to be unreasonable or foolish, can often hurt people.

Motivation for Reading Tell your students that the ballad is a conversation between ravens about dining on the corpse of a tollen knight. Ask what atmosphere is suggested by such a scene.

Thematic Idea Another poem about death is "In Memoriam, A. H. H.," by Tennyson, page 809.

Purpose-Setting Question What view of human life and death does the ballad present? Is it pessimistic, optimistic, or realistic? What word would you use to describe the view and mood?

Teaching to Ability Levels You might read the poem to **less advanced** students and have them follow in the text. **More advanced** students might enjoy translating it into modern English for discussion.

Master Teacher Note The word *corbie* is a chiefly Scottish term for a carrion crow or raven. Many of the folk ballads are Scottish in origin.

1 **Enrichment** Death by murder or accident is one of the most common themes of ballads. Treating this theme by the device of a conversation between two ravens makes "The Two Corbries" one of the more distinctive medieval ballads.

2 **Literary Focus** A ballad traditionally has no introduction. It begins *in medias res.* This ballad is an exception. What motive might its author have had?

3 **Discussion** What is your response to the device of having two ravens discuss their dining plans?

4 **Critical Thinking and Reading** In an English version of the poem, a "lady full of woe" discovers the body, buries him, and dies before evening. Which ending do you prefer? Why?

1 # The Twa Corbies[1]

2 As I was walking all alane,
I heard twa corbies making a mane.[2]
The tane unto the tither did say,
3 "Whar sall we gang and dine the day?"

"In behint yon auld fail dyke,[3]
I wot[4] there lies a new-slain knight;
And naebody kens[5] that he lies there
But his hawk, his hound, and his lady fair.

"His hound is to the hunting gane,
His hawk to fetch the wild-fowl hame,
His lady's ta'en anither mate,
So we may mak our dinner sweet.

"Ye'll sit on his white hause-bane,[6]
And I'll pike out his bonny blue e'en;[7]
Wi' ae lock o' his gowden hair
We'll theek[8] our nest when it grows bare.

4 "Mony a one for him maks mane,
But nane sall ken whar he is gane.
O'er his white banes, when they are bare,
The wind sall blaw for evermair."

1. **Twa Corbies:** Two ravens.
2. **mane:** Moan.
3. **fail dyke:** Bank of earth.
4. **wot:** know.
5. **kens:** knows.
6. **hause-bane:** Neck-bone.
7. **e'en:** Eyes.
8. **theek:** Thatch.

THINKING ABOUT THE SELECTION

Recalling

1. (a) Where is the knight lying? (b) In what condition is he?
2. Who besides the ravens knows what has happened to the knight?
3. Why is the knight's lady not interested in his fate?
4. What does one of the ravens suggest doing with the knight's golden hair?

Interpreting

5. (a) How would you describe the tone of the ballad? (b) How does the tone add to the ballad's impact?
6. What effect would be lost if the incident were described by a human speaker rather than as a conversation between two ravens?

Applying

7. Stories told from the point of view of an animal are unusual but by no means rare. What other story or stories do you recall that present the viewpoint of an animal?

Answers

ANSWERS TO THINKING ABOUT THE SELECTION

Recalling

1. (a) The knight lies on a bank of earth. (b) He is dead.
2. Nobody knows but the knight's hawk, hound, and lady.
3. The lady has another mate already.
4. The raven wants to use it to insulate their nest.

Interpreting

5. (a) There is sadness and pathos in the poem's tone. (b) Since the poem is presented by the hungry ravens and not a sympathetic onlooker, the impact to the ballad is greater.
6. The poem would lose the objectivity that is so often a part of ballads. It would also lose its strange, haunting quality.

Applying

7. Answers will differ. *Watership Down*, by Richard Adams, is one possibility.

Thematic Idea This ballad can be usefully compared with Shakespeare's "Fear No More the Heat o' the Sun," which also adopts an unusual perspective toward death.

1 # Barbara Allan

It was in and about the Martinmas time,[1]
When the green leaves were a-fallin';
That Sir John Graeme in the West Country
Fell in love with Barbara Allan.

He sent his man down through the town
To the place where she was dwellin':
"O haste and come to my master dear,
Gin[2] ye be Barbara Allan."

O slowly, slowly rase[3] she up,
To the place where he was lyin',
And when she drew the curtain by:
"Young man, I think you're dyin'."

"O it's I'm sick, and very, very sick,
And 'tis a' for Barbara Allan."
"O the better for me ye sal[4] never be,
Though your heart's blood were a-spillin'.

2 "O dinna ye mind,[5] young man," said she,
"When ye the cups were fillin',
That ye made the healths gae round and round,
And slighted Barbara Allan?"

He turned his face unto the wall,
And death with him was dealin':
"Adieu, adieu, my dear friends all,
And be kind of Barbara Allan."

And slowly, slowly rase she up,
And slowly, slowly left him;
And sighing said she could not stay,
Since death of life had reft[6] him.

She had not gane a mile but twa,[7]
When she heard the dead-bell knellin',
And every jow[8] that the dead-bell ga'ed[9]
It cried, "Woe to Barbara Allan!"

3 "O mother, mother, make my bed,
O make it soft and narrow:
Since my love died for me today,
I'll die for him tomorrow."

1. **Martinmas time:** November 11.

2. **gin:** If.

3. **rase:** Rose.

4. **sal:** Shall.

5. **dinna ye mind:** Don't you remember.

6. **reft:** Deprived.

7. **not . . . twa:** Gone but two miles.

8. **jow:** Stroke.

9. **ga'ed:** Made.

Motivation for Reading No ballad has generated more adaptations and changes than this one. It has had over a dozen titles and is spoken in countless local accents. A ballad historian found ninety-two versions in Virginia alone, many of them presenting strikingly different texts.

In literature, love and death are often closely connected. Discuss what there is about this combination that can stimulate so much interest.

Master Teacher Note "Barbara Allan" can be found in many albums of folk music. Play a recording for your students before you begin the lesson. Ask the students what is universal about the theme.

Thematic Idea Another selection that deals with the union of love and death is Elizabeth Bowen's story "The Demon Lover," on page 1016.

Purpose-Setting Question How do you explain Barbara Allan's premonition of her tragic Fate?

1 **Literary Focus** As you read, note the presence of several common ballad elements in "Barbara Allan": narrative, dialogue, tragic theme, cryptic elements, and ballad stanza.

2 **Discussion** Of what does Barbara Allan accuse her lover? Is there any explanation given for his action?

3 **Enrichment** Ballads sometimes employ code language. For example, asking that one's bed be made "soft and narrow" indicates that the speaker is dying.

Challenge Invite your students to reconstruct the story that underlies "Barbara Allan."

Humanities Note

Fine art, *Veronica Veronese,* 1872, by Dante Gabriel Rossetti (1828–1882). Dante Gabriel Rossetti was born in London of Italian parents. He began his training as a painter at the Royal Academy but left to apprentice with the British painter Ford Madox Brown. Rossetti, a poet as well as a painter, was a founding member of the Pre-Raphaelite Brotherhood. This was a group of young artists who admired and sought to emulate the work of the Italian painters who preceded Raphael. The Pre-Raphaelite style of painting paid close attention to natural detail and dealt with romantic, moral, and religious subjects. Although the brotherhood was short-lived, lasting only five years, their mode of painting set in motion lasting changes in British art.

The painting *Veronica Veronese* was described by Rossetti as a young woman in a "passionate reverie." The skin tones and red hair glow against the green background and lush velvet texture of her gown, giving her countenance a startling beauty. The pose is one of abstracted thought. The fluid motion of the arms, the scarf, and the branch in the birdcage all serve to draw the eye back to the haunting face. The care given to even the tiniest details, such as the chain about her neck or the tassels on her belt, are an earmark of Rossetti's technique.

You might discuss the following with your class:

1. Does the woman in the painting seem to have the same strength of character as Barbara Allen in the poem?
2. Why do you think this painting was chosen to illustrate this poem? Do you think it is an apt illustration?

VERONICA VERONESE, ROSSETTI
Dante Gabriel
Delaware Art Museum

THINKING ABOUT THE SELECTION

Recalling

1. Why does Sir John Graeme want Barbara Allan to visit him?
2. What are Barbara Allan's first words when she sees Sir John?
3. According to Sir John, why is he "sick, and very, very sick"?
4. What reason does Barbara Allan give for acting unconcerned about his plight?
5. (a) When does Barbara Allan admit how she feels about Sir John? (b) How does she feel?

Interpreting

6. (a) At what point does the ballad make you critical of Barbara Allan? (b) When does it make you sympathize with her?
7. One critic thinks that Sir John acts "like a spineless lover who gave up the ghost without a struggle." How would you answer that criticism?

Applying

8. "Barbara Allan," like most ballads, leaves out things you might like to know. If you were adding a stanza to it (not necessarily at the end), what information would you include?

CRITICAL THINKING AND READING

Interpreting Symbols in Folk Ballads

Ballads are generally concise and direct, but sometimes their words and phrases function as symbols, thereby suggesting more than is immediately evident. A **symbol** is a word, person, or object that stands for something beyond itself. For example, the events in "Barbara Allan" (as well as in "Get Up and Bar the Door") occur "about the Martinmas time." Martinmas, a Christian festival on November 11 in honor of St. Martin, gradually came to symbolize both revelry and a warm, Indian-summer break in the autumn weather. A balladeer, by making use of a well-understood symbol like Martinmas, could add meaning to a brief story without adding an excessive number of words.

1. The literal meaning of in line 18, "When ye the cups were fillin'," is that Sir John was filling people's glasses with drinks. What is the symbolic meaning?
2. When Barbara Allan asks her mother to "make my bed . . . soft and narrow," lines 33 and 34, what kind of "bed" is probably being symbolized?

SPEAKING AND LISTENING

Sharing Folk Ballads

1. "Barbara Allan" is one of the most widely recorded ballads in history, sometimes under the name "Bawbie Allan," "Bonnie Barbara Allan," or a similar title. It was brought to America in the earliest days of settlement. Today there are many recorded American versions as well as many English and Scottish versions of the song. As a class project, find at least five recorded versions of "Barbara Allan" and bring them to class. Play them all, noting the differences in wording from one recording to another. Decide which version the class prefers, and why.
2. Look through some poetry anthologies or collections of ballads to find a ballad you like. Read it to the class. Try to give your reading the expression and intonation it would have been given by the balladeers who first sang it.

THINKING AND WRITING

Writing About a Folk Ballad

Choose one of the four folk ballads you have read. Reread it until you are sure you understand it fully. Make notes. Write the first draft of a composition, explaining the events in the ballad and noting any details that are implied but not directly stated. Point out the literary techniques —such as rhyme, dialogue, repetition—that heighten the dramatic effect of the ballad. Go over your first draft carefully, paying close attention to what you have written. Make any changes needed. Then write the final draft.

Answers

ANSWERS TO THINKING ABOUT THE SELECTION

Recalling

1. He wants to see her again before he dies.
2. Her words are "Young man, I think you're dyin'."
3. He is sick because Barbara Allan rejected him.
4. She feels that Sir John slighted her at a party he gave.
5. (a) She admits he was her love at the end of the poem, line 35. (b) She feels like dying for him.

Interpreting

6. (a) Barbara Allan seems unsympathetic when she visits the young man. (b) The reader begins to feel sympathy for her as the bells begin to toll.
7. Answers will differ. Many students will agree.

Applying

8. Answers will differ. Some possible information to be added is what actually happened at the party. Why did it happen? How long had the separation lasted?

ANSWERS TO CRITICAL THINKING AND READING

1. Sir John was hosting a party.
2. The "soft and narrow" bed symbolizes a coffin.

ANSWERS TO SPEAKING AND LISTENING

1. Choices will differ.
2. You might allow students to give a choral reading, with the dialogue being read by two individuals.

THINKING AND WRITING

For help with this assignment, students can refer to Lesson 12, "Writing About a Poem," in the Handbook of Writing About Literature.

Publishing Student Writing Invite students to read or summarize their explanations. Try to cover all four of the folk ballads.

Writing Across the Curriculum Have the students choose an incident from history and then write a ballad about it, imitating the characteristics of a genuine folk ballad. They should use the typical rhyme scheme *abcb* and select a conventional ballad theme, such as lost love, tragic death, or heroic death. They might use archaic language, if they wish. You might wish to let history teachers know of this assignment. They may be able to suggest appropriate historical incidents.

More About the Author In April of 1388, when Chaucer was in his forties, he actually made a pilgrimage to Canterbury. He was not looking for material, but he was struck by the mixed company assembled at the Tabard Inn at Southwark. He remembered them ten years later when he began to write the "cavalcade of fourteenth century English life" in *The Canterbury Tales,* a work which earned him the title "the father of English poetry and perhaps the prince of it." What does the second part of this title imply about Chaucer?

GEOFFREY CHAUCER

1343[?]–1400

In his own lifetime Geoffrey Chaucer was considered the greatest English poet, and the centuries have not dimmed his reputation. With the single exception of William Shakespeare, no English writer has surpassed Chaucer's achievements. His unfinished masterpiece, *The Canterbury Tales,* ranks as one of the world's finest works of literature. It also provides the best contemporary picture we have of fourteenth century England.

Although the exact date of Geoffrey Chaucer's birth is unknown, official records furnish many of the details of his active life as a public servant. His father was a well-to-do wine merchant in London, a man with sufficient influence to get young Geoffrey a position as a page in a household connected to that of King Edward III. As a page Chaucer's duties were humble, but the job provided him an opportunity to observe the ruling aristocracy, thus broadening his knowledge of the various classes of society. In 1359, while serving in the English army in France, he was captured and held prisoner. The king paid a £16 ransom for his release. In 1366 Chaucer married a lady-in-waiting to the queen.

Throughout his life Chaucer served in key government positions. He was a controller of customs, a justice of the peace, and a one-term member of Parliament. He spent time in France and Italy on diplomatic missions, served as a supervisor of construction and repairs at Westminster Abbey and the Tower of London, and, late in life, acted as a subforester of the king's forest.

It might seem as if Chaucer would have had little time for writing, but in fact he wrote a great deal. He began producing poetry in his twenties and continued to do so for the rest of his life. Moreover, as he grew older, his literary works showed increasing depth and sophistication. In *Troilus and Criseyde,* a long poem dealing with themes from classical antiquity, he displays the dramatic flair and penetrating insight into human character that are his hallmarks. *The Canterbury Tales,* of which only 24 of the projected 124 tales were completed, shows Chaucer's absolute mastery of the storyteller's art.

Chaucer was the first person to be buried in what is now the Poet's Corner of Westminster Abbey.

THE CANTERBURY TALES

People in medieval England sometimes made pilgrimages to sacred shrines. One such shrine was the cathedral in Canterbury, a town about fifty miles southeast of London, where archbishop Thomas a Becket had been murdered in 1170. The pilgrims often traveled in groups for the sake of companionship and protection. Chaucer's masterpiece, *The Canterbury Tales,* introduces a group of "nine and twenty" pilgrims, one of whom is Chaucer himself. These pilgrims appear first at the Tabard Inn in Southwark, near London, and later on the road to Canterbury.

The Canterbury Tales is a frame story; that is, a story that includes, or frames, another story or stories. Chaucer's frame is the pilgrimage, which he originally planned as a round trip but which remained incomplete at his death. Within this frame are the 24 individual stories the pilgrims tell. Chaucer did not invent the frame-story device. The same structural scheme had been used centuries earlier in *The Thousand and One Nights;* and Boccaccio, an Italian contemporary of Chaucer, used it in the *Decameron,* published about 1350.

Chaucer's handling of his pilgrimage frame is brilliant. The stories are mostly old familiar ones, superbly retold. Perhaps even more impressive than the stories are the storytellers. Chaucer's pilgrims, all of whom are introduced briefly in his Prologue, are memorable, vividly drawn individuals whose personalities are unique but whose character traits are universal. The pilgrims interact with one another. Clashes erupt among them as one pilgrim takes offense at another's tale and proceeds to retaliate with his or her own story.

By using the vehicle of the pilgrimage, Chaucer brings together people from the three main segments of medieval society—the church, the court, and the common people. His pilgrims are drawn from the class structure of feudalism (a knight, a squire, a reeve, for example) as well as from the more open classes in the emerging cities (a merchant, an innkeeper) and the powerful, hierarchical church of the time (a nun, a friar, a pardoner). Chaucer's interest in all these people and the shrewd but affectionate pictures he draws of them make them stand out in such distinct detail that they seem real, alive, and almost modern in their foibles and concerns.

More About *The Canterbury Tales* Another pilgrim joins the group after they leave the Tabard Inn, making a total of thirty-two persons in the company. Whether Chaucer ever had any intention of writing 124 tales is questionable. Along the road one of the Host's remarks seems to suggest that Chaucer might have halved his proposed number, but this is by no means clear. In any event, Chaucer left twenty-two finished tales, one unfinished, and another barely begun. While Chaucer made his own contribution as a writer of rhymed fiction, most of the stories did not originate with him. *The Knight's Tale* and *The Monk's Tale* are abbreviated versions of Boccaccio's stories. *The Reeve's Tale* is a version of a French fabliau. *The Man of Law's Tale* is borrowed from John Gower. Ovid and Livy are also sources for the tales. Indeed, Chaucer borrowed the framework for the Canterbury Tales itself. What is the advantage of employing a frame for a collection of narratives?

Master Teacher Note After the class has read the General Prologue, place Art Transparency 3, *The Traveling Companions,* by Augustus Leopold Egg, on the overhead projector. Conduct a class discussion on what this painting implies about how traveling changed from Chaucer's time to the nineteenth century. What other social changes come to mind when this painting is considered in relation to Chaucer's poetry?

GUIDE FOR READING

The Prologue *from* The Canterbury Tales

Writer's Techniques

Characterization. Characterization refers to the personality of a fictional character as well as to the methods by which a writer creates that personality. Writers use a number of methods of characterization. Sometimes a writer makes a **direct** statement about a person: "Phil was hard to get to know, but those who knew him liked him." More often an author reveals character in an **indirect** way, through action, thoughts, and dialogue: "I should really study harder," Joan thought, laying the novel aside. "If I did, I could probably pass the test." Character can also be revealed through comments about the person by others in the story: "He's the kind of guy," said Linda, "who thinks football is the most important thing in life." A character's physical appearance and habits can help to reveal personality: "Doris wore the same threadbare dress she had worn to the party, but today she stood straighter, her shoulders squared." In defining a character, a writer will often combine these techniques to create a lifelike picture.

Look For

Chaucer uses a variety of methods to bring his Canterbury pilgrims to life. As you read "The Prologue," look for the methods of characterization he employs.

Writing

Jot down a few notes for a physical description of a fictional character. Choose a name for your character. Then note the following details: (1) facial features, (2) typical expression, (3) body structure, (4) typical posture, (5) clothing, (6) physical surroundings. Try to list details that not only describe the character but also help to reveal personality.

Vocabulary

Knowing the following words will help you as you read "The Prologue" from *The Canterbury Tales*.

solicitous (sə lis′ ə təs) *adj.*: Showing care or concern (l. 147)

garnished (gär′ nisht) *adj.*: Decorated; trimmed (l. 197)

preferment (pri fʉr′ mənt) *n.*: Advancement in rank (l. 301)

screeds (skrēdz) *n.*: Long, tiresome pieces of writing (l. 336)

sanguine (san′ gwin) *adj.*: Of cheerful temperament (l. 343)

avouches (ə vouch′ ez) *v.*: Asserts positively; affirms (l. 377)

whelks (hwelkz) *n.*: Pimples (l. 640)

prevarication (pri var ə kā′ shən) *n.*: Evasion of truth (l. 682)

Literary Focus Chaucer was unique among writers of his time in his ability to create the look and spirit of people and to turn characteristics into character. His dramatis personae are sharply individual, exact, and unmistakable. Through tricks of gesture, generality, accents, and complexion and by showing vices and virtues, with no ulcer or wart omitted, Chaucer carefully draws his characters. Several of the characters represent idealized people, but they all show us the values of the Medieval period. What do you discover about the ideals of the Middle Ages from reading *The Canterbury Tales?*

Look For Help the students to see the Knight, the Parson, the Plowman, and even the Cleric as idealized individuals whose virtues represent the ideals of the day. Have them note that direct statements are made to bring attention to their virtue.

Writing You might try using the directed-questioning technique here. Ask the students the questions and allow them a minute or so to freewrite the answer.

Vocabulary You might consider reproducing the list on the board or as a handout so students do not have to flip back and forth as they are reading.

Teaching to Ability Levels You might read the Middle English version aloud to **less advanced** students. For **more advanced** students, you might ask them what is the most notable pronunciation difference between Middle and Modern English. Pick out some spelling differences, e.g. *flour* for *flower, martir* for *martyr, seke* for *seek,* etc. Ask them to formulate general rules from these instances. (For instance, the *i* and *e* are sometimes transposed.)

Objectives

1 To understand characterization
2 To make inferences about character
3 To understand similes

Teaching Portfolio: Support Materials

Teacher Backup, p. 000

Vocabulary Check, p. 00

Usage and Mechanics Worksheet, p. 00

Analyzing Literature Worksheet, p. 00

Critical Thinking and Reading Worksheet, p. 00

Selection Test, p. 00

Art Transparency 3, *The Traveling Companions,* August Leopold Egg

The Prologue

Geoffrey Chaucer
translated by Nevill Coghill

When that Aprill with his shourës sootë
The droghte of March hath percëd to the rootë
And bathëd every veyne in swich licour
Of which vertu engendrëd is the flour,
Whan Zephirus eek with his sweetë breeth
Inspirëd hath in every holt and heeth
The tendrë croppës, and the yongë sonnë
Hath in the Ram his half cours y-ronnë,
And smalë fowelës maken melodyë
That slepen al the nyght with open eye,
So priketh hem Nature in hir corages,
Than longen folk to goon on pilgrymages,
And palmeres for to seken straungë strondës,
To fernë halwës kouthe in sondry londës.
And specially, from every shirës endë
On Engelond, to Caunterbury they wendë,
The holy, blisful martir for to seke
That hem hath holpen whan that they were seekë.

When in April the sweet showers fall
And pierce the drought of March to the root, and all
The veins are bathed in liquor of such power
As brings about the engendering of the flower,
When also Zephyrus[1] with his sweet breath
Exhales an air in every grove and heath
Upon tender shoots, and the young sun
His half-course in the sign of the Ram[2] has run,
And the small fowl are making melody
That sleep away the night with open eye
(So nature pricks them and their heart engages)
Then people long to go on pilgrimages
And palmers[3] long to seek the stranger strands[4]
Of far-off saints, hallowed in sundry lands,
And specially, from every shire's end
In England, down to Canterbury they wend
To seek the holy blissful martyr,[5] quick
To give his help to them when they were sick.

1. Zephyrus (zef′ ər əs): The west wind.

2. Ram: Aries, the first sign of the zodiac. The pilgrimage began on April 11, 1387.

3. palmers: Pilgrims who wore two crossed palm leaves to show that they had visited the Holy Land.

4. strands: Shores.

5. martyr: St. Thomas à Becket, the Archbishop of Canterbury, who was murdered in the Canterbury Cathedral in 1170.

Motivation for Reading Imagine that you, along with twenty-five or thirty others, were to take an eighty-mile journey on horseback. Your companions are from all walks of life. The only common bond among them, besides the desire to make the trip, is their competence in their various professions. With no television, radio, Walkman, or magazines for entertainment, what might the company do to entertain themselves? What would you anticipate might happen among the members of the group?

Purpose-Setting Question A significant part of Chaucer's greatness lies in his universality and his profound understanding of human nature. As you read, look for character types that are still recognizable today.

1 **Master Teacher Note** Point out that the rhythm and rhyme arrangement is the iambic pentameter couplet. Chaucer introduced this form into English verse. It is seen in its most sophisticated form in the eighteenth-century verse essays of Alexander Pope. Note that Chaucer favors an open rather than a closed couplet. This means that his sentences do not necessarily end at the conclusion of the couplet but rather run over into subsequent lines.

Have **more advanced** students compare both versions in a line-by-line analysis. How does the rhythm of the modernization compare with that of the original?

2 **Literary Focus** Chaucer is describing the rebirth of the year and its accompanying wanderlust. Medieval man had very limited options for satisfying this desire for travel; individual journeys were extremely hazardous, and the most available type of group expedition was the religious pilgrimage. Why would a religious pilgrimage be so popular?

Humanities Note

Fine art, *The Tabard Inn,* 1946, by Arthur Szyk. Szyk (1894–1951), a Polish-born American artist, did much in his lifetime to revive the lost Medieval art of miniature illumination painting. His art education at the Academy of Fine Art in Krakow, Poland, and at the Beaux Arts Academy in Paris gave him the background in academic art necessary to pursue this exacting form of painting. His most famous work is a series of miniatures of the life of George Washington presented to President Franklin D. Roosevelt by the President of Poland in 1934.

The painting *The Tabard Inn,* done for *The Canterbury Tales* in 1946, was painted in miniature in the style of a medieval monk illuminating a manuscript. Despite the miniature format, this painting is rich in color and detail. The innkeeper stands proudly at the door and surveys the colorful assembly of pilgrims arriving on horseback. The expressions of the group are painted with a touch of humor that allows a glimpse into their personalities. The piety of the knight, the cunning of the friar, and the foppishness of the squire are apparent.

You may wish to ask the following questions to encourage discussion:

1. Is the humorous nature of this painting in keeping with Chaucer's attitude?
2. What does the expression and stance of the innkeeper convey?

3 **Master Teacher Note** Note that, after a rather formal, impersonal, high-flown opening, Chaucer descends to a simpler level: direct, informal narrative.

4 **Clarification** Since Southwark was a suburb at the southern end of the London Bridge, it was a logical starting point for a journey to Canterbury, about eighty miles southeast of London.

THE TABARD INN
Arthur Szyk for the Canterbury Tales
The George Macy Companies

3 It happened in that season that one day
4 In Southwark[6], at The Tabard,[7] as I lay
Ready to go on pilgrimage and start
For Canterbury, most devout at heart,
At night there came into that hostelry
Some nine and twenty in a company
Of sundry folk happening then to fall
In fellowship, and they were pilgrims all
That towards Canterbury meant to ride.

6. Southwark (suth' ərk): A suburb of London at the time.
7. The Tabard (ta' bərd): An inn.

The rooms and stables of the inn were wide;
They made us easy, all was of the best.
And shortly, when the sun had gone to rest,
By speaking to them all upon the trip
I soon was one of them in fellowship
And promised to rise early and take the way
To Canterbury, as you heard me say.
But nonetheless, while I have time and space,
Before my story takes a further pace,
It seems a reasonable thing to say
What their condition was, the full array
Of each of them, as it appeared to me
According to profession and degree,
And what apparel they were riding in;
And at a Knight I therefore will begin. 5
There was a *Knight*, a most distinguished man,
Who from the day on which he first began
To ride abroad had followed chivalry, 6
Truth, honor, generousness and courtesy.
He had done nobly in his sovereign's war
And ridden into battle, no man more,
As well in Christian as heathen places,
And ever honored for his noble graces.
When we took Alexandria,[8] he was there.
He often sat at table in the chair
Of honor, above all nations, when in Prussia.
In Lithuania he had ridden, and Russia,
No Christian man so often, of his rank.
When, in Granada, Algeciras sank
Under assault, he had been there, and in
North Africa, raiding Benamarin;
In Anatolia he had been as well
And fought when Ayas and Attalia fell,
For all along the Mediterranean coast
He had embarked with many a noble host.
In fifteen mortal battles he had been
And jousted for our faith at Tramissene
Thrice in the lists, and always killed his man.
This same distinguished knight had led the van
Once with the Bey of Balat, doing work 7
For him against another heathen Turk;
He was of sovereign value in all eyes.
And though so much distinguished, he was wise
And in his bearing modest as a maid.
He never yet a boorish thing had said
In all his life to any, come what might;
He was a true, a perfect gentle-knight.

8. Alexandria: The site of one of the campaigns fought by Christians against groups who posed a threat to Europe during the fourteenth century. The place names that follow refer to other battlesites in these campaigns, or crusades.

5 **Enrichment** Since the Knight possesses the highest social standing among the pilgrims, it is appropriate that he be the first described.

6 **Enrichment** When Chaucer describes the Knight as the epitome of chivalry, he is talking about an ideal from the past. By the 1380's when Chaucer began this work, feudalism and chivalry, its accompanying social code for the nobility, were all but gone.

7 **Critical Thinking and Reading** Although the Knight is always considered one of Chaucer's most admirable characters, indeed so admirable that he seems idealized rather than realistic, these lines suggest a somewhat less attractive side to his character. In what way do they do so?

8 **Discussion** What do these comments on the Knight's appearance reveal about his nature?

9 **Reading Strategy** What is the Knight's purpose in joining the pilgrimage? As you learn about the other pilgrims, watch for their motives, usually less noble than that of the knight.

10 **Critical Thinking and Reading** What seems to motivate the Squire to do well in battle? What other lines suggest his preoccupation in this same area?

11 **Discussion** How does the Squire's appearance differ from his father's? From the various references to it, what does this physical description reveal about the Squire's character?

12 **Discussion** What do we learn about the education of a well-born young man in the fourteenth century?

13 **Reading Strategy** How does Chaucer regard the Squire? Is he idealized like his father or is he more realistic, with both faults and virtues? Almost all the pilgrims will combine moral strength and weakness. Suggest that the students should be alert for this combination as they read.

14 **Critical Thinking and Reading** The description of the Yeoman concentrates primarily on his physical appearance, and there is little sense of the kind of man he is. Why do you think Chaucer has neglected any indication of his inner nature?

15 **Literary Focus** Who does the Yeoman look like? Point out that the Robin Hood resemblance is generally noted, and that the original Robin Hood was presumably a late twelfth-century figure but woodmen's garb would have changed little during the intervening years.

Speaking of his equipment, he possessed
Fine horses, but he was not gaily dressed.
8 He wore a fustian[9] tunic stained and dark
With smudges where his armor had left mark;
9 Just home from service, he had joined our ranks
To do his pilgrimage and render thanks.
He had his son with him, a fine young *Squire*,
A lover and cadet, a lad of fire
With locks as curly as if they had been pressed.
He was some twenty years of age, I guessed.
In stature he was of a moderate length,
With wonderful agility and strength.
He'd seen some service with the cavalry
In Flanders and Artois and Picardy[10]
10 And had done valiantly in little space
Of time, in hope to win his lady's grace.
He was embroidered like a meadow bright
And full of freshest flowers, red and white.
11 Singing he was, or fluting all the day;
He was as fresh as is the month of May.
Short was his gown, the sleeves were long and wide;
He knew the way to sit a horse and ride.
He could make songs and poems and recite,
12 Knew how to joust and dance, to draw and write.
He loved so hotly that till dawn grew pale
He slept as little as a nightingale.
13 Courteous he was, lowly and serviceable,
And carved to serve his father at the table.
14 There was a *Yeoman*[11] with him at his side,
No other servant; so he chose to ride.
This Yeoman wore a coat and hood of green,
15 And peacock-feathered arrows, bright and keen
And neatly sheathed, hung at his belt the while
—For he could dress his gear in yeoman style,
His arrows never drooped their feathers low—
16 And in his hand he bore a mighty bow.
His head was like a nut, his face was brown.
He knew the whole of woodcraft up and down.
A saucy brace[12] was on his arm to ward
It from the bow-string, and a shield and sword
Hung at one side, and at the other slipped
A jaunty dirk,[13] spear-sharp and well-equipped.
A medal of St. Christopher[14] he wore
17 Of shining silver on his breast, and bore
A hunting-horn, well slung and burnished clean,
That dangled from a baldric[15] of bright green.
He was a proper forester I guess.

9. fustian (fus' chən): A coarse cloth of cotton and linen.

10. Flanders . . . Picardy: Regions in Belgium and France.

11. *Yeoman* (yō' mən) *n.*: Attendant.

12. brace: Bracelet.

13. dirk *n.*: A short, straight dagger.

14. St. Christopher: The patron saint of forests and travelers.

15. baldric *n.*: A belt worn over one shoulder and across the chest to support a sword.

16 **Literary Focus** There are several references to the Yeoman's professional skill. Suggest that the students find these references. Almost all of Chaucer's pilgrims are good at what they do. He has created not only a cross-section of medieval society but a group of skilled practitioners of medieval occupations.

17 **Enrichment** The fact that he wears a St. Christopher medal does not necessarily suggest that the Yeoman is pious. St. Christopher medals were commonplace among Medieval travelers.

There also was a *Nun,* a Prioress.[16]
Her way of smiling very simple and coy.
Her greatest oath was only "By St. Loy!"[17]
And she was known as Madam Eglantyne.
And well she sang a service,[18] with a fine
Intoning through her nose, as was most seemly,
And she spoke daintily in French, extremely,
After the school of Stratford-atte-Bowe;[19]
French in the Paris style she did not know.
At meat her manners were well taught withal;
No morsel from her lips did she let fall,
Nor dipped her fingers in the sauce too deep;
But she could carry a morsel up and keep
The smallest drop from falling on her breast.
For courtliness she had a special zest,
And she would wipe her upper lip so clean
That not a trace of grease was to be seen
Upon the cup when she had drunk; to eat,
She reached a hand sedately for the meat.
She certainly was very entertaining,
Pleasant and friendly in her ways, and straining
To counterfeit a courtly kind of grace,
A stately bearing fitting to her place,
And to seem dignified in all her dealings.
As for her sympathies and tender feelings,
She was so charitably solicitous
She used to weep if she but saw a mouse
Caught in a trap, if it were dead or bleeding.
And she had little dogs she would be feeding
With roasted flesh, or milk, or fine white bread.
And bitterly she wept if one were dead
Or someone took a stick and made it smart;
She was all sentiment and tender heart.
Her veil was gathered in a seemly way,
Her nose was elegant, her eyes glass-gray;
Her mouth was very small, but soft and red,
Her forehead, certainly, was fair of spread,
Almost a span[20] across the brows, I own;
She was indeed by no means undergrown.
Her cloak, I noticed, had a graceful charm.
She wore a coral trinket on her arm,
A set of beads, the gaudies[21] tricked in green,
Whence hung a golden brooch of brightest sheen
On which there first was graven a crowned A,
And lower, *Amor vincit omnia.*[22]
Another *Nun,* the chaplain at her cell,
Was riding with her, and *three Priests* as well.

16. Prioress *n.*: In an abbey, the nun ranking just below the abbess. 18
17. St. Loy: St. Eligius, patron saint of goldsmiths and courtiers. 19 20
18. service: Daily prayer.

19. Stratford-atte-Bowe: A nunnery near London.

21

22

THE YEOMAN
Arthur Szyk for the Canterbury Tales
The George Macy Companies

23

20. span: Nine inches.

21. gaudies: Large green beads that marked certain prayers on a set of prayer beads.
22. *Amor vincit omnia* (ä môr′ wink′ it ôm′ nē ä): "Love conquers all" (Latin). 24

Humanities Note

Fine art, *The Yeoman,* 1946, by Arthur Szyk. In this miniature painted in 1946 for *The Canterbury Tales,* the artist shows a fully equipped medieval yeoman. He appears ready for any occurrence in the forest, from the appearance of game to an attack by highwaymen. He is portrayed as a sturdy fellow with a serious expression on his face. In painting these miniatures, Arthur Szyk, with patience and meticulous care, imitates monkish manuscript painters. Through this painstaking effort, he succeeds in capturing the charm and medieval flavor of that art.

1. How does Szyk's depiction of the yeoman compare with your image of him?
2. How closely does this depiction match Chaucer's description in lines 105–121?

18 **Enrichment** Chaucer introduces here the first of his various ecclesiastical pilgrims and his first woman. Of the thirty pilgrims who set out from Southwark, three are women, and of these three two are nuns.

19 **Clarification** An oath "by St. Loy" would have been mild and inoffensive.

20 **Critical Thinking and Reading** Since "Eglantyne" was the name of several clinging-vine heroines in Medieval romances, what comment does Chaucer seem to be making about the Prioress?

21 **Discussion** What does Chaucer's use of the verb *counterfeit* suggest?

22 **Discussion** Is Chaucer commending her tenderness of heart or mocking it? Although his tone in describing the Prioress is quite consistently satiric, Chaucer likes her. Why then might he use a satiric tone?

23 **Clarification** The Prioress would have taken a vow of poverty when she entered religious life. This vow would have precluded her owning a luxury such as little dogs. What do you think of their diet? Is it appropriate? What about the "coral trinket"? Frequently Chaucer's descriptions can be understood in two ways. Does the inscription *"Amor vincit omnia"* refer to secular or spiritual love?

24 **Master Teacher Note** The other nun mentioned here, her companion, is the second woman on the pilgrimage. The three priests mentioned prevent the number of pilgrims from adding up to thirty. It has been conjectured that Chaucer left this line unfinished and that someone else filled it in. It should be remembered that no manuscript for *The Canterbury Tales* exists today that Chaucer could have seen. All are copies by fifthteenth-century scribes; the earliest dates back to about 1410; Chaucer died in 1400.

25 **Clarification** The Monk, another ecclesiastical pilgrim, held a position in his monastery somewhat like the Prioress's in her convent. Both were figures of some authority.

26 **Discussion** What was the Monk's attitude toward the rules of his order?

27 **Master Teacher Note** Here is one of the infrequent instances in the Prologue in which the narrator directly injects his own personality and opinion. It should be remembered that the "I" of the Prologue is not really Chaucer but an imaginary character, one who is far more naïve and impressionable than the real, urbane, tolerant, sophisticated author himself.

28 **Discussion** What kind of activity was expected of a Monk? What did this Monk choose to do instead?

29 **Clarification** To be fat in the Middle Ages was a status symbol. Only the rich had more than enough to eat; thus obesity suggested affluence.

30 **Discussion** Do you believe that this Monk observed the vow of poverty that he, like the Prioress, would have taken upon entering monastic life? A second vow required of the religious was a vow of obedience. How well did he fulfill these vows?

31 **Enrichment** Unlike monks, whose work lay within a monastery, friars were itinerant ecclesiastics whose begging supported schools, hospitals, and other church-related institutions. This Friar exemplifies the corruption to which many in these mendicant orders had sunk by Chaucer's time.

25 A *Monk* there was, one of the finest sort
Who rode the country; hunting was his sport.
A manly man, to be an Abbot able;
Many a dainty horse he had in stable.
His bridle, when he rode, a man might hear
Jingling in a whistling wind as clear,
Aye, and as loud as does the chapel bell
Where my lord Monk was Prior of the cell.
The Rule of good St. Benet or St. Maur[23]
As old and strict he tended to ignore;
26 He let go by the things of yesterday
And took the modern world's more spacious way.
He did not rate that text at a plucked hen
Which says that hunters are not holy men
And that a monk uncloistered is a mere
Fish out of water, flapping on the pier,
That is to say a monk out of his cloister.
That was a text he held not worth an oyster;
And I agreed and said his views were sound;
Was he to study till his head went round
27 Poring over books in cloisters? Must he toil
As Austin[24] bade and till the very soil?
Was he to leave the world upon the shelf?
Let Austin have his labor to himself.
This Monk was therefore a good man to horse;
Greyhounds he had, as swift as birds, to course.
28 Hunting a hare or riding at a fence
Was all his fun, he spared for no expense.
I saw his sleeves were garnished at the hand
With fine gray fur, the finest in the land,
And on his hood, to fasten it at his chin
He had a wrought-gold cunningly fashioned pin;
Into a lover's knot it seemed to pass.
His head was bald and shone like looking-glass;
So did his face, as if it had been greased.
29 He was a fat and personable priest;
His prominent eyeballs never seemed to settle.
They glittered like the flames beneath a kettle;
Supple his boots, his horse in fine condition.
30 He was a prelate fit for exhibition,
He was not pale like a tormented soul.
He liked a fat swan best, and roasted whole.
His palfrey[25] was as brown as is a berry.
There was a *Friar*, a wanton[26] one and merry,
31 A Limiter,[27] a very festive fellow.
In all Four Orders[28] there was none so mellow
So glib with gallant phrase and well-turned speech.

23. St. Benet or St. Maur: St. Benedict, author of monastic rules, and St. Maurice, one of his followers. Benet and Maur are French versions of Benedict and Maurice.

24. Austin: English version of St. Augustine, who criticized lazy monks.

25. palfrey: Saddle horse.
26. wanton: Jolly.
27. Limiter: A friar who is given begging rights for a certain limited area.
28. Four Orders: There were four orders of friars who supported themselves by begging: Dominicans, Franciscans, Carmelites, and Augustinians.

THE MONK
Arthur Szyk for the Canterbury Tales
The George Macy Companies

Humanities Note

Fine art, *The Monk,* 1946, by Arthur Szyk. In this miniature, Szyk shows the massive and richly robed monk described in the Prologue. His wealth is apparent from his fine fur-trimmed robes, gold brooch, elaborate sword, and tooled wallet. His expression is one of haughty self-satisfaction. Szyk painted the worldly cleric with humor and wit, emphasizing the incongruity between the trappings of wealth and the man's humble vocation.

1. How does Szyk's pictorial representation of the monk compare with Chaucer's description?
2. Does this depiction look realistic or exaggerated?

32 Master Teacher Note The implication here is that the Friar found husbands and dowries for women he himself had seduced. Since the third vow that religious took was the vow of chastity, his moral laxity is clear.

33 Clarification The Friar had received from his order a license to hear confessions without gaining permission from local priests and to give absolution for more serious sins than parish priests could. The friars were often charged with laxity in imposing penances. This Friar, in effect, allowed people to pay for having their sins forgiven.

34 Clarification A soft white neck was considered a mark of licentiousness.

35 Reading Strategy Read to discover what the Friar's attitude toward priestly duties is. What was his great talent?

He'd fixed up many a marriage, giving each
32 Of his young women what he could afford her.
He was a noble pillar to his Order.
Highly beloved and intimate was he
With County folk within his boundary,
And city dames of honor and possessions;
For he was qualified to hear confessions,
Or so he said, with more than priestly scope;
He had a special license from the Pope.
Sweetly he heard his penitents at shrift[29]
With pleasant absolution, for a gift.
He was an easy man in penance-giving
Where he could hope to make a decent living;
33 It's a sure sign whenever gifts are given
To a poor Order that a man's well shriven,[30]
And should he give enough he knew in verity
The penitent repented in sincerity.
For many a fellow is so hard of heart
He cannot weep, for all his inward smart.
Therefore instead of weeping and of prayer
One should give silver for a poor Friar's care.
He kept his tippet[31] stuffed with pins for curls,
And pocket-knives, to give to pretty girls.
And certainly his voice was gay and sturdy,
For he sang well and played the hurdy-gurdy.[32]
At sing-songs he was champion of the hour.
34 His neck was whiter than a lily-flower
But strong enough to butt a bruiser down.
He knew the taverns well in every town
And every innkeeper and barmaid too
Better than lepers, beggars and that crew,
For in so eminent a man as he
It was not fitting with the dignity
Of his position, dealing with a scum
Of wretched lepers; nothing good can come
Of dealings with the slum-and-gutter dwellers,
But only with the rich and victual-sellers.
35 But anywhere a profit might accrue
Courteous he was and lowly of service too.
Natural gifts like his were hard to match.
He was the finest beggar of his batch,
And, for his begging-district, payed a rent;
His brethren did no poaching where he went.
For though a widow mightn't have a shoe,
So pleasant was his holy how-d'ye-do
He got his farthing from her just the same
Before he left, and so his income came

29. shrift: Confession.

30. well shriven: Absolved of his sins.

31. tippet: Hood.

32. hurdy-gurdy: A stringed instument played by cranking a wheel.

To more than he laid out. And how he romped,
Just like a puppy! He was ever prompt
To arbitrate disputes on settling days
(For a small fee) in many helpful ways,
Not then appearing as your cloistered scholar
With threadbare habit hardly worth a dollar,
But much more like a Doctor or a Pope.
36 Of double-worsted was the semi-cope[33]
Upon his shoulders, and the swelling fold
About him, like a bell about its mold
When it is casting, rounded out his dress.
He lisped a little out of wantonness
To make his English sweet upon his tongue.
When he had played his harp, or having sung,
His eyes would twinkle in his head as bright
As any star upon a frosty night.
This worthy's name was Hubert, it appeared.
There was a *Merchant* with a forking beard
And motley dress; high on his horse he sat,
37 Upon his head a Flemish[34] beaver hat
And on his feet daintily buckled boots.
He told of his opinions and pursuits
In solemn tones, and how he never lost.
The sea should be kept free at any cost
38 (He thought) upon the Harwich-Holland range,[35]
He was expert at currency exchange.
This estimable Merchant so had set
39 His wits to work, none knew he was in debt,
He was so stately in negotiation,
Loan, bargain and commercial obligation.
He was an excellent fellow all the same;
To tell the truth I do not know his name.
40 An *Oxford Cleric,* still a student though,
One who had taken logic long ago,
41 Was there; his horse was thinner than a rake,
And he was not too fat, I undertake,
But had a hollow look, a sober stare;
The thread upon his overcoat was bare.
He had found no preferment in the church
42 And he was too unworldly to make search
For secular employment. By his bed
He preferred having twenty books in red
And black, of Aristotle's[36] philosophy,
To having fine clothes, fiddle or psaltery.[37]
Though a philosopher, as I have told,
He had not found the stone for making gold.[38]
Whatever money from his friends he took

33. semi-cope: Cape.

34. Flemish: From Flanders.

35. Harwich-Holland range: The North Sea between England and Holland.

36. Aristotle's (ar′ is tot′ əlz): Referring to the Greek philosopher (384–322 B.C.).

37. psaltery (sôl′ tər ē): An ancient stringed instrument.

38. stone . . . gold: At the time alchemists believed that a "philosopher's stone" existed that could turn base metals into gold.

36 **Critical Thinking and Reading** How did his clothing reflect his character?

37 **Enrichment** The "motley" dress, made of multi-colored cloth woven in designs, suggests affluence, as do the imported beaver hat and daintily buckled boots. The Merchant is a very wealthy man.

38 **Literary Focus** "Kept free from pirates" is the implication and it reflects the Merchant's special-interest bias: the government should spare no expense in employing public funds to protect his business ventures. Does this kind of special-interest bias still exist?

39 **Discussion** Does concealment of his debts suggest that the merchant is dishonest? Does Chaucer make a moral judgment? Note that Chaucer tends to make very few explicit moral judgments. He seems extremely tolerant of human frailty.

40 **Enrichment** The term "cleric" referred to any ecclesiastical student as well as to a priest, and Oxford University in the 14th century was essentially a training ground for the religious. Chaucer's Oxford Cleric was evidently a very advanced student. Although not an ordained priest, he had undoubtedly completed most of the required course of study.

41 **Clarification** The thinness of both the Cleric and his horse as well as the threadbare condition of his coat all attest to his poverty.

42 **Clarification** It was common for men of clerical training to seek employment outside the Church. This cleric was not aggressive or materialistic enough to have found it.

Humanities Note

Fine art, *The Student,* 1946, by Arthur Szyk. In the miniature *The Student,* Szyk cleverly shows the student's preference for intellectual attainment over worldly matters. His drab tunic and patched knees contrast with his intent expression as he reads his book. He absently gestures with his left hand as if in conversation with himself, unaware of the picture he presents to others. Although not as decorative as the other, more richly dressed characters illustrated by Szyk, the student is detailed with care and skill.

1. Do you think Szyk's miniature captures the personality of the student as Chaucer has portrayed him?
2. Does Szyk's student remind you of any young scholar you have ever seen?

THE STUDENT
Arthur Szyk for the Canterbury Tales
The George Macy Companies

He spent on learning or another book
43 And prayed for them most earnestly, returning
Thanks to them thus for paying for his learning.
His only care was study, and indeed
He never spoke a word more than was need,
Formal at that, respectful in the extreme,
Short, to the point, and lofty in his theme.
The thought of moral virtue filled his speech
44 And he would gladly learn, and gladly teach.
45 A *Sergeant at the Law* who paid his calls,
Wary and wise, for clients at St. Paul's[39]
There also was, of noted excellence.
Discreet he was, a man to reverence,
Or so he seemed, his sayings were so wise.
He often had been Justice of Assize
By letters patent, and in full commission.
His fame and learning and his high position
Had won him many a robe and many a fee.
There was no such conveyancer[40] as he;
46 All was fee-simple[41] to his strong digestion,
Not one conveyance could be called in question.
Nowhere there was so busy a man as he;
But was less busy than he seemed to be.
He knew of every judgment, case and crime
Recorded, ever since King William's time.
He could dictate defenses or draft deeds;
No one could pinch a comma from his screeds,
And he knew every statute off by rote.
He wore a homely parti-colored coat
47 Girt with a silken belt of pin-stripe stuff;
Of his appearance I have said enough.
There was a *Franklin*[42] with him, it appeared;
48 White as a daisy-petal was his beard.
A sanguine man, high-colored and benign,
He loved a morning sop[43] of cake in wine.
He lived for pleasure and had always done,
For he was Epicurus'[44] very son,
In whose opinion sensual delight
Was the one true felicity in sight.
As noted as St. Julian[45] was for bounty
He made his household free to all the County.
His bread, his ale were the finest of the fine
And no one had a better stock of wine.
49 His house was never short of bake-meat pies,
Of fish and flesh, and these in such supplies
It positively snowed with meat and drink
And all the dainties that a man could think.

39. St. Paul's: A London cathedral outside of which lawyers often met to discuss their cases.

40. conveyancer: One who draws up documents for transferring ownership of property.

41. fee-simple: Restricted ownership.

42. *Franklin:* Wealthy landowner.

43. sop: Piece.

44. Epicurus' (ep' i kyoor' əs): Referring to a Greek philosopher (342?–370 B.C.) who believed that happiness is the most important goal in life.

45. St. Julian: Patron saint of hospitality.

43 **Discussion** Do you think the Cleric took advantage of his friends by allowing them to contribute to his upkeep? Could he repay them in any way?

44 **Enrichment** This Oxford Cleric is considered to be one of the handful of idealized characters introduced in the Prologue. He is the model of what a student should be rather than a portrait of what a student generally is. He represents the passion for learning that was already stirring in Europe. The description "gladly would he learn and gladly teach" is an often-quoted encomium for the dedicated scholar.

45 **Enrichment** The term "Sergeant at the Law" referred to a member of a small, chosen group of lawyers—one who had at least sixteen years experience, was the King's legal servant, acted as judge, and was among the most eminent members of his profession. In Chaucer's day there were about twenty in this exclusive group.

46 **Discussion** Is the lawyer a skillful practitioner of his profession? What evidence is there of his skill?

47 **Enrichment** The fact that his coat was "parti-colored" suggests luxury. Less expensive fabric would be dyed a single color. A belt of silk would also suggest affluence, since silk would have to be imported from the Orient.

48 **Clarification** A franklin was a landholder of free but not noble birth. He seemed, however, to have been regarded as a gentleman with a social position equal to a knight, squire, or sergeant at law. Chaucer's Franklin is certainly a man of wealth and dignity. He corresponds to the country squire of a later period.

49 **Discussion** For what is the Franklin noted? What is his greatest joy in life? How admirable is this occupation?

50 Critical Thinking and Reading What might Chaucer be suggesting about the Franklin's source of delicacies by abruptly ending the description with a reference to his role as Sheriff and auditor?

51 Enrichment In England the term *haberdasher* means "a dealer in small wares or notions." In this country it refers to a dealer in men's furnishings.

52 Reading Strategy Read to discover what four of the five guildsmen have in common.

53 Master Teacher Note Why did their wives think they should be aldermen? Is a woman's social position today determined by her husband's? Note that we learn more about the wives' characters than about the guildsmen's characters.

54 Literary Focus There is only one physically descriptive fact given about the Cook, and it is somewhat unappetizing. Students might theorize as to Chaucer's reason for including it.

55 Critical Thinking and Reading What does Chaucer imply when he says the Skipper "rode . . . as best he could"?

According to the seasons of the year
Changes of dish were ordered to appear.
He kept fat partridges in coops, beyond,
Many a bream and pike were in his pond.
Woe to the cook whose sauces had no sting
Or who was unprepared in anything!
And in his hall a table stood arrayed
And ready all day long, with places laid.
As Justice at the Sessions[46] none stood higher;
He often had been Member for the Shire.[47]
A dagger and a little purse of silk
Hung at his girdle, white as morning milk.
50 As Sheriff he checked audit, every entry.
He was a model among landed gentry.
51 A *Haberdasher*, a *Dyer*, a *Carpenter*,
52 A *Weaver* and a *Carpet-maker* were
Among our ranks, all in the livery
Of one impressive guild-fraternity.
They were so trim and fresh their gear would pass
For new. Their knives were not tricked out with brass
But wrought with purest silver, which avouches
A like display on girdles and on pouches.
Each seemed a worthy burgess,[48] fit to grace
A guild-hall with a seat upon the dais.
Their wisdom would have justified a plan
To make each one of them an alderman;
They had the capital and revenue,
53 Besides their wives declared it was their due.
And if they did not think so, then they ought;
To be called "*Madam*" is a glorious thought,
And so is going to church and being seen
Having your mantle carried like a queen.
They had a *Cook* with them who stood alone
For boiling chicken with a marrow-bone,
Sharp flavoring-powder and a spice for savor.
He could distinguish London ale by flavor,
And he could roast and seethe and broil and fry,
Make good thick soup and bake a tasty pie.
But what a pity—so it seemed to me,
54 That he should have an ulcer on his knee.
As for blancmange,[49] he made it with the best.
There was a *Skipper* hailing from far west;
He came from Dartmouth, so I understood.
55 He rode a farmer's horse as best he could,
In a woolen gown that reached his knee.
A dagger on a lanyard[50] falling free
Hung from his neck under his arm and down.
The summer heat had tanned his color brown,

46. Sessions: Court sessions.

47. Member . . . Shire: Parliamentary representative for the county.

48. burgess: A member of a legislative body.

49. blancmange (blə mänj'): At the time, a creamy chicken dish.

50. lanyard: A loose rope around the neck.

And certainly he was an excellent fellow.
Many a draught of vintage, red and yellow,
He'd drawn at Bordeaux, while the trader snored.
The nicer rules of conscience he ignored.
If, when he fought, the enemy vessel sank,
He sent his prisoners home; they walked the plank.
As for his skill in reckoning his tides,
Currents and many another risk besides,
Moons, harbors, pilots, he had such dispatch
That none from Hull to Carthage was his match.
56 Hardy he was, prudent in undertaking;
His beard in many a tempest had its shaking,
And he knew all the havens as they were
From Gottland to the Cape of Finisterre,
And every creek in Brittany and Spain;
The barge he owned was called *The Maudelayne.*
  A *Doctor* too emerged as we proceeded;
57 No one alive could talk as well as he did
On points of medicine and of surgery,
For, being grounded in astronomy,
He watched his patient's favorable star
58 And, by his Natural Magic, knew what are
The lucky hours and planetary degrees
For making charms and magic effigies.
The cause of every malady you'd got
He knew, and whether dry, cold, moist or hot;[51]
He knew their seat, their humor and condition.
He was a perfect practicing physician.
These causes being known for what they were,
He gave the man his medicine then and there.
59 All his apothecaries[52] in a tribe
Were ready with the drugs he would prescribe,
And each made money from the other's guile;
They had been friendly for a goodish while.
In his own diet he observed some measure;
There were no superfluities for pleasure,
Only digestives, nutritives and such.
60 He did not read the Bible very much.
In blood-red garments, slashed with bluish-gray
And lined with taffeta,[53] he rode his way;
61 Yet he was rather close as to expenses
And kept the gold he won in pestilences.
Gold stimulates the heart, or so we're told.
He therefore had a special love of gold.
  A worthy *woman* from beside *Bath*[54] city
62 Was with us, somewhat deaf, which was a pity.
In making cloth she showed so great a bent
She bettered those of Ypres and of Ghent.[55]

51. The cause . . . hot: It was believed that the body was composed of four "humors" (cold and dry, hot and moist, hot and dry, cold and moist) and that diseases resulted from a disturbance of one of these "humors."

52. apothecaries (ə päth′ ə ker′ ēz): Persons who prepared drugs.

53. taffeta (taf′ i tə): A fine silk fabric.

54. *Bath*: An English resort city.

55. Ypres (ē′ prə) **and of Ghent** (gent): Flemish cities known for wool making.

56 **Clarification** Like most of the other pilgrims, he was extremely adept at his job. The breadth of his maritime skill is suggested in specific geographical terms, as "from Hull to Carthage," *i.e.*, from northern England to northern Africa, and from "Gottland to the Cape of Finisterre," *i.e.*, Sweden to Spain. The name Finisterre is literally translated "the end of the earth."

57 **Reading Strategy** Read to see the excellent picture Chaucer gives of the practice of medicine in 14th-century England.

58 **Master Teacher Note** Astronomy really means astrology here; the divination of the supposed influences of the stars on human events. Medieval medicine relied heavily on the belief of a relationship between planetary influences and disease. The "charms and magic effigies" could have been either wax representations of the patients—like benign voodoo dolls—or talismans representing signs of the Zodiac. Both were used by physicians. "Natural Magic" was regarded as a legitimate science, as opposed to black magic or necromancy.

59 **Discussion** What sharp practice between the physician and the apothecaries is suggested here? Might anything like it exist in modern medicine?

60 **Master Teacher Note** Doctors were commonly regarded as irreligious skeptics, especially those that followed the school of the great twelfth-century Arabian physician Averroës. A comparison has often been made between this line and the proverb "Ubi tres medici, duo athei" or "Where there are three doctors, two are atheists." Is this conflict between religion and science still in existence?

61 **Discussion** The fabric and the color of the physician's garment suggest affluence. Do you get the sense that he is a free spender?

62 **Enrichment** Her deafness came from a blow on the ear administered by her fifth husband because she had torn several pages out of an antifeminist book he insisted on reading to her.

Humanities Note

Fine art, *The Wife of Bath,* 1946, by Arthur Szyk. In this miniature the artist shows the good wife of Bath to be an imposing and decorative figure. The provocative posture and bold eyes are in keeping with Chaucer's description of her. The tiny details of dress, such as the gold buttons and the heart pattern on her belt, show the extreme skill of the artist in executing a painting on such a small scale. When discussing this painting with your class, point out the similarities in Szyk's portrait of the wife of Bath and Chaucer's written account of her.

1. What impression of the wife's personality does the painting express?
2. What does Chaucer's description of her convey that the painting does not?

THE WIFE OF BATH
Arthur Szyk for the Canterbury Tales
The George Macy Companies

In all the parish not a dame dared stir
Towards the altar steps in front of her,
63 And if indeed they did, so wrath was she
As to be quite put out of charity.
Her kerchiefs were of finely woven ground;[56]
I dared have sworn they weighed a good ten pound,
The ones she wore on Sunday, on her head.
64 Her hose were of the finest scarlet red
And gartered tight; her shoes were soft and new.
Bold was her face, handsome, and red in hue.
A worthy woman all her life, what's more
She'd had five husbands, all at the church door,
Apart from other company in youth;
No need just now to speak of that, forsooth.
And she had thrice been to Jerusalem,
Seen many strange rivers and passed over them;
She'd been to Rome and also to Boulogne,
St. James of Compostella and Cologne,[57]
And she was skilled in wandering by the way.
65 She had gap-teeth, set widely, truth to say.
Easily on an ambling horse she sat
66 Well wimpled[58] up, and on her head a hat
As broad as is a buckler[59] or a shield;
She had a flowing mantle that concealed
Large hips, her heels spurred sharply under that.
In company she liked to laugh and chat
67 And knew the remedies for love's mischances,
An art in which she knew the oldest dances.
68 A holy-minded man of good renown
There was, and poor, the *Parson* to a town,
Yet he was rich in holy thought and work.
He also was a learned man, a clerk,
Who truly knew Christ's gospel and would preach it
Devoutly to parishioners, and teach it.
Benign and wonderfully diligent,
And patient when adversity was sent
(For so he proved in great adversity)
He much disliked extorting tithe[60] or fee,
69 Nay rather he preferred beyond a doubt
Giving to poor parishioners round about
From his own goods and Easter offerings.
He found sufficiency in little things.
Wide was his parish, with houses far asunder,
Yet he neglected not in rain or thunder,
In sickness or in grief, to pay a call
On the remotest, whether great or small,
Upon his feet, and in his hand a stave.

56. ground: A composite fabric.

57. Jerusalem . . . Rome . . . Boulogne . . . St. James of Compostella . . . Cologne: Famous pilgrimage sites at the time.

58. wimpled: Wearing a scarf covering the head, neck, and chin.

59. buckler: A small, round shield.

60. tithe (tīth): One tenth of a person's income, paid as a tax to support the church.

63 **Clarification** People went up to the altar to make their offerings in order of social precedence. Arguments over this precedence are stock examples in Medieval literature of the sin of pride.

64 **Reading Strategy** Read for the various references to her appearance. Describe the Wife of Bath. What sense do you have about her age? What evidence does Chaucer present of her affluence?

65 **Master Teacher** Note Medieval physiognomists believed there was a connection between character and physical features. A gap between teeth was regarded not only as a sign that a person would be lucky and would travel extensively, but also that this person was bold, false, gluttonous, and lascivious.

66 **Enrichment** The traditional garments or habits of those modern nuns who wear habits are simple Medieval dress. While secular styles changed, theirs did not. The cloth covering the hair, ears, and neck is the wimple that all married women wore in the Middle Ages. Nuns were considered married women, the brides of Christ.

67 **Discussion** Why is it no surprise to us that the Wife of Bath has an outgoing personality and is an expert on love?

68 **Master Teacher Note** The Parson, or parish priest, is another idealized pilgrim, one who stands in sharp contrast to those other clergy on the pilgrimage who are either worldly or corrupt. His virtues are those on which Wycliffe and other reformers laid emphasis.

69 **Discussion** What were his attitude toward and his actions regarding tithes? The penalty of excommunication was often imposed for their nonpayment.

70 Discussion Here lies the essence of the Parson's virtue. What does he regard as his most important function?

71 Reading Strategy Read to discover the practices in which the admirable Parson does not engage. The Parson's goodness reveals what unethical practices of the clergy were common at the time.

72 Master Teacher Note Like his brother, the Plowman, a small tenant farmer, is an idealized character, described with great sympathy. Most frequently in medieval literature the peasant was treated satirically or contemptuously.

73 Critical Thinking and Reading What specific virtues does the Plowman demonstrate?

70 This noble example to his sheep he gave,
First following the word before he taught it,
And it was from the gospel he had caught it.
This little proverb he would add thereto
That if gold rust, what then will iron do?
For if a priest be foul in whom we trust
No wonder that a common man should rust;
The true example that a priest should give
Is one of cleanness, how the sheep should live.
He did not set his benefice to hire[61]
And leave his sheep encumbered in the mire
71 Or run to London to earn easy bread
By singing masses for the wealthy dead,
Or find some Brotherhood and get enrolled.
He stayed at home and watched over his fold
So that no wolf should make the sheep miscarry.
He was a shepherd and no mercenary.
Holy and virtuous he was, but then
Never contemptuous of sinful men,
Never disdainful, never too proud or fine,
But was discreet in teaching and benign.
His business was to show a fair behavior
And draw men thus to Heaven and their Savior,
Unless indeed a man were obstinate;
And such, whether of high or low estate,
He put to sharp rebuke to say the least.
I think there never was a better priest.
He sought no pomp or glory in his dealings,
No scrupulosity had spiced his feelings.
Christ and His Twelve Apostles and their lore
He taught, but followed it himself before.
72 There was a *Plowman* with him there, his brother.
Many a load of dung one time or other
He must have carted through the morning dew.
He was an honest worker, good and true,
Living in peace and perfect charity,
And, as the gospel bade him, so did he,
Loving God best with all his heart and mind
And then his neighbor as himself, repined
73 At no misfortune, slacked for no content,
For steadily about his work he went
To thrash his corn, to dig or to manure
Or make a ditch; and he would help the poor
For love of Christ and never take a penny
If he could help it, and, as prompt as any,
He paid his tithes in full when they were due
On what he owned, and on his earnings too.

61. set . . . hire: Pay someone else to perform his parish duties.

74 He wore a tabard[62] smock and rode a mare.
There was a *Reeve,*[63] also a *Miller,* there,
A College *Manciple*[64] from the Inns of Court,
A papal *Pardoner*[65] and, in close consort,
A Church-Court *Summoner,*[66] riding at a trot,
And finally myself—that was the lot.
75 The *Miller* was a chap of sixteen stone,[67]
76 A great stout fellow big in brawn and bone.
He did well out of them, for he could go
And win the ram at any wrestling show.
Broad, knotty and short-shouldered, he would boast
He could heave any door off hinge and post,
Or take a run and break it with his head.
His beard, like any sow or fox, was red
And broad as well, as though it were a spade;
And, at its very tip, his nose displayed
A wart on which there stood a tuft of hair.
Red as the bristles in an old sow's ear.
His nostrils were as black as they were wide.
He had a sword and buckler at his side,
His mighty mouth was like a furnace door.
77 A wrangler and buffoon, he had a store
Of tavern stories, filthy in the main.
His was a master-hand at stealing grain.
He felt it with his thumb and thus he knew
Its quality and took three times his due—
A thumb of gold, by God, to gauge an oat!
He wore a hood of blue and a white coat.
He liked to play his bagpipes up and down
And that was how he brought us out of town.
The *Manciple* came from the Inner Temple;
All caterers might follow his example
In buying victuals; he was never rash
Whether he bought on credit or paid cash.
78 He used to watch the market most precisely
And go in first, and so he did quite nicely.
Now isn't it a marvel of God's grace
That an illiterate fellow can outpace
The wisdom of a heap of learned men?
His masters—he had more than thirty then—
All versed in the abstrusest legal knowledge,
Could have produced a dozen from their College
79 Fit to be stewards in land and rents and game
To any Peer in England you could name,
And show him how to live on what he had
Debt-free (unless of course the Peer were mad)

62. tabard: A loose jacket.
63. *Reeve:* An estate manager.
64. *Manciple:* A buyer of provisions.
65. *Pardoner:* One who dispenses papal pardons.
66. *Summoner:* One who serves summonses to church courts.
67. sixteen stone: 224 pounds. A stone equals 14 pounds.

74 **Clarification** A mare was an extremely humble steed.

75 **Enrichment** A miller ground wheat into flour, and he was traditionally paid with a percentage of the ground grain.

76 **Enrichment** Chaucer devotes considerable space to a physical description of the Miller. Medieval physiognomists would have associated his short-shouldered, stocky figure, his bushy red beard, and his warty nose with the traits of shamelessness, loquacity, belligerence, and lecherousness.

77 **Reading Strategy** After you read, be prepared to review the Miller's character.

78 **Discussion** What was the Manciple's purchasing technique?

79 **Discussion** How did he "outpace" or outsmart his employers? What is the narrator's attitude toward this? Why do you think he admires such skullduggery? What kind of men were the Manciple's employers? Did they deserve to be cheated?

80 Master Teacher Note A reeve was generally a subordinate estate-manager. Chaucer's Reeve evidently had greater power and was more like a chief manager or steward. His choleric complexion would have denoted to physiognomists sharpness of wit, irascibility, and wantonness. Which of these traits does his description in the Prologue include?

81 Clarification His short hair indicated his servile position.

82 Discussion What specific indicators of his competency are cited? Why was he so unpopular with his inferiors?

83 Literary Focus He could please his lord by lending him some of the lord's own possessions, thus garnering thanks plus a reward. Why might he have more ready cash than his lord?

84 Literary Focus It is interesting to note that the Reeve chose his place in the cavalcade farthest away from the Miller, who led the procession. There was a traditional enmity between the two occupations. Why?

85 Enrichment His hideous skin condition was known as alopecia, a form of leprosy. Chaucer lists the most popular remedies of the day.

Or be as frugal as he might desire,
And they were fit to help about the Shire
In any legal case there was to try;
And yet this Manciple could wipe their eye.
80 The *Reeve* was old and choleric and thin;
His beard was shaven closely to the skin,
His shorn hair came abruptly to a stop
81 Above his ears, and he was docked on top
Just like a priest in front; his legs were lean,
Like sticks they were, no calf was to be seen.
He kept his bins and garners[68] very trim;
No auditor could gain a point on him.
And he could judge by watching drought and rain
The yield he might expect from seed and grain.
His master's sheep, his animals and hens,
Pigs, horses, dairies, stores and cattle-pens
Were wholly trusted to his government.
82 And he was under contract to present
The accounts, right from his master's earliest years.
No one had ever caught him in arrears.
No bailiff, serf or herdsman dared to kick,
He knew their dodges, knew their every trick;
Feared like the plague he was, by those beneath.
He had a lovely dwelling on a heath,
Shadowed in green by trees above the sward.[69]
A better hand at bargains than his lord,
He had grown rich and had a store of treasure
83 Well tucked away, yet out it came to pleasure
His lord with subtle loans or gifts of goods,
To earn his thanks and even coats and hoods.
When young he'd learnt a useful trade and still
He was a carpenter of first-rate skill.
The stallion-cob he rode at a slow trot
Was dapple-gray and bore the name of Scot.
He wore an overcoat of bluish shade
And rather long; he had a rusty blade
Slung at his side. He came, as I heard tell,
From Norfolk, near a place called Baldeswell.
His coat was tucked under his belt and splayed.
84 He rode the hindmost of our cavalcade.
There was a *Summoner* with us in the place
Who had a fire-red cherubinnish face.[70]
Black, scabby brows he had, and a thin beard.
Children were afraid when he appeared.
85 No quicksilver, lead ointments, tartar creams,
Boracic, no, nor brimstone, so it seems,
Could make a salve that had the power to bite,

68. garners *n.*: Buildings for storing grain.

69. sward *n.*: Turf.

70. fire-red . . . face: In the art of the Middle Ages, the faces of cherubs, or angels, were often painted red.

Clean up or curve his whelks of knobby white.
He wore a garland set upon his head
Large as the holly-bush upon a stake
Outside an ale-house, and he had a cake,
A round one, which it was his joke to wield
As if it were intended for a shield.
86 He and a gentle *Pardoner* rode together,
A bird from Charing Cross of the same feather,
Just back from visiting the Court of Rome.
He loudly sang "*Come hither, love, come home!*"
The Summoner sang deep seconds to this song,
No trumpet ever sounded half so strong.
This Pardoner had hair as yellow as wax,
Hanging down smoothly like a hank of flax.
In driblets fell his locks behind his head
Down to his shoulders which they overspread;
Thinly they fell, like rat-tails, one by one.
He wore no hood upon his head, for fun;
The hood inside his wallet had been stowed,
He aimed at riding in the latest mode;
But for a little cap his head was bare
87 And he had bulging eyeballs, like a hare.
He'd sewed a holy relic on his cap;
His wallet lay before him on his lap,
Brimful of pardons come from Rome all hot.
He had the same small voice a goat has got.
His chin no beard had harbored, nor would harbor,
Smoother than ever chin was left by barber.
I judge he was a gelding, or a mare.
As to his trade, from Berwick down to Ware
There was no pardoner of equal grace,
For in his trunk he had a pillowcase
Which he asserted was Our Lady's veil.
He said he had a gobbet[71] of the sail
Saint Peter had the time when he made bold
To walk the waves, till Jesu Christ took hold.
88 He had a cross of metal set with stones
And, in a glass, a rubble of pigs' bones.
And with these relics, any time he found
Some poor up-country parson to astound,
On one short day, in money down, he drew
More than the parson in a month or two,
And by his flatteries and prevarication
Made monkeys of the priest and congregation.
But still to do him justice first and last
In church he was a noble ecclesiast.
How well he read a lesson or told a story!

71. gobbet: Piece.

86 **Clarification** Pardoners were sellers of papal indulgences. Some were laymen, many wholly unauthorized, and their tricks and abuses were condemned by Church authority. Chaucer's Pardoner seems to have taken at least minor orders.

87 **Master Teacher Note** The physical description of the Pardoner would have suggested to the Medieval reader familiar with the science of physiognomy that the man was effeminate, deceptive, gluttonous, drunken, and treacherous. What physical characteristics might indicate that type of character? Do you think such characteristics are a reliable indicator of character?

88 **Discussion** How did the Pardoner take advantage of the simple country priest? Why is this chicanery particularly distasteful?

89 Discussion In what way is he a "noble ecclesiast"? Is this term bestowed on him naively by the pilgrim Chaucer, ironically by the poet Chaucer, or a combination of both?

90 Reading Strategy Review the narrator's original intentions in describing the pilgrims. Has he kept it? What aspects of life has he described in the Prologue? What classes of society does he criticize and why? What class does he favor and why?

91 Reading Strategy As you read, look for the two disclaimers Chaucer makes in these lines. What authority does he cite in support of his honesty? What kind of criticism is he anticipating and preventing? Why is it clear that the pilgrim rather than the poet Chaucer is speaking?

But best of all he sang an Offertory,[72]
For well he knew that when that song was sung
89 He'd have to preach and tune his honey-tongue
And (well he could) win silver from the crowd.
That's why he sang so merrily and loud.
Now I have told you shortly, in a clause,
The rank, the array, the number and the cause
90 Of our assembly in this company
In Southwark, at that high-class hostelry
Known as *The Tabard*, close beside *The Bell.*
And now the time has come for me to tell
How we behaved that evening; I'll begin
After we had alighted at the inn,
Then I'll report our journey, stage by stage,
All the remainder of our pilgrimage.
But first I beg of you, in courtesy,
Not to condemn me as unmannerly
If I speak plainly and with no concealings
And give account of all their words and dealings,
Using their very phrases as they fell.
For certainly, as you all know so well,
He who repeats a tale after a man
Is bound to say, as nearly as he can,
Each single word, if he remembers it,
91 However rudely spoken or unfit,
Or else the tale he tells will be untrue,
The things invented and the phrases new.
He may not flinch although it were his brother,
If he says one word he must say the other.
And Christ Himself spoke broad[73] in Holy Writ,
And as you know there's nothing there unfit,
And Plato[74] says, for those with power to read,
"The word should be as cousin to the deed."
Further I beg you to forgive it me
If I neglect the order and degree
And what is due to rank in what I've planned.
I'm short of wit as you will understand.
Our *Host* gave us great welcome; everyone
Was given a place and supper was begun.
He served the finest victuals you could think,
The wine was strong and we were glad to drink.
A very striking man our Host withal,
And fit to be a marshal in a hall.
His eyes were bright, his girth a little wide;
There is no finer burgess in Cheapside.[75]
Bold in his speech, yet wise and full of tact,
There was no manly attribute he lacked,
What's more he was a merry-hearted man.

72. Offertory: The song that accompanies the collection of the offering at a church service.

73. broad: Bluntly.

74. Plato: A Greek philosopher (427?-347? B.C.).

75. Cheapside: A district in London.

After our meal he jokingly began
To talk of sport, and, among other things
After we'd settled up our reckonings,
He said as follows: "Truly, gentlemen,
You're very welcome and I can't think when
—Upon my word I'm telling you no lie—
I've seen a gathering here that looked so spry,
No, not this year, as in this tavern now.
I'd think you up some fun if I knew how.
And, as it happens, a thought has just occurred
And it will cost you nothing, on my word.
You're off to Canterbury—well, God speed!
Blessed St. Thomas answer to your need!
And I don't doubt, before the journey's done
You mean to while the time in tales and fun.
Indeed, there's little pleasure for your bones
Riding along and all as dumb as stones.
So let me then propose for your enjoyment,
Just as I said, a suitable employment.
And if my notion suits and you agree
And promise to submit yourselves to me
Playing your parts exactly as I say
Tomorrow as you ride along the way,
Then by my father's soul (and he is dead)
If you don't like it you can have my head!
Hold up your hands, and not another word."
Well, our consent of course was not deferred,
It seemed not worth a serious debate;
We all agreed to it at any rate
And bade him issue what commands he would.
"My lords," he said, "now listen for your good,
And please don't treat my notion with disdain.
This is the point. I'll make it short and plain.
Each one of you shall help to make things slip
By telling two stories on the outward trip
To Canterbury, that's what I intend,
And, on the homeward way to journey's end
Another two, tales from the days of old;
And then the man whose story is best told,
That is to say who gives the fullest measure
Of good morality and general pleasure,
He shall be given a supper, paid by all,
Here in this tavern, in this very hall,
When we come back again from Canterbury.
And in the hope to keep you bright and merry
I'll go along with you myself and ride
All at my own expense and serve as guide.
I'll be the judge, and those who won't obey

92 **Reading Strategy** From reading Chaucer's descriptions of the pilgrims, which one do you think will tell the best story? Why?

Shall pay for what we spend upon the way.
Now if you all agree to what you've heard
Tell me at once without another word,
And I will make arrangements early for it."
   Of course we all agreed, in fact we swore it
Delightedly, and made entreaty too
That he should act as he proposed to do,
Become our Governor in short, and be
Judge of our tales and general referee,
And set the supper at a certain price.
We promised to be ruled by his advice
Come high, come low; unanimously thus
We set him up in judgment over us.
More wine was fetched, the business being done;
We drank it off and up went everyone
To bed without a moment of delay.
   Early next morning at the spring of day
Up rose our Host and roused us like a cock,
Gathering us together in a flock,
And off we rode at slightly faster pace
Than walking to St. Thomas' watering-place;[76]
And there our Host drew up, began to ease
His horse, and said, "Now, listen if you please,
My lords! Remember what you promised me.
If evensong and matins will agree[77]
Let's see who shall be first to tell a tale.
And as I hope to drink good wine and ale
I'll be your judge. The rebel who disobeys,
92 However much the journey costs, he pays.
Now draw for cut and then we can depart;
The man who draws the shortest cut shall start."

76. St. Thomas' watering-place: A brook two miles from the inn.

77. If evensong . . . agree: If what you said last night holds true this morning.

THINKING ABOUT THE SELECTION

Recalling

1. What does Chaucer say that people long to do when spring comes?
2. Which pilgrim is described as being (a) "modest as a maid"? (b) "all sentiment and tender heart"? (c) "a very festive fellow"?
3. Which pilgrim is described as having (a) "a special love of gold"? (b) "gap-teeth"? (c) "a store of tavern stories"?
4. How does Chaucer say he will report the events of the pilgrimage?
5. What entertainment on the journey does the host propose?

Interpreting

6. Chaucer pokes gentle fun at some of the pilgrims. What is his opinion of the Nun's singing voice and of her French?
7. Although the Friar and the Parson are both religious men, they are very different. What are some of the ways in which they differ?
8. What, if anything, does Chaucer seem to dislike about (a) the Skipper? (b) the Doctor?

Applying

9. If Chaucer were writing *The Canterbury Tales* today, what three kinds of pilgrims do you think he might consider adding to the group?

ANALYZING LITERATURE

Understanding Characterization

Chaucer sometimes makes direct statements about a character: "He was an honest worker, good and true." More often he reveals character indirectly, often through action: "She used to weep if she but saw a mouse/Caught in a trap." There is not much dialogue in the Prologue, but Chaucer frequently uses physical appearance to suggest character. Compare the appearance of the Miller ("A great stout fellow big in brawn and bone") with that of the Reeve ("old and choleric and thin"). Their looks match their personalities.

1. What nouns does Chaucer use to characterize the Squire?
2. How does Chaucer mainly characterize (a) the Doctor? (b) the Host?

CRITICAL THINKING AND READING

Making Inferences About Characters

If you are to understand fictional characters fully, you must make inferences about them. You must draw conclusions based on what the writer has told you about their actions, thoughts, words, and appearance. When Chaucer writes of the Parson, "That if gold rust, what will iron do?" you can infer that the Parson realizes he should be a model of behavior for his parishioners. What can you infer about the Pardoner from the information in lines 670–675?

UNDERSTANDING LANGUAGE

Using Similes

A **simile** is a comparison of two unlike things using *like* or *as:*

His mighty mouth was *like* a furnace door.
White *as* a daisy-petal was his beard.

The usual purpose of a simile is to give the reader an apt and striking picture of the person or object being described.

1. What three similes appear in lines 646–656 of the sketch of the Pardoner?
2. Try to find at least five other similes in the Prologue. What are they?

THINKING AND WRITING

Writing a Pilgrim's Tale

Now that you know something about each of Chaucer's pilgrims, write a tale you think one of them might tell. Choose a pilgrim and study his or her sketch carefully. When you are sure you understand the pilgrim's character, write a tale that he or she might tell. You may modernize the tale, if you wish, setting it in the present. But make sure the message of the tale fits the character of the pilgrim.

Answers

ANSWERS TO THINKING ABOUT THE SELECTION

Recalling

1. People long to go on pilgrimages.
2. The pilgrims described are (a) the Knight, (b) the Prioress, and (c) the Friar.
3. The pilgrims described are (a) the Doctor, (b) the Wife of Bath, and (c) the Miller.
4. He will report it stage by stage —plainly, concealing nothing.
5. The host proposes that each pilgrim tell two tales going and two more on the return. The best shall receive a free dinner.

Interpreting

6. Her voice is too nasal. Her French would be incomprehensible to a Parisian.
7. The Friar does not take his religious vows seriously; he prefers worldly pleasures and catering to the wealthy. The Parson is all that a good priest should be.
8. (a) Chaucer dislikes the Skipper because he disregards the rules of conscience—stealing wine and forcing prisoners to walk the plank. (b) The Doctor cares more about gold than his patients; he and his apothecaries worked together selling drugs at inflated prices. Also, he did not read the Bible much.

Applying

9. Answers will differ. Some possibilities are astronaut, stockbroker, professional athlete, and physical-fitness instructor.

ANSWERS TO ANALYZING LITERATURE

1. The Squire is a "lover," a "cadet," and "a lad of fire."
2. (a) Chaucer characterizes the Doctor indirectly, through action mainly. (b) Chaucer uses action, description, and several direct statements to characterize the Host.

ANSWERS TO CRITICAL THINKING AND READING

The Pardoner appears to be something of a con man.

ANSWERS TO UNDERSTANDING LANGUAGE

1. Three similes are hair "as yellow as wax," hanging "like a hank of wax," and fell "like rats-tails."
2. Answers will differ. There are many possibilities such as "as loud as does the chapel bell" (line 175), "not pale like a tormented soul" (line 209), "as brown as a berry" (line 211), "just like a puppy" (line 264), "like a bell about its mould" (line 272), "as broad as is a buckler or a shield" (line 475).

THINKING AND WRITING

For help with this assignment, students can refer to Lesson 19, "Writing a Short Story," in the Handbook of Writing About Literature.

Publishing Student Writing Ask the students to read their papers to the class. Alternatively, you might read them without revealing the writers. Ask the class to determine which pilgrim is "telling" the tale. Discuss why they thought so.

Literary Focus That greed is the root of all evil is exemplified by this story. What moral weaknesses besides greed do the rioters have? Suggest that your students look for them. This tale has been called the perfect short story. Does it deserve this praise? What short-story qualities does it contain? You might want to review the generally accepted short-story criteria.

Look For Review the meaning of irony and paradox with the students to help them analyze the mood of the tale.

Writing Have the students freewrite about the anecdote for five minutes and then share what they have with the class.

Vocabulary Read to the class the lines in which the vocabulary words appear. Ask students to discover the meaning from the context.

Teaching to Ability Levels All levels would benefit from reading aloud. For **less advanced** students you might alternate reading with the students. Since Chaucer intended the tales as entertainment, encourage **more advanced** students to read with feeling and drama.

GUIDE FOR READING

The Pardoner's Tale
from The Canterbury Tales

Writer's Techniques

Exemplum. An anecdote is a brief account of an incident or event. Although "The Pardoner's Tale" may seem rather long for an anecdote, it is a special kind of anecdote—a 238-line anecdote within a sermon, something the Pardoner would have called an *exemplum,* or example. While anecdotes are often personal or biographical, the *exemplum* in "The Pardoner's Tale" is intended to establish the truth of a moral.

The idea for "The Pardoner's Tale" did not originate with Chaucer; it goes back to antiquity. The Pardoner uses this simple but powerful anecdote as an *exemplum* to prove the maxim, *"Radix malorum est cupiditas,"* or "Greed is the root of all evil."

Look For

As you read "The Pardoner's Tale," notice how closely its structure resembles that of a short story, even though it is written in verse. Notice, too, the mood the tale conveys.

Writing

You have heard many sayings similar to "Greed is the root of evil." List at least five such sayings. Try to think of ones for which a good exemplum might be written.

Vocabulary

Knowing the following words will help you as you read "The Pardoner's Tale" from *The Canterbury Tales.*

rioters (rī′ ət ərz) *n.*: Loud, dissolute bullies (l. 1)
stile (stīl) *n.*: A step or set of steps used in climbing over a fence or wall (l. 52)
pallor (pal′ ər) *n.*: Unnatural lack of color; paleness (l. 80)
hoary (hôr′ ē) *adj.*: White or gray with age (l. 85)
prating (prāt′ iŋ) *v.*: Talking much and foolishly (l. 106)
tarry (tar′ ē) *v.*: To delay, linger, be tardy (l. 195)
apothecary (ə päth′ ə ker ē) *n.*: Pharmacist or druggist (l. 196)

Objectives

1 To understand anecdote and exemplum
2 To make inferences based on the narrator's words
3 To read Middle English aloud
4 To write an analysis

Teaching Portfolio: Support Materials

Teacher Backup, pp. 00-00

Vocabulary Check, p. 00

Usage and Mechanics Worksheet, p. 00

Analyzing Literature Worksheet, p. 00

Critical Thinking and Reading Worksheet, p. 00

Language Worksheet, p. 00

Selection Test, p. 00

from The Pardoner's Tale

Geoffrey Chaucer

translated by Nevill Coghill

During their journey to Canterbury, each of the pilgrims tells a tale. After the Knight, the Miller, the Reeve, the Nun, and the narrator have finished, the Pardoner entertains the others with a tale that supports his claim that "greed is the root of all evil."

It's of three rioters I have to tell
1 Who long before the morning service bell[1]
Were sitting in a tavern for a drink.
And as they sat, they heard the hand-bell clink
Before a coffin going to the grave;
2 One of them called the little tavern-knave[2]
And said "Go and find out at once—look spry!—
Whose corpse is in that coffin passing by;
And see you get the name correctly too."
"Sir," said the boy, "no need, I promise you;
Two hours before you came here I was told.
He was a friend of yours in days of old,
3 And suddenly last night, the man was slain,
Upon his bench, face up, dead drunk again.
There came a privy[3] thief, they call him Death,
Who kills us all round here, and in a breath
He speared him through the heart, he never stirred.
And then Death went his way without a word.
4 He's killed a thousand in the present plague,[4]
And, sir, it doesn't do to be too vague
5 If you should meet him; you had best be wary.
Be on your guard with such an adversary,
Be primed to meet him everywhere you go,
That's what my mother said. It's all I know."
The publican[5] joined in with, "By St. Mary.
What the child says is right; you'd best be wary,
This very year he killed, in a large village
A mile away, man, woman, serf at tillage,[6]
Page in the household, children—all there were.
Yes, I imagine that he lives round there.
It's well to be prepared in these alarms,
He might do you dishonor." "Huh, God's arms!"

1. long before . . . bell: Long before 9:00 A.M.

2. tavern-knave: Serving boy.

3. privy: Secretive.

4. plague: The Black Death, which killed over a third of the population of England in 1348 and 1349.

5. publican: Innkeeper.

6. tillage: Plowing.

Motivation for Reading Explain that this tale takes place during a plague. The pestilence, we know now, was not one disease but two occurring simultaneously. The bubonic plague sent the victim's fever soaring and caused ugly pustules in armpit and groin but, in many cases, did not kill. The other illness was the pneumonic plague, which attacked the victim's lungs, was much more contagious, and was almost always fatal. A plague death is the impetus that begins the tale.

Master Teacher Note This tale would be an excellent choice for a reader's theater production. Students could write their own adaptions and present them to the class.

Purpose-Setting Question Why is it hypocritical that the Pardoner should tell a tale with the theme Greed is the root of all evil? Recalling Chaucer's description of him in the Prologue, do you find any redeeming qualities in him?

1 **Literary Focus** The bibulous nature of these "rioters" is quickly established. They have started drinking very early. What purpose does this fact serve in the exemplum?

2 **Literary Focus** What is the paradox in these lines? Another paradox is having the Pardoner preach such a moral tale. Why do you think Chaucer does this?

3 **Reading Strategy** How is it both prophetic and appropriate that it is their friend and fellow-rioter who has died?

4 **Enrichment** During sixteen months in 1348–49, the Black Plague reduced England's population from approximately four million to perhaps two million five hundred thousand.

5 **Reading Strategy** What advice is given to the rioters? Will they follow this good advice?

Thematic Idea Another selection that deals with the theme of sin and false friends is "The Poison Tree" by William Blake, page 626. The excerpt from Pepy's *Diary* on page 524 is a remarkable account of a later English plague.

6 **Discussion** What vow do they swear together? Note the emphasis on their sense of brotherhood. Does this vow make sense? Or is it a result of their inebriation? Should you accept the vow literally?

7 **Literary Focus** Not only are these rioters drunken and profane, but they are also excessively rude and churlish. What purpose does this serve in a story conceived as an exemplum?

8 **Master Teacher Note** Why has the old man lived so long? For whom has he been seeking? This old man seems to be either a symbol of Death or of Old Age, Death's Messenger. Which of these interpretations seems more likely?

The rioter said, "Is he so fierce to meet?
I'll search for him, by Jesus, street by street.
God's blessed bones! I'll register a vow!
6 Here, chaps! The three of us together now,
Hold up your hands, like me, and we'll be brothers
In this affair, and each defend the others,
And we will kill this traitor Death, I say!
Away with him as he has made away
With all our friends. God's dignity! To-night!"
They made their bargain, swore with appetite,
These three, to live and die for one another
As brother-born might swear to his born brother.
And up they started in their drunken rage
And made towards this village which the page
And publican had spoken of before.
Many and grisly were the oaths they swore,
Tearing Christ's blessed body to a shred;[7]
"If we can only catch him, Death is dead!"
When they had gone not fully half a mile,
Just as they were about to cross a stile,
They came upon a very poor old man
Who humbly greeted them and thus began,
"God look to you, my lords, and give you quiet!"
To which the proudest of these men of riot
7 Gave back the answer, "What, old fool? Give place!
Why are you all wrapped up except your face?
Why live so long? Isn't it time to die?"
The old, old fellow looked him in the eye
And said, "Because I never yet have found,
8 Though I have walked to India, searching round
Village and city on my pilgrimage,
One who would change his youth to have my age.
And so my age is mine and must be still
Upon me, for such time as God may will.
"Not even Death, alas, will take my life;
So, like a wretched prisoner at strife
Within himself, I walk alone and wait
About the earth, which is my mother's gate,
Knock-knocking with my staff from night to noon
And crying, 'Mother, open to me soon!
Look at me, mother, won't you let me in?
See how I wither, flesh and blood and skin!
Alas! When will these bones be laid to rest?
Mother, I would exchange—for that were best—
The wardrobe in my chamber, standing there
So long, for yours! Aye, for a shirt of hair[8]
To wrap me in!' She has refused her grace,
Whence comes the pallor of my withered face.

7. Tearing . . . shred: Their oaths included expressions such as "God's arms" (line 32) and "God's blessed bones" (line 35).

8. shirt of hair: Here, a shroud.

"But it dishonored you when you began
To speak so roughly, sir, to an old man,
Unless he had injured you in word or deed.
It says in holy writ, as you may read,
'Thou shalt rise up before the hoary head
And honor it,' And therefore be it said
'Do no more harm to an old man than you,
Being now young, would have another do
When you are old'—if you should live till then.
And so may God be with you, gentlemen,
For I must go whither I have to go."
"By God," the gambler said, "you shan't do so,
You don't get off so easy, by St. John!
I heard you mention, just a moment gone,
A certain traitor Death who singles out
And kills the fine young fellows hereabout.
And you're his spy, by God! You wait a bit.
Say where he is or you shall pay for it,
By God and by the Holy Sacrament!
I say you've joined together by consent
To kill us younger folk, you thieving swine!"
"Well, sirs," he said, "if it be your design
To find out Death, turn up this crooked way
Towards that grove. I left him there today
Under a tree, and there you'll find him waiting.
He isn't one to hide for all your prating.
You see that oak? He won't be far to find.
And God protect you that redeemed mankind,
Aye, and amend you!" Thus that ancient man.
At once the three young rioters began
9 To run, and reached the tree, and there they found
A pile of golden florins[9] on the ground,
New-coined, eight bushels of them as they thought.
No longer was it Death those fellows sought,
For they were all so thrilled to see the sight,
The florins were so beautiful and bright,
That down they sat beside the precious pile.
The wickedest spoke first after a while.
"Brothers," he said, "you listen to what I say.
I'm pretty sharp although I joke away.
It's clear that Fortune has bestowed this treasure
To let us live in jollity and pleasure.
Light come, light go! We'll spend it as we ought.
God's precious dignity! Who would have thought
10 This morning was to be our lucky day?
"If one could only get the gold away,
Back to my house, or else to yours, perhaps—
For as you know, the gold is ours, chaps—
We'd all be at the top of fortune, hey?

9. florins: Coins.

9 Reading Strategy What do you predict that they will do now?

10 Reading Strategy What is the irony here?

11 Discussion Is the motive for sending one of the young men back to town alone honest and believable?

Humanities Note

Fine art, *The Pardoner,* 1946, by Arthur Szyk. The illustration uses Chaucer's description of the Pardoner in the *Prologue* to interpret his character. The stringy yellow hair, the wallet bulging with relics, and the cap upon his head are all taken from that description. The sanctimonious expression and gesture of forgiveness are from the imagination of Arthur Szyk. This miniature is finely detailed and painted in subtle glowing colors. In discussing Szyk's miniatures with your students, you may wish to mention that the costumes portrayed are close in style to those actually worn in England in Chaucer's time. Ask your students if the impression of the Pardoner that they get from this illustration is similar to or different from the impression of him they got from the Prologue.

But certainly it can't be done by day.
People would call us robbers—a strong gang,
So our own property would make us hang.
No, we must bring this treasure back by night
Some prudent way, and keep it out of sight.
And so as a solution I propose
11 We draw for lots and see the way it goes.
The one who draws the longest, lucky man,
Shall run to town as quickly as he can
To fetch us bread and wine—but keep things dark—
While two remain in hiding here to mark
Our heap of treasure. If there's no delay,
When night comes down we'll carry it away,

THE PARDONER
Arthur Szyk for the Canterbury Tales
The George Macy Companies

All three of us, wherever we have planned."
He gathered lots and hid them in his hand
Bidding them draw for where the luck should fall.
It fell upon the youngest of them all,
And off he ran at once towards the town.
As soon as he had gone, the first sat down
And thus began a parley[10] with the other:
"You know that you can trust me as a brother;
Now let me tell you where your profit lies;
You know our friend has gone to get supplies
And here's a lot of gold that is to be
Divided equally amongst us three.
Nevertheless, if I could shape things thus
So that we shared it out—the two of us—
Wouldn't you take it as a friendly turn?"
"But how!" the other said with some concern,
"Because he knows the gold's with me and you;
What can we tell him? What are we to do?'
"Is it a bargain," said the first, "or no?
For I can tell you in a word or so
What's to be done to bring the thing about."
12 "Trust me," the other said, "you needn't doubt
My word. I won't betray you, I'll be true."
"Well," said his friend, "you see that we are two,
And two are twice as powerful as one.
Now look; when he comes back, get up in fun
To have a wrestle; then, as you attack,
I'll up and put my dagger through his back
While you and he are struggling, as in game;
Then draw your dagger too and do the same.
Then all this money will be ours to spend,
Divided equally of course, dear friend.
Then we can gratify our lusts and fill
The day with dicing at our own sweet will."
Thus these two miscreants[11] agreed to slay
The third and youngest, as you heard me say.
The youngest, as he ran towards the town,
Kept turning over, rolling up and down
Within his heart the beauty of those bright
New florins, saying, "Lord, to think I might
Have all that treasure to myself alone!
Could there be anyone beneath the throne
Of God so happy as I then should be?"
And so the Fiend,[12] our common enemy,
Was given power to put it in his thought
That there was always poison to be bought,
And that with poison he could kill his friends.

10. parley (pär′ lē): Discussion.

11. miscreants (mis′ krē ənts): Villains.

12. Fiend: Satan.

12 **Literary Focus** Note in this passage the repeated use of words and phrases such as *trust, brother, I won't betray you,* and *I'll be true.* What is the irony here?

Challenge Does your view of the Pardoner change as a result of hearing his tale?

To men in such a state the Devil sends
Thoughts of this kind, and has a full permission
To lure them on to sorrow and perdition;[13]
For this young man was utterly content
To kill them both and never to repent.
And on he ran, he had no thought to tarry,
Came to the town, found an apothecary
And said, "Sell me some poison if you will,
I have a lot of rats I want to kill
And there's a polecat too about my yard
That takes my chickens and it hits me hard;
But I'll get even, as is only right,
With vermin that destroy a man by night."
The chemist answered, "I've a preparation
Which you shall have, and by my soul's salvation
If any living creature eat or drink
A mouthful, ere he has the time to think,
Though he took less than makes a grain of wheat,
You'll see him fall down dying at your feet;
Yes, die he must, and in so short a while
You'd hardly have the time to walk a mile,
The poison is so strong, you understand."
This cursed fellow grabbed into his hand
The box of poison and away he ran
Into a neighboring street, and found a man
Who lent him three large bottles. He withdrew
And deftly poured the poison into two.
He kept the third one clean, as well he might,
For his own drink, meaning to work all night
Stacking the gold and carrying it away.
And when this rioter, this devil's clay,
Had filled his bottles up with wine, all three,
Back to rejoin his comrades sauntered he.
Why make a sermon of it? Why waste breath?
Exactly in the way they'd planned his death
They fell on him and slew him, two to one.
Then said the first of them when this was done,
"Now for a drink. Sit down and let's be merry,
For later on there'll be the corpse to bury."
And, as it happened, reaching for a sup,
He took a bottle full of poison up
And drank; and his companion, nothing loth,
Drank from it also, and they perished both.
There is, in Avicenna's long relation[14]
Concerning poison and its operation,
Trust me, no ghastlier section to transcend
What these two wretches suffered at their end.
Thus these two murderers received their due,
So did the treacherous young poisoner too.

13. perdition: Damnation.

14. Avicenna's (a′ və sen′ əz) **long relation:** A book on medicines written by Avicenna (980–1037), an Arab physician, which contains a chapter on poisons.

THINKING ABOUT THE SELECTION

Recalling

1. What do the three rioters pledge to do?
2. (a) What does the old man tell the rioters they will find under a tree? (b) What do they actually find there?
3. How do the two rioters decide to increase their share of the gold? Explain their plan.
4. What does the youngest rioter do when he goes to town for bread and wine?

Interpreting

5. In line 39, Death is presented as a traitor. Do you think this description appropriate? Explain you answer.
6. Do the rioters keep the pledge they made in the tavern? Why or why not?
7. Does the old man know that in directing the three rioters to the oak tree he is sending them to their deaths? Explain.

Applying

8. What person in the news today, or in the recent past, has shown character traits similar to those of the Pardoner?

FOCUS ON LITERATURE

Understanding an Anecdote (Exemplum)

"The Pardoner's Tale" is an *exemplum,* a brief moral story that the Pardoner tells the pilgrims. In medieval times an *exemplum* was often included in a sermon.

1. How does the young rioter's dialogue with the chemist help to characterize both the rioter and his two companions?
2. What moral does this exemplum establish?
3. In what ways does "The Pardoner's Tale" differ from a short story?

CRITICAL THINKING AND READING

Making Inferences

In the Prologue Chaucer makes the point that he is reporting the pilgrims' tales, "using their very phrases." Therefore, although the narrator of *The Canterbury Tales* is Chaucer, the narrator of each individual tale is a particular pilgrim. You can make judgments about the Pardoner based on his own narration. Since Chaucer has already commented in the Prologue on the Pardoner's character, you have a chance to compare Chaucer's view of the Pardoner with the Pardoner's view of himself.

1. Does the topic the Pardoner chooses for his *exemplum* reflect his own interests? Explain.
2. Considering Chaucer's Prologue, how seriously do you think the Pardoner takes his moral that "Greed is the root of evil"? Explain.

SPEAKING AND LISTENING

Reading Middle English Aloud

After the Norman conquest of England in 1066, there were two languages in daily use: the French of the invaders and the Old English of the natives. As time passed, the English language began to change. By about 1150 the changes in English were notable enough for later scholars to identify the start of a new period; Middle English lasted roughly from 1150 to 1500.

Middle English is much easier to read than is Old English, but there are differences between it and the language we use today. In reading Middle English, you pronounce every syllable: *bathed* is /bath′ ed/; *soote* is /sō′ t /. Some consonants that today are silent were sounded in Middle English: *k* in *k*nyght; *g* in *g*nawe; *l* in fo*l*k; and *gh* in drou*gh*te.

Read aloud ll. 1–25 on page 115.

THINKING AND WRITING

Writing an Analysis

Write an essay analyzing "The Pardoner's Tale." An analysis is not a plot summary; it is an explanation of how the various elements in a literary work fit together. In analyzing Chaucer's tale, consider at least three of these elements: characters, plot, dialogue, moral, rhyme scheme, similes, symbolism.

Answers

ANSWERS TO THINKING ABOUT THE SELECTION

Recalling

1. They swear to live and die for one another
2. (a) The old man tells them they will find Death under the tree. (b) They find a pile of gold florins.
3. The two rioters decide to kill their companion by stabbing him in the back while wrestling.
4. The youngest buys poison to murder the two others.

Interpreting

5. It is appropriate inasmuch as Death betrays people, robs them of life, and hands them over to the grave.
6. Actually they do because they all die together. However, it was not the intention of the oath that they would murder each other.
7. Yes, he probably does. The old man is either Death himself or his messenger, Old Age.

Applying

8. Answers will differ. Some politicians or celebrities might be appropriate.

ANSWERS TO ANALYZING LITERATURE

1. The youngest rioter calls his companions vermin that destroy a man by night, although the apothecary assumes he is talking of rats and a polecat.
2. The moral is that greed is the root of evil.
3. It is shorter, a single episode, and the characters are completely symbolic. Moreover, it is more concerned with illustrating an idea than with re-creating experience.

ANSWERS TO CRITICAL THINKING AND READING

1. Yes, the Pardoner is a convincing preacher who wants his audience, recognizing the evil of greed, to donate money to him.
2. He takes it very seriously—as a means of satisfying his own greed.

ANSWERS TO UNDERSTANDING LANGUAGE

You might choose to read aloud a few lines before the students attempt to read the lines. Review the material about heroic couplets to help them read effectively.

THINKING AND WRITING

Publishing Student Writing After the students have completed their compositions, have them evaluate their work in writing groups. Ask them to choose one member who seems most knowledgeable about "The Pardoner's Tale" to represent the group in a panel discussion of all seven elements of the exemplum. After the panel members have presented the elements in their papers, allow the class to ask questions.

More About the Poem Although there are theories about the authorship of *Sir Gawain and the Green Knight,* no solid evidence exists to attribute authorship to anyone in particular. The author, called the Pearl Poet after another of his poems, was a contemporary of Chaucer's, but his work is so much more difficult to read in the original that only scholars can translate him.

GUIDE FOR READING

1375 [?]

Audiences in the Middle Ages enjoyed tales of adventure and fantasy, featuring heroes and rogues, magicians and monsters. One of the finest of these medieval romances, *Sir Gawain and the Green Knight,* was written by an unknown bard who lived at the time of Chaucer. "Master Anonymous," as the *Gawain* poet has been called, tells an unforgettable tale about one of the legendary knights of King Arthur's Round Table.

Although the poet is unknown, the *Gawain* manuscript (of which the British Museum owns the only copy) suggests something of its creator's background. The poet probably lived in northwestern England, judging by the poem's dialect and by its old-fashioned alliterative verse, neither of which reflects the fashion in Chaucer's London. Nevertheless, the poet is familiar with life at court and, like Chaucer, may have been connected to an aristocratic household. The poet also seems to have read widely in Latin and French as well as in English.

Sir Gawain's plot elements date back many centuries. In ancient vegetation myths, beheading is a ritual death intended to ensure the return of spring and the growth of new crops. More in line with Sir Gawain's adventure, a ninth century Irish narrative recounts a beheading contest as the supreme test of courage. Twelfth century French romances tell a similar tale, while the temptations faced by young Gawain may owe something to early French stories.

Arthurian legends, popular throughout Europe, developed orally over a long period of time. Despite this lengthy tradition, *Sir Gawain* is an original and masterful work. Not only is it excitingly told, but the poet introduces a high degree of realism into the setting. Most medieval romances take place with Camelot shimmering in the bright days of spring or summer. Not this poem. Sir Gawain's adventures occur in the bleakness of winter, with the chill desolation reinforcing the hero's trials. Nor is the hero himself without fault, as he is in so many other tales of knights and ladies. Sir Gawain is admirable but not invulnerable, which lends a psychological dimension to this medieval story. As one critic put it, the hero "gains in human credibility what he loses in ideal perfection."

Objectives

1 To understand a medieval romance
2 To make inferences about chivalric ideals
3 To understand abstract words
4 To evaluate a medieval romance

Teaching Portfolio: Support Materials

Teacher Backup, pp. 00-00

Vocabulary Check, p. 00

Usage and Mechanics Worksheet, p. 00

Analyzing Literature Worksheet, p. 00

Critical Thinking and Reading Worksheet, p. 00

Language Worksheet, p. 00

Selection Test, p. 00

from Sir Gawain and the Green Knight

Literary Forms

Medieval Romance. From the twelfth to the fifteenth century, medieval romances were the popular literature of England. Based on the feudal ideal of chivalry and imbued with adventure, love, and the supernatural, medieval romances typically feature kings, knights, and damsels in distress. The earliest romances were always in verse, but later ones were sometimes in prose.

The enduring popularity of these tales of romance stems in part from their glamorous portrayal of castle life—the festivals, the feasts, the knights in armor, the courtly love. Medieval romances were for many generations the stock in trade of professional storytellers, some of whom were employed in noble households, others of whom made the rounds of modest inns and taverns. As literacy increased, the status of the minstrel declined, but the romances, preserved in written form, continue to have appeal even today.

Of all the medieval romances, the best known are those about King Arthur and his Knights of the Round Table. Arthur, who may have been a Welsh chieftain in the fifth or sixth century, is the central figure in early Arthurian romances. In later ones King Arthur's knights, such as Sir Gawain and Sir Lancelot, assume the principal roles.

Look For

As you read the excerpt from *Sir Gawain and the Green Knight,* notice the extent to which Sir Gawain lives up to the ideals of chivalry—bravery, honor, courtesy, fairness to enemies, respect for women—and the extent to which he fails.

Writing

In a few sentences, comment on the following statement by Charles Kingsley, nineteenth century English historian and writer: "Some say that the spirit of chivalry is past, that the spirit of romance is dead. The age of chivalry is never past, so long as there is a wrong left unredressed on earth."

Vocabulary

Knowing the following words will help you as you read the excerpt from *Sir Gawain and the Green Knight.*

assay (as ā′) *v.*: To prove or test (l. 68)

haft (haft) *n.*: A handle of a weapon or tool (l. 105)

adjure (ə joor′) *v.*: To appeal to earnestly (l. 152)

recreant (rek′ rē ənt) *adj.*: Cowardly (l. 226)

caviled (kav′ ′ld) *v.*: Raised trivial objections (l. 370)

largesse (lär jes′) *n.*: Nobility of spirit (l. 472)

Literary Focus *Sir Gawain and the Green Knight* has been called the best English example of the medieval romance, one of the most charming romances ever written anywhere, and a literary work of the highest quality, surpassed or equaled only by Chaucer's *Troilus and Criseyde.* Among the qualities for which it is admired are its picturesque language, vivid descriptions, penetrating characterizations, skillful structure, and sensitive recreation of the drama, color, and pageantry of medieval life. Although the selection presented here is brief, it exhibits many of the cited qualities. Which qualities do you find in this excerpt?

Look For Discuss the chivalric code and Arthur's establishment of the Round Table. (*Age of Faith,* by Anne Fremantle, for Time-Life Books is an excellent source.) Have the students trace the code throughout this tale.

Writing Before you ask students to comment upon the statement, you might discuss it with them to make sure they understand chivalry and romance. You might ask them what evidence they see of these ideals today.

Vocabulary Review the words with the students before they read the selection. You might put the words and definitions on the board or reproduce them so students will not need to flip back and forth as they read.

Teaching to Ability Levels For **less advanced** students you might want to give an overall synopsis of the story so they can follow the plot as they read. For **more advanced** students, you might reproduce for them more of the poem; especially valuable might be Part Two.

from Sir Gawain and the Green Knight

translated by Marie Borroff

The work begins at the start of a New Year's Eve feast at King Arthur's Court in Camelot. Before anyone has started eating, the festivities are interrupted by an immense green knight who suddenly appears at the hall door. The knight rides a green horse and is armed with a gigantic ax.

This horseman hurtles in, and the hall enters;
Riding to the high dais,[1] recked he no danger;
1 Not a greeting he gave as the guests he o'erlooked,
Nor wasted his words, but "Where is," he said,
"The captain of this crowd? Keenly I wish
To see that sire with sight, and to himself say my say."
He swaggered all about
To scan the host so gay;
He halted, as if in doubt
Who in that hall held sway.

There were stares on all sides as the stranger spoke,
For much did they marvel what it might mean
That a horseman and a horse should have such a hue,
Grow green as the grass, and greener, it seemed.
Then green fused on gold more glorious by far.
All the onlookers eyed him, and edged nearer,
And awaited in wonder what he would do,
For many sights had they seen, but such a one never,
2 So that phantom and fairy the folk there deemed it,
Therefore chary[2] of answer was many a champion bold,
And stunned at his strong words stone-still they sat
In a swooning silence in the stately hall.
As all were slipped into sleep, so slackened their speech
apace.
Not all, I think, for dread,
But some of courteous grace
Let him who was their head
Be spokesman in that place.

Then Arthur before the high dais that entrance beholds,
And hailed him, as behooved, for he had no fear,

1. **dais** (dā' is) *n.*: Platform.

2. **chary** (cher' ē) *adj.*: Not giving freely.

Motivation for Reading After a brief explanation of Arthur and the Round Table, read to the students the beginning of the poem, which is not included in this selection. (You might use *Sir Gawain and the Green Knight* translated by Brian Stone for The Penguin Classics.) Emphasize the glorious feast, the noble crowd, and the merry entertainments. Then ask the class what they anticipate will happen.

Thematic Idea Another selection that deals with the theme of chivalry is *Morte d'Arthur,* by Sir Thomas Malory, page 65.

Master Teacher Note This is a wonderful unit for projects; one possibility is a Medieval Fair. This project crosses the curriculum to bring in art, music, drama, and history. Food, games, and costumes can be researched.

Purpose-Setting Question What lesson does Sir Gawain learn in this encounter?

1 **Master Teacher Note** What does this poetry sound like? Students should recognize its similarity to Anglo-Saxon poetry in alliteration, four-beat line, indeterminate number of unaccented syllables, and placement of caesura. *Sir Gawain and the Green Knight,* written about 1370, three hundred years after the Norman invasion, combines Anglo-Saxon poetic techniques with Anglo-French rhyme and a fixed number of syllables. The result is a poem written largely in a loose, alliterating meter with rhyming verses at intervals.

Sir Gawain and the Green Knight creates alliteration through the use of stock synonyms. Numerous equivalents for commonly used words like *horse, weapons, king,* and *bravery* were available to the author and these words were interchanged at will.

2 **Discussion** What effect does the Green Knight's appearance have on the assembled court? Why are they silent? Explain that "As all" (line 23) should be understood as "as if all."

FROM THE ROMANCE OF KING ARTHUR AND HIS KNIGHTS OF THE ROUND TABLE
Arthur Rackham
Weathervane Books

Humanities Note

Illustration, by Arthur Rockham. The English illustrator Arthur Rackham (1867–1936) was born in London. He studied drawing at the Lambeth School of Art there. He worked as an illustrator of magazines and books for most of his life. Many of his original drawings are now in the collection of the Tate Gallery in London.

Arthur Rackham's style of drawing reflects his interest in prints of the German Renaissance. Although more modern in approach, his works maintain the detail and angular grace of that school. This illustration of a castle was done for a book entitled *The Romance of King Arthur.* Ever a lover of fairy-tales and scenes of fantasy, Rackham enjoyed drawing such scenes as this castle.

Consider discussing the following with your students: Does this castle convey a feeling of hospitality or does it seem forbidding? Explain.

3 Discussion Why has the Green Knight come? He states his purpose, a game, after a string of compliments and a disclaimer of warlike intent.

4 Reading Strategy Read to discover the Green Knight's attitude toward the assembled knights. Note the contempt he shows in words like "beardless" and "puny." This contemptuous tone is continued in lines 85–91.

5 Master Teacher Note Describe the game that the Green Knight proposes. Here the poet introduces the first main story element, traditionally called the "Beheading Game." This, like the other two story elements that he includes, was not his original invention. In fact, they all derive from folklore. He was, however, the first to combine them. What was the Court's immediate response to the Green Knight's proposal?

And said "Fellow, in faith you have found fair welcome;
The head of this hostelry Arthur am I;
Leap lightly down, and linger, I pray,
And the tale of your intent you shall tell us after."
"Nay, so help me," said the other, "He that on high sits,
To tarry here any time, 'twas not mine errand;
But as the praise of you, prince, is puffed up so high,
And your court and your company are counted the best,
Stoutest under steel-gear on steeds to ride,
Worthiest of their works the wide world over,
And peerless to prove in passages of arms,
And courtesy here is carried to its height,
And so at this season I have sought you out.
3 You may be certain by the branch that I bear in hand
That I pass here in peace, and would part friends,
For had I come to this court on combat bent,
I have a hauberk[3] at home, and a helm beside,
A shield and a sharp spear, shining bright,
And other weapons to wield, I ween well, to boot,
But as I willed no war, I wore no metal.
But if you be so bold as all men believe,
You will graciously grant the game that I ask by right."
Arthur answer gave
And said, "Sir courteous knight,
If contest here you crave,
You shall not fail to fight."

"Nay, to fight, in good faith, is far from my thought;
There are about on these benches but beardless children,
4 Were I here in full arms on a haughty[4] steed,
For measured against mine, their might is puny.
And so I call in this court for a Christmas game,
For 'tis Yule, and New Year, and many young bloods about;
If any in this house such hardihood claims,
Be so bold in his blood, his brain so wild,
As stoutly to strike one stroke for another,
I shall give him as my gift this gisarme[5] noble,
This ax, that is heavy enough, to handle as he likes,
And I shall bide the first blow, as bare as I sit.
If there be one so wilful my words to assay,
5 Let him leap hither lightly, lay hold of this weapon;
I quitclaim it forever, keep it as his own,
And I shall stand him a stroke, steady on this floor,
So you grant me the guerdon to give him another, sans blame.[6]
In a twelvemonth[7] and a day
He shall have of me the same;
Now be it seen straightway
Who dares take up the game."

3. hauberk (hô' bərk) *n.*: Coat of armor.

4. haughty (hôt' ē) *adj.*: Lofty.

5. gisarme (gi zärm') *n.*: Battle-ax.

6. I . . . blame: I will stand firm while he strikes me with the ax provided that you reward me with the opportunity to do the same to him without being blamed for it.

7. twelvemonth: A year.

If he astonished them at first, stiller were then
All that household in hall, the high and the low;
The stranger on his green steed stirred in the saddle,
And roisterously his red eyes he rolled all about,
Bent his bristling brows, that were bright green,
Wagged his beard as he watched who would arise.
When the court kept its counsel he coughed aloud,
And cleared his throat coolly, the clearer to speak:
"What, is this Arthur's house," said that horseman then,
"Whose fame is so fair in far realms and wide?
Where is now your arrogance and your awesome deeds,
Your valor and your victories and your vaunting words?
Now are the revel and renown of the Round Table
Overwhelmed with a word of one man's speech,
For all cower and quake, and no cut felt!"
With this he laughs so loud that the lord grieved;
The blood for sheer shame shot to his face, and pride.
With rage his face flushed red,
And so did all beside.
Then the king as bold man bred
Toward the stranger took a stride.

And said, "Sir, now we see you will say but folly,
Which whoso has sought, it suits that he find.
No guest here is aghast of your great words.
Give to me your gisarme, in God's own name,
And the boon you have begged shall straight be granted."
He leaps to him lightly, lays hold of his weapon;
The green fellow on foot fiercely alights.
Now has Arthur his ax, and the haft grips,
And sternly stirs it about, on striking bent.
The stranger before him stood there erect,
Higher than any in the house by a head and more;
With stern look as he stood, he stroked his beard,
And with undaunted countenance drew down his coat,
No more moved nor dismayed for his mighty dints
Than any bold man on bench had brought him a drink of wine.
6 Gawain by Guenevere
Toward the king doth now incline:
"I beseech, before all here,
That this melee may be mine."

"Would you grant me the grace," said Gawain to the king,
"To be gone from this bench and stand by you there,
7 If I without discourtesy might quit this board,
And if my liege lady[8] misliked it not,
I would come to your counsel before your court noble.

8. liege (lēj) **lady:** Guenevere, the wife of the lord, Arthur, to whom Gawain is bound to give service and allegiance.

6 **Enrichment** Sir Gawain was the son of Arthur's half-sister, the Queen of Orkney.

7 **Reading Strategy** Read for the characteristics of chivalry that Sir Gawain exhibits in this speech.

8 Discussion When the Green Knight asks Sir Gawain to repeat the terms of the agreement, what one point omitted by Sir Gawain does the Green Knight emphasize?

For I find it not fit, as in faith it is known,
When such a boon is begged before all these knights,
Though you be tempted thereto, to take it on yourself
While so bold men about upon benches sit,
That no host under heaven is hardier of will,
Nor better brothers-in-arms where battle is joined;
I am the weakest, well I know, and of wit feeblest;
And the loss of my life would be least of any;
That I have you for uncle is my only praise;
My body, but for your blood, is barren of worth;
And for that this folly befits not a king,
And 'tis I that have asked it, it ought to be mine,
And if my claim be not comely let all this court judge in
sight."
The court assays the claim,
And in counsel all unite
To give Gawain the game
And release the king outright.

Then the king called the knight to come to his side,
And he rose up readily, and reached him with speed,
Bows low to his lord, lays hold of the weapon,
And he releases it lightly, and lifts up his hand,
And gives him God's blessing, and graciously prays
That his heart and his hand may be hardy both.
"Keep, cousin," said the king, "what you cut with this day,
And if you rule it aright, then readily, I know,
You shall stand the stroke it will strike after."
Gawain goes to the guest with gisarme in hand,
And boldly he bides there, abashed not a whit.
Then hails he Sir Gawain, the horseman in green:
"Recount we our contract, ere you come further.
First I ask and adjure you, how you are called
That you tell me true, so that trust it I may."
"In good faith," said the good knight, "Gawain am I
Whose buffet befalls you,[9] whate'er betide after,
And at this time twelvemonth take from you another
With what weapon you will, and with no man else alive."
The other nods assent:
"Sir Gawain, as I may thrive,
8 I am wondrous well content
That you this dint[10] shall drive."

"Sir Gawain," said the Green Knight, "By God, I rejoice
That your fist shall fetch this favor I seek,
And you have readily rehearsed, and in right terms,
Each clause of my covenant with the king your lord,

9. **Whose . . . you:** Whose blow you will receive.

10. **dint:** Blow.

Save that you shall assure me, sir, upon oath,
That you shall seek me yourself, wheresoever you deem
My lodgings may lie, and look for such wages[11]
As you have offered me here before all this host."
"What is the way there?" said Gawain, "Where do you dwell?"
I heard never of your house, by Him that made me,
Nor I know you not, knight, your name nor your court.
But tell me truly thereof, and teach me your name,
And I shall fare forth to find you, so far as I may,
And this I say in good certain, and swear upon oath."
"That is enough in New Year, you need say no more,"
Said the knight in the green to Gawain the noble,
"If I tell you true, when I have taken your knock,
And if you handily have hit, you shall hear straightway
Of my house and my home and my own name;
Then follow in my footsteps by faithful accord.
And if I spend no speech, you shall speed the better:
You can feast with your friends, nor further trace my tracks.[12]
Now hold your grim tool steady
And show us how it hacks."
"Gladly, sir; all ready,"
Says Gawain; he strokes the ax.

The Green Knight upon ground girds him with care:
Bows a bit with his head, and bares his flesh:
His long lovely locks he laid over his crown,
Let the naked nape for the need be shown.
Gawain grips to his ax and gathers it aloft—
The left foot on the floor before him he set—
Brought it down deftly upon the bare neck,
That the shock of the sharp blow shivered the bones
And cut the flesh cleanly and clove it in twain,[13]
That the blade of bright steel bit into the ground.
9 The head was hewn off and fell to the floor;
Many found it at their feet, as forth it rolled;
The blood gushed from the body, bright on the green,
Yet fell not the fellow, nor faltered a whit,
But stoutly he starts forth upon stiff shanks,
And as all stood staring he stretched forth his hand,
Laid hold of his head and heaved it aloft,
Then goes to the green steed, grasps the bridle,
Steps into the stirrup, bestrides his mount,
And his head by the hair in his hand holds,
And as steady he sits in the stately saddle
As he had met with no mishap, nor missing were his head.

11. **wages:** A blow.

12. **If I tell you . . . tracks** (lines 178–183): The Green Knight tells Gawain that he will let him know where he lives after he has taken the blow. If he is unable to speak following the blow, there will be no need for Gawain to know.

13. **clove it in twain:** Split it in two.

9 **Literary Focus** These lines are a good example of the concreteness and realism of description that contribute to *Sir Gawain and the Green Knight*'s excellence. Why does the result of Sir Gawain's blow to the Green Knight evoke more terror in him and the Court than if he had failed?

10 Literary Focus The picture of the disembodied head turned toward the audience and speaking is particularly vivid and gruesome. What purpose does it serve in the romance?

11 Discussion Why did King Arthur keep his composure and resume activities after the Green Knight left?

His bulk about he haled,
That fearsome body that bled;
There were many in the court that quailed
Before all his say was said.

For the head in his hand he holds right up;
10 Toward the first on the dais directs he the face,
And it lifted up its lids, and looked with wide eyes,
And said as much with its mouth as now you may hear:
"Sir Gawain, forget not to go as agreed,
And cease not to seek till me, sir, you find,
As you promised in the presence of these proud knights.
To the Green Chapel come, I charge you, to take
Such a dint as you have dealt—you have well deserved
That your neck should have a knock on New Year's morn.
The Knight of the Green Chapel I am well-known to many,
Wherefore you cannot fail to find me at last;
Therefore come, or be counted a recreant knight."
With a roisterous rush he flings round the reins,
Hurtles out at the hall door, his head in his hand,
That the flint fire flew from the flashing hooves.
Which way he went, not one of them knew
Nor whence he was come in the wide world so fair.
The king and Gawain gay
Make a game of the Green Knight there,
Yet all who saw it say
'Twas a wonder past compare.

11 Though high-born Arthur at heart had wonder,
He let no sign be seen, but said aloud
To the comely queen, with courteous speech,
"Dear dame, on this day dismay you no whit;
Such crafts are becoming at Christmastide,
Laughing at interludes, light songs and mirth,
Amid dancing of damsels with doughty knights.
Nevertheless of my meat now let me partake,
For I have met with a marvel, I may not deny."
He glanced at Sir Gawain, and gaily he said,
"Now, sir, hang up your ax, that has hewn enough,"
And over the high dais it was hung on the wall
That men in amazement might on it look,
And tell in true terms the tale of the wonder.
Then they turned toward the table, those two together,
The good king and Gawain, and made great feast,
With all dainties double, dishes rare,
With all manner of meat and minstrelsy both,
Such happiness wholly had they that day in hold.

Now take care, Sir Gawain,
That your courage wax not cold
When you must turn again
To your enterprise foretold.

The following November, Sir Gawain sets out to fulfill his promise to the Green Knight. For weeks he travels alone through the cold, threatening woods of North Wales. Then, after he prays for shelter, he comes upon a wondrous castle on Christmas Eve, where he is greeted warmly by the lord of the castle and his lady. Sir Gawain inquires about the location of the Green Chapel, and the lord assures him that it is nearby and promises to provide him with a guide to lead him there on New Year's Day. Before the lord and Sir Gawain retire for the night, they agree to exchange whatever they receive during the next three days. Sir Gawain keeps his pledge for the first two days, but on the third day he does not give the lord the magic green girdle that the lady gives him because she promises that the girdle will protect him from any harm. The next day, Gawain sets out for the Green Chapel. His guide urges him not to proceed, but Gawain refuses to take this advice. He feels that it would be dishonorable not to fulfill his pledge. He is determined to accept his fate; however, he does wear the magic green girdle that the lady had given him. 12

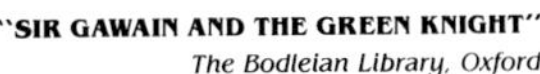
"SIR GAWAIN AND THE GREEN KNIGHT"
The Bodleian Library, Oxford

12 Master Teacher Note Another of the traditional main story elements that the poet has utilized is touched on in this summary, the "Exchange of Winnings." The third element, extremely important in the plot, is the "Temptation Story," in which the lady of the castle tries to tempt Sir Gawain.

Humanities Note

Illuminated manuscript, "Sir Gawain and the Green Knight." Medieval illuminated manuscripts were produced in monasteries by cloistered monks and by specially hired laymen. They were painted on hand-lettered vellum manuscripts to decorate and often illustrate a part of the text. Works of both a religious and secular nature were produced. Today, they provide an invaluable literary and visual historic record.

The miniature painting, *Gawain Departs Guenivere and Arthur,* is from an illuminated manuscript. The content of this manuscript is an account of the adventures of Sir Gawain. This charming painting is executed in the calligraphic, flat style that is typical of medieval art. The format, three separate scenes on a single plane, can be compared to that of today's comic strip. This lively, brightly colored account of the knight's adventures is a welcome message from the past to today's reader of ancient works.

You may wish to ask your students the following questions:

1. How does the artist show the King and Queen reacting to Gawain's departure?
2. How does this compare with the written account?

13 **Reading Strategy** Describe the Chapel Green. How does its appearance affect Sir Gawain's spirits?

14 **Discussion** What is the "barbarous din" he hears? What is the effect on the reader? On Sir Gawain?

He puts his heels to his horse, and picks up the path;
Goes in beside a grove where the ground is steep,
Rides down the rough slope right to the valley;
And then he looked a little about him—the landscape was
  wild,
And not a soul to be seen, nor sign of a dwelling,
But high banks on either hand hemmed it about,
With many a ragged rock and rough-hewn crag;
The skies seemed scored by the scowling peaks.
Then he halted his horse, and hoved there a space,
And sought on every side for a sight of the Chapel,
But no such place appeared, which puzzled him sore,
Yet he saw some way off what seemed like a mound,
A hillock high and broad, hard by the water,
Where the stream fell in foam down the face of the steep
And bubbled as if it boiled on its bed below.
The knight urges his horse, and heads for the knoll;
Leaps lightly to earth; loops well the rein
Of his steed to a stout branch, and stations him there.
He strides straight to the mound, and strolls all about,
Much wondering what it was, but no whit the wiser;
It had a hole at one end, and on either side,
And was covered with coarse grass in clumps all without,
And hollow all within, like some old cave,
Or a crevice of an old crag—he could not discern aright.
13 "Can this be the Chapel Green?
Alack!" said the man, "Here might
The devil himself be seen
Saying matins[14] at black midnight!"

"Now by heaven," said he, "it is bleak hereabouts;
This prayer house is hideous, half covered with grass!
Well may the grim man mantled in green
Hold here his orisons,[15] in hell's own style!
Now I feel it is the Fiend, in my five wits,
That has tempted me to this tryst,[16] to take my life;
This is a Chapel of mischance, may the mischief take it!
As accursed a country church as I came upon ever!"
With his helm on his head, his lance in his hand,
He stalks toward the steep wall of that strange house.
Then he heard, on the hill, behind a hard rock,
Beyond the brook, from the bank, a most barbarous din:
Lord! it clattered in the cliff fit to cleave it in two,
As one upon a grindstone ground a great scythe!
14 Lord! it whirred like a mill-wheel whirling about!
Lord! it echoed loud and long, lamentable to hear!
Then "By heaven," said the bold knight, "That business up
  there
Is arranged for my arrival, or else I am much misled.

14. matins *n.*: Morning prayers.

15. orisons *n.*: Prayers.

16. tryst (trist) *n.*: Meeting.

Let God work! Ah me!
All hope of help has fled!
Forfeit my life may be
But noise I do not dread."

Then he listened no longer, but loudly he called,
"Who has power in this place, high parley to hold?
For none greets Sir Gawain, or give him good day;
If any would a word with him, let him walk forth
And speak now or never, to speed his affairs."
"Abide," said one on the bank above over his head,
"And what I promised you once shall straightway be given."
Yet he stayed not his grindstone, nor stinted its noise,
But worked awhile at his whetting before he would rest,
And then he comes around a crag, from a cave in the rocks,
Hurtling out of hiding with a hateful weapon,
15 A Danish ax[17] devised for that day's deed,
With a broad blade and bright, bent in a curve,
Filed to a fine edge—four feet it measured
By the length of the lace that was looped round the haft.
And in form as at first, the fellow all green,
His lordly face and his legs, his locks and his beard,
Save that firm upon two feet forward he strides,
Sets a hand on the ax-head, the haft to the earth;
When he came to the cold stream, and cared not to wade,
He vaults over on his ax, and advances amain
On a broad bank of snow, overbearing and brisk of mood.
Little did the knight incline
When face to face they stood;
Said the other man, "Friend mine,
It seems your word holds good!"

"God love you, Sir Gawain!" said the Green Knight then,
"And well met this morning, man, at my place!
And you have followed me faithfully and found me betimes,
And on the business between us we both are agreed:
Twelve months ago today you took what was yours,
And you at this New Year must yield me the same.
And we have met in these mountains, remote from all eyes:
There is none here to halt us or hinder our sport;
Unhasp your high helm, and have here your wages;
Make no more demur than I did myself
When you hacked off my head with one hard blow."
"No, by God," said Sir Gawain, "that granted me life,
I shall grudge not the guerdon,[18] grim though it prove;
And you may lay on as you like till the last of my part be paid."

17. Danish ax: A long-bladed ax.

18. guerdon: Reward.

15 Enrichment The Danish ax was named for the Vikings who used it. It was a kind of battle-ax with a very long blade, and usually without a spike on the back. The Green Knight's weapon, the gisarme, was a battle-ax complete with a spike.

16 Discussion Although a hero, Sir Gawain is humanized primarily through two actions. What are they? What is the effect of these failings on the reader? On the Green Knight? Compare this presentation of the hero with that of Beowulf. Which do you prefer and why?

17 Discussion How does the author maintain suspense in this scene? Is Sir Gawain's anger justified?

He proffered, with good grace,
His bare neck to the blade,
And feigned a cheerful face:
He scorned to seem afraid.

Then the grim man in green gathers his strength,
Heaves high the heavy ax to hit him the blow.
With all the force in his frame he fetches it aloft,
With a grimace as grim as he would grind him to bits;
Had the blow he bestowed been as big as he threatened,
A good knight and gallant had gone to his grave.
16 But Gawain at the great ax glanced up aside
As down it descended with death-dealing force,
And his shoulders shrank a little from the sharp iron.
Abruptly the brawny man breaks off the stroke,
And then reproved with proud words that prince among knights.
"You are not Gawain the glorious," the green man said,
"That never fell back on field in the face of the foe,
And now you flee for fear, and have felt no harm:
Such news of that knight I never heard yet!
I moved not a muscle when you made to strike,
Nor caviled at the cut in King Arthur's house;
My head fell to my feet, yet steadfast I stood,
And you, all unharmed, are wholly dismayed—
Wherefore the better man I, by all odds, must be."
Said Gawain, "Strike once more;
I shall neither flinch nor flee;
But if my head falls to the floor
There is no mending me!"

"But go on, man, in God's name, and get to the point!
Deliver me my destiny, and do it out of hand,
For I shall stand to the stroke and stir not an inch
Till your ax has hit home—on my honor I swear it!"
"Have at thee then!" said the other, and heaves it aloft,
And glares down as grimly as he had gone mad.
He made a mighty feint, but marred not his hide;
Withdrew the ax adroitly before it did damage.
Gawain gave no ground, nor glanced up aside,
But stood still as a stone, or else a stout stump
17 That is held in hard earth by a hundred roots.
Then merrily does he mock him, the man all in green:
"So now you have your nerve again, I needs must strike;
Uphold the high knighthood that Arthur bestowed,
And keep your neck-bone clear, if this cut allows!"
Then was Gawain gripped with rage, and grimly he said.

"Why, thrash away, tyrant, I tire of your threats;
You make such a scene, you must frighten yourself."
Said the green fellow, "In faith, so fiercely you speak
That I shall finish this affair, nor further grace allow."
He stands prepared to strike
And scowls with both lip and brow;
No marvel if the man mislike
Who can hope no rescue now.

He gathered up the grim ax and guided it well:
Let the barb at the blade's end brush the bare throat;
He hammered down hard, yet harmed him no whit
Save a scratch on one side, that severed the skin;
The end of the hooked edge entered the flesh,
And a little blood lightly leapt to the earth.
And when the man beheld his own blood bright on the snow,
He sprang a spear's length with feet spread wide,
Seized his high helm, and set it on his head,
Shoved before his shoulders the shield at his back,
Bares his trusty blade, and boldly he speaks— 18
Not since he was a babe born of his mother
Was he once in this world one half so blithe—
"Have done with your hacking—harry me no more!
I have borne, as behooved, one blow in this place;
If you make another move I shall meet it midway
And promptly, I promise you, pay back each blow with brand.
One stroke acquits me here;
So did our covenant stand
In Arthur's court last year—
Wherefore, sir, hold your hand!"

He lowers the long ax and leans on it there,
Sets his arms on the head, the haft on the earth,
And beholds the bold knight that bides there afoot,
How he faces him fearless, fierce in full arms,
And plies him with proud words—it pleases him well.
Then once again gaily to Gawain he calls,
And in a loud voice and lusty, delivers these words:
"Bold fellow, on this field your anger forbear!
No man has made demands here in manner uncouth,
Nor done, save as duly determined at court.
I owed you a hit and you have it; be happy therewith!
The rest of my rights here I freely resign.
Had I been a bit busier, a buffet, perhaps,
I could have dealt more directly; and done you some harm.

18 **Discussion** When the Green Knight finally delivers the blow, what does it amount to? How does Gawain react when he sees his own blood on the snow?

19 **Literary Focus** The Green Knight discloses that his first and second feints, or pretended blows, did not touch Sir Gawain because, in their promised exchange of winnings, Sir Gawain had in fact given back to the Knight what he had won that day—in each case, a kiss from the Green Knight's wife. However, because Sir Gawain had kept the girdle that would guard him from harm and thus had not lived up to his bargain, he received the third blow, although it was only a token blow, a scratch. What is the Green Knight's assessment of Sir Gawain's overall behavior? Do you blame Sir Gawain for his act of deception? Does Sir Gawain blame himself?

First I flourished with a feint, in frolicsome mood,
And left your hide unhurt—and here I did well
By the fair terms we fixed on the first night;
And fully and faithfully you followed accord:
Gave over all your gains as a good man should.
A second feint, sir, I assigned for the morning
You kissed my comely wife—each kiss you restored.
For both of these there behooved but two feigned blows by
right.
True men pay what they owe;
No danger then in sight.
You failed at the third throw,
So take my tap, sir knight.

"For that is my belt about you, that same braided girdle,
My wife it was that wore it; I know well the tale,
And the count of your kisses and your conduct too,
And the wooing of my wife—it was all my scheme!
She made trial of a man most faultless by far
Of all that ever walked over the wide earth;
As pearls to white peas, more precious and prized,
So is Gawain, in good faith, to other gay knights.
19 Yet you lacked, sir, a little in loyalty there,
But the cause was not cunning, nor courtship either,
But that you loved your own life; the less, then, to blame."
The other stout knight in a study stood a long while,
So gripped with grim rage that his great heart shook.
All the blood of his body burned in his face
As he shrank back in shame from the man's sharp speech.
The first words that fell from the fair knight's lips:
"Accursed be a cowardly and covetous heart!
In you is villainy and vice, and virtue laid low!"
Then he grasps the green girdle and lets go the knot,
Hands it over in haste, and hotly he says:
"Behold there my falsehood, ill hap betide it!
Your cut taught me cowardice, care for my life,
And coveting came after, contrary both
To largesse and loyalty belonging to knights.
Now am I faulty and false, that fearful was ever
Of disloyalty and lies, bad luck to them both! and greed.
I confess, knight, in this place,
Most dire is my misdeed;
Let me gain back your good grace,
And thereafter I shall take heed."

Then the other laughed aloud, and lightly he said,
"Such harm as I have had, I hold it quite healed.

GAWAIN RECEIVING THE GREEN GIRDLE
Woodcut by Fritz Kredel from Gardner
The Complete Works of the Gawain Poet, 1965
The University of Chicago

Humanities Note

Fine art, *Gawain Receiving the Green Girdle,* by Fritz Kredel. Fritz Kredel (1900–1973) was a German-born American artist. He was educated in Germany at the Realgymnasium in Darmstadt and the Kunstgewerbeschule in Offenbach. Kredel worked chiefly in woodcuts, prints made from designs cut into wooden blocks. He has won many awards both in the United States and in Europe for his book illustrations.

This woodcut is done in the ancient method of a medieval woodcut. Kredel has maintained the straightforward vitality of the artists of that time. You could mention to your students that if the illustration were compared with a medieval woodcut, it would be difficult to tell, from style alone, which is contemporary.

Kredel made a point of thoroughly studying a text before he illustrated it. He felt that in illustration the artist should strive to glorify the author's work, not to overshadow it. This philosophy is a success in *Gawain.* The simple lines and sparse detail give an accurate portrayal of the characters without distracting our focus of attention from the poem.

1. Tell why you think the style and overall effect of the woodcut is or is not well suited to the poem.
2. Do you feel that highly realistic oil or watercolor paintings are usually preferable to line drawings on woodcuts such as this? Explain your answer.

20 Discussion Why must Sir Gawain go through this ordeal? What does the ordeal achieve for Sir Gawain? In what way is the ordeal symbolic? Note the time of year. How does this add to the symbolism?

You are so fully confessed, your failings made known,
And bear the plain penance of the point of my blade,
I hold you polished as a pearl, as pure and as bright
As you had lived free of fault since first you were born.
And I give you, sir, this girdle that is gold-hemmed
20 And green as my garments, that, Gawain, you may
Be mindful of this meeting when you mingle in throng
With nobles of renown—and known by this token
How it chanced at the Green Chapel, to chivalrous knights.
And you shall in this New Year come yet again
And we shall finish out our feast in my fair hall, with cheer."

THINKING ABOUT THE SELECTION

Recalling

1. What kind of challenge does King Arthur at first think the Green Knight has in mind?
2. The Green Knight's challenge has two parts. (a) What is Sir Gawain to do immediately? (b) What is he to do a year later?
3. What does Sir Gawain do at the Green Chapel to cause the Green Knight to question his valor?
4. Why does the Green Knight only scratch Sir Gawain with his ax?

Interpreting

5. The Green Knight laughs at the members of the Round Table in line 92. Why?
6. When Sir Gawain sees the Green Chapel, who does he think the Green Knight may be?
7. In lines 465–477 why is Sir Gawain upset?

Applying

8. What modern occupation do you think comes closest to matching the duties and ideals of the Knights of the Round Table? Explain your answer.

ANALYZING LITERATURE

Understanding Medieval Romances

Most medieval romances

- Embody the ideals of chivalry
- Are set in a remote time or place
- Emphasize rank and social distinctions
- Convey a sense of the supernatural
- Present a hero engaged in pure adventure
- Have a loose structure, lacking in unity
- Include love as a major plot element
- Feature spontaneous, unmotivated fighting

1. Which of these characteristics does *Sir Gawain and the Green Knight* NOT display?
2. In medieval romances, a hero seldom admits failure. Does Sir Gawain follow this tradition? Explain.

CRITICAL THINKING AND READING

Making Inferences About Chivalry

Human actions and motivations reflect the ideals of the society in which people live. Today a community leader might laugh off the kind of challenge the Green Knight hurls at King Arthur. You can infer from the way Arthur and Sir Gawain react, however, that in the age of chivalry one took seriously such challenges to one's courage.

1. What ideals of medieval society can you infer from Sir Gawain's offer to accept the challenge made to Arthur?
2. What ideals can you infer from Sir Gawain's distress at the end of the poem, even after he has withstood the blow of the ax?

UNDERSTANDING LANGUAGE

Using Abstract Words

An **abstract word** expresses a quality that cannot be directly perceived through the senses. For example, although you can see a *knight* or an *ax* (concrete words), you cannot see, hear, touch, taste, or smell *chivalry, courage,* or *loyalty*. Often the best way to define an abstract word is with a specific example:

> Sir Gawain set out for the Green Chapel even though he was certain it meant death. That is what I call *bravery*.

Write a specific example that shows the meaning of each of the following abstract words.

1. grandeur
2. temerity
3. perspicacity
4. flightiness

THINKING AND WRITING

Evaluating the Medieval Romance

One of the world's most famous novels, *Don Quixote* by Miguel de Cervantes, satirizes medieval romances like *Sir Gawain and the Green Knight*. What aspects of the medieval romance do you think Cervantes may have felt deserved satire? Jot down your answers to this question. Arrange your answers in a logical order for development in an essay. Write the essay. Make any revisions that seem necessary.

Answers

ANSWERS TO THINKING ABOUT THE SELECTION

Recalling

1. Arthur thinks that the Green Knight wants a joust or fight.
2. (a) Sir Gawain is to strike a blow with an ax at the Green Knight. (b) A year later he is to find the Green Knight and receive a blow from an ax in return.
3. At the first blow, Sir Gawain flinches a little.
4. The Green Knight wounds him because Sir Gawain has failed to keep the third day's bargain; he did not give up the green girdle.

Interpreting

5. He laughs insultingly because he finds Arthur's brave knights cowardly.
6. Sir Gawain thinks that the Green Knight might be Satan.
7. He is upset at himself for being false, greedy, cowardly, and disloyal to his code.

Applying

8. Answers will differ. Perhaps the police, firefighters, paramedics, and the military might be mentioned.

ANSWERS TO ANALYZING LITERATURE

1. *Sir Gawain and the Green Knight*'s plot has unity, and the fighting is not spontaneous or unmotivated. Some students might not recognize the love element since it is a part of the summary.
2. Sir Gawain admits his failure by telling the Green Knight and later King Arthur of his greed and cowardice. Therefore, he does not follow tradition.

ANSWERS TO CRITICAL THINKING AND READING

1. Loyalty and fealty to the king can be inferred, as well as courage.
2. Courage, loyalty, and honesty were values that he felt upset about violating. He also decried his covetousness.

ANSWERS TO UNDERSTANDING LANGUAGE

Answers will differ. For example (1) After viewing the Grand Canyon for the first time, I understood the grandeur of nature. (2) John criticized his boss and the company's hiring policy in front of the president. That is temerity. (3) The fact that she sold her stocks before the market fell sharply showed her perspicacity. (4) Pat switches from one guru's religion to another popular philosophy every other week. That is flightiness.

THINKING AND WRITING

For help with this assignment, students can refer to Lesson 20, "Writing a Short Dramatic Sketch," in the Handbook of Writing About Literature.

Writing Across the Curriculum

Once the students have decided what deserved satire in Medieval romances, give them the option of writing a play that actually satirizes *Sir Gawain and the Green Knight* or another poem. They might work with the drama department to prepare their plays for presentation to the class.

More About the Selection The morality play, of which *Everyman* is the finest example, emerged in English drama in the fifteenth century. Basically a dramatized sermon appealing more to the intellect than to the emotions, it strove to answer the question "How can man save his soul?" Written in the form of an allegory, the typical morality play tended to be somewhat dull and didactic. Consequently, it was often enlivened by humor, particularly in the portrayal of the evil characters. *Everyman*, however, was compelling enough to do without slapstick comedy to enthrall audiences. It has been performed by both amateur and professional actors for more than four centuries. What forms of literature or popular entertainment do we use today to teach lessons and promote values?

GUIDE FOR READING

1475 [?]

English theater began with what are called miracle plays, sometimes referred to as mystery plays. The aim of a miracle play is to dramatize an incident from the Bible. Morality plays, which came later, deal with the human struggle between virtues and vices. They feature characters that represent abstract qualities such as Beauty, Good Deeds, Knowledge, and Death. The most famous and sophisticated of the morality plays is *Everyman*, written by an unknown playwright.

The English theater originated in the medieval church. To make religious services more meaningful and impressive, the clergy began inserting bits of dialogue into the mass. These miniature dramas, much expanded, became miracle plays. The plays moved outdoors, lost their direct connection with the church, and became a popular form of entertainment. The miracle plays were performed on wagons that moved from place to place within a town or city. Each wagon stopped at designated stations, presenting the same play over and over. A viewer could sometimes see as many as fifty miracle plays by staying in one place throughout the day and watching as the procession of wagons passed by.

Morality plays such as *Everyman* grew out of these miracle plays and also out of medieval allegories, not all of them English, in which the characters are abstractions—Fear, Courtesy, Greed, Delight, and so on. *Everyman* resembles an earlier Dutch morality play, *Elckerlijk*, but since the subject matter of the two plays, the summoning of death, is so common, both may come from a single source. The theme of *Everyman* is the salvation of the soul as death approaches. When Everyman is summoned by Death, he finds that none of his friends and relatives—Fellowship, Cousin, Kindred, or Goods—will keep him company. As he makes his descent into the grave, only Good Deeds will go with him.

This play has enjoyed extraordinary success since its appearance in the fifteenth century. The allegory has been translated into many languages, has been used by later writers as the basis of their plays, and has often been performed, both as an academic revival and a commercial production, on the twentieth-century stage.

Objectives

1. To understand morality plays
2. To interpret names as symbols
3. To perform a play
4. To discuss a morality play

Teaching Portfolio: Support Materials

Teacher Backup, pp. 00-00

Vocabulary Check, p. 00

Usage and Mechanics Worksheet, p. 00

Analyzing Literature Worksheet, p. 00

Critical Thinking and Reading Worksheet, p. 00

Language Worksheet, p. 00

Selection Test, p. 00

from Everyman

Literary Forms

Morality Play. Medieval morality plays have a singleness of purpose, to dramatize the conflict between the power of good and evil for control of one's soul. Although the plays are intended to entertain audiences, they also seek to teach strict lessons of right and wrong. Essentially religious, morality plays are allegories in which characters appear as abstract virtues and vices. By their very nature the characters are one-dimensional, lacking the complexity found in characters in more sophisticated drama. The plays were originally produced for a middle-class town audience, many of whose members could neither read nor write. For the most part the plays are anonymously written. This may seem strange to you, because *Everyman* and other moralities came into being at a time when records were kept. A main reason for the anonymity of writers is (as the morality plays teach) that worldly ambition counted for little in the church-dominated culture of that era. Lack of credit for individual achievement was the order of the day. No one knows, for instance, who designed the magnificent Gothic cathedrals or created the stained glass and statues that adorn them. The medieval architect and sculptor, like the medieval playwright, worked primarily for the glory of God.

Look For

As you read the excerpt from *Everyman,* look for the message that is stated explicitly at the beginning and end of the play. Notice how it is reiterated throughout.

Writing

Assume you are writing a play to dramatize a principle such as "Honesty is the best policy" or "Haste makes waste." Write the principle. Then list at least five characters you would cast in the play. Give them abstract names like Deceit or Punctuality.

Vocabulary

Knowing the following words will help you as you read the excerpt from *Everyman.*

reverence (rev′ ər əns) *n.*: Deep respect or awe (l. 2)
transitory (tran′ sə tôr ē) *adj.*: Temporary; fleeting (l. 6)
tempests (tem′ pistz) *n.*: Violent outbursts (l. 48)
respite (res′ pit) *n.*: Postponement; delay (l. 100)
terrestrial (tə res′ trē əl) *adj.*: Of this world; earthly (l. 155)
caitiff (kāt′ if) *n.*: An evil person (l. 171)

Literary Focus Review the characteristics of allegory. What will the title character represent?

Look For As you read the play, your **less advanced** students may have difficulty with the language in the beginning. They might benefit from reading aloud and frequently summarizing what has occurred.

Writing Choose one of the given principles and suggest a character or two who might appear in the play. Then have students suggest other suitable characters. The class might discuss some of the actions these characters might perform that match their names.

Vocabulary Review the vocabulary with your students before reading. You might inform them that *caitiff* as an adjective means "mean" and "cowardly."

Motivation for Reading Imagine that you knew that Death was coming for you. In fact, you even had the opportunity to talk to Death. What would you say to him? What would you request of him? The title character in this play is faced with this situation.

Thematic Idea Another selection that deals with the theme of saving the soul is *Tragical History of Doctor Faustus,* by Christopher Marlowe, page 185.

Purpose-Setting Question The Messenger, whose speech serves as a prologue, opens the play with a brief summary of what it proposes to convey. What is that message?

1 **Reading Strategy** Define *transitory.* What theme is implied?

2 **Reading Strategy** Before your students read God's speech, ask them to keep the following questions in mind: How does God characterize man and the condition of the world? What has man forgotten? With what is he preoccupied? Is he improving?

from Everyman

Here beginneth a treatise[1] how the High Father of Heaven sendeth DEATH *to summon every creature to come and give account of their lives in this world, and is in manner of a moral play.*

[*Enter* MESSENGER.]

MESSENGER. I pray, you all give your audience,
And hear this matter with reverence,
By figure[2] a moral play.
The Summoning of Everyman called it is,
1 That of our lives and ending shows
How transitory we be all day.[3]
The matter is wonder precious,
But the intent of it is more gracious
And sweet to bear away.
The story saith: Man, in the beginning
Look well, and take good heed to the ending,
Be you never so gay.
You think sin in the beginning full sweet,
Which in the end causeth the soul to weep,
When the body lieth in clay.
Here shall you see how fellowship and jollity,
Both strength, pleasure, and beauty,
Will fade from thee as flower in May.
For ye shall hear how our Heaven-King
Calleth Everyman to a general reckoning.
Give audience and hear what he doth say.

2 [*Exit* MESSENGER. *Enter* GOD.]

GOD. I perceive, here in my majesty,
How that all creatures be to me unkind,[4]
Living without dread in worldly prosperity.
Of ghostly[5] sight the people be so blind,
Drowned in sin, they know me not for their God.
In worldly riches is all their mind:
They fear not of my righteousness the sharp rod;
My law that I showed when I for them died
They forget clean, and shedding of my blood red.
I hanged between two,[6] it cannot be denied:
To get them life I suffered to be dead.
I healed their feet, with thorns hurt was my head.
I could do no more than I did, truly—
And now I see the people do clean forsake me.

1. **treatise:** Narrative.
2. **by figure:** In form.
3. **all day:** Always.
4. **unkind:** Thoughtless.
5. **ghostly:** Spiritual.
6. **two:** The two thieves between whom Christ was crucified.

3 They use the seven deadly sins damnable,
As pride, coveitise,[7] wrath, and gluttony
Now in the world be made commendable.
And thus they leave of angels the heavenly company.
Every man liveth so after his own pleasure,
And yet of their life they be nothing sure.
I see the more that I them forbear,
The worse they be from year to year:
All that liveth appaireth[8] fast.
4 Therefore I will, in all the haste,
Have a reckoning of every man's person.
For, and[9] I leave the people thus alone
In their life and wicked tempests,
Verily they will become much worse than beasts;
For now one would by envy another up eat.
Charity do they all clean forgeet.
I hoped well that every man
In my glory should make his mansion,
And thereto I had them all elect.[10]
But now I see, like traitors deject,[11]
They thank me not for the pleasure that I to[12] them
  meant,
Nor yet for their being that I them have lent.
I proffered the people great multitude of mercy,
And few there be that asketh it heartily.[13]
They be so cumbered[14] with worldly riches
That needs on them I must do justice—
On every man living without fear.
5 Where art thou, Death, thou mighty messenger?

[*Enter* DEATH.]

DEATH. Almighty, God, I am here at your will,
  Your commandment to fulfull.
6 GOD. Go thou to Everyman,
  And show him, in my name,
  A pilgrimage he must on him take,
  Which he in no wise may escape;
7 And that he bring with him a sure reckoning
  Without delay or any tarrying.
DEATH. Lord, I will in the world go run over all,[15]
  And cruelly out-search both great and small.

[*Exit* GOD.]

Everyman will I beset that liveth beastly
Out of God's laws, and dreadeth not folly.
He that loveth riches I will strike with my dart,
His sight to blind, and from heaven to depart[16]—
Except that Almsdeeds[17] be his good friend—
In hell for to dwell, world without end.

7. coveitise: Avarice.

8. appaireth: Degenerates.

9. and: If.

10. elect: Chosen.

11. deject: Abased.

12. to: For.

13. heartily: Sincerely.

14. cumbered: Encumbered.

15. over all: Everywhere.

16. depart: Separate.

17. Almsdeeds: Deeds of mercy; good deeds.

3 **Enrichment** The Seven Deadly Sins as stated by the Church are pride, covetousness, lust, anger, gluttony, envy, and sloth.

4 **Discussion** In the midst of this indictment, God decides to "have a reckoning of every man's person." What does this mean?

5 **Literary Focus** What quality of allegory is demonstrated here?

6 **Clarification** Note that God here refers for the first time to Everyman as a specific person. Before this, he has used the term generally.

7 **Literary Focus** Again the reckoning is mentioned. Death is instructed to tell Everyman to bring it on his projected journey. What is that journey?

8 Master Teacher Note Point out how natural this conversation between Death and Everyman is. Everyman reacts in most predictable ways. He admits he is unready, offers a bribe, begs for a twelve-year postponement, is then willing to settle for a single day, looks for ameliorating conditions, and despairs. Is that realistic?

9 Discussion What is Death's rationale for refusing Everyman's bribe?

Lo, yonder I see Everyman walking:
Full little he thinketh on my coming;
His mind is on fleshly lusts and his treasure,
And great pain it shall cause him to endure
Before the Lord, Heaven-King.

[*Enter* EVERYMAN.]

Everyman, stand still! Whither art thou going
Thus gaily? Hast thou thy Maker forgeet?
EVERYMAN. Why askest thou?
Why wouldest thou weet?[18]
DEATH. Yea, sir, I will show you:
In great haste I am sent to thee
From God out of his majesty.
EVERYMAN. What! sent to me?
DEATH. Yea, certainly.
Though thou have forgot him here,
He thinketh on thee in the heavenly sphere,
As, ere we depart, thou shalt know.
EVERYMAN. What desireth God of me?
DEATH. That shall I show thee:
A reckoning he will needs have
Without any longer respite.
EVERYMAN. To give a reckoning longer leisure I crave.
This blind[19] matter troubleth my wit.
DEATH. On thee thou must take a long journay:
Therefore thy book of count[20] with thee thou bring,
8 For turn again thou cannot by no way.
And look thou be sure of thy reckoning,
For before God thou shalt answer and shew
Thy many bad deeds and good but a few—
How thou hast spent thy life and in what wise,
Before the Chief Lord of Paradise.
Have ado that we were in that way,[21]
For weet thou well thou shalt make none attornay.[22]
EVERYMAN. Full unready I am such reckoning to give.
I know thee not. What messenger art thou?
DEATH. I am Death that no man dreadeth,[23]
For every man I 'rest,[24] and no man spareth;
For it is God's commandment
That all to me should be obedient.
EVERYMAN. O Death, thou comest when I had thee least in mind.
In thy power it lieth me to save:
Yet of my good[25] will I give thee, if thou will be kind,
Yea, a thousand pound shalt thou have—
And defer this matter till another day.
9 **DEATH.** Everyman, it may not be, by no way.

18. weet: Know.

19. blind: Unexpected.

20. count: Accounts.

21. Have ado . . . way: Let us get started.

22. none attornay: None appear in your place.

23. that no man dreadeth: That fears no one.

24. 'rest: Arrest.

25. good: Goods.

I set nought by[26] gold, silver, nor riches,
Nor by pope, emperor, king, duke, nor princes,
For, and I would receive gifts great,
All the world I might get.
But my custom is clean contrary:
I give thee no respite. Come hence and not tarry!
EVERYMAN. Alas, shall I have no longer respite?
I may say Death giveth no warning.
To think on thee it maketh my heart sick,
For all unready is my book of reckoning.
But twelve year and I might have a biding,[27]
My counting-book I would make so clear
That my reckoning I should not need to fear.
Wherefore, Death, I pray thee, for God's mercy,
Spare me till I be provided of remedy.
DEATH. Thee availeth not to cry, weep, and pray;
But haste thee lightly[28] that thou were gone that journay,
And prove[29] thy friends, if thou can.
For weet thou well the tide[30] abideth no man,
And in the world each living creature
For Adam's sin must die of nature.[31]
EVERYMAN. Death, if I should this pilgrimage take
And my reckoning surely make,
Show me, for saint[32] charity,
Should I not come again shortly?
DEATH. No, Everyman. And thou be once there,
Thou mayst never more come here,
Trust me verily.
EVERYMAN. O gracious God in the high seat celestial,
Have mercy on me in this most need!
10 Shall I have company from this vale terrestrial
Of mine acquaintance that way me to lead?
DEATH. Yea, if any be so hardy
That would go with thee and bear thee company.
Hie[33] thee that thou were gone to God's magnificence,
Thy reckoning to give before his presence.
What, weenest[34] thou thy life is given thee,
And thy worldly goods also?
EVERYMAN. I had weened so, verily.
DEATH. Nay, nay, it was but lent thee.
For as soon as thou art go,
Another a while shall have it and then go therefro,
Even as thou hast done.
Everyman, thou art mad! Thou hast thy wits[35] five,
And here on earth will not amend thy live![36]
For suddenly I do come.
EVERYMAN. O wretched caitiff! Whither shall I flee
That I might 'scape this endless sorrow?

26. set nought by: Care nothing for.

27. twelve year . . . biding: If I might have a twelve-year delay.

28. lightly: Quickly.

29. prove: Test.

30. tide: Time.

31. of nature: Naturally.

32. saint: Holy.

33. Hie: Hasten.

34. weenest: Suppose.

35. wits: Senses.

36. thy live: In thy life.

10 **Reading Strategy** Everyman is allowed company on his journey. Who might conceivably travel the entire distance with him?

11 **Master Teacher Note** Notice the theological lesson implicit here: No one knows when Death will arrive; therefore, it behooves everyone to be prepared at all times.

12 **Clarification** In the summary Everyman first calls on the physical and material comforts of the world to accompany him. Then he appeals to things of the spirit.

13 **Discussion** Why is Good Deeds the only companion to enter the grave with Everyman? Why can Knowledge only accompany him to its brink?

Now, gentle Death, spare me till tomorrow,
That I may amend me
11 With good advisement.[37]
DEATH. Nay, thereto I will not consent,
Nor no man will I respite,
But to the heart suddenly I shall smite,
Without any advisement.
And now out of thy sight I will me hie:
See thou make thee ready shortly,
For thou mayst say this is the day
That no man living may 'scape away.
[*Exit* DEATH.]

12 *Everyman calls on Fellowship, Cousin, Kindred, and Goods (his friends, relatives, and wealth) to accompany him on his journey, but they all refuse and desert him. Everyman then summons his Good Deeds and Knowledge, and Knowledge leads him to Confession, who comforts him. Following his meeting with Confession, Everyman is assisted by Good Deeds, Knowledge, Beauty, Strength, Five-Wits (Five Senses), and Discretion (the attributes that make up an integrated person) in making up his book of accounts. Then each one, except for Good Deeds and Knowledge, leaves him as he makes final preparations for his journey to the grave.*

EVERYMAN. O Jesu, help, all hath forsaken me!
GOOD DEEDS. Nay, Everyman, I will bide with thee:
I will not forsake thee indeed;
Thou shalt find me a good friend at need.
EVERYMAN. Gramercy,[38] Good Deeds! Now may I true friends see.
They have forsaken me every one—
I loved them better than my Good Deeds alone.
Knowledge, will ye forsake me also?
KNOWLEDGE. Yea, Everyman, when ye to Death shall go,
But not yet, for no manner of danger.
EVERYMAN. Gramercy, Knowledge, with all my heart!
13 **KNOWLEDGE.** Nay, yet will I not from hence depart
Till I see where ye shall become.[39]
EVERYMAN. Methink, alas, that I must be gone
To make my reckoning and my debts pay,
For I see my time is nigh spent away.
Take example, all ye that this do hear or see,
How they that I best loved do forsake me,
Except my Good Deeds that bideth truly.
GOOD DEEDS. All earthly things is but vanity.

37. advisement: Preparation.

38. Gramercy: Good thanks.

39. where ye shall become: What shall become of you.

Beauty, Strength, and Discretion do man forsake,
Foolish friends and kinsmen that fair spake—
All fleeth save Good Deeds, and that am I.

EVERYMAN. Have mercy on me, God most mighty,
And stand by me, thou mother and maid, holy Mary!

GOOD DEEDS. Fear not: I will speak for thee.

EVERYMAN. Here I cry God mercy!

GOOD DEEDS. Short our end, and 'minish our pain.[40]
Let us go, and never come again.

EVERYMAN. Into thy hands, Lord, my soul I commend:
Receive it, Lord, that it be not lost.
As thou me boughtest,[41] so me defend,
And save me from the fiend's boast,
That I may appear with that blessed host
That shall be saved at the day of doom.
In manus tuas, of mights most,
Forever *commendo spiritum meum.*[42]

[EVERYMAN *and* GOOD DEEDS *descend into the grave.*]

KNOWLEDGE. Now hath he suffered that we all shall endure,
The Good Deeds shall make all sure.
Now hath he made ending,
Methinketh that I hear angels sing
And make great joy and melody
Where Everyman's soul received shall be.

ANGEL. [*within*] Come, excellent elect spouse to Jesu![43]
Here above thou shalt go
Because of thy singular virtue.
Now the soul is taken the body fro,
Thy reckoning is crystal clear:
Now shalt thou into the heavenly sphere—
Unto the which all ye shall come
That liveth well before the day of doom.

[*Enter Doctor.*[44]]

DOCTOR. This memorial[45] men may have in mind:
Ye hearers, take it of worth, old and young,
And forsake Pride, for he deceiveth you in the end.
And remember Beauty, Five-Wits, Strength, and
Discretion,
They all at the last do Everyman forsake,
Save his Good Deeds there doth he take—
But beware, for and they be small,
14 Before God he hath no help at all—
None excuse may be there for Everyman.
Alas, how shall he do than?[46]
For after death amends may no man make,
For then mercy and pity doth him forsake.

40. Short . . . pain: Make our death quick and diminish our pain.

41. boughtest: Redeemed.

42. *In manus . . . meum:* "Into thy hands, O greatest of powers, I commend my spirit forever." (Latin)

43. spouse to Jesu: Everyman's soul is referred to as the bride of Jesus.

44. doctor: A learned theologian.

45. memorial: Reminder.

46. than: Then.

14 **Literary Focus** The Doctor summarizes the message of the play in this concluding speech. Why is he chosen for that role?

Humanities Note

Fine Art, *The Old Man and Death,* Joseph Wright of Derby.

Joseph Wright of Derby (1734–1797) called himself "of Derby" to distinguish himself from another painter who worked at the same time, Richard Wright. Joseph Wright was a precociously talented child. He later studied portrait painting with Thomas Hudson and traveled to Italy to continue his study of art. Joseph Wright of Derby is remembered for his genre and landscape paintings.

This painting, *The Old Man and Death,* was completed about 1774. It is a commentary on man's fear of death. The choice of a subject that expressed a strong emotion shows Wright's attraction to Romanticism in art. A skillful painter, Wright was able to convey the terror of the old man and the eerie mood of the setting of the painting.

You might ask the following questions:

1. What comment is the artist making about death?
2. Explain why this painting is an appropriate illustration for *Everyman.*

If his reckoning be not clear when he doth come,
God will say, "*Ite, maledicti, in ignem eternum!*"[47]
And he that hath his account whole and sound,
High in heaven he shall be crowned,
Unto which place God bring us all thither,
That we may live body and soul togither.
Thereto help, the Trinity!
Amen, say ye, for saint charity.

47. *Ite . . . eternum:* "Depart, ye cursed, into everlasting fire." (Latin)

THE OLD MAN AND DEATH, C.1774
Joseph Wright of Derby
Wadsworth Atheneum

THINKING ABOUT THE SELECTION

Recalling

1. On what mission does God send Death?
2. What does Everyman request when he first learns the purpose of Death's visit?
3. (a) How does Good Deeds respond to Everyman's plea for companionship? (b) How does Knowledge respond?
4. According to the Doctor, what can be done after death to make up for mistakes or oversights in life? Explain.

Interpreting

5. What is God's main complaint about the way people on earth are behaving?
6. Death repeatedly refuses to give Everyman any additional time. Why?
7. What does Death tell Everyman about the ownership of worldly goods?

Applying

8. How do you account for the fact that stage productions of *Everyman* have continued to be successful up to the present day?

FOCUS ON LITERATURE

Understanding a Morality Play

The basic question in a morality play is, "What must I do to be saved?" A struggle occurs between good and evil, virtues and vices, for the possession of one's soul. The characters are persons presented as abstractions: Death, Pride, Strength, Beauty, Knowledge. *Everyman's* plot is restricted to the last part of a typical morality play—the arrival of Death.

1. Find two places in *Everyman* (not at the very beginning or end) where a line or lines directly express the play's message. Write the lines.
2. Which characters represent categories of people rather than abstract qualities?

CRITICAL THINKING AND READING

Interpreting Names as Symbols

The name of a character in literature can be used as a symbol. A **symbol** is a word, person, or object that stands for something beyond itself. For example, a star can stand for achievement. In a morality play like *Everyman,* a character is simply called Achievement, but the star symbol can be used as a character's name for the same purpose—e.g., Brenda Starr. Achievement can also be suggested by a name like Mark Winner. Choose two of the following fictional names and make them into appropriate morality play names. (Example: Mr. Bumble = Stupidity) (1) Mr. Gradgrind (2) Holly Golightly (3) Jack Armstrong (4) Lady Sneerwell (5) Tess Truehart (6) Flem Snopes (7) Daddy Warbucks.

SPEAKING AND LISTENING

Performing in a Play

When you act in a play, you must fully understand your part as the playwright intends it. You must go beyond a mere reading of lines. What is the character's personality? What is his or her motivation?

Go to the library and borrow a recording of a play for which you can also borrow the text. Choose a scene and read it a few times. Then listen to the professional actor read it. Note the stress, the pauses, the emotion. Compare the professional performance with your own.

Next, select a passage from *Everyman* and read it until you understand its meaning and purpose completely. Rehearse it until you know how you want to say every word. If possible, practice it with a tape recorder. Be prepared to read the passage in class.

THINKING AND WRITING

Discussing a Morality Play

Write an essay in which you discuss the playwright's answer in *Everyman* to the morality play question about the conduct of life. Give your opinion of the play's effectiveness. Is the play dramatic? Persuasive? Would it be better if Everyman escaped Death? Explain.

Answers

ANSWERS TO THINKING ABOUT THE SELECTION

Recalling

1. Death is sent to bring Everyman to his reckoning.
2. He requests an extension.
3. (a) Good Deeds will follow him all the way. (b) Knowledge will follow him to the grave but no farther.
4. No man can make up for his mistakes after death. There is no mercy or pity after death. If his reckoning is sound, he goes to Heaven; if not, Hell.

Interpreting

5. God's main complaint is that people have forsaken him, forgetting his sacrifice.
6. Death refuses because time waits for no man.
7. Material things are simply lent man during his lifetime.

Applying

8. Answers will differ. One possible answer is that *Everyman* is a continuing success because it deals with the universal question of death and the afterlife.

ANSWERS TO ANALYZING LITERATURE

1. Choices may differ. Here are two possible answers: "For weet thou well the tide abideth no man,/ And in the world each living creature/ For Adam's sin must die of nature (lines 144–146, spoken by Death)." "All earthly things is but vanity./. . . All fleeth save Good Deeds . . . (lines 203–206, spoken by Good Deeds)."
2. The characters are Fellowship, Cousin, and Kindred. The Doctor may be considered a representative of theologians, or religious philosophere.

ANSWERS TO CRITICAL THINKING AND READING

Answers will differ. Some possibilities are Pedantary, Amorousness, Courage or Strength, Snobbery, Loyalty or Faithfulness, Laziness, and Wealth or Greed.

SPEAKING AND LISTENING

You might consider placing students in groups and giving each group a section of the play. Have them present their portion of the play to the class in a dramatic reading or as a reader's-theater presentation.

THINKING AND WRITING

For help with this assignment, students can refer to Lesson 14, "Writing About Drama," in the Handbook of Writing About Literature.

Publishing Student Writing In writing groups have the students read one another's essays. After all essays have been read, the students should reach a consensus about the effectiveness of the play. By reading excerpts from the group's papers, students can present to the class the decision of the group and the reasons. Establish the consensus of the class.

The writing assignments on page 150 have students write creatively, while those on page 151 have them think about the selections and write critically.

YOU THE WRITER *Guidelines for Evaluating Assignment 1*

1. Has the student imitated a medieval ballad or narrative, emulating the style and form of the model?
2. Has the student created a "medieval" plot, characters, and setting?
3. Is the story written in a clear, interesting, well-organized manner?
4. Could the imitation almost pass for an authentic medieval ballad or narrative?
5. Is the imitation free from grammar, usage, and mechanics errors?

Guidelines for Evaluating Assignment 2

1. Does the monologue present the thoughts about life of a character from medieval literature?
2. Are there sufficient references and details in the monologue to convey the speaker's ideas and create the impression that a medieval character is speaking?
3. Has the student made the monologue sound authentic by modeling it after the selections in the unit?
4. Is the monologue well-organized and consistent in style?
5. Is the monologue free from grammar, usage, and mechanics errors?

Guidelines for Evaluating Assignment 3

1. Has the student established a viewpoint for his or her letter about an episode from medieval literature?
2. Has the student based his or her style on the selections in this unit in order to create a medieval flavor?
3. Apart from the style, is the letter a conventional personal letter?
4. Are the details vividly expressed?
5. Is the letter free from grammar, usage, and mechanics errors?

YOU THE WRITER

Assignment

1. Many English poets have written imitations of medieval ballads and narratives. Write your own imitation of a poem in this unit. Make your poem medieval in content as well as in form and style.

Prewriting. First think of the "medieval" plot, characters, and setting you will use in your poem. Prepare a map outlining these features. Then examine your model for the structure, verse form, and other literary aspects you will imitate.

Writing. When you write your first draft, concentrate on getting the story down on paper in a clear, interesting, well-organized way. Write in verse, but do not try to refine the poetry yet.

Revising. You may now concentrate on emulating the style and form of your model. Work on your poem until it could almost pass for an authentic medieval ballad or narrative. Read it aloud. How would it sound if it were accompanied by a musical instrument?

Assignment

2. Write a monologue in prose or verse in which one of the characters you have encountered in medieval literature presents his or her thoughts about the kind of life he or she has led or about life in general.

Prewriting. First select your character. Then decide what main idea or ideas your character will express. Then think of the references to medieval experience your character will use to illustrate and support these ideas.

Writing. Try to make your monologue sound authentically medieval by modeling it on the selections you have read in this unit. Make sure your narrator's personality shines clearly through his or her words.

Revising. Try to improve the details of the monologue so they both aptly convey the speaker's ideas and create the impression that a medieval character is speaking. Finally, make any improvements you can in the organization and style of the monologue.

Assignment

3. Imagine that you are a medieval man or woman who has witnessed any episode presented in the selections of this unit. Write a letter to a friend or relative in which you tell what you witnessed.

Prewriting. First establish your viewpoint: Where were you in relation to the characters and events? What exactly did you observe?

Writing. Try to think of yourself as a medieval person as you write your letter. Base your style of writing on the selections in this unit. Apart from the style, your letter should be a conventional personal letter.

Revising. Can you in any way express more vividly the details of what you witnessed? Can you give the letter a more medieval flavor? Revise in the light of these questions.

YOU THE CRITIC

Assignment

1. The literature of past societies provides clues to what life might have been like for the ordinary person. Write an essay in which you present your impressions of medieval life based on the selections in this unit.

Prewriting. Ask yourself, "Judging by the literature I have read, how would I have felt living in medieval England? What would have been the troubles and the advantages of living in those days?"

Writing. Your essay should basically answer the preceding questions. Be sure you refer to the clues you found in the selections you read.

Revising. First check that your essay is faithful to your sense of how you would have responded to life in the Middle Ages. Then revise it for organization, style, and grammatical correctness.

Assignment

2. The literature of the past sometimes presents ideas, values, or customs that would be useful to life today. Write an essay in which you explain how one such medieval idea, value, or custom would enhance present-day life.

Prewriting. First decide what the details of the literature you have read reveal about life and how they illustrate the quality about which you are concerned. Then list your reasons for wanting to see this quality revived or maintained today.

Writing. Write an essay that first describes the idea, value, or custom; then illustrates it by reference to literature; and finally argues for its relevance to the present.

Revising. Make sure the organization of your essay allows for adequate treatment of the description, illustration, and argumentation mentioned above. Check for lapses in style and usage.

Assignment

3. Choose the selection from medieval literature that you liked best, and write an essay in which you explain why you consider it superior to other selections in the unit.

Prewriting. First choose one or two other works of medieval literature with which you can appropriately compare the selection you have chosen. Then list your reasons for preferring it to the others.

Writing. Write an essay based on your prewriting work. Illustrate and support your reasons by apt references to the literature. Aim to make your reader see the excellence you perceive in the work of your choice.

Revising. Concentrate on making your evaluation fair and balanced. Tone down any excessive claims for the preferred work or against the others. Finally, look for and correct any errors in grammar or lapses in style.

YOU THE CRITIC
Guidelines for Evaluating Assignment 1

1. Has the student written an essay that explains how he or she would have felt living in medieval England and identified the troubles and advantages of living at that time?
2. Does the student use examples from the literature to support his or her points about life in the Middle Ages?
3. Is the essay well-organized and consistent in style?
4. Is the essay free from grammar, usage, and mechanics errors?

Guidelines for Evaluating Assignment 2

1. Does the essay begin with a description of the medieval idea, value, or custom the student feels would be useful today?
2. Does the student illustrate his or her point by references to medieval literature?
3. Does the student effectively argue for the relevance of the value, idea, or custom to the present?
4. Is the essay well-organized and free from grammar, usage, and mechanics errors?

Guidelines for Evaluating Assignment 3

1. Does the essay explain why the chosen selection of medieval literature is superior to others?
2. Does the student illustrate and support his or her thesis by references to the literature?
3. Is the evaluation fair and balanced while showing the excellence of the student's choice?
4. Is the essay free from grammar, usage, and mechanics errors?

Humanities Note

Fine art, *Queen Elizabeth and Sir Walter Raleigh,* by Charles Edouard Boutibonne. This picture, painted two centuries after Sir Walter Raleigh's death, is a fanciful depiction of Raleigh's presentation of booty from his exploits to Queen Elizabeth I. Raleigh was, with the exception of a period of disgrace that resulted from an injudicious marriage, a long-lasting favorite of the queen. A soldier, explorer, colonizer, courtier, poet, philosopher, and historian, he exemplified the ideal Renaissance man. His fortunes fell drastically, however, when James I ascended to the throne, for the newly-crowned king feared Raleigh was part of a conspiracy against him. Condemned to death in 1603, he was executed in 1616. Cool and composed to the end, he is reported to have commented on the sharpness of the executioner's axe, saying "This is a sharp medicine, but it is a physician for all diseases."

QUEEN ELIZABETH AND SIR WALTER RALEIGH
Charles Edouard Boutibonne
Three Lions

THE ENGLISH RENAISSANCE
1485–1625

This royal throne of kings, this sceptered isle,
This earth of majesty, this seat of Mars,
This other Eden, demi-paradise,
This fortress built by Nature for herself
Against infection and the hand of war,
This happy breed of men, this little world,
This precious stone set in the silver sea,
Which serves it in the office of a wall,
Or as a moat defensive to a house,
Against the envy of less happier lands,
This blessed plot, this earth, this realm, this England.

William Shakespeare

153

1 **Enrichment** Because the earliest books printed in England, including those by Chaucer and Malory, were written in the East Midland or London dialect, this particular regional speech became the standard.

The ending of the Wars of the Roses and the founding of the Tudor dynasty in 1485 opened a new era in English life. Monarchs assured stability by increasing their own power and undercutting the strength of the nobles. At the same time, they dramatically changed England's religious practices. They also helped to transform England from a small, insular nation into one of the world's great powers. In this way the English people gained a new pride and sense of nationhood, clearly reflected in the patriotic lines by William Shakespeare (1564–1616) on the previous page.

THE COMING OF THE RENAISSANCE

The Renaissance was a flowering of literary, artistic, and intellectual development that began in Italy in the fourteenth century. The movement was inspired by the arts and scholarship of ancient Greece and Rome, which were rediscovered during the Crusades. Classical learning lived again as new generations of scholars and artists explored and extended the achievements of the ancients. Among the key characteristics of the Renaissance were:

- The religious devotion of the Middle Ages, with its emphasis on the afterlife, gave way to a new interest in the human being's place here on earth.
- Universities introduced a new curriculum called the humanities, which included history, geography, poetry, and modern languages.
- The invention of printing from movable type made books available to more people than ever before. A German printer, Johann Gutenberg, published a Bible in the 1450's that is believed to be the first book printed in the new manner.
- While scholars used Greek and Latin to study the ancients and students learned those languages in school, more and more writers began working in the vernacular—the local language. In
1 England, the English language shed some of its regional differences and became increasingly standardized.

The Slow Spread of Renaissance Ideas

The Renaissance did not jump the Channel into England until the final two decades of the fifteenth century. At that time, Renaissance ideas had already been spreading across the European continent for more than a century. Because the Renaissance began in Italy, many of the leading Renaissance figures were Italian. Among them were the poet Dante Alighieri (1265–1321), author of *The Divine Comedy;* Francesco Petrarca, known as Petrarch (1304–1374), who wrote lyric poetry in a new fourteen-line form called the sonnet; and the painter, sculptor, architect, engineer, and scientist Leonardo da Vinci (1452–1519). Because of the scope of his interests and talents, Da Vinci typifies what we call the Renaissance man—a person of broad education and interests whose curiosity knew no bounds.

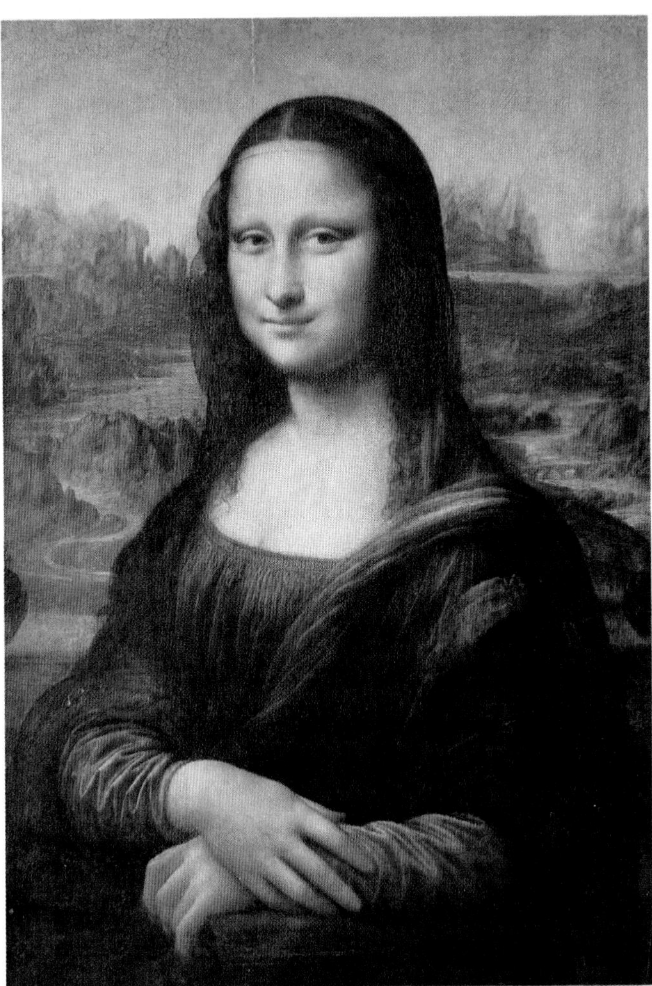

MONA LISA
Leonardo Da Vinci
Three Lions

The Age of Exploration

The Renaissance thirst for knowledge had many practical consequences, one of which was a great burst of exploration. The Crusades had opened routes to Asia, but the merchants of the Italian city-states quickly monopolized trade over the new routes by sea and land. Seeking their own path to the riches of Asia, navigators representing Portugal and Spain began seeking an all-sea route. Aided by the development of the compass and by advances in astronomy, which freed them from the need to cling closely to the ocean's shores, these navigators ventured far and

Humanities Note

Fine art, *Mona Lisa,* by Leonardo da Vinci. Born in 1452 in the town of Vinci, Leonardo was an engineer, inventor, and artist. The most famous of his portraits, *Mona Lisa* amazed the artist's contemporaries with its delicate use of light and shadow. Famous not only for the subtlety of its technique, the portrait has also fascinated viewers who are intrigued by the mysterious psychology of the sitter. Why is this smiling face so compelling? The smile not only echoes a mood but also suggests a timeless, symbolic expression. Her face embodies the quality of maternal tenderness that is Leonardo's essence of womanhood. Even the rocky landscape in the background suggests elementary generative forces. The *Mona Lisa* serves as a superb example of the artist's goal in painting: to depict the "intention of man's soul."

BRITISH EVENTS

c. 1500	*Everyman* first performed.
1512	First masque performed.
1516	Thomas More publishes *Utopia*.
1520	Bowling becomes popular in London.
1534	Henry VIII issues Act of Supremacy.
	Nicholas Udall writes *Ralph Roister Doister*, first English comedy.
	Church of England established.
1535	Thomas More executed.
1541	John Knox leads Calvinist reformation in Scotland.
1547	Henry VIII dies.
1549	Book of Common Prayer issued.
1558	Elizabeth I becomes queen.
1560	Thomas Tallis publishes English cathedral music.
1563	Over 20,000 Londoners die in plague.
1576	Francis Drake returns from circumnavigating the globe.
c. 1582	**Sir Philip Sidney** writes *Astrophel and Stella*.
c. 1586	**Christopher Marlowe** writes *Tamburlaine the Great*.
1587	Mary, Queen of Scots executed.
	Christopher Marlowe completes *The Tragical History of Doctor Faustus*.
1588	English navy defeats Spanish Armada.

Sir Thomas More with His Family

Queen Elizabeth I

The Last Supper

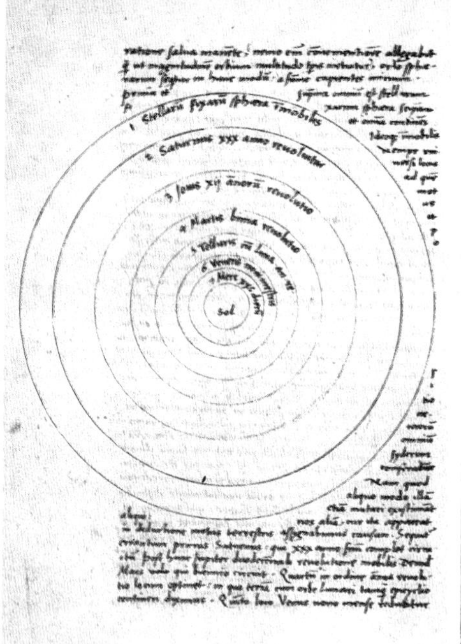
Copernicus's Treatise of Astronomy

Columbus Sets Sail from Spain

English Navy Attacking Spanish Armada

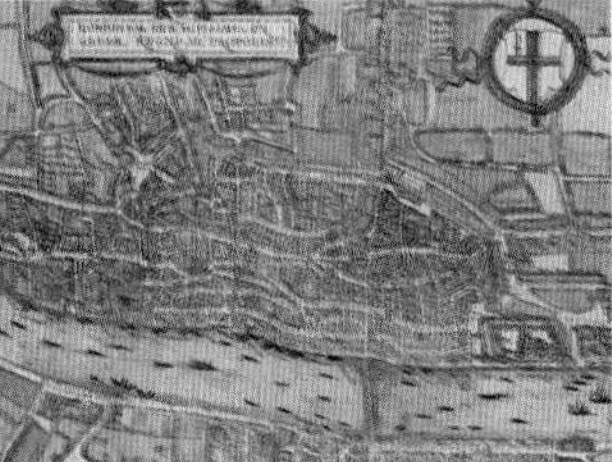
London c. 1558

Francisco Pizarro

WORLD EVENTS

1490 Italy: Ballet introduced.

1492 Columbus lands in New World.

1495 Italy: Leonardo da Vinci paints *The Last Supper*.

1497 North America: John Cabot explores northeastern coast.

Africa: Vasco da Gama rounds Cape of Good Hope.

1500 Italy: Michelangelo sculpts *David*.

1503 Italy: Leonardo da Vinci paints *Mona Lisa*.

1506 Italy: Construction on St. Peter's Cathedral begins.

1509 Italy: Michelangelo paints ceiling of Sistine Chapel.

1510 Japan: Ports opened to European ships.

1513 North America: Ponce de Leon explores Florida.

Balboa sights Pacific Ocean.

1518 Africa: Algiers and Tunisia founded.

1519-1522 Magellan sails around the world.

1520 Spain: Chocolate first introduced to Europe.

1521 Mexico: Cortez conquers Aztecs.

Italy: Pope Leo X excommunicates Martin Luther.

1530 Poland: Copernicus completes treatise on astronomy.

1532 Peru: Pizarro conquers Incas.

France: Rabelais publishes *Gargantua and Pantagruel*, Book I.

BRITISH EVENTS

1590 **Edmund Spenser** publishes *The Faerie Queene*, Part I.

1594 **Shakespeare** composes *Romeo and Juliet*.

1595 **Shakespeare's** *A Midsummer Night's Dream* first performed.

1599 Globe Theatre opens.

1600 East India Company founded.

1602 Bodeleian Library opens at Oxford.

1603 Elizabeth I dies; James I becomes king.

1605 Guy Fawkes executed for Gunpowder Plot.

Shakespeare's *Macbeth* first performed.

1606 **Ben Jonson** publishes *Volpone*.

1609 **Shakespeare's** *Sonnets* published.

1611 King James Bible published.

1616 *Collected Works of Ben Jonson* published.

1620 **Francis Bacon** publishes *Novum Organum*.

1623 First patent laws passed.

1625 James I dies.

Globe Theatre

Galileo

Cervantes

The Pilgrims Land at Plymouth Rock

William Shakespeare

The Wedding Dance

Abkar the Great

WORLD EVENTS

1534 Spain: St. Ignatius Loyola founds Jesuit brotherhood.

1554 Italy: Cellini completes bronze statue of Perseus.

1556 India: Akbar the Great comes to power.

1565 Malta: Knights of St. John fight off Turkish invasion.

1566 Belgium: Bruegel paints *The Wedding Dance*.

1567 South America: 2,000,000 Indians die of typhoid.

Brazil: Rio de Janeiro founded by Portuguese.

1580 France: Montaigne's *Essays* published.

1582 Italy: Pope Gregory XIII introduces new calendar.

1595 South America: Sir Walter Raleigh explores Orinoco River.

1605 Spain: Cervantes publishes Part I of *Don Quixote*.

1607 North America: British colony established at Jamestown.

1609 Italy: Galileo builds first telescope.

North America: French colony of Quebec established.

1618 Germany: Kepler proposes laws of planetary motion.

1620 North America: Pilgrims land at Plymouth Rock.

Humanities Note

Fine art, Portrait of Erasmus, by Hans Holbein. Holbein the Younger (1497–1543) grew up in Augsburg, a center for international commerce in southern Germany that was particularly responsive to Italy's Renaissance movements. At eighteen, he moved to Switzerland, where he became a leading artist of Basel. Most probably a gift for Thomas Moore, this portrait of Erasmus was painted soon after Holbein's move to Switzerland. A truly memorable picture of a Renaissance man, it is an intimate yet monumental photographic likeness of the great doctor of humane letters. The portrait conveys his philosophical turn of mind as well as his intellectual authority. When Holbein traveled to England to avoid the turmoil of the Protestant Reformation in Basel, Erasmus recommended him to Thomas Moore. Moore responded to Erasmus' recommendation in a letter that stated, "Your friend is a wonderful artist."

2 **Master Teacher Note** To review this concept of clerical abuse, you might remind students of the Pardoner from the Prologue to Chaucer's *Canterbury Tales,* (page 91).

PORTRAIT OF ERASMUS
Hans Holbein
National Gallery, Parma
Scala New York/Florence

wide. Their explorations culminated in Columbus's discovery of the New World in 1492. Soon, European powers were establishing colonies in the Americas and extracting great wealth from the new lands.

England's participation in this Age of Exploration began in 1497, when the Italian-born explorer John Cabot, sailing for an English company, reached Newfoundland (an island off the east coast of what is now Canada) and perhaps also the mainland. Cabot thus laid the basis for future English claims in North America. However, English leaders would not exploit those claims until near the end of the English Renaissance.

The Protestant Reformation

Hand in hand with commercial expansion came a growing sense of nationalism, which, along with the new Renaissance spirit, led many Europeans to question the universal authority of the Roman Catholic Church. Many people had grievances against the church. Some objected to the sale of indulgences—remissions of
2 punishment for sins, for which people made payments that often went straight into the pockets of corrupt church officials. Critics also objected to other forms of payment to the church, viewing them as a form of taxation. Other people argued that church leaders played favorites by supporting Mediterranean powers against more northerly countries. Still others—scholars who were influenced by the growth of independent thinking in the universities—questioned church teachings and the church hierarchy.

One critical scholar was the great Dutch thinker Desiderius Erasmus (1466–1536), whose edition of the New Testament raised serious questions about standard church interpretations of the Bible. Erasmus studied and taught in England. Through his friendship with such English writers as Thomas More (1478–1535), Erasmus focused attention on issues of morality and religion, which remained as central concerns of the English Renaissance, often overshadowing the artistic concerns that dominated the Italian Renaissance.

Although Erasmus himself remained a Roman Catholic, he helped to pave the way for a split in the Roman Church that began in 1517, when a German monk named Martin Luther (1483–1546) nailed a list of dissenting beliefs (his "ninety-five theses") to the door of a German church. Luther's protest was aimed only at reforming the Roman Catholic Church, but it ended by dividing that church and introducing a new form of Christian belief known as Protestantism. The process that Luther started has come to be called the Protestant Reformation.

Fueled by political discontent, the Protestant Reformation swept through much of Europe. It led to frequent wars between European nations whose rulers had opposing religious beliefs. Protestants and Catholics both suffered persecution, depending on where they happened to live and which religion their ruler supported. Protestants themselves divided, and in Germany the followers of Luther (called Lutherans) persecuted the followers of another Protestant reformer, John Calvin of Geneva. Calvin's ideas (called Calvinism) found a foothold in Switzerland, England, and Scotland, however, and helped bring about the establishment of the Puritan and Presbyterian sects.

ENGLAND UNDER THE TUDORS

The Tudor dynasty ruled England from 1485 to 1603. Looking back, we see this period as a time of stability and economic expansion. English wool growers were finding new markets abroad. English investors were forming trading companies to tap the riches of far-off places like India. London had grown into a metropolis of more than 180,000 people. However, those who lived in Tudor times often saw economic changes as a threat to the old familiar ways, and memories of the Wars of the Roses caused many people to fear new outbreaks of civil strife.

Henry VII and Henry VIII

The first Tudor monarch, Henry VII, inherited an England that had been depleted and exhausted by years of civil war. By the time he died in 1509, he had rebuilt the nation's treasury and established law and order. In doing so, he had restored the prestige of the monarchy and had set the stage for his successors.

Henry VII was succeeded by his handsome and athletic son,

MARTIN LUTHER FASTENING HIS 95 THESES ON THE DOOR OF ALL SAINTS CHURCH, WITTENBURG, GERMANY, ON 31 OCTOBER, 1517
19th-Century Engraving
The Granger Collection

Humanities Note

Fine art, Martin Luther fastening his 95 Theses on the door of All Saints Church, Wittenburg, Germany, on 31 October, 1517. Outraged by Johann Tetzel's selling of indulgences, Martin Luther posted 95 theses, or questions for debate, on the door of the Wittenburg castle church, as this engraving shows. There is a certain irony in this piece of art because the Reformation initiated violent feelings against religious images, and many works of art were destroyed. Luther himself disapproved of the destruction and, condemning only their idolatrous use, stated that pictures were neither good nor bad; only people's misuse of the art made it evil.

Humanities Note

Fine art, *King Henry VIII of England,* by Hans Holbein. In 1526, Hans Holbein the Younger (1497–1543) left Basel, Switzerland for England where he hoped to receive commissions from Henry VIII. He was successful in receiving commissions from not only the king but also influential members of the court. This portrait of Henry VIII is among Holbein's most famous. The portrait shows the king, grown gross with self-indulgence. The artist painted Henry in rigid frontality conveying the authority of an absolute ruler. The immobile pose suggests an air of unapproachability while the display of precisely rendered jewels and gold embroidery creates the overwhelming sensation of Henry VIII's ruthless, commanding presence.

3 **Historical Context** Henry's oldest son, Arthur, who predeceased his father, had been the first husband of Catherine of Aragon. It was on the basis of this former marriage that Henry sought his annulment.

4 **Enrichment** Robert Bolt's play *A Man for All Seasons* (Random House, 1966) presents a beautifully written and highly sympathetic picture of More.

5 **Historical Context** Edward's devout Protestantism was more the product of his Seymour relatives' influence than that of his father's; doctrinally, Henry remained Catholic all his life.

6 **Historical Context** In order to prevent the Catholic Mary from succeeding to power upon Edward's death, his advisor Northumberland put Lady Jane Grey, Edward's first cousin, on the throne after marrying her to his son. The reign lasted nine days and ended with execution in the Tower.

KING HENRY VIII OF ENGLAND
Hans Holbein
The Granger Collection

Henry VIII. Like his father, Henry VIII was a practicing Catholic. He even wrote a book against Luther, for which a grateful pope granted him the title "Defender of the Faith."

Henry VIII's relationship with the pope did not last, however. Because his marriage with Catherine of Aragon had not produced a son, Henry tried to obtain an annulment from the pope so that he could marry Anne Boleyn. When the pope refused, Henry remarried anyway. This defiance of papal authority led to an open break with the Roman Catholic Church. Under the Act of Supremacy (1534), 3
the king assumed full control of the church in England and severed all ties with Rome. Henry became supreme head of the new Church of England (or Anglican Church). He seized the Catholic Church's English property and dissolved the powerful monasteries, selling some of their lands to benefit the royal treasury and granting the rest as gifts to loyal friends.

Although the Protestant Reformation was not directly responsible for Henry's break with Rome, it helped to pave the way. Many people in England had resented Roman dominance, and the break helped to stir new feelings of national pride. Henry used ruthless measures to suppress opposition among monks, friars, and a few others. He even had his former friend and leading advisor, Thomas More, executed, because More had refused to renounce his faith.

Henry married six times in all. His first two marriages produced 4
two daughters, Mary and Elizabeth. His third wife, Jane Seymour, bore a son, Edward, who was but a frail child when Henry died in 1547.

Edward VI and Mary I

Henry VIII's son, Edward VI, became king at the age of nine and died at the age of fifteen. During his brief reign, a series of parliamentary acts were instituted that dramatically changed the nation's religious practices. English replaced Latin in church ritual, 5
and the Anglican prayer book, or *Book of Common Prayer,* became required in public worship. By Edward's death in 1553, England was well on its way to becoming a Protestant nation.

Roman Catholicism made a turbulent comeback, however, when Edward's half-sister, Mary, took the throne. Mary I was herself 6
Catholic, and she restored Roman practices to the Church of England. She also restored the authority of the pope over the English church and insisted on marrying her Spanish cousin, Philip II, thus seeming to make England a minor appendage to the powerful Spanish state. In a time of growing national feeling, many people found these acts extremely unpatriotic. People were also disturbed by Mary's violent repression of Protestants. Ordering the execution of some 200 Protestants, she earned the nickname Bloody Mary and strengthened anti-Catholic sentiment within England.

Elizabeth I

When Mary I died after a five-year reign, her half-sister, Elizabeth I, came to the throne. She would be the last of the Tudors, dying unmarried and childless, after a long and successful reign.

Strong and clever, Elizabeth was probably England's ablest monarch since William the Conqueror. She received a Renaissance education and read widely in the Greek and Latin classics. She became a great patron of the arts, gathering around her a flock of courtiers that included most of the best writers of her day. Many of the era's greatest literary works bear a dedication to the queen, and the word *Elizabethan* has come to signify the English Renaissance at its height.

Elizabeth also put an end to the religious turmoil that had existed during Mary I's reign. She reestablished the monarch's supremacy in the Church of England and restored the *Book of Common Prayer,* and she instituted a policy of religious moderation that enjoyed great popular support, although it failed to please many devout Catholics and Protestants.

Often working with England's Catholic factions were France and Spain, Europe's strongest powers at the start of Elizabeth's reign. Both nations sought to dominate England, but each was anxious that the other should not. Elizabeth and her counselors adroitly played one side against the other, dangling offers of marriage to the queen as bait. Elizabeth's clever maneuvering of French and Spanish royalty allowed England a period of peace during which commercial and maritime interests prospered.

If Elizabeth had one outstanding problem, it was her Catholic cousin Mary Stuart, queen of Scotland by birth and (as great-granddaughter of Henry VII) next in line for the throne of England. Because Catholics did not recognize Henry VIII's marriage to Elizabeth's mother, Anne Boleyn, they considered Mary Stuart the queen of England. As a prisoner in England for nineteen years, Mary became the center of numerous Catholic plots against Elizabeth. While punishing the plotters, Elizabeth let her royal cousin live. Finally, however, a court convicted Mary of plotting to murder Elizabeth, and Parliament insisted on Mary's execution. Mary went to the block in 1587, a Catholic martyr. Her famous motto, "In my end is my beginning," took on new meaning when her death led Catholic Spain to declare war on England.

Defeat of the Spanish Armada

The quarrels between Spain and England went beyond the execution of Mary. Spain rejected most English claims to territory in the Americas and resented the fact that English adventurers, known as privateers, had been attacking and plundering Spanish ships. In theory, privateers like John Hawkins and Francis Drake operated on their own, but in reality they acted on the authority of Queen Elizabeth.

QUEEN ELIZABETH I OF ENGLAND c. 1588
by or after George Gower
The Granger Collection

Humanities Note

Fine art, *Queen Elizabeth I of England,* by George Gower. During the English Renaissance, art, unlike music, literature, and drama, was little appreciated. Sixteenth century English art suffered from the lack of enlightened court patronage. The Tudor monarchs, Elizabeth I especially, were adverse to expenditures either on buildings or pictures; only portraits were valued. George Gower's portrait of Elizabeth captures her regal mein. Her richly decorated and jeweled clothing attests to her position. The interest in portraits can be explained by the Protestant and Puritan emphasis on individuality, an outcome of the Reformation.

Humanities Note

Fine art, *Queen Elizabeth I knighting Francis Drake.* This illustration, created centuries after Drake's circumnavigation of the globe, depicts his knighting as the first Englishman to accomplish that feat. Pictured is the Sir Francis Drake known in legend as a piratical hero and master navigator who was called Queen Elizabeth of England's "heaven-born navigator."

Humanities Note

Fine art, The launching of fireships against the Spanish Armada. As the Spanish Armada approached the southern coast of England, it encountered a bombardment by the English navy's long guns. The British guns inflicted serious casualties. The Spanish fled to Calais where the next night the English sent eight vessels armed with explosives as fireships into the crowded harbor. These sixteenth-century torpedoes caused heavy damage to the Armada, which was compounded by collisions during frantic maneuvers to escape the onslaught. This event in which the Spanish fleet was badly mauled is celebrated in this picture. The result of this victory was a natural upsurge in morale. The defeat of the Invincible Armada raised England to a first-class sea power; it ranks as one of the most decisive battles in history.

QUEEN ELIZABETH I KNIGHTING FRANCIS DRAKE ON BOARD THE *GOLDEN HIND* AT DEPTFORD, 4 APRIL, 1581
19th-Century Engraving
The Granger Collection

Spain's King Philip II, already infuriated by the sea pirates, considered Mary's execution the last straw. He prepared a Spanish fleet, or armada, of 130 warships and sent it to attack England. In an eight-day battle in the English Channel in 1588, English sailors outfought and outmaneuvered the Spanish fleet. The defeat of the Spanish armada marked the decline of Spain and the emergence of England as a great sea power.

STUARTS AND PURITANS

The English Renaissance continued after Elizabeth died in 1603, although a new dynasty—the Stuarts—came to the throne of England. Determined that the end of the Tudor line should not bring a dispute over the throne and a return of civil strife, Elizabeth named Scotland's King James VI as her successor. James's claim to England's throne rested on his descent from King Henry VII through his mother, Mary Stuart, Elizabeth's old antagonist. Unlike Mary, however, James was a Protestant.

THE LAUNCHING OF FIRESHIPS AGAINST THE SPANISH ARMADA
National Maritime Museum, Greenwich, England

The years of the new Stuart king (1603–25), who became England's James I, are sometimes described as the Jacobean era, from Jacobus, the Latin word for *James*. On the surface, the era seemed to be merely an extension of the Elizabethan age. Like his predecessor, James I was a strong supporter of the arts. He also took measures to further England's position as a world power, sponsoring the establishment of England's first successful American colony—Jamestown, Virginia.

During James's reign, however, a conflict began developing that would later erupt into war. Guided by the medieval idea of the "divine right of kings," James I often treated the Parliament with contempt. He and Parliament became involved in a power struggle, quarreling over taxes and foreign wars. James I also persecuted the Puritans, who were strongly represented in the House of Commons. Prompted by James's religious intolerance, a group of Puritans migrated to America, and established the Plymouth Colony in 1621.

ACHIEVEMENTS OF THE ENGLISH RENAISSANCE

The Elizabethan Age produced an explosion of cultural energy. English architects designed and constructed beautiful mansions. Composers turned out new hymns to fit the Anglican service and popularized the English madrigal, a love song sung without musical accompaniment, often by several harmonizing voices. Painters and sculptors were busy, too. While the Renaissance masters generally were not English, some—like the German artist Hans Holbein the Younger (1497?–1543), court painter to Henry VIII—did move to England. 7

Meanwhile, the Renaissance spurred the growth of English educational institutions. Instead of depending on tutors, wealthy families began sending their sons to public schools (that is, schools outside the home—they were actually what Americans call private secondary schools). At the same time, the universities at Oxford and Cambridge were improved and expanded.

Literature in Early Tudor Times

The years from 1485 to 1558 served as a prelude to the great age of Elizabethan literature. Many major writers, such as Thomas More, continued to work in Latin. More's *Utopia* (1516) is a powerful vision of a society free of medieval superstition and prejudice. More and more writers, however, were using the vernacular—English.

7 **Master Teacher Note** To make this colorful period even more pictorially vivid, you might show students some of Holbein's portraits, particularly those of the royal family.

Humanities Note

Fine art, *Sir Walter Raleigh,* by Nicholas Hilliard. Elizabethan genius ran to music and literature not toward the visual arts. In general, the demand for portraits, the only art form appreciated by the Elizabethans, was filled by foreign artists visiting England. One notable exception was Nicholas Hilliard (1547–1619). A goldsmith by training, he specialized in fine jewelry and miniature portraits on parchment. These were tiny keepsakes often worn by their owners as jewelry.

This portrait of Sir Walter Raleigh is such a miniature. It is noteworthy for the amount of detail, particularly in Raleigh's collar.

8 **Literary Movement** See Wyatt's sonnet "Whoso List to Hunt," page 171.

9 **Literary Movement** See Sonnets 31 and 39 from *Astrophel and Stella,* pages 176–178.

10 **Literary Movement** Spenser's sonnet sequence, the *Amoretti,* is represented by Sonnets 1, 26, and 75, pages 197–199.

11 **Literary Movement** See Shakespeare's sonnets, pages 204–212.

SIR WALTER RALEIGH
N. Hillard
Three Lions

The poet Thomas Wyatt (1503–42), who had traveled widely on the
continent, introduced the sonnet to England. Wyatt translated or 8
adapted many of the sonnets of the Italian Renaissance poet
Petrarch. A second early Tudor poet, Henry Howard, Earl of Surrey
(1517–47), experimented with the sonnet form and was the first to
use blank verse, the unrhymed ten-syllable lines that would later be
the tool of the great Elizabethan dramatists.

Elizabethan Poetry

During the lengthy reign of Elizabeth I, English literature came of age. Many of the most significant literary developments came in the area of poetry. Favoring lyric poetry, rather than the narrative poems favored by their medieval redecessors, the Elizabethan poets perfected the sonnet and began experimenting with other poetic forms.

One of the most popular literary forms during the Elizabethan
age was the sonnet cycle, a series of sonnets that fit loosely
together to form a story. The first of the great Elizabethan sonnet
cycles was *Astrophel and Stella* by Philip Sidney (1554–86). As a
member of a poetry club called Areopagus, Sidney also helped to 9
adapt classical verse forms to fit the English language.

Another major Elizabethan poet was Edmund Spenser (1552?
–99). Spenser wrote intricate verse filled with rich imagery. Although
Spenser wrote many fine sonnets, his most famous work, *The Faerie* 10
Queen, is an imaginative epic, or long heroic poem, dedicated to
Queen Elizabeth. Spenser wrote his epic in complex nine-line units,
now called Spenserian stanzas.

Christopher Marlowe (1564–93), a noted playwright, was also a gifted lyric poet. Marlowe helped popularize pastoral verse, which idealizes the rustic simplicity of rural life, in such poems as "The Passionate Shepherd to His Love."

Marlowe's poem inspired Sir Walter Raleigh (1552?–1618) to write a famous response, "The Nymph's Reply to the Shepherd." Poet, historian, courtier, soldier, and explorer, Raleigh was a typical Renaissance man whose adventurous life mirrored the restless spirit of his day.

Another brilliant lyric poet, the famous playwright William Shakespeare, brought the Elizabethan sonnet to new heights. In composing his sonnet cycle, Shakespeare varied the pattern and rhyme 11
schemes of the Petrarchan, or Italian, sonnet, employing a form now
known as the English, or Shakespearean, sonnet.

Elizabethan Drama

During the Elizabethan age, English drama also came into full bloom. Playwrights turned away from religious subjects and began writing more complex and sophisticated plays. Drawing upon the classical models of ancient Greece and Rome, writers reintroduced tragedies—plays in which disaster befalls a hero or heroine—and comedies—originally, plays in which a humorous situation leads to a happy resolution. Playwrights also began writing their plays in carefully crafted blank verse, using rich language, filled with vivid imagery.

Since Elizabethan dramas were almost entirely in verse, it is not surprising that many of the age's best poets were also its leading playwrights.
12 Christopher Marlowe became the first major Elizabethan dramatist in the 1580s, writing such plays as *Tamburlaine the Great* and *The Tragical History of Doctor Faustus*. Had Marlowe lived past the age of thirty, he might well have rivaled Shakespeare as England's greatest playwright.

Shakespeare began his involvement with the theater as an actor. By 1592 he was a popular playwright, his works even having been performed at Elizabeth's court. After the Globe Theater was built in 1599, many of Shakespeare's plays were performed there. Shakespeare wrote thirty-seven plays, among them many of the greatest plays of all time. He wrote nine tragedies, including *Romeo and Juliet, Hamlet,* and *Macbeth*; several comedies, including *A Merchant of Venice* and *A Midsummer Night's Dream*; several histories, including *Richard II, Richard III*, and *Henry V*; and a number of plays often classified as "romances" or "tragic comedies." Filled with powerful and beautiful language, his plays display his deep understanding of human nature and his compassion toward all types and classes of people. Because of their eloquent language and their depth and complexity, Shakespeare's plays
13 have retained their popularity for centuries. As the seventeenth-century writer Ben Jonson said of Shakespeare: "He was not of an age but for all time."

WILLIAM SHAKESPEARE
Artist Unknown
Three Lions

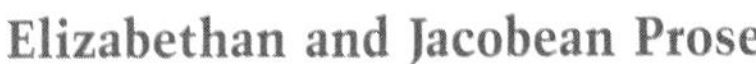

Elizabethan and Jacobean Prose

Prose took a back seat to poetry and drama in the English Renaissance. Scholars still preferred to write in Latin, and their English prose had a Latin flavor. Because they used long words and ornate sentences their work was often difficult to read.

Several Elizabethan poets contributed major works of prose however. Philip Sidney's *Defence of Poesie* (about 1582) is one of the earliest works of English literary criticism. Thomas Nashe's *Unfortunate Traveler* (1594), a fictional adventure, was a forerunner of the novel.
14 Another important work of prose, *History of the World* was written by Walter Raleigh during his years of confinement in the Tower of London (for allegedly plotting against James I).

Perhaps the leading prose writer of the English Renaissance was Francis Bacon, a high government official under James I. "I

Humanities Note

Fine art, *William Shakespeare.* Over the years, Shakespeare and his plays, like Queen Elizabeth, have inspired hundreds of drawings, paintings, engravings, and other works of art. This portrait of Shakespeare by an unknown artist would have been painted during his London years, when he became well known, even outside the theater world. Queen Elizabeth admitted to being "a great admirer of the immortal Shakespeare." Shakespeare's company, The Lord Chamberlain's Men, were often summoned to Elizabeth's court at Richmond, Greenwich, or Whitehall, to participate in the festivals of the seasons. Shakespeare himself included many flattering references to the queen which were graciously accepted by her.

12 **Literary Movement** An excerpt from *The Tragical History of Doctor Faustus* begins on page 185.

13 **Literary Movement** See "To the Memory of My Beloved Master, William Shakespeare," page 395.

14 **Historical Context** Raleigh was eventually executed by James I, an action that increased the King's unpopularity among his subjects.

Humanities Note

Title page of the first edition of the King James Bible, London, 1611. On July 22, 1604, after considering an initial proposal from Puritan elements, James I announced that he had "appointed certain learned men, to the number four and fifty, for translating the Bible." The first edition appeared from the press of Robert Barker, the king's printer, in 1611. Barker issued many copies; some with the title page reproduced here and others with a woodcut title page he had used for the earlier Bishop's Bible (1602) which introduces the new Testament in this the first Authorized Version. After the title page comes a fulsome dedication to James, a superb preface which defends the principles of vernacular Bibles, various tables including genealogies, and a map of Canaan. Chapters were illustrated with richly engraved borders and elaborate first letters reminiscent of the illuminated manuscripts of the Middle Ages. (See page 389 for a title page reminiscent of the illuminated manuscripts of the Middle Ages. (See page 389 for a title page from the New Testament.) The King James Bible was never officially authorized; nevertheless, because of its merit, majesty of language, and music of its rhythm, it became the most generally used version and a monument to the English language.

15 **Literary Movement** See the excerpt from *Novum Organum,* page 365.

16 **Literary Movement** See the selections from the King James Bible, pages 370–373.

TITLE PAGE OF THE FIRST EDITION OF THE KING JAMES *BIBLE*
London, 1611
The Granger Collection

have taken all knowledge to be my province," Bacon wrote, and his
literary output reflects his scholarship in many fields. His greatest
work, the *Novum Organum* (1620), written in Latin, made major
contributions to natural science and philosophy. Bacon is also 15
known for his formal essays—short prose works focusing on single
topics. His essays, including "Of Students" and "Of Ambition,"
highlight the rational detachment of his clever, inquiring mind.

The most monumental prose achievement of the entire English
Renaissance is undoubtedly the English translation of the Bible
commissioned by King James on the advice of Protestant clergymen. Fifty-four scholars labored for three years to bring this
magnificent work to fruition. The King James Bible, or Authorized 16
Version, is among the most widely quoted and influential works in
the English language.

The English Renaissance moved England out of its medieval past and into the modern world. No writers since have surpassed the literary achievements of Shakespeare or the majestic language of the King James Bible. These provide the standard against which all English literature has been judged right down to the present time.

ENGLISH VOICES

Quotations by Prominent Figures of the Period

They (in Utopia) wonder much to hear that gold, which in itself is so useless a thing, should be everywhere so much esteemed.

Sir Thomas More, *Utopia*

I know I have the body of a weak and feeble woman, but I have the heart and stomach of a king, and of a king of England too.

Elizabeth I, speech to the troops on the approach of the Armada

Was this the face that launched a thousand ships,
And burnt the topless towers of Iliumo?

Christopher Marlowe, *The Tragical History of Doctor Faustus*

Now is the winter of our discontent
Made glorious summer by this sun of York.

William Shakespeare, *Richard III*

The quality of mercy is not strained,
It droppeth as the gentle rain from heaven
Upon the place beneath: it is twice blessed;
It blesseth him that gives and him that takes. . . .

William Shakespeare, *The Merchant of Venice*

The fault, dear Brutus, is not in our stars,
But in ourselves, that we are underlings.

William Shakespeare, *Julius Caesar*

Something is rotten in the state of Denmark.

William Shakespeare, *Hamlet*

The world's mine oyster.

William Shakespeare, *The Merry Wives of Windsor*

Of one that loved not wisely but too well.

William Shakespeare, *Othello*

How sharper than a serpent's tooth it is
To have a thankless child!

William Shakespeare, *King Lear*

Reading Critically The information on this page is designed to help students read critically the literature of the English Renaissance. It is designed to help students place a literary work in its historical context, understand the literary movements of the time, and appreciate the writers' techniques used to convey the ideas of the period.

Discuss the information on this page with your students, and explain that the selection that accompanies this page, "Whoso List to Hunt," by Sir Thomas Wyatt, is a model for reading critically the literature of this period. It contains in the side column notes that draw attention to elements that reflect the historical context, the influence of literary movements, and the writer's techniques. Have students pay attention to these notes and suggest that they make their own critical comments as they read the selection.

To give students further practice with the process of reading critically, use the selection in the Teaching Portfolio, "Sonnet 61," by Michael Drayton page 000, following the Teacher Backup which students can annotate themselves. Encourage students to use these strategies as they read the literature in this unit.

READING CRITICALLY

The Literature of 1485–1625

Historical Context

During the years from 1485 to 1625, English life changed dramatically. The feudal system disappeared, and overseas commerce transformed England into a wealthy and powerful nation. The English navy became one of the world's strongest military forces, and through exploration and colonization Britain developed into a large, rapidly expanding empire. Religious life in England also underwent a major transformation during this period. Refusing to accept the Pope's decision not to allow him to divorce his wife, King Henry VIII severed the country's connection with the Roman Catholic Church and established the Church of England, appointing himself as the church's leader.

Literary Movements

It was during this period that English literature came into full bloom. A cultural movement known as the Renaissance swept through the European continent, eventually making its way into England. Responding to this movement, Queen Elizabeth I actively supported education, science, and the arts. Her support helped to generate a tremendous amount of literary activity. Influenced by the classical works of ancient Rome and Greece, writers explored new literary forms and created some of the finest works the country has ever produced.

Writers' Techniques

The most significant developments of the period came in the areas of poetry and drama. Turning away from the long narrative poems of the Middle Ages, poets introduced a new poetic form, the lyric, into English literature. Lyrics are short, tightly structured poems in which the speaker generally focuses on conveying his or her thoughts or feelings. Most often, during this period lyrics were written in sonnet form, and they frequently dealt with the subject of love. Sonnets were often written in sequences and were generally filled with energetic, musical language. Dramas during this period were also known for their beautiful language. Written in carefully crafted verse, these dramas delve into complex characters and themes, frequently offering important insights about human nature.

On the following pages is a selection by poet Sir Thomas Wyatt. The notes in the side column should help you to place the selection in its historical context.

Objectives

1 To understand the Petrarchan sonnet
2 To interpret figurative meaning
3 To read aloud a classic poem
4 To respond to criticism

Teaching Portfolio: Support Material

Teacher Backup, p. 000

Reading Actively, p. 00

Usage and Mechanics Worksheet, p. 00

Analyzing Literature Worksheet, p. 00

Critical Thinking and Reading Worksheet, p. 00

Language Worksheet, p. 00

MODEL

VIEW OF A PARK, WITH HUNTSMEN AND DEER
Peter Tillemans
Victoria & Albert Museum Trustees

Whoso List[1] to Hunt

Sir Thomas Wyatt

Whoso list to hunt, I know where is an hind,[2]
But as for me, alas, I may no more:
The vain travail hath wearied me so sore.

Writer's Technique: This poem is a Petrarchan sonnet with an *abbaabba cddcee* rhyme scheme.

1. **Whoso list:** Whoever wants.
2. **hind:** Doe.

Humanities Note

Fine art, *View of a Park, with Huntsmen and Deer* by Peter Tillemans. Tillemans (1684-1734), a Flemish-English sporting and topographical artist, came to England in 1708 to copy old masters for an art dealer in London. He remained there until his death. He is best known for his horse and racing "portraits" and for paintings of stately homes. He was one of the first English artists to incorporate sporting scenes with panoramic landscape painting.

The painting *View of a Park With Huntsmen and Deer* is a small watercolor. It is a neat and formal scene painted with a matter-of-fact perspective. The wealth of detail painted into such a small format speaks of Tillemans's skill as an artist. The huntsmen with their dogs, the tree studded park land, and the running and grazing deer contribute to a very lovely rendering of the English countryside of the time.

Consider using these questions for discussion:

1. Do you feel that the artist idealized this landscape?
2. Is this watercolor a straightforward rendering of what the artist saw or might it have a deeper meaning? Explain.

Motivation for Reading Have students imagine that they are among the first readers of this poem, that they are observing the sonnet for the first time. How might they react? Explain that the reading public of the period was small and well-educated and that it enjoyed allusions; many nursery rhymes, for example, contained allusions to royal and political figures.

Purpose-Setting Question How do you know that this sonnet is talking about more than hunting a deer—that it is alluding to Ann Boleyn?

Clarification Line 9 means "I'll put an end to any doubts he may have."

Clarification The "Caesar" referred to in line 13 is Henry VIII.

More About the Author This sonnet is an adaptation of one written by Petrarch—a further indication of his powerful influence on Wyatt. Wyatt's credit for introducing the sonnet to our language does much for his reputation. How might literary history have been affected if Wyatt did not introduce the sonnet to England in the sixteenth century?

Literary Movement: The deer represents a woman whom the speaker loves. During this period literature frequently explored the subject of love.
Writer's Technique: Wyatt uses lively, musical language.
Historical Context: The woman to whom Wyatt is referring is Anne Boleyn, who soon became King Henry VIII's second wife.

I am of them that farthest cometh behind;
Yet may I, by no means, my wearied mind
Draw from the deer, but as she fleeth afore,
Fainting I follow. I leave off therefore,
Since in a net I seek to hold the wind.
Who list her hunt, I put him out of doubt,
As well as I, may spend his time in vain.
And graven with diamonds in letters plain
There is written, her fair neck round about,
"*Noli me tangere*,[3] for Caesar's I am,[4]
And wild for to hold, though I seem tame."

---

3. *Noli me tangere*: "Don't touch me"; words spoken by the resurrected Jesus in John 20:17.
4. Caesar's I am: At the time in which the poem was written, it was believed that Caesar attached collars inscribed with the words "Do not touch me, for I am Caesar's" to his deer to protect them from hunters.

Sir Thomas Wyatt (1503?–1542) was a diplomat and courtier in the service of King Henry VIII as well as a poet. Born in Kent, Wyatt lived an eventful and sometimes dangerous life. In 1527 while on a government mission in Italy, he became deeply interested in the works of Petrarch, the great fourteenth-century Italian poet. Already a master of traditional English lyrics, Wyatt became, under Petrarch's influence, a skillful writer of sonnets and introduced this form into England.

Wyatt was born in Kent in the castle of his father, a member of Henry's Privy Council and an executor of his will. Following in his father's footsteps, young Thomas took his place in court as a page at Princess Mary's christening. He entered Cambridge University in 1516, and married Elizabeth Brook, the daughter of Lord Cobden, in 1520.

Wyatt's poetry has been praised for its vigor and drama but is sometimes criticized for its roughness of meter. He was fortunate to have found in Petrarch an excellent form—the sonnet—which gave artistic shape to the sincerity and depth of emotion he felt when writing about love. The sonnet "Whoso List to Hunt," illustrates both the virtues of his poetry and his debt to Petrarch. It also has a special biographical interest, for it is almost certainly about his relationship with Anne Boleyn, later the wife of Henry VIII.

Sir Thomas Wyatt was the first important poet of the English Renaissance. He introduced to England a poetic form used by numerous great poets, including Shakespeare, for nearly five centuries. He ushered in the first great age of English lyric poetry. Finally, he wrote a number of poems that have a permanent place in English literature.

THINKING ABOUT THE SELECTION

Recalling

1. On the literal level, what realization has the speaker come to?
2. Tell why you think his feelings are or are not in complete harmony with this realization.
3. What are his cautionary remarks to other hunters?

Interpreting

4. (a) If this poem on the figurative level is about the poet's love for Anne Boleyn, then what does hunting a hind represent? (b) Whom does Caesar stand for?
5. What special meaning does "Noli me tangere" have?

Applying

6. Wyatt lived and wrote four and a half centuries ago. Do the feelings in "Whoso List to Hunt" seem to be outdated? Tell why you think that this poem does or does not speak to people today.

ANALYZING LITERATURE

Understanding the Petrarchan Sonnet

A sonnet is a fourteen-line poem in iambic pentameter with a fixed rhyme scheme. In the **Petrarchan sonnet** you have just read, the rhyme scheme of the octave is *abbaabba;* that of the sestet is *cddcee.*

1. To what extent is the two-part structure of the sonnet reflected in the thought content?
2. The sonnet was originally used almost exclusively for love poetry. Is there something about the sonnet form that makes it more suitable for this subject than for others? Explain your answer.

CRITICAL THINKING AND READING

Interpreting the Figurative Meaning

A poet will sometimes write a poem that has both a literal and a **figurative meaning.** "Whoso List to Hunt" is such a poem. On the literal level it is about hunting a hind. On the figurative level it is about the speaker's frustrated love for a lady. In general, you should view a poem as having a figurative meaning only when there is either internal or external evidence for such a view. Internal evidence refers to the details of a poem that clearly suggest an intended meaning beyond the literal one. External evidence refers to knowledge about the poet's life, artistic beliefs, and so on, that likewise suggests a meaning beyond the literal.

1. What external evidence do you have for interpreting Wyatt's poem as an account of his love for Anne Boleyn?
2. What internal evidence indicates that the sonnet is a love poem?

SPEAKING AND LISTENING

Reading Aloud Classic British Poems

Reading aloud older British poems may be more difficult than reading more recent poems. In older poetry you will encounter more archaic, obsolete, and unfamiliar words. The sentence structure may be more complicated and twisted. Historical references may be obscure. Such difficulties impede reading.

Practice reading "Whoso List to Hunt" aloud.

THINKING AND WRITING

Responding to Criticism

A critic of Wyatt's, J. W. Lever, remarked in his book *The Elizabethan Love Sonnet* that "Wyatt's best love poetry was really out-of-love poetry." In a brief essay, show why you think that "Whoso List to Hunt" could or could not be used as evidence to support Lever's statement.

First go over the poem carefully looking for details that help you answer the question "Is this a love poem or an out-of-love poem?" Then decide on an effective order in which to present your analyses and conclusions. When you revise, be sure you have relied on what is actually in the poem and have not read anything into it. Assume that you are writing for people who enjoy reading intelligent, well-written literary criticism.

to be presented in the octave and the speaker's thoughts and feelings about the situation to be presented in the sestet. This makes the form especially well suited to love poetry, though it can be equally effective. for other subjects.

ANSWERS TO CRITICAL THINKING AND READING

1. It was rumored he was romantically involved with her. He was imprisoned with others when Anne's later infidelities were discovered.
2. The poem speaks of the pursuit of a single doe, but it makes no mention of weapons or the kill. "Her fair neck roundabout" hardly conjures the image of a deer; rather, it suggests interest in a woman.

SPEAKING AND LISTENING

Consider having students practice their readings in groups, where group members can give feedback and suggestions. Then have volunteers read aloud the sonnet to the class.

THINKING AND WRITING

Publishing Student Writing After students have written their essays, you might have them take sides: those who believe that this is an "out-of-love" poem and those who do not. Have several students from each side read their essays while you list on the board the major support for each side. Perhaps you might have an informal debate about the issue to see if one side can convince the other.

Answers

ANSWERS TO THINKING ABOUT THE SELECTION

Recalling

1. The speaker realizes that he is physically unable to continue the hunt.
2. His feelings are not in harmony with this realization because his mind continues the pursuit.
3. He remarks that all is hopeless. The hind is the property of another.

Interpreting

4. (a) Hunting a hind would represent his futile pursuit of Ann Boleyn. (b) Caesar would represent Henry VIII.
5. The Latin words imply "I am already spoken for."

Applying

6. Suggested Response: The poem remains widely read because it reflects a human condition that will continue to exist.

ANSWERS TO ANALYZING LITERATURE

1. In the first part of the sonnet, the speaker addresses his situation. In the second part he gives advice to others based on what he has learned.
2. The two-part structure of the sonnet allows for a romantic situation

More About the Author Sidney's Defence of Poesy was in part a response to Stephen Gosson's 1579 publication of The School of Abuse, a Puritanical attack on drama and poetry. It distills Classical and Renaissance literary-critical theory as it rebuts attacks and evaluates the writing of the period.

SIR PHILIP SIDNEY

1554–1586

Sir Philip Sidney wrote the first great sonnet sequence in English, *Astrophel and Stella.* Before Sidney, Sir Thomas Wyatt and the Earl of Surrey had written excellent sonnets, but Sidney was the first to write a series of sonnets linked by subject matter and theme. In addition, his *Defence of Poesy* marks the beginning of English literary criticism.

Sidney was born at Penshurst, the country home of his aristocratic family. After studying at Oxford and Cambridge he traveled extensively in Europe. Back in England he became a favorite at court, where his charm, intelligence, and good judgment were recognized and admired. In 1575 he made the acquaintance of Penelope Devereux, the daughter of Lord Essex. She was then thirteen. They became engaged, but the engagement was later broken off and Penelope became the wife of Lord Rich. She is the Stella of *Astrophel and Stella.*

In 1580 he fell out of favor with the court for writing a letter to Queen Elizabeth urging her not to marry the Duke of Anjou. He then retired to his sister's home, where he wrote part of *Arcadia,* a pastoral romance. Eventually he regained his status with the queen and was knighted in 1583. In 1586 during a military engagement against the Spanish Catholics in Holland, Sidney was wounded. As he lay on the ground, he refused the water offered him, insisting that it be given to another wounded soldier. Twenty-six days later Sidney died, to the great grief of his country.

During his life Sir Philip Sidney was widely revered as a courtier, soldier, scholar, and poet—a model gentleman of the English Renaissance. Today he is acknowledged as the first important literary critic in English. He is also recognized as the poet who inspired the sonnet sequences of later Renaissance poets and as the author of a number of eloquent sonnets that stand with the best poetry of this period.

Objectives

1 To understand a sonnet sequence
2 To write a letter of response

Teaching Portfolio: Support Materials

Teacher Backup, p. 000

Vocabulary Check, pp. 00

Usage and Mechanics Worksheet, p. 00

Analyzing Literature Worksheet, p. 00

Critical Thinking and Reading Worksheet, p. 00

Language Worksheet, p. 00

Selection Test, p. 000

GUIDE FOR READING

Sonnet 31; Sonnet 39

Literary Forms

The Sonnet Sequence. A sonnet sequence is a group of sonnets linked by theme or subject. The form was brought to perfection by the fourteenth-century Italian poet Petrarch, whose *Sonnets to Laura* directly or indirectly inspired the sequences of later poets.

Again and again certain conventions appear in sonnet sequences: The lady is golden-haired, with cheeks like roses or lilies. She is proud. She cruelly rebuffs her poet-lover. The lover is unfailingly faithful. He fears her scorn and rejection but hopes for her love. Hence he describes himself as alternately freezing and burning. He is like a ship tossed by the sea. He calls upon sleep to ease his cares. Through his poetry his lady will be given eternal fame.

The widespread reliance of English Renaissance poets on such conventions makes their poetry seem somewhat artificial. In real life, love is seldom as it is depicted in poetry that makes use of Petrarchan conventions. Nevertheless, the sonnet sequences were enormously popular in their day, and the best of them are still read today.

Look For

As you read the following sonnets from *Astrophel and Stella,* look for the conventions mentioned above. Do the sonnets seem too conventional and artificial? Do they contain real feelings? Remember that Stella is based on a real woman, Penelope Devereaux.

Writing

Do love stories of today (in books, films, and TV shows) make use of widely recurring conventional ideas about men, women, and the course of love? List as many as you can recall.

Vocabulary

Knowing the following words will help you as you read "Sonnet 31" and "Sonnet 39."

wan (wän) *adj.*: sickly pale (p. 176, l. 2)

languished (laŋ′gwisht) *v.*: made weak or sickly looking (p. 176, l. 7)

balm (bäm) *n.*: anything healing or soothing (p. 178, l. 2).

Literary Focus You might mention that the major Elizabethan poets and, to a lesser degree, John Donne were all at least indirectly indebted to earlier, Continental poets, such as Dante, Petrarch, Boccaccio, and Ronsard. The courtly, Petrarchan love literature of the Elizabethan age owes its themes, attitudes, and conventions to these earlier Italian and French authors.

Look For Make students aware that they are learning about writers who are changing the course of English poetry. They are introducing forms still in use 400 years later. As they read the sonnets, have them compare Sidney's work with Wyatt's. The differences are clear.

Teaching to Ability Levels Make *Astrophel and Stella* available to those wishing to read more or all of it. For **less advanced** students, suggest that linking sonnets together by subject matter might be like finding a noted popular music writer linking 20 or more of his songs—that each could be sung on its own, but if all were done in sequence in concert, let's say, there would emerge a larger story from them.

Writing Have students consider poem or story ideas that link together yet are able to stand alone.

Vocabulary Have students observe how much more contemporary is Sidney's use of the language than Wyatt's. English as we know it is dramatically changing during this period.

Motivation for Reading Compare these sonnets with Wyatt's regarding style, language, content. Wyatt is sometimes criticized for his rough meter. Are these smoother? Why?

Master Teacher Notes Point out that the entire sonnet is in the form of an apostrophe—a figure of speech in which a speaker addresses someone absent as if he or she were present or (as here) an inanimate object as if it could reply.

Purpose-Setting Question What evidence suggests a connection or link in the content of the two sonnets?

1 **Literary Focus** Apostrophe is employed throughout, as the poet addresses the moon. His purpose, however, is to express his feelings about his earthly love.

2 **Clarification** Cupid is the busy archer. Ask students to paraphrase lines 3-4.

3 **Discussion** What are long-with-love-acquainted eyes? Whose are they? What is a lover's case? For *case*, read "condition." How does the poet know the moon's feelings?

4 **Discussion** Having established in the octave, that he and the moon share similar feelings, the poet poses a lengthy question in the sestet. Have students paraphrase the question (Are women there as proud, contemptuous, and ungrateful as they are here? Is constancy there considered some form of idiocy?).

Sonnet 31

Sir Philip Sidney

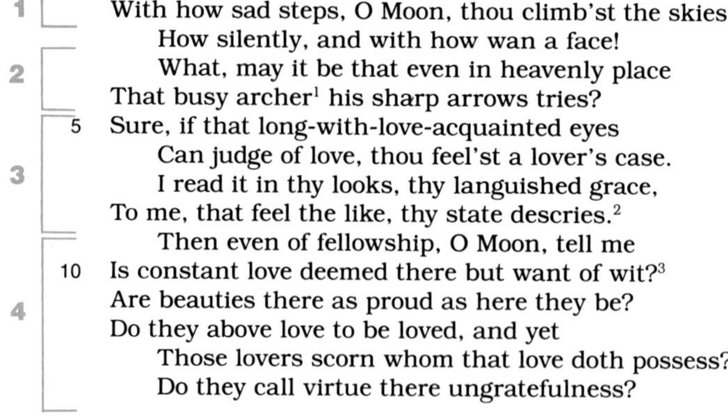

1 With how sad steps, O Moon, thou climb'st the skies!
How silently, and with how wan a face!
2 What, may it be that even in heavenly place
That busy archer[1] his sharp arrows tries?
Sure, if that long-with-love-acquainted eyes
3 Can judge of love, thou feel'st a lover's case.
I read it in thy looks, thy languished grace,
To me, that feel the like, thy state descries.[2]
Then even of fellowship, O Moon, tell me
Is constant love deemed there but want of wit?[3]
4 Are beauties there as proud as here they be?
Do they above love to be loved, and yet
Those lovers scorn whom that love doth possess?
Do they call virtue there ungratefulness?

1. busy archer: Cupid, the Roman god of love.
2. descries: Reveals.
3. wit: Intelligence.

THINKING ABOUT THE SELECTION

Recalling

1. What four lover's complaints are expressed in the sestet?
2. Describe the appearance of the moon.

Interpreting

3. What is the connection between the appearance of the moon and the thoughts the speaker utters?
4. Paraphrase lines 3–4 and lines 5–8.
5. Judging by what is said in the sonnet, what do you infer about the speaker's relationship with his lady?

Applying

6. How would you answer the speaker's question to the moon: "O Moon, tell me/Is constant love deemed there but want of wit"? How is constancy in love viewed in the modern world? Explain your answer.

SHEPHERDS UNDER A FULL MOON
Samuel Palmer
Ashmolean Museum, Oxford

Humanities Note

Fine art, *Shepherds Under a Full Moon* by Samuel Palmer. Samuel Palmer (1805–1881), a British painter, is best known for the small, intense landscapes he painted during a seven-year period in Shoreham, Kent. A self-taught artist, Palmer was influenced by the works and person of William Blake. He belonged to a group of artists called "The Ancients," who worked with the sincerity and purity of artists in the Middle Ages. His landscapes combined direct approach and deep color with poetic vision and pantheistic joy.

Shepherds Under a Full Moon was painted during the Shoreham years, 1826–1833. Moonlit landscape were a favorite subject of Samuel Palmer. He loved the magical transformation of shapes and forms by the cool gray light. The shepherds become ancient draped statues; the sheep become silvered forms carved from the dark, mysterious landscape. The dreamlike beauty of the scene and the mystical mood of the painting are qualities found in all the Shoreham paintings of Samuel Palmer.

You might use these questions for discussion:

1. Do the figures in the painting seem to be addressing questions to the moon as Sidney does in this sonnet?
2. How do you think the painter feels about the moon?
3. How does the painter's feelings compare with the poet's feelings about the moon?

Answers

ANSWERS TO THINKING ABOUT THE SELECTION

Recalling

1. Constancy is treated as a form of idiocy; beauties are too proud; they scorn those who love them; and they consider their own ingratitude a virtue.
2. It climbs into the sky silently with sad steps and wan face.

Interpreting

3. The moon looks to him the way he feels, prompting his questions.
4. Lines 3-4: "Tell me, does Cupid fire his arrows even in the heavenly place where you dwell?" Lines 5-8: "If one long acquainted with love is seeing right, your appearance and manner are those of one in love."
5. He hardly suggests a joyous romance.

Applying

6. "No, constant love is not considered stupidity." In general, people value and admire constancy in love.

Motivation for Reading Ask students if they have ever felt a strange desire for sleep not because they were physically tired but because they were oppressed by cares or worries. This poem is based on the idea that sleep may offer escape from life's unhappiness.

Master Teacher Note A number of structural and content similarities exist between Sonnet 31 and Sonnet 39. Look for and discuss them, beginning with the similar first lines.

Purpose-setting Question Why does the poet seek sleep?

Purpose-setting Question What helps and comforts does Sidney attribute to sleep?

1 **Discussion** How is sleep viewed by the poet? Is this a narrow view? The phrase "poor man's wealth" is a paradox, an apparent contradiction that in fact makes sense. What does this paradox mean?

2 **Discussion** The poet continues to struggle against despair. Tribute (line 8) here means some form of payment. What good tribute might the poet offer?

3 **Discussion** Challenge your students to paraphrase the sestet. To help them, point out that the poet offers to give sleep all the things that make for a sound rest.

Sonnet 39

Sir Philip Sidney

Come sleep, O sleep, the certain knot of peace,
1 The baiting place[1] of wit, the balm of woe,
The poor man's wealth, the prisoner's release,
The indifferent judge between the high and low;
With shield of proof[2] shield me from out the prease[3]
2 Of those fierce darts Despair at me doth throw:
O make in me those civil wars to cease;
I will good tribute pay, if thou do so.
Take thou of me smooth pillows, sweetest bed,
A chamber deaf to noise, and blind to light,
3 A rose garland, and a weary head:
And if these things, as being thine by right,
Move not thy heavy grace, thou shalt in me,
Livelier then elsewhere, Stella's image see.

---

1. **baiting place:** A place for refreshment.
2. **proof:** Proven strength.
3. **prease:** Crowd.

THINKING ABOUT THE SELECTION

Recalling

1. What six benefits does the speaker attribute to sleep in lines 1–4?

Interpreting

2. Literally, what are the fierce darts that Despair hurls (line 6)?
3. What might the metaphor "civil wars" (line 7) signify?
4. In what sense could sleep see Stella's image in the speaker?
5. Why is the speaker addressing sleep?

Applying

6. What psychological truth about people's desire for sleep is the basis for the speaker's calling upon sleep?

ANALYZING LITERATURE

Understanding a Sonnet Sequence

The names Astrophel and Stella mean "star-lover" and "star." Since it is known that Sidney's sequence of 108 sonnets plus 11 songs is based on his love for Penelope Devereux, we know that Astrophel represents Sidney and Stella represents Penelope. The 108 sonnets do not present a love story in narrative form. Rather, they offer reflections on the course of Astrophel's love. A reader, however, can detect the story that underlies the sequence.

Since *Astrophel and Stella* makes extensive use of the love-poem conventions present in Petrarch's *Sonnets to Laura,* the sequence seems to mix the artificial and the real, convention and sincerity. In the best of Sidney's poems, the Petrarchan conventions produce an effect of courtly grace and charm, while allowing the lover's real feelings to show through.

1. Do Sidney's two sonnets seem to you primarily sincere or primarily artificial? Give reasons for your opinion.
2. Why do you suppose a poet would decide to use an elaborate set of conventional ideas and images in love poetry, rather than write of love in a realistic way?

THINKING AND WRITING

Writing a Letter of Response

If Stella had received Sonnets 31 and 39 as a gift from Sidney, how might she have responded to them? What might she have said to him in a letter acknowledging that she had received and read the sonnets? Write the letter you think Stella might have written.

First reread the material in the Guide for Reading to review the way ladies were depicted in sonnet sequences. Then decide what Stella would have said in her letter. Assume that she "got the message" Sidney's poems contain. How would she have expressed her thanks for the poems? What might she have said about what the poems imply about her and her treatment of Astrophel? When you revise, make the style of your letter as suitable as you can to the courtly, Petrarchan love depicted in Sidney's sonnets.

Answers

ANSWERS TO THINKING ABOUT THE SELECTION

Recalling

1. The six benefits of sleep described in lines 1-4 are the following: it assures one of peace; it restores the keen mind; it heals sorrows; it is the poor man's wealth; it allows the prisoner to wander far and wide in his dreams; and it treats all people the same.

Interpreting

2. The fierce darts of despair felt by the poet are likely the pains brought on by his feelings for Stella.
3. The "civil wars" of line 7 suggest strong internal arguments, conflicting opinions, and indecision.
4. Sleep will see Stella's image when the poet dreams of her.
5. The poet addresses sleep because he longs for all of sleep's benefits, and he longs to dream of Stella.

Applying

6. Sleep is a form of escape for people. Also, in dreams people can escape to worlds and places where their lives will not take them.

ANSWERS TO ANALYZING LITERATURE

1. Students will take sides—that the poems seem artificial and that they show strong sincerity. That they are sincere is suggested by the convincing power of language employed by Sidney in each sonnet.
2. Discuss the fact that poetry, through the use of metaphorical language, intensifies feelings and images; that the conventions used by Petrarch proved themselves to be wonderfully inspiring in Italian. In following Petrarch's lead, Sidney was using conventions of form and meaning that his English readers would expect in love poetry and would respond to favorably.

More About the Author It has also been claimed that Marlowe was actually more of what we'd call a free thinker than an athiest in an age of orthodoxy. Shakespeare was to learn much about play construction from him. Marlowe's stunning use of blank verse established it as the dramatic form to follow.

CHRISTOPHER MARLOWE

1564–1593

Though not the first English poet to write in blank verse (unrhymed iambic pentameter), Christopher Marlowe's brilliant use of it in his plays established blank verse as the preeminent meter for verse drama and ultimately for epic poetry in English. Marlowe is the author of one of the world's immortal tragedies, *Dr. Faustus,* as well as several other notable plays and poems.

Born in Canterbury, Marlowe was the son of a shoemaker. He went to Cambridge University on a scholarship usually awarded to students studying for the ministry. However, he spent much of his time writing plays and serving as a government agent. He never took holy orders. He is, indeed, reputed to have been an atheist, or at least to have held highly unorthodox religious views.

While at Cambridge Marlowe wrote *Tamburlaine,* the play that made the public aware of his dazzling abilities. It dramatizes the exploits of a fourteenth-century Scythian shepherd who conquered much of the known world. As Marlowe portrays him, Tamburlaine personifies energy and ambition and is thus a character eminently suited for the dramatist's powerful blank verse. In the remaining six years of his life, Marlowe wrote five more plays, including *Dr. Faustus* and a sequel to *Tamburlaine*. On May 30, 1593, he was killed by a dagger thrust in a tavern. His death may have been the result of a fight over the bill, or it may have been a political assassination.

Marlowe's fame rests primarily on his plays, especially on his "mighty line," as Ben Jonson described his dramatic blank verse. *Dr. Faustus* has been a classic of dramatic literature for four hundred years. However, Marlowe's nondramatic poetry alone would be enough to secure him a permanent place in English literature. His *Hero and Leander* is one of the finest narrative poems ever written in English, and "The Passionate Shepherd to His Love" is one of the best-known and most popular lyrics of the English Renaissance.

Objectives

1. To appreciate lyric poetry
2. To infer cultural attitudes
3. To write an invitation in verse

Teaching Portfolio: Support Material

Teacher Backup, p. 000

Vocabulary Check, pp. 00

Analyzing Literature Worksheet, pp. 00

Critical Thinking and Reading Worksheet, pp. 00

Selection Test, pp. 00

GUIDE FOR READING

The Passionate Shepherd to His Love

Literary Forms

Pastoral Poetry. A lyric poem is a poem that expresses personal thoughts and feelings. As the word lyric suggests, such a poem may have some of the characteristics of a song. It is often brief and written in rhymed verse with a pronounced rhythm. Many lyric poems have, in fact, been set to music, such as the one you are about to read. Ballads, sonnets, odes, songs, and elegies are some of the more common types of lyric poetry.

"The Passionate Shepherd to His Love" is one of the most famous examples of pastoral poetry. A *pastoral poem* is a lyric that celebrates the beauty and pleasures of country life. As a tradition in English literature, pastoral poetry often makes use of a number of conventions. The speaker in a pastoral poem is frequently a shepherd. He either addresses or speaks about a shepherdess or other country maiden with whom he is in love. The world of nature is idealized. The goodness and happiness of a life in harmony with such a world are valued above all else. Pastoral poetry was especially popular during the English Renaissance, but the tradition extends from the classical era of Greece and Rome to the present.

Look For

As you read "The Passionate Shepherd to His Love," look for its lyrical and its pastoral qualities. How like a song is the poem? To what extent does the poem conform to the pastoral conventions described above?

Writing

Think of the most appealing country place you know. If you wanted to persuade a friend to visit the place, which features would you mention? List five or six and briefly describe them.

Vocabulary

Knowing the following words will help you as you read "The Passionate Shepherd to His Love."

dales (dālz) *n.*: Hollows, valleys (p. 182, l. 3)

madrigals (mad′ri gəlz) *n*: Songs with parts for several voices with no musical accompaniment (p. 182, l. 8)

posies (pō′ zēz) *n.*: Bouquets (p. 183, l. 10)

swains (swānz) *n.*: Country youths (p. 183, l. 25)

Literary Focus This was an era of singing. One was not educated without learning to sing and play an instrument. Lyric poems such as "The Passionate Shepherd to His Love" were often printed in songbooks before they were published elsewhere.

Look For Suggest that students read the poem to a tune in their minds. Suggest something with an old Christmas-carol quality to it, so they may savor its musical quality.

Writing Have students develop lists of words and phrases that create strong and appealing country images. Have students in class select the best of them to be used by all in a paragraph or other written piece.

Vocabulary If these few words are reviewed before reading the poem, students will have little difficulty comprehending the sense.

Motivation for Reading Read to your students some good examples of pastoral poetry from an anthology of Elizabethan poetry.

Master Teacher Note You might point out that pastoral lyrics such as Marlowe's represent a very old tradition in Western poetry. The classical Greek and Roman poets established the tradition, which poets today have not yet abandoned.

Thematic Idea This poem should be read in conjunction with Raleigh's "Nymph's Reply to the Shepherd."

Purpose-Setting Question Why do you think this pastoral lyric was one of the most famous of Elizabethan songs?

1 **Literary Focus** This flawless lyric gained great popularity in its own day and elicited many "replies." Have students note the four-beat line, which is much quicker than a sonnet's five-beat line.

2 **Discussion** The idyllic setting and descriptions ignore reality. Why might a love poem present an idealized version of nature?

Humanities Note

Fine art, *The Hireling Shepherd* by William Holman Hunt. William Holman Hunt (1827–1910) was a British painter. Educated at the Schools of the Royal Academy in London, Hunt rebelled against the stifling academic atmosphere and became one of the original founding members of the Pre-Raphaelite Brotherhood. The Pre-Raphaelites endeavored through their painting to return art to the pure simplicity and honesty of the early Christian painters before Raphael. In his paintings, William Holman Hunt combined realistic treatment with romantic themes from literature, history, and the Bible.

1 The Passionate Shepherd to His Love

Christopher Marlowe

2 Come live with me, and be my love,
And we will all the pleasures prove[1]
That hills and valleys, dales and fields,
And all the craggy mountains yields.

And we will sit upon the rocks,
Seeing the shepherds feed their flocks,
By shallow rivers, to whose falls
Melodious birds sings madrigals.

1. **prove:** Experience.

THE HIRELING SHEPHERD
William Holman Hunt
The Manchester City Art Galleries

The Hireling Shepherd was painted in 1853. Hunt's approach to the traditional romantic subject matter is original in composition. Painted with carefully detailed realism, the colors of the work are bright and fresh. Hunt approached each painting with passion and sincerity. He strove to exalt the viewer and to record nature faithfully.

You may wish to ask the following questions:

1. Does the shepherd in the painting appear to be sincere? Explain.
2. Is the shepherd in the poem sincere?
3. Does the woman in this painting appear to believe the promises the shepherd is making? Explain.

And I will make thee beds of roses,
And a thousand fragrant posies,
A cap of flowers and a kirtle[2]
Embroidered all with leaves of myrtle;

A gown made of the finest wool,
Which from our pretty lambs we pull;
Fair lined slippers for the cold,
With buckles of the purest gold;

A belt of straw and ivy buds,
With coral clasps and amber studs;
And if these pleasures may thee move,
Come live with me, and be my love.

Thy silver dishes for thy meat,
As precious as the gods do eat,
Shall on an ivory table be
Prepared each day for thee and me.

The shepherd swains shall dance and sing 3
For thy delight each May morning;
If these delights thy mind may move,
Then live with me, and be my love.

---

2. kirtle: Skirt.

THINKING ABOUT THE SELECTION

Recalling

1. Describe the kind of life the shepherd is offering his love.

Interpreting

2. How realistic is his representation of the kind of life he and his love will lead? Explain.

Applying

3. If a poet of today were to write a contemporary version of this poem, how might the details differ from Marlowe's?

ANALYZING LITERATURE

Appreciating Pastoral Poems

A **pastoral poem** idealizes the rustic life. Such poetry often contains an implied contrast between the good life of nature and the corrupt life of a court or city.

1. Read Marlowe's poem aloud. What qualities of it might inspire someone to set it to music?
2. Since a shepherd, not Marlowe, is the speaker, in what sense can the poem be said to express personal thoughts and feelings?
3. Would you infer from "The Passionate Shepherd to His Love" that Marlowe's Elizabethan readers valued the pastoral life because England was becoming more urbanized? Why or why not?

3 **Discussion** Have students notice that only the month of May is mentioned, not January or February. Why?

Master Teacher Note After students have read and discussed "The Passionate Shepherd to His Love," place Gainsborough's painting of Mrs. Sheridan on the overhead projector. Have your class compare the mood and overall effect of the painting with the mood and effect of the poem. What are the obvious differences? Are there any similarities? What might a viewer infer about Gainsborough's feelings about his subject?

Answers

ANSWERS TO THINKING ABOUT THE SELECTION

Recalling

1. The shepherd is offering his love a form of the good life, filled with pleasures, treasures, eternal spring, and continued happiness.

Interpreting

2. The offerings of the shepherd generate a limited picture. Real life simply isn't that way. The shepherd speaks of rosebuds and May, neglecting the rest of the year. He speaks of sitting about while others care for the sheep.

Applying

3. A contemporary version of this poem might give less stress to wearing apparel and more to the continued peace and quiet of this pastoral setting away from the loud and hurried world we live in today.

ANSWERS TO ANALYZING LITERATURE

1. The smooth, easy flow of the words call for it to be sung, which it was.
2. At expresses the personal thoughts and feelings of an imaginary character, the shepherd.
3. Life in the cities of the period left something to be desired, certainly. This is certainly escapist verse that implies Elizabethan awareness of the possible benefits of rural living.

Literary Focus The Broadway musical *Damned Yankees* is a modern popular example of the many variations on this fascinating theme. Gounod's opera *Faust,* first sung in 1859, is still regularly presented around the world today.

Look For Introduce the grasping-for-straws idea that dominates this powerful final scene of the play.

Writing Acknowledge the challenge, if not impossibility, for most of us of creating a written record of the emotions accompanying not only imminent death but also an awareness of eternity in Hell. This aside, ask students to write about how they would spend their last hour if they were Dr. Faustus.

Vocabulary Review the vocabulary words in the list before reading the selection

GUIDE FOR READING

from The Tragical History of the Life and Death of Doctor Faustus

Historical Context

The Faust Legend. The Faust legend is one of the most important legends of western civilization. Numerous writers have seen it as a profound revelation of the consequences of aspiring to rise above the ordinary human condition.

The legend derives from the life and activities of an actual German scholar and magician, Johann Faust (or Faustus), who lived from about 1480 to 1540. He traveled widely, performed magic, and died under mysterious circumstances. Many Germans of the time considered him a fraud, but Martin Luther, the founder of Protestantism, believed that he had Satanic powers. Even during Faust's life he was the subject of legends. According to many of them, he had sold his soul to the devil for youth, knowledge, and magical powers.

In 1587 a crude, unreliable biography of Faust appeared. The unknown author incorporated into it many legends of other magicians. The biography concludes with Faust going to hell at the end of his life. This volume appeared in an English translation titled *The History of the Damnable Life and Deserved Death of Doctor John Faustus.* It is the immediate source of Marlowe's play, which was probably written in 1588.

Look For

As you read the excerpt from *Dr. Faustus,* look for vivid expressions of the terror and despair of Faustus as he approaches eternal damnation in hell. What details are especially effective in conveying Faustus's emotions?

Writing

Create an imaginary experience you would anticipate with dread—for example, a test of some kind, a visit to a doctor or dentist, or a confrontation. What would be your thoughts and feelings as the time of the experience neared? Write a monologue that presents your thoughts as they pass through your mind. Try to write the monologue in a way that expresses your feelings without naming them.

Vocabulary

Knowing the following words will help you as you read from *The Tragical History of the Life and Death of Doctor Faustus.*

firmament (fʉr′mə mənt) *n.*: The sky, viewed poetically as a solid arch or vault (p. 185, l. 14)

nativity (nə tiv′ə tē′) *n.*: Birth, especially in regard to place and time (p. 185, l. 25)

incessant (in ses′'nt) *adj.*: aever ceasing (p. 186, l. 36)

engendered (in jen′dərd) *v.*: Brought into being (p. 186, l. 48)

Objectives

1 To understand the historical context of the legend

2 To make inferences about characters

Teaching Portfolio: Support Material

Teacher Backup, p. 000

Vocabulary Check, pp. 00

Usage and Mechanics Worksheet, pp. 00

Analyzing Literature Worksheet, pp. 00

Critical Thinking and Reading Worksheet, pp. 00

Selection Test, pp. 00

from # The Tragical History of the Life and Death of Doctor Faustus

Christopher Marlowe

Early in the play, Dr. Faustus, the main character, contracts his soul to the devil for special powers of the mind. Now, facing death, he makes a desperate attempt to repent and save his soul.

FAUST. Ah, Faustus,
1 Now hast thou but one bare hour to live
And then thou must be damned perpetually!
Stand still, you ever-moving spheres of heaven,
That time may cease and midnight never come;
Fair Nature's eye, rise, rise again, and make
2 Perpetual day; or let this hour be but
A year, a month, a week, a natural day,
That Faustus may repent and save his soul!
O lente lente currite noctis equi.[1]
The stars move still,[2] time runs, the clock will strike,
The devil will come, and Faustus must be damned.
O, I'll leap up to my God! Who pulls me down?
See, see, where Christ's blood streams in the firmament!
One drop would save my soul—half a drop! ah, my Christ!
Rend not my heart for naming of my Christ;
Yet will I call on him—O, spare me, Lucifer!
Where is it now? 'Tis gone; and see where God
3 Stretcheth out his arm and bends his ireful brows.
Mountains and hills, come, come and fall on me
And hide me from the heavy wrath of God,
No, no—
Then will I headlong run into the earth:
Earth, gape! O no, it will not harbor me.
You stars that reigned at my nativity,
Whose influence hath allotted death and hell,
Now draw up Faustus like a foggy mist

1. ***O lente . . . equi:*** "Slowly, slowly run, O horses of the night," adapted from a line in Ovid's *Amores.*
2. **still:** Always.

Motivation for Reading Clarify as vividly as you can the prospect before Faustus. Ask students to try to imagine the near-absolute terror he must feel.

Master Teacher Note With **more advanced** students, you might read the sermon on the eternal pains of hell in James Joyce's *A Portrait of the Artist as a Young Man.*

Thematic Idea Consider Dylan Thomas' poem "Do Not Go Gentle into That Good Night," on pp. 1120

Purpose-Setting Question How does absolute despair run through these lines?

1 **Discussion** The very idea of eternal perpetuity is startling to us, as everything we know of has a beginning and an end. How does perpetual damnation affect Faustus?

2 **Discussion** Have students observe Marlowe's images of time relentlessly pulling Faustus toward the final moment. Why is it a powerful emotional device?

3 **Discussion** What avenues does Faustus seek to avoid his confrontation?

4 **Discussion** Having failed to gain some way to avoid eternal Hell, what does he ask next?

5 **Discussion** But what does he conclude?

6 **Discussion** Note that he at least partially accepts the blame for what is about to happen.

Humanities Note

Woodcut, *Faust Conjuring Up the Devil*. The earliest form of type printing in Europe was the fifteenth-century block woodcut. Designs and letters were cut into wood, inked, and pressed onto paper. This wood block print is from the title page of the 1624 edition of *Doctor Faustus*. The primitively executed design was prepared by an unknown artist for a London printer. This scene of Dr. Faustus conjuring up the devil is one of the earliest European examples of printed book illustration.

Into the entrails of yon laboring cloud
That when you vomit forth into the air,
My limbs may issue from your smoky mouths,
So that my soul may but ascend to heaven.

[*The watch strikes.*]

Ah, half the hour is past; 'twill all be past anon.
O God,
If thou wilt not have mercy on my soul,
Yet for Christ's sake whose blood hath ransomed me
4 Impose some end to my incessant pain:
Let Faustus live in hell a thousand years,
A hundred thousand, and at last be saved!
5 O, no end is limited to damnèd souls!
Why wert thou not a creature wanting soul?
Or why is this immortal that thou hast?
Ah, Pythagoras' *metempsychosis*[3]—were that true,
This soul should fly from me, and I be changed
Unto some brutish beast. All beasts are happy,
For when they die
Their souls are soon dissolved in elements,
But mine must live still to be plagued in hell.
Cursed be the parents that engendered me!
No, Faustus, curse thyself, curse Lucifer
6 That hath deprived thee of the joys of heaven.

[*The clock strikes twelve.*]

3. metempsychosis: The supposed passing of the soul at death into another body; from the philosophy of Pythagoras, an ancient Greek philosopher and mathematician, who lived in the sixth century B.C.

FAUST CONJURING UP THE DEVIL (WOODCUT)
Artist Unknown
The Bettmann Archive

It strikes, it strikes! Now, body, turn to air
Or Lucifer will bear thee quick[4] to hell!

[*Thunder and lightning.*]

O soul, be changed to little water drops
And fall into the ocean, ne'er be found.
My God, my God, look not so fierce on me!

[*Enter* DEVILS.]

Adders and serpents, let me breathe awhile!
Ugly hell, gape not—come not, Lucifer—
I'll burn my books—ah, Mephistophilis!

[*Exit* DEVILS *with* FAUSTUS.]

---

4. quick: Alive.

THINKING ABOUT THE SELECTION

Recalling

1. What vain hopes and longings pass through Faustus's mind as midnight approaches?

Interpreting

2. Explain his exclamation "O, I'll leap up to my God! Who pulls me down? / See, see, where Christ's blood streams in the firmament!"
3. What does Faustus request of the stars in lines 25–31?
4. Paraphrase lines 40–46.
5. Analyze Marlowe's poetic technique in the excerpt. How does he convey Faustus's terror and despair?

Applying

6. Can you imagine another situation that would cause someone to feel terror and despair equal to Faustus's? Explain why you do or do not think that Faustus's terror and despair are unsurpassable.

ANALYZING LITERATURE

Understanding Historical Context

Marlowe's *Dr. Faustus* is the first great literary treatment of the Faust legend. In the centuries that have followed, a number of major writers have used the legend as the basis for literary works. The greatest of these is Goethe's poetic drama *Faust*.

The importance of the Faust legend is that it embodies what some thinkers see as an enduring impulse in western civilization from the Renaissance to the present: the drive to go beyond ordinary bounds of knowledge and power, even at the cost of one's own soul.

1. What impression do you get of Faustus's character and personality from his speech?
2. What moral values and attitudes does the speech implicitly uphold?
3. Name one character from history who could be termed "Faustian." Explain the similarity between this character and Faust.
4. Explain why the quest for knowledge would be an appropriate theme during the English Renaissance.

7 **Discussion** Even as the clock strikes, how does Faustus continue to react? What dramatic effect does this have?

Answers

ANSWERS TO THINKING ABOUT THE SELECTION

Recalling

1. He asks that time cease and midnight never come, so he may repent and save his soul. He seeks but one drop of Christ's blood, when he is restrained from leaping up to Heaven; he hopes the earth will cover him; he wants to be drawn into the entrails of a cloud; and, saving all that, he would as soon have no soul at all to avoid his fate.

Interpreting

2. He wishes to leap up to God, but to no avail: he feels as if someone were pulling him down. The blood of Christ is believed to have been shed to save the souls of all mankind.
3. He asks that the stars draw him up into the clouds, and when they spit out the pieces his soul will have burst free to ascend to Heaven.
4. He would rather be a brutish beast whose soul is dissolved into elements than remain himself and face his fate.
5. Marlowe uses vivid and detailed imagery to depict Faustus's state of mind. He also exploits the rhythmic possibilities of blank verse to intensify the emotional level of the speech.

Applying

6. Some students might suggest that the prospect of death as a total extinction of one's being could cause one to feel as much terror and despair as Faustus feels.

ANSWERS TO ANALYZING LITERATURE

1. His speech shows Faustus to be gifted with vivid imagination, grand notions, and the ability to convey his thoughts and images with power and sensitivity.
2. It upholds the need to live within the confines of traditional morality and not to sacrifice one's soul for the more-than-human powers that evil—on the devil—can bestow.
3. Answers will vary. Encourage students to tell how the character they select went beyond the bounds of morality and ethical restraint.
4. The humanistic spirit of the Renaissance made the quest for knowledge a hallmark of Elizabethan culture. Writers would have naturally been attracted to the theme, and readers and playgoers would have responded vigorously to works that made use of it.

More About the Author Much of Raleigh's verse was published anonymously, the main reason for much of it's being lost. His lyrics were often written in an unconventional style, being more free in form than other verse of the period.

SIR WALTER RALEIGH

1552–1618

Most people remember Sir Walter Raleigh as the courtier who supposedly covered a puddle with his cloak so that Queen Elizabeth I would not get her feet wet. Raleigh was much more than a dashing gallant, however. He is renowned as the founder of the colony of Virginia and the man who introduced tobacco to Europe. In his own time he was honored as a soldier, an explorer, and a poet. Today his actions often receive more attention than his words, but Raleigh's poems, few of which have survived, are rich and complex, reflecting the vicissitudes of his own life.

Raleigh, born into a well to-do family in Devonshire, served as a soldier for the Huguenots in France, attended Oxford briefly, and then, with others, outfitted a fleet purportedly for exploration but in fact to attack Spanish shipping. Returning to England in 1581, he gained an introduction to court and, making the most of his proud, handsome bearing and forceful personality, quickly became a favorite of Queen Elizabeth I. She showered him with honors, bestowed upon him vast estates in Ireland, and put him in charge of expeditions to colonize America, including the one that ended with the "Lost Colony" at Roanoke, Virginia.

Trouble began for Raleigh when the queen learned of his secret marriage to one of her maids of honor. His brief imprisonment at that time foreshadowed a much longer imprisonment under King James I. Accused by James of treason and convicted in an unfair trial, Raleigh spent many of the last years of his life in the Tower of London. There, surrounded by family and servants, he wrote his *History of the World,* a work intended to show God's judgment on the wicked. Released when he was past sixty, he made one final voyage to South America in search of gold. The expedition failed, and upon his return the Spanish ambassador accused him of burning a Spanish settlement. The old charge of treason was revived. Raleigh was convicted, and after calmly composing his own epitaph on October 28, 1618, he went to his execution the next day.

Raleigh's reputation as a writer is difficult to assess because so little of his work has survived. What does survive suggests a mature poetic talent. His lyrics convey realism, humor, and largeness of spirit, with occasional flashes of bitterness that his cruel fate would seem to have warranted.

Objectives

1. To identify the speaker in a poem
2. To understand the tone of a poem

Teaching Portfolio: Support Material

Teacher Backup, p. 000

Vocabulary Check, pp. 00

Usage and Mechanics Worksheet, pp. 00

Analyzing Literature Worksheet, pp. 00

Critical Thinking and Reading Worksheet, pp. 00

Selection Test, pp. 00

GUIDE FOR READING

The Nymph's Reply to the Shepherd; To His Son

Writer's Techniques

The Speaker. The speaker in a poem is comparable to the narrator in prose fiction. He or she is the one—not usually the poet—who presumably is delivering the lines of the poem. In Marlowe's "The Passionate Shepherd to His Love," for instance, the speaker is a love-obsessed shepherd, not the historical and very unrustic Christopher Marlowe. This distinction is important. It is easy to make the mistake of regarding the poet as the speaker when in fact poets use all sorts of speakers in their poems: kings, knights, shepherds, lovers, Greek gods, mythological heroes, and historical figures, not to mention clouds, animals, and so on. Identifying the speaker and evaluating the purpose of the speaker in a poem can help you understand poetry better.

Look For

As you read these two poems by Sir Walter Raleigh, decide who the speaker is in each one. Also see how much you can infer about the character and attitudes of each speaker.

Writing

Think of an issue or event about which you have strong feelings. It may be the lyrics of a song you dislike. It may be an aspect of school that you think could be improved. It may be a political situation that you think presents problems for your community, state, or nation. Using the cluster technique, jot down your thoughts on the issue.

Vocabulary

Knowing the following words will help you as you read "The Nymph's Reply to the Shepherd" and "To His Son."

fold (fōld) *n.*: A pen in which to keep sheep (p. 190, l. 5).
wanton (wän't'n) *adj.*: Luxuriant: said of vegetation (p. 190, l. 9).
gall (gôl) *n.*: Something bitter or distasteful (p. 190, l. 11).
folly (fäl'ē) *n.*: Foolishness (p. 190, l. 16).
apace (ə pās') *adv.*: Swiftly: with speed (p. 192, l. 1).
asunder (ə sun'dər) *adv.*: Apart; in separate directions (p. 192, l. 2).
betokeneth (bi tō'k'n eth) *v.*: To be a sign of; to indicate (p. 192, l. 8).
frets (fretz) *v.*: Eats away (p. 192, l. 12).
halter (hôl'tər) *n.*: A rope for hanging; hangman's noose (p. 192, l. 12).

Literary Focus Have students look back over poems they have already read to determine who the speakers are and how the authors expressed the personalities and attitudes of those speakers.

Look For The speakers in each of the two poems assume a serious tone—one repudiating the romantic enticements of the shepherd, the other issuing a rather sobering warning to his son.

Writing Alternatively, have students write a paragraph or two, issuing a serious warning to their "sons."

Vocabulary Explain how the word *fold* has taken on its broader meaning relating to people. Explain the more familiar definitions of *wanton:* "uncontrolled," "malicious," "dissolute."

Motivation for Reading Have students compare this reply line by line with Marlowe's poem. Have them note how closely Raleigh follows the original poem in his response.

Master Teacher Note John Donne's "The Bait" and Robert Herrick's "To Phyllis, to Love and Live with Him" are two other answers to the Marlowe poem.

Purpose-Setting Question How does the nymph's attitude toward life and love compare with the shepherd's, in Marlowe's poem?

1 **Literary Focus** This is probably the most famous of the replies to Marlowe's poem, and is Raleigh's most often-quoted poem.

2 **Literary Focus** The very first word, *if*, is the most important word in the poem. What happy but unreal situations are linked to it here?

3 **Discussion** Explain how the word *time* is used here.

4 **Literary Focus** Challenge **more advanced** students to paraphrase this couplet. Point out that the prose syntax of these lines would be "A honey tongue is fancy's spring, but a heart of gall is sorrow's fall.

5 **Discussion** Explain the meaning of this line. How does it affect the tone of the poem?

6 **Discussion** Under what conditions would the nymph come to live with the shepherd? What is the reader to infer about the view of life that underlies the poem?

The Nymph's Reply to the Shepherd

Sir Walter Raleigh

1 *This poem was written by Raleigh as a response to the invitation presented in Christopher Marlowe's "The Passionate Shepherd to His Love."*

If all the world and love were young,
2 And truth in every shepherd's tongue,
These pretty pleasures might me move
To live with thee, and be thy love.

3 Time drives the flocks from field to fold,
When rivers rage and rocks grow cold,
And Philomel[1] becometh dumb,
The rest complains of cares to come.

The flowers do fade, and wanton fields
To wayward winter reckoning yields;
4 A honey tongue, a heart of gall,
Is fancy's spring, but sorrow's fall.

Thy gowns, thy shoes, thy beds of roses,
Thy cap, thy kirtle,[2] and thy posies
Soon break, soon wither, soon forgotten,
5 In folly ripe, in reason rotten.

Thy belt of straw and ivy buds,
Thy coral clasps and amber studs,
All these in me no means can move
To come to thee and be thy love.

But could youth last and love still breed,
6 Had joys no date[3] nor age no need,
Then these delights my mind might move,
To live with thee and be thy love.

---

1. **Philomel:** The nightingale.
2. **kirtle:** Skirt.
3. **date:** Ending.

Answers

ANSWERS TO THINKING ABOUT THE SELECTION

Recalling

1. (a) The speaker is the nymph wooed by the shepherd in Marlowe's "The Passionate Shepherd to His Love." (b) The shepherd is addressed. (c) They are taken from "The Passionate Shepherd to His Love."
2. The first suggestion comes in the *if* clause of line 1.

Interpreting

3. She thinks the gifts are ephemeral and therefore of little value.
4. She would accept his offer if youth could last, love and joy never end, and age bring no grief.
5. Both poems are written in iambec tetrameter quatrains rhyming *aabb*.

Applying

6. Answers will vary. Idealists will probably side with the amorous shepherd, skeptics with the negativistic nymph.

ANSWERS TO ANALYZING LITERATURE

1. (a) She is skeptical toward it. (b) She seems cool and self-possessed.
2. Raleigh's conceiving the reply sug-

THINKING ABOUT THE SELECTION

Recalling

1. (a) Who is the speaker in this poem? (b) Who is the person being addressed? (c) From what literary work are these two characters taken?
2. How does the speaker first suggest that the shepherd may be making unrealistic promises?

Interpreting

3. What does the speaker think about the gifts being offered her in the previous poem?
4. Under what circumstances might the speaker accept the shepherd's offer?
5. In what ways does the form of Raleigh's poem resemble that of Marlowe's?

Applying

6. If the shepherd and the nymph were to debate the question "What is love?" whose side would you take? Why?

ANALYZING LITERATURE

Identifying the Speaker in a Poem

The **speaker** in a poem is the character portrayed as delivering the lines. In "The Nymph's Reply to the Shepherd," the speaker is a nymph—the same nymph whom Marlowe's shepherd addresses in "The Passionate Shepherd to His Love" (page 182). The speaker in a poem should not be confused with the poet. In Raleigh's poem the nymph is the speaker; she is obviously not Raleigh himself. Sometimes the beliefs and attitudes of the speaker are the same as those of the poet, but not always.

1. (a) What is the speaker's attitude toward the shepherd's proposal? (b) How would you describe her emotional state?
2. Do you think Sir Walter Raleigh's own view of the shepherd's proposal is probably the same as or different from that of the nymph? Support your answer.

CRITICAL THINKING AND READING

Making Inferences About Tone

Tone is the attitude shown by a writer toward his or her subject, characters, or audience. It is often expressed as an adjective: cheerful, sarcastic, amused, lofty, sad, or any of dozens of other possibilities. The tone of "The Passionate Shepherd to His Love" might be described as optimistic. Tone is created through choice of words and details.

1. How would you describe the tone of "The Nymph's Reply to the Shepherd"?
2. What words in the poem help to convey this tone? Find at least five words.

THINKING AND WRITING

Writing an Invitation in Verse

Write a four-line or eight-line poem to invite a group of friends to a picnic in the country. Use a four-beat line and an aabb rhyme scheme. First think of some of the most appealing aspects of the picnic, such as the guests, the foods that will be served, and the scenic features of the picnic area. Then describe them in verse. You might conclude your invitation by repeating all or part of your opening line.

When you revise, try to make the tone of your verses lighthearted and pleasant. If you wish, idealize the pleasures of the picnic. Read the invitation aloud to check that the rhythm and rhyme sound right.

For help with this assignment, students can refer to Lesson 18, "Writing a Poem," in the Handbook of Writing About Literature.

THINKING AND WRITING

Writing Your Own Reply

Using either Marlowe's (page 182) or Raleigh's poem as a model, write a poetic response of your own to one or both of the poets' views of love. Begin by making notes on what the poet says; then make a few notes on what you will say. Write your poem trying to match the form of Marlowe's or Raleigh's poem. As you revise your poem, be sure you have made your views clear. The tone of your poem can be humorous, if you wish.

For help with this assignment, studets can again refer to Lesson 18, "Writing a Poem," in the Handbook of Writing About Literature.

gests that his view of the shepherd's proposal is probably the same as the nymph's.

ANSWERS TO CRITICAL THINKING AND READING

1. The tone is self-assured and somewhat scornful, with a hint of regret in the last stanza.
2 Some words that convey the tone are *If* (line 1), *cold* (line 6), *cares* (line 8), *gall* (line 11), and *rotten,* (line 16).

Motivation for Reading Ask students to observe how this poetic advice to his son reflects Raleigh's experiences with life's realities

Master Teacher Note With **less advanced** students, point out that the "three things" that the poem is about are a gallows tree, the string of a hangman's bag, and a boy sentenced to hang.

Purpose-Setting Question What do you think Raleigh's son is like?

1 **Literary Focus** This poem is written in the Shakespearean, or English, sonnet form of three quatrains and a couplet. Observe how each section expresses its own idea.

2 **Discussion** What happens when the three things that grow up apart come together?

3 **Discussion** The third quatrain describes what the three things do before they meet and after they meet. Explain.

4 **Discussion** Paraphrase the hope expressed in the closing couplet.

1 To His Son

Sir Walter Raleigh

Three things there be that prosper up apace
2 And flourish, whilst they grow asunder far,
But on a day, they meet all in one place,
And when they meet, they one another mar;
And they be these: the wood, the weed, the wag.[1]
The wood is that which makes the gallow tree;
The weed is that which strings the hangman's bag;
The wag, my pretty knave, betokeneth thee.
Mark well, dear boy, whilst these assemble not,
3 Green springs the tree, hemp grows, the wag is wild,
But when they meet, it makes the timber rot;
It frets the halter, and it chokes the child.
4 Then bless thee, and beware, and let us pray
We part not with thee at this meeting day.

1. **wag** *n.*: A mischievous young boy.

THINKING ABOUT THE SELECTION

Recalling

1. (a) Who is the speaker in this poem? (b) Who is the person being spoken to?
2. What happens when the wood, the weed, and the wag meet?
3. Who is the wag in the poem?
4. What is the speaker's main concern?

Interpreting

5. Given the speaker's concern, what conclusion can you draw about the behavior of the speaker's son? Explain.
6. How would you describe the poem's tone?

Applying

7. The German writer Goethe wrote, "Behavior is the mirror in which everyone displays his own image." Discuss the meaning of this quotation.

CRITICAL THINKING AND READING

Making Inferences About Purpose

A poet's purpose in writing a poem involves more than just subject and theme. **Purpose** is a broad term that covers whatever the writer intends to communicate to the reader. To infer purpose, you must understand the poem's central idea and you must experience its emotional impact. When you fully understand the meaning of "The Nymph's Reply to the Shepherd," for instance, you can infer that Raleigh's purpose is to refute Marlowe's idealistic and simplistic view of love and to present a more realistic view.

What do you think was Raleigh's purpose in writing this poem to his son?

Answers

ANSWERS TO THINKING ABOUT THE SELECTION

Recalling

1. (a) The speaker is a father, who may or may not be Raleigh. (b) He is addressing his potentially wayward or free-spirited son.
2. When wood, weed, and wag meet, they mar each other.
3. The wag is the son.
4. The speaker's main concern is that his son not be hanged.

Interpreting

5. We must conclude that the son has at least the potential for finding himself in serious trouble. Such a serious and strong warning would hardly be given otherwise.
6. The tone is serious and moralistic.

Applying

7. Answers will differ, though the general sense might be that how we behave reflects what we think of ourselves.

ANSWERS TO CRITICAL THINKING AND READING

Raleigh's purpose was probably to keep his son out of trouble.

PORTRAIT OF AN UNKNOWN MAN
Nicholas Hilliard
Victoria & Albert Museum Trustees

Humanities Note

Fine art, *Portrait of an Unknown Man* by Nicholas Hilliard. Nicholas Hilliard (1547–1619) was the premier miniaturist of Elizabethan England. He was apprenticed to the Queen's jewelers and soon began producing miniatures, tiny portraits often mounted in gold and worn as jewelry. In time he was appointed limner (portraitists were called "limners") and goldsmith to Queen Elizabeth I.

This miniature portrait, also called "Young Man Among the Roses," is thought to be a portrait of Robert Devereaux, Second Earl of Essex. Approximately 5½ by 3 inches, it is not very small for a miniature. Executed on parchment glued to pasteboard, the miniature is a copy of a figure in a fresco Hilliard saw in France. With his fancy attire and handsome face, this young nobleman appears to be the perfect English court dandy.

You might use these questions for discussion:

1. Does the young man in this miniature appear to be in need of guidance and advice like that offered by Sir Walter Raleigh to his son? Explain.
2. What is it about the young man in the portrait that makes him seem unworldly and callow?

More About the Author He has been called the poet's poet because so many have learned from his artistry. He blended Platonism, Puritanism, and patriotism in the content of his work, bringing to it Heavenly love and beauty, a moral tone and his fierce sense of pride and devotion for what he saw as England's destiny.

EDMUND SPENSER

1552–1599

Edmund Spenser, the "poet's poet," is considered the finest non-romantic poet of the English Renaissance. An imaginative experimenter in verse forms, he invented the Spenserian stanza and the Spenserian sonnet, which exerted a powerful influence on the poets who followed him.

Unlike many poets of the time, Edmund Spenser was born into a working-class family. His father was a clothmaker, and Edmund attended the Merchant Taylors' School on a scholarship for a poor man's son. He went on to Cambridge University as a "sizar," a student who was required to work his way through school. During Spenser's first year at Cambridge, his earliest poems were published.

Graduating with an M.A. degree in 1576, Spenser served in a variety of positions with wealthy noblemen, including that of secretary to the Earl of Leicester, a favorite of Queen Elizabeth I. While in Leicester's service, he became friends with Sir Philip Sidney, and the two of them formed the core of a select literary group.

In 1580 Spenser took a position as secretary to the Lord Deputy of Ireland. Thereafter he spent most of his life in Ireland, acquiring Kilcolman Castle, an Irish estate, where he did much of his writing. Sir Walter Raleigh visited him at Kilcolman Castle and was so impressed by Spenser's unfinished *The Faerie Queen* that he persuaded Spenser to take the first three books to London for publication.

The Faerie Queen established Spenser's reputation as the leading poet of his day. This great work, intentionally written in an archaic style, combines two literary forms, the romance and the epic, into an allegory about "the twelve moral virtues." Dedicated to Queen Elizabeth I, *The Faerie Queen* brought Spenser a small pension but no position at court.

In 1594 Spenser married Elizabeth Boyle, whom his sonnet sequence *Amoretti* commemorates. *Amoretti,* which means "little cupids" or "little love poems," is unique in the English Renaissance for being addressed to the poet's wife.

Irish rebels destroyed Spenser's castle during an uprising, and Spenser returned to London. He died on January 13, 1599, and is buried in what is now the Poet's Corner of Westminster Abbey.

Objectives

1 To understand the Spenserian stanza
2 To understand the Sparserian sonnet
3 To understand personification
4 To compare and contrast sonnets

Teaching Portfolio: Support Material

Teacher Backup, pp. 00

Vocabulary Check, pp. 00

Usage and Mechanics Worksheet, pp. 00

Analyzing Literature Worksheet, pp. 00

Language Worksheet, pp. 00

Selection Test, pp. 00

GUIDE FOR READING

from The Faerie Queen; Sonnet 1; Sonnet 26; Sonnet 75

Writer's Techniques

Spenserian Poetry. Edmund Spenser had a lifelong interest in theories of poety, and he is recognized as one of the great innovators in English verse forms. Two of his innovations are especially notable.

When Spenser wrote *The Faerie Queen,* he created a new type of stanza that was named for him. A *Spenserian stanza* consists of nine lines, the first eight of which are in iambic pentamenter. The ninth line has two additional syllables and is called an *alexandrine.* The rhyme scheme of a Spenserian stanza is *ababbcbcc.*

Although most sonnets follow either the Petrarchan or the Shakespearean form, there is a third type called the Spenserian sonnet. A *Spenserian sonnet* has fourteen lines, but its rhyme scheme differs from that of other sonnets. The rhyme scheme is *abab bcbc cdcd ee.* Often there is no break in a Spenserian sonnet between the octave (first eight lines) and sestet (last six lines).

Look For

As you read these poems by Edmund Spenser, look for similarities in the rhyme schemes. Also consider the effect that an alexandrine at the end of every stanza might have in a long narrative poem.

Writing

Spenser intended *The Faerie Queen,* a lengthy allegory, to consist of twelve books, but he completed only six. In each a hero representing a moral virtue was to have a series of adventures, fighting off such enemies as Envy, Pride, and Despair. Among the virtues in Spenser's plan are Holiness, Friendship, Justice, and Courtesy. All twelve books were to be unified by the presence of the legendary Prince Arthur and by Gloriana, who represents Queen Elizabeth I.

Select either a virtue such as truth or honesty or a fault such as pride or envy. Freewrite about it.

Vocabulary

Knowing the following words will help you as you read the excerpt from *The Faerie Queen* and the sonnets by Spenser.

ycladd (i klad') *pp.*: Clothed, dressed (p. 196, l. 2)

curbe (kʉrb) *n.*: A chain or strap around a horse's lower jaw attached to the bit to check the horse (p. 196, l. 7)

deigne (dān) *v.*: To condescend; lower oneself (p. 197, l. 6)

moly (mō'lē) *n.*: European wild garlic (p. 198, l. 8)

coveted (kuv'it əd) *v.*: Wanted eagerly (p. 198, l. 10)

assay (a sā') *v.*: To try, attempt (p. 199, l. 5)

eternize (i tʉr'nīz) *v.*: To make everlasting (p. 199, l. 11)

Literary Focus Because the alexandrine, or ninth line, of the Spenserian stanza can impede an easy flow from stanza to stanza in longer works, he often repeated the final line or continued the *c* rhyme scheme as the *a* rhyme in the next stanza.

Look For Have students consider what, if any, differences are created by the change in rhyme scheme from the other sonnet forms studied.

Writing Select one of the topics students think of and have the class discuss what allegorial figure might be used to represent it.

Vocabulary Make students aware that *ycladd* is an old form of *clad*, that *curbe* is currently *curb chain,* and that *deigne* is presently *deign.*

Master Teacher Note Point out that an Elizabethan reader would have responded to Spenser's verse much as a reader of today responds to late-nineteenth-century poetry. The Elizabethan would have considered Spenser's language beautiful but antiquated.

1 **Literary Focus** Note that the spelling is somewhat archaic with the final silent *e* remaining on many of the words that have since lost it.

2 **Clarification** *Chide* here means "objected to." His spirited horse objected to the inhibiting bit and curb chain.

Answers

ANSWERS TO THINKING ABOUT THE SELECTION

Recalling

1. (a) The knight is wearing battered armor. (b) He carries a silver shield. (c) He is riding across a plain.

Interpreting

2. His armor bears the blows of many battles, even though he is untested in combat.
3. The knight might be described as noble.

Applying

4. Answers will vary. The type of person a student chooses is less important than the reasons he or she gives for the choice.

ANSWERS TO ANALYZING LITERATURE

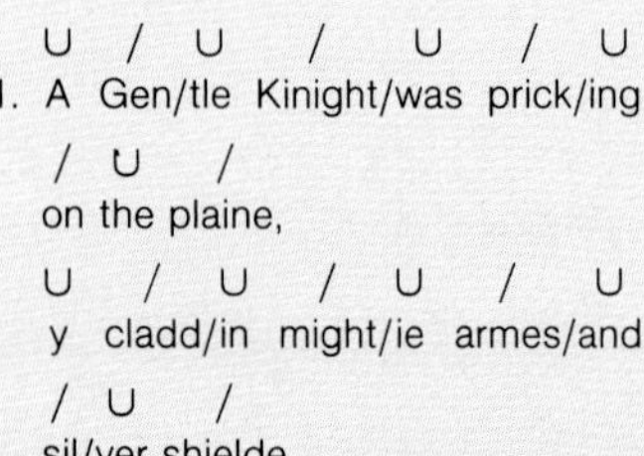

U / U / U / U
1. A Gen/tle Kinight/was prick/ing
/ U /
on the plaine,
U / U / U / U
y cladd/in might/ie armes/and
/ U /
sil/ver shielde,

U / U / U / U
Wherein/olddints/ofdeep/wounds
/ U /
did/remaine . . .

2. The rhyme scheme is *ababbcbcc*.

from # The Faerie Queen

Edmund Spenser

This excerpt from Spenser's epic, The Faerie Queene, *is a description of the Redcrosse Knight, the hero of Book 1, who represents the virtue of holiness.*

1 A Gentle Knight was pricking[1] on the plaine,
Ycladd in mightie armes[2] and silver shielde,
Wherein old dints of deepe wounds did remaine,
The cruell markes of many a bloudy fielde;
Yet armes till that time did he never wield:[3]
2 His angry steede did chide his foming bitt,
As much disdayning to the curbe to yield:
Full jolly[4] knight he seemd, and faire did sitt,
As one for knightly giusts[5] and fierce encounters fitt.

---

1. pricking: Cantering.
2. armes: Armor.
3. Wherein . . . wield: The knight wears the armor of the Christian man, which bears the dents of every Christian's fight against evil. However, Redcrosse is wearing the armor for the first time.
4. jolly: Gallant.
5. giusts: Jousts.

THINKING ABOUT THE SELECTION

Recalling

1. (a) What is the knight wearing? (b) What is he carrying? (c) What is he doing?

Interpreting

2. What is strange about the knight's armor?
3. The knight is described as gentle and jolly (gallant). What one adjective do you think might sum up the knight's character?

Applying

4. If you were to pick a character to represent the moral virtue of truth, what kind of person would you choose?

ANALYZING LITERATURE

Understanding the Spenserian Stanza

The first eight lines of a Spenserian stanza are in iambic pentameter, or ten syllables with a pattern of alternating stressed and unstressed syllables. The ninth line, called the alexandrine, has two additional syllables.

1. Choose three lines of the stanza from *The Faerie Queen* and mark them, for stressed and unstressed syllables and for feet. Use ∪ to indicate an unstressed syllable and / to indicate a stressed syllable.
2. What is the rhyme scheme of this stanza?

Sonnet 1

Edmund Spenser

1 Happy ye leaves when as those lily hands,
which hold my life in their dead doing[1] might,
Shall handle you and hold in love's soft bands,
Like captives trembling at the victor's sight,
And happy lines, on which with starry light,
Those lamping[2] eyes will deigne sometimes to look
And read the sorrows of my dying spright,[3]
Written with tears in heart's close[4] bleeding book.
And happy rhymes bathed in the sacred brook,
2 Of Helicon[5] whence she derived is,
When ye behold that angel's blessed look,
My soul's long lacked food, my heaven's bliss.
3 Leaves, lines, and rhymes, seek her to please alone,
Whom if ye please, I care for other none.

---

1. **doing:** Killing.
2. **lamping:** Flashing.
3. **spright:** Spirit.
4. **close:** Secret.
5. **sacred . . . Helicon:** From Greek mythology, the Hippocrene, the fountain from which the waters of poetic inspiration flowed, located on Mt. Helicon, the sacred home of the Muses.

Motivation for Reading The 88 sonnets in Spenser's *Amoretti* adhere to the Platonic Idea of Beauty and Goodness, giving them a moral beauty and dignity beyond other sonnets studied in this unit.

Purpose-Setting Question In this first of the 88 sonnets, what is the poet's sole purpose for writing it?

1 **Clarification** For *leaves,* read *pages of a book.* What other happy things does the poet address? Why are they happy?

2 **Discussion** Why does he say his beloved is derived from or comes from Helicon?

3 **Discussion** How are the final two lines of the sonnet used?

THINKING ABOUT THE SELECTION

Recalling

1. What three listeners does the speaker address in "Sonnet 1"?

Interpreting

2. Who is *she* in line 10 and *her* in line 13?
3. What is the speaker asking the listeners to do?
4. (a) To what objects does Spenser give human qualities? (b) How does Spenser tie this personification to the main idea of the sonnet?

Applying

5. What animal would you choose to personify pride? Why?

ANALYZING LITERATURE

Understanding the Spenserian Sonnet

The rhyme scheme of a Spenserian sonnet differs from that of the more familiar Petrarchan sonnet. The Spenserian rhyme Scheme is *abab bcbc cdcd ee.* Does this rhyme Scheme seem easier or harder for a poet to work with? Explain.

UNDERSTANDING LANGUAGE

Interpreting Personification

A writer who attributes human qualities to objects or animals is using **personification.** When Spenser calls the leaves in line 1 "happy," he is personifying them. Sometimes, as in allegory, personification even extends to abstract words. An idea such as beauty or honor, for example, is given human qualities.

Answers

ANSWERS TO THINKING ABOUT THE SELECTION

Recalling

1. The poet addresses leaves (pages of a book), lines, and rhymes in the sonnet.

Interpreting

2. *She* and *her* are references to his beloved; it is she who is his inspiration.
3. He asks them to seek to please her alone.
4. (a) He gives human qualities to leaves, lives, and rhymes. (b) He tells them to please his beloved. To please her is the point of the sonnet.

Applying

4. Answers will vary. The animal chosen, however, is less important than the reasons students give for their choices.

ANSWERS TO ANALYZING LITERATURE

1. Since the writer of a Petrarchan sonnet can use any rhyme scheme for the restet, the Spenserian rhyme scheme may be somewhat more difficult.

ANSWERS TO UNDERSTANDING LANGUAGE

1. Spenser also gives human qualities to tunes and rhymes.
2. The personification is essential to the sonnet, as he addresses the three art forms in it.

Purpose-Setting Question How does this poem justify the mixture of life's delights and disappointments?

1 **Discussion** What identical point is the poet making in each of these eight lines? (He states it directly in line 9.)

2 **Discussion** What further points does he make about the union of "sweet with sour"?

3 **Critical Thinking and Reading** Relate this concluding couplet to the implied love affair.

Answers

ANSWERS TO THINKING ABOUT THE SELECTION

Recalling

1. He uses "Sweet is the . . . , but . . ." in each of the first seven lines and a nearly identical pattern in line 8.
2. Spenser observes that tempering sweet with sour only makes it more desirable.

Interpreting

3. No pain, no gain.

Applying

4. Answers will vary. Some Twelfth graders may mention graduation, which is sweet inasmuch as it represents the culmination of their high-school years and sour inasmuch as it represents the end of a phase of their lives.
5. Students should consult a book on Chinese philosophy.

Sonnet 26

Edmund Spenser

Sweet is the rose, but grows upon a briar;
Sweet is the juniper, but sharp his bough;
Sweet is the eglantine,[1] but pricketh near;
Sweet is the fir bloom, but his branches rough;
1 Sweet is the cypress, but his rynd is tough,
Sweet is the nut, but bitter is his pill;[2]
Sweet is the broom flower, but yet sour enough;
And sweet is moly, but his root is ill.
So every sweet with sour is tempered still,[3]
That maketh it be coveted the more:
2 For easy things that may be got at will,
Most sorts of men do set but little store.
Why then should I account of little pain,
3 That endless pleasure shall unto me gain.

1. **eglantine:** A European rose with hooked spines.
2. **pill:** Core.
3. **still:** Always.

THINKING ABOUT THE SELECTION

Recalling

1. In what ways are the lines in the octave of "Sonnet 26" similar?
2. According to Spenser, what is the effect of tempering every "sweet with sour"?

Interpreting

3. How would you express in today's English what Spenser says in the closing couplet?

Applying

4. List other examples from life where the sweet is offset by the sour.
5. Find information on the Chinese principle of yin and yang.

Sonnet 75

Edmund Spenser

BODEGO BAY, CALIFORNIA, PACIFIC OCEAN
© Peter Arnold

One day I wrote her name upon the strand,[1]
But came the waves and washèd it away:
Again I wrote it with a second hand,
But came the tide, and made my pains his prey.
1 "Vain man," said she, "that dost in vain assay,
A mortal thing so to immortalize,
For I myself shall like to this decay,
And eek[2] my name be wipèd out likewise."
"Not so," quod[3] I, "let baser things devise.
To die in dust, but you shall live by fame:
My verse your virtues rare shall eternize,
2 And in the heavens write your glorious name.
Where whenas death shall all the world subdue,
Our love shall live, and later life renew."

1. **strand:** Beach.
2. **eek:** Also.
3. **quod:** Said.

THINKING ABOUT THE SELECTION

Recalling

1. What two events occur twice in the first quatrain of "Sonnet 75"?
2. (a) Who begins speaking in line 5? (b) Who begins speaking in line 9?

Interpreting

3. (a) Why does the poet believe his love's name will not be washed away by the tide? (b) Has time proven him right?

Applying

4. How do the three sonnets from Spenser's *Amoretti*—1, 26, and 75—fit the definition of a sonnet sequence?

THINKING AND WRITING

Comparing and Contrasting Sonnets

Reread "Sonnet 26" and "Sonnet 75" noting their similarities and differences. Write a composition in which you compare and contrast the form, tone, and meaning of the two sonnets. Begin with a chart:

	Form	Tone	Meaning
Sonnet 26			
Sonnet 75			

Use the chart as a basis for writing the first draft of your composition. Remember that to **compare** means to examine similiarities; to **contrast** means to discuss differences. When you have finished, read your first draft carefully for organization, content, grammar, mechanics, and style. Revise it as necessary.

Master Teacher Note The "eternalizing" power of poetry is a theme that has its roots in classical poetry.

1 **Discussion** Describe the poet's actions and his lady's opinion of them. Why does she call his efforts vain?

2 **Discussion** How does the poet explain why his lady is wrong? Should this explanation be taken seriously, or is it merely a graceful, witty compliment?

Answers

ANSWERS TO THINKING ABOUT THE SELECTION

Recalling

1. Twice the speaker wrote his lady's name in the sand; twice the waves washed it away.
2. (a) The lady speaks in line 5. (b) The poet answers in line 9.

Interpreting

3. (a) Her name shall live forever in the lines of his verse. (b) As we are still reading this sonnet 400 years later, he seems to have been correct.

Applying

4. All three are linked together as part of a poetic account of a love relationship.

More About the Author This might be a good time to note that so many of the authors of this period, like Nashe, died young. Nashe lived but 34 years.

THOMAS NASHE

1567–1601

Although Thomas Nashe is best known today for his novel *The Unfortunate Traveler,* the Elizabethans knew him better as a brash, opinionated writer of pamphlets. His personality made him stand out from his contemporaries. While they were writing lyrical poetry or plays, he was carrying on violent written arguments with the Puritans, whom he despised. In addition to his notoriety as a warring pamphleteer, he acquired a modest literary reputation as a poet, novelist, and playwright.

Nashe, the sheltered son of an English churchman, attended Cambridge as a sizar—a scholarship student who worked to defray expenses. Upon graduation he traveled briefly in France and Italy, then settled in London as a writer. He soon began turning out breezy but acidic criticisms of current literary trends and Puritan pamphleteers. At one point his running argument with Gabriel Harvey, a satirical versifier, became so heated that the government ordered both men to cease and desist.

Using material from daily life, Nashe wrote novels and roguish adventures that are filled with spirit and wit. *The Unfortunate Traveler,* published in 1594, is a remarkable work of its kind and helped to establish the adventure novel in England. As a dramatist, often in collaboration with other writers, Nashe achieved less success. One of his comedies, *The Isle of Dogs,* the text of which is now lost, so angered the authorities that Nashe was sent to Fleet prison for a time. Nashe's poetry is not as sensational as his prose, but like his prose it relies on everyday life for inspiration.

As a lyric poet Nashe is often linked with certain other sixteenth-century writers who are not widely read today. Among these excellent but less familiar poets are John Skelton, Sir Edward Dyer, Robert Southwell, and Thomas Campion. Except for the prolific Campion, most of them, like Nashe, are known for only a few poems.

Objectives

1 To understand a litany
2 To learn to generalize from a set of assumptions
3 To write about the concerns of a people

Teaching Portfolio: Support Material

Teacher Backup, p. 000

Vocabulary Check, pp. 00

Usage and Mechanics Worksheet, pp. 00

Analyzing Literature Worksheet, pp. 00

Critical Thinking and Reading Worksheet, pp. 00

Language Worksheet, p. 000

Selection Test, p. 000

GUIDE FOR READING

A Litany in Time of Plague

Writer's Techniques

Litany. Strictly speaking, the word *litany* is a religious rather than a literary term. A litany is a prayer that consists of a series of alternating appeals by a minister or priest and responses by the congregation or choir. The term is sometimes applied to a poem, chant, or other recital that is echoic and repetitive.

Look For

As you read "A Litany in Time of Plague," decide which lines would be read by the minister or priest and which ones are a response by the congregation.

Writing

At the time Nashe was writing, the bubonic plague and black plague (or Black Death), two forms of the same infection, had ravaged Europe periodically. The mortality rate ran as high as 90 percent among those infected. The causes of the plague were unknown, and even the quarantining of victims had only limited effectiveness against the frightening menace. Jot down two or three threats to modern life for which a litany might be an appropriate literary form. Freewrite briefly about one of them.

Vocabulary

Knowing the following words will help you as you read "A Litany in Time of Plague."

ope (ōp) *v.*: Open (1.25)

wantonness (wän't'n nis) *n.*: State of being reckless or undisciplined (1. 29)

vain (vān) *adj.*: Foolish; worthless (1. 33)

degree (di grē') *n.*: social class (1. 36)

Literary Focus The word litany comes from the Greek and Latin, meaning "to pray." Its use is appropriate, as the speaker faces certain death while taking a prayerful look backward and forward.

Look For Note that the first line of each stanza establishes its content, and that each moves toward the final and obvious resolution of solace in the promise of heaven.

Writing Help your students to brainstorm aloud for several possibilities.

Vocabulary Your **less advanced** students may find other Elizabethan words and expressions difficult. You may wish to point out and explain such expressions before reading the poem.

1 **Master Teacher Note** This poem is generally regarded by critics as one of the finest examples of the "plain style" of Elizabethan poetry–as distinguished from the richer, more complex style of Sidney and Spenser.

Purpose-Setting Question How might a plague radically change one's values and beliefs?

Discussion Each of the first five stanzas in this litany cites a particular aspect of life that will inevitably fall prey to death. Name them.

2 **Discussion** What does this line mean?

3 **Discussion** What is the gate that earth holds open?

4 **Clarification** For 'wit with his wantonness' read 'the extravagant enjoyment of the intellect

5 **Literary Focus** Note that the word *therefore* marks the transition from the series of somber comments on the ephemeral quality of life to a supplication for action. What action is the poet calling for?

6 **Thematic Idea** This metaphor for life appears in its most famous form in *Macbeth*, Act V, scene v.

1 A Litany in Time of Plague

Thomas Nashe

Adieu, farewell earth's bliss,
This world uncertain is;
Fond[1] are life's lustful joys,
Death proves them all but toys,[2]
2 None from his darts can fly.
I am sick, I must die.
Lord, have mercy on us!

Rich men, trust not in wealth,
Gold cannot buy you health;
Physic[3] himself must fade,
All things to end are made.
The plague full swift goes by;
I am sick, I must die.
Lord, have mercy on us!

Beauty is but a flower
Which wrinkles will devour;
Brightness falls from the air,
Queens have died young and fair,
Dust hath closed Helen's[4] eye.
I am sick, I must die.
Lord, have mercy on us!

Strength stoops unto the grave,
Worms feed on Hector[5] brave,
Swords may not fight with fate.
Earth still holds ope her gate; 3
Come! come! the bells do cry.
I am sick, I must die.
Lord, have mercy on us!

Wit with his wantonness 4
Tasteth death's bitterness;
Hell's executioner
Hath no ears for to hear
What vain art can reply.
I am sick, I must die.
Lord, have mercy on us!

Haste, therefore, each degree, 5
To welcome destiny.
Heaven is our heritage,
Earth but a player's stage; 6
Mount we unto the sky.
I am sick, I must die.
Lord, have mercy on us!

1. **fond:** Foolish.
2. **toys:** Trifles.
3. **physic:** Doctor.
4. **Helen's:** Referring to Helen of Troy, the legendary wife of the king of Sparta, whose abduction led to the start of the Trojan War.
5. **Hector:** A Trojan hero killed by Achilles in Homer's *Iliad*.

THINKING ABOUT THE SELECTION

Recalling

1. (a) What does the speaker believe must inevitably happen to him? (b) What line states the basis for this belief?
2. According to the speaker, what is the fate of (a) beauty? (b) strength?

Interpreting

3. After beginning a stanza with a general statement, how does the poet emphasize the truth of the statement?
4. (a) Is the speaker in despair because he must die? (b) Why or why not?
5. Do you think the speaker is suggesting that nothing on earth endures? Explain.

Applying

6. "A Litany in Time of Plague" was presented before the Archbishop of Canterbury in 1592. How does this fact indicate that the speaker in the poem—the "I"—is not Thomas Nashe himself?

ANALYZING LITERATURE

Understanding a Litany

A **litany** is a form of prayer in which appeals to God alternate with responses by the congregation. The word *litany,* when applied to a literary work, often has a meaning defined by the work itself, one that may differ from the religious meaning. In "A Litany in Time of Plague," however, there does appear to be a statement—response pattern in each stanza.

1. When this poem was presented to the Archbishop of Canterbury, it was as part of a play. What lines in each stanza do you think would be spoken in the play as a response to the "priest"?
2. What features of the poem make it appropriate for presentation as a statement—response litany?

CRITICAL THINKING AND READING

Generalizing from a Set of Assumptions

A **generalization** is a general idea, principle, or rule that you assume to be true. It is based on inductive reasoning. To make a generalization, you must look at a number of specific cases and draw conclusions from them. A *valid generalization* is one based on a sufficient amount of supporting evidence. The more evidence you have, the more reliable your generalization will be, but sometimes generalizations must be made on limited evidence or on a set of assumptions. Any assumptions you make—any guesses based on evidence—must be as sound and sensible as possible if the generalization you draw from them is to be valid.

1. What generalization can you make about the concerns of the people in London at the time Nashe wrote this poem?
2. What assumptions did you make that led you to this generalization?

THINKING AND WRITING

Writing About the Concerns of a People

What was London like in the late sixteenth century? What did people worry about? Based on your reading of "A Litany in Time of Plague" and your answers in the Critical Thinking and Reading section, write a composition explaining your answers. Use quotes from the poem to support your conclusion, and find additional evidence if you can.

Answers

ANSWERS TO THINKING ABOUT THE SELECTION

Recalling

1. (a) The speaker is anticipating death. (b) Line 5 state's the basis for this belief.
2. (a) Beauty will wither and die away. (b) Strength declines.

Interpreting

3. After each stanza's general statement, the speaker supports it with vivid examples.
4. (a) No, he is not. (b) Because the speaker looks forward to heaven after life on earth, he accepts the inevitability of death.
5. It is too strong a statement to suggest that he thinks nothing on earth endures, but he suggests that so many of the things and qualities we humans prize are as frail as life itself.

Applying

6. The speaker in the poem is dying of the plague.

ANSWERS TO ANALYZING LITERATURE

1. The refrain "I am sick, I must die./ Lord, have mercy on us!" would be the response.
2. The first five lines of each stanza are appropriate words from a member of the clergy for his parishioners, while the final two lines are clearly response lines.

ANSWERS TO CRITICAL THINKING AND READING

1. Londoners might have been concerned about how transitory and impermanent life is.
2. Answers will vary. Suggested response: Literature reflects the general concerns of a people.

More About the Author By all accounts Shakespeare is the greatest writer in the English language. While his plays account for most of the boundless praise of his work, the sonnets should not be overlooked. While we have the magnificence of his works to enrich us, segments of his life have mystified scholars for centuries. The story line or sequence of the sonnets poses many of those unanswered questions. Who are the young man, the rival poet, and the dark lady? Are parts of the sequence autobiographical? We do not know.

WILLIAM SHAKESPEARE

1564–1616

Because of his profound understanding of the many aspects of human nature, his compassion toward all types and classes of people, and the power and beauty of his language, William Shakespeare is generally regarded as the greatest writer of English literature. More than 350 years after his death, Shakespeare's plays continue to be read widely and produced frequently throughout the world. His plays have the same powerful impact on audiences today as they did when they were first staged.

Shakespeare was born in a small country town, Stratford-on-Avon, in April (probably April 23) 1564. His father was a successful businessman who held a number of positions in the town government. Presumably educated at the Stratford grammar school, Shakespeare acquired a basic understanding of Latin, but he did not attend a university. Shakespeare married Anne Hathaway in 1582, and the couple had a daughter, Susanna, in 1583 and twins, Hamnet and Judith, in 1585. Very little is known about Shakespeare's life from the date the twins were born to his appearance in a London acting company seven years later.

By that time, however, he had already developed a reputation as an actor and had written several plays. It was not unusual for members of theater companies to do a number of different jobs, from writing to acting to designing costumes to taking care of advertising, theater arrangements, and finances. By 1594 Shakespeare was a part owner and the principal playwright of the Lord Chamberlain's Men, one of the most successful theater companies in London. In 1599 the company built the famous Globe Theater, where most of Shakespeare's plays were performed. When James I became king in 1603, following Queen Elizabeth I's death, he took control of the Lord Chamberlain's Men and renamed the company The King's Men. In about 1610 Shakespeare retired to Stratford, though he continued to write plays. Six years later, on April 23, he died and was buried in Holy Trinity Church in Stratford.

Because Shakespeare wrote his plays to be performed, not published, no one knows exactly when each of the plays was written. However, through extensive research, scholars have been able to chart several periods in Shakespeare's development as a playwright. During his early years (through most of the 1590's) Shakespeare wrote a number of comedies (including *The Comedy of Errors, Love's Labor Lost, The Merchant of Venice,* and *A Midsummer Night's Dream*), several histories (including *Richard II, Richard III,* and *Henry IV*), and two tragedies *(Titus Andronicus and Romeo and Juliet).* Shakespeare then wrote several of his finest romantic comedies *(As You Like It, Twelfth Night,* and *Much Ado About Nothing)* just before the turn of the century. During the first decade of the seventeenth century, Shakespeare created his greatest tragedies *(Hamlet, Othello, King Lear, Macbeth, Antony and Cleopatra,* and *Coriolanus).* Finally, toward the end of his life, Shakespeare wrote several plays referred to as "romances" or "tragicomedies" *(The Winter's Tale, Cymbeline,* and *The Tempest).*

In addition to his 37 plays, Shakespeare wrote 154 sonnets and two narrative poems. He probably worked on his sonnets from 1592 through 1598, a time when sonneteering was in vogue in London. It is likely that he wrote many of them in 1592 when the London theater was closed because of a plague.

Below is a list of Shakespeare's poems and plays in roughly chronological order.

Poems

Venus and Adonis
The Rape of Lucrece
Sonnets
The Phoenix and the Turtle

Plays

The Comedy of Errors
Love's Labor's Lost
2 Henry VI
3 Henry VI
1 Henry VI
Richard III
Titus Andronicus
The Taming of the Shrew
The Two Gentlemen of Verona
The Tragedy of Romeo and Juliet
Richard II
A Midsummer Night's Dream
King John
The Merchant of Venice
1 Henry IV
2 Henry IV
Much Ado About Nothing
Henry V
The Tragedy of Julius Caesar
As You Like It
Twelfth Night
Hamlet
The Merry Wives of Windsor
Troilus and Cressida
All's Well That Ends Well
Othello
Measure for Measure
King Lear
Macbeth
Antony and Cleopatra
Timon of Athens
Coriolanus
Pericles
Cymbeline
The Winter's Tale
The Tempest
Henry VIII

Literary Focus As he did throughout his career, Shakespeare took an existing form and made it his own. It has been noted that the sonnet form is so restrictive that few perfect or near perfect examples exist. Too often the final couplet fails to conclude or answer adequately within its confines. But, when it works, the sonnet soars.

Look For The four examples are really quite different in tone. Despite this, have students seek to find qualities in them that mark them the work of one author, and more importantly, the work of a great writer.

Writing As Sonnet 130 is considered a satire on the Petrarchan form, as an alternative assignment have students write a gentle satire on one of the other sonnets. Set guidelines and limits for their one- or two- paragraph exercise.

Vocabulary *Haply* is considered archaic. Discuss the possible ways words might fall out of use and gain this label. Ask students to consider words they know that may be archaic someday.

GUIDE FOR READING

Sonnet 29; Sonnet 73; Sonnet 116; Sonnet 130

Writer's Techniques

Shakespearean Sonnet. During the Elizabethan period, the sonnet sequence, a group of sonnets unified by a common theme, became a popular literary form. Shakespeare's 154 sonnets, like those in other sonnet sequences, are numbered and fit loosely together to form a story. Most of the sonnets are addressed to a handsome, talented young man, urging him at first to marry and have children who can carry on his talents. The speaker also warns the young man about the destructive powers of time, age, and moral weakness. Midway through the sequence, the sonnets focus on a rival poet who has also addressed poems to the young man. Twenty-five of the later sonnets are addressed to a "dark lady," who is romantically involved with both the speaker and the young man. The focus of these later sonnets is on the grief she causes by her betrayal of the speaker.

William Shakespeare did not invent what is now called the Shakespearean sonnet (Sir Thomas Wyatt and the Earl of Surrey did), but Shakespeare is its greatest master. A Shakespearean sonnet, fourteen lines in iambic pentameter, consists of three quatrains and a rhyming couplet. The usual rhyme scheme is *abab cdcd efef gg*. Shakespeare's sonnets ordinarily present a problem or premise in the first twelve lines and offer a solution or conclusion (sometimes a statement of the theme) in the final couplet.

Look For

As you read the following sonnets by Shakespeare, pay close attention to their form, looking for the problem or premise and the solution or conclusion.

Writing

Shakespeare's sonnets reflect on various aspects of life, such as personal relationships, the passing of time, and the relationship between human beings and nature. Jot down your thoughts on three aspects of life that you might consider writing about in a sonnet. Then list some of the ideas and emotions you associate with each one.

Vocabulary

Knowing the following words will help you as you read the sonnets by Shake peare.

haply (hap′lē) *adv.*: By chance (p. 207, l. 10)
sullen (sul′ən) *adj.*: Gloomy; dismal (p. 207, l. 12)
tempests (tem′pistz) *n.*: Violent storms (p. 210, l. 6)
dun (dun) *adj.*: Dull grayish brown (p. 211, l. 3)
belied (bi līd′) *v.*: Proved false; contradicted (p. 211, l. 14)

Objectives

1 To understand the Shakespearen sonnet
2 To compare and contrast sonnets

Teaching Portfolio: Support Material

Teacher Backup, p. 000

Vocabulary Check, pp. 00

Usage and Mechanics Worksheet, pp. 00

Analyzing Literature Worksheet, pp. 00

Language Worksheet, pp. 00

Selection Test, pp. 00

Sonnet 29

William Shakespeare

When in disgrace with fortune and men's eyes,
I all alone beweep my outcast state,
1 And trouble deaf heaven with my bootless[1] cries,
And look upon myself and curse my fate,
Wishing me like to one more rich in hope,
2 Featured like him, like him with friends possessed,
Desiring this man's art, and that man's scope,
3 With what I most enjoy contented least.
Yet in these thoughts myself almost despising,
Haply I think on thee, and then my state,
4 Like to the lark at break of day arising
From sullen earth, sings hymns at heaven's gate;
   For thy sweet love remembered such wealth brings
   That then I scorn to change my state with kings.

1. bootless: Futile.

THINKING ABOUT THE SELECTION

Recalling

1. With whom or what is the speaker in disfavor?
2. What are three things the speaker wishes for?
3. When the speaker thinks of the person to whom the sonnet is addressed, how does his attitude change?

Interpreting

4. How would you describe the mood (a) of the first eight lines of this sonnet? (b) of the last six lines?
5. Why is the comparison with the lark an appropriate one for the speaker to make?
6. How do the last two lines summarize the theme of the sonnet?

Applying

7. If you were to give this sonnet a title, what would it be?

ANALYZING LITERATURE

Understanding Shakespearean Sonnets

"Sonnet 29" is a Shakespearean sonnet consisting of three quartains and a couplet. It has the usual rhyme scheme of such a sonnet, *abab cdcd efef gg*. In a Shakespearean sonnet, the poet typically presents a problem or premise in the first twelve lines followed by a solution or conclusion in the last two. In "Sonnet 29," however, a change in direction occurs at line 9, as it does in a Petrarchan sonnet.

1. Each of the first two quatrains expresses a distinct but related thought. In your own words, what are these two thoughts?
2. What rhyming words represent (a) the *b*'s in the rhyme scheme? (b) the *e*'s? (c) the *g*'s?
3. How does the thought expressed in the last two lines of the sonnet relate to what is said in the first eight lines?
4. What is your reaction to this sonnet's theme?

Motivation for Reading Make students aware that the sonnet describes feelings each of us experiences from time to time. While our reactions to those feelings will vary, the concerns here are universal.

Master Teacher Note Though consisting of three quotations and a couplet, this sonnet is organized like a Petrarchan sonnet: an unhappy situation is presented in the octave, a response and solution in the sestet.

Purpose-Setting Question What or who is able to restore the speaker's self-esteem?

1 **Clarification** 'Trouble deaf heaven' means 'I pray, but God doesn't hear me.'

2 **Discussion** When in this state of mind, what aspects of others does the speaker envy?

3 **Clarification** Read 'enjoy' as 'possess'. What does this line mean? How would you summarize the situation presented in the octave?

4 **Discussion** Discuss the tone of the sestet. What causes this dramatic change in the speaker's mood? Note how the powerful and positive imagery of the simile in lines 11-12 changes the mood.

Answers

ANSWERS TO THINKING ABOUT THE SELECTION

Recalling

1. The speaker's fortunes are going badly and others look upon him unfavorably.
2. He wishes he might have greater hopes and prospects, that he might have better physical features, and that he might have many friends.
3. When he thinks of the person, he is so happy that he would not change his state with kings.

Interpreting

4. (a) The first eight lines describe periods when the speaker is filled with self-pity; the mood of the lines reflects this feeling. (b) The mood of the last six lines reflects the rising spirits of the speaker when he is reminded of the person to whom the poem is addressed.
5. He becomes like the lark, rising up from his sullen mood to a state of joy.
6. The final couplet says that his love brings him wealth beyond that of a king.

ANSWERS TO ANALYZING LITERATURE

1. The main thought in the first quatrain is one of extreme dissatisfaction with oneself. In the second it is envy of the happier lot in life of others.
2. (a) *State* and *fate* are the *b*'s in the rhyme scheme. (b) *Despising* and *arising* are the *e* rhymes. (c) *Brings* and *kings* are the *g* rhymes.
3. The thought in the last two lines refutes the first eight lines.
4. Answers will differ, though many students are likely to respond favorably to the idea that the thought of one's beloved can bring joy to living.

Humanities Note

Fine art, *The Sonnet* by William Mulready. William Mulready (1786–1863) was an English painter born in Ireland. At fifteen he was supporting himself by illustrating books and by painting sets for theaters. He later attended the School of the Royal Academy in London and thereafter remained faithful to the academic training he received there.

The painting *The Sonnet* was finished in 1839. It shows Mulready's fascination with the refinement of the Dutch School of painting. This is a narrative painting, one that tells a story. The woman's expression suggests that she is moved by what she is reading. The title of the painting and the humble attitude of the man both suggest that he is the author of the sonnet.

You might use these questions for discussion:

1. What do you imagine could be the subject of the sonnet that the woman is reading?
2. How might you interpret the man's expression?

THE SONNET
William Mulready
Victoria & Albert Museum Trustees

Answers

ANSWERS TO THINKING ABOUT THE SELECTION
Recalling

1. The speaker compares himself to autumn.
2. The speaker compares himself to twilight.
3. In the third quatrain, the speaker

Sonnet 73

William Shakespeare

That time of year thou mayst in me behold
1 When yellow leaves, or none, or few, do hang
Upon those boughs which shake against the cold,
Bare ruined choirs where late the sweet birds sang.
In me thou see'st the twilight of such day
As after sunset fadeth in the west,
2 Which by and by black night doth take away,
Death's second self that seals up all in rest.
In me thou see'st the glowing of such fire,
3 That on the ashes of his youth doth lie,
As the deathbed whereon it must expire,
Consumed with that which it was nourished by.[1]
This thou perceivest, which makes thy love more
4 strong,
To love that well which thou must leave ere long.

1. Consumed . . . by: Choked by the ashes of that which fueled its flame.

THINKING ABOUT THE SELECTION

Recalling

1. To what season of the year does the speaker compare himself?
2. To what time of day does the speaker compare himself?
3. What comparison does the speaker make in the third quatrain?

Interpreting

4. How does the speaker resemble the three things to which he compares himself?
5. In the "bare ruin'd choirs" of line 4, the word *choirs* refers literally to the loft where church singers perform. What does it mean as Shakespeare uses it here?
6. Explain the meaning of "Death's second self" in line 8.
7. How does the thought in the final couplet relate to the rest of the sonnet?

Applying

8. Many people regret growing old. How do you think the speaker in this sonnet feels about it? Support your answer with details from the sonnet.

(Answers begin on p. 208.)

Motivation for Reading Observe how Shakespeare deals in rich poetic terms with aging, creating in the process a splendid sonnet.

Master Teacher Note Each of the three quatrains opens with the same idea: You can see in me . . . All three parallel one another in structure and sense.

Purpose-setting Question What mood and tone do the powerful images of the first twelve lines convey?

1 **Literary Focus** What is the speaker saying about himself? Late fall is frequently used in poetry as an image of old age and winter as an image of death. Discuss the beautiful metaphor Shakespeare creates here. Note that *choir* here refers to the place rather than the singers.

2 **Discussion** What new image of impending death does this quatrain introduce? In what way is night "death's second self"?

3 **Discussion** What is the third image of impending death? What might be the reason for presenting the three sets of images in this particular order? Would a different order be as effective?

4 How does the speaker's age demonstrate the strength of the other's love?

compares his life to a fire that now consists of a few glowing embers on top of ashes.

Interpreting

4. The speaker resembles the three things he describes in that, like them, an end is near for him.
5. Shakespeare sees the silhouetted bare branches as resembling the ruined choir of some ancient abbey.
6. He refers to night as death's second self.
7. The "thou" who is addressed perceives all that the speaker has described in the three quatrains and therefore loves him all the more.

Applying

8. He may regret growing old, but the compensation is that his aging increases his beloved's love for him.

Motivation for Reading What is love? Though it cannot be defined to everyone's satisfaction, Shakespeare here offers one of the most famous definitions of love in world literature.

Master Teacher Note Have students concentrate on the implications of the two metaphors in lines 5-8.

Purpose-setting Question What is Shakespeare's idea of the essence of love?

1 **Clarification** For "marriage of true minds" read "true love." Ask students to paraphrase the opening sentence.

2 **Discussion** What does the second sentence mean? **Less advanced** students may need help in paraphrasing line 4.

3 **Discussion** In this quatrain, what metaphors does Shakespeare employ to show the constancy of true love? Explain them.

4 **Discussion** *Fool* in line 9 means "jester" or "plaything." Why is love *not* "Time's fool"?

Sonnet 116

William Shakespeare

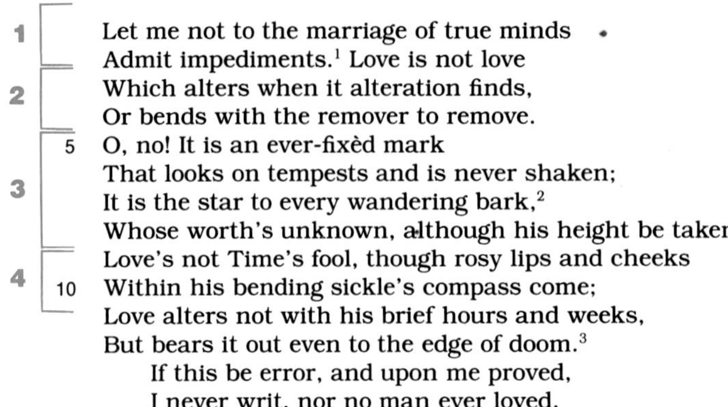

1 Let me not to the marriage of true minds
Admit impediments.[1] Love is not love
2 Which alters when it alteration finds,
Or bends with the remover to remove.
O, no! It is an ever-fixèd mark
That looks on tempests and is never shaken;
3 It is the star to every wandering bark,[2]
Whose worth's unknown, although his height be taken.
4 Love's not Time's fool, though rosy lips and cheeks
Within his bending sickle's compass come;
Love alters not with his brief hours and weeks,
But bears it out even to the edge of doom.[3]
If this be error, and upon me proved,
I never writ, nor no man ever loved.

1. **impediments:** Reasons why a marriage should not be allowed to take place.
2. **star . . . bark:** The star that guides every wandering ship; the North Star.
3. **doom:** Judgment Day.

THINKING ABOUT THE SELECTION

Recalling

1. According to the speaker, what are three things that love is not?
2. To what is love compared in the second quatrain?

Interpreting

3. What are the points of similarity between true love and the North Star?
4. The speaker notes that "Love's not Time's fool." (a) What does he mean? (b) How does this idea fit in with the central theme of the sonnet?
5. Ordinarily, the final couplet in a Shakespearean sonnet offers a summary or solution. This final couplet is a bit different. What point does it make about the content of the rest of the sonnet?

Applying

6. What is your opinion of the speaker's concept of true love? Explain your answer.

ANSWERS TO THINKING ABOUT THE SELECTION

Recalling

1. Love isn't true love if it can be altered when it finds changes in the other person. It isn't true love if it gives in to whoever or whatever tries to end it. It isn't true love if it is shaken by troubles.
2. It is likened to a sea-mark and to the North Star, which unlike all the other stars remains constant in the heavens.

Interpreting

3. True love and the North Star are constant and unchanging. Like the North Star, true love is a steadfast guide in one's life.
4. (a) The speaker uses the word *fool to mean "court jester" or "clown". Time, he says, cannot make love into something laughable or contemptible. It is serious and long-lived, if not eternal. (b) This idea is one more expression of the theme that true love is unchanging and undying.*
5. In the final couplet he in essence says that his argument is as indisputable as his own existence and career as a writer.

Applying

6. Answers will vary, though most should see that what he is saying is perhaps the most commonly held notion of what love is.

Sonnet 130

William Shakespeare

My mistress' eyes are nothing like the sun;
Coral is far more red than her lips' red;
If snow be white, why then her breasts are dun;
If hairs be wires, black wires grow on her head.
I have seen roses damasked,[1] red and white,
1 But no such roses see I in her cheeks;
And in some perfumes is there more delight
Than in the breath that from my mistress reeks.[2]
I love to hear her speak. Yet well I know
That music hath a far more pleasing sound.
I grant I never saw a goddess go;[3]
My mistress, when she walks, treads on the ground.
2 And yet, by heaven, I think my love as rare
As any she belied with false compare.

1. **damasked:** Variegated.
2. **reeks:** Emanates.
3. **go:** Walk.

THINKING ABOUT THE SELECTION

Recalling

1. What is less than perfect about the mistress's (a) lips? (b) cheeks? (c) breath? (d) voice?

Interpreting

2. "Sonnet 130" is often called an anti-Petrarchan sonnet. What do you think is meant by "anti-Petrarchan"?
3. There are indications even before the final couplet that the speaker loves his mistress despite her supposed imperfections. What is one such indication?

Applying

4. Would you like to have this kind of sonnet written about you, or would you prefer the more traditional kind with its idealized comparisons? Give your reasons.

THINKING AND WRITING

Comparing and Contrasting Sonnets

Choose the Shakespeare sonnet you like best. Then choose a sonnet by another writer —Wyatt, Sidney, or Spenser. Write an essay in which you compare and contrast the form, tone, and meaning of the two sonnets. Set up a chart for taking notes. Write the first draft of your essay, keeping in mind that to **compare** means to examine similarities; to **contrast** means to discuss differences.

As you write, try to incorporate direct quotations from the sonnets into your paper. When you have finished your first draft, reread it, paying special attention to the way you have punctuated direct quotations. Make any changes needed before completing your final draft. Then share it with your classmates.

Motivation for Reading Exaggerated praise of one's beloved was traditional in Elizabethan poetry, including Shakespeare's. Here, however, he satirizes conventional love poetry.

Master Teacher Note A conventional Elizabethan beauty in love poetry should be bright-eyed, red-lipped, blonde-haired, and red-cheeked.

Purpose-Setting Question Is Shakespeare insulting his beloved, just having fun, or complimenting her?

Thematic Idea This poem can be read in conjunction with Sidney's and Spenser's sonnets, with which it is in marked contrast.

1 **Literary Focus** The conventional ideas of beauty expressed in Elizabethan poetry all derive ultimately from Petrarch, whose beloved Laura was, in appearance, all that Shakespeare's "dark lady" is not. The references to the sun, coral, snow, roses, perfumes, music, and a goddess are also Petrarchan stereotypes.

2 The last line means "as any woman falsely depicted with unjustifiable comparisons." What are the speaker's feelings about his lady's appeal?

Answers

ANSWERS TO THINKING ABOUT THE SELECTION

Recalling

1. (a) They are not as red as coral. (b) Her cheeks aren't like damasked roses. (c) Perfumes offer more delight than her breath. (d) Her voice is less pleasing than music.

Interpreting

2. In this context, *anti-Petrarchan* means repudiating the Petrachan ideal of feminine beauty.
3. He says that he loves to hear her speak. Further, the tone throughout is good-humored and kind, not sarcastic and cruel.

Applying

4. Answers will vary, though most will probably prefer more traditional forms of praise.

Literary Focus Aside from their strong entertainment value, the songs helped define the tone or mood of a scene, character or situation. Only rarely, as with the first song here, do they have a direct bearing on the plot itself.

Look For As students read these songs, look for phrasing and word clusters that strongly suggest they were meant to be sung.

Writing Alternatively, have students consider a light story line all or most are familiar with from class, TV or film. Have them select areas along that story line where songs might be appropriate. More advanced students might sketch out timely lyrics.

Vocabulary Have students read the words aloud and discuss current use or non-use of them, with examples.

GUIDE FOR READING

Tell Me Where Is Fancy Bred? It Was a Lover and His Lass; Fear No More the Heat o' the Sun

Writer's Techniques

Shakespearean Songs. Music and song were important aspects of life during the English Renaissance. Serenades, street songs, pastoral invitations, nonsense songs, ballads—all were popular at every level of English society. Shakespeare included 124 songs in his plays. The songs serve specific purposes in the plays in which they appear; they were not added merely to capitalize on the appeal of music. Although Shakespeare's songs were sung on stage as part of the productions, none of the original printed versions of the plays includes the music. As a consequence, much of the original music has been lost. Nevertheless, the lyrics can be enjoyed as poems without music. They can also be appreciated outside the context of the plays. William Shakespeare, unparalleled playwright and poet, was also one of England's great songwriters.

Look For

As you read the following songs from Shakespeare's plays, look for the thought and feeling underlying each one.

Writing

Take some or all of the lyrics of a popular song and rewrite them in your own way. Your song can be as playful or as serious as you wish. It can be on any subject that interests you.

Vocabulary

Knowing the following words will help you as you read the songs by Shakespeare.

begot (bi gät′) *v.*: Brought into being (p. 213)
engendered (in jen′dərd) *v.*: Caused to exist (p. 213)
knell (nel) *n.*: Sound of a bell, especially one rung slowly, as at a funeral (p. 213)
prime (prīm) *n.*: Best, most mature period (p. 214)
exorciser (ek′sôr sīz′ər) *n.*: Sorcerer; magician (p. 216)
consummation (kän′sə mā′ hən) *n.*: State of fulfillment or completion (p. 216)

Objectives

1 To understand Shakespearian songs
2 To find details that develop mood
3 To find details that support purpose
4 To write about Shakespeare's songs

Teaching Portfolio: Support Material

Teacher Backup, pp. 00

Vocabulary Check, pp. 00

Usage and Mechanics Worksheet, pp. 00

Analyzing Literature Worksheet, pp. 00

Critical Thinking and Reading Worksheet, pp. 00

Language Worksheet, pp. 00

Selection Test, pp. 00

Tell Me Where Is Fancy[1] Bred

William Shakespeare

This song is sung in The Merchant of Venice *(Act III, Scene ii) while Bassanio is trying to choose between the caskets of gold, silver, and lead, knowing that only by making the correct choice will he be able to win Portia as his wife.*

Tell me where is fancy bred,
1 Or in the heart or in the head?
How begot, how nourishèd?
    Reply, reply.
It is engendered in the eyes,
2 With gazing fed; and fancy dies
In the cradle where it lies.
    Let us all ring fancy's knell:
3 I'll begin it—Ding, dong, bell.
Ding, dong, bell.

1. **Fancy:** Love.

Motivation for Reading As he does here, Shakespeare often uses a question to deal with a significant philosophical, moral, or other kind of issue. Here the question is, Where in us does love arise?

Master Teacher Note Bassanio chooses the casket of lead—the one least appealing to the eye—and thereby wins Portia.

Purpose-setting Question What is the answer to the question raised in the song?

1 **Discussion** What questions are asked by these lines?

2 **Discussion** What answers are given to them? What is implied here about the longevity of love?

3 **Discussion** Do these lines imply that love cannot long endure?

THINKING ABOUT THE SELECTION

Recalling

1. What two possible sources of fancy are mentioned at the beginning of the song?
2. Where does the reply to the two questions place the origin of fancy?

Interpreting

3. The word *fancy* is central to the meaning of the poem. It means "love," to be sure, but a superficial kind of love—a love based only on outward appearances. Why is this distinction important?
4. What is it that helps fancy flourish?
5. Why do you think the speaker says that fancy dies in the cradle?
6. What does it mean to "ring fancy's knell"?

Applying

7. Bassanio must choose the correct one of three caskets if he is to win Portia. Two of the caskets are of glittering gold and silver; one is of plain lead. Bassanio chooses the lead casket. Using the words of the song as clues, why do you think he makes that choice?

Answers

ANSWERS TO THINKING ABOUT THE SELECTION

Recalling

1. Fancy might come from the heart or from the mind.
2. The answer says it is engendered in the eyes.

Interpreting

3. These lines address not the kind of true love written about in the sonnets but mere infatuation. The song says that fancy is neither of the heart nor the mind but of the eyes; it is superficial and fleeting.
4. Fancy is fed through gazing. It feeds on visual stimuli.
5. With nothing more than appearances to nourish fancy, it will be short-lived. Our eyes will look elsewhere.
6. The speaker is telling us that fancy is not enough, that we must go beyond outward appearances. Hence the line means that fancy is to be repudiated.

Applying

7. He chooses as he does to avoid being deceived by attractive appearances.

Motivation for Reading Since this song is being sung to a couple about to be wed, students can anticipate its tone and spirit.

Master Teacher Note The refrains in this poem are common to many Elizabethan songs.

Thematic Idea Compare this song with Marlowe's "Passionate Shepherd . . ." on page 182.

Purpose-setting Question Why is springtime important to the tone, mood, and theme of this song?

1 **Literary Focus** In all stanzas only lines 1 and 3 change. The others constitute refrains dealing with the traditional relationships between lovers, weddings, springtime, and birdsongs.

2 **Literary Focus** Here Shakespeare is drawing on the classical *carpe diem* ("seize the day") theme. It is based on the assumption that since life is so brief one should seize the day of pleasure and joy while one can.

3 **Discussion** Students should be asked to paraphrase this line.

It Was a Lover and His Lass

William Shakespeare

This song, from As You Like It *(Act V, Scene iii), is sung by two pages to Touchstone, a clown, and Audrey, a country maid, on the day before their marriage.*

It was a lover and his lass,
    With a hey, and a ho, and a hey nonino,
1 That o'er the green cornfield did pass
    In the springtime, the only pretty ringtime,[1]
When birds do sing, hey ding a ding, ding.
Sweet lovers love the spring.

Between the acres of the rye,
    With a hey, and a ho, and a hey nonino,
These pretty country folks would lie,
    In the springtime, the only pretty ringtime,
When birds do sing, hey ding a ding, ding.
Sweet lovers love the spring.

This carol they began that hour,
    With a hey, and a ho, and a hey nonino,
How that life was but a flower
    In the springtime, the only pretty ringtime,
2 When birds do sing, hey ding a ding, ding.
Sweet lovers love the spring.

And therefore take the present time,
    With a hey, and a ho, and a hey nonino,
3 For love is crownèd with the prime
    In the springtime, the only pretty ringtime,
When birds do sing, hey ding a ding, ding.
Sweet lovers love the spring.

---

1. **ringtime:** Wedding season.

THE WOODCUTTER COURTING THE MILKMAID
Thomas Gainsborough
Woburn Abbey

THINKING ABOUT THE SELECTION

Recalling

1. What do lovers love?
2. To what do lovers compare life?

Interpreting

3. Why do you think springtime is called "the only pretty ringtime"?
4. What recommendation about love is made in the last stanza?

Applying

5. Love songs have always been popular. What modern love song do you think comes closest to having the same message as "It Was a Lover and His Lass"?

CRITICAL THINKING AND READING

Finding Details That Develop Mood

The **mood** of a piece of writing is the atmosphere or emotion it conveys. Mood can be created through descriptive details and word choice. For example, a dark sky, rolling thunder, and howling wind can create an eerie mood. Such words as *shivering, aghast, oppressive,* and *helplessness* can add to it.

1. How would you describe the mood in this song?
2. (a) What descriptive details help convey the mood? (b) What words help convey it?

Humanities Note

Fine art, *The Woodcutter Courting the Milkmaid*, 1775, by Thomas Gainsborough. Thomas Gainsborough (1727–1788), an English painter, was educated at the St. Martin Lane Academy in London. He embarked on his career as a painter in Ipswich and the fashionable resort of Bath, where his fame as a portraitist was established. He moved to London and became one of England's most popular portrait painters. His subjects were the wealthy and noble, whose features he idealized and beautified. He was the favorite painter of King George III and later of Queen Charlotte.

Gainsborough loved landscape painting and for his own pleasure painted what he termed "fancy pictures." These were imaginary rural landscapes with peasants, which were influenced by the French bucolic painters of his day. *The Woodcutter Courting the Milkmaid* was painted early in his career in Ipswich. The delicate pastoral scene is painted in the soft strokes of color wash that are the trademark of a Gainsborough landscape. The scene is dominated by a dying oak tree painted in sensitive detail. The figures of the milkmaid and the woodcutter are dressed more in the style of French peasants, showing the influence of the French painters Gainsborough admired. This rural scene shows Gainsborough's love for the idealized country life.

You might ask the following questions for discussion:

1. What story does this painting tell?
2. In what ways does this painting illustrate this poem?

Answers

ANSWERS TO THINKING ABOUT THE SELECTION

Recalling

1. Lovers love the spring.
2. Life is compared to a flower.

Interpreting

3. Springtime is the time for love and marriage, nature's time of renewal.
4. The singer urges the hearer to take advantage of the present time, as it is joyous but all too brief.

Applying

5. Answers will vary depending on what rock and popular songs your students are currently enjoying.

ANSWERS TO CRITICAL THINKING AND READING

1. The mood is light, happy, and promising.
2. (a) Warm descriptions of spring's activities with birds singing, acres of rye (in which pretty country folk do lie), and green cornfields all suggest the mood. (b) The words *sweet lovers, green, pretty ringtime, birds . . . sing,* and *flower* are among those helping to create the mood of the song.

Motivation for Reading Here is a lament. As such it should express regret for the loss of the loved one while noting the sad compensations to be found on such an occasion.

Master Teacher Note By mistake, Imogen drinks a potion that causes a death-like trance. Ultimately she is reconciled with her lover. Hence, this song is ironic. Two characters from the play sing it in alternating stanzas or lines.

Purpose-Setting Question What composite comment does the song make about life? Does it suggest that the loved one is better off now?

1 **Literary Focus** The first three stanzas of this tender lyric follow a definite pattern: three lines that comfort the dead by specifying ills they need no longer suffer, a line stating a philosophic truth, and two lines reiterating that death awaits us all. Lines 5-6 are often quoted. Ask students to explain the witty meaning of this simile.

2 **Discussion** What does this line mean?

3 **Literary Focus** The final stanza departs from the others in content and form to become a personal prayer for the safekeeping of the dead girl's spirit. What do the singers pray for?

Fear No More the Heat o' the Sun

William Shakespeare

This song, from Cymbeline *(Act IV, Scene ii), is a lament for Imogen, the heroine, who is supposed to be dead.*

Fear no more the heat o' the sun,
    Nor the furious winter's rages;
Thou thy worldly task hast done,
1 Home art gone, and ta'en thy wages.
Golden lads and girls all must,
As[1] chimney sweepers, come to dust.

Fear no more the frown o' the great;
    Thou art past the tyrant's stroke;
Care no more to clothe and eat;
2 To thee the reed is as the oak:
The scepter, learning, physic,[2] must
All follow this, and come to dust.

Fear no more the lightning flash,
    Nor the all-dreaded thunder stone;[3]
Fear not slander, censure rash;
    Thou hast finished joy and moan:
All lovers young, all lovers must
Consign to thee, and come to dust.

No exorciser harm thee!
Nor no witchcraft charm thee!
Ghost unlaid forbear thee!
3 Nothing ill come near thee!
Quiet consummation have;
And renownèd be thy grave!

---

1. **As:** Like.
2. **scepter, learning, physic:** Kings, scholars, doctors.
3. **thunder stone:** At the time it was believed that the sound of thunder was caused by falling meteorites.

THINKING ABOUT THE SELECTION

Recalling

1. What are five aspects of life that the deceased no longer has to worry about?
2. What will happen to young lovers?

Interpreting

3. In the last stanza, what do the three concerns mentioned have in common?
4. Judging by the things the deceased no longer has to fear, what status in life do you think she held?

Applying

5. If this song were to be sung today, where would a person be most likely to hear it? Explain your answer.

ANALYZING LITERATURE

Understanding Shakespeare's Songs

The songs in Shakespeare's plays are functional; that is, each serves a specific purpose. In "Fear No More the Heat o' the Sun," the purpose is to convince the audience to look upon Imogen's death as a release from the pain and sorrow of life. The details in the song all stress the idea that Imogen has no further need to fear these troubling aspects of existence.

1. What are some of the details that support the purpose of the song?
2. Suppose the lament were to take exactly the opposite approach—with the details chosen to emphasize life's vanished joys. What might some of the specific details be?

THINKING AND WRITING

Writing About Shakespeare's Songs

Write an essay about Shakespeare's songs, commenting on their themes, tone, and language. Explain how the songs do or do not match your general impression of Shakespeare's works. Begin by rereading the songs and making notes on them. Then write a thesis sentence that states the main idea you intend to develop. In writing your first draft, try to work in appropriate quotations from the songs. Reread the first draft making sure the paper is logically developed and reads smoothly. Write a final draft incorporating all changes and corrections.

Answers

ANSWERS TO THINKING ABOUT THE SELECTION

Recalling

1. Five aspects of life the deceased need not contend with are the heat of the sun, winter's rages, the frowns of the great, the lightning's flash, and the thunder's clap.
2. All young lovers will eventually die.

Interpreting

3. All are part of the supernatural and refer to harm.
4. In the play, Imogen is the daughter of the king, a fact that may not be conveyed by the words of the song, as it suggests that being clothed and eating are part of life's chores along with frowns of the great.

Applying

5. A person might hear it at an unconventional funeral service.

ANSWERS TO ANALYZING LITERATURE

1. The details include the following: the heat of the sun, the writer's rages, the displeasure of the powerful, punishments inflicted by tyrants, ordinary cases, thunder and lightning, slander, and censure. These details are what Mogen need no longer fear.
2. Answers will vary. Vanished joys might include friendship, love, family happiness, the beauties of nature, success, admiration, and so on.

THINKING AND WRITING

For help with this assignment, students can refer to Lesson 12, "Writing About a Poem," in the Handbook of Writing About Literature.

Master Teacher Note In conjunction with this section on the Elizabethan Theater, you might show one of the films or filmstrips available on the subject. Two possibilities are *Theater in Shakespeare's Time,* BFA, or *World of Shakespeare Series,* "Shakespeare's Theater," CCM. Information on these films would be available in media catalogs.

Enrichment Traveling theater companies performed in many locations. They also used temporary stages in bear and bull baiting arenas. They put on plays in court, in great halls of artistocratic homes, in law courts, and at universities.

Enrichment In the Elizabethan theaters, costumes were conventional. Therefore, a king could be identified by his robe, crown, and scepter, while a fool always wore motley.

Enrichment Elizabethan plays compensated for lack of scenery with abundant noise. The theatergoers seemed to enjoy sounds. The texts of plays of the time abound with directions for various trumpet calls—sennets, tuckets, and flourishes. Royal personages always enter the stage with a flourish on the trumpets. Battle scenes were accompanied by all sorts of noises, such as alarams and retreats.

THE ELIZABETHAN THEATER

English drama came of age during the reign of Elizabeth I, developing into a sophisticated and very popular art form. While playwrights like Shakespeare were mainly responsible for the great theatrical achievements of the time, the importance of actors, audiences, and theater buildings should not be underestimated.

Before the reign of Elizabeth I, theater companies traveled about the country putting on plays wherever they could find an audience, often performing in the open courtyards of inns. Spectators watched from the ground or from the inn windows. The system persisted for years, but inns as theaters had a number of disadvantages. A permanent building solely for the production of plays was sorely needed.

England's First Playhouse

When Shakespeare was twelve years old, an actor named James Burbage built London's first theater, called The Theater, just beyond the city walls in Shoreditch. Actors—even prominent and well-to-do actors like Burbage—occupied an anomalous place in society. Despite the growing popularity of plays, actors of the time, however prosperous, were widely regarded as rogues and vagabonds. An act of Parliament in 1572 required acting companies to operate under the patronage of a respectable person or organization, and a London ordinance two years later imposed a number of licensing restrictions on theatrical groups and productions. Burbage's acting company enjoyed the patronage of the Earl of Leicester, but Burbage financed the new theater himself. His theater, once completed, proved a success, and its design set the pattern for the theaters that followed, including the famous Globe Theater in Southwark, built in 1599, where many of Shakespeare's plays were performed.

The Globe Theater

The Globe was an octagonal structure with an unroofed yard in the center where the "groundlings" stood. Groundlings were members of the audience who paid a mere penny to attend. Three tiers of seats, the galleries, rose around the perimeter of the yard and were protected by a thatched roof. Theatergoers in the galleries looked down on a rectangular wooden stage, raised a few feet off the ground, that jutted out into the yard. The groundlings were closer to the stage than were members of the gallery audience, but they had a less satisfactory view.

Permanence, however, allowed many refinements. At the back of the main stage were two doors that led to a dressing room and were used for most of the actors' entrances and exits. Built into the main stage were one or more trapdoors leading to an area below the stage. Actors playing ghosts or witches would appear and disappear through the trapdoors. Behind the main stage was a curtained recess, or inner stage, that was used (with the curtain opened) for

the presentation of indoor scenes. Directly over the inner stage was an upper stage, often used as a bedroom or a balcony. Above that—at the height of the top tier of seats—was a small building known as "the heavens" where the stage crew could produce thunder and other sound effects.

Although the Globe was not a large theater, it could accommodate more than two thousand spectators, about eight hundred of whom stood in the yard. Performances were given in the afternoon, the stage being lit by daylight. Costumes were colorful and often expensive, but the sets were simple, and scenery as we think of it today was hardly used at all. The companies strove for special effects, however, such as birds and goddesses descending from the roof by means of ropes and pulleys.

Women's roles in the plays were acted by men or, more commonly, by boys. Partly because of the absence of scenery to change and the absence of a curtain across the main stage, the plays proceeded at a brisk pace. Actors spoke their lines more rapidly than they do today. A good voice and excellent diction were imperative, and Elizabethan audiences spoke of "hearing" plays rather than "seeing" them. To a theatergoer of the time, the vocabulary of Shakespeare was familiar and easily grasped. Even so, the plays had to have dramatic power to hold a popular and sometimes unruly audience. Shakespeare's plays surely had that power. They still do.

Enrichment There is only one contemporary picture of an Elizabethan stage. This is a sketch made from memory by a Dutch traveler named Johannes de Witt, who visited London in 1596. In addition to making notes, he made a sketch of the interior of a theater. His notes, translated from Latin, include the following description: "Of all the theatres, however, the largest and most magnificent is that one of which the sign is a swan, called in the vernacular the Swan Theatre; for it accommodates in its seats three thousand persons, and it is built of a mass of flint stones (of which there is a prodigious supply in London), and supported by wooden columns painted in such excellent imitation of marble that it is able to deceive even the most cunning. Since its form resembles that of a Roman work, I have made a sketch of it above."

Humanities Note

Reconstruction of the Second Globe Theatre at London. This drawing shows a view of the stage of the Globe Theatre. The stage juts out into the yard, surrounded on three sides by seats or standing room for spectators. The "shadow," which is located over the stage and supported by pillars, protected players from the rain. Behind the stage is an inner recess, often called the "tiring house," used for indoor scenes. On the second level is the "chamber," with a balcony. The chamber was used to represent walls of a castle or town or a bedchamber in a dwelling. On the third level is another chamber, usually used by musicians. The fourth level is the turret, known as "the heavens," containing a bell, and other means of creating sound effects.

In this scene, Faustus is raising Mephistopheles through a trap, from Christopher Marlowe's play *The Tragical History of the Life and Death of Doctor Faustus.*

Enrichment A tragedy in the classical sense is a type of drama in which the major character undergoes a morally significant struggle that ends disastrously. According to Aristotle in the *Poetics,* the purpose of a tragedy is to arouse the emotions of pity and fear in the audience and thus to produce a catharsis of these emotions.

Enrichment Two important factors in tragedy are the role of chance or fate and the hero's tragic flaw. The hero of a tragedy has a flaw—some character defect that helps to bring about his downfall; otherwise, he would be afflicted with entirely undeserved suffering. The hero has ordinary human failings or limitations and falls short of ultimate perfection.

SHAKESPEAREAN TRAGEDY

The Tragedy of Macbeth

Macbeth is one of Shakespeare's great tragedies, a compelling and timeless drama about the success, treachery, and disintegration of a brave but flawed human being. Its diagnosis of evil is as apt today as it was when The King's Men first presented the play.

Shakespeare completed *Macbeth* in 1606, not long after the appearance of his other great tragedies—*Hamlet, Othello,* and *King Lear.* Intended as a tribute to King James I, *Macbeth* may have been first performed before the royal family at Hampton Court, a palace twelve miles from the center of London. King James, who already wore the crown of Scotland when he ascended the throne of England, would have found *Macbeth* especially intriguing. The play is set in Scotland in the eleventh century, when James's family, the Stuarts, first came to the Scottish throne. One of the strongest and most virtuous characters in the play, Banquo, is said to have been the father of the first of the Stuart kings.

Shakespeare derived the basic plot for *Macbeth* from an account of eleventh-century Scottish history in Raphael Holinshed's *Chronicles of England, Scotland, and Ireland.* In writing his play, Shakespeare altered and expanded Holinshed's history, reshaped the personalities, and invented some new characters.

The central character in *Macbeth,* as in other Elizabethan (and Greek) tragedies, is a tragic hero, a person of high rank and personal quality. Because of a fatal weakness, a tragic flaw, the hero becomes involved in a series of events that lead to his eventual downfall and destruction.

At the beginning of Shakespeare's play, the hero, Macbeth, is pictured as courageous, trustworthy, and loyal. By the end of the play, his ambition has driven him to commit a series of horrendous acts that, once begun, he is powerless to stop. While the audience is repelled by Macbeth's actions, it also pities him, understanding Macbeth's anguish and knowing how easy it is to fall prey to uncontrolled ambition or greed.

The temptations Macbeth faces are ones that have confronted people throughout time. These universal lures—along with Shakespeare's suspense-filled plot, superbly drawn characters, and masterful use of language—have contributed to the play's continuing popularity from Elizabethan days to the present.

The Whole Play

A great play like *Macbeth* weaves a variety of elements into a unified whole. No matter how impressive the individual speeches or how memorable the incidents, the play must be judged on its total effect. If the playwright has successfully blended plot, character, setting, atmosphere, diction, and imagery—and if the actors have then captured the entire rich tapestry on stage—the result is an intensely satisfying drama.

Plot

Basic to every plot is conflict, or struggle. External conflict occurs when a character struggles against another person or an outside force. In *Macbeth* there is external conflict between Macbeth and Macduff. Internal conflict is that which occurs within the mind of a character. Macbeth's agonizing over whether or not to kill Duncan is an example of internal conflict.

Character

Nothing is more important in a work of literature than the portrayal of character. *Macbeth* is a masterpiece of characterization. Macbeth, the tragic hero, is shown as being destroyed because of a tragic flaw.

Setting

Setting is the time and place in which the events in a literary work take place. The general setting of *Macbeth* is Scotland (and briefly England) in the tenth and eleventh centuries. Specific scenes are set at Inverness, on a desolate heath, in the royal palace at Forres, and so on. Because of the limited scenery in Elizabethan drama, Shakespeare often has his characters describe their surroundings.

Atmosphere

The atmosphere in *Macbeth* is one of doom and foreboding. Much of the action takes place in foul weather or in the "thick night" of darkened castles. The witches and apparitions cast a pall whenever they appear. Except for the porter's brief speech, there is little in the play resembling lightheartedness.

Diction

The term *diction* has two meanings. It can mean the pronunciation of words by an actor or other speaker. It can also mean the writer's choice of words, which in a play are delivered by the actors. A writer chooses words with care, making sure they are appropriate to the character, theme, and atmosphere of the literary work. For example, King Duncan in *Macbeth* uses language suitable for a king, while the porter speaks in a more earthy style.

Imagery

Imagers is usually visual, but it can evoke responses from any of the senses. Images, wrote one critic, like those of ". . . pouring the sweet milk of concord into hell; of the earth shaking in fever; . . . of the tale told by an idiot . . . —all keep the imagination moving 'on a wild and violent sea.' . . ."

Enrichment Unlike modern audiences, Elizabethan writers and playgoers did not care if a plot was original. Many of Shakespeare's plays are based on familiar stories or readily available source material. For *Macbeth* Shakespeare took the names of his characters from Raphael Holinshed's *Chronicles,* but he was not interested in historical accuracy as he wrote. He used the events as he wanted to make a play that could be performed in two or three hours. He invented, expanded, and linked historically unconnected events in order to create this powerful tragedy.

Master Teacher Note As students read *Macbeth,* have them keep a notebook in which they jot down their thoughts and comments as they read. They might use the categories on these pages: plot, character, setting, atmosphere, diction, imagery. In addition to thoughts and comments, students might also record significant quotations from the play.

Literary Focus If students have read any of the sonnets in this text, they are already familiar with iambic pentameter. Advise them to note that as they read, the verse format will come to seem as natural as prose after a page or two.

Look For Have **more advanced** students observe where and how Shakespeare turns phrases around, changes nouns into verbs, and otherwise alters structure to maintain the meter on occasion.

Writing Have two or more students write sentences about any subject on the board. Then have the class change each around to conform to iambic pentameter.

Vocabulary Some of the words here and in the next four acts will seldom if ever be used by students. *Liege* is an example. Note, however, that *refurbish* and *prophecy* are two of today's commonly used words.

GUIDE FOR READING

The Tragedy of Macbeth, Act I

Writer's Techniques

Blank Verse. Like all of Shakespeare's plays, *Macbeth* is written mainly in blank verse. Blank verse is composed of unrhymed lines of iambic pentameter. Iambic pentameter has five feet, or beats, per line, and every other syllable is stressed. The following two lines are an example of blank verse from Act I of *Macbeth*.

∪ / ∪ / ∪ / ∪ / ∪ /
Your face my thane, is as a book where men
∪ / ∪ / ∪ / ∪ / ∪ /
May read strange manners. To beguile the time,

Blank verse, which was introduced into English literature by the Earl of Surrey, can be stately and dignified, but it can also produce an effect of smooth, natural speech more effectively than most other metrical patterns. It is one of the most flexible and versatile verse forms, a favorite not only of the poets during the English Renaissance, but of many later poets.

Look For

C. S. Lewis wrote, "Gratitude looks to the past and love to the present; fear, avarice, lust and ambition look ahead." As you read *Macbeth,* look for how the witches' predictions for Macbeth's future affect him.

Writing

Because of its versatility, blank verse can be used to reproduce all kinds of speech. Listen carefully to a discussion, or think of a conversation you have recently had. Reshape this speech into dialogue written in blank verse. Try to make it sound as natural as possible.

Vocabulary

Knowing the following words will help you as you read *Macbeth,* Act I.

furbished (fur'bisħd) *adj.*: Brightened; polished (Sc. ii, l. 32)
prophetic (prə fet'ik) *adj.*: Having the power to predict or foreshadow (Sc. iii, l. 78)
surmise (sər mīz') *v.*: To form an opinion from inconclusive evidence (Sc. iii, l. 141)
liege (lēj) *n.*: Lord or king (Sc. iv, l. 3)
chastise (chas tīz') *v.*: To condemn sharply; scold (Sc. v, l. 28)
metaphysical (met ə fiz'i k'l) *adj.*: Very abstract (Sc. v, l. 30)
sovereign (säv'rən) *adj.*: Supreme in power, rank, or authority (Sc. v, l. 72)

Objectives

1. To read and understand blank verse
2. To make inferences about characters
3. To read blank verse aloud
4. To compare and contrast characters

Teaching Portfolio: Support Material

Teacher Backup, p. 000

Vocabulary Check, p. 00

Usage and Mechanics Worksheet, pp. 00

Analyzing Literature Worksheet, pp. 00

Critical Thinking and Reading Worksheet, pp. 00

Language Worksheet, pp. 00

Selection Test, pp. 00

The Tragedy of Macbeth

William Shakespeare

CHARACTERS

Duncan, King of Scotland
Malcolm, **Donalbain** — his sons
Macbeth, **Banquo**, **Macduff**, **Lennox**, **Ross**, **Menteith**, **Angus**, **Caithness** — noblemen of Scotland
Fleance, son to Banquo
Siward, Earl of Northumberland, general of the English forces
Young Siward, his son
Seyton, an officer attending on Macbeth
Son to Macduff
An English Doctor
A Scottish Doctor
A Porter
An Old Man
Three Murderers
Lady Macbeth
Lady Macduff
A Gentlewoman attending on Lady Macbeth
Hecate
Witches
Apparitions
Lords, Officers, Soldiers, Attendants, and Messengers

Setting: Scotland; England

Act I

Scene i. *An open place.*
1 [*Thunder and lightning. Enter* THREE WITCHES.]

FIRST WITCH. When shall we three meet again?
In thunder, lightning, or in rain?

SECOND WITCH. When the hurlyburly's done,
When the battle's lost and won.

2 THIRD WITCH. That will be ere the set of sun.

FIRST WITCH. Where the place?

SECOND WITCH. Upon the heath.

THIRD WITCH. There to meet with Macbeth.

Motivation for Reading Explain that the first act of a play provides much of the exposition—introducing the story and characters while establishing mood, tone, and direction. As the curtain falls, however, the audience should be eager to see how all that has been laid down so far will further develop and conclude.

Master Teacher Note Have your students observe the recurring juxtaposition of opposites that begins in line 4. Such opposites occur again and again throughout. Everything seems turned upside down throughout the play—with its characters, its events, and with nature itself.

1 **Literary Focus** Scene i is unusually short and powerful. Opening scenes so often plod through necessary set-up information. Remind the students that the play was written to be seen, and as such makes a powerful visual opening.

2 **Discussion** Why will the witches meet again? When and where? What do you expect will be happening with the introduction of witches, storms, and so on?

Humanities Note

Fine art, *The Three Witches* by Henry Fuseli. Henry Fuseli (1741–1825), a Swiss-born English artist, was initially a writer, but with encouragement from Sir Joshua Reynolds, the head of the Royal Academy of Art, he began to paint seriously. His formal art education consisted of an eight-year sojourn in Rome, where he studied the art of the Italian master Michelangelo. The style in which Fuseli painted is a combination of romanticism, fantasy, and a fascination with the grotesque. Throughout his career Fuseli was influenced by literature, especially the works of William Shakespeare.

The painting *The Three Witches* was done to illustrate *Macbeth*. Fuseli's love for the weird and fantastic is apparent in this painting. The spectral quality of the three figures and the ominous skull-headed insect are like something from a nightmare. The strong composition is enhanced by the rhythm of the three outstretched arms ending in talonlike hands.

You might ask your students these questions:

1. How does this painting communicate the message that these three beings are not of this world?
2. Does this painting give you a better understanding of the fright felt by the characters upon encountering the witches?

3 **Clarification** Forres is the site of Duncan's castle.

4 **Literary Focus** Duncan's second word is *blood*, one of the important motifs of the play.

THE THREE WITCHES
Henry Fuseli
Courtauld Institute Galleries, London

FIRST WITCH. I come, Graymalkin.[1]

SECOND WITCH. Paddock[2] calls.

THIRD WITCH. Anon![3]

ALL. Fair is foul, and foul is fair.
Hover through the fog and filthy air. [*Exit.*]

1. **Graymalkin:** The first witch's helper, a gray cat.
2. **Paddock:** The second witch's helper, a toad.
3. **Anon:** At once.

3 ***Scene ii.*** *A camp near Forres, a town in northeast Scotland.* [*Alarum within.*[1] *Enter* KING DUNCAN, MALCOLM, DONALBAIN, LENNOX, *with* ATTENDANTS, *meeting a bleeding* CAPTAIN.]

1. **Alarum within:** Trumpet call offstage.

4 **KING.** What bloody man is that? He can report,
As seemeth by his plight, of the revolt
The newest state.

MALCOLM. This is the sergeant[2]
Who like a good and hardy soldier fought
'Gainst my captivity. Hail, brave friend!
Say to the king the knowledge of the broil[3]
As thou didst leave it.

CAPTAIN. Doubtful it stood,
As two spent swimmers, that do cling together
And choke their art.[4] The merciless Macdonwald—
Worthy to be a rebel for to that
The multiplying villainies of nature
5 Do swarm upon him—from the Western Isles[5]
Of kerns and gallowglasses[6] is supplied;
And fortune, on his damnèd quarrel[7] smiling,
Showed like a rebel's whore:[8] but all's too weak:
For brave Macbeth—well he deserves that name—
Disdaining fortune, with his brandished steel,
Which smoked with bloody execution,
6 Like valor's minion[9] carved out his passage
Till he faced the slave;
Which nev'r shook hands, nor bade farewell to him,
Till he unseamed him from the nave to th' chops,[10]
And fixed his head upon our battlements.

KING. O valiant cousin! Worthy gentleman!

CAPTAIN. As whence the sun 'gins his reflection[11]
Shipwracking storms and direful thunders break,
So from that spring whence comfort seemed to come
Discomfort swells. Mark, King of Scotland, mark:
7 No sooner justice had, with valor armed,
Compelled these skipping kerns to trust their heels
But the Norweyan lord,[12] surveying vantage,[13]
With furbished arms and new supplies of men,
Began a fresh assault.

KING. Dismayed not this
Our captains, Macbeth and Banquo?

CAPTAIN. Yes;
As sparrows eagles, or the hare the lion.
If I say sooth,[14] I must report they were
As cannons overcharged with double cracks;[15]
So they doubly redoubled strokes upon the foe.
Except[16] they meant to bathe in reeking wounds,
Or memorize another Golgotha,[17]
I cannot tell—
But I am faint; my gashes cry for help.

2. sergeant: Officer.

3. broil: Battle.

4. choke their art: prevent each other from swimming.

5. Western Isles: The Hebrides, off Scotland.

6. Of kerns and gallowglasses: With lightly armed Irish foot soldiers and heavily armed soldiers.

7. damnèd quarrel: Accursed cause.

8. Showed . . . whore: Falsely appeared to favor Macdonwald.

9. minion: Favorite.

10. unseamed . . . chops: Split him open from the navel to the jaws.

11. 'gins his reflection: Rises.

12. Norweyan lord: King of Norway.

13. surveying vantage: Seeing an opportunity.

14. sooth: Truth.

15. cracks: Explosives.

16. except: Unless.

17. memorize . . . Golgotha (gol' gə thə): Make the place as memorable for slaughter as Golgotha, the place where Christ was crucified.

5 **Historical Focus** Holinshed suggests that Duncan's gentle nature prompted the uprising by Macdonwald.

6 **Discussion** What do we learn of Macbeth's prowess in battle?

7 **Discussion** What discomfort swells? Why?

8 Discussion What does Cawdor do? How does this battle conclude?

9 Clarification "Dollars" would have been Dutch thalers or Spanish pieces-of-eight.

KING. So well thy words become thee as thy wounds;
They smack of honor both. Go get him surgeons.
[*Exit* CAPTAIN, *attended.*]

[*Enter* ROSS *and* ANGUS.]

Who comes here?

MALCOLM. The worthy Thane[18] of Ross.

LENNOX. What a haste looks through his eyes! So should he look
That seems to[19] speak things strange.

ROSS. God save the king!

KING. Whence cam'st thou, worthy Thane?

ROSS. From Fife, great King;
Where the Norweyan banners flout the sky
And fan our people cold.
Norway[20] himself, with terrible numbers,
Assisted by that most disloyal traitor
8 The Thane of Cawdor, began a dismal[21] conflict;
Till that Bellona's bridegroom, lapped in proof,[22]
Confronted him with self-comparisons,[23]
Point against point, rebellious arm 'gainst arm,
Curbing his lavish[24] spirit: and, to conclude,
The victory fell on us.

KING. Great happiness!

ROSS. That now
Sweno, the Norways' king, craves composition;[25]
Nor would we deign him burial of his men
9 Till he disbursèd, at Saint Colme's Inch,[26]
Ten thousand dollars to our general use.

KING. No more that Thane of Cawdor shall deceive
Our bosom interest:[27] go pronounce his present[28] death,
And with his former title greet Macbeth.

ROSS. I'll see it done.

KING. What he hath lost, noble Macbeth hath won.
[*Exit.*]

Scene iii. *A heath near Forres.*
[*Thunder. Enter the* THREE WITCHES.]

FIRST WITCH. Where hast thou been, sister?

SECOND WITCH. Killing swine.[1]

THIRD WITCH. Sister, where thou?

18. Thane: A Scottish title of nobility.

19. seems to: Seems about to.

20. Norway: The King of Norway.

21. dismal: Threatening.

22. Bellona's . . . proof: Macbeth is called the mate of Bellona, the goddess of war, clad in tested armor.

23. self-comparisons: Counter movements.

24. lavish: Insolent.

25. composition: Terms of peace.

26. St. Colme's Inch: Island near Edinburgh, Scotland.

27. our bosom interest: My heart's trust.

28. present: Immediate.

1. Killing swine: It was commonly believed that witches killed domestic animals.

FIRST WITCH. A sailor's wife had chestnuts in her lap,
And mounched, and mounched, and mounched.
"Give me," quoth I.
10 "Aroint thee,[2] witch!" the rump-fed ronyon[3] cries.
Her husband's to Aleppo[4] gone, master o' th' Tiger:
But in a sieve[5] I'll thither sail,
And, like a rat without a tail,[6]
I'll do, I'll do, and I'll do.

SECOND WITCH. I'll give thee a wind.

FIRST WITCH. Th' art kind.

THIRD WITCH. And I another.

FIRST WITCH. I myself have all the other;
And the very ports they blow,[7]
All the quarters that they know
I' th' shipman's card.[8]
I'll drain him dry as hay:
Sleep shall neither night nor day
11 Hang upon his penthouse lid;[9]
He shall live a man forbid:[10]
Weary sev'nights[11] nine times nine
Shall he dwindle, peak,[12] and pine:
Though his bark cannot be lost,
Yet it shall be tempest-tossed.
Look what I have.

SECOND WITCH. Show me, show me.

FIRST WITCH. Here I have a pilot's thumb,
Wracked as homeward he did come.
[*Drum within.*]

THIRD WITCH. A drum, a drum!
Macbeth doth come.

ALL. The weird[13] sisters, hand in hand,
12 Posters[14] of the sea and land,
Thus do go about, about:
Thrice to thine, and thrice to mine,
And thrice again, to make up nine.
Peace! The charm's wound up.

[*Enter* MACBETH and BANQUO.]

13 **MACBETH.** So foul and fair a day I have not seen.

BANQUO. How far is 't called to Forres? What are these
So withered, and so wild in their attire,
That look not like th' inhabitants o' th' earth,
And yet are on 't? Live you, or are you aught

2. Aroint thee: Be off.
3. rump-fed ronyon: Fat-rumped, scabby creature.
4. Aleppo: A trading center in Syria.
5. sieve: It was commonly believed that witches often sailed in sieves.
6. rat . . . tail: According to popular belief, witches could assume the form of any animal, but the tail would always be missing.
7. they blow: To which the winds blow.
8. card: Compass.
9. penthouse lid: Eyelid.
10. forbid: Cursed.
11. sev'nights: Weeks.
12. peak: Waste away.
13. weird: Destiny-serving.
14. Posters: Swift travelers.

10 Literary Focus The power and malevolence of the witches is demonstrated by the havoc created upon the sailor-husband of this selfish woman.

11 Literary Focus Sleeplessness is a recurring theme throughout the play.

12 Clarification *Wyrd* is the Anglo-Saxon word for fate, and that is the way *weird* is used here.

13 Discussion Notice that Macbeth echoes the words of the witches from scene i. Why is it foul and fair?

14 Literary Focus It is likely that mature and whiskered males, rather than young men, who normally played female parts, played the roles of the haglike witches.

15 Literary Focus Prophesies since earliest times have been ambiguous—this to save the necks of prophets who were regularly consulted before battles and on other occasions in ancient times. Prophesies in Greek mythology and literature were most often cloaked with ambiguity for reasons of the story.

That man may question? You seem to understand me,
By each at once her choppy[15] finger laying
14 Upon her skinny lips. You should be women,
And yet your beards forbid me to interpret
That you are so.

MACBETH. Speak, if you can: what are you?

FIRST WITCH. All hail, Macbeth! Hail to thee, Thane of Glamis!

SECOND WITCH. All hail, Macbeth! Hail to thee, Thane of Cawdor!

THIRD WITCH. All hail, Macbeth, that shalt be King hereafter!

BANQUO. Good sir, why do you start, and seem to fear
Things that do sound so fair? I' th' name of truth,
Are you fantastical,[16] or that indeed
Which outwardly ye show? My noble partner
You greet with present grace[17] and great prediction
Of noble having[18] and of royal hope,
That he seems rapt withal:[19] to me you speak not.
If you can look into the seeds of time,
And say which grain will grow and which will not,
Speak then to me, who neither beg nor fear
Your favors nor your hate.

FIRST WITCH. Hail!

SECOND WITCH. Hail!

THIRD WITCH. Hail!

FIRST WITCH. Lesser than Macbeth, and greater.

15 SECOND WITCH. Not so happy,[20] yet much happier.

THIRD WITCH. Thou shalt get kings, though thou be none.
So all hail, Macbeth and Banquo!

FIRST WITCH. Banquo and Macbeth, all hail!

MACBETH. Stay, you imperfect[21] speakers, tell me more:
By Sinel's[22] death I know I am Thane of Glamis;
But how of Cawdor? The Thane of Cawdor lives,
A prosperous gentleman; and to be King
Stands not within the prospect of belief,
No more than to be Cawdor. Say from whence
You owe[23] this strange intelligence?[24] Or why
Upon this blasted heath you stop our way
With such prophetic greeting? Speak, I charge you.
[WITCHES *vanish.*]

15. choppy: chapped.
16. fantastical: Imaginary.
17. grace: Honor.
18. having: Possession.
19. rapt withal: Entranced by it.
20. happy: Fortunate.
21. imperfect: Incomplete.
22. Sinel's (si' nəlz): Macbeth's father's.
23. owe: Own.
24. intelligence: Information.

MACBETH AND THE WITCHES
Clarkson Stanfield
Leicestershire Museums

Humanities Note

Fine art, *Macbeth and the Witches* by Clarkson Stanfield. William Clarkson Stanfield (1793–1867) was an English painter who began his life as a sailor. To pass time while on board ship, Stanfield drew marine views and made scenery for the sailors' play productions. Upon discharge from the navy, Stanfield took a job as a scene painter in a London theater. In subsequent years he gained an outstanding reputation for his painted scenery and worked for many theaters.

This watercolor sketch, *Macbeth and the Witches*, was done for a production of *Macbeth* at one of the theaters for which Stanfield worked. It was painted between the years 1813 and 1829. A skillful stage design, it serves to explain the popularity of Stanfield in theater circles. You may wish to ask your students this question: Does this sketch help you to visualize the impact of this scene on a theater audience?

16 Clarification Ross is not sure whether Cawdor aligned himself with Norway or Macdonwald. In either case he is being held for treason.

BANQUO. The earth hath bubbles as the water has,
And these are of them. Whither are they vanished?

MACBETH. Into the air, and what seemed corporal[25] melted
As breath into the wind. Would they had stayed!

BANQUO. Were such things here as we do speak about?
Or have we eaten on the insane root[26]
That takes the reason prisoner?

MACBETH. Your children shall be kings.

BANQUO. You shall be King.

MACBETH. And Thane of Cawdor too. Went it not so?

BANQUO. To th' selfsame tune and words. Who's here?

[*Enter* ROSS *and* ANGUS.]

ROSS. The King hath happily received, Macbeth,
The news of thy success; and when he reads[27]
Thy personal venture in the rebels' fight,
His wonders and his praises do contend
Which should be thine or his.[28] Silenced with that,
In viewing o'er the rest o' th' selfsame day,
He finds thee in the stout Norweyan ranks,
Nothing afeard of what thyself didst make,
Strange images of death.[29] As thick as tale
Came post with post,[30] and every one did bear
Thy praises in his kingdom's great defense,
And poured them down before him.

ANGUS. We are sent
To give thee, from our royal master, thanks;
Only to herald thee into his sight,
Not pay thee.

ROSS. And for an earnest[31] of a greater honor,
He bade me, from him, call thee Thane of Cawdor;
In which addition,[32] hail, most worthy Thane!
For it is thine.

BANQUO. [*Aside*] What, can the devil speak true?

MACBETH. The Thane of Cawdor lives: why do you dress me
In borrowed robes?

ANGUS. Who was the thane lives yet,
But under heavy judgment bears that life
16 Which he deserves to lose. Whether he was combined[33]

25. corporal: Real.

26. insane root: Henbane or hemlock, believed to cause insanity.

27. reads: Considers.

28. His wonders . . . his: His admiration contends with his desire to praise you.

29. Nothing . . . death: Killing, but not being afraid of being killed.

30. As thick . . . post: As fast as could be counted came messenger after messenger.

31. earnest: Pledge.

32. In which addition: With this new title.

33. combined: Allied.

With those of Norway, or did line[34] the rebel
With hidden help and vantage,[35] or that with both
He labored in his country's wrack,[36] I know not;
But treasons capital, confessed and proved,
Have overthrown him.

MACBETH. [*Aside*] Glamis, and Thane of Cawdor:
The greatest is behind.[37] [*To* ROSS *and* ANGUS]
Thanks for your pains.
[*Aside to* BANQUO] Do you not hope your children
shall be kings,
When those that gave the Thane of Cawdor to me
Promised no less to them?

BANQUO. [*Aside to* MACBETH] That, trusted home,[38]
Might yet enkindle you unto[39] the crown,
Besides the Thane of Cawdor. But 'tis strange:
And oftentimes, to win us to our harm,
17 The instruments of darkness tell us truths,
Win us with honest trifles, to betray 's
In deepest consequence.
Cousins,[40] a word, I pray you.

MACBETH. [*Aside*] Two truths are told,
As happy prologues to the swelling act
Of the imperial theme.[41]—I thank you,
gentlemen.—
[*Aside*] This supernatural soliciting
Cannot be ill, cannot be good. If ill,
Why hath it given me earnest of success,
18 Commencing in a truth? I am Thane of Cawdor:
If good, why do I yield to that suggestion[42]
Whose horrid image doth unfix my hair
And make my seated[43] heart knock at my ribs,
Against the use of nature?[44] Present fears
Are less than horrible imaginings.
My thought, whose murder yet is but fantastical
Shakes so my single[45] state of man that function
19 Is smothered in surmise, and nothing is
But what is not.

BANQUO. Look, how our partner's rapt.

20 **MACBETH.** [*Aside*] If chance will have me King, why,
chance may crown me,
Without my stir.

BANQUO. New honors come upon him,
Like our strange[46] garments, cleave not to their
mold
But with the aid of use.

34. line: support.
35. vantage: Assistance.
36. wrack: Ruin.

37. behind: Still to come.

38. home: fully.
39. enkindle you unto: Encourage you to hope for.

40. Cousins: Often used as a term of courtesy between fellow noblemen.

41. swelling . . . theme: Stately idea that I will be King.

42. suggestion: Thought of murdering Duncan.
43. seated: Fixed.
44. Against . . . nature: In an unnatural way.

45. single: Unaided, weak.

46. strange: New.

17 **Discussion** What warning does Banquo offer Macbeth?

18 **Discussion** With Ross's words hardly out, Macbeth is already thinking of murder. What does the thought of it do to him?

19 **Literary Focus** Here Macbeth expresses that what is, is not—a constantly recurring theme.

20 **Discussion** What decision does Macbeth seem to come to here?

21 Discussion Ask the students how they might rephrase these lines?

22 Discussion How did Cawdor meet his death? In doing so, how did he seem to treat his life?

23 Discussion Duncan's comment here is most significant to Duncan and to the play. What does he say?

24 Literary Focus Note the irony of Macbeth's entrance as Duncan utters these words.

21 MACBETH. [*Aside*] Come what come may,
Time and the hour runs through the roughest day.

BANQUO. Worthy Macbeth, we stay upon your leisure.[47]

MACBETH. Give me your favor.[48] My dull brain was wrought
With things forgotten. Kind gentlemen, your pains
Are registered where every day I turn
The leaf to read them. Let us toward the King.
[*Aside to* BANQUO] Think upon what hath chanced, and at more time,
The interim having weighed it,[49] let us speak
Our free hearts[50] each to other.

BANQUO. Very gladly.

MACBETH. Till then, enough. Come, friends. [*Exit.*]

47. **stay upon your leisure:** Await your convenience.
48. **favor:** Pardon.
49. **The interim . . . it:** When we have had time to think about it.
50. **Our free hearts:** Our minds freely.

Scene iv. *Forres. The palace.*

[*Flourish.*[1] *Enter* KING DUNCAN, LENNOX, MALCOLM, DONALBAIN, *and* ATTENDANTS.]

KING. Is execution done on Cawdor? Are not
Those in commission[2] yet returned?

MALCOLM. My liege,
They are not yet come back. But I have spoke
With one that saw him die, who did report
That very frankly he confessed his treasons,
Implored your Highness' pardon and set forth
A deep repentance: nothing in his life
22 Became him like the leaving it. He died
As one that had been studied[3] in his death,
To throw away the dearest thing he owed[4]
As 'twere a careless[5] trifle.

KING. There's no art
To find the mind's construction[6] in the face:
23 He was a gentleman on whom I built
An absolute trust.

24 [*Enter* MACBETH, BANQUO, ROSS, *and* ANGUS.]

O worthiest cousin!
The sin of my ingratitude even now
Was heavy on me: thou art so far before,
That swiftest wing of recompense is slow
To overtake thee. Would thou hadst less deserved,
That the proportion both of thanks and payment
Might have been mine![7] Only I have left to say,
More is thy due than more than all can pay.

1. **Flourish:** Trumpet fanfare.
2. **in commission:** Commissioned to oversee the execution.
3. **studied:** Rehearsed.
4. **owed:** Owned.
5. **careless:** Worthless.
6. **mind's construction:** A person's character.
7. **Would . . . mine:** If you had been less worthy, my thanks and payment could have exceeded the rewards you deserve.

MACBETH. The service and the loyalty I owe,
In doing it, pays itself.[8] Your Highness' part
Is to receive our duties: and our duties
Are to your throne and state children and servants;
25 Which do but what they should, by doing every thing
Safe toward[9] your love and honor.

KING. Welcome hither.
I have begun to plant thee, and will labor
To make thee full of growing. Noble Banquo,
That hast no less deserved, nor must be known
No less to have done so, let me enfold thee
And hold thee to my heart.

BANQUO. There if I grow,
The harvest is your own.

KING. My plenteous joys,
Wanton[10] in fullness, seek to hide themselves
In drops of sorrow. Sons, kinsmen, thanes,
And you whose places are the nearest, know,
We will establish our estate upon
26 Our eldest, Malcolm,[11] whom we name hereafter
The Prince of Cumberland: which honor must
Not unaccompanied invest him only,
But signs of nobleness, like stars, shall shine
On all deservers. From hence to Inverness,[12]
And bind us further to you.

MACBETH. The rest is labor, which is not used for you.[13]
I'll be myself the harbinger,[14] and make joyful
The hearing of my wife with your approach;
So, humbly take my leave.

KING. My worthy Cawdor!

MACBETH. [*Aside*] The Prince of Cumberland! That is a
step
27 On which I must fall down, or else o'erleap,
For in my way it lies. Stars, hide your fires;
Let not light see my black and deep desires:
The eye wink at the hand;[15] yet let that be
Which the eye fears, when it is done, to see. [*Exit.*]

KING. True, worthy Banquo; he is full so valiant,
And in his commendations I am fed;
28 It is a banquet to me. Let's after him,
Whose care is gone before to bid us welcome.
It is a peerless kinsman. [*Flourish. Exit.*]

8. pays itself: Is its own reward.

9. Safe toward: With sure regard for.

10. Wanton: Unrestrained.

11. Establish . . . Malcolm: Make Malcolm the heir to my throne.

12. Inverness: Macbeth's castle.

13. The rest . . . you: Anything not done for you is laborious.

14. harbinger: An advance representative of the army or royal party who makes arrangements for a visit.

15. wink at the hand: Be blind to the hand's deed.

25 **Literary Focus** Note the irony of these lines.

26 **Discussion** Where does Duncan's announcement leave "chance" as a factor in Macbeth's being king?

27 **Discussion** What is Macbeth's state of mind by this time?

28 **Literary Focus** Consider the irony of this speech. How do these words relate to lines 12–14?

29 Literary Focus In order to share the contents of the letter, Lady Macbeth must read it aloud. What techniques might be used in today's stage and film productions where letters remain important parts of stories?

30 Discussion What is Lady Macbeth's reaction to the prophesy? What is her concern about Macbeth in this regard? How does she describe him?

31 Literary Focus Note the words *mad* in line 31 and *dead* in line 36 used in what would otherwise be stage-business dialogue. Death and madness prevail here.

Scene v. *Inverness. Macbeth's* castle.
[Enter MACBETH'S WIFE, *alone, with a letter.*]

LADY MACBETH. [*Reads*] "They met me in the day of
success; and I have learned by the perfect'st report
they have more in them than mortal knowledge.
When I burned in desire to question them further, they made themselves air, into which they vanished. Whiles I stood rapt in the wonder of it, came
29 missives[1] from the King, who all-hailed me 'Thane
of Cawdor'; by which title, before, these weird sisters
saluted me, and referred me to the coming on
of time, with 'Hail, King that shalt be!' This have I
thought good to deliver thee,[2] my dearest partner of
greatness, that thou mightst not lose the dues of
rejoicing, by being ignorant of what greatness is
promised thee. Lay it to thy heart, and farewell."

Glamis thou art, and Cawdor, and shalt be
What thou art promised. Yet do I fear thy nature;
It is too full o' th' milk of human kindness
To catch the nearest[3] way. Thou wouldst be great,
Art not without ambition, but without
The illness[4] should attend it. What thou wouldst highly,
That wouldst thou holily; wouldst not play false,
30 And yet wouldst wrongly win. Thou'dst have, great Glamis,
That which cries "Thus thou must do" if thou have it;
And that which rather thou dost fear to do
Than wishest should be undone.[5] Hie thee hither,
That I may pour my spirits in thine ear,
And chastise with the valor of my tongue
All that impedes thee from the golden round[6]
Which fate and metaphysical aid doth seem
To have thee crowned withal.

[*Enter* MESSENGER.]

What is your tidings?

MESSENGER. The King comes here tonight.

LADY MACBETH. Thou'rt mad to say it!
Is not thy master with him, who, were't so,
Would have informed for preparation?

31 **MESSENGER.** So please you, it is true. Our thane is coming.
One of my fellows had the speed of him,[7]
Who, almost dead for breath, had scarcely more
Than would make up his message.

1. **missives:** Messengers.

2. **deliver thee:** Report to you.

3. **nearest:** Quickest.

4. **illness:** Wickedness.

5. **that which . . . undone:** What you are afraid of doing you would not wish undone once you have done it.

6. **round:** Crown.

7. **had . . . him:** Overtook him.

LADY MACBETH. Give him tending;
He brings great news. [*Exit* MESSENGER.]
32 The raven himself is hoarse
That croaks the fatal entrance of Duncan
Under my battlements. Come, you spirits
That tend on mortal[8] thoughts, unsex me here,
And fill me, from the crown to the toe, top-full
Of direst cruelty! Make thick my blood,
Stop up th' access and passage to remorse[9]
33 That no compunctious visitings of nature[10]
Shake my fell[11] purpose, nor keep peace between
Th' effect[12] and it! Come to my woman's breasts,
And take my milk for gall,[13] you murd'ring minis-
ters,[14]
Wherever in your sightless[15] substances
You wait on[16] nature's mischief! Come, thick night,
And pall[17] thee in the dunnest[18] smoke of hell,
34 That my keen knife see not the wound it makes,
Nor heaven peep through the blanket of the dark,
To cry "Hold, hold!"

[*Enter* MACBETH.]

Great Glamis! Worthy Cawdor!
Greater than both, by the all-hail hereafter!
Thy letters have transported me beyond
This ignorant[19] present, and I feel now
The future in the instant.[20]

MACBETH. My dearest love,
Duncan comes here tonight.

LADY MACBETH. And when goes hence?

MACBETH. Tomorrow, as he purposes.

LADY MACBETH. O, never
Shall sun that morrow see!
Your face, my Thane, is as a book where men
May read strange matters. To beguile the time,[21]
Look like the time; bear welcome in your eye,
35 Your hand, your tongue: look like th' innocent flower,
But be the serpent under 't. He that's coming
Must be provided for: and you shall put
This night's great business into my dispatch;[22]
Which shall to all our nights and days to come
Give solely sovereign sway and masterdom.

36 **MACBETH.** We will speak further.

LADY MACBETH. Only look up clear.[23]
37 To alter favor ever is to fear.[24]
38 Leave all the rest to me. [*Exit.*]

8. **mortal:** Deadly.
9. **remorse:** Compassion.
10. **compunctious . . . nature:** Natural feelings of pity.
11. **fell:** Savage.
12. **effect:** Fulfillment.
13. **milk for gall:** Kindness in exchange for bitterness.
14. **ministers:** Agents.
15. **sightless:** Invisible.
16. **wait on:** Assist.
17. **pall:** Enshroud.
18. **dunnest:** Darkest.
19. **ignorant:** Unknowing.
20. **instant:** Present.
21. **beguile the time:** Deceive the people tonight.
22. **dispatch:** Management.
23. **look up clear:** Appear innocent.
24. **To alter . . . fear:** To show a disturbed face will arouse suspicion.

32 **Clarification** The raven was considered a bird of evil omen and was thought to foretell death with its croaking.

33 **Discussion** Compare the Macbeth we know so far with the Lady Macbeth of these few lines.

34 **Literary Focus** Note the parallel between Macbeth's prayer for a shroud of darkness in scene iv, lines 50-53, and her pleas. How are they similar and how are they different? What do they suggest about the two of them?

35 **Literary Focus** The need for deception arises again. She fears his face will tell all.

36 **Discussion** What does Macbeth's four-word answer suggest about his feelings for the murder his wife so ardently desires?

37 **Discussion** How does Lady Macbeth react to his answer?

38 **Literary Focus** Duncan has already declared Malcolm to be his heir. At this point Lady Macbeth doesn't know this. It has been suggested that explanatory lines may be missing here and throughout this play, which is Shakespeare's shortest.

39 Literary Focus Point out the dramatic irony here—summer, birth, delicate air are all observed by Duncan and Banquo, while the audience knows it to be a place of deception and imminent death.

40 Discussion Why is Duncan's simple, warm speech ironic?

Scene vi. *Before Macbeth's castle.*

[*Hautboys.*[1] *Torches. Enter* KING DUNCAN, MALCOLM, DONALBAIN, BANQUO, LENNOX, MACDUFF, ROSS, ANGUS, *and* ATTENDANTS.]

KING. This castle hath a pleasant seat;[2] the air
Nimbly and sweetly recommends itself
Unto our gentle[3] senses.

BANQUO. This guest of summer,
39 The temple-haunting martlet,[4] does approve[5]
By his loved mansionry[6] that the heaven's breath
Smells wooingly here. No jutty,[7] frieze,
Buttress, nor coign of vantage,[8] but this bird
Hath made his pendent bed and procreant cradle.[9]
Where they most breed and haunt,[10] I have observed
The air is delicate.

[*Enter* LADY MACBETH.]

KING. See, see, our honored hostess!
40 The love that follows us sometime is our trouble,
Which still we thank as love. Herein I teach you
How you shall bid God 'ield us for your pains
And thank us for your trouble.[11]

LADY MACBETH. All our service
In every point twice done, and then done double,
Were poor and single business[12] to contend
Against those honors deep and broad wherewith
Your Majesty loads our house: for those of old,
And the late dignities heaped up to them,
We rest your hermits.[13]

KING. Where's the Thane of Cawdor?
We coursed[14] him at the heels, and had a purpose
To be his purveyor:[15] but he rides well,
And his great love, sharp as his spur, hath holp[16] him
To his home before us. Fair and noble hostess,
We are your guest tonight.

LADY MACBETH. Your servants ever
Have theirs, themselves, and what is theirs, in
compt,[17]
To make their audit at your Highness' pleasure,
Still[18] to return your own.

KING. Give me your hand.
Conduct me to mine host: we love him highly,
And shall continue our graces towards him.
By your leave, hostess. [*Exit.*]

1. Hautboys: Oboes announcing the arrival of royalty.
2. seat: Location.
3. gentle: Soothed.
4. temple-haunting martlet: The martin, a bird that usually nests in churches. In Shakespeare's time *martin* was a slang term for a person who is easily deceived.
5. approve: Show.
6. mansionry: Nests.
7. jutty: Projection.
8. coign of vantage: Advantageous corner.
9. procreant (prō′ krē ənt) **cradle:** Nest where the young are hatched.
10. haunt: Visit.
11. The love . . . trouble: Though my visit inconveniences you, you should ask God to reward me for coming, because it was my love for you that prompted my visit.
12. single business: Feeble service.
13. rest your hermits: Remain your dependents bound to pray for you. Hermits were often paid to pray for another person's soul.
14 coursed: Chased.
15. purveyor: Advance supply officer.
16. holp: Helped.
17. compt: Trust.
18. Still: Always.

Scene vii. *Macbeth's castle.*

[*Hautboys. Torches. Enter a* SEWER,[1] and diverse SERVANTS with dishes and service over the stage. Then enter MACBETH.]

MACBETH. If it were done[2] when 'tis done, then 'twere well
It were done quickly. If th' assassination
Could trammel up the consequence, and catch,
With his surcease, success;[3] that but this blow
Might be the be-all and the end-all—here,
But here, upon this bank and shoal of time,
We'd jump the life to come.[4] But in these cases
We still have judgment here; that we but teach
Bloody instructions, which, being taught, return
To plague th' inventor: this even-handed[5] justice
Commends[6] th' ingredients of our poisoned chalice[7]
To our own lips. He's here in double trust:
First, as I am his kinsman and his subject,
41 Strong both against the deed; then, as his host,
Who should against his murderer shut the door,
Not bear the knife myself. Besides, this Duncan
Hath borne his faculties[8] so meek, hath been
So clear[9] in his great office, that his virtues
Will plead like angels trumpet-tongued against
The deep damnation of his taking-off;
And pity, like a naked newborn babe,
Striding the blast, or heaven's cherubin[10] horsed
Upon the sightless couriers[11] of the air,
Shall blow the horrid deed in every eye,
That tears shall drown the wind. I have no spur
To prick the sides of my intent, but only
Vaulting ambition, which o'erleaps itself
And falls on th' other—

[*Enter* LADY MACBETH.]

42 How now! What news?

LADY MACBETH. He has almost supped. Why have you left the chamber?

MACBETH. Hath he asked for me?

LADY MACBETH. Know you not he has?

MACBETH. We will proceed no further in this business:
43 He hath honored me of late, and I have bought[12]
Golden opinions from all sorts of people,
Which would be worn now in their newest gloss,
Not cast aside so soon.

LADY MACBETH. Was the hope drunk

1. **sewer:** Chief butler.

2. **done:** Over and done with.

3. **If . . . success:** If the assassination could be done successfully and without consequence.

4. **We'd . . . come:** I would risk life in the world to come.

5. **even-handed:** Impartial.

6. **commends:** Offers.

7. **chalice:** Cup.

8. **faculties:** Powers.

9. **clear:** Blameless.

10. **cherubin:** Angels.

11. **sightless couriers:** Unseen messengers (the wind).

12. **bought:** Acquired.

41 **Discussion** In Macbeth's first soliloquy, what arguments does he present against the murder and what argument or arguments in its favor? Given this argument, how, logically, should he respond?

42 **Discussion** Ask the students why is it significant that Lady Macbeth should enter at this moment?

43 **Discussion** Macbeth's words of reluctance to Lady Macbeth lack the force of his reasons in the soliloquy. Why?

44 Literary Focus The adage of the cat getting its feet wet foreshadows the later sleepwalking scene in which Lady Macbeth's "paws" become stained.

45 Literary Focus Manliness and masculinity as related to courage enter here. Lady Macbeth, who earlier prayed to be "un-sexed," suggests he is afraid to get his "feet wet."

46 Clarification She is challenging his manhood by, in effect saying, "When you dared to do it, then you were a real man. If you are now reluctant, you are no man."

47 Discussion While this question indicates he will go along with the plan, what does it say of Macbeth's enthusiasm for it?

48 Discussion What is Lady Macbeth's plan?

49 Discussion What does Macbeth mean by this statement?

Wherein you dressed yourself? Hath it slept since?
And wakes it now, to look so green and pale
At what it did so freely? From this time
Such I account thy love. Art thou afeard
To be the same in thine own act and valor
As thou art in desire? Wouldst thou have that
Which thou esteem'st the ornament of life,[13]
And live a coward in thine own esteem,
44 Letting "I dare not" wait upon[14] "I would,"
Like the poor cat i' th' adage? [15]

45 **MACBETH.** Prithee, peace!
I dare do all that may become a man;
Who dares do more is none.

46 **LADY MACBETH.** What beast was 't then
That made you break[16] this enterprise to me?
When you durst do it, then you were a man;
And to be more than what you were, you would
Be so much more the man. Nor time nor place
Did then adhere,[17] and yet you would make both.
They have made themselves, and that their[18] fitness now
Does unmake you. I have given suck, and know
How tender 'tis to love the babe that milks me:
I would, while it was smiling in my face,
Have plucked my nipple from his boneless gums,
And dashed the brains out, had I so sworn as you
Have done to this.

47 **MACBETH.** If we should fail?

LADY MACBETH. We fail?
But[19] screw your courage to the sticking-place[20]
And we'll not fail. When Duncan is asleep—
Whereto the rather shall his day's hard journey
Soundly invite him—his two chamberlains
Will I with wine and wassail[21] so convince,[22]
48 That memory, the warder of the brain,
Shall be a fume, and the receipt of reason
A limbeck only:[23] when in swinish sleep
Their drenchèd natures lies as in a death,
What cannot you and I perform upon
Th' unguarded Duncan, what not put upon
His spongy[24] officers, who shall bear the guilt
Of our great quell? [25]

MACBETH. Bring forth men-children only;
49 For thy undaunted mettle[26] should compose
Nothing but males. Will it not be received,
When we have marked with blood those sleepy two

13. ornament of life: The crown.

14. wait upon: Follow.

15. poor . . . adage: From an old proverb about a cat who wants to eat fish but is afraid of getting its paws wet.

16. break: Reveal.

17. Did then adhere: Was then suitable (for the assassination).

18. that their: Their very.

19. But: Only.

20. sticking-place: The notch that holds the bowstring of a taut crossbow.

21. wassail: Carousing.

22. convince: Overpower.

23. That . . . only: That memory, the guardian of the brain, will be confused by the fumes of the drink, and the reason become like a still, distilling confused thoughts.

24. spongy: Sodden.

25. quell: Murder.

26. mettle: Spirit.

SCENE FROM MACBETH
Cattermole
By permission of The Folger Shakespeare Library

Humanities Note

Fine art, *Scene from Macbeth* by George Cattermole. George Cattermole (1800–1868), a British painter of literary and historic scenes, began his career as an architectural draftsman but became caught up in the wave of the English Romantic movement in art. He is one of the leading representatives of the painting of the past in scenes of chivalry, religion, and literary sentiment.

Scene from Macbeth is one of numerous paintings based on the plays of Shakespeare that Cattermole produced in the 1850's. The figures in the scene are described with spirit and accuracy. Cattermole had the ability to make scenes like this come alive to the viewer.

You might ask students this question: Many artists have been inspired by the works of Shakespeare. What element from *Macbeth* inspired this artist?

50 **Literary Focus** Again a reference to reality and appearance.

Of his own chamber, and used their very daggers,
That they have done 't?

LADY MACBETH. Who dares receive it other,[27]
As we shall make our griefs and clamor roar
Upon his death?

MACBETH. I am settled, and bend up
Each corporal agent to this terrible feat.
50 Away, and mock the time[28] with fairest show:
False face must hide what the false heart doth know.
[*Exit.*]

27. **other:** Otherwise.

28. **mock the time:** Mislead the world.

THINKING ABOUT THE SELECTION

Recalling

1. (a) What does the Captain tell King Duncan about Macbeth's battlefield deeds? (b) What does the King learn from Ross about the Thane of Cawdor's activities? (c) What reward for victory does Macbeth receive almost immediately from the King?
2. What do the three witches predict (a) for Macbeth? (b) for Banquo?
3. How does Macbeth react to the witches' hailing him as Thane of Cawdor?
4. (a) What happens to the Thane of Cawdor? (b) Why, despite the witches' predictions, does Macbeth have reason to doubt he will succeed Duncan as king?
5. (a) How does Lady Macbeth first learn of the witches' predictions regarding Macbeth? (b) What in Macbeth's personality does she fear may thwart his ambition?
6. (a) What action does Lady Macbeth plan to take during the King's visit? (b) How does she intend to accomplish it? (c) How does she advise Macbeth to act in King Duncan's presence?

Interpreting

7. Both the witches and Macbeth make statements about "foul" and "fair." (a) What are two possible meanings for the witches' words? (b) What does Macbeth mean by his remark?
8. Macbeth and Banquo respond differently to the witches' predictions. (a) After becoming Thane of Cawdor, how does Macbeth react to the thought of becoming king? (b) How does Banquo view the witches' predictions?
9. In Scene vi, what is the irony in the description of the air surrounding Macbeth's castle?
10. Why is Macbeth indecisive about the idea of killing the King?
11. How does Lady Macbeth's knowledge of her husband's character help her to convince him that the murder plot should be carried out?

Applying

12. How do you think that Macbeth should have answered Lady Macbeth when, speaking of the planned murder, she said, "What beast was't then / That made you break this enterprise to me?"

ANALYZING LITERATURE

Understanding Blank Verse

Most of the lines in Shakespeare's plays are written in **blank verse,** or unrhymed iambic

Answers

ANSWERS TO THINKING ABOUT THE SELECTION

Recalling

1. (a) He recounts Macbeth's fearless bravery and leadership. (b) Ross tells Duncan of Cawdor's traitorous deeds during the battles and of his defeat. (c) In the same breath that Duncan orders Cawdor's execution, he bestows the title Theme of Cawdor upon Macbeth.
2. The three witches predict (a) that Macbeth will become Thane of Cawdor and King, (b) and that Banquo shall beget kings.
3. He is startled and fearful.
4. (a) The Thane of Cawdor is executed for his misdeeds. (b) Macbeth, already swelled with ambition because of the predictions, sees Malcolm, Duncan's son and declared heir to the throne, as the obstacle to his becoming King.
5. (a) Lady Macbeth reads her husband's letter to her describing the encounter with the witches. (b) She shows concern that his nature, filled with the milk of human kindness, may thwart his ambition.
6. (a) Lady Macbeth plans to murder Duncan in his bed and (b) lay the blame upon Duncan's servants, made drunk for this purpose and smeared with Duncan's blood as they sleep. (c) She warns Macbeth to hide his intents beneath a show of warm hospitality toward the happy King.

Interpreting

7. (a) The entire play turns on these reversals, here introduced in the first minutes. The great victory spells death for Duncan. Lady

pentameter. Each line has ten syllables, with the stress falling on every second syllable.

U / U / U / U / U /
The King hath happily received, Macbeth,

U / U / U / U / U
The news of thy success; and when he

/
reads

Blank verse approximates the rhythm of spoken conversation. To keep the lines from becoming monotonous, Shakespeare sometimes varies the pattern of unstressed and stressed syllables or writes a shorter or longer line. Pauses at different places in the lines also help to prevent a singsong rhythm from developing.

1. *Scansion* is the analysis of verse according to its meter. Write the following lines marking stressed and unstressed syllables.

   But here, upon this bank and shoal of time,
   We'd jump the life to come. But in these cases

2. What variation does the second line show?
3. Find two successive lines in Act 1 that are in perfect iambic pentameter. Write them marking stressed and unstressed syllables.

CRITICAL THINKING AND READING

Making Inferences About Characters

When you read or see a play by Shakespeare, you must make inferences about the major characters. You have to draw your own conclusions about their personalities and motivations. Since Shakespeare's characters are complex, you should avoid hasty conclusions. For instance, Macbeth at first appears to be brave, resolute, and loyal. But later in Act I you begin to see him in a different light. Always wait until you have sufficient evidence before making inferences about an important Shakespearean character.

1. In Scene iii, from line 70 to the end, Shakespeare presents a vivid picture of Macbeth. Based on the accumulating evidence, what inferences can you draw about Macbeth's character?
2. What can you infer about Banquo from the more limited evidence in Scene iii, lines 120–126?

UNDERSTANDING LANGUAGE

Reading Blank Verse Aloud

Since the blank-verse pattern of stressed and unstressed syllables is a natural one, you are likely to find it easier and more comfortable to read Shakespeare's plays aloud than to read rigidly rhymed verse. With blank verse you will not be tempted into the singsong trap set by rhyme. When reading blank verse, allow the meaning of the passage—and its punctuation—to guide your reading. Listening to professional actors reading Shakespeare can be highly valuable.

Choose a passage of about ten lines from Act I. Read it until you understand it fully. Then practice reading it aloud. Stop at the end of a line only when the punctuation calls for it. When you are ready, read the passage in class so that the meaning comes through clearly to your audience.

THINKING AND WRITING

Comparing and Contrasting Characters

Write a composition comparing and contrasting the character of Macbeth with that of Lady Macbeth. Find at least two passages spoken by each character that illustrate and support the points you intend to make. Include these in your first draft. When you revise, make sure the quoted passages fit logically into what you have written.

(Answers begin on p. 240.)

ANSWERS TO ANALYZING LITERATURE

1. Scansion:

   U / U / U / /
   But here, upon this bank and

   / U /
   shoal of time,

   U / U / U / U /
   We'd jump the life to come. But in

   U / U
   these cases
2. The second line ends with an additional, unstressed syllable.
3. Answers will differ widely, of course. One possible choice is Scene vii, lines 60-61:

   U / U / U / U
   But screw your courage to the

   / U /
   sticking-place

   U / U / U / U /
   And we'll not fail. When Duncan is

   U /
   a sleep—

ANSWERS TO CRITICAL THINKING AND READING

1. Macbeth appears to be instantly and dramatically fascinated with the possibilities given by the witches—this in contrast to Banquo's reaction. When he is told of the first prediction's truth, he immediately envisions murdering the king. Even though the thought unnerves him, we now share this ambitious and murderous side of Macbeth's nature.
2. While Macbeth's mind soars to grand and sordid heights, Banquo cooly wonders why these foul forces have tempted them with these predictions. Do they not have some greater evil planned, he wonders.

Challenge At this point in the play, is tragedy inevitable?

THINKING AND WRITING

Suggest that students refer to Lesson 9, "Writing About Character," in the Handbook of Writing About Literature.

Macbeth, wife of the great warrior shows greater evil than her warrior husband, Macbeth. The promise of the crown is fulfilled but brings only pain and death. (b) Macbeth appears to be referring to the awful weather and the great victory.

8. (a) Ambition surges through Macbeth, filling his mind with the possibilities of wearing the crown. (b) Banquo wonders if the "instruments of darkness" aren't tempting them with promises only to bring harm and pain to them in the end.
9. The scene outside Macbeth's castle is deceptive—nature shows itself in its best light, disarming the king as he enters the place where the darkest deeds are being planned.
10. Macbeth's ambition struggles with his sense of decency and logic. As bad as all this is, the idea of harming your own guest makes the thought even more troublesome. Then, too, he is aware that Malcolm must be dealt with, and that a great cry will go up at the death of this kind and good man.
11. She questions his manhood when he hesitates, and thereby spurs him on.

Applying

12. He might reply that the beast of logic holds him back. The planned action is evil, holds greater dangers than the rewards, and that haste serves no purpose.

Literary Focus Stress the three means by which an author can create atmosphere—setting, word choice, and specific details. Make the students aware of how limited the stage setting and detail possibilities were for Shakespeare, whose plays were presented on a nearly bare stage in daylight. Make the students aware that the images created in their minds as they read the play arise from the power of language alone.

Look For Have the students note scenes where powerful atmosphere is created. Determine what words or images are responsible.

Writing If you or your students are using a thesaurus, perform the same exercise with verbs. Have the students note how powerful the right verb can be in a sentence.

Vocabulary Have your students use these words in sentences of their own making.

GUIDE FOR READING

Macbeth, Act II

Writer's Techniques

Atmosphere. The atmosphere in a work of literature is its general mood or feeling. Atmosphere can often be described in one word: *fateful,* for example, or *melancholy* or *cheerful.* A writer creates atmosphere mainly through setting, word choice, and selection of specific details. Since realistic scenery was minimal and since lighting could not be controlled on the Elizabethan stage, Shakespeare often had to rely on dialogue to describe settings. His precise wording and choice of details help build the prevailing mood in each play. A great deal of the atmosphere in *Macbeth* and other Elizabethan plays depends on speech—on what the characters say. Shakespeare, like most great writers, is a master at creating atmosphere.

Look For

As you read *Macbeth,* Act II, look for indications of atmosphere and try to determine what word or words best describe it.

Writing

Choose an adjective that describes mood—*lively, dismal,* or *scary,* for example—and freewrite a passage that creates the intended atmosphere. Choose words that help to emphasize the mood. You may find it helpful to look in a thesaurus under the adjective you have chosen.

Vocabulary

Knowing the following words will help you as you read *Macbeth,* Act II.

augment (ôg ment′) *v.*: To make greater; enlarge (Sc. i, l. 27)
palpable (pal′pə b′l) *adj.*: Capable of being touched or felt (Sc. i, l. 40)
stealthy (stel′thē) *adj.*: Sly; furtive (Sc. i, l. 54)
multitudinous (mul′tə to͞od′′n əs) *adj.*: Existing in great numbers (Sc. ii, l. 61)
equivocate (i kwiv′ə kāt′) *v.*: Tell falsehoods (Sc. iii, l. 11)
anointed (ə noint′id) *adj.*: Declared sacred (Sc. iii, l. 57)
predominance (pri däm′ə nans) *n.*: Superiority (Sc. iv, l. 8)

Objectives

1 To understand atmosphere in a play
2 To interpret symbols

Teaching Portfolio: Support Material

Teacher Backup, p. 000

Vocabulary Check, p. 00

Usage and Mechanics Worksheet, p. 00

Analyzing Literature Worksheet, p. 00

Critical Thinking and Reading Worksheet, p. 00

Language Worksheet, p. 00

Selection Test, p. 00

Act II

Scene i. *Inverness. Court of Macbeth's castle.*
[*Enter* BANQUO, *and* FLEANCE, *with a torch before him.*]

1 **BANQUO.** How goes the night, boy?

FLEANCE. The moon is down; I have not heard the clock.

BANQUO. And she goes down at twelve.

FLEANCE. I take't, 'tis later, sir.

BANQUO. Hold, take my sword. There's husbandry[1] in
heaven.
Their candles are all out. Take thee that[2] too.
A heavy summons[3] lies like lead upon me,
2 And yet I would not sleep. Merciful powers,
Restrain in me the cursèd thoughts that nature
Gives way to in repose!

[*Enter* MACBETH, *and a* SERVANT with a torch.]

Give me my sword!
Who's there?

MACBETH. A friend.

BANQUO. What, sir, not yet at rest? The King's a-bed:
He hath been in unusual pleasure, and
3 Sent forth great largess to your offices:[4]
This diamond he greets your wife withal,
By the name of most kind hostess; and shut up[5]
In measureless content.

MACBETH. Being unprepared,
Our will became the servant to defect,
Which else should free have wrought.[6]

BANQUO. All's well.
4 I dreamt last night of the three weird sisters:
To you they have showed some truth.

MACBETH. I think not of them.
Yet, when we can entreat an hour to serve,
We would spend it in some words upon that business,
If you would grant the time.

BANQUO. At your kind'st leisure.

MACBETH. If you shall cleave to my consent, when 'tis,[7]
It shall make honor for you.

1. **husbandry:** Thrift.

2. **that:** Probably his sword belt.

3. **summons:** Weariness.

4. **largess . . . offices:** Gifts to your servants' quarters.

5. **shut up:** Retired.

6. **Being . . . wrought:** Because we did not have enough time to prepare, we were unable to entertain as lavishly as we wanted to.

7. **cleave . . . 'tis:** Join my cause when the time comes.

Motivation for Reading The stage has been set for the murder of Duncan. Have your students watch for its effects upon the already shaken Macbeth and the steely nerved Lady Macbeth.

Master Teacher Notes The imagery created during this act utilizes the three ideas or motifs of night, blood, and water that continue through the play. Have the students observe how the three are used to intensify the impact of this act. How do Macbeth and Lady Macbeth deal with them or treat them?

Purpose-setting Question What is revealed about the minds and characters of Macbeth and Lady Macbeth in this act?

1 **Literary Focus** Much of the action of this play happens in darkness. Do you see a connection between this setting and the events of the play?

2 **Discussion** Notice that Banquo has had trouble sleeping. What do you suppose are his "cursed thoughts"?

3 **Discussion** How might Macbeth inwardly react to Banquo's observation of Duncan's excessive pleasure at this visit?

4 **Discussion** Banquo acknowledges that thoughts of the witches and their prophesies have been weighing on his mind. What might he be considering?

5 **Discussion** How does this statement differ from Macbeth's response to the prophesies?

6 **Historical Focus** This play was probably written in honor of, and performed before, James I, a direct descendent of Banquo. Given that fact, Banquo's portrayal as a totally honorable man is understandable, despite a less attractive image painted by Holinshed.

7 **Literary Focus** This famous soliloquy is among Shakespeare's most notable. In it Macbeth's vivid imagination again surfaces in the form of a bloody dagger and other morbid imagery. In him imagination is a controlling force.

5 **BANQUO.** So[8] I lose none
In seeking to augment it, but still keep
6 My bosom franchised[9] and allegiance clear,
I shall be counseled.

MACBETH. Good repose the while!

BANQUO. Thanks, sir. The like to you!
[*Exit* BANQUO *with* FLEANCE.]

MACBETH. Go bid thy mistress, when my drink is ready,
She strike upon the bell. Get thee to bed.
[*Exit* SERVANT.]

Is this a dagger which I see before me,
The handle toward my hand? Come, let me clutch thee.
I have thee not, and yet I see thee still.
Art thou not, fatal vision, sensible[10]
To feeling as to sight, or art thou but
A dagger of the mind, a false creation,
Proceeding from the heat-oppressèd brain?
I see thee yet, in form as palpable
As this which now I draw.
Thou marshal'st[11] me the way that I was going;
And such an instrument I was to use.
Mine eyes are made the fools o' th' other senses,
Or else worth all the rest. I see thee still;
7 And on thy blade and dudgeon[12] gouts[13] of blood,
Which was not so before. There's no such thing.
It is the bloody business which informs[14]
Thus to mine eyes. Now o'er the one half-world
Nature seems dead, and wicked dreams abuse[15]
The curtained sleep; witchcraft celebrates
Pale Hecate's offerings;[16] and withered murder,
Alarumed by his sentinel, the wolf,
Whose howl's his watch, thus with his stealthy pace,
With Tarquin's[17] ravishing strides, towards his design
Moves like a ghost. Thou sure and firm-set earth,
Hear not my steps, which way they walk, for fear
Thy very stones prate of my whereabout,
And take the present horror from the time,
Which now suits with it.[18] Whiles I threat, he lives:
Words to the heat of deeds too cold breath gives.
[*A bell rings.*]
I go, and it is done: the bell invites me.
Hear it not, Duncan, for it is a knell
That summons thee to heaven, or to hell. [*Exit.*]

8. So: Provided that.

9. bosom franchised: Heart free (from guilt).

10. sensible: Able to be felt.

11. marshal'st: Leads.

12. dudgeon: Wooden hilt.
13. gouts: Large drops.
14. informs: Takes shape.
15. abuse: Deceive.

16. Hecate's (hĕk'ə tēz) **offerings:** Offerings to Hecate, the Greek goddess of witchcraft.
17. Tarquin's: Of Tarquin, sixteenth-century Roman tyrant.

18. take . . . it: Remove the horrible silence which suits this moment.

ELLEN TERRY AS LADY MACBETH
J. S. Sargent
Tate Gallery, on Loan to National Portrait Gallery, London

Scene ii. *Macbeth's castle.*
[*Enter* LADY MACBETH.]

LADY MACBETH. That which hath made them drunk hath made me bold;
8 What hath quenched them hath given me fire. Hark! Peace!
9 It was the owl that shrieked, the fatal bellman,
Which gives the stern'st good-night.[1] He is about it.
The doors are open, and the surfeited grooms[2]
Do mock their charge with snores. I have drugged their possets,[3]
That death and nature do contend about them,
Whether they live or die.

1. bellman . . . good-night: It was customary for a bell to be rung at midnight outside of a condemned person's cell on the night before an execution.
2. surfeited grooms: Overfed servants.
3. possets: Warm bedtime drinks.

Humanities Note

Fine art, *Ellen Terry as Lady Macbeth,* 1889, by John Singer Sargent. Sargent (1856–1925) was born in Italy of American parents. After training as a painter at the Paris studio of Carolus-Duran, he settled in London and was much sought after as a painter of portraits. He is considered to be the most notable portraitist of his day.

The brilliant actress Ellen Terry is one of the many famous and socially prominent people portrayed by Sargent. In executing this portrait, Sargent did not strive as much to show Lady Macbeth as to reveal the dynamic actress behind the character.

The pose in this painting is appropriately theatrical and impressive. The drapery of the costume is painted in many tones and scintillating textures that convey a richness suitable for nobility. Although the crown was not part of the original costume, Sargent used it in the painting for dramatic effect.

You might use the following questions for discussion:

1. What might the character be thinking as she holds the crown above her head?
2. Although richly dressed and regal in pose, does this woman seem suited to be a queen?
3. How does this artist's concept of Lady Macbeth compare with the other paintings of the character used to illustrate this play?

8 **Discussion** What has she done?

9 **Clarification** It was believed the sound of an owl foretold death.

10 **Literary Focus** We see here the first crack in the icy armor of Lady Macbeth. Till now she has uttered not a single word about the human factor in this awful deed.

11 **Discussion** What mood or atmosphere do these short lines create?

12 **Discussion** What is Macbeth's mood here? Is he addressing Lady Macbeth or is he not quite in contact with her after the bloody deed? What words seem to verify your answer?

13 **Historical Note** In Shakespeare's time, the hangman also tore out the vital organs of victims as part of public executions.

14 **Discussion** Of what significance is it that he is unable to say Amen? Is it significant if he is left in a spiritual void?

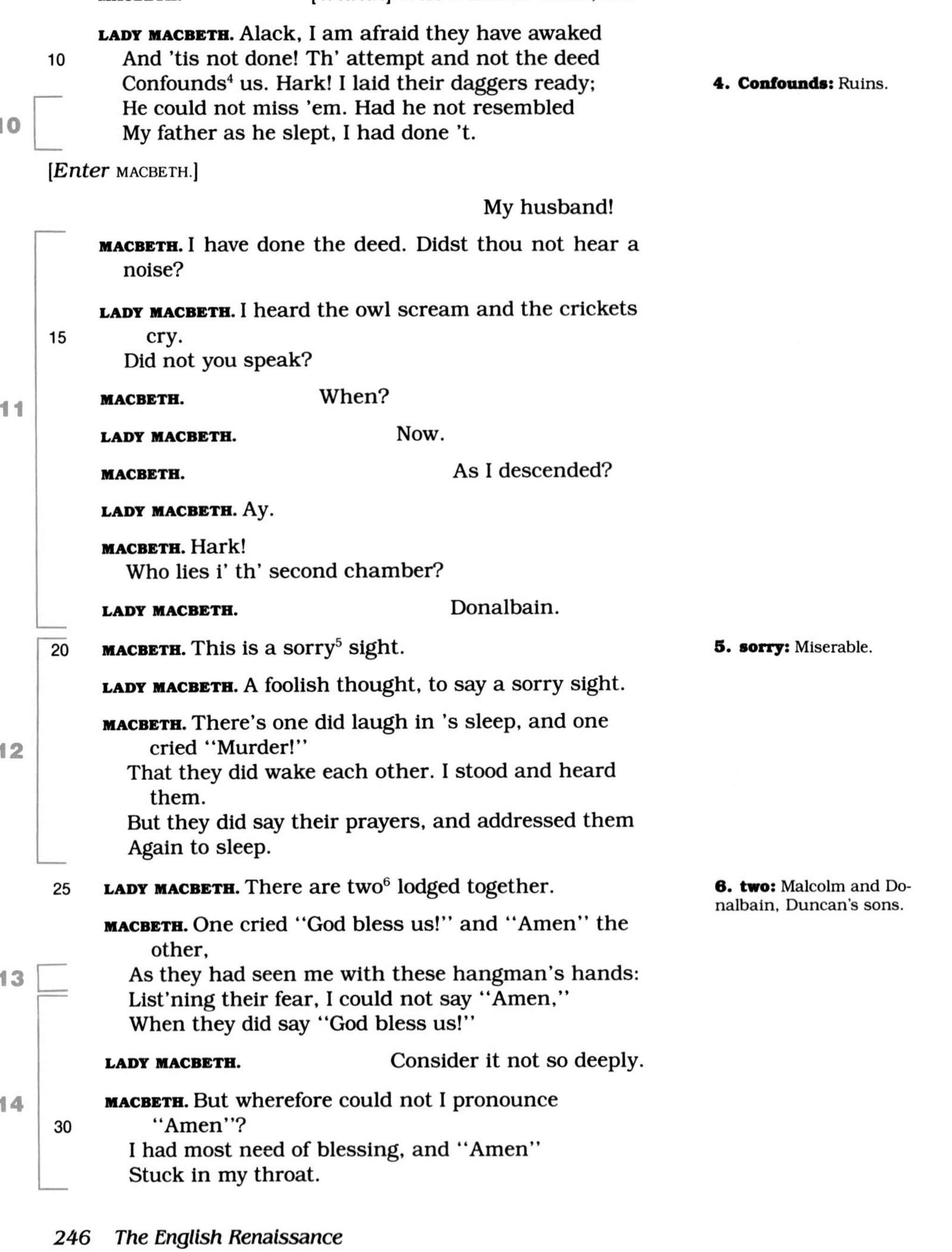

MACBETH. [*Within*] Who's there? What, ho?

LADY MACBETH. Alack, I am afraid they have awaked
And 'tis not done! Th' attempt and not the deed
Confounds[4] us. Hark! I laid their daggers ready;
He could not miss 'em. Had he not resembled
10 My father as he slept, I had done 't.

[*Enter* MACBETH.]

My husband!

MACBETH. I have done the deed. Didst thou not hear a noise?

LADY MACBETH. I heard the owl scream and the crickets cry.
Did not you speak?

11 MACBETH. When?

LADY MACBETH. Now.

MACBETH. As I descended?

LADY MACBETH. Ay.

MACBETH. Hark!
Who lies i' th' second chamber?

LADY MACBETH. Donalbain.

MACBETH. This is a sorry[5] sight.

LADY MACBETH. A foolish thought, to say a sorry sight.

MACBETH. There's one did laugh in 's sleep, and one
12 cried "Murder!"
That they did wake each other. I stood and heard them.
But they did say their prayers, and addressed them
Again to sleep.

LADY MACBETH. There are two[6] lodged together.

MACBETH. One cried "God bless us!" and "Amen" the other,
13 As they had seen me with these hangman's hands:
List'ning their fear, I could not say "Amen,"
When they did say "God bless us!"

LADY MACBETH. Consider it not so deeply.

14 MACBETH. But wherefore could not I pronounce "Amen"?
I had most need of blessing, and "Amen"
Stuck in my throat.

4. **Confounds:** Ruins.

5. **sorry:** Miserable.

6. **two:** Malcolm and Donalbain, Duncan's sons.

LADY MACBETH. These deeds must not be thought
15 After these ways; so, it will make us mad.

MACBETH. Methought I heard a voice cry "Sleep no more!
Macbeth does murder sleep"—the innocent sleep,
Sleep that knits up the raveled sleave[7] of care,
The death of each day's life, sore labor's bath,
Balm of hurt minds, great nature's second course,[8]
16 Chief nourisher in life's feast—

LADY MACBETH. What do you mean?

MACBETH. Still it cried "Sleep no more!" to all the house:
"Glamis hath murdered sleep, and therefore Cawdor
Shall sleep no more: Macbeth shall sleep no more."

LADY MACBETH. Who was it that thus cried? Why, worthy
Thane,
You do unbend[9] your noble strength, to think
So brainsickly of things. Go get some water,
17 And wash this filthy witness[10] from your hand.
Why did you bring these daggers from the place?
They must lie there: go carry them, and smear
The sleepy grooms with blood.

MACBETH. I'll go no more.
I am afraid to think what I have done;
Look on 't again I dare not.

LADY MACBETH. Infirm of purpose!
Give me the daggers. The sleeping and the dead
Are but as pictures. 'Tis the eye of childhood
That fears a painted devil. If he do bleed,
18 I'll gild[11] the faces of the grooms withal,
For it must seem their guilt. [*Exit. Knock within.*]

MACBETH. Whence is that knocking?
How is 't with me, when every noise appalls me?
What hands are here? Ha! They pluck out mine eyes!
Will all great Neptune's ocean wash this blood
Clean from my hand? No; this my hand will rather
19 The multitudinous seas incarnadine,[12]
Making the green one red.

[*Enter* LADY MACBETH.]

LADY MACBETH. My hands are of your color, but I shame
To wear a heart so white. [*Knock.*] I hear a knocking
At the south entry. Retire we to our chamber.
A little water clears us of this deed:
How easy is it then! Your constancy
Hath left you unattended.[13] [*Knock.*] Hark! more
knocking.

7. knits . . . sleave: Straightens out the tangled threads.
8. second course: The main course; sleep.

9. unbend: Relax.

10. witness: Evidence.

11. gild: Paint.

12. incarnadine (in kär′ nə din): Redden.

13. Your constancy . . . unattended: Your firmness of purpose has left you.

15 **Literary Focus** The remark is another indication of Lady Macbeth's potential vulnerability.

16 **Literary Focus** Macbeth acknowledges the madness of his act and predicts the destruction of anything resembling a normal life after this night. What benefits of sleep are specified here?

17 **Discussion** It is said Macbeth has too much imagination and Lady Macbeth too little. How do these lines and her following speeches seem to verify that opinion?

18 **Literary Focus** *Gild* is a grim pun here.

19 **Discussion** What do these lines mean both literally and figuratively?

20 Discussion What does Macbeth wish? Why?

21 Literary Focus The preceding scene could hardly have been more dramatic and tension-filled for audiences. The introduction of the drunken porter here breaks the tension and carries the play forward. His references to these wrongs were surely meaningful and worthy of a laugh to the audiences of the day.

22 Enrichment Thomas de Quincey's essay "On the Knocking at the Gate in Macbeth" provides interesting insights into this character.

23 Clarification He is undoubtedly holding his hand out for a tip.

24 Literary Focus From this point on Macduff plays a major role in the events of the drama. That he does not appear before now gives credence to those who believe sections of the play may be missing.

Get on your nightgown, lest occasion call us
And show us to be watchers.[14] Be not lost
So poorly in your thoughts.

MACBETH. To know my deed, 'twere best not know myself. [*Knock.*]
20 Wake Duncan with thy knocking! I would thou couldst! [*Exit.*]

Scene iii. *Macbeth's castle.*

[*Enter a* PORTER.[1] *Knocking within.*]

PORTER. Here's a knocking indeed! If a man were porter
of hell gate, he should have old[2] turning the key.
[*Knock.*] Knock, knock, knock! Who's there, i' th'
name of Beelzebub?[3] Here's a farmer, that
21 hanged himself on th' expectation of plenty.[4] Come
in time! Have napkins enow[5] about you; here you'll
sweat for 't. [*Knock.*] Knock, knock! Who's there, in
th' other devil's name? Faith, here's an equivocator,
that could swear in both the scales against
either scale;[6] who committed treason enough for
God's sake, yet could not equivocate to heaven. O,
22 come in, equivocator. [*Knock.*] Knock, knock, knock!
Who's there? Faith, here's an English tailor come
hither for stealing out of a French hose:[7]
come in, tailor. Here you may roast your goose.[8]
[*Knock.*] Knock, knock; never at quiet! What are you?
But this place is too cold for hell. I'll devil-porter it no
further. I had thought to have let in some of all
professions that go the primrose way to th'
everlasting bonfire. [*Knock.*] Anon, anon! [*Opens an*
23 *entrance.*] I pray you, remember the porter.

[*Enter* MACDUFF *and* LENNOX.]

24 **MACDUFF.** Was it so late, friend, ere you went to bed, That you do lie so late?

PORTER. Faith, sir, we were carousing till the second cock:[9] and drink, sir, is a great provoker . . .

MACDUFF. I believe drink gave thee the lie[10] last night.

PORTER. That it did, sir, i' the very throat on me: but I requited him for his lie, and, I think, being too strong for him, though he took up my legs sometime, yet I make a shift to cast[11] him.

MACDUFF. Is thy master stirring?

[*Enter* MACBETH.]

14. watchers: Up late.

1. porter: Doorkeeper.

2. should have old: Would have plenty of.

3. Beelzebub (bē el′ zə bub): The chief devil.

4. A farmer . . . plenty: A farmer who hoarded grain, hoping that the prices would come up as a result of a bad harvest.

5. enow: Enough.

6. an equivocator . . . scale: A liar who could make two contradictory statements and swear that both were true.

7. stealing . . . hose: Stealing some cloth from the hose while making them.

8. goose: Pressing iron.

9. second cock: 3:00 A.M.

10. gave thee the lie: Laid you out.

11. cast: Vomit.

Our knocking has awaked him; here he comes.

LENNOX. Good morrow, noble sir.

MACBETH. Good morrow, both.

MACDUFF. Is the king stirring, worthy Thane?

25 MACBETH. Not yet.

MACDUFF. He did command me to call timely[12] on him:
I have almost slipped the hour.

MACBETH. I'll bring you to him.

MACDUFF. I know this is a joyful trouble to you;
But yet 'tis one.

MACBETH. The labor we delight in physics pain.[13]
This is the door.

MACDUFF. I'll make so bold to call,
For 'tis my limited service.[14] [*Exit* MACDUFF.]

LENNOX. Goes the king hence today?

MACBETH. He does: he did appoint so.

LENNOX. The night has been unruly. Where we lay,
Our chimneys were blown down, and, as they say,
Lamentings heard i' th' air, strange screams of death,
26 And prophesying with accents terrible
Of dire combustion[15] and confused events
New hatched to th' woeful time: the obscure bird[16]
Clamored the livelong night. Some say, the earth
Was feverous and did shake.

27 MACBETH. 'Twas a rough night.

LENNOX. My young remembrance cannot parallel
A fellow to it.

[*Enter* MACDUFF.]

MACDUFF. O horror, horror, horror! Tongue nor heart
Cannot conceive nor name thee.

MACBETH AND LENNOX. What's the matter?

MACDUFF. Confusion[17] now hath made his masterpiece.
Most sacrilegious murder hath broke ope
The Lord's anointed temple,[18] and stole thence
The life o' th' building.

MACBETH. What is 't you say? The life?

LENNOX. Mean you his Majesty?

12. timely: Early.

13. labor . . . pain: Labor that we enjoy cures discomfort.

14. limited service: Assigned duty.

15. combustion: Confusion.

16. obscure bird: Bird of darkness, the owl.

17. Confusion: Destruction.

18. The Lord's anointed temple: The King's body.

25 **Literary Focus** Note the dramatic irony here.

26 **Literary Focus** The horror of the night before was matched by an unnatural series of storms and howlings, all seeming to prophesy some terrible event. Shakespeare again intensifies dramatic events with corresponding natural phenomena. Further, the murder of an anointed king would be viewed by Elizabethans as a most heinous crime against nature itself.

27 **Literary Focus** Note the understatement.

Humanities Note

Fine art, *Lady Macbeth,* 1812, by Henry Fuseli. Fuseli (1741–1825), a Swiss-born English painter and instructor at London's Royal Academy, was an eccentric man with a fascination for the strange and the fantastic. This interest is apparent in the surreal quality of his paintings. Inspired by the works of Shakespeare, Fuseli contributed nine paintings based on the playwright's works to Boydell's Shakespeare Gallery in London. These paintings are considered to be Fuseli's best works.

The painting *Lady Macbeth* was done from a drawing Fuseli made in 1760 after seeing actor David Garrick and actress Mrs. Pritchard in a performance of *Macbeth.* This painting of the scene immediately after the murder of Duncan shows the horror of Macbeth at what he has done and the unshaken control of Lady Macbeth. The scene has a dreamlike quality that reflects the psychological disorder of the characters.

You may wish to ask the following questions:

1. Why do you suppose the painter made the figures appear ghostlike?
2. How does this portrayal of Lady Macbeth compare with your conception of her?
3. Is the painter's sparse use of color effective in creating the mood for this scene? Explain.

LADY MACBETH SEIZING THE DAGGERS
Henry Fuseli
The Tate Gallery, London

MACDUFF. Approach the chamber, and destroy your sight
With a new Gorgon:[19] do not bid me speak;
See, and then speak yourselves. Awake, awake!
[*Exit* MACBETH *and* LENNOX.]
Ring the alarum bell. Murder and Treason!
Banquo and Donalbain! Malcolm! Awake!
Shake off this downy sleep, death's counterfeit,
And look on death itself! Up, up, and see
The great doom's image![20] Malcolm! Banquo!
As from your graves rise up, and walk like sprites,[21]
To countenance[22] this horror. Ring the bell.

[*Bell rings. Enter* LADY MACBETH.]

19. Gorgon: Medusa, a mythological monster whose appearance was so ghastly that those who looked at it turned to stone.

20. great doom's image: Likeness of Judgment Day.

21. sprites: Spirits.

22. countenance: Be in keeping with.

LADY MACBETH. What's the business,
That such a hideous trumpet calls to parley[23]
The sleepers of the house? Speak, speak!

MACDUFF. O gentle lady,
'Tis not for you to hear what I can speak:
The repetition, in a woman's ear,
Would murder as it fell.

[*Enter* BANQUO.]

O Banquo, Banquo!
Our royal master's murdered.

LADY MACBETH. Woe, alas!
What, in our house?

BANQUO. Too cruel anywhere.
Dear Duff, I prithee, contradict thyself,
And say it is not so.

[*Enter* MACBETH, LENNOX, *and* ROSS.]

MACBETH. Had I but died an hour before this
chance,
I had lived a blessèd time; for from this instant
30 There's nothing serious in mortality:[24]
All is but toys.[25] Renown and grace is dead,
The wine of life is drawn, and the mere lees[26]
Is left this vault[27] to brag of.

[*Enter* MALCOLM *and* DONALBAIN.]

DONALBAIN. What is amiss?

MACBETH. You are, and do not know 't.
The spring, the head, the fountain of your blood
Is stopped; the very source of it is stopped.

MACDUFF. Your royal father's murdered.

MALCOLM. O, by whom?

LENNOX. Those of his chamber, as it seemed, had
done 't:
Their hands and faces were all badged[28] with blood;
So were their daggers, which unwiped we found
Upon their pillows. They stared, and were distracted.
No man's life was to be trusted with them.

MACBETH. O, yet I do repent me of my fury,
31 That I did kill them.

MACDUFF. Wherefore did you so?

23. parley: A war conference.

24. serious in mortality: Worthwhile in mortal life.

25. toys: Trifles.

26. lees: Dregs.

27. vault: World.

28. badged: Marked.

28 **Discussion** Why are these lines to Lady Macbeth so ironic?

29 **Discussion** Is this comment from Lady Macbeth believable? Is it helpful in establishing her innocence? Note Banquo's sharp reply.

30 **Discussion** What is the irony about this passionate speech? How does it reflect his words of the night before?

31 **Discussion** What do we see happening to Macbeth and the direction of his actions following the murder of Duncan? What more can we expect?

32 Discussion Discuss the visible reactions of Macbeth and Lady Macbeth the morning after the murder. What do these reactions imply about each of them at this point?

33 Discussion What reason does Macbeth give for killing the grooms? What is the real reason?

34 Discussion What does he mean?

35 Literary Focus Lady Macbeth faints. Scholars argue about the legitimacy of this action. Is she fainting or is she pretending to faint? Which seems more likely? Why?

36 Discussion Why do Malcolm and Donalbain decide to flee?

MACBETH. Who can be wise, amazed, temp'rate and furious,
Loyal and neutral, in a moment? No man.
The expedition[29] of my violent love
Outrun the pauser, reason. Here lay Duncan,
32 His silver skin laced with his golden blood,
And his gashed stabs looked like a breach in nature
For ruin's wasteful entrance: there, the murderers,
33 Steeped in the colors of their trade, their daggers
Unmannerly breeched with gore.[30] Who could refrain,
That had a heart to love, and in that heart
Courage to make 's love known?

LADY MACBETH. Help me hence, ho!

MACDUFF. Look to the lady.

MALCOLM. [*Aside to* DONALBAIN] Why do we hold our tongues,
That most may claim this argument for ours?[31]

DONALBAIN. [*Aside to Malcolm*] What should be spoken here,
34 Where our fate, hid in an auger-hole,[32]
May rush, and seize us? Let's away:
Our tears are not yet brewed.

MALCOLM. [*Aside to* DONALBAIN] Nor our strong sorrow
Upon the foot of motion. [33]

35 **BANQUO.** Look to the lady.
[LADY MACBETH *is carried out.]*
And when we have our naked frailties hid,[34]
That suffer in exposure, let us meet
And question[35] this most bloody piece of work,
To know it further. Fears and scruples[36] shake us.
In the great hand of God I stand, and thence
Against the undivulged pretense[37] I fight
Of treasonous malice.

MACDUFF. And so do I.

ALL. So all.

MACBETH. Let's briefly[38] put on manly readiness,
And meet i' th' hall together.

ALL. Well contented.
[*Exit all but* MALCOLM *and* DONALBAIN.]

MALCOLM. What will you do? Let's not consort with them.
36 To show an unfelt sorrow is an office[39]
Which the false man does easy. I'll to England.

29. expedition: Haste.

30. breeched with gore: Covered with blood.

31. That most . . . ours: Who are the most concerned with this topic.

32. auger-hole: Tiny hole, an unsuspected place because of its size.

33. Our tears . . . motion: We have not yet had time for tears nor to turn our sorrow into action.

34. when . . . hid: When we have put on our clothes.

35. question: Investigate.

36. scruples: Doubts.

37. undivulged pretense: Hidden purpose.

38. briefly: Quickly.

39. office: Function.

DONALBAIN. To Ireland, I; our separated fortune
Shall keep us both the safer. Where we are
There's daggers in men's smiles; the near in blood,
The nearer bloody.[40]

MALCOLM. This murderous shaft that's shot
Hath not yet lighted,[41] and our safest way
Is to avoid the aim. Therefore to horse;
And let us not be dainty of leave-taking,
But shift away. There's warrant[42] in that theft
Which steals itself[43] when there's no mercy left.
[*Exit.*]

40. the near . . . bloody: The closer we are in blood relationship to Duncan, the greater our chance of being murdered.
41. lighted: Reached its target.
42. warrant: Justification
43. that theft . . . itself: stealing away.

Scene iv. Outside Macbeth's castle.

[*Enter* ROSS *with an* OLD MAN.]

OLD MAN. Threescore and ten I can remember well:
37 Within the volume of which time I have seen
Hours dreadful and things strange, but this sore[1]
night
Hath trifled former knowings.

ROSS. Ha, good father,
Thou seest the heavens, as troubled with man's act,
Threatens his bloody stage. By th' clock 'tis day,
And yet dark night strangles the traveling lamp:[2]
38 Is 't night's predominance, or the day's shame,
That darkness does the face of earth entomb,
When living light should kiss it?

39 **OLD MAN.** 'Tis unnatural,
Even like the deed that's done. On Tuesday last
A falcon, tow'ring in her pride of place,[3]
40 Was by a mousing owl hawked at and killed.

ROSS. And Duncan's horses—a thing most strange
and certain—
Beauteous and swift, the minions of their race,
Turned wild in nature, broke their stalls, flung out,
Contending 'gainst obedience, as they would make
War with mankind.

OLD MAN. 'Tis said they eat[4] each other.

ROSS. They did so, to th' amazement of mine eyes,
That looked upon 't.

[*Enter* MACDUFF.]

Here comes the good Macduff.
How goes the world, sir, now?

MACDUFF. Why, see you not?

1. sore: Grievous.
2. traveling lamp: The sun.
3. tow'ring . . . place: Soaring at its summit.
4. eat: Ate.

37 **Literary Focus** The first half of this brief scene recapitulates nature's upheaval mentioned previously. In past ages, it was widely believed that chaos in the social and political orders of life was reflected in the natural and cosmic orders.

38 **Literary Focus** Day is night. Again the reference to disorder and unnatural events.

39 **Literary Focus** The old man refers here to the rumor that Duncan's sons were responsible for his death.

40 **Literary Focus** Have your students take note that it is a female hawk that was pulled from its high place by an owl. What might this suggest?

41 **Literary Focus** The latter part of this short scene establishes that Duncan's sons, having fled, are the prime suspects, and that Macbeth is already named to succeed Duncan.

ROSS. Is 't known who did this more than bloody deed?

MACDUFF. Those that Macbeth hath slain.

ROSS. Alas, the day!
What good could they pretend? [5]

41
MACDUFF. They were suborned:[6]
Malcolm and Donalbain, the king's two sons,
Are stol'n away and fled, which puts upon them
Suspicion of the deed.

ROSS. 'Gainst nature still.
Thriftless ambition, that will ravin up[7]
Thine own life's means! Then 'tis most like
The sovereignty will fall upon Macbeth.

MACDUFF. He is already named, and gone to Scone[8]
To be invested.

ROSS. Where is Duncan's body?

MACDUFF. Carried to Colmekill,
The sacred storehouse of his predecessors
And guardian of their bones.

ROSS. Will you to Scone?

MACDUFF. No, cousin, I'll to Fife. [9]

ROSS. Well, I will thither.

MACDUFF. Well, may you see things well done there. Adieu,
Lest our old robes sit easier than our new!

ROSS. Farewell, father.

OLD MAN. God's benison[10] go with you, and with those
That would make good of bad, and friends of foes!
[*Exit.*]

5. pretend: Hope for.

6. suborned: Bribed.

7. ravin up: Devour greedily.

8. Scone (skōōn): Where Scottish kings were crowned.

9. Fife: Where Macduff's castle is located.

10. benison: Blessing.

Answers

ANSWERS TO THINKING ABOUT THE SELECTION

Recalling

1. (a) Macbeth sees a dagger, which becomes covered with blood. (b) When the bell rings at the end of scene i, Macbeth leaves to kill Duncan.
2. (a) Lady Macbeth would have killed him herself, except that he resembled her father as he lay asleep. (b) Macbeth still holds the daggers after the murder. (c) Lady Macbeth is concerned about Macbeth's reaction to the killing, part of which is his maintaining the bloody knives. She fears his reaction may spoil their plan. (d) She takes the knives and the responsibility for the details after the murder.
3. (a) The porter imagines he stands at the gates of hell observing the entrants, whom he describes as they pass. (b) Macbeth now wishes the knocking could awaken Duncan. (c) Macduff and Lennox knock, as they were obliged to awaken the King.
4. (a) Macduff enters the King's chamber to find him slaughtered. (b) Macbeth rushes in and kills the blood-smeared grooms. (c) Malcolm and Donalbain flee for fear that their lives are in jeopardy, too, as they realize there is a killer among them.
5. (a) The assumption is made that the grooms killed the King, at the orders of Malcolm and Donalbain. That would explain why they fled as they did.

Interpreting

6. Simply, he will sleep no more, because the thoughts of his horri-

THINKING ABOUT THE SELECTION

Recalling

1. (a) What is it that Macbeth thinks he sees in his "fatal vision"? (b) When the bell rings at the end of Scene i, what does Macbeth do?
2. (a) Why, according to Lady Macbeth, did she not kill the King herself? (b) What does Macbeth do with the daggers after the murder? (c) Why does this bother Lady Macbeth? (d) What action does she take?
3. (a) What does the drunken porter imagine he is doing in response to the knocking at the door? (b) What does Macbeth wish the knocking could do? (c) Who is doing the knocking? Why?
4. (a) Who first learns that a murder has taken place? (b) What action does Macbeth take against the grooms? (c) Why do Malcolm and Donalbain leave Macbeth's castle?
5. (a) Who does Macduff say has killed King Duncan? Why do Malcolm and Donalbain fall under suspicion, according to Macduff?

Interpreting

6. What does Macbeth mean by saying he has "murdered sleep"?
7. What is ironic about Lady Macbeth's remark "A little water clears us of this deed"?
8. (a) Why do you think critics consider the porter's speech to be comic relief? (b) How do the porter's comments on the people arriving at "hell gate" mirror Macbeth's dilemma?
9. What do you think causes Lady Macbeth to faint?
10. (a) Why does Ross have doubts about accepting the grooms as the murderers? (b) Why is Macduff concerned that "our old robes" may fit "easier than our new"?

Applying

11. In his soliloquy in Scene i, Macbeth speaks of "vaulting ambition." (a) How can vaulting ambition bring with it great success? (b) How can it bring with it destruction?

ANALYZING LITERATURE

Understanding Atmosphere

Atmosphere is the general mood or feeling in a literary work. In *Macbeth* the murder of the King occurs on an unusually dark, moonless night. The blackness of the night, which is conveyed through dialogue, matches the blackness of the deed. The grim, foreboding atmosphere reinforces the emotional states of the characters.

1. What is eerie about Macbeth's soliloquy in Scene i?
2. Reread Lennox's description of the night, Scene iii, lines 43–50. How does this description add to the atmosphere of the scene?
3. (a) How do the strange natural occurrences mentioned in Scene iv affect the atmosphere? (b) How do they relate to the night's events at Inverness Castle?

CRITICAL THINKING AND READING

Interpreting Symbols

A **symbol** is a word, person, object, or action that stands for something beyond itself. A flag, for example, is more than a piece of cloth; it stands for a country, its people, its ideals. Similarly, the ringing of the bell in Scene i is more than just a sound. It symbolizes an imminent death, much like the bell announcing an execution at London's Newgate prison or the small handbell that was rung outside a condemned person's cell at midnight to urge repentance.

1. In Scene ii, Lady Macbeth compares an owl's shriek to the "fatal bellman." How does this comparison extend the symbol of the bell?
2. Blood and water function as symbols in Scene ii, lines 44–68. (a) What does each symbolize? (b) What indication is there that Macbeth is less impressed by this symbolism than his wife is?
3. It has been suggested that the Old Man in Scene iv is a symbol for the people of Scotland. What is there about the Old Man that makes this suggestion plausible?

(Answers begin on p. 254.)

gained. (b) "Vaulting ambition" entails risks, including the possibility of failure and death.

ANSWERS TO ANALYZING LITERATURE

1. The description tells of an unruly night, filled with the sounds of lamentings and strange screams of death and prophesying. Confusion reigns. "Some say, the earth did . . . shake." It is such a night within the castle, as well.
2. (a) Day is night. The world is turned upside down, or so it seems. (b) All of the unnatural natural events reflect the murder of the King. So heinous an act is the killing of a monarch that the forces of the world are being wrenched by it.

ANSWERS TO CRITICAL THINKING AND READING

1. With this comparison, the owl's screeches become like the bell —fatal signals.
2. (a) Blood symbolizes murder and the stain of quilt; water symbolizes the removal of quilt. (b) Macbeth argues that the stain of blood is so great that his hands will turn the ocean red.
3. He certainly can be a symbol for all good people. He abhors the terrible deed of the night before; he has witnessed good and bad in this land for many years; and he wishes success for Ross and MacDuff, who refer to him as father.

ble deed will never leave him or allow him any peace.

7. Unlike her husband, she believes, or would like to believe, that a bit of scrubbing will wash away this deed as it does the blood. Later in the play during her sleepwalking scene, she will utter "out damned spot" as the stains of this deed persist.
8. (a) There isn't much doubt of its being comic relief—critics have differed about its appropriateness here. It is generally agreed Shakespeare injected the drunken porter as an effective way to alter the mood from the horror and power of the preceding scene. (b) The imagined characters entering hell are all liars and cheats who thought they could get away with their misdeeds. In the end, each must pay.
9. Critics argue about her fainting. Some think she does, and others think she pretends in order to demonstrate her shock over Duncan's death. Shakespeare doesn't tell us. If she really faints, it could be a first sign of the instability that destroys her. Have students discuss the possibilities.
10. (a) Ross wonders what the grooms had to gain by killing the King. (b) Macduff suggests that unless they do things well and carefully from here on, they could end up dead, also.

Applying

11. (a) Nothing ventured, nothing

Literary Focus Point out to the students that authors of stories or plays about historical figures or events often use dramatic irony because they can presuppose readers' or viewers' knowledge of the events. A story about a couple meeting and falling in love aboard the Titanic might be an obvious and overworked example. Have students give examples of their own.

Look For Have students find examples of irony and be able to label them as dramatic, situational, or verbal.

Writing Have **less-advanced** students sketch out ironic situations.

Vocabulary Suggest that students use a good dictionary to find the origins and meanings of the roots of these words.

GUIDE FOR READING

Macbeth, Act III

Writer's Techniques

Irony. In general, irony is a contrast between what is said and what is meant or between what is expected and what occurs. There are three kinds of irony in literature, all of which occur in *Macbeth*.

Dramatic irony exists when the words or acts of a character in a play carry a meaning the character does not understand but the audience does. An example of dramatic irony occurs in *Macbeth* at the beginning of Act I, Scene vi, when Banquo and Duncan discuss the pleasant and delicate air as they arrive at Inverness. The audience knows, but Banquo and Duncan do not, that a murderous plot is being hatched behind the castle walls.

Situational irony occurs when the expected results of an action or situation differ from the actual results.

Verbal irony exists when a speaker says one thing and means the opposite. In a famous speech in Shakespeare's *Julius Caesar,* for example, when Mark Antony says of the assassins of Caesar, "So are they all, all honorable men," he means exactly the opposite of what he says. To him, the assassins are *not* honorable men. Antony's words are therefore verbal irony.

Look For

As you read *Macbeth,* Act III, look for examples of verbal irony —situations in which the speaker means almost exactly the opposite of what he or she says.

Writing

At this point in *Macbeth,* you know a great deal about the major characters—more, in fact, than they know about themselves. Based on your knowledge, make notes on what you think will happen to the following characters by the end of the play: Macbeth, Lady Macbeth, Banquo, Macduff.

Vocabulary

Knowing the following words will help you as you read *Macbeth,* Act III.

indissoluble (in di säl'yoo b'l) *adj.*: Not able to be dissolved or undone (Sc.i, l. 17)
dauntless (dônt'lis) *adj.*: Fearless (Sc. i, l. 52)
jocund (jäk'ənd) *adj.*: Cheerful; jovial (Sc. ii, l. 40)
infirmity (in fʉr'mə tē) *n.*: Physical or mental defect; illness (Sc. iv, l. 87)
malevolence (mə lev'ə ləns) *n.*: Ill will; spitefulness (Sc. vi, l. 28)

Objectives

1 To understand irony
2 To interpret connotative meanings
3 To write a speculative essay

Teaching Portfolio: Support Material

Teaching Backup, p. 000

Vocabulary Check, p. 00

Usage and Mechanics Worksheet, p. 00

Analyzing Literature Worksheet, p. 00

Critical Thinking and Reading Worksheet, p. 00

Language Worksheets, p. 00

Language Worksheet, p. 00

Selection Test, p. 00

Act III

Scene i. *Forres. The palace.*
[*Enter* BANQUO.]

BANQUO. Thou hast it now: King, Cawdor, Glamis, all,
As the weird women promised, and I fear
Thou play'dst most foully for 't. Yet it was said
It should not stand[1] in thy posterity,
1 But that myself should be the root and father
Of many kings. If there come truth from them—
As upon thee, Macbeth, their speeches shine—
Why, by the verities on thee made good,
May they not be my oracles as well
And set me up in hope? But hush, no more!

[*Sennet*[2] *sounded. Enter* MACBETH *as King,* LADY MACBETH, LENNOX, ROSS, LORDS, *and* ATTENDANTS.]

MACBETH. Here's our chief guest.

LADY MACBETH. If he had been forgotten,
It had been as a gap in our great feast,
And all-thing[3] unbecoming.

MACBETH. Tonight we hold a solemn[4] supper, sir,
And I'll request your presence.

BANQUO. Let your Highness
Command upon me, to the which my duties
Are with a most indissoluble tie
For ever knit.

MACBETH. Ride you this afternoon?

BANQUO. Ay, my good lord.

MACBETH. We should have else desired your good advice
(Which still hath been both grave and prosperous[5])
2 In this day's council; but we'll take tomorrow.
Is 't far you ride?

BANQUO. As far, my lord, as will fill up the time
'Twixt this and supper. Go not my horse the better,[6]
I must become a borrower of the night
For a dark hour or twain.

MACBETH. Fail not our feast.

BANQUO. My lord, I will not.

MACBETH. We hear our bloody cousins are bestowed
In England and in Ireland, not confessing
3 Their cruel parricide, filling their hearers
With strange invention.[7] But of that tomorrow,

1. **stand:** Continue.

2. **Sennet:** Trumpet call.

3. **all-thing:** Altogether.

4. **solemn:** Ceremonious.

5. **grave and prosperous:** Weighty and profitable.

6. **Go not . . . better:** Unless my horse goes faster than I expect.

7. **invention:** Lies.

Motivation for Reading The King is dead and Macbeth now rules Scotland. What complications will arise? They should make themselves known in this act.

Purpose-setting Question What is Macbeth's state of mind in Act III?

1 **Discussion** In Banquo's brief soliloquy, he clearly voices his suspicions of Macbeth. He also speculates about the witches' prophesies for him. How much time has passed? Why do you think Banquo has told no one about the prophesies?

2 **Discussion** What will Banquo be doing during this day?

3 **Discussion** Who are "our bloody cousins"?

4 Discussion How does all that follows hinge upon the meaning of this line? What does it imply about Macbeth's character?

5 Discussion The soliloquy is divided into two parts, with Macbeth's reasons for fearing Banquo in the first part and, in the second, Macbeth's resentment of Banquo's prophecy. What is the chief reason he feels Banquo is a threat to him? What is the source of the resentment about the prophecy? Does it seem likely that Banquo might try to wrench the throne from him, or is this more of Macbeth's fevered imagination?

6 Discussion What does this challenge indicate about Macbeth's state of mind at this point?

When therewithal we shall have cause of state
Craving us jointly.[8] Hie you to horse. Adieu,
Till you return at night. Goes Fleance with you?

BANQUO. Ay, my good lord: our time does call upon 's.

MACBETH. I wish your horses swift and sure of foot,
And so I do commend you to their backs.
Farewell. [*Exit* BANQUO.]
Let every man be master of his time
Till seven at night. To make society
The sweeter welcome, we will keep ourself
Till suppertime alone. While[9] then, God be with you!

[*Exit* LORDS *and all but* MACBETH *and a* SERVANT.]

Sirrah,[10] a word with you: attend those men
Our pleasure?

ATTENDANT. They are, my lord, without the palace gate.

MACBETH. Bring them before us. [*Exit* SERVANT.]
4 To be thus[11] is nothing, but[12] to be safely thus—
Our fears in Banquo stick deep,
And in his royalty of nature reigns that
Which would be feared. 'Tis much he dares;
And, to[13] that dauntless temper of his mind,
He hath a wisdom that doth guide his valor
To act in safety. There is none but he
Whose being I do fear: and under him
My genius is rebuked,[14] as it is said
Mark Antony's was by Caesar. He chid[15] the sisters,
When first they put the name of King upon me,
And bade them speak to him; then prophetlike
5 They hailed him father to a line of kings.
Upon my head they placed a fruitless crown
And put a barren scepter in my gripe,[16]
Thence to be wrenched with an unlineal hand,
No son of mine succeeding. If 't be so,
For Banquo's issue have I filed[17] my mind;
For them the gracious Duncan have I murdered;
Put rancors in the vessel of my peace
Only for them, and mine eternal jewel[18]
Given to the common enemy of man,[19]
To make them kings, the seeds of Banquo kings!
Rather than so, come, fate, into the list,
6 And champion me to th' utterance![20] Who's there?

[*Enter* SERVANT *and* TWO MURDERERS.]

Now go to the door, and stay there till we call.
[*Exit* SERVANT.]
Was it not yesterday we spoke together?

8. cause . . . jointly: Matters of state demanding our joint attention.

9. While: Until.

10. Sirrah: A common address to an inferior.

11. thus: King.
12. but: Unless.

13. to: Added to.

14. genius is rebuked: Guardian spirit is cowed.
15. chid: Scolded.

16. gripe: Grip.

17. filed: Defiled.

18. eternal jewel: Soul.
19. common . . . man: The Devil.

20. champion me to th' utterance: Fight against me to the death.

MURDERERS. It was, so please your Highness.

MACBETH. Well then, now
Have you considered of my speeches? Know
That it was he in the times past, which held you
So under fortune,[21] which you thought had been
Our innocent self: this I made good to you
In our last conference; passed in probation[22] with you,
How you were born in hand,[23] how crossed, the instruments,
Who wrought with them, and all things else that might
7 To half a soul[24] and to a notion[25] crazed
Say "Thus did Banquo."

FIRST MURDERER. You made it known to us.

MACBETH. I did so; and went further, which is now
Our point of second meeting. Do you find
Your patience so predominant in your nature,
That you can let this go? Are you so gospeled,[26]
To pray for this good man and for his issue,
Whose heavy hand hath bowed you to the grave
And beggared yours for ever?

FIRST MURDERER. We are men, my liege.

MACBETH. Ay, in the catalogue ye go for[27] men;
As hounds and greyhounds, mongrels, spaniels, curs,
8 Shoughs, water-rugs[28] and demi-wolves, are clept[29]
All by the name of dogs: the valued file[30]
Distinguishes the swift, the slow, the subtle,
The housekeeper, the hunter, every one
According to the gift which bounteous nature
Hath in him closed,[31] whereby he does receive
Particular addition,[32] from the bill
That writes them all alike: and so of men.
Now if you have a station in the file,[33]
Not i' th' worst rank of manhood, say 't,
And I will put that business in your bosoms
Whose execution takes your enemy off,
Grapples you to the heart and love of us,
Who wear our health but sickly in his life,[34]
Which in his death were perfect.

SECOND MURDERER. I am one, my liege,
Whom the vile blows and buffets of the world
9 Hath so incensed that I am reckless what
I do to spite the world.

21. held . . . fortune: Kept you from good fortune.
22. passed in probation: Reviewed the proofs.
23. born in hand: Deceived.
24. half a soul: A halfwit.
25. notion: Mind.
26. gospeled: Ready to forgive.
27. go for: Pass as.
28. Shoughs (shuks), **water-rugs:** Shaggy dogs, long-haired dogs.
29. clept: Called.
30. valued file: Classification by valuable traits.
31. closed: Enclosed.
32. addition: Distinction (to set it apart from other dogs).
33. file: Ranks.
34. wear . . . life: Are sick as long as he lives.

7 **Discussion** Note that there is little subtlety here in labeling these two as murderers. This is a second meeting. What has Macbeth suggested about Banquo to stimulate their anger?

8 **Literary Focus** Note that Macbeth, in attacking their manhood, uses the same argument as did Lady Macbeth against him.

9 **Discussion** How does the Second Murderer assess his rank among men and how does he react?

10 Discussion Paraphrase this statement. Does it sound sincere?

11 Discussion What reason does Macbeth give for not being able to openly use his power as king to punish Banquo?

12 Discussion Notice that Macbeth mentions Fleance almost as an afterthought. How important to Macbeth is Fleance's death? Why?

FIRST MURDERER. And I another
So weary with disasters, tugged with fortune,
10 That I would set[35] my life on any chance,
To mend it or be rid on 't.

MACBETH. Both of you
Know Banquo was your enemy.

BOTH MURDERERS. True, my lord.

MACBETH. So is he mine, and in such bloody distance[36]
That every minute of his being thrusts
Against my near'st of life:[37] and though I could
With barefaced power sweep him from my sight
And bid my will avouch[38] it, yet I must not,
For certain friends that are both his and mine,
11 Whose loves I may not drop, but wail his fall[39]
Who I myself struck down: and thence it is
That I to your assistance do make love,
Masking the business from the common eye
For sundry weighty reasons.

SECOND MURDERER. We shall, my lord,
Perform what you command us.

FIRST MURDERER. Though our lives—

MACBETH. Your spirits shine through you. Within this hour at most
I will advise you where to plant yourselves,
Acquaint you with the perfect spy o' th' time,
The moment on 't;[40] for 't must be done tonight,
And something[41] from the palace; always thought[42]
That I require a clearness:[43] and with him—
To leave no rubs[44] nor botches in the work—
Fleance his son, that keeps him company,
Whose absence is no less material to me
12 Than is his father's, must embrace the fate
Of that dark hour. Resolve yourselves apart:[45]
I'll come to you anon.

MURDERERS. We are resolved, my lord.

MACBETH. I'll call upon you straight.[46] Abide within.
It is concluded: Banquo, thy soul's flight,
If it find heaven, must find it out tonight. [*Exit.*]

Scene ii. *The palace.*
[*Enter* MACBETH'S LADY *and a* SERVANT.]

LADY MACBETH. Is Banquo gone from court?

SERVANT. Ay, madam, but returns again tonight.

35. set: Risk.

36. distance: Disagreement.

37. near'st of life: Most vital parts.

38. avouch: Justify.

39. wail his fall: (I must) bewail his death.

40. the perfect . . . on 't: The exact information of the exact time.

41. something: Some distance.

42. thought: Remembered.

43. clearness: Freedom from suspicion.

44. rubs: Flaws.

45. Resolve yourselves apart: Make your own decision.

46. straight: Immediately.

LADY MACBETH. Say to the King, I would attend his
leisure
For a few words.

SERVANT. Madam, I will. [*Exit.*]

LADY MACBETH. Nought's had, all's spent,
13 Where our desire is got without content:
'Tis safer to be that which we destroy
14 Than by destruction dwell in doubtful joy.

[*Enter* MACBETH.]

How now, my lord! Why do you keep alone,
Of sorriest fancies your companions making,
15 Using those thoughts which should indeed have died
With them they think on? Things without all remedy
Should be without regard: what's done is done.

MACBETH. We have scotched[1] the snake, not killed it:
She'll close[2] and be herself, whilst our poor malice
Remains in danger of her former tooth.[3]
But let the frame of things disjoint,[4] both the worlds[5]
suffer,
Ere we will eat our meal in fear, and sleep
In the affliction of these terrible dreams
That shake us nightly: better be with the dead,
16 Whom we, to gain our peace, have sent to peace,
Than on the torture of the mind to lie
In restless ecstasy.[6] Duncan is in his grave;
After life's fitful fever he sleeps well.
Treason has done his worst: nor steel, nor poison,
Malice domestic, foreign levy,[7] nothing,
Can touch him further.

LADY MACBETH. Come on.
Gentle my lord, sleek o'er your rugged looks;
Be bright and jovial among your guests tonight.

MACBETH. So shall I, love; and so, I pray, be you:
Let your remembrance apply to Banquo;
17 Present him eminence,[8] both with eye and tongue:
Unsafe the while, that we must lave[9]
Our honors in these flattering streams
And make our faces vizards[10] to our hearts,
Disguising what they are.

LADY MACBETH. You must leave this.

MACBETH. O, full of scorpions is my mind, dear wife!
Thou know'st that Banquo, and his Fleance, lives.

LADY MACBETH. But in them nature's copy's not eterne.[11]

1. **scotched:** Wounded.
2. **close:** Heal.
3. **in . . . tooth:** In as much danger as before.
4. **frame of things disjoint:** Universe collapse.
5. **both the worlds:** Heaven and earth.
6. **ecstasy:** Frenzy.
7. **Malice . . . levy:** Civil and foreign war.
8. **Present him eminence:** Honor him.
9. **Unsafe . . . lave:** We are unsafe as long as we have to wash.
10. **vizards** (viz′ ərdz): Masks.
11. **nature's . . . eterne:** Nature's lease is not eternal.

13 **Discussion** Paraphrase the first line of this telling statement. When she says "we destroy," what does she mean? What did they destroy?

14 **Literary Focus** It was indicated earlier that Lady Macbeth has no imagination; we are seeing the results of the lack here. What would seem glaringly obvious to most people she is only now coming to realize—too late.

15 **Literary Focus** Note how she tries to cover her own depression in trying to elevate her husband's spirits, advising him to do what she herself, in private, cannot.

16 **Discussion** What is Macbeth suggesting might be better than the terrible dreams that torment him nightly? Who is "sleeping" more soundly than he?

17 **Discussion** In assuring Lady Macbeth that he will strike the proper mood at the party, what do we learn about Macbeth and his relationship with his wife at this point through these few lines?

Humanities Note

Fine art, *Banquo at the Gate*, by Sir John Gilbert. Sir John Gilbert (1817–1897) was a British painter and illustrator. Gilbert drew with incredible ability while still a young child. He studied drawing with the artist George Lance, but his greatest training was the self-imposed habit of continuously sketching.

Sir John Gilbert was known for his paintings of historical subjects. This woodcut, *Banquo at the Gate,* from Mackey's *Shakespeare,* is based on a drawing Gilbert did for that book. The composition is satisfying, with the lit figures on the left balanced by the dark, lurking forms of the murderers on the right. Although it is a depiction of a night scene, there is a richness of detail in the dark areas. Gilbert loved to draw narrative scenes and did so with an appealing vivacity and spirit.

You might use these questions for discussion:

1. Although the figures at the gate are smaller in scale than the murderers, they are the focal point of this drawing. How does the artist draw your attention to these figures?
2. How does the artist give an ominous or evil air to the dark figures?

18 Literary Focus Note the increasingly lyrical quality of Macbeth's lines.

19 Discussion Macbeth hints at the foul deed he has planned, choosing to keep it from Lady Macbeth. What does line 54 suggest?

WOOD ENGRAVING AFTER SIR JOHN GILBERT
The Granger Collection

MACBETH. There's comfort yet; they are assailable.
Then be thou jocund. Ere the bat hath flown
18 His cloistered flight, ere to black Hecate's summons
The shard-borne[12] beetle with his drowsy hums
Hath rung night's yawning peal, there shall be done
A deed of dreadful note.

LADY MACBETH. What's to be done?

MACBETH. Be innocent of the knowledge, dearest chuck,[13]
Till thou applaud the deed. Come, seeling[14] night,
Scarf up[15] the tender eye of pitiful day,
And with thy bloody and invisible hand
Cancel and tear to pieces that great bond[16]
Which keeps me pale! Light thickens, and the crow
Makes wing to th' rooky[17] wood.
Good things of day begin to droop and drowse,
Whiles night's black agents to their preys do rouse.
19 Thou marvel'st at my words: but hold thee still;
Things bad begun make strong themselves by ill:
So, prithee, go with me. [*Exit.*]

12. shard-borne: Borne on scaly wings.

13. chuck: A term of endearment.

14. seeling: Eye-closing. Falconers sometimes sewed a hawk's eyes closed in order to train it.

15. Scarf up: Blindfold.

16. great bond: Between Banquo and fate.

17. rooky: Full of rooks, or crows.

Scene iii. *Near the palace.*

20 [*Enter* THREE MURDERERS.]

FIRST MURDERER. But who did bid thee join with us?

THIRD MURDERER. Macbeth.

SECOND MURDERER. He needs not our mistrust; since he delivers
Our offices[1] and what we have to do
To the direction just.[2]

FIRST MURDERER. Then stand with us.
The west yet glimmers with some streaks of day.
Now spurs the lated traveler apace
To gain the timely inn, and near approaches
The subject of our watch.

THIRD MURDERER. Hark! I hear horses.

BANQUO. [*Within*] Give us a light there, ho!

SECOND MURDERER. Then 'tis he. The rest
That are within the note of expectation[3]
Already are i' th' court.

FIRST MURDERER. His horses go about.[4]

THIRD MURDERER. Almost a mile: but he does usually—
So all men do—from hence to th' palace gate
Make it their walk.

21 [*Enter* BANQUO *and* FLEANCE, *with a torch.*]

SECOND MURDERER. A light, a light!

THIRD MURDERER. 'Tis he.

FIRST MURDERER. Stand to 't.

BANQUO. It will be rain tonight.

FIRST MURDERER. Let it come down.

[*They set upon* BANQUO.]

BANQUO. O, treachery! Fly, good Fleance, fly, fly, fly! [*Exit* FLEANCE.]
22 Thou mayst revenge. O slave! [*Dies.*]

THIRD MURDERER. Who did strike out the light?

23 **FIRST MURDERER.** Was't not the way?[5]

THIRD MURDERER. There's but one down; the son is fled.

SECOND MURDERER. We have lost best half of our affair.

FIRST MURDERER. Well, let's away and say how much is done. [*Exit.*]

1. **offices:** Duties.
2. **direction just:** Exact detail.
3. **within . . . expectations:** On the list of expected guests.
4. **His . . . about:** His horses have been taken to the stable.
5. **way:** Thing to do.

20 **Literary Focus** Enter the third murderer. He has beguiled scholars for centuries. He has been variously described as a messenger from Macbeth, as Macbeth himself, an emissary of the witches, and someone friendly to Banquo's cause. Have the students give their opinions.

21 **Literary Focus** Banquo and Fleance carry a torch, indicating darkness, in keeping with that theme.

22 **Discussion** In the melee, Fleance escapes. Does this seem likely, considering the odds and Fleance's youth and inexperience? How might the light have been put out?

23 **Literary Focus** Some critics believe that the exact climax of the play occurs with the stage direction "*Exit* FLEANCE." Whether or not this assessment is correct, why is Fleance's escape extremely important?

24 Literary Focus Macbeth's conversation with the Murderer would take place at the side of the stage, presumably out of sight and out of earshot of the guests.

25 Literary Focus It has also been argued that this is the climax, when Macbeth learns of the escape of Fleance.

26 Discussion Was he in fact as whole as marble and as well as these lines imply? Why or why not?

27 Clarification *Worm* held a broader meaning in Shakespeare's time, often referring to a snake.

Scene iv. *The palace.*
[*Banquet prepared. Enter* MACBETH, LADY MACBETH, ROSS, LENNOX, LORDS, *and* ATTENDANTS.]

MACBETH. You know your own degrees;[1] sit down:
At first and last, the hearty welcome.

LORDS. Thanks to your Majesty.

MACBETH. Ourself will mingle with society[2]
And play the humble host.
Our hostess keeps her state,[3] but in best time
We will require[4] her welcome.

LADY MACBETH. Pronounce it for me, sir, to all our friends,
For my heart speaks they are welcome.

[*Enter* FIRST MURDERER.]

MACBETH. See, they encounter thee with their hearts' thanks.
Both sides are even: here I'll sit i' th' midst:
Be large in mirth; anon we'll drink a measure[5]
The table round. [*Goes to* MURDERER] There's blood upon thy face.

24 **MURDERER.** 'Tis Banquo's then.

MACBETH. 'Tis better thee without than he within.[6]
Is he dispatched?

MURDERER. My lord, his throat is cut; that I did for him.

MACBETH. Thou art the best o' th' cutthroats.
Yet he's good that did the like for Fleance;
If thou didst it, thou art the nonpareil.[7]

25 **MURDERER.** Most royal sir, Fleance is 'scaped.

MACBETH. [*Aside*] Then comes my fit again: I had else been perfect,
26 Whole as the marble, founded as the rock,
As broad and general as the casing[8] air:
But now I am cabined, cribbed, confined, bound in
To saucy[9] doubts and fears.—But Banquo's safe?

MURDERER. Ay, my good lord: safe in a ditch he bides,
With twenty trenchèd[10] gashes on his head,
The least a death to nature.[11]

MACBETH. Thanks for that.
27 [*Aside*] There the grown serpent lies; the worm that's fled

1. **degrees:** Ranks. At state banquets guests were seated according to rank.
2. **society:** The company.
3. **keeps her state:** Remains seated on her throne.
4. **require:** Request.
5. **measure:** Toast.
6. **thee . . . within:** You outside than him inside.
7. **nonpareil:** Without equal.
8. **as . . . casing:** As unrestrained as the surrounding.
9. **saucy:** Insolent.
10. **trenchèd:** Trenchlike.
11. **nature:** Natural life.

Hath nature that in time will venom breed,
No teeth for th' present. Get thee gone. Tomorrow
We'll hear ourselves[12] again. [*Exit* MURDERER.]

LADY MACBETH. My royal lord,
You do not give the cheer.[13] The feast is sold
That is not often vouched, while 'tis a-making,
'Tis given with welcome.[14] To feed were best at home;
From thence, the sauce to meat is ceremony;[15]
Meeting were bare without it.

[*Enter the* GHOST OF BANQUO, *and sits in* MACBETH'S *place*.]

MACBETH. Sweet remembrancer!
Now good digestion wait on appetite,
And health on both!

LENNOX. May 't please your Highness sit.

MACBETH. Here had we now our country's honor roofed,[16]
Were the graced person of our Banquo present—
Who may I rather challenge for unkindness
Than pity for mischance![17]

ROSS. His absence, sir,
Lays blame upon his promise. Please 't your Highness
To grace us with your royal company?

MACBETH. The table's full.

LENNOX. Here is a place reserved, sir.

MACBETH. Where?

LENNOX. Here, my good lord. What is 't that moves your Highness?

MACBETH. Which of you have done this?

28 **LORDS.** What, my good lord?

MACBETH. Thou canst not say I did it. Never shake
Thy gory locks at me.

ROSS. Gentlemen, rise, his Highness is not well.

LADY MACBETH. Sit, worthy friends. My lord is often thus,
And hath been from his youth. Pray you, keep seat.
The fit is momentary; upon a thought[18]
He will again be well. If much you note him,
You shall offend him and extend his passion.[19]
Feed, and regard him not.—Are you a man?

MACBETH. Ay, and a bold one, that dare look on that
Which might appall the devil.

12. **hear ourselves:** Talk it over.

13. **give the cheer:** Make the guests feel welcome.

14. **The feast . . . welcome:** The feast at which the host fails to make the guests feel welcome while the food is being prepared is no more than a bought dinner.

15. **From . . . ceremony:** Ceremony adds a pleasant flavor to the food.

16. **our . . . roofed:** The most honorable men in the country under one roof.

17. **Who . . . mischance:** Whom I hope I may reproach for being absent due to discourtesy rather than pity because he has had an accident.

18. **upon a thought:** In a moment.

19. **passion:** Suffering.

28 **Literary Focus** The stage direction for the entrance of the ghost suggests a ghostlike figure appearing on the Elizabethan stage. In modern productions, the seat usually remains empty, the ghost being a figment of Macbeth's imagination. In contrast, the ghost of Hamlet's father appears nightly on the battlements, where he is seen by the guards as well as by Hamlet himself.

29 Literary Focus These lines would not be overheard by the guests.

30 Literary Focus His efforts to make her see the ghost are futile, as it is visible only in his mind.

31 Literary Focus Note that she again questions his manhood in order to snap him out of his distraction.

32 Discussion What happens that makes the ghost reappear for Macbeth?

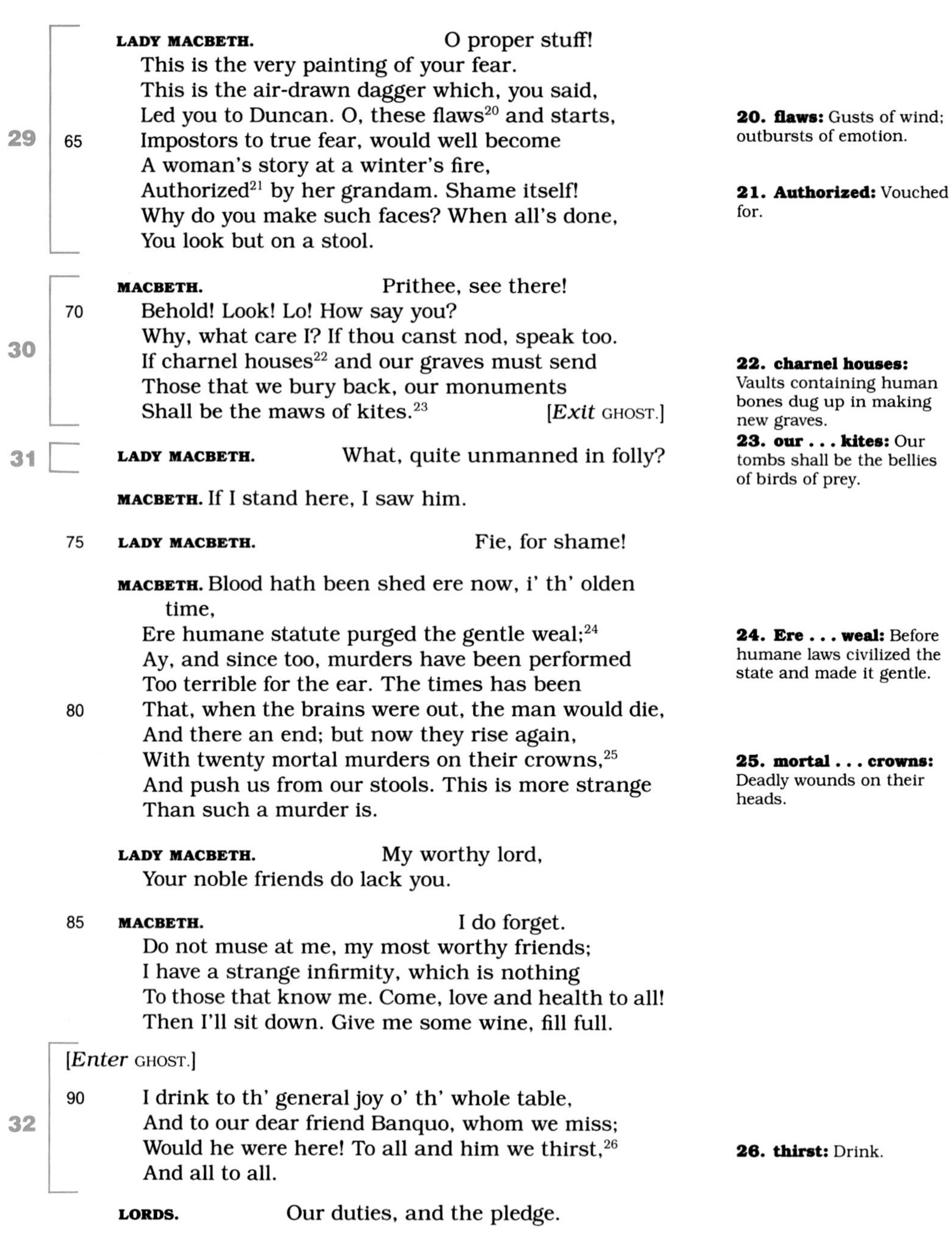

LADY MACBETH. O proper stuff!
This is the very painting of your fear.
This is the air-drawn dagger which, you said,
Led you to Duncan. O, these flaws[20] and starts,
29 Impostors to true fear, would well become
A woman's story at a winter's fire,
Authorized[21] by her grandam. Shame itself!
Why do you make such faces? When all's done,
You look but on a stool.

MACBETH. Prithee, see there!
Behold! Look! Lo! How say you?
30 Why, what care I? If thou canst nod, speak too.
If charnel houses[22] and our graves must send
Those that we bury back, our monuments
Shall be the maws of kites.[23] [*Exit* GHOST.]

31 **LADY MACBETH.** What, quite unmanned in folly?

MACBETH. If I stand here, I saw him.

LADY MACBETH. Fie, for shame!

MACBETH. Blood hath been shed ere now, i' th' olden time,
Ere humane statute purged the gentle weal;[24]
Ay, and since too, murders have been performed
Too terrible for the ear. The times has been
That, when the brains were out, the man would die,
And there an end; but now they rise again,
With twenty mortal murders on their crowns,[25]
And push us from our stools. This is more strange
Than such a murder is.

LADY MACBETH. My worthy lord,
Your noble friends do lack you.

MACBETH. I do forget.
Do not muse at me, my most worthy friends;
I have a strange infirmity, which is nothing
To those that know me. Come, love and health to all!
Then I'll sit down. Give me some wine, fill full.

[*Enter* GHOST.]

I drink to th' general joy o' th' whole table,
32 And to our dear friend Banquo, whom we miss;
Would he were here! To all and him we thirst,[26]
And all to all.

LORDS. Our duties, and the pledge.

20. flaws: Gusts of wind; outbursts of emotion.

21. Authorized: Vouched for.

22. charnel houses: Vaults containing human bones dug up in making new graves.

23. our . . . kites: Our tombs shall be the bellies of birds of prey.

24. Ere . . . weal: Before humane laws civilized the state and made it gentle.

25. mortal . . . crowns: Deadly wounds on their heads.

26. thirst: Drink.

MACBETH. Avaunt![27] and quit my sight! Let the earth hide thee!
Thy bones are marrowless, thy blood is cold;
Thou hast no speculation[28] in those eyes
Which thou dost glare with.

LADY MACBETH. Think of this, good peers,
But as a thing of custom, 'tis no other.
Only it spoils the pleasure of the time.

MACBETH. What man dare, I dare.
Approach thou like the rugged Russian bear,
The armed rhinoceros, or th' Hyrcan[29] tiger;
33 Take any shape but that,[30] and my firm nerves
Shall never tremble. Or be alive again,
And dare me to the desert[31] with thy sword.
If trembling I inhabit[32] then, protest me
The baby of a girl. Hence, horrible shadow!
Unreal mock'ry, hence! [*Exit* GHOST.]
Why, so: being gone,
I am a man again. Pray you, sit still.

LADY MACBETH. You have displaced the mirth, broke the good meeting,
With most admired[33] disorder.

MACBETH. Can such things be,
And overcome us[34] like a summer's cloud,
Without our special wonder? You make me strange
Even to the disposition that I owe,[35]
When now I think you can behold such sights,
And keep the natural ruby of your cheeks,
When mine is blanched with fear.

ROSS. What sights, my lord?

LADY MACBETH. I pray you, speak not: He grows worse and worse;
Question enrages him: at once, good night.
Stand not upon the order of your going,[36]
But go at once.

LENNOX. Good night; and better health
Attend his Majesty!

LADY MACBETH. A kind good night to all!
[*Exit* LORDS.]

MACBETH. It will have blood, they say: blood will have blood.
Stones have been known to move and trees to speak;

27. Avaunt: Be gone!

28. speculation: sight.

29. Hyrcan (hər′ kən): From Hyrcania, a province of the ancient Persian and Macedonian empires south of the Caspian Sea.

30. that: Banquo's shape.

31. desert: A place where neither of us could escape.

32. inhabit: Remain indoors.

33. admired: Amazing.

34. overcome us: Come over us.

35. disposition . . . owe: My own nature.

36. Stand . . . going: Do not wait to depart in order of rank.

33 **Discussion** Might this be a kind of response to Lady Macbeth's suggestion that he is "unmanned"?

34 Clarification What time is it? (Almost morning.)

35 Literary Focus Macbeth has established a kind of police state with paid informers in the houses of important people.

36 Clarification "For mine own good . . . way" means "My own interests and needs take precedence over all else." Is this a proper attitude for a king?

37 Discussion He then indicates that at this point retreating would be as difficult as going ahead with more bloodletting. Is that true? Would it even be possible to retreat at this point?

38 Discussion How does he rationalize the appearance of the ghost?

39 Literary Focus This scene is almost unanimously regarded as spurious and is generally considered not to have been written by Shakespeare. Because Elizabethan audiences so thoroughly enjoyed the witches, it is thought that Thomas Middleton wrote and injected this scene, which contributes nothing to the action of the play. In 1612 Middleton wrote a play entitled *The Witch.*

Augures and understood relations[37] have
By maggot-pies and choughs[38] and rooks brought
forth
The secret'st man of blood.[39] What is the night?

34 LADY MACBETH. Almost at odds[40] with morning, which is
which.

MACBETH. How say'st thou, that Macduff denies his
person
At our great bidding?

LADY MACBETH. Did you send to him, sir?

MACBETH. I hear it by the way, but I will send:
35 There's not a one of them but in his house
I keep a servant fee'd.[41] I will tomorrow,
And betimes[42] I will, to the weird sisters:
More shall they speak, for now I am bent[43] to know
By the worst means the worst. For mine own good
36 All causes shall give way. I am in blood
Stepped in so far that, should I wade no more,
37 Returning were as tedious as go o'er.
Strange things I have in head that will to hand,
Which must be acted ere they may be scanned.[44]

LADY MACBETH. You lack the season of all natures,[45]
sleep.

MACBETH. Come, we'll to sleep. My strange and self-
38 abuse[46]
Is the initiate fear that wants hard use.[47]
We are yet but young in deed. [*Exit.*]

Scene v. *A witches' haunt.*
39 [*Thunder. Enter the* THREE WITCHES, *meeting* HECATE.]

FIRST WITCH. Why, how now, Hecate! you look angerly.

HECATE. Have I not reason, beldams[1] as you are,
Saucy and overbold? How did you dare
To trade and traffic with Macbeth
In riddles and affairs of death;
And I, the mistress of your charms,
The close contriver[2] of all harms,
Was never called to bear my part,
Or show the glory of our art?
And, which is worse, all you have done
Hath been but for a wayward son,
Spiteful and wrathful; who, as others do,
Loves for his own ends, not for you.
But make amends now: get you gone,

37. Augures and understood relations: Omens and the relationship between the omens and what they represent.

38. maggot-pies and choughs (chufs): Magpies and crows.

39. man of blood: Murderer.

40. at odds: Disputing.

41. fee'd: Paid to spy.

42. betimes: Quickly.

43. bent: Determined.

44. scanned: Examined.

45. season . . . natures: Preservative of all living creatures.

46. My . . . self-abuse: My strange delusion.

47. initiate . . . use: Beginner's fear that will harden with experience.

1. beldams: Hags.

2. close contriver: secret inventor.

And at the pit of Acheron[3]
Meet me i' th' morning: thither he
Will come to know his destiny.
Your vessels and your spells provide,
Your charms and everything beside.
I am for th' air; this night I'll spend
Unto a dismal and a fatal end:
Great business must be wrought ere noon.
Upon the corner of the moon
There hangs a vap'rous drop profound;
I'll catch it ere it come to ground:
And that distilled by magic sleights[4]
Shall raise such artificial sprites[5]
As by the strength of their illusion
Shall draw him on to his confusion.[6]
He shall spurn fate, scorn death, and bear
His hopes 'bove wisdom, grace, and fear:
And you all know security[7]
Is mortals' chiefest enemy.

[*Music and a song.*]

Hark! I am called; my little spirit, see,
Sits in a foggy cloud and stays for me. [*Exit.*]

[*Sing within,* "Come away, come away," *etc.*]

FIRST WITCH. Come, let's make haste; she'll soon be back again. [*Exit.*]

40 ***Scene vi.*** *The palace.*

[*Enter* LENNOX *and another* LORD.]

LENNOX. My former speeches have but hit[1] your thoughts,
Which can interpret farther.[2] Only I say
Things have been strangely borne.[3] The gracious Duncan
Was pitied of Macbeth: marry, he was dead.
And the right-valiant Banquo walked too late;
Whom, you may say, if 't please you, Fleance killed,
For Fleance fled. Men must not walk too late.
41 Who cannot want the thought,[4] how monstrous
It was for Malcolm and for Donalbain
To kill their gracious father? Damnèd fact![5]
How it did grieve Macbeth! Did he not straight,
In pious rage, the two delinquents tear,
That were the slaves of drink and thralls[6] of sleep?
Was not that nobly done? Ay, and wisely too;
For 'twould have angered any heart alive
To hear the men deny 't. So that I say

3. Acheron (ak' ə ron'): Hell; in Greek mythology the river of Hades.

4. sleights: Devices.

5. artificial sprites: Spirits created by magic.

6. confusion: Ruin.

7. security: Overconfidence.

1. hit: Coincided.

2. Which . . . farther: From which you can draw your own conclusions.

3. borne: Managed.

4. cannot . . . thought: Can fail to think.

5. fact: Deed.

6. thralls: slaves.

40 Literary Focus This scene is totally expository, allowing the audience insight into what is happening in Scotland under Macbeth's rule. Some scholars suggest the scene should follow rather than precede Act IV, scene i. Seek student's thoughts as you read on.

41 Discussion Do we detect sarcasm here? What is Lennox really saying?

42 Discussion What does this line tell us of their feelings?

43 Discussion Where has Macduff gone? Why?

44 Discussion How is Macbeth reacting to all this?

45 Clarification Read as "You'll be sorry."

He has borne all things well: and I do think
That, had he Duncan's sons under his key—
As, an 't[7] please heaven, he shall not—they should find
What 'twere to kill a father. So should Fleance.
But, peace! for from broad[8] words, and 'cause he failed
42 His presence at the tyrant's feast, I hear,
Macduff lives in disgrace. Sir, can you tell
Where he bestows himself?

LORD. The son of Duncan,
From whom this tyrant holds the due of birth,[9]
Lives in the English court, and is received
43 Of the most pious Edward[10] with such grace
That the malevolence of fortune nothing
Takes from his high respect.[11] Thither Macduff
Is gone to pray the holy King, upon his aid[12]
To wake Northumberland and warlike Siward;[13]
That by the help of these, with Him above
To ratify the work, we may again
Give to our tables meat, sleep to our nights,
Free from our feasts and banquets bloody knives,
Do faithful homage and receive free honors:[14]
All which we pine for now. And this report
44 Hath so exasperate the King that he
Prepares for some attempt of war.

LENNOX. Sent he to Macduff?

LORD. He did: and with an absolute "Sir, not I,"
The cloudy[15] messenger turns me his back,
45 And hums, as who should say "You'll rue the time
That clogs[16] me with this answer."

LENNOX. And that well might
Advise him to a caution, t' hold what distance
His wisdom can provide. Some holy angel
Fly to the court of England and unfold
His message ere he come, that a swift blessing
May soon return to this our suffering country
Under a hand accursed!

LORD. I'll send my prayers with him.
[*Exit.*]

7. an 't: If it.

8. broad: Unguarded.

9. due of birth: Birthright, claim to the throne.

10. Edward: Edward the Confessor, King of England 1042–1066.

11. with . . . respect: Does not diminish the high respect he is given.

12. upon his aid: To aid Malcolm.

13. To . . . Siward: To call to arms the commander of the English forces, the Earl of Northumberland, and his son Siward.

14. free honors: Honors given to free men.

15. cloudy: Disturbed.

16. clogs: Burdens.

Answers

ANSWERS TO THINKING ABOUT THE SELECTION

Recalling

1. (a) Because the prophecies have come true for Macbeth, he wonders if they will indeed come true for him as well, making him the father of a line of kings. (b) Macbeth is now concerned that the blood he has spilled will serve the heirs of Banquo, as Macbeth is childless.
2. (a) The murderers are instructed by Macbeth to kill Banquo and his son, Fleance. (b) The death of Fleance is important to Macbeth's plans and wishes in order to halt the possible succession to the throne of Banquo's heirs.
3. The plans partially fail as Fleance escapes.
4. (a) In scene iv, Macbeth is tormented by the vision of the dead Banquo sitting in his place at the banquet table. (b) Lady Macbeth explains to the guests that Macbeth suffers from a childhood affliction that occasionally overtakes him.
5. (a) Macbeth seeks out the witches again to learn where all this killing is going to lead—to learn the worst, as he says. (b) Lady Macbeth urges him to get some sleep, which he has sorely lacked and by which he may regain his wits.
6. (a) Macduff lives in disgrace for failing to attend Macbeth's banquet. (b) Macduff has gone off to England to seek the aid of the king, Northumberland, and his son, Siward, in an effort to dethrone Macbeth and free Scotland from his tyranny.

Interpreting

7. The moral decline of Macbeth is evident. Prior to Duncan's murder, he was driven by raw ambition, which would have been checked

THINKING ABOUT THE SELECTION

Recalling

1. (a) In Scene i, what are Banquo's thoughts about the witches' prophecies? (b) What are Macbeth's thoughts about the prophecies?
2. (a) What two people are the murderers told to kill? (b) Why is it necessary to kill both?
3. What goes wrong with the murderers' plans?
4. (a) In Scene iv, why does Macbeth not sit down at the banquet table? (b) How does Lady Macbeth explain his behavior?
5. (a) Why does Macbeth want to see the witches again? (b) What does Lady Macbeth think Macbeth needs most?
6. (a) In Scene vi, what reason does Lennox give for Macduff's being in disgrace? (b) What is Macduff trying to accomplish in England?

Interpreting

7. Macbeth's soliloquy in Scene i shows that his attitude toward those who stand in his way has changed. Recall the soliloquy prior to Duncan's murder. What change or changes have occurred?
8. How does Macbeth's technique of persuading the murderers resemble Lady Macbeth's earlier method of persuading Macbeth?
9. How has the relationship between Macbeth and Lady Macbeth changed?
10. Events at the banquet show that Macbeth can no longer pretend to be innocent. What evidence is there that he will continue to kill those who threaten him?

Applying

11. By the end of Act III, Macbeth is in desperate trouble. What advice would you give him concerning his best course of action?

ANALYZING LITERATURE

Understanding Irony

In *verbal irony* there is a contrast between what is said and what is meant. An example of verbal irony occurs in Act III, Scene i, when Macbeth says to Banquo, "Here's our chief guest," knowing that Banquo will be murdered on his orders before the great feast begins.

1. What three additional examples of verbal irony can you find in the conversation in Scene i between Macbeth and Banquo?
2. In Scene vi Lennox appears to accept Macbeth's version of the various murders. (a) How can you tell from what Lennox says that he does not really believe in Macbeth's innocence? (b) What are three examples of verbal irony in Lennox's opening speech?

CRITICAL THINKING AND READING

Interpreting Connotative Meanings

The **connotation** of a word is what is suggested by the word in addition to its literal meaning, or denotation. For instance, the denotation of the word *home* is "the place where one lives." The associations of *home* give the word its *connotative meanings:* "warmth, love, peace." Shakespeare, like all good writers, chooses words for their connotative meanings.

1. When the ghost of Banquo exits (Scene iv, line 108), Macbeth says, "I am a man again." What are the connotative meanings of *man*?
2. When Macbeth is talking to the murderers (Scene i, lines 90–91), he says, "Whose heavy hand hath bowed you to the grave / And *beggared* yours forever?" What are the connotative meanings of *beggared*?

THINKING AND WRITING

Who Is the Third Murderer?

Shakespeare never reveals the identity of the third murderer. Who do you think the third murderer might be? Write an essay supporting your theory of his or her identity. Reread Scene iii carefully. Then build a logical case using facts and lines from the play to support your theory. Use the process of elimination to exonerate some of the major characters. Remember, though, that the third murderer may have been sent by someone—even the witches—for a specific purpose (perhaps the killing of Banquo or the escape of Fleance). In revising your paper, make sure you have left no logical holes in your argument. Proofread and prepare a final draft.

(Answers begin on p. 270.)

by his natural decency, had it not been for Lady Macbeth. Now he coldly plans the deaths of Banquo and Fleance because of the witches' predictions and because he is childless. In this soliloquy we find no evidence of decency or compassion.

8. Macbeth implies that they are less than men if they choose to stand by and let the wrongs of Banquo—most likely fabricated by Macbeth—go unpunished. Lady Macbeth's implications were similar when her husband seriously questioned the wisdom of their awful plan.
9. Macbeth has drawn into himself. Lady Macbeth is not apprised of, much less consulted about, his plans for Banquo and Fleance. His letter to her early in the play suggests much communication and sharing before all this.
10. He says that he is so deep in blood now that there is no turning back, implying that future sacrifices will be made to protect their bloody gains.

Applying

11. Answers will vary. However, given Macbeth's character and situation it seems likely that the only advice he would heed would be to continue along his murderous—and tragic—course. Advice grounded in traditional morality would, no doubt, be of no avail with Macbeth.

ANSWERS TO ANALYZING LITERATURE

1. In lines 13–14 Macbeth again requests Banquo's presence, not knowing that his ghost will indeed attend. In line 22 Macbeth says that he will seek Banquo's good advice tomorrow, knowing there will be no tomorrow for Banquo. In line 28, Banquo assures Macbeth he will not fail to attend the banquet. In fact, his ghost attends.
2. (a) His equivocations and exaggerations lead one to question immediately his true meaning, for example in line 7. The language seems purposely bloated and overdone, suggesting that he means the opposite of what he says. Finally, he refers to Macbeth as the tyrant, leaving no doubt of his true meaning. (b) Lennox says that Macbeth pitied the murdered Duncan, that it was monstrous of Malcolm and Donalbain to murder their gracious father, and that Macbeth's killing of the servants was understandable under the circumstances.

ANSWERS TO CRITICAL THINKING AND READING

1. When Macbeth says he is a "man" again, he is saying he is strong, fearless, composed, clear-headed, of good humor, and clever.
2. He is saying Banquo has put these two in a state where they will become beggars, a level of human life frightening and disturbing to everyone, as it saps people of their dignity.

THINKING AND WRITING

Publishing Student Writing Students might enjoy hearing one another's essays. Ask for volunteers to share their essays with the class.

Literary Focus By now most students know about plot. For those who do not, explain that plot is what you tell someone when you explain the story line of a TV show or movie to a friend. Draw a line on the board moving from left to right that swings upward, then downward. At the point where the line turns downward is the climax. You might want to mark points along the line that correspond with actions of the play so far.

Look For As the climax has already occurred, have students look for the way the plot winds downward toward a resolution.

Writing Have students discuss why, in a work of literary merit, the characters drive the plot, and not the other way around. To be sure students understand this important concept, ask them to explain how the character of Lady Macbeth dictates the shape of a segment of the plot of the play. What if Macbeth had married the woman who became Lady Macduff? How would she have reacted to his letter in the beginning of Act II?

Vocabulary Have your students use each of these words in a sentence of their own.

GUIDE FOR READING

Macbeth, Act IV

Writer's Techniques

Plot Development. The plot of a literary work is the sequence of related events that create and then resolve a conflict. Conflict is the struggle, or interplay of forces, that takes place within the story. The main character may be in conflict with another person, with a value system, with fate, or with nature. Certain background information is necessary for an understanding of the action. This information is called **exposition,** and it usually appears early in the story. The plot movement at the beginning is one of *rising action* toward a climax. The *climax,* or *crisis,* is the peak of tension, a dramatic turning point. In a tragedy like *Macbeth,* the climax often occurs near the middle of the play. Then comes a period of *falling action,* which, in tragedy, shows the downfall of the tragic hero. The falling action leads finally to the *resolution,* or *denouement,* the point at which the conflict ends and the outcome is made clear.

Look For

As you read *Macbeth,* Act IV, consider the plot progression up to this point. Think about the climax—which has already occurred. What is happening to Macbeth's personality and character as he is caught up in the vortex of events?

Writing

Plot is closely intertwined with character. Indeed, in a work of literary merit, you will find that character largely drives the plot, not the other way around. Make some notes analyzing that character of Macbeth. List his virtues as well as his faults, for the complexity of Macbeth's character lies at the heart of his difficulties.

Vocabulary

Knowing the following words will help you as you read *Macbeth, Act IV.*

pernicious (pər nish′ əs) *adj.*: Evil; wicked (Sc. i, l. 131)
judicious (jo͞o di′ əs) *adj.*: Showing good judgment (Sc. ii, l. 6)
sundry (sun′ drē) *adj*: Various; miscellaneous (Sc. iii, l. 48)
imtemperance (in tem′ pər əns) *n.*: Lack of restraint (Sc. iii, l. 66)
avarice (av′ ər is) *n.*: Greed (Sc. iii, l. 78)
credulous (drej′ o͞o ləs) *adj.*: Tending to believe too readily (Sc. iii, l. 120)

Objectives

1. To understand plot development
2. To read between the lines
3. To understand the idea of the tragic flaw

Teaching Portfolio: Support Material

Teacher Backup, p. 000

Vocabulary Check, p. 00

Usage and Mechanics Worksheet, p. 00

Analyzing Literature Worksheet, p. 00

Critical Thinking and Reading Worksheet, pp. 00

Language Worksheet, p. 00

Selection Test, pp. 00

Act IV

Scene i. *A witches' haunt.*
[*Thunder. Enter the* THREE WITCHES.]

FIRST WITCH. Thrice the brinded[1] cat hath mewed.

SECOND WITCH. Thrice and once the hedge-pig[2] whined.

1, 2 THIRD WITCH. Harpier[3] cries. 'Tis time, 'tis time.

FIRST WITCH. Round about the caldron go:
In the poisoned entrails throw.
Toad, that under cold stone
Days and nights has thirty-one
Swelt'red venom sleeping got,[4]
Boil thou first i' th' charmèd pot.

ALL. Double, double, toil and trouble;
Fire burn and caldron bubble.

SECOND WITCH. Fillet of a fenny snake,
In the caldron boil and bake;
Eye of newt and toe of frog,
Wool of bat and tongue of dog,
Adder's fork[5] and blindworm's[6] sting,
Lizard's leg and howlet's[7] wing,
For a charm of pow'rful trouble,
Like a hell-broth boil and bubble.

3 ALL. Double, double, toil and trouble;
Fire burn and caldron bubble.

THIRD WITCH. Scale of dragon, tooth of wolf,
Witch's mummy, maw and gulf[8]
Of the ravined[9] salt-sea shark,
Root of hemlock digged i' th' dark, . . .
Slivered in the moon's eclipse,
Nose of Turk and Tartar's lips,
Finger of birth-strangled babe
Ditch-delivered by a drab,
Make the gruel thick and slab:[10]
Add thereto a tiger's chaudron,[11]
For th' ingredience of our caldron.

ALL. Double, double, toil and trouble;
Fire burn and caldron bubble.

SECOND WITCH. Cool it with a baboon's blood,
Then the charm is firm and good.

[*Enter* HECATE *and the other* THREE WITCHES.]

4 HECATE. O, well done! I commend your pains;

1. **brinded:** Striped.
2. **hedge-pig:** Hedgehog.
3. **Harpier:** One of the spirits attending the witches.
4. **Swelt'red . . . got:** Venom sweated out while sleeping.
5. **fork:** Forked tongue.
6. **blindworm's:** Small, limbless lizard's.
7. **howlet's:** A small owl's.
8. **maw and gulf:** Stomach and gullet.
9. **ravined:** Ravenous.
10. **slab:** sticky.
11. **chaudron** (shō′ drən): Entrails.

Motivation for Reading We are now beyond the climax of the play. Observe how this entire act leads downward, step by step, for Macbeth.

Master Teacher Note As you read and discuss Act IV, suggest that your students note, or perhaps list, all plot developments and other details that seem to prepare for the culminating events in Act V.

Purpose-setting Question How do the events of Act IV prepare for the concluding events in Act V?

1 **Literary Focus** Harpier is the Third Witch's familiar, or spirit servant. In Act I, scene i, we learned that Graymalkin and Paddock are the familiars of the First and Second Witches, respectively.

2 **Discussion** What is it time for? Why?

3 **Literary Focus** The witches proceed to throw all kinds of incredibly disgusting and unwholesome ingredients into the caldron to increase the potion's evil powers. What effect do these lines have on you?

4 **Literary Focus** The entrance of Hecate and her companions here has little to do with the action of the play, and is considered in the same light as the previous witch scene. Compare these passages with the witch scenes of Act I.

5 **Literary Focus** Note the irony in the witches' evaluation of Macbeth.

6 **Discussion** What does this greeting imply about Macbeth?

7 **Discussion** Macbeth demands an answer to his questions, no matter what the consequences. What possible consequences does he conjure up? What does this speech tell us about his kingly qualities? What should a leader's first consideration be?

And every one shall share i' th' gains:
And now about the caldron sing,
Like elves and fairies in a ring,
Enchanting all that you put in.

[*Music and a song:* "Black Spirits," *etc. Exit* HECATE *and the other* THREE WITCHES.]

SECOND WITCH. By the pricking of my thumbs,
Something wicked this way comes:
Open, locks,
Whoever knocks!

[*Enter* MACBETH.]

6 **MACBETH.** How now, you secret, black, and midnight hags!
What is 't you do?

ALL. A deed without a name.

MACBETH. I conjure you, by that which you profess,
Howe'er you come to know it, answer me:
Though you untie the winds and let them fight
Against the churches; though the yesty[12] waves
Confound[13] and swallow navigation up;
Though bladed corn be lodged[14] and trees blown down;
7 Though castles topple on their warders' heads;
Though palaces and pyramids do slope[15]
Their heads to their foundations; though the treasure
Of nature's germens[16] tumble all together,
Even till destruction sicken, answer me
To what I ask you.

FIRST WITCH. Speak.

SECOND WITCH. Demand.

THIRD WITCH. We'll answer.

FIRST WITCH. Say, if th' hadst rather hear it from our mouths,
Or from our masters?

MACBETH. Call em, let me see 'em.

FIRST WITCH. Pour in sow's blood, that hath eaten
Her nine farrow;[17] grease that's sweaten
From the murderer's gibbet[18] throw
Into the flame.

ALL. Come, high or low,
Thyself and office[19] deftly show!

12. yesty: Foamy.

13. Confound: Destroy.

14. lodged: Beaten down.

15. slope: Bend.

16. nature's germens: Seeds of all life.

17. farrow: Young pigs.

18. gibbet (jib' it): Gallows.

19. office: Function.

[*Thunder.* FIRST APPARITION: *an Armed Head.*[20]]

MACBETH. Tell me, thou unknown power—

FIRST WITCH. He knows thy thought:
Hear his speech, but say thou nought.

FIRST APPARITION. Macbeth! Macbeth! Macbeth! Beware
8 Macduff!
Beware the Thane of Fife. Dismiss me: enough.
[*He descends.*]

MACBETH. Whate'er thou art, for thy good caution thanks:
Thou hast harped[21] my fear aright. But one word more—

FIRST WITCH. He will not be commanded. Here's another,
More potent than the first.

[*Thunder.* SECOND APPARITION: *a Bloody Child.*[22]]

SECOND APPARITION. Macbeth! Macbeth! Macbeth!

MACBETH. Had I three ears, I'd hear thee.

SECOND APPARITION. Be bloody, bold, and resolute! Laugh
9 to scorn
The pow'r of man, for none of woman born
Shall harm Macbeth. [*Descends.*]

MACBETH. Then live, Macduff: what need I fear of thee?
10 But yet I'll make assurance double sure,
And take a bond of fate.[23] Thou shalt not live;
That I may tell pale-hearted fear it lies,
And sleep in spite of thunder.

[*Thunder.* THIRD APPARITION: *a Child Crowned, with a tree in his hand.*[24]]

What is this,
That rises like the issue of a king,
And wears upon his baby-brow the round
And top of sovereignty?[25]

ALL. Listen, but speak not to 't.

THIRD APPARITION. Be lion-mettled, proud, and take no care
Who chafes, who frets, or where conspirers are:
Macbeth shall never vanquished be until
11 Great Birnam Wood to high Dunsinane Hill
Shall come against him. [*Descends.*]

20. an Armed Head: A symbol of Macduff.

21. harped: Hit upon.

22. a Bloody Child: A symbol of Macduff at birth.

23. take . . . fate: Get a guarantee from fate (by killing Macduff).

24. a Child . . . hand: A symbol of Malcolm.

25. top of sovereignty: Crown.

8 **Discussion** What is the first of the three messages?

9 **Discussion** What does the second apparition predict?

10 **Discussion** How does Macbeth react? Why doesn't he pause to consider if the prediction might have some hidden meaning? What precaution will he take?

11 **Discussion** What is the third prophecy?

275

12 Discussion Why is Macbeth pleased with this prophecy's content, and what does he conclude?

13 Clarification Hautboys are wooden pipe-like instruments.

14 Discussion What does Macbeth learn from the appearance of the kings and Banquo? What should he learn about the prophecies, but apparently does not?

MACBETH. That will never be.
Who can impress[26] the forest, bid the tree
Unfix his earth-bound root? Sweet bodements,[27]
good!
Rebellious dead, rise never, till the Wood
12 Of Birnam rise, and our high-placed Macbeth
Shall live the lease of nature,[28] pay his breath
To time and mortal custom.[29] Yet my heart
Throbs to know one thing. Tell me, if your art
Can tell so much: shall Banquo's issue ever
Reign in this kingdom?

ALL. Seek to know no more.

MACBETH. I will be satisfied. Deny me this,
And an eternal curse fall on you! Let me know.
Why sinks that caldron? And what noise is this?

13 [*Hautboys.*]

FIRST WITCH. Show!

SECOND WITCH. Show!

THIRD WITCH. Show!

ALL. Show his eyes, and grieve his heart;
Come like shadows, so depart!

[*A show of eight* KINGS *and* BANQUO, *last* KING *with a glass*[30] *in his hand.*]

MACBETH. Thou art too like the spirit of Banquo. Down!
Thy crown does sear mine eyelids. And thy hair,
Thou other gold-bound brow, is like the first.
A third is like the former. Filthy hags!
Why do you show me this? A fourth! Start, eyes!
What, will the line stretch out to th' crack of doom?
14 Another yet! A seventh! I'll see no more.
And yet the eighth appears, who bears a glass
Which shows me many more; and some I see
That twofold balls and treble scepters[31] carry:
Horrible sight! Now I see 'tis true;
For the blood-boltered[32] Banquo smiles upon me,
And points at them for his.[33] What, is this so?

FIRST WITCH. Ay, sir, all this is so. But why
Stands Macbeth thus amazedly?
Come, sisters, cheer we up his sprites,
And show the best of our delights:
I'll charm the air to give a sound,
While you perform your antic round,[34]
That this great king may kindly say
Our duties did his welcome pay.

26. impress: Force into service.

27. bodements: Prophecies.

28. lease of nature: Natural lifespan.

29. mortal custom: Natural death.

30. glass: Mirror.

31. twofold . . . scepters: Coronation emblems and insignia of the kingdoms of England, Scotland, and Ireland, united in 1603 when James VI of Scotland became James I of England.

32. blood-boltered: With his hair matted with blood.

33. his: His descendants.

34. antic round: Grotesque circular dance.

MACBETH AND THE WITCHES
Engraved by Thew after Reynolds
Royal Academy of Arts, London

[*Music.* THE WITCHES *dance, and vanish.*]

MACBETH. Where are they? Gone? Let this pernicious
hour
Stand aye accursèd in the calendar!
Come in, without there!

[*Enter* LENNOX.]

LENNOX. What's your Grace's will?

MACBETH. Saw you the weird sisters?

LENNOX. No, my lord.

MACBETH. Came they not by you?

LENNOX. No indeed, my lord.

MACBETH. Infected be the air whereon they ride,
And damned all those that trust them! I did hear
The galloping of horse. Who was 't came by?

Humanities Note Fine art, *Macbeth and the Witches,* engraved by Robert Thew. Robert Thew (1758–1802), a British engraver, had little formal training as an artist. He was, however, a man of great natural ability and motivation. He taught himself the art of engraving and attained excellence in it. He used this art to create shop bills and business cards until a stroke of good fortune won him an introduction to the eminent publisher and engraver John Boydell (1719–1804). Boydell enlisted Thew's services on a large project involving the engraving of twenty-two paintings on Shakespearean subjects by England's leading artists for a subscription series of prints.

The engraving *Macbeth and the Witches* published in 1802, was done after a painting by Sir Joshua Reynolds (1723–1792), who was one of England's most respected portrait painters. Boydell's employment of Robert Thew was considered an endorsement of the engraver's considerable talents and thereby established his fame.

You might use the following question in your discussion:

1. How does this artist's conception of the witches differ from the common stereotype of a witch?
2. What about this engraving makes it seem like a painting?

15 **Discussion** What does this decision tell us about Macbeth's continuing moral decline? In what way are these murders worse than those he has already committed?

16 **Discussion** To whom is Lady Macduff referring?

17 **Discussion** What argument does she make against his flight?

LENNOX. 'Tis two or three, my lord, that bring you word
Macduff is fled to England.

MACBETH. Fled to England?

LENNOX. Ay, my good lord.

MACBETH. [*Aside*] Time, thou anticipat'st[35] my dread exploits.
The flighty purpose never is o'ertook
Unless the deed go with it.[36] From this moment
The very firstlings of my heart[37] shall be
The firstlings of my hand. And even now,
To crown my thoughts with acts, be it thought and
15 done:
The castle of Macduff I will surprise;
Seize upon Fife; give to th' edge o' th' sword
His wife, his babes, and all unfortunate souls
That trace[38] him in his line. No boasting like a fool;
This deed I'll do before this purpose cool:
But no more sights!—Where are these gentlemen?
Come, bring me where they are. [*Exit.*]

35. anticipat'st: Foretold.

36. The flighty . . . it: The fleeting plan is never fulfilled unless it is carried out at once.

37. firstlings . . . heart: First thoughts, impulses.

38. trace: Succeed.

Scene ii. *Macduff's castle.*
[*Enter* MACDUFF'S WIFE, *her* SON, *and* ROSS.]

16 LADY MACDUFF. What had he done, to make him fly the land?

ROSS. You must have patience, madam.

LADY MACDUFF. He had none:
His flight was madness. When our actions do not,
Our fears do make us traitors.

ROSS. You know not
Whether it was his wisdom or his fear.

LADY MACDUFF. Wisdom! To leave his wife, to leave his babes,
His mansion and his titles,[1] in a place
From whence himself does fly? He loves us not;
17 He wants the natural touch:[2] for the poor wren,
The most diminutive of birds, will fight,
Her young ones in her nest, against the owl.
All is the fear and nothing is the love;
As little is the wisdom, where the flight
So runs against all reason.

ROSS. My dearest coz,[3]
I pray you, school[4] yourself. But, for your husband,
He is noble, wise, judicious, and best knows

1. titles: possessions.

2. wants . . . touch: Lacks natural affection.

3. coz: Cousin.

4. school: Control.

The fits o' th' season.[5] I dare not speak much further:
But cruel are the times, when we are traitors
And do not know ourselves;[6] when we hold rumor
From what we fear,[7] yet know not what we fear,
18 But float upon a wild and violent sea
Each way and move. I take my leave of you.
Shall not be long but I'll be here again.
Things at the worst will cease, or else climb upward
To what they were before. My pretty cousin,
Blessing upon you!

19 **LADY MACDUFF.** Fathered he is, and yet he's fatherless.

ROSS. I am so much a fool, should I stay longer,
It would be my disgrace and your discomfort.[8]
I take my leave at once. [*Exit* ROSS.]

LADY MACDUFF. Sirrah, your father's dead;
And what will you do now? How will you live?

SON. As birds do, mother.

LADY MACDUFF. What, with worms and flies?

20 **SON.** With what I get, I mean; and so do they.

LADY MACDUFF. Poor bird! thou'dst never fear the net nor lime,[9]
The pitfall nor the gin.[10]

SON. Why should I, mother? Poor birds they are not set for.
My father is not dead, for all your saying.

LADY MACDUFF. Yes, he is dead: how wilt thou do for a father?

SON. Nay, how will you do for a husband?

LADY MACDUFF. Why, I can buy me twenty at any market.

SON. Then you'll buy 'em to sell[11] again.

LADY MACDUFF. Thou speak'st with all thy wit, and yet i' faith,
With wit enough for thee.[12]

SON. Was my father a traitor, mother?

LADY MACDUFF. Ay, that he was.

SON. What is a traitor?

LADY MACDUFF. Why, one that swears and lies.[13]

SON. And be all traitors that do so?

5. fits o' th' season: Disorders of the time.

6. when . . . ourselves: When we are treated as traitors but do not know of any treason.

7. when . . . fear: Believe rumors based on our fears.

8. It . . . discomfort: I would disgrace myself and embarrass you by weeping.

9. lime: Birdlime, a sticky substance smeared on branches to catch birds.

10. gin: Trap.

11. sell: Betray.

12. for thee: For a child.

13. swears and lies: Takes an oath and breaks it.

18 **Discussion** What is the temper of the country and its people?

19 **Discussion** Explain this paradoxical line.

20 **Literary Focus** This exchange between Lady Macduff and her son is one of the few tender and witty passages in the play. Little Macduff is a precocious child who is doted on by his mother. Our knowledge of Macbeth's intentions makes the scene doubly poignant. Why might Shakespeare have included this scene?

Humanities Note

Fine art: Drawing of Lady Macduff by Sir John Gilbert. Sir John Gilbert (1817–1897) did this drawing of Lady Macduff and the murderers for Mackey's *Shakespeare*, an illustrated book in a series that won him great popularity as an illustrator. The ease with which the figures are drawn and the scene composed shows the superior sketching ability that Gilbert achieved through continuous practice. This drawing is dramatic, narrative, and spirited. It appeals even to today's viewer.

You might use the following questions for discussion:

1. A narrative drawing is one that tells a story. What story does this drawing tell?
2. How does the artist portray the fear and tension of this scene?

21 **Discussion** Of what significance is this discussion of traitors beyond showing us how clever and bright the young Macduff is?

WOOD ENGRAVING AFTER SIR JOHN GILBERT
The Granger Collection

LADY MACDUFF. Every one that does so is a traitor, and must be hanged.

21 **SON.** And must they all be hanged that swear and lie?

LADY MACDUFF. Every one.

SON. Who must hang them?

LADY MACDUFF. Why, the honest men.

SON. Then the liars and swearers are fools; for there are liars and swearers enow[14] to beat the honest men and hang up them.

LADY MACDUFF. Now, God help thee, poor monkey! But how wilt thou do for a father?

SON. If he were dead, you'd weep for him. If you would not, it were a good sign that I should quickly have a new father.

LADY MACDUFF. Poor prattler, how thou talk'st!

[*Enter a* MESSENGER.]

MESSENGER. Bless you, fair dame! I am not to you known,
Though in your state of honor I am perfect.[15]
I doubt[16] some danger does approach you nearly:
If you will take a homely[17] man's advice,
Be not found here; hence, with your little ones.
To fright you thus, methinks I am too savage;
To do worse to you were fell[18] cruelty,
Which is too nigh your person. Heaven preserve you!
I dare abide no longer. [*Exit* MESSENGER.]

LADY MACDUFF. Whither should I fly?
I have done no harm. But I remember now
I am in this earthly world, where to do harm
22 Is often laudable, to do good sometime
Accounted dangerous folly. Why then, alas,
Do I put up that womanly defense,
To say I have done no harm?—What are these faces?

[*Enter* MURDERERS.]

MURDERER. Where is your husband?

LADY MACDUFF. I hope, in no place so unsanctified
Where such as thou mayst find him.

MURDERER. He's a traitor.

SON. Thou li'st, thou shag-eared[19] villain!

MURDERER. What, you egg!

[*Stabbing him.*]

Young fry[20] of treachery!

SON. He has killed me, mother:
Run away, I pray you! [*Dies.*]

[*Exit* LADY MACDUFF *crying "Murder!"*
followed by MURDERERS.]

14. enow: Enough.

15. in . . . perfect: I am fully informed of your honorable rank.

16. doubt: Fear.

17. homely: Simple.

18. fell: Fierce.

19. shag-eared: Hairy-eared.

20. fry: Offspring.

22 **Discussion** What can we judge of Lady Macduff's character from this and earlier comments? Compare her to Lady Macbeth.

23 **Historical Focus** The English court to which Malcolm earlier fled, and the scene of this meeting with Macduff, is the court of Edward the Confessor. The action of this play would have concluded in the year 1054, when Malcolm III, called Malcolm Canmore, ascended the Scottish throne. His daughter Matilda married Henry I of England.

24 **Discussion** What does his initial suggestion to Macduff suggest about Malcolm's character? Is this judgment compatible with his behavior earlier in the play?

25 **Discussion** Compare the tone of Macduff's response. Why is it appropriate to what we know about Macduff?

26 **Discussion** What concern does Malcolm voice?

27 **Discussion** Why is Macduff's simple answer not convincing to Malcolm?

28 **Literary Focus** The theme of appearances and realities is continued here. In this case how is Malcolm dealing with them?

29 **Discussion** Why does the fact that Macduff left his family unprotected in Scotland give Malcolm doubts?

23 ***Scene iii.*** *England. Before the King's palace.*
[*Enter* MALCOLM *and* MACDUFF.]

24 MALCOLM. Let us seek out some desolate shade, and there
Weep our sad bosoms empty.

25 MACDUFF. Let us rather
Hold fast the mortal[1] sword, and like good men
Bestride our down-fall'n birthdom.[2] Each new morn
New widows howl, new orphans cry, new sorrows
Strike heaven on the face, that it resounds
As if it felt with Scotland and yelled out
Like syllable of dolor.[3]

MALCOLM. What I believe, I'll wail;
What know, believe; and what I can redress,
As I shall find the time to friend,[4] I will.
What you have spoke, it may be so perchance.
This tyrant, whose sole[5] name blisters our tongues,
Was once thought honest:[6] you have loved him well;
26 He hath not touched you yet. I am young; but something
You may deserve of him through me;[7] and wisdom[8]
To offer up a weak, poor, innocent lamb
T' appease an angry god.

MACDUFF. I am not treacherous.

MALCOLM. But Macbeth is.
A good and virtuous nature may recoil
In an imperial charge.[9] But I shall crave your pardon;
27 That which you are, my thoughts cannot transpose:[10]
28 Angels are bright still, though the brightest[11] fell:
Though all things foul would wear[12] the brows of grace,
Yet grace must still look so.[13]

MACDUFF. I have lost my hopes.

29 MALCOLM. Perchance even there where I did find my doubts.
Why in that rawness[14] left you wife and child,
Those precious motives, those strong knots of love,
Without leave-taking? I pray you,
Let not my jealousies[15] be your dishonors.
But mine own safeties.[16] You may be rightly just
Whatever I shall think.

MACDUFF. Bleed, bleed, poor country:
Great tyranny, lay thou thy basis sure,

1. mortal: Deadly.
2. Bestride . . . birthdom: Protectively stand over our native land.
3. Like . . . dolor: A similar cry of anguish.
4. to friend: Be friendly.
5. sole: Very.
6. honest: Good.
7. deserve . . . me: Earn by betraying me to Macbeth.
8. wisdom: It is wise.
9. recoil . . . charge: Give way to a royal command.
10. transpose: Transform.
11. the brightest: Lucifer.
12. would wear: Desire to wear.
13. so: Like itself.
14. rawness: Unprotected state or condition.
15. jealousies: Suspicions.
16. safeties: Protections.

For goodness dare not check thee: wear thou thy
wrongs:
The title is affeered.[17] Fare thee well, lord:
I would not be the villain that thou think'st
For the whole space that's in the tyrant's grasp
And the rich East to boot.

MALCOLM. Be not offended:
I speak not as in absolute fear of you.
I think our country sinks beneath the yoke;
It weeps, it bleeds, and each new day a gash
Is added to her wounds. I think withal
There would be hands uplifted in my right;[18]
And here from gracious England[19] have I offer
Of goodly thousands: but, for all this,
When I shall tread upon the tyrant's head,
Or wear it on my sword, yet my poor country
Shall have more vices than it had before,
More suffer, and more sundry ways than ever,
By him that shall succeed.

MACDUFF. What should he be?

30 **MALCOLM.** It is myself I mean, in whom I know
All the particulars of vice so grafted[20]
That, when they shall be opened,[21] black Macbeth
Will seem as pure as snow, and the poor state
Esteem him as a lamb, being compared
With my confineless harms.[22]

MACDUFF. Not in the legions
Of horrid hell can come a devil more damned
In evils to top Macbeth.

MALCOLM. I grant him bloody,
Luxurious,[23] avaricious, false, deceitful,
Sudden,[24] malicious, smacking of every sin
That has a name: but there's no bottom, none,
In my voluptuousness: your wives, your daughters,
Your matrons and your maids, could not fill up
The cistern of my lust, and my desire
All continent impediments[25] would o'erbear,
That did oppose my will. Better Macbeth
Than such an one to reign.

31 **MACDUFF.** Boundless intemperance
In nature[26] is a tyranny; it hath been
Th' untimely emptying of the happy throne,
And fall of many kings. But fear not yet
To take upon you what is yours: you may
Convey[27] your pleasures in a spacious plenty,

17. affeered: Legally confirmed.

18. in my right: On behalf of my claim.

19. England: The King of England.

20. grafted: Implanted.

21. opened: In bloom.

22. confineless harms: Unbounded evils.

23. luxurious: Lecherous.

24. Sudden: Violent.

25. continent impediments: Restraints.

26. nature: Man's nature.

27. Convey: Secretly manage.

30 **Discussion** Malcolm suggests that he is worse than Macbeth. What three specific evils does he accuse himself of in the lines that follow? Do these self-accusations seem believable?

31 **Discussion** How does Macduff address the first of Malcolm's claims to evil?

32 Discussion How does he compare the second failing with Malcolm's first? How does he suggest it be overcome?

33 Discussion What does Malcolm say he has none of?

34 Clarification For *concord,* read "harmony."

35 Discussion What is Macduff's reaction to Malcolm's third failing?

And yet seem cold, the time you may so hoodwink.
We have willing dames enough. There cannot be
That vulture in you, to devour so many
As will to greatness dedicate themselves,
Finding it so inclined.

MALCOLM. With this there grows
In my most ill-composed affection[28] such
A stanchless[29] avarice that, were I King,
I should cut off the nobles for their lands,
Desire his jewels and this other's house:
And my more-having would be as a sauce
To make me hunger more, that I should forge
Quarrels unjust against the good and loyal,
Destroying them for wealth.

MACDUFF. This avarice
Sticks deeper, grows with more pernicious root
Than summer-seeming[30] lust, and it hath been
32 The sword of[31] our slain kings. Yet do not fear.
Scotland hath foisons[32] to fill up your will
Of your mere own.[33] All these are portable,[34]
With other graces weighed.

33 **MALCOLM.** But I have none: the king-becoming graces,
As justice, verity, temp'rance, stableness,
Bounty, perseverance, mercy, lowliness,
Devotion, patience, courage, fortitude,
I have no relish of them, but abound
In the division of each several crime,[35]
Acting it many ways. Nay, had I pow'r, I should
34 Pour the sweet milk of concord into hell,
Uproar the universal peace, confound[36]
All unity on earth.

MACDUFF. O Scotland, Scotland!

MALCOLM. If such a one be fit to govern, speak:
I am as I have spoken.

MACDUFF. Fit to govern!
No, not to live. O nation miserable!
With an untitled[37] tyrant bloody-sceptered,
35 When shalt thou see thy wholesome days again,
Since that the truest issue of thy throne[38]
By his own interdiction[39] stands accursed,
And does blaspheme his breed?[40] Thy royal father
Was a most sainted king: the queen that bore thee,
Oft'ner upon her knees than on her feet,
Died[41] every day she lived. Fare thee well!
These evils thou repeat'st upon thyself

28. affection: Character.
29. stanchless: Never-ending.
30. summer-seeming: Summerlike.
31. of: That killed.
32. foisons (foi′ zənz): Plenty.
33. mere own: Own property.
34. portable: Bearable.
35. division . . . crime: Variations of each kind of crime.
36. confound: Destroy.
37. untitled: Having no right to the throne.
38. truest . . . throne: Child of the true king.
39. interdiction: Exclusion.
40. blaspheme his breed: Slander his ancestry.
41. Died: Prepared for heaven.

Hath banished me from Scotland. O my breast,
Thy hope ends here!

MALCOLM. Macduff, this noble passion,
Child of integrity, hath from my soul
Wiped the black scruples, reconciled my thoughts
To thy good truth and honor. Devilish Macbeth
By many of these trains[42] hath sought to win me
Into his power; and modest wisdom[43] plucks me
From over-credulous haste: but God above
Deal between thee and me! For even now
I put myself to thy direction, and
Unspeak mine own detraction,[44] here abjure
The taints and blames I laid upon myself,
36 For[45] strangers to my nature. I am yet
Unknown to woman, never was forsworn,
Scarcely have coveted what was mine own,
At no time broke my faith, would not betray
The devil to his fellow, and delight
No less in truth than life. My first false speaking
Was this upon myself. What I am truly,
Is thine and my poor country's to command:
Whither indeed, before thy here-approach,
Old Siward, with ten thousand warlike men,
Already at a point,[46] was setting forth.
Now we'll together, and the chance of goodness
Be like our warranted quarrel![47] Why are you silent?

MACDUFF. Such welcome and unwelcome things at once
'Tis hard to reconcile.

[*Enter a* DOCTOR.]

MALCOLM. Well, more anon. Comes the King forth, I pray
you?

DOCTOR. Ay, sir. There are a crew of wretched souls
That stay[48] his cure: their malady convinces
The great assay of art;[49] but at his touch,
Such sanctity hath heaven given his hand,
They presently amend.[50]

MALCOLM. I thank you, doctor.
[*Exit* DOCTOR.]

MACDUFF. What's the disease he means?

MALCOLM. 'Tis called the evil:[51]
A most miraculous work in this good King,
37 Which often since my here-remain in England
I have seen him do. How he solicits heaven,
Himself best knows: but strangely-visited people,

42. trains: Enticements.
43. modest wisdom: Prudence.
44. detraction: Slander.
45. For: As.
46. at a point: Prepared.
47. the chance ... quarrel: May our chance of success equal the justice of our cause.
48. stay: Wait for.
49. convinces ... art: Defies the efforts of medical science.
50. presently amend: Immediately recover.
51. evil: Scrofula (skrof′ yə lə), a skin disease called "the king's evil" because it was believed that it could be cured by the king's touch.

36 **Literary Focus** Here Malcolm explains that he was testing Macduff. He goes on to give him some good news. What is it?

37 **Historical Focus** This brief scene with the doctor is a digression, presumably written to compliment James I. Edward the Confessor supposedly had the power to cure the disease scrofula with his saintly touch. This power and the kings' use of it to cure their subjects appeared to come to an end with James I, who was reluctant to continue the practice until persuaded by his ministers. These lines praise his decision.

38 Discussion Why is Ross reluctant to share the news of Macduff's family? What added meaning can this line carry?

All swoll'n and ulcerous, pitiful to the eye,
The mere[52] despair of surgery, he cures,
Hanging a golden stamp[53] about their necks,
Put on with holy prayers: and 'tis spoken,
To the succeeding royalty he leaves
The healing benediction. With this strange virtue
He hath a heavenly gift of prophecy,
And sundry blessings hang about his throne
That speak him full of grace.

[*Enter* ROSS.]

MACDUFF. See, who comes here?

MALCOLM. My countryman; but yet I know him not.

MACDUFF. My ever gentle[54] cousin, welcome hither.

MALCOLM. I know him now: good God, betimes[55] remove
The means that makes us strangers!

ROSS. Sir, amen.

MACDUFF. Stands Scotland where it did?

ROSS. Alas, poor country!
Almost afraid to know itself! It cannot
Be called our mother but our grave, where nothing[56]
But who knows nothing is once seen to smile;
Where sighs and groans, and shrieks that rent the air,
Are made, not marked, where violent sorrow seems
A modern ecstasy.[57] The dead man's knell
Is there scarce asked for who,[58] and good men's lives
Expire before the flowers in their caps,
Dying or ere they sicken.

MACDUFF. O, relation
Too nice,[59] and yet too true!

MALCOLM. What's the newest grief?

ROSS. That of an hour's age doth hiss the speaker;[60]
Each minute teems[61] a new one.

MACDUFF. How does my wife?

ROSS. Why, well.

MACDUFF. And all my children?

ROSS. Well too.

MACDUFF. The tyrant has not battered at their peace?

38 **ROSS.** No; they were well at peace when I did leave 'em.

52. mere: Utter.
53. stamp: Coin.
54. gentle: Noble.
55. betimes: Quickly.
56. nothing: No one.
57. modern ecstasy: Ordinary emotion.
58. The dead . . . who: People can no longer keep track of Macbeth's victims.
59. nice: Exact.
60. That . . . speaker: The report of the grief of an hour ago is hissed as stale news.
61. teems: Gives birth to.

MACDUFF. Be not a niggard of your speech: how goes 't?

ROSS. When I came hither to transport the tidings,
Which I have heavily borne, there ran a rumor
Of many worthy fellows that were out;[62]
Which was to my belief witnessed[63] the rather,
For that I saw the tyrant's power[64] afoot.
Now is the time of help. Your eye in Scotland
Would create soldiers, make our women fight,
39 To doff[65] their dire distresses.

MALCOLM. Be 't their comfort
We are coming thither. Gracious England hath
Lent us good Siward and ten thousand men;
An older and a better soldier none
That Christendom gives out.

ROSS. Would I could answer
This comfort with the like! But I have words
That would be howled out in the desert air,
Where hearing should not latch[66] them.

MACDUFF. What concern they?
The general cause or is it a fee-grief[67]
Due to some single breast?

ROSS. No mind that's honest
But in it shares some woe, though the main part
Pertains to you alone.

MACDUFF. If it be mine,
Keep it not from me, quickly let me have it.

ROSS. Let not your ears despise my tongue for ever,
Which shall possess them with the heaviest sound
That ever yet they heard.

MACDUFF. Humh! I guess at it.

ROSS. Your castle is surprised; your wife and babes
Savagely slaughtered. To relate the manner,
Were, on the quarry[68] of these murdered deer,
To add the death of you.

MALCOLM. Merciful heaven!
What, man! Ne'er pull your hat upon your brows;
Give sorrow words. The grief that does not speak
Whispers the o'er-fraught[69] heart and bids it break.

MACDUFF. My children too?

ROSS. Wife, children, servants, all
That could be found.

62. out: In rebellion.
63. witnessed: Confirmed.
64. power: Army.
65. doff: Put off.
66. latch: Catch.
67. fee-grief: Personal grief.
68. quarry: Heap of game slain in a hunt.
69. o'er-fraught: Overburdened.

39 **Literary Focus** Ross turns to Malcolm to tell him that his presence in Scotland would support an uprising against Macbeth, who is by now nothing short of a tyrant. Only after Malcolm's response does he painfully and haltingly return to the terrible news about Macduff's family.

40 Literary Focus Macduff's struggle to absorb this terrible news adds emotional power and realism to this scene.

41 Discussion What does Macduff mean by this line?

42 Discussion Whom does Macduff blame? Why?

43 Literary Focus Explain this metaphor.

44 Literary Focus The imagery of night and day returns again. The evil associated with this play has occurred mostly at night. It is fitting and conscious that this last line of Act IV acknowledges that day will follow even the longest of nights. Even as we struggle with these most mindless of murders, one senses that the struggle will soon be over.

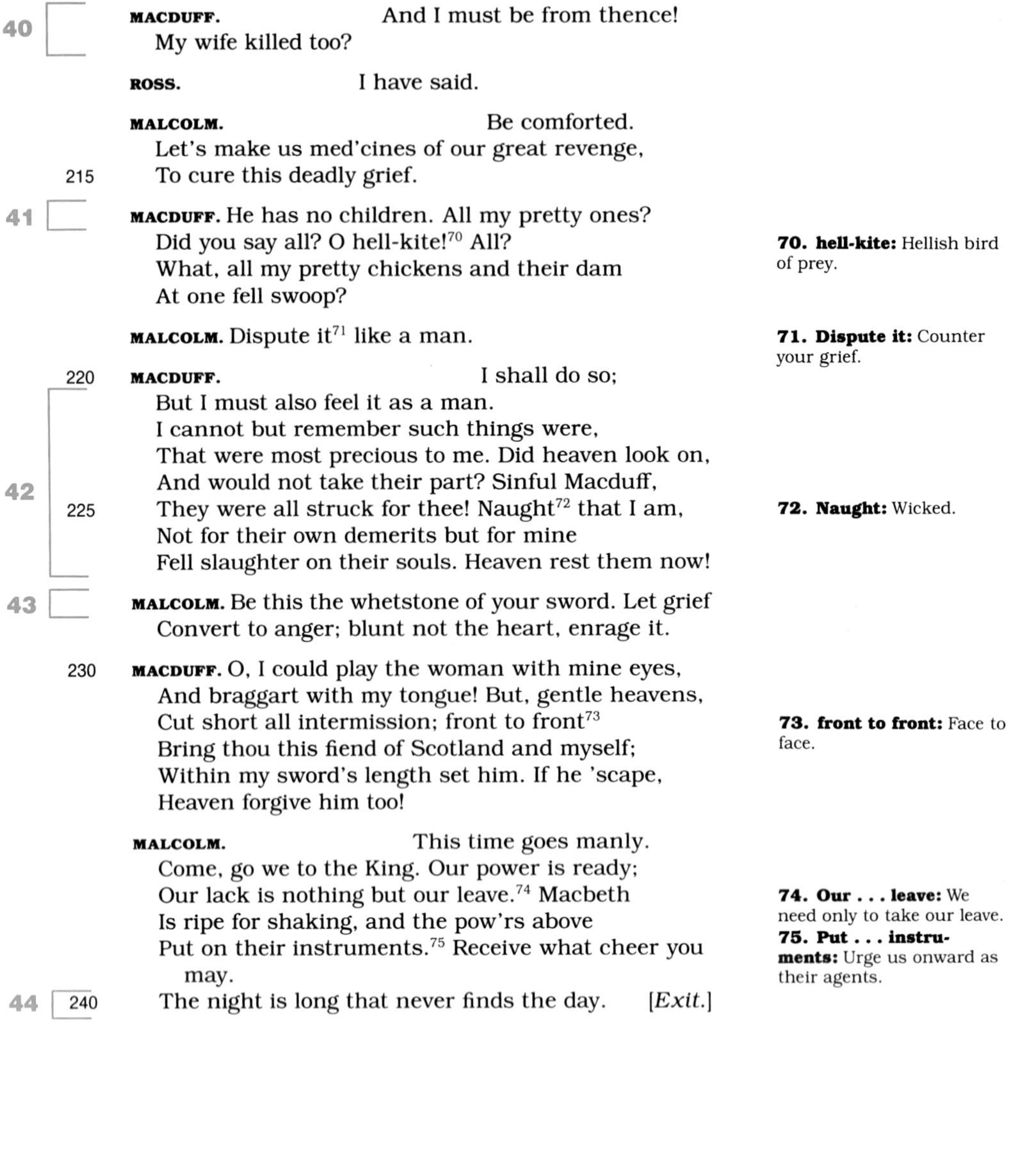

40 MACDUFF. And I must be from thence!
My wife killed too?

ROSS. I have said.

MALCOLM. Be comforted.
Let's make us med'cines of our great revenge,
To cure this deadly grief.

41 MACDUFF. He has no children. All my pretty ones?
Did you say all? O hell-kite![70] All?
What, all my pretty chickens and their dam
At one fell swoop?

MALCOLM. Dispute it[71] like a man.

MACDUFF. I shall do so;
42 But I must also feel it as a man.
I cannot but remember such things were,
That were most precious to me. Did heaven look on,
And would not take their part? Sinful Macduff,
They were all struck for thee! Naught[72] that I am,
Not for their own demerits but for mine
Fell slaughter on their souls. Heaven rest them now!

43 MALCOLM. Be this the whetstone of your sword. Let grief
Convert to anger; blunt not the heart, enrage it.

MACDUFF. O, I could play the woman with mine eyes,
And braggart with my tongue! But, gentle heavens,
Cut short all intermission; front to front[73]
Bring thou this fiend of Scotland and myself;
Within my sword's length set him. If he 'scape,
Heaven forgive him too!

MALCOLM. This time goes manly.
Come, go we to the King. Our power is ready;
Our lack is nothing but our leave.[74] Macbeth
Is ripe for shaking, and the pow'rs above
Put on their instruments.[75] Receive what cheer you
may.
44 The night is long that never finds the day. [*Exit.*]

70. hell-kite: Hellish bird of prey.

71. Dispute it: Counter your grief.

72. Naught: Wicked.

73. front to front: Face to face.

74. Our . . . leave: We need only to take our leave.

75. Put . . . instruments: Urge us onward as their agents.

Answers

ANSWERS TO THINKING ABOUT THE SELECTION
Recalling

1. (a) The first apparition tells Macbeth to beware of Macduff. (b) The second apparition says that none of woman born shall harm Macbeth, who naturally assumes Macduff is of woman born. (c) The third apparition tells Macbeth that he'll not be vanquished till Burnam Wood comes to his castle, Dunsinane.
2. Macbeth seeks to know if Banquo's descendants will rule Scotland. The witches do not tell him, but (b) they do generate images of future kings and the dead Banquo to prove that his offspring become kings.
3. (a) Lennox tells Macbeth that Macduff has fled to England. (b) He decides to slay Macduff's wife, children, and others at the unprotected castle.
4. (a) Malcolm is testing Macduff's loyalty to Scotland and his abhorrence of Macbeth and his plots when he claims to be worse than Macbeth. (b) Upon hearing of Malcolm's proclaimed failings, Macduff says he cannot support him in his quest to rule his beloved Scotland. With this Malcolm admits his ruse.

THINKING ABOUT THE SELECTION

Recalling

1. (a) What does the first apparition tell Macbeth? (b) How does the prophecy of the second apparition seem to contradict that of the first? (c) What does the third apparition promise?
2. (a) What question do the witches refuse to answer? (b) What vision do they parade before Macbeth?
3. (a) Where does Lennox say Macduff has gone? (b) On learning of Macduff's absence, what does Macbeth decide to do to Macduff's family?
4. (a) In his conversation with Macduff, why does Malcolm pretend to have all of Macbeth's vices and more? (b) What convinces Malcolm that Macduff is trustworthy?
5. (a) What good news about "gracious England" does Ross bring Malcolm? (b) What bad news does Ross bring Macduff?

Interpreting

6. Why does Macbeth readily accept the predictions made by the second and third apparitions?
7. (a) In the witches' procession of kings, why do some kings carry double and triple scepters? (b) Why does Banquo carry a mirror?
8. (a) What is Macbeth's reason for killing Macduff's wife and child? (b) How do these murders differ from the previous ones?
9. How would you describe Macbeth's character at this point in the play?
10. How is Malcolm's character revealed in the dialogue with Macduff in Scene iii?
11. Based on Macduff's reaction to the murder of his wife and son, how would you describe Macduff's character?

Applying

12. In staging *Macbeth,* some producers eliminate Scene ii, the murder of Lady Macduff and her son. (a) What reasons do you think they give for doing so? (b) What is your reaction to that kind of cut?

ANALYZING LITERATURE

Understanding Plot Development

Plot is a series of related incidents progressing through a period of *rising action* to a *climax.*

1. How do the apparitions' prophecies in Scene i prepare the audience for the plot developments to follow?
2. By the end of Act IV, the character of each major living participant—Macbeth, Lady Macbeth, Malcolm, Macduff, even Ross—has been made clear. How has this portrayal of character laid the groundwork for later events?

CRITICAL THINKING AND READING

Reading Between the Lines

In a play as carefully crafted as *Macbeth,* there are very few insignificant lines. For instance, in Act IV when one of the witches says, "'Tis time, 'tis time," the reader should think, "Time for what? Time for the witches to exact their price from Macbeth?"

Even today, critics have differing opinions about the character of Ross, a man who can be evaluated only by reading between the lines. What is your opinion of Ross's character—is he a toadying politician, a loyal Scot, or something else? Defend your assessment.

THINKING AND WRITING

Writing About Macbeth's Tragic Flaw

Macbeth is a tragic hero, a person of high rank who is brought to eventual ruin by a flaw in his character. Macbeth's tragic flaw is his ambition, which leads him into a series of bloody and increasingly indefensible acts. Write a composition in which you relate Macbeth's character to the plot development of the play. First make some notes on how Macbeth's personality and motivations get him into trouble and prevent him from getting out. Then write a first draft. When you revise, make sure each of your major points ties Macbeth's character to a plot element.

(Answers begin on p. 287.)

5. (a) Ross tells Malcolm that England has provided ten thousand soldiers to fight against Macbeth. (b) Then he sadly tells Macduff about the murder of his family and household.

Interpreting

6. Macbeth knows that the predictions made earlier came true; therefore he assumes these predictions are accurate, too. Rather than wonder if they are in some riddle form, however, he quickly assumes he is safe till he dies of old age.
7. (a) The double and triple scepters are the insignia of the Kingdoms of England, Scotland, and Ireland, united in 1603 when James VI of Scotland, Banquo's heir, became James I of England. (b) The eighth king carries a mirror to show images of more kings—including perhaps King James—beyond him in whom Banquo's blood will flow.
8. (a) They pose little or no threat to Macbeth, but as the castle is unprotected, and he was warned to beware Macduff, he feels he should act quickly against his enemy's family. (b) There is no sensible reason for these murders. As twisted as the logic was for the other killings, we can understand why they happened.
9. Macbeth is mentally unstable at this point. He has become a despot.
10. While Malcolm claims a great list of character flaws, his speeches hardly confirm his claims. He seems a good and caring man. Then upon learning of the murders of Macduff's family, he demonstrates his strength of character and good sense.
11. *Admirable* seems an appropriate word to describe Macduff's character as it is shown when he struggles with the knowledge of the loss of his family. He behaves nobly under the crushing reality.

Applying

12. (a) One good reason would be that the slaughter is melodramatic and pitiful, not tragic. (b) Answers will vary.

ANSWERS TO ANALYZING LITERATURE

1. Macbeth is warned to beware of Macduff. Knowing his deteriorating state of mind, we can assume he will try to act against Macduff or his family. He seems to read the other predictions as an assurance that he will live out his life uncontested. Given this, he now feels he can do whatever he likes, which he seems to be doing. This behavior is leading to an uprising.
2. If character development dictates plot, as it should, a confrontation between good and evil is imminent. Malcolm and Macduff have rallied their forces. Macbeth has armed himself with prophecies that he reads as making him immune to being overcome. Lady Macbeth will likely continue her passage away from center stage as her actions continue to destroy her from within.

ANSWERS TO CRITICAL THINKING AND READING

As critics differ in their opinions, so will you find varying answers from student readers. His loyalties remain ambiguous, it seems, until he is sure about where the power will lie. A character such as he opens possibilities for lively discussion.

GUIDE FOR READING

Macbeth, Act V

Writer's Techniques

Theme. The theme of a literary work is its central idea, an idea that can usually be expressed as a general statement about life. Every element in a work of literature—plot, character, setting, and so on—contributes to the theme. In many works of literature, including *Macbeth,* the theme pertains not only to the lives of the characters on stage but also, and more importantly, to the lives of the members of the audience. Sometimes it is possible to state a theme in one sentence, although complex literary works may require a lengthier explanation. A theme may be directly stated, but more commonly it is implied.

Look For

As you read *Macbeth,* Act V, identify the play's theme, the central idea evolving from the events in the drama. Consider first the fate of Macbeth himself; then consider its application to people in general.

Writing

Jot down a few lines from Act V of *Macbeth* (and perhaps from earlier acts) that seem to imply the theme of the play. While the theme is not directly stated, the dialogue gives many indications that you will find helpful. Remember that the theme cannot be expressed in a single word or phrase. It requires at least a complete sentence and often more.

Vocabulary

Knowing the following words will help you as you read *Macbeth,* Act V.

perturbation (pʉr′tər bā′ shən) *n.*: Disorder (Sc. i, l. 9)
pristine (pris′tēn) *adj.*: Pure; untouched; unspoiled (Sc. iv, l. 53)
clamorous (klam′ər əs) *adj.*: Noisy (Sc. vi, l. 10)
harbingers (här′bin jərz) *n.*: Forerunners (Sc. vi, l. 10)

Literary Focus You might have students practice identifying the themes of applicable stories recently studied, as theme identification can be elusive. While it is usually more complex, a theme can be likened to the moral of a fable.

Look For Look for actions in this final act that support the theme of the play, and consider how they do so.

Writing Alternatively, identify a worthy story, possibly a recent popular film, known to everyone in the class. Have the students identify its theme and give some explanation to support their answers.

Vocabulary Ask students to use each of these words in a phrase or sentence.

Motivation for Reading Everything is in place for the conclusion of the play. Have the students recall that Macbeth pins his hopes for a lengthy reign as king upon ambiguous prophecies.

Master Teacher Note As you discuss Act V, point out how earlier incidents, events, foreshadowings, and images are culminated here.

Purpose-Setting Question What is your final judgment on Macbeth and the outcome of his deeds?

Objectives

1. To understand the theme
2. To read Shakespearean English

Teaching Portfolio: Support Material

Teacher Backup, p. 000

Vocabulary Check, p. 00

Usage and Mechanics Worksheet, pp. 00

Analyzing Literature Worksheet, p. 00

Critical Thinking and Reading Worksheet, p. 00

Language Worksheet, p. 00

Act V

1 ***Scene i.*** *Dunsinane. In the castle.*

[*Enter a* DOCTOR OF PHYSIC *and a* WAITING-GENTLEWOMAN.]

DOCTOR. I have two nights watched with you, but can perceive no truth in your report. When was it she last walked?

2, 3 **GENTLEWOMAN.** Since his Majesty went into the field.[1] I have seen her rise from her bed, throw her nightgown upon her, unlock her closet,[2] take forth paper, fold it, write upon 't, read it, afterwards seal it, and again return to bed; yet all this while in a most fast sleep.

DOCTOR. A great perturbation in nature, to receive at once the benefit of sleep and do the effects of watching![3] In this slumb'ry agitation, besides her walking and other actual performances, what, at any time, have you heard her say?

GENTLEWOMAN. That, sir, which I will not report after her.

DOCTOR. You may to me, and 'tis most meet[4] you should.

4 **GENTLEWOMAN.** Neither to you nor anyone, having no witness to confirm my speech.

[*Enter* LADY MACBETH, *with a taper.*]

Lo you, here she comes! This is her very guise,[5] and, upon my life, fast asleep! Observe her; stand close.[6]

DOCTOR. How came she by that light?

5 **GENTLEWOMAN.** Why, it stood by her. She has light by her continually. 'Tis her command.

DOCTOR. You see, her eyes are open.

GENTLEWOMAN. Ay, but their sense[7] are shut.

DOCTOR. What is it she does now? Look, how she rubs her hands.

6 **GENTLEWOMAN.** It is an accustomed action with her, to seem thus washing her hands: I have known her continue in this a quarter of an hour.

LADY MACBETH. Yet here's a spot.

DOCTOR. Hark! She speaks. I will set down what comes from her, to satisfy[8] my remembrance the more strongly.

1. **field:** Battlefield.
2. **closet:** Chest.
3. **effects of watching:** Deeds of one awake.
4. **meet:** Suitable.
5. **guise:** Custom.
6. **close:** Hidden.
7. **sense:** Powers of sight.
8. **satisfy:** Support.

1 **Literary Focus** Notice that this scene takes place at Dunsinane, the castle cited in the prophecy, and that nearby is Birnam Wood. Does Macbeth seem to be tempting fate to fortify himself here? Why might he have little concern about this detail?

2 **Literary Focus** Notice that this scene is written almost entirely in prose. Blank verse was not used for the language of servants and other working folk.

3 **Discussion** Why are these two characters here?

4 **Literary Focus** Point out how with only a few lines of dialogue even a minor character can be developed. What does this answer tell us about the gentlewoman?

5 **Discussion** Why is it ironic that Lady Macbeth is now afraid of the dark?

6 **Literary Focus** The same Lady Macbeth, who in Act II, scene ii said, "A little water clears us of this deed" now cannot clean the blood from her hands.

291

Humanities Note

Fine art, *Mrs. Siddons as Lady Macbeth,* 1812, by George Henry Harlow. George Harlow (1787–1819), was British, a painter of historical scenes and landscapes as well as a clever and apt portraitist. He studied painting and drawing with several leading British painters. His knack for capturing an individual's personality on canvas led to many portrait commissions from famous people, including artists Benjamin West and Henry Fuseli and the actress Sarah Siddons.

Mrs. Siddons as Lady Macbeth was commissioned to commemorate the farewell performance of the actress in the play *Macbeth.* In this portrait, Sarah Siddons has a glowing, ethereal quality that seems almost supernatural. Her features are delineated with beauty and grace. It is an appropriate tribute to the leading tragic actress of the day.

In discussing this portrait with your class, you may wish to compare this artist's rendition of the character with those of the other two artists, Fuseli and Sargent, who painted Lady Macbeth. You might use the following questions for discussion:

1. Which portrait is most in keeping with your concept of Lady Macbeth?
2. Which portrait is the least effective illustration for the play? Why?
3. Do you feel that the use of portraits of legendary actresses to illustrate this play has enriched your study of it?

MRS. SIDDONS AS LADY MACBETH
Garrick Club
E. T. Archive

LADY MACBETH. Out, damned spot! Out, I say! One: two: why, then 'tis time to do 't. Hell is murky. Fie, my lord, fie! A soldier, and afeard? What need we fear who knows it, when none can call our pow'r to accompt?[9] Yet who would have thought the old man to have had so much blood in him?

DOCTOR. Do you mark that?

9. **to accompt:** Into account.

LADY MACBETH. The Thane of Fife had a wife. Where is she now? What, will these hands ne'er be clean? No more o' that, my lord, no more o' that! You mar all with this starting.

DOCTOR. Go to, go to! You have known what you should not.

GENTLEWOMAN. She has spoke what she should not, I am sure of that. Heaven knows what she has known.

LADY MACBETH. Here's the smell of the blood still. All the perfumes of Arabia will not sweeten this little hand. Oh, oh, oh!

DOCTOR. What a sigh is there! The heart is sorely charged.[10]

GENTLEWOMAN. I would not have such a heart in my
7 bosom for the dignity[11] of the whole body.

DOCTOR. Well, well, well—

GENTLEWOMAN. Pray God it be, sir.

DOCTOR. This disease is beyond my practice. Yet I have known those which have walked in their sleep who have died holily in their beds.

LADY MACBETH. Wash your hands; put on your nightgown; look not so pale! I tell you yet again, Banquo's buried. He cannot come out on 's[12] grave.

DOCTOR. Even so?

LADY MACBETH. To bed, to bed! There's knocking at the gate. Come, come, come, come, give me your hand! What's done cannot be undone. To bed, to bed, to bed! [*Exit* LADY MACBETH.]

DOCTOR. Will she go now to bed?

GENTLEWOMAN. Directly.

DOCTOR. Foul whisp'rings are abroad. Unnatural deeds
Do breed unnatural troubles. Infected minds
8 To their deaf pillows will discharge their secrets.
More needs she the divine than the physician.
God, God forgive us all! Look after her;
9 Remove from her the means of all annoyance,[13]
And still keep eyes upon her. So good night.
My mind she has mated[14] and amazed my sight:
I think, but dare not speak.

GENTLEWOMAN. Good night, good doctor. [*Exit.*]

10. charged: Burdened.

11. dignity: Worth.

12. on 's: Of his.

13. annoyance: Injury.

14. mated: Baffled.

7 Discussion Pick out the specific events that Lady Macbeth's fragementary speech recalls through line 69.

8 Discussion Is there some wisdom in the doctor's conclusion that she has more need of spiritual help than medical or physical help? What signs existed that pointed toward a mental collapse?

9 Discussion What does the doctor mean when he tells the gentlewoman to remove the means of all annoyance? What does he anticipate?

10 Literary Focus In this largely expository scene, the thanes who enter are obviously the Scottish rebels referred to in Act IV, scene iii.

11 Discussion What is about to happen at Birnam Wood? Why is this significant?

12 Literary Focus Take note of the simile.

10 ***Scene ii.*** *The country near Dunsinane.*
[*Drum and colors. Enter* MENTEITH, CAITHNESS, ANGUS, LENNOX, SOLDIERS.]

MENTEITH. The English pow'r[1] is near, led on by
Malcolm,
His uncle Siward and the good Macduff.
Revenges burn in them; for their dear causes
Would to the bleeding and the grim alarm
Excite the mortified man.[2]

11 ANGUS. Near Birnam Wood
Shall we well meet them; that way are they coming.

CAITHNESS. Who knows if Donalbain be with his
brother?

LENNOX. For certain, sir, he is not. I have a file[3]
Of all the gentry: there is Siward's son,
And many unrough[4] youths that even now
Protest[5] their first of manhood.

MENTEITH. What does the tyrant?

CAITHNESS. Great Dunsinane he strongly fortifies.
Some say he's mad; others, that lesser hate him,
Do call it valiant fury: but, for certain,
He cannot buckle his distempered cause
Within the belt of rule.[6]

ANGUS. Now does he feel
His secret murders sticking on his hands;
Now minutely revolts upbraid his faith-breach.[7]
Those he commands move only in command,
Nothing in love. Now does he feel his title
12 Hang loose about him, like a giant's robe
Upon a dwarfish thief.

MENTEITH. Who then shall blame
His pestered[8] senses to recoil and start,
When all that is within him does condemn
Itself for being there?

CAITHNESS. Well, march we on,
To give obedience where 'tis truly owed.
Meet we the med'cine of the sickly weal,[9]
And with him pour we, in our country's purge,
Each drop of us.[10]

LENNOX. Or so much as it needs
To dew the sovereign flower and drown the weeds.[11]
Make we our march towards Birnam.
[*Exit, marching.*]

1. pow'r: Army.

2. Would . . . man: Would incite a dead man to join the bloody and grim call to arms.

3. file: List.

4. unrough: Beardless.

5. Protest: Assert.

6. rule: Self-control.

7. minutely . . . faith-breach: Every minute revolts rebuke his disloyalty.

8. pestered: Tormented.

9. med'cine . . . weal: Malcolm and his supporters are "the med'cine" that will heal "the sickly" commonwealth.

10. Each . . . us: Every last drop of our blood.

11. dew . . . weeds: Water the royal flower (Malcolm) and drown the weeds (Macbeth).

Scene iii. *Dunsinane. In the castle.*

[*Enter* MACBETH, DOCTOR, *and* ATTENDANTS.]

MACBETH. Bring me no more reports; let them fly all![1]
Till Birnam Wood remove to Dunsinane
I cannot taint[2] with fear. What's the boy Malcolm?
Was he not born of woman? The spirits that know
All mortal consequences[3] have pronounced me thus:
13 "Fear not, Macbeth; no man that's born of woman
Shall e'er have power upon thee." Then fly, false thanes,
And mingle with the English epicures.[4]
The mind I sway[5] by and the heart I bear
Shall never sag with doubt nor shake with fear.

[*Enter* SERVANT.]

The devil damn thee black, thou cream-faced loon.[6]
Where got'st thou that goose look?

SERVANT. There is ten thousand—

14 **MACBETH.** Geese, villain?

15 **SERVANT.** Soldiers, sir.

16 **MACBETH.** Go prick thy face and over-red thy fear.
Thou lily-livered boy. What soldiers, patch?[7]
Death of thy soul! Those linen[8] cheeks of thine
Are counselors to fear. What soldiers, whey-face?

SERVANT. The English force, so please you.

MACBETH. Take thy face hence. [*Exit* SERVANT.]
Seyton!—I am sick at heart.
When I behold—Seyton, I say!—This push[9]
Will cheer me ever, or disseat[10] me now.
17 I have lived long enough. My way of life
18 Is fall'n into the sear,[11] the yellow leaf,
19 And that which should accompany old age,
As honor, love, obedience, troops of friends,
I must not look to have; but, in their stead,
Curses not loud but deep, mouth-honor, breath,
Which the poor heart would fain deny, and dare not.
Seyton!

[*Enter* SEYTON.]

SEYTON. What's your gracious pleasure?

MACBETH. What news more?

SEYTON. All is confirmed, my lord, which was reported.

1. **let . . . all:** Let them all desert me!
2. **taint:** Become infected
3. **mortal consequences:** Future human events.
4. **epicures:** Gluttons.
5. **sway:** Move.
6. **loon:** Fool.
7. **patch:** Fool.
8. **linen:** Pale as linen.
9. **push:** Effort.
10. **disseat:** Unthrone.
11. **the sear:** A withered state.

13 **Discussion** Macbeth sums up the situation in these lines. What is happening as he prepares for battle? Why does he claim no fear? Do you think he is sincere?

14 **Clarification** The loon is a large diving, fish-eating northern waterfowl whose weird laughing cry has an almost insane human quality about it.

15 **Literary Focus** Notice the array of insulting epithets about the servant's pallor. How do you account for this extravagantly offensive behavior?

16 **Discussion** Paraphrase lines 16–17.

17 **Clarification** Seyton, his attendant, is off stage. Macbeth raises his voice to summon him; otherwise, this brief soliloquy is spoken quietly.

18 **Literary Focus** Point out Macbeth's subdued behavior now that he is alone. Does this speech elicit our sympathy? Shakespeare wants to remind us that this is a tragedy, and that the audience is witnessing the fall of a once great man.

19 **Clarification** For *mouth-honor* (line 27), read "lip service."

20 Discussion What does it indicate about Macbeth's state of mind that he will don his armor before it is needed? Remember, eleventh-century armor was quite heavy, cumbersome, and tiring to wear.

21 Discussion When Macbeth asks the doctor if he can "minister to a mind diseased" and otherwise attend to what might seem to be Lady Macbeth's problems, does he hope some cure might exist for him, too?

22 Literary Focus Point out the hysterical quality of this speech as Macbeth speaks with the doctor while showing impatience with Seyton about his armor.

23 Literary Focus One must sympathize with the doctor, whose house call embroils him in a deadly confrontation.

24 Literary Focus Note that the rebels have joined with the British forces.

MACBETH. I'll fight, till from my bones my flesh be
hacked.
Give me my armor.

20 SEYTON. 'Tis not needed yet.

MACBETH. I'll put it on.
Send out moe[12] horses, skirr[13] the country round.
Hang those that talk of fear. Give me mine armor.
How does your patient, doctor?

DOCTOR. Not so sick, my lord,
As she is troubled with thick-coming fancies
That keep her from her rest.

MACBETH. Cure her of that.
Canst thou not minister to a mind diseased,
Pluck from the memory a rooted sorrow,
21 Raze out[14] the written troubles of the brain,
And with some sweet oblivious antidote
Cleanse the stuffed bosom of that perilous stuff
Which weighs upon the heart?

DOCTOR. Therein the patient
Must minister to himself.

MACBETH. Throw physic[15] to the dogs, I'll none of it.
Come, put mine armor on. Give me my staff.
Seyton, send out.—Doctor, the thanes fly from
me.—
Come, sir, dispatch. If thou couldst, doctor, cast
22 The water[16] of my land, find her disease
And purge it to a sound and pristine health,
I would applaud thee to the very echo,
That should applaud again.—Pull 't off,[17] I say.—
What rhubarb, senna, or what purgative drug,
Would scour these English hence? Hear'st thou of
them?

DOCTOR. Ay, my good lord; your royal preparation
Makes us hear something.

MACBETH. Bring it[18] after me.
I will not be afraid of death and bane[19]
Till Birnam Forest come to Dunsinane.

23 DOCTOR. [*Aside*] Were I from Dunsinane away and clear,
Profit again should hardly draw me here. [*Exit.*]

24 ***Scene iv.*** *Country near Birnam Wood.*
[*Drum and colors. Enter* MALCOLM, SIWARD, MACDUFF, SIWARD'S SON, MENTEITH, CAITHNESS, ANGUS, *and* SOLDIERS, *marching.*]

12. moe: More.
13. skirr: Scour.
14. Raze out: Erase.
15. physic: Medicine.
16. cast the water: Diagnose the illness.
17. Pull 't off: Pull off a piece of armor which has been put on incorrectly in Macbeth's haste.
18. it: His armor.
19. bane: Destruction.

MALCOLM. Cousins, I hope the days are near at hand
That chambers will be safe.[1]

MENTEITH. We doubt it nothing.

SIWARD. What wood is this before us?

MENTEITH. The Wood of Birnam.

MALCOLM. Let every soldier hew him down a bough
25 And bear 't before him. Thereby shall we shadow[2]
The numbers of our host, and make discovery[3]
Err in report of us.

SOLDIERS. It shall be done.

SIWARD. We learn no other but the confident tyrant
Keeps still in Dunsinane, and will endure
Our setting down before 't.[4]

MALCOLM. 'Tis his main hope,
For where there is advantage to be given
26 Both more and less[5] have given him the revolt,
And none serve with him but constrainèd things
Whose hearts are absent too.

MACDUFF. Let our just censures
Attend the true event,[6] and put we on
Industrious soldiership.

SIWARD. The time approaches,
That will with due decision make us know
What we shall say we have and what we owe.[7]
Thoughts speculative their unsure hopes relate,
But certain issue strokes must arbitrate:[8]
Towards which advance the war.[9] [*Exit, marching.*]

1. **That . . . safe:** That people will be safe in their own homes.
2. **shadow:** Conceal.
3. **discovery:** Those who see us.
4. **setting down before 't:** Laying siege to it.
5. **more and less:** People of high and low rank.
6. **our . . . event:** True judgment await the actual outcome.
7. **owe:** Own.
8. **strokes . . . arbitrate:** Fighting must decide.
9. **war:** Army.

Scene v. *Dunsinane. Within the castle.*
[*Enter* MACBETH, SEYTON, *and* SOLDIERS, *with drum and colors.*]

MACBETH. Hang out our banners on the outward walls.
The cry is still "They come!" Our castle's strength
Will laugh a siege to scorn. Here let them lie
27 Till famine and the ague[1] eat them up.
Were they not forced[2] with those that should be ours,
We might have met them dareful,[3] beard to beard,
And beat them backward home.
[*A cry within of women.*]
What is that noise?

SEYTON. It is the cry of women, my good lord. [*Exit.*]

1. **ague:** Fever.
2. **forced:** Reinforced.
3. **dareful:** Boldly.

25 Discussion How does this order recall the prophecy made to Macbeth?

26 Discussion Why doesn't Macbeth meet these opposing forces in battle, rather than let them lay siege to the castle?

27 Discussion What is Macbeth's claim as the siege begins? Is this realistic or more bravado?

28 Discussion When in the play was this true?

29 Discussion How do you interpret the first line of this speech? Is he being totally callous or is he suggesting that her death at any other time would allow him time for sympathy?

30 Literary Focus Here is Macbeth's most notable speech in the play, a powerful expression of life's futility as he is being crushed from all sides. Is Macbeth's story "a tale . . . full of sound and fury/ signifying nothing"?

31 Discussion Macbeth is now told of Birnam Wood's moving toward Dunsinane. How does he react? Why?

32 Clarification *Equivocation* means "the ambiguous language of the prophecy."

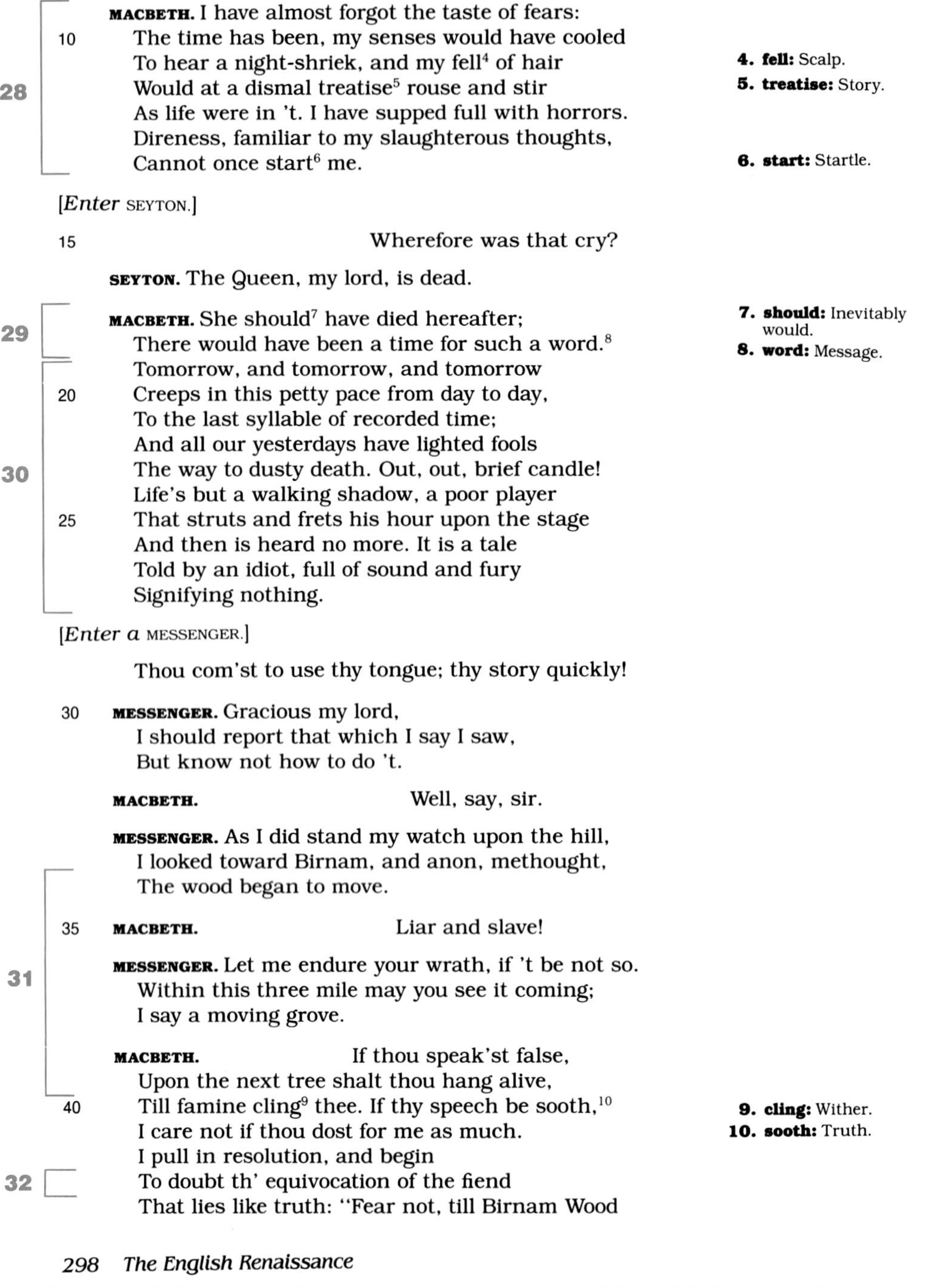

28 MACBETH. I have almost forgot the taste of fears:
The time has been, my senses would have cooled
To hear a night-shriek, and my fell[4] of hair
Would at a dismal treatise[5] rouse and stir
As life were in 't. I have supped full with horrors.
Direness, familiar to my slaughterous thoughts,
Cannot once start[6] me.

[*Enter* SEYTON.]

Wherefore was that cry?

SEYTON. The Queen, my lord, is dead.

29 MACBETH. She should[7] have died hereafter;
There would have been a time for such a word.[8]

30 Tomorrow, and tomorrow, and tomorrow
Creeps in this petty pace from day to day,
To the last syllable of recorded time;
And all our yesterdays have lighted fools
The way to dusty death. Out, out, brief candle!
Life's but a walking shadow, a poor player
That struts and frets his hour upon the stage
And then is heard no more. It is a tale
Told by an idiot, full of sound and fury
Signifying nothing.

[*Enter a* MESSENGER.]

Thou com'st to use thy tongue; thy story quickly!

MESSENGER. Gracious my lord,
I should report that which I say I saw,
But know not how to do 't.

MACBETH. Well, say, sir.

MESSENGER. As I did stand my watch upon the hill,
31 I looked toward Birnam, and anon, methought,
The wood began to move.

MACBETH. Liar and slave!

MESSENGER. Let me endure your wrath, if 't be not so.
Within this three mile may you see it coming;
I say a moving grove.

MACBETH. If thou speak'st false,
Upon the next tree shalt thou hang alive,
Till famine cling[9] thee. If thy speech be sooth,[10]
I care not if thou dost for me as much.
I pull in resolution, and begin
32 To doubt th' equivocation of the fiend
That lies like truth: "Fear not, till Birnam Wood

4. fell: Scalp.
5. treatise: Story.
6. start: Startle.
7. should: Inevitably would.
8. word: Message.
9. cling: Wither.
10. sooth: Truth.

Do come to Dunsinane!'' And now a wood
Comes toward Dunsinane. Arm, arm, and out!
If this which he avouches[11] does appear,
There is nor flying hence nor tarrying here.
33 I 'gin to be aweary of the sun,
And wish th' estate o' th' world were now undone.
Ring the alarum bell! Blow wind, come wrack!
At least we'll die with harness[12] on our back. [*Exit.*]

11. avouches: Asserts.

12. harness: Armor.

34 ***Scene vi.*** *Dunsinane. Before the castle.*
[*Drum and colors. Enter* MALCOLM, SIWARD, MACDUFF, *and their army, with boughs.*]

MALCOLM. Now near enough. Your leavy[1] screens throw down,
And show like those you are. You, worthy uncle,
Shall, with my cousin, your right noble son,
Lead our first battle.[2] Worthy Macduff and we
Shall take upon 's what else remains to do,
According to our order.[3]

SIWARD. Fare you well.
Do we but find the tyrant's power[4] tonight,
Let us be beaten, if we cannot fight.

MACDUFF. Make all our trumpets speak; give them all breath,
Those clamorous harbingers of blood and death.
[*Exit. Alarums continued.*]

1. leavy: Leafy.

2. battle: Battalion.

3. order: Plan.

4. power: Forces.

Scene vii. *Another part of the field.*
[*Enter* MACBETH.]

MACBETH. They have tied me to a stake; I cannot fly,
35 But bearlike I must fight the course.[1] What's he
That was not born of woman? Such a one
Am I to fear, or none.

[*Enter* YOUNG SIWARD.]

YOUNG SIWARD. What is thy name?

MACBETH. Thou'lt be afraid to hear it.

YOUNG SIWARD. No; though thou call'st thyself a hotter name
Than any is in hell.

MACBETH. My name's Macbeth.

YOUNG SIWARD. The devil himself could not pronounce a title
More hateful to mine ear.

MACBETH. No, nor more fearful.

1. bearlike . . . course: Like a bear chained to a stake being attacked by dogs, I must fight until the end.

33 Literary Focus He wearies of life. Further, we witness one more reference to the day-night theme.

34 Literary Focus The action in these final three scenes is continuous, focusing in turn on different groups of soldiers and different parts of the battlefield.

35 Discussion What are Macbeth's chances at this point? What does he see as his only hope?

36 Discussion Is it surprising that Macbeth so easily destroys Siward? What force is driving him? Notice how he and Macduff narrowly miss a confrontation.

37 Clarification *Kerns* were "hired Irish foot soldiers."

38 Discussion What is the outcome by the end of this scene? How have Macbeth's soldiers been fighting?

39 Discussion What decision does Macbeth make about how he will accept the loss of the battle and the kingdom?

40 Discussion Why has Macbeth avoided Macduff during the battle? Does it suggest he has some feelings about what he did?

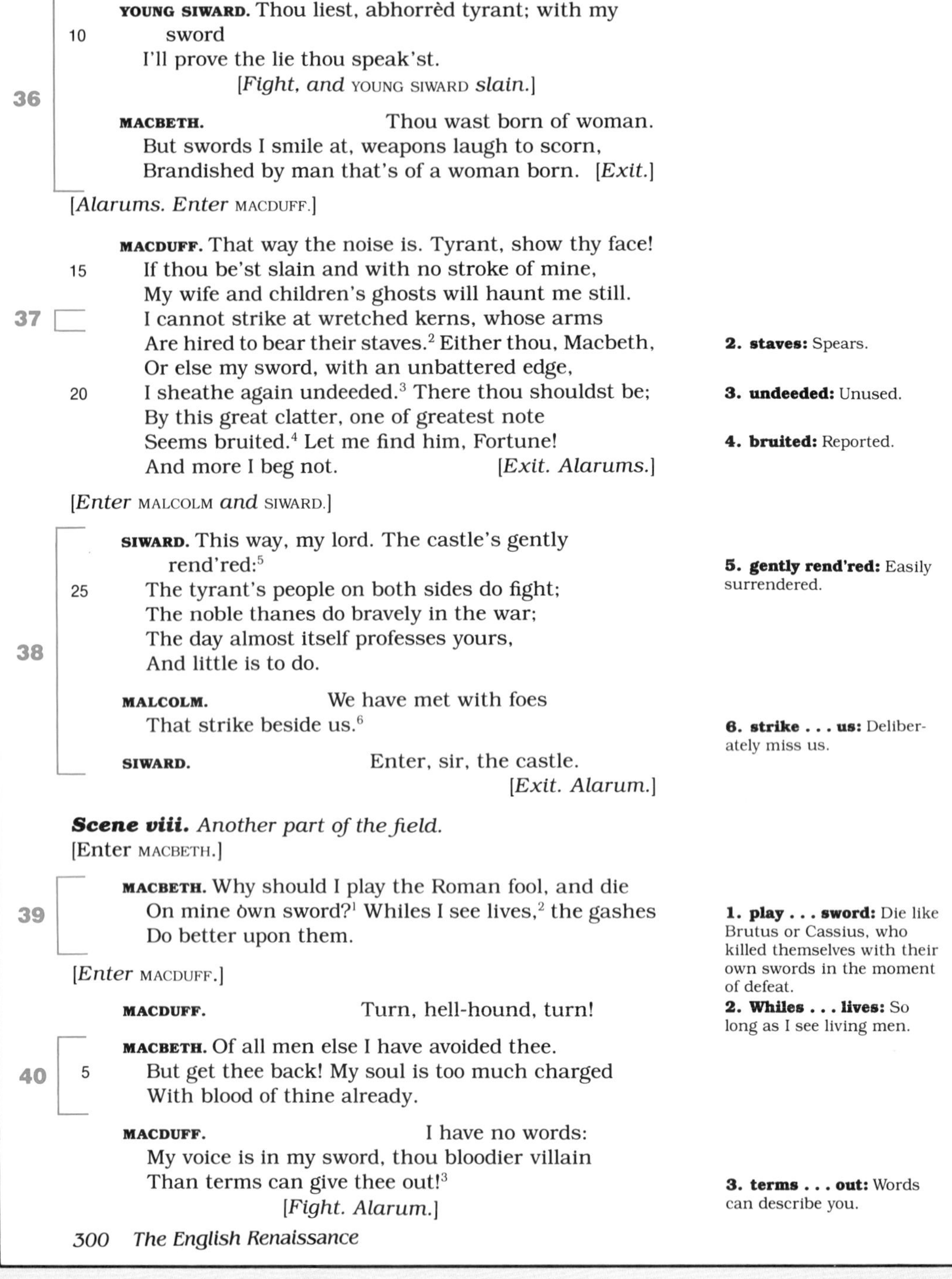

YOUNG SIWARD. Thou liest, abhorrèd tyrant; with my
sword
I'll prove the lie thou speak'st.
36 *[Fight, and* YOUNG SIWARD *slain.]*

MACBETH. Thou wast born of woman.
But swords I smile at, weapons laugh to scorn,
Brandished by man that's of a woman born. *[Exit.]*

[Alarums. Enter MACDUFF.*]*

MACDUFF. That way the noise is. Tyrant, show thy face!
If thou be'st slain and with no stroke of mine,
My wife and children's ghosts will haunt me still.
37 I cannot strike at wretched kerns, whose arms
Are hired to bear their staves.[2] Either thou, Macbeth,
Or else my sword, with an unbattered edge,
I sheathe again undeeded.[3] There thou shouldst be;
By this great clatter, one of greatest note
Seems bruited.[4] Let me find him, Fortune!
And more I beg not. *[Exit. Alarums.]*

[Enter MALCOLM *and* SIWARD.*]*

SIWARD. This way, my lord. The castle's gently
rend'red:[5]
The tyrant's people on both sides do fight;
The noble thanes do bravely in the war;
38 The day almost itself professes yours,
And little is to do.

MALCOLM. We have met with foes
That strike beside us.[6]

SIWARD. Enter, sir, the castle.
[Exit. Alarum.]

Scene viii. *Another part of the field.*
[Enter MACBETH.]

MACBETH. Why should I play the Roman fool, and die
39 On mine own sword?[1] Whiles I see lives,[2] the gashes
Do better upon them.

[Enter MACDUFF.*]*

MACDUFF. Turn, hell-hound, turn!

MACBETH. Of all men else I have avoided thee.
40 But get thee back! My soul is too much charged
With blood of thine already.

MACDUFF. I have no words:
My voice is in my sword, thou bloodier villain
Than terms can give thee out![3]
[Fight. Alarum.]

2. staves: Spears.

3. undeeded: Unused.

4. bruited: Reported.

5. gently rend'red: Easily surrendered.

6. strike . . . us: Deliberately miss us.

1. play . . . sword: Die like Brutus or Cassius, who killed themselves with their own swords in the moment of defeat.

2. Whiles . . . lives: So long as I see living men.

3. terms . . . out: Words can describe you.

MACBETH. Thou losest labor:
As easy mayst thou the intrenchant[4] air
With thy keen sword impress[5] as make me bleed:
Let fall thy blade on vulnerable crests;
I bear a charmèd life, which must not yield
To one of woman born.

41 **MACDUFF.** Despair thy charm,
And let the angel[6] whom thou still hast served
Tell thee, Macduff was from his mother's womb
Untimely ripped.[7]

MACBETH. Accursèd be that tongue that tells me so,
For it hath cowed my better part of man![8]
And be these juggling fiends no more believed,
That palter[9] with us in a double sense;
42 That keep the word of promise to our ear,
And break it to our hope. I'll not fight with thee.

MACDUFF. Then yield thee, coward,
And live to be the show and gaze o' th' time:[10]
43 We'll have thee, as our rarer monsters[11] are,
Painted upon a pole,[12] and underwrit,
"Here may you see the tyrant."

MACBETH. I will not yield,
To kiss the ground before young Malcolm's feet,
And to be baited with the rabble's curse.
Though Birnam Wood be come to Dunsinane,
And thou opposed, being of no woman born,
44 Yet I will try the last. Before my body
I throw my warlike shield. Lay on, Macduff;
And damned be him that first cries "Hold, enough!"
[Exit, fighting. Alarums.]

[Re-enter fighting, and MACBETH *slain. Exit* MACDUFF, *with* MACBETH. *Retreat and flourish.*[13] *Enter, with drum and colors,* MALCOLM, SIWARD, ROSS, THANES, *and* SOLDIERS.]

MALCOLM. I would the friends we miss were safe arrived.

45 **SIWARD.** Some must go off;[14] and yet, by these I see,
So great a day as this is cheaply bought.

MALCOLM. Macduff is missing, and your noble son.

ROSS. Your son, my lord, has paid a soldier's debt:
He only lived but till he was a man;
The which no sooner had his prowess confirmed
In the unshrinking station[15] where he fought,
But like a man he died.

SIWARD. Then he is dead?

4. **intrenchant:** Incapable of being cut.
5. **impress:** Make a dent in.
6. **angel:** Fallen angel, fiend.
7. **his . . . ripped:** Macduff's mother died before giving birth to him.
8. **better . . . man:** Courage.
9. **palter:** Juggle.
10. **gaze o' th' time:** Spectacle of the age.
11. **monsters:** Freaks.
12. **Painted . . . pole:** Pictured on a banner stuck on a pole by a showman's booth.
13. **Retreat and flourish:** Trumpet call to withdraw and fanfare.
14. **go off:** Die.
15. **unshrinking station:** Place where he stood firmly.

41 **Discussion** What does Macbeth tell Macduff about a confrontation between them? How does Macduff crush Macbeth's final hope?

42 **Discussion** What is he saying about the witches here?

43 **Discussion** If Macbeth gives himself up, what does Macduff suggest they will do with him?

44 **Literary Focus** In his final lines, Macbeth at least redeems himself as a brave and determined warrior.

45 **Discussion** Paraphrase these lines.

46 Clarification Wounds in the back would suggest a cowardly death during flight. His wounds in front tell the story that he died bravely.

47 Discussion How does the old soldier, Siward, react to his son's death? Is he being heartless, or is there another explanation?

48 Literary Focus The "newer comfort" is Macbeth's head, a compelling reason for the actual killing to take place off stage.

49 Literary Focus The final upbeat speech that closes the play is typical of Shakespeare's tragedies. It is intended to resolve any questions that may remain. Lines 70–71 confirm that Lady Macbeth took her own life. Was there an indication of this given earlier?

ROSS. Ay, and brought off the field. Your cause of sorrow
Must not be measured by his worth, for then
It hath no end.

46 **SIWARD.** Had he his hurts before?

ROSS. Ay, on the front.

SIWARD. Why then, God's soldier be he!
Had I as many sons as I have hairs,
I would not wish them to a fairer death:
And so his knell is knolled.

MALCOLM. He's worth more sorrow,
And that I'll spend for him.

SIWARD. He's worth no more:
47 They say he parted well and paid his score:
48 And so God be with him! Here comes newer comfort.

[*Enter* MACDUFF, *with* MACBETH'S *head.*]

MACDUFF. Hail, King! for so thou art: behold, where stands
Th' usurper's cursèd head. The time is free.[16]
I see thee compassed with thy kingdom's pearl,[17]
That speak my salutation in their minds,
Whose voices I desire aloud with mine:
Hail, King of Scotland!

ALL. Hail, King of Scotland!

[*Flourish.*]

MALCOLM. We shall not spend a large expense of time
Before we reckon with your several loves,[18]
And make us even with you.[19] My thanes and kinsmen,
Henceforth be earls, the first that ever Scotland
In such an honor named. What's more to do,
Which would be planted newly with the time[20]—
As calling home our exiled friends abroad
49 That fled the snares of watchful tyranny,
Producing forth the cruel ministers
Of this dead butcher and his fiendlike queen,
Who, as 'tis thought, by self and violent hands
Took off her life—this, and what needful else
That calls upon us, by the grace of Grace
We will perform in measure, time, and place:[21]
So thanks to all at once and to each one,
Whom we invite to see us crowned at Scone.
[*Flourish. Exit all.*]

16. The . . . free: Our country is liberated.

17. compassed . . . pearl: Surrounded by the noblest people in the kingdom.

18. reckon . . . loves: Reward each of you for your devotion.

19. make . . . you: Pay what we owe you.

20. What's . . . time: What remains to be done at the beginning of this new age.

21. in measure . . . place: Fittingly at the appropriate time and place.

Answers

ANSWERS TO THINKING ABOUT THE SELECTION

Recalling

1. (a) The gentlewoman has observed Lady Macbeth walking in her sleep on several occasions prior to seeking the doctor's help. (b) She will not tell him the troubling words she has overheard.
2. (a) She refers to the murders of Duncan, Banquo, and Macduff's family. (b) She comes back again and again to the murder of Duncan, the only one she participated in and because of which all the others followed.
3. (a) The four Scottish lords are crossing over to the other side to assist in the overthrow of Macbeth. (b) They will meet the English forces by Birnam Wood.
4. (a) He tells Macbeth that Lady

THINKING ABOUT THE SELECTION

Recalling

1. (a) Why are the doctor and the gentlewoman watching Lady Macbeth? (b) What does the gentlewoman refuse to tell the doctor?
2. (a) While Lady Macbeth is sleepwalking, to to what three prior events does she refer? (b) To which event does she keep coming back?
3. (a) In Scene ii what are the four Scottish lords preparing to do? (b) Where will they meet the English forces?
4. (a) What news does Seyton bring Macbeth in Scene v? (b) What in the messenger's report makes Macbeth fear that the apparitions' second prophecy is coming true?
5. (a) In Scene viii why does Macbeth tell Macduff he does not wish to fight him? (b) What does Macduff tell Macbeth concerning the apparitions' third prophecy?
6. (a) Whom does Macbeth kill in the encounter with the English forces? (b) Whom does Macduff kill? (c) At the end of the play, who is to be crowned King of Scotland?

Interpreting

7. Why do you think it is an "accustomed action" for Lady Macbeth to wash her hands while sleepwalking?
8. (a) Why does Macbeth remain confident of surviving the battle with Malcolm's army despite his own troops' desertion? (b) Judging by the way Macbeth behaves in Scene iii, describe his state of mind.
9. What changes in his personality is Macbeth describing in Scene v, lines 9–14?
10. Why does Macbeth say, "She should have died hereafter," upon learning of the death of Lady Macbeth?
11. Macbeth, mad and murderous though he is, shows certain admirable traits to the very end. What are some of his better traits?

Applying

12. If Macbeth had defeated Malcolm's forces and remained King of Scotland, what actions do you think he would have taken in regard to (a) Malcolm? (b) the rebellious Scottish lords? (c) the witches?

ANALYZING LITERATURE

Understanding Theme

Theme is the central or dominating idea in a literary work. In a tragedy the theme is based on the actions of a tragic hero—a basically moral person, often of noble stature, whose downfall usually results from a bad choice. The bad choice stems from a tragic flaw in the hero's character.

1. What is the tragic flaw in Macbeth's character? Support your answer.
2. What is the theme of *Macbeth?* State the theme. Your statement should be in the form of a universal truth, not restricted to Macbeth's tragic flaw and its consequences.
3. What events in Act V show Macbeth's downfall to be complete and irreversible?

UNDERSTANDING LANGUAGE

Reading Shakespearean English

The language of Shakespeare is Early Modern English, the direct ancestor of our own Modern English. Around the year 1500, Middle English, the language of Chaucer, began to undergo a number of gradual, systematic changes. One was the elimination of the vowel sound at the end of many words. The word *name,* for example, had two syllables in Middle English but only one by Shakespeare's time. Other changes occurred. The so-called "Great Vowel Shift" resulted in many changes in pronunciation: *he* in Middle English had sounded like *hey, mouse* like *moose,* and *moon* like *moan*. The renewed interest in Greek and Latin added many words of classical origin to the language. Certain consonants, such as the *l* in *would* and *could,* were still pronounced in Shakespeare's day. The pronouns *thou* and *thee* were in common use, as were the verbs *hath* and *doth* and the expressions *anon, prithee,* and *fie.*

1. In Scene iii, lines 35–37, find and list three examples of how Shakespearean English differs from today's.
2. In Scene v, lines 38–41, find and list three more examples of these differences.

(Answers begin on p. 302.)

Macbeth is dead. (b) The messenger tells Macbeth that Birnam Wood seems to be moving toward the castle.

5. (a) He does not wish to fight Macduff, he says, because enough of Macduff's family's blood has already been spilled. (b) Macduff startles Macbeth with the news that he was taken from his mother's womb—he was, therefore, not born, in the strict sense of the word.
6. (a) Macbeth kills the young Siward in battle. (b) Macduff in turn kills Macbeth. (c) Malcolm is to be crowned king of Scotland.

Interpreting

7. Lady Macbeth is haunted by the terrible deed she helped commit contrary to her initial belief that "a little water" would wash away the blood. The blood is the guilt that she obsessively tries to wash away.
8. (a) Macbeth believes he is shielded by the substance of the prophecies. (b) Macbeth is struggling with his emotions here. He is almost unstrung, judging by his words and actions.
9. Here we see Macbeth's emotions taking a swing all the way back. He seems now unable to respond at all to the terrible sounds he hears.
10. (a) This line could be interpreted in more than one way. It suggests that he would wish it to have happened at another time, when he could properly mourn, or possibly he's saying she would have died soon, anyway, so what difference does her death make?
11. Macbeth chooses to die doing battle, like a soldier, even though all is lost. He will not kill himself, nor will he simply give himself up. In this he shows his bravery and courage.

Applying

12. Answers will vary. (a) He almost certainly would have slain Malcolm. (b) He might have punished them or attempted to win back their loyalty. (c) He might have forgotten about them or occasionally consulted them.

ANSWERS TO ANALYZING LITERATURE

1. Answers will differ. Ruthless ambition might be considered the flaw, since this drives Macbeth to commit the crime that ultimately eventuates in his death.
2. The theme of Macbeth might be stated thus: Succumbing to a lust for power at any cost will inevitably lead to turmoil and destruction.
3. In Act V we learn that the unlikely prophecies of moving forests and a man not of woman born come true. We see an army laying siege to Macbeth's castle as his own forces abandon him and those who remain show no will to resist. Further, Macbeth shows no remorse or repentence.

ANSWERS TO UNDERSTANDING LANGUAGE

1. The words *moe* for *more, skirr* for *scour,* and *mine* for *my* are clear examples of the differences.
2. The use of *thou* for *you, speak'st* for *speak* and *shalt* for *shall* are three more examples.

Enrichment As compared with tragedy, comedy is a lighter form of drama that aims to amuse and that ends happily. Aristotle pointed out that psychologically there is a very fine line of distinction between great comedy and great tragedy. For the Elizabethans a play was a comedy if it ended happily for the major characters, even though other elements might tend to be tragic.

SHAKESPEAREAN COMEDY

The Tempest

A comedy is a literary work that begins in adversity and ends in good fortune. Since a comedy is meant to amuse, the protagonist always solves the problem with which he or she is confronted. In *The Tempest,* a play that came at the end of Shakespeare's writing career, Prospero has lost his kingdom through the treachery of both Antonio, his brother, and Alonso, the king of Naples. Now an enchanter on a distant island, Prospero conjures up a storm that transports his enemies to his realm. There, through magical intervention, Prospero unites his daughter Miranda with Ferdinand, the son of the king of Naples, and reconciles with Antonio and Alonso, thereby regaining his kingdom. Although this play ends in good fortune, characteristic of comedy, its themes are so rich and its insights so profound that some critics hesitate to simply call it comedy. They classify it instead as tragicomedy, since it contains both the hope that characterizes comedy and the illumination that characterizes tragedy.

The Tempest may be the last play that Shakespeare completed. Because of this, some see it as a farewell address from Shakespeare to his art. They identify him as Prospero, comparing Prospero's magic to Shakespeare's craft and the breaking of Prospero's wand to the end of Shakespeare's career. Others, though they do not deny the possibility of this reading, say that the play is far too complex for this interpretation only. Instead, they claim that the richness of the play comes from its ambiguities, which suggest that life is not simple, but full of complex meanings and significances.

The Whole Play

Just as a Shakespearean play is made up of five acts, it also consists of a number of elements. Among these elements are plot, character, setting, atmosphere, diction, and imagery. It is possible to analyze each element separately, just as the five acts can be examined individually. However, in a successful play, the elements work together to form a unified whole.

Plot

The Tempest involves a series of separations and reconciliations—Prospero from and to Antonio, Miranda from and to

Ferdinand, and Alonso from and to Ferdinand. In *The Tempest,* the major conflict is between Prospero and his enemies, who stripped him of his title and sent him to what they hoped would be a watery grave. The resolution of the main plot in *The Tempest* suggests that Prospero forgives all who tried to harm him.

Character

Character is usually less developed in a comedy than in a tragedy. Nevertheless, many of the characters in *The Tempest,* Prospero in particular, are very well drawn. Prospero is considered a round character—a well-developed, three-dimensional figure. Minor characters, such as Trinculo and Stephano, who provide comic relief, are generally flat characters. A specific type of flat character is the stock character, or stereotype—a familiar, predictable character who appears repeatedly in similar plays or literary works. Stock characters, like the sprite Ariel and the monster Caliban, may have important roles in the play, but they usually lack the complexity of major characters. However, in *The Tempest,* even the monster Caliban takes on symbolic meaning.

Setting

The action in a literary work takes place in a particular place and time. The setting of *The Tempest,* is a desert island in the Mediterranean, somewhere between Tunis and Naples. Shakespeare wrote the play to be contemporary with his day. The entire play takes place on an enchanted island, following a storm at sea.

Atmosphere

In *The Tempest,* the atmosphere is charged with a mystical force. Prospero uses his magical powers to make the other characters unsure that what they see and do is real.

Diction

The Tempest contains some of Shakespeare's finest verse. Ariel's lyrical verses increase the effect of all the elements of the play. Caliban's ominous, foreboding verses add to the elements as well.

Imagery

Literary imagery—comparisons, descriptions, and figures of speech—help a reader or listener to envision a work in their mind. In *The Tempest* Ariel's speeches and song create a sense of goodness and light. On the other hand, the imagery in Caliban's verses creates a feeling of evil and darkness.

Master Teacher Note As students read *The Tempest,* have them keep a notebook in which they jot down their thoughts and comments as they read. They might use the categories on these pages for their notes: plot, character, setting, atmosphere, diction, imagery. In addition to thoughts and comments, students might also record significant quotations from the play.

Master Teacher Note *The Tempest* has been greatly loved by audiences and readers alike. Coleridge called it a "most miraculous drama." To emphasize its tremendous appeal to the imagination, explore how it was partially the inspiration for such diverse poems as Milton's "Comus," T.S. Eliot's "The Waste Land," and W. H. Auden's "The Sea and the Mirror."

Literary Focus The complex interweaving of the conflicts of the plot and subplots in *The Tempest* is as convoluted as any in today's soap operas. The isolation of the island both intensifies and forces us to focus on these conflicts. Shakespeare recognizes the possible tedium in the exposition as Prospero sorts out all of the events and relationships for Miranda. He relieves what could be the monotony of his discourse by constantly checking with Miranda, hence with us, to see if she is listening and understanding. Students could be reminded to do the same as they read.

Look For Your **less advanced** students may have difficulty keeping the events and characters of the exposition straight. Have these students make a chart or map of the characters and their relationships that they fill in as they read. Their chart will help them answer the questions in the Critical Thinking and Reading section at the end of this act.

Writing You might have students offer their conflicts in class. You could then lead the class in a discussion of the idea that without conflict a dramatic story is impossible.

Vocabulary Remind students to make good use of their dictionaries and the glosses to the text of the play as they read. Often comprehension of an entire passage depends on understanding the meaning of one word or phrase.

GUIDE FOR READING

The Tempest, Act I

The Writer's Techniques

Exposition and Conflict. Two important elements of plot are exposition and conflict. Exposition is the part of a literary work that reveals background information. Because of the importance of exposition, writers include it as early in the narrative as possible, blending it into the ongoing action so as not to slow down the narrative. Conflict is the struggle between two opposing persons or forces in a literary work. A conflict may be an external or an internal one, the most obvious being a conflict between one character and another. A character may also struggle against fate, society, nature, or self. Whatever the kind of conflict—and there may be more than one conflict and more than one kind of conflict in a literary work—the tension created by it usually contributes to the development of the plot.

Look For

As you read *The Tempest,* Act I, notice how quickly and smoothly Shakespeare provides the rather complex background needed to understand the play. Notice, too, the different kinds of conflicts that are introduced almost immediately.

Writing

List five kinds of conflict you have seen developed in novels, movies, or situation comedies on television. Identify the characters or forces that opposed each other in each conflict. Also comment on the theory that "without conflict there would be no story."

Vocabulary

Knowing the following words will help you as you read *The Tempest,* Act I.

tempest (tem' pist) *n.*: A violent storm accompanied by rain; any violent commotion or tumult, an uproar (the title of the play)

boatswain (bō' s'n) *n.*: A warrant officer or petty officer in charge of a ship's deck crew, rigging, and anchors (Sc. i, l. 1)

blasphemous (blăs' fə məs) *adj.*: Disrespectful of God; impious (Sc. i, l. 41)

inquisition (ĭn' kwə zish' ən) *n.*: Any investigation that violates the privacy or rights of individuals (Sc. ii, l. 35)

perfidious (pər fid'ē əs) *adj.*: Disloyal; treacherous (Sc. ii, l. 68)

manifold (man'ə fōld') *adj.*: Of many kinds; varied (Sc. ii, l. 264)

abhorred (əb hôrd') *adj.*: Something that is regarded with horror or loathing (Sc. ii, l. 273, l. 352)

unmitigable (un mit'i gə b'l) *adj.*: Not able to be diminished in intensity (Sc. ii, l. 276)

Objectives

1. To understand the use of exposition and conflict in drama
2. To diagram plot development
3. To write about conflict in a play

Teaching Portfolio: Support Material

Teacher Backup, p. 00

Vocabulary Check, p. 00

Usage and Mechanics Worksheet, p. 00

Analyzing Literature Worksheet, p. 00

Critical Thinking and Reading Worksheet, p. 00

Language Worksheet, p. 00

Selection Test, p. 00

The Tempest

William Shakespeare

CHARACTERS

The Scene: An uninhabited island.

Alonso, King of Naples
Sebastian, his brother
Prospero, the right Duke of Milan
Antonio, his brother, the usurping Duke of Milan
Ferdinand, son to the King of Naples
Gonzalo, an honest old councilor
Adrian and Francisco, lords
Caliban, a savage and deformed slave
Trinculo, a jester
Stephano, a drunken butler

Master of a ship
Boatswain
Mariners
Miranda, daughter to Prospero
Ariel, an airy spirit
Iris, **Ceres**, **Juno**, **Nymphs**, **Reapers** — [presented by] spirits
[**Other Spirits attending on Prospero**]

Act I

Scene i. *On a ship at sea.*

1 [*A tempestuous noise of thunder and lightning heard. Enter a* SHIPMASTER *and a* BOATSWAIN.]

MASTER. Boatswain!

BOATSWAIN. Here, master. What cheer?[1]

MASTER. Good,[2] speak to th' mariners! Fall to't yarely,[3] or we run ourselves aground. Bestir, bestir! [*Exit.*]

[*Enter* MARINERS.]

BOATSWAIN. Heigh, my hearts! Cheerly, cheerly, my hearts! Yare, yare! Take in the topsail! Tend to th' master's

1. What cheer? What is your will? What do you wish?
2. Good: Good fellow.
3. yarely: Vigorously; briskly; quickly.

Motivation for Reading Imagine that you have been informed that you are of royal blood. Try to project how this would affect the way you view yourself and your world.

Thematic Idea Shakespeare begins *The Tempest* with the classic conflict of man against nature. Writers before and after him, notably Emily Brontë and Thomas Hardy, set their stories around the same theme. In "The Tempest," Shakespeare shifts from a direct confrontation between man and nature to the more subtle confrontation between the civilized, or "nurtured," man and the natural man.

Purpose-Setting Question What parts do exposition and conflict play in Act I of "The Tempest"?

1 **Enrichment** Shakespeare may have been influenced in the selection of setting and plot for "The Tempest" by two printed pamphlets and a manuscript letter written in 1610. They were about an expedition of the Virginia Company that set sail from Plymouth, England, on July 2, 1609. All of the vessels, except the flagship that carried Sir George Somers and the future governor of Virginia, Sir Thomas Gates, arrived safely in Jamestown in August. The flagship *Sea Adventure* was presumed lost, but on May 23, 1610, Somers and his men found their way to Jamestown. They had run around on the island of Bermuda, an island that was carefully avoided by sailors because of dire reports that circulated concerning it, causing it to be called the Isle of Devils. The shipwrecked Englishmen found no devils there; instead they found the island to be delightful, providing them with food, shelter, and wood to build boats in which to continue their voyage.

2 **Discussion** Why is the boatswain angry with Antonio and Gonzalo?

3 **Discussion** How does the boatswain feel about his royal passengers?

whistle![4] Blow till thou burst thy wind, if room enough![5]

[*Enter* ALONSO, SEBASTIAN, ANTONIO, FERDINAND, GONZALO, *and others.*]

ALONSO. Good boatswain, have care. Where's the master? Play the men.[6]

BOATSWAIN. I pray now, keep below.

ANTONIO. Where is the master, bos'n?

2 **BOATSWAIN.** Do you not hear him? You mar our labor. Keep your cabins; you do assist the storm.

GONZALO. Nay, good, be patient.

BOATSWAIN. When the sea is. Hence! What cares these roarers[7] for the name of king? To cabin! Silence! Trouble us not!

GONZALO. Good, yet remember whom thou hast aboard.

3 **BOATSWAIN.** None that I more love than myself. You are a councilor; if you can command these elements to silence and work the peace of the present,[8] we will not hand[9] a rope more. Use your authority. If you cannot, give thanks you have lived so long, and make yourself

4. whistle: A high-pitched whistle used to give orders.

5. Blow . . . enough: This is addressed to the wind and means, "blow until you split or burst as long as we are in the open sea and have room to maneuver."

6. Play the men: Make the men work.

7. roarers: Loud, noisy characters (here referring either to the waves or to Alonso, Antonio, and Gonzalo).

8. command . . . present: Order the raging storm to stop and bring peace to the present (as in the function or job of the kings's councilor).

9. hand: handle.

3 ready in your cabin for the mischance of the hour, if it so hap. Cheerly,[10] good hearts! Out of our way, I say. [*Exit.*]

4 **GONZALO.** I have great comfort from this fellow. Methinks he hath no drowning mark upon him; his complexion is perfect gallows.[11] Stand fast, good Fate, to his hanging! Make the rope of his destiny our cable, for our own doth little advantage.[12] If he be not born to be hanged, our case is miserable. [*Exit with the rest.*]

[*Enter* BOATSWAIN.]

BOATSWAIN. Down with the topmast! Yare! Lower, lower! Bring her to try with main course.[13] [*A cry within.*] A plague upon this howling! They are louder than the weather or our office.[14]

[*Enter* SEBASTIAN, ANTONIO, *and* GONZALO.]

Yet again? What do you here? Shall we give o'er[15] and drown? Have you a mind to sink?

SEBASTIAN. A pox o' your throat,[16] you bawling, blasphemous, incharitable dog!

BOATSWAIN. Work you, then.

ANTONIO. Hang, cur! Hang, you insolent noisemaker! We are less afraid to be drowned than thou art.

GONZALO. I'll warrant him for[17] drowning, though the ship were no stronger than a nutshell and as leaky as an unstanched[18] wench.

BOATSWAIN. Lay her ahold, ahold! Set her two courses! Off to sea again! Lay her off![19]

[*Enter* MARINERS *wet.*]

MARINERS. All lost! To prayers, to prayers! All lost! [*Exit.*]

5 **BOATSWAIN.** What, must our mouths be cold?

GONZALO. The King and Prince at prayers! Let's assist them,
For our case is as theirs.

SEBASTIAN. I am out of patience.

6 **ANTONIO.** We are merely[20] cheated of our lives by drunkards.
This wide-chopped[21] rascal—would thou mightst lie drowning
The washing of ten tides![22]

10. Cheerly: Quickly.

11. no drowning . . . gallows: This alludes to a popular proverb, "He that's born to be hanged need fear no drowning."

12. for . . . advantage: Our own (destiny) will not save us from drowning.

13. Bring . . . course: A nautical term meaning "Bring the ship about to try to hold the course."

14. They . . . office: The passengers are noisier than the storm or our work.

15. give o'er: give up.

16. pox . . . throat: A plague or curse on your throat.

17. warrant him for: Guarantee him against.

18. unstanched: Not checked or stopped.

19. Lay . . . off: Get control. Bring her back on course. Get the ship out to sea. Get her away from shore.

20. merely: Totally; completely; absolutely; wholly; entirely.

21. wide-chopped: Big-mouthed; talkative.

22. ten tides: Pirates were tied down on the shore and left to drown by the washing of tides over them, usually three.

4 **Reading Strategy** This passage—especially the allusion to the proverb and the personification of fate—points out the importance of having a good background in history, mythology, and literature or the ability to research references to those areas when reading Shakespeare. Have students keep a record of all allusions they encounter as they read this play.

5 **Discussion** What does the boatswain mean in this line?

6 **Reading Strategy** The reader or the audience again must know what the "washing of ten tides" means in order to understand this passage fully. Point out to students that good readers pay close attention to the glosses to the text and immediately incorporate the information found there into their reading.

7 Discussion Have students compare and contrast Antonio, Sebastian, and Gonzalo. What do we learn about these three characters in this exchange?

8 Literary Focus Miranda's first speech reveals her tender and sweet spirit and her complete dependence on her father. Because she understands so little about her world, Shakespeare has Prospero deliver the exposition of the play as an explanation to Miranda about who she is and how she got where she is.

9 Reading Strategy Discuss the multileveled interpretations of the word *fraughting* in line 13 and their effect on the text. Good readers look for all the meanings and interpretations of words and phrases so as not to miss any of the writer's meaning.

GONZALO. He'll be hanged yet,
Though every drop of water swear against it
And gape at wid'st to glut him.

[*A confused noise within*] "Mercy on us!"
"We split, we split!" "Farewell, my wife and children!"
"Farewell, brother!" "We split, we split, we split!"
[*Exit* BOATSWAIN.]

ANTONIO. Let's all sink wi' th' King.

SEBASTIAN. Let's take leave of him.
[*Exit with* ANTONIO.]

7 **GONZALO.** Now would I give a thousand furlongs of sea for an acre of barren ground—long heath,[23] brown furze,[24] anything. The wills above be done, but I would fain[25] die a dry death.
[*Exit.*]

Scene ii. *The island. In front of Prospero's cell.*

[*Enter* PROSPERO *and* MIRANDA.]

MIRANDA. If by your art, my dearest father, you have
Put the wild waters in this roar, allay them.
The sky, it seems, would pour down stinking pitch
But that the sea, mounting to th' welkin's cheek,[1]
Dashes the fire out. O, I have suffered
With those that I saw suffer! A brave[2] vessel
8, 9 (Who had no doubt some noble creature in her)
Dashed all to pieces! O, the cry did knock
Against my very heart! Poor souls, they perished!
Had I been any god of power, I would
Have sunk the sea within the earth or ere[3]
It should the good ship so have swallowed and
The fraughting[4] souls within her.

PROSPERO. Be collected.
No more amazement.[5] Tell your piteous[6] heart
There's no harm done.

MIRANDA. O, woe the day!

PROSPERO. No harm.
I have done nothing but in care of thee,
Of thee my dear one, thee my daughter, who
Art ignorant of what thou art, naught knowing
Of whence I am, nor that I am more better[7]
Than Prospero, master of a full poor cell,
And thy no greater father.[8]

MIRANDA. More to know
Did never meddle[9] with my thoughts.

23. heath: Heather, a shrub that grows on barren soil.
24. furze: Gorse, a shrub that puts forth yellow flowers.
25. fain: Rather.

1. welkin's cheek: Sky's clouds.

2. brave: Splendid.

3. ere: Before.

4. fraughting: Laden, referring back to the ship which is loaded with a cargo of souls.
5. amazement: Bewilderment; alarm; consternation.
6. piteous: Filled with pity; compassionate.

7. more better: Of higher rank.
8. thy . . . father: Your father, who is no greater than master of a poor cave.
9. meddle: Mix.

PROSPERO. 'Tis time
I should inform thee farther. Lend thy hand
And pluck my magic garment from me. So.
[*Lays down his robe.*]
Lie there, my art. Wipe thou thine eyes; have comfort.
The direful spectacle of the wrack,[10] which touched
The very virtue[11] of compassion in thee,
I have with such provision[12] in mine art
So safely ordered that there is no soul—
No, not so much perdition[13] as an hair
Betid[14] to any creature in the vessel
Which thou heard'st cry, which thou saw'st sink.
Sit down;
For thou must not know farther.

MIRANDA. You have often
Begun to tell me what I am; but stopped
And left me to a bootless[15] inquisition,
Concluding, "Stay; not yet."

10. wrack: Wreck.

11. virtue: Essence.

12. provision: Prevision; foresight.

13. perdition: Loss.

14. Betid: Befell; happened.

15. bootless: Pointless; fruitless; useless.

10 Discussion What confuses Miranda in this exchange with her father? How does Prospero clear up the confusion?

11 Discussion What issue is Miranda asking her father to clear up for her? Notice the background information Prospero presents in the speeches that follow.

PROSPERO. The hour's now come;
The very minute bids thee ope thine ear.
Obey, and be attentive. Canst thou remember
A time before we came unto this cell?
I do not think thou canst, for then thou wast not
Out[16] three years old.

MIRANDA. Certainly, sir, I can.

PROSPERO. By what? By any other house or person?
Of anything the image tell me that
Hath kept with thy remembrance.

MIRANDA. 'Tis far off,
And rather like a dream than an assurance
That my remembrance warrants. Had I not
Four or five women once that tended me?

PROSPERO. Thou hadst, and more, Miranda. But how is it
That this lives in thy mind? What seest thou else
In the dark backward and abysm of time?[17]
If thou remeb'rest aught ere thou cam'st here,
How thou cam'st here thou mayst.

MIRANDA. But that I do not.

PROSPERO. Twelve year since, Miranda, twelve year since,
Thy father was the Duke of Milan and
A prince of power.

10 **MIRANDA.** Sir, are not you my father?

PROSPERO. Thy mother was a piece of virtue,[18] and
She said thou wast my daughter; and thy father
Was Duke of Milan; and his only heir
And princess, no worse issued.[19]

MIRANDA. O the heavens!
11 What foul play had we that we came from thence?
Or blessèd was't we did?

PROSPERO. Both, both, my girl!
By foul play, as thou say'st, were we heaved thence,
But blessedly holp[20] hither.

MIRANDA. O, my heart bleeds
To think o' th' teen[21] that I have turned you to,
Which is from[22] my remembrance! Please you, farther.

PROSPERO. My brother and thy uncle, called
Antonio—
I pray thee mark me—that a brother should
Be so perfidious!—he whom next thyself
Of all the world I loved, and to him put

16. out: Beyond; past; more than.

17. abysm of time: Depths of the past.

18. piece of virtue: Example of perfection and purity.

19. no worse issued: No less royal.

20. holp: Helped.

21. teen: Misery.

22. from: Gone from.

The manage of my state, as at that time
Through all the signories[23] it was the first,
And Prospero the prime duke, being so reputed
In dignity, and for the liberal arts
Without a parallel. Those being all my study,
The government I cast upon my brother
And to my state grew stranger, being transported
And rapt in secret studies. Thy false uncle—
Dost thou attend me?

MIRANDA. Sir, most heedfully.

PROSPERO. Being once perfected[24] how to grant suits,
How to deny them, who t' advance, and who
To trash for overtopping,[25] new-created
The creatures that were mine, I say—or changed 'em,
Or else new-formed 'em[26]—having both the key
Of officer and office, set all hearts i' th' state
To what tune pleased his ear, that now he was
The ivy which had hid my princely trunk
And sucked my verdure[27] out on't. Thou attend'st not?

MIRANDA. O, good sir, I do.

PROSPERO. I pray thee mark me.
I thus neglecting worldly ends, all dedicated
To closeness[28] and the bettering of my mind—
With that which, but by being so retired,
O'erprized all popular rate, in my false brother
Awaked an evil nature,[29] and my trust,
Like a good parent, did beget of him
A falsehood in its contrary as great
As my trust was, which had indeed no limit,
A confidence sans bound. He being thus lorded—
Not only with what my revenue yielded
But what my power might else exact, like one
Who having into truth—by telling of it,[30]
Made such a sinner of his memory
To credit[31] his own lie, he did believe
He was indeed the Duke, out o' th' substitution
And executing th' outward face of royalty
With all prerogative.[32] Hence his ambition growing—
Dost thou hear?

12 **MIRANDA.** Your tale, sir, would cure deafness.

PROSPERO. To have no screen between this part he played
And him he played it for, he needs will be
Absolute Milan.[33] Me (poor man) my library
13 Was dukedom large enough. Of temporal[34] royalties
He thinks me now incapable; confederates

23. signories: Feudal estates; seigneuries; principalities.

24. perfected: Skilled at.

25. trash for overtopping: Hold back for going too fast or being too ambitious; "trash" refers to a cord or leash used in training dogs.

26. new-created . . . 'em: He remade my staff—either by replacing those I had chosen with others loyal to him or by turning my people against me.

27. verdure: Green vegetation—health and vigor.

28. closeness: Seclusion.

29. With . . . nature: By devoting myself to higher things, which is beyond popular understanding, I aroused evil in my brother.

30. like . . . it: Like one truly entitled to what my power commanded by simply claiming the right.

31. credit: Believe.

32. out . . . prerogative: By substituting for me and pretending he was royalty with all its rights and privileges.

33. Absolute Milan: Duke in fact, not just in pretense.

34. temporal: In time, of this world.

12 **Discussion** What does Miranda mean by this remark?

13 **Discussion** Given what you have learned about Prospero thus far, what does he value and in what order of priority would he put his values?

(So dry he was for sway[35]) wi' th' King of Naples
To give him annual tribute, do him homage,
Subject his coronet to his crown, and bend
The dukedom, yet unbowed (alas, poor Milan!),
To most ignoble stooping.

MIRANDA. O the heavens!

PROSPERO. Mark his condition,[36] and th' event;[37] then tell
me
If this might be a brother.

MIRANDA. I should sin
To think but nobly of my grandmother.
Good wombs have borne bad sons.

PROSPERO. Now the condition.
This King of Naples, being an enemy
To me inveterate, hearkens my brother's suit;
Which was, that he, in lieu o' th' premises[38]
Of homage and I know not how much tribute,
Should presently extirpate me and mine
Out of the dukedom and confer fair Milan,
With all the honors, of my brother. Whereon,
A treacherous army levied, one midnight
Fated to th' purpose, did Antonio open
The gates of Milan; and, i' th' dead of darkness,
The ministers[39] for th' purpose hurried thence
Me and thy crying self.

MIRANDA. Alack, for pity!
I, not rememb'ring how I cried out then,
Will cry it o'er again; it is a hint[40]
That wrings mine eyes to't.

PROSPERO. Hear a little further,
And then I'll bring thee to the present business
Which now's upon's; without the which this story
Were most impertinent.[41]

MIRANDA. Wherefore did they not
That hour destroy us?

PROSPERO. Well demanded, wench.
My tale provokes that question. Dear, they durst not,
So dear the love my people bore me; nor set
A mark so bloody on the business; but,
With colors fairer, painted their foul ends.
In few,[42] they hurried us aboard a bark;
Bore us some leagues to sea, where they prepared
A rotten carcass of a butt,[43] not rigged,
Nor tackle, sail, nor mast; the very rats

35. dry . . . sway: Thirsty for power, we would say "Hungry for power."

36. condition: The terms of agreement with Naples.

37. event: The outcome.

38. in lieu o' th' premises: In return for promises.

39. ministers: Agents.

40. hint: Occasion.

41. impertinent: Inappropriate; not pertinent; beside the point.

42. In few: With little explanation; using few words.

43. butt: A contemptuous reference to a ship; a tub.

Instinctively have quit it. There they hoist us,
To cry to th' sea that roared to us; to sigh
To th' winds, whose pity, sighing back again,
Did us but loving wrong.

14 **MIRANDA.** Alack, what trouble
Was I then to you!

PROSPERO. O, a cherubin
Thou wast that did preserve me! Thou didst smile,
Infused with a fortitude from heaven,
When I have decked the sea with drops full salt,[44]
Under my burden groaned; which raised in me
An undergoing stomach,[45] to bear up
Against what should ensue.

MIRANDA. How came we ashore?

PROSPERO. By providence divine.
Some food we had, and some fresh water, that
A noble Neapolitan, Gonzalo,
Out of his charity, who being then appointed
Master of this design, did give us, with
15 Rich garments, linens, stuffs, and the necessaries
Which since have steaded much.[46] So, of his gentleness,
Knowing I loved my books, he furnished me
From mine own library with volumes that
I prize above my dukedom.

MIRANDA. Would I might
But ever see that man!

PROSPERO. Now I arise.
Sit still, and hear the last of our sea sorrow.
Here in this island we arrived; and here
Have I, thy schoolmaster, made thee more profit
Than other princess' can,[47] that have more time
For vainer hours, and tutors not so careful.

MIRANDA. Heavens thank you for't! And now I pray you,
sir—
For still 'tis beating in my mind—your reason
For raising this sea storm?

PROSPERO. Know thus far forth.
By accident most strange, bountiful Fortune
(Now my dear lady[48]) hath mine enemies
16 Brought to this shore; and by my prescience[49]
I find my zenith[50] doth depend upon
A most auspicious star, whose influence
If now I court not, but omit,[51] my fortunes
Will ever after droop. Here cease more questions.

44. decked . . . salt: Decorated the sea with tears.

45. undergoing stomach: Underlying courage.

46. steaded . . . much: Been of much use.

47. princess' can: Princesses have.

48. Now . . . lady: Now my supporter.

49. prescience: Knowledge before an event; foreknowledge.

50. zenith: Highest fortune.

51. omit: Ignore.

14 **Reading Strategy** This statement summarizes Miranda and her relationship with her father. Based on this and what you have read so far, describe Miranda's character. What virtue is implied by her remark here?

15 **Literary Focus** As the exposition continues, we find that Prospero's tale is indeed filled with strange and incredible happenings. Have students list the details of his tale they find most strange.

16 **Clarification** Notice another event "most strange."

17 Enrichment *The Tempest* was presented, along with Thomas Campion's *The Lords' Masque,* at the celebration held in honor of the marriage of Lady Elizabeth, James I's daughter, to the Elector Palatine. In a watercolor sketch of the costumes, Indigo Jones portrayed the fiery spirits that appeared in both plays—Ariel in *The Tempest*—is dressed apparently in flames, with fiery wings and bases, carrying in each hand a torch of wax.

Thou art inclined to sleep. 'Tis a good dullness,
And give it way. I know thou canst not choose.
[MIRANDA *sleeps.*]

Come away,[52] servant, come! I am ready now.
Approach, my Ariel! Come!

[*Enter* ARIEL.]

17

ARIEL. All hail, great master! Grave sir, hail! I come
To answer thy best pleasure; be't to fly,
To swim, to dive into the fire, to ride
On the curled clouds. To thy strong bidding task
Ariel and all his quality.[53]

PROSPERO. Hast thou, spirit,
Performed to point,[54] the tempest that I bade thee?

ARIEL. To every article.
I boarded the King's ship. Now on the beak,
Now in the waist, the deck,[55] in every cabin,
I flamed amazement.[56] Sometime I'd divide
And burn in many places; on the topmast,
The yards, and boresprit[57] would I flame distinctly,[58]
Then meet and join. Jove's lightnings, the precursors
O' th' dreadful thunderclaps, more momentary
And sight-outrunning were not. The fire and cracks
Of sulfurous roaring the most mighty Neptune
Seem to besiege, and make his bold waves tremble;
Yea, his dread trident shake.

PROSPERO. My brave spirit!
Who was so firm, so constant, that this coil[59]
Would not infect his reason?

ARIEL. Not a soul
But felt a fever of the mad and played
Some tricks of desperation. All but mariners
Plunged in the foaming brine and quit the vessel,
Then all afire with me. The King's son Ferdinand,
With hair up-staring[60] (then like reeds, not hair),
Was the first man that leapt; cried "Hell is empty,
And all the devils are here!"

PROSPERO. Why, that's my spirit!
But was not this nigh shore?

ARIEL. Close by, my master.

PROSPERO. But are they, Ariel, safe?

ARIEL. Not a hair perished.
On their sustaining[61] garments not a blemish,
But fresher than before; and as thou bad'st me,

52. Come away: Come here.

53. quality: Others like Ariel who make up his band of spirits.

54. to point: To the smallest detail; with absolute precision.

55. Now . . . deck: Now on the prow, now amidships, now on the rear deck or poop.

56. flamed amazement: Caused terror by appearing as fire.

57. boresprit: Bowsprit.

58. distinctly: In distinct or separate places.

59. coil: Tumult; uproar.

60. up-staring: Standing up on end.

61. sustaining: Supporting by keeping them afloat.

In troops I have dispersed them 'bout the isle.
The King's son have I landed by himself,
Whom I left cooling of the air with sighs
In an odd angle of the isle, and sitting,
His arms in this sad knot. [*Illustrates with a gesture.*]

PROSPERO. Of the King's ship,
The mariners, say how thou hast disposed,
And all the rest o' th' fleet.

18 **ARIEL.** Safely in harbor
Is the King's ship; in the deep nook where once
Thou call'dst me up at midnight to fetch dew
From the still-vexed Bermoothes,[62] there she's hid;
The mariners all under hatches stowed,
Who, with a charm joined to their suff'red labor,[63]
I have left asleep. And for the rest o' th' fleet,
Which I dispersed, they all have met again,
And are upon the Mediterranean flote[64]
Bound sadly home for Naples,
Supposing that they saw the King's ship wracked
And his great person perish.

PROSPERO. Ariel, thy charge
Exactly is performed; but there's more work.
What is the time o' th' day?

ARIEL. Past the mid season.[65]

62. Bermoothes: Bermudas.

63. suff'red labor: The work they had done.

64. flote: Sea.

65. mid season: Noon.

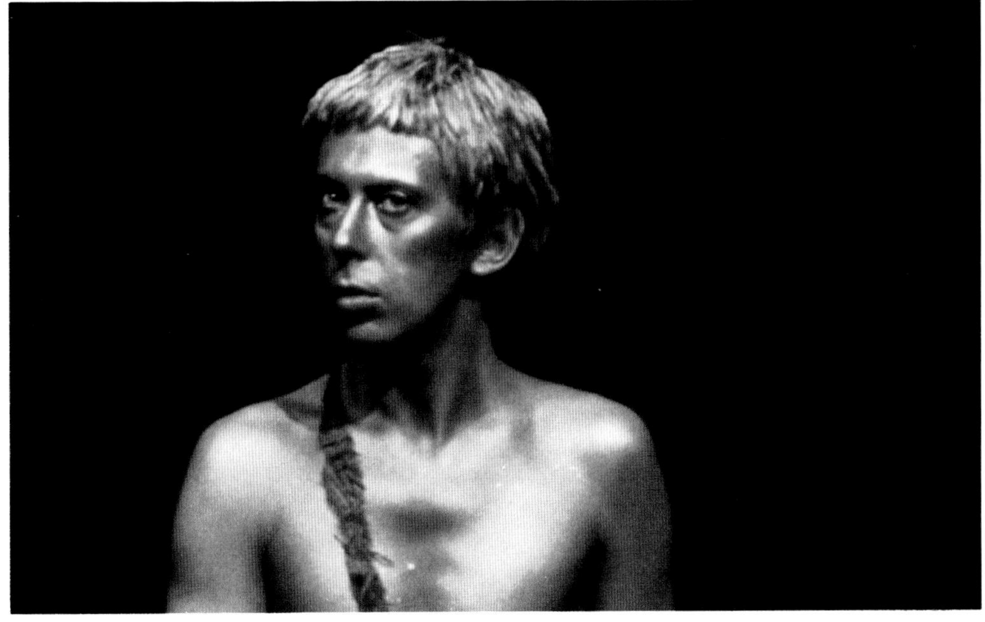

18 **Discussion** The scene is now set. Have students predict what conflicts or problems might now arise.

19 Enrichment The theme of slavery versus freedom runs through this play. Have students keep track of other incidences of this theme as they read.

PROSPERO. At least two glasses.[66] The time 'twixt six and now
Must by us both be spent most preciously.

19 ARIEL. Is there more toil? Since thou dost give me pains,[67]
Let me remember[68] thee what thou hast promised,
Which is not yet performed me.

PROSPERO. How now? Moody?
What is't thou canst demand?

ARIEL. My liberty.

PROSPERO. Before the time be out? No more!

ARIEL. I prithee,
Remember I have done thee worthy service,
Told thee no lies, made thee no mistakings, served
Without or grudge or grumblings. Thou did promise
To bate me a full year.[69]

PROSPERO. Dost thou forget
From what a torment I did free thee?

ARIEL. No.

PROSPERO. Thou dost; and think'st it much to tread the ooze
Of the salt deep,
To run upon the sharp wind of the North,
To do me business in the veins[70] o' th' earth
When it is baked[71] with frost.

ARIEL. I do not, sir.

PROSPERO. Thou liest, malignant thing! Hast thou forgot
The foul witch Sycorax,[72] who with age and envy[73]
Was grown into a hoop? Hast thou forgot her?

ARIEL. No, sir.

PROSPERO. Thou hast. Where was she born? Speak! Tell me!

ARIEL. Sir, in Argier.[74]

PROSPERO. O, was she so? I must
Once in a month recount what thou hast been,
Which thou forget'st. This damned witch Sycorax,
For mischiefs manifold, and sorceries terrible
To enter human hearing, from Argier,
Thou know'st, was banished. For one thing she did
They would not take her life. Is not this true?

ARIEL. Ay, sir.

66. two glasses: Two o'clock; the turning of two hourglasses.

67. pains: Hard work.

68. remember: Remind.

69. bate . . . year: Reduce my servitude by a full year.

70. veins: Underground streams.

71. baked: Hardened.

72. Sycorax: The name of the witch, possibly made up from two or more Greek words.

73. envy: Spite.

74. Argier: Algiers in North Africa.

PROSPERO. This blue-eyed hag was hither brought with child
And here was left by th' sailors. Thou, my slave,
As thou report'st thyself, wast then her servant.
And, for thou wast a spirit too delicate
To act her earthy and abhorred commands,
Refusing her grand hests,[75] she did confine thee,
By help of her more potent ministers,[76]
20 And in her most unmitigable rage,
Into a cloven pine; within which rift
21 Imprisoned thou didst painfully remain
A dozen years; within which space she died
And left thee there, where thou didst vent thy groans
As fast as millwheels strike. Then was this island
(Save for the son that she did litter here,
A freckled whelp, hagborn) not honored with
A human shape.

ARIEL. Yes, Caliban her son.

PROSPERO. Dull thing, I say so! He, that Caliban
Whom now I keep in service. Thou best know'st
What torment I did find thee in; thy groans
Did make wolves howl and penetrate the breasts
Of ever-angry bears. It was a torment
To lay upon the damned, which Sycorax
Could not again undo. It was mine art,
When I arrived and heard thee, that made gape
The pine, and let thee out.

ARIEL. I thank thee, master.

PROSPERO. If thou more murmur'st, I will rend an oak
22 And peg thee in his knotty entrails till
Thou hast howled away twelve winters.

ARIEL. Pardon, master.
I will be correspondent[77] to command
And do my spriting gently.[78]

PROSPERO. Do so; and after two days
I will discharge thee.

ARIEL. That's my noble master!
What shall I do? Say what? What shall I do?

PROSPERO. Go make thyself like a nymph o' th' sea. Be subject
To no sight but thine and mine, invisible
To every eyeball else. Go take this shape
And hither come in't. Go! Hence with diligence!
[*Exit* ARIEL.]

75. hests: Orders.

76. more potent ministers: More powerful agents.

77. correspondent: Obedient.

78. gently: Graciously.

20 **Discussion** What was it about Ariel's character that forced the witch to imprison him?

21 **Discussion** What is the difference between Prospero's treatment of Ariel and Sycorax's treatment? Do you agree with the poet and critic Samuel Taylor Coleridge that the contrast of treatment makes us "sensible that the liberated spirit ought to be grateful"? Explain.

22 **Discussion** Why might Prospero threaten Ariel here?

23 Master Teacher Note You might have students research further the costumes used in Shakespeare's plays—from his time to the present—to depict such characters as Ariel and Caliban. In addition, students could present drawings of these characters as they would have them appear on stage.

24 Discussion What does Caliban's speech suggest about him?

25 Enrichment Another recurrent theme is sovereignty versus conspiracy. Have students compare Caliban's situation with Prospero's.

Awake, dear heart, awake! Thou hast slept well.
Awake!

MIRANDA. The strangeness of your story put
Heaviness[79] in me.

PROSPERO. Shake it off. Come on.
We'll visit Caliban, my slave, who never
Yields us kind answer.

MIRANDA. 'Tis a villain, sir,
I do not love to look on.

PROSPERO. But as 'tis,
We cannot miss[80] him. He does make our fire,
Fetch in our wood, and serves in offices
That profit us. What, ho! Slave! Caliban!
Thou earth, thou! Speak!

CALIBAN. [*Within*] There's wood enough within.

PROSPERO. Come forth, I say! There's other business for thee.
23 Come, thou tortoise! When?

[*Enter* ARIEL *like a water nymph.*]

Fine apparition! My quaint[81] Ariel,
Hark in thine ear. [*Whispers.*]

ARIEL. My lord, it shall be done. [*Exit.*]

PROSPERO. Thou poisonous slave, got by the devil himself
Upon thy wicked dam, come forth!

[*Enter* CALIBAN.]

CALIBAN. As wicked dew as e'er my mother brushed
With raven's feather from unwholesome fen
24 Drop on you both! A southwest[82] blow on ye
And blister[83] you all o'er!

PROSPERO. For this, be sure, tonight thou shalt have cramps,
Side-stitches that shall pen thy breath up. Urchins[84]
Shall, for that vast of night that they may work,[85]
All exercise on thee; thou shalt be pinched
As thick as honeycomb, each pinch more stinging
Than bees that made 'em.

CALIBAN. I must eat my dinner.
25 This island's mine by Sycorax my mother,
Which thou tak'st from me. When thou cam'st first,
Thou strok'st me and made much of me; wouldst give me

79. Heaviness: Sleepiness.

80. miss: Manage without.

81. quaint: Clever; ingenious.

82. southwest: A wind believed to carry the plague.

83. blister: Boils associated with the Bubonic Plague or Black Death.

84. Urchins: Goblins.

85. vast . . . work: The long period of the night when goblins are permitted to do as they wish.

Water with berries in't, and teach me how
26 To name the bigger light, and how the less,
That burn by day and night. And then I loved thee
And showed thee all the qualities o' th' isle,
The fresh springs, brine pits, barren place and fertile.
Cursed be I that did so! All the charms
Of Sycorax—toads, beetles, bats, light on you!
27 For I am all the subjects that you have,
Which first was mine own king; and here you sty[86] me
In this hard rock,[87] whiles you do keep from me
The rest o' th' island.

PROSPERO. Thou most lying slave,
Whom stripes[88] may move, not kindness! I have used thee
28 (Filth as thou art) with humane care, and lodged thee
In mine own cell till thou didst seek to violate
The honor of my child.

CALIBAN. O ho, O ho! Would't had been done!
Thou didst prevent me; I had peopled else
This isle with Calibans.

MIRANDA. Abhorrèd slave,
Which any print of goodness wilt not take,
Being capable of all ill[89] I pitied thee,
Took pains to make thee speak, taught thee each hour
One thing or other. When thou didst not, savage,
Know thine own meaning, but wouldst gabble like
A thing most brutish, I endowed thy purposes
With words that made them known. But thy vile race,
Though thou didst learn, had that in't which good natures
Could not abide to be with. Therefore wast thou
Deservedly confined into this rock, who hadst
Deserved more than a prison.

CALIBAN. You taught me language, and my profit on't
Is, I know how to curse. The red plague rid[90] you
For learning[91] me your language!

PROSPERO. Hagseed, hence!
Fetch us in fuel. And be quick, thou'rt best,[92]
To answer other business. Shrug'st thou, malice?
If thou neglect'st or dost unwillingly
What I command, I'll rack thee with old cramps,
Fill all thy bones with aches, make thee roar
That beasts shall tremble at thy din.

CALIBAN. No, pray thee.
[*Aside*] I must obey. His art is of such pow'r

86. sty: Lodge or pen up, as in a pig sty.
87. rock: Cave.

88. stripes: Whiplashes.

89. print . . . ill: Impression of goodness will not take since you are capable only of making an evil impression.

90. rid: Destroy.
91. learning: Teaching.

92. thou'rt best: You'd better.

26 **Discussion** What might the bigger light be?

27 **Discussion** What was Caliban's position on the island before Prospero and Miranda arrived?

28 **Discussion** Why did Prospero cease treating Caliban kindly?

29 Master Teacher Note Robert Johnson, lutenist to the king, composed music for this song and for "Where the bee sucks, there suck I," which still exist. It is thought that he supplied the music for the rest of the play as well. Students may enjoy hearing recorded versions of these two songs. To what earlier event does Ariel's song allude?

It would control my dam's god, Setebos,[93]
And make a vassal of him.

PROSPERO. So, slave; hence! [*Exit* CALIBAN.]

[*Enter* FERDINAND; *and* ARIEL *(invisible), playing and singing.*]

Ariel's song.

Come unto these yellow sands,
And then take hands
Curtsied when you have and kissed
The wild waves whist,[94]
Foot it featly[95] here and there;
And, sweet spirtes, the burden bear.
Hark, hark!
[*Burden, dispersedly.*[96]] Bow, wow!
The watchdogs bark.
[*Burden, dispersedly.*] Bow, wow!
Hark, hark! I hear
The strain of strutting chanticleer[97]
Cry cock-a-diddle-dow.

FERDINAND. Where should this music be? I' th' air or th' earth?
It sounds no more; and sure it waits upon
Some god o' th' island. Sitting on a bank,
Weeping again the King my father's wrack,
This music crept by me upon the waters,
Allaying both their fury and my passion[98]
With its sweet air. Thence I have followed it,
Or it hath drawn me rather; but 'tis gone.
No, it begins again.

Ariel's song.

Full fathom five[99] thy father lies
Of his bones are coral made;
Those are pearls that were his eyes;
29 Nothing of him that doth fade
But doth suffer a sea change
Into something rich and strange.
Sea nymphs hourly ring his knell:
[*Burden.*] Ding-dong.
Hark! Now I hear them—ding-dong bell.

FERDINAND. The ditty does remember my drowned father.
This is no mortal business, nor no sound
That the earth owes.[100] I hear it now above me.

PROSPERO. The fringed curtains of thine eye advance[101]
And say what thou seest yond.

93. Setebos: The name of a South American Indian god who was mentioned in a travel book by a sixteenth-century Englishman.

94. kissed . . . whist: Kissed the wild waves into silence.

95. featly: Nimbly.

96. *Burden; dispersedly:* A stage direction calling for a background sound of dogs and later of a crowing rooster.

97. chanticleer: Rooster, originally the name of the rooster character in popular medieval fables.

98. passion: Emotion; sorrow.

99. Full fathom five: Fully or completely at a depth of 30 feet in water.

100. owes: Owns; possesses.

101. eye advance: Look up.

MIRANDA. What is't? A spirit?
Lord, how it looks about! Believe me, sir,
It carries a brave form. But 'tis a spirit.

PROSPERO. No, wench; it eats, and sleeps, and hath such senses
As we have, such. This gallant which thou seest
Was in the wrack; and, but he's something stained
With grief (that's beauty's canker), thou mightst call him
A goodly person. He hath lost his fellows
And strays about to find 'em.

MIRANDA. I might call him
A thing divine; for nothing natural
I ever saw so noble.

PROSPERO. [*Aside*] It goes on, I see,
As my soul prompts it. Spirit, fine spirit, I'll free thee
Within two days for this.

FERDINAND. Most sure, the goddess
On whom these airs attend! Vouchsafe my prayer
May know if you remain[102] upon this island,
And that you will some good instruction give
How I may bear me[103] here. My prime request,
Which I do last pronounce, is (O you wonder!)
If you be maid or no?

MIRANDA. No wonder, sir,
But certainly a maid.

FERDINAND. My language? Heavens!
I am the best of them that speak this speech,
Were I but where 'tis spoken.

PROSPERO. How? The best?
What wert thou if the King of Naples heard thee?

FERDINAND. A single[104] thing, as I am now, that wonders
To hear thee speak of Naples. He does hear me;
And that he does I weep. Myself am Naples,
30 Who with mine eyes, never since at ebb, beheld
The King my father wracked.

MIRANDA. Alack, for mercy!

FERDINAND. Yes, faith, and all his lords, the Duke of Milan
And his brave son being twain.[105]

PROSPERO. [*Aside*] The Duke of Milan
And his more braver daughter could control[106] thee,
If now 'twere fit to do 't. At the first sight

102. remain: Live; dwell.

103. bear me: Behave; conduct myself.

104. single: Helpless; alone; solitary.

105. twain: Two.

106. control: Disprove; prove wrong.

30 Discussion What does Ferdinand mean when he calls himself Naples? In what ways is the ruler of a country equivalent to the country?

31 Critical Thinking and Reading Why do you think that Prospero "speaks . . . ungently"? How will his doing so further his plans and, hence the main plot of the play?

32 Discussion Do you agree with Prospero's sentiments here? Explain.

They have changed eyes.[107] Delicate Ariel,
I'll set thee free for this. [*To* FERDINAND] A word, good sir.
I fear you have done yourself some wrong.[108] A word!

MIRANDA. Why speaks my father so ungently? This
31 Is the third man that e'er I saw; the first
That e'er I sighed for. Pity move my father
To be inclined my way!

FERDINAND. O, if a virgin,
And your affection not gone forth, I'll make you
The Queen of Naples.

PROSPERO. Soft, sir! One word more.
[*Aside*] They are both in either's pow'rs. But this swift business
32 I must uneasy make, lest too light winning
Make the prize light. [*To* FERDINAND] One word more! I charge thee
That thou attend me. Thou dost here usurp
The name thou ow'st[109] not, and hast put thyself
Upon this island as a spy, to win it
From me, the lord on't.

FERDINAND. No, as I am a man!

MIRANDA. There's nothing ill can dwell in such a temple.
If the ill spirit have so fair a house,
Good things will strive to dwell with't.

PROSPERO. Follow me.
[*To* MIRANDA] Speak not you for him; he's a traitor. [*To* FERDINAND] Come!
I'll manacle thy neck and feet together;
Sea water shalt thou drink; thy food shall be
The fresh-brook mussels, withered roots, and husks
Wherein the acorn cradled. Follow!

FERDINAND. No.
I will resist such entertainment till
Mine enemy has more pow'r.
[*He draws, and is charmed from moving.*]

MIRANDA. O dear father,
Make not too rash a trial of him, for
He's gentle and not fearful.[110]

PROSPERO. What, I say,
My foot my tutor?[111] [*To* FERDINAND] Put thy sword up, traitor—
Who mak'st a show but dar'st not strike, thy conscience

107. changed eyes: Exchanged glances like lovers.

108. done . . . wrong: Spoken falsely.

109. ow'st: Own.

110. gentle . . . fearful: Of good birth and courageous.

111. My . . . tutor? Am I to be taught by one so far below me?

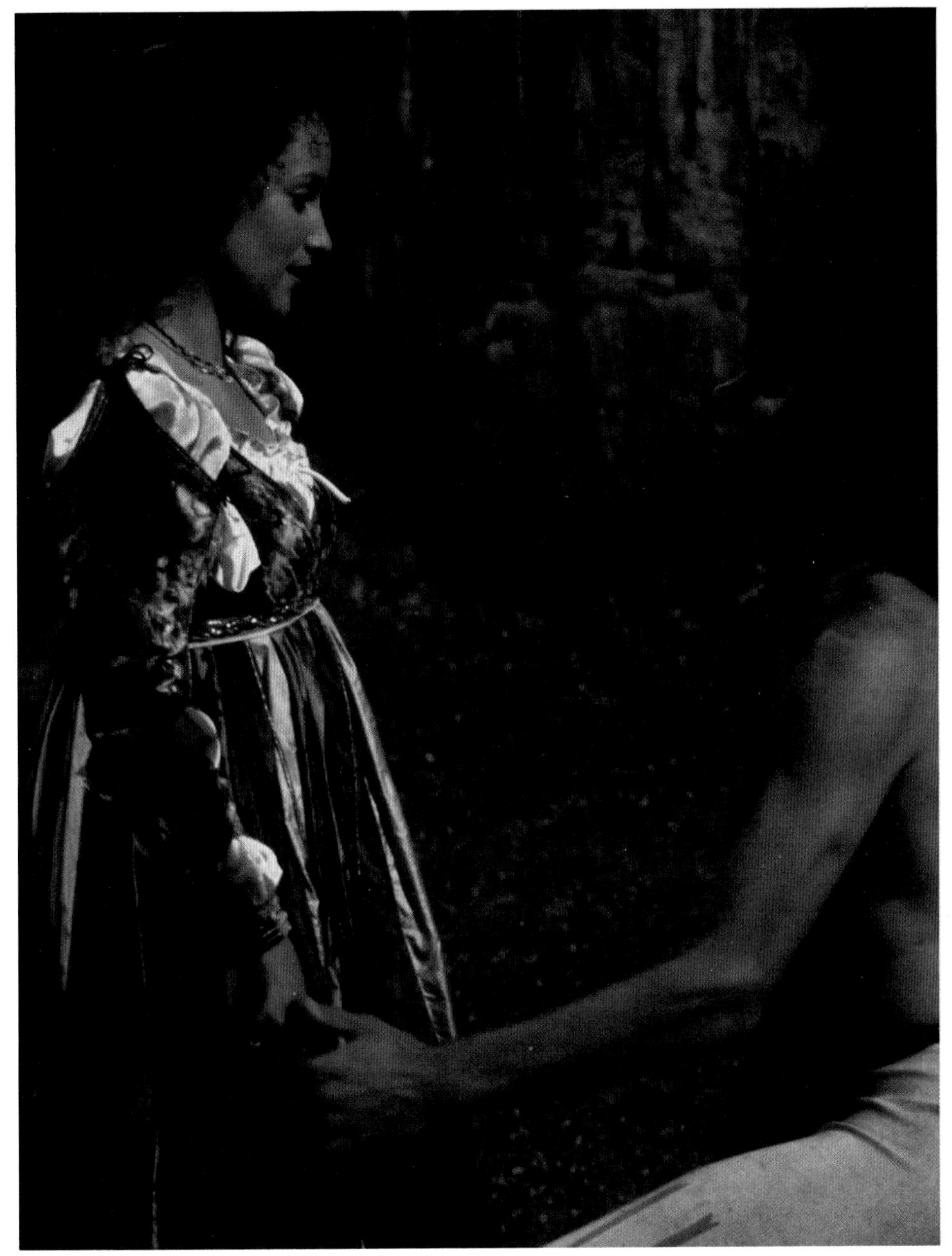

33 **Discussion** How does Ferdinand feel about what has happened to him? How does he feel about Miranda?

Is so possessed with guilt! Come, from thy ward![112]
For I can here disarm thee with this stick[113]
And make thy weapon drop.

MIRANDA. Beseech you, father!

PROSPERO. Hence! Hang not on my garments.

MIRANDA. Sir, have pity.
I'll be his surety.

PROSPERO. Silence! One word more
Shall make me chide thee, if not hate thee. What,
An advocate for an impostor? Hush!
Thou think'st there is no more such shapes as he,
Having seen but him and Caliban. Foolish wench!
To th' most of men this is a Caliban,
And they to him are angels.

MIRANDA. My affections
Are then most humble. I have no ambition
To see a goodlier man.

PROSPERO. [*To* FERDINAND] Come on, obey!
Thy nerves[114] are in their infancy again
And have no vigor in them.

33

FERDINAND. So they are.
My spirits, as in a dream, are all bound up.
My father's loss, the weakness which I feel,
The wrack of all my friends, nor this man's threats
To whom I am subdued, are but light to me,
Might I but through my prison once a day
Behold this maid. All corners else o' th' earth
Let liberty make use of.[115] Space enough
Have I in such a prison.

PROSPERO. [*Aside*] It works. [*To* FERDINAND] Come on.
[*To* ARIEL] Thou hast done well, fine Ariel! [*To* FERDINAND] Follow me.
[*To* ARIEL] Hark what thou else shalt do me.

MIRANDA. Be of comfort.
My father's of a better nature, sir,
Than he appears by speech. This is unwonted
Which now came from him.

PROSPERO. Thou shalt be as free
As mountain winds; but then[116] exactly do
All points of my command.

ARIEL. To th' syllable.

PROSPERO. [*To* FERDINAND] Come, follow. [*To* MIRANDA]
Speak not for him. [*Exit.*]

112. ward: Position of defense.

113. stick: Prospero's magic wand.

114. nerves: Sinews; muscles; strength.

115. All . . . of: Let freedom be in all the rest of the world.

116. but then: Until then.

Answers

ANSWERS TO THINKING ABOUT THE SELECTION

Recalling

1. (a) The ship apparently sinks with all hands on board. (b) Prospero assures Miranda that the crew and passengers are all safe.
2. (a) Prospero is the banished Duke of Milan, who has spent his years on the desert island learning to use white magic from his books. (b) Prospero's title and dukedom were taken away by his brother Antonio with the support of the king, Alonso, and his entourage—all of whom are on the ship.
3. (a) Ariel is a good spirit who serves Prospero because Prospero released him from the tree-prison in which he had been placed by a witch who died. (b) Prospero designs the plans for using his magical powers or "art." As Prospero's servant, Ariel carries out any tasks that need to be done to complete the plans.

Interpreting

4. (a) Gonzalo thinks that the boatswain looks like a man that will die by hanging, not drowning. He doesn't like the fact that the boatswain doesn't treat him and his party with respect. (b) The boatswain thinks that Gonzalo and his party are useless because they know nothing about sailing, and he wants them out of his way so that he and his men can work.
5. Miranda's father is her sole source of love and information. She is certain that he can do anything; hence

THINKING ABOUT THE SELECTION

Recalling

1. (a) What is the apparent fate of the ship at the end of Scene i? (b) What is the fate of the ship, according to Prospero?
2. (a) Who is Prospero, and what is his "art"? (b) What is the conflict between Prospero and some of the passengers on the ship caught in the tempest?
3. (a) Who is Ariel, and why is he at Prospero's beck and call? (b) What part does Ariel play in Prospero's "art"?

Interpreting

4. (a) What is Gonzalo's attitude toward the boatswain? (b) What is the boatswain's attitude Gonzalo?
5. How does Miranda feel about her father and his "art"?
6. What characteristics do Caliban and Ariel have in common? How are they different?
7. How does Shakespeare let us know that he is well aware that his exposition in Scene ii is, by necessity, lengthy and, therefore, fairly undramatic?
8. Based on your reading of Act I, why do you think that Shakespeare gave this play the title *The Tempest?*

Applying

9. Miranda says of Ferdinand, "There's nothing ill can dwell in such a temple./If the ill spirit have so fair a house,/Good things will strive to dwell with't." First interpret Miranda's words. Do you agree with the sentiment expressed? Explain.

ANALYZING LITERATURE

Exposition and Conflict

Exposition and conflict are two of the major elements of *The Tempest,* and both are introduced early—in Act I. In Scene ii, Shakespeare presents all the background information about the major characters and their conflicts as Prospero explains to his daughter, Miranda, how they came to live on the island. Conflict, the struggle between two opposing characters or forces, is an integral part of the play from the beginning of Scene i as the mariners battle the storm.

1. What do you learn about Miranda and her real station in life as Prospero describes the events of the past?
2. What do you learn about Prospero, Ariel, and Caliban during Prospero's confrontations with each servant in Scene ii?

CRITICAL THINKING AND READING

Diagraming Plot Development

An alert viewer or reader of a play assesses the part each character plays in the plot.

1. Draw a diagram showing Prospero's relationship to each of the major characters presented in Scene i and their relationships to each other.
2. Draw a diagram showing Prospero's relationship to each of the major characters in Scene ii and their relationships to each other.

THINKING AND WRITING

Writing About Conflict

Suppose you are writing a syndicated advice column and you receive the following letter:

Dear Helping Hand:

A few years ago, my brother did something very unkind to me. He put my three-year-old daughter and me out to sea in a ship that he knew wouldn't last very long on the open water. When he thought I wouldn't return he took my title, Duke of Milan. Now there seems to be a chance for me to return his "favor." I have learned how to make people and things do what I want them to. Should I use my power to seek my revenge or forgive him?

—Confused on a desert island

Write a response to Confused on a desert island (Prospero, that is) giving your view of the conflict between Prospero and Antonio and suggesting a sensible alternative for the distraught letter writer. Use any relevant information from the play to help you formulate your advice. As you revise the first draft of your letter, check it for tone. Your response should appear concerned, informal, nonjudgmental, and practical.

(Answers begin on p. 326 .)

she begs him to calm to storm.

6. Caliban and Ariel are both supernatural beings under the control of Prospero. However, Ariel is a delightful creature of the air who has a childlike simplicity, while Caliban is a monster most foul who is entirely of the earth. While Ariel is spiritual, Caliban is base and earthy.
7. Shakespeare has Prospero interrupt the exposition to check with Miranda—and also the audience—to make certain that she is listening and that she understands.
8. The play begins on a ship at sea in a tempest. The tempest continues on the island as the characters try to work out their conflicts with each other.

Applying

9. This question should spark a lively discussion. Some students may agree with Miranda that appearance reveals the true person, while others may argue for the sentiment that beauty is only skin deep.

Challenge Some students may have read Rostand's *Cyrano du Bergerac* or may have seen the movie *Roxanne* based on this play. Have them discuss the theme of his work with Miranda's statement about appearance and goodness: "There's nothing ill can dwell in such a temple . . ."

ANSWERS TO ANALYZING LITERATURE

1. Miranda, who at one time had women to wait on her, is the daughter of a duke. She is a young woman of noble birth, not just a castaway on an island with no family connections or property.
2. Prospero is a powerful master who will deal with people fairly if they deal fairly with him. Ariel is a faithful servant who, although he wants to be free from servitude, is pleasant and loyal. Caliban, who also wants to be free from serving Prospero instead is vicious in his verbal attacks and complains constantly about his duties.

Challenge For Miranda, what are the advantages and disadvantages of being raised with Prospero as her only source of knowledge and love and her only human contact?

ANSWERS TO CRITICAL THINKING AND READING

For both questions, Prospero—the master of the island and the real Duke of Milan—should appear in the center of the diagram. For question 1, the characters to be connected with him in the diagram include Ferdinand, Sebastian, Gonzalo, Antonio, and Alonso. For question 2, the characters are Miranda, Ariel, Caliban, and Ferdinand.

Writing Across the Curriculum You might work with the history department in having students prepare background papers on the exploration that was going on in the New World at the time that Shakespeare wrote *The Tempest.* Your students could also research the information in the pamphlets and letter referred to in the first

Enrichment note on page 307.

Literary Focus To emphasize the function of stock characters in drama, discuss stock characters that students are familiar with in television shows, movies, plays, or books that they have recently read. Emphasize that a stock character shows no development during the story and has the same function throughout.

Look For You might create a two-column chart on the chalkboard. Label one column *Round Characters* and the other *Stock Characters.* As students read, have them fill in the chart.

Writing Alternatively, have students freewrite their reactions to a play that has no stock characters in it and one that has nothing but stock characters.

Vocabulary Your **more advanced** students may enjoy tracing the history and development of such words from the play as *spendthrift.* Have them report their findings to the group.

GUIDE FOR READING

The Tempest, Act II

Writer's Techniques

Stock Character. A stock character, also called a stereotype, is a type of literary character who has become familiar to audiences through repetition. Such a character does not grow or develop as major characters should do. He or she is predictable. Indeed, the effectiveness of a stock character may depend upon the audience recognizing the character's traits and anticipating his or her actions. A stock character usually, but not always, plays a minor role in the play. Among the most common stock characters are the self-effacing best friend of the hero or heroine, the admiring Dr. Watson-type sidekick in a traditional mystery, and the ignorant, good-natured GI who is the butt of jokes in a war story. Shakespeare often uses a stock character—usually a servant—in his tragedies for comic relief. In Act II of *The Tempest,* Shakespeare introduces Stephano, the king's butler, and Trinculo, the king's jester and Stephano's sidekick, who provide a comic relief subplot that parallels the more serious subplot involving Antonio and Sebastian.

Look For

As you read *The Tempest,* Act II, give some thought to which of the characters in the play are round characters—that is, three-dimensional figures who are fully developed or who have the potential to develop—and which are stock characters, or stereotypes.

Writing

In addition to the kinds of stock characters just described, think of at least three other kinds you have noticed in plays or stories. Jot them down, noting the function that each plays.

Vocabulary

Knowing the following words will help you as you read *The Tempest,* Act II.

spendthrift (spend′thrift′) *n.*: A person who spends money wastefully or foolishly (Sc. i, l. 26).

beseech (bi sēch′) *v.*: To ask earnestly; entreat; implore (Sc. i, l. 105).

importune (im′ pôr to͞on′) *v.*: To press with frequent requests; ask insistently (Sc. i, l. 134).

supplant (sə plant′) *v.*: To take the place of; supersede (Sc. i, l. 274).

credulous (krej′o͞o ləs) *adj.*: Tending to believe too readily; guillible (Sc. ii, l. 153).

Objectives

1. To recognize use and function of stock characters in drama
2. To understand how diction helps create a dramatic character
3. To write about the function of a character in a dramatic work

Teaching Portfolio: Support Material

Teacher Backup, p. 00

Vocabulary Check, p. 00

Usage and Mechanics Worksheet, p. 00

Analyzing Literature Worksheet, p. 00

Critical Thinking and Reading Worksheet, p. 00

Language Worksheet, p. 00

Selection Test, p. 00

Scene i. *Another part of the island.*

[*Enter* ALONSO, SEBASTIAN, ANTONIO, GONZALO, ADRIAN, FRANCISCO, *and others.*]

GONZALO. Beseech you, sir, be merry. You have cause
(So have we all) of joy; for our escape
Is much beyond our loss. Our hint of[1] woe
Is common; every day some sailor's wife,
The master of some merchant,[2] and the merchant,
Have just our theme of woe. But for the miracle,
I mean our preservation, few in millions
Can speak like us. Then wisely, good sir, weigh
Our sorrow with our comfort.

ALONSO. Prithee, peace.

SEBASTIAN. [*Aside to* ANTONIO] He receives comfort like cold
porridge.[3]

ANTONIO. [*Aside to* SEBASTIAN] The visitor[4] will not give him
o'er so.[5]

1 **SEBASTIAN.** Look, he's winding up the watch of his wit; by
and by it will strike.

GONZALO. Sir—

SEBASTIAN. [*Aside to* ANTONIO] One. Tell.[6]

GONZALO. When every grief is entertained, that's offered
Comes to th' entertainer—

SEBASTIAN. A dollar.[7]

2 **GONZALO.** Dolor[8] comes to him, indeed. You have spoken
truer than you purposed.

SEBASTIAN. You have taken it wiselier[9] than I meant you
should.

GONZALO. Therefore, my lord—

ANTONIO. Fie, what a spendthrift is he of his tongue!

ALONSO. I prithee, spare.[10]

3 **GONZALO.** Well, I have done. But yet—

SEBASTIAN. He will be talking.

ANTONIO. Which, of he or Adrian, for a good wager, first
begins to crow?

1. **hint of:** Occasion for.

2. **master . . . merchant:** Captain of a ship owned by a merchant.

3. **porridge:** A kind of thick soup made with peas; hence there is an indirect pun on the word "peace."

4. **visitor:** A person who "visits" the sick or elderly and offers comfort.

5. **give . . . so:** Give up so easily; quickly stop offering unwanted comfort.

6. **One. Tell:** That's the first. Keep count.

7. **dollar:** English pronunciation of the German *taler*, silver coin.

8. **Dolor:** A Latin word meaning "pain" or "grief." The word was pronounced very much like "dollar."

9. **wiselier:** More wittily; more cleverly.

10. **prithee, spare:** Please spare me all this cleverness; please shut up.

Motivation for Reading Tell students to imagine, as they read Act II, that they are to set up the ideal society for their family and friends. Have them take note of the characters and their speeches in Act II, particularly in Scene i, as they present their arguments for their ideal society.

Master Teacher Note Your students may enjoy reading Montaigne's "Of the Cannibals" and discovering those parts that must have been of interest to Shakespeare, because they are reflected in *The Tempest.*

Purpose-Setting Question What effect does each have on the plot and subplots?

1 **Reading Strategy** Understanding imagery is critical to the comprehension of Shakespearean drama. What information is the image of the watch meant to convey?

2 **Reading Strategy** Understanding puns will enhance comprehension. Discuss the use of *dollar* and *dolor* and the intended relationship between their meanings and their use.

3 **Discussion** This passage is typical of extended exchanges among the members of the king's party. Why is their exchange apparently so lighthearted? What do you learn about Gonzalo, Sebastian, and Antonio in this exchange?

SEBASTIAN. The old cock.[11]

ANTONIO. The cock'rel.

SEBASTIAN. Done! The wager?

ANTONIO. A laughter.

SEBASTIAN. A match!

ADRIAN. Though this island seem to be desert—

ANTONIO. Ha, ha, ha!

SEBASTIAN. So, you're paid.

ADRIAN. Uninhabitable and almost inaccessible—

SEBASTIAN. Yet—

ADRIAN. Yet—

ANTONIO. He could not miss't.

ANDRIAN. It must needs be of subtle, tender, and delicate temperance.[12]

11. old cock: Old rooster, Gonzalo.

12. temperance: Mild climate. Also, moderation, and among Puritans, the name of a woman, as in the next line.

ANTONIO. Temperance was a delicate wench.

SEBASTIAN. Ay, and a subtle, as he most learnedly delivered.

ANDRIAN. The air breathes upon us here most sweetly.

SEBASTIAN. As if it had lungs, and rotten ones.

4 **ANTONIO.** Or as 'twere perfumed by a fen.

GONZALO. Here is everything advantageous to life.

ANTONIO. True; save means to live.

SEBASTIAN. Of that there's none, or little.

GONZALO. How lush and lusty the grass looks! How green!

ANTONIO. The ground indeed is tawny.

SEBASTIAN. With an eye of green[13] in't.

ANTONIO. He misses not much.

SEBASTIAN. No; he doth but mistake the truth totally.

GONZALO. But the rarity of it is—which is indeed almost beyond credit—

SEBASTIAN. As many vouched rarities are.

GONZALO. That our garments, being, as they were, drenched in the sea, hold, notwithstanding, their' freshness and glosses, being rather new-dyed than stained with salt water.

ANTONIO. If but one of his pockets could speak, would it not say he lies?[14]

SEBASTIAN. Ay, or very falsely pocket up his report.[15]

GONZALO. Methinks our garments are now as fresh as when we put them on first in Afric, at the marriage of the King's fair daughter Claribel to the King of Tunis.

SEBASTIAN. 'Twas a sweet marriage, and we prosper well in our return.

ADRIAN. Tunis was never graced before with such a paragon to[16] their queen.

GONZALO. Not since widow Dido's time.

5 **ANTONIO.** Widow? A pox o' that! How came that 'widow'' in? Widow Dido!

SEBASTIAN. What if he had said ''widower Aeneas''[17] too? Good Lord, how you take it!

13. eye of green: Patch of green here and there in the parched earth.

14. If . . . lies? If one of Gonzalo's pockets could speak, wouldn't it prove him a liar by being water stained?

15. pocket . . . report: Cover up Gonzalo's lie by not being stained. Gonzalo can't win either way.

16. to: For.

17. Widow Dido . . . widower Aeneas: An allusion to a great love story in the national epic of Rome, the *Aeneid* by Virgil.

4 **Enrichment** A fen (line 52) is a low-lying piece of land that is swampy or marshy and because of the stagnant water can give off an unpleasant odor. Most of the fens in England have since this time been reclaimed, much as the lowland in the Netherlands has been, with a system of canals running about the level of the ground throughout the area. The fens arguably provide some of the richest soil in Great Britain and, according to those who live there, now offer fresh and truly ''perfumed'' air.

5 **Master Teacher Note** To fully understand Shakespeare's allusion here to Roman mythology, have a volunteer summarize the story of Aeneas and Dido for the rest of the group.

6 **Enrichment** The theme of separation runs through this play. For this and other reasons, some critics feel *The Tempest* contains the subject matter of tragedy. Have students trace the development of this theme as they read. Then have them relate this theme to the story of Dido and Aeneus.

ADRIAN. "Widow Dido," said you? You make me study of that. She was of Carthage, not of Tunis.

GONZALO. This Tunis, sir, was Carthage.

ADRIAN. Carthage?

GONZALO. I assure you, Carthage.

ANTONIO. His word is more than the miraculous harp.[18]
SEBASTIAN. He hath raised the wall and houses too.

ANTONIO. What impossible matter will he make easy next?

SEBASTIAN. I think he will carry this island home in his pocket and give it his son for an apple.

ANTONIO. And, sowing the kernels of it in the sea, bring forth more islands.

GONZALO. Ay!

ANTONIO. Why, in good time.

GONZALO. [*To* ALONSO] Sir, we were talking that our garments seem now as fresh as when we were at Tunis at the marriage of your daughter, who is now Queen.

ANTONIO. And the rarest that e'er came there.

SEBASTIAN. Bate,[19] I beseech you, widow Dido.

ANTONIO. O, widow Dido? Ay, widow Dido!

GONZALO. Is not, sir, my doublet as fresh as the first day I wore it? I mean, in a sort.[20]

ANTONIO. That "sort" was well fished for.

GONZALO. When I wore it at your daughter's marriage.

6

ALONSO. You cram these words into mine ears against
The stomach of my sense.[21] Would I had never
Married my daughter there! For, coming thence,
My son is lost; and, in my rate,[22] she too,
Who is so far from Italy removed
I ne'er again shall see her. O thou mine heir
Of Naples and of Milan, what strange fish
Hath made his meal on thee?

FRANCISCO. Sir, he may live.
I saw him beat the surges under him
And ride upon their backs. He trod the water,
Whose enmity he flung aside, and breasted
The surge most swol'n that met him. His bold head
'Bove the contentious waves he kept, and oared

18. miraculous harp: The harp of Amphion, son of the Greek god Zeus, was played so perfectly that the stones for the walls of the city of Thebes slid into place by themselves. Gonzalo's words are more miraculous than the harp because they created a whole city by mistakenly identifying ancient Carthage with modern Tunis.

19. Bate: With the exception of.

20. in a sort: In a manner of speaking.

21. You . . . sense: You force comfort upon me so that it revolts against common sense.
22. rate: View; opinion.

Himself with his good arms in lusty stroke
To th' shore, that o'er his wave-worn basis bowed,
As stooping to relieve him. I no doubt
He came alive to land.

ALONSO. No, no, he's gone.

SEBASTIAN. [*To* ALONSO] Sir, you may thank yourself for this great loss,
That would not bless our Europe with your daughter,
But rather loose her to an African,
Where she, at least, is banished from your eye
Who hath cause to wet the grief on't.

ALONSO. Prithee, peace.

SEBASTIAN. You were kneeled to and importuned otherwise
By all of us; and the fair soul herself
Weighed, between loathness and obedience, at
Which end o' th' beam should bow.[23] We have lost your son,
I fear, forever. Milan and Naples have
Moe[24] widows in them of this business' making
Than we bring men to comfort them.
The fault's your own.

ALONSO. So is the dear'st[25] o' th' loss.

8 **GONZALO.** My Lord Sebastian,
The truth you speak doth lack some gentleness,
And time to speak it in. You rub the sore
When you should bring the plaster.

SEBASTIAN. Very well.

ANTONIO. And most chirurgeonly.[26]

SEBASTIAN. [*To* ALONSO] It is foul weather in us all, good sir,
When you are cloudy.

SEBASTIAN. [*Aside to* ANTONIO] Foul weather?

ANTONIO. [*Aside to* SEBASTIAN] Very foul.

GONZALO. Had I plantation[27] of this isle, my lord—

ANTONIO. He'd sow't with nettle seed.

SEBASTIAN. Or docks, or mallows.

GONZALO. And were the king on't, what would I do?

SEBASTIAN. Scape being drunk for want of wine.

9 **GONZALO.** I' th' commonwealth I would by contraries[28]
Execute all things. For no kind of traffic[29]
Would I admit; no name of magistrate;

23. Which . . . bow: To which should she yield.

24. Moe: More.

25. dear'st: Costliest.

26. chirurgeonly: As a surgeon might.

27. plantation: The right of colonization.

28. by contraries: Against prevailing customs.

29. traffic: Trade or business.

7 **Discussion** For what is Gonzalo criticizing Sebastian in this passage?

8 **Clarification** The word *plaster* is still used in Great Britain today as something that covers a wound, like a band-aid.

9 **Enrichment** The following passage about early American Indian society from Montaigne's "Of the Cannibals" is the source for Gonzalo's description of his ideal commonwealth.

"It is a nation, would I answer Plato, that hath no kind of traffic [commerce], no knowledge of letters, no intelligence of numbers, no name of magistrate, nor of politic superiority; no use of service, of riches, or of poverty; no contracts, no successions, no partitions, no occupation but idle; no respect of kindred but common, no apparel but natural, no manuring of lands, no use of wine, corn, or metal." Is Gonzalo's vision of the ideal commonwealth realistic?

10 Discussion How does Ariel's bringing on sleep further the plot of the play? When was this device used earlier? What effect did it have then?

Letters[30] should not be known; riches, poverty,
And use of service,[31] none; contract, succession,[32]
Bourn, bound of land, tilth, vineyard, none;[33]
No use of metal, corn, or wine, or oil;
No occupation; all men idle, all;
And women too, but innocent and pure;
No sovereignty.[34]

SEBASTIAN. Yet he would be king on't.

ANTONIO. The latter end of his commonwealth forgets the beginning.

GONZALO. All things in common nature should produce
Without sweat or endeavor. Treason, felony,
Sword, pike, knife, gun, or need of any engine[35]
Would I not have; but nature should bring forth,
Of it[36] own kind, all foison,[37] all abundance,
To feed my innocent people.

SEBASTIAN. No marrying 'mong his subjects?

ANTONIO. None, man, all idle—knaves.

GONZALO. I would with such perfection govern, sir,
T' excel the Golden Age.

SEBASTIAN. [*Loudly*] Save his Majesty!

ANTONIO. [*Loudly*] Long live Gonzalo!

GONZALO. And—do you mark me, sir?

ALONSO. Prithee, no more. Thou dost talk nothing to me.

GONZALO. I do well believe your Highness; and did it to minister occasion[38] to these gentlemen, who are of such sensible[39] and nimble lungs that they always use to laugh at nothing.

ANTONIO. 'Twas you we laughed at.

GONZALO. Who is this kind of merry fooling am nothing to you; so you may continue, and laugh at nothing still.

ANTONIO. What a blow was there given!

SEBASTIAN. And it had not fall'n flatlong.[40]

GONZALO. You are gentlemen of brave mettle; you would lift the moon out of her sphere if she would continue in it five weeks without changing.

[*Enter* ARIEL (*invisible*) *playing solemn music.*]

10 **SEBASTIAN.** We would so, and then go a-batfowling.[41]

ANTONIO. Nay, good my lord, be not angry.

30. Letters: Education; learning.
31. service: Servants.
32. succession: Inheritance.
33. Bourn . . . none: No boundaries or enclosures of land, farms, vineyards.
34. I' th' commonwealth . . . sovereignty: This entire speech by Gonzalo represents a rejection of the civilization of Shakespeare's day. Many of the ideas and even words are very close to an English translation of an essay by the great French writer Montaigne. The essay presented an idealized picture of American Indian life. It also was an early depiction of life in which has come to be called the "state of nature."
35. engine: Weapon.
36. it: Its.
37. foison: Rich harvest.
38. minister occasion: Offer an opportunity.
39. sensible: Sensitive.
40. flatlong: The flat side of the sword.
41. We . . . a-batfowling: We would use the light of the moon to hunt birds at night attracted by light and knock them down with bats or clubs.

GONZALO. No, I warrant you; I will not adventure my discretion so weakly.[42] Will you laugh me asleep? For I am very heavy.

ANTONIO. Go sleep, and hear us.

[*All sleep except* ALONSO, SEBASTIAN, *and* ANTONIO.]

ALONSO. What, all so soon asleep? I wish mine eyes
Would, with themselves, shut up my thoughts. I find
They are inclined to do so.

SEBASTIAN. Please you, sir,
Do not omit the heavy offer of it.
It seldom visits sorrow; when it doth,
It is a comforter.

ANTONIO. We too, my lord,
Will guard your person while you take your rest,
And watch your safety.

ALONSO. Thank you. Wondrous heavy.
[ALONSO *sleeps. Exit* ARIEL.]

SEBASTIAN. What a strange drowsiness possesses them!

ANTONIO. It is the quality o' th' climate.

SEBASTIAN. Why
Doth it not then our eyelids sink? I find not
Myself disposed to sleep.

ANTONIO. Nor I: my spirits are nimble.
They fell together all, as by consent.
They dropped as by a thunderstroke. What might,
Worthy Sebastian—O, what might?—No more!
And yet methinks I see it in thy face,
What thou shouldst be. Th' occasion speaks thee,[43] and
11 My strong imagination sees a crown
Dropping upon thy head.

SEBASTIAN. What? Art thou waking?

ANTONIO. Do you not hear me speak?

SEBASTIAN. I do; and surely
It is a sleepy language, and thou speak'st
Out of thy sleep. What is it thou didst say?
This is a strange repose, to be asleep
With eyes wide open; standing, speaking, moving,
And yet so fast asleep.

ANTONIO. Noble Sebastian,
Thou let'st thy fortune sleep—die, rather; wink'st[44]
Whiles thou art waking.

42. not adventure . . . weakly: I will not risk my reputation by responding to such weak wit.

43. occasion speaks thee: Opportunity offers you.

44. wink'st: Close your eyes.

11 Critical Thinking and Reading
Have the students discuss the two themes of *The Tempest* which are apparent here. Have them discuss natural man versus nurtured man and reality versus illusion, the attributes of each character, and the situation that furthers these themes.

12 Discussion Why do people sometimes deny or mock what they most want? What do we mean by the term "sour grapes"? What evidence do you find in everyday life of the tendency to diminish what you want but fear you cannot have?

13 Enrichment Ask for a volunteer to locate Aesop's fable of the fox and the sour grapes. Have this student share this fable with the class.

14 Discussion Why was the question of succession to the throne so important to people living during the English Renaissance?

15 Discussion What are Antonio's rationales for Sebastian's taking over the kingdom?

SEBASTIAN. Thou dost snore distinctly;
There's meaning in thy snores.

ANTONIO. I am more serious than my custom. You
Must be so too, if heed me; which to do
Trebles thee o'er.[45]

SEBASTIAN. Well, I am standing water.[46]

ANTONIO. I'll teach you how to flow.

SEBASTIAN. Do so. To ebb
Hereditary sloth instructs me.

ANTONIO. O,
If you but knew how you the purpose cherish
12 Whiles thus you mock it; how, in stripping it,
13 You more invest it![47] Ebbing men, indeed,
Most often do so near the bottom run
By their own fear or sloth.

SEBASTIAN. Prithee, say on.
The setting of thine eye and cheek proclaim
A matter[48] from thee; and a birth, indeed,
Which throes thee much[49] to yield.

ANTONIO. Thus, sir:
Although this lord of weak remembrance, this
Who shall be of as little memory
When he is earthed,[50] hath here almost persuaded
(For he's a spirit of persuasion, only
Professes to persuade[51]) the King his son's alive,
'Tis as impossible that he's undrowned
As he that sleeps here swims.

SEBASTIAN. I have no hope
That he's undrowned.

ANTONIO. O, out of that no hope
What great hope have you! No hope that way is
Another way so high a hope that even
Ambition cannot pierce a wink beyond,
But doubt discovery there.[52] Will you grant with me
That Ferdinand is drowned?

SEBASTIAN. He's gone.

ANTONIO. Then tell me,
14 Who's the next heir of Naples?

SEBASTIAN. Claribel.

ANTONIO. She that is Queen of Tunis; she that dwells
15 Ten leagues beyond man's life;[53] she that from Naples
Can have no note—unless the sun were post;[54]

45. Trebles thee o'er: Triples your present power.
46. standing water: Still water; not moving water, as between the tides.
47. in stripping . . . invest it: While seeming to deny ambition, you shape it all the more.
48. matter: Something of importance.
49. throes thee much: Gives you much pain.
50. earthed: Buried.
51. For . . . persuade: For he [Gonzalo] is the very spirit of conviction and is nothing more than a professional persuader.
52. Ambition . . . there: The eye of ambition cannot see beyond the present, and even doubts what it sees there.
53. Ten . . . life: Ten leagues [infinitely] farther than one could travel in a lifetime.
54. post: Mail courier.

The man i' th' moon's too slow—till newborn chins
Be rough and razorable;[55] she that from whom
We all were sea-swallowed, though some cast[56] again,
And by that destiny, to perform an act
Whereof what's past is prologue, what to come,
In yours and my discharge.

SEBASTIAN. What stuff is this? How say you?
'Tis true my brother's daughter's Queen of Tunis;
So is she heir of Naples; 'twixt which regions
There is some space.

ANTONIO. A space whose ev'ry cubit
Seems to cry out "How shall that Claribel
Measure us back to Naples? Keep in Tunis,
And let Sebastian wake!" Say this were death
That now hath seized them, why, they were no worse
Than now they are. There be that can rule Naples
As well as he that sleeps; lords that can prate
As amply and unnecessarily
As this Gonzalo; I myself could make
A chough of as deep chat.[57] O, that you bore
The mind that I do! What a sleep were this
For your advancement! Do you understand me?

SEBASTIAN. Methinks I do.

ANTONIO. And how does your content
Tender[58] your own good fortune?

SEBASTIAN. I remember
16 You did supplant your brother Prospero.

ANTONIO. True.
And look how well my garments sit upon me,
Much feater[59] than before. My brother's servants
Were then my fellows; now they are my men.

SEBASTIAN. But, for your conscience—

ANTONIO. Ay, sir, where lies that? If 'twere a kibe,[60]
'Twould put me to my slipper; but I feel not
This deity in my bosom. Twenty consciences
That stand 'twixt me and Milan, candied be they
And melt, ere they molest! Here lies your brother,
No better than the earth he lies upon—
17 If he were that which now he's like, that's dead—
Whom I with this obedient steel (three inches of it)
Can lay to bed forever; whiles you, doing thus,
To the perpetual wink for aye might put
This ancient morsel, this Sir Prudence, who
Should not upbraid our course. For all the rest,
They'll take suggestion as a cat laps milk;

55. till . . . razorable: Until newborn babes grow beards and have to shave.

56. cast: Cast up on shore; survive.

57. I . . . chat: I myself could make a crow sound as profound as Gonzalo.

58. Tender: Think of.

59. feater: More attractively; more fittingly.

60. kibe: An inflammation of the heel caused by cold.

16 **Reading Strategy** Have students prepare a semantic map showing the conspiracies that run through *The Tempest.* Ask them to add to this map as they read.

17 **Discussion** What does this speech reveal about Antonio? What example of irony can you find in this speech?

They'll tell the clock[61] to any business that
We say befits the hour.

SEBASTIAN. Thy case, dear friend,
Shall be my precedent. As thou got'st Milan,
I'll come by Naples. Draw thy sword. One stroke
Shall free thee from the tribute which thou payest,
And I the King shall love thee.

ANTONIO. Draw together;
And when I rear my hand, do you the like,
To fall it on Gonzalo. [*They draw.*]

SEBASTIAN. O, but one word!

[*Enter* ARIEL (*invisible*) *with music and song.*]

ARIEL. My master through his art foresees the danger
That you, his friend, are in, and sends me forth
(For else his project dies) to keep them living.
[*Sings in* GONZALO'*s ear.*]

While you here do snoring lie,
Open-eyed conspiracy
His time doth take.
If of life you keep a care,
Shake off slumber and beware.
Awake, awake!

ANTONIO. Then let us both be sudden.

SEBASTIAN. [*Wakes*] Now good angels
Preserve the King! [*The others wake.*]

ALONSO. Why, how now? Ho, awake! Why are you drawn?
Wherefore this ghastly looking?

GONZALO. What's the matter?

SEBASTIAN. Whiles we stood here securing your repose,
Even now, we heard a hollow burst of bellowing
Like bulls, or rather lions. Did't not wake you?
It struck mine ear most terribly.

ALONSO. I heard nothing.

ANTONIO. O, 'twas a din to fright a monster's ear,
To make an earthquake! Sure it was the roar
Of a whole herd of lions.

ALONSO. Heard you this, Gonzalo?

GONZALO. Upon mine honor, sir, I heard a humming,
And that a strange one, too, which did awake me.
I shaked you, sir, and cried. As mine eyes opened,
I saw their weapons drawn. There was a noise,

61. tell the clock: Agree to.

That's verily.[62] 'Tis best we stand upon our guard,
Or that we quit this place. Let's draw our weapons.

ALONSO. Lead off this ground, and let's make further search
For my poor son.

GONZALO. Heavens keep him from these beasts!
For he is, sure, i' th' island.

ALONSO. Lead away.

ARIEL. Prospero my lord shall know what I have done.
So, King, go safely on to seek thy son. [*Exit.*]

Scene ii. *Another part of the island.*

18 [*Enter* CALIBAN *with a burden of wood. A noise of thunder heard.*]

19 **CALIBAN.** All the infections that the sun sucks up
From bogs, fens, flats, on Prosper fall, and make him
By inchmeal[1] a disease! His spirits hear me,
And yet I needs must curse. But they'll nor pinch,
Fright me with urchin shows,[2] pitch me i' th' mire,
Nor lead me, like a firebrand,[3] in the dark
Out of my way, unless he bid 'em. But
For every trifle are they set upon me;
Sometime like apes that mow[4] and chatter at me,
And after bite me; then like hedgehogs which
Lie tumbling in my barefoot way and mount
Their pricks at my footfall; sometime am I
All wound with adders, who with cloven tongues
Do hiss me into madness.

[*Enter* TRINCULO.]

Lo, now, lo!
Here comes a spirit of his, and to torment me
For bringing wood in slowly. I'll fall flat.
Perchance he will not mind me. [*Lies down.*]

20 **TRINCULO.** Here's neither bush nor shrub to bear off[5] any weather at all, and another storm brewing; I hear it sing i' th' wind. Yond same black cloud, yond huge one, looks like a foul bombard[6] that would shed his liquor. If it should thunder as it did before, I know not where to hide my head. Yond same cloud cannot but fall by pailfuls. What have we here? A man or a fish? Dead or alive? A fish! He smells like a fish; a very ancient and

62. **verily:** The truth.

1. **By inchmeal:** Inch by inch.
2. **urchin shows:** Visions of hobgoblins.
3. **Nor . . . firebrand:** Nor lead me astray with such illusions as the will-o'-the-wisp.
4. **mow:** Make faces.

5. **bear off:** Protect against.

6. **bombard:** A large jug made of leather.

18 **Discussion** How is the atmosphere of the opening scene of Act II different from the atmosphere of the last scene of Act I?

19 **Enrichment** To further emphasize the struggle between natural man and nurtured man and as an indication of the effect that Montaigne's essay had on Shakespeare, he uses a near anagram of the word cannibal—Caliban—as the name of the most "natural" of his characters. *Cannibal* comes from the word *Carib,* meaning "strong men," the name of the Indians that explorers found in the West Indies and after whom the Caribbean Sea was named. Originally the word had no connection with the eating of flesh.

20 **Literary Focus** What is there in Trinculo's opening speech that indicates that he is probably a stock character?

21 **Literary Focus** What is there in Stephano's opening lines that indicates that he is probably a stock character?

22 **Discussion** Compare Caliban's reaction to seeing men with Miranda's reaction to seeing Ferdinand.

fishlike smell; a kind of not of the newest Poor John.[7] A strange fish! Were I in England now, as once I was, and had but this fish painted,[8] not a holiday fool there would but give a piece of silver. There would this monster make a man;[9] any strange beast there makes a man. When they will not give a doit[10] to relieve a lame beggar, they will lay out ten to see a dead Indian. Legged like a man! And his fins like arms! Warm, o' my troth! I do now let loose my opinion, hold it no longer. This is no fish, but an islander, that hath lately suffered by a thunderbolt. [*Thunder.*] Alas, the storm is come again! My best way is to creep under his gaberdine; there is no other shelter hereabout. Misery acquaints a man with strange bedfellows. I will here shroud[11] till the dregs of the storm be past. [*Creeps under* CALIBAN'*s garment.*]

[*Enter* STEPHANO, *singing,* (*a bottle in his hand*).]

21

STEPHANO. I shall no more to sea, to sea;
Here shall I die ashore.

This is a very scurvy[12] tune to sing at a man's funeral. Well, here's my comfort. [*Drinks.*]

The master, the swabber, the boatswain, and I,
The gunner, and his mate,
Loved Mall, Meg, and Marian, and Margery,
But none of us cared for Kate.
For she had a tongue with a tang,
Would cry to a sailor "Go hang!"
She loved not the savor of tar nor of pitch;
Yet a tailor might scratch her where'er she did itch.
Then to sea, boys, and let her go hang!

This is a scurvy tune too; but here's my comfort. [*Drinks.*]

22

CALIBAN. Do not torment me! O!

STEPHANO. What's the matter? Have we devils here? Do you put tricks upon 's with savages and men of Inde, ha? I have not scaped drowning to be afeard now of your four legs. For it hath been said, "As proper a man as ever went on four legs cannot make him give ground"; and it shall be said so again, while Stephano breathes at' nostrils.

CALIBAN. The spirit torments me. O!

STEPHANO. This is some monster of the isle, with four legs, who hath got, as I take it, an ague.[13] Where the devil should he learn our language? I will give him some

7. **Poor John:** A type of fish similar to codfish.

8. **painted:** A shopkeeper's sign at the market.

9. **make a man:** Make a person's fortune.

10. **doit:** A coin of the lowest value.

11. **shroud:** Cover myself.

12. **scurvy:** Despicable.

13. **ague:** A feverish ailment characterized by violent shivering, similar to malaria.

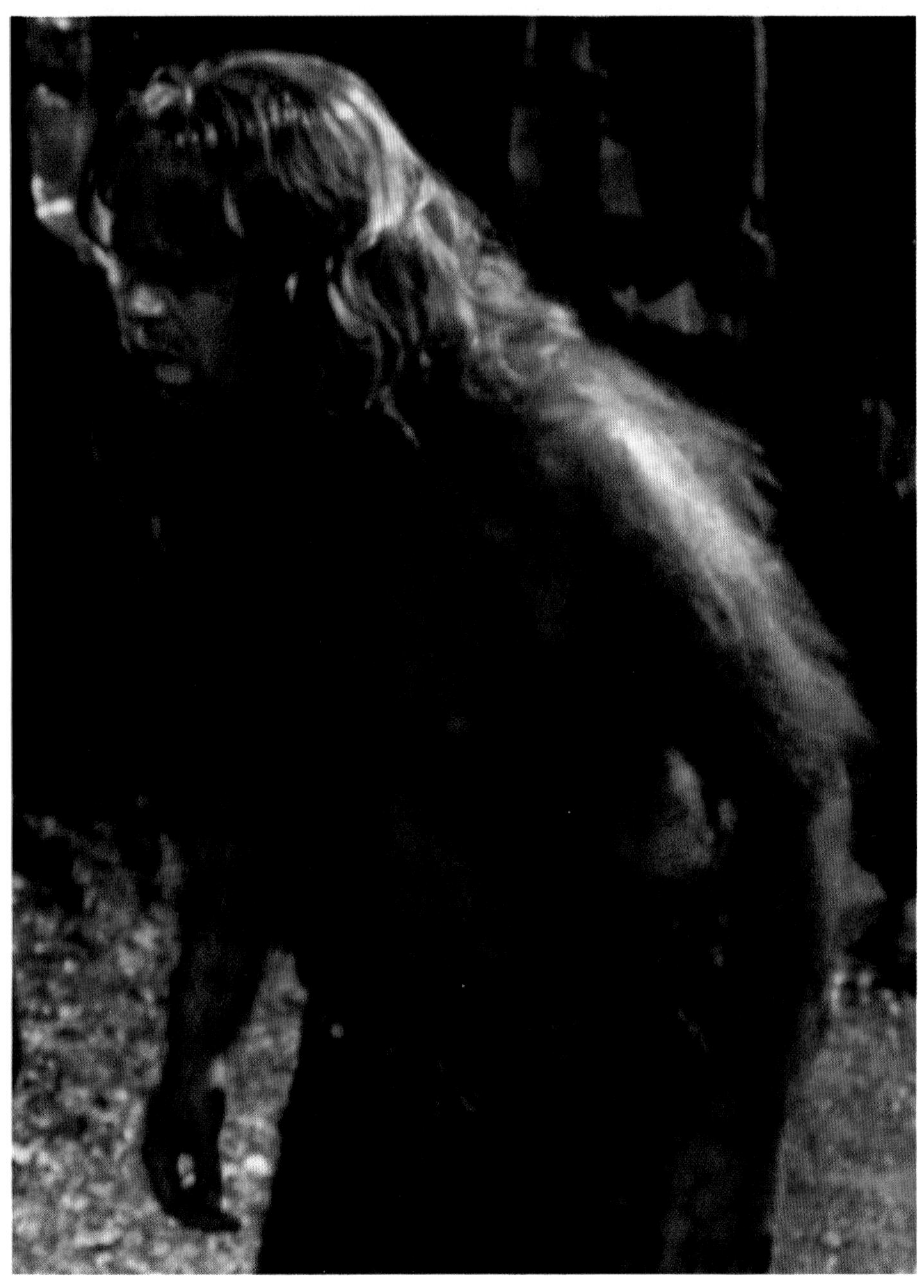

23 **Enrichment** Some critics see in the giving of drink to Caliban by Stephano and Trinculo an allusion to the settlers giving of drink, or fire water, to the native Americans.

relief, if it be but for that. If I can recover[14] him, and keep him tame, and get to Naples with him, he's a present for any emperor that ever trod on neat's leather.[15]

CALIBAN. Do not torment me, prithee; I'll bring my wood home faster.

STEPHANO. He's in his fit now and does not talk after the wisest. He shall taste of my bottle; if he have never drunk wine afore, it will go near to remove his fit. If I can recover him and keep him tame, I will not take too much for him.[16] He shall pay for him that hath him, and that soundly.

CALIBAN. Thou dost me yet but little hurt. Thou wilt anon;[17] I know it by thy trembling. Now Prosper works upon thee.

STEPHANO. Come on your ways, open your mouth; here is that which will give language to you, cat.[18] Open your mouth. This will shake your shaking, I can tell you, and that soundly. [*Gives* CALIBAN *drink.*] You cannot tell who's your friend. Open your chaps[19] again.

TRINCULO. I should know that voice. It should be—but he is drowned; and these are devils. O, defend me!

23 **STEPHANO.** Four legs and two voices—a most delicate monster! His forward voice now is to speak well of his friend; his backward voice is to utter foul speeches and to detract. If all the wine in my bottle will recover him, I will help his ague. Come! [*Gives drink.*] Amen! I will pour some in thy other mouth.

TRINCULO. Stephano!

STEPHANO. Doth thy other mouth call me? Mercy, mercy! This is a devil, and no monster. I will leave him; I have no long spoon.[20]

TRINCULO. Stephano! If thou beest Stephano, touch me and speak to me; for I am Trinculo—be not afeard—thy good friend Trinculo.

STEPHANO. If thou beest Trinculo, come forth. I'll pull thee by the lesser legs. If any be Trinculo's legs, these are they. [*Draws him out from under* CALIBAN'*s garment.*] Thou art very Trinculo indeed! How cam'st thou to be the siege[21] of this mooncalf?[22] Can he vent Trinculos?

TRINCULO. I took him to be killed with a thunderstroke. But art thou not drowned, Stephano? I hope now thou art not drowned. Is the storm overblown? I hid me under

14. recover: Cure.

15. trod on neat's leather: Walked on cowhide; an ancient folk saying.

16. I . . . him: However much I get for him will not be enough.

17. anon: Soon.

18. cat: An allusion to a popular saying of the day: "Ale will make a cat talk."

19. chaps: Slang for mouth.

20. spoon: Another allusion to a proverb: "He who eats with the devil must have a long spoon."

21. siege: Human waste; excrement.

22. mooncalf: Monster.

the dead mooncalf's gaberdine for fear of the storm. And art thou living, Stephano? O, Stephano! two Neapolitans scaped!

STEPHANO. Prithee do not turn me about; my stomach is not constant.

CALIBAN. [*Aside*] These be fine things, and if they be not sprites.
24 That's a brave god and bears celestial liquor.
I will kneel to him.

STEPHANO. How didst thou scape? How cam'st thou hither? Swear by this bottle how thou cam'st hither. I escaped upon a butt of sack which the sailors heaved o'erboard—by this bottle which I made of the bark of a tree with mine own hands since I was cast ashore.

CALIBAN. I'll swear upon that bottle to be thy true subject, for the liquor is not earthly.

STEPHANO. Here! Swear then how thou escap'dst.

TRINCULO. Swum ashore, man, like a duck. I can swim like a duck, I'll be sworn.

25 **STEPHANO.** Here, kiss the book. [*Gives him drink.*] Though thou canst swim like a duck, thou art made like a goose.

TRINCULO. O Stephano, hast any more of this?

STEPHANO. The whole butt,[23] man. My cellar is in a rock by th' seaside, where my wine is hid. How now, mooncalf? How does thine ague?

CALIBAN. Hast thou not dropped from heaven?

STEPHANO. Out o' th' moon, I do assure thee. I was the Man i' th' Moon when time was.[24]

CALIBAN. I have seen thee in her, and I do adore thee. My mistress showed me thee, and thy dog, and thy bush.[25]

26 **STEPHANO.** Come, swear to that; kiss the book. [*Gives him drink.*] I will furnish it anon with new contents. Swear. [CALIBAN *drinks.*]

TRINCULO. By this good light, this is a very shallow monster! I afeard of him? A very weak monster. The Man i' th' Moon? A most poor credulous monster! Well drawn,[26] monster, in good sooth!

CALIBAN. I'll show thee every fertile inch o' th' island; and I will kiss thy foot. I prithee, be my god.

23. butt: A large cask of wine.

24. when time was: Once upon a time; in time past.

25. thee . . . bush: According to popular legend, the man in the moon was exiled there because he gathered firewood on Sunday, a day of rest and prayer. Gathering firewood was considered work. His dog was with him at the time.

26. Well drawn: Good long drink of wine.

24 **Discussion** Why is Caliban so eager to see Stephano as a god?

25 **Discussion** What does Stephano mean when he says "kiss the book"?

26 **Discussion** What effect does Stephano's joke about being the "Man i' th' Moon" have on Caliban?

27 Discussion Why does Stephano assume that the king and his party are drowned?

28 Discussion Why does Caliban shout that he is free?

29 Enrichment The word *brave* comes from the Latin word *barbarus*, which meant "barbarous." Ask for a student volunteer to trace the growth in meaning of the word *brave* in an unabridged dictionary or the *Oxford English Dictionary.* Have this student report on his or her findings to the class.

TRINCULO. By this light, a most perfidious and drunken monster! When's god's asleep, he'll rob his bottle.

CALIBAN. I'll kiss thy foot. I'll swear myself thy subject.

STEPHANO. Come on then. Down, and swear!

TRINCULO. I shall laugh myself to death at this puppy-headed monster. A most scurvy monster! I could find in my heart to beat him—

STEPHANO. Come, kiss.

TRINCULO. But that the poor monster's in drink. An abominable monster!

CALIBAN. I'll show thee the best springs; I'll pluck thee berries;
I'll fish for thee, and get thee wood enough.
A plague upon the tyrant that I serve!
I'll bear him no more sticks, but follow thee,
Thou wondrous man.

TRINCULO. A most ridiculous monster, to make a wonder of a poor drunkard!

CALIBAN. I prithee let me bring thee where crabs[27] grow;
And I with my long nails will dig thee pignuts,[28]
Show thee a jay's nest, and instruct thee how
To snare the nimble marmoset.[29] I'll bring thee
To clust'ring filberts,[30] and sometimes I'll get thee
Young scamels[31] from the rock. Wilt thou go with me?

27 STEPHANO. I prithee now, lead the way without any more talking. Trinculo, the King and all our company else being drowned, we will inherit here. Here, bear my bottle. Fellow Trinculo, we'll fill him by and by again. [CALIBAN *sings drunkenly.*]

CALIBAN. Farewell, master; farewell, farewell!

TRINCULO. A howling monster! A drunken monster!

CALIBAN.
No more dams I'll make for fish,
Nor fetch in firing
At requiring,
Nor scrape trenchering,[32] nor wash dish
'Ban, 'Ban, Ca—Caliban
Has a new master. Get a new man!

28 Freedom, high day! High day, freedom! Freedom, high day, freedom!

29 STEPHANO. O brave monster! Lead the way. [*Exit.*]

27. crabs: Crabapples.
28. pignuts: Roots or other underground tubers; earthnuts.
29. marmoset: A small New World monkey found in Central America.
30. filberts: Hazel trees.
31. scamels: An unknown word. Perhaps a misspelling of "seamels" or "sea mews," a sea gull, which often builds its nest on the rocks that line the shore.
32. trenchering: Wooden platters used as dishes for food.

Answers

ANSWERS TO THINKING ABOUT THE SELECTION
Recalling

1. Sebastian feels that if Alonso had not insisted on this marriage, against everyone's advice, they would not be shipwrecked on the island.
2. (a) Prospero sends Ariel to put a sleeping charm on Sebastian and Antonio. This turns out to be a device to get them to reveal their true selves. (b) Sebastian and Antonio plot to kill Alonso and put Sebastian, his brother, in his place as king. (c) Alonso and Gonzalo are told that Sebastian and Antonio have heard a terrible roar, probably a "whole herd of lions," and that they have drawn their swords to protect Gonzalo and Alonso. The king and his councilor believe their story.
3. Caliban hides under his garment when he hears Trinculo coming and Trinculo hides under the garment with him when he hears Sebastian, who is in a drunken stupor, coming. Neither one of them covers his feet, hence four feet appear to be coming from one body.
4. (a) Stephano, the king's butler, has floated to safety on the barrel in which the liquor supply was kept. He evidently got thirsty on the trip. (b) He believes that Stephano is powerful and bears celestial liquor. Caliban wants so desperately to be out from under Prospero's power that he is willing to serve anyone else whom he thinks can take him away from Prospero. (c) Caliban promises to show him all the natural resources on the island, basically the same thing that he did to win Prospero's favor.

THINKING ABOUT THE SELECTION

Recalling

1. Who does Sebastian hold responsible for their misfortune and why?
2. (a) Why do Gonzalo and Alonso fall asleep? (b) What do Sebastian and Antonio attempt to do while the king and his councilor are asleep? (c) When they wake up, what do Alonso and Gonzalo believe has happened?
3. Describe how Caliban and Trinculo end up looking like a four-legged monster.
4. (a) Why is Stephano drunk? (b) Why does Caliban believe him to be a god? (c) What does Caliban promise to do for Stephano?

Interpreting

5. One of the conflicts in *The Tempest* is between two theories—the first that "natural" man is man at his best and the second theory that "nurtured" (or civilized) man is man at his best. Put each of the characters who has been introduced thus far into one of the categories and label each character as either good or evil.
6. The main plot and several subplots are already being developed by Act II of *The Tempest*. Draw a chart showing the main plot and subplots, indicating how the various subplots are related to the main plot.
7. Antonio and Sebastian appear to be good men who are loyal to the king. What is the reality of the situation?

Applying

8. The American writer Margaret Fuller wrote, "The civilized man is a larger mind but a more imperfect nature than the savage." React to this statement.

ANALYZING LITERATURE

Understanding Stock Characters

The kind of character who is familiar and predictable because of having appeared under different names in many different literary works is called a stock character, or stereotype. In *The Tempest*, there are several characters who could be considered stock characters. Stephano, the drunken buffoon of a servant to the king, is a recurring character type in plays and stories. Stephano's function is to offer comic relief to what is quickly becoming a potentially dangerous situation for the major characters.

1. Ariel, despite his winning ways, is a stock character. Why?
2. Evil monsters are commonly found in literature; however, Caliban is not a stock character. Why not?

UNDERSTANDING LANGUAGE

Recognizing Diction as a Character Trait

The words and phrases a character uses can show a great deal about the character. Ariel's musical rhyming speech, for example, helps convey the aery quality and goodness of this cheery sprite. By contrast, the speech of Caliban, particularly at the beginning of Act II, Scene ii, portrays him as primarily an evil and soulless animallike being, whom Prospero taught to speak but who only learned to "curse."

1. How does Gonzalo's diction help to characterize him as a man of goodness? Use examples from the play to support your answer.
2. How does Antonio's diction help to characterize him as a man of selfishness and evil? Use examples from the play.

THINKING AND WRITING

Writing About a Character's Function

In *The Tempest*, Trinculo and Stephano offer comic relief as they parallel the actions of Antonio and Sebastian. Ariel, also a stock character, serves his own function. Write a composition in which you explain what Ariel does in Act II to move the plot, develop character, convey theme, or otherwise add interest to the play. First, reread Ariel's part, asking yourself what dramatic function this lyrical spirit serves. Take notes, organize them, and write a first draft of your paper. Be certain that you have answered the basic question: What does Ariel, a stock character, do that makes his appearance in the paper important? When you revise your paper, check it for spelling errors. The names of some of the characters are easy to misspell.

Interpreting

5. Suggested response: Prospero—nurtured, good; Miranda—nurtured, good; Ferdinand—nurtured, good; Alonso—nurtured, in question; Gonzalo—nurtured, good; Antonio—nurtured, evil; Sebastian—nurtured, evil; Caliban—natural, evil; Ariel—supernatural, good, Stephano—in question; Trinculo—in question.

6. Plot: Prospero seeks to punish those who took his dukedom away.
   Subplot: Ferdinard and Miranda are trying to get together.
   Subplot: Antonio and Sebastian are plotting to kill Alonso.
   Subplot: Trinculo, Stephano, and Caliban are plotting to kill Prospero.
   Subplot: Ariel and Caliban are both working to win their freedom.

7. Sebastian and Antonio want power and control for themselves. They will stoop to anything, including murder, to get what they want.

Applying

8. This statement supports the idea of the noble savage. Some students will agree, claiming that human beings are instrinsically good, while others will disagree, claiming that human beings are flawed and so must be civilized.

(Answers begin on p. 344.)

Challenge Prepare a formal classroom debate on the topic of nature versus nurture.

ANSWERS TO ANALYZING LITERATURE

1. Ariel is a stock character because he doesn't change or develop personally during the play.
2. Caliban is more than a stock character because, even though he doesn't develop much as a character he shows potential for being different from what he is. This potential gives him more dimension than the standard stock character.

ANSWERS TO CRITICAL THINKING AND READING

1. (a) Prospero has Ariel put a charm on them so that they will fall asleep, thereby creating an opportunity for Sebastian and Antonio to reveal their true characters. (b) Antonio convinces Sebastian that the fates must have given them this chance to kill the king and his party, giving the crown to Sebastian.
2. Sebastian and Antonio want power and control for themselves and will do anything, including committing murder, to get it.

ANSWERS TO UNDERSTANDING LANGUAGE

1. Suggested Response: Gonzalo's speech is characterized by his attempts to make peace among his companions (Scene i, lines 1–9) and his desire for the ideal society, (Scene i, lines 152–169).
2. Suggested Response: Antonio's speech is characterized by his attempts to find the negative in every situation (Scene i, lines 145–148) and his plotting to gain control and power, (Scene i, lines 207–224).

THINKING AND WRITING

Publishing Student Writing You might have a group of student edit and publish a booklet called *Commentaries on the Tempest.* These editors would select the best examples of students' critical writing to appear in this booklet.

Literary Focus Characters are an important part of drama. Just as writers use comparison and contrast as a way of putting their characters and ideas in sharper focus, so can readers use comparison and contrast to enhance their understanding of a literary work. By comparing and contrasting characters and events of the work with people and situations in other literary works or in their own lives, readers can increase their comprehension.

Look For Some students benefit from "mapping" the information that they are to learn. As they read, give them the option of making a four-column chart with the major characters in the first column and a list of their characteristics in the second column. In the third column, have them put the name of a character from a story or a person that they know who is like that character, and in the fourth column, the name of someone who represents the opposite.

Writing With **less advanced** students, you may wish to make this a class-discussion activity, listing the comparisons and contrasts on the blackboard.

Vocabulary The phoenix myth is one of the most important in Shakespearean and Elizabethan literature. You might have one of your students give an oral report on this fabulous bird and its significance in literature. **More advanced** students can be directed to Shakespeare's strange metaphysical funeral poem, "The Phoenix and the Turtle."

GUIDE FOR READING

The Tempest, Act III

The Writer's Techniques

Characters. As the plots and subplots of a play unfold during the rising action, the circumstances in which the major characters find themselves become increasingly complex. The reactions of these characters help shed light not only on the characters themselves but on the course of the plot and subplots. As a character develops, the audience and reader learn to predict what that character will do in new situations and in different situations based on what that character has done in the past. To make the development of a character more clear, writers often compare and contrast that character and his or her actions to another character. For example, in Act III, Scene i, Shakespeare clearly portrays Ferdinand's goodness and Caliban's hatefulness by contrasting Ferdinand's willingness to haul logs for Prospero with Caliban's anger at having to perform the same task in Act II, Scene ii.

Look For

As you read *The Tempest,* Act III, watch for the use of comparison and contrast to describe and develop the characters.

Writing

List some of the ways the following characters were compared and contrasted in Acts I and II: Caliban and Ariel, Prospero and Antonio, and the boatswain and Gonzalo. Include what you learned about each character from what was compared and contrasted.

Vocabulary

Knowing the following words will help you as you read *The Tempest,* Act III.

odious (ō′ dē ə s) *adj.*: Exciting repugnance or aversion; abhorrent; hateful (Sc. i, l. 5).
jocund (jäk′ ənd) *adj.*: Cheerful; pleasant (Sc. ii, l. 122).
phoenix (fē′ niks) *n.*: A fabled bird of Arabia said to consume itself by fire every five hundred years and to rise renewed from its own ashes (Sc. iii, l. 23).
surfeit (sur′ fit) *n.*: Too much of something; an excess (Sc. iii, l. 55).

Objectives

1. To understand characters in drama
2. To recognize plays on words
3. To choose the meaning that fits the context
4. To compare and contrast characters

Teaching Portfolio

Teacher Backup, p. 00

Vocabulary Check, p. 00

Usage and Mechanics Worksheet, p. 00

Analyzing Literature Worksheet, p. 00

Critical Thinking and Reading Worksheet, p. 00

Understanding Language Worksheet, p. 00

Selection Test, p. 00

Art Transparency 5, *The Storm, Antigonus Pursued by the Bear* by Joseph Wright, p. 00

Act III

1 **Scene i.** *In front of Prospero's cell.*

[*Enter* FERDINAND, *bearing a log.*]

FERDINAND. There be some sports are painful, and their labor
Delight in them sets off;[1] some kinds of baseness
Are nobly undergone, and most poor matters
Point to rich ends. This my mean task
Would be as heavy to me as odious, but
2 The mistress which I serve quickens[2] what's dead
And makes my labors pleasures. O, she is
Ten times more gentle than her father's crabbed;
And he's composed of harshness. I must remove
Some thousands of these logs and pile them up,
Upon a sore injunction.[3] My sweet mistress
Weeps when she sees me work, and says such baseness
Had never like executor. I forget;[4]
But these sweet thoughts do even refresh my labors,
Most busiest when I do it.[5]

[*Enter* MIRANDA; *and* PROSPERO *(behind, unseen).*]

MIRANDA. Alas, now pray you,
Work not so hard! I would the lightning had
Burnt up those logs that you are enjoined to pile!
Pray set it down and rest you. When this burns,
'Twill weep[6] for having wearied you. My father
Is hard at study; pray now rest yourself;
He's safe for these three hours.

FERDINAND. O most dear mistress,
The sun will set before I shall discharge
What I must strive to do.

MIRANDA. If you'll sit down,
3 I'll bear your logs the while. Pray give me that;
I'll carry it to the pile.

FERDINAND. No, precious creature,
I had rather crack my sinews, break my back,
Than you should such dishonor undergo
While I sit lazy by.

MIRANDA. It would become me
As well as it does you; and I should do it
With much more ease; for my good will is to it,
And yours it is against.

1. sets off: Cancels or balances the pain.

2. quickens: Enlivens; animates; brings to life.

3. Upon a sore injunction: Upon a threat of harsh punishment.

4. I forget: I neglect my chores.

5. Most . . . it: A corrupted text, generally interpreted to mean "my thoughts of my mistress are busiest when I am hardest at work."

6. weep: Ooze a resinous sap.

Motivation for Reading Tell students that they are going to be encountering a different, very human conflict in each of the three scenes in Act III. As they determine what each conflict is, have them compare and contrast each with a conflict that they have read about elsewhere in literature.

Master Teacher Note Point out that in the structure of Act III, Shakespeare makes use of sharply contrasting scenes. Those involving Caliban, Stephano, and Trinculo contain much comic relief, in contrast with the serious scenes involving other characters, especially Miranda and Ferdinand.

Purpose-Setting Question How does Shakespeare use comparisons and contrasts to further the plot and subplots and the development of the characters?

1 **Reading Strategy** Have a volunteer summarize the action in Act II, scene ii. Remind students as they read, to compare this scene of Act III with the previous scene.

2 **Literary Focus** What is the comparison in this passage and how does the comparison help develop Ferdinand's and Miranda's characters?

3 **Clarification** Miranda's offer to help carry the logs for Ferdinand, who is now tantamount to a servant, stands in stark contrast to what was an acceptable activity for a woman of her station at that time. This contrast shows us even more clearly how unaffected by society's rules Miranda is and how honestly she acts from her heart.

Master Teacher Note After the class has read and discussed the first two acts of *The Tempest,* display Art Transparency 5, *The Storm, Antiqonus Pursued by the Bear* by Joseph Wright, on the overhead projector. Mention that this painting is based on a scene in another late play of Shakespeare's, *The Winter's Tale.* Ask your students whether the overall impression they get from this painting resembles the impression they have gotten from their reading of *The Tempest.* Is there any aspect of the painting that recalls a scene from the play? Which one?

PROSPERO. [*Aside*] Poor worm, thou art infected!
This visitation[7] shows it.

MIRANDA. You look wearily.

FERDINAND. No, noble mistress, 'tis fresh morning with me
When you are by at night. I do beseech you,
Chiefly that I might set it in my prayers,
What is your name?

MIRANDA. Miranda. O my father,
I have broke your hest to say so!

FERDINAND. Admired Miranda![8]
Indeed the top of admiration, worth
What's dearest to the world! Full many a lady
I have eyed with best regard, and many a time
Th' harmony of their tongues hath into bondage
4 Brought my too diligent ear. For several virtues
Have I liked several women; never any
With so full soul but some defect in her
Did quarrel with the noblest grace she owed,
And put it to the foil.[9] But you, O you,
So perfect and so peerless, are created
Of every creature's best.

MIRANDA. I do not know
One of my sex; no woman's face remember,
Save, from my glass, mine own. Nor have I seen
More that I may call men than you, good friend,
And my dear father. How features are abroad
I am skilless[10] of; but, by my modesty
(The jewel in my dower), I would not wish
Any companion in the world but you;
Nor can imagination form a shape,
Besides yourself, to like of. But I prattle
5 Something too wildly, and my father's precepts
I therein do forget.

FERDINAND. I am, in my condition,
A prince, Miranda; I do think, a king
(I would not so), and would no more endure
This wooden slavery than to suffer
The fleshfly blow[11] my mouth. Hear my soul speak!
The very instant that I saw you, did
My heart fly to your service; there resides,
To make me slave to it; and for your sake
Am I this patient log-man.

MIRANDA. Do you love me?

7. visitation: Visit.

8. Admired Miranda: "Admire" comes from the Latin *to wonder* and the name "Miranda" derives from the Latin *mirandus* meaning "wonderful."

9. put it to the foil: Put it to the test, which it failed.

10. skilless: Ignorant.

11. blow: Befoul; contaminate; pollute.

4 **Discussion** What does Ferdinand tell Miranda and reveal to you about his past in this passage?

5 **Discussion** The story of Ferdinand and Miranda was especially treasured during Victorian times. Why would an age that is often characterized by its sentimentality so favor this love story?

6 Discussion Miranda again shows her openness. Why does she weep? What does she ask of Ferdinand? What does she promise to do if his answer is "no"?

7 Discussion The name Miranda is based on the Latin word *mirandus*, meaning "wonderful or strange." Why is this name appropriate for this character?

FERDINAND. O heaven, O earth, bear witness to this sound,
And crown what I profess with kind event
If I speak true! If hollowly, invert
What best is boded me[12] to mischief! I,
Beyond all limit of what else i' th' world,
Do love, prize, honor you.

MIRANDA. I am a fool
To weep at what I am glad of.

PROSPERO. [*Aside*] Fair encounter
Of two most rare affections! Heavens rain grace
On that which breeds between 'em!

FERDINAND. Wherefore weep you?

MIRANDA. At mine unworthiness, that dare not offer
What I desire to give, and much less take
What I shall die to want.[13] But this is trifling;[14]
6 And all the more it seeks to hide itself,
The bigger bulk it shows. Hence, bashful cunning,
And prompt me, plain and holy innocence!
I am your wife, if you will marry me;
If not, I'll die your maid. To be your fellow[15]
You may deny me; but I'll be your servant,
Whether you will or no.

FERDINAND. My mistress, dearest,
And I thus humble ever.

MIRANDA. My husband then?

FERDINAND. Ay, with a heart as willing
7 As bondage e'er of freedom.[16] Here's my hand.

MIRANDA. And mine, with my heart in't; and now farewell
Till half an hour hence.

FERDINAND. A thousand thousand!
[*Exit* (FERDINAND *and* MIRANDA *in different directions*).]

PROSPERO. So glad of this as they I cannot be,
Who are surprised withal;[17] by my rejoicing
At nothing can be more. I'll to my book;
For yet ere suppertime must I perform
Much business appertaining.[18] [*Exit.*]

Scene ii. *Another part of the island.*

[*Enter* CALIBAN, STEPHANO, *and* TRINCULO.]

STEPHANO. Tell me not! When the butt is out, we will drink water; not a drop before. Therefore bear up and board 'em![1] Servant monster, drink to me.

12. What . . . me: What good fortune will be given me.

13. want: Lack; be without.

14. But . . . trifling: But words cannot express my feelings.

15. fellow: Partner.

16. as willing . . . freedom: As eagerly as a prisoner is to gain his freedom.

17. withal: By it all.

18. appertaining: Relating (to my plans).

1. bear . . . 'em: An old seaman's expression meaning "drink up."

TRINCULO. Servant monster? The folly of this island! They say there's but five upon this isle; we are three of them. If th' other two be brained like us, the state totters.

STEPHANO. Drink, servant monster, when I bid thee; thy eyes are almost set in thy head.

TRINCULO. Where should they be set else? He were a brave monster indeed if they were set in his tail.

STEPHANO. My man-monster hath drowned his tongue in sack.[2] For my part, the sea cannot drown me. I swam, ere I could recover the shore, five-and-thirty leagues off and on, by this light. Thou shalt be my lieutenant, monster, or my standard.[3]

TRINCULO. Your lieutenant, if you list;[4] he's no standard.

STEPHANO. We'll not run, Monsieur Monster.

TRINCULO. Nor go neither; but you'll lie like dogs, and yet say nothing neither.

STEPHANO. Mooncalf, speak once in thy life, if thou beest a good mooncalf.

CALIBAN. How does thy honor? Let me lick thy shoe. I'll not serve him; he is not valiant.

8 **TRINCULO.** Thou liest, most ignorant monster; I am in case to justle a constable.[5] Why, thou deboshed[6] fish thou, was there ever man a coward that hath drunk so much sack as I today? Wilt thou tell a monstrous lie, being but half a fish and half a monster?

CALIBAN. Lo, how he mocks me! Wilt thou let him, my lord?

TRINCULO. "Lord" quoth he? That a monster should be such a natural![7]

CALIBAN. Lo, lo, again! Bite him to death, I prithee.

STEPHANO. Trinculo, keep a good tongue in your head. If you prove a mutineer—the next tree![8] The poor monster's my subject, and he shall not suffer indignity.

CALIBAN. I thank my noble lord. Wilt thou be pleased to hearken once again to the suit I made to thee?

STEPHANO. Marry,[9] will I. Kneel and repeat it; I will stand, and so shall Trinculo.

9 [*Enter* ARIEL, *invisible.*]

CALIBAN. As I told thee before, I am subject to a tyrant,
A sorcerer, that by his cunning hath
Cheated me of the island.

2. **sack:** A white wine.

3. **standard:** Standard bearer, but Caliban can barely stand.

4. **if you list:** If you wish. In sailor's jargon, "list" means "lean to one side," as an injured ship or a drunken man.

5. **I am . . . constable:** I am in good enough condition to fight a policeman.

6. **deboshed:** Drunken; debauched.

7. **natural:** Fool; idiot.

8. **the next tree:** An elliptical expression for "You'll hang from the next tree."

9. **Marry:** An exclamation meaning "By the Virgin Mary!"

8 **Critical Thinking and Reading** Discuss with the students the humor in the use of the word *monstrous* regarding a lie that is being told by someone who is only half monster. Point out that lines such as these are even more humorous when delivered on stage by a comic actor who can add gestures and timing to his delivery.

9 **Enrichment** Some modern productions of this play have sought to emphasize its other-worldly aspects. One production at Yale University, for example, set the play in a spaceship. Ask students to discuss how they would stage the play to emphasize its miraculous qualities.

10 Discussion How do Ariel's interruptions complicate matters for Caliban, Stephano, and Trinculo?

11 Reading Strategy Relate this passage to any comedy routine done by a group of comedians, such as the Three Stooges. The students' prior knowledge and experience with such a performance will help them to understand more fully the comic effect of this passage.

10 **ARIEL.** Thou liest.

CALIBAN. Thou liest, thou jesting monkey
thou!
I would my valiant master would destroy thee.
I do not lie.

STEPHANO. Trinculo, if you trouble him any more in's tale,
11 by this hand, I will supplant some of your teeth.

TRINCULO. Why, I said nothing.

STEPHANO. Mum then, and no more. Proceed.

CALIBAN. I say by sorcery he got this isle;
From me he got it. If thy greatness will
Revenge it on him—for I know thou dar'st,
But this thing[10] dare not—

10. this thing: Trinculo.

STEPHANO. That's most certain.

CALIBAN. Thou shalt be lord of it, and I'll serve thee.

STEPHANO. How now shall this be compassed?
Canst thou bring me to the party?

CALIBAN. Yea, yea, my lord! I'll yield him thee asleep,
Where thou mayst knock a nail into his head.

ARIEL. Thou liest; thou canst not.

CALIBAN. What a pied[11] ninny's this! Thou scurvy patch![12]
I do beseech thy greatness, give him blows
And take his bottle from him. When that's gone,
He shall drink naught but brine, for I'll not show him
Where the quick freshes[13] are.

STEPHANO. Trinculo, run into no further danger! Interrupt the monster one word further and, by this hand, I'll turn my mercy out o' doors and make a stockfish[14] of thee.

TRINCULO. Why, what did I? I did nothing. I'll go farther off.

STEPHANO. Didst thou not say he lied?

ARIEL. Thou liest.

STEPHANO. Do I so? Take thou that! [*Strikes* TRINCULO.] As you like this, give me the lie another time.

TRINCULO. I did not give the lie. Out o' your wits, and hearing too? A pox o' your bottle! This can sack and drinking do. A murrain[15] on your monster, and the devil take your fingers!

CALIBAN. Ha, ha, ha!

STEPHANO. Now forward with your tale. [*To* TRINCULO] Prithee, stand further off.

CALIBAN. Beat him enough. After a little time
I'll beat him too.

STEPHANO. Stand farther. Come, proceed.

CALIBAN. Why, as I told thee, 'tis a custom with him
I' th' afternoon to sleep. There thou mayst brain him,
Having first seized his books, or with a log
12 Batter his skull, or paunch[16] him with a stake,
Or cut his wezand[17] with thy knife. Remember
First to possess his books; for without them
He's but a sot,[18] as I am, nor hath not

11. pied: Many colored.
12. patch: Jester.
13. freshes: Fresh water streams.
14. stockfish: Dried and salted codfish.
15. murrain: Cattle disease.
16. paunch: Stab him in the belly.
17. wezand: Throat; windpipe.
18. sot: Fool.

12 **Discussion** Even Caliban, the epitome of the "natural" man, thinks he knows from where Prospero's power comes. What does he plan to do with Prospero's source of power?

13 Critical Thinking and Reading Discuss the understatement and the irony in this description of Miranda—she is indeed beautiful, more beautiful than a witch.

14 Discussion Discuss how this statement highlights Caliban's base nature. In what way does Caliban serve as a foil to Ferdinand?

One spirit to command. They all do hate him
As rootedly as I. Burn but his books.
He has brave utensils[19] (for so he calls them)
Which, when he has a house, he'll deck withal.
And that most deeply to consider is
The beauty of his daughter. He himself
Calls her a nonpareil.[20] I never saw a woman
13 But only Sycorax my dam and she;
But she as far surpasseth Sycorax
As great'st does least

STEPHANO. Is it so brave a lass?

CALIBAN. Ay, lord. She will become thy bed, I warrant,
14 And bring thee forth brave brood.

STEPHANO. Monster, I will kill this man. His daughter and I will be King and Queen—save our Graces!—And Trinculo and thyself shall be viceroys. Dost thou like the plot, Trinculo?

TRINCULO. Excellent.

STEPHANO. Give me thy hand. I am sorry I beat thee; but while thou liv'st, keep a good tongue in thy head.

CALIBAN. Within this half hour will he be asleep.
Wilt thou destroy him then?

STEPHANO. Ay, on mine honor.

ARIEL. This will I tell my master.

CALIBAN. Thou mak'st me merry; I am full of pleasure.
Let us be jocund. Will you troll the catch[21]
You taught me but whilere?[22]

STEPHANO. At thy request, monster, I will do reason, any reason. Come on, Trinculo, let us sing. [*Sings.*]

Flout 'em and scout[23] 'em
And scout 'em and flout 'em!
Thought is free.

CALIBAN. That's not the tune.
[ARIEL *plays the tune on a tabor*[24] *and pipe.*]

STEPHANO. What is this same?

TRINCULO. This is the tune of our catch, played by the picture of Nobody.[25]

STEPHANO. If thou beest a man, show thyself in thy likeness. If thou beest a devil, take't as thou list.

TRINCULO. O, forgive me my sins!

19. utensils: Household furnishings.

20. nonpareil: From the French, meaning "without equal."

21. Will . . . catch: Will you sing the tune?

22. but whilere: Just now.

23. scout: Mock.

24. tabor: Small drum.

25. picture of Nobody: Possibly an allusion to a comedy called *No-body and Some-body.*

STEPHANO. He that dies pays all debts. I defy thee. Mercy upon us!

CALIBAN. Art thou afeard?

STEPHANO. No, monster, not I.

CALIBAN. Be not afeard; the isle is full of noises,
Sounds and sweet airs that give delight and hurt not.
Sometimes a thousand twangling instruments
Will hum about mine ears; and sometimes voices
15 That, if I then had waked after long sleep,
Will make me sleep again; and then, in dreaming,
The clouds methought would open and show riches
Ready to drop upon me, that, when I waked,
I cried to dream again.

STEPHANO. This will prove a brave kingdom to me, where I shall have my music for nothing.

CALIBAN. When Prospero is destroyed.

STEPHANO. That shall be by and by; I remember the story.

TRINCULO. The sound is going away; let's follow it, and after do our work.

STEPHANO. Lead, monster; we'll follow. I would I could see this taborer; he lays it on.

TRINCULO. [*To* CALIBAN] Wilt come? I'll follow Stephano.
[*Exit.*]

Scene iii. *Another part of the island.*

[*Enter* ALONSO, SEBASTIAN, ANTONIO, GONZALO, ADRIAN, FRANCISCO, *etc.*]

GONZALO. By'r Lakin,[1] I can go no further, sir;
My old bones aches. Here's a maze trod indeed
Through forthrights and meanders.[2] By your patience,
I needs must rest me.

ALONSO. Old lord, I cannot blame thee,
Who am myself attached[3] with weariness
To th' dulling of my spirits. Sit down and rest.
Even here I will put off my hope, and keep it
16 No longer for my flatterer. He is drowned
Whom thus we stray to find; and the sea mocks
Our frustrate search on land. Well, let him go.

17 **ANTONIO.** [*Aside to* SEBASTIAN] I am right glad that he's so out of hope.

1. **By'r Lakin:** Dialect, meaning "By our Lady."

2. **forthrights and meanders:** Straight and wandering paths.

3. **attached:** Afflicted; seized.

15 **Enrichment** Caliban tells Prospero at one point that the only benefit he has for having learned language is that he has learned to curse, a skill of which he makes good use. Caliban is given this passage to speak, one of the loveliest, most lyrical of the play because he is associated with the background of this magic island, which is created largely by poetry.

16 **Discussion** Why is Alonso willing to allow Gonzalo to stop and rest?

17 **Discussion** When do Sebastian and Antonio expect to carry out their plan?

18 **Discussion** How does Shakespeare use music to maintain the magical quality of this play?

19 **Discussion** What does this speech reveal about Antonio?

20 **Discussion** What does this speech reveal about Gonzalo?

21 **Discussion** What does Prospero mean in his comment?

Do not for one repulse forgo the purpose
That you resolved t' effect

SEBASTIAN. [*Aside to* ANTONIO] The next advantage
Will we take throughly.

ANTONIO. [*Aside to* SEBASTIAN] Let it be tonight;
For, now they are oppressed with travel, they
Will not nor cannot use such vigilance
As when they are fresh.

SEBASTIAN. [*Aside to* ANTONIO] I say tonight. No more.

18 *[Solemn and strange music; and* PROSPERO *on the top*[4] *(invisible). Enter several strange* SHAPES, *bringing in a banquet; and dance about it with gentle actions of salutations; and, inviting the King etc. to eat, they depart.*]

ALONSO. What harmony is this? My good friends, hark!

GONZALO. Marvelous sweet music!

ALONSO. Give us kind keepers,[5] heavens! What were these?

SEBASTIAN. A living drollery.[6] Now I will believe
That there are unicorns; that in Arabia
There is one tree, the phoenix' throne; one phoenix
At this hour reigning there.

19 **ANTONIO.** I'll believe both;
And what does else want credit, come to me,
And I'll be sworn 'tis true. Travelers ne'er did lie,
Though fools at home condemn 'em.

20 **GONZALO.** If in Naples
I should report this now, would they believe me
If I should say I saw such islanders?
(For certes[7] these are people of the island)
Who, though they are of monstrous shape, yet note,
Their manners are more gentle, kind, than of
Our human generation you shall find
Many—nay, almost any.

21 **PROSPERO.** [*Aside*] Honest lord,
Thou hast said well; for some of you there present
Are worse than devils.

ALONSO. I cannot too much muse[8]
Such shapes, such gesture, and such sound, expressing
(Although they want the use of tongue) a kind
Of excellent dumb discourse.

PROSPERO. [*Aside*] Praise in departing.[9]

4. on the top: A stage direction indicating that Prospero is to stand at the rear of the stage or possibly on a structure above it so as to seem invisible to the characters onstage.

5. kind keepers: Good protectors or guardian angels.

6. living drollery: A puppet show, such as Punch 'n' Judy, but using live actors; perhaps a masque.

7. certes: Certain; sure.

8. muse: Wonder at; ponder.

9. Praise in departing: Keep your praise until you leave.

FRANCISCO. They vanished strangely.

SEBASTIAN. No matter, since
They have left their viands[10] behind; for we have stomachs.
Will't please you taste of what is here?

ALONSO. Not I.

GONZALO. Faith, sir, you need not fear. When we were boys,
Who should believe that there were mountaineers
Dewlapped[11] like bulls, whose throats had hanging at 'em
Wallets of flesh? Or that there were such men
Whose heads stood in their breasts? Which now we find
Each putter-out of five for one will bring us
Good warrant of.[12]

ALONSO. I will stand to, and feed;
Although my last, no matter, since I feel
The best is past. Brother, my lord the Duke,
Stand to, and do as we.

22 *[Thunder and lightning. Enter* ARIEL, *like a harpy;*[13] *claps his wings upon the table; and with a quaint device*[14] *the banquet vanishes.]*

ARIEL. You are three men of sin, whom destiny—
That hath to instrument[15] this lower world
And what is in't—the never-surfeited sea
Hath caused to belch up you and on this island,
Where man doth not inhabit, you 'mongst men
Being most unfit to live. I have made you mad;
And even with suchlike valor men hang and drown
Their proper selves.[16]
[ALONSO, SEBASTIAN, *etc. draw their swords.*]
You fools! I and my fellows
23 Are ministers of Fate. The elements,
Of whom your swords are tempered,[17] may as well
Wound the loud winds, or with bemocked-at stabs
Kill the still-closing waters, as diminish
One dowle that's in my plume.[18] My fellow ministers
Are like invulnerable.[19] If you could hurt,
Your swords are now too massy for your strengths[20]
And will not be uplifted. But remember
(For that's my business to you) that you three
From Milan did supplant good Prospero;
Exposed unto the sea, which hath requit it,[21]
Him and his innocent child; for which foul deed
The pow'rs, delaying, not forgetting, have
Incensed the seas and shores, yea, all the creatures,

10. viands: Food.

11. Dewlapped: Loose skin hanging from the neck of certain animals, such as cows and bulls.

12. Each . . . warrant of: Ordinary travelers (who take out insurance at which they are repaid five-to-one) confirm nowadays that such fanciful creatures actually exist.

13. harpy: A harpy is a mythical figure from ancient Greece who pursued those guilty of wrongdoing.

14. a quaint device: A stage mechanism, such as a puff of smoke and a trap door, that aids the banquet hidden by Ariel's harpy wings to "vanish."

15. to instrument: As its instrument.

16. even with . . . selves: With courage granted by madness men kill themselves.

17. tempered: Made.

18. dowle . . . plume: Fluffy little feather in my covering of feathers.

19. My fellow . . . invulnerable: My companions are as incapable of being harmed (as I am).

20. If you . . . strengths: But even if you could hurt us, your swords are too heavy for your strength.

21. requit it: Avenged that wrong.

22 **Discussion** Why is it appropriate that Ariel appears like a harpy?

23 **Discussion** Whom does Ariel address? What is each guilty of?

24 Discussion What does this speech reveal about Alonso?

25 Reading Strategy Have students summarize the events in the play up to this point.

Against your peace. Thee of thy son, Alonso,
They have bereft; and do pronounce by me
Ling'ring perdition (worse than any death
Can be at once) shall step by step attend
You and your ways; whose wraths to guard you from,
Which here, in this most desolate isle, else falls
Upon your heads, is nothing but heart's sorrow[22]
And a clear life ensuing.

[*He vanishes in thunder; then, to soft music, enter the* SHAPES *again, and dance with mocks and mows,*[23] *and carrying out the table.*]

PROSPERO. Bravely the figure of this harpy hast thou
Performed, my Ariel; a grace it had, devouring.[24]
Of my instruction hast thou nothing bated
In what thou hadst to say. So, with good life
And observation strange, my meaner ministers
Their several kinds have done.[25] My high charms work,
And these, mine enemies, are all knit up
In their distractions. They now are in my pow'r;
And in these fits I leave them, while I visit
Young Ferdinand, whom they suppose is drowned,
And his and mine loved darling. [*Exit above.*]

GONZALO. I' th' name of something holy, sir, why stand you
In this strange stare?

ALONSO. O, it is monstrous, monstrous!
Methought the billows spoke and told me of it;
The winds did sing it to me; and the thunder,
24 That deep and dreadful organ pipe, pronounced
The name of Prosper; it did bass my trespass.[26]
Therefore my son i' th' ooze is bedded; and
I'll seek him deeper than e'er plummet sounded
And with him there lie mudded. [*Exit.*]

SEBASTIAN. But one fiend at a time,
I'll fight their legions o'er![27]

ANTONIO. I'll be thy second.

[*Exit* SEBASTIAN *and* ANTONIO.]

GONZALO. All three of them are desperate; their great guilt,
Like poison given to work a great time after,
Now 'gins to bite the spirits. I do beseech you,
25 That are of suppler joints, follow them swiftly
And hinder them from what this ecstasy[28]
May not provoke them to.

ADRIAN. Follow, I pray you.

[*Exit all.*]

22. nothing . . . sorrow: Nothing but sincere repentance (will protect you from the wrath of the avenging powers).

23. mocks and mows: Derisive gestures and grimaces.

24. a grace . . . devouring: Your performance had an all-consuming grace.

25. with good life . . . done: With true-to-life acting and close attention to my wishes, your lower ranking companions—my agents—have performed their parts according to their natures.

26. bass my trespass: The bass part of nature's thunderous music made clear to me the wrong I did Prospero.

27. But one fiend . . . o'er: If they but put one devil against me at a time, I'll fight their armies to the last demon.

28. ecstasy: Insanity.

Answers

ANSWERS TO THINKING ABOUT THE SELECTION

Recalling

1. Ferdinand takes great pleasure in hauling logs because they will be used to warm his love, Miranda.
2. Because he wants Miranda and Ferdinand to fall in love, he listens in on their conversation to be certain that nothing goes wrong with his plan.
3. Alonso, Gonzalo, Sebastian, and Antonio are all astonished at the appearance of the spirits and the feast. Alonso is doubtful and has to be convinced that he should eat. When the food disappears, they are frightened and draw their swords to protect themselves.
4. Prospero compliments Ariel on a job well done, recognizes that his own charms have worked well, and tells Ariel that he must go check on Ferdinand and Miranda.

Interpreting

5. Prospero is delighted because their falling in love is part of his plan for making Miranda happy and resolving the conflicts between himself and Alonso.
6. Because Caliban sees him as a god and wants him to take over the island, Stephano becomes the

THINKING ABOUT THE SELECTION

Recalling

1. Why is Ferdinand happy to be carrying logs?
2. Explain why Prospero makes himself invisible and eavesdrops on the conversation between Miranda and Ferdinand.
3. Explain the reactions of each character to the banquet. What happens to it before they can begin eating?
4. What message does Prospero give Ariel near the end of Act III?

Interpreting

5. Explain how Prospero feels about Miranda and Ferdinand falling in love.
6. Describe the part that Stephano, Trinculo, and Caliban each play in the relationship of this unlikely trio.
7. How does the harpy's message help Prospero gain control over his adversaries?

Applying

8. Sebastian, Alonso, and Antonio realize that confronting one's own mistakes is a difficult thing to do. Why is it difficult to admit to being wrong?

ANALYZING LITERATURE

Understanding Characters

Writers compare and contrast characters in order to provide their readers and audience with a clear picture of what each represents.

1. Compare and contrast Stephano, Trinculo, and Caliban. Why does each decide to kill Prospero?
2. Compare and contrast the behavior of Sebastian and Antonio to that of Stephano and Trinculo.

CRITICAL THINKING AND READING

Recognizing Plays on Words

Writers often use plays on words to convey humor. Puns—plays on words based on the similarity of sound between two words with different meanings—offer a light way to send two messages, one seemingly serious, the other humorous. Irony—a figure of speech in which the actual intent is expressed in words that carry the opposite meaning—can be used the same way. The effectiveness of irony comes partly from the impression it gives of great restraint.

1. Identify the pun in Scene ii, ll. 34–35. What are the intended meanings?
2. Discuss the irony in Scene ii, ll. 5–7. What do you expect Trinculo to say? What does he say?
3. Discuss the irony in the exchange about Miranda between Caliban and Stephano in Scene ii, ll. 90–109.

UNDERSTANDING LANGUAGE

Finding Meaning That Fits the Context

The specific meanings of many words are determined by context. The word *foil* (Scene i, l. 46) has a number of possible meanings. When Ferdinand says, ". . . And put it to the foil," you know what kind of foil he means.

Use the context to determine the meaning of each of the following italicized words.

1. ". . . 'Twill *weep* for having wearied you." Scene i, l. 19
2. ". . . Did *quarrel* with the noblest grace she owed; . . ." Scene i, l. 45)
3. (". . . And *crown* what I profess with kind event . . ." (Scene i, l. 69)

THINKING AND WRITING

Writing About Comparison and Contrast

Write an essay that compares and contrasts Lady Macbeth and Miranda, the two major female characters in Shakespeare's plays *Macbeth* and *The Tempest*. Before you write, review each play, looking for each appearance of the women. Take notes on the characteristics of each one each time she appears. As you tell how they are similar and how they are different, include your own assessment of each character. When you go over your final draft, make sure you have included enough information so a reader who has not read either or both of the plays will understand what you have written.

(Answers begin on p. 358.)

leader while Caliban becomes a willing servant. Trinculo is happy to be a part of whatever his friend Stephano wants to do.

7. Alonso is already weakened because he believes that his precious son has drowned. The guilt he feels because of the harpy's message makes him even more vulnerable to Prospero's power. Sebastian and Antonio respond angrily to being made to feel guilty and rush off to challenge whatever is threatening them. They are out of control and desperate, and therefore vulnerable to Prospero's magic.

Applying

8. This question should provoke a lively class discussion. Although students' responses will differ, they should include vanity, self-esteem, and simple embarrassment.

ANSWERS TO ANALYZING LITERATURE

1. Stephano and Trinculo are both simple, lantish men who enter the plot mainly because they have been drinking too much. They are earthy and common without being as base as Caliban. Although Caliban is inhuman, more a monster than a man, he does display a sense of wonder that is lacking in Stephano and Trinculo. His motive for entering the plot is to gain his freedom, although, in fact, he would simply be trading one master for another.
2. Sebastian, Antonio, Stephano, and Trinculo all want to murder someone in order to take control—Sebastian and Antonio want to kill Alonso to take over his kingdom and Stephano and Trinculo want to kill Prospero to take over his island. Sebastian and Antonio are basically evil men who have both done this sort of thing before while Stephano and Trinculo are basically gentle men who are involved primarily because they are drunk.

ANSWERS TO CRITICAL THINKING AND READING

1. The word *natural* in lines 30-31 means "fool, idiot." It is also a reference to Caliban as representative of natural man as opposed to nurtured man—one of the themes of the play.
2. Normally, we expect people to praise themselves and their abilities; instead Trinculo says they are all in trouble if the other two people they know on the island are as dim-witted as the three of them.
3. Caliban tells Stephano that Miranda's beauty is unequaled—in fact, she is more beautiful than the only other woman he has seen, his mother, who was a witch. Caliban also comments on her bravery by saying that she is brave enough to marry Stephano, indicating that she must be brave indeed.

Challenge Have students find examples of other plays on words in Acts I, II, and III. Have them add to this list as they read Acts IV and V.

ANSWERS TO UNDERSTANDING LANGUAGE

1. Exude water or other liquid, as a wound
2. Dispute heatedly
3. Honor, dignify

THINKING AND WRITING

Publishing Student Writing Have students submit their essays to the booklet they submitted earlier called *Commentaries on the Tempest.*

Literary Focus The most effective incidents in a story are those that spring naturally from the characters. The most effective plot will present struggles that would be naturally engaged in by those characters. The function of a plot, therefore, is to translate a character or characters into action. In *The Tempest,* each character is translated into action by the main plot as well as by his or her own subplot. The interweaving of the plot and subplots results in the resolution of each of the plots, thus the resolution of the conflicts between the characters.

Look For Some of your students may benefit from graphically portraying the development of the plot and subplots. Have them draw a story map for each plot, indicating the climax and the denouement by event.

Writing Later, after the students have discovered the resolution of a plot, have them freewrite an alternative resolution of their own. If their prediction was different from the actual resolution, have them use that as the basis for their freewriting.

Vocabulary Have students select at least four of the five words and use them to write a paragraph describing two of the characters in the play and the relationship between them.

GUIDE FOR READING

The Tempest, Act IV

The Writer's Techniques

Resolution of Plot. The resolution of a plot (or subplot), sometimes called the denouement, occurs at the end of the falling action. The conflict with which the plot is concerned is resolved, and the outcome is made clear. The resolution does not necessarily tie up all the loose ends, however; that can come later. The resolution is seldom an instantaneous occurrence. When a plot has many subplots, the process of unraveling them all may take some time. If there are subplots, they may be resolved before or after the resolution of the main plot. As you know, *The Tempest* has a main plot and several subplots.

Main plot: concerns the conflict between Prospero and the men who took away his dukedom and put him in danger.

Subplot: concerns the ever-increasing love between Ferdinand and Miranda.

Subplot: concerns the plan that Caliban, Stephano, and Trinculo have cooked up to kill Prospero.

Subplot: concerns the plan that Antonio and Sebastian have to kill Alonso and put Sebastian in his place.

Subplot: concerns Ariel's desire to be free.

Look For

As you read *The Tempest,* Act IV, watch carefully for the resolution of the plot or any of the subplots. Notice what is—and what is not—resolved by the end of the act.

Writing

Jot down your predictions about how each of the plots will be resolved. Remember that because this is a comedy, there will be a happy ending. Remember, too, that not every plot will be resolved in Act IV. You may have to wait until Act V to find out whether some of your predictions are correct.

Vocabulary

Knowing the following words will help you read *The Tempest,* Act IV.

austere (ô stir′) *adj.*: Having a stern personality or appearance; somber (Sc. i, l. 1)

vexation (vek sā′ shən) *n.*: An annoyance (Sc. i, l. 5)

ardor (är′ dər) *n.*:Great warmth or intensity of passion, emotion, desire, and so forth (Sc. i, l. 56)

temperate (tem′pər it) *adj.*: Exercising moderation and self-restraint (Sc. i, l. 132)

canker (kaŋ′ kər) *n.*: An ulcer-like sore on the lips or in the mouth (Sc. i, l. 192)

Objectives

1. To recognize and predict the resolution of a plot
2. To understand cause-and-effect relationships in a plot
3. To write a resolution to a plot

Teaching Portfolio: Support Material

Teacher Backup, p. 00

Vocabulary Check, p. 00

Usage and Mechanics Worksheet, p. 00

Analyzing Literature Worksheet, p. 00

Critical Thinking and Reading Worksheet, p. 00

Language Worksheet, p. 00

Selection Test, p. 00

Scene i. *In front of Prospero's cell.*

[*Enter* PROSPERO, FERDINAND, *and* MIRANDA.]

PROSPERO. If I have too austerely punished you,
Your compensation makes amends; for I
Have given you here a third of mine own life,
1 Or that for which I live; who once again
I tender to thy hand. All thy vexations
Were but my trials of thy love, and thou
Hast strangely[1] stood the test. Here, afore heaven,
I ratify this my rich gift. O Ferdinand,
Do not smile at me that I boast her off,[2]
For thou shalt find she will outstrip all praise
And make it halt[3] behind her.

FERDINAND. I do believe it
Against an oracle.[4]

PROSPERO. Then, as my gift, and thine own acquisition
Worthily purchased, take my daughter. But
If thou dost break her virgin-knot before
All sanctimonious[5] ceremonies may
With full and holy rite be minist'red,
2 No sweet aspersion[6] shall the heavens let fall
To make this contract grow;[7] but barren hate,
Sour-eyed disdain, and discord shall bestrew
The union of your bed with weeds so loathly
That you shall hate it both. Therefore take heed,
As Hymen's lamps shall light you.[8]

FERDINAND. As I hope
For quiet days, fair issue, and long life,
With such love as 'tis now, the murkiest den,
The most opportune place, the strong'st suggestion
Our worser genius can,[9] shall never melt
Mine honor into lust, to take away
The edge[10] of that day's celebration
When I shall think or Phoebus' steeds[11] are foundered[12]
Or Night kept chained below.[13]

PROSPERO. Fairly spoke.
Sit then and talk with her; she is thine own.
What, Ariel![14] My industrious servant, Ariel!

[*Enter* ARIEL.]

ARIEL. What would my potent master? Here I am.

1. strangely: Wonderfully.
2. boast her off: Praise her to the sky.
3. halt: Limp.
4. I do . . . oracle: I believe you even if a prophet should say otherwise.
5. sanctimonious: Sacred; holy.
6. aspersion: Ritual sprinkling of water, as in a religious ceremony.
7. this contract grow: This marriage develop into a family.
8. As . . . you: As the lamps of the god of marriage burn clearly to light your way at the wedding ceremony.
9. worser genius can: Bad demon can make. (In medieval times, everyone had a good demon and a bad demon or set of angels watching over him or her. This was an inheritance from the ancient Greeks, who believed everyone had a personal demon.)
10. The edge: Intense pleasure.
11. Phoebus' steeds: The horses of Apollo the sun god. They pulled the sun god's chariot across the sky from dawn to dusk.
12. foundered: Made lame.
13. below: Below the horizon.
14. What, Ariel!: Here, Ariel! Come here, Ariel!

Motivation for Reading Humans make mistakes, some of which cause problems for others. How we react to making mistakes and to those who cause trouble for us plays an important role in what kind of character we develop. Have students think about an experience in which mistakes were involved. How did the person or persons affected by the mistakes react? How were the problems ultimately resolved?

Master Teacher Note Our first knowledge of *The Tempest* comes from its production at court on November 1, 1611, a year after the pamphlets about the *Sea Adventure* became available in England. In the winter of 1612–13, the play was presented again at court, this time as an appropriate part of the celebration of the marriage of James I's daughter, Princess Elizabeth, to Frederick the Elector Palatine. **More advanced** students might research and present an account of the festivities, including reactions to the presentation of *The Tempest.*

Speaking and Listening Have volunteers present the masque in Act IV as a readers' theater or as a staged play with costumes.

Purpose-Setting Question Which conflicts and plots are resolved in this act, and how are they resolved?

1 **Discussion** What leads Prospero to give his permission for Ferdinand and Miranda to marry?

2 **Discussion** Why does Prospero threaten Ferdinand?

3 Discussion Who are the "rabble" of whom Prospero speaks?

4 Discussion What is revealed about Ariel's character in the last line of this verse?

5 Literary Focus The following play within a play is part of the denouement of the young-love plot. The climax has come earlier, when Prospero recognized the love between Ferdinand and Miranda and gave his permission for them to marry. This subplot will finally be resolved when Alonso is made aware of the relationship and approves.

6 Enrichment Some critics feel that this marriage masque was added in honor of the marriage of Princess Elizabeth, daughter of King James, to Frederick the Elector Palatine. Why might Shakespeare have added material to please King James?

7 Discussion What is the meaning behind this line?

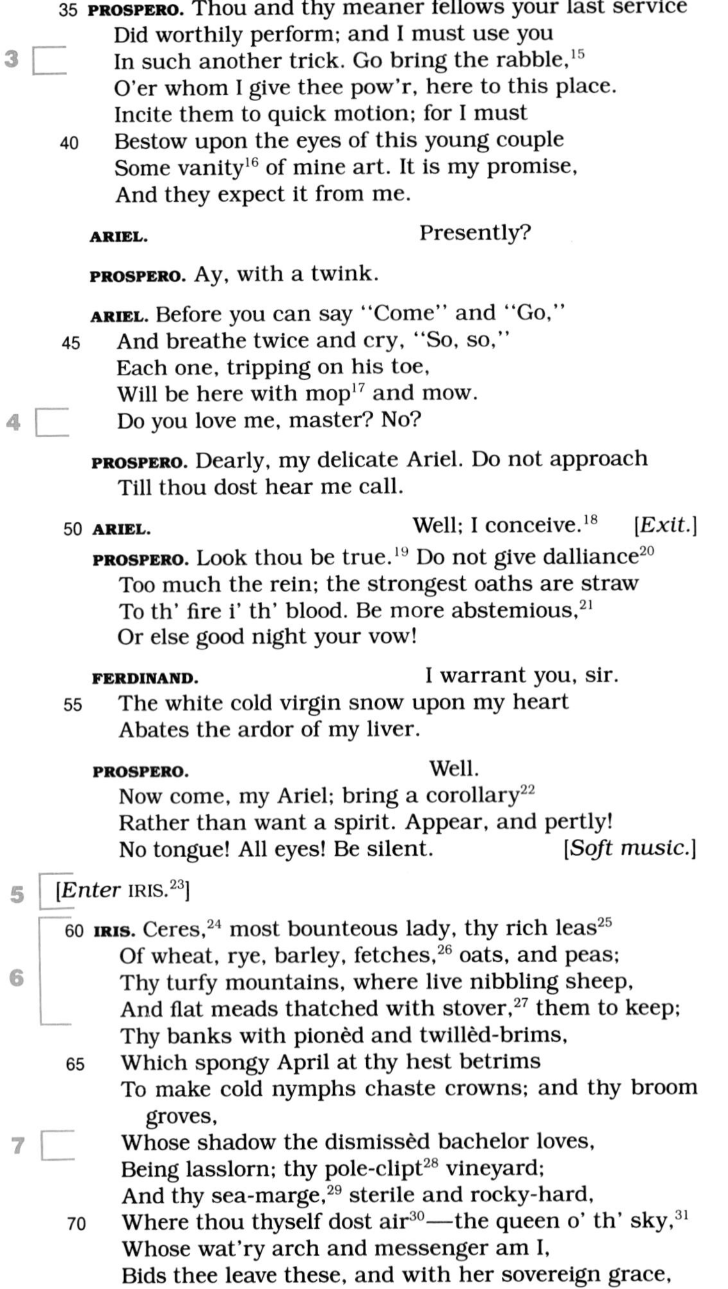

PROSPERO. Thou and thy meaner fellows your last service
Did worthily perform; and I must use you
3 In such another trick. Go bring the rabble,[15]
O'er whom I give thee pow'r, here to this place.
Incite them to quick motion; for I must
Bestow upon the eyes of this young couple
Some vanity[16] of mine art. It is my promise,
And they expect it from me.

ARIEL. Presently?

PROSPERO. Ay, with a twink.

ARIEL. Before you can say "Come" and "Go,"
And breathe twice and cry, "So, so,"
Each one, tripping on his toe,
Will be here with mop[17] and mow.
4 Do you love me, master? No?

PROSPERO. Dearly, my delicate Ariel. Do not approach
Till thou dost hear me call.

ARIEL. Well; I conceive.[18] [*Exit.*]

PROSPERO. Look thou be true.[19] Do not give dalliance[20]
Too much the rein; the strongest oaths are straw
To th' fire i' th' blood. Be more abstemious,[21]
Or else good night your vow!

FERDINAND. I warrant you, sir.
The white cold virgin snow upon my heart
Abates the ardor of my liver.

PROSPERO. Well.
Now come, my Ariel; bring a corollary[22]
Rather than want a spirit. Appear, and pertly!
No tongue! All eyes! Be silent. [*Soft music.*]

5 [*Enter* IRIS.[23]]

6 IRIS. Ceres,[24] most bounteous lady, thy rich leas[25]
Of wheat, rye, barley, fetches,[26] oats, and peas;
Thy turfy mountains, where live nibbling sheep,
And flat meads thatched with stover,[27] them to keep;
Thy banks with pionèd and twillèd-brims,
Which spongy April at thy hest betrims
To make cold nymphs chaste crowns; and thy broom groves,
7 Whose shadow the dismissèd bachelor loves,
Being lasslorn; thy pole-clipt[28] vineyard;
And thy sea-marge,[29] sterile and rocky-hard,
Where thou thyself dost air[30]—the queen o' th' sky,[31]
Whose wat'ry arch and messenger am I,
Bids thee leave these, and with her sovereign grace,

15. rabble: The lower ranking spirits; mob or disorderly collection of lower-class individuals.

16. vanity: Trifle; small, unimportant thing.

17. mop: Grin or gesture.

18. conceive: Comprehend; understand.

19. Look . . . true: [Addressed to Ferdinand and Miranda, who were embracing] Stop that! Be faithful to your promise.

20. dalliance: Amorous play; playful lovemaking.

21. abstemious: Moderate; sparing; restrained; controlled; temperate.

22. corollary: An extra spirit.

23. Iris: In classical mythology, a goddess who served as a messenger of the gods. Iris rode the rainbow to deliver her messages.

24. Ceres: The Roman goddess of the earth and agriculture.

25. leas: Meadows.

26. fetches: Vegetables, also clover, alfalfa, and soybeans.

27. meads . . . stover: Meadows having grasses used to feed cattle or sheep.

28. pole-clipt: Pruned.

29. sea-marge: The margin of the sea; seashore.

30. Where . . . air: Where you yourself stroll on holiday.

31. queen o' th' sky: Juno, the Roman goddess, queen of the gods.

362 *The English Renaissance*

[JUNO *descends.*[32]]

Here on this grass plot, in this very place,
To come and sport; her peacocks fly amain.[33]
Approach, rich Ceres, her to entertain.

[*Enter* CERES.]

CERES. Hail, many-colored messenger, that ne'er
Dost disobey the wife of Jupiter,[34]
Who, with thy saffron wings, upon my flow'rs
Diffusest honey drops, refreshing show'rs,
And with each end of thy blue bow dost crown
My bosky[35] acres and my unshrubbed down,
Rich scarf to my proud earth. Why hath thy queen
Summoned me hither to this short-grassed green?

IRIS. A contract of true love to celebrate
And some donation freely to estate[36]
On the blessed lovers.

CERES. Tell me, heavenly bow,
If Venus[37] or her son,[38] as thou dost know,
Do now attend the Queen? Since they did plot
The means that dusky Dis[39] my daughter got,[40]
Her and her blind boy's[41] scandaled[42] company
I have forsworn.

32. *Juno descends:* A stage direction indicating that Juno is slowly lowered from the ceiling of the stage.

33. amain: Speedily. (Juno's chariot was drawn by peacocks.)

34. Jupiter: In Roman mythology, the ruler of the gods.

35. bosky: Woodsy.

36. estate: Bestow.

37. Venus: The Roman goddess of love.

38. her son: Cupid, the Roman god of love.

39. Dis: The Roman god of the underworld.

40. my daughter got: An allusion to the classical myth of the abduction of Proserpine. Proserpine, the daughter of Ceres, was carried off by Dis to his underworld kingdom where he made her queen.

41. blind boy's: Cupid, who was often shown blindfolded.

42. scandaled: Scandalous.

8 **Reading Strategy** Have students give a brief character sketch of each of the major characters in the play within a play.

9 **Reading Strategy** Have students summarize the action in this marriage masque.

IRIS. Of her society
Be not afraid; I met her Deity
Cutting the clouds towards Paphos,[43] and her son
Dove-drawn with her. Here thought they to have done
Some wanton charm upon this man and maid,
Whose vows are, that no bed-right shall be paid
Till Hymen's torch be lighted. But in vain;
Mars's hot minion[44] is returned again;[45]
Her waspish-headed son[46] has broke his arrows,
Swears he will shoot no more, but play with sparrows
And be a boy right out.[47]

[JUNO *alights.*]

CERES. Highest queen of state,
8 Great Juno, comes; I know her by her gait.

JUNO. How does my bounteous sister? Go with me
To bless this twain, that they may prosperous be
And honored in their issue.

[*They sing.*]

JUNO. Honor, riches, marriage blessing,
Long continuance, and increasing,
Hourly joys be still[48] upon you!
Juno sings her blessings on you.
[CERES.] Earth's increase, foison plenty,
9 Barns and garners never empty,
Vines with clust'ring bunches growing,
Plants with goodly burden bowing;
Spring come to you at the farthest
In the very end of harvest.[49]
Scarcity and want shall shun you,
Ceres' blessing so is on you.

FERDINAND. This is a most majestic vision, and
Harmonious charmingly. May I be bold
To think these spirits?

PROSPERO. Spirits, which by mine art
I have from their confines called to enact
My present fancies.

FERDINAND. Let me live here ever!
So rare a wond'red[50] father and a wise
Makes this place Paradise.

[JUNO *and* CERES *whisper, and send* IRIS *on employment.*]

PROSPERO.. Sweet now, silence!
Juno and Ceres whisper seriously.
There's something else to do. Hush and be mute,
Or else your spell is marred.

43. Paphos: A major center for the worship of Venus, on Cyprus.

44. Mars's hot minion: Venus, who was the mistress of Mars, the Roman god of war.

45. returned again: Returned home to Paphos.

46. waspish-headed son: Cupid, who was thought of as having a sharp sting like a wasp because of his arrows.

47. boy right out: An ordinary boy, like all other boys.

48. still: Forever; always.

49. Spring . . . harvest: As summer ends may spring begin—in other words, may there never be a winter in your lives.

50. wond'red: Wonderful.

IRIS. You nymphs, called Naiades,[51] of the windring[52] brooks,
With your sedged crowns and ever-harmless looks,
Leave your crisp[53] channels, and on this green land
Answer your summons; Juno does command.
Come, temperate nymphs, and help to celebrate
A contract of true love; be not too late.

[*Enter certain* NYMPHS.]

You sunburned sicklemen, of August weary,
Come hither from the furrow and be merry.
Make holiday; your rye-straw hats put on,
And these fresh nymphs encounter everyone
In country footing.[54]

10 [*Enter certain* REAPERS, *properly habited. They join with the* NYMPHS *in a graceful dance; towards the end whereof* PROSPERO *starts suddenly and speaks;*[55] *after which, to a strange, hollow, and confused noise, they heavily*[56] *vanish.*]

PROSPERO. [*Aside*] I had forgot that foul conspiracy
Of the beast Caliban and his confederates
Against my life. The minute of their plot
Is almost come. [*To the* SPIRITS] Well done! Avoid![57] No more!

FERDINAND. This is strange. Your father's in some passion
That works him strongly.

MIRANDA. Never till this day
Saw I him touched with anger so distempered.[58]

PROSPERO. You do look, my son, in a movèd sort,[59]
As if you were dismayed; be cheerful, sir.
Our revels now are ended. These our actors,
As I foretold you, were all spirits and
Are melted into air, into thin air;
And, like the baseless fabric of this vision,
11 The cloud-capped towers, the gorgeous palaces,
12 The solemn temples, the great globe itself,
Yea, all which it inherit,[60] shall dissolve,
And, like this insubstantial pageant faded,
Leave not a rack[61] behind. We are such stuff
As dreams are made on, and our little life
Is rounded with a sleep. Sir, I am vexed.
Bear with my weakness; my old brain is troubled.
Be not disturbed with my infirmity.
If you be pleased, retire into my cell
And there repose. A turn or two I'll walk
To still my beating mind.

51. Naiades: Water nymphs, minor goddesses of classical mythology who were usually represented as lovely young women.
52. windring: Wandering.
53. crisp: Having little waves.
54. footing: Dancing.
55. speaks: Prospero breaks the spell, which required silence.
56. heavily: Reluctantly.
57. Avoid: Depart.
58. distempered: Fierce; intense.
59. moved sort: Troubled state of mind.
60. it inherit: Inhabit it.
61. rack: Windswept cloud.

10 **Enrichment** Point out to students that the masque was a form of entertainment with a mythological and allegorical theme popular during the sixteenth and seventeenth centuries. In it, characters wore elaborate costumes. Ask students what contemporary word is related to masque (masquerade). The masque lasted in popularity until 1642, when the Civil War put an end to all theatrical performances.

11 **Enrichment** This passage is considered to be one of the greatest in all of Shakespeare. Discuss its message—that what we assume is concrete physical reality will also be an illusion—and the relationship of the message to the illusion-versus-reality theme of the play.

12 **Discussion** Discuss whether or not this speech supports the view that Shakespeare himself might be Prospero.

13 **Reading Strategy** In their own words, have students describe what Ariel has charmed Trinculo, Stephano, and Caliban into doing.

14 **Critical Thinking and Reading** For every effect, there is a cause. What has caused these three to find themselves in such a predicament?

FERDINAND, MIRANDA. We wish your peace.
[*Exit* FERDINAND *with* MIRANDA.]

PROSPERO. Come with a thought! I thank thee, Ariel. Come.

[*Enter* ARIEL.]

ARIEL. Thy thoughts I cleave to. What's thy pleasure?

PROSPERO. Spirit,
We must prepare to meet with Caliban.

ARIEL. Ay, my commander. When I presented[62] Ceres,
I thought to have told thee of it, but I feared
Lest I might anger thee.

PROSPERO. Say again, where didst thou leave these varlets?[63]

13

ARIEL. I told you, sir, they were red-hot with drinking;
So full of valor that they smote the air
For breathing in their faces, beat the ground
For kissing of their feet; yet always bending[64]
Towards their project. Then I beat my tabor;
At which like unbacked[65] colts they pricked their ears,
Advanced[66] their eyelids, lifted up their noses
As they smelt music. So I charmed their ears
That calflike they my lowing followed through
Toothed briers, sharp furzes, pricking goss,[67] and thorns,
Which ent'red their frail shins. At last I left them
I' th' filthy mantled[68] pool beyond your cell,
There dancing up to th' chins, that the foul lake
O'erstunk their feet.

PROSPERO.. This was well done, my bird.
Thy shape invisible retain thou still.
The trumpery[69] in my house, go bring it hither
For stale[70] to catch these thieves.

ARIEL. I go, I go. [*Exit.*]

PROSPERO. A devil, a born devil, on whose nature
Nurture can never stick; on whom my pains,
Humanely taken, all, all lost, quite lost!
And as with age his body uglier grows,
So his mind cankers. I will plague them all,
Even to roaring.

[*Enter* ARIEL, *loaden with glistering apparel, etc.*]

Come, hang them on this line.[71]

14

[PROSPERO *and* ARIEL *remain, invisible. Enter* CALIBAN, STEPHANO, *and* TRINCULO, *all wet.*]

62. presented: This is ambiguous. It could mean that Ariel acted the part of Ceres, or in the role of Iris, introduced Ceres and the entire pageant.

63. varlets: Low, vile rascals.

64. bending: Heading.

65. unbacked: Untrained and hence unsaddled.

66. Advanced: Raised.

67. goss: Shrubs.

68. mantled: Covered, as with a polluted foam or scum.

69. trumpery: Fancy looking, gaudy, cheap clothes.

70. stale: Bait.

71. line: A linden tree.

CALIBAN. Pray you tread softly, that the blind mole may not
Hear a foot fall. We now are near his cell.

STEPHANO. Monster, your fairy, which you say is a harmless fairy, has done little better than played the Jack[72] with us.

TRINCULO. Monster, I do smell all horse piss, at which my nose is in great indignation.

STEPHANO. So is mine. Do you hear, monster? If I should take a displeasure against you, look you—

TRINCULO. Thou wert but a lost monster.

CALIBAN. Good my lord, give me thy favor still.
Be patient, for the prize I'll bring thee to
Shall hoodwink[73] this mischance. Therefore speak softly.
All's hushed as midnight yet.

TRINCULO. Ay, but to lose our bottles in the pool—

STEPHANO. There is not only disgrace and dishonor in that, monster, but an infinite loss.

TRINCULO. That's more to me than my wetting. Yet this is your harmless fairy, monster.

STEPHANO. I will fetch off my bottle, though I be o'er ears[74] for my labor.

CALIBAN. Prithee, my king, be quiet. Seest thou here?
This is the mouth o' th' cell. No noise, and enter.
Do that good mischief which may make this island
Thine own forever, and I, thy Caliban,
For aye thy footlicker.

STEPHANO. Give me thy hand. I do begin to have bloody thoughts.

TRINCULO. O King Stephano! O peer![75] O worthy Stephano, look what a wardrobe here is for thee!

CALIBAN. Let it alone, thou fool! It is but trash.

TRINCULO. O, ho, monster! We know what belongs to a frippery.[76] O King Stephano!

15 **STEPHANO.** Put off that gown, Trinculo! By this hand, I'll have that gown!

TRINCULO. Thy Grace shall have it.

CALIBAN. The dropsy[77] drown this fool! What do you mean
To dote thus on such luggage?[78] Let't alone,

72. Jack: Knave; also will-o'-the-wisp.

73. hoodwink: Hide.

74. o'er ears: Underwater [in the polluted pool].

75. O King . . . peer: Alludes to a popular song.

76. a frippery: A shop selling old, second-hand clothes.

77. dropsy: An ailment caused by excessive accumulation of fluid in the body.

78. luggage: Encumbrance; burdens.

15 **Discussion** From this exchange, who would represent nurtured man and who would represent natural man?

16 Reading Strategy Have students summarize the action in and around the pond.

17 Discussion Do you think that the punishment of Caliban, Stephano, and Trinculo fits their crime? Explain.

18 Discussion From Prospero's point of view, what is now the situation on the island?

And do the murder first. If he awake,
From toe to crown he'll fill our skins with pinches,
Make us strange stuff.

STEPHANO. Be you quiet, monster. Mistress line, is not this my jerkin?[79] [*Takes it down.*] Now is the jerkin under the line.[80] Now, jerkin, you are like to lose your hair and prove a bald jerkin.[81]

TRINCULO. Do, do![82] We steal by line and level,[83] and't like[84] your Grace.

STEPHANO. I thank thee for that jest. Here's a garment for't. Wit shall not go unrewarded while I am king of this country. "Steal by line and level" is an excellent pass of pate.[85] There's another garment for't.

TRINCULO. Monster, come put some lime[86] upon your fingers, and away with the rest.

CALIBAN. I will have none on't. We shall lose our time
And all be turned to barnacles,[87] or to apes
With foreheads villainous low.

STEPHANO. Monster, lay-to your fingers; help to bear this away where my hogshead of wine is, or I'll turn you out of my kingdom. Go to, carry this.

TRINCULO. And this.

STEPHANO. Ay, and this.

[*A noise of hunters heard. Enter divers* SPIRITS *in shape of dogs and hounds, hunting them about;* PROSPERO *and* ARIEL *setting them on.*]

PROSPERO. Hey, Mountain, hey!

ARIEL. Silver! There it goes, Silver!

PROSPERO. Fury, Fury! There, Tyrant, there! Hark, hark!

16 [CALIBAN, STEPHANO, *and* TRINCULO *are driven out.*]

Go, charge my goblins that they grind their joints
With dry convulsions,[88] shorten up their sinews
17 With agèd cramps,[89] and more pinch-spotted make
them
Than pard or cat o' mountain.[90]

ARIEL. Hark, they roar!

PROSPERO. Let them be hunted soundly. At this hour
18 Lies at my mercy all mine enemies.
Shortly shall all my labors end, and thou
Shalt have the air at freedom. For a little,
Follow, and do me service. [*Exit.*]

79. jerkin: A sleeveless, hip-length jacket.

80. under the line: Under the linden tree. Also a play on the word "line," which can refer to the line on maps marking the equator—see the next sentence.

81. Now . . . bald jerkin: Sailors crossing the equator were believed to lose their hair from high fevers contracted in the tropics.

82. Do, do: Fine, fine.

83. line and level: Plumb line and carpenter's level, tools used as rules for making straight lines.

84. and't like: And if it please.

85. pass of pate: Thrust of wit.

86. lime: Birdlime, a sticky substance used to trap birds—thieves are supposed to have sticky fingers.

87. barnacles: North European geese that breed in the frigid arctic.

88. dry convulsions: Violent spasms that cause bones to grind against one another.

89. aged cramps: Cramps such as the elderly might get.

90. pard . . . mountain: Leopard or wildcat.

THINKING ABOUT THE SELECTION

Recalling

1. What does Prospero give Ferdinand at the beginning of Act IV?
2. (a) In the play that Ariel puts on for the young lovers, who are Iris, Ceres, and Juno? (b) Explain what they are coming together to celebrate.
3. Describe how Ariel stops Caliban and his cohorts from harming Prospero.

Interpreting

4. (a) Explain why Prospero has Ariel put on the play within a play. (b) Explain why Prospero stops Ariel's play before the end.
5. Why does Ceres want to make certain that Venus and her son do not attend the celebration?
6. How does Ariel know Stephano and Trinculo will wear the weird clothing he has hung for them in the tree?

Applying

7. Stephano and Trinculo are no different as the play nears an end from how they were when they were first introduced. What other character in fiction does not change? Explain whether that character does not change because he or she can be no other way or because the character has worked hard to become so and is satisfied.

ANALYZING LITERATURE

Resolution of Plot

The resolution, or denouement, of a plot takes place after the climax and shows how the conflict is decided, or resolved. By the end of Act IV of *The Tempest,* you know the resolution to two of the subplots—the outcome of the love between Ferdinand and Miranda and the outcome of the plot of Caliban, Stephano, and Trinculo to kill Prospero. You do not know the outcomes of the main plot and the other subplots. Review your predictions of the resolutions of the plots. Also, write down any new information that you have gathered in Act IV that will bring you closer to predicting the outcome of each of the other plots. Change your predictions if necessary.

CRITICAL THINKING AND READING

Understanding Cause and Effect

That *The Tempest* is a fantasy does not lessen the need for cause-and-effect relationships within the play. There has to be a reason—a cause—for Ferdinand and Miranda to fall in love, for Caliban to want to kill Prospero, for Stephano and Trinculo to end up in a pond of filth, for Prospero to want revenge. Readers or viewers will accept most effects, even startling and fantastic ones, if an acceptable cause has been presented. People in Shakespeare's time commonly accepted the intervention of supernatural beings in the lives of human beings. Consequently, such actions, especially in a comedy, would seem reasonable to theatergoers. Within the realm of magic, however, Ariel's and Prospero's actions must have believable causes and effects. Shakespeare took much care to match acceptable dramatic effects with plausible causes.

1. What causes Prospero to bestow his blessings on Ferdinand and Miranda?
2. What causes Prospero to be "touched with anger so distempered"?
3. What causes Caliban, Stephano, and Trinculo to make such fools of themselves?

THINKING AND WRITING

Write an essay proposing your resolution to the main plot. Explain why you have predicted what you have, offering examples from the play. Describe those characteristics in Prospero that led you to your prediction as well as the actions of his adversaries that helped you determine what Prospero's final action would be. Make notes before you write, and use these notes in writing your draft. Include those quotations from the play that you think are appropriate. Evaluate your first draft carefully, being certain you have made clear the reasons for your prediction. Make any changes in the first draft that seem necessary, then write your final draft. Check to see that it has no errors in grammar, spelling, or punctuation.

Answers

ANSWERS TO THINKING ABOUT THE SELECTION

Recalling

1. Prospero gives Ferdinand permission to marry his daughter, Miranda.
2. (a) Iris is a messenger for the gods; Ceres is the Roman goddess of the earth and agriculture; and Juno is the wife of Jupiter, the ruler of the gods. (b) They are gathering to celebrate the marriage of a young couple who are truly in love.
3. Ariel charmed the trio into wallowing in a foul-smelling lake. He then left gaudy, ridiculous clothes for them to put on, which they do.

Interpreting

4. (a) Prospero has promised to demonstrate to Ferdinand and Miranda some of his "art" and chooses to pay tribute to them and their love by having supernatural beings present a classic play about true love. (b) Prospero stops the play because he remembers that there is a plot against his life.
5. Ceres wanted to be certain that Venus and Cupid, who are the Roman goddess and god of love, did not influence the young couple to be unfaithful to each other.
6. Prospero knows that because since these men live for the moment and are wet and filthy, they

(Answers begin on p. 368.)

will unthinkingly seize the clothes and put them on.

Applying

7. Student's responses will differ, but students should offer as an example a character who is truly a stock character, such as the absent-minded professor or the bespeckled librarian, and should provide adequate support for their opinions.

ANSWERS TO ANALYZING LITERATURE

Students' predictions will differ, but they should be solidly based on what has happened so far. Make sure students understand that their predictions may be logical but still not turn out to be true.

ANSWERS TO CRITICAL THINKING AND READING

1. Prospero bestows his blessings on their love because Ferdinand has passed all of Prospero's trials and proven that he is now worthy of Miranda.
2. Prospero becomes angry because he remembers that Trinculo, Stephano, and Caliban are on their way to kill him.
3. Stephano, Trinculo, and Caliban act the way they do partially because they have consumed so much liquor and partially because they are shallow characters and are thus incapable of truly changing their behavior.

Challenge Have students write an essay comparing the use of the supernatural in *The Tempest* with the use of the supernatural in a modern play or screenplay.

Writing Across the Curriculum In cooperation with the history department, have students write fictionalized historical accounts of the celebration surrounding the marriage of Princess Elizabeth to Frederick the Elector Palatine in the winter of 1612–13. Have them make certain that the historical detail is accurate and that the character type could have existed and the events taken place.

Literary Focus Point out to your students that a number of Shakespeare's comedies, including *The Tempest,* are comic primarily in the sense that they end happily, not in the sense that they are largely funny. In drama, the theme is an abstract concept that is made concrete through its representation in the characters, in the actions and in the imageries of the work. Because *The Tempest* is one of his last plays, Shakespeare interweaves several themes into it, themes that had been important to him throughout his writing.

Look For Have those students who used story maps to track the main plot and subplots, have them add the theme that follows each plot. Their maps should graphically portray a network of the plots and themes of *The Tempest.*

Writing Those students that used story mapping as a technique by which to sort out the plots and the themes of *The Tempest* will want to use those maps to direct their freewriting.

Vocabulary Have your students use the vocabulary words in sentences that describe characters, situations, or actions that they imagine.

GUIDE FOR READING

The Tempest, Act V

Writer's Techniques

Shakespearean Comedy and Theme. Shakespearean comedy follows no set formula; the plays are all distinctive. Each comedy has a theme, and that theme is always less serious than that in a tragedy. *The Tempest,* Shakespeare's last complete play, has more than one theme: When is illusion reality and reality illusion? Which is superior, the natural man or the "nurtured" man? Should one seek revenge or strive to forgive? What is natural and what is supernatural? When should one submit to servitude and when should one seek freedom? Although critics disagree as to the importance of each of these themes, readers and viewers are enriched by following each theme and, as they do, each plot through to its individual resolution.

Look For

As you read *The Tempest,* Act V, think about the thematic elements that have been evident throughout the play. In Act V, look for information that will help you understand how Shakespeare felt about these themes.

Writing

Freewrite about the intertwined plots of *The Tempest.* See if you can tie them all to a central theme that can be expressed as a general statement. Keep in mind that the title of a literary work often gives an indication of the general theme.

Vocabulary

Knowing the following words will help you as you read *The Tempest,* Act V.

penitent (pen′ ə tənt) *adj.*: Feeling or showing sorrow for one's misdeeds or sins (Sc. i, l. 28)

abjure (əb joor′) *v.*: To vow to give up; repudiate (Sc. i, l. 51)

wrangle (raŋ′g′l) *v.*: To argue noisily and angrily; bicker (Sc. i, l. 173)

rectify (rek′tə fī) *v.*: To set right; correct (Sc. i, l. 244)

Objectives

1. To understand Shakespearean comedy and its themes
2. To distinguish between *comic* and *funny*
3. To write about themes in dramatic works

Teaching Portfolio: Support Material

Teacher Backup, p. 00

Vocabulary Check, p. 00

Usage and Mechanics Worksheet, p. 00

Analyzing Literature Worksheet, p. 00

Critical Thinking and Reading Worksheet, p. 00

Language Worksheet, p. 00

Selection Test, p. 00

Act V

Scene i. *In front of Prospero's cell.*

[*Enter* PROSPERO *in his magic robes, and* ARIEL.]

PROSPERO. Now does my project gather to a head.
My charms crack not, my spirits obey, and time
Goes upright with his carriage.[1] How's the day?

ARIEL. On the sixth hour, at which time, my lord,
1 You said our work should cease.

PROSPERO. I did say so
When first I raised the tempest. Say, my spirit,
How fares the King and 's followers?

ARIEL. Confined together
In the same fashion as you gave in charge,
Just as you left them—all prisoners, sir,
In the line grove which weather-fends[2] your cell.
They cannot budge till your release.[3] The King,
His brother, and yours abide all three distracted,
And the remainder mourning over them,
2 Brimful of sorrow and dismay; but chiefly
Him that you termed, sir, the good old Lord Gonzalo.
His tears runs down his beard like winter's drops
From eaves of reeds.[4] Your charm so strongly works 'em,
That if you now beheld them, your affections
Would become tender.

PROSPERO. Dost thou think so, spirit?

ARIEL. Mine would, sir, were I human.

PROSPERO. And mine shall.
Hast thou, which art but air, a touch, a feeling
Of their afflictions, and shall not myself,
One of their kind, that relish all as sharply,
Passion as they, be kindlier moved than thou art?
Though with their high wrongs I am struck to th' quick,
Yet with my nobler reason 'gainst my fury
Do I take part. The rarer action is
In virtue than in vengeance. They being penitent,
The sole drift of my purpose doth extend
3, 4 Not a frown further. Go, release them, Ariel.
My charms I'll break, their senses I'll restore,
And they shall be themselves.

ARIEL. I'll fetch them, sir.
[*Exit.*]

1 carriage: Burden.

2. weather-fends: Protects from inclement weather.

3. till your release: Until you free them.

4. eaves of reeds: Thatched roofs.

Motivation for Reading Ask your students to remember a favorite detective or mystery story and the clues that helped them figure out how the case was solved. Point out that in *The Tempest* there have been clues—based on the characteristics of the major players themselves—all through the play as to what will happen to each character. Have your students share their predictions revealing what fate awaits each of the major characters.

Master Teacher Note Have volunteers research several critical analyses of Shakespeare's intent in the Epilogue of *The Tempest*. Is he, for instance, bidding farewell to the theater? Have them debate the various possibilities, asking the rest of the group to determine which arguments are the most plausible and convincing.

Purpose-Setting Question What are the themes that are demonstrated in the resolution of the conflicts in Act V?

1 **Discussion** In his respectful way, what is Ariel hinting at in this speech?

2 **Literary Focus** Which theme does Gonzalo's attitude support?

3 **Discussion** Discuss the process Prospero goes through to recognize what he will do about his adversaries.

4 **Literary Focus** How does Prospero's attitude support the same theme as Gonzalo's attitude does?

5 Enrichment You may wish to mention that some critics have interpreted this speech as Shakespeare's symbolic farewell to the theater. What is it about the speech that might justify this interpretation? Other critics see it as Shakespeare's comment on the relation of art to life. What evidence justifies this interpretation? Ask students to discuss which interpretation they favor.

6 Reading Strategy Have volunteers paraphrase this passage and explain whom Prospero is talking to this time.

7 Discussion Why does Prospero, in lines 84–86, indicate that he will change apparel?

PROSPERO. Ye elves of hills, brooks, standing lakes, and groves,
And ye that on the sands with printless foot
Do chase the ebbing Neptune, and do fly him[5]
When he comes back; you demi-puppets that
By moonshine do the green sour ringlets[6] make,
Whereof the ewe not bites; and you whose pastime
Is to make midnight mushrumps,[7] that rejoice
To hear the solemn curfew; by whose aid
(Weak masters[8] though ye be) I have bedimmed
The noontide sun, called forth the mutinous winds,
5 And 'twixt the green sea and the azured vault
Set roaring war; to the dread rattling thunder
Have I given fire and rifted Jove's stout oak
With his own bolt; the strong-based promontory
Have I made shake and by the spurs[9] plucked up
The pine and cedar; graves at my command
Have waked their sleepers, oped, and let 'em forth
By my so potent art. But this rough magic
I here abjure; and when I have required
Some heavenly music (which even now I do)
To work mine end upon their senses that[10]
This airy charm is for, I'll break my staff,
Bury it certain fathoms in the earth,
And deeper than did ever plummet sound
I'll drown my book. [*Solemn music.*]

[*Here enters* ARIEL *before; then* ALONSO, *with a frantic gesture, attended by* GONZALO; SEBASTIAN *and* ANTONIO *in like manner, attended by* ADRIAN *and* FRANCISCO. *They all enter the circle which* PROSPERO *had made, and there stand charmed; which* PROSPERO *observing, speaks.*]

A solemn air, and the best comforter
To an unsettled fancy, cure thy brains,
Now useless, boiled within thy skull! Three stand,
For you are spell-stopped.
Holy Gonzalo, honorable man,
Mine eyes, ev'n sociable to show of thine,
6, 7 Fall fellowly drops.[11] The charm dissolves apace;
And as the morning steals upon the night,
Melting the darkness, so their rising senses
Begin to chase the ignorant fumes that mantle
Their clearer reason. O good Gonzalo,
My true preserver, and a loyal sir
To him thou follow'st, I will pay thy graces
Home[12] both in word and deed. Most cruelly

5. fly him: Race with him.

6. green sour ringlets: Small circles of grass that grow around spreading fungi.

7. mushrumps: Mushrooms.

8. Weak masters: Not powerful magicians.

9. spurs: Roots.

10. their senses that: The senses of those whom.

11. sociable . . . drops: Identifying with the tears in your eyes, mine also drop tears in sympathy.

12. pay . . . home: Repay your kindness fully.

Didst thou, Alonso, use me and my daughter.
Thy brother was a furtherer in the act.
Thou art pinched for't now, Sebastian. Flesh and blood,
You, brother mine, that entertained ambition,
Expelled remorse and nature;[13] whom, with Sebastian
(Whose inward pinches therefore are most strong),
Would here have killed your king, I do forgive thee,
Unnatural though thou art. Their understanding
Begins to swell, and the approaching tide
Will shortly fill the reasonable shore,
That now lies foul and muddy. Not one of them
That yet looks on me or would know me. Ariel,
Fetch me the hat and rapier in my cell.
I will discase[14] me, and myself present
As I was sometime Milan. Quickly, spirit!
Thou shalt ere long be free.

[*Exit* ARIEL *and returns immediately.*]

[ARIEL *sings and helps to attire him.*]

8 Where the bee sucks, there suck I;
In a cowslip's bell I lie;
There I couch when owls do cry.
On the bat's back I do fly
After summer merrily.
Merrily, merrily shall I live now
Under the blossom that hangs on the bough.

PROSPERO. Why, that's my dainty Ariel! I shall miss thee,
But yet thou shalt have freedom; so, so, so.
To the King's ship, invisible as thou art!
There shalt thou find the mariners asleep
Under the hatches. The master and the boatswain
Being awake, enforce them to this place,
And presently,[15] I prithee.

ARIEL. I drink the air before me, and return
Or ere your pulse twice beat. [*Exit.*]

GONZALO. All torment, trouble, wonder, and amazement
Inhabits here. Some heavenly power guide us
Out of this fearful country!

PROSPERO. Behold, sir King,
The wrongèd Duke of Milan, Prospero.
For more assurance that a living prince
Does now speak to thee, I embrace thy body,
And to thee and thy company I bid
A hearty welcome.

9 **ALONSO.** Whe'r[16] thou be'st he or no,

13. nature: Natural feeling (of brotherly affection and loyalty).

14. discase: Disrobe.

15. presently: Quickly.

16. Whe'r: Whether.

8 **Discussion** Of what does Ariel sing here? To what is he looking forward?

9 **Literary Focus** Which theme does the speech support and why? Find other evidence of this theme as you continue reading.

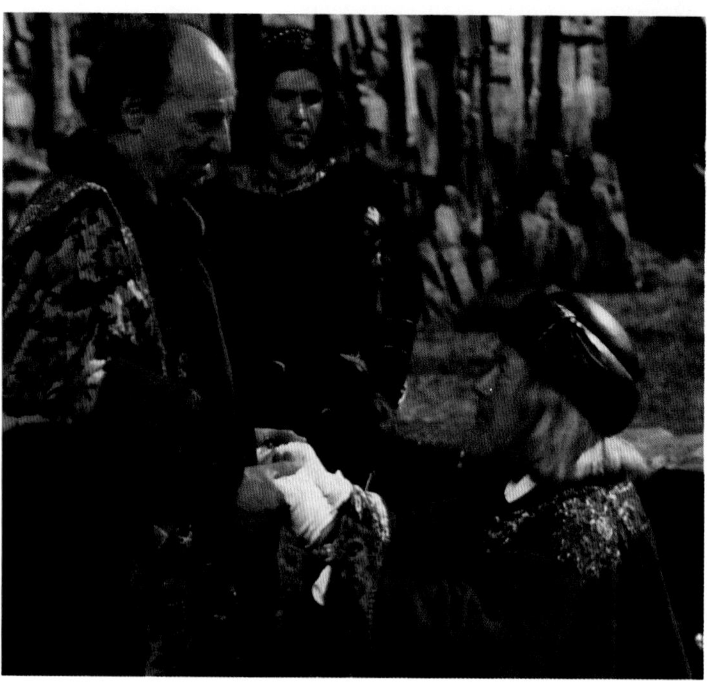

Or some enchanted trifle[17] to abuse me,
As late I have been, I not know. Thy pulse
Beats, as of flesh and blood; and, since I saw thee,
Th' affliction of my mind amends, with which,
I fear, a madness held me. This must crave[18]
(And if this be at all[19]) a most strange story.
Thy dukedom I resign and do entreat
Thou pardon me my wrongs. But how should Prospero
Be living and be here?

PROSPERO. First, noble friend,
Let me embrace thine age, whose honor cannot
Be measured or confined.

GONZALO. Whether this be
Or be not, I'll not swear.

PROSPERO. You do yet taste
Some subtleties[20] o' th' isle, that will not let you
Believe things certain. Welcome, my friends all.
[*Aside to* SEBASTIAN *and* ANTONIO] But you, my brace of lords, were I so minded,
I here could pluck his Highness' frown upon you,

17. trifle: A ghost.

18. crave: Yearn for; desire intensely.

19. And . . . all: And if this be real.

20. taste some subtleties: Sense some deceptions, an allusion to popular pastries made to look like castles, ships, and the like.

And justify[21] you traitors. At this time
I will tell no tales.

10 **SEBASTIAN.** [*Aside*] The devil speaks in him.

PROSPERO. No.
For you, most wicked sir, whom to call brother
Would even infect my mouth, I do forgive
Thy rankest fault—all of them; and require
My dukedom of thee, which perforce I know
Thou must restore.

ALONSO. If thou beest Prospero,
Give us particulars of thy preservation;
How thou hast met us here, whom three hours since
Were wracked upon this shore; where I have lost
(How sharp the point of this remembrance is!)
My dear son Ferdinand.

PROSPERO. I am woe[22] for't, sir.

ALONSO. Irreparable is the loss, and patience
Says it is past her cure.

PROSPERO. I rather think
You have not sought her help, of whose soft grace
For the like loss I have her sovereign aid
And rest myself content.

ALONSO. You the like loss?

PROSPERO. As great to me, as late,[23] and supportable
To make the dear loss, have I means much weaker
Than you may call to comfort you; for I
Have lost my daughter.

ALONSO. A daughter?
O heavens, that they were living both in Naples,
The King and Queen there! That they were, I wish
Myself were mudded in that oozy bed
Where my son lies. When did you lose your daughter?

PROSPERO. In this last tempest. I perceive these lords
At this encounter do so much admire
That they devour their reason, and scarce think
Their eyes do offices[24] of truth, their words
11 Are natural breath. But, howsoev'r you have
Been justled from your senses, know for certain
That I am Prospero, and that very duke
Which was thrust forth of Milan, who most strangely
Upon this shore, where you were wracked, was landed
To be the lord on't. No more yet of this;
For 'tis a chronicle of day by day,

21. justify: Prove.

22. woe: Sorry.

23. As . . . late: As great a loss to me as to you, and as recent a one.

24. do offices: Perform the functions.

10 Discussion What beliefs of the period are behind Sebastian's comment?

11 Discussion How does Prospero deceive Alonso a bit here and why do you think that he does so?

12 **Enrichment** Shakespeare allows Prospero a little ironic humor and cynicism here as Prospero, with tongue in cheek, remarks that Miranda's wonder at the humans is only because they are new to her. This dry remark is as far as the comic spirit is allowed to go in Prospero.

Not a relation for a breakfast, nor
Befitting this first meeting. Welcome sir;
This cell's my court. Here have I few attendants,
And subjects none abroad.[25] Pray you look in.
My dukedom since you have given me again,
I will requite you with as good a thing,
At least bring forth a wonder to content ye
As much as me my dukedom.

[*Here* PROSPERO *discovers*[26] FERDINAND *and* MIRANDA *playing at chess.*]

MIRANDA. Sweet lord, you play me false.

FERDINAND. No, my dearest love,
I would not for the world.

MIRANDA. Yes, for a score of kingdoms you should wrangle,
And I would call it fair play.[27]

ALONSO. If this prove
A vision of the island, one dear son
Shall I twice lose.

SEBASTIAN. A most high miracle!

FERDINAND. Though the seas threaten, they are merciful.
I have cursed them without cause. [*Kneels.*]

ALONSO. Now all the blessings
Of a glad father compass thee about!
Arise, and say how thou cam'st here.

MIRANDA. O, wonder!
How many goodly creatures are there here!
12 How beauteous mankind is! O brave new world
That has such people in't!

PROSPERO. 'Tis new to thee.

ALONSO. What is this maid with whom thou wast at play?
Your eld'st[28] acquaintance cannot be three hours.
Is she the goddess that hath severed us
And brought us thus together?

FERDINAND. Sir, she is mortal;
But by immortal providence she's mine.
I chose her when I could not ask my father
For his advice, nor thought I had one. She
Is daughter to this famous Duke of Milan,
Of whom so often I have heard renown
But never saw before; of whom I have
Received a second life; and second father
This lady makes him to me.

25. abroad: Elsewhere on this island.

26. discovers: Reveals.

27. for a score . . . play: If we were really playing for high stakes and you cheated me, I'd call it fair play.

28. eld'st: Longest.

ALONSO. I am hers.
But, O, how oddly will it sound that I
Must ask my child forgiveness!

PROSPERO. There, sir, stop.
Let us not burden our remembrance with
A heaviness that's gone.

GONZALO. I have inly wept,
Or should have spoke ere this. Look down, you gods,
And on this couple drop a blessèd crown!
For it is you that have chalked forth the way
Which brought us hither.

ALONSO. I say amen, Gonzalo.

GONZALO. Was Milan thrust from Milan that his issue
Should become kings of Naples? O, rejoice
Beyond a common joy, and set it down
With gold on lasting pillars. In one voyage
13 Did Claribel her husband find at Tunis,
And Ferdinand her brother found a wife
Where he himself was lost; Prospero his dukedom
In a poor isle; and all of us ourselves
When no man was his own.

ALONSO. [*To* FERDINAND *and* MIRANDA] Give me your hands.
Let grief and sorrow still embrace his heart
That doth not wish you joy.

GONZALO. Be it so! Amen!

[*Enter* ARIEL, *with the* MASTER *and* BOATSWAIN *amazedly following.*]

O, look, sir; look, sir! Here is more of us!
I prophesied if a gallows were on land,
This fellow could not drown. Now, blasphemy,
That swear'st grace o'erboard,[29] not an oath on shore?
Hast thou no mouth by land? What is the news?

BOATSWAIN. The best news is that we have safely found
Our king and company; the next, our ship,
Which, but three glasses[30] since, we gave out split,
Is tight and yare[31] and bravely rigged as when
We first put out to sea.

ARIEL. [*Aside to* PROSPERO] Sir, all this service
14 Have I done since I went.

PROSPERO. [*Aside to* ARIEL] My tricksy spirit!

ALONSO. There are not natural events; they strengthen
From strange to stranger. Say, how came you hither?

29. blasphemy . . . o'erboard: Irreverent curses that threw salvation into the sea.

30. glasses: Hours.
31. yare: Shipshape.

13 **Literary Focus** Which themes are addressed in Gonzalo's speech?

14 **Discussion** How has Ariel and Prospero's relationship developed during the play? What do you anticipate will soon happen to it?

377

15 Reading Strategy What is the play on words in the phrase *dead of sleep?*

16 Discussion To which master does Caliban refer?

BOATSWAIN. If I did think, sir, I were well awake,
15 I'd strive to tell you. We were dead of sleep
And (how we know not) all clapped under hatches;
Where, but even now, with strange and several noises
Of roaring, shrieking, howling, jingling chains,
And moe diversity of sounds, all horrible,
We were awaked; straightway at liberty;
Where we, in all our trim, freshly beheld
Our royal, good, and gallant ship, our master
Cap'ring to eye her.[32] On a trice, so please you,
Even in a dream, were we divided from them
And were brought moping[33] hither.

ARIEL. [*Aside to* PROSPERO] Was't well done?

PROSPERO. [*Aside to* ARIEL] Bravely, my diligence. Thou shalt be free.

ALONSO. This is as strange a maze as e'er men trod,
And there is in this business more than nature
Was ever conduct[34] of. Some oracle
Must rectify our knowledge.

PROSPERO. Sir, my liege,
Do not infest your mind with beating on
The strangeness of this business. At picked leisure,
Which shall be shortly, single I'll resolve you
(Which to you shall seem probable) of every
These happened accidents;[35] till when, be cheerful
And think of each thing well. [*Aside to* ARIEL] Come hither, spirit.
Set Caliban and his companions free.
Untie the spell. [*Exit* ARIEL.] How fares my gracious sir?
There are yet missing of your company
Some few odd lads that you remember not.

[*Enter* ARIEL, *driving in* CALIBAN, STEPHANO, *and* TRINCULO, *in their stolen apparel.*]

STEPHANO. Every man shift for all the rest, and let no man take care for himself; for all is but fortune. *Coraggio,*[36] bully-monster, *coraggio!*

TRINCULO. If these be true spies which I wear in my head, here's a goodly sight.

CALIBAN. O Setebos, these be brave spirits indeed!
16 How fine my master is! I am afraid
He will chastise me.

SEBASTIAN. Ha, ha!
What things are these, my Lord Antonio?
Will money buy 'em?

32. master . . . her: Our captain dancing to see her.
33. moping: Dazed.

34. conduct: Conductor.

35. accidents: Occurrences.

36. *Coraggio:* Italian, courage.

ANTONIO. Very like. One of them
Is a plain fish and no doubt marketable.

PROSPERO. Mark but the badges[37] of these men, my lords,
Then say if they be true.[38] This misshapen knave,
His mother was a witch, and one so strong
That could control the moon, make flows and ebbs,
And deal in her command without her power.[39]
These three have robbed me, and this demi-devil
(For he's a bastard one) had plotted with them
To take my life. Two of these fellows you
Must know and own; this thing of darkness I
Acknowledge mine.

CALIBAN. I shall be pinched to death.

ALONSO. Is not this Stephano, my drunken butler?

SEBASTIAN. He is drunk now. Where had he wine?

ALONSO. And Trinculo is reeling ripe. Where should they
Find this grand liquor that hath gilded 'em?
How cam'st thou in this pickle?

17 **TRINCULO.** I have been in such a pickle, since I saw you last, that I fear me will never out of my bones. I shall not fear flyblowing.[40]

SEBASTIAN. Why, how now, Stephano?

STEPHANO. O, touch me not! I am not Stephano, but a cramp.

PROSPERO. You'd be king o' the isle, sirrah?

STEPHANO. I should have been a sore[41] one then.

ALONSO. This is a strange thing as e'er I looked on.

PROSPERO. He is as disproportioned in his manners
As in his shape. Go, sirrah, to my cell;
Take with you your companions. As you look
To have my pardon, trim it handsomely.

18 **CALIBAN.** Ay, that I will; and I'll be wise hereafter,
And seek for grace. What a thrice-double ass
Was I to take this drunkard for a god
And worship this dull fool!

PROSPERO. Go to! Away!

ALONSO. Hence, and bestow your luggage where you found it.

SEBASTIAN. Or stole it rather.

[*Exit* CALIBAN, STEPHANO, *and* TRINCULO.]

37. badges: Insignia worn by servants to indicate the master they serve.
38. true: Honest.

39. without her power: Without the moon's authority.

40. flyblowing: Pickling is a way to preserve meat from maggots.

41. sore: Pained or angry.

17 **Reading Strategy** What is the double meaning intended in this passage? Discuss the modern usage of the expression "in a pickle."

18 **Literary Focus** Which theme does Caliban's comment support and what do we learn about Caliban?

19 Discussion What does Prospero plan to do with his future?

20 Literary Focus Which theme does the Epilogue support? What do you learn about Prospero here and what might you infer about Shakespeare?

PROSPERO. Sir, I invite your Highness and your train
To my poor cell, where you shall take your rest
For this one night; which, part of it, I'll waste[42]
With such discourse as, I not doubt, shall make it
Go quick away—the story of my life,
19 And the particular accidents gone by
Since I came to this isle. And in the morn
I'll bring you to your ship, and so to Naples,
Where I have hope to see the nuptial
Of these our dear-beloved solemnizèd;
And thence retire me to my Milan, where
Every third thought shall be my grave.

ALONSO. I long
To hear the story of your life, which must
Take[43] the ear strangely.

PROSPERO. I'll deliver[44] all;
And promise you calm seas, auspicious gales,
And sail so expeditious that shall catch
Your royal fleet far off. [*Aside to* ARIEL] My Ariel, chick,
That is thy charge. Then to the elements
Be free, and fare thou well! [*To the others*] Please you,
draw near. [*Exit all.*]

42. waste: Spend.

43. Take: Hold; sound.

44. deliver: Tell.

EPILOGUE

Spoken by Prospero

Now my charms are all o'erthrown,
And what strength I have's mine own,
Which is most faint. Now 'tis true
I must be here confined by you,
Or sent to Naples. Let me not,
Since I have my dukedom got
And pardoned the deceiver, dwell
In this bare island by your spell;
But release me from my bands[1]
20 With the help of your good hands.[2]
Gentle breath[3] of yours my sails
Must fill, or else my project fails,
Which was to please. Now I want
Spirits to enforce, art to enchant;
And my ending is despair
Unless I be relieved by prayer,[4]
Which pierces so that it assaults
Mercy itself and frees all faults.
As you from crimes would pardoned be,
Let your indulgence[5] set me free. [*Exit.*]

FINIS

1. bands: Pledges; promises.
2. hands: Applause.
3. Gentle breath: Approving comments.

4. prayer: My plea, request, or petition.

5. indulgence: Generosity; also, remission from sins according to Roman Catholic doctrine.

Answers

ANSWERS TO THINKING ABOUT THE SELECTION

1. Ariel wants to hurry and get everything resolved so that he can be freed.
2. Prospero chooses virtue, or to forgive those that did him harm, because he believes that they are penitent and seek forgiveness from him.
3. Prospero says that he will break his staff, bury it deep in the earth, and drop his book into the deep sea.
4. Prospero removes his charm of invisibility and puts on a hat and a rapier that make him look more like himself when he was the Duke of Milan.

THINKING ABOUT THE SELECTION

Recalling

1. What is Ariel's first priority as the play winds to a close?
2. Which does Prospero choose, virtue or vengeance, and why?
3. How does Prospero let us know he is through using his magic?
4. How does Prospero change his appearance to meet his adversaries?
5. Describe Gonzalo's and Alonso's reactions to Prospero's appearance.
6. (a) What does Prospero mean when he tells Alonso that he, like Alonso, "lost" a child in the tempest? (b) How does Alonso discover what Prospero means?
7. Explain how the boatswain finds the king and his party.
8. What change takes place in Caliban?
9. What is Ariel's last act as Prospero's servant?

Interpreting

10. Explain what Miranda represents in the play.
11. If Prospero is the "voice" of Shakespeare, what message does Shakespeare want to leave his audience with at the end of the play? At the end of the Epilogue?

Applying

12. With which character in *The Tempest* did you most identify? Explain your choice, providing lines from his or her speeches to support your choice.

ANALYZING LITERATURE

Shakespearean Comedy and Theme

Shakespeare's comedies, though less serious in intent than his tragedies, nevertheless have definite themes. A theme, as you know, is the central idea of a literary work. The themes of *The Tempest,* while not directly stated, are all strongly supported by speeches and incidents in the play.

1. What do you think is the most important theme in *The Tempest?* (State the theme in one sentence. Your statement should be in the form of a universal truth, not restricted just to the characters and circumstances of this play.)
2. What one speech in Act V comes closest to expressing the theme you have selected as most important?

UNDERSTANDING LANGUAGE

Distinguishing Between Words

The words *comic* and *funny* are not exact synonyms, although they have a shared meaning element—"provoking laughter or mirth." The difference is that *funny* is a general term for anything amusing or laughable, while *comic* pertains to the elements of comedy. If something is comic, it exhibits wit and humor and tends to be amusing in a thoughtful way. It may be side-splittingly funny in parts, but it does not have to be. *The Tempest* has a sampling of both. The antics of Stephano, Trinculo, and Caliban, as they try to plot Prospero's death—with Ariel offering undetected suggestions—is reminiscent of the Three Stooges. On the other hand, Prospero's trickery and sleight-of-hand offer the more subtle humor that is labeled comic.

1. Explain what characteristics of Stephano, Trinculo, and Caliban make them the comic characters they are.
2. Sometimes a situation is comic if the character believes something to be true while the audience knows what is really happening. How does Prospero use this technique to have one last bit of "fun" with Alonso?

THINKING AND WRITING

Recognizing Themes

Write an essay in which you defend your choice of the most important theme in *The Tempest.* Before beginning to write, you will find it helpful to make notes on the speeches and events that support your choice. Organize these notes into an informal outline. When you revise your first draft, check those notes to make certain you have used everything you need to defend your choice of theme. Proofread your essay and prepare a final draft.

(Answers begin on p. 380.)

5. Alonso feels that he has gone mad when he first sees Prospero and begs Prospero's forgiveness, returning to him his dukedom. When Prospero thanks him for his bravery and his help earlier, Gonzalo is modest and has difficulty remembering his part in protecting and supplying Prospero and Miranda when they were first put to sea.
6. (a) Prospero means that he lost his daughter to the love of a young man, Ferdinand. (b) Prospero reveals Ferdinand and Miranda playing chess.
7. Ariel awakens the ship's master, the boatswain, and the crew by making weird shrieking and jingling noises and spiriting them onto the island and to the place where everyone is gathered.
8. Caliban says that he was foolish to believe that a drunken fool was a god and promises that he will be wise hereafter and seek for grace.
9. Prospero asks Ariel to calm the seas so that Alonso's ship will have a safe journey.

Interpreting

10. Suggested response: Miranda represents Shakespeare's dream of an ideal—innocent, pure love.
11. Shakespeare wants his audience to understand how important he believes forgiveness and reconciliation are. In the Epilogue, he lets us know that this play, too, has been an illusion, and he has Prospero ask to be released from the stage and the illusion. Some critics believe that Shakespeare was also presenting his farewell to the stage.

Applying

12. Answers will differ. Students might, alternatively, be asked to name the character whose role they would be most eager to take if they were actors.

ANSWERS TO ANALYZING LITERATURE

1. Answers will differ. Possibilities include the theme of illusion and reality, of reconciliation and forgiveness, and of nature versus nurture.
2. Answers will differ. All these themes are touched on in the speeches of Act V.

Challenge Have students write an essay analyzing the use of the theme that they have chosen as most important in *The Tempest* and, if possible, in another play or story that they have seen or read.

ANSWERS TO UNDERSTANDING LANGUAGE

1. Suggested response: Stephano, Trinculo, and Caliban share the inability to see below the surface of a situation. They don't understand what motivates them or what motivates anyone else, so they have no control over what they do and what happens to them. Their actions become comic because they are so out of control.
2. Prospero told Alonso that his daughter was "lost," too, even though Prospero and the audience know that she is "lost" to Ferdinand and is playing chess with him just out of view.

THINKING AND WRITING

Publishing Student Writing Have students submit their essays to the class booklet *Commentaries on The Tempest.*

More About the Author It is said no figure in English history has been so grandly praised while being at the same time harshly criticized. He was both wise and base. Pope called him "the wisest, brightest and meanest of mankind." For all his brilliance —and that is the proper word —Bacon could not live within his means. His extravagances put him continually in need of funds to allay ever-pursuing creditors.

Literary Focus Because Bacon's writing style is not easy, have students seek to isolate and understand the aphorisms from each paragraph. He leads into them fairly clearly.

Look For Have students look for lines such as ". . . which is this:" which lead them into the aphoristic insights.

Writing Have students write down one or more insights beyond the confines listed here.

Vocabulary Discuss these words with students, putting those in common use into current language. Affectations, antiquity and prudence are the obvious three.

GUIDE FOR READING

from Novum Organum: Idols of the Cave

Sir Francis Bacon (1561–1626) was born in London, the son of Sir Nicholas Bacon, Lord Keeper of the Great Seal. Although he made no discoveries in natural science and proposed no new scheme of philosophy, he gave to the seventeenth century something that it lacked, a "science of science" and a "philosophy of philosophy." Bacon's *Essays,* fifty-eight in all, appeared between 1597 and 1625. Full of practical wisdom and noted for their style, they reflect the experiences of Bacon's own life.

Writer's Techniques

Aphorism. An aphorism is a short statement that expresses a wise or clever observation about life. The term comes from Hippocrates's *Aphorisms,* a collection of tersely worded medical principles written by an early Greek physician. Hippocrates's opening sentence is a famous example of an aphorism: "Life is short, art is long, opportunity fleeting, experimenting dangerous, reasoning difficult."

Look For

As you read Bacon's "Idols of the Cave" from *Novum Organum,* look for the aphorisms. What insights about life do they provide?

Writing

Write the following headings across the top of a piece of paper: *Being a teenager, Being a student, Being a friend, Being a son or daughter.* Under each heading write two or more observations you have made or facts you have learned from your experience.

Vocabulary

Knowing the following words will help you as you read "Idols of the Cave" from *Novum Organum.*

constitution (kän'stə to͞o' shən) *n.*: Makeup (of a person) (p. 383)
habituated (hə bich'o͞o wāt'id) *v.*: Accustomed to (p. 383)
contentious (kən te 'shəs) *adj.*: Of questionable validity (p. 383)
discursive (dis kur'siv) *adj.*: Reaching conclusions by a series of logical steps, as opposed to intuitive (p. 383)
antiquity (an tik'wə tē) *n.*: Ancient times (p. 383)
affectations (af'ek tā'shənz) *n.*: Pretenses (p. 384)
felicity (fə lis'ə tē) *n.*: Apt expression or thought (p. 384)
prudence (pro͞od''ns) *n.*: Care in avoiding errors; discretion (p. 384)

Objectives

1 To understand aphorisms
2 To reason from facts to generalizations
3 To understand words based on Latin roots
4 To write aphorisms

Teaching Portfolio: Support Material

Teacher Backup, p. 000

Vocabulary Check, pp. 00

Usage and Mechanics Worksheet, pp. 00

Analyzing Literature Worksheet, pp. 00

Critical Thinking and Reading Worksheet, pp. 00

Selection Test, pp. 00

from Novum Organum[1]

1 Idols[2] of the Cave

Sir Francis Bacon

53

2 The *Idols of the Cave* take their rise in the peculiar constitution, mental or bodily, of each individual; and also in education, habit and accident. Of this kind there is a great number and variety; but I will instance those the pointing out of which contains the most important caution, and which have most effect in disturbing the clearness of the understanding.

54

3 Men become attached to certain particular sciences[3] and speculations, either because they fancy themselves the authors and inventors thereof, or because they have bestowed the greatest pains upon them and become most habituated to them. But men of this kind, if they betake themselves to philosophy and contemplations of a general character, distort and color them in obedience to their former fancies; a thing especially to be noticed in Aristotle,[4] who made his natural philosophy a mere bondservant to his logic, thereby rendering it contentious and well nigh useless. The race of chemists[5] again out of a few experiments of the furnace have built up a fantastic philosophy, framed with reference to a few things; and Gilbert[6] also, after he had employed himself most laboriously in the study and observation of the loadstone,[7] proceeded at once to construct an entire system in accordance with his favorite subject.

55

There is one principal and, as it were, radical distinction between different minds, in respect of philosophy and the sciences, which is this: that some minds are stronger and apter to mark the differences of things, others to mark their resemblances. The steady and acute mind can fix its contemplations and dwell and fasten on the subtlest distinctions: the lofty and discursive mind recognizes and puts together the finest and most general resemblances. Both kinds however easily err in excess, by catching the one at gradations, the other in shadows. 4

56

There are found some minds given to an extreme admiration of antiquity, others to an extreme love and appetite for novelty; but few so duly tempered that they can hold the mean, neither carping at what has been well 5

---

1. **Novum Organum:** The New Instrument of Learning.
2. **Idols:** Misleading images of truth.
3. **sciences:** Ideas.
4. **Aristotle:** Ancient Greek philosopher (384–322 B.C.).
5. **chemists:** Alchemists; people who practiced alchemy, an early form of chemistry, involving the study of philosophical and magical associations.
6. **Gilbert:** William Gilbert (1540?–1603), an English physician, known for his studies of magnetic force.
7. **loadstone** *n*: A strongly magnetic variety of the mineral magnetite.

Motivation for Reading Bacon draws attention to four obstacles to clear thinking. Have students seek them out and identify each.

Master Teacher Note Introduce several more contemporary aphorisms and their creators—Mark Twain, Yogi Berra, and Will Rogers, among others, might be good choices.

Purpose-Setting Question What four obstacles to clear thinking does Bacon discuss in this work?

1 **Clarification** Many students are familiar with the definition of *idol* as a "god" or "false god." The less-used definition applies here —*idol* as "a false or misleading idea or fallacy."

2 **Discussion** Bacon suggests that many fallacies of the mind exist and for many reasons. Which of them will he discuss here?

3 **Discussion** Why do men become particularly attached to certain views or viewpoints? What happens when these men turn their attentions to other, more general fields of thought?

4 **Discussion** What does Bacon see as the main distinction between the scientific and the philosophic mind? How is each inclined to go too far?

5 **Discussion** What two extreme attitudes does Bacon criticize? What is the ideal, instead? Where does he feel truth can be found?

6 **Discussion** What problems arise in the study of nature and bodies? What does Bacon see as the ideal way to study them?

7 **Discussion** What, then, are the four reasons for the growth of the Idols of the Cave? Note that this section summarizes the previous four. What should every student of nature take as his general rule?

laid down by the ancients, nor despising what is well introduced by the moderns. This however turns to the great inquiry of the sciences and philosophy; since these affectations of antiquity and novelty are the humors of partisans rather than judgments;
5 and truth is to be sought for not in the felicity of any age, which is an unstable thing, but in the light of nature and experience, which is eternal. These factions therefore must be abjured, and care must be taken that the intellect be not hurried by them into assent.

57

Contemplations of nature and of bodies in their simple form break up and distract the understanding, while contemplations of nature and bodies in their composition and
6 configuration overpower and dissolve the understanding:[8] a distinction well seen in the school of Leucippus and Democritus[9] as compared with the other philosophies. For that school is so busied with the particles that it hardly attends to the structure; while the others are so lost in admiration of the structure that they do not penetrate to the simplicity of nature. These kinds of contemplation should therefore be alternated and taken by turns; that so the understanding may be rendered at once penetrating and comprehensive, and the inconveniences above mentioned with the idols which proceed from them, may be avoided.

58

Let such then be our provision and contemplative prudence for keeping off and dislodging the *Idols of the Cave*, which grow for the most part either out of the predominance of a favorite subject, or out of an excessive tendency to compare or to distinguish, or out of partiality for particular ages,
or out of the largeness or minuteness of the 7
objects contemplated. And generally let every student of nature take this as a rule—that whatever his mind seizes and dwells upon with peculiar satisfaction is to be held in suspicion, and that so much the more care is to be taken in dealing with such questions to keep the understanding even and clear.

8. contemplations . . . understanding: Neither reducing nature to the most basic principles nor trying to observe all of nature's particulars can produce a true understanding of it.

9. Leucippus and Democritus: Ancient Greek philosophers.

THINKING ABOUT THE SELECTION

Recalling

1. In 53 what four sources of the "Idols of the Cave" does Bacon identify?
2. What two reasons are mentioned in 54 for people becoming attached to certain ideas?
3. What is the main distinction noted in 55 between different minds?
4. According to Bacon in 57, what is the main fault with the philosophy of Leucippus and Democritus?

Interpreting

5. In your own words, what does Bacon think is wrong with Aristotle's philosophy?
6. (a) If Bacon were to put himself into one of the two categories in 55, which one would it be? (b) Why?
7. In both 55 and 56, Bacon warns against going to extremes. How does he suggest doing it?
8. What purpose does the advice in 58 serve?

Applying

9. (a) In your own words, what is the rule Bacon recommends in 58 for a "student of nature"? (b) What is your opinion of the rule? (c) What, if any, instances can you think of in your personal experience where it might apply?

Answers

ANSWERS TO THINKING ABOUT THE SELECTION

Recalling

1. Bacon identifies the mental or bodily constitution of an individual, along with education, habit, and accident as four sources of the

ANALYZING LITERATURE

Understanding Aphorism

An **aphorism** is a concise statement expressing a wise or clever observation about life. In a very few words it summarizes a great deal of information or experience. Explaining the meaning of an aphorism requires many more words than those in the aphorism. Sometimes an example helps to make the meaning of an aphorism clear. In your own words, give the meaning of each of the following aphorisms from the works of Sir Francis Bacon.

1. "Revenge is a kind of wild justice, which the more man's nature seems to run to, the more ought law to weed it out."
2. "Virtue is like a rich stone—best plain set."
3. "There is no excellent beauty that hath not some strangeness in the proportion."
4. "Prosperity is not without many fears and distastes; and adversity is not without comforts and hopes."

CRITICAL THINKING AND READING

Reasoning

Before Bacon's time, science was based on *deductive reasoning*—the process of applying an already accepted general principle to specific facts. Bacon considered that method to be backwards. He argued that true science requires *inductive reasoning*—the process of examining specific facts in order to derive a general principle. From "some good quantity of observation" Bacon created his aphorisms in *Novum Organum*. Bacon's aphorisms therefore demonstrate in style as well as content the method of inductive reasoning.

When inductive reasoning is carried out logically, it results in a *valid generalization*—a statement, supported by evidence, that holds true in a large number of cases. If you make a generalization on the basis of only a few examples, without taking exceptions or qualifying facts into account, you produce a *hasty generalization*. A hasty generalization may be valid but only by accident, since the process of reaching it is flawed.

Read the following examples and decide which are valid generalizations and which are hasty generalizations.

1. I did worse on today's calculus test than I did on the three previous ones. I'm going to get a bad grade in calculus.
2. In the ninth inning I struck out with the bases loaded. I'll never be a good baseball player.
3. I helped my aunt run her day-care center for six toddlers this summer. I worked every day for two months. It takes skill and patience to care for young children.
4. It rained on my birthday for the last two years. It's almost sure to rain on it this year, too.

UNDERSTANDING LANGUAGE

Words from Latin Roots

Many words in the English language came from Latin. Sometimes the entire word was borrowed—*senator,* for example—but more often the Latin base, or root, was used in combination with something else to create a new word.

Use each of the following Latin roots to make at least two English words. If necessary, use a dictionary. You may have to change the spelling of the Latin root when you write the English word. For example, the Latin root *aer* (air) gives us *airplane* and *airmail*.

1. *omni* (all)
2. *viv* (live)
3. *flex* (bend)
4. *avis* (bird)
5. *sect* (cut)
6. *fid* (faith)
7. *rupt* (break)
8. *aqua* (water)
9. *grat* (thank)
10. *locut* (speak)

THINKING AND WRITING

Writing Aphorisms

Choose three of the observations that you made for the Writing assignment. Rewrite each observation in the form of an aphorism. Be sure that your aphorism, like those of Sir Francis Bacon, is a valid generalization. This requires that your observation be based on sufficient evidence to make the resulting aphorism express a general truth, one that cannot be easily disproved.

(Answers begin on p. 384.)

Idols of the Cave.

2. Two reasons people become attached to certain ideas are that they consider themselves the authors or inventors of them, or that they've spent great time and trouble with them, making them their own.
3. Some minds are able to note differences in things, while others note similarities or resemblances in things.
4. The school of Leucippus and Democritus was so concerned with the particles of things that it overlooked the structure of things.

Interpreting

5. Suggested Response: Bacon felt Aristotle's philosophy was made a bondservant to his logic; that is, his logic kept his philosophy within very tight limits.
6. (a) Suggested Response: Bacon considered his mind to be lofty and discursive. It is possible he considered himself of both minds, however. (b) He dealt with resemblances.
7. He suggests that the intellect not allow itself to be hurried into extreme decisions.
8. The advice in 58 summarizes the four points he made earlier. It also leads to a generalization that students of nature should beware of thoughts or ideas the mind is content or satisfied with.

Applying

9. (a) Suggested Response: The rule is to be suspicious of whatever notion one's mind finds special. (b) Answers will vary, though at least some students should argue for its usefulness. (c) Answers again will vary, though some should mention the applicability of the rule to interpersonal relationships.

ANSWERS TO ANALYZING LITERATURE

1. Legal punishments for revenge should increase in intensity and severity in direct proportion to its occurrence.
2. Virtue needs little beyond its own richness and luster to make its value known.
3. The most prized kind of beauty has at least a touch of strangeness to it.
4. The rich fear losing their wealth; the poor can hope to attain riches.

ANSWERS TO CRITICAL THINKING AND READING

1. This is a valid generalization, as the student has flunked four tests and seems to be getting worse as the course progresses.
2. This is a hasty generalization. Striking out once is no indication of a batter's ability.
3. This is a valid generalization, arrived at through solid experience.
4. This is a hasty generalization, of course.

ANSWERS TO UNDERSTANDING LANGUAGE

1. omniscient, omnipresent
2. revive, vivacious
3. flexible, reflexes
4. aviary, aviation
5. intersect, section
6. fidelity, confidence
7. interrupt, rupture
8. aquatic, aquarium
9. gratitude, grateful, ingrate
10. elocution, eloquent

THINKING AND WRITING

Publishing Student Writing The best efforts of your students can be printed in enlarged form and displayed on a bulletin board.

THE KING JAMES BIBLE

1611

King James I, son of Mary Queen of Scots, ascended the English throne upon the death of Queen Elizabeth I. One of the first demands the new king faced was that of the Puritans for a uniform English version of the Bible. At the Hampton Court Conference in 1604, James accepted their demand. He commissioned fifty-four English scholars and clergymen to compare all extant texts of the Bible and to produce a definitive English edition. They succeeded perhaps beyond their expectations. The King James Version of the Holy Bible, published in 1611, has been called "the only classic ever created by a committee." From its earliest appearance until the present day it has been regarded as one of the great works of English literature.

The Bible, a collection of books developed over a period of more than twelve hundred years, consists of two main parts, the Old Testament and the New Testament. The Old Testament was originally written in Hebrew, the New Testament in Greek. In A.D. 382, St. Jerome translated the Bible into Latin, and his translation, called the Vulgate Version, remained the standard Bible in the West for centuries. An English reformer, John Wyclif, along with his followers, produced the first English translation from Latin in the late 1300's.

It was the Reformation in the 1500's, however—and the growing use of Gutenberg's movable type—that increased the demand for a Bible in the vernacular, or common language of the people. William Tyndale, a Protestant chaplain and tutor, decided to prepare a new English translation from Hebrew and Greek. Faced with clerical opposition at home, he went to Germany, where he translated and printed the New Testament in English. Arrested for heresy while at work on the Old Testament, Tyndale was executed near Brussels, Belgium, in 1536. The importance of Tyndale's New Testament is that the King James committee, impressed by its diction and rhythm, followed it more closely than any other translation in working on their 1611 masterpiece.

Other Bibles preceded the King James Version. None had the immense impact of the King James or Authorized Version, which in fact was never officially "authorized." It won its acceptance through use. Generations of people in Great Britain and the United States grew up reading its text and adding its wisdom to the common store of knowledge. Hundreds of expressions—"swords into plowshares," "fat of the land," "out of the mouths of babes"—are familiar to nearly every English-speaking person, while the magnificent rhythms of the Bible have influenced English prose and poetry throughout its history.

Objective

1. To recognize a psalm

Teaching Portfolio: Support Material

Teacher Backup, p. 00-00

Vocabulary Check, p. 00

Usage and Mechanics Worksheet, pp. 00

Critical Thinking and Reading Worksheet, p. 00

Language Worksheet, p. 00

Selection Test, p. 00

GUIDE FOR READING

Psalm 23; The Parable of the Prodigal Son; I Corinthians 13

Literary Forms

Psalm and Parable. The Bible, particularly the Old Testament, contains a wide variety of literary forms in both prose and poetry. Many of them are already familiar to you, but two may not be. A psalm is a song or lyric poem in praise of God. Psalms were originally meant to be sung to the accompaniment of a stringed instrument. Today the word *psalm* generally refers to one of the 150 poetic pieces in the Old Testament Book of Psalms. Although the Hebrew authors of the psalms are mostly unknown, King David is often credited with having composed a few of them. The subject matter of the psalms varies widely. Some are hymns for public worship; others tell of historical events; still others portray everyday life in the Holy Land.

A parable is a short, simple story, usually about a common kind of occurrence, from which a moral or religious lesson can be drawn. Some parables, such as that of the unproductive vineyard, appear in the Old Testament. In the New Testament, Jesus often answers a question by telling a brief story based on an experience familiar to his listeners. Among the best known New Testament parables are those of the good Samaritan, the mustard seed, and the prodigal son.

Look For

As you read the following selections from the King James Version of the Bible, look for the differences in form among them.

Writing

Think of an incident that would make a good parable. It should be an everyday occurrence whose outcome conveys a moral lesson. Jot down some notes about what happened. Indicate why you think the incident you have chosen fits the requirements for a parable.

Vocabulary

Knowing the following words will help you as you read the selections from the King James Bible.

righteousness (rī′chəs nis) *n.*: Doing what is fair and just (p. 388)

prodigal (präd′i gəl) *adj.*: Addicted to wasteful expenditure (p. 389)

entreated (in trēt′id) *v.*: Begged; pleaded (p. 390)

transgressed (trans grest′) *v.*: overstepped or broke (a law or commandment) (p. 390)

iniquity (in ik′wə tē) *n.*: Wickedness (p. 391)

Literary Focus Among the literary devices used most effectively in the King James Bible is parallelism, the repetition of phrases that are similar in structure. Another is imagery.

Look For Have students look for examples of parallelism and for powerful imagery in the three examples given.

Writing You might suggest, as an alternative, that when your students have read the Parable of the Prodigal Son they write an essay about the father and his two sons aimed at bringing some insight to the parable. They might, for example, concentrate on the universal implications of the story.

Vocabulary Have students use these words in sentences of their own making.

Motivation for Reading Ask students to enjoy the poetic rhythms and imagery of this best known of the psalms before seeking to analyze its meanings.

Master Teacher Note Discuss with your class why this poem is a traditional element in burial services for both Christians and Jews.

Purpose-Setting Question How does the psalm carry the Lord-as-shepherd image through from beginning to end?

1 **Discussion** How do these lines enhance the shepherd idea? How do they go beyond it?

2 **Discussion** How is the speaker supported and comforted by this guidance?

3 **Discussion** What future benefits does the speaker anticipate?

Psalm 23

The Lord is my shepherd; I shall not want.
He maketh me to lie down in green pastures: he leadeth me
1 beside the still waters.
He restoreth my soul: he leadeth me in the paths of
righteousness for his name's sake.
Yea, though I walk through the valley of the shadow of
death, I will fear no evil: for thou art with me; thy rod and
2 thy staff they comfort me.
Thou preparest a table before me in the presence of mine
enemies; thou anointest my head with oil; my cup
runneth over.
3 Surely goodness and mercy shall follow me all the days of
my life: and I will dwell in the house of the Lord forever.

THINKING ABOUT THE SELECTION

Recalling

1. In the first part of the psalm, what images carry out the idea of the Lord as a shepherd?
2. At what point does the psalmist change from speaking of the Lord as a shepherd to viewing Him as a host preparing a feast?

Interpreting

3. Why would the Lord's (shepherd's) rod and staff comfort the psalmist (sheep)?
4. Why is it significant that the table is prepared "in the presence of mine enemies"?

Applying

5. Two years before the King James Bible appeared, the Douay Version, an English translation from Latin, was published in France. Following are the last three lines of Psalm 23 in the Douay Bible. What stylistic features of the King James Version distinguish it from the Douay Version?

Thou hast fatted my head with oil,
and my chalice inebriating how
goodly is it!
And thy mercy shall follow me
all the days of my life
And that I may dwell in the house
of the Lord in longitude of days.

ANALYZING LITERATURE

Recognizing a Psalm

A **psalm** is a sacred song or lyric poem. The psalms in the Book of Psalms, originally in Hebrew, were meant to be sung to the accompaniment of a stringed instrument. Since none of the Biblical translations really advanced that purpose, the paraphrasing of psalms into metrical verse began during the Reformation. This rephrasing, which permitted the psalms to be sung by congregations, emphasized the lyrical nature of the original compositions.

What qualities of Psalm 23 make it especially lyrical?

Answers

ANSWERS TO THINKING ABOUT THE SELECTION

Recalling

1. The Lord provides for the speaker; he guides him to places where there is plenty; he restores his inner well-being; he helps him lead a righteous life; and he protects him from the fears of death and evil.
2. The change occurs with the line that begins "Thou preparest a table . . . ," the speaker refers to the Lord as a host.

Interpreting

3. The rod and staff, or the lord's power, will be used to protect the psalmist.
4. A point is made that all, even the psalmist's enemies, are aware of the protection and sustenance offered by the lord.

Applying

5. The King James Version is simpler. It avoids such Latinate phrases as "chalise inebriating" and "longitude of days."

ANSWERS TO ANALYZING LITERATURE

Suggested Response: Its rythmn and phrasin make it lyrical.

Luke 15:11–32

The Parable of the Prodigal Son

A certain man had two sons. And the
younger of them said to his father, "Father,
1 give me the portion of goods that falleth to
me." And he divided unto them his living.
And not many days after the younger
son gathered all together, and took his journey into a far country, and there wasted his
substance with riotous living. And when he
had spent all, there arose a mighty famine in
that land; and he began to be in want. And
he went and joined himself to a citizen of
2 that country; and he sent him into his fields
to feed swine. And he would fain[1] have filled
his belly with the husks that the swine did
eat and no man gave unto him.
And when he came to himself, he said,
"How many hired servants of my father's
have bread enough and to spare, and I perish with hunger! I will arise and go to my
father, and will say unto him, "Father, I
have sinned against heaven, and before
3 thee, and am no more worthy to be called
thy son. Make me as one of thy hired servants."
And he arose, and came to his father.
But when he was yet a great way off, his
father saw him, and had compassion and
ran, and fell on his neck, and kissed him.
And the son said unto him, "Father, I have
sinned against heaven, and in thy sight, and
am no more worthy to be called thy son."

KING JAMES BIBLE, 1611
Title page of the New Testament
The Folger Shakespeare Library

1. **fain** *adv.*: Gladly.

Motivation for Reading Have students discuss why a well-told parable can teach a lesson more effectively than an argumentative or expository form of expression.

Master Teacher Note Explain that parables—didactic stories—are a universal means of teaching in comparatively unsophisticated or unschooled societies. Since Christ's hearers were often simple country people, it was inevitable that he should use parables to teach them.

Purpose-setting Question Have students keep in mind as they read that a moral or spiritual lesson is being taught. What is it? Is the older son justified in his unhappiness? What point is expressed in the last three paragraphs?

1 **Clarification** Be sure students understand the roles of elder and younger sons in a landholding family: that the elder son will take over the land and titles—a condition that remains in many situations even today.

2 **Discussion** Why do you suppose he does not return to the home of his family?

3 **Discussion** Under what conditions does he at last allow himself to return?

Humanities Note:

King James Bible, 1611, title page of the New Testament. This frontispiece appeared in the first edition of the English Bible of 1611, known as the King James Version. The art for the title page was executed by an unknown artist in the employ of Robert Barker (d.1645). Robert Barker held the office of King's printer, which entitled him to a royally granted monopoly on the printing of English bibles, prayer books, statutes, and proclamations. This handsome page with the classically depicted biblical figures appeared in both of the editions issued in 1611. These books were the most noteworthy issue of the Barker family.

You may wish to ask your students what the style of the drawing indicates about the content of the book.

4 **Clarification** To kill and feast upon the fatted calf bestows great honor upon an event or people for whom it is done. Even the killing of a baby goat, a kid, as mentioned below, was done for some festive occasion.

5 **Discussion** Why does the father say that his son "was dead"?

But the father said to his servants,
"Bring forth the best robe, and put it on
him; and put a ring on his hand, and shoes
4 on his feet; and bring hither the fatted calf,
and kill it; and let us eat, and be merry: for
this my son was dead, and is alive again; he
was lost, and is found." And they began to
be merry.

Now his elder son was in the field; and as he came and drew nigh to the house, he heard music and dancing. And he called one of the servants, and asked what these things meant. And he said unto him, "Thy brother is come; and thy father hath killed the fatted calf, because he hath received him safe and sound."

And he was angry, and would not go in: therefore came his father out, and entreated him. And he answering said to his father, "Lo, these many years do I serve thee, neither transgressed I at any time thy commandment; and yet thou never gavest me a kid, that I might make merry with my friends; but as soon as this thy son was come, which hath devoured thy living, thou hast killed for him the fatted calf."

And he said unto him, "Son, thou art
ever with me, and all that I have is thine. It
was meet[2] that we should make merry, and
be glad: for this thy brother was dead, and is 5
alive slain; and was lost, and is found."

2. **meet** *adj.*: Fitting.

THINKING ABOUT THE SELECTION

Recalling

1. What happens to the younger son's money?
2. (a) Why does the younger son decide to return home? (b) What does he intend to say to his father?
3. How does the father react to the return of his younger son?
4. (a) Why is the older son angry? (b) How does his father answer the complaint?

Interpreting

5. From the limited evidence given in the parable, how repentant do you think the younger son is?
6. Why is the father happy rather than unhappy at the sight of his younger son?
7. To what extent do you think the older son is justified in being angry at the treatment given his brother?

Applying

8. A parable is meant to teach a moral or spiritual lesson. What lesson do you draw from this one?
9. Sometimes this parable is called "The Parable of the *Lost* Son." How might that title affect your reaction to it?

Answers

ANSWERS TO THINKING ABOUT THE SELECTION

1. He spends it foolishly in extravagant ways.
2. (a) He is forced to take menial work to barely survive, and decides he can work as a hired servant at home and avoid starvation. (b) He intends to admit he has sinned against heaven, beg his father's forgiveness for squandering his money, and seek to work as a servant.
3. His father, elated with his son's return, orders a feast in his honor.
4. (a) The older son is angry that his brother is honored despite his failings, while he receives little recognition for his own hard work and clean living. (b) He tells his older son that everything of the father's is his, and that they should be glad that the younger brother, whom they considered literally or figuratively dead, has returned.

Interpreting

5. The evidence is very limited, indeed. He has at least tasted hard times and suffering.
6. The father had given his son up for dead, or at least had feared he would never see him again.
7. There is an implication that the older son is as hard working and obedient as the younger son was unwise and extravagant, and perhaps the feelings expressed have been long held by the obedient brother. A suggestion of "he always liked you better" seems possible.

Applying

8. Suggested Response: One lesson might be that it is never too late to repent and reform oneself.
9. The word *lost* would emphasize the loss of the son to his family. The word *prodigal* on the other hand, emphasizes the son's moral failings.

I Corinthians 13

Though I speak with the tongues of men
and of angels, and have not charity, I am
become as sounding brass, or a tinkling
cymbal. And though I have the gift of prophecy, and understand all mysteries, and all
1 knowledge; and though I have all faith, so
that I could remove mountains, and have not
charity, I am nothing. And though I bestow
all my goods to feed the poor, and though I
give my body to be burned, and have not
charity, it profiteth me nothing. Charity
suffereth long, and is kind; charity envieth
not; charity vaunteth not itself, is not puffed
up, doth not behave itself unseemly, seeketh
not her own, is not easily provoked, think-
2 eth no evil; rejoiceth not in iniquity, but
rejoiceth in the truth; beareth all things,
believeth all things, hopeth all things,
endureth all things. Charity never faileth:
but whether there be prophecies, they shall
fail; whether there be tongues, they shall
cease; whether there be knowledge, it shall
vanish away. For we know in part, and we
prophesy in part. But when that which is
perfect is come, then that which is in part 3
shall be done away. When I was a child, I
spoke as a child; but when I became a man,
I put away childish things. For now we see
through a glass darkly; but then face to
face: now I know the part; but then shall I
know even as also I am known. And now
abideth faith, hope, charity, these three;
but the greatest of these is charity.

THINKING ABOUT THE SELECTION

Recalling

1. In each of the first three sentences, the apostle Paul mentions some impressive personal achievements. (a) What are they? (b) In each case, if he lacks charity, what is the result?
2. The sentence beginning "Charity suffereth long" describes the nature of charity. (a) What does charity do? (b) What does it not do?
3. This passage is a letter to the Corinthians. In it Paul advises them to prepare for the coming perfect times with God. What analogy does he use to make his point clear?

Interpreting

4. Knowing what Paul means by *charity* is vital to an understanding of the passage. He does *not* mean "human kindness" or "doing good." What does the word *charity* mean, as Paul uses it? Context clues can help, but you may also need to consult a dictionary.
5. (a) Given this definition of *charity*, how do faith and hope relate to charity? (b) Why is charity "the greatest of these"?
6. (a) Find two uses of parallelism. (b) Does the use of parallelism make the writing more or less effective? Explain.

Applying

7. The apostle Paul is giving advice to the Corinthians on how to live a spiritual life. How, if at all, do you think it would be possible to know whether a person is following Paul's advice concerning charity?

Motivation for Reading Although this part of a letter to the church in Corinth is written in prose, it contains some of the most poetic, lyrical lines in the English language. Ask students to tell their ideas of the nature of charity, the subject of this passage.

Master Teacher Note Before studying this passage closely, read it aloud so that your students can respond to its rhythms and imagery.

Purpose-Setting Question Paul places great importance upon the expression of charity. What, in fact is he saying about it?

1 **Discussion** What significance does the speaker attribute to charity in human relationships?

2 **Discussion** How does the speaker define charity both by what it is and by what it is not?

3 **Discussion** How does the word and the definition of *part* fit into a clear understanding of the entire passage? How do the lines dealing with childhood and adulthood apply?

Answers

ANSWERS TO THINKING ABOUT THE SELECTION

1. (a) He speaks with the tongues of people and of angels; he has the gift of prophecy, understands all mysteries and all knowledge, and has faith enough to be able to remove mountains: and he bestows all his goods to the poor, and gives his body to be burned. (b) In each case he is as nothing without charity.
2. (a) (b) Charity is long suffering, is kind, is without envy, does not vaunt or puff itself up, is not unseemly, isn't easily provoked, doesn't think in evil ways, rejoices in the truth and disdains iniquity. It bears all things, believes, hopes, and endures, and it never fails.
3. He uses the analogy of a child speaking as a child and an adult putting away childish ways. He also suggests that the time before God is like looking through a glass darkly, while the future will be a matter of looking face to face.

Interpreting

4. Charity, as he intends it, has a broad meaning to include leniency, brotherly love, and tolerance.
5. (a) The combined faith in God, hope for the future, and charity in the present, he suggests, are cornerstones for the kind of life all people desire and deserve. (b) He does not explain why charity is the greatest, though perhaps he assumes that it is because it is, in essence, love.

Applying

6. Suggested Response: One would have to judge from a person's actions, although even then the element of charity in them might be difficult to discern.

The writing assignments on page 392 have students write creatively, while those on page 393 have them think about the selections and write critically.

YOU THE WRITER
Guidelines for Evaluating Assignment 1

1. Has the student written a sonnet that is modeled on one from this unit?
2. Has the student devoted the octave to one main idea and used the sestet to comment upon it?
3. Does the sonnet have fourteen five-beat lines and a rhyme scheme like that of the model?
4. Is the sonnet free from grammar, usage, and mechanics errors?

Guidelines for Evaluating Assignment 2

1. Has the student written a scene showing two individuals in conflict, which is modeled on the dialogue of Marlowe or Shakespeare?
2. Does the scene reveal the nature of the conflict and aspects of their personalities?
3. Does the scene begin slowly and gradually build the conflict?
4. Is the scene free from grammar, usage, and mechanics errors?

Guidelines for Evaluating Assignment 3

1. Has the student written ten personifications modeled on figurative speech found in Elizabethan poetry?
2. Is each of the personifications expressed in a complete sentence?
3. Are the personifications appropriate and clear?
4. Is each of the personification free from grammar, usage, and mechanics errors?

YOU THE WRITER

Assignment

1. Write a sonnet modeled on any one contained in this unit. Your poem should have fourteen five-beat lines and the same rhyme scheme as your model.

Prewriting. Before you write, make a list of subjects that interest you—places, sports, hobbies, people you know, and so on. Then, from this list, choose the topic that appeals to you most and freewrite about it.

Writing. Write the first draft of your sonnet. You might devote the octave to one main idea and use the sestet to comment on it.

Revising. When you revise, check to see that your sonnet has fourteen five-beat lines and a rhyme scheme like that of one of the sonnets you have read.

Assignment

2. Write a scene modeled on the dramatic literature of this period, showing two individuals in conflict. As the characters talk, have them reveal the nature of the conflict between them and aspects of their personalities.

Prewriting. Before you write, make notes on the conflict between the characters. What is it about? How will it develop? How will it conclude?

Writing. Start the scene off slowly and gradually build the conflict. Although you need not use blank verse, try to emulate the style of the speeches in Marlowe or Shakespeare.

Revising. See if you can improve the way you developed and concluded the conflict. Then read the dialogue aloud. Can you improve the style of the speeches? Have you followed the conventions of drama in writing your scene?

Assignment

3. One of the most effective types of figurative language is personification. When a poet uses personification, he or she speaks about a nonhuman thing as if it were a person, maybe by saying something like "The sun is smiling." Write ten examples of personification modeled on the use of this figure of speech in Elizabethan poetry.

Prewriting. Before you write, look around you at the objects in your room, on the street outside your window, in your back yard. Let your imagination picture some of the objects you see doing things that human beings might do—singing, dancing, smiling, and so on.

Writing. Now, using the ideas you obtained by letting your imagination work, write your ten examples of personification.

Revising. When you revise, be sure that each of your examples is expressed in a complete sentence and that the personification is appropriate and clear.

YOU THE CRITIC

Assignment

1. Choose a character from a play in this unit and write an essay discussing the changes he or she undergoes. Tell (1) what the character was like at first, (2) what caused him or her to change, and (3) what he or she was like after the change.

Prewriting. Scan the play of your choice for a character who undergoes a change. When you have found this character, divide a sheet of paper into three columns and make notes on the three focal points mentioned above.

Writing. In your opening paragraph, state your main idea about the change the character undergoes. In the paragraphs that follow, discuss each of the focal points. In your concluding paragraph, restate your main idea in an interesting way.

Revising. When you revise, see if you can improve the organization and style of your essay.

Assignment

2. The theme of a poem is the central idea or insight the poem presents. Choose two poems from this section and write an essay stating the theme of each. In addition, identify the images, lines, and figures of speech that helped the author of each poem to express the theme.

Prewriting. Reread two of the poems you liked best. As you read each poem, ask yourself this question: What is the main idea this poem is expressing? The answer to this question is the theme. Now ask yourself how the poet developed and expressed the theme by using images, figures of speech, and other poetic devices.

Writing. Discuss each poem separately. For each poem state the theme and identify the specific devices that the poet used to develop it.

Revising. When revising, check that your remarks are clear and well supported by apt references to the literature.

Assignment

3. Write an essay about a sonnet from this section, discussing the following: (1) the subject of the sonnet, (2) the poet's attitude toward this subject, and (3) the passages in the poem where this attitude is revealed most clearly.

Prewriting. Reread the poem and try to grasp the author's tone of voice, for this tone reveals the poet's attitude. Where do you hear this tone most clearly—in what lines, words, images?

Writing. In your opening paragraph, identify the subject of the poem and the author's attitude toward it. Then in the body paragraphs, discuss in detail the specific lines in the poem where this attitude is revealed most clearly.

Revising. Revise to improve the clarity and organization of your essay. Then correct any errors in grammar and style that you find.

YOU THE CRITIC

Guidelines for Evaluating Assignment 1

1. Does the student begin the essay by stating his or her thesis about the change the character undergoes?
2. Does the body of the essay discuss what the character was like at first, what caused him or her to change, and what he or she was like after the change?
3. Does the concluding paragraph restate the main idea in an interesting way?
4. Is the essay well-organized and free from grammar, usage, and mechanics errors?

Guidelines for Evaluating Assignment 2

1. Does the student discuss separately the theme of two poems from the Elizabethan period?
2. Has the student explained how images, lines, and figures of speech have contributed to the development of the theme?
3. Has the student supported his or her ideas with sufficient references to the literature?
4. Is the essay free from grammar, usage, and mechanics errors?

Guidelines for Evaluating Assignment 3

1. Has the student identified the subject of the poem and the author's attitude toward it in the opening paragraph?
2. Does the body of the essay discuss with clarity and in detail the specific lines in the poem where this attitude is clearly revealed?
3. Is there a satisfactory concluding paragraph?
4. Is the essay well-organized and free from grammar, usage, and mechanics errors?

Humanities Note

Fine art, *The Thames at Westminster Stairs,* by Claude de Jongh. Little is known about the life of the Dutch painter Claude de Jongh (c. 1600–1663). He worked in Utrecht during the 1620's and 1630's and later traveled to London. It was there that he painted scenes of the Thames River and London Bridge.

The Thames at Westminster Stairs is one of his views of the London Bridge and the Thames during the seventeenth century. In this view the thickly developed bank of the Thames is in sharp contrast with the openness in the distance.

THE THAMES AT WESTMINSTER STAIRS
Claude de Jongh, c. *1600-1663*
Yale Center for British Art, Paul Mellon Collection

THE SEVENTEENTH CENTURY
1625–1660

During the time men live without a common power to keep them all in awe, they are in that condition which is called war, and such a war as is of every man against every man. . . . In such condition there is no place for industry, because the fruit thereof is uncertain, and consequently no culture of the earth; no navigation, nor use of the commodities that may be imported by sea; no commodious building; . . . no arts; no letters; no society; and, which is worst of all, continual fear, and danger of violent death; and the life of man, solitary, poor, nasty, brutish, and short. 1

Thomas Hobbes

1 **Enrichment** This passage from Hobbes is derived from his famous political treatise, *Leviathan.*

In the passage above, Thomas Hobbes pictures the terrible condition of people who lived before there were kings to bring order to society. Without rulers to keep people "in awe," Hobbes insisted, society would dissolve in chaos, and life would be "poor, nasty, brutish, and short." Hobbes claimed he was writing about a "state of nature" that existed before the dawn of history. But, in 1651, he had good reason to worry about the breakdown of society. The English had shocked the world by beheading their king in 1649 and abolishing the monarchy. Perhaps England had not quite reverted to the state of nature Hobbes imagined. But Hobbes, like many conservatives, believed that the violence would continue until the English again had "a common power to keep them all in awe."

It is difficult to believe that civil war followed so closely on the Golden Age of Elizabeth, with its triumphant defeat of the Spanish Armada and its brilliant literary achievements. Looking back, we see the English Renaissance as a time of unsurpassed accomplishments, but to people at the time, the age was one of frightening doubts as well as great expectations.

In science, philosophy, religion, and politics, long-held beliefs and ideas were discredited. The Ptolemaic world view—according to which Earth is the center of a finite universe—was giving way to the Copernican theory of an infinite universe in which the Earth is merely one planet in one of countless solar systems, and not even at the center of its own solar system. William Gilbert's studies of magnetism and William Harvey's discovery of the circulation of the blood opened new realms to the human imagination as well as to the human understanding. Sir Francis Bacon's writings popularized a reliance on observation and experimentation, as opposed to ancient authority, in scientific and intellectual pursuits. And, later in the century, Sir Isaac Newton created the classical physics that remained unchallenged until our own century. The triumph of the modern scientific spirit in the seventeenth century is symbolized by the establishment of the Royal Society in 1662.

Moreover, religious and political grievances, masked by the brilliance of Elizabeth I, began to emerge in the reign of the first Stuart king, James I. During the reign of Charles I, they led to a full-scale civil war. The Civil War unleashed new forces in English society, challenging the most basic ideas of order, even the monarchy itself. It swept away the rigid structure of the old society, in which the court was the center of political power and literary activity. In its place grew a new, competitive society, with a looser social structure and greater freedom in religion and politics.

THE ROOTS OF CIVIL CONFLICT

The roots of the religious and political conflicts that underlay the Civil War stretched back many years. Under Elizabeth the Anglican

Church held to a middle course between Catholicism and Calvinism. Puritans still worshiped and held positions in the Anglican Church, even though they disagreed with some of the church's practices. That situation started to change after James I became king in 1603. James made no secret of his hostility toward Calvinism. He used his power as head of the Anglican Church to dismiss Puritan clergymen.

Charles I

In 1625, Charles I inherited all the religious problems his father had faced—and made them worse. He was married to the daughter of the king of France, a Catholic. That fact alone alarmed the people of England, most of whom were firmly Protestant.

Like his father, Charles had little love for Puritans. The king wholeheartedly supported Archbishop Laud, the reactionary leader of the anti-Puritans. Laud insisted that clergymen "conform," or observe all the church ceremonies, including those the Puritans disliked. In this way, Laud pulled the Anglican Church back toward Catholicism. Laud retreated so far from Protestantism, in fact, that the pope offered to make him a Catholic bishop. Laud refused, but many Protestants still saw him as a Catholic in all but name.

Money Troubles

Charles I was like his father in another way. He was determined, in the words of Charles Dickens, "to be a high and mighty king not to be called to account by anybody." This attitude put Charles on a collision course with Parliament, and the crash came quickly over a basic question: money.

Charles had instigated wars against Spain and France and needed money to fight both enemies. Under English law, the money had to be granted to him by Parliament. But Parliament supported neither venture, and the king had to turn elsewhere. From his wealthy subjects Charles extorted loans by threatening them with prison. Charles lost popularity with commoners by pressing the poor into service as soldiers and sailors.

The king's abuse of his power angered many subjects. When Parliament met in 1628, its members boldly stood up to the king by passing the Petition of Right. This document spelled out the basic rights of Englishmen—at the time women had no political rights. Charles unhappily accepted the Petition of Right in order to get approval for new revenues. He soon showed that he had no intention of abiding by it. When leaders of Parliament protested, Charles had them arrested and then dissolved Parliament. For the next eleven years, Charles ruled without so much as calling Parliament into session.

BRITISH EVENTS

1625 Full-bottomed wigs come into fashion.

1627 **Sir Francis Bacon** publishes *The New Atlantis*.

1628 William Harvey explains blood circulation.

1633 **John Donne's** *Poems* published.

George Herbert's *The Temple* published.

1634 Covent Garden Market opens.

1635 Public mail service established.

1637 Charles I summons Long Parliament.

John Milton publishes *Lycidas*.

1640 **John Donne's** *Devotions upon Emergent Occasions* published.

1642 English Civil War begins.

Puritans close theaters.

1644 **John Milton** writes *Areopagitica*.

1645 **John Milton** publishes *Poems*.

1646 **John Suckling** publishes *Fragmenta Aurea*.

1647 First newspaper ad appears.

1648 George Fox founds Society of Friends (Quakers).

Robert Herrick publishes *Hesperdes*.

1649 Charles I beheaded.

Richard Lovelace publishes *Lucasta*.

1651 Thomas Hobbes publishes *Leviathan*.

1653 Oliver Cromwell becomes Lord Protector.

1658 Oliver Cromwell dies.

1659 Puritan government collapses.

1660 Monarchy restored.

Theaters reopened.

Sir Francis Bacon

Execution of Charles I

The Night Watch

John Milton

Covent Garden Market

New Amsterdam

Molière

King Louis XIV

Andrew Marvell

WORLD EVENTS

1626 North America: Dutch found New Amsterdam.

1630 France: Beginning of public advertising.

North America: William Bradford begins writing *Of Plymouth Plantation*.

Boston founded by John Winthrop.

1636 North America: Rhode Island founded by Roger Williams.

Harvard University founded.

France: Corneille publishes *Le Cid*.

1637 Japan: All Europeans expelled.

1639 India: English settlement established at Madras.

1640 North America: *Bay Psalm Book* published in Massachusetts.

Italy: First European cafe opens in Venice.

Holland: Rembrandt paints *Self-Portrait*.

1642 Holland: Rembrandt paints *Night Watch*.

North America: Education becomes compulsory in Massachusetts.

1643 France: Molière founds Comédie Française.

1644 France: Descartes publishes *Principia Philosophicae*.

China: Ming Dynasty ends.

1647 North America: Massachusetts establishes free public schools.

1651 North America: William Bradford finishes *Of Plymouth Plantation*.

1654 France: Louis XIV becomes king.

1657 France: First stockings manufactured.

1659 France: Molière publishes "The Flying Doctor."

1660 South Africa: First Dutch settlers arrive.

Humanities Note

Fine art, *Portrait of Charles I,* c. 1635, by Anthony van Dyck. Anthony van Dyck (1599–1641) was an important Baroque artist, who attained international stature. He was court painter in England to Charles I from 1632 to 1644. He is best known for the portraits he painted during this time. The flourishing aristocratic society of this period was charmed by this handsome painter, friend of Charles I.

Van Dyck created a new aristocratic portrait tradition that continued into the late eighteenth century. He had the ability to capture a vivid likeness but with an elegant style. This portrait of Charles I hunting shows the king at ease in a less rigid pose than a formal state portrait, but hardly less grand. The fluid backdrop with landscape, horse, and two grooms contrasts with the elegance of the king's pose.

PORTRAIT OF CHARLES I
Anthony van Dyck
The Louvre, Paris

Conflict with the Puritans

Many English subjects were disgusted with Charles, but none more so than the Puritans. The king's ally, Archbishop Laud, had stepped up his persecution of these Calvinist "dissenters." In brutal public ceremonies, Puritan leaders had their noses slit, their cheeks branded, and their ears cropped off. The Puritans often displayed such faith and resolve during these mutilations that they won the hearts of onlookers. "The more I am beaten down, the more I am lifted up!" exclaimed one Puritan as a torturer finished his work.

It was no accident that Laud and the "High Church" Anglicans supported the king, while most Puritans opposed him. The Puritan religious outlook had implications for politics. Radical Puritans wanted to do away with bishops and the whole hierarchy of the Anglican Church. They believed that each congregation, or group of worshipers, had the right to choose its own minister. As you can see, this belief resembled democracy in politics.

Most Puritans were dead set against the idea of a king's "divine right" to rule, on which Charles I insisted. One Puritan put the matter plainly: "A King is a thing men have made for their own sakes." It was only a short step further to the idea that men could *un*make a king. James I had understood this danger and summed it up in the curt phrase, "No bishop, no king."

The Long Parliament

The policies of Charles and Archbishop Laud were unpopular enough in England. But when the king and archbishop tried to force conformity on Scottish Calvinists, the Scots rose up in defiance. In 1639, King Charles had to lead an army north to put down the rebellion. With the war stalemated, Charles returned to London, once again desperate for funds.

Parliament, however, was in no mood to grant the king's request without guarantees in return. Among other things, Parliament demanded the trial of Laud and Thomas Wentworth, the hated leader of the king's army. Both were tried and later executed. The legislators also insisted on reforms to limit the power of the king. As the session went on in the stormy atmosphere of London, one demand led to another. At last, in 1642, Parliament condemned Charles as a tyrant.

Charles struck back by sending armed men into Parliament to seize the opposition leaders. The leaders escaped, and Parliament began raising its own army. Charles fled north, rallying loyalists to his side. For the next eleven years, the "Long Parliament" ruled England. The Civil War had begun.

The Civil War

When war came, the people of England were forced to choose sides. The king's supporters were called Cavaliers, since many of

2 **Historical Context** According to Divine Right belief, power comes *down* from God to the king; according to Puritan belief, power rises *up* from the people to the king.

Humanities Note

Print, *The Execution of Charles I of England.* Charles I was brought to trial by the lower house of Parliament—elected men who decided they should rule. His execution sent horror throughout Europe; his was the first state execution of a monarch.

This woodcut, colored by hand, shows the execution scene. Woodblock prints are made by cutting the lines of the picture into a block of wood, which is then inked and pressed onto paper. The simple lines are obvious in this print. The artist has made the executioner's ax prominent, while the halberds of those surrounding the platform seem to reflect it.

3 **Historical Context** Cromwell's New Model Army, known as "Ironsides," was probably the finest fighting force in Europe.

4 **Historical Context** Charles's execution was not popular. When his severed head was displayed to the huge crowd in attendance, they uttered a groan "such as I never heard before and desire I may never hear again," according to a contemporary diarist.

THE EXECUTION OF KING CHARLES I OF ENGLAND AT WHITEHALL, LONDON, JANUARY 30, 1649
Colored woodcut from Contemporary Ballad-Sheet
The Granger Collection

these aristocrats were skilled horsemen, or cavalry. They generally lived in the countryside. Parliament drew its followers from London and the towns, where Puritanism ran strong. Because these austere Calvinists cut their hair short, they were known as Roundheads.

The same grit Puritans had shown under the torturer's hand
3 made them fierce enemies. The dour Puritan leader Oliver Cromwell took charge of Parliament's forces. He drilled them into an unparalleled fighting machine called the New Model Army. At the Battle of Marston Moor, the New Model Army showed the power of its training. The next year, in 1645, Cromwell's troops defeated a Cavalier army and captured Charles I.

Meanwhile, a battle of another kind was going on in Parliament. There, members of the different Protestant factions were struggling for power. Gradually, the most radical Puritans won out. In 1648, they shut the doors on moderate members. Then the radicals brought Charles I to trial. With no moderates to oppose them, the
4 radical Puritans found the king guilty of treason. Charles I was beheaded on January 1, 1649. Parliament, or the few members who remained, declared that the monarchy was over and that England was a republic.

From Commonwealth to Protectorate

The monarchy was gone, but what would replace it? Oliver Cromwell became leader of the new English Commonwealth, as the new government was called. Cromwell, ruling with the radicals left in Parliament, faced the hopeless task of uniting a nation divided not into two but numerous factions. Many subjects had turned against Parliament after the execution of Charles I. A popular poem of the time lamented:

On Tuesday last his Grace,
Cheerfully, cheerfully,
Went to his dying place,
to end all strife,
Where many a weeping eye,
With groans unto the skie,
To see his Majesty,
There end his life.

Discontent among the English people was fueled by the severe policies of the Puritans. They outlawed gambling, horse racing, newspapers, fancy clothes, public dancing, and theater. Cromwell faced perils from outside England, too. In Scotland, rebels rallied to Charles II, son of the executed king. In Ireland, Catholics had risen
against Protestant landowners. Cromwell himself led the force that 5
savagely repressed that rebellion. In addition, England was at war against Spain and Holland.

These disorders forced Cromwell to give up even the pretense of republican government. In 1653, he dissolved Parliament and named himself Lord Protector. He ruled as a virtual dictator until his death in 1658, when his son became Lord Protector. By then the English people were thoroughly sick of the endless taxations, violence, and disorder. Parliament reconvened and asked Charles II to become king. In 1660, the monarchy was restored. Though Cromwell inspired as much fear and hatred as love and reverence, he always remained true to his own high moral purposes. The measures he resorted to as ruler of England were stern and painful, yet they were probably necessary to achieve order in such a troubled, disorderly period of English history.

LITERATURE OF A TURBULENT AGE

The reign of Charles I and the Interregnum, or period between reigns, that followed were a time of intense religious and political conflict. Under Charles I, the court remained the center of literary life. Poets upheld the traditional courtly values of loyalty to crown and church and the strict code of honor. Not surprisingly, the poets often fought on the side of the king.

The literature of the turbulent years from 1625 to 1660 in part continues the styles of the Renaissance and in part reflects changing conditions. Although Ben Jonson and others wrote plays that were more popular than Shakespeare's, the period is not remembered for its drama. Rather, it is an age that produced some of the best-loved poems in English—Jonson's crystalline lyrics and digni-

5 **Historical Context** Cromwell's name still lives in infamy in Ireland.

Humanities Note

Fine art, *Oliver Cromwell,* by Sir Peter Lely. Peter Lely was a Flemish school portrait painter. Upon arriving in England, he studied the paintings of Van Dyck (who had just died), and his earlier portraits often approach the great master's style. During the Civil War, Lely received portrait commissions from members of both political parties.

Oliver Cromwell (1599–1658), the powerful military leader, foe of Charles I, and "Lord Protector" of Britain, headed a virtual dictatorship under a constitution drafted by officers of the army. Lely painted this portrait showing Cromwell in military garb, but not with the sternness and implacability often associated with him. During the period known as the Restoration, Charles II knighted Lely and appointed him court painter.

OLIVER CROMWELL
Sir Peter Lely (Peter Van Der Faes)
Firenze, Galleria Palatina
Art Resource

fied, longer poems modeled after classical precedents; John Donne's brilliant, intellectually ingenious, amorous and religious verses; and Andrew Marvell's lyrics combining the classical polish of Jonson and the intellectual brilliance of Donne. Appropriate to a society cleft by civil war, the literature of the age had another side. The Puritan writers John Milton and John Bunyan produced deeply religious works very much different in style and substance from those of Jonson, Donne, and their followers.

Jonson's Life

The most influential writer of the early 1600s was Ben Jonson. Jonson's life is a mirror of the tensions of his time. Jonson rose from humble origins—his stepfather was a bricklayer. The family lived near Westminster Abbey, however, and Jonson was lucky enough to attend its school. There he read the Greek and Latin authors that shaped so much of his own later writing. Although he hoped to attend college, the young Jonson found himself laying bricks. But he refused to give up his ambitions. One friend described him as having "a trowel in his hand . . . and a book in his pocket."

Jonson set down his trowel to become a soldier, and later turned up as an actor in London. One of his earliest works, a satirical play, was condemned as slanderous and landed Jonson in jail. A later play was well received, but Jonson had little chance to bask in the praise. He argued with an actor, killed him in a duel, and was once again imprisoned. There Jonson converted to Catholicism, though he later returned to the Anglican church—another sign of the changeable times he lived in.

Ultimately, Jonson became a great favorite of James I and was friendly with many noblemen and with other writers—including Shakespeare, who acted in one of Jonson's earliest plays and is the subject of one of his finest poems. By the 1620s Jonson was the best-known poet in a city of poets. As one admirer said, Jonson was the "fairest light in no darke time."

THE SCHOOLS OF JONSON AND DONNE

Jonson's Work

6 In Jonson's life we can see the turmoil of his age—violence, persecution, religious conflict. But in his writing Jonson strove for the perfection and harmony he found in his beloved classical authors, turning away from the ornate style of Elizabethan times. Although Jonson was steeped in, and greatly influenced by, the classics, he was not an imitator. He created his own voice, which people of the time recognized as distinctively modern and strong.

Jonson took seriously the role of poet. He believed, in fact, that no other profession could compare to it. Poets, he wrote, encourage "young men to all good disciplines, inflame grown men to all great virtues, [and] keep old men in their best and supreme state." A person could not be "the good poet without first being a good man," he asserted. Jonson lived up to this moral duty in several ways: by giving good advice in some poems; by honoring worthy men and
7 women in others; and, in his plays, by satirizing corruption and immorality.

The School of Donne

The other great poet of the early 1600's was John Donne (1572?–1631). Whereas Jonson did all he could to raise the prestige of poets, and personally oversaw the printing of his poems, Donne

BEN JONSON
The Granger Collection

Humanities Note

Fine art, *Portrait of Ben Jonson.* Portraiture was the most common and respected form of art in the seventeenth century. The sober, restrained style of this portrait of Ben Jonson reflects the artistic trends following the Reformation and the strength of Protestant, and particularly Puritan, beliefs in the country.

6 **Literary Movement** This classical clarity is evident in the lyrics "On My First Son," page 446; "Song: to Celia," page 447; and "Still to Be Neat," page 448.

7 **Enrichment** Jonson's plays *Volpone* and *The Alchemist,* for example, both satirize avarice.

8 Enrichment These early poems generally share the cynical Cavalier attitude toward love.

9 Literary Movement See Holy Sonnets 10 and 14, pages 422–424, which exemplify this deep religious commitment.

10 Enrichment It was T. S. Eliot's critical essays that revived interest in Donne and the other metaphysical poets in the twentieth century.

never tried to make writing a career. His poems, in fact, were not published until two years after his death. But manuscripts of his work circulated at court, and his witty, cerebral poems created a widely admired style in English literature: metaphysical poetry.

Donne's life, like Jonson's, reflected his turbulent age. Donne was raised a Roman Catholic. After studying at Oxford, he traveled
abroad, fighting against the Spanish in the 1590's. As a young man,
8 Donne took an active part in the life of the court and composed
many fine love poems. (According to Ben Jonson, Donne wrote "all
his best pieces ere he was twenty-five.") Later, Donne turned to the Protestant faith. In 1615, he was ordained as an Anglican minister. His sermons in St. Paul's Cathedral, which often lasted for hours, held hundreds of listeners at rapt attention. They are among the finest prose works of the century. After the death of his wife, Donne withdrew from society. In contrast to the fervent love poems of his youth, Donne's later poetry expresses intense religious feeling, often penitential in character. Given Donne's evolution from courtier
9 to minister, it is not surprising that his poetry often embodies the
conflict between the spirit and the world.

More than any other poet,Donne is associated with the metaphysical school of poetry. Metaphysical poetry is characterized by an unusual degree of intellectualism. Even in his love poems, Donne will base his images and figures of speech on material drawn from law, medieval theology and philosophy, natural science, metalurgy, medicine, astronomy, old legends, and other sources that more conventional poets seldom make use of. Moreover, Donne's poems are frequently structured like ingenious, subtle arguments involving
complicated—and often witty—reasoning. Finally, they often em-
10 ploy a type of metaphor termed a *conceit*. A conceit is a comparison
in which the subject is likened to something that would never normally be associated with it. In Donne's most famous conceit, for example, he likens his and his beloved's souls to the legs of a geometrician's compass:

> If they be two, they are two so
>   As stiff twin compasses are two;
> Thy soul, the fixed foot, makes no show
>   To move, but doth if the other do.
>
> And though it in the center sit,
>   Yet, when the other far doth roam,
> It leans and hearkens after it,
>   And grows erect as that comes home.

The Sons of Ben

Jonson and Donne were the dominant poets of their age. Later poets of the seventeenth century are usually classified as being

JOHN DONNE
The Granger Collection

disciples of either Jonson or Donne. Like all such categorizations, these are only partly correct. The "Sons of Ben" were influenced by Donne's work, and the "School of Donne" read and admired Ben Jonson. The basic distinction is useful nonetheless.

Among the best-known sons of Ben were Robert Herrick, Sir John Suckling, and Richard Lovelace. These Sons of Ben are also called Cavalier poets, since they are identified with the king's cause. Robert Herrick (1591–1674) was probably closest to Jonson in style and temperament. Although he lived through the Civil War and Interregnum, Herrick's poetry gives little evidence of these worldly disturbances. He concentrated instead on things that could not
touched be touched by war: "I sing of Brooks, of Blossomes, Birds, 11

Humanities Note

Fine art, *Portrait of John Donne.* This seventeenth-century portrait of Donne presents Donne's complex nature, as he was both highly intellectual and deeply emotional. The formal quality of the portrait and the serene expression reflect Donne's religious devotion.

11 **Enrichment** Herrick's "To the Virgins, to Make Much of Time," page 454, is a *carpe diem* poem: literally, "seize the day;" enjoy the moment because life is fleeting.

12 Literary Movement Both "The Constant Lover," page 458, and "Song," page 459, echo an attitude prevalent among the Cavalier poets: cynicism about love.

13 Master Teacher Note To dramatize the diametrically different attitudes toward love of the Elizabethans and the Cavaliers, you might ask students to compare "The Constant Lover," page 458, with Shakespeare's Sonnet 116, page 210.

14 Literary Movement See "To Lucasta, on Going to the Wars," page 460, and "To Althea, from Prison," page 461, both of which voice these views.

15 Literary Movement Herbert's "Man," page 435, contains a number of conceits, as do "Virtue," page 432, and "Easter Wings," page 434, to a lesser degree.

16 Enrichment T. S. Eliot showed his great admiration for "To His Coy Mistress," page 440, by quoting and paraphrasing passages from it in both "The Love Song of J. Alfred Prufrock" and "The Waste Land." Marvell's poem is another example of the *carpe diem* tradition.

and Bowers; /Of April, May, of June and July-Flowers." Herrick, who became an Anglican minister, also wrote graceful religious poems.

Sir John Suckling (1609–1642), an admirer of Jonson's style but not of his moral severity, was also influenced by Donne's early love poems. Suckling, the perfect courtier, was everything the Puritans
12 despised. A gambler, cardsharp, and pleasure seeker, he is
13 remembered today for his love poems. In 1639, Suckling marched north with Charles I to put down the Scottish rebellion. He fled England two years later after becoming involved in a political intrigue and died in France at a young age.

Richard Lovelace (1618–1656?) was, like Suckling, a luminary of Charles I's court. A strikingly handsome man, Lovelace wrote
14 about themes near the heart of the Cavaliers: honor, bravery, true love, and stoical resolve. Lovelace also fought for the king's cause and went to prison for it. It was there that he wrote many of his finest poems.

The School of Donne

The most notable followers of John Donne were George Herbert (1593–1633) and Andrew Marvell (1621–1678). Herbert's mother was a friend of Donne's, and in many ways the life of Herbert parallels Donne's. He keenly felt the tension between religious and worldly drives. At first intending to enter the church, Herbert was tempted for a time to enjoy the sparkling life at the court of James I. Later Herbert became an Anglican deacon and gave himself to the care of his parish. Like Donne, Herbert excelled at the conceit and
15 the other stylistic features of metaphysical poetry. However, Herbert's best poems are almost all religious lyrics. When read together, in his volume *The Temple*, they reveal a greater range of religious feelings than are found in Donne's religious verse.

Andrew Marvell was born later than the other metaphysical and Cavalier poets and is in many ways a figure of transition. Marvell was still a young man when the Civil War began and had little connection with the court. In fact, for three years Marvell tutored the daughter of a Puritan leader. Later Marvell became the assistant of John Milton, the greatest of the Puritan poets. When the monarchy was restored in 1660, Marvell used his influence at court to prevent Milton's execution for treason.

Marvell's best lyrics blend the metaphysical brilliance of Donne and Herbert and the classical finish of Jonson and Herrick. They offer observations on nature, love, and God that, at first, seem urbane and conventional but on closer inspection, prove profound
16 and problematical. His best-known poem, "To His Coy Mistress," is one of the very best lyrics in English literature.

GEORGE HERBERT
The Granger Collection

THE PURITAN WRITERS

So far we have been looking at poets connected with the court of the Stuarts. But perhaps the greatest poet of the seventeenth century was a Puritan, not a Cavalier: John Milton. The Puritan movement also produced the best-selling prose writer of the century, John Bunyan. Only the Bible sold more copies than Bunyan's religious narrative *The Pilgrim's Progress*.

John Milton

In John Milton (1608–1674) the streams of the Renaissance and the Reformation flow together. Like Ben Jonson, he was a learned disciple of the Greek and Latin authors. But unlike Elizabethan humanists and the Cavalier poets, Milton was a profound Calvinist who studied the Old Testament in Hebrew.

Humanities Note

Fine art, *Portrait of George Herbert.* This portrait presents Herbert in the garb of a parish priest, the life he chose over his career in court. His serenity is offset by a penetrating gaze, reflecting an intense intellectual commitment as well as deep religious convictions.

17 Literary Movement See Milton's sonnet "When I Consider How My Light Is Spent," page 466.

18 Enrichment When Bunyan went to prison for refusing to refrain from preaching Puritan doctrine, he took two books with him: Foxe's *Book of Martyrs* and the Bible. They provided his inspiration for *The Pilgrim's Progress*.

19 Literary Movement An excerpt from *The Pilgrim's Progress* begins on page 482.

Milton was born in London to a prosperous middle-class family. He got a good basic education, studied at Cambridge, and spent six years after college reading and studying on his own. In the 1640's, Milton was working as a private tutor in London. As the battle between Charles I and Parliament grew hotter, Milton began writing political pamphlets for the Roundhead cause. His part in the "pamphlet wars" produced *Areopagitica,* a ringing call for freedom of the press.

Milton supported the Commonwealth and Protectorate and even defended the execution of Charles I. As Cromwell's rule turned to a dictatorship, however, Milton lost hope in the possibility of
17 forming a just society on earth. Milton, who went completely blind by 1652, set about composing an epic that would offer a poetic explanation as to why God allows suffering and unhappiness in this world.

Paradise Lost, published in 1667, reflects Milton's humanistic love of poetry and his Puritan devotion to God. In Book I of *Paradise Lost,* Milton voices his poetic ambition: to create "things unattempted yet in Prose or Rhyme." A few lines later he asserts his religious aim: to "justify the ways of God to men." The poem is both a heroic epic that recounts the expulsion of Adam and Eve from Eden and a vindication of God's wisdom.

John Bunyan

After decades of political activity, Milton concluded that the best humans could hope for was to lead their individual lives blamelessly. That was the premise that John Bunyan began with. Unlike Milton, Bunyan had little education beyond reading the Bible, but what his reading and studies lacked in variety they made up for in profundity. A tinker by trade, Bunyan wandered from town to town in rural England, preaching wherever people would listen. After the
18 restoration of Charles II, Bunyan was imprisoned, and it was there he wrote *The Pilgrim's Progress*.

The simplicity of the work in form and style was no small factor in its success. The allegory tells the story of a man who flees sin to lead a holy life. In his "apology" for the work Bunyan tells his readers:

19 This book will make a traveller of thee,
If by its counsel thou wilt ruled be;
It will direct thee to the Holy Land,
If thou wilt its directions understand.

Bunyan and Milton produced the greatest literary works of the Puritan revolution. The Commonwealth had failed, but left behind a new culture that was neither courtly nor Puritan. The next age would belong to professional writers, journalists, and playwrights, not to courtly poets or Puritan proselytizers. The revolution that had begun in the mid-seventeenth century would continue in the eighteenth.

ENGLISH VOICES

Quotations by Prominent Figures of the Period

No man is an Island, entire of itself; . . . any man's death diminishes me, because I am involved in Mankind; and therefore never send to know for whom the bell tolls; it tolls for thee.

John Donne, "Meditation XVII"

Art hath an enemy called Ignorance.

Ben Jonson, "Every Man Out of His Humor"

Drink to me only with thine eyes
And I will pledge with mine.

Ben Jonson, "To Celia"

Gather ye rosebuds while ye may,
Old Time is still a-flying.

Robert Herrick, "To the Virgins to Make Much of Time"

They also serve who only stand and wait.

John Milton, "Sonnet: On His Blindness"

But at my back I always hear
Time's winged chariot hurrying near.

Andrew Marvell, "To His Coy Mistress"

I have laid aside business, and gone a-fishing.

Izaak Walton, *The Compleat Angler*

Stone walls do not a prison make,
Nor iron bars a cage.

Richard Lovelace, "To Althea, from Prison"

Reading Critically The purpose of this page is to guide students in the critical reading of seventeenth century English literature. The information offered here will allow students to place a work of literature in its historical context, identify literary movements of the time, and appreciate the techniques used by writers of the period.

As you discuss the information on the page with the class, explain that the poem "To the Memory of My Beloved Master, William Shakespeare" by Ben Jonson beginning on page 413, is a model for reading critically. The side columns contain notes that draw students' attention to elements that reflect the historical context, the influence of the literary movements, and the writer's techniques.

To give students further practice with the process of reading critically, use the selection in the Teaching Portfolio, page 000, which students can annotate themselves. Encourage students to use these strategies as they read the literature in this unit.

Teaching to Ability Levels For **less advanced** students, you might review any difficult vocabulary words with the class before reading. Also, summarize the poem for the class before they read. **More advanced** students might appreciate reading the poem aloud.

READING CRITICALLY

The Literature of 1625–1660

When you read literature, it is important to place it in its historical context. Doing so will help you to understand influences on the writer's ideas and techniques.

Historical Context

During the years from 1625 to 1660, England suffered from tremendous political and religious unrest. Shortly after Charles I inherited the throne in 1625, he became involved in a power struggle with the Parliament, whose members strongly objected to his efforts to limit Parliamentary authority. Charles I's continuing suppression of Puritans also aroused a great deal of anger among certain members of the Parliament, many of whom were Puritans. This controversy resulted in a civil war that began in 1642 and brought about the temporary downfall of the monarchy in 1649. Oliver Cromwell, a Puritan member of Parliament, ruled the nation for nine years before dying in 1658 and leaving the country in the hands of his son, Richard. Richard proved to be an ineffective ruler, however, and in 1660 the monarchy was restored.

Literary Movements

The writers from this period can be divided essentially into two groups: the metaphysical poets and the Sons of Ben. A group consisting of John Donne and several of his followers, the metaphysical poets are known for their intellectual verse filled with complex, elaborate, and striking comparisons. In contrast, the Sons of Ben, led by the influential poet Ben Jonson, are known for their precise, witty, and elegant poetry. However, John Milton, probably the most significant writer of the period, did not fit into either of these categories. Drawing upon a variety of literary traditions, Milton produced a range of different types of works.

Writers' Techniques

Among the metaphysical poets, the conceit, an especially striking type of metaphor, was a popular literary device. Influenced by the works of the ancient Greeks and Romans, the Sons of Ben relied on classical poetic forms and often used allusions in their works. Milton, on the other hand, made extensive use of both metaphors and allusions.

On the following pages is a poem by Ben Jonson. The notes in the side column should help you to place the poem in its historical context.

Objectives

1. To analyze allusions
2. To analyze the effect of allusions
3. To write an informal letter offering an opinion

Teaching Portfolio: Support Materials

Teacher Backup, p.

Reading Critically, p. 00

Usage and Mechanics Worksheet, p. 00

Analyzing Literature Worksheet, p. 00

Critical Thinking and Reading Worksheet, p. 00

Language Worksheet, p. 00

Selection Test, p. 00

MODEL

To the Memory of My Beloved Master, William Shakespeare

Ben Jonson

To draw no envy, Shakespeare, on thy name,
Am I thus ample[1] to thy book and fame:
While I confess thy writings to be such
As neither man nor Muse can praise too much.
'Tis true, and all men's suffrage.[2] But these ways
Were not the paths I meant unto thy praise:
For silliest[3] ignorance on these may light,
Which, when it sounds at best, but echoes right;
Or blind affection,[4] which doth ne'er advance
The truth, but gropes, and urgeth all by chance;
Or crafty malice, might pretend this praise,
And think to ruin, where it seemed to raise . . .
But thou art proof against them, and indeed
Above the ill fortune of them, or the need.
I, therefore will begin. Soul of the age!
The applause! delight! the wonder of our stage!
My Shakespeare, rise; I will not lodge thee by
Chaucer, or Spenser, or bid Beaumont[5] lie
A little further, to make thee a room:
Thou art a monument, without a tomb,
And art alive still, while thy book doth live,
And we have wits to read, and praise to give.

Historical Context: This poem first appeared in the opening pages of the first edition of Shakespeare's collected plays, published in 1623.

Literary Movement: Jonson stresses a rational, intellectual examination of Shakespeare's achievements.

Writer's Technique: Jonson uses apostrophe, directly addressing Shakespeare in the poem.

Literary Movement: Jonson uses the type of strong and elegant yet simple and precise language that characterized the poetry of the Sons of Ben.

---

1. **ample:** Liberal.
2. **suffrage:** Agreement.
3. **silliest:** Simplest.
4. **blind affection:** Prejudice.
5. **Beaumont:** Francis Beaumont (1584–1616), a playwright who was one of Shakespeare's contemporaries. Chaucer, Spenser, and Beaumont were buried in Westminster Abbey; Shakespeare was buried in Stratford. Jonson believes that it is proper for Shakespeare to be buried apart from these other important writers.

Motivation for Reading Imagine that you were given the assignment of writing an introduction to a collection of Shakespeare's plays. What would you say about them? In what literary form would you choose to write? Ben Jonson, a follower of Shakespeare, was in that position. He wrote a poem.

Purpose-Setting Question Jonson was not only a poet but also a playwright. This introduction seems particularly generous because Shakespeare's plays were competing with and receiving more acclaim than Jonson's. What does this praise of Shakespeare indicate about Jonson's character?

Enrichment A close intimacy sprang up between Shakespeare and Jonson. Together they drew a great circle of friends around them. The company often met at the Mermaid Tavern, which boasted about entertaining "the tribe of Ben."

Clarification In line 19, Jonson is referring to the south transept of Westminster Abbey, the Poets' Corner. Many of England's greatest poets are buried there; among them Geoffrey Chaucer, Edmund Spenser, John Dryden, Thomas Gray, Alfred Tennyson, and Robert Browning. Nearby lie the men of letters.

Look For For Herbert, the formal perfection of a poem reflected the perfection of God's creation, and Herbert's poems are well-known for their formal virtuosity. Note that the 164 poems in *The Temple* display some 140 different stanzaic patterns.

Writing Have **less advanced** students write a brief essay explaining how their motto is appropriate to the picture they chose.

Vocabulary Dicuss with **less advanced** students the meanings of unfamiliar words in their vocabulary list.

Objectives

1. To understand Herbert's use of emblems and symbols
2. To analyze Herbert's style
3. To write about emblematic images

Motivation for Reading Have students imagine and then describe feeling a sense of intimacy and cooperation with God. How would they express this intimacy? What objects might they choose as symbols to help them describe their feeling?

Writer's Technique: Jonson uses regular rhyme and rhythm throughout the poem.

Writer's Technique: Jonson alludes to classical Greek and Roman tragic playwrights.

That I not mix thee so, my brain excuses,
I mean with great, but disproportioned[6] Muses;
For, if I thought my judgment were of years,
I should commit thee surely with thy peers,
And tell, how far thou didst our Lyly outshine,
Or sporting Kyd, or Marlowe's[7] mighty line.
And though thou hadst small[8] Latin, and less Greek,
From thence to honor thee, I would not seek
For names; but call forth thund'ring Aeschylus,
Euripides, and Sophocles to us,
Paccuvius, Accius,[9] him of Cordova dead,[10]
To life again, to hear thy buskin[11] tread,
And shake a stage: Or, when thy socks[12] were on,

---

6. disproportioned: Not comparable.
7. Lyly . . . Kyd . . . Marlowe: Elizabethan playwrights who influenced Shakespeare.
8. small: A limited knowledge of.
9. Aeschylus (es′ *k*ə ləs)**, Euripides** (yoo rip′ ə dēz′) **. . . Sophocles** (sof′ ə klēz′) **. . . Paccuvius** (pə ko͞o′ vē əs), **Accius** (ak′ ē əs): Classical Greek and Roman tragic playwrights.
10. him . . . dead: Classical Roman playwright, Seneca, born in Cordova, Spain.
11. buskin: Symbolizes tragedy. Tragic actors wore shoes with thick "buckskin" soles.
12. socks: Symbolize comedy. Comic actors wore thin-soled shoes called "socks."

Leave thee alone, for the comparison
Of all, that insolent Greece, or haughty Rome
Sent forth, or since did from their ashes come.
Triumph, my Britain, thou hast one to show,
To whom all scenes[13] of Europe homage owe.
He was not of an age, but for all time!
And all the Muses still were in their prime,
When like Apollo[14] he came forth to warm
Our ears, or like a Mercury[15] to charm!
Nature herself was proud of his designs,
And joyed to wear the dressing of his lines!
Which were so richly spun, and woven so fit,[16]
As, since, she will vouchsafe no other wit.
The merry Greek, tart Aristophanes,
Neat Terence, witty Plautus,[17] now not please,
But antiquated, and deserted lie
As they were not of Nature's family.
Yet must I not give Nature all; thy art,
My gentle Shakespeare, must enjoy a part.
For though the poet's matter nature be,
His art doth give the fashion.[18] And, that he
Who casts[19] to write a living line, must sweat,
(Such as thine are) and strike the second heat
Upon the Muse's anvil; turn the same,
(And himself with it) that he thinks to frame,
Or for the laurel[20] he may gain a scorn;
For a good poet's made, as well as born.
And such wert thou. Look how the father's face
Lives in his issue, even so, the race
Of Shakespeare's mind, and manners brightly shines
In his well torned, and true filèd[21] lines;
In each of which, he seems to shake a lance,[22]
As brandished at the eyes of ignorance.

Writer's Technique: Jonson alludes to figures from Greek and Roman mythology.

Writer's Technique: Jonson alludes to classical Greek and Roman comic dramatists. Jonson's frequent use of allusions to classical Greece and Rome reflects the influence of classical writing and ideas on his work.

Writer's Technique: Jonson uses the work of a blacksmith as a metaphor for the tasks of a poet.

Literary Movement: Jonson stresses the importance of education and hard work in shaping a poet's talent.

---

13. scenes: Stages.
14. Apollo: In Greek and Roman mythology, the god of light, music, and poetry.
15. Mercury: In Roman mythology, the messenger of the gods and the god of cleverness.
16. fit: Appropriately.
17. Aristophanes (ar′ is tof′ ə nēz′) **. . . Terence** (ter′ əns) **. . . Plautus** (plô′ təs): Classical Greek and Roman comic playwrights.
18. fashion: Form.
19. casts: Undertakes.
20. laurel: Fame.
21. true filèd: Accurately polished.
22. shake a lance: A pun on Shakespeare's name.

Master Teacher Note It is fairly well established that Shakespeare acted in Jonson's play *Every Man in His Humor.* Some have suggested that Shakespeare's portrait in the 1623 folio shows him in the part of Old Knowell.

For Further Study Biographical information on Jonson appears on page 444, and other poems by him are on pages 446-448.

2. Jonson refers to many classical dramatists: Aeschylus, Euripides, Sophocles, Paccavius, Accius, Seneca, Aristophanes, Terence, Plautus.
3. When Jonson compares Shakespeare to Apollo, he suggests that Shakespeare is a creator of music and poetry. His allusion to Mercury, the trickster of Olympus, compliments Shakespeare's sense of humor and wit.

ANSWERS TO CRITICAL THINKING AND READING

1. Answers will differ. Suggested response: By understanding the greatness of the playwrights or the characteristics of the gods in the allusions, the reader can recognize how great Jonson feels Shakespeare actually is.
2. Jonson suggests that Shakespeare is the greatest of all dramatists by writing that Shakespeare is a peer of or superior to classical and contemporary playwrights.
3. Jonson's allusions demonstrate his knowledge and interest. He would have expected his audience also to recognize the allusions.

THINKING AND WRITING

Publishing Student Writing Read a few letters to the class. Ask the class to respond to the criticism. Determine the class's consensus on Jonson's opinion about Shakespeare and about writing.

ANSWERS TO ANALYZING LITERATURE

1. Jonson alludes to Lyly, Kyd, and Marlow.

Answers

ANSWERS TO THINKING ABOUT THE SELECTION

Recalling

1. The wrong reasons for praising Shakespeare are simple ignorance which will make the praise sound empty, affectionate prejudice which will disregard the truth, or malice which would attempt to ruin while pretending to flatter.
2. Jonson would place Shakespeare with the greatest of classical Greek and Roman playwrights and rank him ahead of the contemporary writers such as Marlow or Kyd.
3. Shakespeare's ideas and style shine through in his lines, enlightening all who read and hear them.
4. Since Shakespeare's death, the stage has mourned and despaired.

Interpreting

5. Jonson suggests that Shakespeare's genius is universal; his works will have meaning throughout time.
6. Jonson is comparing the effort of writing to a blacksmith's forging iron. Like a blacksmith, a writer must work and rework a line until it is right.
7. (a) The poem reveals Jonson's great admiration and respect for Shakespeare. (b) To Jonson, writing is difficult. Although one may have a talent, it must be shaped and disciplined by hard work and "sweat."

Applying

8. Answers will differ. Suggested Response: A writer can be immortalized because his or her ideas live on in the works. Future generations will have the opportunity to explore a writer's opinions and thoughts, thus keeping alive aspects of the writer.

Sweet swan of Avon![23] what a sight it were
To see thee in our waters yet appear,
And make those flights upon the banks of Thames
That so did take Eliza and our James![24]
But stay, I see thee in the hemisphere
Advanced, and made a constellation there!
Shine forth, thou star of poets, and with rage[25]
Or influence, chide, or cheer the drooping stage,
Which, since thy flight from hence, hath mourned like
night,
And despairs day, but for thy volume's light.

Historical Context: Jonson refers to Queen Elizabeth I and King James I, who encouraged and supported Shakespeare and other writers.

23. Avon: The river on which Shakespeare's home town, Stratford, is located.
24. Eliza . . . James: Queen Elizabeth I and King James I.
25. rage: Poetic inspiration.

THINKING ABOUT THE SELECTION

Recalling

1. According to lines 1–12, what are the wrong reasons for praising Shakespeare?
2. According to the final two lines, how has the stage reacted since Shakespeare's death?

Interpreting

3. What does Jonson mean when he comments that Shakespeare was "not of an age, but for all time"?
4. What is the meaning of the metaphor in lines 57–59?
5. (a) What does this poem reveal about Jonson's attitude toward Shakespeare? (b) What does it reveal about his attitudes concerning the art of writing?
6. (a) How does your awareness of the meaning of the allusions contribute to your overall understanding of Jonson's poem? (b) How does Jonson's use of allusions help to give you a sense of Shakespeare's place in literary history?
7. How do Jonson's allusions reflect his interest in classical Greek and Roman literature?

Applying

8. In this poem, Jonson expresses the idea that a writer can be immortalized through his or her work. Explain whether you agree with this suggestion.

THINKING AND WRITING

Writing a Letter

Write a letter to Ben Jonson in which you tell him whether you agree with the attitudes he expresses concerning Shakespeare and the art of writing. Reread the poem, focusing on Jonson's attitudes. Brainstorm about your own attitudes on these subjects. Then express your opinions in personal letter. Use an informal, conversational writing style, but be sure to support your opinions. When you revise, make sure you have not included any unnecessary information. Proofread your letter and prepare a final draft.

The Schools of Donne and Jonson

GREENWICH PALACE FROM THE NORTHEAST WITH A MAN-OF-WAR AT ANCHOR (detail) c. 1630
National Maritime Museum

Humanities Note

Fine art, *Greenwich Palace from the Northeast with a Man-of-War at Anchor,* c. 1630. The influence of the Dutch landscape painters is evident in dark and somber coloring of this painting by an unknown artist. The peaceful mood reflects the pride and security the English navy provided for the nation during this time. The navy was among the strongest in the world. It enabled the English to expand its territories abroad. The prominent position of the flag reflects the pride and patriotism associated with the navy, despite the political and religious turmoil in the country.

More About the Author Although a great church man, John Donne was known in his youth for his love poems, which were circulated in manuscript but were not published until years later. Donne's love poetry is more intimate and personal than that of his predecessors. This song is a farewell, or valedictory, poem, written on the occasion of an impending departure from his wife. Ask students to consider the feelings husband and wife might have as they anticipate the separation. What might be their concerns?

JOHN DONNE

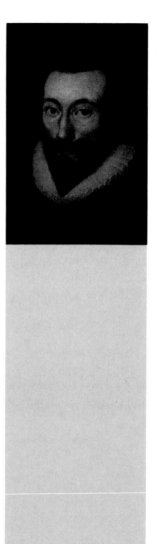

1572(?)–1631

John Donne's reputation has changed over time. He was very popular during his own lifetime, but his writings went out of favor soon after his death. At the beginning of the twentieth century, however, interest in his works revived. Now Donne occupies a major position in literature. Modern critics place him with William Shakespeare and John Milton at the very pinnacle of English poetry.

Donne was raised by his widowed mother, who was a devout Catholic and a member of the family of St. Thomas More. At the time, being Catholic was difficult, for Roman Catholics were severely discriminated against in Queen Elizabeth's England. Indeed, Donne later recanted his Catholicism and joined the Anglican Church. Scholars are divided as to his motives. They wonder whether he experienced a genuine conversion or made a shrewd move to try and gain advancement in courtly society.

Donne's life is generally described as falling into two parts. The first is often thought of as the "wild youth of Jack Donne, ambitious man about town." Bright, clever, and charming, Donne was welcomed into the most exclusive courtly circles and served as private secretary to one of the Queen's highest-ranking officials. He was so charming that he wooed and won the hand in marriage of Anne More, his employer's niece.

As with his religious conversion, some scholars have questioned Donne's motives. Cynics thought that through this marriage Donne had made a shrewd move to advance his career. However, the marriage did not work out that way. Because of the opposition of Anne's father, Donne's marriage ruined his chances for advancement. As a consequence, the devoted couple and their many children experienced seventeen years of poverty, illness, and despair. During these years Donne eked out a living as a writer of religious tracts and as the temporary secretary of several aristocrats. He also became during this difficult period one of the most widely read and influential poets of the age.

Later Donne was ordained and made dean of St. Paul's Cathedral in London. He now entered the second part of his life, which has been described as the "sacred calling of Dr. John Donne, Dean of St. Paul's." From this time until his death, Donne was the most popular preacher in England; his meditations and sermons were published during his life and went through several editions.

We should not, however, emphasize too much the differences between the younger and older Donne. All of his writings, whether on love or faith, were written with the same intensity and wit.

Objectives

1. To understand paradox
2. To understand metaphysical conceits
3. To follow an argument
4. To write about a philosophical argument

Teaching Portfolio: Support Material

Teacher Backup, p. 000

Vocabulary Check, p. 00

Usage and Mechanics Worksheet, p. 00

Analyzing Literature Worksheet, p. 00

Critical Thinking and Reading Worksheet, p. 00

Language Worksheet, p. 00

Selection Test, p. 00

GUIDE FOR READING

Song, Holy Sonnet 10, Holy Sonnet 14

The Writer's Techniques

Donne was a leading writer of what has come to be called *metaphysical poetry* because of its concern with philosophical and religious issues. This kind of poetry is characterized by the extensive use of paradoxes and conceits.

Paradox. In literature, a paradox is an apparent self-contradiction that reveals a kind of truth. One of the most famous literary paradoxes is present in Donne's "Holy Sonnet 14": "Take me to You, imprison me, for I, / Except You enthral me, never shall be free." Finding "freedom" in prison or in slavery would seem to many people a contradiction. But here, "prison" and "enthral" (enslave) are metaphors for submissive devotion to God, which to the deeply religious person represents true freedom.

Metaphysical Conceit. A conceit is an extended, fanciful metaphor that makes a surprising or unexpected comparison. In the sixteenth century, the Elizabethans fell in love with long, elaborate conceits, as in Sir Philip Sidney's comparison of the moon with a languishing lover in "Sonnet 31." The metaphysical poets, such as John Donne and Andrew Marvell, wrote ingenious, often shocking conceits in which very dissimilar objects are compared.

Look For

As you read "Song," "Holy Sonnet 10," and "Holy Sonnet 14," notice Donne's use of paradoxes and metaphysical conceits; keep in mind that an entire poem can be based on a conceit, and that one or two words as well as a full sentence can seem self-contradictory.

Writing

Write a short composition in which you use metaphors to explain yourself. Try to convince someone of an unusual experience you have had. Find objects, ideas, or common experiences that you can compare with your own experience and explain the connections.

Vocabulary

Knowing the following words will help you as you read Donne's poems.

divining (də vīn′ iŋ) *adj.*: Guessing; intuitive (p. 421, l. 33)

forethink (for think′) *v.*: Foretell; predict (p. 421, l. 34)

usurped (yo͞o sʉrp'd′) *adj.*: Wrongfully seized (p. 424, l. 5)

chaste (chāst) *adj.*: Pure; untainted; unblemished (p. 424, l. 14)

ravish (rav′ ish) *v.*: Violate; (p. 424, l. 14)

Literary Focus Students may find paradox a difficult concept. Ask them to explain the common saying, "The more things change, the more they stay the same."

Look For Students may have difficulty grasping the literal meaning of Donne's conceits. Ask them to read aloud any passages they find puzzling and to provide a paraphrase.

Writing Ask students to choose one of the metaphors they write and use this metaphor as the basis for writing their own metaphysical conceit.

Vocabulary Ask students to point out unfamiliar words and words used in unfamiliar ways. Ask volunteers to provide meanings and paraphrases.

Teaching to Ability Levels Have **more advanced** students read Donne's other famous valedictory poems, "A Valediction Forbidding Mourning" and "A Valediction of Weeping." Have them write a report comparing these poems and "Song."

Motivation for Reading Ask students to imagine that they are departing on a long and possibly dangerous journey. Ask them what they might want to say to someone they love to keep him or her from mourning the separation.

Master Teacher Note Ask students to discuss which of Donne's arguments they find most compelling.

Thematic Idea Another farewell poem to a lover is Lovelace's "To Lucasta, on Going to the Wars," page 460.

Purpose-Setting Question The poem is structured as a series of arguments. How does each stanza present a new reason for Donne's wife not to mourn his departure?

1 **Discussion** What fears does the speaker address in the first four lines?

2 **Discussion** In what way is Donne's departure a "feigned death"? Note that death, like love, was a favorite topic in poetry and drama in the early 17th century.

3 **Discussion** What is the purpose behind Donne's reference to the sun? How does he tie the sun's actions to his own? What "wings and spurs" does the poet have?

4 **Discussion** What is the relationship between good fortune and time? What good can come of bad fortune?

5 **Literary Focus** This stanza, with its complicated, obscure imagery, is the most metaphysical in the poem. What is the literal meaning of the stanza? How does the meaning express a paradox?

Song

John Donne

Sweetest love, I do not go,
1 For weariness of thee,
Nor in hope the world can show
A fitter love for me;
But since that I
Must die at last, 'tis best
To use[1] myself in jest,
2 Thus by feigned[2] deaths to die.

Yesternight the sun went hence,
And yet is here today;
He hath no desire nor sense,
3 Nor half so short a way;
Then fear not me,
But believe that I shall make
Speedier journeys, since I take
More wings and spurs than he.

O how feeble is man's power,
That if good fortune fall,
Cannot add another hour,
4 Nor a lost hour recall!
But come bad chance,
And we join to it our strength,
And we teach it art and length,
Itself o'er us to advance.

When thou sigh'st, thou sigh'st not wind,
But sigh'st my soul away;
When thou weep'st, unkindly kind,
5 My life's blood doth decay.
It cannot be
That thou lovest me as thou say'st,
If in thine my life thou waste,
That art the best of me.

---

1. **use:** Condition.
2. **feigned:** Imagined.

Let not thy divining heart
Forethink me any ill,
Destiny may take thy part,
And may thy fears fulfill;
But think that we
Are but turned aside to sleep.
They who one another keep
Alive, ne'r parted be.

THINKING ABOUT THE SELECTION

Recalling

1. What are the speaker's reasons for leaving his beloved?
2. What does the speaker say happens when "bad chance" comes (ll. 21–24)?
3. How do the beloved's sighs and tears affect the speaker?
4. How does the speaker suggest his beloved think of their parting?

Interpreting

5. To what is the sun in stanza 2 compared?
6. Of what is the speaker trying to convince his beloved? How would you outline the speaker's argument?
7. What is the tone of the poem? Is it angry, beseeching, reassuring, uncertain, mocking?

Applying

8. The speaker in this poem resorts to exaggeration as an instrument of persuasion. Do you think that exaggerating in order to win is a valid persuasive technique? Explain your answer.
9. Although this is a love poem, it is cast in the form of an argument. Why is that appropriate?

ANALYZING LITERATURE

Understanding Paradox

A paradox is an apparent self-contradiction that reveals a truth. A very well-known one is the statement of Jesus in Matthew 16:25, "For whosoever will save his life shall lose it." A related paradox can be found in Donne's "Holy Sonnet 10": ". . . poor death, nor yet canst thou kill me." In this example, the speaker says death cannot kill him because as a devout Christian he will have eternal life. Our very puzzlement adds zest to our understanding once we have figured out the meaning of the paradox, which is why religious leaders and writers so often employ them.

Donne's "Song" contains a couple of paradoxes. Explain why the following quote is a paradox, what it means, and how it works in the poem: "when thou weep'st, unkindly kind" (line 27).

6 Discussion What does Donne's wife fear? What is Donne's attitude toward this fear?

Answers

ANSWERS TO THINKING ABOUT THE SELECTION

Recalling

1. He says that his departure is a preparation for his ultimate departure in death.
2. By our actions, we make misfortune worse.
3. They weaken him.
4. He asks her to think that as long as two people remember each other, they are not really parted but rather separated, as in sleep.

Interpreting

5. As the sun disappears and returns predictably each day, so too will the speaker return.
6. He asks her not to grieve over their separation by offering the following arguments: that his departure will be a rehearsal for his death; that like the sun, he will inevitably return; that his beloved's grieving weakens him; and that she should think of them as merely turned aside in sleep.
7. The tone is tender and reassuring.

Applying

8. Answers will differ. Suggested response: Although it is often tempting to exaggerate the facts of an argument, exaggeration can undermine credibility. On the other hand, as in this poem, exaggeration can sometimes make arguments more vivid and compelling.
9. The speaker's purpose is to persuade his beloved not to grieve over their separation. Marlowe's "The Passionate Shepherd to His Love" and Raleigh's "The Nymph's Reply to the Shepherd" taken together constitute debate on love.

ANSWERS TO ANALYZING LITERATURE

The speaker's wife is "kind" because she mourns his departure. But the speaker sees this grieving as actually unkind because her grieving "wastes" and weakens him. "Unkindly kind" is an oxymorom, a figure of speech that is a short, self-contradictory phrase, an abbreviated paradox.

Challenge "Song" comes full circle by returning at the end to the theme of death. Why is this structure appropriate to the theme of departure in the poem?

Speaking and Listening Although Donne is often accused of being irregular and harsh in his versification, here he has used regular, melodious meter and smooth diction. Have volunteers rehearse and then read the poem aloud. Discuss why the rhythm, structure, and diction should make the title "Song" appropriate.

Motivation for Reading Point out that John Gunther used the opening words of this sonnet as the title for his book *Death Be Not Proud* about the death of his son. Why should Gunther, like many others, have looked to this poem as a source of comfort?

Master Teacher Note Point out that, like "Song" and many of his other poems, Donne develops this sonnet through a series of discrete arguments, each developed in a separate quatrain.

Thematic Idea Other selections on death that might be compared to this sonnet are Browning's "Prospice," page 834, and Thomas's "Do Not Go Gentle into That Good Night," page 1120.

Purpose-Setting Question Why does Donne begin the poem with a challenge? How do the first four words set the tone for the rest of the poem?

1 **Enrichment** This sonnet begins with an apostrophe, the figure of speech in which an absent person or a personified object or quality is addressed directly.

2 **Discussion** How does stating that Death must be pleasurable deflate its power?

3 **Literary Focus** An even more vigorous attack is launched here. In what way is Death the slave of fate? of chance? of kings? of desperate men?

4 **Discussion** In what way does the couplet represent the climax of the poem? What is the tone of the poem? Is it somber and funereal? Or is it instead contemptuous and superior? Is the tone of the poem what you would expect in a poem on death?

Holy Sonnet 10

John Donne

1 Death be not proud, though some have called thee
Mighty and dreadful, for thou art not so;
For those whom thou think'st thou dost overthrow,
Die not, poor death, nor yet canst thou kill me.
From rest and sleep, which but thy pictures[1] be,
2 Much pleasure; then from thee much more must flow,
And soonest our best men with thee do go,
Rest of their bones, and soul's delivery[2]
3 Thou art slave to fate, chance, kings, and desperate men,
And dost with poison, war, and sickness dwell,
And poppy,[3] or charms can make us sleep as well
And better than thy stroke; why swell'st[4] thou then?
4 One short sleep past, we wake eternally,
And death shall be no more; Death, thou shalt die.

---

1. pictures: Images.
2. And . . . delivery: Our best men go with you to rest their bones and find freedom for their souls.
3. poppy: Opium.
4. swell'st: Swell with pride.

THINKING ABOUT THE SELECTION

Recalling

1. In the first four lines, why does the speaker say that death should not be proud?
2. Why does the speaker say in lines 5–8 that death is pleasant? What within these lines indicates that death is a source of pleasure?
3. How does the speaker characterize death in lines 9–12?
4. Why does the speaker say that death shall be no more?

Interpreting

5. (a) What does the speaker mean when he says in lines 3–4: "For those whom thou think'st thou dost overthrow, / Die not, poor death, nor yet canst thou kill me"? (b) In what way is this meaning reinforced by the last two lines?
6. (a) What does the paradox "Death, thou shalt die" mean? What makes it paradoxical? (b) In what way does the final paradox serve as the conclusion to the argument of the poem?

Applying

7. In the poem, the speaker gives human characteristics to death. This is called *personification.* Death has often been personified in art and literature, sometimes as the grim reaper carrying a scythe, at other times as an angel with black wings and a net, and at still other

Answers

ANSWERS TO THINKING ABOUT THE SELECTION

Recalling

1. In reality Death has no power.
2. Rest and sleep are pleasant, and since death resembles a deep sleep, it must be even more pleasant. Death rests the body and delivers the soul to heaven.
3. Death is paired with ugly and sor-

SIR THOMAS ASTON AT THE DEATHBED OF HIS WIFE
John Souch
Manchester City Art Galleries

times as a fierce horseman whose head is often a skull. Think of other ways you may have seen death personified in literature or art. Discuss with your classmates what each of these images implies about our attitudes toward death. How does Donne's poem address these attitudes?

ANALYZING LITERATURE

Understanding Metaphysical Conceit

The term "conceit" comes from the Italian word *concetto,* meaning "conception." Metaphysical poets often worked out complex, far-fetched conceits, and Donne was among the best of them. Sometimes a metaphysical conceit is an elaborate image; sometimes it can be just a line or two, as we saw earlier. And sometimes it can be an underlying idea. What is essential to all metaphysical conceits, however, is the startling conjunction of dissimilar concepts, ideas, images, or objects.

The underlying conceit of "Holy Sonnet 10" is that Death's overweening pride is wholly undeserved.

1. What are the images in the poem that illustrate the conceit?
2. How do they relate with each other to form a single image of a powerless Death?

Humanities Note

Fine art, *Sir Thomas Aston at the Deathbed of His Wife,* by John Souch. Souch was a British portrait painter who was active from 1617 to 1636. He gained his training as a painter during an apprenticeship under a painter of heraldry, (coats of arms), named Randle Holme.

Of the few portraits of Souch that survive, *Sir Thomas Aston at the Deathbed of His Wife,* is the most important. Painted in 1635, this group portrait of the high sheriff of Cheshire, Thomas Aston, and one of his children at the deathbed of his first wife, Magdalene, is interesting for Souch's use of the medieval device of portraying Lady Aston simultaneously as dead, on her deathbed, and alive, on the bottom right of the painting. The artificial pose of the figures is relieved by the concentration of skill used to paint the heads. The mood and personality of each person is captured by the artist's depiction of their countenance. The work is painted in high-gloss colors that give the jewel-like appearance of an enamelled miniature. This work was most likely commissioned as a memorial to the first Lady Aston.

You might use the following questions for discussion:

1. In what ways does this painting reflect the ideas of the sonnet?
2. What do you think the artist meant to convey by the dual portrait of Lady Aston?

did things.

4. We will awaken to be with God.

Interpreting

5. (a) Those whom Death thinks it has taken are really not dead. (b) The last two lines explain how this paradox can be so: the dead will awaken to eternal life.
6. (a) Death will be powerless and meaningless. The statement is paradoxical because only Death has the power to kill and thus will be killing itself. (b) The final paradox is the logical culmination of the argument premised on the Christian belief in life after death.

Applying

7. Suggested Response: Each of these images shows death as frightening and powerful. Donne shows death as pleasant (a deep sleep), powerless, and even pitiable.

ANSWERS TO ANALYZING LITERATURE

1. Death is merely a form of sleep and not even as good a form as can be gained with medication or hypnosis. Death is a "slave" since it can be summoned by anyone. Death keeps company with such unsavory elements as poison and sickness. Most important, it is only a temporary condition before entering eternal life.
2. Each image belittles death.

Challenge What does Donne gain by addressing Death directly, rather than describing it in the third person?

Motivation for Reading Discuss with students situations where they have wanted to do, or to stop doing, something, but have been unable to do it.

Master Teacher Note Ask students what kinds and degrees of emotion they can find in the sonnet—for example, anger, guilt, and desperation. What words and passages do they find most intensely emotional? Why?

Thematic Idea Other selections that deal with man's attempt to reach God are *Everyman,* page 142, and *Pilgrim's Progress,* page 482.

Purpose-Setting Question What is the effect of Donne's unusual reliance on action verbs in the sonnet?

1 **Discussion** What image is Donne suggesting with words like "batter," "shine," "bend your force," "break," "blow," and "burn"? Note that Donne sees God as a tinker, smithy, or mender of pottery and himself as a broken vessel in need of repair. Point out that there are fourteen verbs in this quatrain. What cumulative tone emerges from them? Note that the verbs are clumped in threes to further develop the triune quality of God. What is the effect of alliteration in the quatrain?

2 **Discussion** What image does this quatrain evoke with words like "usurped town," "viceroy," and "captived"? What tone do these words suggest? What is the soul trying to do? How is its attempt being frustrated?

3 **Discussion** A third image emerges here with words like "love," "betrothed," "divorce," and "knot." What is it?

4 **Literary Focus** This line contains the central paradox of the poem. In what way can imprisonment lead to freedom?

Holy Sonnet 14

John Donne

Batter my heart, three-personed God;[1] for You
1 As yet but knock, breathe, shine, and seek to mend;
That I may rise, and stand, o'erthrow me, and bend
Your force, to break, blow, burn and make me new.
I, like an usurped town, to another due,
2   Labor to admit You, but O, to no end,
Reason Your viceroy[2] in me, me should defend,
But is captived, and proves weak or untrue.
Yet dearly I love You, and would be loved fain,
3 But am betrothed unto Your enemy.
Divorce me, untie, or break that knot again;
Take me to You, imprison me, for I,
4 Except You enthral[3] me, never shall be free,
5 Nor ever chaste, except You ravish me.

---

1. **three-personed God:** The Trinity: the Father, the Son, and the Holy Ghost.
2. **viceroy:** Deputy.
3. **enthral:** Enslave.

5 **Literary Focus** The image of Christ as a bridegroom is traditional. Nevertheless, Donne's treatment of the image is quite startling. Why? How does it represent a culmination of the imagery elsewhere in the poem?

THINKING ABOUT THE SELECTION

Recalling

1. In the first four lines what does the speaker ask God to do?
2. (a) To what does the speaker compare himself in line 5? (b) Of what does the speaker complain in lines 6–8? (c) How is reason characterized in lines 7 and 8?
3. (a) How does the speaker describe his condition in lines 9 and 10? (b) What does the speaker ask God to do in lines 11–12? (c) What reason does he give for his request in lines 13–14?

Interpreting

4. In line 2 why does the speaker complain of God's gentleness? Why does the speaker want God to treat him violently?
5. What are the paradoxes in lines 3, 13, and 14? What do they mean? How do they affect you, the reader?
6. Who is the "enemy" to whom the speaker is "betrothed"?
7. What is the tone in this poem? Is it belligerent, argumentative, pleading, arrogant, or contemptuous?

Applying

8. In the poem the speaker wants to be overwhelmed with emotion. There are many instances when a person might want to experience a deep emotion. What are some of these instances?

CRITICAL THINKING AND READING

Following an Argument

Metaphysical poets were said to combine "passion with reason." Reason is the chief tool of philosophy, and arguments are the chief tools of reason. A philosophical argument—which is much different from the shouting match we usually think of—is a logical or reasonable demonstration of how certain facts or ideas can or must lead to a conclusion. When you say, "I believe such and such because of this, that, and the other," you are offering an *argument* for your beliefs.

But of course, few if any literary works display their "arguments" as nakedly as we have just done. For example, if we think of "Holy Sonnet 14" as an argument—rather than as a prayer or an appeal, which is another way to view the poem—then we might ask why the speaker is saying, in effect, "God, please beat down my resistance so that I can worship you." After reflection, we might come up with the proposition: "Suffering overwhelms doubt and leads to the love of God."

Reread "Holy Sonnet 14" and support the proposition with the images and metaphors of the poem. First state the proposition or thesis, then give evidence supporting the proposition. Finally restate the proposition as a conclusion in such a way as to indicate it follows from the evidence.

THINKING AND WRITING

Writing a Philosophical Argument

Take your argument—thesis or proposition, supporting evidence, and conclusion—for Donne's poem and discuss it in a 500-word composition. Make sure you express your opinion of Donne's argument. Include in your discussion evidence supporting your opinion.

Take off from Donne's poem and write your own philosophical argument. For example, "Holy Sonnet 14" might suggest questions about the difficulty of making a commitment or of feeling an attachment to a transcendent or abstract idea. Freewrite, exploring your answer to this question. After you have arrived at an answer to your question, take that as your thesis or proposition. Develop supporting evidence, take into account opposing views, if there are any, answer them, and present your conclusion. When you revise, keep in mind that when writing an argumentative essay, you have to persuade your readers that your views are correct. Are your supporting details arranged so that they will have a powerful effect? Have you provided enough support? Proofread your essay and prepare a final draft.

Answers

ANSWERS TO THINKING ABOUT THE SELECTION

Recalling

1. He wants God to force him to have faith and thus make him new.
2. (a) He compares himself to a town that has been seized by force. (b) He complains that his reason, which should convince him to be faithful, is ineffective. (c) Reason is personified as the imprisoned deputy of God.
3. (a) He would gladly love God but is betrothed to the devil.
   b. He wants God to take him by force from the devil.
   c. He thinks that unless he is completely possessed by God he cannot be Free of evil.

Interpreting

4. God's attempts are too weak to help the speaker attain salvation. He thinks that he can only be faithful if God forces him to have faith.
5. The speaker can only rise if God knocks him down; he can only be free if God imprisons him; he can only be chaste if he is taken passionately by God. In each case he is begging God to take control of him so that he can be faithful.
6. He is "betrothed" to the devil.
7. The tone is passionately pleading and argumentative.

Applying

8. We might wish that we could return greater love to someone who loves us. We might wish that we could more fully appreciate the objects and interests that are important to the people close to us. We might wish that we could feel deeper religious faith.

ANSWER TO CRITICAL THINKING AND READING

Proposition: Suffering overwhelms doubt and leads to the love of God.

Evidence: (images of suffering) Speaker asks that God use Force to overcome doubt—"batter my heart," "bend/Your force, to break, blow, burn and make me new," "am betrothed to Your enemy," "imprison me," and "except You ravish me."

Conclusion: The speaker desires that doubt and temptation be forcibly removed so that the speaker is free to love God.

Challenge Rewrite the poem using different verbs, for example, "strike" or "hit" instead of "Batter," or "attached" instead of "betrothed," and so forth. How would the effect of the poem change?

THINKING AND WRITING

For help with this assignment, students can refer to Lesson 21, "Writing a Personal Essay," in the Handbook of Writing About Literature.

Publishing Student Writing You might read aloud several of the better arguments and use them as models for other students in revising their arguments.

Literary Focus Help students phrase the themes of "Holy Sonnet 10"—Death has no cause to be haughty because the dead will enter into eternal life—and "Holy Sonnet 14"—God needs to force us into faithfulness.

Look For Help your **less advanced** students understand the concept of theme by discussing the themes of some current films.

Writing Suggest that students develop their number one idea as the theme of a composition, using their own experience as evidence to support the theme.

Vocabulary Have **less advanced** students use the more common vocabulary words —*piety, covetousness, affliction,* and *tribulation*—in their own sentences.

GUIDE FOR READING

Meditation 17

The Writer's Techniques

Theme. The central or main idea of a literary work is its *theme*. In some works, the theme is stated directly. At the beginning of Sir Francis Bacon's "Idols of the Cave," for example, he says that prejudices derived from "education, habit, and accident" may interfere with the ability to understand things clearly. More often, though, the theme of a literary work is presented indirectly. An example of this can be found in John Donne's "Song." We can say the theme of the poem is something like: "Separation may seem like death, but it is really more like sleep, and lovers would suffer less if they viewed their separation this way."

Many works of literature have more than one theme. When they do, there is usually one dominant or controlling idea and several secondary or subordinate ones. For example, the major theme of *Macbeth* is the effects of ruthless ambition. This is not, however, the only theme in the play. To it can be added as secondary themes: cruelty by rulers causes rebellion; illegitimate power will be overthrown; and evil deeds bring their own punishment.

No matter the kind of writing, themes arise from the elements of the work. In a poem, for example, metaphor, image, and choice of words frequently develop the theme; in a play or novel, plot, character, and dialogue usually illustrate the theme; and in an essay, subordinate ideas and the ways in which language is used.

Look For

As you read "Meditation 17," notice the way Donne uses subordinate ideas and repeated words, phrases, and sentences to reinforce his theme.

Writing

Jot down ideas as they come to you while reading Donne's meditation. Then assign numbers to your jottings according to their importance to you. Number one will be your main theme.

Vocabulary

Knowing the following words will help you as you read Donne's "Meditation 17."

contention (kən ten′shən) *n.*: Controversy; dispute, p. 427
piety (pī′ə tē) *n.*: Devotion, p. 427
application (ap′lə kā′shən) *n.*: Specific act or case, p. 427
intermit (in tər mit′) *v.*: Stop for a time, p. 428
promontory (präm′ən tôr′ē) *n.*: Land that juts out into a body of water, p. 428
covetousness (kuv′it əs nəs) *n.*: Greediness, p. 428
affliction (ə flik′shən) *n.*: Pain; suffering, p. 428

Objectives

1 To recognize main and subordinate themes
2 To recognize Donne's argument through analogy
3 To write about theme

Teaching Portfolio: Support Material

Teacher Backup, p.

Vocabulary Check, p. 00

Usage and Mechanics Worksheet, p. 00

Analyzing Literature Worksheet, p. 00

Critical Thinking and Reading Worksheet, p. 00

Language Worksheet, p. 00

Selection Test, p. 00

Meditation 17

John Donne

Nunc lento sonitu dicunt, Morieris.

(Now, this bell tolling softly for another, says to me, Thou must die.)

Perchance he for whom this bell tolls may be so ill as that he knows not it tolls for him;
1 and perchance I may think myself so much better than I am as that they who are about me and see my state may have caused it to toll for me, and I know not that. The church is catholic, universal, so are all her actions; all that she does belongs to all. When she baptizes a child, that action concerns me; for that child is thereby connected to that head which is my head too, and ingrafted into that body[1] whereof I am a member. And when she buries a man, that action concerns me: all mankind is of one author and
2 is one volume; when one man dies, one chapter is not torn out of the book, but translated[2] a better language; and every chapter must be so translated. God employs several translators; some pieces are translated by age, some by sickness, some by war, some by justice; but God's hand is in every translation, and his hand shall bind up all our scattered leaves again for that library where every book shall lie open to one another. As therefore the bell that rings to a sermon calls not upon the preacher only, but upon the congregation to come, so this bell calls us all; but how much more me, who am brought so near the door by this sickness. There was a contention as far as a suit[3] (in which both piety and dignity, religion and estimation,[4] were mingled) which of the religious orders should ring to prayers first in the morning; and it was determined that they should ring first that rose earliest. If we understand aright the dignity of this bell that tolls for our evening prayer, we would be glad to make it ours by rising early, in that application, that it might be ours as well as his whose indeed it is. The bell doth

1. body: The Catholic church.
2. translated: Carried across on a spiritual level from one sphere to another.

3. suit: Lawsuit.
4. estimation: Self-esteem.

Motivation for Reading Everyone at some time has contemplated his or her own death. In "Holy Sonnet 10," Donne confronts the idea in a self-assured apostrophe to Death. How is his attitude toward death different now?

Master Teacher Note From what students know of Donne's poetry, ask them what they expect to find in the meditation. Answers should include a series of metaphysical conceits, paradox, and a series of arguments.

Thematic Idea Another selection in which someone contemplates his own death is Keats's "When I Have Fears that I May Cease to Be," page 729.

Purpose-Setting Question How does Donne maintain the bell motif throughout the meditation?

1 **Enrichment** The tradition of tolling the church bell to indicate a death is an old one. Students might find out where this custom originated.

2 **Literary Focus** Recall that a conceit is an extended metaphor comparing two basically dissimilar things. In this meditation, Donne uses several conceits. The first sees people as chapters in a book. What is the second? The third?

3 Enrichment The passage beginning "No man is an island" contains some of the most quoted prose in English literature. Ernest Hemingway, for example, borrowed from it his title *For Whom the Bell Tolls*.

4 Discussion What does Donne mean when he says that "affliction is a treasure"? Note that a similar idea appears in "Song," lines 21-24. Do you agree? Explain his parallel between tribulation and money.

toll for him that thinks it doth; and though it intermit again, yet from that minute that that occasion wrought upon him, he is united to God. Who casts not up his eye to the sun when it rises? but who takes off his eye from a comet when that breaks out? Who bends not his ear to any bell which upon any occasion rings? but who can remove it from that bell which is passing a piece of himself out of this world? No man is an island, entire of itself; every man is a piece of the continent, a part of the main.[5] If a clod be washed away by the sea, Europe is the less, as well
3 as if a promontory were, as well as if a manor of thy friend's or of thine own were. Any man's death diminishes me because I am involved in mankind, and therefore never send to know for whom the bell tolls; it tolls for thee. Neither can we call this a begging of misery or a borrowing of misery, as though we were not miserable enough of ourselves but must fetch in more from the next house, in taking upon us the misery of our neighbors. Truly it were an excusable covetousness if we did; for affliction is a treasure, and scarce any man hath enough of it. No man hath affliction enough that is not matured and ripened by it, and made fit for God by that affliction. If a man carry treasure in bullion, or in a wedge of gold, 4
and have none coined into current money, his treasure will not defray him as he travels. Tribulation is treasure in the nature of it, but it is not current money in the use of it, except we get nearer and nearer our home, heaven, by it. Another man may be sick too, and sick to death, and this affliction may lie in his bowels as gold in a mine and be of no use to him; but this bell that tells me of his affliction digs out and applies that gold to me, if by this consideration of another's danger, I take mine own into contemplation and so secure myself by making my recourse to my God, who is our only security.

5. main: Mainland.

THINKING ABOUT THE SELECTION

Recalling

1. In "Meditation 17," what are the circumstances that cause church bells to toll?
2. Why does Donne say the tolling bell applies to him as well as to others?
3. At the conclusion, why does Donne say that contemplation of the tolling bell brings one close to God?

Interpreting

4. To what do the metaphors "chapter," "book," "language," and "translated" refer?
5. What is meant by "No man is an island entire of itself; every man is a piece of the continent"?

Applying

6. At the beginning of the Second World War, Donne's phrase "No man is an island" became widely used as a slogan by those fighting Nazi Germany. It served to explain why Great Britain went to war in defense of Poland and France, and why the United States helped Britain in its most difficult times. Given this historical context, how did the meaning of the phrase match the meaning intended by Donne?
7. What is Donne's attitude toward death in "Meditation 17"? How does it compare with his view of death in "Holy Sonnet 10"?

ANALYZING LITERATURE

Recognizing Themes

Themes are the central ideas of literary works. Some works have several themes in the same piece, one dominant and others subordinate. The subordinate ideas usually play a supporting role by backing up or reinforcing the main idea.

1. In the following list of ideas from "Meditation 17," which one is central and which are secondary?
   a. Death comes to everyone.
   b. There is life after death.
   c. All humans share the same experiences.
   d. Contemplation of another's death and suffering can prepare one for life after death.
   e. By empathizing with another's suffering, we recognize our common humanity.
   f. No individual exists alone.
2. Explain how the secondary ideas support the main one, and show how Donne's theme controls the other ideas.

CRITICAL THINKING AND READING

Arguing Through Analogy

An **analogy** is a comparison pointing up the resemblance between two or more things, ideas, or people. For example, one might draw an analogy between a teacher, who takes students through the difficulties of a subject, and a guide who takes travelers over some difficult or dangerous terrain.

Analogies are often used to explain complicated ideas or argue difficult points. As a rule, an analogy compares an unusual or abstract concept to something familiar or concrete. A frequent analogy, for example, is the comparison of the effect of a person's attractiveness to the action of a magnet on metal, as when we talk of an individual's "magnetism."

To "prove" that there is an afterlife and that death is not final, Donne draws an analogy. What is that analogy? How does this analogy contribute to the overall argument of "Meditation 17"?

THINKING AND WRITING

Writing About the Theme of a Work

Take the idea that you chose in Analyzing Literature as central to "Meditation 17" and discuss how Donne developed it. Show how he hammered away at certain ideas through repetition. Also show how one idea supported another in an almost pyramidal fashion, with Donne's major theme at the apex.

Answers

ANSWERS TO THINKING ABOUT THE SELECTION

Recalling

1. The bell tolls to signal a death.
2. The death of one person affects everyone.
3. The tolling bell reminds one of one's own death and the necessity of assuring one's salvation.

Interpreting

4. Donne compares humankind to a book and individual people to the chapters. When a person dies, however, the chapter is not removed from the book but "translated" or transferred to a "better language," in other words, to be with God.
5. No one is isolated but is connected to everyone else.

Applying

6. It matched Donne's intended meaning: that we are all involved with one another.
7. Donne sees the death of others as a useful reminder that we are not isolated and that we should make ourselves closer to God. In "Holy Sonnet 10," he sees death as haughty and ultimately powerless.

ANSWERS TO ANALYZING LITERATURE

1. Though all of these ideas are present in "Meditation 17," the idea that contemplating another's death and suffering can bring us closer to God is perhaps central.
2. The other ideas are implied in the central one. Donne's language —as in the "No man is an island" passage—relates these other ideas to the central idea and, thereby, to his main purpose: to encourage believing Christians to contemplate death and turn to God as their "only security."

The central theme of "Meditation 17" is that by empathizing with another's suffering, we recognize our common humanity. The other themes listed are secondary.

ANSWERS TO CRITICAL THINKING AND READING

Donne compares dying with being "translated" from one language to another. When one chapter of the volume to which we all belong is torn out, the loss affects us all and reminds us of our closeness to God.

Challenge Which is Donne's most effective metaphor? Why?

THINKING AND WRITING

For help with this assignment, students can refer to Lesson 11, "Writing About Theme,"in the Handbook of Writing About Literature.

More About the Author According to his biographer, Izaak Walton, on the night of his installation as a country pastor, George Herbert told a friend, "I now look back upon my aspiring thoughts and think myself more happy than if I had attained what then I so ambitiously thirsted for." What different kinds of satisfactions might one find upon moving from an active life in the city to life in a rural village? What might be one's interests and priorities?

GEORGE HERBERT

1593–1633

Herbert was born to a wealthy and influential aristocratic family. Instead of becoming a high-ranking official at the English court, however, he became a country parson at one of the smallest rural churches in England. There he served the poor and wrote the poems that gained him fame.

Like many wealthy young men, George Herbert first looked toward worldly success. He served as spokesman for Cambridge University, usually a steppingstone to high public office, and became a favorite of King James I. It was during this period of great promise that Herbert also served for two years as a Member of Parliament. With the deaths of his mother and several patrons, he withdrew from London. In 1630 he accepted a parish assignment in a remote part of England. For the remaining three years of his life he devoted himself to his church: He restored the church buildings at his own expense, tended to his parishioners, performed music for his congregation, and composed his devotional poems.

In many ways, Herbert's poetry shows the influence of John Donne. This is understandable, since Donne was older and a good family friend. Herbert's temperament, however, was very different from that of his doubt-ridden, anxious mentor. The poetry Herbert wrote is graceful, pious verse intended to instill devotion by giving pleasure. As he himself put it: "A verse may find him who a sermon flies, / And turn delight into a sacrifice."

Herbert organized his poems in a particular sequence and called his collection *The Temple.* Just before his death, he sent the manuscript of *The Temple* to a profoundly religious friend named Nicholas Ferrar with a special request. If Ferrar found the poems worthy, then he should have them published; if not, they should be burned. Fortunately, Ferrar found the poems worthy. *The Temple,* as it turned out, was enormously popular throughout the seventeenth century.

Herbert had carefully given his collection of 160 very different poems a unifying concept. Taken together, all the poems represent the experience of attending church. *The Temple* opens with the rather long poem, "The Church Porch," and then, in a wide variety of verse forms, represents parts of a church building, religious services, sacred objects, and private devotions. We can glimpse the large assortment of forms and themes present in Herbert's collection of poems by examining the three reprinted in this volume.

Objectives

1. To understand Herbert's use of emblems and symbols
2. To analyze Herbert's style
3. To write about emblematic images

Teaching Resource Portfolio: Support Material

Teacher Backup, p.

Vocabulary Check, p. 00

Usage and Mechanics Worksheet, p. 00

Analyzing Literature Worksheet, p. 00

Critical Thinking and Reading Worksheet, p. 00

Language Worksheet, p. 00

Selection Test, p. 00

GUIDE FOR READING

Virtue, Easter Wings, Man

The Writer's Techniques

Emblematic Images. Emblems were usually pictures accompanied by mottoes or labels and poems connecting or explaining the pictures and the mottoes. In some instances the poem itself was shaped so as to serve as picture, motto, and explanation. George Herbert's "Easter Wings" is such a poem. Verses of this type are called *emblematic images* or *emblem poems*.

Emblem poems were written so that visual image and verbal image could reinforce one another. "Easter Wings," for example, is concerned with the resurrection of the spirit, and angelic wings may well help the troubled soul to rise and take flight. When this poem was first published, it was printed on its side. In this way, the poem *looked* as if an angel or bird were flying, wings spread apart.

Shaped poems, such as "Easter Wings," have been produced intermittently since ancient times. An ancient Roman, writing about a sea fight, had the lines of his poems written so that they made pictures of ships at battle. Shaped poems were not produced after the classical period until their revival at the beginning of the Renaissance. Then they became popular. One Renaissance poet wrote a drinking song shaped like a bottle. Other poets wrote their verses so as to make shapes of crosses, altars, hearts, tears, and so forth. Shaped poems are still being written today, and they often still serve a kind of emblematic purpose.

Look For

As you read "Virtue," "Easter Wings," and "Man," notice the way Herbert arranges his lines so as to emphasize his meaning.

Writing

Write the name of a picture that appeals to you. For example, you might choose the painting of *Mona Lisa* by Leonardo da Vinci or the photograph of the Beatles dressed as *Sergeant Pepper's Lonely Hearts Club Band*. Use the name as the motto and write a short comment for motto and picture.

Vocabulary

Knowing the following words will help you as you read Herbert's "Virtue," "Easter Wings," and "Man."

compacted (kəm pakt′d) *v.*: Put together, p. 432

virtuous (vur′cho͞o wəs) *adj.*: Pure, righteous, p. 432

harmoniously (här mō′nē əs le) *adv.*: In a manner that is in accordance, p. 434

affliction (ə flik′shən) *n.*: Suffering, p. 434

habitation (hab′ə tā′shən) *n.*: Home; dwelling, p. 435

symmetry (sim′ə trē) *n.*: Balance of form, p. 435

amity (am′ə tē) *n.*: Peaceful relationships, p. 435

Literary Focus Herbert viewed the poet's task as uncovering God's hidden meanings. As God created emblems, or meaningful pictures, for man to discover, the writer created poetry that reflected these symbols. Poetry thus represented for Herbert the highest form of praise for God.

Look For For Herbert, the formal perfection of a poem reflected the perfection of God's creation, and Herbert's poems are well-known for their formal virtuosity. Note that the 164 poems in *The Temple* display some 140 different stanzaic patterns.

Writing Have **less advanced** students write a brief essay explaining how their motto is appropriate to the picture they chose.

Vocabulary Discuss with **less advanced** students the meanings of unfamiliar words in their vocabulary list.

Motivation for Reading Have students imagine and then describe feeling a sense of intimacy and cooperation with God. How would they express this intimacy? What objects might they choose as symbols to help them describe their feeling?

Master Teacher Note Although Herbert was known for his saintliness and deep devotion to the church, his poetry is neither sentimental nor pompous. Instead, it is unusual and inventive. Herbert delighted in odd forms and patterns. Discuss examples of this combination of piety and playfulness in his poetry—for example the refrain in "Virtue," the shape of "Easter Wings," and the image of the canopied bed in "Man," lines 31-32.

Thematic Idea Another devotional poet who may be compared with Herbert is Gerard Manley Hopkins, pages 852–859.

Purpose-Setting Question What is the theme of each poem?

1 **Enrichment** In the Prologue to *Canterbury Tales,* Chaucer uses the word vertu to mean "power" or "strength." What meanings does *Virtue* have in Herbert's poem?

2. **Discussion** How is the day "the bridal of the earth and sky"?

3 **Discussion** Why does Herbert make the last line of each stanza shorter than the rest?

4 **Discussion** Why does the beauty of the rose bring tears to the gazer's eyes? Why is the gazer "rash"?

5 **Discussion** How does the spring represent the culmination of the images of the previous stanzas? To what senses does this stanza appeal?

1 # Virtue

George Herbert

Sweet day, so cool, so calm, so bright,
2 The bridal of the earth and sky;
The dew shall weep thy fall tonight;
3 For thou must die.

Sweet rose, whose hue angry and brave[1]
4 Bids the rash gazer wipe his eye:
Thy root is ever in its grave,
And thou must die.

5 Sweet spring, full of sweet days and roses,
A box where sweets[2] compacted lie;
My music shows ye have your closes,[3]
And all must die.

6 Only a sweet and virtuous soul,
Like seasoned timber, never gives;
But though the whole world turn to coal,[4]
Then chiefly lives.

1. **angry and brave:** Red (the hue of anger) and splendid.
2. **sweets:** Perfumes.
3. **closes:** The concluding sounds.
4. **turn to cinder:** Be reduced to cinder and ash by the fires of the Last Judgment (see II Peter 3:10).

THINKING ABOUT THE SELECTION

Recalling

1. In the first three stanzas of "Virtue," what happens to "sweet day," "sweet rose," and "sweet spring"?
2. In the last stanza, what happens to the "sweet and virtuous soul"?

Interpreting

3. (a) What do the last lines of each of the four stanzas say? (b) How is the last line in the fourth stanza different from the other three? (c) When combined, what additional meaning do they gain?
4. How is the thought that all of nature dies but the soul lives eternally shown in this poem?
5. If death means a permanent end to existence, in what sense can one say that *days, roses,* and *spring* actually die?
6. Mark the rhyme scheme of the poem. What rhyming sound is most often repeated? What rhyming sound replaces this in the last stanza? In what way does the rhyme emphasize the theme or main point of the poem?

6 **Discussion** What other adjective is added to "sweet" in this stanza? Why is the soul like "seasoned timber"? Help students see the difference in durability between green and seasoned wood.

Answers

ANSWERS TO THINKING ABOUT THE SELECTION

Recalling

1. They all must die.
2. It lives eternally.

Interpreting

3. a. Taken together, they state that everything dies except the soul.

THE MILKMAID
Myles Birket Foster
Victoria & Albert Museum Trustees

Applying

7. Basically, this poem says that the virtuous soul need not fear death. What other poem in this book imparts a similar message?

ANALYZING LITERATURE

Understanding Emblematic Images

Although emblematic images are usually associated with pictures and shaped verse, it is sometimes possible to see a kind of emblematic impulse in more traditionally formed poems. To see the emblematic image in a poem such as "Virtue," for example, we need to probe the meaning of the word *emblem*. The word comes into English from the Latin meaning "inlaid," as in mosaic pictures, which are made of little pieces of stone put together according to a pattern that forms an image. From this use it came to mean "symbol," one thing standing for another.

In early Renaissance emblems, poems were written to comment on or explain pictorial symbols. After a while, poems and pictures became separated and the reader of an emblematic poem had to imagine the symbolic picture to which it related.

Explain the symbolism of "sweet day," "sweet rose," and "sweet spring." Then explain what "seasoned timber" might represent and how it relates to the sweet day, rose, and spring symbols. Describe the pictorial image you think this poem might fit.

Humanities Note

Fine art, *The Milkmaid* by Myles Birket Foster. Miles Birket Foster (1825–1899), a British watercolorist, showed a precocious talent for drawing and was encouraged by his family. At the age of sixteen, he was apprenticed to a wood engraver for five years. He subsequently worked as a book illustrator and painter. His reputation was established in a bizarre way. When his father died, the death was mistaken for his, and art critics wrote flowery eulogies praising his talent and mourning the great loss to the world of art. When this confusion was cleared up, he was famous and remained so.

Foster loved to paint dainty, rustic scenes of rural England. He is best known for watercolors of gentle subjects painted with charm, grace, and fresh color. *The Milkmaid* is one of these paintings. It shows Foster's leaning toward the Pre-Raphaelite style in his careful attention to detail and the romantic mood of the subject. The stippled application of paint, uniquely his, creates a dreamy effect.

You may wish to use the following questions for discussion:

1. What is the difference between what the poet Herbert and the painter Foster see in the glory of spring?
2. Why is this painting a suitable illustration for this contemplative poem?

b. The first three stanzas culminate in the words "must die"; the fourth, with the word "lives."
c. They gain the meaning that a virtuous soul triumphs over death.

4. The poem presents three examples of things that die, followed by an example of something that does not.
5. They cease to be.
6. The rhyme scheme is *abab, cbcb, dbdb, efef.* The long *i* sound is repeated in the first three stanzas. The *ives* sound replaces it in stanza four. The main rhyme is based on the word "die." The idea of the living soul is associated with a different rhyme.

Applying

7. Donne's Holy Sonnet 10 has a similar theme.

ANSWERS TO ANALYZING LITERATURE

"Sweet day," "Sweet rose," and "Sweet spring" are three symbols of the beauty and mortality of merely natural life. "Seasoned timber" symbolizes something natural that has been prepared to survive death. Seasoned timber, therefore, contrasts with the three preceding symbols. The pictorial image implied is that of sound, lasting wood in a natural setting where all other things are drooping or already dead.

1 **Discussion** What is the significance of the title? Point out that for Christians, Easter is the day of resurrection, the time of Christ's rising from the dead. The poet wishes to rise above sin and spiritual poverty. Note the references to flight in the poem.

2 **Literary Focus** Notice how the physical shape of the poem reflects its content. For example, line 1 deals with the abundance with which man was created; in line 2, some of that abundance has been lost; and in line 3, there is further decay, until line 5, with "Most poor." Then, after line 6, "With thee," spiritual growth begins. The same progression of ideas occurs in the second stanza. See if students can trace the debilitating effects of sorrow, sickness, shame, and sin, with the same mid-stanza reversal in stanza 2.

3 **Discussion** To what "victory" does the speaker refer?

4 **Enrichment** In the Bible, Malachi says, "Son of man shall rise with feeling in his wings." Isaiah says, "through affliction we shall rise on wings." Have students compare these images with the last two lines of this poem and with the similar statement at the end of Donne's "Meditation 17" that adversity helps us better appreciate God's gifts.

1 Easter Wings

George Herbert

2
Lord, who createdst man in wealth and store,[1]
Though foolishly he lost the same,
Decaying more and more,
Till he became
Most poor:
With thee
O let me rise
As larks, harmoniously,
And sing this day thy victories:
Then shall the fall further the flight in me.

My tender age in sorrow did begin.
And still with sickness and shame
Thou didst so punish sin,
That I became
Most thin.
With thee
3 Let me combine
And feel this day thy victory:
For, if I imp[2] my wing on thine,
4 Affliction shall advance the flight in me.

---

1. **store:** Abundance.
2. **imp:** Graft.

THINKING ABOUT THE SELECTION

Recalling

1. At the end of the poem, why does the speaker say he wants to "combine" with God? In what way does this echo lines 6–10?

Interpreting

2. (a) In line 11, what does the speaker mean when he says: "My tender age in sorrow did begin"? Why should he have begun in sorrow? (b) How does this line echo lines 1–5?
3. In what way is line 10 a paradox?
4. How are the title and shape of the poem appropriate to its meaning or theme?

Applying

5. George Herbert was sickly as a child and remained in frail health throughout his rather short life. He also moved from the pomp of the royal court to the poverty of a rural church. In what way are these personal experiences reflected in "Easter Wings"?

Answers

ANSWERS TO THINKING ABOUT THE SELECTION

Recalling

1. He thinks that if he can "combine" with God, he can imitate Christ's suffering and thereby rise to God. In both passages, he wants to praise Christ's "victory" of rising from the dead.

Interpreting

2. a. He had been ill and frail since an early age.
   b. Lines 1-5 state that humankind in general has been afflicted with pain; lines 11-15 say how the speaker himself was afflicted with pain.
3. The speaker states that the Fall will make him rise closer to God.
4. The wing-like shape of the poem is an emblem for its title. At Easter, the spirit is reborn and able to fly to God.

Applying

5. Herbert refers directly to his personal "sickness and shame," and also implies his religiosity and prayerful spirituality.

Man

George Herbert

My God, I heard this day,
That none doth build a stately habitation,
But he that means to dwell therein.
1 What house more stately hath there been,
Or can be, than is man? to whose creation
All things are in decay.[1]

For Man is every thing,
And more: He is a tree, yet bears more fruit;
A beast, yet is, or should be more:[2]
Reason and speech we only bring.[3]
Parrots may thank us, if they are not mute,
They go upon the score.[4]

Man is all symmetry,
Full of proportions, one limb to another,
And all to all the world besides:
2 Each part may call the furthest, brother:
For head with foot hath private amity,
And both with moons and tides.

Nothing hath got so far,
But man hath caught and kept it, as his prey.
His eyes dismount the highest star:
He is in little all the sphere.
3 Herbs gladly cure our flesh; because that they
Find their acquaintance there.

For us the winds do blow,
The earth doth rest, heaven move, and fountains flow.
Nothing we see, but means our good,
As our delight, or as our treasure:
The whole is, either our cupboard of food,
Or cabinet of pleasure.

---

1. to . . . decay: In comparison to created man, all other things are in decay.
2. For . . . more: Man has an animal, vegetable, and spiritual nature.
3. Reason . . . bring: Man alone is capable of speaking and using reason.
4. Parrots . . . score: Parrots may also seem to be able to speak, but only because man has taught them how.

1 **Enrichment** Here Herbert expresses the theory of the nature of man common to the Renaissance: in a hierarchy man is at the top of creation next to God.

2 **Enrichment** Note that man's "symmetry" is not only internal so that the parts of his body operate in unity with each other, but also external so that he operates in unity with all the world, including the moon and tides.

3 **Discussion** How is man "in little all the sphere"?

4 **Discussion** What is the image created in lines 31-32?

5 **Discussion** Who are the innumerable servants who wait on man? What is the other world that attends man?

4 The stars have us to bed;
Night draws the curtain, which the sun withdraws;
Music and light attend our head.
All things unto our flesh are kind
In their descent and being; to our mind
In their ascent and cause.

Each thing is full of duty:
Waters united are our navigation;
Distinguished, our habitation;
Below, our drink; above, our meat;
Both are our cleanliness. Hath one such beauty?
Than how are all things neat?[5]

More servants wait on man,
Than he'll take notice of: in every path
5 He treads down that which doth befriend him,
When sickness makes him pale and wan.[6]
Oh mighty love! Man is one world, and hath
Another to attend him.

Since then, my God, thou hast
So brave a palace built; O dwell in it,
That it may dwell with thee at last!
Till then, afford us so much wit;
That, as the world serves us, we may serve thee,
And both thy servants be.

5. Each . . . neat: Each element serves man in a number of ways. Water is used as an example. Oceans are used for navigation; dividing waters created the earth that man inhabits (Genesis 1:6-7); water provides man with food and drink; and water allows man to cleanse himself. If one element can serve man so well, how beautiful is the sum of the elements.
6. He . . . won: Man treads down the herb that can cure him when he is sick.

THINKING ABOUT THE SELECTION

Recalling

1. In the first stanza of "Man," what question does the speaker ask?
2. How is man described in lines 7–24?
3. In lines 25–42, what does the speaker say is the relation of nature to man?
4. As shown in the next-to-last stanza, how does man behave toward nature?
5. In the final stanza, what are the two requests the speaker makes?

Interpreting

6. To what specific categories do each of the items mentioned in lines 7–10 belong? In broad general terms, how is man characterized in these lines?
7. To what does the "brave palace" of line 50 refer? In what way does this metaphor recall lines 4 and 5? How does this echoing serve to conclude or "close" the poem?

Applying

8. In a certain sense, this poem can be read as a criticism of human disregard for the rich bounties of nature. If modern environmentalists were to make the same criticism, as they often do, what would they say? To whom would they address their pleas? How would they present their position or viewpoint?

THINKING AND WRITING

Writing About Emblematic Images

Properly speaking, an emblem consisted of a picture, a motto, and a poem. Over time, however, picture and poem came to be separated. As a result, many poems were written as if they contained their own picture, as in "Easter Wings," for example, or as if they were written to explain or comment on a picture in the poet's mind, as might be said of "Virtue" or of "Man."

Reread "Man" and describe the picture that might have been in Herbert's mind or that could accompany the poem today. Explain your description by referring to the details of the poem. When you revise, make sure you have included vivid details from the poem. Proofread your description and prepare a final draft.

CRITICAL THINKING AND READING

Analyzing Herbert's Style

1. Describe Herbert's style in this poem.
2. How is it appropriate to his theme?

The word *style* refers to the characteristic way in which an individual does something, such as dressing, swimming, painting a picture, or writing a poem. In literature, style refers specifically to the way an individual uses language.

When we analyze a literary style, we examine a writer's characteristic choice of words, use of figures of speech, arrangement of sentences, organization of paragraphs, and, in poetry, treatment of rhythm and rhyme. Sometimes we also look at an author's use of certain literary devices —such as paradox, imagery, or symbolism —and his or her seeming preference for certain subjects or themes. John Donne, for example, seems to prefer themes that reflect anxiety, uncertainty, or suffering. He often uses exaggerated language when treating these difficult matters, thereby creating discomfort and heightening the emotional response to his writing. Donne's style could thus be described as highly provocative.

George Herbert stands in marked contrast to Donne. The poems Herbert wrote tend to make the reader feel comfortable, perhaps even soothed, as if listening to the gentle murmur of continuous prayer. Herbert's diction, or vocabulary, is essentially quiet, never clangorous as is Donne's on many occasions. Even when dealing with so potentially traumatic a subject as the Fall of Man, or his own approaching death, Herbert's words are mild, almost as if spoken in a whisper.

Reread "Easter Wings" and look closely at the way Herbert uses language. For example, notice the way he uses rhyme (in Herbert's day, "poor" rhymed with "more" and "store"); notice also that in the second half of each stanza, the only perfect rhyme for "thee" is "me," and "thee" of course refers to God. Describe Herbert's style in this poem and show how it complements his main idea. In addition to his use of rhyme, take into account his choice of words, his changes in line lengths, and his treatment of metaphors and similes.

Answers

ANSWERS TO THINKING ABOUT THE SELECTION

Recalling

1. Why would anyone build a grand home unless he planned to live there?
2. Man is better than trees or beasts; his body is in perfect harmony; and he is in perfect command of nature.
3. Everything in nature exists for man's nourishment or pleasure.
4. Man is arrogant and wasteful of nature, which he dominates.
5. The speaker wants God to dwell with him so that he may eventually dwell with God; in the meantime, he asks for the intelligence and perception to serve God while he is on earth.

Interpreting

6. The tree represents the vegetable kingdom, the beast the animal kingdom, reason and speech the realm of human beings. Man is connected to all other living creatures but superior to them.
7. The "palace" is the human person. Herbert begins the poem with the metaphor of a fine house to represent the human person. The poem comes full circle with its return to the opening metaphor.

Applying

8. Herbert believes that nature exists for man's use and should be respected as such. Modern environmentalists stress that the earth is an ecosystem with all forms of life existing interdependently. They address their pleas to people who think that nature exists only for their use and would exploit it. They usually express their views in speeches, and in newspaper and magazine articles, although occasionally in poetry.

ANSWERS TO CRITICAL THINKING AND READING

Students might point out, among other things, that Herbert's elaborate rhymes and complex but regularly recurring metrical patterns are especially appropriate in a poem that celebrates man's special place in a complex but orderly and purposeful universe maintained by God. The scientific and cosmological references, along with the generally intellectual manner of the poem, are in harmony with the poem's rational theology: Herbert's view of man in relation to the universe and God is rooted in centuries of orthodox Christian theology and thought.

THINKING AND WRITING

Publishing Student Writing Have students share their emblematic images by reading them aloud.

Challenge Think of additional images of things that die which could be added to the series of images in "Virtue." Would the additional images improve the poem?

More About the Author Andrew Marvell was an intensely private man whose lyric poetry remained almost unknown in his own time. After his death, he was chiefly remembered as a member of Parliament and as a political writer. It was only in the late nineteenth century that Marvell was rediscovered as a poet. What are some reasons that a writer's work would be neglected and then rediscovered?

ANDREW MARVELL

1621–1678

Although seemingly easy and relaxed in style, Andrew Marvell was actually tough in poetry and politics. Beneath his graceful lyrics lie somber ideas and rigorous structures. Alongside his ready adaptability resided a firm attachment to his friends and beliefs.

Marvell was the son of a Puritan minister who was appointed to a church in Hull, a small town on the Humber River in northern England. There young Andrew remained until he entered Cambridge University at the age of twelve. While at Cambridge, he wrote several poems in Greek and Latin that were published by the university in a volume dedicated to King Charles I. After his father's death, Marvell traveled in Europe, where he learned to speak several modern European languages.

During his stay in Europe, the English Parliament, dominated by Puritans, rebelled against the king. On first returning to England, Marvell established friendships with royalist supporters of Charles I. At this time he wrote several verses commemorating these friends, among whom was the poet Richard Lovelace. Somewhat later, he was hired by Lord Fairfax, the commanding general of the anti-royalist Parliamentary army, to teach his daughter foreign languages. Marvell held this position for about two years, at which time he may have written most of the poems for which he is now famous.

Several years after ceasing to teach Fairfax's daughter, Marvell became tutor to the ward of Oliver Cromwell, leader of the Puritan rebellion and ruler of England. Shortly afterward, Marvell served as unofficial court poet to Cromwell himself. Obviously capable, Marvell gained the attention and sponsorship of the great English poet John Milton, who was at the time Latin Secretary to Cromwell's Council of State. Several years later, Marvell became Milton's assistant. Throughout this period, Marvell wrote several political and commemorative poems.

In 1659, after Cromwell's death and shortly before the monarchy was restored, Marvell was elected the Member of Parliament from Hull. He was regularly returned to Parliament until his death, almost twenty years later. It is believed that while a member, he was mainly responsible for saving Milton from a long imprisonment and possible death sentence.

Marvell showed an extraordinary ability to adjust to the realities of his time. He also displayed, however, an equal firmness of principle. After the Restoration of Charles II, Marvell wrote political satires and prose pamphlets attacking the abuses of monarchy and defending democratic concepts.

Objectives

1 To recognize couplets and hidden quatrains in the poems
2 To analyze tone
3 To compare and contrast authors' styles

Teaching Resource Portfolio: Support Material

Teacher Backup, p.

Vocabulary Check, p. 00

Usage and Mechanics Worksheet, p. 00

Analyzing Literature Worksheet, p. 00

Critical Thinking and Reading Worksheet, p. 00

Language Worksheet, p. 00

Selection Test, p. 00

GUIDE FOR READING

To His Coy Mistress, The Picture of Little T. C. in a Prospect of Flowers

The Writer's Techniques

Couplets and Quatrains. Two of the most common structural elements in poetry are couplets and quatrains. Two lines rhyming together are called a *couplet,* and four lines rhyming in various ways are called a *quatrain.* Here is an example of a couplet and a quatrain. The example is by Andrew Marvell, who used these forms in an early poem that he wrote as a debate between the Soul and Pleasure.

Quatrain:

PLEASURE

Wilt thou all the glory crave *a*
That war or peace commend? *b*
Half the world shall be thy slave, *a*
The other half thy friend. *b*

Couplet:

SOUL

What friends, if to my self untrue! *c*
What slaves, unless I captive you! *c*

Although both the couplet and the quatrain are often used as complete stanzas by themselves, they are also frequently used as parts of longer stanzas.

Look For

As you read "To His Coy Mistress" and "The Picture of Little T. C. in a Prospect of Flowers," notice Marvell's use of the couplet.

Writing

Write two lines that rhyme, then write several more two-line rhymes. If four of these rhyming lines seem related, perhaps because they deal with the same subject or central idea, join them together. Now write four new lines in which the rhymes alternate. You might then have one quatrain rhyming *a b a b* and another rhyming *a a b b.*

Vocabulary

Knowing the following words will help you as you read.

coy (koi) *adj.*: Reluctant to make a commitment; it is important to recognize that the modern sense of "pretending to be shy" is absent from the poem (p. 440, title)

hew (hyo͞o) *n.*: Color; hue (p. 440, l. 33)

nymph (nimf) *n.*: In classical mythology, a minor nature goddess usually shown as a lovely young girl (p. 442, l. 2)

compound (käm′pound) *v.*: Join; combine (p. 442, l. 17)

parley (pär′lē) *v.*: Talk; converse (p. 442, l. 18)

prime (prīm) *n.*: best stage or time (p. 443, l. 37)

Literary Focus In the English sonnet, the concluding couplet provides a sense of closure, often summarizing the material that has preceded it. Couplets also lend themselves to aphorism—short, witty sayings that express a general truth. A couplet such as Marvell's, "The grave's a fine and private place,/ But none I think do there embrace" displays the pithy wit of an aphorism.

Look For Have **less advanced** students identify the rhyme scheme and stanzaic pattern in "Little T.C."

Writing Have **more advanced** students choose one of the quatrains they wrote for their freewriting assignment. Have them complete a poem of several stanzas that continues the same rhyme scheme.

Vocabulary Discuss with **more advanced** students why Marvell might have chosen to use in "Little T.C." such words as "ere" which was already archaic in his time, three of which are, "aspect," and "parley," all very formal words. Point out that Marvell's style throughout this poem is elegant and distanced, in contrast to the flippancy of "To His Coy Mistress."

Motivation for Reading Both "To His Coy Mistress" and "Little T.C." focus on the value of youth. How do we regard youth in our culture? Why? How is this similar or different from the way Marvell presents youth?

Master Teacher Note Explain the Ovidian tradition of *carpe diem,* or "seize the day," which urges taking advantage of the pleasures of the moment. Discuss whether this philosophy is a sound one.

Thematic Idea Other poems on the theme of *carpe diem* are Raleigh's "The Nymph's Reply to the Shepherd" on page 190 and Herrick's "To the Virgins, to Make Much of Time," page 454. Marvell can also be compared with Wordsworth, whom he anticipates in his appreciation of the open air and countryside.

Purpose-Setting Question Which words signal shifts in focus or time frame? ("But" and "Now" in "To His Coy Mistress"; "Meantime" in "Little T.C.")

1 **Discussion** Why does the speaker call his love "vegetable"?

2 **Enrichment** Praise of the lover's body was a poetic convention called a "blazon." Here it is satirized by Marvell. Students might compare this passage to Shakespeare's Sonnet 130.

3 **Literary Focus** Point out the use of personification in these lines. "Time's winged chariot" is a classical image, many of which appear in Marvell's poetry.

4 **Discussion** How do these lines express the theme of *carpe diem?*

To His Coy Mistress

Andrew Marvell

Had we but world enough, and time,
This coyness lady were no crime.
We would sit down, and think which way
To walk, and pass our long love's day.
Thou by the Indian Ganges' side
Should'st rubies find; I by the tide
Of Humber[1] would complain. I would
Love you ten years before the Flood,
And you should if you please refuse
Till the conversion of the Jews.[2]
1 My vegetable love should grow
Vaster than empires, and more slow;
An hundred years should go to praise
Thine eyes, and on thy forehead gaze;
2 Two hundred to adore each breast,
But thirty thousand to the rest;
An age at least to every part,
And the last age should show your heart.
For, lady, you deserve this state,[3]
Nor would I love at lower rate.
3 But at my back I always hear
Time's winged chariot hurrying near:
And yonder all before us lie
Deserts of vast eternity.
Thy beauty shall no more be found,
Nor, in thy marble vault, shall sound
My echoing songs; then worms shall try
That long-preserved virginity,
And your quaint honor turn to dust,
And into ashes all my lust:
The grave's a fine and private place,
But none I think do there embrace.
Now therefore, while the youthful hew
4 Sits on thy skin like morning dew,
And while thy willing soul transpires[4]
At every pore with instant fires,

---

1. **Humber:** River flowing through Hull, Marvell's home town.
2. **conversion of the Jews:** According to Christian tradition, the Jews were to be converted immediately before the Last Judgment.
3. **state:** Dignity.
4. **transpires:** Breathes out.

Now let us sport us while we may,
And now, like amorous birds of prey,
Rather at once our time devour
Than languish in his slow-chapped[5] power.
Let us roll all our strength, and all
Our sweetness, up into one ball,
And tear our pleasures with rough strife
Thorough[6] the iron gates of life:
5 Thus, though we cannot make our sun
Stand still, yet we will make him run.

5. slow-chapped: Slow-jawed.
6. thorough: Through.

THINKING ABOUT THE SELECTION

Recalling

1. According to line 1 of "To His Coy Mistress," under what conditions would the lady's coyness not be a crime?
2. In lines 3–7, what would the lady and the speaker each do, separately and together?
3. Starting at the end of line 7 and continuing to line 20, how does the speaker express his love?
4. In lines 21–24, what does the speaker hear at his back, and what lies before him and the lady?
5. In what place does the action described in lines 25–32 occur?
6. In lines 33–40, why does the speaker urge the lady to act "now"?
7. In conclusion (lines 41–46), what does the speaker say that he and the lady should do?

Interpreting

8. If you had to state the speaker's objections to the lady's resistance in one sentence, what would that sentence be?
9. Since time is central to the poem, how is it expressed? Point to the word pictures or images and to the comparisons or metaphors that stand for and represent time.

Applying

10. The lines "But at my back I always hear / Time's winged chariot hurrying near" have a great deal of meaning. What is the modern experience that these lines express?

ANALYZING LITERATURE

Recognizing Couplets and Quatrains

Couplets are two lines that rhyme and quatrains are four lines that rhyme in various ways. One of the ways to make a quatrain is to join two couplets that deal with one idea, word picture, or comparison. This is sometimes done in long poems, although the quatrain may thus be "hidden."

There are indeed several hidden quatrains in this poem made up entirely of couplets. For example, look at lines 21–24.

These four lines make a single unit, a quatrain. The preceding lines all deal with praising the beauty of the lady; the following lines describe what happens to the body after death. By contrast, the quatrain deals directly with the experience of time.

Find at least one other hidden quatrain. Explain how Marvell's ideas, word pictures, and comparisons move through his couplets.

5 **Clarification** For "we will make him run" read "we'll give him a run for his money!"

Answers

ANSWERS TO THINKING ABOUT THE SELECTION

Recalling

1. If the lovers had all space and time in which to live and love, then her coyness would not matter.
2. Together they would sit and think about which way to walk; on opposite sides of the world, she would find rubies and he would lament.
3. He expresses his love in terms of how much time he would use to praise her.
4. He hears Time at his back, reminding him of his death ahead.
5. These lines describe what it's like in a grave.
6. He wants her to act now while she is still young, beautiful, and full of vitality.
7. He wants them to seize all the pleasure they can, while they can.

Interpreting

8. She keeps wasting time rather than taking advantage of her youth.
9. Marvell uses the following images: the lovers thinking about which way to walk; references to the flood and "the conversion of the Jews"; description of love as "vegetable"; the hyperbolic description of the lady; "Time's winged chariot"; time personified as having "slow-chapped power"; and the sun.

Applying

10. These lives express the feeling that death and extinction are imminent.

ANSWERS TO ANALYZING LITERATURE

Hidden quatrains include lines 13–17, 33–36, 37–40, and 41–44. Within each of the three verse paragraphs, the images and ideas are linked by association—they simply fit together to express ideas. However, the three verse paragraphs taken together have a logical structure that may be summarized thus: If we had all of time and space at our command, your coyness would be acceptable (Paragraph 1). However, we don't (Paragraph 2). Therefore, let us enjoy life and love while we can (Paragraph 3).

1 **Clarification** T.C. was possibly Theophilia Cornewall, a young girl who may have been seven or eight when Marvell wrote the poem. The name "Theophilia" can be translated from the Greek as "God's beloved," in which connection see line 10, "This darling of the gods."

2 **Enrichment** The adjective "golden" indicates the era that Marvell is describing—a golden age of perfection.

3 **Enrichment** Before the Fall, Eve also named the flowers.

4 **Discussion** What does T.C.'s life seem to represent?

5 **Enrichment** Cupid, personified as "The wanton love," was often shown carrying a bow and arrows as his insignia.

6 **Discussion** Note the development of the word "enemy" into a military conceit. What weapon does T.C. use in this war? Note the double meaning of "glancing wheels" in line 20.

7 **Discussion** Why would she more despise those that yield?

8 Why does the poet wish to watch from the shade?

9 **Discussion** How does the mood change at the end of the poem?

1 The Picture of Little T. C. in a Prospect[1] of Flowers

Andrew Marvell

2 See with what simplicity
This nymph begins her golden days!
In the green grass she loves to lie,
3 And there with her fair aspect tames
The wilder flowers and gives them names,
But only with the roses play,
And them does tell
What color best becomes them, and what smell.
4 Who can foretell for what high cause
This darling of the gods was born!
5 Yet this is she whose chaster laws
The wanton love shall one day fear,
And, under her command severe
See his bow broke and ensigns[2] torn.
Happy who can
6 Appease this virtuous enemy of man!
O then let me in time compound
And parley with those conquering eyes
Ere they have tried their force to wound,
Ere, with their glancing wheels, they drive
In triumph over hearts that strive,
7 And them that yield but more despise:
Let me be laid,
8 Where I may see thy glories from some shade.
Meantime, whilst every verdant[3] thing
Itself does at thy beauty charm,
Reform the errors of the spring;
Make that the tulips may have share
Of sweetness, seeing they are fair;
And roses of their thorns disarm:
But most procure

---

1. prospect: Landscape.
2. ensigns: Flags.
3. verdant *adj.*: Green.

That violets may a longer age endure.
But O, young beauty of the woods,
Whom nature courts with fruits and flowers,
Gather the flowers, but spare the buds,
Lest Flora[4] angry at thy crime
To kill her infants in their prime,
9 Do quickly make th' example yours;
And ere we see,
Nip in the blossom all our hopes and thee.

---

4. Flora: The Roman goddess of flowers.

THINKING ABOUT THE SELECTION

Recalling

1. What is the nymph doing in stanza 1?
2. In stanza 2, what will Love fear?
3. Why does the speaker, in stanza 3, want to converse with "those conquering eyes"?
4. To whom are stanzas 4 and 5 addressed?
5. What is asked for in the fourth stanza?
6. Of what is the "young beauty" warned in the last stanza?

Interpreting

7. Nymphs are pretty young nature goddesses from classical mythology. They were often depicted in art and literature as rejecting ardent lovers, many of whom were gods. What details in the poem identify little T.C. with a wood nymph?
8. The speaker at first addresses someone outside the poem, then suddenly shifts and addresses directly little T.C. Where in the poem does this shift occur? What word signals the shift?

Applying

9. Each stanza of this poem ends in a couplet, two lines that rhyme together. What other poems that you have read in this volume end their stanzas with couplets?
10. In a sense, "The Picture of Little T. C. in a Prospect of Flowers" can be thought of as an emblem poem such as George Herbert might have written. Emblems were pictures with mottoes and poems. What sort of picture do you think would be appropriate for this poem by Marvell?

THINKING AND WRITING

Comparing and Contrasting Styles

A literary style is a distinctive use of language. Individual writers have their own style, true enough, but sometimes groups of writers also share a common style. The metaphysical poets were such a group. Among the stylistic traits shared by these poets were a fondness for conceits (extended, farfetched comparisons), paradoxes (apparent contradictions), arguments (efforts at persuasion), and obscure bits of knowledge. Choose two metaphysical writers. List the characteristics of their style. Write an essay comparing and contrasting their styles. When you revise make sure you have included details from their poems to support your ideas.

Answers

ANSWERS TO THINKING ABOUT THE SELECTION

Recalling

1. She is lying on the grass in a flower garden.
2. Love will fear her rejection.
3. He wants to flirt with her before she becomes wise to her womanly powers.
4. They are addressed to the girl.
5. He asks that she make the flowers more perfect.
6. She is warned not to antagonize the goddess of flowers.

Interpreting

7. She is associated throughout with nature; in addition, the speaker fears that she will one day spurn love.
8. The shift occurs at the beginning of the fourth stanza with the word *thy*.

Applying

9. English sonnets such as Shakespeare's, Spenser's sonnets, and Raleigh's "To His Son." end their final stanza with a couplet.
10. Little T.C. might be shown lying on the grass, fingering the abundance of flowers surrounding her. The background would be lush and highly decorated. Cupid might be waiting in the background on one side; Flora might be jealously watching on the other.

THINKING AND WRITING

For help with this assignment, students can refer to Lesson 12, "Writing About a Poem," in the Handbook of Writing About Literature.

Publishing Student Writing You might read aloud the better papers to stimulate further discussion of Donne's themes.

Challenge In both "To His Coy Mistress" and "Little T.C.," Marvell creates perfect worlds that are belied by reality. Describe these perfect worlds. Why can't they be attained?

More About the Author Ben Jonson was vain, pugnacious, and given to excessive drinking, as well as enormously charismatic and revered as a writer. In the Preface to his play *Volpone,* he wrote of "the impossibility of any man's being a good poet without first being a good man." What do you think Jonson meant by this statement? Do you agree with it?

BEN JONSON

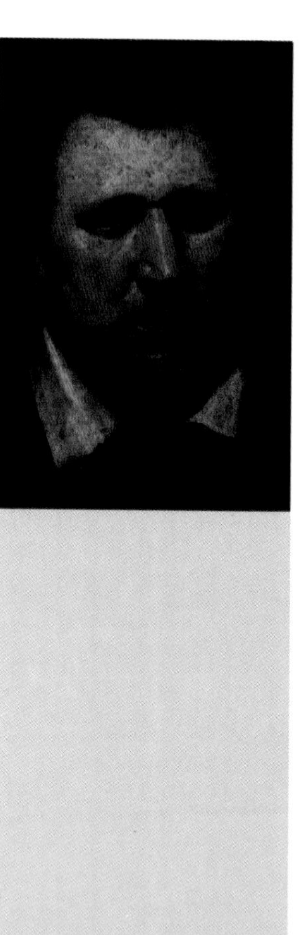

1572–1637

From bricklayer to literary dictator, Ben Jonson's life story is the perfect tale of rags to riches. Not only does his life suggest myth, his physique does too. He was a large man with boundless energy and enormous courage. Friend of Shakespeare and Donne, Jonson was their chief rival in drama and lyric. In addition, Jonson was a classical scholar, an astute critic, a superb prose stylist, a skillful translator, and the chief arbiter of taste for an entire generation of writers.

Adopted when an infant by a bricklayer, Jonson worked for his stepfather a number of years while attending the equivalent of high school under one of the leading teachers of the age. Too poor to pursue his education further, Jonson enlisted in the army and fought in the wars for Dutch independence from Spain. At one point as a soldier, he fought in single combat the champion of the enemy before the massed armies of Holland and Spain. Jonson won.

On returning to England, Jonson went on the stage as an actor. His early years in the theater were stormy ones: He was jailed one time for taking part in a "seditious and slanderous" play; another time he was almost hanged for killing a fellow actor in a duel; and still later he was suspected of having a part in a plot on the life of King James I. Despite the turbulence of his life, however, Jonson learned his stagecraft well and became a major dramatist in his own right. His first play had William Shakespeare in a major role, and his later plays were performed by the chief acting companies of the day, including Shakespeare's.

Jonson was so successful he was granted a handsome pension by King James I and treated as if he were poet laureate of England. Over many years he had written masques, elaborate entertainments, for the royal court, where he was a favorite writer. During these years he was enormously influential, functioning as virtual dictator over the literary efforts of the day.

A number of the brightest and best of the young courtly writers flocked about Jonson and called themselves the "Sons" or "Tribe of Ben." Among the outstanding Sons of Ben can be counted Robert Herrick and John Suckling. Although not himself one of the "Sons," Richard Lovelace was also much influenced by Jonson. Indeed, Jonson's direct influence extended beyond these poets to the end of the seventeenth century and into the eighteenth. It is still felt today. What Jonson said of Shakespeare can be said of him as well: "He was not of an age, but for all time."

Objectives

1. To understand apostrophe
2. To infer the author's purpose
3. To write a letter defending the lady in "Still to Be Neat"

Teaching Portfolio: Support Material

Teacher Backup, p. 00

Vocabulary Check, p. 00

Usage and Mechanics Worksheet, . 00

Analyzing Literature Worksheet, p. 00

Critical Thinking and Reading Worksheet, p. 00

Language Worksheet, p. 00

Selection Test, p. 00

GUIDE FOR READING

On My First Son, Song: To Celia, Still to Be Neat

The Writer's Techniques

Apostrophe. An apostrophe is a figure of speech in which an abstract idea or quality, a place or inanimate thing, or a dead or absent person is addressed as if present and able to hear and understand what is said. Ben Jonson used an apostrophe when he directly addressed William Shakespeare, who had been dead for several years, in his poem "To the Memory of My Beloved Master, William Shakespeare."

Apostrophes have been used since very early times by the ancient Greeks and Romans. Here is the opening line to Homer's *Odyssey:*

Tell me, Muse, of the man of many ways. . . .

Although it is rare to find a modern poet apostrophizing, it does sometimes occur. Dylan Thomas apostrophized part of his anatomy in his poem "All All and All the Dry World's Lever."

Know, O my bone, the jointed lever.

For the most part, though, use of the apostrophe today sounds old-fashioned, which brings to mind an ancient Roman apostrophe.

O time! O custom!

Look For

As you read "On My First Son," "Song: To Celia," and "Still to Be Neat," notice Jonson's use and non-use of the apostrophe. What feelings does the poet express about the person each poem addresses?

Writing

Often people have unfinished conversations with others, conversations that they complete many times over in the privacy of their homes. Complete an unfinished conversation.

Vocabulary

Knowing the following words will help you as you read Jonson's "On My First Son," "Song: To Celia," and "Still to Be Neat."

lament (lə ment') *v.*: Mourn; wail; bemoan (p. 446, l. 6)

presumed (pri zo͞om'd') *v.*: Supposed (p. 448, l. 4)

Literary Focus Jonson began the edition of his poetry called *The Works* with the following apostrophe:

To the Reader
Pray thee, take care, that tak'st my book in hand,
To read it well: that is, to understand.

Discuss Why Jonson might have begun the book this way and the significance of his use of the word *understand.*

Look For Have **less advanced** students find examples of apostrophe in other poems in their texts.

Writing Have **more advanced** students write a short poem to complete the apostrophes they wrote for their freewriting assignment.

Teaching to Ability Levels Have **more advanced** students read and write a brief report on *Volpone* or *The Alchemist.*

On My First Son

Ben Jonson

Farewell, thou child of my right hand,[1] and joy;
　　My sin was too much hope of thee, loved boy,
Seven years thou wert lent to me, and I thee pay,
1 　　Exacted by thy fate, on the just[2] day.
O, could I lose all father,[3] now. For why
　　Will man lament the state he should envy?
To have so soon scaped world's, and flesh's rage,
　　And, if no other misery, yet age?
Rest in soft peace, and, asked, say here doth lie
2 　　Ben Jonson his best piece of poetry.
For whose sake, henceforth, all his vows be such,
3 　　As what he loves may never like too much.

---

1. child . . . hand: The literal translation of the Hebrew name Benjamin. Jonson's son was born in 1596 and died in 1603.
2. just: Exact.
3. lose . . . father: Give up all thoughts of being a father.

THINKING ABOUT THE SELECTION

Recalling

1. What is the epitaph Jonson has composed for his son in lines 9–12? What vow does Jonson make as part of the epitaph?

Interpreting

2. How would you rephrase the "sin" Jonson attributes to himself in line 2? What details in the poem support this reading?
3. Why does Jonson say in line 6 that his son's death is enviable?

Applying

4. Compare Jonson's poem on his son's death with Donne's meditation and sonnet. Does Jonson express as much anguish or suffering as Donne?

ANALYZING LITERATURE

Understanding Apostrophes

The apostrophe is a literary convention that allows an author to bring vividly to the mind of a reader the subject of the apostrophe. It endows that subject with a degree of life it might not otherwise have and thereby makes it easier for the reader to share the writer's emotion.

1. To whom is this poem addressed?
2. What question does Jonson ask in lines 5–8?
3. Explain how the device of the apostrophe allows him to clearly express his emotions.

Motivation for Reading Jonson's writings were firmly grounded in classical tradition—polished, formal, and understated. Jonson's was a public voice, unlike the more private and overtly emotional voices of some of his immediate predecessors. Point out that these qualities look ahead to the poetry of the eighteenth century.

Master Teacher Note Quote Jonson's comment from *Conversations with Drummond* that "verses stand by sense, without either colors or accent." Discuss what kind of poetry this aesthetic ideal would produce.

Thematic Idea Another poem that deals with the death of a beloved young man is Tennyson's *In Memoriam*, page 809.

Purpose-Setting Question How does Jonson's poetry differ in style and tone from the poetry of Donne, Herbert, and Marvell? Does Jonson use metaphysical conceits? paradox?

1 **Clarification** For *"O could,"* read "if only I could."

2 **Discussion** In what way is the child his father's "best piece of poetry"? What figure of speech is this?

3 **Clarification** "Like" and "love" were used interchangeably in the Renaissance.

Answers

ANSWERS TO THINKING ABOUT THE SELECTION

Recalling

1. "Rest in soft peace, and, asked say here doth lie/ Ben Jonson his best piece of poetry./ For whose sake, henceforth, all his vows be such,/ As what he loves may never like too much." The speaker vows that he will never again love anything so much.

Interpreting

2. "My sin" might be rephrased as "the cause of my pain." He says that the cause of his pain was to love his son too much, that he wishes he could forget that he had been a father, that death is preferable to life because life is so painful, that his son was "his best piece of poetry," and that he will never allow himself to love anything else so much.
3. The dead have escaped the pain of this world, the decay of the flesh, and the misery of old age.

Applying

4. Donne argues in "Holy Sonnet 10" that death has no meaning because life is eternal; he states in "Meditation 17" that the death of one person affects us all and that suffering brings us closer to God. Jonson's style seems less emotional than Donne's, but is possibly more moving because it is understated.

ANSWERS TO ANALYZING LITERATURE

1. It is addressed to his son.
2. The question is "Why does man lament death, which brings escape from all the miseries of life?"
3. Addressing his dead son gives Jonson a rational pretext for expressing his feelings.

Song: To Celia

Ben Jonson

Drink to me only with thine eyes,
And I will pledge with mine;
Or leave a kiss but in the cup,
And I'll not look for wine.
The thirst that from the soul doth rise,
Doth ask a drink divine:
But might I of Jove's[1] nectar sup,
I would not change for thine.

I sent thee late[2] a rosy wreath,
Not so much honoring thee,
As giving it a hope, that there
It could not withered be.
But thou thereon did'st only breathe,
And sent'st it back to me;
Since when it grows and smells, I swear,
Not of itself, but thee.

---

1. Jove's: Jupiter's. In Roman mythology, Jupiter is the ruler of the gods.
2. late: Recently.

THINKING ABOUT THE SELECTION

Recalling

1. What does the speaker ask for in the first four lines of "Song: To Celia"?
2. In the next four lines, what does the speaker say the soul requires and what substitutes does it desire?
3. (a) Why, according to lines 11–12, did the speaker send the "rosy wreath" to Celia? (b) In lines 14–16, what does the speaker say happened to the wreathe?

Interpreting

4. The speaker says a number of times that he prefers expressions of love to drink, whether wine or nectar. (a) What does love give him that drink cannot? (b) In which lines does he say this?

Applying

5. Many of Jonson's songs were updated versions of classical Latin and Greek poems. It seems, therefore, only fair to do the same to him. If you were asked to update "Song: To Celia," how would you do so?
6. In your opinion, why has this song been so popular down through the centuries?

Enrichment Jonson developed this song from some prose pieces written by Philostratus, a Greek letter writer of the third century. Set to music, it has been a familiar and popular song for almost four hundred years. Jonson's lyrics owe a great deal to Roman and Greek lyrics with their sense of proportion, structural beauty, lucidity and conciseness of style, and freedom from extravagance.

Answers

ANSWERS TO THINKING ABOUT THE SELECTION

Recalling

1. He asks that Celia toast him with her eyes and send him a kiss.
2. The soul asks for divine love; but even if the speaker could have the food of the gods, he would prefer Celia's love.
3. (a) He says that the wreath would not wither if it were in Celia's presence. (b) Celia sent it back to the speaker, but it acquired Celia's scent.

Interpreting

4. (a) Love gives him greater delight. (b) He implies this in lines 7-8.

Applying

5. Answers will differ but students might make the following points: one might modernize the language and change the reference to Jove, and one might also change the extravagant conceit about the wreath and possibly focus on the modern uneasiness with the idea of perfect love or on the dynamics between the man and woman.
6. The song is charming, rhythmic, and accessible. It deals with the always interesting topics of flirting, wine, and devoted love.

Master Teacher Note You might wish to compare the affection expressed in "To Celia" with that depicted in *Abelard Soliciting the Hand of Heloise,* by Angelica Kauffmann. You may wish to explain that Pierre Abelard was a notable twelfth-century thinker and teacher and that Heloise was at first his student and later his wife. The story of their love is one of the most famous in history. Ask your students to tell what feelings the scene implies. Are the feelings in "To Celia" similar or different?

1 **Discussion** What does the speaker presume is the reason for a woman to dress elaborately and use make-up and perfume?

2 **Clarification** For "look," read "appearance."

3 **Clarification** For the "adulteries of art" we should read "adulterations"—debasements by the addition of foreign or inferior substances. However, the more commonly understood suggestion of unfaithfulness in marriage can also be inferred.

4 **Discussion** How does the last line pull the poem together?

Still to Be Neat

Ben Jonson

Still to be neat, still to be dressed,
As, you were going to a feast;
Still to be powdered, still perfumed:
1 Lady, it is to be presumed,
Though arts hid causes are not found,
All is not sweet, all is not sound.

2 Give me a look, give me a face,
That makes simplicity a grace;
Robes loosely flowing, hair as free:
Such sweet neglect more taketh me,
3 Then all th'adulteries of art.
4 They strike mine eyes, but not my heart.

THINKING ABOUT THE SELECTION

Recalling

1. To whom is the first stanza of "Still to Be Neat" addressed?
2. In stanza 1, what is the speaker saying about the Lady's appearance?
3. What does the speaker ask for in the second stanza?

Interpreting

4. The speaker's tone in the first stanza is one of complaint and criticism. What words convey this tone?
5. Where does the speaker say that art raises questions about the good and the true?
6. Essentially, the poem says that art is false, and that naturalness is both more truthful and more appealing. What statements in the poem support this theme or main idea?
7. A modern writer once said, "Nature imitates art." What does this statement reveal about modern attitudes toward art and nature, and how does it contrast with the attitude expressed by Jonson?

Answers

ANSWERS TO THINKING ABOUT THE SELECTION

Recalling

1. It is addressed to a lady.
2. He says that she is too elaborately dressed and made up.
3. He asks that she dress simply and artlessly.

Interpreting

4. The repetition of "still" suggests annoyance.
5. In lines 5-6 he says that artfulness leaves the impression that something is wrong.
6. In stanza 2, he says that simplicity is "a grace" and that artfulness has no emotional appeal.

Applying

7. The statement presumes that the work of humans is better than the work of nature. Jonson would say that art should imitate nature and would praise art for simplicity and fidelity to nature.

Challenge Given Jonson's taste for simplicity in art, as suggested in "Still to Be Neat," how do you think he would regard a poem like "Easter Wings"?

MARRIAGE À LA MODE IV: THE COUNTESS'S MORNING LEVÉE
William Hogarth
National Gallery, London

THINKING AND WRITING

Responding to Criticism

Imagine that you are either the Lady or the Lady's friend and are called upon to respond to the speaker's criticism. Write a letter to the speaker defending the Lady, the virtue of neatness, and the truthfulness of art. Remember, you do not want to offend the speaker; if possible, you would like to persuade him that he is mistaken. It would be a nice touch if you could write your letter as a poem, but prose will do as well.

Humanities Note

Fine art, Detail from *Marriage á la Mode IV: The Countess's Morning Levée* by William Hogarth. William Hogarth (1697–1764), a British painter, portraitist, and engraver, studied art at the Cheron and Vanderbeck's Academy of St. Martin's Lane in London. Although successful as a portraitist, Hogarth's true fame came from his paintings and engravings of "conversation pieces," commentaries on moral subjects of his time executed with satiric wit. This work made him the leading British artist of the first half of the eighteenth century.

The painting *Marriage á la Mode: The Countess's Morning Leveé* (1745), is from a series of six paintings entitled *Marriage á la Mode, a modern comic tale.* They deal with the deterioration of a marriage of convenience between a merchant's daughter and the son of an earl. In this, the fourth painting of the series, the countess is shown having her hair dressed in preparation for her day. These paintings are thought to be Hogarth's most polished and careful works. They were very popular as a set of engravings.

You might use the following questions for discussion:

1. What attitudes toward women are expressed in both the painting and the poem?
2. Hogarth employs symbolism to make his point in the painting; does Jonson use this same device in his poem? Elaborate.

More About the Author While a young man living in London, Robert Herrick was a "Son of Ben," one of the followers of Ben Jonson. Many people feel that Herrick surpassed his master in charm, craftsmanship, and spontaneity. What might be some of the advantages and disadvantages for a young artist of having an older mentor, or more experienced advisor?

ROBERT HERRICK

1591–1674

Called the greatest songwriter of the English language, Herrick's verses please the ear more than the mind. Although he lived through one of the most controversial periods of English history, little of this is reflected in his poetry. His poems are light, whimsical, highly polished, and extremely artificial. They are also a joy to read and hear.

Born to a wealthy goldsmith in London who died when Robert was young, Herrick was apprenticed to his even wealthier uncle, who was also a goldsmith. Although there are no records of his early education, Herrick went up to Cambridge when he was 22 and graduated when he was 29 with a master's degree. Shortly afterward he was ordained a minister and served as a chaplain with English troops fighting in France. On his return from France he was assigned a rural parish in southwestern England. At first unhappy at his "internal exile," Herrick soon adjusted to the lovely countryside and easy life of a country parson. There he wrote his charming verse that celebrated equally the passage of time, the beauty of nature, the joys of love, the pleasures of paganism, and the modesty of Christian devotion.

Although not politically active, Herrick was evicted from his parish by triumphant Puritans after the final defeat of Charles I. Returning to his native and much-loved London, Herrick published his poems in a single, thick little volume with two titles: *Hesperides* and *Noble Numbers*. *Hesperides,* which is the classical Greek name for a mythological garden at the western edge of the world, contained Herrick's secular poems, for which he is best known today. *Noble Numbers* contained his religious verse. Published at a politically turbulent time in London, Herrick's light and graceful poems were ignored by his contemporaries. Interest in them was revived in the nineteenth century, and they are highly regarded today.

With the Restoration in 1660, Herrick went back to his parish in the west country and remained there until his death. When he was young, he had been one of the most ardent disciples of Ben Jonson. From the older poet, Herrick had learned the virtues of a light touch, of a polished surface, and of a restrained manner. He carried his lessons well into his exile, where he sang "of brooks, of blossoms, birds, and bowers: / Of April, May, of June, and July flowers."

Objectives

1. To understand symbols
2. To make inferences about the *carpe diem* tradition
3. To write a reply in verse to "To the Virgins . . ."
4. To write about the thinking process

Teaching Portfolio: Support Material

Teacher Backup, p. 00

Vocabulary Check, p. 00

Usage and Mechanics Worksheet, p. 00

Analyzing Literature Worksheet, p. 00

Critical Thinking and Reading Worksheet, p. 00

Understanding Language Worksheet, p. 00

Selection Test, p. 00

GUIDE FOR READING

An Ode for Him, to the Virgins, to Make Much of Time

The Writer's Techniques

Symbols. A symbol stands for something other than itself while at the same time making us aware of itself. For example, although we realize that the American flag is a piece of cloth, we also recognize that it stands for the United States, its system of government, and the kinds of freedom that are enjoyed here. Writers often use symbols because they are such economical ways of expressing complex ideas. For example, the rose is used frequently to express the idea of the swift passage of time and the short duration of beauty and freshness. Feasts or meals often symbolize sharing, affection, community, and close companionship. The rose and the feast are central symbols in the following two poems by Herrick.

Look For

As you read the following poems, notice the symbols that Herrick uses and the way he builds on them.

Writing

Write the name of an object, such as a flag, a flower, a football, a catcher's mitt, a sewing needle, or a rolling pin. First describe the object as it actually exists: the way it looks, what it is used for. Then write down all the associations you have with the object.

Vocabulary

Knowing the following words will help you as you read "An Ode for Him" and "To the Virgins, to Make Much of Time."

ode (ōd) *n.*: A poem of varying line lengths and usually several stanzas, often addressed to someone; in classical literature, a poem to be sung, usually in praise of someone (p. 452, title)

lyric (lir′ik) *n.*: A poem, one of the major categories of poetry; in classical literature, a song accompanied by a lyre (p. 452, l. 4)

clusters (klus′tərz) *n.*: Groups, gatherings; bunches, as of grapes for wine (p. 452, l. 7)

frolic (fräl′ik) *adj.*: Merry (p. 452, l. 10)

wit (wit) *n.*: Intelligence, wisdom (p. 452, l. 14)

overplus (ō′vər plus′) *n.*: Surplus, abundance; enough over for others (p. 452, l. 14)

talent (tal′ənt) *n.*: A biblical unit of money; native ability (p. 452, l. 17)

succeed (sək sēd′) *v.*: Follow; come after (p. 454, l. 12)

former (fôr′mər) *adj.*: Earlier; coming before (p. 454, l. 12)

coy (koi) *adj.*: Unwilling to make a commitment, *not* the modern sense of "pretending to be shy" (p. 454, l. 13)

prime (prīm) *n.*: Youth (p. 454, l. 15)

tarry (tar′ē) *v.*: Linger, abide; continue in the same condition (p. 454, l. 16)

Discussion The term *ode* implies a poem that is serious, formal, and dignified, usually written to commemorate a person or event. Odes often have an elaborate stanzaic pattern. Does Herrick's poem fit this definition?

2 **Discussion** What is meant by "lyric feasts"?

3 **Discussion** What is meant by "nobly wild"?

4 **Discussion** "Stock" is a metaphor for what commodity referred to in the poem? How is that image developed throughout?

1 An Ode for Him (Ben Jonson)

Robert Herrick

Ah Ben!
Say how, or when
Shall we thy guests
2 Meet at those lyric feasts,
Made at the Sun,
The Dog, the Triple Tun?[1]
Where we such clusters had,
3 As made us nobly wild, not mad;
And yet each verse of thine
Outdid the meat, outdid the frolic wine.

My Ben
Or[2] come again:
Or send to us,
Thy wits great overplus;
But teach us yet
Wisely to husband[3] it;
Lest we that talent spend:
And having once brought to an end
4 That precious stock; the store
Of such a wit the world should have no more.

---

1. Sun . . . Dog . . . Triple Tun: The names of taverns where "The Tribe of Ben" (see p. 444) would gather.
2. or: Either.
3. husband: Conserve.

THINKING ABOUT THE SELECTION

Recalling

1. What question is asked in the first six lines?
2. In lines 7–10, what does the speaker say took place at Ben Jonson's favorite taverns?
3. (a) In lines 11–16, what does the speaker ask of Ben? (b) In lines 17–20, what risks does the speaker describe if Ben does not respond?

Interpreting

4. In what way were the speaker and others Ben Jonson's guests?
5. The tone of this poem is melancholy. What words, phrases, and thoughts contribute to setting this melancholy tone?

Applying

6. "An Ode for Him" is a poem praising Ben Jonson. Today, there are many occasions when we speak words of praise. What are those occasions and how would you express yourself on such occasions?

CRITICAL THINKING AND READING

Knowing Differences Among Synonyms

A **synonym** is a word that has the same or similar meaning as another word, as for example, *error* and *mistake*. Sometimes, several words are synonyms, such as *error, mistake, slip-up,* and *blunder*. They all mean "incorrectness" or "inaccuracy," but there are slight differences among them. *Error* often implies that the incorrectness is the result of *stubborness,* as when we say, "That was an error in judgment." In contrast, *mistake* is much less harsh in implication. It does not, for example, suggest *willfulness,* as does *error*. The word *mistake* also often suggests that the incorrectness or inaccuracy is minor, as when we say, "Oh well, he just made a mistake." We would never use the word *error* in that sentence.

We might, though, use the word *slip-up* if we felt the mistake was a result of carelessness. *Slip-up* is even less formal than *mistake* and would not be used in a report to the top boss of a corporation, for instance. On the other hand, *blunder,* which is far more formal than *slip-up* and *mistake,* is much farther from *error* in its associated meanings than the other two. The senses of *stupidity, clumsiness,* and *sloppiness* are part of the meaning of *blunder*.

If we were to arrange our three words according to how close they are to the word *error,* we would put them in the following order:
error, (1) mistake, (2) slip-up, and (3) blunder. Do the same with the following synonyms taken from "An Ode for Him." Look each word up in the dictionary, number them according to how close they are to the main word, and explain how they differ from one another.

1. *feast:* meal, banquet, religious celebration
2. *wild:* uncivilized, uncontrolled, impassioned
3. *teach:* guide, train, instruct

THINKING AND WRITING

Writing About Thinking

Imagine that you are writing a letter to a friend explaining how you arranged the synonyms. In your letter, answer the following questions. What was the basis for the order in which you placed the synonyms? Did you first look in the dictionary to find out what the words mean? How did you know the dictionary definition was correct? Did you try to make up sentences to fit the definitions? Did you try out the definitions and sentences on people you know? What was their reaction? Did you check out the order of the synonyms with these people? How did they react to that? Did they confirm your judgment? If not, what did you do? At the end of your letter, ask your friend what he thinks the order of the synonyms should be and why. Revise your letter and prepare a final draft.

Answers

ANSWERS TO THINKING ABOUT THE SELECTION

1. When will the Tribe of Ben meet again?
2. The Tribe of Ben ate, drank, recited poetry, and became "nobly wild."
3. (a) He asks that Ben either return or send them his surplus talent. (b) The risk is that they might waste the talent that Ben has lent them.

Interpreting

4. Ben entertained them with his verse and wit; this was his hospitality.
5. The tone is set first of all by the fact that Jonson is dead. The indications of Jonson's talent also contribute to the tone of melancholy.

Applying

6. Answers will differ, but students are probably familiar with awards ceremonies at school, with media awards like the Academy Awards, and with the presentation of honorary degrees at a university. At these occasions speeches are delivered praising the person honored.

ANSWERS TO CRITICAL THINKING AND READING

1. *banquet:* a large, elaborate meal usually implying a meal commemorating a formal occasion.
2. *religious celebration:* a feast to commemorate a holy day or event.
3. *meal:* simply the food served and eaten in one sitting

wild, living or found in a natural state

1. *uncontrolled:* lacking discipline, as though found in a natural state
2. *uncivilized:* not conforming to the rules of civilized behavior (Both uncontrolled and uncivilized are somewhat derogatory.)
3. *impassioned:* filled with intense feeling (This is probably closest to Herrick's meaning.)

teach, to provide knowledge or instruction

1. *instruct:* to convey knowledge or skill to; more formal than *teach*
2. *train:* to teach systematically, as for a profession or athletic event
3. *guide:* to lead carefully through

Motivation for Reading Ask students to imagine that they are song-writers. What would they say in a song (a) urging young women to take advantage of their youth and energy before they get old and (b) commemorating a dead friend, teacher, and drinking partner?

Master Teacher Note Ask students how many have heard the line "Gather ye rosebuds while ye may." Ask them to explain this line. Why is it so famous?

Thematic Idea Other poems on the theme of *carpe diem* are "The Nymph's Reply to the Shepherd" on page 190 and "To His Coy Mistress" on page 440. Another commemorative poem is Jonson's "To the Memory of My Beloved Master."

Discussion Describe the rhyme scheme and rhythm of the poem. How do they contribute to the poem's overall effect?

To the Virgins, to Make Much of Time

Robert Herrick

Gather ye rosebuds while ye may,
Old time is still a-flying;
And this same flower that smiles today
Tomorrow will be dying.

The glorious lamp of heaven, the sun,
The higher he's a-getting,
The sooner will his race be run,
And nearer he's to setting.

That age is best which is the first,
When youth and blood are warmer;
But being spent, the worse, and worst
Times still succeed the former.

Then be not coy, but use your time,
And, while ye may, go marry;
For, having lost but once your prime,
You may forever tarry.[1]

1. **tarry** (tar'ē) *v.*: Delay.

THINKING ABOUT THE SELECTION

Recalling

1. In stanza 1, why does the speaker advise the girls to gather the rosebuds while they may?
2. In the second stanza, what happens to the sun as it gets higher in the sky?
3. According to the third stanza, what is the best age and what happens when it is passed?
4. In stanza 4, why does the speaker suggest that the young girls stop delaying and marry?

Interpreting

5. The central theme or idea of this poem is the swift passage of time. What images or mental pictures express this theme?

Applying

6. This poem is in one sense advice to young women to marry while still young. In what way does it also express the "carpe diem" or "seize the day" tradition? Why do you think

Answers

ANSWERS TO THINKING ABOUT THE SELECTION

Recalling

1. The rosebuds—the joys of youth—last a very short time.
2. It gets closer to setting.
3. The best age is youth and after that things get worse and worse.
4. If they don't marry now, maybe they never will.

Interpreting

5. Images that express the passage of time are the rosebuds, the sun, and the different stages of life.

Applying

6. Throughout, the poem expresses the idea that time flies and pleasures must be seized while they are available. This is the essence of the "carpe diem" theme. One special reason for the popularity of the tradition is that it is a staple of Classical poetry, which most English poets of this time knew well and admired.

ANSWERS TO ANALYZING LITERATURE

1. Symbols of time include rosebuds, flowers that smile today and die tomorrow, and the course of the sun.
2. These symbols work together to create a vivid impression of the

THREE LADIES ADORNING A TERM OF HYMEN
Sir Joshua Reynolds
The Tate Gallery, London

this tradition was so popular during the seventeenth century?

ANALYZING LITERATURE

Understanding Symbols

Symbols are at the same time themselves and stand for something else. The poets of the sixteenth and seventeenth centuries loved playing with the conventions of their art. One of the most popular conventions of the period was the combination of a swiftly passing time and an urgent need to love. Robert Herrick was one of the most successful players of this conventional game.

1. Point to all the symbols of time in "To the Virgins, to Make Much of Time."
2. How do these symbols work together to suggest "blossoming youth" and "decaying age"?

transience of all young, lovely growing things.

THINKING AND WRITING

Publishing Student Writing Possible arguments that might be included in a response to Herrick are: love can be enjoyed at any time in life; mature love is deeper than youthful love; and youthful love is often merely infatuation. You might consider having students' share their responses in a class magazine.

Humanities Note

Fine art, *Three Ladies Adorning a Term of Hymen,* 1773, by Sir Joshua Reynolds. An English painter, Sir Joshua Reynolds (1723–1792) began his artistic education as an apprentice to the artist Thomas Hudson. His education continued as he traveled to Italy where he studied the works of the masters, particularly Rubens and Michelangelo. After his return to England, he became famous for his portraits of the British upper class done with classical themes and backgrounds of ancient landscapes and architecture. He was instrumental in the formation of the Royal Academy and became its first president.

The painting, *Three Ladies Adorning a Term of Hymen,* was posed for by three daughters of a London gentleman. It was painted as more of a "conversation piece" than as a portrait. The three young women, in classical drapery, are shown holding a garland of flowers before a term (stone figure used by ancient Romans to mark boundries) of the god of marriage. The classical theme is further carried out in the details of the amphora and shield to the right. The pose is artificial and theatrical in a good-natured way. When viewing this painting with your students, you might mention that although the painting was produced more than a century after the poem was written, the sentiments expressed in both are the same.

Master Teacher Note After reading Herrick's "To the Virgins, to Make Much of Time," place *Young Girl and Death,* by Marianne Stokes, on the overhead projector. Ask your students to summarize the "message" of Herrick's poem. Then ask them to suggest what underlying similarity of idea is present in Stokes's strange painting. If necessary, you might prompt discussion by pointing out that even for young girls life does not last forever.

More About the Authors Both John Suckling and Richard Lovelace inherited great sums of money. Both loyally supported the king against the rebel Puritans. From what you know of their lives, what way of life would you say that Suckling and Lovelace represent? How would you expect this way of life to be expressed in their poetry?

BIOGRAPHIES

Sir John Suckling (1609–1642)

Richard Lovelace (1618–1657)

The works of Suckling and Lovelace have been linked together as the prime examples of the courtly lyrics known as *Cavalier poetry*. Both poets wrote a light and easy kind of verse associated with the court of Charles I. Both affected a tone of gentlemanly nonchalance in their poems; both were courtiers under Charles.

Suckling came from an extremely wealthy family and used up his inheritance in extravagant living. At one point he hired one hundred fighting men, dressed them up in fancy uniforms, went off to fight for the king in Scotland, and was roundly beaten by the sullen, unfashionably dressed Scots. When he was not engaged in futile fights, he wasted his wealth in gambling. However, he was also a serious patron of many excellent poets, wrote four plays that were spectacularly staged and published at his own exorbitant cost, and composed the delicate lyrics that have gained him fame for over 300 years. As Parliament rebelled against King Charles and gained control of the government, Suckling joined in a conspiracy to free a Royalist leader from the Tower of London. The plot was exposed and Suckling fled to France. There he died impoverished and in despair.

Also from an extremely wealthy family, Lovelace was the pretty boy of Cavalier poetry. He was so handsome that the king and queen ordered that he be granted a master's degree before he completed his studies at Oxford. He was, however, also talented. While at Oxford he wrote a play, painted some fine pictures, and performed credibly on several musical instruments. Perhaps because he was so attractive, Lovelace was chosen by the Royalists to present to Parliament a demand for the restoration of the king's right to absolute authority. Lovelace was immediately arrested. It was while imprisoned that he wrote "To Althea" as a justification for siding with the king even though it meant being confined in jail. After his release from prison, he rejoined Charles's forces in the civil war and spent most of his fortune to help equip the king's army. Upon Charles's defeat in 1645, Lovelace went to France and fought against Holland. Returning to England some while later, he was once again imprisoned by the Puritans. It was during this second imprisonment that he prepared for publication the volume of poems that included "To Lucasta." Although no one knows for certain, it is believed that he died in poverty.

Objectives

1. To write about tone
2. To understand the effect of connotative meaning
3. To compare and contrast the poetry of Suckling and Lovelace

Teaching Portfolio: Support Material

Teacher Backup, p. 000

Vocabulary Check, p. 00

Usage and Mechanics Worksheet, p. 00

Analyzing Literature Worksheet, p. 00

Critical Thinking and Reading Worksheet, p. 00

Language Worksheet, p. 00

Selection Test, p. 00

GUIDE FOR READING

The Constant Lover; Song; To Lucasta, on Going to the Wars; To Althea, from Prison

The Writer's Techniques

Tone. In literature, *tone* refers to the attitude expressed by an author toward his or her subject or audience. A writer's attitude is conveyed through language, characterization, setting, point of view, and details of appearance, voice, location, and the like. Whether in prose or poetry, recognizing the writer's tone is essential to an understanding of the work. Without this recognition, we cannot tell if an author is serious or playful, mocking or admiring, angry or joking, laughing or crying. Very often the tone of a piece of writing can shift from one quality to another.

Look For

As you read the poems of Suckling and Lovelace, notice the tone of each work. Pay special attention to their choice of words, images, metaphors (comparisons), and sound patterns such as rhyme and rhythm.

Writing

Describe the way you feel about something. Your subject can be either serious or trivial. The important thing about your writing is that you reveal how you feel through the words and details you choose. Do not say directly how you feel; do not say, "I am angry," "I am amused," "I am proud," or "I am sorry."

Vocabulary

Knowing the following words will help you as you read the poems of Suckling and Lovelace.

constant (kän′stənt) *adj.*: Faithful; unchanging; unceasing (p. 458, title)
molt (mōlt) *v.*: Cast off; shed, as skin or feathers (p. 458, l. 5)
wan (wän) *adj.*: [Archaic] Gloomy, not the modern sense of sickly pale (p. 459, l. 1)
fond (fänd) *adj.*: [Archaic] Foolish, not the modern sense of having affection for someone or something (p. 459, l. 1)
nunnery (nun′ər ē) *n.*: Convent, a dwelling place for nuns (p. 460, l. 2)
inconstancy (in kän′stən sē) *n.*: Fickleness; changeableness (p. 460, l. 9)
grates (grāts) *n.*: A frame of metal bars used as a partition (p. 461, l. 4)
fettered (fet′ər′d) *adj.*: Chained; confined (p. 461, l. 6)
hermitage (hur′mit ij) *n.*: A retreat suitable for meditation; originally, a hermit's dwelling (p. 462, l. 28)

Literary Focus One tone of voice that will be familiar to students is sarcasm. Ask volunteers to repeat the words "Nice catch" seriously and then sarcastically.

Look For Discuss details that a reader would need to know to pick up the tone of "Nice catch" accurately. Do you think that it is easier to convey tone in poetry or in prose? What devices does a poet have for conveying tone that a prose writer lacks? What devices does a prose writer have?

Writing Have students read aloud the descriptions they wrote for their freewriting assignment. Have members of the class guess the tone each description is trying to convey.

Vocabulary Discuss with **less advanced** students the meaning of the following additional vocabulary words: *prithee* "please," *allay* "reduce," *tipple* "drink alcohol."

Motivation for Reading Love is the major theme of the poetry of Suckling and Lovelace, but it is often regarded cynically. Notice how the subject of love is treated with less reverence and greater facetiousness than in the love poetry you have read previously.

Master Teacher Note A lyric poem is commonly defined as a short, songlike poem expressing the poet's personal thoughts and feelings. Discuss how the poems of Suckling and Lovelace fit this definition. Note the songlike structure, the elegant and direct style, and the regular rhythms.

Purpose-Setting Question What literary devices do Suckling and Lovelace use?

1 **Clarification** For "Out upon it!" read "Can you believe it?"

2 **Discussion** What does the speaker mean by "If it prove fair weather"?

3 **Clarification** For "had made no stays," read: "wouldn't have lasted."

Humanities Note

Fine art, *The Interrupted Sleep* by François Boucher. Boucher (1703–1770), was a French painter and engraver. Many commissions for his work came from his friend and patron, Madame Pompadour. In 1765 Boucher was named "first painter" to the King of France.

The Interrupted Sleep is pervaded with the voluptuousness that typifies Boucher's work. His lush, decorative, rococo art suited the taste of the self-delighted society of France under Louis XV.

You may use the following questions for discussion:

1. The theme of both the painting and the poem is love. Contrast or compare the poet's and the artist's attitude about love.
2. Does the word *frivolous* apply to this painting? Explain.

The Constant Lover

Sir John Suckling

1 Out upon it! I have loved
Three whole days together;
And am like to love three more,
2 If it prove fair weather.

Time shall molt away his wings,
Ere he shall discover
In the whole wide world again
Such a constant lover.

But the spite on 't is, no praise
Is due at all to me:
3 Love with me had made no stays,
Had it any been but she.

Had it any been but she,
And that very face,
There had been at least ere this
A dozen dozen in her place.

THE INTERRUPTED SLEEP
François Boucher
The Metropolitan Museum of Art

THINKING ABOUT THE SELECTION

Recalling

1. In the first stanza of "The Constant Lover," how long has the speaker loved?
2. According to lines 3 and 4, what conditions are necessary for the speaker to continue to love?
3. In the second stanza, how long will it be before Time will find a lover as faithful as the speaker?
4. According to stanza 3, why is praise not due the speaker?
5. In the last stanza, what reason does the speaker give for not leaving his lady for another "dozen dozen" women?

Interpreting

6. The poem is an elaborate compliment to a lady. What are the elements that contribute to this compliment?
7. When an inanimate object or an abstract idea, such as Time or Death, is given human characteristics, it is called *personification*. What is personified in stanza 2 and how does it work in the poem?
8. (a) What attitude toward love and the woman are evident? (b) In what way is the word *constant* in the title ironic?

Applying

9. What qualities do you think characterize a *constant* lover?

Answers

ANSWERS TO THINKING ABOUT THE SELECTION

Recalling

1. The speaker has loved for three days.
2. He will continue to love if the weather stays good.
3. It will be forever before Time discovers a lover so faithful.
4. He would not have been constant with any other lover.
5. He has been constant because this lady is special.

Interpreting

6. The elements that contribute to this compliment are the hyperbolic images of Time's wings melting and "a dozen dozen women," as well as the confession that he would have left her if she had been anyone else.
7. Time is personified. The personification expresses a hyperbolic idea: Time will cease to exist before such a constant lover as the speaker can be found.
8. (a) The speaker is lighthearted about love in general, but seriously infatuated with the woman. (b) This lover is not at all constant, except—for the moment—with his current lady.

Applying

9. Answers will vary, although all students should include faithfulness, or a similar quality.

Song 1

Sir John Suckling

FAIR IS MY LOVE
Edwin A. Abbey
The Harris Museum and Art Gallery, Preston

Why so pale and wan, fond lover?
    Prithee, why so pale?
Will, when looking well can't move her,
    Looking ill prevail?
    Prithee, why so pale? 2

Why so dull and mute, young sinner?
    Prithee, why so mute?
Will, when speaking well can't win her,
    Saying nothing do't?
    Prithee, why so mute?

Quit, quit, for shame; this will not move,
    This cannot take her.
If of herself she will not love, 3
    Nothing can make her:
    The devil take her!

THINKING ABOUT THE SELECTION

Recalling

1. In the first stanza of "Song," how does the lover look?
2. What is the question the speaker asks in the second stanza?
3. What advice to the lover does the speaker give in the third stanza?

Interpreting

4. The third stanza is different from the two preceding ones. In what way is it different?
5. What has caused the "fond" lover to look and behave in the way described by the speaker?
6. What do you think is the lover's emotional state? Explain your answer.

Applying

7. This poem is in a sense an early example of advice to the lovelorn. If a good friend broke up with a loved one, what sort of advice would you give? What would you say and how would you say it?

THINKING AND WRITING

Writing About Tone

Write an essay in which you discuss the tone of Suckling's "Song." Imagine that you will deliver this paper to a scholarly audience. For this audience you will want to discuss the use of irony and wit as instruments for expressing the poet's attitude toward his subject.

1 **Discussion** In what ways is the poem a song?

2 **Enrichment** In the tradition of Petrarch, the Italian sonneteer, the lover became pale and silently wasted away for want of his beloved.

3 **Discussion** What is the speaker's attitude toward love?

Humanities Note

Fine art, *Fair is My Love,* by Edwin Austin Abbey. Abbey (1852-1911) was an expatriate American painter, muralist, and illustrator who lived in England. An apt and clever draftsman in pen and ink, Abbey had a definite attraction for scenes from the British middle ages. The painting *Fair is My Love* was done after 1890 during a period when Edwin Abbey turned to the medium of oil paint. A sweet and charming scene, set in a castle garden, it is historically correct in every detail.

You might use these questions for discussion:

1. How would you describe this painting?
2. In what ways does the painting illustrate Suckling's poem?

ANSWERS TO THINKING ABOUT THE SELECTION

Recalling

1. The lover looks ill.
2. Why is the lover so silent?
3. His advise is to forget about the girl.

Interpreting

4. The third stanza consists of commands rather than questions.
5. He is unhappy that he cannot win his lady.
6. The lover is depressed.

Applying

7. Answers will differ, but common advice might be to find another lover.

1 **Discussion** What image does "nunnery" suggest? Why are Lucasta's breast and mind a nunnery?

2 **Discussion** In what sense is the war the speaker's "new mistress"?

3 **Discussion** How do you think Lovelace would define honor?

Humanities Note

Fine art, *Going to the Battle,* 1858, by Sir Edward Coley Burne-Jones. Burne-Jones (1833–1898), a British painter, abandoned studies in theology to become a painter. After a brief apprenticeship with Dante Gabriel Rossetti, a founding member of the Pre-Raphaelite brotherhood, he began his lifetime work as a painter. His work exemplifies the Pre-Raphaelite style in its use of subjects from medieval times, allegory and myth, careful attention to detail and purity of color and form.

Going to the Battle is a pen and ink study of a medieval theme. The graceful maidenly figures are formalized in the manner of a carved frieze. The draped folds and rich patterns of their clothing add to the enchantment of the scene.

Consider using these questions for discussion:

1. What seems to be the attitude of the knight in this drawing?
2. What aspects of the poem are reflected in this drawing?

WOMAN SEATED BY POOL, HEAD ON HAND
W. Crane
New York Public Library

To Lucasta, on Going to the Wars

Richard Lovelace

1 Tell me not, Sweet, I am unkind,
That from the nunnery
Of thy chaste breast, and quiet mind,
To war and arms I fly.

2 True, a new mistress now I chase,
The first foe in the field;
And with a stronger faith embrace
A sword, a horse, a shield.

Yet this inconstancy is such,
As you too shall adore;
I could not love thee, Dear, so much,
3 Loved I not honor more.

THINKING ABOUT THE SELECTION

Recalling

1. In the first stanza of "To Lucasta, on Going to the Wars," from whom is the speaker going and toward what is he "flying"?
2. In the second stanza, whom does the speaker chase and what will he embrace?
3. According to the last stanza, why will the abandoned lady "adore" the speaker's "inconstancy"?

Interpreting

4. What is the "new mistress" the speaker refers to in the second stanza?
5. What do you believe is the "stronger faith" mentioned by the speaker in line 7?
6. What does the speaker mean when he says in lines 11–12, "I could not love thee, Dear, so much / Loved I not honor more"?
7. This poem is an argument made by the speaker to his lady-love in an effort to convince her to accept his leaving her for war. What details in the poem support this interpretation?

Applying

8. If you were to leave a loved one to go off to fight, what would you say to convince that person to accept your departure?
9. In "Song" (pp. 420–421), John Donne also wrote an argument trying to persuade his beloved to accept his leaving her. Compare the poems by Donne and Lovelace. How do they differ? In what one respect are they similar?

Answers

ANSWERS TO THINKING ABOUT THE SELECTION

Recalling

1. He is leaving his beloved and going to war.
2. He is chasing the enemy and embracing weapons.
3. She will recognize how admirable his sense of honor is.

Interpreting

4. The "new mistress" is honor and loyalty to the king.
5. The "stronger faith" is faith in the justness of his political beliefs.
6. I am only capable of such deep love for you because I am a man honorable enough to put my own desires second to my loyalty to the king.
7. He asks that his lover not see him as unkind and argues that she should love him all the more because he is fighting for an honorable cause.

Applying

8. Answers will differ, but will probably make a point of the cause being worthy.
9. The poems differ in the emphasis they place on the reason for departure, the emphasis they place on the lady and her feelings, and the number and complexity of the arguments. Both apostrophize the lady.

To Althea, from Prison

Richard Lovelace

When love with unconfined wings
Hovers within my gates,
And my divine Althea brings
To whisper at the grates;
When I lie tangled in her hair
And fettered to her eye,
The gods[1] that wanton[2] in the air
Know no such liberty. 1

When flowing cups run swiftly round,
With no allaying Thames,[3]
Our careless heads with roses bound,
Our hearts with loyal flames;
When thirsty grief in wine we steep,
When healths[4] and drafts[5] go free,
Fishes that tipple in the deep,
Know no such liberty. 2

When, like committed linnets,[6] I
With shriller throat shall sing
The sweetness, mercy, majesty,
And glories of my King;
When I shall voice aloud how good
He is, how great should be,
Enlarged[7] winds that curl the flood,
Know no such liberty. 3

---

1. **gods:** The word *gods* is replaced by *birds* in some versions of this poem.
2. **wanton:** Play.
3. **cups . . . Thames** (temz): Wine that has not been diluted by water (from the river Thames).
4. **healths:** Toasts.
5. **drafts:** Drinks.
6. **committed linnets:** Caged finches.
7. **enlarged:** Released.

1 **Literary Focus** In this stanza Lovelace makes use of the literary device of paradox. What is the paradox? What are the paradoxes in the following stanzas?

2 **Discussion** Why are fish appropriate symbols of liberty here?

3 **Discussion** Why are winds an appropriate symbol here?

4 **Discussion** Why are the angels an appropriate symbol here?

Answers

ANSWERS TO THINKING ABOUT THE SELECTION

Recalling

1. (a) The god is hovering within the prison gates. (b) She is whispering outside the bars of his cell.
2. (a) Being with Althea gives him the greatest freedom. (b) Celebrating with friends gives him the greatest freedom.
3. Praising King Charles gives him the greatest liberty.
4. (a) He needs freedom for his mind, heart, and soul. (b) Gods, fish, winds, and angels will experience no greater freedom than he. (c) He compares his freedom to that of an angel.
5. (a) He moves from love of a woman, to celebrating with his friends, to love for the king, or from personal to public pleasures. (b) Freedom doesn't depend on where you are but on whether the heart and mind are free.

Interpreting

6. (a) The poem is about what constitutes true freedom. (b) Each stanza focuses on one expression of liberty: love, friendship, and love of one's country.
7. Answers will differ but students might note that the title and the fact that the speaker returns to the idea of love at the end argue that it is a love poem. The fact that the speaker is not complaining while in prison suggests that the poem is an expression of devotion for the king.

Applying

8. Answers will differ but students might point out that the sentiment is reassuring and pithily expressed.

Stone walls do not a prison make,
    Nor iron bars a cage;
Minds innocent and quiet take
    That for an hermitage;
If I have freedom in my love,
    And in my soul am free,
4 Angels alone that soar above,
    Enjoy such liberty.

THINKING ABOUT THE SELECTION

Recalling 4B, I; 2A, B

1. (a) According to lines 1–4, where is the god Love hovering? (b) Where is the "divine Althea" whispering?
2. (a) In lines 5–8, what does the speaker say gives him the greatest freedom? (b) What conditions does the speaker describe in the second stanza as yielding the greatest freedom?
3. In the third stanza, when will the speaker know the greatest "liberty"?
4. (a) What, in the last stanza, does the speaker say is required to enable him to enjoy the maximum freedom? (b) What or whom, does the speaker say in the first three stanzas, will experience no greater freedom than he? (c) To what does the speaker compare his freedom in the last stanza?

Interpreting 2A, B; 3B, F, G; 4B, C, E, F, H

5. (a) The conditions for the speaker's freedom form a progressive movement in the first three stanzas. What is that movement? (b) Summarize the speaker's conception of freedom.
6. In seventeenth-century England, part of the conflict between King Charles I and his rebellious Parliament was over freedom. Charles wanted to rule by "divine right," which meant basically that he could do as he wished. Parliament wished to take that right away from him. To Charles, this meant a loss of freedom. The Puritans in Parliament, on the other hand, felt that Charles had tried to take away their freedom of religion. From their point of view, it was either his freedom or their freedom that was at stake.

   (a) In what way does Lovelace's poem, "To Althea," reflect this issue? (b) Why does each stanza turn on the idea of "liberty"?
7. Some critics have called "To Althea" a love poem; others have said it was an expression of devotion to King Charles. Which do you believe is right and why?

Applying 2A, B; 3F; 4B, C, E, F, H

8. The first two lines of the fourth stanza of "To Althea" are very famous. They have been repeated down through the ages, often by people who did not know their source. Aside from their poignancy, why, in your opinion, have these lines been so very popular?

The Puritan Age

THE FARRIER'S SHOP, c. 1620–1687
Gael Barend
Guildhall Art Gallery, London

Humanities Note

Fine art, *The Farrier's Shop,* Gael Barend (c. 1600–1663). During the latter part of the seventeeth century, other forms of painting besides portraiture emerged, perhaps influenced by the art of Holland and France. At the same time, interest was growing in genre scenes, scenes of everyday life in the country, like the scene in *The Farrier's Shop.* A farrier is one who shoes horses or one who treats them medically. This scene centers on the farrier about his business, a common scene in village life of the seventeenth century.

More About the Author John Milton was known in his time as a fiery revolutionary and writer of political tracts as well as a poet. Toward the end of his life, poor and blind, with his cause lost, he retired to his writing, hoping to "leave something to aftertimes as they should not willingly let die." What does this quotation reveal about Milton's view of himself as a poet?

JOHN MILTON

1608–1674

Ranked with William Shakespeare and Geoffrey Chaucer as one of the greatest poets of the English language, John Milton actually produced very few poems. The major part of his life he spent either studying literature or writing political tracts. Yet *Paradise Lost* by itself would have been enough to earn him a place among the immortals of English literature.

Born in London to a middle-class family, Milton grew up in a highly cultured environment. His father was a composer and musician of considerable ability as well as a professional scribe or notary. Milton's father was also deeply religious and devoted to the Protestant cause. Educated first at home by tutors, Milton started his formal education in the equivalent of high school when he was about thirteen. While a student at this school he mastered Greek, Latin, and Hebrew as well as several modern European languages. Then he went on to college.

It was while at Cambridge University that Milton decided to prepare himself for a career as a great poet ("God's poet," was how he described it). From this point onward until the English Civil War broke out, Milton devoted himself to a life of study. After earning his degrees from Cambridge, he withdrew to his father's house at Horton for five years, where he is reputed to have read everything that was written in the ancient and modern languages that he knew. It was during this long period of study that Milton wrote "L'Allegro," "Il Penseroso," and "Lycidas" which by themselves would have earned him a lasting position as a major poet. Following his stay at Horton, he went on the Grand European Tour for two years.

While Milton was in Europe, Parliament rebelled against King Charles I; learning of the revolt, Milton cut short his trip and rushed back to England. There, he immediately took up the cudgels in defense of the Parliamentary and Puritan cause. It was in this role that he took part in the pamphlet war of the time and became a leading exponent of republican principles. As a result of his brilliant writings, Oliver Cromwell made Milton Latin Secretary of the Commonwealth. It was in this job that he went blind. Upon restoration of the monarchy, he was at first imprisoned and then released. Andrew Marvell, his former assistant and now Member of Parliament, may have argued on his behalf.

After Milton's release and the loss of most of his property, he withdrew into his blindness and poverty to write *Paradise Lost,* the greatest epic of the English language.

Objectives

1. To recognize the Italian sonnet
2. To understand multiple meaning of words
3. To explain an allusion in poetry and use an allusion in writing
4. To compare and contrast the English and the Italian sonnet

Teaching Portfolio: Support Material

Teacher Backup, pp. 00-00

Vocabulary Check, p. 00

Usage and Mechanics Worksheet, p. 00

Analyzing Literature Worksheet, p. 00

Critical Thinking and Reading Worksheet, p. 00

Language Worksheet, p. 00

Selection Test, p. 00

GUIDE FOR READING

When I Consider How My Light Is Spent; On His Having Arrived at the Age of Twenty-Three

The Writer's Techniques

The Italian Sonnet. The sonnet is one of the major forms of English poetry, but it was invented by the Italians in the thirteenth century. It was imported into England by Wyatt and Surrey in the middle of the sixteenth century. The Italian sonnet is a fourteen-line lyric poem. It is usually divided into two segments, an octave of eight lines and a sestet of six lines. According to the sonnet convention, the octave is supposed to present a situation or problem and the sestet is supposed to offer an answer or response. The rhyme scheme also follows a fairly strict pattern. The octave rhymes *abbaabba* and the sestet usually varies, although within a fairly narrow range. In English, sonnets, whether Italian or not, are written in ten-syllable lines, five beats to the line with a stress pattern that goes like this:

∪ / ∪ / ∪ / ∪ / ∪ /
open unto the fields and to the sky.

Look For

As you read Milton's sonnets, notice his rhyme scheme and the shift in tone between the octave and the sestet.

Writing

Jot down some ideas on reaching whatever age you might now be—16, 17, 18. Try to include some ideas reflecting your view of your accomplishments to date and what you expect from the future.

Vocabulary

Knowing the following words will help you as you read the following two poems.

spent (spent) *adj.*: Used up; gone (p. 466, l. 1)
bent (bent) *adj.*: Determined; resolved (p. 466, l. 4)
chide (chīd) *v.*: Scold; rebuke (p. 466, l. 6)
exact (ig zakt′) *v.*: Demand; compel (p. 466, l. 7)
yoke (yōk) *n.*: A wooden contrivance joining the heads of two draft animals, such as oxen, to make them capable of pulling heavier loads (p. 466, l. 11)
subtle (sut′ ′l) *adj.*: Cunning; ingenious (p. 468, l. 1)
semblance (sem′ bləns) *n.*: Appearance; image (p. 468, l. 5)
measure (mezh′ ər) *n.*: Quantity, dimensions, size (p. 468, l. 10)
even (ē′ vən) *adj.*: Parallel; on the same level with; conforming to (p. 468, l. 10)
grace (grās) *n.*: God's favor or approval (p. 468, l. 13)

Literary Focus Almost every major poet, even into the twentieth century, has tried his or her hand at writing sonnets. What do you think writers and readers find so appealing about the sonnet? Why should it be such a popular form?

Look For Ask students to point out which words signal the shifts in tone between the octave and sestet in Milton's sonnets. Then note that the shift occurs midway in the ninth line of "When I Consider . . ." rather than at the end of the eighth. Point out that "but" and "yet" are very common signal words in Italian sonnets.

Writing Have **less advanced** students write about their accomplishments in prose.

Vocabulary Have **less advanced** students paraphrase the sonnets using definitions from their vocabulary lists.

Motivation for Reading Although the sonnet is an intricate and highly disciplined form of poetry, it is often used by poets to express very personal feelings. In many of Milton's writings, such as *Paradise Lost,* he speaks as an impersonal narrator. These sonnets, however, are highly personal responses to events in his life: his twenty-third birthday and his blindness. What events in your own life might you consider writing a poem or story about?

Master Teacher Note Ask students by what age they expect to have "made it." Discuss what it means to have "made it." Which goals could they not accomplish if they were suddenly blinded? What would their feelings be?

Thematic Idea Another sonnet on the theme of accomplishment is Keats's "When I have fears that I may cease to be," p. 729

Purpose-Setting Question What is the mood of the octaves in Milton's two sonnets? What is the mood of the sestets? How is the shift in mood similar in both sonnets? What causes the shift in mood in both?

1 **Clarification** Since Milton became totally blind at the age of forty-five, his reference to his life being half over is reasonable, if not entirely accurate.

2 **Discussion** Read aloud to students the parable of the talents. What bearing does the parable have on the poem?

3 **Reading Strategy** Ask students to paraphrase this line.

4 **Literary Focus** Point out the use of personification in this line.

5 **Discussion** What conclusion does Milton draw at the end of the sonnet?

When I Consider How My Light Is Spent

John Milton

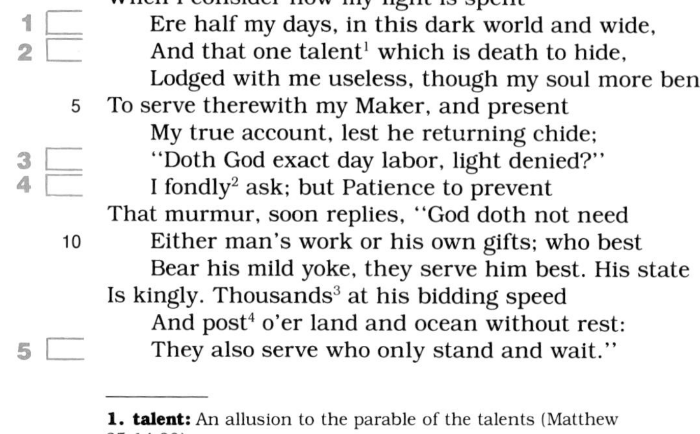

When I consider how my light is spent
1 Ere half my days, in this dark world and wide,
2 And that one talent[1] which is death to hide,
Lodged with me useless, though my soul more bent
To serve therewith my Maker, and present
My true account, lest he returning chide;
3 "Doth God exact day labor, light denied?"
4 I fondly[2] ask; but Patience to prevent
That murmur, soon replies, "God doth not need
Either man's work or his own gifts; who best
Bear his mild yoke, they serve him best. His state
Is kingly. Thousands[3] at his bidding speed
And post[4] o'er land and ocean without rest:
5 They also serve who only stand and wait."

1. talent: An allusion to the parable of the talents (Matthew 25:14-30).
2. fondly: Foolishly.
3. thousands: Thousands of angels.
4. post: Travel.

THINKING ABOUT THE SELECTION

Recalling

1. According to lines 1–2, at what point in the speaker's life does his eyesight fail?
2. What three qualities does the second speaker attribute to God?

Interpreting

3. The first speaker in this poem expresses a sense of failure. What is the nature of that failure?
4. Why, in your opinion, might Milton have felt that his blindness made his talent "useless?"
5. Explain the last line of the poem: "They also serve who only stand and wait."
6. This sonnet, unlike most other sonnets, is like the dialogue in a play. How does this unusual formal arrangement affect your understanding of the poem?

Applying

7. Do you feel it is necessary for people to use their talents? Explain your answer.

Answers

ANSWERS TO THINKING ABOUT THE SELECTION

Recalling

1. It fails halfway through his life.
2. God is accepting, wise, and merciful.

Interpreting

3. He is unable to write.
4. Answers will differ, but one important possibility is that he would not be able to use visual observations in his poetry.
5. Patient acceptance of God's will, even if unaccompanied by action, is pleasing to God.
6. Suggested answer: it makes the speaker's conflicting feelings more vividly dramatic.

Applying

7. Answers will vary, though it might be argued that not to use one's talents is ultimately harmful to the individual.

ANALYZING LITERATURE

Understanding Italian Sonnets

The rhyme scheme of Milton's sonnet on his blindness is *abbaabba cdecde,* which is common to the Italian sonnet. To emphasize their rhyme scheme, most sonneteers end-stop their lines. When a natural pause occurs at the end of a line, the line is called *end-stopped.* An example of end stopping is the third line of Milton's "When I Consider . . ." This can be contrasted with the next line, the normal reading of which carries one over to the following or fifth line. This kind of carry-over is called *enjambment* or a *run-on line.* Run-on lines tend to obscure end rhymes and thereby make the rhyme scheme more subtle than it might otherwise be. There are a number of run-on lines in Milton's poem.

Another characteristic of the sonnet is the change that takes place between the first eight lines or octave and the following six lines or sestet. Most often the change is very subtle in the Italian sonnet. In Milton's "When I Consider . . ." it is very obvious.

1. Which rhyme sounds are end-stopped and which run-on in the octave?
2. How many end-stopped lines are there in the sestet?
3. Did you read the run-on lines as if you were reading prose? Explain your answer.
4. Which seemed more natural to you, the end-stopped lines or the run-on ones? Which more artificial?
5. What shift in tone did you experience between the octave and sestet when reading aloud? How do you account for this shift?

UNDERSTANDING LANGUAGE

Understanding Multiple Meanings

Most words have more than one meaning. Picking the word *friend* at random, one dictionary indicates five different meanings; another indicates seven.

Poets often use words in such a way as to exploit several meanings of a word at the same time. In this way they enrich an image or a poem.

1. What are the two meanings of the word *talent?*
2. Which is the primary one in the poem?
3. How does the secondary one reinforce the meaning of the primary sense of *talent?*
4. In Milton's mind, what was his chief, perhaps only, talent? What had he spent most of his early life preparing for?
5. What kind of "death" might Milton have experienced if he "hid" or did not use his talent?

ANSWERS TO ANALYZING LITERATURE

1. End-stopped lines: 2, 3, 6, 7
   Run-on lines: 1, 4, 5, 8
2. There are only two end-stopped lines in the sestet, lines 13 and 14.
3. The lines still have the rhythm of poetry and read as such.
4. The run-on lines seem more natural because they follow natural speech patterns; the end-stopped lines seem more artificial.
5. The tone changes from anxiety to assurance. The shift occurs because the speakers change.

ANSWERS TO UNDERSTANDING LANGUAGE

1. Talent is a natural ability and is also an ancient coin.
2. The primary meaning is "ability."
3. The secondary meaning emphasizes the worth of his talent by comparing it to a valuable coin.
4. His chief talent is as a writer. He had spent most of his early life preparing to be a writer.
5. He would have experienced a spiritual death.

1 **Enrichment** Actually, Milton had already produced a respectable amount of writing, including the famous poems "L'Allegro" and "Il Penseroso."

2 **Discussion** What do we gather about Milton's physical appearance at this time?

3 **Clarification** The antecedent of "it" is "inward ripeness."

4 **Clarification** For "even," read "adequate."

5 **Discussion** By using the term "Great Taskmaster" for God, Milton seems to see God in what light?

On His Having Arrived at the Age of Twenty-Three

John Milton

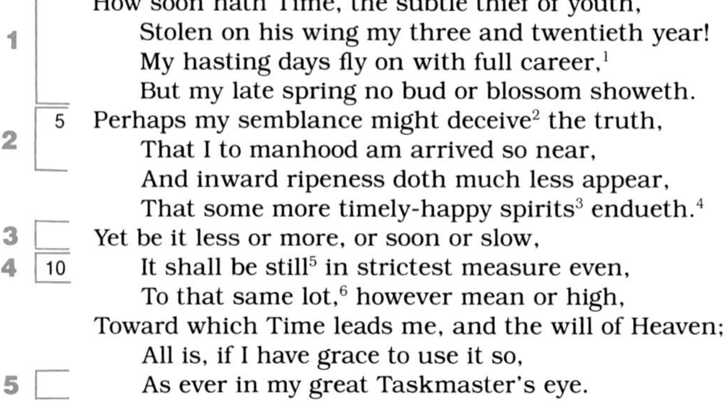

How soon hath Time, the subtle thief of youth,
1 Stolen on his wing my three and twentieth year!
My hasting days fly on with full career,[1]
But my late spring no bud or blossom showeth.
2 Perhaps my semblance might deceive[2] the truth,
That I to manhood am arrived so near,
And inward ripeness doth much less appear,
That some more timely-happy spirits[3] endueth.[4]
3 Yet be it less or more, or soon or slow,
4 It shall be still[5] in strictest measure even,
To that same lot,[6] however mean or high,
Toward which Time leads me, and the will of Heaven;
All is, if I have grace to use it so,
5 As ever in my great Taskmaster's eye.

1. **career:** Speed.
2. **deceive:** Prove false.
3. **timely-happy spirits:** Other people who seem to be more accomplished poets at the age of twenty-three.
4. **endueth:** Endoweth.
5. **still:** Always.
6. **lot:** Fate.

THINKING ABOUT THE SELECTION

Recalling

1. According to the first line, who or what is the "subtle thief of youth"?
2. According to the second line, what was stolen?
3. What, according to line 3, flies on swiftly?
4. In line 4, what is not shown?
5. In lines 5–6, what is the speaker's image that "might deceive the truth"?
6. According to lines 7–8, what does not appear that others seem to have?
7. According to lines 8–12, to what will the speaker's accomplishments eventually conform?
8. What, according to lines 13–14, is forever in the "great Taskmaster's eye"?

Interpreting

9. A metaphor is a comparison of two unlike things. In line 4, Milton uses two metaphors: one for the advanced stage of his youth, the other to represent the early or full development of his poetic ability. Which words are the metaphors?
10. Compare and contrast the concerns of the first four and second four lines of the poem.
11. Overall, what concerns the speaker in the first eight lines?
12. How do the last six lines answer the concern expressed in the first eight lines?

Applying

13. One reason Milton may have felt he hadn't achieved much is that he hadn't yet decided on a career. He had first thought of entering the church and becoming a minister, but by the time he was twenty-three had decided against it. How many people do you know who have made career decisions by the time they were twenty-three? Why do you think it is so difficult to do this?

THINKING AND WRITING

Comparing and Contrasting Sonnets

Write an essay comparing and contrasting the Italian and English sonnets. Imagine you are writing this explanation for your school newspaper.

The English sonnet, which is also commonly known as the Shakespearean sonnet, is markedly different from the Italian form. The sonnet was first developed by the Italians as a fourteen-line love poem with a strict rhyme scheme and structure. The structure is divided into an eight-line octave and a six-line sestet.

The English sonnet, which derives from the Italian, has an entirely different structure and rhyme scheme. In this instance, the sonnet is divided into three four-line quatrains and a concluding two-line couplet. Each of these units has a different set of rhymes and a slightly different thought or image.

Use Shakespeare's "Sonnet 73" (pages 208–209) and Milton's "On His Having Arrived at the Age of Twenty-Three" as your models. Analyze the rhyme scheme for both poems and explain the shifts in thought and image for both poems. Also describe the subjects of both poems. In what way are the subjects similar? How are they different? When you revise, make sure you have arranged your information in logical order. Proofread your essay and prepare a final draft.

THINKING AND WRITING

For help with this assignment, students can refer to Lesson 16, "Writing a Comparative Evaluation," in the Hankbook of Writing About Literature.

Publishing Student Writing After reading the essays, you may want to read several of the best to your class as models of thoughtful, well-organized comparisons.

Answers

ANSWERS TO THINKING ABOUT THE SELECTION

Recalling

1. Time is the "subtle thief of youth."
2. His twenty-third year was stolen.
3. His life flies on swiftly.
4. No buds or blossoms are shown.
5. His appearance, or "semblance," might "deceive the truth."
6. An "inward ripeness" does not seem to appear.
7. They will eventually conform to what he should accomplish according to his age and God's will.
8. God's eye envisions Milton's destiny as a poet.

Interpreting

9. The bud represents youth, the blossom his poetic development.
10. In the first stanza, he is concerned that so much time has passed and that he has accomplished so little. In the second stanza, he is concerned that his outward appearance does not reflect his inward maturity. Both stanzas use horticultural metaphors, such as bud, blossom, and ripeness.
11. He is concerned about his lack of accomplishments.

Applying

13. Answers will differ. Students might mention that many who make career decisions early in life change their careers in the future.

Literary Focus Since students will find the syntax of Milton's sentences exceptionally complex and the sense, therefore, difficult to grasp, point out that Milton was deliberately writing in what was known as the "high style"—a dignified style that made use of sentence forms modeled on Latin grammar.

Look For You might occasionally stop to analyze a grammatically complex passage so as to help your students with the sense of the lines. You might also read extended passages aloud, after encouraging your students to listen to the verbal music of the blank verse and not to worry about understanding everything that Milton is saying.

Writing You may wish to read relevant passages from Genesis.

Vocabulary If you choose to examine closely selected passages from the poem, you may wish to have your students use context clues to figure out the meanings of the unfamiliar words.

GUIDE FOR READING

from Paradise Lost

The Writer's Techniques

Epic Poetry. An epic is a long narrative poem written in an elevated style. It tells the story of a major cultural hero and reflects the values of the society in which it was produced. The early English epic *Beowulf* exhibits the values of the Anglo-Saxon warriors for whom it was composed. John Milton's epic *Paradise Lost* expresses the values of Christian England in the late seventeenth century. It also expresses, however, ideas that are so universal that the poem has become *the* epic of the English-speaking world.

Milton based his poem on the biblical story of Adam and Eve and his style on the classical epics of ancient Greece and Rome. Like the *Aeneid,* the epic of classical Rome, Milton divided *Paradise Lost* into twelve books. He wrote the poem in blank verse, which no one writing in English had done before except in plays, at that time a low-class art form. Milton chose blank verse, which uses an unrhymed iambic pentameter line, because the great epics of ancient Greece and Rome did not rhyme.

Look For

As you read, look for the ways Milton uses traditional forms in an original way so as to create a unique and powerful work of art.

Writing

Jot down all the information you remember of the Biblical story of the fall of Adam and Eve.

Vocabulary

Knowing the following words will help you as you read our selection from the beginning of *Paradise Lost.*

oracle (ôr'ə k'l) *n.*: In classical antiquity, the shrine in which a god spoke through a priest or priestess (l. 12)
illumine (i lo͞o' min) *v.*: Light up (l. 23)
transgress (trans' gres) *v.*: Violate a law or command (l. 31)
guile (gīl) *n.*: Artful trickery; cunning (l. 34)
impious (im' pē əs) *adj.*: Disrespectful; irreverent, ungodly (l. 43)
obdurate (äb' do͞or ət) *adj.*: Stubborn, unyielding (l. 58)
tempestuous (tem pes' cho͞o wəs) *adj.*: Turbulent; violently stormy (l. 77)
transcendent (tran sen' dənt) *adj.*: Surpassing, exceeding, beyond all limits (l. 86)
myriads (mir' ē ədz) *n.*: Tens of thousands (l. 87)
suppliant (sup' lē ənt) *adj.*: Beseeching prayerfully; imploring (l. 112)
ignominy (ig'nə min' ē) *n.*: Humiliation; dishonor; disgrace (l. 115)
apostate (ə pas tāt') *adj.*: Denying former religious conviction (l. 125)

Objectives

1 To understand the conventions and style of Milton's epic.
2 To practice reading comprehension skills with difficult poetic language.

Teaching Portfolio: Support Material

Teacher Backup, pp. 00-00

Vocabulary Check, p. 00

Usage and Mechanics Worksheet, p. 00

Analyzing Literature Worksheet, p. 00

Critical Thinking and Reading Worksheet, p. 00

Language Worksheet, p. 00

Selection Test, p. 00

from Paradise Lost

John Milton

Of man's first disobedience, and the fruit
Of that forbidden tree, whose mortal[1] taste
Brought death into the world, and all our woe,
With loss of Eden, till one greater Man[2]
Restore us, and regain the blissful seat,
Sing Heavenly Muse,[3] that on the secret top
Of Oreb, or Sinai,[4] didst inspire
That shepherd, who first taught the chosen seed,
In the beginning how the Heavens and Earth
Rose out of Chaos: or if Sion hill[5]
Delight thee more, and Siloa's brook[6] that flowed
Fast[7] by the oracle of God, I thence
Invoke thy aid to my adventurous song,
That with no middle flight intends to soar
Above the Aonian mount,[8] while it pursues
1 Things unattempted yet in prose or rhyme.
And chiefly thou O Spirit,[9] that dost prefer
Before all temples the upright heart and pure,
Instruct me, for thou know'st; thou from the first
Wast present, and with mighty wings outspread
Dovelike sat'st brooding on the vast abyss
And mad'st it pregnant: what in me is dark
Illumine, what is low raise and support;
That to the height of this great argument[10]

---

1. mortal: Deadly.
2. one . . . Man: Christ.
3. Heavenly Muse: Urania, the muse of astronomy and sacred poetry in Greek mythology. Here, Milton associates Urania with the holy spirit that inspired Moses ("That shepherd,") to receive and interpret the word of God for the Jews ("the chosen seed"). To convey the message of God to his people, Moses wrote the first five books of the Bible, including Genesis. Genesis is the book on which *Paradise Lost* is based.
4. Oreb (ôr′ ĕb) **. . . Sinai** (sī′ nī′): Alternate names for the mountain where God communicated the laws to Moses.
5. Sion (sī′ ən) **hill:** The hill near Jerusalem on which the temple ("the oracle of God,") stood.
6. Siloa's (sī lō′ əz) **brook:** A stream near Sion hill.
7. fast: Close.
8. Aonian (ā ō′ nē ən) **Mount:** Mount Helicon in Greek mythology, home of the Muses. Milton is drawing a comparison between the epic he is now presenting and the epics written by the classical Greek poets, Homer and Virgil.
9. Spirit: The Holy Spirit, the voice that provided inspiration for the Hebrew prophets.
10. argument: Theme.

Motivation for Reading Ask students to describe their own images of Satan and Hell.

Master Teacher Note Read aloud the Biblical description of the Fall (Genesis 2 and 3).

Thematic Idea Another selection that deals with the theme of evil is Shakespeare's *Macbeth.*

Purpose-Setting Question In what ways does Milton portray Satan as a fully realized character?

1 **Discussion** What are the "Things unattempted yet in prose or rhyme"?

2 Discussion Ask students what they think Milton might mean in this line.

3 Reading Strategy The epic, like its Classical predecessors, begins *in medias res,* in the middle of things. Ask students to discuss what action has preceded this section.

I may assert Eternal Providence,
2 And justify the ways of God to men.
 Say first, for Heaven hides nothing from thy view
Nor the deep tract of Hell, say first what cause
Moved our grand[11] parents in that happy state,
Favored of Heaven so highly, to fall off
From their Creator, and transgress his will
For[12] one restraint,[13] lords of the world besides?[14]
Who first seduced them to that foul revolt?
The infernal Serpent; he it was, whose guile
Stirred up with envy and revenge, deceived
The mother of mankind, what time his pride
Had cast him out from Heaven, with all his host
Of rebel angels, by whose aid aspiring
To set himself in glory above his peers,
He trusted to have equaled the Most High,
If he opposed; and with ambitious aim
Against the throne and monarchy of God
Raised impious war in Heaven and battle proud
With vain attempt. Him the Almighty Power
Hurled headlong flaming from the ethereal sky
With hideous ruin and combustion down
To bottomless perdition, there to dwell
In adamantine[15] chains and penal fire.
Who durst defy the Omnipotent to arms.
Nine times the space that measures day and night
To mortal men, he with his horrid crew
Lay vanquished, rolling in the fiery gulf,
Confounded though immortal. But his doom
Reserved him to more wrath; for now the thought
3 Both of lost happiness and lasting pain
Torments him; round he throws his baleful eyes
That witnessed[16] huge affliction and dismay,
Mixed with obdurate pride and steadfast hate.
At once as far as angels' ken,[17] he views
The dismal situation waste and wild:
A dungeon horrible, on all sides round,
As one great furnace flamed, yet from those flames
No light, but rather darkness visible
Served only to discover sights of woe,
Regions of sorrow, doleful shades, where peace

---

11. grand: First in importance and in time.
12. for: Because of.
13. one restraint: That Adam and Eve should not eat of the fruit of the tree of knowledge.
14. besides: In every other respect.
15. adamantine (ad′ ə man′ tēn) *adj*: Unbreakable.
16. witnessed: Gave evidence of.
17. ken: Can see.

And rest can never dwell, hope never comes
That comes to all; but torture without end
Still urges,[18] and a fiery deluge, fed
With ever-burning sulfur unconsumed:
Such place eternal justice had prepared
For these rebellious, here their prison ordained
In utter darkness, and their portion set
As far removed from God and light of Heaven
As from the center thrice to the utmost pole.[19]
O how unlike the place from whence they fell!
There the companions of his fall, o'erwhelmed
With floods and whirlwinds of tempestuous fire,
He soon discerns, and weltering by his side
One next himself in power, and next in crime,
Long after known in Palestine, and named
Beelzebub.[20] To whom the archenemy,
And thence in Heaven called Satan, with bold words
Breaking the horrid silence thus began:
    "If thou beest he; but O how fallen! how changed
From him, who in the happy realms of light
Clothed with transcendent brightness didst outshine
Myriads though bright: if he whom mutual league,
United thoughts and counsels, equal hope
And hazard in the glorious enterprise,
Joined with me once, now misery hath joined
In equal ruin: into what pit thou seest
From what height fallen, so much the stronger proved
He with his thunder:[21] and till then who knew
The force of those dire arms? Yet not for those,
Nor what the potent Victor in his rage
Can else inflict, do I repent or change,
Though changed in outward luster, that fixed mind
And high disdain, from sense of injured merit,
That with the Mightiest raised me to contend,
And to the fierce contention brought along
Innumerable force of spirts armed
That durst dislike his reign, and me preferring,
His utmost power with adverse power opposed
In dubious battle on the plains of Heaven,
And shook his throne. What though the field be lost?
All is not lost; the unconquerable will,

18. urges: Afflicts.
19. center . . . pole: Three times the distance from the center of the universe (earth) to the outermost sphere of the universe.
20. Beelzebub (bē el' zə bub'): Traditionally, the chief devil, or Satan. In this poem, Satan's chief lieutenant among the fallen angels.
21. He . . . thunder: God.

4 Discussion In line 106, Satan states that all is not lost. What do they still have?

5 Discussion Contrast Beelzebub's attitude toward his banishment with Satan's.

And study[22] of revenge, immortal hate,
4 And courage never to submit or yield:
And what is else not to be overcome?
That glory never shall his wrath or might
Extort from me. To bow and sue for grace
With suppliant knee, and deify his power
Who from the terror of this arm so late
Doubted[23] his empire, that were low indeed,
That were an ignominy and shame beneath
This downfall; since by fate the strength of gods
And this empyreal substance[24] cannot fail,
Since through experience of this great event,
In arms not worse, in foresight much advanced,
We may with more successful hope resolve
To wage by force or guile eternal war
Irreconcilable, to our grand Foe,
Who now triumphs, and in the excess of joy
Sole reigning holds the tyranny of Heaven."
    So spake the apostate angel, though in pain,
Vaunting aloud, but racked with deep despair;
And him thus answered soon his bold compeer.[25]
    "O prince, O chief of many throned Powers,
That led the embattled Seraphim[26] to war
Under thy conduct, and in dreadful deeds
Fearless, endangered Heaven's perpetual King,
And put to proof his high supremacy,
Whether upheld by strength, or chance, or fate!
Too well I see and rue the dire event[27]
That with sad overthrow and foul defeat
Hath lost us Heaven, and all this mighty host
5 In horrible destruction laid thus low,
As far as gods and heavenly essences
Can perish: for the mind and spirit remains
Invincible, and vigor soon returns,
Though all our glory extinct, and happy state
Here swallowed up in endless misery.
But what if he our conqueror (whom I now
Of force[28] believe almighty, since no less
Than such could have o'erpowered such force as ours)
Have left us this our spirit and strength entire
Strongly to suffer and support our pains,

---

22. study: Pursuit.
23. doubted: Feared for.
24. empyreal (em pir′ ē əl) **substance:** The indestructible substance of which Heaven, or the empyrean, is composed.
25. compeer: Comrade, equal.
26. Seraphim (sĕr′ ə fim): The highest order of angels.
27. event: Outcome.
28. of force: Necessarily.

That we may so suffice[29] his vengeful ire,
Or do him mightier service as his thralls
By right of war, whate'er his business be
Here in the heart of Hell to work in fire,
Or do his errands in the gloomy deep?
What can it then avail though yet we feel
Strength undiminished, or eternal being
To undergo eternal punishment?"
Whereto with speedy words the Archfiend replied:
"Fallen cherub, to be weak is miserable,
Doing or suffering:[30] but of this be sure,
To do aught[31] good never will be our task,
But ever to do ill our sole delight,
As being the contrary to his high will
Whom we resist. If then his providence
Out of our evil seek to bring forth good,
Our labor must be to pervert that end,
And out of good still[32] to find means of evil;
Which oft times may succeed, so as perhaps
Shall grieve him, if I fail not,[33] and disturb
His inmost counsels from their destined aim.
But see the angry Victor[34] hath recalled
His ministers of vengeance and pursuit
Back to the gates of Heaven: the sulfurous hail
Shot after us in storm, o'erblown hath laid
The fiery surge, that from the precipice
Of Heaven received us falling, and the thunder,
Winged with red lightning and impetuous rage,
Perhaps hath spent his shafts, and ceases now
To bellow through the vast and boundless deep.
Let us not slip[35] the occasion, whether scorn,
Or satiate[36] fury yield it from our Foe.
Seest thou yon dreary plain, forlorn and wild,
The seat of desolation, void of light,
Save what the glimmering of these livid flames
Casts pale and dreadful? Thither let us tend
From off the tossing of these fiery waves,
There rest, if any rest can harbor there,
And reassembling our afflicted powers,[37]
Consult how we may henceforth most offend

---

29. suffice: Satisfy.
30. doing or suffering: Whether one is active or passive.
31. aught: Anything.
32. still: Always.
33. if . . . not: Unless I am mistaken.
34. angry Victor: God.
35. slip: Fail to take advantage of.
36. satiate: Satisfied.
37. afflicted powers: Overthrown armies.

Humanities Note

Fine art, Engraving by Jacob Tonson. This engraving was produced as an illustration for *Paradise Lost.* It is from a lavish folio published in 1688 by Jacob Tonson (1656–1736), a London printer. This engraving reflects the baroque style in art (elaborate decoration characterized by overuse of the curve) that was in full flower in England at the time. Grotesque and nightmarish, this engraving is an appropriate visualization of the subject it illustrates.

Listed below are questions for class discussion of this illustration:

1. Do you think this artist's concept of Satan agrees with Milton's characterization of him? Explain.
2. Is this illustration an accurate visualization of Milton's text? Explain.

Our Enemy, our own loss how repair,
How overcome this dire calamity,
What reinforcement we may gain from hope,
If not what resolution from despair."

6
Thus Satan talking to his nearest mate,
With head uplift above the wave, and eyes
That sparkling blazed; his other parts besides,
Prone on the flood, extended long and large,

From the British Library

Lay floating many a rood,[38] in bulk as huge
As whom the fables name of monstrous size,
Titanian, or Earthborn, that warred on Jove,
Briareos or Typhon,[39] whom the den
By ancient Tarsus[40] held, or that sea beast
Leviathan,[41] which God of all his works
Created hugest that swim the ocean stream:
Him haply slumbering on the Norway foam
The pilot of some small night-foundered skiff,
Deeming some island, oft, as seamen tell,
With fixed anchor in his scaly rind
Moors by his side under the lee, while night
Invests[42] the sea, and wished morn delays:
So stretched out huge in length the Archfiend lay
Chained on the burning lake, nor ever thence
Had risen or heaved his head, but that the will
And high permission of all-ruling Heaven
Left him at large to his own dark designs,
7 That with reiterated crimes he might
Heap on himself damnation, while he sought
Evil to others, and enraged might see
How all his malice served but to bring forth
Infinite goodness, grace and mercy shown
On man by him seduced, but on himself
Treble confusion, wrath and vengeance poured.
Forthwith upright he rears from off the pool
His mighty stature; on each hand the flames
Driven backward, slope their pointing spires, and rolled
In billows leave in the midst a horrid vale.
Then with expanded wings he steers his flight
Aloft, incumbent[43] on the dusky air
That felt unusual weight, till on dry land
He lights, if it were land that ever burned
With solid, as the lake with liquid fire;
And such appeared in hue, as when the force
8 Of subterranean wind transports a hill
Torn from Pelorus, or the shattered side

38. rood: An old unit of measure, equal to seven or eight yards.
39. Titanian (tī tā′ nē ən) **. . . Earthborn . . . Briareos** (brī ăr′ ē əs) **. . . Typhon** (tī′ fən): In classical mythology, both the Titans, led by Briareos, who had a hundred hands, and the Giants (Earthborn), led by Typhon, a hundred-headed serpent monster, fought with Jove. As punishment for their rebellion, both Briareos and Typhon were thrown into the underworld.
40. Tarsus (tär′ səs): The capital of Cilicia (sə lish′ ə). Typhon is said to have lived in Cilicia near Tarsus.
41. Leviathan (lə vī′ ə thən): A great sea monster.
42. invests: Covers.
43. incumbent: Lying.

6 Discussion How will Satan's plan for destruction be thwarted by Heaven?

7 Discussion How do Satan and his mate escape the flames? Note the epic simile here.

9 Discussion Explain Satan's philosophy in these lines.

10 Discussion Ask students if they are surprised at Satan's decision to exclude the others from his Kingdom. Why or why not?

Of thundering Etna,[44] whose combustible
And fueled entrails thence conceiving fire,
Sublimed[45] with mineral fury, aid the winds,
And leave a singed bottom all involved[46]
With stench and smoke: such resting found the sole
Of unblessed feet. Him followed his next mate,
Both glorying to have scaped the Stygian[47] flood
As gods, and by their own recovered strength,
Not by the sufferance[48] of supernal[49] power.
"Is this the region, this the soil, the clime,"
Said then the lost Archangel, "this the seat
That we must change[50] for Heaven, this mournful gloom
For that celestial light? Be it so, since he
Who now is sovereign can dispose and bid
What shall be right: farthest from him is best,
Whom reason hath equaled, force hath made supreme
Above his equals. Farewell happy fields,
Where joy forever dwells. Hail horrors! Hail
Infernal world! and thou, profoundest Hell
Receive thy new possessor, one who brings
A mind not to be changed by place or time.
The mind is its own place, and in itself
Can make a Heaven of Hell, a Hell of Heaven.
What matter where, if I be still the same,
And what I should be, all but less than he
Whom thunder hath made greater? Here at least
We shall be free; the Almighty hath not built
Here for his envy, will not drive us hence:
9 Here we may reign secure, and in my choice
To reign is worth ambition though in Hell:
Better to reign in Hell than serve in Heaven.
But wherefore[51] let we then our faithful friends,
The associates and copartners of our loss
Lie thus astonished[52] on the oblivious[53] pool,
10 And call them not to share with us their part
In this unhappy mansion, or once more
With rallied arms to try what may be yet
Regained in Heaven, or what more lost in Hell?"

---

44. Pelorus (pə lôr′ əs) **. . . Etna:** Volcanic mountains in Sicily.
45. sublimed: Vaporized.
46. involved: Enveloped.
47. Stygian (stij′ ē ən): Of the river Styx, which, in Greek mythology, encircled Hades, the home of the dead.
48. sufferance: Permission.
49. supernal: Heavenly.
50. change: Exchange.
51. wherefore: Why.
52. astonished: Stunned.
53. oblivious: Causing forgetfulness.

THINKING ABOUT THE SELECTION

Recalling

1. The first five lines of *Paradise Lost* tell the biblical story of Adam and Eve and their expulsion from Paradise. What are the five elements of the story that Milton chooses to emphasize?
2. Lines 6–26 are the invocation to the muse. Which lines state the help that Milton is seeking?
3. In lines 29–36, Milton fills out a bit of the story of Adam and Eve. What new element does he introduce here?
4. (a) Lines 34–53 tell of another, earlier Fall from Grace. Who fell that earlier time? (b) What caused that earlier Fall?
5. Lines 59–74 describe Hell. What are its main features?
6. (a) In lines 84–155 Satan addresses Beelzebub and speaks of eternal rebellion and war against God. What are his motives for continuing the war? (b) Explain Beelzebub's advice.
7. From lines 193 to 209, Milton describes the size of Satan. To what creatures is Satan compared?

Interpreting

8. Throughout his invocation, from the first line to the twenty-sixth, Milton mixes references to the Hebrew Bible and classical mythology. What effect is created by Milton's combination of Hebrew and Greek-Roman elements?
9. In what ways are the Fall of Adam and Eve paralleled by the Fall of Satan and his cohorts? Point out the parallels in the poem.
10. Between lines 200 and 208 Milton uses an epic simile in which he compares Satan to the sea beast Leviathan. How does Milton convey the huge size of Leviathan, the point of the comparison?
11. From lines 242 until the end of this excerpt at line 270, Satan expresses simultaneously his despair at losing heaven and his resolve to glory in his lost condition. What words, phrases, and lines show Satan's feelings?
12. How would you describe Satan's character? Is he petty, mean, grand, self-pitying, heroic, stubborn, weak, or rebellious? You may combine several of these characterizations, but support your choices with references to the poem.

Applying

13. The eighteenth-century poet William Blake said "Milton was of the Devil's party." What do you think this statement means. Explain why you agree or disagree with this statement. Find evidence from the poem to support your answer.

ANALYZING LITERATURE

Understanding Epic Poetry

Epic poems express the values of their cultures through stories of heroes and villains in conflict. As in any other kind of story, the conflict is central and can be of many different kinds. Some conflicts are between characters, some are between a character and the environment, and some are within a character's mind.

The conflict in *Paradise Lost* is essentially between Satan and God, and the arena in which the struggle takes place is in the heart and mind first of Eve and then of Adam. The most illuminating insights into the struggle, however, come from the mind of Satan, which is always conscious of the beauty of goodness as it plans evil.

1. What causes Satan the greatest mental anguish?
2. How does he view Heaven? Contrast this to his view of Hell.
3. Interpret his statement: "The mind is its own place, and in itself / Can make a Heaven of Hell, a Hell of Heaven."

Answers

ANSWERS TO THINKING ABOUT THE SELECTION

Recalling

1. Milton emphasizes Adam and Eve's disobedience, their eating of the apple, the death and evil that their disobedience caused, the loss of Eden, and the salvation of man through Christ.
2. Lines 22-26 state the help.
3. Milton writes that Satan deceived Eve out of revenge on God for casting him out of heaven.
4. (a) Satan himself fell earlier. (b) Satan fell because he challenged God's sovereign rule.
5. Hell is dark, eternally burning, and filled with tortured souls who have no hope of relief.
6. (a) Satan wants to continue the war because God has humiliated him and because the experience of the last rebellion has made them stronger and wiser. (b) Beelzebub's advice is to accept the fact that God is almighty and therefore cannot be overthrown by the powers of hell.
7. Satan is compared to the Titans and to the Leviathan.

Interpreting

8. The references place the poem on a grand scale because the poem seems to encompass all Western cultures.
9. Adam and Eve, like Satan, question God's sovereignty. God punished Satan by exiling him from heaven and punished Adam and Eve by exiling them from Eden. Both had been God's favorites.
10. Milton conveys his size by telling how the pilot of a small boat might mistake him for an island.
11. Students may select different lines, but a good choice might be lines 249-251 or line 263.
12. Satan is certainly rebellious and stubborn—Beelzebub speaks of Satan's "fixed mind," line 97—but he is also courageous in refusing to be conquered.

Applying

13. Blake felt that Milton—at least subconciously—admired Satan's energy, heroic qualities, and rebelliousness against a God who is depicted as rational and authoritarian.

ANSWERS TO ANALYZING LITERATURE

1. Satan's greatest mental anguish is caused by his humiliation at having been cast out of heaven.
2. Satan views Heaven as the place of all goodness. He views Hell as the place of all evil.
3. The statement suggests that Heaven and Hell, or good and evil, are merely states of mind.

More About the Author John Bunyan began *The Pilgrim's Progress* as a distraction while in prison. His intention had been to write an autobiographical account of the problems that beset the faithful when he began to write allegory. He continued the allegory that became *The Pilgrim's Progress* as a distraction from his main task. How often do you think successful books get written "by accident"? Have you ever written something successful that was very different from what you had originally intended?

JOHN BUNYAN

1628–1688

Perhaps the most widely read book by any English author, *The Pilgrim's Progress* was written by an ill-educated traveling tinker or mender of pots, pans, and other household utensils. John Bunyan's father had been a tinker before him and had trained him in his craft. As a child John received some education at the local grammar school. After marriage, Bunyan educated himself by reading two religious tracts that his wife brought as a dowry and the Bible. On the basis of this background he wrote a great many religious books and tracts, culminating in the most popular, *The Pilgrim's Progress*.

Born and raised near Bedford in central England, he left there at sixteen to join the Parliamentary army and did not return until a number of years later. At twenty-one he married and at twenty-five he started to preach after several years of an intense spiritual struggle in the dark night of the soul. Bunyan had joined a nonconformist sect and was an unlicensed preacher to its congregation at Bedford. Upon the restoration of the Stuart monarchy, Bunyan, as well as many other nonconformist preachers, was arrested. Refusing to renounce his faith, he remained imprisoned for twelve years, during which time he wrote a fairly large number of religious works. Upon his release as a result of a general amnesty, Bunyan returned to Bedford as a licensed preacher. Except for a short period during which he was imprisoned again, Bunyan remained in Bedford for the rest of his life. There he preached to his congregation and an increasing audience in the barn that served as his church and continued to work at his trade as a tinker. During his second imprisonment, Bunyan wrote the first part of *The Pilgrim's Progress*. Several years later he wrote the second part of this work and a number of other fairly successful books. Altogether Bunyan wrote and published nearly sixty works, yet at his death he was almost as poor as when he was born.

From the seventeenth century through the nineteenth, *The Pilgrim's Progress* was the most successful Christian text written by an Englishman. It was translated into well over 100 languages. Once you have read it, you can understand why the book was so popular. Bunyan was a superb storyteller. He wrote with humor; drew vivid, easily understandable characters; provided suspense and action; and sent a clear, unambiguous message. Moreover, his language, though simple and colloquial, is charged with echoes of the Bible. In essence, Bunyan's tale reflected the main cultural values of his audience.

Objectives

1 To recognize allegory
2 To interpret the author's point of view
3 To use the Oxford English Dictionary
4 To write an allegory

Teaching Portfolio: Support Material

Teacher Backup, p. 000

Vocabulary Check, p. 00

Usage and Mechanics Worksheet, p. 00

Analyzing Literature Worksheet, p. 00

Critical Thinking and Reading Worksheet, p. 00

Understanding Language Worksheet, p. 00

Selection Test, p. 00

GUIDE FOR READING

from *The Pilgrim's Progress*

The Writer's Techniques

Allegory. When the plot, characters, and setting of a story clearly represent abstract ideas, the narrative is called an *allegory.* An allegory can be prose or poetry. It operates on at least two levels: an on-the-surface level and a beneath-the-surface level.

The interest in allegory goes back very far in human history. In fact, the word itself comes from ancient Greece. However, allegory as a way of creating literature hit its stride in the Middle Ages. Medieval writers developed several kinds of allegories. *The Faerie Queene,* for example, is primarily a social allegory, although it has religious, moral, and political elements as well. *Everyman,* on the other hand, is almost entirely a moral allegory, and *The Pilgrim's Progress* is almost entirely a religious one.

The purpose of all allegory is to teach entertainingly. As Bunyan put it in his preface to *The Pilgrim's Progress:*

> [Fish] must be groped for, and tickled too,
> Or they will not be catch'd, whate'er you do.

To make their instruction clear, writers of allegories draw simple, one-dimensional characters and settings, which are then assigned the names of their governing traits. For example, *The Pilgrim's Progress* is an allegory of Christian redemption and salvation. The hero's name is Christian. He leaves the City of Destruction (this world) and goes toward the Celestial City (the place of salvation or heaven). Some of the characters on his journey are Obstinate, Faithful, and Mr. Worldly Wiseman. Some of the place names are Slough of Despond, House Beautiful, and Valley of Humiliation.

Look For

As you read "Vanity Fair," take note of the way Bunyan develops the actions, characters, and settings of his story.

Writing

Jot down the names of several traits, such as Happy, Dour, Mr. Cynic, or Miss Know-it-All. Then write little scenes in which characters bearing these names display the traits.

Vocabulary

Knowing the following words will help you as you read the "Vanity Fair" episode from *The Pilgrim's Progress.*

vanity (van′ ə tē) *n.*: A trifle, knickknack, or other insignificant thing (p. 482, subtitle)
knaves (nāvz) *n.*: Scoundrels; cheaters (p. 482)
reverence (rev′ ər əns) *n.*: Great respect (p. 484)
raiment (rā′ mənt) *n.*: Clothing (p. 484)
traffic (traf′ ik) *n.*: Business (p. 484)
carriages (kar′ ij iz) *n.*: Ways of bearing oneself; deportment (p. 484)

Literary Focus Students should be familiar with allegory from such popular stories as "The Fox and the Grapes." Have students describe this story and its meaning. Have them describe other well-known allegories that they are familiar with.

Look For Bunyan's settings are vivid and concrete in their use of detail. Read aloud his description of the things sold at the fair and point out his use of specific and realistic detail. In addition, his characters and their actions are true to everyday life. Preview the final scene in the selection by describing how the pilgrims enter town, create a "hubbub" because of their odd dress, speech, and behavior, and are immediately distrusted.

Writing Divide **more advanced** students into small groups. Have them write brief scenes in which the characters from their freewriting assignments meet and share an adventure.

Vocabulary Have **less advanced** students locate the vocabulary words in the selection and substitute the given meaning for each word.

Motivation for Reading *Pilgrim's Progress* is a largely autobiographical account of the adventures and dangers a Christian encounters in his passage through life. Have students imagine that they are allegorical characters named "Student." What adventures and dangers might they encounter on their journey toward their diplomas? What characters might they meet along the way?

Master Teacher Note Discuss the "vanities" of the modern world.

Thematic Idea Another selection that deals with the Christian's passage through the world is *Everyman*, p. 000.

Purpose-Setting Question In what ways does Bunyan show what it means to be a pilgrim? In what ways are we all pilgrims?

1 **Enrichment** The full title of the book is *The Pilgrim's Progress from This World to That Which Is to Come: Delivered under the Similitude of a Dream.* What is the "pilgrim's progress"? What is he progressing toward? Why do you think Bunyan uses the device of a dream to tell his story?

2 **Clarification** The "ware of Rome" is the Roman Catholic Church, which England had broken away from.

1

from The Pilgrim's Progress

John Bunyan

Vanity Fair

This is probably the best-known episode of The Pilgrim's Progress. *The book's hero, Christian, and his companion, Faithful, pass through the town of Vanity during the season of the local fair. Local fairs were an important British tradition, giving people the opportunity to buy wares sold by merchants from all over Europe. At the same time, these fairs involved a good deal of eating and drinking and offered a wide variety of entertainment. In this selection, Bunyan uses the fair to demonstrate how worldly attractions can corrupt religious life.*

Then I saw in my dream, that when they were got out of the wilderness, they presently saw a town before them, and the name of that town is Vanity; and at the town there is a fair kept, called Vanity Fair. It is kept all the year long. It beareth the name of Vanity Fair, because the town where it is kept, is lighter than vanity, and also, because all that is there sold, or that cometh thither, is vanity; as is the saying of the wise, "All that cometh is vanity" (Ecclesiastes 1:2, 14; 2:11, 7; 11:8; Isaiah 11:17).

This fair is no new-erected business, but a thing of ancient standing. I will show you the original of it.

Almost five thousand years ago, there were pilgrims walking to the Celestial City,[1] as these two honest persons are; and Beelzebub,[2] Apollyon,[3] and Legion,[4] with their companions, perceiving by the path that the pilgrims made, that their way to the city lay through this town of Vanity, they contrived here to set up a fair; a fair wherein should be sold all sorts of vanity, and that it should last all the year long. Therefore at this fair are all such merchandise sold as houses, lands, trades, places, honors, preferments,[5] titles, countries, kingdoms, lusts, pleasures, and delights of all sorts, as harlots, wives, husbands, children, masters, servants, lives, blood, bodies, souls, silver, gold, pearls, precious stones, and what not.

And moreover, at this fair there is at all times to be seen jugglings, cheats, games, plays, fools, apes, knaves, and rogues, and that of every kind.

Here are to be seen, too, and that for nothing, thefts, murders, adulteries, false swearers, and that of a blood-red color.

And as, in other fairs of less moment, there are the several rows and streets under

---

1. Celestial City: The source of salvation.
2. Beelzebub (bē el′ zə bub): Prince of the devils (Matthew 12:24).
3. Apollyon (a pol′ yən): The angel of the bottomless pit (Revelation 9:11).
4. Legion: The unclean spirit (Mark 5:9).

5. preferments: Appointments and promotions to political or ecclesiastical positions.

their proper names, where such and such wares are vended; so here likewise you have the proper places, rows, streets (namely, countries and kingdoms), where the wares of this fair are soonest to be found. Here is the Britain Row, the French Row, the Italian Row, the Spanish Row, the German Row, where several sorts of vanities are to be sold. But as in other fairs some one commodity is as the chief of all the fair, so the ware of Rome and her merchandise is greatly promoted in this fair; only our English nation, with some others, have taken a dislike thereat.

Now, as I said, the way to the Celestial City lies just through this town where this lusty[6] fair is kept; and he that would go to the city, and yet not go through this town, "must needs go out of the world" (I Corinthians 5:10). The Prince of princes himself, when here, went through this town to his own country, and that upon a fair day too;[7] yea, and, as I think, it was Beelzebub, the

6. lusty: Merry.
7. The Prince . . . too: Refers to the temptation of Christ in the wilderness (Matthew 4:1–11).

PILGRIM'S PROGRESS
Angels/Pilgrim/Knight Figures
John Bunyan
The British Library

Humanities Note

Illustration for *The Pilgrim's Progress.* This illustration was made for the first edition of the second part of *The Pilgrim's Progress,* published in 1682. The identity of the artist is unknown. It is a woodcut engraving, a printing process by which prints are made from designs cut into wooden blocks that are inked and pressed onto paper, thereby transferring the design. The subject is a depiction of an episode from Bunyan's text involving the character Christian on his pilgrimage.

You may wish to use the following questions for discussion:

1. This art deals with a religious subject, as does the art used to illustrate the King James Version of the Bible, (page 389). How do the styles of the two examples of art compare?
2. Do you feel that the difference in styles is a reflection of the difference in religious outlook of the two eras in English history? Explain.

3 Discussion How do you think the pilgrims were dressed?

4 Discussion What is the significance of the pilgrims' degradation? How does it recall Christ's humiliation by the Romans?

chief lord of this fair, that invited him to buy of his vanities; yea, would have made him lord of the fair, would he but have done him reverence as he went through the town. Yea, because he was such a person of honor, Beelzebub had him from street to street, and showed him all the kingdoms of the world in a little time, that he might, if possible, allure that Blessed One to cheapen[8] and buy some of his vanities; but he had no mind to the merchandise, and, therefore, left the town without laying out so much as one farthing upon these vanities. This fair, therefore, is an ancient thing of long standing, and a very great fair.

Now these pilgrims, as I said, must needs go through this fair. Well, so they did; but, behold, even as they entered into the fair, all the people in the fair were moved, and the town itself, as it were, in a hubbub about them, and that for several reasons: for

3 First, the pilgrims were clothed with such kind of raiment[9] as was diverse from the raiment of any that traded in that fair. The people, therefore, of the fair made a great gazing upon them: some said they were fools, some they were bedlams[10] and some they were outlandish men[11] (I Corinthians 2:7,8).

Secondly, and as they wondered at their apparel, so they did likewise at their speech; for few could understand what they said. They naturally spoke the language of Canaan,[12] but they that kept the fair were the men of this world; so that, from one end of the fair to the other, they seemed barbarians each to the other (Job 12:4; I Corinthians 4:9).

Thirdly, but that which did not a little amuse the merchandisers was that these pilgrims set very light by their wares; they cared not so much as to look upon them; and if they called upon them to buy, they would put their fingers in their ears, and cry, "Turn away mine eyes from beholding vanity," and look upwards, signifying that their trade and traffic was in heaven (Psalms 129:37; Philippians 3:19, 20).

One chanced mockingly, beholding the carriages of the men, to say unto them, "What will ye buy?" But they, looking gravely upon him, said, "We buy the truth" (Proverbs 23:23). At that there was an occasion taken to despise the men the more; some mocking, some taunting, some speaking reproachfully, and some calling upon others to smite them. At last things came to a hubbub and great stir in the fair, insomuch that all order was confounded. Now was word presently brought to the great one of the fair, who quickly came down, and deputed some of his most trusty friends to take these men into examination, about whom the fair was almost overturned. So the men were brought to examination; and they that sat upon[13] them, asked them whence they came, whither they went, and what they did there, in such an unusual garb? The men told them that they were pilgrims and strangers in the world, and that they were going to their own country, which was the Heavenly Jerusalem (Hebrews 11:13–16); and that they had given no occasion to the men of the town, nor yet to the merchandisers, thus to abuse them, and to let[14] them in their journey, except it was for that, when one asked them what they would buy, they said they would buy the truth. But they that were appointed to examine them did not believe them to be any other than bedlams and mad, or else such as came to put all things into a confusion in the fair. Therefore 4
they took them and beat them, and besmeared them with dirt, and then put them into the cage, that they might be made a spectacle to all the men of the fair.

8. cheapen: Ask the price of.
9. raiment: Clothing.
10. bedlams: Lunatics from Bethlehem Hospital, the insane asylum in London.
11. outlandish men: Foreigners.
12. Canaan: The Promised Land. The "language of Canaan" is the language of the Bible.

13. sat upon: Interrogated and tried them.
14. let: Hinder.

THINKING ABOUT THE SELECTION

Recalling

1. In *The Pilgrim's Progress,* on what path or route is the town of Vanity located?
2. When in time was the fair established at Vanity?
3. Who were the ones that first set up the fair?
4. What can be seen at the fair?
5. Which individuals *must* go through the town and hence through the fair as well?
6. What were the three reasons the two pilgrims caused such a stir at the fair?
7. What did the pilgrims say that led to their being examined by "the great one's trusty friends"?

Interpreting

8. Why do the travelers have to pass through the fair to reach their destination?
9. What does the fair represent?
10. Why were the pilgrims so uppity toward the inhabitants of the fair?

Applying

11. "Vanity Fair," as well as the whole of *The Pilgrim's Progress,* represents a level and type of writing that is no longer common. If you were to write something like "Vanity Fair" today, how would you go about it?

ANALYZING LITERATURE

Recognizing Allegory

Everything in an **allegory** is geared toward delivering a message. The plot, characters, dialogue, and setting all contribute to the same end—to make the author's ideas immediately understandable.

1. How does the allusion to the temptation of Jesus in the wilderness relate to the purpose of the fair at Vanity?
2. Why is the town and its fair astride the path the true Christian must follow?
3. Why is the fair run by Beelzebub?
4. In relation to Christian virtue, what does the fair represent?

CRITICAL THINKING AND READING

Interpreting the Author's Point of View

Point of view refers to the way a story is told. Stories are told by *someone* and that someone or narrator is represented by a grammatical form or person. The first-person narrator is the character in the story who says "I," like the dreamer in *The Pilgrim's Progress.* The third-person narrator is the one who says "he," "she," or "it." In *The Pilgrim's Progress* the dreamer is also a third-person narrator.

In this excerpt from the "Vanity Fair" episode, there is a first-person and third-person narrator.

1. Point out where each occurs and what the function of the narrator is in any one circumstance.
2. Describe which kind of third-person narrator is being used.
3. Discuss the effect that using two kinds of narrators has on Bunyan's story.
4. In what way might this device suit Bunyan's purpose and allow him the freedom to express his own point of view?

THINKING AND WRITING

Writing an Allegory for Today's World

Allegories generally use one-dimensional characters and situations to present clear ideas about religious, moral, political, or social issues. Write an allegory about the modern world for your fellow students. Remember, allegories are stories, and all stories have conflict. In allegories, this conflict is between characters representing abstract ideas. You should have one central character that the reader can identify with. Do not forget to choose a particular point of view when writing your narrative. You may wish to use a first-person or third-person narrator, or you may wish to alternate between the two, as Bunyan did.

Answers

ANSWERS TO THINKING ABOUT THE SELECTION

Recalling

1. Vanity is on the road to the Celestial City.
2. The fair was set up "almost five thousand years ago."
3. The devils Beelzebub, Apollyon, and Legion set up the fair.
4. Everything corrupt and with the potential to corrupt can be seen at the fair.
5. Everyone must go through the fair.
6. The pilgrims created a stir because of their clothes, their speech, and their lack of interest in the wares.
7. The pilgrims said, "We buy the truth."

Interpreting

8. They have to face and conquer temptation before they can reach salvation.
9. The fair represents worldly corruption.
10. The pilgrims felt superior because they were on the road to salvation and the others were not.

Applying

11. Answers will differ, but students would probably approach such a task using more rounded characters and realistic situations.

ANSWERS TO ANALYZING LITERATURE

1. The fair represents worldly temptations such as the devil offered Jesus.
2. Like Christ, the Christian must be tested in order to prove his true resolve.
3. Beelzebub is the most appropriate figure to preside over a collection of temptations because he represents the greatest evil.
4. The fair represents everything that might corrupt Christian virtue.

ANSWERS TO CRITICAL THINKING AND READING

The excerpt begins with a first-person narrator, then shifts to a story told by a third-person narrator. The first-person narrator provides a link to the rest of the book by tying the adventures together and helps the allegory seem more personal. The third-person narrator gives Bunyan the scope to tell a story outside the experience of his central character.

THINKING AND WRITING

For help with this assignment, students can refer to Lesson 19, "Writing a Short Story," in the Handbook of Writing About Literature.

Challenge Both Milton and Bunyan were writers with strong religious beliefs that were reflected in their works. Compare the place of faith in their works, their purpose in writing, their use of the Bible, and their views of God and the devil.

The writing assignments on page 486 have students write creatively, while those on page 487 have them think about the selections and write critically.

YOU THE WRITER
Guidelines for Evaluating Assignment 1

1. Has the student written a personal letter that a seventeenth-century poet might have written?
2. Does the letter paraphrase the poem in contemporary language?
3. Does the letter capture the personality, style, and tone of the poet?
4. Is the letter free from grammar, usage, and mechanics errors?

Guidelines for Evaluating Assignment 2

1. Has the student written a brief fictional narrative in which the main character is an author from the unit?
2. Has the student given the reader a glimpse of the author's life?
3. Does the narrative have a beginning, middle, and end?
4. Is the narrative free from grammar, usage, and mechanics errors?

Guidelines for Evaluating Assignment 3

1. Has the student modeled his or her poem about a person on a seventeenth-century poem?
2. Does the poem follow the rhythm, rhyme scheme, and stanza pattern of the model?
3. Does the poem stand alone as a satisfactory imitation of seventeenth-century poetry?
4. Is the poem free from grammar, usage, and mechanics errors?

YOU THE WRITER

Assignment

1. Several poems in this unit are addressed to a person. Select one of these poems and turn it into a personal letter such as the poet might have conceivably written.

Prewriting. Write a line-by-line paraphrase of the poem. Then decide how this material should be developed in prose.

Writing. When you write the letter, use modern English, but try to capture the personality and tone of your seventeenth-century author.

Revising. Think of the purpose or main point of your letter. What changes can you make to improve the letter's effectiveness? See if you can add to its seventeenth-century style and tone.

Assignment

2. Many of the authors in this unit led adventurous lives. Write a brief short story in which the main character is an author from this unit.

Prewriting. Review the author's biography and his works. Jot down notes about this author. List details that make him come alive. Then use your imagination. In what scene or situation can you picture him? What other characters are present? How does the scene or situation conclude? Make a map outlining the events in your short story.

Writing. Write the first draft of your short story. Aim to give the reader a glimpse of the author's personality and style. Your narrative should have a beginning, middle, and end. Arrange events in chronological order.

Revising. Make whatever changes will enhance the seventeenth-century character of your narrative. Does the dialogue sound appropriate to the time and place? Then see if you can improve the narrative flow and style.

Assignment

3. Several poems in this unit are about specific people. Write a poem about a person you know, modeling your verses on one of the seventeenth-century poems.

Prewriting. Think of the person your poem will be about and jot down whatever comes to mind about him or her. Then select thoughts and images that can be linked in a poem structured like your seventeenth-century model.

Writing. You might first write a prose passage that contains all the ideas you wish to express. Then turn the passage into verse, following the rhythm, rhyme scheme, and stanza pattern of your model.

Revising. Rewrite your verses until they can stand alone as a satisfactory imitation of seventeenth-century poetry. Read it aloud. Listen to the way it sounds.

YOU THE CRITIC

Assignment

1. Jacobean poetry is distinguished by the presence of striking, highly imaginative figures of speech. Write an essay in which you develop this point by citing and analyzing such figures in the work of three Jacobean poets.

Prewriting. Review the poems you have read and scan them for figures of speech. Analyze the figures to determine what makes them effective vehicles of meaning.

Writing. Write the first draft of your essay. Discuss the figures of speech in a systematic way to prove and illustrate the idea that striking and imaginative figures of speech are a distinctive characteristic of seventeenth-century poetry.

Revising. First check that your separate analyses all relate to and support your main point. Then look for and correct lapses in grammar and style.

Assignment

2. Write an essay in which you compare one humorous and one serious love poem from this unit. Show how each presents a distinctive attitude toward love or the poet's beloved.

Prewriting. Once you have chosen the poems you plan to write about, find the lines, words, ideas, and images that create the humorous or serious tone of each poem.

Writing. Begin with a topic sentence that sums up the different attitude toward love seen in each poem. Then write about each poem separately, supporting your thesis sentence with the evidence you gathered in your prewriting work.

Revising. First check that you have compared the poems in a way that shows clearly the different feelings and attitudes they express. Then look for and correct errors in grammar and style.

Assignment

3. How does seventeenth-century English literature in general differ from the literature of earlier periods? Write an essay in which you answer this question.

Prewriting. First think of one or two differences in subject matter between seventeenth-century and earlier English literature. Then think of one or two differences in style or artistic technique. What specific works or parts of works would you cite to support your views?

Writing. You might first discuss the differences in subject matter and then the differences in style or technique. Be sure to refer to specific works or passages to support your ideas.

Revising. Pay particular attention to improving the organization of your essay so that the characteristics you are concerned with emerge clearly and vividly.

YOU THE CRITIC
Guidelines for Evaluating Assignment 1

1. Does the essay develop the ideas that Jacobean poetry is distinguished by the presence of striking, highly imaginative figures of speech?
2. Is the thesis supported by examples from the literature?
3. Are the points developed systematically?
4. Is the essay free from grammar, usage, and mechanics errors?

Guidelines for Evaluating Assignment 2

1. Does the essay begin with a statement that sums up the different attitudes toward love seen in two seventeenth-century poems?
2. Does the student write about each poem separately while supporting the thesis with evidence from the poems?
3. Has the student offered lines, words, ideas, and images to show clearly the humorous and serious tones of the poems?
4. Is the essay free from grammar, usage, and mechanics errors?

Guidelines for Evaluating Assignment 3

1. Does the essay demonstrate the difference between seventeenth-century English literature and earlier works?
2. Does the student base the comparison on differences in subject matter, style, and technique?
3. Does the student refer to specific works and passages to clarify and illustrate his or her ideas?
4. Is the essay free from grammar, usage, and mechanics errors?

Humanities Note

Fine art, *Morville Hall, Shropshire,* by John Inigo Richards. Richards (c. 1720–1810) was a theatrical scene painter and landscapist.

Throughout the eighteenth century, a "rediscovery" of England was taking place. This interest in the country was manifested in a profusion of illustrated town histories, finely engraved maps, and pictorial records of travel in various regions. The countryside was changing: Open land was disappearing; farm land was being developed, land values were growing, and common land was being enclosed. There was a desire to record the disappearing way of life.

John Inigo Richards wavered between an imitative classical landscape and the reality of the English countryside. In this painting of a Shropshire scene, he has created a fine open vista, no doubt influenced by his experience with theatrical scene painting.

MORVILLE HALL, SHROPSHIRE, 1720?-1810
John Inigo Richards
Roy Miles Fine Paintings, London

488

THE RESTORATION AND THE EIGHTEENTH CENTURY

1660–1798

All Nature is but art, unknown to thee,
All chance, direction which thou canst not see;
All discord, harmony not understood;
All partial evil, universal good. 1

Alexander Pope

1 **Enrichment** These lines from Alexander Pope's *Essay on Man* express the kind of optimism that his French contemporary Voltaire mocked in his famous satire *Candide.*

2 Literary Movement See the excerpt from Daniel Defoe's *Journal of the Plague Year,* page 532, a vivid recreation of the Black Death's emergence in England in 1665. Defoe's *Journal* reads like an eyewitness account although Defoe was only five years old when it occurred.

In 1660, England stood at the threshold of a new age. The religious conflicts that had brought on the Civil War had been settled, and a king once again sat on the throne. The people of England could look forward to a period of stability, order, and progress.

This happy prospect was reinforced by the ideas of a scientific revolution then sweeping Europe. From their close observation of nature, Isaac Newton and other scientists concluded that harmony and order underlay all the events in the world. They also believed that human beings were capable of discovering and understanding that order.

The Scientific Revolution ushered in a new era called the Age of Reason, or the Enlightenment. During the Enlightenment, confidence in human reason spread beyond the realm of science. In the verses quoted above, for example, Alexander Pope asserted that everything in nature has a design and purpose. Disharmony is an illusion—no more than "harmony not understood." Like scientists, Pope believed, poets must struggle to see beneath the superficial chaos and grasp the underlying harmony of the world.

The Enlightenment thus put great emphasis on order, harmony, and stability. At the same time, however, it was an age that believed in progress, and progress meant change. Great changes indeed overtook England between 1660 and the late 1700's. As Parliament restricted the power of the monarch, England improved what was already an admirably democratic political system in Europe. Even more profound changes took place in the economic sphere. English merchants were accumulating great wealth, in part because of their trade with England's colonial empire. In the late 1700s they began to invest in the first factories of the Industrial Revolution. By 1800, Britain had surpassed its ancient rival, France, as the foremost military and economic power in Europe.

From 1660 to the late 1700's, British literature continued to exhibit order and harmony in spite of, or perhaps because of, the rapid transformation of British society. Before discussing the literature of the period, however, it will be helpful to look in more detail at the political, social, and economic developments that took place in England from 1660 to the end of the 1700's.

THE GROWTH OF ENGLISH DEMOCRACY

The Restoration of Monarchy

Soon after Oliver Cromwell's death, in 1658, Parliament offered the crown to the exiled son of Charles I. In 1660, he became Charles II. Most English people fervently hoped that the restoration of the House of Stuart would end the fighting between Puritans and Anglicans and between Parliament and the Crown.

The omens in the first years of Charles II's reign were not good.
2 In 1665, a plague swept the city of London, killing 70,000 people. A

year later, the Great Fire destroyed over half the city's houses. Yet these calamities were quickly overcome. London was rebuilt on a grander scale under the direction of the brilliant architect Christopher Wren (1632–1723). Profits from the global trade carried on by British merchants furthered London's growth.

Charles II had lived in Paris during Cromwell's Protectorship. In sharp contrast to the drab Puritan leaders, Charles II enjoyed elegance. His court copied the plush clothing, rich jewelry, and elaborate wigs of Paris. An avid patron of the arts, Charles also invited Italian composers and Dutch painters to live and work in London. In 1662 he advanced the scientific spirit of the age by chartering the Royal Society, devoted to the study of natural science.

Although some critics said Charles cared more about pleasure than power, he was a shrewd ruler. He kept his Catholic convictions to himself even while accepting money from the Catholic king of France. The problem of having a Catholic king rule a Protestant nation could not, however, be kept in check forever. After Charles II died, James, son of Charles I, became king. James II was a stubborn ruler and a devout Catholic. Trouble loomed when James appointed Catholics to high offices and dismissed Parliament for failing to obey his wishes.

A Glorious Revolution

The crisis came in 1688, when James II's wife gave birth to a son. To the people of England, this meant that another Catholic king would someday sit on the throne. Parliament reacted quickly. Several leaders invited Mary, the Protestant daughter of James II, to rule England jointly with her husband, William of Orange. William was a prince of Holland and a champion of Protestantism in Europe. 3

When William and Mary arrived in England, they were prepared to fight for the throne if necessary. But James, recalling the fate of his father, escaped to France. The people of England hailed the event as a "Glorious Revolution," since not a drop of blood had been shed. The next year, William and Mary agreed to respect a Bill of Rights passed by Parliament. Among other things, it guaranteed Parliament the right to approve all taxes and said that a king could not suspend the law. With the Bill of Rights, England attained a limited, or constitutional, monarchy. Although it was far from being a democracy in the modern sense, England was among the most democratic nations of Europe. 4

Political Parties Emerge

After William of Orange followed his wife Mary to the grave in 1702, Mary's sister Anne, a Protestant, became queen. Under Queen Anne, England grew stronger and more united. One important act of her reign was the joining of the realms of England and Scotland. The Act of Union, passed in 1707, created the nation of Great Britain, with a central government in London.

3 **Historical Context** James's two daughters, offspring of his first marriage, were safely Protestant. It was his second marriage to the Catholic Mary of Modena that produced the Catholic son who so threatened Parliament.

4 **Historical Context** William and Mary were joint monarchs. They were first cousins, both grandchildren of Charles I (William through Charles's daughter Mary), both with royal Stuart blood in their veins. Thus when Mary died, William retained the throne.

BRITISH EVENTS

1660 **Samuel Pepys** begins *Diary*.

1662 Royal Society chartered.

1663 Drury Lane Theater opens.

1666 Great Fire of London.

First cheddar cheese produced.

1667 **John Milton's** *Paradise Lost* published.

1668 **John Dryden** publishes *An Essay of Dramatic Poesy*.

1685 James II becomes king.

1687 Isaac Newton publishes *Philosophiae Naturalis Principia Mathematica*.

1688 Glorious Revolution.

1689 Bill of Rights becomes law.

1690 John Locke publishes *Essay Concerning Human Understanding*.

1700 William Congreve publishes *The Way of the World*.

1701 Act of Settlement.

1702 English enters War of the Spanish Succession.

First daily newspaper begins publication.

1707 Great Britain created by Act of Union.

1709 First Copyright Act.

First literary magazine, *The Tatler*, begins publication.

1712 **Alexander Pope** publishes *The Rape of the Lock*.

1714 George I becomes king.

1719 First organized cricket match takes place.

Daniel Defoe publishes *Robinson Crusoe*.

Palace at Versailles

The Syndics

Samuel Pepys

John Locke

The Great Fire of London

La Salle Visits Indian Village

Major Port for Trade with China

Johann Sebastian Bach

WORLD EVENTS

1661 Holland: Rembrandt paints *The Syndics*.

1662 France: Louis XIV begins palace at Versailles.

1664 North America: Britain seizes New Netherlands.

1665 Holland: Vermeer paints *The Artist's Studio*.

1666 Italy: Stradivari labels first violin.

1669 France: Molière's *Tartuffe* first performed.

1677 France: Racine's *Phèdre* first performed.

1678 North America: La Salle explores Great Lakes.

1680 Dodo becomes extinct.

1685 China: All ports opened to foreign trade.

1690 India: Calcutta founded by British.

1700 Japan: Kabuki Theater developed.

1703 Russia: Peter the Great begins building St. Petersburg.

1714 Holland: Fahrenheit constructs mercury thermometer.

1715 France: Louis XV succeeds to throne.

1721 Germany: Bach composes *Brandenburg Concertos*.

1727 Brazil: First coffee planted.

1728 Pacific: Behring explores Alaskan waters.

1735 Russia: Ballet school opens in St. Petersburg.

1740 Prussia: Frederick the Great succeeds to throne.

1748 France: Montesquieu publishes *The Spirit of the Law*.

1749 Portugal: Sign language invented.

BRITISH EVENTS

1726 **Jonathan Swift** publishes *Gulliver's Travels*.

1735 William Hogarth paints *The Rake's Progress*.

1745 Last Jacobite rebellion in Scotland.

1749 Henry Fielding publishes *Tom Jones*.

1750 **Thomas Gray** publishes "Elegy in a Country Churchyard".

1755 **Samuel Johnson** publishes *Dictionary of the English Language*.

1756 Britain enters Seven Years' War.

1766 **Oliver Goldsmith** publishes *The Vicar of Wakefield*.

1775 Actress Sarah Siddons debuts at Drury Lane Theater.

1786 **Robert Burns** publishes *Poems Chiefly in Scottish Dialect*.

1789 **William Blake** publishes *Songs of Innocence*.

1791 **James Boswell** publishes *The Life of Samuel Johnson*.

1793 England goes to war with France.

1798 Admiral Nelson defeats French at Aboukir Bay.

Illustration from *Gulliver's Travels*

The American Revolution Begins

Robert Burns

Johnson and Boswell

Captain Cook Explores the South Pacific

The Storming of the Bastille

Benjamin Franklin

Mozart

The Boston Tea Party

WORLD EVENTS

1752	North America: Benjamin Franklin invents lightning rod.
1759	Canada: British troops capture Québec.
1765	North America: Stamp Act imposed.
1769	Pacific: Captain Cook explores New Zealand and Australia (to 1770).
1772	France: Diderot publishes *Encyclopédie*.
1773	Austria: Waltz introduced.
	North America: Boston Tea Party.
1774	France: Louis XVI succeeds to throne.
	Germany: Goethe publishes *The Sorrows of Young Werther*.
1775	United States: Revolution begins.
1776	United States: Thomas Jefferson writes Declaration of Independence.
1780	Peru: Rebellion against Spanish rule.
1781	France: Rousseau's *Confessions* published.
	Germany: Kant publishes *Critique of Pure Reason*.
1784	France: First school for the blind established.
1786	Austria: Mozart's *Marriage of Figaro* first performed.
1789	France: Revolution begins with storming of Bastille.
1791	Austria: Haydn composes *Surprise Symphony*.
1793	France: Reign of Terror begins.
1795	Africa: Mungo Park explores Niger River.

During Anne's reign, there was another important political development. Once again, France and Britain were at war. The war helped to crystallize two political factions in Parliament, the Tories and the Whigs. The Tories included aristocrats and lesser landowners. As a group, they were conservatives who were against the changes taking place in Britain. Most Tories opposed the war with France as a waste of tax money. Whigs, on the other hand, supported the war. Many Whigs came from Britain's growing class of merchants, who made handsome profits supplying war goods. They also wanted Britain to crush France once and for all and become the undisputed trade leader of Europe. The split between Tories and Whigs would remain a basic fact of British politics for many decades.

Favoring the Tories, Queen Anne signed a treaty to end the war in 1713, the same year she fell ill. Earlier, Parliament had passed a law stipulating that only a Protestant could inherit the throne. When
5 Anne died in 1714, the throne passed to a little-known relative of James I who ruled a small principality in Hanover, Germany.

QUEEN ANNE AND THE KNIGHTS OF THE GARTER, 1713
Peter Angelis
The Granger Collection

Humanities Note

Fine art, *Queen Anne and the Knights of the Garter,* by Peter Angelis. The Flemish painter Peter Angelis (1685–1734) was born in Dunkirk (his original name, Pierre Angillis, has become Anglicized among English-speaking writers). After traveling in Flanders, he lived in England between about 1719 and 1727. Angelis is admired for his carefully executed pastoral scenes and pleasingly decorative genre paintings, showing ordinary people in simple, domestic settings. Angelis also painted more formal scenes, such as this court scene of Queene Anne in a ceremonial role, installing the Knights of the Garter in 1713.

5 **Historical Context** Although Ann had many children, they all predeceased her. Thus her successor was George of Hanover, a great-grandson of James I through his daughter Elizabeth.

A Cabinet and Prime Minister

The new king, George I, spoke no English and had little interest in the affairs of Britain. He seemed an unlikely figure to advance democracy in Britain, but in fact he did. George I relied on ministers, chosen from Parliament, to run the country. This group of ministers was called the cabinet, and the chief among them came to be known as the prime minister. Robert Walpole, a brilliant and energetic Whig was the first man to unify the cabinet government in the person of the prime minister. Thus began the cabinet system still used in Britain today. Through the cabinet, Parliament gained a greater voice in the nation's policies.

In 1760, another Hanoverian king came to the British throne. Born in Britain, George III thought of himself as an Englishman, not a German. He was a strong-willed man who took his mother seriously when she said, "George, be a king." Using his wealth and influence, the king packed Parliament with men loyal to him. He then set about pursuing his own policies. His strong-headed handling of the American colonies helped bring about the American Revolution.

The king's disastrous policies toward America angered Parliament. In 1782, a fiery twenty-four-year-old became prime minister. William Pitt, the youthful Tory leader, had great plans for reform of the British government. Before he had a chance to put them into effect, however, France erupted in revolution. Soon thereafter, Britain and France were at war again, putting off any chance of reform.

KING GEORGE III OF ENGLAND, c. 1760
Allan Ramsay
The Granger Collection

THE TRANSFORMATION OF BRITAIN'S ECONOMY

An Agricultural Revolution

After the Restoration, Britain's system of government became gradually more democratic. Gradual changes also occurred in the economic life of the nation.

In 1660, the vast majority of the British people were farmers. Most either rented their fields from a landlord or cultivated a patch of common land. By the late 1600s, however, new economic forces were changing life in the countryside. New farm tools made it possible for farmers to plant and harvest a much bigger crop. As a result, landlords began to fence in the land they had once rented out, hiring laborers to work the land for them. 6

Bigger, more efficient estates replaced the small holdings of earlier times. By the mid-1700's, British farms were producing much more food. With more food available, the population of the small island surged upward. Since fewer farmhands were needed, many people left the countryside. In the growing towns, they became the factory hands who ran the machines of the early Industrial Revolution.

Humanities Note

Fine art, *George III of England,* c. 1760, by Allan Ramsay. Scottish-born Allan Ramsay (1713–1784) studied painting in Italy. In the 1730's he settled in London, where he became a well-known portrait painter. Ramsay cultivated a style of depicting some of his subjects in the costume or the pose of a famous ancient person or statue, such as that of Apollo. His works done in a simpler manner are less formal and, at least to modern tastes, more appealing.

Through Ramsay's patron, the Prince of Wales's tutor, the artist received commissions to paint a portrait of the Prince (1757) and, about 1760, when the young monarch ascended to the throne, of King George III. In 1761 Ramsay was appointed painter-in-ordinary to the king.

6 **Enrichment** These "Enclosure Acts," driving people off the land, provide the background for Oliver Goldsmith's famous poem, "The Deserted Village." Goldsmith himself, whose poem "Woman" appears on page 605, has the unique distinction of having created a literary masterpiece in three separate fields: poetry, the drama with *She Stoops to Conquer,* and the novel with *The Vicar of Wakefield.*

The Industrial Age Dawns

The Industrial Revolution began in Britain. A series of British inventions after 1750 made the spinning and weaving of cloth much more efficient. At the same time, the steam engine was perfected and adapted to run a power loom. These machines were brought together in factories, which were soon producing vast quantities of cotton cloth. Merchants sold the goods all over the world, adding more gold to the nation's coffers.

Although the Industrial Revolution happened first in England, the nation did not become predominantly industrial until the 1800's. As late as the 1790's, a majority of British people still earned their living as farmers. Yet the economic changes of the 1700's had major significance. They profoundly affected ways of thinking about the world.

NEW IDEAS FOR A NEW AGE

The Enlightenment

In a sense, the Industrial Revolution began when British inventors found practical ways to apply the ideas of the Scientific Revolution. The Scientific Revolution led to other developments as well. Works by Enlightenment thinkers in many other fields can all be considered its offspring.

In 1687, Sir Isaac Newton published his monumental study of gravity and the movement of the planets. Popular awareness of Newton's achievement is reflected in this couplet from a poem by Alexander Pope:

> Nature and Nature's laws lay hid in night:
> God said, Let Newton be! and all was light.

Each breakthrough in astronomy, physics, and chemistry seemed to affirm the hope that human beings would someday perfect their knowledge of the world. Thinkers in other fields tried to make their studies as orderly and rational as the studies of a scientist. In *The Wealth of Nations,* for example, Adam Smith suggested that economic life is ruled by laws as discoverable as scientific laws.

One of the greatest figures of the Enlightenment was John Locke, a British philosopher and political theorist. After the Glorious Revolution, Locke brought the rationalism of the age to his study of government. Kings, said Locke, did not have a "divine right" to hold power. Rather, a monarch's authority came from the consent of the people. If the monarch abuses his subjects, they "are thereupon absolved from any further obedience." Locke's enlightened ideas about government helped shape the arguments of the American colonists during their disputes with George III.

The scientific advances of the Enlightenment established the

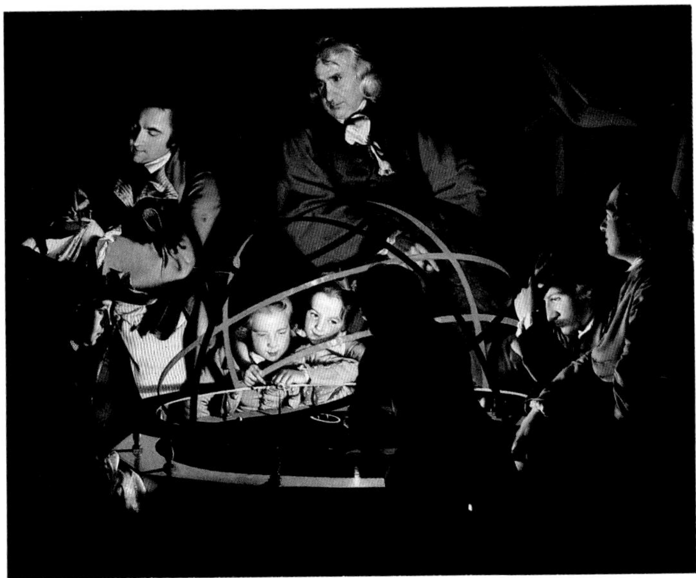

A PHILOSOPHER LECTURING ON THE ORRERY
Joseph Wright of Derby
Derby Art Gallery

basis for the new technology of the Industrial Revolution. But beyond that, a new confidence in human ability encouraged inventors to experiment with new devices, and capitalists to risk their money on untested ideas. Hence, the Industrial Revolution both grew out of and reinforced the new scientific spirit.

The Neoclassical Ideal

Everywhere they looked, the Enlightenment thinkers discerned what they took to be evidence of the world's harmony and order. When Alexander Pope and others sought kindred spirits in the past, they often found them among the writers of ancient Greece and Rome. In the works of Homer, Virgil, Horace, and other classical authors, Enlightenment thinkers and artists discovered harmony, restraint, and clarity—the very qualities they admired most.

English writers of the Enlightenment are often called *neoclassical* because they emulated classical styles. The features of neoclassicism are easy to identify. One feature is the frequent use of classical allusions—that is, references to the myths, gods, and heroes of ancient times. Another is an inclination to generalize about the world rather than to describe it from a particular individual's point of view. John Dryden, Alexander Pope, and Samuel Johnson often put their generalizations about the world in the form of *aphorisms*—short, quotable sentences, such as "The proper study of mankind is man." (See the quotations on page XXX.)

Humanities Note

Fine art, *A Philosopher Lecturing on the Orrery,* by Joseph Wright of Derby. Joseph Wright of Derby (1734–1797) studied in London with the master painter Joshua Reynolds. He first became a portrait painter but later devoted himself to landscape and genre painting. He made many sketches of flame effects and has been called a painter of light.

His interest in the effects of light are obvious in this painting. The focus of the picture is the orrery, a mechanical apparatus for illustrating, with balls of various sizes, the movements and phases of the planets in the solar system. It was named after Charles Boyle, Earl of Orrery, for whom one was made.

7 **Literary Movement** See Samuel Johnson's "Letter to Lord Chesterfield," page 578, as a comment on and a repudiation of patrons. This letter was said to have broken the patronage system; subsequent writers looked more to public support than to private encouragement.

8 **Master Teacher Note** To help students gain a better understanding of the position of poet laureate, you might ask them to research all the poets laureate up to the present. You might also ask them to research America's recent recognition of poets with the establishment of a laureateship here.

One other feature of neoclassicism makes the work of Pope and others lively and amusing: a fondness for satire, the literary ridicule of the vices, follies, and stupidities of society. Such classical poets as Horace, Juvenal, and Martial provided the English poets of the eighteenth century with superb models of the genre.

Most of the satires of the time were mild and inoffensive, usually written in a formal, neoclassical style. Pope, for example, wrote a long poem, *The Dunciad,* in a high-flown, heroic style—but the poem is a satirical celebration of stupidity. Other satirists, such as Jonathan Swift, were less polite. His *Gulliver's Travels* includes savage attacks on lawyers, princes, and mankind in general. In *A Modest Proposal,* Swift suggests a way "for preventing the children of poor people in Ireland from being a burden to their parents or country." Swift's ironic solution—to eat them—is the modest proposal at the heart of a bitter satire directed against the English absentee landlords who were destroying Ireland.

The Literary World Expands

As Britain grew wealthier, more men and women could afford an education. The number of people who could read grew, as did the number who could spend money on books. This change had several results. Daily newspapers began to appear. The first real magazine, the *Gentleman's Magazine,* began publication in 1731. The first private lending libraries, which charged their members a fee, also opened in the early 1700's.

In London, coffeehouses and clubs became popular places for middle-class men to stop in, read the newspapers, and chat about politics. Expanding literacy presented writers with a real opportuni-
7 ty. No longer did they have to rely on a few wealthy patrons for their livelihood. For the first time, writers could at least survive on the money they made from their books and articles. The modern world of publishers, copyright laws, and royalties began to take shape in London during the 1700's.

THREE LITERARY AGES

The literature of the Restoration and eighteenth century may be thought of as comprising three broad divisions, or "ages": the Age of Dryden, the Age of Pope and Swift, and the Age of Johnson.

The Age of Dryden

The Age of Dryden in literature extends from the year of the restoration of Charles II, 1660, to 1700, the year of Dryden's death. In history, this forty-year period is called the Restoration. Dryden,
8 whose works included poems, plays, and essays, dominated the period. He was named poet laureate, England's official poet, by Charles II.

Among Dryden's most famous works are his satirical poems,

THE RAKE'S PROGRESS: NO. 5, THE MARRIAGE
William Hogarth
The Granger Collection

especially *Mac Flecknoe,* written in 1682. These satires included unflattering portraits of real people of his time. Although the poems employ lofty, heroic language, they actually ridicule their "heroes." For this reason they are often called mock heroic poems, or mock epics. Dryden also created several celebratory poems for royal and other public events. These poems, in true Enlightenment spirit, hail
the achievements of humanity. A famous example is "A Song for St. 9
Cecelia's Day," an ode in honor of music.

The Restoration was also noted for its drama, especially comedies. When he became king, Charles II reopened the London
theaters, which the disapproving Puritans had closed. The Restora- 10
tion theaters, fancier and more costly than those of Shakespeare's time, did a thriving business. Dryden himself wrote the best tragedy of the period. Entitled *All for Love,* it recounts the ill-fated romance of Antony and Cleopatra.

Humanities Note

Fine art, *The Rake's Progress: No. 5, the Marriage,* 1735, by William Hogarth. Hogarth (1697–1764) was a man of social vision, who thought that the purpose of painting was to teach the reward of virtue and the wages of sin. He painted this series showing a rake's progress from profligacy and idleness to crime and death. Each picture in the series presents a dramatic scene from the rake's life. In this picture the rake has just been saved from debtors' prison by Sarah Young. He is marrying a one-eyed old woman for her money. In the background, with her infant in her arms, Sarah Young protests the marriage. The condition of the church reflects the squalor of the transaction.

9 **Literary Movement** John Dryden's "A Song for St. Cecilia's Day," page 517, is one of two odes he wrote to honor this saint, traditionally considered the inventor of the pipe organ. In both, Dryden unifies sound and sense with great skill.

10 **Enrichment** When the theaters reopened, women were seen for the first time on the English stage, according to Samuel Pepys's diary.

11 Literary Movement See the excerpt from Dryden's "An Essay on Dramatic Poesy," page 512, written in the precise and graceful style that earned him the title, "father of modern English prose." It was in these critical essays that Dryden established Chaucer's and Shakespeare's modern reputations.

12 Literary Movement The excerpt from Pepys's diary, page 524, not only records in accurate detail the major events of London life in the 1660's but also contains many interesting personal observations. Pepys was extremely frank because his diary was written in a code that was not deciphered until almost one hundred years after his death.

13 Literary Movement See the excerpt from Pope's *The Rape of the Lock,* page 560, which not only satirizes the folly of man but also mocks the elaborate and stylized conventions of the epic form.

14 Enrichment Samuel Richardson's *Pamela,* published more than twenty years later, is often considered the first modern English novel.

11 Prose writing also flourished in the Restoration. Dryden wrote a series of essays about drama that laid the foundation for British literary criticism. These, along with his translations of Plutarch and other prose compositions, represent what many literary historians consider the first modern prose. They are clear, plain, direct,
12 colloquial in tone, and—for people of today—easy to read. Probably the most fascinating prose work of the period, however, was the diary kept by Samuel Pepys (1633–1703). Pepys kept his journal for nine years, beginning in 1660. With remarkable frankness he recorded the daily events in London during those turbulent years, including the deadly plague of 1665 and the Great Fire.

The Age of Pope and Swift

During the reign of Queen Anne in the early 1700's, one of the most admired writer's in London was Alexander Pope. Pope's poetry is a shining example of neoclassical style, exhibiting wit, elegance, and moderation. All these qualities show forth in his most famous work,
13 *The Rape of the Lock,* a mock-heroic poem that satirizes, the absurdities of a war between the sexes.

Pope also had enormous influence as a literary critic. His principles found eloquent expression in *An Essay on Criticism,* a long verse essay in heroic couplets. Many well-known aphorisms can be traced to that work, including the following couplet:

True wit is Nature to advantage dress'd;
What oft was thought, but ne'er so well express'd.

Pope, a Tory, was a special favorite of Queen Anne. When George I came to power in 1714, the Tories fell out of favor, and Pope retired to his country house. There he wrote *An Essay on Man,* a long poem that asserts the essential order and goodness of the universe and the rightness of humanity's place in it.

Another Tory writer of the time was Jonathan Swift (1667–1745). Swift, a close friend of Pope's, wrote mild satires while Queen Anne reigned. After her death and the fall of the Tories, Swift grew increasingly bitter. The behavior of the rising merchants, whom he viewed as shameless money grubbers, enraged Swift. *Gulliver's Travels* and *A Modest Proposal* date from this later period. Swift stood apart from many of his contemporaries by his antagonism to the idea that human nature is essentially good. In his great satires he presents the older view that human nature is deeply flawed, and that improvement must begin with a recognition of our intellectual and moral limitations.

One book that enjoyed a huge success at the time told about a shipwrecked British sailor struggling to survive on a deserted
14 island. The work, *Robinson Crusoe,* has been called the first novel in English. It was such a success that its author, Daniel Defoe, immediately set to work on other novels. Defoe's experiments with

the novel opened up a new form of fiction that, in the 1800's, would become the favorite reading matter of the middle classes.

England's first literary periodicals, *The Tatler* and *The Spectator,*
also appeared in the early 1700's. Written by Joseph Addison
(1672–1719) and Richard Steele (1672–1729), these one-page 15
papers included crisply written reflective essays and news. The
essays quickly became models for other prose writers.

The Age of Johnson

Alexander Pope died in 1744, and Jonathan Swift the following year. The dominant literary figure of the next generation was Samuel Johnson. Like many young writers after him, Johnson honed his writing style by working as a journalist. He later published his own magazine, *The Rambler.* Johnson also wrote poetry, literary criticism, and a novel. His most important work, however, was the
Dictionary of the English Language, published in 1755. It was the
first dictionary that could be considered a standard and authorita- 16
tive reference work on English.

Samuel Johnson dominated his age not only by his writings but also by his conversation and acquaintanceships. A brilliant and inexhaustible talker, he was friendly with most of the writers, painters, and actors of his time. His wise advice helped nurture the careers of many younger talents.

One reason we know so much about Samuel Johnson is that
one of those younger talents, James Boswell (1740–1795), wrote his
biography. Boswell followed his friend and mentor from club to
coffeehouse to dinner party, faithfully recording Johnson's com- 17
ments and witticisms. The result, Boswell's *Life of Samuel Johnson,*
was the first modern biography written in English. It gives a vivid
portrait not only of Johnson but of life in London in the 1700's.

The Age of Johnson saw other literary accomplishments. On the stage, the Restoration tradition of satire was carried on by Oliver Goldsmith and other comic playwrights. Among the many important works of prose, Edward Gibbon's history of Rome stands out. And novelists, working in the tradition begun by Defoe, produced a spate of popular books. Among the best were Samuel Richardson's *Pamela* and *Clarissa*, Fanny Burney's *Evelina,* Henry Fielding's *Tom Jones* and *Joseph Andrews*, and Lawrence Sterne's *Tristram Shandy*.

THE ECLIPSE OF THE ENLIGHTENMENT

By 1750 Britain was launched on a course of rapid industrialization. In the new industrial towns, mills and factories belched smoke into the country air. Inside the factories, men, women, and children toiled at machines for twelve and fourteen hours a day. Every year

15 Literary Movement See the examples of Addison and Steele's essays, pages 552 and 555; these famous literary partners are given credit for creating the familiar essay. Steele was considered the more original thinker, Addison the more polished writer.

16 Literary Movement See the excerpts from Johnson's Preface, page 580, and from his dictionary proper, page 583. His dictionary is extremely idiosyncratic and often strongly colored by the author's own biases.

17 Literary Movement See the excerpts from Boswell's *Life of Samuel Johnson,* page 588, a work to which he dedicated thirty years. It was Dryden who first defined the word *biography* as "the history of particular men's lives."

Humanities Note

Fine art, *Sir Isaac Newton,* c. 1726, by John Vanderbank. Vanderbank (c. 1694–1730) painted during the first part of the eighteenth century. This portrait of Sir Isaac Newton is considered one of his best works. Newton is shown in a studious pose with an open book in front of him, an appriately symbolic scene for the Age of Reason.

18 **Literary Movement** Although Gray's "Elegy Written in a Country Churchyard," page 598, exhibits some of the emotion and language of the revolt against neo-classicism, Gray is very much a transitional figure who retains formal and impersonal eighteenth-century diction and a modified heroic couplet. He is more revolutionary and "romantic" in his content: sympathy for the common person.

19 **Literary Movement** Blake's lyrics, on pages 620–626, taken from his *Songs of Innocence* and his *Songs of Experience,* reveal his preoccupation with "contraries": the contrasts between the innocence of childhood and the wisdom of experience as well as the necessity for both.

SIR ISAAC NEWTON, c. 1726
Attributed to John Vanderbank
The Granger Collection

more poor people crowded into the towns and cities, unable to find regular work and barely able to survive.

As a result of these changes, writers and intellectuals began to lose faith in the ability of human reason to solve every problem. The thinkers in the Age of Reason looked to science to make life better for humanity. Yet by the late 1700's, "progress" seemed to be bringing misery to millions.

As they began to doubt the basic assumptions of the Enlightenment, writers turned away from the standards of neoclassicism. Instead of using the impersonal, high-flown style of the early 1700's, some wrote in the common language of everyday life. Departing from the spirit of rationalism, they charged their poems with powerful emotions. Thomas Gray's *Elegy in a Country Churchyard,*
completed in 1750 exemplifies the transition from the formal,
classical poetic styles of the early eighteenth century to the more 18
emotional manner of the Romantic era.

William Blake broke even more sharply with the ideas and
attitudes of Pope and the neoclassicists. In simple language, he 19
conveyed mystical ideas and biting attacks on what England was
becoming. In one poem he derided those who held to a complacent faith in human rationality, while ignoring the spiritual side of human existence:

> You don't believe—I won't attempt to make ye;
> You are asleep—I won't attempt to wake ye.
> Sleep on! Sleep on! while in your pleasant dreams
> Of Reason you may drink of Life's clear streams.
> Reason and Newton, they are quite two things;
> For so the swallow and the sparrow sings.

The Age of Reason, with its unbounded faith in human intelligence, was coming to an end. New voices were being raised, and they no longer spoke in the clipped and polished language of rationalist neoclassicism. They would make the 1800's a new literary age.

ENGLISH VOICES

Quotations by Prominent Figures of the Period

Errors, like straws, upon the surface flow;
He who would search for pearls must dive below.

John Dryden, *All for Love*

Titles are shadow, crowns are empty things,
The good of subjects is the end of kings.

Daniel Defoe, "The True-Born Englishman"

Satire is a sort of glass, wherein beholders do generally discover everybody's face but their own.

Jonathan Swift, "The Battle of the Books"

Proper words in proper places, make the true definition of a style.

Jonathan Swift, "Letter to a Young Clergyman"

Sweet are the slumbers of the virtuous man.

Joseph Addison, "Cato"

Reading is to the mind what exercise is to the body.

Richard Steele, *The Tatler*

The noblest motive is the public good.

Richard Steele, *The Spectator*

To err is human, to forgive divine.

Alexander Pope, *An Essay on Criticism*

Fools rush in where angels fear to tread.

Alexander Pope, *An Essay on Criticism*

When a man is tired of London, he is tired of life.

Samuel Johnson, Quoted by James Boswell in *The Life of Samuel Johnson*

The paths of glory lead but to the grave.

Thomas Gray, "Elegy in a Country Churchyard"

The best laid plans o' mice and men
Gang aft a-gley.

Robert Burns, To a Mouse.

Reading Critically The purpose of this page is to guide students in the critical reading of literature written between 1660-1798. The information here will enable students to place a work of literature in its historical context, identify the literary movements of the time, and appreciate the techniques used by writers to convey the ideas of the period.

As you discuss this information with your class, explain that the poem "Holy Thursday" by William Blake beginning on the facing page is a model for reading critically. The side columns contain notes that draw students' attention to elements that reflect the historical context, the influence of the literary movements, and the writer's techniques.

To give students further practice with the process of reading critically, use the excerpt from Pepys's *Diary* (Coronation of Charles II) in the **Teaching Portfolio,** page 000, which students can annotate themselves. Encourage students to use these strategies as they read the literature in this unit.

Teaching to Ability Levels For **less advanced** students, you might discuss the meaning of the title before reading the poem. (See clarification note on page 507.) **More advanced** students might wish to interpret the title's significance before reading the poem.

READING ACTIVELY

The Literature of 1660–1798

When you read literature, it is important to place it in its historical context. Doing so will help you to see how it was shaped by the dominant attitudes of the period and to appreciate the techniques the writer used to convey these attitudes.

Historical Context

During the years from 1660 to 1798, English life was dominated by a desire for social and political stability. The nation had been severely shaken by the events of the civil war and the Puritan dictatorship and sought to reestablish a sense of order and security. Although the monarchy had been restored, the Parliament developed into the nation's supreme ruling force. Despite this shift in power, the English people generally remained complacent. The nation prospered financially and its citizens tended to be patriotic and optimistic. This sense of optimism resulted in part from scientific and philosophical advances that helped create a belief that everything in the universe could be explained.

Literary Movements

The literature written between 1660 and 1798 generally reflects the faith in reason and the desire for stability that characterized English life at the time. Strongly influenced by the works of classical Greek and Roman writers, writers generally displayed their intelligence, education, and sense of discipline in their works. Their works also conveyed their faith in English traditions and captured the elegance of English aristocratic life at the time. Toward the end of the eighteenth century, however, some writers, who are often referred to as Pre-romantics, began to react against the emphasis on reason and the intellect by writing emotional verse.

Writers' Techniques

During this period English prose flourished. Writers wrote formal essays on a variety of subjects, presenting logical, scientific arguments. The literary letter became a popular form; the first modern biography was written; and literary criticism and fiction flourished. In poetry, writers generally turned away from the lyric and wrote formally structured poems, often filled with classical allusions. Writers often displayed their wit by satirizing the society of their day in both poems and essays. The Preromantic poets, however, disregarded the tastes of the time and reestablished the lyric.

On the following page is a poem by William Blake, a Preromantic poet. The notes in the side column should help you to place the selection in its historical context.

Objectives

1. To analyze sound devices
2. To analyze the effect of sound devices
3. To respond to criticism

Teaching Portfolio: Support Materials

Teacher Backup, pp. 00-00

Reading Critically, p. 00

Usage and Mechanics Worksheet, p. 00

Analyzing Literature Worksheet, p. 00

Critical Thinking and Reading Worksheet, p. 00

Language Worksheet, p. 00

Selection Test, p. 00

MODEL

Holy Thursday

William Blake

Is this a holy thing to see,
In a rich and fruitful land,
Babes reduced to misery,
Fed with cold and usurious[1] hand?

Is that trembling cry a song?
Can it be a song of joy?
And so many children poor?
It is a land of poverty!

And their sun does never shine,
And their fields are bleak and bare,
And their ways are filled with thorns;
It is eternal winter there.

For where-e'er the sun does shine,
And where-e'er the rain does fall,
Babe can never hunger there,
Nor poverty the mind appall.

---

1. usurious (yo͞o zho͝or′ ē əs) *adj.*: Lending money at a high rate of interest.

Motivation for Reading Ask the students to discuss injustices that they see in today's society. Problems of homelessness, and poverty are examples. Explain that such problems are not unique to our society and era but were also common during the Pre-Romantic period during which William Blake wrote. A courageous man both physically and mentally, Blake wrote "Holy Thursday" attacking a serious social problem of his day, which is still a familiar one today.

Master Teacher Note An engraver by profession, Blake, with the help of his wife, published his poetry in a unique way. Instead of using a printing press, his poems were drawn on metal plates with varnish and designs sketched into the margins. The metal plates were plunged into acid baths, which ate away the unvarnished portions. The letters and illustrations stood out like engravings. Blake and his wife then painstakingly colored them, sometimes with gold leaf. The process is remarkable because, in order to appear correct to the reader, the letters had to be written backward. Most of Blake's books were prepared in this manner.

For examples of this work, see pages 621, 622 and 626.

Purpose-Setting Question Blake uses sound devices to reinforce his outrage about the inhumane conditions suffered by the children of the poor. How effective is his use of sound devices in emphasizing his theme?

Clarification The title refers to the Ascension, or visible departure of Jesus Christ from the earth, which occurred on Holy Thursday.

For Further Study Biographical information on Blake appears on page 618, and other poems by him are on pages 620-626.

Answers

ANSWERS TO THINKING ABOUT THE SELECTION

Recalling

1. Blake characterizes England as a rich and fruitful land in the first stanza. (b) In the second stanza he brands the country a land of poverty.
2. The poor never see the sun shine, they own bleak and bare fields, and have thorns filling their paths. They live in an eternal winter.
3. Where the sun shines and the rain falls, babies can never be hungry, and poverty will never horrify.

Interpreting

4. Suggested response: Because Holy Thursday is a happy day, the title is ironic. Blake uses the title to point out the contrast between the way things are and the way they should be.
5. (a) A suggested response: Lines 13 and 14 are parallel. (b) The parallel structure of these lines recalls the parallel structure of the lines 9, 10, and 11. This underscores the contrast between the poverty and the ideal.
6. (a) In "Holy Thursday" Blake is decrying miserable conditions forced upon the urban poor, especially the children, during the Industrial Revolution. (b) By writing the poem, he hoped to bring attention to the problem, thereby creating an impetus to rectify the miserable situation.

Applying

7. Answers will differ. Suggested response: Yes, this poem might be applied to the contemporary United States. There are many homeless people—many of them children. The poor are often malnourished and hungry, while many more affluent people live in comfort.

Challenge Write a protest poem about a problem you see in American society.

THINKING ABOUT THE SELECTION

Recalling

1. (a) How does Blake characterize England in the first stanza? (b) How does he characterize the country in the second stanza?
2. What observations about the poor does Blake make in the third stanza?
3. According to the final stanza, what can never happen "where-e'er the sun does shine" and "the rain does fall"?

Interpreting

4. Holy Thursday is another name for Ascension Day, the day on which Jesus' ascension into heaven is celebrated. Why do you think Blake used this name as the title of his poem?
5. (a) Find one example of Blake's use of parallelism—the repetition of phrases, clauses, or sentences that are similar in meaning or structure? (b) How does his use of parallelism reinforce the meaning of the poem?
6. (a) What is the theme, or main point, of the poem? (b) What was Blake's purpose in writing the poem?

Applying

7. Do you think this poem could be applied to contemporary American society? Why or why not?

ANALYZING LITERATURE

Using Sound Devices

Alliteration, consonance, and assonance are three sound devices used in poetry. Alliteration is the repetition of consonant sounds at the beginnings of words or accented syllables. For example, the *th* sound is repeated in line 1 of "Holy Thursday": "Is *th*is a holy *th*ing to see." Consonance is the repetition of consonant sounds at the ends of words or accented syllables. Notice the repetition of the *d* sound in line 4 of Blake's poem: "Fe*d* with col*d* an*d* usurious han*d*." Assonance is the repetition of vowel sounds. For example, the short *i* sound is repeated in "*i*s," "th*i*s," "*i*n," and "r*i*ch" in the first two lines of "Holy Thursday."

1. Find another example of alliteration in "Holy Thursday."
2. Find another example of consonance.
3. Find another example of assonance.

CRITICAL THINKING AND READING

Analyzing the Effect of Sound Devices

Sound devices cause poetry to have a musical quality. The repetition of sounds also adds emphasis to certain words and reinforces the meaning of a poem.

1. Find two cases in which Blake's use of a sound device adds emphasis to important words.
2. How does the emphasis of these words reinforce the meaning of the poem?

THINKING AND WRITING

Responding to Criticism

A critic has stated that Blake had "the ability to establish direct contact with readers, however remote in time or space." Write an essay in which you discuss this comment in relation to "Holy Thursday." Consider the meaning of the critic's comment. Reread the poem with the critic's statement in mind. Prepare a thesis statement. Then write your essay, using evidence from the poem to support your thesis. When you revise, make sure you have not included any unnecessary information.

ANSWERS TO ANALYZING LITERATURE

1. Another example of alliteration is "And their *s*un does never *sh*ine . . ."
2. Another example of consonance in "Babe can neve*r* hunge*r* the*r*e . . ."
3. Another example of assonance is "And their f*ie*lds are bl*ea*k & bare . . ."

ANSWERS TO CRITICAL THINKING AND READING

1. The "b" sounds in line 10 and the long "e" sounds in the same line add emphasis to the words.
2. These sounds are harsh sounds, sounds of crying and sadness. They reinforce the misery being presented in the poem.

THINKING AND WRITING

Publishing Student Writing

Using writing groups, have students choose one essay that their group likes the best from essays written by another group. Have a member of the group read the essay to the class. After all choices have been read, discuss the points made. Determine whether the class agrees with the critic's statement.

The Restoration

THE ELECTION—THE POLLING, 1697–1764
William Hogarth
Sir John Soane's Museum, London

Humanities Note

Fine art, *The Election—the Polling*. 1755, by William Hogarth. Hogarth (1697–1764) was first apprenticed to a silver plate engraver but later studied painting, learning the decorative style of James Thornhill. He emerged as a painter of portraits and conversation pieces but later turned to paintings of moral subjects. His most famous works were those in which he painted a dramatic series scenes with a moral point.

The Election—the Polling is one painting in the last series that Hogarth painted. It is possible that Hogarth was inspired by the lively scenes that marked the election of 1754.

More About the Author Looking back on the last half of the seventeenth century in England, which had seen political upheaval and civil strife, followed by the folly and indulgence of the Restoration, John Dryden wrote: "Thy wars brought nothing about/Thy lovers were all untrue./'Tis well an old age is out,/And time to begin a new." Dryden's answer to the excesses of the earlier seventeenth century was to praise the virtues of order, balance, and harmony, words which appear often in his writing. As the most influential poet of his time, he, more than any other single person, brought about a change in intellectual attitudes that led to a new age in literature. Do you think it is possible for a single individual today to have such a pronounced effect on the attitudes of this country? If so, support your answer with examples. If not, explain your answer.

JOHN DRYDEN

1631–1700

John Dryden dominated the literary scene in the last quarter of the seventeenth century. The most accomplished poet of the period, he also ranks high in English letters as a dramatist, essayist, satirist, and critic. His versatility and professionalism helped to establish writing as a legitimate career in England. The poet T. S. Eliot has maintained that Dryden "is the ancestor of nearly all that is best in the poetry of the eighteenth century," while the poet Matthew Arnold observed, "Here at last we have the true English prose, a prose such as we would all gladly use if only we knew how."

Born at the vicarage of Aldwinkle All Saints, Northamptonshire, where his father was a country gentleman, young Dryden studied at Westminster School. He graduated from Trinity College, Cambridge, in 1654, and five years later published his first important poem, *Heroic Stanzas*. The poem commemorates the death of Oliver Cromwell, under whose protectorate Dryden seems to have held a minor political post. A year later, in *Astraea Redux,* he did a political about-face and hailed the return to the throne of King Charles II. While in his fifties, Dryden, who had once been a Puritan and then an Anglican, became a convert to Roman Catholicism.

Dryden first came to prominence as a playwright, producing blank-verse tragedies and comedies. He was appointed poet laureate in 1668, a position that was supposed to pay an annual salary of two hundred pounds, but because of problems in the Royal Treasury, he received only half. His best play, *All for Love* (1677), is a rewriting of Shakespeare's *Antony and Cleopatra* in a clear, simple style. He displays his full power in *Absalom and Achitophel,* a political poem published in 1681. This poem was followed a year later by the equally impressive *The Medall,* also on politics.

After the Revolution of 1688 in England, which brought the Protestants William and Mary to the throne, Dryden lost his laureateship. He was replaced by Thomas Shadwell, whom Dryden had satirized a few years earlier in the poem *Mac Flecknoe.* To compensate for his lost income, Dryden increased his literary output, translating classical writers and writing prologues and miscellaneous pieces. The last of these efforts, his *Fables, Ancient and Modern*—translations from Chaucer, Boccaccio, and Ovid —appeared the year he died.

As a writer, Dryden was uniquely a man of his era. He expressed himself on virtually every important issue of the day. His friend William Congreve, a fellow playwright, pays tribute to Dryden's talents, saying that "no man hath written in our language so much . . . and in so various manners so well. . . ."

Objectives

1. To understand formal and informal essays
2. To chart an analysis of an essay
3. To write an evaluation of an analysis

Teaching Portfolio: Support Material

Teacher Backup, pp. 00-00

Vocabulary Check, p. 00

Usage and Mechanics Worksheet, p. 00

Analyzing Literature Worksheet, p. 00

Critical Thinking and Reading Worksheet, p. 00

Language Worksheet, p. 00

Selection Test, p. 000

GUIDE FOR READING

from An Essay of Dramatic Poesy

Literary Forms

Essay. An essay is a prose composition that expresses the writer's viewpoint on a limited topic. Essays vary in length from several paragraphs to the equivalent of an entire book. Modern essays are generally short, but in the eighteenth century, when the essay flourished as a popular literary form, essays were considerably longer. Dryden's complete essay on dramatic poesy—about thirty-five printed pages—is of average length for the time. Essays can be classified as formal or informal. A *formal essay* is one that deals with a serious subject in a carefully organized and often lofty way. An *informal essay,* or *personal essay,* is lighter and less structured than a formal essay. It may be humorous, and —even though classified as nonfiction—it may stretch the truth considerably or abandon it entirely. An informal essay is generally written in a conversational tone, reflecting the personality of the author and displaying distinctly personal touches.

Look For

As you read the excerpt from "An Essay of Dramatic Poesy," be alert to the language Dryden uses to express his views on the relative merits of Shakespeare and Ben Jonson.

Writing

When you read a work of fiction, what do you look for? An exciting plot? Well-developed, believable characters? Insights into human nature? List at least five characteristics that you think a work of fiction should have. Then make a second list in which you include the characteristics that detract from a work of fiction—for example, dull characters or an unbelievable plot.

Vocabulary

Knowing the following words will help you as you read the excerpt from "An Essay of Dramatic Poesy."

insipid (in sip′id) *adj.*: Not exciting or interesting; dull; lifeless (p. 512)

dotages (dōt′ ij əz) *n.*: Second childhoods; states of senility (p. 512)

judicious (jo͞o dish′əs) *adj.*: Having or showing good judgment (p. 512)

laboriously (lə bôr′ē əs lē) *adv.*: In a manner involving much hard work (p. 514)

Literary Focus Have students bring in examples of articles from newspapers and magazines that fit the definitions of formal and informal essays. Under each type, make a list of the essay subjects brought in. Discuss whether some subjects are better treated in a formal or informal manner.

Look For Suggest that students look for Dryden's overall opinion of each writer.

Writing Have students think of a work of fiction they read recently. Have **less advanced** students write a few sentences explaining whether or not the work exhibits one of the positive characteristics they listed. Challenge **more advanced** students to write a brief essay on two characteristics, using examples to support their points.

Vocabulary Write the vocabulary words on the chalkboard and have a different student pronounce each word and use it in a sentence that illustrates its meaning.

Motivation for Reading Point out that Dryden is not only one of the greatest English literary critics but also the first great master of prose in modern English. Ask your class if they think that a critical essay may be considered a work of art, as other kinds of essays often are.

Master Teacher Note As a writer deeply steeped in the classics, Dryden should perhaps have preferred Jonson to Shakespeare. The fairness of his judgments on both is a credit to his critical objectivity.

Thematic Idea This essay might be compared and contrasted with Hazlett's essay on *Macbeth,* page 756.

Purpose-Setting Question Which does Dryden think is the more admirable characteristic in a poet—natural genius or an ability to follow the rules?

1 **Enrichment** John Dryden wrote *An Essay on Dramatic Poesy* "without the help of books or the advice of friends," he said. This was due to the fact that he, along with hundreds of others, had fled to the country to escape the London plague of 1665.

2 **Clarification** *An Essay on Dramatic Poesy* was written as a discussion among four people in dialogue form about such subjects as the comparison of Elizabethan, French, and Restoration plays, the place of rhyme in drama, and the value of dramatic "rules." The last is discussed in this excerpt.

3 **Literary Focus** How does the opening statement reflect Dryden's informal style?

4 **Discussion** What do you think Dryden means by the word *soul?*

5 **Discussion** What are Shakespeare's faults?

1, 2

from An Essay on Dramatic Poesy

John Dryden

Shakespeare and Ben Jonson Compared

3 To begin, then, with Shakespeare. He was the man who of all modern, and perhaps ancient poets, had the largest and
4 most comprehensive soul. All the images of nature were still present to him, and he drew them, not laboriously, but luckily; when he describes anything, you more than see it, you feel it too. Those who accuse him to have wanted[1] learning, give him the greater commendation: he was naturally learned; he needed not the spectacles of books to read nature; he looked inwards, and found her there. I cannot say he is everywhere alike; were he so, I should do him injury to compare him with the greatest of mankind. He is many times flat, insipid; his comic wit
5 degenerating into clenches,[2] his serious swelling into bombast. But he is always great, when some great occasion is presented to him; no man can say he ever had a
6 fit subject for his wit, and did not then raise himself as high above the rest of poets,

7

> *Quantum lenta solent inter viburna cupressi*[3]

8

The consideration of this made Mr. Hales of Eton say that there was no subject of which any poet ever writ, but he would produce it much better done in Shakespeare; and however others are now generally preferred before him, yet the age wherein he lived, which had contemporaries with him Fletcher[4] and Jonson, never equaled them to him in their esteem: and in the last
king's court, when Ben's reputation was at 9
highest, Sir John Suckling, and with him the greater part of the courtiers, set our Shakespeare far above him. . . .

As for Jonson, to whose character I am now arrived, if we look upon him while he was himself (for his last plays were but his
dotages), I think him the most learned and 10
judicious writer which any theater ever had. He was a most severe judge of himself, as well as others. One cannot say he wanted
wit, but rather that he was frugal of it. In his 11
works you find little to retrench[5] or alter. Wit, and language, and humor also in some measure, we had before him; but something of art was wanting to the drama till he came.

1. **wanted:** Lacked.
2. **clenches:** Puns.
3. ***Quantum . . . cupressi:*** As do cypresses among the bending shrubs. From Virgil's *Eclogues* 1:25.
4. **Fletcher:** John Fletcher (1579–1625), an Elizabethan playwright.
5. **retrench:** Delete.

6 **Clarification** Dryden conceived of wit as a balancing of genius and art, of imagination and judgment.

7 **Discussion** Why do you think Dryden uses Latin here?

8 **Reading Strategy** Summarize Dryden's view of Shakespeare.

9 **Clarification** The last king's court refers to the court of Charles I, who was executed in 1649.

10 **Discussion** What was Dryden's opinion of Jonson's last plays?

11 **Discussion** Explain what Dryden meant by these lines.

SHAKESPEARE AND HIS CONTEMPORARIES
John Faed
From the Collection of Mr. and Mrs. Sandor Korein

Humanities Note

Fine art, *Shakespeare and His Contemporaries* by John Faed. John Faed (1820–1902) was a Scottish painter and miniaturist. Born into an artistically talented family, he is considered a self-taught artist. At the age of eleven, he was successfully painting miniature portraits. He continued doing so for forty years before switching to larger-format canvases. In these larger works, he preferred subjects from Shakespeare, the Bible, and Scottish history.

The painting *Shakespeare and his Contemporaries (at the Mermaid Tavern),* was painted after 1862. John Faed's detailed style of portraiture reflects his experience as a miniaturist. Although his paintings are carefully finished, they lack interesting color and atmosphere. Narrative, historic subjects like this were favored in Victorian England. This painting inspired an engraving by John Faed's brother, James, which was widely circulated as a popular print.

You may wish to discuss the following with your class:

1. What does this painting show about Shakespeare's character?
2. What does it reveal about Elizabethan life?
3. The painter Faed and the writer Dryden are artists from different eras. Despite this, what do you think their works have in common?

12 Discussion Restate this sentence in your own words.

13 Discussion Explain what Dryden means by idiom.

14 Clarification Homer was a Greek epic poet traditionally believed to have been the author of the *Iliad* and the *Odyssey*. Virgil was a Roman poet, author of the epic poem the *Aeneid*. To Dryden, both were to be admired for the order, balance, and harmony of their writings.

15 Discussion What value judgments are implied in the words *admire* and *love*?

12 He managed his strength to more advantage than any who preceded him. You seldom find him making love in any of his scenes or endeavoring to move the passions; his genius was too sullen and saturnine[6] to do it gracefully, especially when he knew he came after those who had performed both to such a height. Humor was his proper sphere: and in that he delighted most to represent mechanic people.[7] He was deeply conversant in the ancients, both Greek and Latin, and he borrowed boldly from them: there is scarce a poet or historian among the Roman authors of those times whom he has not translated in *Sejanus* and *Catiline*.[8] But he has done his robberies so openly, that one may see he fears not to be taxed by any law. He invades authors like a monarch; and what would be theft in other poets is only victory in him. With the spoils of these writers he so represents old Rome to us, in its rites, ceremonies, and customs, that if one of their poets had written either of his tragedies, we had seen less of it than in him. If there was any fault in his language, 'twas that he weaved it too closely and laboriously, in his serious plays; perhaps, too, he did a little too much Romanize our tongue, leaving the words which he translated almost as much Latin as he found them, wherein, though he learnedly followed the idiom of their language, he did not enough comply 13
with the idiom of ours. If I would compare him with Shakespeare, I must acknowledge him the more correct poet, but Shakespeare the greater wit. Shakespeare was the Homer, or father of our dramatic poets; Jon- 14
son was the Virgil, the pattern of elaborate writing; I admire him, but I love 15
Shakespeare. . . .

6. **saturnine:** Heavy.
7. **mechanic people:** Artisans.
8. ***Sejanus* and *Catiline*:** Two of Jonson's plays.

THINKING ABOUT THE SELECTION

Recalling

1. How does Dryden respond to the criticism that Shakespeare lacked learning?
2. What was the opinion of Shakespeare held by Mr. Hales of Eton?
3. According to Dryden, what was missing from English drama before Ben Jonson started writing?
4. Far from accusing Jonson of theft, what does Dryden say about his borrowing from classical writers?

Interpreting

5. In your own words, what does Dryden mean by saying that Shakespeare "had the largest and most comprehensive soul"?
6. Dryden uses a Latin quotation from Virgil to describe Shakespeare's achievement. How does this quotation relate to the comment that immediately precedes it?
7. In what sense does Dryden mean that Shakespeare was not a "correct poet"?

Applying

8. Assume that the virtues of Shakespeare and Jonson represent the qualities Dryden admired in all writers. (a) What qualities would Dryden's perfect writer have? (b) What writer, in your opinion, comes closest to having those qualities? Explain the reasons for your choice.

514

ANALYZING LITERATURE

Understanding an Essay

An **essay** is a prose composition, usually short, that deals with one topic. Typically, the writer of an essay states his or her personal views on the topic. A formal essay is serious and dignified. An informal essay is lighter and more conversational. Dryden's "Essay of Dramatic Poesy," written more than three hundred years ago, may not seem like an informal essay, but it is. It is written in the form of a conversation among four friends as they are boating on the Thames. One of them, named Neander, represents Dryden. He is the person speaking in the excerpt included in this book.

1. Two signs of informality in writing are (a) the occasional use of sentence fragments and (b) the occasional use of a conjunction to start a sentence. Find an example of each of these in the excerpt from Dryden's essay.
2. Compare Dryden's essay with Bacon's "Idols of the Cave" (pages 383–384). What are three noticeable differences in prose style between the two essays. (In examining prose style, look at sentence structure, sentence length, rhetorical devices, word choice, and so on.)

CRITICAL THINKING AND READING

Charting an Analysis

Dryden's "An Essay of Poesy" is an analysis of the literary merits of William Shakespeare and Ben Jonson. The essay contains a number of specific statements praising, criticizing, or comparing the two writers. On a sheet of paper, list as many properties of a writer as you can find in Dryden's essay. These properties can be good or bad. Beside each property on your list, state in a phrase or short sentence how Dryden rates each writer in regard to it. For example, you might list "Education" as a property. Your entry for Shakespeare might then read, "Lacked formal education but was thoroughly self-educated."

Property	Shakespeare	Jonson
1. Education	Lacked formal education but was thoroughly self-educated	

If nothing is said about one of the two writers in regard to a particular property, write, "No comment." Complete your chart with a statement summarizing Dryden's overall opinion of Shakespeare and Jonson as writers.

THINKING AND WRITING

Writing an Evaluation of an Analysis

Review the chart you prepared on Shakespeare and Jonson. Also review the lists you made before reading. Use these materials as the basis for an essay in which you evaluate Dryden's analysis of the literary merits of Shakespeare and Jonson. Take into account your own opinion of Shakespeare and Jonson as well. Is Dryden fair to Shakespeare? Does Dryden overrate Jonson? These and other questions should occur to you as you write the first draft. When you are ready to revise, reread the Dryden excerpt to be sure you are interpreting his opinions accurately. Be sure you have supported your own opinions well. Make any needed changes. Then write your final draft.

ANSWERS TO ANALYZING LITERATURE

1. Answers will differ. Suggested responses:
   (a) Dryden opens with a sentence fragment: "To begin, then, with Shakespeare." (b) The sentence that begins "But he is always great . . ." begins with a conjunction.
2. Dryden's sentences are shorter than Bacons's; they are simpler in grammatical structure; the vocabulary is less Latinate and formal.

ANSWERS TO CRITICAL THINKING AND READING

Answers will differ. Students should conclude by mentioning that Dryden admired Jonson, but loved Shakespeare.

THINKING AND WRITING

Publishing Student Writing Students could exchange essays and evaluate each other's.

Answers

ANSWERS TO THINKING ABOUT THE SELECTION

Recalling

1. He felt that Shakespeare's lack of learning was an advantage that enabled him to have better communion with nature.
2. Hales thought that Shakespeare was unequalled as a poet.
3. Before the arrival of Jonson, English drama lacked true artistry.
4. He borrowed openly, and what he borrowed he improved upon because he was so adept a writer.

Interpreting

5. Shakespeare's soul was in closer communication with nature, i.e. he showed more imagination than other poets.
6. Shakespeare's ability placed him higher than other poets, as the cypress rises above bending shrubs.
7. Shakespeare did not always follow the rules of correct drama; he was more interested in imaginative expression.

Applying

8. (a) Dryden's perfect writer would have the wit and imagination of Shakespeare and the discipline of Jonson. (b) Answers will differ.

Literary Focus Make sure that students grasp the essential idea of an ode: a poem on a dignified subject in a formal and elevated style. You might also mention that Dryden's ode was set to music by Handel.

Look For A brief reading aloud of two or three of the opening sections will help students to grasp the high tone of Dryden's verses.

Writing Lead the class in brainstorming for suitable subjects.

Vocabulary Have students think of a synonym and an antonym for the vocabulary word.

GUIDE FOR READING

A Song for St. Cecilia's Day

Literary Forms

Ode. An ode is a lyric poem, usually rhymed, that addresses and praises a person, an object, or a quality. Most odes are dignified or exalted in subject matter and style. The word *ode* comes from a Greek word meaning "song." The earliest odes, dating back to ancient Greece, were elaborate chants with themes and responses sung by a divided choir. Pindar, a Greek poet of the fifth century B.C., refined the form, becoming one of its great masters. The form he devised has been considerably changed over the centuries. Although Dryden patterned his odes loosely on classical models, later writers varied the form in many ways. Once recognizable by its shape, the ode today is more a matter of tone and intention than of structure.

Look For

As you read "A Song for St. Cecilia's Day," notice the poet's use of exalted language to pay homage to the memory of St. Cecilia, patron saint of music.

Writing

Jot down some thoughts on a person, thing, or event you think deserves to be honored. Then free-write a short tribute, either in a paragraph or in a few lines of poetry, in which you make clear the qualities of the person, thing, or event that you believe justify the tribute.

Vocabulary

Knowing the following word will help you as you read "A Song for St. Cecilia's Day."

sequacious (si kwā′shəs) *adj.*: *Archaic.* Tending to follow dutifully; in service of (p. 519, l. 50)

Objectives

1. To understand the ode as a literary form
2. To understand the effect of sound in poetry
3. To write an ode

Teaching Portfolio: Support Material

Teacher Backup, pp. 00-00

Vocabulary Check, p. 00

Usage and Mechanics Worksheet, p. 00

Analyzing Literature Worksheet, p. 00

Critical Thinking and Reading Worksheet, p. 00

Language Worksheet, p. 00

Selection Test, p. 000

A Song for St. Cecilia's Day[1]

John Dryden

1

From harmony, from heavenly harmony
This universal frame[2] began;
When Nature underneath a heap
Of jarring atoms[3] lay, 1
And could not heave her head,
The tuneful voice was heard from high,
"Arise, ye more than dead."

Then cold and hot and moist and dry[4]
In order to their stations leap,
And Music's power obey.
From harmony, from heavenly harmony
This universal frame began:
From harmony to harmony
Through all the compass of the notes it ran,
The diapason[5] closing full in Man. 2

2

What passion cannot Music raise and quell? 3
When Jubal[6] struck the chorded shell,
His listening brethren stood around,
And, wondering, on their faces fell
To worship that celestial sound.

---

1. "A Song for St. Cecilia's Day" was composed for the Festival of St. Cecilia on November 22, 1687. According to legend, St. Cecilia was an early Christian martyr, who became the patron saint of music.
2. universal frame: The structure of the universe.
3. jarring atoms: The chaos that preceded the creation of the universe.
4. cold . . . dry: Earth, fire, water, and air, the four elements out of which everything was composed, according to the ancient Greeks.
5. diapason (dī ′ ə pā′ zən): The entire range of tones on a musical scale. Dryden is also making reference to the Chain of Being, the ordered creation from inanimate nature up to man.
6. Jubal: In Genesis 4:21, Jubal is said to be the inventor of the lyre and the pipe.

Motivation for Reading Play for students some dramatically different types of music that evoke different moods. Then discuss how music can affect our emotions.

Master Teacher Note Dryden's ode dramatizes the ancient conception of the universe as a harmony created by God of the warring elements of chaos. The spheres that encased the planets and stars were believed to create a divine music inaudible to humans.

Purpose-Setting Question How does the poet use sound to enhance the poem's meaning?

1 **Discussion** What figure of speech is used in these lines?

2 **Discussion** What does man represent?

3 **Clarification** Dryden centers his poem on this line.

Humanities Note

Fine art, *The Music of a Bygone Age,* by John Melhuish Strudwick. Strudwick (1849–1937) was a British painter of the Pre-Raphaelite school (painters who emulated the works of primitive Christian painters before Raphael, the Italian Renaissance master). He left the Schools of the Royal Academy to assist at the studios of eminent Pre-Raphaelite artists, Spencer-Stanhope and Burne-Jones. The works of these men and Strudwick's admiration for Italian art greatly influenced his style.

The Music of a Bygone Age was painted in 1890. The influence of his teachers is apparent in the poetic subject matter, the classically draped clothing, and the resemblance of the figures to angels from Italian religious paintings. The almost startling detail and the clear glowing colors of this painting are trademarks of the Pre-Raphaelite style.

You might use the following questions for discussion:

1. Which instruments appear in both the painting and the poem?
2. Is the angelic appearance of the figures in this painting appropriate to this poem? Explain.
3. What sort of music would you expect to hear from the musicians in this painting?

THE MUSIC OF A BYGONE AGE
John Melhuish Strudwick
Art Resource

Less than a god they thought there could not dwell
Within the hollow of that shell
That spoke so sweetly, and so well.
What passion cannot Music raise and quell?

3

The trumpet's loud clangor
Excites us to arms
With shrill notes of anger
And mortal alarms. 4
The double double double beat
Of the thundering drum
Cries, "Hark! the foes come:
Charge, charge, 'tis too late to retreat."

4

The soft complaining flute
In dying notes discovers[7] 5
The woes of hopeless lovers,
Whose dirge is whispered by the warbling lute.

5

Sharp violins proclaim
Their jealous pangs and desperation.
Fury, frantic indignation, 6
Depth of pains and height of passion,
For the fair, disdainful dame.

6

But Oh! What art can teach,
What human voice can reach
The sacred organ's praise? 7
Notes inspiring holy love,
Notes that wing their heavenly ways
To mend the choirs above.

8

7

Orpheus[8] could lead the savage race,
And trees unrooted left their place,
Sequacious of the lyre:
But bright Cecilia raised the wonder higher:

---

7. discovers: Reveals.
8. Orpheus (ôr′ fē əs): In Greek mythology, a poet and musician whose magic musical powers enabled him to charm rocks, trees, and wild beasts by playing his lyre.

4 **Discussion** What passion is referred to in this stanza? Are the instruments referred to appropriate symbols for this passion?

5 **Discussion** How does this stanza contrast in mood with the previous stanza?

6 **Discussion** Is the violin an appropriate instrument to represent the "Depth of pains and height of passion"? Why or why not?

7 **Discussion** With what passion does Dryden associate the organ?

8 **Reading Strategy** Stanzas three through six describe the four passions that music can "raise and quell." What are they?

9 Discussion Explain the paradox in this line?

When to her organ vocal breath was given,
An angel heard, and straight appeared
   Mistaking earth for heaven.

GRAND CHORUS

As from the power of sacred lays[9]
   The spheres began to move.[10]
And sung the great Creator's praise
   To all the blessed above;
   So when the last and dreadful hour
This crumbling pageant[11] *shall devour,*
The trumpet shall be heard on high,[12]
9 *The dead shall live, the living die,*
And Music shall untune the sky.

---

9. lays: Songs.
10. *spheres . . . move:* According to legend, the celestial bodies (spheres) were put into motion by angelic song. The motion of the spheres was believed to produce harmonious music, a hymn of "praise" for the "Creator," sung by the created.
11. *pageant:* The universe.
12. *trumpet . . . high:* From I Corinthians 15:52, the last trumpet that will announce the Last Judgment, or the end of the universe.

THINKING ABOUT THE SELECTION

Recalling

1. According to the first stanza, what was the condition of Nature when the universe took shape?
2. In addition to the corded shell, what musical instruments are mentioned in the poem?
3. What does Dryden claim an angel did upon hearing Cecilia play the organ?
4. What instrument will announce Judgment Day?

Interpreting

5. The word *harmony* dominates the first stanza. What meaning, or meanings, does it have as Dryden uses it?
6. (a) What musical instrument does Dryden suggest is the most heavenly? (b) In view of the day the poem celebrates, why is this praise especially appropriate?
7. Why will music "untune the sky" in "the last and dreadful hour"?

Applying

8. Dryden is often called an "occasional" poet, because he wrote in response to major news events, literary developments, and, as in this poem, to celebrate special days. Occasional poetry is no longer popular. What do people do today to commemorate special events and heroes?

ANALYZING LITERATURE

Recognizing an Ode

An **ode** is a lyrical poem that pays homage to a person, thing, or quality. The earliest odes are from classical times, such as those of the Greek poet Pindar (522?–443 B.C.) and the Latin poet Horace (65–8 B.C.). The Greek ode, which is the ancestor of the odes written by Dryden, is composed of three-part stanzas called *triads*. Each triad is made up of a *strophe* (sung by one half the singers in a choir), an *antistrophe* (sung by the other half), and an *epode* (sung by the entire choir). Dryden and other poets of the seventeenth century use a much looser prosodic system than Pindar's, as do later writers.

1. In "A Song for St. Cecilia's Day," how many lines are (a) in each numbered stanza? (b) in the Grand Chorus?
2. (a) Which stanzas have regular patterns of rhyme? (b) What are these patterns? (Use a, b, c, and so on, to show patterns.)
3. Why do you think Dryden uses such an irregular stanza and rhyme scheme for his poem?

CRITICAL THINKING AND READING

Understanding the Effect of Sound

Dryden's words carry meaning not only in a lexical, or dictionary, sense but also through their sound. For example, in the third stanza, the word *shrill* echoes—that is, imitates the sound of—the insistent cry of the trumpet. The word *double*, while not in itself echoic of a drum, becomes so when repeated like a drumbeat—"double, double, double."

1. What word in the third stanza besides *double* has a sound that echoes the pounding of the drum?
2. What words in the fourth stanza have sounds that echo the melodic flute and lute?
3. What sounds in the fifth stanza echo the piercing tone of the violin?

THINKING AND WRITING

Writing an Ode

Choose one of the following topics and write an ode concerning it. You may decide on the number of stanzas and the length of lines, but try to follow at least two of the rhyme patterns used by Dryden in "A Song for St. Cecilia's Day." Also, use as many echoic, or sound-imitative, devices as you can. Read your ode aloud to judge its effect. After revising, proofread it and prepare a final draft.

1. The United States
2. A season of the year
3. A brother or sister
4. Honesty

Answers

ANSWERS TO THINKING ABOUT THE SELECTION

Recalling

1. Nature was buried under a heap of jarring atoms.
2. The musical instruments mentioned are the trumpet, drum, flute, lute, violin, organ, and lyre.
3. Hearing the sound an angel appeared, thinking earth was heaven.
4. The trumpet will announce it.

Interpreting

5. The word *harmony* refers to musical sweetness and also to order and symmetry.
6. (a) Dryden thinks the organ is the most heavenly instrument. (b) Since St. Cecilia is regarded as the inventor of the organ, his praise is especially appropriate.
7. When the universe ends, on the biblical Judgment Day, there will no longer be harmony.

Applying

8. To commemorate events and heroes people stay home from work and enjoy themselves. A feast or parade is often involved.

ANSWERS TO ANALYZING LITERATURE

1. (a) There are, respectively, fifteen, nine, eight, four, five, six, and seven lines in each numbered stanza. (b) There are nine lines in the Grand Chorus.
2. (a) There are no regular patterns of rhyme; each stanza has a different pattern. (b) 1a, b, c, d, e, f, e, f, c, d, a, b, a, b, b; 2a, a, b, a, b, a, a, a, a; 3a, b, a, c, d, e, e, d; 4a, b, b, a; 5a, b, b, b, a; 6a, a, b, c, b, c; 7a, a, b, b, c, d, c; chorus a, b, a, c, d, d, e, e, e
3. Answers will differ. A possible answer is: The first stanza is highly irregular to show the emergence of harmony out of chaos. The second stanza consists mostly of couplets to suggest the sweet harmony described. The other stanzas are irregular to suggest the different instruments being described. In the Grand Chorus, a highly irregular pattern is again used as chaos returns.

ANSWERS TO CRITICAL THINKING AND READING

1. The word *thundering* echoes the drum's pounding.
2. The words *soft, woes, whispered,* and *warbling* have sounds that echo the flute and lute.
3. The words *proclaim, pangs, desperation, indignation, pains,* and *passion* echo the tone of the violin.

Challenge What figure of speech uses words with sounds that imitate or suggest their meanings?

ANSWERS TO THINKING AND WRITING

For help with this assignment, students can refer to Lesson 18, "Writing a Poem," in the Handbook of Writing About Literature.

Publishing Student Writing Suggest that students submit their odes to the school literary magazine for publication. Alternatively, you might prepare a class magazine with students' odes.

More About the Author In addition to being a man of action, Samuel Pepys was quite a scholar. He had a good working knowledge of several languages—Latin, Greek, French, Spanish, and some Italian—and he sometimes put these languages to use in his diary. He and Mrs. Pepys frequently spoke French, and Pepys liked to read books in Latin, especially the scientific and philosophical works of his favorite writer, Sir Francis Bacon. What does Pepys's classical education and proficiency in languages tell you about the education of the day? Do you think he was atypical of other men of his station in life?

SAMUEL PEPYS

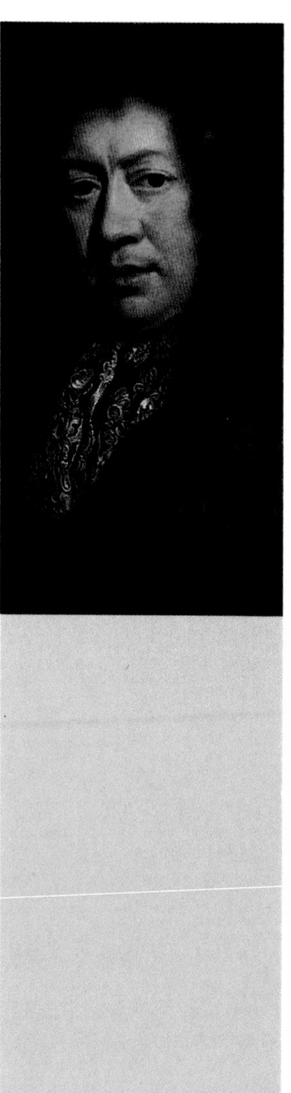

1633–1703

Samuel Pepys (pēpz) is an unusual figure in English literature, not so much because his fame rests on a single work but rather the one work, his *Diary,* was never intended for publication. This *Diary,* which Pepys kept in shorthand and in his own private code, was not deciphered until the nineteenth century.

The man who painted this vivid portrait of his times was a "very worthy, industrious, and curious person," according to his friend John Evelyn. Born in London, the son of a tailor, Pepys studied at St. Paul's School and Magdalene College, Cambridge. Upon graduation in 1653, he became secretary to his influential cousin Sir Edward Montagu, later the Earl of Sandwich. Two years later he married Elizabeth St. Michel, a girl of fifteen. The *Diary* contains many details of their strife-ridden union, which survived Pepys' countless infidelities and lasted until her early death in 1669.

Pepys began his career as a naval man—as well as his famous *Diary*—in 1660, when he was appointed clerk of the King's ships and clerk of the privy seal. His advancement, as the *Diary* notes, was rapid, and with each new position, Pepys grew richer. Yet his life was not without its tragedies. In the same year his wife died, Pepys's failing eyesight caused him to stop keeping the *Diary.* In 1679 he was imprisoned briefly in the Tower of London, accused of popery and treason, and in 1690 he once again spent some time in prison on charges of intrigue.

The *Diary,* originally in six manuscript volumes, remained in cipher until 1819 when a student at Magdalene College, Cambridge, began transcribing it. Published in 1825, the *Diary* proved a fascinating mix of candid private revelations and keenly observed public scenes. The 1660's, during which the diary was kept, saw Pepys' personal rise in the world from obscure clerk to highly regarded public servant. It also saw—and through Pepys's eyes modern readers can see—the coronation of King Charles II, the devastating London plague of 1665, and the Great Fire of 1666.

In the centuries since his death, some readers have dismissed Pepys as a shallow figure and his observations as mere gossip. But the Samuel Pepys who emerges from between the lines of the *Diary* is more than just a government careerist with a roving eye. He is a man of intelligence and great diplomacy, much admired by the people of his time, and evidently deserving of that admiration. He is also a diarist of exceptional honesty and perception. Readers of today who wish to know about life in seventeenth-century London are greatly in his debt.

Objective

1 To understand the diary as a literary form

Teaching Portfolio: Support Material

Teacher Backup, pp. 00-00

Vocabulary Check, p. 00

Usage and Mechanics Worksheet, p. 00

Analyzing Literature Worksheet, p. 00

Critical Thinking and Reading Worksheet, p. 00

Language Worksheet, p. 00

Selection Test, p. 000

GUIDE FOR READING

from The Diary

Literary Forms

Diary. A diary is a personal day-by-day record of events, experiences, and observations. Perhaps you think of a diary as simply a collection of notes about the small details in one's life, such as what the diarist had for breakfast. Many diaries fit that definition but not all. The diaries that become literature are usually those that provide insights into important historical events or periods. *The Diary of Anne Frank,* for instance, gives readers a poignant glimpse of a young Jewish girl's ultimately futile attempt to escape Nazi persecution by hiding with her family in Nazi-occupied Netherlands in World War II. The events have an importance beyond Anne Frank's individual fate. Moreover, as with most diaries that are regarded as literature, it is exceptionally well written.

Look For

As you read the excerpts from *The Diary* of Samuel Pepys, look for examples of the writer's insights into the events he is describing. How does he make seventeenth-century London come alive for you?

Writing

Make some notes about an especially memorable event you have experienced. These notes can be in the form of a diary entry; that is, they do not have to be written in grammatically complete sentences or arranged in an orderly sequence.

Vocabulary

Knowing the following words will help you as you read the excerpts from Samuel Pepys's *Diary.*

apprehensions (ap rə hen′ shənz) *n.*: Fears, concerns (p. 524)

abated (ə bāt′id) *v.*: Lessened (p. 524)

lamentable (lam′ən tə b′l) *adj.*: Distressing (p. 525)

discoursing (dis kôrs′iŋ) *v.*: Talking about; discussing (p. 528)

Literary Focus Ask students how many of them keep or have kept a diary. Discuss whether they would like others to read their diaries.

Look For Why are the events as told through Pepys's eyes more interesting than if they were presented strictly factually?

Writing Suggest that **more advanced** students write a poem about the event and compare the effect of the two literary forms.

Vocabulary After reviewing the vocabulary words, ask students to consider whether they would be likely to use any of the words in a diary of their own. Why or why not? What do the words tell about Pepys and the time in which he was writing?

Motivation for Reading Ask students to imagine what it would be like to be involved in a huge disaster, such as a fire or an epidemic. Assuming they were not yet personally involved, what would their first reaction be: to try to get away or to help those in need?

Master Teacher Note Pepys's travel experiences, intellectual interests, and governmental activities make his diary an important historical document. His candid revelations of private personal experience make the diary a fascinating human document of great psychological interest.

Purpose-Setting Question As you read, decide whether Pepys wrote his diary for personal information or if he had in mind a larger audience at some time.

Thematic Idea Read and discuss Thomas Nashe's "A Litany in Time of Plague," on page 202, in conjunction with the excerpts from Pepys' work.

1 **Discussion** What can you infer about Pepys's position in the community?

2 **Discussion** Why were public funerals not allowed during the plague?

3 **Discussion** What does this tell you about Pepys's personality?

4 **Discussion** What was Pepys's job at this time?

5 **Discussion** Why is Pepys both elated and disturbed by news about the plague?

6 **Critical Thinking and Reading** List five specific examples that Pepys uses to back up his growing fear of the plague.

from **The Diary**

Samuel Pepys

The Plague

Sept. 3, 1665. (Lord's Day.) Church
being done, my Lord Bruncker, Sir J. Min-
nes, and I up to the vestry[1] at the desire of
1 the Justices of the Peace, Sir Theo. Biddulph
and Sir W. Boreman and Alderman Hooker,
in order to the doing something for the keeping of the plague from growing; but Lord! to
consider the madness of the people of the
town, who will (because they are forbid)
2 come in crowds along with the dead corps[2]
to see them buried; but we agreed on some
orders for the prevention thereof.[3] Among
other stories, one was very passionate, methought, of a complaint brought against a man in the town for taking a child from London from an infected house. Alderman Hooker told us it was the child of a very able citizen in Gracious Street, a saddler,[4] who had buried all the rest of his children of the plague, and himself and wife now being shut up and in despair of escaping, did desire only to save the life of this little child; and so prevailed to have it received stark-naked into the arms of a friend, who brought it (having put it into new fresh clothes) to Greenwich; where upon hearing the story, we did agree it should be permitted to be
received and kept in the town. Thence with
my Lord Bruncker to Captain Cocke's,
where we mighty merry and supped, and 3
very late I by water to Woolwich, in great
apprehensions of an ague. . . .

Sept. 14, 1665. When I come home I spent some thoughts upon the occurrences of this day, giving matter for as much content on one hand and melancholy on another, as any day in all my life. For the first; the
finding of my money and plate,[5] and all safe
at London, and speeding in my business of 4
money this day. The hearing of this good
news to such excess, after so great a despair
of my Lord's doing anything this year; adding to that, the decrease of 500 and more,
which is the first decrease we have yet had
in the sickness since it begun: and great
hopes that the next week it will be greater. 5
Then, on the other side, my finding that
though the bill[6] in general is abated, yet the
city within the walls is increased, and likely
to continue so, and is close to our house
there. My meeting dead corpses of the
plague, carried to be buried close to me at
noonday through the city in Fanchurch 6
Street. To see a person sick of the sores,
carried close by me by Grace church in a

1. **vestry** (ves' trē) *n.*: A church meeting room.
2. **corps:** corpses.
3. **but we . . . thereof:** Funeral processions were forbidden in London during the plague. However, the law was often ignored.
4. **saddler** *n.*: A person who makes, sells, and repairs saddles.
5. **plate:** Valuable serving dishes and flatware.
6. **bill:** Weekly list of burials.

hackney coach.[7] My finding the Angell Tavern at the lower end of Tower Hill, shut up, and more than that, the alehouse at the Tower Stairs, and more than that, the person was then dying of the plague when I was last there, a little while ago, at night, to write a short letter there, and I overheard the mistress of the house sadly saying to her husband somebody was very ill, but did not think it was of the plague. To hear that poor Payne, my waiter, hath buried a child, and is dying himself. To hear that a laborer I sent but the other day to Dagenhams, to know how they did there, is dead of the plague; and that one of my own watermen, that carried me daily, fell sick as soon as he had landed me on Friday morning last, when I had been all night upon the water (and I believe he did get his infection that day at Brainford), and is now dead of the plague. To hear that Captain Lambert and Cuttle are killed in the taking these ships; and that Mr. Sidney Montague is sick of a desperate fever at my Lady Carteret's, at Scott's Hall. To
7 hear that Mr. Lewes hath another daughter sick. And, lastly, that both my servants, W. Hewer and Tom Edwards, have lost their fathers, both in St. Sepulcher's parish, of the plague this week, do put me into great apprehensions of melancholy, and with good reason. But I put off the thoughts of sadness as much as I can, and the rather to keep my wife in good heart and family also. After supper (having eat nothing all this day) upon a fine tench[8] of Mr. Shelden's taking, we to bed.

The Fire of London

Sept. 2, 1666. (Lord's day.) Some of our maids sitting up late last night to get things ready against our feast today, Jane called us up about three in the morning, to tell us of a great fire they saw in the city. So I rose and slipped on my night-gown, and went to her window, and thought it to be on the back side of Mark Lane at the farthest; but, being unused to such fires as followed, I thought it far enough off; and so went to bed again and to sleep. About seven rose again to dress myself, and there looked out at the window, and saw the fire not so much as it was and farther off. So to my closet to set things to rights after yesterday's cleaning. By and by Jane comes and tells me that she hears that above 300 houses have been burned down tonight by the fire we saw, and that it is now burning down all Fish Street, by London Bridge. So I made myself ready presently, and walked to the Tower,[9] and there got up upon one of the high places, Sir J. Robinson's little son going up with me; and there I did see the houses at that end of the bridge all on fire, and an infinite great fire on this and the other side the end of the bridge; which, among other people, did trouble me 8
for poor little Michell and our Sarah on the bridge. So down, with my heart full of trouble, to the Lieutenant of the Tower, who tells me that it begun this morning in the King's baker's house in Pudding Lane, and that it hath burned St. Magnus's Church and most part of Fish Street already. So I down to the waterside, and there got a boat and through bridge, and there saw a lamentable fire. Poor Michell's house, as far as the Old Swan, already burned that way, and the fire running farther, that in a very little time it got as far as the steel yard, while I was there. Everybody endeavoring to remove their goods, and flinging into the river or bringing them into lighters that lay off; poor people staying in their houses as long as till the very fire touched them, and then running into boats, or clambering from one pair of stairs by the waterside to another. And
among other things, the poor pigeons, I perceive, were loth to leave their houses, but 9
hovered about the windows and balconies

7. hackney coach: A carriage for hire.
8. tench *n.*: A type of fish.

9. Tower: The Tower of London.

7 Discussion What does Pepys achieve by briefly listing those who have died rather than developing a single story?

8 Discussion Give examples that illustrate that Pepys is a man of action.

9 Discussion What does the fact that Pepys noticed the plight of the pigeons tell you about the man?

525

Humanities Note

Fine art, *The Great Fire of London, 1666.* This painting of *The Great Fire of London,* by an unknown artist hangs in the Museum of London, England. Even today this spectacle of an uncontrolled inferno is terrifying to behold. Paintings such as this and accounts such as the diary of Samuel Pepys give an idea of the effect of this disaster upon the inhabitants of the seventeenth-century city.

You may wish to ask the following questions:

1. What line from Pepys's account of the fire would be an appropriate caption for this painting?
2. Do you think the artist of this painting was an eyewitness to this fire? Explain.

THE GREAT FIRE OF LONDON, 1666
The Museum of London

till they were, some of them burned, their wings, and fell down. Having stayed, and in an hour's time seen the fire rage every way, and nobody, to my sight, endeavoring to quench it, but to remove their goods, and leave all to the fire, and having seen it get as far as the steel yard, and the wind mighty high and driving it into the city; and everything, after so long a drought, proving combustible, even the very stones of churches, and among other things the poor steeple by which pretty Mrs.— lives, and whereof my old schoolfellow Elborough is parson, taken fire in the very top, and there burned till it fell down. I to Whitehall (with a gentleman with me who desired to go off from the Tower, to see the fire, in my boat), and there up to the King's closet in the chapel, where people come about me, and I did give them an account dismayed them all, and word was carried in to the King. So I was called for, and did tell the King and Duke of York what I saw, and that unless his Majesty did command houses to be pulled down nothing could stop the fire. They seemed much troubled, and the King commanded me to go to my Lord Mayor from him, and command him to spare no houses, but to pull down before the fire every way. The Duke of York bid me tell him that if he would have any more soldiers he shall; and so did my Lord Arlington afterwards, as a great secret. Here meeting with Captain Cocke, I in his coach, which he lent me, and Creed with me to Paul's,[10] and there walked along Watling Street, as well as I could, every creature coming away loaden with goods to save, and here and there sick people carried away in beds. Extraordinary good goods carried in carts and on backs. At last met my Lord Mayor in Canning Street, like a man spent,

10. Paul's: St. Paul's Cathedral.

with a handkerchief about his neck. To the King's message he cried, like a fainting woman, "Lord! what can I do? I am spent: people will not obey me. I have been pulling
10 down houses; but the fire overtakes us faster than we can do it." That he needed no more soldiers; and that, for himself, he must go and refresh himself, having been up all night. So he left me, and I him, and walked home, seeing people all almost distracted, and no manner of means used to quench the fire. The houses, too, so very thick thereabouts, and full of matter for burning, as pitch and tar, in Thames Street; and warehouses of oil, and wines, and brandy, and other things. Here I saw Mr. Isaake Houblon, the handsome man, prettily dressed and dirty, at his door at Dowgate, receiving some of his brothers' things, whose houses were on fire; and, as he says, have been removed twice already; and he doubts (as it soon proved) that they must be in a little time removed from his house also, which was a sad consideration. And to see the churches all filling with goods by people who them-
11 selves should have been quietly there at this time. By this time it was about twelve o'clock; and so home. Soon as dined, and walked through the city, the streets full of nothing but people and horses and carts loaden with goods, ready to run over one another, and removing goods from one burned house to another. They now removing out of Canning Street (which received goods in the morning) into Lumbard Street, and farther; and among others I now saw my little goldsmith, Stokes, receiving some friend's goods, whose house itself was burned the day after. I to Paul's Wharf, where I had appointed a boat to attend me, and took in Mr. Carcasse and his brother, whom I met in the street, and carried them below and above bridge to and again to see the fire, which was now got farther, both below and above, and no likelihood of stopping it. Met with the King and Duke of York in their barge, and with them to Queenhithe, and there called Sir Richard Browne to them. Their order was only to pull down houses apace, and so below bridge at the waterside; but little was or could be done, the fire coming upon them so fast. Good hopes there was of stopping it at the Three Cranes above, and at Buttolph's Wharf below bridge, if care be used; but the wind carries it into the city, so as we know not by the waterside what it do there. River full of lighters and boats taking in goods, and good goods swimming in the water, and only I observed that hardly one lighter or boat in three that had the goods of a house in, but there was a pair of virginals[11] in it. Having seen as much as I could now, I away to Whitehall by appointment, and there walked to St. James's Park, and there met my wife and Creed and Wood and his wife, and walked to my boat; and there upon the water again, and to the fire up and down, it still increasing, and the wind great. So near the fire as we could for smoke; and all over
the Thames, with one's face in the wind, 12
you were almost burned with a shower of firedrops. This is very true; so as houses were burned by these drops and flakes of fire, three or four, nay, five or six houses, one from another. When we could endure no more upon the water, we to a little alehouse on the Bankside, over against the Three Cranes, and there stayed till it was dark almost, and saw the fire grow; and, as it grew darker, appeared more and more, and in corners and upon steeples, and between churches and houses, as far as we could see up the hill of the city, in a most horrid
malicious bloody flame, not like the fine 13
flame of an ordinary fire. Barbary and her husband away before us. We stayed till, it being darkish, we saw the fire as only one entire arch of fire from this to the other side the bridge, and in a bow up the hill for an arch of above a mile long: it made me weep to see it. The churches, houses, and all on fire and flaming at once; and a horrid noise the flames made, and the cracking of houses

11. virginals *n.*: Small, legless harpsichords.

10 **Enrichment** Look at pictures of London in 1666. Notice the closeness of the buildings and the wooden structures.

11 **Discussion** What seems to be the primary activity during the fire?

12 **Discussion** Why do they find it difficult to remain on the river?

13 **Literary Focus** How does Pepys's description differ from, say, a newspaper account of the fire?

14 Discussion Why would Pepys's iron chests be safe in his cellar?

at their ruin. So home with a sad heart, and there find everybody discoursing and lamenting the fire; and poor Tom Hater come with some of his few goods saved out of his house, which is burned upon Fish Street Hill. I invited him to lie at my house, and did receive his goods, but was deceived in his lying there, the news coming every moment of the growth of the fire; so as we were forced to begin to pack up our own goods, and prepare for their removal; and did by moonshine (it being brave dry, and moonshine, and warm weather) carry much of my goods into the garden, and Mr. Hater and I did
14 remove my money and iron chests into my cellar, as thinking that the safest place. And got my bags of gold into my office, ready to carry away, and my chief papers of accounts also there, and my tallies into a box by themselves. So great was our fear, as Sir W. Batten hath carts come out of the country to fetch away his goods this night. We did put Mr. Hater, poor man, to bed a little; but he got but very little rest, so much noise being in my house, taking down of goods.

3rd. About four o'clock in the morning, my Lady Batten sent me a cart to carry away all my money, and plate, and best things, to Sir W. Rider's at Bednall Green. Which I did, riding myself in my nightgown in the cart; and, Lord! to see how the streets and the highways are crowded with people running and riding, and getting of carts at any rate to fetch away things. I find Sir W. Rider tired with being called up all night, and receiving things from several friends. His house full of goods, and much of Sir W. Batten's and Sir W. Pen's. I am eased at my heart to have my treasure so well secured. Then home, with much ado to find a way, nor any sleep all this night to me nor my poor wife.

THINKING ABOUT THE SELECTION

Recalling

1. In his entry for September 3, 1665, Pepys tells a story of a saddler's family. What is the story of the last living child?
2. In his entry for September 14, 1665, Pepys gives two reasons for feeling content. One is that his valuables are safe. What is the other?
3. (a) When does Pepys first learn of the great fire? (b) When Pepys looks out his window at seven in the morning on September 2, 1666, what does he observe about the fire?
4. (a) What does Pepys recommend to the King and the Duke of York? (b) What is the reply?
5. Summarize Pepys's actions on September 3, 1666.

Interpreting

6. In the entry for September 14, 1665, Pepys states that he has despaired "of my Lord's doing anything this year." (a) What does he mean by the statement? (b) What does it show about Pepys's beliefs?
7. On September 2, 1666, Pepys sees "the churches all filling with goods by people who themselves should have been quietly there at this time." (a) Why do you think people are storing goods in churches? (b) Why do you think they themselves should have been there at the time?
8. From the evidence of these diary entries, how would you describe Pepys's character and personality?

Applying

9. (a) In Pepys's London, which do you think was the greater disaster—the plague or the great fire? Explain. (b) What disasters in modern times, if any, compare with the London plague of 1665 and the great fire of 1666?

Answers

ANSWERS TO THINKING ABOUT THE SELECTION

Recalling

1. A saddler and his wife, who had lost all but one of their children to the plague and feared for their own lives, asked a friend to take the child to safety. It was agreed by Pepys and his friends that the child should be allowed to stay in the town.
2. The number of plague victims had decreased by more than 500.
3. (a) Pepys first learns of the fire at three in the morning of Sept. 2, 1666. (b) He observes that the fire had diminished and was farther away.
4. (a) Pepys recommended that houses be torn down to stop the advance of the fire. (b) The King asked Pepys to command the Mayor to tear down houses in the fire's path.
5. At four A.M. Pepys used a borrowed cart to take his valuables to a friend's house which was safe from the fire. Then he found his way home, but got no sleep.

Interpreting

6. (a) Pepys had given up hope of the King allocating more money for the navy that year. (b) This shows that Pepys was concerned about doing a good job in his business.
7. (a) People were storing goods in churches because they were usually made of stone, which is not inflammable. (b) The people should have been in church praying to God for safety from the fire.
8. Pepys was a vigorous, friendly, curious, religious, and compassionate man, apparently well-liked and respected.

Applying

9. Answers will differ. Possible answers include:
(a) The greater disaster was probably the fire, which not only destroyed lives but property as well.
(b) The Great Fire of San Francisco, caused by an earthquake, resulted in many deaths and much damage.

The Age of Pope and Swift

CONVERSTiON IN A PARK
Thomas Gainsborough
The Louvre, Paris

Humanities Note

Fine art, *Conversation in a Park,* by Thomas Gainsborough. Gainsborough (1727–1788) was an English painter of portraits, landscapes, and genre subjects. He studied in London and was influenced by the Dutch naturalistic manner and the French rococo style. He became a member of the Royal Academy in 1768. By 1780 Gainsborough was receiving portrait commissions from the Royal family. Although he became the favorite portraitist of British high society, Gainsborough often said that his heart was in landscapes not portraits.

This painting, *Conversation in a Park,* combines portraiture with landscape. It has also been called *Lady and Gentleman in Landscape* and *Thomas Sandby and Wife,* but it may well be the painter and his wife. In the background is an English landscape garden. These gardens were carefully planned to appear natural and picturesque. Little temples and artificial ruins were used to show the superiority of the ancients.

This portrait was painted during Gainsborough's Suffolk period. He presumably settled in Suffolk about 1748, where he painted many portraits of unidentified sitters.

More About the Author After his experience at the pillory, a form of punishment usually reserved for the lowest classes, Defoe seemed to abandon his political conscience. Trying to recover from a bankruptcy that he blamed on his political mishaps, he wrote for whoever would pay him, regardless of the politics of the issue or his own personal convictions. Do you think Defoe's concern in his later writing for the negative effect of civilization on moral and social life might have stemmed from his own experiences? Do you think that the end ever justifies the means? Explain.

DANIEL DEFOE

1660–1731

Although Daniel Defoe produced an impressive number of pamphlets, essays, and poems throughout his life, he was nearly sixty years old before he began writing the novels that established him as a writer of genius. Defoe's *Robinson Crusoe,* a book that recounts the mostly imaginary adventures of a real person, marked the beginning of the modern English novel. Defoe's realistic, almost documentary narrative of a man marooned on a desert island was something new in English literature. It established a genre.

Defoe's life was an odd mixture of business, politics, religion, and journalism. Born to a middle-class family named Foe (he added the "De" later), Defoe attended a school run by the Dissenters, a loosely knit group that refused to accept the principles set down by the Church of England. He considered entering the Presbyterian ministry but instead turned his attention to commerce. He invested heavily and not always well in a variety of ventures—a ship, diving bells, wines, civet cats. The scope of his activities is shown by the size of his debt. When he declared bankruptcy in 1692, he owed his creditors 17,000 pounds.

At that point, he turned to writing (and to patrons for his writing) to try to improve his fortunes. His pen, however, also got him into trouble. After enjoying brief success with *The True-Born Englishman* (1701), a defense of King William III against his detractors, he wrote an ill-advised satire, *The Shortest Way with the Dissenters* (1702), that landed him in jail and in the pillory. Published anonymously, this pamphlet condemned the very religious group Defoe favored. Its irony amused neither the Dissenters nor members of the Church of England, but Defoe had enough popularity to attract cheering supporters rather than rock throwers at his pillory appearance.

Late in life Defoe turned to writing books that purported to be memoirs, among them *Robinson Crusoe* (1719) and *Moll Flanders* (1722). As published, these books were not novels in the strict sense, since they were sold as nonfiction. Although Defoe has been accused "of forging a story, and imposing it on the world for truth," these books are generally regarded as novels today—and as outstanding novels at that.

Defoe's journalistic talents served him well in writing *A Journal of the Plague Year* (1722). He studied official documents, interviewed survivors of the plague, and may have drawn upon his own memories as a young child. The vivid historical re-creation of the plague is a triumph of Defoe's energetic, detailed style in a genre that set English fiction upon a new path.

Objective

1 To understand first-person narrative

GUIDE FOR READING

from A Journal of the Plague Year

Writer's Techniques

First-person Narrative. Fiction is written from one of two main points of view—first person or third person. The narrator's perspective can vary somewhat in each of them. A third-person narrator, for example, can be *omniscient* (all-knowing) or *limited* (restricted to the mind of one character). A first-person narrator ("I") can be a *participant* (directly involved in the action) or an *observer* (reporting on the actions of another, as Watson reports on Sherlock Holmes). From a writer's standpoint, first-person narration imposes severe limitations. The narrator must be physically present at all times and involved in most of the important action. Everything must be observed through the eyes and mind of that narrator; there can be no omniscience, no multiple viewpoints. If the first-person narrator is a participant, the story will sound very much like a personal memoir or an autobiography. If the writing is highly realistic and plausible, you may think (unless told otherwise) that you are reading nonfiction. In *A Journal of the Plague Year,* that is exactly what Defoe had in mind.

Look For

As you read the excerpt from *A Journal of the Plague Year,* notice the specific details the first-person narrator uses. How do they lend credibility to Defoe's fictional account?

Writing

Choose an imaginary setting for a description, such as a new planet inhabited by an unfamiliar species or your own community at a time in the distant past or future. Using that setting, list some of the specific details you would include in a first-person narrative.

Vocabulary

Knowing the following words will help you as you read the excerpt from *A Journal of the Plague Year.*

distemper (dis tem′pər) *n.*: An infectious disease, in this case the plague (p. 533)

oppressed (ə prest′) *v.*: Burdened (p. 534)

importuning (im pôr to͞on′iŋ) *v.*: Begging; urging (p. 534)

promiscuously (prə mis′kyo͞o wəs lē) *adv.*: Without care or thought (p. 534)

prodigious (prə dij′əs) *adj.*: Enormous; huge (p. 535)

Literary Focus Review with students the view of the plague depicted in Samuel Pepys's *Diary.* Discuss whether the limitations of a first-person participant narrator overshadowed the benefits of reading about the plague through Pepys's eyes. Have students give examples to support their opinions.

Look For Write the word *apple* on the chalkboard. Then ask students to think of adjectives that describe the apple. Discuss how adjectives help to create an image in the mind of how an apple looks, tastes, feels, and smells. In the same way, details supplied by a narrator create a clearer image and add a greater sense of reality to a work of fiction.

Writing Remind students to use sensory words to provide a clearer image of their imaginary setting.

Vocabulary Review the vocabulary words by calling on different students to pronounce the words and use them in sentences.

Motivation for Reading Sir Walter Scott said of the *Journal*: "The subject is hideous almost to disgust, yet . . . we go . . . reading to the end of the volume, while we nod over many a more elegant subject." Encourage students to discuss Scott's observation and to reflect on why movies and books about such subjects have proven popular.

Purpose-Setting Question Neither the life of the time nor even the life of the plague occurred in quite the way Defoe presented it in the *Journal*. What incidents do you think might be fictitious?

Thematic Idea Read and discuss Nashe's "A Litany in Time of Plague," page 202, and the excerpts from Pepys' *Diary*, page 524, in conjunction with this selection. For a brilliant modern fictional account of a plague, see Albert Camus's *The Plague*. Encourage your **more advanced** students to read this Defoe-influenced work.

1 **Literary Focus** How does Defoe's trick of qualifying his statement, as if it were important to be perfectly accurate, affect the realism of the narrative?

2 **Literary Focus** How does first-person narration help to accomplish this?

3 **Discussion** Why didn't people mourn publicly for their friends?

4 **Literary Focus** Explain how the author elaborates the image of the "voice of mourning."

5 **Enrichment** Increasing indifference to others is a central moral issue in the *Journal*. As concern for the plague spreads, concern for the plight of others decreases.

from A Journal of the Plague Year

Daniel Defoe

The face of London was now indeed
strangely altered, I mean the whole mass of
buildings, city, liberties, suburbs, Westminster, Southwark, and altogether; for as to
1 the particular part called the city, or within
the walls, that was not yet much infected.

JOURNAL OF THE PLAGUE YEAR: THE DEAD CART
The British Library

But in the whole the face of things, I say, was
much altered; sorrow and sadness sat upon
every face; and though some parts were not
yet overwhelmed, yet all looked deeply concerned; and as we saw it apparently coming
on, so everyone looked on himself and his
family as in the utmost danger. Were it
possible to represent those times exactly to
those that did not see them, and give the
reader due ideas of the horror that every- 2
where presented itself, it must make just
impressions upon their minds and fill them
with surprise. London might well be said to
be all in tears; the mourners did not go
about the streets indeed, for nobody put on
black or made a formal dress of mourning 3
for their nearest friends; but the voice of
mourning was truly heard in the streets.
The shrieks of women and children at the
windows and doors of their houses, where
their dearest relations were perhaps dying,
or just dead, were so frequent to be heard as 4
we passed the streets, that it was enough to
pierce the stoutest heart in the world to hear
them. Tears and lamentations were seen
almost in every house, especially in the first
part of the visitation; for toward the latter
end men's hearts were hardened, and death
was so always before their eyes, that they
did not so much concern themselves for the 5
loss of their friends, expecting that themselves should be summoned the next
hour. . . .

I went all the first part of the time freely

Humanities Note

Wood engraving: *The Dead Cart.* The wood engraving *The Dead Cart* was done by an unknown artist for an early edition of Daniel Defoe's *A Journal of the Plague Year,* first published in 1722. The wood engraving was one of the earliest means of reproducing illustrations in the printed book.

You might use the following questions for discussion:

1. For what was the dead cart used?
2. What seems to be the attitude of the artist toward his subject matter?
3. How does this illustration reinforce the extent to which the plague affected society?

about the streets, though not so freely as to run myself into apparent danger, except 6 when they dug the great pit in the churchyard of our parish of Aldgate. A terrible pit it was, and I could not resist my curiosity to go and see it. As near as I may judge, it was about forty feet in length, and about fifteen or sixteen feet broad, and, at the time I first looked at it, about nine feet deep; but it was said they dug it near twenty feet deep afterwards in one part of it, till they could go no deeper for the water; for they had, it seems, dug several large pits before this. For though the plague was long a-coming to our parish, yet, when it did come, there was no parish in or about London where it raged with such 7 violence as in the two parishes of Aldgate and Whitechapel.

I say they had dug several pits in another ground, when the distemper began to spread in our parish, and especially when the dead carts began to go about, which was not, in our parish, till the beginning of August. Into these pits they had put perhaps fifty or sixty bodies each; then they made larger holes, wherein they buried all that the cart brought in a week, which, by the middle to the end of August, came to from 200 to 400 a week; and they could not well dig them larger, because of the order of the magistrates confining them to leave no bodies within six feet of the surface; and the water 8 coming on at about seventeen or eighteen feet, they could not well, I say, put more in one pit. But now, at the beginning of September, the plague raging in a dreadful manner, and the number of burials in our parish increasing to more than was ever buried in any parish about London of no larger extent, they ordered this dreadful gulf to be dug, for such it was rather than a pit.

They had supposed this pit would have supplied them for a month or more when they dug it, and some blamed the churchwardens for suffering[1] such a frightful thing, telling them they were making preparations to bury the whole parish, and the like; but time made it appear the churchwardens knew the condition of the parish better than they did, for the pit being finished the 4th of September, I think, they began to bury in it the 6th, and by the 20th, which was just two weeks, they had thrown into it 1114 bodies, when they were obliged to fill it up, the bodies being then come to lie within six feet of the surface. I doubt not but there may be some ancient persons alive in the parish who can justify the fact of this, and are able to show even in what place of the churchyard the pit lay better than I can. The mark of it also was many years to be seen in the churchyard on the surface, lying in length parallel with the passage which goes by the west wall of the churchyard out of 9 Houndsditch, and turns east again into Whitechapel, coming out near the Three Nuns' Inn.

It was about the 10th of September that my curiosity led, or rather drove, me to go and 10 see this pit again, when there had been near 400 people buried in it; and I was not content to see it in the daytime, as I had done before, for then there would have been nothing to have been seen but the loose earth; for all the bodies that were thrown in were immediately covered with earth by those they called the buriers, which at other times were called bearers; but I resolved 11 to go in the night and see some of them thrown in.

There was a strict order to prevent people coming to those pits, and that was only to prevent infection. But after some time that order was more necessary, for people that were infected and near their end, and delirious also, would run to those pits, wrapped in blankets or rugs, and throw themselves in, and, as they said, bury themselves. I cannot say that the officers suffered any willingly to lie there; but I have heard that in a great pit in Finsbury, in the parish of Cripplegate, it lying open then to the fields, for it was not then walled about,

1. **suffering:** Allowing.

6 **Discussion** Do you think it was strange that the narrator wanted to see the pit? Explain.

7 **Literary Focus** How does the use of proper names add to the realism of the narrative?

8 **Literary Focus** What is the effect of citing dates and numbers of bodies?

9 **Literary Focus** What purpose does this seemingly useless detail serve?

10 **Literary Focus** What is the effect of the narrator's correcting himself?

11 **Discussion** Why were buriers sometimes called "bearers"?

12 **Discussion** Why does the narrator feel that "no tongue can express" the dreadful condition?

13 **Discussion** What "uses" do you think the narrator might find for what he was about to see?

14 **Discussion** Why would the pit be a "sermon"?

15 **Discussion** What do you think the sexton meant by "voice" and "speaking sight"?

16 **Discussion** What happens to strengthen the narrator's resolve to see the pit?

17 **Discussion** What is the effect of including the story of the desperate mourner?

Master Teacher Note Toward the end of the *Journal* the narrator comments on the susceptibility of the city to plague. "The Plague like a great Fire, if a few Houses only are contiguous where it happens, can only burn a few Houses; or if it begins in a single, or as we call it a lone House, can only burn that lone House where it begins: but if it begins in a close built Town, or city, and gets a Head, there its fury encreases, it rages over the whole Place, and consumes all it can reach." How does this comment apply to what you know about the devastating London fire described in Samuel Pepys's *Diary*?

[some] came and threw themselves in, and expired there, before they threw any earth upon them; and that when they came to bury others, and found them there, they were quite dead, though not cold.

This may serve a little to describe the dreadful condition of that day, though it is impossible to say anything that is able to give a true idea of it to those who did not see it, other than this, that it was indeed very,
12 very, very dreadful, and such as no tongue can express.

I got admittance into the churchyard by being acquainted with the sexton who attended, who, though he did not refuse me at all, yet earnestly persuaded me not to go, telling me very seriously, for he was a good, religious, and sensible man, that it was indeed their business and duty to venture, and to run all hazards, and that in it they might hope to be preserved; but that I had no apparent call to it but my own curiosity, which, he said, he believed I would not pretend was sufficient to justify my running that hazard. I told him I had been pressed in my mind to go, and that perhaps it might be an instructing sight, that might not be with-
13 out its uses. "Nay," says the good man, "if you will venture upon that score, name of God go in; for, depend upon it, 't will be a
14 sermon to you, it may be, the best that ever you heard in your life. 'T is a speaking
15 sight," says he, "and has a voice with it, and a loud one, to call us all to repentance"; and with that he opened the door and said, "Go, if you will."

His discourse had shocked my resolution a little, and I stood wavering for a good while, but just at that interval I saw two links[2] come over from the end of the Minories, and
16 heard the bellman, and then appeared a dead cart, as they called it, coming over the streets; so I could no longer resist my desire of seeing it, and went in. There was nobody, as I could perceive at first, in the churchyard, or going into it, but the buriers and the fellow that drove the cart, or rather led the horse and cart; but when they came up to the pit they saw a man go to and again,[3] muffled up in a brown cloak, and making motions with his hands under his cloak, as if he was in a great agony, and the buriers immediately gathered about him, supposing he was one of those poor delirious or desperate creatures that used to pretend, as I have said, to bury themselves. He said nothing as he walked about, but two or three times groaned very deeply and loud, and sighed as he would break his heart.

When the buriers came up to him they soon found he was neither a person infected and desperate, as I have observed above, or a person distempered in mind, but one oppressed with a dreadful weight of grief indeed, having his wife and several of his children all in the cart that was just come in with him, and he followed in an agony and
excess of sorrow. He mourned heartily, as it 17
was easy to see, but with a kind of masculine grief that could not give itself vent by tears; and calmly defying the buriers to let him alone, said he would only see the bodies thrown in and go away, so they left importuning him. But no sooner was the cart turned round and the bodies shot into the pit promiscuously, which was a surprise to him, for he at least expected they would have been decently laid in, though indeed he was afterwards convinced that was impracticable; I say, no sooner did he see the sight but he cried out aloud, unable to contain himself. I could not hear what he said, but he went backward two or three steps and fell down in a swoon. The buriers ran to him and took him up, and in a little while he came to himself, and they led him away to the Pie Tavern over against the end of Houndsditch, where, it seems, the man was known, and where they took care of him. He looked into the pit again as he went away,

2. **links:** Torches.

3. **to and again:** To and fro.

but the buriers had covered the bodies so immediately with throwing in earth, that though there was light enough, for there were lanterns, and candles in them, placed all night round the sides of the pit, upon heaps of earth, seven or eight, or perhaps more, yet nothing could be seen.

This was a mournful scene indeed, and affected me almost as much as the rest; but the other was awful and full of terror. The cart had in it sixteen or seventeen bodies; some were wrapped up in linen sheets, some in rags, some little other than naked, or so loose that what covering they had fell from them in the shooting out of the cart, and they fell quite naked among the rest; but the matter was not much to them, or the indecency much to anyone else, seeing they were all dead, and were to be huddled together into the common grave of mankind, as we may call it, for here was no difference made, but poor and rich went together; there was no other way of burials, neither was it possible there should, for coffins were not to be had for the prodigious numbers that fell in such a calamity as this. 18

THINKING ABOUT THE SELECTION

Recalling

1. (a) Describe the great pit in the churchyard of Aldgate parish. (b) What was the purpose of the pit?
2. (a) What limited the depth to which the pit could be dug? (b) What restriction did an order of the magistrates put on the use of the pit?
3. How many bodies does the narrator say were buried in the great pit between September 6 and September 20?
4. (a) What prompts the narrator to visit the pit? (b) Why does he go at night?
5. (a) What kind of person did the buriers at first suppose the man in the brown cloak to be? (b) Summarize the incident concerning the man in the brown cloak.

Interpreting

6. Why do you think the narrator describes the great pit in such a specific and detailed way?
7. Judging by the tone of this excerpt and the narrator's reason for visiting the pit, what kind of person do you think the narrator is?
8. Why does the sexton at the churchyard say that visiting the pit will "be a sermon to you . . . a voice . . . to call us all to repentence"?
9. What causes the "masculine grief" of the man in the brown cloak to turn suddenly to anguish?

Applying

10. Many writers have written fictional accounts of great disasters or have used disasters as backgrounds for their fiction. Why do you think disasters have this fictional appeal?

ANALYZING LITERATURE

Recognizing First-person Narrative

A **first-person narrative** is one told by an "I" narrator—a person present at the events being described. A first-person narrator can be either a participant or an observer in the main action. Defoe's *A Journal of the Plague Year* claims to be a first-person narrative of a London resident, one "H. F.," written during the great plague of 1665. In reality, it is a fictional reconstruction written by Defoe more than fifty years later.

1. Why do you think Defoe chose a first-person narrator, an "eyewitness," to present this account of the plague year?
2. Defoe has been called the father of modern journalism. (a) If "H. F.'s" first-person account of the plague were true, what features would qualify it as good journalism? (b) What features would you not find in the usual modern news story?

18 Enrichment In reality, most of the plague's victims were London's poor; it was even called "the Poors Plague."

Interpreting

6. By emphasizing the size of the pit, the narrator is trying to convey the horrible reality of the plague.
7. The narrator is a curious person, in this case morbidly so, who wants to see things for himself, rather than hear about them second-hand. He feels pity for the plague victims, but is able to view the horror somewhat dispassionately, as a news reporter might do.
8. The sexton wants the narrator to be reminded of his own mortality and to repent for his sins.
9. The man sees the bodies of his loved ones thrown into the pit, instead of being gently placed there. This brings home the reality of their deaths.

Applying

10. Answers will differ. Suggested answer: Disasters have fictional appeal because they offer a naturally exciting plot and are an excellent backdrop for illustrating human nature. The dread of sudden, violent death and widespread social disintegration is a universal fear and a subject which is likely to sell books.

Answers

ANSWERS TO THINKING ABOUT THE SELECTION

Recalling

1. (a) The pit was about forty feet in length, about fifteen or sixteen feet wide, and about nine feet deep. (b) The pit served as a grave for the plague victims.
2. (a) Water limited the depth. (b) The pit could be filled with bodies no closer than six feet from the surface.
3. The narrator says 1,114 bodies were buried.
4. (a) His curiosity prompted him to visit the pit. (b) By day the bodies had already been covered with dirt. He wanted to see the bodies thrown into the pit.
5. They thought the man in the brown cloak was a victim of the plague who wanted to bury himself. (b) Quietly mourning the deaths of his wife and children, the man came to the pit to watch their burial. But when he saw their bodies dumped unceremoniously into the pit he cried aloud and fainted. When he revived, the buriers took him to a tavern where he was looked after by friends.

ANSWERS TO ANALYZING LITERATURE

1. An eyewitness account gives a much greater sense of immediacy to the events; the reader feels a greater sense of involvement. It also adds credibility.
2. (a) The fact that it is an eyewitness account of a newsworthy event qualifies it as good journalism. There is also scrupulous attention to accuracy. (b) The narrator would not be present, nor would the narrator's personal reactions to the events. The reader would not be mentioned in a news story.

Challenge Encourage your students to write a fictional account of a plague in their school or community.

More About the Author In a letter to his friend Alexander Pope, written in 1725, Jonathan Swift declared that "the chief end I propose to myself in all my labors is to vex the world rather than divert it." In spite of this dour credo, *Gulliver's Travels*, when it came out, was "the conversation of the whole town [London] . . . the whole impression [edition] sold in a week . . .." After you read the excerpts here, think about whether his readers might have missed the bitter satire of his book, and simply mistook it for amusing fiction, or that, however vexing Swift hoped to be, people find satire entertaining? In other words with what motive do people read satire? Do they hope to better themselves? Or do they hope simply to find themselves shaking their heads in wry agreement with the author? Can you think of any present day works, written or visual, that seem to be created with the intention of "vexing the world"? And does the public generally find this type of work vexing, or entertaining?

JONATHAN SWIFT

1667–1745

The life of Jonathan Swift is a tale of thwarted ambition coupled with brilliant literary achievement. In the Church of England and in British politics, he sometimes seemed on the verge of great success, only to have an unkind fate baffle his expectations. In literature, on the other hand, he achieved an almost unparalleled triumph with *Gulliver's Travels,* a book that can be read—and has been read since its publication—as a children's story, a fantasy, a parody of travel books, and a sophisticated satire on English politics.

Jonathan Swift was born in Dublin, Ireland, to English parents. His father died before he was born, and young Jonathan, through the assistance of relatives, attended Kilkenny Grammar School and Trinity College, Dublin. Later he joined the household of Sir William Temple, a retired diplomat, who lived at Moor Park, Surrey, England. Swift read, studied, and wrote for the next few years. Receiving none of the hoped-for political support from Sir William, he decided on a career in the church.

After Temple's death in 1699, Swift, was given a small parish near London. The satirical writing he had done while in the Temple household was somewhat out of character for a clergyman, but its brilliance was widely acknowledged when it appeared as two separate books in 1704. Published anonymously, *A Tale of a Tub* satirizes excesses in religion and learning, while *The Battle of the Books* describes a comic encounter between ancient and modern literature.

Although *A Tale of a Tub* dashed his hopes for advancement to the rank of bishop in the Church of England, Swift remained a defender of the Anglican faith. In 1710, he changed his political allegiance from the conservative Whig party to the Tory party favored by Queen Anne. He benefited immediately from this switch. As the leading party writer for the government, he wrote many pamphlets and wielded considerable political influence. The glory was short-lived, however. Anne died in 1714; the Whigs regained power; and Swift, embittered, returned to Ireland as dean of St. Patrick's Cathedral, a position he held for more than thirty years.

Back in Ireland, he continued to write satires, including *Drapier Letters* (1724) and *A Modest Proposal* (1729), which championed the Irish cause. With the publication of *Gulliver's Travels* (1726), he reached the height of his literary power. In his later years, he suffered what was probably Ménière's disease, marked by a serious loss of memory and balance. His death in 1745 deprived the world of one of its great writers—a generous and learned man who despised the fanaticism, selfishness, and pride of people in general but admired individual human beings.

Objectives

1. To familiarize the student with satirical writing and its usual targets
2. To understand generalizations
3. To acquaint the student with words derived from literature

Teaching Portfolio: Support Material

Lesson Plan, p. 00

Vocabulary Check, p. 00

Usage and Mechanics Worksheet, p. 00

Analyzing Literature Worksheet, p. 00

Critical Thinking and Reading Worksheet, p. 00

Language Worksheet, p. 00

Selection Test, p. 00

Art Transparency 7, *St. Michael's Mount, Cornwall,* Arthur Joseph Meadows

GUIDE FOR READING

from Gulliver's Travels

Writer's Techniques

Satire. Satire is writing that uses wit and humor to ridicule vices, follies, stupidities, and abuses. Irony is often an element in satire, as is sarcasm. Satire can take the form of prose, poetry, or drama. Satirists, by directing their barbs toward those they view as offenders, hope to improve the situation—to reform individuals, groups, or humanity as a whole. Satire may be gentle and amusing or it may be cruel and even vicious. Whatever its tone, satire is usually subtle enough to require the reader to make at least a small mental leap to connect it with its target.

Look For

As you read the excerpts from *Gulliver's Travels,* watch for Swift's use of wit and irony. Pay attention to whom and what he is ridiculing.

Writing

Think about current social or political problems or situations that might be suitable subjects for satire. Try to suggest at least two. Jot these ideas down. After each subject, give one aspect of it that is particularly open to ridicule.

Vocabulary

Knowing the following words will help you as you read the excerpts from *Gulliver's Travels.*

conjecture (kən jek'chər) *v.*: To guess (p. 538)
fomented (fō ment'id) *v.*: Stirred up; incited (p. 539)
expostulate (ik späs'chə lāt) *v.*: To reason earnestly with (p. 539)
schism (siz''m) *n.*: A division into groups or factions (p. 539)
expedient (ik spē'dē ənt) *n.*: A device used in an emergency (p. 540)
encomiums (en kō'mē əmz) *n.*: Formal expressions of praise or tribute (p. 541)
habituate (hə bich'oo wāt') *v.*: To make used to (p. 542)
perfidiousness (pər fid'ē əs nis) *n.*: Betrayal of trust (p. 543)
panegyric (pan'ə jir'ik) *n.*: A speech giving praise (p. 543)
odious (ō'dē əs) *adj.*: Hateful; disgusting (p. 543)

Literary Focus Satire walks a shaky tightrope between cynicism and idealism. In tone it is often ironic, sarcastic or even despairing. Our impression of the writer may be the rather off-putting one of a bitterly disgusted person. But at its best satire does more than ridicule, it hopes to change a situation. Behind the anger we may catch glimpses of a wistfulness for the world that should be.

Look For Have students notice the tone in the following two selections. Does it seem the same in each, or different?

Writing Another source for situations to satirize might come from political cartoons. Suggest that your students collect several that please them, then let them consider if they could translate visual indignation into a written satire.

Vocabulary As a preview, you may wish to ask your class to scan the selection, searching for the vocabulary words. When a student finds one, he or she could read its definition aloud to the class, then read the sentence in which it was discovered.

Motivation for Reading Have students imagine that they live in a time, live in a land, or work in a company where great injustices have been done. But it is dangerous to speak out against these villainies. At best they might lose their friends and their jobs; at worst they might lose their liberty or even their lives. If they still felt that they had to say something, how might they couch their criticism for maximum deniability, and yet still get their point across? Might they veil their criticism behind a satirical fable? You might relate this idea to the saying "If the shoe fits, wear it."

Master Teacher Note As your students are reading the excerpts from *Gulliver's Travels,* place Art Transparency 7, *St. Michael's Mount, Cornwall* by Arthur Joseph Meadows, on the overhead projector. Explain that this painting suggests what Gulliver's sea journeys would have been like. Ask your students what it might have felt like to be on one of the boats in such a turbulent sea. Discuss whether people today who travel across an ocean can get an accurate impression of the power and might of the sea, or whether modern vessels prevent travelers from really feeling what the sea can be like.

Purpose-Setting Question Who is Swift satirizing in this piece? Who do the Lilliputians represent, and who are the Blefuscudians?

Thematic Idea Compare Swift's satirical methods and targets with those of Pope in "The Rape of the Lock," page 560.

from Gulliver's Travels

Jonathan Swift

In Gulliver's Travels, *Swift exposes the corruption and defects in England's political, social, and economic institutions. The work centers on the four imaginary voyages of Lemuel Gulliver, the narrator, a well-educated but unimaginative ship's surgeon. Each of these voyages takes Gulliver to a different remarkable and bizarre world. During his stays in these imaginary lands, Gulliver is led toward realizations about the flawed nature of the society from which he had come, and he returns to England filled with disillusionment.*

from A Voyage to Lilliput

After being shipwrecked, Gulliver swims to shore and drifts off to sleep. When he awakens, he finds that he has been tied down by the Lilliputians (lil' ə pyōō' shənz), a race of people who are only six inches tall. Though he is held captive and his sword and pistols are taken from him, Gulliver gradually begins to win the Lilliputians' favor because of his mild disposition, and he is eventually granted his freedom. Through Gulliver's exposure to Lilliputian politics and court life, the reader becomes increasingly aware of the remarkable similarities between the English and Lilliputian affairs of state. The following excerpt begins during a discussion between the Lilliputian Principal Secretary of Private Affairs and Gulliver concerning the affairs of the Lilliputian empire.

We are threatened with an invasion from the island of Blefuscu,[1] which is the other great empire of the universe, almost as large and powerful as this of his Majesty. For as to what we have heard you affirm, that there are other kingdoms and states in the world, inhabited by human creatures as large as yourself, our philosophers are in much doubt, and would rather conjecture that you dropped from the moon, or one of the stars; 1
because it is certain, that an hundred mortals of your bulk would, in a short time, destroy all the fruits and cattle of his Majesty's dominions. Besides, our histories of six thousand moons make no mention of any other regions, than the two great empires of Lilliput and Blefuscu. Which two mighty powers have, as I was going to tell you, been engaged in a most obstinate war for six and thirty moons past. It began upon the following occasion. It is allowed on all hands, that the primitive way of breaking eggs before we eat them, was upon the larger end; but his 2
present Majesty's grandfather, while he was a boy, going to eat an egg, and breaking it according to the ancient practice, happened to cut one of his fingers. Whereupon the Emperor, his father, published an edict,

1. **Blefuscu:** Represents France.

1 **Discussion** Although Swift's main target in this piece is religious schism, here he aims a swipe at a different group. Who is he satirizing? Have a student explain the irony of "Besides, our histories . . . make no mention . . ."

2 **Discussion** Although Swift has a specific conflict in mind, what does the cause of the war between Blefuscu and Lilliput suggest about all wars?

commanding all his subjects, upon great penalties, to break the smaller end of their eggs. The people so highly resented this law that our histories tell us there have been six rebellions raised on that account; wherein one emperor lost his life, and another his crown.[2] These civil commotions were constantly fomented by the monarchs of Blefuscu; and when they were quelled, the exiles always fled for refuge to that empire. It is computed that eleven thousand persons have, at several times, suffered death rather than submit to break their eggs at the smaller end. Many hundred large volumes have been published upon this controversy; but the books of the Big-Endians have been long forbidden, and the whole party rendered incapable by law of holding employments.[3] During the course of these troubles, the emperors of Blefuscu did frequently expostulate by their ambassadors, accusing us of making a schism in religion, by offending
3 against a fundamental doctrine of our great prophet Lustrog, in the fifty-fourth chapter of the *Brundecral* (which is their Alcoran[4]). This, however, is thought to be a mere strain upon the text, for the words are these: That all true believers shall break their eggs at
4 the convenient end; and which is the convenient end, seems, in my humble opinion, to be left to every man's conscience, or at least in the power of the chief magistrate[5] to determine. Now the Big-Endian exiles have found so much credit in the Emperor of Blefuscu's court, and so much private assistance and encouragement from their party here at home, that a bloody war hath been carried on between the two empires for six and thirty moons with various success; during which time we have lost forty capital ships, and a much greater number of smaller vessels, together with thirty thousand of our best seamen and soldiers; and the damage received by the enemy is reckoned to be somewhat greater than ours. However, they have now equipped a numerous fleet, and are just preparing to make a descent upon us; and his Imperial Majesty, placing great confidence in your valor and strength, hath commanded me to lay this account of his affairs before you.

I desired the Secretary to present my humble duty to the Emperor, and to let him know, that I thought it would not become me, who was a foreigner, to interfere with parties; but I was ready, with the hazard of my life, to defend his person and state against all invaders.

The empire of Blesfuscu is an island
situated to the north-northeast side of Lilliput, from whence it is parted only by a channel of eight hundred yards wide. I had not yet seen it, and upon this notice of an intended invasion, I avoided appearing on that side of the coast, for fear of being discovered by some of the enemy's ships, who had received no intelligence of me, all intercourse between the two empires having been strictly forbidden during the war, upon pain of death, and an embargo laid by our Emperor upon all vessels whatsoever. I communicated to his Majesty a project I had formed of seizing the enemy's whole fleet; which, as our scouts assured us, lay at anchor in the harbor ready to sail with the first fair wind. I consulted the most experienced seamen upon the depth of the channel, which they had often plumbed, who told me, that in the middle at high water it was seventy *glumgluffs* deep (which is about six 5
feet of European measure), and the rest of it 6
fifty *glumgluffs* at most. I walked to the northeast coast over against Blefuscu, where, lying down behind a hillock, I took out my small pocket perspective-glass, and

2. It is allowed . . . crown: Here, Swift satirizes the dispute in England between the Catholics (Big-Endians) and Protestants (Little-Endians). King Henry VIII who "broke" with the Catholic church, King Charles I who "lost his life," and King James who lost his "crown" are each referred to in the passage.

3. the whole party . . . employments: The Test Act (1673) prevented Catholics from holding office.

4. Alcoran: Koran, the sacred book of the Moslems.

5. chief magistrate: Ruler.

3 **Discussion** Note that clergyman Swift does not equate the Lilliputians's sacred book with the Bible. This puts him two steps removed from the true object of his satire. Does that insulation perhaps make him feel safer?

4 **Literary Focus** Have a student explain the irony of this sentence. Swift also seems to be saying that there may not be so much difference between religions as some men think, and also, that at least some matters of religion might be best left to each man's conscience. Would that have been a daring opinion for a clergyman to hold in that day and age?

5 **Enrichment** France lies east-southeast of England. Separating the two countries is the English Channel, twenty-one miles wide at its narrowest point.

6 **Discussion** What is the effect of including words such as *glumgluffs* that are unique to the Lilliputian vocabulary?

7 **Literary Focus** Notice that in the account of Gulliver's taking of the fleet, satire is overpowered by narrative. It returns immediately, however, once he ceases his solitary labors and returns to the Lilliputian shore.

Humanities Note

Fine art: Illustration for *Gulliver's Travels* by Willy Pogany.

William Andrew Pogany (1882–1955), nicknamed Willy, was born in Hungary and became an American citizen in 1921. Pogany studied art in many art schools throughout Europe. An artist of great versatility, he is remembered not only for his illustrations but also for his costume and set designs, his murals, sculptures, and portraits, as well as his accomplishments as art director for various Hollywood studios.

Between 1940 and 1951, Willy Pogany illustrated more than 150 books. The drawings for *Gulliver's Travels* were done for a 1947 edition for children, published in New York. Pogany chose the medium of pen and ink to execute these narrative drawings. This drawing shows Gulliver towing a Lilliputian warship to Blefescu. The style shows Pogany's command of figure drawing and provides a visualization of the text in a simple way.

You may wish to discuss this question: What does this drawing tell you about the size of Gulliver?

viewed the enemy's fleet at anchor, consisting of about fifty men of war, and a great number of transports. I then came back to my house and gave order (for which I had a warrant) for a great quantity of the strongest cable and bars of iron. The cable was about as thick as packthread, and the bars of the length and size of a knitting-needle. I trebled the cable to make it stronger, and for the same reason I twisted three of the iron bars together, bending the extremities into a hook. Having thus fixed fifty hooks to as many cables, I went back to the northeast coast and, putting off my coat, shoes, and stockings, walked into the sea in my leath-
7 ern jerkin, about half an hour before high
water. I waded with what haste I could, and swam in the middle about thirty yards until I felt ground; I arrived at the fleet in less than half an hour. The enemy was so frightened when they saw me, that they leaped out of their ships, and swam to shore, where there could not be fewer than thirty thousand souls. I then took my tackling, and, fastening a hook to the hole at the prow of each, I tied all the cords together at the end. While I was thus employed, the enemy discharged several thousand arrows, many of which struck in my hands and face and, besides the excessive smart, gave me much disturbance in my work. My greatest apprehension was for my eyes, which I should have infallibly lost, if I had not suddenly thought of an expedient. I kept among other little necessaries a pair of spectacles in a private pocket, which, as I observed before, had escaped the Emperor's searchers. These I took out and fastened as strongly as I could upon my nose and thus armed went on boldly with my work in spite of the enemy's arrows, many of which struck against the glasses of my spectacles, but without any other effect further than a little to discompose them. I had now fastened all the hooks

Illustration by Willy Pogany
The Donnell Library Children's Room, New York Public Library

and, taking the knot in my hand, began to pull; but not a ship would stir, for they were all too fast held by their anchors, so that the boldest part of my enterprise remained. I therefore let go the cord, and, leaving the hooks fixed to the ships, I resolutely cut with my knife the cables that fastened the anchors, receiving above two hundred shots in my face and hands; then I took up the knotted end of the cables to which my hooks were tied and, with great ease, drew fifty of the enemy's largest men-of-war after me.

The Blefuscudians, who had not the least imagination of what I intended, were at first confounded with astonishment. They had seen me cut the cables and thought my design was only to let the ships run adrift or fall foul on each other; but when they perceived the whole fleet, moving in order, and saw me pulling at the end, they set up such a scream of grief and despair that it is almost impossible to describe or conceive. When I had got out of danger, I stopped a while to pick out the arrows that stuck in my hands and face, and rubbed on some of the same ointment that was given me at my first arrival, as I have formerly mentioned. I then took off my spectacles, and, waiting about an hour until the tide was a little fallen, I waded through the middle with my cargo and arrived safe at the royal port of Lilliput.

The Emperor and his whole court stood on the shore expecting the issue of this great adventure. They saw the ships move forward in a large half-moon but could not discern me, who was up to my breast in water. When I advanced to the middle of the channel, they were yet more in pain, because I was under water to my neck. The Emperor concluded me to be drowned, and that the enemy's fleet was approaching in a hostile manner; but he was soon eased of his fears; for, the channel growing shallower every step I made, I came in a short time within hearing, and holding up the end of the cable by which the fleet was fastened, I cried in a loud voice, Long live the most puissant[6] Emperor of Lilliput! This great prince received me at my landing with all possible encomiums and created me a *Nardac* upon the spot, which is the highest title of honor among them.

His Majesty desired I would take some other opportunity of bringing all the rest of his enemy's ships into his ports. And so unmeasurable is the ambition of princes, that he seemed to think of nothing less than reducing the whole empire of Blesfuscu into a province and governing it by a viceroy; of destroying the Big-Endian exiles and compelling that people to break the smaller end of their eggs, by which he would remain sole monarch of the whole world. But I endeavored to divert him from this design by many arguments drawn from the topics of policy as well as justice, and I plainly protested that I would never be an instrument of bringing a free and brave people into slavery. And when the matter was debated in 8
council, the wisest part of the ministry were of my opinion.

This open bold declaration of mine was so opposite to the schemes and politics of his Imperial Majesty that he could never forgive me; he mentioned it in a very artful manner at council, where I was told that some of the wisest appeared, at least, by their silence, to be of my opinion; but others, who were my secret enemies, could not forbear some expressions, which by a sidewind reflected on me. And from this time began an intrigue between his Majesty and a junta 9
of ministers maliciously bent against me, which broke out in less than two months and had like to have ended in my utter destruction. Of so little weight are the greatest services to princes when put into the balance with a refusal to gratify their passions.

from A Voyage to Brobdingnag 10

Gulliver's second voyage leads him to

6. **puissant** (pyo͞o′ i sənt): Powerful.

8 **Discussion** Why does Gulliver acquire many enemies after this feat?

9 **Clarification** A *junta* is a Spanish word meaning "an assembly or council, or a group of political intriguers." This is one of the earliest known usages of the word in the English language.

10 **Master Teacher Note** To introduce "A Voyage to Brobdingnag," locate reproductions of three works by Goya—a painting and an etching each entitled *The Giant*, and an etching from the Caprichos, no. 43, *The Sleep Of Reason Produces Monsters*. The first two works relate directly to this selection. In the notes that come with the third, the artist sets down a credo with which Swift would surely have agreed. "A universal language. The artist dreaming. His sole intention is to banish harmful errors and perpetuate with this work of Caprichos the solid testimony of truth."

11 Literary Focus Ask a student to define apprehension, as it is used in this context. Discuss the word *apprehend* derived from the Latin *apprehendere*, "to take hold of." Note how the word has evolved from its first two meanings of (a) "to take into custody, to arrest or capture" and (b) "to grasp mentally" into (c) "a feeling of foreboding or anxious dread"?

12 Literary Focus Ask one of your students to define *copious*.

13 Discussion Do you think that Swift intends his reference to "our noble country" to be ironical? What syllable might you emphasize if you were an actor reading this line aloud?

14 Discussion The King seems refreshingly naïve when he wants to know at what age gaming is outgrown. Is Swift suggesting that, in an ideal world, gaming might be an unworthy pursuit for true adults? From Swift's mention of this pastime, what might we infer about gambling's place in English society?

15 Discussion This is very plain speaking indeed. Can your students think of any reasons why Swift might let the King have these lines, rather than let Gulliver think or speak them?

Brobdingnag (brob′ ding nag′), an island located near Alaska that is inhabited by giants twelve times as tall as Gulliver. After being sold to the Queen of Brobdingnag, Gulliver describes the English social and political institutions to the king, who reacts to his description with contempt and disgust.

It is the custom that every Wednesday (which, as I have before observed, was their Sabbath), the King and Queen, with the royal issue of both sexes, dine together in the apartment of his Majesty, to whom I was now become a favorite; and at these times my little chair and table were placed at his left hand before one of the saltcellars. This prince took a pleasure in conversing with me, inquiring into the manners, religion, laws, government, and learning of Europe, wherein I gave him the best account I was
11 able. His apprehension was so clear, and his judgment so exact, that he made very wise reflections and observations upon all I said. But I confess, that after I had been a little too
12 copious in talking of my own beloved country, of our trade, and wars by sea and land, of our schisms in religion, and parties in the state, the prejudices of his education prevailed so far, that he could not forbear taking me up in his right hand, and stroking me gently with the other, after an hearty fit of laughing, asked me whether I were a Whig or a Tory.[7] Then turning to his first minister, who waited behind him with a white staff, near as tall as the mainmast of the *Royal Sovereign*,[8] he observed how contemptible a thing was human grandeur, which could be mimicked by such diminutive insects as I. And yet, said he, I dare engage, those creatures have their titles and distinctions of honor, they contrive little nests and burrows, that they call houses and cities; they make a figure in dress and equipage;[9] they love, they fight, they dispute, they cheat, they betray. And thus he continued on, while my color came and went several times,
with indignation to hear our noble country, 13
the mistress of arts and arms, the scourge of France, the arbitress of Europe, the seat of virtue, piety, honor and truth, the pride and envy of the world, so contemptuously treated. . . .

He laughed at my odd kind of arithmetic (as he was pleased to call it) in reckoning the numbers of our people by a computation drawn from the several sects among us in religion and politics. He said he knew no reason why those who entertain opinions prejudicial to the public should be obliged to change or should not be obliged to conceal them. And, as it was tyranny in any government to require the first, so it was weakness not to enforce the second; for, a man may be allowed to keep poisons in his closets, but not to vend them about as cordials.

He observed, that among the diversions of our nobility and gentry[10] I had mentioned
gaming.[11] He desired to know at what age 14
this entertainment was usually taken up, and when it was laid down. How much of their time it employed; whether it ever went so high as to affect their fortunes. Whether mean vicious people by their dexterity in that art might not arrive at great riches, and sometimes keep our very nobles in dependence, as well as habituate them to vile companions, wholly take them from the improvment of their minds, and force them, by the losses they received, to learn and practice that infamous dexterity upon others.

He was perfectly astonished with the historical account I gave him of our affairs during the last century, protesting it was
only an heap of conspiracies, rebellions, 15
murders, massacres, revolutions, banishments, the very worst effects that avarice,

7. Whig . . . Tory: British political parties.
8. ***Royal Sovereign:*** One of the largest ships in the British Navy.
9. equipage (ek′ wə pij): Horses and carriages.

10. gentry: The class of landowning people ranking just below the nobility.
11. gaming: Gambling.

faction, hypocrisy, perfidiousness, cruelty, rage, madness, hatred, envy, lust, malice, and ambition could produce.

His Majesty in another audience was at the pains to recapitulate the sum of all I had spoken; compared the questions he made with the answers I had given; then taking me into his hands, and stroking me gently, delivered himself in these words, which I shall never forget, nor the manner he spoke them in. "My little friend Grildrig, you have made a most admirable panegyric upon your country. You have clearly proved that ignorance, idleness, and vice are the proper ingredients for qualifying a legislator. That laws are best explained, interpreted, and applied by those whose interest and abilities lie in perverting, confounding, and eluding them. I observe among you some lines of an institution, which in its original might have been tolerable, but these half erased, and the rest wholly blurred and blotted by corruptions. It doth not appear from all you have said how any one perfection is required toward the procurement of any one station among you, much less that men are ennobled on account of their virtue, that priests are advanced for their piety or learning, soldiers for their conduct or valor, judges for their integrity, senators for the love of their country, or counselors for their wisdom. As for yourself, continued the King, who have spent the greatest part of your life in traveling, I am well disposed to hope you may hitherto have escaped many vices of your country. But, by what I have gathered from your own relation, and the answers I have with much pains wringed and extorted from you, I cannot but conclude the bulk of your natives to be the most pernicious race of little odious vermin that nature ever suffered to crawl upon the surface of the earth."

Nothing but an extreme love of truth
16 could have hindered me from concealing
this part of my story. It was in vain to discover my resentments, which were always turned into ridicule; and I was forced to rest with patience while my noble and most beloved country was so injuriously treated. I am heartily sorry as any of my readers can possibly be that such an occasion was given, but this prince happened to be so curious and inquisitive upon every particular that it could not consist either with gratitude or good manners to refuse giving him what satisfaction I was able. Yet thus much I may be allowed to say in my own vindication that I artfully eluded many of his questions and gave to every point a more favorable turn by many degrees than the strictness of truth would allow. For I have always borne that laudable partiality to my own country, which Dionysius Halicarnassensis[12] with so much justice recommends to an historian. I would hide the frailties and deformities of
my political mother and place her virtues 17
and beauties in the most advantageous light. This was my sincere endeavor in those many discourses I had with that mighty monarch, although it unfortunately failed of success.

But great allowances should be given to a king who lives wholly secluded from the rest of the world, and must therefore be altogether unacquainted with the manners and customs that most prevail in other nations: the want of which knowledge will ever
produce many prejudices, and a certain nar- 18
rowness of thinking, from which we and the politer countries of Europe are wholly exempted. And it would be hard indeed, if so remote a prince's notions of virtue and vice were to be offered as a standard for all mankind.

To confirm what I have now said, and further to show the miserable effects of a confined education, I shall here insert a passage which will hardly obtain belief. In hopes to ingratiate myself farther into his Majesty's favor, I told him of an invention discovered between three and four hundred

12. **Dionysius** (dī′ ə nish′ əs) **Halicarnassensis** (hal′ ə kär na sen′ sis): A Greek writer who lived in Rome and attempted to persuade the Greeks to submit to their Roman conquerors.

16 **Discussion** The phrase "an extreme love of truth" has a double meaning. On the ironical level, Gulliver protests too much that only his love for the truth lets him pass on the King's painfully frank opinions. On another level entirely, it is Swift's indignant love of truth that inspires him to write of his country's iniquities.

17 **Literary Focus** Why is it necessary for Gulliver to insist on his loyalty to his country?

18 **Critical Thinking and Reading** Discuss the scathing irony of this paragraph.

19 **Discussion** What is Gulliver offering to make for the King?

20 **Enrichment** Gunpowder *is* a very simple compound, consisting of sulfur, saltpeter, and charcoal.

Humanities Note

Fine art: Illustration for *Gulliver's Travels* by Willy Pogany.

Willy Pogany was much admired as an illustrator. His drawings for *Gulliver's Travels* were produced during a prolific period (1940–1951) in his career, in which he illustrated more than 150 books. This pen-and-ink drawing is a visualization of Gulliver explaining the use of gunpowder to the King of Brobdingnag. The humor of the situation is emphasized by the horrified expression on the face of the King. In these illustrations Pogany made every effort to present simple, pleasing drawings that a child would find appealing.

Consider asking the following question: Swift employed humor to make his point in *Gulliver's Travels*. How does the artist use this same device in his drawing?

Master Teacher Note Bring in copies of *Mad* Magazine and *National Lampoon*, and also satirical comic strips such as *Doonesbury* or *Bloom County*. Also bring in some satirical columns by Art Buchwald or Russell Baker. Allow your students to work in groups and ask them to identify the topics being satirized by the artists and writers, then to share their findings with the class. Ask them also to decide on the tone of each satirical piece. Is it a bitter satire? a funny or gentle one? You might let the class vote on which satire they think is most effective in getting its point across.

years ago, to make a certain powder, into an heap of which the smallest spark of fire falling, would kindle the whole in a moment,
19 although it were as big as a mountain, and make it all fly up in the air together, with a noise and agitation greater than thunder. That a proper quantity of this powder rammed into an hollow tube of brass or iron, according to its bigness, would drive a ball of iron or lead with such violence and speed as nothing was able to sustain its force. That the largest balls, thus discharged, would not only destroy whole ranks of an army at once, but batter the strongest walls to the ground, sink down ships, with a thousand men in each, to the bottom of the sea; and when linked together by a chain, would cut through masts and rigging, divide hundreds of bodies in the middle, and lay all waste before them. That we often put this powder into large hollow balls of iron, and discharged them by an engine into some city we were besieging, which would rip up the pavement, tear the houses to pieces, burst and throw splinters on every side, dashing out the brains of all who came near. That I knew the ingredients very well, which were
cheap, and common; I understood the manner of compounding them, and could direct 20
his workmen how to make those tubes of a size proportionable to all other things in his Majesty's kingdom, and the largest need not be above two hundred foot long; twenty or thirty of which tubes, charged with the proper quantity of powder and balls, would batter down the walls of the strongest town

Illustration by Willy Pogany
The Donnell Library Children's Room, New York Public Library

in his dominions in a few hours, or destroy the whole metropolis, if ever it should pretend to dispute his absolute commands. This I humbly offered to his Majesty as a small tribute of acknowledgment in return of so many marks that I had received of his royal favor and protection.

21 The King was struck with horror at the description I had given of those terrible engines and the proposal I had made. He was amazed how so impotent and groveling an insect as I (these were his expressions) could entertain such inhuman ideas, and in so familiar a manner as to appear wholly unmoved at all the scenes of blood and desolation which I had painted as the common effects of those destructive machines; whereof he said some evil genius, enemy to mankind, must have been the first contriver. As for himself, he protested that although few things delighted him so much as new discoveries in art or in nature, yet he would rather lose half his kingdom than be privy to such a secret, which he commanded me, as I valued my life, never to mention any more.

THINKING ABOUT THE SELECTION

Recalling

1. (a) Describe the conflict between Lilliput and Blefuscu over the breaking of eggs. (b) How many people have died as a result?
2. (a) How does Gulliver capture the Blefuscudian fleet? (b) What problem do the enemy arrows cause him? (c) How does he solve the problem?
3. (a) What are some of the words the king of Brobdingnag uses to describe English history over the preceding hundred years? (b) How does he describe the English people?
4. (a) What invention does Gulliver describe to the King of Brobdingnag? (b) What is the King's reaction to the invention?

Interpreting

5. In the dispute between English Catholics and Protestants, what does Swift's attitude seem to be? Explain.
6. Why does Gulliver lose favor with the Lilliputian King in spite of having captured the Blefuscudian fleet?
7. If the views of the King of Brobdingnag represent Swift's own views, what is Swift's general opinion of recent English history and politics?
8. (a) Why do you think Gulliver supposes that his gunpowder proposal to the King of Brobdingnag will be regarded favorably? (b) How is it regarded? (c) Why?

Applying

9. Why do you think Swift makes one of the races Gulliver visits tiny in comparison with him and the other race gigantic?

ANALYZING LITERATURE

Understanding Satire

Satire is writing that uses wit and humor to expose and ridicule human vice and folly. Instead of praising the ideal, the satirist focuses on what is false, despicable, or foolish. Since people perceive things differently, not everyone will agree on what deserves to be satirized. Yet effective satire is so ingenious in its presentation and, at the same time, so clear in its purpose that most readers will appreciate the writing and grasp the point, regardless of their personal

21 **Discussion** What is the King's reaction to Gulliver's offer? Why is it necessary for the satire that the King react this way?

ANSWERS TO THINKING ABOUT THE SELECTION

Recalling

1. (a) The Emperor of the Lilliputians ordered his subjects to break the small end of their eggs. The Blefuscudians have supported the Lilliputian rebels who wished to continue breaking their eggs at the large end. (b) Some forty-one thousand Lilliputians have died as a result of this edict.
2. (a) Gulliver captures the fleet by cutting their anchor cables, then towing them away. (b) The arrows smart, and they threaten his eyes. (c) He puts on a pair of spectacles.
3. (a) He calls it a "heap of conspiracies, rebellions, murders [and] massacres . . . the very worst effects that avarice . . . cruelty [and] malice could produce." (b) He describes the English as "the most pernicious race of little odious vermin that nature ever suffered to crawl upon the surface of the earth."
4. (a) Gulliver describes gunpowder to the King. (b) The King is horrified, and bids Gulliver never mention it again, if he values his life.

Interpreting

5. Swift seems to think that the dispute is as silly as the dispute over the proper way to break an egg. He seems to suggest that the matter might at best be left to each man's conscience, or failing that, to his own monarch's decision.
6. He refuses to help him enslave the Blefuscudians.
7. Swift's general opinion of recent English history seems to be that it has been foolish, bloody, and barbaric.
8. (a) Gulliver supposes that the King will be interested in his gunpowder proposal because, in Gulliver's experience, monarchs delight in owning and using lethal weapons. (b) In fact, the King regards his proposal with horror. (c) He values gains in science or art, rather than technological advances in "destructive machinery."

Applying

9. Swift may have several reasons for making one of his races tiny, and the other gigantic. First, this gives us variety and symmetry, both distinguishing and yet uniting these two stories. Second, it is interesting that, each time, the criticized race is the smaller one. "To act small" is a phrase of contempt. Third, does Swift perhaps wish to avoid directly condemning the Protestant–Catholic disputes? Notice that the religious idiocies are assigned to the Lilliputians. The other vices and actions are laid directly at the door of the English, by the King of Brobdingnag.

ANSWERS TO ANALYZING LITERATURE

1. Swift is satirizing domestic and international schisms in religion, and people's belligerence and cruelty to people in general.
2. It varies from warily ironic Lilliput to savagely ironic in Brobdingnag.
3. (a) In "A Voyage to Lilliput," the Principal Secretary of Private Affairs notes that the philosophers of Lilliput doubt that Gulliver comes from somewhere on earth, since their histories make no mention of any countries besides Lilliput and Blefuscu. The irony here is directed against closed minds, to which if a thing is not known, it is judged not to exist at all. (b) When Gulliver maintains, in his accounts to the King of Brobdingnag, that he "gave every point a more favorable turn . . . than the strictness of truth would allow," he is being ironic, for his gloss of the truth is enough to horrify that ruler. (c) In the following paragraph, Swift refers to the King's "narrowness of thinking, from which we and the politer countries of Europe are wholly exempted."

ANSWERS TO CRITICAL THINKING AND READING

1. The King observes "how contemptible a thing was human grandeur, which could be mimicked by such diminutive insects as [Gulliver]."
2. The King makes the following generalizations about (a) legislators —"that ignorance, idleness and vice are the proper" qualifications to become one. (b) priests—are not "advanced for their piety or learning" (c) soldiers—are not promoted "for their conduct or their valor" (d) judges—are not hired "for their integrity" nor are (e) senators—chosen "for the love of their country."
3. He concludes that the bulk of the human race is "an odious vermin."

ANSWERS TO UNDERSTANDING LANGUAGE

1. Yahoo: Any of a race of brutish, degraded creatures; degraded, vicious humans
2. Lilliputian: Tiny, or narrow minded and petty
3. Brobdingnagian: Of gigantic proportions

THINKING AND WRITING

Publishing Student Writing Give your students the opportunity to read aloud and listen to one another's stories.

views. Satire can be light and good-humored, or it can be bitter and unsparing. An important ingredient of much satire is irony—that is, a contrast between what is said and what is meant. For example, when Gulliver says that his "color came and went several times, with indignation to hear our noble country . . . the seat of virtue, piety, honor . . . the pride and envy of the world, so contemptuously treated," you can be quite sure that Swift is being ironic.

1. What is Swift satirizing in *Gulliver's Travels?*
2. From the excerpts you have read, how would you describe the tone of Swift's prose?
3. Point out at least three examples of irony in the excerpts from *Gulliver's Travels.*

CRITICAL THINKING AND READING
Understanding Generalizations

A **generalization** is a conclusion based on the accumulation of evidence. This evidence may come in the form of facts, statistics, incidents, and so on. In the excerpt from *A Voyage to Lilliput,* Gulliver uses a single striking example as the basis for this generalization: "Of so little weight are the greatest services to princes when put into the balance with a refusal to gratify their passions." In *A Voyage to Brobdingnag,* the King makes a number of generalizations about the English and other Europeans based on what Gulliver tells him.

1. What generalization does the King make to his first minister after Gulliver, sitting at a little table and chair . . . before one of the salt cellars," has told him about European manners, religion, laws, government, and learning? Is the generalization valid, or sound in light of the information the king has? Explain your answer.
2. After listening to Gulliver's historical account of "our affairs during the last century," what generalization does the King make about each of the following groups?
   a. legislators
   b. priests
   c. soldiers
   d. judges
   e. senators
3. What broader generalization does the King make about *all* the groups listed above?

UNDERSTANDING LANGUAGE
Using Words from Literature

Sometimes the names invented by writers become so closely associated with certain character traits or behaviors that they enter the language as standard English words. The word *lilliputian,* for example, can be found in most dictionaries. Several other words from *Gulliver's Travels* have joined the mainstream of modern English. Look up each of the following words in a standard dictionary. On a sheet of paper, write (a) each word you find and (b) its definition(s). Indicate capitalization where needed.

1. yahoo 2. lilliputian 3. brobdingagian

THINKING AND WRITING
Writing a New Adventure for Gulliver

In addition to his trips to Lilliput and Brobdingnag, Lemuel Gulliver journeys to a place called Laputa and to the land of the Houyhnhnms. In Laputa, Swift's satire is directed against learned fools, impractical professors who, among other silly enterprises, are trying to extract sunshine from cucumbers. In the land of the Houyhnhnms, he encounters a race of noble, intelligent horses that are served by vile, humanlike Yahoos. Create a fifth land for Gulliver to visit. Remember the types of creatures he has already encountered and the things he has learned along the way. In a narrative passage of a page or two, write your version of a new voyage by Gulliver. Give the land a name. Give its inhabitants names and characteristics. Include the truths about humans that Gulliver hears uttered by his hosts in this strange land. When you revise, make sure you have told your tale in chronological order.

GUIDE FOR READING

from Thoughts on Various Subjects

Writer's Techniques

Epigram. The word *epigram* has two meanings. An epigram can be a short poem with a witty or satirical point, or it can be a brief, clever statement that often pairs opposite thoughts. This pairing of opposite thoughts is called *antithesis.* In an epigram, terseness is vital—the writer must state the point as concisely as possible.

Look For

As you read the excerpts from Swift's "Thoughts on Various Subjects," note the humor in the epigrams. Also look for examples of antithesis.

Writing

Think of a well-known short story or choose one of the stories in this book. Consider the theme of the story. Then write a one-sentence summary of the theme. Make it as concise and epigrammatic as possible.

Vocabulary

Knowing the following words will help you as you read this excerpt from "Thoughts on Various Topics."

solicit (sə lis′ it) *v.*: Ask for; plead for (p. 548)

inconsistencies (in′ kən sis′ tən sez) *n.*: contradictions (p. 548)

fluency (flo͞o′ ən sē) *n.*: Easy flow; smoothness (p. 548)

diversion (də vər′ zhən) *n.*: Pastimes; amusements (p. 549)

Literary Focus You might like to point out to students that they know quite a few epigrams already. Folk sayings and mothers' admonitions are often epigrammatic. Consider "Pretty is as pretty does"; "All that glitters is not gold"; and "His eyes were bigger than his stomach." See if the class can contribute other examples.

Look For Your **less advanced** students may have problems with the concept of antithesis. Suggest that they first look for the word *but* in any of the epigrams, and then try to spot two words or ideas within that epigram that seem to have opposite meanings; for example, fat and thin. For your **more advanced** students, ask them to explain the phrase "We're from the government, and we're here to help you." Why do most adults find this amusing? Is this statement antithetical?

Writing You might suggest that your students approach this exercise as if they were wittling a block of wood. Ask them to first "rough in" the theme in three or four declarative sentences. Then see if they can introduce an antithesis into their short paragraph. Is there a "but" within their rough theme? Then ask them to reduce their theme to one declarative sentence. At that point, after they have dealt with the content of their epigram, they should be ready to shape it into its final, epigrammatic form and to polish it. For your **less advanced** students, a good source for their themes might be *Aesop's Fables*, since each of those is constructed rather tightly around a particular lesson. A second source for clear-cut themes might be Kipling's *Just So* stories.

Vocabulary Have some of your **less advanced** students use the vocabulary words in sentences.

from Thoughts on Various Subjects

Jonathan Swift

Thoughts on Various Subjects developed out of an agreement between Alexander Pope and Swift to record their passing thoughts. The following are some of Swift's ideas and impressions, which were included in his commonplace book, or book of collected passages.

1 We have just enough religion to make us hate, but not enough to make us love one another.

2 When we desire or solicit anything, our minds run wholly on the good side or circumstances of it; when 'tis obtained, our minds run wholly on the bad ones.

When a true genius appears in the world, you may know him by this sign: that the dunces are all in confederacy against him.

3 It is in disputes as in armies where the weaker side sets up false lights and makes a great noise to make the enemy believe them more numerous and strong than they really are.

I have known some men possessed of good qualities which were very serviceable to others but useless to themselves, like a sundial on the front of a house, to inform the neighbors and passengers but not the owner within.

If a man would register all his opinions upon love, politics, religion, learning, etc. beginning from his youth, and so go on to old age, what a bundle of inconsistencies and contradictions would appear at last. 4

Ambition often puts men upon doing the meanest offices; so climbing is performed in the same posture with creeping. 5

Ill company is like a dog who dirts those most whom he loves best.

No wise man ever wished to be younger.

The common fluency of speech in many men and most women is owing to a scarcity of matter and scarcity of words; for whoever is a master of language and hath a mind full of ideas, will be apt, in speaking, to hesitate upon the choice of both; whereas common speakers have only one set of ideas and one set of words to clothe them in, and these are always ready at the mouth: So people come faster out of a church when it is almost empty than when a crowd is at the door.

Motivation For Reading An idea can be one of the most enduring artifacts in the world. Thoughts that endure have two characteristics. They are short, and they offer a truth that holds good through the centuries. If the thought is a funny one, it is that much more memorable. Let the students imagine that they want to do one of three things: They want to pass on a piece of wisdom to a beloved grandchild. They want to write an epitaph for a friend's grave. They want to insult an enemy in a way that no one will ever forget. And for each of these, they want their words, to be remembered. Have them devise a sentence of twenty words or fewer that accomplishes their purpose.

Master Teacher Note Because he was learned in the classics, Swift was inclined toward the classical ideal of giving terse, pointed expression to his thoughts. The epigrammatic tradition in English poetry and prose issues from the great writers of ancient Greece and Rome.

Purpose-Setting Question Which of the following "Thoughts" apply to what you have observed of life?

1 **Discussion** How might this epigram be applied to the religious differences and wars in the Middle East and in Ireland? Can the class think of other disputes that this saying brings to mind?

2 **Discussion** Do you think this is true? Could you give an example from your own experience?

3 **Reading Strategy** Ask one of your students to rephrase this epigram in his or her own words.

4 **Discussion** What do your students think about this? Have they noticed any great changes in their own thoughts yet? Have their opinions changed as to what would make them happy? As to what they'd like to be when they grow up? As to where they might like to go to college?

5 **Literary Focus** Could this epigram be applied to Macbeth? Explain.

ANSWERS TO THINKING ABOUT THE SELECTION
Recalling

1. Swift compares armies to disputes. In this usage, those engaged in arguement might be either individuals or groups.
2. Swift says that no wise man ever wished to be younger.
3. He says that most forms of play resemble fighting.

6 Dignity, high station, or great riches are in some sort necessary to old men in order to keep the younger at a distance who are otherwise too apt to insult them upon the score of their age.

7 Every man desires to live long, but no man would be old.

Most sorts of diversion in men, children, and other animals are an imitation of fighting. 8

Very few men, properly speaking, live at present but are providing to live another time. 9

THINKING ABOUT THE SELECTION

Recalling

1. To what does Swift compare armies that attempt to confuse the enemy by means of false lights and great noise?
2. According to Swift, what does a wise man never wish?
3. What does Swift say that most forms of play resemble?

Interpreting

4. The American writer Ralph Waldo Emerson observed, "A foolish consistency is the hobgoblin of little minds." Of which Swift epigram does Emerson's thought remind you?
5. In your own words, what is Swift's view of the difference between the speaking habits of a master of language and a common speaker?

Applying

6. Using a standard book of quotations arranged by subject matter, find other epigrams on three of the subjects dealt with by Swift.

THINKING AND WRITING

Writing Epigrams

In an epigram, as in lyric poetry, every word counts. The aim is to express an original thought in a brief, witty, memorable way. Review the epigrams from Swift's *Thoughts on Various Subjects,* paying close attention to how Swift uses wit and antithesis. Then write three epigrams of your own. Take your time in planning and writing the epigrams. Revise carefully. Although a good epigram looks simple, it requires considerable thought and imagination.

6 **Discussion** Do you think that the young tend to insult the old about their age, or is it perhaps that the existence of youth in itself is an insult to the aged? Ask students to defend one side or the other of that question.

7 **Discussion** Compare this epigram with the one which says "No wise man ever wished to be younger." Is there another epigram here that would explain the seeming inconsistency between these two thoughts?

8 **Discussion** Ask your students for examples to illustrate this epigram, and also to refute it. Do they agree with Swift or disagree?

9 **Discussion** You might relate this epigram to the present day by saying "Life is not a dress rehearsal." You might also relate Swift's thought to these lines of John Greenleaf Whittier, "For all sad words of tongue or pen, the saddest are these: 'It might have been.'"

Writing Across the Curriculum For an extra credit assignment, have your students compare Swift's *Thoughts on Various Subjects* with Ben Franklin's maxims in *Poor Richard's Almanack.* Ask them to write a short essay comparing the personality of each writer as revealed through the tone of his epigrams. The eighteenth century was considered an age of great optimism, an age that celebrated mankind's rationality and believed in its perfectability. Which man seems more atuned to his century's outlook? One man was a statesman and the other a clergyman. Judging by the works your students have read by each man, who do they feel was best suited to his profession and why?

Interpreting

4. Swift's epigram concerning the "inconsistencies and contradictions" of a man's belief over the span of his lifetime is very nearly the antithesis of Emerson's observation; but perhaps Swift has in mind an intelligent man, such as himself.
5. A common speaker, having only a small repertoire of thoughts and vocabulary, is able to choose his response quickly. A master of language has so many possible responses that he hesitates before speaking.

Applying

6. Answers will differ. Possibilities are (a) Swift—"Every man desires to live long . . ." A long life may not be good enough, but a good life is long enough. (b) Swift—"Ambition often puts men upon doing the meanest offices . . ." Sell not virtue to purchase wealth, nor liberty to purchase power. (c) Swift—"Ill company is like a dog . . ." Act uprightly and despise calumny; dirt may stick to a mud wall, but not to polished marble. (d) Swift—"I have known some men possessed of good qualities . . ." Great good nature, without prudence, is a great misfortune.

(All the examples are by Benjamin Franklin, *Poor Richard's Almanack.*)

More About the Authors The first issue of the *Spectator* appeared two months after the *Tatler* was discontinued. Instead of trying to duplicate the *Tatler*, which the authors felt had tried to do too many things, they limited the *Spectator* to discussions of literature, manners, and morals. Each issue of the paper was limited to a single theme, the purpose of which was "to enliven morality with wit, and to temper wit with morality." Joseph Addison and Richard Steele delivered their opinions through an imaginary spokesman, the Spectator, whose signature appeared on every essay. From a position of amused detachment, the Spectator gently satirized the extravagances of fashionable life and gave sensible advice about how to correct them. Do you think a paper like the *Spectator* would be popular today? Why or why not?

BIOGRAPHIES

Joseph Addison (1672–1719)
Sir Richard Steele (1672–1729)

Although great writing seldom results from a team effort, the collaboration of Joseph Addison and Richard Steele is an exception to the general rule. Addison and Steele's work on two precedent-setting periodicals, *The Tatler* and *The Spectator,* has earned both authors a permanent place in literary history.

The two men, born a few weeks apart, were opposites in many ways. Joseph Addison, dignified, shy, and rather cold, enjoyed a reputation as a Latin scholar. Richard Steele, energetic, witty, and outgoing, was a man-about-town. Nevertheless, for most of their lives they were close friends, temperamentally different but sharing similar aims and values. Addison, born in a village in Wiltshire, England, and Steele, born in Dublin, Ireland, met as classmates at the Charterhouse School in London. They then went on to Oxford, where Addison graduated but Steele did not.

Instead, Steele took a commission in the army and immersed himself in the London literary scene. Steele had a tendency to live beyond his means, and in 1709, to earn some extra money, he started *The Tatler,* a periodical dealing with "gallantry, pleasure and entertainment." *The Tatler* proved highly popular in London coffeehouses, appearing three times a week from April 1709 to January 1711.

Since his undergraduate days, Addison had pursued a different path from that of Steele's. An outstanding student, he became a Fellow of Magdalen College, Oxford, and was invited by John Dryden to do translations of Virgil. After four years of European study and travel, he produced a hugely successful epic poem, "The Campaign," celebrating the Duke of Marlborough's victory at the Battle of Blenheim. In 1706 Addison was named undersecretary of state, and two yea s later was elected to the House of Commons, where he remained until his death.

In 1709, while serving briefly as secretary to the Lord Lieutenant of Ireland, he began reading the newly published *Tatler.* Despite Steele's pen name, "Isaac Bickerstaff," Addison recognized the writing as that of his old friend, and he began to submit contributions, notes, and suggestions. *The Tatler,* mostly the work of Steele, was succeeded by *The Spectator,* issued daily except Sunday from March 1711 to December 1712, and revived briefly in 1714. *The Spectator* was mostly the work of Addison, although Steele contributed regularly.

Objectives

1. To understand the informal essay
2. To write an informal essay

Teaching Portfolio: Support Material

Teacher Backup, pp. 00-00

Vocabulary Check, p. 00

Usage and Mechanics Worksheet, p. 00

Analyzing Literature Worksheet, p. 00

Critical Thinking and Reading Worksheet, p. 00

Language Worksheet, p. 00

Selection Test, p. 000

GUIDE FOR READING

Country Manners; Thoughts in Westminster Abbey

Literary Forms

Informal Essay. An *informal essay,* like a formal essay, presents the observations and opinions of its author, but it does so in a more relaxed and conversational manner. The informal essay is sometimes called a *familiar essay,* a *personal essay,* or, when printed in a magazine or newspaper, a *periodical essay.* The eighteenth century was a time in which the formal essay flourished. The formal essay was first used in England by Sir Francis Bacon. The informal essay, introduced by the sixteenth-century French writer Michel de Montaigne, had its English antecedents in John Dryden. An informal essay, less structured than a formal essay, is written in a personal, often anecdotal, sometimes humorous way.

The informal essays of Addison and Steele were published regularly in *The Tatler* and *The Spectator.* These two publications, which comprise the bulk of Addison and Steele's literary output, are notable for their wide-ranging, nonpolitical content and their graceful tone and style. Steele was the more imaginative writer, Addison the better craftsman. Both set a high standard for later periodical essayists and journalists to follow.

Look For

As you read the following two informal essay, notice the conversational style of the language. (Bear in mind that conversation in the eighteenth century was more formal than it is today.)

Writing

Think of a topic on which opinion varies. It should be a topic about which you have strong opinions of your own. Jot down notes about this topic. These notes should include not only support for your own viewpoint but also evidence that helps to refute the opposing viewpoint. Save these notes for later use.

Vocabulary

Knowing the following words will help you as you read "Country Manners" and "Thoughts in Westminster Abbey."

deferences (def′ər ən sez) *n.*: Courtesies (p. 552)
complaisance (kəm plā′z′ns) *n.*: Desire to be agreeable (p. 552)
modish (mōd′ish) *adj.*: Fashionable (p. 552)
superfluities (so͞o′pər flo͞o′ə tēz) *n.*: Excesses (p. 552)
precedency (pres′ə dən sē) *n.*: Priority because of rank (p. 552)
rostral (räs′trəl) *adj.*: Having a beaklike projection, or rostrum, as at the prow of a ship (p. 557)
repository (ri päz′ə tôr ē) *n.*: A center for accumulation and storage (p. 557)
timorous (tim′ər əs) *adj.*: Fearful; timid (p. 557)
inordinate (in ôr′d′n it) *adj.*: Beyond reasonable limits (p. 557)

Literary Focus In the *Spectator* Addison wrote about the disadvantages of the informal essay over a long, formal literary work. "We must immediately fall into our Subject, and treat every part of it in a lively Manner, or our Papers are thrown by as dull and insipid: Our Matter must lie close together, and either be wholly new in itself, or in the Turn it receives from our Expressions. . . . it is often expected that every Sheet should be a kind of Treatise, and make out in thought what it wants in Bulk; that a Point of Humour should be worked up in all its Parts; and a subject touched upon in its most essential articles, without the Repetitions, Tautologies, and Enlargements that are indulged to longer Labours. An Essay Writer must . . . give the Virtue of a full draught in a few Drops." Discuss whether you agree with Addison's points.

Look For Write the following sentence from the *Spectator* on the chalkboard: "There has happened another revolution in the point of good breeding which relates to the conversation among men of mode and which I cannot but look upon as very extraordinary." To emphasize the difference between informal language in the eighteenth century and today, have students reword the sentence, using informal English.

Writing Ask your students to tell what topics they have thought of. Select a few for class discussion. Then invite the class to offer *pro* and *con* opinions.

Vocabulary Have students study the vocabulary words on their own. Discuss any words that need further explanation. Then have students think of antonyms for all the words except *rostral* and *repository.* Ask students which set of words they would use to describe people in high society, and which set of words would describe ordinary people.

Motivation for Reading Have students discuss this quotation "good breeding shows itself most where to an ordinary eye it appears the least." Explain that it is taken from the excerpt they are about to read.

Master Teacher Note Bring in pictures illustrating changes in fashion over the centuries. Discuss how attitudes toward fashion change.

Purpose-Setting Question Look for ways in which the authors reveal themselves in the essay.

1 **Discussion** Define deferences, condescensions, and submissions and explain why they would not be part of blunt and natural behavior.

2 **Discussion** Why do country people have manners of the last age? Why is an excess of good breeding evidence of its lack?

3 **Discussion** Which group—justices' wives or duchesses—would one normally expect to show excesses of good breeding? What point is being made here?

4 **Literary Focus** What does the statement about "rural politeness" tell you about the personality of the author? Do you think the anecdotes that follow are exaggerated? What element do the anecdotes add to the essay? Summarize the author's statements about good breeding up to this point.

Country Manners

Joseph Addison and Richard Steele

The Spectator, July 17, 1711

The first and most obvious reflections which arise in a man who changes the city for the country are upon the different manners of the people whom he meets with in those two different scenes of life. By manners I do not mean morals, but behavior and good breeding as they show themselves in the town and in the country.

And here, in the first place, I must observe a very great revolution that has happened in this article of good breeding.
1 Several obliging deferences, condescensions, and submissions, with many outward forms and ceremonies that accompany them, were first of all brought up among the politer part of mankind, who lived in courts and cities and distinguished themselves from the rustic part of the species (who on all occasions acted bluntly and naturally) by such a mutual complaisance and intercourse of civilities. These forms of conversation by degrees multiplied and grew troublesome; the modish world found too great a constraint in them, and have therefore thrown most of them aside. Conversation was so encumbered with show and ceremony that it stood in need of a reformation to retrench its superfluities and restore its natural good sense and beauty. At present, therefore, an unconstrained carriage and a certain openness of behavior are the height of good breeding. The fashionable world is grown free and easy; our manners sit more loose upon us; nothing is so modish as an agreeable negligence. In a word, good breeding shows itself most where to an ordinary eye it appears the least.

If after this we look on the people of mode in the country, we find in them the manners of the last age. They have no sooner fetched themselves up to the fashion of a polite world, but the town has dropped 2
them, and are nearer to the first stage of nature than to those refinements which formerly reigned in the court and still prevail in the country. One may now know a man that never conversed in the world by his excess of good breeding. A polite country squire[1] shall make you as many bows in half an hour as would serve a courtier[2] for a week. There is infinitely more to do about place and precedency in a meeting of justices' 3
wives than in an assembly of duchesses.

This rural politeness is very troublesome to a man of my temper who generally takes the chair that is next me and walks first or last, in the front or in the rear, as chance directs. I have known my friend Sir Roger's dinner almost cold before the company could adjust the ceremonial and be prevailed upon to sit down; and have hearti- 4
ly pitied my old friend when I have seen him forced to pick and cull his guests, as they sat at the several parts of his table, that he might drink their healths according to their respective ranks and qualities. Honest Will Wimble, who I should have thought had

1. squire n.: A country gentleman or landed proprietor.
2. courtier (kôr′ tē ər) *n.*: An attendant at a royal court.

been altogether uninfected with ceremony, gives me abundance of trouble in this particular. Though he has been fishing all the morning, he will not help himself at dinner till I am served. When we are going out of the hall, he runs behind me; and last night, as we were walking in the fields, stopped short at a stile till I came up to it and, upon my making signs to him to get over, told me, with a serious smile, that sure I believed they had no manners in the country.

There has happened another revolution in the point of good breeding which relates to the conversation among men of mode and which I cannot but look upon as very extraordinary. It was certainly one of the first distinctions of a well-bred man to express everything that had the most remote appearance of being obscene in modest terms and distant phrases; whilst the clown, who had no such delicacy of conception and ex-
5 pression, clothed his ideas in those plain homely terms that are the most obvious and natural. This kind of good manners was perhaps carried to an excess so as to make conversation too stiff, formal, and precise; for which reason (as hypocrisy in one age is generally succeeded by atheism in another) conversation is in a great measure relapsed into the first extreme; so that at present several of our men of the town, and particularly those who have been polished in
6 France, make use of the most coarse, uncivilized words in our language and utter themselves often in such a manner as a clown would blush to hear.

This infamous piece of good breeding, which reigns among the coxcombs[3] of the town, has not yet made its way into the country; and as it is impossible for such an irrational way of conversation to last long among a people that makes any profession of religion or show of modesty, if the country gentlemen get into it, they will certainly be left in the lurch. Their good breeding will come too late to them, and they will be thought a parcel of lewd clowns, while they fancy themselves talking together like men of wit and pleasure.

As the two points of good breeding, which I have hitherto insisted upon, regard behavior and conversation, there is a third which turns upon dress. In this too the country are very much behindhand. The rural beaus are not yet got out of the fashion that took place at the time of the Revolution[4] but ride about the country in red coats and laced hats; while the women in many parts are still trying to outvie one another in the height of their headdresses.

But a friend of mine, who is now upon the western circuit, having promised to give me an account of the several modes and fashions that prevail in the different parts of the nation through which he passes, I shall defer the enlarging upon this last topic till I have received a letter from him, which I expect every post.

---

3. coxcombs *n.*: Silly, vain people.

4. the Revolution: The "Glorious Revolution" of 1688, during which James II was expelled from the throne.

5 **Clarification** As it is used here, the word *clown* means an "uncouth person," or a "yokel." To what group is the clown's language comparable?

6 **Discussion** What does the author think about this latest example of good breeding? What is ironic about such an expression of "good breeding"?

Reading Strategy Summarize the three points of good breeding the essay discusses.

THINKING ABOUT THE SELECTION

Recalling

1. (a) What happened in the first "great revolution . . . of good breeding"? (b) Where did the revolution occur? (c) What brought about the change?
2. How did "country gentlemen" react to the change in city manners?
3. What annoys the writer about the behavior of (a) Sir Roger? (b) Honest Will Wimble?
4. (a) What did the second revolution in good breeding involve? (b) Where did it occur? (c) Why might its effects make "a clown . . . blush"?
5. (a) How has the country reacted to the revolution in conversation? (b) In what other area of good breeding may country gentlemen someday react?

Interpreting

6. Why do you think the country lags behind the city in manners?
7. Why would a city dweller who had once expected an "excess of good breeding" now be annoyed by it?
8. (a) To which group mentioned in the essay does the writer belong? (b) Why must he await a letter before he can comment on the fashion prevailing in the country?

Applying

9. In the United States today, what are the differences, if any, between country manners and city manners? Explain.
10. In nineteenth-century America, Walt Whitman wrote, "To the real artist in humanity, what are called bad manners are often the most picturesque and significant of all." How do you think Addison and Steele would have reacted to Whitman's comment? Explain your answer.

ANALYZING LITERATURE

Understanding Informal Essay

As its name implies, an informal essay expresses the observations and opinions of its author in a personal, conversational way. The informal essay is less rigid than the formal essay. The views stated can be highly individual, even outrageous. Although Addison and Steele are seldom outrageous, they do express unequivocal, thought-provoking opinions.

1. For each of the three "points of good breeding" in "Country Manners," find one statement that you consider highly opinionated.
2. A personal essay shows clear signs of having been written by the specific individual whose opinions it expresses. What are three such signs in "Country Manners"?

THINKING AND WRITING

Writing an Informal Essay

Use the topic that you chose for Writing, page 551, or else select a new topic on which opinions vary. Possible general topic areas include politics, sports, arts, and leisure. If you are using the topic you chose earlier, you have existing notes for it. If not, begin by stating your opinion clearly in one sentence. Then jot down notes before you start to write. When writing the first draft of your informal essay, use a personal, conversational style. In revising the first draft, pay close attention to tone. A good conversational style is friendly and down-to-earth but not overly clever.

Answers

ANSWERS TO THINKING ABOUT THE SELECTION

Recalling

1. (a) Members of polite society introduced mannerisms into conversation that distinguished them from rustics. (b) The revolution occurred in the courts and cities. (c) Modish society rejected the forms of conversation as too complicated and troublesome.
2. Country gentlemen retained the conversational mannerisms after they had been rejected by city folk.
3. (a) Sir Roger lets his dinner grow cold while he follows outmoded ceremonies of politeness. (b) Will Wimble insists on deferring to his guest at the dinner table and even in the fields.
4. (a) The second revolution involved abandoning polite words in favor of obscene ones. (b) It occurred first in France and was brought to London. (c) The words were so obscene and uttered in such a manner that even a boor would blush.
5. (a) The country has ignored it. (b) Country gentlemen may someday react to a change in dress.

Interpreting

6. New ideas usually begin in centers of intellectual activity; in the country, people are more concerned with simple pleasures.
7. Styles have changed; the excesses of good breeding are now perceived for exactly what they are—ridiculous conventions that stand in the way of common sense.
8. (a) The writer considers himself a member of the "politer part of mankind." (b) He is unaware of what is in vogue in different parts of the nation.

Applying

9. Answers will differ. A possible answer is that modern transportation and communication have helped to bridge the gap between country and city; as a result, the differences are far less pronounced.

ANSWERS TO ANALYZING LITERATURE

1. Three highly opinionated statements are (1) ". . . good breeding shows itself most where to an ordinary eye it appears the least." (2) ". . . as it is impossible for such an irrational way of conversation to last long among a people that makes any profession of religion or show of modesty, if the country gentlemen get into it, they will certainly be left in the lurch." (3) "The rural beaus are not yet got out of the fashion that took place at the time of the Revolution . . ."
2. Three signs are (1) "I have known my friend Sir Roger's dinner almost cold . . ." (2) Honest Will Wimble . . . gives me abundance of trouble in this particular." (3) ". . . I shall defer the enlarging upon this last topic until I have received a letter from him, which I expect every post."

Thoughts in Westminster Abbey[1]

Joseph Addison and Richard Steele

The Spectator, March 30, 1711

When I am in a serious humor, I very often walk by myself in Westminster Abbey; where the gloominess of the place, and the
1 use to which it is applied, with the solemnity of the building, and the condition of the people who lie in it, are apt to fill the mind with a kind of melancholy, or rather thoughtfulness, that is not disagreeable. I yesterday passed a whole afternoon in the churchyard, the cloisters, and the church, amusing myself with the tombstones and inscriptions that I met with in those several regions of the dead. Most of them recorded nothing else of the buried person, but that he was born upon one day, and died upon another: the whole history of his life being comprehended in those two circumstances, that are common to all mankind. I could not but look upon these registers of existence,
2 whether of brass or marble, as a kind of satire upon the departed persons; who had left no other memorial of them, but that they were born and that they died. They put me in mind of several persons mentioned in the
3 battles of heroic poems, who have sounding names given them, for no other reason but that they may be killed, and are celebrated for nothing but being knocked on the head.

Upon my going into the church, I entertained myself with the digging of a grave; and saw in every shovelful of it that was thrown up, the fragment of a bone or skull intermixed with a kind of fresh moldering earth that some time or other had a place in the composition of a human body. Upon this I began to consider with myself what innumerable multitudes of people lay confused together under the pavement of that ancient cathedral; how men and women, friends and enemies, priests and soldiers, monks and prebendaries,[2] were crumbled amongst 4
one another, and blended together in the same common mass; how beauty, strength, and youth, with old age, weakness, and deformity, lay undistinguished in the same promiscuous heap of matter.

After having thus surveyed this great magazine of mortality, as it were, in the 5
lump; I examined it more particularly by the accounts which I found on several of the monuments which are raised in every quarter of that ancient fabric. Some of them were covered with such extravagant epitaphs that, if it were possible for the dead person to be acquainted with them, he would blush at the praises which his friends have bestowed upon him. There are others so excessively modest, that they deliver the character of the person departed in Greek or

1. **Westminster Abbey:** A famous church in Westminster, England, where English monarchs are crowned, and where English monarchs and many famous writers and statesmen are buried.

2. **prebendaries** (preb′ ən der′ ēz) *n.*: In the Church of England, honorary clergymen.

Motivation for Reading Ask students if they have ever wandered through a cemetery and read the inscriptions on the gravestones. Discuss the kinds of inscriptions they read and how those on older tombstones differed from more modern inscriptions.

Master Teacher Note Have students look at the painting of Westminster Abbey on page 556. Point out that because authors had to be invited to be buried in Poets' Corner and had to pay a fee, it was a very prestigious place. Ben Jonson, for example, was invited but did not have the money. He asked them to give him half a space, which was all he could afford, and he would be buried standing up. Supposedly, this was done. His stone is only half the size of the others.

Purpose-Setting Question How is the author affected by his meditative ramblings? How does he come to view the activities that engross most people?

Thematic Idea You might read this essay in conjunction with Gray's "Elegy Written in a Country Churchyard," page 598.

1 **Discussion** Why does the Abbey have the effect the author mentions?

2 **Discussion** Why does the author call the inscriptions a "satire"?

3 **Literary Focus** What element of an informal essay is found in these lines?

4 **Critical Thinking and Reading** What is the effect of the accumulation of similar phrases and words in these lines?

5 **Literary Focus** What does the author mean by "magazine of mortality"?

Challenge Encourage your **more advanced** students to read the Talk of the Town pages of the *New Yorker.* Invite them to report, either orally or in writing, on the similarities and differences between the informal essays of the *Spectator* and those of the *New Yorker.*

6 Discussion What does this mean in light of what you have learned about Poets' Corner?

7 Discussion How would a foreigner draw conclusions about a nation's ignorance or politeness from its tombstones?

8 Discussion According to the author, what is incongruous about this picture?

Humanities Note

Fine art, *St. Edmunds Chapel in Westminster Abbey,* John Fulleylove. The British artist John Fulleylove (1845–1908) specialized in painting and drawing landscapes, gardens, buildings, and interiors. He traveled through England, France, and Italy in search of subjects. His works were exhibited for sale at various galleries and societies in England.

In 1904 a group of excellent pencil sketches were exhibited at the Gouper Gallery in London. Among them was this view of the St. Edmunds Chapel in Westminster Abbey. Always noteworthy as a fine architectural draftsman, Fullylove shows his skill in this drawing. Every detail of the carvings, arches, and tombs is confidently and solidly drawn with perfect perspective. This drawing was reproduced in color in 1907 as an illustration in a guidebook. The accuracy and detail of Fullylove's works made them particularly desirable as illustrations.

You might ask the following questions:

1. What information about Westminster Abbey does this drawing give?
2. How is a drawing like this similar to and different from a photograph? Which do you think is more effective? Why?

Hebrew, and by that means are not understood once in a twelvemonth. In the poetical
quarter, I found there were poets who had no
6 monuments, and monuments which had no
poets. I observed, indeed, that the present war[3] had filled the church with many of these uninhabited monuments, which had been erected to the memory of persons whose bodies were perhaps buried in the plains of Blenheim,[4] or in the bosom of the ocean.

I could not but be very much delighted with several modern epitaphs, which are written with great elegance of expression and justness of thought, and therefore do
honor to the living as well as to the dead. As
7 a foreigner is very apt to conceive an idea of
the ignorance or politeness of a nation, from the turn of their public monuments and inscriptions, they should be submitted to the perusal of men of learning and genius, before they are put in execution. Sir Cloudesly Shovel's[5] monument has very often given me great offense: instead of the brave rough English admiral, which was the distinguishing character of that plain gallant man, he is represented on his tomb by
the figure of a beau, dressed in a long peri-
wig,[6] and reposing himself upon velvet cush- 8
ions under a canopy of state. The inscription is answerable to the monument; for instead of celebrating the many remarkable actions he had performed in the service of his country, it acquaints us only with the manner of his death, in which it was impossible for him to reap any honor. The Dutch,

3. the present war: The War of the Spanish Succession, in which England and several other European nations fought against an alliance led by the French and Spanish.
4. Blenheim (blen′ əm): Village in western Bavaria that was the site of an important battle (1704) during the War of the Spanish Succession.

5. Sir Cloudesly Shovel (1650–1707): English admiral and commander of the British fleet.
6. periwig (per′ ə wig′) *n.*: A type of wig often worn by men during the seventeenth and eighteenth centuries.

ST. EDMUND'S CHAPEL, WESTMINSTER ABBEY
John Fulleylove

whom we are apt to despise for want of
genius, show an infinitely greater taste of
antiquity and politeness in their buildings
9 and works of this nature, than what we
meet with in those of our own country. The
monuments of their admirals, which have
been erected at the public expense, represent them like themselves; and are adorned
with rostral crowns and naval ornaments,
with beautiful festoons of seaweed, shells,
and coral.
10 But to return to our subject. I have left
the repository of our English kings for the
contemplation of another day, when I shall
find my mind disposed for so serious an
amusement. I know that entertainments of
this nature are apt to raise dark and dismal
thoughts in timorous minds and gloomy imaginations; but for my own part, though I am
11 always serious, I do not know what it is to be
melancholy; and can therefore take a view of
nature in her deep and solemn scenes, with
the same pleasure as in her most gay and
delightful ones. By this means I can improve
myself with those objects which others con- 12
sider with terror. When I look upon the
tombs of the great, every emotion of envy
dies in me; when I read the epitaphs of the
beautiful, every inordinate desire goes out;
when I meet with the grief of parents upon
a tombstone, my heart melts with compassion; when I see the tomb of the parents themselves, I consider the vanity of
grieving for those whom we must quickly follow: when I see kings lying by those
who deposed them, when I consider rival wits 13
placed side by side, or the holy men that
divided the world with their contests and
disputes, I reflect with sorrow and astonishment on the little competitions, factions,
and debates of mankind. When I read the
several dates of the tombs, of some that died
yesterday, and some six hundred years ago,
I consider that great day when we shall all
of us be contemporaries, and make our appearance together.

9 **Discussion** What irony is implied here?

10 **Literary Focus** What is the effect of the sentence fragment?

11 **Discussion** What is the difference between being serious and melancholy?

12 **Discussion** Why might objects that fill others with terror affect the author in a different way?

13 **Literary Focus** You might wish to read the latter part of this paragraph aloud. The prose style here blends richness and depth of feeling with neoclassical balance and elegance. Ask your students what the "great day" is that the author alludes to.

THINKING ABOUT THE SELECTION

Recalling

1. (a) At what times does the author say he visits Westminster Abbey? (b) Why does he go then?
2. (a) Who was Sir Cloudsley Shovel? (b) What kind of man was he? (b) Why does the author object to Shovel's monument?
3. On what does the author reflect with "sorrow and astonishment"?

Interpreting

4. What two kinds of epitaphs seem to offend the author most?
5. The author states that some modern epitaphs "do honor to the living as well as to the dead." (a) What does he mean? (b) Why does he think proposed monuments and epitaphs should be reviewed by "men of learning and genius"?
6. What does the author mean by "that great day when we shall all of us be contemporaries"?

Applying

7. At the end of the essay the author lists a number of ironies he sees in Westminster Abbey. (a) Which of them seems the most poignant to you? (b) What ironies can you think of that might be added to the list?

Answers

ANSWERS TO THINKING ABOUT THE SELECTION

Recalling

1. (a) The author goes to Westminster Abbey when he is feeling serious. (b) He goes then because the place fills his mind with an agreeable thoughtfulness.
2. (a) Sir Cloudesly Shovel was an English admiral. (b) He was a brave, plain, and gallant man who had served his country well. (c) The picture on the monument bears no resemblance to the man and the inscription honors his death rather than his life.
3. He reflects with "sorrow and astonishment" on the competitions, factions, and debates of mankind.

Interpreting

4. The author is annoyed by overly extravagant or excessively modest epitaphs.
5. (a) Good epitaphs honor the person who has died and do not offend those who read them. (b) Men of learning and genius would presumably make sure that poorly written epitaphs did not appear on tombstones.
6. He means Judgment Day, when the dead shall arise from their graves.

Applying

7. Answers will differ. Possible answers are: (a) The most poignant concerns meeting with the grief of parents upon a tombstone. (b) Other ironies include beggars' lying next to the wealthy, murderers next to those murdered, and the religious next to atheists.

More About the Author Alexander Pope was the first English poet to support himself solely by his writings. Being a Catholic prevented him both from holding public office and from seeking out a wealthy patron—means by which many other artists had gotten support so they might continue their work. Today the role of government aid for the arts is hotly debated. Ask students for their views on whether government should support the arts.

ALEXANDER POPE

1688–1744

From the age of eight or nine, Alexander Pope knew that he wanted to become not just a poet but a great poet. Before he was twenty-one, his *Essay on Criticism* had brought him to the attention of the leading literary figures of England. His satiric *The Rape of the Lock,* probably the best pseudo-epic poem in English, followed when he was twenty-four. Despite a crippling childhood disease and persistent ill health, Pope triumphantly achieved his boyhood ambition. A brilliant satirist in verse, he gave his name (the Age of Pope and Swift) to the literary era in which he lived and wrote.

Born into the Roman Catholic family of a London linen merchant, Pope had to struggle for position. After the expulsion of King James II, English Catholics could not legally vote, hold office, attend a university, or live within ten miles of London. To comply with the rule of residency, his family moved to Binfield, near Windsor Forest, a rural setting where Pope spent his formative years writing poetry, studying the classics, and becoming broadly self-educated. Pope's physical problems were as severe as his religious ones. Deformed by tuberculosis of the spine, Pope stood only about four and a half feet tall—"the little Alexander whom the women laugh at," he said—and he suffered from nervousness and excruciating headaches throughout his life. In 1718 Pope moved to a five-acre estate at Twickenham (twit′ nam), a village on the Thames, where he lived until his death.

Although Pope, "the Wasp of Twickenham," is more often remembered for his quarrels than for his cordiality, he became friends, and remained so for life, with members of a Tory group that included Jonathan Swift, John Gay, and Lord Bolingbroke. Pope instigated the formation of the Scriberlus Club, the purpose of which was to ridicule what its members regarded as "false tastes in learning." The satiric emphasis of the club probably gave some impetus to the writing of Swift's *Gulliver's Travels,* Gay's *Beggar's Opera,* and Pope's *The Dunciad*—a "burlesque heroick" attack on Pope's literary enemies (most of whom are now forgotten).

In the 1730's Pope's writing turned increasingly philosophical. He embarked on a massive work concerning morality and government, but completed only *An Essay on Man* and *Moral Essays*. Nevertheless, the entire body of his work is sufficient for critics today to accord him exceptionally high praise. The twentieth-century poet Edith Sitwell calls Pope "perhaps the most flawless artist our race has yet produced."

Objectives

1. To introduce the mock epic as a literary form
2. To infer the author's purpose in writing
3. To write about tone in a mock epic

Teaching Portfolio: Support Material

Teacher Backup, pp. 000

Vocabulary Check, p. 00

Usage and Mechanics Worksheet, p. 00

Analyzing Literature Worksheet, p. 00

Critical Thinking and Reading Worksheet, p. 00

Language Worksheet, p. 00

Selection Test, p. 000

GUIDE FOR READING

from The Rape of the Lock

Literary Forms

Mock Epic. A mock epic is a long, humorous narrative poem that treats a trivial subject in the grand, elevated style of a true epic such as the *Odyssey* or *Paradise Lost*. Sometimes called a *mock-heroic* poem, this literary form reached the height of its popularity in the eighteenth century. The *conventions,* or standard elements, of an epic require both the characters and the action to be of heroic proportions. The theme of a true epic concerns fundamental human problems. In a classical epic, gods and goddesses oversee and sometimes intervene in human affairs. When these conventions of an epic are satirically applied to a subject of little consequence, the result can be highly amusing.

Look For

As you read the excerpts from *The Rape of the Lock,* look for the conventions of a true or classical epic that Pope uses satirically.

Writing

Freewrite about an incident you have heard or read about that you think has been magnified beyond its importance. In your writing, carry the incident to an illogical extreme, as the writer of a mock epic would do.

Vocabulary

Knowing the following words will help you as you read the excerpts from *The Rape of the Lock.*

obliquely (ə blēk'lē) *adv.*: At a slant (III, l. 20)
plebian (pli bē'ən) *adj.*: Common; ordinary (III, l. 54)
destitute (des'tə to͞ot) *adj.*: Lacking (III, l. 63)
refulgent (ri ful'jənt) *adj.*: Shining; radiant (III, l. 77)
desist (di zist') *v.*: Stop (III, l. 121)
assignations (as'ig nā'shənz) *n.*: Appointments to meet (III, l. 169)
doughty (dout'ē) *adj.*: Brave (V, l. 33)

Literary Focus Explain to all of your students, but especially to the **less advanced,** that the essence of a mock epic is the incongruity between style and subject: the style is dignified and elevated; the subject is ordinary, and even trivial.

Look For In reading the excerpts, students should be aware of these conventions of a true epic and the substitutions that Pope employs: A feminine protagonist replaces the male hero. A card game replaces the epic battle. Sylphs and gnomes replace the gods and goddesses who intervene in the events.

Writing In writing about the incident, remind students of Swift's admonition to satirists: ridicule the foible and not the person.
". . . malice never was his aim;
He lash'd the vice, but spar'd
the name:
No individual could resent,
Where thousands equally were
meant.
His satire points at no defect
But what all mortals may
correct . . ."
[from "Verses on the Death of
Dr. Swift," by Jonathan Swift]

Vocabulary Choose one student to lead the class in a discussion of the words and their meanings.

Motivation for Reading What social manners and human behavior are ripe for satirizing today? What literary form would seem appropriate as a vehicle for such satire?

Master Teacher Note Pope first published the poem in 1712 in two cantos. Two years later he expanded the work to five cantos. This later version included the supernatural elements. These were taken from Rosicrucian mythology, in which the four elements—earth, air, fire, and water—were inhabited by sylphs and gnomes. Even though invisible, they were active in human affairs—sylphs as guardian spirits and gnomes as mischief makers. In this poem Ariel is the chief sylph and Belinda's guardian.

Reading Strategy Most poetry—and certainly the mock epic—benefits from being read aloud. Pick two accomplished readers to take the parts of Belinda and the Baron in Canto V. Choose a third student to act as the narrator. Have this canto read aloud by the three students, interpreting the lines as they might be delivered on stage.

Purpose-Setting Question What elements of an epic do you find in these excerpts?

1 **Literary Focus** Note the use of zeugma (zo͞og'me), a figure of speech Pope was fond of employing. This is a device in which a word—in this case, *fall*—modifies or governs two or more words, although it makes sense with only one. The word *take,* in line 8, is another example of the figure. Ask students to be alert for this rhetorical device in the poem.

from # The Rape of the Lock

Alexander Pope

The Rape of the Lock, *a mock epic, or a humorous poem written in the style of and recalling situations from the famous epic poems of Homer, Virgil, and Milton, is based on an actual incident. When Lord Petre, a wealthy baron, cut a lock of hair from the head of the beautiful Arabella Fermor, a great quarrel developed between the lady's family and the family of Lord Petre. Following the incident, Pope's friend John Caryll suggested that Pope write a poem mocking the trivial incident to point out the absurdity of the families' reactions. In writing* The Rape of the Lock, *however, Pope went far beyond the ridiculous incident that inspired it. The poem, filled with allusions to the great literary works of the past, is a poignant appraisal of the social manners and human behavior of the time.*

The first of the poem's five cantos opens with a formal statement of theme and an invocation to the Muse for poetic inspiration. Then Belinda, the poem's heroine, receives a warning from the sylph Ariel that a dreadful event will take place in her immediate future. In Canto II, during a boat ride on the Thames, an adventurous baron admires Belinda's hair and is determined to cut two bright locks from her head and keep them as a prize. Aware of the baron's desires, Ariel urges the spirits to protect Belinda.

Canto III

Close by those meads, forever crowned with flowers,
Where Thames with pride surveys his rising towers,
There stands a structure of majestic frame,[1]
Which from the neighboring Hampton takes its name.
Here Britain's statesmen oft the fall foredoom
Of foreign tyrants, and of nymphs at home;
Here thou, great Anna![2] whom three realms obey,

---

1. structure . . . frame: Hampton Court, a royal palace near London.

2. Anna: Queen Anne, who ruled England, Ireland, and Scotland from 1702 through 1714.

THE BARGE, 1895–96
Aubrey Beardsley

Dost sometimes counsel take—and sometimes tea.
    Hither the heroes and the nymphs resort,
To taste awhile the pleasures of a court;
In various talk th' instructive hours they passed,
Who gave the ball, or paid the visit last;
One speaks the glory of the British Queen,
And one describes a charming Indian screen;
A third interprets motions, looks, and eyes;
At every word a reputation dies.

Humanities Note

Fine art, *The Barge* by Aubrey Beardsley. The British illustrator Aubrey Beardsley (1872–1898) achieved in his six productive years a strange and wonderful style that would have taken many artists a lifetime. His only formal art training was one year of lessons at the Westminster School of Art in London. His lifelong illness, tuberculosis, did not leave him the strength to explore oil painting or any form of artistic expression other than the pen-and-ink drawing for which he is remembered. He received his first illustration commission by chance through a bookseller he frequented. This commission led to many others and to fame as an illustrator. His career ended abruptly with his death at the age of twenty-six.

The illustrations for Alexander Pope's "The Rape of the Lock" were done for an 1896 edition of that work. *The Barge* is one of the nine pen-and-ink drawings Beardsley produced. In executing this drawing, he introduced a technique of using dots to give texture and variety to his usually severe lines. Embellished decoratively, this drawing still demonstrates Beardsley's elegance of form and his grasp of the formal rules of good composition.

You might want to use this question for discussion: Has the artist approached this drawing of Belinda with sincerity or satire? Explain.

2 **Discussion** What kind of world does Belinda live in? How "instructive" are the subjects Belinda and her friends talk about?

3 Discussion What elements of a card game are appropriate for imitating a battle?

4 Clarification Belinda leads with the ace of spaces. Nine tricks make up the game. To win, one person must take at least five.

5 Clarification She plays the two of spades.

Snuff, or the fan,[3] supply each pause of chat,
With singing, laughing, ogling, and all that.
    Meanwhile, declining from the noon of day,
The sun obliquely shoots his burning ray;
The hungry judges soon the sentence sign,
And wretches hang that jurymen may dine;
The merchant from th' Exchange[4] returns in peace,
And the long labors of the toilet[5] cease.
Belinda now, whom thirst of fame invites,
Burns to encounter two adventurous knights,
At omber[6] singly to decide their doom;
And swells her breast with conquests yet to come.
Straight the three bands prepare in arms to join,
Each band the number of the sacred nine.[7]
Soon as she spreads her hand, th' aerial guard
Descend, and sit on each important card:
First Ariel perched upon a Matadore,[8]
Then each, according to the rank they bore;
3 For sylphs, yet mindful of their ancient race,
Are, as when women, wondrous fond of place.
    Behold, four kings in majestry revered,
With hoary whiskers and a forky beard;
And four fair queens whose hands sustain a flower,
Th' expressive emblem of their softer power;
Four knaves in garbs succinct,[9] a trusty band,
Caps on their heads, and halberts[10] in their hand;
And particolored troops, a shining train,
Draw forth to combat on the velvet plain.
    The skilful nymph reviews her force with care:
Let spades be trumps! she said, and trumps they were.
    Now move to war her sable Matadores,
In show like leaders of the swarthy Moors.
4 Spadillio[11] first, unconquerable Lord!
Led off two captive trumps, and swept the board.
5 As many more Manillio[12] forced to yield,
And marched a victor from the verdant field.[13]

---

3. snuff . . . fan: At the time, gentlemen commonly took snuff, and ladies usually carried a fan.
4. Exchange: The London financial center where merchants, bankers, and brokers conducted business.
5. toilet: Dressing tables.
6. omber: A popular card game.
7. sacred nine: A reference to the nine Muses of Greek mythology.
8. Matadore: A powerful card that could take a trick.
9. succinct (sək siŋkt′): Belted.
10. halberts: Long-handled weapons.
11. Spadillio: The ace of spades.
12. Manillio: The two of spades.
13. verdant field: The card table, covered with a green cloth.

Him Basto[14] followed, but his fate more hard 6
Gained but one trump and one plebeian card.
With his broad saber next, a chief in years, 7
The hoary majesty of spades appears,
Puts forth one manly leg, to sight revealed,
The rest, his many-colored robe concealed.
The rebel knave, who dares his prince engage,
Proves the just victim of his royal rage.
Even mighty Pam,[15] that kings and queens o'erthrew
And mowed down armies in the fights of loo,
Sad chance of war! now destitute of aid,
Falls undistinguished by the victor spade!
　　Thus far both armies to Belinda yield;
Now to the baron fate inclines the field.
His warlike Amazon her host invades, 8
Th' imperial consort of the crown of spades.
The club's black tyrant first her victim died,
Spite of his haughty mien, and barbarous pride.
What boots[16] the regal circle on his head,
His giant limbs, in state unwieldy spread;
That long behind he trails his pompous robe,
And, of all monarchs, only grasps the globe?
　　The baron now his diamonds pours apace; 9
Th' embroidered king who shows but half his face,
And his refulgent queen, with powers combined 10
Of broken troops an easy conquest find.
Clubs, diamonds, hearts, in wild disorder seen,
With throngs promiscuous strew the level green.
Thus when dispersed a routed army runs,
Of Asia's troops, and Afric's sable sons,
With like confusion different nations fly,
Of various habit, and of various dye,
The pierced battalions disunited fall,
In heaps on heaps; one fate o'erwhelms them all.
　　The knave of diamonds tries his wily arts, 11
And wins (oh shameful chance!) the queen of hearts.
At this, the blood the virgin's cheek forsook,
A livid paleness spreads o'er all her look;
She sees, and trembles at th' approaching ill,
Just in the jaws of ruin, and codille.[17]
And now (as oft in some distempered state)
On one nice trick depends the general fate.

14. Basto: The ace of clubs.
15. Pam: The knave of clubs, the highest card in the game called "100."
16. what boots: Of what benefit is.
17. codille: A term meaning the defeat of a hand of cards.

6 Clarification She plays the ace of clubs, the third highest card.

7 Clarification She plays the king of spades and wins her fourth trick. But this uses up the last of her trump cards.

8 Clarification She plays the king of clubs, which the Baron trumps with his queen of spades.

9 Clarification The Baron plays his high diamonds, for Belinda is out of trump cards.

10 Clarification He takes a trick with the queen of diamonds

11 Clarification His jack of diamonds takes her queen of hearts, since she cannot follow suit.

12 **Clarification** The Baron plays his ace of hearts. Since hearts are not trumps, though, this card is worth less than the face cards of the heart suit. Belinda wins.

Humanities Note

Fine art, *The Rape of the Lock* by Aubrey Beardsley. The drawing entitled *The Rape of the Lock* is one of the nine produced by Aubrey Beardsley for an 1896 edition of Alexander Pope's comic poem of the same name. The satiric nature of the poem appealed to Beardsley's sense of the burlesque. He depicts the incident of the cutting of the hair with a mocking humor comparable to Pope's. The rococo extravagance of the drawing room and attire of the figures also matches the satiric exaggeration of the situation by Pope. The artist's appreciation of the poet's wit and humor adds an extra element to these drawings.

You may wish to discuss the following with your class: In his poem Pope glorifies a trivial incident. Would you say that the artist does the same in his drawing? Explain.

12 An ace of hearts steps forth; the king unseen
Lurked in her hand, and mourned his captive queen.
He springs to vengeance with an eager pace,
And falls like thunder on the prostrate ace.
The nymph exulting fills with shouts the sky;
The walls, the woods, and long canals reply.
Oh thoughtless mortals! ever blind to fate,
Too soon dejected, and too soon elate.
Sudden, these honors shall be snatched away,
And cursed forever this victorious day.

THE RAPE OF THE LOCK, 1895–96
Aubrey Beardsley

Fo lo! the board with cups and spoons is crowned,
The berries crackle, and the mill turns round;[18]
On shining altars of Japan[19] they raise
The silver lamp; the fiery spirits blaze;
From silver spouts the grateful liquors glide,
While China's earth[20] receives the smoking tide.
At once they gratify their scent and taste,
And frequent cups prolong the rich repast.
Straight hover round the fair her airy band;
Some, as she sipped, the fuming liquor fanned,
Some o'er her lap their careful plumes displayed,
Trembling, and conscious of the rich brocade.
Coffee (which makes the politician wise,
And see through all things with his half-shut eyes)
Sent up in vapors to the baron's brain
New stratagems, the radiant lock to gain.
Ah cease, rash youth! desist ere 'tis too late,
Fear the just gods, and think of Scylla's fate![21]
Changed to a bird, and sent to flit in air,
She dearly pays for Nisus' injured hair!
But when to mischief mortals bend their will,
How soon they find fit instruments of ill!
Just then, Clarissa drew with tempting grace 13
A two-edged weapon from her shining case:
So ladies in romance assist their knight,
Present the spear, and arm him for the fight.
He takes the gift with reverence, and extends
The little engine[22] on his fingers' ends;
This just behind Belinda's neck he spread,
As o'er the fragrant steams she bends her head.
Swift to the lock a thousand sprites repair,
A thousand wings, by turns, blow back the hair;
And thrice they twitched the diamond in her ear;
Thrice she looked back, and thrice the foe drew near.
Just in that instant, anxious Ariel sought
The close recesses of the virgin's thought;
As on the nosegay in her breast reclined, 14
He watched th' ideas rising in her mind,
Sudden he viewed, in spite of all her art,
An earthly lover lurking at her heart.[23]

18. the berries . . . round: The coffee beans are ground in a hand mill at the table.
19. altars of Japan: Small imported lacquer tables.
20. China's earth: Earthenware cups imported from China.
21. Scylla's (sil′ əz) **fate:** Scylla, the daughter of King Nisus, was turned into a sea bird because she cut off the lock of her father's hair on which his safety depended and sent it to his enemy.
22. engine: Instrument.
23. earthly lover . . . heart: If in her heart Belinda wants the baron to succeed, they cannot protect her.

13 Clarification Clarissa is an unidentified friend of Belinda. What purpose does Clarissa have?

14 Clarification Note that Ariel loses his power, for Belinda's thoughts are now possessed by an earthly lover.

15 **Literary Focus** Note the use of zeugma.

16 **Discussion** What is the victor's "glorious prize"?

Amazed, confused, he found his power expired,
Resigned to fate, and with a sigh retired.
The peer now spreads the glittering forfex[24] wide,
T' enclose the lock; now joins it, to divide.
Even then, before the fatal engine closed,
A wretched sylph too fondly interposed;
Fate urged the shears, and cut the sylph in twain,
(But airy substance soon unites again).
The meeting points the sacred hair dissever
From the fair head, forever, and forever!
Then flashed the living lightning from her eyes,
And screams of horror rend th' affrighted skies.
Not louder shrieks to pitying heaven are cast,
15 When husbands, or when lap dogs breathe their last;
Or when rich China vessels fallen from high,
In glittering dust, and painted fragments lie!
16 "Let wreaths of triumph now my temples twine,"
The victor cried, "the glorious prize is mine!"
While fish in streams, or birds delight in air,
Or in a coach and six the British Fair,
As long as *Atalantis*[25] shall be read,
Or the small pillow grace a lady's bed,
While visits shall be paid on solemn days,
When numerous wax lights in bright order blaze,
While nymphs take treats, or assignations give,
So long my honor, name, and praise shall live!
What time would spare, from steel receives its date,[26]
And monuments, like men, submit to fate!
Steel could the labor of the gods destroy,
And strike to dust th' imperial towers of Troy;
Steel could the works of mortal pride confound,
And hew triumphal arches to the ground.
What wonder then, fair nymph! thy hairs should feel,
The conquering force of unresisted steel?

from Canto V

In Canto IV, *after Umbriel, "a dusky, melancholy sprite," empties a bag filled with "the force of female lungs, sighs, sobs, and passions, and the war of tongues" onto Belinda's head, the lady erupts over the loss of her lock. Then she "bids her beau," Sir Plume, to "demand the precious hairs," but Plume is unable to persuade the baron to return the hair.*

---

24. forfex: Scissors.
25. *Atalantis:* A popular book of scandalous gossip.
26. receives its date: Is destroyed.

In the beginning of Canto V, *Clarissa, a level-headed nymph, tries to bring an end to the commotion, but rather than being greeted with applause, her speech is followed by a battle cry.*

"To arms, to arms!" the fierce virago[27] cries,
And swift as lightning to the combat flies.
All side in parties, and begin th' attack;
Fans clap, silks rustle, and tough whalebones crack;
Heroes' and heroines' shouts confusedly rise,
And bass and treble voices strike the skies.
No common weapons in their hands are found,
Like gods they fight, nor dread a mortal wound.
So when bold Homer makes the gods engage,
And heavenly breasts with human passions rage;
'Gainst Pallas, Mars, Latona, Hermes[28] arms; 17
And all Olympus[29] rings with loud alarms:
Jove's[30] thunder roars, heaven trembles all around,
Blue Neptune[31] storms, the bellowing deeps resound;
Earth shakes her nodding towers, the ground gives way,
And the pale ghosts start at the flash of day!
Triumphant Umbriel on a sconce's height[32]
Clapped his glad wings, and sat to view the fight;
Propped on their bodkin spears,[33] the sprites survey
The growing combat, or assist the fray.
While through the press enraged Thalestris[34] flies,
And scatters death around from both her eyes,
A beau and witling[35] perished in the throng,
One died in metaphor, and one in song.
"O cruel nymph! a living death I bear,"
Cried Dapperwit, and sunk beside his chair.
A mournful glance Sir Fopling[36] upwards cast,
"Those eyes are made so killing"—was his last.

---

27. virago (və rā' gō): Scolding woman.
28. Pallas . . . Hermes: Gods who directed the Trojan War. Pallas and Hermes supported the Greeks, while Mars and Latona sided with the Trojans.
29. Olympus: The mountain which was supposed to be the home of the gods.
30. Jove's: Referring to Jupiter, the ruler of the Gods in Roman mythology; identified with Zeus in Greek mythology.
31. Neptune: The Roman god of the sea; identified with Poseidon in Greek mythology.
32. sconce's height: A candleholder attached to the wall.
33. bodkin spears: Large needles.
34. Thalestris (thə lēs' tris): An Amazon (a race of female warriors supposed to have lived in Scythia) who played a role in the medieval tales of Alexander the Great.
35. witling: A person who fancies himself or herself a wit.
36. Dapperwit, Sir Fopling: Names of amusing characters in comedies of the time.

17 **Discussion** How is the battle similar to accounts of epic battles? What are the ladies' weapons?

18 Discussion How does Belinda subdue the Baron?

Thus on Maeander's[37] flowery margin lies
Th' expiring swan, and as he sings he dies.
When bold Sir Plume had drawn Clarissa down,
Chloe[38] stepped in, and killed him with a frown;
She smiled to see the doughty hero slain,
But, at her smile, the beau revived again.
Now Jove suspends his golden scales in air,
Weighs the men's wits against the lady's hair;
The doubtful beam long nods from side to side;
At length the wits mount up, the hairs subside.
See, fierce Belinda on the baron flies,
With more than usual lightning in her eyes;
18 Nor feared the chief th' unequal fight to try,
Who sought no more than on his foe to die.
But this bold lord with manly strength endued,
She with one finger and a thumb subdued:
Just where the breath of life his nostrils drew,
A charge of snuff the wily virgin threw;
The gnomes direct, to every atom just,
The pungent grains of titillating dust.
Sudden with starting tears each eye o'erflows,
And the high dome re-echoes to his nose.
"Now meet thy fate," incensed Belinda cried,
And drew a deadly bodkin[39] from her side . . .
"Boast not my fall," he cried, "insulting foe!
Thou by some other shalt be laid as low.
Nor think, to die dejects my lofty mind;
All that I dread is leaving you behind!
Rather than so, ah let me still survive,
And burn in Cupid's flames—but burn alive."
"Restore the lock!" she cries; and all around
"Restore the lock!" the vaulted roofs rebound.
Not fierce Othello in so loud a strain
Roared for the handkerchief that caused his pain.[40]
But see how oft ambitious aims are crossed,
And chiefs contend till all the prize is lost!
The lock, obtained with guilt, and kept with pain,
In every place is sought, but sought in vain.
With such a prize no mortal must be blessed,
So Heaven decrees! with Heaven who can contest?

---

37. Maeander's: Referring to a river in Asia.
38. Chloe (klō′ ē): The heroine of the ancient Greek pastoral romance, *Daphnis and Chloe.*
39. bodkin: An ornamental pin shaped like a dagger.
40. not . . . pain: In Shakespeare's *Othello,* the hero is convinced that his wife is being unfaithful to him when she cannot find the handkerchief that he had given her. Actually, the handkerchief had been taken by the villain, Iago, who uses it as part of his evil plot.

THE BATTLE OF THE BEAUX AND BELLES
Aubrey Beardsley

Humanities Note

Fine art, *The Battle of the Beaux and the Belles* by Aubrey Beardsley. This drawing is one of the nine pen-and-ink drawings by Beardsley for the 1896 edition of Alexander Pope's "The Rape of the Lock." This rococo scene is executed with the skill and mocking wit for which Beardsley is noted. The abundance of ruffles and flounces and the extravagance of embroidery and pattern serve to emphasize the silliness of the situation depicted. Beardsley's satiric style appropriately illustrates this social parody by Pope.

You may wish to ask this question: Do you feel that the elaborate decorative style of the drawing is similar to the language of the poem? Explain.

19 Discussion What happens, finally, to the lock of Belinda's hair? In light of the poem, is this an appropriate resolution? Why, or why not?

Some thought it mounted to the lunar sphere,
Since all things lost on earth are treasured there.
There heroes' wits are kept in ponderous vases,
And beaux' in snuffboxes and tweezer cases.
There broken vows and deathbed alms are found,
And lovers' hearts with ends of riband bound . . .

19
But trust the Muse—she saw it upward rise,
Though marked by none but quick, poetic eyes . . .
A sudden star, it shot through liquid[41] air
And drew behind a radiant trail of hair . . .[42]

Then cease, bright Nymph! to mourn thy ravished hair,
Which adds new glory to the shining sphere!
Not all the tresses that fair head can boast,
Shall draw such envy as the lock you lost.
For, after all the murders of your eye,[43]
When, after millions slain, yourself shall die;
When those fair suns shall set, as set they must,
And all those tresses shall be laid in dust,
This lock, the Muse shall consecrate to fame,
And midst the stars inscribe Belinda's name.

41. liquid: Clear.
42. trail of hair: The word "comet" comes from a Greek word meaning "long-haired."
43. murders . . . eye: Lovers struck down by her glances.

THINKING ABOUT THE SELECTION

Recalling

1. (a) In what activity is Belinda engaged during the first half of Canto III? (b) What is the outcome?
2. (a) What is the group doing when the "berries crackle, and the mill turns round"?
3. (a) What is the "two-edged weapon" that Clarissa gives the baron? (b) How many times does the baron fail to get the lock of hair? (c) How does Belinda respond when he does get it? (d) How does the baron react?
4. (a) In Canto V, what noises accompany the attack that follows Belinda's cry of "To arms, to arms!"? (b) With what weapon does Belinda threaten the baron's life? (c) What does she demand that he do?
5. (a) Who has possession of the lock at the end of Canto V? (b) What do some people think has happened to it?

Interpreting

6. Why do you think Pope precedes the trivial episodes in Canto III with such a grisly image as "wretches hang that jurymen may dine"?
7. What similarity is there between Pope's description of the omber game and his description of the events following the theft of the lock?

8. Lines 79–88 in Canto V are "elegant spoofing," according to one critic. Yet in a sense Pope made the poem's extravagant claim come true. How did he do it?

Applying

9. Pope based *The Rape of the Lock* on an actual incident. What incident in the news today might provide the basis for a similar mock epic? (Your freewriting on page 559 may supply an answer to this question.)

ANALYZING LITERATURE

Understanding Mock Epic

A **mock epic** is a humorous narrative poem done in the manner of a true epic. It may resemble classical epics such as the *Odyssey* or the *Iliad*. It may contain elements of English epics such as *Beowulf* or *Paradise Lost*. Or, as in *The Rape of the Lock*, a mock epic may show traces of both types. In either case it will have characters who perform what appear to be heroic deeds. It may also contain references from mythology and include impossible or supernatural events.

1. (a) What are three trivial incidents in *The Rape of the Lock* that Pope presents in a heroic manner? (b) What are three characteristics of the heroic manner that the poem exhibits?
2. What are some of the mythical creatures, including deities and muses, mentioned in the poem? Try to find at least seven.

CRITICAL THINKING AND READING

Inferring the Author's Purpose

Up to a point, you know the author's purpose in writing *The Rape of the Lock*. Pope is mocking the overwrought reaction of two noble families to a hair-cutting prank. In his own words, Pope is "using a vast force to lift a feather." But that is not his only intent. The author has a more serious purpose than just memorializing a silly incident. To understand what it is, you have to read between the lines—to infer—what Pope believes about human behavior and social manners. The following lines from the poem give clues to the author's purpose. First interpret the lines in your own words. Then write a general statement expressing what you believe to be Pope's purpose in writing the poem.

1. Oh thoughtless mortals! ever blind to fate,/Too soon dejected, and too soon elate. (Canto III, lines 101–102)
2. But when to mischief mortals bend their will,/ How soon they find fit instruments of ill! (Canto III, lines 125–126)
3. But see how oft ambitious aims are crossed,/ And chiefs contend till all the prize is lost! (Canto V, lines 63–64)

THINKING AND WRITING

Writing About Tone

Tone is sometimes easier to recognize than to describe. You can easily see that the tone of *The Rape of the Lock* is high-flown and heroic. But what are the features of Pope's language that lend the poem its distinctive tone? Ask yourself these questions. You will find it helpful to take notes in answering them.

1. How do the words in the poem differ from the words you use in ordinary speaking and writing? (Consider figurative as well as literal meanings of words.)
2. How does the arrangement of words in sentences differ from that in most sentences in everyday English? (Pay attention to inverted elements, modifier placement, parallelism, and so on.)
3. More broadly, what is the total effect of Pope's language? (Look at his overstatement, allusions, choice of details—indeed, anything that makes the poem high-flown and mock heroic.)

Use your answers to these questions to write a composition on the tone of *The Rape of the Lock*. Begin by stating what you believe the tone of the poem to be. Support that statement by citing examples from the poem. Use quotations. Revise, checking especially your organization and coherence.

Answers

ANSWERS TO THINKING ABOUT THE SELECTION

Recalling

1. (a) Belinda is engaged in a social "hour," which includes a card game. (b) Belinda beats the Baron at omber, the card game.
2. They are reflecting on the outcome of the card game.
3. (a) Clarissa gives the Baron a pair of scissors. (b) The Baron fails three times. (c) She screams with horror. (d) The Baron cries out in glee.
4. (a) The shouts of people, the rustling of their clothes, and handclaps are likened to thunder, roaring gods, and the ringing of loud alarms. (b) Belinda threatens the Baron with a hairpin. (c) She demands that he return the lock of hair.
5. (a) In the end the lock flies heavenward. (b) It changes into a star in the heavens, bearing Belinda's name.

Interpreting

6. Answers will differ but should include the idea that such biting satire is quite typical of Pope.
7. Answers will differ but should include the idea that both are elevated to the dignity of a true epic by the use of innumerable allusions.
8. Answers will differ but should include the notion that Pope, by immortalizing Belinda in this poem, made good on his extravagent claim.

Applying

9. Answers will differ. Some students may find an incident involving celebrities.

ANSWERS TO ANALYZING LITERATURE

1. (a) Pope presents in a heroic manner the card game, the theft of the lock, and the battle scene following it. (b) The poem includes a hero[ine], a battle scene, and the intervention of gods and goddesses [sylphs and gnomes] in human affairs.
2. Among the creatures listed are Scylla, Pallas, Hermes, Olympus, Jove, Neptune, Muses, and Cupid.

ANSWERS TO CRITICAL THINKING AND READING

1. Most people do not consider the long-term ramifications of an action, so they either celebrate, or mourn, its hoped-for ends before the results are really known.
2. People are usually quite ingenious in devising ways to get what they want and in rationalizing the means they use to gain the desired end.
3. Selfish ambition keeps people from compromising, preferring instead to see that no one wins if they themselves do not.

Students will express differently Pope's purpose, but they all should see that it is primarily moral and aims to uphold conventional norms of conduct and behavior.

Challenge Have students compare the satiric style of Swift and of Addison and Steele with that of Pope. Which is the most biting? Which the cleverest? Which has the most telling impact?

THINKING AND WRITING

Publishing Student Writing You may want several students volunteer to read aloud their compositions.

Literary Focus Select a few more heroic couplets to illustrate the form. Among those of Pope's most often quoted are

A little learning is a dangerous thing;
Drink deep, or taste not the Pierian spring . . .

Honor and shame from no condition rise;
Act well your part; there all the honor lies.

'Tis education forms the common mind:
Just as the twig is bent, the tree's inclined.

Hope springs eternal in the human breast:
Man never is, but always to be blest.

Look For Students are more likely to respond to Pope's witty couplets if they hear them read aloud.

Writing You might provide your students with some brief, witty quotations from Bartlett's or some other collection of quotations. They can then versify them.

Vocabulary Ask individual students to use each of the words in a sentence.

GUIDE FOR READING

from An Essay on Man

Writer's Techniques

Heroic Couplet. A heroic couplet is a rhyming pair of lines in iambic pentameter. Since it requires the clear thought and precise wording admired by classically inspired writers, it was a favorite verse form among Restoration and eighteenth-century poets. Dryden, Swift, and Pope are among the best-known users of the form. The heroic couplet, concise and quotable, is often used in satire. The following lines from Pope's *The Rape of the Lock* are a heroic couplet.

∪ / ∪ / ∪ / ∪ / ∪ /
He springs to vengeance with an eager pace,
∪ / ∪ / ∪ / ∪ / ∪ /
And falls like thunder on the prostrate ace.

Look For

As you read the excerpt from *An Essay on Man,* look for Pope's use of heroic couplets.

Writing

Many of Pope's heroic couplets are closed couplets—that is, their two lines represent a complete thought.

True wit is Nature to advantage dress'd,
What oft was thought, but ne'er so well expressed.

That couplet, a complete thought, is from Pope's *Essay on Criticism.* Create a closed couplet; it will consist of two rhyming lines with ten syllables each, the stress falling on every second syllable. As a closed couplet, it will make a complete, understandable statement, ideally in an effective and memorable way.

Vocabulary

Knowing the following words will help you as you read the excerpt from *An Essay on Man.*

isthmus (is'məs) *n.*: A narrow strip of land, with water on each side, connecting two larger land masses (l. 3)

stoic (stō'ik) *n.*: A person indifferent to pleasure or pain (l. 6)

disabused (dis'ə byo͞ozd') *adj.*: Freed from false ideas (l. 14)

Objectives

1. To introduce the heroic couplet as a literary form
2. To generalize about emotion and intellect
3. To respond to neoclassical criticism

Teaching Portfolio: Support Material

Teacher Backup, pp. 000

Vocabulary Check, p. 00

Usage and Mechanics Worksheet, p. 00

Analyzing Literature Worksheet, p. 00

Critical Thinking and Reading Worksheet, p. 00

Language Worksheet, p. 00

Selection Test, p. 00

from # An Essay on Man

Alexander Pope

An Essay on Man *is an examination of human nature, society, and morals. In describing the work, Pope comments that it is "a general map of man, marking out . . . the greater parts, their extent, their limits, and their connection." The following excerpt is from the second epistle, in which Pope attempts to show how it is possible for man to achieve a psychological harmony through self-understanding and self-love.*

Know then thyself, presume not God to scan;
The proper study of mankind is man.
Placed on this isthmus of a middle state,
A being darkly wise, and rudely great:
With too much knowledge for the skeptic side, 1
With too much weakness for the stoic's pride,
He hangs between; in doubt to act, or rest;
In doubt to deem himself a god, or beast; 2
In doubt his mind or body to prefer;
Born but to die, and reasoning but to err;
Alike in ignorance, his reason such,
Whether he thinks too little, or too much: 3
Chaos of thought and passion, all confused;
Still by himself abused, or disabused;
Created half to rise, and half to fall;
Great lord of all things, yet a prey to all;
Sole judge of truth, in endless error hurled:
The glory, jest, and riddle of the world! 4

Motivation for Reading Challenge your students to find any statement here that is not a wise and memorable description of the human condition.

Master Teacher Note Pope's *Essay on Man* was never completed. It's purpose was, in his own words, "to vindicate the ways of God to man." The *Essay,* or the part of it that was completed, is made up of four Epistles. The first deals with the order and goodness of the world and the right of man to be a part of it. The third deals with man in the society he created; and the fourth deals with happiness.

Purpose-Setting Question Pope's poetry is noted for its compression of language—for the clarity, glitter, beauty, and exactness of his phrasing. Which couplets do you find remarkable for these qualities? Which might you wish to memorize?

1 **Discussion** How does the poet show that man's condition is a middle state?

2 **Discussion** What purpose does the repetition of *doubt* serve in reinforcing the poet's point of view?

3 **Discussion** What is Pope's view of our mental powers? In general, how would you sum up Pope's description of man in these lines? Do you agree or disagree with his view?

Challenge It has been said that Pope has been kept alive as a poet more because of his way with words than by his philosophy. Do these lines suggest that he was a shallow-thinker?

4 **Discussion** Reread the closing line. Give an example of present-day man as the glory of the world, as the jest of the world, and as the riddle of the world. What actions might portray man in each of these phrases?

THINKING ABOUT THE SELECTION

Recalling

1. What does Pope say should be the object of man's study?
2. According to Pope, what prevents man from being (a) a skeptic? (b) a stoic?
3. What word, repeated three times, suggests the world of chaos and error in which human beings exist?

Interpreting

4. Pope writes that man stands on an "isthmus of a middle state." He describes the middle state in detail. In a single word, what is (a) at one end of the isthmus? (b) at the other end?
5. What do you think Pope means by the line, "In doubt his mind or body to prefer"?
6. "Know then thyself," writes Pope. How can a person "in mindless error hurled" achieve that goal?

Applying

7. Most writers today reject the idea of literature presenting an obvious moral. Pope believed just the opposite. He felt that poetry has a didactic, or instructional, role to play. What do you think?

ANALYZING LITERATURE

Understanding a Heroic Couplet

A heroic couplet is a pair of rhymed lines in iambic pentameter. An *iamb* is a metrical foot consisting of one short syllable followed by one long syllable or one unstressed syllable followed by one stressed syllable. The word *apply* (ə plī′), for instance, could function as an iamb:

∪ /
apply

1. Find one word that functions as an iamb in each of the following lines: 1, 2, 7, 8, 11.
2. Since it is a heroic couplet, lines 7–8 should rhyme, but they seem not to. (a) What explanation can you suggest for this apparent mistake? (Hint: Look up in a dictionary the pronunciation of the adjective *bestial.*) (b) Find five similarly nonrhyming pairs of words in *The Rape of the Lock*. How can you explain them?

CRITICAL THINKING AND READING

Generalizing

To some extent—except for stable religious convictions—each era sets its own moral and intellectual standards. What is viewed as acceptable in one century may seem outrageous in another. For example, the word *leg* (referring to that part of the human anatomy) was considered so scandalous by Victorians that even chairs and tables were said to have *limbs*. Today the word *leg* seems innocuous.

1. If Pope's observations represent the thought of his day, how did people in the eighteenth century view the relationship between the intellect and the emotions?
2. What differences, if any, do you see in that relationship today?

THINKING AND WRITING

Responding to Neoclassical Criticism

In the preface to his poem "Religio Laici," John Dryden offers his critical opinion of how poetry should be written:

> The expressions of a poem designed purely for instruction ought to be plain and natural, and yet majestic; for the poet is . . . a kind of lawgiver, and those three qualities which I have named are proper to the legislative style.

In an essay of no more than one page, state (1) whether you agree with Dryden as to how a poem "purely for instruction" should be written, and (2) whether you think *An Essay on Man* (based on the excerpt you have read) has the three elements named. Draw freely from the poem to support your opinion. When you revise, make sure you have provided adequate support for your opinion.

Answers

ANSWERS TO THINKING ABOUT THE SELECTION

Recalling

1. The proper study of mankind, says Pope, is man.
2. (a) Too much knowledge keeps man from becoming a skeptic. (b) Too much weakness keeps man from becoming a stoic.
3. The word *doubt* suggests a world of chaos and error.

Interpreting

4. (a) At one end of the isthmus is the skeptic (or beast); (b) on the other is the stoic (or god).
5. The line suggests that man has trouble deciding whether to be ruled by his mind or by his passions.
6. Answers will differ but may include the idea that a person should always be as self-critical as possible, knowing that great care must be exercised to avoid errors of judgment.

Applying

7. Answers will differ. However, encourage your students to support their opinions with reasons and, if possible, references to works of didactic literature.

ANSWERS TO ANALYZING LITERATURE

1. The words *thyself* and *presume* (line 1), *mankind* (line 2), *between* (line 7), *himself* (line 8), and *alike* (line 11) function as iambs.
2. (a) In lines 7–8 the words *rest* and *beast* are examples of near rhyme, in which there are changes within the vowel sounds of words meant to rhyme. (b) In the "Rape of the Lock" lines 5-6, 7-8, 27-28, 29-30, 45-46, 49-50, and 111-112 in Canto III are near rhymes. In Canto V lines 7-8, 69-70, 79-80, and 81-82 are examples. Near rhyme is a perfectly acceptable technique in poetry.

ANSWERS TO CRITICAL THINKING AND READING

1. Answers will differ but should include the idea that in Pope's time people believed in a rational order of things and in their willingness to subordinate their emotions to the intellect.
2. Answers will differ but will likely include the idea that today people are more trusting in the free expression of emotion.

THINKING AND WRITING

Publishing Student Writing Students with differing opinions might read their essays to the class. Classmates could then evaluate their essays.

The Age of Jonson

Oliver Goldsmith, James Boswell, And Samuel Johnson At The Mitre Tavern
Nineteenth-century colored engraving
The Granger Collection

Humanities Note

Engraving, *Oliver Goldsmith, James Boswell, and Samuel Johnson at the Mitre Tavern.* This engraving presents three men of the period who frequently spent time in conversation. Johnson is on the right in this picture, the admiring Boswell in the back, and Oliver Goldsmith, the playwright and poet, is on the left.

More About the Author Samuel Johnson's "theme of themes," as it has been called, is expressed in the title of his poem "The Vanity of Human Wishes." By this Johnson means the hunger of imagination which preys upon life to make us see things as we wish they were rather than as they are—a representative eighteenth-century viewpoint. What relevance does Johnson's view hold for the present day?

SAMUEL JOHNSON

1709–1784

Many readers know Samuel Johnson only through the biography written by his contemporary and ardent admirer, James Boswell. That is unfortunate, because the Samuel Johnson who is revealed through his own writings is a man with much to say on a variety of subjects—a man who, despite the excellence of Boswell's portrait, is best read firsthand. During his own lifetime, Johnson was widely recognized as the most influential literary figure of his day as well as a brilliant and witty conversationalist. Indeed, the second half of the eighteenth century is often called the Age of Johnson.

Johnson's success was hard-won. The son of a bookseller in Lichfield, a small town north of Birmingham, he grew up in poverty. He described himself as a "poor diseased infant." A series of childhood illnesses left him physically weak and facially disfigured. A brilliant child who read *Hamlet* at the age of eight, Johnson feared that insanity would deprive him of his single advantage, his intellect. He entered Pembroke College, Oxford, in 1728, but was forced to leave after fourteen months because of a lack of funds. For six years thereafter, until deciding to pursue a literary career in earnest, he was a Lichfield bookseller and schoolmaster, reading widely and occasionally working on translations. At the age of twenty-six he married a widow much older than he, to whom he remained devoted until her death.

In 1737 he moved to London. Despite critical praise for his early writing, he failed to gain a large audience. It was Johnson's *Dictionary of the English Language,* published in 1755, that earned him a permanent place in English letters. For the next two years, he wrote *The Idler,* a series of articles for a weekly newspaper, in addition to completing one of his best-loved works, *Rasselas,* a moral romance.

Johnson was awarded an annual pension of three hundred pounds in 1762, which made him something of a man of leisure. The next year he and twenty-three-year-old James Boswell met for the first time in the back parlor of Tom Davis's bookshop. It was a fateful meeting, one that led, after many further meetings, to Boswell's *Life of Johnson,* a book generally regarded as the finest biography in English.

In 1765 Johnson published an acclaimed edition of Shakespeare. His last important work, *The Lives of the Poets,* appeared in ten volumes between 1779 and 1781. It is a group of fifty-two critical biographies that cover about two hundred years of English literary history. Late in life Johnson received honorary degrees from Oxford and from Trinity College, Dublin—thus the "Dr." that often precedes his name. He is buried in Westminster Abbey.

Objectives

1. To understand diction and style in prose writings
2. To compare and contrast writing styles
3. To make inferences about tone
4. To write dictionary entries

Teaching Portfolio: Support Material

Teacher Backup, pp. 000

Vocabulary Check, p. 00

Usage and Mechanics Worksheet, p. 00

Analyzing Literature Worksheet, p. 00

Critical Thinking and Reading Worksheet, p. 00

Language Worksheet, p. 00

Selection Test, p. 00

GUIDE FOR READING

Letter to Lord Chesterfield; *from* The Preface to A Dictionary of the English Language; *from* A Dictionary of the English Language

Writer's Techniques

Diction and Style. In written communication, *diction* means word choice. A careful writer chooses words that are clear, correct, and effective. The words that are chosen are at the same time combined in phrases, sentences, and paragraphs. The distinctive way in which words are combined is called *style*. Diction and style change over the years, just as fashion changes. Writing tends to be more casual today than it was two hundred years ago, although formal situations still require formal diction and style. The intended audience for a piece of writing helps to determine appropriate diction and style.

Look For

As you read the following selections, look at Johnson's diction and style. All are crafted with great care and skill.

Writing

In your local newspaper, find a letter to the editor with which you disagree. Jot down your points of disagreement. Then write the opening paragraph of a response. Try to match your diction and style to that of the published letter you have chosen.

Vocabulary

Knowing the following words will help you as you read the excerpts from Johnson's works.

patron (pā'trən) *n.*: One who gives financial aid to an artist or writer (p. 578)
encumbers (in kum'bər z) *v.*: Weighs down with a load (p. 578)
asperity (as per'ə tē) *n.*: Ill temper; irritability (p. 579)
lexicographer (lek'sə käg'rə fər) *n.*: One who compiles a dictionary (p. 580)
recompense (rek'əm pens) *n.*: Reward; payment (p. 580)
caprices (kə prē'sis) *n.*: Whims (p. 580)
propagators (präp'ə gāt'ərz) *n.*: Those who cause something to happen or to spread (p. 581)
protracted (prō trak'tid) *v.*: Drawn out; prolonged (p. 581)
unctuous (uŋk'choo wəs) *adj.*: Oily (p. 583)

Literary Focus Review diction and style as they are reflected in the works of Swift, page 538, whose own style is noted for its simplicity. As an example of present-day formal writing, a governmental proclamation will prove useful. Point out that Johnson's usual diction and style are formal—too formal for the taste of most readers today. Although no one now is likely to imitate Johnson's prose, exposure to his craftsmanship can be beneficial to those trying to write with dignity and elegance.

Look For Students should also look for the strong feelings channeled through the dignified and restrained style.

Writing Have students compare the diction and style of several letters to the editor. Choose from serious, angry, bewildered, and humorous letters.

Vocabulary Write the words on the chalkboard and ask individual students to use them in original sentences.

Motivation for Reading Suppose you received belated praise and encouragement from someone who had earlier rejected your pleas for aid. Would you resent these belated offers and honors? How would you express your resentment?

Master Teacher Note You might point out that this letter implicitly teaches a most valuable lesson about how to express anger and resentment. Ask your students to decide what the lesson is.

Purpose-Setting Question Among its attributes, Johnson's style is noted for the balanced construction of phrases and clauses, carefully controlled rhythmns, and use of Latinate, often many-syllabled words. Which of these characteristics do you find in his letter?

Enrichment Despite the tone of Johnson's letter, Lord Chesterfield thought enough of it to show it to his friends as an example of good writing. Chesterfield himself was the author of a series of letters to his son, which are still looked upon as models of letters describing society and behavior of the time.

Reading Strategy To help students get the full impact of Johnson's diction, style, and tone read the letter aloud at least once.

1 **Discussion** Why did Johnson take the trouble to write the letter? What do you learn of the background to the letter?

2 **Discussion** What might the first sentence of the paragraph mean? What is Johnson's view of patrons? What is he implying about belated recognition? N.B.: The word *solitary* is a reference to the fact that he is a widower; Johnson's wife died in 1752.

Letter to Lord Chesterfield

Samuel Johnson

Shortly after the completion of the Dictionary, *Lord Chesterfield published two articles praising it. He had earlier ignored Johnson's appeals for financial assistance for the writing of the* Dictionary.

To the Right Honorable
the Earl of Chesterfield

February 7, 1755

My Lord:

I have been lately informed by the proprietor of the *World*[1] that two papers in which my *Dictionary* is recommended to the public were written by your Lordship. To be so distinguished is an honor which, being very little accustomed to favors from the great, I know not well how to receive, or in what terms to acknowledge.

When upon some slight encouragement
1 I first visited your Lordship, I was overpowered like the rest of mankind by the enchantment of your address,[2] and could not forbear to wish that I might boast myself "*Le vainqueur du vainqueur de la terre*";[3] that I might obtain that regard for which I saw the world contending, but I found my attendance so little encouraged that neither pride nor modesty would suffer me to continue it. When I had once addressed your Lordship in public, I had exhausted all the art of pleasing which a retired and uncourtly scholar can possess. I had done all that I could; and no man is well pleased to have his all neglected, be it ever so little.

Seven years, my Lord, have now passed since I waited in your outward rooms or was repulsed from your door, during which time I have been pushing on my work through difficulties of which it is useless to complain and have brought it at last to the verge of publication without one act of assistance, one word of encouragement, or one smile of favor. Such treatment I did not expect, for I never had a patron before.

The shepherd in Virgil grew at last acquainted with love, and found him a native of the rocks.[4] "Is not a patron, my Lord, one who looks with unconcern on a man struggling for life in the water and when he has
reached ground encumbers him with help. 2
The notice which you have been pleased to take of my labors, had it been early, had been kind; but it has been delayed till I am indifferent and cannot enjoy it, till I am solitary and cannot impart it, till I am known and do not want[5] it.

---

1. **the *World*:** A newspaper in which Lord Chesterfield had praised Johnson's *Dictionary*.
2. **address:** Conversation.
3. ***Le vainqueur du vainqueur de la terre*** (lə van kər′ dyo͞o van kər′ də lä ter′): French for "the conqueror of the conqueror of the earth."
4. **The shepherd . . . rocks:** In Virgil's *Eclogue*, a shepherd complains that love must have been born among jagged rocks.
5. **want:** Need.

3 I hope it is no very cynical asperity not to confess obligation where no benefit has been received, or to be unwilling that the public should consider me as owing that to a patron which Providence has enabled me to do for myself.

Having carried on my work thus far with so little obligation to any favorer of learning, I shall not be disappointed though I should conclude it, if less be possible, with less; for I have been long wakened from that dream of hope, in which I once boasted myself with so much exultation, my Lord,

Your Lordship's most humble,
most obedient servant, 4
Samuel Johnson

3 Discussion Restate this one-sentence paragraph in your own words.

4 Discussion What is the tone of the closing?

THINKING ABOUT THE SELECTION

Recalling

1. (a) How did Johnson learn of Lord Chesterfield's articles in the *World*? (b) Why does he feel the need to respond?
2. How much time has passed since Johnson first tried to get financial assistance from Lord Chesterfield for work on the *Dictionary*?
3. What does Johnson say will not cause him any disappointment at this point?

Interpreting

4. How does the definition of a patron in the fourth paragraph apply to Johnson's experience with Lord Chesterfield?
5. From Johnson's remarks in the next to last paragraph, what misinformation do you think Chesterfield may have conveyed in his *World* articles concerning his relationship with Johnson?

Applying

6. Suppose Lord Chesterfield had assisted Johnson throughout the development of his dictionary. How do you think Johnson would then have responded to the articles in the *World*?

ANALYZING LITERATURE

Diction and Style

Diction in writing is word choice. **Style** is the overall effect of a writer's choice and arrangement of words. In fact, Lord Chesterfield once called style "the dress of thought." Diction and style are influenced by purpose, audience, and the period in which the writing is done. In his "Letter to Lord Chesterfield," Samuel Johnson intends his diction and style to deliver an unmistakable message.

1. (a) What is the purpose of the letter? (b) What is its audience? (c) How does Johnson feel about the audience?
2. What are ten words that you consider to be especially well chosen for the point Johnson wants to make and the way in which he wants to make it?
3. What are three stylistic devices that Johnson uses effectively? Give one example of each from the letter. (Among the possibilities, consider parallelism, understatement, overstatement, and quotation.)

Answers

ANSWERS TO THINKING ABOUT THE SELECTION

Recalling

1. (a) The owner of the *World* told Johnson. (b) He does not wish anyone to think he was obligated to Chesterfield for the latter's help, which never was forthcoming.
2. Seven years have passed.
3. At this point Johnson will not be disappointed that he has had no encouragement, no financial help.

Interpreting

4. Johnson was rejected by Lord Chesterfield; the definition is quite personal.
5. The earl may have suggested he had encouraged and abetted Johnson all along.

Applying

6. Answers will differ but should include the idea that Johnson would no doubt have responded with a finely phrased expression of humble gratitude.

ANSWERS TO ANALYZING LITERATURE

1. (a) The purpose of the letter is to express his disapproval at Chesterfield's misleading praise for his work. (b) His audience is Lord Chesterfield himself, then anyone else who had the good fortune to read the letter. (c) Johnson is not pleased with Chesterfield's actions.
2. Answers will differ. Possibilities are *overpowered, neglected, repulsed, patron, struggling, encumbers, labors, delayed, indifferent, obligation.*
3. Answers will differ. Possibilities are overstatement as in sentence 1 of paragraph 2, parallelism as at the end of sentence 1 of paragraph 3, and the allusion to Virgil's shepherd in sentence 1 of paragraph 4.

Motivation for Reading Can you imagine having to write, read, and speak English without having a dictionary for a reference tool? How would you find the meanings of unfamiliar words? How would you know the correct spelling, or pronunciation?

Master Teacher Note Johnson's efforts to compile his dictionary were truly heroic. Today such work would be carried out by numerous committees overseeing staffs of specialists, and with the aid of computers. Suggest that your students read Johnson's "Preface" with the aim of discerning some of the difficulties he had to overcome.

Purpose-Setting Question While a writer's style may remain constant, the tone often changes from selection to selection, depending on its audience and its purpose. How does the tone of the "Preface" differ from that of the letter to Lord Chesterfield?

1 **Discussion** Do you agree with this point of view?

2 **Discussion** Explain how this passage could be considered hyperbole. What other examples do you find in the "Preface"?

3 **Enrichment** Like the French and Italian academies, which had produced dictionaries, Johnson at first wanted to "fix" the language; he looked upon change with suspicion; he felt change was likely to corrupt the language.

4 **Discussion** Do you agree? Besides writers, what other groups of people might be included in the term *authors*? Explain your choices.

from The Preface to A Dictionary of the English Language

Samuel Johnson

1 It is the fate of those who toil at the lower employments of life, to be rather driven by the fear of evil, than attracted by the prospect of good; to be exposed to censure, without hope of praise; to be disgraced by miscarriage, or punished for neglect, where success would have been without applause, and diligence without reward.

2 Among these unhappy mortals is the writer of dictionaries; whom mankind have considered, not as the pupil, but the slave of science, the pioneer of literature, doomed only to remove rubbish and clear obstructions from the paths through which learning and genius press forward to conquest and glory, without bestowing a smile on the humble drudge that facilitates their progress. Every other author may aspire to praise; the lexicographer can only hope to escape reproach, and even this negative recompense has been yet granted to very few.

I have, notwithstanding this discouragement, attempted a dictionary of the English language, which, while it was employed in the cultivation of every species of literature, has itself been hitherto neglected; suffered to spread under the direction of chance, into wild exuberance; resigned to the tyranny of time and fashion: and exposed to the corruptions of ignorance and caprices of innovation.

3 When I took the first survey of my undertaking, I found our speech copious without order and energetic without rule: wherever I turned my view, there was perplexity to be disentangled and confusion to be regulated; choice was to be made out of boundless variety, without any established principle of selection; adulterations were to be detected, without a settled test of purity; and modes of expression to be rejected or received, without the suffrages of any writers of classical reputation or acknowledged authority.

Having therefore no assistance but from general grammar, I applied myself to the perusal of our writers; and noting whatever might be of use to ascertain or illustrate any word or phrase, accumulated in time the materials of a dictionary, which, by degrees, I reduced to method, establishing to myself, in the progress of the work, such rules as experience and analogy suggested to me; experience, which practice and observation were continually increasing; and analogy, which, though in some other words obscure, was evident in others . . .

In hope of giving longevity to that which its own nature forbids to be immortal, I have devoted this book, the labor of years, to the honor of my country, that we may no longer yield the palm of philology, without a contest to the nations of the continent. The chief glory of every people arises from its authors. 4 Whether I shall add anything by my own writings to the reputation of English literature, must be left to time. Much of my life has been lost under the pressures of disease; much has been trifled away; and much has always been spent in provision for the day that was passing over me; but I shall not think my employment useless or ignoble, if by my assistance foreign nations and distant ages gain access to the propagators of knowledge, and understand the teachers of truth; if my labors afford light to the repositories of science, and add celebrity to Bacon, to Hooker, to Milton, and to Boyle.[1]

When I am animated by this wish, I look with pleasure on my book, however defective, and deliver it to the world with the spirit of a man that has endeavored well. That it will immediately become popular, I have not promised to myself. A few wild blunders, and risible absurdities, from which no work of such multiplicity was ever free, may for a time furnish folly with laughter, and harden ignorance into contempt; but useful diligence will at last prevail, and there never can be wanting some who distinguish desert; who will consider that no dictionary of a living tongue ever can be
5 perfect, since, while it is hastening to publication, some words are budding, and some falling away; that a whole life cannot be spent upon syntax and etymology, and that even a whole life would not be sufficient; that he, whose design includes whatever language can express, must often speak of what he does not understand; that a writer will sometimes be hurried by eagerness to the end, and sometimes faint with weariness under a task which Scaliger[2] compares to the labors of the anvil and the mine; that what is obvious is not always known, and what is known is not always present; that sudden fits of inadvertency will surprise vigilance, slight avocations[3] will seduce attention, and casual eclipses of the mind will darken learning; and that the writer shall often in vain trace his memory at the moment of need, for that which yesterday he knew with intuitive readiness, and which will come uncalled into his thoughts tomorrow.

In this work, when it shall be found that much is omitted, let it not be forgotten that much likewise is performed; and though no book was ever spared out of tenderness to the author, and the world is little solicitous to know whence proceed the faults of that which it condemns; yet it may gratify curiosity to inform it, that the *English Dictionary* was written with little assistance of the learned, and without any patronage of the
great; not in the soft obscurities of retire- 6
ment, or under the shelter of academic bowers, but amidst inconvenience and distraction, in sickness and in sorrow. It may repress the triumph of malignant criticism to observe that if our language is not here fully displayed, I have only failed in an attempt which no human powers have hitherto completed. If the lexicons of ancient tongues, now immutably fixed and comprised in a few volumes, be yet, after the toil of successive ages, inadequate and delusive; if the aggregated knowledge and cooperating diligence of the Italian academicians did not secure them from the censure of Beni;[4] if the embodied critics of France, when fifty years had been spent upon their work, were obliged to change its economy[5] and give their second edition another form, I may surely be contented without the praise of perfection, which, if I could obtain, in this gloom of solitude, what would it avail me? I have protracted my work till most of those whom I wished to please have sunk into the grave,[6] and success and miscarriage are empty sounds: I therefore dismiss it with frigid tranquility, having little to fear or hope from censure or from praise.

---

1. Bacon . . . Boyle: Writers quoted by Johnson in the *Dictionary*.
2. Scaliger: Joseph Justus Scaliger (1540–1609), a scholar who suggested that criminals should be condemned to writing dictionaries.
3. avocation: Something that calls one away or distracts one from something.
4. Beni: Paolo Beni severely criticized the first Italian dictionary.
5. economy: Organization.
6. sunk . . . grave: Johnson's wife had died three years earlier.

5 **Enrichment** Here, Johnson admits that language cannot be "fixed"; rather it is a living thing, constantly changing.

6 **Discussion** Under what conditions did Johnson write the *Dictionary*?

Enrichment Boswell had this to say about Johnson's monumental project: "The world contemplated with wonder [a work] achieved by one man, while other countries had thought such undertakings fit only for whole academies." To produce his *Dictionary*, Johnson labored alone for seven years. By way of comparison, to complete the authoritative *Dictionary* of the French Academy required the labors of forty scholars for forty years.

Answers

ANSWERS TO THINKING ABOUT THE SELECTION

Recalling

1. (a) Writers of dictionaries are among those "who toil at the lower employments of life." (b) The lexicographer's "negative recompense" is "to escape reproach."
2. (a) Among other things, Johnson found English to be lacking in order and in rules. (b) General grammar was his only assistance.
3. Johnson devoted his *Dictionary* to the honor of England.
4. Any living tongue is constantly changing—adding words, dropping words, changing meanings, and so on.

Interpreting

5. (a) Johnson wrote the *Dictionary* to help codify English—that is, put some order into the language. (b) Students' answers will differ, but it can be inferred that previous dictionary-making was not effective.
6. Johnson collected words by reading the principal writers of his and earlier times.
7. Students' answers will differ, but it is quite likely that Johnson was both hopeful and pessimistic about his work. The final words of the "Preface" have a mock-serious tone about them.

Applying

8. Johnson would likely have a low opinion of today's dictionary writers, many of whom look upon themselves as reporters of the language and its usage rather than arbiters of good taste and correctness in language.
9. Computers have simplified the organization of information, the storage of information, and the changing or updating of information.

THINKING AND WRITING

Publishing Student Writing Students comparing or contrasting styles of the same authors might be interested in reading each other's essays.

THINKING ABOUT THE SELECTION

Recalling

1. (a) Among what class of workers does Johnson place writers of dictionaries? (b) What is the lexicographer's "negative recompense"?
2. (a) When Johnson "took the first survey," what did he find English speech to be lacking? (b) What gave him his only assistance?
3. To whom or what does Johnson say he has "devoted this book"?
4. Why, according to "The Preface," can "no dictionary of a living tongue ever be perfect"?

Interpreting

5. (a) What is Johnson's reason for having undertaken the task of writing a dictionary of English? (b) What can you conclude about prior dictionary-making in England?
6. How did Johnson collect the words for his dictionary?
7. Johnson seems to have mixed feelings about his efforts. (a) Do you think he is hopeful or pessimistic (or perhaps both) about the fate of his dictionary? Explain. (b) How have his efforts held up against the test of time?

Applying

8. What opinion do you think Johnson would have of today's unabridged English dictionaries?
9. How have computers changed the role of dictionary makers?

THINKING AND WRITING

Comparing and Contrasting Styles

A **writer's style** is the distinctive way that he or she uses language. No two writers have exactly the same style, although you may notice obvious similarities, especially among writers of the same era. Think about other writers' works that you have read so far in this book. Which writer has a style the most like—or, if you prefer, the least like—that of Samuel Johnson? To answer the question, you will need to consider diction, sentence structure, tone, and point of view. Style is a complex matter; parallels can be difficult. Once you have made your choice, write a short essay in which you compare and contrast the style of Johnson with that of the other writer you have chosen. Take notes before you start to do your first draft. Be specific as to the similarities and differences between the two styles you are comparing. When you revise for your final draft, go back to make sure that your observations about style are accurate and that your quoted excerpts are correct.

from A Dictionary of the English Language

Samuel Johnson

1 **athle'tick.** Strong of body; vigorous; lusty; robust.

Science distinguishes a man of honor from one of those *athletick* brutes, whom underservedly we call heroes. Dryden.

bang. A blow; a thump; a stroke: a low word.

I am a bachelor. That's to say, they are fools that marry; you'll bear me a *bang* for that. Shakespeare, *Julius Caesar.*

to ba'rbecue. A term used in the West Indies for dressing a hog whole; which, being split to the backbone, is laid flat upon a large gridiron, raised about two foot above a charcoal fire, with which it is surrounded.

Oldfield, with more than harpy throat endu'd,
Cries, send me, gods, a whole hog *barbecu'd.* Pope.

bu'ffleheaded. A man with a large head, like a buffalo; dull; stupid; foolish.

cream. The unctuous or oily part of milk, which, when it is cold, floats on the top, and is changed by the agitation of the churn into butter; the flower of milk.

electri'city. A property in some bodies, whereby, when rubbed so as to grow warm, they draw little bits of paper, or such like substances, to them. Quincy.

Such was the account given a few years ago of electricity; but the industry of the present age, first excited by the experiments of Gray, has discovered in electricity a multitude of philosophical wonders. Bodies electrified by a sphere of glass, turned nimbly round, not only emit flame, but may be fitted with such a quantity of the electrical vapor as, if discharged at once upon a human body, would endanger life. The force of this vapor has hitherto appeared instantaneous, persons at both ends of a long chain seeming to be struck at once. The philosophers are now endeavoring to intercept the strokes of lightning.

to fu'rnace. To throw out as sparks from a furnace. A bad word.

He *furnaces*
The thick sighs from him. Shakespeare's *Cymbeline.*

gang. A number herding together; a troop; a company; a tribe; a herd. It is seldom used but in contempt or abhorrence.

ha'tchet-face. An ugly face; such, I suppose, as might be hewn out of a block by a hatchet.

Motivation for Reading Ask students why dictionaries are important.

Purpose-Setting Question Johnson's is a highly personal dictionary, quite unlike modern works. As such, you can expect the tone of his entries to be affected by his attitude toward the words. Try to describe the tone of each entry as you read it.

1 **Enrichment** Note that unlike modern dictionaries, Johnson's offers no help in pronouncing words.

2 **Discussion** What is the meaning of this word today?

3 **Discussion** Having read the letter to Lord Chesterfield, is this the definition you would have expected? Why, or why not?

4 **Discussion** What is the present-day spelling of this word?

5 **Enrichment** Note that Johnson identifies verbs by the use of the word *to*.

An ape his own dear image will embrace;
An ugly beau adores a *hatchet-face*. Dryden.

lifegua'rd. The guard of a king's person.

2 **mo'dern.** In Shakespeare, vulgar; mean; common.

We have our philosophical persons to make *modern* and familiar things supernatural and causeless. Shakespeare.

3 **pa'tron.** One who countenances, supports or protects. Commonly a wretch who supports with insolence, and is paid with flattery.

pi'ckle. Condition; state. A word of contempt and ridicule.

How cam'st though in this *pickle?* Shakespeare.

plu'mper. Something worn in the mouth to swell out the cheeks.

She dex'trously her *plumpers* draws,
That serve to fill her hollow jaws. Swift's *Miscellanies.*

shill-I-shall-I. A corrupt reduplication of *shall I?* The question of a man hesitating. To stand *shill-I-shall-I*, is to continue hesitating and procrastinating. 4

I am somewhat dainty in making a resolution, because when I make it, I keep it; I don't stand *shill-I-shall-I* then; if I say't, I'll do't. Congreve's *Way of the World.*

to sneeze. To emit wind audibly by the nose. 5

wi'llow. A tree worn by forlorn lovers.

to wipe. To cheat; to defraud.

The next bordering lords commonly encroach one upon another, as one is stronger, or lie still in wait to *wipe* them out of their lands. Spenser, *On Ireland.*

you'ngster, you'nker. A young person. In contempt.

youth. The part of life succeeding to childhood and adolescence; the time from fourteen to twenty-eight.

THINKING ABOUT THE SELECTION

Recalling

1. What is Johnson's definition of (a) *lifeguard* and (b) *modern?*
2. According to Johnson, what is (a) a "tree worn by forlorn lovers"? (b) a person "from fourteen to twenty-eight"?

Interpreting

3. How does Johnson indicate that a word is a verb?
4. Why do you think the word *electricity* receives such a long definition?
5. Given what you know of Johnson's life, how do you account for his comment about *patron:* "a wretch who supports with insolence, and is paid with flattery"?
6. (a) In a modern dictionary, how is the entry for *shill-I-shall-I* spelled? (b) What inferences do you make about Johnson based on his definition?

Applying

7. Dictionaries are generally scientific, objective works. Johnson's dictionary, however, is filled with opinions and value judgments. What are three conspicuous examples of the kind of wording that would not appear in a modern dictionary?

CRITICAL THINKING AND READING

Making Inferences About Tone

Tone, the manner in which a writer communicates, shows the writer's attitude toward his or her subject. It often displays traces of the writer's personality or set of values. When tone seems to be completely straightforward, as in a newspaper report, a reader will tend to accept the writer's message at face value. If tone appears to be ironic or sarcastic, as in a satirical essay, a reader will be on guard for less obvious meanings. Tone can usually be described by one or two adjectives. Review Johnson's definitions of the following words. Then, in a brief paragraph, tell what you can infer from them about Johnson's tone.

1. bang
2. cream
3. to furnace
4. hatchet-face
5. youngster

THINKING AND WRITING

Writing Johnsonian Dictionary Entries

Take a look once again at the entries from Johnson's *Dictionary.* Pay close attention to exactly how they are written. Then search through a standard modern dictionary of the English language and find at least five words that might be imaginatively redefined through Johnson's eyes. Finally, write Johnsonian definitions for these words. Follow his style in every way possible, including accenting, diction, and outspokenness.

Answers

ANSWERS TO THINKING ABOUT THE SELECTION

Recalling

1. (a) According to Johnson, a *lifeguard* is the guard of a king's person. (b) The word *modern* means "vulgar," "mean," or "common."
2. (a) According to Johnson, "a tree worn by forlorn lovers" is a willow; (b) a person "from fourteen to twenty-eight" is a youth.

Interpreting

3. Johnson indecates verbs by using the word *to.*
4. The entry for *electricity* is quite long, perhaps in order to explain it in detail, thinking that most people would be completely unfamiliar with the term.
5. Johnson's definition of *patron* is in keeping with his experiences with Lord Chesterfield.
6. (a) The word is spelled *shilly-shally.* (b) Johnson may either have had difficulty making decisions, or he may have felt contempt for indecisive people.

Applying

7. Students' answers will differ, but should include the entries for words like *electricity, gang,* and *youngster.*

ANSWERS TO CRITICAL THINKING AND READING

1. The tone of *bang* is pejorative.
2. The tone of *cream* is matter-of-fact.
3. The tone of *to furnace* is pedantic.
4. The tone of *hatchet-face* is matter-of-fact.
5. The tone of *youngster* is matter-of-fact.

Challenge Have students compile a dictionary of present-day slang they commonly use. Their definitions should be as subjective as those Johnson used.

THINKING AND WRITING

Publishing Student Writing Students' definitions could be collected in a dictionary.

More About the Author It is ironic that a man who had such an inferiority complex should write what is regarded as the finest biography ever. It is doubly ironic that thanks to the discovery of James Boswell's personal papers in the 1920's, more is known today about Boswell himself than about the great man he so admired. Give an example of irony in your own life or the life of someone you know.

JAMES BOSWELL

(1740–1795)

Not until the twentieth century did James Boswell rise from the fringes of literary history to take his place as perhaps the greatest biographer in English literature. Best known for his biography of Samuel Johnson, Boswell wrote with vigor, training his eye now on the picturesque, now on the grotesque.

Born into an aristocratic family in Edinburgh, Scotland, Boswell was educated at the University of Glasgow, the University of Edinburgh, and the University of Utrecht. Although he received his degree in law and was admitted to the bar in both Scotland and England, Boswell's true passion was literature. His father, a prominent judge, was angered by what he saw as his son's "shallow" values. The extremely sensitive young Boswell interpreted this dissatisfaction as rejection, which led in turn to feelings of inferiority. In an effort to overcome his low self-esteem and at the same time find a suitable father figure, Boswell became a celebrity chaser, seeking out the acquaintanceship of the great men and women of his day. To his credit, many of them became his lifelong friends.

Among these was the writer Samuel Johnson, whom Boswell met while visiting London in 1763. After his acceptance into the prestigious Literary Club, Boswell devoted thirty years to compiling detailed records of Johnson's activities and conversations. From these assorted bits and pieces he distilled his famous work, *The Life of Samuel Johnson,* a precise yet wonderfully intimate portrait of the colorful poet. "The great art of biography," Boswell wrote, "is to keep the person whose life we are giving always in the reader's view." This he does by depicting Johnson variously as "a rhinoceros, in a kind of good humoured growl," and as "blowing out his breath like a whale" following an argument.

In addition to his portrait of Johnson, Boswell wrote numerous personal journals. *An Account of Corsica* (1768) is a sympathetic report of his meeting with the Corsican patriot Paoli and of Corsica's struggle for independence. His *Journal of a Tour in the Hebrides* (1785), published after Johnson's death, tells of the trip he made with the sage to Scotland.

During his lifetime Boswell's popularity was stifled by the biting criticism leveled at his work by the poet Thomas Gray, who caustically noted that "any fool may write a valuable book by chance, if he will only tell what he heard and saw. . . ." It is only since the 1920's, in fact, when a batch of Boswell's private papers were discovered in Malahide Castle, that the reading public has had any real awareness of this often-rowdy, often-vain young gentleman who gave the world its closest look at Samuel Johnson.

Objectives

1. To understand a *biography*
2. To recognize subjective information
3. To write from Samuel Johnson's point of view

Teaching Portfolio: Support Material

Teacher Backup, pp. 000

Vocabulary Check, p. 00

Usage and Mechanics Worksheet, p. 00

Analyzing Literature Worksheet, p. 00

Critical Thinking and Reading Worksheet, p. 00

Language Worksheet, p. 00

Selection Test, p. 000

GUIDE FOR READING

from The Life of Samuel Johnson

Literary Forms

Biography. A biography is an account of a person's life, usually written, though sometimes communicated orally, by another person. Effective biography will represent the subject's life accurately and thoroughly. A good biography, in other words, paints a complete portrait, giving as much space to the subject's flaws and limitations as to his or her most admirable traits. An important milestone in the writing of biography was James Boswell's legendary *The Life of Samuel Johnson.* In his work Boswell displayed an impressive grasp of Johnson's character by presenting countless particular details rather than a distant and generalized view of the man. The art of the biography has continued into the present century with such monumental works as Carl Sandburg's massive work on the life of Abraham Lincoln, which spans several volumes.

Look For

As you read the excerpts from *The Life of Samuel Johnson,* look for Boswell's impartiality as he presents both the virtues and weaknesses of the man he held in such high esteem.

Writing

Imagine that you were able to interview a person whom you greatly admire. The person in question may be an athlete, film star, author, or the like. Prepare a list of questions that you think would reveal the individual behind the public mask.

Vocabulary

Knowing the following words will help you as you read the excerpts from *The Life of Samuel Johnson.*

abasement (ə bās′ mənt) *n.*: Condition of being put down or humbled (p. 588)

animadversion (an′ə mad vʉr′ zhən) *n.*: Unfavorable comment (p. 590)

chimerical (ki mir′i k'l) *adj.*: Imaginary; unreal (p. 590)

credulity (krə do͞o′ lə tē) *n.*: Tendency to believe too readily (p. 591)

malignity (mə lig′nə tē) *n.*: Strong desire to harm others (p. 592)

impetuous (im pech′o͞o wəs) *adj.*: Acting rashly (p. 592)

petulance (pech′o͞o ləns) *n.*: Insolent behavior (p. 592)

tincture (tiŋk′chər) *n.*: Tint (p. 593)

pernicious (pər nish′əs) *adj.*: Causing serious injury; deadly (p. 593)

inculcated (in kul′kāt id) *v.*: Impressed upon the mind by frequent repetition (p. 593)

Literary Focus Discuss the term *biography* and ask students what biographies they have read. Ask them whether the biography gave an intimate picture of the individual or whether it presented a distant and generalized view. Which is preferable in a biography and why?

Look For Suggest that students think, as they read through the excerpts, of how they would describe Johnson if they were writing a brief encyclopedia entry about him.

Writing Boswell stated that his aim in writing a biography of Johnson was "to write, not his panegyrick, which must be all praise, but his Life; which, great and good as he was, must not be supposed to be entirely perfect . . . in every picture there should be shade as well as light." Discuss whether reporters have an obligation to present both "shade" and "light" when they write about a public person. Where does a celebrity's private life end and his or her public life begin? What kinds of questions, if any, should an interviewer avoid?

Vocabulary Make sure students understand the pronunciations and meanings of the vocabulary words. Challenge **more advanced** students to think of a synonym for each vocabulary word. If necessary, suggest that they use a dictionary or a thesaurus for help.

Motivation for Reading Discuss whether a biography should necessarily tell about a person's entire life. What kinds of information should be included? What should be left out?

Master Teacher Note Johnson disliked biography because he believed that "he that recounts the life of another, commonly dwells most upon conspicuous events, lessens the familiarity of his tale to increase its dignity, shews his favourite at a distance decorated and magnified like the ancient actors in their tragick dress, and endeavours to hide the man that he may produce a hero." Johnson's ideal for biography is clear —the less distance between reader and subject the better. Discuss what techniques a biographer might use to lessen the distance between reader and subject.

Purpose-Setting Question A critic once said that Boswell's *Life of Samuel Johnson* was an accidental masterpiece, produced by a fool who happened to have a perfect subject. When you have read this excerpt, tell whether you think Boswell was little more than a skillful reporter? Support your answer.

1 **Discussion** What impression of Boswell does this paragraph give the reader?

2 **Discussion** Does the description of Boswell's first meeting with Johnson illuminate as much about Boswell's personality as it does about Johnson's? Explain.

3 **Literary Focus** At the time Boswell wrote his biography, the literary form had been only recently developed. What differences can you perceive in the opening paragraphs between this biography and more modern examples?

from The Life of Samuel Johnson

James Boswell

Boswell Meets Johnson

1763

This is to me a memorable year; for in it I had the happiness to obtain the acquaintance of that extraordinary man whose memoirs I am now writing; an acquaintance which I shall ever esteem as one of the most fortunate circumstances in my life. Though then but two-and-twenty, I had for several
1 years read his works with delight and instruction, and had the highest reverence for their author, which had grown up in my fancy into a kind of mysterious veneration, by figuring to myself a state of solemn elevated abstraction, in which I supposed him to live in the immense metropolis of London. . . .

Mr. Thomas Davies[1] the actor, who then kept a bookseller's shop in Russel Street, Covent Garden, told me that Johnson was very much his friend, and came frequently to his house, where he more than once invited me to meet him; but by some unlucky accident or other he was prevented from coming to us.

At last, on Monday the 16th day of May, when I was sitting in Mr. Davies's back
2,3 parlor, after having drunk tea with him and Mrs. Davies, Johnson unexpectedly came into the shop; and Mr. Davies having perceived him through the glass door in the room in which we were sitting, advancing towards us—he announced his aweful[2] approach to me, somewhat in the manner of an actor in the part of Horatio, when he addresses Hamlet on the appearance of his father's ghost, "Look, my Lord, it comes,"[3] I found that I had a very perfect idea of Johnson's figure, from the portrait of him painted by Sir Joshua Reynolds[4] soon after he had published his *Dictionary,* in the attitude of sitting in his easy chair in deep meditation, which was the first picture his friend did for him, which Sir Joshua very kindly presented to me, and from which an engraving has been made for this work. Mr. Davies mentioned my name, and respectfully introduced me to him. I was much agitated; and recollecting his prejudice against the Scotch, of which I had heard much, I said to Davies, "Don't tell where I come from." "From Scotland," cried Davies roguishly. "Mr. Johnson," said I, "I do indeed come from Scotland, but I cannot help it." I am willing to flatter myself that I meant this as light pleasantry to sooth and conciliate him, and not as an humiliating abasement at the expense of my country. But however that might be, this speech was somewhat

1. Thomas Davies: An English bookseller and unsuccessful actor (1712–1785).

2. aweful: Awe-inspiring.

3. Horatio " . . . it comes": From Shakespeare's *Hamlet* (Act I, Scene iv).

4. Sir Joshua Reynolds: A celebrated portrait painter at the time (1723–1792).

JOHNSON AND BOSWELL

Humanities Note

Engraving, *Johnson and Boswell.* This engraving of the ghost of Samuel Johnson haunting his biographer, Boswell, appeared in the 1803 edition of the play *The Way of the World* by William Congreve. The artist, whose identity is unknown, was in the employ of the publisher, C. Bestland of West End, Hempstead, England. William Congreve (1670–1729) was known to Boswell and Johnson, who admired him greatly.

You may wish to use the following questions for discussion.

1. Boswell allows in his biography that he himself was a silly fop next to the stern and stately Johnson. Does this comparison come across in the illustration? Explain.
2. What facts did Boswell reveal about Johnson that may have made him return to "haunt" his biographer, as shown in this illustration?

4 Discussion What does Johnson mean by this statement?

5 Discussion How, according to Johnson, does Providence preserve equality among mankind?

6 Literary Focus What does this statement tell you about Johnson's view of the monarchy? of punishment for sedition?

unlucky; for with that quickness of wit for which he was so remarkable, he seized the expression "come from Scotland," which I used in the sense of being of that country; and, as if I had said that I had come away from it, or left, retorted, "That, Sir, I find, is what a very great many of your countrymen cannot help." This stroke stunned me a good deal; and when we had sat down, I felt myself not a little embarrassed, and apprehensive of what might come next. He then addressed himself to Davies: "What do you think of Garrick?[5] He has refused me an order for the play for Miss Williams, because he knows the house will be full, and that an order would be worth three shillings." Eager to take any opening to get into conversation with him, I ventured to say, "O, Sir, I cannot think Mr. Garrick would grudge such a trifle to you." "Sir," said he, with a stern look, "I have known David Garrick longer than you have done: and I know no right you have to talk to me on the subject." Perhaps I deserved this check; for it was rather presumptuous in me, an entire stranger, to express any doubt of the justice of his animadversion upon his old acquaintance and pupil. I now felt myself much mortified, and began to think that the hope which I had long indulged of obtaining his acquaintance was blasted. And, in truth, had not my ardor been uncommonly strong, and my resolution uncommonly persevering, so rough a reception might have deterred me forever from making any further attempts. Fortunately, however, I remained upon the field not wholly discomfited; and was soon rewarded by hearing some of his conversation, of which I preserved the following short minute,[6] without marking the questions and observations by which it was produced.

"People," he remarked, "may be taken in once, who imagine that an author is greater in private life than other men. Uncommon parts require uncommon opportunities for their exertion." 4

"In barbarous society, superiority of parts is of real consequence. Great strength or great wisdom is of much value to an individual. But in more polished times there are people to do everything for money; and then there are a number of other superiorities, such as those of birth and fortune, and rank, that dissipate men's attention, and leave no extraordinary share of respect for personal and intellectual superiority. This is wisely ordered by Providence, to preserve some equality among mankind." 5

"Sir, this book (*The Elements of Criticism*,[7] which he had taken up) is a pretty essay, and deserves to be held in some estimation, though much of it is chimerical."

Speaking of one[8] who with more than ordinary boldness attacked public measures and the royal family, he said, "I think he is safe from the law, but he is an abusive scoundrel; and instead of applying to my Lord Chief Justice to punish him, I would send half a dozen footmen and have him well ducked."[9] 6

"The notion of liberty amuses the people of England, and helps to keep off the *taedium vitae*.[10] When a butcher tells you that his heart bleeds for his country, he has, in fact, no uneasy feeling."

"Sheridan[11] will not succeed at Bath with his oratory. Ridicule has gone down before him, and, I doubt,[12] Derrick[13] is his enemy."

---

5. Garrick: David Garrick (1717–1779), a famous actor who had been educated by Johnson. Garrick was also one of the managing partners of the Drury Lane Theater in London.

6. minuten: Note.

7. *Elements of Criticism*: One of the works of Scottish philosophical writer Henry Home (1696–1782).

8. one: John Wilkes (1727–1797), an English political agitator.

9. ducked: Tied to a chair at the end of a plank and plunged into water.

10. *taedium vitae* (tī'dē əm vē' tī): Boredom.

11. Sheridan: Thomas Sheridan (1719–1788), an Irish actor and author. At the time, Sheridan was reading lectures at the Oratory at Bath.

12. doubt: Fear.

13. Derrick: The Master of Ceremonies of the Oratory at Bath.

"Derrick may do very well, as long as he can outrun his character; but the moment his character gets up with him, it is all over."

It is, however, but just to record, that some years afterwards, when I reminded
7 him of this sarcasm, he said, "Well, but Derrick has now got a character that he need not run away from."

I was highly pleased with the extraordinary vigor of his conversation, and regretted that I was drawn away from it by an engagement at another place. I had, for a part of the evening, been left alone with him, and had ventured to make an observation now and then, which he received very civilly; so that I was satisfied that though there was a roughness in his manner, there was no ill nature in his disposition. Davies followed me to the
8 door, and when I complained to him a little of the hard blows which the great man had given me he kindly took upon him to console me by saying, "Don't be uneasy. I can see he likes you very well."

Johnson's Character

The character of Samuel Johnson has, I trust, been so developed in the course of this work, that they who have honored it with a perusal, may be considered as well acquainted with him. As, however, it may be expected that I should collect into one view the capital and distinguishing features of this extraordinary man, I shall endeavor to acquit myself of that part of my biographical undertaking, however difficult it may be to do that which many of my readers will do
9 better for themselves.

His figure was large and well formed, and his countenance of the cast of an ancient statue; yet his appearance was rendered strange and somewhat uncouth by convulsive cramps, by the scars of that distemper[14] which it was once imagined the royal touch could cure,[15] and by a slovenly mode of dress. He had the use only of one eye; yet so much does mind govern and even supply the deficiency of organs, that his visual perceptions, as far as they extended, were uncommonly quick and accurate. So morbid was his temperament, that he never knew the natural joy of a free and vigorous use of his limbs: when he walked, it was like the struggling gait of one in fetters; when he rode, he had no command or direction of his horse, but was carried as if in a balloon. That with his constitution and habits of life he should have lived seventy-five years, is a proof that an inherent *vivida vis*[16] is a powerful preservative of the human frame.

Man is, in general, made up of contradictory qualities; and these will ever show themselves in strange succession, where a consistency in appearance at least, if not in reality, has not been attained by long habits of philosophical discipline. In proportion to the native vigor of the mind, the contradictory qualities will be the more prominent, and more difficult to be adjusted; and, therefore, we are not to wonder that Johnson exhibited an eminent example of this remark which I have made upon human nature. At different times, he seemed a different man, in some respects; not, however, in any great
or essential article, upon which he had fully 10
employed his mind, and settled certain principles of duty, but only in his manners and in the display of argument and fancy in his talk. He was prone to superstition, but not to credulity. Though his imagination might incline him to a belief of the marvelous and the mysterious, his vigorous reason examined the evidence with jealousy.[17] He was a sincere and zealous Christian, of high Church of England and monarchical princi-

14. distemper *n.*: Scrofula, a type of tuberculosis that causes swelling and scarring of the neck.

15. royal touch . . . cure: It was at one time believed that the touch of an English monarch had the power to heal. As a child Johnson was taken to Queene Anne to receive her touch in the hope that it would cure him.

16. *vivida vis*: Lively force.

17. jealousy: Suspicion.

7 Literary Focus What does this statement show about Johnson's flexibility?

8 Discussion How is Boswell's sense of inferiority revealed here?

9 Discussion Do you think this is false modesty?

10 Discussion What one characteristic of Johnson's always remained the same?

11 **Critical Thinking and Reading** How does Boswell excuse Johnson's many prejudices?

12 **Critical Thinking and Reading** How does Boswell excuse Johnson's "hasty and satirical sallies even against his best friends"?

13 **Discussion** Considering Pope, Swift, and other writers of the time, why do you think satirists were in such vogue during the "Age of Enlightenment"?

14 **Critical Thinking and Reading** How does the manner in which Boswell presents Johnson's weaknesses help to lessen their seriousness?

ples, which he would not tamely suffer to be questioned; and had, perhaps, at an early period, narrowed his mind somewhat too much, both as to religion and politics. His being impressed with the danger of extreme latitude in either, though he was of a very independent spirit, occasioned his appearing somewhat unfavorable to the prevalence of that noble freedom of sentiment which is the best possession of man. Nor can it be denied, that he had many prejudices; which,
11 however, frequently suggested many of his pointed sayings that rather show a playfulness of fancy than any settled malignity. He was steady and inflexible in maintaining the obligations of religion and morality; both from a regard for the order of society, and from a veneration for the Great Source of all order; correct, nay, stern in his taste; hard to please, and easily offended; impetuous and irritable in his temper, but of a most humane and benevolent heart, which showed itself not only in a most liberal charity, as far as his circumstances would allow, but in a thousand instances of active benevolence. He was afflicted with a bodily disease, which made him often restless and fretful; and with a constitutional melancholy, the clouds of which darkened the
12 brightness of his fancy, and gave a gloomy cast to his whole course of thinking: we,
13 therefore, ought not to wonder at his sallies of impatience and passion at any time; especially when provoked by obtrusive ignorance, or presuming petulance; and allowance must be made for his uttering hasty and satirical sallies even against his best friends. And, surely, when it is considered, that, "amidst sickness and sorrow," he exerted his faculties in so many works for the benefit of mankind, and particularly that he achieved the great and admirable Dictionary of our language, we must be astonished at his resolution. The solemn text, "of him to whom much is given, much will be required," seems to have been ever present to his mind, in a rigorous sense, and to have made him dissatisfied with his labors and acts of goodness, however comparatively great; so that the unavoidable consciousness of his superiority was, in that respect, a cause of disquiet. He suffered so much from this, and from the gloom which perpetually haunted him and made solitude frightful, that it may be said of him, "If in this life only 14
he had hope, he was of all men most miserable."[18] He loved praise, when it was brought to him; but was too proud to seek for it. He was somewhat susceptible of flattery. As he was general and unconfined in his studies, he cannot be considered as master of any one particular science; but he had accumulated a vast and various collection of learning and knowledge, which was so arranged in his mind, as to be ever in readiness to be brought forth. But his superiority over other learned men consisted chiefly in what may be called the art of thinking, the art of using his mind; a certain continual power of seizing the useful substance of all that he knew and exhibiting it in a clear and forcible manner; so that knowledge, which we often see to be no better than lumber[19] in men of dull understanding, was, in him, true, evident, and actual wisdom. His moral precepts are practical; for they are drawn from an intimate acquaintance with human nature. His maxims carry conviction; for they are founded on the basis of common sense, and a very attentive and minute survey of real life. His mind was so full of imagery, that he might have been perpetually a poet; yet it is remarkable, that, however rich his prose is in this respect, his poetical pieces, in general, have not much of that splendor, but are rather distinguished by strong sentiment and acute observation, conveyed in harmonious and energetic verse, particularly in heroic couplets. Though usually grave, and even aweful, in his deportment, he possessed uncommon and peculiar powers of wit and humor; he frequently indulged himself in colloquial pleasantry; and the hearti-

18. "If . . . miserable": From I Corinthians 15:19.
19. lumber: Rubbish.

est merriment was often enjoyed in his company; with this great advantage, that as it was entirely free from any poisonous tincture of vice or impiety, it was salutary to those who shared in it. He had accustomed himself to such accuracy in his common conversation, that he at all times expressed his thoughts with great force, and an elegant choice of language, the effect of which was aided by his having a loud voice, and a slow deliberate utterance. In him were united a most logical head with a most fertile imagination, which gave him an extraordinary advantage in arguing: for he could reason close or wide, as he saw best for the moment. Exulting in his intellectual strength and dexterity, he could, when he pleased, be the greatest sophist[20] that ever contended in the lists of declamation; and, from a spirit of contradiction and a delight in showing his powers, he would often maintain the wrong side with equal warmth and ingenuity; so that, when there was an audience, his real opinions could seldom be gathered from his talk; though when he was in company with a single friend, he would discuss a subject with genuine fairness: but he was too conscientious to make error permanent and pernicious, by deliberately writing it; and, in all his numerous works, he earnestly inculcated what appeared to him to be the truth; his piety being constant, and the ruling principle of all his conduct.

Such was Samuel Johnson, a man 15
whose talents, acquirements, and virtues, were so extraordinary, that the more his character is considered the more he will be regarded by the present age, and by posterity, with admiration and reverence.

20. sophist (säf' ist) *n.*: One who makes misleading arguments.

15 **Reading Strategy** Summarize the contradictory qualities Boswell found fascinating in Johnson.

593

Answers

ANSWERS TO THINKING ABOUT THE SELECTION

Recalling

1. His body cramped convulsively; he was scared; his clothes were slovenly; one eye was useless; and he walked with a struggling gait.
2. (a) He was superstitious but not gullible. (b) He was a zealous Christian. (c) He loved praise. (d) He was somewhat susceptible to flattery.

Interpreting

3. (a) The art of using his mind and his powers of wit and humor explain his sarcastic remark. (b) He was charitable and actively benevolent. (c) He was impatient when provoked by ignorance.
4. Answers will differ. A possible answer is: Boswell's inferiority complex, which led him to become a celebrity chaser, probably led him to exaggerate Johnson's brilliance and wit, although the man undoubtedly had a good measure of both.

Applying

5. Answers will differ. Possible answers are: (a) "Man is, in general, made up of contradictory qualities . . ."; "At different times, he seemed a different man . . ."; ". . . he had many prejudices . . ."; and "He was somewhat susceptible to flattery." (b) No, because they help to form a complete picture of the man.
6. Answers will differ. Possible answers are: (a) Most celebrities seem to enjoy attention and to assume they are welcome to "drop in" on friends and acquaintances. They also assume that whatever they have to say is important. (b) One difference between Johnson and celebrities today is that today's celebrities would not generally appear in public in "a slovenly mode of dress."

ANSWERS TO ANALYZING LITERATURE

Answers will differ.

1. Boswell was so impressed by Johnson even before he met him and so anxious to impress him when he did that he probably could not have been impartial.
2. The statements provide a good picture of Johnson even without the questions and observations that led up to them.

ANSWERS TO CRITICAL THINKING AND READING

Answers will differ. Students should provide support for their choices.

THINKING AND WRITING

For help with this assignment, students can use Lesson 10, "Writing About Point of View," in the Handbook of Writing About Literature.

THINKING ABOUT THE SELECTION

Recalling

1. What aspects of Johnson's appearance prompt Boswell to describe him as "strange and somewhat uncouth"?
2. (a) What, according to the selection, was Johnson's position on superstition? (b) On religion? (c) On praise? (d) On flattery?

Interpreting

3. (a) What details of Johnson's personality described in this excerpt explain his sarcastic remark about Scotland in "Boswell Meets Johnson"? (b) His desire to obtain a free theater ticket for a friend? (c) His harsh reply to Boswell's comment on Garrick?
4. What do you learn about Boswell himself from this passage? Support your comments with evidence.

Applying

5. (a) Which of the observations presented in this excerpt do you think apply more or less to most people? (b) Do you think the inclusion of these details detracts from the integrity of Boswell's biography? Explain your answer.
6. (a) What similarities do you detect between the lifestyles and habits of celebrities of the eighteenth century and those of our own age? (b) What differences do you detect?

ANALYZING LITERATURE

Understanding Biography

A **biography** is a history of a person told or written by others. A good biography meets several criteria. It presents (1) the subject in an impartial light; (2) a complete and unified picture of the subject; (3) the subject against the backdrop of the times in which he or she lived. Based on the excerpt from Boswell's *The Life of Samuel Johnson,* state how well you think the work stacks up against these criteria. In making your assessment, consider the following questions.

1. Can Boswell's statement that he "was much agitated" upon meeting Johnson be taken as an admission that he was not in a frame of mind to report facts impartially? Why?
2. On page 590, Boswell notes that he preserved Johnson's observations "without marking the questions and observations" that led up to them. Does this suggest a lack of completeness? Why?

CRITICAL THINKING AND READING

Recognizing Subjective Information

Subjective information is information colored by a person's own attitudes and feelings. *Objective* information is information that preserves some widely held truth. The statement "I like to eat chicken" is a piece of subjective information. The statement "Chicken is a source of protein" is a piece of objective information. Biography, if it is interesting, will usually contain a mixture of subjective and objective statements.

Bearing in mind what you read about Boswell in the biographical sketch of him on page 586, which of the details presented in this excerpt do you suspect of being the most subjective? Explain your answer.

THINKING AND WRITING

Writing from Johnson's Point of View

Write an account of the meeting described in this excerpt from Samuel Johnson's point of view. Before beginning, review Boswell's quotations of Johnson in order to help you form an impression of the older man's prose style and general attitude toward life. Feel free to add original details that may have escaped Boswell's attention.

Pre-Romantic Poetry

HAYMAKERS, 1785
George Stubbs
The Granger Collection

Humanities Note

Fine art, *Haymakers,* 1785, by George Stubbs. George Stubbs (1724–1806), most famous for his numerous paintings of horses, hunters, and equestrian scenes, brought to his work an understanding of anatomy, a subject he studied with much enthusiasm. In 1766 his book *Anatomy of the Horse* was published; a later book, *Comparative Exposition of the Structure of the Human Body with that of a Tiger and Common Fowls,* was unfinished when he died.

Stubbs's paintings reveal his commitment to portraying animals subjects with great realism. Both animal and human figures are portrayed in *Haymakers,* a pasoral scene evocative of the growing romantic interest in simple peasant life.

More About the Author Thomas Gray remains one of the best known and respected of all English poets, yet his reputation rests entirely on the basis of three major poems and three or four short lyrics. Ask students to discuss the relative value of quality versus quantity in determining ranking in any field. Should a person who has contributed only, say, two or three admittedly brilliant poems—or songs, or books, etc.—be ranked with artists who have contributed much more—even if the latters' works are not all first rate?

THOMAS GRAY

(1716–1771)

Although Thomas Gray produced precious little poetry during his lifetime, his scant output was more a result of his perfectionism than it was of any lack of ideas. Gray was a scholar, with interests ranging from literature to art to science and beyond. Had he lived in an era more compatible with the romantic yearnings of his soul, he might, as the poet Matthew Arnold suggested, have been capable of far greater things.

Gray was born in the Cornhill section of London. Gray himself suffered from convulsions, a condition that forced his mother on at least one occasion to open a vein in his head to relieve pressure on his brain. He was educated at Eton and Cambridge and, after completing his studies, traveled through Europe with his friend Horace Walpole.

At the end of three years, Gray returned to England and lived for a time with his mother and sister in the village of Stoke Poges. It was in this sleepy hamlet during the summer of 1742 that he wrote his first important poems—"On the Spring," "On a Distant Prospect of Eton College," and "Hymn to Adversity." It was also around this time that Gray penned his most famous poetic work, "Elegy Written in a Country Churchyard." A copy of the elegy that he sent to Walpole accidentally fell into the hands of a dishonest editor. Ultimately it was retrieved, though only after a great struggle, which adds a touch of irony to Gray's having refused to accept payment for the poem when at last it was published.

After reaching the age of thirty, Gray lived an increasingly quiet country life, becoming something of a hermit. A confirmed bachelor, he busied himself with books and experimented with new poetic forms, while conducting private studies in classical literature at Cambridge. His work of this period, which includes the odes "The Bard" (1757) and "The Descent of Odin" (1761), reflects his love of Celtic and Norse mythology and his interest in history and language. In 1771 while planning a visit to a friend in Switzerland, the poet suffered a violent attack of gout and died on July 30. Seven years after his death, a monument honoring him was erected in Westminster Abbey.

Although Gray was a less than energetic poet, the small body of works that he left behind is notable for its juxtaposing of established forms and novel sentiments. His "Elegy in a Country Churchyard," in particular, combines masterfully the neoclassical style of his own century with the Romantic ideals of the next one.

Objectives

1. To understand the elegy as a literary form
2. To evaluate the effect of inverted sentences in verse
3. To appreciate vivid verbs in verse
4. To write an elegy

Teaching Portfolio: Support Material

Teacher Backup, pp. 00-00

Vocabulary Check, p. 00

Usage and Mechanics Worksheet, p. 00

Analyzing Literature Worksheet, p. 00

Critical Thinking and Reading Worksheet, p. 00

Language Worksheet, p. 00

Selection Test, p. 00

GUIDE FOR READING

Elegy Written in a Country Churchyard

Literary Forms

Elegy. An elegy is a lyric poem or musical composition that laments a death. The form, which dates back to ancient Greece and Rome, flourished during the European Renaissance that spanned the fourteenth through the sixteenth centuries. Although an elegy usually mourns the death of an individual, it may also address the ravages of time or may function as a meditation on the nature of loss. The elegy, while conforming to no rigid structural guidelines, often opens with an expression of grief and moves gradually toward a philosophical acceptance of the loss. Thomas Gray's "Elegy Written in a Country Churchyard," inspired by the death of the poet's close friend Richard West, marks one of two highpoints of the elegiac form in English literature, the other being Tennyson's *In Memoriam,* composed a century later.

Look For

As you read "Elegy Written in a Country Churchyard," look for evidence that the poet is mourning not an individual, but an aspect of the human condition.

Writing

Gray's elegy ends with an epitaph, a poetic inscription intended to appear on a gravestone. Often an epitaph mentions a property or trait of the deceased for which he or she might best be remembered. Write an epitaph for yourself or for a friend. Focus, using as few words as possible, on the individual's most memorable quality.

Vocabulary

Knowing the following words will help you as you read "Elegy Written in a Country Churchyard."

knell (nel) *n.*: Sound of a bell rung slowly (p. 598, l. 1)
jocund (jäk'ənd) *adj.*: Cheerful (p. 599, l. 27)
pregnant (preg'nənt) *adj.*: Full of ideas; inventive (p. 600, l. 46)
penury (pen'yə rē) *n.*: Poverty (p. 600, l. 51)
inglorious (in glôr'ē əs) *adj.*: Little-known (p. 600, l. 59)
circumscribed (sʉr'kəm skrīb'd) *v.*: Limited; confined (p. 600, l. 65)
ingenuous (in jen'yoo wəs) *adj.*: Naive; simple (p. 601, l. 69)
tenor (ten'ər) *n.*: General tendency or course (p. 601, l. 76)

Literary Focus Stress the fact that the elegy is a meditative poem lamenting the death of a particular person. Gray's elegy, however, laments not the death of a specific person, but dwells on death as the ultimate fate of all people, rich and poor alike.

Look For Many students will try to make Gray himself the persona. The person meditating in the poem may be best thought of as a persona perhaps not unlike Gray, but likely not Gray himself.

Writing You might lead your students in writing a group epitaph in the form of a quatrain rhyming *abab.* Begin with the formula phrase *Here lies . . .*

Vocabulary Go over the vocabulary words as a class. Have students use them in sentences of their own.

Motivation for Reading Suggest that your students look for the democratic spirit that pervades this poem. What seems to be Gray's attitude toward the ordinary, humble man and woman.

Master Teacher Note Gray is a transitional figure, a bridge between the eighteenth-century classical ideals and the Romantic movement of the nineteenth century. As his "Elegy . . ." reveals, Gray reflects the former in his respect for established literary forms and in his knowledge of Greek and Roman culture. At the same time elements of Romanticism are revealed—in the subject matter and in the dignified tone of the poem.

Purpose-Setting Question Whom does the poet lament in this elegy?

Thematic Idea Compare Gray's poem with the excerpt from John Donne's "Meditation XVII," on page 427. How are they similar in content; how are they different? A similar comparison may be made with "Thoughts in Westminster Abbey," page 555.

1 **Literary Focus** Note that the poem is written in iambic-pentameter quatrains, with an alternating rhyme scheme, *abab.* This is a typical eighteenth-century elegiac form.

2 **Reading Strategy** Have students sum up the content of the opening three stanzas. Note how they establish the setting and mood of the poem. What time of day is it? Where is the speaker? How do you know it is set in the country? What is the mood of these stanzas?

3 **Literary Focus** In line 13 the speaker shifts attention to the graveyard and its inhabitants. This stanza and the next nineteen offer some general reflections prompted by the setting.

Elegy Written in a Country Churchyard

Thomas Gray

The curfew tolls the knell of parting day,
1 The lowing herd winds slowly o'er the lea,[1]
The plowman homeward plods his weary way,
And leaves the world to darkness and to me.

Now fades the glimmering landscape on the sight,
And all the air a solemn stillness holds,
Save where the beetle wheels his droning flight,
And drowsy tinklings lull the distant folds;

Save that from yonder ivy-mantled tower,
2 The moping owl does to the moon complain
Of such as, wandering near her secret bower,
Molest her ancient solitary reign.

3 Beneath those rugged elms, that yew tree's shade,
Where heaves the turf in many a moldering heap,
Each in his narrow cell forever laid,
The rude[2] forefathers of the hamlet sleep.

The breezy call of incense-breathing morn,
The swallow twittering from the straw-built shed,
4, 5 The cock's shrill clarion, or the echoing horn,[3]
No more shall rouse them from their lowly bed.

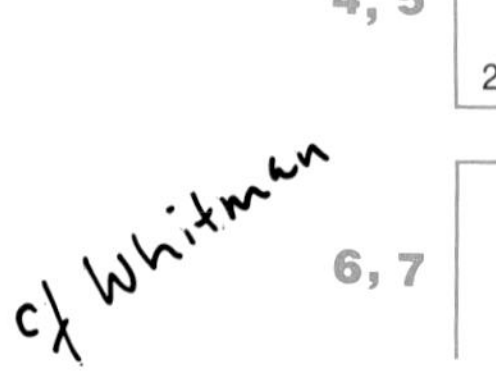

For them no more the blazing hearth shall burn,
6, 7 Or busy housewife ply her evening care:
No children run to lisp their sire's return,
Or climb his knees the envied kiss to share.

1. **lea:** Meadow.
2. **rude:** Uneducated.
3. **horn:** The hunter's horn.

4 **Clarification** A clarion is trumpet-like sound.

5 **Discussion** Note the morning sounds described in lines 17–20. How are they different from the evening sounds in the first three stanzas?

6 **Discussion** Lines 21–28 illustrate activities in the daily lives of these simple people. What kinds of activities are mentioned? How did they feel about their work? Does the speaker sympathize with or mock their lives?

7 **Literary Focus** Gray's sympathy with common people and his sense that working close to nature is both joyful and ennobling are Romantic attitudes.

Oft did the harvest to their sickle yield,
    Their furrow oft the stubborn glebe[4] has broke;
How jocund did they drive their team afield!
    How bowed the woods beneath their sturdy stroke!

Let not Ambition mock their useful toil,
    Their homely joys, and destiny obscure;
Nor Grandeur hear with a disdainful smile
    The short and simple annals of the poor.

The boast of heraldry,[5] the pomp of power,
    And all that beauty, all that wealth e'er gave,
Awaits alike the inevitable hour.
    The paths of glory lead but to the grave.

8 Literary Focus In lines 29–44 the speaker shifts to talk about the inevitability of death—even for the mighty. Note the formal style.

9 Literary Focus Line 36 is one of the many lines often quoted from this poem. Note the use of personification in this line.

---

4. glebe: Soil.
5. heraldry: Noble descent.

10 Clarification "Hands, that the rod of empire might have swayed" means "mighty ruler." "Or waked to ecstasy the living lyre" is a way of saying "poet."

11 Discussion What kept these dead from realizing their potential? Point out that the word *rage* means "ardor or enthusiasm." The phrase *genial current* means "natural potentialities."

12 Literary Focus Lines 53–56 are often quoted. In your own words summarize the meaning. How apt are the lines, considering the theme of the poem?

13 Clarification Lines 61–72 might be summarized as "Their lot in life prevented them from becoming great statesmen and benefactors, but it also prevented them from becoming tyrants." Explain that the phrase *ingenuous shame* might mean "the shame a good person feels when he or she doesn't live up to ideals."

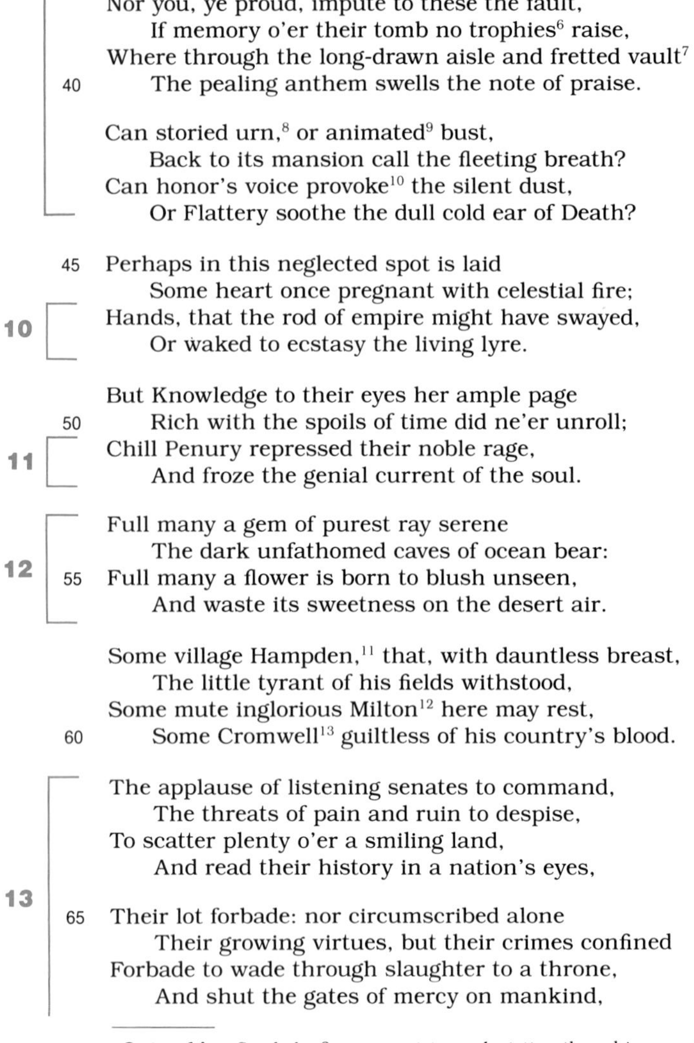

Nor you, ye proud, impute to these the fault,
If memory o'er their tomb no trophies[6] raise,
Where through the long-drawn aisle and fretted vault[7]
The pealing anthem swells the note of praise.

Can storied urn,[8] or animated[9] bust,
Back to its mansion call the fleeting breath?
Can honor's voice provoke[10] the silent dust,
Or Flattery soothe the dull cold ear of Death?

Perhaps in this neglected spot is laid
Some heart once pregnant with celestial fire;
10 Hands, that the rod of empire might have swayed,
Or waked to ecstasy the living lyre.

But Knowledge to their eyes her ample page
Rich with the spoils of time did ne'er unroll;
11 Chill Penury repressed their noble rage,
And froze the genial current of the soul.

12 Full many a gem of purest ray serene
The dark unfathomed caves of ocean bear:
Full many a flower is born to blush unseen,
And waste its sweetness on the desert air.

Some village Hampden,[11] that, with dauntless breast,
The little tyrant of his fields withstood,
Some mute inglorious Milton[12] here may rest,
Some Cromwell[13] guiltless of his country's blood.

13 The applause of listening senates to command,
The threats of pain and ruin to despise,
To scatter plenty o'er a smiling land,
And read their history in a nation's eyes,

Their lot forbade: nor circumscribed alone
Their growing virtues, but their crimes confined
Forbade to wade through slaughter to a throne,
And shut the gates of mercy on mankind,

6. trophies: Symbolic figures or pictures depicting the achievements of the dead man.
7. fretted vault: A church ceiling decorated with intersecting lines.
8. storied urn: A funeral urn with an epitaph inscribed on it.
9. animated: Lifelike.
10. provoke: Call forth.
11. Hampden: John Hampden (1594–1643), an English statesman who defied King Charles I by resisting the king's efforts to revive the obsolete tax of ship-money without the authority of Parliament.
12. Milton: English poet, John Milton (1608–1674).
13. Cromwell: Oliver Cromwell (1599–1658), English revolutionary leader and Lord Protector of the Commonwealth from 1653 to 1658.

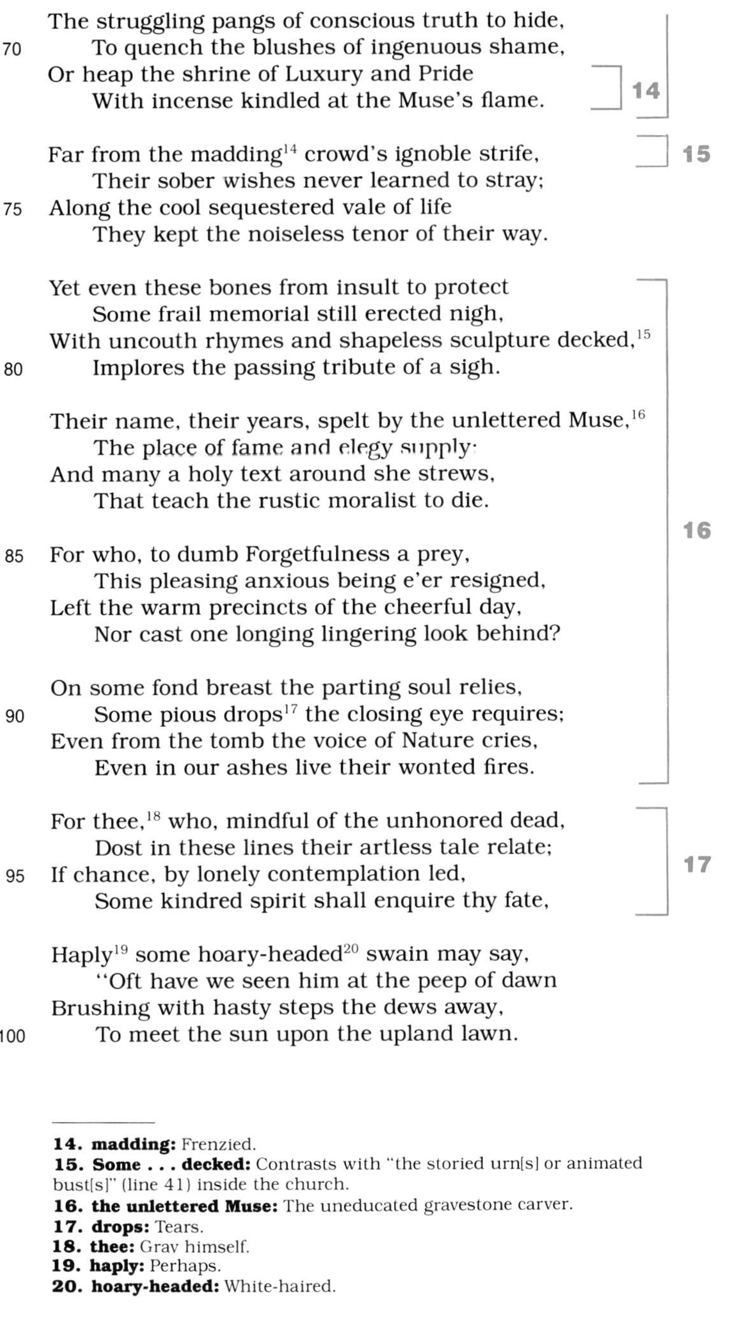

The struggling pangs of conscious truth to hide,
    To quench the blushes of ingenuous shame,
Or heap the shrine of Luxury and Pride
    With incense kindled at the Muse's flame.

Far from the madding[14] crowd's ignoble strife,
    Their sober wishes never learned to stray;
Along the cool sequestered vale of life
    They kept the noiseless tenor of their way.

Yet even these bones from insult to protect
    Some frail memorial still erected nigh,
With uncouth rhymes and shapeless sculpture decked,[15]
    Implores the passing tribute of a sigh.

Their name, their years, spelt by the unlettered Muse,[16]
    The place of fame and elegy supply:
And many a holy text around she strews,
    That teach the rustic moralist to die.

For who, to dumb Forgetfulness a prey,
    This pleasing anxious being e'er resigned,
Left the warm precincts of the cheerful day,
    Nor cast one longing lingering look behind?

On some fond breast the parting soul relies,
    Some pious drops[17] the closing eye requires;
Even from the tomb the voice of Nature cries,
    Even in our ashes live their wonted fires.

For thee,[18] who, mindful of the unhonored dead,
    Dost in these lines their artless tale relate;
If chance, by lonely contemplation led,
    Some kindred spirit shall enquire thy fate,

Haply[19] some hoary-headed[20] swain may say,
    "Oft have we seen him at the peep of dawn
Brushing with hasty steps the dews away,
    To meet the sun upon the upland lawn.

14. madding: Frenzied.
15. Some . . . decked: Contrasts with "the storied urn[s] or animated bust[s]" (line 41) inside the church.
16. the unlettered Muse: The uneducated gravestone carver.
17. drops: Tears.
18. thee: Gray himself.
19. haply: Perhaps.
20. hoary-headed: White-haired.

14 Clarification Lines 71–72 are an allusion to people who write poetry that extols the vices of powerful people.

15 Literary Focus Thomas Hardy chose "Far from the madding crowd" as the title of one of his novels.

16 Literary Focus In lines 77–92 the speaker shifts focus to the desire of humble people for some kind of immortality in the minds of the living. Lines 85–92 offer a reason why these people need a memorial of some kind. What is that reason? Explain that the phrase *this pleasing anxious being* means "the living human body."

17 Clarification The *thee* is the *me* of line 4. The speaker is addressing himself, imagining the death of the kind of person he is. *If chance* means "if it happens that."

601

18 Clarification The heath is wasteland too poor to farm.

19 Literary Focus This imaginary epitaph is written for a person very much like Gray himself, although it does not appear on the poet's own gravestone. Even after the "Elegy . . ." was published and brought him fame, Gray remained both indifferent to and suspicious of it. Explain how the epitaph is a logical summation of the poem.

Challenge Explain why passages like lines 3, 8, and 88 have been acclaimed for their blend of sound and sense. What other memorable passages did you find? Explain your choices.

"There at the foot of yonder nodding beech,
That wreathes its old fantastic roots so high,
His listless length at noontide would he stretch,
And pore upon the brook that babbles by.

"Hard by yon wood, now smiling as in scorn,
Muttering his wayward fancies he would rove;
Now drooping, woeful wan, like one forlorn,
Or crazed with care, or crossed in hopeless love.

"One morn I missed him on the customed hill,
18 Along the heath, and near his favorite tree;
Another came; nor yet beside the rill,[21]
Nor up the lawn, nor at the wood was he;

"The next, with dirges due in sad array
Slow through the churchway path we saw him borne.
Approach and read (for thou canst read) the lay
Graved on the stone beneath yon aged thorn."[22]

The Epitaph

Here rests his head upon the lap of Earth
A youth, to Fortune and to Fame unknown.
Fair Science[23] *frowned not on his humble birth,*
And melancholy marked him for her own.

19 *Large was his bounty, and his soul sincere,*
Heaven did a recompense as largely send:
He gave to misery (all he had) a tear,
He gained from Heaven ('twas all he wished) a friend.

No farther seek his merits to disclose,
Or draw his frailties from their dread abode
(There they alike in trembling hope repose),
The bosom of his Father and his God.

---

21. rill: Brook.
22. thorn: Hawthorn tree.
23. Science: Learning.

Answers

ANSWERS TO THINKING ABOUT THE SELECTION
Recalling

1. (a) The speaker is in a country graveyard. (b) It is evening, or twilight.
2. They will no longer enjoy the warmth of a house filled with loving children, or the joys of honest work.

THINKING ABOUT THE SELECTION

Recalling

1. The first four stanzas establish the setting of the poem. (a) Where is the speaker? (b) What time of day is it?
2. According to lines 21–25, what pleasure will these "rude forefathers" no longer partake of?
3. What sorts of lives does the speaker speculate, in lines 57–60, that these people might have led under other circumstances?
4. To whom is "The Epitaph" in the last three stanzas dedicated?

Interpreting

5. (a) What do you think is meant by "the inevitable hour" in line 35? (b) By "its mansion" in line 42?
6. (a) How would you summarize the sentiment expressed in lines 53–56? (b) In lines 77–92?

Applying

7. (a) Tell who or what the poet is elegizing. (b) State whether you share his sense of loss, giving reasons for your answer.

ANALYZING LITERATURE

Understanding an Elegy

An **elegy** is a lyric poem that expresses mourning. Usually the object of this mourning is the death of an individual, though an elegy can also grieve the toll that time's passage takes on youth or beauty. Typically the elegy begins solemnly, with the poet's expression of sadness over his or her loss, and ends with an insight that enables the poet to cope with this loss.

1. (a) Whom does the poet grieve in "Elegy Written in a Country Churchyard"? (b) What do these people seem to represent to the poet? (c) What words express the poet's sadness?
2. (a) Does the poet come to accept his loss by the end of the poem? Explain your answer. (b) What insight helps him to reach this acceptance? (c) What ideas or thoughts bridge his grief and his acceptance?

CRITICAL THINKING AND READING

Evaluating Inverted Sentences

In English the most common sentence structure is "subject-verb-object." That is, the "doer" of the action is usually named first, the word specifying the action appears second, and the recipient of the action comes last. In poetry the parts of the sentence are sometimes **inverted,** or reversed, to emphasize a particular idea. In line 90, for example, the poet places the object *some pious drops* before both the subject and verb of the sentence, to focus the reader's attention on the idea of tears. Locate the following lines, and identify the order of the sentence parts. Then tell what idea is being stressed.

1. Line 5
2. Lines 13–16
3. Lines 49–50
4. Lines 81–82

UNDERSTANDING LANGUAGE

Appreciating Vivid Verbs

The words a poet uses can help convey the poem's mood and can influence the feelings the poem arouses in the reader. In the opening stanzas of Gray's "Elegy," the mood is one of quiet solemnity. To carry this feeling across to the reader, the poet chooses **vivid,** or highly descriptive, verbs. Notice, for instance, Gray's use of the verb *plod* in line 3, to suggest slow and weary movement. Imagine how bland the line would have seemed if the poet had instead chosen the verb *goes*.

Find five vivid verbs in this elegy and explain the effect of each.

THINKING AND WRITING

Writing an Elegy

Using the epitaph you created for the Writing activity on page 597 as a starting point, write an elegy. Imitate as many of the features of Gray's "Elegy" as you can, including inverted sentence structure and vivid verbs. Remember to begin your elegy with an expression of your grief and to end it with a statement of acceptance.

(Answers begin on p. 602.)

3. These people, under other circumstances, might have been great leaders—in letters and in politics, for example.
4. "The epitaph" is dedicated to all the humble, unknown people buried in the churchyard.

Interpreting

5. (a) The "inevitable hour" is the moment of death. (b) "Its mansion" is life itself.
6. (a) Answers will differ but should include the idea that many wonderful things in nature go unnoticed. (b) Answers will differ but should include the idea that the humble people long for some kind of immortality in the minds of the living.

Applying

7. (a) The poet is elegizing the death of all people, the mighty and the common. (b) Answers will differ.

ANSWERS TO ANALYZING LITERATURE

1. The poet grieves for the common people, whose lives go unnoticed. They seem to represent the Romantic attitude that working close to nature is both joyful and ennobling. Answers to the last question in this item will differ.
2. The poet accepts his loss, believing that these dead repose in heaven with God. Answers to the last question in this item will differ.

ANSWERS TO CRITICAL THINKING AND READING

1. Line 5 is verb-subject. Here the poet stresses the word *fades*.
2. Lines 13–16 begin with a series of subordinate clauses, and end with a subject-verb arrangement. The poet uses the subordinate clauses to build the reader's emotions, climaxing with the final, main clause.
3. Lines 49–50 offer a similar arrangement. Subordinate matter precedes the subject; more intervening subordinate matter follows the subject; and the lines end with the verb.
4. Lines 81–82 offer a subordinate clause, with its modifiers, followed by the subject and verb; again the poet reverses the normal word order to build emotional suspense.

ANSWERS TO UNDERSTANDING LANGUAGE

Answers will differ. Possibilities include

1. In line 8 the verb *lull* helps build a mood of somnolence.
2. In line 14 the verb *heaves* helps build a mood of energetic motion.
3. In line 23 the verb *lisp* helps build a mood of playful innocence and love.
4. In line 28 the verb *bowed* helps build a mood of aquiescence.
5. In line 40 the verb *swells* helps build a mood of pride.
6. In line 50 the verb *unroll* helps build a mood of regret or disappointment.

Challenge Ask students to consider whether it is better to lead a quiet, obscure life, or one in which the person is famous. Once they have marshalled their ideas pro and con, have them write a paper of four or five paragraphs defending their choice.

THINKING AND WRITING

Publishing Student Writing Invite students to read their elegies in class.

More About the Author The poem "Woman" is from Oliver Goldsmith's novel the *Vicar of Wakefield*. In 1762, Dr. Samuel Johnson, a good friend of Goldsmith, learned that Goldsmith had been arrested for not paying his rent. When Johnson arrived at the scene, Goldsmith admitted that his only asset was the unpublished manuscript of the novel. Johnson was able to sell the manuscript to a publisher for enough money to keep Goldsmith out of jail. On another occasion Goldsmith gambled away most of his passage money for a planned trip to America and gave the rest to a poor woman with eight children. What do these anecdotes tell you about Goldsmith's personality and in particular, his ability to handle money?

Literary Focus How do the theme and open pattern of the poem "Woman" show Goldsmith's transition from a neoclassicist—a believer in the orderly rationality of ancient Greece and Rome—to a Romantic poet?

Teaching to Ability Levels Review with **less advanced** students the poetic structure of such closed-pattern forms as a sonnet and a ballad. A sonnet has fourteen iambic pentameter lines rhyming according to one of two general schemes. A ballad has four lines of poetry with a rhyme scheme *abcb*. You may also want to review meter.

Look For Ask students to determine whether the two-stanza structure of the poem reflects a two-part thought content.

Writing For inspiration students may read several advice columns.

Vocabulary Suggest that **more advanced** students write a couplet using the vocabulary words.

GUIDE FOR READING

Woman

Oliver Goldsmith (1728–1774) was generally regarded as an essayist of the highest standing. Much of what is known of the first half of Goldsmith's life is known through his own accounts. In 1766, four years after the publication of an important collection of essays titled *Citizen of the World,* he produced his first and only novel, *The Vicar of Wakefield.* Later, Goldsmith turned to poetry and enjoyed both critical and financial success with poems typified by their lively descriptions and easy manner.

The Writer's Technique

Poetic Structure. Poetic structure is the pattern or formal design of a poem. Several factors determine a poem's structure: number of stressed syllables per line, line length, and rhyme scheme. Also grouped under the heading of structure are such considerations as the size and shape of the stanzas and the relationship among ideas, images, and sound devices used by the poet. Generally poems are categorized, in terms of their structure, as either closed-pattern or open-pattern. Closed-pattern poems are those that exhibit some or all of the properties of a well-defined traditional poetic form; sonnets and ballads are two examples of closed-pattern poems. Open-pattern poems exhibit no such properties. Oliver Goldsmith's "Woman" is an example of an open-pattern poem.

Look For

As you read "Woman," look for the structural elements used by the poet, as well as the relationship between structure and content.

Writing

Imagine that you write an advice column for a local newspaper. You have received a letter from a young man or woman who is heartbroken. Write a response in the form of a poem offering original suggestions that will help the person get through this difficult period.

Vocabulary

Knowing the following words will help you as you read "Woman."

folly (fäl'ē) *n.*: Foolish action or belief (l. 1)

melancholy (mel'ən käl'ē) *n.*: Sadness; lowness of spirit (l. 3)

Objectives

To understand poetic structure

Teaching Portfolio: Support Material

Teacher Backup, pp. 00-00

Vocabulary Check, p. 00

Usage and Mechanics Worksheet, p. 00

Analyzing Literature Worksheet, p. 00

Critical Thinking and Reading Worksheet, p. 00

Language Worksheet, p. 00

Selection Test, p. 00

Woman

Oliver Goldsmith

When lovely woman stoops to folly,
  And finds too late that men betray, 1
What charm can soothe her melancholy?
  What art can wash her tears away?

The only art her guilt to cover,
  To hide her shame from every eye, 2
To give repentance to her lover,
  And wring his bosom is—to die.

THINKING ABOUT THE SELECTION

Recalling

1. What has made the woman in the poem melancholy?
2. (a) What question does the speaker ask? (b) What answer does he give?

Interpreting

3. Judging from its usage in lines 4 and 5, what do you think is meant by the term "art"?
4. Do you think the poet is being serious in his solution for melancholy of the sort described in the poem? Explain why you feel as you do?

Applying

5. What does the poet's addressing this poem exclusively to women suggest about the values of his era?

ANALYZING LITERATURE

Understanding Poetic Structure

Poetic structure is the shape or general pattern of a poem. The elements that determine a poem's structure include the number of beats per line, line length, rhyme scheme, and stanza size. Depending on their structure, poems fall into either the closed-pattern or open-pattern category. Closed-pattern poems are those that follow a well-defined set of structural rules. The sonnet, which is required among other things to have exactly fourteen lines, is an example of a closed-pattern poetic form. Open-pattern poems, by contrast, are free of such rigid constraints. The structure a poet chooses for a particular poem is often a function of the poem's content and theme.

1. (a) What aspects of the content and theme in "Woman" do you think led the poet to choose an open pattern for the poem? (b) Why do you think he wrote his poem in a total of two four-line stanzas?
2. What effect is created by the short, almost abrupt, lines?
3. What other factors can you think of that may have led to the poet's use of rhyming lines and a regular number of stressed syllables? Support your answer.

Motivation for Reading Ask students if men and women differ in their reaction to heartbreak.

Master Teacher Note In overstatement a writer exaggerates, not to deceive the reader but to create a special effect. In understatement a writer says less than what he or she means. To illustrate the difference compare two poems with the same theme. You might wish to use Robert Burns's "A Red, Red Rose" to illustrate overstatement and Robert Frost's "The Rose Family" to illustrate understatement.

Thematic Idea You might precede a reading of Goldsmith's lyric with a reading of Suckling's "The Constant Lover," on page 458.

Purpose-Setting Question What is the tone of the poem?

1 **Discussion** Does men mean "several men" or "men in general"?

2 **Literary Focus** What is the rhyme scheme? How many stressed syllables are there per line?

Answers

ANSWERS TO THINKING ABOUT THE SELECTION

Recalling

1. The woman has been betrayed by her lover.
2. (a) The speaker asks what will make her feel better. (b) The only way she can feel better is to die.

Interpreting

3. By "art" Goldsmith means "skillful use of the imagination."
4. Answers will differ. A possible answer is that the light tone of the poem suggests that the poet is offering an exaggerated solution to feelings that are exaggerated.

Applying

5. Answers will differ. A possible answer is that there were two sets of values in Goldsmith's era—one for women, who were expected to be faithful, and one for men, who were expected to be otherwise.

ANSWERS TO ANALYZING LITERATURE

1. Answers will differ. Possible answers are: (a) The open pattern reinforces the woman's folly—she sought to escape the bounds of tradition. (b) The two four-line stanzas suggest the duality between men and women. The first stanza establishes the problem, the second suggests the solution.
2. The short, lines suggest that the poet did not consider the problem worth discussing at length.
3. Answers will differ. The rhyme pattern (*abab, cdcd)* is simple, perhaps to emphasize the triviality of the problem in the poet's eyes. The four stressed syllables may reflect the beating of the heart.

More about the Author Although Robert Burns liked to portray himself as an artist whose work came naturally from his emotions, he was actually quite well educated by the time he started to write. Similarly, although his public image was that of a simple Scottish farmer (he was called the "Peasant Poet"), his work won him acceptance into Edinburgh high society, and he spent a great deal of time in that city enjoying his literary and social success. But at the height of his popularity Burns decided to leave Edinburgh and return to farming. He said, "I see the time not distant far when the popular tide shall recede with silent celerity and leave me a barren waste of sand." What did Burns mean by these words? Can you think of any modern-day examples of personalities for whom "the popular tide receded"?

ROBERT BURNS

1759–1796

No other name is more synonymous with the title "The voice of Scotland" than that of the poet Robert Burns. A farmer and a farmer's son, Burns was born at Alloway, in Ayrshire, and spent his early years in the two-room clay cottage his father had built. Although poverty prevented Burns from receiving a formal education, with his father's encouragement he read widely, studying the Bible, Shakespeare, and Alexander Pope on his own. His mother, though herself illiterate, instilled in him a love of Scottish folk songs, legends, and proverbs.

In 1786 Burns published his first collection of poems at a small local press. Although the collection, which included "To a Mouse," was successful, Burns only first came to the attention of the public at large the following year when a fuller collection, *Poems: Chiefly in Scottish,* was published at Edinburgh. He was invited to the Scottish capital, where he was swept into the social scene, if only as something of a rustic curiosity. He left Edinburgh in 1788, to explore the English border region and the Highlands.

Later that year he married Jean Armour, his sweetheart of many years, and returned to the farm to work the land. The soil proved unproductive, however, and so to supplement his income he took a position with the Excise Service—Scotland's department of taxation. All the while he continued to refine his poetic style, turning out some of his finest verses. At the outbreak of the French Revolution, he became an outspoken supporter of the republican cause, a move that threatened his job and alienated many of his friends. His spirits low and his health taxed by a weak heart he had had since childhood, Burns contracted a fever from which he never recovered. Thousands of people from all social levels followed his coffin to the grave, and he was acclaimed the national poet of Scotland.

Burns's numerous adventures produced many lyrics that figure among the most natural and spontaneous the English language has produced. His poems, written for the most part in dialect, are characterized by innocence, honesty, and simplicity. First and last a people's poet, Burns crafted poetic "melodies" that speak to "the sons and daughters of labor and poverty"—and for them. Though some of the poet's work had its origins in folk tunes, "it is not," as James Douglas wrote, "easy to tell where the vernacular ends and the personal magic begins."

Objectives

1 To understand Robert Burns's use of dialect
2 To recognize satire as a form of humor
3 To compare and contrast two poems in writing
4 To write about dialect

Teaching Portfolio: Support Material

Teacher Backup, pp. 00-00

Vocabulary Check, p. 00

Usage and Mechanics Worksheet, p. 00

Analyzing Literature Worksheet, p. 00

Critical Thinking and Reading Worksheet, p. 00

Language Worksheet, p. 00

Selection Test, p. 00

GUIDE FOR READING

To a Mouse; To a Louse; Afton Water; John Anderson, My Jo

The Writer's Technique

Dialect. Dialect is the language, and particularly the speech habits, of a particular social class, region, or group. A dialect may vary from the standard form of a language in grammar, in pronunciation, and in the use of certain expressions. In literature it can serve to establish character, tone, and setting. The use of dialect by a writer or poet can also add to the immediacy and familiarity of a piece of literature.

In the eighteenth century, the belief was widespread among writers that only formal diction was acceptable in poetry. Rules were thus developed concerning the subjects and styles that were thought to be appropriate for poetry. Common life and colloquial language were almost always excluded from the poet's domain. Robert Burns rebelled against these rules, both with his use of Scottish dialect and his celebration of the rural and working life. Like so many poets of the age that ushered in the Romanticism of the next generation, Burns strived to capture in words the language and experiences of the human heart.

Look For

As you read the four poems by Robert Burns, look for his use of dialect to express variously such emotions as tenderness (as in "Afton Water") and mild anger (as in the satirical "To a Louse").

Writing

Write an account titled A Day in the Life of a ________, filling in the blank with one of the following: dog, cat, bird, squirrel, goldfish, or gerbil. Try to get inside the mind of the subject of your narrative, imagining the triumphs, defeats, fears, and hopes your creature experiences on a typical day.

Vocabulary

Knowing the following words will help you as you read the four poems by Robert Burns.

keen (kēn) *adj.*: Having a sharp edge or point (p. 609, l. 24)

drear (drir) *adj.*: Dreary; melancholy (p. 610, l. 46)

impudence (im′ pyo͞o dəns) *n.*: Quality of being rash or contrary (p. 611, l. 2)

kindred (kin′drid) *n.*: Relatives; relations (p. 611, l. 15)

rills (rilz) *n.*: Little brooks (p. 614, l. 10)

wanton (wän′t′n) *adj.*: Frisky; playful (p. 615, l. 19)

stems (stemz) *v.*: Stops; dams up (p. 615, l. 20)

lays (lāz) *n.*: Short poems to be sung (p. 615, l. 22)

Literary Focus Ask students to consider what aspects of Robert Burns's life and work made him stand out from poets and prose writers who preceded him.

Look For A friend described Burns this way, "When animated in company he was a man of a million; his swarthy features glowed, his eyes kindled up till they were all but lighted; his plowman stoop vanished; and his voice—deep, manly, and musical—added its sorcery of pathos or of wit, till the dullest owned the enchantment of his genius." How is Burns's personality, as described here, evident in his poems?

Writing Ask students about movies or television shows they have seen or stories they have read which are told from an animal's point of view. Discuss whether the author was successful in getting "inside the mind" of the animal. If the author was successful, suggest that they use similar techniques in writing their own accounts.

Vocabulary Have **less advanced** students read the words and their definitions aloud. Call on a different student to use each word in a sentence.

Motivation for Reading To help familiarize students with the Scottish dialect and to make it easier for them to understand, play a recording of the poem or read it aloud.

Master Teacher Note One of Burns's many Romantic qualities is his original metrical form. Breaking away from the heroic couplet in both this poem and "To a Louse," he employs a six line stanza with lines 1, 2, 3, and 5 all rhyming and written in iambic tetrameter; lines 4 and 6, written in iambic dimeter, provide a second rhyme sound.

Purpose-Setting Question How does Burns's use of dialect add to the poem's appeal?

1 **Discussion** What does Burns's sympathy for the mouse's situation tell you about the man himself?

To a Mouse

On Turning Her up in Her Nest with the Plow, November, 1785

Robert Burns

1
Wee, sleekit,[1] cow'rin', tim'rous beastie,
O, what a panic's in thy breastie!
Thou need na start awa sae hasty,
        Wi' bickering brattle![2]
I wad be laith[3] to rin an' chase thee
        Wi' murd'ring pattle![4]

---

1. **sleekit:** Sleek.
2. **Wi' . . . brattle:** In sudden flight.
3. **wad be laith:** Would be loath.
4. **pattle:** Paddle for cleaning a plow.

I'm truly sorry man's dominion
Has broken Nature's social union,
An' justifies that ill opinion,
Which makes thee startle,
At me, thy poor, earth-born companion,
An' fellow-mortal!

I doubt na, whyles,[5] but thou may thieve;
What then? poor beastie, thou maun[6] live!
A daimen icker in a thrave[7]
'S a sma' request:
I'll get a blessin' wi' the lave,[8]
And never miss't!

Thy wee bit housie, too, in ruin!
Its silly wa's[9] the win's are strewin'!
An' naething, now, to big[10] a new ane,
O' foggage[11] green!
An' bleak December's winds ensuin',
Baith snell[12] an keen!

Thou saw the fields laid bare and waste,
An' weary winter comin' fast,
An' cozie here, beneath the blast,
Thou thought to dwell,
Till crash! the cruel coulter[13] past
Out through thy cell.

That wee bit heap o' leaves an' stibble,
Has cost thee mony a weary nibble!
Now thou's turned out, for a' thy trouble,
But[14] house or hald,[15]
To thole[16] the winter's sleety dribble,
An' cranreuch[17] cauld!

---

5. whyles: At times.
6. maun: Must.
7. A . . . thrave: An occasional ear of grain in a bundle.
8. lave: Rest.
9. silly wa's: Feeble walls.
10. big: Build.
11. foggage: Rough grass.
12. snell: Sharp.
13. coulter: Plow blade.
14. But: Without.
15. hald: Property.
16. thole: Withstand.
17. cranreuch (krən′ rəkh): Frost.

2 Discussion What is the speaker apologizing for?

3 Discussion Why is the destruction of the mouse's house so serious?

4 Literary Focus Here Burns seems to be viewing the situation from the mouse's point of view.

5 **Literary Focus** At this point the poet changes focus. From a specific account of a small, poignant incident Burns moves to a general statement that relates to the human experience. John Steinbeck borrowed from this stanza the title *Of Mice and Men* for his novel that treats of plans gone fatally awry.

Answers

ANSWERS TO THINKING ABOUT THE SELECTION

Recalling

1. (a) The poem takes place on Burns's farm in Scotland in November.
2. The speaker apologizes to the mouse for frightening it.
3. The speaker has plowed under the moss the mouse needs to build a home.
4. The mouse's problem is one it must deal with now. The speaker has both past misfortunes and future problems to worry about.

Interpreting

5. The "social union" refers to the balance among natural things.
6. The sentiment suggests that the speaker believes that the end justifies the means.
7. (a) "The best laid schemes o' mice an' men Gang aft a-gley" carries the poem's theme. (b) You cannot always count on things working out the way you expect them to.

Applying

8. Answers will differ but students should support their positions.

ANSWERS TO ANALYZING LITERATURE

1. (a) The dialect suggests that the speaker is uneducated and low in social standing. (b) Both the speaker and the mouse are poor, lowly creatures subject to life's twists and turns.
2. (a) Answer will differ but may include the following. Final consonants are dropped in *cowrin'* (cowring) and *sma'* (small), and *wi'* (with). (b) The letter *o* is replaced by *a* in *hald* (holding), *lane* (alone), and *canna* (cannot).
3. The poem would lack the intimacy it now possesses, the flavor of the place and the speaker.

But, Mousie, thou art no thy lane,[18]
In proving foresight may be vain:
The best laid schemes o' mice an' men
Gang aft a-gley,[19]
An' lea'e us nought but grief an' pain,
For promised joy.

5

Still thou art blest, compared wi' me!
The present only toucheth thee:
But, och! I backward cast my e'e
On prospects drear!
An' forward, though I canna see,
I guess an' fear!

18. no thy lane: Not alone.
19. Gang aft a-gley: Go often awry.

THINKING ABOUT THE SELECTION

Recalling

1. What is the setting of the poem?
2. For what reason does the speaker apologize to the mouse?
3. Why is the mouse unable to build a new home?
4. Why does the speaker say that, compared with him, the mouse is blessed?

Interpreting

5. To what "social union" do you think the speaker is referring in line 7?
6. What does the sentiment in lines 13–14 suggest about the speaker's own moral code?
7. (a) What famous line in the poem carries the poem's theme? (b) How might you state this theme in your own words?

Applying

8. What value do you place on foresight? Explain your answer.

ANALYZING LITERATURE

Recognizing Dialect

Dialect is a collection of speech habits and patterns belonging to a specific group, class, or region. Often, a dialect will possess its own unique grammar, pronunciation, and vocabulary. One of the first poets to write using the Scottish dialect of English, Robert Burns placed himself in direct opposition to the poetic standards of the eighteenth century.

1. (a) What does the use of dialect in this poem suggest about the speaker's social station? (b) How does it help carry across the poem's theme?
2. Like the standard language, dialects of a language follow rules. Find at least two examples in the poem of each of the following pronunciation rules for Scottish English. (a) Final consonants are dropped. (b) The letter *o* is replaced by either *ae* or *a*.
3. How would the effect of this poem have been different if it had been written in standard English?

1 # To a Louse

On Seeing One on a Lady's Bonnet at Church

Robert Burns

Ha! whare ye gaun, ye crowlin' ferlie![1]
Your impudence protects you sairly:[2]
2 I canna say but ye strunt[3] rarely,
Owre gauze and lace;
Though faith! I fear ye dine but sparely
On sic a place.

Ye ugly, creepin', blastit wonner,[4]
Detested, shunned by saunt an' sinner,
How dare ye set your fit[5] upon her,
3 Sae fine a lady?
Gae somewhere else, and seek your dinner
On some poor body.

Swith![6] in some beggar's haffet[7] squattle;[8]
There ye may creep, and sprawl, and sprattle[9]
4 Wi' ither kindred, jumping cattle,
In shoals and nations:
Whare horn nor bane[10] ne'er dare unsettle
Your thick plantations.

Now haud[11] ye there, ye're out o' sight,
Below the fatt'rels,[12] snug an' tight;
Na, faith ye yet![13] ye'll no be right
Till ye've got on it,
The vera tapmost, tow'ring height
O' Miss's bonnet.

---

1. **crowlin' ferlie:** Crawling wonder.
2. **sairly:** Sorely.
3. **strunt:** Strut.
4. **blastit wonner:** Blasted wonder.
5. **fit:** Foot.
6. **swith:** Swift.
7. **haffet:** Locks.
8. **squattle:** Sprawl.
9. **sprattle:** struggle.
10. **horn nor bane:** Comb nor poison.
11. **haud:** Hold.
12. **fatt'rels:** Ribbon ends.
13. **Na faith ye yet!:** Confound you!

Motivation for Reading Ask students how they might react if they saw a louse on a lady's hat in a church.

Literary Focus Although this poem shares many of the Romantic characteristics of "To a Mouse," its satiric tone puts it at least partly in the neo-classical tradition.

Master Teacher Note Have students look up the word *lousy* in a good dictionary and note the various meanings of the word ("infested with lice"; "mean"; "painful"; "inferior"; "abundantly supplied"). How do the meanings of the word, which derives from the word *louse,* reflect the message of this poem?

Purpose-Setting Questions How does this poem illustrate Burns's sense of humor? How do the number of stanzas and the rhyme scheme in this poem compare with "To a Mouse"?

1 **Clarification** Explain that in Burns's time lice—small, wingless creatures that suck the blood of animals and humans—were quite common. Today, better standards of hygiene have helped to keep the insects under control.

2 **Discussion** What is the speaker's attitude toward the louse?

3 **Literary Focus** These lines reflect Burns's satiric tone. Is he saying that the louse should be on a poor person or that it is a common expectation that lice will be on poor people? This idea is repeated in lines 31–36.

4 **Discussion** Burns pursues this idea with great originality here, suggesting several reasons why the louse would be happier on a poor person's head. What are those reasons?

5 **Literary Focus** Point out that this stanza echoes the second stanza.

6 **Literary Focus** This stanza marks a change in the poem. Instead of speaking to the louse, the speaker addresses Jenny.

7 **Discussion** As in "To a Mouse," Burns moves from the specific to the general. Is he generalizing the folly of the louse or humans or both? Explain.

My sooth! right bauld ye set your nose out,
As plump and gray as onie grozet;[14]
O for some rank, mercurial rozet,[15]
        Or fell,[16] red smeddum,[17]
I'd gie you sic a hearty dose o't,
        Wad dress your droddum![18]

I wad na been surprised to spy
You on an auld wife's flannen toy;[19]
5 Or aiblins some bit duddie boy,[20]
        On's wyliecoat;[21]
But Miss's fine Lunardi![22] fie,
        How daur ye do't?

O, Jenny, dinna toss your head,
An' set your beauties a' abread![23]
6 Ye little ken what cursèd speed
        The blastie's[24] makin'!
Thae[25] winks and finger-ends, I dread,
        Are notice takin'!

O wad some Pow'r the giftie gie us
To see oursels as ithers see us!
7 It wad frae monie a blunder free us
        And foolish notion:
What airs in dress an' gait wad lea'e us,
        And ev'n devotion!

---

14. onie grozet (grŏz′ it): Any gooseberry.
15. rozet (rŏz′ it): Rosin.
16. fell: Sharp.
17. smeddum: Powder.
18. Wad . . . droddum: Would put an end to you.
19. flannen toy: Flannel cap.
20. Or . . . boy: Or perhaps on some little ragged boy.
21. wyliecoat (wī′ lē kōt′): Undershirt.
22. Lunardi: A balloon-shaped bonnet, named for Vincenzo Lunardi, a balloonist of the late 1700's.
23. abread: Abroad.
24. blastie's: Creature's.
25. Thae: Those.

THINKING ABOUT THE SELECTION

Recalling

1. (a) What is the louse doing? (b) What does the speaker command it to do instead?
2. What does the speaker say he would like to do in lines 27–30?
3. (a) Whom does the speaker address in the seventh stanza? (b) What does he warn her against?

Interpreting

4. (a) What conclusions can you draw about Jenny's character? (b) What evidence supports these assumptions?
5. What is the poet's tone—that is, his attitude toward his subject?
6. Like "To a Mouse," this poem contains a famous line that suggests the poem's theme. (a) What is that line? (b) What is the poem's theme?

Applying

7. William Hazlitt wrote, "Life is the art of being well deceived." How do you think Burns would respond to this statement? Explain your answer.

CRITICAL THINKING AND READING

Recognizing Satire

Satire is writing that uses humor and wit to expose folly and flaws of humans or institutions. Popular since ancient Greek and Roman times, satire has long been an effective tool of both writers and reformers. In order to recognize the target of the poet's satire, reread the brief biography of Robert Burns on page 606. Based on information you find there and on the poem itself, answer the following questions about "To a Louse."

1. (a) What do you imagine to be the social class of the speaker? Why? (b) Of Jenny? Why?
2. (a) What is the louse's "crime"? What does the speaker have in common with those to whom he seems to feel the louse belongs? (b) What is ironic about this?

THINKING AND WRITING

Comparing and Contrasting Two Poems

"To a Mouse" and "To a Louse" are often considered to be companion poems. Indeed, both poems address creatures of nature, and both are written in the Scottish dialect. Apart from these obvious similarities, consider other traits the poems share in common, as well as features that set the two apart. Consider in particular the theme of the poems and the attitude of the poet toward society. Discuss your findings with your classmates. Then write an essay comparing and contrasting the two poems. When you revise, make sure you have presented both similarities and differences. Proofread your essay and prepare a final draft.

Answers

ANSWERS TO THINKING ABOUT THE SELECTION

Recalling

1. (a) The louse is crawling on a lady's hat while she is sitting in church. (b) The speaker commands the louse to find its dinner on the head of some beggar.
2. He would like to kill it by giving it a dose of deadly red powder.
3. (a) The speaker addresses Jenny, the woman wearing the bonnet. (b) He warns her against shaking her head.

Interpreting

4. (a) In the speaker's opinion, Jenny is vain. There is the suggestion that she comes to church to be seen, rather than to worship. (b) In the last stanza Burns suggests that people could save themselves from many a blunder if they could see themselves as others see them. He specifically refers to "airs in dress an' gait."
5. The poet's tone is one of quiet anger and gentle ridicule.

Applying

6. (a) The line that suggests the poem's theme is "O wad some Pow'r the giftie gie us/To see oursels as ithers see us!" (b) The theme is that people who put on airs are seen as foolish by others.

Challenge Do you agree or disagree with Burns's message in the poem?

ANSWERS TO CRITICAL THINKING AND READING

1. The dialect suggests that the speaker is from a low social class. Jenny is probably an upper-class woman, since the speaker calls her a fine lady.
2. The louse's crime is that it chose a fine bonnet to crawl on rather than some "poor body." Like those he feels the louse belongs on, the speaker is poor. The irony is that the louse chose the body of someone with social standing, rather than the kind of body it would be expected to be on.

Afton[1] Water

Robert Burns

Flow gently, sweet Afton, among thy green braes,[2]
1 Flow gently, I'll sing thee a song in thy praise;
My Mary's asleep by thy murmuring stream,
Flow gently, sweet Afton, disturb not her dream.

Thou stock-dove whose echo resounds through the glen,
2 Ye wild whistling blackbirds in yon thorny den,
Thou green-crested lapwing, thy screaming forbear,
I charge you, disturb not my slumbering fair.

How lofty, sweet Afton, thy neighboring hills,
Far marked with the courses of clear, winding rills;
There daily I wander as noon rises high,
My flocks and my Mary's sweet cot[3] in my eye.

---

1. Afton: The Afton is a river in Ayrshire, a former county in Southwestern Scotland.
2. braes (brāz): Slopes.
3. cot: Cottage.

Motivation for Reading Since this is a lyric poem meant to be set to music, you may want to play a recording of the song based on the poem. Ask students what picture of Scotland they get from the poem. Would they like to visit Burns's homeland?

Master Teacher Note This poem exemplifies Burns's transitional role to the Romantic period. Here he foreshadows the Romantics and their return to the rustic, simple joys of life.

Purpose-Setting Question How does the absence of dialect affect your response to this poem?

Thematic Idea This poem might be compared and contrasted with Marlowe's "Passionate Shepherd to His Love," on page 182, for tone, mood, and overall effect.

1 **Discussion** What meter and rhyme scheme does Burns use? How do they enhance the musical aspect of the poem?

2 **Discussion** Do you think the speaker believes that the birds will stop making their noises in answer to his charge? Why or why not?

Humanities Notes

Fine art, *View of the River Dee Near Eaton Hall* Richard Wilson. The British landscape painter Richard Wilson (1714–1782) is often referred to as the "father of British landscape painting". Classically educated by his father, a country rector, Wilson studied painting in London and Italy. Wilson was revered by fellow painters, but because of a royal affront, his estrangement from the King kept him from fame and fortune in his lifetime.

View of the River Dee Near Eaton Hall shows the sensitivity with which Wilson treated nature. He uses the French device of a dark foreground to frame the light on the landscape to a stunning effect. The sky and atmosphere of the painting are spacious and clear, the colors subtle and harmonious.

You might use the following questions for discussion:

1. What feelings do both the poet and the painter share regarding nature?
2. What feature of this painting makes it particularly suitable as an illustration for this poem?

How pleasant thy banks and green valleys below,
Where wild in the woodlands the primroses blow;
There oft as mild evening weeps over the lea,[4]
The sweet-scented birk[5] shades my Mary and me.

Thy crystal stream, Afton, how lovely it glides,
And winds by the cot where my Mary resides;
How wanton thy waters her snowy feet lave,
As gathering sweet flowerets she stems thy clear wave.

Flow gently, sweet Afton, among thy green braes,
Flow gently, sweet river, the theme of my lays; 3
My Mary's asleep by thy murmuring stream,
Flow gently, sweet Afton, disturb not her dream.

4. **lea:** Meadow.
5. **birk:** Birch.

THINKING ABOUT THE SELECTION

Recalling

1. (a) Why does the speaker ask the Afton to "flow gently"? (b) What other three things does he command to be silent?
2. What is the speaker's occupation?

Interpreting

3. (a) What is the poem's mood—the feeling it conveys to the reader? (b) What words and phrases help achieve this mood?
4. (a) What assumptions can you make about Mary based on the poem? (b) About the speaker's feelings toward her?
5. Do you think the author, in composing these lines, had any purpose in mind other than to entertain? Explain your answer.

Applying

6. What songs or lullabies are you familiar with that carry the same message as this poem?

3 **Discussion** Why is the repetition of the phrase *Flow gently* especially appropriate to the thought content of the poem?

Answers

ANSWERS TO THINKING ABOUT THE SELECTION

Recalling

1. (a) The speaker wants the Afton to flow gently so as not to wake up Mary. (b) The speaker wants the stock-doves, the blackbirds, and the lapwings to be silent.
2. The speaker is a shepherd.

Interpreting

3. (a) The poem's mood is one of peace and contentment. (b) Words such as *gently, murmuring, sweet, pleasant, mild, sweet-scented,* and *glides* help to achieve this mood.
4. (a) We can assume that Mary is the speaker's love and that she is content enough with him to fall asleep by the stream. (b) The speaker is in love with Mary, whom he calls "my Mary." He is also protective of her.
5. In addition to entertaining, Burns wanted to celebrate love and the beauties of nature, a typically Romantic concept.

Applying

6. Answers will differ. Possible answers include "The Brahms Lullaby" and "Rock-a-Bye-Baby."

Motivation for Reading Play a Beatles' recording of "When I'm Sixty-Four" from their *Sergeant Pepper's Lonely Hearts Club Band* album. Ask students why someone in love might ask this question.

Purpose-Setting Question What does the poem suggest about Burns's attitude toward old age?

John Anderson, My Jo[1]

Robert Burns

John Anderson, my jo, John,
    When we were first acquent,
Your locks were like the raven,
    Your bonnie[2] brow was brent;[3]
But now your brow is beld,[4] John,
    Your locks are like the snow;
But blessings on your frosty pow,[5]
    John Anderson, my jo.

John Anderson, my jo, John,
    We clamb[6] the hill thegither;
And monie[7] a canty[8] day, John,
    We've had wi' ane anither:
Now we maun[9] totter down, John,
    And hand in hand we'll go,
And sleep thegither at the foot,
    John Anderson, my Jo.

We're a dry wi' drinking o't,
    We're a dry wi' drinking o't;
The minister kiss'd the fiddler's wife,
    An' could na preach for thinkin' o't.

---

1. **jo:** Joy.
2. **bonnie:** Pretty.
3. **brent:** Unwrinkled.
4. **beld:** Bald.
5. **pow:** Head.
6. **clamb:** Climbed.
7. **monie:** Many.
8. **canty:** Cheerful.
9. **maun:** Must.

THINKING ABOUT THE SELECTION

Recalling

1. (a) How does the speaker say John Anderson looked when she and he first met? (b) How does he look now?
2. What does the speaker say she and John Anderson will do now?

Interpreting

3. What do you suppose to be the relationship between the speaker and John Anderson? Explain your assumption.
4. (a) How would you paraphrase what the speaker is saying in the first four lines of the second stanza? (b) In the last four lines?

Applying

5. It has been noted that "John Anderson, My Jo" reveals Robert Burns's great talent for writing romantic poetry. Explain why you agree or disagree with this observation.

THINKING AND WRITING

Writing About Dialect

Three of the four poems you have read by Robert Burns are written in dialect. In an essay, explain how you believe the impact of these poems would have been altered had the poet chosen to write them instead in standard English. Before writing consider the following questions. What factors do you think influenced Burns's decision to use dialect? What qualities of tone are communicated through the use of dialect? Of theme? What aspects of the message in "Afton Waters" may have prompted the poet to write in standard English?

Answers

ANSWERS TO THINKING ABOUT THE SELECTION

Recalling

1. (a) When she first met him he had dark hair and a smooth, unwrinkled brow. (b) Now John is balding, with white hair.
2. They will grow old together.

Interpreting

3. The speaker and John Anderson are husband and wife.
4. (a) When we were young we spent many happy days together. (b) Now that we are old we will enjoy each other until we die.

Applying

5. Answers will differ. Suggested response: Love is a constant theme in Romantic poetry. While most Romantic poets extoll the virtues of young love or unrequited love, Burns extolls a happy love that has reached old age. The poem is direct, natural, and passionate—all indicative of his great talent.

THINKING AND WRITING

Publishing Student Writing You might have students meet in small groups and choose one essay from the group to be read aloud to the class.

More About the Author William Blake's belief in a union of opposites is reflected in his famous "Doctrine of Contraries": "Without Contraries," he wrote, "is no progression. Attraction and repulsion, reason and energy, love and hate, are necessary to human existence." Do you agree with this view? Explain.

WILLIAM BLAKE

1757–1827

When William Blake was four years old, he screamed because he saw God at his window. At age eight, while walking in the fields, he saw a tree filled with angels. To outside observers, Blake's "spells" might have seemed a cause for grave concern. In the home of his parents—themselves followers of the mystical teachings of Emanuel Swedenborg—the boy's "gift of vision" was something to be revered and nurtured. At least partly as a result of the family's way of life, the century and the world received a painter and a poet whose contributions are as rare as they are brilliant.

Blake was born in London, where his father ran a hosiery shop. He was never sent to school but instead, after expressing a desire to become a painter, was apprenticed to an engraver. Ultimately self-taught, he found his way into art and literature.

Between the ages of twelve and twenty, Blake wrote a series of poems, *Poetical Sketches,* that followed the tradition of English lyric poetry, while bringing a new innocence to his subject matter. When he was thirty-two, he published his *Songs of Innocence,* which he had composed when he was younger, and which explored his favorite subject—the destiny of the human spirit. Instead of printing the collection, he developed a unique process whereby the words and illustrations were etched on metal plates with varnish, then painted in by hand. Because the process was time-consuming, few books could be produced, and so to support himself, Blake hired himself out to other authors as an illustrator and sold what he could of his own works for one pound apiece. He also continued to write and in 1794 brought out a companion to *Songs of Innocence* titled *Songs of Experience.*

In *Songs of Innocence* Blake had suggested that by recapturing the imagination and wonderment of childhood, we could achieve the goal of self-awareness. The poems thus present views of the world as filtered through the eyes and mind of a child. In *Songs of Experience* he now insisted that a return to innocence was not, at least by itself, sufficient to an awareness of our true identity—that we must also recognize and attempt to understand the evils around us. Thus Blake's credo was that there must be a union of opposites, a fusion of innocence and experience.

Unrecognized by his peers and living only slightly above poverty level, Blake spent his seventy years in constant creative activity. Only later, many years after his death, was the system behind his work understood. His poetry operates on two levels, one of them symbolic, the other literal. Both of them address a single purpose—the renewal of the human spirit.

Objectives

1 To recognize symbolism
2 To write about William Blake's symbolism as illustrated in his poetry

Teaching Portfolio: Support Material

Teacher Backup, pp. 00-00

Vocabulary Check, p. 00

Usage and Mechanics Worksheet, p. 00

Analyzing Literature Worksheet, p. 00

Critical Thinking and Reading Worksheet, p. 00

Language Worksheet, p. 00

Selection Test, p. 000

GUIDE FOR READING

The Lamb; The Tiger; The Human Abstract; Infant Sorrow; A Poison Tree

The Writer's Technique

Symbolism. Symbolism is the use of a person, an object, a place, or an idea to represent itself and something beyond itself at the same time. Two well-known examples of symbolism are the use of the Stars and Stripes to represent the United States and the use of a skull and crossbones to represent something poisonous. While symbolism occurs in all types of literature, poetry, by virtue of its purity as an art form, is an especially natural vehicle for the presentation of ideas in symbolic form. Symbolism also permits the poet to introduce in relatively little space concepts and ideas that would ordinarily require more extensive treatment. In "The Tiger," William Blake uses the jungle cat as a symbol for the savage and untamed forces in the world that prompt human beings to perform evil actions.

Look For

As you read the six poems by Blake, look for the poet's use of both universal symbols—those that have a clear and generalized meaning, and private symbols—those whose meanings are indicated by their context.

Writing

Imagine that suddenly you were four or five years old again. Look around you, at the people and objects in your presence, and attempt to describe in a paragraph what you see. Try to use words that you believe would be appropriate to a small child, and remember that much which you take for granted would seem new and wonderful to someone a good deal younger.

Vocabulary

Knowing the following words will help you as you read the six poems by Blake.

vales (vālz) *n.*: Valleys (p. 620, l. 8)

symmetry (sim'ə trē) *n.*: Beauty resulting from balance of form (p. 623, l. 4)

aspire (ə spīr') *v.*: Rise high (p. 623, l. 7)

sinews (sin'yo͞oz) *n.*: Muscular power; force (p. 623, l. 10)

abstract (ab'strakt) *n.*: Brief summary stating main points (p. 624, title)

swaddling (swäd'liŋ) *adj.*: Long, narrow bands of cloth wrapped around newborn babies (p. 625, l. 6)

Literary Focus Distinguish between a sign and a symbol. Point out that a sign—such as a traffic light or stop sign—has a single, distinct meaning. A symbol, however, may have an indefinable meaning, a number of different meanings, or a meaning that can vary from one interpreter to another.

Look For Tell students that the details of the poems should suggest the meanings of the basic symbols.

Writing In writing about innocence, Blake was describing a mystical state, rather than childhood, but he identifies the two so closely that his poems seem to be spoken by the very children themselves. He does not look at children; he actually enters their minds and speaks through their mouths.

Vocabulary Review the vocabulary words orally. Challenge **more advanced** students to use all of the words in sentences.

Motivation for Reading Ask students if important ideas can be expressed in simple words. Have students give examples.

Master Teacher Note You may want to consider teaching the "The Lamb" and "The Tiger" together, as they suggest such totally different attributes of the same God. Taken together the two poems exemplify Blake's belief in contrasts.

Purpose-Setting Question What symbols does Blake use in the poem? What do they stand for?

1 **Discussion** Note that the words in the poem are mostly monosyllabic and extremely simple, as is the rhyme scheme. Why do you think Blake uses such simple diction?

2 **Discussion** What is the rhyme scheme? How does it enhance the meaning of the poem?

3 **Clarification** Jesus was described as "the Lamb" by John the Baptist in the Bible, in John 1:20 and Revelations 5:18. In what special sense was Christ the Lamb of God?

4 **Discussion** Who is the speaker in the poem?

The Lamb

William Blake

Little Lamb, who made thee?
Dost thou know who made thee?
Gave thee life, and bid thee feed,
By the stream and o'er the mead;
1, 2 Gave thee clothing of delight,
Softest clothing, woolly, bright;
Gave thee such a tender voice,
Making all the vales rejoice?
Little Lamb, who made thee?
Dost thou know who made thee?

Little Lamb, I'll tell thee,
Little Lamb, I'll tell thee.
He is callèd by thy name,
3 For He calls Himself a Lamb.
He is meek, and He is mild;
He became a little child.
4 I a child, and thou a lamb,
We are callèd by His name.
Little Lamb, God bless thee!
Little Lamb, God bless thee!

THINKING ABOUT THE SELECTION

Recalling

1. (a) What questions does the speaker ask in the first stanza? (b) What answer does he give in the second?
2. How does the speaker identify himself in the second stanza?

Interpreting

3. Blake uses repetition to create a mood, or overall feeling, in this poem. (a) What types of words does he repeat? (b) What feeling is created?
4. (a) How would you characterize the creator imagined in this poem? (b) Find at least three words that support your opinion.

Applying

5. Assume that you were asked to illustrate this poem. (a) What kinds of images would you use to represent the words? (b) What style of drawing might you use?

ANALYZING LITERATURE

Recognizing Symbolism

A **symbol** is a thing, idea, person, or place that has a meaning in and of itself but also stands for more. An old, bent man with a scythe symbolizes the end of the year. In poetry, symbolism—the systematic use of symbols—adds particular clarity to a poet's point. In "The Lamb," Blake offers two separate but related symbolic representations for the animal named in the title.

1. What two things does the lamb symbolize? What properties of the lamb suggest its use as a symbol? What is the origin of the symbolic interpretation of the lamb in the second stanza?
2. Restate "The Lamb" in purely literal language. What is the poet's message? How is that message altered, if at all, by restating the poem in literal terms?

Answers

ANSWERS TO THINKING ABOUT THE SELECTION

Recalling

1. (a) The speaker asks the Lamb who its maker was, who fed and clothed it, and who gave it its voice. (b) God made the Lamb.
2. The speaker identifies himself as a child and a Christian.

Interpreting

3. (a) The words *Little Lamb, thee, He,* and *God* are repeated. (b) The feeling is that all the creatures in the world are one with God, the creator. The repetition also suggest a child's limited vocabulary.
4. Answers will differ. Possible answers are: (a) The creator is gentle and compassionate. (b) The creator provided the Lamb with soft, bright clothing and a tender voice—signs of compassion. The speaker calls the creator "meek" and "mild."

Applying

5. Answers will differ. Possible answers are: (a) An image of a child playing with a lamb in the country would be an appropriate image. (b) The style should be soft, perhaps painted in watercolors or drawn in pastels.

The Lamb
Little Lamb who made thee?
Dost thou know who made thee
Gave thee life & bid thee feed.
By the stream & o'er the mead;
Gave thee clothing of delight,
Softest clothing wooly bright;
Gave thee such a tender voice,
Making all the vales rejoice;
Little Lamb who made thee
Dost thou know who made thee
Little Lamb I'll tell thee,
Little Lamb I'll tell thee:
He is called by thy name,
For he calls himself a Lamb:
He is meek & he is mild,
He became a little child:
I a child & thou a lamb,
We are called by his name.
Little Lamb God bless thee.
Little Lamb God bless thee.

Humanities Note

Fine art; Illustration from a manuscript of "The Lamb" by William Blake. William Blake was a visionary painter as well as a poet. As a child Blake was subject to divine visions and claimed to have "seen" God on many occasions. These visions recurred throughout his life and had a profound influence on his artistic and literary works. He is best remembered for the books that he composed, printed, and illustrated himself.

The page *The Lamb* comes from his book entitled *Songs of Innocence,* published in 1789. Only twenty-seven of these books were made by Blake. This page incorporates a hand-lettered version of the poem with an illustration. Lightly printed in brown ink, Blake hand-colored the page with watercolor. Executed in the expressive style that is singularly Blake's, this delicate drawing, filled with symbolism, perfectly illustrates the symbolic language of his poem.

Consider these questions for your discussion of this work of art:

1. Does this drawing seem frivolous or lighthearted? Explain your answer.
2. How does this compare to the language of the poem?

ANSWERS TO ANALYZING LITERATURE

1. The lamb symbolizes innocence and Christ. The lamb is a gentle, harmless creature, clothed in white. The lamb as a symbol for Christ originated in the Bible.
2. The message is that through achieving a childlike innocence we can become closer to God. The message is the same, but it is less memorable when stated in literal terms.

Humanities Note

Fine Art, *The Tiger,* 1794, by William Blake. The engraving "The Tiger," lightly printed in brown ink and hand-colored with watercolor, was done by Blake himself. Note how the trees in the print repeat the straight symmetry of the tiger's stripes. The simplicity of the drawing complements the simple language of the poem. You might ask the students whether the drawing as well as the poem is meant to convey a more complex meaning.

Enrichment It has been suggested that Blake's choice of the tiger symbol may have been a reflection of the times. The tiger seemed to be an image that often came to English minds in a effort to describe the French Revolution, which coincided with Blake's work on his *Songs of Innocence. The London Times* of January 7, 1792, tells us that the French people are now "loose from all restraints, and in many instances, more vicious than wolves and tigers." Another comment stated that the "mob were barbarous beyond the tiger's cruelty." Years later Wordsworth looked back on the Paris of 1792 as "a place of fear . . . Defenceless as a wood where tigers roam."

The Tiger

William Blake

Tiger! Tiger! burning bright
In the forests of the night,
1 What immortal hand or eye
Could frame thy fearful symmetry?

2 In what distant deeps or skies
Burnt the fire of thine eyes?
On what wings dare he aspire?
What the hand dare seize the fire?

3 And what shoulder, and what art,
Could twist the sinews of thy heart?
And when thy heart began to beat,
What dread hand? and what dread feet?

4 What the hammer? what the chain?
In what furnace was thy brain?
What the anvil? what dread grasp
Dare its deadly terrors clasp?

5 When the stars threw down their spears,
And watered heaven with their tears,
6 Did he smile his work to see?
Did he who made the Lamb make thee?

7 Tiger! Tiger! burning bright
In the forests of the night,
What immortal hand or eye
Dare frame thy fearful symmetry?

THINKING ABOUT THE SELECTION

Recalling

1. (a) What question is raised in the first stanza? (b) In the second stanza? (c) In the fifth stanza?

Interpreting

2. (a) What properties of the tiger are suggested by the images mentioned in the fourth stanza? (b) What emotional impact is created by those images?
3. (a) What do you suppose to be the answer to the central question of the poem? (b) Is it the same answer as that given in "The Lamb"? Explain.

Applying

4. "The Lamb" was included in *Songs of Innocence;* "The Tiger" in *Songs of Experience.* What does the use of the tiger as a symbol of the world of experience suggest about Blake's view of that world?

Motivation for Reading Tell your students that this poem, from *Songs of Experience,* is the companion to "The Lamb." As the lamb symbolizes innocence, the tiger symbolizes experience. In what way are these two "opposite states of being," as Blake called them? Challenge the class to try to figure out what overarching meaning arises from the two poems taken together.

1 **Discussion** How is this question the same as the question asked in the first stanza of "The Lamb"? How is it different?

2 **Literary Focus** Note the repetition of the word *fire* and the use of fire-related words here and elsewhere in the poem. How is fire an appropriate image for the tiger?

3 **Literary Focus** Note the repetition of the words *dare* and *dread* in the poem. How do the words apply to the tiger? to the experience—as opposed to innocence—that the tiger represents?

4 **Literary Focus** How do the words *twist, hammer, chain, furnace,* and *anvil* serve as a metaphor of the tiger's place of origin?

5 **Discussion** What figure of speech is used in these lines? What do you think the lines mean?

6 **Discussion** Is the answer to this question provided in the poem? What question about the nature of existence is Blake really asking?

7 **Discussion** How does this stanza differ from the first? Does "The Tiger," like "The Lamb," answer the central question posed in the poem?

Purpose-Setting Question Can you think of another symbol that Blake might have used instead of a tiger? Would, say, a lion or a wolf be as effective? Why or why not?

Answers

ANSWERS TO THINKING ABOUT THE SELECTION

Recalling

1. (a) In the first stanza the tiger is asked who created its frame. (b) In the second stanza the same question is asked about its eyes. (c) In the fifth stanza the tiger is asked whether the creator was pleased with his work.

Interpreting

2. (a) The images suggest the tiger's ferociousness, its cruelty, and its ability to terrify. (b) The images arouse fear.
3. (a) God created the tiger. (b) The same God who made the lamb made the tiger, since God created all things.

Applying

4. Blake believed that the world was full of opposites and that to become closer to God, to our true identify, we must understand both sides.

Master Teacher Note The simplicity of the poem's structure—its short lines and symmetrical meter—is like that of nursery rhymes. You may want to use examples to emphasize this point.

Motivation for Reading Read the Biblical version of the creation, which describes Adam and Eve's fall from grace as a result of eating fruit from the tree of knowledge. Discuss what happened after they ate the fruit. Tell students to keep the symbolism of the Biblical account in mind as they read "The Human Abstract."

Master Teacher Note This poem is from *Songs of Experience.* Its complement in *Songs of Innocence* is "The Divine Image," which celebrates mercy, pity, peace, and love. "The Human Abstract" shows their antitheses: exploitation, cruelty, conflict, and hypocritical humility.

Purpose-setting Question Does this poem seem to belong in *Songs of Innocence* or *Songs of Experience?* Support your choice by referring to specific statements in the poem.

1 **Discussion** Do you think Blake is being sarcastic here? Why or why not?

2 **Discussion** Who do you think Blake means by "we"?

3 **Discussion** Give a modern political example of how selfish love can affect peace.

4 **Discussion** What figure of speech is employed here?

5 **Discussion** Why would the raven choose the tree's thickest shade to make its nest?

6 **Literary Focus** What does Nature symbolize?

The Human Abstract

William Blake

1 Pity would be no more,
If we did not make somebody Poor;
2 And Mercy no more could be,
If all were as happy as we;

3 And mutual fear brings peace,
Till the selfish loves increase;
Then Cruelty knits a snare,
And spreads his baits with care.

4 He sits down with holy fears,
And waters the ground with tears;
Then Humility takes its root
Underneath his foot.

Soon spreads the dismal shade
Of Mystery over his head;
And the Caterpillar and Fly
Feed on the Mystery.

And it bears the fruit of Deceit,
Ruddy and sweet to eat;
And the Raven his nest has made 5
In its thickest shade.

The Gods of the earth and sea,
Sought through Nature to find this Tree, 6
But their search was all in vain:
There grows one in the Human Brain.

THINKING ABOUT THE SELECTION

Recalling

1. (a) What, according to the first stanza, would happen if no one in the world were poor? (b) If everyone were happy?
2. A tree is described in the third and following stanzas? Where is this tree said to grow?

Interpreting

3. In the fifth stanza Blake writes of "the fruit of Deceit." (a) What do you think this phrase is intended to symbolize? (b) What other symbols are present in the poem? (c) How do they expand the poem's meaning?

Applying

4. (a) What does the title suggest about the poet's outlook? (b) Do you agree with the view he presents here? Explain your answer.

Answers

ANSWERS TO THINKING ABOUT THE SELECTION

Recalling

1. (a) If no one were poor, there would be no pity. (b) If everyone were happy, there would be no mercy.
2. The tree of Humility grows under the feet of Cruelty.

Interpreting

3. (a) The fruit of Deceit suggests the apple that caused Eve to lie to Adam and resulted in her fall from grace. (b) The Tree of Mystery symbolizes the tree of knowledge, or experience; the seed of the fatal tree is man's cruelty, its root is false humility, and its fruit is deceit. The caterpillar and the fly symbolize the evil in life that feeds on man's weaknesses, and the raven is a symbol for death. (c) The symbols point out the dangers of experience; it can bring about people's downfall.

Applying

4. (a) Blake calls this image of a tree which is life-destroying a "Human Abstract" because it is false and unnatural, existing only in the human mind—unlike nature, the impulse of life, which is concrete and real. (b) Answers will differ.

Infant Sorrow

William Blake

My mother groaned, my father wept, 1
Into the dangerous world I leapt;
Helpless, naked, piping loud,
Like a fiend hid in a cloud. 2

Struggling in my father's hands,
Striving against my swaddling bands,
Bound and weary, I thought best 3
To sulk upon my mother's breast.

THINKING ABOUT THE SELECTION

Recalling

1. (a) How does the speaker describe each of his parents in the opening stanza? (b) The world?
2. What event has just occurred?

Interpreting

3. How would you describe this poem's tone —the feelings it awakens in the reader? What words contribute to these feelings?
4. (a) In what sense do you think the speaker is "bound," as he describes himself in line 7? (b) Where do you suppose he would prefer to be?

Applying

5. In which of the two volumes, *Songs of Innocence* or *Songs of Experience,* do you think this poem was included? Explain your assumption.

Motivation for Reading Blake was born into a very poor family and grew up in a poverty-stricken section of London. How do you think his early experiences are reflected in the poem "Infant Sorrow"?

Master Teacher Note "Infant Sorrow" is from *Songs of Experience.* The corresponding poem in *Songs of Innocence* is "Infant Joy":

"I have no name:
I am but two days old."
What shall I call thee?
"I happy am,
Joy is my name."
Sweet joy befall thee!

Purpose-setting Question How would you describe the unusual view of birth presented in the poem?

1 **Discussion** How do the parents' reactions to the child's birth affect the mood of the poem? Why do you think they felt the way they did?

2 **Discussion** What do you think Blake meant by the simile?

3 **Discussion** Why does the speaker decide to sulk on his mother's breast?

Answers

ANSWERS TO THINKING ABOUT THE SELECTION

Recalling

1. (a) His mother groaned and his father wept. (b) The world was dangerous.
2. The speaker was born.

Interpreting

3. The tone awakens feelings of helplessness, depression and suffering. The words *groaned, wept, helpless, struggling, swaddling, bound, weary,* and *sulk* contribute to these feelings.
4. (a) The speaker is bound by the limits the world imposes, as well as by the "swaddling bands." (b) He would prefer to be free, in heaven.

Applying

5. This poem was included in *Songs of Experience,* since it deals with the evil in the world. It shows the contrast between innocence and the world's evils.

Motivation for Reading Have students discuss the last time they felt anger. How did they deal with it? Discuss whether it is better to express anger or to repress it.

Purpose-setting Question How does the tree here resemble the tree in "The Human Abstract"?

Master Teacher Note This poem may be interpreted as a symbolic depiction of the psychology of unresolved enmity. When anger and animosity are cultivated, like a tree, they can kill.

1 **Discussion** What is the meter of the first three lines of the stanza? The last line?

2 **Literary Focus** What do you think the apple symbolizes?

3 **Literary Focus** What does the garden symbolize?

4 **Literary Focus** What does this image symbolize? How does Blake use mixed meters in this concluding stanza to build and then relieve tension?

A Poison Tree

William Blake

1 I was angry with my friend:
I told my wrath, my wrath did end.
I was angry with my foe:
I told it not, my wrath did grow.

And I watered it in fears,
Night and morning with my tears;
And I sunnèd it with smiles,
And with soft deceitful wiles.

And it grew both day and night,
2 Till it bore an apple bright.
And my foe beheld it shine,
And he knew that it was mine,

3 And into my garden stole
When the night had veiled the pole;[1]
In the morning glad I see
4 My foe outstretched beneath the tree.

1. **pole:** Sky.

Humanities Note

Fine art, Illustration from a manuscript of "A Poison Tree" by William Blake. William Blake was a painter as well as a poet of mystic vision. His apprenticeship to an engraver gave him the background necessary to produce the bound volumes of his poems. In these books, Blake composed both the text and illustrations, which were printed simultaneously on a single page that he later hand-tinted with watercolor. These beautiful, lyrical books, laboriously produced in a small number, are considered to be Blake's finest effort.

The page "A Poison Tree" is from one of Blake's handmade books entitled *Songs of Experience,* published in 1794. The illustrations and poems for this work are of a darker nature than those done for *Songs of Innocence.* The tortured, evil-looking tree symbolizes the growth of the nurtured anger mentioned in the poem. The written poem becomes an integral part of the visual design of this page.

You may wish to discuss the following:

1. Does this drawing accurately depict the anguish of the speaker in the poem? Explain your answer.
2. What is it about this drawing that gives it an ominous mood?
3. How does the mood of this page compare to the page done for "The Lamb" shown on page 621?

THINKING ABOUT THE SELECTION

Recalling

1. (a) What does the speaker say occurred when he revealed his anger? (b) When he did not?
2. What "grows" out of the speaker's anger?

Interpreting

3. What sort of person do you find the speaker of this poem to be? What evidence can you find in support of your view?
4. (a) What symbols are used in the poem? How effective do you find them to be?

Applying

5. In what other famous piece of literature does an apple appear as a symbol? What relationship can you detect between its symbolic value there and here?
6. (a) Which of the other five poems by Blake printed here is this one most reminiscent of in theme, structure, and symbolism? (b) Which of the two poems do you think states its message most clearly? Give your reasons.

THINKING AND WRITING

Writing About Symbolism

Blake wrote to communicate his deeply mystical belief that coming of age forces a child to leave "Eden and struggle with a world that has lost its Paradise." For Blake, the uniting of innocence and experience carries with it an awareness of the inseparability of good and evil. His poems make extensive use of symbolism to convey that notion. List the symbols used by Blake in the six poems to represent these opposing forces of good and evil. Then in an essay discuss how these symbols clarify and add dimension to the notion underlying the poems. When you revise, make sure you have included adequate examples. Proofread your essay and prepare a final draft.

Answers

ANSWERS TO THINKING ABOUT THE SELECTION

Recalling

1. (a) When he revealed his anger to a friend, the wrath ended. (b) When he did not reveal his anger to a foe, it grew.
2. A tree of wrath grew out of the speaker's anger.

Interpreting

3. The speaker is a person who refuses to resolve his enmity with a foe. The second stanza offers evidence of the speaker's active cultivation of wrath.
4. (a) The chief symbols are the tree and the apple. The tree is a symbol of nurtured, cultivated enmity. The apple is a symbol of the fruit, or consequence, of hatred—death.

Applying

5. The apple is a symbol in the story from Genesis about man's fall from grace. God banished Adam and Eve from the Garden of Eden after they had eaten of the apple. Here the foe is banished from the garden by death.
6. (a) This poem is most reminiscent of "The Human Abstract" in theme, structure, and symbolism. (b) "A Poison Tree" states its message more clearly because the symbols are more universal. In "The Human Abstract" many of the symbols refer to Blake's private philosophy and their interpretation is more uncertain.

THINKING AND WRITING

Publishing Student Writing Student essays could be collected in a booklet and displayed in the classroom.

The writing assignments on page 627 have students write creatively, while those on page 628 have them think about the selections and write critically.

YOU THE WRITER
Guidelines for Evaluating Assignment 1

1. Has the student written additional stanzas for an eighteenth-century poem that are consistent with the original in content?
2. Has the student followed the model's meter and rhyme?
3. Is the style of the student's lines appropriate?
4. Are the new stanzas free from grammar, usage, and mechanics errors?

Guidelines for Evaluating Assignment 2

1. Has the student written a narrative or essay modeled on one of the selections of eighteenth-century literature that has content reflecting the ideas and beliefs of the period?
2. Has the student written the essay with the values and outlook of an author in mind?
3. Has the student chosen an appropriate style that is consistent with the author's?
4. Is the essay free from grammar, usage, and mechanics errors?

Guidelines for Evaluating Assignment 3

1. Does the letter express thoughts about a major event or concern of the eighteenth century?
2. Does the letter maintain an eighteenth-century outlook, character, and flavor?
3. Has the student written the letter in a clear, well-organized way?
4. Is the letter free from grammar, usage, and mechanics errors?

YOU THE WRITER

Assignment

1. Select a poem from this unit and write a stanza or two that could be added onto the end as a continuation of the original. Your additional lines should follow the verse form and style of the original.

Prewriting. Freewrite, exploring the meaning of the original poem. Decide what you might say that would be in harmony with the content of the original. Then study the meter and rhyme of this poem.

Writing. Write your lines in verse, trying to keep to the meter and rhyme of the original. Your first concern, however, should be with the content.

Revising. Refine your verse. Have you followed your model's meter and rhyme? Is the style of your lines appropriate? Finally, check over the content. Does it seem in keeping with that of the original?

Assignment

2. Write a prose narrative or essay modeled on one of the selections in this unit. The content should reflect the ideas and beliefs of the period. The style should closely follow that of your model.

Prewriting. Reread the selection you have chosen. Decide what subject matter, ideas, and viewpoint would make your narrative or essay a close imitation of the original.

Writing. When you write your first draft, try to keep within the mind and outlook of the author whose work you are following. As well as you can, follow his style.

Revising. First check that the content of your writing is in keeping with the era of the original. Then check that the style is also appropriate. Finally, look for and correct any lapses in grammar and style.

Assignment

3. Imagine you are a young lady or gentleman of the eighteenth century. Write a letter to a friend in which you express your thoughts on any major event or concern of the day.

Prewriting. Review the introduction to this unit and any other information you have gathered about the era. Select your subject from this material. Then outline what you will say to your friend. Remember that you are an eighteenth-century person and your comments should reflect the standards and concerns of this time.

Writing. When you write your letter, concentrate on expressing your thoughts in a clear, well-organized way. Try, however, to maintain an eighteenth-century outlook.

Revising. See if you can enhance the eighteenth-century character and flavor of your letter. Although your letter is to a friend, it should have a somewhat formal tone. Make sure your language is appropriate. Then correct any errors in grammar that you notice.

YOU THE CRITIC

Assignment

1. The era called Restoration and the Eighteenth century makes up one of the great periods of English prose. Write a descriptive essay in which you compare and contrast the prose of the period with the prose you find in magazines and newspapers of today.

Prewriting. First decide what you find especially admirable in one or two of the selections you have read. What adjectives would you use to describe this quality? What passages would you cite to illustrate it? How is the prose of today different?

Writing. Write an essay based on your prewriting work. Strive to be clear and precise in your descriptions.

Revising. Ask yourself, "Am I conveying clearly the qualities I see in the prose? Am I using comparison and contrast effectively to differentiate eighteenth-century prose from the prose of today?"

Assignment

2. A line from Alexander Pope, "What oft was thought, but ne'er so well expressed," could be applied to some of the best literature of this period. Choose at least two works from this unit and show how they express traditional ideas both elegantly and memorably.

Prewriting. Review selections you have read and find statements or passages that could stand alone as memorable quotations. Jot down notes about the meaning of each passage. Then decide in what order you will quote and comment on them.

Writing. First write a topic sentence that sums up your general opinion of the style and content of the lines and passages you are concerned with. Then present your quotations with comments on their literary effectiveness.

Revising. Look for and correct any lapses in the style and organization of your essay or in grammar.

Assignment

3. Literature reflects the times in which it is created. Write an essay showing how the literature you have read in this unit reflects the historical developments and trends of the period.

Prewriting. Review the introduction to the unit and any other related knowledge you may have. Which of the selections you have read comes to mind during your review? How do they reflect their times? Freewrite, exploring your answers.

Writing. Write an essay based on your prewriting work. You might first mention a historical development or trend and then describe how it is reflected in one of the works you have read.

Revising. Check that your essay is well organized and unified by a topic sentence, and that your explanations are clear and well developed. Finally, correct any errors in grammar or style.

YOU THE CRITIC

Guidelines for Evaluating Assignment 1

1. Has the student used comparison and contrast to write a descriptive essay about eighteenth-century prose and prose found in magazines and newspapers today?
2. Has the student described what is admirable about eighteenth-century prose?
3. Has the student provided clear and precise evidence to support the main idea?
4. Is the essay free from grammar, usage, and mechanics errors?

Guidelines for Evaluating Assignment 2

1. Does the student begin the essay with a statement that sums up his or her general opinion of the style and content of the lines and passages chosen?
2. Does the student present the quotations chosen from eighteenth-century literature and comment on their literary effectiveness?
3. Does the student prove that eighteenth-century authors expressed traditional ideas elegantly and memorably?
4. Is the essay free from grammar, usage, and mechanics errors?

Guidelines for Evaluating Assignment 3

1. Has the student begun the essay by describing an historical development or trend of the eighteenth century?
2. Does the student describe how the development or trend is reflected in one of the works of the period?
3. Has the student used sufficient evidence from the work to support his or her main idea?
4. Is the essay free from grammar, usage, and mechanics errors?

Humanities Note

Fine art, *View in Hampshire,* by Patrick Nasmyth. Patrick Nasmyth (1787–1831) was born in Edinburgh, Scotland, one of eleven children of the landscape painter Alexander Nasmyth. In 1807 Patrick moved to London. He overcame the handicap of an injury to his right hand by learning to use his left hand with as much skill as if he had been left-handed.

View in Hampshire, like many of Nasmyth's oils, is in the style of Dutch landscape painters, whose works are marked by somber colors, emphasis on light and shadow, careful attention to detail, and, generally, a sense of quiet calmness. *View in Hampshire,* showing a rural scene in a locality southwest of London, is characterized in particular by its simplicity and gentleness. The most significant figure against the rustic background is the grazing horse. It is the sort of pastoral scene that has come to be associated with the Romantics.

VIEW IN HAMPSHIRE
Patrick Nasmyth

THE ROMANTIC AGE
1798–1832

One impulse from a vernal wood
  May teach you more of man,
Of moral evil and of good,
  Than all the sages can.

Sweet is the lore which Nature brings;
  Our meddling intellect
Misshapes the beauteous forms of things—
  We murder to dissect.

Enough of Science and of Art;
  Close up those barren leaves;
Come forth, and bring with you a heart
  That watches and receives.

from "The Tables Turned"
William Wordsworth

Humanities Note

Fine art, *Capture of the Bastille, 14 July, 1789,* by Claude Cholat. The Bastille was originally built, in the 1370's, as a fortified gate to protect the French against British attack. Over the centuries the fortification was added to, until it had eight towers 100 feet high, surrounded by an 80-foot moat. In the seventeenth century, under Cardinal Richelieu, chief minister to King Louis XIII, political prisoners were sent to the Bastille for the first time; even banned books were kept within its walls.

At the time of the storming of the Bastille, only seven prisoners were being held. The original intention of the crowd was to ask that arms kept in the Bastille be distributed. Angered at the arrogant response of the prison head, however, they forced their way in. Two days later the legislative assembly in Paris decided that the Bastille must be torn down—a procedure that took several years. In any event, the structure, in Paris, had become the symbol of the tyranny of the French monarchy and aristocracy.

1 **Enrichment** The young poet Shelley shared much of the radical William Godwin's revolutionary ardor and eventually became his son-in-law, marrying Mary Godwin after the suicide of his young wife.

CAPTURE OF THE BASTILLE, JULY 14, 1789
Claude Cholat
The Granger Collection

The preceding stanzas from "The Tables Turned," written in 1798, capture some of the main sentiments of a new age in British literature, an age in which writers "turned the tables" on eighteenth century thinking, insisting that the world be viewed through the heart, not the mind. During this period, which was named the Romantic Age by historians during the late 1800's, nearly all the attitudes and tendencies of eighteenth-century classicism and rationalism were redefined or changed dramatically. To understand how these changes occurred, it is necessary to examine not only the impact of events in Britain, but also the effects of the social and political upheaval that began taking place in other parts of the world.

REVOLUTION AND REACTION

Toward the end of the eighteenth century, two revolutions occurred outside England that indirectly threatened the stability of the British political and social systems. During the 1770's the American colonies revolted against British rule, eventually winning their independence and forming a government based on the principles of freedom and equality. While the American Revolution divided British public opinion and aroused some awareness of the need for reform, its impact on British society was not nearly as great as that of the French Revolution, which demonstrated that it was possible for a long-standing government to be successfully challenged on its own soil.

The French Revolution began on July 14, 1789, when a group of French citizens stormed the Bastille, a Paris prison for political prisoners. In the weeks that followed, the revolutionaries placed limits on the powers of King Louis XVI, established a new government, and approved a document called the Declaration of the Rights of Man, affirming the principles of "liberty, equality, and fraternity." France became a constitutional monarchy.

Opposing Views

From the start, the revolution evoked strong reactions from both liberals and conservatives throughout the rest of Europe. In England the ruling class felt threatened by the implications of the events in France, while most intellectuals, including several of the most important and influential writers of the Romantic Age, enthusiastically supported the revolution and the democratic ideals on which it was grounded. One ardent supporter of the revolution was Charles James Fox, leader of the Whig party, who declared, "How much the greatest event it is that ever happened in the world! and how much the best!" Poet William Wordsworth also spoke out in support of the
1 revolution, and philosopher and novelist William Godwin (1756–1836) reacted to the revolution by writing *An Enquiry Concerning Social Justice* (1793), in which he predicted that British society

would evolve peacefully into a nation characterized by freedom and equality. In contrast, Whig political thinker Edmund Burke (1729–1797), who had sympathized with the American Revolution, condemned the events in France. In *Reflections on the Revolution in France* (1790), he argued that the French, unlike the Americans, were attacking the very fabric of their society with complete disregard for their roots and ancestry. Burke warned that the revolution was bound to grow violent and mourned that "the age of chivalry is gone . . . and the glory of Europe is extinguished forever."

THE REIGN OF TERROR

Burke's views did not win wide acceptance in Britain until his dire predictions began coming true. As royalists, moderates, and radicals jockeyed for power, the French Revolution became more and more chaotic. In 1792, France declared war on Austria, touching off an invasion by Austrian and Prussian troops, whose leader proclaimed the intention of restoring the French king to full authority. Fuming with patriotic indignation, a radical group called the Jacobins gained control of the French legislative assembly, abolished the monarchy, and declared the nation a republic. Mobs attacked and killed many prisoners—including former aristocrats and priests—and soon French refugees began pouring into England with tales of these bloody "September massacres." Within weeks the revolutionaries had tried and convicted Louis XVI on a charge of treason. When Louis XVI went to the guillotine early in 1793, a revolutionary leader, Georges Danton, exclaimed: "The kings of Europe would challenge us. We throw them the head of a king!"

Following the execution, revolutionary violence reached its peak, as the Jacobins, under the leadership of Maximilien Robespierre, began what is called the Reign of Terror. Before the terror ended in the summer of 1794, revolutionary authorities had imprisoned thousands of royalists, moderates, and even radicals, sending 2
some 4000 of them—including Danton and finally Robespierre himself—to the guillotine.

British Reaction

The September massacres and the Reign of Terror were so shocking that even Britons who had sympathized with the French Revolution now turned against it. Conservative Britons, already hostile to the Revolution, demanded a crackdown on reformers within Britain, whom they denounced as dangerous Jacobins. Adding to British alarm was the success of France's new "citizen army," which expelled the Austrian and Prussian invaders and then set out to "liberate" other European nations from despotic rule. British leaders did not want France or any other nation to win dominance on the European continent. In 1793, France took the initiative by declaring war on Britain. Thus began a series of wars

2 **Master Teacher Note** For a vivid recreation of the Reign of Terror, you might suggest that students read Charles Dickens's *A Tale of Two Cities,* Dickens's only historical novel.

BRITISH EVENTS

1798 **William Wordsworth** and **Samuel Taylor Coleridge** publish *Lyrical Ballads*.

Wolfe Tone Rebellion in Ireland.

1801 Act of Union creates United Kingdom of Great Britain and Ireland.

Union Jack becomes official flag.

1802 J.M.W. Turner's *Calais Pier* exhibited in London.

1803 Henry Shrapnel invents exploding shell.

1805 Battle of Trafalgar.

1807 Thomas Moore writes *Irish Melodies*.

1811 King George III declared permanently insane.

1812 **Byron** publishes *Childe Harold's Pilgrimage*.

1813 Waltz becomes acceptable in London ballrooms.

Jane Austen publishes *Pride and Prejudice*.

1814 George Stephenson constructs first successful steam locomotive.

Walter Scott publishes *Waverley*.

1815 John MacAdam constructs roads of crushed stone.

1817 **William Hazlitt** writes *Characters of Shakespeare's Plays*.

1818 Thomas Bowdler publishes censored edition of Shakespeare's plays.

Mary Wollstonecraft Shelley publishes *Frankenstein, or the Modern Prometheus*.

William Wordsworth

George Stephenson's

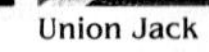

Union Jack

Jane Austen

Rosetta Stone

Sir Walter Scott and Robert Burns

634

Locomotive

Napoleon

Beethoven

Robert Fulton's Steamboat

WORLD EVENTS

1799 France: Napoleon becomes head of revolutionary government.

Egypt: Rosetta Stone, key to deciphering hieroglyphics, discovered.

1800 Italy: Volta builds first electric battery.

Spain: Goya paints *The Two Majas*.

1802 Haiti: Toussaint L'Ouverture leads rebellion against French rule.

1803 United States: Louisiana Territory purchased from France.

Germany: French occupy Hanover.

1804 Germany: Beethoven composes *Symphony No. 3*.

France: Napoleon crowns himself emperor.

1805 Eastern Europe: Napoleon defeats allies at Austerlitz.

1807 United States: Fulton's steamboat navigates Hudson River.

1808 Italy: Excavation of Pompeii begins.

Germany: Goethe publishes *Faust*, Part I.

1809 United States: Washington Irving writes "Rip Van Winkle."

1810 South America: Simón Bolívar leads rebellions against Spanish rule.

1812 Russia: Napoleon loses hundreds of thousands of troops in retreat from Moscow.

Spain: Wellington drives French from Madrid.

United States: War with Britain declared.

1813 Germany: Allies defeat Napoleon at Leipzig.

Mexico: Independence declared.

BRITISH EVENTS

1819 Peterloo Massacre in Manchester.

Percy Bysshe Shelley publishes "Ode to the West Wind".

1820 King George III dies.

John Keats publishes "Ode on a Grecian Urn".

1821 *Manchester Guardian* begins publication.

John Constable paints *The Grove*

1823 **Charles Lamb** publishes *Essays of Elia*.

1824 First labor unions permitted.

1825 Horse-drawn buses begin operating in London.

John Nash completes rebuilding of Buckingham Palace.

1827 System for purifying London water installed.

1829 Catholic Emancipation Act passed.

Robert Peel establishes Metropolitan Police in London.

1830 Liverpool-Manchester railway opens.

1831 Michael Faraday demonstrates electromagnetic induction.

1832 First Reform Act extends voting rights.

John Keats

The Grove

London in the 1820's

Charles Lamb

Liverpool-Manchester

The Peterloo Massacre

THE

LAST OF THE MOHICANS.

BY

JAMES FENIMORE COOPER.

NEW YORK:
D. APPLETON AND COMPANY, PUBLISHERS.

The Last of the Mohicans

Savannah, the First Steamer to Cross the Atlantic

Railway

Edgar Allan Poe

WORLD EVENTS

1814 France: Napoleon abdicates and is exiled to Elba.

1815 France: Napoleon returns for "Hundred Days."

Belgium: Napoleon defeated at Waterloo.

France: Napoleon exiled to St. Helena.

1816 Italy: Rossini composes *The Barber of Seville*.

1817 United States: William Cullen Bryant publishes "Thanatopsis."

Germany: Hegel publishes *Encyclopedia of the Philosophical Sciences*.

1818 First steamship crosses Atlantic.

1821 Greece: War with Turkey begins.

Germany: Heinrich Heine publishes *Poems*.

1822 Austria: Schubert begins *Symphony No. 8* ("Unfinished Symphony").

Russia: Aleksandr Pushkin publishes *Eugene Onegin*.

1823 United States: Monroe Doctrine closes Americas to further European colonization.

1825 Russia: Bolshoi Ballet established.

1826 Germany: Mendelssohn composes *Overture to A Midsummer Night's Dream*.

United States: James Fenimore Cooper publishes *The Last of the Mohicans*.

1827 France: Alexandre Dumas publishes *The Three Musketeers*.

1830 France: Stendhal publishes *The Red and the Black*.

1831 United States: Edgar Allan Poe publishes *Poems*.

France: Victor Hugo publishes *The Hunchback of Notre Dame*.

Humanities Note

Fine art, *The Battle of Trafalgar,* c. 1823, by J.M. W. Turner. John Mallord William Turner had a precocious talent and exhibited his first painting at the Royal Academy when he was fifteen. He became very successful, frequently exhibiting paintings there. In 1823, Turner was commissioned to paint a vast representation of the Battle of Trafalgar. This piece now hangs in the National Maritime Museum in Greenwich, England. In this work Turner projected all his patriotism and his love of the sea. However, he was unable to meet the criticisms of the seaman who wanted complete historical accuracy. Like most of Turner's work, this one is large in scope, showing a dramatic sea and sky. In true Romantic fashion, the natural elements are emphasized over the human ones.

that would drag on for twenty-two years, creating fear and rigidity within Britain and effectively squelching during that time all hope of reform within British society.

The Tory government led by William Pitt (the Younger) began the reaction by outlawing all talk of parliamentary reform outside the halls of Parliament, banning public meetings, and suspending certain basic rights. Later, Pitt's government crushed a rebellion in Ireland. Liberal-minded Britons had no political outlet for their hopes and dreams. Many turned to literature and art as a way to find in the pristine world of romanticized nature the source of beauty and truth.

The Napoleonic Wars

Britain's battles against France took a new turn after 1799, when a military leader named Napoleon Bonaparte came to power in Paris. Napoleon had grandiose plans for French military expansion, and he was an able leader. After a brief break in French-British hostilities in 1802–03, war resumed in earnest. Napoleon, who had declared himself emperor of France, planned an invasion of Britain, but had to abandon the plan after a British fleet under Lord Nelson defeated the French fleet at the Battle of Trafalgar, off Spain, in 1805. Napoleon's armies fought well against Britain's European allies, however, and by 1807 they controlled almost all of Europe as far east as the borders of Russia. Britain ruled the ocean, but Napoleon ruled Europe.

In 1812 Napoleon finally overextended himself by invading Russia. There his armies suffered a series of bloody defeats. At the same time, Napoleon was experiencing reverses in the west. His forces were defeated in the Peninsular War (1808–13) in Portugal

THE BATTLE OF TRAFALGAR
J. M. W. Turner
The Granger Collection

and Spain and, in 1814, British and allied armies closed in on him and forced him to abandon his crown. Napoleon was not finished, however. Exiled to the Mediterranean island of Elba, he plotted a return, and in 1815 he managed to escape to France, assemble an army, and resume rule for a period known as the Hundred Days. Napoleon's attempt to regain his former glory ended on the battlefield at Waterloo, Belgium, in 1815, when the Duke of Wellington, British hero of the Peninsular War, led an allied army to a decisive victory.

All over Britain, people celebrated the end of the Napoleonic Wars with bonfires and other festivities. Royalists hailed the restoration of monarchical authority throughout Europe, while radicals mourned the failure of the revolutionary ideals of liberty and equality.

COPING WITH SOCIETY'S PROBLEMS

Throughout the long wars with France, Britain's government kept a tight lid on domestic dissent. It ignored the problems caused by the Industrial Revolution—including the overcrowding of factory towns, the unpleasant and unsafe working conditions in the factories, and the long working hours, and low pay experienced by the workers—and the problems only got worse.

Rumblings Among the People

Britain's government claimed to be following a hands-off policy, but in fact it sided openly with employers against workers even helping to crush the workers' attempts to form unions. Meanwhile, the working class grew steadily larger and more restless. In the factory towns of northern England, workers protested the loss of jobs to new machinery in the violent Luddite Riots (1811–13). In Manchester, mounted soldiers charged a peaceful mass meeting of cotton workers and killed several of them in what came to be known as the Peterloo Massacre (1819). To many, it seemed that British society was splitting into two angry camps—the working classes, who demanded reform, and the ruling classes, who resisted fiercely.

Beginnings of Reform

During this time, Britain had a series of weak and ineffective royal heads. George III, long subject to bouts of insanity, went irretrievably mad in 1811. His eldest son, the scandal-plagued and unpopular George, Prince of Wales, ruled as Regent from 1811 to 1820—a period known as the Regency. Then the old king died and
3 the Regent became George IV. When he died in 1830, his brother took over as William IV—an old and weak but amiable king, who ruled until 1837.

The weakness of these kings helped to enhance the power of the prime ministers—in theory named by the king, but in practice

NAPOLEON (THE CAMPAIGN IN FRANCE, 1814)
J. L. E. Meissonier
The Granger Collection

KING WILLIAM IV OF ENGLAND
Sir Martin Archer Shee
The Granger Collection

3 **Historical Context** The Victorian novelist William Thackeray characterized him as "the last and worst of all the Georges" because of his extravagance and his treatment of his consort. The poet Leigh Hunt was sentenced to a two-year prison term for calling him a "fat Adonis."

Humanities Note

Fine art, 1864, Napoleon *(The Campaign in France, 1814)*, by J. L. E. Meissonier. Jean Louis Ernest Meissonier (1815–1891) accompanied Napoleon III, Napoleon Bonaparte's nephew, to Italy in the 1850's. Meissonier did a series of paintings of Napoleon I. This detail of *The Campaign in France, 1814* shows the French general in a typical pose, leading his troops on a light-colored horse. The invasion of France by Britain and Spain in 1814 led to the downfall of the emperor, and thus the painting depicts a great leader whose defeat is imminent.

Humanities Note

Fine art, *King William IV of England* by Sir Martin Archer Shee. When he was nineteen Martin Archer Shee (1769–1850), who had studied art in his native Dublin, went to London, at the urging of the famous American portrait painter Gilbert Stuart. Through influential connections, Shee entered the Royal Academy, in 1790, and later became a successful portrait painter whose subjects included members of the royal family.

Shee's full-length portrait of the King William IV is a typical formal pose of a monarch. It was painted by a man whose conservative views on art were expressed in two poems Shee wrote: "Rhymes on Art, or the Remonstrance of a Painter" (1805) and "Elements of Art" (1809). Shee's interest in both painting and literature led his friend the poet Lord Byron, perhaps satirically, to write: "And here let Shee and genius find a place,/Whose pen and pencil yield an equal grace. . . ."

SKETCH FOR HADLEIGH CASTLE, c. 1828–9
John Constable
The Granger Collection

chosen by the strongest party in Parliament. The Tory leaders who held power during and immediately after the Napoleonic Wars rejected all suggestions of reform. A new generation of Tories emerged in the 1820's, however, and a trickle of reforms began. however, A law was passed in 1824 permitting Britain's first labor unions to organize; and in 1829 the Catholic Emancipation Act restored economic and religious freedoms to Roman Catholics.

The trickle grew into a stream of reforms following a Whig victory in the election of 1830. The Reform Law of 1832 brought sweeping changes to British political life. By extending voting rights to the small but important middle class (males only), this law threatened the traditional dominance of land-owning aristocrats in Parliament. Moreover, in 1833 Parliament passed the first law governing factory safety. That same year, it also abolished slavery.

THE BEGINNINGS OF ROMANTICISM

Writers of the Romantic Age reacted strongly to the events of their time. They felt stirrings of excitement or repulsion as they 4
contemplated the French Revolution. They saw the dramatic changes being wrought by the Industrial Revolution and longed for the simplicity and purity of the past. They sensed the rumblings of discontent and desperation that could not be silenced, even by the repressive measures of the war years. Those who had applauded the French Revolution, envisioning a new age of democracy and 5
equality in Britain, were left in a state of bitter disappointment. They turned their attention to literary endeavors, creating a Romantic style that offered a new perspective on the world—a perspective that focused on nature and "the common people."

New Literary Concerns

Just as the French revolutionaries had at first discarded the customs and procedures that had traditionally governed French society, the Romantic writers abandoned many of the dominant attitudes and principles of eighteenth-century literature. New literary concerns emerged, many of which had been shaped either by the French revolutionary spirit or by the effects of the Industrial Revolution. The Romantic writers' interest in the trials and dreams of common people and their desire for radical change developed out of the democratic idealism that characterized the early part of the French Revolution, while their deep attachment to nature was a response to the consequences of industrialization. These and other characteristics of Romantic literature represent a distinct departure from the concerns associated with eighteenth-century classicism and rationalism. Because of this dichotomy, the prevailing ideas and attitudes of Romanticism are most easily grasped when viewed in contrast to those of the eighteenth century. The following chart identifies some of the contrasting tendencies.

Humanities Note

Fine art, Sketch for *Hadleigh Castle,* c. 1828–9, by John Constable. All of the paintings of John Constable (1776–1837) show familiar and realistic scenes of the English countryside. Constable wanted to paint what he saw with his own eyes, for he believed that landscape painting must be based on observable facts. He went out into the countryside to make sketches from nature and painted final versions in his studio. This working sketch for *Hadleigh Castle* is an example of his work in progress. This detail shows a literal rendering, with freshness in color resulting from working in natural light outdoors.

4 **Enrichment** Wordsworth in particular among the older Romantic poets supported the French Revolution, although both Coleridge and Southey were ardent revolutionaries in their youth.

5 **Literary Movement** Wordsworth's "London, 1802," page 666, expresses his reaction to the disappointing outcome of the French Revolution and the growing reactionary spirit in England.

	CLASSICISM AND RATIONALISM	ROMANTICISM
SOURCES OF INSPIRATION	scientific observation of the outer world; logic	examination of inner feelings, emotions; imagination
	classical Greek and Roman literature	the literature of the Middle Ages
ATTITUDES AND INTERESTS	pragmatic	idealistic
	interested in science, technology	interested in the mysterious and supernatural
	concerned with general, universal experiences	concerned with the particular
	believed in following standards and traditions	sought to develop new forms of expression
	felt optimistic about the present	romanticized the past
	emphasized moderation and self-restraint	tended toward excess and spontaneity
	appreciated elegance, refinement	appreciated folk traditions
SOCIAL CONCERNS	valued stability and harmony	desired radical change
	favored a social hierarchy	favored democracy
	interested in maintaining the aristocracy	concerned with common people
	concerned with society as a whole	concerned with the individual
	believed that nature should be controlled by humans	felt that nature should be untamed

It is customary to set the beginning of Britain's Romantic Age in 1798, the year in which William Wordsworth and Samuel Taylor Coleridge published the *Lyrical Ballads,* establishing the Romantic principles that would dominate British literature for several decades. However, the ideas of Romanticism arose on continental Europe well before the turn of the century. Even in Britain a handful of poets—most notably Thomas Gray, Robert Burns, and William Blake—had displayed some of the characteristics of Romantic thinking before *Lyrical Ballads* was published.

Jean-Jacques Rousseau

Though he died before the start of the Romantic Age, Swiss-born writer Jean-Jacques Rousseau (1712–1778), a leading philosopher of eighteenth-century France, planted one of the seeds from

RAIN, STEAM, AND SPEED—THE GREAT WESTERN RAILWAY, BEFORE 1844
J. M. W. Turner
The Granger Collection

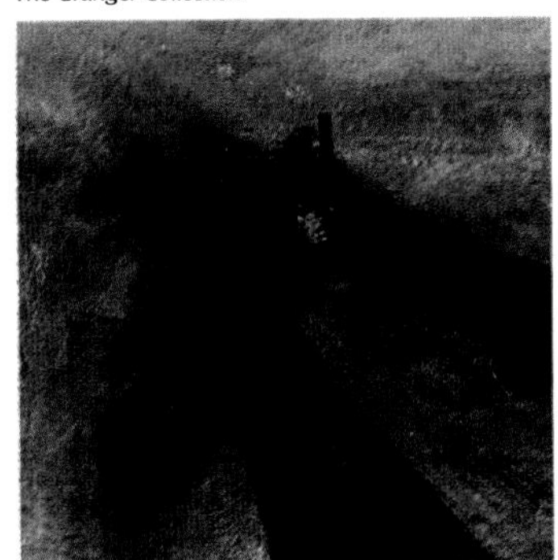

Humanities Note

Fine art, *Rain, Steam, and Speed —the Great Western Railway,* 1844, by J. M. W. Turner. In the latter part of his life, Turner was experimenting more with color and light. *Rain, Steam, and Speed* is a view of a steam engine crossing a bridge over the Thames in a rainstorm. There is almost no separation between the water and the sky. The effect is almost impressionistic. Turner inserted a playful touch with the hare running along the track in front of the train.

Humanities Note

Fine art, *Portrait of Goethe,* Josef Karl Stieler. The portrait of Goethe, by Josef Karl Stieler (1781–1853), a German painter, shows the famous poet, playwright, and philosopher as a middle-aged man. His sturdy bearing and his look of strength and dignity suggest a person well established, respected, and admired. At the same time, his expressive eyes, looking to the right rather than directly at the viewer, convey a sense of searching or inquiry, almost even of impatience. The papers Goethe holds in his hand are, presumably, symbols of his literary interests and his prolific intellectual output. His ideas were to strongly influence the thinkers of the Romantic Age.

6 **Enrichment** All the English Romantics read Rousseau enthusiastically; if the Romantic movement was somewhat unbalanced—an over-correction of eighteenth-century neo-classicism—so was Rousseau himself, whose last years were threatened by insanity.

7 **Enrichment** Romanticism began in Germany and moved in a generally chronological pattern to England, then Russia, then France, then both North and South America. Its progress, however, was not strictly regular; Burns and Blake were employing Romantic characteristics in Britain in the 1780's.

8 **Enrichment** Among other Romantic painters were the French Eugène Delacroix (1799–1863) and the German Caspar David Friedrich (1774–1840).

PORTRAIT OF GOETHE
Joseph Karl Stieler
Three Lions

which Romanticism grew. Rousseau saw society as a force of evil that infringed on personal liberty and human happiness. "Man is born free," he wrote, "and everywhere he is in chains." He reasoned that humanity should revert to its natural state, abandoning its stifling social institutions and outworn philosophies and listening instead to nature, instinct, and intuition.

Rousseau prepared the way for political revolution. The Americans who declared their independence in 1776 quoted Rousseau often, and the French revolutionaries of 1789 quoted him even more frequently. Rousseau also prepared the way for a new artistic movement, Romanticism. During the latter part of the eighteenth century, in the German-speaking areas of Europe, which were not yet a unified nation and often suffered from the repressive policies of powerful Prussia and Austria, a group of nationalistically minded writers began incorporating Rousseau's ideas into major works of poetry, drama, and fiction.

Johann Wolfgang von Goethe

The most influential of this group was Johann Wolfgang von Goethe (1749–1832). In search of inspiration, Goethe turned to the German literature of the Middle Ages, early vernacular works filled with myth and superstition, adventure and passion, not unlike the Anglo-Saxon *Beowulf.* In these works Goethe found not only a source of pride for a new generation of German writers but also a primitive simplicity much in keeping with Rousseau's ideas and values. A fascination with medieval times—the same Middle Ages that "enlightened" thinkers had despised—soon became characteristic of the emerging artistic movement. In fact, the movement would later be named the Romantic Age because of its interest in medieval *romances*—imaginary tales of adventure written in one of the Roman dialects, the early forms of languages derived from Latin.

THE ROMANTIC AGE IN BRITISH POETRY

Romanticism was a movement that affected not only literature but all the arts. In music, it produced such brilliant European composers as Germany's Ludwig van Beethoven (1770–1827) and Austria's Franz Schubert (1797–1828), but no one of comparable stature in Britain. In painting, it influenced the intensely personal and warmly spontaneous rural landscapes of Britain's John Constable (1776–1837) and J. M. W. Turner (1775–1851). However, it is for literature, and especially for poetry, that Britain's Romantic Age is most famous.

Wordsworth and Coleridge: A Break with the Past

When William Wordsworth (1770–1850) asked his friend Samuel Taylor Coleridge (1772–1834) to collaborate with him in the publication of *Lyrical Ballads,* he was well aware that their collection

CALAIS PIER: AN ENGLISH PACKET ARRIVING
J. M. W. Turner
The Granger Collection

of poetry would make a distinct break with the past. To underscore that break, Wordsworth included in the second (1800) and third (1802) editions of *Lyrical Ballads* a preface explaining the new poetic principles he and Coleridge had employed. That preface defined poetry as "the spontaneous overflow of powerful feelings" and explained that poetry "takes its origin from emotion recollected in tranquillity." An emphasis on the emotions, then, was central to the new Romantic poetry the two men were creating.

Equally important was subject matter. According to the preface, poetry should deal with "incidents and situations from common life" over which the poet throws "a certain coloring of imagination, whereby ordinary things should be presented . . . in an unusual way." Wordsworth's poems gave "the charm of novelty to things of every day," as Coleridge later said. Coleridge, on the other hand,
9 provided the "coloring of imagination," creating imaginative settings and mysterious sequences of events.

Finally, Wordsworth's preface spoke about incorporating human passions with "the beautiful and permanent forms of nature."
10 An emphasis on nature would become another important characteristic of British Romantic verse, and Wordsworth would frequently be described as a "nature poet."

The Romantic view of nature was quite different from that of most eighteenth-century literature. Nature was not a force to be
11 tamed and analyzed scientifically; rather, it was a wild, free force that could inspire poets to instinctive spiritual understanding. In "The Tables Turned," Wordsworth advised readers to

> Come forth into the light of things,
> Let Nature be your Teacher.

SAMUEL TAYLOR COLERIDGE
Peter Vandyke
The Granger Collection

Humanities Note

Fine art, *Calais Pier, with French Poissards preparing for sea: an English packet arriving.* 1803, by J. M. W. Turner. Turner's vision of the world was a fantastic one, bathed in dramatic light filled with dazzling pageantries. In many of his pictures, like *Calais Pier,* he crowded in every effect that would make them more dazzling and striking. He shows the power of nature, which is not always kind to humans. Here Turner presents dazzling light in stark contrast with the dark shadows of the storm clouds. The viewer can feel the rush of the wind and the impact of the waves, against which the humans struggle.

Humanities Note

Fine art, *Samuel Taylor Coleridge,* 1795, by Peter Vandyke. A native of the Netherlands, Peter Vandyke (b. 1729; death date uncertain) was asked to come to England by Sir Joshua Reynolds, the widely acclaimed British portrait painter. In England Vandyke assisted Reynolds, and he also painted portraits of his own; he exhibited some of them in London in the 1760's.

It was at the invitation of a publisher that Vandyke painted his portrait of Samuel Taylor Coleridge, which now hangs in London's National Portrait Gallery. The portrait of Coleridge is formal —perhaps in something of the "grand style" favored by Reynolds—and yet it displays warmth and humanity, especially in the expressiveness of the subject's eyes.

9 **Literary Movement** Coleridge's "The Rime of the Ancient Mariner," page 670, is considered to be his one complete and perfectly executed masterpiece. Coleridge planned many works, but his temperament prevented their completion; his fragment "Kubla Khan," page 695, a rich and evocative dream picture, gives evidence of the abortive nature of much of his inspiration.

10 **Literary Movement** Wordsworth's "Lines Composed a Few Miles Above Tintern Abbey," page 654, and "My Heart Leaps Up When I Behold," page 660, give a personal history of his own commitment to Nature. Both these poems are prefatory to his great "Ode: Intimations of Immortality from Recollections of Early Childhood."

11 **Literary Movement** In Wordsworth's "The World Is Too Much with Us," page 667, the poet truly sees untamed Nature as an elemental spiritual force.

12 Enrichment Wordsworth became so extremely conservative, even reactionary, in his old age that his ideas came to be denounced by younger writers. The Victorian poet Robert Browning, for example, in his poem "The Lost Leader," mourned Wordsworth's decline from liberalism.

13 Enrichment Although Byron was an outstandingly attractive man, he did have one physical flaw: a clubfoot.

14 Enrichment Byron's "English Bards and Scotch Reviewers" treats all three "first generation Romantics" with contempt; he calls Wordsworth idiotic, Coleridge turgid, and Southey long-winded.

15 Literary Movement Both Emily Brontë's *Wuthering Heights* and Charlotte Brontë's *Jane Eyre* (excerpts from which can be found on page 912 and page 924, respectively) contain Byronic heroes in the characters of Heathcliff and Rochester.

16 Literary Movement See the excerpt from Byron's *Don Juan*, page 707, for a work whose satirical tone is definitely anti-Romantic.

17 Enrichment Although Shelley was a political radical, his self-imposed exile was based more on his personal than his political unpopularity. The English public was unforgiving of his abandonment of his wife, her subsequent suicide, and his immediate remarriage to a woman who had already borne him two children.

Use your judgment in deciding whether to share this sort of sensitive material with your students.

In idealizing unspoiled nature, Wordsworth and the other Romantics were not merely abandoning the philosophies of classicism and rationalism; they were condemning the Industrial Revolution and its encroachment on the English countryside.

Lyrical Ballads met a cool reception at first, but with time it came to be regarded as the cornerstone of Britain's Romantic Age. Also with time, Wordsworth and Coleridge became respected members of Britain's literary establishment. Their literary ideas began to seem
12 less radical than they once had, and their political thinking—deeply marked by events in France—grew more conservative.

The Second Generation of Romantic Poets

Wordsworth and Coleridge blazed the way for a new generation of British Romantic poets—the so-called "second generation" of poets, which included Byron, Shelley, and Keats. Coming of age during the Napoleonic era and the Regency, these younger poets rebelled even more strongly than Wordsworth and Coleridge against the British conservatism of the time. All three died abroad after tragically short lives, and their viewpoints were those of disillusioned outsiders.

George Gordon, Lord Byron (1788–1824), did not begin life as an outsider. On the contrary, he was part of the British aristocracy —a member of the House of Lords, an intimate of high-born men and women. Although critics responded unfavorably to his early poetry, Byron persisted and finally achieved success when he published *Childe Harold's Pilgrimage* (1812). Handsome, egotisti-
13 cal, and aloof, Byron became the darling of elegant society—but not for long. Shocked by Byron's radical politics and scandalous love affairs, London hostesses began to shun him, and Byron left Britain in 1816, never to return. He died of a fever while fighting with Greek revolutionaries in their struggle to win independence from Turkey.

Because they had abadoned their democratic ideals, Byron
14 wrote scornfully about Wordsworth and Coleridge. However much of his work reflects their Romantic style. His long narrative poems
15 often feature brooding, passionate, rebellious figures. Such "Byronic" heroes and heroines became a common feature of the literature of the Romantic Age. On the other hand, some of Byron's work —such as his poem *Don Juan* (1819–24)—owes more to
16 eighteenth-century mock epics than it does to Wordsworth and Coleridge.

Byron's friend Percy Bysshe Shelley (1792–1822) was also well-born and politically radical—more consistently radical, in fact, than Byron. In poems such as "Song to the Men of England" (1819), Shelley urged England's lower classes to rebel.

Like Byron, Shelley was shunned for his radical ideas; he left
17 Britain for good in 1818. Unlike Byron, however, Shelley did not

18 attain fame in his own lifetime. Yet he is now remembered for the fervor he brought to lyric poetry in such intensely personal and emotional verses as "To a Skylark" (1821).

John Keats (1795–1821), the third great figure in the second generation of Romantic poets, was also a master of lyrical poetry. Unlike Byron and Shelley, Keats was born outside elegant society, the son of a London stable keeper. Keats trained to be a doctor, then abandoned his medical career to pursue his passion for poetry. He produced many of his greatest poems in a burst of creativity during the first nine months of 1819—works like *Fall of*
19 *Hyperion* and "Ode on a Grecian Urn." Unfortunately however, Keats was already struggling against tuberculosis. Hoping to recuperate in a warmer climate he traveled to Italy, where he died at the age of twenty-five. By his own request, his epitaph reads: "Here lies one whose name was writ in water."

JOHN KEATS
Joseph Severn
The Granger Collection

THE ROMANTIC AGE IN BRITISH PROSE

Poetry was the dominant literary form during the Romantic Age, but not the only one. Many significant prose works also appeared, mainly in the form of essays and novels. This was a dry period for drama; only two theaters were licensed to produce plays, and they tended to feature popular spectacles rather than serious plays. However, Shelley and other poets did write closet dramas, verse works intended to be read rather than produced on the stage.

The Romantic Essayists

20 British readers of the Romantic Age could find brilliant literary criticism and topical essays in a variety of new periodicals. The earliest of these periodicals reflected the conservative and neoclassical ideals of an earlier age; they roundly condemned the Romantic poets and their work. In time, however, periodicals that were more sympathetic to the Romantics came into being. One such publication, *The London Magazine,* although it appeared only from 1820 to 1829, attracted major contributions from the three greatest essayists of the era: Charles Lamb (1775–1834), William Hazlitt (1778–
21 1830), and Thomas De Quincey (1785–1859). Lamb, in particular, transformed the informal essay of the eighteenth century into a more personal, more introspective Romantic composition.

The Romantic Novelists

Unlike the Romantic poets, the novelists of the Romantic Age did not make a sharp break with the past. In fact, the three main types of Romantic novels—the Gothic novel, the novel of manners, and the historical romance—all represented elaborations on earlier forms.

The Gothic novel first appeared in the middle of the eighteenth

Humanities Note

Fine art, *John Keats,* 1818, by Joseph Severn. In 1820, when Keats was suffering from tuberculosis, his publisher arranged for the poet to go to Rome, to a warmer climate. Joseph Severn (1793–1879), a painter who had been a close friend of Keats for several years, accompanied the poet to Italy and took care of him until Keats died.

The portrait of Keats depicts the poet in a subdued, pensive mood—perhaps not what one would imagine of the poet who produced such intensely creative works within such a short period of time. Another portrait Severn made of Keats, a charcoal drawing, has a more expressive look. Probably done more rapidly than the painting, the drawing captures the poet in a more spontaneous pose.

18 **Literary Movement** See Shelley's "To a Skylark," page 718, and his "Ode to the West Wind," page 714, for examples of his consummate poetic skill and great lyric beauty.

19 **Literary Movement** See "Ode on a Grecian Urn," page 736, for the famous statement that epitomizes Keats's passionate commitment to beauty.

20 **Enrichment** Most of the Romantic writers were strongly criticized when their poetry first appeared. The *Edinburgh Review* was particularly harsh; its negative tone inspired Byron's retort, "English Bards and Scotch Reviewers." The critics' savaging, in the *Quarterly Review,* has popularly but erroneously been considered a contributory cause for Keats's early death at the age of twenty-six.

21 **Literary Movement** Charles Lamb's essay, "Dream Children," page 750, reveals both his gentle nature and the disappointments of a life that precluded domestic happiness: Because his sister Mary had killed their mother in a fit of insanity, Lamb was afraid to marry and have children.

Humanities Note

Fine art, *Sir Walter Scott/ Abbotsford Family,* by Sir David Wilkie. Some of the earlier works of David Wilkie (1785–1841), such as *The Blind Fiddler* (1807), are in the tradition of seventeenth-century Dutch genre painting—they depict, with great technical skill, the everyday lives of ordinary people. Wilkie's unsentimental, unpretentious scenes of village life, painted on a small scale, were quite popular and influential in his day. Wilkie helped establish a style of painting that suggested a "story," possibly with an implied moral.

Wilkie, who had left his native Scotland in 1805 to go to London, returned to the north for a visit in 1817. He stayed, at that time, with Sir Walter Scott. Some six years earlier Scott had purchased land in Roxburghshire, Scotland, and, between 1817 and 1824, had his house, called Abbotsford, built for him. In Wilkie's painting, Scott is shown with people from the village. The writer, who limped as a result of childhood polio, holds a cane. The work is a tribute both to a famous literary man and to the simple people among whom he lived.

22 **Literary Movement** See the introduction to Mary Shelley's *Frankenstein,* page 744, a story she reportedly devised when the Shelleys and Byron were whiling away a rainy evening together in Italy during their exiles.

23 **Literary Movement** See the excerpt from Jane Austen's *Pride and Prejudice,* page 762, unarguably the finest novel of the Romantic period, a masterpiece of insightful character development and gentle satire.

SIR WALTER SCOTT/ABBOTSFORD FAMILY, 1804
Sir David Wilkie
The Granger Collection

century. It featured a number of standard ingredients, including brave heroes and heroines, threatening scoundrels, vast eerie castles, and ghosts. The Romantic fascination with mystery and the supernatural made such novels quite popular during the Romantic
22 Age. One of the most successful was *Frankenstein, or the Modern Prometheus* (1818), written by Shelley's wife, Mary Wollstonecraft Shelley (1797–1851).

The Romantic novel of manners carried on in the tradition of earlier writers by turning a satirical eye on British customs. The most highly regarded writer of novels of manners was Jane Austen
23 (1775–1817) whose works include *Sense and Sensibility* (1811) and *Pride and Prejudice* (1813). Her incisive portrayals of character are more reflective of the classical sensibility of the eighteenth century than the Romantic notions of the new age.

Historical romances—imaginative works of fiction built around a real person or historical event—had appeared long before the Romantic Age, but they attained their peak of popularity in the work of Sir Walter Scott (1771–1832). Passionately devoted to his native Scotland, Scott wrote about the days of knights and chivalry. Although he expressed a Scottish nationalism not unlike the nationalism of Germany's Romantic writers, Scott remained popular with England's ruling class, who apparently did not view his tales of a bygone age as a threat to the status quo.

The close of Britain's Romantic Age is usually set in 1832, the year of the passage of the First Reform Bill. However, the ideas of Romanticism remained a strong influence on many writers from following generations. In fact, even today we can detect elements of Romanticism in many major works of contemporary fiction and poetry as well as in TV dramas, movies, and popular songs.

ENGLISH VOICES

Quotations by Prominent Figures of the Period

Bliss was it on that dawn to be alive . . .
France standing on the top of golden hours
And human nature seemed born again.

William Wordsworth, *The Prelude*

But yet I know, where'er I go.
That there hath past away a glory from the earth . . .
nothing can bring back the hour
Of splendor in the grass, of glory in the flower.

William Wordsworth, Ode: "Intimations of Immortality from Recollections of Early Childhood"

Poetry is not the proper antithesis to prose, but to science.

Samuel Taylor Coleridge, *Definitions of Poetry*

One half the world cannot understand the pleasures of the other.

Jane Austen, *Emma*

It is a truth universally acknowledged that a man in possession of a good fortune must be in want of a wife.

Jane Austen, *Pride and Prejudice*

Clear writers, like fountains, do not seem so deep as they are.

Charles Lamb, *Imaginary Conversation*

I love not man the less, but Nature more.

George Gordon, Lord Byron, *Childe Harold's Pilgrimage*

If Winter comes, can Spring be far behind?

Percy Bysshe Shelley, "Ode to the West Wind"

The poetry of earth is never dead.

John Keats, "Sonnet: On the Grasshopper and the Cricket"

"Beauty is truth, truth beauty"—that is all
Ye know on earth, and all ye need to know.

John Keats, "Ode on a Grecian Urn"

Reading Critically The purpose of this page is to guide students in the critical reading of literature of the Romantic Age. The information offered here will allow students to place a work of literature in its historical context, identify literary movements of the time, and appreciate the techniques used by writers of the period.

As you discuss the information on the page with the class, explain that the poem "The Solitary Reaper" by William Wordsworth beginning on page 649, is a model for reading critically. The side columns contain notes that draw students' attention to elements that reflect the historical context, the influence of the literary movements, and the writer's techniques.

To give students further practice with the process of reading critically, use the selection in the **Teaching Portfolio,** "I Am" by John Clare, page 000, following the Teacher Backup which students can annotate themselves. Encourage students to use these strategies as they read the literature in this unit.

Teaching to Ability Levels For **less advanced** students, discuss any difficult vocabulary words before reading. You might wish to have them read the poem aloud after they have read it silently.

READING CRITICALLY

The Literature of 1798–1832

When you read literature, it is important to place it in its historical context. Doing so will help you to see how it reflects the dominant ideas of its time and appreciate the techniques the writer used in conveying these ideas.

Historical Context

During the years from 1798 to 1832, English life was dramatically influenced by the aftereffects of the French Revolution and the realities of industrialization. While many English intellectuals supported the democratic ideals upon which the French Revolution was grounded, the English ruling class took measures to ensure that a similar revolution could not occur in England. At the same time, the industrial revolution was having a profound social and economic impact on the nation. English cities grew rapidly and became the nation's economic centers. Factory workers labored long hours for extremely low wages, and young children often had to work to help support their families. It became increasingly clear that new governmental policies were needed to accommodate these changes. Yet few political changes occurred until 1832, when the First Reform Bill was passed.

Literary Movements

Toward the end of the eighteenth century, an artistic movement known as Romanticism developed as a reaction against the dominant ideas and standards of Rationalism. Unlike the Rationalists, who stressed logic and reason, the Romantics emphasized emotions and the imagination. The Romantics also possessed a strong belief in democracy, an interest in mystery and the supernatural, a belief in excess and spontaneity, a concern for common people, and a love of nature.

Writers' Techniques

The Romantic period was an age in which poetry flourished. Using the language of common people, the Romantics wrote lyric poems that generally focused on ordinary situations and ordinary people. Although poetry was the major form of literary expression during the period, a number of significant novels and essays were also produced. Like Romantic poetry, these works reflect the dominant ideas and attitudes of the age.

On the following pages is a poem by William Wordsworth, a major Romantic poet. The annotations in the side column should help you to place the selection in its historical context.

Objectives

1. To analyze diction
2. To appreciate sound devices
3. To write a poem

Teaching Portfolio: Support Materials

Teacher Backup, p. 000

Reading Critically, *"I Am"* by John Clare, p. 00

Usage and Mechanics Worksheet, p. 00

Analyzing Literature Worksheet, p. 00

Critical Thinking and Reading Worksheet, p. 00

Language Worksheet, p. 00

Selection Test, p. 00

MODEL

The Solitary Reaper

William Wordsworth

This poem was inspired by a passage from Thomas Willkinson's Tour of Scotland *(1824): "Passed a female who was reaping alone; she sung in Erse (Scottish Gaelic) as she bended over her sickle; the sweetest human voice I ever heard: her strains were tenderly melancholy, and felt delicious long after they were heard no more."*

Behold her, single in the field,
Yon solitary Highland lass!
Reaping and singing by herself;
Stop here, or gently pass!
Alone she cuts and binds the grain,
And sings a melancholy strain;
O listen! for the vale profound
Is overflowing with the sound.

Literary Movement: Wordsworth uses his imagination to transform a passage from Wilkinson's book into a poem. The poem's subject reflects the Romantic interest in common people and rural life.

No nightingale did ever chaunt
More welcome notes to weary bands
Of travelers in some shady haunt,
Among Arabian sands;
A voice so thrilling ne'er was heard
In springtime from the cuckoo-bird,
Breaking the silence of the seas
Among the farthest Hebrides.

Literary Movement: Wordsworth's references to the songs of birds reflect the Romantic love of nature.

Will no one tell me what she sings?—
Perhaps the plaintive numbers flow
For old, unhappy, far-off things,
And battles long ago;
Or is it some more humble lay,
Familiar matter of today?
Some natural sorrow, loss, or pain,
That has been, and may be again?

Writer's Technique: The poem is a lyric written in octaves, or eight-line stanzas, using an *ababccdd* rhyme scheme.

Writer's Technique: The poem is written in common, everyday language.

Whate'er the theme, the maiden sang
As if her song could have no ending;

649

Literary Movement: The speaker examines his inner feelings and explores the emotional impact of the experience.

I saw her singing at her work,
And o'er the sickle bending;
I listened, motionless and still;
And, as I mounted up the hill,
The music in my heart I bore,
Long after it was heard no more.

THINKING ABOUT THE SELECTION

Recalling

1. What is the "solitary Highland lass" doing when the speaker sees her?
2. To what does the speaker compare the woman's singing in the second stanza?
3. What possible subjects of the woman's song does the speaker imagine?
4. What does the speaker bear in his heart as he continues his walk?

Interpreting

5. What do the comparisons in the second stanza suggest about the woman's song?
6. What does the final stanza reveal about the impact of the experience on the speaker?

Applying

7. In what ways does the type of life portrayed in the poem contrast with the type of life you would imagine the nineteenth-century factory workers must have lead?

ANALYZING LITERATURE

Appreciating a Writer's Diction

Diction refers to a writer's choice of words. A writer uses language appropriate for the subject and characters.

1. In this poem Wordsworth uses simple, direct language. Why is this type of language appropriate?
2. Why would the poem be less effective if it were written using elegant, ornate language?

CRITICAL THINKING AND READING

Understanding Sound Devices

In "The Solitary Reaper," Wordsworth uses a number of sound devices to give the poem a musical quality. For example, he uses alliteration —the repetition of consonant sounds at the beginnings of words—in line 9, repeating the *n* sound: "*N*o *n*ightingale did ever chant." Wordsworth also uses assonance, or the repetition of similar vowel sounds. Notice the repetition of the *i* sound in line 1: "Behold her, s*i*ngle *i*n the field."

1. Find two more examples of alliteration.
2. Find two more examples of assonance.
3. How does the poem's musical quality reflect its meaning?

THINKING AND WRITING

Writing a Poem

Write a poem in which the Highland lass describes the experience that Wordsworth's speaker observes. Use your imagination to develop her character. When writing your poem, make sure it conveys the character you have developed. In your poem, reveal the subject of her song and present her impressions of the speaker of Wordsworth's poem. When you revise, make sure you have used concrete images, or word pictures.

Master Teacher Note In his lyrics Wordsworth freely used conversational language in contrast to traditional poetic speech. This conversation-like diction tightened Wordsworth's lyrics, and, combined with Wordsworth's kinship with nature, helped create poems with a frank and noble simplicity.

For Further Study Biographical information on Wordsworth appears on page 652, and other poems by him are on pages 654–667.

Answers

ANSWERS TO THINKING ABOUT THE SELECTION

Recalling

1. The Lass is singing and reaping wheat.
2. Wordsworth compares the woman's singing to the songs of a nightingale and a cuckoo-bird.
3. The speaker feels she might be singing an old, sad ballad about battles or a less noble song about the sorrows human beings feel.
4. The speaker bore the music of her song in his heart.

Interpreting

5. The comparisons suggest that her singing is a part of nature, and they imply that the song is very welcome and beautiful.
6. The woman's song had a tremendous impact on the speaker because he would remember the experience forever.

Applying

7. Answers will differ. Suggested Response: The factory workers of the period worked under horrible conditions, laboring many grueling hours in factories with no health or safety regulations. They had little time to enjoy the outdoors and certainly had little opportunity to work in a natural environment.

ANSWERS TO ANALYZING LITERATURE

1. Wordsworth's simple language is appropriate because he is writing about commonplace subjects and events.
2. Since the poem was written to show the charm of everyday things, elegant language would conflict with the ordinariness of the setting.

ANSWERS TO CRITICAL THINKING AND READING

1. Two possibilities are "*B*reaking the *s*ilence of the *s*eas" and "*P*erhaps the *p*laintive numbers flow."
2. One possibility is . . . b*a*nds of tr*a*velers . . ."; another is . . . h*ea*rd no m*o*re."
3. Since the poem is about a woman's beautiful singing, the musical quality mirrors the subject of the poem.

THINKING AND WRITING

For help with this assignment, students can refer to Lesson 18, "Writing a Poem," in the Handbook of Writing About Literature.

Publishing Student Writing Have the students make posters of their poems by illustrating their poems with original art, photographs, or pictures from magazines. Display the posters.

Poetry

SALISBURY CATHEDRAL
John Constable
Musea de Arte, Sao Paulo, Art Resource

Humanities Note

Fine art, *Salisbury Cathedral,* by John Constable. Constable (1776–1837) is one of Britain's supreme landscape painters. He studied art in London as a young man and exhibited his first landscape in 1803. Constable preferred to go out into the countryside to make sketches and then return to his studio to make final versions. Sketching live outside enabled him to capture individuality in movement, light, and atmosphere, which were the elements that interested him. *Salisbury Cathedral* emphasizes the cathedral by bathing it in light, while the foreground, in shadow, presents a dramatic frame.

More About the Author Not only is William Wordsworth generally acclaimed as one of the five or six greatest English poets of all time, he is also one of the most quoted. As they read the selections, have students point out those lines that are most memorable to them. Ask them to look for the basis of Wordsworth's great reputation.

WILLIAM WORDSWORTH

1770–1850

William Wordsworth is among the small group of writers and poets who truly deserve the title "pioneer." His name is almost synonymous with the movement known as *Romanticism.* Wordsworth demonstrated that poetry was a free—a *living*—form of artistic expression, a view that contrasted sharply with that held by the generation writing before him. Whereas the Neoclassicists, as these earlier poets were called, insisted that poetry address a narrow range of topics and be rigidly structured, Wordsworth's poems were written for the common people—and in a common language.

Born in the beautiful Lake District of England, Wordsworth loved to roam the hills and sit and meditate by the streams. He was well-suited to country living and in later years found nature to be the source of his poetic inspiration and internal peace. Though his parents died when he was young—his mother when he was eight, his father when he was thirteen—Wordsworth's education was seen to, and in 1787 he entered Cambridge. After graduation he traveled through Europe, spending considerable time in France. Here he became caught up in the popular side of the French Revolution, with its emphasis on the rights of the individual. He also found time to fall in love with a young woman named Annette Vallon.

Wordsworth's involvement in the Revolution and his affair with Annette ended abruptly, however, when England declared war on France in 1793 and he was forced to return to his homeland. A year later, the Revolution was halted altogether with the execution of its leader, Robespierre. Wordsworth, seeing his ideals dashed, lapsed into a deep depression. Two people who came to his spiritual rescue were his sister Dorothy and his good friend Samuel Taylor Coleridge.

With Coleridge, Wordsworth composed *Lyrical Ballads* (1798), a collection of poems that reflected his "revolutionary" approach to poetry. In the preface to the collection, Wordsworth put forth his view that poetry should deal with common people and ordinary experiences—that its style and form should reflect "a spontaneous overflow of emotion." Though the book was not received favorably at first, it eventually gained recognition as a major poetic work and is seen today as one of the most influential works on poetic theory ever written in the English language.

Objectives

1. To understand Romanticism
2. To compare and contrast experiences
3. To write about Romanticism
4. To interpret a paradox
5. To write a nature poem

Teaching Portfolio: Support Material

Teacher Backup, p. 000

Vocabulary Check, p. 00

Usage and Mechanics Worksheet, p. 00

Analyzing Literature Worksheet, p. 00

Critical Thinking and Reading Worksheet, p. 00

Language Worksheet, p. 00

Selection Test, p. 000

GUIDE FOR READING

Lines Composed a Few Miles Above Tintern Abbey; My Heart Leaps Up When I Behold

The Writer's Technique

Romanticism. Romanticism was a literary movement in Europe in the late eighteenth century. It grew out of a negative reaction to the rigid, formal guidelines and forced subject matter that typified the poetry and art of the previous age. Whereas rationalism and a reliance on scientific doctrine were highly valued by the earlier Neoclassicists, Romanticists believed in the virtues of the imagination and fantasy. The Romantic writer was not only permitted, but encouraged, to give vent to his or her emotions—to write spontaneously, from the heart. Love of nature and an idealization of rural life were naturals for the Romantic poet. Many of these aspects of the Romantic credo figure in the poems of William Wordsworth. Subjectivity in particular is clearly visible in his "Lines Composed a Few Miles Above Tintern Abbey."

Look For

As you read these two poems, look for the poet's focus on nature and personal experience.

Writing

Think about a place you have been that made a vivid impression on you. You might choose a place you visited on vacation or one where you lived. Close your eyes and try to visualize this locale, concentrating on details. Then, freewrite, describing everything you "see."

Vocabulary

Knowing the meanings of the following words will help you as you read "Lines Composed a Few Miles Above Tintern Abbey."

repose (ri pōz′) *v.*: Lie back (p. 654)
tuft (tuft) *n.*: Grouping of fibers such as hair or grass (p. 654)
pastoral (pas′tər əl) *adj.*: Pertaining to country life (p. 654)
recompense (rek′ əm pens′) *n.*: Payment in return (p. 657)
perchance (pər chans′) *adv.*: Perhaps, possibly (p. 657)
genial (jēn′ yəl) *adj.*: Kindly, cordial (p. 658)

Literary Focus Students should realize that while Romanticism arose from a negative reaction to the rigidities of the Restoration and Eighteenth Century, it was hardly a time of complete anarchy. Indeed the literary changes occurred more in poetic diction than in the literary forms poets used to express their thoughts and feelings. "Lines Composed a Few Miles Above Tintern Abbey," for one, is written in blank verse. Regular meters, rhyme schemes, and the use of the sonnet form, all of which are traditional poetic devices, are also evident in the selections by Wordsworth.

Writing Wordsworth, devastated by the way the French Revolution was turning out, returned to Tintern Abbey, a place he loved in youth, as a way to help regain his peace of mind. Suggest that students write a description of a place they go to in order to find peace of mind.

Vocabulary Go over the words with your **less advanced** students so they will be familiar with them as they read the poem. Stress that the meanings reflect the context in which the words appear in the poem.

Motivation for Reading Have students think of a place they knew and loved as a child. What was it about the place that fascinated them then? Now, have them suppose that after several years they are to return to the place. Will they expect the place to be the same? Will they expect their feelings about it to be the same? Do they think they can—or would want to—recapture their original feelings about the place?

Purpose-Setting Question What evidences of Wordsworth's suggestion that one should "Let Nature be your teacher" do you find in the poem?

1 **Discussion** What sort of scene is described in these lines? Is anything missing from the scene? If so, what?

2 **Copse** (line 14) are thickets of small trees.

3 **Reading Strategy** The poem artfully develops by introducing new ideas at key junctures. These occur at lines 22, 49, 57-8, and 111. Have students summarize the main idea in a section before they move on to the next.

4 **Discussion** Why is the simile of the blind man's eye so effective?

5 **Discussion** In lines 26-41, the poet tells how scenes of the Abbey have influenced him over the past five years. How have they done so? Where has he spent those years?

Lines Composed a Few Miles Above Tintern Abbey

William Wordsworth

This poem was written in 1798 during Wordsworth's second visit to the valley of the River Wye and the ruins of Tintern Abbey, once a great medieval church, in Wales. Having passed through the region alone five years earlier, Wordsworth brought his sister with him to share the experience this time. Of this experience and the poem it inspired, Wordworth wrote, "No poem of mine was composed under circumstances more pleasant for one to remember than this."

Five years have past; five summers, with the length
Of five long winters! and again I hear
These waters, rolling from their mountain springs
With a soft inland murmur. Once again
Do I behold these steep and lofty cliffs,
That on a wild secluded scene impress
Thoughts of more deep seclusion; and connect
The landscape with the quiet of the sky.
The day is come when I again repose
Here, under this dark sycamore, and view
1, 2 These plots of cottage ground, these orchard tufts,
Which at this season, with their unripe fruits,
Are clad in one green hue, and lose themselves
'Mid groves and copses. Once again I see
These hedgerows, hardly hedgerows, little lines
Of sportive wood run wild: these pastoral farms,
Green to the very door; and wreaths of smoke
Sent up, in silence, from among the trees!
With some uncertain notice, as might seem
Of vagrant dwellers in the houseless woods,
Or of some hermit's cave, where by his fire
The hermit sits alone.

3 These beauteous forms,
4 Through a long absence, have not been to me
As is a landscape to a blind man's eye:
5 But oft, in lonely rooms, and 'mid the din
Of towns and cities, I have owed to them

TINTERN ABBEY
Samuel Palmer
Victoria & Albert Museum, London

Humanities Note

Fine art, *Tintern Abbey* by J. M. W. Turner. Joseph Mallord William Turner (1775-1851) was a premier British landscape painter. A precocious talent, Turner exhibited his first paintings at the age of fifteen. He subsequently studied at the Schools of the Royal Academy and took lessons from an architectural draftsman. Upon completion of his education, he toured England on foot and made watercolors of regional scenes, which he sold to an appreciative public. He later developed his unique, almost abstract approach to painting the light and atmosphere of a landscape, for which he became notable.

The watercolor *Tintern Abbey* was painted early in his career on one of his sketching tours. The skilled depiction of the architectural elements of this painting reflect his training with the draftsman. Romantic, pretty, and decorative, it appealed to the picture-buying public of his day.

Consider using these questions for class discussion:

1. What feature, do you think, inspired Turner to paint this ruin?
2. What adjectives would you use to describe the style?

In hours of weariness, sensations sweet,
Felt in the blood, and felt along the heart;
And passing even into my purer mind,
With tranquil restoration—feelings too
Of unremembered pleasure: such, perhaps,
As have no slight or trivial influence
On that best portion of a good man's life.
His little, nameless, unremembered, acts
Of kindness and of love. Nor less, I trust,
To them I may have owed another gift,
Of aspect more sublime; that blessed mood,
In which the burthen[1] of the mystery,
In which the heavy and the weary weight
Of all this unintelligible world,
Is lightened—that serene and blessed mood,
In which the affections gently lead us on—
Until, the breath of this corporeal frame[2]
And even the motion of our human blood
Almost suspended, we are laid asleep
In body, and become a living soul;
While with an eye made quiet by the power
Of harmony, and the deep power of joy,
We see into the life of things.

If this
Be but a vain belief, yet, oh! how oft—
In darkness and amid the many shapes
Of joyless daylight; when the fretful stir
Unprofitable, and the fever of the world,
Have hung upon the beatings of my heart—
How oft, in spirit, have I turned to thee,
O sylvan[3] Wye! thou wanderer through the woods,
How often has my spirit turned to thee!

And now, with gleams of half-extinguished thought,
With many recognitions dim and faint,
And somewhat of a sad perplexity,
The picture of the mind revives again;
While here I stand, not only with the sense
Of present pleasure, but with pleasing thoughts
That in this moment there is life and food
For future years. And so I dare to hope,
Though changed, no doubt, from what I was when first
I came among these hills; when like a roe[4]

---

1. burthen: Burden.
2. corporeal (kôr pôr′ ē əl) **frame:** Body.
3. sylvan (sil′ vən): Wooded.
4. roe: A type of deer.

I bounded o'er the mountains, by the sides
Of the deep rivers, and the lonely streams,
Wherever nature led: more like a man
Flying from something that he dreads, than one
Who sought the thing he loved. For nature then
(The coarser pleasures of my boyish days,
And their glad animal movements all gone by)
To me was all in all—I cannot paint
What then I was. The sounding cataract 6
Haunted me like a passion; the tall rock,
The mountain, and the deep and gloomy wood,
Their colors and their forms, were then to me
An appetite; a feeling and a love,
That had no need of a remoter charm,
By thought supplied, nor any interest
Unborrowed from the eye. That time is past,
And all its aching joys are now no more,
And all its dizzy raptures. Not for this
Faint[5] I, nor mourn nor murmur; other gifts
Have followed; for such loss, I would believe,
Abundant recompense. For I have learned
To look on nature, not as in the hour
Of thoughtless youth; but hearing oftentimes
The still, sad music of humanity,
Nor harsh nor grating, though of ample power
To chasten and subdue. And I have felt
A presence that disturbs me with the joy
Of elevated thoughts; a sense sublime
Of something far more deeply interfused, 7
Whose dwelling is the light of setting suns,
And the round ocean and the living air,
And the blue sky, and in the mind of man;
A motion and a spirit, that impels
All thinking things, all objects of all thought,
And rolls through all things. Therefore am I still
A lover of the meadows and the woods
And mountains; and of all that we behold
From this green earth; of all the mighty world
Of eye, and ear—both what they half create,
And what perceive; well pleased to recognize
In nature and the language of the sense, 8
The anchor of my purest thoughts, the nurse,
The guide, the guardian of my heart, and soul 9
Of all my moral being.

Nor perchance.
If I were not thus taught, should I the more

5. faint: Lose heart.

6 Clarification A cataract is a waterfall.

7 Discussion What is the "something" the poet refers to?

8 Clarification The word *sense* means "senses."

9 Discussion Ask students to tell in their own words what the poet recognizes in nature? Help **less advanced** students to paraphrase these metaphors.

10 **Discussion** Explain the reason for the poet's sister's presence in the poem.

11 **Master Teacher Note** This work is written in blank verse—lines of unrhymed iambic pentameter, five metrical feet to each line. It is a verse form often used with serious, even stately, works. Students might compare Wordsworth's use of blank verse with that of Shakespeare in *Macbeth,* page 223 and *The Tempest,* page 306.

Suffer[6] my genial spirits[7] to decay;
For thou art with me here upon the banks
Of this fair river; thou my dearest Friend,[8]
My dear, dear Friend, and in thy voice I catch
The language of my former heart, and read
My former pleasures in the shoooting lights
Of thy wild eyes. Oh! yet a little while
May I behold in thee what I was once,
10 My dear, dear Sister! and this prayer I make,
Knowing that Nature never did betray
The heart that loved her; 'tis her privilege,
Through all the years of this our life, to lead
From joy to joy; for she can so inform
The mind that is within us, so impress
With quietness and beauty, and so feed
With lofty thoughts, that neither evil tongues,
Rash judgments, nor the sneers of selfish men,
Nor greetings where no kindness is, nor all
The dreary intercourse of daily life,
Shall e'er prevail against us, or disturb
Our cheerful faith, that all which we behold
Is full of blessings. Therefore let the moon
Shine on thee in thy solitary walk;
And let the misty mountain winds be free
To blow against thee: and, in after years,
When these wild ecstasies shall be matured
Into a sober pleasure; when thy mind
Shall be a mansion for all lovely forms,
Thy memory be as a dwelling place
For all sweet sounds and harmonies; oh! then,
If solitude, or fear, or pain, or grief,
Should be thy portion, with what healing thoughts
Of tender joy wilt thou remember me,
And these my exhortations! Nor, perchance—
If I should be where I no more can hear
Thy voice, nor catch from thy wild eyes these gleams
Of past existence—wilt thou then forget
That on the banks of this delightful stream
We stood together; and that I, so long
A worshipper of Nature, hither came
Unwearied in that service: rather say
With warmer love—oh! with far deeper zeal
Of holier love. Nor wilt thou then forget,
That after many wanderings, many years

---

6. suffer: Allow.
7. genial spirits: Creative powers.
8. Friend: His sister Dorothy.

Of absence, these steep woods and lofty cliffs,
And this green pastoral landscape, were to me
More dear, both for themselves and for thy sake!

THINKING ABOUT THE SELECTION

Recalling

1. In "Lines Composed a Few Miles Above Tintern Abbey," how have the poet's memories of his first visit to the Wye valley altered him?
2. (a) Apart from his pleasure at the moment, what does the poet hope to gain from his second visit to the valley? (b) What does he hope his sister will gain?

Interpreting

3. (a) At what time of year does the poet make his second visit to the area near Tintern Abbey? (b) Find evidence in the poem that supports your answer.
4. In line 35 of the poem, the poet mentions "another gift" which his contact with this rural scene has bestowed upon him. Briefly describe this gift.
5. To what is the poet referring in line 109 as the "anchor of my purest thoughts?"

Applying

6. Do you think it was Wordsworth's wish that everyone attempt to share his experience with and attitudes toward nature? Do you think he believed everyone was capable? Explain.

ANALYZING LITERATURE

Understanding Romanticism

Romanticism stressed the importance of emotion and imagination as tools of the artist. To Wordsworth, one of the movement's foremost practitioners, Romanticism also meant a return to nature and an escape from the contamination of modern cívilization. Wordsworth urged the poet to explore his or her innermost feelings—to become attuned to the stirrings of the soul. For this reason, much of Romantic art and poetry has a spiritual, at times almost mystical, quality about it.

Look again at "Lines Composed a Few Miles Above Tintern Abbey," and as you read be on the lookout for the words *soul, heart,* and *spirit.* Paraphrase (state in your own words) each of the poet's thoughts that contains one or more of these words. Explain how each thought relates to the ideals of the Romantic movement.

CRITICAL THINKING AND READING

Comparing and Contrasting Experiences

A careful reading of "Tintern Abbey" reveals that even as a young man Wordsworth was a sensitive and perceptive person. And yet the poem details certain differences between his first and second trips to the Wye valley. Skim the poem for details and then describe:

1. the differences in the poet's behavior.
2. the differences and similarities in his thoughts and attitudes.

THINKING AND WRITING

Writing About Romanticism

The twentieth-century American writer Thomas Wolfe defined the true Romantic feeling as "not the desire to escape life, but to prevent life from escaping you." Freewrite, exploring the meaning of this quotation. Then write an essay explaining how "Tintern Abbey" typifies the true Romantic feeling as defined by Wolfe. When you revise make sure you have supported your opinion with details from the poem.

Answers

ANSWERS TO THINKING ABOUT THE SELECTION

Recalling

1. He has changed from a youth charged with the wild ecstacy of his love for nature into a mature person who cherishes the solace nature now affords him.
2. (a) He hopes to reinforce his sense of the solace nature provides in such a way that it will carry through his entire life. (b) He hopes that his sister will experience the same feelings for nature that he now has.

Interpreting

3. (a) The time of year is summer. (b) We learn this from lines 10-14.
4. The gift is the ability nature has to ease our burdened minds.
5. He refers to nature and the language of the senses.

Applying

6. Suggested Response: By implication rather than direct statement, the poet not only wishes that everyone would try to share his experiences and attitudes towards nature, he also believes everyone is capable of doing so. The many suggestions to likenesses between man and nature bear this out.

ANSWERS TO ANALYZING LITERATURE

Responses will differ; however, responses should come from lines 28, 54-57, 110, 117, and 123.

ANSWERS TO CRITICAL THINKING AND READING

1. The poet experienced nature as a youth with the boundless energy of the young; he never stopped to contemplate what nature means; rather, full of "aching joys" and "dizzy raptures," he merely enjoyed nature for its own sake. As a mature adult, the poet casts off that boundless energy to replace it with a serious contemplative attitude.
2. As a boy the poet experienced nature as an object of pure sensual pleasure. As a mature person he observes it as the heart and soul of all his moral being. The similarity is that his abiding love for nature has not altered; only the way in which he expresses that love has changed.

THINKING AND WRITING

Publishing Student Writing Post the papers written as a result of the Thinking and Writing activity on a bulletin board for several days. Have students vote for the papers that they think are best. Present these to the school newspaper for possible publication.

My Heart Leaps Up When I Behold

William Wordsworth

My heart leaps up when I behold
    A rainbow in the sky:
So was it when my life began;
So is it now I am a man;
So be it when I shall grow old,
    Or let me die!
1 The child is father of the Man;
And I could wish my days to be
Bound each to each by natural piety.[1]

1. **natural piety:** Devotion to nature.

LANDSCAPE WITH RAINBOW
Joseph Wright of Derby
Derby Art Gallery

Motivation for Reading Have students discuss their experience with rainbows. When have they seen them? Under what circumstances? What thoughts have they had in connection with rainbows?

Discussion Ask students to explain line 7 in their own words and cite examples of its truth from present-day life.

Purpose-Setting Question How important are the early years in forming the beliefs one holds as an adult?

1 **Enrichment** "My heart leaps up . . ." provided the seed of Wordsworth's eloquent "Ode: Intimations of Immortality from Recollections of Early Childhood." In later editions of the Ode, first published in 1807, lines 7-9 of "My heart leaps up . . ." were used as an epitaph to the Ode.

Humanities Note

Fine art, *Landscape with Rainbow: View Near Chesterfield,* Joseph Wright of Derby. The British painter Joseph Wright of Derby (1734-1797) called himself "of Derby" to be distinguished from a contemporary, also a painter, named Richard Wright. He is remembered chiefly for his paintings of scientific subjects and of figures lit by candle or firelight. He has also produced landscapes and portraits of note.

Joseph Wright of Derby maintained a life-long interest in natural phenomena that were related to light. In this painting, *Landscape With Rainbow: View Near Chesterfield,* painted about 1794-5, he explores this interest. Being of a scientific frame of mind, he no doubt sought to reproduce this ephemeral event as an item for study. The relation between romantic art and science demonstrated by Wright shows the early effects of the industrial revolution upon art.

You may wish to ask students the following question: Both the artist and the poet, Wordsworth, were inspired by nature. What is the difference in the basis for each artist's inspiration?

THINKING ABOUT THE SELECTION

Recalling

1. What is the poet's hope in the poem "My Heart Leaps Up"?

Interpreting

2. What general statement might the poet have used in place of the first two lines?
3. What do you think the poet means when he speaks of "natural piety"?

Applying

4. (a) What interest of yours would you like to share with other people? (b) How best might you communicate this to them?

CRITICAL THINKING AND READING

Interpreting a Paradox

A **paradox** is a statement that makes sense in spite of an apparent contradiction. "Youth is wasted on the young," for example, is paradoxical. However, it makes perfect sense when we consider that hindsight, or the experience of age, can help us better appreciate the value of what we have when we are young.

1. The statement, "The child is Father of the Man" is one of the most famous paradoxes in literature. Explain how this seeming contradiction can be true.
2. Explain what belief of the Romantic movement this paradox illustrates.

THINKING AND WRITING

Writing a Nature Poem

Write a short poem about the joy you find in some aspect of nature. The poem need not rhyme, but should contain ample description of the source of your pleasure, as well as an account of precisely how this aspect of nature makes you feel.

When you revise, make sure you have used sensory details to make your description of nature vivid. Have you chosen words that carry the appropriate connotations?

Answers

ANSWERS TO THINKING ABOUT THE SELECTION

Recalling

1. His hope is that his emotional love of nature will remain with him all his life.

Interpreting

2. Answers will differ. Suggested response: The poet might have used an expression such as "Events of nature excite me."
3. The poet probably means innate goodness as well as the goodness one acquires from maintaining a close relationship with nature.

Applying

4. (a) Answers will differ. (b) Answers will differ, though students might well mention written and oral communication.

ANSWERS TO CRITICAL THINKING AND READING

1. Suggested Response: What one is as a child generates what one is as an adult.
2. Suggested Response: This paradox illustrates the belief in the natural goodness of things, of the natural goodness in a child that might be lost in an adult.

THINKING AND WRITING

For help with this assignment, students can refer to Lesson 18, "Writing a Poem," in the Handbook of Writing About Literature.

Publishing Student Writing Encourage students to volunteer to read their poems aloud. You might have the class select the best to submit to your school's literary magazine.

Challenge Think back on your own life. What beliefs that you hold now were formed in those early years? Organize your thoughts into an essay of three or four paragraphs.

Literary Focus Except for "It is a Beauteous Evening," all of the following sonnets are Petrarchan, with an octave rhyme scheme of *a b b a a b b a*.

Purpose-Setting Question Are there aspects of nature that a big city, at certain times, may display?

Master Teacher Note The first line of the poem states Wordsworth's subject—the beauty of London. The remainder of the poem expands upon his theme—the natural beauty of London.

GUIDE FOR READING

Composed Upon Westminster Bridge, September 3, 1802; It Is a Beauteous Evening, Calm and Free; London, 1802; The World Is Too Much with Us

Literary Forms

The Sonnet. A sonnet is a fourteen-line poem in which each line contains five strong beats and five weak beats. While most sonnets follow one of two general rhyme schemes—the Shakespearean (or English) and the Petrarchan (or Italian)—many poets adapt the rhyme to fit their own needs. The sonnet occupies a particular place of distinction among the poems of Wordsworth. Though a champion of freedom and spontaneity in poetry, Wordsworth nevertheless recognized the importance of order and discipline. The sonnet, as a relatively short and decisive poetic statement, was the logical vehicle for treating such subjects as the human condition and the importance of nature to the human spirit. "Scarcely one of my poems," Wordsworth wrote, "does not aim to direct attention to some moral sentiment." His purpose, as he saw it, was "to console the afflicted" and "to add sunshine to daylight by making the happy happier." These and related other goals could best be served, he felt, through the sonnet.

Look For

As you read Wordsworth's sonnets, look for the manner in which he uses this highly stylized poetic form to advance his views on the state of the human race and his feelings toward nature.

Writing

Think of a topic that holds importance for you. The topic could range from such social issues as finding shelter for the homeless of our country to such personal ones as the love between a pet and a person. Write down specific details of your topic that might be covered in a poem.

Vocabulary

Knowing the following words will help you as you read the four sonnets by Wordsworth.

steep (stēp) *v.*: Become saturated with (p. 663)

stagnant (stag′nənt) *adj.*: Standing still, as water (p. 666)

sordid (sor′did) *adj.*: Unclean, dirty (p. 667)

boon (bo͞on) *n.*: Something good or pleasant that is given, like a blessing (p. 667)

Composed Upon Westminster Bridge

September 3, 1802

William Wordsworth

Earth has not anything to show more fair:
Dull would he be of soul who could pass by
A sight so touching in its majesty;
This City now doth, like a garment, wear
The beauty of the morning; silent, bare,
Ships, towers, domes, theaters, and temples, lie
Open unto the fields, and to the sky;
All bright and glittering in the smokeless air,
Never did sun more beautifully steep
In his first splendor, valley, rock, or hill;
Ne'er saw I, never felt, a calm so deep!
The river glideth at his own sweet will:
Dear God! the very houses seem asleep:
And all that mighty heart is lying still!

THINKING ABOUT THE SELECTION

Recalling

1. At what time of day is the poem "Composed Upon Westminster Bridge" set?
2. What sights does the poet see around him?

Interpreting

3. In lines 9–10, the poet sums up his reaction to his own description of the first eight lines. State this reaction in your own words.
4. Paraphrase the last four lines of this poem.

Applying

5. In what way is this poem contrary to some of the ideas expressed by Wordsworth in "My Heart Leaps Up"? How can you account for these differences? With which attitude are you more in sympathy? Explain your answer.

Enrichment Along with Shakespeare, Milton, and Keats, Wordsworth reigns with the best English sonneteers. On the day in 1801 that his sister, Dorothy, read Milton's sonnets to him, Wordsworth composed three of his own. These were the first of well over 500 that he eventually wrote. "Composed upon Westminster Bridge," he explained, was written in 1802 "on the roof of a coach on my way to France."

1 **Discussion** Does this description of London surprise you, coming as it does from Wordsworth, a poet of nature? Explain why or why not.

2 **Discussion** What qualities of nature does the poet find in London?

Answers

ANSWERS TO THINKING ABOUT THE SELECTION

Recalling

1. The poem is set "at first light" —dawn.
2. The poet sees the sights of the city—ships, towers, domes, and temples—lying "bright and glittering in the smokeless air."

Interpreting

3. Answers may differ, but should include the general interpretation that London has never looked so beautiful.

Applying

4. Answers will differ, but should include the point that this poem presents a city scene *vs.* a rural scene, yet the city is presented *before* it awakens, before the hustle and bustle of any great city overwhelms its similarities to a rural, natural setting.

Answers

ANSWERS TO THINKING ABOUT THE SELECTION

Recalling

1. The poem is set "at first light" —dawn.

1 Discussion List the words in the first five lines that describe the evening's mood.

2 Clarification *Being* here refers to "the sea."

3 Clarification The "Dear Child" is Wordsworth's daughter Caroline.

4 Clarification *Abraham's bosom* means "heaven."

5 Clarification The "inner shrine" is the "inner recess of the Jerusalem Temple, which is entered only on the Day of Atonement."

6 Literary Focus As a sonnet with an octave–sestet structure, this poem raises a question or an issue in the first eight lines and addresses it in the closing six. Explain what the issue is and how it is resolved.

It Is a Beauteous Evening, Calm and Free

William Wordsworth

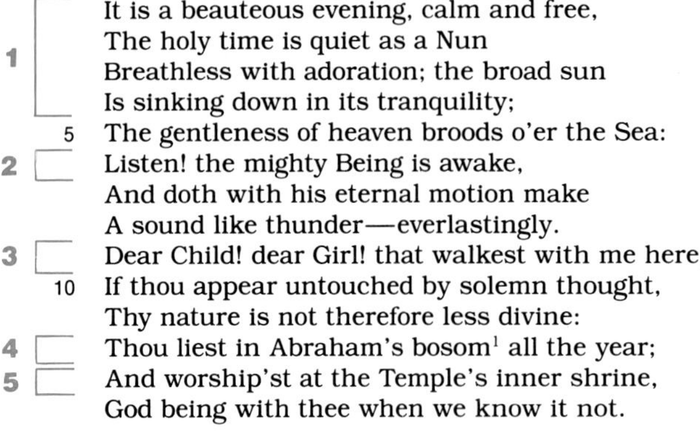

1 It is a beauteous evening, calm and free,
The holy time is quiet as a Nun
Breathless with adoration; the broad sun
Is sinking down in its tranquility;
The gentleness of heaven broods o'er the Sea:
2 Listen! the mighty Being is awake,
And doth with his eternal motion make
A sound like thunder—everlastingly.
3 Dear Child! dear Girl! that walkest with me here,
If thou appear untouched by solemn thought,
Thy nature is not therefore less divine:
4 Thou liest in Abraham's bosom[1] all the year;
5 And worship'st at the Temple's inner shrine,
God being with thee when we know it not.

1. **Abraham's bosom:** Heaven (Luke 16:22).

THINKING ABOUT THE SELECTION

Recalling

1. Describe the setting of "It Is a Beauteous Evening."
2. Who is the poet's companion?

Interpreting

3. What is meant by "eternal motion" and "thunder"?
4. How does the poet's response to the scene differ from that of the child?
5. (a) How would you summarize the poet's advice to the child? (b) to the reader?

Applying

6. What differences in the last six lines of the poem might you expect if they were addressed to another adult? Explain.

CORNFIELD BY MOONLIGHT
Samuel Palmer
British Museum

ANALYZING LITERATURE

Recognizing a Sonnet

A **sonnet** is a poem with fourteen lines, each with five strong and five weak beats. Sonnets are generally divided into two main types, Shakespearean or Petrarchan, on the basis of rhyme scheme and stanza division. The Shakespearean sonnet is divided into three *quatrains* (or stanzas of four lines) and a closing *couplet* (pair of lines). Its rhyme scheme is most often *abab cdcd efef gg*. The Petrarchan sonnet, by contrast, is composed of a group of eight lines (called an *octet*), followed by a group of six (the *sestet*). The rhyme scheme is usually *abbaabba cdecde,* though variations exist in the sestet.

1. Which kind of sonnet is "It Is a Beauteous Evening, Calm and Free"?
2. What is its rhyme scheme?
3. (a) What is the subject matter of the first eight lines? (b) What is the subject matter of the last six lines? (c) Explain how both parts complement each other.

Humanities Note

Fine art, *Cornfield by Moonlight,* 1830, by Samuel Palmer. Samuel Palmer (1805–1881), an English Romantic painter, was a precocious artist, exhibiting paintings at the Royal Academy when he was fourteen. His works—visionary, idealized landscapes and pastorals—were influenced by the English mystic poet and painter William Blake. Palmer became a member of "the Ancients," a group of artists who sought to return art to the state of purity it attained in the Middle Ages. This group settled in Shoreham, Kent. There Palmer painted what are considered to be his finest works. *Cornfield by Moonlight* exemplifies the work achieved by Palmer at Shoreham.

Inspired by the beautiful summer evening, Palmer translated his mystical feelings into a painted scene, executed in watercolor and gouache, which is opaque watercolor. Lit by the moon and a magical evening star, the harvested sheaves of wheat seem to symbolize all that is bountiful and good in the world. The figure, gilded with moonlight, seems to be in total harmony with the landscape.

You might point out to the students that Samuel Palmer revered nature, and ask them why this reverence makes this painting a suitable illustration for Wordsworth's poem.

Answers

ANSWERS TO THINKING ABOUT THE SELECTION

Recalling

1. The poem is set by the ocean on a calm, quiet evening.
2. The poet's companion is a little child, a girl.

Interpreting

3. The "eternal motion" is the movement of the sea; the "thunder" is the roar of the surf.
4. The poet is moved to solemn thoughts about nature and life; the child, so young, is unaware of such things.
5. (a) Answers will differ, but they should include the ideas that although the child is unaware of the majesty of the scene she is no less divine a creature, and that (b) all creatures, young and old, are possessed of an innate goodness.

Applying

6. Answers may differ, but they should include the idea that in talking to another adult rather than a child, the poet would likely have stressed the adult's knowledge of God's presence in nature.

ANSWERS TO ANALYZING LITERATURE

1. "It Is a Beauteous Evening, Calm and Free" is a Petrarchan sonnet.
2. Its rhyme scheme is abba, abba, cde cde.
3. (a) The subject of the octet is the lovely, moving evening. (b) The subject of the sestet is the speaker's awareness of the divine nature of the child with him. (c) The speaker sees the divine presence as manifested in the evening reflected in the child.

Motivation for Reading When Wordsworth wrote this sonnet, he had just returned from a trip to France, then suffering the ravages of the Revolution. The poet was struck with "the vanity and parade of our own country" as contrasted with "the desolation that the Revolution had produced in France." What evidence in the poem shows this attitude?

Purpose-Setting Question What qualities in John Milton, to whom the poem is addressed, does Wordsworth admire?

1 **Enrichment** Wordsworth calls on Milton not only as the great poet and upholder of freedom, but also as foreign secretary to the Council of State, a government post he held in the seventeenth century.

2 **Discussion** These lines suggest what the English have given up. What are these qualities?

3 **Discussion** What qualities in Milton's life did Wordsworth most admire?

Challenge Consider having students look up William Blake's "London," written at about the same time, to compare and contrast both poets' views of the city.

London, 1802

William Wordsworth

1 Milton! thou shouldst be living in this hour:
England hath need of thee: she is a fen[1]
Of stagnant waters: altar, sword, and pen,
Fireside, the heroic wealth of hall and bower,
2 Have forfeited their ancient English dower
Of inward happiness. We are selfish men;
Oh! raise us up, return to us again;
And give us manners, virtue, freedom, power.
Thy soul was like a Star, and dwelt apart,
Thou hadst a voice whose sound was like the sea:
3 Pure as the naked heavens, majestic, free,
So didst thou travel on life's common way,
In cheerful godliness; and yet thy heart
The lowliest duties on herself did lay.

1. fen: Bog.

THINKING ABOUT THE SELECTION

Recalling

1. (a) What other poet does Wordsworth address in "London, 1802"? (b) What does he ask that poet to do?

Interpreting

2. According to the poet, in what way is England like a "fen/Of stagnant waters"?
3. Which individuals do you think are represented by the terms "altar," "sword," "pen," and "fireside"?

Applying

4. (a) In what ways does the poet's image of London differ with that expressed in "Composed Upon Westminster Bridge," written in the same year? (b) How might Wordsworth explain these differences?

Answers

ANSWERS TO THINKING ABOUT THE SELECTION

Recalling

1. (a) Wordsworth addresses Milton. (b) He wants Milton to restore proper values to the English people.

Interpreting

2. England has become too rich, its people living too lavishly; it has become a selfish nation.
3. The term *altar* suggests the clergy; *sword*, the military; *pen*, writers and intellectuals; and *fireside*, the common people.

Applying

4. (a) In "London, 1802" the poet sees a city, a country, that has lost its virtues, has turned into a nation of selfish people. "Westminster Bridge," on the other hand, portrays the city—and, by implication, the people—as the fairest, most majestic city on Earth. (b) Wordsworth's trip to France, where he saw first-hand the ravages of the Revolution, made him aware of how self-centered the English had become.

The World Is Too Much with Us

William Wordsworth

The world is too much with us; late and soon,
Getting and spending, we lay waste our powers:
Little we see in Nature that is ours;
We have given our hearts away, a sordid boon![1]
This sea that bares her bosom to the moon;
The winds that will be howling at all hours,
And are upgathered now like sleeping flowers; 1
For this, for everything, we are out of tune;
It moves us not.—Great God! I'd rather be
A Pagan suckled in a creed outworn; 2
So might I, standing on this pleasant lea,[2]
Have glimpses that would make me less forlorn;
Have sight of Proteus[3] rising from the sea;
Or hear old Triton[4] blow his wreathèd horn.

---

1. boon: Favor.
2. lea: Meadow.
3. Proteus (prō' tyo͞os): In Greek mythology, a sea god who could change his appearance at will.
4. Triton: In Greek mythology, a sea god with the head and upper body of a man and the tail of a fish.

THINKING ABOUT THE SELECTION

Recalling

1. In "The World Is Too Much with Us," what does the poet say "we" have given away?

Interpreting

2. Explain what the poet means by the words *world* and *Nature*.
3. (a) Why would the poet rather be "A Pagan suckled in a creed outworn"? (b) How would even a "creed outworn" be preferable to the materialistic faith Wordsworth observed?

Applying

4. In 1955 in the United States, Erich Fromm wrote, "We live in a world of things, and our only connection with them is that we know how to manipulate or to consume them." How do you think Wordsworth would respond to this contemporary viewpoint?

Enrichment This sonnet, written four years after "London 1802," reinforces Wordsworth's dismay at the growth in materialism that accompanied the French Revolution.

1 **Discussion** The poet states that "we are out of tune." With what are they out of tune? Note that line 8 does not follow the regular rhythm one expects in a sonnet. Why is it appropriate that this line is irregular?

2 **Discussion** Explain the relevance of the reference to paganism expressed in line 10.

Master Teacher Note This sonnet offers an opportunity to discuss diction. Like all great poets, Wordsworth sought out the most meaningful words, which does not always mean the noblest or most beautiful words. Try substituting "buying and selling" for "getting and spending" (line 2), "dozing" for "sleeping" (line 7), and "visions" for "glimpses" (line 12). Which is the better word choice in each case? Why?

Answers

ANSWERS TO THINKING ABOUT THE SELECTION

Recalling

1. We have given away our hearts, that is, our feelings for the natural world.

Interpreting

2. By *world* the poet means the everyday material concerns of humans. By *nature* he means the natural world.
3. Suggested Responses: (a) A pagan's belief might at least allow one to respond to nature and the divine presence in it. (b) A "creed outworn" might have more integrity then the materialistic faith he observes.

Applying

4. Suggested Response: Wordsworth would probably agree with Fromm.

More About the Author Coleridge's plan to start an ideal community, which he conceived with the poet Robert Southey, was to have been a "pantisocracy"—Coleridge's term—on the banks of the Susquehanna River in Pennsylvania. It was to be, as he wrote, an "experiment in human perfectability." Their scheme collapsed at the start when Southey's aunt refused to underwrite the project.

See if your students can recall any other attempts to set up ideal communities. Ask whether or not they feel human perfectability is attainable.

SAMUEL TAYLOR COLERIDGE

1772–1834

Samuel Taylor Coleridge is the classic case of the gifted writer whose genius was hampered by lifelong problems, among them self-doubt and poor health. Coleridge was born in Ottery St. Mary on the Devon coast of England, the last of fourteen children, only four of whom survived. Spoiled by his father, Coleridge withdrew into a world of books and fantasy. At age nine, after his father died, Coleridge was sent to school in London. There the boy excelled and began developing an ability to speak on such matters as philosophy in a way that left his fellow students spellbound.

In 1791 Coleridge entered Cambridge University on a scholarship, but left before he graduated. He discussed plans with several other thinkers of the age to start up a colony in America whose members would live on a high intellectual plane. It was agreed that each member would have a wife. Though the plans for the community fell through, Coleridge's marriage plans did not, and in 1795 he married Sara Fricker.

With his wife, Coleridge moved in 1797 to Somerset, where he developed a close friendship with William Wordsworth, an important poet of the period. In 1798 the two turned out *Lyrical Ballads,* a joint collection of their work. The four poems that make up Coleridge's contribution to the volume deal with matters of the spiritual world and include his masterpiece, "The Rime of the Ancient Mariner." Though at first public response to this collection of poems was lukewarm, the book slowly gained critical attention, ultimately causing a revolution in poetic style and thought and firmly establishing the movement known as Romanticism.

As Coleridge's fame grew, his marriage, his health, and his friendship with Wordsworth all gradually failed. He suffered increasingly from asthma and rheumatism, and he began to rely heavily on painkillers, which dulled his creative powers. Still, Coleridge managed to turn out a good deal of work in the years left him, and in a variety of areas. He worked variously as a journalist, as a lecturer on Shakespeare and Milton, as an essayist, and as a playwright, earning a tidy sum of money in 1812 with his tragedy *Remorse.* And all the time, despite his personal hardships, Coleridge continued to make himself available to visitors, which ultimately proved to have a great impact on the young crop of Romanticists writing at that time.

Perhaps Coleridge's greatest legacy was the insight he affords his reader on the role of imagination in literature. His belief that literature is a magical blend of thought and emotion is at the very heart of his greatest works, in which the unreal is often made to seem real.

GUIDE FOR READING

The Rime of the Ancient Mariner

The Writer's Technique

Sound Devices. The relationship between poetry and music has often been noted. Just as music achieves its effect through rhythms and harmonies, so poetry achieves its effect through sound devices, or techniques that enhance the meter and rhyme of a poem.

Chief among the sound devices available to the poet is *alliteration,* the repetition of a given consonant sound at the beginning of words or accented syllables that occur close together. Notice, for example, the repeated *f* sound in these lines from "The Rime of the Ancient Mariner": "The *f*air breeze blew, the white *f*oam *f*lew,/ The *f*urrow *f*ollowed *f*ree. . . ."

Consonance, a device related to alliteration, is the repetition of a given consonant sound at the end of words or accented syllables appearing close by. Consider another line from Coleridge, this one capitalizing on the *v* sound: "When the i*v*y tod is hea*v*y with snow . . ."

In the sound device known as *assonance,* it is a vowel sound that is repeated in nearby words or syllables. In the following passage, the long *a* sound is so treated: "The western w*a*ve was all afl*a*me./ The d*a*y was well-nigh done!"

Internal rhyme, a fourth sound device, features rhyming words within the space of a single line. As an example, note the following line: "With heavy *thump,* a lifeless *lump* . . ."

Look For

As you read "The Rime of the Ancient Mariner," look to the poet's use of sound devices and the effect he achieves with them.

Writing

Imagine a contest: A friend has dreamed of a skeleton ship manned by spectral figures. You and a group of friends decide to flesh out the dream. The best narrative will win the contest. Write your tale of this skeleton ship.

Vocabulary

Knowing the following words will help you as you read "The Rime of the Ancient Mariner."

averred (ə vʉrd′) *v.*: Stated to be true (p. 674)

sojourn (sō′ jʉrn) *v.*: Stay for a while (p. 681)

expiated (ĕk′ spē āt əd) *v.*: Forgiven; absolved (p. 687)

reverence (rĕv′ ər əns) *n.*: Respect (p. 692)

Literary Focus Sound goes hand in hand with sense in this poem. Provide students with examples of poetic sound devices such as alliteration, onomatopoeia, consonance, assonance, and rhyme.

Look For Your **less advanced** students may have difficulty identifying assonance and consonance. Consider pointing out a few examples of each from the poem before they begin to read.

Writing Have students discuss Coleridge's belief that poetry involves a "willing suspension of disbelief for the moment." Once the discussion has run its course, students should sum up in their own words, in writing, what the statement means to them.

Vocabulary Go over the words with the class before beginning the study of the poem to be certain that students understand the meanings of the words as they are used in the poem.

Objectives

1. To understand the use of sound devices in poetry
2. To analyze the effects of sound devices
3. To recognize archaic words and their meanings
4. To write a response to a statement by the poet

Teaching Portfolio: Support Material

Teacher Backup, p. 000

Vocabulary Check, p. 00

Usage and Mechanics Worksheet, p. 00

Analyzing Literature Worksheet, p. 00

Critical Thinking and Reading Worksheet, p. 00

Language Worksheet, p. 00

Selection Test, p. 000

1

The Rime of the Ancient Mariner

Samuel Taylor Coleridge

The Rime of the Ancient Mariner, *based on a dream of Coleridge's friend, John Cruikshank, was originally planned as a collaboration between Coleridge and Wordsworth. Eventually Wordsworth dropped out of the project, but not before making a number of valuable suggestions, including the shooting of the albatross and the navigation of the ship by the dead men. Several years after the poem was first published in* Lyrical Ballads *(1798), Coleridge added the prose explanations in the margins to aid the reader in understanding the poem's meaning.*

Argument

How a Ship having passed the Line[1] was driven by storms to the cold Country towards the South Pole: and how from
2 thence she made her course to the tropical Latitude of the Great Pacific Ocean; and of the strange things that befell: and in what manner the Ancyent Marinere came back to his own Country.

Part I

An ancient Mariner meeteth three Gallants bidden
3 to a wedding feast and
detaineth one.

It is an ancient Mariner,
And he stoppeth one of three.
4 "By thy long gray beard and glittering eye,
Now wherefore stopp'st thou me?

"The Bridegroom's doors are opened wide,
And I am next of kin;
5 The guests are met, the feast is set:
May'st hear the merry din."

1. **Line:** Equator.

Motivation for Reading Coleridge based this poem on a deep human experience—the sense of isolation and guilt. Ask students if they recall any characters from fiction they have read whose story is based on the same human experience. Did the character overcome those feelings? If so, how?

Master Teacher's Note Charles Lamb, in a letter to Wordsworth, had this to say about the poem:

"For me, I was never so affected with any human Tale. After first reading it, I was totally possessed with it for many days—I dislike all the miraculous part of it, but the feelings of the man under the operation of such scenery dragged me along like Tom Piper's magic whistle."

Purpose-Setting Question How important are literary devices that emphasize sound to establishing the mood and sense of a poem?

1 **Enrichment** This poem was the opening selection in Wordsworth's and Coleridge's famous *Lyrical Ballads* (1798). Later, Wordsworth expressed doubt about placing the poem first, thinking it would put readers off with its mystical and supernatural feeling. Wordsworth's own "Tintern Abbey," page 654, was the final poem in the collection.

2 **Reading Strategy** Since the poem is a narrative it has all the elements of fiction—characters, setting, plot, conflict, point of view, and theme. Students should be aware of this as they read.

3 **Enrichment** Sometime between 1798 and 1817, when the poem reappeared, Coleridge added the marginal notes.

4 **Clarification** The "glittering eye" suggests that the Mariner is a hypnotist.

5 **Discussion** The account of the Wedding Guest's reactions in Part I serves as a frame for the Mariner's tale. Why do you think the poet has chosen a wedding, normally a happy occasion, against which to relate the tale?

The Wedding Guest is spellbound by the eye of the old seafaring man and constrained to hear his tale.

He holds him with his skinny hand,
"There was a ship," quoth he.
"Hold off! unhand me, graybeard loon!"
Eftsoons[2] his hand dropped he.

He holds him with his glittering eye—
The Wedding Guest stood still,
And listens like a three years' child:
The Mariner hath his will.

The Wedding Guest sat on a stone:
He cannot choose but hear;
And thus spake on that ancient man,
The bright-eyed Mariner.

The Mariner tells how the ship sailed southward with a good wind and fair weather till it reached the Line.

"The ship was cheered, the harbor cleared,
Merrily did we drop
Below the kirk,[3] below the hill,
Below the lighthouse top.

"The Sun came up upon the left,
Out of the sea came he!
And he shone bright, and on the right
Went down into the sea.

"Higher and higher every day,
Till over the mast at noon[4]—"
The Wedding Guest here beat his breast,
For he heard the loud bassoon.

The Wedding Guest heareth the bridal music; but the Mariner continueth his tale.

The bride hath paced into the hall.
Red as a rose is she;
Nodding their heads before her goes
The merry minstrelsy.

The Wedding Guest he beat his breast,
Yet he cannot choose but hear;
And thus spake on that ancient man
The bright-eyed Mariner.

The ship driven by a storm toward the South Pole.

"And now the Storm blast came, and he
Was tyrannous and strong:
He struck with his o'ertaking wings,
And chased us south along.

---

2. eftsoons: Immediately.
3. kirk: Church.
4. over . . . noon: The ship has reached the equator.

Reading Strategy Students will need to identify speakers at points where characters other than the Mariner are speaking. Stress this at the opening of the tale. See also lines 80, 224, 345, 400, 410, and 527.

6 **Literary Focus** Another sound device prominent in the poem is onomatopoeia. Line 61 offers a fine example of this device. Be sure students are aware of the importance of onomatopoeia in the poem.

7 **Enrichment** It was Wordsworth, not Coleridge, who thought of the albatross.

"With sloping masts and dipping prow,
As who pursued with yell and blow
Still treads the shadow of his foe,
And forward bends his head,
The ship drove fast, loud roared the blast,
And southward aye[5] we fled.

"And now there came both mist and snow.
And it grew wondrous cold;
And ice, mast-high, came floating by,
As green as emerald.

The land of ice, and of fearful sounds, where no living thing was to be seen.

"And through the drifts the snowy clifts[6]
Did send a dismal sheen;
Nor shapes of men nor beasts we ken[7]—
The ice was all between.

"The ice was here, the ice was there,
The ice was all around;
It cracked and growled, and roared and howled,
6 Like noises in a swound![8]

Till a great sea bird, called the Albatross, came through the snow-fog, and was received with great joy and hospitality.

7 "At length did cross an Albatross,
Thorough[9] the fog it came;
As if it had been a Christian soul,
We hailed it in God's name.

"It ate the food it ne'er had eat,[10]
And round and round it flew.
The ice did split with a thunder-fit;
The helmsman steered us through!

And lo! the Albatross proveth a bird of good omen, and followeth the ship as it returned northward through fog and floating ice.

"And a good south wind sprung up behind;
The Albatross did follow,
And every day, for food or play,
Came to the mariner's hollo!

"In mist or cloud, on mast or shroud,[11]
It perched for vespers[12] nine;
Whiles all the night, through fog-smoke white,
Glimmered the white Moonshine."

---

5. **aye:** Ever.
6. **clifts:** Icebergs.
7. **ken:** knew.
8. **swound:** swoon.
9. **thorough:** Through.
10. **eat** (et): Old form of *eaten.*
11. **shroud** *n.*: Ropes stretching from the ship's side to the masthead.
12. **vespers:** Evenings.

ENGRAVING BY GUSTAV DORÉ FOR THE RIME OF THE ANCIENT MARINER
by Samuel Taylor Coleridge

Humanities Note

Fine art, illustration, 1875, by Gustave Doré. The French illustrator Gustave Doré (1832–1883) began his career as a cartoonist and caricaturist in Paris. His fame spread, and he was soon established as one of the best illustrators in Paris. Doré was self-taught; he refined his technique through independent study of engravings at the National Library in Paris.

Inspired by "The Rime of the Ancient Mariner," Doré published a set of illustrations for the poem in 1875. Doré's obsession with this poem led to some of his most eerie and disturbing images. Although this illustrated volume of Coleridge's poem was not a commercial success, it is considered to be an artistic triumph for Gustave Doré.

This engraving was intended to illustrate the first two lines of the poem. The surprise of the wedding guest and the desperation of the Mariner are both skillfully portrayed by Doré. His mastery of figure drawing and composition are evident in this drawing.

You might discuss the following with your students.

1. What can you say about the eye of the Mariner in this engraving?
2. How does the artist accurately portray the reluctant demeanor of the wedding guest?

8 **Discussion** What significant event happens at the end of Part I?

9 **Reading Strategy** Have students summarize the events of Part I.

10 **Literary Focus** Note the use of alliteration and internal rhyme in these lines.

11 **Discussion** What is the immediate consequence of the Mariner's actions? What soon follows? How does the crew feel about the Mariner?

The ancient Mariner inhospitably killeth the pious bird of good omen.

"God save thee, ancient Mariner!
From the fiends, that plague thee thus!—
Why look'st thou so?"[13] "With my crossbow
I shot the Albatross."

Part II

"The Sun now rose upon the right:[14]
Out of the sea came he,
Still hid in mist, and on the left
Went down into the sea.

"And the good south wind still blew behind,
But no sweet bird did follow.
Nor any day for food or play
Came to the mariners' hollo!

His shipmates cry out against the ancient Mariner for killing the bird of good luck.

"And I had done a hellish thing,
And it would work 'em woe:
For all averred, I had killed the bird
That made the breeze to blow.
Ah wretch! said they, the bird to slay,
That made the breeze to blow!

But when the fog cleared off, they justify the same, and thus make themselves accomplices in the crime.

"Nor dim nor red, like God's own head,
The glorious Sun uprist;[15]
Then all averred, I had killed the bird
That brought the fog and mist.
'Twas right, said they, such birds to slay,
That bring the fog and mist.

The fair breeze continues; the ship enters the Pacific Ocean, and sails northward, even till it reaches the Line.

"The fair breeze blew, the white foam flew,
The furrow[16] followed free;
We were the first that ever burst
Into that silent sea.

The ship hath been suddenly becalmed.

"Down dropped the breeze, the sails dropped
down,
'Twas sad as sad could be;
And we did speak only to break
The silence of the sea!

---

13. God . . . so: Spoken by the Wedding Guest.
14. The Sun . . . right: The ship is now headed north.
15. uprist: Arose.
16. furrow: Ship's wake.

ENGRAVING BY GUSTAV DORÉ FOR THE RIME OF THE ANCIENT MARINER
by Samuel Taylor Coleridge

Humanities Note

Fine art, illustration, 1875, by Gustave Doré. Doré's engraving of the shooting of the albatross is created with skill and imagination. Ask the students why the artist might have chosen to illustrate the moment before the arrow struck the bird.

Humanities Note

Fine art, illustration, 1875, by Gustave Doré. Doré's engraving of the ship tossing on a heavy sea evokes the sense of hopelessness that a person at the mercy of the sea must feel.

You might ask the following questions.

1. What details convey the peril of the ship in this engraving?
2. What mood does this illustration evoke?

ENGRAVING BY GUSTAV DORÉ FOR THE RIME OF THE ANCIENT MARINER
by Samuel Taylor Coleridge

"All in a hot and copper sky,
The bloody Sun, at noon,
Right up above the mast did stand,
No bigger than the Moon.

"Day after day, day after day,
We stuck, nor breath nor motion;
As idle as a painted ship
Upon a painted ocean.

And the Albatross begins to be avenged.

"Water, water, everywhere,
And all the boards did shrink;
Water, water, everywhere,
Nor any drop to drink.

"The very deep did rot: O Christ!
That ever this should be!
Yea, slimy things did crawl with legs
Upon the slimy sea.

"About, about, in reel and rout[17]
The death fires[18] danced at night;
The water, like a witch's oils,
Burned green, and blue and white.

A Spirit had followed them; one of the invisible inhabitants of this planet, neither departed souls nor angels. They are very numerous, and there is no climate or element without one or more.

"And some in dreams assurèd were
Of the Spirit that plagued us so;
Nine fathom deep he had followed us
From the land of mist and snow.

"And every tongue, through utter drought, 12
Was withered at the root;
We could not speak, no more than if
We had been choked with soot.

The shipmates, in their sore distress, would fain throw the whole guilt on the ancient Mariner: in sign whereof they hang the dead sea bird round his neck.

"Ah! well a-day! what evil looks
Had I from old and young!
Instead of the cross, the Albatross
About my neck was hung.

13

17. rout: Disorderly crowd.
18. death fires: St. Elmo's fire, a visible electrical discharge from a ship's mast, believed by sailors to be an omen of disaster.

12 **Discussion** Lines 135-6 tell of the sailors' punishment. Why was it so terrible?

13 **Reading Strategy** Have students summarize the events of Part II.

Part III

"There passed a weary time. Each throat
Was parched, and glazed each eye.
A weary time! a weary time!
How glazed each weary eye,
When looking westward, I beheld
A somethling in the sky.

The ancient Mariner beholdeth a sign in the element afar off.

"At first it seemed a little speck,
And then it seemed a mist;
It moved and moved, and took at last
A certain shape, I wist.[19]

"A speck, a mist, a shape, I wist!
And still it neared and neared:
As if it dodged a water sprite,
It plunged and tacked and veered.

At its nearer approach, it seemeth him to be a ship; and at a dear ransom he freeth his speech from the bonds of thirst.

"With throats unslaked, with black lips baked,
We could nor laugh nor wail;
Through utter drought all dumb we stood!
I bit my arm, I sucked the blood,
And cried, A sail! a sail!

"With throats unslaked, with black lips
  baked,
Agape they heard me call:

A flash of joy;

Gramercy![20] they for joy did grin,
And all at once their breath drew in,
As they were drinking all.

And horror follows. For can it be a ship that comes onward without wind or tide?

"See! see! (I cried) she tacks no more!
Hither to work us weal;[21]
Without a breeze, without a tide,
She steadies with upright keel!

"The western wave was all aflame.
The day was well nigh done!
Almost upon the western wave
Rested the broad bright Sun;
When that strange shape drove suddenly
Betwixt us and the Sun.

---

19. wist: Knew.
20. Gramercy (grə mur′ sē): Great thanks.
21. work us weal: Assist us.

It seemeth him but the skeleton of a ship.

"And straight the Sun was flecked with bars,
(Heaven's Mother send us grace!)
As if through a dungeon grate he peered
With broad and burning face.

And its ribs are seen as bars on the face of the setting Sun. The Specter Woman and her Death-mate, and no other on board the skeleton ship.

"Alas! (thought I, and my heart beat loud)
How fast she nears and nears!
Are those *her* sails that glance in the Sun,
Like restless gossameres?[22]

"Are those *her* ribs through which the Sun
Did peer, as through a grate?
And is that Woman all her crew?
Is that a Death? and are there two?
Is Death that woman's mate?

Like vessel, like crew!

Death and Life-in-Death have diced for the ship's crew, and she (the latter) winneth the ancient Mariner.

"*Her* lips, were red, *her* looks were free,
Her locks were yellow as gold;
Her skin was as white as leprosy,
The Nightmare Life-in-Death was she, 14
Who thicks man's blood with cold.

"The naked hulk alongside came,
And the twain were casting dice;
'The game is done! I've won! I've won!' 15
Quoth she, and whistles thrice.

No twilight within the courts of the Sun.

"The Sun's rim dips; the stars rush out:
At one stride comes the dark;
With far-heard whisper, o'er the sea,
Off shot the specter bark.

At the rising of the Moon,

"We listened and looked sideways up!
Fear at my heart, as at a cup,
My lifeblood seemed to sip!
The stars were dim, and thick the night,
The steersman's face by his lamp gleamed white;
From the sails the dew did drip—
Till clomb[23] above the eastern bar
The hornèd[24] Moon, with one bright star
Within the nether tip.

---

22. gossameres: Floating cobwebs.
23. clomb: Climbed.
24. hornèd: Crescent.

14 Discussion What do you make of the term "Life-in-Death" for the specter who gambled and won the souls of the crew? How apt is the name?

15 Clarification She won the lives of the crew, except for the Mariner, who will live on to suffer.

16 Reading Strategy Have students summarize the events in Part III.

17 Literary Focus Note the alliteration and assonance in lines 232-235, which give this stanza a haunting, mournful sound.

18 Literary Focus Note the simile in line 247. Ask students to tell what is implied by it?

One after another,

"One after one, by the star-dogged Moon,[25]
Too quick for groan or sigh,
Each turned his face with a ghastly pang,
And cursed me with his eye.

His shipmates drop down dead.

"Four times fifty living men,
(And I heard nor sigh nor groan)
With heavy thump, a lifeless lump,
They dropped down one by one.

But Life-in-Death begins her work on the ancient Mariner.

"The souls did from their bodies fly—
They fled to bliss or woe!
And every soul, it passed me by,
Like the whizz of my crossbow!"

16

Part IV

The Wedding Guest feareth that a Spirit is talking to him;

"I fear thee, ancient Mariner!
I fear thy skinny hand!
And thou art long, and lank, and brown,
As is the ribbed sea sand.

"I fear thee and thy glittering eye,
And thy skinny hand, so brown."

But the ancient Mariner assureth him of his bodily life, and proceedeth to relate his horrible penance.

"Fear not, fear not, thou Wedding Guest!
This body dropped not down.

17

"Alone, alone, all, all alone,
Alone on a wide wide sea!
And never a saint took pity on
My soul in agony.

He despiseth the creatures of the calm,

"The many men, so beautiful!
And they all dead did lie:
And a thousand thousand slimy things
Lived on; and so did I.

And envieth that they should live, and so many lie dead.

"I looked upon the rotting sea,
And drew my eyes away;
I looked upon the rotting deck,
And there the dead men lay.

"I looked to heaven, and tried to pray;
But or[26] ever a prayer had gushed,
A wicked whisper came, and made
18 My heart as dry as dust.

---

25. star-dogged Moon: An omen of impending evil to sailors.
26. or: Before.

"I closed my lids, and kept them close,
And the balls like pulses beat;
For the sky and the sea and the sea and the
  sky
Lay like a load on my weary eye,
And the dead were at my feet.

But the curse liveth for him in the eye of the dead men.

"The cold sweat melted from their limbs,
Nor rot nor reek did they;
The look with which they looked on me
Had never passed away.

"An orphan's curse would drag to hell
A spirit from on high;
But oh! more horrible than that
Is the curse in a dead man's eye!
Seven days, seven nights, I saw that curse,
And yet I could not die.

In his loneliness and fixedness he yearneth towards the journeying Moon, and the stars that still sojourn, yet still move onward; and everywhere the blue sky belongs to them, and is their appointed rest, and their native country and their own natural homes, which they enter unannounced, as lords that are certainly expected and yet there is a silent joy at their arrival.

"The moving Moon went up the sky,
And nowhere did abide:
Softly she was going up,
And a star or two beside—

"Her beams bemocked the sultry main,[27]
Like April hoarfrost spread;
But where the ship's huge shadow lay,
The charmèd water burned alway
A still and awful red.

By the light of the Moon he beholdeth God's creatures of the great calm.

"Beyond the shadow of the ship,
I watched the water snakes:
They moved in tracks of shining white,
And when they reared, the elfish light
Fell off in hoary flakes.

"Within the shadow of the ship
I watched their rich attire:
Blue, glossy green, and velvet black,
They coiled and swam; and every track
Was a flash of golden fire. **19**

Their beauty and their happiness.

"O happy living things! no tongue
Their beauty might declare:
A spring of love gushed from my heart,
And I blessed them unaware; **20**

He blesseth them in his heart.

Sure my kind saint took pity on me,
And I blessed them unaware.

---

27. main: Open sea.

19 Discussion How might the Mariner's change in attitude lead to his salvation?

20 Discussion What might be the significance of line 285 as a step in the Mariner's salvation?

21 Reading Strategy Have students summarize the events in Part IV.

22 Enrichment Lines 292-293 are often quoted. Have students identify lines elsewhere in the poem they think are memorable.

The spell begins to break.

"The selfsame moment I could pray;
21 And from my neck so free
The Albatross fell off, and sank
Like lead into the sea.

Part V

22 "Oh sleep! it is a gentle thing,
Beloved from pole to pole!
To Mary Queen the praise be given!
She sent the gentle sleep from Heaven,
That slid into my soul.

By grace of the holy Mother, the ancient Mariner is refreshed with rain.

"The silly[28] buckets on the deck,
That had so long remained,
I dreamed that they were filled with dew;
And when I awoke, it rained.

"My lips were wet, my throat was cold,
My garments all were dank;
Sure I had drunken in my dreams,
And still my body drank.

"I moved, and could not feel my limbs:
I was so light—almost
I thought that I had died in sleep,
And was a blessèd ghost.

He heareth sounds and seeth strange sights and commotions in the sky and the element.

"And soon I heard a roaring wind:
It did not come anear;
But with its sound it shook the sails,
That were so thin and sere.[29]

"The upper air burst into life!
And a hundred fire flags sheen,[30]
To and fro they were hurried about!
And to and fro, and in and out,
The wan stars danced between.

"And the coming wind did roar more loud,
And the sails did sigh like sedge;[31]
And the rain poured down from one black
  cloud;
The Moon was at its edge.

---

28. silly: Empty.
29. sere: Dried up.
30. fire flags sheen: The aurora australis, or southern lights, shone.
31. sedge *n.*: A rushlike plant that grows in wet soil.

ENGRAVING BY GUSTAV DORÉ FOR THE RIME OF THE ANCIENT MARINER
by Samuel Taylor Coleridge

Humanities Note

Fine art, illustration, 1875, by Gustave Doré. Doré's engraving of the haunted, ice-bound ship is an unforgettable, eerie vision. Trapped in a frozen sea, the cursed ship glitters with ice. It seems to be lit from within by an evil light.

You might ask the following questions.

1. The poet uses words to create and describe situations. How does this artist visually describe the situation?
2. If you had seen this illustration before reading the poem, what mood would it evoke?

"The thick black cloud was cleft, and still
The Moon was at its side:
Like waters shot from some high crag,
The lightning fell with never a jag,
A river steep and wide.

The bodies of the ship's crew are inspired[32] and the ship moves on;

"The loud wind never reached the ship,
Yet now the ship moved on!
Beneath the lightning and the Moon
The dead men gave a groan.

"They groaned, they stirred, they all uprose,
Nor spake, nor moved their eyes;
It had been strange, even in a dream,
To have seen those dead men rise.

"The helmsman steered, the ship moved
on:
Yet never a breeze up-blew;
The mariners all 'gan work the ropes,
Where they were wont[33] to do;
They raised their limbs like lifeless tools—
We were a ghastly crew.

"The body of my brother's son
Stood by me, knee to knee;
The body and I pulled at one rope,
But he said nought to me.

"I fear thee, ancient Mariner!"

But not by the souls of the men, nor by demons of earth or middle air, but by a blessed troop of angelic spirits, sent down by the invocation of the guardian saint.

"Be calm, thou Wedding Guest!
'Twas not those souls that fled in pain,
Which to their corses[34] came again,
But a troop of spirits blessed:

"For when it dawned—they dropped their
arms,
And clustered round the mast;
Sweet sounds rose slowly through their
mouths,
And from their bodies passed.

32. inspired: Inspirited.
33. wont: Accustomed.
34. corses: Corpses.

"Around, around, flew each sweet sound,
Then darted to the Sun;
Slowly the sounds came back again,
Now mixed, now one by one.

"Sometimes a-dropping from the sky
I heard the skylark sing;
Sometimes all little birds that are,
How they seemed to fill the sea and air
With their sweet jargoning![35]

"And now 'twas like all instruments,
Now like a lonely flute;
And now it is an angel's song,
That makes the heavens be mute.

"It ceased; yet still the sails made on
A pleasant noise till noon,
A noise like of a hidden brook
In the leafy month of June,
That to the sleeping woods all night
Singeth a quiet tune.

"Till noon we quietly sailed on,
Yet never a breeze did breathe;
Slowly and smoothly went the ship,
Moved onward from beneath.

The lonesome Spirit from the South Pole carries on the ship as far as the Line, in obedience to the angelic troop, but still requireth vengeance.

"Under the keel nine fathom deep, 23
From the land of mist and snow,
The spirit slid; and it was he
That made the ship to go.
The sails at noon left off their tune,
And the ship stood still also.

"The Sun, right up above the mast,
Had fixed her to the ocean:
But in a minute she 'gan stir,
With a short uneasy motion—
Backwards and forwards half her length
With a short uneasy motion.

"Then like a pawing horse let go,
She made a sudden bound:
It flung the blood into my head,
And I fell down in a swound. 24

---

35. jargoning: Singing.

23 Clarification A fathom is equal to six feet; therefore, water which is "nine fathom deep" is water that is fifty-four feet deep.

24 Clarification A swound is a swoon or faint.

25 Discussion What fate remains in store for the Mariner?

26 Reading Strategy Have students summarize the events in Part V.

The Polar Spirit's fellow demons, the invisible inhabitants of the element, take part in his wrong; and two of them relate, one to the other, that penance long and heavy for the ancient Mariner hath been accorded to the Polar Spirit, who returneth southward.

"How long in that same fit I lay,
I have not to declare;
But ere my living life returned,
I heard and in my soul discerned
Two voices in the air.

" 'Is it he?' quoth one, 'Is this the man?
By him who died on cross,
With his cruel bow he laid full low
The harmless Albatross.

" 'The spirit who bideth by himself
In the land of mist and snow,
He loved the bird that loved the man
Who shot him with his bow.'

"The other was a softer voice,
As soft as honeydew:
25 Quoth he, 'The man hath penance done,
And penance more will do.'

26

Part VI

FIRST VOICE

" 'But tell me, tell me! speak again,
Thy soft response renewing—
What makes that ship drive on so fast?
What is the ocean doing?'

SECOND VOICE

" 'Still as a slave before his lord,
The ocean hath no blast;
His great bright eye most silently
Up to the Moon is cast—

"If he may know which way to go;
For she guides him smooth or grim.
See, brother, see! how graciously
She looketh down on him.'

FIRST VOICE

The Mariner hath been cast into a trance; for the angelic power causeth the vessel to drive northward faster than human life could endure.

" 'But why drives on that ship so fast,
Without or wave or wind?'

SECOND VOICE

"'The air is cut away before,
And closes from behind.

"Fly, brother, fly! more high, more high!
Or we shall be belated;
For slow and slow that ship will go,
When the Mariner's trance is abated.'

The super-natural motion is retarded; the Mariner awakes, and his penance begins anew.

"I woke, and we were sailing on
As in a gentle weather;
'Twas night, calm night, the moon was high;
The dead men stood together.

"All stood together on the deck,
For a charnel dungeon[36] litter;
All fixed on me their stony eyes,
That in the Moon did glitter.

"The pang, the curse, with which they died,
Had never passed away;
I could not draw my eyes from theirs,
Nor turn them up to pray.

The curse is finally expiated.

"And now this spell was snapped; once more
I viewed the ocean green,
And looked far forth, yet little saw
Of what had else been seen—

"Like one, that on a lonesome road
Doth walk in fear and dread,
And having once turned round walks on,
And turns no more his head;
Because he knows, a frightful fiend
Doth close behind him tread.

"But soon there breathed a wind on me,
Nor sound nor motion made:
Its path was not upon the sea,
In ripple or in shade.

"It raised my hair, it fanned my cheek
Like a meadow-gale of spring—
It mingled strangely with my fears,
Yet it felt like a welcoming.

27

36. charnel dungeon: Vault where corpses or bones are deposited.

27 **Literary Focus** Note the simile in lines 456-7. Why is the reference to a meadow especially significant?

28 Discussion Explain how the Mariner's ship returns home. Is it a normal sailing, or one with miraculous overtones?

29 Literary Focus Note the simile in line 472. Is it effective, or is it trite and unimaginative?

28
"Swiftly, swiftly flew the ship,
Yet she sailed softly too:
Sweetly, sweetly blew the breeze—
On me alone it blew.

And the ancient Mariner beholdeth his native country.

"Oh! dream of joy! is this indeed
The lighthouse top I see?
Is this the hill? is this the kirk?
Is this mine own countree?

"We drifted o'er the harbor bar,
And I with sobs did pray—
O let me be awake, my God!
Or let me sleep alway.

29
"The harbor bay was clear as glass,
So smoothly it was strewn![37]
And on the bay the moonlight lay,
And the shadow of the Moon.

"The rock shone bright, the kirk no less,
That stands above the rock;
The moonlight steeped in silentness
The steady weathercock.

The angelic spirits leave the dead bodies,

"And the bay was white with silent light,
Till rising from the same,
Full many shapes, that shadows were,
In crimson colors came.

And appear in their own forms of light.

"A little distance from the prow
Those crimson shadows were;
I turned my eyes upon the deck—
Oh, Christ! what saw I there!

"Each corse lay flat, lifeless and flat,
And, by the holy rood![38]
A man all light, a seraph[39] man,
On every corse there stood.

"This seraph band, each waved his hand:
It was a heavenly sight!
They stood as signals to the land,
Each one a lovely light;

37. strewn: spread.
38. rood: Cross.
39. seraph: Angel.

"This seraph band, each waved his hand,
No voice did they impart—
No voice; but oh! the silence sank
Like music on my heart.

"But soon I heard the dash of oars,
I heard the Pilot's cheer;
My head was turned perforce away
And I saw a boat appear.

"The Pilot and the Pilot's boy,
I heard them coming fast:
Dear Lord in Heaven! it was a joy
The dead men could not blast.

"I saw a third—I heard his voice:
It is the Hermit good!
He singeth loud his godly hymns
That he makes in the wood. 30
He'll shrieve[40] my soul, he'll wash away
The Albatross's blood.

Part VII 31

The Hermit of the Wood,

"This Hermit good lives in that wood
Which slopes down to the sea.
How loudly his sweet voice he rears!
He loves to talk with mariners
That come from a far countree.

"He kneels at morn, and noon, and eve—
He hath a cushion plump:
It is the moss that wholly hides
The rotted old oak-stump.

"The skiff boat neared; I heard them talk.
'Why, this is strange, I trow![41]
Where are those lights so many and fair,
That signal made but now?'

Approacheth the ship with wonder.

" 'Strange, by my faith!' the Hermit said—
'And they answered not our cheer!
The planks looked warped! and see those
sails,
How thin they are and sere!
I never saw aught like to them,
Unless perchance it were

40. shrieve (s-hrēv): Absolve from sin.
41. trow: Believe.

30 **Discussion** In the final stanza of Part VI the Mariner's words imply a fervent wish. What is that wish?

31 **Reading Strategy** Have students summarize the events of Part VI.

"'Brown skeletons of leaves that lag
My forest brook along;
When the ivy tod[42] is heavy with snow,
And the owlet whoops to the wolf below,
That eats the she-wolf's young.'

"'Dear Lord! it hath a fiendish look'
(The Pilot made reply)
'I am a-feared'—'Push on, push on!'
Said the Hermit cheerily.

"The boat came closer to the ship,
But I nor spake nor stirred;
The boat came close beneath the ship,
And straight[43] a sound was heard.

The ship suddenly sinketh.

"Under the water it rumbled on,
Still louder and more dread;
It reached the ship, it split the bay;
The ship went down like lead.

The ancient Mariner is saved in the Pilot's boat.

"Stunned by that loud and dreadful sound,
Which sky and ocean smote,
Like one that hath been seven days drowned
My body lay afloat;
But swift as dreams, myself I found
Within the Pilot's boat.

"Upon the whirl, where sank the ship,
The boat spun round and round;
And all was still, save that the hill
Was telling of the sound.

"I moved my lips—the Pilot shrieked
And fell down in a fit;
The holy Hermit raised his eyes,
And prayed where he did sit.

"I took the oars; the Pilot's boy,
Who now doth crazy go,
Laughed loud and long, and all the while
His eyes went to and fro.
'Ha! ha!' quoth he, 'full plain I see,
The Devil knows how to row.'

---

42. tod: Bush.
43. straight: Immediately.

690

"And now, all in my own countree,
I stood on the firm land!
The Hermit stepped forth from the boat,
And scarcely he could stand.

The ancient Mariner earnestly entreateth the Hermit to shrieve him; and the penance of life falls on him.

"'O shrieve me, shrieve me, holy man!'
The Hermit crossed his brow.[44]
'Say, quick,' quoth he, 'I bid thee say—
What manner of man art thou?'

"Forthwith this frame of mine was wrenched
With a woful agony,
Which forced me to begin my tale;
And then it left me free.

And ever and anon through out his future life an agony constraineth him to travel from land to land;

"Since then, at an uncertain hour,
That agony returns;
And till my ghastly tale is told,
This heart within me burns.

"I pass, like night, from land to land;
I have strange power of speech;
That moment that his face I see,
I know the man that must hear me:
To him my tale I teach.

"What loud uproar bursts from that door!
The wedding guests are there;
But in the garden bower the bride
And bridemaids singing are;
And hark the little vesper bell,
Which biddeth me to prayer!

"O Wedding Guest! this soul hath been
Alone on a wide wide sea:
So lonely 'twas, that God himself
Scarce seemed there to be.

"O sweeter than the marriage feast,
'Tis sweeter far to me,
To walk together to the kirk
With a goodly company!— 32

44. crossed his brow: Made the sign of the cross on his forehead.

32 **Discussion** In these lines the Mariner admits that the company of living people is the sweetest blessing he can seek. Why does he feel this way?

33 Discussion These lines reveal the theme, or moral, of the tale. Restate that theme in your own words. What other lines in the poem can you find that relate to the moral?

34 Reading Strategy Have students summarize the events in Part VII.

Challenge How does the blend of Christian and pagan imagery extend the poet's intention to write a poem that deals with the supernatural? The imagery in the poem, while often eerie, is always quite vivid. What images stand out as most forceful?

Thematic Idea Turn back to the ballad "Sir Patrick Spens," page 78. What similarities do you see in form and style between that ballad and this one? What are the chief differences, aside from length?

"To walk together to the kirk,
And all together pray,
While each to his great Father bends,
Old men, and babes, and loving friends
And youths and maidens gay!

And to teach, by his own example, love and reverence to all things that God made and loveth.

"Farewell, farewell! but this I tell
To thee, thou Wedding Guest!
He prayeth well, who loveth well
Both man and bird and beast.

33
"He prayeth best, who loveth best
All things both great and small;
For the dear God who loveth us,
He made and loveth all."

The Mariner, whose eye is bright,
Whose beard with age is hoar,
Is gone; and now the Wedding Guest
Turned from the bridegroom's door.

He went like one that hath been stunned
And is of sense forlorn;
A sadder and a wiser man,
He rose the morrow morn.

34

THINKING ABOUT THE SELECTION

Recalling

1. (a) What happens to the ship as a result of the storm? (b) What change occurs when the Albatross appears?
2. (a) What "hellish thing" does the Mariner do? (b) How do the other sailors at first react to this deed? (c) What changes their minds?
3. (a) Who is the crew of the strange ship that appears in Part III? (b) What happens to the Mariner's shipmates soon after the appearance of this ship?
4. (a) What changes take place in the Mariner in Part IV? (b) What burden is he freed of as a result of these changes?
5. (a) According to the margin notes in Part V, what force causes the ship to move? (b) Who serves as the crew of the ship on this leg of its journey? (c) What force takes control of the ship at the equator?
6. What does the Mariner hope the Hermit will do for him?
7. What is the Mariner's lifelong penance?

Interpreting

8. What do you think the Albatross symbolizes, or stands for? Find evidence to support your answer.
9. In what ways might the journey of the Mariner be seen as spiritual as well as actual?
10. Some of the events Coleridge describes are

Answers

ANSWERS TO THINKING ABOUT THE SELECTION
Recalling

1. (a) The storm drove the ship south into an ice field. (b) The ice split, a good south wind blew up, and the ship headed back north.
2. (a) The Mariner shoots the Albatross with a crossbow. (b) At first the other sailors think the Mariner has done a good thing. (c) They change their minds when the ship is becalmed.
3. (a) The Specter Woman and her Death-mate are the crew. (b) One after another, the Mariner's shipmates drop dead.
4. (a) The Mariner's initial feelings of dismay, envy, and anger change to those of love when he finds he can pray. (b) The Mariner having learned to pray, the Albatross falls off him.
5. (a) The Polar Spirit from the South carries the ship on its way. (b) A troop of angelic spirits make up the crew. (c) Fellow demons of the Polar Spirit take over the ship once it reaches the equator.
6. The Mariner hopes the hermit will absolve him of his sin.
7. His penance is to wander the

real and some are supernatural. Why do you think he includes both kinds in this poem?

Applying

11. Reread lines 614–617. How might this advice be useful for today's world?
12. What do we mean when we say that some past action stays with a person "like an albatross around his or her neck"?

ANALYZING LITERATURE

Understanding Sound Devices

Alliteration, consonance, assonance, and internal rhyme are four sound devices used to enhance the meaning and create the mood of a poem. **Alliteration** is the repetition of a first consonant sound in words or accented syllables ("the owlet *w*hoops to the *w*olf"). **Consonance** is the repetition of a final consonant sound in words or accented syllables ("thy skin*ny* ha*nd*, so brow*n*"). **Assonance** is the repetition of a vowel sound ("the Sun's r*i*m d*i*ps"). **Internal rhyme** is a rhyme within a line ("on the b*ay* the moonlight l*ay*").

Identify the sound device or devices in each of the following lines from "The Rime of the Ancient Mariner."

1. lines 7–8
2. lines 31–32
3. lines 121–122
4. lines 236–237
5. lines 452–453
6. lines 478–479

CRITICAL THINKING AND READING

Analyzing the Effects of Sound Devices

Sound devices in poetry please the ear and also reinforce meaning and create moods. In lines 41–44, for example, the repetition of the *s* sound, through both alliteration and consonance, enables us almost to hear the hissing of the sea foam as the ship is tossed about.

1. Reread lines 331–340. Identify the sound devices used and explain how they add to the eerie mood of the scene.
2. Reread lines 472–483. State the feeling you think Coleridge was trying to establish in his reader. Tell whether, in your opinion, his use of sound devices helps, and give your reasons.

UNDERSTANDING LANGUAGE

Using Archaic Words and Meanings

To give his poem the feeling of something written long ago, Coleridge used archaic, or outdated, language in "The Rime of the Ancient Mariner." Old verb forms such as *stoppeth* (line 2), Middle English words such as *eftsoons* (line 12), and earlier meanings of familiar words, such as *silly* to mean "empty" (line 297) all sounded as odd to Coleridge's original audience as they do to us today.

Find at least one other example each of old verb forms, Middle English words, and former word meanings in the poem. State whether you feel they help achieve the feeling Coleridge was striving after.

THINKING AND WRITING

Responding to a Statement

Coleridge wrote that successful poetry is poetry that will arouse "the sympathy of the reader by a faithful adherence to the truth of nature" while, at the same time, "giving the interest of novelty by the modifying colors of imagination." In an essay, argue whether or not you feel Coleridge met these standards in "The Rime of the Ancient Mariner." Begin by defining *sympathy* and *interest* as you believe he has used the words here. Support your claims by quoting passages from the poem. When you revise make sure you have included details from the poem to support your judgment. Proofread your essay and prepare a final draft.

earth telling his tale and teaching love and reverence for all things.

Interpreting

8. Suggested Response: The Albatross symbolizes nature as an evocation or test of human moral responses.
9. The Mariner's journey can also be thought of as an allegory of one's passage through life—from innocence through sin to grace and penitence. Sin makes an outcast of the person; Grace and penitence readmit the person back into society.
10. Answers will differ. Suggested Response: Including the real and the supernatural results in a poem whose images are more vivid and lasting, as well as more credible.

Applying

11. Answers may differ but should include the idea that the moral of the poem is to love all things, both great and small. Certainly applying this moral to the world today would lessen tensions between people and nations.
12. "Having an albatrass around one's neck" means that a person is unable to escape the effects of the past action.

ANSWERS TO ANALYZING LITERATURE

1. Lines 7-8 contain internal rhyme and consonance.

(Answers begin on p. 692.)

2. Lines 31-32 contain internal rhyme, alliteration, assonance, and consonance.
3. Lines 121-122 contain alliteration and assonance.
4. Lines 236-237 contain alliteration, assonance, and consonance.
5. Lines 452-453 contain alliteration, assonance, and consonance.
6. Lines 478-479 contain alliteration.

ANSWERS TO CRITICAL THINKING AND READING

1. In lines 331-340 the use of alliteration and assonance—especially the long *o* sound in the latter—reinforces the eeriness of the scene.
2. In lines 472-483 the poet succeeds in evoking a ghostly feeling through the use of sound devices, especially alliteration and assonance. Students' reasons should refer to the effects of specific sound devices.

ANSWERS TO UNDERSTANDING LANGUAGE

Examples of archaic words abound in the poem; they include *hath, spake, ken, o'ertaking, swound, look'st, uprist, reel* and *rout, wist, gramercy, nigh, twain, quoth, clomb, anear, corses, singeth, bideth, looketh,* and *shrieve,* all of which add to the supernatural, otherworldly effect that permeates the tale.

Writing Across the Curriculum
Today many people are concerned with preserving the delicate ecological balance that allows all life to co-exist. How does the Mariner's philosophy support the concerns of scientists? Of ordinary citizens? Consider working with the science department on this question. Science teachers might contribute current information on ecological concerns.

Challenge Compare and contrast the Mariner's philosophy with the Renaissance concept of the "Great Chain of Being."

Literary Focus Point out that although Romanticism is most often thought of as an attempt to return to nature, a concern with the exotic, the strange, the far-away is a powerful strain in all forms of Romantic art. "Kubla Khan" is one of the greatest expressions of this form of Romanticism.

Look for You might have students look for lines in "The Rime of the Ancient Mariner" that relate to one or more of the five senses as a way of alerting students to Coleridge's employment of such sensory details in his poems.

Writing Have students discuss the term *exotic* in an attempt to define it and to give examples. They can then complete the writing activity.

Vocabulary Go over the words before reading the poem. Consider adding these words to the list: *damsel* (young girl, maiden); *decree* (official decision, law); *tumult* (violent disturbance, confusion, or excitement).

GUIDE FOR READING

Kubla Khan

Literary Movements

Romanticism. Romanticism was a literary and artistic movement that began in Europe toward the end of the eighteenth century. A rebellion against the cold rationalism and strict adherence to form that typified the earlier Neoclassical movement, Romanticism stressed imagination and subjectivity as key literary virtues. The Romantic writer was free to express his or her personal views in a spontaneous and nonlogical fashion. The goal of the Romantics thus was to bring people to an awareness of their "oneness" with all other living things. It was in the spirit of this movement and its goal that Coleridge gave his poem "Kubla Khan" the subtitle "A Vision in a Dream." The word *vision* here reminds us that the Romantics were fond of mysticism and fantasy—the stuff of visions. The word *dream* calls to mind a freedom from the rules and logical order of the day-to-day world—traits that were at the very heart of Romanticism.

Look For

As you read "Kubla Khan," be alert to the many details related to the five senses, which help you imagine the exotic and fantastic landscape. In particular, pay attention in the last stanza to Coleridge's comment on the power of imagination.

Writing

Recall as best you can a dream you had in which you made a trip to a strange place. Alternatively, think about an actual distant and exotic land, possibly in the Orient, that you visited, perhaps on vacation or perhaps only in your imagination. Write a vivid description of that real or imagined place. Use as many details of sight, sound, touch, taste, and smell as you are able.

Vocabulary

Knowing the following words will help you as you read "Kubla Khan."

sinuous (sin′ yo͞o əs) adj.: Winding, twisting (p. 695)

tumult (to͞o′ mult) *n.*: Noisy confusion (p. 696)

prophesying (prŏf′ ə sī iŋ) *v.*: Predicting (p. 696)

Objective

1. To understand the beliefs of Romanticism

Teaching Portfolio: Support Material

Lesson plan, p. 00-00

Vocabulary Check, p. 00

Usage and Mechanics Worksheet, p. 00

Analyzing Literature Worksheet, p. 00

Critical Thinking and Reading Worksheet, p. 00

Language Worksheet, p. 00

Selection Test, p. 00

Kubla Khan 1

Samuel Taylor Coleridge

This poem was inspired by a passage about Kubla Khan (kōō' ble kän), the founder of the Mongol dynasty in China in the thirteenth century, in Samuel Purchas's Purchas His Pilgrimage *(1613): "Here the Khan Kubla commanded a palace to be built, and a stately garden thereunto. And thus ten miles of fertile ground were inclosed with a wall." Coleridge claims to have fallen asleep while reading this passage due to the effects of medication he was taking for an illness at the time (1797). Three hours later, he awoke from a dream, finding his mind was filled with two to three hundred lines of poetry, which were an elaboration of the description he had read immediately before drifting off to sleep. Coleridge immediately began to write down the lines that filled his head, but when he was interrupted by a visitor, he forgot the lines that he had not yet transcribed. As a result, he was unable to complete the poem.*

In Xanadu[1] did Kubla Khan
A stately pleasure dome decree:
Where Alph,[2] the sacred river, ran
Through caverns measureless to man
    Down to a sunless sea.
So twice five miles of fertile ground 2
With walls and towers were girdled round;
And there were gardens bright with sinuous rills,[3]
Where blossomed many an incense-bearing tree;
And here were forests ancient as the hills,
Enfolding sunny spots of greenery.

But oh! that deep romantic chasm which slanted
Down the green hill athwart[4] a cedarn cover![5]
A savage place! as holy and enchanted
As e'er beneath a waning moon was haunted 3
By woman wailing for her demon lover!
And from this chasm, with ceaseless turmoil seething,
As if this earth in fast thick pants were breathing.

---

1. **Xanadu** (zan' ə dōō): An indefinite area in China.
2. **Alph:** Probably derived from the Greek river Alpheus, the waters of which, it was believed in Greek mythology, joined with a stream to form a fountain in Sicily.
3. **rills:** Brooks.
4. **athwart:** Across.
5. **cedarn cover:** Covering of cedar trees.

Motivation for Reading Ask students to imagine they have just awakened from a vivid dream of some exotic place. Would they try to hold onto the images the dream evoked? Why or why not?

Master Teacher Note Scholars have discovered that passages in the poem derive from about eight travel writers besides Purchas, as well as landscapes that Coleridge himself had seen.

Purpose-Setting Question What evidence of passion, mysticism, and fantasy do you find in "Kubla Khan"?

1 **Enrichment** Coleridge said that Lord Byron convinced him to publish "Kubla Khan," which he did, "rather as a psychological curiosity, than on the ground of any supposed *poetic* merits."

2 **Literary Focus** The indefinite Oriental setting exemplifies Romantic fascination with the exotic, strange, and faraway. However, the "measureless" caverns, the gardens, and the ancient forests recall the more conventional Romantic interest in nature. You might read these lines aloud and ask your students to describe the mood and atmosphere they create.

3 **Discussion** With **more advanced,** or more mature, students, you may wish to point out the mixture of savagery, holiness, enchantment, passion, and demonolatry in these lines. Imagery and connotation combine to make these verses especially memorable. Ask what feelings this place seems to stir in the poet.

4 **Discussion** What makes this line such an effective description of the sacred river? Help your **less advanced** students to see that alliteration (the *m* sound) and rhythm together make the verse imitate the motion of the river.

5 **Discussion** What new emotion is introduced in lines 29–30? Point out that in lines 31–36 the delicacy of the "pleasure dome" is suggested and therefore its vulnerability to war.

6 **Literary Focus** Point out that the abrupt transition to the damsel is typical of the free-flowing nature of a dream. Coleridge's use of a non-logical structure in "Kubla Khan" is characteristically Romantic. Classical and neoclassical poets, conversely, tend to rely on a logical structure in their poems.

7 **Discussion** Point out that the poem becomes personal at the end. Ask students to summarize the poet's vision of himself here. In what sense would he "build that dome in air"? You may need to explain that line 51 describes a magical ritual intended to protect the inspired, frenzied poet from intrusion. The image of the poet as a divinely inspired madman is common in some of the more extreme forms of Romanticism.

A mighty fountain momently was forced;
Amid whose swift half-intermitted burst
Huge fragments vaulted like rebounding hail,
Or chaffy grain beneath the thresher's flail;
And 'mid these dancing rocks at once and ever
It flung up momently the sacred river.
4 Five miles meandering with a mazy motion
Through wood and dale the sacred river ran,
Then reached the caverns measureless to man,
5 And sank in tumult to a lifeless ocean:
And 'mid this tumult Kubla heard from far
Ancestral voices prophesying war!
The shadow of the dome of pleasure
Floated midway on the waves;
Where was heard the mingled measure
From the fountain and the caves.
It was a miracle of rare device.[6]
A sunny pleasure dome with caves of ice!

6 A damsel with a dulcimer[7]
In a vision once I saw:
It was an Abyssinian[8] maid,
And on her dulcimer she played.
Singing of Mount Abora.[9]
7 Could I revive within me
Her symphony and song,
To such a deep delight 'twould win me,
That with music loud and long,
I would build that dome in air,
That sunny dome! those caves of ice!
And all who heard should see them there,
And all should cry, Beware! Beware!
His flashing eyes, his floating hair!
Weave a circle round him thrice,
And close your eyes with holy dread,
For he on honeydew hath fed,
And drunk the milk of Paradise.

---

6. **device:** Design.
7. **dulcimer:** (dul' sə mər) *n.*: A musical instrument with metal strings which produce sounds when struck by two small hammers.
8. **Abyssinian** (ab ə sin' ē ən): Ethiopian.
9. **Mount Abora:** Probably Mount Amara in Abyssinia.

Answers

ANSWERS TO THINKING ABOUT THE SELECTION

Recalling

1. The pleasure dome was "twice five miles" in size.
2. "A mighty fountain" was forced up.

CHINESE SILK ALBUM LEAF, YUAN DYNASTY, KUBLAI KHAN
The Granger Collection

THINKING ABOUT THE SELECTION

Recalling

1. What was the size of the palatial estate that Kubla Khan ordered built?
2. What, according to the second stanza, was forced up through "that deep romantic chasm"?
3. What did Kubla Khan hear in the noise made by the river emptying into the ocean?
4. (a) According to the last stanza, what did the speaker once see in a vision? (b) What part of that vision does the speaker wish he could revive?

Interpreting

5. Using your own words, what does the speaker say would happen to him and "all who heard" if he were able to revive his vision?
6. What statement do you think Coleridge is making here about the power of imagination?
7. (a) Find one example each of Coleridge's use of alliteration and assonance. (b) Explain how each example enhances the meaning or mood of the words.
8. (a) Do you feel that Coleridge's imagination and "music" combine to make his vision seem real for the reader? (b) Support your answer with quotations from the poem.

Applying

9. Do you think people should be governed more by their emotions or their reason? Do you think there should be a balance between the two? Explain your answer.

Humanities Note

Fine art, illuminated manuscript. The Persian illuminated manuscripts were generally concerned with nonreligious subjects, as portrayal of the sacred was forbidden. Artists, who were often retained by princes, recorded historical scenes, accounts of battles, hunting scenes, and so on, to be shown as public record. This miniature of Kubla Khan is from such an illuminated manuscript. It is typical of the work of these Islamic artists. The emphasis is on the outline of the forms without much attempt at a three-dimensional effect. The colors are bright, the composition lively, and the overall effect decorative. This miniature, from Marco Polo's *Book of the Traveler,* narrates the meeting of the explorer with the great Kubla Khan.

You may wish to ask the following questions:

1. How does the artist's conception of the great Kubla Khan compare with Coleridge's?
2. Could the artist's image of the castle in this miniature be the "pleasure dome" from the poem? Explain.

(Answers begin on p. 696.)

3. Kubla heard "Ancestral voices prophesying war!"
4. (a) The speaker once saw a "damsel with a dulcimer." (b) The speaker wishes he could revive "Her symphony and song." (c) The vision would win him over to build the sunny pleasure dome.

Interpreting

5. He would re-create in his imagination Kubla Khan's pleasure dome and the cover of ice. Those who heard him would look upon him as an inspired madman and seal him off from ordinary people.
6. Answers will differ but should mention that imagination has the power to create a vision that amounts to a kind of reality. Coleridge is also suggesting that the imagination is a form of divinely inspired lunacy.
7. (a) Line 4 contains alliteration; line 6 contains assonance. (b) Alliteration in line 4 draws the reader's attention to the key words *measureless* and *man.* In line 6 the long *i* sound "lifts" the tone of the poem from the depths—of sound as well as sense—of the preceding lines.
8. (a) Answers will differ but should affirm that imagination and music do indeed combine to make the vision seem real. (b) Students' supporting quotations will differ. However, the descriptions of the caverns, the "deep romantic chasm," the sacred river, and the maid with the dulcimer would be appropriate choices.

Applying

9. Answers will differ. In their answers students should cite the advantages and disadvantages of being governed by emotion and reason.

Challenge More than one critic has noted that "Kubla Khan" oscillates between giving and taking away, between what the critic Elisabeth Schneider, for example, describes as "bright affirmation and sunless negation." Defend or attack this interpretation, citing specific passages from the poem to support your view.

More About the Author Lord Byron was once as celebrated for his lifestyle as for the remarkable quality of his works. Indeed, he gave rise to the term *Byronic hero*—a kind of hero as outcast, a person in whom, as Byron himself once suggested, there is much to admire and much to hate. Ask students to discuss any public figures they think might qualify as Byronic heroes.

GEORGE GORDON, LORD BYRON

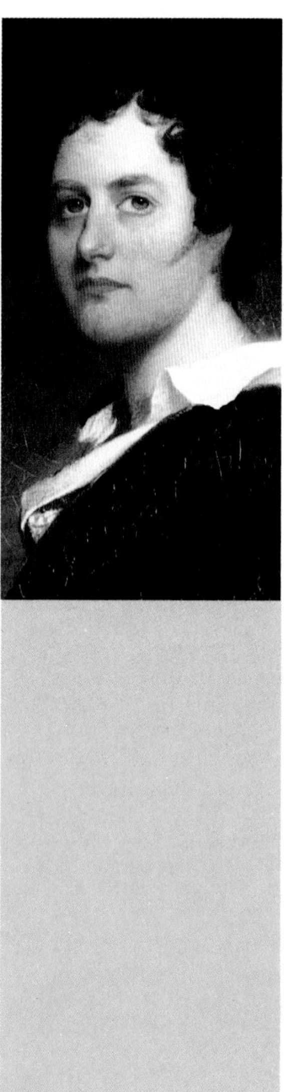

1788–1824

In his life as well as in his work, George Gordon, Lord Byron typified the Romanticist's zest for life. As much a public figure as a literary genius, Byron lived life "in the fast lane"—a point that was looked on with disapproval by his contemporaries.

Whether distasteful behavior is purely a matter of example is open to debate. Nevertheless, it is significant to note that Byron was born in London to a father whose good looks—which his son inherited—made him irresistible to women. The father, John Byron, died when his son was three. When the young Byron was ten, the death of a great-uncle brought him the title of Baron, along with an estate at Newstead. Here the boy and his mother went to live until, at seventeen, Byron left home to attend Trinity College at Cambridge. At college, Byron made many friends, played many sports, and spent much money. He also published his first book of poems, *Hours of Idleness* (1807), which received harsh criticism from the *Edinburgh Review.* He was hurt but not crushed by this attack on his work, and two years later he came out with *English Bards and Scotch Reviewers,* a poem poking fun at the magazine.

That same year, Byron journeyed to the Near East, and spent the next two years traveling. When he returned home, he brought with him two sections of a book-length poem titled *Childe Harold,* which depicted a young hero not unlike himself—moody, reckless, sensitive, and adventuresome. The work was received with great enthusiasm, and Byron became a very popular figure in important English circles. So great was his popularity, in fact, that his next published work, *The Corsair,* sold 10,000 copies in one day.

During this period Byron saw a great many women. In 1815 he married Ann Isabella Milbanke, with whom he had a daughter. The couple seemed mismatched from the start and, after about a year, separated. Hurt by nasty gossip, Byron left England, never to return. It was in Italy that he began work on his most ambitious opus, *Don Juan* (pronounced "JOO-en"), a mock epic of the Romantic hero.

It was also at this point that tragedy struck, and then struck again—first with the death of his daughter, later with that of his friend, the poet Shelley. In 1823 Byron joined a group of revolutionaries seeking to free Greece from Turkish rule. Before the revolt got underway, however, Byron died of rheumatic fever, at the age of 36.

Although Byron openly spurned the works of other Romantics, including Wordsworth and Coleridge, his independence was a hallmark of the Romantic movement.

GUIDE FOR READING

She Walks in Beauty; So We'll Go No More A-Roving; Apostrophe to the Ocean

The Writer's Technique

Figurative Language. Figurative language is the name given to a class of literary conventions that purposely distorts language to make ideas more interesting and memorable. As opposed to literal language, or language "by the rules," figurative language is not to be taken at face value. When a poet writes, for instance, of trees "standing by the side of the road like sentinels," he or she is attempting to get the reader to picture trees that are very upright, much like soldiers.

Look For

As you read the following three poems by Byron, be alert to his use of figurative language to place ideas and thoughts in a new light.

Writing

Develop a list of about twenty adjectives and descriptive phrases, such as *blue, filled with holes, slippery,* and so on. Randomly choose three entries from your list, and write them at the top of a sheet of paper. Then try to think of two objects that share each of the three traits. Write a sentence that compares one of the objects to the other. Try this with at least four pairs of objects.

Vocabulary

Knowing the following words will help you as you read the next three poems by Byron.

gaudy (gôd′ ē) *adj.*: Showy in a tasteless way (p. 700)
impaired (im per′ 'd) *v.*: Diminished (p. 700)
tress (tres) *n.*: Lock of human hair (p. 700)
eloquent (el′ ə kwənt) *adj.*: Very expressive (p. 700)
armaments (är mə mənts) *n.*: Arms, weapons (p.703)
arbiter (är′ bə tər) *n.*: Judge, umpire (p. 703)
torrid (tôr′ id) *adj.*: Hot, scorching (p. 704)

Literary Focus With **less advanced** students, explain that literal language means what it says, whereas figurative language says one thing but means much more. Presenting several metaphors to illustrate how figurative language works should prove helpful.

Look for Your **less advanced** students may have difficulty recalling the various figures of speech referred to. Consider previewing Analyzing Literature (page 705) so they can refresh their understanding.

Writing Give the class an example to help them get started: for a snowy evening write, "An infinity of down blanketed the sleeping earth." Have a few students volunteer their figurative descriptions.

Vocabulary Review the words as a class before taking up the study of the poems.

Objectives

1. To analyze figurative language
2. To evaluate a poem

Teaching Portfolio: Support Material

Teacher Backup, p. 000

Vocabulary Check, p. 00

Usage and Mechanics Worksheet, p. 00

Analyzing Literature Worksheet, p. 00

Critical Thinking and Reading Worksheet, p. 00

Language Worksheet, p. 00

Selection Test, p. 000

Art Transparency 7, *Arran* by Henry Moore, p. 000

Motivation for Reading Inform the class that this is one of the most famous descriptions of womanly beauty in English poetry. Challenge them to describe in prose Lady Horton's beauty.

Master Teacher Note The poem was published in Byron's *Hebrew Melodics,* which was written to be set to adaptations of traditional Jewish times.

Purpose-Setting Question: What figures of speech and images does Byron use to express his sense of the lady's beauty?

Thematic Idea Compare and contrast this poem with Shakespeare's Sonnet 130, (p. 211).

1 **Enrichment** Byron wrote this lyric for Lady Horton as soon as he had returned to his room following a dance at which he saw her.

2 **Discussion** The opening simile is justly famous. How apt is it? How is Lady Horton like the night?

3 **Discussion** Does Byron's picture emphasize the physical or the spiritual aspect of the lady?

Challenge Compare the rhythm, the meter, and the rhyme scheme in this poem to those in the heroic couplets of Pope's "Rape of the Lock," page 560.

1 She Walks in Beauty

George Gordon, Lord Byron

This poem, written to be set to music, was inspired by Byron's first meeting with Lady Wilmot Horton, his cousin by marriage, who wore a black mourning gown with spangles.

2 She walks in beauty, like the night
Of cloudless climes and starry skies;
And all that's best of dark and bright
Meet in her aspect and her eyes:
Thus mellowed to that tender light
Which heaven to gaudy day denies.

One shade the more, one ray the less,
Had half impaired the nameless grace
Which waves in every raven tress,
Or softly lightens o'er her face;
Where thoughts serenely sweet express
How pure, how dear their dwelling place.

3 And on that cheek, and o'er that brow,
So soft, so calm, yet eloquent,
The smiles that win, the tints that glow,
But tell of days in goodness spent,
A mind at peace with all below,
A heart whose love is innocent!

THINKING ABOUT THE SELECTION

Recalling

1. In "She Walks in Beauty," to what does the speaker of the poem compare the lady's beauty?
2. What color is the lady's hair?

Interpreting

3. What do you think is the meaning of "that tender light" in line 5?
4. What does the speaker believe the woman's appearance reveals about her character?

Applying

5. (a) Why was nature a logical choice for Byron as something with which to compare a lady's beauty? (b) Why would it be a logical choice for any comparison by Byron?

Answers

ANSWERS TO THINKING ABOUT THE SELECTION

Recalling

1. The speaker compares the lady's beauty to a starry night.
2. Her hair is black.

Interpreting

3. "Tender light" refers to the lady's fair complexion.
4. Her appearance suggests a character imbued with peace and innocent love.

Applying

5. Suggested Responses: (a) Putting aside Byron's place among Romantic poets, nature was a logical choice for Byron's comparison because nature offers various images of beauty. (b) It would be logical because Byron, living in the great age of nature poetry, would naturally have been predisposed to look to nature for figurative comparisons.

So We'll Go No More A-Roving

George Gordon, Lord Byron

This poem was included in a letter to Thomas Moore, written from Venice on February 28, 1817. Carnival season had just passed and Byron, at the age of twenty-nine, found himself in a prolonged period of reflection. The poem is based on the refrain of the Scottish song, "The Jolly Beggar."

So we'll go no more a-roving
    So late into the night,
Though the heart be still as loving,
    And the moon be still as bright.

1 For the sword outwears its sheath,
    And the soul wears out the breast,
And the heart must pause to breathe,
    And Love itself have rest.

Though the night was made for loving,
    And the day returns too soon,
2 Yet we'll go no more a-roving
    By the light of the moon.

THINKING ABOUT THE SELECTION

Recalling

1. What does the speaker say that "Love itself" must have?

Interpreting

2. (a) What do you think is meant by the line "And the soul wears out the breast"? (b) Why must the heart "pause to breathe"?
3. (a) Why will the speaker "go no more a-roving"? (b) How might you summarize in one sentence the speaker's message?

Applying

4. Which properties of the Romantic spirit are evident in this poem?

Master Teacher Note Byron wrote to Moore "I find 'the sword wearing out the scabbard,' though I have but just turned the corner of twenty-nine." You may want to tell **less advanced** students that Byron had been "living it up" wildly in the days preceding the composition of this poem.

Purpose-Setting Question In what sense does the sword outwear the sheath and the soul outwear the breast?

1 **Discussion** What statement does the first stanza make? Stanza two offers an explanation of the statement. What is it?

2 **Discussion** Although the poem has a rhythm that suggests dancing and, perhaps, singing, what tone does it convey?

Challenge Would you consider this a young man's poem? Why, or why not?

Answers

ANSWERS TO THINKING ABOUT THE SELECTION

Recalling

1. "Love itself" must have rest.

Interpreting

2. Suggested Responses: (a) "The soul wears out the breast" suggests that the physical being, or body, is not as strong as the spirit, or desire. (b) there is a time—a need—in life to reflect on one's actions.
3. (a) The speaker will "go no more a-rowing" because the active time of his life has passed, and a time of reflection is at hand. (b) Suggested Response: There is an appropriate time for everything in life.

Applying

4. Properties of the Romantic spirit found in the poem include simple language, an interest in common people, free use of one's imagination, and a subjective point of view towards one's subject.

Motivation for Reading Have students imagine they are face to face with the aspect of nature that impresses them most. What thoughts and impressions would they have? How might they try to express those feelings?

Purpose-Setting Question What view of the ocean does Byron present?

1 **Enrichment** In 1809–11 Byron made a grand tour of Greece, Turkey, and Albania, following which he published a travel poem of his experiences. When the public learned that Byron himself was the hero of *Childe Harold's Pilgrimage,* he quickly became the most talked about and sought after poet of his day. In his own words Byron said, "I awoke one morning and found myself famous."

2 **Master Teacher Note** Students should be aware that apostrophe is a literary device by which a writer addresses an absent person, place, or thing, or an inanimate object as if it could hear the writer's words. Refer to Shelley's "A Dirge," on page 00, which includes the lines "Rough wind, that moanest loud/Grief too sad for song," and to Burns's "Afton Water," on page 000, which includes the lines "Flow gently, sweet Afton! among thy green braes."

3 **Discussion** What paradoxical qualities of the ocean are introduced in the first stanza? Explain how line 5 is an expression of the Romantic spirit.

4 **Discussion** Line 10 is one of Byron's most quoted lines. Why do you think it is?

5 **Discussion** Who is the "he" referred to in line 17? Who is the "thy"?

1 *from* Childe Harold's Pilgrimage

2 Apostrophe to the Ocean

George Gordon, Lord Byron

There is a pleasure in the pathless woods,
There is a rapture on the lonely shore,
There is society, where none intrudes,
By the deep sea, and music in its roar;
3 I love not man the less, but nature more,
From these our interviews, in which I steal
From all I may be, or have been before,
To mingle with the universe, and feel
What I can ne'er express, yet cannot all conceal.

4 Roll on, thou deep and dark blue ocean—roll!
Ten thousand fleets sweep over thee in vain;
Man marks the earth with ruin—his control
Stops with the shore; upon the watery plain
The wrecks are all thy deed, nor doth remain
A shadow of man's ravage, save[1] his own,
When, for a moment, like a drop of rain,
5 He sinks into thy depths with bubbling groan,
Without a grave, unknelled, uncoffined, and unknown.

His steps are not upon thy paths—thy fields
Are not a spoil for him—thou dost arise
And shake him from thee; the vile strength he wields
For earth's destruction thou dost all despise,
Spurning him from thy bosom to the skies,
And send'st him, shivering in thy playful spray
And howling, to his gods, where haply[2] lies
His petty hope in some near port or bay,
And dashest him again to earth—there let him lay.[3]

1. **save:** Except.
2. **haply:** Perhaps.
3. **lay:** A note on Byron's proof suggests that he intentionally made this grammatical error for the sake of the rhyme.

SHIPWRECK
J.C.C. Dahl
Munich Neue Pinakothek/Kavaler

The armaments which thunderstrike the walls
Of rock-built cities, bidding nations quake,
And monarchs tremble in their capitals,
The oak leviathans,[4] whose huge ribs make
Their clay creator[5] the vain title take
Of lord of thee, and arbiter of war—
These are thy toys, and, as the snowy flake,
They melt into thy yeast of waves, which mar
Alike the Armada's[6] pride or spoils of Trafalgar.[7] 6

Thy shores are empires, changed in all save thee—
Assyria, Greece, Rome, Carthage, what are they?
Thy waters washed them power while they were free,
And many a tyrant since; their shores obey

---

4. leviathans (lə vī′ ə thənz): Monstrous sea creatures, described in the Old Testament. Here the word means giant ships.
5. clay creator: Human beings.
6. Armada's: Refers to the Spanish Armada, defeated by the English in 1588.
7. Trafalgar: The battle in 1805 during which the French and Spanish fleets were defeated by the British fleet led by Lord Nelson.

Humanities Note

Fine art: *The Shipwreck,* J.C.C. Dahl. Johann Christian Clausen Dahl (1788-1857) was a Norwegian naturalist painter. In the principles of naturalism, an offshoot of Romanticism, a landscape should not simply mimic nature but should endeavor to convey a deeper meaning. Dahl traveled extensively throughout Europe continually learning and pursuing his art. His ceaseless observation of nautre prepared him to paint the masterly studies of it that make his art so noteworthy.

The fierce elemental forces of nature were a point of ceaseless fascination for J.C.C. Dahl. Although the subject of *The Shipwreck* is a typical romantic theme, Dahl gives it added dimension through his treatment of the sea and sky. A master of portraying the essence of scenes of nature, Dahl imbued this scene with a sense of immediacy and drama.

You might wish to ask students the following questions:

1. Byron speaks of the sea with "music in its roar." Do you think the artist has succeeded in visually communicating the sound of the ocean? Explain.
2. The poet is expressing his feelings about the ocean in this poem; in this painting, the artist, too, expresses his feelings about the ocean. How do you think the artist feels about the ocean?

6 **Enrichment** In 1588 storms destroyed more than half the Spanish Armada. In 1805 a similar fate met the French ships. Each date marks one of England's greatest sea victories.

7 **Discussion** What characteristic of the ocean is described in lines 44–45?

8 **Discussion** Throughout the poem, the speaker creates an image of the ocean as all powerful and relentless. Yet in the last stanza he expresses great love and delight in the ocean. Why is this not surprising?

Master Teacher Note After reading Byron's "Apostrophe to the Ocean," you might wish to place Art Transparency 8, Henry Moore's *Arran,* on your overhead projector. Arran is an island in the Firth of Clyde, in southwest Scotland. Ask your students to examine how Moore has depicted the water. What impression was he trying to convey? How well has he succeeded? Compare this painting with Byron's poem. What do you think Byron's intention was? How does it compare with Moore's?

The stranger, slave, or savage; their decay
Has dried up realms to deserts—not so thou,
Unchangeable, save to thy wild waves' play.
7 Time writes no wrinkle on thine azure brow;
Such as creation's dawn beheld, thou rollest now.

Thou glorious mirror, where the Almighty's form
Glasses[8] itself in tempests; in all time,
Calm or convulsed—in breeze, or gale, or storm,
Icing the pole, or in the torrid clime
Dark-heaving—boundless, endless, and sublime;
The image of eternity, the throne
Of the Invisible; even from out thy slime
The monsters of the deep are made; each zone
Obeys thee; thou goest forth, dread, fathomless, alone.

8 And I have loved thee, ocean! and my joy
Of youthful sports was on thy breast to be
Borne, like thy bubbles, onward; from a boy
I wantoned with thy breakers—they to me
Were a delight; and if the freshening sea
Made them a terror—'twas a pleasing fear,
For I was as it were a child of thee,
And trusted to thy billows far and near,
And laid my hand upon thy mane—as I do here.

8. **glasses:** Mirrors.

THINKING ABOUT THE SELECTION

Recalling

1. How does the speaker of the poem say the ocean makes him feel?
2. How does he say the ocean treats such things as warships and sea monsters?
3. What childhood memories of the ocean does the speaker have?

Interpreting

4. In line 10, the speaker describes the movement of ships over the ocean as "in vain." What might he mean by this?
5. What property of the ocean does the speaker admire in the fifth stanza?
6. What double meaning might the speaker have intended in his reference to the ocean as a glorious mirror in line 46?

Applying

7. Do you believe it is still true today that humans control of the planet "stops with the shore," as Byron puts it in "Apostrophe to the Ocean"? Explain.

ANALYZING LITERATURE

Understanding Figurative Language

Figurative language is language that links, in one way or another, things or ideas that are generally unrelated. Also known as figures of speech, figurative language is actually a category heading for a number of literary devices. Simile, among the best known of these, is a comparison using a word such as like or as. The line "the sheen of their spears was like stars on the sea" contains a simile.

Metaphor, often thought of as a companion to the simile, compares two objects without making use of a linking word. The line "The moon was a ghostly galleon tossed upon cloudy seas" contains a metaphor.

A third device, personification, gives human characteristics to nonhuman subjects. The line "The moon peeked out from behind a cloud" contains an example of personification.

Identify the type of figurative language in each quotation, and express in your own words what it adds to the poem.

1. She walks in beauty, like the night . . . (p. 682)
2. . . . the heart must pause to breathe . . . (p. 683)
3. . . . like a drop of rain,/He sinks into thy depths . . . (p. 684)
4. These are thy toys, and, as the snowy flake,/ They melt into the yeast of waves . . . (p. 685)
5. Thou glorious mirror, where the Almighty's form/Glasses itself . . . (p. 686)

THINKING AND WRITING

Evaluating a Poem

When you read a review of a film or book in a newspaper, you are reading an evaluation. Write an evaluation of one of the three poems by Byron. First jot down ideas about this poem. Then write your first draft. Mention such things as language, style, and subject matter, and conclude with your personal reactions to the piece, giving conclusive reasons for why you feel as you do. When you revise make sure that your arguments are sound. Proofread your essay and prepare a final draft.

Writing Across the Curriculum
Ask students to find passages from a science book describing the ocean, or one phase of it, such as storms or tides. Science teachers might suggest sources. Have students contrast the scientific approach to describing the ocean to the poet's.

Answers

ANSWERS TO THINKING ABOUT THE SELECTION

Recalling

1. The ocean fills the speaker with emotion to the point that he cannot express himself.
2. The ocean treats warships and sea monsters with disdain.
3. He remembers the ocean as a wonderful, if at times terror-filled, place to swim and play.

Interpreting

4. No matter how important the fleets of warships are to men, they cannot challenge the ocean nor can they damage it.
5. The speaker admires the ocean's being unchangeable.
6. The poet may be using the term *mirror* in the sense of "reflecting" and also in the sense of a reflection of life as a whole.

Applying

7. Answers will differ but should include ideas about recent, and not so recent, attempts to control the sea, as in Holland, through the use of elaborate dykes, as in dredging harbor inlets, and as in experiments with "farming" the sea for minerals.

ANSWERS TO ANALYZING LITERATURE

1. This image is a simile.
2. This image personifies the heart.
3. This image is a simile.
4. The images here are metaphors and a simile.
5. The image is a metaphor.

Answers about the effect of each type of figurative language will differ but should include the idea that figurative language makes any work more interesting and vivid, as well as easier to understand.

Thinking and Writing

For help with this assignment, students can refer to Lesson 15, "Evaluating a Literary Work," in the Handbook of Writing About Literature.

Look for Your **less advanced** students to have trouble grasping the concept of mock epic. Consider reviewing the mock epic poetry of Alexander Pope (pages 560-570) before beginning the study of this poem.

Writing Pick one of these activities, and ask students to suggest pompous and inflated descriptions that might apply to it. For example, walking a dog could be described as "perambulating with my pooch."

Literary Focus *Don Juan* (pronounced Jo͞o ən) was begun in July of 1818, and Byron worked on it almost until his death, in 1824. He had read the Italian seriocomic versions of medieval chivalric romances, and from them learned how to manage the ottava-rima stanza, with its *ababab* rhyme scheme. He also learned how effective an alternation of sublimity and ridiculousness could be in a mock epic.

Vocabulary Although the vocabulary in the excerpt is not especially difficult, you may want to list on the board and define some of the other words that **less advanced** students may have difficulty with.

GUIDE FOR READING

from Don Juan

Literary Forms

Mock Epic. A mock epic is a long poem that mocks, or pokes fun at, a trivial subject by treating it in the grand style of epic poetry. The epic poem, which found its loftiest expression in such timeless works as The *Iliad,* the *Odyssey,* and *Paradise Lost,* was defined not only by its style but also by certain regular features. The poem usually began, for example, with an *invocation,* or request for inspiration and guidance from a muse or deity, and it was usually divided into long sections called *cantos* or books. In addition, the epic generally contained lengthy and carefully worded speeches by heroes, and included descriptions of battles fought by noble warriors. In a mock epic, this combination of ingredients—a lofty style and a base subject—leads to humorous results. When, for example, the romantic adventures of a beautiful young man are narrated in a grand fashion, as is the case in Don Juan, the end product is hilarious.

Look For

As you read the excerpt from *Don Juan,* look for ways in which this mock epic satirizes the aging poet who narrates this poem.

Writing

Think of an activity that is especially trivial or commonplace, such as walking a dog or going to the supermarket for groceries. Now think of several adjectives that might be used—or *misused*—to describe this activity in an heroic manner. Finally, write a "mini-mock epic" that paints a lofty picture of this routine task.

Vocabulary

Knowing the following words will help you as you read the excerpt from *Don Juan.*

retort (ri tôrt′) *n.*: Come back with a smart answer or wisecrack (p. 707)

credulous (krej′ o͞o ləs) *adj.*: Willing to believe (p. 708)

copious (kō′ pē əs) *adj.*: Abundant, plentiful (p. 708)

avarice (av′ ər is) *n.*: Greed (p. 708)

Objective

1 To write about the Byronic hero

Teaching Portfolio: Support Material

Lesson plan, pp. 00-00

Vocabulary Check, p. 00

Usage and Mechanics Worksheet, p. 00

Analyzing Literature Worksheet, p. 00

Critical Thinking and Reading Worksheet, p. 00

Understanding Language Worksheet, p. 00

Selection Test, p. 00

from Don Juan

George Gordon, Lord Byron

Though it is unfinished, Don Juan *is generally regarded as Byron's finest work. The long poem, a mock epic that was described by Shelley as being "something wholly new and relative to the age," satirizes the political and social problems of Byron's time.*

Traditionally the character of Don Juan, the poem's hero, had been portrayed as being a wicked and immoral man driven solely by his obsession with beautiful women. In Byron's work Don Juan is depicted as an innocent young man whose physical beauty, charm, and spirit prove to be extremely alluring for ladies, leading him into many difficult situations.

Many people feel that what makes Don Juan *such a great poem are the lapses in the story, during which the speaker drifts away from the subject. During these lapses the speaker comments on the issues of the time and on life in general. In this excerpt the speaker abandons his hero to reflect on old age and death.*

But now at thirty years my hair is gray
    (I wonder what it will be like at forty?
I thought of a peruke[1] the other day)—
    My heart is not much greener; and, in short, I
Have squandered my whole summer while 'twas May,
    And feel no more the spirit to retort; I
Have spent my life, both interest and principal,
And deem not, what I deemed, my soul invincible. 1, 2

No more—no more—Oh! never more on me
    The freshness of the heart can fall like dew,
Which out of all the lovely things we see
    Extracts emotions beautiful and new,
Hived in our bosoms like the bag o' the bee: 3
    Think'st thou the honey with those objects grew?
Alas! 'twas not in them, but in thy power
To double even the sweetness of a flower.

No more—no more—Oh! never more, my heart,
    Canst thou be my sole world, my universe!

1. **peruke** (pə ro͞ok'): Wig.

Motivation for Reading Ask your students to tell how it might feel to think that the best of life is already in the past and the future promises very little that seems to matter.

Master Teacher Note Consider introducing the poem by reading Herrick's "To the Virgins . . .," on page 454, to awaken students to the notion of youth as something that quickly passes.

Purpose-Setting Question What evidence do you see that Byron is poking fun at his subject?

1 **Enrichment** *Don Juan* is written in ottava rima, an Italian stanza form of eight iambic pentameter lines with a rhyme scheme of *abababcc.*

2 **Discussion** Explain the aptness of the word *greener* in line 4. What does the color green often symbolize? As a symbol of a stage of life, what would its opposite color be?

3 **Literary Focus** Note the simile in line 13. What is being compared to what?

4 **Enrichment** Stanzas three and four represent Byron's version of Wordsworth's famous "Ode: Intimations of Immortality. . . ." In lines 22–23 what does the poet tell us has replaced frivolous emotions?

5 **Discussion** How did the poet manage to lose his ambition?

6 **Discussion** According to the poet, what is the end of fame? Do you agree with his view?

7 **Thematic Idea** Compare the allusion to Cheops with Shelley's poem "Ozymandias," on page 712.

Once all in all, but now a thing apart,
    Thou canst not be my blessing or my curse:
The illusion's gone forever, and thou art
    Insensible, I trust, but none the worse,
And in thy stead I've got a deal of judgment,
Though heaven knows how it ever found a lodgment.

4 My days of love are over; me no more
    The charms of maid, wife, and still less of widow
Can make the fool of which they made before—
    In short, I must not lead the life I did do;
The credulous hope of mutual minds is o'er,
    The copious use of claret is forbid too,
So for a good old-gentlemanly vice,
I think I must take up with avarice.

5 Ambition was my idol, which was broken
    Before the shrines of Sorrow and of Pleasure;
And the two last have left me many a token
    O'er which reflection may be made at leisure:
Now, like Friar Bacon's brazen head, I've spoken,
    "Time is, Time was, Time's past,"[2] a chymic[3] treasure
Is glittering youth, which I have spent betimes—
My heart in passion, and my head on rhymes.

6 What is the end of fame? 'tis but to fill
    A certain portion of uncertain paper:
Some liken it to climbing up a hill,
    Whose summit, like all hills, is lost in vapor;
For this men write, speak, preach, and heroes kill,
    And bards burn what they call their "midnight taper,"
To have, when the original is dust,
A name, a wretched picture, and worse bust.

7 What are the hopes of man? Old Egypt's King
    Cheops erected the first pyramid
And largest, thinking it was just the thing
    To keep his memory whole, and mummy hid:
But somebody or other rummaging
    Burglariously broke his coffin's lid:
Let not a monument give you or me hopes,
Since not a pinch of dust remains of Cheops.

---

2. Friar Bacon . . . Time's past": In Robert Greene's comedy *Friar Bacon and Friar Burgandy* (1594), these words are spoken by a bronze bust, made by Friar Bacon.
3. chymic (kim′ ik): Alchemic; counterfeit.

But I, being fond of true philosophy,
Say very often to myself, "Alas!
All things that have been born were born to die,
And flesh (which Death mows down to hay) is grass; 8
You've passed your youth not so unpleasantly,
And if you had it o'er again—'twould pass—
So thank your stars that matters are no worse,
And read your Bible, sir, and mind your purse."

But for the present, gentle reader! and
Still gentler purchaser! the bard—that's I—
Must, with permission, shake you by the hand,
And so your humble servant, and good-bye!
We meet again, if we should understand
Each other; and if not, I shall not try
Your patience further than by this short sample—
'Twere well if others followed my example.

"Go, little book, from this my solitude!
I cast thee on the waters—go thy ways!
And if, as I believe, thy vein be good,
The world will find thee after many days."[4]
When Southey's read, and Wordsworth understood,
I can't help putting in my claim to praise—
The four first rhymes are Southey's, every line:
For God's sake, reader! take them not for mine!

4. "Go . . . days": The lines are from the last stanza of Robert Southey's (1774–1843) *Epilogue to the Lay of the Laureate.*

THINKING ABOUT THE SELECTION

Recalling

1. What causes the speaker to think of a peruke?
2. (a) What does the speaker say has been his "sole world" and "universe" up until now? (b) With what "old-gentlemanly vice" will he replace it?

Interpreting

3. In the fifth stanza, the speaker notes that youth is a "chymic," or counterfeit, "treasure." In what way do you think he means this?
4. Summarize in your own words the point the speaker is making in his mention of Cheops.
5. What do you think is meant by the remark "flesh . . . is grass" in line 60?

THINKING AND WRITING

Writing about the Byronic Hero

As a young man Byron saw himself—and was eager for others to see him—as melancholy, sensitive, opposed to order, fearless, given to mood swings, and hungry for new adventures. This list of traits, which the poet applied to many of the heroes he created, came to be identified as those of the "Byronic hero." Think of main characters you have read about in other works of fiction, and choose one that comes close to fitting this description. In a brief essay, explain in what ways this character is, and is not, a Byronic hero. When you revise make sure you have provided adequate support for your main idea.

8 **Discussion** Describe the tone in this stanza.

Answers

ANSWERS TO THINKING ABOUT THE SELECTION

Recalling

1. Growing older makes the speaker think of growing bald, and so the need for a wig.
2. (a) His heart—his passion—has been his whole world—his universe. (b) He will take up avarice.
3. As metaphors of fame the poet chooses a biographical account on the page of a book or other publication. and climbing a hill whose crest is obscured.

Interpreting

4. Answers will differ but might include the idea that youth is full of dreams and misdirected ambitions or that it quickly passes.
5. Answers will differ but should include the idea that nothing man builds does, or hopes for remains long after he has died.
6. Flesh, like grass, will be cut down in death.

Applying

7. (a) Answers will differ. (b) Answers will differ.

Thinking and Writing

For help with this assignment, students can refer to Lesson 9, "Writing About Character," in the Handbook of Writing About Literature.

More About the Author Percy Bysshe Shelley was not appreciated for his poetry during his lifetime. At his death, most of his volumes of poetry remained unsold. Yet William Wordsworth, a contemporary, called Shelley "one of the best artists of us all: I mean in workmanship and style." Ask students to consider why such a great artist might not be appreciated until after his death. Can they think of other examples of poets and other artists who did not achieve fame until after their deaths?

PERCY BYSSHE SHELLEY

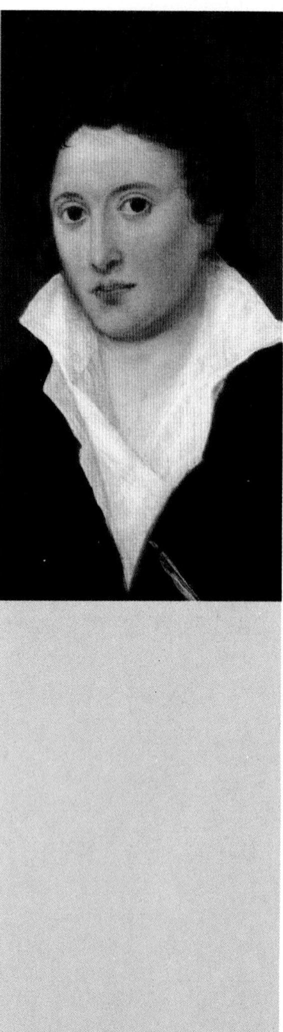

1792–1822

When he died in a boating accident at age thirty, Percy Bysshe Shelley was eulogized by his friend Byron as "without exception the best and least selfish man I ever knew." This seems strange praise indeed, considering it was directed at a man whose disenchantment with the world was at least as great as his appreciation of its beauties. At once modest and intense, Shelley was a poet of rare gift. He was also a self-appointed reformer who believed that humankind was capable of attaining a more perfect society.

Shelley was born in Sussex and raised on a fine country estate where he spent a quiet childhood. He was sent to excellent schools—first Eton, a prestigious boarding school, and later Oxford—but was never able to settle into the routine of a student. Instead he preferred to wander over the countryside or perform private scientific experiments. At Oxford Shelley became friends with a young man named Thomas Jefferson Hogg, whose political views were as strong as his own. The friendship further fueled Shelley's rebellious nature, and when with Hogg's support he wrote a pamphlet titled *The Necessity of Atheism;* both were expelled.

The incident led to trouble between Shelley and his father, and instead of going home Shelley headed for London. There he met sixteen-year-old Harriet Westbrook, who played on his sympathy for the underdog by describing her miserable situation at home and at school. The two married and went to Ireland, where Shelley tried unsuccessfully to "deliver the Irish people from tyranny."

In 1813 he completed his first important poem, "Queen Mab," a philosophical work that explored some of the ideas he had read about in Godwin's *Political Justice.* The view that Shelley put forth—that government and institutions should be reshaped to better conform to the will of the people—was evident in much of his poetry, even in his nature poems.

Shelley's marriage, meanwhile, was in trouble. Harriet felt she could not keep up with her husband, whose political ideals, in any case, she had come to question. Shelley was unhappy too, and after divorcing Harriet in 1814 he married Mary Wollstonecraft Godwin.

Shelley spent the last four years of his life in Italy, where he became close friends with Byron. Here Shelley wrote some of his best poetry, including "Ode to the West Wind" and "Prometheus Unbound," the second of these a long poem predicting that someday humanity would be free of tyranny.

Shelley has been called the perfect poet of the Romantic era. One need only consider his emotional response to life and his belief in personal freedom to appreciate how fitting that title is.

GUIDE FOR READING

Ozymandias; Ode to the West Wind; To a Skylark; To—; A Dirge

Literary Forms

The Ode. Poetic structure is the framework or blueprint on which a poem is built. The structure takes into account the number of stanzas, the rhyme scheme, and the rhythmic patterns to be used.

An *ode* is a lyrical poem that pays homage to a person, a quality, or a thing. The first odes were written in Classical times by the Greek poet Pindar (552?–443? B.C.) and the Latin poet Horace (65–8 B.C.) The Pindaric ode, which is the more often imitated of the two, consists mainly of three-line stanzas called *triads*. Shelley's "Ode to the West Wind" is a Pindaric ode.

Look For

As you read the next five poems by Shelley, look for elements of style which make the poems interesting and add to your appreciation of them.

Writing

Think of several individuals, objects, and qualities which you hold in high regard. To get yourself started, you might think of people who do important work in your community, and who have such character traits as honesty and reliability. Write each at the top of a sheet of paper and under it jot down some of your thoughts.

Vocabulary

Knowing the following words will help you as you read the next five poems by Shelley.

visage (viz'ij) *n.*: A person's face or facial expression (p. 712, l. 4)
pestilence (pes't'l əns) *n.*: Highly contagious disease, such as plague (p. 714, l. 5)
verge (vʉrj) *n.*: Edge, rim (p. 715, l. 21)
sepulcher (sep''l kər) *n.*: Tomb (p. 715, l. 25)
cleave (klēv) *v.*: Split apart, especially in two (p. 716, l. 38)
despoil (di spoil') *v.*: Take away one's possessions (p. 716, l. 42)
tumult (to͞o'mult) *n.*: Commotion, disturbance (p. 716, l. 59)
impetuous (im pech' o͞o wəs) *adj.*: Tending to act impulsively, without thinking (p. 717, l. 62)
blithe (blīth) *adj.*: Cheerful (p. 718, l. 1)
profuse (prə fyo͞os') *adj.*: Abundant, pouring out (p. 718, l. 5)
vaunt (vônt) *v.*: Speak boastfully (p. 720, l. 69)
languor (laŋ' gər) *n.*: Weakness, fatigue (p. 720, l. 77)
satiety (sə tī'ə tē) *n.*: State of being filled to excess (p. 720, l. 80)
dirge (dʉrj) *n.*: Song of mourning (p. 723, title)

Literary Focus Originally, an ode was a poem meant to be sung. However, in English poetry an ode is a lyric poem with two primary characteristics: a dignified theme and a formal, elevated style.

Look For It may be helpful for your **less advanced** students to review poetic forms and such elements as rhyme, rhythm, and stanzas.

Writing Have students bring to class articles about people who have made admirable achievements. Make a list of those people on the chalkboard, and have students who brought in the articles write their achievements under the names on the board. Students may then proceed to make their own lists.

Vocabulary Give students ten minutes to study the vocabulary words as you write the words on the chalkboard. Give a quiz in which you supply the definition and students choose the word being defined from among the words on the board. Your **less advanced** students may need help with these additional words: *colossal* (page 712), *azure* (page 714), and *unpremeditated* (page 718).

Objectives

1. To understand the poetic structure of a poem
2. To understand the ode
3. To recognize an author's style
4. To write an ode
5. To compare and contrast views of nature

Teaching Portfolio: Support Material

Teacher Backup, p. 000

Vocabulary Check, p. 00

Usage and Mechanics Worksheet, p. 00

Analyzing Literature Worksheet, p. 00

Critical Thinking and Reading Worksheet, p. 00

Language Worksheet, p. 00

Selection Test, p. 000

Motivation for Reading Ask students to review the term *irony,* a contrast between an expected outcome and the actual outcome or between appearance and reality. Then ask if they think the term applies to Shelley's life. For example, Shelley died unexpectedly at a very young age, before his work received recognition. Ask if they can think of any examples of irony in their own lives. Tell them that irony is an important device in the poem "Ozymandias."

Master Teacher Note In conjunction with this poem you may want to teach the poem "Ozymandias Revisited," a parody by Morris Bishop.

Purpose-Setting Question What generalization about grand human achievements might a reader draw from this poem?

1 **Enrichment** Ozymandias was a pharoah who ruled Egypt during the thirteenth century B.C. He was known for his extensive building programs and as the pharoah who oppressed the Israelites. He was responsible for the largest statue in Egypt, on which were carved the words: "I am Ozymandias, king of kings; if anyone wishes to know what I am and where I lie, let him surpass me in some of my exploits."

Speaking and Listening Remind students that poetry is meant to be read aloud. Choose a volunteer to read "Ozymandias" aloud to the class.

1 # Ozymandias[1]

Percy Bysshe Shelley

I met a traveler from an antique land
Who said: Two vast and trunkless legs of stone
Stand in the desert. Near them, on the sand,
Half sunk, a shattered visage lies, whose frown,
And wrinkled lip, and sneer of cold command,
Tell that its sculptor well those passions read
Which yet survive, stamped on these lifeless things,
The hand that mocked them and the heart that fed:
And on the pedestal these words appear:
"My name is Ozymandias, king of kings:
Look on my works, ye Mighty, and despair!"
Nothing beside remains. Round the decay
Of that colossal wreck, boundless and bare,
The lone and level sands stretch far away.

---

1. Ozymandias (ōz ī män′ dē əs): The Greek name for Ramses. Ramses II, the king referred to in the poem, was a pharoah who ruled Egypt during the thirteenth century B.C. and built many great palaces and statues. One statue was inscribed with the words: "I am Ozymandias, king of kings, if anyone wishes to know what I am and where I lie, let him surpass me in some of my exploits."

THINKING ABOUT THE SELECTION

Recalling

1. (a) Whom has the speaker met? (b) What sight does this person describe?

Interpreting

2. What sort of person is suggested by the visage that is described?
3. Think of the words on the pedestal. (a) Why is it ironic that the statue has crumbled? (b) Why is it ironic that it is surrounded by desert?
4. What is the theme of this poem?

Applying

5. (a) What is your definition of power? (b) What is your definition of pride? (c) In what way do the two complement each other?

ANALYZING LITERATURE

Understanding Poetic Structure

The poetic structure of a poem is the plan on which it is built. Poetic structure includes such elements as rhyme, rhythm, and number of stanzas. Analyze the poetic structure of "Ozymandias." State whether or not you feel this structure enhances the poem's message. When you revise make sure you have provided adequate support for your main idea.

Answers

ANSWERS TO THINKING ABOUT THE SELECTION

Recalling

1. (a) The speaker met a traveler from an antique (ancient) land. (b) In the desert are the crumbling remains of a statue of the Egyptian pharaoh Ozymandias.

Interpreting

2. The person suggested is cold, cruel, and conceited.
3. (a) It is ironic that the statue of a ruler who claimed great works is now surrounded by emptiness. (b) This is another irony; the crumbling statue mocks the pride of the once great ruler.
4. Answers will differ. Suggestions include "How the mighty have fallen," Don't get too big for your britches," and "A man's pride shall bring him low."

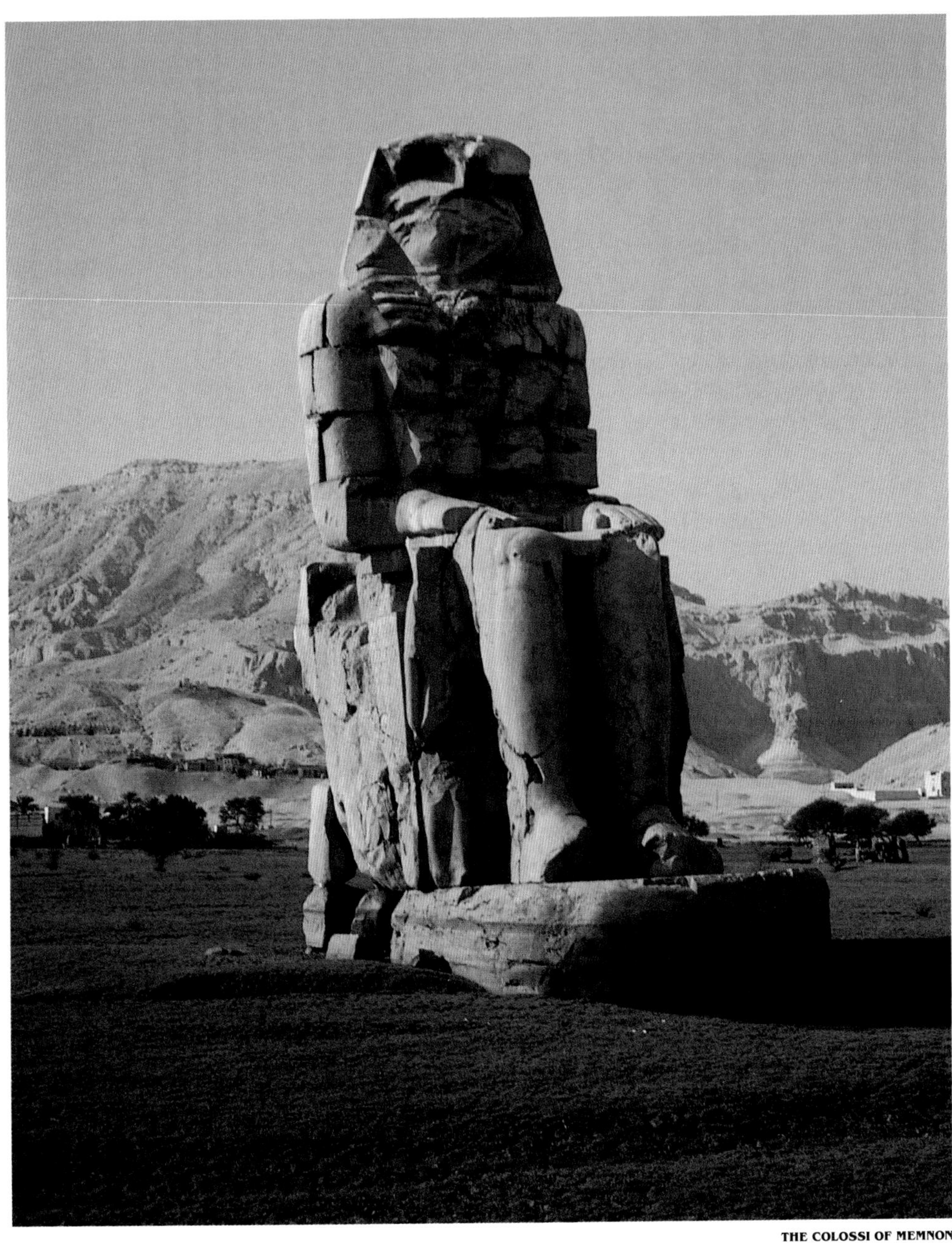

THE COLOSSI OF MEMNON
Diane Rawson
Photo Researchers

Applying

5. Answers will differ. Suggested responses: (a) Power is authority. (b) Pride is a sense of one's self respect. (c) Power and pride in proper proportions can balance each other.

ANSWERS TO ANALYZING LITERATURE

"Ozymandias" is a sonnet. Its fourteen lines, written in iambic pentameter, are divided into two parts in which the first eight lines, the octave, describe the statue of Ozymandias, and the last six lines, the sestet, bring out the irony implicit in the wreckage. It was appropriate for Shelley to choose this traditional structure, since it helps to emphasize his message—the first part of the poem strikes the reader with the image of the ruined statue, while the second part reinforces the irony of the statue's condition. The sonnet format presents a challenge to a poet. Shelley more than met the challenge by incorporating an unconventional—and difficult—rhyme scheme. Perhaps he wanted to show that he could in fact surpass Ozymandias in his exploits by creating a great work of art that, unlike the statue, would last forever.

Challenge Tell why you think that this poem should or should not be considered a Romantic poem.

Literary Focus Point out that the entire ode is in the form of an apostrophe—an address to an inanimate object as if it could reply. Each of the first three sections, it should be pointed out, has a single main clause, "oh, hear." In the last two sections the poet expresses what he wants the west wind to hear.

Motivation for Reading Discuss the Romantic idea of nature's power. Ask students why Shelley would choose to write an ode to the west wind. What is it about the west wind that he would admire?

Master Teacher Note You may want to review personification—a metaphor in which an inanimate object, an animal, or an abstraction is compared to a person and given human characteristics. Point out that Shelley uses personification as well as apostrophe throughout the poem. You may also wish to point out that Shelley's verse form in "Ode to the West Wind" is a modification of terza rima, a three-line stanza form rhyming *aba bcb cdc,* etc. Dante's "Divine Comedy" is also written in this verse form. Shelley's modification is to conclude each section with a couplet.

Purpose-Setting Question As you read the poem, consider how its structure and rhyme scheme enhance its meaning.

1 **Discussion** How are the first three sections of the poem tied together?

Ode to the West Wind

Percy Bysshe Shelley

Shelley composed this poem in the woods near Florence, Italy. He described the day of its composition as one "when that tempestuous wind, whose temperature is at once mild and animating, was collecting the vapors which pour down the autumnal rains."

I

O wild West Wind, thou breath of Autumn's being,
Thou, from whose unseen presence the leaves dead
Are driven, like ghosts from an enchanter fleeing,

Yellow, and black, and pale, and hectic red,
Pestilence-stricken multitudes: O thou,
Who chariotest to their dark and wintry bed

The wingèd seeds, where they lie cold and low,
Each like a corpse within its grave, until
Thine azure sister of the Spring[1] shall blow

Her clarion[2] o'er the dreaming earth, and fill
1 (Driving sweet buds like flocks to feed in air)
With loving hues and odors plain and hill:

Wild Spirit, which art moving everywhere;
Destroyer and preserver; hear, oh, hear!

II

Thou on whose stream, 'mid the steep sky's commotion,
Loose clouds like earth's decaying leaves are shed,
Shook from the tangled boughs of Heaven and Ocean,

Angels[3] of rain and lightning: there are spread
On the blue surface of thine aery surge,
Like the bright hair uplifted from the head

---

1. **sister of Spring:** The south wind.
2. **clarion:** *n.*: A trumpet producing clear, sharp, shrill tones.
3. **angels:** Messengers.

CIRRUS CLOUD STUDY
John Constable
Victoria & Albert Museum, Trustees

Of some fierce Maenad,[4] even from the dim verge
Of the horizon to the zenith's height,
The locks of the approaching storm. Thou dirge

Of the dying year, to which this closing night
Will be the dome of a vast sepulcher,
Vaulted with all thy congregated might

Of vapors, from whose solid atmosphere
Black rain, and fire, and hail will burst: oh, hear!

III

Thou who didst waken from his summer dreams
The blue Mediterranean, where he lay,
Lulled by the coil of his crystalline streams,

---

4. Maenad (mē′ nad): A priestess of Bacchus, the Greek and Roman god of wine and revelry.

Humanities Note

Fine art, *Cirrus Cloud Study*, 1882, by John Constable. England's John Constable (1776–1937) is one of that country's most notable landscape painters. His paintings differed from those of his contemporaries in their fresh, vibrant use of color and in their close observance of nature. A lover of the outdoors, Constable was ever conscious of the effects of light, weather, and season upon the landscape.

Cirrus Cloud Study was painted in 1822. He felt that as the sky was a large and important part of a landscape painting, it was very important to paint it realistically and effectively. Studies such as this caught the effects of light, cloud, wind, and sky with consummate mastery.

You might ask the following questions:

1. The wind is an invisible force; we can only see its effect. How has the artist allowed us to "see" the wind in this painting?
2. What do you think are the artist's feelings about the wind?

2 Discussion How do the last two sections differ from the first three? What function do they serve?

3 Discussion Does the poem end on an optimistic or a pessimistic note? Explain.

Beside a pumice[5] aisle in Baiae's bay,[6]
And saw in sleep old palaces and towers
Quivering within the wave's intenser day,

All overgrown with azure moss and flowers
So sweet, the sense faints picturing them! Thou
For whose path the Atlantic's level powers

Cleave themselves into chasms, while far below
The sea-blooms and the oozy woods which wear
The sapless foliage of the ocean, know

Thy voice, and suddenly grow gray with fear,
And tremble and despoil themselves: oh, hear!

IV

If I were a dead leaf thou mightest bear;
If I were a swift cloud to fly with thee;
A wave to pant beneath thy power, and share

The impulse of thy strength, only less free
Than thou, O uncontrollable! If even
I were as in my boyhood, and could be

The comrade of thy wanderings over Heaven,
As then, when to outstrip thy skyey speed
Scarce seemed a vision; I would ne'er have striven

As thus with thee in prayer in my sore need.
Oh, lift me as a wave, a leaf, a cloud!
2, 3 I fall upon the thorns of life! I bleed!

A heavy weight of hours has chained and bowed
One too like thee: tameless, and swift, and proud.

V

Make me thy lyre,[7] even as the forest is:
What if my leaves are falling like its own!
The tumult of thy mighty harmonies

---

5. pumice (pum′ is) *n.*: Volcanic rock.
6. Baiae's (bā′ yēz) **bay:** An ancient Roman resort near Naples.
7. lyre: Aeolian (ē o′ lē ən) lute, or wind harp, a stringed instrument which produces musical sounds when the wind passes over it.

Will take from both a deep, autumnal tone,
Sweet though in sadness. Be thou, Spirit fierce,
My spirit! Be thou me, impetuous one!

Drive my dead thought over the universe
Like withered leaves to quicken a new birth!
And, by the incantation of this verse,

Scatter, as from an extinguished hearth
Ashes and sparks, my words among mankind!
Be through my lips to unawakened earth

The trumpet of a prophecy! O Wind,
If Winter comes, can Spring be far behind?

THINKING ABOUT THE SELECTION

Recalling

1. According to the poem, with what season is the west wind associated?
2. (a) What does the wind do to dead leaves? (b) What does it do to the ocean?
3. What does the speaker ask of the wind in section V of the poem?

Interpreting

4. In what sense is the wind a "destroyer and preserver"?
5. (a) How, according to section IV, has the speaker changed? (b) What caused this change?
6. Whose "new birth" (line 65) do you think the speaker wishes to bring about?
7. (a) Interpret the last line of this poem. (b) How does this famous last line tie the poem together?

Applying

8. In what way is the message in this poem related to Shelley's lifelong mission?

ANALYZING LITERATURE

Understanding the Ode

An ode is a poem that honors an individual, a thing, or a trait. The form dates back to Classical times, when it was written to be sung at a festival or as part of a play. Many features of the Classical ode are to be found in "Ode to the West Wind." Find evidence in Shelley's poem of each of the following properties.

1. Direct form of address to the individual, trait, or thing being honored.
2. An almost fearful reverence for the thing or person being honored.
3. Dignified and lofty language and examples.

Answers

ANSWERS TO THINKING ABOUT THE SELECTION

Recalling

1. The west wind is associated with autumn.
2. (a) The wind drives the dead leaves. (b) It forms waves on the ocean.
3. The speaker asks the wind to scatter his thoughts and words among mankind.

Interpreting

4. The west wind brings winter, which destroys plant life. But it also preserves seeds which come to life in the spring.
5. (a) In section IV the speaker loses some of his awe of the wind and wishes to share its power and freedom. (b) The speaker has experienced the thorns, or pains, of life.
6. The speaker is seeking a new age of freedom for all people.
7. Suggested Response: The west wind brings winter, or death, but after winter spring brings new life. In other words, there is hope that some day people will be free.

Applying

8. Suggested Response: Shelley was against any kind of tyranny; he believed strongly in personal freedom for all people. In this poem Shelley proclaims his faith that there can be a society free from oppression and unjust authority.

Challenge In his essay "A Defense of Poetry," Shelley wrote that "poets are the unacknowledged legislators of the world." How does "Ode to the West Wind" help to explain what Shelley meant?

ANSWERS TO ANALYZING LITERATURE

1. Answers will differ. Suggested response: Shelley addresses the wind directly in the opening line of the poem: "O wild West Wind. . . ."
2. Answers will differ. Suggested response: Shelley calls the wind "O uncontrollable!"
3. Suggested Response: Shelley compares "the locks" of an approaching storm carried on the wind to the "bright hair uplifted from the head/Of some fierce Maenad."

Motivation for Reading Discuss with students what freedom means to them. Ask students to come up with their own symbol for freedom.

Purpose-Setting Question As you read the poem, compare its form with that of "Ode to the West Wind." Consider how the form enhances the poem's message.

Thematic Idea: Compare and contrast the "Ode to the West Wind" (page 714) and "To a Skylark" for what they imply about the individual in relation to society.

1 **Discussion** Why does the speaker say the skylark is not a bird?

To a Skylark

Percy Bysshe Shelley

1 Hail to thee, blithe spirit!
Bird thou never wert,
That from heaven, or near it,
Pourest thy full heart
In profuse strains of unpremeditated art.

Higher still and higher,
From the earth thou springest
Like a cloud of fire;
The blue deep thou wingest,
And singing still dost soar, and soaring ever singest.

In the golden lightning
Of the sunken sun,
O'er which clouds are brightening,
Thou dost float and run;
Like an unbodied joy whose race is just begun.

The pale purple even[1]
Melts around thy flight;
Like a star of heaven,
In the broad daylight
Thou art unseen, but yet I hear thy shrill delight,

Keen as are the arrows
Of that silver sphere,[2]
Whose intense lamp narrows
In the white dawn clear,
Until we hardly see—we feel that it is there.

All the earth and air
With thy voice is loud,
As, when night is bare,
From one lonely cloud
The moon rains out her beams, and Heaven is overflowed.

---

1. even: Evening.
2. silver sphere: The morning star.

CLOUD STUDY, 1821
John Constable
Yale Center for British Art

What thou art we know not;
  What is most like thee?
From rainbow clouds there flow not
  Drops so bright to see,
As from thy presence showers a rain of melody.

Like a poet hidden
  In the light of thought,
Singing hymns unbidden,
  Till the world is wrought
To sympathy with hopes and fears it heeded not:

Like a highborn maiden
  In a palace tower,
Soothing her love-laden 2
  Soul in secret hour
With music sweet as love, which overflows her bower:

Like a glowworm golden
  In a dell of dew,
Scattering unbeholden
  Its aerial hue
Among the flowers and grass, which screen it from the view!

Humanities Note

Fine art, *Sky Study,* 1821, by John Constable. John Constable (1776–1837) is one of Britain's most noteworthy landscape painters. Educated at the Royal Academy, Constable disagreed with some of the artificial academic techniques of painting and sought to paint landscapes with truth and originality. His works were painted outdoors instead of in a studio, and he used bright colors that were closer to nature. He painted the landscape in all lights and seasons, paying close attention to changes brought about by weather conditions.

Sky Study, a study of strato-cumulus cloud formations, was painted in 1821. It is one of a group of small oil sketches that Constable did in order to study the effects of weather, time of day, and time of year on the sky. He carefully noted the weather conditions, time, and date on each study. This intense preparation, which resulted in the painting of this lovely patch of sky, is one of the many reasons John Constable was able to paint such successful landscapes.

You may wish to ask the following questions.

1. Which lines from Shelley's poem do you feel this painting illustrates best?
2. How does the poet's appreciation of nature differ from the painter's?

2 **Discussion** What is the central element of each simile in these stanzas?

Like a rose embowered
In its own green leaves,
By warm winds deflowered,[3]
Till the scent it gives
Makes faint with too much sweet those heavy-wingèd thieves.[4]

Sound of vernal showers
On the twinkling grass,
Rain-awakened flowers,
All that ever was
Joyous, and clear, and fresh, thy music doth surpass:

Teach us, sprite or bird,
What sweet thoughts are thine:
I have never heard
Praise of love or wine
That panted forth a flood of rapture so divine.

Chorus Hymeneal,[5]
Or triumphal chant,
Matched with thine would be all
But an empty vaunt,
A thing wherein we feel there is some hidden want.

What objects are the fountains[6]
Of thy happy strain?
What fields, or waves, or mountains?
What shapes of sky or plain?
What love of thine own kind? what ignorance of pain?

With thy clear keen joyance
Languor cannot be;
Shadow of annoyance
Never came near thee;
Thou lovest—but ne'er knew love's sad satiety.

Waking or asleep,
Thou of death must deem[7]
Things more true and deep
Than we mortals dream,
Or how could thy notes flow in such a crystal stream?

---

3. deflowered: Fully open.
4. thieves: The "warm winds."
5. Chorus Hymeneal (hī′ mə nē′ əl): Marriage song, named after Hymen, the Greek god of marriage.
6. fountains: Sources, inspiration.
7. deem: Know.

We look before and after,
And pine for what is not;
Our sincerest laughter
With some pain is fraught;
Our sweetest songs are those that tell of saddest thought.

Yet if[8] we could scorn
Hate, and pride, and fear;
If we were things born
Not to shed a tear,
I know not how thy joy we ever should come near. 3

Better than all measures
Of delightful sound,
Better than all treasures
That in books are found,
Thy skill to poet were,[9] thou scorner of the ground!

Teach me half the gladness
That thy brain must know,
Such harmonious madness
From my lips would flow,
The world should listen then, as I am listening now.

8. if: Even if.
9. were: Would be.

3 **Discussion** Even if these conditions suggested in this stanza were met, why couldn't man hope to experience the joy of the skylark?

THINKING ABOUT THE SELECTION

Recalling

1. At what time of day does the "blithe spirit" fly?
2. (a) To what four things does the speaker compare the bird in lines 36–55? (b) In what ways does he say the bird is like these things?

Interpreting

3. Why does the poet say of the bird, "Bird thou never wert"?
4. What do you suppose the speaker means in line 80 by "love's sad satiety"?
5. (a) How is the poet's song different from the bird's song? (b) Why can the bird's song "flow in such a crystal stream"?
6. (a) What does the speaker ask the skylark to teach him? (b) What effect does he think this would have on the world? (c) Why does he feel this way?

Applying

7. The twentieth century poet W. H. Auden wrote, "A verbal art like poetry is reflective; it stops to think. Music is immediate; it goes on to become." Discuss the meaning of this quotation.

Answers

ANSWERS TO THINKING ABOUT THE SELECTION

Recalling

1. The "blithe spirit" flies at sundown.
2. (a) The speaker compares the bird to a poet, a high-born maiden, a glowworm, and a rose. (b) Like these things, the bird is artless; it performs for itself alone.

Interpreting

3. The bird's song is full of joy; it has not experienced the pains of life that mortals must endure.
4. Loving too much can bring sadness.
5. (a) The bird's song is for itself alone while the poet's song is intended to be delivered to an audience. (b) The bird's song flows "in such a crystal stream" because its source is pure.
6. (a) The speaker asks the bird to teach him how to enjoy life. (b) The world would learn how to live in harmony. (c) The bird's song is so full of gladness that he is sure the world would listen, just as he has.

Applying

7. Answers will differ. Students might suggest that the appreciation of poetry takes time, while the melodies of music provide immediate gratification.

Motivation for Reading Discuss why memories are so important to us.

Purpose-Setting Question How do the simple rhyme scheme and short lines add to the poem's effectiveness?

1 **Discussion** What three images are mentioned in the first six lines of the poem?

2 **Discussion** How is the fourth image like the first three?

Answers

ANSWERS TO THINKING ABOUT THE SELECTION

Recalling

1. Thoughts of his love will remain in his memory.

Interpreting

2. Music, odors, and roses all have lingering qualities that live on in memory.
3. Love never dies.

Applying

3. Answers will differ. Suggested Response: Like the music, odors, and roses in the poem, poetry with its sensory language and rhythmic sound, has qualities that linger in memory. Some of these qualities are lost in prose.

ANSWERS TO CRITICAL THINKING AND READING

Answers will differ depending on the poem chosen, but students should mention the rhythmic pattern of the sentences, arrangement of words, and sentence and line length. All points should be supported with examples from Shelley's poems.

THINKING AND WRITING

For help with this assignment, students can refer to Lesson 18, "Writing a Poem," in the Handbook of Writing About Literature.

To ———

Percy Bysshe Shelley

Music, when soft voices die,
Vibrates in the memory—
Odors, when sweet violets sicken,
1 Live within the sense they quicken.

Rose leaves, when the rose is dead,
Are heaped for the belovèd's bed;
2 And so thy thoughts,[1] when thou art gone,
Love itself shall slumber on.

1. **thy thoughts:** Thoughts of thee.

THINKING ABOUT THE SELECTION

Recalling

1. What does the speaker of the poem say will happen to "thy thoughts, when thou art gone"?

Interpreting

2. Explain how music, odors, and roses will live on.
3. What idea about love is the speaker communicating?

Applying

3. How differently would this idea come across if it were presented in simple prose rather than as a poem? Explain.

CRITICAL THINKING AND READING

Recognizing Author's Style

Style is the way an author chooses and arranges words to express ideas. Just as no two personalities are identical, no two writing styles are identical. Sentence length, variation in sentence patterns, and word usage are among the features that define a writer's style. Carefully reread "To ———" and any other poem of your choice by Shelley, noting stylistic similarities in the areas mentioned above. Briefly describe this style, and tell whether or not you like it, and why. When you revise make sure you have included details from the poems to support your thesis.

THINKING AND WRITING

Writing an Ode

Select one of the objects about which you jotted down some thoughts before you read these poems by Shelley. Examine the observations you made regarding that person, thing, or trait, and decide whether you want to change, add, or remove any of these observations. Then write an ode to that person, quality, or thing. When you revise make sure you have created a vivid description.

A Dirge

Percy Bysshe Shelley

Rough wind, that moanest loud
    Grief too sad for song;
Wild wind, when sullen cloud
    Knells all the night long;
Sad storm, whose tears are vain,
Bare woods, whose branches strain,
Deep caves and dreary main,—
    Wail, for the world's wrong!

THINKING ABOUT THE SELECTION

Recalling

1. What does the speaker of the poem ask the wind, a storm, and bare branches to do?

Interpreting

2. What do you think the speaker means by "the world's wrong"?
3. What effect is created by calling upon the natural elements to bemoan the world's wrong? How does this device help portray the poet's sense of moral indignation?

Applying

4. If Shelley were living in the contemporary world, what aspects of life might he bemoan?

THINKING AND WRITING

Comparing and Contrasting Nature Views

Select a poem by one of the other Romantic poets you have read so far, and compare that poet's view of nature with Shelley's. Start by jotting down notes about each poem. Use quotes from each of the poems to illustrate similarities and differences. When you revise make sure you have presented your information in a logical order.

Literary Focus Ask students to list the verbs and adjectives in the poem which determine the poem's mood.

Master Teacher Note This poem, like "Ode to the West Wind" and "To a Skylark" is in the form of an apostrophe to several different natural phenomena.

Purpose-Setting Question What two figures of speech are primary in the poem?

1 **Clarification** The word *dirge* means "a mournful song, often accompanying a funeral." It can also refer to something, such as a poem, that has the qualities of a dirge.

2 **Discussion** After reading the poem aloud, ask your students to tell how the sound of the poem, especially the rhymes, matches the description of the natural forces. Why does the poet ask nature to wail?

Answers

ANSWERS TO THINKING ABOUT THE SELECTION

Recalling

1. The speaker asks them to wail.

Interpreting

2. The speaker sees the world as full of hypocrisy and injustice.
3. The poet sees the natural elements as superior to conditions developed by humans. Therefore, it is appropriate that the natural take the world to task for its wrongs.

Applying

4. Answers will differ. Students might mention excessive materialism, war, and the threat of nuclear destruction.

Challenge In this poem Shelley illustrates his belief that nature has compassion for man, or at least can be responsive to his situation. Do you think man has compassion for nature? Why or why not?

More About the Author Unlike his fellow poets Wordsworth, Byron, and Shelley, Keats was not occupied with revolutionary social and political ideals. Indeed, references to these ends are hardly ever in his works.

Have students discuss whether the proper aim of poetry is to further such beliefs, or is it simply "art for art's sake".

JOHN KEATS

1795–1821

Despite his early death and the fact that the most important of his works were composed in the space of two years, John Keats remains one of the major influences on English poetry. Known as a pure artist, Keats saw the appreciation of beauty as an end in itself and made the pursuit of beauty the goal of his poetry. As Keats himself so eloquently put it, "Beauty is truth, truth beauty."

Born in London of working-class parents, Keats was unusually handsome and active as a child. He developed a reputation for fighting, not so much out of rowdiness as from a readiness to take sides in a worthy cause. It was not until he became a close friend of his schoolmaster's son, Charles Cowden Clarke, that Keats developed an interest in poetry and became an avid reader.

In 1815 Keats began the study of medicine at a London hospital. By this time he had already begun writing poetry, and though his studies earned him a pharmacist's license, he ultimately abandoned medicine for a career as a poet. His first major effort, *Endymion,* published in the spring of 1818, was severely attacked by the journals of the day. Part of the reason for the harsh criticism was Keats's association with Leigh Hunt, a radical poet, but much of it had to do with the verse itself. Far from being crushed by the assault, Keats began the second of his long poems, *Hyperion,* which was never completed.

The end of the year found Keats mourning the loss of his brother Tom to tuberculosis. It also found the poet deliriously happy over his engagement to Fanny Brawne, a lively 18-year-old who was a light in Keats's life. The following year, 1819, was when Keats turned out his finest work, including "The Eve of St. Agnes," "The Eve of St. Mark," and his famous odes. This might have been only the beginning, but Keats's health took a turn for the worse. He moved to Italy, which promised a warmer climate, but to no avail. After a long battle with tuberculosis, the disease that had claimed his brother, he died at 25.

Though Keats and Shelley knew each other, their visions of what the poet should be could not have been more different. Keats did not share Shelley's rebellious spirit, not did he feel that poetry was the proper vehicle for political statements. Rather Keats sought to refine his idea of beauty, and in so doing, refined ours. His extraordinary sensitivity enabled him to see beauty in the most ordinary of circumstances, while his mastery of verse enabled him to unveil that beauty to the world.

Objectives

1. To understand the technical aspects of the sonnet form
2. To compare and contrast sonnets

Teaching Portfolio: Support Material

Teacher Backup, p. 000

Vocabulary Check, p. 00

Usage and Mechanics Worksheet, p. 00

Analyzing Literature Worksheet, p. 00

Critical Thinking and Reading Worksheet, p. 00

Language Worksheet, p. 00

Selection Test, p. 000

GUIDE FOR READING

On First Looking into Chapman's Homer; Bright Star! Would I Were Steadfast as Thou Art; When I Have Fears That I May Cease to Be

Literary Forms

The Sonnet. The sonnet is a poem of fourteen lines arranged according to a specific rhyme scheme, with five strong beats and five weak beats per line. In each of the two basic types of sonnet, Petrarchan and Shakespearean, a portion of the poem is used to present a problem or ask a question, and another portion to resolve it. Despite the demands of its form, the successful sonnet is one that flows smoothly, creates powerful impressions, and delivers an important message without sounding forced. These features are hallmarks of the sonnets written by Keats.

Look For

As you read the three sonnets by Keats, look for the way in which the poet draws your attention away from the external elements of the form and toward rich impressions and thoughts.

Writing

Think about a book you have read or a film or work of art you have seen that in some way has changed your life. Consider what particular features of the work led to this change. Then freewrite, comparing this experience to other moving experiences people have.

Vocabulary

Knowing the following words will help you as you read the three sonnets by Keats.

expanse (ik spans′) *n.*: Wide, continuous stretch, as of land (p. 726, l. 5)
ken (ken) *n.*: Range of sight or knowledge (p. 726, l. 10)
surmise (sər mīz′) *v.*: Guess, assume (p. 726, l. 13)
ablution (ab lo͞o′ shən) *n.*: Washing or cleansing of the body (p. 728, l. 6)
gleaned (glēnd) *v.*: Picked from, as crops—in this case thoughts (p. 729, l. 2)
teeming (tēm′ iŋ) *adj.*: Filled to overflowing (p. 729, l. 2)

Literary Focus Preview the technical aspects of each kind of sonnet with students.

Look for Your **less advanced** students may need additional work with the Petrarchan and Shakespearean sonnet forms in order to be able to distinguish between the two. Reread, as needed, sonnets by Shakespeare, Milton, and Wordsworth, pointing out differences between the Petrarchan and Shakespearean forms.

Writing Lead a discussion in which students contribute experiences with media or art that have influenced them. Then have them do the writing activity.

Vocabulary Go over the new words as a class before beginning the study of the sonnets.

Motivation for Reading Have students recall a time when they were awed by some discovery, perhaps quite by accident. What were their impressions?

Master Teacher Note Students should hear this poem read aloud to get the full impact of the masterly blend of rhythm and meaning. Read the poem aloud yourself, or play a recording of it.

Purpose-Setting Question How apt is the sonnet form for the meaning the poet wishes to convey?

Literary Focus Note Keats's use of diction. Point out the archaic words in the octave—*goodly, bards, fealty, demesne*—which suggest the dignified antiquity of classical poetry and Homer. Compare this archaic diction to the simple language in the sestet which suggests the excitement of the discoveries of a planet and the Pacific.

1 **Discussion** Are the travels Keats talks about in the octave real or imaginary? What are the "realms of gold" in line 1? What does Homer's demesne contain?

2 **Discussion** What two similes does Keats use to compare the sense of excitement at reading Chapman for the first time? How apt are these similes? Does the fact that Balboa, not Cortez, discovered the Pacific weaken the poem? Why or why not?

On First Looking into Chapman's Homer

John Keats

When Keats was twenty-one, his former teacher, Charles Cowden Clarke, introduced him to a translation of Homer by Elizabethan poet George Chapman. The two men spent the evening reading this book, and early the next morning Keats presented this sonnet to Clarke.

Much have I traveled in the realms of gold,
And many goodly states and kingdoms seen;
Round many western islands have I been
1 Which bards in fealty to Apollo[1] hold.
Oft of one wide expanse had I been told
That deep-browed Homer ruled as his demesne;[2]
Yet did I never breathe its pure serene[3]
Till I heard Chapman speak out loud and bold:
Then felt I like some watcher of the skies
2 When a new planet swims into his ken;
Or like stout Cortez[4] when with eagle eyes
He stared at the Pacific—and all his men
Looked at each other with a wild surmise—
Silent, upon a peak in Darien.[5]

---

1. **Apollo:** In Greek and Roman mythology, the god of music, poetry, and medicine.
2. **demesne** (di mān'): Realm.
3. **serene:** Clear air.
4. **Cortez:** Here, Keats was mistaken. The Pacific was discovered in 1513 by Balboa, not Cortez.
5. **Darien** (dä ryĕn'): The Isthmus of Panama.

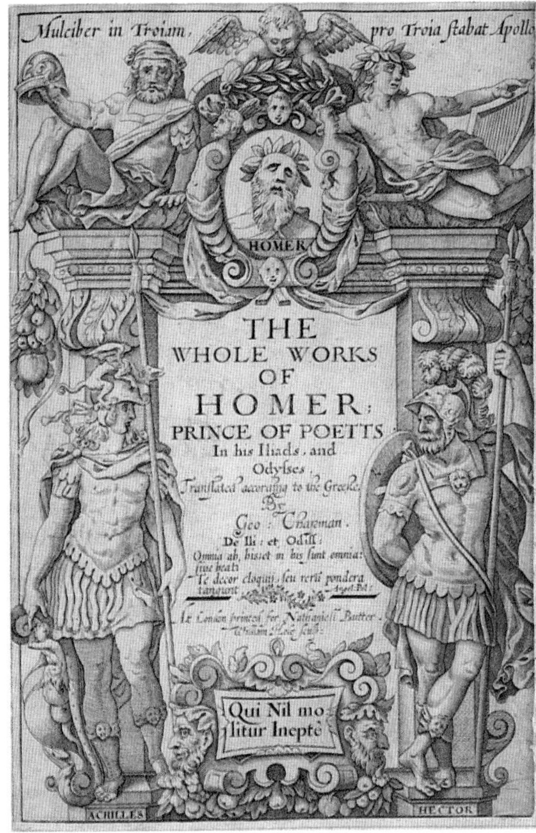

FRONTISPIECE, HOMER'S ILIAD AND ODYSSEY, 1612
G. Chapman
The British Library

THINKING ABOUT THE SELECTION

Recalling

1. What does the speaker of the poem claim he missed before reading Chapman?

Interpreting

2. (a) What transportation did the speaker use in his "travels"? (b) To what does he compare his new-found wonderment?
3. Dante Gabriel Rossetti, a poet of the nineteenth century, wrote that "A Sonnet is a coin: its face reveals/The soul—it converse, to what Power tis due." (a) How would you describe Keats's "soul," as it is revealed in "On First Looking into Chapman's Homer"? (b) What is the "power" to which that soul owes its due?

Applying

4. Do you think books can change people's lives? Explain your answer.

Humanities Note

Fine art, Engraving, Frontispiece by William Hole. The frontispiece to the 1612 edition of George Chapman's *The Whole Works of Homer, Prince of Poetts* (sic) was designed and engraved by William Hole (or Holle, fl. 1600–1630). William Hole, one of the earliest English engravers, is noteworthy for his engravings of sheet music, authors' portraits, and title pages for volumes of works by Gibbons, Coryat, and Chapman, among others.

The architectural frame surrounding the title reflects the classic style of the famous architect of the day, Inigo Jones. The two columns are protected by Hector and Achilles, figures from Greek mythology. A portrait medallion of Homer wreathed in laurel, the leave used by the ancients to crown heros and honored ones, surmounts the whole. This engraving is a flowery presentation that shows the beginnings of the Baroque style.

You may wish to discuss the following with your students:

1. From the design of this engraving what would you predict about the content of the book?
2. Keats felt Homer to come alive for him after reading this translation by George Chapman. Do you feel that the artist of this engraving also felt that way about the work of Chapman? Explain.

Answers

ANSWERS TO THINKING ABOUT THE SELECTION

Recalling

1. The speaker missed the true import, as well as the beauty and majesty, of Homer's works.

Interpreting

2. (a) The speaker has traveled figuratively—through books. (b) He compares his new-found wonderment to that of an astronomer discovering a star and an explorer discovering the Pacific.
3. Suggested Responses: (a) Keats's soul is open to new ideas and impressions and is capable of awe-struck appreciation. (b) That "power" might be ideas found in books.

Applying

4. Answers will differ but should include the idea that one should always be open to new ideas and new interpretations, and these can be found in books.

Master Teacher Note Keats wrote the sonnet in the first days of his engagement to Fanny Brawne. This was shortly after the death of his brother Tom from tuberculosis.

Purpose-Setting Question Although this is a Shakespearean sonnet in form, its ideas are divided into an octave and a sestet. What are the poet's thoughts in the octave? What are they in the sestet?

1 **Literary Focus** Note the use of apostrophe in line 1. What does "steadfast" mean?

2 **Discussion** Explain why the two sights that the star sees —ablution and snow—suggest innocence.

3 **Discussion** Lines 9–14, which function as a sestet, reveal the circumstances under which the poet wishes to remain steadfast. What are those circumstances?

Answers

ANSWERS TO THINKING ABOUT THE SELECTION

Recalling

1. The star watches the moving waters of the oceans and the snows upon the mountains and the moors.

Interpreting

2. (a) The poet wishes to be unchangeable. (b) At the same time the poet does not want to be isolated. He wants to be with his love forever.
3. By "sweet unrest" the poet suggests a state of sleepless ecstacy.
4. Suggested Responses: (a) In the octave, the poet expresses the desire to be firm and unchanging in purpose. (b) In the sestet, he responds that he wants to be able to live with his love, experiencing every aspect of her life. (c) The word that signals the response is "No."

Bright Star, Would I Were Steadfast as Thou Art

John Keats

1 Bright star, would I were steadfast as thou art—
Not in lone splendor hung aloft the night
And watching, with eternal lids apart,
Like nature's patient, sleepless Eremite,[1]
The moving waters at their priestlike task
Of pure ablution round earth's human shores,
2 Or gazing on the new soft-fallen mask
Of snow upon the mountains and the moors—
No—yet still steadfast, still unchangeable,
Pillowed upon my fair love's ripening breast,
3 To feel forever its soft fall and swell,
Awake forever in a sweet unrest,
Still, still to hear her tender-taken breath,
And so live ever—or else swoon to death.

1. **Eremite** (ĕr′ ə mīt′): Hermit.

THINKING ABOUT THE SELECTION

Recalling

1. What two things does the speaker say the star watches from its position in the sky?

Interpreting

2. (a) In what ways does the speaker wish to be like the star? (b) In what ways does he wish to be different?
3. What do do think is meant by "sweet unrest" in line 12?
4. In a Petrarchan, or Italian, sonnet, the first eight lines pose a question or problem, while the last six lines offer a solution or comment on or extend the issue. (a) What question or problem is presented in the octave, or first eight lines? (b) What response is given in the sestet, or next six lines? (c) What word signals this response?

Applying

5. Based on this poem, describe Keats's attitudes toward nature and emotion. Explain how these attitudes are typical of the Romantic movement.

When I Have Fears That I May Cease to Be

John Keats

When I have fears that I may cease to be
Before my pen has gleaned my teeming brain,
1 Before high-piled books, in charactery,[1]
Hold like rich garners[2] the full ripened grain;
When I behold, upon the night's starred face,
Huge cloudy symbols of a high romance,
2 And think that I may never live to trace
Their shadows, with the magic hand of chance;[3]
And when I feel, fair creature of an hour,
3 That I shall never look upon thee more,
Never have relish in the fairy power
Of unreflecting love—then on the shore
Of the wide world I stand alone, and think
4 Till love and fame to nothingness do sink.

1. **charactery:** Written or printed letters of the alphabet.
2. **garners:** Storehouses for grain.
3. **chance:** Inspiration.

JOHN KEATS, 1821
J. Severn
By Courtesy of the National Portrait Gallery, London

THINKING ABOUT THE SELECTION

Recalling

1. (a) What does the speaker say he fears missing in lines 1–8? (b) In lines 9–12?

Interpreting

2. What do you think is meant by "cloudy symbols of a high romance" in line 6?
3. Whom is the speaker addressing in line 10?
4. How does the speaker resolve his fears?

Applying

5. What does this poem suggest about Keats's views on death? Do you feel these views would be held by the other Romantic poets you have read? Why or why not?

THINKING AND WRITING

Comparing and Contrasting Sonnets

Choose one of the sonnets by William Wordsworth (pages 663–667). On a sheet of paper take notes on how this sonnet is similar to and different from the sonnets of Keats in form (Shakespearean vs. Petrarchan), subject matter, word usage, and theme. In an essay of one page or more write about your findings. When you revise make sure you have included details from the poems as support.

Motivation for Reading You might discuss with students whether at graduation time they will have any regrets about goals unreached. In this poem, Keats expresses his fears of not accomplishing all that he would like.

Thematic Idea Compare the subject and theme of this sonnet with Byron's "So We'll Go No More A Roving" on page 701.

Literary Focus Compare the structure of this sonnet to "On First Looking into Chapman's Homer," a Petrarchan sonnet.

1 **Enrichment** Written in 1818, before he met Fanny Brawne, this is the first of Keats's Shakespearean sonnets. The use of "I" reveals this to be a very personal lyric. In lines 1–4 what does Keats say he fears he will not have time to do before his death?

2 **Discussion** In lines 5–9 Keats tells what he fears he will never do. What is that?

3 **Literary Focus** Note the change in imagery in the lyric—when Keats talks about the products of his mind he uses concrete images; when he talks about products of his spirit, he uses more amorphous images. In lines 9–12 Keats tells of a third fear. What is this third fear? Note that *unreflecting* (line 12) means "untroubled by any need to think."

4 **Discussion** The final two lines of a Shakespearean sonnet usually offer a conclusion. What is the conclusion Keats reaches here?

Answers

ANSWERS TO THINKING ABOUT THE SELECTION

Recalling

1. (a) The poet fears not having the time to write all that is in his mind and not being able to write everything his imagination can conceive. (b) The poet fears he will never experience reciprocal love.

Interpreting

2. By "cloudy symbols of high romance" the poet may mean his imagination or images and thoughts that inspire him.
3. "Thee" refers to someone he loves or might come to love.
4. The poet realizes that in the larger sense personal love and fame are of little account.

Applying

5. Answers will differ, but based on the meaning and contents of this sonnet, it appears that Keats is not concerned with the idea of an afterlife. This would seem somewhat out of character with the other Romantics, all of whom embraced personal beliefs of eternity and afterlife. Throughout his poetry, however, Keats's views of eternity seem clouded with moods of doubt and mystery.

Literary Focus After discussing imagery review the ode form before beginning a study of the poem. See Shelley's "Ode to the West Wind" on page 714. While Shelley's ode is in the Pindaric mode, Keats devised his own stanza form. This ode is written in ten-line stanzas of essentially iambic pentameter, except that the eighth line in each stanza is iambic trimeter. Keats's rhyme scheme is *ababcdecde.* Point out the heavy use of allusion in the ode. Note that authors who use allusions assume a certain knowledge on the part of their readers.

Look For Select a few of the more imagistic passages, and read them aloud to illustrate the kind of rich, lush imagery Keats uses.

Writing Have students tell what images they thought of to describe the various features.

Vocabulary With **less advanced** students, be prepared to list and define additional words from the poems that may prove difficult.

GUIDE FOR READING

Ode to a Nightingale; Ode on a Grecian Urn; To Autumn

The Writer's Technique

Imagery. Imagery is language that helps a reader form a mental picture of an object or idea by appealing to one or more of the five senses. Taken by itself the word *bread,* for example, is nothing more than just that—a word. When, however, the word is part of the image "warm loaf of freshly baked bread," our sense of sight and especially our sense of smell are both called into play. In his odes, Keats used imagery with a degree of skill that few poets before or since have achieved.

Look For

As you read the next three poems by Keats, be alert to the poet's use of imagery and to the sense or senses to which each image appeals.

Writing

Picture a setting in nature with which you are very familiar—a park, a wooded area, or the like. On a sheet of paper jot down as many physical features of the scene as you can. You might, for instance, mention trees, grass, rocks, and sky. Lastly, think up an image for each feature you mentioned that would enable a reader to develop a strong mental picture.

Vocabulary

Knowing the following words will help you as you read the next three poems by Keats.

opiate (ō' pe it) *n.*: Something that brings on relaxation or sleep (p. 731, l. 3)
vintage (vin'tij) *n.*: Wine or nectar of high quality (p. 731, l. 11)
requiem (rek'wē əm) *n.*: Musical composition or service honoring the dead (p. 734, l. 60)
unravished (un rav'ishd) *adj.*: Undisturbed, unspoiled (p. 736, l. 1)
cloyed (kloid) *adj.*: Made sick by an overdose (p. 737, l. 29)

Ode to a Nightingale

John Keats

Keats composed the following ode in 1819, while living in Hampstead with his friend Charles Brown. Brown wrote the following description about how the ode was composed: "In the spring of 1819 a nightingale had built her nest near my house. Keats felt a tranquil and continued joy in her song; and one morning he took his chair from the breakfast table to the grass plot under the plum tree, where he sat for two or three hours. When he came into the house, I perceived he had some scraps of paper in his hand, and these he was quietly thrusting behind the books. On inquiry, I found those scraps, four or five in number, contained his poetic feeling on the song of our nightingale."

I

My heart aches, and a drowsy numbness pains
    My sense, as though of hemlock[1] I had drunk,
Or emptied some dull opiate to the drains
    One minute past, and Lethe-wards[2] had sunk:
'Tis not through envy of thy happy lot,
    But being too happy in thine happiness,—
        That thou, light-wingèd Dryad[3] of the trees,
            In some melodious plot
    Of beechen green, and shadows numberless,
        Singest of summer in full-throated ease.

1

2

II

O, for a draft[4] of vintage! that hath been
    Cooled a long age in the deep-delved earth,
Tasting of Flora[5] and the country green,
    Dance, and Provençal[6] song, and sunburnt mirth!

3, 4

1. **hemlock:** A poisonous herb.
2. **Lethe-wards:** Toward Lethe, the river of forgetfulness in Hades, the underworld, in classical mythology.
3. **Dryad** (drī′ əd): In classical mythology, a wood nymph.
4. **draft:** Drink.
5. **Flora:** In classical mythology, the goddess of flowers, or the flowers themselves.
6. **Provençal** (prō′ vən säl′): Pertaining to Provence, a region in southern France, renowned in the late Middle Ages for its troubadours, who composed and sang love songs.

Master Teacher Note This poem is an example of what Keats termed "negative capability" —one of the most famous and elusive phrases ever uttered by a great poet. Part of its meaning may be stated thus: the capability of a poet to negate himself or herself and enter fully into his or her subject so as it represent it with an especially rich and vibrant objectivity.

Purpose-Setting Question What thoughts and feelings in the poet does the nightingale evoke?

1 **Discussion** As the poem opens, what is the poet's state of mind?

2 **Clarification** The word *thy* refers to the nightingale.

3 **Discussion** In stanza two the poet says he longs to leave the world behind to join the nightingale. By what means would he accomplish this?

4 **Discussion** What senses does Keats appeal to in stanza two?

Humanities Note

Fine art, *Small Bird on a Flowering Plum Branch,* attributed to Ma Lin. This delicate Chinese painting on silk shows a bird perched on a branch. The serenity of the scene suggest the freedom from earthly concerns for which Shelley longs in his "Ode to a Nightingale."

As students read the poem and look at the art, you might use these questions for discussion.

1. How has the artist suggested peacefulness and serenity in this painting?
2. What "among the leaves hast [the bird] never known"?
3. What elements of Beauty would Shelley admire in this painting?

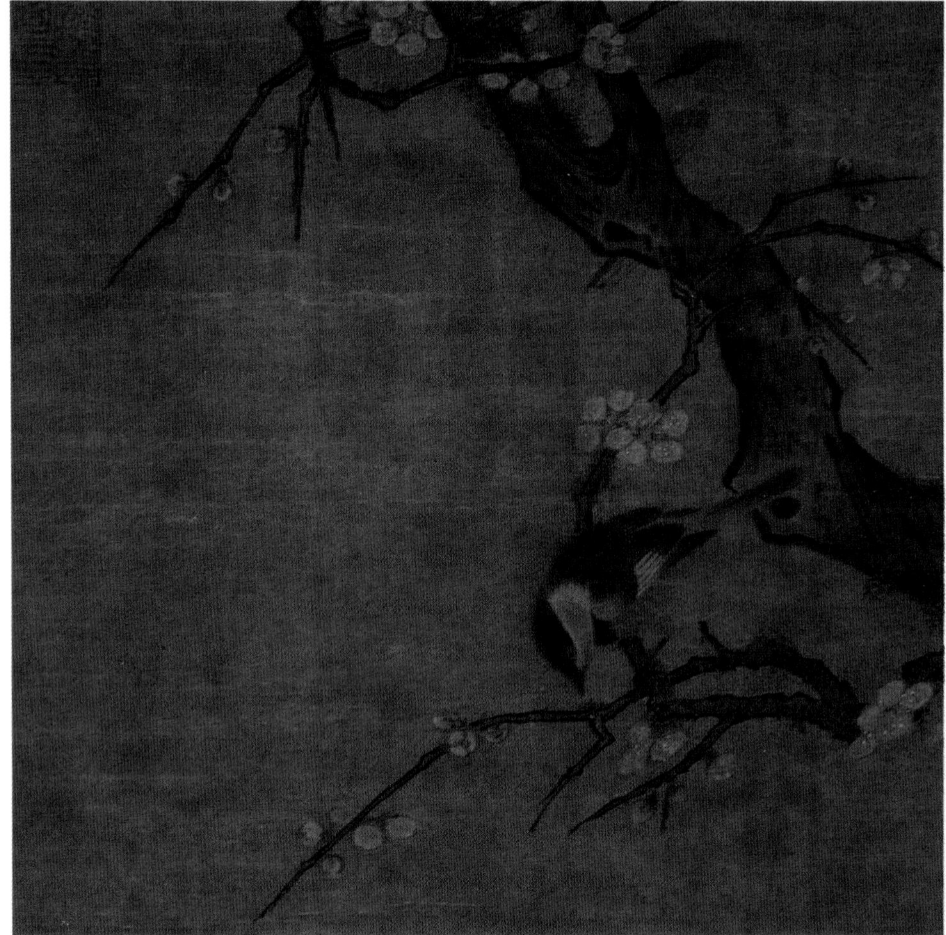

SMALL BIRD ON A FLOWERING PLUM BRANCH
The Goto Museum

O for a beaker full of the warm South,
Full of the true, the blushful Hippocrene,[7]
With beaded bubbles winking at the brim,
And purple-stained mouth;
That I might drink, and leave the world unseen,
And with thee fade away into the forest dim:

7. Hippocrene (hĭp′ ə krēn′): In classical mythology, the fountain of the Muses on Mt. Helicon. From this fountain flowed the waters of inspiration.

III

Fade far away, dissolve, and quite forget
What thou among the leaves hast never known,
The weariness, the fever, and the fret
Here, where men sit and hear each other groan;
Where palsy shakes a few, sad, last gray hairs, 5
Where youth grows pale, and specter-thin, and dies;[8]
Where but to think is to be full of sorrow
And leaden-eyed despairs,
Where Beauty cannot keep her lustrous eyes,
Or new Love pine at them beyond tomorrow.

IV

Away! away! for I will fly to thee,
Not charioted by Bacchus[9] and his pards,
But on the viewless[10] wings of Poesy,[11]
Though the dull brain perplexes and retards:
Already with thee! tender is the night, 6, 7
And haply[12] the Queen-Moon is on her throne,
Clustered around by all her starry Fays;[13]
But here there is no light,
Save what from heaven is with the breezes blown
Through verdurous[14] glooms and winding mossy ways.

V

I cannot see what flowers are at my feet,
Nor what soft incense hangs upon the boughs,
But, in embalmed[15] darkness, guess each sweet
Wherewith the seasonable month endows
The grass, the thicket, and the fruit-tree wild; 8
White hawthorn, and the pastoral eglantine;[16]
Fast fading violets covered up in leaves;
And mid-May's eldest child,
The coming musk-rose, full of dewy wine,
The murmurous haunt of flies on summer eves.

---

8. youth . . . dies: Keats is referring to his brother, Tom, who had died from tuberculosis the previous winter.
9. Bacchus (băk′ əs): In classical mythology, the god of wine, who was often represented in a chariot drawn by leopards ("pards").
10. viewless: Invisible.
11. Poesy: Poetic fancy.
12. haply: Perhaps.
13. Fays: Fairies.
14. verdurous: Green-foliaged.
15. embalmed: Perfumed.
16. eglantine (eg′ lən tīn′): Sweetbrier or honeysuckle.

5 **Discussion** In stanza three the poet says he would like to fade into the forest trees with the nightingale. What advantage does he see in this?

6 **Discussion** In stanza four the poet chooses his vehicle of escape. What is it?

7 **Enrichment** The phrase "tender is the night" (line 35) was borrowed by F. Scott Fitzgerald as the title of one of his novels.

8 **Enrichment** Stanza five is justly acclaimed as a beautifully lyrical evocation of the scents and sounds of an early summer woodland evening. Point out how much of the stanza consists of rich, sensuous imagery. The word *sweet* (line 43) means "sweet smells."

9 **Discussion** If, as the poet says in stanza six, he should die, what would happen to the nightingale's song?

10 **Discussion** Stanza seven develops one of Keats's basic beliefs—the permanence and changelessness of beauty. In what sense was the nightingale "not born for death"? How does he use the nightingale's song to express this idea?

11 **Discussion** In stanza eight the poet is brought back to reality from his reverie. What meaning do lines 73–74 hold? Note that *fancy* (line 73) means "imagination."

VI

Darkling[17] I listen; and, for many a time
I have been half in love with easeful Death,
Called him soft names in many a mused[18] rhyme,
To take into the air my quiet breath;
Now more than ever seems it rich to die,
9 To cease upon the midnight with no pain,
While thou art pouring forth thy soul abroad
In such an ecstasy!
Still wouldst thou sing, and I have ears in vain—
To thy high requiem become a sod.

VII

Thou wast not born for death, immortal Bird!
No hungry generations tread thee down;
The voice I hear this passing night was heard
In ancient days by emperor and clown:
Perhaps the selfsame song that found a path
10 Through the sad heart of Ruth,[19] when, sick for home,
She stood in tears amid the alien corn;
The same that ofttimes hath
Charmed magic casements, opening on the foam
Of perilous seas, in fairylands forlorn.

VIII

Forlorn! the very word is like a bell
To toll me back from thee to my sole self!
Adieu! the fancy cannot cheat so well
As she is famed[20] to do, deceiving elf.
11 Adieu! adieu! thy plaintive anthem[21] fades
Past the near meadows, over the still stream,
Up the hillside; and now 'tis buried deep
In the next valley-glades:
Was it a vision, or a waking dream?
Fled is that music:—Do I wake or sleep?

17. darkling: In the dark.
18. mused: Meditated.
19. Ruth: In the Bible (Ruth 2:1–23), a widow who left her home and went to Judah to work in the corn (wheat) fields.
20. famed: Reported.
21. anthem: Hymn.

THINKING ABOUT THE SELECTION

Recalling

1. What is the speaker's mood in stanza I?
2. (a) What wish does the speaker express at the end of stanza II and at the beginning of stanza III? (b) According to stanza IV, how will he accomplish this wish?
3. What effect does the word "forlorn" have on the speaker in stanza VIII?

Interpreting

4. (a) What is the "draught of vintage" the speaker craves in stanza II? (b) What would it help him to escape?
5. (a) What differences between the speaker's world and the bird's are described in stanza IV? (b) What is meant in line 38 by "here there is no light"? (c) What problem does this lack create?
6. (a) What does the speaker find tempting in stanza VI? (b) What changes his mind in stanza VII?

Applying

7. The poem ends with a question. What is its relevance, both to the poem and to the spirit of the Romantic movement?
8. The twentieth-century American novelist F. Scott Fitzgerald took the title of one of his novels from line 35: "Already with thee! Tender is the night." (a) In what way can the night be tender? (b) Why are the words "tender is the night" especially appropriate for one who has been "half in love with easeful Death"?

ANALYZING LITERATURE

Using Imagery

Imagery is language that appeals to the senses and, by so doing, creates a vivid picture in the reader's mind. The phrase "blustery, windswept day" provides the reader with a strong impression that the simple phrase "cold day" does not. Such is the impact of imagery. Find an everyday equivalent for each of the following images from "Ode to a Nightingale." Then state which of Keats's words are central to his image.

1. "With beaded bubbles winking at the brim,/ And purple-stained mouth;" (lines 17–18)
2. "Where palsy shakes a few, sad, last gray hairs,/Where youth grows pale, and specter-thin, and dies;" (lines 25–26)
3. The coming musk-rose, full of dewy wine,/The murmurous haunt of flies on summer eves." (lines 49–50)

Answers

ANSWERS TO THINKING ABOUT THE SELECTION

Recalling

1. The poet's mood can be described as one of sadness, even depression.
2. (a) The poet wishes to leave the world behind and join the nightingale. (b) He wishes to leave the world and fade into the forest with the nightingale.
3. The word *forlorn* brings the poet out of his reverie.

Interpreting

4. (a) The poet craves a draft of wine. (b) The wine, he thinks, will help him leave the real world.
5. (a) The real world is one in which the brain is perplexed and dulled; the nightingale's world is one of permanence, through his song. (b) The line suggests the real world lacks the joy, as well as brightness, of nature's world, as exemplified by the nightingale.
6. (a) The poet finds the idea of death tempting. (b) The nightingale's song evokes the idea of immortality.

Applying

7. Suggested Response: The question means "Was my reverie of the nightingale a dream—a form of sleep—or is my return to ordinary thoughts and feelings a kind of sleep?" For both the poem and the entire Romantic movement, the poet's vision is a kind of awakening to intenser life; a return to ordinary living is, by comparison, a sleep.

ANSWERS TO ANALYZING LITERATURE

1. The image in lines 17–18 refers to a glass of wine.
2. The image in lines 25–26 refers to the process of aging and death.
3. The image in lines 49–50 refers to rosebuds about to burst, with insects hovering about them.

   In all of the images, the nouns and adjectives—and to a lesser extent the verbs—are of central expressive importance. The other words are little more than connectives.

Challenge Trace each of the mythological allusions in a handbook such as Bullfinch's. Then explain the aptness of each allusion.

Enrichment This ode was likely inspired by the poet's contemplating the Elgin marbles. Acquired by the British Museum in 1816, the marbles are a group of relief sculptures from the Parthenon in Athens that depict various scenes from Greek mythology. Just which urn—if indeed it ever existed—Keats used as his model is not known.

Literary Focus Again Keats uses a ten-line stanza of iambic pentameter lines. The rhyme scheme in the first seven lines is *ababcde;* the last three are variations—*dce, ced,* or *cde.*

1 **Discussion** What scene is depicted in the opening stanza? Why does Keats address the urn as the "still unravished bride of quietness," as the "foster child of silence and slow time," and as a "sylvan historian"? What conclusions can you draw from Keats's pictures in the opening stanza?

2 **Discussion** What does Keats mean by lines 11–12? To what melodies is he referring? What advantages are there for the participants in this scene? what disadvantages?

3 **Discussion** In stanzas two and three Keats begins to answer the questions he raised in the opening stanza. What are his answers? What is the difference between real life and life as depicted on the urn?

Ode on a Grecian Urn

John Keats

I

Thou still unravished bride of quietness,
Thou foster child of silence and slow time,
Sylvan[1] historian, who canst thus express
A flowery tale more sweetly than our rhyme:
1 What leaf-fringed legend haunts about thy shape
Of deities or mortals, or of both,
In Tempe[2] or the dales of Arcady?[3]
What men or gods are these? What maidens loath?[4]
What mad pursuit? What struggle to escape?
What pipes and timbrels?[5] What wild ecstasy?

II

2 Heard melodies are sweet, but those unheard
Are sweeter; therefore, ye soft pipes, play on;
Not to the sensual[6] ear, but, more endeared,
Pipe to the spirit ditties of no tone:
Fair youth, beneath the trees, thou canst not leave
Thy song, nor ever can those trees be bare;
Bold Lover, never, never canst thou kiss,
Though winning near the goal—yet, do not grieve;
3 She cannot fade, though thou hast not thy bliss,
Forever wilt thou love, and she be fair!

III

Ah, happy, happy boughs! that cannot shed
Your leaves, nor ever bid the Spring adieu;
And, happy melodist, unwearied,
Forever piping songs forever new;

---

1. **sylvan:** Rustic, representing the woods or forest.
2. **Tempe** (tem′ pē): A beautiful valley in Greece that has become a symbol of supreme rural beauty.
3. **Arcady** (är′ kə dē): A region in Greece that has come to represent supreme pastoral contentment.
4. **loath:** Unwilling.
5. **timbrels:** Tambourines.
6. **sensual:** Involving the physical sense of hearing.

More happy love! more happy, happy love!
    Forever warm and still to be enjoyed,
      Forever panting, and forever young;
All breathing human passion far above,
    That leaves a heart high-sorrowful and cloyed,
      A burning forehead, and a parching tongue.

IV

Who are these coming to the sacrifice?
    To what green altar, O mysterious priest,
Lead'st thou that heifer lowing at the skies,
    And all her silken flanks with garlands dressed?
4 What little town by river or seashore,
    Or mountain-built with peaceful citadel,
      Is emptied of this folk, this pious morn?
And, little town, thy streets forevermore
    Will silent be; and not a soul to tell
      Why thou art desolate, can e'er return.

COLUMN KRATER (CALLED THE "ORCHARD VASE"), SIDE A: WOMEN GATHERING APPLES
The Metropolitan Museum of Art

4 **Discussion** What pictures does Keats draw in stanza four? Note the fantasy that Keats creates about the town—that it is eternally empty since all its residents are frozen in time on the urn.

Humanities Note

The Column Krater (Orchard Vase): Women Gathering Apples. Artifacts from the early Greek period include many painted vessels, called vases or urns. In spite of their utilitarian function, these vases were in many cases works of art. The highly individual drawings on them show scenes from mythology, legend, and everyday life. This vase, in the red-figured style, shows a common scene. The women are in profile with well-proportioned and realistic features.

As students look at this typical Greek vase, you might ask these questions.

1. What common activity is happening in this painting?
2. To what aspects of an urn like this might Shelley be referring in his ode?
3. What rhetorical questions might Shelley have posed about this particular vase?

5 **Discussion** In the last stanza Keats steps back to summarize his contemplations. What message does the urn have? Consider the antecedent of *that* to be all of lines 46–49. Then the message might be that the beauty of the urn shall comfort future generations with its linking of truth and beauty.

Enrichment Keats wrote in a letter that what the imagination seizes as beauty must be truth. Critic Harold Bloom extends this statement to speculate that "the urn's beauty is truth because age cannot waste it; our woes cannot consume it. The urn's truth, its existence out of time, is beauty because such freedom is beautiful to us. The condition of man, for Keats, is such that all we shall ever know we know on earth, and the sum of our knowledge is the identity of beauty and truth, when beauty is defined as what gives joy forever, and truth is what seizes upon us as beauty."

5

V

O Attic[7] shape! Fair attitude! with brede[8]
Of marble men and maidens overwrought,[9]
With forest branches and the trodden weed;
Thou, silent form, dost tease us out of thought
As doth eternity: Cold[10] Pastoral!
When old age shall this generation waste,
Thou shalt remain, in midst of other woe
Than ours, a friend to man, to whom thou say'st,
"Beauty is truth, truth beauty,"—that is all
Ye know on earth, and all ye need to know.

7. **Attic:** Attica was the region of Greece in which Athens was located; a region characterized by grace and simplicity.
8. **brede:** An interwoven pattern.
9. **overwrought:** All over.
10. **cold:** Unchanging.

THINKING ABOUT THE SELECTION

Recalling

1. As the speaker studies the scene on a Grecian urn, it takes hold of his imagination. (a) Whom does the speaker address in stanza II of the poem? (b) Whom does he address in stanza III?
2. What ritual is described in the first four lines of stanza IV?

Interpreting

3. (a) In what way is the urn a "Sylvan historian"? (b) How can it tell its "flowery tale more sweetly than our rhyme"?
4. (a) Interpret lines 11–12: "Heard melodies are sweet, but those unheard/Are sweeter . . ." (b) What do these lines indicate about the power of the imagination?
5. (a) Why might the lover in stanza II grieve? (b) Why does the speaker advise him not to grieve?
6. (a) What is the "Cold Pastoral" mentioned in line 45? (b) With what does the speaker contrast it?

Applying

7. (a) Explain the meaning of the last two lines of the poem. (b) In what ways might this finish have been appropriate to "Ode to a Nightingale"?
8. In *Endymion,* John Keats wrote, "A thing of beauty is a joy forever;/Its loveliness increases; it will never/Pass into nothingness." Compare and contrast the idea of beauty expressed in these lines with that expressed in lines 49–50 of "Ode on a Grecian Urn".

Answers

ANSWERS TO THINKING ABOUT THE SELECTION

Recalling

1. (a) In stanza two the speaker addresses the "fair youth" who is pursuing his love. (b) In stanza three the poet addresses the trees and a musician.
2. The ritual is the sacrifice of an animal to the gods.

Interpreting

3. The "sylvan historian" is the forest itself which stands witness to the events the poem depicts.
4. (a) "Unheard melodies" are those of the imagination. (b) The power of the imagination is very strong. Things that do not exist in the senses can exist in the imagination.
5. (a) The lover might grieve because he never catches his love. (b) The lover should not grieve because his love will always be strong and the maiden always fair and young.
6. (a) The "Cold Pastoral" is the scene frozen in time by art. (b) It is contrasted with real life.

Applying

7. (a) Answers will differ but should suggest that truth and beauty are linked. (b) Answers will differ but should suggest that in "Ode to a Nightingale" the beauty associated with nature constitutes truth for the poet.
8. Answers will differ but students should point out that in both passages that beauty is universal and lasting.

1 # To Autumn

John Keats

I

Season of mists and mellow fruitfulness,
Close bosom-friend of the maturing sun;
Conspiring with him how to load and bless
With fruit the vines that round the thatch-eves run;
2 To bend with apples the mossed cottage-trees,
And fill all fruit with ripeness to the core;
To swell the gourd, and plump the hazel shells
With a sweet kernel; to set budding more,
And still more, later flowers for the bees,
Until they think warm days will never cease,
For Summer has o'er-brimmed their clammy cells.

II

4 Who hath not seen thee oft amid thy store?
Sometimes whoever seeks abroad may find
Thee sitting careless on a granary floor,
Thy hair soft-lifted by the winnowing[1] wind;
Or on a half-reaped furrow sound asleep,
Drowsed with the fume of poppies, while thy hook[2]
5 Spares the next swath and all its twined flowers:
And sometimes like a gleaner thou dost keep
Steady thy laden head across a brook;
Or by a cider-press, with patient look,
6 Thou watchest the last oozings hours by hours.

III

Where are the songs of Spring? Ay, where are they?
Think not of them, thou hast thy music too—
7 While barred clouds bloom the soft-dying day,
And touch the stubble-plains with rosy hue;
Then in a wailful choir the small gnats mourn
Among the river sallows,[3] borne aloft
Or sinking as the light wind lives or dies;

---

1. **winnowing:** Fanning; winnowing is a process in which the chaff is fanned from the grain.
2. **hook:** Scythe.
3. **sallows:** Willow trees.

Enrichment Two days after completing the ode, Keats wrote in a letter to a friend; "How beautiful the season is now—How fine the air . . . I never liked stubble fields so much as now—Aye better than the chilly green of the spring. Somehow a stubble plain looks warm—in the same way that some pictures look warm—this struck me so much in my Sunday's walk that I composed upon it."

1 **Literary Focus** Note that the entire poem is an apostrophe—the poet speaks directly to autumn.

2 **Discussion** What words in the opening stanza suggest fulness? Why is this an appropriate description for the season? Note that the word *clammy* means "heavily liquid."

4 **Discussion** Who is *thee* referred to in line 12? What kind of figure of speech does it prepresent?

5 **Clarification** A swath is a path cut by a scythe or sickle.

6 **Literary Focus** Note the use of onomatopoeia in *oozings*. What is the dominant tone of the whole stanza?

7 **Discussion** Explain how the poet achieves the hint of melancholy in the third stanza. What sights and sounds are evoked?

Challenge Point out examples of the poet's use of tactile images in the ode.

Answers

ANSWERS TO THINKING ABOUT THE SELECTION

Recalling

1. (a) The season is conspiring to ripen the fruit and all the harvests, and to fooling the bees into thinking that summer will never end. (b) The season is conspiring with the sun to accomplish these ends.
2. Songs of autumn include choirs of gnats, the bleat of lambs, and the songs of hedge-crickets and of birds.

Interpreting

3. Autumn can be described as "a close bosom-friend of the maturing sun" because it is in conjunction with the sun that the season has produced its bountiful harvest.
4. (a) The activities include harvesting and pressing fruit for cider. (b) These activities create an impression of pleasantness and productivity.
5. The poet suggests the sounds of spring are hardly formidable compared to the varied songs of autumn.

Applying

6. Answers will differ but should include the idea that Keats likely disliked winter because of its association with death and decay.

SPEAKING AND LISTENING

Consider having students present their readings with music to the class.

THINKING AND WRITING

For help with this assignment, students can refer to Lesson 12, "Writing About a Poem," in the Handbook of Writing About Literature.

And full-grown lambs loud bleat from hilly bourn;[4]
Hedge-crickets sing; and now with treble soft
The red-breast whistles from a garden croft;[5]
And gathering swallows twitter in the skies.

---

4. **bourn:** Region.
5. **croft:** An enclosed plot of farm land.

THINKING ABOUT THE SELECTION

Recalling

1. (a) In stanza I of the poem, what is the season described as "doing"? (b) With whom is the season "conspiring"?
2. What are some of the songs of autumn?

Interpreting

3. In what way can Autumn be described as a "close bosom-friend of the maturing sun"?
4. (a) What activities frequently associated with the season are described in the second stanza? (b) What impression of Autumn is created by mentioning these activities?
5. Why do you think the speaker mentions the songs of Spring in stanza III?

Applying

6. What do you suppose was Keats's attitude toward winter? Explain your answer in terms of the three odes you have just read.

SPEAKING AND LISTENING

Selecting Music to Accompany a Poem

In "To Autumn," Keats mentions the songs of Spring and of Autumn. Many of the images he presents in the poem, in fact, suggest music. Find a piece of music that you feel would provide good background to Keats's poem about autumn. Try reading the poem aloud as the music plays. If possible, bring a recording of the music you select to class.

THINKING AND WRITING

Comparing and Contrasting Odes

Choose one of the odes by Shelley that you read. Reread it, noting such features as word choice, stanza structure, and overall message. In a one-page composition, discuss the ways in which the three odes by Keats are similar to and different from that of Shelley. Include mention of whose work you like better and state your reasons.

Prose

FISHERMAN UPON A LEE SHORE
J. M. W. Turner
The Iveagh Bequest, Kenwood, Bridgeman/Art Resource

Humanities Note

Fine art, *Fisherman Upon a Lee Shore,* 1802, by J. M. W. Turner. John Mallord William Turner exhibited his first painting at the Royal Academy when he was fifteen. He became very successful, frequently exhibiting paintings there. Turner was stirred by wild and dramatically romantic scenes, like this. Many aspects of this piece are typical of Turner's work—filled with striking effects: an awe-inspiring storm, a battle with the raging seas, dazzling light and shadows. In Turner's work, nature reflects and expresses human emotions—the humans are small and overwhelmed in the face of powers beyond control.

More About the Author Even had she not written *Frankenstein* and several other novels, Mary Wollstonecraft Shelley would probably still have become famous merely by association. Her father, William Godwin, was a brilliant political thinker; her mother, Mary Wollstonecraft, was a celebrated feminist, who wrote *A Vindication of the Rights of Women;* her husband, Percy Shelley, is now recognized as one of the finest Romantic poets; and she counted among her close friends another poetic genius, Lord Byron. In an age when a woman's role was often confined to the home, what influence do you think these people had on Mary Shelley's life?

MARY SHELLEY

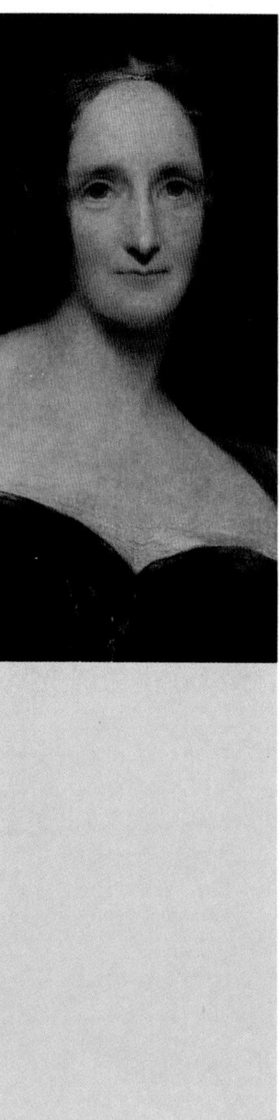

1797–1851

Even the most serious and dedicated of writers have their lighter moments. It is interesting to note that had it not been for such a moment involving two of English literature's most gifted writers, one of the most celebrated Gothic novels of all time might never have seen the light of day. More interesting still, the novel in question, *Frankenstein,* was penned by neither of the aforementioned greats —the poets Percy Bysshe Shelley and Lord Byron—but by the wife of the former, Mary Shelley.

Born in London, Mary Wollstonecraft Godwin was the daughter of William Godwin, a political thinker and writer given to radical ideas. One of her father's books, *Political Justice,* managed to attract the attention of the young and equally radically minded Percy Shelley, who became one of Godwin's disciples. Mary Godwin in turn became a great admirer of the young poet, and the two of them eloped to Switzerland when she was seventeen.

Mary Shelley's first piece of writing, *Journal of a Six Weeks' Tour* (1817), was a collaborative effort with her husband. Her first solo work—the novel with which her name is most often associated today—grew, quite innocently, out of idle conversation between Byron and another friend during a visit to the Shelleys' home on Lake Geneva in 1816. As a result of the conversation, it was suggested as a means of passing the time that each of the four friends attempt to write a ghost story. Though the results of the contest were largely unremarkable, Mary Shelley's horrific tale of the creation of a monster so impressed the gathering that her husband later urged her to develop it into a full-length novel. Thus was born *Frankenstein* (1818), and the creature that has thrilled countless readers and fueled the imaginations of generations of film makers.

After *Frankenstein,* Mary Shelley produced five more novels: *Valperga* (1823) and *Perkin Warbeck* (1830), which are historical works; the autobiographical *Lodore* (1835); *Falkner* (1837), a complicated mystery tale; and *The Last Man* (1826).

If *Frankenstein* is, as scholars have noted, structurally weak, it is nevertheless a "good read." More important from a historical perspective, the novel was the first in a long line of works to explore the potential dangers of technology that falls into the wrong hands.

Objectives

1. To recognize the Gothic tradition
2. To write in the Gothic tradition

Teaching Portfolio: Support Material

Teacher Backup, p. 000

Vocabulary Check, p. 00

Usage and Mechanics Worksheet, p. 00

Analyzing Literature Worksheet, p. 00

Critical Thinking and Reading Worksheet, p. 00

Language Worksheet, p. 00

Selection Test, p. 000

GUIDE FOR READING

Introduction to *Frankenstein*

Literary Movements

Gothic Tradition. The Gothic novel was a late eighteenth-century revival of the tale of terror, which has its roots in antiquity. Gothic fiction, or *Gothicism,* is formally defined by two elements—the historical and the "wonderful," or supernatural. One of the earliest and best-known Gothic novels was Horace Walpole's *The Castle of Otranto* (1765), a hair-raising account of a castle terrorized by a giant. Within the pages of Walpole's thriller, paintings and statues come to life for the first time in fiction. The next important contributor to the "renaissance of wonder" was Clara Reeve, a critic, whose *The Old English Baron* (1777) was, in her own humble opinion, an improvement on Walpole's haunted castle story. The Gothic tradition was refined considerably in the hands of Matthew Gregory Lewis, who, at the age of twenty, published *The Monk* (1796), a cleverly conceived and simply told tale of a Spanish friar who enters into a contract with the devil. The first novel to depict its horrors in graphic terms, *The Monk* paved the way for Mary Shelley's *Frankenstein* (1818), whose main character breathes life into one of the best-known and most terrifying monsters of all time.

Look For

As you read Mary Shelley's "Introduction to *Frankenstein,*" be alert to the elements that she describes as being responsible for her tale's appeal.

Writing

Give some thought to ideas that might be incorporated into a tale of terror. Well-used but always-dependable possibilities include graveyards at night, dark winding staircases, and ghosts. Sketch a rough outline to a story that contains some of these ideas.

Vocabulary

Knowing the following words will help you as you read "Introduction to *Frankenstein.*"

appendage (ə pen'dij) *n.*: Something added on (p. 744)
ungenial (un jēn'yəl) *adj.*: Unfriendly; characterized by bad weather (p. 744)
acceded (ak sēd'id) *v.*: (With *to*) Yielded to; agreed upon (p. 745)
platitude (plat'ə to͞od') *n.*: Statement lacking originality (p. 745)
phantasm (fan' taz'm) *n.*: Supernatural form or shape (p. 746)
incitement (in sīt'mənt) *n.*: Cause to perform; encouragement (p. 747)
progeny (präj' ə nē) *n.*: Offspring; child (p. 747)

Literary Focus The complete title to Mary Shelley's work is *Frankenstein; or, the Modern Prometheus.* The literary reference is to the mythological figure central to her husband's poem "Prometheus Unbound"—the Greek Titan who was chained and tortured by the god Zeus for stealing fire from heaven and giving it to humans. Prometheus was a popular figure in Romantic poetry, for he had the full range of Romantic moral sensibility and the full Romantic capacity for creation and destruction.

Have students make a list of Gothic novels they have read. Which ones are by modern writers? Which ones were written before the twentieth century? What aspects do these novels share?

Look For Suggest that **more advanced** students read *Frankenstein* as well as other stories written in the gothic tradition, including those mentioned in the Guide for Reading. Have them prepare a list of common characteristics.

Writing Have your students brainstorm about other gothic-terror devices. The class might also attempt to suggest a skeletal plot outline.

Vocabulary For **less advanced** students, you may wish to read passages from the excerpt in class and use context clues to guide students toward an understanding of other difficult words.

Motivation for Reading Most likely, some students in your class will have seen a movie version sion of Mary Shelley's novel *Frankenstein.* Ask them to briefly discuss the movie's premise and postulate why the story of Frankenstein is still popular after so many years.

Master Teacher Note Suggest that students read the Greek myth about Prometheus and Percy Shelley's poem "Prometheus Unbound." Then have them speculate on the appropriateness of the full title to Mary Shelley's work.

Purpose-Setting Question What influences of the Romantic age are evident in the work?

1 **Discussion** What does this paragraph tell you about Mary Shelley's personality?

2 **Clarification** This is a reference to Lord Byron's poem "Childe Harold's Pilgrimage," a travelogue written in Spenserian stanzas that made him the toast of London society.

3 **Discussion** What element(s) in these ghost stories can be found in the typical ghost story?

Introduction to *Frankenstein*

Mary Wollstonecraft Shelley

In this introduction to the third edition of Frankenstein, *published in 1831, Mary Shelley recalls the circumstances that led her to write the novel during the summer of 1816.*

The Publishers of the Standard Novels, in selecting Frankenstein for one of their series, expressed a wish that I should furnish them with some account of the origin of the story. I am the more willing to comply, because I shall thus give a general answer to the question, so very frequently asked me:
1 "How I, then a young girl, came to think of, and to dilate upon, so very hideous an idea?" It is true that I am very averse to bringing myself forward in print; but as my account will only appear as an appendage to a former production, and as it will be confined to such topics as have connection with my authorship alone, I can scarcely accuse myself of a personal intrusion. . . .

In the summer of 1816, we[1] visited Switzerland, and became the neighbors of Lord Byron. At first we spent our pleasant hours on the lake or wandering on its shores; and Lord Byron, who was writing
2 the third canto of *Childe Harold,* was the only one among us who put his thoughts upon paper. These, as he brought them successively to us, clothed in all the light and harmony of poetry, seemed to stamp as divine the glories of heaven and earth, whose influences we partook with him.

But it proved a wet, ungenial summer, and incessant rain often confined us for days to the house. Some volumes of ghost stories, translated from the German into French,[2] fell into our hands. There was "The History of the Inconstant Lover,"[3] who, when he thought to clasp the bride to whom he had pledged his vows, found himself in the arms of the pale ghost of her whom he had deserted. There was the tale of the sinful founder of his race,[4] whose miserable doom it was to bestow the kiss of death
on all the younger sons of his fated house, 3
just when they reached the age of promise. His gigantic, shadowy form, clothed like the ghost in Hamlet, in complete armor but with the beaver[5] up, was seen at midnight, by the moon's fitful beams, to advance slowly along the gloomy avenue. The shape was lost beneath the shadow along the gloomy avenue. The shape was lost beneath the shadow of the castle walls; but soon a gate swung back, a step was heard, the door of the chamber opened, and he advanced to the couch of the blooming youths, cradled in healthy sleep. Eternal sorrow sat upon his face as he bent down and kissed the fore-

1. we: Mary Shelley, her husband Percy Bysshe Shelley, and their two children.

2. volumes . . . French: *Fantasmagoriana,* or *Collected Stories of Apparitions of Specters, Ghosts, Phantoms, Etc.,* published anonymously in 1812.

3. "The History . . . Lover": The true name of the story is "The Dead Fiancée."

4. the tale . . . race: "Family Portraits."

5. beaver: The hinged piece of armor that covers the face.

A VIEW OF CHAMONIX AND MT. BLANC
Julius Schnon von Carolsfeld
Austrian Gallery, Vienna

heads of the boys, who from that hour withered like flowers snapped upon the stalk. I have not seen these stories since then, but their incidents are as fresh in my mind as if I had read them yesterday.

"We will each write a ghost story," said Lord Byron; and his proposition was acceded to. There were four of us.[6] The noble author began a tale, a fragment of which he printed at the end of his poem of Mazeppa. Shelley, more apt to embody ideas and sentiments in the radiance of brilliant imagery, and in the music of the most melodious
4 verse that adorns our language, than to invent the machinery of a story, commenced one founded on the experiences of his early life. Poor Polidori had some terrible idea about a skull-headed lady, who was so punished for peeping through a keyhole—what to see I forget—something very shocking and wrong of course; but when she was reduced to a worse condition than the renowned Tom of Coventry,[7] he did not know what to do with her, and was obliged to despatch her to the tomb of the Capulets,[8] the only place for which she was fitted. The illustrious poets also, annoyed by the platitude of prose, speedily relinquished their uncongenial task.

I busied myself *to think of a story*— a story to rival those which had excited us to this task. One which would speak to the mysterious fears of our nature and awaken thrilling horror—one to make the reader dread to look round, to curdle the blood, and
quicken the beatings of the heart. If I did not 5
accomplish these things, my ghost story would be unworthy of its name. I thought and pondered—vainly. I felt that blank in-

6. four of us: Byron, the two Shelleys, and John William Polidori, Byron's physician.

7. Tom of Coventry: "Peeping Tom" who, according to legend, was struck blind for looking at Lady Godiva as she rode naked through Coventry.

8. tomb of the Capulets: Where Romeo and Juliet died.

Humanities Note

Fine art, *A View of Chamonix and M. Blanc,* 1824, Julius Schnon von Carolsfeld. Carolsfeld (1794–1872) was a German Nazarene painter. The Nazarenes were a group of Viennese artists who sought a return to the art of the Middle Ages. In their efforts to achieve the proper atmosphere, they occupied an abandoned monastery in Rome and worked as artist-monks. Their art was romantic, sentimental, and realistic.

The academically trained Julius von Carolsfeld often expressed this Nazarene form of Romanticism in landscape painting. *A View of Chamonix and Mt. Blanc* was painted in 1824. Beautifully detailed, it is a moonlit view of a famous glacier-covered mountain and a small village in the French Alps. As is common in German Romanticism, the painting has a weird or mysterious feeling to it, perhaps because of the extreme realism. This weirdness is the very quality that makes this painting appropriate as an illustration for the environment in which Mary Shelley wrote the horror classic *Frankenstein.*

You might wish to use the following questions as a basis for class discussion.

1. How would you describe the setting of this painting?
2. Does this setting match the setting of the story?
3. What mood does this painting instill in you?

4 **Discussion** What did Mary Shelley think of her husband's storytelling ability?

5 **Discussion** Why might Mary Shelley have had such a hard time thinking of a story?

6 **Discussion** How is the Romantic concern about the nature of creativity reflected here?

7 **Discussion** What insight do these observations give into the personalities of Byron and Shelley?

8 **Discussion** Would the Romantics have admired or deplored Mary Shelley's imaginative reverie? Why?

9 **Enrichment** The twentieth-century writer W. Somerset Maugham wrote, "Reverie is the groundwork of creative imagination; it is the privilege of the artist that with him it is not as with other men an escape from reality, but the means by which he accedes to it." Have students discuss the meaning of this quotation. How does it relate to Mary Shelley's reverie?

capability of invention which is the greatest misery of authorship, when dull Nothing replies to our anxious invocations. *Have you thought of a story?* I was asked each morning, and each morning I was forced to reply with a mortifying negative. . . .

Many and long were the conversations between Lord Byron and Shelley, to which I was a devout but nearly silent listener. During one of these, various philosophical doctrines were discussed, and among others the nature of the principle of life and whether there was any probability of its ever being discovered and communicated. They talked of the experiments of Dr. Darwin[9] (I speak
6, 7 not of what the Doctor really did or said that he did, but, as more to my purpose, of what was then spoken of as having been done by him), who preserved a piece of vermicelli in a glass case till by some extraordinary means it began to move with voluntary motion. Not thus, after all, would life be given. Perhaps a corpse would be reanimated: galvanism[10] had given token of such things. Perhaps the component parts of a creature might be manufactured, brought together, and endued with vital warmth.

Night waned upon this talk, and even the witching hour had gone by, before we retired to rest. When I placed my head on my pillow, I did not sleep, nor could I be said to think. My imagination, unbidden, possessed and guided me, gifting the successive images that arose in my mind with a vividness
8 far beyond the usual bounds of reverie. I saw—with shut eyes but acute mental vision—I saw the pale student of unhallowed arts kneeling beside the thing he had put together. I saw the hideous phantasm of a man stretched out, and then, on the working of some powerful engine, show signs of life and stir with an uneasy, half vital motion. Frightful must it be, for supremely frightful would be the effect of any human endeavor to mock the stupendous mechanism of the Creator of the world. His success would terrify the artist; he would rush away from his odious handiwork, horror-stricken. He would hope that, left to itself, the slight spark of life which he had communicated would fade; that this thing, which had received such imperfect animation, would subside into dead matter; and he might sleep in the belief that the silence of the grave would quench forever the transient existence of the hideous corpse which he had looked upon as the cradle of life. He sleeps; but he is awakened; he opens his eyes; behold the horrid thing stands at his bedside, opening his curtains, and looking on him with yellow, watery, but speculative eyes.

I opened mine in terror. The idea so possessed my mind, that a thrill of fear ran through me, and I wished to exchange the ghastly image of my fancy for the realities around. I see them still: the very room, the dark parquet,[11] the closed shutters, with the moonlight struggling through, and the sense I had that the glassy lake and white high Alps were beyond. I could not so easily get rid of my hideous phantom: still it haunted me. I must try to think of something else. I recurred to my ghost story—my tiresome unlucky ghost story! O! if I could only contrive one which would frighten my reader as I myself had been frightened that night!

Swift as light and as cheering was the idea that broke in upon me. "I have found it! What terrified me will terrify others, and I need only describe the specter which had haunted my midnight pillow." On the morrow I announced that I had *thought of a story.* I began that day with the words, *It was on a dreary night of November,* making only a transcript of the grim terrors of my waking dream.

At first I thought but of a few pages—of 9

9. Dr. Darwin: Erasmus Darwin (1731–1802), physician, natural scientist, and poet.

10. galvanism: The use of electric current to induce twitching in dead muscles.

11. parquet (pär kā'): Flooring made of wooden pieces arranged in a pattern.

a short tale—but Shelley urged me to develop the idea at greater length. I certainly did not owe the suggestion of one incident, nor scarcely of one train of feeling, to my husband, and yet but for his incitement, it would never have taken the form in which it was presented to the world. From this declaration I must except the preface. As far as I can recollect, it was entirely written by him.

And now, once again, I bid my hideous progeny go forth and prosper. I have an 10
affection for it, for it was the offspring of 11
happy days, when death and grief were but words, which found no true echo in my heart. Its several pages speak of many a walk, many a drive, and many a conversation, when I was not alone; and my companion was one who, in this world, I shall never see more. But this is for myself: my readers have nothing to do with these associations.

THINKING ABOUT THE SELECTION

Recalling

1. What question does the author say people frequently ask her?
2. (a) What forced the author, her husband, and their friends to stay indoors? (b) What did they do to pass the time?
3. What was Byron's proposition?
4. (a) What provided the author with inspiration for her story? (b) What "vision" came to the author after she retired for the night?

Interpreting

5. What do the goals the author sets for herself in writing her ghost story suggest about her as a person?
6. Based on her description of her "vision," what seems to be the author's attitude toward work of the sort carried out by Dr. Darwin?

Applying

7. Many areas of scientific investigation carry both potential benefits and potential dangers for humankind. (a) What such areas in our own age can you name? (b) Which areas do you believe human beings should never have become involved in? Give reasons for your answer.

ANALYZING LITERATURE

Recognizing Gothic Tradition

The Gothic tradition of the horror story, which began in the eighteenth century, traces back to ancient times. In *The Spirit of the Public Journals,* a 1797 pamphlet, a "recipe" for the Gothic novel is given. Among the "ingredients" listed are: an old castle, a long gallery with secret doors, three freshly murdered bodies, assorted skeletons, and "noises, whispers, and groans." In *Frankenstein,* Mary Shelley endeavored to improve slightly on that formula.

1. Based on your reading of her introduction, what most likely is the theme of *Frankenstein?*
2. Based on the French translations of ghost stories Shelley mentions, what other "ingredients" might be added to the above list?

THINKING AND WRITING

Writing in the Gothic Tradition

Review the ideas and outline you developed for the assignment under Writing on page 743. Then write an original story or episode that follows the Gothic tradition. You may add as many of the elements mentioned. If you can, build a theme into your horror story. When you revise make sure you have told your tale in chronological order.

10 **Discussion** Explain why the author says she has "an affection" for her horror story.

11 **Clarification** The name Frankenstein is commonly associated with the monster. It, in fact, refers to the creator.

Answers

ANSWERS TO THINKING ABOUT THE SELECTION

Recalling

1. She says that people ask her: How did a young girl conceive such a hideous idea?
2. (a) Rainy weather drove them indoors. (b) To pass the time they read ghost stories.
3. Byron proposed that each of them write a ghost story.
4. (a) Her inspiration was a discussion between Byron and Shelley about whether life could be manufactured. (b) She dreamed about a man who had created human life.

Interpreting

5. They suggest a somewhat insecure person. The presence of Shelley and Byron probably made her feel this way. She was not content to settle for "secondbest"—her ghost story had to be worthy of its name.
6. She saw any human attempt to create life as a mockery of the Creator.

Applying

7. (a) Answers will differ. Possible answers include the following: The attempt to create life in a test tube and experiments with nuclear energy are two examples of scientific investigation that carry both potential benefits and dangers. (b) Answers will differ; though nuclear weapons will be mentioned by many, because of their potential for destruction.

Challenge What other works of literature have been inspired by dreams?

ANSWERS TO ANALYZING LITERATURE

1. The theme of *Frankenstein* is that man should not try to interfere with the work of God.
2. She thought that a horror story should be terrifying, that death should be a prominent theme, and that the central character should atone for a sin by suffering a terrible fate.

THINKING AND WRITING

Publishing Student Writing Horror stories have always been popular with people of all ages. Suggest that students compile the best ghost stories into a book that might serve as a class fundraiser at Halloween.

More About the Author Some critics believe that Charles Lamb's best essays were written under the pen name "Elia." "Dream Children: A Reverie" is one example of Elia's work. A.C. Ward noted "As Elia, Lamb was rarely dull . . . yet, as Lamb, his pen at times drags wearily." Do you think that by becoming someone else in his imagination, Lamb felt freer to express himself and to deal with the unhappier aspects of his life? Why?

CHARLES LAMB

1775–1834

A personal friend of most of the great English writers of his day, Charles Lamb was considered one of the foremost prose writers of the Romantic Era—a distinction he has retained through the present time.

The son of a clerk and the grandson of a housekeeper, Lamb was born in London. He was educated at Christ's Hospital, a school for poor children, where he met and became lifelong friends with a fellow student, Samuel Taylor Coleridge, who later became a well-known poet and critic. At seventeen Lamb left school and took a job with the South Sea House, a large London trading company. He soon received a better position as an accountant at a rival firm, the East India House, where he remained employed for thirty-three years.

In 1796 an event occurred that shadowed the rest of Lamb's life. His sister Mary, given to brief fits of insanity, killed their mother. After this, Lamb, always a loving brother, devoted himself to Mary's care and protection. Upon his retirement from East India House, he was granted a comfortable pension and after his sister's confinement to an asylum, took her to live in the country.

Throughout most of his life, Lamb wrote to supplement his regular income. Although he composed a number of poems and plays, it was with his essays and literary criticism that he made his mark as a writer. In 1808 he published a book on Elizabethan dramatic poets that established his reputation as a critic. Thereafter, he began to contribute essays to periodicals such as the *Examiner,* the *Quarterly Review,* the *London Magazine,* and the *Reflector,* a magazine published by the poet Leigh Hunt.

It was in the *London Magazine* that Lamb's series of personal essays written under the name Elia first appeared in printed form. Later these essays were collected and published in the volumes *Essays of Elia* (1832) and *Last Essays of Elia* (1833). Lamb also collaborated with his sister Mary on a number of works, including the ever-popular *Tales from Shakespeare* (1807), a collection designed to introduce young readers to Shakespeare's plays.

Many of Lamb's essays are autobiographical, with characters modeled on his father, his grandmother, his brother John, and other relatives. Though they are known for their gentle humor, the essays often display an undercurrent of great sadness, the result of the tragedies that Lamb experienced in his life.

Objectives

1. To understand the familiar essay
2. To infer a writer's tone
3. To recognize multiple meanings of words
4. To analyze a writer's attitudes.

Teaching Portfolio: Support Material

Teacher Backup, p. 000

Vocabulary Check, p. 00

Usage and Mechanics Worksheet, p. 00

Analyzing Literature Worksheet, p. 00

Critical Thinking and Reading Worksheet, p. 00

Language Worksheet, p. 00

Selection Test, p. 000

GUIDE FOR READING

Dream Children: A Reverie

The Writer's Technique

Familiar Essay. An essay is a short prose composition that focuses on a single subject. A familiar or informal essay is a loosely constructed essay that uses conversational English to communicate a writer's thoughts in a manner that will interest or entertain the reader. Since familiar essays frequently include details from the author's own life, they are sometimes referred to as "personal" essays.

The familiar essay has its origins in the writings of Michel de Montaigne, a French author of the sixteenth century. It was Montaigne who first used the term *essai*—French for "attempt"—to describe the somewhat rambling, often amusing compositions in which he communicated highly personal thoughts to his readers.

Look For

As you read "Dream Children: A Reverie," look for the qualities of the familiar essay displayed in it, as well as to ways in which it differs from the formal essays of writers such as Francis Bacon (pages 383–384) and John Dryden (pages 512–520).

Writing

Choose a fairly light topic that allows some room for opinion, such as whether the school week should be shortened or lengthened. Freewrite, expressing your opinion on this topic, defending your position with abundant examples from your own life and experience.

Vocabulary

Knowing the following words will help you as you read "Dream Children: A Reverie."

reverie (rev′ər ē) *n.*: Daydream (p. 750)
upbraiding (up brād′iŋ) *n.*: Scolding (p. 750)
tawdry (tô′drē) *adj.*: Cheap; gaudy (p. 750)
desisted (di zist′əd) *v.*: Stopped (p. 750)
apparition (ap′ə rish′ən) *n.*: Ghost (p. 751)
impertinent (im pʉr′ t'n ənt) *adj.*: Rude; disrespectful (p. 751)
mettlesome (met′'l səm) *adj.*: High-spirited (p. 751)

Literary Focus Ask students to explain the meaning of the word *reverie* and to give examples of daydreams they have had. Point out that an informal essay, being loosely structured, is an especially appropriate form for the material of a reverie.

Look For Reviewing the highly formal structure of an essay such as Bacon's "Of Studies" will point up the differences in Lamb's essay.

Writing Allow your students a few minutes to offer their reasons for their opinion.

Vocabulary Have **more advanced** students study the vocabulary words on their own. Call on **less advanced** students to write the vocabulary words and their definitions on the chalkboard.

Motivation for Reading Ask for student volunteers to share a story about their grandparents' childhoods. Discuss why people find stories about their elders so appealing.

Master Teacher Note You may wish to mention that the seventeenth-century prose writers greatly influenced Lamb's style.

Thematic Idea Have students compare the ideas on reverie in this selection with those in Mary Wollstonecraft Shelley's "Introduction to *Frankenstein*," p. 744.

Purpose-Setting Question What details in the essay might have come from Lamb's own life?

1 **Critical Thinking and Reading** What is the tone of the first paragraph? How does it set the stage for the rest of the essay?

2 **Discussion** The narrator repeats the phrase "Then I told . . ." several times. What do such repetitions do to the pace of the story?

3 **Discussion** At the end of each of the first three paragraphs, the author describes the reaction of one of the children. What effect does this create?

Dream Children: A Reverie

Charles Lamb

Children love to listen to stories about their elders when *they* were children; to stretch their imagination to the conception of a traditionary great-uncle, or grandame whom they never saw. It was in this spirit that my little ones crept about me the other evening to hear about their great-grandmother Field,[1] who lived in a great house in Norfolk (a hundred times bigger than that in which they and papa lived) which had been the scene—so at least it
1 was generally believed in that part of the country—of the tragic incidents which they had lately become familiar with from the ballad of "The Children in the Wood."[2] Certain it is that the whole story of the children and their cruel uncle was to be seen fairly carved out in wood upon the chimney piece of the great hall, the whole story down to the Robin Redbreasts;[3] till a foolish rich person pulled it down to set up a marble one of modern invention in its stead, with no story upon it. Here Alice put out one of her dear mother's looks, too tender to be called upbraiding.

Then I went on to say, how religious and how good their great-grandmother Field was, how beloved and respected by everybody, though she was not indeed the mistress of this great house, but had only the charge of it (and yet in some respects she might be said to be the mistress of it too) committed to her by the owner, who preferred living in a newer and more fashionable mansion which he had purchased somewhere in the adjoining county; but still she lived in it in a manner as if it had been her own, and kept up the dignity of the great house in a sort while she lived, which afterwards came to decay, and was nearly pulled down, and all its old ornaments stripped and carried away to the owner's other house, where they were set up, and looked as awkward as if someone were to carry away the old tombs they had seen lately at the Abbey, and stick them up in Lady C.'s tawdry gilt drawing room. Here John smiled, as much as to say, "that would be foolish indeed."

And then I told how, when she came to die, her funeral was attended by a concourse 2
of all the poor, and some of the gentry too, of the neighborhood for many miles round, to show their respect for her memory, because she had been such a good and religious woman; so good indeed that she knew all the Psaltery[4] by heart, ay, and a great part of the Testament besides. Here little Alice spread her hands. 3

Then I told what a tall, upright, graceful person their great-grandmother Field once was; and how in her youth she was esteemed the best dancer—here Alice's little right foot played an involuntary movement, till, upon my looking grave, it desisted—the

1. **great-grandmother Field:** Mary Field, Lamb's grandmother.
2. **"The Children in the Wood":** A popular ballad of the time about the mysterious disappearance of two children.
3. **Robin Redbreasts:** At the end of the story, the robin buries the bodies of the children with leaves.

4. **Psaltery** (sôl′ tə rē): The Psalms of David.

best dancer, I was saying, in the county, till a cruel disease, called a cancer, came, and bowed her down with pain; but it could never bend her good spirits, or make them stoop, but they were still upright, because she was so good and religious.

Then I told how she was used to sleep by herself in a lone chamber of the great lone house; and how she believed that an apparition of two infants was to be seen at midnight gliding up and down the great staircase near where she slept, but she said "those innocents would do her no harm"; and how frightened I used to be, though in those days I had my maid to sleep with me, because I was never half so good or religious as she—and yet I never saw the infants. Here John expanded all his eyebrows and tried to look courageous.

Then I told how good she was to all her grandchildren, having us to the great house in the holidays, where I in particular used to spend many hours by myself, in gazing upon the old busts of the Twelve Caesars that had
4 been Emperors of Rome, till the old marble heads would seem to live again, or I to be turned into marble with them; how I never could be tired with roaming about that huge mansion, with its vast empty rooms, with their worn-out hangings, fluttering tapestry, and carved oaken panels, with the gilding almost rubbed out—sometimes in the spacious old-fashioned gardens, which I had almost to myself, unless when now and then a solitary gardening man would cross me—and how the nectarines and peaches hung upon the walls, without my ever offer-
5 ing to pluck them, because they were forbidden fruit, unless now and then—and because I had more pleasure in strolling about among the old melancholy-looking yew trees, or the firs, and picking up the red berries, and the fir apples,[5] which were good for nothing but to look at—or in lying about upon the fresh grass, with all the fine garden smells around me—or basking in the orangery, till I could almost fancy myself ripening too along with the oranges and the limes in that grateful warmth—or in watching the dace that darted to and fro in the fishpond, at the bottom of the garden, with here and there a great sulky pike hanging midway down the water in silent state, as if it mocked at their impertinent friskings—I had more pleasure in these busy-idle diversions than in all the sweet flavors of peaches, nectarines, oranges, and such like common baits of children. Here John slyly deposited back upon the plate a bunch of grapes, which, not unobserved by Alice, he had meditated dividing with her, and both seemed willing to relinquish them for the present as irrelevant.

Then in somewhat a more heightened tone, I told how, though their great-grandmother Field loved all her grandchildren, yet in an especial manner she might be said to love their uncle, John L—,[6] because he was so handsome and spirited a youth, and a king to the rest of us; and, instead of moping about in solitary corners, like some of us, he would mount the most mettlesome horse he could get, when but an imp no bigger than themselves, and make it carry him half over the county in a morning, and join the hunters when there were any out—and yet he loved the old great house and gardens too, but had too much spirit to be always pent up within their boundaries—and how their uncle grew up to man's estate as brave as he was handsome, to the admiration of everybody, but of their great-grandmother Field most especially; and how he used to carry me upon his back when I was a lame-footed boy—for he was a good bit older than me—many a mile when I could not walk for pain; and how in after life he became lame-footed too, and I did not always (I fear) make allowances enough for him when he was impatient, and in pain, nor remember sufficiently how considerate he had been to me when I was lame-footed;

5. fir apples: Fir cones.

6. John L—: John Lamb, Charles's brother.

4 **Discussion** How do these lines illustrate the chief purpose of a familiar essay?

5 **Discussion** What do these lines express about Lamb's attitude toward nature?

6 Clarification His brother John died not long before Charles wrote this essay.

7 Discussion Do you think the narrator wishes for "what might have been"? Why or why not?

8 Discussion How does the world in which the narrator finds himself differ from the world of his daydreams?

and how when he died, though he had not been dead an hour, it seemed as if he had died a great while ago, such a distance there is betwixt life and death; and how I bore his death as I thought pretty well at first, but afterwards it haunted and haunted me; and though I did not cry or take it to heart as some do, and as I think he would have done 6 if I had died, yet I missed him all day long, and knew not till then how much I had loved him. I missed his kindness, and I missed his crossness, and wished him to be alive again, to be quarreling with him (for we quarreled sometimes) rather than not have him again, and was as uneasy without him, as he their poor uncle must have been when the doctor took off his limb. Here the children fell a-crying, and asked if their little mourning which they had on was not for uncle John, and they looked up, and prayed me not to go on about their uncle, but to tell them some stories about their pretty dead mother.

Then I told how for seven long years, in hope sometimes, sometimes in despair, yet persisting ever, I courted the fair Alice W—n;[7] and, as much as children could understand, I explained to them what coyness, and difficulty, and denial meant in maidens—when suddenly, turning to Alice, the soul of the first Alice looked out at her eyes with such a reality of representment, that I became in doubt which of them stood there before me, or whose that bright hair was; and while I stood gazing, both the children gradually grew fainter to my view, receding, and still receding till nothing at last but two mournful features were seen in the uttermost distance, which, without speech, strangely impressed upon me the effects of speech: "We are not of Alice, nor of thee, nor are we children at all. The children of Alice called Bartrum father. We are nothing; less than nothing, and dreams. We are only what might have been, and must wait 7 upon the tedious shores of Lethe[8] millions of ages before we have existence, and a name"—and immediately awaking, I found myself quietly seated in my bachelor armchair, where I had fallen asleep, with the faithful 8 Bridget[9] unchanged by my side—but John L. (or James Elia) was gone forever.

7. Alice W—n: Alice Winterton, name given to Ann Simmons, whom Lamb loved in his earlier years.

8. Lethe (lē′ thē): In classical mythology, the river of forgetfulness, flowing through Hades, the land of the dead.

9. Bridget: Name given to Lamb's sister, Mary.

THINKING ABOUT THE SELECTION

Recalling

1. (a) According to the opening paragraph, who is listening to the narrator's story? (b) Why are these listeners interested in hearing about great-grandmother Field?
2. (a) Besides his grandmother, which relative does the narrator speak of with deep affection? (b) What has happened to this relative?
3. (a) Who was Alice W—n? (b) According to the final paragraph, who closely resembles her?
4. (a) What is revealed about the narrator's audience in the final paragraph? (b) What is revealed about Alice W—n?

Interpreting

5. Why do you suppose the narrator's listeners are named John and Alice?
6. Identify three details in the essay that make the young John and Alice seem real.

Answers

ANSWERS TO THINKING ABOUT THE SELECTION

1. (a) The narrator's children are listening to the story. (b) Children like to listen to stories about their elders as children, to try to imagine what they were like when they were young.
2. (a) The narrator speaks of John L—, his brother and the grandchild of great-grandmother Field. (b) John L— has died.
3. (a) Alice was a woman whom the narrator courted. In reality, she was the woman (Ann Simmons) Charles Lamb loved but never married. (b) Alice, the child of the narrator, closely resembles Alice W—n.
4. (a) The narrator imagined the children in a daydream. (b) Alice W—n married a man named Bartrum and bore his children.

Interpreting

5. The narrator named his listeners after people he loved—his brother John and Alice Winterton.
6. Answers will differ. Possible answers include the following: The narrator describes Alice's reactions

7. In what ways does the apparition seen by great-grandmother Field **foreshadow**—that is, give the reader an advance glimpse of—the events at the end of the essay?
8. (a) What does this essay reveal about Charles Lamb's feelings toward his being unmarried and childless? (b) Why might such feelings be prompted by thoughts of his own childhood and especially of his brother John?

Applying

9. Do you think it is always important to know details of an author's life to fully appreciate the author's work? Explain.

ANALYZING LITERATURE

Understanding the Familiar Essay

A **familiar,** or informal, **essay** is a loosely constructed piece of prose that deals with a single topic and uses conversational English. Although a familiar essay may contain some short story elements, such as plot and character, it is nevertheless considered to be nonfiction, since its chief purpose is to communicate its author's thoughts and feelings, and not those of imaginary characters.

1. Which characters in Lamb's essay are real? Which are imaginary?
2. Which elements in the essay make it seem like a short story? Give several examples.
3. In what ways is the author's style characteristic of a familiar essay?

CRITICAL THINKING AND READING

Inferring Tone

The **tone** of a story, poem, or essay is the attitude the writer takes with respect to the audience, a character, or a situation. In much the way a person's tone of voice will affect how his or her words are understood, so the tone of a literary selection helps shape the reader's reaction toward it. Determine the tone Lamb takes with respect to each of the following, and describe its effect on you.

1. Great-grandmother Field.
2. Young Alice and John.
3. The great house.
4. Alice W—n.

UNDERSTANDING LANGUAGE

Using Multiple Meaning of Words

While good authors as a rule use words precisely, they occasionally use words with second and even third meanings to enrich a thought or sentiment. A writer might, for instance, describe a character's state of mind as "cloudy," with the intention of conveying both the meanings "confused" and "bleak or unhappy." In "Dream Children: A Reverie," Charles Lamb uses several words in this fashion. For each sentence, give two meanings for the italicized word, and describe its impact.

1. "Then I told what a tall, *upright,* graceful person their great-grandmother . . . was." (page 750)
2. ". . . upon my looking *grave,* it desisted . . ." (page 750)
3. ". . . two mournful features . . . without speech, *strangely* impressed upon me the effects of speech. . . ." (page 752)

THINKING AND WRITING

Analyzing a Writer's Attitudes

Lamb's attitude toward his personal fantasy world and his attitude toward reality, as expressed in the essay, appear to be different. Discuss this difference in terms of his blend of factual and fictional details. Ask: What, exactly, is Lamb escaping from? What is he escaping to? What is his view of himself in the fantasy role of father? What relationship does this view bear to his real role as brother? Organize your thoughts and write the first draft of a brief essay. When you revise make sure you have included adequate details to support your main idea.

(Answers begin on p. 752.)

to his words, in such ways as "Alice put out one of her dear mother's looks" and "Alice spread her hands." He also describes John's reactions: "Here John smiled. . . ."

7. Great-grandmother Field saw the apparitions of two infants at midnight, which foreshadows the disclosure at the end of the essay that the children Alice and John are imaginary.
8. (a) The essay suggests that Lamb wished he had married Alice and that they had had children. (b) His memories caused him to feel nostalgic about his family and rueful about his bachelorhood.

Applying

9. Answers will differ. Suggested response: Knowing details about an author's life and his or her attitudes can add to the appreciation of some works. However, in most cases the works can be appreciated on their own merit, without any special knowledge of the author.

ANSWERS TO ANALYZING LITERATURE

1. The characters of great-grandmother Field, John L—, and Alice W—n, and Bridget are real. The grandchildren Alice and John are imaginary.
2. Answers will differ. Possible answers include the following: The opening lines suggest that the piece will be a short story. The setting is established by the description of great-grandmother Field's house. Characters are introduced and brought to life. There is no firm plot, but the suggestion of a plot is there; for example, when the narrator talks about his brother John. There is a resolution to the story when the narrator wakes up.
3. The personal nature and rambling structure of the essay and the use of character, description, and colloquial language, including the frequent use of parentheses, are all characteristic of a familiar essay.

Challenge William Wordsworth claimed that poetry should have its origin in "emotion recollected in tranquillity." How do you think Wordsworth would react to this essay? Explain your answer.

ANSWERS TO CRITICAL THINKING AND READING

Answers will differ. Possible answers follow.

1. Great-grandmother Field is described with loving admiration and respect.
2. Young Alice and John are described with gentle amusement and affection.
3. The house is described with a tone that is a combination of wonder and nostalgia.
4. Alice W—n is described in a sad and regretful tone.

ANSWERS TO UNDERSTANDING LANGUAGE

1. *Upright* means "erect." *Upright* can also mean "honest" or "just," which adds an admirable dimension to great-grandmother's character.
2. *Grave* means "solemn." The word *grave* can also refer to a tomb, which carries greater impact due to the description of great-grandmother Field's funeral in the preceding sentences.
3. The word *strangely* means "oddly." It can also suggest "in an extraordinary way," which adds to the impact of the dream.

More About the Author In addition to being a literary and theatrical critic, William Hazlitt wrote about such widely diverse topics as politics, philosophy, economics, painting, and prize-fighting. Although he was greatly admired for his opinionated essays, he was not nearly as successful in his personal life. He alienated many of his acquaintances, and both of his marriages ended in separation. Ask students what qualitities that served Hazlitt well as a critic might have interfered with his personal relationships.

WILLIAM HAZLITT

1778–1830

Second only to Coleridge as a critic of the Romantic era, William Hazlitt was known in his day and is remembered in ours for his brisk and direct writing style. In addition Hazlitt was a true Romantic who lived life as he wrote about it—with gusto.

The son of a Unitarian minister who sympathized with the colonists during the American Revolution, Hazlitt sailed with his family to America when he was five and remained there for three years. He planned, like his father, to enter the clergy and was admitted to Hackney Theological Seminary in London. A difficulty in expressing himself both orally and on paper, however, forced him to abandon his goal and he returned to his family in Shropshire.

It was there in 1798 that Hazlitt met the poet Samuel Taylor Coleridge, who at the time was a house guest of Hazlitt's father. Recognizing Hazlitt's brilliance, Coleridge introduced the young man to his friends Wordsworth and Charles Lamb, who also found Hazlitt impressive.

Hazlitt, meanwhile, was still frustrated by his inability to communicate his ideas in writing, and at twenty-one he journeyed again to London, this time to study painting with his brother. Finding that his talents in this area were limited as well, he tried his hand once more at writing, and in 1805 published his first book, *An Essay on the Principles of Human Action.* In the six years that followed, he married, wrote two more books, and delivered a series of lectures on philosophy.

The year 1812 found Hazlitt penniless and his spirit broken. He took a paying job as a parliamentary reporter for a London newspaper and—much to his surprise and delight—he developed a following as a writer on a variety of subjects. In 1817 he published *Characters in Shakespeare's Plays,* which he followed up a year later with *A View of the English Stage,* a collection of drama criticism. At last, fame and respect had arrived!

Long an eccentric who judged everyone and everything according to his own rigid system of values, Hazlitt became more bitter and opinionated with age. He turned his talented pen to angry attacks on less liberal journalists than himself, as well as on poets and politicians, and in so doing made many enemies. Only the younger Romantic poets like Shelley and Keats admired Hazlitt's work of this period, and then only because of its intensity and dedication to the philosophy of Rousseau.

While to the modern mind Hazlitt's criticism tends to be overly subjective, scholars nevertheless respect him as one of the leading critics of Elizabethan and Romantic literature. Above all else Hazlitt is remembered for his ability to cut to the heart of an issue and to state his views firmly and honestly.

Objectives

1. To understand the purpose of a critical essay
2. To find main ideas and supporting details
3. To evaluate and write about literary criticism

Teaching Portfolio: Support Material

Teacher Backup, p. 000

Vocabulary Check, p. 00

Usage and Mechanics Worksheet, p. 00

Analyzing Literature Worksheet, p. 00

Critical Thinking and Reading Worksheet, p. 00

Language Worksheet, p. 00

Selection Test, p. 000

GUIDE FOR READING

Macbeth

Literary Forms

Critical Essay. A critical essay is an essay that evaluates the merits of a given topic, usually artistic. While such an essay expresses the personal views and observations of its author, the essay will, if it is fair and honest, also appeal to some universal standard. Literary criticism, an area that gives rise to one of the best-known forms of critical essay, the literary essay, began with the Greek philosopher Plato and was later refined by Aristotle. From the fall of Rome through the Renaissance in the late fourteenth century, literary criticism was neglected in favor of church-related issues. With the Romantic movement came the first modern examples of the critical literary essay, as typified by the writings of Samuel Taylor Coleridge, Charles Lamb, and William Hazlitt.

Look For

As you read Hazlitt's essay on *Macbeth,* look for instances of both the author's perceptiveness as a critic and his lack of objectivity in considering his subject.

Writing

Imagine that you have been asked to review a play for your school newspaper. Make a list of the details of which you would need to take notice. Keep in mind that, in addition to such literary matters as character and theme, you would need to pay attention to how well the actors projected their voices, how effective the lighting was, and so on.

Vocabulary

Knowing the following words will help you as you read Hazlitt's essay on *Macbeth.*

preternatural (prēt'ər nach'ər əl) *adj.*: Outside the natural or normal order (p. 756)
tumultuous (too͝ mul'choo͞ wəs) *adj.*: Disorderly; violent (p. 757)
vehemence (vē'ə məns) *n.*: Strength of feeling and emotion (p. 757)
obdurate (äb' door ət, äb dyoor ət) *adj.*: Hardened against what is good or moral (p. 757)
ascendancy (ə send' ən sē) *n.*: Major or dominating influence (p. 757)
inexorable (in ek'sər ə b'l) *adj.*: Ongoing, with no sign of stopping (p. 757)
baneful (bān' fəl) *adj.*: Full of harm; destructive (p. 757)
compunctious (kəm punk shəs) *adj.*: Sorrowful; regretful (p. 758)
gratuitous (grə to͞o'ə təs) *adj.*: Undeservedly or without reason (p. 758)
servile (sur' v'l) *adj.*: Slavelike (p. 758)
malignity (mə lig' nə tē) *n.*: Deadliness (p. 758)
aggrandizement (ə gran' diz mənt) *n.*: Increase in power (p. 758)

Literary Focus Explain that Hazlitt uses the present tense to write about his subject. As they read the essay, have students think about why Hazlitt chose the present tense and what effect this has on their reaction to his criticism.

Look For Remind students that Hazlitt's essays have been criticized for being too subjective; that is, he often stated opinions without supporting them. Have students look for examples of opinions that are not supported by evidence in the form of examples or quotations from the play.

Writing Hazlitt wrote this essay in reaction to seeing the play *Macbeth* performed in London. For extra credit, your **more advanced** students might enjoy writing a critical essay on a play, movie, or television show they have seen. Have them discuss the likenesses and differences between two major characters.

Vocabulary Have your **less advanced** students use each of the vocabulary words in a sentence that illustrates its meaning.

Master Teacher Note Discuss the purpose of critical essays. This essay might be used to lend insight into the study of *Macbeth,* pages 223–303.

Motivation for Reading Ask students to name a play, movie, or television program they have seen recently and select one seen by a majority of students for discussion. Have several different students explain why they liked or disliked the play, movie, or television program. Encourage them to support their opinions with evidence.

Then discuss the role of the critic. What do they think a critic should tell about the work of literature or program? Why does the word *critic* carry a negative connotation?

Thematic Idea You might have students compare the ideas set form in this essay with those in George Bernard Shaw's "Preface to *Pygmalion.*" p. 1124.

Purpose-Setting Question How would you describe Hazlitt's style in this essay? What aspects of the play is he most interested in?

1 **Discussion** Have one student read aloud the opening lines to Hazlitt's essay, taken from Shakespeare's *Midsummer Night's Dream,* and discuss their meaning.

2 **Discussion** How does Hazlitt's description of Shakespeare's plays relate to the quote at the beginning of the essay?

3 **Critical Thinking and Reading** What main idea do the quotations from the play help to support?

Macbeth

William Hazlitt

"The poet's eye in a fine
frenzy rolling
Doth glance from heaven to
earth, from earth to heaven;
1 *And as imagination bodies forth*
The forms of things
unknown, the poet's pen
Turns them to shape, and
gives to airy nothing
A local habitation and a name."[1]

Macbeth and *Lear, Othello* and *Hamlet,* are usually reckoned Shakespeare's four principal tragedies. *Lear* stands first for the profound intensity of the passion; *Macbeth* for the wildness of the imagination and the rapidity of the action; *Othello* for the progressive interest and powerful alternations of feeling; *Hamlet* for the refined development of thought and sentiment. If the force of genius shown in each of these works is astonishing, their variety is not less so. They are like different creations of the same mind, not one of which has the slightest reference to the rest. This distinctness and originality is indeed the necessary consequence of truth and nature. Shakespeare's genius alone appeared to possess the resources of nature. He is "your only *tragedy maker.*" His plays have the force of things upon the mind. What he represents is brought home to the bosom as a part of our
2 experience, implanted in the memory as if we had known the places, persons, and things of which he treats. *Macbeth* is like a record of a preternatural and tragical event. It has the rugged severity of an old chronicle with all that the imagination of the poet can engraft upon traditional belief. The castle of Macbeth, round which "the air smells wooingly," and where "the temple-haunting martlet builds," has a real subsistence in the mind; the Weird Sisters meet us in person on "the blasted heath"; the "air-drawn 3
dagger" moves slowly before our eyes; the "gracious Duncan," the "blood-boltered Banquo" stand before us; all that passed through the mind of Macbeth passes, without the loss of a tittle,[2] through ours. All that could actually take place, and all that is only possible to be conceived, what was said and what was done, the workings of passion, the spells of magic, are brought before us with the same absolute truth and vividness.

Shakespeare excelled in the openings of his plays: that of *Macbeth* is the most striking of any. The wildness of the scenery, the sudden shifting of the situations and characters, the bustle, the expectations excited, are equally extraordinary. From the first entrance of the Witches and the description of them when they meet Macbeth:

What are these
So wither'd and so wild
in their attire,
That look not like the
inhabitants of th' earth
And yet are on't?

the mind is prepared for all that follows.

This tragedy is alike distinguished for the lofty imagination it displays, and for the

1. **"The poet's eye . . . name":** From Shakespeare's *A Midsummer Night's Dream,* Act V, Scene i.

2. **tittle** *n.:* A very small particle.

tumultuous vehemence of the action; and the one is made the moving principle of the other. The overwhelming pressure of preternatural agency urges on the tide of human passion with redoubled force. Macbeth himself appears driven along by the violence of his fate like a vessel drifting before a storm: he reels to and fro like a drunken man; he staggers under the weight of his own purposes and the suggestions of others; he stands at bay with his situation; and from the superstitious awe and breathless suspense into which the communications of the Weird Sisters throw him is hurried on with daring impatience to verify their predictions, and with impious and bloody hand to tear aside the veil which hides the uncertainty of the future. He is not equal to the struggle with fate and conscience. He now "bends up each corporal instrument to the terrible feat"; at other times his heart mis-
4 gives him, and he is cowed and abashed by his success. "The deed, no less than the attempt, confounds him." His mind is assailed by the stings of remorse, and full of "preternatural solicitings." His speeches and soliloquies are dark riddles on human life, baffling solution, and entangling him in their labyrinths. In thought he is absent and perplexed, sudden and desperate in act, from a distrust of his own resolution. His energy springs from the anxiety and agitation of his mind. His blindly rushing forward on the objects of his ambition and revenge, or his recoiling from them, equally betrays the harassed state of his feelings. This part of his character is admirably set off by being brought in connection with that of Lady Macbeth, whose obdurate strength of will and masculine firmness give her the ascendancy over her husband's faltering virtue.
5 She at once seizes on the opportunity that offers for the accomplishment of all their wished-for greatness, and never flinches from her object till all is over. The magnitude of her resolution almost covers the magnitude of her guilt. She is a great bad woman, whom we hate, but whom we fear more than we hate. She does not excite our loathing and abhorrence like Regan and Goneril.[3] She is only wicked to gain a great end and is perhaps more distinguished by her commanding presence of mind and inexorable self-will, which do not suffer her to be diverted from a bad purpose, when once formed, by weak and womanly regrets, than by the hardness of her heart or want of natural affections. The impression which her lofty determination of character makes on the mind of Macbeth is well described where he exclaims:

Bring forth men children only;
For thy undaunted mettle should
compose
Nothing but males!

Nor do the pains she is at to "screw his courage to the sticking-place," the reproach to him, not to be "lost so poorly in himself," the assurance that "a little water clears them of this deed," show anything but her greater consistency in depravity. Her strong-nerved ambition furnishes ribs of steel to "the sides of his intent"; and she is herself wound up to the execution of her
baneful project with the same unshrinking 6
fortitude in crime, that in other circumstances she would probably have shown patience in suffering. The deliberate sacrifice of all other considerations to the gaining "for their future days and nights sole sovereing sway and masterdom," by the murder of Duncan, is gorgeously expressed in her invocation on hearing of "his fatal entrance under her battlements":

Come all you spirits
That tend on mortal
thoughts, unsex me here:
And fill me, from the
crown to th' toe, top-full
Of direst cruelty; make
thick my blood,
Stop up the access and
passage to remorse,

---

3. Regan and Goneril: King Lear's evil daughters in Shakespeare's *King Lear.*

4 Discussion Would this description of Macbeth be as effective if it were written in the past tense? Why or why not?

5 Discussion Contrast the personalities of Macbeth and Lady Macbeth, as described by Hazlitt. What does Hazlitt mean when he calls Lady Macbeth "a great bad woman"? Can you think of any other literary characters who might fit this description?

6 Discussion Do you agree with Hazlitt's assumption that Lady Macbeth would probably have been patient in suffering? Why or why not?

7 Discussion What contrasts does Hazlitt see between the Witches and Lady Macbeth?

8 Enrichment According to the Gaelic tradition of tanistry, succession to the throne went to the most "worthy" kinsmen. Thus, in fact, Macbeth did have some claim to the throne. What might be some of the results of the custom of tanistry?

9 Reading Strategy Ask students to prepare a list of the contrasts Hazlitt sees in the play and challenge them to add contrasts of their own to the list.

That no compunctious visitings of nature
Shake my fell purpose, nor keep peace between
The effect and it. Come to my woman's breasts,
And take my milk for gall, you murthering ministers,
Wherever in your sightless substances
You wait on nature's mischief. Come, thick night!
And pall thee in the dunnest smoke of hell,
That my keen knife see not the wound it makes,
Nor heav'n peep through the blanket of the dark,
To cry, hold, hold!

When she first hears that "Duncan comes there to sleep" she is so overcome by the news, which is beyond her utmost expectations, that she answers the messenger, "Thou 'rt mad to say it"; and on receiving her husband's account of the predictions of the Witches, conscious of his instability of purpose, and that her presence is necessary to goad him on to the consummation of his promised greatness, she exclaims:

Hie thee hither,
That I may pour my spirits in thine ear,
And chastise with the valor of my tongue
All that impedes thee from the golden round,
Which fate and metaphysical aid doth seem
To have thee crowned withal.

This swelling exultation and keen spirit
7 of triumph, this uncontrollable eagerness of anticipation, which seems to dilate her form and take possession of all her faculties, this solid, substantial flesh and blood display of passion, exhibit a striking contrast to the cold, abstracted, gratuitous, servile malignity of the Witches, who are equally instrumental in urging Macbeth to his fate for the mere love of mischief, and from a disinterested delight in deformity and cruelty. They are hags of mischief, obscene panders to iniquity, malicious from their impotence of enjoyment, enamored of destruction, because they are themselves unreal, abortive, half-existences, who become sublime from their exemption from all human sympathies and contempt for all human affairs, as Lady Macbeth does by the force of passion! Her fault seems to have been an excess of that strong principle of self-interest and family aggrandizement, not amenable to the common feelings of compassion and justice, 8
which is so marked a feature in barbarous nations and times. A passing reflection of this kind, on the resemblance of the sleeping king to her father, alone prevents her from slaying Duncan with her own hand. . . .

Macbeth (generally speaking) is done upon a stronger and more systematic principle of contrast than any other of Shakespeare's plays. It moves upon the verge of an abyss, and is a constant struggle between life and death. The action is desperate and the reaction is dreadful. It is a huddling together of fierce extremes, a war of opposite natures which of them shall destroy the other. There is nothing but what has a violent end or violent beginnings. The lights and shades are laid on with a determined 9
hand; the transitions from triumph to despair, from the height of terror to the repose of death, are sudden and startling; every passion brings in its fellow-contrary, and the thoughts pitch and jostle against each other as in the dark. The whole play is an unruly chaos of strange and forbidden things, where the ground rocks under our feet. Shakespeare's genius here took its full swing, and trod upon the farthest bounds of nature and passion.

Answers

ANSWERS TO THINKING ABOUT THE SELECTION

Recalling

1. "*Lear* stands first for the profound intensity of passion; *Macbeth* for the wildness of the imagination and the rapidity of the action; *Othello*

THINKING ABOUT THE SELECTION

Recalling

1. According to Hazlitt, what does each of Shakespeare's "four principal tragedies" embody?
2. Which of these plays does Hazlitt say has the best dramatic opening? Why?
3. On pages 757–58, Hazlitt quotes a long passage spoken by Lady Macbeth that begins with the words, "Come all you spirits." What aspect of her character does he say this passage reveals?
4. In Hazlitt's opinion, what "systematic principle" sets *Macbeth* apart from Shakespeare's other plays?

Interpreting

5. On page 756, Hazlitt states that Shakespeare is "your only *tragedy maker.*" (a) What do you think he means by this? (b) What do you think is the significance of the quotation marks around this phrase?
6. What two qualities does Hazlitt claim advance the action in the play, and what effect do they have on the characters of Macbeth and Lady Macbeth?
7. Hazlitt concludes his essay with the observation that in *Macbeth* Shakespeare's genius "took its full swing, and trod upon the farthest bounds of nature and passion." What evidence does he offer in support of this view?

Applying

8. How does Hazlitt's writing style compare with modern editorial style? Tell which you prefer and why you prefer it.

ANALYZING LITERATURE

Understanding a Critical Essay

A **critical essay** is a prose piece that reviews or critiques a work of art or literature. In the present day, standards for objective criticism have been established by experts. In the eighteenth century, by contrast, these standards varied pretty much from critic to critic. The essays of William Hazlitt, in particular, are marked by a tendency toward subjective, highly personal observations, although these observations are often supported with examples and quotations from the work. Reread Hazlitt's essay on *Macbeth,* and locate the following:

1. Three opinions that are supported by examples or quotes from the play.
2. Three opinions that are not supported.
3. Three phrases that demonstrate Hazlitt's enthusiasm for Shakespeare's writing in general and for *Macbeth* in particular.

CRITICAL THINKING AND READING

Finding Main Ideas

The **main idea** in a paragraph is the key point the author wishes to get across to the reader. Each main idea is backed up by one or more **supporting details.** Read the following quotations from Hazlitt's essay on *Macbeth.* Each is a supporting detail. Find the paragraph from which it was taken, and state the main idea of that paragraph.

1. "The wildness of the scenery, the sudden shifting of the situations and characters . . . are equally extraordinary." (page 756)
2. "The action is desperate and the reaction is dreadful." (page 758)
3. "The whole play is an unruly chaos of strange and forbidden things, where the ground rocks under our feet." (page 758)

THINKING AND WRITING

Evaluating Literary Criticism

In a magazine or newspaper, find a review of a book you have read or a play you have seen. As you read the review, ask yourself the following questions: What facts does the critic present? Which statements are opinions? What details does the critic offer in support of his or her opinions? Does the critic convey any strong feeling for the work? How interesting is the review?

After you have organized your thoughts regarding these and other questions that might occur to you, write an essay evaluating the review. When you revise make sure you have included adequate supporting details.

for the progressive interest and powerful alternations of feeling; *Hamlet* for the refined development of thought and sentiment."

2. *Macbeth* has the best dramatic opening because of its wild scenery, the sudden shifts of situations and characters, the bustle, and the fact that it excites the reader's expectations.
3. The passage reveals Lady Macbeth's firmness of purpose and her "consistency in depravity."
4. *Macbeth* is set apart by its "systematic principle of contrast."

Interpreting

5. (a) Hazlitt calls Shakespeare the "only *tragedy maker*" because the characters and events in his plays seem to spring from real life, like a force of nature. (b) The quotation marks signify a kind of irony —through his plays Shakespeare "makes" tragedies happen; in life, however, tragedies result from seemingly unavoidable events.
6. Imagination and vehemence advance the action of the play. Although Macbeth is bothered by his conscience, he is too weak-willed to resist his wife's passionate ambition. Her determined wickedness undoes them both.
7. In the concluding paragraph Hazlitt offers no concrete evidence in the form of examples or quotes from the play to support this view. However, his view is very much in keeping with, and supported by, much of what precedes.

(Answers begin on p. 758.)

Applying

8. Answers will differ. Students should see that Hazlitt's style is more dramatic and emotional than that of most modern literary critics.

ANSWERS TO ANALYZING LITERATURE

1. Answers will differ. Suggested answers may include the following. Hazlitt quotes the description of the Witches to support his opinion that the first entrance of the Witches prepares the mind for what follows. That Lady Macbeth is steadfastly intent on the murder of Duncan is supported by quoting her words when she hears that Duncan had made his fatal entrance. That Lady Macbeth feels she is necessary to goad Macbeth to greatness is supported by a quotation.
2. Answers will differ. Suggested answers may include the following. Hazlitt does not support these three opinions: First, the plays *Macbeth, Lear, Othello,* and *Hamlet* are "like different creations of the same mind. . . ." Second, the Witches "are equally instrumental in urging Macbeth to his fate. . . ." Third, Lady Macbeth is "a woman . . . whom we fear more than we hate."
3. Answers will differ. Suggested answers may include the following. Hazlitt's enthusiasm for Shakespeare's writing is demonstrated by such phrases as "force of genius," "lofty imagination," and "absolute truth and vividness."

ANSWERS TO CRITICAL THINKING AND READING

1. Macbeth has the most striking opening of any of Shakespeare's plays.
2. In *Macbeth* Shakespeare pushes nature and passion to their limits by emphasizing extreme contrasts.
3. See #2 above.

THINKING AND WRITING

Publishing Student Writing

Using their essays as the basis, have students carry out a roundtable discussion of the role of critics in today's society and the validity of contemporary criticism.

More About the Author Jane Austen developed her critical faculties at an early age. At fourteen, she wrote parodies of the popular novel that showed her sure grasp of the weaknesses of the genre. Discuss with your class how early observations of life in a small town may have contributed to her later writing. Discuss parallels between the drawing of caricatures to mock or to portray a known personality and Austen's use of the written sketch.

JANE AUSTEN

1775–1817

If nothing else, the life and work of Jane Austen explode the myth that it is impossible to produce a great novel without having first sampled a broad range of life experiences. Her social comedies are considered by critics today to be masterpieces of character portrayal and dialogue.

Born at Steventon in southwestern England to loving parents of modest means, Austen was the seventh of eight children. From an early age she enjoyed writing, and entertained her family with parodies, or humorous sendups, of the syrupy, sentimental fiction and drama that were fashionable at the time. When she was in her late teens she began her first novel, *Sense and Sensibility,* which is the story of two sisters. Prior to its completion, however, she put it aside to concentrate on another novel, *First Impressions.* Written as a series of letters, the work that would eventually be reshaped into her highly acclaimed *Pride and Prejudice* rapidly became the family favorite. So certain, in fact, was her father of its merits that he offered the work to a book publisher, who rejected it. Not easily discouraged, Austen plunged into a third novel, *Northanger Abbey,* a mock horror tale, which she finished in 1797.

In 1801 the family relocated to Bath, near the sea, where Austen for the first time in her life experienced unhappiness. In letters she described herself as an "exile" from the rural surroundings that she loved so much. When her father died in 1806, the family, or what remained of it—by now all the male children had married—left Bath for a cottage on an estate outside London. On the death of his wife, Austen's brother Edward and his eleven children came to live on the estate, and once again Austen found herself surrounded by relatives in a bustling household. The writer's block that had plagued her during her period of sadness vanished, and she eagerly returned to work, revising her early novels and completing three new ones.

Sense and Sensibility, the first to be published, appeared in 1811. It was followed two years later by *Pride and Prejudice,* and a year after that by *Mansfield Park.* In 1816 Austen became ill but continued to write, completing two more novels, *Persuasion* and *Northanger Abbey,* before her death. Her brother Henry saw to the publication of both works, including a biographical sketch of his sister, who during her life had insisted on anonymity.

Because in her writing Austen places intellect above emotion, she is seen by some as more neoclassical than Romantic. What all critics seem to be in agreement on, however, is her ranking as one of the greatest English novelists writing in any period.

Objectives

1. To recognize the elements of the novel
2. To see the novel as a mirror of a society's customs and attitudes
3. To use context clues to understand words
4. To write fiction mirroring some aspect of present day society

Teaching Portfolio: Support Material

Teacher Backup, p. 000

Vocabulary Check, p. 00

Usage and Mechanic's Worksheet, p. 00

Analyzing Literature Worksheet, p. 00

Critical Thinking and Reading Worksheet, p. 00

Language Worksheet, p. 00

Selection Test, p. 00

GUIDE FOR READING

from Pride and Prejudice

Literary Forms

The Novel. A novel is a book-length prose narrative with fictitious characters shown in various types of situations. The elements of the novel are generally the same as those of the short story: character, setting, plot, point of view, and theme. In addition to a plot, a novel may have one or more subplots, or lesser sequences of events, that relate to the main one.

The novel is the youngest literary form, dating back in English literature just over two hundred years. The first English novels took the form of a series of letters or of biography. Although conservative ministers preached that reading novels was wasteful and immoral, the form gained popularity during the Romantic era. The two most important novelists of this period were Sir Walter Scott, whose stories combined history with romance, and Jane Austen, who was the first to write highly crafted fiction. While Austen's novels are often parodies, or comedic takeoffs, on the stuffy "novels of manners" written by most of her contemporaries, her works reflect her attitudes toward the middle-class concerns of her times.

Look For

As you read the excerpt from *Pride and Prejudice,* pay close attention to how Jane Austen uses action and dialogue to reveal the personalities of her characters. Notice also her skillful use of irony as she comments on the behavior of her social group.

Writing

Think about an aspect of American society today that you feel could stand to be improved. You might comment on overcrowding in our schools or the sorrowful quality of life in many major urban centers. Select such an aspect and, on a sheet of paper, make some notes about the subject and your feelings toward it.

Vocabulary

Knowing the following words will help you as you read the excerpt from *Pride and Prejudice.*

overscrupulous (ō′vər skro͞o′ pyə ləs) *adj.*: Overly concerned about details (p. 764)

caprice (kə prēs′) *n.*: Tendency to act on whim (p. 764)

circumspection (sʉr′ kəm spek′ shən) *n.*: Caution (p. 765)

tumult (to͞o′ mult) *n.*: Uproar (p. 765)

conjecturing (kən jek′chər iŋ) *v.*: Guessing (p. 765)

fastidious (fas tid′ ē əs) *adj.*: Hard to please (p. 767)

Literary Focus Austen's work often took the form of parody or of gently mocking social commentary. What does this tell us about her own personality?

Look For Have the students notice the ways in which characterization is developed. How often does Austen use description to tell us facts about a character? How often does she utilize dialogue to develop character?

Some of the characters in this selection take themselves quite seriously, and some do not. Have the class find examples of each type of personality. Which type might be closest to Austen's own outlook? Does the hero or heroine of a novel usually mirror its author's views?

Writing You might suggest such an aspect and then invite students to offer their thoughts about it. Alternatively, have your students list human qualities that lend themselves to satirization, for example, stupidity, hypocrisy, self-righteousness, good intentions, greed, pride, gluttony, and self-delusion. If irony is the contrast between appearance and reality or between an expected outcome and the actual outcome, which of these qualities might be used as the basis for ironic comment? Have them imagine ways that a particular quality could be mocked in a humorous fashion, or in a savagely indignant fashion.

Vocabulary Have your **more advanced** students watch for words or phrases within the selection that have acquired a different usage since Austen's day, for example, *engage, design, develop,* and *handsome.*

Motivation for Reading Have your female students imagine that they live in a world where the only road to security is a successful marriage. Let your male students imagine what it would be like to be a young man of wealth, who may be judged more for his income than his personal qualities. Have students discuss how their expectations would be different from what they are today.

Master Teacher Note Discuss famous first lines of books, from "Call me Ishmael" to "It was a dark and stormy night." What makes some sentences so memorable and so resonant? Can the students think of any examples from their own favorite books? Have a selection of popular and classic novels available, and compare their opening sentences. Is Austen's opening sentence an epigram or a hook? Does it seem foreshadow the following action or drag the reader into it? Can the students detect any change of pace between how books opened in Austen's time and today? If they do, what do they think accounts for the difference?

Purpose-Setting Question What is the author's attitude to her characters? Does she approve of some more than others? Which ones?

1 **Discussion** What might the eligible man think of this attitude? What might his response tell us about his personality?

2 **Literary Focus** Discuss how characterization is achieved through dialogue. Contrast Mr. and Mrs. Bennet's styles of speaking—taciturn vs. loquacious, flat vs. exclamatory, and cool vs. hot. Could we make judgments about their personalities by the end of the first page?

3 **Clarification** When Austen's father died in 1805, his wife and two daughters were left to survive on an income of 450 pounds per year, a sum which was barely adequate for that time.

from Pride and Prejudice

Jane Austen

Pride and Prejudice *is a satirical examination of social relationships and economic concerns in upper-class society in early nineteenth-century England. The novel relates the story of the Bennet family—Mr. and Mrs. Bennet and their five daughters. In this excerpt from the beginning of the novel, the Bennets are introduced, and Mrs. Bennet's intentions are made apparent.*

It is a truth universally acknowledged that a single man in possession of a good fortune must be in want of a wife.

1 However little known the feelings or views of such a man may be on his first entering a neighborhood, this truth is so well fixed in the minds of the surrounding families that he is considered as the rightful property of some one or other of their daughters.

"My dear Mr. Bennet," said his lady to him one day, "have you heard that Netherfield Park is let at last?"

Mr. Bennet replied that he had not.

"But it is," returned she; "for Mrs. Long has just been here, and she told me all about it."

2 Mr. Bennet made no answer.

"Do not you want to know who has taken it?" cried his wife impatiently.

"*You* want to tell me, and I have no objection to hearing it."

This was invitation enough.

"Why, my dear, you must know, Mrs. Long says that Netherfield is taken by a young man of large fortune from the north of England; that he came down on Monday in a chaise and four[1] to see the place, and was so much delighted with it that he agreed with Mr. Morris immediately; that he is to take possession before Michaelmas,[2] and some of his servants are to be in the house by the end of next week."

"What is his name?"

"Bingley."

"Is he married or single?"

"Oh! single, my dear, to be sure! A single man of large fortune; four or five thousand a year. What a fine thing for our girls!" 3

"How so? how can it affect them?"

"My dear Mr. Bennet," replied his wife, "how can you be so tiresome! You must know that I am thinking of his marrying one of them."

"Is that his design in settling here?"

"Design! nonsense, how can you talk so! But it is very likely that he *may* fall in love with one of them, and therefore you must visit him as soon as he comes."

"I see no occasion for that. You and the girls may go, or you may send them by themselves, which perhaps will be still better, for as you are as handsome as any of them, Mr. Bingley might like you the best of the party."

"My dear, you flatter me. I certainly *have* had my share of beauty, but I do not pretend to be anything extraordinary now.

1. chaise and four: A lightweight carriage drawn by four horses.
2. Michaelmas: The feast of the archangel Michael, celebrated on September 29.

"LADY COLVILLE"
Sir Henry Raeburn
The Bridgeman Art Library/Art Resource

Humanities Note

Fine art, *Lady* Coleville, by Sir Henry Raeburn. Raeburn (1756–1823) was a notable Scottish portrait painter. First a jeweler's apprentice who worked in miniature, he is considered to be a self-taught artist. He later traveled to London and then to Rome where association with other artists enriched his technique. He established a studio when he returned to Edinburgh and soon gained considerable reputation both there and in London as a portrait painter.

During his career as a portraitist, Raeburn painted more than seven hundred portraits. As in this portrait of *Lady Coleville,* he took a simple and direct approach to the painting of a likeness. He was a clever observer of character and was able to paint personality as well as features. This bold directness, coupled with his shrewd eye for the idiosyncracies of his sitter, places his work among the best of the British portrait painters. Before his death he was appointed His Majesty's Limner, or portraitist, for Scotland. He was knighted by King George V.

You may wish to ask the following questions.

1. What would you say is the personality of the lady in this portrait?
2. How do you think the painter felt about his subject?

4 **Critical Thinking and Reading** As the Bennets discuss their children, note what qualities each of them considers a virtue in a young woman. What is Bennet's opinion of girls in general? Ask the students if they think that is his own opinion or the general attitude of males of that period.

5 **Discussion** In a letter to her sister, Austen once referred to the "playfulness and epigrammatism of the general style" of this novel. An epigram is defined as a terse, witty, and pointed statement, often antithetical. Mr. Bennet's description of his wife's nerves fits this definition. Ask the students to find other examples of Austen's playfulness, or "epigrammatism".

6 **Reading Strategy** Ask your students to find examples of the Bennets' qualities of temperment as summarized by Austen in this paragraph. Students may want to check the definition of caprice in the Guide For Reading.

7 **Discussion** Based on their previous knowledge of him, ask students to suggest why Mr. Bennet refrains from immediately telling his wife of the visit to Mr. Bingley. Does this make Mr. Bennett a more or less believable character?

8 **Critical Thinking and Reading** What does Mrs. Bennet's outburst tell us about the customs of the period? What does it say about the position of women within the social structure?

9 **Discussion** This is the first time that Elizabeth speaks in the novel. Contrast her attitude with that of her mother in the paragraph above. What conclusions can be drawn already about Elizabeth's character? Make sure that students notice that Austen generally uses dialogue to create character, while description is used to summarize it.

When a woman has five grown-up daughters, she ought to give over thinking of her own beauty."

"In such cases, a woman has not often much beauty to think of."

"But, my dear, you must indeed go and see Mr. Bingley when he comes into the neighborhood."

"It is more than I engage for, I assure you."

"But consider your daughters. Only think what an establishment it would be for one of them. Sir William and Lady Lucas are determined to go merely on that account, for in general you know they visit no newcomers. Indeed you must go, for it will be impossible for *us* to visit him if you do not."

"You are overscrupulous surely. I dare say Mr. Bingley will be very glad to see you; and I will send a few lines by you to assure him of my hearty consent to his marrying whichever he chooses of the girls; though I must throw in a good word for my little Lizzy."

"I desire you will do no such thing. Lizzy is not a bit better than the others; and I am sure she is not half so handsome as Jane, nor half so good humored as Lydia. But you
4 are always giving *her* the preference."

"They have none of them much to recommend them," replied he; "they are all silly and ignorant like other girls; but Lizzy has something more of quickness than her sisters."

"Mr. Bennet, how can you abuse your own children in such a way? You take delight in vexing me. You have no compassion on my poor nerves."

"You mistake me, my dear. I have a high respect for your nerves. They are my old
5 friends. I have heard you mention them with consideration these twenty years at least."

"Ah! you do not know what I suffer."

"But I hope you will get over it and live to see many young men of four thousand a year come into the neighborhood."

"It will be no use to us if twenty such should come since you will not visit them."

"Depend upon it, my dear, that when there are twenty, I will visit them all."

Mr. Bennet was so odd a mixture of quick parts, sarcastic humor, reserve, and caprice, that the experience of three and twenty years had been insufficient to make his wife understand his character. *Her* mind was less difficult to develop. She was a 6
woman of mean understanding, little information, and uncertain temper. When she was discontented she fancied herself nervous. The business of her life was to get her daughters married; its solace was visiting and news.

Mr. Bennet was among the earliest of those who waited on Mr. Bingley. He had always intended to visit him, though to the
last always assuring his wife that he should 7
not go; and till the evening after the visit was paid, she had no knowledge of it. It was then disclosed in the following manner. Observing his second daughter employed in trimming a hat, he suddenly addressed her with,

"I hope Mr. Bingley will like it, Lizzy."

"We are not in a way to know *what* Mr.
Bingley likes," said her mother resentfully, 8
"since we are not to visit."

"But you forget, mama," said Elizabeth, "that we shall meet him at the assemblies,
and that Mrs. Long has promised to intro- 9
duce him."

"I do not believe Mrs. Long will do any such thing. She has two nieces of her own. She is a selfish, hypocritical woman, and I have no opinion of her."

"No more have I," said Mr. Bennet; "and I am glad to find that you do not depend on her serving you."

Mrs. Bennet deigned not to make any reply; but unable to contain herself, began scolding one of her daughters.

"Don't keep coughing so, Kitty, for heaven's sake! Have a little compassion on my nerves. You tear them to pieces."

"Kitty has no discretion in her coughs," said her father; "she times them ill."

"I do not cough for my own amusement," replied Kitty fretfully.

"When is your next ball to be, Lizzy?"

"Tomorrow fortnight."

"Aye, so it is," cried her mother, "and Mrs. Long does not come back till the day before; so, it will be impossible for her to introduce him, for she will not know him herself."

"Then, my dear, you may have the advantage of your friend, and introduce Mr. Bingley to *her.*"

"Impossible, Mr. Bennet, impossible, when I am not acquainted with him myself; how can you be so teasing?"

"I honor your circumspection. A fortnight's acquaintance is certainly very little. 10 One cannot know what a man really is by the end of a fortnight. But if *we* do not venture, somebody else will; and after all, Mrs. Long and her nieces must stand their chance; and therefore, as she will think it an act of kindness, if you decline the office, I will take it on myself."

The girls stared at their father. Mrs. Bennet said only, "Nonsense, nonsense!"

"What can be the meaning of that emphatic exclamation?" cried he. "Do you consider the forms of introduction and the stress that is laid on them as nonsense? I cannot quite agree with you *there.* What say you, Mary? for you are a young lady of deep reflection I know, and read great books, and make extracts."

Mary wished to say something very sensible but knew not how.

"While Mary is adjusting her ideas," he continued, "let us return to Mr. Bingley."

"I am sick of Mr. Bingley," cried his wife.

"I am sorry to hear *that;* but why did not you tell me so before? If I had known as much this morning, I certainly would not have called on him. It is very unlucky; but as I have actually paid the visit, we cannot escape the acquaintance now."

The astonishment of the ladies was just what he wished; that of Mrs. Bennet perhaps surpassing the rest; though when the first tumult of joy was over, she began to declare that it was what she had expected all the while.

"How good it was in you, my dear Mr. Bennet! But I knew I should persuade you at last. I was sure you loved your girls too well to neglect such an acquaintance. Well, how pleased I am! and it is such a good joke, too, that you should have gone this morning and never said a word about it till now."

"Now, Kitty, you may cough as much as you choose," said Mr. Bennet; and, as he spoke, he left the room, fatigued with the raptures of his wife.

"What an excellent father you have, girls," said she, when the door was shut. "I do not know how you will ever make him amends for his kindness; or me either, for that matter. At our time of life, it is not so pleasant, I can tell you, to be making new acquaintance every day; but for your sakes, we would do anything. Lydia, my love, though you *are* the youngest, I dare say Mr. Bingley will dance with you at the next ball."

"Oh!" said Lydia stoutly, "I am not afraid; for though I *am* the youngest, I'm the tallest."

The rest of the evening was spent in conjecturing how soon he would return Mr. Bennet's visit, and determining when they should ask him to dinner.

Not all that Mrs. Bennet, however, with the assistance of her five daughters, could ask on the subject was sufficient to draw from her husband any satisfactory description of Mr. Bingley. They attacked him in various ways; with barefaced questions, ingenious suppositions, and distant surmises; but he eluded the skill of them all; and they were at last obliged to accept the secondhand intelligence of their neighbor, Lady Lucas. Her report was highly favorable. Sir William had been delighted with him. He was quite young, wonderfully handsome, extremely agreeable, and to crown the whole, he meant to be at the next assembly

10. *Fortnight* is a term much more widely used in Great Britain than in the United States. It refers to a period of two weeks.

11 Discussion Discuss the parallels between dancing and courtship and between finding a partner for the dance and a partner for life. Compare Bingley's and Darcy's attitudes towards dancing, and their choice or refusal of partners. Could this foreshadow their acceptance or rejection of love?

12 Literary Focus Ask your students to discuss irony and humor, contrasting the ever dwindling reports of the size of Bingley's party to its final reality. Also ask your students to note how Austen shows us the importance of rumor and gossip in small-town life.

13 Discussion Do your students think that the ladies' first preference for Darcy over Mr. Bingley is an objective one, or might it be related to his reported income? How does their impression of his appearance change once his pride has wounded them?

with a large party. Nothing could be more delightful! To be fond of dancing was a cer-
11 tain step towards falling in love; and very lively hopes of Mr. Bingley's heart were entertained.

"If I can but see one of my daughters happily settled at Netherfield," said Mrs. Bennet to her husband, "and all the others equally well-married, I shall have nothing to wish for."

In a few days Mr. Bingley returned Mr. Bennet's visit and sat about ten minutes with him in his library. He had entertained hopes of being admitted to a sight of the young ladies of whose beauty he had heard much; but he saw only the father. The ladies were somewhat more fortunate, for they had the advantage of ascertaining from an upper window that he wore a blue coat and rode a black horse.

An invitation to dinner was soon afterwards dispatched; and already had Mrs. Bennet planned the courses that were to do credit to her housekeeping, when an answer arrived which deferred it all. Mr. Bingley was obliged to be in town the following day and consequently unable to accept the honor of their invitation, etc. Mrs. Bennet was quite disconcerted. She could not imagine what business he could have in town so soon after his arrival in Hertfordshire;[3] and she began to fear that he might be always flying about from one place to another and never settled at Netherfield as he ought to be. Lady Lucas quieted her fears a little by starting the idea of his being gone to London only to get a large party for the ball; and a report soon followed that Mr. Bingley was to bring twelve ladies and seven gentlemen with him to the assembly. The girls grieved over such a number of ladies; but were
12 comforted the day before the ball by hearing that, instead of twelve, he had brought only six with him from London, his five sisters and a cousin. And when the party entered the assembly room, it consisted of only five, altogether: Mr. Bingley, his two sisters, the husband of the eldest, and another young man.

Mr. Bingley was good-looking and gentlemanlike; he had a pleasant countenance and easy, unaffected manners. His sisters were fine women, with an air of decided fashion. His brother-in-law, Mr. Hurst, merely looked the gentleman; but his friend Mr. Darcy soon drew the attention of the room by his fine, tall person, handsome features, noble mien; and the report which was in general circulation within five minutes after his entrance of his having ten thousand a year. The gentlemen pronounced him to be a fine figure of a man, the ladies declared he was much handsomer than Mr. Bingley, and he was looked at with great admiration for about half the evening, till his manners gave a disgust which turned the tide of his popularity; for he was discov- 13
ered to be proud, to be above his company, and above being pleased; and not all his large estate in Derbyshire[4] could then save him from having a most forbidding, disagreeable countenance, and being unworthy to be compared with his friend.

Mr. Bingley had soon made himself acquainted with all the principal people in the room; he was lively and unreserved, danced every dance, was angry that the ball closed so early, and talked of giving one himself at Netherfield. Such amiable qualities must speak for themselves. What a contrast between him and his friend! Mr. Darcy danced only once with Mrs. Hurst and once with Miss Bingley, declined being introduced to any other lady, and spent the rest of the evening in walking about the room, speaking occasionally to one of his own party. His character was decided. He was the proudest, most disagreeable man in the world, and everybody hoped that he would never come there again. Amongst the most violent

---

3. Hertfordshire (här′ fərd shir): A county in southeastern England.

4. Derbyshire (dur′ bē shir): A county in central England.

against him was Mrs. Bennet, whose dislike of his general behavior was sharpened into particular resentment by his having slighted one of her daughters.

Elizabeth Bennet had been obliged, by the scarcity of gentlemen, to sit down for
4 two dances; and during part of that time, Mr. Darcy had been standing near enough for her to overhear a conversation between him and Mr. Bingley, who came from the dance for a few minutes to press his friend to join it.

"Come, Darcy," said he, "I must have you dance. I hate to see you standing about by yourself in this stupid manner. You had much better dance."

"I certainly shall not. You know how I
5 detest it, unless I am particularly acquainted with my partner. At such an assembly as this, it would be insupportable. Your sisters are engaged, and there is not another woman in the room whom it would not be a punishment to me to stand up with."

"I would not be so fastidious as you are," cried Bingley, "for a kingdom! Upon my honor, I never met with so many pleasant girls in my life as I have this evening; and there are several of them you see uncom-
6 monly pretty."

"*You* are dancing with the only handsome girl in the room," said Mr. Darcy, looking at the eldest Miss Bennet.

"Oh! she is the most beautiful creature I ever beheld! But there is one of her sisters sitting down just behind you, who is very pretty, and I dare say, very agreeable. Do let me ask my partner to introduce you."

"Which do you mean?" and turning around, he looked for a moment at Elizabeth, till catching her eye, he withdrew his own and coldly said, "She is tolerable; but not handsome enough to tempt *me;* and I am in no humor at present to give consequence to young ladies who are slighted by other
7 men. You had better return to your partner and enjoy her smiles, for you are wasting your time with me."

Mr. Bingley followed his advice. Mr. Darcy walked off; and Elizabeth remained with no very cordial feelings towards him. She told the story however with great spirit
among her friends; for she had a lively, 18
playful disposition, which delighted in anything ridiculous.

The evening altogether passed off pleasantly to the whole family. Mrs. Bennet had seen her eldest daughter much admired by the Netherfield party. Mr. Bingley had
danced with her twice, and she had been 19
distinguished by his sisters. Jane was as much gratified by this as her mother could be, though in a quieter way. Elizabeth felt Jane's pleasure. Mary had heard herself mentioned to Miss Bingley as the most accomplished girl in the neighborhood; and Catherine and Lydia had been fortunate enough to be never without partners, which was all that they had yet learned to care for at a ball. They returned therefore in good spirits to Longbourn, the village where they
lived, and of which they were the principal 20
inhabitants. They found Mr. Bennet still up. With a book he was regardless of time; and on the present occasion he had a good deal of curiosity as to the event of an evening which had raised such splendid expectations. He had rather hoped that all his wife's views on the stranger would be disappointed; but he soon found that he had a very different story to hear.

"Oh! my dear Mr. Bennet," as she entered the room, "we have had a most delightful evening, a most excellent ball. I wish you had been there. Jane was so admired, nothing could be like it. Everybody said how well she looked; and Mr. Bingley thought her quite beautiful and danced with her twice. Only think of *that* my dear; he actually danced with her twice; and she was the only creature in the room that he asked a second time. First of all, he asked Miss Lucas. I was so vexed to see him stand up with her; but, however, he did not admire her at all: indeed, nobody can, you know; and he seemed quite struck with Jane as she was going down the dance. So, he inquired who she

14 **Enrichment** Of Austen's six brothers, two were in the navy and one was in the militia. Although politics rarely intrudes into the Bennet's world, *Pride and Prejudice* takes place within the period of the Napoleonic Wars. A shortage of young men is hardly remarkable and may in part account for the energy with which women seek marriage partners.

15 **Discussion** From this statement ask the class if they can draw any conclusion about Darcy's character which might mitigate his obvious pride.

16 **Literary Focus** How is character revealed through dialogue in these paragraphs? What does each man's attitudes about the women in the room reveal about himself?

17 **Discussion** Darcy's speaking such words within Elizabeth's hearing would be an impardonable offense, even for a gentleman of questionable manners. Ask your class to discuss any reason why the author might include this scene, even though she pushes credibility by including it.

18 **Reading Strategy** Have students describe other ways in which a woman might have reacted to this analysis of her charms.

19 **Literary Focus** Discuss the phrase "had been distinguished." What does that use of the word mean here? What are some other uses of *distinguish?*

20 **Critical Thinking and Reading** What can the students conclude about a society where one family is considered the principal one within a town? Do they feel that this differs from life in their own town today, and if so, how?

21 **Discussion** Contrast Mrs. Bennet's reaction to Darcy's slight with Elizabeth's. Which reaction do students find most admirable?

22 **Enrichment** A nephew's account of Austen describes her as "very attractive . . . tall and slender . . . her whole appearance expressive of health and animation." She dearly loved to dance and was considered by her family to be something of a flirt. Of all her creations, Elizabeth Bennet was her favorite heroine; Elizabeth's character as revealed in this selection suggests that she was Austen's literary alter ego.

was, and got introduced, and asked her for the two next. Then, the two third he danced with Miss King, and the two fourth with Maria Lucas, and the two fifth with Jane again, and the two sixth with Lizzy, and the Boulanger—"

"If he had had any compassion for *me*," cried her husband impatiently, "he would not have danced half so much! Say no more of his partners. Oh! that he had sprained his ankle in the first dance!"

"Oh! my dear," continued Mrs. Bennet, "I am quite delighted with him. He is so excessively handsome! and his sisters are charming women. I never in my life saw any thing more elegant than their dresses. I dare say the lace upon Mrs. Hurst's gown—"

Here she was interrupted again. Mr. Bennet protested against any description of finery. She was therefore obliged to seek another branch of the subject, and related, with much bitterness of spirit and some 2
exaggeration, the shocking rudeness of Mr. Darcy.

"But I can assure you," she added, "that Lizzy does not lose much by not suiting *his* fancy; for he is a most disagreeable, horrid man, not at all worth pleasing. So high and so conceited that there was no enduring him! He walked here, and he walked there, fancying himself so very great! Not handsome enough to dance with! I wish you had 2
been there, my dear, to have given him one of your set-downs. I quite detest the man."

THINKING ABOUT THE SELECTION

Recalling

1. (a) Who is the new young man in the neighborhood? (b) Why is Mrs. Bennet eager for her husband to pay him a visit?
2. (a) Why is Mr. Bingley unable to accept the Bennets' invitation to dinner? (b) How does Mrs. Bennet react?
3. (a) At the ball, who receives the most attention from Mr. Bingley? (b) Why does Mr. Darcy refuse to dance with Elizabeth?

Interpreting

4. What character traits of Mr. and Mrs. Bennet emerge from their conversations?
5. (a) What does Mr. Bennet's "joke" on his wife reveal about his feelings toward her? (b) What does it reveal about the author's feelings toward her characters and their values?
6. (a) What kind of person is Mr. Darcy? (b) What reasons might Jane Austen have had for including such a character?

Applying

7. (a) In what ways have women changed since Jane Austen's time? (b) In what ways have men changed? (c) What choices do women have today that were unavailable to them then?

ANALYZING LITERATURE

Understanding the Novel

A **novel** is a long fictional prose narrative that often contains many characters and several conflicts. Besides the main plot, there may be one or more subplots. The action in a novel may take place over an extended period of time and in many different locations. Based on the excerpt of *Pride and Prejudice* you have read, answer the following questions.

1. Which of the characters do you think will turn out to be central to the novel? Why?
2. What conflicts are clear from the excerpt? How do you suppose they will be resolved?
3. What possible subplots can you imagine?

Answers

ANSWERS TO THINKING ABOUT THE SELECTION

Recalling

1. (a) Mr. Bingley is the new gentleman. (b) She wishes to introduce him to her marriageable daughters.
2. (a) He will be in London that day. (b) She fears that he may be a gadabout and, therefore, not good husband material.
3. (a) Jane Bennet receives the most attention. (b) Elizabeth is not handsome enough to tempt him, and he's not in the mood to dance with wallflowers.

Interpreting

4. Mr. Bennet is sarcastic, teasing, and whimsical. Mrs. Bennet is humorless, literal, and conventional.
5. (a) He enjoys teasing and surprising her. His unpredictability also may allow him to feel superior. (b) Austen seems to feel that their preoccupation with "the forms" may be over-stressed but is essentially sensible.
6. (a) He is proud, aloof, and perhaps shy. (b) Like Elizabeth, he stands apart from society and allows Austen to comment on its foibles. He is Elizabeth's complement, having brains and tact without humor. She has humor, brains, and little tact.

Applying

7. (a) Answers will differ. Students should see that for most women today marriage is not the only goal. (b) Answers will differ. Students should see that most men feel less superior intellectually and less omnipotent. (c) Women may meet whom they please, may support themselves, and may marry or not.

ANSWERS TO ANALYZING LITERATURE

1. Elizabeth and Mr. Darcy will be central to the novel, as will Mr. and Mrs. Bennet. Austen has set up conflicts between these couples that will drive the plot.
2. Conflicts exist between the "feelings or views" of two young men of large fortune and the matrimonial intentions of the women of Hertfordshire. They also arise between Mr. and Mrs. Bennet on a domestic level and between Elizabeth and Darcy. The Bennets resolve their differences to some degree by uniting to ensure their daughters' well-being. The other conflicts will be resolved through love and marriage.
3. A subplot between the beautiful Jane and Mr. Bingley seems likely.

CRITICAL THINKING AND READING

Viewing a Novel as a Mirror of Society

Novels are not written in vacuums, but by people whose thoughts and attitudes are influenced to some degree by the time and place in which they are writing. The following quotations from *Pride and Prejudice* provide insight into social attitudes and customs of Jane Austen's day. Read the quotations and tell what each reveals about the custom or attitude that is shown after it in parentheses.

1. "Do you consider the forms of introduction and the stress that is laid on them nonsense? I cannot agree with you there." (manners)
2. "If I can see but one of my daughters happily settled at Netherfield . . . and all the others equally well-married, I shall have nothing to wish for." (marriage)
3. ". . . his friend Mr. Darcy soon drew the attention of the room by his fine, tall person, handsome features, [and] noble mien. . . ." (physical appearance)

UNDERSTANDING LANGUAGE

Using Context Clues

Often the meaning of an unfamiliar word can be guessed from its **context**—that is, from the words and phrases around it. Using context clues, attempt to figure out the meaning of the italicized words in the following sentences. To see the word in a still larger context, turn back to the page on which it appears. Check your guesses in a good dictionary.

1. "Is that his *design* in settling here?" (page 762)
2. "You take delight in *vexing* me. You have no compassion on my poor nerves." (page 764)
3. The business of her life was to get her daughters married; its *solace* was visiting and news. (page 764)
4. "I do not know how you will ever make him *amends* for his kindness." (page 764)
5. They attacked him in various ways: with barefaced questions, ingenious suppositions, and distant *surmises*. (page 765)

THINKING AND WRITING

Writing Fiction

Review the notes you took under Writing on page 761. Write a short story that addresses the topic and mirrors your feelings about it. Include at least three characters, each with a different personality, and then decide on the conflict that will divide them. Plan a sequence of events that will lead to a high point in the story, to be followed by a resolution of the conflict. Then write your first draft. When you revise your draft, make sure you have related events in chronological order. Be prepared to present your story to the class.

THINKING AND WRITING

Writing Across the Curriculum

You might want to inform the history department of your study of this selection. A supplementary assignment could be to relate the historical and social concept of the Protestant Ethic—that virtue is rewarded in this life by financial success—with the deference and admiration that are shown to young men of income in this novel.

ANSWERS TO CRITICAL THINKING AND READING

1. Although Bennet mocks his wife when he says this, these words are a central tenet of Austen's novel and are an accepted truism of her day. Social harmony and stability were greatly valued. This is an aspect of a class society that may seem alien to your students. Manners were a way of both maintaining barriers and allowing for social intercourse between one class and another and between sexes. Introductions served to identify those with whom it was permissible to associate.
2. "Well married" meant marrying class and money. Happiness and romantic love were not given the emphasis that they have in present-day society.
3. Appearance was of great importance. Nobility and even virtue were closely associated with visual impact.

ANSWERS TO UNDERSTANDING LANGUAGE

1. *Design* means "purpose" or "intention."
2. *Vexing* means "annoying" or "irritating."
3. *Solace* means "comfort."
4. *Amends* means "something done to make up for an injury."
5. *Surmises* means "guesses."

The writing assignments on page 770 have students write creatively, while those on page 771 have them think about the selections and write critically.

YOU THE WRITER

Guidelines for Evaluating Assignment 1

1. Has the student written an original ode on an inspirational topic related to the current age?
2. Is the ode at least three stanzas?
3. Has the student used vivid words?
4. Is the ode free from grammar, usage, and mechanics errors?

Guidelines for Evaluating Assignment 2

1. Has the student written a letter in response to a submission by a Romantic poet to an eighteenth-century literary magazine?
2. Has the student expressed his or her feelings about the letter and given reasons why he or she likes or dislikes the submission?
3. Is the letter one page in length?
4. Is the letter free from grammar, usage, and mechanics errors?

Guidelines for Evaluating Assignment 3

1. Has the student written a 500-word essay on a topic that is timely and of general interest to the community?
2. Has the student written two drafts?
3. Is any casual language general enough to be understood by the audience?
4. Is the essay free from grammar, usage, and mechanics errors?

YOU THE WRITER

Assignment

1. If there was one poetic form that permitted the Romantic poet to pour out his or her heart, it was the ode, a poem that pays tribute to an individual, quality, or place. Of course, the particular subject a poet chose for an ode was to an extent limited by circumstances of the times. Had Shelley and Keats lived in our present era of high technology, they might well have dedicated odes to the vastness of our universe.

Prewriting. Brainstorm to come up with an inspirational topic related to the current age, perhaps organ implants or high-speed electronic computers.

Writing. Write an original ode of at least three stanzas that expresses your awe for this modern wonder.

Revising. Review what you have written, making sure you have used vivid words. Check troublesome spellings.

Assignment

2. The Romantic movement grew out of an opposition to the tightly structured view of art and the reliance on scientific doctrine that typified writers of the previous age. The Romantic poet was concerned with emotions and concentrated on natural topics. Imagine you are the editor of a literary magazine and you have just received a poem by an unknown poet named Wordsworth or Coleridge (or any Romantic you have read).

Prewriting. List the tasks you think a magazine editor might be responsible for. Make notes for a response letter to this new poet.

Writing. Write a one-page letter explaining your feelings. State why you like or dislike this new submission.

Revising. Reread your letter for coherence and punctuation. Make sure you have maintained a single tone throughout.

Assignment

3. Essays, whether formal or personal, present the views of their authors in a well-organized and readable manner, sometimes using casual language to enhance a point. Imagine you are living during the Romantic Age. You are invited to write a guest column of approximately 500 words for a local newspaper.

Prewriting. Get your mind spinning to come up with a topic that is both timely and of general interest to the inhabitants of your city or community. Jot down notes to test your knowledge.

Writing. Do at least two drafts of your essay—one to develop the general structure and a second to iron out rough spots.

Revising. Check your essay for continuity. Be sure that any casual language you have used is general enough to be understood by your audience.

YOU THE CRITIC

Assignment

1. In the preface to the second edition of his *Lyrical Ballads,* William Wordsworth stated that his goal was "to choose incidents . . . from common life" and make them "interesting by tracing in them . . . the primary laws of our nature." It might be argued that this statement fairly summarized the goal of all Romantics. Write an essay demonstrating that the work of a Romantic poet of your choosing fits the above description.

Prewriting. Before you begin to write, make sure you understand all parts of the Wordsworth statement. Decide in particular what you believe the phrase "primary laws of our nature" means.

Writing. Write the first draft of your essay. Quote specific poems that illustrate your claim.

Revising. Check to see that main subpoints of your essay support the thesis statement. Correct any run-on sentences or fragments.

Assignment

2. A writer's style is like a personal stamp that uniquely identifies his or her work. Style is determined by such features as word choice and sentence length. Evaluate the prose styles of two of the Romantic writers you have read and, in a comparative essay, tell which of the works you find more enjoyable.

Prewriting. Plan your essay by comparing and contrasting the features mentioned above, along with such considerations as fit of style to subject matter. Organize your presentation of similarities and differences.

Writing. Quote freely from the two writers' works. Devote one paragraph to a clear statement of preference, including reasons for your feelings.

Revising. Reread your essay for internal consistency. Be sure you have anticipated and addressed any opposing views.

Assignment

3. Most of the major literary figures of the Romantic movement were supporters of the rebel cause in the French Revolution. Coleridge, for instance, while still in school, composed an ode celebrating the storming of the Bastille, the prison where "enemies" of the French state had been sent. In an expository paper, discuss what aspects of the Romantic temperament would logically lead to such a political stance.

Prewriting. Divide a sheet of paper into two columns. In one, list traits of the liberal mind; in the other, list aspects of the Romantic world view. Draw lines connecting corresponding traits.

Writing. Write your first draft. In the first paragraph include a definitive statement of your purpose in writing.

Revising. Make sure you have adequately supported your main idea. Proofread your paper for possible errors and omissions.

YOU THE CRITIC
Guidelines for Evaluating Assignment 1

1. Does the essay begin with a thesis that conveys the student's opinion about the applicability of Wordsworth's statement?
2. Do the subpoints of the essay support the thesis statement?
3. Has the student used quotations from specific poems to support his or her claim?
4. Is the essay free from grammar, usage, and mechanics errors?

Guidelines for Evaluating Assignment 2

1. Has the student written an essay comparing and contrasting two Romantic poets?
2. Has the student expressed a clear preference for one of the poets?
3. Has the student quoted freely from the two writers' works?
4. Has the student anticipated and addressed any opposing views?
5. Is the essay free from grammar, usage, and mechanics errors?

Guidelines for Evaluating Assignment 3

1. Has the student begun the essay with a definitive statement of purpose?
2. Has the student shown the aspects of the Romantic temperament that would logically lead to support for the French Revolution?
3. Has the main idea been adequately supported by evidence from the literature?
4. Is the essay free from grammar, usage, and mechanics errors?

Humanities Note

Fine art, *Queen Victoria's Visit to Cherbourg,* by Jules Achille Noel. Noel (1815–1881) was an English painter who worked during the Victorian Age. In his painting *Queen Victoria's Visit to Cherbourg,* he celebrates one of the events during her sixty-three year reign with the pomp and pageantry typical of the period.

Respect for the throne increased dramatically under Victoria's rule as Great Britain reached the height of its power. Although it was under her rule that the power of the British throne became largely symbolic, she aroused in the British people deep feelings of affection and admiration.

BIG BEN
Derain Troyes
Private Collection

THE VICTORIAN AGE
(1833–1901)

The year's at the spring
And the day's at the morn;
Morning's at seven;
The hillside's dew-pearled;
The lark's on the wing;
The snail's on the thorn;
God's in his heaven—
All's right with the world!*

From the song of an Italian urchin in "Pippa Passes"
Robert Browning

773

Humanities Note

London's Crystal Palace. Prosperity and growth marked the Victorian Age. This was clearly seen with the erection of London's Crystal Palace, which housed the Great Exhibition of 1851. Designed by Sir Joseph Paxton, the Crystal Palace was of iron-frame and glass-panel construction. Covering almost nineteen acres, the Crystal Palace was the first prefabricated structure with standardized sections constructed in the factory and assembled at the building site.

Queen Victoria reigned for sixty-four years, from 1837 to 1901—the longest reign of any British monarch. With occasional exceptions, those were years of prosperity for Britain. Robert Browning's lines on the preceding page echo the ringing optimism and self-assurance that marked the Victorian Age. The Victorians recognized that, in fact, all was not really "right with the world," and they worked hard to make improvements. Yet they firmly believed that theirs was the best nation in the best era history had yet produced.

LIVING IN THE VICTORIAN AGE

Britain's booming economy and rapid expansion encouraged great optimism. Profiting from its early industrial revolution, Britain became the world leader in manufacturing. Factories dotted the land. Factory towns grew into large cities. Banks, retail shops, and other businesses expanded. These changes in turn spurred the growth of two important classes—an industrial working class and a modern middle class, able to live a better life because of the low cost and large variety of mass-produced factory goods.

As its industry and commerce prospered, Britain expanded its merchant fleet and its powerful navy. Economic and military power helped Britain to acquire new colonies in far-flung parts of the globe. Victorians could quite literally boast that "the sun never sets on the British empire."

Yet, for all its smug self-satisfaction, the Victorian Age was also a time of social concern. Victorian writers exposed a dark underside of the industrial age—brutal factory conditions and stinking slums that bred poverty and disease. Goaded by reformers and radicals of many sorts, Victorian leaders took steps to expand democracy and better the lot of the poor. By the time Victoria died in 1901, Britain had shed some of its smugness and was grappling with the social and economic problems industrialization had caused.

PAINTING OF LONDON'S CRYSTAL PALACE, DONE FOR THE GREAT EXHIBITION OF 1851
The British Museum

Victoria and Albert

Victoria became queen at the age of eighteen. She impressed the members of Parliament with her grace and self-assurance, but she could also be very stubborn. In 1840 she insisted on marrying a first cousin, a minor German princeling named Albert of Saxe-Coburg-Gotha. Many Britons disliked the marriage: What if Prince Albert filled the queen's head with "European" notions of absolute rule? As it turned out, Albert understood the limited powers of British royalty. His wisdom and impartial advice did much to soften the personality of the queen. (It was she who reigned; Albert was not king but *prince consort*—the monarch's husband.)

Victoria and Albert produced a large family and restored to the monarchy a sense of decorum, sadly lacking since the madness of George III and the scandalous behavior of his sons. The twentieth century would tend to look back on Victoria as prim to the point of prudishness. However, we must remember that her restrained behavior came in reaction to those earlier royal excesses.

When Albert died of typhoid fever in 1861, Victoria went into deep mourning. For a time she was almost a recluse, leaving day-to-day government in the hands of her prime ministers. Victoria's limited involvement in political affairs helped to turn Britain into the modern constitutional monarchy it is today, in which the duties of the sovereign are largely ceremonial.

Victorian Politics

The prime ministers who govern Britain serve at the sufferance of Parliament, and can be dismissed at any time by a vote of no confidence. Such a system produces a more rapid turnover of leadership than does our own presidential system.

The years of Victoria's reign brought a change in the policies and even the names of the two parties that had dominated eighteenth-century politics. The Whig party formerly had championed Britain's commercial dominance and colonial empire. Gradually, the Whigs adopted new attitudes and became known as the Liberal party. Liberals often attacked colonial expansion and, under the leadership of William Gladstone, pressed for reforms at home and in Ireland. Meanwhile, the Tory party began to abandon its old stance of isolationism in foreign affairs and stubborn resistance to social change. The Tories (or Conservatives, as they came to be called) now supported imperialism—the expansion of empire. Under leaders like Benjamin Disraeli, the Conservatives also supported electoral reform. It was Disraeli who helped push through the Second Reform Bill of 1867, doubling the electorate by granting voting rights to tenant farmers and to better-paid male workers.

The Liberals and Conservatives alternated in power. Each party had its die-hard followers, but each had to compete for the same middle-of-the-road "swing" voters. As a result, Victorian politics emphasized compromise and slow reform.

BRITISH EVENTS

1833 Slavery abolished in British empire.

1837 Victoria becomes queen.

Charles Dickens writes *The Pickwick Papers* and *Oliver Twist*.

Thomas Carlyle writes *The French Revolution*.

1840 Michael Faraday experiments with electric currents.

1843 **William Wordsworth** becomes poet laureate.

1844 George Williams founds YMCA.

1845 Irish Potato Famine begins.

1847 Factory Act passed.

Charlotte Brontë publishes *Jane Eyre*.

Emily Brontë publishes *Wuthering Heights*.

1848 First Public Health Act.

Women begin attending University of London.

1850 Public Libraries Act.

Elizabeth Barrett Browning publishes *Sonnets from the Portuguese*.

1854 Britain enters Crimean War.

Parliament abolishes religious restrictions for university attendance.

1856 Henry Bessemer introduces steelmaking process.

1859 Charles Darwin publishes *On the Origin of Species*.

1860 Florence Nightingale founds school for nurses.

Food and Drugs Act passed.

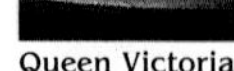

Queen Victoria

Charles Darwin

Battle from

Charlotte Brontë

Charles Dickens

Karl Marx

the Crimean War

Samuel Morse

Sepoy Mutiny

Richard Wagner

WORLD EVENTS

1836 United States: Ralph Waldo Emerson publishes *Nature*.

1841 South Pacific: New Zealand becomes a British colony.

United States: Edgar Allan Poe publishes "The Murders in the Rue Morgue."

1842 Asia: Hong Kong becomes a British colony.

France: Honoré de Balzac publishes *The Human Comedy*.

1844 America: Samuel F. B. Morse patents telegraph.

1846 America: Elias Howe patents sewing machine.

France: Pierre Joseph Proudhon publishes *The Philosophy of Poverty*.

1848 France: Revolution establishes new republic under Louis Napoleon.

Belgium: Marx and Engels publish *Communist Manifesto*.

1850 France: Life insurance introduced.

Germany: Wagner's opera *Lohengrin* first performed.

1851 Australia: Gold discovered in New South Wales.

1853 Eastern Europe: Beginning of Crimean War.

1854 Japan: Trade with West reopened.

United States: Henry David Thoreau publishes *Walden*.

1856 France: Gustave Flaubert publishes *Madame Bovary*.

1857 India: Sepoy Mutiny against British.

1858 India: Political power of East India Company abolished.

BRITISH EVENTS

1863 Construction of London Underground begins.

1864 **Robert Browning** publishes *The Ring and the Book*.

1865 Joseph Lister initiates antiseptic surgery.

London Fire Department established.

Lewis Carroll publishes *Alice's Adventures in Wonderland*.

1867 **Matthew Arnold** publishes "Dover Beach."

1869 Debtors' prisons abolished.

1878 Salvation Army established.

1879 **George Meredith** publishes *The Egoist*.

1880 Joseph Swan installs first electric lighting.

1883 **Robert Louis Stevenson** publishes *Treasure Island.*

1884 First edition of *Oxford English Dictionary* published.

1886 English Lawn Tennis Association founded at Wimbledon.

1887 First Sherlock Holmes tale published.

1888 Jack the Ripper stalks London's East End.

1891 **Thomas Hardy** publishes *Tess of the d'Urbervilles*.

1892 **Rudyard Kipling** publishes *Barrack-room Ballads*.

1895 Oscar Wilde publishes *The Importance of Being Earnest*.

1896 **A. E. Housman** publishes *A Shropshire Lad*.

1901 Queen Victoria dies.

Illustration from *Treasure Island*

Robert Browning

Alice's Adventures

Suez Canal

Alexander Graham Bell

Civil War Begins

in Wonderland

Anton Chekhov

Boxer Rebellion

WORLD EVENTS

1861 United States: Civil War begins.

1865 Russia: Leo Tolstoy publishes *War and Peace*.

Austria: Gregor Mendel proposes laws of heredity.

1866 Europe: Seven Weeks' War leads to unification of modern Germany.

1869 Egypt: Suez Canal completed.

1873 France: Jules Verne publishes *Around the World in Eighty Days*.

1876 United States: Alexander Graham Bell patents telephone.

1877 United States: Thomas Edison patents phonograph.

1878 Afghanistan: British troops fight Second Afghan War.

1879 South Africa: Zulu War against British.

1880 Russia: Feodor Dostoevsky publishes *The Brothers Karamazov*.

1882 Egypt: Britain invades and conquers nation.

1884 United States: Mark Twain publishes *The Adventures of Huckleberry Finn*.

1885 Belgium: van Gogh paints *The Potato Eaters*.

1894 Asia: Sino-Japanese War begins.

1896 Greece: First modern Olympics held.

1898 China: Boxer Rebellion against foreign influence.

France: Marie and Pierre Curie discover radium.

1899 Russia: Anton Chekhov publishes *Uncle Vanya*.

Humanities Note

Fine art, *Warrington High Street,* by T. Hesketh. Realism was the dominant movement in art during the later part of the nineteenth century and marks the style of T. Hesketh's *Warrington High Street.* Realist painters sought to present scenes from life, not from imagination. They expanded the usual subject matter of paintings to include all levels of society, not just the wealthy and the aristocracy. Capturing local color as Hasketh does in this detail was important to the Realists, who sought to achieve verisimilitude in all images.

WARRINGTON HIGH STREET
T. Hesketh
Warrington Museum and Art Gallery

Domestic Problems and Reforms

Two key issues—trade policy and electoral reform—dominated domestic politics during the first half of the Victorian era. Trade debate centered on the Corn Laws, which had long slapped high tariffs on "corn" (grain). This discouraged food imports and helped British landlords and farmers. However, it also tended to keep food prices high, which angered consumers and the poorer classes. At stake was not just money but life itself, as became evident in 1845, when a failure of Ireland's potato crop caused a massive famine in which as many as one million Irish people died.

Seeking to increase the supply of food, Parliament repealed the Corn Laws in 1846. Over the following decade, Parliament changed other trade laws, putting an end to the policy of protectionism (restriction of imports to protect domestic producers). Instead, Britain now adopted a policy of free trade (allowing imports and exports with few or no restrictions). The new policy reflected the interests of rising British industries, which prospered by importing raw materials and exporting finished goods. Times had changed, and Britain was fast becoming an industrial rather than an agricultural nation.

Many Britons thought that the second issue—electoral reform—had been settled in 1832, when the Reform Law gave the vote to middle-class males. They were wrong; working-class people wanted further reform. In 1837, a group of radicals drew up a "People's Charter" demanding, among other things, universal suffrage for males. This so-called Chartist movement fizzled out after a decade or so, but new demands for electoral change led to the Second Reform Bill of 1867 and to almost complete male suffrage in 1885.

The urge for reform also affected many other areas. Women, although still not eligible to vote, began to attend universities. Parliament passed laws to reduce the working day for women and children, to establish a system of free grammar schools, and to legalize trade unions. It voted to improve public sanitation and to regulate factories and housing. Still, such measures did not go far enough to suit everyone, and agitation continued for further reform.

One of the most important issues left unresolved in the Victorian Age was the future of Ireland, where widespread poverty had bred bitter opposition to British control. In the 1880's and 1890's the Liberal leader William Gladstone supported Irish demands for home rule (self-government). However, a hard-line faction of Liberals joined Conservatives to block action on Gladstone's proposals.

EMPIRE AND FOREIGN POLICY

Britain was not alone in its drive to form a world empire in the Victorian Age. Other European powers were grabbing colonies too. British diplomats tried to protect and expand the British empire while promoting a balance of power within Europe.

The Imperialist Urge

Victorian Britons who supported a policy of imperialism could cite a long list of arguments: Colonies would provide raw materials and markets for British industry. They would offer a home for British settlers. Britain had no choice; if it didn't seize a territory, one of its European rivals would do so. Perhaps the clinching argument was the writer Rudyard Kipling's notion of "the white man's burden." Victorians tended to believe that Western civilization—commonly perceived as white, Christian, and progressive—was superior to all other cultures. This attitude led many Victorians to look condescendingly on non-Westerners as people in need of assistance. What could be more noble than to help those "natives" by offering them the protection of the British empire? While such an argument seems faintly ridiculous by today's lights, many Victorians sincerely believed it.

Britain's empire had two sorts of land—"settled" territories, where whites made up a large part of the population, and outright colonies, in which few whites lived. During the Victorian Age Britain granted considerable self-government to "settled" territories such as Canada, Australia, and New Zealand. On the other hand, it exercised strict rule over places such as Hong Kong (acquired from China in 1841). After a rebellion in 1856 by sepoys (Indian troops under British command), Britain shouldered aside the British East India Company and took direct control of India. Victoria would thus add "Empress of India" to her formal titles.

The Crimean War

The Victorian years were generally peaceful. Britain fought only one major European war—the Crimean War (1854–56), so called because it took place on the Crimean peninsula in southern Russia. Britain, France, and Turkey teamed up to thwart Russian expansion, but the battles were largely inconclusive. Today we remember the war mainly for the brave but disastrous charge of Britain's Light Brigade. This was commemorated in a famous poem by Alfred, Lord Tennyson, including these lines:

> Theirs not to make reply,
> Theirs not to reason why,
> Theirs but to do and die.

Britain as a World Power

In the last three decades of Victoria's rule, Britain reached new heights of wealth and power. It gained control of the new Suez Canal in Egypt. It acquired Cyprus, an island in the eastern Mediterranean. It joined other European powers in a scramble to carve up Africa, acquiring such territories as Kenya, Uganda, Nigeria, and Rhodesia (Zimbabwe). Also, Britain expanded its control over what is now South Africa, defeating Dutch settlers there in the Boer War of 1899–1902.

THE TRIUMPHS OF THE BRITISH ARMY AND NAVY, 1897
COMMEMORATING THE DIAMOND JUBILEE OF QUEEN VICTORIA
English Lithograph, 1897
The Granger Collection

Humanities Note

Fine art, *The Triumphs of the British Army and Navy,* 1897. This lithograph commemorates the Diamond Jubilee of Queen Victoria, or the sixtieth year of her reign. It shows the triumphs of the British Army and Navy at Balaclava in the Crimea and in the Sudan.

The armed forces of Great Britain, France, Turkey, and Sardinia fought the Russian forces for control of the Holy Lands. However, the underlying causes of the war were based on conflicting commercial interests, politics, and dynastic rivalries. This lithograph indicates the high level of patriotism felt by the British.

Even in those years of expansion, however, Britons could not help worrying about the future. Other nations, especially the United States and Germany, were rapidly building up industry and competing with Britain in world markets. How long could Britain maintain its economic superiority? How would economic changes affect the balance of power? For how long would Britain's navy "rule the waves"? By the end of Victoria's reign in 1901, British leaders had many disturbing questions to ponder.

VICTORIAN THOUGHT

Victorian thinkers often disagreed on the crucial issues of their times, but they shared a deep confidence in humanity's ability to better itself. "Man is not the creature of circumstances," said Benjamin Disraeli. "Circumstances are the creatures of man." This spirit of optimism prevailed up to the closing years of the Victorian era.

Responses to Industrialization

The changes brought about by the industrial revolution stirred conflicting feelings among Victorian thinkers. On the one hand, they admired the material benefits industrialization had brought. On the other, they deplored the brutality of factory life and of industrial slums.

We can divide into three groups the political and economic theories Victorians employed for dealing with the changed conditions of the industrial age:

Theories

- **Laissez-faire theory.** This theory holds that government should avoid meddling in the affairs of business—should "let it be" (the meaning of the French term). When allowed full freedom, the theory goes, industry will use the most efficient techniques and reach the highest possible level of prosperity.
- **Reformist liberalism.** Those who held this theory believed that rapid change brings problems that *laissez-faire* policies cannot solve. They argued that government intervention and regulation were sometimes necessary to protect the rights of the weak against the strong.
- **Socialism.** Some thinkers and activists favored a more far-reaching policy, ending private ownership of major industries and substituting public ownership. Supporters of socialism also called for sweeping government measures to promote equality and help the poor.

Religion and Science

At the same time they were debating the political problems posed by industrialization, the Victorians were grappling with the religious and philosophical implications of modern life. A religious movement called evangelicalism influenced many Victorians. The movement linked strict personal morality with a strong commitment to social reform, leading to the founding of such institutions as the Young Men's Christian Association (YMCA) and the Salvation Army. The Liberal leader William Gladstone was among those inspired by evangelicalism to devote his life to public service and social reform. The Oxford Movement expressed a second strain of religious thought, seeking a return to more traditional church ritual.

Other Victorians turned to science for answers. The theory of evolution proposed by Charles Darwin (1809–82) in *On the Origin of Species* (1859) stirred bitter controversy. Some Victorian thinkers saw Darwin's theory as a direct challenge to Biblical truth and traditional religious faith. Some accepted both Darwin's theory and religion, striving to reconcile scientific and religious insights.

Darwin believed that a process called natural selection guides evolution. By this process, some organisms survive (because they can adapt to changing conditions) and some die out (because they cannot adapt). A social scientist named Herbert Spencer (1820–1903) applied Darwin's idea—which Spencer called "the survival of the fittest"—to social life. In Spencer's harsh philosophy, called Social Darwinism, the "fittest" humans achieve social and economic success while the "unfit" fail. Neither government nor private charities should attempt to interfere with this "natural" process, said the Social Darwinists—applying *laissez-faire* theory to social as well as economic life.

VICTORIAN LITERATURE

The ideas of the Victorian Age—political and moral, scientific and religious—helped to shape the works you will read in this unit. Indeed, they helped to define the Victorians themselves. Education was spreading in the Victorian Age, and as literacy increased, so did the impact of the written word. Probably at no other time before or since did books enjoy such enormous popularity and influence.

Romanticism, Realism, and Naturalism

The Romantic movement continued to influence writers of the Victorian Age, but new styles of writing came into vogue. Romanticism had begun as a radical departure from literary practice; now it was part of mainstream culture, safe but slightly stale. A new generation of writers, coming of age in a time of rapid technological change, began to examine the social effects of that change. The heroes of the new generation's literature would be ordinary people

783

Humanities Note

Fine art, *Dudley Street, Seven Dials, London,* 1872, by Gustave Doré. Gustave Doré (1832–83) was an enormously popular illustrator of the mid-nineteenth century. Born in France, Doré illustrated some of the world's greatest classics, including the Bible, Dante's *Divine Comedy,* Tennyson's *Idylls of the King,* and Coleridge's "The Rime of the Ancient Mariner." As seen in this detail, his work is informed by his taste for romantic realism and reflects his taste for the dramatic.

DUDLEY STREET, SEVEN DIALS, LONDON, 1872
Gustave Doré
The Granger Collection

facing the day-to-day problems of life. Life would be presented as it is, rather than as it might be. We call this new literary movement realism, because it sought to portray human life realistically, as it is actually lived, without sugar coating.

Romantic thinking had lent itself to poetic language, and we study the Romantic Age chiefly for its poetry. Realism, on the other hand, focused on more down-to-earth or prosaic events especially suited to prose. The shift in style helped to make the Victorian Age the great age of the British novel.

By focusing on ordinary people, realist literature reflected the nineteenth-century trend to democracy and appealed to a growing middle-class audience. Realist writing often dealt with family relationships, religion and morality, social change, and social reform —topics of special interest to middle-class readers.

New ideas in science also made their mark on Victorian literature. A movement known as naturalism—an outgrowth of realism—sought to apply the techniques of scientific observation to writing about life in the industrial age. Naturalists crammed their novels with details—the sour smells of poverty, the harsh sounds of factory life—often with the aim of promoting social reform. Naturalist writers directly contradicted the romantic view of nature as kindly and benevolent. To naturalists, the idea that nature mirrored human feelings was false—a "pathetic fallacy." Instead, naturalist writers portrayed nature as harsh and indifferent to the human suffering it often caused.

It would be a mistake to assume that Victorian writers abandoned romanticism altogether. Some writers blended romanticism with realism or naturalism; others sought to revive romanticism as the radical force it once had been. Two Victorian literary movements deserve special mention here. One is a group of painters and poets known as the Pre-Raphaelite Brotherhood. Formed about 1850, this short-lived group sought to ignore the ugliness of industrial life by portraying nature with the fidelity found in medieval Italian art, before the Renaissance painter Raphael (1483–1520). The leading Pre-Raphaelite was Dante Gabriel Rossetti (1828–82), who excelled both as a painter and as a poet. The second group, known as the aesthetic movement, appeared toward the end of the Victorian Age. Aesthetes like the writer Oscar Wilde (1854–1900) turned away from the everyday world and sought to create "art for art's sake"—works whose sole reason for being was their perfection or beauty.

Victorian Poetry

The Victorian Age produced a large and diverse body of poetry. The Romantic style predominated at first, but realism and naturalism gained force as time went on.

The most popular poet of the era, however, was a romantic —Alfred, Lord Tennyson (1809–92). Influenced by earlier romantic poets, especially Walter Scott, Tennyson wrote many long narrative poems on ancient and medieval themes like the King Arthur legend. His verse displays a keen sense of the music of language, and some of his more sentimental lyrics reappeared in popular songs. Yet Tennyson also revealed a deeper, more thoughtful side in such powerful poems as "Ulysses" (1842) and "In Memorium" (1850). Tennyson became poet laureate after Wordsworth died in 1850.

Robert Browning (1812–89) produced a body of poetry as diverse as Tennyson's, although in his lifetime he never achieved equal public acclaim. Many of Browning's poems display Romantic attitudes. Others, however, show the influence of realism in seeking to portray individuals with un-Romantic authenticity. Critics have especially admired Browning's use of the dramatic monologue—a long speech by an imaginary character—to expose pretense and

BEATA BEATRIX, c. 1863
Dante Gabriel Rossetti
The Granger Collection

Humanities Note

Fine art, *Beata Beatrix,* c. 1863, by Dante Gabriel Rossetti. Dante Gabriel Rossetti (1828–82) was one of the founding members of the Pre-Raphaelite Brotherhood. This group of painters turned away from the materialism and ugliness they perceived in the industrialized world and toward the spirituality and idealism they associated with the past, especially the Middle Ages and the early Renaissance.

Humanities Note

Alfred Lord Tennyson, Caricature, 1871, by Carlo Pellegrini. Caricature is a type of art that exaggerates the physical characteristics or mannerisms of its subject. Caricature is often used to poke fun at elevated subjects, such as the poet laureate.

This caricature of Tennyson gives great emphasis to certain characteristics. You might have students determine what the caricaturist is poking fun at.

ALFRED, LORD TENNYSON, CARICATURE, 1871
Carlo Pellegrini
The Granger Collection

reveal a character's inner self. In 1846, Browning plunged into one of literature's most famous romances when he eloped with the poet Elizabeth Barrett, whose father had forbidden the marriage. At the time, Elizabeth was a more famous poet than Robert. History has since reversed that verdict, but Elizabeth Barrett Browning (1806–61) is still remembered for the beautiful love poems she wrote her husband.

A number of other Victorian poets also worked in the Romantic vein. You have already read of the Pre-Raphaelites, who include Dante Gabriel Rossetti; his sister, Christina Rossetti (1830–94); and George Meredith (1828–1909). Another poet with a Romantic style was Emily Brontë (1818–48), who often described characters and settings from the imaginative world of her own childhood.

Matthew Arnold (1822–88) was probably the first Victorian poet to focus on "the bewildering confusion" of the industrial age. Many of Arnold's poems deal with alienation: separation from nature, isolation from other human beings. In his most famous poem, "Dover Beach" (1867), he breaks with poetic tradition and employs free verse—poetry with no fixed rhythm—to portray the confusion and loss of faith of his times. Arnold was a forerunner of the more pessimistic naturalist writers.

Late Victorian naturalism found its strongest voice in Thomas Hardy (1840–1928), whose poetry, like his prose, focuses on workers and farmers overwhelmed by the forces of nature and society. Life's disappointments were also a frequent subject of A. E. Housman (1859–1936), whose quiet lyrics speak of personal loss and rural change.

Rudyard Kipling (1865–1936), who wrote fiction and children's stories as well as poetry, gained great popularity in the 1890's. Kipling created action-packed narrative poems such as "Gunga Din" (1892) and many short lyric poems that became popular songs. He employs the dialect of working-class soldiers in realist poems such as "Tommy" (1892):

> For it's Tommy this, an' Tommy that, an' "Chuck 'im out, the brute!"
> But it's "Savior of 'is Country" when the guns begin to shoot.

One final Victorian poet, Gerard Manley Hopkins (1844–89), remained unpublished during his own century but would later inspire twentieth-century poets. Hopkins, a Catholic priest, wrote deeply religious verse influenced by the earlier Romantic poets and the philosopher Duns Scotus. He was also an innovative craftsman, introducing a rhythmic pattern called sprung rhythm that abandoned traditional metric feet.

Victorian Drama

Compared to poetry, drama in the Victorian Age seemed pale and uninspired. Playhouses were few in number and hemmed in by government restrictions. Only toward the end of the century did the theater begin to show some sparkle, with serious dramas like Sir Arthur Wing Pinero's *The Second Mrs. Tanqueray* (1893) and satirical ones like Oscar Wilde's *The Importance of Being Earnest* (1895).

Victorian Fiction

If one form of literature can be seen as quintessentially Victorian, it is the novel. Members of the new middle class were avid readers, and they loved novels—especially novels that reflected the main social issues of the day. Responding to the demand, weekly and monthly magazines published novels chapter by chapter, in serial form. Curious readers had to keep buying the magazine to learn what happened next. Most of the best novelists of the day wrote, at one time or another, for the magazines.

Romanticism heavily influenced early Victorian novels, especially those written by three sisters—Emily Brontë (1818–48), Charlotte Brontë (1816–55), and the lesser-known Anne Brontë (1820–49). Emily's classic *Wuthering Heights* (1847) tells the poetic tale of the doomed passions of Catherine Earnshaw and of Heathcliff, one of English fiction's outstanding Byronic heroes. Charlotte's famous *Jane Eyre* (1847) recounts the adventures of a governess who falls in love with her mysterious employer, Mr. Rochester. Nevertheless, both works also contain elements of the new realism—as in *Jane Eyre*'s vivid portrait of the heroine's harsh childhood.

The realistic elements of *Jane Eyre* probably owe much to the influence of Charles Dickens (1812–70), who surpassed all other Victorian novelists in popularity. Dickens never forgot his impoverished childhood, filling his novels with poignant details that dramatized the problems of a grimy industrial England. Although Dickens treated social problems realistically and became an outspoken voice for social reform, he tempered his criticism with humor. Many of his characters are comic caricatures in which a particular human foible or vice is exaggerated. Dickens also showed a sentimental

BAYSWATER OMNIBUS
G. W. Joy
Museum of London

Humanities Note

Fine art, *Bayswater Omnibus,* by G. W. Joy. George William Joy (1844–1925) was a British painter who painted realistic scenes of everyday life. This scene in a public conveyance reflects the concerns of the social realists, showing the rapidly growing middle class.

Humanities Note

Fine art, *Hyde Park near Grosvenor Gate,* 1842, by Thomas Shotter Boys. Thomas Shotter Boys (1803–72) was a British painter who sought to present everyday life in a realistic fashion. This painting captures the pageant of Victorian life in an age of opulence. The setting, Hyde Park, was an appropriate place to show Victorian people at leisure.

HYDE PARK NEAR GROSVENOR GATE, 1842
Thomas Shotter Boys
Guildhall Art Gallery

side, providing happy endings for many of his plucky heroes and heroines.

Other Victorian realists were less sentimental in their portraits of people and society. George Meredith, already mentioned as a romantic poet, produced careful psychological studies of characters and their motives in novels such as *The Egoist* (1879). Mary Ann Evans, writing under the pen name George Eliot (1819–80), examined moral issues and personal relationships in novels such as *Adam Bede* (1859). Also choosing realistic themes were William Makepeace Thackeray (1811–63), Anthony Trollope (1815–82), Elizabeth Gaskell (1810–65), and Samuel Butler (1835–1902).

As the century drew to a close, British novelists leaned more and more to naturalism. Thomas Hardy was the most highly regarded of late Victorian naturalists. Hardy set his fiction in western England, which he called by its old Saxon name, Wessex. His pessimistic novels often portray rural characters who have been disappointed in life and love.

Such downbeat themes did not attract the enthusiastic reception for naturalist novels that earlier realist novels had won. Late Victorian readers tended to prefer the action-packed adventure stories of writers like Robert Louis Stevenson (1850–94) and Rudyard Kipling or the Sherlock Holmes mysteries of Sir Arthur Conan Doyle (1859–1930).

Nonfiction Prose

Novels, of course, were only one of the many types of prose available to Victorian readers. British writers poured out a steady stream of histories, biographies, essays, and criticism.

Greatest of the historians were Thomas Carlyle (1795–1881) and Thomas Babington Macaulay (1800–59). Carlyle also wrote historical biographies. Perhaps the outstanding literary biography of the era was Elizabeth Gaskell's *Life of Charlotte Brontë* (1857), still a primary source of information on the Brontë family.

All the great Victorian thinkers produced influential prose works. Matthew Arnold, for example, made a sharp attack on the British class system in *Culture and Anarchy* (1869), his most famous work of social criticism. Other influential works included *Modern Painters* (1843) by John Ruskin (1819–1900), *On Liberty* (1859) by John Stuart Mill (1806–73), *The Idea of a University Defined* (1873) by John Henry Newman (1801–90), and *Studies in the History of the Renaissance* (1873) by Walter Pater (1839–94).

All in all, the Victorian Age produced a diverse body of literature—entertaining, scholarly, humorous, profound. Because the era is so close to our own times—and because in it we see the beginnings of our own problems, many of them still unresolved—Victorian literature has a special relevance to readers in the twentieth century. In addition, the Victorian writers were brilliant storytellers, and we read their works not only for literary appreciation and historical understanding but for pure reading pleasure.

ENGLISH VOICES

Quotations by Prominent Figures of the Period

Man is a tool-making animal.

Thomas Carlyle, *Sartor Resartus*

Youth is a blunder; manhood a struggle; old age a regret.

Benjamin Disraeli, *Coningsby*

If thou must love me, let it be for naught
Except for love's sake only.

Elizabeth Barrett Browning, *Sonnets from the Portuguese*

The only purpose for which power can be rightfully exercised over any member of a civilized community, against his will, is to prevent harm to others.

John Stuart Mill, *On Liberty*

You cannot fight against the future. Time is on our side.

William E. Gladstone, Speech on the Second Reform Bill

It's them as take advantage
that get advantage i'
this world.

George Eliot, *Adam Bede*

'Tis better to have loved and lost
Than never to have loved at all.

Alfred, Lord Tennyson, "In Memoriam A.H.H."

A man's reach should exceed his grasp,
Or what's a heaven for?

Robert Browning, "Andrea del Sarto"

He had used the word in its Pickwickian sense.

Charles Dickens, *The Pickwick Papers*

Reading Critically The information on this page is designed to help students read critically the literature of the Victorian Age. This information guides students to place a work of literature in its historical context, recognize the literary movements of the time, and appreciate the writers' techniques in conveying the ideas of the period.

As you discuss this information with your students, explain that the poem on the following pages, "Ulysses" by Alfred, Lord Tennyson, is a model for reading critically. The notes in the side column draw students' attention to the aspects of the poem that reflect the historical context, the literary movements, and Tennyson's techniques. Have students pay attention to the notes and make their own critical comments as they read the poem.

To give students further practice with the process of reading critically, use the selection in the Teaching Portfolio, "The Subjection of Women" by John Stuart Mill, page 000, which students can annotate themselves. Encourage students to use these strategies as they read the literature in this unit.

READING CRITICALLY

The Literature of 1832–1901

When you read literature it is important to place it in its historical context. Doing so will help you to see how the writer was influenced by the dominant ideas and attitudes of the time and how the work fits into a particular literary movement.

Historical Context

The Victorian Age was a period marked by industrial and scientific advances, social progress, political stability, and economic prosperity. When the period began, England was the world's wealthiest and most powerful nation, and the British Empire spanned the globe. As the age progressed, the nation continued to flourish, as industrial growth and development strengthened its economy and its empire reached its peak. With the expansion of industry, the middle class became a dominant force in British society, whose belief in hard work and strict morality came to represent the age. The middle class also possessed a sense of social responsibility that helped to bring about reforms that gradually improved the living and working conditions of the lower classes.

Literary Movements

The dominant attitudes and beliefs of the Victorian period are reflected in the literature of the time. While some writers embodied the Victorian ideals, others reacted against them. Many Victorian works conveyed the optimism and conservativism that characterized the age. Other works explored the problems that arose from industrialization and confronted the materialism, hypocrisy, and social pretense that accompanied the nation's prosperity. Because of the contrasting approaches of writers of the time, Victorian literature is extremely varied and diverse.

Writers' Techniques

The English novel came of age during the Victorian period. Often published in serial form, Victorian novels are generally characterized by their episodic plots and their realistic portrayal of nineteenth-century life. In poetry, writers displayed a wide array of voices and styles. However, Victorian poets were generally more detached and objective than their predecessors from the Romantic Age.

On the following pages is a poem by Alfred, Lord Tennyson, a major Victorian poet. The notes in the side column should help you to place the selection in its historical context.

Objectives

1. To understand a dramatic monologue
2. To understand a character's motivation
3. To write a continuation of the poem

Teaching Portfolio: Support Material

Teacher Backup, p. 000

Reading Critically, p. 00

Usage and Mechanics Worksheet, p. 00

Analyzing Literature Worksheet, p. 00

Critical Thinking and Reading Worksheet, p. 00

Language Worksheet, p. 00

Selection Test, p. 00

MODEL

Ulysses

Alfred, Lord Tennyson

In Homer's epic poem, the Odyssey, *Ulysses (yo͞o lĭs ēz), the hero of the poem, sets out for his home in Ithaca after ten years of fighting in the Trojan War. The journey is long and filled with adventure. Another decade passes before Ulysses finally reaches his destination. The story of Ulysses is continued in Tennyson's poem, as Ulysses finds himself growing restless years after his return to Ithaca, and he contemplates making a final voyage.*

It little profits that an idle king,
By this still hearth, among these barren crags,
Matched with an aged wife, I mete and dole[1]
Unequal[2] laws unto a savage race,
That hoard, and sleep, and feed, and know not me.
I cannot rest from travel; I will drink
Life to the lees.[3] All times I have enjoyed
Greatly, have suffered greatly, both with those
That loved me, and alone; on shore, and when
Through scudding drifts the rainy Hyades[4]
Vexed the dim sea. I am become a name;
For always roaming with a hungry heart
Much have I seen and known—cities of men
And manners, climates, councils, governments,
Myself not least, but honored of them all—
And drunk delight of battle with my peers,
Far on the ringing plains of windy Troy.
I am a part of all that I have met;
Yet all experience is an arch wherethrough
Gleams that untraveled world, whose margin fades
Forever and forever when I move.

Writer's Technique: Tennyson's poem is a dramatic monologue a poem in which the speaker addresses one or more listeners whose replies are not given. The dramatic monologue was a popular poetic form during the Victorian age.

Writer's Technique: The poem is written in blank verse, or unrhymed lines of iambic pentameter.

Writer's Technique: Tennyson's imagery recalls Ulysses's adventures in Homer's *Iliad* and *Odyssey*.

1. **mete and dole:** Measure and give out.
2. **unequal:** Unfair.
3. **lees:** Sediment.
4. **Hyades** (hī′ ə dēz): A group of stars whose rising was assumed to be followed by rain.

Motivation for Reading Ask students to imagine that they have lived a life as a great adventurer. They have fame and respect around the world. What would it be like to grow old? How might aging change their lives? Relate this imagined situation to that of the great Greek hero Odysseus, also known as Ulysses.

Master Teacher Note Review with students the major episodes of the *Odyssey*, which they have probably read in an earlier grade. Elicit the heroic qualities of Odysseus, known as Ulysses to the Romans. Ask students to speculate on his life after the events of the *Odyssey*. Then tell them that in this poem Tennyson imagines the thoughts of Ulysses years after his return to Ithaca.

Purpose-Setting Question What force or need drives Ulysses?

Humanities Note

Fine art, *Ulysses* by Jean Auguste Dominique Ingres. Ingres (1780–1867), a French painter of historical subjects and portraits, was exposed to art as a child by his father, a sculptor. He first studied music, but his interest in art proved stronger. He studied with various French artists, the foremost of whom was the classicist David. His travels to Italy exposed him to the works of Raphael, the Renaissance artist, by whom he was strongly influenced.

The painting *Ulysses* was completed in 1827. It demonstrates the commitment of Ingres to classicism (unemotional aesthetic principles in art imitating those of ancient Rome and Greece) in the beauty of line and restraint of color. Technically perfect, it is a formal, pure, graceful composition that shows Ingres's attraction to the monumental sculptures of ancient Rome and Greece.

You might use these questions for class discussion:

1. Does this seem to be a portrait of a man longing for adventure? Explain.
2. How does the formal, somewhat cold classicism of this painting compare to the language of Tennyson's poem?

ULYSSES
Jean-Auguste-Dominique Ingres
National Gallery of Art, Washington

How dull it is to pause, to make an end,
To rust unburnished, not to shine in use!
As though to breathe were life. Life piled on life
Were all too little, and of one to me
Little remains; but every hour is saved
From that eternal silence, something more,
A bringer of new things; and vile it were
For some three suns to store and hoard myself,
And this gray spirit yearning in desire
To follow knowledge like a sinking star,
Beyond the utmost bound of human thought.

This is my son, mine own Telemachus,
To whom I leave the scepter and the isle[5]
Well-loved of me, discerning to fulfill
This labor, by slow prudence to make mild
A rugged people, and through soft degrees
Subdue them to the useful and the good.
Most blameless is he, centered in the sphere
Of common duties, decent not to fail
In offices of tenderness, and pay
Meet[6] adoration to my household gods,
When I am gone. He works his work, I mine.
There lies the port; the vessel puffs her sail;
There gloom the dark broad seas. My mariners,
Souls that have toiled and wrought, and thought with me—
That ever with a frolic welcome took
The thunder and the sunshine, and opposed
Free hearts, free foreheads—you and I are old;
Old age hath yet his honor and his toil;
Death closes all; but something ere the end,
Some work of noble note, may yet be done,
Not unbecoming men that strove with Gods.
The lights begin to twinkle from the rocks;
The long day wanes; the slow moon climbs; the deep
Moans round with many voices. Come, my friends,
'Tis not too late to seek a newer world.
Push off, and sitting well in order smite
The sounding furrows; for my purpose holds
To sail beyond the sunset, and the baths
Of all the western stars, until I die.
It may be that the gulfs will wash us down;
It may be we shall touch the Happy Isles,
And see the great Achilles,[8] whom we knew.
Though much is taken, much abides; and though
We are not now that strength which in old days
Moved earth and heaven, that which we are, we are—
One equal temper of heroic hearts,
Made weak by time and fate, but strong in will
To strive, to seek, to find, and not to yield.

Historical Context: Ulysses's efforts to "subdue" the people of Ithaca parallels the efforts of the British Empire to "civilize" the natives of many of its colonies.

Literary Movement: Ulysses's desires reflect the Victorian work ethic.

Writer's Technique: The sunset symbolizes Ulysses's advancing age and the approach of his death.

Literary Movement: Ulysses's assertion reflects the sense optimism and self-assurance that characterizes Victorian life.

---

5. isle: Ithaca, an island off the coast of Greece.
6. meet: Appropriate.
7. Happy Isles: Elysium, or the Islands of the Blessed; in classical mythology, the place where heroes went after death.
8. Achilles (ə' kil' ēz): The Greek hero of the Trojan War.

Enrichment This monologue occurs on the island of Ithaca, where Ulysses is now king. At the moment of the monologue, he is preparing to set sail for his legendary last voyage. It was predicted in the *Odyssey* that the hero would make a final voyage. During medieval times, Dante tells in the "Inferno" canto XXVI, how Ulysses makes a fatal voyage into the unknown in his search for knowledge.

For Further Study Biographical information on Tennyson appears on page 796, and additional poems by him are on pages 798–820.

THINKING ABOUT THE SELECTION

Recalling

1. (a) How does Ulysses describe his current situation? (b) What past experiences does he describe?
2. What work is Ulysses leaving to Telemachus?
3. According to lines 58–61, what is Ulysses's purpose?
4. What comments does Ulysses make about his present condition in the final six lines?

Interpreting

5. How does Ulysses's current situation contrast with his previous experiences?
6. (a) What is Ulysses's attitude toward his experiences and accomplishments? (b) What are his feelings about aging? (c) What is his attitude toward life in general?
7. How is Telemachus different from his father?
8. What is the poem's theme?

Applying

9. Do you think that most people share Ulysses's feelings about aging? Why or why not?

ANALYZING LITERATURE

Understanding Dramatic Monologues

A dramatic monologue is a poem in which one character speaks to one or more silent listeners at a critical point in the speaker's life. The speaker's comments reveal the circumstances surrounding the conversation and offer insights into his or her personality. For example, in Tennyson's poem Ulysses reveals his attitudes concerning old age and death.

1. Why is the occasion of this poem a critical point in Ulysses's life?
2. What do Ulysses's comments reveal about his view concerning his purpose in life?
3. What are the dominant traits of Ulysses's personality?

CRITICAL THINKING AND READING

Understanding a Character's Motivation

In portraying any type of character, a writer must provide a motivation, or a stated or implied reason for the character's behavior, to make the character's actions believable. The motivation is the cause for the action. The ensuing action is the effect, or result. For example, in "Ulysses" Tennyson makes it clear that Ulysses's desire to make a final voyage is partly the result of his disenchantment with his current situation.

1. Name one other motivation for Ulysses's desire to make a final voyage.
2. How is this motivation conveyed in the poem?

THINKING AND WRITING

Writing a Continuation of the Poem

Write a dramatic monologue in which Ulysses describes the final voyage that he contemplates in Tennyson's poem. Brainstorm about the details and outcome of the journey. Arrange the details in chronological order. Then write your poem, using formal, dignified language similar to the language Tennyson uses in "Ulysses." When you revise, make sure you have used concrete details in describing the voyage. After you have finished revising, proofread your poem and share it with your classmates.

Answers

ANSWERS TO THINKING ABOUT THE SELECTION

Recalling

1. (a) Ulysses describes his situation as "barren," ruling an uncaring "savage race" who do not know him. (b) He describes his past experiences in the Trojan Wars and his travels among "cities of men" where he has encountered all sorts of people, governments, and scenes.
2. To Telemachus, he leaves the ruling of Ithaca and the paying of homage to the household gods.
3. His purpose, stated in lines 58-61, is to "sail beyond the sunset . . . until I die."
4. He comments that his physical strength has faded but his will "To strive, to seek, to find, and not to yield" is strong.

Interpreting

5. In his previous experiences, Ulysses was a strong, clever, heroic adventurer. In contrast, his life as ruler of Ithaca is uneventful; he is unknown and unappreciated there, and he longs for the old days of fame and adventure.
6. (a) Ulysses is proud of his past accomplishments. (b) Ulysses is feeling restless as he ages, yearning for one more chance to find knowledge and glory before he dies. (c) In general, Ulysses sees life as an opportunity for adventure.
7. Telemachus is attentive to his duties, content to live an ordered life.
8. Suggested Response: The theme might be that a hero continues to face life courageously even when aging and weary.

Applying

9. Answers will differ. Students might suggest that most people do not share the feelings of Ulysses about aging. Most people are content to reduce activities as they grow older.

ANSWERS TO ANALYZING LITERATURE

1. At this point in his life, Ulysses feels that he has little time left, that this is his last chance for knowledge of the world.
2. He feels that his purpose in life is to seek knowledge, glory, and fame.
3. The major traits that Ulysses reveals in this poem are a strong will, determination, pride, and confidence in his abilities.

ANSWERS TO CRITICAL THINKING AND READING

1. Another motive for Ulysses desire to make a final voyage in his great yearning for knowledge of the world.
2. This belief is stated directly in lines 30-32, suggested in his memories of his past adventures, and evident in his urging to his companions "to seek a newer world" in line 57.

THINKING AND WRITING

Publishing Student Writing After students have written their poems, you might have them read their poems aloud in small groups. Each group can decide on the most effective poem and designate one person to read that poem to the class.

Major Victorian Poets

FAIR, QUIET AND SWEET REST
Luke Fildes
Warrington Museum and Art Gallery

795

More About the Author Alfred, Lord Tennyson's early education under the supervision of his father included a thorough immersion in classical literature. By the age of seven, Tennyson had not only read, but memorized, all of the odes written by the Latin poet Horace. How might Tennyson's classical education be related to his success as a poet?

ALFRED, LORD TENNYSON

1809–1892

When Alfred Tennyson was named baron by Queen Victoria in 1883, he was doubly honored—first by the title "Lord," second by being the first English writer so titled. The honor seemed fitting for one whom most Victorians regarded as the poetic voice of their age. His commitment to responsible action and his belief in the inherent goodness of people were just two of many traits that made Tennyson the object of his contemporaries' admiration and affection. Yet, beyond these qualities was the man himself, forever struggling to overcome shyness and self-doubt, his mind keenly attuned to the problems of his century. Tennyson's best poems reflect both the inner and outer being, expressing through a clear and richly haunting music those certainties that sustain the human spirit.

Tennyson was born in the rural town of Somersby in Lincolnshire, the fourth of twelve children. His father, a rector, had a large library and personally supervised his son's early education. In 1827 Tennyson entered Trinity College, Cambridge, where he became close friends with Arthur Henry Hallam, the son of a noted historian and a great fan of Tennyson's early efforts at poetry. In 1830, with Hallam's encouragement, Tennyson published *Poems, Chiefly Lyrical,* which he followed up two years later with the simply titled *Poems*. When Hallam died suddenly in Vienna in 1833, the loss left a void in Tennyson's life that nearly destroyed him.

Grief, however, was ultimately to prove to be the inspiration behind some of the poet's greatest work. Relatively soon after Hallam's death, Tennyson began work on a collection of memorial poems dedicated to his friend. When the lengthy tribute, titled *In Memoriam,* finally appeared in 1850, the Queen's husband, Prince Albert, was so impressed that he encouraged the Queen to appoint Tennyson next Poet Laureate of England. For the next forty years Tennyson continued to publish regularly. Among his most celebrated works was *Idylls of the King,* a series of poems based on the legend of King Arthur, which began appearing in 1859 and was completed in 1885.

Modern scholars are in general agreement that there is much of lasting value in Tennyson's works. Certainly, there is no denying what the twentieth-century poet and critic T. S. Eliot has called the "abundance, variety, and complete competence" in Tennyson's poetry. Nor can one ignore the number of "quotable lines" Tennyson has added to the language, among them "'Tis better to have loved and lost, than never to have loved at all." These aspects of his verse and others have earned Tennyson yet another honor—that of being one of the best-known poets of any age.

Objectives

1. To recognize meter and stanza structure
2. To understand the author's purpose
3. To find meanings that fit the context
4. To write a description of the poet's style

Teaching Portfolio: Support Material

Teacher Backup, p. 000

Vocabulary Check, p. 00

Usage and Mechanics Worksheet, p. 00

Analyzing Literature Worksheet, p. 00

Critical Thinking and Reading Worksheet, p. 00

Language Worksheet, p. 00

Selection Test, p. 000

GUIDE FOR READING

The Lady of Shalott; Tears, Idle Tears; The Splendor Falls

The Writer's Technique

Meter and Stanza Structure. Meter is the regular pattern of stressed and unstressed syllables in poetry. Stanza structure is a term that takes into account the meter, rhyme scheme, line length, and number of lines within each stanza of a poem. Through the structure of the stanza, the poet establishes unity, of both form and thought, within a poem.

For "The Lady of Shalott," a poem inspired by Arthurian legend, Tennyson appropriately chose a meter and stanza structure that recalled medieval romances—tales in verse that described the deeds of knights and ladies. The stanza of these romances, known as a "tail-rhyme stanza," was traditionally six lines long and composed of two pairs of rhyming lines, each followed by a short third line, or "tail." The rhyming lines, moreover, customarily contained four stressed syllables, or beats, while the tail contained three. Tennyson, as will be seen, altered this traditional pattern somewhat in "The Lady of Shalott," and in so doing, lent his poem a magical, almost dreamlike quality.

Look For

As you read "The Lady of Shalott," be alert to the steady rhythm of the meter as well as to the persistent echoing of the rhymes in each stanza.

Writing

Imagine that the only view of the world you had was a reflection of it, as through a mirror. Freewrite, describing what sensations you would miss in not experiencing life firsthand, and tell how this would make you feel.

Vocabulary

Knowing the following words will help you as you read the next three poems by Tennyson.

casement (kās′ mənt) *n.*: Window that is hinged at the sides. (p. 798, l. 25)

burnished (bʉr′ nisʰhd) *adj.*: Made shiny by daily use. (p. 801, l. 101)

waning (wān′iŋ) *v.*: Gradually becoming dimmer. (p. 801, l. 119)

prow (prou) *n.*: Front of a boat. (p. 802, l. 125)

feigned (fānd) *v.*: Pretended. (p. 804, l. 17)

cataract (kat′ ə rakt′) *n.*: Waterfall. (p. 806, l. 4)

glens (glenz) *n.*: Valleys. (p. 806, l. 11)

Literary Focus Point out that Tennyson was a restless and inventive poet, with a keen ear for the music of poetry. Tell students that all of these factors may have influenced his adaptation of the tail-rhyme stanza.

Look For Your **less advanced** students may become sidetracked by the focus on meter and stanza structure. Have them read each poem once, focusing on content. Then have them reread each poem, focusing on structure.

Writing Carry out the assignment literally by inviting student volunteers to sit facing a corner of the classroom in which a mirror has been set up. Ask them to record their impressions of the proceedings in the room over the space of five minutes. Discuss the results of the experiment.

Vocabulary Have your **less advanced** students read the words *prow* and *feigned* aloud to make sure they have mastered the pronunciations.

Motivation for Reading Have students discuss what they know about Arthurian legend and the Knights of the Round Table. Have them volunteer names and roles of such key characters as Sir Lancelot. What did King Arthur and his knights see as their purpose? What did they do to accomplish this purpose?

Master Teacher Note Tell students that the poem they are about to read involves a woman who has been placed under a curse. Elicit details of other stories, fables, and fairy tales they know of in which people are under spells or curses. Make a list of these details on the board. Generate a discussion about what happens in these tales when the spell is broken.

Thematic Idea Another selection that focuses on the legend of King Arthur is the excerpt from *Morte Darthur* by Thomas Malory (p. 65).

Purpose-Setting Question What sorts of problems might confront a person whose life is devoted to creating art?

1 **Literary Focus** What is the rhyme scheme of the first stanza? How many accented syllables are there in each line?

2 **Discussion** What are the connotations of the word *gray*? What does the use of this word suggest about the Lady's existence?

The Lady of Shalott

Alfred, Lord Tennyson

Part I

1
On either side the river lie
Long fields of barley and of rye,
That clothe the wold[1] and meet the sky;
And through the field the road runs by
To many-towered Camelot,[2]
And up and down the people go,
Gazing where the lilies blow[3]
Round an island there below,
The island of Shalott.

Willows whiten, aspens quiver,
Little breezes dusk and shiver
Through the wave that runs forever
By the island in the river
Flowing down to Camelot.
2
Four gray walls, and four gray towers,
Overlook a space of flowers,
And the silent isle imbowers
The Lady of Shalott.

By the margin, willow-veiled.
Slide the heavy barges trailed
By slow horses; and unhailed
The shallop[4] flitteth silken-sailed
Skimming down to Camelot:
But who hath seen her wave her hand?
Or at the casement seen her stand?
Or is she known in all the land,
The Lady of Shalott?

Only reapers, reaping early
In among the bearded barley,
Hear a song that echoes cheerly,

1. wold: Rolling plains.
2. Camelot: A legendary English town where King Arthur had his court and Round Table.
3. blow: Bloom.
4. shallop: A light open boat.

From the river winding clearly,
Down to towered Camelot:
And by the moon the reaper weary,
Piling sheaves in uplands airy,
Listening, whispers, " 'Tis the fairy
Lady of Shalott."

Part II

There she weaves by night and day
A magic web with colors gay.
She has heard a whisper say,
A curse is on her if she stay 3
To look down to Camelot.
She knows not what the curse may be,
And so she weaveth steadily,
And little other care hath she,
The Lady of Shalott.

THE LADY OF SHALOTT
John Waterhouse
The Tate Gallery, London

3 **Reading Strategy** What impression do you have of the Lady so far? What details prompt this interpretation?

Humanities Note

Fine art, *The Lady of Shalott,* 1888, by John W. Waterhouse. John William Waterhouse (1849–1917) studied and exhibited at the Royal Academy in London. He is considered to be both a Classical and pre-Raphaelite painter of mainly romantic and poetic subjects. Much of his work was inspired by the poetry of Tennyson and Keats.

This painting, beautifully detailed and executed, was done in iridescent colors that lend a supernatural feel to it. The painting is rich in symbolism. The chain in the Lady's hand, for instance, represents her bondage to fate, and the guttering candle her soon-to-be-extinguished flame of life. Note, too, the Lady's grief-stricken expression, which registers her resignation to her fate.

Some additional points for class discussion include the following:

1. How true to the details of the poem do you feel the artist kept?
2. Do you feel that the mood of the painting effectively mirrors that of the poem?
3. What additional symbols can you locate in the painting? What do they represent?

4 Discussion How do the descriptions of these people differ from that of the Lady?

5 Reading Strategy What do you think the Lady might do about her plight?

6 Discussion How does the repetition of the *b* sound at the beginning of many of the stressed syllables enhance the description of Lancelot?

7 Discussion Compare the use of color in these lines with its use in line 15.

And moving through a mirror[5] clear
That hangs before her all the year,
Shadows of the world appear.
There she sees the highway near
Winding down to Camelot:
There the river eddy whirls,
And there the surly village churls,
And the red cloaks of market girls,
Pass onward from Shalott.

4 Sometimes a troop of damsels glad,
An abbot on an ambling pad,[6]
Sometimes a curly shepherd lad,
Or long-haired page in crimson clad,
Goes by to towered Camelot;
And sometimes through the mirror blue
The knights come riding two and two:
She hath no loyal knight and true,
The Lady of Shalott.

But in her web she still delights
To weave the mirror's magic sights,
For often through the silent nights
A funeral, with plumes and lights
And music, went to Camelot:
Or when the moon was overhead,
5 Came two young lovers lately wed;
"I am half sick of shadows," said
The Lady of Shalott.

Part III

A bow-shot from her bower eaves,
6 He rode between the barley sheaves,
The sun came dazzling through the leaves,
And flamed upon the brazen greaves[7]
Of bold Sir Lancelot.
A red-cross knight[8] forever kneeled
To a lady in his shield,
7 That sparkled on the yellow field,
Beside remote Shalott.

---

5. mirror: Weavers placed mirrors in front of their looms, so that they could view the progress of their work.
6. pad: An easy-paced horse.
7. greaves: Armor that protects the legs below the kneecaps.
8. red-cross knight: Refers to the Redcrosse Knight from *The Faerie Queene* by Edmund Spenser. In Spenser's work, the knight represents St. George, the patron saint of England, in addition to being a symbol of holiness.

The gemmy[9] bridle glittered free,
Like to some branch of stars we see
Hung in the golden Galaxy.[10]
The bridle bells rang merrily
As he rode down to Camelot:
And from his blazoned baldric[11] slung
A mighty silver bugle hung,
And as he rode his armor rung,
Beside remote Shalott.

All in the blue unclouded weather
Thick-jeweled shone the saddle leather,
The helmet and the helmet feather
Burned like one burning flame together,
As he rode down to Camelot.
As often through the purple night,
Below the starry clusters bright,
Some bearded meteor, trailing light,
Moves over still Shalott.

His broad clear brow in sunlight glowed;
On burnish'd hooves his war horse trode;
From underneath his helmet flowed
His coal-black curls as on he rode,
As he rode down to Camelot.
From the bank and from the river
He flashed into the crystal mirror,
"Tirra lirra," by the river
Sang Sir Lancelot.

She left the web, she left the loom,
She made three paces through the room,
She saw the waterlily bloom,
She saw the helmet and the plume,
She looked down to Camelot.
Out flew the web and floated wide;
The mirror cracked from side to side;
"The curse is come upon me," cried
The Lady of Shalott.

8

Part IV

In the stormy east wind straining,
The pale yellow woods were waning,

9. gemmy: Jeweled.
10. Galaxy: The Milky Way.
11. blazoned baldric: A decorated sash worn diagonally across the chest.

8 Reading Strategy What do you think will happen to the Lady now?

9 Discussion Mischance is 'bad luck.' Whose bad luck is referred to here, and what is the nature of that bad luck?

10 Discussion How does the Lady's song compare with that of Lancelot in line 107?

The broad stream in his banks complaining,
Heavily the low sky raining
    Over towered Camelot;
Down she came and found a boat
Beneath a willow left afloat,
And round about the prow she wrote
    The Lady of Shalott.

And down the river's dim expanse
Like some bold seër in a trance,
9 Seeing all his own mischance—
With a glassy countenance
    Did she look to Camelot.
And at the closing of the day
She loosed the chain, and down she lay;
The broad stream bore her far away,
    The Lady of Shalott.

Lying, robed in snowy white
That loosely flew to left and right—
The leaves upon her falling light—
Through the noises of the night
    She floated down to Camelot:
And as the boathead wound along
The willowy hills and fields among,
They heard her singing her last song,
    The Lady of Shalott.

10 Heard a carol, mournful, holy,
Chanted loudly, chanted lowly,
Till her blood was frozen slowly,
And her eyes were darkened wholly,
    Turned to towered Camelot.
For ere she reached upon the tide
The first house by the waterside,
Singing in her song she died,
    The Lady of Shalott.

Under tower and balcony,
By garden wall and gallery,
A gleaming shape she floated by,
Dead-pale between the houses high,
    Silent into Camelot.
Out upon the wharfs they came,
Knight and burgher, lord and dame,
And round the prow they read her name,
    The Lady of Shalott.

Who is this? and what is here?
And in the lighted palace near
Died the sound of royal cheer; 11
And they crossed themselves for fear,
All the knights at Camelot:
But Lancelot mused a little space;
He said, "She has a lovely face;
God in his mercy lend her grace, 12
The Lady of Shalott."

THINKING ABOUT THE SELECTION

Recalling

1. (a) According to the poem, where does the Lady live? (b) How do the people of Camelot know of her existence?
2. What does the Lady spend all of her time doing, and why?
3. Where does she glimpse "shadows of the world"?
4. (a) What action does the Lady take when she sees Sir Lancelot in the mirror? (b) What happens to her as a result?

Interpreting

5. In line 42, the speaker says the Lady "knows not what the curse may be." Explain the curse in your own words?
6. Critics have seen this poem as a commentary on the plight of the artist. In the light of this interpretation, what is meant by the Lady's complaint in lines 71–72?
7. (a) Why do you think the author devotes so much space to his description of Sir Lancelot? (b) How does it relate to the Lady's action and to the overall meaning of the poem?

Applying

8. Why do you find the legend of King Arthur an especially effective—or especially poor—vehicle for the author's commentary on art and the artist in "The Lady of Shalott"?

ANALYZING LITERATURE

Recognizing Meter and Stanza Structure

Meter is a pattern of stressed and unstressed syllables that creates a predictable rhythm in a poem. Meter is expressed in terms of units called *feet,* each consisting of one stressed beat and one or more unstressed beats. Meter is but one ingredient in a poem's **stanza structure,** which also takes into account such matters as variation in line length, overall number of lines, and rhyme scheme. In "The Lady of Shalott," Tennyson adapted—or altered to suit his needs—an ancient stanza form that had the following structure: 1. Six lines per stanza; 2. Four feet in lines 1, 2, 4, and 5; 3. Three feet in lines 3 and 6; 4. The rhyme scheme *aabccb* (where repeated letters represent rhyming words).

Examine several stanzas of "The Lady of Shalott." Note the ways in which the stanza structure differs from the one above. Tell how the changes add to the poem's chantlike effect.

CRITICAL THINKING AND READING

Understanding the Author's Purpose

It has been suggested that Tennyson's purpose in writing "The Lady of Shalott" was to show how the past reflects the problems of the present day.

1. Which events or statements in the poem point to a possible problem?
2. What is the nature of that problem?
3. What specific instances of this problem are evident in modern society?

11 **Enrichment** King Arthur and the Knights of the Round Table are favorite subjects for students. Suggest further readings, such as T. H. White's *Once and Future King.*

12 **Reading Strategy** Ask students whether they suspect Lancelot was aware of his role in the death of the Lady.

Answers

ANSWERS TO THINKING ABOUT THE SELECTION

Recalling

1. (a) She lives in a tower on the island of Shalott. (b) Only reapers know of her existence and only through the song she sings.
2. She weaves a magic web to avoid invoking a curse that has been placed on her.
3. She sees them in a mirror.
4. (a) She boards a boat bound for Camelot. (b) She dies.

Interpreting

5. Suggested Response: The Lady is forbidden from glimpsing the real world.
6. Suggested Response: The complaint expresses dissatisfaction with the contrived world of art and a desire for human contact.
7. (a) The extensive description is intended perhaps to provide a glimpse of the dazzling colors of the real world. (b) It is precisely this world that the artist forsakes for the contrived world of art.

Applying

8. Answers will differ. Students may find the setting effective because the artist's gift is elusive and mystical, like the legend.
Challenge In what ways might the artist's life be considered richer than that of the non-artistic person?

ANSWERS TO ANALYZING LITERATURE

1. Each stanza contains nine lines.
2. Lines 1–8 each contain four beats.
3. Line 9 contains three beats.
4. The rhyme scheme is *aaaabcccb.* The additional rhyming lines, along with the invariable repetition of "Camelot" at the end of the fifth line and "Shalott" at the end of the ninth, conspire to lend the poem the character of a ritual chant.

ANSWERS TO CRITICAL THINKING AND READING

1. Suggested Response: The Lady's feelings of entrapment, artistic considerations aside, are indicative of a problem.
2. Suggested Response: The problem is that of alienation from society in an age of high technology. We must remember that the era in which Tennyson lived was marked by significant industrial advances that tended to minimize the self-worth of the individual.
3. Suggested Reponse: In the twentieth century this alienation is manifest in the devastating legions of the homeless found in inner cities.

Motivation for Reading Ask students whether they have ever had the experience of feeling especially happy or especially sad without knowing exactly why. Ask them to attempt to recall what ran through their minds on such an occasion. Were they simply content to submit to the feeling? Did they attempt to get to the root of it? Did they try to lose themselves in some mindless activity?

Master Teacher Note Have students look at the painting of Tintern Abbey, page 655. What feelings does the image of the ruined church evoke? Explain that a similar view of this church prompted the poem students are about to read.

Thematic Idea Another selection that deals with the passage of time and the impermanence of human life is "Ozymandias" by Percy Bysshe Shelley (p. 712).

Purpose-Setting Question What are the advantages and disadvantages of our ability to remember the past?

1 **Discussion** What do autumn fields represent to the speaker?

2 **Discussion** What is meant by "friends up from the underworld"? What clues support your interpretation?

3 **Enrichment** The reference to "casement" here and "autumn fields" in the first stanza are explained in a note from the poet as harking directly to his view of the woods "yellowing with autumn seen through the ruined windows" of Tintern Abbey.

from The Princess

Alfred, Lord Tennyson

The Princess *(1847) is a long narrative poem that contains a number of songs. Some of these songs, including the two that follow, are considered to be among the finest of Tennyson's lyrics.*

Tears, Idle Tears

Tears, idle tears, I know not what they mean,
Tears from the depth of some divine despair
Rise in the heart, and gather to the eyes,
1 In looking on the happy autumn fields,
And thinking of the days that are no more.

Fresh as the first beam glittering on a sail,
2 That brings our friends up from the underworld,
Sad as the last which reddens over one
That sinks with all we love below the verge;
So sad, so fresh, the days that are no more.

Ah, sad and strange as in dark summer dawns
The earliest pipe of half-awakened birds
To dying ears, when unto dying eyes
3 The casement slowly grows a glimmering square;
So sad, so strange, the days that are no more.

Dear as remembered kisses after death,
And sweet as those by hopeless fancy feigned
On lips that are for others; deep as love,
Deep as first love, and wild with all regret;
O Death in Life, the days that are no more.

THINKING ABOUT THE SELECTION

Recalling

1. According to the first stanza, what causes the tears to rise?
2. In what three ways does the speaker describe "the days that are no more."

Interpreting

3. Why are the tears described as "idle"?
4. What do you think is meant in line 2 by "some divine despair"?
5. What comment is Tennyson making about our ability to remember things past?
6. A refrain is a repeated line or phrase in a poem or song. Identify the refrain in this poem, and explain how you think it was intended to make the reader feel.

Applying

7. (a) Why do you think people feel nostalgia for "days that are no more"? (b) In what way is nostalgia bittersweet?

UNDERSTANDING LANGUAGE

Fitting the Context

Words have great versatility. Often they can be used as more than one part of speech and have several different meanings. For example, consider the word *fancy* in line 17: "And sweet as those by hopeless fancy feigned." In this line, fancy is a noun that means "imagination." However, one dictionary provides twenty different meaning for the word *fancy* and shows it used as four parts of speech.

For each sentence below, find the meaning of fancy that fits the context and tell as what part of speech the word is being used.

1. She refused to wear clothing with fancy trimming.
2. He didn't fancy the way the painting captured his likeness.
3. The young people took a fancy to each other.
4. "Well, fancy that!" exclaimed elderly Mrs. Kane.

THINKING AND WRITING

Describing the Poet's Style

A poet's **style** is the way he or she strings together words and ideas to communicate a particular image or message. In "Tears, Idle Tears," Tennyson's style includes the abundant use of repetition and the contrast between positive and negative impressions (such as "sad" and "fresh" in the second stanza). Write an essay explaining how Tennyson's style relates to his theme. Begin by stating the theme of the poem. Use quotations freely to illustrate the points you cover. When you revise, make sure you have quoted exactly and punctuated your quotations accurately.

Answers

ANSWERS TO THINKING ABOUT THE SELECTION

Recalling

1. Thoughts of "the days that are no more" cause the tears to rise.
2. He describes them as "so sad, so fresh," "so sad, so strange," and as "Death in life."

Interpreting

3. Suggested Response: The tears are described as "idle" because they are part of a lingering sadness.
4. Answers may differ. Students may interpret this phrase as meaning either a grievous loss or an inexplicable sadness of larger-than-human proportions.
5. Suggested Response: He is claiming that our ability to recall condemns us to recall happy bygone times wistfully—that this ability is, thus, a bittersweet phenomenon.
6. The refrain is "the days that are no more." The line was intended to evoke a melancholy feeling.

Applying

7. (a) Suggested Response: People feel nostalgia for "days that are no more" because they tend to romanticize the past. (b) It is bittersweet because it makes us feel happy to have experienced the times we are remembering but at the same time makes us feel sad that those times have passed.

Challenge Do you feel it would be an oversimplification, based on the message in this poem, to declare Tennyson a pessimist? Why or why not?

ANSWERS TO UNDERSTANDING LANGUAGE

1. fancy *adj.*: ornamental
2. fancy *v.*: Have a liking for
3. fancy *n.*: Liking
4. fancy *v.*: Can you imagine (that)

THINKING AND WRITING

Publishing Student Writing

After students have completed the assignment, go through the roll alphabetically asking each student as you call his or her name to provide one word describing the poet's style. Each time a new word is mentioned, write it on the board. When each student has spoken, determine, by a show of hands, which students have covered the most terms in their essays. Have three or four of them read their essays to the class.

Motivation for Reading Ask students to offer impressions of exotic places to which they have been or to imagine places they would like to go. What qualities of these places were—or would be—most memorable? Apart from photographs, what mementos help us remember places we have been? What kinds of sounds and sights tend to come to mind when we think of these places?

Master Teacher Note Ask a student who plays trumpet or bugle to bring the instrument to class. Have these students describe the sorts of tones the instrument produces. If possible, arrange a demonstration. Then tell your students that the poem they are about to read was partly inspired by the sounds of a bugle the poet heard on a visit to Lake Killarney, in Ireland.

Thematic Idea Another selection that deals with the immortality of beauty is Keats's "Ode on a Grecian Urn," page 736.

Purpose-Setting Question What does the speaker hear, see, and ask?

1 **Discussion** What feeling, or mood, is established in the first stanza? What words and images create this mood?

2 **Reading Strategy** What is the effect of the repetition of the word *dying*?

3 **Clarification** Elfland is another name for fairyland, which to the Irish borders the "real" world.

4 **Discussion** What is meant by "our echoes?"

The Splendor Falls

Alfred, Lord Tennyson

The splendor falls on castle walls
1 And snowy summits old in story;
The long light shakes across the lakes,
And the wild cataract leaps in glory.
2 Blow, bugle, blow, set the wild echoes flying,
Blow, bugle; answer, echoes, dying, dying, dying.

O hark, O hear! how thin and clear,
And thinner, clearer, farther going!
O sweet and far from cliff and scar[1]
3 The horns of Elfland faintly blowing!
Blow, let us hear the purple glens replying;
Blow, bugle; answer, echoes, dying, dying, dying.

O love, they die in yon rich sky,
They faint on hill or field or river:
4 Our echoes roll from soul to soul,
And grow forever and forever.
Blow, bugle, blow, set the wild echoes flying,
And answer, echoes, answer, dying, dying, dying.

---

1. **scar:** Mountainside.

THINKING ABOUT THE SELECTION

Recalling

1. Where exactly, according to the poem, does the splendor fall?
2. What do the bugles "set flying"?

Interpreting

3. (a) What do you think is the meaning of the phrase "horns of Elfland" in line 10? (b) Of "wild echoes" in lines 5 and 17?

Applying

4. (a) This poem was published in 1847. What "splendor" do you suppose Tennyson had in mind that he felt was "dying" from the world around him? (b) What "splendor" might a contemporary poet have in mind in writing about today's world?

Answers

ANSWERS TO THINKING ABOUT THE SELECTION

Recalling

1. The splendor falls on castle walls and snowy summits.
2. They set the wild echoes flying.

Interpreting

3. (a) The suggestion is that the speaker is so taken with the beauty of the moment that the horns seem almost to emanate from a mystical region. (b) The suggestion is that the echoes are part of a world untainted by worldliness.

Applying

4. (a) Suggested Response: He might have felt that the unspoiled beauty of nature was disappearing. (b) Suggested Response: A contemporary poet might also write about the unspoiled beauty of nature.

Challenge This poem captures the poet's response to beauty. To what extent do you find the saying "Beauty is in the eye of the beholder" to apply in this case?

THE BARD
John Martin
Yale Center for British Art

Humanities Note

Fine art, *The Bard,* 1817, by John Martin. John Martin (1789–1854) was a British painter of landscapes and historical scenes. He began his artistic endeavors painting heraldry on coaches and decorating china, activities that supported him while he studied painting in London. He eventually gained recognition for his paintings. He chose to paint historical scenes because it was the quickest and surest way to gain eminence and honors.

The painting *The Bard,* completed in 1817, exemplifies Martin's unique approach to the painting of historical events. He emphasized the landscape over the historical figures, an unheard-of choice in history painting at the time. This painting was inspired by a poem of the same name (written by Thomas Grey, 1757). It refers to an incident in the life of King Edward I. The figures are dwarfed by the vast, towering mountains and the magnificent, glowing castle. John Martin made this landscape into something astonishing and beautiful.

You may wish to use the following questions for discussion:

1. Although this painting was not specifically painted to illustrate this poem, which visual elements match Tennyson's descriptive phrases? There are at least four.
2. Tennyson refers to Elfland in his poem. Do you feel that this painting illustrates the magical allusions in the poem? Explain.

Literary Focus Elegy is a fairly straightforward concept, and it might suffice here simply to point out to students that the form carries into music, where it is known also as requiem. The concept of symbolism can be reinforced by asking students to suggest some common symbols—the Statue of Liberty and Cupid are obvious choices—and to tell what each represents.

Look For You may want to read through the poems with your **less advanced** students, highlighting the use of symbols.

Writing As an alternative, divide the class into three groups, assigning one of the three emotions mentioned to each. After the groups have had a chance to brainstorm, a spokesperson can report the group's findings to the class.

Vocabulary Have your students write sentences using each of the vocabulary words.

GUIDE FOR READING

from In Memoriam A. H. H.; The Lotos Eaters; Crossing the Bar

Literary Forms

Elegy. An elegy is any poem that mourns the passing of an individual. The writing of elegies traces back to ancient times and, since the Renaissance, has been an enduring tradition among English poets. Tennyson's *In Memoriam* is widely acknowledged as one of the finest elegies ever written. The poem not only laments the death of Tennyson's closest friend, Arthur Henry Hallam, but also provides a "chronicle" of the poet/speaker's emotions as he moves gradually away from sheer grief and doubt, and ultimately toward understanding, acceptance, and faith. In this sense *In Memoriam* is more about life, love, and hope than it is about death, anger, and despair.

The Writer's Technique

A *symbol* is a person, place, object, or action that represents an idea in addition to its usual meaning. For example, a parent might be a symbol of authority and a spring flower might be a symbol of rebirth. Poets often use symbols to fill images with a deeper significance. In "The Lady of Shalott," for instance, Tennyson uses the web and mirror respectively as symbols for art and the artist's tendency to experience life secondhand.

Look For

As you read Tennyson's poetry, look for his use of symbols.

Writing

The sudden death of a friend or relative, especially a young one, can stir up a wide range of emotions in the survivors, including despair, anger, and doubt. Describe what in particular might lead to these feelings about such a loss.

Vocabulary

Knowing the following words will help you as you read the following poems by Tennyson.

divers (dī' vərz) *adj.*: Varied; having many parts (archaic spelling) (p. 809, l. 2)
chrysalis (Kris' əs) *n.*: Cocoon of a butterfly (p. 811, l. 36)
diffusive (di fyōō'siv) *adj.*: Spread out (p. 811, l. 51)
languid (laŋ'gwid) *adj.*: Slow, lacking energy (p. 813, l. 5)
slumbrous (slum'brəs) *adj.*: Peaceful, suggesting sleep (p. 813, l. 13)
consumed (kən sōōm'd') *adj.*' Overtaken, overwhelmed (p. 814, l. 57)
perpetual (pər pech'ōō wəl) *adj.*: Constant, unending (p. 815, l. 61)
waxing (waks'iŋ) *v.*: Growing, ripening (p. 815, l. 77)
reconcile (rek'ən sīl') *v.*: Make up with (p. 816, l. 125)
doleful (dōl'fəl) *adj.*: Filled with sadness (p. 818, l. 161)

Objectives

1 To understand an elegy
2 To make inferences about the subject of an elegy
3 To recognize importance of allusions
4 To find antonyms
5 To recognize symbols
6 To compare attitudes
7 To write about symbols

Teaching Portfolio: Support Material

Teacher Backup, p. 000

Vocabulary Check, p. 00

Usage and Mechanics Worksheet, p. 00

Analyzing Literature Worksheet, p. 00

Critical Thinking and Reading Worksheet, p. 00

Language Worksheet, p. 00

Selection Test, p. 000

Art Transparency 10, *Tours; Sunset* by J. M. W. Turner

from In Memoriam A. H. H.

Alfred, Lord Tennyson

In Memoriam A.H.H. *is an elegiac poem that conveys Tennyson's feelings and reflections about the death of his close friend Arthur Hallam, a talented young man who died suddenly at the age of twenty-two. Though Milton's* Lycidas *and Shelley's* Adonais *also lamented the deaths of promising young men, the structure of Tennyson's poem is quite different from these earlier elegies. Unlike the earlier elegies,* In Memoriam A.H.H. *is made up of 131 seemingly self-sustaining lyrics that were composed over a period of seventeen years, as the poet struggled to come to terms with the feelings of doubt and despair that stemmed from his friend's early death.*

1

I held it truth, with him who sings
  To one clear harp in divers tones,
  That men may rise on stepping stones 1
Of their dead selves to higher things.

But who shall so forecast the years
  And find in loss a gain to match?
  Or reach a hand through time to catch
The far-off interest of tears?

Let Love clasp Grief lest both be drowned,
  Let darkness keep her raven gloss. 2
  Ah, sweeter to be drunk with loss,
To dance with death, to beat the ground,

Than that the victor Hours should scorn
  The long result of love, and boast,
  "Behold the man that loved and lost,
But all he was is overworn."

7

Dark house, by which once more I stand
  Here in the long unlovely street,
  Doors, where my heart was used to beat 3
So quickly, waiting for a hand,

Motivation for Reading Have students discuss the various ways in which people cope with the death of a loved one. Are there any common phases through which all people pass in this situation? If so, what are these phases?

Master Teacher Note If possible, arrange for the class to listen to recorded excerpts of several famous requiems—perhaps those by Faure, Verdi, and Berlioz. Direct their attention to the slow tempo, mournful mood, and occasional melodic surges found in each of the compositions. Ask what emotions these musical elements seem to correspond to.

Thematic Idea Another selection that deals with the subject of loss is Thomas Gray's "Elegy Written in a Country Churchyard," page 598.

Purpose-Setting Question What does this poem reveal about the nature of grief?

1 **Reading Strategy** Have students state this bit of conventional wisdom in their own words.

2 **Discussion** Personification is the ascribing of human traits to a nonhuman entity. What is the poet personifying here?

3 **Critical Thinking and Reading** What qualities of the speaker's relationship with his friend might lead to the feelings implied here?

Humanities Note

Fine art, *Nocturne: Grey and Gold—Chelsea Snow,* 1878, by James McNeill Whistler. Whistler (1834–1903) was an American painter who lived and worked in London. Both countries, England and the United States, claim him as their artist. His formal education as a painter consisted of a brief period of training in drawing and etching as a U.S. coastal surveyer and cartographer. It continued in Paris through close association with prominent French "modern" artists of his day. Whistler moved to London permanently in 1859 to paint.

The painting *Nocturne: Grey and Gold—Chelsea Snow* is one of a group of night scenes painted by Whistler. He used the musical term *nocturne* to suggest the poetic mood and subtle evening tones of the paintings. Whistler used the darkness of night to simplify and abstract shapes. The space in this painting is broken down into three simple shapes: the sky, the snow, and the dark mass of buildings and trees. The lone figure walking on the glowing snow seems to disappear into the darkness of the building.

You may wish to use the following questions for discussion:

1. What is the effect of the glowing lights in the window? Do they seem cheerful, or do they enhance the desolation of the scene?
2. Why might the person be walking alone in the dark?
3. What is the mood of the figure walking in the cold?

NOCTURNE: GREY AND GOLD—CHELSEA SNOW
James McNeill Whistler
The Fogg Art Museum, Cambridge, Mass.

A hand that can be clasped no more—
Behold me, for I cannot sleep,
And like a guilty thing I creep 4
At earliest morning to the door.

He is not here; but far away
The noise of life begins again,
And ghastly through the drizzling rain 5
On the bald street breaks the blank day.

82

I wage not any feud with Death
For changes wrought on form and face;
No lower life that earth's embrace
May breed with him, can fright my faith.

Eternal process moving on,
From state to state the spirit walks;
And these are but the shattered stalks, 6
Or ruined chrysalis of one. 7

Nor blame I Death, because he bare
The use of virtue out of earth;
I know transplanted human worth 8
Will bloom to profit, otherwhere.

For this alone on Death I wreak
The wrath that garners in my heart;
He put our lives so far apart
We cannot hear each other speak.

130

Thy voice is on the rolling air;
I hear thee where the waters run;
Thou standest in the rising sun,
And in the setting thou art fair. 9

What art thou then? I cannot guess;
But though I seem in star and flower
To feel thee some diffusive power,
I do not therefore love thee less.

My love involves the love before;
My love is vaster passion now;
Though mixed with God and Nature thou,
I seem to love thee more and more.

Far off thou art, but ever nigh;
I have thee still, and I rejoice; 10
I prosper, circled with thy voice;
I shall not lose thee though I die.

4 **Discussion** What might prompt feelings of guilt in the speaker?

5 **Reading Strategy** Have students describe the speaker's emotional state at this point.

6 **Clarification** The term *these* refers to the forms of lower life mentioned in line 30.

7 **Critical Thinking and Reading** Why is the use of the term *crysalis* especially appropriate in light of Hallam's age when he died?

8 **Discussion** How might you state this sentiment in your own words?

9 **Reading Strategy** Have students compare the speaker's response to his loss here with those of the previous three stanzas.

10 **Discussion** What is the meaning of this line?

Answers

ANSWERS TO THINKING ABOUT THE SELECTION

Recalling

1. He now doubts that men may rise to higher things by treading on "their dead selves."
2. He is standing before the home of his late friend.
3. He is angry with death for making it impossible to speak with his friend.
4. It has increased.

Interpreting

5. (a) The corporeal, or bodily, manifestation is gone. (b) Hallam's spirit will live on in his friend's cherished memories.
6. Suggested Response: It means that although Hallam has disappeared from the physical world, his spirit remains embedded in the speaker's heart.
7. Students will note that in the first two excerpts, the speaker is still in deep pain. In the third and fourth, by contrast, he is respectively angry and resigned.

Applying

8. (a) Encourage students, in formulating answers, to avoid such clichés as "Time heals all wounds." (b) Answers will differ. Students may insist that their ideas would be close to those expressed in the poem.
9. (a) It means that people live on in the memories of others. (b) Hallam lives on in the speaker's memory.

ANSWERS TO ANALYZING LITERATURE

1. Answers will differ. Students may cite Tennyson's vigil before his late friend's home as something quite private and personal. His anger at death for making communication impossible with his friend is also a facet of his private loss.
2. Suggested Response: Tennyson's view of the world as a cold and bleak place (lines 26–28) is a typical manifestation of the human reaction to grief.
3. Suggested Response: The speaker's rejoicing and prospering (lines 58–59) are indications that he has come a long way toward acceptance. As a poet he is able to concretize his thoughts so as to make them accessible to future generations who may, thus, benefit by his experience.

ANSWERS TO CRITICAL THINKING AND READING

1. The implication is that Hallam was a warm and sincere man, perhaps with a firm and friendly grasp.
2. The reference suggests that Hallam had great potential that was not fully realized.
3. One might infer that Hallam was a man who managed to make his presence felt.

THINKING ABOUT THE SELECTION

Recalling

1. In Part 1, what truth does the speaker say he once held but now doubts?
2. Where is the speaker standing in Part 7?
3. For what one thing, in Part 82, does the speaker "wreak the wrath" in his heart on death?
4. In Part 130, what does the speaker say has happened to his love for his friend?

Interpreting

5. (a) According to the excerpts, what part of his friend does the poet finally accept is lost forever? (b) What part does he come to recognize will live forever?
6. Explain the paradox in line 57: "Far off thou art, but ever nigh."
7. Compare the first two excerpts with the last two. How have the poet's emotions changed?

Applying

8. (a) If you had to console someone who had lost a loved one, what advice might you give to help that person cope? (b) How close would your ideas be to those implied in the last excerpt of *In Memoriam?*
9. The English novelist Samuel Butler has written, "To die completely, a person must not only forget but forgotten, and he who is not forgotten is not dead." (a) Discuss the meaning of this quotation. (b) How does it relate to *In Memorium*?

ANALYZING LITERATURE

Understanding an Elegy

An **elegy** is a poem or song that laments a death, usually recent. *In Memoriam* is an especially strong elegy since, as Tennyson himself put it, the poem is "rather the cry of the whole human race than mine. In the poem altogether private grief swells out into thought of, and hope for, the whole world."

1. Which details in the four excerpts seem particularly "private"?
2. Which seem to apply to "the whole human race"?
3. What hope for future generations is implied in the final excerpt.

CRITICAL THINKING AND READING

Making Inferences About the Subject

In *In Memoriam* Tennyson never actually describes his friend directly but rather drops clues as to the man's personality. The reader must thus **infer,** or piece together from these clues, a picture of the man. What personality traits can you infer from the following?

1. Tennyson's reminiscence in Part 7 of his friend's hand clasp.
2. His comparing of his friend's remains to a "ruined crysalis."
3. His sensing in Part 130 of his friend's "diffusive power" in a star and flower.

The Lotos-Eaters

Alfred, Lord Tennyson

During their long voyage homeward in Homer's Odyssey, *the Greek veterans of the Trojan War come to the land of the Lotos-Eaters, where, upon consuming the lotos's honeyed fruit, they are tempted by the desire to abandon their journey. Instead, the men wanted to forget about going home and stay in the land of the Lotos-Eaters forever.*

In "The Lotos-Eaters," Tennyson expands upon Homer's brief account of the men's stay in the land of the Lotos-Eaters, delving into the men's desire for rest and the feelings of guilt that grew out of this desire.

"Courage!" he[1] said, and pointed toward the land,
"This mounting wave will roll us shoreward soon."
In the afternoon they came unto a land
In which it seemed always afternoon.
All round the coast the languid air did swoon,
Breathing like one that hath a weary dream.
Full-faced above the valley stood the moon;
And like a downward smoke, the slender stream
Along the cliff to fall and pause and fall did seem. 1

A land of streams! some, like a downward smoke,
Slow-dropping veils of thinnest lawn[2] did go;
And some through wavering lights and shadows broke,
Rolling a slumbrous sheet of foam below.
They saw the gleaming river seaward flow
From the inner land: far off, three mountaintops,
Three silent pinnacles of aged snow,
Stood sunset-flushed; and, dewed with showery drops,
Up clomb the shadowy pine above the woven copse.

The charmed sunset lingered low adown
In the red West: through mountain clefts the dale
Was seen far inland, and the yellow down[3]
Bordered with palm, and many a winding vale
And meadow, set with slender galingale;[4]
A land where all things always seemed the same!

---

1. he: Odysseus (ō dis' ē as) (or Ulysses), the hero of the *Odyssey*.
2. lawn *n.*: A fine, thin linen.
3. down *n.*: An expanse of open, high, grassy land.
4. galingale *n.*: A plant similar in appearance to tall grass.

Motivation for Reading Have students discuss the role of work in people's lives. How would it feel never to have to do work of any sort? How would it feel to be totally free of all responsibility? Would never-ending leisure eventually become tiresome?

Master Teacher Note Write the name *Odysseus* on the board. Ask students how much they know about this figure from Greek mythology. What modern English word is derived from the character's name? What is an odyssey? Inform students that they are about to read about one of Odysseus's adventures as seen through the eyes of a Victorian poet.

Thematic Idea Another selection that deals with the temptation of escape from the responsibilities of life is "Ode to a Nightingale" by John Keats, on page 731.

Purpose-Setting Question What qualities of modern life might make the prospect of escape tempting?

1 **Discussion** What qualities of the land strike you as particularly soothing and seductive?

2 Discussion What is the mental and physical state of the sailors? What circumstances do you suppose may have brought about these feelings?

3 Critical Thinking and Reading What island is the home of the sailors?

4 Discussion What is the effect of the repetition of the *s* sound in this passage?

5 Reading Strategy What does the speaker mean by his reference to "we" as "the first of things" (line 60) and as "the roof and crown of things" (line 68)?

And round about the keel with faces pale,
Dark faces pale against that rosy flame,
The mild-eyed melancholy Lotos-eaters came.

Branches they bore of that enchanted stem,
Laden with flower and fruit, whereof they gave
To each, but whoso did receive of them,
And taste, to him, the gushing of the wave
Far far away did seem to mourn and rave
On alien shores; and if his fellow spake,
His voice was thin, as voices from the grave;
And deep asleep he seemed, yet all awake,
And music in his ears his beating heart did make.

They sat them down upon the yellow sand,
Between the sun and moon upon the shore;
And sweet it was to dream of Fatherland,
2 Of child, and wife, and slave; but evermore
Most weary seemed the sea, weary the oar,
Weary the wandering fields of barren foam.
Then someone said, "We will return no more";
And all at once they sang, "Our island home[5]
3 Is far beyond the wave; we will no longer roam."

Choric Song[6]

I

There is sweet music here that softer falls
Than petals from blown roses on the grass,
4 Or night dews on still waters between walls
Of shadowy granite, in a gleaming pass;
Music that gentler on the spirit lies,
Than tired eyelids upon tired eyes;
Music that brings sweet sleep down from the blissful skies.
Here are cool mosses deep.
And through the moss the ivies creep,
And in the stream the long-leaved flowers weep,
And from the craggy ledge the poppy hangs in sleep.

II

Why are we weighed upon with heaviness
And utterly consumed with sharp distress,
While all things else have rest from weariness?
All things have rest: why should we toil alone,
5 We only toil, who are the first of things,

5. home: Ithaca, an island off the coast of Greece.
6. Choric Song: Sung by the Greek travelers in chorus.

And make perpetual moan,
Still from one sorrow to another thrown;
Nor ever fold our wings,
And cease from wanderings,
Nor steep our brows in slumber's holy balm;
Nor harken what the inner spirit sings,
"There is no joy but calm!"
Why should we only toil, the roof and crown of things?[7]

III

Lo! in the middle of the wood,
The folded leaf is wooed from out the bud
With winds upon the branch, and there
Grows green and broad, and takes no care,
Sun-steeped at noon, and in the moon
Nightly dew-fed; and turning yellow
Falls, and floats adown the air.
Lo! sweetened with the summer light,
The full-juiced apple, waxing over-mellow,
Drops in a silent autumn night.
All its allotted length of days,
The flower ripens in its place,
Ripens and fades, and falls, and hath no toil,
Fast-rooted in the fruitful soil.

IV

Hateful is the dark-blue sky,
Vaulted o'er the dark-blue sea.
Death is the end of life; ah, why
Should life all labor be?
Let us alone. Time driveth onward fast,
And in a little while our lips are dumb.
Let us alone. What is it that will last?
All things are taken from us, and become
Portions and parcels of the dreadful Past.
Let us alone. What pleasure can we have
To war with evil? Is there any peace
In ever climbing up the climbing wave?
All things have rest, and ripen toward the grave
In silence; ripen, fall and cease:
Give us long rest or death, dark death, or dreamful ease.[8]

6

7

---

7. Why . . . things?: This line echoes the following passage from Edmund Spenser's *Faerie Queene*: "Why then dost thou, O man, that of them all/Art Lord, and eke of nature Soveraine/willfully . . . waste thy joyous hours in needless pain . . . ?"
8. All . . . ease: This passage echoes the following lines in Spenser's *Faerie Queene*: "Sleep after toyle, port after stormie seas/Ease after war, death after life does greatly please."

6 **Discussion** The phrase *Let us alone* is repeated. With whom are the sailors arguing?

7 **Critical Thinking and Reading** What is the effect of the allusion to Spenser's *Faerie Queen*?

8 **Reading Strategy** How does the speaker's mood here differ from that implied in lines 85–97? What does this mood swing tell you?

9 **Discussion** How would you state the speaker's thoughts here in your own words? What point is he driving at?

10 **Critical Thinking and Reading** Explain the allusion in this line.

11 **Clarification** The "pilot stars" were fixed celestial points used by sailors in ancient times for purposes of navigation.

V

How sweet it were, hearing the downward stream,
With half-shut eyes ever to seem
Falling asleep in a half dream!
To dream and dream, like yonder amber light,
Which will not leave the myrrh[9] bush on the height;
8 To hear each other's whispered speech;
Eating the Lotos day by day,
To watch the crisping[10] ripples on the beach,
And tender curving lines of creamy spray;
To lend our hearts and spirits wholly
To the influence of mild-minded melancholy;
To muse and brood and live again in memory,
With those old faces of our infancy
Heaped over with a mound of grass,
Two handfuls of white dust, shut in an urn of brass!

VI

Dear is the memory of our wedded lives,
And dear the last embraces of our wives
9 And their warm tears; but all hath suffered change;
For surely now our household hearths are cold,
Our sons inherit us, our looks are strange,
And we should come like ghosts to trouble joy.
Or else the island princes[11] over-bold
Have eat our substance, and the minstrel sings
10 Before them of the ten years' war in Troy,
And our great deeds, as half-forgotten things.
Is there confusion in the little isle?
Let what is broken so remain.
The Gods are hard to reconcile;
'Tis hard to settle order once again.
There *is* confusion worse than death,
Trouble on trouble, pain on pain,
Long labor unto aged breath,
Sore task to hearts worn out by many wars
11 And eyes grown dim with gazing on the pilot stars.

---

9. myrrh (mur) *n.*: A plant that produces a fragrant gum resin used in making incense and perfume.
10. crisping *adj.*: Curling.
11. princes: Suitors who were courting Odysseus' (Ulysses') wife, Penelope.

VII

But, propped on beds of amaranth[12] and moly,[13]
How sweet (while warm airs lull us, blowing lowly)
With half-dropped eyelid still,
Beneath a heaven dark and holy,
To watch the long bright river drawing slowly
His waters from the purple hill—
To hear the dewy echoes calling
From cave to cave through the thick-twined vine—
To watch the emerald-colored water falling
Through many a woven acanthus[14] wreath divine!
Only to hear and see the far-off sparkling brine,
Only to hear were sweet, stretched out beneath the pine.

---

12. amaranth (am′ ə ranth′) *n.*: An imaginary flower that never fades or dies.

13. moly (mō′ lē) *n.*: In classical mythology, an herb of magic powers. In the Odyssey, (Ulysses) uses moly to protect himself from the incantation of Circe (sər′ sē), an enchantress who turned men into swine.

14. acanthus (ə kan′ thəs) *n.*: A thistlelike plant.

CARVED GEM OF LIGHT BROWN SARDONYX
Roman 3rd to 2nd Century BC, Ulysses Mourning for Home
Staatliche Museen zu Berlin

12 Discussion What facts is the speaker reporting in these lines?

13 Enrichment Have students read the episode of *The Odyssey* that tells of Odysseus's adventures in the land of the Lotos-Eaters. Ask them to compare and contrast the two writers' of the subject.

VIII

The Lotos blooms below the barren peak,
The Lotos blows by every winding creek;
12 All day the wind breathes low with mellower tone;
Through every hollow cave and alley lone
Round and round the spicy downs the yellow Lotos dust is blown.
We have had enough of action, and of motion we,
Rolled to starboard, rolled to larboard, when the surge was seething free,
Where the wallowing monster spouted his foam fountains in the sea.
Let us swear an oath, and keep it with an equal mind,
In the hollow Lotos land to live and lie reclined
On the hills like Gods together, careless of mankind.
For they lie beside their nectar, and the bolts[15] are hurled
Far below them in the valleys, and the clouds are lightly curled
Round their golden houses, girdled with the gleaming world;
Where they smile in secret, looking over wasted lands,
Blight and famine, plague and earthquake, roaring deeps and fiery sands,
Clanging fights, and flaming towns, and sinking ships, and praying hands.
But they smile, they find a music centered in a doleful song.
Steaming up, a lamentation and an ancient tale of wrong,
Like a tale of little meaning though the words are strong;
Chanted from an ill-used race of men that cleave the soil,
Sow the seed, and reap the harvest with enduring toil,
Storing yearly little dues of wheat, and wine and oil;
Till they perish and they suffer—some, 'tis whispered—down in hell
Suffer endless anguish, others in Elysian valleys[16] dwell,
Resting weary limbs at last on beds of asphodel.[17]
Surely, surely, slumber is more sweet than toil, the shore
13 Than labor in the deep mid-ocean, wind and wave and oar;
Oh rest ye, brother mariners, we will not wander more.

---

15. bolts: Thunderbolts.
16. Elysian (i lizh′ ən) **valleys:** In Greek mythology, heroes went to Elysia after death.
17. asphodel (as′ fə del′): A plant with yellow or white lilylike flowers.

THINKING ABOUT THE SELECTION

Recalling

1. What strange property of the land is mentioned in lines 4 and 24 of the poem?
2. (a) How do the men describe this new land in the poem's "choric song"? (b) How do they describe the lives they had led up till now? (c) What reasons do they give for wanting to remain?

Interpreting

3. (a) What do the men find so appealing about the land of the lotos-eaters? (b) What nagging concerns haunt them in spite of the effect of the lotos plants?
4. (a) What differences can you find between the odd-numbered and even-numbered stanzas of the poem's "choric song"? (b) What do these differences suggest about the decision the men have made?

Applying

5. To what extent do you think Tennyson is "prescribing" the sailors' decision in "The Lotos-Eaters" as a solution for problems of life in his time? Explain your answer.

CRITICAL THINKING AND READING

Recognizing Allusions

An **allusion** is a reference to a person, place, statement, or event in another work of art or cultural work. Writers use allusions to help the reader grasp a greater truth. Suppose that Tennyson had written "The Lotos-Eaters" without any of its allusions to classical mythology.

1. What general truth might have been missed?
2. What qualities of the poem would have been lost?
3. What other qualities might have been more evident?

UNDERSTANDING LANGUAGE

Finding Antonyms

Antonyms are words that have opposite, or nearly opposite meanings. For example, in line 155 Tennyson writes, "On the hills like Gods together, careless of man kind." An antonym for the word *careless* is *concerned.*

Choose an antonym for each of the italicized words below.

1. "This *mounting* wave will roll us shoreward soon."
   a. swelling b. climbing c. falling d. dramatic
2. "And some through *wavering* lights and shadows broke . . ."
   a. uncertain b. trembling c. bright d. steady
3. "The charmed sunset *lingered* low adown . . ."
   a. faltered b. departed
   c. operated d. remained
4. "The mild-eyed *melancholy* Lotus-eaters came."
   a. sad b. lonely c. beautiful d. joyful
5. "The folded leaf is *wooed* from out the bud . . ."
   a. coaxed b. wed
   c. shunned d.humored

Answers

ANSWERS TO THINKING ABOUT THE SELECTION

Recalling

1. Things are always the same; it is perpetual afternoon.
2. (a) The new land is a dreamy place that lulls the soul with sweet music. (b) Their lives thus far have been marked by constant wandering and toil. (c) They seek respite from their weariness.

Interpreting

3. (a) Students may note both physical features of the place and its allure as an environment free from the strife of the real world. (b) They are nagged by obligations to their families.
4. (a) The stanzas depict alternately the tranquil state the sailors have now achieved and the miseries of the life they have led to this point. (b) The arrangement reflects the sailors' ambivalence concerning their decision.

Applying

5. Answers will differ. Students may feel they detect a note of advocacy in the poem, especially in terms of its conclusion.

ANSWERS TO CRITICAL THINKING AND READING

1. Suggested Response: The idea that people can easily be torn between a desire to escape from the responsibilities of life and an awareness of the implications of doing so.
2. Suggested Response: The poem would have lost its richness, its feeling of adventure, and its grounding in the past.
3. Suggested Response: The poem might have seemed newer and fresher.

ANSWERS TO UNDERSTANDING LANGUAGE

1. c 2. d
3. b 4. d
5. c

Master Teacher Note Place Art Transparency 10, J. M. W. Turner's *Tours; Sunset,* on the overhead projector. Invite your students to express their impressions of the scene depicted and of Turner's artistry. You might then have them compare the subject and mood of this painting with the subject and mood of "Crossing the Bar." Is Turner's painting a good illustration for Tennyson's poem? Invite your students to discuss this question.

Thematic Idea Another poem that confronts the subject of death is "Prospice" by Robert Browning, page 834.

Purpose-Setting Question What are the speaker's feelings concerning death?

1 **Discussion** From whom do you think the speaker receives this "one clear call"?

2 **Critical Thinking and Reading** What thoughts do the words "evening bell" bring to mind?

3 **Discussion** How would you describe the speaker's outlook?

Humanities Note

Fine art, *The Angry Sea,* ca. 1880, by James Abbott McNeill Whistler (1834–1903). Whistler was an American artist who lived and worked in London. Although he had little formal training as a painter, his close association with leading Parisian "Modern" artists brought forth his talent. In 1859 he moved permanently to London and began to establish his reputation.

The Angry Sea reveals the strong influence of Japanese art on Whistler. In a few fluid strokes he captures the essence of the sea, sky, and sand with details such as the white waves and the ship.

Crossing the Bar

Alfred, Lord Tennyson

Tennyson requested that this poem, written three years before his death, be printed at the end of all editions of his poetry.

1 Sunset and evening star,
And one clear call for me!
And may there be no moaning of the bar,[1]
When I put out to sea,

But such a tide as moving seems asleep,
Too full for sound and foam,
When that[2] which drew from out the boundless deep
Turns again home.

2 Twilight and evening bell,
And after that the dark!
And may there be no sadness of farewell,
When I embark;

3 For though from out our bourne[3] of Time and Place
The flood may bear me far,
I hope to see my Pilot face to face
When I have crossed the bar.

1. bar: Sandbar.
2. that: The soul.
3. bourne: Boundary.

THE ANGRY SEA
James McNeill Whistler
Freer Gallery of Art, Smithsonian Institution

When discussing this painting with your students, point out that the subtle colors are in keeping with the reflective tone of the poem. Further points for class discussion include:

1. The artist used economy of line to express his visual message. Might the same be said of the poet and his use of words? Explain.
2. Although simple in form, this painting is quite dramatic. Is this in keeping with the mood of the poem? why or why not?

THINKING ABOUT THE SELECTION

Recalling

1. What does the speaker of the poem request in lines 3–4 and again in lines 11–12?

Interpreting

2. What do you think is actually meant by the phrase "crossing the bar"?
3. Who do you think the "Pilot" is?

Applying

4. Which excerpt from *In Memoriam* do you think is most in keeping with the attitude Tennyson expresses in "Crossing the Bar"? Explain why you feel as you do.

ANALYZING LITERATURE

Recognizing Symbols

A **symbol** is a thing, person, place, or idea whose meaning transcends, or goes beyond, its usual literal definition. When the reader of "Crossing the Bar" recognizes that the sea journey described in the poem is in actuality the "journey" everyone must make at life's end, the symbolic meaning of many of the ideas and images becomes obvious. State the meaning symbolized by each of the following ideas.

1. moaning of the bar.
2. putting out to sea.
3. twilight.
4. the dark.
5. the flood bearing one far.

CRITICAL THINKING AND READING

Comparing Attitudes

Writers may write about the same subject but take quite different positions. Read each statement below about death. Explain which one you feel comes closest to the attitude Tennyson expresses in "Crossing the Bar."

1. Oliver Wendell Holmes: "Death tugs at my ear and says: 'Live, I am coming.'"
2. John Dryden: "To die is landing on some distant shore."
3. Genesis 3:19: "Dust thou art, and unto dust shalt thou return."
4. Ralph Waldo Emerson: "Our fear of death is like our fear that summer will be short, but when we will have had our swing of pleasure, our fill of fruit, and our swelter of heat, we say we have had our day."
5. William Hazlitt: "Our repugnance to death increases in proportion to our consciousness of having lived in vain."

THINKING AND WRITING

Writing About Symbols

In "Crossing the Bar" Tennyson uses a series of interrelated symbols to deliver his thoughts on the issues of serenity at life's end and faith in an afterlife. He might, of course, have selected a different set of symbols to express these thoughts. Choose a symbolic vehicle other than a boat trip that could stand for the journey at life's end. Some possibilities are a walk up a hill, or the writing of the last chapter of a book. Make notes on the various details that might be used in such a symbolic representation. Then express Tennyson's ideas, in either a poem or brief story that uses this set of symbols.

Answers

ANSWERS TO THINKING ABOUT THE SELECTION

Recalling

1. He asks that there be no hesitation or sadness when he leaves.

Interpreting

2. The phrase refers to death.
3. The Pilot is God.

Applying

4. Answers will differ, but most students will probably agree that the last excerpt they read is most like this poem in its affirmation of the poet's faith.

ANSWERS TO ANALYZING LITERATURE

1. Suggested Response: The phrase symbolizes mourning.
2. This is another symbol for dying.
3. The phrase represents the end of life.
4. Suggested Response: The dark signifies the finality of death.
5. Suggested Response: The flood symbolizes the journey to the afterlife.

ANSWERS TO CRITICAL THINKING AND READING

Suggested Response: The attitude expressed by Dryden is most similar to Tennyson's attitude. Like Tennyson, Dryden views death as a journey to a distant, unknown world.

Writing Across the Curriculum
As an alternative, suggest that students choose an important event in history, possibly a war, and create a string of related symbols to represent facets of it. You might want to inform the history department about this assignment. History teachers might be able to aid the students in researching the event they choose.

More About the Author Robert Browning's relationship with the poet Elizabeth Barrett began with a series of letters, the first of which Browning wrote in 1844, before he himself had achieved any renown. The two maintained their correspondence for more than a decade before they finally met in person. What facet of Robert Browning's personality is revealed in this detail of his life? Why might such a character trait be important for a writer?

ROBERT BROWNING

1812–1889

In Victorian England, clubs to promote the works of the giants of English literature were fairly common. In 1881, a group of amateur scholars banded together to found another such club, the Browning Society. What made this literary club unique was that the poet it paid tribute to was *living.* Yet, if honor in this form came unusually early to Robert Browning, then fame came unusually late, for it was not until nearly a half century after the publication of his first book that the public came to recognize his genius.

Robert Browning was born in London and spent the first twenty-eight years of his life there. Like Tennyson, he was educated mainly at home, spending much of his time during his early years in his father's large library. Here he immersed himself in art, history, literature, philosophy, religion, music, medicine, and zoology. At twenty-one, Browning published his first book, *Pauline,* a highly personal record of his religious skepticism, no doubt influenced by the writings of Shelley. Discouraged by the book's poor critical reception, Browning tried his hand next at something less personal, publishing *Paracelsus,* a long dramatic poem, in 1835. Failing again to please the critics, he turned to drama and two years later produced *Strafford,* which closed. after five performances.

Despite his inability to establish himself in the public eye as a writer to be reckoned with, Browning was all the while shaping the distinctive dramatic voice that would ensure his eventual fame. In *Dramatic Lyrics* (1842), *Dramatic Romances and Lyrics* (1845), and *Men and Women* (1855) he reveals a rich and varied talent in both the short lyrical poem and the dramatic monologue.

In 1846 he married Elizabeth Barrett, a poet whose fame greatly exceeded his own. They established a home in Florence, Italy, a setting that figured in many of Browning's works. The marriage was an extremely happy one, and when his wife died in 1861, Browning, unable to face constant reminders of her in Florence, returned to London. Here, he soon became a popular figure, especially among university students, who were attracted to his next book, *Dramatis Personnae* (1864). This was followed by his masterpiece, *The Ring and the Book* (1868), which was hailed as the most "profound spiritual treasure that England had produced since the days of Shakespeare." Based on an actual seventeenth-century Italian murder trial, this long poem includes ten dramatic monologues.

Browning's dramatic monologues have greatly influenced many twentieth-century poets. Today, he is admired not only for these complex psychological portraits, but also for his masterful blending of natural speech rhythms with strict poetic forms.

Objectives

1. To understand a dramatic monologue
2. To make inferences about the speaker
3. To appreciate diction
4. To write a dramatic monologue
5. To interpret tone
6. To write a comparison of two places
7. To make inferences about a poet's attitudes
8. To write a comparison of two poems

Teaching Portfolio: Support Material

Teacher Backup, p. 000

Vocabulary Check, p. 00

Usage and Mechanics Worksheet, p. 00

Analyzing Literature Worksheet, p. 00

Critical Thinking and Reading Worksheet, p. 00

GUIDE FOR READING

My Last Duchess; Home-Thoughts, from Abroad; Love Among the Ruins; Prospice

Literary Forms

Dramatic Monologue. A dramatic monologue is a dramatic poem by a single speaker, much like a speech from a play. Unlike a play, however, where each speech is preceded by the name of its speaker, the dramatic monologue contains no such outward label. Rather, the identity of the speaker is revealed through his or her words. In "My Last Duchess," we learn, strictly through the speaker's conversation with an unnamed companion, the setting of the poem and—more importantly—the inner conflict that prompts the character's speech.

Look For

As you read "My Last Duchess," be alert to clues in the speaker's words as to his identity and true character.

Writing

Write a brief fictional account of *your* life in the Oval Office titled "I, The President." Focus not on affairs of state but on the day-to-day routine in your household—your relationship with your family and friends, the stress that your job places on those relationships, and so on. Be sure to answer, somewhere in your account, the question "How has power changed me?"

Vocabulary

Knowing the following words will help you as you read the next four poems by Browning.

countenance (koun'tə nəns) *n.*: Face (p. 824, l. 7)
officious (ə fish'əs) *adj.*: Overly eager to please *(obsolete meaning)* (p. 824, l. 27)
munificence (myo͞o nif'ə s'ns) *n.*: Great generosity (p. 826, l. 49)
pretense (pri tens') *n.*: Claim *(British spelling)* (p. 826, l. 50)
dowry (dôu'rē) *n.*: Property that a woman brings to her husband at marriage (p. 826, l. 51)
avowed (ə voud') *v.*: Swore (p. 826, l. 52)
verdure (vʉr'jər) *n.*: Green plants (p. 830, l. 15)
vestige (ves'tij) *n.*: Trace; bit (p. 830, l. 29)
turret (tʉr'it) *n.*: Small tower projecting from a building (p. 831, l. 37)
sublime (sə blīm') *adj.*: Inspiring admiration through greatness or beauty (p. 831, l. 44)
minions (min'yənz) *n.*: Attendants or agents (p. 831, l. 47)
brazen (brā'z'n) *adj.*: Made of brass (p. 832, l. 75)
sheaf (shēf) *n.*: Bundle of twigs or fibers (p. 829, l. 5)
bole (bōl) *n.*: Tree trunk (p. 829, l. 6)
dower (dou'ər) *n.*: Gift (p. 829, l. 19)
rapture (rap'chər) *n.*: Expression of great joy (p. 829, l. 16)
guerdon (gʉr'd'n) *n.*: Reward (p. 834, l. 11)

Literary Focus To help the students understand the concept, refer them to one of the longer soliloquies in *Macbeth.* Point out that a dramatic monologue is essentially a soliloquy that is entirely self-contained.

Look For In a dramatic monologue, the speaker addresses one or more listeners, whose replies are not given. To whom is "My Last Duchess" addressed?

Writing As an alternative assignment, have students freewrite about their feelings concerning being away from home for an extended period of time.

Vocabulary Have your **more advanced** students write a short composition in which they use all of the vocabulary words.

Language Worksheet, p. 00

Selection Test, p. 000

Art Transparency 11, *Goodbye on the Mersea* by Tissot

Motivation for Reading Ask students what titles such as *Duke* and *Count* conjure up in their minds. What kinds of lives do such individuals live? What are their homes like? How does one come to have such a title?

Thematic Idea Another selection that focuses on a member of the nobility is the excerpt from *Don Juan* by Lord Byron, on page 707.

Purpose-Setting Question What does the monologue reveal about the speaker's personality?

1 **Critical Thinking and Reading** What pattern of rhyme does Browning establish in the first several lines?

2 **Discussion** What is the effect of the speaker's hesitation in this sentence?

3 **Literary Focus** What do these lines reveal about the speaker's personality?

My Last Duchess

Robert Browning

This poem, set in the sixteenth century in a castle in northern Italy, is based on events from the life of the Duke of Ferrara, an Italian nobleman, whose first wife died after only three years of marriage. Following his wife's death, the Duke began making arrangements to remarry. In Browning's poem, the Duke is showing a painting of his first wife to an agent who represents the father of the woman he hopes to marry.

1 That's my last Duchess painted on the wall,
Looking as if she were alive. I call
That piece a wonder, now: Frà Pandolf's[1] hands
Worked busily a day, and there she stands.
Will 't please you sit and look at her? I said
"Frà Pandolf" by design, for never read
Strangers like you that pictured countenance,
The depth and passion of its earnest glance,
But to myself they turned (since none puts by
The curtain I have drawn for you, but I)
And seemed as they would ask me, if they durst,[2]
How such a glance came there; so, not the first
Are you to turn and ask thus. Sir, 'twas not
Her husband's presence only, called that spot
Of joy into the Duchess' cheek: perhaps
Frà Pandolf chanced to say "Her mantle laps
Over my lady's wrist too much," or "Paint
Must never hope to reproduce the faint
Half-flush that dies along her throat"; such stuff
Was courtesy, she thought, and cause enough
For calling up that spot of joy. She had
2 A heart—how shall I say?—too soon made glad,
Too easily impressed; she liked whate'er
She looked on, and her looks went everywhere.
Sir, 'twas all one! My favor at her breast,
The dropping of the daylight in the West,
3 The bough of cherries some officious fool
Broke in the orchard for her, the white mule
She rode with round the terrace—all and each

1. Frà Pandolf's: The work of Brother Pandolf, an imaginary painter.
2. durst: Dared.

PARMIGIANINO: ANTEA NAPOLI
Capodimonte
Art Resource

Humanities Note

Fine art, *Antea Napoli* by Parmigianino. Parmigianino (1503–1540) was the last true northern Italian High Renaissance painter. He painted with mannered realism.

In this painting also called *La Bella,* Parmigianino's expert draftmanship is apparent. The lady's wealth and refinement are obvious through the artist's depiction of her rich clothing and graceful gesture. The artist has sacrificed emphasis on her femininity in favor of portraying elegance. This emphasis on cold elegance in his canvases, in lieu of emotion, is a trait often criticized today.

When viewing this work with your students, you may wish to ask the following questions:

1. Do you feel this lady in the painting could be the one referred to in Browning's poem?
2. What do you think is the painter's attitude toward women?
3. How does the artist's attitude compare with the attitude of the Duke toward women?

4 **Reading Strategy** Have students predict what the speaker might have done.

5 **Discussion** What do you think is meant by the line "I gave commands"?

Would draw from her alike the approving speech,
Or blush, at least. She thanked men—good! but thanked
Somehow—I know not how—as if she ranked
My gift of a nine-hundred-years-old name
4 With anybody's gift. Who'd stoop to blame
This sort of trifling? Even had you skill
In speech—(which I have not)—to make your will
Quite clear to such an one, and say, "Just this
Or that in you disgusts me; here you miss,
Or there exceed the mark"—and if she let
Herself be lessoned so, nor plainly set
Her wits to yours, forsooth,[3] and made excuse,
—E'en then would be some stooping; and I choose
Never to stoop. Oh sir, she smiled, no doubt,
Whene'er I passed her; but who passed without
5 Much the same smile? This grew; I gave commands;
Then all smiles stopped together. There she stands
As if alive. Will 't please you rise? We'll meet
The company below, then. I repeat,
The Count your master's known munificence
Is ample warrant that no one just pretense
Of mine for dowry will be disallowed;
Though his fair daughter's self, as I avowed
At starting, is my object. Nay, we'll go
Together down, sir! Notice Neptune,[4] though,
Taming a sea horse, thought a rarity,
Which Claus of Innsbruck[5] cast in bronze for me!

3. **forsooth:** In truth.
4. **Neptune:** In Roman mythology, the god of the sea.
5. **Claus of Innsbruck:** An imaginary Austrian sculptor.

THINKING ABOUT THE SELECTION

Recalling

1. (a) Where are the speaker and his companion? (b) What are they looking at?
2. What was the Duke's "gift" to his wife?

Interpreting

3. (a) What question are we to understand the speaker's companion to have asked. (b) What is the speaker's reply?
4. (a) What aspects of the Duke's personality are revealed in his keeping the painting behind a curtain? (b) What aspects are revealed in his being the only one allowed to draw the curtain?
5. (a) What has happened to the "last" Duchess? (b) Where in the poem is this revealed?
6. (a) How would you state the sentiment expressed in lines 21–22? (b) What examples does the speaker give as an illustration of this trait? (c) What feelings did it stir up in him?

Answers

ANSWERS TO THINKING ABOUT THE SELECTION

Recalling

1. (a) They are in the speaker's home, a castle. (b) They are looking at a portrait of the speaker's late wife.
2. He gave her his nine-hundred-year-old name.

Interpreting

3. (a) The speaker has apparently assumed that the man was about to ask about the lifelike expression on the face in the painting. (b) The speaker informs his listener that the "spot of joy" on the Duchess's face appeared there often and that his presence was not the sole occasion for it.
4. (a) Students might insist that this reveals his protectiveness over his possessions. (b) Suggested Response: This suggests that he orders his life in a rigorous fashion and that he sets rigid rules for those around him.
5. (a) She has apparently been killed. (b) In line 46 by the words "all smiles stopped," the speaker intimates that he had her killed.
6. (a) Suggested Response: The Duchess was indiscriminate in her appreciation of things, lumping together the finer things that came her way with the baser ones. (b) She was equally pleased by the sunset, by a bough of cherries, and by a mule. (c) The trait was extremely irritating to the Duke.

Applying

7. The eighteenth century English statesman and writer Edmund Burke has written, "The greater the power, the more dangerous the abuse." What are your reactions to this statement?

ANALYZING LITERATURE

Dramatic Monologue

A **dramatic monologue** is a poem that reveals a character's personality through what he or she says in a dramatic situation. In most dramatic monologues, the character addresses another character who is merely a silent listener. By drawing conclusions based on the character's words, the reader can piece together the poem's setting, the situation that prompts the character to speak, and the character's motives and actions.

1. Imagine that this dramatic monologue is part of a play or movie that you are directing. Describe the setting and the situation that prompts the Duke's speech.
2. What tone of voice do you think the Duke uses? Explain your answer.
3. What motives do you suppose the Duke has for showing the Count's agent the portrait of his dead wife?
4. The Count's agent never speaks. How do you imagine he acts when he learns of the Duke's displeasure with his wife?
5. (a) What makes this kind of poem an especially strong vehicle for conveying information about a character? (b) How differently would you see the Duke if Browning had written "My Last Duchess" as a short story?

CRITICAL THINKING AND READING

Making Inferences About the Speaker

An **inference** is a conclusion arrived at through known facts or evidence. In "My Last Duchess," Browning never directly describes the Duke's personality. Rather, he relies upon the reader to make inferences, from selected information, about the sort of man the Duke is. Find evidence in the poem that the Duke is: (1) jealous, (2) overly proud, (3) determined to have things his way, (4) preoccupied with possessions, (5) a stern boss.

UNDERSTANDING LANGUAGE

Revealing Diction

The **diction,** or choice of words, in "My Last Duchess" is an important ingredient of the Duke's character. To show that the man is a member of the nobility and, therefore, schooled in the social graces, Browning has the Duke use such formal constructions as "Will't please you sit and look at her?" Yet, there are clues in his speech habits that suggest the Duke's good manners are only skin-deep. Locate examples of language in the poem that demonstrate:

1. that the Duke is rude and insulting to his staff.
2. that he wants to appear humble.
3. that he thinks of himself as reasonable.

THINKING AND WRITING

Writing a Dramatic Monologue

Assume for the moment that the Duke has presented an accurate description of his last Duchess. List as many of her personality traits as you can. Then write an original dramatic monologue in which the Duchess reveals her impressions of her husband. In planning your monologue, consider the setting you want to convey and the occasion that prompts the speech. When you revise, make sure you have created a consistent picture of the Duchess.

Applying

7. Answers will differ. Students may comment that they agree with Burke's statement, because the actions of powerful people can have a tremendous impact on the lives of others.

Challenge How do you think Browning wants the reader to feel toward the Duke? Find evidence in support of your claim.

ANSWERS TO ANALYZING LITERATURE

1. Suggested Response: The setting is a gallery in the Duke's castle. The Duke and the agent are seated on a red velvet banquette. The Duke rises and draws a brocade curtain revealing a portrait.
2. Suggested Response: His tone of voice is arrogant and proud.
3. Suggested Response: He shows the portrait, because it provides him with an occasion to convey his expectations of a wife.
4. Suggested Response: He probably reports back to the Count that the Duke is an unfit suitor for the Count's daughter.
5. (a) Suggested Response: In a dramatic monologue we can learn about a character directly

(Answers begin on p. 826.)

through his or her comments. (b) Suggested Response: We would probably learn about the Duke's personality through his actions as well as his comments.

ANSWERS TO CRITICAL THINKING AND READING

1. The Duke's jealousy is manifest in his reaction to his wife and her "bad habit."
2. His feeling that it would be "stooping" to point out the Duchess's annoying habits is indicative of his pride.
3. This is shown in his high expectations from his wife and in his strict control.
4. His art collection and his treatment of his wife as a possession suggest this trait.
5. His reference to his gardener as an "officious fool" suggests that he is perhaps a stern boss.

ANSWERS TO UNDERSTANDING LANGUAGE

1. Suggested Response: He refers to his gardener as "some officious fool."
2. Suggested Response: Line 36 contains a self-effacing aside —"(which I have not)."
3. Suggested Response: His reference to the dowry in lines 48-51 conveys his belief that he is reasonable.

THINKING AND WRITING

For help with this assignment, students can refer to Lesson 18, "Writing a Poem," in the Handbook of Writing About Literature.

Publishing Student Writing After reading student compositions, choose two or three that best satisfy the terms of the assignment. Have the writer of each arrange an in-class presentation of the monologue complete with props.

Humanities Note

Fine art, *In Early Spring* by John William Inchbold. Inchbold (1830–1888) was a British landscape painter and etcher. John W. Inchbold received art training through his apprenticeship to a London lithography company and through a series of watercolor lessons. He was sympathetic to the precepts of the Pre-Raphaelite painters—a group of painters who emulated the primitive Italian artists who worked before Raphael. He was the first painter to bring the Pre-Raphaelite style to landscape painting.

This painting, *In Early Spring,* was completed in 1855. This depiction of tufts of grass breaking through the rich brown earth, early buds and flowers, and the new lambs of spring is realistically detailed. When first exhibited, it was highly praised for its strict attention to the minute details of nature. Inchbold saw the poetic possibilities of the English landscape and painted it with the truth, meticulous detail, and fresh colors of his Pre-Raphaelite beliefs.

You may wish to use the following questions for classroom discussion:

1. What feelings do both the artist and the poet share about England?
2. Could this be the English spring countryside that the poet longs for? Explain.

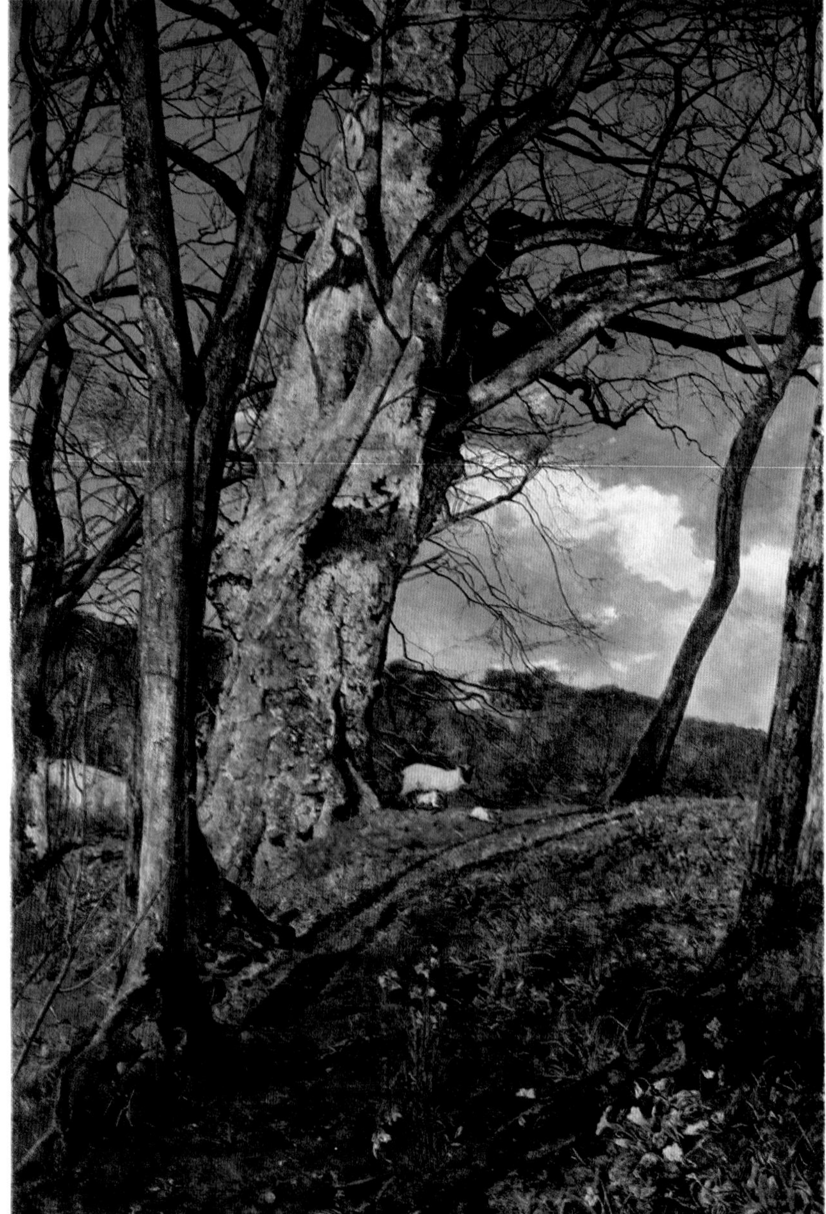

In Early Spring
Inchbod
Ashmolean Museum, Oxford

Home-Thoughts, from Abroad

Robert Browning

Oh, to be in England
Now that April's there, 1
And whoever wakes in England
Sees, some morning, unaware,
That the lowest boughs and the brushwood sheaf
Round the elm-tree bole are in tiny leaf,
While the chaffinch[1] sings on the orchard bough
In England—now! 2

And after April, when May follows,
And the whitethroat[2] builds, and all the swallows!
Hark, where my blossomed pear tree in the hedge
Leans to the field and scatters on the clover
Blossoms and dewdrops—at the bent spray's edge—
That's the wise thrush; he sings each song twice over. 3
Lest you should think he never could recapture
The first fine careless rapture!
And though the fields look rough with hoary dew,
All will be gay when noontide wakes anew
The buttercups, the little children's dower 4
—Far brighter than this gaudy melon flower![3]

1. **chaffinch** (chaf′ finch′) *n.*: A small European songbird.
2. **whitethroat** *n.*: Bird having white around the throat.
3. **melon flower:** The large, yellow flower of melon plants, native to a warm climate.

THINKING ABOUT THE SELECTION

Recalling

1. What time and place does the poem celebrate?
2. List four birds and six plants that the speaker says "whoever wakes in England" sees.

Interpreting

3. (a) Where do you suppose the speaker of the poem is? (b) What details of the poem provide clues?
4. How do you think the speaker is using the phrase "the little children's dower" in line 19?
5. Browning wrote this poem in England, following a trip to Italy. Why do you think he chose to write the poem as though he were far away at the time?

Applying

6. Think of a time when you were homesick, or try to imagine what it would be like. What details of home do you think would come to mind for you?

Motivation for Reading Ask whether any of your students spent summers at overnight camp when they were younger. Have them attempt to recall what the experience was like. Were they homesick? What in particular did they miss?

Master Teacher Note After discussing the poem, place Art Transparency 11, Tissot's *Good-bye on the Mersey,* on the overhead projector. Let your students get a sense of the Victorian atmosphere of the scene, and then ask them to compare the painting and the poem for mood and spirit. You might even wish to discuss the question of which medium, poetry or painting, can more effectively express feelings and emotions.

Thematic Idea Another poem that deals with the poet's love for his British homeland is Rupert Brooke's "The Soldier," page 1068.

Purpose-Setting Question What does the term *home* mean to the speaker?

1 **Enrichment** Though he spent many years in Florence, Browning was not actually abroad in 1845, the year he wrote this poem.

2 **Discussion** Does the speaker present a slanted view here?

3 **Discussion** What is the speaker's state of mind?

4 **Clarification** The word *gaudy* means "overly showy" or "flashy."

Answers

ANSWERS TO THINKING ABOUT THE SELECTION

Recalling

1. The poem celebrates England in the springtime.
2. The four birds mentioned are the chaffinch, the whitethroat, the swallow, and the thrush. The six plants are the brushwood, the elm tree, the melon, the pear tree, clover, and the buttercup.

Interpreting

3. (a) The supposition is that the speaker is in a warm climate. (b) The mention of the melon flower, a mostly tropical flower, suggests this.
4. Students might either interpret this metaphorically—as though the bright flowers are, in their childlike simplicity, gifts *from* children—or literally: buttercups are popular flowers among children, hence, nature's gift to them.
5. Suggested Response: It was an effective means for communicating his love for his country.

Applying

6. Answers will differ. Students might mention their favorite restaurants, shopping centers, and parks.

Love Among the Ruins

Robert Browning

This poem presents the contrast between past and present through the eyes of a shepherd, anxious to return to his waiting wife. The ruins that the shepherd and his wife live among may be the remains of ancient Babylon or Nineveh or one of the Etruscan cities of Italy.

Where the quiet-colored end of evening smiles,
        Miles and miles
1 On the solitary pastures where our sheep
        Halt asleep
2 Tinkle homeward through the twilight, stray or stop
        As they crop—
Was the site once of a city great and gay
        (So they say),
Of our country's very capital, its prince
        Ages since
Held his court in, gathered councils, wielding far
        Peace or war.

Now—the country does not even boast a tree,
        As you see,
To distinguish slopes of verdure, certain rills
        From the hills
Intersect and give a name to (else they run
        Into one),
Where the domed and daring palace shot its spires
        Up like fires
3 O'er the hundred-gated circuit of a wall
        Bounding all,
Made of marble, men might march on nor be pressed,
        Twelve abreast.

And such plenty and perfection, see, of grass
4   Never was!
Such a carpet as, this summertime, o'erspreads
        And embeds
Every vestige of the city, guessed alone,[1]
        Stock or stone—

1. guessed alone: Because the site of the city is now covered with grass, one can only guess where it was.

Motivation for Reading Ask students to volunteer what they know about empires that no longer exist. If there are students in your class who have visited the crumbling ancient forums of Rome or Greece, have them describe what they saw. What causes a civilization to vanish? Is it irreverent to walk on the ruins of a vanished civilization? Why or why not?

Master Teacher Note Obtain a photograph of the Parthenon. (A shot of the ruin appears on page 95 of H. W. Janson's *History of Art*, Prentice-Hall/Abrams). Ask students what feelings the sight of the ancient Greek temple evokes in them. Ask them to explain these feelings.

Thematic Idea Another selection that deals with the ephemeral nature of greatness is "Ozymandias" by Percy Bysshe Shelley, on page 712.

Purpose-Setting Question What lessons can we learn from the mistakes of the past?

1 **Discussion** Where is the poem set? At what time of day?

2 **Clarification** The word *tinkle* adds an audial detail to this vividly described scene. The sound is made by bells around the necks of the sheep.

3 **Discussion** Contrast the image in these lines with that of the first sixteen lines.

4 **Critical Thinking and Reading** What do the words *plenty and perfection* suggest about the speaker's feelings toward the current state of the land? Toward its former state?

Where a multitude of men breathed joy and woe
Long ago;
Lust of glory pricked their hearts up, dread of shame
Struck them tame;
And that glory and that shame alike, the gold
Bought and sold. 5

Now—the single little turret that remains
On the plains,
By the caper[2] overrooted, by the gourd
Overscored,
While the patching houseleek's[3] head of blossom winks
Through the chinks—
Marks the basement whence a tower in ancient time
Sprang sublime,
And a burning ring, all round, the chariots traced
As they raced,
And the monarch and his minions and his dames
Viewed the games.

---

2. caper *n.*: A prickly, trailing Mediterranean bush.
3. houseleek *n.*: A plant with yellow, pink, or red flowers and compact rosettes of thick, fleshy leaves.

Italian Ruins
Nattes
Victoria & Albert Museum Trustees

Humanities Note

Fine art, *Italian Ruins,* by John Claude Nattes. The English watercolor artist, John Claude Nattes (1765–1822) was born of Irish parents. His work is among that of the early English topographical painters—descriptive painters of towns, parishes, ruins, tracts of land, estates, and buildings. He published books describing Scotland, England, France, and Italy, which he illustrated with his watercolor paintings.

The undated watercolor entitled *Italian Ruins* was probably painted in the years between 1781 and 1784. It is done in the style Nattes preferred, sepia details tinted with color. The ruined temple or building rises out of an Italian urban scene. A tree grows in the center, showing the degree of decay to which the ruin has succumbed. The descriptive scene has a romantic air and a poetic charm.

You may discuss the following with your students:

1. Which phrase in the first line of Browning's poem describes the style of this painting?
2. What is it about ruins that both Browning and Nattes found inspiring?

5 **Reading Strategy** Have students note that lines 35–36 provide a clue about why the civilization may have fallen.

6 **Discussion** What is ironic about a shepherd and his wife living in one of the remnants of the castle?

7 **Reading Strategy** Have students summarize in their own words what they believe happened to the empire and why it happened.

8 **Discussion** What is the meaning of the final line?

And I know, while thus the quiet-colored eve
Smiles to leave
To their folding, all our many-tinkling fleece
In such peace,
And the slopes and rills, in undistinguished gray
Melt away—
That a girl with eager eyes and yellow hair
Waits me there
6 In the turret whence the charioteers caught soul
For the goal,
When the king looked, where she looks now, breathless, dumb
Till I come.

But he looked upon the city, every side,
Far and wide,
All the mountains topped with temples, all the glades'
Colonnades,[4]
All the causeys,[5] bridges, aqueducts—and then,
All the men!
When I do come, she will speak not, she will stand,
Either hand
On my shoulder, give her eyes the first embrace
Of my face,
Ere we rush, ere we extinguish sight and speech
Each on each.

In one year they sent a million fighters forth
South and North,
7 And they built their gods a brazen pillar[6] high
As the sky,
Yet reserved a thousand chariots in full force—
Gold, of course.
Oh heart! oh blood that freezes, blood that burns!
Earth's returns
For whole centuries of folly, noise and sin!
Shut them in,
With their triumphs and their glories and the rest!
8 Love is best.

---

4. Colonnades (käl′ ə nādz′) *n.*: Series of columns set at regular intervals; here, groups of trees surrounding an open area.
5. causeys *n.*: Causeways or raised roads.
6. brazen pillar: Built from the brass of captured chariots.

THINKING ABOUT THE SELECTION

Recalling

1. (a) What does the speaker say once stood where sheep pastures now stand? (b) What single trace remains?
2. What does the speaker say awaits him on the pastures at twilight?

Interpreting

3. What do you suppose is the identity of the speaker?
4. (a) How would you summarize the speaker's comments on the civilization mentioned in lines 33–36? (b) How would you describe his feelings toward this civilization?
5. (a) What do you think is the purpose of the speaker's noting in line 67 that his companion "will not speak" when he arrives? (b) What might he expect his companion to say?
6. (a) What do you think is the meaning of the speaker's lament in lines 81–82? (b) To what "folly" might he be referring?
7. Explain why "Love Among the Ruins" is or is not an appropriate title for the poem.

Applying

8. Reread "Ozymandias" by Shelley on page 712. (a) What similarities do you see between the messages in the two poems? (b) What differences do you see in the conclusions reached by the two poets?

CRITICAL THINKING AND READING

Interpreting Tone

Tone is the author's attitude toward his or her subject or audience. A work may have a tone that is lighthearted or serious, ironic or sincere, or any of numerous other possibilities. Just as a person's tone of voice can affect the way a remark is interpreted by others, so the tone of a literary work affects how the reader perceives the author's purpose.

1. (a) How would you describe the tone of the speaker of "Love Among the Ruins" with respect to the ruined splendor? (b) With respect to the civilization? (c) With respect to his companion?
2. Consider what other tone Browning might have used to make the point he makes here. Would another tone strengthen or weaken the poem's impact? Explain your answer.

THINKING AND WRITING

Comparing and Contrasting Two Places

Think about how your town or city might have appeared 100 years ago. Write a description of the "two faces" of your city. Begin by listing ways in which the locale has undoubtedly changed, as well as ways in which it has probably remained the same, over the century. In writing your description, use vivid details so that your audience will be able to picture both the "old" city and the "new" one.

Answers

ANSWERS TO THINKING ABOUT THE SELECTION

Recalling

1. (a) He says a great city stood there. (b) All that remains are scattered ruins—a turret and a chariot track.
2. A "girl with eager eyes and yellow hair" awaits him.

Interpreting

3. The speaker is a shepherd.
4. (a) The suggestion is that these people succumbed to base desires and greed. (b) Suggested Response: The speaker feels contempt for this civilization.
5. (a) Suggested Response: He wants to convey the fact that they have a deep understanding of each other and do not need to speak. (b) He expects her to say nothing.
6. (a) Suggested Response: The lament seems to be over the treacheries of the human heart. (b) The folly refers to the mistakes that brought about the destruction of the empire.
7. Suggested Response: It is an appropriate title, because the poem captures the ability of love to survive among the ruins that result from base desires.

Applying

8. (a) Answers will differ. Students should note that both poems deal with edifices of stone, now crumbled, that once demonstrated the power and invincibility of an individual or of a people. (b) Suggested Response: The difference is chiefly one of tone. Browning laments the folly that led to the fall of a civilization, while Shelley approaches his subject with a note of scorn, almost of triumph.

Challenge The metric pattern of the poem—a line of six feet followed by a line of two—seems almost playful. How well does this pattern relate to the poem's theme?

ANSWERS TO CRITICAL THINKING AND READING

1. (a) He seems to lament, though for the most part in a subdued fashion, the ruined splendor. (b) His tone toward the civilization is slightly more bitter—as though he feels the fate of the people was well-deserved. (c) His tone toward his wife is passionate—"a girl with eager eyes and yellow hair."
2. Suggested Response: Browning might have written the poem in an outwardly angry or outwardly mournful fashion. If this were the case, its subtle shadings and mild irony would have been lost.

Writing Across the Curriculum
You might permit students to develop as an alternative topic the "two faces" of our planet—the earth today contrasted with the earth 1,000 years ago. Inform your science department about this assignment. Science teachers may be able to provide students with important details concerning the earth's appearance.

Motivation for Reading Remind students that we humans are the only creatures on earth to have a knowledge of our own mortality. What are the advantages and disadvantages of possessing this knowledge?

Thematic Idea Another poem that presents the poet's view of his own death is "Crossing the Bar" by Alfred, Lord Tennyson, on page 820.

Purpose-Setting Question What is the speaker's attitude toward death?

1 **Reading Strategy** Have students pause and consider other metaphors Browning might have used here.

2 **Critical Thinking and Reading** What is the speaker's attitude toward the struggle he describes?

3 **Discussion** What gradual steps is the speaker describing? Which of these steps do you think corresponds to the end of the "journey" mentioned in line 9?

4 **Discussion** What two meanings can you attach to the word *rest* as it is used here?

Prospice

Robert Browning

This poem, the title of which means "look forward," was written by Browning after the death of his wife. It is the classic expression of Browning's feelings about death.

Fear death?—to feel the fog in my throat,
    The mist in my face,
When the snow begins, and the blasts denote
    I am nearing the place,
The power of the night, the press of the storm,
1   The post of the foe;
Where he stands, the Arch Fear in a visible form,
    Yet the strong man must go.
For the journey is done and the summit attained,
    And the barriers fall,
Though a battle's to fight ere the guerdon be gained,
2   The reward of it all.
I was ever a fighter, so—one fight more,
    The best and the last!
I would hate that death bandaged my eyes, and forbore,
    And bade me creep past.
No! let me taste the whole of it, fare like my peers,
    The heroes of old,
Bear the brunt, in a minute pay glad life's arrears
    Of pain, darkness, and cold.
For sudden the worst turns the best to the brave,
    The black minute's at end,
And the elements' rage, the fiend-voices that rave,
3   Shall dwindle, shall blend,
Shall change, shall become first a peace out of pain,
    Then a light, then thy breast,
Oh thou soul of my soul![1] I shall clasp thee again,
4   And with God be the rest!

1. **soul of my soul:** Browning's wife.

THINKING ABOUT THE SELECTION

Recalling

1. (a) With what question does the speaker open the poem? (b) What is his answer in line 17?
2. (a) To what, in lines 1–14, does the speaker compare the process of dying? (b) Who, in lines 17–18, does the speaker say are his peers?

Interpreting

3. (a) What opposing forces does the speaker suggest are fighting at the moment of death? (b) What, according to line 21, is ironic about the nature of this battle?
4. (a) Whom do you think Browning is addressing in line 27 as "thou soul of my soul"? (b) What does this suggest about his belief in an afterlife?
5. In what way is this poem a look forward?

Applying

6. Browning has sometimes been criticized for being overly optimistic about situations in which others would be more skeptical. (a) Do you think this is true of his views in "Prospice?" Why or why not? (b) What other poets have you read who seem to share his attitudes?

CRITICAL THINKING AND READING

Making Inferences About Attitudes

Students of literature are warned repeatedly of the dangers of misidentifying the first-person narrator of a work with the work's author. Yet, in dealing with "Prospice," scholars generally assume that the attitudes reflected in the poem are precisely those of its author.

1. Based on what you have read about Robert Browning and his attitudes, how justified do you think scholars are in making this assumption?
2. What subjects besides death might an author choose to address without the use of a fictitious narrator? What poems are stories that fit this description.

THINKING AND WRITING

Comparing and Contrasting Two Poems

Both Tennyson's "Crossing the Bar" and Browning's "Prospice" express the poet's deepest feelings about dying. Reread the two poems, and think about the similarities and differences between them. Consider especially the following questions as you plan an essay comparing and contrasting the poems: What do Tennyson's image of the tide and Browning's image of the battle reveal about each poet's attitudes toward dying? How do the poet's notions of the afterlife differ? Which poem seems more effective to you? Begin your essay by summarizing your conclusions. Support your opinions by quoting freely from the poems. When you revise, make sure you have quoted precisely and have punctuated your sentences accurately.

Answers

ANSWERS TO THINKING ABOUT THE SELECTION

Recalling

1. (a) The question is "Fear death?" (b) His answer is a firm "No!"
2. (a) He compares it variously to struggling through a storm and to a battle. (b) He identifies himself with "the heroes of old."

Interpreting

3. (a) Suggested Response: The fear of death and the desire to continue living battles with the desire to surrender to death. (b) Suggested Response: The irony, in the speaker's view, is that something positive emerges out of this negative struggle.
4. (a) He is addressing his late wife. (b) The clear indication is that he believes in such a state.
5. It is a "look forward" to the poet's own death.

Applying

6. (a) Answers will differ. Many students may feel that Browning's view is overly optimistic. (b) Suggested Response: Tennyson expresses a similar view in "Crossing the Bar."

ANSWERS TO CRITICAL THINKING AND READING

1. Students should be in general agreement that this assumption is warranted. First, the poem fits the image presented in the biography of Browning as a perseverer—a man who refused to take "no" for an answer when his first publishing efforts failed. Second, the timeliness of the poem—its publication shortly after the death of the poet's wife—would indicate a personal stake in these sentiments.
2. Answers will differ. Students might suggest such subjects as war, nature, and industrialization.

THINKING AND WRITING

For help with this assignment, students can refer to Lesson 16, "Writing a Comparative Evaluation," in the Handbook of Writing About Literature.

More About the Author When Matthew Arnold's first volume of poems appeared in 1849 his sister commented that the book "almost like a new Introduction to him . . . I felt there was so much more of . . . practical questioning in Matt's book than I was prepared for. . . ." Is it surprising that Arnold's poetry revealed aspects of his personality of which those close to him had previously been unaware? Why or why not?

MATTHEW ARNOLD

1822–1888

Of all the great Victorian poets, Matthew Arnold strikes twentieth-century readers as the most modern. The persistent theme of his poems—people's isolation and alienation from nature and from one another—has been echoed by many writers and thinkers of our own age. His pessimistic outlook too—that "there is everything to be endured, nothing to be done"—coincides with the view of many today that we are a generation of lost souls.

Matthew Arnold was born in Laleham, Middlesex, and educated at Rugby School, where his father, a believer in the good of social change, was headmaster. After entering Oxford in 1841, Arnold startled his contemporaries by dressing and behaving like an aristocratic dandy. Yet, behind this Byronic mask was developing the serious and sensitive social conscience that was to guide Arnold's career as a public servant, poet, and literary critic.

In 1851 Arnold accepted the post of Inspector of Schools, which he held until two years before his death. In this job he traveled through England and the Continent, and published reports that did much to improve public education in Great Britain. All the while, he remained a poet at heart, though his first two books, published in 1849 and 1851, met with little success.

His fortunes changed in 1853, with the publication of *Poems: A New Edition,* which included a long preface that established Arnold as a writer of clear critical prose as well as of quality poetry. With *New Poems* (1867), which contained his celebrated "Dover Beach," Arnold felt that he had expressed everything he had to say through poetry. From that point forward, he thus focused his creative energies on literary criticism.

The melancholy outlook of his poems, Arnold himself noted, was unrelieved by hope. Nevertheless, it was his belief that the role of literature was to "inspirit and rejoice the reader: that it shall convey a charm and infuse delight." In such critical works as *Culture and Anarchy* (1869), Arnold argued also that literature should train us to open our minds to what is true and valuable in life. For Arnold, then, literature's truth and cultural value lay in its ability to enlarge and develop humanity's "moral and social passion for doing good." Even his critical examinations of the classics and of Dante and Shakespeare were in part attempts to help readers of his day find permanent values in an industrialized society that Arnold viewed as increasingly materialistic and self-serving.

Despite his own opinions regarding the shortcomings of his poetic vision, Arnold's "dark" poems are a mirror of his critical beliefs: They charm and delight audiences, as well as point out enduring truths.

Objectives

1 To understand imagery and mood
2 To write about imagery and mood
3 To use figurative language
4 To write about a Victorian poet

Teaching Portfolio: Support Material

Teacher Backup, p. 000

Vocabulary Check, p. 00

Usage and Mechanics Worksheet, p. 00

Analyzing Literature Worksheet, p. 00

Critical Thinking and Reading Worksheet, p. 00

Language Worksheet, p. 00

Selection Test, p. 000

GUIDE FOR READING

To Marguerite—Continued; Self-Dependence; Dover Beach

The Writer's Technique

Imagery and Mood. Imagery is language that appeals to one or more of the senses. Poets rely on imagery to help establish *mood,* the overall feeling that a poem awakens in the reader. For example, if a poet wishes to create a mood of frustration, he or she may rely on imagery associated with a summer traffic jam—the sight of countless cars gleaming in the sunshine, the sound of motors humming, the feel of the heat rising from the pavement, the smell and perhaps even the taste of exhaust fumes. The same imagery, however, can be used to convey a mood of excitement and energy when the focus of the poem becomes a raceway, where roaring cars zoom past cheering spectators.

Figurative Language. Figurative language is the name applied to a group of literary devices that use words and phrases in an unorthodox way to create interesting effects. Figurative language is not to be taken literally. Among the many "figures of speech" used by poets are *apostrophe,* in which the poet directly addresses an absent person or some object or idea, and *personification,* the assigning of human qualities to nonhuman things. Both of these devices are used by Matthew Arnold in "Self-Dependence."

Look For

As you read "To Marguerite—Continued," look for the poet's use of island images and the mood he is attempting to convey by his use of them. As you read "Self-Dependence," be alert to the author's use of apostrophe and personification and to the objects on which he uses these devices.

Writing

Imagine yourself on a beach, watching the ebb and flow of the ocean. Freewrite, exploring the thoughts that spring to mind.

Vocabulary

Knowing the following words will help you as you read the three poems by Matthew Arnold.

severance (sev'ər əns) *n.*: State of being kept separate (p. 838, l. 22)

compose (kəm pōz') *v.*: Get oneself together emotionally; calm (p. 840, l. 8)

tremulous (trem'yoo ləs) *adj.*: Trembling; timid (p. 842, l. 13)

turbid (tur'bid) *adj.*: Muddy or cloudy; confused. (p. 842, l. 17)

certitude (sur'tə tood) *n.*: Certainty (p. 843, l. 34)

Literary Focus Reinforce the notion of imagery by reading off a list of images and having students identify the senses to which each one appeals.

Look For Your **less advanced** students may have difficulty with the concept of apostrophe. Help them grasp the notion by reviewing the use of the device in such poems as "Death, Be not Proud" by Donne and "Apostrophe to the Ocean" by Byron.

Writing Before students complete the writing activity, discuss the thoughts and feelings they associate with the ocean.

Vocabulary Have your **more advanced** students attempt to use as many of the five vocabulary words as possible in a single, well-formed sentence. Accept a minimum of four.

Motivation for Reading Ask students whether they feel it is possible to be part of a crowd and yet feel alone. If so, what types of people are likely to experience this sensation? What might be some of the causes of these feelings.

Thematic Idea Another selection that deals with the isolation of an individual within the bounds of a large society is George Orwell's memoir, *Shooting an Elephant,* on page 1034.

Purpose-Setting Question What is the speaker's unfulfilled wish?

1 **Clarification** *Enisled* is a verb meaning "made into an island."

2 **Literary Focus** What change in mood do you detect at the beginning of the second stanza?

3 **Discussion** How do the details in this passage develop the metaphor of the "sea of life"?

4 **Discussion** For what is the speaker wishing?

5 **Reading Strategy** Have students explain how the message here would have differed had the speaker mentioned "God," rather than "*a* God."

To Marguerite—Continued

Matthew Arnold

1 Yes! in the sea of life enisled,
With echoing straits between us thrown,
Dotting the shoreless watery wild,
We mortal millions live *alone.*
The islands feel the enclasping flow,
2 And then their endless bounds they know.

But when the moon their hollows lights,
And they are swept by balms of spring,
And in their glens, on starry nights,
3 The nightingales divinely sing;
And lovely notes, from shore to shore,
Across the sounds and channels pour—

Oh! then a longing like despair
Is to their farthest caverns sent;
For surely once, they feel, we were
Parts of a single continent!
Now round us spreads the watery plain—
4 Oh might our marges meet again!

Who ordered, that their longing's fire
Should be, as soon as kindled, cooled?
Who renders vain their deep desire?
5 A God, a God their severance ruled!
And bade betwixt their shores to be
The unplumbed, salt, estranging sea.

---

1. enisled (in ild′) *adj.*: Isolated, as if placed on an island.

THINKING ABOUT THE SELECTION

Recalling

1. Where and how, according to lines 1–4, do "we mortal millions live?"
2. (a) According to lines 7–14, what sights and sounds seem to trigger "a longing like despair?" (b) What true cause for this longing is explained in lines 15–18?
3. According to the last stanza, who ordered that this longing's "fire" be "cooled?"

Interpreting

4. To what or whom do you think Arnold is comparing the islands?
5. What human condition is Arnold lamenting in this poem?
6. (a) Who do you suppose the "god" mentioned in line 22 might be? (b) What evidence do you have that this is not a "good" god?

Applying

7. John Donne wrote, "No man is an island entire of itself; every man is a piece of the continent, a part of the main." Arnold's "Yes!" at the beginning of this poem seems to be a flat contradiction of Donne's view. Which poet's view do you agree with more? Why?

ANALYZING LITERATURE

Creating Imagery and Mood

An **image** is a word or phrase that appeals to one or more of the five senses. Poets string together images to create a particular **mood,** or emotional response in the reader. In "To Marguerite—Continued," the dominant imagery is intended to help the reader form a mental picture of islands in a vast ocean. Arnold contrasts this imagery, however, with images of springtime in the second stanza.

1. What mood does Arnold establish with the island imagery in the first stanza? How do the sounds of the words themselves contribute to this mood?
2. What mood is suggested by the springtime images in the second stanza? How does the third stanza destroy this mood? How does this intentional undermining of a positive mood fit in with the theme of the poem?

THINKING AND WRITING

Writing About Imagery and Mood

The image of an island is an almost perfect vehicle for suggesting a mood of loneliness and, in the case of Arnold's poem, for a commentary on human isolation. Consider other images Arnold might have chosen that would have created a similar mood and been equally well suited to his theme. Make notes on one such image and on the senses to which it would appeal. Then write a brief poem or prose narrative that carries the message of "To Marguerite—Continued." When you revise, make sure you have used as many descriptive words as you can to enhance the vividness of your imagery and to sharpen the focus of the piece's mood.

Answers

ANSWERS TO THINKING ABOUT THE SELECTION

Recalling

1. We live on islands, all alone.
2. (a) Moonlight, spring breezes, and the song of the nightingales trigger this longing. (b) The longing arises out of a desire that humanity might once again be single united race.
3. A God ordered the separation.

Interpreting

4. He is comparing the islands to human souls; each individual is an island.
5. He is alluding to the coldness and alienation that have developed among humans in these modern, technologically oriented times.
6. (a) Students will note that this is the "God of modern industry." (b) That the god is not a benevolent presence is indicated by his act of cooling the longing for togetherness with indifference.

Applying

7. Answers will differ. Those who agree with Donne will take the position that total independence is neither possible nor desirable, while those who side with Arnold will contend that solidarity is desirable but unattainable.

ANSWERS TO ANALYZING LITERATURE

1. He establishes a mood of cold isolation. The repetition of the ō contributes to this mood.
2. The mood in the second stanza is one of quietude and tranquility. The third stanza destroys the mood by opening with a plaintive cry and the mention of a "longing like despair". The subverting of the positive mood is appropriate to the theme because it is precisely what the poet ascribes to the "God" of industry in line 22.

THINKING AND WRITING

For help with this assignment, students can refer to Lesson 4, "Writing About Imagery," in the Handbook of Writing About Literature.

Motivation for Reading Ask students to comment on what they see when they look up at the stars at night. Do they merely see pretty twinkling lights, or do they entertain more profound thoughts? What associations might the stars and the vastness of the nighttime sky have had for thinkers of past generations?

Thematic Idea Another poem that deals with the concept of human self-sufficiency is "Not Waving, But Drowning" by Stevie Smith, on page 1316.

Purpose-Setting Question What credo does the speaker come to adopt through the experience he describes?

1 **Discussion** Have students discuss what "end" the poet might be referring to here and what this reveals about his intentions.

2 **Literary Focus** What are the objects of the apostrophe in these lines?

3 **Clarification** The word *unaffrighted* means "not frightened."

4 **Literary Focus** What human traits are ascribed to the stars and ocean in this passage?

5 **Enrichment** You might wish to have students read Arnold's short poem "The Last Word," which explores in more detail the "fever" that tends to erupt among "differing souls."

6 **Reading Strategy** Have students restate these thoughts in their own words.

Self-Dependence

Matthew Arnold

Weary of myself, and sick of asking
What I am, and what I ought to be,
At this vessel's prow I stand, which bears me
Forwards, forwards, o'er the starlit sea.

And a look of passionate desire
O'er the sea and to the stars I send:
1 "Ye who from my childhood up have calmed me,
Calm me, ah, compose me to the end!

"Ah, once more," I cried, "ye stars, ye waters,
2 On my heart your mighty charm renew;
Still, still let me, as I gaze upon you,
Feel my soul becoming vast like you!"

From the intense, clear, star-sown vault of heaven,
Over the lit sea's unquiet way,
In the rustling night air came the answer:
"Wouldst thou *be* as these are? *Live* as they.

3 "Unaffrighted by the silence round them,
Undistracted by the sights they see,
4 These demand not that the things without them
Yield them love, amusement, sympathy.

"And with joy the stars perform their shining,
And the sea its long moon-silvered roll;
5 For self-poised they live, nor pine with noting
All the fever of some differing soul.

"Bounded by themselves, and unregardful
In what state God's other works may be,
In their own tasks all their powers pouring,
These attain the mighty life you see."

O air-born voice! long since, severely clear,
A cry like thine in mine own heart I hear:
6 "Resolve to be thyself; and know that he,
Who finds himself, loses his misery!"

THINKING ABOUT THE SELECTION

Recalling

1. (a) What emotional state do we find the speaker in at the poem's beginning? (b) Where does the speaker say he is standing and going?
2. (a) What does the poet ask of the sea and the stars? (b) What answer does he receive in line 16?
3. What characteristics of the sea and stars enable them to "attain the mighty life" the speaker so admires?
4. What cry does the speaker finally hear in his own heart?
5. Why do you think the poet calls this poem "Self-Dependence," not "Independence"?

Interpreting

6. (a) In your own words, identify the problem that Arnold presents in the first two lines of the poem. (b) Identify the solution offered in the last two lines.
7. Lines 7–12 mention the speaker's childhood. What does the passage imply that the speaker has lost?
8. What do you suppose is the source of the "air-born voice" in the poem?
9. What is meant by "the fever of some differing soul" in line 24?

Applying

10. According to lines 19–20, nature is self-dependent because it does not require love, amusement, or sympathy. Do you think it is possible for human beings to attain such self-dependence? Explain your answer.

ANALYZING LITERATURE

Using Figurative Language

Figurative language is language not to be taken at face value. Many devices used by poets fall into the category of figurative language. In one such device, apostrophe, the poet directly addresses an absent human being or some object or idea. In personification, another device, human qualities are assigned to a nonhuman object. Both of these devices, or "figures of speech," are used by Arnold in "Self-Dependence."

1. In which lines does Arnold use apostrophe? What or whom is he addressing?
2. What does Arnold personify in the poem? What human characteristics does he assign to these nonhuman things?
3. What reason might Arnold have had for using apostrophe and personification in this poem? How would the poem have been different had he not chosen to use these devices?

Answers

ANSWERS TO THINKING ABOUT THE SELECTION

Recalling

1. (a) He is weary and full of self-doubt. (b) He is standing on the prow of a ship headed out to sea.
2. (a) He asks them to calm and compose him, as they did when he was younger. (b) He is told that if he would be like the sea and stars, he must live like them.
3. They are totally self-sufficient —needing neither love nor sympathy, nor concerned for the opinions of others.
4. He hears his own heart state, that we are less miserable when we at least know our true selves.
5. The poem focuses on self-sufficiency rather than on independence.

Interpreting

6. (a) Students will note that the problem is one of discontent with the modern world and with what it has done to human relations. (b) The solution is to understand our own identities.
7. Suggested Response: He has lost his innocence.
8. Suggested Response: It is the voice of the heavens.
9. The phrase refers to the angry arguments of one whose opinion differs.

Applying

10. Answers will differ. Students may comment that they do believe that such self-dependence is possible.

Challenge Does the message in this poem conflict in any way with the message in "To Marguerite —Continued"? If so, how?

ANSWERS TO ANALYZING LITERATURE

1. Apostrophe is used in lines 7–12, and again in lines 29–30. In the first instance he is addressing the sea and stars, and in the second the air-born voice.
2. He personifies the sea and stars. The characteristics he assigns them include fear, distraction, sight, love, amusement, sympathy, joy, poise, pining, and arguing.
3. Answers will differ. Students might note that Arnold needed a nonhuman entity with which to compare what he saw as typical human behavior and that, in this regard, personification, at least, was virtually unavoidable.

Motivation for Reading Have students discuss the associations that they have with the ocean. What are their positive associations? What are their negative associations.

Thematic Idea Another work which attempts to help us see through the illusions of modern life is "The Lagoon" by Joseph Conrad, page 962.

Purpose-Setting Question What is the speaker's assessment of the state of the race?

1 **Reading Strategy** Have students review Arnold's references to the sea in "To Marguerite—Continued" (p. 838) and "Self-Dependence" (p. 840).

2 **Discussion** How would you describe the mood in this stanza? How does it compare with the mood in the first stanza?

3 **Reading Strategy** Have students determine the antecedent of "it" in this line.

4 **Clarification** The "Sea of Faith" refers to religious faith, which had been badly shaken for many Victorians, including Arnold, by Darwin's theory of evolution. People at this time felt they had to choose between science and religion.

Dover Beach

Matthew Arnold

The sea is calm tonight.
1 The tide is full, the moon lies fair
Upon the straits:[1] on the French coast the light
Gleams and is gone; the cliffs of England stand,
Glimmering and vast, out in the tranquil bay.
Come to the window, sweet is the night air!
Only, from the long line of spray

Where the sea meets the moon-blanched land,
Listen! you hear the grating roar
Of pebbles which the waves draw back, and fling,
2 At their return, up the high strand,[2]
Begin, and cease, and then again begin,
With tremulous cadence slow, and bring
The eternal note of sadness in.

Sophocles[3] long ago
3 Heard it on the Aegaean,[4] and it brought
Into his mind the turbid ebb and flow
Of human misery; we
Find also in the sound a thought,
Hearing it by this distant northern sea.

The Sea of Faith
Was once, too, at the full, and round earth's shore
4 Lay like the folds of a bright girdle furled.
But now I only hear
Its melancholy, long, withdrawing roar,
Retreating, to the breath
Of the night wind, down the vast edges drear
And naked shingles[5] of the world.

---

1. **straits:** Strait of Dover, between England and France.
2. **strand:** Shore.
3. **Sophocles** (säf′ ə klēz′): A Greek tragic dramatist (496?–406 B.C.)
4. **Aegaean** (ē jē′ ən): The arm of the Mediterranean Sea between Greece and Turkey.
5. **shingles** *n.*: Beaches covered with large, coarse, waterworn gravel.

Ah, love, let us be true
5 To one another! for the world, which seems
To lie before us like a land of dreams,
So various, so beautiful, so new,
Hath really neither joy, nor love, nor light,
Nor certitude, nor peace, nor help for pain;
And we are here as on a darkling[6] plain
Swept with confused alarms of struggle and flight,
Where ignorant armies clash by night.

---

6. darkling *adj.*: In the dark.

5 **Discussion** To whom do you think these lines are addressed? Explain your answer.

THINKING ABOUT THE SELECTION

Recalling

1. (a) According to the first stanza, what does the speaker see and hear from his window? (b) What does the "tremulous cadence" of the pebbles against the beach "bring in?" (c) Who else does the speaker say "long ago" heard this same sound?
2. What, according to lines 21–28, has happened to the "Sea of Faith?"
3. What sad reality does the speaker describe for his companion in lines 30–34?

Applying

4. A symbol is a thing, person, or place that stands for something beyond itself. (a) What might the "cliffs of England" symbolize in line 4? (b) The "naked shingles of the world" in line 28? (c) "Night" in line 37?
5. (a) What effect do you think Arnold aimed to achieve by varying the length of lines and using an irregular rhyme scheme? (b) How do these poetic devices relate to the theme?
6. (a) How is the battle image in the last three lines a fitting conclusion to this poem? (b) How would you state the message of these lines in your own words?

Applying

7. (a) To what extent does Arnold's plea to "be true to one another" in lines 29–30 provide a satisfactory solution to the "ebb and flow of human misery" he sees in the world? (b) Where does this solution break down?
8. (a) State the similarities in theme and imagery you find between this poem and "To Marguerite—Continued" on page 838. (b) State the differences.

THINKING AND WRITING

Writing About a Victorian Poet

From what you know of Victorian society and of Arnold's career, which attitudes of the Victorian Age do you think his poem's reflect? Consider, among other things, the effects that industrialization and science had on nineteenth-century England—both positive and negative. Comment on the effects of such forces in an essay that identifies Arnold's place as a poet of his time. When you revise, make sure you have mentioned mood and theme in your treatment of the topic.

Answers

ANSWERS TO THINKING ABOUT THE SELECTION

Recalling

1. (a) He sees and hears the ebb and flow of the tide. (b) It brings in "the eternal note of sadness." (c) He says that Sophocles heard the sound.
2. It has retreated.
3. He describes the world as a place without joy, love, light, certitude, peace, or help for pain.

Interpreting

4. (a) They might stand for England itself, or for mankind. (b) This is the world stripped of its illusion. (c) Night here represents the darkness of reality.
5. (a) The metric structure and rhyme scheme of the poem are uneven, like the ebb and flow of the tides. (b) Suggested Response: They reflect the opposing forces upon which the poem focuses.
6. (a) It sums up Arnold's view of the current state of the world and contrasts sharply with the opening lines. (b) Suggested Response: The message is that the human race is in hopeless turmoil.

Applying

7. (a) Answers will differ. Students might note that this plea echoes the cry the speaker of "Self-Dependence" hears in his own heart at the end of that poem. (b) The solution breaks down inasmuch as honesty enables us to recognize, but not to deal with, the problems of the world delineated in the poem.
8. (a) Answers will differ. Students will note in particular the use of sea imagery and the conclusion that we are a race of lost and isolated souls. (b) The differences should include the views that "Dover Beach" is a more diffused and outwardly philosophical poem and that the metaphorical use of sea here (line 21) is much more direct.

Writing Across the Curriculum
As an alternative assignment, have students focus on the principles set down by Darwin and its effects on the artistic community in Victorian England at large. Science teachers may be able to aid students in conducting their research.

More About the Author At the age of sixteen Thomas Hardy was apprenticed to an architect. Following what for a time appeared to be his life's career path, he followed up this early training with formal study in London, ultimately winning a prize for his architectural work from the Royal Institute. What aspects of the study of architecture might prove useful to a writer and poet?

THOMAS HARDY

1840–1928

Both a novelist and a poet, Thomas Hardy is sometimes called "the last of the great Victorians." Like Matthew Arnold, Hardy held a pessimistic view of the world. In his great novels he depicted people striving against overwhelming odds within a society and universe that were uncaring. Unlike Arnold, however, who sought to improve society, Hardy remained a passive observer of the ills of his century; if he offered comfort at all, it was in the uncertain hope that the future would be at least different, if not better.

Thomas Hardy was born in Dorset, a region in southwest England noted for its agriculture and, perhaps more importantly, for its ruins which date to Anglo-Saxon and Roman times. This "Wessex," as Hardy fictionalized the region in his poems and novels, is the setting for the works that established Hardy's reputation as a writer. In *Far from the Madding Crowd* (1874), *The Return of the Native* (1878), *The Mayor of Casterbridge* (1886), *Tess of the D'Urbervilles* (1891), and his masterpiece, *Jude the Obscure* (1895), Hardy's characters move against a haunting landscape that is at once ancient and modern, starkly beautiful yet indifferent to the tragic lives of its inhabitants.

Despite the undeniable greatness of Hardy's novels, the bleak view they presented was distressing to a public who much preferred the life-affirming optimism of Tennyson and Browning. So intense, in fact, was the angry response to *Jude the Obscure* upon its publication that Hardy thought it wise to abandon the novel in favor of his first literary love, poetry. An epic verse drama about the Napoleonic Wars, *The Dynasts* (1904–1908), earned Hardy immense public acclaim. With each book of verse that he produced over the next two decades, his reputation as a man of letters grew. When he died, the world honored him by burying his ashes in the Poet's Corner of Westminster Abbey, though, as a token to the region that he loved, his heart was buried in Dorset.

Hardy's poetry marks a bridge between the Victorian Age and the Modernist movement of the twentieth century. In his use of strict meters and stanza structure, Hardy was unmistakably Victorian. One contemporary critic called him "the most fertile inventor of stanza-forms in all English literature." And yet, another critic, Leonard Woolf, viewed Hardy as one of the spiritual parents of the modern generation. Hardy's use of "nonpoetic" language and odd rhymes, coupled with his fatalistic outlook, were both source and inspiration to numerous twentieth-century writers, among them such important figures as Virginia Woolf, Siegfried Sassoon, and Robert Graves.

Objectives

1. To use similes and metaphors
2. To prepare an oral report on Wessex
3. To understand irony
4. To write a response to a poem

Teaching Portfolio: Support Material

Teacher Backup, pp. 00–00

Vocabulary Check, p. 00

Usage and Mechanics Worksheet, p. 00

Analyzing Literature Worksheet, p. 00

Critical Thinking and Reading Worksheet, p. 00

Language Worksheet, p. 00

Selection Test, p. 000

GUIDE FOR READING

The Darkling Thrush; The Man He Killed; "Ah, Are You Digging on My Grave?"

The Writer's Technique

Simile and Metaphor. A simile is a figure of speech that compares two unlike things, using an explicit word such as *like* or *as*. In "Love Among the Ruins," Robert Browning uses a simile to compare the towers on a castle to flames: ". . . the doomed and daring palace shot its spires/Up *like* fires. . . ." A metaphor is a figure of speech that compares two unlike things directly, without the use of an intervening word. In "London, 1802," William Wordsworth laments the sorrowful state of affairs in the England of his day by comparing the country metaphorically to a swamp: "England hath need of thee: she is a fen/Of stagnant waters. . . ." Poets use similes and metaphors to broaden the meanings of their images by making surprising connections between generally unrelated things and ideas.

The Writer's Technique

Irony. Irony is the intentional difference between expectation and reality in a poem or story. In *situational irony* the outcome of an event or situation is different from what the author has led the reader to predict. By using situational irony in "'Ah, Are You Digging on My Grave?,'' Hardy communicates an especially strong message to the reader.

Look For

As you read "The Darkling Thrush," look for the poet's use of similes and metaphors in his descriptions of the weather and landscape. As you read "'Ah, Are You Digging on My Grave?,'' look for the contrast between what the speaker believes to be the reason for the digging and the actual reason.

Writing

Write an account of an occasion when something relatively unimportant managed to change your mood entirely. Consider possibilities such as a beautiful flower growing through a crack in the pavement of a city sidewalk. Give details of how you felt before and after the mood-changing experience.

Vocabulary

Knowing the following words will help you as you read "The Darkling Thrush."

terrestrial (tə res'trē əl) *adj.*: Of the earth; worldly (p. 846, l. 27)

gaunt (gônt) *adj.*: Thin (p. 846, l. 21)

Literary Focus To clarify the notion of situational irony, give students examples of the phenomenon as it occurs in everyday life. Then ask them to come up with their own examples of situational irony.

Look For In order to help your **less advanced** students grasp the distinction between simile and metaphor, present them with a list of well-known similes—such as "busy as a bee"—and have them convert each to a metaphor—such as "a busy bee."

Writing If students are unable to come up with an actual example, ask them to invent an experience that fits the description of the assignment.

Vocabulary Make sure that your students are familiar with the following additional words from "The Darkling Thrush": *desolate, crypt,* and *fervorless.*

Motivation for Reading Have students discuss the idea of omens and portents, such as the belief that the groundhog's ability to see its shadow on February 2 ensures six more weeks of winter. Why do many people hold to such beliefs? What would life be like if everyone believed in exactly the same things?

Thematic Idea Another poem which deals with a message implicit in a bird's song is "To a Skylark" by Percy Bysshe Shelley, on page 718.

Purpose-Setting Question What change in the speaker's outlook does the song of the thrush bring about?

1 **Discussion** What seems to be the speaker's mood?

2 **Literary Focus** The simile in line 6 includes the phrase "broken lyres." Why is the image of a broken musical instrument especially fitting here?

3 **Enrichment** The word *haunted* is intended to mean both "roamed" and "wandered gloomily, like a ghost."

4 **Literary Focus** What figures of speech are used in these lines?

5 **Clarification** *Illimited* is an alternate form of the word *unlimited.*

6 **Discussion** What has brought about the change in the speaker's mood?

7 **Discussion** Would you describe this ending as optimistic? Why or why not?

The Darkling[1] Thrush

Thomas Hardy

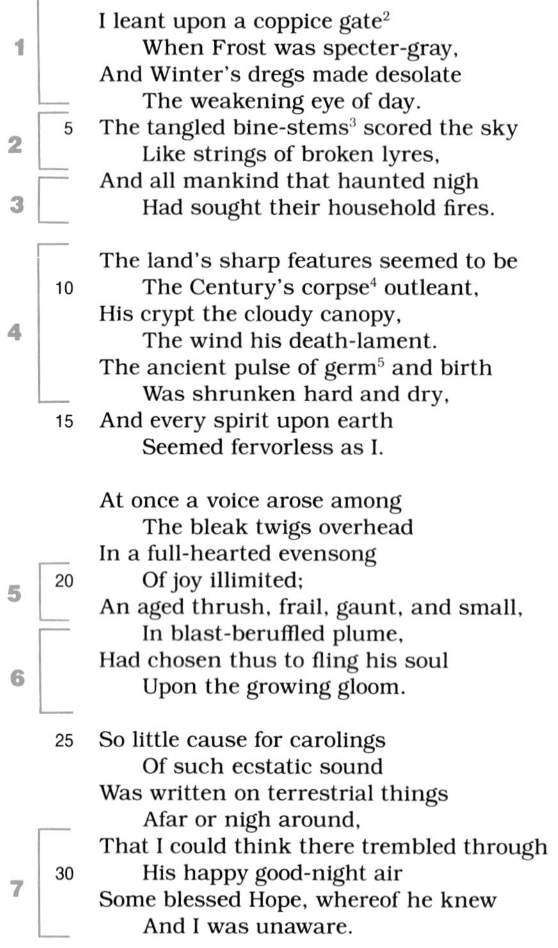

1 I leant upon a coppice gate[2]
When Frost was specter-gray,
And Winter's dregs made desolate
The weakening eye of day.
2 The tangled bine-stems[3] scored the sky
Like strings of broken lyres,
3 And all mankind that haunted nigh
Had sought their household fires.

4 The land's sharp features seemed to be
The Century's corpse[4] outleant,
His crypt the cloudy canopy,
The wind his death-lament.
The ancient pulse of germ[5] and birth
Was shrunken hard and dry,
And every spirit upon earth
Seemed fervorless as I.

At once a voice arose among
The bleak twigs overhead
In a full-hearted evensong
5 Of joy illimited;
An aged thrush, frail, gaunt, and small,
6 In blast-beruffled plume,
Had chosen thus to fling his soul
Upon the growing gloom.

So little cause for carolings
Of such ecstatic sound
Was written on terrestrial things
Afar or nigh around,
7 That I could think there trembled through
His happy good-night air
Some blessed Hope, whereof he knew
And I was unaware.

1. **darkling** *adj.*: In the dark.
2. **coppice** (kop′ is) **gate:** Gate leading to a thicket, or small wood.
3. **bine-stems:** Twining stems.
4. **Century's corpse:** This poem was written on December 31, 1900, the last day of the nineteenth century.
5. **germ:** Seed or bud.

THINKING ABOUT THE SELECTION

Recalling

1. In what season of the year and at what time of day is the poem set?
2. What do the "land's sharp features" suggest to the speaker?
3. (a) What does the speaker suddenly hear in the third stanza? (b) What does the speaker think about as a result of this experience?

Interpreting

4. (a) What mood does the poet establish in the first two stanzas? (b) What images contribute to this mood? (c) With what does the poet contrast these images in the last two stanzas?
5. (a) Why do you think the poet characterizes the thrush as he does in lines 21–22? (b) What might the thrush symbolize?

Applying

6. Depressed people react in different ways to others who display "joys illimited." The poem describes one possible reaction. What are some other possibilities?
7. Reread "To a Skylark" by Shelley on page 000. (a) What similarities are evident in the speaker's response to the thrush in this poem? (b) What differences do you detect?

ANALYZING LITERATURE

Using Simile and Metaphor

A **simile** is a figure of speech that compares basically dissimilar things, using such connective words as *like* or *as.* Consider the following simile from Tennyson's "The Lotos-Eaters," which makes use of the connective word *than:* "There is sweet music here that softer falls/Than petals from blown roses on the grass. . . ." A **metaphor** compares basically dissimilar things as well, but without the use of a connective word. When, again in "The Lotos-Eaters," Tennyson refers to the ocean as "fields of barren foam," he is speaking in metaphorical terms. Similes and metaphors are used by poets to heighten the meanings of their images.

1. Identify each of the following italicized images from "The Darkling Thrush" as either a simile or a metaphor. Tell what two objects are being compared in each case.
   a. Winter's *dregs* made desolate/The *weakening eye of day.* (Lines 3–4)
   b. The tangled bine-stems *scored* the sky/ Like *strings of broken lyres. . . .* (Lines 5–6)
   c. An aged thrush . . . /Had chosen to *fling his soul*/Upon the *growing gloom.* (Lines 21–24)
2. To what are the land's sharp features compared in lines 9–11? Explain why this metaphor is especially appropriate for the time and place in which the poem is set.

SPEAKING AND LISTENING

Preparing an Oral Report on Wessex

Hardy's novels and many of his poems are set in "Wessex," his fictional name for the Dorset countryside that he loved. Using reference books, biographies of Hardy, histories of the Victorian Age, and Hardy's own works, prepare a five-to-ten-minute oral report on some aspect of Hardy's Wessex. You might consider one of the following topics:

a. the geography of Wessex (Dorset)
b. the history of the region (prehistoric, Roman, Anglo-Saxon)
c. Wessex life in Victorian times
d. Wessex as depicted in Hardy's works

Answers

ANSWERS TO THINKING ABOUT THE SELECTION

Recalling

1. It is wintertime and toward the close of day.
2. They suggest the corpose of the century laid out.
3. (a) He hears a thrush overhead. (b) He speculates on whether there is perhaps some hope in store.

Interpreting

4. (a) The mood is one of unrelieved gloom and pessimism. (b) Students might note such death-related images as "specter" and such decay-related images as "dregs," "weakening," and "tangled." (c) He contrasts them with slightly more upbeat images—"carolings" and "happy good-night air."
5. (a) Answers will differ. Students will perhaps note that this adds to the irony of the bird's song. (b) Suggested Response: The bird might symbolize the indomitability of the human spirit even in the most cheerless of times.

Applying

6. Answers will differ. Students may be acquainted with the tendency in some persons to bristle and lash out angrily at good cheer in others when their own spirits are low. Yet another possibility is that of a lapse still further into a depressed state.
7. (a) As in Shelley's poem, the speaker here is looking for a cause for at least guarded optimism. (b) The optimism in Shelley's poem is more direct and heartfelt, as though it were that of the poet himself.

ANSWERS TO ANALYZING LITERATURE

1. (a) The first is a metaphor comparing the end of a winter's day to dregs of wine; the second is a metaphor comparing the end of day to an eye losing its sight.
   (b) The first is a metaphor comparing the appearance of a network of twigs against the sky to the sky's having been crisscrossed or scored; the second is a simile comparing the above effect to the disconnected strings of a broken instrument.
   (c) The first is a metaphor comparing the act of singing to the flinging of a soul; the second is a metaphor comparing the oncoming darkness of day to increasing gloom.
2. They are compared respectively to a corpse, a crypt, and a dirge. The metaphors are apt insofar as the century is gloomily and unceremoniously winding down.

The Man He Killed

Thomas Hardy

"Had he and I but met
By some old ancient inn,
1 We should have sat us down to wet
Right many a nipperkin![1]

"But ranged as infantry,
And staring face to face,
I shot at him as he at me,
And killed him in his place.

2 "I shot him dead because—
Because he was my foe,
Just so: my foe of course he was;
That's clear enough; although

"He thought he'd 'list,[2] perhaps,
Off-hand like—just as I—
3 Was out of work—had sold his traps—
No other reason why.

"Yes; quaint and curious war is!
You shoot a fellow down
You'd treat if met where any bar is,
Or help to half-a-crown."[3]

---

1. **nipperkin** *n.*: A small glass for beer or wine.
2. **'list:** Enlist.
3. **half-a-crown:** A British coin.

Motivation for Reading Write the expression "All's fair in love and war" on the board. Ask if students have ever heard this expression. Do students find the saying true? Are there some aspects of war that strike them as blatantly unfair? What other expressions do they know of that comment on war?

Master Teacher Note Distribute among your students a photograph of the *Marseillaise,* the sculpture by François Rude that crowns the Arc de Triomphe in Paris. (One appears on page 487 of H. W. Janson's *History of Art,* Prentice-Hall/Abrams.) Tell your students that this represents soldiers marching off to war, urged on by the Genius of Liberty, the figure at the top. Ask them whether this gives a realistic image of war. What problems arise out of the glorification of war?

Thematic Idea Another poem depicts the horrors of war is Stephen Spender's "What I Expected," page 1108.

Purpose-Setting Question What attitude toward war does the poem express?

1 **Discussion** What impression do you have of the age of the speaker? Of the other man? Why?

2 **Discussion** How would you describe the speaker's tone?

3 **Discussion** What was the speaker's reason for enlisting? How does this add to the poem's irony?

THINKING ABOUT THE SELECTION

Recalling

1. (a) What does the speaker suggest might have happened had he and the other man met "by some old ancient inn"? (b) Where did they meet instead? (c) What happened?
2. What similarities between himself and the other man does the speaker note in lines 13–16?

Interpreting

3. (a) What do you think is the significance of the quotation marks in each stanza? (b) Who do you suppose the speaker is? (c) To whom do you think the poem is addressed?
4. Why do you think the speaker hesitates at the end of line 9?
5. (a) What point about the nature of war is Hardy making in this poem? (b) In what way is war "quaint and curious," as his speaker notes in line 17?
6. Do you think Hardy is writing about a specific war or about war in general? Explain your answer.

Applying

7. Why is it easier for an enemy to be faceless than to have a face?

AT THE WINDOW, 1960
Jacob Kainen

Answers

ANSWERS TO THINKING ABOUT THE SELECTION

Recalling

1. (a) They might have shared some refreshment together. (b) They met on the battlefield. (c) The speaker shot and killed the other man.
2. Both enlisted on an offhand manner; neither was a patriot.

Interpreting

3. (a) They indicate that the words are spoken by a character, not the poet. (b) The speaker is a soldier. (c) It is addressed to the world at large, to express the speaker's casual—and the poet's all-consuming—horror over this event.
4. Students will observe that the speaker needs to remind himself —or persuade himself—of the rationale behind his wanton act. The hesitation also adds a natural lifelike quality to the narration.
5. (a) Suggested Response: He is pointing up the absurdity of a disagreement between major powers manifesting itself in the loss of innocent lives. (b) Suggested Response: War might be thought of as "quaint" because it often involves young, inexperienced people; it might be thought of as "curious" because these innocents are often the casualties.
6. Suggested Response: He is writing about war in general.

Applying

7. (a) Suggested Response: It is easier for the enemy to be faceless, because it makes it seem as if the deaths of enemy soldiers are in some way unreal.

Humanities Note

Fine art: *At The Window,* 1960, by Jacob Kainen. The American painter and graphic artist Jacob Kainen was born in 1909. Kainen felt his most valuable education came from association with other artists. As curator of the Department of Prints and Drawings of the National Collection of Fine Arts, he single-handedly built and expanded this collection during his twenty years in the position.

As a painter, Jacob Kainen has worked in many styles. *At the Window* is a figural abstraction. The painting is an amalgam of loose geometric shapes that represent a room, a window, and a man. The colors have no correspondence to reality but were used for their emotional impact on the viewer. The mood of the painting is one of depression, created in part by the prevalent low intensity blue. The unifying element in this and all of Kainen's work is the value uniformity of the colors.

Consider these questions for discussion:

1. What is the mood or effect of this painting?
2. In what ways does it illustrate "The Man He Killed"?

Motivation for Reading Ask students to describe, without naming names, the characteristics shared by most vain people. What makes people vain? Is vanity an easy flaw to correct? How do most people feel toward others who are vain?

Thematic Idea Another poem that explores the subject of human vanity is "To a Louse" by Robert Burns, page 611.

Purpose-Setting Question What is the unexpected answer to the title question of the poem?

1 **Reading Strategy** Caution students to pay strict attention to opening and closing quotation marks, signaling a change in speakers.

2 **Reading Strategy** Have students note that two key possibilities have now been eliminated. Are they able to identify the speaker?

3 **Clarification** The word *tendance,* an alternate form of *tending,* means "the acting of maintaining, as a garden."

4 **Discussion** Is it a natural state of affairs to have enemies? If not, what does this perhaps suggest about the deceased?

5 **Discussion** What other popular expression are you aware of that summarized this sentiment?

"Ah, Are You Digging on My Grave?"

Thomas Hardy

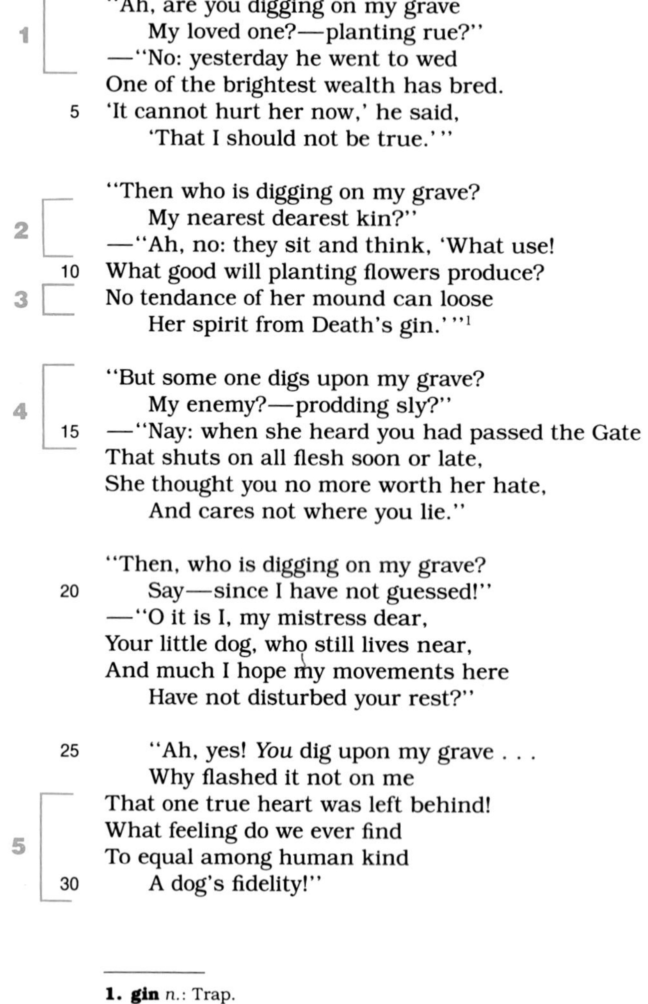

"Ah, are you digging on my grave
1 My loved one?—planting rue?"
—"No: yesterday he went to wed
One of the brightest wealth has bred.
'It cannot hurt her now,' he said,
'That I should not be true.' "

"Then who is digging on my grave?
2 My nearest dearest kin?"
—"Ah, no: they sit and think, 'What use!
What good will planting flowers produce?
3 No tendance of her mound can loose
Her spirit from Death's gin.' "[1]

"But some one digs upon my grave?
4 My enemy?—prodding sly?"
—"Nay: when she heard you had passed the Gate
That shuts on all flesh soon or late,
She thought you no more worth her hate,
And cares not where you lie."

"Then, who is digging on my grave?
Say—since I have not guessed!"
—"O it is I, my mistress dear,
Your little dog, who still lives near,
And much I hope my movements here
Have not disturbed your rest?"

"Ah, yes! *You* dig upon my grave . . .
Why flashed it not on me
That one true heart was left behind!
What feeling do we ever find
5 To equal among human kind
A dog's fidelity!"

1. **gin** *n.*: Trap.

"Mistress, I dug upon your grave
To bury a bone, in case
I should be hungry near this spot
When passing on my daily trot.
I am sorry, but I quite forgot
It was your resting-place."

THINKING ABOUT THE SELECTION

Recalling

1. (a) In the first stanza, who does the dead woman suspect is digging on her grave? (b) In the second stanza? (c) In the third stanza? (d) What response does she receive?
2. (a) Who in fact is doing the digging? (b) How does the woman react when she learns the answer to this question? (c) What reason does the digger give for disturbing the grave?

Interpreting

3. (a) At what point do you begin to suspect the identity of the voice responding to the woman's questions? (b) What effect does Hardy achieve by withholding this information?
4. (a) What mood does Hardy create by having a dead person speak? (b) How does this mood change once the digger is identified?
5. What point about human vanity and self-esteem is Hardy making in this poem?

Applying

6. (a) Of "The Darkling Thrush," "The Man He Killed," and this poem, which strikes you as the most pessimistic? (b) The least pessimistic? (c) Why?

ANALYZING LITERATURE

Understanding Irony

Irony is a purposeful contrast between expectation and reality. In "'Ah, Are You Digging on My Grave?'" Hardy uses situational irony. That is, he leads the reader to expect one kind of outcome but instead delivers another.

1. What is ironic about the voice in the last four lines of each of the first three stanzas?
2. What emotions does the dead woman express when she learns the identity of the digger? How do the digger's final words ironically alter the woman's emotional expectations?
3. Irony is often related to tone—the author's attitude toward the subject or audience. Explain how the irony in this poem is related to Hardy's pessimism and lack of sentimentality.

THINKING AND WRITING

Writing a Response to a Poem

In "'Ah, Are You Digging on My Grave?'" Hardy delivers pessimistic pronouncements on two different but related topics—human self-worth and human apathy. Consider your reaction to Hardy's views on these subjects by asking yourself questions such as the following. To what extent are Hardy's attitudes typical only of the era in which he lived? To what degree are tributes to the dead really tributes to the living? How thoroughly do we know the feelings others have toward us? How well do we understand our own feelings toward others? In an essay, sum up your response to the views Hardy presents. When you revise, make sure you have provided adequate support for your opinion.

Answers

ANSWERS TO THINKING ABOUT THE SELECTION

Recalling

1. (a) She believes it is her widower. (b) She believes it is her relatives. (c) She believes it is her enemy. (d) The response each time is negative.
2. (a) The digger is her dog. (b) She responds in essence that a dog is more loyal than any human. (c) The dog replies that it was burying a bone and quite forgot that this was his mistress's grave site.

Interpreting

3. (a) Answers will differ. Students may comment that they first begin to suspect the identity of the voice in the third stanza. (b) He builds suspense and creates humor.
4. (a) Suggested Response: He creates a mock-melancholic mood. (b) By the time the digger's identity is made known, any pretense of mourning has been cast aside.
5. Suggested Response: People are never as important as they think they are.

Applying

6. Answers will differ depending on particular tastes and emotional reactions. The majority of the students will probably name "The Darkling Thrust" as most pessimistic because of its somber air, and "'Ah, Are You Digging on My Grave'" as least pessimistic because of its humor.

ANSWERS TO ANALYZING LITERATURE

1. The irony is that the voice is a dog—the very last soul, literally, that the dead woman might guess.
2. She seems consoled slightly that at least someone might mourn her. Her expectations are overturned when it is revealed that not even the dog has remembered her.
3. The irony is a function of Hardy's outlook. It thus stands to reason that the tone of a poem treating the subject of vanity will have a mocking, scornful tone.

THINKING AND WRITING

After students have completed their compositions, divide them into groups and have them read their rough drafts to one another and suggest ways in which they could be improved.

More About the Author As a student and, later, as a teacher, Gerard Manley Hopkins was a stickler for detail and organization. Intolerant of his own limitations, and even more so of those in others, he found it difficult to make and keep friends. How can such personality traits harm a writer? How can they help a writer?

GERARD MANLEY HOPKINS

1844–1889

Though Gerard Manley Hopkins saw none of his work published during his lifetime, he was nevertheless the most innovative poet of the Victorian Age. Born in Essex, just outside of London, Hopkins was the oldest of nine children in a well-educated and prosperous family. While still in grammar school, Hopkins began writing poetry, a practice that he maintained throughout his years at Oxford, where he also studied the classics.

It was during his third year at Oxford that Hopkins decided to become a Catholic, much to the dismay of his parents, who were devout Anglicans. Upon being accepted into the Society of Jesus in 1868, he symbolically burned his early poems, resolving "to write no more." Though he remained true to his word for the next seven years, Hopkins continued to keep detailed notebooks—as he had done ever since childhood—that recorded his fascination with words and his love of nature.

In 1874, as part of his preparation for the priesthood, Hopkins went to St. Bueno's College in Wales to study theology. There he learned to speak Welsh. He also began again to write poetry, though of a sort that was different not only from his earlier verse but from anything ever before done in English. Encouraged by a Jesuit superior, Hopkins wrote a long poem about a tragic shipwreck in which five nuns had drowned. "The Wreck of the Deutschland," apart from the great emotional power packed into it, was the first poem in which Hopkins used what he called "sprung rhythm." This was a technique that unleashed a flood of imagery by discarding certain "unnecessary" sentence parts, such as prepositions and conjunctions. Despite the intensity of the feeling behind the words, the Jesuit magazine rejected the poem.

In 1877, the year he was ordained a priest, Hopkins wrote some of his best and best-known poems, including "God's Grandeur," "Pied Beauty," and "Hurrahing in Harvest." Like most of Hopkins's poems, the goal of these was to reveal and glorify the individual essence—or "inscape," as he called it—of everything in nature.

Hopkins served as a parish priest and missionary preacher among the poor in London, Liverpool, and Glasgow. Despite his total dedication to his calling, long hours and a tendency toward perfectionism left him depressed and in poor health. He died of typhoid fever one month before his forty-fifth birthday.

Objectives

1. To write a reply by a character in a poem

Teaching Portfolio: Support Material

Teacher Backup, p. 000

Vocabulary Check, p. 00

Usage and Mechanics Worksheet, p. 00

Analyzing Literature Worksheet, p. 00

Critical Thinking and Reading Worksheet, p. 00

Language Worksheet, p. 00

Selection Test, p. 000

GUIDE FOR READING

God's Grandeur; Hurrahing the Harvest; Pied Beauty; Spring and Fall

The Writer's Technique

Rhythm and Rhyme. Rhythm is the pattern of stressed and unstressed syllables in a line of poetry. Every poem has rhythm, but not every poem has meter, a regular, predictable rhythmic pattern made up of units called "feet." Each foot consists of one stressed syllable and a fixed number of unstressed syllables. In the 1870's, Gerard Manley Hopkins created a new kind of rhythm that resembled natural speech. In *sprung rhythm,* as Hopkins termed his creation, the number of unstressed syllables varies from foot to foot. Precisely which syllables received stress, moreover, is not accidental but carefully planned to help convey meaning and emotion. Finally, sprung rhythm calls for the innovative use of language, for the combining of existing words, the extending of word meanings, the invention of new words, and the elimination of words that do not add to the desired effect. As applied by Hopkins, the rules of sprung rhythm often produced startling and remarkably original results.

Rhyme is the repetition of the same or similar sounds in two or more words. When rhyme occurs at the ends of lines in a poem it is called "end rhyme." When rhyme occurs within a single line it is called "internal rhyme." Again breaking with tradition, Hopkins used both types of rhyme, as well as "approximate rhyme," or rhyme that relates words similar in function or meaning.

Look For

As you read, look for the use of sprung rhythm and curious rhymes to enhance the meaning and emotion in each poem.

Writing

Write the name of a prized possession, much-loved pastime, or favorite season at the top of a sheet of paper. Taking your cue to begin from someone with a watch, write whatever words and phrases come to mind for a period of at least two minutes. When you are told to stop, read over what you have written. Note phrases and words whose *sounds* seem to relate to your topic.

Vocabulary

Knowing the following words will help you as you read.

barbarous (bär'bər əs) *adj.*: Primitive; uncivilized (p. 857, l. 1)

azurous (az'ər əs) *adj.*: Purple-blue (p. 857, l. 9)

dappled (dap''ld) *adj.*: Speckled; having more than one color (p. 858, l. 1)

fickle (fik''l) *adj.*: Unfaithful (p. 858, l. 8)

blight (blīt) *n.*: Condition of withering (p. 859, l. 15)

Literary Focus Inform students that, in a number of his poems, Hopkins added accent marks to show which syllables receive stress.

Look For Exemplify approximate or slant rhyme by having students read several poems by Emily Dickinson, including "I Never Saw a Moor." Have them note, in particular, the slant rhymes "Heaven" and "given."

Writing After students have completed the assignment, have them compare results. Students whose lists seem less creative should be encouraged to make another attempt.

Vocabulary Your **less advanced** students might work in groups when learning these vocabulary words.

Motivation for Reading Have students ponder the question of what the planet earth would be like if the human species had never come to inhabit it. In what ways would the planet be worse off? In what ways would it be better off? What tolls has human industry exacted on our planet? Who are the victims?

Master Teacher Note Make available to your students a photograph of the detail of the ceiling of the Sistine Chapel that depicts God's creation of Adam. (One appears on page 360 of H. W. Janson's *History of Art,* Prentice-Hall/Abrams.) Ask students to look carefully at the photo to determine what is happening. Have them note that the finger of God is not quite touching that of Adam. Ask them what significance might be attached to this detail.

Thematic Idea Another poem that celebrates the wonder and mystique of God's creation is "The Tiger" by William Blake, on page 622.

Purpose-Setting Question How does God's grandeur make itself felt?

1 **Discussion** What force of nature do you normally associate with the word *charge?* What is the effect of the word here?

2 **Literary Focus** What is the rhyme scheme of the first stanza?

3 **Discussion** How might you express the sentiment of lines 8–9 in your own words?

4 **Enrichment** This poem is a sonnet. Have students review the form and content of other sonnets they have read. In what ways is this one different?

God's Grandeur

Gerard Manley Hopkins

1 The world is charged with the grandeur of God.
It will flame out, like shining from shook foil;[1]
It gathers to a greatness, like the ooze of oil
Crushed.[2] Why do men then not reck his rod?[3]
2 Generations have trod, have trod, have trod;
And all is seared with trade; bleared, smeared with toil;
And wears man's smudge and shares man's smell: the soil
Is bare now, nor can foot feel, being shod.

3 And for all this, nature is never spent;
There lives the dearest freshness deep down things;
And though the last lights off the black West went
Oh, morning, at the brown brink eastward, springs—
Because the Holy Ghost over the bent
4 World broods with warm breast and with ah! bright wings.

1. **foil** *n.*: Tinsel.
2. **crushed:** Squeezed from olives.
3. **reck his rod:** Heed God's authority.

THINKING ABOUT THE SELECTION

1. According to this poem, with what is the world charged?

Recalling

2. (a) According to lines 5–8, what has humankind done to God's grandeur? (b) According to line 9, what difference has man's behavior made? Explain.
3. (a) What is the Holy Ghost compared to in the last two lines? (b) What verb describes what it does? (c) What two adjectives describe it?

Interpreting

4. What kind of emotional response do you suppose Hopkins hoped to awaken in the reader of lines 1–4? Do you think he succeeds?
5. What do you think is the meaning of the question raised in line 4?
6. (a) What effect do you think the poet hoped to achieve by the repetition in line 5? (b) By the alliteration, or consonant repetition, of *sm* in lines 6–7?

Answers

ANSWERS TO THINKING ABOUT THE SELECTION

Recalling

1. The world is charged with the "grandeur of God."
2. (a) We have trod and smeared it. (b) In spite of our incursions, God's grandeur is undiminished, since, as is stated in line 9, "nature is never spent."
3. (a) It is compared to a great bird. (b) The verb *broods* is used. (c) The adjectives *warm* and *bright* are used.

Interpreting

4. Suggested Response: He is trying to awaken a sense of awe and admiration.
5. Suggested Response: He is asking why, considering the omnipotence of God, we do not heed his word.

BIRD'S NEST
Ros W. Jenkins
Warrington Museum and Art Gallery

7. "God's Grandeur" is a sonnet, a poetic form with very specific rhyme requirements. Note, for instance, the number of words rhyming with *God* and *foil* in the first eight lines.
   (a) Why do you suppose Hopkins chose so rigid a poetic form for this poem? In what way does the form reinforce his message? (b) What effect do you think Hopkins wanted to achieve by the sounds of the words *ooze, oil,* and *crushed* in lines 3 and 4? By the repetition of *d* sounds in line 10? Of *b* sounds in the last two lines?

Applying

8. (a) Although Hopkins notes many abuses in this poem, do you think his overall outlook is optimistic or pessimistic? Explain. (b) How would you define the difference between an optimist and a pessimist?

Humanities Note

Fine art, *Bird's Nest,* by Ros. W. Jenkins. Ros. W. Jenkins was a British watercolorist of the Victorian era. In his painting, *Bird's Nest,* Jenkins was influenced by the works of the British painter William Henry Hunt. Jenkin's employs Hunt's technique of building up layers of pure color and then creating detail with a method of stippling (applying dots of color) and crosshatching (using a grid of intersecting lines to create texture). This technique produces a beautifully textured and realistically colored effect. The influence of the Pre-Raphaelite Movement (artists who sought a return in painting to the purity of the middle ages) is also apparent in this work. Jenkins employs the Pre-Raphaelite precepts of truth to nature and intense detail. Decorative paintings such as this depiction of bird's nests filled with eggs resting on a forest floor, were a great delight to the Victorians and were likely to be found prominently displayed in an ornate parlor.

You might ask your students these questions:

1. How does this artist regard nature?
2. How does this painting reflect Hopkins's ideas in "God's Grandeur"?

6. (a) Suggested Response: The repetition almost carries the sense of the soil being trampled underfoot. (b) Suggested Response: Again, the repetition of the *sm* sounds carries the suggestion of smudging or smearing.
7. (a) Suggested Response: The form reflects the dignity of the poem's message. (b) Suggested Response: In each case the repetition of sound echoes the image being created.

Applying

8. (a) Answers will differ. Students will perhaps feel for the most part that the poem is optimistic. (b) Suggested Response: An optimist is a person who looks for the positive side of a situation, while a pessimist looks for the negative side.

Challenge Do you find the image of God implied in the first several lines of the poem inconsistent with that presented in the last two lines? Why or why not?

Humanities Note

Fine Art, *Harvest Field with Gleaners* by George Robert Lewis. Lewis (1782–1871) was an English portrait, genre, and landscape painter. He studied at the School of the Royal Academy, in London. He made his living painting portraits and illustrating travel books with descriptive landscape aquatints (an etching process that produces prints that look like watercolor paintings).

Harvest Field With Gleaners, Haywood, Herefordshire (1815), was painted in an area of England where Lewis completed many works. He shows the earth yielding its bounty to sturdy English peasants. A versatile artist, Lewis demonstrates in this work his narrative skill and his enthusiasm for nature.

You may wish to use the following questions for discussion:

1. What do you think are the artist's feelings about the bounty of nature?
2. How do the artist's feelings compare to those of Hopkins about the bounty of nature?

THINKING ABOUT THE SELECTION

Recalling

1. (a) In line 4, what does the speaker see on the ground? (b) In the sky? (c) How are these two things alike for the speaker?
2 (a) What does the speaker do in line 5? (b) What does he see?
3. According to the last stanza, what happens to someone who beholds nature's beauties?

Interpreting

4. How would you describe the speaker's emotional state in the poem? Support your answer

Answers

ANSWERS TO THINKING ABOUT THE SELECTION

Recalling

1. (a) He sees stacks of drying corn on the ground. (b) He sees fluffy clouds in the sky. (c) Both hold exquisite beauty for him.
2. (a) He walks and lifts up his heart and eyes. (b) He takes in the beauty that God has provided.
3. It knocks such a person off his or her feet.

Interpreting

4. Students will use such terms as *happy, ecstatic, delighted, rapturous.* Students might cite, among other possibilities, the exclamation in line 2, his rhetorical questions in lines 3–4, and lines 7–8.
5. The question here, like that in lines 3–4, is a rhetorical one. One possible paraphrase students might offer is: What greeting by a loved one could be more exhilarating to the senses than this one?
6. (a) The reference is to the observer of nature's bounty. (b) Students might paraphrase what is happening with the well-known expression: The person is being "knocked off his feet."

Applying

7. (a) Students should recall that the

Hurrahing in Harvest 1

Gerard Manley Hopkins

Summer ends now; now, barbarous in beauty, the stoks[1]
  arise 2
    Around; up above, what wind-walks! what lovely
      behavior 3
    Of silk-sack clouds! has wilder, wilful-wavier
Meal-drift molded ever and melted across skies? 4

I walk, I lift up, I lift up heart, eyes,
    Down all that glory in the heavens to glean our Savior;
    And, éyes, héart, what looks, what lips yet gave you a 5
Rapturous love's greeting of realer, of rounder replies?

And the azurous hung hills are his world-wielding shoulder
    Majestic—as a stallion stalwart, very-violet-sweet!—
These things, these things were here and but the beholder
    Wanting; which two when they once meet, 6
The heart rears wings bold and bolder
    And hurls for him, O half hurls earth for him off under
      his feet.

1. **stoks** *n.*: Sheaves of corn stacked together on end to dry.

HARVEST FIELD WITH GLEANERS, HAYWOOD, HEREFORDSHIRE
George Robert Lewis
The Tate Gallery, London

---

with quotations.

5. In your own words, what question does the speaker ask in lines 7–8?
6. (a) Who is "him" in line 14? (b) What does the speaker say is happening to "him?"

Applying

7. (a) In what ways is this poem more typical of the Romantic than the Victorian period? (b) In what ways is it typical of neither?

Motivation for Reading Ask students what the term *harvest* conjures up in their minds? At what time of year does harvesting take place? Where does it take place? What is harvested? What colors does the word summon up? Finally ask them what kind of mood they would expect in a poem that conveys the poet's impressions of the harvest.

Thematic Idea Another selection that pays homage to the fall is "To Autumn" by John Keats, on page 739.

Purpose-Setting Question What is the speaker celebrating?

1 **Critical Thinking and Reading** The title, like many of the lines of the poem, contains alliteration.

2 **Discussion** Where is the speaker located?

3 **Critical Thinking and Reading** What do you think the speaker means by "wind-walks"? Why is this an especially effective image?

4 **Clarification** The question here is a rhetorical one: The speaker is not expecting a reply.

5 **Discussion** Why is the word *glean* particularly appropriate here?

6 **Clarification** The syntax of these lines may be confusing to the students. Explain that "and but the beholder/Wanting" means "all that was missing was someone to behold these things."

Romantics extolled the virtues of nature, unlike the Victorians who often wrote of doom and gloom. (b) The poem is typical of neither in its use of invented words and a highly personalized syntax.

Challenge How many examples of alliteration can the students come up with?

Master Teacher Note Procure a copy of the etching by Dutch graphic artist M. C. Escher titled *Day and Night* and make it available to the class. (A reproduction of the woodcut appears on page 252 of Douglas R. Hofstadter's Pulitzer Prize-winning book *Gödel, Escher, Bach: An Eternal Braid,* Basic Books, New York, 1970.) Ask for student commentary on the artwork, whose background and foreground of flying birds meld into one another. What does the work suggest to them about life? About nature?

Thematic Idea Another poem that deals with the inexplicable contrasts in nature is "The Tiger" by William Blake, page 622.

Purpose-Setting Question What comment is the speaker offering on the subject of variety?

1 **Clarification** The word *pied* means "having blotches in two or more colors."

2 **Discussion** What is the speaker asking for in this poem?

3 **Discussion** What change in emotion is evident between the first stanza and these lines?

1 # Pied Beauty

Gerard Manley Hopkins

2 Glory be to God for dappled things—
For skies of couple-color as a brinded[1] cow;
For rose-moles all in stipple[2] upon trout that swim;
Fresh-firecoal chestnut-falls;[3] finches' wings;
Landscape plotted and pieced—fold, fallow, and plow;
And áll trádes, their gear and tackle and trim.

3 All things counter,[4] original, spare, strange;
Whatever is fickle, freckled (who knows how?)
With swift, slow; sweet, sour; adazzle, dim;
He fathers-forth whose beauty is past change:
Praise him.

1. **brinded** *adj.*: Having a gray or tawny coat streaked with a darker color.
2. **stipple** *n.*: Dots or small spots.
3. **fresh-firecoal chestnut-falls:** Roasted chestnuts.
4. **counter:** Contrary.

THINKING ABOUT THE SELECTION

Recalling

1. What five "dappled things" does the speaker name in the first five lines?
2. What does the speaker ask the reader to do in line 11?

Interpreting

3. (a) What do you think is the meaning of "couple-color" in line 2? (b) Why do you think Hopkins chose this, rather than a more conventional way, of expressing the thought?
4. What difference can you see between the "dappled things" of the first stanza and the sorts of things hinted at in the second?
5. What significance do you attach to meaning of the words in parentheses in line 8?
6. What do you think is meant by the phrase "whose beauty is past change" in line 10?

Applying

7. Compare "Pied Beauty" with "God's Grandeur." (a) In what ways are the two poems similar? (b) How are they different in their outlook on the world as altered by humans? (c) How might Hopkins have explained this apparent paradox, or self-contradiction.

Answers

ANSWERS TO THINKING ABOUT THE SELECTION

Recalling

1. He mentions skies, trout, finches, plowed fields, and all trades.
2. He is asking us, in hymn fashion, to praise the Lord.

Interpreting

3. (a) The meaning of this inverted term is clearly "having two colors." (b) Students will observe that this is yet another instance of the poet's beloved alliteration.
4. The items in the second stanza are of a more abstract nature—they are simply traits.
5. Students might suggest that the poet is expressing his wonderment in these words.
6. The indication is that God is a constant, unchanging force.

Applying

7. (a) Both poems, students will note, celebrate the natural beauty God has produced. (b) Whereas "God's Grandeur" laments the way in which humans have "bleared and smeared" the landscape with their toils, "Pied Beauty" celebrates "all trades" in line 6. (c) The paradox may be understood if we accept that "Pied Beauty" is merely a less specific poem. Rather than dwell on humans' incursions on God's grandeur, the poem accepts the good along with the bad ("whatever is fickle . . . sour") as manifestations of God's greatness.

Spring and Fall
To a Young Child
Gerard Manley Hopkins

Márgarét, you are grieving
Over Goldengrove unleaving?
Leáves, like the things of man, you
With your fresh thoughts care for, can you?
Ah! ás the heart grows older
It will come to such sights colder
By and by, nor spare a sigh
Though worlds of wanwood[1] leafmeal[2] lie;
And yet you will weep and know why.
Now no matter, child, the name:
1 Sórrow's springs áre the same.
Nor mouth had, no nor mind, expressed
What heart heard of, ghost[3] guessed:
2 It is the blight man was born for,
It is Margaret you mourn for.

1. **wanwood** (wän′ wood): Pale wood.
2. **leafmeal:** Ground-up decomposed leaves.
3. **ghost:** Spirit.

A MOTHER AND CHILD ON THE ISLE OF WIGHT
James Collinson
Yale Center for British Art

THINKING ABOUT THE SELECTION
Recalling

1. According to the speaker, in what way will Margaret change as she grows older?

Interpreting

2. What do you think is meant by "fresh thoughts" in line 4? By "worlds of wanwood leafmeal" in line 8?
3. What is the theme?

Applying

4. (a) What is the relevance of the title "Spring and Fall?" (b) What might "spring" stand for? (c) What second meaning of "fall" might be relevant to the speaker's advice to the child?

THINKING AND WRITING
Writing Margaret's Reply

Imagine that you are Margaret. Try to put yourself in the position of a child who has just suffered a grave disappointment over something an adult would find trivial. Now write a response to the adult speaker of "Spring and Fall" that gives the child's view of the world and defends the child's right to his or her feelings, however inappropriate they might seem to an adult. Your response may take the form of either a poem or prose piece, but it should offer some insight on how children view the world of grownups.

Humanities Note

Fine art, *A Mother and Child on the Isle of Wight* by James Collinson. Collinson (1825–1881) was a British painter. He studied at the Schools of the Royal Academy. He was one of the seven original members of the Pre-Raphaelite Brotherhood, a group of English artists who rebelled against the rules of the academy and sought a return in painting to the purity of style of the early Christian painters who worked before Raphael, the Italian Renaissance master.

Although James Collinson faithfully followed the technical precepts of the Pre-Raphaelite Brotherhood, he lacked the poetic inspiration of many of its members. Collinson preferred to paint sweet domestic scenes that usually involved children.

The painting *A Mother and Child on the Isle of Wight,* done in 1849–51, is typical of Collinson's choice of sentimental subjects. The Pre-Raphaelite influence is shown in the use of clear, bright color and in the abundance of detail.

You might discuss the following with your students:

1. Does the mood of this painting suit the tone of the poem?
2. Both the poem and the painting were produced during the same period in English history. What qualities do they have in common?

Purpose-Setting Question For what is the young girl in the poem grieving?

1 **Discussion** What double meaning might you attach to the word *springs?*

2 **Discussion** What do you suppose is the "blight of man"?

Answers

ANSWERS TO THINKING ABOUT THE SELECTION
Recalling

1. Her heart will grow colder.

Interpreting

2. (a) Students will understand "fresh thoughts" to be young, undeveloped thoughts—thoughts that are new with each generation of the species. (b) The clear implication is that decay is as much a part of life as birth. It is something that Margaret will have to learn to accept.
3. Suggested Response: All things human must die.

Applying

4. (a) Students may draw a number of associations, including the Biblical reference, i.e., the Fall of Man. (b) Spring in this instance stands for the season and for the rebirth that accompanies it. (c) Fall is both the season and the fall alluded to earlier in this answer.

THINKING AND WRITING

For help with this assignment, students can refer to Lesson 18, "Writing a Poem," in the Handbook of Writing About Literature.

More About the Author Although most of the poems in *A Shropshire Lad,* A. E. Housman's best-known volume, center on rural life in the village of Shropshire, all of them were composed in the Highgate section of London, where Housman lived between 1886 and 1905. What does this fact reveal about the capabilities of the artistic mind?

A. E. HOUSMAN

1859–1936

A foremost classical scholar of his age, Alfred Edward Housman devoted his life to teaching and translating the great Latin poets. And, yet, most modern readers who know Housman, know him as the author of three slender volumes of poetry that are as romantic and melancholy as any ever written.

Housman was born in Worcestershire, the oldest of seven children in a middle-class family. His carefree childhood came to an end when his mother died, following a long illness, on his twelfth birthday. Money became a problem for the family, but Housman, a bright and resourceful young man, won a scholarship to Oxford, where he studied classical literature and philosophy. Though he was a brilliant student, his intolerance of any error by himself or others left him with few friends.

While at Oxford, Housman fell secretly in love with a young woman who was interested only in his friendship. His despair over this relationship combined with his unhappy teen years seems to have darkened the rest of Housman's life and gave his poetry its bitter undertones.

Upon leaving Oxford, Housman went to work in the Patent Office. Determined to prove himself in the classics, he studied Greek and Latin at night and wrote scholarly articles for academic journals. In 1892, his hard-earned reputation as an expert in his field led to his appointment as professor of Latin at University College in London.

Though Housman spent the balance of his life engaged in scholarly pursuits, he found time to write poetry. His first and most famous collection of verse, *A Shropshire Lad* (1896), has as its fictitious narrator a homesick farmboy living in the city. In simple, precise language and brisk, regular rhythms, Housman focuses on the grim realities and fleeting joys of life. Housman paid for the first publication of *A Shropshire Lad* out of his own pocket, but it soon became highly popular. More than twenty-five years later, *Last Poems* (1922) was an instant best seller. After Housman's death, his brother Laurence edited and published *More Poems* (1936).

In a famous lecture that he delivered in 1933, Housman, who worked at projecting a public image as an emotionless intellectual, stated that the goal of poetry is to "transfuse emotion," not to transmit thought. A well-written poem, he maintained, makes a physical impact on the reader, like a shiver down the spine or a punch in the stomach. It is because of this impact in much of his own work that the best of A. E. Housman's poems have been marked for immortality.

Objectives

1 To recognize the theme of a poem
2 To write a response to literary criticism

Teaching Portfolio: Support Material

Teacher Backup, pp. 00–00

Vocabulary Check, p. 00

Usage and Mechanics Worksheet, p. 00

Analyzing Literature Worksheet, p. 00

Critical Thinking and Reading Worksheet, p. 00

Language Worksheet, p. 00

Selection Test, p. 000

GUIDE FOR READING

To an Athlete Dying Young; Loveliest of Trees; When I Was One-and-Twenty; With Rue My Heart Is Laden

The Writer's Technique

Theme. The theme in a literary work is the insight into life that it communicates to the reader. One of several recurring themes in Housman's verse is the bittersweet notion that youth is beautiful but that, like beauty itself, it passes too quickly. Even in those upbeat instances where Housman is describing happiness and glory, the reader senses an undercurrent of doom and a concern with the courage and endurance that will be required to face it. The charming, easy rhymes in his poems contrast sharply with his melancholy themes, which reflect both the pessimism of the late Victorian Age and the sadness in his own life.

Look For

As you read the five poems by A. E. Housman, look for his recurring themes of love, exile, and death.

Writing

Reflect on a topic to which you have a strong response—both positive and negative. Possibilities might include the promise of the future mixed with its uncertainties, or bittersweet memories of a favorite afterschool gathering spot that no longer exists. Freewrite, attempting to capture—using vivid details—the happy and sad sides of your topic.

Vocabulary

Knowing the following words will help you as you read the poems by Housman.

rout (rout) *n.*: Overwhelming defeat (p. 862, l. 17)

lintel (lin't'l) *n.*: Beam over a door (p. 862, l. 23)

rue (ro͞o) *n.*: Sorrow (p. 866, l. 1)

laden (lād''n) *v.*: Burdened; weighed down (p. 866, l. 1)

Literary Focus A common pitfall among students is to confuse theme with topic. To highlight the difference, list a number of topics on the board and ask students to develop related themes. For example, you might write "Youth," and the students might suggest the theme, "Youth is wasted on the young."

Look For To help your **less advanced** students pick up on these themes, have them make a checklist of words that relate to the topics of love and death—for example, *joy, sadness, friendship,* and *beauty.* Urge them to consult this checklist periodically as they read.

Writing Have students prepare for the writing assignment by plotting out on a chart their positive and negative responses to a prospective topic. This will enable them to determine whether there is sufficient "grist" for development in this topic.

Vocabulary Students should also be familiar with the following words: *rout, garland,* and *threescore.*

Motivation for Reading Discuss the effects of aging on professional athletes. How does the public's attitude toward athletes change as the athletes grow older? What psychological effects might this change in attitude have on the athletes? How does the public respond to the early death of certain athletes?

Thematic Idea Another poem that presents the poet's response to death is "Do Not Go Gentle into That Good Night" by Dylan Thomas, on page 1120.

Purpose-Setting Question What is the speaker's attitude toward death?

1 **Discussion** How does the meaning of "home" in this stanza differ from that implied in the first stanza?

2 **Discussion** What is the tone of the poem?

3 **Clarification** *Betimes* is an archaic word meaning "early."

4 **Discussion** Lintels are not ordinarily low. What else might the speaker have in mind?

5 **Clarification** This is an inverted sentence; its subject is "the strengthless dead."

To an Athlete Dying Young

A. E. Housman

The time you won your town the race
We chaired you through the marketplace;
Man and boy stood cheering by,
And home we brought you shoulder-high.

1 Today, the road all runners come,
Shoulder-high we bring you home,
And set you at your threshold down,
Townsman of a stiller town.

Smart lad, to slip betimes away
2,3 From fields where glory does not stay
And early though the laurel[1] grows
It withers quicker than the rose.

Eyes the shady night has shut
Cannot see the record cut,
And silence sounds no worse than cheers
After earth has stopped the ears:

Now you will not swell the rout
Of lads that wore their honors out,
Runners whom renown outran
And the name died before the man.

So set, before its echoes fade,
The fleet foot on the sill of shade,
4 And hold to the low lintel up
The still-defended challenge cup.

And round that early-laureled head
5 Will flock to gaze the strengthless dead,
And find unwithered on its curls
The garland briefer than a girl's.

1. **laurel:** A symbol of victory.

THINKING ABOUT THE SELECTION

Recalling

1. (a) In what sport did the athlete excel? (b) What did the townspeople do to show their admiration for the athlete following the contest mentioned in the first stanza?
2. (a) Where is the athlete "today"? (b) What does the speaker say the athlete will not have to be concerned about "now"?

Interpreting

3. (a) What visual image presented in the first stanza is repeated in the second stanza? (b) How is the meaning of the image different in the second stanza. (c) How does this difference affect the mood, or reader's emotional reaction?
4. (a) How would you summarize the speaker's comments in lines 9–20? (b) What is meant by "the name died before the man"?
5. (a) In what way is the challenge cup mentioned in line 24 "still-defended"? (b) What double meaning might the poet have intended for the word "still"?

Applying

6. Tell whether you agree or disagree with the speaker in this poem. Give reasons for your answer.
7. What advice would you give an athlete who is concerned about growing old and losing his or her "glory"?

ANALYZING LITERATURE

Finding the Theme

The **theme** in a poem is its insight into life. A poem's theme should not be confused with its subject, which can usually be described in a single word, such as "love" or "war." Rather, the theme reflects the author's thoughts on that subject—for instance, "love is blind," "love is a battlefield." Since poets seldom state the theme directly, the reader must *infer,* or figure out, the theme from the events and descriptions in the poem. One effective way of doing this is by constructing a series of meaningful questions that take into account the facts of the poem, as well as such features as its setting, tone, and mood. Answer the following questions on "To an Athlete Dying Young." Then state the poem's theme.

1. (a) Who is the "main character" in the poem? (b) What is the character's main accomplishment?
2. (a) What has happened to this character that is the occasion for this poem? (b) What details in the second stanza alert you to this happening? (c) What is the speaker's tone—that is, what seems to be his true feelings toward this happening?
3. (a) What does the speaker assume in lines 9–20 might have happened to the main character in later years? (b) On what evidence does the speaker most likely base this assumption?
4. (a) What generalization might be made about the relationship between accomplishment and praise? (b) To what other areas of life might this generalization apply?
5. What is the speaker's attitude toward life and death?
6. What is the theme of the poem?

Answers

ANSWERS TO THINKING ABOUT THE SELECTION

Recalling

1. (a) He was a runner. (b) They carried him home on their shoulders.
2. (a) He is being carried to his grave. (b) He will not have to be concerned about his glory fading.

Interpreting

3. (a) The repeated image is that of the athlete being carried shoulder-high. (b) In the second stanza he is being carried by pall-bearers. (c) Students should express a feeling of being taken aback the second time.
4. (a) A possible summary might be the following: The athlete is wise to die before his reputation is worn out or his glory is diminished by the excellence of successive generations. (b) It means that the athletes were forgotten before their deaths.
5. (a) It is still-defended in the sense that the athlete has died before anyone had a chance to beat his record. (b) Students might note the use of *still* in the second stanza to designate the realm of the dead. The cup here is in the possession of the dead athlete.

Applying

6. Answers will differ. Many students may feel that the speaker's attitude is too pessimistic.
7. Answers will differ. Students might suggest that such an athlete could look forward to new "victories" off the playing field, rather than dwell on old ones on it.

ANSWERS TO ANALYZING LITERATURE

1. (a) The main character is a runner. (b) He has won a race for his town.
2. (a) The runner has died. (b) He is being carried to his grave. (c) Suggested Response: The tone is melancholy yet resolved.
3. (a) He assumes that the athlete's record would have been broken and his glory would have faded. (b) This often happens to athletes as they grow older.
4. (a) Suggested Response: The speaker suggests that praise does not come without accomplishment. (b) Suggested Response: The generalization can be applied to nearly all areas of life.
5. Suggested Response: The speaker seems to accept death as a natural part of the cycle of life.
6. Suggested Response: Glory does not last.

Motivation for Reading Ask students to volunteer what they know about various trees and flowers. Which flowers have a particularly strong fragrance? Which do the students find most pleasant? Which trees tend to produce flowers? Ask if anyone in the class is familiar with the flowers produced by the cherry tree. What color are its flowers?

Thematic Idea Another poem that treats the subject of nature and its beauty is "God's Grandeur" by Gerard Manley Hopkins, page 854.

Purpose-Setting Question What motivates the speaker to roam the woodlands and admire the trees?

1 **Clarification** *Ride* is another word for "road" or "path."

2 **Enrichment** The Biblical estimate of a man's lifespan is "three score years and ten"—or seventy years.

3 **Discussion** What do you think the speaker is implying in his claim that fifty years provides "little room" to "look at things in bloom"?

Loveliest of Trees

A. E. Housman

Loveliest of trees, the cherry now
Is hung with bloom along the bough,
1 And stands about the woodland ride
Wearing white for Eastertide.

2 Now, of my threescore years and ten,
Twenty will not come again,
And take from seventy springs a score,
It only leaves me fifty more.

And since to look at things in bloom
3 Fifty springs are little room,
About the woodlands I will go
To see the cherry hung with snow.

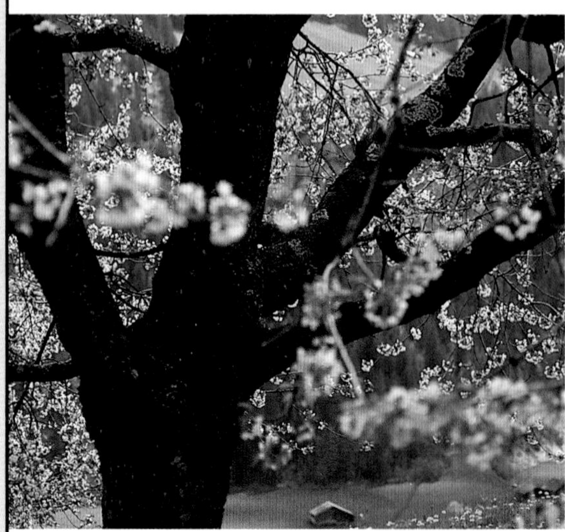

THINKING ABOUT THE SELECTION

Recalling

1. (a) During what season of the year is the poem set? (b) How can you tell?
2. What is the speaker of the poem doing?
3. (a) How old is the speaker? (b) To what age does he expect to live?

Interpreting

4. What realization does the speaker come to in the second stanza?
5. In the third stanza the speaker makes a resolution for himself. Do you think this resolution has to do only with trees? Explain.

Applying

6. (a) What is the theme of the poem? (b) Judging from this theme, what would you guess is the speaker/poet's attitude toward an afterlife?

Answers

ANSWERS TO THINKING ABOUT THE SELECTION

Recalling

1. (a) The poem is set during the springtime. (b) That is when Easter takes place.
2. He is walking about the woodlands, admiring the cherry trees.
3. (a) He is twenty. (b) He expects to live to seventy.

Interpreting

4. He realizes that if his life expectancy is seventy years and he has lived twenty of those years, he has precious little time left—relative to the enjoyment of the pursuit—to admire nature.
5. Answers will differ. Students should be aware that the probable intent of this line is that the speaker intends to make good use of his time in all pursuits.

Applying

6. (a) The theme is that we should spend our days wisely since we are allotted so few. (b) Students might speculate that, based on his emphasis on enjoying the here and now, he perhaps does not believe in an afterlife.

1 # When I Was One-and-Twenty

A. E. Housman

When I was one-and-twenty
    I heard a wise man say,
2 "Give crowns and pounds and guineas[1]
    But not your heart away;
3 Give pearls away and rubies
    But keep your fancy free."
But I was one-and-twenty,
    No use to talk to me.

When I was one-and-twenty
    I heard him say again,
"The heart out of the bosom
    Was never given in vain;
'Tis paid with sighs a plenty
    And sold for endless rue."
4 And I am two-and-twenty,
    And oh, 'tis true, 'tis true.

1. **crowns . . . guineas:** Denominations of money.

THINKING ABOUT THE SELECTION

Recalling

1. (a) What does the speaker say he "heard a wise man say" when he was "one-and-twenty?" (b) What, according to lines 7–8, was the speaker's reaction to this advice?
2. What is the speaker's comment in the last line on the wise man's second piece of advice?

Interpreting

3. With what is the speaker/poet equating the age of one-and-twenty in this poem? Explain your answer.
4. (a) What is significant about the fact that the speaker has twice received advice? (b) How is this relevant in light of the poem's theme?
5. What do you suppose happened to the speaker that changed his mind?

Applying

6. What event in Housman's life may have prompted the writing of this poem?

Motivation for Reading Inform students that there is an ancient Indian saying: "Fool me once—a curse on you! Fool me twice—a curse on me!" Have they ever refused good advice, not once, but twice? How did they feel ultimately about having done this? What lesson did they learn?

Thematic Idea Another poem that deals with the theme of love between two individuals is "When I Have Fears that I May Cease to Be" by John Keats, page 729.

Purpose-Setting Question What lesson has the speaker learned through experience?

1 **Reading Strategy** Ask students, all of whom are still several years shy of this age, what being twenty-one must be like? What do they expect to know when they have reached this age?

2 **Enrichment** At the time Housman was writing, a crown would have been worth about $1.25; pounds and guineas were both worth about $5.

3 **Discussion** State in your own words the advice this wise man is giving.

4 **Reading Strategy** Based on what the speaker states here, what has apparently happened to him in the previous year?

Answers

ANSWERS TO THINKING ABOUT THE SELECTION

Recalling

1. (a) He heard the wise man advise him to give away money and jewels but not his heart. (b) He ignored it.
2. He now realizes that it was good advice.

Interpreting

3. Students will appreciate that the age is being equated with youth and inexperience. They might cite in support of this claim the message in lines 7–8.
4. (a) It is significant since he has ignored it both times. (b) It is relevant inasmuch as the speaker was evidently so consumed with love that he was twice—and may have been hundreds of times—unable to take the advice.
5. He was apparently jilted or his love was not returned.

Applying

6. (Answers will differ.) Students may recall that he himself was a victim of unrequited love.

Motivation for Reading Ask whether there are any students in the class who have moved from one city to another. Who among them were saddened by the experience? What was the saddest part of leaving? How long did the sadness last? How did these feelings change over time?

Thematic Idea Another selection that deals with the realities facing the aging is "Sonnet 73" by Shakespeare, page 209.

Purpose-Setting Question What is the cause of the speaker's sadness?

1 **Enrichment** Housman wrote that Shakespeare's songs were a major influence on his poetry. Indeed the adjective "golden" here in conjunction with the references to "maiden" and "lad" echoes Shakespeare's song "Fear No More the Heat o' the Sun."

2 **Discussion** What do you think is the age of the speaker? Why?

With Rue My Heart Is Laden

A. E. Housman

With rue my heart is laden
  For golden friends I had,
1 For many a rose-lipped maiden
  And many a lightfoot lad.

By brooks too broad for leaping
  The lightfoot boys are laid;
2 The rose-lipped girls are sleeping
  In fields where roses fade.

THINKING ABOUT THE SELECTION

Recalling

1. What has happened to the speaker's friends?

Interpreting

2. What is meant by "golden" in line 2?
3. What do the adjectives "rose-lipped" and "lightfoot" suggest about the speaker's memories of his friends?
4. (a) What do you suppose is the meaning of the phrase "too broad for leaping" in line 4? (b) By the phrase "where roses fade" in line 8?
5. The subjects of this poem are "youth" and "beauty." What statement is the poet making about those subjects?

Applying

6. In what ways do you think young people and adults view the passage of time differently?

THINKING AND WRITING

Responding to Criticism

William Archer, a critic and contemporary of Housman, wrote in a review of *A Shropshire Lad* that "there is nothing whining about Mr. Housman's melancholy" in his verse. "Rather," the critic continued, "it is bracing, invigorating . . ." In an essay, state whether you agree or disagree with this assessment. Quote freely from the poems to support your view and to defend against the opposing view. In either case, respond to Archer's criticism as, itself, a product of the Victorian Age. Ask yourself what difference there might have been in his statements had they not been made at a time when the public was up in arms about the writings of such pessimists as Thomas Hardy. When you revise, make sure you have provided adequate support for your opinions.

Answers

ANSWERS TO THINKING ABOUT THE SELECTION

Recalling

1. They have died.

Interpreting

2. The word means "valuable" or "precious."
3. Both adjectives suggest that the speaker has retained images of his friends from the days when they were young and vital.
4. (a) Students might make the connection between the image and the boundaries between life and death. The brooks are too broad in the sense that the speaker's friends can never jump back from the Great Beyond. (b) The same inference may be made with respect to this image.
5. He appears to be saying that both youth and beauty inexorably end.

Applying

6. Suggested Response: Young people tend to be less aware of the passage of time, because they are not yet concerned with their advancing age.

THINKING AND WRITING

For help with this assignment, students can refer to Lesson 15, "Evaluating a Literary Work," in the Handbook of Writing About Literature.

Publishing Student Writing After students have completed the assignment, divide the class into teams based on their position with respect to the subject, and stage a debate. Allow each side time to prepare and consolidate their information.

Other Victorian Poets

TEMPERANTIA, 1872
Sir Edward Burne-Jones
Christie's, London

More About the Authors When **Elizabeth Barrett Browning** was thirteen years old, her father printed fifty copies of her poem *Battle of Marathon.* What effect do you think an honor of this sort might have on the typical child writer?

Dante Gabriel Rossetti had a great passion for collecting things, including pets. At one point, his brother reported, he had as many as two dozen animals living on the grounds of his home, among them a zebra, a raccoon, and a kangaroo. In what way might the poet's bizarre habit have been yet another manifestation of his genius?

BIOGRAPHIES

Elizabeth Barrett Browning (1806–1861)

One of the best-known woman poets of her own or any time, Elizabeth Barrett was the oldest of twelve children in an upper middle class family. She received no formal education, but a zest for knowledge enabled her to learn eight languages on her own.

Barrett began writing poetry as a child and, by the time she reached adulthood, had published four immensely popular volumes of verse. Though she met many of the leading writers of the day, a longtime illness made her something of a recluse.

Then, in 1845, she began to receive letters from the poet Robert Browning, who, after five months of correspondence, paid her a visit. Her doctors suggested that she spend the winter of 1846 in Italy, which offered a warmer climate. When her stern father refused to allow her to leave, she and Browning eloped there.

In 1849 their son was born, whom they nicknamed "Pen." A year later, Mrs. Browning revised and published *Sonnets from the Portuguese,* a sequence of 44 love poems written to her husband. *Aurora Leigh* (1857), a love story in blank verse, was completed during the second of two trips she made back to London.

Dante Gabriel Rossetti (1828–1882)

A successful painter as well as a poet, Dante Gabriel Rossetti was the son of an Italian patriot who had been exiled from his homeland. Growing up in a bilingual household under the watchful eye of parents who, themselves, were devoted to literature and the arts, Rossetti began writing plays and poetry at the age of five.

In 1837 he was sent to King's College School, but when money became a problem for the family, the young Rossetti was encouraged to pursue a more lucrative career as a painter. He was admitted to the Royal Academy, a prestigious art school, but could not adjust to a structured education and left after two years to study privately.

At twenty Rossetti founded the Pre-Raphaelite Brotherhood, a group of painters and writers who favored a return to the styles of artists who had lived before the time of the Italian Renaissance artist Raphael. In 1860 he married Elizabeth Siddal, a model who had posed for him. She became the subject of many of the poems in *The House of Life* (1870), a sequence of sonnets reflecting different aspects of love. When his wife died, he buried his poems with her, but later had them retrieved.

Rossetti's poems, like his paintings, are filled—sometimes to the point of crowding—with color and pictorial detail. The despair in his later poems anticipated the pessimism of many modern writers.

Objectives

1 To recognize sonnet form

Teaching Portfolio: Support Material

Teacher Backup, p. 000

Vocabulary Check, p. 00

Usage and Mechanics Worksheet, p. 00

Analyzing Literature Worksheet, p. 00

Critical Thinking and Reading Worksheet, p. 00

Language Worksheet, p. 00

Selection Test, p. 000

GUIDE FOR READING

Sonnet 43; Silent Noon

Literary Forms

The Sonnet. A sonnet is a lyric poem that has fourteen lines and a fixed rhyme scheme. Of the two most common forms of sonnet, the Italian and English, the Italian is the older, dating back to the thirteenth century. The form, also known as the Petrarchan sonnet, reached its height in the hands of Francesco Petrarch (1304–1374), who wrote over three hundred sonnets to a woman named Laura. The Italian sonnet has two parts—the *octave,* consisting of eight lines, which asks a question or raises a problem; and the *sestet,* consisting of six lines, which answers the question or resolves the problem. Though the rhyme scheme of the sestet varies, the octave always has the rhyme scheme *abbaabba.*

Despite occasional lapses in its popularity, the sonnet has surfaced again and again throughout the ages as the poetic form of choice among poets. In the nineteenth century, Elizabeth Barrett Browning and Dante Gabriel Rossetti, writing independently, revived the *sonnet cycle,* a series of sonnets loosely connected by subject or theme. Both of these cycles treat, in their own fashion, the subject of love.

Look For

As you read "Sonnet 43" and "Silent Noon," be alert to the questions raised in the octave and answered in the sestet, as well as to any differences in rhyme scheme.

Writing

Write the word "love" at the top of a sheet of paper. Then write ten complete sentences that explore your thoughts and feelings on the subject. Avoid mentioning specific names of individuals. When you have finished writing, read over your work and decide which of your impressions might be unique to you and could, therefore, be expanded into a poem or series of personal reflections.

Vocabulary

Knowing the meanings of the following words will help you as you read "Silent Noon."

amass (ə mas′) *v.*: Gather together (p. 871, l. 4)

dower (dou′ər) *n.*: Gift (p. 871, l. 12)

inarticulate (in′är tik′ yə lit) *adj.*: Not able to speak (p. 871, l. 13)

Literary Focus Challenge your **more advanced** students to try their hand at this time-honored poetic form. Have them share their efforts with the class.

Look For Prepare your **less advanced** students for an analysis of the sestet rhyme scheme by alerting them to three commonly used formulas: *cdcdcd, cdeecd,* and *cdecde.*

Writing Remind students that love has its good side and its bad side. You might suggest, in fact, that they divide their paper into two sections—one for each "side" of the emotion—before they begin taking notes.

Vocabulary Have students write two sentences using each of the vocabulary words.

Master Teacher Note Tell students that the poem they are about to read was part of a cycle presented by the poet to her husband shortly after breakfast one morning in 1847. Add that the poems held a meaning for Mrs. Browning so deep and private that it was only after much persuasion that she agreed to let her husband publish them, and then only under the title *Sonnets from the Portuguese,* which suggests that the poems were not originals but translations.

Purpose-Setting Question How well does the rigid form of the sonnet fit the poet's intentions?

1 **Clarification** Provide students with more details about the poet's health, explaining that she was plagued throughout her life with pain from a spine injury she sustained when she was fifteen.

Sonnet 43

Elizabeth Barrett Browning

How do I love thee? Let me count the ways.
I love thee to the depth and breadth and height
My soul can reach, when feeling out of sight
For the ends of Being and ideal Grace.
I love thee to the level of every day's
Most quiet need, by sun and candlelight.
I love thee freely, as men strive for Right;
I love thee purely, as they turn from Praise.
1 I love thee with the passion put to use
In my old griefs, and with my childhood's faith.
I love thee with a love I seemed to lose
With my lost saints—I love thee with the breath,
Smiles, tears, of all my life!—and, if God choose,
I shall but love thee better after death.

THINKING ABOUT THE SELECTION

Recalling

1. (a) What question does the speaker ask? (b) How many answers to this question does she give?
2. What does the speaker say she will do "if God choose"?

Interpreting

3. (a) What do you think the speaker means in lines 9–10 by "with the passion put to use/In my old griefs"? (b) By "with a love I seemed to lose/With my lost saints" in lines 11–12?
4. What effect is created by the repetition of the words "I love thee" throughout the poem?

Applying

5. Consult the list of ten sentences you wrote for the Writing assignment on page 869. What thoughts and feelings of your own might you add to those expressed by Elizabeth Barrett Browning in this poem?

ANALYZING LITERATURE

Understanding a Sonnet

A **sonnet** is a fourteen-line lyric poem with a fixed pattern of rhyme. The Italian sonnet has two parts. The first part, the octave, poses a question or presents a problem in eight lines. The second part, the sestet, answers that question or problem in six lines.

1. What line in the octet (first eight lines) ends with an irregular rhyming word? How might this irregularity be explained?
2. What is the rhyme scheme of the sestet?
3. Based on what you have learned about the Italian sonnet, tell in what critical way Sonnet 43 violates the rules. How does this violation help the poem to deliver its message?

Answers

ANSWERS TO THINKING ABOUT THE SELECTION

Recalling

1. (a) She asks herself in what ways she loves her husband. (b) She gives a total of seven answers.
2. She says that she will love her husband better after death.

Interpreting

3. (a) If students accept that this is a reference to the poet's infirmity, they may note the amount of energy a handicapped person must put into the simple routines of daily life. (b) Perhaps this again harks back to the poet's infirmity; in other words, her illness may have compromised religious convictions that she held till that time.
4. Students might view this either as a means of separating items in a catalogue or as the speaker's desire to repeat her feelings again and again for impact.

Applying

5. Answers will differ. One possibility is: I love you with every fiber of my body and soul (11 words).

ANSWERS TO ANALYZING LITERATURE

1. Alert students will note that the word "Grace" (line 4) ends in a different sibilant sound from the words ending lines 1, 5, and 8. Perhaps at the time the poem was written the pronunciation of the word was slightly different from that we give it today.
2. The rhyme scheme is *cdcdcd.*
3. The poem does not follow the formal division into octet and sestet. That is, the question raised in the octet is also answered, in part, in the octet—specifically in lines 2–8. Students may infer from this violation that the poet was intentionally emphasizing the complexity of the answer to her question by allowing it to occupy most of the space of the poem.

Silent Noon

Dante Gabriel Rossetti

Your hands lie open in the long fresh grass—
The finger-points look through like rosy blooms:
Your eyes smile peace. The pasture gleams and glooms 1
'Neath billowing skies that scatter and amass.
All round our nest, far as the eye can pass,
Are golden kingcup fields with silver edge
Where the cow-parsley skirts the hawthorn hedge.
'Tis visible silence, still as the hourglass.

Deep in the sun-searched growths the dragonfly
Hangs like a blue thread loosened from the sky— 2
So this winged hour is dropped to us from above.
Oh! clasp we to our hearts, for deathless dower,
This close-companioned inarticulate hour
When twofold silence was the song of love.

"WAY" CHINTZ
William Morris
The Granger Collection

THINKING ABOUT THE SELECTION

Recalling

1. (a) Where are the speaker and his companion? (b) What time of day is it? (c) What time of year? (d) How can you tell?

Interpreting

2. (a) What do you think the speaker means when he says the "pasture gleams and glooms"? (b) How might this detail be related to his training as an artist?
3. Is it possible for silence to be "visible," as the speaker states in line 8? Explain.
4. How do you explain the paradox in the last line?

Applying

5. Under what circumstances does silence have an effect opposite to the one described? What details might the poet have used to "paint" an impression of that kind of silence?

Thematic Idea Another poem that explores deeply-felt emotions is "When I Have Fears that I May Cease to Be" by John Keats, page 729.

Purpose-Setting Question What is the relationship between the speaker and the person to whom the poem is addressed?

1 **Discussion** Can eyes smile? Can a person smile a message?

2 **Discussion** What do you suppose the speaker means in stating that this hour is "dropped to us from above"?

Humanities Note

Fabric design, "Way" Chintz, by William Morris. Morris (1834–1896) was an English painter, designer, craftsman and poet. In 1861, William Morris set up a firm that produced decorative crafts such as furniture, wallpaper, and fabric. Inspired by the Pre-Raphaelite ideals, he sought to revive the "lost" medieval spirit of design, simplicity, good materials, sound workmanship, and rich decoration.

The fabrics such as the "Way Chintz" (of printed cotton, velveteen, and woven silk) designed by William Morris exploited the natural beauty of the fiber as part of the creation of the design. He looked to nature for his patterns, combining plant form with a strong structure.

Consider these questions for discussion:

1. What do both the fabric design and the poem glorify?
2. Can you accept this fabric as an art form? Explain.

Answers

ANSWERS TO THINKING ABOUT THE SELECTION

Recalling

1. (a) They are lying in the grass. (b) It is noontime. (c) It is either spring or summer. (d) Flowers and plants are in bloom.

Interpreting

2. (a) Students should recognize this is a poetic way of describing the effects of the sunshine on the pasture, as it passes behind and emerges again from clouds. (b) Suggested Response: Artists have a deep awareness of the importance of light.
3. Suggested Response: Yes, silence is sometimes so pronounced that we feel as if we can almost see it.
4. Suggested Response: The paradox rests within the reference to silence as a "song" of love. While a song is defined in part by the presence of sound, the song in this instance is sounded out not in words, but in the message contained within the lovers' eyes and hearts.

Applying

5. Students should have no difficulty imagining circumstances under which silence communicates anger or hurt. As to what details might suggest this kind of silence, possibilities include mute staring, a frigid climate, and dagger-like eyes.

More About the Authors Between the years of 1862 and 1864, **George Meredith** shared a house in London with two prominent poets of his generation, A. C. Swinburne and Dante Gabriel Rossetti. How might this living arrangement both have helped and hindered Meredith's poetic career?

Despite the serious tone and religious themes that characterize much of her work, **Christina Rossetti** was so amused by a parody of her poem "A Birthday" that she pasted it into her copy of her *Poems* (1875). What does this action reveal about her personality?

Rudyard Kipling's two children, for whom he wrote his first *Jungle Book,* both died when they were young. How might these tragic events have shaped Kipling's vision as a writer?

One of **Robert Louis Stevenson's** more popular and well-known works is *A Child's Garden of Verses,* published in 1885. Written in a simple style, the poems in this volume present the world through a child's imagination. What qualities must a writer possess in order to appeal to both adults and children?

BIOGRAPHIES

George Meredith (1828–1909)

Meredith was born in the coastal city of Portsmouth. When his first volume of verse *Poems* (1851) failed to sell, he turned to fiction but, again, enjoyed little success. It was not until the publication of *The Egoist* in 1879 that Meredith received the public recognition he had been seeking. Though Meredith is known primarily as a novelist, he always thought of himself first and foremost as a poet. Indeed, his best poems evoke the power of nature and the joy of humanity's relationship to it.

Christina Rossetti (1830–1894)

The younger sister of the poet Dante Gabriel Rossetti, Christina Rossetti is considered by some critics to be the greatest woman poet in all of English literature. In 1871 Rossetti fell victim to a disease that disfigured her and left her an invalid. In spite of this, she continued to write, turning out in the space of her lifetime five collections of verse, a book of poems for children, a book of prayers, and a book of religious meditations. Her simple lyrical poems exhibit a grace and precision that is rare.

Rudyard Kipling (1865–1936)

Rudyard Kipling was equally skillful as a poet and writer of prose. Born in Bombay, India, to English parents, Kipling was placed, when he was five, in a foster home in England. Kipling returned to India in 1882 to work as a journalist. During the next seven years, he published a number of witty poems and stories, and by the time he visited London in 1890, he was a celebrity. Kipling wrote several books that have since become children's classics: *The Jungle Books* (1895), *Captains Courageous* (1897), and *Kim* (1905).

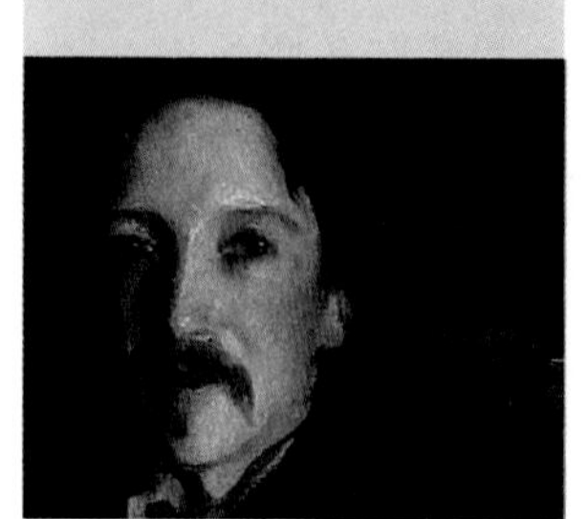

Robert Louis Stevenson (1850–1894)

Robert Louis Stevenson was born in Edinburgh, Scotland. An essayist, poet, dramatist, and novelist, he is perhaps best remembered for such thrilling tales of suspense and adventure as *The Strange Case of Dr. Jekyll and Mr. Hyde, The Master of Ballantrae, Kidnapped,* and *Treasure Island.* Traveling constantly for his health, Stevenson died in Samoa, where he was buried "under the wide and starry sky."

Objectives

1. To understand how imagery is used in poetry
2. To write about a poem's historical context

Teaching Portfolio: Support Material

Teacher Backup, p. 000

Vocabulary Check, p. 00

Usage and Mechanics Worksheet, p. 00

Analyzing Literature Worksheet, p. 00

Critical Thinking and Reading Worksheet, p. 00

Language Worksheet, p. 00

Selection Test, p. 000

GUIDE FOR READING

Lucifer in Starlight; A Birthday; Recessional; Requiem

The Writer's Technique

Imagery. Imagery is language, often in the form of poetic details, that appeals to one or more of the five senses. Poets use imagery to communicate experience vividly, to make you see, feel, hear, smell, and taste the ideas they present to you in words. Since imagery is often visual, images are often thought of as "word pictures." The Pre-Raphaelite poets included images in their poems that would ordinarily go unnoticed, such as shadows on a wall or the scraping sound of chairs pushed across a floor. The poems of George Meredith and Christina Rossetti show influences of the Pre-Rapaelite movement. The sense-related details and elaborate word pictures in their verse provide a sharp contrast to the more stately images of Kipling's "Recessional."

Look For

As you read "Lucifer By Starlight" and "A Birthday," look for the specific details that permit the mind's eye to glimpse bright and contrasting colors. As you read "Recessional," look for the very different sort of imagery used by Kipling.

Writing

Try to recall an experience you had that created vivid sense impressions, such as weathering a violent storm, or attempting to sleep on a blisteringly hot night without the aid of a fan or air conditioner. Freewrite about your experience, using as many images as you can. Focus, if possible, on all, or at least several, of the five senses.

Vocabulary

Knowing the meanings of the following words will help you as you read the next three poems.

dominion (də min′ yən) *n.*: Place of rule; home territory (p. 874, l. 2)
specter (spek′tər) *n.*: Ghost or ghost-like appearance (p. 874, l. 4)
careened (kə rēnd) *v.*: Leaned to one side (p. 874, l. 7)
halcyon (hal′sē ən) *adj.*: Calm (p. 875, l. 6)
dais (dā′is) *n.*: Throne (p. 875, l. 9)
vair (ver) *n.*: Gray and white fur (p. 875, l. 10)
contrite (kən trīt′) *adj.*: Willing to repent or atone (p. 876, l. 10)
requiem (rek′wē əm) *n.*: A dirge or mass for the dead (p. 878, title)

Literary Focus Reinforce the notion of imagery by creating—and then having your students create—images related to several objects in the classroom.

Look For Have your **less advanced** students review several poems in this unit that are rich in imagery. For example, you might choose "To Marguerite—Continued," page 838, and "The Darkling Thrush," page 846.

Writing Have students share their freewriting with the other members of the class.

Vocabulary Have students write a paragraph in which they use all of the vocabulary words.

Motivation for Reading Ask students to name and describe their favorite terrifying creatures from film and fiction. Through a discussion, elicit what traits are common to these fantastic creations. If students were going to fashion a fiend of their own creation, what additional features would they incorporate to enhance its fright appeal?

Thematic Idea Another selection that deals with the fall of Satan is the excerpt from *Paradise Lost* by John Milton, page 470.

Purpose-Setting Question What does Satan encounter upon his rise?

1 **Clarification** The name *Lucifer* means "light-bearer."

2 **Discussion** What do these lines suggest about the size of the creature?

3 **Discussion** What do you suppose to be the meaning of "Awe"?

Answers

ANSWERS TO THINKING ABOUT THE SELECTION

Recalling

1. (a) He was tired of his dark dominion. (b) He rises up above the world.
2. (a) He looks at the stars that are the "brain of heaven." (b) He sinks once again.

Interpreting

3. It signifies earth.
4. Students might note that he has wings and that he is large enough to cast a shadow over much of a continent.
5. His scars were probably caused by his struggling against his descent from Paradise.
6. (a) The army is made up of the forces that represent the side of righteousness. (b) The inherent goodness of mankind is unalterable.
7. (a) The problem raised in the octet is that of Lucifer attempting to reassert his supremacy. (b) The response in the sestet is that the forces of good will rally to forestall such a rise.
8. Suggested Response: The allusion makes it clear that Lucifer is seeking revenge. The "old revolt from Awe" refers to the actions that caused him to be cast out of heaven.
9. Answers will differ. Students may comment that this knowledge creates another possible interpretation of the poem.

Applying

10. Answers will differ. Some students may observe that the vastness of the sky suggests to them the infiniteness of the universe and of God's work—the very idea perhaps that came to Meredith's mind.

1 # Lucifer in Starlight

George Meredith

On a starred night Prince Lucifer uprose.
Tired of his dark dominion swung the fiend
Above the rolling ball in cloud part screened,
Where sinners hugged their specter of repose.
Poor prey to his hot fit of pride were those.
And now upon his western wing he leaned,
2 Now his huge bulk o'er Afric's sands careened,
Now the black planet shadowed Arctic snows.
Soaring through wider zones that pricked his scars
3 With memory of the old revolt from Awe,
He reached a middle height, and at the stars,
Which are the brain of heaven, he looked, and sank.
Around the ancient track marched, rank on rank,
The army of unalterable law.

THINKING ABOUT THE SELECTIONS

Recalling

1. (a) Why does Prince Lucifer rise up? (b) Where does he go?
2. (a) What does he look at when he reaches "the middle height?" (b) What is his reaction to what he sees?

Interpreting

3. What do you understand "the rolling ball in cloud part screened" in line 3 to signify?
4. What are you able to gather about the appearance of "the fiend" from lines 6–9?
5. What do you think has caused Lucifer's scars, mentioned in line 9?
6. (a) Who or what makes up "the army of unalterable law"? (b) What situation is unalterable?
7. "Lucifer in Starlight" is a sonnet. (a) What question or problem is raised in the octet? (b) What answer or resolution is provided in the sestet?
8. In Milton's *Paradise Lost,* Satan (also known as Lucifer) is an angel who has fallen from grace and has, thus, been cast out of Heaven. How might this allusion explain Lucifer's feelings and "mission" in "Lucifer in Starlight?" What might be the meaning of "old revolt from Awe" in line 10?
9. In classical mythology, Lucifer (which means "lightbearer") was the morning star—that is, the planet Venus at dawn. The rising of Prince Lucifer, thus, also refers to the appearance of Venus on the horizon. How does knowing this enhance your appreciation of the poem?

Applying

10. Meredith may have come upon the idea for this poem while gazing up at a nighttime sky. What thoughts come to you when you gaze up at the stars? What themes might the vastness of the sky suggest?

A Birthday

Christina Rossetti

My heart is like a singing bird
Whose nest is in a watered shoot: 1
My heart is like an apple tree
Whose boughs are bent with thickset fruit;
My heart is like a rainbow shell
That paddles in a halcyon sea;
My heart is gladder than all these
Because my love is come to me.

Raise me a dais of silk and down;
Hang it with vair[1] and purple dyes; 2
Carve it in doves and pomegranates,
And peacocks with a hundred eyes;
Work it in gold and silver grapes,
In leaves and silver fleurs-de-lys;[2]
Because the birthday of my life
Is come, my love is come to me.

---

1. **vair** *n.*: Squirrel fur.
2. **fleurs-de-lys** (flʉr′ də lēz′) *n:* Emblems resembling lilies or irises.

THINKING ABOUT THE SELECTION

Recalling

1. (a) To what three things does the speaker compare her heart in the first stanza? (b) Why does she feel as she does?
2. (a) What does the speaker ask for in the second stanza? (b) What does she say has come?

Interpreting

3. (a) What feeling does the poem convey? (b) Find three images that contribute to that feeling.
4. The poet makes abundant use of repetition, especially in the first stanza. How does this affect the mood of the poem?
5. What possible meanings might you attach to the phrase "the birthday of my life?"

Applying

6. The second stanza of "A Birthday" has been called a "fully Pre-Raphaelite word-picture." Using what you have learned about the Pre-Raphaelite movement along with evidence from the poem explain why you think this is so.

Master Teacher Note Have students examine several artistic renderings of the Madonna and Child reprinted in H. W. Janson's *History of Art* (Prentice-Hall/Abrams). You might choose in particular those of Domenico Veneziano, Colorplate 31, and Parmigianino, Colorplate 43. Ask students what attributes of the birth of Christ are common to these paintings. What similar traits might they expect in anyone "reborn" into a new religion? What events can they name that might affect an individual in the same way as a spiritual rebirth?

Thematic Idea Another poem that deals with spiritual rebirth is "Easter Wings" by George Herbert, page 434.

Purpose-Setting Question What is the source of the speaker's ecstasy?

1 **Discussion** What ideas are commonly associated with the image of a singing bird?

2 **Literary Focus** What qualities are suggested by these images?

Answers

ANSWERS TO THINKING ABOUT THE SELECTION

Recalling

1. (a) She compares it to a singing bird, an apple tree, and a rainbow shell. (b) She feels this way because her "love" has come to her.
2. (a) She asks for an elaborate dais. (b) She says that the "birthday of my life" has come.

Interpreting

3. (a) Students will observe that the poem conveys a feeling of ecstasy. (b) The images in the first stanza suggest that feeling.
4. Suggested Response: The repetition reinforces the mood.
5. Students might understand the poet to be referring to her discovery of the central religious force in her life.

Applying

6. Students may recall that the Pre-Raphaelite movement was an effort to restore art to its state of glory by emphasizing the color and light suggestive of the works of the High Renaissance. This portion of the poem fairly dazzles with its colors and painstaking imagery.

Motivation for Reading Ask students what they know of the famous pleasure ship, the *Titanic*. Ask what other phenomena they can think of that were thought to be indestructible but proved such thinking to be flawed. What do these phenomena reveal about earthly ambition?

Thematic Idea Another poem that deals with the vanity of a fallen empire is "Love Among the Ruins" by Robert Browning, page 830.

Purpose-Setting Question What is the speaker instructing his audience to remember?

1 **Clarification** As it is used here, the word *awful* means "inspiring awe."

2 **Reading Strategy** The phrase "lest we forget" is repeated not only within the line, but at the end of the first two stanzas. Look ahead to determine if it is repeated throughout. What effect does repetition of this the phrase create?

Recessional[1]

Rudyard Kipling

In 1897 a national celebration called the "Diamond Jubilee" was held in honor of the sixtieth anniversary of Queen Victoria's reign. The occasion prompted a great deal of boasting about the strength and greatness of the empire. Kipling responded to the celebration by writing this poem, reminding the people of England that the British empire might not last forever.

God of our fathers, known of old—
    Lord of our far-flung battle-line—
1 Beneath whose awful Hand we hold
    Dominion over palm and pine—
Lord God of Hosts, be with us yet
Lest we forget—lest we forget!

The tumult and the shouting dies—
    The Captains and the Kings depart—
Still stands Thine ancient Sacrifice,
    An humble and a contrite heart.[2]
Lord God of Hosts, be with us yet,
Lest we forget—lest we forget!

Far-called, our navies melt away—
    On dune and headland sinks the fire[3]—
Lo, all our pomp of yesterday
    Is one with Nineveh[4] and Tyre![5]
Judge of the Nations, spare us yet,
2 Lest we forget—lest we forget!

---

1. **recessional** *n.*: A hymn sung at the end of a religious service.
2. **An . . . heart:** An allusion to the Bible (Psalms 51:17): "The sacrifices of God are a broken spirit: a broken and contrite heart, O God, thou wilt not despise."
3. **On . . . fire:** Bonfires were lit on high ground all over Britain as part of the opening ceremonies of the Jubilee celebration.
4. **Nineveh** (nin′ ə və): The ancient capital of the Assyrian Empire, the ruins of which were discovered buried in desert sands in the 1850's.
5. **Tyre** (tīr): Once a great port and the center of ancient Phoenician culture, now a small town in Lebanon.

If, drunk with sight of power, we loose
    Wild tongues that have not Thee in awe—
Such boasting as the Gentiles use
    Or lesser breeds without the Law[6]— 3
Lord God of Hosts, be with us yet,
Lest we forget—lest we forget!

For heathen heart that puts her trust
    In reeking tube[7] and iron shard[8]—
All valiant dust that builds on dust,
    And guarding calls not Thee to guard— 4
For frantic boast and foolish word,
Thy mercy on Thy People, Lord!

---

6. Such boasting . . . Law: An allusion to the Bible (Romans 2:14): "For when the Gentiles, which have not the law, do by nature things contained in the law, these, having not the law, are a law unto themselves."
7. tube: The barrel of a gun.
8. shard: Fragment of a bombshell.

THINKING ABOUT THE SELECTION

Recalling

1. (a) To whom is this poem addressed? (b) To whom is Kipling really speaking?
2. What does the speaker suggest, in lines 15–16, happens to "our pomp of yesterday?"
3. What does the speaker beg in the last line?

Interpreting

4. What qualities and actions does the poem condemn? Support your answer.
5. What is the poem's theme?

Applying

6. What differences do you detect in the images used by Kipling in "Recessional" and those used by George Meredith in "Lucifer in Starlight"? Which poet's imagery do you find more effective? Explain.

THINKING AND WRITING

Writing About Historical Context

Kipling's "Recessional" may be seen as a rejection of some of the values of the England in which he lived. Supplement what you have learned about Victorian England by consulting an encyclopedia or other historical reference. Note, in addition to the economic, political, and religious climates of the period, specific events that may have shaped the thoughts of the citizenry. Weigh all possible influences on Kipling at the time during which he composed this poem in 1897 and discard those that are irrelevant. Then write an explanatory paper in which you identify "Recessional" as a product of its period. Refer to specific lines of the poem to strengthen your thesis. When you revise, make sure your essay is organized in a logical order.

3 **Discussion** What does the speaker ask for in this stanza?

4 **Discussion** What effect is created by altering the last line here?

Answers

ANSWERS TO THINKING ABOUT THE SELECTION

Recalling

1. (a) From the first line it might be construed that the poet is addressing his thoughts to God. (b) The message is actually directed toward the people of England.
2. He is suggesting that it will ultimately crumble into either nothingness or obscurity, as did these ancient capitals respectively.
3. He asks for the mercy of God on his people.

Interpreting

4. Students should have no trouble citing the poem's disparaging of pridefulness and haughty behavior. They may use as examples the lessons on Nineveh and Tyre (line 16) and the boastings of the Gentiles (line 21), among others.
5. Suggested Response: People and nations should conduct themselves with moderation and humility.

Applying

6. Answers will differ. Both poets make use of powerful images —Meredith the imagery of a fiendish presence rising, Kipling that of war machines crumbling—to convey the central ideas of their poems. Ask students to pinpoint images that are especially palpable.

THINKING AND WRITING

After students have completed the assignment, divide them into groups and have them read their rough drafts to one another and suggest ways in which they can be improved.

Motivation for Reading Have students discuss the purpose of epitaphs. What should an epitaph convey about a deceased individual?

Purpose-Setting Question How does the speaker wish to be remembered?

Answers

ANSWERS TO THINKING ABOUT THE SELECTION

Recalling

1. The speaker wishes to be buried "under the wide and starry sky."
2. The speaker approaches his death "gladly" and "with a will."

Interpreting

3. Suggested Response: The speaker's epitaph is appropriate because he has lived his life fully and happily and sees death and the grave as coming home to rest after his full and happy life.

Applying

4. Answers will differ. Suggested Response: People like to write their own epitaphs because they want others who come after them to know how they perceived their lives or perceived life in general.
5. Answers will differ. Students should highlight their most important qualities.

Requiem

Robert Louis Stevenson

Under the wide and starry sky
Dig the grave and let me lie.
Glad did I live and gladly die.
  And I laid me down with a will.

This be the verse you grave for me:
Here he lies where he longed to be;
Home is the sailor, home from sea,
  And the hunter home from the hill.

THINKING ABOUT THE SELECTION

Recalling

1. Where does the speaker wish to be buried?
2. How does the speaker approach his death?

Interpreting

3. Explain why the speaker's epitaph is appropriate.

Applying

4. Explain why you think people like to write their own epitaphs.
5. What epitaph would you create for yourself? Explain the reason for your choice.

Prose

A SUMMER DAY IN HYDE PARK
John Ritchie
Museum of London

More About the Author From his earliest years, when he went to work in a factory and took to wandering the streets of London, Charles Dickens absorbed not only the sights and sounds of urban life but also its bleak and oppressive spirit. He knew early-modern industrial civilization at first hand, and when he matured into a writer of fiction he expressed his poetic and prophetic sense of urban and industrial life with a degree of depth and insight few writers have ever equaled. Hence, though his dates of birth and death place him squarely in the Victorian age, as an artist he seems almost contemporary.

CHARLES DICKENS

(1812–1870)

No other writer since Shakespeare has occupied a more important place in popular culture than Charles Dickens. From his own time on, his works, with their unforgettable characters, have held special appeal for both scholars and the reading public at large, and have been transformed time and again into plays and films.

Dickens was born in Portsmouth on England's southern coast. Except for a few happy years at Chatham, east of London, his childhood was darkened by his father's wavering economic status. After years of eluding creditors, his father was finally sent to debtor's prison. Dickens in the meantime was sent to a "prison" of his own—to a factory where he worked long hours pasting labels. These experiences and other ills of the newly industrialized society figure prominently in his novels.

After becoming a law clerk at the age of fifteen, Dickens taught himself shorthand and became a court reporter. At twenty-one he began applying his keen powers of observation to humorous literary sketches of everyday life in London while reporting on the Parliamentary debates. A collection of these, *Sketches by Boz* (1835–36), earned him a small following, which he built up considerably with his first novel *The Pickwick Papers,* published in 1837.

Next came such favorites as *Oliver Twist* (1837), *Nicholas Nickleby* (1839), and, after a trip to America where his fame had already spread, *A Christmas Carol* (1843). In these early novels, which paint a sweeping satiric picture of Victorian England, Dickens displayed both a passion for social reform and a unique ability to combine humor with horror—themes and techniques that became the hallmark of all his fiction. He also developed his lifelong practice of writing for serial publications. Paid by the word, he wove elaborate plots with vast numbers of characters.

A turn toward more serious planning and characterization of greater psychological depth are evident in *Dombey and Son* (1848) and *David Copperfield* (1850), which also contain social criticism that is more direct and less optimistic. In the later novels Dickens blended these elements together most successfully, and the results were his masterpieces: *Bleak House* (1853), *Hard Times* (1854), and *Great Expectations* (1861). "The Signalman" was published in 1866 in a collection including several other railway stories.

Dickens never gave up journalism as a second outlet for his social conscience. In later life, the work load imposed by his many writing responsibilities coupled with his exhausting public reading tours took its toll on his health. In 1870, while at work on a novel, *The Mystery of Edwin Drood,* he died of a stroke.

Objectives

1 To appreciate plot in a ghost story
2 To be able to distinguish between realistic and supernatural detail
3 To select the correct meaning of a word for its context

Teaching Portfolio: Support Material

Teacher Backup, pp. 00-00

Vocabulary Check, p. 00

Usage and Mechanics Worksheet, p. 00

Analyzing Literature Worksheet, p. 00

Critical Thinking and Reading Worksheet, p. 00

Language Worksheet, p. 00

Selection Test, p. 00

GUIDE FOR READING

The Signalman

The Writer's Technique

Plot in a Ghost Story. Plot is the ordered arrangement of happenings that make up a story or novel. Plot can be structured in a straight *chronological* progression, from the earliest event in time to the latest, or it can jump backwards and forward in time. In either case, plot generally builds on some *conflict,* or struggle between characters and/or forces, until it reaches a *climax,* or height of tension. The portion of the story from this point to the end, during which all remaining problems are solved, is called the *resolution.*

In a ghost story, the plot is built around *supernatural* elements —events beyond the normal order of things. The conflict is often between these supernatural forces and the human beings whose world they have invaded. At times, however, the conflict takes the form of a difference of opinion between two characters as to the explanation of certain mysterious events. In "The Signalman," for example, the first-person narrator attempts to explain away in rational terms the "ghost" that is plaguing a railroad employee.

Look For

As you read "The Signalman," look for the suspense and air of mystery Dickens creates through his narrator's repeated efforts to persuade the signalman that the latter has been a victim of his senses.

Writing

Prepare the groundwork for an original ghost story. Consider the story's setting and characters by asking yourself questions such as the following: Is the story to take place in the here and now? What form will the "ghost" take? Who will be the person haunted by the ghost, and what will be the ghost's purpose? Jot down your answers to these and related questions.

Vocabulary

Knowing the following words will help you as you read "The Signalman."

foreshortened (fôr shôr't'nd) *adj.*: Narrowed by observer's angle of vision (p. 882)

precipitate (pri sip'ə tit) *adj.*: Steep (p. 882)

gesticulate (jes tik' yə lāt') *v.*: Communicate excitedly by gestures (p. 886)

saturnine (sat'ər nīn) *adj.*: Sluggish or gloomy (p. 883)

ruminate (ro͞o' mə nāt) *v.*: Think over; meditate (p. 888)

subordinate (sə bôr' də nit) *adj.*: Beneath another in rank (p. 888)

Literary Focus Dickens is considered to be a great portrait painter as well as a masterly maker of plots. This short story highlights his psychological acumen as well. You might mention that in some of the best ghost stories, such as *The Turn of the Screw,* by Henry James, the psychological and the supernatural are often closely connected.

Look For Have students identify clues within the story which suggest a peculiar relationship between the narrator and the Signalman.

Writing You might have your students discuss or speculate about how a psychological condition might lead to a person's seeing a ghost or some other supernatural phenemenon.

Vocabulary Ask students to take apart as many of these vocabulary words as possible. Examine roots, suffixes, and prefixes. Look up the origins of whatever words cannot be treated in this way.

Motivation for Reading Tell students that "The Signalman" is a modern story of supernatural mystery. Mention, however, that psychological elements play a role in the plot.

Challenge Encourage students to solve or explain the mystery.

Master Teacher Note In the periodical literature of Dickens's day, there was a good deal of debate about spiritialism, dreams, and the supernatural. Curiously, Dickens wrote articles critical of spiritualist pretensions, yet published stories based upon the supernatural. "The Haunted House" is one such story.

Thematic Idea Point out that Joseph Conrad uses a split or mysterious personality in *The Secret Sharer.* Dickens may be employing a similar method here.

Purpose-Setting Question How might the apparition in this story be explained?

1 **Reading Strategy** Who speaks the opening line of the story?

2 **Discussion** In what way might the spatial relation between the signalman and the narrator be significant?

3 **Critical Reading and Thinking** Why is the signalman reluctant to point out the path?

4 **Discussion** What elements of the setting suggest to the narrator that he has left the "natural world"?

The Signalman

Charles Dickens

1 "Halloa! Below there!"

When he heard a voice thus calling to him, he was standing at the door of his box, with a flag in his hand, furled round its short pole. One would have thought, considering the nature of the ground, that he could not have doubted from what quarter the voice came; but instead of looking up to where I stood on the top of the steep cutting nearly over his head, he turned himself about, and looked down the Line. There was something remarkable in his manner of doing so, though I could not have said for my life what. But I know it was remarkable enough to attract my notice, even though his figure was foreshortened and shadowed, down in the deep trench, and mine was high above him, so steeped in the glow of an angry sunset, that I had shaded my eyes with my hand before I saw him at all.

"Halloa! Below!"

From looking down the Line, he turned
2 himself about again, and, raising his eyes, saw my figure high above him.

"Is there any path by which I can come down and speak to you?"

He looked up at me without replying, and I looked down at him without pressing him too soon with a repetition of my idle question. Just then there came a vague vibration in the earth and air, quickly changing into a violent pulsation, and an oncoming rush that caused me to start back, as though it had force to draw me down. When such vapor as rose to my height from this rapid train had passed me and was skimming away over the landscape, I looked down again, and saw him refurling the flag he had shown while the train went by.

I repeated my inquiry. After a pause, during which he seemed to regard me with fixed attention, he motioned with his rolled-up flag towards a point on my level, some two or three hundred yards distant. I called down to him, "All right!" and made for that point. There, by dint of looking closely about me, I found a rough zigzag descending path notched out, which I followed.

The cutting was extremely deep, and unusually precipitate. It was made through a clammy stone, that became oozier and wetter as I went down. For these reasons, I
found the way long enough to give me time to 3
recall a singular air of reluctance or compulsion with which he had pointed out the path.

When I came down low enough upon the zigzag descent to see him again, I saw that he was standing between the rails on the way by which the train had lately passed, in an attitude as if he were waiting for me to appear. He had his left hand at his chin, and that left elbow rested on his right hand, crossed over his breast. His attitude was one of such expectation and watchfulness, that I stopped a moment, wondering at it.

I resumed my downward way, and stepping out upon the level of the railroad, and drawing nearer to him, saw that he was a dark sallow man, with a dark beard and rather heavy eyebrows. His post was in as solitary and dismal a place as ever I saw. On either side, a dripping-wet wall of jagged stone, excluding all view but a strip of sky;
the perspective one way only a crooked pro- 4
longation of this great dungeon; the shorter perspective in the other direction terminating in a gloomy red light, and the gloomier

entrance to a black tunnel, in whose massive architecture there was a barbarous, depressing, and forbidding air. So little sunlight ever found its way to this spot, that it had an earthy, deadly smell; and so much cold wind rushed through it, that it struck chill to me, as if I had left the natural world.

Before he stirred, I was near enough to him to have touched him. Not even then removing his eyes from mine, he stepped back one step, and lifted his hand.

This was a lonesome post to occupy (I said), and it had riveted my attention when I looked down from up yonder. A visitor was a rarity, I should suppose; not an unwelcome rarity, I hoped? In me, he merely saw a man who had been shut up within narrow limits all his life, and who, being at last set free,
5 had a newly awakened interest in these great works. To such purpose I spoke to him; but I am far from sure of the terms I used; for, besides that I am not happy in opening any conversation, there was something in the man that daunted me.

He directed a most curious look towards the red light near the tunnel's mouth, and looked all about it, as if something were missing from it, and then looked at me.

That light was part of his charge? Was it not?

He answered in a low voice, "Don't you know it is?"

The monstrous thought came into my mind, as I perused the fixed eyes and the saturnine face, that this was a spirit, not a man. I have speculated since, whether there may have been infection in his mind.

In my turn, I stepped back. But in making the action, I detected in his eyes some latent fear of me. This put the monstrous thought to flight.

"You look at me," I said, forcing a smile, "as if you had a dread of me."

"I was doubtful," he returned, "whether I had seen you before."

"Where?"

He pointed to the red light he had looked at.

"There?" I said.

Intently watchful of me, he replied (but without sound), "Yes."

"My good fellow, what should I do there? However, be that as it may, I never was there, you may swear."

"I think I may," he rejoined. "Yes, I am sure I may."

His manner cleared, like my own. He replied to my remarks with readiness, and in well-chosen words. Had he much to do there? Yes; that was to say, he had enough responsibility to bear; but exactness and watchfulness were what was required of him, and of actual work—manual labor—he had next to none. To change that signal, to trim those lights, and to turn this iron handle now and then, was all he had to do under that head. Regarding those many long and lonely hours of which I seemed to make so much, he could only say that the routine of his life had shaped itself into that form, and he had grown used to it. He had taught himself a language down here—if only to know it by sight, and to have formed his own crude ideas of its pronunciation, could be called learning it. He had also worked at fractions and decimals, and tried a little algebra; but he was, and had been as a boy, a poor hand at figures. Was it necessary for him when on duty always to remain in that channel of damp air, and could he never rise into the sunshine from between those high stone walls? Why, that depended upon times and circumstances. Under some conditions there would be less upon the Line than under others, and the same held good as to certain hours of the day and night. In bright weather, he did choose occasions for getting a little above these lower shadows; but, being at all times liable to be called by his electric bell, and at such times listening for it with redoubled anxiety, the relief was less than I would suppose.

He took me into his box, where there was a fire, a desk for an official book in which he had to make certain entries, a telegraphic instrument with its dial, face, and needles, and the little bell of which he had spoken. On my trusting that he would excuse the

5 **Discussion** What explanation does the narrator give for his interest in the tunnel and the signalman?

Humanities Note

Fine art, *Two Tunnels,* 1975, by Guy Worsdell. The British wood engraver and painter Guy Worsdell was born in 1908. He studied at the Central school of Art and Design and with the wood engraver John Beedham. Worsdell is well known for his wood engraving prints. He did much to promote the creative aspects of the technique.

Wood engraving involves incising designs into a block of wood. This block is then inked and pressed onto paper, leaving a black and white image. It is an exacting art that requires strength and precision. The engraving *Two Tunnels* shows the degree of refinement in this technique attained by Guy Worsdell. In this sharp black-and-white image of a train, he has captured a sense of movement through his composition. The rich details of the landscape and train display a wide variety of textures and shading. Masterful wood engravings such as this helped to establish the technique as a fine art form.

You might use these questions for discussion:

1. Do you find the absence of color in this black and white image a benefit to this illustration? Explain
2. What mood does this engraving evoke? Is it appropriate to "The Signalman"? Explain.
3. Does this sharp, direct image compare favorably with the language of the story?

TWO TUNNELS, 1975
Guy Worsdell

remark that he had been well educated, and (I hoped I might say without offense) perhaps educated above that station, he observed that instances of slight incongruity in such wise would rarely be found wanting among large bodies of men; that he had heard it was so in workhouses, in the police force, even in that last desperate resource, the army; and that he knew it was so, more or less, in any great railway staff. He had been, when young (if I could believe it, sitting in that hut—he scarcely could), a student of natural philosophy, and had attended lectures; but he had run wild, misused his opportunities, gone down, and never risen again. He had no complaint to offer about that. He had made his bed, and he lay upon it. It was far too late to make another.

All that I have here condensed, he said in a quiet manner, with his grave dark regards divided between me and the fire. He threw in the word, "Sir," from time to time, and especially when he referred to his youth, as though to request me to understand that he claimed to be nothing but what I found him. He was several times interrupted by the little bell, and had to read off messages, and send replies. Once he had to stand without the door, and display a flag as a train passed, and make some verbal communication to the driver. In the discharge of his duties, I observed him to be remarkably exact and vigilant, breaking off his discourse at a syllable, and remaining silent until what he had to do was done.

In a word, I should have set this man down as one of the safest of men to be employed in that capacity, but for the circumstance that while he was speaking to me he twice broke off with a fallen color, turned his face towards the little bell when it did NOT ring, opened the door of the hut (which was kept shut to exclude the un-
6 healthy damp), and looked out towards the red light near the mouth of the tunnel. On both of those occasions, he came back to the fire with the inexplicable air upon him which I had remarked, without being able to define, when we were so far asunder.

Said I, when I rose to leave him, "You almost make me think that I have met with a contented man."

(I am afraid I must acknowledge that I said it to lead him on.)

"I believe I used to be so," he rejoined, in the low voice in which he had first spoken; "but I am troubled, sir, I am troubled."

He would have recalled the words if he could. He had said them, however, and I took them up quickly.

"With what? What is your trouble?"

"It is very difficult to impart, sir. It is very, very difficult to speak of. If ever you make me another visit, I will try to tell you."

"But I expressly intend to make you another visit. Say, when shall it be?"

"I go off early in the morning, and I shall be on again at ten tomorrow night, sir."

"I will come at eleven."

He thanked me, and went out at the door with me. "I'll show my white light, sir," he said, in his peculiar low voice, "till you have found the way up. When you have found it, don't call out! And when you are at the top, don't call out!"

His manner seemed to make the place strike colder to me, but I said no more than, "Very well."

"And when you come down tomorrow 7
night, don't call out! Let me ask you a parting question. What made you cry, 'Halloa! Below there!' tonight?"

"Heaven knows," said I. "I cried something to that effect—"

"Not to that effect, sir. Those were the very words. I know them well."

"Admit those were the very words. I said them, no doubt, because I saw you below."

"For no other reason?"

"What other reason could I possibly have?"

"You had no feeling that they were conveyed to you in any supernatural way?"

"No."

He wished me good night, and held up his light. I walked by the side of the down Line of rails (with a very disagreeable sensation of a train coming behind me) until I found the path. It was easier to mount than to descend, and I got back to my inn without any adventure.

Punctual to my appointment, I placed my foot on the first notch of the zigzag next night, as the distant clocks were striking eleven. He was waiting for me at the bottom, with his white light on. "I have not called out," I said, when we came close together; "may I speak now?" "By all means, sir." "Good night, then, and here's my hand." "Good night, sir, and here's mine." With that we walked side by side to his box, entered it, closed the door, and sat down by the fire.

"I have made up my mind, sir," he began, bending forward as soon as we were seated, and speaking in a tone but a little above a whisper, "that you shall not have to ask me twice what troubles me. I took you for someone else yesterday evening. That troubles me."

"That mistake?"

"No. That someone else."

"Who is it?"

"I don't know."

"Like me?"

"I don't know. I never saw the face. The

6 Reading Strategy What does this curious action suggest about the signalman?

7 Discussion What one request does the signalman make of the narrator on his return visit?

left arm is across the face, and the right arm is waved—violently waved. This way."

I followed his action with my eyes, and it was the action of an arm gesticulating, with the utmost passion and vehemence, "For God's sake, clear the way!"

"One moonlight night," said the man, "I was sitting here, when I heard a voice cry, 'Halloa! Below there!' I started up, looked from that door, and saw this Someone else standing by the red light near the tunnel, waving as I just now showed you. The voice seemed hoarse with shouting, and it cried, 'Look out! Look out!' And then again, 'Halloa! Below there! Look out!' I caught up my lamp, turned it on red, and ran towards the figure, calling, 'What's wrong? What has happened? Where?' It stood just outside the blackness of the tunnel. I advanced so close upon it that I wondered at its keeping the sleeve across its eyes. I ran right up at it, and had my hand stretched out to pull the sleeve away, when it was gone."

"Into the tunnel," said I.

"No. I ran on into the tunnel, five hundred yards. I stopped, and held my lamp above my head, and saw the figures of the measured distance, and saw the wet stains stealing down the walls and trickling through the arch. I ran out again faster than I had run in (for I had a mortal abhorrence of the place upon me), and I looked all round the red light with my own red light, and I went up the iron ladder to the gallery top of it, and I came down again, and ran back here. I telegraphed both ways, 'An alarm has been given. Is anything wrong?' The answer came back, both ways, 'All well.'"

Resisting the slow touch of a frozen finger tracing out my spine, I showed him how that this figure must be a deception of his sense of sight; and how that figures, originating in disease of the delicate nerves that minister to the functions of the eye, were known to have often troubled patients, some of whom had become conscious of the nature of their affliction, and had even proved it by experiments upon themselves. "As to an imaginary cry," said I, "do but listen for a moment to the wind in this unnatural valley while we speak so low, and to the wild harp it makes of the telegraph wires!"

That was all very well, he returned, after we had sat listening for a while, and he ought to know something of the wind and the wires—he who so often passed long winter nights there, alone and watching. But he would beg to remark that he had not finished.

I asked his pardon, and he slowly added these words, touching my arm:

"Within six hours after the Appearance, the memorable accident on this Line happened, and within ten hours the dead and wounded were brought along through the tunnel over the spot where the figure had stood."

A disagreeable shudder crept over me, but I did my best against it. It was not to be denied, I rejoined, that this was a remarkable coincidence, calculated deeply to impress his mind. But it was unquestionable that remarkable coincidences did continually occur, and they must be taken into account in dealing with such a subject. Though to be sure I must admit, I added (for I thought I saw that he was going to bring the objection to bear upon me), men of common sense did not allow much for coincidences in making the ordinary calculations of life.

He again begged to remark that he had not finished.

I again begged his pardon for being betrayed into interruptions.

"This," he said, again laying his hand upon my arm, and glancing over his shoulder with hollow eyes, "was just a year ago. Six or seven months passed, and I had recovered from the surprise and shock, when one morning, as the day was breaking, I, standing at the door, looked towards the red light, and saw the specter again." He stopped, with a fixed look at me.

"Did it cry out?"

"No. It was silent."

"Did it wave its arm?"

"No. It leaned against the shaft of the light, with both hands before the face. Like this."

Once more I followed his action with my eyes. It was an action of mourning. I have seen such an attitude in stone figures on tombs.

"Did you go up to it?"

"I came in and sat down, partly to collect my thoughts, partly because it had turned me faint. When I went to the door again, daylight was above me, and the ghost was gone."

"But nothing followed? Nothing came of this?"

He touched me on the arm with his forefinger twice or thrice, giving a ghastly nod each time:

8 "That very day, as a train came out of the tunnel, I noticed, at a carriage window on my side, what looked like a confusion of hands and heads, and something waved. I saw it just in time to signal the driver, Stop! He shut off, and put his brake on, but the train drifted past here a hundred and fifty yards or more. I ran after it, and, as I went along, heard terrible screams and cries. A beautiful young lady had died instantaneously in one of the compartments, and was brought in here, and laid on this floor between us."

Involuntarily I pushed my chair back, as I looked from the boards at which he pointed to himself.

"True, sir. True. Precisely as it happened, so I tell it you."

I could think of nothing to say, to any purpose, and my mouth was very dry. The wind and the wires took up the story with a long lamenting wail.

9 He resumed. "Now, sir, mark this, and judge how my mind is troubled. The specter came back a week ago. Ever since, it has been there, now and again, by fits and starts."

"At the light?"

"At the Danger light."

"What does it seem to do?"

He repeated, if possible with increased passion and vehemence, that former gesticulation of, "For God's sake, clear the way!"

Then he went on. "I have no peace or rest for it. It calls to me, for many minutes together, in an agonized manner, 'Below there! Look out! Look out!' It stands waving to me. It rings my little bell—"

I caught at that. "Did it ring your bell yesterday evening when I was here, and you went to the door?"

"Twice."

"Why, see," said I, "how your imagination misleads you. My eyes were on the bell, and my ears were open to the bell, and if I am a living man, it did NOT ring at those times. No, nor at any other time, except when it was rung in the natural course of physical things by the station communicating with you."

He shook his head. "I have never made a mistake as to that yet, sir. I have never confused the specter's ring with the man's. The ghost's ring is a strange vibration in the bell that it derives from nothing else, and I have not asserted that the bell stirs to the eye. I don't wonder that you failed to hear it. But *I* heard it."

"And did the specter seem to be there, when you looked out?"

"It WAS there."

"Both times?"

He repeated firmly: "Both times."

"Will you come to the door with me, and look for it now?"

He bit his under lip as though he were somewhat unwilling, but arose. I opened the door, and stood on the step, while he stood in the doorway. There was the Danger light. There was the dismal mouth of the tunnel. There were the high, wet stone walls of the cutting. There were the stars above them.

"Do you see it?" I asked him, taking particular note of his face. His eyes were prominent and strained, but not very much more so, perhaps, than my own had been when I had directed them earnestly towards the same spot.

8 **Discussion** What two events had followed the previous appearances of the apparition?

9 **Discussion** Why is the Signalman presently so troubled?

10 Discussion What is the signalman's predicament?

"No," he answered. "It is not there."

"Agreed," said I.

We went in again, shut the door, and resumed our seats. I was thinking how best to improve this advantage, if it might be called one, when he took up the conversation in such a matter-of-course way, so assuming that there could be no serious question of fact between us, that I felt myself placed in the weakest of positions.

"By this time you will fully understand, sir," he said, "that what troubles me so dreadfully is the question, What does the specter mean?"

I was not sure, I told him, that I did fully understand.

"What is its warning against?" he said, ruminating, with his eyes on the fire, and only by times turning them on me. "What is the danger? Where is the danger? There is danger overhanging somewhere on the Line. Some dreadful calamity will happen. It is not to be doubted this third time, after what has gone before. But surely this is a cruel haunting of *me.* What can *I* do?"

He pulled out his handkerchief, and wiped the drops from his heated forehead.

"If I telegraph Danger, on either side of me, or on both, I can give no reason for it," he went on, wiping the palms of his hands. "I should get into trouble, and do no good.
10 They would think I was mad. This is the way it would work: Message: "Danger! Take care!" Answer: "What Danger? Where?" Message: "Don't know. But for God's sake, take care!" They would displace me. What else could they do?"

His pain of mind was most pitiable to see. It was the mental torture of a conscientious man, oppressed beyond endurance by an unintelligible responsibility involving life.

"When it first stood under the Danger light," he went on, putting his dark hair back from his head, and drawing his hands outward across and across his temples in an extremity of feverish distress, "why not tell me where that accident was to happen—if it must happen? Why not tell me how it could be averted—if it could have been averted? When on its second coming it hid its face, why not tell me, instead, "She is going to die. Let them keep her at home"? If it came, on those two occasions, only to show me that its warnings were true, and so to prepare me for the third, why not warn me plainly now? And I, Lord help me! A mere poor signalman on this solitary station! Why not go to somebody with credit to be believed, and power to act?"

When I saw him in this state, I saw that for the poor man's sake, as well as for the public safety, what I had to do for the time was to compose his mind. Therefore, setting aside all question of reality or unreality between us, I represented to him that whoever thoroughly discharged his duty must do well, and that at least it was his comfort that he understood his duty, though he did not understand these confounding Appearances. In this effort I succeeded far better than in the attempt to reason him out of his conviction. He became calm; the occupations incidental to his post as the night advanced began to make larger demands on his attention: and I left him at two in the morning. I had offered to stay through the night, but he would not hear of it.

That I more than once looked back at the red light as I ascended the pathway, that I did not like the red light, and that I should have slept but poorly if my bed had been under it, I see no reason to conceal. Nor did I like the two sequences of the accident and the dead girl. I see no reason to conceal that either.

But what ran most in my thoughts was the consideration how ought I to act, having become the recipient of this disclosure? I had proved the man to be intelligent, vigilant, painstaking, and exact; but how long might he remain so, in his state of mind? Though in a subordinate position, still he held a most important trust, and would I (for

DETAIL OF RED VIRGINIA CREEPER
Edvard Munch
Three Lions

instance) like to stake my own life on the chances of his continuing to execute it with precision?

Unable to overcome a feeling that there would be something treacherous in my communicating what he had told me to his superiors in the Company, without first being plain with himself and proposing a middle course to him, I ultimately resolved to offer to accompany him (otherwise keeping his secret for the present) to the wisest medical practitioner we could hear of in those parts, and to take his opinion. A change in his time of duty would come round next night, he had apprised me, and he would be off an hour or two after sunrise, and on again soon after sunset. I had appointed to return accordingly.

Humanities Note

Fine art, *Red Virginia Creeper* by Edvard Munch. Munch (1863–1944), a Norwegian painter and graphic artist, studied art at the School of Arts and Crafts in Oslo and in Paris. Munch's unique and complex psychological style is considered a forerunner of expressionism (nonobjective use of symbols and stereotypes, to give objective expression to inner experience).

The painting *Red Virginia Creeper* was painted in 1899–1900, during a period in Munch's life when he turned his focus outward to other people and the world around him. This, along with other paintings done at this time, was a motif he wished to use for a series of large decorative murals entitled "The Frieze of Life." The large house, covered with the red growth of the vine, has an air of mystery. The lonely figure in the foreground is surrounded by an aura of despair. The viewer is given no clue to the reasons behind his despair. Executed in a rhythmic, flowing style, this painting expresses isolation and spiritual unease.

You might use these questions for discussion:

1. How does the artist view the human condition?
2. How does this compare to Dickens's view of the human condition?

11 Discussion What is the significance of the description of the signalman's face as "quite composed"?

12 Discussion How was the signalman killed?

13 Discussion Why was the engine driver seen in the same position as the ghost?

Next evening was a lovely evening, and I walked out early to enjoy it. The sun was not yet quite down when I traversed the field-path near the top of the deep cutting. I would extend my walk for an hour, I said to myself, half an hour on and half an hour back, and it would then be time to go to my signalman's box.

Before pursuing my stroll, I stepped to the brink, and mechanically looked down, from the point from which I had first seen him. I cannot describe the thrill that seized upon me, when, close at the mouth of the tunnel, I saw the appearance of a man, with his left sleeve across his eyes, passionately waving his right arm.

The nameless horror that oppressed me passed in a moment, for in a moment I saw that this appearance of a man was a man indeed, and that there was a little group of other men, standing at a short distance, to whom he seemed to be rehearsing the gesture he made. The Danger light was not yet lighted. Against its shaft, a little low hut, entirely new to me, had been made of some wooden supports and tarpaulin. It looked no bigger than a bed.

With an irresistible sense that something was wrong—with a flashing self-reproachful fear that fatal mischief had come of my leaving the man there, and causing no one to be sent to overlook or correct what he did—I descended the notched path with all the speed I could make.

"What is the matter?" I asked the men.

"Signalman killed this morning, sir."

"Not the man belonging to that box?"

"Yes, sir."

"Not the man I know?"

"You will recognize him, sir, if you knew
11 him," said the man who spoke for the others, solemnly uncovering his own head, and raising an end of the tarpaulin, "for his face is quite composed."

"O, how did this happen, how did this happen?" I asked, turning from one to another as the hut closed in again.

"He was cut down by an engine, sir. No man in England knew his work better. But somehow he was not clear of the outer rail. It was just at broad day. He had struck the
light, and had the lamp in his hand. As the 12
engine came out of the tunnel, his back was towards her, and she cut him down. That man drove her, and was showing how it happened. Show the gentleman, Tom."

The man, who wore a rough dark dress, stepped back to his former place at the mouth of the tunnel.

"Coming round the curve in the tunnel, sir," he said, "I saw him at the end, like as if I saw him down a perspective-glass. There was no time to check speed, and I knew him to be very careful. As he didn't seem to take heed of the whistle, I shut it off when we were running down upon him, and called to him as loud as I could call."

"What did you say?"

"I said, 'Below there! Look out! Look out! For God's sake, clear the way!' "

I started.

"Ah! it was a dreadful time, sir. I never
left off calling to him. I put this arm before 13
my eyes not to see, and I waved this arm to the last; but it was no use."

Without prolonging the narrative to dwell on any one of its curious circumstances more than on any other, I may, in closing it, point out the coincidence that the warning of the Engine Driver included, not only the words which the unfortunate Signalman had repeated to me as haunting him, but also the words which I myself—not he—had attached and that only in my own mind, to the gesticulation he had imitated.

THINKING ABOUT THE SELECTION

Recalling

1. (a) How does the signalman behave during his first meeting with the narrator? (b) What explanation for this behavior is given in the second meeting?
2. (a) What tragedy followed the specter's first appearance? (b) Its second appearance? (c) How has it been warning the signalman lately?
3. What happens to the signalman?

Interpreting

4. Do you think the narrator is totally convinced of his own explanations of the events on the railroad line? Explain.
5. (a) What do you think is the narrator's view of the supernatural? (b) What evidence are you given that the events he narrates have changed his views?

Applying

6. In light of his description of the signalman's job, how does this story serve Dickens's goal of promoting social change in England?

ANALYZING LITERATURE

Following the Plot in a Ghost Story

The **plot** is the series of events in a story or novel that answers the question "What happens?" Plot usually involves a conflict, or clash between characters or opposing forces, that builds to a high point called the climax. In a ghost story, the plot revolves around supernatural—or "otherworldly"—elements.

1. What supernatural elements are featured in "The Signalman"? How do these elements tie in directly to the story's plot?
2. The story features several different conflicts. Identify:
   a. The conflict between the narrator and the signalman.
   b. The signalman's inner conflict.
   c. The narrator's inner conflict.

CRITICAL THINKING AND READING

Separating Details

Like any good ghost story, "The Signalman" is filled with details that lend themselves to both realistic and supernatural interpretation. What the signalman, for example, identifies as the specter's cry, the narrator "writes off" as the sound of the wind whistling through the telegraph wires. Yet not all details in the story can be explained away so simply. Identify the realistic and supernatural significance of each of the following details.

1. The ringing of the bell.
2. The words "For God's sake, clear the way!"
3. A figure with its left sleeve across its face and its right arm waving frantically.

UNDERSTANDING LANGUAGE

Fitting the Context

Occasionally writers use words that, in a given context, are *ambiguous*, or open to more than one interpretation. In each case, give the intended meaning of the italicized word, and identify a second possible reading.

1. . . . an oncoming rush . . . caused me to *start* back . . . (page 882)
2. . . . in [the tunnel's] architecture there was a . . . forbidding *air*. (page 883)
3. That light was part of his *charge*? (page 883)
4. I have seen such an *attitude* in stone figures on tombs. (page 887)

THINKING AND WRITING

Writing a Ghost Story

Using the notes you developed earlier, write an original ghost story. Before you proceed, map out your story's plot. Ask: What will happen in the story, and in what order will you report the events? What is the conflict, and who does it involve? How will the conflict be resolved? When you have answered these questions, you may begin your first draft.

Answers

ANSWERS TO THINKING ABOUT THE SELECTION

Recalling

1. (a) During his first meeting with the narrator, the signalman acts troubled. (b) In the second meeting, the signalman explains that he took the narrator for someone else.
2. (a) Within six hours after the specter's first appearance, there was a train crash. (b) After its second appearance, a young woman was killed. (c) Lately, it has been ringing a bell to warn the signalman.
3. The signalman is killed by a train.

Interpreting

4. The narrator does not seem to be totally convinced by his own explanations of the events on the railroad line. He concludes by speaking of "curious" circumstance and coincidence.
5. (a) At first, the narrator is doubtful of the supernatural. (b) The events he witnesses cause him to be uncertain of the meaning of the events.

Applying

6. Dickens's description of the signalman's job points up its hardships and dangers, thus contributing to his goal of promoting social change in England.

ANSWERS TO ANALYZING LITERATURE

1. "The Signalman" features a mysterious apparition, a series of warnings, and sudden tragedies.
2. (a) The narrator and the signalman are not certain whether or not to trust one another. (b) The signalman doesn't know if he should trust his feelings about the strange goings on at the train tunnel. (c) The narrator is in conflict over whether or not to believe the signalman.

ANSWERS TO CRITICAL THINKING AND READING

1. The narrator maintains the bell did not ring. The signalman points out that "the ghost's ring is a strange vibration in the bell that it derives from nothing else. . . ."
2. These are the words the narrator has mentally used. He hears them mysteriously repeated by a man who says they were uttered by the apparition.
3. The signalman as well as the apparition is said to assume this pose.

UNDERSTANDING LANGUAGE

1. to pull back—return
2. mood—smell
3. duty—obligation
4. appearance—facade
5. job—watch

THINKING AND WRITING

For help with this assignment, students can refer to Lesson 19 "Writing a Short Story," in the Handbook of Writing About Literature.

More About the Author Because Thomas Hardy was considered to be the greatest novelist of his generation, when he died he was buried in Poet's Corner in Westminster Abbey in London. At his own request, however, his heart was buried in the churchyard in Stinsford, the town of his birth. The family cottage just outside Stinsford very much resembles the cottage that he describes in "The Three Strangers" and is still occupied by people who live off the land. Hardy loved the Dorset countryside in which he grew up, and said that he used the rural setting because its stark simplicity gave his novels the same dramatic intensity and sharpness of focus that the Greek theater gave to the Greek plays.

THOMAS HARDY

1840–1928

In addition to being a highly regarded poet, Thomas Hardy was one of the most important fiction writers of the Victorian Age. Set in the imaginary region of Wessex, Hardy's novels and stories focused on the plight of the underdog in an unfeeling society.

Hardy was born in the Dorset countryside in southwestern England, the area upon which his fictional setting of Wessex is based. After leaving school at the age of fifteen, Hardy was trained to be an architect. He developed a strong interest in fiction and poetry, however, and eventually decided to focus his energy on writing. His first novel, *Desperate Remedies,* was published annonymously in 1871. The following year he achieved success as a novelist with the publication of *Under the Greenwood Tree.* Hardy went on to produce several more novels, but when his book *Jude the Obscure* (1896) prompted a hostile reaction, he turned to writing poetry.

In his novels and stories, Hardy often depicted characters whose destinies were shaped by forces beyond their control. Many of his works, including "The Three Strangers," also contain an element of mystery, resulting in part from the rough, unforgiving landscape that serves as their setting.

Objectives

1. To understand the use and importance of setting and mood in a short story
2. To make inferences about the author's attitude toward fate
3. To read and understand the use of dialect in a short story
4. To describe a setting

Teaching Portfolio: Support Material

Teacher Backup, pp. 00-00

Vocabulary Check, p. 00

Usage and Mechanics Worksheet, p. 00

Analyzing Literature Worksheet, p. 00

Critical Thinking and Reading Worksheet, p. 00

Language Worksheet, p. 00

Selection Test, p. 00

GUIDE FOR READING

The Writer's Technique

Setting and Mood. Setting is the time when and place where a story takes place. This information is sometimes vital to a story's *mood,* or the feelings it stirs in the reader. If, for example, the story is set in a crowded, bustling city, the mood will be tense and hectic. If, on the other hand, the story is set on a lush tropical island, the mood will be calm and tranquil.

Look For

As you read "The Three Strangers," be alert to details of the story's setting and to the mood it creates.

Writing

Imagine that a stranger appeared at the front door of your home one evening. Letting your imagination run free, describe this person's appearance, as well as yours and your family's initial reaction to him or her. Finally, state the reason for the stranger's visit.

Vocabulary

Knowing the following words will help you as you read "The Three Strangers."

inimical (in im′ i k'l) *adj.*: Unfriendly (p. 894)
salient (sāl′ yənt) *adj.*: Striking; easily noticeable (p. 897)
desultory (dez′ 'l tôr ē) *adj.*: Jumping from point to point (p. 898)
alacrity (ə lak′ r tē) *n.*: Willingness (p. 902)
baleful (bāl fəl) *adj.*: Of or with evil intent (p. 905)

Literary Focus Point out that Hardy is sometimes considered a regional novelist because he consistently used the geographic area known as Wessex as the setting for his stories. His affection for this region and for those characters whose roots are there is in sharp contrast with his generally pessimistic view of life. Hardy's philosophical determinism as expressed in his novels is similar to the Greek view of fate as expressed in Classical Tragedy, which Hardy knew well.

Look For Have your less advanced students compile a list of the words and phrases that describe parts of the countryside. Have them separate their words and phrases into two columns—those that create a positive impression and those that create a negative one.

Writing For an alternative exercise, have students discuss the similarities and differences between the reactions of rural Victorian society to strangers, as described in "The Three Strangers," and the reactions of modern urban society. Then have them complete the freewriting assignment, taking into consideration the points raised in the discussion.

Vocabulary Discuss the denotative and connotative meanings of each of the vocabulary words and how each affects the overall tone of the selection.

Motivation for Reading Tell students that "The Three Strangers" is a mystery, complete with a musical riddle. As they read, have them jot down clues to the true identities of each of the strangers and mark the clue that finally tells them the identity of each.

Master Teacher Note The movie based on Thomas Hardy's *Far from the Madding Crowd* graphically captures the mood and tone created by Hardy's use of setting. Students might view it on their own or as a group and then discuss the importance of the setting.

Thematic Idea Point out that both Charles Dickens and Emily Brontë in the selections included in this book use setting to determine the mood and tone of their works. Dickens uses the deplorable living conditions in urban London, and Brontë uses the rugged Yorkshire countryside in winter.

Purpose-Setting Question What role does setting play in this story?

1 **Literary Focus** What effect does the setting have on the mood of the story? What is the mood in the opening paragraphs?

2 **Discussion** Discuss the setting of the shepherd's house. Why had this particular spot proven good for a dwelling? Why is it a good location for a story called "The Three Strangers"?

The Three Strangers

Thomas Hardy

Among the few features of agricultural England which retain an appearance but little modified by the lapse of centuries, may be reckoned the long, grassy and furzy downs, coombs,[1] or ewe-leases, as they are called according to their kind, that fill a large area of certain counties in the south and southwest. If any mark of human occupation is met with hereon, it usually takes the form of the solitary cottage of some
1 shepherd.

Fifty years ago such a lonely cottage stood on such a down, and may possibly be standing there now. In spite of its loneliness, however, the spot, by actual measurement, was not three miles from a county town. Yet that affected it little. Three miles of irregular upland, during the long inimical seasons, with their sleets, snows, rains, and mists, afford withdrawing space enough to isolate a Timon[2] or a Nebuchadnezzar;[3] much less, in fair weather, to please that less repellent tribe, the poets, philosophers, artists, and others who "conceive and meditate of pleasant things."

Some old earthen camp or barrow,[4] some clump of trees, at least some starved fragment of ancient hedge is usually taken
2 advantage of in the erection of these forlorn dwellings. But, in the present case, such a kind of shelter had been disregarded. Higher Crowstairs, as the house was called, stood quite detached and undefended. The only reason for its precise situation seemed to be the crossing of two footpaths at right angles hard by, which may have crossed there and thus for a good five hundred years. Hence the house was exposed to the elements on all sides. But, though the wind up here blew unmistakably when it did blow, and the rain hit hard whenever it fell, the various weathers of the winter season were not quite so formidable on the down as they were imagined to be by dwellers on low ground. The raw rimes[5] were not so pernicious as in the hollows, and the frosts were scarcely so severe. When the shepherd and his family who tenanted the house were pitied for their sufferings from the exposure, they said that upon the whole they were less inconvenienced by "wuzzes and flames" (hoarses and phlegms) than when they had lived by the stream of a snug neighboring valley.

The night of March 28, 182– was precisely one of the nights that were wont to call forth these expressions of commiseration. The level rainstorm smote walls, slopes, and hedges like the clothyard shafts of Senlac and Crecy.[6] Such sheep and outdoor animals as had no shelter stood with their buttocks to the winds; while the tails of little birds trying to roost on some scraggy thorn were blown inside out like umbrellas. The gable-end of the cottage was stained with wet, and the eavesdroppings flapped against the wall. Yet never was commiseration for the shepherd more misplaced. For that cheerful rustic was entertaining a large

---

1. coombs (ko͞oms) *n:* Deep, narrow valleys.
2. Timon (tī'mən): A fifth-century Greek hermit who lived in a cave.
3. Nebuchadnezzar (neb' yə kəd nez' ər): A Babylonian king who isolated himself in the fields after becoming insane.
4. barrow *n.*: A heap of earth or rocks marking a grave.

5. rimes (rīmz) *n:* White frost.
6. clothyard . . . Crecy (krā sē'): Yard-long arrows used in battles fought in England (at Senlac) and France (at Crecy).

party in glorification of the christening of his second girl.

The guests had arrived before the rain began to fall, and they were all now assembled in the chief or living room of the dwelling. A glance into the apartment at eight o'clock on this eventful evening would have resulted in the opinion that it was as cozy and comfortable a nook as could be wished for in boisterous weather. The calling of its inhabitant was proclaimed by a number of highly polished sheep crooks without stems that were hung ornamentally over the fire-
3 place, the curl of each shining crook varying from the antiquated type engraved in the patriarchal pictures of old family Bibles to the most approved fashion of the last local sheep fair. The room was lighted by half a dozen candles, having wicks only a trifle smaller than the grease which enveloped them, in candlesticks that were never used but at high days, holy days, and family feasts. The lights were scattered about the room, two of them standing on the chimney piece. This position of candles was in itself significant. Candles on the chimney piece always meant a party.

On the hearth, in front of a backbrand to give substance, blazed a fire of thorns, that crackled "like the laughter of the fool."

Nineteen persons were gathered here. Of these, five women, wearing gowns of various bright hues, sat in chairs along the wall; girls shy and not shy filled the window bench; four men, including Charley Jake the hedge carpenter, Elijah New the parish clerk, and John Pitcher, a neighboring dairyman, the shepherd's father-in-law,
4 lolled in the settle; a young man and maid, who were blushing over tentative *pourparlers*[7] on a life companionship, sat beneath the corner cupboard; and an elderly engaged man of fifty or upward moved restlessly about from spots where his betrothed was not to the spot where she was. Enjoyment was pretty general, and so much the more prevailed in being unhampered by conventional restrictions. Absolute confidence in each other's good opinion begat perfect ease, while the finishing stroke of manner, amounting to a truly princely serenity, was lent to the majority by the absence of any expression or trait denoting that they wished to get on in the world, enlarge their minds, or do any eclipsing thing whatever —which nowadays so generally nips the bloom and *bonhomie*[8] of all except the two extremes of the social scale.

Shepherd Fennel had married well, his wife being a dairyman's daughter from a vale at a distance, who brought fifty guineas in her pocket—and kept them there, till they should be required for ministering to the needs of a coming family. This frugal woman had been somewhat exercised as to the character that should be given to the gathering. A sit-still party had its advantages; but an undisturbed position of ease in chairs and settles was apt to lead on the men to such an unconscionable deal of toping[9] that they would sometimes fairly drink the house dry. A dancing party was the alternative; but this, while avoiding the foregoing objection on the score of good drink,
had a counterbalancing disadvantage in the 5
matter of good victuals, the ravenous appetites engendered by the exercise causing immense havoc in the buttery. Shepherdess Fennel fell back upon the intermediate plan of mingling short dances with short periods of talk and singing, so as to hinder any ungovernable rage in either. But this scheme was entirely confined to her own gentle mind: the shepherd himself was in the mood to exhibit the most reckless phases of hospitality.

The fiddler was a boy of those parts, about twelve years of age, who had a wonderful dexterity in jigs and reels, though his fingers were so small and short as to necessitate a constant shifting for the high notes, from which he scrambled back to the first

7. *pourparlers* (po͞or′ pär lā′): Informal discussions (French).

8. *bonhomie* (bän′ ə mē′): Good nature (French).
9. toping: Drinking.

3 Discussion Compare and contrast the conditions inside and outside the cottage.

4 Discussion How do the people in the cottage feel about themselves and each other? Why?

5 Discussion You might mention that fennel is an herb of the parsley family. What is most appealing about Mrs. Fennel? What is least appealing?

Humanities Note

Fine art, *Summer, Afternoon After a Shower* by John Constable. John Constable (1776–1837), a noteworthy British landscape painter was educated at the schools of the Royal Academy. he began his career in 1802 as a portrait and landscape painter. He is remembered today for his innovation of working out-of-doors and his resulting landscapes of vibrant color and light.

Summer, Afternoon After a Shower demonstrates Constable's constant interest in the effects of weather upon the landscape. Constable painted the skies in all atmospheric conditions. In this painting he attempts to describe truthfully the tempers of weather. The freshness and color of the wind-tossed landscape suffused with a vifid light were unknown qualities in his day, when formalized, studio versions of nature were the accepted mode.

You might use the following questions for discussion:

1. What features of this painting make it appropriate as an illustration for this story?
2. What is the mood of this painting?
3. Does it match the mood of the story?

SUMMER, AFTERNOON AFTER A SHOWER
John Constable
The Tate Gallery, London

position with sounds not of unmixed purity of tone. At seven the shrill tweedle-dee of this youngster had begun, accompanied by a booming ground bass from Elijah New, the parish clerk, who had thoughtfully brought with him his favorite musical instrument, the serpent.[10] Dancing was instantaneous, Mrs. Fennel privately enjoining the players on no account to let the dance exceed the length of a quarter of an hour.

But Elijah and the boy in the excitement of their position quite forgot the injunction. Moreover, Oliver Giles, a man of seventeen, one of the dancers, who was enamored of his partner, a fair girl of thirty-three rolling years, had recklessly handed a new crown-piece to the musicians, as a bribe to keep going as long as they had muscle and wind. Mrs. Fennel seeing the steam begin to generate on the countenances of her guests, crossed over and touched the fiddler's elbow and put her hand on the serpent's mouth. But they took no notice, and fearing she might lose her character of genial hostess if she were to interfere too markedly, she retired and sat down helpless. And so the dance whizzed on with cumulative fury, the performers moving in their planet-like courses, direct and retrograde,[11] from apogee to perigee,[12] till the hand of the well-kicked clock at the bottom of the room had traveled over the circumference of an hour.

While these cheerful events were in course of enactment within Fennel's pastoral dwelling an incident having considerable bearing on the party had occurred in the gloomy night without. Mrs. Fennel's concern about the growing fierceness of the dance corresponded in point of time with the ascent of a human figure to the solitary hill of Higher Crowstairs from the direction of the distant town. This personage strode on through the rain without a pause, following the little-worn path which, further on in its course, skirted the shepherd's cottage.

It was nearly the time of full moon, and on this account, though the sky was lined with a uniform sheet of dripping cloud, ordi-

---

10. serpent *n.*: An obsolete, coiled bass wind instrument.

11. direct and retrograde: Orbital directions.
12. from apogee to perigee: From the points in orbit farthest from and nearest to the earth.

nary objects out of doors were readily visible. The sad wan light revealed the lonely pedestrian to be a man of supple frame; his gait suggested that he had somewhat passed the period of perfect and instinctive agility, though not so far as to be otherwise than rapid of motion when occasion required. At a rough guess, he might have been about forty years of age. He appeared tall, but a recruiting sergeant, or other person accustomed to the judging of men's heights by the eye, would have discerned that this was chiefly owing to his gauntness, and that he was not more than five-feet-eight or nine.

Notwithstanding the regularity of his tread there was caution in it, as in that of one who mentally feels his way; and despite the fact that it was not a black coat nor a dark garment of any sort that he wore, there was something about him which suggested that he naturally belonged to the black-coated tribes[13] of men. His clothes were of fustian,[14] and his boots hobnailed, yet in his progress he showed not the mud-accustomed bearing of hobnailed and fustianed peasantry.

By the time that he had arrived abreast of the shepherd's premises the rain came down, or rather came along, with yet more determined violence. The outskirts of the little settlement partially broke the force of wind and rain, and this induced him to stand still. The most salient of the shepherd's domestic erections was an empty sty at the forward corner of his hedgeless garden, for in these latitudes the principle of
6 masking the homelier features of your establishment by a conventional frontage was unknown. The traveler's eye was attracted to this small building by the pallid shine of the wet slates that covered it. He turned aside, and, finding it empty, stood under the pent roof for shelter.

While he stood the boom of the serpent within the adjacent house, and the lesser strains of the fiddler, reached the spot as an accompaniment to the surging hiss of the flying rain on the sod, its louder beating on the cabbage leaves of the garden, on the straw hackles of eight or ten beehives just discernible by the path, and its dripping from the eaves into a row of buckets and pans that had been placed under the walls of the cottage. For at Higher Crowstairs, as at all such elevated domiciles, the grand difficulty of housekeeping was an insufficiency of water; and a casual rainfall was utilized by turning out, as catchers, every utensil that the house contained. Some queer stories might be told of the contrivances for economy in suds and dishwaters that are absolutely necessitated in upland habitations during the droughts of summer. But at this season there were no such exigencies; a mere acceptance of what the skies bestowed was sufficient for an abundant store.

At last the notes of the serpent ceased and the house was silent. This cessation of activity aroused the solitary pedestrian from the reverie into which he had lapsed, and, emerging from the shed, with an apparently new intention, he walked up the path to the house door. Arrived here, his first act was to kneel down on a large stone beside the row of vessels, and to drink a copious draft from one of them. Having quenched his thirst he rose and lifted his hand to knock, but paused with his eye upon the panel. Since the dark surface of the wood revealed absolutely nothing, it was evident that he must be mentally looking through the door, as if he wished to measure thereby all the possibilities that a house of this sort might include, and how they might bear upon the question of his entry.

In his indecision he turned and surveyed the scene around. Not a soul was anywhere visible. The garden path stretched downward from his feet, gleaming like the track of a snail; the roof of the little well (mostly dry), the well cover, the top rail of the garden gate, were varnished with the same dull liquid glaze; while, far away in the vale, a faint whiteness of more than usual extent

13. black-coated tribes: Middle class.
14. fustian (fus'chən) *n.*: A coarse cotton cloth.

6 **Critical Thinking and Reading**
What part does fate play in this stranger's actions? What part did the man's own free will play?

7 Reading Strategy Based on what you have read so far, how would you react to the knock at the door if you were a guest at the party? What do you anticipate is going to happen because the shepherd has let a stranger into his house?

8 Discussion What is your first impression of the man? What do you think is the first impression of the party guests?

9 Discussion Why is it odd that the man has misplaced some objects? What are other reasons that he doesn't have his pipe and tobacco box with him?

showed that the rivers were high in the meads. Beyond all this winked a few bleared lamplights through the beating drops —lights that denoted the situation of the county town from which he had appeared to come. The absence of all notes of life in that direction seemed to clinch his intentions, and he knocked at the door.

Within, a desultory chat had taken the place of movement and musical sound. The hedge carpenter was suggesting a song to the company, which nobody just then was inclined to undertake, so that the knock
7 afforded a not unwelcome diversion.

"Walk in!" said the shepherd promptly.

The latch clicked upward, and out of the night our pedestrian appeared upon the doormat. The shepherd arose, snuffed two of the nearest candles, and turned to look at him.

Their light disclosed that the stranger was dark in complexion and not unprepossessing as to feature. His hat, which for a moment he did not remove, hung low over his eyes, without concealing that they were large, open, and determined, moving with a flash rather than a glance around the room. He seemed pleased with his survey, and, baring his shaggy head, said, in a rich deep voice, "The rain is so heavy, friends, that I ask leave to come in and rest awhile."

"To be sure, stranger," said the shep-
8 herd. "And faith, you've been lucky in choosing your time, for we are having a bit of a fling for a glad cause—though, to be sure, a man could hardly wish that glad cause to happen more than once a year."

"Nor less," spoke up a woman. "For 'tis best to get your family over and done with, as soon as you can, so as to be all the earlier out of the fag o't."[15]

"And what may be this glad cause?" asked the stranger.

"A birth and christening," said the shepherd.

The stranger hoped his host might not be made unhappy either by too many or too few of such episodes, and being invited by a gesture to a pull at the mug, he readily acquiesced. His manner, which, before entering, had been so dubious, was now altogether that of a careless and candid man.

"Late to be traipsing athwart this coomb —hey?" said the engaged man of fifty.

"Late it is, master, as you say.—I'll take a seat in the chimney corner, if you have nothing to urge against it, ma'am; for I am a little moist on the side that was next the rain."

Mrs. Shepherd Fennel assented, and made room for the self-invited comer, who, having got completely inside the chimney corner, stretched out his legs and his arms with the expansiveness of a person quite at home.

"Yes, I am rather cracked in the vamp,"[16] he said freely, seeing that the eyes of the shepherd's wife fell upon his boots, "and I am not well fitted either. I have had some rough times lately, and have been forced to pick up what I can get in the way of wearing, but I must find a suit better fit for working days when I reach home."

"One of hereabouts?" she inquired.

"Not quite that—farther up the country."

"I thought so. And so be I; and by your tongue you come from my neighborhood."

"But you would hardly have heard of me," he said quickly. "My time would be long before yours, ma'am, you see."

This testimony to the youthfulness of his hostess had the effect of stopping her cross-examination.

"There is only one thing more wanted to make me happy," continued the newcomer. "And that is a little baccy,[17] which I am sorry to say I am out of."

"I'll fill your pipe," said the shepherd. 9

"I must ask you to lend me a pipe likewise."

"A smoker, and no pipe about 'ee?"

15. **fag o't:** Fatigue of it.

16. **vamp** *n.*: The part of a shoe or boot covering the instep.

17. **baccy:** Tobacco.

COTTAGE AND POND, MOONLIGHT
Thomas Gainsborough
Victoria & Albert Museum Trustees

"I have dropped it somewhere on the road."

The shepherd filled and handed him a new clay pipe, saying, as he did so, "Hand me your baccy box—I'll fill that too, now I am about it."

The man went through the movement of searching his pockets.

"Lost that too?" said his entertainer, with some surprise.

"I am afraid so," said the man with some confusion. "Give it to me in a screw of paper." Lighting his pipe at the candle with a suction that drew the whole flame into the bowl, he resettled himself in the corner and bent his looks upon the faint steam from his damp legs, as if he wished to say no more.

Meanwhile the general body of guests had been taking little notice of this visitor by reason of an absorbing discussion in which they were engaged with the band about a tune for the next dance. The matter being settled, they were about to stand up when an interruption came in the shape of another knock at the door.

At sound of the same the man in the chimney corner took up the poker and began stirring the brands as if doing it thoroughly were the one aim of his existence; and a second time the shepherd said, "Walk in!" In a moment another man stood upon the straw-woven doormat. He too was a stranger.

This individual was one of a type radically different from the first. There was more of the commonplace in his manner, and a certain jovial cosmopolitanism sat upon his features. He was several years older than the first arrival, his hair being slightly frosted, his eyebrows bristly, and his whiskers cut back from his cheeks. His face was rather full and flabby, and yet it was not altogether a face without power. A few grog blossoms marked the neighborhood of his

Humanities Note

Fine art, *Cottage and Pond, Moonlight* by Thomas Gainsborough. Thomas Gainsborough (1727–1788), an important English painter of portraits and landscapes, was educated at St. Martins Lane Academy in London. Gainsborough slowly gained fame as a portrait painter. Although portraits were his main source of income, he preferred to paint landscapes. His progression in his art gained him considerable fame and the honor of being the favorite painter of King George III and Queen Charlotte. He is remembered today as the most accomplished and innovative painter of eighteenth-century England.

The painting *Cottage and Pond, Moonlight* is something of a curiosity. It is painted in transparent color on a foot-square pane of glass. It was intended for use in an invention of Gainsborough's, a candle-lit viewing box that he called "Gainsborough's Peep Show," which he used to amuse his family and friends. Gainsborough did a series of these paintings on glass of varying landscape subjects, ten of which are known to exist. Of the ten, this is perhaps the most effective. The cozy lit windows and the glowing sunset sky lend a dramatic air to the scene. These slides are exhibited, backlit in a darkened hallway, in the Victoria and Albert Museum in London.

Below are questions you may use for discussion of this painting with your students:

1. In what ways does this painting visualize the setting of the story?
2. What is the effect of the lights pouring from the cottage windows? Is it one of invitation or hostility? Explain.

10 Clarification Hardy uses the name Casterbridge to refer to Dorchester, a town he knew very well, in the south of England. He uses Casterbridge again in his novel *The Mayor of Casterbridge.*

11 Discussion What is Mrs. Fennel's reaction to the two strangers?

nose. He flung back his long drab greatcoat, revealing that beneath it he wore a suit of cinder-gray shade throughout, large heavy seals, of some metal or other that would take a polish, dangling from his fob as his only personal ornament. Shaking the water drops from his low-crowned glazed hat, he
10 said, "I must ask for a few minutes' shelter, comrades, or I shall be wetted to my skin before I get to Casterbridge."

"Make yourself at home, master," said the shepherd, perhaps a trifle less heartily than on the first occasion. Not that Fennel had the least tinge of niggardliness in his composition; but the room was far from large, spare chairs were not numerous, and damp companions were not altogether desirable at close quarters for the women and girls in their bright-colored gowns.

However, the second comer, after taking off his greatcoat, and hanging his hat on a nail in one of the ceiling beams as if he had been specially invited to put it there, advanced and sat down on the table. This had been pushed so closely into the chimney corner, to give all available room to the dancers, that its inner edge grazed the elbow of the man who had ensconced himself by the fire; and thus the two strangers were brought into close companionship. They nodded to each other by way of breaking the ice of unacquaintance, and the first stranger handed his neighbor the family mug—a huge vessel of brown ware, having its upper edge worn away like a threshold by the rub of whole generations of thirsty lips that had gone the way of all flesh, and bearing the following inscription burnt upon its rotund side in yellow letters:

THERE IS NO FUN
UNTiLL i CUM

11 The other man, nothing loth,[18] raised the mug to his lips, and drank on, and on, and on—till a curious blueness overspread the countenance of the shepherd's wife, who had regarded with no little surprise the first stranger's free offer to the second of what did not belong to him to dispense.

"I knew it!" said the toper to the shepherd with much satisfaction. "When I walked up your garden before coming in, and saw the hives all of a row, I said to myself, 'Where there's bees there's honey, and where there's honey there's mead.' But mead of such a truly comfortable sort as this I really didn't expect to meet in my older days." He took yet another pull at the mug, till it assumed an ominous elevation.

"Glad you enjoy it!" said the shepherd warmly.

"It is goodish mead," assented Mrs. Fennel, with an absence of enthusiasm which seemed to say that it was possible to buy praise for one's cellar at too heavy a price. "It is trouble enough to make—and really I hardly think we shall make any more. For honey sells well, and we ourselves can make shift with a drop o' small mead and metheglin[19] for common use from the comb-washings."

"O, but you'll never have the heart!" reproachfully cried the stranger in cinder gray, after taking up the mug a third time and setting it down empty. "I love mead, when 'tis old like this, as I love to go to church o' Sundays, or to relieve the needy any day of the week."

"Ha, ha, ha!" said the man in the chimney corner, who, in spite of the taciturnity induced by the pipe of tobacco, could not or would not refrain from this slight testimony to his comrade's humor.

Now the old mead of those days, brewed of the purest first-year or maiden honey, four pounds to the gallon—with its due complement of white of eggs, cinnamon, ginger, cloves, mace, rosemary, yeast, and processes of working, bottling, and cellaring—tasted remarkably strong; but it did not taste so strong as it actually was. Hence,

18. nothing loth: Not reluctant.

19. small mead and metheglin: Weaker types of mead.

presently, the stranger in cinder gray at the table, moved by its creeping influence, unbuttoned his waistcoat, threw himself back in his chair, spread his legs, and made his presence felt in various ways.

"Well, well, as I say," he resumed, "I am going to Casterbridge, and to Casterbridge I must go. I should have been almost there by this time; but the rain drove me into your dwelling, and I'm not sorry for it."

"You don't live in Casterbridge?" said the shepherd.

"Not as yet; though I shortly mean to move there."

"Going to set up in trade, perhaps?"

"No, no," said the shepherd's wife. "It is
12 easy to see that the gentleman is rich, and don't want to work at anything."

The cinder-gray stranger paused, as if to consider whether he would accept that definition of himself. He presently rejected it by answering, "Rich is not quite the word for me, dame. I do work, and I must work. And even if I only get to Casterbridge by midnight I must begin work there at eight tomorrow morning. Yes, het or wet, blow or snow, famine or sword, my day's work tomorrow must be done."

"Poor man! Then, in spite o' seeming,
12 you be worse off than we?" replied the shepherd's wife.

"'Tis the nature of my trade, men and maidens. 'Tis the nature of my trade more than my poverty. . . . But really and truly I must up and off, or I shan't get a lodging in the town." However, the speaker did not move, and directly added, "There's time for one more draft of friendship before I go; and I'd perform it at once if the mug were not dry."

"Here's a mug o' small," said Mrs. Fennel. "Small, we call it, though to be sure 'tis only the first wash o' the combs."

"No," said the stranger disdainfully. "I won't spoil your first kindness by partaking o' your second."

"Certainly not," broke in Fennel. "We don't increase and multiply every day, and I'll fill the mug again." He went away to the dark place under the stairs where the barrel stood. The shepherdess followed him.

"Why should you do this?" she said reproachfully, as soon as they were alone. "He's emptied it once, though it held enough for ten people; and now he's not contented wi' the small, but must needs call for more o' the strong! And a stranger unbeknown to any of us. For my part, I don't like the look o'
the man at all." 13

"But he's in the house, my honey; and 'tis a wet night, and a christening. Daze it, what's a cup of mead more or less? There'll be plenty more next bee-burning."

"Very well—this time, then," she answered, looking wistfully at the barrel. "But what is the man's calling, and where is he one of, that he should come in and join us like this?"

"I don't know. I'll ask him again."

The catastrophe of having the mug drained dry at one pull by the stranger in cinder gray was effectually guarded against this time by Mrs. Fennel. She poured out his allowance in a small cup, keeping the large one at a discreet distance from him. When he had tossed off his portion, the shepherd renewed his inquiry about the stranger's occupation.

The latter did not immediately reply, and the man in the chimney corner, with sudden demonstrativeness, said, "Anybody 14
may know my trade—I'm a wheelwright."

"A very good trade for these parts," said the shepherd.

"And anybody may know mine—if they've the sense to find it out," said the stranger in cinder gray.

"You may generally tell what a man is by his claws," observed the hedge carpenter, looking at his own hands. "My fingers be as full of thorns as an old pincushion is of pins."

The hands of the man in the chimney corner instinctively sought the shade, and he gazed into the fire as he resumed his pipe. The man at the table took up the hedge carpenter's remark, and added smartly,
"True; but the oddity of my trade is that, 15

12 Reading Strategy Understanding irony will help students comprehend the author's message. How does Mrs. Fennel reveal how she feels about the second stranger in these ironic statements?

13 Discussion What does Hardy reveal about Mr. and Mrs. Fennel in this exchange under the stairs?

14 Reading Strategy What can you infer from this passage about the stranger's reluctance to discuss his trade?

15 Discussion What clue does the stranger provide in the last sentence of this bracketed section?

16 **Enrichment** Although this musical riddle is certainly not the finest example of Hardy's poetry, he did consider himself a better poet than a novelist. In fact, he considered poetry to be far more important than fiction and hoped that he would be remembered as a poet.

17 **Discussion** How do the guests react to the second stranger's song and why?

18 **Discussion** What might make the first stranger ask for a second verse of the song?

19 **Discussion** What does the second stranger's song reveal about his profession?

instead of setting a mark upon me, it sets a mark upon my customers."

No observation being offered by anybody in elucidation of this enigma the shepherd's wife once more called for a song. The same obstacles presented themselves as at the former time—one had no voice, another had forgotten the first verse. The stranger at the table, whose soul had now risen to a good working temperature, relieved the difficulty by exclaiming that, to start the company, he would sing himself. Thrusting one thumb into the armhole of his waistcoat, he waved the other hand in the air, and, with an extemporizing gaze at the shining sheep crooks above the mantelpiece, began:

"O my trade it is the rarest one,
Simple shepherds all—
My trade is a sight to see;
16 *For my customers I tie, and*
take them up on high,
And waft 'em to a far countree!"

The room was silent when he had finished the verse—with one exception, that of the man in the chimney corner, who, at the singer's word, "Chorus!" joined him in a deep bass voice of musical relish—

"And waft 'em to a far countree!"

17 Oliver Giles, John Pitcher the dairyman, the parish clerk, the engaged man of fifty, the row of young women against the wall, seemed lost in thought not of the gayest kind. The shepherd looked meditatively on the ground, the shepherdess gazed keenly at the singer, and with some suspicion; she was doubting whether this stranger were merely singing an old song from recollection, or was composing one there and then for the occasion. All were as perplexed at the obscure revelation as the guests at Belshazzar's Feast,[20] except the man in the chimney corner, who quietly said, "Second verse, stranger," and smoked on.

The singer thoroughly moistened himself from his lips inwards, and went on with the next stanza as requested:

"My tools are but common ones,
Simple shepherds all—
My tools are no sight to see: 19
A little hempen string, and a post
whereon to swing,
Are implements enough for me!"

Shepherd Fennel glanced round. There was no longer any doubt that the stranger was answering his question rhythmically. The guests one and all started back with suppressed exclamations. The young woman engaged to the man of fifty fainted halfway, and would have proceeded, but finding him wanting in alacrity for catching her she sat down trembling.

"Oh, he's the—!" whispered the people in the background, mentioning the name of an ominous public officer. "He's come to do it! 'Tis to be at Casterbridge jail tomorrow—the man for sheep-stealing—the poor clockmaker we heard of, who used to live away at Shottsford and had no work to do—Timothy Summers, whose family were a-starving, and so he went out of Shottsford by the high road, and took a sheep in open daylight, defying the farmer and the farmer's wife and the farmer's lad, and every man jack among 'em. He' (and they nodded towards the stranger of the deadly trade) 'is come from up the country to do it because there's not enough to do in his own county town, and he's got the place here now our own county man's dead; he's going to live in the same cottage under the prison wall."

The stranger in cinder gray took no notice of this whispered string of observations, but again wetted his lips. Seeing that his friend in the chimney corner was the only one who reciprocated his joviality in any way, he held out his cup towards that appreciative comrade, who also held out his own. They clinked together, the eyes of the rest of

20. as the . . . Belshazzar's (bel shaz′ərz) **Feast:** In the Old Testament, writing appeared on the wall during a feast held by the king of Babylon warning him of defeat (Ezekiel 5:1).

the room hanging upon the singer's actions. He parted his lips for the third verse; but at that moment another knock was audible upon the door. This time the knock was faint and hesitating.

The company seemed scared; the shepherd looked with consternation towards the entrance, and it was with some effort that he resisted his alarmed wife's deprecatory glance, and uttered for the third time the welcoming words, "Walk in!"

The door was gently opened, and another man stood upon the mat. He, like those who had preceded him, was a stranger. This time it was a short, small personage, of fair complexion, and dressed in a decent suit of dark clothes.

"Can you tell me the way to—?" he began; when, gazing round the room to observe the nature of the company amongst whom he had fallen, his eyes lighted on the stranger in cinder gray. It was just at the instant when the latter, who had thrown his mind into his song with such a will that he scarcely heeded the interruption, silenced all whispers and inquiries by bursting into his third verse:

"Tomorrow is my working day,
Simple shepherds all—
Tomorrow is a working day for me:
For the farmer's sheep is slain,
and the lad who did it ta'en,
And on his soul may God ha' merc-y!"

The stranger in the chimney corner, waving cups with the singer so heartily that his mead splashed over on the hearth, repeated in his bass voice as before:—

21 *"And on his soul may God ha' merc-y!"*

All this time the third stranger had been standing in the doorway. Finding now that he did not come forward or go on speaking,
22 the guests particularly regarded him. They noticed to their surprise that he stood before them the picture of abject terror—his knees trembling, his hand shaking so violently that the door latch by which he supported himself rattled audibly; his white lips were parted, and his eyes fixed on the merry officer of justice in the middle of the room. A moment more and he had turned, closed the door, and fled.

"What a man can it be?" said the shepherd.

The rest, between the awfulness of their late discovery and the odd conduct of this third visitor, looked as if they knew not what to think, and said nothing. Instinctively they withdrew farther and farther from the grim gentleman in their midst, whom some of them seemed to take for the Prince of Darkness himself, till they formed a remote
circle, an empty space of floor being left 23
between them and him—. . . *circulus, cujus centrum diabolus.*[21] The room was so silent—though there were more than twenty people in it—that nothing could be heard but the patter of the rain against the window shutters, accompanied by the occasional hiss of a stray drop that fell down the chimney into the fire, and the steady puffing of the man in the corner, who had now resumed his pipe of long clay.

The stillness was unexpectedly broken. The distant sound of a gun reverberated through the air—apparently from the direction of the county town.

"Be jiggered!" cried the stranger who had sung the song, jumping up.

"What does that mean?" asked several.

"A prisoner escaped from the jail —that's what it means."

All listened. The sound was repeated, and none of them spoke but the man in the chimney corner, who said quietly, "I've often been told that in this county they fire a gun at such times; but I never heard it till now."

"I wonder if it is *my* man?" murmured
the personage in cinder gray. 24
"Surely it is!" said the shepherd invol-

21. *circulus . . . diabolus:* A circle with the devil at its center.

20 **Critical Reading and Thinking** Fate is at work again in the arrival of the third stranger. What part does it play in the passage?

21 **Reading Strategy** Understanding irony increases reading comprehension. What is ironic about the first stranger's statement 'And on his soul may God ha' merc-y!'

22 **Discussion** What is the third stranger's reaction to the assembled group?

23 **Critical Reading and Thinking** Describe the part that fate plays in setting the tone of this passage.

24 **Discussion** What conclusions do the party guests reach about the third stranger? What has gone on before that contributes to their jumping to these conclusions?

25 **Discussion** Why were these men so eager to begin the hunt for the third stranger?

untarily. "And surely we've zeed him! That little man who looked in at the door by now, and quivered like a leaf when he zeed ye and heard your song!"

"His teeth chattered, and the breath went out of his body," said the dairyman.

"And his heart seemed to sink within him like a stone," said Oliver Giles.

"And he bolted as if he'd been shot at," said the hedge carpenter.

"True—his teeth chattered, and his heart seemed to sink; and he bolted as if he'd been shot at," slowly summed up the man in the chimney corner.

"I didn't notice it," remarked the hangman.

"We were all a-wondering what made him run off in such a fright," faltered one of the women against the wall, "and now 'tis explained!"

The firing of the alarm gun went on at intervals, low and sullenly, and their suspicions became a certainty. The sinister gentleman in cinder gray roused himself. "Is there a constable here?" he asked, in thick tones. "If so, let him step forward."

The engaged man of fifty stepped quavering out from the wall, his betrothed beginning to sob on the back of the chair.

"You are a sworn constable?"

"I be, sir."

"Then pursue the criminal at once, with assistance, and bring him back here. He can't have gone far."

"I will, sir, I will—when I've got my staff. I'll go home and get it, and come sharp here, and start in a body."

"Staff!—never mind your staff; the man'll be gone!"

"But I can't do nothing without my staff—can I, William, and John, and Charles Jake? No; for there's the king's royal crown a painted on en in yaller and gold, and the lion and the unicorn, so as when I raise en up and hit my prisoner, 'tis made a lawful blow thereby. I wouldn't 'tempt to take up a man without my staff—no, not I. If I hadn't the law to gie me courage, why, instead o' my taking up him he might take up me!"

"Now, I'm a king's man myself, and can give you authority enough for this," said the formidable officer in gray. "Now then, all of ye, be ready. Have ye any lanterns?"

"Yes—have ye any lanterns?—I demand it!" said the constable.

"And the rest of you able-bodied—

"Able-bodied men—yes—the rest of ye!" said the constable.

"Have you some good stout staves and pitchforks—"

"Staves and pitchforks—in the name o' the law! And take 'em in yer hands and go in quest, and do as we in authority tell ye!"

Thus aroused, the men prepared to give chase. The evidence was, indeed, though circumstantial, so convincing, that but little argument was needed to show the shepherd's guests that after what they had seen 25
it would look very much like connivance if they did not instantly pursue the unhappy third stranger, who could not as yet have gone more than a few hundred yards over such uneven country.

A shepherd is always well provided with lanterns; and, lighting these hastily, and with hurdle staves in their hands, they poured out of the door, taking a direction along the crest of the hill, away from the town, the rain having fortunately a little abated.

Disturbed by the noise, or possibly by unpleasant dreams of her baptism, the child who had been christened began to cry heartbrokenly in the room overhead. These notes of grief came down through the chinks of the floor to the ears of the women below, who jumped up one by one, and seemed glad of the excuse to ascend and comfort the baby, for the incidents of the last half-hour greatly oppressed them. Thus in the space of two or three minutes the room on the ground floor was deserted quite.

But it was not for long. Hardly had the sound of footsteps died away when a man returned round the corner of the house from the direction the pursuers had taken. Peeping in at the door, and seeing nobody there, he entered leisurely. It was the stranger of the chimney corner, who had gone out with the rest. The motive of his return was shown by his helping himself to a cut piece of skimmer cake that lay on a ledge beside where he had sat, and which he had apparently forgotten to take with him. He also poured out half a cup more mead from the quantity that remained, ravenously eating and drinking these as he stood. He had not finished when another figure came in just as quietly—his friend in cinder gray.

"O—you here?" said the latter, smiling. "I thought you had gone to help in the capture." And this speaker also revealed the object of his return by looking solicitously round for the fascinating mug of old mead.

"And I thought you had gone," said the other, continuing his skimmer cake with some effort.

"Well, on second thoughts, I felt there were enough without me," said the first confidentially, "and such a night as it is, too. Besides, 'tis the business o' the government to take care of its criminals—not mine."

"True; so it is. And I felt as you did, that there were enough without me."

"I don't want to break my limbs running over the humps and hollows of this wild country."

"Nor I neither, between you and me."

"These shepherd people are used to it —simple-minded souls, you know, stirred
27 up to anything in a moment. They'll have
him ready for me before the morning, and no trouble to me at all."

"They'll have him, and we shall have saved ourselves all labor in the matter."

"True, true. Well, my way is to Casterbridge; and 'tis as much as my legs will do to take me that far. Going the same way?"

"No, I am sorry to say! I have to get home over there" (he nodded indefinitely to the right), "and I feel as you do, that it is quite enough for my legs to do before bedtime."

The other had by this time finished the mead in the mug, after which, shaking hands heartily at the door, and wishing each other well, they went their several ways.

In the meantime the company of pursuers had reached the end of the hog's-back elevation which dominated this part of the down. They had decided on no particular plan of action; and, finding that the man of the baleful trade was no longer in their company, they seemed quite unable to form any such plan now. They descended in all directions down the hill, and straightway several of the party fell into the snare set by Nature for all misguided midnight ramblers over this part of the cretaceous formation. The 'lanchets,' or flint slopes, which belted the escarpment at intervals of a dozen yards, took the less cautious ones unawares, and losing their footing on the rubbly steep they slid sharply downwards, the lanterns rolling from their hands to the bottom, and there lying on their sides till the horn was scorched through.

When they had again gathered themselves together the shepherd, as the man
who knew the country best, took the lead, 28
and guided them round these treacherous inclines. The lanterns, which seemed rather to dazzle their eyes and warn the fugitive than to assist them in the exploration, were extinguished, due silence was observed; and in this more rational order they plunged into the vale. It was a grassy, briery, moist defile, affording some shelter to any person who had sought it; but the party perambulated it in vain, and ascended on the other side. Here they wandered apart, and after an interval closed together again to report progress. At the second time of closing in they found themselves near a lonely ash, the single tree on this part of the coomb, probably sown there by a passing bird some fifty years before. And here, standing a little to one side of the trunk, as motionless as the trunk itself, appeared the man they were in quest of, his outline being well defined against the sky beyond. The band noiselessly drew up and faced him.

26 Discussion What are the reactions of the first two strangers to the search for the third?

27 Master Teacher Note In regard to the second stranger's referring to the people as "simple-minded souls," you might want to point out that pride is a common fatal flaw in Greek tragedy. Pride is standing in the way of the second stranger's accomplishing his task. Because he is looking down his nose at the peasants, he fails to see what is in front of him.

28 Literary Focus Setting plays an important part in the development of Hardy's plots. Discuss how setting controls the action of this passage.

29 **Discussion** What are the true identities of the first and second strangers? Have students tell when they first suspected who each man was.

"Your money or your life!" said the constable sternly to the still figure.

"No, no," whispered John Pitcher. "'Tisn't our side ought to say that. That's the doctrine of vagabonds like him, and we be on the side of the law."

"Well, well," replied the constable impatiently; "I must say something, mustn't I? and if you had all the weight o' this undertaking upon your mind, perhaps you'd say the wrong thing too! Prisoner at the bar, surrender, in the name of the Father—the Crown, I mane!"

The man under the tree seemed now to notice them for the first time, and, giving them no opportunity whatever for exhibiting their courage, he strolled slowly towards them. He was, indeed, the little man, the third stranger; but his trepidation had in a great measure gone.

"Well, travelers," he said, "did I hear ye speak to me?"

"You did; you've got to come and be our prisoner at once!" said the constable. "We arrest 'ee on the charge of not biding in Casterbridge jail in a decent proper manner to be hung tomorrow morning. Neighbors, do your duty, and seize the culpet!"

On hearing the charge the man seemed enlightened, and, saying not another word, resigned himself with preternatural civility to the search party, who, with their staves in their hands, surrounded him on all sides, and marched him back towards the shepherd's cottage.

It was eleven o'clock by the time they arrived. The light shining from the open door, a sound of men's voices within, proclaimed to them as they approached the house that some new events had arisen in their absence. On entering they discovered the shepherd's living room to be invaded by two officers from Casterbridge jail, and a well-known magistrate who lived at the nearest county seat, intelligence of the escape having become generally circulated.

"Gentlemen," said the constable, "I have brought back your man—not without risk and danger; but everyone must do his duty! He is inside this circle of able-bodied persons, who have lent me useful aid, considering their ignorance of Crown work. Men, bring forward your prisoner!" And the third stranger was led to the light.

"Who is this?" said one of the officials.

"The man," said the constable.

"Certainly not," said the turnkey; and the first corroborated his statement.

"But how can it be otherwise?" asked the constable. "Or why was he so terrified at sight o' the singing instrument of the law who sat there?" Here he related the strange behavior of the third stranger on entering the house during the hangman's song.

"Can't understand it," said the officer coolly. "All I know is that it is not the condemned man. He's quite a different character from this one; a gauntish fellow, with dark hair and eyes, rather good-looking, and with a musical bass voice that if you heard it once you'd never mistake as long as you lived."

"Why, souls—'twas the man in the chimney corner!"

"Hey—what?" said the magistrate, coming forward after inquiring particulars from the shepherd in the background. "Haven't you got the man after all?"

"Well, sir," said the constable, "he's the man we were in search of, that's true; and yet he's not the man we were in search of. For the man we were in search of was not the man we wanted, sir, if you understand my everyday way; for 'twas the man in the chimney corner!"

"A pretty kettle of fish altogether!" said the magistrate. "You had better start for the other man at once."

The prisoner now spoke for the first time. The mention of the man in the chimney corner seemed to have moved him as nothing else could do. "Sir," he said, stepping forward to the magistrate, "take no 29
more trouble about me. The time is come when I may as well speak. I have done nothing; my crime is that the condemned

man is my brother. Early this afternoon I left home at Shottsford to tramp it all the way to Casterbridge jail to bid him farewell. I was benighted, and called here to rest and ask the way. When I opened the door I saw before me the very man, my brother, that I thought to see in the condemned cell at Casterbridge. He was in this chimney corner; and jammed close to him, so that he could not have got out if he had tried, was the executioner who'd come to take his life, singing a song about it and not knowing that it was his victim who was close by, joining in to save appearances. My brother threw a glance of agony at me, and I knew he meant, 'Don't reveal what you see; my life depends on it.' I was so terror-struck that I could hardly stand, and, not knowing what I did, I turned and hurried away."

The narrator's manner and tone had the stamp of truth, and his story made a great impression on all around. "And do you know where your brother is at the present time?" asked the magistrate.

"I do not. I have never seen him since I closed this door."

"I can testify to that, for we've been between ye ever since," said the constable.

"Where does he think to fly to? What is his occupation?"

"He's a watch-and-clock-maker, sir."

"'A said 'a was a wheelwright—a wicked rogue," said the constable.

"The wheels of clocks and watches he meant, no doubt," said Shepherd Fennel. "I thought his hands were palish for's trade."

"Well, it appears to me that nothing can be gained by retaining this poor man in custody," said the magistrate; "your business lies with the other, unquestionably."

And so the little man was released offhand; but he looked nothing the less sad on that account, it being beyond the power of magistrate or constable to raze out the written troubles in his brain, for they concerned another whom he regarded with more solicitude than himself. When this was done, and the man had gone his way, the night was found to be so far advanced that it was deemed useless to renew the search before the next morning.

Next day, accordingly, the quest for the clever sheep stealer became general and keen, to all appearance at least. But the intended punishment was cruelly disproportioned to the transgression, and the sympathy of a great many country folk in that district was strongly on the side of the fugitive. Moreover, his marvelous coolness and daring in hob-and-nobbing with the hangman, under the unprecedented circumstances of the shepherd's party, won their admiration. So that it may be questioned if all those who ostensibly made themselves so busy in exploring woods and fields and lanes were quite so thorough when it came to the private examination of their own lofts and outhouses. Stories were afloat of a mysterious figure being occasionally seen in some old overgrown trackway or other, remote from turnpike roads; but when a search was instituted in any of these suspected quarters nobody was found. Thus the days and weeks passed without tidings. 30

In brief, the bass-voiced man of the chimney corner was never recaptured. Some said that he went across the sea, others that he did not, but buried himself in the depths of a populous city. At any rate, the gentleman in cinder gray never did his morning's work at Casterbridge, nor met anywhere at all, for business purposes, the genial comrade with whom he had passed an hour of relaxation in the lonely house on the slope of the coomb.

The grass has long been green on the graves of Shepherd Fennel and his frugal wife; the guests who made up the christening party have mainly followed their entertainers to the tomb; the baby in whose honor they all had met is a matron in the sere and yellow leaf. But the arrival of the three strangers at the shepherd's that night, and the details connected therewith, is a story as well known as ever in the country about Higher Crowstairs. 31

30 **Discussion** What factors contribute to the sympathy toward the sheep thief? What can be inferred from his remaining free?

31 **Reading Strategy** What ironies have made this tale an interesting study of human nature? Have students compare this story to Thomas Hardy's poem "The Man He Killed."

THINKING ABOUT THE SELECTION

Recalling

1. (a) Where and when does the story take place? (b) What event is being celebrated?
2. (a) Describe the appearance of the first stranger. (b) Of the second stranger.
3. (a) What is the second stranger's occupation? (b) How is this revealed?
4. (a) Whom does Shepherd Fennel assume the third stranger to be? (b) Why?

Interpreting

5. What do the speech habits of the Fennels and their guests reveal about them?
6. (a) How early on did you guess the identity of the first stranger? (b) The second? (c) The third? (d) What clues did you use?

Applying

7. What does this story suggest about its author's respect for institutions such as the law in nineteenth-century England? Explain.

ANALYZING LITERATURE

Setting and Mood

The setting of a story is when and where the action occurs. In addition to such "factual" details as place names and historical references, setting also accounts for time of day, season, weather conditions, and the like. Aspects of setting, especially of the latter type help determine a story's mood—the emotional response it excites in its readers. Read the following details of setting from "The Three Strangers." Tell the mood suggested by each detail and by all of them taken together. Explain why each detail creates the mood it does.

1. Fifty years ago such a lonely cottage stood.
2. The level rainstorm smote walls, slopes, and hedges . . . ; the tails of little birds trying to roost on some scraggy thorn were blown inside out like umbrellas. The gable-end of the cottage was stained wet.
3. The room was lighted by half a dozen candles. . . . On the hearth . . . blazed a fire of thorns that crackled.

CRITICAL THINKING AND READING

Inferring the Author's Attitude

In "The Three Strangers" fate plays an important—and sometimes fickle—role. Had fate, for instance, not decreed a rainstorm, the sheep-stealer might never have come face-to-face with his executioner. And it is the same fateful rainstorm that enables the guilty man to escape capture by his pursuers. From these and other events in the story, attempt to **infer,** or arrive at an understanding of, Hardy's attitude toward the role of fate. Ask yourself: Does he seem to feel that fate governs our lives? To what extent does he believe that we can and should alter fate by exercising our own free will?

UNDERSTANDING LANGUAGE

Reading Dialect

Most of the characters in the story speak with a particular **dialect,** or manner of speech that typifies a particular region or group. The use of dialect in a story adds to both its realism and its local flavor. Restate each of the following quotations in standard English.

1. "Late to be traipsing athwart this coomb—hey?" (page 898)
2. "A smoker, and no pipe about 'ee?" (page 898)
3. ". . . That little man . . . quivered . . . when he zeed ye . . . !" (page 904)
4. "'A said 'a was a wheelwright . . ." (page 907)

THINKING AND WRITING

Describing a Place

Choose a place that you know well—perhaps the neighborhood you live in or a city that you have visited often. On a sheet of paper jot down as many details of the place as you can think of. Try to include in your list features that make the location unique, or at least easy to visualize. Then convert your notes into a description that would enable a stranger to picture it with little difficulty. Be prepared to share your description with your class.

Answers

ANSWERS TO THINKING ABOUT THE SELECTION

Recalling

1. (a) It takes place in and around a shepherd's cottage in Wessex on March 24, 182–. (b) a christening.
2. (a) The first stranger is about forty years old, gaunt, five-feet-eight or nine, dressed in a black coat. (b) The second stranger is several years older with slightly frosted hair, bristly eyebrows, and whiskers; his face is full and flabby with a nose marked by grog blossoms; he wears a cinder-grey suit and a greatcoat.
3. (a) The second stranger is a hangman. (b) He reveals his identity by singing a song about himself.
4. Fennel assumes he is the sheep-stealer because of the terrified look on his face when he discovers who the hangman is.

Interpreting

5. They indicate that they are humble workers of the land.
6. Answers will differ.

Applying

7. Suggested response: Hardy's respect was limited.

Challenge How do you think Hardy wants you to feel toward the sheep stealer? Include evidence from the selection that supports your answer.

ANSWERS TO ANALYZING LITERATURE

Suggested response: Hardy's description of the outside of the cottage and the rain falling on the farm buildings and the surrounding downs creates a picture of bleak loneliness. This somber mood is alleviated and contrasted by his warm description of the convivial atmosphere inside the cottage.

ANSWERS TO CRITICAL THINKING AND READING

Suggested response: Hardy seems to demonstrate his belief in the supremacy of man's free will over fate when the criminal uses the hangman's pride against him and tricks him, thereby making escape possible.

ANSWERS TO UNDERSTANDING LANGUAGE

Suggested responses:

1. "It is rather late to be wandering around these barren hills, isn't it?"
2. "If you are a smoker, why don't you have a pipe?"
3. "That little man shook all over with fright when he saw you."
4. "He said that he was a wheelwright."

The Victorian Novel

WAITING, 1854
Sir John Everett Millais
Birmingham City Art Gallery

Humanities Note

Fine art, *Waiting,* 1854, by Sir John Everett Millais. Sir John Everett Millais (1829–96) rebelled against the proposed subject matter of the Realists and helped found the Pre-Raphaelite Brotherhood. He chose as his subject matter religious, historical, and literary topics. Known for his tightly executed works, Millais was called by the poet Baudelaire "the painter of meticulous detail."

More About the Author Emily Brontë was the most reclusive of the surviving Brontë children. While Charlotte, Anne, and the ill-fated Branwell, were able to work and live in the world, Emily could not endure the regulation and what she saw as the subjugation that so-called "normal" life entailed. A surprisingly competent homemaker, Emily, throughout her life, craved the freedom of her beloved moors as sustenance for her imaginative and, to a certain extent, her physical life. A gifted poet and novelist, Emily Brontë was clever about monetary matters and, without benefit of the drawing lessons her brother enjoyed, produced competent sketches of wild and domestic creatures. What other authors do you know of that have chosen to live as recluses? Why does creativity seem often to require this?

EMILY BRONTË

1818–1848

The daughter of an Irish clergyman, Emily Brontë whose efforts gave the world *Wuthering Heights* in 1847 was one of the three novel-writing sisters. Charlotte wrote *Jane Eyre* and Anne wrote *Agnes Grey*.

Born in the Yorkshire town of Hartshead-cum-Clifton, Brontë was raised, along with her brother and four sisters, by an aunt, following the early death of their mother. As children the Brontës were often left to themselves. For recreation they walked the bleak moors near Haworth, where the family had moved from Hartshead, and invented imaginary "histories" for toy soldiers, a pastime they continued to pursue up through their teen years. In 1842 Emily went to Brussels with her sister Charlotte, to study at the Pensionnat Heger, in the hopes of starting their own school. The death of their aunt, however, brought the sisters prematurely back to Yorkshire.

In 1845 Charlotte accidentally discovered some poems that Emily had composed. The discovery led in turn to the revelation that Charlotte and Anne had secretly been writing poetry as well, and in 1846 the three talented Brontës published at their own expense a book of verses by "Currer, Ellis, and Acton Bell," the pen names that kept the sisters' initials but hid their real names. The book sold only two copies, but the venture had stoked the sisters' creative fires and each began work on a novel.

For her project, Emily chose to write about the Yorkshire countryside she knew so well. And she chose to write about it with the same poetic voice that typified the romantic tales she had produced as a child. The result, *Wuthering Heights,* is a tale of love, revenge, and redemption that comments on the tensions of nineteenth-century society. Unlike Charlotte's *Jane Eyre,* which became an instant success, *Wuthering Heights* failed in its day to gain the recognition it deserved.

Emily, meanwhile, was in poor health, having long suffered from a respiratory condition. Her breathing became extremely labored with the death of her brother in 1848, and before the year was over she died at the age of thirty.

That Emily Brontë may have intended her masterpiece as a visionary work is suggested by a study of her poetry, which expresses her impatience with social order and her yearning for a "dazzling sea" of infinity. As some contemporary critics have suggested, *Wuthering Heights* clouds rather than explains the mysteries of Brontë's brief life, yet there is no denying the enormous imaginative power behind the words.

Objectives

1 To understand the significance of the first-person point of view
2 To write about point of view as a narrative technique

Teaching Portfolio: Support Material

Teacher Backup, pp. 00-00

Vocabulary Check, p. 00

Usage and Mechanics Worksheet, p. 00

Analyzing Literature Worksheet, p. 00

Critical Thinking and Reading Worksheet, p. 00

Language Worksheet, p. 00

Selection Test, p. 00

GUIDE FOR READING

from Wuthering Heights

The Writer's Technique

First-Person Narrator (Observer). The first-person narrator in a work of fiction is the story-teller who narrates events from the "I" or "we" point of view. Unlike the third-person narrator, who is a disembodied voice that reports the events of the story from a remote position, the first-person narrator is a full-fledged character, subject to limitations and flaws.

The first-person narrator may stand in any of various relations to the events being described, ranging from being at the center of those events to being merely an observer or witness to them. It is important to recognize that even when the first-person narrator speaks purely as an observer, his or her comments and interpretations are *subjective,* that is, colored by his or her own perceptions and values.

Look For

As you read the excerpt from *Wuthering Heights,* look for Brontë's use of a first-person narrator and to the effects she intentionally achieves.

Writing

Think of a familiar fairy tale or folk tale such as "Cinderella" or "The Three Little Pigs." Invent a new character to serve as first-person narrator in the role of observer. Consider what sort of individual your narrator is—what sorts of values he or she embraces—and what slant he or she might bring to the telling of the tale.

Vocabulary

Knowing the following words will help you as you read the excerpt from *Wuthering Heights*.

misanthropist (mis an′ thrə pist) *n.*: One who hates or mistrusts others (p. 912)
soliloquized (sə lil′ ə kwīzd′) *v.*: Talked to oneself (p. 912)
impertinence (im pʉr′t'n əns) *n.*: Rudeness (p. 913)
physiognomy (fiz′ ē äg′nə mē) *n.*: Facial features thought to reveal character or disposition (p. 914)
sagacity (sə gas′ə tē) *n.*: Wisdom; judgment (p. 917)
virulency (vir′yoo lən sē) *n.*: Harmfulness (p. 920)
assiduity (as ə dyoo′ə tē) *n.*: Diligence (p. 916)

Literary Focus Point of view in *Wuthering Heights* is extraordinarily complex. In this excerpt we are presented with an observing first-person narrator. Shortly, however, Lockwood ceases to report what he sees and begins to tell us what he hears from Nelly Dean, the housekeeper. The story of *Wuthering Heights* is retold through the double filter of one who saw first-hand what happened—Nelly—and an agent from the outside world—Lockwood.

Look For Your **less advanced** students may have some difficulty in distinguishing between subjective and objective information. Have them practice stating facts about the plot, characters, and style of *Wuthering Heights,* as an objective exercise; then encourage them to express their feelings and opinions about the same topic as a subjective exercise.

Writing Have students list or discuss two sets of topics: i.e. those that lend themselves to first-person treatment and those that seem to call for third-person narration. There may be some overlap. Discuss reasons for assigning subjects to one or the other list. Then have students complete the freewriting assignment, keeping the points raised during discussion in mind.

Vocabulary Ask students to use each of the words correctly in a sentence.

Motivation for Reading Tell students that *Wuthering Heights* presents a character at once repulsive and compelling. Challenge students to outline their evolving reactions to Heathcliff.

Master Teacher Note Tell students that when *Wuthering Heights* first appeared, Heathcliff was seen as shocking and brutal. Heathcliff is Emily's version of a "Byronic hero," that is, a character inspired by the poet Lord Byron. Typically, the Byronic hero is dark, brooding, and unpredictable.

Purpose-Setting Question Why might Brontë have someone like Lockwood narrate the story of *Wuthering Heights?*

1 **Reading Strategy** Mr. Lockwood believes that he and Heathcliff have much in common. Ask students to determine as they read whether or not Lockwood was correct in his initial assumption.

2 **Discussion** Compare and contrast the names of the narrator and his landlord. What was Brontë's purpose in creating these names?

3 **Discussion** Compare and contrast the styles Lockwood and Heathcliff use to address one another. What does his manner of speech reveal about each character?

4 **Critical Reading and Thinking** What part might Lockwood's view of Heathcliff play in the narration of the story?

5 **Critical Reading and Thinking** What assumptions does Lockwood make in this passage?

from Wuthering Heights

Emily Brontë

1801—I have just returned from a visit to my landlord—the solitary neighbor that I shall be troubled with. This is certainly a beautiful country! In all England, I do not believe that I could have fixed on a situation so completely removed from the stir of society. A perfect misanthropist's Heaven: and
1 Mr. Heathcliff and I are such a suitable pair to divide the desolation between us. A capital fellow! He little imagined how my heart warmed towards him when I beheld his black eyes withdraw so suspiciously under their brows, as I rode up, and when his fingers sheltered themselves, with a jealous resolution, still further in his waistcoat, as I announced my name.

"Mr. Heathcliff?" I said.

A nod was the answer.

"Mr. Lockwood your new tenant, sir. I do myself the honor of calling as soon as possible after my arrival, to express the hope that I have not inconvenienced you by my perse-
2 verance in soliciting the occupation of
3 Thrushcross Grange: I heard yesterday you had had some thoughts . . ."

"Thrushcross Grange is my own, sir," he interrupted, wincing. "I should not allow anyone to inconvenience me, if I could hinder it—walk in!"

The "walk in" was uttered with closed teeth, and expressed the sentiment, "Go to the deuce";[1] even the gate over which he leaned manifested no sympathizing movement to the words; and I think that circumstance determined me to accept the invitation: I felt interested in a man who seemed 4
more exaggeratedly reserved than myself.

When he saw my horse's breast fairly pushing the barrier, he did pull out his hand to unchain it, and then sullenly preceded me up the causeway, calling, as we entered the court, "Joseph, take Mr. Lockwood's horse, and bring up some wine."

"Here we have the whole establishment of domestics, I suppose," was the reflection,
suggested by this compound order. "No 5
wonder the grass grows up between the flags, and cattle are the only hedgecutters."

Joseph was an elderly, nay, an old man —very old, perhaps, though hale and sinewy. "The Lord help us!" he soliloquized in an undertone of peevish displeasure, while relieving me of my horse: looking, meantime, in my face so sourly that I charitably conjectured he must have need of divine aid to digest his dinner, and his pious ejaculation had no reference to my unexpected advent.

Wuthering Heights is the name of Mr. Heathcliff's dwelling. "Wuthering" being a significant provincial adjective, descriptive of the atmospheric tumult to which its station is exposed in stormy weather. Pure, bracing ventilation they must have up there at all times, indeed: one may guess the power of the north wind blowing over the edge, by the excessive slant of a few stunted firs at the end of the house; and by a range of gaunt thorns all stretching their limbs one way, as if craving alms of the sun. Happily, the architect had foresight to build it strong:

---

1. Go to the deuce: An exclamation of annoyance.

Master Teacher Note A favorite theme in the nineteenth century was man's fall from innocence and privilege into the world of experience and pain. Wordsworth in *The Prelude* and Coleridge in *The Rime of the Ancient Mariner* presented this myth in poetry. In *Wuthering Heights,* Emily Brontë similarly presents two contrasting worlds: the Heights, where the Earnshaws and Heathcliff live, and the Grange, the home of the Lintons.

the narrow windows are deeply set in the wall, and the corners defended with large jutting stones.

Before passing the threshold, I paused to admire a quantity of grotesque carving lavished over the front, and especially about the principal door; above which, among a wilderness of crumbling griffins[2] and shameless little boys, I detected the date "1500" and the name "Hareton Earn-
6 shaw." I would have made a few comments, and requested a short history of the place from the surly owner; but his attitude at the door appeared to demand my speedy entrance, or complete departure, and I had no desire to aggravate his impatience previous to inspecting the penetralia.[3]

One step brought us into the family sitting room, without any introductory lobby or passage: they call it here "the house" pre-eminently. It includes kitchen and parlor, generally; but I believe at Wuthering Heights the kitchen is forced to retreat altogether into another quarter: at least I distinguished a chatter of tongues, and a clatter of culinary utensils, deep within; and I observed no signs of roasting, boiling, or baking, about the huge fireplace; nor any glitter of copper saucepans and tin colanders on the walls. One end, indeed, reflected splendidly both light and heat from ranks of immense pewter dishes, interspersed with silver jugs and tankards, towering row after row, on a vast oak dresser, to the very roof. The latter had never been underdrawn: its entire anatomy lay bare to an inquiring eye, except where a frame of wood laden with oatcakes and clusters of legs of beef, mutton, and ham, concealed it. Above the chimney were sundry villainous old guns, and a couple of horse-pistols; and, by way of ornament, three gaudily painted canisters disposed along its ledge. The floor was of smooth, white stone; the chairs, high-backed, primitive structures, painted green; one or two heavy black ones lurking in the shade. In an arch under the dresser, reposed a huge, liver-colored pointer, surrounded by a swarm of squealing puppies; and other dogs haunted other recesses.

The apartment and furniture would have been nothing extraordinary as belonging to a homely, northern farmer, with a stubborn countenance, and stalwart limbs set out to advantage in knee breeches and gaiters.[4] Such an individual seated in his
armchair, his mug of ale frothing on the 7
round table before him, is to be seen in any circuit of five or six miles among these hills, if you go at the right time after dinner. But Mr. Heathcliff forms a singular contrast to his abode and style of living. He is a dark-skinned gypsy in aspect, in dress and manners a gentleman: that is, as much a gentleman as many a country squire: rather slovenly, perhaps, yet not looking amiss with his negligence, because he has an erect and handsome figure; and rather morose. Possibly, some people might suspect him of a degree of underbred pride; I have a sympathetic chord within that tells me it is nothing of the sort: I know, by instinct, his reserve springs from an aversion to showy
displays of feeling—to manifestations of 8
mutual kindliness. He'll love and hate equally under cover, and esteem it a species of impertinence to be loved or hated again. No, I'm running on too fast: I bestow my own attributes over liberally on him. Mr. Heathcliff may have entirely dissimilar reasons for keeping his hand out of the way when he meets a would-be acquaintance, to those which actuate me. Let me hope my constitution is almost peculiar: my dear mother used to say I should never have a comfortable home; and only last summer I proved myself perfectly unworthy of one.

While enjoying a month of fine weather 9

2. griffins *n*: Mythological animals with the body and hind legs of a lion and the head and wings of an eagle.

3. penetralia (pen′ ə trā′ lē ə) *n*: The innermost parts.

4. gaiters *n*.: Cloth coverings for the instep and lower leg.

6 **Clarification** Hareton Earnshaw was the original owner of Wuthering Heights and an early ancestor of the Mr. Earnshaw who brought the orphaned Heathcliff to Wuthering Heights.

7 **Discussion** Ask students to explain the observation that Mr. Heathcliff's person and personality sharply contrast with his style of living.

8 **Reading Strategy** What causes Lockwood to reverse his initial belief that Heathcliff and he have much in common? Is he more or less correct here than at his story's beginning?

9 **Discussion** Explain how the narrator's digression about the girl at the seacoast relates to his interest in Heathcliff.

10 **Discussion** How does the description of the canine attack evoke humor?

11 **Critical Reading and Thinking** What is the effect of such language as *fiends, devil, possessed swine,* and *spirits*? Can you find later examples that continue this metaphor?

12 **Reading Strategy** Why does Heathcliff grin at Lockwood? Ask students to determine as they read if Heathcliff maintains this same attitude towards Lockwood.

at the seacoast, I was thrown into the company of a most fascinating creature: a real goddess in my eyes, as long as she took no notice of me. I "never told my love" vocally; still, if looks have language, the merest idiot might have guessed I was over head and ears: she understood me at last, and looked a return—the sweetest of all imaginable looks. And what did I do? I confess it with shame—shrunk icily into myself, like a snail; at every glance retired colder and farther; till finally the poor innocent was led to doubt her own senses, and, overwhelmed with confusion at her supposed mistake, persuaded her mamma to decamp.[5] By this curious turn of disposition I have gained the reputation of deliberate heartlessness; how undeserved, I alone can appreciate.

I took a seat at the end of the hearthstone opposite that towards which my landlord advanced, and filled up an interval of silence by attempting to caress the canine mother, who had left her nursery, and was sneaking wolfishly to the back of my legs, her lip curled up, and her white teeth watering for a snatch. My caress provoked a long, guttural gnarl.

"You'd better let the dog alone," growled Mr. Heathcliff in unison, checking fiercer demonstrations with a punch of his foot. "She's not accustomed to be spoiled—not kept for a pet." Then, striding to a side door, he shouted again, "Joseph!"

Joseph mumbled indistinctly in the depths of the cellar, but gave no intimation of ascending; so his master dived down to him, leaving me *vis-à-vis*[6] the ruffianly dog and a pair of grim shaggy sheepdogs, who shared with her a jealous guardianship over all my movements. Not anxious to come in contact with their fangs, I sat still; but, imagining they would scarcely understand tacit insults, I unfortunately indulged in winking and making faces at the trio, and some turn of my physiognomy so irritated madam, that she suddenly broke into a fury, and leapt on my knees. I flung her back, and hastened to interpose the table between us. This proceeding roused the whole hive. Half a dozen four-footed fiends, of various sizes and ages, issued from hidden dens to the common center. I felt my heels and coat laps peculiar subjects of assault; and, parrying
off the larger combatants as effectually as I 10
could with the poker, I was constrained to demand, aloud, assistance from some of the household in reestablishing peace.

Mr. Heathcliff and his man climbed the cellar steps with vexatious phlegm:[7] I don't think they moved one second faster than usual, though the hearth was an absolute tempest of worrying and yelping. Happily, an inhabitant of the kitchen made more dispatch: a lusty dame, with tucked-up gown, bare arms, and fire-flushed cheeks, rushed into the midst of us flourishing a frying pan; and used that weapon, and her tongue, to such purpose, that the storm subsided magically, and she only remained, heaving like a sea after a high wind, when her master entered on the scene.

"What the devil is the matter?" he asked, eyeing me in a manner I could ill
endure after this inhospitable treatment. 11

"What the devil, indeed!" I muttered. "The herd of possessed swine could have had no worse spirits in them than those animals of yours, sir. You might as well leave a stranger with a brood of tigers!"

"They won't meddle with persons who touch nothing," he remarked, putting the bottle before me, and restoring the displaced table. "The dogs do right to be vigilant. Take a glass of wine?"

"No thank you."

"Not bitten, are you?"

"If I had been, I would have set my signet[8] on the biter."

Heathcliff's countenance relaxed into a grin. 12

---

5. decamp *v.*: Leave suddenly.
6. vis-à-vis (vē' zə vē'): Face to face with.

7. phlegm (flem) *n.*: Sluggishness.
8. signet *n.*: Seal.

"Come, come," he said, "you are flurried, Mr. Lockwood. Here, take a little wine. Guests are so exceedingly rare in this house that I and my dogs, I am willing to own, hardly know how to receive them. Your health, sir!"

I bowed and returned the pledge; beginning to perceive that it would be foolish to sit sulking for the misbehavior of a pack of curs;[9] besides, I felt loath to yield the fellow further amusement at my expense; since his humor took that turn. He—probably swayed by prudential considerations of the folly of offending a good tenant—relaxed a little in the laconic style of chipping off his pronouns and auxiliary verbs, and introduced what he supposed would be a subject of interest to me—a discourse on the advantages and disadvantages of my present place of retirement. I found him very intelligent on the topics we touched; and before I went home, I was encouraged so far as to volunteer another visit tomorrow. He evidently wished no repetition of my intrusion. I shall go, notwithstanding. It is astonishing how sociable I feel myself compared with him.

Yesterday afternoon set in misty and cold. I had half a mind to spend it by my study fire, instead of wading through heath and mud to Wuthering Heights. On coming up from dinner, however (*N.B.*—I dine between twelve and one o'clock; the housekeeper, a matronly lady, taken as a fixture along with the house, could not, or would not, comprehend my request that I might be served at five), on mounting the stairs with this lazy intention, and stepping into the room, I saw a servant girl on her knees, surrounded by brushes, and coal scuttles; and raising an infernal dust as she extinguished the flames with heaps of cinders. This spectacle drove me back immediately; I took my hat, and, after a four miles' walk, arrived at Heathcliff's garden gate just in time to escape the first feathery flakes of a snow shower.

On that bleak hilltop the earth was hard with a black frost, and the air made me shiver through every limb. Being unable to remove the chain, I jumped over, and, running up the flagged causeway bordered with straggling gooseberry bushes, knocked vainly for admittance, till my knuckles tingled, and the dogs howled.

"Wretched inmates!" I ejaculated, mentally, "you deserve perpetual isolation from your species for your churlish inhospitality. At least, I would not keep my doors barred in the daytime. I don't care—I will get in!" So resolved, I grasped the latch and shook it vehemently. Vinegar-faced Joseph projected his head from a round window of the barn.

"Whet are ye for?" he shouted. "T' maister's dahn i' t' fowld. Goa rahnd by th' end ut' laith, if yah went tuh spake tull him."

"Is there nobody inside to open the door?" I hallooed, responsively.

"They's nobbut t' missis; and shoo'll nut oppen 't an ye mak yer flaysome dins till neeght."

"Why? cannot you tell her who I am, eh, Joseph?"

"Nor-ne me! Aw'll hae noa hend wi't," muttered the head vanishing.

The snow began to drive thickly. I seized the handle to essay another trial; when a young man without coat, and shouldering a pitchfork, appeared in the yard behind. He hailed me to follow him, and, after marching through a wash-house, and a paved area containing a coal shed, pump, and pigeon cote, we at length arrived in the huge, warm, cheerful apartment, where I was formerly received. It glowed delightfully in the radiance of an immense fire, compounded of coal, peat, and wood; and near the table, laid for a plentiful evening meal, I was pleased to observe the "missis," an individual whose existence I had never previously suspected. I bowed and waited, thinking she would bid me take a seat. She looked at me, leaning

---

9. curs *n.*: Dogs of mixed breed.

13 **Clarification** Juno is the name of the principal goddess in Roman mythology. The wife of Jupiter, she is the patroness of marriage and the well-being of women.

14 **Discussion** How do Lockwood's continual mistakes, like this one over the rabbits, make him appear?

back in her chair, and remained motionless and mute.

"Rough weather!" I remarked. "I'm afraid, Mrs. Heathcliff, the door must bear the consequence of your servants' leisure attendance: I had hard work to make them hear me!"

She never opened her mouth. I stared —she stared also. At any rate, she kept her eyes on me in a cool, regardless manner, exceedingly embarrassing and disagreeable.

"Sit down," said the young man, gruffly. "He'll be in soon."

13 I obeyed; and hemmed, and called the villain Juno, who deigned, at this second interview, to move the extreme tip of her tail, in token of owning my acquaintance.

"A beautiful animal!" I commenced again. "Do you intend parting with the little ones, madam?"

"They are not mine," said the amiable hostess, more repellingly than Heathcliff himself could have replied.

14 "Ah, your favorites are among these!" I continued, turning to an obscure cushion full of something like cats.

"A strange choice of favorites!" she observed scornfully.

Unluckily, it was a heap of dead rabbits. I hemmed once more, and drew closer to the hearth, repeating my comment on the wildness of the evening.

"You should not have come out," she said, rising and reaching from the chimneypiece two of the painted canisters.

Her position before was sheltered from the light; now, I had a distinct view of her whole figure and countenance. She was slender, and apparently scarcely past girlhood: an admirable form, and the most exquisite little face that I have ever had the pleasure of beholding: small features, very fair; flaxen ringlets, or rather golden, hanging loose on her delicate neck; and eyes, had they been agreeable in expression, they would have been irresistible: fortunately for my susceptible heart, the only sentiment they evinced hovered between scorn and a kind of desperation, singularly unnatural to be detected there.

The canisters were almost out of her reach; I made a motion to aid her; she turned upon me as a miser might turn if anyone attempted to assist him in counting his gold.

"I don't want your help," she snapped; "I can get them for myself."

"I beg your pardon," I hastened to reply.

"Were you asked to tea?" she demanded, tying an apron over her neat black frock, and standing with a spoonful of the leaf poised over the pot.

"I shall be glad to have a cup," I answered.

"Were you asked?" she repeated.

"No," I said, half smiling. "You are the proper person to ask me."

She flung the tea back, spoon and all; and resumed her chair in a pet,[10] her forehead corrugated, and her red underlip pushed out, like a child's, ready to cry.

Meanwhile, the young man had slung onto his person a decidedly shabby upper garment, and, erecting himself before the blaze, looked down on me, from the corner of his eyes, for all the world as if there were some mortal feud unavenged between us. I began to doubt whether he were a servant or not: his dress and speech were both rude, entirely devoid of the superiority observable in Mr. and Mrs. Heathcliff; his thick, brown curls were rough and uncultivated, his whiskers encroached bearishly over his cheeks, and his hands were embrowned like those of the common laborer; still his bearing was free, almost haughty, and he showed none of a domestic's assiduity in attending on the lady of the house. In the absence of clear proofs of his condition, I deemed it best to abstain from noticing his curious conduct; and, five minutes afterwards, the entrance of Heathcliff relieved me, in some measure, from my uncomfortable state.

---

10. pet: A fit of peevishness.

WUTHERING HEIGHTS
Fritz Eichenberg

"You see, sir, I am come, according to promise!" I exclaimed, assuming the cheerful; "and I fear I shall be weather-bound for half an hour, if you can afford me shelter during that space."

"Half an hour?" he said, shaking the white flakes from his clothes; "I wonder you should select the thick of a snowstorm to ramble about in. Do you know that you run a risk of being lost in the marshes? People familiar with these moors often miss their road on such evenings; and, I can tell you, there is no chance of a change at present."

"Perhaps I can get a guide among your lads, and he might stay at the Grange till morning—could you spare me one?"

"No, I could not."

"Oh, indeed! Well, then, I must trust to my own sagacity."

"Umph!"

"Are you going to mak' th' tea?" demanded he of the shabby coat, shifting his ferocious gaze from me to the young lady.

"Is *he* to have any?" she asked, appealing to Heathcliff.

"Get it ready, will you?" was the answer uttered so savagely that I started. The tone in which the words were said, revealed a genuine bad nature. I no longer felt inclined to call Heathcliff a capital fellow. When the preparations were finished, he invited me with: "Now, sir, bring forward your chair." And we all, including the rustic youth, drew round the table; an austere silence prevailing while we discussed our meal.

I thought, if I had caused the cloud, it was my duty to make an effort to dispel it. They could not every day sit so grim and

Humanities Note

Illustration for *Wuthering Heights* by Fritz Eichenberg. The expatriate German artist Fritz Eichenberg (b. 1901) arrived in New York City in 1933. His excellence in the black-and-white wood-engraving technique that he learned in Germany (Kunstgewerbeschule, Cologne and State Academy of Graphic Design, Leipzig) immediately earned him many illustration commissions. He has illustrated more than sixty books with wood engravings. His talent is highly respected in the art world, and he has exhibited his works nationally.

The technique of wood engraving is the process of incising lines into a block of boxwood using a sharp instrument. The block is then inked and pressed onto a paper, forming a black-and-white image. Eichenberg used this technique for the illustrations that he did in 1943 for *Wuthering Heights*. He felt it was particularly effective in producing the dark atmosphere and tortured landscapes necessary to this tale. These drawings are visually effective in their strong linear effects and overtones of dramatic emotion.

You might use these questions for discussion:

1. How does the lack of color in this illustration heighten the visual impact of the image?
2. Which details of this illustration do you find particularly effective?

15 **Discussion** What mistakes of identity does Mr. Lockwood make concerning the young woman?

16 **Reading Strategy** What does this remark reveal about Lockwood? How does Lockwood view himself? Is there any difference between the way he appears to the folk at the Heights and the way he sees himself?

17 **Clarification** Hareton Earnshaw is named after the original owner of Wuthering Heights, the man whose name is inscribed on its principal gate. This young Hareton is the son of Hindley Earnshaw, who tormented Heathcliff when he was a young, orphan boy. By belittling Hareton as he does, Heathcliff revenges what happened to him, or so he hopes.

taciturn; and it was impossible, however ill-tempered they might be, that the universal scowl they wore was their everyday countenance.

"It is strange," I began, in the interval of swallowing one cup of tea and receiving another; "it is strange how custom can mold our tastes and ideas: many could not imagine the existence of happiness in a life of such complete exile from the world as you spend, Mr. Heathcliff; yet, I'll venture to say, that, surrounded by your family, and with your amiable lady as the presiding genius over your home and heart . . ."

"My amiable lady!" he interrupted, with an almost diabolical sneer on his face. "Where is she—my amiable lady?"

"Mrs. Heathcliff, your wife, I mean."

15 "Well, yes—Oh! you would intimate that her spirit has taken the post of ministering angel, and guards the fortunes of Wuthering Heights, even when her body is gone. Is that it?"

Perceiving myself in a blunder, I attempted to correct it. I might have seen that there was too great a disparity between the ages of the parties to make it likely that they were man and wife. One was about forty; a period of mental vigor at which men seldom cherish the delusion of being married for love by girls: that dream is reserved for the solace of our declining years. The other did not look seventeen.

Then it flashed upon me: "The clown at my elbow, who is drinking his tea out of a basin and eating his bread with unwashed hands, may be her husband. Heathcliff, junior, of course. Here is the consequence of being buried alive: she has thrown herself away upon that boor, from sheer ignorance that better individuals existed! A sad 16 pity—I must beware how I cause her to regret her choice." The last reflection may seem conceited; it was not. My neighbor struck me as bordering on repulsive; I knew, through experience, that I was tolerably attractive.

"Mrs. Heathcliff is my daughter-in-law," said Heathcliff, corroborating my surmise. He turned, as he spoke, a peculiar look in her direction, a look of hatred unless he has a most perverse set of facial muscles that will not, like those of other people, interpret the language of his soul.

"Ah, certainly—I see now: you are the favored possessor of the beneficent fairy," I remarked, turning to my neighbor.

This was worse than before: the youth grew crimson, and clenched his fist, with every appearance of a meditated assault. But he seemed to recollect himself, presently; and smothered the storm in a brutal curse, muttered on my behalf; which, however, I took care not to notice.

"Unhappy in your conjectures, sir!" observed my host; "we neither of us have the privilege of owning your good fairy; her mate is dead. I said she was my daughter-in-law, therefore, she must have married my son."

"And this young man is . . ."

"Not my son, assuredly!"

Heathcliff smiled again, as if it were rather too bold a jest to attribute the paternity of that bear to him.

"My name is Hareton Earnshaw," growled the other; "and I'd counsel you to 17 respect it!"

"I've shown no disrespect," was my reply, laughing internally at the dignity with which he announced himself.

He fixed his eye on me longer than I cared to return the stare, for fear I might be tempted either to box his ears, or render my hilarity audible. I began to feel unmistakably out of place in that pleasant family circle. The dismal spiritual atmosphere overcame, and more than neutralized the glowing physical comforts round me; and I resolved to be cautious how I ventured under those rafters a third time.

The business of eating being concluded, and no one uttering a word of sociable conversation, I approached a window to examine the weather. A sorrowful sight I saw:

dark night coming down prematurely, and sky and hills mingled in one bitter whirl of wind and suffocating snow.

"I don't think it possible for me to get home now, without a guide," I could not help exclaiming. "The roads will be buried already; and, if they were bare, I could scarcely distinguish a foot in advance."

"Hareton, drive those dozen sheep into the barn porch—they'll be covered if left in the fold all night—and put a plank before them," said Heathcliff.

"How must I do?" I continued, with rising irritation.

There was no reply to my question; and on looking round I saw only Joseph bringing in a pail of porridge for the dogs, and Mrs. Heathcliff leaning over the fire, diverting herself with burning a bundle of matches which had fallen from the chimneypiece as she restored the tea canister to its place. The former, when he had deposited his burden, took a critical survey of the room; and, in cracked tones, grated out:

"Aw woonder hagh yah can faishion tuh stand thear i' idleness un war, when all on 'em's goan aght! Bud yah're a nowt, and it's noa use talking—yah'll niver mend uh yer ill ways; bud, goa raight tuh t' divil, like yer mother afore ye!"

I imagined, for a moment, that this piece of eloquence was addressed to me; and, sufficiently enraged, stepped towards the aged rascal with an intention of kicking him out of the door. Mrs. Heathcliff, however, checked me by her answer.

"You scandalous old hypocrite!" she replied. "Are you not afraid of being carried away bodily, whenever you mention the devil's name? I warn you to refrain from provoking me, or I'll ask your abduction as a special favor.
18 Stop, look here, Joseph," she continued, taking a long, dark book from a shelf. "I'll show you how far I've progressed in the Black Art: I shall soon be competent to make a clear house of it. The red cow didn't die by chance; and your rheumatism can hardly be reckoned among providential visitations!"

"Oh, wicked, wicked!" gasped the elder; "may the Lord deliver us from evil!"

"No, reprobate! you are a castaway—be off, or I'll hurt you seriously! I'll have you all modeled in wax and clay; and the first who passes the limits I fix, shall—I'll not say what he shall be done to—but, you'll see! Go, I'm looking at you!"

The little witch put a mock malignity into her beautiful eyes, and Joseph, trembling with sincere horror, hurried out praying and ejaculating "wicked" as he went. I thought her conduct must be prompted by a species of dreary fun; and, now that we were alone, I endeavored to interest her in my distress.

"Mrs. Heathcliff," I said, earnestly, "you must excuse me for troubling you—I presume, because, with that face, I'm sure you cannot help being good-hearted. Do point out some landmarks by which I may know my way home: I have no more idea how to get there than you would have how to get to London!"

"Take the road you came," she answered, ensconcing herself in a chair, with a candle, and the long book open before her. "It is brief advice, but as sound as I can give."

"Then, if you hear of me being discovered dead in a bog or a pit full of snow, your conscience won't whisper that it is partly your fault?"

"How so? I cannot escort you. They wouldn't let me go to the end of the garden wall."

"*You!* I should be very sorry to ask you to cross the threshold, for my convenience, on such a night," I cried. "I want you to *tell* me my way, not to *show* it; or else to persuade Mr. Heathcliff to give me a guide."

"Who? There is himself, Earnshaw, Zillah, Joseph, and I. Which would you have?"

"Are there no boys at the farm?"

"No, those are all."

18 Discussion How do these remarks characterize their speaker as well as the household?

19 **Reading Strategy** How has the picture Lockwood presents of himself changed since the first paragraph of the novel?

"Then, it follows that I am compelled to stay."

"That you may settle with your host. I have nothing to do with it."

"I hope it will be a lesson to you, to make no more rash journeys on these hills," cried Heathcliff's stern voice from the kitchen entrance."As to staying here, I don't keep accommodations for visitors: you must share a bed with Hareton, or Joseph, if you do."

"I can sleep on a chair in this room," I replied.

"No, no! A stranger is a stranger, be he rich or poor: it will not suit me to permit any one the range of the place while I am off guard!" said the unmannerly wretch.

With this insult, my patience was at an end. I uttered an expression of disgust, and pushed past him into the yard, running against Earnshaw in my haste. It was so dark that I could not see the means of exit; and, as I wandered round, I heard another specimen of their civil behavior amongst each other. At first, the young man appeared about to befriend me.

"I'll go with him as far as the park," he said.

"You'll go with him to hell!" exclaimed his master, or whatever relation he bore. "And who is to look after the horses, eh?"

"A man's life is of more consequence than one evening's neglect of the horses: somebody must go," murmured Mrs. Heathcliff, more kindly than I expected.

"Not at your command!" retorted Hareton. "If you set store on him, you'd better be quiet."

"Then I hope his ghost will haunt you; and I hope Mr. Heathcliff will never get another tenant, till the Grange is a ruin!" she answered sharply.

"Hearken, hearken, shoo's cursing on em!" muttered Joseph, towards whom I had been steering.

He sat within earshot, milking the cows by the light of a lantern, which I seized unceremoniously, and, calling out that I would send it back on the morrow, rushed to the nearest postern.

"Maister, maister, he's staling t' lantern!" shouted the ancient, pursuing my retreat. "Hey, Gnasher! Hey, dog! Hey, Wolf, holld him, holld him!"

On opening the little door, two hairy monsters flew at my throat, bearing me down and extinguishing the light; while a mingled guffaw, from Heathcliff and Hareton, put the copestone[11] on my rage and humiliation. Fortunately, the beasts seemed more bent on stretching their paws, and yawning, and flourishing their tails, than devouring me alive; but they would suffer no resurrection, and I was forced to lie till their malignant masters pleased to deliver me: then hatless, and trembling with wrath, I ordered the miscreants to let me out—on their peril to keep me one minute longer—with several incoherent threats of retaliation that, in their indefinite depth of virulency, smacked of King Lear.[12]

The vehemence of my agitation brought on a copious bleeding at the nose, and still Heathcliff laughed, and still I scolded. I don't know what would have concluded the scene, had there not been one person at hand rather more rational than myself, and more benevolent than my entertainer. This was Zillah, the stout housewife; who at length issued forth to inquire into the nature of the uproar. She thought that some of them had been laying violent hands on me; and, not daring to attack her master, she turned her vocal artillery against the younger scoundrel.

"Well, Mr. Earnshaw," she cried, "I wonder what you'll have agait next! Are we going to murder folk on our very doorstones? 19
I see this house will never do for me—look at t' poor lad, he's fair choking! Wisht, wisht! you mun'n't go on so. Come in, and

11. copestone: Here, finishing touch.
12. King Lear: The hero of Shakespeare's *King Lear* who is betrayed and mistreated by his two scheming daughters.

I'll cure that. There now, hold ye still."

With these words she suddenly splashed a pint of icy water down my neck, and pulled me into the kitchen. Mr. Heathcliff followed, his accidental merriment expiring quickly in his habitual moroseness.

I was sick exceedingly, and dizzy and faint; and thus compelled, perforce, to accept lodgings under his roof. He told Zillah to give me a glass of brandy, and then passed on to the inner room; 20 while she condoled with me on my sorry predicament, and having obeyed his orders, whereby I was somewhat revived, ushered me to bed.

THINKING ABOUT THE SELECTION

Recalling

1. (a) Who is the narrator of the story? (b) What is his relationship to Heathcliff?
2. Why is Heathcliff's home named "Wuthering Heights?"
3. (a) What qualities does Lockwood at first believe he shares with Heathcliff? (b) What changes that impression?
4. (a) Why does Lockwood attempt to return home without a guide after his second visit? (b) What happens to him? (c) Who rescues him?

Interpreting

5. After his unfriendly reception and the first incident with the dogs, why do you think Lockwood decides to visit Heathcliff a second time?
6. (a) Judging from their interraction with one another and with their guest, how would you describe each of the residents of Wuthering Heights? (b) What factors may have made these people the way they are?

Applying

7. What does this passage reveal about life and social customs in nineteenth-century England?

ANALYZING LITERATURE

Reporting First-Person Narration

A **first-person narrator** in a novel or story reports the events first-hand. As opposed to a third-person narrator, the "I" or "we" story-teller is involved to some extent in what happens. Whether that involvement is as a direct participant in the action or a mere observer will affect the *credibility,* or believableness, of the narrator's summary of events and views on other characters.

On a scale of 1 to 10, where 1 signifies total involvement and 10 signifies a lack of involvement, rate the first-person narrator of *Wuthering Heights.* Then determine his credibility by considering the following:

1. The extent to which he is responsible for the first attack by the dogs, and his response to that attack.
2. How his reception by Mrs. Heathcliff might color his perception of her.
3. What prompts Joseph to order the dogs on him a second time.

THINKING AND WRITING

Writing About the Narrative Technique

Suppose that you located an earlier version in manuscript form of *Wuthering Heights* in which Brontë had used a third-person narrator. In an explanatory essay, tell in what ways the excerpt you have read was different. Mention, in particular, the balance between subjective and objective information, and differences in the portrayal of the character Lockwood. Feel free, if you like, to "quote" passages from this literary find.

20 Critical Reading and Thinking In what ways has the relationship between Lockwood's subjective and objective opinions altered?

Answers

ANSWERS TO THINKING ABOUT THE SELECTION

Recalling

1. (a) Mr. Lockwood is the story's narrator. (b) Lockwood occupies Thrushcross Grange as Heathcliff's tenant.
2. Heathcliff's dwelling is called Wuthering Heights because, as Joseph explains, its elevated location exposes it to stormy weather or "wuthering."
3. (a) Lockwood believes that he and Heathcliff share a dislike of mankind and a preference for solitude. (b) Heathcliff's cruelty to man and beast leads Lockwood to feel that they have less in common than he at first supposed.
4. (a) Lockwood attempts to return home without a guide after his second visit because he is thoroughly disgusted with all the inhabitants of the Grange and cannot bear the thought of spending a night there. (b) Joseph sets the dogs on Lockwood, for "staling t' lantern!" (c) Zillah, the housewife, saves Lockwood from choking on a nosebleed.

Interpreting

5. Lockwood probably decides to visit Heathcliff a second time because the first meeting raised so many unanswered questions.
6. (a) The inhabitants of Wuthering Heights seem, each in her or his own way, sullen, angry, and disappointed. (b) All the characters seem to suffer from a disinheritance—a loss of money, power, privilege, or love.

Applying

7. The passage emphasizes the extreme hierarchical nature of life and social customs in nineteenth-century England.

Challenge Why do you suppose Brontë created a character so ordinary as Lockwood to witness and relate the fantastic scene at Wuthering Heights?

ANSWERS TO ANALYZING LITERATURE

Suggested response: Lockwood cannot be described as "totally involved" in what happens during his first two visits to the Heights because, for most of the time that he is there, he misreads everyone he meets. His involvement is superficial and accidental. On a scale of one-to-ten, he might be rated a five.

1. Lockwood is almost completely responsible for the first attack by the dogs. He provokes the dogs by acting foolishly and irresponsibly. Afterwards, he is outraged and blames others.
2. Mrs. Heathcliff's aloof manner makes Lockwood ill at ease. He behaves like a fool and then resents her amusement.
3. Joseph thinks Lockwood is stealing a lantern.

More About the Author As late as the mid-nineteenth century, it was believed that most women were incapable of writing serious poetry and prose. So that their work might be at least considered for publication, Charlotte Brontë and her sisters adopted pseudonyms that preserved the initials of their Christian names even as they disguised their gender. Charlotte, Emily, and Anne Brontë became, respectively, Currer, Ellis, and Acton Bell. Charlotte Brontë was fascinated by the role of author, and she depicted her character, Jane Eyre, as more than just a narrator or storyteller. Repeatedly, in the course of the novel, Jane addresses her audience as "Dear Reader," thus making it clear that she is presenting herself as the author of the story of her own life. Brontë affords her character two qualities at the time reserved for men, i.e., the ability to write and to gain control over a narrative and the ability to shape one's own destiny and thereby to achieve autonomy. Try to recall other first-person narratives you have read; Dickens provides some good examples. What relationship do you see between the first-person narrator's ability to look back upon his or her life and make sense of it and that same narrator's ability to grow and mature as a character?

CHARLOTTE BRONTË

1816–1855

Charlotte Brontë, older sister of Emily Brontë (see page 910), produced in her brief lifetime four novels of which the best known is *Jane Eyre*. Charlotte was one of six children born to Patrick Brontë, a clergyman, and Maria Branwell. After the death of her mother to cancer and of her two older sisters to tuberculosis, Charlotte and the three remaining Brontë children were placed in the care of an aunt. To combat the loneliness and drudgery of their isolated life on the Yorkshire moors, the children created the fantasy worlds of Angria and Gondal on paper.

At the age of nineteen, Charlotte accepted the post of governess for two separate families, rounding out an already hectic schedule as a schoolteacher. She traveled to Belgium to study foreign languages and further refine her teaching skills, but all the while she was secretly writing poetry. When it was revealed that her sisters were also dabbling in verse, the three jointly published a book of their poems under the pen name "Bell."

After this each sister began independent work on a novel. Although Emily's book, *Wuthering Heights,* and Anne's *Agnes Grey* were accepted readily for publication, Charlotte was unable to generate interest in *The Professor,* a novel about the growth of an orphaned young man who goes to teach at a Belgian school. Her next effort, the fictionalized autobiography of an orphan girl, was immediately accepted by a publisher in 1847 and became an overnight sensation among readers of the popular Victorian novel. This was her masterpiece *Jane Eyre*.

It was shortly after she had started her third novel, *Shirley,* that Brontë's life was shattered, first by the death of her brother, and then, within the space of a year, by the passing of her two sisters. As a means of coping with her grief and loneliness, she continued to work on the book and edited the writings her sisters had left behind.

In 1854, the year after Brontë completed her fourth and, as it was to be, final novel she married Arthur Bell Nicholls, her father's curate. She died a year later, of complications connected with pregnancy.

Despite her limited literary output, Brontë influenced the development of the novel with her close examination of women's inner battles and their frustrations with restricted lives. Her presentation of the individual's feelings under confining circumstances is powerful and realistic, anticipating later psychological character studies.

Objectives

1. To report first-person narration
2. To make inferences about the narrator
3. To use context clues
4. To write a continuation of an excerpt

Teaching Portfolio: Support Material

Teacher Backup, pp. 00-00

Vocabulary Check, p. 00

Usage and Mechanics Worksheet, p. 00

Analyzing Literature Worksheet, p. 00

Critical Thinking and Reading Worksheet, p. 00

Language Worksheet, p. 00

Selection Test, p. 00

GUIDE FOR READING

from Jane Eyre

The Writer's Technique

First-Person Narration (Participant). The first-person narrator as participant is not merely the "I" or "we" from whose point of view the story is told, but is an integral part of the story. As is true of any character in a tale, the participating first-person narrator has the power to affect the outcome and the fate of all other characters. The story, as seen through the eyes of this participant, takes on an immediacy that is otherwise not possible. The readers are made party to the narrator's innermost thoughts and feelings while being permitted simultaneously to evaluate those feelings in terms of the narrator's biases and restricted understanding of events. In *Jane Eyre,* which has its roots in the fictionalized autobiographical style of novels of the eighteenth century, the participating first-person narrator permits the reader to glimpse her inner struggles, while offering her views of the events and characters that figure in her life.

Look For

As you read the excerpt from *Jane Eyre,* look for how the writer uses first-person narration to show Jane's feelings and create sympathy for her.

Writing

Over the course of several days keep a fictionalized journal written by an individual from an alien civilization who is being permitted to share in the events of your life. Before you begin, consider what the alien's routine includes and ways in which your routine might differ. In your account attempt to capture the alien's surprise and awe at some of our "strange" customs.

Vocabulary

Knowing the following words will help you as you read the excerpt from *Jane Eyre.*

sprightly (sprīt′lē) *adj.*: Lively (p. 924)
vignettes (vin yets) *n.*: Decorative designs or borderless pictures in a book (p. 926)
crimped (krimpd) *v.*: Shaped; creased (p. 926)
diffidence (dif′ə dəns) *n.*: Shyness; hesitation (p. 926)
rummage (rum′ij) *v.*: Search by thoroughly examining (p. 927)

Literary Focus Not only is *Jane Eyre* one of the earliest successful novels by a woman, it is also one of the first major novels to employ a first-person female narrator. Jane Eyre faces some of the same problems as her creator, Charlotte Brontë; each, for example, finds herself an outsider in a world to which she would like to belong—the one an orphan in a landscape of entitlement and the other a woman in a predominantly male profession.

Look For Less advanced students may be better able to appreciate the complexity of first-person participant narration if they try to rewrite a paragraph of *Jane Eyre* from a third-person omniscient point of view. Take turns reading these student versions aloud. Discuss the ways in which a change in point of view alters a story.

Writing You can help your students get started by having the class brainstorm about the alien and his or her civilization and routines. What earthly events might the alien be involved in? Again, have the students suggest possibilities.

Vocabulary Have students look up these vocabulary words in the dictionary. Remark upon their derivation as well as their early use in English. Have students make up sentences using these words.

Motivation for Reading Discuss with students what it means to be an outsider. Ask for examples of famous outsiders in history and literature. Make a list of the feelings and attitudes one associates with the role of outsider.

Master Teacher Note *Jane Eyre* is, in many ways, a grown-up fairy tale. Analyze the fairy-tale elements in the excerpt, and relate them to classic tales. Project the possible direction of Jane's narrative based on the opening scene.

Purpose-Setting Question Why is it essential that *Jane Eyre* be told in the first person?

1 **Discussion** What do we learn about the narrator in these opening paragraphs of her life's story?

2 **Reading Strategy** Have students visualize this scene. Why does Brontë set her first-person narrator in this position, that is, between the drear November outside and the warm, scarlet within? What does this contrast say about the conflict Jane experiences?

3 **Clarification** *Bewick's History of British Birds* was a popular, illustrated guide—somewhat like our field guides.

4 **Critical Thinking and Reading** Presumably *Bewick's* contains a variety of illustrations. What can we infer about Jane's mood from the particular passages to which she is drawn?

from Jane Eyre

Charlotte Brontë

Chapter 1

There was no possibility of taking a walk that day. We had been wandering, indeed, in the leafless shrubbery an hour in the morning; but since dinner (Mrs. Reed, when there was no company, dined early) the cold winter wind had brought with it clouds so somber, and a rain so penetrating, that further outdoor exercise was now out of the question.

I was glad of it: I never liked long walks, especially on chilly afternoons: dreadful to me was the coming home in the raw twilight, with nipped fingers and toes, and a heart saddened by the chidings of Bessie,
1 the nurse, and humbled by the consciousness of my physical inferiority to Eliza, John, and Georgiana Reed.

The said Eliza, John, and Georgiana were now clustered round their mama in the drawing room: she lay reclined on a sofa by the fireside, and with her darlings about her (for the time neither quarreling nor crying) looked perfectly happy. Me, she had dispensed from joining the group; saying, "She regretted to be under the necessity of keeping me at a distance; but that until she heard from Bessie, and could discover by her own observation that I was endeavoring in good earnest to acquire a more sociable and childlike disposition, a more attractive and sprightly manner—something lighter, franker, more natural as it were—she really must exclude me from privileges intended only for contented, happy, little children."

"What does Bessie say I have done?" I asked.

"Jane, I don't like cavilers or questioners; besides, there is something truly forbidding in a child taking up her elders in that manner. Be seated somewhere; and until you can speak pleasantly, remain silent."

A small breakfast room adjoined the drawing room. I slipped in there. It contained a bookcase; I soon possessed myself of a volume, taking care that it should be one stored with pictures. I mounted into the window seat; gathering up my feet, I sat cross-legged, like a Turk; and, having drawn the red moreen[1] curtain nearly close, I was shrined in double retirement.

Folds of scarlet drapery shut in my view
to the right hand; to the left were the clear 2
panes of glass, protecting, but not separating me from the drear November day. At intervals, while turning over the leaves of my book, I studied the aspect of that winter afternoon. Afar, it offered a pale blank of mist and cloud; near, a scene of wet lawn and storm-beat shrub, with ceaseless rain sweeping away wildly before a long and lamentable blast.

I returned to my book, *Bewick's History
of British Birds;* the letterpress[2] thereof I 3
cared little for, generally speaking; and yet there were certain introductory pages that,
child as I was, I could not pass quite as a 4

1. **moreen** *adj.*: Made from heavy woolen material.
2. **letterpress** *n.*: Print.

Thematic Idea Point out that the first-person participating narrator has often been used to depict the growth of a character from youth, through crisis, to young adulthood. Dickens's *David Copperfield* and James Joyce's *Portrait of the Artist as a Young Man* are other examples. In *Jane Eyre,* Charlotte Brontë uses the first-person participating narrator to portray a young girl's development from childhood to maturity.

JANE EYRE
Fritz Eichenberg

Humanities Note

Illustration for *Jane Eyre* by Fritz Eichenberg. Fritz Eichenberg, born in 1901, is a German-American wood engraver and illustrator. Born in Cologne, Germany, Eichenberg studied art there and at the State Academy of Graphic Design in Leipzig. During his student days he fell in love with the black-and-white medium of wood engraving, a technique of incising lines into a boxwood block with a sharp instrument, called a burin, to create a design. This block is then inked and pressed onto paper; the incised lines print a black image.

Eichenberg fled Nazi Germany to the United States in 1933. He settled in New York City and soon became an award-winning book illustrator. The illustrations for *Jane Eyre* were done in 1943. His extreme skill in the wood-engraving technique resulted in the interesting variety of textures and lights and darks that comprise this vivid illustration. As well as illustrating numerous books and exhibiting his works nationally, Fritz Eichenberg has taught at many prestigious schools of art and has become the head of the Pratt Institute in Brooklyn, New York.

You might ask your students the following questions:

1. Does this illustration inspire sympathy in you? Explain.
2. How does the artist achieve the emotional effect of this illustration?

5 **Enrichment** *Pamela* and *Henry, Earl of Moreland* were novels popular with Charlotte Brontë's contemporaries. Of special interest is *Pamela,* a first-person epistolary novel that tells the story of a young woman whose position in life is analogous to Jane's.

6 **Discussion** Imagine this moment in Jane's story as a scene in a play. What is the effect of John Reed's intrusion upon Jane's daydreams? Why is it significant that he appears upon the scene at the moment that he does?

7 **Discussion** How old do you think Jane is as she tells her story? This first-person narrative is retrospective. How does looking back upon life's adventures allow one to understand and shape them?

blank. They were those which treat of the haunts of seafowl: of "the solitary rocks and promontories" by them only inhabited; of the coast of Norway, studded with isles from its southern extremity, the Lindeness, or Naze, to the North Cape:

Where the Northern Ocean, in
vast whirls,
Boils round the naked, melancholy
isles
Of farthest Thule; and the Atlantic
surge
Pours in among the stormy
Hebrides.

4 Nor could I pass unnoticed the suggestion of the bleak shores of Lapland, Siberia, Spitzbergen, Nova Zembla, Iceland, Greenland, with "the vast sweep of the Arctic Zone, and those forlorn regions of dreary space—that reservoir of frost and snow, where firm fields of ice, the accumulation of centuries of winters, glazed in Alpine heights above heights, surround the pole, and concenter the multiplied rigors of extreme cold." Of these death-white realms I formed an idea of my own: shadowy, like all the half-comprehended notions that float dim through children's brains, but strangely impressive. The words in these introductory pages connected themselves with the succeeding vignettes, and gave significance to the rock standing up alone in a sea of billow and spray; to the broken boat stranded on a desolate coast; to the cold and ghastly moon glancing through bars of cloud at a wreck just sinking.

I cannot tell what sentiment haunted the quiet solitary churchyard, with its inscribed headstone, its gate, its two trees, its low horizon, girdled by a broken wall, and its newly risen crescent, attesting the hour of eventide.

The two ships becalmed on a torpid sea, I believed to be marine phantoms.

The fiend pinning down the thief's pack behind him, I passed over quickly: it was an object of terror.

So was the black, horned thing seated aloof on a rock, surveying a distant crowd surrounding a gallows.

Each picture told a story; mysterious often to my undeveloped understanding and imperfect feelings, yet ever profoundly interesting—as interesting as the tales Bessie sometimes narrated on winter evenings, when she chanced to be in good humor; and when, having brought her ironing table to the nursery hearth, she allowed us to sit about it, and while she got up Mrs. Reed's lace frills, and crimped her nightcap borders, fed our eager attention with passages of love and adventure taken from old fairy tales and older ballads, or (as at a later period I discovered) from the pages of *Pamela,* and *Henry, Earl of Moreland.* 5

With Bewick on my knee, I was then happy: happy at least in my way. I feared nothing but interruption, and that came too soon. The breakfast room door opened.

"Boh! Madame Mope!" cried the voice of John Reed. Then he paused: he found the room apparently empty. 6

"Where the dickens is she?" he continued. "Lizzy! Georgy!" calling to his sisters, "Jane is not here. Tell mama she is run out into the rain—bad animal!"

"It is well I drew the curtain," thought I; and I wished fervently he might not discover my hiding place; nor would John Reed have found it out himself: he was not quick either of vision or conception; but Eliza just put her head in at the door, and said at once:

"She is in the window seat, to be sure, Jack."

And I came out immediately, for I trembled at the idea of being dragged forth by the said Jack.

"What do you want?" I asked, with awkward diffidence.

"Say, 'What do you want, Master Reed?'" was the answer. "I want you to come here," and seating himself in an armchair, he intimated by a gesture that I was to approach and stand before him.

John Reed was a schoolboy of fourteen years old; four years older than I, for I was 7 but ten; large and stout for his age, with a dingy and unwholesome skin; thick lineaments in a spacious visage, heavy limbs and large extremities. He gorged himself habitually at table, which made him bilious, and gave him a dim and bleared eye and flabby cheeks. He ought now to have been at school; but his mama had taken him home for a month or two, "on account of his delicate health." Mr. Miles, the master, affirmed that he would do very well if he had fewer cakes and sweetmeats sent him from home; but the mother's heart turned from an opinion so harsh, and inclined rather to the more refined idea that John's sallowness was owing to overapplication and, perhaps, to pining after home.

John had not much affection for his mother and sisters, and an antipathy to me. He bullied and punished me; not two or three times in the week, nor once or twice in the day, but continually; every nerve I had feared him, and every morsel of flesh on my bones shrank when he came near. There were moments when I was bewildered by the terror he inspired, because I had no appeal whatever against either his menaces or his inflictions: the servants did not like to offend their young master by taking my part against him, and Mrs. Reed was blind and deaf on the subject: she never saw him
8 strike or heard him abuse me, though he did both now and then in her very presence; more frequently, however, behind her back.

Habitually obedient to John, I came up to his chair. He spent some three minutes in thrusting out his tongue at me as far as he could without damaging the roots. I knew he would soon strike, and while dreading the blow, I mused on the disgusting and ugly appearance of him who would presently deal it. I wonder if he read that notion in my face; for, all at once, without speaking, he struck suddenly and strongly. I tottered, and on regaining my equilibrium retired back a step or two from his chair.

"That is for your impudence in answering mama awhile since," said he, "and for your sneaking way of getting behind curtains and for the look you had in your eyes two minutes since, you rat!"

Accustomed to John Reed's abuse, I never had an idea of replying to it; my care was how to endure the blow which would certainly follow the insult.

"What were you doing behind the curtain?" he asked.

"I was reading."

"Show the book."

I returned to the window and fetched it thence.

"You have no business to take our books; you are a dependent, mama says; you have no money; your father left you none; you ought to beg, and not to live here with gentlemen's children like us, and eat the same meals we do, and wear clothes at our mama's expense. Now, I'll teach you to rummage my bookshelves, for they *are* mine 9
—all the house belongs to me, or will do in a few years. Go and stand by the door, out of the way of the mirror and the windows."

I did so, not at first aware what was his intention, but when I saw him lift and poise the book and stand in act to hurl it, I instinctively started aside with a cry of alarm; not soon enough, however: the volume was flung, it hit me, and I fell, striking my head against the door and cutting it. The cut bled, the pain was sharp, my terror had passed its climax, other feelings succeeded.

"Wicked and cruel boy!" I said. "You are like a murderer, you are like a slave driver, you are like the Roman emperors!"

I had read Goldsmith's *History of Rome*, and had formed my opinion of Nero, Caligula, etc. Also I had drawn parallels in silence,
which I never thought thus to have declared 10
aloud. 11

"What! what!" he cried. "Did you say that to me? Did you hear her, Eliza and Georgiana? Won't I tell mama? but first . . ."

He ran headlong at me. I felt him grasp my hair and my shoulder; he had closed with a desperate thing. I really saw in him a tyrant, a murderer. I felt a drop or two of blood from my head trickle down my neck, and was sensible of somewhat pungent suf-

8 **Critical Thinking and Reading** Although Mrs. Reed appears only briefly in this scene, what can we infer about her character from the description of her treatment of John and Jane?

9 **Discussion** What do these remarks of John Reed's tell us about Jane? What sorts of feelings might arise as a result of being called a "dependent"?

10 **Enrichment** Nero and Caligula were Roman emperors famed for their savage cruelty.

11 **Critical Thinking and Reading** What can you infer about Jane as a result of her ability to draw a parallel between John Reed and the portraits of Nero and Caligula?

ferings. These sensations for the time predominated over fear, and I received him in frantic sort. I don't very well know what I did with my hands, but he called me "rat! rat!" and bellowed out aloud. Aid was near him: Eliza and Georgiana had run for Mrs. Reed, who was gone upstairs; she now came upon the scene, followed by Bessie and her maid Abbot. We were parted: I heard the words:

"Dear! dear! What a fury to fly at Master John!"

"Did ever anybody see such a picture of passion?"

Then Mrs. Reed subjoined:

"Take her away to the red room, and lock her in there." Four hands were immediately laid upon me, and I was borne upstairs.

THINKING ABOUT THE SELECTION

Recalling

1. (a) Where are the Reed children at the beginning of the selection? (b) Why has Jane not been invited to join them? (c) What does she do to entertain herself?
2. (a) How does the fight between John and Jane start? (b) What happens to Jane as a result of the fight?

Interpreting

3. (a) How would you describe Jane's treatment by Mrs. Reed? (b) By the Reed children?
4. What do Jane's reactions to the Reed children, and especially John, reveal about her?

Applying

5. (a) If you were in Jane's situation, would you react as she does? (b) In what ways might you react differently?
6. (a) What does Jane's situation suggest about the era in which she lived? (b) How would things be different for a child in the same situation today?

ANALYZING LITERATURE

Reporting First-Person Narration

The participating first-person narrator is more than simply an observer or reporter of facts; rather, he or she is a vital part of the story. When seen from the vantage point of this participant, the story becomes more immediate and vivid for the reader than it otherwise could. Because of the skill with which Charlotte Bronte developed her first-person narrator in *Jane Eyre,* we are almost able at times to experience firsthand the child's emotional state. For each of the following portions of the narrative in the excerpt you read, describe what you believe young Jane was feeling.

1. Not being permitted to join the Reeds after dinner.
2. Curling up in the window seat with the curtains drawn.
3. Being ordered by John to address him as "Master Reed."
4. Being struck with the book.
5. Being taken to the "red room" by "four hands."

CRITICAL THINKING AND READING

Making Inferences About the Narrator

Much of what we learn about Jane's physical appearance, personality, and so on we learn not through direct statements but through **inferences,** or conclusions, that we draw based on her actions and habits. What details about the narrator can you infer from each of the following:

1. Her choosing a book "stored with pictures?"
2. Her "mounting into" the window seat?
3. Her reactions to the words and pictures in the book on birds?
4. Her seeing a relationship between Goldsmith's *History of Rome* and John Reed?

UNDERSTANDING LANGUAGE

Using Context Clues

Clues to the meaning of an unfamiliar word are often supplied by the **context—**that is, by nearby words and sentences. Such clues may take the form of a direct definition, or they may be words that are either opposite or similar in meaning to the unknown word.

Use context to figure out the words in italics in the following sentences. Tell which word or words in each sentence provides the strongest clue to the word's meaning. Check your answers in a dictionary.

1. "Jane, I don't like *cavilers* or questioners."
2. The two ships [were] becalmed on a *torpid* sea . . .
3. John had not much affection for his mother and sisters, and an *antipathy* for me.
4. I tottered, and on regaining my *equlibrium* retired back a step or two.
5. "You are a *dependent,* mama says; you have no money."

THINKING AND WRITING

Continuing the Novel

Continue Jane Eyre's first-person account of her life by writing Chapter 2. Begin with what happens to Jane after she is taken to the "red room." You may be as creative as you like and introduce new characters, but try to preserve the tone and atmosphere Charlotte Brontë has created up to this point. When you revise your first draft, make sure you have related events in chronological order. Proofread your final draft and share it with your classmates.

Answers

ANSWERS TO THINKING ABOUT THE SELECTION

Recalling

1. (a) At the beginning of the story the Reed children are in the drawing room before the fire. (b) Jane has not been invited to join them because Mrs. Reed maintains that she is unsociable and not childlike. (c) To entertain herself, Jane withdraws to a windowsill to read.
2. (a) John seems to attack Jane more or less for the fun of it. (b) As a result of the fight, Jane is exiled to the red room.

Interpreting

3. (a) Mrs. Reed is cruel and insensitive to Jane. (b) The Reed children are similarly thoughtless and sadistic towards their orphaned cousin.
4. Jane's reactions to the Reed children, particularly John, reveal her to be perceptive and passionate.

Applying

5. (a) Answers may differ. (b) Answer may differ. Some might react more aggressively, and somer.
6. (a) Jane's situation suggests that orphaned young girl's were regarded as burdens by their relatives. (b) Things would probably not be particularly different today.

ANSWERS TO ANALYZING LITERATURE

1. Suggested answer: She probably felt humbled and sad.
2. Suggested answer: She probably felt safe, secure, and temporarily free from humiliation.
3. Suggested answer: She probably felt embarrassed, resentful, and contemptuous of John, but also docile and unsure of herself.
4. Suggested answer: Besides physical pain, she feels anger.
5. Suggested answer: She probably felt perplexed, powerless, and humiliated.

ANSWERS TO CRITICAL THINKING AND READING

Suggested responses:

1. From her choosing a book "stored with pictures" we can infer that Jane seeks solace in her imagination.
2. Jane's "mounting into" the window seat suggests that she withdraws from the world in order to sort out her feelings.
3. From Jane's reactions to the words and pictures in the book on birds we can infer that she is unusually sensitive and creative.
4. Jane's noting of a relationship between John Reed and Goldsmith's *History of Rome* shows that she is intelligent and, for a girl, particularly well-read.

ANSWERS TO UNDERSTANDING LANGUAGE

1. fault-finders ("questioners")
2. motionless ("becalmed")
3. dislike ("not much affection")
4. balance ("tottered," "regaining")
5. a person who relies on someone else's support ("no money")

THINKING AND WRITING

For help with this assignment, students can refer to Lesson 19, "Writing a Short Story," in the Handbook of Writing About Literature.

The writing assignments on page 930 have students write creatively, while those on page 931 have them think about the selections and write critically.

YOU THE WRITER
Guidelines for Evaluating Assignment 1

1. Does the imaginary conversation between a Victorian poet and the student include the answers to three good questions about the poet's works or about life in Victorian England?
2. Does the dialogue include vivid details about the appearance of the poet and the setting of the conversation?
3. Are the poet's responses consistent with his or her writing style?
4. Is the dialogue lifelike and interesting with many vivid words?
5. Is the conversation free from grammar, usage, and mechanics errors?

Guidelines for Evaluating Assignment 2

1. Has the student written a chapter that extends a work of Victorian fiction or creates a new episode in the life of one of the characters?
2. Are any additions of character or setting reasonable in terms of the original story?
3. Is the addition consistent in the words and the actions of the main character?
4. Is the addition free from grammar, usage, and mechanics errors?

Guidelines for Evaluating Assignment 3

1. Has the student written an original poem in the style of a Victorian poet?
2. Has the student kept in mind the Victorian poets' tendency to be pessimistic?
3. Has the student been faithful to the line length, rhyme scheme, word choice, type of images used, and meter of the poet he or she imitated?
4. Is the poem free from grammar, usage, and mechanics errors?

YOU THE WRITER

Assignment

1. Suppose you had traveled back in time to Victorian England and met one of the poets whose works you have read. Record an imaginary conversation between you and that poet in which you asked and received answers to three good questions about his or her poetry or about life in the Victorian era.

Prewriting. Brainstorm to develop questions that will provide some insight into the art of the poet or into the social climate as reflected by the works and background material you have read.

Writing. Include in your composition details about the appearance of the poet and the setting of your conversation. Attempt to word the poet's responses in a manner consistent with his or her writing style.

Revising. Read your composition to see whether your description and dialogue are lifelike and interesting. Replace dull words with vivid ones.

Assignment

2. Choose one of the fiction selections you read and enjoyed in this unit, and write either a brief chapter that extends the action of the original or an entirely new episode in the life of one of the characters. Tell your story as you think the author of the original might have done.

Prewriting. Before you begin to write, make a study of the characters, paying particular attention to such details as physical appearance and speech habits. Familiarize yourself also with the author's style of narration.

Writing. Add new characters and settings, if you like, but make sure your additions are reasonable in terms of the original story. Strive for consistency in your characters' words and actions.

Revising. Compare the punctuation of your dialogue with that of the original, and correct any errors. Look for inconsistencies.

Assignment

3. Although every literary period has its outstanding poets, none rivals the Victorian era in the individuality of its poetic voices. This was the age when Browning was experimenting with his dramatic monologues, Hopkins with his sprung rhythm, Tennyson with his elaborate stanza forms. Write an original poem that imitates the style of one of the poets from this unit.

Prewriting. Get your creative juices flowing by considering possible subjects for a poem. Bear in mind that the majority of Victorian poets were quite pessimistic in their outlook on life.

Writing. As you write, be mindful of such details as line length, rhyme scheme, word choice, types of images used, and meter.

Revising. Adjust any weaknesses in structure and rhyme. Check the spellings of any words of which you are unsure.

YOU THE CRITIC

Assignment

1. Vivian de Sola Pinto, a scholar on Victorian literature, wrote that Thomas Hardy, unlike most other Victorian poets, was out "to produce a dramatic, rather than a pictorial or musical effect." Write an essay that either addresses this commentary on Hardy or explores the goals of another Victorian poet you have read.

Prewriting. Consider the possible meanings of the word "dramatic" as it is used in this sense. Scan the works by the poet you intend to focus on, and jot down words or phrases.

Writing. Open your essay with a clear thesis statement. Support each point you make with quotations from the poems or the background material on your poet.

Revising. Assess the first draft f your essay for la ity and coherence. Look out for any unwanted shifts in tense in the course of your discussion.

Assignment.

2. A writer in the *Edinburgh Review* for July 1858 described the nineteenth century as an "age of transition—a period when changes, deeply and permanently affecting the whole condition of mankind, are occurring more rapidly . . . than at any prior time in human history." Extending the statement to include our own time, write a paper that agrees or disagrees.

Prewriting. On a sheet of paper note what you have learned about the history of the Victorian era, with specific regard to technological advances. On a second sheet make notes about similar advances in our own time.

Writing. Convert your notes into an essay. Back up each change with examples of the effects it has had on the human race, explaining in wh t way th e effects are irreversible.

Revising. Examine your paper for evidence of faulty logic or grammar.

Assignment

3. The Victorian period is often regarded as one of pessimism. One need only recall the poetry of Arnold or Hardy to understand why. Yet at least two of the Victorians you read, Browning and Hopkins, were quite positive, or at least hopeful, most of the time. Select one pessimistic Victorian and one nonpessimistic one, and write an essay that compares and contrasts the two.

Prewriting. Begin by rereading the poetry of each of the poets you choose. As you read, jot down on separate sheets of paper thoughts and feelings the poem awakens in you.

Writing. State the purpose of your essay in your first paragraph. Quote specific lines and images from the poems to support the claims you make.

Revising. Proofread your paper to ensure that all your sentences make sense.

YOU THE CRITIC
Guidelines for Evaluating Assignment 1

1. Does the essay begin with a clear thesis statement about the goals of Hardy or another Victorian poet?
2. Is each point supported with quotes from the poems or background material on the poet?
3. Has the student commented on the dramatic aspects of the poet's works?
4. Is the essay free from grammar, usage, and mechanics errors?

Guidelines for Evaluating Assignment 2

1. Has the student agreed or disagreed with extending the statement to include our own time?
2. Has the student backed up each change mentioned with examples of the effects it has had on the human race, explaining in what ways those effects are irreversible?
3. Is the essay at least 250 words long?
4. Is the essay free from grammar, usage, and mechanics errors?

Guidelines for Evaluating Assignment 3

1. Does the student state the purpose of the essay, comparing a pessimistic and an optimistic poet, in the beginning of the paper?
2. Has the student quoted specific lines and images from the poems to support the claims made?
3. Has the student written a satisfying conclusion?
4. Is the essay free from grammar, usage, and mechanics errors?

Humanities Note

Fine art, *Big Ben,* 1905–06, by André Derain. French painter André Derain (1880–1954) traveled to England in the early 1900's and completed a series of very personal paintings of London. For Derain, that city had an undeniable charm, and he used dabs of paint in bright, almost playful colors to convey his sense of the liveliness of the scene. The massive architecture of England's Houses of Parliament and the familiar sight of the clock, "Big Ben," are made more human by Derain's light-hearted use of color, by the twirls of paint, by the deliberately decorative design of the sails of the boat passing by.

This painting is typical of Derain's early work. He went on to become one of the first Fauvists. The French word *fauve* means "wild beast" and the derisive name was hurled at Derain and other young artists, who cheerfully adopted it. The Fauvists painted in an expressionist style, characterized by bold distortion of forms and exhuberant color. The beginnings of that color can be seen in this early work.

BIG BEN, 1905–1906
André Derain
Art Resource

THE MODERN PERIOD

1901–1945

Turning and turning in the widening gyre
The falcon cannot hear the falconer;
Things fall apart; the center cannot hold;
Mere anarchy is loosed upon the world,
The blood-dimmed tide is loosed, and everywhere
The ceremony of innocence is drowned.

from "The Second Coming,"
William Butler Yeats

933

Humanities Note

Fine art, *An English Rose,* by Joseph Clark. Clark (1834–1926) was an English painter who worked in oils. Born in Dorset, he came to London at eighteen to study. He was a genre painter, using a realistic style to portray subjects from everyday life. The portrait called *An English Rose* captures a woman of the Edwardian Age. The light focused on the face and neck of this young woman gives her an almost luminous quality, and she appears relaxed, though expectant. There is a soft, almost affectionate treatment of the subject. This feeling is accomplished, in part, by the emphasis on rounded forms and proportions, ranging from the soft modeling of the features of the face, to the wave of the hair, to the shape and texture of the flowers. Harsh, angular lines are absent and there is a wispy, youthful quality to the rendering of her dress.

A complacent world floated into the twentieth century on a mood of hope and anticipation. Science and technology were off and soaring. "Progress" was the word on everyone's lips. What could possibly go wrong?

Plenty, as it turned out. While advances in communications and transportation drew the world closer together, modern warfare —William Butler Yeats's "blood-dimmed tide"—nearly destroyed it. World War I (1914–18) killed more than eight million people. World War II (1939–45) took an even higher toll. The wars, and the economic and moral upheaval they caused, shattered countless illusions.

British literature of the modern period (1901–1945) reflects these historical events, riding a swinging pendulum of hope and despair. First, the new century spurred a spirit of innovation in all the arts. Then World War I caused a backswing of disillusionment. Those two spirits, innovation and disillusionment, prompted modern writers to reject many of the traditions of nineteenth-century literature. It was time to experiment with fresh themes, fresh literary styles. "Make it new," exhorted American poet Ezra Pound, the London representative of Chicago's *Poetry* magazine. Pound's advice became the rallying cry of a generation of writers on both sides of the Atlantic.

THE EDWARDIAN AGE

AN ENGLISH ROSE
Joseph Clark
Gallerie George, London

When Queen Victoria died in 1901, her eldest son succeeded her as Edward VII. We call the years from 1901 to 1914 the Edwardian Age (although Edward died in 1910).

The rigid class distinctions and moral certainties of Victorian times lingered on into the Edwardian Age. We can read about the English country manors of this era in the novels of the American-born Henry James (1843–1916). James vividly portrays the opulence, the pampered gentry, the armies of servants. At the beginning of the century, one Briton in every six worked as a servant.

The rapid pace of change doomed this outdated way of life. Electricity became the "silent servant." It powered household appliances and made many of the jobs of servants obsolete. Telephones (and later radios) brought news from distant places. Automobiles (and later airplanes) opened new possibilities for travel.

As people gained new knowledge and greater sophistication, they began to question Victorian values and ideas. Women marched for the right to vote. A new Labor party, demanding greater rights for the working class, challenged the dominance of the existing Liberal and Conservative parties. In Ireland and in Britain's colonies, nationalists agitated for home rule or independence. By the time George V came to the throne in 1910, the nineteenth-century way of life was fading into memory.

A STAR SHELL, c. 1916
Christopher Richard Wynne Nevinson
Tate Gallery

THE FIRST WORLD WAR AND ITS CONSEQUENCES

World War I erupted suddenly, but pressure had been building since the nineteenth century. Then, Britain and France had grabbed colonial empires, while Germany lagged behind. When the Germans later sought colonies of their own, their desires clashed with established British and French interests. The nations of Europe chose sides. Tensions grew. All it took was a spark to ignite the war—and the assassination in 1914 of Austria-Hungary's Archduke Ferdinand provided the spark.

Britain went to war in a light-hearted and confident spirit. Many had the romantic notion that the war would offer "good sport" and end in a few weeks. Sir Edward Grey, the foreign minister, saw more clearly. Gazing out on a London street at dusk, he said: "The lamps are going out all over Europe. We shall not see them lit again in our lifetime."

Poisonous gas, massive artillery barrages, and machine guns turned the fields of France and Belgium into a killing ground. Heroic cavalry charges and chivalrous hand-to-hand combat had little place in this first modern war. For four grim years of stalemate, the opposing armies slugged it out. The slaughter decimated a generation of young men and shredded the very fabric of British society. Poets perished by the scores. Many posthumously published poems tell the horrors of trench warfare and mourn the loss of heroic ideals.

Humanities Note

Fine art, *A Star Shell,* c. 1916 by Christopher Richard Wynne Nevinson. Nevinson (1889–1946) was an English painter, strongly influenced by the Italian futurists and their angular, explosive work, which often idealized danger, war, and the machine age.

He was a landscape and figure artist, an etcher, and a lithographer who served as motor mechanic, ambulance driver, hospital orderly, and official war artist during World War I. During that time, the battlefield was his landscape. He used the principles of futurism to portray a dramatic view of modernized warfare, but he did not glorify it as the futurists had. He saw in the cubes and angles of futurism the perfect tools with which he could depict the rifles, trenches, and fences of war. *A Star Shell* is full of force; it is dramatic, exciting, and sinister. In this painting, as well as others, Nevinson experimented with kaleidoscopic patterns of color, designed to startle. The cast shadows promote the painting's starkness and immediacy.

BRITISH EVENTS

1901 Edward VII becomes king.

1902 **Joseph Conrad** publishes *Heart of Darkness*.

1903 Emmeline Pankhurst founds women's suffrage organization.

1904 **Saki** publishes his first stories.

1905 First London motor buses appear.

1908 Boy Scouts founded.

London hosts Olympic games.

1910 George V becomes king.

1912 **George Bernard Shaw** publishes *Pygmalion*.

1913 **D.H. Lawrence** publishes *Sons and Lovers*.

1914 Britain enters World War I.

1916 Easter Rebellion in Ireland.

1917 **Siegfried Sassoon** publishes *Counter-Attack and Other Poems*.

1918 Women achieve right to vote.

Rupert Brooke's *Collected Poems* published.

1919 Britain joins League of Nations.

Lady Astor becomes first female member of Parliament.

1920 **Katherine Mansfield** publishes *Bliss and Other Stories*.

1921 Irish free state formed.

BBC begins regular radio broadcasts.

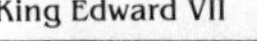

King Edward VII

Joseph Conrad

King George V and His Family

1908 Olympic Games

Battle Scene from World War I

Flight of the Wright Brothers at Kitty Hawk

Albert Einstein

Mohandas Gandhi

"STARS AND STRIPES NAILED TO THE NORTH POLE"
DR. FREDERICK A. COOK
APRIL 21 1908
APRIL 6 1909
COMMANDER ROBERT E. PEARY
TWO DAUNTLESS AMERICANS WHO REACHED THE GOAL OF A THOUSAND YEARS AND PLANTED THE STARS AND STRIPES UPON THE AXIS OF THE WORLD.

Postcard Commemorating Discovery of North Pole

WORLD EVENTS

1901 United States: Ragtime music develops.

Germany: Thomas Mann publishes *Buddenbrooks*.

1903 United States: Orville and Wilbur Wright build first successful airplane.

1904 Asia: Russo-Japanese War begins.

1905 Germany: Albert Einstein proposes theory of relativity.

1909 Arctic: Explorers reach North Pole.

1911 China: Republic established under Sun Yat-sen.

Antarctic: Explorers reach South Pole.

Atlantic: *R.M.S. Titanic* sinks.

1913 Africa: Albert Schweitzer opens hospital in Congo.

France: Marcel Proust publishes *Remembrance of Things Past*.

1914 Europe: Archduke Ferdinand assassinated; World War I begins.

Central America: Panama Canal opens.

1917 Russia: Tsar overthrown; Bolsheviks seize power.

Austria: Sigmund Freud publishes *Introduction to Psychoanalysis*.

1920 Switzerland: League of Nations holds first meeting.

India: Gandhi leads nonviolent protests.

1921 Italy: Luigi Pirandello publishes *Six Characters in Search of an Author*.

BRITISH EVENTS

1922 **T.S. Eliot** publishes *The Waste Land*.

1924 First British airline begins regular operations.

E.M. Forster publishes *A Passage to India*.

1925 John L. Baird transmits first television pictures.

1927 **Virginia Woolf** publishes *To the Lighthouse*.

1928 Shakespeare Theatre opens in Stratford-upon-Avon.

W.B. Yeats writes "Sailing to Byzantium."

1930 **W.H. Auden** publishes *Poems*.

1934 **Dylan Thomas** writes "The Force That Through the Green Fuse. . . ."

1935 Radar developed by British physicists.

1936 First BBC television broadcast.

1937 **Louis MacNeice** writes "The Sunlight on the Garden."

1938 **Graham Greene** publishes *Brighton Rock*.

1939 Britain enters World War II.

1940 Winston Churchill becomes prime minister.

Bombing of Britain begins.

1945 **George Orwell** publishes *Animal Farm*.

Elizabeth Bowen writes "The Demon Lover."

London After Bombing by Germans

Winston Churchill

Charles Lindbergh

George VI and His Family

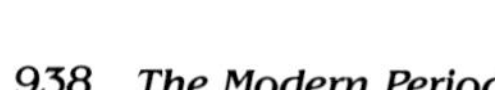

Mandolin and Guitar

T.S. Eliot

Dylan Thomas

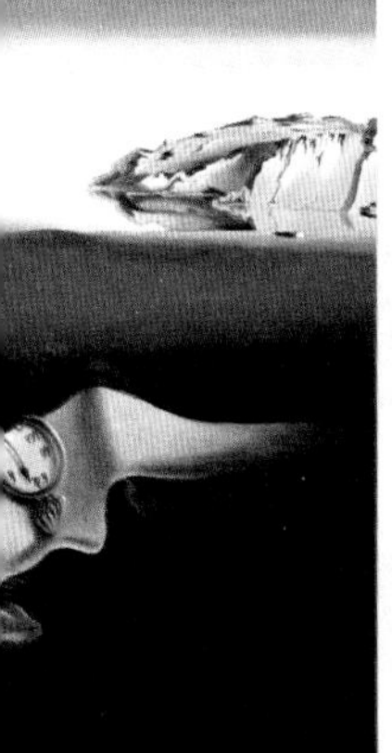
Persistence of Memory

Adolf Hitler

WORLD EVENTS

1922 Italy: Mussolini forms fascist government.

France: James Joyce publishes *Ulysses*.

1923 France: Le Corbusier publishes *Towards a New Architecture*.

1924 Soviet Union: Lenin dies; Stalin comes to power.

1925 Germany: Adolf Hitler publishes *Mein Kampf*, part I.

Austria: Franz Kafka's *The Trial* published.

1927 Charles Lindbergh crosses the Atlantic.

1928 France: Sixty-five nations sign Kellogg-Briand pact outlawing war.

1929 Beginning of worldwide depression.

1931 China: Japanese invade Manchuria.

France: Salvador Dali paints *Persistence of Memory*.

1932 Soviet Union: Famine kills 5 million.

1933 Germany: Hitler comes to power.

United States: Franklin D. Roosevelt becomes President.

1935 Africa: Mussolini invades Ethiopia.

1936 Spain: Civil War begins.

1937 France: Spanish artist Pablo Picasso creates *Guernica* mural.

1938 Europe: Hitler annexes Austria.

1939 Europe: Hitler invades Poland; World War II begins.

1941 Pacific: Pearl Harbor bombed; America enters war.

1945 Japan: Atomic bombs dropped on Hiroshima and Nagasaki.

Humanities Note

Fine art, *Over the Top (at Marcoing, December 1917)* by John Nash. Nash was a twentieth-century British wood engraver and an oil and watercolor painter of landscapes and still lifes. Born in 1893, he had no formal art training but was encouraged by his elder brother Paul, a prominent painter, engraver, illustrator, and theater designer. John Nash lived in the country and was a passionate gardener and botanist. In 1918, during World War I, he became an official war artist.

Over the Top shows the men of the regiment he served with in France, climbing out of their trench and walking, heads down, into the smoke of the barrage. There is power in the slow upward and forward movement, and the viewer sees the simultaneous fear and determination of the advancing soldiers.

1 **Enrichment** This Easter Rebellion prompted one of Yeats's finest poems, "Easter, 1916," in which he voices his own ambivalence about the revolutionaries themselves and the wisdom of the uprising.

2 **Literary Movement** George Orwell's essay, "Shooting an Elephant," page 1034, illuminates the strained relationship between English colonial authority and Burmese natives.

The Russian Revolution

Meanwhile, the war was toppling empires and convulsing whole societies. Russia's tottering monarchy collapsed in the spring of 1917. A democratic government took over and kept Russia in the war as an ally of Britain and France. Overwhelmed by the miserable conditions at the front, however, many Russian soldiers simply refused to fight on. Later in 1917, in a second spasm of revolution, Lenin's Bolsheviks ousted Russia's democratic leadership and set up the world's first Communist state. Russia's was the first of many European monarchies that the war would sweep away. Within a short time, the German and Austro-Hungarian monarchies vanished as well.

The Irish Rebellion

Meanwhile, unrest festered in Ireland. The Irish, predominantly
Roman Catholic, had long resented British rule. At Easter of 1916
Irish nationalists in Dublin launched a rebellion that British troops
quickly smashed. However, by executing the rebel leaders, Britain 1
turned them into martyrs. Irish men and women who had previously
held back—including major literary figures like William Butler Yeats
(1865–1939)—now rallied to the cause of Irish independence.

The surge of Irish nationalism led to a hard-fought guerrilla war. In 1921 Britain capitulated. It granted independence to the Irish Free State. The new nation included all of Ireland except six mainly Protestant counties of the province of Ulster, in the north, which gained home rule but remained part of the United Kingdom. Violent disputes continue to this day over the future of the six counties of Northern Ireland.

OVER THE TOP (AT MARCOING, DECEMBER 1917)
John Nash

The Peace

In 1917 the United States entered the war on the side of Britain and France. World War I finally ground to a halt as Germany, starved and wracked by internal disputes, sued for peace. On armistice day—November 11, 1918—the guns fell silent. A year later, negotiators signed the Treaty of Versailles, calling for Germany to disarm and to pay huge reparations for war damages. "This is not peace," prophesied France's Marshal Ferdinand Foch. "This is an armistice for twenty years." The world would have to bear the legacy of bitterness spawned by the Great War and the Petty Peace, as writer H. G. Wells (1866–1946) called them.

BETWEEN THE WARS

European civilization struggled to recover from the war as
hunger and hardship persisted into the 1920's. In Britain, strikes and
unrest kept industry in turmoil. Although Britain's overseas empire 2
remained intact, stirrings of discontent began to trouble the tranquili-

ty of colonies like India and Burma. More and more angry voices questioned the right of European powers to rule distant lands.

The Lost Generation

For years, "progress" had been undermining old traditions and values. World War I had added to the damage, exposing the sham of heroic myths and fostering an attitude of cynicism and despair. What modern values or rituals could fill the emptiness? In his poem *The
Waste Land (1922), T. S. Eliot expressed a widely felt disillusion- 3
ment with twentieth-century life:

> You know only
> A heap of broken images, where the sun beats,
> And the dead tree gives no shelter, the cricket no relief,
> And the dry stone no sound of water. . . .
> I think we are in rats' alley
> Where the dead men lost their bones.

People spoke of the disillusioned youth of postwar Europe as a "lost generation." Some drowned their cares in the pursuit of pleasure. They drove fast cars, danced to wild new jazz tunes, and experimented with many passing fads. Having won the right to vote in 1918, British women displayed a startling sense of independence. "Flappers" bobbed their hair short and wore low-waisted and daringly brief dresses. This postwar decade of extravagant behavior came to a shuddering halt when the New York Stock Market crash of 1929 began the worldwide Great Depression.

The Rise of Fascism

Hungry Europeans—people without jobs or future prospects —pinned their hopes on political extremes. Some embraced communism. Others, more numerous, leaned toward fascism—first in Italy under dictator Benito Mussolini, then in Germany under another dictator, Adolf Hitler.

As the 1930's wore on, the menace of fascism grew. Hitler built up Germany's military strength. Italy invaded Ethiopia. The two fascist dictators aided the rightist side in Spain's civil war, allied themselves with Japan, and threatened their neighbors.

A crucial moment came in 1938, when Hitler demanded territory from Czechoslovakia. Czechoslovakia's allies, Britain and France, agreed to the transfer of territory after Hitler promised he would make no more demands. "I believe it is peace for our time . . . peace with honor," British Prime Minister Neville Chamberlain proclaimed on returning from a meeting with Hitler in Munich, Germany, that September.

However, appeasement failed. In March 1939, Hitler seized what was left of Czechoslovakia. His invasion of Poland in September 1939 touched off World War II. Marshal Foch had been right: The armistice lasted barely twenty years.

3 **Literary Movement** This sense of disillusionment is evident in Eliot's "The Hollow Men," page 1081, in which he focuses on the spiritual emptiness of modern man.

THE SECOND WORLD WAR

The Second World War was, if anything, more destructive than the First. Hitler's "final solution" to "the Jewish problem" brought death to six million Jews. A German invasion of Russia killed soldiers and civilians by the millions. Battles raged all the way from Europe to North Africa, from the mountains of Burma and China to Hawaii. Massive bombing campaigns turned cities like London, Dresden, and Tokyo into raging infernos. Finally, in the waning days of the war in 1945, American atomic bombs blasted two Japanese cities, Hiroshima and Nagasaki, into cinder and ash. The war's death toll has been estimated at 35 million—not counting the millions who died in German concentration camps.

Somehow, Britain muddled through. The darkest days came in 1940, when France had fallen and Britain alone bore the brunt of German attacks. Inspired by Prime Minister Winston Churchill's ringing oratory, and joined in 1941 by two allies, the United States and Russia, Britain fought on to victory. However, it was a bitter, draining victory, ousting Britain from the ranks of first-rate powers and marking an end to Britain's long age of imperial glory.

MODERNISM AND THE INTERNATIONAL ARTISTIC COMMUNITY

Against this backdrop of chaos and violence, writers and other artists put forth a burst of creative energy. Often they left their own countries to work abroad—some as refugees from war, some by choice. Cultural centers like London, Paris, New York, and Berlin developed communities of painters, composers, architects, and writers—people who had come from many different lands. More than ever before, a truly international artistic community took shape.

This community of artistic people responded to the spirit of the times with a frenzy of innovation. How many ways were there to "make it new"? The ways seemed endless—and often puzzling. Controversy raged over radical new techniques in painting, music, architecture, and literature. What did the odd shapes and figures of cubist painters like Pablo Picasso of Spain and Georges Braque of France actually mean? Why did the Russian composer Igor Stravinsky put so much discordance into his *Rite of Spring* (1913)? Could people actually live and work in the modernistic buildings of architects such as France's Le Corbusier or Spain's Antonio Gaudí or in the glass-and-steel structures of Germany's Bauhaus school? Why did modern writers focus so much attention on human weakness and social decay?

In all fields of artistic life, innovators sought to create new art forms appropriate for the twentieth century. They all seemed to have one motto: "Out with the old, in with the new." Today we group the various schools and movements of this generation under the heading of modernism.

942

THE IDEAS OF MODERNISM

Although the specific movements that composed modernism were frequently short-lived, they shared a number of characteristics. First, all sought to be new and different, to experiment with new forms, to innovate, to startle, even to shock. In his poem "L'Art 1910," the American Ezra Pound (1885–1972) described a modernist painting:

> Green arsenic smeared on an egg-white cloth,
> Crushed strawberries! Come, let us feast our eyes.

Pound's poem illustrates some of the principles of a technique called imagism, which Pound helped introduce to British and American poetry. It uses *images*—details that can be perceived by the senses—to communicate its message. It employs *precise language.* It abandons nineteenth-century "poetic" diction for the vocabulary of *everyday speech.* It uses *free verse* instead of the fixed rhythm, or meter, of most nineteenth-century poetry. Finally, it *suggests* its message instead of stating it directly. Nowhere does Pound tell us that art in 1910 was startling. He merely implies it through words like "smeared" and through the juxtaposition of clashing images like "arsenic" and "strawberries."

One of the chief influences on modernism was the symbolist movement of the late nineteenth century. Symbolism originated with French poets like Charles Baudelaire (1821–67) and Stéphane Mallarmé (1842–98), whose methods then influenced such late Victorian writers as Oscar Wilde (1854–1900) and Algernon Swinburne (1837–1909). The symbolists rejected naturalism. Their poetry was deeply emotional and personal, like earlier romantic poetry, but it was at times far more subtle. It presented an array of imaginative symbols, seeking to evoke emotions in readers' minds.

EZRA POUND, 1938–39
Wyndham Lewis
The Granger Collection

Humanities Note

Fine art, *Ezra Pound,* 1938–9 by Wyndham Lewis. Controversial American poet Ezra Pound (1885–1972) and British painter and author Wyndham Lewis (b. Maine 1886 – d. England 1957) were good friends, brought together in England in the early part of the twentieth century, as founders and champions of the short-lived radical art movement Vorticism. In painting, the vorticists used color as a means of expression of its own; the world of machines was as real to them as the world of nature, and they simplified forms into machine-like angularity. In writing, the Vorticists wanted to free post-Victorian verse from its confining structure. Pound was a major force in the shaping of twentieth-century poetry, and encouraged young writers such as James Joyce and T. S. Eliot.

By the time Lewis painted this arresting portrait, his own work had become more conventional, though forceful line and construction remained. There is great strength in the diagonal movement, set up by the lines of the figure. Pound himself seems entirely self-sufficient, indifferent to the viewer, and there is a definite sense of bones beneath the flesh of the face. The image of Pound at rest is a sharp contrast to the impending drama of his life. Pound broadcast Fascist propaganda for the Italians during World War II, and at the end of the war was brought to the United States to stand trial as a traitor. He was found mentally unfit to answer the charges and was hospitalized for more than a decade. Pound remains one of the most controversial literary figures of this century.

4 **Enrichment** Naturalism, whose ambition, according to the critic George Saintsbury, was to mention the unmentionable, was a technique established by the French novelist Emile Zola in the late nineteenth century. Its chief proponents in English literature were George Moore and George Gissing, neither of whom is widely read today. Moore is more importantly remembered as a cofounder, with Yeats and Edward Martyn, of the Irish Literary Theatre, later called the Abbey Theatre.

The use of images as subtle symbols would become characteristic of modernist poetry by Yeats and Eliot as well as the imagists.

A second characteristic of modernist art and literature was a tendency to present human experiences in fragments that viewers or readers had to piece together in their own minds. For example, Picasso's cubist paintings broke things into component parts. They showed the angles and planes that made up an object, an action, or a human form. The dadaists, who came after the cubists, saw the world as a meaningless jumble. One method of dadaist composition was simply to cut up words, dump them in a hat, and remove them in haphazard order to form a "poem." The message was not in the poem but in the method.

4 A third characteristic was the use of the techniques of realism and naturalism. Often this meant taking up subjects previously considered too trivial or too unpleasant for art and literature. Realism focused on the details of everyday life. Naturalism examined social and economic problems of the working class.

A fourth characteristic was attention to the new psychological insights of Austria's Sigmund Freud, Switzerland's Carl Jung, and other pioneer psychologists. Psychological realism—called expressionism in drama—sought to duplicate the inner workings of characters' minds, rather than merely to capture outer actions and experiences as earlier realism had done. Psychologist William James, brother of the American author Henry James, observed that the human mind works not in chronological order but in a series of associations. The mind leaps from thought to thought in what William James called the stream of consciousness.

LITERATURE OF THE MODERN PERIOD

British writing of the period 1900–45 does not fall into clear-cut categories or movements. However, we can divide the period into three broad stages: before 1910, from 1910 to 1930, and from 1930 to 1945. In the first, or Edwardian, stage, writers used the techniques of realism and naturalism to examine the social problems caused by rapid change. The most radical and characteristic works of modernism appeared during the second stage—especially in the years of disillusionment at the end of World War I. After 1930, writers tried to cope with the enormous problems posed by the Great Depression, the rise of fascism, and World War II. During this third stage a more direct, even somewhat didactic literature of conscience came into prominence.

Cutting across these three stages was an Irish Literary Revival, spurred by the explosion of nationalism in Ireland. The Revival—also called the Irish Literary Renaissance or Celtic Renaissance—began in late Victorian times. It sought to revive the dying Gaelic language, to explore early Celtic history and literature, and to express the Irish spirit.

THE ARTIST'S GARDEN AT DURBINS, c. 1915
Roger Fry
Yale Center for British Art, Paul Mellon Fund

Achievements in Poetry

The stages of the modern period appear clearly in poetry, and even within the evolving styles of individual poets. William Butler Yeats, a leading light of the Irish Literary Revival, provides an example. Yeats's early poetry (he was born in 1865) blends a Romantic love of nature with an interest in the myths and mysticism of Celtic antiquity. It follows strict rhyme schemes. In later years, Yeats abandoned Romanticism and relaxed the strictness of his form, often adopting the free verse so popular with the modernists. He employed symbolic images to delve into troubling questions of history and modern life. By the time of Yeats's death in 1939, many 5 considered him the finest English-language poet of the twentieth century.

A Romantic strain also persisted in other British poetry of the early twentieth century. Even some of the brutally realistic poems that developed from World War I reflected romantic longings—to flee battle for the peace and beauty of the English countryside, for example. Among the best-known poets to die in the Great War was 6 Rupert Brooke (1887–1915). The many other poets of World War I included Siegfried Sassoon (1886–1967), Ivor Gurney (1890–1937), Wilfred Owen (1893–1918), and Robert Graves (1895–1985).

Many of the poets who survived the war went on to express the attitudes of the "lost generation" in the modernist poetry of the 1920's. An important influence on these poets was the Victorian writer Gerard Manley Hopkins (1844–89), whose verse appeared posthumously in 1918. Hopkins used what he called sprung rhythm instead of more traditional metric patterns. Hopkins prepared the way for the modernists' use of free verse.

Preeminent among modernist poets of the 1920's was T. S. Eliot, whose verse displays a keen interest in Freud and modern psychology. His "Love Song of J. Alfred Prufrock" (1917), for example, takes the form of a dramatic monologue. It offers the

Humanities Note

Fine art, *The Artist's Garden at Durbins,* c. 1915, by Roger Fry. Roger Fry (1866–1934) was an influential British art critic, still life and landscape painter. Born in London, he earned a degree in natural science at Cambridge. His scientist's curiosity was reflected in his art criticism and in his painting.

Fry drew as a child, and after attending Cambridge his interest in art was encouraged by several friends. He studied in London and Paris and introduced the French master Paul Cezanne and the post-impressionists to England. From 1905 to 1910 he was curator of paintings at New York's Metropolitan Museum of Art.

This painting depicts the view from the big windows in the country house Fry designed himself. A special feeling for simple, classic design structures the composition and guides the viewer, in an organized way, into the pleasant scene of the life in Surrey. The freedom in this painting is in the color and forms, which have movement and life independent of the objects they represent.

5 **Literary Movement** Typical of the images that Yeats employed in his mature poetry is the golden bird in "Sailing to Byzantium," page 1054, symbolic of unaging art.

6 **Literary Movement** See Rupert Brooke's "The Soldier," page 1068, and "The Great Lover," page 1069, for this romantic strain. Although Brooke was eventually a victim of World War I, he died before he ever reached the front, and his poetry contains none of the bitterness and disillusionment of other World War I poets like Siegfried Sassoon or Wilfred Owen.

7 **Enrichment** Eliot's verse play, *Murder in the Cathedral,* emerged from his belief that only a living faith could give meaning to life.

8 **Literary Movement** References to the disequilibrium of the political universe are also present in Auden's "In Memory of W. B. Yeats," page 1076; Yeats died in January, 1939, just a few months before the outbreak of World War II.

9 **Literary Movement** See Dylan Thomas's "Fern Hill," page 1116, for a celebration of the innocence and joy of life in childhood; see his "The Force That Through the Green Fuse Drives the Flower," page 1114, for an expression of the contention between the forces of life and death; see his "Do Not Go Gentle into That Good Night," page 1120, as an exhortation to his father to fight against encroaching annihilation.

10 **Enrichment** It is interesting to note that since Shakespeare, most of the great British writers of comedy have been Irish: William Congreve during the Restoration, Richard Brinsley Sheridan and Oliver Goldsmith in the eighteenth century, Oscar Wilde in the Victorian Age, and George Bernard Shaw in the twentieth century. Possibly their position as outsiders enabled them to see more clearly than insiders could the mockable faults of the society they depicted.

11 **Enrichment** Eliot's *Murder in the Cathedral* borrows from techniques of the past: a verse play combining the chorus of the Greek drama with the allegorical representations of the medieval morality play.

12 **Enrichment** The Abbey Theatre, along with the Moscow Art Theatre, was considered one of the two great theaters of the world in the early twentieth century. Although it still exists in Dublin, its stature has diminished.

fragmentary interior thoughts of a character's stream of consciousness. Eliot's long poem *The Waste Land* (1922) stands as a monument to the despair and bitterness of the "lost generation."
7 Only later did Eliot shed some of his skepticism and find solace within the Anglican church.

In the 1930's and 1940's, poets showed greater interest in political and social topics. W. H. Auden (1907–73), Louis MacNeice (1907–63), Stephen Spender (born 1909), and Henry Reed (born 1914) continued to employ subtle symbolism and imagery. However,
8 they also made direct statements of social protest. Consider these lines from Auden's famous "September 1, 1939," meditating on the eruption of World War II:

> I and the public know
> What all schoolchildren learn;
> Those to whom evil is done
> Do evil in return.

Romanticism did not die out completely, even in the latter years of the modern period. It flared into a wild brilliance in the verses
9 of Dylan Thomas (1914–53), a Welsh poet who often focused on themes of life and death, as in "When, Like a Running Grave" (1934).

Achievements in Drama

10 The towering figure of late Victorian and modern drama is Irish-born George Bernard Shaw (1856–1960). Shaw was delving into the problems of a changing society even before the Edwardian Age. Blending realism with witty satire, he evoked laughter while prodding theatergoers to think about social issues such as class prejudice, the role of women, education, poverty, and war.

The Edwardian Age produced other important dramatists as well. James Matthew Barrie (1860–1937) wrote the classic children's fantasy *Peter Pan* (1904). John Galsworthy (1867–1933) wrote plays that each focus on a timely social problem. *Strife* (1909), for example, deals with labor-management relations. *Justice* (1910) looks at the prison system.

In the Depression years of the 1930's, Noel Coward (1899–1973) won attention for a series of smartly sophisticated dramas and musicals. The poet T. S. Eliot attempted to revive verse drama
11 with works like *Murder in the Cathedral* (1935), a play about Thomas Becket, an archbishop of twelfth-century England.

12 The Irish Literary Revival led to the founding in 1904 of an Irish national theater (the Abbey Theater of Dublin) and produced some of the modern period's finest plays. John Millington Synge (1871–1909) vividly captures Irish rural life in plays like *Riders to the Sea* (1904). Sean O'Casey (1884–1964) turned to urban themes. He depicts the life of the poor in violence-torn Dublin in tragicomedies like *The Shadow of a Gunman* (1925).

Achievements in Fiction

We cannot fit the fiction of the modern period into neat, clear categories. The fiction swings between romanticism and realism, between misty fantasy and cynical disillusionment. Sometimes it probes the human mind, dwelling on the neuroses and longings of isolated individuals. Sometimes it sweeps across the vastness of history, pondering the mystery of human achievement and human suffering.

Arnold Bennett (1867–1931) was among several fiction writers of the Edwardian Age who produced brilliant works of realism and naturalism. In books such as *The Old Wives' Tale* (1901), Bennett depicted the working-class life of industrial England. He avoided authorial intrusion—the nineteenth-century practice of inserting the author's asides and opinions into a tale. Like Bennett, other modernist fiction writers want readers to draw their own conclusions about characters and events.

A second Edwardian novelist, Joseph Conrad (1857–1924), pioneered in the use of psychological realism. The Polish-born Conrad settled in London after learning English as a sailor on a British ship. He explored the individual's struggle with nature in tales of the sea such as *Lord Jim* (1900) and attacked colonialism in the brooding short novel *Heart of Darkness* (1902). Conrad's tales helped to popularize the short novel, or novella. 13

The British short story, earlier overshadowed by the Russian, the French, and the American short story, gained new attention in the modern period. Among the first masters of modern British short stories was the humorist H. H. Munro (1870–1916), who wrote under the pen name Saki. Another talented short-story writer was New Zealand-born Katherine Mansfield (1888–1923), who crafted sensitive tales of middle-class life.

The class system and the plight of the industrial worker emerged as key themes in the short stories and novels of D. H. Lawrence (1885–1930). Lawrence was a naturalist, but he had a Romantic abhorrence for the march of factories across the rural landscape. 14 His savage hatred of conventional British manners and morals gives bite to novels like *Sons and Lovers* (1913) and the notorious *Lady Chatterley's Lover* (1928–29). 15

Perhaps the greatest pioneer of modernist fiction was the Irish writer James Joyce (1882–1941). Joyce revolutionized the form and structure of both the short story and the novel. In *The Dubliners* (1914), he presents a group of realistic short tales about working-class life in Dublin. Joyce tries to have each story achieve what he calls an epiphany—a flash of awareness in which all the story elements come together and the reader grasps the story's meaning. Joyce's brilliant novel *Ulysses* (1922) was one of the first works of fiction to employ stream of consciousness. Joyce labored for years on this book, using an immense variety of techniques and symbols to pair an ancient Greek myth with a tale of twentieth-century Dublin.

STUDLAND BEACH
Vanessa Bell
The Tate Gallery

Humanities Note

Fine art, *Studland Beach,* 1911, by Vanessa Bell. Vanessa Bell (1879–1961) was a bold innovator in English art. She was the elder sister of writer Virginia Woolf who believed there was "something uncompromising" about her sister's art.

Bell painted figures and still lifes in oil. Her subjects are presented in broad masses—dramatically, directly, clearly and in an ordered fashion. In her work, there is bold division of the painted surface into simple, interrelated blocks of color. As in *Studland Beach* a strong diagonal divides the design, and all objects are integrated into it. She gives equal force to the blocks of color between the figures and to the figures themselves. Bell's interest in form and color led to a period of work that was completely abstract.

There is a strangeness to *Studland Beach* filled with faceless figures all intently focused on something the viewer cannot see. The painting is extreme and jarring: the figures are rooted, intensely, in a scene where, to the viewer, nothing seems to be happening.

13 **Enrichment** Eliot's poem, "The Hollow Men," uses as one of its epigraphs a line from Conrad's *Heart of Darkness:* "Mistah Kurtz—he dead." Both works emphasize the tragic result of spiritual emptiness.

14 **Master Teacher Note** To demonstrate the way poets from totally different time periods and backgrounds can treat a similar theme, you might compare Lawrence's "Snake," page 1057, with Coleridge's "The Rime of the Ancient Mariner," page 670, particularly the section on the water-snakes.

15 **Literary Movement** See Lawrence's "The Rocking Horse Winner," page 996, for a bitter indictment of the destructive power of materialism in English society.

Humanities Note

Fine art, *The Mud Bath,* 1914, by David Bomberg. Bomberg (1890–1957) was a British painter of figures, landscapes, and still lifes in oil and water color. He studied in England and met Pablo Picasso in Paris. Bomberg wanted to translate the motion of life in urban times in an expressive, not a photographic, manner. He was influenced by the Cubists, but while many were painting machines, he preferred to use their techniques to paint figures and comment on modern life.

The starkly rigid, abstracted figures of *The Mud Bath* are animated by fierce energy, concretizing Bomberg's fascination with the harshness and vitality of urban existence. The clusters of figures are reduced to the most spare equations of brilliant color and form, symbols participating in a hectic drama borne from twentieth-century existence.

16 **Literary Movement** Graham Greene, better known for his novels than for his short stories, is almost always concerned in his serious works (as opposed to his popular adventure stories or "entertainments") with the problems of good and evil. See his "Across the Bridge," page 1024, for a development of this theme.

THE MUD BATH
David Bomberg
The Tate Gallery

Another writer famous for capturing the stream of consciousness in fiction is Virginia Woolf (1882–1941). Woolf's major works include *Mrs. Dalloway* (1922) and *To the Lighthouse* (1927). She was the most distinguished member of a group of modernists known as the Bloomsbury set, named for the London neighborhood in which they congregated. E. M. Forster (1879–1970) also formed part of the Bloomsbury set. Forster portrayed the tragic clash of British and Indian cultures in his most famous novel, *A Passage to India* (1924).

As we have seen, social and political issues gained new attention in the 1930's and 1940's. In his futuristic novel *Brave New World* (1932), Aldous Huxley (1894–1963) used biting satire to criticize the misuse of science in totalitarian states. George Orwell (1903–50) ridiculed communism in his modern fable *Animal Farm* (1945) and in *1984* (1949). Like other dystopian novels, *1984* depicts a frightening future society, seeking to warn readers of the horror that may result from current trends. Other noteworthy British fiction writers of the era include Graham Greene (born 1904), Evelyn
16 Waugh (1903–66), Nancy Mitford (1904–73), C. P. Snow (1905–80), and the Irish writer Elizabeth Bowen (1899–1973).

It is probably too soon to evaluate fully the achievements of the modern period, but clearly the writers of the era had an enormous influence on those who would follow them. Writers such as Joyce and Woolf revolutionized the novel by developing new techniques suited to the chaotic confusions and groping skepticisms of modern times. Writers such as Yeats, Eliot, and Auden crafted new poetic tools and prepared a firm foundation for all subsequent twentieth-century verse. Moreover, the plays of Shaw and of the Irish Literary Revival became classics of the British theater, opening up new subject matter that would serve as a starting point for further innovation in later generations. The literature of the years 1900–1945 remains profoundly relevant in our contemporary period, in a world still chaotic, still torn by doubts, where people of talent are still eager to "make it new."

ENGLISH VOICES

Quotations by Prominent Figures of the Period

The greatest of evils and the worst of crimes is poverty.

George Bernard Shaw, *Major Barbara*

Vanity plays lurid tricks with our memory.

Joseph Conrad, *Lord Jim*

And what rough beast, its hour come round at last,
Slouches towards Bethlehem to be born?

William Butler Yeats, "The Second Coming"

Nothing could have been more obvious to the peoples of the early twentieth century than the rapidity with which war was becoming impossible. And as certainly they did not see it. They did not see it until the atomic bombs burst in their fumbling hands.

H. G. Wells, *The World Set Free*

Only two classes of books are of universal appeal: the very best and the very worst.

Joseph Conrad, *No More Parades*

I cannot forecast to you the actions of Russia. It is a riddle wrapped in a mystery inside an enigma.

Sir Winston Churchill, Radio broadcast

I have nothing to offer but blood, toil, tears, and sweat. . . .

Winston Churchill, First speech as Prime Minister

Impropriety is the soul of wit.

William Somerset Maugham, *The Moon and Sixpence*

Ireland is the old sow that eats her farrow.

James Joyce, *A Portrait of the Artist as a Young Man*

It is a symbol of Irish art. The cracked looking glass of a servant.

James Joyce, *Ulysses*

Women have served all these centuries as looking glasses possessing the magic and delicious power of reflecting the figure of man at twice its natural size.

Virginia Woolf, *A Room of One's Own*

Reading Critically The purpose of this page is to guide students in reading critically the modern literature of England. The information here is intended to help students place a work of literature in its historical context, recognize the literary movements of the time, and appreciate the writers' techniques used to present the ideas of the period.

As you discuss the information on this page with your students, explain that the short story on the following pages, "A Dill Pickle" by Katherine Mansfield, is a model for reading critically. It contains notes in the side column that draw attention to elements that reflect the historical context, the influence of the literary movements, and the writer's techniques.

To give students further practice with the process of reading critically, use the selection in the Teaching Portfolio, "A Singing Lesson," by Katherine Mansfield, page 000, following the Teacher Backup, which students can annotate themselves. Encourage students to use these strategies as they read the literature in this unit.

READING CRITICALLY

The Literature of 1901–1945

When you read literature it is important to place it in its historical context. Doing so will help you to see how it was shaped by the events and attitudes of the time.

Historical Context

The Modern Age was one of the most turbulent and traumatic periods in British history. Numerous British colonies were granted their independence, and the British Empire was gradually transformed into the British Commonwealth, an association of self-governing countries. The country suffered through two tragic wars that caused the deaths of thousands of its citizens and experienced an economic depression that resulted in a startlingly high unemployment rate. At the same time, technological advances occurred that significantly changed the nature of people's lives. As a result of these events, there was a dramatic shift in the dominant attitudes and sentiments of the English people, as the sense of optimism and self-assurance that characterized the Victorian Age was replaced by a sense of uncertainty, disjointedness, and disillusionment.

Literary Movements

As the nation's attitude shifted, a new literary movement developed called Modernism. Rejecting previous literary traditions, the Modernists sought to capture the essence of modern life in both the form and content of their work. Delving into the minds of their characters, writers explored the sense of isolation, uncertainty, and disillusionment that had come to characterize modern life. The disjointedness of modern life was also reflected in the form of typical Modernist works, which often lack the expositions, resolutions, transitions, and explanations used in traditional works.

Writers' Techniques

During the Modern Age, writers explored a number of new literary techniques. Poets created works using free verse; fiction writers used shifting points of view; and both poets and fiction writers experimented with the stream-of-consciousness technique, attempting to recreate the natural flow of their characters' thoughts. At the same time, modern writers relied heavily on such traditional devices as symbols and allusions, often using these devices in conveying the themes of their works.

On the following pages is a short story by Katherine Mansfield, a prominent modern fiction writer. The notes in the side column should help you to place the selection in its historical context.

Objectives

1. To understand dialogue
2. To make inferences based on dialogue

Teaching Portfolio: Support Material

Teacher Backup, p. 000

Reading Critically, "A Singing Lesson" by Katherine Mansfield, p. 00

Usage and Mechanics Worksheet, p. 00

Analyzing Literature Worksheet, p. 00

Critical Thinking and Reading Worksheet, p. 00

Language Worksheet, p. 00

Selection Test, p. 00

MODEL

A Dill Pickle

Katherine Mansfield

And then, after six years, she saw him again. He was seated at one of those little bamboo tables decorated with a Japanese vase of paper daffodils. There was a tall plate of fruit in front of him, and very carefully, in a way she recognized immediately as his "special" way, he was peeling an orange.

Literary Movement: Like most modern short stories, this story begins without an exposition, and background information is revealed as the story progresses.

He must have felt that shock of recognition in her for he looked up and met her eyes. Incredible! He didn't know her! She smiled; he frowned. She came toward him. He closed his eyes an instant, but opening them his face lit up as though he had struck a match in a dark room. He laid down the orange and pushed back his chair, and she took her little warm hand out of her muff and gave it to him.

"Vera!" he exclaimed. "How strange. Really, for a moment I didn't know you. Won't you sit down? You've had lunch? Won't you have some coffee?"

She hesitated, but of course she meant to.

"Yes, I'd like some coffee." And she sat down opposite him.

"You've changed. You've changed very much," he said, staring at her with that eager, lighted look. "You look so well. I've never seen you look so well before."

"Really?" She raised her veil and unbuttoned her high fur collar. "I don't feel very well. I can't bear this weather, you know."

"Ah, no. You hate the cold. . . ."

"Loathe it." She shuddered. "And the worst of it is that the older one grows . . ."

Writer's Technique: Vera's character is revealed through her actions and comments.

He interrupted her. "Excuse me," and tapped on the table for the waitress. "Please bring some coffee and cream." To her: "You are sure you won't eat anything? Some fruit, perhaps. The fruit here is very good."

"No, thanks. Nothing."

"Then that's settled." And smiling just a hint too broadly he took up the orange again. "You were saying—the older one grows—"

Motivation for Reading Have students imagine running into someone they have not seen for a long time and this person does not recognize them. How would they react? Then tell them that this person is a former boyfriend or girlfriend. How would they react to this added information? Point out that this is the situation in "A Dill Pickle."

Purpose-Setting Question How does the dialogue in this story develop the characters, the theme, and the plot?

Critical Thinking and Reading You might point out that the male character in this story is referred to only as "him" or "he." What effect does this have on the story?

"The colder," she laughed. But she was thinking how well she remembered that trick of his—the trick of interrupting her—and of how it used to exasperate her six years ago. She used to feel then as though he, quite suddenly, in the middle of what she was saying, put his hand over her lips, turned from her, attended to something different, and then took his hand away, and with just the same slightly too broad smile, gave her his attention again. . . . Now we are ready. That is settled.

"The colder!" He echoed her words, laughing too. "Ah, ah. You still say the same things. And there is another thing about you that is not changed at all—your beautiful voice—your beautiful way of speaking." Now he was very grave; he leaned toward her, and she smelled the warm, stinging scent of the orange peel. "You have only to say one word and I would know your voice among all other voices. I don't know what it is—I've often wondered—that makes your voice such a—haunting memory. . . . Do you remember that first afternoon we spent together at Kew Gardens? You were so surprised because I did not know the names of any flowers. I am still just as ignorant for all your telling me. But whenever it is very fine and warm, and I see some bright colors—it's awfully strange—I hear your voice saying: 'Geranium, marigold and verbena.' And I feel those three words are all I recall of some forgotten, heavenly language. . . . You remember that afternoon?"

Writer's Technique: Mansfield interrupts the sequence of events in the story by presenting flashbacks in which Vera reminisces about previous events. The use of this technique reflects the Modernist perception of life as fragmented and disjointed.

"Oh, yes, very well." She drew a long, soft breath, as though the paper daffodils between them were almost too sweet to bear. Yet, what had remained in her mind of that particular afternoon was an absurd scene over the tea table. A great many people taking tea in a Chinese pagoda, and he behaving like a maniac about the wasps—waving them away, flapping at them with his straw hat, serious and infuriated out of all proportion to the occasion. How delighted the sniggering tea drinkers had been. And how she had suffered.

But now, as he spoke, that memory faded. His was the truer. Yes, it had been a wonderful afternoon, full of geranium and marigold and verbena, and—warm sunshine. Her thoughts lingered over the last two words as though she sang them.

In the warmth, as it were, another memory unfolded. She saw herself sitting on a lawn. He lay beside her, and suddenly, after a long silence, he rolled over and put his head in her lap.

"I wish," he said, in a low, troubled voice, "I wish that I had taken poison and were about to die—here now!"

952

At that moment a little girl in a white dress, holding a long, dripping water lily, dodged from behind a bush, stared at them, and dodged back again. But he did not see. She leaned over him.

"Ah, why do you say that? I could not say that."

But he gave a kind of soft moan, and taking her hand he held it to his cheek.

"Because I know I am going to love you too much—far too much. And I shall suffer so terribly, Vera, because you never, never will love me."

He was certainly far better looking now than he had been then. He had lost all that dreamy vagueness and indecision. Now he had the air of a man who has found his place in life, and fills it with a confidence and an assurance which was, to say the least, impressive. He must have made money, too. His clothes were admirable, and at that moment he pulled a Russian cigarette case out of his pocket.

Writer's Technique: The man's personality is revealed through Vera's impressions of his appearance.

"Won't you smoke?"

"Yes, I will." She hovered over them. "They look very good."

"I think they are. I get them made for me by a little man in St. James's Street. I don't smoke very much. I'm not like you—but when I do, they must be delicious, very fresh cigarettes. Smoking isn't a habit with me; it's a luxury—like perfume. Are you still so fond of perfumes? Ah, when I was in Russia . . ."

She broke in: "You've really been to Russia?"

"Oh, yes. I was there for over a year. Have you forgotten how we used to talk of going there?"

"No, I've not forgotten."

He gave a strange half laugh and leaned back in his chair. "Isn't it curious. I have really carried out all those journeys that we planned. Yes, I have been to all those places that we talked of, and stayed in them long enough to—as you used to say, 'air oneself' in them. In fact, I have spent the last three years of my life traveling all the time. Spain, Corsica, Siberia, Russia, Egypt. The only country left is China, and I mean to go there, too, when the war is over."

As he spoke, so lightly, tapping the end of his cigarette against the ashtray, she felt the strange beast that had slumbered so long within her bosom stir, stretch itself, yawn, prick up its ears, and suddenly bound to its feet, and fix its longing, hungry stare upon those faraway places. But all she said was, smiling gently: "How I envy you."

Writer's Technique: Mansfield uses a third-person limited point of view, focusing on Vera's thoughts and feelings. The use of a limited point of view reflects the Modernist belief that reality is shaped by people's perceptions.

He accepted that. "It has been," he said, "very wonderful

Master Teacher Note Mansfield's stories reflect the confusion and complexity of the modern age. She writes not about neat, controlled incidents but about common, fragmented incidents; her technique is to reveal the significance gradually of these incidents. "A Dill Pickle" is an example of such an incident.

Enrichment The Volga River is the longest river in Europe, flowing more than two thousand miles. It flows entirely within what was once Russia and now is part of the Soviet Union.

—especially Russia. Russia was all that we had imagined, and far, far more. I even spent some days on a river boat on the Volga. Do you remember that boatman's song that you used to play?"

"Yes." It began to play in her mind as she spoke.

"Do you ever play it now?"

"No, I've no piano."

He was amazed at that. "But what has become of your beautiful piano?"

She made a little grimace. "Sold. Ages ago."

"But you were so fond of music," he wondered.

"I've no time for it now," said she.

He let it go at that. "That river life," he went on, "is something quite special. After a day or two you cannot realize that you have ever known another. And it is not necessary to know the language—the life of the boat creates a bond between you and the people that's more than sufficient. You eat with them, pass the day with them, and in the evening there is that endless singing."

She shivered, hearing the boatman's song break out again loud and tragic, and seeing the boat floating on the darkening river with melancholy trees on either side. . . . "Yes, I should like that," said she, stroking her muff.

Historical Context: The story occurs prior to the Russian Revolution of 1917.

"You'd like almost everything about Russian life," he said warmly. "It's so informal, so impulsive, so free without question. And then the peasants are so splendid. They are such human beings—yes, that is it. Even the man who drives your carriage has—has some real part in what is happening. I remember the evening a party of us, two friends of mine and the wife of one of them, went for a picnic by the Black Sea. We took supper and champagne and ate and drank on the grass. And while we were eating the coachman came up. 'Have a dill pickle,' he said. He wanted to share with us. That seemed to me so right, so—you know what I mean?"

Writer's Technique: Mansfield captures Vera's stream of consciousness as her mind drifts through a series of thoughts loosely connected by her natural associations. The use of the stream-of-consciousness technique was prompted by the developments of modern psychology.

And she seemed at that moment to be sitting on the grass beside the mysteriously Black Sea, black as velvet and rippling against the banks in silent, velvet waves. She saw the carriage drawn up to one side of the road, and the little group on the grass, their faces and hands white in the moonlight. She saw the pale dress of the woman outspread and her folded parasol, lying on the grass like a huge pearl crochet hook.

Writer's Technique: Vera's comment is ironic, or surprising, because she has a false impression of the dill pickle.

Apart from them, with his supper in a cloth on his knees, sat the coachman. "Have a dill pickle," said he, and although she was not certain what a dill pickle was, she saw the greenish glass jar with a red chili like a parrot's beak glimmering through. She sucked in her cheeks; the dill pickle was terribly sour. . . .

"Yes, I know perfectly what you mean," she said.

In the pause that followed they looked at each other. In the past when they had looked at each other like that they had felt such a boundless understanding between them that their souls had, as it were, put their arms round each other and dropped into the same sea, content to be drowned, like mournful lovers. But now, the surprising thing was that it was he who held back. He who said:

"What a marvelous listener you are. When you look at me with those wild eyes I feel that I could tell you things that I would never breathe to another human being."

Was there just a hint of mockery in his voice or was it her fancy? She could not be sure.

"Before I met you," he said, "I had never spoken of myself to anybody. How well I remember one night, the night that I brought you the little Christmas tree, telling you all about my childhood. And of how I was so miserable that I ran away and lived under a cart in our yard for two days without being discovered. And you listened, and your eyes shone, and I felt that you had even made the little Christmas tree listen too, as in a fairy story."

But of that evening she had remembered a little pot of caviar. It had cost seven and sixpence. He could not get over it. Think of it—a tiny jar like that costing seven and sixpence. While she ate it he watched her, delighted and shocked.

"No, really, that is eating money. You could not get seven shillings into a little pot that size. Only think of the profit they must make. . . ." And he had begun some immensely complicated calculations. . . . But now good-bye to the caviar. The Christmas tree was on the table, and the little boy lay under the cart with his head pillowed on the yard dog.

"The dog was called Bosun," she cried delightedly.

But he did not follow. "Which dog? Had you a dog? I don't remember a dog at all."

"No, no. I mean the yard dog when you were a little boy." He laughed and snapped the cigarette case to.

"Was he? Do you know I had forgotten that. It seems such ages ago. I cannot believe that it is only six years. After I had recognized you today—I had to take such a leap—I had to take a leap over my whole life to get back to that time. I was such a kid then." He drummed on the table. "I've often thought how I must have bored you. And now I understand so

Literary Movement: Modernist writers often explore the difficulty of establishing successful relationships in the modern world.

Literary Movement: The contrast in their recollections of the evening reflects the Modernist belief in the subjectivity of human experience.

Writer's Technique: The man's character is revealed through his comments.

Writer's Technique What does the dill pickle suggest about the relationship between these two people?

perfectly why you wrote to me as you did—although at the time that letter nearly finished my life. I found it again the other day, and I couldn't help laughing as I read it. It was so clever—such a true picture of me." He glanced up. "You're not going?"

She had buttoned her collar again and drawn down her veil.

"Yes, I am afraid I must," she said, and managed a smile. Now she knew that he had been mocking.

"Ah, no, please," he pleaded. "Don't go just for a moment," and he caught up one of her gloves from the table and clutched at it as if that would hold her. "I see so few people to talk to nowadays, that I have turned into a sort of barbarian," he said. "Have I said something to hurt you?"

Writer's Techniques: Vera refuses to admit that his comments have hurt her, though it is clear from her actions that they have.

"Not a bit," she lied. But as she watched him draw her glove through his fingers, gently, gently, her anger really did die down, and besides, at the moment he looked more like himself of six years ago. . . .

"What I really wanted then," he said softly, "was to be a sort of carpet—to make myself into a sort of carpet for you to walk on so that you need not be hurt by the sharp stones and the mud that you hated so. It was nothing more positive than that—nothing more selfish. Only I did desire, eventually, to turn into a magic carpet and carry you away to all those lands you longed to see."

As he spoke she lifted her head as though she drank something; the strange beast in her bosom began to purr. . . .

Literary Movement: The man's comment reflects the sense of pessimism that often characterizes modern life.

"I felt that you were more lonely than anybody else in the world," he went on, "and yet, perhaps, that you were the only person in the world who was really, truly alive. Born out of your time," he murmured, stroking the glove, "fated."

What had she done! How had she dared to throw away her happiness like this. This was the only man who had ever understood her. Was it too late? Could it be too late? *She* was that glove that he held in his fingers. . . .

"And then the fact that you had no friends and never had made friends with people. How I understood that, for neither had I. Is it just the same now?"

"Yes," she breathed. "Just the same. I am as alone as ever."

"So am I," he laughed gently, "just the same."

Suddenly with a quick gesture he handed her back the glove and scraped his chair on the floor. "But what seemed to me so mysterious then is perfectly plain to me now. And to you, too, of course. . . . It simply was that we were such egoists, so self-engrossed, so wrapped up in ourselves that we hadn't a corner in our hearts for anybody else. Do you know," he cried, naive and hearty, and dreadfully like another side of that old self again, "I began studying a Mind System when I was in Russia, and I found that we were not peculiar at all. It's quite a well known form of . . ."

Historical Context: Psychology was a common interest in the Modernist period.

She had gone. He sat there, thunderstruck, astounded beyond words. . . . And then he asked the waitress for his bill.

"But the cream has not been touched," he said. "Please do not charge me for it."

Literary Movement: Like most Modernist stories, the story ends abruptly, without a resolution.

Katherine Mansfield (1888-1923) was born Kathleen Mansfield Beauchamp in Wellington, New Zealand. At the age of fifteen she headed to London where she studied for three years at Queens College. In London she became acquainted with a number of literary figures, the most significant of whom were D. H. Lawrence and Virginia Woolf. It was the latter who, along with her husband, published Mansfield's first book of short stories, *Preludes,* in 1917. The overall bittersweet tone of the volume anticipated her second and more ambitious collection, *The Garden Party and Other Stories* (1922), in which she successfully combined her angry and sentimental impulses in portraits of impoverished single women.

Her writing brought her into contact with the literary critic J. Middleton Murray, whom she married. The two lived a nomadic and at times penniless life, moving back and forth between the Continent and London. Increasingly ill with tuberculosis, Mansfield spent the last few years of her life in and out of clinics and hospitals before the disease finally claimed her in 1923.

Critics credit Mansfield with having greatly refined the art of the short story. Her works have often been compared to those of Joyce and the Russian writer Chekhov, whom she greatly admired. When called upon to describe her motivation as a writer, Katherine Mansfield replied that she wrote out of both a sense of joy and a sense of doom. Indeed, her short stories—which alternately express cynicism toward the corruption of modern English society and recall fond memories of a blissful childhood—reflect this dual outlook.

THINKING ABOUT THE SELECTION

Recalling

1. (a) How does Vera's friend react when he first sees her? (b) How does this make Vera feel?
2. (a) What does the man remember about the first afternoon they spent together? (b) What does Vera remember?
3. Where has the man been for the past six years?
4. (a) What does Vera begin to feel toward the end of the story, as her friend explains their mutual loneliness? (b) What changes her mind?

More About the Author Katherine Mansfield's first major collection of stories, *Prelude,* which she wrote as a response to her brother's death early in World War I, uses as a backdrop Mansfield's memories of her native New Zealand. *Prelude* was published in 1918 and *Bliss,* which secured her reputation as a serious short story writer, in 1920. Her prose style is almost poetic, and her stories are centered on the psychological conflicts and frustrations of her characters, who reveal themselves through their conversations. Ask students to think of other authors whom they have studied this year who seem more interested in the psychological conflicts of their characters than they are in plot.

Answers

ANSWERS TO THINKING ABOUT THE SELECTION

Recalling

1. (a) He can't remember her at first. (b) She is amazed that he doesn't know her.
2. (a) He remembers the bright colors and perfume of the flowers and her voice naming the flowers. (b) Vera remembers his making a ridiculous scene about some wasps and her being embarrassed.
3. He says he has traveled to Russia, Spain, Corsica, Siberia, and Egypt.
4. (a) She wonders why she threw away her chance at happiness with "the only man who had ever understood her." (b) She realizes that, despite his insistence that the two of them are the same, they are not. She is not the egoist he is; she doesn't purposely or inadvertently hurt people; she doesn't manipulate people. She does not want to get sucked into his game again; he can manipulate her feelings so well that she knows she must leave.

(Answers begin on p. 957.)

Interpreting

5. (a) He is very impressed with himself and is very caught up with impressing others. It is also clear that their love affair made a huge impression on her but not on him. (b) He sees none of his own faults and vanities. He tries to romanticize events after they happen, but she remembers the realities of what happened—in this instance, his obsession with the cost of the caviar.
6. Her decision that his memories are truer than hers shows that she *wants* it to have been that romantic—not that it was. It also indicates that she has a hard time not being taken in by his manipulation of her—now as in the days of their affair.
7. Suggested Response: Vera's action symbolizes her ambivalence towards him and her indecision whether to stay or go.
8. Suggested Response: The man truly seems to be an egoist: all of his conversation focuses on himself and his view of the world. Vera, however, seems to be able to think about and talk about people and events outside herself.
9. (a) Suggested Response: The title might be significant because of the man's reaction to the dill pickle, which reveals his condescension towards others, his egoism, his romanticizing of events for manipulative purposes. The dill pickle also symbolizes the man himself and what he offers to Vera—something sour rather than the sweetness and light that he thinks he offers. (b) Because of what it symbolizes, the title seems very appropriate for the story.

Applying

10. Answers will differ. Suggested Response: Unselfishness and a willingness to take risks are among the qualities necessary for people to be open to love.

ANSWERS TO ANALYZING LITERATURE

1. Suggested Response: This passage gives an impression of Vera through her feeling about cold, but, even more, the author indicates Vera's concern with aging.
2. Suggested Response: The author shows in this one phrase that they had an intimate relationship and that he knew many things about her.
3. Suggested Response: The author shows that the young man is affected and in love with his perception of himself. The passage also shows condescension toward the peasants.
4. Suggested Response: The author shows the young man again as a flatterer and a manipulator. The words are also ironic because he does so much more talking than she that she can't help being a listener.

ANSWERS TO CRITICAL THINKING AND READING

Suggested Response: He thinks he is an expert on almost every subject, including what is good and what people ought to do: His statement "You are sure you won't eat anything? . . . The fruit here is very good" shows this.

He is overly dramatic and tries to manipulate people's emotions through this flattery and overdramatization. He is insincere; for example, he says "I wish that I had taken poison and were about to die—here now!"

He is tight with money. For example, he says "But the cream has not been touched. . . . Please do not charge me for it." In con-

---

Interpreting

5. (a) What difference between Vera and her friend is revealed in the first two paragraphs of the story? (b) What difference is revealed through their attitudes toward the pot of caviar?
6. Vera decides that her friend's recollections of the afternoon at Kew Gardens are "truer" than hers. What does this reveal about her?
7. What action do you think is symbolized by Vera's unbuttoning and buttoning her collar?
8. Do you think Vera's and the man's behavior reveal the truth of his statement about their being egoists? Support your answer with details from the story.
9. (a) What do you think is the significance of the story's title? (b) Do you think the title is an appropriate one? Explain.

Applying

10. The man claims that Vera and he were so wrapped up in themselves that they didn't have room in their hearts for anyone else. What qualities do you think are necessary for a person to be open to love?

ANALYZING LITERATURE

Understanding Dialogue

Dialogue is conversation that takes place between two or more characters in a literary work. One key purpose of dialogue is to present information about the characters in a direct and interesting manner. Knowing precisely when to let a character speak for himself or herself through dialogue and when to speak *for* that character requires great skill on the part of a writer.

Locate the following passages from the story, and read the paragraphs that precede and follow each. In each case explain what effect you feel the author achieves through dialogue that would be lost through direct narration.

1. "Loathe it." She shuddered. "And the worst of it is that the older one grows . . ." (page 951)
2. "The colder!" He echoed her words, laughing too. "Ah, ah. You still say the same things." (page 952)
3. "And while we were eating, the coachman came up. 'Have a dill pickle," he said. He wanted to share with us. That seemed to me so right, so—you know what I mean?" (page 954)
4. "What a marvelous listener you are . . ." (page 955)

CRITICAL THINKING AND READING

Making Inferences Based on Dialogue

It has been said that language is "a window on the mind." If we accept this observation as true, then we can use dialogue to learn a great deal about the workings of a character's mind. Notice, for instance, Vera's tendency to speak in very short, almost clipped sentences—a habit that might lead us to infer that she is a guarded, cautious person which, in fact, as the narrator assures us, she is. Her friend, too, reveals much about his thoughts, feelings, and ideas through his dialogue, though in this instance we receive no additional clues from the narrator. Explain what each of the following lines of dialogue reveals about the man's personality.

What impression do you form of the narrator from what he says? Find lines of dialogue to back up your answer.

Prose

GARDENS IN THE POUND, COOKHAM, 1936
Stanley Spencer
Leeds City Art Galleries

Humanities Note

Fine art, *Gardens in the Pound, Cookham,* 1936, by Stanley Spencer. Stanley Spencer (1891–1959), trained in academic art at the prestigious Slade School in London. He lived his entire life in the small village of Cookham, near London. He considered it his "paradise on earth." Spencer is remembered for his landscapes of Cookham and paintings of mythical-religious fantasy set in Cookham.

Gardens in the Pound demonstrates Spencer's considerable skill as an artist. The natural detail is sensitively handled with a fresh point of view. The carefully rendered tones and textures of the vegetation and sunlight create interesting and random patterns. Spencer loved every aspect of Cookham, from alleyways to gardens and spent many hours recording them in paint.

text, this statement also shows how little real feeling he has for Vera since she has just left and being charged for the cream is all he can think about.

More About the Author Joseph Conrad was the son of a Polish nobleman, who lived in exile in northern Russia. Growing up in the Ukraine, the young Conrad was isolated by language, culture, and customs from those around him. Both of his parents died when he was young, and this increased his isolation. How might Conrad's isolation have affected his writing?

JOSEPH CONRAD

1857–1924

To become one of the most distinguished novelists of one's age would be accomplishment enough for most writers. To do so in a language other than one's own native tongue, as Joseph Conrad did, is an achievement without parallel.

Born in Poland to a scholarly father, Josef Teodor Konrad Nalecz Korzeniowski was orphaned at the age of ten. He fled his Russian-occupied homeland to France and England when he was sixteen, and spent the next dozen years as an apprentice seaman. The voyages that he made to exotic corners of the globe—Asia, Africa, and South America—were later put to use as the vivid settings for much of his fiction. In 1886, he became a ship's captain and an English citizen.

It was not until he was thirty-eight that Conrad published his first novel, *Almayer's Folly.* That year, 1895, also marked his marriage and his retirement from the sea. In the next few years, Conrad so far overcame the difficulties of writing in an adopted tongue (English was actually his third language; Polish and Russian were his first and second) that he became one of the masters of Modernist prose. In 1897 he published his first important novel, *The Nigger of The Narcissus,* and within the next seven years produced three masterpieces: *Lord Jim* (1900), *Youth,* a collection of shorter pieces that includes his well-known "Heart of Darkness" (1902), and the ambitious *Nostromo* (1904).

After a brief collaboration with novelist Ford Maddox Ford, Conrad came out with two novels about revolutionaries, *The Secret Agent* (1907) and *Under Western Eyes* (1911). Remaining active through the end of his life, he was at work on *Suspense,* an ambitious historical novel in the classic tradition, when he died in 1924.

Conrad often used the tradition of the sea yarn to create what, on the surface, were thrilling adventure tales. His serious thematic concerns, however, are readily apparent. Almost invariably the notion of "voyage" in a Conrad novel translates to a voyage of self-discovery. The menacing jungles and vast oceans that confront his characters become metaphors for the hidden depths of the self; the requirement for loyalty among crew members of a ship, often unmet, symbolizes the frailty of human relationships in a world filled with deception, corruption, and betrayal.

If Conrad's themes were Modernist, his technical treatments of those themes were even more so. Often, and memorably, as in "The Lagoon," he shifts the point of view from which the story is told.

GUIDE FOR READING

The Lagoon

The Writer's Technique

Shifting Point of View and Theme. Point of view is the vantage point from which an author elects to narrate a story. Traditionally, writers have narrated stories from either the first-person point of view, in which the speaker is also a character, or the third-person point of view, in which the speaker is not specifically identified by name. With the arrival of the Modernist movement in the early twentieth century, a third option was available—that of using both points of view within the space of a single narrative. By so doing, the writer was able to "move" the narrator from the foreground to the background as the action dictated. In "The Lagoon" Joseph Conrad shifts between a third- and first-person narrator with the additional purpose of emphasizing the story's theme, or central idea, that the line between reality and illusion is often blurred.

Look For

As you read "The Lagoon," be alert to shifts in point of view and to the effects those shifts have on your overall impression of the story.

Writing

Try to recall, or invent, an occasion when a friend took you into his or her confidence and shared a problem with you. In a paragraph, describe the emotions you experienced as you listened to your friend. Note in particular whether you were sympathetic to your friend's dilemma, whether you were able to offer any useful advice, and whether there were implications of the problem that applied to yourself and others.

Vocabulary

Knowing the following words will help you as you read "The Lagoon."

portals (pôr′t'lz) *n.*: Doors; gateways (p. 962)
invincible (in vin′səb'l) *adj.*: Unconquerable (p. 963)
propitiate (prə pish′ē āt′) *v.*: Ease the burden of; appease (p. 964)
conflagration (kän′flə grā′ shən) *n.*: Great fire (p. 965)
august (ô gust′) *adj.*: Worthy of great respect (p. 966)

Literary Focus First-person point of view gives the reader access to the inner thoughts of the character, while third person narration allows other characters to speak their thoughts. Ask the students to keep in mind the central idea that even external realities can be illusions as they observe the point-of-view shift from first-person to third-person.

Look For Ask students to provide reasons Conrad might have for telling a story within a story.

Writing Ask the **less advanced** students to compare themselves to the white man as a friendly listener. Discuss sympathetic listening and compassion. Your **more advanced** students can analyze the way the white man serves as a bridge between the particular story of Arsat and the universal story of mankind, or the way he functions as a chorus.

Vocabulary Ask the students to find the place the captain enters *portals* in the story, and ask the students to look for the larger symbolism of portals in "The Lagoon." Have your **more advanced** students look at the connotation of *portals* to see whether the white man and the lagoon become *portals.* Have your **less advanced** students read *conflagration, invincible, propitiate,* aloud and use them in sentences so that you can be sure they can pronounce and understand these words. Discuss *august, conflagration,* and *invincible* in terms of Conrad's use of romantic imagery.

Objectives

1. To understand shifting points of view and theme
2. To make inferences about a moral code
3. To set up a reader's theater
4. To respond to theme

Teaching Portfolio: Support Material

Teacher Backup, pp. 00-00

Vocabulary Check, p. 00

Usage and Mechanics Worksheet, p. 00

Analyzing Literature Worksheet, p. 00

Critical Thinking and Reading Worksheet, p. 00

Understanding Language Worksheet, p. 00

Selection Test, p. 00

The Lagoon

Joseph Conrad

The white man, leaning with both arms over the roof of the little house in the stern of the boat, said to the steersman—

"We will pass the night in Arsat's clearing. It is late."

The Malay[1] only grunted, and went on looking fixedly at the river. The white man rested his chin on his crossed arms and gazed at the wake of the boat. At the end of the straight avenue of forests cut by the intense glitter of the river, the sun appeared unclouded and dazzling, poised low over the water that shone smoothly like a band of metal. The forests, somber and dull, stood motionless and silent on each side of the broad stream. At the foot of big, towering trees, trunkless nipa palms rose from the mud of the bank, in bunches of leaves enormous and heavy, that hung unstirring over the brown swirl of eddies. In the stillness of the air every tree, every leaf, every bough,
1 every tendril of creeper and every petal of minute blossoms seemed to have been bewitched into an immobility perfect and final. Nothing moved on the river but the eight paddles that rose flashing regularly, dipped together with a single splash; while the steersman swept right and left with a periodic and sudden flourish of his blade describing a glinting semicircle above his head. The churned-up water frothed along-
2 side with a confused murmur. And the white man's canoe, advancing up stream in the short-lived disturbance of its own making, seemed to enter the portals of a land from which the very memory of motion had forever departed.

The white man, turning his back upon the setting sun, looked along the empty and broad expanse of the sea-reach. For the last three miles of its course the wandering, hesitating river, as if enticed irresistibly by the freedom of an open horizon, flows straight into the sea, flows straight to the east—to the east that harbors both light and darkness. Astern of the boat the repeated call of some bird, a cry discordant and feeble, skipped along over the smooth water and lost itself, before it could reach the other shore, in the breathless silence of the world.

The steersman dug his paddle into the stream, and held hard with stiffened arms, his body thrown forward. The water gurgled aloud; and suddenly the long straight reach seemed to pivot on its center, the forests swung in a semicircle, and the slanting beams of sunset touched the broadside of the canoe with a fiery glow, throwing the slender and distorted shadows of its crew upon the streaked glitter of the river. The white man turned to look ahead. The course of the boat had been altered at right-angles to the stream, and the carved dragonhead of its prow was pointing now at a gap in the fringing bushes of the bank. It glided through, brushing the overhanging twigs, and disappeared from the river like some

1. **Malay** (mā' lā): A native of the Malay peninsula in Southeast Asia.

Motivation For Reading Ask the students to imagine a terrible conflict or moral dilemma. For example, what would be the price of abandoning brotherhood for love or abandoning personal honor and dignity for passionate love? Discuss Arsat and Diamelen as outcasts. What did Arsat hope to gain? What do Arsat and Diamelen actually lose?

Master Teacher Note You might mention to your class that Conrad is sometimes termed an impressionistic writer inasmuch as his style of writing often seeks to capture the atmosphere and texture of reality. To clarify students' understanding of impressionism, place Art Transparency 13, *The Bridge, Etaples* by Philip Wilson Steer, on the overhead projector. Point out that the painting does not aim for a photographic reproduction of a scene. Rather it conveys the mood and atmosphere of it. You might encourage your students to discuss the advantages and disadvantages of impressionism in art and literature.

Purpose-Setting Question Joseph Conrad wrote "My task which I am trying to achieve is, by the power of the written word, to make you hear, to make you feel —it is, before all to make you *see*. . . . If I succeed, you shall find there according to your deserts; encouragement, consolation, fear, charm—all you demand, and perhaps, also that glimpse of truth for which you have forgotten to ask." Does Arsat give the white man a glimpse of "the truth"? Does "The Lagoon" make the reader *see?*

1 **Discussion** What effect is created by the immobility described here?

2 **Clarification** *Portals* probably refers to portals of the mind. Conrad indicates a voyage of self-discovery here.

Enrichment "The Lagoon" was published in 1898. Between 1883 and 1888 Joseph Conrad sailed in Eastern waters as a British merchant seaman. The Eastern seas provided inspiration to Conrad for the brilliant color and atmosphere of the setting for "The Lagoon." Observe the busy, realistic details of the native life contrast with the quiet, eerie quality of the isolated lagoon.

slim and amphibious creature leaving the water for its lair in the forests.

3 The narrow creek was like a ditch: tortuous, fabulously deep; filled with gloom under the thin strip of pure and shining blue of the heaven. Immense trees soared up, invisible behind the festooned draperies of creepers. Here and there, near the glistening blackness of the water, a twisted root of some tall tree showed amongst the tracery of small ferns, black and dull, writhing and motionless, like an arrested snake. 4 The short words of the paddlers reverberated loudly between the thick and somber walls of vegetation. Darkness oozed out from between the trees, through the tangled maze of the creepers, from behind the great fantastic and unstirring leaves; the darkness, mysterious and invincible; the darkness scented and poisonous of impenetrable forests.

The men poled in the shoaling[2] water. The creek broadened, opening out into a wide sweep of a stagnant lagoon. The forests receded from the marshy bank, leaving a level strip of bright green, reedy grass to frame the reflected blueness of the sky. A fleecy pink cloud drifted high above, trailing the delicate coloring of its image under the floating leaves and the silvery blossoms of the lotus. A little house, perched on high piles, appeared black in the distance. Near it, two tall nibong palms, that seemed to have come out of the forests in the background, leaned slightly over the ragged roof, with a suggestion of sad tenderness and care in the droop of their leafy and soaring heads.

2. **shoaling:** Shallow.

3 **Discussion** What mood does this description create?

4 **Discussion** What does the imagery suggest about the forest?

5 **Discussion** Why do the polers dislike stopping at Arsat's hut?

6 **Reading Strategy** Ask the students to summarize what the natives don't like, and to predict the role of "invisible dangers" or fate in this story.

7 **Enrichment** "Tuan" means lord and it is a malay term of respect which probably refers to Captain Jim Lingard, who was a local hero and father figure at the time Conrad sailed in the Malayan settlements. Lingard was the first European to establish a very isolated tracking post up the Berau river.

The steersman, pointing with his paddle, said, "Arsat is there. I see his canoe fast between the piles."

The polers ran along the sides of the boat glancing over their shoulders at the end of the day's journey. They would have preferred to spend the night somewhere else than on this lagoon of weird aspect and ghostly reputation. Moreover, they disliked Arsat, first as a stranger, and also because
5 he who repairs a ruined house, and dwells in it, proclaims that he is not afraid to live amongst the spirits that haunt the places abandoned by mankind. Such a man can disturb the course of fate by glances or words; while his familiar ghosts are not easy to propitiate by casual wayfarers upon whom they long to wreak the malice of their human master. White men care not for such things, being unbelievers and in league with the Father of Evil, who leads them unharmed through the invisible dangers of
6 this world. To the warnings of the righteous they oppose an offensive pretense of disbelief. What is there to be done?

So they thought, throwing their weight on the end of their long poles. The big canoe glided on swiftly, noiselessly, and smoothly, toward Arsat's clearing, till, in a great rattling of poles thrown down, and the loud murmurs of "Allah[3] be praised!" it came with a gentle knock against the crooked piles below the house.

The boatmen with uplifted faces shouted discordantly, "Arsat! O Arsat!" Nobody came. The white man began to climb the rude ladder giving access to the bamboo platform before the house. The juragan[4] of the boat said sulkily, "We will cook in the sampan,[5] and sleep on the water."

"Pass my blankets and the basket," said the white man curtly.

He knelt on the edge of the platform to receive the bundle. Then the boat shoved off, and the white man, standing up, confronted Arsat, who had come out through the low door of his hut. He was a man young, powerful, with a broad chest and muscular arms. He had nothing on but his sarong.[6] His head was bare. His big, soft eyes stared eagerly at the white man, but his voice and demeanor were composed as he asked, without any words of greeting—

"Have you medicine, Tuan?"[7] 7

"No," said the visitor in a startled tone. "No. Why? Is there sickness in the house?"

"Enter and see," replied Arsat, in the same calm manner, and turning short round, passed again through the small doorway. The white man, dropping his bundles, followed.

In the dim light of the dwelling he made out on a couch of bamboos a woman stretched on her back under a broad sheet of red cotton cloth. She lay still, as if dead; but her big eyes, wide open, glittered in the gloom, staring upward at the slender rafters, motionless and unseeing. She was in a high fever, and evidently unconscious. Her cheeks were sunk slightly, her lips were partly open, and on the young face there was the ominous and fixed expression—the absorbed, contemplating expression of the unconscious who are going to die. The two men stood looking down at her in silence.

"Has she been long ill?" asked the traveler.

"I have not slept for five nights," answered the Malay, in a deliberate tone. "At first she heard voices calling her from the water and struggled against me who held her. But since the sun of today rose she hears nothing—she hears not me. She sees nothing. She sees not me—me!"

He remained silent for a minute, then asked softly—

---

3. Allah (al' ə): The Moslem name for God.
4. juragan (jo͞o rä' gän): Captain or master.
5. sampan: A small flat-bottomed boat with a cabin formed by mats.

6. sarong: A long, brightly colored strip of cloth worn like a skirt.
7. Tuan (twan): Malayan for "sir."

"Tuan, will she die?"

"I fear so," said the white man sorrowfully. He had known Arsat years ago, in a far country in times of trouble and danger, when no friendship is to be despised. And since his Malay friend had come unexpectedly to dwell in the hut on the lagoon with a strange woman, he had slept many times there, in his journeys up and down the river. He liked the man who knew how to keep faith in council and how to fight without fear by the side of his white friend. He liked
8 him—not so much perhaps as a man likes
his favorite dog—but still he liked him well enough to help and ask no questions, to think sometimes vaguely and hazily in the midst of his own pursuits, about the lonely man and the long-haired woman with audacious face and triumphant eyes, who lived together hidden by the forests—alone and feared.

The white man came out of the hut in time to see the enormous conflagration of sunset put out by the swift and stealthy shadows that, rising like a black and impal-
9 pable vapor above the treetops, spread over
the heaven, extinguishing the crimson glow of floating clouds and the red brilliance of departing daylight. In a few moments all the stars came out above the intense blackness of the earth, and the great lagoon gleaming suddenly with reflected lights resembled an
10 oval patch of night sky flung down into the
hopeless and abysmal night of the wilderness. The white man had some supper out of the basket, then collecting a few sticks that lay about the platform, made up a small fire, not for warmth, but for the sake of the smoke, which would keep off the mosquitos. He wrapped himself in his blankets and sat with his back against the reed wall of the house, smoking thoughtfully.

Arsat came through the doorway with noiseless steps and squatted down by the fire. The white man moved his outstretched legs a little.

"She breathes," said Arsat in a low voice, anticipating the expected question. "She breathes and burns as if with a great fire. She speaks not; she hears not—and burns!"

He paused for a moment, then asked in a quiet, incurious tone—

"Tuan . . . will she die?"

The white man moved his shoulders uneasily, and muttered in a hesitating manner—

"If such is her fate."

"No, Tuan," said Arsat calmly. "If such is my fate. I hear, I see, I wait. I remember . . . Tuan, do you remember the old days? Do you remember my brother?"

"Yes," said the white man. The Malay rose suddenly and went in. The other, sitting still outside, could hear the voice in the hut. Arsat said: "Hear me! Speak!" His words were succeeded by a complete silence. "O Diamelen!" he cried suddenly. After that cry there was a deep sigh. Arsat came out and sank down again in his old place.

They sat in silence before the fire. There was no sound within the house, there was no sound near them; but far away on the lagoon they could hear the voices of the boatmen ringing fitful and distinct on the calm water. The fire in the bows of the sampan shone faintly in the distance with a hazy red glow. Then it died out. The voices ceased. The land and the water slept invisible, unstirring and mute. It was as though there had been nothing left in the world but the glitter of stars streaming, ceaseless and vain, through the black stillness of the night.

The white man gazed straight before him into the darkness with wide-open eyes. The fear and fascination, the inspiration and the wonder of death—of death near, unavoidable, and unseen, soothed the unrest of his race and stirred the most indis- 11
tinct, the most intimate of his thoughts. The ever-ready suspicion of evil, the gnawing suspicion that lurks in our hearts, flowed out into the stillness round him—into the stillness profound and dumb, and made it appear untrustworthy and infamous, like

8 **Critical Thinking and Reading** Contrast Arsat and the white man in their attitudes toward friendship. What can you infer about Conrad from the narrator's ironical aside about the white man?

9 **Enrichment** The intense colors show the influence of the brilliant colors and heightened atmosphere of Conrad's tropical voyages.

10 **Discussion** What does the lagoon reflect?

11 **Discussion** Ask the students how the pairs of adjectives work.

12 **Master Teacher Note** Ask the students to observe the shift in person and atmosphere in this passage. The mysterious, "phantom-filled" struggle refers to the primitive feelings or the subconscious part of man. During the early decades of the twentieth century studies of Freud and others who studied the human unconscious, made a deep impact on the arts. Conrad's writing shows a fascination for the workings of the subconscious. Many of his primitive journeys and his primitive characters, like Arsat, can be viewed as symbols of our own primitive natures.

The exploration of the unconscious, along with the shifts in point of view, show why Conrad has been called the father of twentieth-century literature.

13 **Clarification** Conrad describes nature as indifferent to man at the lagoon. Conrad's theory of "moral isolation" claims man's weaknesses take over when a person is isolated. The lagoon also creates an atmosphere of isolation for the white man.

14 **Enrichment** Conrad said "The artist, then, like the thinker or the scientist, seeks the truth and makes his appeal." How does Arsat make both the white man and the reader see the truth?

15 **Reading Strategy** Ask the students to predict the kind of love Arsat will describe.

16 **Discussion** What is the strength of brotherly love and what is its danger?

17 **Clarification** Conrad used facts about local people to enrich all of his Far East stories. Inche Maida was a local married to a chief of Perak. The princess of Perak was described as "light, spare and a little witch like," and probably was the model for Inchi Midah.

the placid and impenetrable mask of an unjustifiable violence. In that fleeting and powerful disturbance of his being the earth enfolded in the starlight peace became a shadowy country of inhuman strife, a battlefield of phantoms terrible and charming, august or ignoble, struggling ardently for
12 the possession of our helpless hearts. An unquiet and mysterious country of inextinguishable desires and fears.

A plaintive murmur rose in the night; a murmur saddening and startling, as if the great solitudes of surrounding woods had
13 tried to whisper into his ear the wisdom of their immense and lofty indifference. Sounds hesitating and vague floated in the air round him, shaped themselves slowly into words; and at last flowed on gently in a murmuring stream of soft and monotonous sentences. He stirred like a man waking up and changed his position slightly. Arsat, motionless and shadowy, sitting with bowed head under the stars, was speaking in a low and dreamy tone—

". . . for where can we lay down the heaviness of our trouble but in a friend's heart? A man must speak of war and of love. You, Tuan, know what war is, and you have seen me in time of danger seek death as other men seek life! A writing may be lost; a
14 lie may be written; but what the eye has seen is truth and remains in the mind!"

"I remember," said the white man quietly. Arsat went on with mournful composure—

15 "Therefore I shall speak to you of love. Speak in the night. Speak before both night and love are gone—and the eye of day looks upon my sorrow and my shame; upon my blackened face; upon my burnt-up heart."

A sigh, short and faint, marked an almost imperceptible pause, and then his words flowed on, without a stir, without a gesture.

"After the time of trouble and war was over and you went away from my country in the pursuit of your desires, which we, men of the islands, cannot understand, I and my brother became again, as we had been before, the sword bearers of the Ruler. You know we were men of family, belonging to a ruling race, and more fit than any to carry on our right shoulder the emblem of power. And in the time of prosperity Si Dendring showed us favor, as we, in time of sorrow, had showed to him the faithfulness of our courage. It was a time of peace. A time of deer hunts and cock fights; of idle talks and foolish squabbles between men whose bellies are full and weapons are rusty. But the sower watched the young rice shoots grow up without fear, and the traders came and went, departed lean and returned fat into the river of peace. They brought news too. Brought lies and truth mixed together, so that no man knew when to rejoice and when to be sorry. We heard from them about you also. They had seen you here and had seen you there. And I was glad to hear, for I remembered the stirring times, and I always remembered you, Tuan, till the time came when my eyes could see nothing in the past, because they had looked upon the one who is dying there—in the house."

He stopped to exclaim in an intense whisper, "O Mara bahia! O Calamity!" then went on speaking a little louder.

"There's no worse enemy and no better friend than a brother, Tuan, for one brother
knows another, and in perfect knowledge is 16
strength for good or evil. I loved my brother. I went to him and told him that I could see nothing but one face, hear nothing but one voice. He told me: 'Open your heart so that she can see what is in it—and wait. Patience is wisdom. Inchi Midah may die or our Ruler may throw off his fear of a woman!' . . . I waited! . . . You remember the lady with the veiled face, Tuan, and the fear of
our Ruler before her cunning and temper. 17
And if she wanted her servant, what could I do? But I fed the hunger of my heart on short glances and stealthy words. I loitered on the path to the bath houses in the daytime, and when the sun had fallen behind the forest I crept along the jasmine hedges of the wom-

en's courtyard. Unseeing, we spoke to one
another through the scent of flowers,
through the veil of leaves, through the
blades of long grass that stood still before
our lips; so great was our prudence, so faint
was the murmur of our great longing. The
time passed swiftly . . . and there were
whispers amongst women—and our enemies watched—my brother was gloomy,
and I began to think of killing and of a fierce
18 death. . . . We are of a people who take what
they want—like you whites. There is a time
19 when a man should forget loyalty and respect. Might and authority are given to rulers, but to all men is given love and strength
and courage. My brother said, 'You shall
take her from their midst. We are two who
are like one.' And I answered, 'Let it be soon,
for I find no warmth in sunlight that does
not shine upon her.' Our time came when
the Ruler and all the great people went to
the mouth of the river to fish by torchlight.
There were hundreds of boats, and on the
white sand, between the water and the forests, dwellings of leaves were built for the
households of the Rajahs.[8] The smoke of
cooking fires was like a blue mist of the
evening, and many voices rang in it joyfully.
While they were making the boats ready to
beat up the fish, my brother came to me and
said, 'Tonight!' I looked to my weapons, and
when the time came our canoe took its place
in the circle of boats carrying the torches.
The lights blazed on the water, but behind
the boats there was darkness. When the
shouting began and the excitement made
them like mad we dropped out. The water
swallowed our fire, and we floated back to
the shore that was dark with only here and
there the glimmer of embers. We could hear
the talk of slave girls amongst the sheds.
Then we found a place deserted and silent.
We waited there. She came. She came running along the shore, rapid and leaving no
trace, like a leaf driven by the wind into the
sea. My brother said gloomily, 'Go and take
her; carry her into our boat.' I lifted her in
my arms. She panted. Her heart was beating
against my breast. I said, 'I take you from
those people. You came to the cry of my
heart, but my arms take you into my boat
against the will of the great!' 'It is right,' said
my brother. 'We are men who take what we
want and can hold it against many. We
should have taken her in daylight.' I said,
'Let us be off'; for since she was in my boat I
began to think of our Ruler's many men.
'Yes. Let us be off,' said my brother. 'We are
cast out and this boat is our country now 20
—and the sea is our refuge.' He lingered
with his foot on the shore, and I entreated
him to hasten, for I remembered the strokes
of her heart against my breast and thought
that two men cannot withstand a hundred.
We left, paddling downstream close to the
bank; and as we passed by the creek where
they were fishing, the great shouting had
ceased, but the murmur of voices was loud
like the humming of insects flying at noonday. The boats floated, clustered together, in
the red light of torches, under a black roof of
smoke; and men talked of their sport. Men
that boasted, and praised, and jeered—men
that would have been our friends in the
morning, but on that night were already our
enemies. We paddled swiftly past. We had no
more friends in the country of our birth. She
sat in the middle of the canoe with covered
face; silent as she is now; unseeing as she is
now—and I had no regret at what I was
leaving because I could hear her breathing
close to me—as I can hear her now."

He paused, listened with his ear turned to the doorway, then shook his head and went on.

"My brother wanted to shout the cry of
challenge—one cry only—to let the people
know we were freeborn robbers who trusted 21
our arms and the great sea. And again I
begged him in the name of our love to be
silent. Could I not hear her breathing close
to me? I knew the pursuit would come quick
enough. My brother loved me. He dipped his
paddle without a splash. He only said,

8. Rajahs (ra′ jəz): Malayan chiefs.

18 Discussion What similarity to the whites is Arsat describing?

19 Discussion What is illusory here and what is real?

20 Discussion Why are they outcasts? How does isolation connect the brothers to the white man? In what way is Conrad an outcast also?

21 Clarification Conrad introduces pirates into "The Lagoon" since his Far East travels frequently brought him to a pirate haunt at that time.

22 **Discussion** In his brother's mind, what would Arsat have to do to become whole again?

23 **Reading Strategy** Predict what is going to happen to Arsat's brother.

24 **Clarification** The secret place Arsat's brother knows is probably a secret navigable channel up the Berau river which Captain Lingard found. Lingard was the only white man living in this very isolated place.

'There is half a man in you now—the other half is in that woman. I can wait. When you are a whole man again, you will come back with me here to shout defiance. We are sons
22 of the same mother.' I made no answer. All my strength and all my spirit were in my hands that held the paddle—for I longed to be with her in a safe place beyond the reach of men's anger and of women's spite. My love was so great, that I thought it could guide me to a country where death was unknown, if I could only escape from Inchi Midah's fury and from our Ruler's sword. We paddled with haste, breathing through our teeth. The blades bit deep into the smooth water. We passed out of the river; we flew in clear channels amongst the shallows. We skirted the black coast; we skirted the sand beaches where the sea speaks in whispers to the land; and the gleam of white sand flashed back past our boat, so swiftly she ran upon the water. We spoke not. Only once I said, 'Sleep, Diamelen, for soon you may want all your strength.' I heard the sweetness of her voice, but I never turned my head. The sun rose and still we went on. Water fell from my face like rain from a cloud. We flew in the light and heat. I never looked back, but I knew that my brother's eyes, behind me, were looking steadily ahead, for the boat went as straight as a bushman's dart, when it leaves the end of the sumpitan.[9] There was no better paddler, no better steersman than my brother. Many times, together, we had won races in that canoe. But we never had put out our strength as we did then—then, when for the last time we paddled together! There was no braver or stronger man in our country than my brother. I could not spare the
23 strength to turn my head and look at him, but every moment I heard the hiss of his breath getting louder behind me. Still he did not speak. The sun was high. The heat clung to my back like a flame of fire. My ribs were ready to burst, but I could no longer get enough air into my chest. And then I felt I must cry out with my last breath. 'Let us rest!' . . . 'Good!' he answered; and his voice was firm. He was strong. He was brave. He knew not fear and no fatigue . . . My brother!"

A murmur powerful and gentle, a murmur vast and faint; the murmur of trembling leaves, of stirring boughs, ran through the tangled depths of the forests, ran over the starry smoothness of the lagoon, and the water between the piles lapped the slimy timber once with a sudden splash. A breath of warm air touched the two men's faces and passed on with a mournful sound—a breath loud and short like an uneasy sigh of the dreaming earth.

Arsat went on in an even, low voice:

"We ran our canoe on the white beach of a little bay close to a long tongue of land that seemed to bar our road; a long wooded cape going far into the sea. My brother knew that place. Beyond the cape a river has its entrance, and through the jungle of that land 24
there is a narrow path. We made a fire and cooked rice. Then we lay down to sleep on the soft sand in the shade of our canoe, while she watched. No sooner had I closed my eyes than I heard her cry of alarm. We leaped up. The sun was halfway down the sky already, and coming in sight in the opening of the bay we saw a prau[10] manned by many paddlers. We knew it at once; it was one of our Rajah's praus. They were watching the shore, and saw us. They beat the gong, and turned the head of the prau into the bay. I felt my heart become weak within my breast. Diamelen sat on the sand and covered her face. There was no escape by sea. My brother laughed. He had the gun you had given him, Tuan, before you went away, but there was only a handful of powder. He spoke to me quickly: 'Run with her along the path. I shall keep them back, for they have

---

9. sumpitan (sump′ ə tăn): A Malayan blowgun which discharges poisonous darts.

10. prau (prou) *n.*: A swift Malayan boat with a large sail.

no firearms, and landing in the face of a man with a gun is certain death for some. Run with her. On the other side of that wood there is a fisherman's house—and a canoe. When I have fired all the shots I will follow. I am a great runner, and before they can come up we shall be gone. I will hold out as long as I can, for she is but a woman—that can neither run nor fight, but she has your
25 heart in her weak hands.' He dropped behind the canoe. The prau was coming. She and I ran, and as we rushed along the path I heard shots. My brother fired—once—twice—and the booming of the gong ceased. There was silence behind us. That neck of land is narrow. Before I heard my brother fire the third shot I saw the shelving shore, and I saw the water again: the mouth of a broad river. We crossed a grassy glade. We ran down to the water. I saw a low hut above the black mud, and a small canoe hauled up. I heard another shot behind me. I thought, 'That is his last charge.' We rushed down to the canoe; a man came running from the hut, but I leaped on him, and we rolled together in the mud. Then I got up, and he lay still at my feet. I don't know whether I had killed him or not. I and Diamelen pushed the canoe afloat. I heard yells behind me, and I saw my brother run across the glade. Many men were bounding after him. I took her in my arms and threw her into the boat, then leaped in myself. When I looked back I saw that my brother had fallen. He fell and was up again, but the men were closing round him. He shouted, 'I am coming!' The men were close to him. I looked. Many men. Then I looked at her. Tuan, I pushed the canoe! I pushed it into deep water. She was kneeling forward looking at me, and I said, 'Take your paddle,' while I struck the water with mine. Tuan, I heard him cry. I heard him cry my name twice; and I heard voices shouting, 'Kill! Strike!' I never turned back. I heard him
26 calling my name again with a great shriek, as when life is going out together with the voice—and I never turned my head. My own name! . . . My brother! Three times he called—but I was not afraid of life. Was she not there in that canoe? And could I not with her find a country where death is forgotten—where death is unknown!"

The white man sat up. Arsat rose and stood, an indistinct and silent figure above the dying embers of the fire. Over the lagoon a mist drifting and low had crept, erasing slowly the glittering images of the stars. And now a great expanse of white vapor covered the land; it flowed cold and gray in the darkness, eddied in noiseless whirls round the tree-trunks and about the platform of the house, which seemed to float upon a restless and impalpable illusion of a sea. Only far away the tops of the trees stood outlined on the twinkle of heaven, like a somber and forbidding shore—a coast deceptive, pitiless and black.

Arsat's voice vibrated loudly in the profound peace.

"I had her there! I had her! To get her I would have faced all mankind. But I had her—and—"

His words went out ringing into the empty distances. He paused, and seemed to listen to them dying away very far—beyond 27
help and beyond recall. Then he said quietly—

"Tuan, I loved my brother."

A breath of wind made him shiver. High above his head, high above the silent sea of mist the drooping leaves of the palms rattled together with a mournful and expiring sound. The white man stretched his legs. His chin rested on his chest, and he murmured sadly without lifting his head—

"We all love our brothers."

Arsat burst out with an intense whispering violence— 28

"What did I care who died? I wanted peace in my own heart."

He seemed to hear a stir in the house—listened—then stepped in noiselessly. The white man stood up. A breeze was coming in fitful puffs. The stars shone paler as if they had retreated into the frozen

25 Discussion Why does Arsat's brother stay behind?

26 Reading Strategy Ask students to explain Arsat's illusion.

27 Clarification Sometimes Arsat breaks off, goes to check on Diamelen, and breaks the story. Thus, the reader experiences the story the same way the narrator does—with glimpses of the changes in Arsat's emotional reality.

28 Literary Focus What is Conrad telling us about choice? Look for proof that this statement is another illusion.

29 Discussion What does the white eagle symbolize?

30 Master Teacher Note Conrad contrasts the lagoon's brilliance with Arsat's deep dark gloom when Diamelen dies. Diamelen has shone like a diamond or false light for Arsat. The realistic picture of the "merciless" sunshine contrasts with the earlier romantic landscape which seemed to sympathize with Arsat. Shifting from a romantic to a realistic point of view within the same story characterizes Conrad as modern, and it conveys Conrad's theme of the real world as illusion.

31 Discussion Relate the levels of meaning in this exchange to the theme of "The Lagoon."

32 Critical Thinking and Reading What does the white man's reaction show about Conrad's moral code?

33 Reading Strategy Ask students to summarize the cost of Arsat's obsession.

34 Discussion What does the darkness represent? What are Arsat's lost illusions?

depths of immense space. After a chill gust of wind there were a few seconds of perfect calm and absolute silence. Then from behind the black and wavy line of the forests a column of golden light shot up into the heavens and spread over the semicircle of the eastern horizon. The sun had risen. The mist lifted, broke into drifting patches, vanished into thin flying wreaths; and the unveiled lagoon lay, polished and black, in the heavy shadows at the foot of the wall of
29 trees. A white eagle rose over it with a slanting and ponderous flight, reached the clear sunshine and appeared dazzlingly brilliant for a moment, then soaring higher, became a dark and motionless speck before it vanished into the blue as if it had left the earth forever. The white man, standing gazing upward before the doorway, heard in the hut a confused and broken murmur of distracted words ending with a loud groan. Suddenly Arsat stumbled out with outstretched hands, shivered, and stood still for some time with fixed eyes. Then he said—

"She burns no more."

Before his face the sun showed its edge above the treetops, rising steadily. The breeze freshened; a great brilliance burst upon the lagoon, sparkled on the rippling water. The forests came out of the clear shadows of the morning, became distinct, as
30 if they had rushed nearer—to stop short in a great stir of leaves, of nodding boughs, of swaying branches. In the merciless sunshine the whisper of unconscious life grew louder, speaking in an incomprehensible voice round the dumb darkness of that human sorrow. Arsat's eyes wandered slowly, then stared at the rising sun.

"I can see nothing," he said half aloud to
31 himself.

"There is nothing," said the white man, moving to the edge of the platform and waving his hand to his boat. A shout came faintly over the lagoon and the sampan began to glide toward the abode of the friend of ghosts.

"If you want to come with me, I will wait
all the morning," said the white man, look- 32
ing away upon the water.

"No, Tuan," said Arsat softly. "I shall not eat or sleep in this house, but I must first see my road. Now I can see nothing—see nothing! There is no light and no peace in
the world; but there is death—death for 33
many. We were sons of the same mother —and I left him in the midst of enemies; but I am going back now."

He drew a long breath and went on in a dreamy tone:

"In a little while I shall see clear enough to strike—to strike. But she has died, and . . . now . . . darkness."

He flung his arms wide open, let them fall along his body, then stood still with unmoved face and stony eyes, staring at the sun. The white man got down into his canoe. The polers ran smartly along the sides of the boat, looking over their shoulders at the beginning of a weary journey. High in the stern, his head muffled up in white rags, the juragan sat moody, letting his paddle trail in the water. The white man, leaning with both arms over the grass roof of the little cabin, looked back at the shining ripple of the boat's wake. Before the sampan passed out of the lagoon into the creek he lifted his eyes. Arsat had not moved. He stood lonely in the searching sunshine; and
he looked beyond the great light of a cloud- 34
less day into the darkness of a world of illusions.

Answers

ANSWERS TO THINKING ABOUT THE SELECTION

Recalling

1. The white man's crew want nothing to do with Arsat because they are afraid of him; he must be dangerously unafraid of the invisible spirits since he lives in a ruined house.
2. When he reaches Arsat's clearing the white man discovers that Diamelen is dying.
3. Arsat's brother was killed by the ruler's henchmen after Diamelen and Arsat desert him in the middle of the enemy.
4. Arsat says he will strike back at the enemies who killed his brother.

Interpreting

5. Arsat is more emotional and primitive than the white man, who is cold and objective. The white man and

THINKING ABOUT THE SELECTION

Recalling

1. Why do the members of the white man's crew want nothing to do with Arsat?
2. What does the white man discover when he reaches Arsat's clearing?
3. What happened to Arsat's brother?
4. At the end of the story, what does Arsat say he will do?

Interpreting

5. Compare and contrast the white man and Arsat.
6. Conrad devotes a good deal of space to descriptions of the sky and air. What events in the story are paralleled by the "conflagration of sunset" (page 965) and the rattling of the palm trees (page 969)?
7. When, following Diamelen's death, Arsat says "I can see nothing," the white man replies, "There is nothing" (page 970). (a) What do you think is meant by this remark? (b) How might it relate to the final line of the story?

Applying

8. (a) What might have been Conrad's purpose in not naming the white man in this story? (b) How does this decision reinforce the theme?

ANALYZING LITERATURE

Shifting Point of View and Theme

Point of view in a story is the vantage point from which the events are narrated. In a first-person narrative, the speaker is either a participant or observer in the story; whereas in a third-person narrative, the speaker is not directly identified. In "The Lagoon" Joseph Conrad narrates most of the story from the third-person point of view, though the "story within a story"—Arsat's tale—is narrated by Arsat himself.

1. What would have been lost if the entire story had been narrated by Arsat?
2. Why do you think Conrad chose to have Arsat narrate his own story?
3. How is the story's theme reinforced by the shift between points of view?

CRITICAL THINKING AND READING

Making Inferences About a Moral Code

When, for the second time in the story, Arsat says "I loved my brother" (page 969), the white man observes that "We all love our brothers." Though the remark might be taken at face value, the theme of the story suggests that its author is stating a larger truth about the "brotherhood" between all human beings and about the rules by which we should, but perhaps do not always, conduct our lives. Tell, based on Arsat's narrative, what you believe to be Conrad's views on the following moral issues:

1. The division of a society into classes.
2. The crossing of class lines in such a society.
3. The defiance of law in any society.
4. The degree to which we should feel free to pursue a goal at any cost.

SPEAKING AND LISTENING

Setting Up a Reader's Theater

Arrange a theatrical reading of "The Lagoon" in class. After assigning the parts of the narrator, the white man, and Arsat (you may wish to have several readers do the longer parts), consider what sound effects you will need and how they might be achieved. The sound of the natives in pursuit might be undertaken by the class as a whole. When you have finished planning and rehearsing, perform your reading.

THINKING AND WRITING

Responding to Theme

A lagoon is a pool of brackish water separated from the sea by sand bars and reefs. Knowing this, write an essay explaining the relevance of the story's title to its theme. Begin by stating the theme. Then develop your essay around the following questions. In Conrad's view of things, what does the lagoon represent? What is represented by the sea beyond? What does a voyage to and from the lagoon represent? Feel free to add and answer questions of your own that you feel clarify the relationship between theme and title.

(Answers begin on p. 970.)

Arsat are both upper class, physically brave men who are used to taking what they want. Each one knows isolation since the captain is isolated from his crew and Arsat has become an outcast on the lagoon.

6. The "conflagration of sunset," is paralleled by the white man's answer to Arsat that Diamelen will probably die. The "rattling of the palm trees" parallels Arsat telling the white man that he loved his brother.
7. Suggested Responses: (a) The "nothing" refers to the world Arsat sees without Diamelen and without the illusions of honor and love. (b) The final line of the story refers to everything in this world as "illusion" or "nothing." It also refers to the godlessness Arsat experiences in his spirit.

Applying

(a) Conrad might have left the white man nameless so he could stand for every man. (b) By not naming the white man Conrad blurs the distinction between Arsat and the white man, softens his reality, and makes him seem almost like an illusion. The lack of a name allows him to enter into Arsat's story for everyone and to work as a bridge to the reader.

ANSWERS TO ANALYZING LITERATURE

1. The perspective on Arsat shed by the native's fear of him and the white man's esteem of him would have been lost if Arsat told the whole story.
2. Answers will differ. Conrad involves the reader's emotions and stirs up suspense and dramatic intensity by having Arsat narrate his own story.
3. The shift in person changes perspective and reinforces Conrad's theme of the uncertain distinction between reality and illusion.

THINKING AND WRITING

For help with this assignment, students can refer to Lesson 11, "Writing About Theme," in the Handbook of Writing About Literature.

Publishing Student Writing Have students share their essays in groups. Each group can compile a composite image of the lagoon and share it with the class.

ANSWERS TO CRITICAL THINKING AND READING

Suggested responses:

1. Conrad was an aristocrat but he associated class with inner worth.
2. Conrad probably saw the crossing of class lines as dangerous in a rigid society.
3. Conrad probably felt the defiance of law was dangerous since society needs the illusion of stability which laws give.
4. Conrad shows that it is extremely dangerous to pursue a goal to the point of obsession.

SPEAKING AND LISTENING

Discuss the possibility of using a mirror for the lagoon and a dark drapery for the sky. Analyze the dramatic strength of using doubles for Arsat and the white man, or identical-looking characters, one dressed in black, one in white. Ask the students to discuss Conrad's setting in terms of moral vulnerability in isolation.

More About the Author As a boy, Saki had a passion for drawing comic scenes with animals. He particularly enjoyed scenes in which pushy woman are devoured by no-nonsense lions. In many of his stories, Saki "lets a wild beast loose in some elegant English drawing room" because Saki enjoyed contrasting the free animal savages with the repressed civilized savages. Ask the students to discuss the savagery that Saki's satire and animal imagery reveal beneath the facade of polite society. Ask them to decide if they feel that Saki's ironies leave any room at all for human sentiment.

SAKI (H. H. MUNRO)

1870–1916

The creation of an individualistic style and the adaptation of form to fit one's material are major challenges for every writer. Few can be said to have met these challenges as skillfully and elegantly as the satirist Saki (H. H. Munro).

Born in Burma, Hector Hugh Munro was raised by two aunts in the English county of Devon. He seems to have spent his childhood under a strict, authoritarian regime, if one is to judge by the satirical portraits of aunts in many of his later short stories. As a young adult, Munro returned to Burma to serve in that colony's military police force. After a couple of years, however, recurrent bouts of ill health forced his return to England where he remained for good. Determined to earn a living as a writer, he settled in London.

The turn of the century found Munro writing a regular column for the *Westminster Gazette.* After a year of writing political satire, he became a foreign news correspondent for the *Morning Post,* taking posts in Poland, Russia, and France. It was not until 1904 that Munro capitalized on his true calling, when he published a collection of short stories titled *Reginald,* writing under the pen name Saki (possibly borrowed from the name of the cupbearer in Edward Fitzgerald's popular poem "The Rubaiyat of Omar Khayyam"). The stories in *Reginald,* seldom over a few pages in length, were comically satirical glimpses of upper-class British society during the Edwardian period. With remarkable economy of language, Saki was able to re-create precisely the manners and costumes, not to mention the snobbery and boorishness, that typified the group.

The success of *Reginald* secured Saki's reputation as a master of the comedy of manners, and in his later collections—*Reginald in Russia* (1910) and *The Chronicles of Clovis* (1911)—he revived some of the zany characters from his original cast. The tone of many of these stories, which might be described as playful yet bitingly ironic, was similar to that used by Alexander Pope in *The Rape of the Lock.* Saki's refraining from serious treatments of his subject matter was probably rooted at least partly in the fact that he was a member of the very social class that he mocked.

With the outbreak of World War I in 1914, Saki enlisted for duty in the British army. Two years later he was killed in action in France. Among the collections of his stories published after his death are *The Toys of Peace* (1919) and *The Square Egg* (1924). Although some readers regard his stories as an acquired taste, Saki remains one of the present century's foremost "cupbearers" in the long tradition of English social satire.

GUIDE FOR READING

The Schartz-Metterklume Method

Literary Forms

Satire. Satire is a mode of writing that exposes faults in human beings or institutions and holds those faults up to ridicule. Although virtually any literary form can be cast in the satiric mode, satire has its roots in the plays of ancient Greece and Rome. In the time between then and now, satire flourished especially in the seventeenth century and especially in such lengthy poems as Alexander Pope's mock-epic *The Rape of the Lock* and Samuel Johnson's intensely bitter "The Vanity of Human Wishes."

Despite the lack of any formal guidelines in the writing of satire, modern satirists make free use of irony, a discrepancy between what is said and what is actually intended or between appearances and reality. In his satirical "The Schartz-Metterklume Method," Saki uses irony, along with a companion device, understatement, to poke innocent fun at the pretentious manners of the English "upper crust" of the early twentieth century.

Look For

As you read "The Schartz-Metterklume Method," look for the ways in which the author uses irony and a light, brisk approach to his subject matter and characters to create subtle humor.

Writing

Imagine that on your way to school one day you were mistaken for someone famous. Suppose, moreover, that despite your assurances to the contrary, the person who mistook your identity refused to be dissuaded. Freewrite, telling who you were mistaken for, and describing the funny sequence of events that followed this initial mistake.

Vocabulary

Knowing the following words will help you as you read "The Schartz-Metterklume Method."

inventory (in′vən tôr′ē) *n.*: List of possessions (p. 974)
provoking (prə vōk′iŋ) *adj.*: Annoying, irritating (p. 974)
cowed (koud) *adj.*: Made to feel timid or fearful (p. 975)
condone (kən dōn′) *v.*: Approve; authorize (p. 975)
castigation (kas′tə gā′shən) *n.*: Punishment (p. 976)
balustrade (bal′ə strād′) *n.*: Railing supported by small pillars of stone or wood (p. 976)

Literary Focus Satire is a type of protest born of anger and indignation. A satirist is a self-appointed guardian of standards, ideals and truths. Saki uses satire to correct, censure, and ridicule the follies and vices of his society. Using contempt and laughter he reveals the cracks beneath society's false facade.

Look For Irony is an intention or attitude opposite to that which is actually stated. Ask the students to look for the irony in the technique of the Schartz-Metterklume method, and in Mrs. Quabarl's and Lady Carlotta's behavior.

Because your **less advanced** students may find irony difficult to grasp, you may wish to ask them to frequently summarize the actual events of the story so that they can follow Saki's ironical and satirical twists.

Writing Have students discuss the tradition of mistaken identity in comedies such as Shakespeare's comedies or television comedies. Then have them complete the writing activity.

Vocabulary Find the sentences the vocabulary words appear in, and write them on the chalk board. Have your **less advanced** students discuss the meaning of the vocabulary words in each sentence so that they will not become confused by Saki's twists of meaning.

Objectives

1. To understand satire
2. To make inferences about tone
3. To understand words with Latin roots
4. To compare and contrast approaches to satire

Teaching Portfolio: Support Material

Lesson Plan, pp. 00–00

Vocabulary Check, p. 00

Usage and Mechanics Worksheet, p. 00

Analyzing Literature Worksheet, p. 00

Critical Thinking and Reading Worksheet, p. 00

Understanding Language Worksheet, p. 00

Selection Test, p. 00

Motivation for Reading Have students imagine being mistaken for someone totally strange, and receiving an invitation based on the mistake. Would they be tempted to play along with it? Does the idea of play-acting or acting out fantasy appeal to most people?

Thematic Idea Another selection in which the writer satirizes aspects of the society of his day is the excerpt from "The Rape of the Lock" by Alexander Pope (p. 560).

Purpose-Setting Question Why does Saki pick out essential characteristics and exaggerate them?

1 **Reading Strategy** Summarize what prompts Lady Carlotta to leave the train? **Less advanced** students may need frequent summaries to understand Saki's irony.

2 **Literary Focus** Discuss the irony in Saki's "doctrine of noninterference." **More advanced** students may relate the "doctrine of noninterference" to both Lady Carlotta's attitude and Saki's overall tone in "The Schartz-Metterklume Method."

3 **Literary Focus** Saki's ironic image of Lady Carlotta sketching while the other lady is attacked by a boar is a satire of the emotional detachment of the upper classes. This scene adds a second ironic dimension by satirizing all of the artists—and perhaps Saki as well—who devote themselves to recording art instead of taking action to help those who suffer.

4 **Discussion** What does her reaction to the departure of the train with her luggage reveal about Lady Carlotta?

5 **Critical Reading and Thinking** Ask the students to discuss the way Saki conveys his own tone toward Mrs. Quabarl by describing her tone and approach.

The Schartz-Metterklume Method

Saki

Lady Carlotta stepped out onto the platform of the small wayside station and took a turn or two up and down its uninteresting length, to kill time till the train should be pleased to proceed on its way. Then, in the roadway beyond, she saw a horse struggling with a more than ample load, and a carter of the sort that seems to bear a sullen hatred
1 against the animal that helps him to earn a
living. Lady Carlotta promptly betook her to the roadway, and put rather a different complexion on the struggle. Certain of her acquaintances were wont to give her plentiful admonition as to the undesirability of interfering on behalf of a distressed animal, such interference being "none of her business." Only once had she put the doctrine of nonin-
2 terference into practice, when one of its
most eloquent exponents had been besieged for nearly three hours in a small and extremely uncomfortable may tree by an angry boar-pig, while Lady Carlotta, on the other
3 side of the fence, had proceeded with the
water-color sketch she was engaged on, and refused to interfere between the boar and his prisoner. It is to be feared that she lost the friendship of the ultimately rescued lady. On this occasion she merely lost the train, which gave way to the first sign of impatience it had shown throughout the journey, and steamed off without her. She bore the desertion with philosophical indifference; her friends and relations were thor-
4 oughly well used to the fact of her luggage
arriving without her. She wired a vague noncommittal message to her destination to say that she was coming on "by another train." Before she had time to think what her next move might be she was confronted by an imposingly attired lady, who seemed to be taking a prolonged mental inventory of her clothes and looks.

"You must be Miss Hope, the governess
I've come to meet," said the apparition, in a 5
tone that admitted of very little argument.

"Very well, if I must I must," said Lady Carlotta to herself with dangerous meekness.

"I am Mrs. Quabarl," continued the lady; "and where, pray, is your luggage?"

"It's gone astray," said the alleged governess, falling in with the excellent rule of life that the absent are always to blame; the luggage had, in point of fact, behaved with perfect correctitude. "I've just telegraphed about it," she added, with a nearer approach to truth.

"How provoking," said Mrs. Quabarl; "these railway companies are so careless.
However, my maid can lend you things for 6
the night," and she led the way to her car.

During the drive to the Quabarl mansion Lady Carlotta was impressively introduced to the nature of the charge that had been thrust upon her; she learned that Claude and Wilfrid were delicate, sensitive young people, that Irene had the artistic temperament highly developed, and that Viola was something or other else of a mold equally commonplace among children of that class and type in the twentieth century.

"I wish them not only to be *taught,*" said

6 **Literary Focus** Ask the students to discuss the situational irony in here.

Mrs. Quabarl, "but *interested* in what they learn. In their history lessons, for instance, you must try to make them feel that they are being introduced to the life stories of men and women who really lived, not merely committing a mass of names and dates to memory. French, of course, I shall expect you to talk at mealtimes several days in the
7 week."

"I shall talk French four days of the week and Russian in the remaining three."

"Russian? My dear Miss Hope, no one in the house speaks or understands Russian."

"That will not embarrass me in the least," said Lady Carlotta coldly.

Mrs. Quabarl, to use a colloquial expression, was knocked off her perch. She was one of those imperfectly self-assured individuals who are magnificent and autocratic as long as they are not seriously opposed. The least show of unexpected resistance goes a long way toward rendering them cowed and apologetic. When the new governess failed to express wondering admiration of the large newly purchased and expensive car, and lightly alluded to the superior advantages of one or two makes which had just been put on the market, the discomfiture of her patroness became almost abject. Her feelings were those which might have animated a general of ancient
8 warfaring days, on beholding his heaviest battle-elephant ignominiously driven off the field by slingers and javelin throwers.

At dinner that evening, although reinforced by her husband, who usually duplicated her opinions and lent her moral support generally, Mrs. Quabarl regained none of her lost ground. The governess not only helped herself well and truly to wine, but held forth with considerable show of critical knowledge on various vintage matters, concerning which the Quabarls were in no wise
9 able to pose as authorities. Previous governesses had limited their conversation on the wine topic to a respectful and doubtless sincere expression of a preference for water. When this one went as far as to recommend a wine firm in whose hands you could not go very far wrong Mrs. Quabarl thought it time to turn the conversation into more usual channels.

"We got very satisfactory references about you from Canon Teep," she observed; 10
"a very estimable man, I should think."

"Drinks like a fish and beats his wife, otherwise a very lovable character," said the governess imperturbably.

"My *dear* Miss Hope! I trust you are exaggerating," exclaimed the Quabarls in unison.

"One must in justice admit that there is some provocation," continued the romancer. "Mrs. Teep is quite the most irritating 11
bridge player that I have ever sat down with; her leads and declarations would condone a certain amount of brutality in her partner, but to souse her with the contents of the only soda-water siphon in the house on a 12
Sunday afternoon, when one couldn't get another, argues an indifference to the comfort of others which I cannot altogether overlook. You may think me hasty in my judgments, but it was practically on account of the siphon incident that I left."

"We will talk of this some other time," said Mrs. Quabarl hastily.

"I shall never allude to it again," said the governess with decision.

Mr. Quabarl made a welcome diversion by asking what studies the new instructress proposed to inaugurate on the morrow.

"History to begin with," she informed him.

"Ah, history," he observed sagely; "now in teaching them history you must take care to interest them in what they learn. You must make them feel that they are being 13
introduced to the life stories of men and women who really lived—"

"I've told her all that," interposed Mrs. Quabarl.

"I teach history on the Schartz- 14
Metterklume method," said the governess loftily.

"Ah, yes," said her listeners, thinking it expedient to assume an acquaintance at 15
least with the name.

7 **Literary Focus** What is ironical about this discussion about languages?

8 **Literary Focus** What is the irony in Saki's comparison here? **Less advanced** students may wish to keep a list of "real" events in Saki's story so they don't get lost in Saki's ironical twists.

9 **Discussion** What does this discussion of wine reveal about Mrs. Quabarl?

10 **Clarification** Saki's names for his leading characters are typical Saki ironies. His fantastic imagination makes the Quabarls sound difficult, the Teeps sound like foolish little birds and Miss Hope sounds like a mishap, which is indeed what Lady Carlotta engineers. The names are appropriate and improbable at the same time.

11 **Critical Thinking and Reading** What does the reader learn about Lady Carlotta as "a romancer?" **More advanced** students may wish to evaluate Saki as a romancer.

12 **Literary Focus** Ask the students to observe the irony and understatement in this delightful passage.

13 **Discussion** What characteristic does Mr. Quabarl reveal?

14 **Reading Strategy** Ask the students to take into consideration Lady Carlotta's behavior and to predict what "the Schartz-Metterklume method" will be like.

15 **Discussion** Why do the Quabarls pretend familiarity with Lady Carlotta's teaching method?

"What are you children doing out here?" demanded Mrs. Quabarl the next morning, on finding Irene sitting rather glumly at the head of the stairs, while her sister was perched in an attitude of depressed discomfort on the window seat behind her, with a wolfskin rug almost covering her.

"We are having a history lesson," came the unexpected reply. "I am supposed to be Rome, and Viola up there is the she-wolf; not a real wolf, but the figure of one that the Romans used to set store by—I forget why. Claude and Wilfrid have gone to fetch the shabby women."

"The shabby women?"

"Yes, they've got to carry them off. They didn't want to, but Miss Hope got one of father's fives bats[1] and said she'd give them a number nine spanking if they didn't, so they've gone to do it."

A loud, angry screaming from the direction of the lawn drew Mrs. Quabarl thither in hot haste, fearful lest the threatened castigation might even now be in process of infliction. The outcry, however, came principally from the two small daughters of the lodge-keeper, who were being hauled and pushed toward the house by the panting and disheveled Claude and Wilfrid, whose task was rendered even more arduous by the incessant, if not very effectual, attacks of the captured maidens' small brother. The governess, fives bat in hand, sat negligently on the stone balustrade, presiding over the scene with the cold impartiality of a goddess of battles. A furious and repeated chorus of "I'll tell muvver" rose from the lodge children, but the lodge mother, who was hard of hearing, was for the moment immersed in the preoccupation of her washtub. After an apprehensive glance in the direction of the lodge (the good woman was gifted with the highly militant temper which is sometimes the privilege of deafness) Mrs. Quabarl flew indignantly to the rescue of the struggling captives.

"Wilfrid! Claude! Let those children go at once. Miss Hope, what on earth is the meaning of this scene?"

"Early Roman history; the Sabine women, don't you know? It's the Schartz- 16
Metterklume method to make children understand history by acting it themselves; fixes it in their memory, you know. Of course, if, thanks to your interference, your boys go through life thinking that the Sabine 17
women ultimately escaped, I really cannot be held responsible."

"You may be very clever and modern, Miss Hope," said Mrs. Quabarl firmly, "but I should like you to leave here by the next train. Your luggage will be sent after you as soon as it arrives."

"I'm not certain exactly where I shall be for the next few days," said the dismissed instructress of youth; "you might keep my luggage till I wire my address. There are only a couple of trunks and some golf clubs and a leopard cub."

"A leopard cub!" gasped Mrs. Quabarl. Even in her departure this extraordinary person seemed destined to leave a trail of 18
embarrassment behind her.

"Well, it's rather left off being a cub; it's more than half grown, you know. A fowl every day and a rabbit on Sundays is what it usually gets. Raw beef makes it too excitable. Don't trouble about getting the car for me, I'm rather inclined for a walk."

And Lady Carlotta strode out of the Quabarl horizon.

The advent of the genuine Miss Hope, who had made a mistake as to the day on which she was due to arrive, caused a turmoil which that good lady was quite unused to inspiring. Obviously the Quabarl family had been woefully befooled, but a certain amount of relief came with the knowledge.

"How tiresome for you, dear Carlotta," said her hostess, when the overdue guest 19
ultimately arrived; "how very tiresome losing your train and having to stop overnight in a strange place."

"Oh dear, no," said Lady Carlotta; "not at all tiresome—for me."

---

1. **fives bats:** Wooden bats used in playing a variation of *fives*, a kind of handball played in England.

16 **Enrichment** *The Rape of the Sabine Women* was an important event in the legendary history of Rome. Romulus instigated this event because he needed wives for his men and he lured away the enemy while his men took Sabine Virgins.

17 **Literary Focus** Does Lady Carlotta ironically provide the kind of history lesson Mrs. Quabarl requested?

18 **Clarification** Remind the students of Saki's delight in freeing the savage to satirize phony civilized conventions.

19 **Literary Focus** Ask the students to observe the understatement in Lady Carlotta's final reply. Saki has been accused of showing contempt for the objects of his satire and Lady Carlotta acts as Saki's spokesman as she shrugs off the entire episode. Were Lady Carlotta's fabrications harmful?

Answers

ANSWERS TO THINKING ABOUT THE SELECTION

Recalling

1. Lady Carlotta misses her train because she interferes on behalf of a distressed horse.
2. (a) Mrs. Quabarl mistakes Lady Carlotta for her new governess, Miss Hope. (b) Lady Carlotta goes along with the idea that she is the governess.
3. The Schartz-Metterklume method makes children understand history by acting it out themselves.
4. (a) The Quabarls dismiss Lady Carlotta because she creates an uproar by threats to spank the chil-

THINKING ABOUT THE SELECTION
Recalling

1. What causes Lady Carlotta to miss her train?
2. (a) What mistake does Mrs. Quabarl make when she sees Lady Carlotta on the platform? (b) How does Lady Carlotta react to this mistake?
3. What is the Schartz-Metterklume Method?
4. (a) Why do the Quabarls dismiss Lady Carlotta? (b) What is her reaction? (c) What request does she make as she is about to leave?
5. How do the Quabarls learn that they have been fooled?

Interpreting

6. (a) How would you describe the Quabarls? (b) How would you describe Lady Carlotta?
7. In your opinion do the characters' names enhance the story's humorous tone? Explain.

Applying

8. A contemporary of Saki, the critic Max Beerbohm remarked that laughter "rejoices in bonds [meaning chains]," if only to break them. Comment on whether you think Saki's humor in this story illustrates the remark.

ANALYZING LITERATURE
Understanding Satire

Satire is writing in which irony, humor, ridicule, or some combination of the three is used to make the reader aware of some evil or folly. In "The Schartz-Metterklume Method" Saki takes satiric aim at customs and attitudes of the English upper-class of his day.

1. Find at least two examples of irony in the story.
2. (a) How is the last sentence of the story an example of understatement? (b) How does the use of understatement bring home the satiric point of the story?
3. Do you think Saki's satire is characterized by biting wit or by more subtle methods? Support your answer.

CRITICAL THINKING AND READING
Making Inferences About Tone

Tone is the attitude taken by the author toward a particular character or subject. Although Saki never directly expresses his feelings about the Quabarls, and particularly Lady Quabarl, the reader has no trouble inferring his tone. Identify the character trait represented by each of the following details. Then, based on the sum of these traits, state Saki's tone.

1. Mrs. Quabarl's taking a "prolonged mental inventory" of Lady Carlotta on the platform
2. Mrs. Quabarl's assuming "in a tone that admitted of very little argument" that Lady Carlotta was the governess
3. Mr. Quabarl's duplicating his wife's opinions
4. The Quabarls' not admitting to never having heard of the Schartz-Metterklume Method

UNDERSTANDING LANGUAGE
Understanding Words with Latin Roots

The following words, which appear in "The Schartz-Metterklume Method," are each based on a Latin root. Look the words up in a good dictionary, noting the precise meaning of the root in each case. Find at least three words that share the root.

1. admonition
2. eloquent
3. abject
4. militant
5. arduous

THINKING AND WRITING
Comparing and Contrasting Approaches

Reread the introduction to and a portion of either *Gulliver's Travels* on page 538 or the excerpts from *The Rape of the Lock* on page 560. When you feel you have regained the flavor of the eighteenth-century work, write an essay in which you highlight the differences and similarities between this early satiric effort and the Saki story. Pay particular attention to language, tone, and theme. Conclude your essay by stating which satire you enjoyed more, giving your reasons. When you revise, make sure you have used details from the selections.

(Answers begin on p. 976.)

dren unless they act out their history lesson. (b) Lady Carlotta asks Mrs. Quabarl to keep her trunks and to feed her leopard cub.

5. The Quabarls discover that they have been fooled when the real governess arrives the next day.

Interpreting

6. Suggested Responses: (a) The Quabarls are pretentious, shallow, snobs. (b) Lady Carlotta is eccentric, sharp, and ironical.
7. Suggested Response: The characters' names enhance the story's humorous tone because they are ironical. The Quabarls are as ridiculous as their quarrelsome name, and "Miss Hope" is funny since she may bring them fresh hope or she may be a mistaken hope. Lady Carlotta does not act like a lady at all, and The Teeps sound like funny little birds.

Applying

8. Saki's humor breaks bonds since it cleanses away the social pretenses of the upper classes and the reader's belief in aristocrats' superiority.

ANSWERS TO ANALYZING LITERATURE

1. Mistaking Lady Carlotta for the governess and treating her high-handedly is situational irony; another example is the discrepancy between the desired and actual results of the living history lesson or the "The Schartz-Metterklume Method."
2. (a) Lady Carlotta's response of "not tiresome" is certainly an understated description of the bizarre events she has precipitated. (b) The understatement emphasizes the advantage Carlotta has taken of the Quabarls.
3. Answers will differ. Students should use details from the story to support their answers.

ANSWERS TO CRITICAL READING AND THINKING

1. Shallowness, superficiality, materialism, and snobbishness.
2. Narrowness of vision; haste in making false assumptions.
3. Shallowness, powerlessness, and lack of imagination.
4. Superficiality and pretentiousness.

Saki's tone is ironical and contemptuous.

Challenge Debate the premise and agree or disagree with the statement "Lady Carlotta escapes Saki's irony entirely because she speaks for the author." Use character traits and evidence of Saki's tone to defend your argument.

ANSWERS TO UNDERSTANDING LANGUAGE

1. *admonitio:* caution; advise against something; *admonish, admonitory, admonishment.*
2. *eloquens:* having the power of fluent and forceful speech; *loquacious, loquacity, eloquence.*
3. *abjectus:* utterly hopeless, or wretched; *abjectly, abjective, abjection.*
4. *militaris:* to have force as evidence; *militancy, militantly, militarism.*
5. *arduus:* requiring great exertion, difficult; *arduously, arduousness, ardor.*

THINKING AND WRITING

Publishing Student Writing Ask for volunteers to share the opinions stated in their essays.

More About the Author Although travel to Italy and Greece contributed setting and characters for many of his works, E. M. Forster spent most of his life in England where he associated with the Bloomsbury group—a group that revolted against the artistic, social, and sexual restrictions of Victorian society. These artists believed in the pleasure of communication and the enjoyment of beauty, and they profoundly affected the development of the avant-garde in literature in Britain. How might Forster's association with this group have affected his writing?

E. M. FORSTER

1879–1970

To understand who E. M. Forster was, it is perhaps best to start with what he was not. He was staunchly opposed to imperialism, to capitalism, to ecclesiasticism, and to just about any other *ism* except for humanism. Forster's ideal, in short, was a civilization in which the rights of the individual are held supreme over those of any collective or organization. It is precisely this message that serves as a theme in most of his novels.

Having lost his father at the age of one, Edward Morgan Forster was raised by his mother and a wealthy aunt. It was the latter's money that made it possible for him to attend the finest schools, beginning with Tonbridge School in Kent, which Forster later attacked as typifying what he called the "materialism of the English school system." In 1897 he entered King's College at Cambridge, which he considered his "spiritual home." After receiving his degree he traveled to Greece and then lived for some time in Italy.

While abroad he penned his first three novels. *Where Angels Fear to Tread* (1905) and *A Room with a View* (1908), set in Italy, examine the conflict between culture and falseness on the one hand, and passion and truth on the other. *The Longest Journey* (1907) recalls Forster's days at his beloved Cambridge, where he returned in 1910 to complete work on an advanced degree. It was in this same year that Forster published *Howard's End,* a carefully drawn portrait of pre-war society in England.

In 1912 Forster visited India. After serving in the International Red Cross during World War I, he returned there in 1921. His experiences and observations provided the inspiration for his most celebrated work, *A Passage to India* (1924). The novel, which treats the difficulties that arise in attempting to establish personal relationships, also delivered a prophetic glimpse of England's relations with India.

Dabbling in criticism and in shorter fiction as well, Forster turned out *Aspects of the Novel* in 1927 and *The External Moment,* a collection of short stories, the following year. He also produced several collections of essays, including *Abinger Harvest* (1936) and *Two Cheers for Democracy* (1951). In 1969 he was named to the Order of Merit.

Although some critics have suggested that Forster's novels deal ultimately with the age-old struggle between good and evil, the situation is more complicated than that. Invariably his villains value possessions over people and appearances over realities. And invariably, as in "The Helping Hand," those villains are made, in the end, to pay for their shallowness.

GUIDE FOR READING

The Helping Hand

The Writer's Technique

Characterization. Characterization is the technique whereby a writer makes known the personality of the characters in a work of fiction. Characterization can be accomplished in one of two ways—directly or indirectly. In direct characterization the writer comments openly on the character's personality, using descriptive phrases and adjectives to telegraph impressions straight to the reader. In indirect characterization the writer permits the reader to make up his or her own mind as to what kind of person the character is. To equip the reader to do this, the writer provides information in the form of one or more of the following: (1) the character's words, including speech habits; (2) the character's actions; (3) the character's appearance; (4) the character's thoughts and feelings; and (5) the views of that character held by other characters in the story. Because it mimics the process we use in life to form impressions and opinions of the people we meet, indirect characterization has the effect of making the characters in a story seem real and lifelike.

Look For

As you read "The Helping Hand," look for the method of characterization used by the author. Notice the way the several different personalities play off one another.

Writing

Write a rough draft of a short poem or story titled "The Borrower." You may, if you wish, base it on a real-life occurrence, but avoid using the real names of individuals. The poem or story should tell about an individual who borrows habitually without ever returning the items borrowed. Include descriptions of the personalities of both the borrower and the lender.

Vocabulary

Knowing the following words will help you as you read "The Helping Hand."

affected (ə fek'tid) *adj.*: In a manner not true to the person (p. 980)

appropriated (ə prō'prē āt'id) *v.*: Borrowed without giving credit (p. 980)

plagiarism (plā'jə riz'm) *n.*: Passing off another's work as one's own (p. 980)

mortification (môr'tə fi kā'shən) *n.*: Feeling of great shock and upset (p. 982)

lucrative (lo͞o'krə tiv) *adj.*: Profitable; rich (p. 982)

Literary Focus In his *Aspects of the Novel* (1927) Forster divides characters into round and flat types. Flat characters derive from stock characters in early Italian comedy and they speak or act repetitively. Round characters are more detailed and diverse. Forster calls his round characters, "ready for extended life."

Look For Students should examine the distinction between round and flat characters in Forster. Round characters are usually shown internally; they express doubts, and they often change their behavior. Flat characters are usually a collection of consistent mannerisms, and the real function of flat character is to throw light on other characters. At the two extremes in "The Helping Hand," you will find the flattened out picture of Lady Anstey contrasted to the well-developed hero, Mr. Henderson. Ask the students to observe the evolution of the character of both Lady Anstey and Mrs. Henderson since their full characterization sheds light on Mr. Henderson and Forster's use of ironical characterization.

Writing Students might prefer to present their characterizations in the form of a short script.

Vocabulary Ask your students to discuss plagiarism in terms of its dictionary meaning and in light of contemporary examples exposed in the media. Make certain that your **less advanced** students understand the pronunciation of each vocabulary word as well as what each word means. To clarify Forster's meaning, ask the students to locate each word in the story and discuss each word in its context.

Objectives

1. To understand characterization
2. To make inferences about character
3. To understand word origins
4. To write about character

Teaching Portfolio: Support Material

Lesson Plan, pp. 00–00

Vocabulary Check, p. 00

Usage and Mechanics Worksheet, p. 00

Analyzing Literature Worksheet, p. 00

Critical Thinking and Reading Worksheet, p. 00

Language Worksheet, p. 00

Selection Test, p. 00

Motivation For Reading Forster uses a great deal of irony in developing the characters in "The Helping Hand." The title of the story is ironical, the central problem is ironical, and the actual outcome is a masterful irony. Ask the students to think about the surprises and complexities underneath Forster's picture of ordinary reality. Ask them to observe the way Forster uses irony to tap into the reality hidden under the surface of things and to show the discrepancy between the inner truth of some of his characters and their external appearance.

Master Teacher Note In *Aspects of the Novel*, Forster describes characterization. He says, "A character in a book is real . . . when the novelist knows everything about it. He may not choose to tell us all he knows . . . But he will give us the feeling that though the character has not been explained, it is explicable, and we get from this a reality of a kind we can never get in daily life." Ask the students to read the story and to evaluate if the character of Mr. Henderson has this kind of reality and if his behavior is consistent in "The Helping Hand."

Thematic Idea Another story in which upper-class society is satirized is "The Schartz-Metterklume Method" by Saki (p. 974).

Purpose-Setting Question What is ironic about the ending of the story?

1 **Literary Focus** How does Mrs. Henderson first appear?

2 **Discussion** What obvious clues did Mrs. Henderson overlook about Lady Anstey's knowledge of da Empoli?

3 **Literary Focus** What does the newspaper move show about Mr. Henderson's inner feelings?

The Helping Hand

E. M. Forster

When Lady Anstey's book on Giovanni da Empoli[1] was published, Mr. Henderson found in it much that needed forgiveness. His friend did not write as charmingly as she talked: a horrid slime of culture oozed over her style, her criticisms were affected, her enthusiasms abominable. This he could have forgiven; but how could he forgive the subject matter? The dear lady had appropriated, without acknowledgement, facts and theories for which he, and he alone, was responsible. He had studied Giovanni da Empoli for years, and the premature fruit of his labors now lay upon the breakfast table—a little apple-green book, four shillings net, being one of Messrs. Angerstein's series of Pocket Painters.

Mrs. Henderson, a devoted wife, was
turning over the leaves with a smile upon
her face, for she was pleased that the words
of Lady Anstey had been printed on such
heavy paper. She knew nothing of the
1 shameful plagiarism, her interest in art
being sympathetic rather than intelligent:
she was always glad when her friends and
her husband got on in it, just as she was
glad when her son got on at school.

"What a long list of books she has read
to write it!" she observed. "Did you know
she could read German? And when did she
2 go to Italy? Wasn't Empoli[2] the place you
made us go to—the dirty hotel where we
had to hunt the chickens out of the bedroom window?"

"Yes," replied Mr. Henderson, remembering with anguish the nights at Empoli which he had spent and Lady Anstey had not.

"Why did we go there? I've forgotten."

"I had things to look up in the archives."
He held up the newspaper as a screen. 3

"I think you look up too much. Here's
Lady Anstey who a little time back knew no
more about Italian art than I do, and yet 4
look! I wish you'd write a little book like this.
I'm sure you could do it."

"I haven't the knack of putting things
brightly." He never said all he thought about
the Pocket Painters and similar editions, 5
believing that anything which induces people to look at pictures has its value.

"Yes: I dare say it's all superficial and wrong."

He answered with some animation, "What makes you think so?"

"Because I mistrust new theories—not that I should have known there was a theory. But she says there is one in the preface."

"Giovanni da Empoli," said Mr. Henderson eagerly, "is one of the great puzzles of
the Quattrocento.[3] It is highly probable from
internal and external evidence that many 6
pictures attributed to other painters should
be given to him."

1. **Giovanni** (jō van′ ē) **da Empoli** (em′ pō lē): A fictional painter.
2. **Empoli:** Town in central Italy.
3. **Quattrocento** (kwät′ trō chen′ tō): The fifteenth century.

4 **Literary Focus** Contrast the indirect characterization of Mrs. Henderson with the direct characterization in the first sentence of the second paragraph.

5 **Critical Thinking and Reading** What does the omission reveal about Mr. Henderson's character?

6 **Discussion** What is the theory that forms the thesis of the book?

"Cut your bread and butter, dear, do not bite it," said Mrs. Henderson to their son.

"If we take one of the Pieros[4] in the
National Gallery, the portrait in the Poldi-
7 Pezzoli at Milan, the so-called Baldovinetti[5]
at Naples, and the *cassoni* attributed to
Pesellino,[6] we notice in all a certain—"

"'Empoli is a quaint old town not untinged with the modern spirit,'" interrupted their son, who was reading out of Lady Anstey's book in the nasal twang that is considered humorous by the young. "'Here in 1409'—then a long note saying why not in 1429—"

"Exactly," said his father.

"'—in 1409 young Giovanni was born,
here, when not on his travels, he lived, and 8
here he died in 1473. Our painter never
married. Of his six children four—'"

"Don't read at meals, dear," said his
mother, taking the book. "This is a great
surprise to me and a great pleasure. I never 9
thought Lady Anstey had it in her."

No more she had. The book was the work of Mr. Henderson. He had no one to blame but himself. Lady Anstey had said, "I want to write a book about Giovanni da Empoli: tell me everything you know," and he had told her, cautiously at first in barren statements, then, as he grew warm, infusing the facts with life, till at last the whole theory stood up before her delighted eyes. "Tell it me again," she said, for she was not quick at following, and he had told it her again and she had made notes of it, and he had placed his own notes at her disposal.

4. Pieros (pye' rōz): Paintings by Italian painter Piero della Francesca (1410 or 1420–1492).
5. Baldovinetti (bäl' dō vē net' tē): Painting by Florentine painter Alessio Baldovinetti (1425–1499).
6. Pesellino (pes ə lē' nō): Francesco Pesellino, an Italian Renaissance painter (1422–1457).

THE NEWSPAPER
Edouard Vuillard
The Phillips Collection

Humanities Note

Fine art, *The Newspaper,* Edouard Vuillard. Vuillard (1868-1940) was a pupil of artist Diogéne Maillart and studied at the Ecole des Beaux Arts and Academie Julien in Paris. He is considered to be a Post-Impressionist, a painter influenced but not guided by the vast changes in art brought about by the Impressionists, and a master Intimist painter, one who paints simple everyday scenes and objects. He was attracted to everyday life and all of its aspects and portrayed the comfortable French middle class in a most charming and decorative way in his paintings.

In this painting, *The Newspaper,* Vuillard shows his talent for finding beauty and poetry in the commonplace. The ordinary image of a man behind a newspaper is turned into a decorative pattern by the flat rhythm of the brush strokes and the pleasing subtle colors. You may point out the Impressionist influence on the painter evidenced in the way the dappling of light breaks up the picture plane. You may also ask the following questions:

1. What do you think the artist was trying to show in this painting?
2. Is the man behind the newspaper actually reading or might he be hiding from something? Explain.
3. Might this be considered a portrayal of the character Mr. Henderson? Explain.

7 **Enrichment** The artists working in Florence at the time in question all influenced one another.

One critic of Forster believes that the group of names in the story suggests that Giovanni da Empoli was Antonio Pollaiuolo rather than a fictional artist. Pollaiuolo, influenced by the revival of antiquity, worked on busts in the ancient manner in the area of Florence. If the artist is indeed Pollaiuolo, what is Forster saying about the need to view his characters in a fully rounded way?

8 **Clarification** Maria Cruttwell, who published the first criticism on Pollaiuolo in 1907, may be Lady Anstey. If so, she helped Forster announce the new information about da Empoli's (Pollaiuolo's) birth. Ask **more advanced** students to discuss the irony in the fact that Cruttwell's criticism of the model for da Empoli was published after Forster reputedly wrote "The Helping Hand," so that Forster was revealing new facts about the artist that he had "stolen" from the critics' notes.

9 **Literary Focus** How does Mrs. Henderson's reaction portray her character?

10 **Critical Thinking and Reading** What do Mrs. Henderson's understatement and Mr. Henderson's silence reveal about the Hendersons?

Does internal and external evidence clarify the truth about Forster's characters in the same ironical way that Mr. Henderson's thesis clarifies the "truth" about da Empoli?

11 **Literary Focus** How do these characters contrast?

12 **Discussion** How does the miniature of the Italian contribute irony?

He reminded himself that facts are universal property, and it is no matter who gives them to the world. But ideas—should there not be some copyright in ideas? He had only meant to stimulate Lady Anstey, not to equip her. However, she had Virgil[7] on her side, and Molière[8] and Shakespeare, and all the ancient Greeks who had taken everything and said nothing to anybody, and splendid fellows they were.

She was perfectly open when they next met, greeting him with "And here is someone else to whom I owe more than I can say." For her book was a success, and Messrs. Angerstein had asked her to do one on Botticelli.[9]

"I'm so glad he's been of use," said Mrs. Henderson, imagining herself to be engaged in conventional civilities. "I never knew he had studied the man." For Mr. Henderson had decided to bear his burden in silence,
10 and neither to his wife nor to anyone else did he give one hint of his mortification. He had in him something of the saint, and knew it would be wrong as well as undignified to repine.

"And now tell me all about Botticelli," said Lady Anstey. But Mr. Henderson told very little about Botticelli. He regarded Lady Anstey with frozen admiration, almost with terror, as a being devoid of conscience and consciousness. They continued great friends, but he saw her as seldom as possible.

Her book, in spite of its popular form, made a considerable impression in artistic circles, and she was soon drawn into the congenial and lucrative atmosphere of controversy. In a fortunate hour Sir William Magnus disagreed with her, and a duel ensued, conducted with courtesy on his side and spirit on hers. Wisely refraining from venturing into new fields, she contented herself with repeating the statements she had made in her book. Mrs. Henderson, who always followed anything personal, was able to write her a hearty letter of congratulation on her victory.

Mr. Henderson did not write. The triumph of his theory gave him no pleasure, for it had triumphed in a mangled form. Lady Anstey had wielded it fairly well, but she had missed all the subtleties, she had spoiled the purity of its outline. Yet she had not spoiled it enough to justify his publishing it anew, under his own name.

He suffered a good deal, though he trained himself to laugh at the irony of the situation. He would like to have found someone to laugh with, but all his friends were 11
embroiled on one side or the other, and he could not trust them to keep silent. As for his wife, she did not believe in irony. Meanwhile the book ran through several editions, and there was a rumor that the powers that be in the National Gallery were troubled, and meditated changing the label on the Piero della Francesca.

By the time Professor Rinaldi came to England, Mr. Henderson was tired of laughing and needed sympathy. Rinaldi, whom Mrs. Henderson called the Italian, was a man of great learning and artistic insight, who had become so disgusted with contro-
versies over beauty that he had left Rome 12
and retired to the curatorship of a small provincial gallery. There he lived, or as others said rotted, studying continually because he could not help it, but avowing his intention of never publishing again.

Here was a man to whom Mr. Henderson could speak freely. They were old friends, and he determined to pay him a visit in London.

"Do," said Mrs. Henderson, "and I will finish off the spring cleaning."

Mr. Henderson left on the Thursday, and Mrs. Henderson turned out the dining room. On Friday she did the drawing room. On Saturday she began at her husband's study, and came across a pasteboard box labeled Giovanni da Empoli.

7. **Virgil:** Classical Roman poet (70–19 B.C.).
8. **Molière** (mōl yer'): French dramatist (1622–1673).
9. **Botticelli** (bät' ə chel' ē): Italian Renaissance painter (1445?–1510).

THE CONVERSATION
Hobson Pittman
The North Carolina Museum of Art, Raleigh, N.C.

Recognizing the name, she opened it and read on the top sheet inside: "Reasons for believing G. to be born in 1409." A strange impulse moved her, and she went for Lady
13 Anstey's book. It gave identical reasons.

Then in one moment the loving wife became a student of art. All Saturday she sat with the book and the papers before her, and discovered that they coincided, not here and there but everywhere. The last paper in the box was a letter from Lady Anstey saying "Many thanks for loan of notes, which have been most acceptable."

All Sunday she thought over the revela-
14 tion, all Monday and all Tuesday she acted on it. Mr. Henderson returned on the Wednesday.

He was looking more cheerful than she had seen him for weeks. "The world is ruled by irony," he observed, and smiled, as if he found the rule easy to bear.

"And how is the Italian?" she asked, rather ill at ease.

"As fine as ever. 'A little less imagination in archaeology and a little more in art' was his advice to Sir William yesterday."

The word "art" gave her an opening, and she exclaimed, "Yes indeed! Yes indeed! Yes indeed!"

"Why this enthusiasm?"

"You dear thing!" she cried, embracing him; "you're too good to be alive!"

"What have I done?" he asked, looking grave.

Humanities Note

Fine art, *The Conversation,* by Hobson Pittman. Pittman (1898–1972) was an American painter, engraver, and teacher. Born in Tarboro, North Carolina, Pittman studied at Pennsylvania State College, the Carnegie Institute, and Columbia University. He also expanded his artistic knowledge with extended travel abroad.

The painting *The Conversation* depicts a narrative subject rendered in a modern, realistic style. It shows the "artistic" interior of a studio, the large window of which shows a view of a spectacular landscape with an approaching storm. Seated before the window, impervious to nature's drama, two figures lean conspiratorialy toward one another. It is painted with an interesting point of view, pleasant colors, and good humor.

You may wish to use the following questions for discussion:

1. Does the humorous and satiric nature of the painting suit the mood of the story? Explain.
2. How does the artist feel about the two women?

13 Discussion How does Mrs. Henderson discover the plagiarism?

14 Critical Thinking and Reading What can we infer from Mrs. Henderson's thinking time as opposed to her action time?

15 **Discussion** Relate the Italian Professor's discovery to Mr. Henderson's statement, "the world is ruled by irony." What ironies exist in this story? What is the irony in the title?

"I've found you out—that you wrote Lady Anstey's book—that she took all your facts and ideas and never said a word. And all these months you've let her talk and become famous and make money. I do admire and love you for it—but do be glad I'm different!"

"What have you been doing?" he said sternly.

"Nothing rude—don't be cross. I only let it out in the course of conversation, or put it in a letter if I was writing one."

"And to whom have you written?"

"Oh, not to Lady Anstey: to Lady Magnus about the vacuum cleaner, and one or two more. And yesterday I met the editor of the *Dudley* and he was horrified. Don't be angry—no, I don't mind if you are angry; it's simple justice I want; she shall *not* pick your brains and no one know; you *shall* have the credit for your own theory."

"Unfortunate," said Mr. Henderson. "Professor Rinaldi has just proved to me that the theory in question is wrong, that the facts are wrong, that the book is wrong, that I am wrong. Unfortunate." 15

THINKING ABOUT THE SELECTION

Recalling

1. (a) How does Mr. Henderson feel when Lady Anstey's book appears? Why? (b) How does his wife feel? Why?
2. (a) What do Lady Anstey's publishers ask her to do following the success of her book? (b) What does she, in turn, ask of Mr. Henderson?
3. (a) What does Mr. Henderson come across during her cleaning? (b) What does she do as a result of this discovery? (c) What is her husband's response to her actions?

Interpreting

4. What is ironic about Lady Anstey's having the title "lady?"
5. Why do you suppose Mr. Henderson decides to "bear his burden in silence?"
6. (a) What does Mrs. Henderson's behavior at the breakfast table reveal about her? (b) What does Lady Anstey's request for information on Botticelli reveal about her?
7. Do you find the title of the story appropriate? Why or why not?

Applying

8. (a) How did you feel at the end of the story? (b) How would you have behaved if you had been Mr. Henderson?

ANALYZING LITERATURE

Understanding Characterization

Characterization is the method a writer uses to reveal the personalities of characters in a story. In direct characterization, the writer tells us directly what sort of person the character is. In indirect characterization, the writer allows us to arrive at our own judgments based on what the character says, does, thinks, and looks like, as well as on how the character is regarded by other characters in the story. In "The Helping Hand," Forster uses a mixture of the two types of characterization. Identify the following characterizations as direct or indirect. For each example of indirect characterization, find the quoted words in the story. Then tell what trait each of the

Answers

ANSWERS TO THINKING ABOUT THE SELECTION

Recalling

1. (a) Mr. Henderson feels angry and mortified when Lady Anstey's book first appears because she has plagiarized his research and his original theory about Giovanni da Empoli. (b) His wife is surprised and impressed that Lady Anstey could learn so much in so short a time.
2. (a) The publishers ask Lady Anstey to do another book using Botticelli as the subject this time. (b) Lady Anstey asks Mr. Henderson to tell her all about Botticelli.
3. (a) During her cleaning, Lady Anstey discovers her husband's box of original notes on da Empoli, and she realizes that Lady Anstey has stolen his research. (b) Mrs. Henderson tells the facts about the plagiarism to an editor. (c) Her husband is upset that she has exposed him as the originator of the theory because the Italian curator has discovered that Mr. Henderson's theory is wrong.

Interpreting

4. Lady Anstey's title is ironical because she does not act at all ladylike when she brashly steals Mr. Henderson's ideas and research.
5. Mr. Henderson is embarrassed and ashamed, and he feels that it would be undignified to expose Lady Anstey—who is one of his social peers—as a fraud.
6. (a) Mrs. Henderson acts foolish, flighty and superficial at the breakfast table. (b) Lady Anstey's request for information on Botticelli reveals her audacity or nerve as well as her total lack of conscience.
7. The title is appropriate because of its irony on three levels. First, because Mr. Henderson gave Lady Anstey his help. Second, because Lady Anstey helped herself to all of Mr. Henderson's research and his original theory. Finally, because Mrs. Henderson wishes him success and she means to be helpful, but she ironically ends up harming Mr. Henderson more than Lady Anstey.

Applying

8. (a) Suggested response: I was amazed and amused by the irony at the end of the story. (b) Suggested response: If I had been Mr. Henderson, I would have exposed Lady Anstey as a plagiarist and a fraud.

Challenge Why doesn't Mr. Henderson get pleasure from the orig-

indirect characterizations reveals and to which character each refers.

1. Mrs. Henderson, a devoted wife, was turning over the leaves with a smile . . . (page 980)
2. "I think you look up too much. . . ." (page 980)
3. He held up the newspaper as a screen. (page 980)
4. "I haven't the knack of putting things brightly." (page 980)
5. . . . he had told her, cautiously at first . . . , then, as he grew warm, infusing the facts with life. . . . (page 981)
6. Wisely refraining from venturing into new fields, she contented herself with repeating the statements she had made in her book. (page 982)
7. "Nothing rude—don't be cross. I only let it out in the course of a conversation, or put it in a letter if I was writing one." (page 984)
8. "Unfortunate," said Mr. Henderson. "Professor Rinaldi has just proved to me that the theory in question is wrong, that the facts are wrong, that the book is wrong, that I am wrong. Unfortunate." (page 984)

CRITICAL THINKING AND READING

Making Inferences About Character

When a writer uses indirect characterization, that writer is leaving it up to the reader to **infer,** or piece together from presented facts, a profile of the character. Read the following profiles of the three main characters in the story. State which of the traits you think are applicable and which are not, backing up your opinions with evidence from the story.

Mr. Henderson: defensive, overly cautious, meek, given to rationalization
Mrs. Henderson: simplistic, shallow, dishonest, a good friend
Lady Anstey: intelligent, poised, treacherous, self-centered

UNDERSTANDING LANGUAGE

Understanding Word Origins

As a rule, the meanings of words change over time. Some word meanings change so much, however, that they leave no trace of the word's original intent. One of the words in the story, *plagiarism*—the passing off of another's writing as one's own—has its roots in a Latin word meaning "kidnap." With the aid of a good dictionary, match up the ancient definitions in the second column with the words from the story.

1. abominable	a. fill with breath, soul
2. theory	b. beginning, first place
3. archives	c. shun as a bad omen
4. animation	d. observe, a viewing

THINKING AND WRITING

Writing About a Character

Choose one of the undeveloped characters in the story—the Hendersons' son, Sir William Magnus, or Professor Rinaldi—and, using the little information provided, create a personality for that character. You may describe the person's appearance and likes and dislikes, but focus the main part of your description on what the person is like. To begin, ask yourself in what ways this person is different from and similar to the other characters in the story. Strive for originality. Then write the first draft of your character sketch. When you revise make sure you have fleshed out your character with vivid details. Proofread your sketch and prepare a final draft.

(Answers begin on p. 984.)

inal success of his theory? How do you predict he will feel about being known as the creator of the theory after Professor Rinaldi's discovery?

ANSWERS TO ANALYZING LITERATURE

Suggested responses:

1. This direct characterization reveals Mrs. Henderson's devoted, sympathetic, generous nature.
2. This indirect characterization reveals that Mrs. Henderson is critical and shallow about her husband's field.
3. This indirect characterization shows that Mr. Henderson feels anguished about Mrs. Anstey's theft of his research.
4. This indirect characterization allows Mr. Henderson to protect his feelings while confirming that he is a scholar rather than a popular writer. It allows him to respond on his wife's shallow level while apparently concealing his contempt for popular books.
5. This indirect characterization reveals Mr. Henderson's passion for his subject.
6. This indirect characterization reveals that although she is not a scholar, Lady Anstey is cunning enough to know how to protect herself.
7. This indirect characterization reveals Mrs. Henderson's naivete and concern.
8. This indirect characterization shows that Mr. Henderson is a man of great restraint with a sense of irony.

ANSWERS TO CRITICAL THINKING AND READING

Mr. Henderson shows that he is defensive and given to rationalization when he says that "he lacks the knack of putting things brightly." His final response shows that he can be seen as meek since he accepts his wife's meddling in his affairs, but his contact with Lady Anstey reveals that he is not overly cautious since he gave away his prized theory.

Mrs. Henderson shows that she is a good friend when she praises Lady Anstey's enterprise in writing the book. Her memories of their trip to Empoli, and her lack of understanding of her husband's work reveal that she is simplistic and shallow. She does not appear dishonest since she takes great pains to reveal the truth about Lady Anstey's fraud.

Lady Anstey has shown her treacherous side by stealing Mr. Henderson's hard work, and she reinforces this with her self-centered behavior when she asks him for new information. Her poise is shown in her ability to conceal her own ignorance in her debates with Sir William Magnus. She has a sly intelligence, like a thief, but she is not an original thinker.

ANSWERS TO UNDERSTANDING LANGUAGE

1. c 2. d 3. b 4. a

THINKING AND WRITING

For help with this assignment, students can refer to Lesson 9, "Writing About Character," in the Handbook of Writing About Literature.

More About the Author The famous intellectual discussions at Bloomsbury brought fresh ideas and attitudes to Virginia Woolf, helping to free her from the reserve of her family's Victorian upbringing. After she and her husband started Hogarth Press, writing, maintaining her delicate nerves, and keeping the comforting friends of Bloomsbury occupied the majority of her time. But Virginia Woolf did have a sensitivity to general social conditions, and particularly to the abuse of women's rights. Her intellectual and her privileged social background allowed her liberal beliefs to flourish. She resented the sexism and corruption of English universities and other aspects of male-dominated Victorian England, and she even refused the honorary degrees of several universities. Her extreme sensitivity and outbreaks of mental illness must have contributed to the feeling of isolation that readers can find in certain of her works.

Ask the students to look for Virginia Woolf's sensitivity to the isolated human condition as they read "The Lady in the Looking Glass: A Reflection." Ask them to also look for examples of Woolf's implied social criticism in this story.

VIRGINIA WOOLF

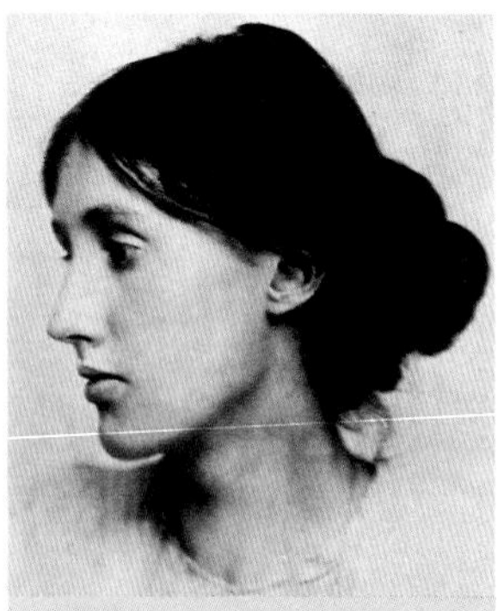

1882–1941

One can scarcely think of twentieth-century trends in fiction without thinking of "stream of consciousness," the technique whereby a character's innermost thoughts, emotions, and memories are woven together into a complex psychological fabric. And one can scarcely think of stream of consciousness without thinking of Virginia Woolf, the brilliant literary pioneer whose novels and short stories introduced this technique to the world.

Ironically for a writer who would become one of the leading lights of Modernism, Virginia Woolf was born into a family of prim and proper Victorians. Her father, Leslie Stephen, who served as the first editor of the renowned *Dictionary of National Biography,* saw to it that his daughter grew up surrounded by books, and at the age of twenty-three Virginia began contributing reviews to the Literary Supplement of *The Times of London.* In 1912 she married Leonard Woolf, an author and social reformer, with whom she founded the Hogarth Press. Their house in the Bloomsbury section of London became an informal meeting place for some of the more important thinkers of the era, attracting such figures as the writers E. M. Forster and Lytton Strachey, the art critic Roger Fry, and the economist John Maynard Keynes.

Woolf's first two novels, *The Voyage Out* (1915) and *Night and Day* (1919) were more or less conventional works. Her third was anything but. *Jacob's Room* (1922), which shattered the conventions of modern fiction-writing, tells the story of a young man's life entirely through an examination of his room and its cluttered contents. Although we never actually meet the title character, we come to know a great deal about him through an artful arrangement of photographs.

In the years between the wars, Woolf continued to refine her fluid, inward-looking style with three more stream-of-consciousness novels—*Mrs. Dalloway* (1925), *To the Lighthouse* (1927), and *The Waves* (1931)—and with four slightly less experimental ones. In her more revolutionary works, she virtually abolished the traditional concept of plot, preferring instead to concentrate on what she called "an ordinary mind on an ordinary day."

For much of her adult life Woolf suffered from painful bouts of depression brought on by poor health and a consuming hatred of war. In 1941, two years after the outbreak of World War II, she ended her life. Today Woolf is recognized, along with James Joyce, whose life span almost exactly paralleled her own, as one of the two most influential shapers of contemporary modern fiction.

GUIDE FOR READING

The Woman in the Looking Glass

The Writer's Technique

Stream of Consciousness. Stream of consciousness is a narrative technique that relies on a character's feelings, memories, and thoughts, as well as associations between the three, to tell a story. Pioneered in the early 1920's by Virginia Woolf, James Joyce, and the American novelist William Faulkner, stream of consciousness marks an attempt to tune in directly to the workings of the character's mind—to capture the random flow of insights and thoughts much as they would naturally occur, moment by moment.

The stream-of-consciousness narrative dispenses with such conventions of traditional fiction as chronological ordering of events and the use of formal transitions. The responsibility for organizing the fragments into a meaningful whole often falls to the reader, who thus becomes more actively involved in the work than is the case with fiction of a more conventional design. The reader must piece together—from memories, unconnected thoughts, and glimpses of the subconscious mind—a meaningful whole. Though its demands on the reader are great, the result of the technique is often an intensely revealing, psychologically complete portrait of a human being.

Look For

As you read "The Woman in the Looking Glass," look for clues to the character's mental and physical makeup.

Writing

Make a list of the contents of a person's room, using your own room at home, the room of someone you know, or one that you have invented for a fictional character. After each item on the list, jot down some notes as to its origin, its physical appearance, and its significance to the occupant.

Vocabulary

Knowing the following words will help you as you read "The Lady in the Looking Glass."

pirouetting (pir′ o͞o wet′ iŋ) *v.*: Dancing or whirling on foot (p. 988)

suffused (sə fyo͞ozd′) *v.*: Filled (p. 988)

transient (tran′ shənt) *adj.*: Person who passes quickly through a place (p. 988)

upbraidings (up brād′ iŋz) *n.*: Stern words of disapproval for an action (p. 990)

evanescence (ev′ ə nes′′ns) *n.*: Gradual disappearance, especially from sight (p. 991)

reticent (ret′ ə s'nt) *adj.*: Laid back; uncommunicati e (p. 991)

Literary Focus Stream-of-consciousness can be understood as an interior dialogue that describes the unspoken thoughts and feelings of characters without resorting to objective description or conventional dialogue. Thus, stream of consciousness concentrates on dreams, thoughts, and emotions of a character. Ask the students if they agree with this method of conveying reality.

Look For You may wish to read through the story with your **less advanced** students to help them appreciate Woolf's use of the stream-of-consciousness technique.

Writing Students might conclude by adding a person to the room they are describing.

Vocabulary Ask your **less advanced** students to read the vocabulary words aloud so that you can be sure they can pronounce them.

Objectives

1. To recognize stream of consciousness
2. To evaluate an author's purpose
3. To use stream of consciousness in writing

Teaching Portfolio: Support Material

Teacher Backup, p. 000

Vocabulary Check, p. 00

Usage and Mechanics Worksheet, p. 00

Analyzing Literature Worksheet, p. 00

Critical Thinking and Reading Worksheet, p. 00

Language Worksheet, p. 00

Selection Test, p. 00

Motivation for Reading Virginia Woolf says, "Examine for a moment an ordinary mind on an ordinary day. The mind receives a myriad of impressions—trivial, fantastic, evanescent, or engraved with the sharpness of steel. From all sides they come, an incessant shower of innumerable atoms; and as they fall . . . they shape themselves." "The Lady in the Looking Glass" takes place in one short period of time. Ask the students to look for the way this story resembles a shower of impressions, both trivial and sharp.

Master Teacher Note Place Art Transparency 14, Cecil Collins's *The Artist and His Daemon,* on the overhead projector. Encourage the class to discuss modernism—the use of new forms and styles—in art and literature, with Collins's painting as representative examples. Do your students like such innovative works? What can they say in favor of, or against, them? Why might writers and painters feel the need to turn from more traditional forms and styles?

Thematic Idea Like Conrad, in "The Lagoon," p. 962, Saki, in "The Schartz-Metterklume Method," p. 974 and Forster, in "The Helping Hand," p. 980, Woolf wished to strip away society's illusion to penetrate the dark reality underneath. Like Forster, Woolf wished to substitute a totally different technique of understanding character, but Woolf's stream-of-consciousness is far more radical than Forster's indirect characterization, and unlike Saki, Conrad, or Forster, Woolf's reality is emotionally colored.

The Lady in the Looking Glass

A Reflection

Virginia Woolf

1 People should not leave looking glasses hanging in their rooms any more than they should leave open checkbooks or letters confessing some hideous crime. One could not help looking, that summer afternoon, in the long glass that hung outside in the hall. Chance had so arranged it. From the depths of the sofa in the drawing room one could see reflected in the Italian glass not only the marble-topped table opposite, but a stretch of the garden beyond. One could see a long grass path leading between banks of tall flowers until, slicing off an angle, the gold rim cut it off.

2 The house was empty, and one felt, since one was the only person in the drawing room, like one of those naturalists who, covered with grass and leaves, lie watching the shyest animals—badgers, otters, kingfishers—moving about freely, themselves unseen. The room that afternoon was full of such shy creatures, lights and shadows, curtains blowing, petals falling—things that never happen, so it seems, if someone is looking. The quiet old country room with its rugs and stone chimney pieces, its sunken bookcases and red and gold lacquer cabinets, was full of such nocturnal creatures. They came pirouetting across the floor, stepping delicately with high-lifted feet and spread tails and pecking allusive beaks as if they had been cranes or flocks of elegant flamingoes whose pink was faded, or peacocks whose trains were veiled with silver. And there were obscure flushes and darkening too, as if a cuttlefish had suddenly suffused the air with purple; and the room had 3 its passions and rages and envies and sorrows coming over it and clouding it, like a human being. Nothing stayed the same for 4 two seconds together.

But, outside, the looking glass reflected the hall table, the sunflowers, the garden path so accurately and so fixedly that they seemed held there in their reality unescapably. It was a strange contrast—all changing here, all stillness there. One could not help looking from one to the other. Meanwhile, 5 since all the doors and windows were open in the heat, there was a perpetual sighing and ceasing sound, the voice of the transient and the perishing, it seemed, coming and going like human breath, while in the looking glass things had ceased to breathe and lay still in the trance of immortality.

Half an hour ago the mistress of the house, Isabella Tyson, had gone down the grass path in her thin summer dress, carrying a basket, and had vanished, sliced off by the gilt rim of the looking glass. She had gone presumably into the lower garden to pick flowers; or as it seemed more natural to

Purpose-Setting Question To what extent does Virginia Woolf eliminate objective description and dialogue in "The Lady in the Looking Glass"?

1 **Discussion** How is a looking glass like a "confession of crime," or an open checkbook?

2 **Literary Focus** In what way is the observer like a naturalist? How does this reference to a naturalist's notes relate to or indirectly characterize stream of consciousness?

3 **Clarification** A cuttlefish is a mollusk that releases a poisonous fluid.

4 **Enrichment** Virginia Woolf used many techniques of poetry to enrich her prose. In this passage she personifies the room giving it access to human emotions. The rapidly changing moods of Isabella's room mirror the rapidly changing states of the human unconscious. Thus even the room seems to have an interior dialogue or stream of consciousness in "The Lady in the Looking Glass."

5 **Discussion** What is real and what is not real in the looking glass? How does the looking glass first function?

THE GARDEN OF LOVE
Walter Richard Sickert
The Fitzwilliam Museum, Cambridge

Humanities Note

Fine art, *The Garden of Love* by Walter Richard Sickert. Sickert (1860–1942) was born in Munich, Germany, but became a British subject. His father, a painter, tried to discourage him from art in favor of a more financially rewarding career, to no avail. Sickert studied at the Slade School of Fine Art in London, but, discouraged by the strict academic atmosphere, he left to work and study at the studio of James McNeill Whistler. Later, in Paris, he studied with the French Impressionist Edgar Degas. Sickert's greatest contribution to British art was his willingness to experiment with, defend, and teach new ideas in art.

The art of Walter Sickert can be described as Impressionistic. *The Garden of Love* exemplifies his style. This study of sunlight on a garden in contrast to a cool interior shows an Impressionist's interest in the effects of different types of light on colors.

You might ask the following questions:

1. How does this garden in the painting compare with the garden in the story?
2. Walter Sickert is notable for exploring new methods and subjects of painting. How does this reputation compare with Virginia Woolf's?

6 Reading Strategy Summarize what has occurred. Why is the observer alone in the room?

7 Discussion What does the imagery in this first impression of Isabella convey?

8 Discussion What does the narrator object to in the comparison of Isabella to the fantastic flower? Can this be seen as social concern about the treatment of women?

9 Discussion Does this pile of facts conflict with stream of consciousness? Is this pile up of facts meant as irony?

10 Discussion According to the observer, what types of things must be in the letters?

suppose, to pick something light and fantastic and leafy and trailing, traveler's-joy, or
6 one of those elegant sprays of convolvulus that twine round ugly walls and burst here and there into white and violet blossoms. She suggested the fantastic and the tremulous convolvulus rather than the upright
7 aster, the starched zinnia, or her own burning roses alight like lamps on the straight posts of their rose trees. The comparison showed how very little, after all these years, one knew about her; for it is impossible that
8 any woman of flesh and blood of fifty-five or sixty should be really a wreath or a tendril. Such comparisons are worse than idle and superficial—they are cruel even, for they come like the convolvulus itself trembling between one's eyes and the truth. There must be truth; there must be a wall. Yet it was strange that after knowing her all these years one could not say what the truth about Isabella was; one still made up phrases like this about convolvulus and traveler's joy. As for facts, it was a fact that she was a spinster; that she was rich; that she had bought this house and collected with her own hands—often in the most obscure corners of the world and at great risk from poisonous stings and Oriental diseases—the rugs, the chairs, the cabinets which now lived their nocturnal life before one's eyes. Sometimes it seemed as if they knew more about her than we, who sat on them, wrote at them, and trod on them so carefully, were allowed to know. In each of these cabinets were many little drawers, and each almost cer-
9 tainly held letters, tied with bows of ribbon, sprinkled with sticks of lavender or rose leaves. For it was another fact—if facts were what one wanted—that Isabella had known many people, had had many friends; and thus if one had the audacity to open a drawer and read her letters, one would find the traces of many agitations, of appointments to meet, of upbraidings for not having met, long letters of intimacy and affection, violent letters of jealousy and reproach, terrible final words of parting—for all those interviews and assignations had led to nothing—that is, she had never married, and yet, judging from the masklike indifference of her face, she had gone through twenty times more of passion and experience than those whose loves are trumpeted forth for all the world to hear. Under the stress of thinking about Isabella, her room became more shadowy and symbolic; the corners seemed darker, the legs of chairs and tables more spindly and hieroglyphic.

Suddenly these reflections were ended violently and yet without a sound. A large black form loomed into the looking glass; blotted out everything, strewed the table with a packet of marble tablets veined with pink and gray, and was gone. But the picture was entirely altered. For the moment it was unrecognizable and irrational and entirely out of focus. One could not relate these tablets to any human purpose. And then by degrees some logical process set to work on them and began ordering and arranging them and bringing them into the fold of common experience. One realized at last that they were merely letters. The man had brought the post.

There they lay on the marble-topped table, all dripping with light and color at first and crude and unabsorbed. And then it was strange to see how they were drawn in and arranged and composed and made part of the picture and granted that stillness and immortality which the looking glass conferred. They lay there invested with a new reality and significance and with a greater heaviness, too, as if it would have needed a chisel to dislodge them from the table. And, whether it was fancy or not, they seemed to have become not merely a handful of casual letters but to be tablets graven with eternal truth—if one could read them, one would 10
know everything there was to be known about Isabella, yes, and about life, too. The pages inside those marble-looking envelopes must be cut deep and scored thick with meaning. Isabella would come in, and take them, one by one, very slowly, and

open them, and read them carefully word by word, and then with a profound sigh of comprehension, as if she had seen to the bottom of everything, she would tear the envelopes to little bits and tie the letters together and lock the cabinet drawer in her determination to conceal what she did not wish to be known.

The thought served as a challenge. Isabella did not wish to be known—but she should no longer escape. It was absurd, it was monstrous. If she concealed so much and knew so much one must prize her open with the first tool that came to hand—the
11 imagination. One must fix one's mind upon her at that very moment. One must fasten her down there. One must refuse to be put off any longer with sayings and doings such as the moment brought forth—with dinners and visits and polite conversations. One must put oneself in her shoes. If one took the phrase literally, it was easy to see the shoes in which she stood, down in the lower garden, at this moment. They were very narrow and long and fashionable—they were made of the softest and most flexible leather. Like everything she wore, they were exquisite. And she would be standing under the high hedge in the lower part of the garden, raising the scissors that were tied to her waist to cut some dead flower, some overgrown branch. The sun would beat down on her face, into her eyes; but no, at the critical moment a veil of cloud covered the sun, making the expression of her eyes doubtful—was it mocking or tender, brilliant or dull? One could only see the indeterminate outline of her rather faded, fine face looking at the sky. She was thinking, perhaps, that she must order a new net for the strawberries; that she must send flowers to Johnson's widow; that it was time
12 she drove over to see the Hippesleys in their new house. Those were the things she talked about at dinner certainly. But one was tired of the things that she talked about at dinner. It was her profounder state of being that one wanted to catch and turn to words, the state that is to the mind what breathing is to the body, what one calls happiness or unhappiness. At the mention of those words it became obvious, surely, that she must be happy. She was rich; she was distinguished; she had many friends;
13 she traveled—she bought rugs in Turkey and blue pots in Persia. Avenues of pleasure radiated this way and that from where she stood with her scissors raised to cut the trembling branches while the lacy clouds veiled her face.

Here with a quick movement of her scissors she snipped the spray of traveler's joy and it fell to the ground. As it fell, surely some light came in too, surely one could penetrate a little farther into her being. Her mind then was filled with tenderness and regret. . . . To cut an overgrown branch sad-
14 dened her because it had once lived, and life was dear to her. Yes, and at the same time the fall of the branch would suggest to her how she must die herself and all the futility and evanescence of things. And then again quickly catching this thought up, with her instant good sense, she thought life had treated her well; even if fall she must, it was to lie on the earth and molder sweetly into the roots of violets. So she stood thinking. Without making any thought precise—for she was one of those reticent people whose minds hold their thoughts enmeshed in clouds of silence—she was filled with thoughts. Her mind was like her room, in which lights advanced and retreated, came pirouetting and stepping delicately, spread their tails, pecked their way; and then
15 her whole being was suffused, like the room again, with a cloud of some profound knowledge, some unspoken regret, and then she was full of locked drawers, stuffed with letters, like her cabinets. To talk of "prizing her open" as if she were an oyster, to use any but the finest and subtlest and most pliable tools upon her was
16 impious and absurd. One must imagine—here was she in the looking glass. It made one start.

11 **Literary Focus** Can you relate this passage to the technique of stream of consciousness?

12 **Clarification** "Interior monologue" has also been used to describe the inner movement of consciousness in a character's mind. What the narrator believes Isabella is thinking provides an indirect characterization of the narrator himself and an ironical comment on stream of consciousness.

13 **Discussion** Why does the narrator assume Isabella is happy?

14 **Literary Focus** What conflicting "thoughts" does Miss Tyson have about cutting the spray of traveler's joy? Are those her thoughts or the narrator's? In what way is this an example of stream of consciousness?

15 **Enrichment** In comparing Isabella's mind to the room, Woolf illustrates stream of consciousness. Virginia Woolf helped to create a revolution when she used stream of consciousness, or described changing thoughts, impressions, memories, and emotions without logical syntax or sequence. How much conventional dialogue takes place in this story? What does this say about the narrator?

16 **Critical Thinking and Reading** What does this passage imply about Woolf and the relationship of stream of consciousness to materialism or psychological realism?

17 Discussion What is ironic in the imagery of Isabella within the still life in the mirror?

18 Discussion How does this passage tie in with the earlier reference to a naturalist? Does this picture seem overly judgmental or harshly realistic in contrast to the narrator's early romantic fantasies?

19 Discussion What is the irony in the letters? What is the greatest irony in the Isabella of the observer's imagination and her reality?

She was so far off at first that one could not see her clearly. She came lingering and pausing, here straightening a rose, there lifting a pink to smell it, but she never stopped; and all the time she became larger and larger in the looking glass, more and more completely the person into whose mind one had been trying to penetrate. One verified her by degrees—fitted the qualities one had discovered into this visible body. There were her gray-green dress, and her long shoes, her basket, and something sparkling at her throat. She came so gradually that she did not seem to derange the pattern in the glass, but only to bring in some new element which gently moved and altered the 17 other objects as if asking them, courteously, to make room for her. And the letters and the table and the grass walk and the sunflowers which had been waiting in the looking glass separated and opened out so that she might be received among them. At last there she was, in the hall. She stopped dead. She stood by the table. She stood perfectly still. At once the looking glass began to pour over her a light that seemed to fix her; that 18 seemed like some acid to bite off the unessential and superficial and to leave only the truth. It was an enthralling spectacle. Everything dropped from her—clouds, dress, basket, diamond—all that one had called the creeper and convolvulus. Here was the hard wall beneath. Here was the woman herself. She stood naked in that pitiless light. And there was nothing. Isabella was perfectly empty. She had no 19 thoughts. She had no friends. She cared for nobody. As for her letters, they were all bills. Look, as she stood there, old and angular, veined and lined, with her high nose and her wrinkled neck, she did not even trouble to open them.

People should not leave looking glasses hanging in their rooms.

THINKING ABOUT THE SELECTION

Recalling

1. Where does the story take place?
2. (a) What has Isabella Tyson gone to do? (b) What arrives while she is out?
3. How does Isabella feel about cutting the flower?
4. What do the letters turn out to be?

Interpreting

5. Who do you think is the narrator of the story? Explain your answer.
6. (a) Based on the information provided, how would you describe Isabella? (b) How would you summarize what the narrator wishes to "prize" from her?
7. The last sentence of the story parrots the first sentence. What is the effect of this repetition, if you consider it together with the story's title and subtitle?
8. What, in your view, is the theme of the story?

Applying

9. Have you ever sought to know what made another person, perhaps a celebrity, "tick" and been disappointed by what you discovered? Give details of your experience and discuss the general truth it suggests.

ANALYZING LITERATURE

Recognizing Stream of Consciousness

Stream of consciousness is a literary technique that attempts to reproduce a character's thought processes as they might naturally occur

Answers

ANSWERS TO THINKING ABOUT THE SELECTION

Recalling

1. The story takes place in a quiet old country room.
2. (a) Isabella Tyson has gone out to the garden to cut flowers. (b) The mail arrives while she is out.
3. Cutting flowers makes Isabella feel sad because it reminds her of life's mortality.
4. The letters turn out to be bills.

Interpreting

5. Suggested response: The narrator sounds like a superficial friend or a writer who has researched many facts about Isabella. Certainly it is someone very well acquainted with the superficial aspects of Isabella's life since the narrator knows that she is a rich spinster who owns her own house with fabulous objects she has collected in travels all over the world. It is also obvious that the narrator is not a close family member or a friend, with a real understanding of Isabella's psyche or her life.
6. (a) Suggested response: Isabella is an elderly, rich, spinster living in lonely unhappy isolation in a quiet old country house. (b) Suggested response: The narrator wishes to "prize" the inner truth or psychological reality of Isabella.
7. The last sentence reaffirms the dangers of mirrors, which are compared to "confessions" of crime in the first sentence and a "reflection" in the subtitle. Confession and reflection indicate personal revelation or the idea of the looking glass as a vehicle of exposure of our private selves. The repetition emphasizes the irony because it simultaneously reflects Isabella, the narrator, and the reader. Thus, the mirror, like literature reflects the eye and imagination of the person looking into it.
8. Suggested response: The theme seems to be the discrepancy between inner reality and superficiality. The story also suggests the isolation of the individual and the need for personal relationships or human communion.

within the human mind. Often fragmented and seemingly unconnected, the thoughts, emotions, and memories that make up a stream-of-consciousness narrative paint a telling portrait of the character when seen from a larger perspective.

Reread carefully the paragraph of the story that begins, "Here with a quick movement of her scissors . . ." (page 991). Then answer the following questions.

1. If one traces her thought patterns from the cutting of the flower through the mention of the "locked drawers" of her mind, how many stages of thought can Isabella be seen to go through? What details of her personality are revealed in this paragraph?
2. What comment on her own technique of stream of consciousness does the author seem to be making in this paragraph?
3. What conclusion about Isabella does the narrator draw from this imaginative examination of Isabella's thoughts?

CRITICAL THINKING AND READING

Evaluating an Author's Purpose

Usually, behind a work of literature is a **purpose,** or intention, that was uppermost in the author's mind when he or she sat down to write. The purpose of some stories, for example, is to impart an understanding about people or life in general, while the purpose of others is merely to entertain. For Virginia Woolf, one ever-present purpose in her writing was to get beyond what she termed "the tyranny of plot"—that is, the requirement of "stylizing" a character's words and actions in accordance with the rules of traditional storytelling.

Give a short synopsis, or summary, of the "plot" implied in "The Lady in the Looking Glass." Then find evidence of the following aspects of Woolf's stream-of-consciousness technique in the story, and tell how they helped her achieve her purpose.

1. The use of random details to develop a character
2. The repetition of details of setting
3. The repetition of specific images, words, and phrases

THINKING AND WRITING

Using Stream-of-Consciousness

Use the list of possessions you developed earlier to tell a story about the occupant of the room. Use a stream-of-consciousness approach, modeling your story on Woolf's. Before you begin to write, map out what happens to the main character, using the time and manner in which the various objects were acquired as a guideline. When you revise make sure you capture the intermingling of conscious thought and memory. Be prepared to share your story with your class.

(Answers begin on p. 992.)

Applying

9. Answers will differ. First appearances are deceptive. People are often quite different than they first appear; when you follow a person's inner thoughts, dreams, beliefs, and fears you come closer to the "reality" of knowing that person.

Challenge What symbolizes the isolation of Isabella in contrast to her gregarious social appearance?

ANSWERS TO ANALYZING LITERATURE

1. Suggested Response: There seem to be approximately four stages here. Isabella feels regret for cutting away the life of the flower because she thinks of life's preciousness. Then she thinks about her own death and life's brevity and its futility. Next she accepts death because she reminds herself that life has treated her well. Isabella reveals that she is sensitive to the flowers, and philosophical or meditative at this point.
2. Woolf shows that the acts that we perform are only superficial outlines of ourselves as deep multidimensional thinking and feeling people. Thus she indicates that the natural thoughts, emotions, and memories which are reproduced in stream-of-consciousness narrative are the only approach to showing a real portrait of a person or character.
3. The narrator concludes that Isabella is reticent but filled with deep feelings, inner thoughts, hidden secrets, and imaginative memories.

ANSWERS TO CRITICAL THINKING AND READING

Suggested response: There is very little plot in the story since Virginia Woolf wished to move away from plot toward a stream-of-consciousness technique.

Isabella has disappeared into the garden; the observer's conception of her is suggested by her delightful home and her luxuriant garden; her wealth implies happiness and success; her silence implies mystery and passion, and the bundle of letters flung on the marble table bear witness to this. But when Isabella reappears in the mirror; the light reveals a different truth of loneliness, indifference, emptiness, and age; the letters are only bills.

1. The random details helped Woolf develop her characters as lifelike. In real life only small illuminations occur and these cumulatively illuminate people to us.
2. The repetition and diffused quality of the images of the setting are lifelike and mirror real life's fragmentation.
3. Woolf repeats images, specific words and phrases into an artistic or musical repetition of impressions which form a collage of Isabella.

THINKING AND WRITING

Publishing Student Writing Read aloud the students' stream-of-consciousness stories and discuss the degree of indirect characterization achieved.

More About the Author D. H. Lawrence was an influential leader in the movement of British literature into the world of modern interests, techniques, and honesty.

Because he was born into the working class, Lawrence was disconnected from the typical writers of the early twentieth century. His parents quarrelled continuously because they were ill-suited to each other. Lawrence's elopement with an older German woman reinforced his sense of isolation; their frequent travels separated him further from the British puritanism and snobbery which he bitterly disliked. Lawrence liked to consider himself a product of a "Mediterranean sensibility" because he looked back to more primitive societies for a wholeness and balance that he felt his contemporary industrial England had lost. As he traveled in search of a utopia, Lawrence studied psychoanalysis and wrote travel books as well as poetry. He had a stormy temperament and his life with his wife had many accusations and break-ups.

D. H. LAWRENCE

1885–1930

D. H. Lawrence occupies a unique position among the leading Modernist writers of the gèneration that came of age before the outbreak of the First World War. The originality of his literary achievements was partly clouded by the explosive controversy attached to his name during his lifetime and for some years after. As with Shelley and Byron before him, the controversy that swirled around Lawrence touched on several points, not the least of which were his unorthodox opinions on politics, society, and morality.

David Herbert Lawrence was born near Nottingham in the English Midlands, the son of a miner. His childhood was marked by poverty, illness, constant bickering between his parents, and his mother's driving ambition to make something of her son. After attending local schools, the young Lawrence spent several years as a teacher before turning to writing as a livelihood.

As a writer Lawrence was deeply influenced by the pioneering psychological theories of Sigmund Freud and by the philosophy of Friedrich Nietzsche. He restlessly searched and researched their writings, seeking confirmation of the underlying moral rightness of his strongest convictions—that the industrial social order was unjust, that open expression of sexuality was healthy, and that human beings could find true fulfillment only by living in harmony with nature.

In 1913, shortly before eloping to Germany with a woman several years older than himself, Lawrence published his first major novel, *Sons and Lovers*—a thinly disguised autobiographical account of his childhood and adolescent years. During World War I, he returned with his wife to England where he published his next major work, *The Rainbow* (1915). His frank treatment of sexuality in the book caused it to be declared obscene.

At the end of the war, the Lawrences left England for extended travels in Italy, Ceylon, Australia, Mexico, and the United States. Lawrence used many of these locales in his fiction: *Kangaroo* (1923), for example, is set in Australia; and *The Plumed Serpent* (1926) is steeped in the mythology of ancient Mexico. It was during his prolonged absence from England that Lawrence found a publisher for one of his greatest novels, *Women in Love* (1921). Ill from tuberculosis, Lawrence completed his last novel, *Lady Chatterley's Lover* (1928), while living in Italy.

In the half century since his death, society's views on Lawrence's writings have changed profoundly. Today, his fiction is almost universally admired for its vivid settings, fine craftsmanship, and psychological insight.

GUIDE FOR READING

The Rocking-Horse Winner

The Writer's Technique

Omniscient Narration. Omniscient narration is another name for the third-person point of view. Unlike the first-person narrator, who doubles as a character, the third-person narrator is strictly an observer who reports the events of the story from a position beyond or outside them. Because of this remote vantage point, the third-person narrator is said to be omniscient, or "all-knowing," privileged with the ability to see into the minds of the characters and to know what fate holds in store for them. While such a narrator is bound by literary convention to remain neutral—is prohibited, that is, from "meddling" in the affairs of the characters—the particular style of the narration often adds another, and sometimes colorful, dimension to the story. In "The Rocking-Horse Winner," for example, D. H. Lawrence adopts a third-person narrative style reminiscent of that used in fairy tales—a choice that is especially well-suited to the curious proceedings in the story.

Look For

As you read "The Rocking-Horse Winner," look for the effect the narrative style has on your understanding of what makes the various characters behave as they do.

Writing

Think about people who believe in such things as superstitions, fortune tellers, and the like. List the qualities that these people have in common. Then attempt to develop a "profile" of the believer in what many others regard as coincidence or chance.

Vocabulary

Knowing the following words will help you as you read "The Rocking-Horse Winner."

discreet (dis krēt′) *adj.*: Wise; prudent (p. 996)
brazening (brā′ z'n iŋ) *v.*: Daring boldly or shamelessly (p. 997)
careered (kə rird′) *v.*: Moved swiftly forward (p. 997)
uncanny (un kan′ ē) *adj.*: Mysterious; hard to explain (p. 1002)
remonstrated (ri män′ strāt id) *v.*: Objected strongly (p. 1003)

Literary Focus The omniscient narrator knows everything. He can enter at will into the mind of any character and tell the reader what the character is thinking. He can move physically and mentally at will. He can be in the present and the past. Using the third-person provides a comfortable form for modern writers because in a real sense the author does "know it all." The flexibility of omniscient narration eliminates limitations since the omniscient narrator can tell us just what the story demands. Although natural to the author, omniscience does not reflect life. We never know everything about other people.

Look For The narrative style suggests a fable or a fairy tale. A fable is a short story designed to convey some useful moral lesson, but often carrying with it associations of the marvelous or mythical. A fairy tale is a simple narrative about enchantment involving magical beings like ogres, witches, and magicians. It is generally told for the amusement of children rather than for their education. Ask your students to decide if "The Rocking-Horse Winner" resembles a fable or a fairy tale.

Writing Before students write, you might engage them in a discussion of the difference between superstition and fate.

Vocabulary Ask the students to discuss the word *uncanny* in relation to fairy tales and ghost stories. Ask them to discuss *brazening* and *discreet* as antonyms, and ask them to provide synonyms for *brazening* and *discreet.* Ask your **more advanced** students to analyze *careered* in terms of its two meanings. Ask them to think about the irony of *careered* as "running at full speed on a course for racing," and "as a profession demanding special preparation," as they read "The Rocking-Horse Winner."

Objectives

1. To understand omniscient narration
2. To understand differences among synonyms
3. To tell the story from a different point of view

Teaching Portfolio: Support Material

Teacher Backup, p. 000

Vocabulary Check, p. 00

Usage and Mechanics Worksheet, p. 00

Analyzing Literature Worksheet, p. 00

Critical Thinking and Reading Worksheet, p. 00

Language Worksheet, p. 00

Selection Test, p. 00

The Rocking-Horse Winner

D. H. Lawrence

There was a woman who was beautiful,
1 who started with all the advantages, yet she
had no luck. She married for love, and the love turned to dust. She had bonny children, yet she felt they had been thrust upon her, and she could not love them. They looked at her coldly, as if they were finding fault with her. And hurriedly she felt she must cover up some fault in herself. Yet what it was that she must cover up she never knew. Nevertheless, when her children were present, she always felt the center of her heart go hard. This troubled her, and in her manner she was all the more gentle and anxious for her children, as if she loved them very much. Only she herself knew that at the
2 center of her heart was a hard little place
that could not feel love, no, not for anybody. Everybody else said of her: "She is such a good mother. She adores her children." Only she herself, and her children themselves, knew it was not so. They read it in each other's eyes.

There were a boy and two little girls. They lived in a pleasant house, with a garden, and they had discreet servants, and felt themselves superior to anyone in the neighborhood.

Although they lived in style, they felt always an anxiety in the house. There was never enough money. The mother had a small income, and the father had a small income, but not nearly enough for the social position which they had to keep up. The father went into town to some office. But though he had good prospects, these prospects never materialized. There was always the grinding sense of the shortage of money, though the style was always kept up.

At last the mother said, "I will see if *I* can't make something." But she did not know where to begin. She racked her brains, and tried this thing and the other, but could not find anything successful. The failure made deep lines come into her face. Her children were growing up, they would have to go to school. There must be more money, there must be more money. The father, who was always very handsome and expensive in his tastes, seemed as if he never *would* be able to do anything worth doing. And the mother, who had a great belief in herself, did not succeed any better, and her tastes were just as expensive.

And so the house came to be haunted by
the unspoken phrase: *There must be more* 3
money! There must be more money! The children could hear it all the time, though nobody said it aloud. They heard it at Christmas, when the expensive and splendid toys filled the nursery. Behind the shining modern rocking horse, behind the smart doll's house, a voice would start whispering: "There *must* be more money! There *must* be more money!" And the children would stop playing, to listen for a moment. They would look into each other's eyes to see if they had all heard. And each one saw in the eyes of the other two that they too had heard. "There *must* be more money! There *must* be more money!"

It came whispering from the springs of

Motivation for Reading *Fate,* like *destiny,* suggests something inevitable without implying good or evil. *Lot* as in lottery or betting suggests the operation of blind chance. Thus, normally betting at a race track symbolizes a gamble on blind chance. But *fate* often means ruin, disaster, and death. There were three goddesses who were supposed to determine the course of human life. *Clotho,* (the Spinner) who spins life's thread; *Lachesis* (Dispenser of Lots), who determines the length; and *Atropos* (Inflexible), who cuts it off. Thus Greek tragedy deals with man's running into his predetermined ruin.

Master Teacher Note Lawrence considered modern man as rootless and cut off from his necessary primitive source of vitality. Lawrence wrote in a letter, "It is our being cut off that is our ailment, and out of this ailment everything bad arises . . . Myself, I suffer badly from being so cut off. But, what is one to do? . . . One has no real human relations—that is so devastating." Alienated from his own country, Lawrence returned only as a visitor.

Lawrence believed literature should "reveal the most secret places of life." What secrets does "The Rocking-Horse Winner" reveal?

Purpose-Setting Question What causes Paul's obsession?

1 **Discussion** How does this opening resemble the conventional opening of a fairy tale, such as "The Sleeping Beauty"?

2 **Critical Reading and Thinking** How do the children know their mother doesn't love them?

3 **Discussion** What does the whispering represent symbolically? Where else do you find haunted houses?

the still-swaying rocking horse, and even the horse, bending his wooden, champing head, heard it. The big doll, sitting so pink and smirking in her new pram,[1] could hear it quite plainly, and seemed to be smirking
4 all the more self-consciously because of it. The foolish puppy, too, that took the place of the teddy bear, he was looking so extraordinarily foolish for no other reason but that he heard the secret whisper all over the house: "There *must* be more money."

Yet nobody ever said it aloud. The whisper was everywhere, and therefore no one spoke it. Just as no one ever says: "We are breathing!" in spite of the fact that breath is coming and going all the time.

"Mother!" said the boy Paul one day. "Why don't we keep a car of our own? Why do we always use uncle's, or else a taxi?"

"Because we're the poor members of the family," said the mother.

"But why *are* we, mother?"

"Well—I suppose," she said slowly and bitterly, "it's because your father has no luck."

The boy was silent for some time.

"Is luck money, mother?" he asked, rather timidly.

"No, Paul! Not quite. It's what causes you to have money."

"Oh!" said Paul vaguely. "I thought when Uncle Oscar said *filthy lucker,* it meant money."

"Filthy lucre does mean money," said the mother. "But it's lucre, not luck."

"Oh!" said the boy. "Then what *is* luck, mother?"

"It's what causes you to have money. If you're lucky you have money. That's why it's better to be born lucky than rich. If
5 you're rich, you may lose your money. But if you're lucky, you will always get more money."

"Oh! Will you! And is father not lucky?"

"Very unlucky, I should say," she said bitterly.

1. **pram:** Baby carriage.

The boy watched her with unsure eyes.

"Why?" he asked.

"I don't know. Nobody ever knows why one person is lucky and another unlucky."

"Don't they? Nobody at all? Does *nobody* know?"

"Perhaps God! But He never tells."

"He ought to, then. And aren't you lucky either, mother?"

"I can't be, if I married an unlucky husband."

"But by yourself, aren't you?"

"I used to think I was, before I married. Now I think I am very unlucky indeed."

"Why?"

"Well—never mind! Perhaps I'm not really," she said.

The child looked at her, to see if she meant it. But he saw, by the lines of her mouth, that she was only trying to hide something from him.

"Well, anyhow," he said stoutly, "I'm a lucky person."

"Why?" said his mother, with a sudden laugh.

He stared at her. He didn't even know 6
why he had said it.

"God told me," he asserted, brazening it out.

"I hope He did, dear!" she said, again with a laugh, but rather bitter.

"He did, mother!"

"Excellent!" said the mother, using one of her husband's exclamations.

The boy saw she did not believe him; or rather, that she paid no attention to his assertion. This angered him somewhere, and made him want to compel her attention.

He went off by himself, vaguely, in a childish way, seeking for the clue to "luck." Absorbed, taking no heed of other people, he went about with a sort of stealth, seeking inwardly for luck. He wanted luck, he wanted it, he wanted it. When the two girls were 7
playing dolls, in the nursery, he would sit on his big rocking horse, charging madly into space, with a frenzy that made the little girls peer at him uneasily. Wildly the horse ca-

4 Discussion Where does the secret whisper originate?

5 Discussion How does Paul's mother define "luck?"

6 Literary Focus What aspect of third-person narration is conveyed by this encounter?

7 Critical Reading and Thinking What can we infer from Paul's frenzied riding? Why does Paul want luck?

997

8 **Enrichment** Uncle Oscar is always joking, and he supplies the whip for the rocking horse and the incentive for Paul to keep wagering. Uncle Oscar implies a reference to Oscar Wilde who published a volume of fairy tales written for his sons in 1888, called *The Happy Prince*. Wilde prefaced his Gothic melodrama, *The Picture of Dorian Gray*, with "there is no such thing as a moral or immoral book." The character of Uncle Oscar includes Wilde's individualism and his lack of morality. The "changeable" name of Paul's horse suggests a reference to Wilde's pen name, which was "Speranza." Wilde firmly believed that art must stand apart from life, and Uncle Oscar stays emotionally aloof like Lawrence's omniscient narrator in this story.

9 **Critical Thinking and Reading** What can you infer about Bassett?

reered, the waving dark hair of the boy tossed, his eyes had a strange glare in them. The little girls dared not speak to him.

When he had ridden to the end of his mad little journey, he climbed down and stood in front of his rocking horse, staring fixedly into its lowered face. Its red mouth was slightly open, its big eye was wide and glassy bright.

"Now!" he would silently command the snorting steed. "Now take me to where there is luck! Now take me!"

And he would slash the horse on the neck with the little whip he had asked Uncle Oscar for. He *knew* the horse could take him to where there was luck, if only he forced it. So he would mount again, and start on his furious ride, hoping at last to get there. He knew he could get there.

"You'll break your horse, Paul!" said the nurse.

"He's always riding like that! I wish he'd leave off!" said his elder sister Joan.

But he only glared down on them in silence. Nurse gave him up. She could make nothing of him. Anyhow he was growing beyond her.

One day his mother and his Uncle Oscar came in when he was on one of his furious rides. He did not speak to them.

"Hallo! you young jockey! Riding a winner?" said his uncle.

"Aren't you growing too big for a rocking horse? You're not a very little boy any longer, you know," said his mother.

But Paul only gave a blue glare from his big, rather close-set eyes. He would speak to nobody when he was in full tilt. His mother watched him with an anxious expression on her face.

At last he suddenly stopped forcing his horse into the mechanical gallop, and slid down.

"Well, I got there!" he announced fiercely, his blue eyes still flaring, and his sturdy long legs straddling apart.

"Where did you get to?" asked his mother.

"Where I wanted to go to," he flared back at her.

"That's right, son!" said Uncle Oscar. "Don't you stop till you get there. What's the horse's name?"

"He doesn't have a name," said the boy. 8

"Gets on without all right?" asked the uncle.

"Well, he has different names. He was called Sansovino last week."

"Sansovino, eh? Won the Ascot.[2] How did you know his name?"

"He always talks about horse races with Bassett," said Joan.

The uncle was delighted to find that his small nephew was posted with all the racing news. Bassett, the young gardener who had been wounded in the left foot in the war, and had got his present job through Oscar Cresswell, whose batman[3] he had been, was a perfect blade of the "turf."[4] He lived in the racing events, and the small boy lived with him.

Oscar Cresswell got it all from Bassett.

"Master Paul comes and asks me, so I 9
can't do more than tell him, sir," said Bassett, his face terribly serious, as if he were speaking of religious matters.

"And does he ever put anything on a horse he fancies?"

"Well—I don't want to give him away—he's a young sport, a fine sport, sir. Would you mind asking him yourself? He sort of takes a pleasure in it, and perhaps he'd feel I was giving him away, sir, if you don't mind."

Bassett was serious as a church.

The uncle went back to his nephew, and took him off for a ride in the car.

"Say, Paul, old man, do you ever put anything on a horse?" the uncle asked.

The boy watched the handsome man closely.

"Why, do you think I oughtn't to?" he parried.

---

2. Ascot: A major English horse race.
3. batman: A British military officer's orderly.
4. blade . . . "turf": Horse-racing fan.

"Not a bit of it! I thought perhaps you might give me a tip for the Lincoln."[5]

The car sped on into the country, going down to Uncle Oscar's place in Hampshire.

"Honor bright?" said the nephew.

"Honor bright, son!" said the uncle.

"Well, then, Daffodil."

"Daffodil! I doubt it, sonny. What about Mirza?"

"I only know the winner," said the boy. "That's Daffodil!"

"Daffodil, eh?"

There was a pause. Daffodil was an obscure horse comparatively.

"Uncle!"

"Yes, son?"

"You won't let it go any further, will you? I promised Bassett."

"Bassett be hanged, old man! What's he got to do with it?"

"We're partners! We've been partners from the first! Uncle, he lent me my first five shillings, which I lost. I promised him, honor bright, it was only between me and him: only you gave me that ten-shilling note I started winning with, so I thought you were
10 lucky. You won't let it go any further, will you?"

The boy gazed at his uncle from those big, hot, blue eyes, set rather close together. The uncle stirred and laughed uneasily.

"Right you are, son! I'll keep your tip private. Daffodil, eh! How much are you putting on him?"

"All except twenty pounds," said the boy. "I keep that in reserve."

The uncle thought it a good joke.

11 "You keep twenty pounds in reserve, do you, you young romancer? What are you betting, then?"

"I'm betting three hundred," said the boy gravely. "But it's between you and me, Uncle Oscar! Honor bright?"

The uncle burst into a roar of laughter.

"It's between you and me all right, you young Nat Gould,"[6] he said, laughing. "But where's your three hundred?"

"Bassett keeps it for me. We're partners."

"You are, are you! And what is Bassett putting on Daffodil?"

"He won't go quite as high as I do, I expect. Perhaps he'll go a hundred and fifty."

"What, pennies?" laughed the uncle.

"Pounds," said the child, with a surprised look at his uncle. "Bassett keeps a bigger reserve than I do."

Between wonder and amusement, Uncle Oscar was silent. He pursued the matter no further, but he determined to take his nephew with him to the Lincoln races.

"Now, son," he said, "I'm putting twenty on Mirza, and I'll put five for you on any horse you fancy. What's your pick?"

"Daffodil, uncle!"

"No, not the fiver on Daffodil!"

"I should if it was my own fiver," said the child.

"Good! Good! Right you are! A fiver for me and a fiver for you on Daffodil."

The child had never been to a race meeting before, and his eyes were blue fire. He pursed his mouth tight, and watched. A Frenchman just in front had put his money on Lancelot. Wild with excitement, he flayed his arms up and down, yelling *"Lancelot! Lancelot!"* in his French accent.

Daffodil came in first, Lancelot second, Mirza third. The child, flushed and with eyes blazing, was curiously serene. His uncle brought him five five-pound notes: four to one.

"What am I to do with these?" he cried, waving them before the boy's eyes.

"I suppose we'll talk to Bassett," said the boy. "I expect I have fifteen hundred now; and twenty in reserve; and this twenty."

---

5. Lincoln: A major English horse race.

6. Nat Gould: A famous English sportswriter and authority on horse racing.

10 Discussion Why makes Paul think that Uncle Oscar is lucky?

11 Discussion How does Uncle Oscar treat the whole affair?

12 **Discussion** What is Paul's connection with Uncle Oscar and Bassett?

13 **Discussion** How would you describe Bassett's attitude toward racing?

14 **Discussion** When are the bets successful?

His uncle studied him for some moments.

"Look here, son!" he said. "You're not serious about Bassett and that fifteen hundred, are you?"

"Yes, I am. But it's between you and me, uncle! Honor bright!"

"Honor bright all right, son! But I must talk to Bassett."

"If you'd like to be a partner, uncle, with Bassett and me, we could all be partners. Only you'd have to promise, honor bright, uncle, not to let it go beyond us three. Bassett and I are lucky, and you must be lucky,
12 because it was your ten shillings I started winning with. . . ."

Uncle Oscar took both Bassett and Paul into Richmond Park for an afternoon, and there they talked.

"It's like this, you see, sir," Bassett said. "Master Paul would get me talking about racing events, spinning yarns, you know, sir. And he was always keen on knowing if I'd made or if I'd lost. It's about a year since, now, that I put five shillings on Blush of Dawn for him—and we lost. Then the luck turned, with that ten shillings he had from you, that we put on Singhalese. And since that time, it's been pretty steady, all things considering. What do you say, Master Paul?"

"We're all right when we're *sure*," said Paul. "It's when we're not quite sure that we go down."

"Oh, but we're careful then," said Bassett.

13 "But when are you *sure?*" smiled Uncle Oscar.

"It's Master Paul, sir," said Bassett, in a secret, religious voice. "It's as if he had it from heaven. Like Daffodil now, for the Lincoln. That was as sure as eggs."

"Did you put anything on Daffodil?" asked Oscar Cresswell.

"Yes, sir. I made my bit."

"And my nephew?"

Bassett was obstinately silent, looking at Paul.

"I made twelve hundred, didn't I, Bassett? I told uncle I was putting three hundred on Daffodil."

"That's right," said Bassett, nodding.

"But where's the money?" asked the uncle.

"I keep it safe locked up, sir. Master Paul, he can have it any minute he likes to ask for it."

"What, fifteen hundred pounds?"

"And twenty! And *forty*, that is, with the twenty he made on the course."

"It's amazing!" said the uncle.

"If Master Paul offers you to be partners, sir, I would, if I were you; if you'll excuse me," said Bassett.

Oscar Cresswell thought about it.

"I'll see the money," he said.

They drove home again, and sure enough, Bassett came round to the garden house with fifteen hundred pounds in notes. The twenty pounds reserve was left with Joe Glee, in the Turf Commission deposit.

"You see, it's all right, uncle, when I'm *sure!* Then we go strong, for all we're worth. Don't we, Bassett?"

"We do that, Master Paul."

"And when are you sure?" said the uncle, laughing.

"Oh, well, sometimes I'm *absolutely* sure, like about Daffodil," said the boy, "and sometimes I have an idea; and sometimes I haven't even an idea, have I, Bassett? Then we're careful, because we mostly go down."

"You do, do you! And when you're sure,
like about Daffodil, what makes you sure, 14
sonny?"

"Oh, well, I don't know," said the boy uneasily. "I'm sure, you know, uncle; that's all."

"It's as if he had it from heaven, sir," Bassett reiterated.

"I should say so!" said the uncle.

But he became a partner. And when the Leger was coming on, Paul was "sure" about Lively Spark, which was a quite inconsiderable horse. The boy insisted on putting a thousand on the horse, Bassett went for five hundred, and Oscar Cresswell two hundred. Lively Spark came in first, and the betting had been ten to one against him. Paul had made ten thousand.

"You see," he said. "I was absolutely sure of him."

Even Oscar Cresswell had cleared two thousand.

"Look here, son," he said, "this sort of thing makes me nervous."

"It needn't, uncle! Perhaps I shan't be sure again for a long time."

"But what are you going to do with your money?" asked the uncle.

"Of course," said the boy, "I started it for mother. She said she had no luck, because father is unlucky, so I thought if *I* was lucky, it might stop whispering."

"What might stop whispering?"

"Our house! I *hate* our house for whispering."

"What does it whisper?"

15 "Why—why"—the boy fidgeted—"why, I don't know! But it's always short of money, you know, uncle."

"I know it, son, I know it."

"You know people send mother writs, don't you, uncle?"

"I'm afraid I do," said the uncle.

"And then the house whispers like people laughing at you behind your back. It's awful, that is! I thought if I was lucky . . ."

"You might stop it," added the uncle.

The boy watched him with big blue eyes, that had an uncanny cold fire in them, and he said never a word.

"Well then!" said the uncle. "What are we doing?"

"I shouldn't like mother to know I was lucky," said the boy.

"Why not, son?"

"She'd stop me."

"I don't think she would."

"Oh!"—and the boy writhed in an odd way— "I *don't* want her to know, uncle."

"All right, son! We'll manage it without her knowing."

They managed it very easily. Paul, at the other's suggestion, handed over five thousand pounds to his uncle, who deposited it with the family lawyer, who was then to inform Paul's mother that a relative had put five thousand pounds into his hands, which sum was to be paid out a thousand pounds at a time, on the mother's birthday, for the next five years. 16

"So she'll have a birthday present of a thousand pounds for five successive years," said Uncle Oscar. "I hope it won't make it all the harder for her later."

Paul's mother had her birthday in November. The house had been "whispering" worse than ever lately, and even in spite of his luck, Paul could not bear up against it. He was very anxious to see the effect of the birthday letter, telling his mother about the thousand pounds.

When there were no visitors, Paul now took his meals with his parents, as he was beyond the nursery control. His mother went into town nearly every day. She had discovered that she had an odd knack of sketching furs and dress materials, so she worked secretly in the studio of a friend who was the chief "artist" for the leading drapers. She drew the figures of ladies in furs 17
and ladies in silk and sequins for the newspaper advertisements. This young woman artist earned several thousand pounds a year, but Paul's mother only made several hundreds, and she was again dissatisfied. She so wanted to be first in something, and she did not succeed, even in making sketches for drapery advertisements.

She was down to breakfast on the morning of her birthday. Paul watched her face as she read her letters. He knew the lawyer's letter. As his mother read it, her face hardened and became more expressionless. Then a cold, determined look came on her mouth. She hid the letter under the pile of others, and said not a word about it.

"Didn't you have anything nice in the post for your birthday, mother?" said Paul. 18

"Quite moderately nice," she said, her voice cold and absent.

She went away to town without saying more.

But in the afternoon Uncle Oscar appeared. He said Paul's mother had had a

15 Critical Thinking and Reading Why does Paul need luck so desperately? What can we infer about Uncle Oscar from this exchange?

16 Critical Thinking and Reading What does Paul's birthday gift to his mother imply about him?

17 Discussion What frustrates Paul's mother? What do Paul and his mother have in common?

18 Discussion What does the reaction of Paul's mother show about her?

19 **Literary Focus** What can we infer about the inevitability of implying some attitude or point of view, even with an omniscient narrator, from this passage? What makes the voices go mad like "a chorus of frogs"?

20 **Discussion** What does Paul's mother infer from his refusal to leave for the seashore? What does this show about her?

21 **Master Teacher Note** "The Rocking-Horse Winner" revolves around the notion of fate, as in a Greek tragedy. Ask the students to relate "The Rocking-Horse Winner" to a Greek tragedy in terms of the working out of the tragic hero's fate, the use of Bassett as an evil spirit, and Uncle Oscar as a chorus.

22 **Literary Focus** How does Paul's "secret within a secret" show the neutrality of the omniscient narrator?

long interview with the lawyer, asking if the whole five thousand could not be advanced at once, as she was in debt.

"What do you think, uncle?" said the boy.

"I leave it to you, son."

"Oh, let her have it, then! We can get some more with the other," said the boy.

"A bird in the hand is worth two in the bush, laddie!" said Uncle Oscar.

"But I'm sure to *know* for the Grand National; or the Lincolnshire; or else the Derby.[7] I'm sure to know for *one* of them," said Paul.

So Uncle Oscar signed the agreement, and Paul's mother touched the whole five thousand. Then something very curious happened. The voices in the house suddenly went mad, like a chorus of frogs on a spring evening. There were certain new furnishings, and Paul had a tutor. He was *really*
19 going to Eton,[8] his father's school, in the following autumn. There were flowers in the winter, and a blossoming of the luxury Paul's mother had been used to. And yet the voices in the house, behind the sprays of mimosa and almond blossom, and from under the piles of iridescent cushions, simply trilled and screamed in a sort of ecstasy: "There *must* be more money! Oh-h-h! There *must* be more money! Oh, now, now-w! now-w-w—there *must* be more money!—more than ever! More than ever!"

It frightened Paul terribly. He studied away at his Latin and Greek with his tutors. But his intense hours were spent with Bassett. The Grand National had gone by: he had not "known," and had lost a hundred pounds. Summer was at hand. He was in agony for the Lincoln. But even for the Lincoln he didn't "know," and he lost fifty pounds. He became wild-eyed and strange, as if something were going to explode in him.

"Let it alone, son! Don't you bother about it!" urged Uncle Oscar. But it was as if the boy couldn't really hear what his uncle was saying.

"I've got to know for the Derby! I've *got* to know for the Derby!" the child reiterated, his big blue eyes blazing with a sort of madness.

His mother noticed how overwrought he was.

"You'd better go to the seaside. Wouldn't you like to go now to the seaside, instead of waiting? I think you'd better," she said, looking down at him anxiously, her heart curiously heavy because of him.

But the child lifted his uncanny blue
eyes. 20

"I couldn't possibly go before the Derby, mother!" he said. "I couldn't possibly!"

"Why not?" she said, her voice becoming heavy when she was opposed. "Why not? You can still go from the seaside to see the Derby with your Uncle Oscar, if that's what you wish. No need for you to wait here. Besides, I think you care too much about these races. It's a bad sign. My family has been a gambling family, and you won't know till you grow up how much damage it has done. But it has done damage. I shall
have to send Bassett away, and ask Uncle 21
Oscar not to talk racing to you, unless you promise to be reasonable about it; go away to the seaside and forget it. You're all nerves!"

"I'll do what you like, mother, so long as you don't send me away till after the Derby," the boy said.

"Send you away from where? Just from this house?"

"Yes," he said, gazing at her. 22

"Why, you curious child, what makes you care about this house so much, suddenly? I never knew you loved it!"

He gazed at her without speaking. He had a secret within a secret, something he had not divulged, even to Bassett or to his Uncle Oscar.

---

7. Grand National . . . Derby: Major English horse races.

8. Eton: A prestigious private school in England.

But his mother, after standing undecided and a little bit sullen for some moments, said:

"Very well, then! Don't go to the seaside till after the Derby, if you don't wish it. But promise me you won't let your nerves go to pieces! Promise you won't think so much about horse racing and *events,* as you call them!"

"Oh, no!" said the boy, casually. "I won't think much about them, mother. You needn't worry. I wouldn't worry, mother, if I were you."

"If you were me and I were you," said his mother, "I wonder what we *should* do!"

"But you know you needn't worry, mother, don't you?" the boy repeated.

"I should be awfully glad to know it," she said wearily.

"Oh, well, you *can,* you know. I mean you *ought* to know you needn't worry!" he insisted.

"Ought I? Then I'll see about it," she said.

23 Paul's secret of secrets was his wooden horse, that which had no name. Since he was emancipated from a nurse and a nursery governess, he had had his rocking horse removed to his own bedroom at the top of the house.

"Surely you're too big for a rocking horse!" his mother had remonstrated.

"Well, you see, mother, till I can have a *real* horse, I like to have *some* sort of animal about," had been his quaint answer.

"Do you feel he keeps you company?" she laughed.

"Oh, yes! He's very good, he always keeps me company, when I'm there," said Paul.

So the horse, rather shabby, stood in an arrested prance in the boy's bedroom.

24 The Derby was drawing near, and the boy grew more and more tense. He hardly heard what was spoken to him, he was very frail, and his eyes were really uncanny. His mother had sudden strange seizures of uneasiness about him. Sometimes, for half an hour, she would feel a sudden anxiety about him that was almost anguish. She wanted to rush to him at once, and know he was safe.

Two nights before the Derby, she was at a big party in town, when one of her rushes of anxiety about her boy, her firstborn, gripped her heart till she could hardly speak. She fought with the feeling, might and main, for she believed in common sense. But it was too strong. She had to leave the dance and go downstairs to telephone to the country. The children's nursery governess was terribly surprised and startled at being rung up in the night.

"Are the children all right, Miss Wilmot?"

"Oh yes, they are quite all right."

"Master Paul? Is he all right?"

"He went to bed as right as a trivet.[9] Shall I run up and look at him?"

"No!" said Paul's mother reluctantly. "No! Don't trouble. It's all right. Don't sit up. We shall be home fairly soon." She did not want her son's privacy intruded upon.

"Very good," said the governess.

It was about one o'clock when Paul's mother and father drove up to their house. All was still. Paul's mother went to her room and slipped off her white fur cloak. She had told her maid not to wait up for her. She heard her husband downstairs, mixing a whisky-and-soda.

And then, because of the strange anxiety at her heart, she stole upstairs to her son's room. Noiselessly she went along the upper corridor. Was there a faint noise? What was it?

She stood, with arrested muscles, outside his door, listening. There was a strange, heavy, and yet not loud noise. Her heart stood still. It was a soundless noise, yet rushing and powerful. Something huge, in violent, hushed motion. What was it? What in God's name was it? She ought to know. She felt that she *knew* the noise. She knew what it was.

---

9. right as a trivet: Perfectly right.

23 Enrichment Discuss the irony of gifts which bring tragedy instead of joy. A rocking-horse is a toy horse. The Trojan horse was another ironical gift of a wooden horse. A Trojan horse was also used by Nazis inside the country of their victims for sabotage. Does Lawrence imply treachery by using a rocking-horse?

24 Reading Strategy An obsession can be defined as "an act of an evil spirit impelling a person from without to action which is detrimental. It is also "a persistent preoccupation with an idea or emotion." Summarize Paul's obsession. What symbolizes his obsession?

25 **Discussion** What does Uncle Oscar's behavior demonstrate about his personality?

26 **Discussion** What simile does Lawrence use? Can a narrator be neutral?

27 **Enrichment** The word *fairy tale* comes from *Fata,* who was one of the Fates in ancient Roman mythology. *Fatum* means "fate," and Fata was a minor supernatural being who could assume diminutive human form and meddle in human affairs. Ask the students to discuss the description of Bassett in terms of his relation to fate or Puck or any imp-like spirit.

28 **Discussion** What is Paul's secret?

29 **Clarification** A bet is a thing staked or pledged between two parties upon the event of a contest. Historically a wager is the act of giving a pledge to abide the event of something. Thus historically one would pledge one's life on the outcome of a duel or battle. Ask the class to discuss these synonyms. How does Lawrence in "The Rocking-Horse Winner" play upon Paul as a "wager" in the ancient meaning of *wage* or "to stake down oneself as security"?

30 **Discussion** What was Paul searching for as he madly rode his rocking-horse? What could have made Paul a "winner"?

Yet she could not place it. She couldn't say what it was. And on and on it went, like a madness.

Softly, frozen with anxiety and fear, she turned the door handle.

The room was dark. Yet in the space near the window, she heard and saw something plunging to and fro. She gazed in fear and amazement.

Then suddenly she switched on the light, and saw her son, in his green pajamas, madly surging on his rocking horse. The blaze of light suddenly lit him up, as he urged the wooden horse, and lit her up, as she stood, blond, in her dress of pale green and crystal, in the doorway.

"Paul!" she cried. "Whatever are you doing?"

"It's Malabar!" he screamed, in a powerful, strange voice. "It's Malabar!"

His eyes blazed at her for one strange and senseless second, as he ceased urging his wooden horse. Then he fell with a crash to the ground, and she, all her tormented motherhood flooding upon her, rushed to gather him up.

But he was unconscious, and unconscious he remained, with some brain fever. He talked and tossed, and his mother sat stonily by his side.

"Malabar! It's Malabar! Bassett, Bassett, I *know* it's Malabar!"

So the child cried, trying to get up and urge the rocking horse that gave him his inspiration.

"What does he mean by Malabar?" asked the heart-frozen mother.

"I don't know," said the father, stonily.

"What does he mean by Malabar?" she asked her brother Oscar.

"It's one of the horses running for the Derby," was the answer.

And, in spite of himself, Oscar Cresswell
25 spoke to Bassett, and himself put a thousand on Malabar: at fourteen to one.

The third day of the illness was critical: they were watching for a change. The boy, with his rather long, curly hair, was tossing
ceaselessly on the pillow. He neither slept
nor regained consciousness, and his eyes
were like blue stones. His mother sat, feeling
her heart had gone, turned actually into a 26
stone.

In the evening, Oscar Cresswell did not come, but Bassett sent a message, saying could he come up for one moment, just one moment? Paul's mother was very angry at the intrusion, but on second thoughts she agreed. The boy was the same. Perhaps Bassett might bring him to consciousness.

The gardener, a shortish fellow with a
little brown moustache and sharp little
brown eyes, tiptoed into the room, touched
his imaginary cap to Paul's mother, and 27
stole to the bedside, staring with glittering,
smallish eyes at the tossing, dying child.

"Master Paul!" he whispered. "Master Paul! Malabar came in first all right, a clean win. I did as you told me. You've made over seventy thousand pounds, you have; you've got over eighty thousand. Malabar came in all right, Master Paul."

"Malabar! Malabar! Did I say Malabar,
mother? Did I say Malabar? Do you think I'm
lucky, mother? I knew Malabar, didn't I?
Over eighty thousand pounds! I call that
lucky, don't you, mother? Over eighty thousand pounds! I knew, didn't I know I knew?
Malabar came in all right. If I ride my horse
till I'm sure, then I tell you, Bassett, you can 28
go as high as you like. Did you go for all you
were worth, Bassett?"

"I went a thousand on it, Master Paul."

"I never told you, mother, that if I can
ride my horse, and *get there,* then I'm absolutely sure—oh, absolutely! Mother, did I
ever tell you? I *am* lucky!" 29

"No, you never did," said the mother.

But the boy died in the night.

And even as he lay dead, his mother
heard her brother's voice saying to her: "My
God, Hester, you're eighty-odd thousand to
the good, and a poor devil of a son to the bad.
But, poor devil, poor devil, he's best gone out 30
of a life where he rides his rocking horse to
find a winner."

Answers

ANSWERS TO THINKING ABOUT THE SELECTION

Recalling

1. The mother blames the father's "bad luck" for the family's lack of money.
2. Paul tries to ride his rocking-horse to discover winners to bet on as a way of changing the family's luck.
3. (a) Paul gives his mother 1000 pounds a year for five years as a birthday present. (b) The mother reacts by wanting all of the money immediately.

THINKING ABOUT THE SELECTION

Recalling

1. Why is the family in the story always short of money?
2. How does Paul try to change the family's luck?
3. (a) What birthday present does Paul give his mother? (b) What is her reaction to it?
4. What does Paul's mother discover upon returning from the big party?

Interpreting

5. What comment does Lawrence seem to be making about the concerns of Paul's parents?
6. On page 997 Paul's mother describes her husband as unlucky? (a) What do you think she means by this? (b) What does the remark reveal about her as a person?
7. What comment about life do you think the author is suggesting in Uncle Oscar's statement on Paul's death at the story's close?
8. Identify Lawrence's theme in this story.

Applying

9. Tell to what extent the problems he addresses are problems primarily of this century.

ANALYZING LITERATURE

Understanding Omniscient Narration

Omniscient narration is narration by a third-person speaker who, "knowing all," is able to "read" the characters' minds and see into their futures. In "The Rocking-Horse Winner," D. H. Lawrence uses a narrative style of the sort ordinarily found in fairy tales. The opening line of the story, for example, has some of the ring of the familiar "Once upon a time" beginning.

1. Identify at least two other features of the story that give it the flavor of a fairy tale. Describe what you feel these features add to the impact of the ending.
2. (a) How different might your overall impression of the story be if Lawrence had used the mother as the narrator? (b) If he had used Uncle Oscar?

UNDERSTANDING LANGUAGE

Understanding Synonyms

Synonyms are words that share a common meaning. The word *luck,* for instance, which appears in one form or another throughout the story has synonyms in the words *fate, fortune,* and *chance,* to name a few. Yet, not all of these words mean the same thing, which suggests that *luck* has several related, but very different, meanings. Reread the section on page 997 where Paul's mother explains luck. Then turn to Paul's final words on page 1004. Tell which synonyms apply to the mother's usage of the word. Then tell which apply to Paul's usage, and explain why that usage is ironic.

THINKING AND WRITING

Telling the Story

Imagine that Paul, and not an omniscient narrator, were telling the story. Try to imagine, based on examples Lawrence provides of the child's language, what words Paul might use to express events. More important, try to envision what takes place inside Paul's mind when he is astride his horse and galloping toward another "victory." Then retell a portion of the story from Paul's point of view. You may wish to concentrate on the section that immediately precedes Paul's lapse into unconsciousness. When you revise make sure you have maintained a consistent point of view. Have you included information Paul would not know? Does your narrator sound like Paul? Proofread your story and prepare a final draft. Read it aloud to your classmates.

4. On returning from the party, the mother finds Paul feverishly riding his rocking-horse.
5. Lawrence seems to be criticizing the indifference and isolation as well as the materialism of Paul's parents.
6. (a) Paul's mother considers her husband unlucky because he has not made her rich. (b) This remark reveals that she is shallow, materialistic, and selfish.
7. Suggested response: Uncle Oscar seems to be saying that the boy was crazy or emotionally stunted so he's better off dead and that the mother is better off with the money.
8. Lawrence's theme might be the irony of greed or the distortion of people's understanding of one another due to their alienation.

Applying

9. Suggested Response: The problem of a desperate need for money and the alienated fragmented family have a definite connection in this century. After industrialization, people left the family farm. Industrial work and the need for money in place of goods changed the nature of life for modern man. The loss of religion and its replacement with material obsession are primarily problems of this century.

Challenge Who are the winners in this story? Who are unlucky?

(Answers begin on p. 1004.)

ANSWERS TO ANALYZING LITERATURE

1. Suggested response: The supernatural powers of the rocking-horse, the anthropomorphic whispering house, plus the fairy tale setting of rich, beautiful, but miserable people with the intervention of the evil spirit Bassett, all give this story the flavor of a fairy tale. The fairy tale features contribute a mythic quality or greater dimension to the ironical end of the story.
2. Suggested Responses: (a) If Lawrence had used the mother as the narrator we would not have been able to see her superficiality or her shabby materialism. Also we could never have followed Paul's reasoning since his mother was oblivious to all but her own concerns. (b) Uncle Oscar would have changed our feeling of compassion for Paul's tragedy since he generally considered life a joke. We would have lost the morality and the social criticism if the narration changed from third-person to either the mother or Uncle Oscar.

ANSWERS TO UNDERSTANDING LANGUAGE

The mother's conversation about luck is based on fortune because she is concerned with money, and she attributes their lack of it to her husband's bad fortune or to chance. When Paul tells his mother that he is lucky, he means that he has wagered or taken a chance and won a fortune. Paul's usage reverses his mother's usage, and it is an ironic reversal. Actually, Paul has run into fate rather than chance and he has lost his life on his lucky wager. The final irony is that Paul and his mother are both entwined by fate and bad luck since the mother's good fortune costs her first-born's life.

THINKING AND WRITING

Divide students into groups, and have them read their rough drafts to one another and suggest ways in which they could be improved.

More About the Author James Joyce's father drank a great deal, which caused him to neglect his affairs and sink first into debt and then poverty. Joyce ended up having to leave the Jesuit boarding school which he attended, and he educated himself for two years. As is the case with other authors, Joyce's background is apparent in much of his writing. Tell students to be on the lookout for references in "Araby" to influences from Joyce's life. Mention that the story itself comes from the collection of short stories "Dubliners." Ask students to discuss what part is played by an author's background in the works of some of the other writers they have read so far this year.

JAMES JOYCE

1882–1941

Although James Joyce left Ireland early in his career to become a leader of the radical literary experimentalists on the Continent, he never lost the respect for tradition that he had learned from his Jesuit teachers. All of his works are set in his native Dublin, and all have firm roots in the literature of the past. If Joyce's innovativeness in the areas of plot, character, and language are undeniable, so then is the notion that part of his greatness was his ability to reinterpret and transform familiar literary forms.

James Joyce was born and educated in Dublin. Choosing, much to the disappointment of his family and teachers, not to enter the priesthood, he briefly considered careers in medicine and singing. His true calling, however, was as a writer, and in 1907 he published *Chamber Music,* a collection of poems. At the time of the book's publication, Joyce was living in Trieste, Italy, where he remained until the outbreak of the First World War.

The year he relocated to Zurich, 1914, also marks the appearance of his landmark volume of short stories *Dubliners.* This collection of deceptively simple tales focuses on people who, on the surface, are quite ordinary but whose minds are filled with raging psychological and emotional conflicts. Each of the main characters in *Dubliners* experiences in some way a growth of self-awareness that leads to a climactic peak in the story.

This process is developed still more fully in *A Portrait of the Artist as a Young Man,* a fictionalized account of Joyce's own life from infancy through age twenty. Like Joyce, Stephen Dedalus, the novel's main character, finds himself in conflict with his family, the Roman Catholic Church, and the nationalistic fervor of his countrymen. The book also reveals a heightened awareness of the power of language and a deeper immersion into the mind of the character. Both these traits are carried forward into *Ulysses* (1922), whose ultimate banning in England and the United States, made Joyce famous if not wealthy. This novel, which roughly parallels Homer's *Odyssey,* analyzes a single day in the life of three Dubliners. The world Joyce depicts, while as solidly three-dimensional as any conjured up by nineteenth-century realists, is nevertheless one in which language can be seen to provide keys to the exploration of truth.

Joyce's last novel, *Finnegan's Wake* (1939), was in many ways the most challenging. Written in what one scholar terms "a dream language of Joyce's own invention," this highly experimental work presents its author's view of human existence as moving through various cycles.

GUIDE FOR READING

Araby

The Writer's Technique

Epiphany. Epiphany (i pif′ ə nē) is a profound mental or spiritual revelation experienced by the hero of a literary work. The term is derived from Greek mythology, where it was used to describe the occasion when a god or goddess, wearing a disguise or concealed in a cloud, would suddenly reveal his or her true divine identity to a mortal. In modern fiction epiphany generally occurs in stories that operate on a mental, or "cerebral," level, rather than on a purely physical level. In such stories the major events are so constructed as to lead up to this dawning, or sudden awareness of an important truth, on the part of a character. What the character *thinks* under circumstances of this sort is more important than what he or she *does.* In his collection of stories *Dubliners,* James Joyce frequently depicts characters who experience epiphany.

Look For

As you read "Araby," one of the short stories in *Dubliners,* look for the moment of insight that constitutes an epiphany for the narrator, as well as to its implications for his future.

Writing

Logan Pearsall Smith wrote, "All mirrors are magical mirrors; never can we see our faces in them." Freewrite, exploring the meaning of the quotation and your reactions to it.

Vocabulary

Knowing the following words will help you as you read "Araby."

imperturbable (im′ pər tʉr′ bə b'l) *adj.*: Calm; not easily ruffled (p. 1009)

litanies (lit″ nēz) *n.*: Form of prayer in which a congregation repeats a fixed response (p. 1010)

garrulous (gar′ ə ləs) *Adj.*: Tending to talk continuously (p. 1011)

derided (di rīd′ id) *v.*: Made fun of; ridiculed (p. 1012)

Objectives

1 To recognize an epiphany
2 To analyze Joyce's attitude toward the narrator
3 To appreciate image-making words
4 To write an extended conversation

Teaching Portfolio: Support Material

Teacher Backup, p. 000

Vocabulary Check, p. 00

Usage and Mechanics Worksheet, p. 00

Analyzing Literature Worksheet, p. 00

Critical Thinking and Reading Worksheet, p. 00

Language Worksheet, p. 00

Selection Test, p. 00

Literary Focus Ask students if they know another context in which the word *epiphany* is used. Explain that the Epiphany, or Twelfth-night, is a Christian holiday celebrated twelve days after Christmas, on January 6. It is the day that the Magi were supposed to have visited the Christ child and the beasts in the stable were able to talk. Explain that religious symbols and references are common in literature, especially in the works of authors such as Joyce, who were heavily influenced by their religion.

Look For As they read "Araby," have students jot down five or six words or phrases to describe the main character so that they may understand the self-revelation that he experiences at the end.

Writing Before they begin writing their paragraphs, have a student read the fifth paragraph of "Araby" beginning with "Her name sprang to my lips . . ." Have students notice the strong verbs and adjectives and concrete nouns Joyce uses to describe his emotions—*sprang, pour, strange prayers and praises, flood from my heart, my confused adoration.* Discuss in some detail the extended simile in the last line. Tell students to describe the emotions they experienced in their moments of epiphany with similar precision and clarity.

Vocabulary Have your **less advanced** students find the prefixes and suffixes in the vocabulary words. Discuss the meanings of the prefixes and suffixes as a means of having the students better understand and remember the words' meanings.

Humanities Note

Fine art, *St. Patrick's Close, Dublin,* by Walter Osborne. Walter Frederick Osborne (1859–1903) was an English landscape painter who lived in Ireland and received his art training there, at the Royal Hibernian Academy. He traveled through England and Europe and was briefly associated with a group of artists known as the Antwerp School in Belgium. His paintings are of urban scenes and the children that inhabited them. He painted the area around St. Patrick's Cathedral in Dublin many times.

The painting *St. Patrick's Close, Dublin,* portrays the poverty and squalor of the neighborhood around the cathedral. The placement of the children leads the eye into the picture plane, allowing it to go from one bleak scene to another. It is an effective portrayal of the indifference of children to the poverty around them.

Following are questions for class discussion:

1. Is this artist merely an observer of this scene or is he making a judgment about it?
2. Could this be a visualization of the street described in Joyce's story? Explain.

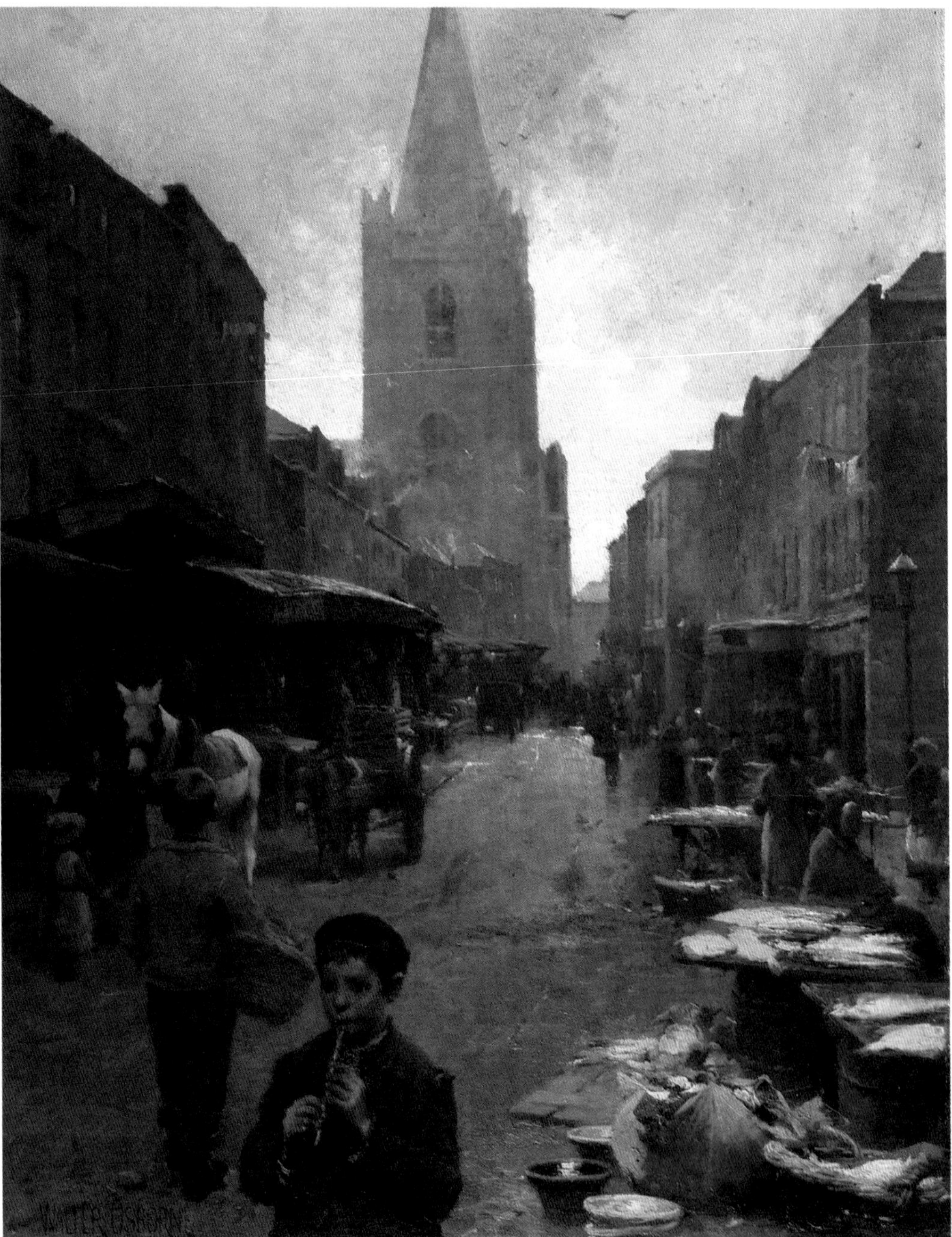

ST. PATRICK'S CLOSE
Walter Osborne
National Gallery of Ireland

Araby

James Joyce

North Richmond Street, being blind,[1]
was a quiet street except at the hour when
the Christian Brothers' School set the boys
free. An uninhabited house of two stories
stood at the blind end, detached from its
neighbors in a square ground. The other
houses of the street, conscious of decent
1 lives within them, gazed at one another with
brown imperturbable faces.

The former tenant of our house, a priest,
had died in the back drawing room. Air,
musty from having been long enclosed,
hung in all the rooms, and the waste room
behind the kitchen was littered with old
useless papers. Among these I found a few
paper-covered books, the pages of which
2,3 were curled and damp: *The Abbot,* by Walter Scott, *The Devout Communicant* and
The Memoirs of Vidocq.[2] I liked the last best
because its leaves were yellow. The wild
garden behind the house contained a central apple tree and a few straggling bushes
under one of which I found the late tenant's
rusty bicycle pump. He had been a very
charitable priest; in his will he had left all
his money to institutions and the furniture
of his house to his sister.

When the short days of winter came
dusk fell before we had well eaten our din-
4 ners. When we met in the street the houses
had grown somber. The space of sky above
us was the color of ever-changing violet and
toward it the lamps of the street lifted their
feeble lanterns. The cold air stung us and we
played till our bodies glowed. Our shouts
echoed in the silent street. The career of our
play brought us through the dark muddy
lanes behind the houses where we ran the
gantlet of the rough tribes from the cottages, 5
to the back doors of the dark dripping gardens where odors arose from the ashpits, to
the dark odorous stables where a coachman
smoothed and combed the horse or shook
music from the buckled harness. When we
returned to the street, light from the kitchen
windows had filled the areas. If my uncle
was seen turning the corner we hid in the
shadow until we had seen him safely
housed. Or if Mangan's sister came out on
the doorstep to call her brother in to his tea
we watched her from our shadow peer up
and down the street. We waited to see
whether she would remain or go in and, if
she remained, we left our shadow and
walked up to Mangan's steps resignedly. 6
She was waiting for us, her figure defined by
the light from the half-opened door. Her
brother always teased her before he obeyed
and I stood by the railings looking at
her. Her dress swung as she moved her body
and the soft rope of her hair tossed from
side to side.

Every morning I lay on the floor in the front parlor watching her door. The blind was pulled down to within an inch of the sash so that I could not be seen. When she came out on the doorstep my heart leaped. I

1. **blind:** Dead end.
2. ***The Abbot . . . Vidocq:*** A historical tale, a religious manual, and the remembrances of a French adventurer, respectively.

Motivation for Reading Have students think of an event that they looked forward to for a long time. Tell them to think specifically of their feelings of anticipation. How did the imagined event and the real event differ?

Purpose-Setting Question What role does epiphany play in this story?

1 **Discussion** Ask students what figure of speech is used in this sentence. Briefly discuss personification.

2 **Critical Thinking and Reading** Ask students why they think Joyce chose a first-person narrator for his story. How would the story differ if it had been told in the third person?

3 **Discussion** Ask students what effect they think living in the same house as a priest might have on the narrator. Tell them to watch for indications of this influence as the story develops.

4 **Discussion** What kind of childhood did the narrator have? About how old are the boys in this story?

5 **Clarification** *Ran the gantlet* refers to an old method of determining someone's guilt or innocence by running between two rows of men with sticks, who would beat the accused. His or her reaction to this *ordeal* would indicate guilt or innocence. Joyce here refers to the boys' having to endure similar treatment from the local bullies.

6 **Discussion** What effect does Mangan's sister have on the boys? How is this effect related to their age?

Master Teacher Note Because Ireland and its internal struggles and conflicts with England are much in the news, have groups of students report briefly on various aspects of Irish history. Suggested topics might be the Battle of the Boyne, the effects of the potato famine of 1846–51, Fenianism, Orangemen, and home rule.

Enrichment In Great Britain, semi-detached houses are like duplexes in the United States and house middle-class people. Terraced houses are like row houses in certain parts of the United States and are the dwellings of working-class people. A detached house is a single house of the upper-middle classes. The neighborhood in "Araby," except for the house on the end, is probably middle or lower-middle class.

Discussion Ask students why Joyce chose the word *litanies* to describe the shouting of boys in the market. Have students skim the paragraph for other words that have church-related connotations. Discuss how this imagery might affect the mood of "Araby." What do the words tell you about the narrator and his feeling for Mangan's sister?

8 **Discussion** What figure of speech is used here? Note that the image fits in with the rest of the religious imagery of the paragraph.

9 **Reading Strategy** How would you describe the narrator's emotional state here?

10 **Clarification** *Araby* is a poetic, and therefore romanticized, form of *Arabia.* During the time period, it was thought of as a mysterious, exotic land. The name of the bazaar, with its romantic connotations, amounts to an advertising ploy.

11 **Critical Thinking and Reading** Discuss the irony of where Mangan's sister wants to go that Saturday and where she will in fact be.

12 **Literary Focus** How might the narrator's first meeting with Mangan's sister be a foreshadowing of his epiphany at the end of the story?

13 **Discussion** What does the narrator think about this romantic version of himself as he recalls this incident?

14 **Reading Strategy** Contrast the attitude of his aunt and uncle toward the bazaar with the narrator's feelings about it. How might their attitudes serve as a foreshadowing of the outcome of the story?

ran to the hall, seized my books and followed her. I kept her brown figure always in my eye and, when we came near the point at which our ways diverged, I quickened my pace and passed her. This happened morning after morning. I had never spoken to her, except for a few casual words, and yet her name was like a summons to all my foolish blood.

Her image accompanied me even in places the most hostile to romance. On Saturday evenings when my aunt went marketing I had to go to carry some of the parcels. We walked through the flaring streets, jostled by drunken men and bargaining women, amid the curses of laborers, the shrill litanies of shopboys who stood on guard by the barrels of pigs' cheeks, the nasal chanting of street singers, who sang a *come-all-you* about O'Donovan Rossa,[3] or a ballad about the troubles in our native land. These noises
7 converged in a single sensation of life for me: I imagined that I bore my chalice safely through a throng of foes. Her name sprang to my lips at moments in strange prayers and praises which I myself did not understand. My eyes were often full of tears (I could not tell why) and at times a flood from my heart seemed to pour itself out into my bosom. I thought little of the future. I did not know whether I would ever speak to her or not or, if I spoke to her, how I could tell her of my confused adoration. But my body was
8 like a harp and her words and gestures were like fingers running upon the wires.

One evening I went into the back drawing room in which the priest had died. It was a dark rainy evening and there was no sound in the house. Through one of the broken panes I heard the rain impinge upon the earth, the fine incessant needles of
9 water playing in the sodden beds. Some distant lamp or lighted window gleamed below me. I was thankful that I could see so little. All my senses seemed to desire to veil themselves and, feeling that I was about to slip from them, I pressed the palms of my hands together until they trembled, murmuring: *"O love! O love!"* many times.

At last she spoke to me. When she addressed the first words to me I was so confused that I did not know what to answer.
She asked me was I going to *Araby.* I forget 10
whether I answered yes or no. It would be a splendid bazaar, she said; she would love to go.

"And why can't you?" I asked.

While she spoke she turned a silver bracelet round and round her wrist. She
could not go, she said, because there would 11
be a retreat[4] that week in her convent.[5] Her brother and two other boys were fighting for their caps and I was alone at the railings. She held one of the spikes, bowing her head towards me. The light from the lamp opposite our door caught the white curve of her neck, lit up her hair that rested there and, falling, lit up the hand upon the railing. It fell over one side of her dress and caught the white border of a petticoat, just visible as she stood at ease.

"It's well for you," she said.

"If I go," I said, "I will bring you something."

What innumerable follies laid waste my
waking and sleeping thoughts after that 13
evening! I wished to annihilate the tedious intervening days. I chafed against the work of school. At night in my bedroom and by day in the classroom her image came between me and the page I strove to read. The syllables of the word *Araby* were called to me through the silence in which my soul luxuriated and cast an Eastern enchantment over me. I asked for leave to go to the bazaar on Saturday night. My aunt was
surprised and hoped it was not some Free- 14
mason[6] affair. I answered few questions in

---

3. ***come-all-you . . . Rossa:*** The opening of a ballad about an Irish hero.

4. **retreat** *n.*: A period of retirement or seclusion for prayer, religious study, and meditation.

5. **convent** *n.*: A school run by an order of nuns.

6. **Freemason:** The Free and Accepted Masons, an international secret society.

class. I watched my master's face pass from amiability to sternness; he hoped I was not beginning to idle. I could not call my wandering thoughts together. I had hardly any patience with the serious work of life which, now that it stood between me and my desire, seemed to me child's play, ugly monotonous child's play.

On Saturday morning I reminded my uncle that I wished to go to the bazaar in the evening. He was fussing at the hallstand, looking for the hat brush, and answered me curtly:

"Yes, boy, I know."

As he was in the hall I could not go into the front parlor and lie at the window. I left the house in bad humor and walked slowly toward the school. The air was pitilessly raw and already my heart misgave me.

When I came home to dinner my uncle had not yet been home. Still it was early. I sat staring at the clock for some time and, when its ticking began to irritate me, I left the room. I mounted the staircase and gained the upper part of the house. The high cold empty gloomy rooms liberated me and I went from room to room singing. From the front window I saw my companions playing below in the street. Their cries reached me weakened and indistinct and, leaning my forehead against the cool glass, I looked over at the dark house where she lived. I may have stood there for an hour, seeing nothing but the brown-clad figure cast by my imagination, touched discreetly by the lamplight at the curved neck, at the hand upon the railings and at the border below the dress.

When I came downstairs again I found Mrs. Mercer sitting at the fire. She was an old garrulous woman, a pawnbroker's widow, who collected used stamps for some pious purpose. I had to endure the gossip of the tea table. The meal was prolonged beyond an hour and still my uncle did not come. Mrs. Mercer stood up to go: she was sorry she couldn't wait any longer, but it was after eight o'clock and she did not like to be out late, as the night air was bad for her. When she had gone I began to walk up and down the room, clenching my fists. My aunt said:

"I'm afraid you may put off your bazaar for this night of Our Lord."

At nine o'clock I heard my uncle's latchkey in the hall door. I heard him talking to himself and heard the hallstand rocking when it had received the weight of his overcoat. I could interpret these signs. When he was midway through his dinner I asked him to give me the money to go to the bazaar. He had forgotten.

"The people are in bed and after their first sleep now," he said.

I did not smile. My aunt said to him energetically:

"Can't you give him the money and let him go? You've kept him late enough as it is."

My uncle said he was very sorry he had forgotten. He said he believed in the old saying: *All work and no play makes Jack a dull boy.* He asked me where I was going and, when I had told him a second time he asked me did I know *The Arab's Farewell to His Steed.*[7] When I left the kitchen he was about to recite the opening lines of the piece to my aunt.

I held a florin[8] tightly in my hand as I strode down Buckingham Street toward the station. The sight of the streets thronged with buyers and glaring with gas recalled to me the purpose of my journey. I took my seat in a third-class carriage of a deserted train. After an intolerable delay the train moved out of the station slowly. It crept onward among ruinous houses and over the twinkling river. At Westland Row Station a crowd of people pressed to the carriage doors; but the porters moved them back, saying that it was a special train for the bazaar. I remained alone in the bare car-

---

7. *The Arab's . . . His Steed:* A popular nineteenth-century poem.

8. florin *n.*: A former two-shilling coin.

15 Clarification The narrator was in such a hurry that he went in at a regular entrance, rather than paying a child's fare, which was much cheaper.

16 Discussion The narrator still uses religious imagery to express his romantic feelings, this time comparing the bazaar to a church. What is the irony of this comparison?

17 Discussion How did the bazaar differ from the narrator's expectations? What side of the bazaar—and life—did the boy confront that night? What does this confrontation make him realize?

18 Literary Focus How does the narrator's moment of epiphany make him feel at the time? How does it make him feel as he recalls it? What does this story tell you about the nature of literary epiphanies?

riage. In a few minutes the train drew up beside an improvised wooden platform. I passed out onto the road and saw by the lighted dial of a clock that it was ten minutes to ten. In front of me was a large building which displayed the magical name.

15 I could not find any sixpenny entrance and, fearing that the bazaar would be closed, I passed in quickly through a turnstile, handing a shilling to a weary-looking man. I found myself in a big hall girdled at half its height by a gallery. Nearly all the stalls were closed and the greater part of the
16, 17 hall was in darkness. I recognized a silence like that which pervades a church after a service. I walked into the center of the bazaar timidly. A few people were gathered about the stalls which were still open. Before a curtain, over which the words *Café Chantant*[9] were written in colored lamps, two men were counting money on a salver.[10] I listened to the fall of the coins.

Remembering with difficulty why I had come I went over to one of the stalls and examined porcelain vases and flowered tea sets. At the door of the stall a young lady was talking and laughing with two young gentlemen. I remarked their English accents and listened vaguely to their conversation.

"O, I never said such a thing!"

"O, but you did!"

"O, but I didn't!"

"Didn't she say that?"

"Yes. I heard her."

"O, there's a . . .fib!"

Observing me the young lady came over and asked me did I wish to buy anything. The tone of her voice was not encouraging; she seemed to have spoken to me out of a sense of duty. I looked humbly at the great jars that stood like Eastern guards at either side of the dark entrance to the stall and murmured:

"No, thank you."

The young lady changed the position of one of the vases and went back to the two young men. They began to talk of the same subject. Once or twice the young lady glanced at me over her shoulder.

I lingered before her stall, though I knew my stay was useless, to make my interest in her wares seem the more real. Then I turned away slowly and walked down the middle of the bazaar. I allowed the two pennies to fall against the sixpence in my pocket. I heard a voice call from one end of the gallery that the light was out. The upper part of the hall was now completely dark.

Gazing up into the darkness I saw myself as a creature driven and derided by vanity; and my eyes burned with anguish and anger. 18

---

9. *Café Chantant:* A café with musical entertainment.
10. salver *n.*: A tray usually used for the presentation of letters or visiting cards.

THINKING ABOUT THE SELECTION

Recalling

1. (a) What does the narrator feel toward Mangan's sister? (b) What are her first words to him?
2. (a) Why is going to the bazaar so important to the narrator? (b) Why is he late getting there? (c) What does he buy?
3. How does the narrator feel at the end of the story?

Interpreting

4. How would you describe the mood, or feeling, established in the opening paragraphs?
5. What might have been the author's reason for

Answers

ANSWERS TO THINKING ABOUT THE SELECTION

Recalling

1. (a) She is his first love; his feelings towards her have a religious fervor to them. (b) She asks if he is going to the bazaar, Araby.
2. (a) He sees it as almost a religious pilgrimage from which he will bring his love a splendid gift. (b) He is late getting to the bazaar because his uncle, to whom the bazaar means nothing, forgets to give him the money for it. (c) The narrator buys nothing at the bazaar, because he suddenly realizes how foolish his romantic aspirations are.
3. (a) He feels silly, his pride is hurt, and he is angry for having put himself in a ridiculous position.

not giving Mangan's sister a name?

6. What makes the narrator feel as he does at the end of the story?
7. (a) Why do you think the author chose "Araby" as a name for the bazaar? (b) As a title for the story? (c) How does it relate to the narrator's experiences?

Applying

8. (a) Look up the meaning of the word *vanity*. Which meaning is intended in the last paragraph of this story? (b) Do you agree with the narrator that he is a "creature driven and derided by vanity"? Support your answer. (c) Do you think vanity is or is not necessary to some degree for survival in today's world? Explain your answer.

ANALYZING LITERATURE

Understanding Epiphany

Epiphany is the sudden recognition of an important truth by a character in a work of fiction. Tracing back to Greek mythology where it referred to the sudden disclosure to one character of a deity's identity, epiphany in contemporary fiction is the unmasking of a truth that was present all along in a character's mind. In the short stories of James Joyce, this truth usually relates to the essential nature of something commonplace—a person, situation, or object—that the character now sees in a new light.

1. Where in "Araby" does the epiphany occur?
2. What does the hero suddenly realize?
3. What suddenly causes him to feel this way?

CRITICAL THINKING AND READING

Analyzing Joyce's Attitude

It is important to keep in mind that, as with any story told from the first-person point of view, the narrator of "Araby" is not the author. Yet as with any such story, the author expresses his attitude toward the character of the narrator through the character's words, thoughts, and actions. Read the following quotes from "Araby." Tell what they reveal, as a whole, about Joyce's attitude toward his narrator's romantic goals.

1. "Every morning I lay on the floor in the parlor watching her door." (page 1009)
2. "Her image accompanied me even in places the most hostile to romance." (page 1010)
3. "Her name sprang to my lips at moments in strange prayers. . . ." (page 1010)
4. "'If I go,' I said, 'I will bring you something.'" (page 1010)

UNDERSTANDING LANGUAGE

Appreciating Image-Making Words

An **image** is a word that appeals to the senses. Joyce is widely recognized as a master of imagery, and "Araby" amply demonstrates why. Identify which words help make each of the following images so vivid, and name the sense or senses to which the image appeals.

1. "The cold air stung us and we played till our bodies glowed." (page 1009)
2. ". . . we ran . . . [to] the dark dripping gardens where odors rose from ashpits, to the dark odorous stables where a coachman smoothed and combed the horse or shook music from the buckled harness." (page 1009)
3. "Her dress swung as she moved her body and the soft rope of her hair tossed from side to side." (page 1009)
4. "The . . . streets thronged with buyers and glaring with gas recalled to me the purpose of my journey." (page 1011)

THINKING AND WRITING

Writing an Extended Conversation

Choose an episode from the story involving the narrator and Mangan's sister—perhaps when he passes her going to school or when they talk about the bazaar. Imagine an extended conversation between them, giving particular emphasis to what they might say and the way in which they would most likely say it. Record this bit of dialogue, permitting yourself ample time to revise any sections that do not ring true.

Interpreting

4. Joyce sets a mood of carefree youth on the verge of adolescence, but the serious and religious side of life—in the guise of the dead priest—is omnipresent.
5. By not naming Mangan's sister, Joyce makes her into a more mysterious, romantic figure—and more symbolic than real.
6. By comparing the reality of the bazaar with his preconceived notions about it, he sees that his devotion to Mangan's sister is silly. He is more in love with his idea of himself in love than he is actually in love with Mangan's sister.
7. (a) *Araby* is an exotic-sounding name that would have excited the imagination of both the boy and other people in the story. (b) The title was probably chosen by Joyce because it mirrors the narrator's concept of himself—that is, *Araby* itself is not as romantic a place as the local people thought it must be. (c) It is by going to the Araby bazaar that the narrator is able to see that his romantic vision of himself is just an illusion.

Applying

8. (a) The intended meaning is "any thing or act that is vain, futile, idle, or worthless." (b) The narrator may be overstating the case, though answers to this question may differ. (c) A measure of vanity is probably unavoidable in all people. Whether it is needed for survival is open to date.

(Answers begin on p. 1012.)

Challenge Is Joyce sympathetic towards the narrator in "Araby"? How does he want the reader to feel both about the narrator and his experience?

ANSWERS TO ANALYZING LITERATURE

1. The epiphany in "Araby" occurs in the final paragraph.
2. The narrator suddenly realizes that his romantic notion of himself is vanity.
3. Imagining the bazaar as a romantic place and seeing it in reality "ignites" the epiphany.

ANSWERS TO CRITICAL THINKING AND READING

1-4. The narrator sees and describes the girl in religious terms because they are probably the only ones, brought up Catholic as he was, that he would be familiar with to describe an emotion. He sees himself as her knight-protector. Joyce is spoofing the narrator's adoloscent romanticism, but in a very gentle way.

ANSWERS TO UNDERSTANDING LANGUAGE

1. *stung:* touch; *glowed:* sight
2. *dripping:* sight, sound; *rose:* sight; *odorous:* smell; *smoothed:* touch; *combed:* touch
3. *swung:* sight; *moved:* sight; *tossed:* sight
4. *thronged: sight; glaring:* sight

THINKING AND WRITING

Writing Across the Curriculum You may want some of the groups who reported on Irish history to write up their reports. You might want to inform the history department of the assignment so that they might provide guidance for research.

More About the Author Elizabeth Bowen's father developed a mental illness when she was only seven. Although her family was well-to-do, her mother moved from the family estate in Ireland to England. When Elizabeth was only twelve, however, her mother died, and Elizabeth spent the rest of her childhood living with relatives on the coast of Kent. She was a teenager during World War I and, during World War II, she worked for the Ministry of Information in London and served as an air raid warden. Ask students what effect they think these biographical facts may have had on the type of novels and short stories Bowen wrote.

ELIZABETH BOWEN

1899–1973

The fiction of Elizabeth Bowen is distinguished by the author's subtle observation of landscape, by her innovative and believable use of the supernatural, and by her haunting portrayal of England during one of the darkest eras of that country's history—the years between 1939 and 1945.

Bowen was born in Dublin and raised in County Cork, Ireland. She published her first novel, *The Hotel,* in 1927. During the 1930s she perfected her craft and in 1938, on the eve of the Second World War, completed one of her best-known works, *The Death of the Heart*. This novel traces the intertwining loves and fortunes of a group of sophisticated but vulnerable Londoners in the 1930s.

During the war Bowen observed England's hardships keenly and with compassion. The brutal realities of the conflict—air raids, blackouts, and espionage—were incorporated into some of her best short stories. Typically she played on the heightening of emotions and perceptions in wartime to probe the inner workings of her characters' minds. Shortly after the end of the war Bowen published another novel, *The Heat of the Day* (1949), which was received with much acclaim. Set in wartime London, the work movingly juxtaposes a tragic love affair with the larger national dilemma of a country's fight for its survival.

After the death of her husband in 1952, Bowen returned to Ireland to live. Although her earlier work was influenced by the psychological realism of Henry James, her later novels—*A World of Love* (1955), *The Little Girls* (1964), and *Eva Trout* (1969)—exhibit a more symbolic, more poetic style. Bowen never fully adopted the stream-of-consciousness technique practiced by her contemporaries, Virginia Woolf and James Joyce. Yet readers may easily sense more than a trace of this technique in Bowen's novels and stories—such is her sensitivity to fine shades of emotion and her eye for small but important detail.

GUIDE FOR READING

The Demon Lover

Historical Context

War and the Ghost Story. Despite the number of times humans have waged warfare on one another throughout history, war has never, happily, become a natural state of affairs for the species. The unnaturalness of a civilization in wartime is especially evident off the battlefield, in the streets of a city. Here the horrors that attend war—loss of life, destruction of property, suffering, fear, and despair—seem ever so much like the work of a band of demonic spirits. The Second World War, in particular, struck individuals living in the war-ravaged cities of Europe as akin to a nightmare. Warning sirens and blackouts were a part of everyday life; whole communities were sometimes evacuated against the danger of an enemy attack, leaving street after street of deserted buildings. These "ghost towns" within metropolises like London impressed some writers as ideal backdrops for stories that deal in events of the supernatural, or ghost stories. One such writer was Elizabeth Bowen, who sought in "The Demon Lover" to pit the horrifying landscape of the battlefield against the still more horrifying landscape closer to home.

Look For

As you read "The Demon Lover," look for the details used by the author to make her ghost story psychologically convincing.

Writing

Imagine that a mysterious letter or other piece of mail that is delivered to your home. In a brief narrative, describe the specific contents of the letter, as well as your and your family's reaction to it. Conclude your account with an explanation of how the mystery was resolved.

Vocabulary

Knowing the following words will help you as you read "The Demon Lover."

parquet (pär kā') *n.*: Wooden floors (p. 1016)

escritoire (es' krə twär') *n.*: Ornamental writing desk (p. 1016)

spectral (spek' trəl) *adj.*: Ghostly (p. 1018)

arboreal (är bôr' ē əl) *adj.*: Situated near or among trees (p. 1019)

circumscribed (sʉr' kəm skrīb'd') *adj.*: Limited; confined (p. 1019)

weal (wēl) *n.*: Discolored ridge on the skin; blister (p. 1020)

aperture (ap' ər chər) *n.*: Opening (p. 1021)

Literary Focus Have students discuss works in which a war setting is used. Suggest *The Red Badge of Courage, All is Quiet on the Western Front, War and Peace, The Guns of Navarone, Gunga Din, The Bridge on the River Kwai, The Bridges at Toko-Ri, Mother Courage, or A Tale of Two Cities* if they need ideas.

Look For Remind students that one of the main elements of a ghost story is suspense. Suspense is created by the mood of a story and by the author's very careful adding of information, piece by piece. Tell students to note the first mention of anything overtly mysterious as they read the story and then reread the story up to that point for words that set the mood of mystery.

Writing You may want the class to brainstorm ideas for the type of letter this might be and then let students come up with their own solutions to the mystery.

Vocabulary Have students write down one or two antonyms for each of the following words: *spectral, circumscribed, aperture.* Have them look up in the dictionary the origins of the words *escritoire* and *parquet*.

Objectives

To understand war and the ghost story

Teaching Portfolio: Support Material

Lesson Plan, pp. 00-00

Vocabulary Check, p. 00

Usage and Mechanics Worksheet, p. 00

Analyzing Literature Worksheet, p. 00

Critical Thinking and Reading Worksheet, p. 00

Understanding Language Worksheet, p. 00

Selection Test, p. 00

The Demon Lover

Elizabeth Bowen

Toward the end of her day in London
1, Mrs. Drover went round to her shut-up
2 house to look for several things she wanted to take away. Some belonged to herself, some to her family, who were by now used to their country life. It was late August; it had been a steamy, showery day: at the moment the trees down the pavement glittered in an escape of humid yellow afternoon sun. Against the next batch of clouds, already piling up ink-dark, broken chimneys and parapets stood out. In her once familiar street, as in any unused channel, an unfamiliar queerness had silted up; a cat wove itself in and out of railings, but no human eye watched Mrs. Drover's return. Shifting some parcels under her arm, she slowly forced round her latchkey in an unwilling
3 lock, then gave the door, which had warped, a push with her knee. Dead air came out to meet her as she went in.

The staircase window having been boarded up, no light came down into the hall. But one door, she could just see, stood ajar, so she went quickly through into the room and unshuttered the big window in there. Now the prosaic woman, looking about her, was more perplexed than she
4 knew by everything that she saw, by traces of her long former habit of life—the yellow smoke stain up the white marble mantelpiece, the ring left by a vase on the top of the escritoire;[1] the bruise in the wallpaper where, on the door being thrown open widely, the china handle had always hit the wall. The piano, having gone away to be stored, had left what looked like claw marks on its part of the parquet.[2] Though not much dust had seeped in, each object wore a film of another kind; and, the only ventilation being the chimney, the whole drawing room smelled of the cold hearth. Mrs. Drover put down her parcels on the escritoire and left the room to proceed upstairs; the things she wanted were in a bedroom chest.

She had been anxious to see how the house was—the part-time caretaker she shared with some neighbors was away this week on his holiday, known to be not yet back. At the best of times he did not look in often, and she was never sure that she trusted him. There were some cracks in the structure, left by the last bombing, on which she was anxious to keep an eye. Not that one could do anything—

A shaft of refracted daylight now lay across the hall. She stopped dead and stared at the hall table—on this lay a letter addressed to her.

She thought first—then the caretaker *must* be back. All the same, who, seeing the house shuttered, would have dropped a letter in at the box? It was not a circular, it was 5
not a bill. And the post office redirected, to the address in the country, everything for her that came through the post. The care-

---

1. **escritoire** (es' krə twär') *n.*: A writing desk or table.

2. **parquet** (pär kā') *n.*: A flooring of inlaid woodwork in geometric forms.

Motivation for Reading Ask students to recall the last mystery or horror movie that they saw. What elements in the movie set up the suspense? Have students discuss the similarities and differences in the building of suspense in a short story and in a movie.

Master Teacher Note Ask students to brainstorm in small groups what they might already know about the ghost story genre. Suggest that they discuss the elements that make up the ghost story; the influence of nineteenth-century romanticism on the genre; and authors—such as Mary Shelley, Emily Brontë, Edgar Allen Poe, and Washington Irving—who used ghostly elements in their writing. Have the groups report on the highlights of their discussion.

Purpose-Setting Question How does war affect the setting of this ghost story?

1 **Reading Strategy** Have students comment on the feelings they have had upon returning to an empty house they have once lived in or even their own house after a long vacation.

2 **Discussion** Why do you suppose Mrs. Drover's house is shut up? Why are they living in the country? Why does the author not reveal why they are in the country at the very beginning of the story?

3 **Discussion** After students have read the first three paragraphs, ask them to skim them again, looking for any words that seem sinister in any way. Ask what the effect of these sinister-sounding words is.

4 **Critical Thinking and Reading** Ask students to explain what *prosaic* means. Ask them why they think the author described Mrs. Drover as *prosaic*. How does describing her thus help set the mood of the story?

5 **Discussion** What inexplicable aspects of the letter's arrival add a sense of mystery?

Thematic Idea Remind students of the elements of a ghost story that are found in the selections from Shelley's *Frankenstein* and Emily Brontë's *Wuthering Heights*.

taker (even if he *were* back) did not know she was due in London today—her call here had been planned to be a surprise—so his negligence in the manner of this letter, leaving it to wait in the dusk and the dust, annoyed her. Annoyed, she picked up the letter, which bore no stamp. But it cannot be important, or they would know . . . She took the letter rapidly upstairs with her, without a stop to look at the writing till she reached what had been her bedroom, where she let in light. The room looked over the garden and other gardens: the sun had gone in; as the clouds sharpened and lowered, the trees and rank lawns seemed already to smoke
6, 7 with dark. Her reluctance to look again at the letter came from the fact that she felt intruded upon—and by someone contemptuous of her ways. However, in the tenseness preceding the fall of rain she read it: it was a few lines.

DEAR KATHLEEN,

You will not have forgotten that today is our anniversary, and the day we said. The years have gone by at once slowly and fast. In view of the fact that nothing has changed, I shall rely upon you to keep your promise. I was sorry to see you leave London, but was satisfied that you would be back in time. You may expect me, therefore, at the hour arranged.

Until then . . . K.

Mrs. Drover looked for the date: it was today's. She dropped the letter onto the bedsprings, then picked it up to see the writing again—her lips, beneath the remains of lipstick, beginning to go white. She felt so much the change in her own face that 8

HOLY BUSH HILL, HAMPSTEAD, 1921
Ethelbert White

6 **Reading Strategy** Ask students why they think Mrs. Drover is reluctant to open the letter. Ask if they think she knows whom the letter is from before she opens it.

7 **Reading Strategy** Based on what they have read so far, whom do students think the letter is from?

8 **Critical Thinking and Reading** Describe Mrs. Drover. What is the effect of waiting until this point of the story to describe her? What is the author's attitude towards her?

Humanities Note

Fine art; *Holy Bush Hill, Hampstead,* 1921, Ethelbert White. White (1891–1972) was a British painter, wood engraver, and print maker. Before the advent of photography, the art of wood engraving fluorished as a means of reproducing pictoral images. It is a process in which lines are incised into wooden blocks, which are then inked and pressed onto paper. This process transfers a black-and-white image of the design.

Ethelbert White is one of the contemporary artists who strove to revive wood engraving as an art form rather than a mere mechanical method of image reproduction. In his wood engraving, *Holy Bush Hill, Hempstead,* White combines modern images, stylized forms, and a variety of interesting textures in this ancient technique. The result is a striking and moody black and white depiction of an English street scene. White's award-winning prints have done much to further wood engraving as an art form.

You might ask your students the following questions:

1. What is the mood of this print? What features create this mood?
2. How does this mood compare with the mood evoked by the story?

9 Clarification A *jumper* is a British word for "a pullover sweater." Be on the lookout for other unfamiliar British usages of commonly used English words.

10 Literary Focus Ask volunteers if they know what literary device is used in the next section. Discuss how flashbacks are used in movies as well as literature.

11 Literary Focus Note that this flashback takes place during World War I and that the rest of the story takes place in the middle of World War II. Ask students what they think the significance of these two time periods is in the story.

12 Discussion What are the sinister aspects of Mrs. Drover's final parting from her fiancé? What does this parting tell the reader about her lover? What do his words indicate about him?

13 Reading Strategy The reader is never told exactly what promise the fiancé extracts from Mrs. Drover? Why? What do you think that promise is?

14 Critical Thinking and Reading Discuss with students what "plight a troth" means. Ask when this archaic term is most commonly used. Ask how the use of the phrase is ironic in the story.

15 Discussion What was her reaction to her fiancé's death? Why do you think "she failed to attract men . . ." Why was marrying Mr. Drover such a relief to her?

she went to the mirror, polished a clear patch in it and looked at once urgently and stealthily in. She was confronted by a woman of forty-four, with eyes starting out under a hatbrim that had been rather carelessly pulled down. She had not put on any more powder since she left the shop where she ate her solitary tea. The pearls her husband had given her on their marriage hung loose round her now rather thinner throat, slipping into the V of the pink wool
9 jumper her sister knitted last autumn as they sat round the fire. Mrs. Drover's most normal expression was one of controlled worry, but of assent. Since the birth of the third of her little boys, attended by a quite serious illness, she had had an intermittent muscular flicker to the left of her mouth, but in spite of this she could always sustain a manner that was at once energetic and calm.

Turning from her own face as precipitately as she had gone to meet it, she went to the chest where the things were, unlocked it, threw up the lid and knelt to search. But as rain began to come crashing down she could not keep from looking over her shoulder at the stripped bed on which the letter lay. Behind the blanket of rain the clock of the church that still stood struck six—with rapidly heightening apprehension she counted each of the slow strokes. "The hour arranged . . . My God," she said, "*What* hour? How should I . . . ? After twenty-five years. . . ."

The young girl talking to the soldier in the garden had not ever completely seen his
10 face. It was dark; they were saying goodbye under a tree. Now and then—for it felt, from not seeing him at this intense moment, as though she had never seen him at all—she verified his presence for these few moments longer by putting out a hand, which he each time pressed, without very much kindness, and painfully, on to one of the breast buttons of his uniform. That cut of the button on the palm of her hand was, principally, what she was to carry away. This was so near the end of a leave from France that she could only wish him already gone. It was August 1916. Being not kissed, being drawn away from and looked at intimidated Kathleen till she imagined spectral glitters in the place of his eyes. Turning away and looking back up the lawn she saw, through branches of trees, the drawing-room window alight; she caught a breath for the moment when 11,
she could go running back there into the safe arms of her mother and sister, and cry: 12
"What shall I do, what shall I do? He has gone."

Hearing her catch her breath, her fiancé said, without feeling: "Cold?"

"You're going away such a long way."

"Not so far as you think."

"I don't understand?"

"You don't have to," he said. "You will. You know what we said."

"But that was—suppose you—I mean, suppose."

"I shall be with you," he said, "sooner or later. You won't forget that. You need do nothing but wait."

Only a little more than a minute later she was free to run up the silent lawn. Looking in through the window at her mother and sister, who did not for the moment perceive her, she already felt that unnatural promise drive down between her and the 13
rest of all humankind. No other way of having given herself could have made her feel so apart, lost and foresworn. She could not 14
have plighted a more sinister troth.

Kathleen behaved well when, some months later, her fiancé was reported missing, presumed killed. Her family not only supported her but were able to praise her courage without stint because they could not regret, as a husband for her, the man they knew almost nothing about. They 15
hoped she would, in a year or two, console herself—and had it been only a question of consolation things might have gone much straighter ahead. But her trouble, behind just a little grief, was a complete dislocation

from everything. She did not reject other lovers, for these failed to appear: for years she failed to attract men—and with the approach of her thirties she became natural enough to share her family's anxiousness on this score. She began to put herself out, to wonder; and at thirty-two she was very greatly relieved to find herself being courted by William Drover. She married him, and the two of them settled down in this quiet, arboreal part of Kensington; in this house the years piled up, her children were born and they all lived till they were driven out by the bombs of the next war. Her movements as Mrs. Drover were circumscribed, and she dismissed any idea that they were still watched.

As things were—dead or living the letter
writer sent her only a threat. Unable, for
some minutes, to go on kneeling with her
back exposed to the empty room, Mrs. Drover rose from the chest to sit on an upright
chair whose back was firmly against the
17 wall. The desuetude of her former bedroom,
her married London home's whole air of
being a cracked cup from which memory,
with its reassuring power, had either evapo-
6 rated or leaked away, made a crisis—and at
just this crisis the letter writer had, knowl-
edgeably, struck. The hollowness of the
house this evening canceled years on years
of voices, habits and steps. Through the
shut windows she only heard rain fall on the
roofs around. To rally herself, she said she
was in a mood—and, for two or three seconds shutting her eyes, told herself that she
had imagined the letter. But she opened
them—there it lay on the bed.

On the supernatural side of the letter's entrance she was not permitting her mind to dwell. Who, in London, knew she meant to call at the house today? Evidently, however, this had been known. The caretaker, *had* he come back, had had no cause to expect her: he would have taken the letter in his pocket, to forward it, at his own time, through the post. There was no other sign that the caretaker had been in—but, if not?

OX HOUSE, SHAFTESBURY, 1932
John R. Biggs

Letters dropped in at doors of deserted houses do not fly or walk to tables in halls. They do not sit on the dust of empty tables with the air of certainty that they will be found. There is needed some human hand—but nobody but the caretaker had a key. Under circumstances she did not care to consider, a house can be entered without a key. It was possible that she was not alone now. She might be being waited for, downstairs. Waited for—until when? Until "the hour arranged." At least that was not six o'clock; six has struck.

She rose from the chair and went over and locked the door.

The thing was, to get out. To fly? No, not
that: she had to catch her train. As a woman
whose utter dependability was the keystone 18
of her family life she was not willing to

Humanities Notes

Wood engraving, *Ox House, Shaftesbury*, 1932, John R. Biggs. In this black-and-white wood block print, the artist John R. Biggs has used the medium effectively to create a scene of haunting quiet. The darkened room with an eerie light shining through the open door creates the feeling of a mysterious presence.

Consider these questions for discussion:

1. What is the mood of this scene?
2. How might this scene relate to the house in "The Demon Lover"?
3. Is this print an effective illustration for "The Demon Lover"? Explain.

---

16 **Literary Focus** How had the letter writer used the circumstances of the war and Mrs. Drover's psychological state against her?

17 **Literary Focus** What kind of figure of speech is this? What does it mean in the story and why is its use here so powerful?

18 **Discussion** How does Mrs. Drover's practicality—her "prosaicness"—work against her?

19 Discussion What do "the complete suspension of her existence" and the fact that she cannot remember his face tell about the fiancé? How does revealing only a little bit at a time about the fiancé affect the story?

20 Reading Strategy What figure of speech is used here and why is it so powerful? In the flashback, the author mentions that Mrs. Drover never clearly saw the fiancé's face. Watch for other references to his face to see how they tie together.

21 Discussion What was the draft that Mrs. Drover felt?

22 Literary Focus How does the atmosphere of war-torn London effect Mrs. Drover's state of mind?

23 Discussion Discuss how the events associated with the taxi heighten the tension to the story's climax when Mrs. Drover screams. Why does she scream?

return to the country, to her husband, her little boys and her sister, without the objects she had come up to fetch. Resuming work at the chest she set about making up a number of parcels in a rapid, fumbling-decisive way. These, with her shopping parcels, would be too much to carry; these meant a taxi—at the thought of the taxi her heart went up and her normal breathing resumed. I will ring up the taxi now; the taxi cannot come too soon; I shall hear the taxi out there running its engine, till I walk calmly down to it through the hall. I'll ring up—But no: the telephone is cut off . . . She tugged at a knot she had tied wrong.

The idea of flight . . . He was never kind to me, not really. I don't remember him kind at all. Mother said he never considered me. He was set on me, that was what it was—not love. Not love, not meaning a person well. What did he do, to make me promise like that? I can't remember—But she found that she could.

She remembered with such dreadful acuteness that the twenty-five years since then dissolved like smoke and she instinc-
19 tively looked for the weal left by the button on the palm of her hand. She remembered not only all that he said and did but the complete suspension of *her* existence during that August week. I was not myself—they all told me so at the time. She
20 remembered—but with one white burning blank as where acid has dropped on a photograph: *under no conditions* could she remember his face.

So wherever he may be waiting, I shall not know him. You have no time to run from a face you do not expect.

The thing was to get to the taxi before any clock struck what could be the hour. She would slip down the street and round the side of the square to where the square gave on the main road. She would return in the taxi, safe, to her own door, and bring the solid driver into the house with her to pick up the parcels from room to room. The idea of the taxi driver made her decisive, bold; she unlocked her door, went to the top of the staircase and listened down.

She heard nothing—but while she was hearing nothing the *passé*[3] air of the staircase was disturbed by a draft that traveled up to her face. It emanated from the basement: down there a door or window was
being opened by someone who chose this 21
moment to leave the house.

The rain had stopped; the pavements steamily shone as Mrs. Drover let herself out by inches from her own front door into the empty street. The unoccupied houses opposite continued to meet her look with their damaged stare. Making toward the thoroughfare and the taxi, she tried not to keep looking behind. Indeed, the silence was so intense—one of those creeks of London silence exaggerated this summer by the damage of war—that no tread could have gained 22
on hers unheard. Where her street debouched on the square where people went on living, she grew conscious of, and checked, her unnatural pace. Across the open end of the square two buses impassively passed each other; women, a perambulator,[4] cyclists, a man wheeling a barrow signalized, once again, the ordinary flow of life. At the square's most populous corner should be—and was—the short taxi rank. This evening, only one taxi—but this, although it presented its blank rump, appeared already to be alertly waiting for her. Indeed, without looking round the driver started his engine as she panted up from behind and put her hand on the door. As she did so, the clock struck seven. The taxi faced
the main road. To make the trip back to her 23
house it would have to turn—she had settled back on the seat and the taxi *had* turned before she, surprised by its knowing movement, recollected that she had not "said where." She leaned forward to scratch

---

3. *passé* (pa sā') *adj.*: Stale.
4. perambulator: A baby carriage.

Answers

ANSWERS TO THINKING ABOUT THE SELECTION
Recalling

1. (a) The story takes place during World War II in London. (b) Mrs. Drover visits her house to pick up some things for her family, who are now living in the countryside to escape the bombing of London.

at the glass panel that divided the driver's head from her own.

The driver braked to what was almost a stop, turned round and slid the glass panel back. The jolt of this flung Mrs. Drover forward till her face was almost into the glass. Through the aperture driver and passenger, not six inches between them, remained for an eternity eye to eye. Mrs. Drover's mouth hung open for some seconds before she could issue her first scream. After that she continued to scream freely and to beat with her gloved hands on the glass all round as the taxi, accelerating without mercy, made off with her into the hinterland of deserted streets.

THINKING ABOUT THE SELECTION

Recalling

1. (a) Where and when does the story take place? (b) Why does Mrs. Drover visit her house in London?
2. (a) Who has written the letter Mrs. Drover discovers? (b) Why is she so upset by it?
3. (a) How does Mrs. Drover plan to escape from the house? (b) Does she succeed in her plan? Explain.

Interpreting

4. In the first paragraph the narrator remarks that "no human eye watched Mrs. Drover's return" to her house? In what way is this remark ironic?
5. (a) What words does the author use to describe Mrs. Drover's reaction to the letter? (b) What feelings do you think the author hoped this description would prompt in the reader?
6. One of the strengths of this short story is its ambiguity. Provide both a supernatural and a rational explanation for (a) the letter, and (b) the cab driver's knowing in which direction to take his passenger before she has spoken up.
7. Why do you think the author devotes so much space to Mrs. Drover's thought processes following the flashback?
8. What do you think is Mrs. Drover's ultimate fate? Explain the basis for your answer.

Applying

9. The story seems to be suggesting that one of the most damaging effects of war is the psychological vulnerability it produces in human beings? Do you agree? Defend your opinion.

ANALYZING LITERATURE

Considering War and the Ghost Story

The devastation that was war-torn London —shells of bombed-out dwellings facing empty streets, periods of blackout, the roar of airplane engines in the sky—provides a choice setting for a story involving the presence of a ghostlike figure. In fact, for the people who lived during that era, the specter was very real, lurking in every darkened doorway and known variously by the names of fear, desperation, and grief. Consider the following war-related details in "The Demon Lover," and explain how each in its own turn adds to the terror the reader feels on the part of Mrs. Drover.

1. The empty house in which the Drovers had lived
2. The break in the routine of mail delivery
3. The prospect of never knowing the fate of a loved one reported "missing in action"
4. The blocks of deserted streets in an evacuated neighborhood

(Answers begin on p. 1020.)

edge is the presence of the ghostly lover. Rational explanations will differ, though students should support their opinions by reference to specific details of the story.

7. By devoting so much space to Mrs. Drover's thinking after the flashback, the reader sees her first rejecting the idea of who the letter writer could be and then coming to the slow realization of who it had to be. The reader also sees her plans to escape and how her own personality helps trap her (her unwillingness to run then and her insistence that she complete the task for which she came). It also increases the tension and suspense because the reader realizes that she doesn't know what he looks like.
8. One interpretation of Mrs. Drover's ultimate fate is that she goes to be the bride of her demon lover. However, if one prefers the psychological approach, it is that she has a nervous breakdown brought on by the war.

Applying

9. Suggested response: It is hard to say which is a worse consequence of war, psychological or physical suffering and damage. Death and destruction of property are terrible things, but the nightmares and psychological damage done to people are no less horrible than death.

ANSWERS TO ANALYZING LITERATURE

1. The empty house, deserted like many houses during the war by Londoners who feared the German bombing, seemed unnatural to Mrs. Drover. It is deserted in the way many "haunted" houses are.
2. The fact that her mail has been rerouted to the house in the country is one of the reasons that she has difficulty figuring out how the letter could have gotten there. The war has caused confusion in even this simple part of life.
3. Not knowing the fate of loved ones is a part of the uncertainty of war that sets the mood of the story.
4. The blocks of deserted streets give the impression of a ghost town —an unnatural setting for a residential neighborhood in London.

2. (a) The letter was written by Mrs. Drover's World War I fiancé. (b) Her fiancé died in the war—if indeed he was ever alive—and had gotten from her some sort of promise, complete with date and hour, to be reunited with him, no matter what happened to him.
3. (a) She plans to escape by leaving the house and returning with a taxi driver to carry her bundles, so she won't be vulnerable to the letter writer. (b) She does not succeed in her plan because the letter writer leaves the house before she does and poses as a taxi driver.

Interpreting

4. The phrase "no human eye watched Mrs. Drover's return" is ironic because an inhuman eye watches her. However, one only sees that this is the author's meaning as other clues about her fiancé mount up. In fact, the author has cleverly mentioned a cat to divert the reader's attention from what she meant by "inhuman."
5. (a) She "dropped the letter," her lips "[went] white," she "felt so much the change in her own face that she went to the mirror," "heightening apprehension" as she listened to the clock. (b) The author hopes this description will make the reader empathize with Mrs. Drover.
6. (a) and (b) The supernatural explanation for both the letter and the cab driver's apparent foreknowl-

More About the Author Graham Greene was intrigued with the omnipresence of evil in the world, the first taste of which he experienced in the school where his father was headmaster. He hated school so much that he ran away, which act resulted in his parents' decision to send him to London to live with and be treated by a psychoanalyst. He later called this time one of the happiest periods of his life. Living with the psychoanalyst probably also accounts for his deep interest in the psychology of the human mind. The influence of Catholicism and his interest in spiritual matters is also reflected in his works, particularly the struggle between good and evil. Have students think of some of the themes that seem to run through the works of other authors they have read, both in class and out.

GRAHAM GREENE

1904–

The search for a source of inner peace, launched earlier in the century by such poets as William Butler Yeats and T. S. Eliot, continues up through our own time in the novels and short stories of Graham Greene. A religious convert like Eliot, Greene writes—like Eliot—of pain, fear, despair, and alienation. His conclusion, which again mirrors the poet's, is that the ultimate key to salvation is a belief in God.

Greene was born in the town of Berkhamstead in Hertfordshire and educated at Berkhamstead School, where his father was headmaster. Though his grades were good enough to earn him admission to Oxford, he disliked school, describing it later as his "first impression of hell."

Much of Greene's early working life was spent as a journalist and travel writer. His training in these areas helped him develop the powers of keen observation, sensitivity to atmosphere, and simplicity of language that have become hallmarks of his fictional style. His journey to Mexico in 1938 provided the setting for his best-known novel, *The Power and the Glory* (1940). His trips to Africa resulted in travelogues as well as two novels, *The Heart of the Matter* (1944) and *A Burnt-Out Case* (1961).

Greene is also an author of books for children, an essayist, and an editor, and has enjoyed considerable success writing films and adapting his own stories for the screen. His cinematic work is tied to yet another outlet for his creativity that Greene has called his "entertainments." These are adventure stories and spy thrillers, often dealing with the secret service and with pursuit. Among these are *Our Man in Havana* (1958) and *The Human Factor* (1978).

Greene's more serious work focuses more on the psychology of human character than on plot. Many of his protagonists are people without roots or beliefs—people in pain. They come across as real and believable individuals in whom good and evil, weakness and strength are intermingled. Though the characters in a Greene story often provide the reader with little reason for finding them likeable, they almost always excite the reader's curiosity and pity—and, almost always, their author treats them with compassion.

The settings for Greene's fiction are usually hot, decaying, and poorly governed places, like the border town in "Across the Bridge." These parched, crumbling landscapes, presented to us in vivid detail, represent the distressed condition of a key character's troubled soul.

Objectives

1 To understand theme and point of view
2 To understand comedy and tragedy
3 To recognize derivational and inflectional suffixes
4 To analyze the effects of point of view

Teaching Portfolio: Support Material

Teacher Backup, p. 000

Vocabulary Check, p. 00

Usage and Mechanics Worksheet, p. 00

Analyzing Literature Worksheet, p. 00

Critical Thinking and Reading Worksheet, p. 00

Understanding Language Worksheet, p. 00

Selection Test, p. 00

GUIDE FOR READING

Across the Bridge

The Writer's Technique

Theme and Point of View. Theme is the central idea of a work of literature. The theme of a work should not be confused with its subject, which can often be summed up in a single word or phrase, such as "love of money." Rather, the theme is a commentary on the subject and is presented in the form of a statement: for example, "The love of money is the root of all evil." Of the many fiction elements that bear on a work's theme, one of the most critical is point of view, or vantage point from which the events of the story are related. By choosing a first-person point of view—telling the story, that is, from the vantage point of "I" or "we"—an author creates an illusion of immediacy which adds emphasis to certain humanistic themes. The theme suggested by the events described in "Across the Bridge," for example, comes home to the reader with special force, partly because those events are related by a firsthand observer of them.

Look For

As you read "Across the Bridge," look for details that hint at the story's theme, as well as the manner in which the author's use of a first-person narrator draws us into the action.

Writing

After obtaining the person's permission, "stake out" a friend or family member for an entire day, perhaps over the course of a weekend. Keep a detailed journal on where this person goes and what he or she does. Note any patterns of behavior in which the person engages, as well as any "strange" moves he or she might make.

Vocabulary

Knowing the following words will help you as you read "Across the Bridge."

forlorn (fər lôrn′) *adj.*: Unhappy; in a pensive mood (p. 1024)

extradition (eks′ trə dish′ ən) *n.*: Release of an accused person into the custody of one state by another state (p. 1024)

awe (ô) *n.*: Fear mixed with great respect (p. 1026)

colossal (kə läs′ ′l) *adj.*: Enormous (p. 1027)

ordure (ôr′ jər) *n.*: Waste matter; excrement (p. 1028)

Literary Focus Have students compare the point of view used in "Araby," "The Demon Lover," and other works of fiction recently read. How does the point of view affect each of these stories?

Look For For your **less advanced** students, you may wish to discuss a simple fairy tale, such as "The Little Red Hen," having them determine its theme from the details in the story.

Writing Before students begin this assignment, have them read a couple of appropriate newspaper articles for the type of journalistic style they ought to use in their writing. Or, if you have any access to diaries, having them look at a diary of a person's daily activities might also help them with this assignment.

Vocabulary Have students use a thesaurus to find several synonyms for *forlorn, awe,* and *colossal.* Have them write the different nuances of the meanings, as well as indicating when they would be used correctly.

Motivation for Reading Tell students that the main figure in this story is a criminal. With that information, have students attempt to describe the main character of the story. They can draw on what they know about criminals from the movies, the newspapers, or any other source. After they have read the first three paragraphs of the story, have them compare Mr. Calloway with their descriptions of a criminal.

Master Teacher Note For students especially interested in Graham Greene or to whet interest for the story, suggest to students that they see one of the many movies that Greene wrote or that were based on his novels. Suggest *The Third Man, This Gun for Hire,* or the spoof of his spy novels, *Our Man in Havana.*

Purpose-Setting Question Why is it important to know the theme of a story?

1 **Reading Strategy** How does the first line of the story pique the reader's curiosity? Who is "he"? What do you know about him? How does this way of describing the character further pique the reader's curiosity in him?

2 **Literary Focus** What is the point of view of the story?

3 **Discussion** Why are the people of the town fascinated with Mr. Calloway? What did they think of him?

4 **Discussion** What purpose does the information about the shoeshine boys serve?

5 **Literary Focus** What is the effect of this simile?

6 **Reading Strategy** Ask students to describe the two towns in the story. How are they alike? How are they different?

Across the Bridge

Graham Greene

1 "They say he's worth a million," Lucia
said. He sat there in the little hot damp
Mexican square, a dog at his feet, with an air
of immense and forlorn patience. The dog
attracted your attention at once; for it was
very nearly an English setter, only something had gone wrong with the tail and the
feathering. Palms wilted over his head, it
was all shade and stuffiness round the
bandstand, radios talked loudly in Spanish
from the little wooden sheds where they
changed your pesos into dollars at a loss. I
could tell he didn't understand a word from
the way he read his newspaper—as I did
2 myself picking out the words which were
like English ones. "He's been here a
month," Lucia said. "They turned him out
of Guatemala and Honduras."

You couldn't keep any secrets for five
hours in this border town. Lucia had only
been twenty-four hours in the place, but she
knew all about Mr. Joseph Calloway. The
only reason I didn't know about him (and I'd
been in the place two weeks) was because I
couldn't talk the language any more than
Mr. Calloway could. There wasn't another
soul in the place who didn't know the story
3 —the whole story of the Halling Investment
Trust and the proceedings for extradition.
Any man doing dusty business in any of the
wooden booths in the town is better fitted by
long observation to tell Mr. Calloway's tale
than I am, except that I was in—literally
—at the finish. They all watched the drama
proceed with immense interest, sympathy
and respect. For, after all, he had a million.

Every once in a while through the long
steamy day, a boy came and cleaned Mr.
Calloway's shoes: he hadn't the right words 4
to resist them—they pretended not to know
his English. He must have had his shoes
cleaned the day Lucia and I watched him at
least half a dozen times. At midday he took a
stroll across the square to the Antonio Bar
and had a bottle of beer, the setter sticking
to heel as if they were out for a country walk
in England (he had, you may remember, one
of the biggest estates in Norfolk). After his
bottle of beer, he would walk down between
the money changers' huts to the Rio
Grande[1] and look across the bridge into the
United States: people came and went constantly in cars. Then back to the square till
lunchtime. He was staying in the best hotel,
but you don't get good hotels in this border
town: nobody stays in them more than a
night. The good hotels were on the other
side of the bridge: you could see their electric
signs twenty stories high from the little 5
square at night, like lighthouses marking
the United States.

You may ask what I'd been doing in so
drab a spot for a fortnight. There was no
interest in the place for anyone; it was just
damp and dust and poverty, a kind of shabby replica of the town across the river: both 6
had squares in the same spots; both had the
same number of cinemas. One was cleaner
than the other, that was all, and more ex-

1. **Rio Grande** (rē′ ō grand′): River that flows between Mexico and Texas.

Thematic Idea Ask students what part the setting plays in the theme of "Araby," "The Demon Lover," "Shooting the Elephant," "The Three Strangers," and "Lagoon." Have them be on the lookout for the answer to this question as they read "Across the Bridge."

pensive, much more expensive. I'd stayed across there a couple of nights waiting for a man a tourist bureau said was driving down from Detroit to Yucatan and would sell a place in his car for some fantastically small figure—twenty dollars, I think it was. I don't know if he existed or was invented by the optimistic half-caste in the agency; anyway, he never turned up and so I waited, not much caring, on the cheap side of the river. It didn't much matter; I was living. One day I meant to give up the man from Detroit and go home or go south, but it was easier not to decide anything in a hurry. Lucia was just waiting for a car going the other way, but she didn't have to wait so long. We waited together and watched Mr. Calloway waiting—for God knows what.

I don't know how to treat this story—it was a tragedy for Mr. Calloway, it was poetic retribution, I suppose, in the eyes of the shareholders he'd ruined with his bogus transactions, and to Lucia and me, at this stage, it was pure comedy—except when he kicked the dog. I'm not a sentimentalist about dogs, I prefer people to be cruel to animals rather than to human beings, but I couldn't help being revolted at the way he'd kick that animal—with a hint of cold-blooded venom, not in anger but as if he 7
were getting even for some trick it had played him a long while ago. That generally happened when he returned from the bridge: it was the only sign of anything resembling emotion he showed. Otherwise he looked a small, set, gentle creature with

7 **Discussion** Why does Mr. Calloway kick his dog every day when he returns from the bridge? What did it show about Mr. Calloway? What does the narrator think about his kicking the dog?

8 **Critical Thinking and Reading** What does the narrator think the dog represents to Calloway? What else might the dog represent to Calloway?

9 **Discussion** This sentence elucidates the townspeople's reaction to Calloway. What did they think about him?

10 **Discussion** What does the policeman whom the narrator meets think about the town? Why is this ironic?

11 **Literary Focus** The narrator can't decide if the story is comedy or tragedy. Ask students why this particular scene is funny. What is the dramatic irony of the scene?

silver hair and a silver moustache, and gold-rimmed glasses, and one gold tooth like a flaw in character.

Lucia hadn't been accurate when she said he'd been turned out of Guatemala and Honduras; he'd left voluntarily when the extradition proceedings seemed likely to go through and moved north. Mexico is still not a very centralized state, and it is possible to get round governors as you can't get round cabinet ministers or judges. And so he waited there on the border for the next move. That earlier part of the story is, I suppose, dramatic, but I didn't watch it and I can't invent what I haven't seen—the long waiting in anterooms, the bribes taken and refused, the growing fear of arrest, and then the flight—in gold-rimmed glasses —covering his tracks as well as he could, but this wasn't finance and he was an amateur at escápe. And so he'd washed up here, under my eyes and Lucia's eyes, sitting all day under the bandstand, nothing to read but a Mexican paper, nothing to do but look across the river at the United States, quite unaware, I suppose, that everyone knew everything about him, once a day kicking his dog. Perhaps in its semi-setter way it reminded him too much of the Norfolk estate
8 —though that, too, I suppose, was the reason he kept it.

And the next act again was pure comedy. I hesitate to think what this man worth a million was costing his country as they edged him out from this land and that. Perhaps somebody was getting tired of the business, and careless; anyway, they sent across two detectives, with an old photograph. He'd grown his silvery moustache since that had been taken, and he'd aged a lot, and they couldn't catch sight of him. They hadn't been across the bridge two hours when everybody knew that there were two foreign detectives in town looking for Mr. Calloway—everybody knew, that is to say, except Mr. Calloway, who couldn't talk Spanish. There were plenty of people who could have told him in English, but they didn't. It wasn't cruelty, it was a sort of awe and respect: like a bull, he was on show,
sitting there mournfully in the plaza with 9
his dog, a magnificent spectacle for which we all had ringside seats.

I ran into one of the policemen in the Bar Antonio. He was disgusted; he had had some idea that when he crossed the bridge life was
going to be different, so much more color 10
and sun, and—I suspect—love, and all he found were wide mud streets where the nocturnal rain lay in pools, and mangy dogs, smells and cockroaches in his bedroom, and the nearest to love, the open door of the Academia Comercial, where pretty mestizo[2] girls sat all the morning learning to typewrite. Tip-tap-tip-tap-tip—perhaps they had a dream, too—jobs on the other side of the bridge, where life was going to be so much more luxurious, refined and amusing.

We got into conversation; he seemed surprised that I knew who they both were and what they wanted. He said: "We've got information this man Calloway's in town."

"He's knocking around somewhere," I said.

"Could you point him out?"

"Oh, I don't know him by sight," I said.

He drank his beer and thought a while. "I'll go out and sit in the plaza. He's sure to pass sometime."

I finished my beer and went quickly off and found Lucia. I said, "Hurry, we're going to see an arrest." We didn't care a thing about Mr. Calloway, he was just an elderly man who kicked his dog and swindled the
poor, and who deserved anything he got. So 11
we made for the plaza; we knew Calloway would be there, but it had never occurred to either of us that the detectives wouldn't recognize him. There was quite a surge of people round the place; all the fruit-sellers and bootblacks in town seemed to have arrived together; we had to force our way through, and there in the little green stuffy

2. mestizo (mes tē′ zō) *adj.*: Of Spanish and Indian parentage.

center of the place, sitting on adjoining seats, were the two plainclothesmen and Mr. Calloway. I've never known the place so silent; everybody was on tiptoe, and the plainclothesmen were staring at the crowd looking for Mr. Calloway, and Mr. Calloway sat on his usual seat staring out over the money-changing booths at the United States.

"It can't go on. It just can't," Lucia said. But it did. It got more fantastic still. Somebody ought to write a play about it. We sat as close as we dared. We were afraid all the time we were going to laugh. The semi-setter scratched for fleas and Mr. Calloway watched the U.S.A. The two detectives watched the crowd, and the crowd watched the show with solemn satisfaction. Then one of the detectives got up and went over to Mr. Calloway. That's the end, I thought. But it wasn't, it was the beginning. For some reason they had eliminated him from their list of suspects. I shall never know why. The man said:

"You speak English?"

"I *am* English," Mr. Calloway said.

Even that didn't tear it, and the strangest thing of all was the way Mr. Calloway came alive. I don't think anybody had spoken to him like that for weeks. The Mexicans were too respectful—he was a man with a million—and it had never occurred to Lucia and me to treat him casually like a human being; even in our eyes he had been magnified by the colossal theft and the worldwide pursuit.

He said: "This is rather a dreadful place, don't you think?"

"It is," the policeman said.

"I can't think what brings anybody across the bridge."

"Duty," the policeman said gloomily. "I suppose you are passing through."

"Yes," Mr. Calloway said.

"I'd have expected over here there'd have been—you know what I mean—life. You read things about Mexico."

"Oh, life," Mr. Calloway said. He spoke firmly and precisely, as if to a committee of shareholders. "That begins on the other side."

"You don't appreciate your own country until you leave it."

"That's very true," Mr. Calloway said. "Very true."

At first it was difficult not to laugh, and then after a while there didn't seem to be 12 much to laugh at; an old man imagining all the fine things going on beyond the international bridge. I think he thought of the town opposite as a combination of London and Norfolk—theaters and cocktail bars, a little shooting and a walk round the field at eve- 13, ning with the dog—that miserable imitation 14 of a setter—poking the ditches. He'd never been across, he couldn't know that it was just the same thing over again—even the same layout; only the streets were paved and the hotels had ten more stories, and life was more expensive, and everything was a little bit cleaner. There wasn't anything Mr. Calloway would have called living—no galleries, no bookshops, just *Film Fun* and the local paper, and *Click* and *Focus* and the tabloids.

"Well," said Mr. Calloway, "I think I'll take a stroll before lunch. You need an appetite to swallow the food here. I generally go down and look at the bridge about now. Care to come, too?"

The detective shook his head. "No," he said, "I'm on duty. I'm looking for a fellow." And that, of course, gave *him* away. As far as Mr. Calloway could understand, there was only one "fellow" in the world anyone was looking for—his brain had eliminated friends who were seeking their friends, husbands who might be waiting for their wives, all objectives of any search but just the one. The power of elimination was what had made him a financier—he could forget the people behind the shares.

That was the last we saw of him for a while. We didn't see him going into the Botica Paris to get his aspirin, or walking back from the bridge with his dog. He simply

12 **Critical Thinking and Reading** Why did the scene lose its humor for the narrator?

13 **Critical Thinking and Reading** What did the town across the bridge represent to Mr. Calloway?

14 **Thematic Idea** Compare Mr. Calloway's romanticized idea of the town across the bridge with the narrator's idea of the bazaar in "Araby."

15 Discussion What does the author mean by this statement?

16 Discussion Why does the narrator suddenly see why Mr. Calloway longs for the town across the bridge? What does this revelation make him feel towards Mr. Calloway?

17 Discussion Why does the narrator feel sorry for Mr. Calloway in this paragraph?

18 Literary Focus What is ironic about the description of Mr. Calloway's "prize" for his efforts to avoid extradition?

19 Literary Focus What is ironic about this sentence? What is the narrator's attitude towards the policemen here?

20 Reading Strategy What is sadly ironic about the fact that everyone in the town speaks English? Why do you think the narrator is ambivalent about telling Mr. Calloway that everyone speaks English? What does this paragraph foreshadow?

21 Critical Thinking and Reading Mr. Calloway has very complex feelings for the dog. Have students discuss those feelings. Does he love or, as he claims, hate the dog?

22 Discussion Why did the two policemen steal Mr. Calloway's dog?

disappeared, and when he disappeared, people began to talk, and the detectives heard the talk. They looked silly enough, and they got busy after the very man they'd been sitting next to in the garden. Then they, too, disappeared. They, as well as Mr. Calloway, had gone to the state capital to see the Governor and the Chief of Police, and it must have been an amusing sight there, too, as they bumped into Mr. Calloway and sat with him in the waiting rooms. I suspect Mr. Calloway was generally shown in first, for everyone knew he was worth a million. Only
15 in Europe is it possible for a man to be a criminal as well as a rich man.

Anyway, after about a week the whole pack of them returned by the same train. Mr. Calloway traveled Pullman,[3] and the two policemen traveled in the day coach. It was evident that they hadn't got their extradition order.

Lucia had left by that time. The car came and went across the bridge. I stood in Mexico and watched her get out at the United States Customs. She wasn't anything in particular but she looked beautiful at a dis-
16 tance as she gave me a wave out of the United States and got back into the car. And I suddenly felt sympathy for Mr. Calloway, as if there were something over there which you couldn't find here, and turning round I saw him back on his old beat, with the dog at his heels.

I said "Good afternoon," as if it had been all along our habit to greet each other. He looked tired and ill and dusty, and I felt sorry
17, 18 for him—to think of the kind of victory he'd been winning, with so much expenditure of cash and care—the prize this dirty and dreary town, the booths of the money changers, the awful little beauty parlors with their wicker chairs and sofas looking like the reception rooms of brothels, that hot and stuffy garden by the bandstand.

He replied gloomily, "Good morning," and the dog started to sniff at some ordure and he turned and kicked it with fury, with depression, with despair.

And at that moment a taxi with the two policemen in it passed us on its way to the bridge. They must have seen that kick; perhaps they were cleverer than I had given them credit for, perhaps they were just sentimental about animals, and thought they'd do a good deed, and the rest happened by accident. But the fact remains—those two
pillars of the law set about the stealing of 19
Mr. Calloway's dog.

He watched them go by. Then he said, "Why don't you go across?"

"It's cheaper here," I said.

"I mean just for an evening. Have a meal at that place we can see at night in the sky. Go to the theater."

"There isn't a chance."

He said angrily, sucking his gold tooth, "Well, anyway, get away from here." He stared down the hill and up the other side. He couldn't see that that street climbing up from the bridge, contained only the same money-changers' booths as this one.

I said, "Why don't *you* go?"

He said evasively. "Oh—business."

I said, "It's only a question of money. You don't *have* to pass by the bridge."

He said with faint interest, "I don't talk Spanish."

"There isn't a soul here," I said, "who doesn't talk English."

He looked at me with surprise. "Is that so?" he said. "Is that so?"

It's as I have said; he'd never tried to talk 20
to anyone, and they respected him too much to talk to him—he was worth a million. I don't know whether I'm glad or sorry that I told him that. If I hadn't he might be there now, sitting by the bandstand having his shoes cleaned—alive and suffering.

Three days later his dog disappeared. I found him looking for it, calling it softly and shamefacedly between the palms of the garden. He looked embarrassed. He said in a 21
low angry voice, "I *hate* that dog. The beast-

3. Pullman: A railroad car with private compartments of seats that can be made into berths for sleeping.

ly mongrel," and called "Rover, Rover" in a voice which didn't carry five yards. He said, "I bred setters once. I'd have shot a dog like that." It reminded him, I *was* right, of Norfolk, and he lived in the memory, and he hated it for its imperfection. He was a man without a family and without friends, and his only enemy was that dog. You couldn't call the law an enemy; you have to be intimate with an enemy.

Late that afternoon someone told him they'd seen the dog walking across the bridge. It wasn't true, of course, but we didn't know that then—they'd paid a Mexican five pesos to smuggle it across. So all that afternoon and the next Mr. Calloway
22 sat in the garden having his shoes cleaned over and over again, and thinking how a dog could just walk across like that, and a human being, an immortal soul, was bound here in the awful routine of the little walk and the unspeakable meals and the aspirin at the botica. That dog was seeing things he
23 couldn't see—that hateful dog. It made him mad—I think literally mad. You must remember the man had been going on for months. He had a million and he was living on two pounds a week, with nothing to spend his money on. He sat there and brooded on the hideous injustice of it. I think he'd have crossed over one day in any case, but the dog was the last straw.

Next day when he wasn't to be seen, I guessed he'd gone across and I went too. The American town is as small as the Mexican. I knew I couldn't miss him if he was there, and I was still curious. A little sorry for him, but not much.

I caught sight of him first in the only drugstore, having a Coca-Cola, and then once outside a cinema looking at the post-
24 ers; he had dressed with extreme neatness, as if for a party, but there was no party. On my third time round, I came on the detectives—they were having Coca-Colas in the drugstore, and they must have missed Mr. Calloway by inches. I went in and sat down at the bar.

"Hello," I said, "you still about." I suddenly felt anxious for Mr. Calloway, I didn't 25
want them to meet.

One of them said, "Where's Calloway?"

"Oh," I said, "he's hanging on."

"But not his dog," he said, and laughed. The other looked a little shocked, he didn't like anyone to *talk* cynically about a dog. Then they got up—they had a car outside.

"Have another?" I said.

"No thanks. We've got to keep moving."

The man bent close and confided to me: "Calloway's on this side."

"No!" I said.

"And his dog."

"He's looking for it," the other said.

"I'm damned if he is," I said, and again one of them looked a little shocked, as if I'd insulted the dog.

I don't think Mr. Calloway was looking for his dog, but his dog certainly found him. There was a sudden hilarious yapping from the car and out plunged the semi-setter and gamboled furiously down the street. One of the detectives—the sentimental one—was into the car before we got to the door and 26
was off after the dog. Near the bottom of the long road to the bridge was Mr. Calloway—I do believe he'd come down to look at the Mexican side when he found there was nothing but the drugstore and the cinemas and the paper shops on the American. He saw the dog coming and yelled at it to go home—"home, home, home," as if they were in Norfolk—it took no notice at all, pelting towards him. Then he saw the police car coming, and ran. After that, everything happened too quickly, but I think the order of events was this—the dog started across the road right in front of the car, and Mr.
Calloway yelled, at the dog or the car, I don't 27
know which. Anyway, the detective swerved—he said later, weakly, at the inquiry, that he couldn't run over a dog, and down went Mr. Calloway, in a mess of broken glass and gold rims and silver hair, and blood. The dog was on to him before any of us could reach him, licking and whimpering and licking. I

23 **Literary Focus** What is the irony Mr. Calloway sees in his situation that makes Mr. Calloway "mad—I think literally mad."

24 **Literary Focus** If you understand the narrator's foreshadowing of events, why is this description of Mr. Calloway ironic?

25 **Discussion** The narrator continues his ambivalent feelings towards Mr. Calloway. Why does he suddenly not want the policemen and Mr. Calloway to meet?

26 **Discussion** What does the dog feel about Mr. Calloway? What does Mr. Calloway think about the dog? Have students back their answers up with passages from the story.

27 **Critical Thinking and Reading** How does Greene set the stage for the sentimental policeman's accidental killing of Mr. Calloway? What is the irony in the policemen's statement at the inquiry?

28 Critical Thinking and Reading What does the narrator mean in this sentence?

29 Discussion Why is the dog's reaction to Mr. Calloway's death a fitting one? Why was it both "comic and . . . pitiable?"

30 Critical Thinking and Reading How might Mr. Calloway have deceived himself? Why does the narrator think that our "capacity for self-deception, our baseless optimism" is "so much more appalling than our despair"?

saw Mr. Calloway put up his hand, and down it went across the dog's neck and the whimper rose to a stupid bark of triumph, but Mr. Calloway was dead—shock and a weak heart.

"Poor old geezer," the detective said, "I bet he really loved that dog," and it's true that the attitude in which he lay looked more like a caress than a blow. I thought it was meant to be a blow, but the detective may have been right. It all seemed to me a little too touching to be true as the old crook lay there with his arm over the dog's neck, dead with his million between the money-changers' huts, but it's as well to be humble in the face of human nature. He had come across the river for something, and it may, after all, have been the dog he was looking for. It sat there, baying its stupid and mongrel triumph across his body, like a piece of sentimental statuary. The nearest he could get to the fields, the ditches, the horizon of his home. It was comic and it was pitiable; but it wasn't less comic because the man was dead. Death doesn't change comedy to tragedy, and if that last gesture was one of affection, I suppose it was only one more indication of a human being's capacity for self-deception, our baseless optimism that is so much more appalling than our despair.

THINKING ABOUT THE SELECTION

Recalling

1. (a) Where does the story take place? (b) What is Mr. Calloway's reason for being there? (c) What is the narrator's reason?
2. (a) Who is Mr. Calloway's constant "companion"? (b) How does he treat this companion?
3. Why do the two detectives not arrest Mr. Calloway at first?
4. (a) What finally brings Mr. Calloway across the bridge? (b) What happens to him?

Interpreting

5. What effect does the repetition of the sentence "He was worth a million" have on you?
6. What trait of Mr. Calloway's personality is revealed by his not knowing that the inhabitants of the town speak English?
7. Both Mr. Calloway and the detectives are disappointed by what they find on the "other side" of the bridge. (a) What proverb does this call to mind? (b) How does this disappointment reflect the story's theme?
8. Consider the role of justice in the story. (a) In what ways is justice served by Mr. Calloway's death? (b) In what way is Mr. Calloway "saved"?

Applying

9. At the end of the story, the narrator says, ". . . I suppose it was only one more indication of a human being's capacity for self-deception, our baseless optimism that is so much more appalling than our despair." Explain your reactions to this statement.

Answers

ANSWERS TO THINKING ABOUT THE SELECTION

Recalling

1. (a) The story takes place in a dirty little Mexican border town on the Rio Grande River. (b) Mr. Calloway is hiding out there, having committed the crime of extortion of trust funds. (c) The narrator is waiting for a ride to the Yucatan peninsula from a man driving down from Detroit.
2. (a) Mr. Calloway's companion is his dog, a rather mangy-looking English setter. (b) He kicks the dog furiously once a day, usually after he looks across the bridge.
3. The two detectives do not recognize Mr. Calloway at first. When they do figure out who he is, they can't arrest him because he is not on American soil. They try to get extradition papers for him, but the governor refuses—the insinuation is that Mr. Calloway buys him off.
4. (a) The detectives steal his dog, and someone tells him that the dog went across the bridge. The narrator indicates that he really goes because he always wanted to see the town on the other side of the bridge. (b) Mr. Calloway is hit by the car of the detectives, who swerve to avoid hitting the dog.
5. The repetition of "he was worth a million" reminds the reader that money and its influence is a central theme of the story, money is what gets Mr. Calloway into his present situation of exile and causes, eventually, his death.
6. Mr. Calloway does not know the townspeople speak English because he feels too superior to them even to notice their bilingualism.
7. (a) The grass is always greener on the other side of the fence. (b) The story's theme centers on the debunking of great expectations—Mr. Calloway thought the town on the other side of the bridge would be wonderful because he was unable to leave the one he was in. Similarly, because of the money he stole, he thought his life would be wonderful; instead he was trapped in a place where he didn't want to be.
8. (a) Because of the money he stole, it seems as if he got his "just deserts." (b) He is "saved" in his doing a noble thing—trying to save the dog and showing his affection for him.

Applying

9. Reactions will vary. You may wish to point out that Greene's Christianity is profoundly rooted in his sense of original sin—the fallen

ANALYZING LITERATURE

Understanding Theme and Point of View

Theme is the insight into life revealed through a literary work. Often misidentified with a story's subject, the theme is a statement about the subject. **Point of view**—the angle from which the story is told—can affect the reader's grasp of the theme. When a story is told, for instance, by a first-person narrator, the reader is made to feel almost a part of the events which in turn brings the theme, or "moral," into sharp focus. Consider the theme of "Across the Bridge." Evaluate the impact that the following "facts" of narration have on the reader's awareness of the theme.

1. The narrator, in the fourth paragraph, gives us his firsthand impressions of the town on the American side.
2. The description of Mr. Calloway's relationship with the dog comes from one who is by his own admission not a lover of dogs.
3. The narrator begins to feel sympathy toward Mr. Calloway.

CRITICAL THINKING AND READING

Understanding Comedy and Tragedy

On page 1025 of the story, the narrator states, "I don't know how to treat this story—it was a tragedy for Mr. Calloway . . . [while to] me, at this stage, it was pure comedy. . . ." Again, at the end, after Mr. Calloway has died, he observes, "It was comic and it was pitiable; but it wasn't less comic because the man was dead. Death doesn't change comedy to tragedy. . . ."

1. In what sense might the death of Mr. Calloway have struck the narrator as comical?
2. Do you agree that death doesn't change comedy to tragedy? Why or why not?
3. The ancient Greeks defined comedy as a play in which the main character triumphs over opposing forces. According to this definition, would you consider "Across the Bridge" more comedy than tragedy, or vice versa? Explain your answer.

UNDERSTANDING LANGUAGE

Learning About Word Completions

Suffixes, the meaning-bearing fragments added to the end of word roots to form new words, fall into two basic types. Derivational suffixes change the part of speech of the word root. The suffix *-al,* which converts the verb *arrive* to the noun *arrival,* is an example of a derivational suffix. Inflectional suffixes affect such matters as number and verb tense without changing the part of speech of the root. The suffix *-es,* which forms the plural noun *churches* from the singular noun *church,* is an example of an inflectional suffix. Identify the italicized part of each of the following words from the story as either a derivational or inflectional suffix. Use each in an original word.

1. pretend*ed*
2. stuff*iness*
3. invest*ment*
4. piti*able*
5. kick*ing*
6. expens*ive*

THINKING AND WRITING

Analyzing the Effects of Point of View

Choose another story that you read in this book, and identify its theme and its narrative point of view. In an essay explain how the point of view affects the theme. Structure your essay on the following questions: Would the impact of the theme have been different had the author used a first-person (or third-person) narrator? What details of narration helped make the theme apparent? What facets of the narrator's character were relevant to the theme? Make sure your essay opens with a clear thesis statement. When you revise make sure you have provided adequate support for your thesis. Proofread your essay and prepare a final draft.

(Answers begin on p. 1030.)

state of the human race—and that this sense may accound for his scorn of "baseless optimism."

ANSWERS TO ANALYZING LITERATURE

1. Through the narrator's eyes, we see the dusty, poverty-filled town as a sort of moral poverty against which the backdrop of Calloway's moral destitution plays. We see the narrator also focusing on money, just as everyone else in the town does—and surely as Mr. Calloway does. So the narrator serves both to interpret the theme and also to represent it.
2. Perhaps the narrator cannot see or understand the relationship of Mr. Calloway and the dog. However, because we see the relationship through the narrator's eyes, he lets us try to figure out the relationship instead of our relying on him. In the same way, reading a piece of literature and figuring out the theme by oneself will have more impact than if one is told exactly what to think. It also brings out one of the themes.
3. The narrator begins to move out of the general human condition of showing no concern for one's fellow man. He starts to see Mr. Calloway as a real person—not perfect, but certainly not all bad.

ANSWERS TO CRITICAL THINKING AND READING

1. The circumstances of Mr. Calloway's death have comic elements—the two policemen missing him yet again in the drugstore, the dog running after him, the policemen chasing the dog, and the car swerving to miss the dog and yet killing Mr. Calloway, which seems ridiculous.
2. Suggested response: Greene thinks there are elements of comedy and tragedy in all parts of life. It is certain that one can be put in the uncomfortable position of laughing at the situation that just preceded Mr. Calloway's death and then feeling as if he or she were laughing at the death itself.
3. Suggested response: The Greeks also believed that the main character in a tragedy is a great person with a tragic flaw. Mr. Calloway is too little a person for his death to qualify as a tragedy—except in the sense that all human life is of value and therefore everyone's death is tragic. However, it does not appear that Mr. Calloway really triumphs over his own misplaced expectations; perhaps he reaches out and loves something—in this case, his dog—more than himself and his aspirations. The story has more comic elements in it than tragic, but it is not a comedy in the classical Greek sense.

ANSWERS TO UNDERSTANDING LANGUAGE

1. inflectional; retained
2. derivational; excessiveness
3. derivational; fulfillment
4. derivational; legible
5. inflectional; accepting
6. derivational; receptive

THINKING AND WRITING

For help with this assignment, students can refer to Lesson 12, "Writing About a Poem," in the Handbook of Writing About Literature.

You may wish to divide students into groups, and have them read their rough drafts to one another and suggest ways in which they could be improved.

More About the Author Because George Orwell felt guilty for letting the stereotypes of race and his position as a police official interfere with his mingling with the Burmese, he spent a period of his life living with the indigent people of Europe. He wore rags, shared quarters with beggars and common laborers in East London and Paris, and tramped around the countryside as a vagrant, working occasionally as a dishwasher, a miner, or a field hand. His years in Burma also changed him politically. His disgust with imperialism and totalitarian governments led him first to anarchism and then to Socialism and libertarianism, systems that, respectively, seek to help the downtrodden and espouse freedom of will and freedom of action for all. Ask students what other famous people they might know—writers or others—whose lives or, in the case of authors, whose writing has been altered by a profound experience such as Orwell had in Burma.

GEORGE ORWELL

1903–1950

Although George Orwell's popular fame is most directly linked to his two novels of political satire, *Animal Farm* and *Nineteen Eighty-Four,* many discerning readers insist that his genius is most readily apparent in his essays and nonfiction. Orwell's prose style, precise yet informal, contributed to making his essays some of the most eloquent short pieces in English writing of the twentieth century.

George Orwell was the pen name chosen by Eric Blair, born in colonial Bengal, an eastern region of India. Schooled in England at Eton, Orwell returned to the East—like H. H. Munro (Saki)—to serve in the Imperial Police in Burma. His experiences in that post, which span the years 1922 to 1927, form the basis of his first novel *Burmese Days* (1934). Disillusioned by his country's policy in the Orient, Orwell left military service to pursue jobs in journalism, publishing, and bookselling in England and France. This period of his life was marked by struggles with poverty, as he recalls in his autobiographical *Down and Out in Paris and London* (1933).

During the 1930's Orwell became deeply involved in social and international causes. *The Road to Wigan Pier* (1937) movingly chronicles the miseries of the English working class during the later phases of the Depression. The coming of the Spanish Civil War (1936–1939) found Orwell firmly committed to the Republican cause. Deploring what he saw as the totalitarianism of the Nationalist victors of the conflict, Orwell paid tribute to the victims in *Homage to Catalonia* (1939).

During World War II Orwell served as literary editor of the *Tribune* from 1943 to 1945 and also contributed political columns to a number of newspapers and journals. In 1945 he published *Animal Farm,* a savage fable that indirectly denounces the evils of both Fascism and Communism. Suffering acutely from the tuberculosis that would ultimately end his life, he completed *Nineteen Eighty-Four* (1948), a grim vision of a future in which language and thought would be everywhere manipulated to serve totalitarian ends.

Orwell's passionate concern for the preservation of political freedom was allied with his efforts to save the English language from "double speak," jargon, and bureaucratic vagueness. In "Politics and the English Language" he dramatically demonstrates how language can be used subtly to conceal political corruption, thereby blinding members of a society to the necessity of moral choice. Although 1984 has come and gone without the fulfillment of Orwell's grim prophecies, his lifelong commitment to political freedom and to the integrity of language as a people's only instrument of communication remain as relevant today as ever.

GUIDE FOR READING

Shooting an Elephant

The Writer's Technique

Tone. Tone is the attitude the writer of a work of fiction takes toward his or her subject, his or her audience, or a character. Just as a speaker's tone of voice can affect the way in which a remark is taken, so the tone of a literary work will help shape the reader's response to it. Tone in a piece of literature is conveyed through the particular words the writer chooses as well as through details of description. For example, a writer who adopts a lighthearted and carefree tone toward the subject of sunshine might refer to the "kiss of warm rays," while the same writer, in approaching the subject with a bitter tone, might make reference to the sun's "cruel, harsh glare." In his essay, "Shooting an Elephant," George Orwell's diction, or word choice, reveals unambiguously his attitude toward the task that has fallen to him as a military police officer in Burma, as well as toward the people to whom he must account for his actions.

Look For

As you read "Shooting an Elephant," look for the tone suggested both by the author's word choice and the details on which he focuses in his narration.

Writing

What is power? Freewrite about the meaning of the word, exploring its effects on both the person who exerts power and the people on whom power is brought to bear.

Vocabulary

Knowing the following words will help you as you read "Shooting an Elephant."

prostrate (präs′ trāt) *adj.*: Defenseless; in a prone or lying position (p. 1034)
despotic (de spät′ ik) *adj.*: Tyrannical (p. 1036)
squalid (skwäl′ id) *adj.*: Miserably poor; wretched (p. 1036)
switch (swich) *n.*: Light whip (p. 1036)
orderly (ôr′ dər lē) *n.*: Soldier assigned to carry out orders of a superior (p. 1036)
senility (si nil′ ə tē) *n.*: Mental and physical decay due to old age (p. 1038)

Literary Focus Remind students that the characters in a story can have many different feelings. For instance, in the first paragraphs of *Shooting an Elephant,* Orwell feels perplexed, upset, insulted, demeaned, and angry; the Burmese feel bitterness, superiority, anger. Tone refers to the *author's* feelings about the subject or characters of his or her story, not how his or her characters feel.

Look For Tone can run the gamut of human emotions. An essay can be serious, light-hearted, emotionally charged, sarcastic, flippant, deprecating, or ecstatic. To understand how many words can be used to describe tone, it might be helpful for students to brainstorm, preferably in small groups, a list of as many emotions, or adjectives describing these emotions, as they can.

Writing It would be useful to have your students discuss the meaning of power and its effects before writing about it.

Vocabulary Have students use their dictionaries or a thesaurus to write a synonym for the first three vocabulary words. Have students write another meaning for the fourth and fifth words, and have them find the meaning of the root of the last word.

Objectives

1 To understand the use and importance of tone in a short story
2 To understand that stereotyping is a form of prejudice
3 To understand word origins
4 To support a written opinion

Teaching Portfolio: Support Material

Teacher Backup, p. 000

Vocabulary Check, pp. 00

Usage and Mechanics Worksheet, p. 00

Analyzing Literature Worksheet, p. 00

Critical Thinking and Reading Worksheet, p. 00

Language Worksheet, p. 00

Selection Test, p. 00

Shooting an Elephant

George Orwell

In Moulmein, in lower Burma, I was hated by large numbers of people—the only time in my life that I have been important enough for this to happen to me. I was subdivisional police officer of the town, and in an aimless, petty kind of way anti-European feeling was very bitter. No one had the guts to raise a riot, but if a European woman went through the bazaars alone somebody would probably spit betel juice over her dress. As a police officer I was an obvious target and was baited whenever it seemed safe to do so. When a nimble Burman tripped me up on the football field and the referee (another Burman) looked the
1 other way, the crowd yelled with hideous laughter. This happened more than once. In the end the sneering yellow faces of young men that met me everywhere, the insults hooted after me when I was at a safe distance, got badly on my nerves. The young Buddhist priests were the worst of all. There were several thousands of them in the town
2 and none of them seemed to have anything to do except stand on street corners and jeer at Europeans.

All this was perplexing and upsetting. For at that time I had already made up my mind that imperialism was an evil thing and the sooner I chucked up my job and got out of it the better. Theoretically—and secretly,
3 of course—I was all for the Burmese and all against their oppressors, the British. As for the job I was doing, I hated it more bitterly than I can perhaps make clear. In a job like that you see the dirty work of Empire at close quarters. The wretched prisoners huddling in the stinking cages of the lockups, the gray, cowed faces of the long-term convicts, the scarred buttocks of the men who had been flogged with bamboos—all these oppressed me with an intolerable sense of guilt. But I could get nothing into perspective. I was young and ill educated and I had had to think out my problems in the utter
silence that is imposed on every Englishman 4
in the East. I did not even know that the British Empire is dying, still less did I know that it is a great deal better than the younger empires that are going to supplant it. All I knew was that I was stuck between my hatred of the empire I served and my rage against the evil-spirited little beasts who tried to make my job impossible. With one part of my mind I thought of the British Raj[1]
as an unbreakable tyranny, as something 5
clamped down, *in saecula saeculorum,*[2] upon the will of prostrate peoples; with another part I thought that the greatest joy in the world would be to drive a bayonet into a Buddhist priest's guts. Feelings like these are the normal byproducts of imperialism; ask any Anglo-Indian official, if you can catch him off duty.

One day something happened which in a roundabout way was enlightening. It was a tiny incident in itself, but it gave me a better glimpse than I had had before of the real

1. Raj (räj): Rule.
2. *in saecula saeculorum* (sē′ ko͞o lə sē′ ko͞o lôr′ əm): Forever and ever.

Motivation for Reading Imagine that you go to a party where you know no one and you are dressed differently from anyone else. One of the people at the party knows someone from your school but doesn't think highly of that person and implies that everyone at your school must be the same way. You are mostly ignored; a few very rude people snicker at your outfit. What feelings do you have at the party? What do you think of the other people who are there? How do you describe the party to your friends?

Master Teacher Note You may wish to have students further their understanding of the essay by asking them to pick one of the following questions to research and answer. How and why did Britain become involved in Burma? What was the outcome of the three Anglo-Burmese Wars? Why did being made a province of India by the British infuriate the Burmese? How did religion fuel the fire of hatred towards the British? What led to the peasant uprising of 1931, which happened shortly after Orwell left Burma? How did Burma eventually become independent? Have them report on their findings in class.

Purpose-Setting Question What is the tone of the essay?

1 **Discussion** How would you feel if you had been treated as Orwell was by the Burmese? Why did the Burmese treat Orwell with contempt? Refer to students' reports in Master Teacher Note or discuss imperialism in general.

2 **Clarification** The Buddhist priests were probably "the worst of all" because, as a province of British-controlled India, the Burmese were subject to the Indian Hindus, whom they disdained.

3 **Literary Focus** What words express Orwell's ambivalent feelings? How do they relate to the tone of the essay? What is the author's attitude towards his subject? Why did he hate his job?

4 **Critical Thinking and Reading** What part did Orwell's age play in his ambivalent feelings towards the Burmese?

5 **Critical Thinking and Reading** Have students keep a list of phrases that Orwell uses to describe the British. Discuss the conflict one would have from representing a government and yet not agreeing with its policies.

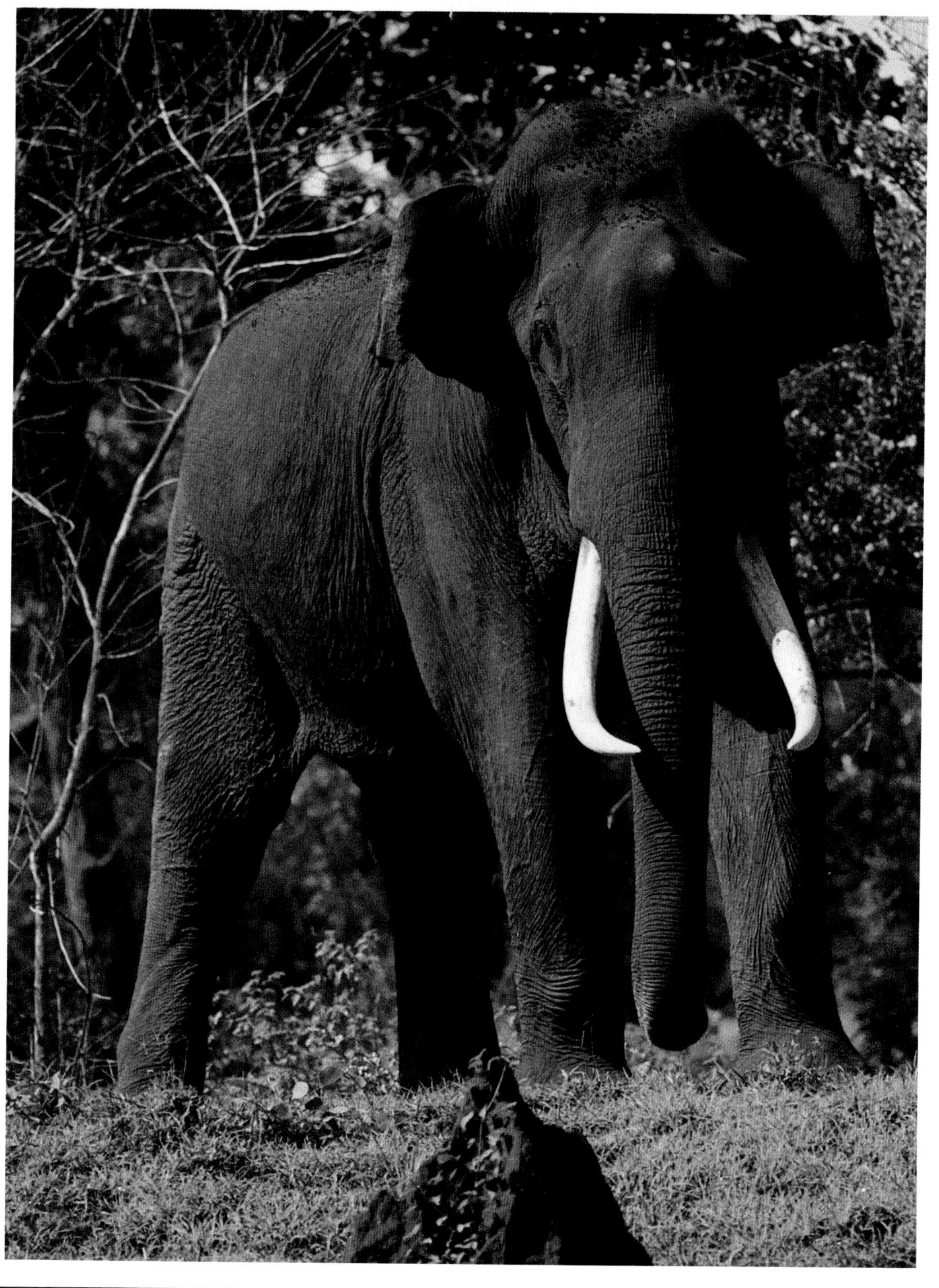

6 Literary Focus How is the atmosphere of the essay—the mood—affected by the comment on the weather?

7 Discussion Orwell sees, though confusedly, that two totally different cultures have great difficulty in understanding one another. What relationship does this comment have to Orwell's feelings of ambivalence about Burma and the inability for westerners to understand the Eastern way?

8 Reading Strategy What effect do you think borrowing the elephant gun will have on the story?

nature of imperialism—the real motives for which despotic governments act. Early one morning the subinspector at a police station the other end of the town rang me up on the phone and said that an elephant was ravaging the bazaar. Would I please come and do something about it? I did not know what I could do, but I wanted to see what was happening and I got onto a pony and started out. I took my rifle, an old .44 Winchester and much too small to kill an elephant, but I thought the noise might be useful *in terrorem.*[3] Various Burmans stopped me on the way and told me about the elephant's doings. It was not, of course, a wild elephant, but a tame one which had gone "must."[4] It had been chained up, as tame elephants always are when their attack of "must" is due, but on the previous night it had broken its chain and escaped. Its mahout,[5] the only person who could manage it when it was in that state, had set out in pursuit, but had taken the wrong direction and was now twelve hours' journey away, and in the morning the elephant had suddenly reappeared in the town. The Burmese population had no weapons and were quite helpless against it. It had already destroyed somebody's bamboo hut, killed a cow and raided some fruit stalls and devoured the stock; also it had met the municipal rubbish van and, when the driver jumped out and took to his heels, had turned the van over and inflicted violences upon it.

The Burmese subinspector and some Indian constables were waiting for me in the quarter where the elephant had been seen. It was a very poor quarter, a labyrinth of squalid bamboo huts, thatched with palm leaf, winding all over a steep hillside. I re-
6 member that it was a cloudy, stuffy morning
at the beginning of the rains. We began
7 questioning the people as to where the elephant had gone and, as usual, failed to get any definite information. That is invariably the case in the East; a story always sounds clear enough at a distance, but the nearer you get to the scene of events the vaguer it becomes. Some of the people said that the elephant had gone in one direction, some said that he had gone in another, some professed not even to have heard of any elephant. I had almost made up my mind that the whole story was a pack of lies, when we heard yells a little distance away. There was a loud, scandalized cry of "Go away, child! Go away this instant!" and an old woman with a switch in her hand came round the corner of a hut, violently shooing away a crowd of naked children. Some more women followed, clicking their tongues and exclaiming; evidently there was something that the children ought not to have seen. I rounded the hut and saw a man's dead body sprawling in the mud. He was an Indian, a black Dravidian[6] coolie,[7] almost naked, and he could not have been dead many minutes. The people said that the elephant had come suddenly upon him round the corner of the hut, caught him with its trunk, put its foot on his back and ground him into the earth. This was the rainy season and the ground was soft, and his face had scored a trench a foot deep and a couple of yards long. He was lying on his belly with arms crucified and head sharply twisted to one side. His face was coated with mud, the eyes wide open, the teeth bared and grinning with an expression of unendurable agony. (Never tell me, by the way, that the dead look peaceful. Most of the corpses I have seen looked devilish.) The friction of the great beast's foot had stripped the skin from his back as neatly as one skins a rabbit. As soon as I saw the dead
man I sent an orderly to a friend's house 8
nearby to borrow an elephant rifle. I had already sent back the pony, not wanting it to

3. ***in terrorem:*** For terror.
4. **must:** Into a dangerous, frenzied state.
5. **mahout** (mə ho͞ot′): An elephant keeper and rider.
6. **Dravidian** (drə vid′ ē ən): Belonging to the race of people inhabiting southern India.
7. **coolie:** Laborer.

go mad with fright and throw me if it smelled the elephant.

The orderly came back in a few minutes with a rifle and five cartridges, and meanwhile some Burmans had arrived and told us that the elephant was in the paddy fields[8] 9 below, only a few hundred yards away. As I started forward practically the whole population of the quarter flocked out of the houses and followed me. They had seen the rifle and were all shouting excitedly that I was going to shoot the elephant. They had not shown much interest in the elephant when he was merely ravaging their homes, but it was different now that he was going to be shot. It was a bit of fun to them, as it would be to an English crowd; besides they wanted the meat. It made me vaguely uneasy. I had no intention of shooting the elephant—I had merely sent for the rifle to defend myself if necessary—and it is always unnerving to have a crowd following you. I marched down the hill, looking and feeling a fool, with the rifle over my shoulder and an ever-growing army of people jostling at my heels. At the bottom, when you got away from the huts, there was a metaled road[9] and beyond that a miry waste of paddy fields a thousand yards across, not yet plowed but soggy from the first rains and dotted with coarse grass. The elephant was standing eight yards from the road, his left side toward us. He took not the slightest notice of the crowd's approach. He was tearing up bunches of grass, beating them against his knees to clean them, and stuffing them into his mouth.

10 I had halted on the road. As soon as I saw the elephant I knew with perfect certainty that I ought not to shoot him. It is a serious matter to shoot a working elephant—it is comparable to destroying a huge and costly piece of machinery—and obviously one ought not to do it if it can possibly be avoided. And at that distance, peacefully eating, the elephant looked no more dangerous than a cow. I thought then and I think now that his attack of "must" was already passing off; in which case he would merely wander harmlessly about until the mahout came back and caught him. Moreover, I did not in the least want to shoot him. I decided that I would watch him for a little while to make sure that he did not turn savage again, and then go home.

But at that moment I glanced round at the crowd that had followed me. It was an immense crowd, two thousand at the least and growing every minute. It blocked the road for a long distance on either side. I looked at the sea of yellow faces above the garish clothes—faces all happy and excited over this bit of fun, all certain that the elephant was going to be shot. 11 They were watching me as they would watch a conjurer about to perform a trick. They did not like me, but with the magical rifle in my hands I was momentarily worth watching. And suddenly I realized that I should have to shoot 12 the elephant after all. The people expected it of me and I had got to do it; I could feel their two thousand wills pressing me forward, irresistibly. And it was at this moment, as I stood there with the rifle in my hands, that I first grasped the hollowness, the futility of the white man's dominion in the East. Here was I, the white man with his gun, standing in front of the unarmed native crowd—seemingly the leading actor of the piece; but in reality I was only an absurd puppet pushed to and fro by the will of those yellow faces behind. I perceived in this moment that when the white man turns tyrant it is his own freedom that he destroys. He becomes a sort of hollow, posing dummy, the conventionalized figure of a sahib.[10] For it is the condition of his rule that he shall spend his life in trying to impress the "natives," and so in every crisis he has got to do what

8. paddy fields: Rice fields.
9. metaled road: A road in which the pavement is reinforced with metal strips.

10. sahib (sä′ ib): Indian word for European gentleman.

9 **Discussion** Why did a crowd form when Orwell set off with the gun? Why did the crowd make him "vaguely uneasy"? How else did it make him feel?

10 **Reading Strategy** Based on what you have read so far, do you think Orwell will shoot the elephant? Why or why not?

11 **Discussion** What does the simile "as they would watch a conjurer about to perform a trick" tell about Orwell's situation with the elephant?

12 **Critical Thinking and Reading** Why does Orwell think he has to kill the elephant? What is the realization he comes to about the real position of power of the British in Burma? What did Orwell fear more than the elephant? Orwell prefaced his essay with the remark that the real motives and nature of imperialism became clear to him in this incident. What are those motives? How did the incident illustrate them? What is the link between Burma and the elephant?

13 Literary Focus What in Orwell's tone tells you how he feels about having shot the elephant?

the "natives" expect of him. He wears a mask, and his face grows to fit it. I had got to shoot the elephant. I had committed myself to doing it when I sent for the rifle. A sahib has got to act like a sahib; he has got to appear resolute, to know his own mind and do definite things. To come all that way, rifle in hand, with two thousand people marching at my heels, and then to trail feebly away, having done nothing—no, that was impossible. The crowd would laugh at me. And my whole life, every white man's life in the East, was one long struggle not to be laughed at.

But I did not want to shoot the elephant. I watched him beating his bunch of grass against his knees with that preoccupied
13 grandmotherly air that elephants have. It seemed to me that it would be murder to shoot him. At that age I was not squeamish about killing animals, but I had never shot an elephant and never wanted to. (Somehow it always seems worse to kill a *large* animal.) Besides, there was the beast's owner to be considered. Alive, the elephant was worth at least a hundred pounds, dead, he would only be worth the value of his tusks, five pounds, possibly. But I had got to act quickly. I turned to some experienced-looking Burmans who had been there when we arrived, and asked them how the elephant had been behaving. They all said the same thing: he took no notice of you if you left him alone, but he might charge if you went too close to him.

It was perfectly clear to me what I ought to do. I ought to walk up to within, say, twenty-five yards of the elephant and test his behavior. If he charged, I could shoot; if he took no notice of me, it would be safe to leave him until the mahout came back. But also I knew that I was going to do no such thing. I was a poor shot with a rifle and the ground was soft mud into which one would sink at every step. If the elephant charged and I missed him, I should have about as much chance as a toad under a steam-roller. But even then I was not thinking particularly of my own skin, only of the watchful yellow faces behind. For at that moment, with the crowd watching me, I was not afraid in the ordinary sense, as I would have been if I had been alone. A white man mustn't be frightened in front of "natives"; and so, in general, he isn't frightened. The sole thought in my mind was that if anything went wrong those two thousand Burmans would see me pursued, caught, trampled on, and reduced to a grinning corpse like that Indian up the hill. And if that happened it was quite probable that some of them would laugh. That would never do. There was only one alternative. I shoved the cartridges into the magazine and lay down on the road to get a better aim.

The crowd grew very still, and a deep, low, happy sigh, as of people who see the theater curtain go up at last, breathed from innumerable throats. They were going to have their bit of fun, after all. The rifle was a beautiful German thing with cross-hair sights. I did not then know that in shooting an elephant one would shoot to cut an imaginary bar running from ear hole to ear hole. I ought, therefore, as the elephant was sideways on, to have aimed straight at his earhole; actually I aimed several inches in front of this, thinking the brain would be further forward.

When I pulled the trigger I did not hear the bang or feel the kick—one never does when a shot goes home—but I heard the devilish roar of glee that went up from the crowd. In that instant, in too short a time, one would have thought, even for the bullet to get there, a mysterious, terrible change had come over the elephant. He neither stirred nor fell, but every line of his body had altered. He looked suddenly stricken, shrunken, immensely old, as though the frightful impact of the bullet had paralyzed him without knocking him down. At last, after what seemed a long time—it might have been five seconds, I dare say—he sagged flabbily to his knees. His mouth slobbered. An enormous senility seemed to have settled upon him. One could have imagined him thousands of years old. I fired again into the same spot. At the second shot he did not collapse but climbed with desperate slowness to his feet and stood weakly upright, with legs sagging and head drooping. I fired a third time. That was the shot that did for him. You could see the agony of it jolt his whole body and knock the last remnant of strength from his legs. But in falling he seemed for a moment to rise, for as his hind legs collapsed beneath him he seemed to tower upward like a huge rock toppling, his trunk reaching skyward like a tree. He trumpeted, for the first and only time. And then down he came, his belly toward me, with a crash that seemed to shake the ground even where I lay.

I got up. The Burmans were already racing past me across the mud. It was obvious that the elephant would never rise again, but he was not dead. He was breathing very rhythmically with long rattling gasps, his great mound of a side painfully rising and falling. His mouth was wide open—I could see far down into caverns of pale pink throat. I waited a long time for him to die, but his breathing did not weaken. Finally I fired my two remaining shots into the spot where I thought his heart must be. The thick blood welled out of him like red velvet, but still he did not die. His body did not even jerk when the shots hit him, the tortured breathing continued without a pause. He was dying, very slowly and in great agony, but in some world remote from
14 me where not even a bullet could damage
him further. I felt that I had got to put an end to that dreadful noise. It seemed dreadful to see the great beast lying there, powerless to move and yet powerless to die, and not even to be able to finish him. I sent back for my small rifle and poured shot after shot into his heart and down his throat. They seemed to make no impression. The tortured gasps continued as steadily as the ticking of a clock.

In the end I could not stand it any longer and went away. I heard later that it took him half an hour to die. Burmans were bringing dahs[11] and baskets even before I left, and I was told they had stripped his body almost to the bones by the afternoon.

Afterward, of course, there were endless discussions about the shooting of the elephant. The owner was furious, but he was only an Indian and could do nothing. Besides, legally I had done the right thing, for a mad elephant has to be killed, like a mad dog, if its owner fails to control it. Among
the Europeans opinion was divided. The 15
older man said I was right, the younger men said it was a shame to shoot an elephant for killing a coolie, because an elephant was worth more than any Coringhee[12] coolie. And afterward I was very glad that the coolie had been killed; it put me legally in the right
and it gave me a sufficient pretext for shoot- 16
ing the elephant. I often wondered whether any of the others grasped that I had done it solely to avoid looking a fool.

11. **dahs** (däz): Knives.
12. **Coringhee** (cor in′ gē): Southern Indian.

14 **Discussion** What does the elephant symbolize to Orwell when he witnesses his painful, slow death "in some world remote from me . . ."? Why is he so upset when the elephant takes a long time to die?

15 **Critical Thinking and Reading** What do you infer from the phrases "only an Indian" and "it was a shame to shoot an elephant for killing a coolie, because an elephant was worth more . . ."?

16 **Critical Thinking and Reading** What is the irony in this statement? How does it further reveal Orwell's confusion and ambivalence about the Burmese?

Answers

ANSWERS TO THINKING ABOUT THE SELECTION

Recalling

1. (a) Orwell was hated simply because he was British and therefore a symbol of British imperialism. (b) He agreed with the Burmese's hatred of imperialism, but their attitude towards him made him angry at them.
2. He sees the mangled and flayed body of the man that the elephant had trampled.
3. (a) He feels that killing the elephant would be murder, since it no longer seemed dangerous; the animal is worth a lot of money; its owner would be angry; although he does not feel squeamish about killing, he seems to have a respect for life that abhors needless slaughter. (b) He knows the crowd expects him to kill the elephant and realizes, as a British official, that he can't "lose face" with the people.
4. The elephant sinks to its knees on the first shot but scrambles up with the second shot. The third shot makes it fall, but the fourth and fifth shots still cannot totally kill it.
5. After the animal is dead, the Burmese strip the meat off its bones.

Interpreting

6. Orwell is confused by his ambivalent feelings towards the Burmese; he agrees with their antipathy for imperialism, but their insulting treatment of him enrages him. The conflict between how he thinks he ought to feel towards the natives and how he actually feels "got badly on [his] nerves." He hates his job because it reveals the "dirty work of the Empire," particularly the wretchedness of prisoners. He therefore feels an overwhelming sense of guilt about his job.
7. The experience with the elephant is enlightening because through it he sees the position of England—and therefore himself—in Burma: that the "oppressors" are not really in charge, as they fancy; the Burmese are. The experience becomes symbolic of the British existence in Burma and through the experience he first understands the cause of his ambivalent feelings.
8. The author goes into great detail about the elephant's death so that the reader will experience the same revulsion as he does and will see the elephant as a symbol of Burma, whose spirit the British are killing just as needlessly and wastefully as he has killed the elephant.
9. (a) The direct language that Orwell uses does not hide the fact that he hates both the British tyranny and the "evil-spirited little beasts"—the Burmese." He also

has a lot of sympathy for the elephant and yet the fact that he feels loyal to his country is evident when he decides, as his country's representative that he cannot appear foolish. (b) The theme of the essay is that man can commit heinous acts to appear "honorable" without looking foolish. Orwell's complex feelings lead him to do something he is morally against, but he has no recourse if he wants to save face. Until this incident, Orwell understands his motivations and actions as little as anyone.

Applying

10. Suggested responses: No, because I am morally against killing animals under any circumstances. Or, yes; I agree with Orwell that it was the only thing he could do if he was to maintain the respect of the people.

ANSWERS TO ANALYZING LITERATURE

Suggested responses:

1. Orwell had ambivalent feelings about the Burmese. On the one hand, he agreed with their hatred of British imperialism and felt that he was a kindred spirit because of his anti-imperialism. ("Theoretically . . . I was all for the Burmese and all against their oppressors, the British.") However, their treatment of him made him so angry that his "greatest joy" would have been to "drive a bayonet into a Buddhist priest's guts." He hated their "sneering faces" and called them "evil-spirited little beasts."
2. He is "all against [the Burmese] oppressors, the British." Again, he probably means theoretically; he can have feelings of patriotism towards his country and still reject its policy decisions. He felt that although the British empire had problems, it was "a great deal better than the younger empires" that came after it.
3. Although Orwell does not feel "squeamish about killing animals," he does not like needless killing. He also feels sorry for the elephant, which is clear in his reference to it as having a "grandmotherly air," and his detailed description of the elephant's death indicates what a impact it has on him.

THINKING ABOUT THE SELECTION

Recalling

1. (a) Why was the narrator hated in Burma? (b) Why were his reactions to this hatred mixed?
2. What grisly sight does the narrator encounter when he arrives in the quarter where the elephant has been seen?
3. (a) What reasons does the narrator give for not wanting to shoot the elephant? (b) Why does he shoot it in spite of these reasons?
4. How many shots does it take to bring the elephant down?
5. What do the Burmans do once the elephant is dead?

Interpreting

6. How would you summarize the sentiments the narrator expresses in the first two paragraphs?
7. What do you think the narrator means when he states at the beginning of the third paragraph that this incident was "enlightening" in "a roundabout way"?
8. What do you think was the narrator's reason for providing his lengthy and detailed description of the elephant's death?
9. (a) What evidence is there in this essay that the narrator was divided in his sympathies. (b) How might the narrator's complex feelings be related to the essay's theme?

Applying

10. If you had been in the narrator's place do you think you would have shot the elephant? Why or why not?

ANALYZING LITERATURE

Identifying Tone

Tone is a writer's attitude toward his or her subject, her or his audience, or a character. In a literary work, tone is communicated through details and the author's choice of words. As a recollection of an incident from a period of George Orwell's life that was "perplexing and upsetting," "Shooting an Elephant" sums up the author's attitude toward several separate but related subjects. In your own words, identify the author's tone toward each of the following subjects, and locate specific words and passages that support your assumption.

1. The Burmans
2. The British Empire
3. Killing and death

CRITICAL THINKING AND READING

Understanding Stereotypes

A **stereotype** is a generalization about a whole group of people that does not apply to all individuals belonging to a certain group. The acceptance and use of stereotypes are forms of prejudice. In "Shooting an Elephant" Orwell explains that he was disliked by Burmans not because of any specific limitation of his own character but because he was European. The Burmans, thus, had a preconceived notion, or stereotype, of the European. What do you think is Orwell's reaction to stereotypes? Explain your answer.

UNDERSTANDING LANGUAGE

Understanding Word Origins

Several words used by Orwell in this selection are "Anglicizations," that is, words from another language which have been given English spellings and pronunciations that imitate the original. In a good dictionary, find each of the following Anglicized words, and trace their origins as far back as you can.

1. raj
2. mahout
3. coolie
4. sahib
5. dahs

THINKING AND WRITING

Supporting an Opinion

In an opinion paper, argue your belief that Orwell was justified, or not justified, in shooting the elephant. Your essay should not only support your own position but should pinpoint and refute arguments that might be raised by the opposition. Draw, if you can, from outside sources to drive home your point. When you revise make sure you have provided adequate support for your opinion.

ANSWERS TO CRITICAL THINKING AND READING

Suggested response: The Burmese stereotypically saw Europeans as despotic and bloodthirsty —as shown by their assumption that Orwell would shoot the elephant.

ANSWERS TO UNDERSTANDING LANGUAGE

1. raj: a Hindi word *raj* from the Sanskrit *rajati*, "he rules."
2. mahout: from Hindi *mahaut, mahawat,* from the Sanskrit *mahamatra* meaning "of great measure," which was originally an honorific title.
3. coolie: Hini *kuli* from *Kuli,* the name of an aboriginal tribe in India.
4. sahib: Hindi *sahib* from Arabic; "master."
5. daks: from Burmese *dā*, "a large heavy knife."

Poetry

HOUSES OF PARLIAMENT, 1903
Claude Monét
The Granger Collection

Humanities Note

Fine art, *Houses of Parliament*, 1903, by Claude Monet. The French painter Monet (1840–1926) was a founder of the impressionist school, and is one of the foremost landscape painters in the history of art. The Impressionists used their broken-color technique to capture the transient variations of light and atmosphere brought on by changes of hour and season. They were interested in the subtle effects of light on form. Monet loosens the brush-strokes, allowing colors to fuse, not on canvas, but in the eye of the viewer. In Impressionism, the actual act of painting becomes visible: every dab and touch is a record of the movement of the brush.

Houses of Parliament is one of 37 views of London's Thames River Monet exhibited in 1904. The painting is mysterious and visionary. Its theme is not the stone architecture, but silhouette and reflections, colored light suspended in air. The cool blue mass of the buildings is markedly contrasted to the fiery pastels of the sky and water, which seem to set the scene ablaze. Volume and depth in the painting are created by the variety of tones of color, which give the atmosphere as tangible a life and breath as that of the solid objects. The boatman in the foreground, moving through the fog, heightens the mysterious mood as do the narrow, tall Gothic towers and spires of the mass of buildings. The colors and technique themselves create a palpable drama.

More About the Author Point out to students that Yeats was an intensely private man who still managed to take an active role in politics and artistic movements. Ask students what, if anything, a person may gain by engaging in activities that seem to go against his or her nature.

WILLIAM BUTLER YEATS

1865–1939

Winner of the Nobel Prize for Literature in 1923, William Butler Yeats (yātz) is generally regarded as one of the finest poets of this century. Born near Dublin, Ireland, Yeats was educated there and in London, but his heart lay to the west, in County Sligo, Ireland, where he spent childhood vacations with his grandparents. In the shadow of Sligo's barren mountains, he became immersed in the mythology and legends of Ireland.

After three years of studying painting in Dublin, Yeats moved to London to pursue a literary career. He became friends with the poet Arthur Symons, who awakened his interest in the symbolic poetry of William Blake and the French Symbolists. Yeats's early poetry shows the Symbolist influence as well as that of the Pre-Raphaelites, a group who believed that art needs a moral center which they felt it had lost nearly three centuries earlier. Symbolism, Pre-Raphaelism, and Irish myth combined in Yeats's first important collection, *The Wanderings of Oisin,* published in 1889.

Yeats led the Irish Literary Revival, helping to establish the Irish Literary Society in London in 1892 and the Irish National Literary Society in Dublin. He was also active in the Irish National Movement, whose members sought Ireland's independence from England. In this, he was spurred by his unrequited love for the beautiful actress and revolutionary, Maud Gonne. To his sorrow—after many refusals of his proposals—she chose a soldier, and Yeats, years later, married another woman.

Near the end of the century, Yeats joined with his friend, Lady Augusta Gregory, in founding the Irish National Theatre Society. He turned his attention to writing plays, among them *The Shadowy Waters* (1900) and *Deirdre* (1907). When he returned to poetry, it was with a new voice, subtler but more powerful than the one he had used before that time. The poems in *The Tower,* published in 1928, show Yeats at the height of his abilities.

In 1922 Yeats was appointed a senator of the new Irish Free State, and on his seventieth birthday he was hailed by his nation as the greatest living Irishman. He continued to write poems until a day or two before his death at Roquebrune, France. One of his last poems contains his famous epitaph: Cast a cold eye / On life, on death. / Horseman, pass by!

Objectives

1. To identify the speaker in a lyric poem
2. To evaluate the use of imagery
3. To write about the use of a speaker

Teaching Portfolio: Support Material

Teacher Backup, p. 000

Vocabulary Check, p. 00

Usage and Mechanics Worksheet, p. 00

Analyzing Literature Worksheet, p. 00

Critical Thinking and Reading Worksheet, p. 00

Language Worksheet, p. 00

Selection Test, p. 000

GUIDE FOR READING

When You Are Old; The Lake Isle of Innisfree; The Wild Swans at Coole; An Irish Airman Foresees His Death

Writer's Techniques

Speaker and Lyric Voice. A lyric poem expresses personal thoughts and feelings on a specific subject. Among the most common subjects are love, death, nature, and war. Sometimes the speaker in a lyric poem—the one whose voice comes through—is, or appears to be, the poet. In Milton's "When I Consider How My Light Is Spent," for example, the speaker seems clearly to be the poet. In Christopher Marlowe's "The Passionate Shepherd to His Love," on the other hand, the speaker is almost certainly not the poet. In many lyric poems, such as William Blake's "The Tiger," you cannot tell for sure whether the speaker is or is not the poet.

Look For

As you read the poems by William Butler Yeats, try to determine who the speaker is in each one.

Writing

Think of a subject about which you have strong feelings, either positive or negative, such as education, friendship, or marriage. Jot down some brief notes that express your feelings on the subject. Then think of a fictional character based either on your reading or your imagination. Write at least three sentences, or three lines of poetry, in which the fictional character expresses your feelings on the subject you have chosen.

Literary Focus Consider telling students that by speculating about the dramatic situation out of which a poem seems to arise, they will be better able to identify the speaker. For example, can they imagine a setting in which these words are spoken? Whom does the speaker seem to be addressing? What events may have led up to this speech?

Look For Have students read each poem aloud before trying to identify the speaker. Simply hearing the poem as a credible speech will give them important clues.

Writing Have students consider why writing about a strong feeling can be helpful.

Motivation for Reading Encourage students to think about someone who disappointed them in rejecting their offer of friendship. What kind of polite response would be appropriate?

Master Teacher Note Elicit from students various meanings for *pilgrim.* Recall with them the pilgrims in Chaucer's *Canterbury Tales* and Pilgrim in Bunyan's *Pilgrim's Progress.* What do these pilgrims have in common? What religious connotations does *pilgrim* have?

Purpose-Setting Question How much self-pity is there in this poem?

Thematic Idea Another selection that you might want to use with this is Matthew Arnold's poem "To Marguerite-Continued," page 838. It is similar to this poem in dealing with unfulfilled love.

1 **Literary Focus** Note that the speaker asks the woman to think about herself before he makes a transition to his own feelings. Why is this method effective?

2 **Discussion** What does Yeats mean by her "pilgrim soul"?

3 **Discussion** What does he mean by "the sorrows of your changing face"?

4 **Literary Focus** What does the imagery suggest about the outcome of this love?

Enrichment It is somewhat ironic for Yeats to be praising his love's "pilgrim soul" when he was adamantly opposed to her revolutionary zeal. He felt that fierce political commitment was unfeminine and unattractive.

When You Are Old

William Butler Yeats

1 When you are old and gray and full of sleep,
And nodding by the fire, take down this book,
And slowly read, and dream of the soft look
Your eyes had once, and of their shadows deep;

2 How many loved your moments of glad grace,
And loved your beauty with love false or true,
But one man loved the pilgrim soul in you,
3 And loved the sorrows of your changing face;

And bending down beside the glowing bars,
4 Murmur, a little sadly, how Love fled
And paced upon the mountains overhead
And hid his face amid a crowd of stars.

THINKING ABOUT THE SELECTION

Recalling

1. What does the speaker ask the person being addressed to do?
2. What happened to Love?

Interpreting

3. Who do you think the "one man" in the second stanza is?
4. What does the phrase "pilgrim soul" suggest about the person being addressed?
5. Why is the word *Love* capitalized in line 10?

Applying

6. When love is not reciprocated, it may be withdrawn, as it apparently was in this poem. Under what circumstances do you think it is right to withdraw love that is not being returned?

ANALYZING LITERATURE

Understanding Speaker and Lyric Voice

The speaker in a lyric poem may or may not be the poet. Sometimes the identity of the speaker is obvious, but often it is hard to be sure. Knowing about the poet's life, while not essential to your enjoyment of a poem, may provide clues to the identity of the speaker.

1. Look back at the biography of Yeats. What event in his life might have prompted him to write this poem?
2. In line 2 the speaker advises the person being addressed to "take down this book." In what way might that advice furnish a clue to the identity of the speaker?

Answers

ANSWERS TO THINKING ABOUT THE SELECTION

Recalling

1. He asks her to read this book and dream about herself as a young woman.
2. Love fled, paced upon the mountains, and hid its face.

Interpreting

3. Suggested Response: The man is the speaker—Yeats himself.
4. Answers will differ. Students may respond that the phrase suggests the woman is a wanderer or seeker.
5. Suggested Response: The speaker is personifying love.

Applying

6. Answers will differ. Students may respond that a person always has the right to withdraw unreciprocated love.

ANSWERS TO ANALYZING LITERATURE

1. Suggested Response: Maud Gonne's choice of a different suitor could have prompted this poem.
2. Suggested Response: One would be reading this poem in a volume of verse, so one can infer that the speaker is a poet.

The Lake Isle of Innisfree

William Butler Yeats

I will arise and go now, and go to Innisfree,
And a small cabin build there, of clay and wattles[1] made:
Nine bean-rows will I have there, a hive for the honeybee,
And live alone in the bee-loud glade.

And I shall have some peace there, for peace comes
dropping slow,
1 Dropping from the veils of the morning to where the cricket
sings;
There midnight's all a glimmer, and noon a purple glow,
And evening full of the linnet's wings.[2]

I will arise and go now, for always night and day
I hear lake water lapping with low sounds by the shore;
2 While I stand on the roadway, or on the pavements gray,
I hear it in the deep heart's core.

OLD HOUSE (IVY COTTAGE), SHOREHAM, 1831–32
Samuel Palmer
Ashmolean Museum, Oxford

---

1. **wattles** *n.*: Stakes interwoven with twigs or branches.
2. **linnet's wings:** The wings of a European singing bird.

THINKING ABOUT THE SELECTION

Recalling

1. (a) What does the speaker want most to find at Innisfree? (b) How will each of the four times of day he mentions contribute to his goal?
2. According to line 11, where is the speaker when he hears the call of Innisfree?
3. Why do you think Innisfree, as the speaker describes it, has so much more appeal for him than where he is now?
4. (a) Do you think the speaker is expressing a wish or a genuine intent to go to Innisfree? (b) What evidence in the poem is there to support your answer?
5. What techniques or devices in the poem help to create a vivid picture of Innisfree?

Applying

6. Popular music sometimes deals with the theme of leaving one place and going to a more desirable place. What song or songs can you think of that have that theme?

Master Teacher Note You might tell students that Yeats had read Thoreau's *Walden* before writing this poem. Remind students that, in his book, Thoreau describes his experiment in living an isolated, self-sufficient life in natural surroundings.

Purpose-Setting Question What is attractive about the way of life that Yeats imagines?

1 **Literary Focus** The metaphors in this stanza contrast with the preceding stanza's literal descriptions.

2 **Literary Focus** Note that stanza three returns to the directness of stanza one. How does this stanza, then, reinforce the message?

Humanities Note

Fine art; *Old House (Ivy Cottage), Shoreham* by Samuel Palmer. Samuel Palmer (1805–1881), was a British visionary painter of pastoral subjects. A precociously talented painter, Palmer exhibited watercolors at London's Royal Academy at the age of fourteen. With the exception of a few lessons, he was a self-taught painter.

The painting *Old House (Ivy Cottage), Shoreham* was completed in 1831–32. The contrast between the motionless shadowed figures and the bright cottage creates a mysterious tension. Even the foliage seems charged and still, as if listening to the words of the group.

You may wish to discuss the following:

1. This painting suggests a simple life, close to nature. How does this compare to the life Yeats writes of in his poem?
2. The artist Samuel Palmer had a deep regard for nature. Do you feel that the poet Yeats shared this regard? Explain.

Answers

ANSWERS TO THINKING ABOUT THE SELECTION

Recalling

1. (a) The speaker desires peace. (b) Morning (mist and cricket song), noon ("a purple glow"), evening (flocks of linnets), and midnight ("all a glimmer") will contribute to the feeling of peace.
2. The speaker is on a city street.

Interpreting

3. Suggested Response: One may infer that the peaceful retreat is in direct contrast to the speaker's more frenetic city life.
4. (a) Suggested Response: The speaker seems to be expressing a deeply felt dream of an ideal type of existance rather than an intent to leave immediately. (b) Throughout the poem, he dwells more on visualizing the ideal than on a plan for departure.
5. Suggested Response: Students may note the repetition of the word "dropping;" the soothing *m*, *n*, and *l* sounds: the concrete, specific images; and the metaphors in the second stanza.

Applying

6. Answers will differ. Students will no doubt suggest currently popular songs.

Motivation for Reading Discuss with students why people think of swans as impressive and unusual birds, and note that the swan has become part of expressions such as *swansong*. What qualities or characteristics do we associate with a swan?

Master Teacher Note You might want to tell students that Coole Park, where this poem is set, was the home of Lady Gregory. She was Yeats's patron and collaborator—they worked together in establishing a national theater. Yeats spent a great deal of time at Coole Park, a large estate with ponds for swans, forest paths, orchards, and so forth.

Thematic Idea Other selections that deal with age and with facing mortality are "Ode to a Nightingale", on page 731, and "Ode on a Grecian Urn", on page 736, both by John Keats.

1 **Discussion** What scene does the poet set? What mood is associated with this scene?

2 **Discussion** What is the effect of the poet's use of exact numbers?

3 **Discussion** The poet shifts the direction of his musings here; he turns from the outward scene to his inner feelings. How *does* he feel? Why is his heart sore? What in particular has changed in the past nineteen years?

4 **Discussion** What does he mean by "passion" and "conquest"? Are these qualities usually associated with the young? Explain.

5 **Discussion** Why does he call the swans "mysterious"?

6 **Discussion** What kind of wakening is he referring to? Why will the swans be gone?

The Wild Swans at Coole

William Butler Yeats

The trees are in their autumn beauty,
The woodland paths are dry,
1 Under the October twilight the water
Mirrors a still sky;
Upon the brimming water among
the stones
Are nine-and-fifty swans.

2 The nineteenth autumn has come
upon me
Since I first made my count;
I saw, before I had well finished,
All suddenly mount
And scatter wheeling in great broken
rings
Upon their clamorous wings.

I have looked upon those brilliant
creatures,
And now my heart is sore.
All's changed since I, hearing at twilight,
3 The first time on this shore,
The bell-beat of their wings above
my head,
Trod with a lighter tread.

Unwearied still, lover by lover,
They paddle in the cold
Companionable streams or climb the air;
4 Their hearts have not grown old;
Passion or conquest, wander where
they will,
Attend upon them still.

But now they drift on the still water,
5 Mysterious, beautiful;
Among what rushes will they build,
By what lake's edge or pool
Delight men's eyes when I awake
6 some day
To find they have flown away?

THINKING ABOUT THE SELECTION

Recalling

1. (a) When did the speaker first begin counting the swans? (b) What did the swans do before he had finished counting?
2. (a) What was the speaker's reaction when he first heard "the bell-beat of their wings"? (b) Why is his reaction different now from what it was then?
3. What will the swans inevitably do?

Interpreting

4. For what thematic purpose does the speaker emphasize the setting in the first two stanzas?
5. In the fourth stanza, how does the speaker suggest that he and the swans are not alike?

Answers

ANSWERS TO THINKING ABOUT THE SELECTION

Recalling

1. (a) He began counting the swans nineteen years ago. (b) The swans flew away before he could finish counting.
2. (a) The speaker was younger then —"trod with a lighter tread"—and was perhaps happier. (b) He is older and tired now, envious of the swans' passion.
3. The swans will fly away.

Interpreting

4. Suggested Response: The speaker emphasizes autumn, generally symbolic of old age and of approaching death.
5. Suggested Response: The swans, in contrast to the speaker, are "unwearied still."
6. Suggested Response: The swans represent eternal youth and enduring love and passion.

Applying

7. Answers will differ but may center on the notion that beauty is fleeting; we know that a beautiful thing will not remain exactly as it is for long.

6. What do you think the swans symbolize to the speaker?

Applying

7. Although the wild swans in their natural setting are beautiful, the speaker feels a sense of sadness and loss. Why does great beauty sometimes arouse those feelings?

CRITICAL THINKING AND READING

Evaluating the Use of Imagery

Imagery in literature is created through the writer's use of words, singly or in combination, to produce a picture in the reader's mind. Images may appeal to any of the five senses. Sometimes they appeal to several senses at once. A writer who refers to "a crisp, shiny, sweet apple" is simultaneously appealing to hearing, sight, and taste. If imagery is to work effectively, readers must be familiar with the key words and their meanings. For example, a reader who has never heard the word *clamorous* will probably not appreciate the imagery of "clamorous wings." The following images are from "The Wild Swans of Coole." Locate each one in the poem and identify the sense or senses to which it appeals.

1. . . . the water/Mirrors a still sky
2. All suddenly mount/And scatter wheeling in great broken rings/Upon their clamorous wings
3. The bell-beat of their wings
4. They paddle in the cold/Companionable streams

ANSWERS TO CRITICAL THINKING AND READING

Suggested Responses: (1) This image appeals to the sense of sight. (2) This image appeals to the senses of sight and hearing. (3) This image appeals to the sense of hearing. (4) This image appeals to the senses of sight and feeling.

Motivation for Reading You may want to spur discussion by asking the following questions. Imagine that you are facing battle in a war. What do you think you would be thinking about?

Purpose-Setting Question Determine what is going through the airman's mind. Is there one central theme or just snatches of thought?

1 **Discussion** Why might the "I" of this poem say that his country is Kiltartan Cross rather than Ireland as a whole?

2 **Discussion** How does the speaker feel about the possible effects of the war?

3 **Discussion** What are the usual reasons that men go to war? Did any of these inspire the narrator? What did inspire him instead? What do you think he means by "A lonely impulse of delight"?

4 **Literary Focus** The final four lines explain why the narrator accepts the death that he foresaw in the two opening lines. Why do you think he values his lonely life and death as a pilot above all else?

An Irish Airman Foresees His Death

William Butler Yeats

Major Robert Gregory, a young Irish artist who was the son of Yeats's friend Lady Augusta Gregory, was killed during World War I while flying over Italy as a member of England's Royal Flying Corps. Gregory's death inspired Yeats to write this poem.

I know that I shall meet my fate
Somewhere among the clouds above;
Those that I fight I do not hate,
Those that I guard I do not love;[1]
1 My country is Kiltartan[2] Cross,
My countrymen Kiltartan's poor,
2 No likely end could bring them loss
Or leave them happier than before.
Nor law, nor duty bade me fight,
Nor public men, nor cheering crowds,
3 A lonely impulse of delight
Drove to this tumult in the clouds;
I balanced all, brought all to mind,
The years to come seemed waste of breath,
4 A waste of breath the years behind
In balance with this life, this death.

---

1. Those . . . love: Because Ireland was under English rule during World War I, many Irish fought as members of the English forces during the war. However, because of their desire for independence many of the Irish felt a great deal of resentment toward the English.
2. Kiltartan: A village near Lady Gregory's estate.

BURNING AIRPLANE
Photri

THINKING ABOUT THE SELECTION

Recalling

1. What does the Irish airman believe will happen to him?
2. (a) How does he feel about those he is fighting against? (b) Why is he fighting them?
3. How does he view (a) his past? (b) his future?

Interpreting

4. The airman does not love those he guards —the English. (a) Do you think his lack of love extends to those he calls his countrymen —Kiltartan's poor? (b) What lines in the poem support your answer?
5. (a) To what extent does the airman seem worried about his fate? (b) How would you describe the airman's character?

Applying

6. Suppose the airman were to survive the war. What do you think he might do with the rest of his life? Explain your answer.

THINKING AND WRITING

Writing About the Use of a Speaker

In writing "An Irish Airman Foresees His Death," Yeats had in mind Major Robert Gregory, the son of Yeats's close friend Lady Augusta Gregory. A volunteer in England's Royal Flying Corps, Major Gregory was killed during World War I while flying over Italy. Think about why Yeats may have chosen to write his poem with Major Gregory as the first-person speaker. Write a brief essay in which you explain why the poem, as written, allows Yeats to express his thoughts about the frailty of life, the futility of war, and the problems of Ireland more powerfully than a third-person point of view would have permitted. When you revise, make sure you have included details from the poem to support your opinion.

Answers

ANSWERS TO THINKING ABOUT THE SELECTION

Recalling

1. He foresees his death.
2. (a) He does not hate those that he fights. (b) He was motivated by "A lonely impulse of delight."
3. (a) and (b) He viewed his past and future as meaningless in comparison to his life and death as a pilot.

Interpreting

4. Suggested Responses: (a) He is sympathetic toward them, but does not believe that loss or victory in the war will change their lot. (b) Lines 7–9 support this response.
5. Suggested Responses: (a) He is not worried about his fate but accepts it. (b) He has a kind of tragic nobility and resignation.

Applying

6. Answers will differ. Some students might respond that he would not do anything constructive. Other students may feel that he would try to help his less fortunate countrymen.

THINKING AND WRITING

Publishing Students Writing You might want to have volunteers read their essays to the class.

Literary Focus It might be helpful for your **less advanced** students to see concrete symbols rather than trying to visualize the concept. Have them bring in, for example, symbols for a season, a holiday, or a sports team.

Look For Suggest that your **less advanced** students look for concrete images that might be symbols.

Writing To explore further the concept of symbols and to trigger their thinking before writing, ask students to think of objects in their own experience that are symbols. Then ask them to choose one symbol to represent themselves—it could be something that represents their interests, their personality, or a specific skill.

Vocabulary Have your students work in groups to imagine situations in which each of these words might be used. Then have the groups propose a sentence for each word.

GUIDE FOR READING

The Second Coming; After Long Silence Sailing to Byzantium

Writer's Techniques

Symbols. In its broadest, most basic sense, a symbol is something that stands for something else. The word *horse* is a symbol for an actual, recognizable animal. In our culture an olive branch is a symbol for peace. A symbol in literature is a word, person, object, or action that stands for something beyond itself. For example, the white whale in Herman Melville's *Moby-Dick* is often said to stand for evil. In the art and literature of the late nineteenth century, the word *symbolism* took on special significance. A group of French artists and poets, reacting against realism, promoted the use of symbols to achieve intensity and complexity in their work, a technique that sometimes approached mysticism. Yeats, an adherent of this type of symbolism in his early poetry, abandoned it later. However, in the last decade of his life, he created an elaborate symbolic system of his own, a system that is largely a curiosity for modern readers. His later poems abound in symbols, but Yeats remains first and foremost a poet, not a system-maker or a philosopher. In his best poems, the symbols do not require mastery of his system, but only the practiced eye of a careful reader.

Look For

As you read the poems by William Butler Yeats, look for his use of symbols and to the possible meanings attached to them.

Writing

If you wished to picture Canada symbolically, you might draw a maple leaf; for Great Britain you might draw a lion and for New York City, an apple. Countries, states, cities, companies, high schools, professional athletic teams—all sometimes develop symbols for easy and perhaps emotional identification. Think about such symbols. Jot down a number of them, identifying what each one symbolizes.

Vocabulary

Knowing the following words will help you as you read "The Second Coming," "After Long Silence," and "Sailing to Byzantium."

anarchy (an′ ər kē) *n.*: Absence of government; confusion, disorder, and violence (p. 1051, l. 4)

conviction (kən vik′ shən) *n.*: Belief in something meaningful, such as a creed (p. 1051, l. 7)

descant (des kant′) *v.*: To talk at length (p. 1053, l. 5)

decrepitude (di krep′ ə to͞od) *n.*: State of being old and broken down (p. 1053, l. 7)

Objectives

1 To recognize and interpret symbols
2 To write a poem about silence

Teaching Portfolio: Support Material

Teacher Backup, p. 000

Vocabulary Check, p. 00

Usage and Mechanics Worksheet, p. 00

Analyzing Literature Worksheet, p. 00

Critical Thinking and Reading Worksheet, p. 00

Language Worksheet, p. 00

Selection Test, p. 000

Art Transparency, p. 000

The Second Coming

William Butler Yeats

"The Second Coming" was inspired by Yeats's belief that history occurs in two-thousand-year cycles, with one civilization passing through stages of development, growth, and decay, before crumbling and giving way to a new civilization that stands in direct opposition to the preceding civilization. The birth of Christ had brought about the end of one civilization and the birth of another, and Yeats believed that the society of the early twentieth century was in a state of decay that would lead to a similar sort of rebirth.

1 Turning and turning in the widening gyre
The falcon cannot hear the falconer;
Things fall apart; the center cannot hold;
Mere anarchy is loosed upon the world,
2 The blood-dimmed tide is loosed, and everywhere
The ceremony of innocence is drowned;
The best lack all conviction, while the worst
Are full of passionate intensity.[1]

Surely some revelation is at hand;
Surely the Second Coming is at hand.
The Second Coming! Hardly are those words out
When a vast image out of *Spiritus Mundi*[2]
Troubles my sight: somewhere in sands of the desert
A shape with lion body and the head of a man,[3]
3 A gaze blank and pitiless as the sun,
Is moving its slow thighs, while all about it
Reel shadows of the indignant desert birds.
The darkness drops again; but now I know
That twenty centuries[4] of stony sleep
Were vexed to nightmare by a rocking cradle,[5]
And what rough beast, its hour come round at last,
Slouches towards Bethlehem to be born?

---

1. **Mere . . . intensity** (lines 4-8): Refers to the Russian Revolution of 1917.
2. ***Spiritus Mundi*** (spir′i təs mo͞on′dē): The Universal Spirit or soul, the Universal Subconscious in which the memories of the entire human race are forever preserved.
3. **A . . . man:** A sphinx.
4. **twenty centuries:** The historical cycle preceding the birth of Christ.
5. **rocking cradle:** The cradle of Jesus Christ.

Motivation for Reading Have students recall movies that they have seen about the fall of Rome or other civilizations, or newscasts about revolutions or anarchy in other countries. What usually followed the upheaval? What did the citizens hope for?

Master Teacher Note Present information about the role of a falconer. Point out the appropriateness of Yeats's choice of a falcon—a small hawk, a predatory bird—as opposed to some other bird in presenting his message.

Purpose-Setting Question What point is Yeats making in this poem?

1 **Discussion** The opening image, the circling flight of the bird, widening and widening until it loses contact with the center to which it should return, is a symbol for disunity. Why is this symbol effective?

2 **Discussion** Yeats speaks of anarchy and the blood-dimmed tide. What might these images represent in the modern world?

3 **Literary Focus** The monstrous threat, in the form of a rough, sphinx-like beast, slouches toward Bethlehem to be born, a frightening travesty of the birth of Christ almost two thousand years earlier.

Enrichment This poem was written in 1919; Yeats felt that the anarchy in the world following World War I heralded the end of the Christian era.

THINKING ABOUT THE SELECTION

Recalling

1. Why does the falcon not return to the falconer, as it ordinarily would in falconry (the hunting of game with falcons)?
2. In the first stanza, what is happening to government and innocence?
3. What does the speaker believe is at hand?
4. (a) What has begun to stir in the desert? (b) How long has it been dormant?
5. What does the speaker say is about to be born?

Interpreting

6. How does Yeats use the unhearing falcon as a symbol of what is happening in the world?
7. What is the imagery in lines 5-6?
8. When did the previous "twenty centuries of stony sleep" occur (that is, before the twentieth century)?
9. (a) What would you expect to appear at the Second Coming? (b) How does that differ from what the speaker suggests will appear?

Applying

10. What historical forces do you think prompt people, including poets, to predict vast upheavals, new civilizations, and even the end of the world?

ANALYZING LITERATURE

Understanding Symbols

A literary **symbol** is a word, person, object, or action that stands for something beyond itself. In "The Second Coming," for instance, the falcon flying in ever-widening circles is more than just a trained hunting bird that has lost its way. It represents something—it symbolizes something. A symbol always requires interpretation. With the falcon, it would help you to know Yeats's theories about "gyres," or cycles, which were a part of his symbolic system, although such knowledge is not really essential to an understanding of the poem.

1. Yeats does not merely talk about twenty centuries of silence. He symbolizes them. (a) What symbol does he use? (b) Why do you think he presents it through a description of its features rather than by naming it outright?
2. (a) What symbolism, if any, do you find in line 6: "The ceremony of innocence is drowned"? (b) What might the "indignant desert birds" in line 17 represent?
3. (a) What symbol does Yeats use to represent the coming era? (b) What characteristics do you associate with this symbol?

Answers

ANSWERS TO THINKING ABOUT THE SELECTION

Recalling

1. The falcon cannot hear its master.
2. Anarchy has been "loosed upon the world," drowning innocence.
3. The speaker believes that "some revelation is at hand."
4. A beast that has been dormant for twenty centuries has begun to stir in the desert.
5. A rough beast is about to be born.

Interpreting

6. Suggested Response: The unhearing falcon is symbolic of the disintegration of the natural order in the universe; it is symbolic of disunity and anarchy; it is a bird not obeying its master.
7. Suggested Response: Innocence is drowned in a bloody tide.
8. The twenty centuries are those following the birth of Christ.
9. (a) Answers will differ. (b) Students should point out differences between their expectations and Yeats's vision of a "shape with a lion body and the head of a man."

Applying

10. Answers will differ. Some students might respond that poets like Yeats may feel that they have important ideas to offer on these subjects.

ANSWERS TO ANALYZING LITERATURE

1. Suggested Responses: (a) He uses the stony, sleeping, sphinx-like creature to symbolize the twenty years of silence (b) Yeats concentrates on its features to emphasize its fearsomeness rather than letting the reader quickly name—and perhaps dismiss it—as a sphinx.
2. Suggested Responses: (a) This image symbolizes the loss of innocence in the modern world. (b) The indignant desert birds could represent those individuals aware of—and alarmed by—a change in the status quo.
3. Suggested Responses: (a) Yeats uses a sphinx-like beast to represent the coming era. (b) Possible characteristics are savagery, loathsomeness, and ugliness, among others.

After Long Silence

William Butler Yeats

Speech after long silence; it is right,
1 All other lovers being estranged or dead,
Unfriendly lamplight hid under its shade,
2 The curtains drawn upon unfriendly night,
3 That we descant and yet again descant
Upon the supreme theme of Art and Song:
4 Bodily decrepitude is wisdom; young
5,6 We loved each other and were ignorant.

THINKING ABOUT THE SELECTION

Recalling

1. What does the speaker say should follow long silence?
2. The speaker describes two things as unfriendly. What are they?
3. What is the "supreme theme" that should be talked about after long silence?
4. Why does the speaker believe the old have more reason than the young to "descant and yet again descant"?

Interpreting

5. (a) What relationship exists between the people who are being urged to speak? (b) How can you tell?
6. What do you suppose was taking place during the period of long silence?
7. The speaker seems to have mixed feelings about old age. How would you describe his feelings?

Applying

8. How fully do you accept the idea that the young cannot talk meaningfully about "Art and Song"? Explain.

THINKING AND WRITING

Writing a Poem About Silence

"After Long Silence" treats the idea of silence symbolically. Silence, according to Yeats, is the time when human beings have little of intellectual importance to communicate to one another. That is one interpretation of silence, but only one. Choose another approach to the subject of silence. Think about it. Write some notes. Then write a poem that expresses your own view of silence. Remember that a poem requires revision just as much as an essay does—perhaps more.

Motivation for Reading Ask students to think about a person who had been a very close friend or relative whom they haven't seen in a long time. What might they talk about if they visited after many long years?

Purpose-Setting Question What is ironical about the speaker's situation?

1 **Discussion** What is the dramatic situation in this brief lyric?

2 **Literary Focus** Note the personifications in the phrases "unfriendly lamplight" and "unfriendly night." Why are lamplight and night unfriendly?

3 **Clarification** *Descant* here means "to talk at considerable length."

4 **Discussion** *Decrepitude* means "the state of being wasted by the infirmities of old age." How are lines 5 and 6 related to line 7?

5 **Discussion** Why, then, were these two ignorant when they were young? Do you think the poet is happier being old and wise?

6 **Discussion** What is the poem's tone?

Publishing Student Writing You may want to have students read their poems aloud in small groups and then discuss the various interpretations of silence that arise. Or you may want to encourage some students to give informal poetry readings to the full class.

Answers

ANSWERS TO THINKING ABOUT THE SELECTION

Recalling

1. Speech should follow long silence.
2. Lamplight and night are unfriendly.
3. The "supreme theme" is Art and Song.
4. The old are wiser in their "decrepitude."

Interpreting

5. Suggested Responses: (a) The two persons had been lovers. (b) In line 2, he says "All other lovers . . .," and in line 8, he says "We loved each other. . . ."
6. Suggested Response: Perhaps they had met and married others.
7. Suggested Response: The speaker deplores the physical infirmities but feels he has gained understanding.

Applying

8. Answers may differ. Students may respond that the young are more interested in action than talk.

THINKING AND WRITING

For help with this assignment, students can refer to Lesson 18, "Writing a Poem," in the Handbook of Writing About Literature.

Motivation for Reading Ask students whether most artists hope that the works they create will survive after their death. Have students consider the motive for this wish. Then tell them that Yeats's "Sailing to Byzantium" deals with this theme.

Purpose-Setting Question What does Byzantium symbolize for Yeats?

Thematic Idea You might want to have students compare the sages in this poem with the Old Masters in Auden's "Musée des Beaux Arts," page 1098.

1 **Discussion** To what "country" is Yeats referring? Is it really a particular country, as England or Ireland would be? Why is the first word of the poem "That" instead of "This"?

2 **Discussion** Explain the figure of speech in this line. How does this figure of speech make the senses seem both positive and negative?

3 **Discussion** What does the poet mean by such "Monuments"? How are they different from "sensual music"?

4 **Discussion** Explain this metaphor.

5 **Enrichment** Yeats was referring to Byzantium (modern Istanbul) in the early sixth century. He believed that Byzantine artists of that time—workers in precious metals, painters, mosaic workers, and so forth—expressed the vision of a whole people rather than their own personal beliefs and emotions. Yeats felt that such an "impersonal" vision was the highest achievement of art.

6 **Discussion** Why does Yeats use the word "artifice" in connection with "eternity"? How is his use of this word linked to his view of Byzantine artists?

Sailing to Byzantium[1]

W. B. Yeats

I

That is no country for old men. The young
In one another's arms, birds in the trees
—Those dying generations—at their song,
The salmon-falls, the mackerel-crowded seas,
Fish, flesh, or fowl, commend all summer long
Whatever is begotten, born, and dies.
Caught in that sensual music all neglect
Monuments of unaging intellect.

II

An aged man is but a paltry thing,
A tattered coat upon a stick, unless
Soul clap its hands and sing, and louder sing
For every tatter in its mortal dress,
Nor is there singing school but studying
Monuments of its own magnificence;
And therefore I have sailed the seas and come
To the holy city of Byzantium.

III

O sages standing in God's holy fire
As in the gold mosaic of a wall,[2]
Come from the holy fire, perne in a gyre,[3]
And be the singing-masters of my soul.
Consume my heart away; sick with desire
And fastened to a dying animal
It knows not what it is; and gather me
Into the artifice of eternity.

---

1. **Byzantium** (bi zan′ shē əm): The ancient capital of the Eastern Roman (or Byzantine) Empire and the seat of the Greek Orthodox Church; today, Istanbul, Turkey. For Yeats, it symbolized the sensual and artistic world as opposed to the natural and biological world.
2. **sages . . . wall:** Wise old men and saints portrayed in gold mosaic on the walls of Byzantine churches.
3. **perne . . . gyre:** Spin in a spiraling motion.

IV

Once out of nature I shall never take
My bodily form from any natural thing,
But such a form as Grecian goldsmiths make
Of hammered gold and gold enameling
To keep a drowsy Emperor awake;
Or set upon a golden bough to sing[4]
To lords and ladies of Byzantium
Of what is past, or passing, or to come.

---

4. To . . . sing: Yeats wrote, "I have read somewhere that in the Emperor's palace at Byzantium was a tree made of gold and silver, and artificial birds that sang."

7 **Discussion** Compare and contrast this realm of artifice with the natural world in the first stanza.

8 **Literary Focus** The golden bird is a symbol of the artist who, through a work of art, has gone beyond the natural world. However, the artist sings about the very world he has transcended—the world of nature, time, and mortality!

You might want to remind students that a paradox is a statement or situation that has contradictory elements. Ask them how the golden bird is a paradoxical symbol.

THINKING ABOUT THE SELECTION

Recalling

1. (a) What do the people of the country referred to in the first stanza "commend"? (b) What do they neglect?
2. How is "an aged man" described in lines 9-10?
3. What does the speaker do in lines 15-16?
4. What does the speaker ask of the sages in the third stanza?
5. What bodily form does the speaker wish to take when he is "out of nature"?

Interpreting

6. How does Byzantium contrast with the country described in the first two stanzas?
7. (a) What do the desires which the speaker expresses in stanzas 3 and 4 reveal about his attitude toward aging and death? (b) How does he hope to immortalize himself?
8. What does this poem suggest about the motives of artists and the purpose of art?

Applying

9. Do you think that most people hope to immortalize themselves in some way? Why or why not?

Answers

ANSWERS TO THINKING ABOUT THE SELECTION

Recalling

1. (a) They commend "Whatever is begotten, born, and dies." (b) They "neglect/Monuments of unaging intellect."
2. "An aged man is . . . /A tattered coat upon a stick. . . ."
3. He sails the seas "To the holy city of Byzantium."
4. He asks them to move in a spiral, teach him to sing, consume his heart, and gather him "Into the artifice of eternity."
5. He wants to be a golden bird.

Interpreting

6. Suggested Response: Byzantium is an eternal, artificial city, not subject to the processes of mortality.
7. Suggested Response: (a) He wants to escape age and death. (b) He wants to immortalize himself by transcending nature. Paradoxically, however, as an artificial, golden bird, he will sing about mortality.
8. Suggested Response: The poem suggests that artists want to somehow escape age and death through their art.

Applying

9. Answers will differ. Students may respond that many people would like to immortalize themselves and that having children can even be viewed as a means to this end.

More About the Author You might tell students that D. H. Lawrence believed a poem should reflect a momentary, spontaneous perception or feeling. Unlike Yeats, he did not view a poem as a carefully constructed, artificial work. Ask students to compare and contrast these two approaches to art. What are the advantages and disadvantages of each?

Literary Focus Consider explaining to students that many poets at the beginning of the century abandoned regular meters because they felt that every poetic expression required its own unique rhythm.

Look For Review with students specific examples of assonance, simile, and onomatopocia.

Writing To open their thinking to a variety of possibilities, have students volunteer samples of "startling sights"—in nature, on a city street, or at a celebration of some kind, for example.

Vocabulary The word *perverse* is based on the Latin root *vertere* (to turn). Have students look up the following words, also based on this root, and explain how they are related to the idea of turning: *obverse, inverse, universe, converse,* and *verse.*

D. H. LAWRENCE

1885–1930

Although D. H. Lawrence is best known for his novels and short stories, he is also a fine poet. His poetry, like his prose, concentrates on the life-giving force of nature, exalting the physical and instinctual over the purely intellectual. Writing in free verse, Lawrence produced a number of powerful and original poems that evoke the "blood consciousness" and "dark gods" he sought. His "belief in the blood" was not merely his philosophy but was the dynamic force, the energy, that fueled his poetic imagination. For a fuller biography of D. H. Lawrence, see page 994.

Snake

The Writer's Techniques

Free Verse. Free verse is poetry that has no clearly defined rhyme scheme or rhythmic pattern. Lines are based on the natural phrasing of the language, and the rhythm follows normal voice cadences. Although no less a poet than Robert Frost has defined the writing of free verse as akin to "playing tennis with the net down," the issue is not that simple. Free verse poems are not merely works of prose laid out to resemble poetry. They *are* poetry, with a long and honored history going back to the Psalms in the Bible. Free verse, never so "free" as prose, has its own rhythmic integrity and commonly makes use of the traditional devices of poetry, such as alliteration (repetition of consonant sounds), assonance (repetition of vowel sounds), and onomatopoeia (words or phrases that imitate the sound being described).

Look For

As you read D. H. Lawrence's "Snake," watch (and listen) for the poetic devices that add color and vitality to the poem.

Writing

Try to recall the most startling sight you have ever come upon. Write a short account of this event. Describe in detail what you were doing when you first became aware of the sight. Explain your feelings at the time. Tell what happened after you began to watch. Describe how the event ended and what your thoughts and feelings were when it was over.

Vocabulary

Knowing the following words will help you as you read "Snake."

perversity (pər vʉr′ sə tē) *n.*: State of being wicked or wrong (l. 32)

convulsed (kən vulst′) *v.*: Shook; moved violently (l. 59)

accursed (ə kʉr′ sid) *adj.*: Hateful (l. 65)

expiate (ek′ spē āt′) *v.*: To make amends for; atone for (l. 74)

Objectives

1. To understand free verse
2. To make inferences about purpose

Teaching Portfolio: Support Material

Teacher Backup, pp. 00–00

Vocabulary Check, p. 00

Usage and Mechanics Worksheet, p. 00

Analyzing Literature Worksheet, p. 00

Critical Thinking and Reading Worksheet, p. 00

Language Worksheet, p. 00

Selection Test, p. 000

Art Transparency, p. 000

Snake

D. H. Lawrence

A snake came to my water-trough
On a hot, hot day, and I in pajamas for the heat,
To drink there.

1 In the deep, strange-scented shade of the great dark carob tree
I came down the steps with my pitcher
And must wait, must stand and wait, for there he was at the trough before me.

He reached down from a fissure in the earth-wall in the gloom
And trailed his yellow-brown slackness soft-bellied down, over the edge of the stone trough
And rested his throat upon the stone bottom,
2 And where the water had dripped from the tap, in a small clearness,
He sipped with his straight mouth,
Softly drank through his straight gums, into his slack long body,
Silently.

Someone was before me at my water-trough,
And I, like a second comer, waiting.

He lifted his head from his drinking, as cattle do,
And looked at me vaguely, as drinking cattle do,
And flickered his two-forked tongue from his lips, and mused a moment,
And stooped and drank a little more,
Being earth-brown, earth-golden from the burning bowels of the earth
On the day of Sicilian July, with Etna[1] smoking.

The voice of my education said to me
He must be killed,
For in Sicily the black, black snakes are innocent, the gold are venomous.

---

1. Etna: A volcanic mountain in eastern Sicily.

Motivation for Reading Ask students why so many people are both fascinated and repelled by snakes and other reptiles. Then tell them that this poem deals with such mixed feelings.

Purpose-Setting Question How do Lawrence's feelings about the snake change?

1 **Discussion** How do the first two stanzas set the scene?

2 **Discussion** Which words in Lawrence's description of the snake communicate his feelings of uneasiness and anxiety?

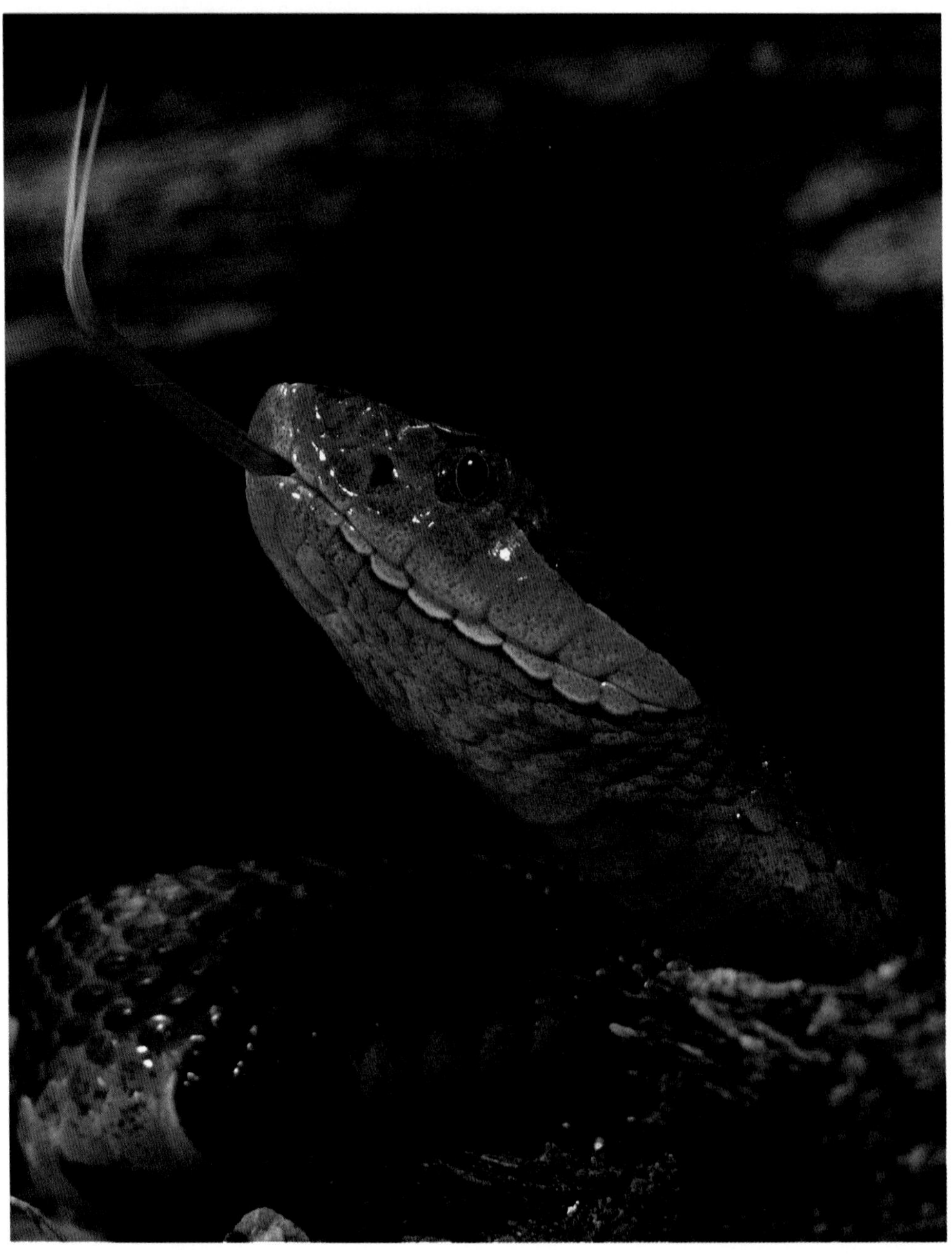

And voices in me said, If you were a man
You would take a stick and break him now, and finish him off.

3 But must I confess how I liked him,
How glad I was he had come like a guest in quiet, to drink at my water-trough
And depart peaceful, pacified, and thankless,
Into the burning bowels of this earth?

Was it cowardice, that I dared not kill him?
Was it perversity, that I longed to talk to him?
4 Was it humility, to feel so honored?
I felt so honored.

And yet those voices:
If you were not afraid, you would kill him!

And truly I was afraid, I was most afraid,
But even so, honored still more
5 That he should seek my hospitality
From out the dark door of the secret earth.

He drank enough
And lifted his head, dreamily, as one who has drunken,
And flickered his tongue like a forked night on the air, so black;
Seeming to lick his lips,
And looked around like a god, unseeing, into the air,
And slowly turned his head,
And slowly, very slowly, as if thrice adream,
Proceeded to draw his slow length curving round
And climb again the broken bank of my wall-face.

And as he put his head into that dreadful hole,
And as he slowly drew up, snake-easing his shoulders, and entered farther,
A sort of horror, a sort of protest against his withdrawing into that horrid black hole,
Deliberately going into the blackness, and slowly drawing himself after,
Overcame me now his back was turned.

6

I looked round, I put down my pitcher,
I picked up a clumsy log
And threw it at the water-trough with a clatter.

3 **Discussion** Explain the conflict that Lawrence experiences.

4 **Literary Focus** What effect does Lawrence create by shortening the fourth line of this stanza?

5 **Discussion** How does Lawrence seem to resolve his conflict?

6 **Discussion** Explain how Lawrence's inner conflict starts up again.

7 **Discussion** Why do you think he compares the snake to the albatross?

8 **Literary Focus** How do the varying line lengths in the final stanza reinforce the contrast between the greatness of the snake and Lawrence's pettiness?

9 **Discussion** How would you describe Lawrence's mood at the conclusion of the poem?

I think it did not hit him,
But suddenly that part of him that was left behind convulsed in undignified haste,
Writhed like lightning, and was gone
Into the black hole, the earth-lipped fissure in the wall-front,
At which, in the intense still noon, I stared with fascination.

And immediately I regretted it.
I thought how paltry, how vulgar, what a mean act!
I despised myself and the voices of my accursed human education.

7 And I thought of the albatross,[2]
And I wished he would come back, my snake.

For he seemed to me again like a king,
Like a king in exile, uncrowned in the underworld,
Now due to be crowned again.

8, 9 And so, I missed my chance with one of the lords
Of life.
And I have something to expiate;
A pettiness.

---

2. **albatross:** In Samuel Taylor Coleridge's "The Rime of the Ancient Mariner," the mariner shoots an albatross, a traditional symbol of good luck.

THINKING ABOUT THE SELECTION

Recalling

1. (a) What is the speaker on his way to do when he first becomes aware of the snake? (b) What is the snake doing?
2. (a) What does the "voice of [his] education" tell the speaker he should do? (b) How does he actually feel about the snake when the "voices" tell him he should kill it?
3. (a) What causes the speaker's horror toward the snake? (b) What does the speaker do? (c) How does he feel about having done it? (d) What three adjectives does he use to characterize his act?

Interpreting

4. In line 65 the speaker mentions "the voices of my accursed education." (a) What are these voices? (b) Why are they accursed?
5. Why does the speaker call the snake "a king in exile" and "one of the lords of life"?
6. The last two lines suggest that the speaker has committed a sin. (a) What is his sin? (b) Why does he call it a "pettiness"?

Answers

ANSWERS TO THINKING ABOUT THE SELECTION

Recalling

1. (a) The speaker is coming to the trough for a drink. (b) The snake is drinking from the trough.
2. (a) The voice says to kill the snake. (b) The speaker likes the snake and is glad it is a guest.
3. (a) The speaker is horrified by the snake disappearing into its hole. (b) He throws a log at the snake. (c) The speaker regrets his action.

Interpreting

4. Suggested Responses: (a) The voices reflect what he has been taught to think about snakes. (b) They are accursed because they direct his thinking and his actions when he would rather respond to his true feelings.
5. Answers will differ. Students may respond that Lawrence views the snake as a symbol or embodiment of a ruler or god from beneath the earth.
6. Suggested Responses: (a) The speaker's sin is trying to kill the snake. (b) The action is petty or mean because the snake is a god-like, sacred animal.

ANSWERS TO ANALYZING LITERATURE

1. Suggested Response: This insistent repetition emphasizes the

Applying

7. Do you agree with the speaker that he has missed his chance? Explain your answer.

ANALYZING LITERATURE

Understanding Free Verse

Poetry with no clearly defined metric pattern or rhyme scheme is called **free verse.** Although inexperienced writers sometimes call their non-poetry "free verse," the truth is that free verse makes use of subtle, varying, but real rhythm as well as other traditional devices of poetry: repetition, alliteration, assonance, and onomatopoeia. It also has, in many cases, a high concentration of symbolism, figurative language, and imagery.

1. Notice how many lines of "Snake" begin with the word *And.* Notice also the repetition of words and phrases in the poem ("hot, hot" in line 2; "as cattle do" . . . "as drinking cattle do" in lines 16–17; and more). What effect do you think Lawrence intends to produce through this insistent repetition?
2. What devices—alliteration, assonance, onomatopoeia, repetition—do you find in each of the following excerpts. Some of them contain more than one device.
   a. In the deep, strange-scented shade of the great dark carobtree
   b. He sipped with his straight mouth,/Softly drank through his straight gums, into his slack long body,/Silently.
   c. And flickered his two-forked tongue from his lips
   d. Was it humility to feel so honored?/I felt so honored.

CRITICAL THINKING AND READING

Making Inferences About Purpose

On the surface "Snake" is a simple poem about Lawrence's (the speaker's/author's) unexpected encounter with a snake at a water-trough on a hot day in Sicily. If you look beneath the surface, however, you will see that his purpose in describing the incident transcends the basic narrative appeal of the poem. Lawrence makes his intent clear—although not his specific message—from his continuing, almost clinical analysis of his reactions to the snake. What underlying statement do you think he is making in "Snake" about human beings in general and himself in particular? Support your answer with quotations from the poem.

strangeness, tension, and urgency of this encounter.

2. Suggested Responses: The poetic devices are (a) Assonance and alliteration (b) alliteration, onomatopoeia, repetition, and assonance (c) alliteration, assonance (d) repetition, alliteration.

ANSWERS TO CRITICAL THINKING AND READING

Answers will differ. Most students will realize that Lawrence is saying that we are educated away from our better, and deeper, impulses: "The voice of my education said to me/He must be killed. . . ."

THINKING AND WRITING

Publishing Student Writing You may want to collect these essays in a book, perhaps with accompanying illustrations.

More About the Author Siegfried Sassoon's poetry changed dramatically as a result of his experiences in the First World War—it became more satiric, realistic, and even shocking. Ask students to consider why his wartime experiences might have influenced his poetry in this way.

SIEGFRIED SASSOON

1886–1967

A decorated, twice-wounded soldier in World War I, Siegfried Sassoon witnessed first-hand the horrors of trench warfare in France. Like a number of other English writers and poets who saw action in the war, he resolved to portray for his own and future generations the grim reality of war, to show graphically its carnage and despair. No one did it better than he. Although Sassoon wrote for almost fifty years after the Armistice, he produced little to match his searing wartime verses that honor and mourn the "citizens of death's gray land."

Sassoon, born into a wealthy Jewish family in London, was something of a dilettante before the war. While attending Marlborough and Clare College, Cambridge, he found that he preferred hunting, cricket, golf, and ballet to more academic pursuits. Poetry aroused his interest also, and he published a number of pastoral poems and parodies while in his early twenties. In 1913, on the eve of World War I, his long poem, *The Daffodil Murderer,* gave evidence of his ability to combine parody with serious self-expression.

When war broke out in 1914, Sassoon joined the army the same day and showed such reckless courage in battle that he earned the nickname "Mad Jack" along with a medal for gallantry. But by the time he was wounded at Arras in April 1917, his attitude toward the supposed glory of war had changed. By then he was writing what he called "trench poems," the starkly realistic, agonized, sometimes horrifying verses on which his reputation rests. *The Old Huntsman* (1917) and *Counter-Attack* (1918) contain most of his memorable poems.

When Sassoon returned to the front in 1918, a British sentry shot him in the head by mistake, and Sassoon spent the rest of the war in a hospital.

After the Armistice, he continued to write, publishing his first prose work, *Memoirs of a Fox-Hunting Man,* in 1928. Billed as a novel, the book is essentially an autobiography, the first of several autobiographical works. Sassoon married at the age of forty-seven and settled down in rural Wiltshire. The literary innovations between the two World Wars passed him by. His niche in English literature had already been secured by a few dozen jarring, outraged, unforgettable poems from the trenches.

Objective

1 To recognize the historical context of a work

Teaching Portfolio: Support Material

Teacher Backup, pp. 00-00

Vocabulary Check, p. 00

Usage and Mechanics Worksheet, p. 00

Analyzing Literature Worksheet, p. 00

Critical Thinking and Reading Worksheet, p. n00

Language Worksheet, p. 00

Selection Test, p. 00

GUIDE FOR READING

Wirers

The Writer's Techniques

Historical Context. Many poems deal with subjects unrelated to a particular time or place. A poem about love, for instance, deals with an emotion that is as old as the human race. But sometimes an historical event will create such an impact that poets feel impelled to comment on, and perhaps to explain, what happened. World War I was such an event. The war's devastation and slaughter, unprecedented at the time, gave rise to millions of words—patriotic, indignant, disillusioned, depending on the views of the writer. Those words were then, and are today, tied to their times. "Black Jack Pershing" was a household name in 1918. Soldiers were *doughboys,* and "Mademoiselle from Armentières" was a song familiar to everyone. Those names and facts are part of the history of World War I. A Siegfried Sassoon poem about World War I is likely to contain words and references unique to the war. As a reader, you must put such words and references into historical context—a perspective required by your distance in time from the events described. Ideally, you would be able to put all of World War I into historical context, but as a practical matter, you know enough about war in general to understand and appreciate a poem about World War I, even if you lack a thorough historical knowledge of the event.

Look For

As you read Siegfried Sassoon's "Wirers," notice the references that place the poem within the historical context of World War I.

Writing

Think of an abstract concept such as anger, betrayal, or loss and relate it to an experience that has affected you deeply. Freewrite about this experience, showing the feelings it caused.

Vocabulary

Knowing the following words will help you as you read "Wirers."

stealthy (stel′ thē) *adj.*: In a quiet, secretive way (l. 4)

desolate (des′ ə lit) *adj.*: Deserted; forlorn (l. 10)

Literary Focus Help students to understand the historical context of the poem and the references to barbed wire and "Boche."

Look For Ask students what image the word *wire* calls up. Remind them that this is a war poem, and help them to eliminate other images such as telephone or electric wires. Offer "barbed wire" if it is not suggested. In what war would this wire have been used?

Writing You might want to divide the class into small groups and have them discuss their experiences before they begin to write.

Motivation for Reading Bring in photographs or other pictures of action at the front lines in World War I, to help set the scene.

Purpose-Setting Question Identify the irony in this poem.

1 **Literary Focus** Note the sudden switch from the blackness of night to "ghastly dawn."

2 **Discussion** What irony is the poet pointing up in the last line?

Wirers[1]

Siegfried Sassoon

"Pass it along, the wiring party's going out"—
And yawning sentries mumble, "Wirers going out."
Unraveling; twisting; hammering stakes with muffled thud,
They toil with stealthy haste and anger in their blood.

The Boche[2] sends up a flare. Black forms stand rigid there,
Stock-still like posts; then darkness, and the clumsy ghosts
Stride hither and thither, whispering, tripped by clutching snare
Of snags and tangles.
Ghastly dawn with vaporous coasts
1 Gleams desolate along the sky, night's misery ended.

2 Young Hughes was badly hit; I heard him carried away,
Moaning at every lurch; no doubt he'll die today.
But *we* can say the front-line wire's been safely mended.

---

1. **wirers:** Soldiers who were responsible for repairing the barbed-wire fences that protected the trenches in World War I.
2. **Boche** (bôsh): German soldier.

THINKING ABOUT THE SELECTION

Recalling

1. What are the wirers getting ready to do at the beginning of the poem?
2. What happens when an enemy flare lights the scene?
3. What does the speaker say will probably be the fate of the soldier named Hughes?

Interpreting

4. How do you think the wirers feel about the job they have to do?
5. (a) What is the speaker's attitude toward what has happened to young Hughes? (b) How do you explain that attitude?

Applying

6. (a) What kinds of nonmilitary jobs may lead to a routine acceptance of the daily presence of danger? (b) What is the difference between those jobs and a soldier's job?

ANALYZING LITERATURE

Historical Context

Actual events provide the historical context of "Wirers." If you knew no history at all, the

Answers

ANSWER TO THINKING ABOUT THE SELECTION

Recalling

1. The wirers are getting ready to lay barbed wire in no man's land.
2. The soldiers stand rigid.
3. Hughes will probably die before the end of the day.

Interpreting

4. Suggested Response: They probably hate their job and are afraid they will be killed.
5. Suggested Response: (a) The speaker is angered by Hughes's death. (b) His anger arises from the fact that a fence is given more importance than a human life.

Applying

6. (a) Answers will differ, but students may mention rescue teams, firemen, and policemen. (b) Answers will differ. One difference is that a soldier is expected to kill others, while civilian workers who take chances are engaged in more constructive activities.

ANSWERS TO ANALYZING LITERATURE

1. Suggested Responses: (a) The setting is not the Civil War because of the Boche. (b) It is probably not

DRAWING OF TANKS, WORLD WAR I
Photo Research Int.

poem—without some kind of textual explanation—would be virtually meaningless to you. However, you know something about the trenches of World War I and about barbed-wire entanglements. You therefore have clues to the historical context of the poem.

1. How can you tell from the poem that its historical context is World War I (1914–18) and not (a) the American Civil War (1861–65)? (b) World War II (1939–45)?
2. A historian has said that in World War I "cavalry was useless" and "artillery was absolutely indispensable." How does the content of the poem support the historian's statement?

Humanities Note

Fine art, *Drawing of Tanks, World War I.* When a country goes to war, all members of society are affected. Artists and writers don soldiers' uniforms along with the professional warriors. Some artists, however, cannot forego expressing themselves through their art even on the battlefield.

This drawing is one unknown artist's comment on the war. Executed in easily portable materials, conté crayon (an oily earth-toned chalk) and paper, it is a quick sketch that gives an unglorified view of a field of battle. Troops advance across a field with trampled grass, blasted trees, and the fallen bodies of other soldiers. The faces of the troops are shocked and haggard as they follow the ominous shapes of the tanks. The sketchy immediacy of the drawing gives the impression that the artist will shortly rejoin the advancing troops. This brief and honest sketch is the work of someone who has experienced the horrors of war and paused to record its reality.

You might use these questions for discussion:

1. What do both the poet and the painter express in their works?
2. How does observation of this sketch affect you?

World War II because barbed wire did not play as large a role in that war.

2. Suggested Response: Cavalry could not have charged across terrain obstructed by barbed wire.

More About the Author Tell students that "The Soldier" is a strongly patriotic poem. Review Rupert Brooke's background. Do you think his comfortable life increased his love of his country? What do you think contributes to a person's patriotism?

RUPERT BROOKE

1887–1915

Although Rupert Brooke had established himself as a poet before World War I, it was the war and Brooke's early death that fostered his almost legendary fame. A handsome, privileged youth, an accomplished athlete and an intellectual, he attracted a host of influential friends who mourned his loss and celebrated his achievements. Brooke's best poems, filled with striking phrases, are exuberant with delight in the simple pleasures of living.

Rupert Brooke was born in Rugby, Warwickshire, and educated at the famous public school there, where his father was an assistant master. He graduated from King's College, Cambridge, and studied for a time in Munich, Germany. A long love affair ended unhappily for Brooke, after which he traveled in the United States, Canada, and the South Pacific, making a pilgrimage to the home of Robert Louis Stevenson in Samoa. His poetry at the time echoes that of John Donne and occasionally Alfred E. Housman.

When war broke out in 1914, Brooke obtained a commission in the Hood Battalion of the Royal Naval Division. "Well, if Armageddon's *on,*" he said at the time, "I suppose one should be there." After participating in the disastrous British expedition to Antwerp, he was ordered to the Dardanelles, where the British hoped to strike a blow against the Turks. He contracted blood poisoning on the way and entered a French military hospital on the Greek island of Skiros in the Aegean Sea. He died there on April 23, St. George's Day.

Brooke's war sonnets, which had appeared a few weeks before his death, gained extraordinary notice in the aftermath. Winston Churchill praised them in the London *Times.* The sonnets, traditional and idealistic, were among the last from the soldier–poets of World War I that expressed an unalloyed patriotism. Brooke had seen little of the trench warfare that so altered the vision of Siegfried Sassoon, Wilfred Owen, and other poets who served in the army.

Impressive as Brooke's poetry is, some of it lacks consistent vision. Contradictions abound. "Impulse was his god," wrote one critic, and it is impossible to speculate on the direction his work might have taken had he survived the war.

Objectives

1. To analyze the theme of patriotism in poetry
2. To understand and appreciate Georgian poetry
3. To appreciate specific words

Teaching Portfolio: Support Material

Teacher Backup, p. 000

Vocabulary Check, p. 00

Usage and Mechanics Worksheet, p. 00

Analyzing Literature Worksheet, p. 00

Critical Thinking and Reading Worksheet, p. 00

Language Worksheet, p. 00

Selection Test, p. 000

Art Transparency 15, *We Are Making a New World* by Paul Nash

GUIDE FOR READING

The Soldier; The Great Lover

The Writer's Techniques

The Theme of Patriotism. Patriotism, the love and loyal support of one's own country, has been a persistent theme in English literature. Shakespeare's lines in *King Richard II* are a stirring patriotic statement: "This royal throne of kings, this sceptered isle . . . This other Eden, demi-paradise . . . This precious stone set in the silver sea . . . This blessed plot, this earth, this realm, this England. . . ." Two centuries later, Sir Walter Scott sounded an equally patriotic note in *The Lay of the Last Minstrel:* "Breathes there the man with soul so dead,/Who never to himself hath said,/This is my own, my native land!" By the time of World War I, Great Britain had reached the height of its power, and Scott's proud boast, "The sun never sets on the immense empire," was the literal truth. At the outbreak of the war, the English were in a buoyantly patriotic mood, and Rupert Brooke's "The Soldier" catches that mood perfectly.

Look For

As you read "The Soldier," look for the words and phrases the poet chooses to express his love for his country.

Writing

Freewrite about an occasion when you felt extreme pride in your country. The occasion might have been a flag-raising ceremony, the celebration of a national holiday, or a time of international crisis. Describe your feelings of patriotism, explaining what life in the United States meant to you at that moment.

Vocabulary

Knowing the following words will help you as you read the poems by Rupert Brooke.

illimitable (i lim′ it ə b'l) *adj.*: Without limit or bounds; immeasurable (p. 1069, l. 4)

inenarrable (in en′ ər ə b'l) *adj.*: Indescribable (p. 1069, l. 5)

benison (ben′ ə z'n) *n.*: Blessing; benediction (p. 1070, l. 39)

sacramented (sak′ rə ment id) *adj.*: Having the properties of religious rites or rituais (p. 1070, l. 62)

covenant (kuv′ ə nənt) *n.*: Solemn, binding agreement (p. 1070, l. 62)

Literary Focus Point out that "The Soldier" is a sonnet. Although the topic is quite different from those of Sidney, Spenser, Shakespeare, or Donne, why is the form appropriate for Brooke's message?

Look For Elicit from students words and phrases they would use to describe love of country. Then have them look for those that Brooke uses.

Writing You might have students focus on the geographical features of the United States that inspire feelings of patriotism —powerful rivers, gorgeous canyons, fertile fields, and so forth.

Vocabulary Have **less advanced** students review these words and use them in sentences before they begin to read.

Master Teacher Note After reading "The Soldier," place Art Transparency 15, *We Are Making a New World* by Paul Nash, on the overhead projector. Ask your students to compare and contrast the poem and the painting for artistic intention, meaning, and overall effectiveness. You might pose this qustion: Which of the two works is more relevant to our situation today?

Motivation for Reading Have students consider the reasons that patriotism can be such a strong emotion. Then tell them that this feeling inspired Rupert Brooke's sonnet "The Soldier."

Purpose-Setting Question Why do you think this poem was praised by Winston Churchill —then a member of the government—during World War I?

Thematic Idea You might want to have students compare the patriotic feelings in this poem with those in Browning's "Home-Thoughts, from Abroad," page 828.

1 **Discussion** Why will the "corner of a foreign field" be "forever England"?

2 **Discussion** What has England given the author?

3 **Discussion** How does the soldier plan to return the gifts of England, even in his death?

Humanities Note

War poster. During both world wars, posters played an important part in communicating government instructions and propaganda to civilian and military communities. In simple, graphic language, these posters urged the people to support the war effort by enlisting, taking war jobs, buying bonds, conserving food and fuel, and above all, by being patriotic.

You might ask these questions:

1. How does the sentiment expressed by this poster relate to that in the poem?
2. Do you feel that such posters would be as effective today? Explain.

WAR POSTER
Photri

The Soldier

Rupert Brooke

If I should die, think only this of me:
    That there's some corner of a foreign field
1 That is forever England. There shall be
    In that rich earth a richer dust concealed;
A dust whom England bore, shaped, made aware,
    Gave, once, her flowers to love, her ways to roam,
2 A body of England's, breathing English air,
    Washed by the rivers, blest by suns of home.

And think, this heart, all evil shed away,
    A pulse in the eternal mind, no less
3   Gives somewhere back the thoughts by England given;
Her sights and sounds; dreams happy as her day;
    And laughter, learnt of friends; and gentleness,
      In hearts at peace, under an English heaven.

THINKING ABOUT THE SELECTION

Recalling

1. How does the speaker ask his readers to remember him if he should die?
2. What are three things that England gave to the speaker?
3. What will the speaker's heart give "somewhere back"?

Interpreting

4. (a) How does the speaker feel toward England? (b) How idealistic, or realistic, do you think his recollections are?
5. What is the "richer dust" that will be found in a foreign field?
6. The speaker says his heart will become a "pulse in the eternal mind." In your own words, what does he mean?

Applying

7. How would you define patriotism?

ANALYZING LITERATURE

Feeling Patriotism

Patriotism is a deep and abiding love for one's country.

1. Why do you think Brooke's war poems, including "The Soldier," are strongly patriotic while many other poems from World War I, such as "Wirers," avoid patriotic sentiments?
2. A number of young English poets died in World War I. One of them, Charles Sorley, said of Rupert Brooke, "He has clothed his attitude in fine words; but he has taken the sentimental attitude." What is your opinion of this remark?

Answers

ANSWERS TO THINKING ABOUT THE SELECTION

Recalling

1. He asks the reader to think of him as being a part of England in foreign soil.
2. England gave flowers to appreciate, paths to roam, air, water, sun, and the laughter of friends.
3. The speaker's heart will give back thoughts of England.

Interpreting

4. Suggested Responses: (a) The speaker feels England is a kind of heaven. (b) The recollections seem generalized and idealized.
5. Suggested Response: The "richer dust" is the dust of the speaker's body.
6. Answers will differ, but students may interpret this statement to mean that the speaker's spirit has joined other heavenly spirits.

Applying

7. Students' answers will differ.

ANSWERS TO ANALYZING LITERATURE

1. Suggested Response: Other poems deal with the grim realities of front-line fighting, which Brooke did not experience.

The Great Lover

Rupert Brooke

I have been so great a lover: filled my days
So proudly with the splendor of Love's praise,
The pain, the calm, and the astonishment,
Desire illimitable, and still content,
1 And all dear names men use, to cheat despair,
For the perplexed and viewless streams that bear
Our hearts at random down the dark of life.
Now, ere the unthinking silence on that strife
Steals down, I would cheat drowsy Death so far,
2 My night shall be remembered for a star
That outshone all the suns of all men's days.
Shall I not crown them with immortal praise
Whom I have loved, who have given me, dared with me
High secrets, and in darkness knelt to see
The inenarrable godhead of delight?
Love is a flame:—we have beaconed the world's night.
3 A city:—and we have built it, these and I.
An emperor:—we have taught the world to die.
So, for their sakes I loved, ere I go hence,
And the high cause of Love's magnificence,
And to keep loyalties young, I'll write those names
Golden forever, eagles, crying flames,
And set them as a banner, that men may know,
To dare the generations, burn, and blow
Out on the wind of Time, shining and streaming. . . .
These I have loved:
White plates and cups, clean-gleaming,
Ringed with blue lines; and feathery, fairy dust;
4, 5 Wet roofs, beneath the lamp-light; the strong crust
Of friendly bread; and many-tasting food;

WHITE CUP AND SAUCER, NO 1016
Fantin-Latour
Fitzwilliam Museum, Cambridge

Motivation for Reading Have students list the simple daily items and activities they enjoy. You might have them share some of these and make a class list. Then point out that Brooke's poem is a tribute to the things he has loved.

Master Teacher Note Review Brooke's life. Why is this poem especially poignant in light of that life?

Purpose-Setting Question How well does the title fit the poem?

1 **Discussion** How do the loves of the speaker enable him to "cheat despair"?

2 **Discussion** Explain what the poet means by the "star."

3 **Discussion** How has the speaker "taught the world to die"?

4 **Critical Thinking and Reading** Make some inferences about the speaker from his list of "loves."

5 **Reading Strategy** In one sentence, summarize what the poet is telling you that he loves in life.

6 **Discussion** What will happen to the speaker's loves as he faces the "gate of Death"?

7 **Discussion** Are these last thoughts optimistic or pessimistic? Support your position with evidence from the poem.

2. Answers will differ. Some students may find the poem intensely sentimental, and others may see it as beautifully patriotic.

Humanities Note

Fine art, *White Cup and Saucer* by Henri Fantin Latour. Henri Fantin Latour (1836–1904) was a French painter. Although Latour enrolled at the Ecole des Beaux Arts in Paris, his studies there were unsuccessful. His self-training, which was more useful, consisted of his friendly association with the Impressionist Manet and the hours spent at the Louvre copying the works of the old masters.

White Cup and Saucer was painted in 1864. It shows the influence of the Impressionists in the simple, objective composition and the importance of the light on the object. A pleasing and direct painting, it shows the artist's awareness of innate beauty in everyday objects.

You might ask the following questions:

1. How do you think Rupert Brooke would feel about this painting?
2. Does this painting suit the thoughtful quality of the poem?

6 Discussion What will happen to the speaker's loves as he faces the "gate of Death"?

7 Discussion Are these last thoughts optimistic or pessimistic? Support your position with evidence from the poem.

Rainbows; and the blue bitter smoke of wood;
And radiant raindrops couching in cool flowers;
And flowers themselves, that sway through sunny hours,
Dreaming of moths that drink them under the moon;
Then, the cool kindliness of sheets, that soon
Smooth away trouble; and the rough male kiss
Of blankets; grainy wood; live hair that is
Shining and free; blue-massing clouds; the keen
Unpassioned beauty of a great machine;
The benison of hot water; furs to touch;
The good smell of old clothes; and others such—
The comfortable smell of friendly fingers,
Hair's fragrance, and the musty reek that lingers
4, 5 About dead leaves and last year's ferns. . . .
Dear names,
And thousand others throng to me! Royal flames;
Sweet water's dimpling laugh from tap or spring;
Holes in the ground; and voices that do sing;
Voices in laughter, too; and body's pain,
Soon turned to peace; and the deep-panting train;
Firm sands; the little dulling edge of foam
That browns and dwindles as the wave goes home;
And washen stones, gay for an hour; the cold
Graveness of iron; moist black earthen mold;
Sleep; and high places; footprints in the dew;
And oaks; and brown horse-chestnuts, glossy-new;
And new-peeled sticks; and shining pools on grass;—
All these have been my loves. And these shall pass,
6 Whatever passes not, in the great hour,
Nor all my passion, all my prayers, have power
To hold them with me through the gate of Death.
They'll play deserter, turn with the traitor breath,
Break the high bond we made, and sell Love's trust
And sacramented covenant to the dust.
—Oh, never a doubt but, somewhere, I shall wake,
And give what's left of love again, and make
New friends, now strangers. . . .
7 But the best I've known
Stays here, and changes, breaks, grows old, is blown
About the winds of the world, and fades from brains
Of living men, and dies.
Nothing remains.

O dear my loves, O faithless, once again
This one last gift I give: that after men
Shall know, and later lovers, far-removed,
Praise you, "All these were lovely"; say, "He loved."

THINKING ABOUT THE SELECTION

Recalling

1. What does the speaker say he will "crown . . . with immortal praise"?
2. What are the first three items in the speaker's list of things he has loved?
3. What does the speaker say will happen to the things he loves after he is gone?
4. The speaker asks one last favor. What is it?

Interpreting

5. The title of this poem, "The Great Lover," might lead you to expect a different kind of poem. (a) In what sense is this not a traditional love poem? (b) In what sense is it a love poem?
6. In line 72 the speaker says, "O faithless." Whom or what is he addressing?
7. Who is being quoted in line 75, "All these were lovely"?
8. Walter de la Mare, the poet, said that Rupert Brooke delighted "in things for themselves." (a) How does this poem support that observation? (b) What properties are shared by (or missing from) all the items on Brooke's list?

Applying

9. If you were compiling a personal list of loves similar to those on Brooke's list, what five items might you add to the ones he includes? Suggest descriptive, image-making words to go with the items—not just "wood smoke," for example, but "the blue bitter smoke of wood."

CRITICAL THINKING AND READING

Identifying The Georgian Poets

Rupert Brooke, Siegfried Sassoon, and D. H. Lawrence, despite their artistic differences, are commonly identified with a group called the Georgian poets. The name stems from the fact that the poets were writing early in the reign of King George V of England. The group's anthology, *Georgian Poetry,* first appeared in 1912. Four more volumes, all featuring contemporary poets, were published biennially through 1922.

1. Georgian poetry has been accused of being "pleasant and almost nonpolitical." T. S. Eliot, a contemporary, said that the poets "insist upon the English countryside and are even positively patriotic." How closely do Brooke's two poems fit those two descriptions?
2. The Georgian poets appeared to be a vital new force in 1912. By 1922 they were clinging to "a tender and prettified Nature, to the false solace of dreams"? Knowing something of Rupert Brooke's life and times, what do you think caused this rapid decline of Georgian poetry?

UNDERSTANDING LANGUAGE

Appreciating Specific Words

Rupert Brooke's choice of words in "The Great Lover" is extraordinarily effective. His words give the reader a vivid mental picture of what he is describing. Rather than merely writing "sheets," for instance (as on a scrawled shopping list), Brooke creates "the cool kindliness of sheets." Those two adjectives—*cool* and *kindliness*—make all the difference. Find ten other specific words in "The Great Lover" that create striking images. (Include entire phrases in your answer, underlining the descriptive word or words. For example: *drowsy* Death.)

ANSWERS TO CRITICAL THINKING AND READING

1. Suggested Response: Both of Brooke's poems are positive about the English countryside and "The Soldier" is explicitly patriotic.
2. Suggested Response: The Georgians themselves may not have greatly changed. However, public attitudes may have been altered as a result of the horrors of World War I. Modernist poets like Pound and Eliot were more attuned to this shift than were the Georgians.

ANSWERS TO UNDERSTANDING LANGUAGE

Answers will differ. Students may include: "*feathery, fairy* dust"; "*many-tasting* food"; "*radiant* raindrops"; "*cool* flowers"; "*sunny* hours"; "*blue-massing* clouds"; and "the *comfortable smell* of *friendly* fingers."

Answers

ANSWERS TO THINKING ABOUT THE SELECTION

Recalling

1. The speaker will crown those he has loved.
2. He first lists white plates and cups trimmed in blue, dust, and wet roofs under lamplight.
3. They will remain but will eventually vanish.
4. The speaker asks to be remembered as having loved.

Interpreting

5. Suggested Responses: (a) This is not a poem of the love of one person for another. (b) It tells what Brooke has loved in his life.
6. Suggested Response: He calls the things he loves "faithless."
7. Suggested Response: Future reader and lovers are being quoted.
8. Suggested Responses: (a) His list indicates an interest in a variety of objects, which he seems to love just "for themselves." (b) All these items are passing sensations and impressions.

Applying

9. Answers will differ.

More About the Author You may want to tell students that T. S. Eliot was a pioneer in taking the urban environment as a subject. At the time he began writing, many poets still assumed that nature was the natural subject for poetry. Ask students what new types of subject matter poets might want to explore today.

T. S. ELIOT

1888–1965

Thomas Stearns Eliot is one of the dominant figures in twentieth-century English literature. A poet, playwright, critic, thinker, and cultural pioneer who changed the consciousness of an entire generation of writers, he emerged in the 1920's as the acknowledged leader of what is now called the Modernist movement. Eliot's work is often difficult to understand, drawing as it does upon a broad range of myth, history, religion, allusion, and symbol. His poems and plays raise fundamental questions about human aspirations and the nature of civilized society.

Eliot has ties to both the United States and Great Britain. Born in St. Louis, Missouri, he was educated at Smith and Milton Academies, Harvard University, the Sorbonne, and Oxford. The outbreak of World War I found Eliot in England, where he remained throughout most of his adult life, eventually acquiring British citizenship. In 1915 he married the sensitive, witty, but highly neurotic Vivienne Haigh-Wood. While writing poetry and critical reviews, Eliot taught school, worked for the banking firm of Lloyd's, and in 1925 took an editorial position with the publishing company that became Faber and Faber.

His earliest work, owing to its unconventional style, was greeted with less than universal acclaim, although the poet Ezra Pound was a vocal supporter from the beginning. Pound saw, as many did not, that Eliot spoke in an authentic new voice and offered an original, if bleak, vision. In *Prufrock and Other Observations* (1917) through *The Waste Land* (1922) and "The Hollow Men" (1925), Eliot pictured the disturbed, fragmented western world wrought by World War I and its aftermath. Then, gradually, came renewed hope through religion, his faith leading him to join the Church of England in 1927. "Journey of the Magi" (1927) and *"Ash Wednesday"* (1930) mark the new religious phase of his life and writing, capped by his poetic masterpiece, *Four Quartets,* published in 1943, during the dark days of World War II.

As he grew older, Eliot turned his attention increasingly to poetic drama and criticism. Although *Murder in the Cathedral* (1935) and *The Cocktail Party* (1950) are often performed, none of his plays have gained the widespread critical admiration accorded his poetry. As a literary critic, Eliot's influence on his contemporaries was profound. His *Notes Towards the Definition of Culture,* one of many noteworthy critical works, appeared in 1948, the same year in which he received the Nobel Prize for Literature. In 1967, on the second anniversary of Eliot's death, a memorial was unveiled in Poet's Corner, Westminster Abbey.

Objectives

1. To recognize and appreciate synecdoche
2. To select music that evokes the mood of a poem
3. To write a poem using synecdoche

Teaching Portfolio: Support Material

Teacher Backup, p. 000

Vocabulary Check, p. 00

Usage and Mechanics Worksheet, p. 00

Analyzing Literature Worksheet, p. 00

Critical Thinking and Reading Worksheet, p. 00

Language Worksheet, p. 00

Selection Test, p. 000

GUIDE FOR READING

Preludes; Journey of the Magi

The Writer's Techniques

Synecdoche. Synecdoche (sĭ nĕk′ də kē) is a figure of speech in which a part stands for the whole, an individual for a class, a material for the thing—or the reverse of any of these. For example, in the sentence, "Give us this day our daily bread," the word *bread* (part) stands for *food* (whole). In the sentence, "The thief knew that a loud noise would bring the law," the word *law* (whole) stands for *police officer* (part). As a poetic device, synecdoche can sometimes make thought-provoking connections that startle and enlighten the reader.

Mood. Mood is the dominant emotion created by a piece of writing. If the mood of a poem is serious and reflective, the reader upon finishing it, will in all likelihood be somber and pensive. If, on the other hand, the mood of a poem is light and whimsical, the reader upon completing it, should be in high spirits and perhaps smiling. Mood must not be confused with either theme or subject matter. For instance, "The Cremation of Sam McGee," a ballad by Robert Service, deals with the death and cremation of a man in the Yukon, but the mood of the ballad is anything but melancholy.

Look For

As you read "Preludes" and "Journey of the Magi," look for the use of synecdoche in the first poem and the mood evoked by the second.

Writing

Look through a newspaper or magazine, for examples of synecdoche. When you have collected ten or more examples, write a brief analysis of the device. In your analysis, indicate (a) which kind of synecdoche occurs most often, and (b) why you think the device came into such common use in English.

Vocabulary

Knowing the following words will help you as you read the poems by T. S. Eliot.

galled (gôld) *adj.*: Injured or made sore by rubbing or chafing (p. 1077, l. 6)

refractory (ri frak′ tər ē) *adj.*: Hard to manage; stubborn (p. 1077, l. 6)

dispensation (dis pən sā′ shən) *n.*: Religious system or belief (p. 1078, l. 41)

Literary Focus Help students to overcome some of their preconceptions about the negative connotations of the word *mood,* connotations that are associated, for instance, with the adjective *moody.* Emphasize that mood involves a state of mind as well as feeling. Have students think of places or events that put a person in a particular mood, for example, a sports event, a private party, a church service, or a graduation. List some of the moods that these places and occasions might inspire.

Look For Your **less advanced** students may need further discussion about the concept of synecdoche. You may want to preview the Analyzing Literature section on page 1076.

Writing Help students to differentiate between a symbol and synecdoche. A police badge, for example, could be a symbol of an officer's authority, whereas the term "the law" stands for all policemen.

Vocabulary You might ask **less advanced** students to read aloud the words and definitions before starting the poems.

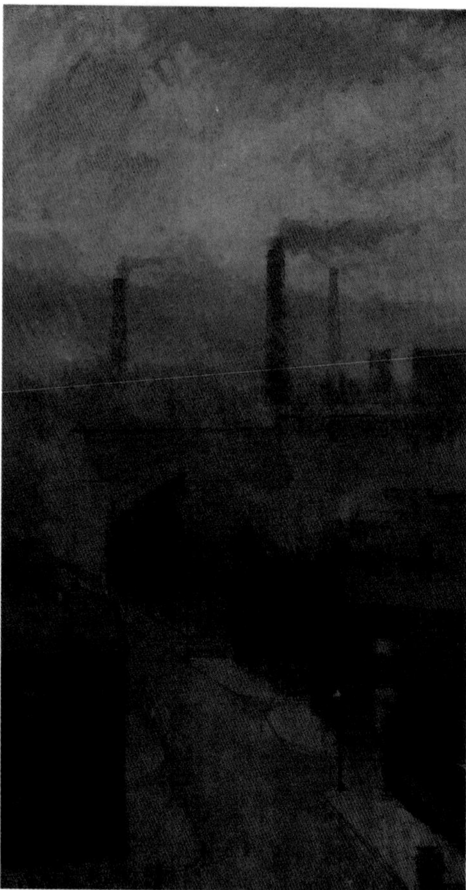

BOLTON, 1938
William Coldstream
The National Gallery of Canada, Ottawa

Preludes

T. S. Eliot

I

The winter evening settles down
With smell of steaks[1] in passageways.
Six o'clock.
The burnt-out ends of smoky days.
And now a gusty shower wraps
The grimy scraps
Of withered leaves about your feet 1
And newspapers from vacant lots;
The showers beat
On broken blinds and chimney-pots,
And at the corner of the street
A lonely cab-horse steams and stamps.
And then the lighting of the lamps.

II

The morning comes to consciousness
Of faint stale smells of beer
From the sawdust-trampled street
With all its muddy feet that press
To early coffee-stands.
With the other masquerades 2
That time resumes,
One thinks of all the hands
That are raising dingy shades
In a thousand furnished rooms.

III

You tossed a blanket from the bed,
You lay upon your back, and waited;
You dozed, and watched the night revealing
The thousand sordid images
Of which your soul was constituted;
They flickered against the ceiling.

1. **steaks:** In 1910, when this poem was composed, steaks were inexpensive and were commonly eaten by members of the lower class.

Motivation for Reading Ask students to recall an evening walk they took and the mood it inspired in them. Tell them that the first of Eliot's "Preludes" evokes a winter evening in a city.

Master Teacher Note You might tell students that at about the time Eliot was writing these poems in America, Ezra Pound was helping to create the Imagist movement in England. That movement generally favored briefer poems, concrete descriptions, deletion of unnecessary words, and the use of free verse rather than traditional meters. Ask students to evaluate "The Preludes" using Imagist criteria.

Purpose-Setting Question How are all these poems related?

1 **Discussion** Note the use of the adjectives in this stanza. What impression do they create?

2 **Discussion** What "masquerades" do you think the poet means?

Humanities Note

Fine art, *Bolton, 1938,* by Sir William Coldstream. The British artist and teacher Sir William Coldstream was born in 1908. He studied at the prestigious Slade School of Art in London. Coldstream dabbled in cinema for a few years and then returned to painting. Along with two other British modern artists, William Coldstream founded the Euston Road School of Drawing and Painting. The guiding principle of this school was that of his art: to speak directly to the viewing public with images that draw upon the simple beauty of the commonplace.

The painting *Bolton, 1938,* demonstrates this guiding principle. Painted in the industrialized North country of England, it is a somewhat romanticized view of a mill and worker's dwellings. The hazy atmosphere lends a mysterious and nostalgic mood to this landscape. Coldstream painted this scene realistically, in subdued colors.

You might use these questions for discussion:

1. In both works of art, the painting and the poem, the artist observes his surroundings. Which observations by the painter match observations by the poet?
2. Compare and contrast the moods evoked by the painting and the poem.

And when all the world came back
And the light crept up between the shutters
And you heard the sparrows in the gutters,
3 You had such a vision of the street
As the street hardly understands;
Sitting along the bed's edge, where
You curled the papers from your hair,
4 Or clasped the yellow soles of feet
In the palms of both soiled hands.

IV

His soul stretched tight across the skies
That fade behind a city block,
Or trampled by insistent feet
At four and five and six o'clock;
And short square fingers stuffing pipes,
And evening newspapers, and eyes
Assured of certain certainties,
The conscience of a blackened street
Impatient to assume the world.

I am moved by fancies that are curled
Around these images, and cling:
5 The notion of some infinitely gentle
Infinitely suffering thing.

Wipe your hands across your mouth, and laugh;
6 The worlds revolve like ancient women
Gathering fuel in vacant lots.

3 Discussion What is the "vision of the street"?

4 Discussion What type of neighborhood is Eliot describing in I, II, and III? What words and phrases indicate this?

5 Discussion What do you think is the "infinitely gentle . . . suffering thing"?

6 Discussion What is the effect of this final image? How does it relate to the rest of "Preludes"?

THINKING ABOUT THE SELECTION

Recalling

1. In Prelude I what is (a) the time of year? (b) the time of day?
2. In Prelude II what is taking place "in a thousand furnished rooms"?
3. What did "you" hear in Prelude III "when all the world came back"?
4. What are the "ancient women" in the simile doing in Prelude IV?

Interpreting

5. (a) To what social class do the people in "Preludes" belong? (b) How can you tell?
6. The symbol of cycles, or cyclic progression, says one critic, "is almost Mr. Eliot's trademark." What cycle do you find in "Preludes"?
7. A musical prelude can introduce a longer work or can stand alone. Each of Eliot's four preludes stands alone, but they all project a similar mood. How would you describe that mood?

Applying

8. "Preludes," written in 1910–11, reflects Eliot's views before the renewal of his religious faith. How might this poem be different if Eliot had written it twenty years later?

ANALYZING LITERATURE

Using Synecdoche

Synecdoche is a figure of speech in which a part stands for the whole ("Five thousand tongues applauded") or the whole for one of its parts ("Wall Street believes that . . ."). In literature, a synecdoche can enable readers to see an idea or an object in a new light. Sometimes, especially in Eliot's poetry, a synecdoche functions as a symbol. In Prelude II Eliot pictures the crowds of people that hurry to get their morning coffee before going to work. Rather than making such a prosaic statement, however, he uses the synecdoche "muddy feet" (line 17), providing the reader with a more visual and revealing image of the faceless morning bustle in a large city. For each of the following lines from "Preludes," (a) identify the synecdoche; (b) tell what the key word stands for; and (c) comment on how it adds to the mood of the poem.

1. The morning comes to consciousness (1. 14)
2. One thinks of all the hands (1. 21)
3. . . . all the world came back (1. 30)
4. You had such a vision of the street/As the street hardly understands (1. 33–34)
5. . . . and eyes/Assured of certain certainties (1. 44–45)

SPEAKING AND LISTENING

Selecting Music That Evokes the Poem

Like much of Eliot's early poetry, "Preludes" implies disenchantment with the twentieth century and reflects a bleak outlook on life. In this respect his poetry has much in common with the music composed in the early twentieth century. Do some library research on modern composers and their music, finding examples of music that expresses a similar disillusionment and seems to complement Eliot's poem. If possible, obtain a tape or tapes of this music to bring to class for listening and discussion.

THINKING AND WRITING

Writing a Poem Using Synecdoche

Choose a theme that interests you and write an original poem on it. You may choose any rhyme scheme and any metric pattern you like, and the poem may be of any reasonable length. Think carefully about how you can work two synecdoches into your poem—one using the part for the whole, the other using the whole for the part. Write the poem, using the synecdoches. Even with good planning, you will find that thoughtful revision is essential to a well-written poem.

Answers

ANSWERS TO THINKING ABOUT THE SELECTION

Recalling

1. The setting is a winter evening.
2. Dingy window shades are being raised.
3. The "you" of the poem "heard the sparrows in the gutters."
4. The ancient women are "Gathering fuel in vacant lots."

Interpreting

5. Suggested Response: The inhabitants of these city streets are laborers in the working class. Clues are broken blinds (line 10), stale smells of beer (15), and dingy shades (22).
6. Suggested Response: The cycle here is evening to day to evening again with little change or variety. The image in the final two lines also suggests a cycle.
7. Suggested Response: The mood is one of futility and dreariness, beneath which a great suffering is occurring.

Applying

8. Answers will differ. Students may respond that Eliot might have presented a more positive outlook and might have found more explicit religious meaning in these scenes.

ANSWERS TO ANALYZING LITERATURE

1. Suggested Response: The *morning* stands for everyone who is waking up. By suggesting a shared consciousness this synecdoche reinforces the impersonality of the poem.
2. Suggested Response: The *hands* represent people who are raising the shades; the image suggests a monotonous sameness.
3. Suggested Response: The *world* coming back refers to the visibility of people and objects in the morning light. This synecdoche implies a cyclic return rather than a renewal.
4. Suggested Response: The *street* refers to the people, objects, and whole life of the street. This synecdoche suggests a spiritual dimension behind the sordid appearances and tired cycles of life.
5. Suggested Response: *Eyes* are the eyes of all these city people. This synecdoche reveals the closed state of mind of people in this environment. By referring to people only as "eyes" or, elsewhere, as feet or fingers, the poet hints at their lack of wholeness.

THINKING AND WRITING

For help with this assignment, students can refer to Lesson 18, "Writing a Poem," in the Handbook of Writing About Literature.

Publishing Student Writing Students may want to read their work to the class and then collect it in a class booklet.

Journey of the Magi

T. S. Eliot

In this poem, the speaker, one of the three wise men who traveled to Bethlehem to pay homage to the baby Jesus, reflects upon the meaning of his journey.

"A cold coming we had of it,
Just the worst time of the year
For a journey, and such a long journey:
The ways deep and the weather sharp,
The very dead of winter."[1]
And the camels galled, sore-footed, refractory,
Lying down in the melting snow.
There were times we regretted
The summer palaces on slopes, the terraces,
And the silken girls bringing sherbet.
Then the camel men cursing and grumbling
And running away, and wanting their liquor and women,
And the night-fires going out, and the lack of shelters,
And the cities hostile and the towns unfriendly
And the villages dirty and charging high prices:
A hard time we had of it.
At the end we preferred to travel all night,
Sleeping in snatches,
With the voices singing in our ears, saying
That this was all folly.

Then at dawn we came down to a temperate valley,
Wet, below the snow line, smelling of vegetation;
With a running stream and a water-mill beating the darkness,
And three trees on the low sky,
And an old white horse galloped away in the meadow.
Then we came to a tavern with vine-leaves over the lintel,
Six hands at an open door dicing for pieces of silver,
And feet kicking the empty wine-skins.

---

1. "A . . . winter.": Adapted from a part of a sermon delivered by 17th-century Bishop Lancelot Adams: "A cold coming they had of it at this time of year, just the worst time of the year to take a journey, and specially a long journey in. The ways deep, the weather sharp, the days short, the sun farthest off . . . the very dead of winter."

Motivation for Reading This journey is more than a physical one. Discuss with students the several connotations of journeys. What have they discovered about themselves and others on "personal" journeys?

Purpose-Setting Question How has the speaker changed as the result of his journey?

1 **Discussion** Describe the conditions of the journey of the Magi.

2 **Discussion** The author says that "this" is all folly. What is "this"?

3 **Discussion** Why do you think the speaker would make the journey again?

4 **Discussion** How is the birth of the savior both a birth and death for the men who witnessed it?

5 **Discussion** Why would the speaker welcome another death? Does his desire show faith or rejection of religion? Explain.

But there was no information, and so we continued
And arrived at evening, not a moment too soon
Finding the place; it was (you may say) satisfactory.

3 All this was a long time ago, I remember,
And I would do it again, but set down
This set down
This: were we led all that way for
Birth or Death? There was a Birth, certainly,
5 We had evidence and no doubt. I had seen birth and death,
But had thought they were different; this Birth was
Hard and bitter agony for us, like Death, our death.
We returned to our places, these Kingdoms,
But no longer at ease here, in the old dispensation,
4 With an alien people clutching their gods.
I should be glad of another death.

THINKING ABOUT THE SELECTION

Recalling

1. What kind of weather did the speaker and his companions have on their journey?
2. What are three other problems they encountered?
3. (a) What did they find when they arrived at the tavern? (b) What did they not find?
4. How had circumstances changed for the speaker and his companions when they returned home?

Interpreting

5. Why did others, and perhaps the wise men themselves, think that "this was all folly"?
6. Why do you think the speaker uses understatement, including the parenthetical "you may say," in line 31?
7. In lines 33–35 the speaker says, and then repeats, the words "set down this." What do you think is the purpose of the repetition?
8. The last line of the poem is ambiguous; there is no single, agreed-upon meaning for it. What do you think it means?

Applying

9. In "Journey of the Magi" Eliot retells the story of the wise men traveling to Bethlehem to visit the newborn Jesus. He adds something of his own to the story. What other biblical stories do you know that Eliot might have treated in a similar way?

ANALYZING LITERATURE

Conveying a Mood

The main feeling or atmosphere a piece of writing conveys is its **mood.** Mood is independent of content and theme, since the same story can be presented in various moods. Indeed, Eliot's "Journey of the Magi" has a different mood from the biblical story on which it is based. Read the original story (Matthew 2: 1–12).

1. How does the mood of Eliot's poem differ from the mood of the biblical story?
2. "Journey of the Magi" was published in 1927. How is the ending of the poem consistent with Eliot's views following his renewal of religious faith in the late 1920's?

Answers

ANSWERS TO THINKING ABOUT THE SELECTION

Recalling

1. The winter weather was cold and sharp.
2. They encountered the following problems: refractory, irritated camels; irresponsible camel drivers; lack of shelter and fires; hostile cities; unfriendly towns; dirty villages; and high prices.
3. At the tavern they found gamblers and drunkards but no information.
4. The speaker and his companion were uneasy at home, feeling alienated from the old forms of worship.

Interpreting

5. Suggested Response: They believed there was no point to this difficult journey.
6. Suggested Response: The understatement gives greater credibility to the speaker's words.
7. Suggested response: The repetition is to emphasize the importance of what follows. It also suggests that someone is taking down his words.
8. Answers will differ. Students might say that the speaker is anticipating his physical death or another spiritual rebirth like the one he experienced.

THINKING AND WRITING

Analyzing Eliot's Use of Ambiguity

Although Eliot's poetry was viewed by his contemporaries as a break from tradition, Eliot maintained, as do critics today, that it is steeped in tradition. The continuing challenge of his poems lies in their many layers of meaning and their seeming lack of connectedness. This intentional complexity grows out of Eliot's deep learning, his conscious use of the literature of the past, and a belief that serious themes demand the "logic of the imagination."

Ambiguity means having the potential for being understood in two or more ways. Once when a magazine editor wished to find out movie actor Cary Grant's age, he sent Grant's agent a telegram: "How old Cary Grant?" The telegraphic response came back: "Old Cary Grant fine." Poets often use ambiguity intentionally and quite seriously, as Eliot does in the last line of "Journey of the Magi." If your class has discussed question 8, you already have some idea of the different possible interpretations of that line. If not, think about them now. There are at least three reasonable and entirely different interpretations. Jot them down—and any others you can think of—before beginning to write. Then write a brief analytical essay in which you state these interpretations and comment on them. Indicate which one or more you think Eliot intended. Give your reasons. Before handing in the final draft of your paper, read it over carefully for logic. Refer to the poem, making sure that what you say is defensible in the context of what Eliot has written.

Applying

9. Answers will differ. Students might refer to the story of Joseph and his brothers.

ANSWERS TO ANALYZING LITERATURE

1. Suggested Response: The mood of Eliot's poem is one of complaint or difficulty rather than joy.
2. Suggested Response: The ending reflects the "death" of one way of thinking and believing and the birth of a new religious consciousness. It also suggests the difficulty of such a change.

THINKING AND WRITING

For help with this assignment students can consult Lesson 13, "Writing About a Poem" in the Handbook of Writing About Literature.

Publishing Student Writing Place students in groups of three or four and assign a recorder for each group. Have students share their interpretations and compile a list of these. Have the recorder report for the group to the class. Students can then note varying interpretations and defenses.

Literary Focus You might want to tell students that reading a poem aloud can often provide a clue to its tone.

Look For Consider asking students to consider how the short lines of this poem affect its tone.

Writing You might want to divide the class into small groups so that students can read the original and revised letters to fellow group members.

Vocabulary Ask students to find three synonyms for the vocabulary word *supplication.*

GUIDE FOR READING

The Hollow Men

The Writer's Techniques

Tone. A speaker uses a certain tone in communicating a message to his or her audience. A writer does much the same thing, but a writer—lacking pitch, stress, and other features of spoken language—must rely on the choice of details, words, and syntax to convey tone. In poetry, tone reveals a great deal about the writer's attitude toward the subject. In fact, identifying the tone of a poem is vital to a full understanding of the poem's meaning.

Look For

As you read "The Hollow Men," pay attention to its tone and to the effect this tone has on Eliot's message.

Writing

Find a short letter to the editor in your local newspaper that is written in a tone that is easy to recognize and describe. Ordinarily you can describe tone with a single word—*outraged,* perhaps, or *reasonable,* or *amused.* Then rewrite the letter in an entirely different tone. If the tone is outraged, make it sweet and pleasant. If the tone is amused, make it bitter and angry.

Vocabulary

Knowing the following words will help you as you read "The Hollow Men."

supplication (sup l ka sh n) *n.*: Act of praying (l. 43)

tumid (too mid) *adj.*: Swollen (l. 60)

Objectives

1 To analyze a poem's tone
2 To interpret allusions
3 To write about tone

Teaching Portfolio: Support Material

Teacher Backup, p. 000

Vocabulary Check, p. 00

Usage and Mechanics Worksheet, p. 00

Analyzing Literature Worksheet, p. 00

Critical Thinking and Reading Worksheet, p. 00

Language Worksheet, p. 00

Selection Test, p. 00

The Hollow Men

T. S. Eliot

Mistah Kurtz[1]*—he dead.*

A penny for the Old Guy[2]

I

We are the hollow men
We are the stuffed men
Leaning together
Headpiece filled with straw. Alas!
Our dried voices, when
We whisper together
1, 2 Are quiet and meaningless
As wind in dry grass
Or rats' feet over broken glass
In our dry cellar

Shape without form, shade without color,
Paralyzed force, gesture without motion;

Those who have crossed
With direct eyes, to death's other Kingdom[3]
Remember us—if at all—not as lost
Violent souls, but only
As the hollow men
The stuffed men.

---

1. Mistah Kurtz: A character in Joseph Conrad's *Heart of Darkness* who travels to Africa hoping to improve the lives of the natives, but finds that, instead, he is corrupted by the worst elements of native life. Horrified by what he had become, Kurtz dies in the jungle.
2. A . . . Guy: A traditional cry used by children on Guy Fawkes Day. Guy Fawkes (1570–1606) was executed for participating in a plot to blow up the king and both Houses of Parliament in 1605. Each year on November 5, children beg for pennies to buy firecrackers which they use to destroy stuffed dummies representing Fawkes.
3. Those . . . Kingdom: An allusion to Dante's *Paradiso*, in which those "with direct eyes" are blessed by God in Heaven.

Motivation for Reading Have students discuss what the phrase "hollow men" means to them. Then tell them that this poem is spoken by figures who call themselves hollow men.

Purpose-Setting Question How do the repetitions in the poem contribute to its meaning?

1 **Literary Focus** How would you describe the tone of this opening stanza?

2 **Discussion** Why does the poet include many *s* sounds in this stanza?

3 **Discussion** Whose "eyes" is the speaker afraid of meeting? Why is the speaker afraid?

4 **Discussion** Why do you think this speaker would want to wear "disguises"?

5 **Discussion** What is "death's other kingdom"?

II

3 Eyes I dare not meet in dreams
In death's dream kingdom
These do not appear:
There, the eyes are
Sunlight on a broken column
There, is a tree swinging
And voices are
In the wind's singing
More distant and more solemn
Than a fading star.

Let me be no nearer
In death's dream kingdom
Let me also wear
Such deliberate disguises
Rat's coat, crowskin, crossed staves
In a field[4]
4 Behaving as the wind behaves
No nearer—

Not that final meeting
In the twilight kingdom

III

This is the dead land
This is cactus land
Here the stone images
Are raised, here they receive
The supplication of a dead man's hand
Under the twinkle of a fading star.

Is it like this
In death's other kingdom
Waking alone
5 At the hour when we are
Trembling with tenderness
Lips that would kiss
Form prayers to broken stone.

---

4. crossed . . . field: Scarecrows.

IV

The eyes are not here
There are no eyes here
In this valley of dying stars
In this hollow valley
This broken jaw of our lost kingdoms

In this last of meeting places
We grope together
And avoid speech
Gathered on this beach of the tumid river[5]

Sightless, unless
The eyes reappear
As the perpetual star[6]
Multifoliate rose[7]
Of death's twilight kingdom
The hope only
6 Of empty men.

V

Here we go round the prickly pear
Prickly pear prickly pear
7 *Here we go round the prickly pear*
At five o'clock in the morning.[8]

Between the idea
And the reality
8 Between the motion
And the act[9]
Falls the Shadow

9 *For Thine is the Kingdom*[10]

---

5. river: From Dante's *Inferno*, the river Archeron, the river which the dead cross over as they pass into Hell.
6. star: A traditional symbol for Christ.
7. Multifoliate rose: In Dante's *Paradiso*, Paradise was described as a "multifoliate rose," or a rose with many leaves. Also, the rose is a traditional symbol for the Virgin Mary.
8. Here . . . morning: Adaptation of a common nursery rhyme. A prickly pear is a cactus.
9. Between . . . act: A reference to *Julius Caesar*, Act II, Scene i, 63–65: "Between the acting of a dreadful thing/And the first motion, all the interim is/Like a phantasma or hideous dream."
10. For . . . Kingdom: From the ending of the Lord's Prayer.

6 **Literary Focus** Is the tone of these lines hopeful? Explain.

7 **Discussion** Explain the significance of the children's song. What do its words and rhythm suggest? How is it appropriate?

8 **Discussion** What do you think Eliot means by "the Shadow"?

9 **Discussion** What is the effect of including the last line of "The Lord's Prayer"?

10 Discussion Explain the effect of the repetition in lines 95–97. How does the repetition add to the meaning of the last line?

Between the conception
And the creation
Between the emotion
And the response
Falls the Shadow

Life is very long[11]

Between the desire
And the spasm
Between the potency
And the existence
Between the essence
And the descent
Falls the Shadow

For Thine is the Kingdom

For Thine is
Life is
For Thine is the

This is the way the world ends
This is the way the world ends
10 *This is the way the world ends*
Not with a bang but a whimper.

---

11. Life . . . long: Quotation from Joseph Conrad's *An Outcast of the Islands.*

THINKING ABOUT THE SELECTION

Recalling

1. How does the speaker say that he and others like him are remembered by those "with direct eyes"?
2. In "death's dream kingdom" what disguise will the speaker wear?
3. What do the hollow men do in the "hollow valley . . . this last of meeting places"?
4. What is it that forever falls between idea and achievement, preventing the hollow men from accomplishing anything?
5. According to the speaker, how does the world end?

Interpreting

6. Although Kurtz was a "hollow sham" and Guy Fawkes was a traitor, the speaker suggests that they were superior to the hollow men. Why were they superior?
7. What aspects of modern life might the "stone images" in part III represent?
8. Both part III and part V suggest a particular kind of landscape in which the hollow men exist. What kind of landscape is it?
9. What do you think "the Shadow" is in part V?

Applying

10. In "The Hollow Men," published in 1925, Eliot presents a bleak picture of his generation. To what extent, if at all, do you think his implied criticism applies to the people of today?

ANALYZING LITERATURE

Conveying Tone

The **tone** of a poem reveals the writer's attitude toward the subject or theme. Tone is conveyed through details and images—hollow men stuffed with straw, a cactus land, a twilight kingdom. It is also carried by words and their connotations—*hollow, meaningless, fading, death, Shadow, whimper.* Syntax, the way in which words are put together, plays a part, too—"Shape without form, shade without color" (parallelism); "The hope only/Of empty men" (ambiguity). How would you describe the tone of "The Hollow Men"? (One adjective can usually describe tone, but since Eliot's poem is more complex than most, you may find it necessary to go into greater detail.)

CRITICAL THINKING AND READING

Interpreting Allusions

An **allusion** in literature is a brief, often indirect reference to a person, a place, an event, or another literary work. "The Hollow Men," is a poem rich in allusions. Choose any three of the following allusions from "The Hollow Men." Explain each one. Tell how the allusion adds meaning to the poem by introducing, as a kind of literary shorthand, a number of associations through the use of only a few words. Try to go somewhat beyond the footnote text.

1. *Mistah Kurtz—he dead.*
2. Those who have crossed/With direct eyes, to death's other Kingdom
3. As the perpetual star/Multifoliate rose
4. Between the motion/And the act
5. *For Thine is the Kingdom*

THINKING AND WRITING

Writing About Tone

Write an essay in which you analyze the tone of T. S. Eliot's poetry. Describe the tone of each of the three Eliot poems in this unit and explain how the tone adds to the meaning of each one. Use quotations from the poems to illustrate and support your points. Follow the three basic steps in the writing process. In prewriting, take notes and make a rough outline. Then write your first draft, using appropriate quotations. In revising, make any major changes that are needed —structural, logical, organizational—as well as checking your grammar and usage. Finally, make any needed proofreading corrections.

Answers

ANSWERS TO THINKING ABOUT THE SELECTION

Recalling

1. He and others are remembered as hollow men and stuffed men.
2. The speaker will be disguised as a scarecrow.
3. The hollow men, sightless, grope together and avoid speech.
4. A shadow falls between the idea and the achievement.
5. The world ends *"Not with a bang but with a whimper."*

Interpreting

6. Suggested Response: These individuals had a direction to their lives and were not afraid of dying.
7. Suggested Response: Stone images could represent skyscrapers or any falsely worshiped material objects.
8. Suggested Response: The landscape is desolate, arid, and unproductive.
9. Answers may differ. Some students may say the Shadow is the fear of taking any action.

Applying

10. Answers will differ. Some students may find this picture too negative; others may feel it is applicable today.

ANSWERS TO ANALYZING LITERATURE

Suggested Response: The tone may be described as bleak, hopeless, enervated, and anxious.

ANSWERS TO CRITICAL THINKING AND READING

1. Suggested Response: The allusion may suggest that even the energetic evil of Kurtz is beyond the capabilities of the hollow men.
2. Suggested Response: These are the eyes of the blessed who see the figures in the poem as hollow.
3. Suggested Response: The only hope of hollow men is some sort of heavenly mercy, perhaps from a compassionate figure like the Virgin Mary.
4. Suggested Response: This phrase from Shakespeare's *Julius Caesar* suggests that all positive action seems dreadful to the hollow men, who are living in a kind of nightmare.
5. Suggested Response: This cut-off phrase from the Lord's Prayer suggests that the hollow men cannot fully pray and therefore cannot get beyond their situation.

THINKING AND WRITING

For help with this assignment, students can refer to Lesson 13, "Writing about a Poem," in the Handbook of Writing About Literature.

Publishing Student Writing Ask student volunteers to read their essays aloud so that students can learn from the variety of points raised.

More About the Author You might want to tell students that Graves preferred a simple life on the island of Majorca to life in England. Ask students what might have motivated Graves to make this choice.

ROBERT GRAVES

1895–

Robert Graves has written successfully in almost every literary form, but he is perhaps best known as the author of the best-selling novel *I, Claudius* (1934), which was made into an outstanding BBC television series a few years ago. Graves achieved his first fame in 1929 with a classic memoir of World War I, *Good-bye to All That*. Despite his prose efforts, however, Graves's true calling is poetry, as he has said. Ever since his first two volumes appeared in 1916, he has been recognized as a major British poet.

The son of a prominent poet, Robert Graves grew up in a London household with an extensive private library, which provided much of his early education. World War I began while he was attending the Charterhouse School and producing his earliest poems. Graves enlisted in the Royal Welsh Fusiliers, the same outfit to which Siegfried Sassoon belonged. Fighting in the trenches, he was severely wounded and reported dead. He later suffered shell shock and received a medical discharge. Graves, like Sassoon, lost all illusions about the glory of war, as shown by his two wartime poetry collections, *Over the Brazier* (1916) and *Fairies and Fusiliers* (1917).

Graves studied at Oxford, received his degree, and in 1927 took a teaching position at the Royal Egyptian University in Cairo. For a number of years he collaborated with the American poet Laura Riding on many writing and publishing projects. In 1929 he and Riding settled in Majorica, an island off the coast of Spain, where he remained except for intervals during the Spanish Civil War, World War II, and a teaching stint at Oxford in the 1960's.

A respected scholar and critic, Graves aroused controversy in 1948 with the publication of *The White Goddess,* a critical study of the origin, value, and history of poetry, whose main thesis—the dominance of a mythic female Muse—is impressively argued but widely questioned. Its influence on Graves' poetry, however, has been substantial and beneficial. His poems, a blend of traditional and modern, sometimes exhibit a deceptive simplicity. According to the American poet Richard Wilbur, they "have the air of being spontaneous answers to actual experience."

Objectives

1 To understand the Modernist Movement
2 To write about the Modernist Movement

Teaching Portfolio: Support Material

Teacher Backup, p. 000

Vocabulary Check, p. 00

Usage and Mechanics Worksheet, p. 00

Analyzing Literature Worksheet, p. 00

Critical Thinking and Reading Worksheet, p. 00

Language Worksheet, p. 00

Selection Test, p. 000

Art Transparency, p. 000

GUIDE FOR READING

Interruption; One Hard Look; She Tells Her Love While Half Asleep

Period Trends

The Modernist Movement. The Modernist movement, or Modernism, followed World War I. Art, architecture, dance, and literature —all were in revolt against the rigid traditional forms of earlier periods. Disillusioned by the war and unhappy with the postwar world, artists sought new forms, new techniques, new subjects. It was a time of ferment. The Modernist writers, like the Georgian poets, demanded a break with the past, but the Modernists were much more radical than the Georgians. The aftermath of war, which doomed the pastoral-minded Georgians, spurred the Modernists to action. Many poets who began as Georgians—D. H. Lawrence, Siegfried Sassoon, Robert Graves—changed and grew. In the 1920's T. S. Eliot in England, James Joyce in Ireland, and E. E. Cummings in the United States experimented in ways that earlier generations would have found incomprehensible.

Look For

As you read the poems by Robert Graves, notice the deeper meanings that are implicit in what appear to be spare and simple lines.

Writing

Choose an everyday object to write about. Set an alarm to go off at the end of five minutes. Then, on a sheet of paper, begin writing nonstop, putting down any thoughts or associations that come to mind in regard to your subject. You need not write full sentences, but try to keep your pen or pencil in motion until the alarm sounds. When your time is up, read over your random jottings. Select the most interesting of them and share them with your classmates.

Vocabulary

Knowing the following words will help you as you read "Interruption."

premonition (prē′ mə nish′ən) *n.*: A warning in advance (l. 5)

gigantified (jī gan′ tə fīd) *adj.*: Made to seem much larger (l. 17)

Literary Focus You may point out that the American poet Ezra Pound was instrumental in creating the Modernist movement in poetry. Influenced by the British novelist Ford Madox Ford and the Philosopher T. E. Hulme, Pound started writing brief poems in free verse that focused on a single image. The group of writers who adopted this approach called themselves Imagists and were active in London before World War I.

Look For Consider telling students that a poem must usually be read several times before it reveals its deeper meanings.

Writing Have students practice thinking by association. Name an item and have a student volunteer an immediate association. Have students continue to associate, for two or three minutes. See where the association leads them. Then assign the writing.

Vocabulary Have **less advanced** students study the words and meanings before they begin reading.

Motivation for Reading Have students think about a time they were sitting quietly, thinking pleasant thoughts. What effect would a loud intrusion have had on their thinking and mood? Tell them that this poem describes an interruption.

Purpose-Setting Question What is modern about this poem?

1 **Discussion** What do the "boots" represent as they trample on the "countryside of thoughtfulness"?

2 **Discussion** What is the effect or power of interruption?

3 **Discussion** Note the imagery in these lines, especially the personification of the interruption. How is this imagery effective?

4 **Discussion** How does the countryside before the interruption compare with this postcard scene?

Interruption

Robert Graves

If ever against this easy blue and silver
Hazed-over countryside of thoughtfulness,
Far behind in the mind and above,
1 Boots from before and below approach trampling,
Watch how their premonition will display
A forward countryside, low in the distance—
A picture-postcard square of June grass;
Will warm a summer season, trim the hedges,
Cast the river about on either flank,
Start the late cuckoo emptily calling,
Invent a rambling tale of moles and voles,
Furnish a path with stiles.
Watch how the field will broaden, the feet nearing,
Sprout with great dandelions and buttercups,
Widen and heighten. The blue and silver
Fogs at the border of this all-grass.
Interruption looms gigantified,
Lurches against, treads thundering through,
2, 3 Blots the landscape, scatters all,
Roars and rumbles like a dark tunnel,
Is gone.
        The picture-postcard grass and trees
Swim back to central: it is a large patch,
It is a modest, failing patch of green,
The postage stamp of its departure,
4 Clouded with blue and silver, closing in now
To a plain countryside of less and less,
Unpeopled and unfeatured blue and silver,
Before, behind, above.

SUN, WIND, AND RAIN
David Cox
The City Museum and Art Gallery, Birmingham

THINKING ABOUT THE SELECTION

Recalling

1. (a) Where does the interruption occur? (b) What time of year is it?
2. With what does the field sprout when the feet near it?
3. What is the sound of the interruption at its height?
4. When the interruption is over, how is the "blue and silver" countryside described?

Interpreting

5. (a) What is the interruption? (b) What is the first indication of the nature of the interruption?
6. Why do you think the interruption is described as being "all-grass"?
7. Why do you think the poet chose to break line 21 abruptly?
8. The meaning, of "Interruption" is not expressed in a series of logically ordered sentences. How is it expressed?

Applying

9. Short stories sometimes have an interruption as their main plot device. (a) What short story do you know that uses this device? (b) What is the nature of the interruption? (c) What precedes and follows the interruption.

Humanities Note

Fine art, *Sun, Wind, and Rain* by David Cox. David Cox (1783–1859), an English landscape painter, learned his craft through various jobs held early in his life—as miniaturist, paint maker, and scene painter. He took a few watercolor lessons from the famous English watercolorist John Varley, after which he taught drawing and sold watercolor sketches for a living. He eventually gained a small reputation as a painter and continued to teach for the rest of his life.

The painting *Sun, Wind, and Rain* was completed in 1845. It was painted in North Wales in oil, a medium that Cox only began to use in 1839. Painted with simple vigor, it is a striking celebration of the caprices of nature.

You might ask the following questions:

1. What do both the poem and the painting describe?
2. Which verbal images in the poem match visual images in the painting?

Answers

ANSWERS TO THINKING ABOUT THE SELECTION

Recalling

1. (a) and (b) The interruption occurs while the speaker is in a "blue and silver" countryside in June. It occurs in the person's thoughts.
2. The field sprouts with dandelions and buttercups.
3. At its height, the sound "Roars . . . like a dark tunnel."
4. The blue and silver countryside is plain, unpeopled, and unfeatured.

Interpreting

5. Suggested Responses: (a) The interruption is the sound of footsteps approaching. (b) The first indication is line 4.
6. Suggested Response: The grass covers the whole landscape.
7. Suggested Response: The break is to emphasize the contrast—the interruption has left, and the summer countryside returns.
8. Suggested Response: It is expressed as a series of associated images.

Applying

9. Answers will differ.

Motivation for Reading Have students think about a time when they saw someone giving another person a hard look. Tell them that this poem considers the effect of such a look.

Purpose-Setting Question How do the short lines of this poem contribute to its meaning?

1 **Clarification** Make sure that students understand this figure of speech is related to the expression, "That's the last straw!"

2 **Reading Strategy** Paraphrase these three lines.

3 **Discussion** What is the theme of this poem?

One Hard Look

Robert Graves

Small gnats that fly
In hot July
And lodge in sleeping ears,
Can rouse therein
A trumpet's din
With Day of Judgment fears.

Small mice at night
Can wake more fright
Than lions at midday;
A straw will crack
The camel's back—
There is no easier way.

One smile relieves
A heart that grieves
Though deadly sad it be,
And one hard look
Can close the book
That lovers love to see.

THINKING ABOUT THE SELECTION

Recalling

1. What does the buzz of a gnat sound like in the ear of a sleeper?
2. What can one hard look do?

Interpreting

3. What is the common characteristic of gnats, mice, and straw that contribute to the meaning of the poem?
4. What main observation does the poem make?

Applying

5. (a) Do you agree with Graves's observation? (b) What experience have you had that supports or casts doubt on what he says?

ANSWERS TO THINKING ABOUT THE SELECTION

Recalling

1. According to the poet a buzz can create a din like a trumpet blaring and cause one to fear death or the day of judgment.
2. A hard look can end a loving relationship.

Interpreting

3. Suggested Response: These are small, usually insignificant items.
4. Suggested Response: Little things can cause major reactions.

Applying

5. (a) Responses will differ. (b) However, most students will be able to relate an experience where a small action caused a strong feeling or reaction.

She Tells Her Love While Half Asleep

She tells her love while half asleep,
    In the dark hours,
        With half-words whispered low:
As Earth stirs in her winter sleep
    And puts out grass and flowers
        Despite the snow,
        Despite the falling snow.

THINKING ABOUT THE SELECTION

Recalling

1. What is the time of day in the poem?
2. "Despite the falling snow," what does the earth do?

Interpreting

3. To what in nature are the "half-words whispered low" compared?
4. What might falling snow represent metaphorically in the relationship between the speaker and the one who "tells her love"?

Applying

5. The flowers of spring are probably the most widely used symbol of rebirth. Why do you think this is so?

THINKING AND WRITING

Writing About the Modernist Movement

The Modernist movement began and peaked in the 1920's. To understand the movement, you need a general understanding of that tumultuous decade. You also should know the works of a few of the major writers—T. S. Eliot, Robert Graves, James Joyce, and Virginia Woolf. Do some library research on the Modernism of the Twenties. Take notes, particularly on the changes in style that Modernism introduced.

Write an essay in which you explain why writers and other artists in that decade felt compelled to strike out in new directions. Include quotations from the sources you have used. When you revise your first draft, check to make sure you have introduced and punctuated the quotations properly.

Motivation for Reading Have students describe a winter field. What is happening to the seeds under the earth? Then tell them that the poet uses the growth of plants as a figure of speech.

Purpose-Setting Question How does the poet feel toward his subject?

1 **Discussion** How are "dark hours" and "winter sleep" similar images?

2 **Discussion** How does the word "falling" add to the snow image? Would the omission of the last line make a difference in the intent of the poem?

Answers

ANSWERS TO THINKING ABOUT THE SELECTION

Recalling

1. The setting is nighttime.
2. The earth begins to grow grass and flowers.

Interpreting

3. Suggested Response: The words are compared to the Earth's stirring.
4. Suggested Response: It may represent a period of waiting or quiescence during which the love is preparing for growth.

Applying

5. Answers will differ. Students may respond that flowers, though dormant in winter, sprout vigorously, beautifully, and trustingly after the winter season.

THINKING AND WRITING

Publishing Student Writing You might want to collect students' essays in a book.

Writing Across the Curriculum You may want to work with the members of the history department to assist students in learning more about the 1920's. Perhaps members of that department could give lectures and suggest movies or other resources to help students place the Modernists in a social context.

More About the Author You might want to tell students that Auden was a virtuoso poet who could imitate Shakespearean songs and the complex prose style of Henry James in the same work. Ask students whether virtuoso artists known for their technique are less likely to produce important or lasting works of art.

W. H. AUDEN

1907–1977

Much as T. S. Eliot became established as the poetic voice of the 1920's, so W. H. Auden emerged as the poetic voice of the 1930's. Born in York, England, Auden moved to the United States at the age of thirty-two and took out citizenship papers, reversing the odyssey of Eliot, who was born in St. Louis, Missouri, and became a British subject. The youthful Auden was greatly influenced by Eliot's *The Waste Land,* but in later life both men replaced their anger and despair with a staunch Christian faith. Versatility, wit, and dazzling technique characterize Auden's poetry.

Wystan Hugh Auden, the son of a doctor, was interested in science as a child and planned to become an engineer. He received his education at St. Edmund's School and Gresham's School, and later attended Oxford University. His first appearance in print was in *Oxford Poetry,* a series of annual collections of verse by the university's undergraduates. The volumes in which his poems appear—1926, 1927, and 1928—also contain poems by Stephen Spender, C. Day Lewis, and Louis MacNeice, all of whom became important poets.

Auden's first published collection, entitled simply *Poems,* appeared in 1930. These poems, innovative and eloquent, struck many readers of the day as strange, even impenetrable. His second volume, *On This Island,* published in 1937, is more down-to-earth and generated greater enthusiasm. He was awarded the King's Poetry Medal that year. In 1939 Auden left England for the United States, where he taught in a number of universities while continuing to write. He became an American citizen in 1946, and his poetry collection, *The Age of Anxiety,* won a Pulitzer Prize in 1948. In 1956, having been elected Professor of Poetry at Oxford University, he returned to England where he remained through 1961.

Auden was a more prolific poet than Eliot, and his output is remarkable for its variety, originality, and craftsmanship. He writes equally well in the current idiom of the street or in the archaic measures of *Beowulf,* in the sing-song manner of a traditional ballad or in the formal cadences of an elegy. He has been called "the most provocative as well as the most unpredictable poet of his generation." With Yeats and Eliot, he shares honors as the most significant British poet of the first half of the twentieth century.

Objectives

1 To understand elegy and figurative language
2 To understand the legacy of an artist
3 To write about paradox

Teaching Portfolio: Support Material

Teacher Backup, p. 000

Vocabulary Check, p. 00

Usage and Mechanics Worksheet, p. 00

Analyzing Literature Worksheet, p. 00

Critical Thinking and Reading Worksheet, p. 00

Language Worksheet, p. 00

Selection Test, p. 000

Art Transparency, p. 000

GUIDE FOR READING

In Memory of W. B. Yeats; Musée des Beaux Arts

The Writer's Techniques

Elegy and Figurative Language. An elegy is a poem of mourning for the dead. The great Greek and Latin elegies, forerunners of elegies in English, were written in distichs. A *distich* is a pair of rhyming lines considered as a unit. The third part of W. H. Auden's "In Memory of W. B. Yeats" is composed of distichs, or couplets, similar to those in a classical elegy. Elegies sum up, often in heroic terms, the lifetime accomplishments of an individual, or, as in Gray's "Elegy Written in a Country Churchyard," a group of people. Elegies frequently make use of figurative language; that is, language rich in figures of speech such as simile, metaphor, and personification. An elegy may also contain literary devices such as paradox and allusion.

Look For

As you read the poems by W. H. Auden, be alert to the use of figures of speech and other literary devices.

Writing

Think of a person, living or dead, whom you greatly admire. This person can be either someone you know (or knew) firsthand or someone famous. Write a few memorial lines for the person, using a figure of speech in each of the lines. Try to use at least one simile, one metaphor, and one personification.

Vocabulary

Knowing the following word will help you as you read "In Memory of W. B. Yeats."

sequestered (si kwes' tərd) *v.*:
Kept apart from others (l. 61)

Literary Focus You may want to point out to students that each section of this elegy has a different form. The first is in free verse, the second uses iambic pentameter, and the third—the most formal section—is cast in quatrains. The meter of the last section is trochaic tetrameter (a trochee foot is the reverse of an iamb).

Look For Consider reviewing **simile** and **metaphor** with less advanced students.

Writing Ask students why they might admire a person. Is it for what the person does? Is it for what they stand for? Is it for their personal qualities of wit, or gentleness, or honesty? Encourage a variety of responses. Then assign the writing.

Vocabulary Ask students to find three synonyms and three antonyms for the vocabulary word *sequestered.*

1 **Discussion** Explain how the death of the poet is kept from his poems.

2 **Discussion** What is the general reaction to this death?

In Memory of W. B. Yeats

W. H. Auden

1

He disappeared in the dead of winter:
The brooks were frozen, the airports almost deserted,
And snow disfigured the public statues;
The mercury sank in the mouth of the dying day.
O all the instruments agree
The day of his death was a dark cold day.

Far from his illness
The wolves ran on through the evergreen forests,
The peasant river was untempted by fashionable quays;[1]
By mourning tongues
1 The death of the poet was kept from his poems.

But for him it was his last afternoon as himself,
An afternoon of nurses and rumors;
The provinces of his body revolted,
The squares of his mind were empty,
Silence invaded the suburbs,
The current of his feeling failed: he became his admirers.

Now he is scattered among a hundred cities
And wholly given over to unfamiliar affections;
To find his happiness in another kind of wood
And be punished by another code of conscience.
The words of a dead man
Are modified in the guts of the living.

But in the importance and noise of tomorrow
When the brokers are roaring like beasts on the floor of the
2 Bourse,[2]
And the poor have the sufferings to which they are fairly
accustomed,

---

1. **quays** (kēz): Wharfs with facilities for loading or unloading ships.
2. **Bourse** (bo͞ors): The Paris Stock Exchange.

And each in the cell of himself is almost convinced of his
  freedom;
2 A few thousand will think of this day
As one thinks of a day when one did something slightly
  unusual.

O all the instruments agree
The day of his death was a dark cold day.

2

You were silly like us: your gift survived it all;
3 The parish of rich women, physical decay,
Yourself; mad Ireland hurt you into poetry.
Now Ireland has her madness and her weather still,
For poetry makes nothing happen: it survives
In the valley of its saying where executives
Would never want to tamper; it flows south
From ranches of isolation and the busy griefs,
Raw towns that we believe and die in; it survives,
A way of happening, a mouth.

4 **3**

Earth, receive an honored guest;
William Yeats is laid to rest:
5 Let the Irish vessel lie
Emptied of its poetry.

Time that is intolerant
Of the brave and innocent,
6 And indifferent in a week
To a beautiful physique,

Worships language and forgives
Everyone by whom it lives;
Pardons cowardice, conceit
Lays its honors at their feet.

Time with this strange excuse
Pardoned Kipling and his views,[3]

---

3. Kipling . . . views: English writer Rudyard Kipling (1865–1936) was a supporter of imperialism.

3 **Literary Focus** Note that the poet is now addressing Yeats directly. What is the effect of this shift?

4 **Literary Focus** Note that Part 3 focuses on the enduring qualities of Yeats's poetry. Why do you think this part of the poem is the most formal?

5 **Literary Focus** How do the shorter stanzas and the use of rhyming couplets—distichs—change the tone?

6 **Discussion** According to the speaker, time worships language and pardons the cowardice of good writers. Do you think either of these concepts is true?

7 Discussion How do these stanzas contrast? What is the role of poetry in the times the poet describes?

8 Discussion Explain the paradox. How can there be a "rapture of distress"?

And will pardon Paul Claudel,[4]
Pardons him for writing well.

In the nightmare of the dark
All the dogs of Europe bark,
And the living nations wait,
Each sequestered in its hate;

Intellectual disgrace
Stares from every human face,
And the seas of pity lie
Locked and frozen in each eye.

7 Follow, poet, follow right
To the bottom of the night,
With your unconstraining voice
Still persuade us to rejoice;

With the farming of a verse
Make a vineyard of the curse,
8 Sing of human unsuccess
In a rapture of distress;

In the deserts of the heart
Let the healing fountain start,
In the prison of his days
Teach the free man how to praise.

---

4. **pardon Paul Claudel** (klō del'): French poet, dramatist, and diplomat. Paul Claudel (1868–1955) had antidemocratic political views, which Yeats at times shared.

THINKING ABOUT THE SELECTION

Recalling

1. What two things were present on Yeats' last afternoon "as himself"?
2. How many people are likely to remember Yeats' death the next day?
3. What was it that "hurt" Yeats into writing poetry?
4. According to the third section of the poem, to whom is time (a) intolerant? (b) indifferent?
5. What does the speaker ask the poet to teach free men?

Interpreting

6. Twice in the first section, the speaker uses the words "all the instruments agree." What instruments might he mean (a) in a literal

Answers

ANSWERS TO THINKING ABOUT THE SELECTION

Recalling

1. Nurses and rumors were present.
2. The speaker says a few thousand may remember Yeats's death.
3. "Mad Ireland" hurt Yeats into writing poetry.
4. Time is intolerant of the brave and innocent and indifferent to a beautiful physique.
5. The speaker asks the poet to teach free men how to praise.

Interpreting

6. Suggested Responses:
   a. The literal instruments are thermometers and barometers. b. Metaphorically the instruments might be the minds and hearts of those who loved the poet's work.
7. Suggested Response: Yeats is in the minds of people in hundreds of cities.
8. Suggested Response: Auden is addressing Yeats in the second section and the Earth and a generic poet in the third section.
9. Suggested Response: a. The speaker says that Europe is full of hatred. b. He feels the poet should "persuade us to rejoice" and teach us how to praise.

sense? (b) in a metaphorical sense?

7. What do you think the poet means by stating in line 18 that Yeats is now "scattered among a hundred cities"?
8. Whom is the speaker addressing in (a) the second section? (b) the third section?
9. (a) How favorably or unfavorably does the speaker view the situation in Europe? (b) How does he think the poet should react to it? Find evidence to support your answer.

Applying

10. This poem is an elegy to William Butler Yeats. Yet, in a sense, it could be addressed to any poet, for Auden sets down the responsibilities and rewards he thinks belong to the poet. What are these responsibilities and rewards?

ANALYZING LITERATURE

Understanding Elegy

An **elegy** is a poem that pays tribute to a person (or, less commonly, more than one person) who has died. Throughout history elegies have been written to immortalize people who, at least in the eyes of the poet, have achieved greatness. Most elegies contain imaginative comparisons—figures of speech such as simile, metaphor, and personification. W. H. Auden uses all three of these kinds of figurative language in "In Memory of W. B. Yeats." Write the line or lines of the poem in which each of the following occurs.

1. Personification in which a day coming to an end is said to display a facial feature,
2. Personification of a body of water as being susceptible to temptation,
3. Metaphor that compares body and mind to geographic areas,
4. Simile in which certain professional people are compared to wild animals,
5. Simile that compares thinking about the death of a great man with thinking about doing something unusual,
6. Personification where something inanimate and abstract has the power to worship and pardon,
7. Metaphor that relates something bad to a place where grapes are grown.

CRITICAL THINKING AND READING

Understanding the Legacy of an Artist

"In Memory of W. B. Yeats" is a poet's tribute not to a lost friend but to a fellow poet. Auden never knew Yeats personally, but he knew of him by reading his poetry. Most poets, as you might suppose, read poetry as well as write it. They are aware of the classics and trends. Poetry —indeed, all literature—is part of an ever-expanding archive, one in which, as in the National Archives, "the past is prologue." Auden, in his elegy, is responding to the loss he believes the world should feel at the loss of a great artist. Yet he is also aware, as the poem makes clear, that while Yeats himself is gone, the poetry of Yeats lives on.

1. What does Auden mean in line 11, "The death of the poet was kept from his poems"?
2. In the third section of the poem, what evidence is there that Auden is mourning the passing of an artist more than the passing of Yeats, the man?

THINKING AND WRITING

Writing About a Paradox

In line 36 Auden observes that "poetry makes nothing happen." But in the next section of the poem he beseeches the poet (any poet) to use his or her gift to lead the human race out of the darkness of hatred. How, you may ask, is it possible for a poet to accomplish this monumental task if "poetry makes nothing happen"? In an essay explain how you might get around this apparent contradiction—this paradox—by drawing upon other insights from the poem. When you revise make sure your essay is well organized and that you have provided adequate support for your thesis.

Applying

10. Answers will differ. Students may indicate that the responsibilities of a poet are to sing about the difficulties and tragedies of life. The rewards are not stated but implied —a poet will live on in his work.

ANSWERS TO ANALYZING LITERATURE

Suggested responses:

1. Line 4
2. Line 9
3. Lines 14, 15
4. Line 25
5. Lines 28, 29
6. Lines 50, 52
7. Line 71

ANSWERS TO CRITICAL THINKING AND READING

1. Suggested Response: The poet is alive in his poems because they still exist.
2. Suggested Response: In line 66 Auden addresses a generic poet and says things that are valid for any poet.

THINKING AND WRITING

Publishing Student Writing Have students volunteer their solutions to the paradox presented. Write the solutions on the chalkboard. Discuss the similarities and differences among them, and find the strength of each, although some may be more workable or valid than others.

Motivation for Reading Ask the students to suppose that they are going to paint a picture to show how society in general reacts to the suffering of others. What scene or images would they choose? Why? Then tell them that Auden's poem deals with this subject.

Master Teacher Note Tell students the story of Daedulus and Icarus. Make sure they know that Bruegel's picture shows the final scene of this story.

Purpose-Setting Question What perspective on human suffering do the Old Masters share?

1 **Discussion** Who are the "Old Masters"?

2 **Discussion** What do the images suggest about suffering?

3 **Discussion** What details in "Bruegel's *Icarus*," as described in the poem, suggest an observation about human suffering?

Musée des Beaux Arts[1]

W. H. Auden

About suffering they were never wrong,
1 The Old Masters: how well they understood
Its human position; how it takes place
While someone else is eating or opening a window or just
walking dully along;
How, when the aged are reverently, passionately waiting
For the miraculous birth, there always must be
Children who did not specially want it to happen, skating
On a pond at the edge of the wood:
2 They never forgot
That even the dreadful martyrdom must run its course
Anyhow in a corner, some untidy spot
Where the dogs go on with their doggy life and the
torturer's horse
Scratches its innocent behind on a tree.

In Brueghel's *Icarus*,[2] for instance: how everything turns
away
Quite leisurely from the disaster; the ploughman may
Have heard the splash, the forsaken cry,
3 But for him it was not an important failure; the sun shone
As it had to on the white legs disappearing into the green
Water; and the expensive delicate ship that must have seen
Something amazing, a boy falling out of the sky,
Had somewhere to get to and sailed calmly on.

---

1. **Musée des Beaux Arts:** The Museum of Fine Arts in Brussels, Belgium.
2. **Brueghel's** (bro͞o′gəlz) ***Icarus:*** *The Fall of Icarus*, a painting by Flemish painter Pieter Brueghel (1522?–1599).

THE FALL OF ICARUS
P.I. Bruegel
Musées Royaux des Beaux-Arts de Belgique

Humanities Note

Fine art, *Landscape With the Fall of Icarus* by Pieter Bruegel. Pieter Bruegel the Elder (1530–1569) was a Flemish painter. He roamed the countryside, often in disguise, to make candid dráwings of peasants at work and play that he would later use for his paintings.

The painting *Landscape With the Fall of Icarus* was influenced by Ovid's tale of Icarus, in which a fisherman, a shepherd, and a peasant go about their daily work oblivious to the drama of the flight and fall of Icarus. Bruegel's painting is composed of little scenes of the events described in Ovid's story. The colors are jewel-like; the detail is exquisite.

You might use the following questions for discussion:

1. In his poem, Auden comments on the indifference of humans to each other's disasters. How does Bruegel show this indifference in this painting?
2. What is the poet's attitude toward this indifference? What is the artist's attitude toward this indifference?

THINKING ABOUT THE SELECTION

Recalling

1. (a) What do the Old Masters show "someone else" doing while suffering occurs? (b) According to the speaker, what do the Old Masters understand about martyrdom?
2. (a) How does the ploughman react to the disaster in the Brueghel painting, *Icarus*? (b) How does the ship respond?

Interpreting

3. What do you think Auden intends the activities in line 4 to represent?
4. What is your understanding of the "miraculous birth" the aged are awaiting?
5. Icarus is a figure in Greek mythology who flies with artificial wings. Coming too close to the sun, the wax of his wings melts, and he falls into the sea and drowns. (a) What does Brueghel mean to imply by calling his painting *Icarus* but showing only Icarus's disappearing legs in the corner of the picture? (b) How closely does Auden's poem adhere to the same theme?

Applying

6. The poem describes an age-old irony. (a) In your own words, what is this irony? (b) What are some examples of it that exist today?

Answers

ANSWERS TO THINKING ABOUT THE SELECTION

Recalling

1. a. Observers to suffering are doing commonplace things such as eating, walking, or opening a window. b. Martyrdom occurs, unremarked, in some "untidy spot."
2. The ploughman ignores Icarus's fall, and the ship sails on.

Interpreting

3. Suggested Response: The activities represent daily, ordinary, somewhat mindless tasks.
4. Suggested Response: The miraculous birth is life after death.
5. Suggested Responses: a. Bruegel implies that people are indifferent to suffering. b. Auden's poem adheres closely to that theme.

Applying

6. Answers will differ, but students may respond as follows: a. The irony is that even the most spectacular sufferings occur in a context of indifference. b. Students should cite examples from literature or experience.

LOUIS MACNEICE

1907–1963

Four members of the "Auden group" at Oxford went on to achieve an honored place in English literature: Auden himself, C. Day Lewis, Stephen Spender, and Louis MacNeice. Of these, MacNeice was generally regarded as the junior member, not because of age but rather because he lacked the artistic certainty and political commitments of the others. A lyric and reflective poet of distinction, he was always modest about the aims of poetry, doubting that poetry could truly change the world. MacNeice's reputation has risen steadily over the years, and today many consider him second only to Auden among the poets of his generation.

MacNeice, the son of a Protestant clergyman, was born in Belfast, Northern Ireland. Surrounded by books as a child, he began to write poetry at the age of seven. By the time he went to Merton College, Oxford, he was familiar with the works of T. S. Eliot and other modern poets. MacNeice's first collection of poems, *Blind Fireworks,* appeared in 1929, while he was still an undergraduate. *Poems,* the collection that established his reputation, came out six years later.

A teacher during the 1930's, MacNeice lectured in Classics at the University of Birmingham from 1930 to 1936 and in Greek at Bedford College for Women from 1936 to 1940. As a writer, he tried his hand at various genres, including drama, but his lasting achievements are in poetry. One of his notable books from the late 1930's, *Letters from Iceland* (1937), co-authored by W. H. Auden, is an unusual travel book in which the poetry outweighs the prose.

In 1941 MacNeice joined the British Broadcasting Company as a feature writer and producer. Among his radio credits are two powerful BBC plays, *Christopher Columbus* (1944) and *The Dark Tower* (1947). He wrote *The Poetry of W. B. Yeats* (1941), a critical summary of that author's work, and produced a number of excellent translations, including Aeschylus' *Agamemnon* and Goethe's *Faust.* MacNeice died in London in 1963 while he was working on his autobiography.

MacNeice's poetry, usually dealing with contemporary life, is restrained and precise, with overtones of melancholy. It is the poetry of a man who, as the poet Edwin Muir put it, "is never swept off his feet."

Objectives

1. To understand scansion
2. To write about the effects of rhyme and rhythm

Teaching Portfolio: Support Material

Teacher Backup, p. 000

Vocabulary Check, p. 00

Usage and Mechanics Worksheet, p. 00

Analyzing Literature Worksheet, p. 00

Critical Thinking and Reading Worksheet, p. 00

Language Worksheet, p. 00

Selection Test, p. 000

Art Transparency, p. 000

GUIDE FOR READING

The Sunlight on the Garden; Sunday Morning

The Writer's Techniques

Scansion. Scansion is the analysis of lines of poetry according to their patterns of rhythm. The key to scansion is meter. Meter is a recurring pattern of stressed and unstressed syllables in poetry. Meter is to poetry approximately what beat is to music. In scansion, stressed syllables are marked with a /; unstressed syllables are marked with a ∪. Each group of syllables makes up a foot. A foot in poetry consists of scansion, feet are marked off a |. In scansion, do not expect to find perfectly regular patterns repeated over and over. After you have identified a metrical foot, look for and expect to find irregularities or breaks from the pattern.

Look For

As you read "The Sunlight on the Garden" and "Sunday Morning," look for the rhythms of the poems. Notice how these rhythms at time force you to focus on key words.

Writing

Choose four lines from any poem that appears earlier in this book. First, mark all the syllables in the lines as either stressed or unstressed. To do this, say the lines aloud. Next, find the pattern of stress that predominates. There are four common patterns:

1. Unstressed/stressed (iambic)
2. Stressed/unstressed (trochaic)
3. Stressed/unstressed/unstressed (dactylic)
4. Unstressed/unstressed/stressed (anapaestic)

Finally, put in the vertical bars that show the end of one foot and the beginning of another. Notice that a vertical bar may divide a word rather than going between two words, as in the second line below from a poem by Robert Browning.

Literary Focus Have students determine the rhythms of their favorite songs. This exercise should give them a greater appreciation of rhythm in poetry.

Look For Your **less advanced** students may be helped to appreciate rhythm by focusing on nursery rhymes, songs associated with holiday times, or camp tunes which have repetitive rhythms that reinforce the message and add to tone as well.

Writing To reinforce the *sounds* of stress patterns, place single words on the board that exemplify a stress pattern, for example, *about*=iambic; *maybe*=trochaic; *finishing*=dactylic; *introduce*=anapestic. Have students volunteer more words and identify stress patterns until students are comfortable with the identifications.

Vocabulary You may want to have students construct their own examples of these various types of metrical feet.

Motivation for Reading Have students think about time passing quickly from year to year. What concerns them most? What do they like to recall from the past?

Purpose-Setting Question What is the tone of this poem?

Master Teacher Note Consider telling students that the fifth line of each stanza is shorter than the others. Have them determine how its meter differs. Also have them consider why the poet chose to insert a shorter line at this point.

1 **Reading Strategy** Offer a one-sentence summary of what this stanza says.

2 **Discussion** What rhyme scheme does MacNeice use?

3 **Discussion** What does the allusion contribute to the meaning of the poem?

4 **Discussion** How do the repetitions contribute to the meaning?

The Sunlight on the Garden

Louis MacNeice

The sunlight on the garden
Hardens and grows cold,
1 We cannot cage the minute
Within its nets of gold,
When all is told
We cannot beg for pardon.

Our freedom as free lances
Advances towards its end;
2 The earth compels, upon it
Sonnets and birds descend;
And soon, my friend,
We shall have no time for dances.

The sky was good for flying
Defying the church bells
And every evil iron
Siren and what it tells:
The earth compels,
3 We are dying, Egypt, dying[1]

And not expecting pardon,
Hardened in heart anew,
4 But glad to have sat under
Thunder and rain with you,
And grateful too
For sunlight on the garden.

1. **We . . . dying:** An allusion to a line spoken by Antony to Cleopatra after he has been mortally wounded in Shakespeare's *Antony and Cleopatra*: "I am dying, Egypt, dying."

OLD THATCHED SUMMER HOUSE
Lilian Stannard
Christopher Wood Gallery, London

Humanities Note

Fine art, *Old Thatched Summer House* by Lillian Stannard. Lillian Stannard (1884–1944) was a British watercolorist. Born into a family of painters, Lillian learned from her mother, Emily, and her father, Henry. Her brother and sister also painted. She specialized in the painting of landscapes, flowers, and gardens.

Old Thatched Summer House was painted at Blackheath. It is a charming rendering of an English garden in full flower. The bright blossoms, flooding sunlight, and thatched hut are painted with sensitivity and dedication to detail. This little-known artist skillfully evokes the true essence of a summer garden through the medium of watercolor.

You might use the following questions for discussion:

1. What do both the poem and this painting celebrate?
2. The purpose of this painting is to provide a pleasant subject to view. How does this purpose compare with that of the poem?

THINKING ABOUT THE SELECTION

Recalling

1. What does the speaker say we shall soon have no time for?
2. What two things does the speaker say he is happy to have experienced?

Interpreting

3. In line 6 and again in line 19 the speaker uses the word *pardon*. From what do you think he is implying there is no pardon?
4. There is an apparent reference to wartime in this poem. What is it?
5. What or whom do you think is dying in this poem—the speaker, a generation, a nation, or something or someone else? Explain your answer.

Applying

6. Death is a familiar theme in poetry. (a) What other poem have you read that conveys an attitude similar to the one expressed here? (b) How does that poem differ from MacNeice's?

ANALYZING LITERATURE

Understanding Scansion

Most poems contain regular rhythmic patterns of stressed and unstressed syllables. The identification of these patterns is called **scansion,** and the act of reading a poem to identify its patterns is called **scanning.**

1. On a sheet of paper, copy "The Sunlight on the Garden." Scan the poem, analyzing it for unstressed and stressed syllables and for feet. Your analysis will show both the recurring patterns and any deviations from them.
2. The poem has an unusual rhyme scheme. Look carefully at the rhyming words MacNeice uses. What makes his rhyme scheme different from that in most poems?

Answers

ANSWERS TO THINKING ABOUT THE SELECTION

Recalling

1. We shall soon have no time for dances.
2. The speaker is happy to have experienced thunder and rain "with you" and sunlight on the garden.

Interpreting

3. Suggested Response: There is no pardon from the passing of time.
4. Suggested Response: The reference occurs in lines 15–16.
5. Suggested Response: Humans in general are dying.

Applying

6. Answers will differ, but students may need to be reminded of poems that express similar attitude so that they can contrast them with MacNeice's poem.

ANSWERS TO ANALYZING LITERATURE

1. Suggested Response: The poem is largely iambic, with trochaic and anapestic feet as variations.
2. Suggested Response: The rhyme scheme is *abcbba,* an unusual pattern.

Motivation for Reading Have students think about what they like to do on a summer Sunday morning. What do their friends like to do? What sorts of activities are different on Sundays from those during the week?

Purpose-Setting Question What feelings does the poet have about Sunday?

Master Teacher Note You may want to have students determine the meter and rhyme scheme of this poem. Then have them consider how the regular form of the poem contributes to its meaning.

1 **Literary Focus** Point out the simile. Note the humor in the comparison.

2 **Discussion** What do the images in these lines suggest about Sunday mornings? Is the metaphor of a "great bazaar" appropriate? Why or why not?

3 **Discussion** Why are the church bells described as "skulls' mouths"? What does their music remind us of?

Sunday Morning

Louis MacNeice

Down the road someone is practicing scales,
1 The notes like little fishes vanish with a wink of tails,
Man's heart expands to tinker with his car
For this is Sunday morning, Fate's great bazaar;
Regard these means as ends, concentrate on this Now,
And you may grow to music or drive beyond Hindhead[1]
2 anyhow,
Take corners on two wheels until you go so fast
That you can clutch a fringe or two of the windy past,
That you can abstract this day and make it to the week of
time
A small eternity, a sonnet self-contained in rhyme.

But listen, up the road, something gulps, the church spire
3 Opens its eight bells out, skulls' mouths which will not tire
To tell how there is no music or movement which secures
Escape from the weekday time. Which deadens and
endures.

---

1. **Hindhead:** A district in the county of Surrey, England.

THINKING ABOUT THE SELECTION

Recalling

1. What are two Sunday-morning activities the speaker mentions?
2. What will "skulls' mouths" never tire of telling?

Interpreting

3. Why do you think the speaker refers to Sunday morning as "Fate's great bazaar"?
4. What does the speaker suggest is required to make the most of a Sunday?
5. The last four lines contrast rather sadly with the first ten. What is the point of the contrast?

Applying

6. "The Sunlight on the Garden" and "Sunday Morning" express a similar futile wish. In your own words, what is that wish?

THINKING AND WRITING

Writing About Rhyme and Rhythm

Modern poets differ in their use of rhyme and rhythm. In "Sunday Morning," MacNeice uses a basic *aabb* rhyme scheme. Scan the poem to determine its metric pattern. Then, in a brief essay, explain what effects the rhyme and rhythm of the poem have on your appreciation of it. Also, try to answer these broader questions: (a) Do you generally prefer rhyming poems to free verse? (b) What effect, if any, does rhyme have on meaning? (c) Do you think subject matter helps to determine the appropriate rhyme and rhythm for a poem?)

Before you start to write, make at least a sketchy outline of the main points you will cover. Your first draft may follow this outline closely or may deviate from it as necessary. When you revise the paper for your final draft, pay special attention to organization. See that your points appear in logical and persuasive order.

Answers

ANSWERS TO THINKING ABOUT THE SELECTION

Recalling

1. Two activities are practicing scales and tinkering with a car.
2. The skulls' mouths tell that there is no escape, whether in music or movement, from deadening weekday time.

Interpreting

3. Suggested Response: Sunday is a day where you can make choices, as at a bazaar, and you may choose to do something that changes your life.
4. Suggested Response: The speaker suggests one should concentrate on the present.
5. Suggested Response: The contrast shows there is no escape from the demands of time.

Applying

6. Suggested Response: Both poems express the wish to hold back time.

THINKING AND WRITING

Publishing Student Writing You might want to divide the class into small groups after they have finished the assignment, so they can discuss their conclusions.

More About the Author Ask students why they might suppose Stephen Spender became interested in political activism?

BIOGRAPHIES

Stephen Spender (1909–   )

No poet of the 1930's has provided posterity with a more detailed and honest picture of the era between the wars than has Stephen Spender. Much of his early poetry deals with the world of the Thirties, that "low dishonest decade" that saw the world lurch from depression to fascism to war. Yet Spender, never a pessimist in the manner of T. S. Eliot, celebrates technology at the same time he confronts the problems of industrial civilization.

The son of a political journalist, Spender was born in London and educated at University College, Oxford, where he met and fell under the spell of W. H. Auden. In 1928, while at Oxford, he hand-printed a limited edition of Auden's *Poems*. Spender contributed his own early poems to *Oxford Poetry*. He lived in Germany in the early 1930's and published his first important book, *Poems*, in 1933, the year Hitler became chancellor of the Third Reich.

Spender, a political activist, traveled to Spain to promote antifascist propaganda during the Spanish Civil War. From 1939 to 1941, he coedited the literary magazine, *Horizon*, and later coedited the political, cultural, and literary review, *Encounter*. In his autobiography, *World Within World* (1951), Spender is candid and perceptive about people, politics, and himself, as he explores and attempts to integrate his lyrical and idealistic vision with the realities of society.

Henry Reed (1914–   )

Although Henry Reed is well-known in England for his many radio plays, his reputation as a poet rests mainly on one slim volume, *A Map of Verona*, published in 1946. In fact, it rests principally on thirty lines in that collection—"Naming of Parts," which is a satirical section of a longer poem, "Lessons of War." Reed's few poems, always precise and assured, vary widely in subject matter, mood, and theme. So do his highly regarded radio plays, among which are an adaptation of *Moby-Dick*, the partly autobiographical *Return to Naples*, and a dramatic prose poem, *The Streets of Pompeii*.

Henry Reed was born in Birmingham, England, and educated at King Edward VI School and the University of Birmingham. After graduation he worked for several years on a biography of Thomas Hardy, then taught school for a year before being drafted into the army in 1941. He received a transfer to the Foreign Office, where he worked in Naval Intelligence. Most of Reed's career since the end of World War II has involved radio drama for the British Broadcasting Corporation (BBC), with some time out for translating and for teaching at the University of Washington in Seattle. His poetic output, though limited, is of high quality.

Objectives

1. To identify the speaker of a poem
2. To compare and contrast two poems

Teaching Portfolio: Support Material

Teacher Backup, p. 000

Vocabulary Check, p. 00

Usage and Mechanics Worksheet, p. 00

Analyzing Literature Worksheet, p. 00

Critical Thinking and Reading Worksheet, p. 00

Selection Test, p. 000

GUIDE FOR READING

What I Expected; Naming of Parts

The Writer's Techniques

Speaker. The speaker in a poem is the poem's narrator. Narration can occur either in the first person *(I, we)* or in the third person *(he, she, it, they).* Often a first-person speaker is a persona created by the poet. Consider, for instance, the first-person speakers who are already dead, as, for example, in Edgar Lee Masters's *Spoon River Anthology*. But even if the speaker is represented as being alive, he or she may not be the poet. In Robert Browning's "My Last Duchess," for example, no one would mistake the speaker (the cruel Duke of Ferrara) for the likable Browning. Sometimes a poet uses a first-person speaker to lend immediacy to the poem's content.

Satire. Satire is writing that uses wit and humor to attack human follies, stupidities, and abuses. It can be directed at a single person or at an entire society. Satire can be written in any genres—novels, short stories, poems, or plays. Always a mixture of humor and criticism, it is intended to persuade the reader, without the use of formal argument, to accept the author's viewpoint. Among the most famous satires in English are Jonathan Swift's *Gulliver's Travels* and George Orwell's *Animal Farm.*

Look For

As you read "What I Expected," look for any clues that suggest whether the first-person speaker and the poet are, or are not, identical. As you read "Naming of Parts," be alert to the evidence of Reed's satiric intent.

Writing

Choose an event in history that happened long before you were born. Possibilities include the signing of the Declaration of Independence, the defense of the Alamo, and the assassination of Abraham Lincoln. Put yourself in the place of a participant in the event. Jot down notes in the first person, just as if you had observed what happened. Include as many details as you can that, prior to your account, were unknown to the general public.

Vocabulary

Knowing the following words will help you as you read "What I Expected."

pulverous (pul′ və rəs) *adj.*: Crumbling (l. 21)

faceted (fas′ ə tid) *adj.*: Having many sides (l. 32)

Literary Focus Discuss with students why determining the speaker's identity is vital to understanding the message of a poem. For example, if the speaker in "What I Expected" were someone complaining about someone else's old age, the message would be quite different. As they read the poem, ask if they empathize with the speaker, pity him, or feel some other emotion.

Look For Your **less advanced** students may have trouble determining the speaker, often assuming the speaker is the poet. It may be helpful to preview the Analyzing Literature discussion on page 1109 to guide their reading.

Writing Have students think about television programs with a "You Are There" type of emphasis. What sorts of first-person accounts are usually presented? Have students think about the details that interested them or that were vital. What sights and sounds were important to convey in such accounts? Then have students do the writing assignment.

Vocabulary Have your **less advanced** students review these words before reading.

Motivation for Reading Discuss with students how people deal with expectations that are not realized? Are some disappointments greater than others? What kinds of expectations that do not come to fruition are the most difficult?

Purpose-Setting Question Who is the speaker in this poem?

1 **Discussion** What inferences about the speaker can be made from his expectations?

2 **Discussion** What surprises the speaker?

3 **Discussion** How are a poem and crystal similar? Why does the speaker assume they are "Exempt from dust"?

What I Expected

Stephen Spender

What I expected, was
Thunder, fighting,
Long struggles with men
And climbing.
1 After continual straining
I should grow strong;
Then the rocks would shake
And I rest long.

What I had not foreseen
Was the gradual day
Weakening the will
Leaking the brightness away,
2 The lack of good to touch,
The fading of body and soul
Smoke before wind,
Corrupt, unsubstantial.

The wearing of Time,
And the watching of cripples pass
With limbs shaped like questions
In their odd twist,
The pulverous grief
Melting the bones with pity,
The sick falling from earth—
These, I could not foresee.

Expecting always
Some brightness to hold in trust
Some final innocence
Exempt from dust,
That, hanging solid,
Would dangle through all
Like the created poem,
3 Or the faceted crystal.

THINKING ABOUT THE SELECTION

Recalling

1. What are four things the speaker says he expected?
2. What are six things he had not foreseen?
3. Besides "Some brightness to hold in trust," what was the speaker always expecting?

Interpreting

4. (a) What do you think is the setting of this poem? (b) What lines in the poem support your answer?
5. In line 12 and again in line 26 the speaker uses the word *brightness*. What do you think this brightness represents?
6. In line 22 the speaker mentions the melting of bones. To whose bones is he referring?

Applying

7. The speaker seems to have been deeply disappointed when reality did not match his expectations. In the eighteenth century, the poet Alexander Pope wrote, "Blessed is he who expects nothing, for he shall never be disappointed." How do you think the speaker would react to this statement? Support your answer.

ANALYZING LITERATURE

Determining the Speaker

The speaker in a poem is the individual who does the telling, the narrator. Speakers fall into two main categories, (1) first person *(I, we),* in which the speaker is in essence a character in the poem; (2) third-person *(he, she, it, they),* in which the speaker is an outsider. Sometimes a first-person speaker is the poet, but more often he or she is not. Rather, the speaker is assuming a particular role to create a desired effect. In determining whether a first-person speaker is probably the poet, it may help you to know something of the poet's life. For instance, you know that Rupert Brooke and the soldier-speaker in "The Soldier" might be one and the same. On the other hand, if you know that Stephen Spender was not a front-line soldier in World War II, you would know he could not have written a first-person battlefield scene except through an assumed identity.

1. Identify the kind of speaker in Stephen Spender's "What I Expected."
2. In view of the subject matter of the poem, why is this kind of speaker a logical one?
3. The speaker and the poet are not one and the same in "What I Expected." How do you know?

THINKING AND WRITING

Comparing and Contrasting Two Poems

Reread Louis MacNeice's "The Sunlight on the Garden," noting in particular the references to flying and to sirens in the third stanza. Some critics have called this a war poem, pointing to "flying" as a reference to fighter planes and to the "evil iron siren" as an air-raid siren. Assuming that this interpretation is correct, write an essay in which you compare and contrast MacNeice's "The Sunlight on the Garden" with Spender's "What I Expected." Concentrate not only on the subject matter of the two poems, but also on their structure—speakers, metric patterns, line lengths, and rhyme schemes. Begin by making notes on both poems. When you write your first draft, quote lines from the poems where appropriate. In revising, be sure you have made your comparisons and contrast clear.

Answers

ANSWERS TO THINKING ABOUT THE SELECTION

Recalling

1. The author lists his expectations in lines 2–8.
2. What he had not foreseen is listed in lines 10–24.
3. The speaker was also always expecting "Some final innocence."

Interpreting

4. Suggested Reponse: There is no specific locale for the poem, but it is set during the speaker's declining years.
5. Suggested Response: The brightness represents ideals or goals to be reached.
6. Suggested Resonse: The speaker refers to his own bones.

Applying

7. Answers will differ. Students may respond that the speaker would not be able to follow Pope's advice.

ANSWERS TO ANALYZING LITERATURE

1. Suggested Response: The speaker is an elderly person, probably a man.
2. Suggested Response: The images of struggles with men and climbing suggest this type of speaker.
3. Suggested Response: The poet *has* created a poem, though the speaker could not.

THINKING AND WRITING

For help with this assignment, students can consult Lesson 16, "Writing a Comparative Evaluation," in the Handbook of Writing About Literature.

Publishing Student Writing Select five or six of the student essays that are representative, and offer them to the school newspaper as poetry reviews.

More About the Author After students have read the biographical sketch, ask them what they suppose would be the topic of Henry Reed's radio drama. What do they find especially fascinating about his varied life?

Motivation for Reading Have students recall a really monotonous, somewhat inane training session of some sort that they went through at some time. Have students share their recollections orally. Then tell them that Henry Reed makes use of such an experience.

Purpose-Setting Question What are the two contrasting scenes in this poem?

1 **Discussion** What are the contrasting settings and situations suggested here?

2 **Literary Focus** How does the repetition of "today" add to the satirical tone?

3 **Discussion** What is the basic contrast represented by the weapons instructor and the description of spring?

4 **Literary Focus** What double meaning is suggested by "Easing the spring"?

5 **Discussion** Note the awkwardness of the repeated clause, "we have not got." What does it emphasize?

Naming of Parts

Henry Reed

Today we have naming of parts. Yesterday,
We had daily cleaning. And tomorrow morning,
We shall have what to do after firing. But today,
1, 2 Today we have naming of parts. Japonica[1]
Glistens like coral in all of the neighboring gardens,
    And today we have naming of parts.

This is the lower sling swivel. And this
Is the upper sling swivel, whose use you will see,
3 When you are given your slings. And this is the piling
  swivel,
Which is your case you have not got. The branches
Hold in the gardens their silent, eloquent gestures,
    Which in our case we have not got.

This is the safety-catch, which is always released
With an easy flick of the thumb. And please do not let me
See anyone using his finger. You can do it quite easy
If you have any strength in your thumb. The blossoms
Are fragile and motionless, never letting anyone see
    Any of them using their finger.

And this you can see is the bolt. The purpose of this
Is to open the breech, as you see. We can slide it
4 Rapidly backwards and forwards: we call this
Easing the spring. And rapidly backwards and forwards
The early bees are assaulting and fumbling the flowers:
    They call it easing the Spring.

They call it easing the Spring: it is perfectly easy
If you have any strength in your thumb: like the bolt,
And the breech, and the cocking-piece, and the point of
  balance,
5 Which in our case we have not got; and the almond-blossom
Silent in all of the gardens and the bees going backwards
  and forwards,
    For today we have naming of parts.

---

1. **japonica** (jə pän′ i kə): A spiny plant with pink or red flowers.

THINKING ABOUT THE SELECTION

Recalling

1. (a) What does the speaker say the members of his group ("we") had yesterday? (b) What will they have tomorrow?
2. What part of the rifle does the speaker not have?
3. What is the purpose of the bolt?
4. What is silent in the gardens?

Interpreting

5. (a) Who are the members of the group identified as "we" in the poem? (b) Why are they having "naming of parts"?
6. (a) In the fourth stanza, what are the two meanings of "easing the Spring"? (b) In the fifth stanza, what are two possible meanings of "the point of balance"?

Applying

7. Suppose you were the instructor giving the "naming of parts" lesson, and you became aware of what is on the mind of the speaker (or second voice). (a) How would you react? (b) How would you rate the chances of the recruit becoming a good soldier?

ANALYZING LITERATURE

Using Satire

Satire is writing that shows the folly or evil of something through the use of wit and humor. In "Naming of Parts," the poet is not directly attacking war or the military, despite the sharp contrast he draws between instruction in rifle parts and the wonders of spring.

1. What specifically is Reed satirizing in the poem?
2. How does he use the repetition of words and phrases to make his point? Give at least two examples.

CRITICAL THINKING AND READING

Comparing and Contrasting Speakers

There may be two speakers in this poem, one the instructor-speaker, the other the trainee-speaker. Or there may be only one speaker who first parrots the dull, mechanical words of the instructor, then gives his own personal thoughts on the attractions of nature in springtime. Whichever way you interpret Reed's method (two different speakers or two opposing voices within the same speaker), the satiric message is the same.

1. (a) Which lines, or parts of lines, in each stanza are the instructor's words or mechanical repetitions of them? (b) Which express the personal feelings of the trainee?
2. Which stanza deviates from this pattern?
3. Describe the similarities and differences between the language of the two voices (or speakers).

THINKING AND WRITING

Writing About Satire

A number of newspaper and magazine columnists write satire. Erma Bombeck's satiric columns on domestic life and Art Buchwald's on politics, among others, have been reprinted in many books. Find a modern satirical column, either original or reprinted, and write an essay analyzing it. Before you start to write, read the column carefully, making a list of devices the writer uses—exaggeration, understatement, analogy, figurative language, and so on. Jot down an example of each device. When you begin to write, first identify the author, topic, and source of the column you are analyzing. Then write the first draft of your essay. Stick to the point; avoid clever but irrelevant comments. When you revise, pay special attention to unity. Every sentence in your essay should relate to the main point you want to make.

Answers

ANSWERS TO THINKING ABOUT THE SELECTION

Recalling

1. The speaker says they had "daily cleaning" and tomorrow they will have "what to do after firing."
2. The piling swivel is not available.
3. The purpose of the bolt is to open the breech.
4. The almond blossom is silent in the garden.

Interpreting

5. Suggested Response: The "we" is a group of young recruits, who are being trained in riflery.
6. Suggested Response: Two meanings of "Easing the spring" are the literal, careful movement of the spring of the rifle and the slow beginning of the season of spring.

Applying

7. Answers will differ. a. Responses will probably note that the instructor would be annoyed or angered at the recruit. b.The chances of the recruit becoming a good soldier are slim.

ANSWERS TO ANALYZING LITERATURE

1. Suggested Response: Reed is satirizing the mechanistic and unproductive instruction.
2. Suggested Response: He uses repetition to point up ironic similarities between the instruction and the emerging spring. See lines 24 and 28.

ANSWERS TO CRITICAL THINKING

1. The instructor's words are lines 7–10, 13–16, 19–22, 25–28; lines of the trainee are 4–6, 10–12, 16–18, 22–24.
2. The final stanza deviates.
3. Suggested Response: The young recruit uses the instructor's words in an ironic context.

THINKING AND WRITING

Publishing Student Writing Have students share their analyses in small groups. They can test their own observations with each other and expand their thinking as well.

More About the Author Dylan Thomas's zest for living shows through in these varied poems. Ask students what they notice about the range of topics and how are they consistent with the person who emerges in the biographical sketch?

DYLAN THOMAS

1914–1953

When Dylan Thomas burst upon the literary scene in 1933, he was barely twenty years old. His poems, romantic, effusive, and melodic, spoke to readers then, as now, in a voice that could be mistaken for no one else's. Despite some critical bewilderment at first, Thomas gained remarkable popularity in his lifetime, probably greater than that of any poet since Byron. The rich, glowing magic of his language propels the reader onward in spite of its often complex imagery, visionary landscapes, and puzzling ambiguities. Stephen Spender called Thomas "a linguistic genius." The critic Louis Untermeyer says that his lines "leap and shout and all but leave the printed page. . . ."

Dylan Thomas was born in Swansea, an industrial city on the southern coast of Wales. His father was a school teacher, and young Dylan, surrounded by his father's books, seems to have spent his childhood in training to be a poet. He attended Swansea Grammar School until 1931, after which he worked intermittently as a newspaper reporter, radio broadcaster, and film scriptwriter. In 1941 he published a collection of stories about his childhood and youth, *Portrait of the Artist as a Young Dog*. He recorded a number of his poems, as well as his "play for voices," *Under Milk Wood,* which premiered in May 1953 at the Fogg Theater of Harvard University, with Thomas reading all the parts.

Thomas did his best work while living in Wales, far from the temptations of London and New York. At work, he was a meticulous craftsman, shy when sober, exercising strict formal control over what on paper seems so spontaneous. But in London, and on his four speaking tours to the United States, he was a different man, flamboyant, childish, hard-drinking, dissolute, an "outlaw defiant." His marriage to the Irish beauty Caitlin Macnamara was stormy but enduring. She was at his side when he died of the effects of alcoholism at St. Vincent's Hospital in New York City.

Poetry, to Thomas, was "the rhythmic, inevitably narrative, movement from an overclothed blindness to a naked vision." That vision is almost always free of the political themes and overtones found in the works of such contemporaries as Auden and Spender. On Thomas's place in literary history, the verdict is mixed. The poet Conrad Aiken sums him up as a "language-lover and language-juggler." The critic David Daiches says that "he was growing in poetic stature to the last" but, more important, "he wrote some poems that the world will not willingly let die."

Objectives

1. To recognize parallelism
2. To differentiate between connotation and denotation
3. To discover etymologies of Middle English words
4. To compose a poem about childhood

Teaching Portfolio: Support Material

Teacher Backup, p. 000

Vocabulary Check, p. 00

Usage and Mechanics Worksheet, p. 00

Analyzing Literature Worksheet, p. 00

Critical Thinking and Reading Worksheet, p. 00

Language Worksheet, p. 00

Selection Test, p. 000

Art Transparency, p. 000

The Force That Through the Green Fuse Drives the Flower; Fern Hill; Do Not Go Gentle into That Good Night

The Writer's Techniques

Parallelism. Parallelism is the matching or contrasting of two or more ideas through the use of similar phrasing. Sometimes parallelism can produce almost a list or catalog, as in *Ecclesiastes* 3:4: "A time to weep, and a time to laugh; a time to mourn, and a time to dance." Another well-known example of this kind of parallelism, also featuring contrasts, is the beginning of Charles Dickens's *A Tale of Two Cities:* "It was the best of times; it was the worst of times. . . ." In poetry, parallelism can appear within a single line, as is Coleridge's "Without a breeze, without a tide." Or it can be within a stanza, as in Shelley's "The seed ye sow, another reaps/The wealth ye find, another keeps." Or it can be from stanza to stanza, as in Byron's "And there lay the steed with his nostril all wide" [stanza four]; "And there lay the rider distorted and pale" [stanza five].

Villanelle. A villanelle is a nineteen-line poem with specific and rather complicated requirements. The first fifteen lines are arranged in three-line stanzas. The first and third lines of the opening stanza are repeated alternately as the closing line of each of the remaining three-line stanzas. They then appear together as a concluding couplet. Only two rhymes are permitted throughout the poem, the rhyme scheme being this: *aba aba aba aba aba abaa*. The villanelle originated in fifteenth-century France, where its aim was to lend a surface simplicity to pastoral poems. Following its revival in the nineteenth century, the villanelle has been used for a broad range of subjects.

Look For

As you read "The Force That Through the Green Fuse Drives the Flower," notice the poet's use of parallelism. Think about the effects he achieves with it.

Writing

Describe a chain of events in your life, beginning each link of the chain with the words, "If it were not for . . ." You might write, for example, "If it were not for my family moving to this city two years ago, I would not have attended this school. If it were not for my attending this school, I would not have met my best friend. If it were not for having met my best friend . . ." and so on. See how far you can take your chain by the end of one page.

Literary Focus Students may find that the form of the villanelle will become clearer when they work through an actual poem. It may be helpful to have students consider why poets are interested in such intricate forms. What, for instance, does repetition and regularity contribute to a poem?

Look For You might want to have students diagram some of the parallel constructions in the poem, after they read it several times.

Writing You might want to divide the class into small groups so they can discuss key events in their lives before they begin to write.

Motivation for Reading Ask students, if they were to think of an image for the driving force of life, what would it be? What contrasting image would they create for death?

Purpose-Setting Question The poet contemplates his mortality. Determine how he feels about it. Look for words or phrases that tell you this feeling.

1 **Literary Focus** What does the color green symbolize in the poem?

2 **Discussion** Explain the paradox of the force as "destroyer."

3 **Discussion** Why do you think the speaker cannot communicate his insight?

4 **Discussion** How are life and death related in this poem?

The Force That Through the Green Fuse Drives the Flower

Dylan Thomas

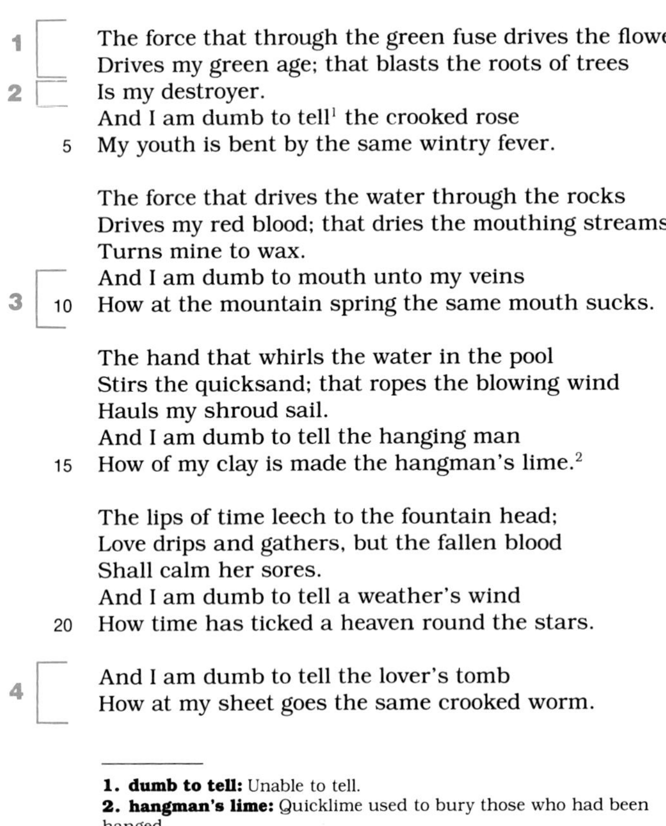

1 The force that through the green fuse drives the flower
Drives my green age; that blasts the roots of trees
2 Is my destroyer.
And I am dumb to tell[1] the crooked rose
My youth is bent by the same wintry fever.

The force that drives the water through the rocks
Drives my red blood; that dries the mouthing streams
Turns mine to wax.
And I am dumb to mouth unto my veins
3 How at the mountain spring the same mouth sucks.

The hand that whirls the water in the pool
Stirs the quicksand; that ropes the blowing wind
Hauls my shroud sail.
And I am dumb to tell the hanging man
How of my clay is made the hangman's lime.[2]

The lips of time leech to the fountain head;
Love drips and gathers, but the fallen blood
Shall calm her sores.
And I am dumb to tell a weather's wind
How time has ticked a heaven round the stars.

4 And I am dumb to tell the lover's tomb
How at my sheet goes the same crooked worm.

---

1. **dumb to tell:** Unable to tell.
2. **hangman's lime:** Quicklime used to bury those who had been hanged.

THINKING ABOUT THE SELECTION

Recalling

1. (a) What does the speaker say he is unable to tell the hangman? (b) What is he unable to tell the lover's tomb?

Interpreting

2. What do you think the speaker means by the phrase (a) "green fuse"? (b) "green age"?
3. (a) What force do you think the speaker has in mind in the first two stanzas? (b) What word does he use in the third stanza to refer to this force?
4. The force in the poem brings about two very different outcomes. In general terms what are they?

Applying

5. To what extent would you describe this poem as one about faith? Explain.

ANALYZING LITERATURE

Using Parallelism

Parallelism, which is a form of repetition, matches or contrasts ideas through the use of similar phrasing or grammatic structures. In "The Force That Through the Green Fuse Drives the Flower," Dylan Thomas uses a complex, interlocking parallelism within stanzas:

The force that drives the green fuse
drives the flower
Drives my green age
that blasts the roots of trees

He also uses parallelism from stanza to stanza.

1. In what way are the second lines of the first three stanzas parallel?
2. In what way are the fourth lines of the first four stanzas parallel?
3. What parallel element exists in the last lines of the last four stanzas?

Answers

ANSWERS TO THINKING ABOUT THE SELECTION

Recalling

1. a. He cannot tell the hanging man that he, the poet, is made of "the hangman's lime." b. The same crooked worm goes at his sheet.

Interpreting

2. Suggested Response: a. The phrase "green fuse" may refer to the stem of a plant. b. The phrase "green age" means a youthful, energetic age.
3. Suggested Response: In these stanzas the speaker means vigorous life forces. b. He uses the word "hand" to refer to this force.
4. Suggested Response: The two outcomes are life and death.

Applying

5. Answers will differ.

ANSWERS TO ANALYZING LITERATURE

1. Suggested Response: Each second line of those stanzas begins with a strong verb-object construction: "Drives my green age"; "Drives my red blood"; and "Stirs the quicksand."
2. The fourth lines of these stanzas all repeat the phrase, "And I am dumb to tell [mouth, in one case] . . . "
3. Suggested Response: Each of these statements begins with the word "How" and explains an interconnection between the poet—except in line 20—and nature or other humans.

Motivation for Reading Ask students: What are some of your best recollections of your childhood? If you could choose one or two adjectives to describe that whole time, what would those adjectives be? Tell them that Thomas writes about his childhood in this poem.

Master Teacher Note You might want to point out to students that the words *green* and *golden* appear often in this poem. Have students consider the connotations of these words. How do these connotations contribute to the theme of the poem.

1 **Discussion** What impression of the speaker's childhood do you get from these lines? Which words and phrases contribute to this impression?

2 **Discussion** What is the meaning of this statement?

3 **Discussion** What is the effect of the repeated use of the word *And*?

4 **Discussion** Where else in the poem does Thomas use personification? How do these personifications contribute to the poem's mood or meaning?

Fern Hill

Dylan Thomas

Now as I was young and easy under the apple boughs
About the lilting house and happy as the grass was green,
The night above the dingle starry,
Time let me hail and climb
Golden in the heydays of his eyes,
1 And honored among wagons I was prince of the apple towns
And once below a time I lordly had the trees and leaves
Trail with daisies and barley
Down the rivers of the windfall light.

And as I was green and carefree, famous among the barns
About the happy yard and singing as the farm was home,
2 In the sun that is young once only,
Time let me play and be
Golden in the mercy of his means,
And green and golden I was huntsman and herdsman, the calves
Sang to my horn, the foxes on the hills barked clear and cold,
And the sabbath rang slowly
In the pebbles of the holy streams.

All the sun long it was running, it was lovely, the hay
Fields high as the house, the tunes from the chimneys, it was air
And playing, lovely and watery
3 And fire green as grass.
And nightly under the simple stars
As I rode to sleep the owls were bearing the farm away,
All the moon long I heard, blessed among stables, the nightjars[1]
Flying with the ricks,[2] and the horses
Flashing into the dark.

And then to awake, and the farm, like a wanderer white
4 With the dew, come back, the cock on his shoulder; it was all

1. nightjars *n.*: Common nocturnal birds, named for the whirring sound which the male makes.
2. ricks *n.*: Haystacks.

THE MAGIC APPLE TREE, c. 1830
Samuel Palmer
Fitzwilliam Museum, Cambridge

Humanities Note

Fine art, *The Magic Apple Tree* by Samuel Palmer. The British painter Samuel Palmer (1805–1881) was influenced by the art and literature of the mystic poet and artist William Blake. Classified by history as a Romantic painter, Palmer took Romanticism one step further toward mysticism. As a member of a group called "the Ancients," who turned to artists of the past for inspiration for their art, Palmer settled in the village of Shoreham, Kent. Here he produced his most memorable works, landscapes full of magic, dreams, and vision.

Samuel Palmer painted *The Magic Apple Tree* while at Shoreham. This is a pastoral in which everything—the hillside, the animals, and the trees—seems to vibrate with a secret life. The sheep seem to be mesmerized by the music played by the boy. The apple tree, bowed with ripe fruit, seems to be leaning toward the pipe-playing boy. Palmer's interpretation of this scene is atmospheric and timeless. It is a worshipful and intense homage to the beauty and goodness of nature.

You might use the following questions for discussion:

1. How does this painting convey a sense of timelessness?
2. How does this timeless quality enhance the painting's suitability as an illustration of Dylan Thomas's childhood reminiscence?
3. What visual elements of this painting match things mentioned in the poem?

5 **Discussion** To which legend or story is this an allusion? How does this allusion add to the poem's meaning?

6 **Discussion** How is the passage of time suggested?

7 **Discussion** Explain the paradox in the phrase "green and dying." How does this paradox relate to the theme of the poem?

5 Shining, it was Adam and maiden,
The sky gathered again
And the sun grew round that very day.
So it must have been after the birth of the simple light
In the first, spinning place, the spellbound horses walking warm
Out of the whinnying green stable
On to the fields of praise.

And honored among foxes and pheasants by the gay house
Under the new made clouds and happy as the heart was long,
In the sun born over and over,
I ran my heedless ways,
My wishes raced through the house-high hay
And nothing I cared, at my sky blue trades, that time allows
In all his tuneful turning so few and such morning songs
Before the children green and golden
Follow him out of grace,

6 Nothing I cared, in the lamb white days, that time would take me
Up to the swallow thronged loft by the shadow of my hand,
In the moon that is always rising,
Nor that riding to sleep
I should hear him fly with the high fields
And wake to the farm forever fled from the childless land.
Oh as I was young and easy in the mercy of his means,
7 Time held me green and dying
Though I sang in my chains like the sea.

THINKING ABOUT THE SELECTION

Recalling

1. What two colors does the speaker use repeatedly to describe himself as a youth?
2. What descriptive words about the hayfields suggest that the speaker was a youngster when observing them?
3. What does the speaker say happened each night as he "rode to sleep"?
4. In the last stanza, where does the speaker suggest that time has taken him?

Interpreting

5. (a) How would you describe the speaker's feelings about his childhood? (b) What are some of the words and phrases that convey this feeling?
6. What do you think is meant in lines 33–34 by "the birth of the simple light/In the first, spinning place"?
7. The mood in the last stanza changes from that in the preceding stanzas. (a) What is the change? (b) What are two lines or phrases earlier in the poem that foreshadow this change?
8. Line 53, "Time held me green and dying," expresses the basic idea of the poem. In your own words, what does the line mean?

Applying

9. Passing from the innocence of childhood to the reality and responsibility of adulthood is the subject of many rituals, proverbs, and literary works. What are a few of these?

CRITICAL READING AND THINKING

Interpreting Connotative Meaning

The **connotation** of a word is the meaning the word has beyond its dictionary definition. For example, *lilting,* in line 2, means "metrical, rhythmic," but, beyond that meaning—or *denotation* —the word has favorable connotations of melodic singing and cheerfulness. By contrast, the word *eurhythmic* has a denotation similar to that of *lilting,* but its connotations, if not actually unfavorable, are rather stuffy and academic. Poets take great care with the connotations of the words they use. (Dylan Thomas is said to have been unhappy with the word *heedless* in line 40, but could not find a word he considered more appropriate for his meaning.)

Find the following words and phrases in "Fern Hill." Explain what connotations you believe the poet intends:
(1) apple towns (l. 6); (2) sun (l. 18); (3) moon (l. 25); (4) sky blue trades (l. 42); (5) lamb white (l. 46); (6) swallow thronged loft (l. 47); (7) in my chains (l. 54); (8) like the sea (l. 54).

UNDERSTANDING LANGUAGE

Using Words from Middle English

Middle English, the English language as it existed from about 1150 to 1500, included many words that are in widespread use today. It also included some that are less familiar—for example, *dingle* (l. 3) and *ricks* (l. 26). "Fern Hill" contains a high percentage of words from Middle English.

1. Using a good dictionary, check the etymologies of *young, easy, green, sabbath, sun, house.*
2. Explain why many of the etymologies show ME (Middle English) being directly preceded by OF (Old French) rather than by OE (Old English) or something else.

THINKING AND WRITING

Writing a Poem About Childhood

The farm in "Fern Hill" belonged to Ann Jones, Dylan Thomas's aunt. As a child, Thomas spent many vacations and holidays there. As an adult, he remembered it as a happy world, an innocent Eden, forever lost. Write a poem about the place where you spent some or all of your childhood. You may have pleasant recollections, like Thomas, or ones that are less pleasant. Write in whatever poetic form you wish. Include as many images as you can to help a reader visualize both the setting and your experiences. Remember that a poem requires prewriting and revision, just as other forms of composition do.

Answers

ANSWERS TO THINKING ABOUT THE SELECTION

Recalling

1. The speaker was green and golden.
2. The hayfields were "high as a house," indicating he was small.
3. He says, figuratively, that owls carried the house away.
4. The speaker suggests that time has taken him to adulthood.

Interpreting

5. Suggested Response: a. The speaker has joyful memories of childhood. b. Numerous words and phrases indicate that joy. Some are "young and easy," "lilting house," "green and carefree," "happy yard," "singing," "playing," "it was all and Shining," "nothing I cared."
6. Suggested Response: That description refers to the creation of the world.
7. a. The change is that the poet begins to express regret for the passing of time. b. Lines 4-5 and 12-14 foreshadow that change.
8. Suggested Response: Even as I was young and growing, I was dying—though I did not know it.

Applying

9. Answers will differ. A confirmation and a Bar Mitzvah are two applicable religious rituals.

ANSWERS TO CRITICAL THINKING AND READING

1. Suggested Response: Small country towns, or places the poet imagined among the apple boughs.
2. Suggested Response: This word seems to mean all the days of his youth.
3. Suggested Response: This word means all the nights of his youth.
4. Suggested Response: This phrase means the innocent, carefree activities of youth.
5. Suggested Response: Innocent days of childhood are suggested.
6. Suggested Response: This phrase may connote aproaching adulthood or an adult's perspective.
7. Suggested Response: This phrase implies that we are all enchained in our dying bodies.
8. Suggested Response: The sea seems wild and free and powerful, yet it is bounded by the land.

ANSWERS TO UNDERSTANDING LANGUAGE

1. young—Middle English; Old English
   easy—Middle English; Old French
   green—Middle English; Old English
   sabbath—Middle English; Old French and Old English
   sun—Middle English; Old English
   house—Middle English; Old English
2. Suggested Response: Many words came into English from French.

THINKING AND WRITING

For help with this assignment, students can consult Lesson 18, "Writing a Poem," in the Handbook of Writing About Literature.

Publishing Student Writing Arrange for students to share their poems in small groups. Encourage them to submit their work to the school literary magazine.

Motivation for Reading Have students think of an older person who is close to them or about whom they care a great deal. If they were to give that person advice on how to face approaching death, what might it be? Tell them that Thomas wrote this poem for his father.

Purpose-Setting Question What is the speaker's advice about facing death?

1 **Discussion** Explain how the metaphors of day and night clarify the meaning of the poem's first line.

2 **Discussion** Each of the middle stanzas characterizes a different kind of person who resists death. Explain how each is categorized and why each type of person struggles.

3 **Discussion** What does the speaker want when he entreats his father to "Curse, bless me now"?

4 **Clarification** Review with students the concept of metonymy—a figure of speech in which a commonly associated feature is used to represent something. Lead them to see that "night" and "light" are metonymic for death and life.

Do Not Go Gentle into That Good Night

Dylan Thomas

Do not go gentle into that good night,
1 Old age should burn and rave at close of day;
Rage, rage against the dying of the light.

Though wise men at their end know dark is right,
Because their words had forked no lightning they
Do not go gentle into that good night.

Good men, the last wave by, crying how bright
Their frail deeds might have danced in a green bay,
Rage, rage against the dying of the light.

2 Wild men who caught and sang the sun in flight,
And learn, too late, they grieved it on its way,
Do not go gentle into that good night.

Grave men, near death, who see with blinding sight
Blind eyes could blaze like meteors and be gay,
Rage, rage against the dying of the light.

And you, my father, there on the sad height,
3 Curse, bless, me now with your fierce tears, I pray.
4 Do not go gentle into that good night.
Rage, rage against the dying of the light.

THINKING ABOUT THE SELECTION

Recalling

1. Starting with the second stanza of this villanelle, what four kinds of men does the speaker describe as they go "into that good night"?

Interpreting

2. (a) In this poem, what does *night* seem to represent? (b) What does *light* represent?
3. Considering the speaker's advice to "rage" against the "dying of the light," why do you think he regards night as "good"?
4. What double meaning does the word *grave* have in line 13?
5. How would you paraphrase the speaker's advice in the final couplet?

Applying

6. Do you think "Do Not Go Gentle into That Good Night" might have been a better poem if Thomas had chosen to work with a less restrictive poetic form than the villanelle? Explain your reasoning.

Answers

ANSWERS TO THINKING ABOUT THE SELECTION

Recalling

1. The speaker describes men who are wise, good, wild, and grave.

Interpreting

2. *Night* represents death; *light* is life.
3. Suggested Response: It might be "good" because it means an end to suffering.
4. Suggested Response: "Grave men" are serious men. Here it could mean approaching the grave.
5. Suggested Response: Do not give up life easily.

Applying

6. Answers will differ. Most students will realize that the repetitions enforced by the villanelle form add to the poem's power.

Drama

SET DESIGN OF COVENT GARDEN FOR PYGMALION
Donald Oenslager
Harvard Theater Collection

More About the Author Music was an integral part of Shaw's household as he was growing up. He began his career as a music critic. Discuss what you think Shaw's reactions might have been to his "didactic drama about phonetics," *Pygmalion,* being turned into a highly successful musical, *My Fair Lady*.

GEORGE BERNARD SHAW

1856–1950

During his ninety-four years, George Bernard Shaw was a novelist, a critic on many subjects, a champion of all sorts of reform, and, finally, a playwright. Original, witty, and opinionated, he often managed to offend people when he was not busy charming them.

Born in Ireland to a family with musical talent but little money, Shaw saw to his own education. At the age of twenty he arrived in London, where he remained for the rest of his life. After trying, and essentially failing, as a writer of fiction, he turned to reviewing—first books, then paintings, and finally music.

Shaw was a restless man, however, with boundless tastes and interests. In 1884 he joined the Fabian Society, an organization whose aim was the peaceful reform of social, economic, and political systems. His personal ambition, as he put it, was "to force the public to reconsider its morals," and toward this end he invested every ounce of his energies. In the process he established himself as a debater and public speaker of some stature.

The enjoyment he derived from crafting lines for his public addresses coupled with his earlier enthusiasm for writing criticism naturally led him in the direction of drama criticism. From there it was a short jump to playwriting itself. Shaw's first play, *Widower's House* (1892), was a rather heavy-handed and ironical exposure of the slum landlord practices and municipal graft that were common ills of the day. His next effort, *Mrs. Warren's Profession* (1894), ran into trouble with official censorship due to its serious treatment f prostitution and the inequities of industrialism. In the same year, *Arms and the Man* enjoyed a limited success.

If people would not attend productions of his plays, Shaw reasoned, they might at least read them. In 1898 he published his first collection, *Plays Pleasant and Unpleasant,* adding the prefaces and epilogues that came to be his trademark.

Shaw's plays, forty-seven in all, continued to challenge the "spiritual sleep" of England's "middle-class morality." When *Pygmalion* was completed in 1913, it was produced in German in Vienna, as a means of avoiding the usual bad press. Its success there led it to London, where, in April of 1914, it opened to immediate acclaim. Like his professor of phonetics, Henry Higgins, Shaw believed in the power of language to break down class barriers. In his will he left a sizable bequest to furthering a system of phonetic spelling. In the interests of spelling simplification, he left out the apostrophe in some contractions, as in this text.

Objectives

1. To understand historical context in drama
2. To use generalizations properly
3. To understand dialect
4. To write about historical context

Teaching Portfolio: Support Material

Teacher Backup, pp. 00-00

Vocabulary Check, p. 00

Usage and Mechanics Worksheet, p. 00

Analyzing Literature Worksheet, p. 00

Critical Thinking and Reading Worksheet, p. 00

Language Worksheet, p. 00

Selection Test, p. 00

Art Transparency 16, *Picadilly Circus* by Charles Ginner

GUIDE FOR READING

Preface to *Pygmalion* and Pygmalion, Act I

Historical Context

The Play. Historical context refers both to the backdrop of historical events against which a work is set and to attitudes and events of the time during which the author lived. The first of these two aspects relates to such matters as when and where the work takes place, to whether the author has used real places and people, and to the degree to which the events have been fictionalized. The second aspect of historical context—the relevance of "current events" and attitudes of the author's day—takes into account any social conditions and values that may have impacted on the subject matter of the work or its execution.

Look For

As you read the "Preface to *Pygmalion*" and Act I of the play, be alert to indications of when and where the play takes place and to references to real and imaginary persons and events.

Writing

To demonstrate the irregularities of English spelling, George Bernard Shaw once suggested that the word *fish* be written *ghoti.* (The *gh,* he explained, was to be pronounced as it is in *rough,* the *o* as in *women,* and the *ti* as in *station.*) Play with English spellings until you have devised three or four "outrageous" words of your own. Show these to your classmates on paper, and see if anyone can read them correctly.

Vocabulary

Knowing the following words will help you as you read the "Preface to *Pygmalion*" and Act I.

conciliatory (ken sil'ē ə tôr' ē) *adj.*: Agreeable (p. 1124)
derisive (di rī' siv) *adj.*: Mocking (p. 1124)
repudiation (ri pyo͞o' dē ā' shən) *n.*: Rejection; denial (p. 1125)
cryptograms (krip' tə gramz) *n.*: Coded messages (p. 1125)
prodigious (prə dij' əs) *adj.*: Large; impressive (p. 1126)
didactic (dī dak' tik) *adj.*: Instructive (p. 1126)
plutocracy (plo͞o tök' rə sē) *n.*: Wealthy governing class (p. 1126)
impertinent (im pʉr' t'n ənt) *adj.*: Bold; impudent (p. 1132)
mendacity (men das' ə tē) *n.*: Lying (p. 1133)
prodigal (präd' i gəl) *adj.*: Wasteful (p. 1136)

Literary Focus Shaw's portrayal of the place of women in society was accurate for the time period in which *Pygmalion* takes place; however, the climate seems to have changed. In the early 1980's, Rex Harrison again played Henry Higgins in a revival of *My Fair Lady;* his speeches that indicated Higgins's ideas of the roles of women were greeted with exclamations of disagreement from the audience.

Look For Have volunteers prepare short presentations on the life and times of late Victorian Britain, including fashion, social habits, royalty, political climate, and other writers.

Writing Remind students that at the bottom of the page in most dictionaries is a guide to the diacritical marks that designate the sounds that words have.

Vocabulary Have your **less advanced** students work in pairs with other students to go over the diacritical marks for each word to learn to pronounce each word correctly.

Motivation for Reading Most romantic stories deal with someone getting his or her heart's desire or fulfilling a dream. Have students think about a heart's desire and freewrite a list of the changes that would be brought about in their lives if they received their heart's desire.

Master Teacher Note Refer students to the story of Pygmalion from Greek mythology and from the Roman poet Ovid's *Metamorphoses.* Discuss the similarities and differences in the stories as the play is read.

Purpose-Setting Question What part does the historical context of *Pygmalion* play in helping Shaw tell his story?

Master Teacher Note In the course of reading *Pygmalion,* you might display Art Transparency 16, *Picadilly Circus* by Charles Ginner, on the overhead projector. Although this painting depicts a time somewhat later than that of Shaw's play, it may give students a sense of the atmosphere of London in the early years of this century. Let the students offer their immediate responses to the painting. What impression of life in London do they get? What impression of it do they get from *Pygmalion?*

Preface to *Pygmalion*

George Bernard Shaw

A Professor of Phonetics

The English have no respect for their language, and will not teach their children to speak it. They cannot spell it because they have nothing to spell it with but an old foreign alphabet of which only the consonants—and not all of them—have any agreed speech value. Consequently no man can teach himself what it should sound like from reading it; and it is impossible for an Englishman to open his mouth without making some other Englishman despise him. Most European languages are now accessible in black and white to foreigners: English and French are not thus accessible even to Englishmen and Frenchmen. The reformer we need most today is an energetic phonetic enthusiast: that is why I have made such a one the hero of a popular play.

There have been heroes of that kind crying in the wilderness for many years past. When I became interested in the subject towards the end of the eighteen-seventies, the illustrious Alexander Melville Bell, the inventor of Visible Speech, had emigrated to Canada, where his son invented the telephone; but Alexander J. Ellis[1] was still a London Patriarch, with an impressive head always covered by a velvet skull cap, for which he would apologize to public meetings in a very courtly manner. He and Tito Pagliardini, another phonetic veteran, were men whom it was impossible to dislike. Henry Sweet,[2] then a young man, lacked their sweetness of character: he was about as conciliatory to conventional mortals as Ibsen[3] or Samuel Butler.[4] His great ability as a phonetician (he was, I think the best of them all at his job) would have entitled him to high official recognition, and perhaps enabled him to popularize his subject, but for his Satanic contempt for all academic dignitaries and persons in general who thought more of Greek than of phonetics. Once, in the days when the Imperial Institute rose in South Kensington, and Joseph Chamberlain[5] was booming the Empire, I induced the editor of a leading monthly review to commission an article from Sweet on the imperial importance of his subject. When it arrived, it contained nothing but a savagely derisive attack on a professor of language and literature whose chair Sweet regarded as proper to a phonetic expert only. The article, being libellous, had to be returned as impossible; and I had to renounce my dream of dragging its author into the limelight. When I met him afterwards, for the first time for many years, I found to my astonishment that he, who had been a quite tolerably presentable young man, had actually managed by sheer scorn to alter his personal appearance until he had become a sort of

1. Alexander J. Ellis: English phonetician and mathematician (1814–1890).

2. Henry Sweet: English phonetician (1845–1912).

3. Ibsen: Norwegian playwright Henrik Ibsen (1828–1906).

4. Samuel Butler: English novelist (1835–1902).

5. Joseph Chamberlain: British statesman (1836–1914).

walking repudiation of Oxford and all its traditions. It must have been largely in his own despite that he was squeezed into something called a Readership[6] of phonetics there. The future of phonetics rests probably with his pupils, who all swore by him; but nothing could bring the man himself into any sort of compliance with the university to which he nevertheless clung by divine right in an intensely Oxonian[7] way. I daresay his papers, if he has left any, include some satires that may be published without too destructive results fifty years hence. He was, I believe, not in the least an ill-natured man: very much the opposite, I should say; but he would not suffer fools gladly; and to him all scholars who were not rabid phoneticians were fools.

Those who knew him will recognize in my third act the allusion to the Current Shorthand in which he used to write postcards. It may be acquired from a four and sixpenny manual published by the Clarendon Press. The postcards which Mrs Higgins describes are such as I have received from Sweet. I would decipher a sound which a cockney would represent by *zerr,* and a Frenchman by *seu,* and then write demanding with some heat what on earth it meant. Sweet, with boundless contempt for my stupidity, would reply that it not only meant but obviously was the word Result, as no other word containing that sound, and capable of making sense with the context, existed in any language spoken on earth. That less expert mortals should require fuller indications was beyond Sweet's patience. Therefore, though the whole point of his Current Shorthand is that it can express every sound in the language perfectly, vowels as well as consonants, and that your hand has to make no stroke except the easy and current ones with which you write m, n, and u, l, p, and q, scribbling them at whatever angle comes easiest to you, his unfortunate determination to make this remarkable and quite legible script serve also as a shorthand reduced it in his own practice to the most inscrutable of cryptograms. His true objective was the provision of a full, accurate, legible script for our language; but he was led past that by his contempt for the popular Pitman system of shorthand, which he called the Pitfall system. The triumph of Pitman was a triumph of business organization: there was a weekly paper to persuade you to learn Pitman: there were cheap textbooks and exercise books and transcripts of speeches for you to copy, and schools where experienced teachers coached you up to the necessary proficiency. Sweet could not organize his market in that fashion. He might as well have been the Sybil[8] who tore up the leaves of prophecy that nobody would attend to. The four and sixpenny manual, mostly in his lithographed handwriting, that was never vulgarly advertized, may perhaps some day be taken up by a syndicate and pushed upon the public as The Times[9] pushed the Encyclopoedia Britannica; but until then it will certainly not prevail against Pitman. I have bought three copies of it during my lifetime; and I am informed by the publishers that its cloistered existence is still a steady and healthy one. I actually learned the system two several times; and yet the shorthand in which I am writing these lines is Pitman's. And the reason is, that my secretary cannot transcribe Sweet, having been perforce taught in the schools of Pitman. In America I could use the commercially organized Gregg shorthand, which has taken a hint from Sweet by making its letters writable (current, Sweet would have called them) instead of having to be geometrically drawn like Pitman's; but all these systems, including

6. Readership *n.*: A position as a lecturer or instructor.
7. Oxonian *adj.*: Pertaining to Oxford University.

8. Sybil: One of the women consulted as prophetesses by the ancient Greeks or Romans.
9. The Times: The *London Times*, a British newspaper.

Sweet's, are spoilt by making them available for verbatim reporting, in which complete and exact spelling and word division are impossible. A complete and exact phonetic script is neither practicable nor necessary for ordinary use; but if we enlarge our alphabet to the Russian size, and make our spelling as phonetic as Spanish, the advance will be prodigious.

Pygmalion Higgins is not a portrait of Sweet, to whom the adventure of Eliza Doolittle would have been impossible; still, as will be seen, there are touches of Sweet in the play. With Higgins's physique and temperament Sweet might have set the Thames on fire. As it was, he impressed himself professionally on Europe to an extent that made his comparative personal obscurity, and the failure of Oxford to do justice to his eminence, a puzzle to foreign specialists in his subject. I do not blame Oxford, because I think Oxford is quite right in demanding a certain social amenity from its nurslings (heavens knows it is not exorbitant in its requirement!); for although I well know how hard it is for a man of genius with a seriously underrated subject to maintain serene and kindly relations with the men who underrate it, and who keep all the best places for less important subjects which they profess without originality and sometimes without much capacity for them, still, if he overwhelms them with wrath and disdain, he cannot expect them to heap honors on him.

Of the later generations of phoneticians I know little. Among them towered Robert Bridges, to whom perhaps Higgins may owe his Miltonic sympathies, though here again I must disclaim all portraiture. But if the play makes the public aware that there are such people as phoneticians, and that they are among the most important people in England at present, it will serve its turn.

I wish to boast that Pygmalion has been an extremely successful play, both on stage and screen, all over Europe and North America as well as at home. It is so intensely and deliberately didactic, and its subject is esteemed so dry, that I delight in throwing it at the heads of the wiseacres who repeat the parrot cry that art should never be didactic. It goes to prove my contention that great art can never be anything else.

Finally, and for the encouragement of people troubled with accents that cut them off from all high employment, I may add that the change wrought by Professor Higgins in the flower-girl is neither impossible nor uncommon. The modern concierge's daughter who fulfills her ambition by playing the Queen of Spain in Ruy Blas[10] at the Théâtre Français is only one of many thousands of men and women who have sloughed off their native dialects and acquired a new tongue. Our West End shop assistants and domestic servants are bilingual. But the thing has to be done scientifically, or the last state of the aspirant may be worse than the first. An honest slum dialect is more tolerable than the attempts of phonetically untaught persons to imitate the plutocracy. Ambitious flower-girls who read this play must not imagine that they can pass themselves off as fine ladies by untutored imitation. They must learn their alphabet over again, and different, from a phonetic expert. Imitation will only make them ridiculous.

10. Ruy Blas (ro͞o ē′ blas′): A play by French writer Victor Hugo (1802–1885).

Note for Technicians. A complete representation of the play as printed in this edition is technically possible only on the cinema screen or on stages furnished with exceptionally elaborate machinery. For ordinary theatrical use the scenes separated by rows of asterisks are to be omitted.

In the dialogue an e upside down indicates the indefinite vowel, sometimes called obscure or neutral, for which, though it is one of the commonest sounds in English speech, our wretched alphabet has no letter.

Pygmalion

CHARACTERS

Henry Higgins	**Eliza Doolittle**	**Taximen**
Colonel Pickering	**Mrs Eynsford Hill**	**Count Nepommuck**
Freddy Eynsford Hill	**Miss Eynsford Hill**	**Host**
Alfred Doolittle	**Mrs Higgins**	**Hostess**
Bystanders	**Mrs Pearce**	**Footmen**
	Parlormaid	**Constables**

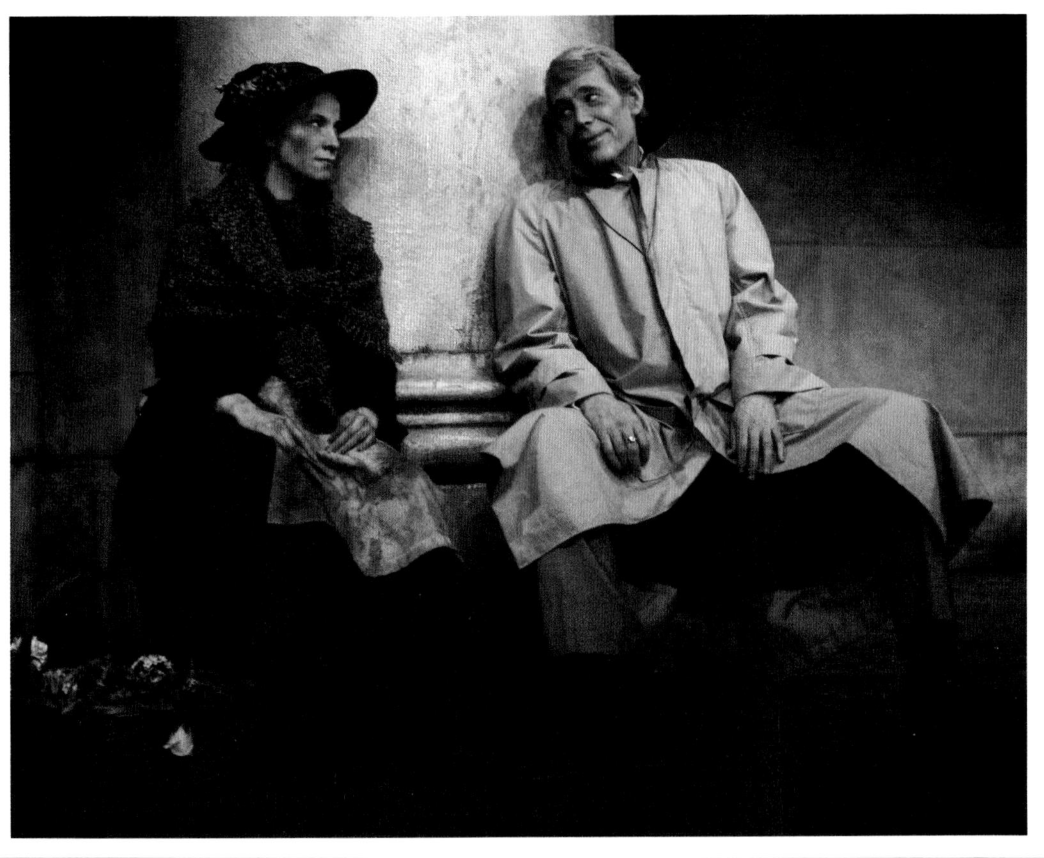

1 **Reading Strategy** Have those students who will benefit from a graphic presentation of information prepare an enlarged map of the part of London in which the play takes place. Being able to locate the centers of activity will help them remember the events that took place in each location. Have them find each place on the map as it is introduced in the play.

2 **Discussion** What classes in London society are brought together in the shelter? How do they reveal their classes? What does the author think of the class presented by the mother? How do you know?

ACT I

London at 11.15 P.M. *Torrents of heavy summer rain. Cab whistles blowing frantically in all directions. Pedestrians running for shelter into the portico of St Paul's church (not Wren's cathedral but Inigo Jones's church in Covent Garden vegetable mar-*
1 *ket), among them a lady and her daughter in evening dress. All are peering out gloomily at the rain, except one man with his back turned to the rest, wholly preoccupied with a notebook in which he is writing.*

The church clock strikes the first quarter.[1]

THE DAUGHTER [*in the space between the central pillars, close to the one on her left*] I'm getting chilled to the bone. What can Freddy be doing all this time? He's been gone twenty minutes.

THE MOTHER [*on her daughter's right*] Not so long. But he ought to have got us a cab by this.

A BYSTANDER [*on the lady's right*] He wont get no cab not until half-past eleven, missus, when they come back after dropping their theatre fares.

THE MOTHER. But we must have a cab. We cant stand here until half-past eleven. It's too bad.

THE BYSTANDER. Well, it ain't my fault, missus.

THE DAUGHTER. If Freddy had a bit of gumption, he would have got one at the theatre door.

THE MOTHER. What could he have done, poor boy?

THE DAUGHTER. Other people got cabs. Why couldn't he?

FREDDY *rushes in out of the rain from the Southampton Street side, and comes between them closing a dripping umbrella. He is a young man of twenty, in evening dress, very wet round the ankles.*

THE DAUGHTER. Well, havnt you got a cab?

FREDDY. Theres not one to be had for love or money.

THE MOTHER. Oh, Freddy, there must be one. You cant have tried.

THE DAUGHTER. It's too tiresome. Do you expect us to go and get one ourselves?

FREDDY. I tell you theyre all engaged. The rain was so sudden: nobody was prepared;
and everybody had to take a cab. Ive been to 2
Charing Cross one way and nearly to Ludgate Circus the other; and they were all engaged.

THE MOTHER. Did you try Trafalgar Square?

FREDDY. There wasn't one at Trafalgar Square.

THE DAUGHTER. Did you try?

FREDDY. I tried as far as Charing Cross Station. Did you expect me to walk to Hammersmith?

THE DAUGHTER. You havnt tried at all.

THE MOTHER. You really are very helpless, Freddy. Go again; and dont come back until you have found a cab.

FREDDY. I shall simply get soaked for nothing.

THE DAUGHTER. And what about us? Are we to stay here all night in this draught,[2] with next to nothing on? You selfish pig—

FREDDY. Oh, very well: I'll go, I'll go. [*He opens his umbrella and dashes off Strandwards, but comes into collision with a flower girl who is hurrying in for shelter, knocking her basket out of her hands. A blinding flash of lightning, followed instantly by a rattling peal of thunder, orchestrates the incident*].

THE FLOWER GIRL. Nah then, Freddy: look wh' y' gowin, deah.

---

1. **first quarter:** Fifteen minutes past the hour.

2. **draught** (draft): Draft.

FREDDY. Sorry [*he rushes off*].

THE FLOWER GIRL [*picking up her scattered flowers and replacing them in the basket*] Theres menners f' yer! Tə-oo banches o voylets trod into the mad. [*She sits down on the plinth*[3] *of the column sorting her flowers, on the lady's right. She is not at all a romantic figure. She is perhaps eighteen, perhaps twenty, hardly older. She wears a little sailor hat of black straw that has long been exposed to the dust and soot of London and has seldom if ever been brushed. Her hair needs washing rather badly: its mousy color can hardly be natural. She wears a shoddy black coat that reaches nearly to her knees and is shaped to her waist. She has a brown skirt with a coarse apron. Her boots are much the worse for wear. She is no doubt as clean as she can afford to be; but compared to the ladies she is very dirty. Her features are no worse than theirs; but their condition leaves something to be desired; and she needs the services of a dentist*].

THE MOTHER. How do you know that my son's name is Freddy, pray?

3 **THE FLOWER GIRL.** Ow, eez yə-ooa, san, is e? Wal, fewd dan y' də-ooty bawmz a mather should, eed now bettern to spawl a pore gel's flahrzn than ran awy athaht pyin. Will ye-oo py me f'them? [*Here, with apologies, this desperate attempt to represent her dialect without a phonetic alphabet must be abandoned as unintelligible outside London*].

THE DAUGHTER. Do nothing of the sort, mother. The idea!

THE MOTHER. Please allow me, Clara. Have you any pennies?

THE DAUGHTER. No. Ive nothing smaller than sixpence.

THE FLOWER GIRL [*hopefully*] I can give you change for a tanner,[4] kind lady.

---

3. plinth: The block at the base of a column.
4. tanner: Slang for a sixpence.

THE MOTHER [*to* CLARA] Give it to me. [CLARA *parts reluctantly*]. Now [*to the* GIRL] This is for your flowers.

THE FLOWER GIRL. Thank you kindly, lady.

THE DAUGHTER. Make her give you the change. These things are only a penny a bunch.

THE MOTHER. Do hold your tongue, Clara. [*To the* GIRL] You can keep the change.

THE FLOWER GIRL. Oh, thank you, lady.

THE MOTHER. Now tell me how you know that young gentleman's name.

THE FLOWER GIRL. I didnt.

THE MOTHER. I heard you call him by it. Dont try to deceive me.

THE FLOWER GIRL [*protesting*] Who's trying to deceive you? I called him Freddy or Charlie same as you might yourself if you was talking to a stranger and wished to be pleasant.

THE DAUGHTER. Sixpence thrown away! Really, mamma, you might have spared Freddy that. [*She retreats in disgust behind the pillar*]. 4

An elderly gentleman of the amiable military type rushes into the shelter, and closes a dripping umbrella. He is in the same plight as FREDDY, *very wet above the ankles. He is in evening dress, with a light overcoat. He takes the place left vacant by* THE DAUGHTER.

THE GENTLEMAN. Phew!

THE MOTHER. [*to the* GENTLEMAN] Oh, sir, is there any sign of its stopping?

THE GENTLEMAN. I'm afraid not. It started worse than ever about two minutes ago [*he goes to the plinth beside the* FLOWER GIRL; *puts up his foot on it; and stoops to turn down his trouser ends*].

THE MOTHER. Oh dear! [*She retires sadly and joins her daughter*].

3 **Speaking and Listening** Have several volunteers give this speech. As a comparison to their work, you might play a recording of this speech from either the play or *My Fair Lady*.

4 **Clarification** A penny, the plural is *pence*, is a coin—originally silver, then copper, and from 1860 bronze. At the time of the play, it was worth ½ of a shilling or 1⁄240 of a pound sterling. A sixpence was equal to six pennies. Now a penny is worth 1⁄100 of a pound sterling.

5 Clarification A sovereign is another name for a pound sterling. A half-a-crown was a coin worth two shillings and sixpence in old money. A shilling was worth twelve pence. A tuppence was equal to two pennies.

6 Discussion How would a pair of boots help the bystander determine that the man was a gentleman?

7 Reading Strategy What clue to the Note Taker's identity does this speech give? What do you guess is the man's occupation?

THE FLOWER GIRL [*taking advantage of the military gentleman's proximity to establish friendly relations with him*] If it's worse, it's a sign it's nearly over. So cheer up, Captain; and buy a flower off a poor girl.

THE GENTLEMAN. I'm sorry. I havnt any change.

THE FLOWER GIRL. I can give you change, Captain.

THE GENTLEMAN. For a sovereign? Ive nothing less.

THE FLOWER GIRL. Garn! Oh do buy a flower off
5 me, Captain. I can change half-a-crown.
Take this for tuppence.

THE GENTLEMAN. Now dont be troublesome: theres a good girl. [*Trying his pockets*] I really havnt any change—Stop: heres three hapence, if thats any use to you [*he retreats to the other pillar*].

THE FLOWER GIRL [*disappointed, but thinking three half-pence better than nothing*] Thank you, sir.

THE BYSTANDER [*to the* GIRL] You be careful: give him a flower for it. Theres a bloke here behind taking down every blessed word youre saying. [*All turn to the man who is taking notes*].

THE FLOWER GIRL [*springing up terrified*] I aint done nothing wrong by speaking to the gentleman. Ive a right to sell flowers if I keep off the kerb. [*Hysterically*] I'm a respectable girl: so help me, I never spoke to him except to ask him to buy a flower off me.

General hubbub, mostly sympathetic to the FLOWER GIRL, *but deprecating her excessive sensibility. Cries of* Dont start hollerin. Who's hurting you? Nobody's going to touch you. Whats the good of fussing? Steady on. Easy, easy, etc., *come from the elderly staid spectators, who pat her comfortingly. Less patient ones bid her shut her head, or ask her roughly what is wrong with her. A remoter group, not knowing what the matter is, crowd in and increase the noise with question and answer:* What's the row? What-she do? Where is he? A tec[5] taking her down. What! him? Yes: him over there: Took money off the gentleman, etc.

THE FLOWER GIRL [*breaking through them to the* GENTLEMAN, *crying wildly*] Oh, sir, dont let him charge me. You dunno what it means to me. Theyll take away my character and drive me on the streets for speaking to gentlemen. They—

THE NOTE TAKER [*coming forward on her right, the rest crowding after him*] There! there! there! there! who's hurting you, you silly girl? What do you take me for?

THE BYSTANDER. It's aw rawt: e's a genleman:
look at his bə-oots. [*Explaining to the* NOTE 6
TAKER] She thought you was a copper's nark, sir.

THE NOTE TAKER [*with quick interest*] Whats a 7
copper's nark?

THE BYSTANDER [*inapt at definition*] It's a—well, it's a copper's nark, as you might say. What else would you call it? A sort of informer.

THE FLOWER GIRL [*still hysterical*] I take my Bible oath I never said a word—

THE NOTE TAKER [*overbearing but good-humored*] Oh, shut up, shut up. Do I look like a policeman?

THE FLOWER GIRL [*far from reassured*] Then what did you take down my words for? How do I know whether you took me down right? You just shew me what youve wrote about me. [*The* NOTE TAKER *opens his book and holds it steadily under her nose, though the pressure of the mob trying to read it over his shoulders would upset a weaker man*]. Whats that? That aint proper writing. I cant read that.

THE NOTE TAKER. I can. [*Reads, reproducing her pronunciation exactly*] "Cheer ap, Keptin; n' baw ya flahr orf a pore gel."

5. **tec:** A slang abbreviation for detective.

THE FLOWER GIRL [*much distressed*] It's because I called him Captain. I meant no harm. [*To the* GENTLEMAN] Oh, sir, dont let him lay a charge agen me for a word like that. You—

THE GENTLEMAN. Charge! I make no charge. [*To the* NOTE TAKER] Really, sir, if you are a detective, you need not begin protecting me against molestation by young women until I ask you. Anybody could see that the girl meant no harm.

THE BYSTANDERS GENERALLY [*demonstrating against police espionage*] Course they could. What business is it of yours? You mind your own affairs. He wants promotion, he does. Taking down people's words! Girl never said a word to him. What harm if she did? Nice thing a girl cant shelter from the rain without being insulted, etc., etc., etc. [*She is conducted by the more sympathetic demonstrators back to her plinth, where she resumes her seat and struggles with her emotion*].

THE BYSTANDER. He aint a tec. He's a blooming busybody: thats what he is. I tell you, look at his bə-oots.

THE NOTE TAKER [*turning on him genially*] And how are all your people down at Selsey?

THE BYSTANDER [*suspiciously*] Who told you my people come from Selsey?

8 **THE NOTE TAKER.** Never you mind. They did. [*To the* GIRL] How do you come to be up so far east? You were born in Lisson Grove.

THE FLOWER GIRL [*appalled*] Oh, what harm is there in my leaving Lisson Grove? It wasnt
9 fit for a pig to live in; and I had to pay four-and-six a week. [*In tears*] Oh, boo —hoo—oo—

THE NOTE TAKER. Live where you like; but stop that noise.

THE GENTLEMAN [*to the* GIRL] Come, come! he cant touch you: you have a right to live where you please.

A SARCASTIC BYSTANDER [*thrusting himself between the* NOTE TAKER *and the* GENTLEMAN] Park Lane, for instance. I'd like to go into the Housing Question with you, I would.

THE FLOWER GIRL [*subsiding into a brooding melancholy over her basket, and talking very low-spiritedly to herself*] I'm a good girl, I am.

THE SARCASTIC BYSTANDER [*not attending to her*] Do you know where *I* come from?

THE NOTE TAKER [*promptly*] Hoxton.

Titterings. Popular interest in the NOTE TAKER*'s performance increases.*

THE SARCASTIC ONE [*amazed*] Well, who said I didnt? Bly me! you know everything, you do.

THE FLOWER GIRL [*still nursing her sense of injury*] Aint no call to meddle with me, he aint.

THE BYSTANDER [*to her*] Of course he aint. Dont you stand it from him. [*To the* NOTE TAKER] See here: what call have you to know about people what never offered to meddle
with you? 10

THE FLOWER GIRL. Let him say what he likes. I dont want to have no truck with him.

THE BYSTANDER. You take us for dirt under your feet, dont you? Catch you taking liberties with a gentleman!

THE SARCASTIC BYSTANDER. Yes: tell him where he come from if you want to go fortune-telling.

THE NOTE TAKER. Cheltenham, Harrow, Cambridge, and India. 11

THE GENTLEMAN. Quite right.

Great laughter. Reaction in the NOTE TAKER*'s favor. Exclamations of* He knows all about it. Told him proper. Hear him tell the toff[6] where he come from? etc.

---

6. toff: English slang for a fashionable person.

8 **Discussion** How does the Note Taker know where the bystander and the girl originated?

9 **Clarification** The Flower Girl paid four shillings and six pence a week in rent.

10 **Critical Thinking and Reading** What generalizations can you make about the Bystander's attitudes and background?

11 **Clarification** The gentleman was brought up in Cheltenham, west of London, in Gloucestershire; went to Harrow, a public (controlled enrollment, privately funded) school for boys; went to university at Cambridge; and served in the military in India.

12 **Discussion** Discuss the difference between the Note Taker's response to the Flower Girl and the Daughter and their responses to him.

13 **Critical Thinking and Reading** How does the exchange support the generalization that the English judge each other as soon as they open their mouths?

THE GENTLEMAN. May I ask, sir, do you do this for your living at a music hall?

THE NOTE TAKER. I've thought of that. Perhaps I shall some day.

The rain has stopped; and the persons on the outside of the crowd begin to drop off.

THE FLOWER GIRL [*resenting the reaction*] He's no gentleman, he aint, to interfere with a poor girl.

THE DAUGHTER [*out of patience, pushing her way rudely to the front and displacing the* GENTLEMAN, *who politely retires to the other side of the pillar*] What on earth is Freddy doing? I shall get pneumownia if I stay in this draught any longer.

THE NOTE TAKER [*to himself, hastily making a note of her pronunciation of "monia"*] Earlscourt.

THE DAUGHTER [*violently*] Will you please keep your impertinent remarks to yourself.

THE NOTE TAKER. Did I say that out loud? I didn't mean to. I beg your pardon. Your mother's Epsom, unmistakeably.

THE MOTHER [*advancing between the* DAUGHTER *and the* NOTE TAKER] How very curious! I was brought up in Largelady Park, near Epsom.

THE NOTE TAKER [*uproariously amused*] Ha! ha! What a devil of a name! Excuse me. [*To the* DAUGHTER] You want a cab, do you?

12 **THE DAUGHTER.** Dont dare speak to me.

THE MOTHER. Oh please, please, Clara. [*Her daughter repudiates her with an angry shrug and retires haughtily*] We should be so grateful to you, sir, if you found us a cab. [*The* NOTE TAKER *produces a whistle*] Oh, thank you. [*She joins her daughter*].
The NOTE TAKER *blows a piercing blast.*

THE SARCASTIC BYSTANDER. There! I knowed he was a plainclothes copper.

THE BYSTANDER. That aint a police whistle: thats a sporting whistle.

THE FLOWER GIRL [*still preoccupied with her wounded feelings*] He's no right to take away my character. My character is the same to me as any lady's.

THE NOTE TAKER. I dont know whether youve noticed it; but the rain stopped about two minutes ago.

THE BYSTANDER. So it has. Why didn't you say so before? and us losing our time listening to your silliness! [*He walks off towards the Strand*].

THE SARCASTIC BYSTANDER. I can tell where you come from. You come from Anwell. Go back there. 13

THE NOTE TAKER [*helpfully*] Hanwell.

THE SARCASTIC BYSTANDER [*affecting great distinction of speech*] Thenk you, teacher. Haw haw! So long [*he touches his hat with mock respect and strolls off*].

THE FLOWER GIRL. Frightening people like that! How would he like it himself?

THE MOTHER. It's quite fine now, Clara. We can walk to a motor bus. Come. [*She gathers her skirts above her ankles and hurries off towards the Strand*].

THE DAUGHTER. But the cab—[*her mother is out of hearing*]. Oh, how tiresome! [*She follows angrily*].

All the rest have gone except the NOTE TAKER, *the* GENTLEMAN, *and the* FLOWER GIRL, *who sits arranging her basket, and still pitying herself in murmurs.*

THE FLOWER GIRL. Poor girl! Hard enough for her to live without being worrited and chivied.[7]

THE GENTLEMAN [*returning to his former place on the* NOTE TAKER*'s left*] How do you do it, if I may ask?

THE NOTE TAKER. Simple phonetics. The science of speech. Thats my profession: also

---

7. **worrited and chivied:** Worried and tormented.

my hobby. Happy is the man who can make a living by his hobby! You can spot an Irishman or a Yorkshireman by his brogue. *I*
can place any man within six miles. I can
15 place him within two miles in London.
Sometimes within two streets.

THE FLOWER GIRL. Ought to be ashamed of himself, unmanly coward.

THE GENTLEMAN. But is there a living in that?

THE NOTE TAKER. Oh yes. Quite a fat one. This is an age of upstarts. Men begin in Kentish Town with £80 a year, and end in Park Lane with a hundred thousand. They want to drop Kentish Town; but they give themselves away every time they open their mouths. Now I can teach them—

THE FLOWER GIRL. Let him mind his own business and leave a poor girl—

THE NOTE TAKER [*explosively*] Woman: cease
this detestable boohooing instantly; or else
16 seek the shelter of some other place of worship.

THE FLOWER GIRL [*with feeble defiance*] Ive a right to be here if I like, same as you.

THE NOTE TAKER. A woman who utters such
depressing and disgusting sounds has no
right to be anywhere—no right to live. Remember that you are a human being with a
17 soul and the divine gift of articulate speech:
that your native language is the language of
Shakespear and Milton and The Bible; and
dont sit there crooning like a bilious pigeon.

THE FLOWER GIRL [*quite overwhelmed, looking up at him in mingled wonder and deprecation without daring to raise her head*] Ah-ah-ah-ow-ow-ow-oo!

THE NOTE TAKER [*whipping out his book*] Heavens! what a sound! [*He writes; then holds out the book and reads, reproducing her vowels exactly*] Ah-ah-ah-ow-ow-ow-oo!

THE FLOWER GIRL [*tickled by the performance, and laughing in spite of herself*] Garn!

THE NOTE TAKER. You see this creature with
her kerbstone English: the English that will
keep her in the gutter to the end of her days.
Well, sir, in three months I could pass that 18
girl off as a duchess at an ambassador's
garden party. I could even get her a place as
lady's maid or shop assistant, which requires better English.

THE FLOWER GIRL. What's that you say?

THE NOTE TAKER. Yes, you squashed cabbage leaf, you disgrace to the noble architecture of these columns, you incarnate insult to the English language: I could pass you off as the Queen of Sheba. [*To the* GENTLEMAN] Can you believe that?

THE GENTLEMAN. Of course I can. I am myself a student of Indian dialects; and—

THE NOTE TAKER [*eagerly*] Are you? Do you know Colonel Pickering, the author of Spoken Sanscrit?

THE GENTLEMAN. I am Colonel Pickering. Who are you?

THE NOTE TAKER. Henry Higgins, author of Higgins's Universal Alphabet.

PICKERING [*with enthusiasm*] I came from India to meet you.

HIGGINS. I was going to India to meet you.

PICKERING. Where do you live?

HIGGINS. 27A Wimpole Street. Come and see me tomorrow.

PICKERING. I'm at the Carlton. Come with me 19
now and lets have a jaw over some supper.

HIGGINS. Right you are.

THE FLOWER GIRL [*to* PICKERING, *as he passes her*] Buy a flower, kind gentleman. I'm short for my lodging.

PICKERING. I really havnt any change. I'm sorry [*he goes away*].

HIGGINS [*shocked at the* GIRL's *mendacity*] Liar. You said you could change half-a-crown.

14 **Discussion** Why is the Note Taker interested in the girl?

15 **Enrichment** London was once a small village surrounded by other small villages. Even though these villages eventually grew together into the large city we call London today, the individual villages and their individual inhabitants have maintained distinct identities, including their own dialects.

16 **Literary Focus** What is there about the Note Taker and the society in which he lives that causes and permits him to be so verbally abusive to this young girl?

17 **Discussion** Compare what you learn about the Note Taker in this speech with what you know about Henry Sweet from reading the Preface.

18 **Discussion** What are the economic side effects of the way the girl speaks?

19 **Enrichment** People of the gentleman's class normally ate a rather extensive breakfast, had a hot, complete meal called *dinner* near noon, had a meal called *tea*—consisting of rather delicate sandwiches and cakes and tea—at 4:00 P.M., and ate a lavish meal called *supper* late in the evening.

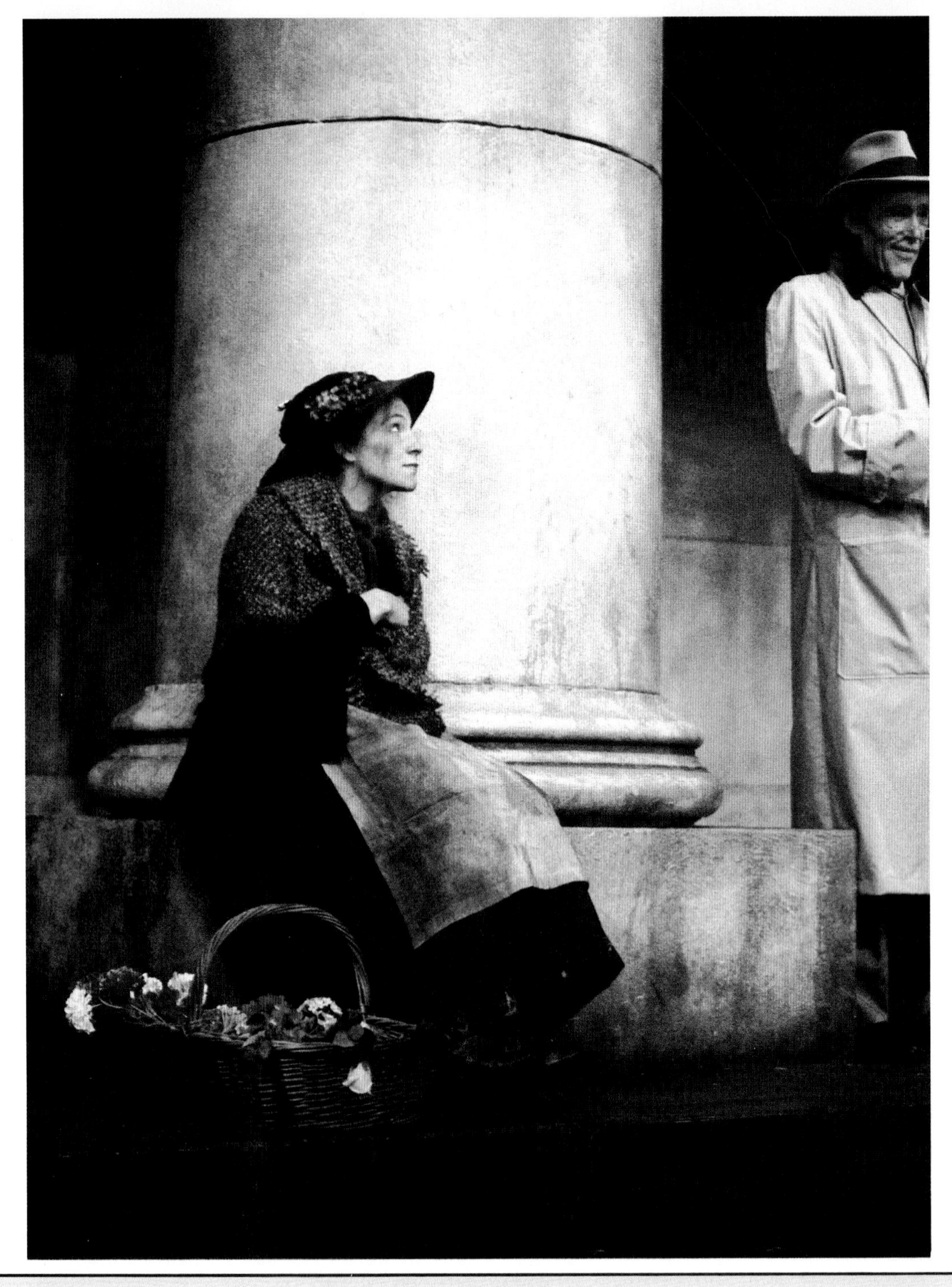

THE FLOWER GIRL [*rising in desperation*] You ought to be stuffed with nails, you ought. [*Flinging the basket at his feet*] Take the whole blooming basket for sixpence.

The church clock strikes the second quarter.

20 **HIGGINS** [*hearing in it the voice of God, rebuking him for his Pharisaic*[8] *want of charity to the poor girl*] A reminder. [*He raises his hat solemnly; then throws a handful of money into the basket and follows* PICKERING].

THE FLOWER GIRL [*picking up a half-crown*] Ah-ow-ooh! [*Picking up a couple of florins*] Aaah-ow-ooh! [*Picking up several coins*] Aaaaah-ow-ooh! [*Picking up a half-sovereign*] Aaaaaaaaaaaah-ow-ooh!!!

FREDDY [*springing out of a taxicab*] Got one at last. Hello! [*To the* GIRL] Where are the two ladies that were here?

THE FLOWER GIRL. They walked to the bus when the rain stopped.

FREDDY. And left me with a cab on my hands! Damnation!

THE FLOWER GIRL [*with grandeur*] Never mind, young man. I'm going home in a taxi. [*She sails off to the cab. The driver puts his hand behind him and holds the door firmly shut against her. Quite understanding his mistrust, she shews him her handful of money*]. A taxi fare aint no object to me, Charlie. [*He grins and opens the door*]. Here. What about the basket?

THE TAXIMAN. Give it here. Tuppence extra.

LIZA. No: I dont want nobody to see it. [*She crushes it into the cab and gets in, continuing the conversation through the window*] Good-bye, Freddy.

FREDDY [*dazedly raising his hat*] Goodbye.

TAXIMAN. Where to?

8. Pharisaic (far′ ə sā′ ik) *adj.*: Referring to the Pharisees, an ancient Jewish party or fellowship that carefully observed the written law; hypocritically self-righteous.

LIZA. Bucknam Pellis [Buckingham Palace].

TAXIMAN. What d'ye mean—Bucknam Pellis?

LIZA. Dont you know where it is? In the Green Park, where the King lives. Goodbye, Freddy. Dont let me keep you standing there. Goodbye. 21

FREDDY. Goodbye [*He goes*].

TAXIMAN. Here? Whats this about Bucknam Pellis? What business have you at Bucknam Pellis?

LIZA. Of course I havnt none. But I wasn't going to let him know that. You drive me home.

TAXIMAN. And wheres home?

LIZA. Angel Court, Drury Lane, next Meiklejohn's oil shop.

TAXIMAN. That sounds more like it, Judy. [*He drives off*].

* * * * * *

Let us follow the taxi to the entrance to Angel Court, a narrow little archway between two shops, one of them Meiklejohn's oil shop. When it stops there, Eliza gets out, dragging her basket with her.

LIZA. How much?

TAXIMAN [*indicating the taximeter*] Cant you read? A shilling.

LIZA. A shilling for two minutes!!

TAXIMAN. Two minutes or ten: it's all the same.

LIZA. Well, I dont call it right. 22

TAXIMAN. Ever been in a taxi before?

LIZA [*with dignity*] Hundreds and thousands of times, young man.

TAXIMAN [*laughing at her*] Good for you, Judy. Keep the shilling, darling, with best love from all at home. Good luck! [*He drives off*].

20 Discussion Why does Higgins throw the girl a handful of money?

21 Enrichment Buckingham Palace, the home of the reigning monarch in London, sits next to Green Park, between Hyde Park and St. James Park—three of the many green spaces maintained as public gardens and parks in London.

22 Discussion What do we learn about the Flower Girl and the Taximan in this exchange between them?

23 **Enrichment** It is still a rather common practice in some homes and boarding houses in Great Britain to have coin-operated gas heaters, water heaters, and lights. The meters allow people to budget carefully the amount of gas, hot water, and electricity that they use.

LIZA [*humiliated*] Impidence!

She picks up the basket and trudges up the alley with it to her lodging: a small room with very old wall paper hanging loose in the damp places. A broken pane in the window is mended with paper. A portrait of a popular actor and a fashion plate of ladies' dresses, all wildly beyond poor ELIZA*'s means, both torn from newspapers, are pinned up on the wall. A birdcage hangs in the window; but its tenant died long ago: it remains as a memorial only.*

These are the only visible luxuries: the rest is the irreducible minimum of poverty's needs: a wretched bed heaped with all sorts of coverings that have any warmth in them, a draped packing case with a basin and jug on it and a little looking glass over it, a chair and table, the refuse of some suburban kitchen, and an American alarum clock on the shelf above the unused fireplace: the whole lighted with a gas lamp with a penny in the slot meter. Rent: four 23
shillings a week.

Here Eliza, chronically weary, but too excited to go to bed, sits, counting her new riches and dreaming and planning what to do with them, until the gas goes out, when she enjoys for the first time the sensation of being able to put in another penny without grudging it. This prodigal mood does not extinguish her gnawing sense of the need for economy sufficiently to prevent her from calculating that she can dream and plan in bed more cheaply and warmly than sitting up without a fire. So she takes off her shawl and skirt and adds them to the miscellaneous bedclothes. Then she kicks off her shoes and gets into bed without any further change.

THINKING ABOUT THE SELECTION

Recalling

1. What kind of reformer does Shaw claim, in the Preface, that "we need most today?"
2. (a) What is the point of Current Shorthand? (b) Why does Shaw find it superior to previous systems?
3. (a) Where and when does the play open? (b) What are the mother and daughter doing?
4. How does The Note Taker amaze the crowd?
5. What feat does The Note Taker say he could accomplish in three months?

Interpreting

6. Based on Shaw's description of Henry Sweet in the Preface, what traits might you say the two men shared?
7. (a) What effect does Shaw achieve by spelling out words according to the speaker's pronunciation? (b) by identifying characters by labels at first?

Applying

8. In the seventh century, Ali ibn-abi-Talib, who was fourth caliph of the Moslems, wrote, "A man is hid under his tongue." (a) Explain the meaning of this quotation. (b) Under what circumstances do you feel that a person's speech habits are important?

ANALYZING LITERATURE

Understanding Historical Context

Historical context refers both to a play's historical validity (if it depicts events at a time other than that at which it was written) and to events and attitudes of the author's day that may have been influential. *Pygmalion* provides us

Answers

ANSWERS TO THINKING ABOUT THE SELECTION

Recalling

1. We need an "energetic phonetic enthusiast"; that was why he made such a man the hero of his play.
2. (a) Current Shorthand made it possible to express every sound—every vowel and consonant—in the English language perfectly. (b) It used "no stroke except the easy and current ones with which you write m, n, and u, l, p, and q."
3. (a) The play opens in the portico of St. Paul's church near the Covent Garden vegetable market in London. It is 11:15 P.M., and it is raining heavily. (b) They are standing in the portico to avoid getting wet, while Freddy, the son, tries to find a taxi to take them home.
4. The Note Taker guesses where several people are from, just by hearing them speak.
5. The Note Taker says that within three months he could pass the Flower Girl off as a duchess at an ambassador's garden party.

Interpreting

6. Shaw says that Higgins is not a portrait of Sweet but that there are touches of Sweet in the play, such as the irascible arrogance with which they both dealt with those they thought to be fools. Shaw also

with a glimpse of English city life shortly after the turn of the century. Tell what the following details from Act I reveal about that lifestyle, and describe any differences you might expect today in your own city.

1. Freddy's searching for a cab while his mother and sister remain sheltered.
2. The crowd's suspicions about The Note Taker.
3. (a) The verbal exchanges between The Note Taker and The Flower Girl. (b) between The Flower Girl and the Taximan.

CRITICAL THINKING AND READING

Generalizing About People

The Note Taker in Act I bases his assumptions about the speech habits of Eliza and the others on well-founded **generalizations,** or observations that apply to classes of people. While such observations, when based on scientific principles as they are here, can be valid, generalizing as a rule is a dangerous practice. Tell what generalizations underlie the following acts, and judge their validity.

1. Shaw's remarking in the Preface that "it is impossible for an Englishman to open his mouth without making some other Englishman despise him."
2. Eliza's assuming that Higgins is a "tec."
3. The crowd's sizing up Pickering as a "toff."
4. The Taximan's holding the door shut against Eliza when she first approaches.

SPEAKING AND LISTENING

Understanding Dialect

A **dialect** is a collection of speech habits that typifies a particular social class or region. A dialect may vary from the standard form of a language in pronunciation, in grammar, and in the use of certain expressions. Whatever its defining features may be, every dialect is *systematic*—or governed by rules. The Cockney accent used by Eliza is used to this day by lower-class inhabitants of London's East End. Arrange for members of the class to read aloud Eliza's speeches on pages 1130 and 1135. After "translating" them into standard English, develop as many rules of pronunciation and grammar as you can for the Cockney dialect.

THINKING AND WRITING

Writing About Historical Context

Reread Shaw's Preface to the play. Then write a short essay evaluating the Preface's contribution to the play's historical context. Begin by asking yourself the following questions. How relevant are Shaw's attitudes about language to the events of Act I? How important is the background information on Henry Sweet? On systems of shorthand? When you revise, make sure you have provided details from the Preface and from Act I to support your thesis. Proofread your essay and prepare a final draft.

says that if Sweet had had Higgins's physique and temperament Sweet might have been more successful in his attempts to change the way that the English looked at their language.

7. (a) Shaw's spelling allows the reader to see and to sound out the differences in the dialects that Higgins is studying. (b) His identification of characters by labels enables the reader to connect the character's speech with his or her profession or role.

Applying

8. Answers will differ, though the general idea of the quotation seems to be that people conceal themselves by what they say.

ANSWERS TO ANALYZING LITERATURE

1. Suggested Response: Men, seen as the stronger sex, were more capable of withstanding rain and were expected to "take care of" women. Today, many women take the initiative in their lives and feel that they can take care of themselves.
2. Suggested Response: The crowd thought that if the Note Taker was watching them carefully he must be a policeman; it seems that policeman were seen as intrusive by this society. This attitude still exists in today's society, although most people would not feel as free to confront such a person as openly and directly as these people did.

(Answers begin on p. 1136.)

3. Suggested Responses: (a) It appears that those of the upper class could speak to everyone else in any way that they might choose; even though, the Flower Girl and some bystanders objected, no one could make the Note Taker stop. Today, there is a real possibility that this confrontation would have gotten violent very quickly and that no one in the crowd would have stepped into help. (b) The Taximan and the Flower Girl are both from the working class and value money in the same way. Only when she showed him that she could pay, did he allow her to get in the taxi. However, when he got to her street, he let her out without paying. Today, it is unlikely that someone would be challenged by Taximan about whether he or she could pay the fare, and it is equally unlikely that the ride would end up being free.

ANSWERS TO CRITICAL THINKING AND READING

1. The generalization that the English judge each other on how they speak is an accurate statement; that they despise each other upon hearing each other speak is an assumption that cannot be made.
2. Eliza became distraught when she assumed that Higgins was a detective; her generalization that anyone taking down notes about his surroundings must be on a case proved to be wrong.
3. That Pickering is a "toff" is an accurate observation; because a toff is a fashionable person whose quality could be easily assessed by anyone who saw him. He dress was that of a gentlemen with class.
4. The Taximan assumed by her manner and by the clothes she wore that Eliza had no money; it turns out that this time his generalization was wrong. She had a fistful of money with which to pay him.

SPEAKING AND LISTENING

Have volunteers put together a list of expressions from the rhyming slang of the Cockneys. Have them present the list orally to the rest of the class, with translations, and have them teach the usage and pronunciation of the expressions.

Literary Focus Remind students what they have learned about round and flat characters and the importance of character development—external and internal—to the development of the story.

Look For Have students who might benefit from a graphic presentation of character development in the play make a chart of the major characters and their characteristics that have been introduced so far. Have them add to the chart when new characters are introduced, when changes occur, or when new characteristics are discovered.

Writing When they have completed their writing, have them exchange their paragraphs with a partner and offer comments that will improve them. Have them return the paragraphs and make whatever changes they feel are necessary.

Vocabulary Have students write down whether these words can be used as other parts of speech; if they can, does the word form change, and does the word meaning change?

GUIDE FOR READING

Pygmalion, Act II

The Writer's Technique

Character Development. Character development is the fleshing out of a character in a work of fiction through confrontations with other characters or forces. Depending upon the extent to which a character changes as a result of these confrontations, he or she is said to be either static or dynamic. A *static character* is one who remains relatively unchanged by events. A *dynamic character,* by contrast, is one who changes considerably, sometimes shedding altogether character traits which he or she possessed earlier in the work. In Shakespeare's *The Taming of the Shrew,* for example, the character Kate begins as a feisty, hot-tempered individual who, through the course of the play, is transformed into a mellow, even-tempered person.

Look For

As you read Act II of *Pygmalion,* look for circumstances that might lead to changes in the characters, as well as to traits in a character that make him or her a candidate for change.

Writing

What motivates people to change? Why do people decide to alter the way they look, behave, or even speak? Freewrite, exploring your thoughts on these questions.

Vocabulary

Knowing the following words will help you as you read Act II of *Pygmalion.*

impetuous (im pech′ oo wəs) *adj.*: Given to doing things on the spur of the moment (p. 1139)

petulance (pech′ oo ləns) *n.*: Peevishness; moodiness (p. 1139)

peremptorily (pə remp′ tə ri lē) *adv.*: Decisively (p. 1141)

zephyr (zef′ ər) *n.*: Gentle wind (p. 1143)

elocution (el′ə kyōō′ shən) *n.*: Art of public speaking (p. 1143)

remonstrance (ri män′ strəns) *n.*: Protest (p. 1144)

presumptuous (pri zump′ choo wəs) *adj.*: Unduly confident or bold (p. 1146)

Objectives

1. To understand character development
2. To make inferences about characters
3. To read dialogue aloud
4. To write comparing and contrasting characters

Teaching Portfolio: Support Material

Teacher Backup, pp. 00-00

Vocabulary Check, p. 00

Usage and Mechanics Worksheet, p. 00

Analyzing Literature Worksheet, p. 00

Critical Thinking and Reading Worksheet, p. 00

Language Worksheet, p. 00

Selection Test, p. 00

ACT II

Next day at 11 A.M. HIGGINS'S *laboratory in Wimpole Street. It is a room on the first floor, looking on the street, and was meant for the drawing room. The double doors are in the middle of the back wall; and persons entering find in the corner to their right two tall file cabinets at right angles to one another against the walls. In this corner stands a flat writing-table, on which are a phonograph, a laryngoscope,*[1] *a row of tiny organ pipes with a bellows, a set of lamp chimneys for singing flames with burners attached to a gas plug in the wall by an indiarubber tube, several tuning-forks of different sizes, a life-size image of half a human head, shewing in section the vocal organs, and a box containing a supply of wax cylinders for the phonograph.*

Further down the room, on the same side, is a fireplace, with a comfortable leather-covered easy-chair at the side of the hearth nearest the door, and a coal-
1 *scuttle. There is a clock on the mantlepiece. Between the fireplace and the phonograph table is a stand for newspapers.*

On the other side of the central door, to the left of the visitor, is a cabinet of shallow drawers. On it is a telephone and the telephone directory. The corner beyond, and most of the side wall, is occupied by a grand piano, with the keyboard at the end furthest from the door, and a bench for the players extending the full length of the keyboard. On the piano is a dessert dish heaped with fruit and sweets, mostly chocolates.

The middle of the room is clear. Besides the easy-chair, the piano bench, and two chairs at the phonograph table, there is one stray chair. It stands near the fireplace. On the walls, engravings: mostly Piranesis[2] *and mezzotint*[3] *portraits. No paintings.*

PICKERING *is seated at the table, putting down some cards and a tuning-fork which he has been using.* HIGGINS *is standing up near him, closing two or three file drawers which are hanging out. He appears in the morning light as a robust, vital, appetizing sort of man of forty or thereabouts, dressed in a professional-looking black frock-coat with a white linen collar and black silk tie. He is of energetic, scientific type, heartily, even violently interested in everything that can be studied as a scientific subject, and careless about himself and other people, including their feelings. He is, in fact, but for his years and size, rather like a very impetuous baby "taking notice" eagerly and loudly, and requiring almost as much watching to keep him out of unintended*
mischief. His manner varies from genial 2
bullying when he is in a good humor to stormy petulance when anything goes wrong; but he is so entirely frank and void of malice that he remains likeable even in his least reasonable moments.

HIGGINS [*as he shuts the last drawer*] Well, I think thats the whole show.

PICKERING. It's really amazing. I havnt taken half of it in, you know.

HIGGINS. Would you like to go over any of it again?

PICKERING [*rising and coming to the fireplace, where he plants himself with his back to the fire*] No, thank you: not now. I'm quite done up for this morning.

HIGGINS [*following him, and standing beside him on his left*] Tired of listening to sounds?

PICKERING. Yes. It's a fearful strain. I rather fancied myself because I can pronounce twenty-four distinct vowel sounds; but your hundred and thirty beat me. I cant hear a bit of difference between most of them.

HIGGINS [*chuckling, and going over to the piano to eat sweets*] Oh, that comes with practice. You hear no difference at first; but you keep on listening, and presently you

---

1. **laryngoscope** (lə riŋ′ gō skōp′) *n.*: An instrument for examining the throat.
2. **Piranesis** (pēr′ ə nā′ zēz): Works of Italian artist Giambattista Piranesi (1720–1778).
3. **mezzotint:** An engraving made from a copper or steel plate.

Motivation for Reading Have students think about, or imagine, a time when they have traveled to a place with which they were totally unfamiliar. Of what kinds of things were they afraid? What kinds of things made them feel welcome? How did they overcome feeling uncomfortable in the new setting? Relate these responses to Liza's feelings as she visits Professor Higgins's laboratory.

Purpose-Setting Question Which characters are dynamic characters, which are static, and what impact does each have on the development of the play?

1 **Master Teacher Note** Students who learn more efficiently visually might draw or construct to scale the set for Higgins's laboratory, based on the description at the beginning of Act II.

2 **Critical Thinking and Reading** What inferences about Higgins's childhood can you make from this description of his behavior?

3 Critical Thinking and Reading What inferences can you make about the part that Mrs. Pearce plays in the Higgins household?

4 Discussion How does Eliza feel about herself?

5 Literary Focus Which of these characters are more likely to be static characters and which are more likely to be dynamic characters as the play progresses?

find theyre all as different as A from B. [MRS PEARCE *looks in; she is* HIGGINS'*s housekeeper*]. Whats the matter?

MRS PEARCE [*hesitating, evidently perplexed*] A young woman asks to see you, sir.

HIGGINS. A young woman! What does she want?

MRS PEARCE. Well, sir, she says youll be glad to see her when you know what she's come about. She's quite a common girl, sir. Very common indeed. I should have sent her away, only I thought perhaps you wanted her to talk into your machines. I hope Ive not done wrong; but really you see such queer people sometimes—youll excuse me, I'm sure, sir—

HIGGINS. Oh, thats all right, Mrs Pearce. Has she an interesting accent?

MRS PEARCE. Oh, something dreadful, sir, really. I dont know how you can take an interest in it.

HIGGINS [*to* PICKERING] Lets have her up. Shew her up, Mrs Pearce [*he rushes across to his working table and picks out a cylinder to use on the phonograph*].

MRS PEARCE [*only half resigned to it*] Very well, sir. It's for you to say. [*She goes downstairs*].

HIGGINS. This is rather a bit of luck. I'll shew you how I make records. We'll set her talking; and I'll take it down first in Bell's Visible Speech; then in broad Romic; and then we'll get her on the phonograph so that you can turn her on as often as you like with the written transcript before you.

MRS PEARCE [*returning*] This is the young woman, sir.

The FLOWER GIRL *enters in state. She has a hat with three ostrich feathers, orange, sky-blue, and red. She has a nearly clean apron, and the shoddy coat has been tidied a little. The pathos of this deplorable figure, with its innocent vanity and consequential air, touches* PICKERING, *who has already straightened himself in the presence of* MRS PEARCE. *But as to* HIGGINS, *the only distinction he makes between men and women is that when he is neither bullying nor exclaiming to the heavens against some feather-weight cross,*[4] *he coaxes women as a child coaxes its nurse when it wants to get anything out of her.*

HIGGINS [*brusquely, recognizing her with unconcealed disappointment, and at once, babylike, making an intolerable grievance of it*] Why, this is the girl I jotted down last night. She's no use: I've got all the records I want of the Lisson Grove lingo; and I'm not going to waste another cylinder on it. [*To the* GIRL] Be off with you: I dont want you.

THE FLOWER GIRL. Dont you be so saucy. You aint heard what I come for yet. [*To* MRS PEARCE, *who is waiting at the door for further instructions*] Did you tell him I come in a taxi?

MRS PEARCE. Nonsense, girl! What do you think a gentleman like Mr Higgins cares 4
what you came in?

THE FLOWER GIRL. Oh, we are proud! He aint above giving lessons, not him: I heard him say so. Well, I aint come here to ask for any compliment; and if my money's not good enough I can go elsewhere.

HIGGINS. Good enough for what?

THE FLOWER GIRL. Good enough for yə-oo. Now you know, dont you? I've come to have lessons, I am. And to pay for em tə-oo: make no mistake.

HIGGINS [*stupent*[5]] Well!!! [*Recovering his breath with a gasp*] What do you expect me 5
to say to you?

THE FLOWER GIRL. Well, if you was a gentleman, you might ask me to sit down, I think. Dont I tell you I'm bringing you business?

---

4. feather-weight cross: A very minor inconvenience.
5. stupent: Astonished.

HIGGINS. Pickering: shall we ask this baggage to sit down, or shall we throw her out of the window?

THE FLOWER GIRL [*running away in terror to the piano, where she turns at bay*] Ah-ah-oh-ow-ow-ow-oo! [*Wounded and whimpering*] I wont be called a baggage when Ive offered to pay like any lady.

Motionless, the two men stare at her from the other side of the room, amazed.

PICKERING [*gently*] But what is it you want?

THE FLOWER GIRL. I want to be a lady in a flower shop stead of sellin at the corner of Tottenham Court Road. But they wont take me unless I can talk more genteel. He said he could teach me. Well, here I am ready to pay him—not asking any favor—and he treats me zif I was dirt.

MRS PEARCE. How can you be such a foolish ignorant girl as to think you could afford to pay Mr Higgins?

THE FLOWER GIRL. Why shouldnt I? I know what lessons cost as well as you do; and I'm ready to pay.

HIGGINS. How much?

THE FLOWER GIRL [*coming back to him, triumphant*] Now youre talking! I thought youd come off it when you saw a chance of getting back a bit of what you chucked at me last night. [*Confidentially*] Youd had a drop in,[6] hadn't you?

HIGGINS [*peremptorily*] Sit down.

THE FLOWER GIRL. Oh, if youre going to make a compliment of it—

6 **HIGGINS** [*thundering at her*] Sit down.

MRS PEARCE [*severely*] Sit down, girl. Do as youre told.

THE FLOWER GIRL. Ah-ah-ah-ow-ow-oo! [*She stands, half rebellious, half bewildered*].

6. **had a drop in:** Been drinking.

PICKERING [*very courteous*] Wont you sit down? [*He places the stray chair near the hearthrug between himself and* HIGGINS].

LIZA [*coyly*] Dont mind if I do. [*She sits down.* PICKERING *returns to the hearthrug*].

HIGGINS. Whats your name?

THE FLOWER GIRL. Liza Doolittle.

HIGGINS [*declaiming gravely*]
Eliza, Elizabeth, Betsy and Bess,
They went to the woods to get a bird's nes':

PICKERING. They found a nest with four eggs 7
in it:

HIGGINS. They took one apiece, and left three in it.

They laugh heartily at their own fun.

LIZA. Oh, dont be silly.

MRS PEARCE [*placing herself behind* ELIZA'*s chair*] You mustnt speak to the gentleman like that.

LIZA. Well, why wont he speak sensible to me?

HIGGINS. Come back to business. How much do you propose to pay me for the lessons?

LIZA. Oh, I know whats right. A lady friend of mine gets French lessons for eighteenpence an hour from a real French gentleman. Well, you wouldnt have the face to ask me the same for teaching me my own language as you would for French; so I wont give more than a shilling. Take it or leave it.

HIGGINS [*walking up and down the room, rattling his keys and his cash in his pockets*] You know, Pickering, if you consider a shilling, not as a simple shilling, but as a percentage of this girl's income, it works out as fully equivalent to sixty or seventy guineas from a millionaire.

PICKERING. How so?

HIGGINS. Figure it out. A millionaire has about £150 a day. She earns about half-a-crown.

6 **Critical Thinking and Reading** What inferences can be made about the relative status and class of these three characters?

7 **Reading Strategy** What is the meaning of this riddle?

1141

8 **Discussion** What is it about Eliza's offer that makes it suddenly attractive to Higgins?

9 **Discussion** What is the bet proposed by Pickering?

10 **Critical Thinking and Reading** What can you infer about the standards of cleanliness in Higgins's class and in Eliza's class?

11 **Reading Strategy** What is ironic about this statement?

12 **Critical Thinking and Reading** What can you infer about Higgins's past experience and philosophy of life from this statement?

LIZA [*haughtily*] Who told you I only—

8 HIGGINS [*continuing*] She offers me two-fifths of her day's income for a lesson. Two-fifths of a millionaire's income for a day would be somewhere about £60. It's handsome. By George, it's enormous! it's the biggest offer I ever had.

LIZA [*rising, terrified*] Sixty pounds! What are you talking? I never offered you sixty pounds. Where would I get—

HIGGINS. Hold your tongue.

LIZA [*weeping*] But I aint got sixty pounds. Oh—

MRS PEARCE. Dont cry, you silly girl. Sit down. Nobody is going to touch your money.

HIGGINS. Somebody is going to touch you, with a broomstick, if you dont stop snivelling. Sit down.

LIZA [*obeying slowly*] Ah-ah-ah-ow-oo-o! One would think you was my father.

HIGGINS. If I decide to teach you, I'll be worse than two fathers to you. Here [*he offers her his silk handkerchief*]!

LIZA. Whats this for?

HIGGINS. To wipe your eyes. To wipe any part of your face that feels moist. Remember: thats your handkerchief; and thats your sleeve. Dont mistake the one for the other if you wish to become a lady in a shop.

LIZA, *utterly bewildered, stares helplessly at him.*

MRS PEARCE. It's no use talking to her like that, Mr Higgins: she doesnt understand you. Besides, youre quite wrong: she doesnt do it that way at all [*she takes the handkerchief*].

LIZA [*snatching it*] Here! You give me that handkerchief. He gev it to me, not to you.

PICKERING [*laughing*] He did. I think it must be regarded as her property, Mrs Pearce.

MRS PEARCE [*resigning herself*] Serve you right, Mr Higgins.

9 PICKERING. Higgins: I'm interested. What about the ambassador's garden party? I'll say youre the greatest teacher alive if you make that good. I'll bet you all the expenses of the experiment you cant do it. And I'll pay for the lessons.

LIZA. Oh, you are real good. Thank you, Captain.

10 HIGGINS [*tempted, looking at her*] It's almost irresistible. She's so deliciously low—so horribly dirty—

LIZA [*protesting extremely*] Ah-ah-ah-ah-ow-ow-oo-oo!!! I aint dirty: I washed my face and hands afore I come, I did.

11 PICKERING. Youre certainly not going to turn her head with flattery, Higgins.

MRS PEARCE [*uneasy*] Oh, dont say that, sir: theres more ways than one of turning a girl's head; and nobody can do it better than Mr Higgins, though he may not always mean it. I do hope, sir, you wont encourage him to do anything foolish.

12 HIGGINS [*becoming excited as the idea grows on him*] What is life but a series of inspired follies? The difficulty is to find them to do. Never lose a chance: it doesnt come every day. I shall make a duchess of this draggle-tailed guttersnipe.

LIZA [*strongly deprecating this view of her*] Ah-ah-ah-ow-ow-oo!

HIGGINS [*carried away*] Yes: in six months—in three if she has a good ear and a quick tongue—I'll take her anywhere and pass her off as anything. We'll start today: now! this moment! Take her away and clean her, Mrs Pearce. Monkey Brand,[7] if it wont come off any other way. Is there a good fire in the kitchen?

MRS PEARCE [*protesting*] Yes; but—

HIGGINS [*storming on*] Take all her clothes off and burn them. Ring up Whitely or some-

7. Monkey Brand: A strong cleaning agent.

body for new ones. Wrap her up in brown paper til they come.

LIZA. Youre no gentleman, youre not, to talk of such things. I'm a good girl, I am; and I know what the like of you are, I do.

13 **HIGGINS.** We want none of your Lisson Grove prudery here, young woman. Youve got to learn to behave like a duchess. Take her away, Mrs Pearce. If she gives you any trouble, wallop her.

LIZA [*springing up and running between* PICKERING *and* MRS PEARCE *for protection*] No! I'll call the police, I will.

MRS PEARCE. But Ive no place to put her.

14 **HIGGINS.** Put her in the dustbin.

LIZA. Ah-ah-ah-ow-ow-oo!

PICKERING. O come, Higgins! be reasonable.

MRS PEARCE [*resolutely*] You must be reasonable, Mr Higgins: really you must. You cant walk over everybody like this.

HIGGINS, *thus scolded, subsides. The hurricane is succeeded by a zephyr of amiable surprise.*

15 **HIGGINS** [*with professional exquisiteness of modulation*] *I* walk over everybody! My dear Mrs Pearce, my dear Pickering, I never had the slightest intention of walking over anyone. All I propose is that we should be kind to this poor girl. We must help her to prepare and fit herself for her new station in life. If I did not express myself clearly it was because I did not wish to hurt her delicacy, or yours.

LIZA, *reassured, steals back to her chair.*

MRS PEARCE [*to* PICKERING] Well, did you ever hear anything like that, sir?

PICKERING [*laughing heartily*] Never, Mrs Pearce: never.

HIGGINS [*patiently*] Whats the matter?

MRS PEARCE. Well, the matter is, sir, that you cant take a girl up like that as if you were picking up a pebble on the beach.

HIGGINS. Why not?

MRS PEARCE. Why not! But you dont know anything about her. What about her parents? She may be married.

LIZA. Garn!

HIGGINS. There! As the girl very properly says, Garn! Married indeed! Dont you know that a woman of that class looks a worn out drudge of fifty a year after she's married?

LIZA. Whood marry me?

HIGGINS [*suddenly resorting to the most thrillingly beautiful low tones in his best elocutionary style*] By George, Eliza, the streets will be strewn with the bodies of men shooting themselves for your sake before Ive done with you.

MRS PEARCE. Nonsense, sir. You mustnt talk like that to her.

LIZA [*rising and squaring herself determinedly*] I'm going away. He's off his chump, he is. I dont want no balmies teaching me. 16

HIGGINS [*wounded in his tenderest point by her insensibility to his elocution*] Oh, indeed! I'm mad, am I? Very well, Mrs Pearce: you neednt order the new clothes for her. Throw her out.

LIZA [*whimpering*] Nah-ow. You got no right to touch me.

MRS PEARCE. You see now what comes of being saucy. [*Indicating the door*] This way, please.

LIZA [*almost in tears*] I didnt want no clothes. I wouldnt have taken them [*she throws away the handkerchief*]. I can buy my own clothes. 17

HIGGINS [*deftly retrieving the handkerchief and intercepting her on her reluctant way to the door*] Youre an ungrateful wicked girl. This is my return for offering to take you out of the gutter and dress you beautifully and make a lady of you.

13 **Reading Strategy** Discuss the irony in walloping a woman to turn her into a duchess.

14 **Clarification** A dustbin is the equivalent of a garbage can or trash barrel in the United States.

15 **Critical Thinking and Reading** What can you infer about Higgins and his own understanding of himself from this passage?

16 **Discussion** What do we learn about Eliza from this remark?

17 **Discussion** What admirable qualities has Eliza demonstrated thus far?

18 **Discussion** Why won't Higgins admit that Eliza has feelings? Do you think that he really does not perceive her as a human being?

19 **Discussion** Has Eliza made an accurate assessment of Higgins's character?

MRS PEARCE. Stop, Mr Higgins. I wont allow it. It's you that are wicked. Go home to your parents, girl; and tell them to take better care of you.

LIZA. I aint got no parents. They told me I was big enough to earn my own living and turned me out.

MRS PEARCE. Wheres your mother?

LIZA. I aint got no mother. Her that turned me out was my sixth stepmother. But I done without them. And I'm a good girl, I am.

HIGGINS. Very well, then, what on earth is all this fuss about? The girl doesnt belong to anybody—is no use to anybody but me. [*He goes to* MRS PEARCE *and begins coaxing*]. You can adopt her, Mrs Pearce: I'm sure a daughter would be a great amusement to you. Now don't make any more fuss. Take her downstairs; and—

MRS PEARCE. But whats to become of her? Is she to be paid anything? Do be sensible, sir.

HIGGINS. Oh, pay her whatever is necessary: put it down in the housekeeping book. [*Impatiently*] What on earth will she want with money? She'll have her food and her clothes. She'll only drink if you give her money.

LIZA [*turning on him*] Oh you are a brute. It's a lie: nobody ever saw the sign of liquor on me. [*To* PICKERING] Oh, sir: youre a gentleman: dont let him speak to me like that.

PICKERING [*in good-humored remonstrance*] Does it occur to you, Higgins, that the girl has some feelings?

HIGGINS [*looking critically at her*] Oh no, I dont think so. Not any feelings that we need bother about. [*Cheerily*] Have you, Eliza?

LIZA. I got my feelings same as anyone else.

HIGGINS [*to* PICKERING, *reflectively*] You see the difficulty?

PICKERING. Eh? What difficulty?

HIGGINS. To get her to talk grammar. The mere pronunciation is easy enough.

LIZA. I dont want to talk grammar. I want to talk like a lady in a flower-shop.

MRS PEARCE. Will you please keep to the point, Mr Higgins. I want to know on what terms the girl is to be here. Is she to have any wages? And what is to become of her when youve finished your teaching? You must look ahead a little.

HIGGINS [*impatiently*] Whats to become of her if I leave her in the gutter? Tell me that, Mrs Pearce.

MRS PEARCE. Thats her own business, not yours, Mr Higgins. 18

HIGGINS. Well, when Ive done with her, we can throw her back into the gutter; and then it will be her own business again; so thats all right.

LIZA. Oh, youve no feeling heart in you: you dont care for nothing but yourself. [*She rises and takes the floor resolutely*]. Here! 19
Ive had enough of this. I'm going [*making for the door*]. You ought to be ashamed of yourself, you ought.

HIGGINS [*snatching a chocolate cream from the piano, his eyes suddenly beginning to twinkle with mischief*] Have some chocolates, Eliza.

LIZA [*halting, tempted*] How do I know what might be in them? Ive heard of girls being drugged by the like of you.

HIGGINS *whips out his penknife; cuts a chocolate in two; puts one half into his mouth and bolts it; and offers her the other half.*

HIGGINS. Pledge of good faith, Eliza. I eat one half: you eat the other. [LIZA *opens her mouth to retort: he pops the half chocolate into it*]. You shall have boxes of them, barrels of them, every day. You shall live on them. Eh?

LIZA [*who has disposed of the chocolate after being nearly choked by it*] I wouldnt have ate it, only I'm too ladylike to take it out of my mouth.

HIGGINS. Listen, Eliza. I think you said you came in a taxi.

LIZA. Well, what if I did? Ive as good a right to take a taxi as anyone else.

HIGGINS. You have, Eliza; and in future you shall have as many taxis as you want. You shall go up and down and round the town in a taxi every day. Think of that, Eliza.

MRS PEARCE. Mr Higgins: youre tempting the
20 girl. It's not right. She should think of the
future.

HIGGINS. At her age! Nonsense! Time enough to think of the future when you havnt any future to think of. No, Eliza: do as this lady does: think of other people's futures; but never think of your own. Think of chocolates, and taxis, and gold, and diamonds.

LIZA. No: I dont want no gold and no diamonds. I'm a good girl, I am. [*She sits down* 21
again, with an attempt at dignity].

HIGGINS. You shall remain so, Eliza, under the care of Mrs Pearce. And you shall marry an officer in the Guards, with a beautiful moustache: the son of a marquis, who will disinherit him for marrying you, but will relent when he sees your beauty and goodness—

PICKERING. Excuse me, Higgins; but I really must interfere. Mrs Pearce is quite right. If this girl is to put herself in your hands for six months for an experiment in teaching, she must understand thoroughly what she's doing.

HIGGINS. How can she? She's incapable of understanding anything. Besides, do any of

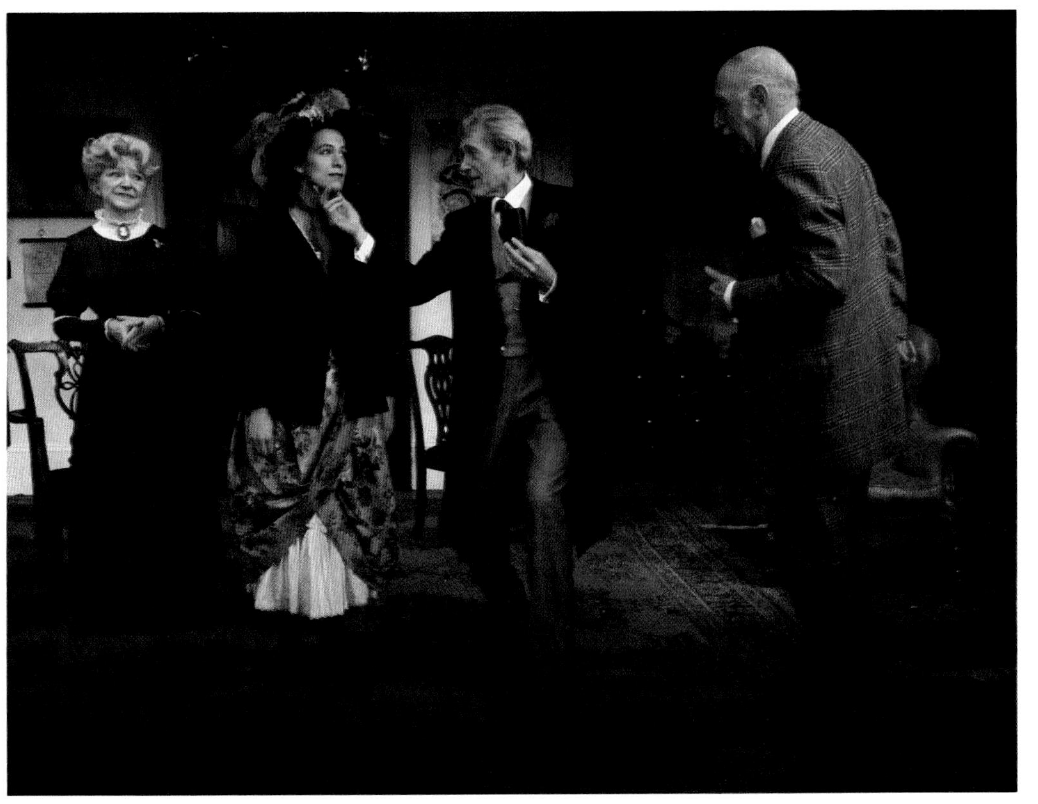

20 **Discussion** On whose side is Mrs. Pearce and why?

21 **Discussion** What does Eliza mean when she repeats, "I'm a good girl, I am"?

22 **Discussion** Is Higgins serious about his plans for Eliza? Explain.

us understand what we are doing? If we did, would we ever do it?

PICKERING. Very clever, Higgins; but not to the present point. [*To* ELIZA] Miss Doolittle—

LIZA [*overwhelmed*] Ah-ah-ow-oo!

22 **HIGGINS.** There! Thats all youll get out of Eliza. Ah-ah-ow-oo! No use explaining. As a military man you ought to know that. Give her her orders: thats enough for her. Eliza: you are to live here for the next six months, learning how to speak beautifully, like a lady in a florist's shop. If youre good and do whatever youre told, you shall sleep in a proper bedroom, and have lots to eat, and money to buy chocolates and take rides in taxis. If youre naughty and idle you will sleep in the back kitchen among the black beetles, and be walloped by Mrs Pearce with a broomstick. At the end of six months you shall go to Buckingham Palace in a carriage, beautifully dressed. If the King finds out youre not a lady, you will be taken by the police to the Tower of London, where your head will be cut off as a warning to other presumptuous flower girls. If you are not found out, you shall have a present of seven-and-sixpence to start life with as a lady in a shop. If you refuse this offer you will be a most ungrateful wicked girl; and the angels will weep for you. [*To* PICKERING] Now are you satisfied, Pickering? [*To* MRS PEARCE] Can I put it more plainly and fairly, Mrs Pearce?

MRS PEARCE [*patiently*] I think youd better let me speak to the girl properly in private. I dont know that I can take charge of her or consent to the arrangement at all. Of course I know you dont mean her any harm; but when you get what you call interested in people's accents, you never think or care what may happen to them or you. Come with me, Eliza.

HIGGINS. Thats all right. Thank you, Mrs Pearce. Bundle her off to the bath-room.

LIZA [*rising reluctantly and suspiciously*] Youre a great bully, you are. I wont stay here if I dont like. I wont let nobody wallop me. I never asked to go to Bucknam Palace, I didnt. I was never in trouble with the police, not me. I'm a good girl—

MRS PEARCE. Dont answer back, girl. You dont understand the gentleman. Come with me. [*She leads the way to the door, and holds it open for* ELIZA].

LIZA [*as she goes out*] Well, what I say is right. I wont go near the King, not if I'm going to have my head cut off. If I'd known what I was letting myself in for, I wouldnt have come here. I always been a good girl; and I never offered to say a word to him; and I dont owe him nothing; and I dont care; and I wont be put upon; and I have my feelings the same as anyone else—

MRS PEARCE *shuts the door; and* ELIZA*'s plaints are no longer audible.*

* * * * * *

Eliza is taken upstairs to the third floor greatly to her surprise; for she expected to be taken down to the scullery.[8] There Mrs Pearce opens a door and takes her into a spare bedroom.

MRS PEARCE. I will have to put you here. This will be your bedroom.

LIZA. O-h, I couldn't sleep here, missus. It's too good for the likes of me. I should be afraid to touch anything. I aint a duchess yet, you know.

MRS PEARCE. You have got to make yourself as clean as the room: then you wont be afraid of it. And you must call me Mrs Pearce, not missus. [*She throws open the door of the dressingroom, now modernized as a bath-room*].

LIZA. Gawd! whats this? Is this where you wash clothes? Funny sort of copper[9] I call it.

---

8. scullery *n.*: A room adjoining the kitchen, where pots and pans are cleaned and stored.
9. copper *n.*: A large metal container or boiler used for washing clothes.

MRS PEARCE. It is not a copper. This is where we wash ourselves, Eliza, and where I am going to wash you.

23 **LIZA.** You expect me to get into that and wet myself all over! Not me. I should catch my death. I knew a woman did it every Saturday night; and she died of it.

MRS PEARCE. Mr Higgins has the gentlemen's bathroom downstairs; and he has a bath every morning, in cold water.

LIZA. Ugh! He's made of iron, that man.

MRS PEARCE. If you are to sit with him and the Colonel and be taught you will have to do the same. They wont like the smell of you if you don't. But you can have the water as hot as you like. There are two taps: hot and cold.

LIZA [*weeping*] I couldnt. I dursnt. Its not natural: it would kill me. I've never had a bath in my life: not what youd call a proper one.

MRS PEARCE. Well, dont you want to be clean and sweet and decent, like a lady? You know you cant be a nice girl inside if youre a dirty slut outside.

LIZA. Boohoo!!!!

MRS PEARCE. Now stop crying and go back into your room and take off all your clothes. Then wrap yourself in this [*Taking down a gown from its peg and handing it to her*] and come back to me. I will get the bath ready.

LIZA [*all tears*] I cant. I wont. I'm not used to it. Ive never took off all my clothes before. It's not right: it's not decent.

MRS PEARCE. Nonsense, child. Dont you take off all your clothes every night when you go to bed?

LIZA [*amazed*] No. Why should I? I should catch my death. Of course I take off my skirt.

MRS PEARCE. Do you mean that you sleep in the underclothes you wear in the daytime?

LIZA. What else have I to sleep in?

MRS PEARCE. You will never do that again as long as you live here. I will get you a proper nightdress.

LIZA. Do you mean change into cold things and lie awake shivering half the night? You want to kill me, you do.

MRS PEARCE. I want to change you from a frowzy slut to a clean respectable girl fit to sit with the gentlemen in the study. Are you going to trust me and do what I tell you or be thrown out and sent back to your flower basket?

LIZA. But you dont know what the cold is to me. You dont know how I dread it.

MRS PEARCE. Your bed won't be cold here: I will put a hot water bottle in it. [*Pushing her into the bedroom*] Off with you and undress.

LIZA. Oh, if only I'd known what a dreadful thing it is to be clean I'd never have come. I didnt know when I was well off. I—[MRS PEARCE *pushes her through the door, but leaves it partly open lest her prisoner should take to flight*].

MRS PEARCE *puts on a pair of white rubber sleeves, and fills the bath, mixing hot and cold, and testing the result with the bath thermometer. She perfumes it with a handful of bath salts and adds a palmful of mustard. She then takes a formidable looking long handled scrubbing brush and soaps it profusely with a ball of scented soap.* 24

ELIZA *comes back with nothing on but the bath gown huddled tightly round her, a piteous spectacle of abject terror.*

MRS PEARCE. Now come along. Take that thing off.

LIZA. Oh I couldnt, Mrs Pearce: I reely couldnt. I never done such a thing.

MRS PEARCE. Nonsense. Here: step in and tell me whether its hot enough for you.

LIZA. Ah-oo! Ah-oo! It's too hot.

23 **Discussion** Why would this statement be valid to Eliza?

24 **Discussion** What surprising information does Eliza reveal about herself as she prepares for her bath? What does this information reveal about the living conditions of the people whom she represents?

25 Discussion Why does Higgins say he is a confirmed bachelor? What reason or reasons would you infer from his behavior?

MRS PEARCE [*deftly snatching the gown away and throwing* ELIZA *down on her back*]. It wont hurt you. [*She sets to work with the scrubbing brush*].

ELIZA*'s screams are heartrending.*

* * * * * *

Meanwhile the Colonel has been having it out with Higgins about Eliza. Pickering has come from the hearth to the chair and seated himself astride of it with his arms on the back to cross-examine him.

PICKERING. Excuse the straight question, Higgins. Are you a man of good character where women are concerned?

HIGGINS [*moodily*] Have you ever met a man of good character where women are concerned?

PICKERING. Yes: very frequently.

HIGGINS [*dogmatically, lifting himself on his hands to the level of the piano, and sitting on it with a bounce*] Well, I havnt. I find that the moment I let a woman make friends with me, she becomes jealous, exacting, suspicious, and a damned nuisance. I find that the moment I let myself make friends with a woman, I become selfish and tyrannical. Women upset everything. When you let them into your life, you find that the woman is driving at one thing and youre driving at another.

PICKERING. At what, for example?

HIGGINS [*coming off the piano restlessly*] Oh, Lord knows! I suppose the woman wants to live her own life; and the man wants to live his; and each tries to drag the other on to the
25 wrong track. One wants to go north and the other south; and the result is that both have to go east, though they both hate the east wind. [*He sits down on the bench at the keyboard*]. So here I am, a confirmed old bachelor, and likely to remain so.

PICKERING [*rising and standing over him gravely*] Come, Higgins! You know what I mean. If I'm to be in this business I shall feel responsible for that girl. I hope it's understood that no advantage is to be taken of her position.

HIGGINS. What! That thing! Sacred, I assure you. [*Rising to explain*] You see, she'll be a pupil; and teaching would be impossible unless pupils were sacred. Ive taught scores of American millionairesses how to speak English: the best looking women in the world. I'm seasoned. They might as well be blocks of wood. *I* might as well be a block of wood. It's—

MRS PEARCE *opens the door. She has* ELIZA*'s hat in her hand.* PICKERING *retires to the easy-chair at the hearth and sits down.*

HIGGINS [*eagerly*] Well, Mrs Pearce is it all right?

MRS PEARCE [*at the door*] I just wish to trouble you with a word, if I may, Mr. Higgins.

HIGGINS. Yes, certainly. Come in. [*She comes forward*]. Dont burn that, Mrs Pearce. I'll keep it as a curiosity. [*He takes the hat*].

MRS PEARCE. Handle it carefully, sir, please. I had to promise her not to burn it; but I had better put it in the oven for a while.

HIGGINS [*putting it down hastily on the piano*] Oh! thank you. Well, what have you to say to me?

PICKERING. Am I in the way?

MRS PEARCE. Not in the least, sir. Mr Higgins: will you please be very particular what you say before the girl?

HIGGINS [*sternly*] Of course. I'm always particular about what I say. Why do you say this to me?

MRS PEARCE [*unmoved*] No, sir: youre not at all particular when youve mislaid anything or when you get a little impatient. Now it doesnt matter before me: I'm used to it. But you really must not swear before the girl.

HIGGINS [*indignantly*] *I* swear! [*Most emphatically*] I never swear. I detest the habit. What the devil do you mean?

1148

MRS PEARCE [*stolidly*] Thats what I mean, sir. You swear a great deal too much. I dont mind your damning and blasting, and what the devil and where the devil and who the devil—

HIGGINS. Mrs Pearce: this language from your lips! Really!

MRS PEARCE [*not to be put off*]—but there is a certain word I must ask you not to use. The girl used it herself when she began to enjoy the bath. It begins with the same letter as bath. She knows no better: she learnt it at her mother's knee. But she must not hear it from your lips.

HIGGINS [*loftily*] I cannot charge myself with having ever uttered it, Mrs Pearce. [*She looks at him steadfastly. He adds, hiding an uneasy conscience with a judicial air*] Except perhaps in a moment of extreme and justifiable excitement.

26 **MRS PEARCE.** Only this morning, sir, you applied it to your boots, to the butter, and to the brown bread.

27 **HIGGINS.** Oh, that! Mere alliteration, Mrs Pearce, natural to a poet.

MRS PEARCE. Well, sir, whatever you choose to call it, I beg you not to let the girl hear you repeat it.

HIGGINS. Oh, very well, very well. Is that all?

MRS PEARCE. No, sir. We shall have to be very particular with this girl as to personal cleanliness.

HIGGINS. Certainly. Quite right. Most important.

MRS PEARCE. I mean not to be slovenly about her dress or untidy in leaving things about.

HIGGINS [*going to her solemnly*] Just so. I intended to call your attention to that. [*He passes on to* PICKERING, *who is enjoying the conversation immensely*]. It is these little things that matter, Pickering. Take care of the pence and the pounds will take care of themselves is as true of personal habits as of money. [*He comes to anchor on the hearthrug, with the air of a man in an unassailable position*].

MRS PEARCE. Yes, sir. Then might I ask you not to come down to breakfast in your dressing-gown, or at any rate not to use it as a napkin to the extent you do, sir. And if you would be so good as not to eat everything off the same plate, and to remember not to put the porridge saucepan out of your hand on the clean tablecloth, it would be a better example to the girl. You know you nearly choked yourself with a fishbone in a jam only last week. 28

HIGGINS [*routed from the hearthrug and drifting back to the piano*] I may do these things sometimes in absence of mind; but surely I dont do them habitually. [*Angrily*] By the way: my dressing-gown smells most damnably of benzine. 29

MRS PEARCE. No doubt it does, Mr Higgins. But if you will wipe your fingers—

HIGGINS [*yelling*] Oh very well, very well: I'll wipe them in my hair in future. 30

MRS PEARCE. I hope youre not offended, Mr Higgins.

HIGGINS [*shocked at finding himself thought capable of an unamiable sentiment*] Not at all, not at all. Youre quite right, Mrs Pearce: I shall be particularly careful before the girl. Is that all?

MRS PEARCE. No, sir. Might she use some of those Japanese dresses you brought from abroad? I really cant put her back into her old things.

HIGGINS. Certainly. Anything you like. Is that all?

MRS PEARCE. Thank you, sir. Thats all. [*She goes out*].

HIGGINS. You know, Pickering, that woman has the most extraordinary ideas about me. Here I am, a shy, diffident sort of man. I've never been able to feel really grown-up and 31

26 **Reading Strategy** What message does Mrs. Pearce wish to convey by using irony?

27 **Discussion** What is Higgins's rationalization for swearing when he finally admits that he does swear?

28 **Critical Thinking and Reading** What can you infer in this passage about how Mrs. Pearce feels about Higgins and about how he feels about her?

29 **Clarification** Benzine is a coal-tar based liquid that is used as a solvent and, in this case, as a cleaning fluid.

30 **Discussion** Is this practice in character for Higgins? If so, why? If not, why not?

31 **Discussion** Do you think Higgins believes what he is saying? Why or why not?

32 Discussion How does the saying "The best defense is a good offense" apply here?

33 Discussion How does Higgins catch Mr. Doolittle off guard?

tremendous, like other chaps. And yet she's firmly persuaded that I'm an arbitrary overbearing bossing kind of person. I cant account for it.

MRS PEARCE *returns.*

MRS PEARCE. If you please, sir, the trouble's beginning already. Theres a dustman[10] downstairs, Alfred Doolittle, wants to see you. He says you have his daughter here.

PICKERING [*rising*] Phew! I say!

HIGGINS [*promptly*] Send the blackguard[11] up.

MRS PEARCE. Oh, very well, sir. [*She goes out*].

PICKERING. He may not be a blackguard, Higgins.

HIGGINS. Nonsense. Of course he's a blackguard.

PICKERING. Whether he is or not, I'm afraid we shall have some trouble with him.

HIGGINS [*confidently*] Oh no: I think not. If theres any trouble he shall have it with me, not I with him. And we are sure to get something interesting out of him.

PICKERING. About the girl?

HIGGINS. No. I mean his dialect.

PICKERING. Oh!

MRS PEARCE [*at the door*] Doolittle, sir. [*She admits* DOOLITTLE *and retires*].

ALFRED *is an elderly but vigorous dustman, clad in the costume of his profession, including a hat with a back brim covering his neck and shoulders. He has well marked and rather interesting features, and seems equally free from fear and conscience. He has a remarkably expressive voice, the result of a habit of giving vent to his feelings without reserve. His present pose is that of wounded honor and stern resolution.*

DOOLITTLE [*at the door, uncertain which of the two gentlemen is his man*] Professor Iggins?

HIGGINS. Here. Good morning. Sit down.

DOOLITTLE. Morning, Governor. [*He sits down magisterially*]. I come about a very serious matter, Governor.

HIGGINS [*to* PICKERING] Brought up in Hounslow. Mother Welsh, I should think. [DOOLITTLE *opens his mouth, amazed.* HIGGINS *continues*] What do you want, Doolittle?

DOOLITTLE [*menacingly*] I want my daughter: thats what I want. See?

HIGGINS. Of course you do. Youre her father, arnt you? You dont suppose anyone else wants her, do you? I'm glad to see you have some spark of family feeling left. She's upstairs. Take her away at once. 32

DOOLITTLE [*rising, fearfully taken aback*] What!

HIGGINS. Take her away. Do you suppose I'm going to keep your daughter for you?

DOOLITTLE [*remonstrating*] Now, now, look here, Governor. Is it reasonable? Is it fairity to take advantage of a man like this? The girl belongs to me. You got her. Where do I come in? [*He sits down again*].

HIGGINS. Your daughter had the audacity to come to my house and ask me to teach her how to speak properly so that she could get a place in a flower-shop. This gentleman and my housekeeper have been here all the time. [*Bullying him*] How dare you come here and attempt to blackmail me? You sent her here on purpose.

DOOLITTLE [*protesting*] No, Governor.

HIGGINS. You must have. How else could you possibly know that she is here?

DOOLITTLE. Don't take a man up like that, Governor.

HIGGINS. The police shall take you up. This is 33
a plant—a plot to extort money by threats. I

---

10. dustman *n.*: A garbage collector.
11. blackguard (blag′ ərd) *n.*: Scoundrel.

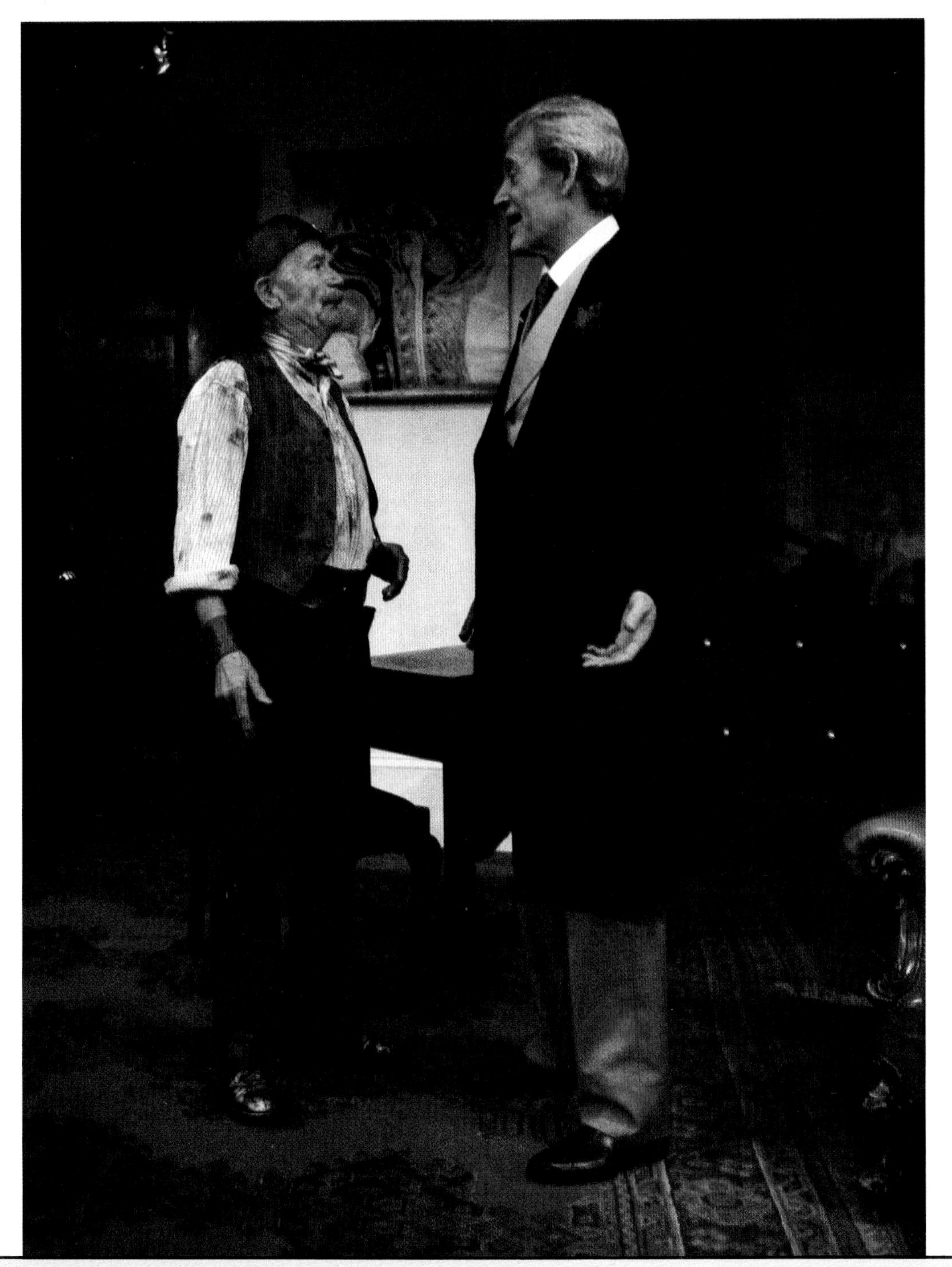

34 Discussion How does Higgins offend Pickering?

shall telephone for the police [*he goes resolutely to the telephone and opens the directory*]

DOOLITTLE. Have I asked you for a brass farthing? I leave it to the gentleman here: have I said a word about money?

HIGGINS [*throwing the book aside and marching down on* DOOLITTLE *with a poser*] What else did you come for?

DOOLITTLE [*sweetly*] Well, what would a man come for? Be human, Governor.

HIGGINS [*disarmed*] Alfred: did you put her up to it?

DOOLITTLE. So help me, Governor. I never did. I take my Bible oath I aint seen the girl these two months past.

HIGGINS. Then how did you know she was here?

DOOLITTLE [*"most musical, most melancholy"*] I'll tell you, Governor, if youll only let me get a word in. I'm willing to tell you. I'm wanting to tell you. I'm waiting to tell you.

34 **HIGGINS.** Pickering: this chap has a certain natural gift of rhetoric. Observe the rhythm of his native woodnotes wild. "I'm willing to tell you: I'm wanting to tell you: I'm waiting to tell you." Sentimental rhetoric! thats the Welsh strain in him. It also accounts for his mendacity and dishonesty.

PICKERING. Oh, please, Higgins: I'm west country myself. [*To* DOOLITTLE] How did you know the girl was here if you didnt send her?

DOOLITTLE. It was like this, Governor. The girl took a boy in the taxi to give him a jaunt. Son of her landlady, he is. He hung about on the chance of her giving him another ride home. Well, she sent him back for her luggage when she heard you was willing for her to stop here. I met the boy at the corner of Long Acre and Endell Street.

HIGGINS. Public house. Yes?

DOOLITTLE. The poor man's club, Governor: why shouldnt I?

PICKERING. Do let him tell his story, Higgins.

DOOLITTLE. He told me what was up. And I ask you, what was my feelings and my duty as a father? I says to the boy, "You bring me the luggage," I says—

PICKERING. Why didnt you go for it yourself?

DOOLITTLE. Landlady wouldnt have trusted me with it, Governor. She's that kind of woman: you know. I had to give the boy a penny afore he trusted me with it, the little swine. I brought it to her just to oblige you like, and make myself agreeable. Thats all.

HIGGINS. How much luggage?

DOOLITTLE. Musical instrument, Governor. A few pictures, a trifle of jewelry, and a bird-cage. She said she didn't want no clothes. What was I to think from that, Governor? I ask you as a parent what was I to think?

HIGGINS. So you came to rescue her from worse than death, eh?

DOOLITTLE [*appreciatively: relieved at being so well understood*] Just so, Governor. That's right.

PICKERING. But why did you bring her luggage if you intended to take her away?

DOOLITTLE. Have I said a word about taking her away? Have I now?

HIGGINS [*determinedly*] Youre going to take her away, double quick. [*He crosses to the hearth and rings the bell*].

DOOLITTLE [*rising*] No, Governor. Dont say that. I'm not the man to stand in my girl's light. Heres a career opening for her, as you might say; and—

MRS PEARCE *opens the door and awaits orders.*

HIGGINS. Mrs Pearce: this is Eliza's father. He has come to take her away. Give her to him. [*He goes back to the piano, with an air of* *washing his hands of the whole affair*].

DOOLITTLE. No. This is a misunderstanding. Listen here—

MRS PEARCE. He cant take her away. Mr Higgins: how can he? You told me to burn her clothes.

DOOLITTLE. Thats right. I cant carry the girl through the streets like a blooming monkey, can I? I put it to you.

HIGGINS. You have put it to me that you want your daughter. Take your daughter. If she has no clothes go out and buy her some.

DOOLITTLE [*desperate*] Wheres the clothes she come in? Did I burn them or did your missus here?

MRS PEARCE. I am the housekeeper, if you please. I have sent for some clothes for your girl. When they come you can take her away. You can wait in the kitchen. This way, please.

DOOLITTLE, *much troubled, accompanies her to the door; then hesitates; finally turns confidentially to* HIGGINS.

DOOLITTLE. Listen here, Governor. You and me is men of the world, aint we?

HIGGINS. Oh! Men of the world, are we? Youd better go, Mrs Pearce.

MRS PEARCE. I think so, indeed, sir. [*She goes, with dignity*].

PICKERING. The floor is yours, Mr Doolittle.

DOOLITTLE [*to* PICKERING] I thank you, Governor. [*To* HIGGINS, *who takes refuge on the piano bench, a little overwhelmed by the proximity of his visitor; for* DOOLITTLE *has a professional flavour of dust about him*]. Well, the truth is, I've taken a sort of fancy to you, Governor; and if you want the girl, I'm not so set on having her back home again but what I might be open to an arrangement. Regarded in the light of a young woman, she's a fine handsome girl. As a daughter she's not worth her keep; and so I tell you straight. All I ask is my rights as a father; and youre the last man alive to expect me to let her go for nothing; for I can see
youre one of the straight sort, Governor. 35
Well, whats a five-pound note to you? and whats Eliza to me? [*He turns to his chair and sits down judicially*].

PICKERING. I think you ought to know, Doolittle, that Mr Higgins's intentions are entirely honorable.

DOOLITTLE. Course they are, Governor. If I thought they wasnt, I'd ask fifty.

HIGGINS [*revolted*] Do you mean to say that you would sell your daughter for £50?

DOOLITTLE. Not in a general way I would; but to oblige a gentleman like you I'd do a good deal, I do assure you.

PICKERING. Have you no morals, man?

DOOLITTLE [*unabashed*] Cant afford them,
Governor. Neither could you if you was as 36
poor as me. Not that I mean any harm, you know. But if Liza is going to have a bit out of this, why not me too?

HIGGINS [*troubled*] I dont know what to do, Pickering. There can be no question that as a matter of morals it's a positive crime to give this chap a farthing. And yet I feel a sort of rough justice in his claim.

DOOLITTLE. Thats it, Governor. Thats all I say. A father's heart, as it were.

PICKERING. Well, I know the feeling; but really it seems hardly right—

DOOLITTLE. Dont say that, Governor. Dont look at it that way. What am I, Governors both? I ask you, what am I? I'm one of the undeserving poor: thats what I am. Think of
what that means to a man. It means that 37
he's up agen middle class morality all the time. If theres anything going, and I put in for a bit of it, it's always the same story: "Youre undeserving; so you cant have it." But my needs is as great as the most deserv-

35 Discussion What is Mr. Doolittle's real motivation for seeking his daughter?

36 Critical Thinking and Reading What can you infer about the lower class from this statement?

37 Literary Focus What is it about Mr. Doolittle that gives him the potential to be a dynamic character?

38 Discussion In your own words, what did "middle class morality" mean during the Victorian period?

39 Discussion How has your view of Mr. Doolittle changed since he was first introduced?

40 Discussion What advice does Mr. Doolittle give Pickering concerning Eliza?

41 Critical Thinking and Reading What can you infer about the place of women in Victorian society from this statement?

ing widows' that ever got money out of six different charities in one week for the death of the same husband. I dont need less than a deserving man: I need more. I dont eat less hearty than him; and I drink a lot more. I want a bit of amusement, cause I'm a thinking man. I want cheerfulness and a song and a band when I feel low. Well, they charge me just the same for everything as they
38 charge the deserving. What is middle class morality? Just an excuse for never giving me anything. Therefore, I ask you, as two gentlemen, not to play that game on me. I'm playing straight with you. I aint pretending to be deserving. I'm undeserving; and I mean to go on being undeserving. I like it; and thats the truth. Will you take advantage of a man's nature to do him out of the price of his own daughter what he's brought up and fed and clothed by the sweat of his brow until she's growed big enough to be interesting to you two gentlemen? Is five pounds unreasonable? I put it to you; and I leave it to you.

HIGGINS [*rising, and going over to* PICKERING] Pickering: if we were to take this man in hand for three months, he could choose between a seat in the Cabinet and a popular pulpit in Wales.

PICKERING. What do you say to that, Doolittle?

DOOLITTLE. Not me, Governor, thank you kindly. Ive heard all the preachers and all the prime ministers—for I'm a thinking man and game for politics or religion or social reform same as all the other amusements—and I tell you it's a dog's life any way you look at it. Undeserving poverty is my line. Taking one station in society with another, it's—it's—well, it's the only one that has any ginger in it, to my taste.

HIGGINS. I suppose we must give him a fiver.

PICKERING. He'll make a bad use of it, I'm afraid.

DOOLITTLE. Not me, Governor, so help me I wont. Dont you be afraid that I'll save it and spare it and live idle on it. There wont be a penny of it left by Monday: I'll have to go to work same as if I'd never had it. It wont pauperize me, you bet. Just one good spree for myself and the missus, giving pleasure to ourselves and employment to others, and satisfaction to you to think it's not been throwed away. You couldn't spend it better.

HIGGINS [*taking out his pocket book and coming between* DOOLITTLE *and the piano*] 39
This is irresistible. Lets give him ten. [*He offers two notes to the* DUSTMAN]

DOOLITTLE. No, Governor. She wouldnt have the heart to spend ten; and perhaps I shouldnt neither. Ten pounds is a lot of money: it makes a man feel prudent like; and then good-bye to happiness. You give me what I ask you, Governor: not a penny more, and not a penny less.

PICKERING. Why dont you marry that missus of yours? I rather draw the line at encouraging that sort of immorality.

DOOLITTLE. Tell her so, Governor: tell her so. *I'm* willing. It's me that suffers by it. Ive no hold on her. I got to be agreeable to her. I got to give her presents. I got to buy her clothes something sinful. I'm a slave to that woman, Governor, just because I'm not her lawful husband. And she knows it too. Catch her marrying me! Take my advice, Governor: marry Eliza while she's young and dont know no better. If you dont youll be sorry for
it after. If you do, she'll be sorry for it after; 41
but better her than you, because youre a man, and she's only a woman and dont know how to be happy anyhow.

HIGGINS. Pickering: if we listen to this man another minute, we shall have no convictions left. [*To* DOOLITTLE] Five pounds I think you said.

DOOLITTLE. Thank you kindly, Governor.

HIGGINS. Youre sure you wont take ten?

DOOLITTLE. Not now. Another time, Governor.

HIGGINS [*handing him a five-pound note*] Here you are.

DOOLITTLE. Thank you, Governor. Good morning. [*He hurries to the door, anxious to get away with his booty. When he opens it he is confronted with a dainty and exquisitely clean young Japanese lady in a simple blue cotton kimono printed cunningly with small white jasmine blossoms.* MRS PEARCE *is with her. He gets out of her way deferentially and apologizes*]. Beg pardon, miss.

THE JAPANESE LADY. Garn! Dont you know your own daughter?

DOOLITTLE	*exclaiming*	Bly me! it's Eliza!
HIGGINS	*simul-*	Whats that? This!
PICKERING	*taneously*	By Jove!

LIZA. Dont I look silly?

HIGGINS. Silly?

MRS PEARCE [*at the door*] Now, Mr Higgins, please dont say anything to make the girl conceited about herself.

HIGGINS [*conscientiously*] Oh! Quite right, Mrs Pearce. [*To* ELIZA] Yes: damned silly.

MRS PEARCE. Please, sir.

HIGGINS [*correcting himself*] I mean extremely silly.

LIZA. I should look all right with my hat on. [*She takes up her hat; puts it on; and walks across the room to the fireplace with a fashionable air*].

HIGGINS. A new fashion, by George! And it ought to look horrible!

DOOLITTLE [*with fatherly pride*] Well, I never thought she'd clean up as good looking as that, Governor. She's a credit to me, aint she?

42 **LIZA.** I tell you, it's easy to clean up here. Hot and cold water on tap, just as much as you like, there is. Woolly towels, there is; and a towel horse[12] so hot, it burns your fingers. Soft brushes to scrub yourself, and a wooden bowl of soap smelling like primroses. Now I know why ladies is so clean. Washing's a treat for them. Wish they could see what it is for the like of me!

HIGGINS. I'm glad the bathroom met with your approval.

LIZA. It didnt: not all of it; and I dont care who hears me say it. Mrs Pearce knows.

HIGGINS. What was wrong, Mrs Pearce?

MRS PEARCE [*blandly*] Oh, nothing, sir. It doesnt matter.

LIZA. I had a good mind to break it. I didnt know which way to look. But I hung a towel over it, I did.

HIGGINS. Over what?

MRS PEARCE. Over the looking-glass, sir.

HIGGINS. Doolittle: you have brought your daughter up too strictly.

DOOLITTLE. Me! I never brought her up at all, except to give her a lick of a strap now and again. Dont put it on me, Governor. She aint accustomed to it, you see: thats all. But she'll soon pick up your free-and-easy ways.

LIZA. I'm a good girl, I am; and I wont pick up no free-and-easy ways.

HIGGINS. Eliza: if you say again that youre a good girl, your father shall take you home.

LIZA. Not him. You dont know my father. All he come here for was to touch you for some money to get drunk on.

DOOLITTLE. Well, what else would I want money for? To put into the plate in church, I suppose. [*She puts out her tongue at him. He is so incensed by this that* PICKERING *presently finds it necessary to step between*

12. towel horse: Towel rack; in this case the rack is heated to dry the towels.

42 **Discussion** How has Eliza's attitude toward bathing changed now that she has taken a bath?

them]. Dont you give me none of your lip; and dont let me hear you giving this gentleman any of it neither, or youll hear from me about it. See?

HIGGINS. Have you any further advice to give her before you go, Doolittle? Your blessing, for instance.

DOOLITTLE. No, Governor: I aint such a mug as to put up my children to all I know myself. Hard enough to hold them in without that. If you want Eliza's mind improved, Governor, you do it yourself with a strap. So long, gentlemen. [*He turns to go*].

HIGGINS [*impressively*] Stop. Youll come regularly to see your daughter. It's your duty, you know. My brother is a clergyman; and he could help you in your talks with her.

DOOLITTLE [*evasively*] Certainly, I'll come, Governor. Not just this week, because I have a job at a distance. But later on you may depend on me. Afternoon, gentlemen. Afternoon, maam. [*He touches his hat to* MRS PEARCE, *who disdains the salutation and goes out. He winks at* HIGGINS, *thinking him probably a fellow-sufferer from* MRS PEARCE'*s difficult disposition, and follows her*].

LIZA. Dont you believe the old liar. He'd as soon you set a bulldog on him as a clergyman. You wont see him again in a hurry.

HIGGINS. I dont want to, Eliza. Do you?

LIZA. Not me. I dont want never to see him again, I dont. He's a disgrace to me, he is, collecting dust,[13] instead of working at his trade.

PICKERING. What is his trade, Eliza?

LIZA. Talking money out of other people's pockets into his own. His proper trade's a navvy;[14] and he works at it sometimes too—for exercise—and earns good money at it. Aint you going to call me Miss Doolittle any more?

PICKERING. I beg your pardon, Miss Doolittle. It was a slip of the tongue.

LIZA. Oh, I dont mind; only it sounded so genteel. I should just like to take a taxi to the corner of Tottenham Court Road and get out there and tell it to wait for me, just to put the girls in their place a bit. I wouldnt speak to them, you know.

PICKERING. Better wait til we get you something really fashionable.

HIGGINS. Besides, you shouldnt cut your old friends now that you have risen in the world. Thats what we call snobbery.

LIZA. You dont call the like of them my friends now, I should hope. Theyve took it out of me often enough with their ridicule when they had the chance; and now I mean to get a bit of my own back. But if I'm to have fashionable clothes, I'll wait. I should like to have some. Mrs Pearce says youre going to give me some to wear in bed at night different to what I wear in the daytime; but it do seem a waste of money when you could get something to shew. Besides, I never could fancy changing into cold things on a winter night.

13. collecting dust: Picking up garbage.
14. navvy (nav′ ē) *n.*: An unskilled laborer.

MRS PEARCE [*coming back*] Now, Eliza. The new things have come for you to try on.

LIZA. Ah-ow-oo-ooh! [*She rushes out*].

MRS PEARCE [*following her*] Oh, dont rush about like that, girl. [*She shuts the door behind her*].

HIGGINS. Pickering: we have taken on a stiff job.

PICKERING [*with conviction*] Higgins: we have.

* * * * * *

There seems to be some curiosity as to what Higgins's lessons to Eliza were like. Well, here is a sample: the first one.

Picture Eliza, in her new clothes, and feeling her inside put out of step by a lunch, dinner, and breakfast of a kind to which it is unaccustomed, seated with Higgins and the Colonel in the study, feeling like a hospital out-patient at a first encounter with the doctors.

Higgins, constitutionally unable to sit still, discomposes her still more by striding restlessly about. But for the reassuring presence and quietude of her friend the Colonel she would run for her life, even back to Drury Lane.

HIGGINS. Say your alphabet.

LIZA. I know my alphabet. Do you think I know nothing? I dont need to be taught like a child.

HIGGINS [*thundering*] Say your alphabet.

PICKERING. Say it, Miss Doolittle. You will understand presently. Do what he tells you; and let him teach you in his own way.

LIZA. Oh well, if you put it like that—Ahyee, bəyee, cəyee, dəyee—

HIGGINS [*with the roar of a wounded lion*] Stop. Listen to this, Pickering. This is what we pay for as elementary education. This unfortunate animal has been locked up for nine years in school at our expense to teach her to speak and read the language of

43 **Discussion** What keeps Eliza from giving up and leaving Higgins's house?

Shakespear and Milton. And the result is Ahyee, Bə-yee, Cə-yee, Dəyee. [*To* ELIZA] Say A, B, C, D.

LIZA [*almost in tears*] But I'm sayin it. Ahyee, Bəyee, Cəyee—

HIGGINS. Stop. Say a cup of tea.

LIZA. A cappətə-ee.

HIGGINS. Put your tongue forward until it squeezes against the top of your lower teeth. Now say cup.

LIZA. C-c-c—I cant. C-Cup.

PICKERING. Good. Splendid, Miss Doolittle.

HIGGINS. By Jupiter, she's done it the first shot. Pickering: we shall make a duchess of her. [*To* ELIZA] Now do you think you could possibly say tea? Not tə-yee, mind: if you ever say bə-yee cə-yee də-yee again you shall be dragged round the room three times by the hair of your head. [*Fortissimo*] T, T, T, T.

LIZA [*weeping*] I cant hear no difference cep that it sounds more genteel-like when you say it.

HIGGINS. Well, if you can hear the difference, what the devil are you crying for? Pickering: give her a chocolate.

PICKERING. No, no. Never mind crying a little, Miss Doolittle: you are doing very well; and the lessons wont hurt. I promise you I wont let him drag you round the room by your hair.

HIGGINS. Be off with you to Mrs Pearce and tell her about it. Think about it. Try to do it by yourself: and keep your tongue well forward in your mouth instead of trying to roll it up and swallow it. Another lesson at half-past four this afternoon. Away with you.

ELIZA, *still sobbing, rushes from the room.*

And that is the sort of ordeal Eliza has to go through for months before we meet her again on her first appearance in London society of the professional class.

THINKING ABOUT THE SELECTION

Recalling

1. (a) Why has Eliza come to see Higgins? (b) With what does she offer to pay him?
2. What are the terms of the bet Pickering proposes?
3. (a) What are Mrs. Pearce's concerns with regard to the arrangement? (b) What are Pickering's?
4. (a) What is the purpose of Alfred Doolittle's visit? (b) How does Higgins respond to his demands?

Interpreting

5. What differences between Higgins and Pickering are pointed out in Act II?
6. (a) What is revealed about the role of women of this era? (b) About middle-class and lower-class ideals?

Applying

7. (a) How does Higgins's treatment of Eliza strike you? (b) Do you think this was Shaw's intention? Explain.

ANALYZING LITERATURE

Understanding Character Development

Character development is the technique of adding depth to characters by causing them to grow by reacting to other characters and events. A static character is essentially unaltered by

Answers

ANSWERS TO THINKING ABOUT THE SELECTION

Recalling

1. (a) Eliza has come to ask Higgins to give her lessons in speaking so that she can speak like a lady and get a proper job in a flower shop. (b) She offers to pay daily with what is approximately half of what she makes in a day.
2. Pickering says that he will pay for all the expenses of having Eliza live at Higgins home and of teaching her if Eliza can pass as a fine lady at an ambassador's garden party.
3. (a) Mrs. Pearce is concerned about how the girl will fit into the household, what the girl's family will think, and then what will happen to the girl after she has finished her lessons. (b) Pickering is concerned about the girl's feelings and the fact that she must thoroughly understand what she is getting herself into.
4. (a) Mr. Doolittle, who says that he has come to get his daughter, has really come to see what monetary benefit he can receive for "allowing" his daughter to live in the Higgins household. (b) Higgins calls his bluff and tells him that he can take his daughter with him immediately.

involvements of plot, whereas a dynamic character is affected, sometimes radically. In order to observe changes in a character, we must have a clear idea of what qualities that character possesses in the first place.

Using at least five adjectives or descriptive phrases, profile each of the five characters appearing in Act II. Then tell which of the characters is static and which is dynamic, giving your reasons for your classifications.

CRITICAL THINKING AND READING

Making Inferences About Characters

Occasionally, in a literary work, we receive conflicting reports on a character's ambitions, motives, and thoughts. This is because, as in real life, a character's self-image often differs drastically from the image other characters hold of her or him. It is the responsibility of the alert reader to consider all information and then to *infer,* or assemble, from it an accurate picture of the character in question. Tell what impression the speaker of each of the following lines hopes to convey, and what impression he or she succeeds in conveying.

1. THE FLOWER GIRL. Did you tell him I come in a taxi? (page 1140)
2. HIGGINS. *I* walk over everybody! My dear Mrs Pearce, my dear Pickering, I never had the slightest intention of walking over anyone. (page 1143)
3. DOOLITTLE. I come about a very serious matter, Governor. (page 1150)

SPEAKING AND LISTENING

Reading Dialogue Aloud

Dialogue consists of lines that represent the actual speech utterances or conversations of the characters in a literary work. In a play, dialogue is everything. Ideally, dialogue should give the impression of actual conversation, not separate speeches. Shaw orchestrated his dialogue like music, varying tempo and intonation to emphasize the ideas and attitudes being expressed. Choose sections of Act II, assign roles, and stage an in-class reading. To make the dialogue as natural and lifelike as possible, readers should consider what they know about each character, including his or her speech habits.

THINKING AND WRITING

Comparing and Contrasting Characters

Using information you have accumulated about the characters thus far, write an essay that explores similarities and differences between any two of the characters in Act II. First select the characters and jot down notes about them. Then write your first draft, remembering to pay attention to underlying motives and stage directions in arriving at an understanding of each character. When you revise, make sure your essay is ordered logically and that you have supported your thesis with details from the play. Proofread your essay and prepare a final draft.

Interpreting

5. Even though Pickering is as single-minded about accomplishing the goal of getting Eliza to speak properly as Higgins is, he appears to be much more aware of the social graces—more genteel—and cares more about others and their feelings.
6. Suggested responses: (a) Women were expected to rely on their men to take care of them, and in turn, men looked on women as more or less their property. Because women were possessions, they could be treated in any way that men chose to treat them, including being beaten if they "needed it." (b) The lower class did what they had to in order to survive and to get some pleasure out of their lives. The middle class tried to maintain a sense of dignity and morality, in some ways emulating the upper class that they aspired to join.

(b) The lower class did what they had to in order to survive and to get some pleasure out of their lives. The middle class tried to maintain a sense of dignity and morality, in some ways emulating the upper class that they aspired to join.

Applying

7. (a) Answers will differ, though students should support their responses with reasons. (b) Answers will again differ. Students should

(Answers begin on p. 1158.)

cite specific aspects of the play to support their interpretations.

ANSWERS TO ANALYZING LITERATURE

Answers will differ. Encourage your students to tell which actions or speeches of characters they had in mind when they formed their views.

ANSWERS TO ANALYZING CRITICAL THINKING AND READING

Suggested responses:

1. Because Eliza equates riding in a taxi with being important, she wants to be certain that Higgins knows that she arrived at his door in a taxi. Higgins, to whom riding in a taxi is commonplace, doesn't care and, therefore, doesn't think any the better of her because she did.
2. Higgins is aghast to find out that anyone thinks that he "walks over anyone." To everyone else it is quite apparent that he does; to Higgins, that is the last thing that he would do.
3. Doolittle is trying to sound serious so that he will be taken seriously; he is not. Higgins will not be blackmailed, so Doolittle must tell him his true intent—to get some money for his own good times from his daughter's good fortune.

Challenge What inferences can you make from about the relationship between Higgins and Eliza in Act II that will help you predict how they will feel about each other by the end of the play?

SPEAKING AND LISTENING

Have students practice in groups before they present their readings to the class.

Writing Across the Curriculum In conjunction with the music department, you might have the students write a critique of the music from *My Fair Lady,* including an analysis of how well the music supported the story.

Literary Focus Shaw is a true satirist. A true satirist is one who is conscious of the fragility of man's institutions and through laughter attempts to improve them, not to tear them down.

Look For After students have decided on the target of Shaw's satire, have them keep a running accounting of statements that satirize that target.

Writing When students have completed this activity, have them read their work aloud to their groups, eliminating all direct references to the subject that they are satirizing. Have the rest of the group discuss the possibilities and guess the subject.

Vocabulary Most of these words have negative connotations. Have students find antonyms for each word, making certain that the antonyms have positive connotations.

GUIDE FOR READING

Pygmalion, Act III

The Writer's Technique

Satire. Satire is a technique that combines humor with criticism to expose flaws and shortcomings in institutions or human beings. Shaw, as an advocate of reform, saw in this brand of "serious comedy" an effective tool. "After all," he wrote, "the salvation of the world depends on the men who will not take evil good-humoredly, and whose laughter destroys the fool instead of encouraging him." The targets, methods, and styles of satire are many and varied. Unfair or outdated laws, pointless rules and regulations, prejudices and mindless conventions, illogical political policies, fads and styles—all have been held up to ridicule in poems, novels, essays, and plays. Today satire flourishes in such diverse media as film, television, cartoons, comic strips, and comedy acts, not to mention, of course, literature. Novels such as George Orwell's *Nineteen Eighty-four,* Evelyn Waugh's *The Loved One,* and Joseph Heller's *Catch-22,* all of them movies as well, satirize many aspects of twentieth-century life.

Look For

As you read Act III of *Pygmalion,* look for the target of Shaw's satire, as well as the balance of bitterness to comedy in his approach.

Writing

Brainstorm in small groups in an effort to come up with a list of styles and habits that you find especially laughable. Attempt to pinpoint the features of your subject that seem silly, unreasonable, or unfair.

Vocabulary

Knowing the following words will help you as you read Act III of *Pygmalion.*

pretension (pri ten′ shən) *n.*: Rank or class (p. 1161)
cynical (sin′ i k′l) *adj.*: Distrustful; sneering (p. 1166)
imprecations (im′ prə kā′ shənz) *n.*: Curses (p. 1167)
somnambulist (säm nam′ byoo list) *n.*: Sleepwalker (p. 1173)
morosely (mə rōs′ lē) *adv.*: Sullenly; in bad humor (p. 1173)
incorrigible (in kôr′ i jə b′l) *adj.*: Not capable of being corrected or of behaving better (p. 1174)

Objectives

1. To recognize satire
2. To compare and contrast attitudes
3. To understand slang
4. To evaluate the effectiveness of satire

Teaching Portfolio: Support Material

Teacher Backup, pp. 00-00

Vocabulary Check, p. 00

Usage and Mechanics Worksheet, p. 00

Analyzing Literature Worksheet, p. 00

Critical Thinking and Reading Worksheet, p. 00

Language Worksheet, p. 00

Selection Test, p. 00

ACT III

It is MRS HIGGINS'*s at-home day.*[1] *Nobody has yet arrived. Her drawing room, in a flat on Chelsea Embankment, has three windows looking on the river; and the ceiling is not so lofty as it would be in an older house of the same pretension. The windows are open, giving access to a balcony with flowers in pots. If you stand with your face to the windows, you have the fireplace on your left and the door in the right-hand wall close to the corner nearest the windows.*

MRS HIGGINS *was brought up on Morris*[2] *and Burne Jones;*[3] *and her room, which is very unlike her son's room in Wimpole Street, is not crowded with furniture and little tables and nicknacks. In the middle of the room there is a big ottoman; and this, with the carpet, the Morris wall-papers, and the Morris chintz window curtains and brocade covers of the ottoman and its cushions, supply all the ornament, and are much too handsome to be hidden by odds and ends of useless things. A few good oil-paintings from the exhibitions in the Grosvenor Gallery thirty years ago (the Burne Jones, not the Whistler*[4] *side of them) are on the walls. The only landscape is a Cecil Lawson*[5] *on the scale of a Rubens.*[6] *There is a portrait of* MRS HIGGINS *as*
1 *she was when she defied the fashion in her youth in one of the beautiful Rossettian*[7] *costumes which, when caricatured by people who did not understand, led to the absurdities of popular estheticism in the eighteen-seventies.*

In the corner diagonally opposite the door MRS HIGGINS, *now over sixty and long past taking the trouble to dress out of the fashion, sits writing at an elegantly simple writing-table with a bell button within reach of her hand. There is a Chippendale chair further back in the room between her and the window nearest her side. At the other side of the room, further forward, is an Elizabethan chair roughly carved in the taste of Inigo Jones.*[8] *On the same side a piano in a decorated case. The corner between the fireplace and the window is occupied by a divan cushioned in Morris chintz.*

It is between four and five in the afternoon.

The door is opened violently; and HIGGINS *enters with his hat on.*

MRS HIGGINS [*dismayed*] Henry! [*Scolding him*] What are you doing here today? It is my at-home day: you promised not to come. [*As* 2 *he bends to kiss her, she takes his hat off, and presents it to him*].

HIGGINS. Oh bother! [*He throws the hat down on the table*].

MRS HIGGINS. Go home at once.

HIGGINS [*kissing her*] I know, mother. I came on purpose.

MRS HIGGINS. But you mustnt. I'm serious, Henry. You offend all my friends: they stop coming whenever they meet you.

HIGGINS. Nonsense! I know I have no small talk; but people dont mind. [*He sits on the settee*]. 3

MRS HIGGINS. Oh! dont they? Small talk indeed! What about your large talk? Really, dear, you mustnt stay.

---

1. at-home day: The day of the week when a lady regularly receives visitors.
2. Morris: William Morris (1834–1896), English poet, artist, and craftsman.
3. Burne Jones: Sir Edward Corley Burne-Jones (1833–1898), English painter and designer.
4. Whistler: James Abbott McNeill Whistler (1834–1903), an American painter who lived in England.
5. Cecil Lawson: Cecil Gordon Lawson (1851–1882), English landscape painter.
6. Rubens: Peter Paul Rubens (1577–1640), a Flemish painter famous for his large paintings.
7. Rossettian: Referring to Dante Gabriel Rossetti (1828–1882), English poet and painter.

8. Inigo Jones: English architect and stage designer (1573–1652).

Motivation for Reading Have students think of a time that they felt out of place at a party, uncomfortable either because they either did not know anyone, because they were dressed incorrectly, or because they did not know how to act. How did they react to the situation? How did those around them seem to react? Relate their responses to Eliza's situation at Mrs. Higgins's at-home day.

Master Teacher Note There are two types of satire—Horatian, which is gentle, urbane, and smiling, and Juvenalian, which is bitter, biting, and angry. Discuss the type that Shaw uses and why.

Thematic Idea One of the themes in Shakespeare's *The Tempest* concerns who is superior —"nurtured" man or natural man. In *Pygmalion,* there is a variation on that theme. Who is superior —upper class ("nurtured") man or lower class (natural) man?

Purpose-Setting Question What is the target of the satire in Act III?

1 **Clarification** In the late nineteenth century, there was a movement to bring art into life. This principle became an affectation that produced the absurdities mentioned here.

2 **Enrichment** The "at home" ritual was very elaborate, made up of such things as leaving calling cards with butlers, wearing white gloves, making polite conversation or gossiping, and delicately sipping tea. Those who participated kept rigorous account of whom they were obligated to visit and of who was obligated to visit them.

3 **Critical Thinking and Reading** Compare and contrast the Higginses' attitudes toward small talk and phonetics.

4 **Critical Thinking and Reading** Compare and contrast the Higginses' attitudes about love.

5 **Master Teacher Note** The spelling of *kerbstone* is indicative of some of the differences between British and American English. Discuss the British spellings of *favour, colour,* and *theatre* and the American words for such British words as *lift* (elevator), *bonnet* (car hood), *boot* (car trunk), *pram* (baby carriage), *mince* (hamburger), and so forth.

HIGGINS. I must. Ive a job for you. A phonetic job.

MRS HIGGINS. No use, dear. I'm sorry; but I cant get round your vowels; and though I like to get pretty postcards in your patent shorthand, I always have to read the copies in ordinary writing you so thoughtfully send me.

HIGGINS. Well, this isn't a phonetic job.

MRS HIGGINS. You said it was.

HIGGINS. Not your part of it. Ive picked up a girl.

MRS HIGGINS. Does that mean that some girl has picked you up?

HIGGINS. Not at all. I dont mean a love affair.

MRS HIGGINS. What a pity!

HIGGINS. Why?

MRS HIGGINS. Well, you never fall in love with anyone under forty-five. When will you discover that there are some rather nice-looking young women about?

HIGGINS. Oh, I cant be bothered with young women. My idea of a lovable woman is some-
4 body as like you as possible. I shall never get into the way of seriously liking young women: some habits lie too deep to be changed. [*Rising abruptly and walking about, jingling his money and his keys in his trouser pockets*] Besides, theyre all idiots.

MRS HIGGINS. Do you know what you would do if you really loved me, Henry?

HIGGINS. Oh bother! What? Marry, I suppose.

MRS HIGGINS. No. Stop fidgeting and take your hands out of your pockets. [*With a gesture of despair, he obeys and sits down again*]. Thats a good boy. Now tell me about the girl.

HIGGINS. She's coming to see you.

MRS HIGGINS. I dont remember asking her.

HIGGINS. You didn't. *I* asked her. If youd known her you wouldnt have asked her.

MRS HIGGINS. Indeed! Why?

HIGGINS. Well, it's like this. She's a common flower girl. I picked her off the kerbstone. 5

MRS HIGGINS. And invited her to my at-home!

HIGGINS [*rising and coming to her to coax her*] Oh, thatll be all right. Ive taught her to speak properly; and she has strict orders as to her behavior. She's to keep to two subjects: the weather and everybody's health—Fine day and How do you do, you know—and not to let herself go on things in general. That will be safe.

MRS HIGGINS. Safe! To talk about our health! about our insides! perhaps about our outsides! How could you be so silly, Henry?

HIGGINS [*impatiently*] Well, she must talk about something. [*He controls himself and sits down again*]. Oh, she'll be all right: dont you fuss. Pickering is in it with me. Ive a sort of bet on that I'll pass her off as a duchess in six months. I started on her some months ago; and she's getting on like a house on fire. I shall win my bet. She has a quick ear; and she's easier to teach than my middle-class pupils because she's had to learn a complete new language. She talks English almost as you talk French.

MRS HIGGINS. Thats satisfactory, at all events.

HIGGINS. Well, it is and it isnt.

MRS HIGGINS. What does that mean?

HIGGINS. You see, Ive got her pronunciation all right; but you have to consider not only how a girl pronounces, but what she pronounces; and that's where—

They are interrupted by the PARLORMAID, *announcing guests.*

THE PARLORMAID. Mrs and Miss Eynsford Hill. [*She withdraws*].

HIGGINS. Oh Lord! [*He rises; snatches his hat from the table; and makes for the door; but before he reaches it his mother introduces him*].

Mrs and Miss Eynsford Hill are the mother and daughter who sheltered from the rain in Covent Garden. The mother is well bred, quiet, and has the habitual anxiety of straitened means. The daughter has acquired a gay air of being very much at home in society: the bravado of genteel poverty.

MRS EYNSFORD HILL [*to* MRS HIGGINS] How do you do? [*They shake hands*].

MISS EYNSFORD HILL. How d'you do? [*She shakes*].

MRS HIGGINS [*introducing*] My son Henry.

MRS EYNSFORD HILL. Your celebrated son! I have so longed to meet you, Professor Higgins.

HIGGINS [*glumly, making no movement in her direction*] Delighted. [*He backs against the piano and bows brusquely*].

MISS EYNSFORD HILL [*going to him with confident familiarity*] How do you do?

HIGGINS [*staring at her*] Ive seen you before somewhere. I havnt the ghost of a notion where; but Ive heard your voice. [*Drearily*] It doesnt matter. Youd better sit down.

6 **MRS HIGGINS.** I'm sorry to say that my celebrated son has no manners. You mustnt mind him.

MISS EYNSFORD HILL [*gaily*] I dont. [*She sits in the Elizabethan chair*].

MRS EYNSFORD HILL [*a little bewildered*] Not at all. [*She sits on the ottoman between her daughter and* MRS HIGGINS, *who has turned her chair away from the writing-table*].

HIGGINS. Oh, have I been rude? I didnt mean to be.

He goes to the central window, through which, with his back to the company, he contemplates the river and the flowers in Battersea Park on the opposite bank as if they were a frozen desert.

The PARLORMAID *returns, ushering in* PICKERING.

THE PARLORMAID. Colonel Pickering. [*She withdraws*].

PICKERING. How do you do, Mrs Higgins?

MRS HIGGINS. So glad youve come. Do you know Mrs Eynsford Hill—Miss Eynsford Hill? [*Exchange of bows. The* COLONEL *brings the Chippendale chair a little forward between* MRS HILL *and* MRS HIGGINS, *and sits down*].

PICKERING. Has Henry told you what weve come for?

HIGGINS. [*over his shoulder*] We were interrupted: damn it!

MRS HIGGINS. Oh, Henry, Henry, really!

MRS EYNSFORD HILL [*half rising*] Are we in the way?

MRS HIGGINS [*rising and making her sit down again*] No, no. You couldnt have come more fortunately: we want you to meet a friend of ours.

HIGGINS [*turning hopefully*] Yes, by George! We want two or three people. You'll do as well as anybody else.

The PARLORMAID *returns, ushering* FREDDY.

THE PARLORMAID. Mr Eynsford Hill.

HIGGINS [*almost audibly, past endurance*] God of Heaven! another of them.

FREDDY [*shaking hands with* MRS HIGGINS] Ahdedo?

MRS HIGGINS. Very good of you to come. [*Introducing*] Colonel Pickering.

FREDDY [*bowing*] Ahdedo?

MRS HIGGINS. I don't think you know my son, Professor Higgins.

FREDDY [*going to* HIGGINS] Ahdedo? 7

HIGGINS [*looking at him much as if he were a pickpocket*] I'll take my oath Ive met you before somewhere. Where was it?

6 **Literary Focus** What about Higgins's manner lets you know that Shaw is going to treat this scene satirically?

7 **Discussion** How does Henry feel about the Eynsford Hills, individually and collectively?

1164

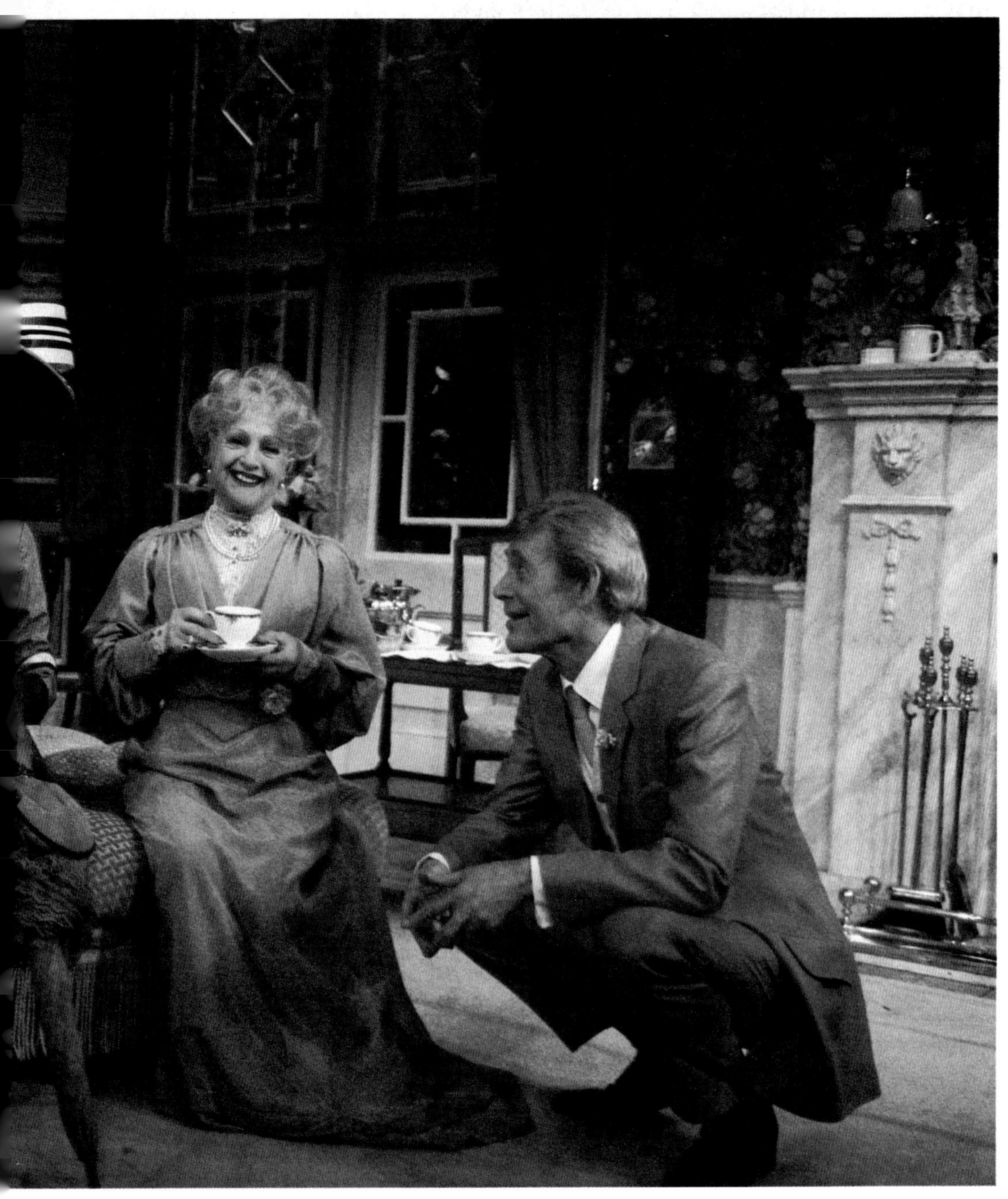

8 **Thematic Idea** Compare and contrast Shakespeare's feelings about civilized and natural man, as represented in *The Tempest,* with Shaw's as shown in this speech.

FREDDY. I dont think so.

HIGGINS [*resignedly*] It dont matter, anyhow. Sit down.

He shakes FREDDY*'s hand, and almost slings him on to the ottoman with his face to the window; then comes round to the other side of it.*

HIGGINS. Well, here we are, anyhow! [*He sits down on the ottoman next* MRS EYNSFORD HILL, *on her left*] And now, what the devil are we going to talk about until Eliza comes?

MRS HIGGINS. Henry: you are the life and soul of the Royal Society's soirées;[9] but really youre rather trying on more commonplace occasions.

HIGGINS. Am I? Very sorry. [*Beaming suddenly*] I suppose I am, you know. [*Uproariously*] Ha, ha!

MISS EYNSFORD HILL [*who considers* HIGGINS *quite eligible matrimonially*] I sympathize. *I* havnt any small talk. If people would only be frank and say what they really think!

HIGGINS [*relapsing into gloom*] Lord forbid!

MRS EYNSFORD HILL [*taking up her daughter's cue*] But why?

HIGGINS. What they think they ought to think is bad enough, Lord knows; but what they really think would break up the whole show. Do you suppose it would be really agreeable if I were to come out now with what *I* really think?

MISS EYNSFORD HILL [*gaily*] Is it so very cynical?

HIGGINS. Cynical! Who the dickens said it was cynical? I mean it wouldnt be decent.

MRS EYNSFORD HILL [*seriously*] Oh! I'm sure you dont mean that, Mr Higgins.

HIGGINS. You see, we're all savages, more or less. We're supposed to be civilized and cultured—to know all about poetry and philosophy and art and science, and so on; but how many of us know even the meanings of these names? [*To* MISS HILL] What do you know of poetry? [*To* MRS HILL] What do you know of science? [*Indicating* FREDDY] What does he know of art or science or anything else? What the devil do you imagine I know of philosophy? 8

MRS HIGGINS [*warningly*] Or of manners, Henry?

THE PARLORMAID [*opening the door*] Miss Doolittle. [*She withdraws*].

HIGGINS [*rising hastily and running to* MRS HIGGINS] Here she is, mother. [*He stands on tiptoe and makes signs over his mother's head to* ELIZA *to indicate to her which lady is her hostess*].

ELIZA, *who is exquisitely dressed, produces an impression of such remarkable distinction and beauty as she enters that they all rise, quite fluttered. Guided by* HIGGINS*'s signals, she comes to* MRS HIGGINS *with studied grace.*

LIZA [*speaking with pedantic correctness of pronunciation and great beauty of tone*] How do you do, Mrs Higgins? [*She gasps slightly in making sure of the H in Higgins, but is quite successful*]. Mr Higgins told me I might come.

MRS HIGGINS [*cordially*] Quite right: I'm very glad indeed to see you.

PICKERING. How do you do, Miss Doolittle?

LIZA [*shaking hands with him*] Colonel Pickering, is it not?

MRS EYNSFORD HILL. I feel sure we have met before, Miss Doolittle. I remember your eyes.

LIZA. How do you do? [*She sits down on the ottoman gracefully in the place just left vacant by* HIGGINS].

MRS EYNSFORD HILL [*introducing*] My daughter Clara.

9. soirées (swä räz′) *n.*: Parties held in the evening.

LIZA. How do you do?

9 CLARA *[impulsively]* How do you do? *[She sits down on the ottoman beside* ELIZA, *devouring her with her eyes]*.

FREDDY *[coming to their side of the ottoman]* Ive certainly had the pleasure.

MRS EYNSFORD HILL *[introducing]* My son Freddy.

LIZA. How do you do?

FREDDY *bows and sits down in the Elizabethan chair, infatuated.*

HIGGINS *[suddenly]* By George, yes: it all comes back to me! *[They stare at him]*. Covent Garden! *[Lamentably]* What a damned thing!

MRS HIGGINS. Henry, please! *[He is about to sit on the edge of the table]* Dont sit on my writing-table: youll break it.

HIGGINS *[sulkily]* Sorry.

10 *He goes to the divan, stumbling into the fender and over the fire-irons on his way; extricating himself with muttered imprecations; and finishing his disastrous journey by throwing himself so impatiently on the divan that he almost breaks it.* MRS HIGGINS *looks at him, but controls herself and says nothing.*

A long and painful pause ensues.

MRS HIGGINS *[at last, conversationally]* Will it rain, do you think?

LIZA. The shallow depression in the west of these islands is likely to move slowly in an easterly direction. There are no indications of any great change in the barometrical situation.

FREDDY. Ha! ha! how awfully funny!

LIZA. What is wrong with that, young man? I bet I got it right.

FREDDY. Killing!

MRS EYNSFORD HILL. I'm sure I hope it wont turn cold. Theres so much influenza about. It runs right through our whole family regularly every spring.

LIZA *[darkly]* My aunt died of influenza: so they said.

MRS EYNSFORD HILL *[clicks her tongue sympathetically]*!!!

LIZA *[in the same tragic tone]* But it's my belief they done the old woman in.

MRS HIGGINS *[puzzled]* Done her in?

LIZA. Y-e-e-e-es, Lord love you! Why should she die of influenza? She come through diphtheria right enough the year before. I saw her with my own eyes. Fairly blue with it, she was. They all thought she was dead; but my father he kept ladling gin down her throat til she came to so sudden that she bit the bowl off the spoon.

MRS EYNSFORD HILL *[startled]* Dear me!

LIZA *[piling up the indictment]* What call would a woman with that strength in her have to die of influenza? What become of her new straw hat that should have come to me? Somebody pinched it; and what I say is, them as pinched it done her in.

MRS EYNSFORD HILL. What does doing her in mean?

HIGGINS *[hastily]* Oh, thats the new small talk. To do a person in means to kill them.

MRS EYNSFORD HILL *[to* ELIZA, *horrified]* You surely dont believe that your aunt was killed?

LIZA. Do I not! Them she lived with would have killed her for a hat-pin, let alone a hat.

MRS EYNSFORD HILL. But it cant have been right for your father to pour spirits down her throat like that. It might have killed her.

LIZA. Not her. Gin was mother's milk to her. Besides, he'd poured so much down his own throat that he knew the good of it. 11

MRS EYNSFORD HILL. Do you mean that he drank?

9 Discussion What do you learn about Clara's character in this speech?

10 Reading Strategy What is the irony between Higgins's image of himself and the display that he puts on here?

11 Discussion Although Eliza's pronunciation might be perfect, what does she lack in her conversation with the Eynsford Hills?

1167

12 Discussion What does it show about the Eynsford Hills when they are so cordially responsive to Eliza's "small talk"? What is the author making fun of here?

LIZA. Drank! My word! Something chronic.

MRS EYNSFORD HILL. How dreadful for you!

LIZA. Not a bit. It never did him no harm what I could see. But then he did not keep it up regular. [*Cheerfully*] On the burst, as you might say, from time to time. And always more agreeable when he had a drop in. When he was out of work, my mother used to give him fourpence and tell him to go out and not come back until he'd drunk himself
12 cheerful and loving-like. Theres lots of women has to make their husbands drunk to make them fit to live with. [*Now quite at her ease*] You see, it's like this. If a man has a bit of conscience, it always takes him when he's sober; and then it makes him low-spirited. A drop of booze just takes that off and makes him happy. [*To* FREDDY, *who is in convulsions of suppressed laughter*] Here! what are you sniggering at?

FREDDY. The new small talk. You do it so awfully well.

LIZA. If I was doing it proper, what was you laughing at? [*To* HIGGINS] Have I said anything I oughtnt?

MRS HIGGINS [*interposing*] Not at all, Miss Doolittle.

LIZA. Well, thats a mercy, anyhow. [*Expansively*] What I always say is—

HIGGINS [*rising and looking at his watch*] Ahem!

LIZA [*looking round at him; taking the hint; and rising*] Well: I must go. [*They all rise.* FREDDY *goes to the door*]. So pleased to have met you. Goodbye. [*She shakes hands with* MRS HIGGINS].

MRS HIGGINS. Goodbye.

LIZA. Goodbye, Colonel Pickering.

PICKERING. Goodbye, Miss Doolittle. [*They shake hands*].

LIZA [*nodding to the others*] Goodbye, all.

FREDDY [*opening the door for her*] Are you walking across the Park, Miss Doolittle? If so—

LIZA [*with perfectly elegant diction*] Walk! Not bloody likely. [*Sensation*]. I am going in a taxi. [*She goes out*].

PICKERING *gasps and sits down.* FREDDY *goes out on the balcony to catch another glimpse of* ELIZA.

MRS EYNSFORD HILL [*suffering from shock*] Well, I really cant get used to the new ways.

CLARA [*throwing herself discontentedly into the Elizabethan chair*] Oh, it's all right, mamma, quite right. People will think we never go anywhere or see anybody if you are so old-fashioned.

MRS EYNSFORD HILL. I daresay I am very old-fashioned; but I do hope you wont begin using that expression, Clara. I have got accustomed to hear you talking about men as rotters, and calling everything filthy and beastly; though I do think it horrible and unladylike. But this last is really too much. Dont you think so, Colonel Pickering?

PICKERING. Dont ask me. Ive been away in India for several years; and manners have changed so much that I sometimes dont know whether I'm at a respectable dinner-table or in a ship's forecastle.

CLARA. It's all a matter of habit. Theres no right or wrong in it. Nobody means anything by it. And it's so quaint, and gives such a smart emphasis to things that are not in themselves very witty. I find the new small talk delightful and quite innocent.

MRS EYNSFORD HILL [*rising*] Well, after that, I think it's time for us to go.

PICKERING *and* HIGGINS *rise.*

CLARA [*rising*] Oh yes: we have three at-homes to go to still. Goodbye, Mrs Higgins. Goodbye, Colonel Pickering. Goodbye, Professor Higgins.

13 **HIGGINS** [*coming grimly at her from the divan, and accompanying her to the door*] Goodbye. Be sure you try on that small talk at the three at-homes. Dont be nervous about it. Pitch it in strong.

CLARA [*all smiles*] I will. Goodbye. Such nonsense, all this early Victorian prudery!

HIGGINS [*tempting her*] Such damned nonsense!

CLARA. Such bloody nonsense!

MRS EYNSFORD HILL [*convulsively*] Clara!

CLARA. Ha! Ha! [*She goes out radiant, conscious of being thoroughly up to date, and is heard descending the stairs in a stream of silvery laughter*].

FREDDY [*to the heavens at large*] Well, I ask you— [*He gives it up, and comes to* MRS HIGGINS]. Goodbye.

MRS HIGGINS [*shaking hands*] Goodbye. Would you like to meet Miss Doolittle again?

FREDDY [*eagerly*] Yes, I should, most awfully.

MRS HIGGINS. Well, you know my days.

FREDDY. Yes. Thanks awfully. Goodbye. [*He goes out*].

MRS EYNSFORD HILL. Goodbye, Mr Higgins.

HIGGINS. Goodbye. Goodbye.

MRS EYNSFORD HILL [*to* PICKERING] It's no use. I shall never be able to bring myself to use that word.

PICKERING. Dont. It's not compulsory, you know. Youll get on quite well without it.

MRS EYNSFORD HILL. Only, Clara is so down on me if I am not positively reeking with the latest slang. Goodbye.

PICKERING. Goodbye [*They shake hands*].

MRS EYNSFORD HILL. [*to* MRS HIGGINS] You mustnt mind Clara. [PICKERING, *catching from her lowered tone that this is not meant for him to hear, discreetly joins* HIGGINS *at the window*]. We're so poor! and she gets so few parties, poor child! She doesn't quite know. [MRS HIGGINS, *seeing that her eyes are moist, takes her hand sympathetically and goes with her to the door*]. But the boy is nice. Dont you think so?

MRS HIGGINS. Oh, quite nice. I shall always be delighted to see him.

MRS EYNSFORD HILL. Thank you, dear. Goodbye. [*She goes out*].

HIGGINS [*eagerly*] Well? Is Eliza presentable [*he swoops on his mother and drags her to the ottoman, where she sits down in* ELIZA'*s place with her son on her left*]?

PICKERING *returns to his chair on her right.*

MRS HIGGINS. You silly boy, of course she's not presentable. She's a triumph of your art and of her dressmaker's; but if you suppose for a moment that she doesn't give herself away in every sentence she utters, you must be perfectly cracked about her.

PICKERING. But dont you think something might be done? I mean something to eliminate the sanguinary[10] element from her conversation. 14

MRS HIGGINS. Not as long as she is in Henry's hands.

HIGGINS [*aggrieved*] Do you mean that my language is improper?

MRS HIGGINS. No, dearest: it would be quite proper—say on a canal barge; but it would not be proper for her at a garden party.

HIGGINS [*deeply injured*] Well I must say—

PICKERING [*interrupting him*] Come, Higgins: you must learn to know yourself. I havnt heard such language as yours since we used to review the volunteers in Hyde Park twenty years ago.

HIGGINS [*sulkily*] Oh, well, if you say so, I suppose I dont always talk like a bishop.

---

10. sanguinary (saŋ′ gwi ner′ ē) *adj.*: Bloody.

13 **Discussion** What is Higgins's motive in encouraging Clara to use the new small talk during her other three visits?

14 **Reading Strategy** What is the intended play on words in this speech? To what is it referring?

15 Discussion What does Higgins reveal about his feelings for Eliza?

16 Discussion Why does Mrs. Pearce end all conversations about Eliza with "You don't think, sir"?

17 Discussion What is Higgins overlooking in this metamorphosis of Eliza?

MRS HIGGINS [*quieting* HENRY *with a touch*] Colonel Pickering: will you tell me what is the exact state of things in Wimpole Street?

PICKERING [*cheerfully: as if this completely changed the subject*] Well, I have come to live there with Henry. We work together at my Indian Dialects; and we think it more convenient—

MRS HIGGINS. Quite so. I know all about that: it's an excellent arrangement. But where does this girl live?

HIGGINS. With us, of course. Where should she live?

MRS HIGGINS. But on what terms? Is she a servant? If not, what is she?

PICKERING [*slowly*] I think I know what you mean, Mrs Higgins.

HIGGINS. Well, dash me if *I* do! Ive had to work
15 at the girl every day for months to get her to her present pitch. Besides, she's useful. She knows where my things are, and remembers my appointments and so forth.

MRS HIGGINS. How does your housekeeper get on with her?

HIGGINS. Mrs Pearce? Oh, she's jolly glad to get so much taken off her hands; for before Eliza came, she used to have to find things and remind me of my appointments. But she's got some silly bee in her bonnet about Eliza. She keeps saying "You dont think, sir": doesn't she, Pick?

PICKERING. Yes: thats the formula. "You dont
16 think, sir." Thats the end of every conversation about Eliza.

HIGGINS. As if I ever stop thinking about the girl and her confounded vowels and consonants. I'm worn out, thinking about her, and watching her lips and her teeth and her tongue, not to mention her soul, which is the quaintest of the lot.

MRS HIGGINS. You certainly are a pretty pair of babies, playing with your live doll.

HIGGINS. Playing! The hardest job I ever tackled: make no mistake about that, mother. But you have no idea how frightfully interesting it is to take a human being and change her into a quite different human being by creating a new speech for her. It's filling up the deepest gulf that separates class from class and soul from soul.

PICKERING [*drawing his chair closer to* MRS HIGGINS *and bending over to her eagerly*] Yes: it's enormously interesting. I assure you, Mrs Higgins, we take Eliza very seriously. Every week—every day almost—there is some new change. [*Closer again*] We keep records of every stage—dozens of gramophone disks and photographs—

HIGGINS [*assailing her at the other ear*] Yes, by George: it's the most absorbing experiment I ever tackled. She regularly fills our lives up: doesn't she, Pick?

PICKERING. We're always talking Eliza.

HIGGINS. Teaching Eliza.

PICKERING. Dressing Eliza.

MRS HIGGINS. What!

HIGGINS. Inventing new Elizas.

HIGGINS.	(*speaking together*)	You know, she has the most extraordinary quickness of ear:
PICKERING.		I assure you, my dear Mrs Higgins, that girl
HIGGINS.		just like a parrot. Ive tried her with every
PICKERING.		is a genius. She can play the piano quite beautifully.
HIGGINS.		possible sort of sound that a human being can make—
PICKERING.		We have taken her to classical concerts and to music
HIGGINS.		Continental dialects, African dialects, Hottentot

PICKERING. (*speaking together*) halls; and it's all the same to her: she plays everything

HIGGINS. clicks, things it took me years to get hold of; and

PICKERING. she hears right off when she comes home, whether it's

HIGGINS. she picks them up like a shot, right away, as if she had

PICKERING. Beethoven and Brahms or Lehar, and Lionel Monckton;

HIGGINS. been at it all her life.

PICKERING. though six months ago, she'd never as much as touched a piano—

MRS HIGGINS [*putting her fingers in her ears, as they are by this time shouting one another down with an intolerable noise*] Sh-sh-sh—sh! [*They stop*].

PICKERING. I beg your pardon. [*He draws his chair back apologetically*].

HIGGINS. Sorry. When Pickering starts shouting nobody can get a word in edgeways.

MRS HIGGINS. Be quiet, Henry. Colonel Pickering: dont you realize that when Eliza walked in Wimpole Street, something walked in with her?

PICKERING. Her father did. But Henry soon got rid of him.

MRS HIGGINS. It would have been more to the point if her mother had. But as her mother didnt something else did.

PICKERING. But what?

MRS HIGGINS. (*unconsciously dating herself by the word*) A problem.

PICKERING. Oh, I see. The problem of how to pass her off as a lady.

HIGGINS. I'll solve that problem. Ive half solved it already.

MRS HIGGINS. No, you two infinitely stupid male creatures: the problem of what is to be done with her afterwards.

HIGGINS. I dont see anything in that. She can go her own way, with all the advantages I have given her.

MRS HIGGINS. The advantages of that poor woman who was here just now! The manners and habits that disqualify a fine lady 19
from earning her own living without giving her a fine lady's income! Is that what you mean?

PICKERING. [*Indulgently, being rather bored*] Oh, that will be all right, Mrs Higgins. [*He rises to go*].

HIGGINS. [*Rising also*] We'll find her some light employment.

PICKERING. She's happy enough. Dont you worry about her. Goodbye. [*He shakes hands as if he were consoling a frightened child, and makes for the door*].

HIGGINS. Anyhow, theres no good bothering now. The thing's done. Goodbye, mother. [*He kisses her, and follows* PICKERING].

PICKERING [*turning for a final consolation*] There are plenty of openings. We'll do whats right. Goodbye.

HIGGINS [*to Pickering as they go out together*] Lets take her to the Shakespear exhibition at Earls Court.

PICKERING. Yes: lets. Her remarks will be delicious.

HIGGINS. She'll mimic all the people for us when we get home. 20

PICKERING. Ripping. [*Both are heard laughing as they go downstairs*].

MRS HIGGINS [*rises with an impatient bounce, and returns to her work at the writing-table. She sweeps a litter of disarranged papers out of the way; snatches a*

18 **Discussion** What dawns on Higgins and Pickering during this exchange?

19 **Discussion** What future problem regarding Eliza does Mrs. Higgins warn her son about?

20 **Discussion** Besides an experiment in phonetics, what has Eliza become to both men?

21 Reading Strategy Predict what this speech may foreshadow.

22 Enrichment *Cockney* can refer to the London working-class dialect or to anyone from London's working class, but it is more specifically anyone in the working class born within the sound of Bow Bells, which are in a church tower in the heart of London.

sheet of paper from her stationery case; and tries resolutely to write. At the third time she gives it up; flings down her pen; grips the table angrily and exclaims] Oh, men! men!! men!!!

* * * * * *

Clearly Eliza will not pass as a duchess yet; and Higgins's bet remains unwon. But the six months are not yet exhausted and just in time Eliza does actually pass as a princess. For a glimpse of how she did it imagine an Embassy in London one summer evening after dark. The hall door has an awning and a carpet across the sidewalk to the kerb, because a grand reception is in progress. A small crowd is lined up to see the guests arrive.

A Rolls-Royce car drives up. Pickering in evening dress, with medals and orders, alights, and hands out Eliza, in opera cloak, evening dress, diamonds, fan, flowers and all accessories. Higgins follows. The car drives off; and the three go up the steps and into the house, the door opening for them as they approach.

Inside the house they find themselves in a spacious hall from which the grand staircase rises. On the left are the arrangements for the gentlemen's cloaks. The male guests are depositing their hats and wraps there.

On the right is a door leading to the ladies' cloakroom. Ladies are going in cloaked and coming out in splendor. Pickering whispers to Eliza and points out the ladies' room. She goes into it. HIggins and Pickering take off their overcoats and take tickets for them from the attendant.

One of the guests, occupied in the same way, has his back turned. Having taken his ticket, he turns round and reveals himself as an important looking young man with an astonishingly hairy face. He has an enormous moustache, flowing out into luxuriant whiskers. Waves of hair cluster on his brow. His hair is cropped closely at the back, and glows with oil. Otherwise he is very smart. He wears several worthless orders. He is evidently a foreigner, guessable as a whiskered Pandour[11] from Hungary; but in spite of the ferocity of his moustache he is amiable and genially voluble.

Recognizing Higgins, he flings his arms wide apart and approaches him enthusiastically.

WHISKERS. Maestro, maestro. [*He embraces* HIGGINS *and kisses him on both cheeks*]. You remember me?

HIGGINS. No I dont. Who the devil are you?

WHISKERS. I am your pupil: your first pupil, your best and greatest pupil. I am little Nepommuck, the marvellous boy. I have made your name famous throughout Europe. You teach me phonetic. You cannot forget ME.

HIGGINS. Why dont you shave?

NEPOMMUCK. I have not your imposing appearance, your chin, your brow. Nobody notice me when I shave. Now I am famous: they call me Hairy Faced Dick.

HIGGINS. And what are you doing here among all these swells?

NEPOMMUCK. I am interpreter. I speak 32 languages. I am indispensable at these international parties. You are great cockney specialist: you place a man anywhere in London the moment he open his mouth. I place any man in Europe. 21, 22

A FOOTMAN *hurries down the grand staircase and comes to* NEPOMMUCK.

FOOTMAN. You are wanted upstairs. Her Excellency cannot understand the Greek gentleman.

NEPOMMUCK. Thank you, yes, immediately.

The FOOTMAN *goes and is lost in the crowd.*

NEPOMMUCK [*to* HIGGINS] This Greek diplomatist pretends he cannot speak nor understand English. He cannot deceive me. He is the son of a Clerkenwell watchmaker. He

11. Pandour: A bodyguard or servant of Hungarian nobles.

speaks English so villainously that he dare not utter a word of it without betraying his origin. I help him to pretend; but I make him pay through the nose. I make them all pay. Ha ha! [*He hurries upstairs*].

PICKERING. Is this fellow really an expert? Can he find out Eliza and blackmail her?

HIGGINS. We shall see. If he finds her out I lose my bet.

ELIZA *comes from the cloakroom and joins them.*

PICKERING. Well, Eliza, now for it. Are you ready?

LIZA. Are you nervous, Colonel?

PICKERING. Frightfully. I feel exactly as I felt before my first battle. It's the first time that frightens.

LIZA. It is not the first time for me, Colonel. I have done this fifty times—hundreds of times—in my little piggery in Angel Court in my day-dreams. I am in a dream now. Promise me not to let Professor Higgins wake me; for if he does I shall forget everything and talk as I used to in Drury Lane.

PICKERING. Not a word, Higgins. [*To* ELIZA] Now, ready?

LIZA. Ready.

PICKERING. Go.

They mount the stairs, HIGGINS *last.* PICKERING *whispers to the* FOOTMAN *on the first landing.*

FIRST LANDING FOOTMAN. Miss Doolittle, Colonel Pickering, Professor Higgins.

SECOND LANDING FOOTMAN. Miss Doolittle, Colonel Pickering, Professor Higgins.

At the top of the staircase the AMBASSADOR *and his* WIFE, *with* NEPOMMUCK *at her elbow, are receiving.*

HOSTESS [*taking* ELIZA*'s hand*] How d'ye do?

HOST [*same play*] How d'ye do? How d'ye do, Pickering?

LIZA [*with a beautiful gravity that awes her hostess*] How do you do? [*She passes on to the drawingroom*].

HOSTESS. Is that your adopted daughter, Colonel Pickering? She will make a sensation.

PICKERING. Most kind of you to invite her for me. [*He passes on*].

HOSTESS [*to* NEPOMMUCK] Find out all about her.

NEPOMMUCK [*bowing*] Excellency—[*he goes into the crowd*].

HOST. How d'ye do, Higgins? You have a rival here tonight. He introduced himself as your pupil. Is he any good?

HIGGINS. He can learn a language in a fortnight—knows dozens of them. A sure mark of a fool. As a phonetician, no good whatever.

HOSTESS. How d'ye do, Professor?

HIGGINS. How do you do? Fearful bore for you this sort of thing. Forgive my part in it. [*He passes on*]. 23

In the drawing room and its suite of salons the reception is in full swing. Eliza passes through. She is so intent on her ordeal that she walks like a somnambulist in a desert instead of a débutante in a fashionable crowd. They stop talking to look at her, admiring her dress, her jewels, and her strangely attractive self. Some of the younger ones at the back stand on their chairs to see.

The Host and Hostess come in from the staircase and mingle with their guests. Higgins, gloomy and contemptuous of the whole business, comes into the group where they are chatting.

HOSTESS. Ah, here is Professor Higgins: he will tell us. Tell us all about the wonderful young lady, Professor.

HIGGINS [*almost morosely*] What wonderful young lady?

HOSTESS. You know very well. They tell me there has been nothing like her in London since people stood on their chairs to look at

23 **Discussion** How do you think the hostess would react to this comment, when Higgins was out of the range of her voice?

24 Reading Strategy Explain the irony in Nepommuck's verdict that Eliza is a fraud.

Mrs Langtry.[12]

NEPOMMUCK *joins the group, full of news.*

HOSTESS. Ah, here you are at last, Nepommuck. Have you found out all about the Doolittle lady?

NEPOMMUCK. I have found out all about her. She is a fraud.

HOSTESS. A fraud! Oh no.

NEPOMMUCK. YES, yes. She cannot deceive me. Her name cannot be Doolittle.

HIGGINS. Why?

NEPOMMUCK. Because Doolittle is an English name. And she is not English.

HOSTESS. Oh, nonsense! She speaks English perfectly.

NEPOMMUCK. Too perfectly. Can you shew me any English woman who speaks English as it should be spoken? Only foreigners who have been taught to speak it speak it well.

24 **HOSTESS.** Certainly she terrified me by the way she said How d'ye do. I had a schoolmistress who talked like that; and I was mortally afraid of her. But if she is not English what is she?

NEPOMMUCK. Hungarian.

ALL THE REST. Hungarian!

NEPOMMUCK. Hungarian. And of royal blood. I am Hungarian. My blood is royal.

HIGGINS. Did you speak to her in Hungarian?

NEPOMMUCK. I did. She was very clever. She said "Please speak to me in English: I do not understand French." French! She pretend not to know the difference between Hungarian and French. Impossible: she knows both.

HIGGINS. And the blood royal? How did you find that out?

NEPOMMUCK. Instinct, maestro, instinct. Only the Magyar races can produce that air of the divine right, those resolute eyes. She is a princess.

HOST. What do you say, Professor?

HIGGINS. I say an ordinary London girl out of the gutter and taught to speak by an expert. I place her in Drury Lane.

NEPOMMUCK. Ha ha ha! Oh, maestro, maestro, you are mad on the subject of cockney dialects. The London gutter is the whole world for you.

HIGGINS [*to the* HOSTESS] What does your Excellency say?

HOSTESS. Oh, of course I agree with Nepommuck. She must be a princess at least.

HOST. Not necessarily legitimate, of course. Morganatic[13] perhaps. But that is undoubtedly her class.

HIGGINS. I stick to my opinion.

HOSTESS. Oh, you are incorrigible.

The group breaks up, leaving HIGGINS *isolated.* PICKERING *joins him.*

PICKERING. Where is Eliza? We must keep an eye on her.

ELIZA *joins them.*

LIZA. I don't think I can bear much more. The people all stare so at me. An old lady has just told me that I speak exactly like Queen Victoria. I am sorry if I have lost your bet. I have done my best; but nothing can make me the same as these people.

PICKERING. You have not lost it, my dear. You have won it ten times over.

HIGGINS. Let us get out of this. I have had enough of chattering to these fools.

PICKERING. Eliza is tired; and I am hungry. Let us clear out and have supper somewhere.

---

12. Mrs. Langtry: Lily Langtry (1852–1929), a beautiful English actress.

13. Morganatic (môr′ gə nat′ ik) *adj.*: Referring to a form of marriage in which a person of royalty or nobility marries a spouse of inferior social status. While such a marriage is considered valid, children produced by it do not inherit titles.

Answers

ANSWERS TO THINKING ABOUT THE SELECTION

1. Mrs. Higgins is upset because she is "at home" that day, and Higgins always offended her friends by refusing to engage in small talk.
2. Eliza is told to talk about the weather and everybody's health.
3. Higgins tells them that Eliza is using the "new small talk," which makes them feel very much behind the times.
4. Nepommuck declares that Eliza is Hungarian of royal, albeit, illegitimate birth.
5. Higgins wins the bet: Eliza passes as a duchess.

Interpreting

6. (a) Eliza goes on at great length about the ill health and eventual death of her gin-guzzling aunt. (b) Nepommuck considers himself an authority on phonetics, Higgins's star pupil. The fact that he is so loud in his pronouncements and so far wrong about Eliza makes Higgins's victory even sweeter.
7. (a) Even though Eliza has been able to fool everyone at the ball, she knows that she is not one of them, and she is well aware that if they knew the truth about her she would not be accepted on any level. (b) He may be suggesting her humble self-knowledge as well as her acute awareness of class differences.

Applying

8. Answers will differ. Such a custom is not generally found in our society.

ANSWERS TO ANALYZING LITERATURE

1. Shaw satirizes the need to make small talk when Eliza discusses the weather and her aunt's influenza in shocking terms, and Higgins tells everyone that she is just being fashionable by using the "new small talk."
2. Shaw satirizes the "at home" custom by having Higgins barge in, unannounced, and tell his mother that he has invited a flower girl of questionable origin to be his mother's guest.
3. Eliza's visit to Mrs. Higgins and her

THINKING ABOUT THE SELECTION

Recalling

1. Why is Mrs. Higgins upset when her son arrives at her house?
2. To what two "safe" topics is Eliza limited?
3. How does Higgins explain Eliza's language to the Eynsford Hills?
4. Who does Nepommuck declare Eliza to be?
5. Explain the outcome of Pickering's bet with Higgins.

Interpreting

6. (a) What humor arises out of Higgins's telling Eliza to limit her conversation to two topics? (b) Out of Nepommuck's "investigation" of Eliza?
7. At the end of the embassy ball Eliza comments that "nothing can make me the same as these people." (a) What do you suppose to be her state of mind as she utters this comment? Why? (b) What is Shaw suggesting about Eliza through this comment?

Applying

8. What parallels to an "at-home day," if any, can you find in modern American social customs? Explain the similarities and point out any differences.

ANALYZING LITERATURE

Using Satire

Satire is a technique that unites comedy and criticism to ridicule an offensive behavior or institution. The targets of satire, since its origins in ancient Greek and Roman drama, have included unjust or overly harsh laws, mindless social customs, and shallow trends. In Act III of *Pygmalion,* Shaw aims his satiric arrows at several customs and foibles of his day that continue to exist in our own. These include

1. the need (of some) to make small talk,
2. proper social etiquette,
3. the effort to pass oneself off as someone one is not.

Locate and describe the places in the act where Shaw pokes fun at each of these human failings.

CRITICAL THINKING AND READING

Comparing and Contrasting Attitudes

In Act III of *Pygmalion,* the characters express a variety of attitudes on a number of topics. Compare and contrast the following characters' views on the topics mentioned, and tell how you believe each of the characters came by those views.

1. Good manners: Higgins, Mrs. Higgins.
2. Love: Higgins, Mrs. Higgins, Freddy.
3. Slang: Mrs. Eynsford Hill, her daughter.
4. The fate of Eliza: Mrs. Higgins, Higgins, Pickering.
5. Formal dress affairs: Eliza, Higgins, Pickering.

UNDERSTANDING LANGUAGE

Understanding Slang

Slang is language used and understood by members of a particular group or culture. Unlike words from the standard language, which change very slowly over long periods of time, slang terms are literally "in" one year, "out" the next. Give the meaning of the following slang terms from Act III. Note any slang used by your own culture—modern-day high school students—to convey the same idea.

1. *Done her in?* (page 1167)
2. Somebody *pinched* it. (page 1167)
3. *On the burst,* as you might say. (page 1168)
4. [And always more agreeable] when he *had a drop in.* (page 1168)

THINKING AND WRITING

Evaluating the Effectiveness of Satire

Satire is a difficult form of comedy to write. A well-conceived satire will neither be so light as to lack punch nor so biting as to lack humor. In a short essay, explain whether or not you find the humor and criticism of Shaw's satire in Act III well-balanced. To get yourself started, answer questions such as the following. What is funny and why? What is being criticized? How clear are Shaw's intentions? When you revise, make sure you have included examples from Act III to back up your theses.

(Answers begin on p. 1174.)

appearance at the ball are both examples of people attempting to be what they are not. The Eynsford Hills are a more subtle example of the same; they are hanging on desperately to the appearance that they belong in the upper class.

ANSWERS TO CRITICAL THINKING AND READING

1. Mrs. Higgins would have been a young woman during the most intensely Victorian years in England, and she was of the class that practiced all the polite customs with precision. Possibly because of her very strict adherence to the rules of etiquette, her son Henry would have nothing to do with them as an adult. He could not be bothered to perform as society would want him to and enjoyed making those who did follow the rules look foolish.
2. Higgins saw love as something that would stand in the way of his doing what he wanted to do, probably because he had grown up not having to do anything for anyone but himself. Mrs. Higgins desperately wanted Henry to find love, probably because she had felt loved by Henry's father and because society demanded that men of Henry's age be married. Freddy sought love because he needed someone to lean on; his mother always let him know how incompetent he was, and he had not learned to rely on himself.
3. Mrs. Eynsford Hill found what she thought was the new slang very difficult to listen to; her daughter thought that using it made her sound chic and used what she thought were slang expressions without understanding what they were or what they meant.
4. Probably because she was a woman and Henry's mother, Mrs. Higgins was worried about Henry mistreating Eliza, using her to his advantage, and forgetting about her. Higgins saw Eliza as an experiment, and because his work was the most important thing in his life he saw nothing wrong with dropping her when he was finished and going on to the next project. Pickering was equally interested in Eliza as a project, but he was also concerned about her feelings; Pickering has a history of helping people in need.
5. Eliza, because she has only dreamed about such events, is enchanted and does not want the evening to end. Higgins hates such formal affairs, probably because he had spent his younger years going to them and is there only because he wants to win the bet. Pickering is a gentleman and enjoys the evening without making a fuss either way; as a military man, he is trained to do his duty.

ANSWERS TO UNDERSTANDING LANGUAGE

Suggested responses:

1. killed, destroyed
2. lifted it; stole it
3. when he felt like; every so often
4. when he was tipsy

Challenge Rewrite Eliza's account of her aunt's influenza in modern slang.

THINKING AND WRITING

Publishing Student Writing Have students write what they think Eliza was thinking as she left the ball with Higgins and Pickering. Have them read their selections to each other aloud, using a British accent and mimicking Eliza's personality as much as possible.

Literary Focus Remind students that a play can have subplots that run parallel to the major plot. Each subplot has its own crisis or climax.

Look For As they read, have those students who benefit from information presented graphically prepare a story map of the major plot and subplots of *Pygmalion.*

Writing Have students brainstorm as a group about what is likely to happen in Act IV.

Vocabulary As they read, have students find other words that they are not sure of and add them to this list.

GUIDE FOR READING

Pygmalion, Act IV

The Writer's Technique

Crisis. Crisis is a highpoint of emotion or action that occurs near the end of a work of fiction. Also known as *climax,* the crisis is one key point in the carefully arranged sequence of elements in a story known as *plot.* Historically the plot contains five such elements, the first of which, the *exposition,* is a playbill of sorts. The exposition tells us who the characters are and what sort of *conflict,* or struggle, they face. Often this conflict is between the characters themselves, although at times an outside force like nature or society is involved. In any event *complications* arise in one form or another, causing the action or emotional intensity to build. Once the crisis, or turning point, has been reached, the work begins to wind down. In this final stage, known as the *resolution* or *denouement,* all problems are solved and any loose ends are tied up. This pattern of elements, first described by the Greek philosopher and theoretician Aristotle, has been abandoned in whole or in part by a number of modern writers. Shaw, in an effort to create a more lifelike drama, deviated somewhat from this formula, especially in his comedies.

Look For

As you read Act IV of *Pygmalion,* be alert to the crisis, to the characters or forces involved in it, and to the conflict that has led to it.

Writing

Imagine you are sitting in a theater watching this play. The curtain has come down on Act III. During intermission, you turn to the person sitting next to you and discuss the play. Create a conversation in which both of you provide ideas on what will happen next.

Vocabulary

Knowing the following words will help you as you read Act IV of *Pygmalion.*

cant (kant) *n.*: Insincere talk (p. 1182)

dudgeon (duj′ ən) *n.*: Angry resentment; rage (p. 1182)

perfunctorily (pər fuŋk′ tə ri lē) *adv.*: Carelessly (p. 1182)

Objectives

1. To explain crisis in a dramatic work
2. To understand cause and effect
3. To understand synonyms and antonyms
4. To write a letter of advice

Teaching Portfolio: Support Material

Teacher Backup, pp. 00-00

Vocabulary Check, p. 00

Usage and Mechanics Worksheet, p. 00

Analyzing Literature Worksheet, p. 00

Critical Thinking and Reading Worksheet, p. 00

Language Worksheet, p. 00

Selection Test, p. 00

ACT IV

The Wimpole Street laboratory. Midnight. Nobody in the room. The clock on the mantelpiece strikes twelve. The fire is not alight: it is a summer night.

Presently HIGGINS *and* PICKERING *are heard on the stairs.*

HIGGINS [*calling down to* PICKERING] I say, Pick: lock up, will you? I shant be going out again.

PICKERING. Right. Can Mrs Pearce go to bed? We dont want anything more, do we?

HIGGINS. Lord, no!

ELIZA *opens the door and is seen on the lighted landing in all the finery in which she has just won* HIGGINS*'s bet for him. She comes to the hearth, and switches on the electric lights there. She is tired: her pallor contrasts strongly with her dark eyes and hair; and her expression is almost tragic. She takes off her cloak; puts her fan and gloves on the piano; and sits down on the bench, brooding and silent.* HIGGINS, *in evening dress, with overcoat and hat, comes in, carrying a smoking jacket which he has picked up downstairs. He takes off the hat and overcoat; throws them carelessly on the newspaper stand; disposes of his coat in the same way; puts on the smoking jacket; and throws himself wearily into the easy-chair at the hearth.* PICKERING, *similarly attired, comes in. He also takes off his hat and overcoat, and is about to throw them on* HIGGINS*'s when he hesitates.*

PICKERING. I say: Mrs Pearce will row if we leave these things lying about in the drawing room.

HIGGINS. Oh, chuck them over the bannisters into the hall. She'll find them there in the morning and put them away all right. She'll think we were drunk.

PICKERING. We are, slightly. Are there any letters?

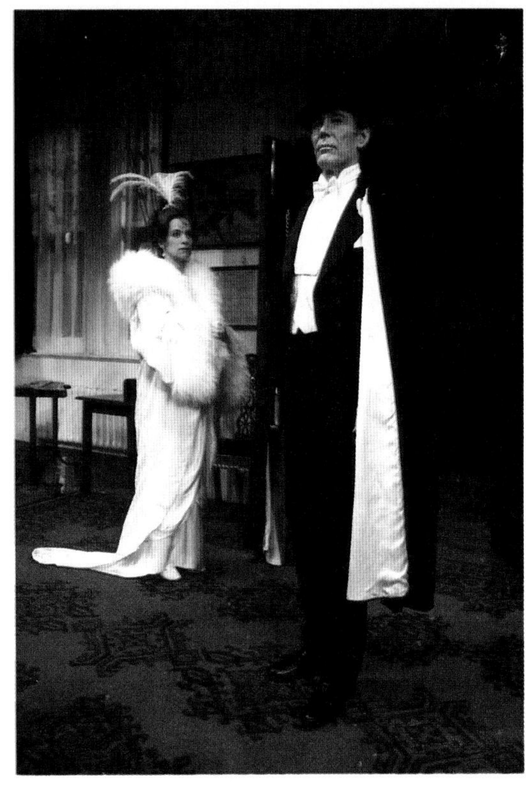

HIGGINS. I didnt look. [PICKERING *takes the overcoats and hats and goes downstairs.* HIGGINS *begins half singing half yawning an air from* La Fanciulla Del Golden West.[1] *Suddenly he stops and exclaims*] I wonder where the devil my slippers are!

1 ELIZA *looks at him darkly; then rises suddenly and leaves the room.*

HIGGINS *yawns again, and resumes his song.*

PICKERING *returns, with the contents of the letter-box in his hand.*

1. **La Fanciulla** (fan choo͞o′ la) **del Golden West:** *The Girl of the Golden West,* an opera by Italian composer Giacomo Puccini (1858–1924).

Motivation for Reading Have students think back to a time when they were caught off guard in an argument and only later came up with the perfect thing to say. Eliza has had plenty of time to think of what she will say if ever the time arises, but she is thrown off course, at times, quite easily. What keeps people from using their best logic and thought in their discussions? What keeps Eliza from remaining logical, strong, and unwaveringly objective in her discussion with Higgins?

Master Teacher Note After students have read Act IV, have them judge who won the debate between Higgins and Eliza, based on logic used, arguments put forth, and points made. Who does Eliza believe won? Who does Higgins believe won? You might show them the same scene from the movie *My Fair Lady* and have them determine the winner of the debate, based on the points above as well as on which actor gave the most convincing performance.

Purpose-Setting Question When does the crisis or climax of the major plot occur?

1 **Reading Strategy** Predict where is.

2 Clarification A fender is a screen-like guard against live coals in front of a fireplace.

3 Literary Focus How does this exchange contribute to the crisis between Higgins and Eliza?

4 Reading Strategy Explain the irony in this speech.

5 Discussion How does Pickering's military career affect his attitude?

6 Discussion What one thing do Pickering and Higgins seem to have forgotten in their joy over their success?

7 Critical Thinking and Reading What do you think finally causes Eliza to break down and to show her true feelings?

2 **PICKERING.** Only circulars, and this coroneted billet-doux[2] for you. [*He throws the circulars into the fender, and posts himself on the hearthrug, with his back to the grate*].

HIGGINS [*glancing at the billet-doux*] Money-lender. [*He throws the letter after the circulars*].

ELIZA *returns with a pair of large down-at-heel slippers. She places them on the carpet before* HIGGINS, *and sits as before without a word.*

HIGGINS [*yawning again*] Oh Lord! What an evening! What a crew! What a silly tomfoolery! [*He raises his shoe to unlace it, and catches sight of the slippers. He stops unlacing and looks at them as if they had appeared there of their own accord*]. Oh! theyre there, are they?

PICKERING [*stretching himself*]. Well, I feel a bit tired. It's been a long day. The garden party, a dinner party, and the reception! Rather too much of a good thing. But youve won your bet, Higgins. Eliza did the trick, and something to spare, eh?

HIGGINS [*fervently*] Thank God it's over!

ELIZA *flinches violently; but they take no notice of her; and she recovers herself and sits stonily as before.*

3 **PICKERING.** Were you nervous at the garden party? *I* was. Eliza didnt seem a bit nervous.

HIGGINS. Oh, she wasnt nervous. I knew she'd be all right. No: it's the strain of putting the job through all these months that has told on me. It was interesting enough at first, while we were at the phonetics; but after that I got deadly sick of it. If I hadnt backed myself to do it I should have chucked the whole thing up two months ago. It was a silly notion: the whole thing has been a bore.

PICKERING. Oh come! the garden party was frightfully exciting. My heart began beating like anything.

HIGGINS. Yes, for the first three minutes. But when I saw we were going to win hands down, I felt like a bear in a cage, hanging about doing nothing. The dinner was worse: sitting gorging there for over an hour, with nobody but a damned fool of a fashionable woman to talk to! I tell you, Pickering, never again for me. No more artificial duchesses. The whole thing has been simple purgatory. 4

PICKERING. Youve never been broken in properly to the social routine. [*Strolling over to the piano*] I rather enjoy dipping into it occasionally myself: it makes me feel young again. Anyhow, it was a great success: an immense success. I was quite frightened once or twice because Eliza was doing it so well. You see, lots of the real people cant do it at all: theyre such fools that they think style comes by nature to people in their position; and so they never learn. Theres always something professional about doing a thing superlatively well. 5

HIGGINS. Yes: thats what drives me mad: the silly people dont know their own silly business. [*Rising*] However, it's over and done with; and now I can go to bed at last without dreading tomorrow.

ELIZA*'s beauty becomes murderous.*

PICKERING. I think I shall turn in too. Still, it's been a great occasion: a triumph for you. Goodnight. [*He goes*].

HIGGINS [*following him*] Goodnight. [*Over his shoulder, at the door*] Put out the lights, Eliza; and tell Mrs Pearce not to make coffee for me in the morning: I'll take tea. [*He goes out*]. 6

ELIZA *tries to control herself and feel indifferent as she rises and walks across to the hearth to switch off the lights. By the time she gets there she is on the point of screaming. She sits down in* HIGGINS*'s chair and holds on hard to the arms. Finally she gives way and flings herself furiously on the floor, raging.* 7

2. **billet-doux** (bil′ ā do͞o′): Love letter.

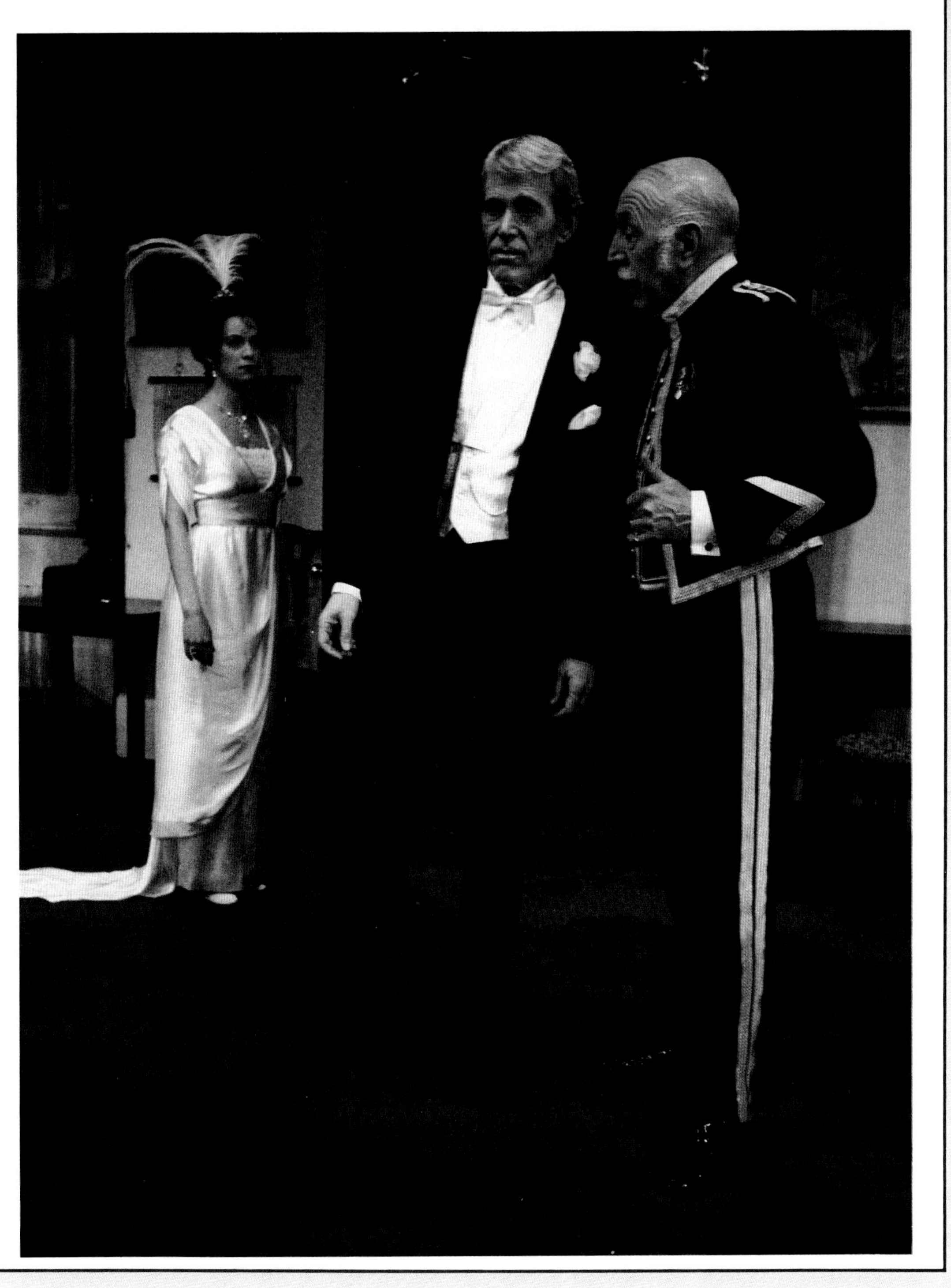

8 Reading Strategy What do Higgins's slippers symbolize to Eliza?

9 Critical Thinking and Reading What causes Higgins to lose a bit of his confidence and to become uneasy?

10 Discussion What does Higgins mean when he says that this "irritation is purely subjective"?

HIGGINS [*in despairing wrath outside*] What the devil have I done with my slippers? [*He appears at the door*].

8 **LIZA** [*snatching up the slippers, and hurling them at him one after the other with all her force*] There are your slippers. And there. Take your slippers; and may you never have a day's luck with them!

HIGGINS [*astounded*] What on earth—! [*He comes to her*]. Whats the matter? Get up. [*He pulls her up*] Anything wrong?

LIZA [(*breathless*] Nothing wrong—with you. Ive won your bet for you, havnt I? Thats enough for you. *I* dont matter, I suppose.

HIGGINS. You won my bet! You! Presumptuous insect! *I* won it. What did you throw those slippers at me for?

LIZA. Because I wanted to smash your face. I'd like to kill you, you selfish brute. Why didnt you leave me where you picked me out of—in the gutter? You thank God it's all over, and that now you can throw me back again there, do you? [*She crisps her fingers*[3] *frantically*].

HIGGINS [*looking at her in cool wonder*] The creature is nervous, after all.

LIZA [*gives a suffocated scream of fury, and instinctively darts her nails at his face*]!!

HIGGINS [*catching her wrists*] Ah! would you? Claws in, you cat. How dare you shew your temper to me? Sit down and be quiet. [*He throws her roughly into the easy-chair*].

LIZA [*crushed by superior strength and weight*] Whats to become of me? Whats to become of me?

HIGGINS. How the devil do I know whats to become of you? What does it matter what becomes of you?

LIZA. You dont care. I know you dont care. You wouldnt care if I was dead. I'm nothing to you—not so much as them slippers.

HIGGINS [*thundering*] Those slippers.

LIZA [*with bitter submission*]. Those slippers. I didnt think it made any difference now.

A pause. ELIZA *hopeless and crushed.* HIGGINS *a little uneasy.* 9

HIGGINS [*in his loftiest manner*] Why have you begun going on like this? May I ask whether you complain of your treatment here?

LIZA. No.

HIGGINS. Has anybody behaved badly to you? Colonel Pickering? Mrs Pearce? Any of the servants?

LIZA. No.

HIGGINS. I presume you dont pretend that *I* have treated you badly?

LIZA. No.

HIGGINS. I am glad to hear it. [*He moderates his tone*]. Perhaps youre tired after the strain of the day. Will you have a glass of champagne? [*He moves towards the door*].

LIZA. No. [*Recollecting her manners*] Thank you.

HIGGINS [*good-humored again*] This has been coming on you for some days. I suppose it was natural for you to be anxious about the garden party. But thats all over now. [*He pats her kindly on the shoulder. She writhes*]. Theres nothing more to worry about.

LIZA. No. Nothing more for you to worry about. [*She suddenly rises and gets away from him by going to the piano bench, where she sits and hides her face*]. Oh God! I wish I was dead.

HIGGINS [*staring after her in sincere surprise*] Why? In heaven's name, why? [*Reasonably, going to her*] Listen to me, Eliza. All this irritation is purely subjective. 10

---

3. crisps her fingers: Clenches her fingers into fists.

LIZA. I dont understand. I'm too ignorant.

HIGGINS. It's only imagination. Low spirits and nothing else. Nobody's hurting you. Nothing's wrong. You go to bed like a good girl and sleep it off. Have a little cry and say your prayers: that will make you comfortable.

LIZA. I heard your prayers. "Thank God it's all over!"

HIGGINS [*impatiently*] Well, dont you thank God it's all over? Now you are free and can do what you like.

LIZA [*pulling herself together in desperation*] What am I fit for? What have you left me fit for? Where am I to go? What am I to do? Whats to become of me?

HIGGINS [*enlightened, but not at all impressed*] Oh, thats whats worrying you, is it? [*He thrusts his hands into his pockets, and walks about in his usual manner, rattling the contents of his pockets, as if condescending to a trivial subject out of pure kindness*]. I shouldnt bother about it if I were you. I should imagine you wont have much difficulty in settling yourself somewhere or other, though I hadnt quite realized that you were going away. [*She looks quickly at him: he does not look at her, but examines the dessert stand on the piano and decides that he will eat an apple*]. You might marry, you know. [*He bites a large piece out of the apple and munches it noisily*]. You see, Eliza, all men are not confirmed old bachelors like me and the Colonel. Most men are the marrying sort [poor devils!]; and youre not bad-looking: it's quite a pleasure to look at you sometimes—not now, of course, because youre crying and looking as ugly as the very devil; but when youre all right and quite yourself, youre what I should call attractive. That is, to the people in the marrying line, you understand. You go to bed and have a good nice rest; and then get up and look at yourself in the glass; and you wont feel so cheap.

ELIZA *again looks at him, speechless, and does not stir.*

The look is quite lost on him: he eats his apple with a dreamy expression of happiness, as it is quite a good one.

HIGGINS [*a genial afterthought occurring to him*] I daresay my mother could find some chap or other who would do very well. 11

LIZA. We were above that at the corner of Tottenham Court Road.

HIGGINS [*waking up*] What do you mean? 12

LIZA. I sold flowers. I didnt sell myself. Now youve made a lady of me I'm not fit to sell anything else. I wish youd left me where you found me.

11 **Reading Strategy** Predict whether Eliza will leave or stay.

12 **Reading Strategy** Discuss the irony in Eliza's statement about her old life.

1181

13 **Discussion** What do you think Eliza would really like Higgins to say at this point?

14 **Discussion** Why is Higgins becoming more and more abusive?

HIGGINS [*slinging the core of the apple decisively into the grate*] Tosh, Eliza. Dont you insult human relations by dragging all this cant about buying and selling into it. You neednt marry the fellow if you dont like him.

LIZA. What else am I to do?

HIGGINS. Oh, lots of things. What about your old idea of a florist's shop? Pickering could set you up in one: he has lots of money. [*Chuckling*] He'll have to pay for all those togs you have been wearing today; and that, with the hire of the jewellery, will make a big hole in two hundred pounds. Why, six months ago you would have thought it the millennium to have a flower shop of your own. Come! youll be all right. I must clear off to bed: I'm devilish sleepy. By the way, I came down for something: I forgot what it was.

LIZA. Your slippers.

HIGGINS. Oh yes, of course. You shied them at me. [*He picks them up, and is going out when she rises and speaks to him*].

LIZA. Before you go, sir—

HIGGINS [*dropping the slippers in his surprise at her calling him Sir*] Eh?

LIZA. Do my clothes belong to me or to Colonel Pickering?

HIGGINS [*coming back into the room as if her question were the very climax of unreason*] What the devil use would they be to Pickering?

LIZA. He might want them for the next girl you pick up to experiment on.

HIGGINS [*shocked and hurt*] Is that the way you feel towards us?

LIZA. I dont want to hear anything more about that. All I want to know is whether anything belongs to me. My own clothes were burnt.

HIGGINS. But what does it matter? Why need you start bothering about that in the middle of the night?

LIZA. I want to know what I may take away with me. I dont want to be accused of stealing.

HIGGINS [*now deeply wounded*] Stealing! You shouldnt have said that, Eliza. That shews a want of feeling.

LIZA. I'm sorry. I'm only a common ignorant girl; and in my station I have to be careful. There cant be any feelings between the like of you and the like of me. Please will you tell me what belongs to me and what doesnt?

HIGGINS [*very sulky*] You may take the whole damned houseful if you like. Except the jewels. Theyre hired. Will that satisfy you? [*He turns on his heel and is about to go in extreme dudgeon*].

LIZA [*drinking in his emotion like nectar, and nagging him to provoke a further supply*] Stop, please. [*She takes off her jewels*]. Will you take these to your room and keep them safe? I don't want to run the risk of their being missing.

HIGGINS [*furious*] Hand them over. [*She puts them into his hands*]. If these belonged to me instead of to the jeweller, I'd ram them down your ungrateful throat. [*He perfunctorily thrusts them into his pockets, unconsciously decorating himself with the protruding ends of the chains*].

LIZA [*taking a ring off*]. This ring isnt the jeweller's: it's the one you bought me in Brighton. I dont want it now. [HIGGINS *dashes the ring violently into the fireplace, and turns on her so threateningly that she crouches over the piano with her hands over her face, and exclaims*] Dont you hit me.

HIGGINS. Hit you! You infamous creature, how dare you accuse me of such a thing? It is you who have hit me. You have wounded me to the heart.

LIZA [*thrilling with hidden joy*] I'm glad. Ive got a little of my own back, anyhow.

15 **HIGGINS** [*with dignity, in his finest professional style*] You have caused me to lose my temper: a thing that has hardly ever happened to me before. I prefer to say nothing more tonight. I am going to bed.

LIZA [*pertly*] Youd better leave a note for Mrs Pearce about the coffee; for she wont be told by me.

HIGGINS [*formally*] Damn Mrs Pearce; and damn the coffee; and damn you; and [*wildly*] damn my own folly in having lavished my hard-earned knowledge and the treasure of my regard and intimacy on a heartless guttersnipe. [*He goes out with impressive decorum, and spoils it by slamming the door savagely*].

16 ELIZA *goes down on her knees on the hearthrug to look for the ring. When she finds it she considers for a moment what to do with it. Finally she flings it down on the dessert stand and goes upstairs in a tearing rage.*

* * * * * *

The furniture of Eliza's room has been increased by a big wardrobe and a sumptuous dressing-table. She comes in and switches on the electric light. She goes to the wardrobe; opens it; and pulls out a walking dress, a hat, and a pair of shoes, which she throws on the bed. She takes off her evening dress and shoes; then takes a padded hanger from the wardrobe; adjusts it carefully in the evening dress; and hangs it in the wardrobe, which she shuts with a slam. She puts on her walking shoes, her walking dress, and hat. She takes her wrist watch from the dressing-table and fastens it on. She pulls on her gloves; takes her vanity bag; and looks into it to see that her purse is there before hanging it on her wrist. She makes for the door. Every movement expresses her furious resolution.

17 She takes a last look at herself in the glass.

She suddenly puts out her tongue at herself; then leaves the room, switching off the electric light at the door.

Meanwhile, in the street outside, Freddy Eynsford Hill, lovelorn, is gazing up at the second floor, in which one of the windows is still lighted.

The light goes out.

FREDDY. Goodnight, darling, darling, darling.

ELIZA *comes out, giving the door a considerable bang behind her.*

LIZA. Whatever are you doing here?

FREDDY. Nothing. I spend most of my nights here. It's the only place where I'm happy. Dont laugh at me, Miss Doolittle.

LIZA. Dont you call me Miss Doolittle, do you hear? Liza's good enough for me. [*She breaks down and grabs him by the shoulders*] Freddy: you dont think I'm a heartless guttersnipe, do you?

FREDDY. Oh no, no, darling: how can you imagine such a thing? You are the loveliest, dearest—

He loses all self-control and smothers her with kisses. She, hungry for comfort, responds. They stand there in one another's arms.

An elderly police constable arrives.

CONSTABLE [*scandalized*] Now then! Now then!! Now then!!!

They release one another hastily.

FREDDY. Sorry, constable. Weve only just become engaged.

They run away.

The constable shakes his head, reflecting on his own courtship and on the vanity of human hopes. He moves off in the opposite direction with slow professional steps.

The flight of the lovers takes them to Cavendish Square. There they halt to consider their next move.

LIZA [*out of breath*] He didnt half give me a fright, that copper. But you answered him proper.

FREDDY. I hope I havnt taken you out of your way. Where were you going? 18

15 **Critical Thinking and Reading** What causes Higgins to change his behavior so abruptly?

16 **Discussion** Why do Higgins and Eliza shift so quickly throughout this exchange from being furious at each other to trying to be kind and back to being furious?

17 **Critical Thinking and Reading** What causes Eliza to stick her tongue out at herself as she leaves?

18 **Discussion** Do you think that Eliza really planned to go to the river? Why or why not?

19 Discussion Would you have felt safe walking about London at night during Victorian times? Why or why not?

20 Enrichment Wimbledon Common is about a forty-five minute ride south and west of London and not a ride usually taken in a taxi.

LIZA. To the river.

FREDDY. What for?

LIZA. To make a hole in it.

FREDDY [*horrified*] Eliza, darling. What do you mean? What's the matter?

LIZA. Never mind. It doesnt matter now. There's nobody in the world now but you and me, is there?

FREDDY. Not a soul.

They indulge in another embrace, and are again surprised by a much younger constable.

SECOND CONSTABLE. Now then, you two! What's this? Where do you think you are? Move along here, double quick.

FREDDY. As you say, sir, double quick.

They run away again, and are in Hanover Square before they stop for another conference.

FREDDY. I had no idea the police were so devilishly prudish.

LIZA. It's their business to hunt girls off the street.

FREDDY. We must go somewhere. We cant wander about the streets all night.

LIZA. Cant we? I think it'd be lovely to wander about for ever.

FREDDY. Oh, darling.

They embrace again, oblivious of the arrival of a crawling taxi. It stops.

TAXIMAN. Can I drive you and the lady anywhere, sir? 19

They start asunder.

LIZA. Oh, Freddy, a taxi. The very thing.

FREDDY. But, damn it, I've no money.

LIZA. I have plenty. The Colonel thinks you should never go out without ten pounds in your pocket. Listen. We'll drive about all night; and in the morning I'll call on old Mrs Higgins and ask her what I ought to do. I'll tell you all about it in the cab. And the police wont touch us there.

FREDDY. Righto! Ripping. [*To the* TAXIMAN] Wimbledon Common. [*They drive off*]. 20

THINKING ABOUT THE SELECTION

Recalling

1. (a) How are Higgins and Pickering feeling as the act opens? (b) How does Eliza feel?
2. What does Higgins suggest when Eliza asks what will become of her?
3. (a) What does Eliza do after Higgins goes to bed? (b) Whom does she run into?

Interpreting

4. (a) What two characters earlier in the play anticipated the concern Eliza expresses here? (b) What was Higgins's response to them?
5. (a) In what ways does Higgins act differently from how he behaved earlier in the play? (b) In what ways is his behavior predictable? (c) What does his behavior reveal about him?

Applying

6. What aspects of being a woman of this era compound Eliza's problems?

ANALYZING LITERATURE

Explaining Crisis

The **crisis** in a work of fiction is the turning point—that moment when the conflict presented

Answers

ANSWERS TO THINKING ABOUT THE SELECTION

Recalling

1. (a) Higgins and Pickering are very proud of themselves and of what they have accomplished by passing Eliza off as royalty. (b) Eliza had a wonderful evening but is very frustrated when the two men give her no credit for the evening's success, when they—in fact—ignore her presence.
2. Higgins says that he doesn't know and he doesn't care what will happen to her.
3. (a) Eliza packs her things and leaves the house. (b) She runs straight into the arms of Freddy, who happens to be watching the house as he does every evening—hoping to catch a glimpse of her.

Interpreting

4. (a) Both Pickering and Mrs. Pearce were concerned from the beginning about what would happen to Eliza after she had learned to be a lady. (b) Higgins alternately said that Eliza could go back where she came from, raged at them for even worrying about the problem, or goodheartedly assured everyone that things would work out fine.
5. (a) Higgins is still as insensitive and abusive as always, but he genuine-

earlier in the work comes to a head. Also referred to as the *climax,* this highpoint, which occurs close to the end of the work, is followed by a resolution of all problems. The crisis in Act IV of *Pygmalion* is quite obviously the outgrowth of a conflict between Higgins and Eliza.

1. What is the nature of that conflict; that is, what has each of the two characters been trying to achieve from the start?
2. What problems mentioned (or raised) in Act IV remain to be resolved? How do you think they will be resolved? Explain why you feel as you do.

CRITICAL THINKING AND READING

Understanding Cause and Effect

Events, both in real life and in fiction, seldom happen in a vacuum. More commonly put, one thing "usually leads to another." Your ride to school does not show up and, therefore, you are late to your first-period class. Because of your lateness, you miss getting down an important assignment due the following day. And so on. An event that leads to a particular result is called a **cause.** The result of the cause is called an **effect.** Most works of fiction are chains of causes and effects.

For each of the following events, supply one cause and one effect.

1. Eliza pays Professor Higgins a visit.
2. Pickering proposes a bet with Higgins.
3. Higgins appears at his mother's "at-home."
4. Eliza throws Higgins's slippers at him.

UNDERSTANDING LANGUAGE

Finding Synonyms and Antonyms

Two words with the same or similar meanings are **synonyms.** *Boy* and *lad* are examples of synonyms. Two words opposite in meaning are **antonyms.** *Light* and *dark* are examples of antonyms. The word in italics to the left of each list appears in Act IV. From each list, select the one synonym and the one antonym. Consult a dictionary if necessary.

1. *resumes:* desists, incites, continues, inures
2. *genial:* reclusive, mystical, cordial, glacial
3. *infamous:* disgraceful, attractive, adorable, obscure
4. *intimacy:* estrangement, confidence, befuddlement, familiarity
5. *oblivious:* apparent, unmindful, self-effacing, self-conscious

THINKING AND WRITING

Writing a Letter of Advice

What do you think about the engagement of Eliza and Freddy? Is she making the right choice? Does she have other options? List any suggestions you would offer Eliza. Then write a letter to her offering advice. When you revise your letter, make sure your advice is practical. Have you presented it in a persuasive manner? Proofread your letter and prepare a final draft.

ly seems to be trying to find a solution to the problem that he has created for Eliza. (b) It is predictable that he is going to be angry, that he will not really understand someone else's needs because he has so few on the personal level, and that he will take all the credit for Eliza's success. (c) It reveals him to be a consistent personality—he is essentially unchanged from what he was at the outset, though he has developed an unacknowledged affection for Eliza.

Applying

6. Most women of the upper class were considered to be little more than decoration on the arms of their men. Because she doesn't have a man to take care of her or an occupation, she is left with nothing to live on.

ANSWERS TO ANALYZING LITERATURE

1. Higgins has devoted all of his energies to seeing that Eliza is mistaken for a lady in polite society so that he will gain recognition as a teacher and so that he can say that he fooled the upper class at their own game. Eliza has been trying to reach the same goal but primarily to better herself and to please Higgins.
2. We don't know whether Eliza will marry Higgins or Freddy, whether Eliza will be found out, or whether Eliza will return to the Higgins's house. Resolutions and reasons for those resolutions will differ.

(Answers begin on p. 1184.)

Challenge How do you predict each conflict will be resolved? Support your answers with details from the play.

ANSWERS TO CRITICAL THINKING AND READING

1. *Cause:* Eliza wants to learn to speak properly.
   Effect: Higgins takes her on as a pupil.
2. *Cause:* Pickering wants to see the girl taken care of.
   Effect: Higgins takes Eliza's life over and makes her into a lady.
3. *Cause:* Higgins wants to see if Eliza can fool a few select people in polite society.
   Effect: Eliza seems to be accepted as upper class, if a little odd.
4. *Cause:* Higgins has been totally insensitive to Eliza's feelings.
   Effect: Eliza makes up her mind to leave Higgins and his lessons.

ANSWERS TO UNDERSTANDING LANGUAGE

1. synonym: continues; antonym: desists
2. synonym: cordial; antonym: reclusive
3. synonym: disgraceful; antonym: adorable
4. synonym: confidence; antonym: estrangement
5. synonym: unmindful; antonym: self-conscious

THINKING AND WRITING

In groups have students read one another's drafts and make suggestions for improvements. The writers can then include suggestions for improvement in their revisions.

Challenge Have students write what they think Eliza was thinking as she listened to Higgins and Pickering congratulate each other after the ball. Have them read their selections to each other aloud, using a British accent and mimicking Eliza's personality as much as possible.

Literary Focus Playwrights must make their work universally true enough to allow the audience to identify with some part of their plays—the characters, the conflicts, the resolutions. Playwrights accomplish this by convincing their audiences that they should trust them to portray life so that it can be understood; they encourage their audiences to "willingly suspend their disbelief" so that their plays can deliver their messages.

Look For Have your students who are preparing story maps complete their maps by adding their descriptions of tone and symbol.

Writing Have students include the resolution of each of the character's conflicts. Then have them choose the combination of resolutions that they prefer and formulate their own endings to the play from those.

Vocabulary All of these words relate to human behavior. Have your **more advanced** students use all those with positive connotations to write a one-paragraph description of a character toward whom they felt positively during the reading of the play. Have them then use all those words with negative connotations to write a one-paragraph description of a character toward whom they felt negatively.

GUIDE FOR READING

Pygmalion, Act V

The Writer's Technique

The Complete Play. A play consists of many elements. The first of these is plot, the sequence of events. Will the plot be structured *chronologically,* moving ever forward in time? Or will it contain flashbacks? Next comes setting, the *when* and *where* of the play. How will time and location be conveyed to the audience? Through speakers' words? Through stage sets? Another element is characters, the people in the action. How many characters will be *round,* that is, complex and true-to-life? How many will be *flat,* one-dimensional figures included purely to advance the plot? Then comes tone, the playwright's attitude toward his or her subject or audience. Will the tone be lighthearted? Serious? A mixture? There is the issue of symbols—people, places, and events that stand for something beyond themselves. Last but not least is theme, the central idea of the play. What message does the play communicate to the audience?

Look For

As you read Act V and the "Epilogue" to *Pygmalion,* be alert to Shaw's answers to questions of plot, setting, character, tone, symbol, and theme regarding the play as a whole.

Writing

Second-guess George Bernard Shaw by drafting out your own ending to the play. What will become of Eliza? Of Higgins? Of Freddy? Be prepared to compare your hunches with those of your classmates.

Vocabulary

Knowing the following words will help you as you read Act V and the "Epilogue" to *Pygmalion.*

resplendently (ri splen′ dənt lē) *adj.*: Splendidly; gorgeously (p. 1188)
vehement (vē′ ə mənt) *adj.*: Energetic; forceful (p. 1188)
magnanimous (mag nan′ ə məs) *adj.*: Generously forgiving (p. 1196)
transfiguration (trans fig′ yoo rā′shən) *n.*: Change in outward appearance (p. 1202)
coquetting (kō ket′ iŋ) *v.*: Flirting (p. 1202)
impetuous (im pech′ oo wəs) *adj.*: Given to rash or hasty action (p. 1203)
transcendence (tran sen′ dəns) *n.*: Rising above (p. 1205)
odious (ō′ dē əs) *adj.*: Hateful; offensive (p. 1207)
pretentious (pri ten′ shəs) *adj.*: Making false claims (p. 1207)

Objectives

1 To understand a complete play
2 To summarize a play
3 To write about the title of a play

Teaching Portfolio: Support Material

Teacher Backup, pp. 00–00

Vocabulary Check, p. 00

Usage and Mechanics Worksheet, p. 00

Analyzing Literature Worksheet, p. 00

Critical Thinking and Reading Worksheet, p. 00

Language Worksheet, p. 00

Selection Test, p. 00

ACT V

MRS HIGGINS's drawing room. She is at her writing-table as before. The PARLORMAID comes in.

THE PARLORMAID [*at the door*] Mr Henry, maam, is downstairs with Colonel Pickering.

MRS HIGGINS. Well, shew them up.

THE PARLORMAID. Theyre using the telephone, maam. Telephoning to the police, I think.

MRS HIGGINS. What!

THE PARLORMAID [*coming further in and lowering her voice*] Mr Henry is in a state, maam. I thought I'd better tell you.

MRS HIGGINS. If you had told me that Mr Henry was not in a state it would have been more surprising. Tell them to come up when theyve finished with the police. I suppose he's lost something.

THE PARLORMAID. Yes, maam [*going*].

MRS HIGGINS. Go upstairs and tell Miss Doolittle that Mr Henry and the Colonel are here. Ask her not to come down til I send for her.

THE PARLORMAID. Yes, maam.

HIGGINS bursts in. He is, as the PARLORMAID has said, in a state.

HIGGINS. Look here, mother: heres a confounded thing!

MRS HIGGINS. Yes, dear. Good morning. [*He checks his impatience and kisses her, whilst the PARLORMAID goes out*]. What is it?

HIGGINS. Eliza's bolted.

MRS HIGGINS [*calmly continuing her writing*] You must have frightened her.

1 **HIGGINS.** Frightened her! nonsense! She was left last night, as usual, to turn out the lights and all that; and instead of going to bed she changed her clothes and went right off: her bed wasnt slept in. She came in a cab for her things before seven this morning; and that fool Mrs Pearce let her have them without telling me a word about it. What am I to do?

MRS HIGGINS. Do without, I'm afraid, Henry. The girl has a perfect right to leave if she chooses.

2 **HIGGINS** [*wandering distractedly across the room*] But I cant find anything. I dont know what appointments Ive got. I'm—[*PICKERING comes in. MRS HIGGINS puts down her pen and turns away from the writing-table*].

PICKERING [*shaking hands*] Good morning, Mrs Higgins. Has Henry told you? [*He sits down on the ottoman*].

HIGGINS. What does that ass of an inspector say? Have you offered a reward?

MRS HIGGINS [*rising in indignant amazement*] You dont mean to say you have set the police after Eliza.

HIGGINS. Of course. What are the police for? What else could we do? [*He sits in the Elizabethan chair*].

PICKERING. The inspector made a lot of difficulties. I really think he suspected us of some improper purpose.

MRS HIGGINS. Well, of course, he did. What right have you to go to the police and give the girl's name as if she were a thief, or a lost umbrella, or something? Really! [*She sits down again, deeply vexed*].

HIGGINS. But we want to find her.

PICKERING. We cant let her go like this, you know, Mrs Higgins. What were we to do?

MRS HIGGINS. You have no more sense, either of you, than two children. Why—

The PARLORMAID comes in and breaks off the conversation.

THE PARLORMAID. Mr Henry: a gentleman wants to see you very particular. He's been sent on from Wimpole Street.

HIGGINS. Oh, bother! I cant see anyone now. Who is it?

Motivation for Reading Have students put themselves in Eliza's place and discuss the following questions. Should I stay with Higgins and Pickering? Should I marry Freddy? Should I go back to being a flower girl? Have them predict what Eliza will do, based on their answers to these questions.

Master Teacher Note When students have finished reading *Pygmalion,* you might show the movie *My Fair Lady,* asking students to compare and contrast the two plays and the effectiveness of each while they watch. Have students write a review explaining which of the two they prefer and why.

Purpose-Setting Question Does Shaw make use of all the elements of a play?

1 **Discussion** Why is Higgins looking for Eliza? Do you think that he's worried about her? Justify your answer based on his past behavior.

2 **Discussion** Discuss the alternative possibilities of why Higgins might be so distracted by Eliza's disappearance.

3 **Reading Strategy** Have students predict what has caused Mr. Doolittle to be dressed so finely and what part Higgins had to play in Doolittle's situation. Have them evaluate their predictions when they discover what has happened.

4 **Discussion** Is Mr. Doolittle's discomfort at not noticing Mrs. Higgins part of his former self or his present self?

THE PARLORMAID. A Mr Doolittle, sir.

PICKERING. Doolittle! Do you mean the dustman?

THE PARLORMAID. Dustman! Oh no, sir: a gentleman.

HIGGINS [*springing up excitedly*] By George, Pick, it's some relative of hers that she's gone to. Somebody we know nothing about. [*To the* PARLORMAID] Send him up, quick.

THE PARLORMAID. Yes, sir. [*She goes*].

HIGGINS [*eagerly, going to his mother*] Genteel relatives! now we shall hear something. [*He sits down in the Chippendale chair*].

MRS HIGGINS. Do you know any of her people?

PICKERING. Only her father: the fellow we told you about.

THE PARLORMAID [*announcing*] Mr Doolittle. [*She withdraws*].

DOOLITTLE *enters. He is resplendently dressed as for a fashionable wedding, and might, in fact, be the bridegroom. A flower in his buttonhole, a dazzling silk hat, and patent leather shoes complete the effect.*
3 *He is too concerned with the business he has come on to notice* MRS HIGGINS. *He walks straight to* HIGGINS, *and accosts him with vehement reproach.*

DOOLITTLE [*indicating his own person*] See here! Do you see this? You done this.

HIGGINS. Done what, man?

DOOLITTLE. This, I tell you. Look at it. Look at this hat. Look at this coat.

PICKERING. Has Eliza been buying you clothes?

DOOLITTLE. Eliza! not she. Why would she buy me clothes?

MRS HIGGINS. Good morning, Mr Doolittle. Wont you sit down?

DOOLITTLE [*taken aback as he becomes conscious that he has forgotten his hostess*] Asking your pardon, maam. [*He approaches her and shakes her proffered hand*]. Thank you. [*He sits down on the ottoman, on* 4
PICKERING*'s right*]. I am that full of what has happened to me that I cant think of anything else.

HIGGINS. What the dickens has happened to you?

DOOLITTLE. I shouldn't mind if it had only happened to me: anything might happen to anybody and nobody to blame but Providence, as you might say. But this is something that you done to me: yes, you, Enry Iggins.

HIGGINS. Have you found Eliza?

DOOLITTLE. Have you lost her?

HIGGINS. Yes.

DOOLITTLE. You have all the luck, you have. I aint found her; but she'll find me quick enough now after what you done to me.

MRS HIGGINS. But what has my son done to you, Mr Doolittle?

DOOLITTLE. Done to me! Ruined me. Destroyed my happiness. Tied me up and delivered me into the hands of middle class morality.

HIGGINS [*rising intolerantly and standing over* DOOLITTLE] Youre raving. Youre drunk. Youre mad. I gave you five pounds. After that I had two conversations with you, at half-a-crown an hour. Ive never seen you since.

DOOLITTLE. Oh! Drunk am I? Mad am I? Tell me this. Did you or did you not write a letter to an old blighter in America that was giving five millions to found Moral Reform Societies all over the world, and that wanted you to invent a universal language for him?

HIGGINS. What! Ezra D. Wannafeller! He's dead. [*He sits down again carelessly*].

DOOLITTLE. Yes: he's dead; and I'm done for. Now did you or did you not write a letter to him to say that the most original moralist at

present in England, to the best of your knowledge, was Alfred Doolittle, a common dustman?

HIGGINS. Oh, after your first visit I remember making some silly joke of the kind.

DOOLITTLE. Ah! You may well call it a silly joke. It put the lid on me right enough. Just give him the chance he wanted to shew that Americans is not like us: that they reckonize and respect merit in every class of life, however humble. Them words is in his
5 blooming will, in which, Henry Higgins, thanks to your silly joking, he leaves me a share in his Predigested Cheese Trust worth [three] thousand a year on condition that I lecture for his Wannafeller Moral Reform World League as often as they ask me up to six times a year.

HIGGINS. The devil he does! Whew! [*Brightening suddenly*] What a lark!

PICKERING. A safe thing for you, Doolittle. They wont ask you twice.

DOOLITTLE. It aint the lecturing I mind. I'll lecture them blue in the face, I will, and not turn a hair. It's making a gentleman of me that I object to. Who asked him to make a gentleman of me? I was happy. I was free. I touched pretty nigh everybody for money when I wanted it, same as I touched you, Enry Iggins. Now I am worrited; tied neck and heels; and everybody touches me for money. It's a fine thing for you, says my solicitor.[1] Is it? says I. You mean it's a good

1. **solicitor** *n.*: A member of the legal profession who is not allowed to plead cases in superior court.

5 **Discussion** What unexpected inheritance did Mr. Doolittle receive? What are its conditions? What role did Higgins play in the inheritance? Compare your predictions to these answers.

6 **Discussion** What does Mr. Doolittle see as advantages and disadvantages of his new status?

7 **Reading Strategy** Discuss the meaning of this allusion and list some of the modern versions, such as "between a rock and a hard place."

8 **Literary Focus** What does the speech say about Higgins as a representative of his class?

thing for you, I says. When I was a poor man and had a solicitor once when they found a pram[2] in the dust cart, he got me off, and got shut of me and got me shut of him as quick as he could. Same with the doctors: used to shove me out of the hospital before I could hardly stand on my legs, and nothing to pay. Now they finds out that I'm not a healthy man and cant live unless they looks after me twice a day. In the house I'm not let do a hand's turn for myself: somebody else must
6 do it and touch me for it. A year ago I hadnt a relative in the world except two or three that wouldn't speak to me. Now Ive fifty, and not a decent week's wages among the lot of them. I have to live for others and not for myself: that middle class morality. You talk of losing Eliza. Dont you be anxious: I bet she's on my doorstep by this: she that could support herself easy by selling flowers if I wasnt respectable. And the next one to touch me will be you, Enry Iggins. I'll have to learn to speak middle class language from you, instead of speaking proper English. Thats where youll come in; and I daresay thats what you done it for.

MRS HIGGINS. But, my dear Mr Doolittle, you need not suffer all this if you are really in earnest. Nobody can force you to accept this bequest. You can repudiate it. Isnt that so, Colonel Pickering?

PICKERING. I believe so.

DOOLITTLE [*softening his manner in deference to her sex*] Thats the tragedy of it, maam. It's easy to say chuck it; but I havnt the nerve. Which of us has? We're all intimidated. Intimidated, maam: thats what we are. What is there for me if I chuck it but the workhouse in my old age? I have to dye my hair already to keep my job as a dustman. If I was one of the deserving poor, and had put by a bit, I could chuck it; but then why should I, acause the deserving poor might as well be millionaires for all the happiness they ever has. They dont know what happiness is. But I, as one of the undeserving poor, have nothing between me and the pauper's uniform but this here blasted three thousand a year that shoves me into the middle class. (Excuse the expression, maam; youd use it yourself if you had my provocation). Theyve got you every way you turn: it's a choice between the Skilly of the
workhouse and the Char Bydis[3] of the mid- 7
dle class; and I havnt the nerve for the workhouse. Intimidated: thats what I am. Broke. Bought up. Happier men than me will call for my dust, and touch me for their tip; and I'll look on helpless, and envy them. And thats what your son has brought me to. [*He is overcome by emotion*].

MRS HIGGINS. Well, I'm very glad youre not going to do anything foolish, Mr Doolittle. For this solves the problem of Eliza's future. You can provide for her now.

DOOLITTLE [*with melancholy resignation*] Yes, maam: I'm expected to provide for everyone now, out of [three] thousand a year.

HIGGINS [*jumping up*] Nonsense! he cant provide for her. He shant provide for her. She
doesnt belong to him. I paid him five pounds 8
for her. Doolittle: either youre an honest man or a rogue.

DOOLITTLE [*tolerantly*] A little of both, Henry, like the rest of us: a little of both.

HIGGINS. Well, you took that money for the girl; and you have no right to take her as well.

MRS HIGGINS. Henry: dont be absurd. If you want to know where Eliza is, she is upstairs.

HIGGINS [*amazed*] Upstairs!!! Then I shall

2. **pram** *n.*: Baby carriage.

3. **Skilly . . . Char Bydis:** Doolittle means Scylla (sil′ ə) and Charybdis (kə rib′ dis), a dangerous rock and whirlpool on either side of the narrow passage between Italy and Sicily. Scylla and Charybdis, personified by the ancient Greeks as two monsters, have come to stand for any two dangers neither of which can be evaded without risking the other.

jolly soon fetch her downstairs. [*He makes resolutely for the door*].

MRS HIGGINS [*rising and following him*] Be quiet, Henry. Sit down.

HIGGINS. I—

MRS HIGGINS. Sit down, dear; and listen to me.

HIGGINS. Oh very well, very well, very well. [*He throws himself ungraciously on the ottoman, with his face towards the windows*]. But I think you might have told us this half an hour ago.

MRS HIGGINS. Eliza came to me this morning. She told me of the brutal way you two treated her.

HIGGINS [*bounding up again*] What!

PICKERING [*rising also*] My dear Mrs Higgins, she's been telling you stories. We didnt treat her brutally. We hardly said a word to her; and we parted on particularly good terms. [*Turning on* Higgins] Higgins: did you bully her after I went to bed?

HIGGINS. Just the other way about. She threw
my slippers in my face. She behaved in the
most outrageous way. I never gave her the
9 slightest provocation. The slippers came
bang into my face the moment I entered the
room—before I had uttered a word. And
used perfectly awful language.

PICKERING [*astonished*] But why? What did we do to her?

MRS HIGGINS. I think I know pretty well what you did. The girl is naturally rather affectionate, I think. Isnt she, Mr Doolittle?

DOOLITTLE. Very tender-hearted, maam. Takes after me.

MRS HIGGINS. Just so. She had become attached to you both. She worked very hard for
you, Henry. I don't think you quite realize
what anything in the nature of brain work
10 means to a girl of her class. Well, it seems
that when the great day of trial came, and
she did this wonderful thing for you without
making a single mistake, you two sat there
and never said a word to her, but talked
together of how glad you were that it was all
over and how you had been bored with the
whole thing. And then you were surprised
because she threw your slippers at you! I
should have thrown the fire-irons at you.

HIGGINS. We said nothing except that we were tired and wanted to go to bed. Did we, Pick?

PICKERING [*shrugging his shoulders*] That was all.

MRS HIGGINS [*ironically*] Quite sure?

PICKERING. Absolutely. Really, that was all.

MRS HIGGINS. You didnt thank her, or pet her, or admire her, or tell her how splendid she'd been.

HIGGINS [*impatiently*] But she knew all about that. We didnt make speeches to her, if thats what you mean.

PICKERING [*conscience stricken*] Perhaps we were a little inconsiderate. Is she very angry?

MRS HIGGINS [*returning to her place at the writing-table*] Well, I'm afraid she wont go back to Wimpole Street, especially now that Mr Doolittle is able to keep up the position you have thrust on her; but she says she is quite willing to meet you on friendly terms and to let bygones be bygones.

HIGGINS [*furious*] Is she, by George? Ho!

MRS HIGGINS. If you promise to behave yourself, Henry, I'll ask her to come down. If not, go home; for you have taken up quite enough of my time.

HIGGINS. Oh, all right. Very well. Pick: you behave yourself. Let us put on our best Sunday manners for this creature that we picked out of the mud. [*He flings himself sulkily into the Elizabethan chair*].

DOOLITTLE [*remonstrating*] Now, now, Enry
Iggins! Have some consideration for my feel- 11
ings as a middle class man.

9 Discussion Decide if Higgins is fooling himself or if he really believes what he is saying and explain your choice.

10 Discussion On whose side is Mrs. Higgins and why?

11 Reading Strategy What is the irony in this statement?

12 **Discussion** Why is it important for Eliza not to know what has happened to her father until after she has made her decision?

13 **Discussion** What causes Higgins to choke?

14 **Literary Focus** If you knew nothing else about Higgins but what you can learn in this speech, how would you describe his character?

MRS HIGGINS. Remember your promise, Henry. [*She presses the bell-button on the writing-table*]. Mr Doolittle: will you be so
12 good as to step out on the balcony for a moment. I dont want Eliza to have the shock of your news until she has made it up with these two gentlemen. Would you mind?

DOOLITTLE. As you wish, lady. Anything to help Henry to keep her off my hands. [*He disappears through the window*].

The PARLORMAID *answers the bell.* PICKERING *sits down in* DOOLITTLE'*s place.*

MRS HIGGINS. Ask Miss Doolittle to come down, please.

THE PARLORMAID. Yes, maam. [*She goes out*].

MRS HIGGINS. Now, Henry: be good.

HIGGINS. I am behaving myself perfectly.

PICKERING. He is doing his best, Mrs Higgins.

A pause. HIGGINS *throws back his head; stretches out his legs; and begins to whistle.*

MRS HIGGINS. Henry, dearest, you dont look at all nice in that attitude.

HIGGINS [*pulling himself together*] I was not trying to look nice, mother.

MRS HIGGINS. It doesnt matter, dear. I only wanted to make you speak.

HIGGINS. Why?

MRS HIGGINS. Because you cant speak and whistle at the same time.

HIGGINS *groans. Another very trying pause.*

HIGGINS [*springing up, out of patience*] Where the devil is that girl? Are we to wait here all day?

ELIZA *enters, sunny, self-possessed, and giving a staggeringly convincing exhibition of ease of manner. She carries a little work-basket, and is very much at home.* PICKERING *is too much taken aback to rise.*

LIZA. How do you do, Professor Higgins? Are you quite well?

HIGGINS [*choking*] Am I— [*He can say no* 13
more].

LIZA. But of course you are: you are never ill. So glad to see you again, Colonel Pickering. [*He rises hastily; and they shake hands*]. Quite chilly this morning, isn't it? [*She sits down on his left. He sits beside her*].

HIGGINS. Dont you dare try this game on me. I taught it to you; and it doesnt take me in. Get up and come home; and dont be a fool.

ELIZA *takes a piece of needlework from her basket, and begins to stitch at it, without taking the least notice of this outburst.*

MRS HIGGINS. Very nicely put, indeed, Henry. No woman could resist such an invitation.

HIGGINS. You let her alone, mother. Let her speak for herself. You will jolly soon see whether she has an idea that I havnt put into her head or a word that I havnt put into her mouth. I tell you I have created this thing 14
out of the squashed cabbage leaves of Covent Garden; and now she pretends to play the fine lady with me.

MRS HIGGINS [*placidly*] Yes, dear; but youll sit down, wont you?

HIGGINS *sits down again, savagely.*

LIZA [*to* PICKERING, *taking no apparent notice of* HIGGINS, *and working away deftly*] Will you drop me altogether now that the experiment is over, Colonel Pickering?

PICKERING. Oh dont. You mustnt think of it as an experiment. It shocks me, somehow.

LIZA. Oh, I'm only a squashed cabbage leaf—

PICKERING [*impulsively*] No.

LIZA [*continuing quietly*]—but I owe so much to you that I should be very unhappy if you forgot me.

PICKERING. It's very kind of you to say so, Miss Doolittle.

1192

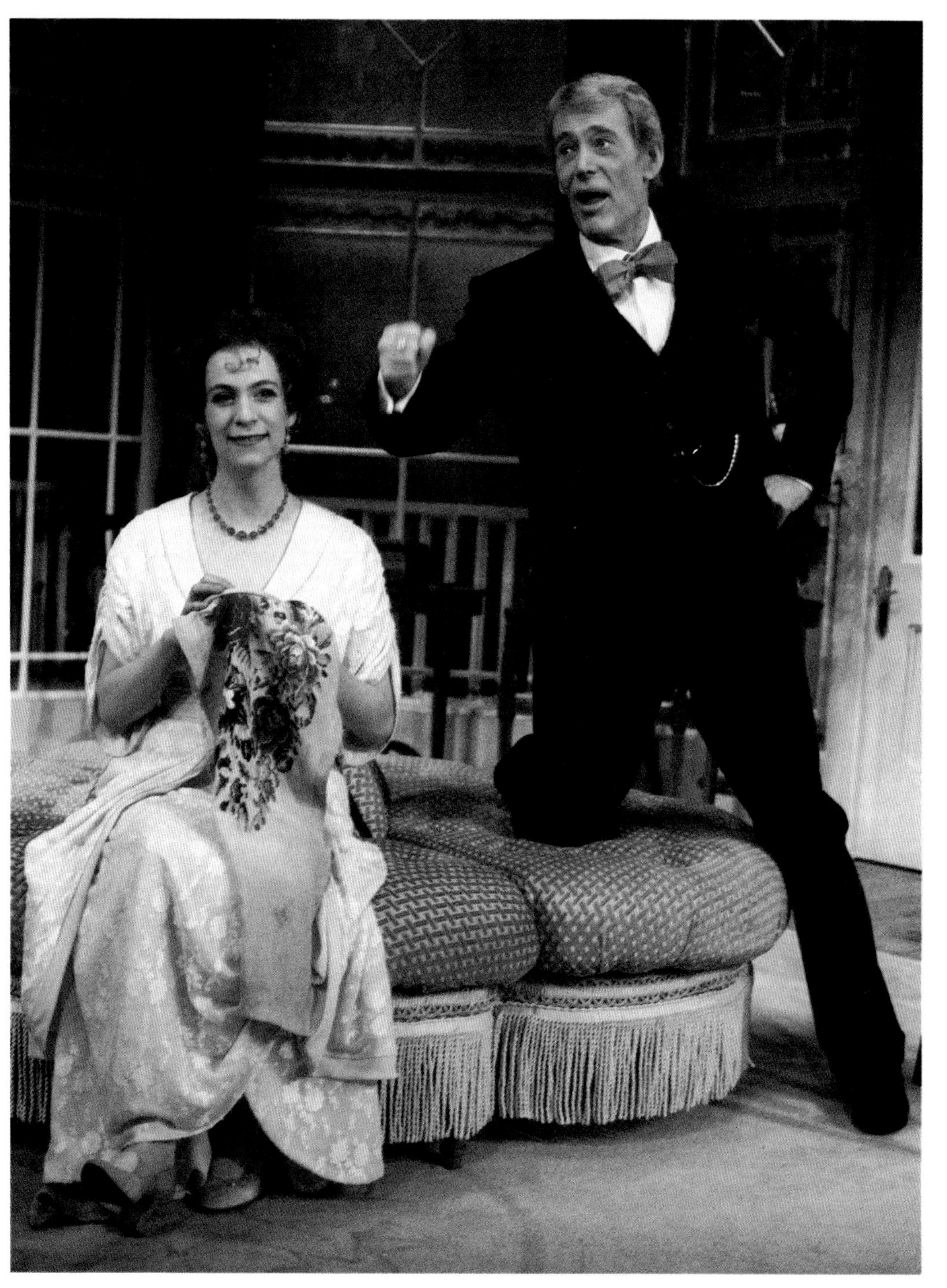

15 **Reading Strategy** What irony is involved in Eliza's explanation to Pickering?

16 **Literary Focus** What effect has having self-respect had on the development of Eliza's character?

17 **Discussion** Of what significance is the fact that Higgins took off his boots in front of Eliza?

18 **Literary Focus** Have students cite examples from the play that support Eliza's observation that the difference between a flower girl and a lady is not in the way that she behaves but in the way that she is treated.

Discussion What has caused the final separation between Eliza's past and present?

15 LIZA. It's not because you paid for my dresses. I know you are generous to everybody with money. But it was from you that I learnt really nice manners; and that is what makes one a lady, isnt it? You see it was so very difficult for me with the example of Professor Higgins always before me. I was brought up to be just like him, unable to control myself, and using bad language on the slightest provocation. And I should never have known that ladies and gentlemen didnt behave like that if you hadnt been there.

HIGGINS. Well!!

PICKERING. Oh, thats only his way, you know. He doesnt mean it.

LIZA. Oh, *I* didnt mean it either, when I was a flower girl. It was only my way. But you see I did it; and thats what makes the difference after all.

PICKERING. No doubt. Still, he taught you to speak; and I couldn't have done that, you know.

LIZA [*trivially*] Of course: that is his profession.

HIGGINS. Damnation!

LIZA [*continuing*] It was just like learning to dance in the fashionable way: there was nothing more than that in it. But do you know what began my real education?

PICKERING. What?

16 LIZA [*stopping her work for a moment*] Your calling me Miss Doolittle that day when I first came to Wimpole Street. That was the beginning of self-respect for me. [*She resumes her stitching*] And there were a hundred little things you never noticed, because they came naturally to you. Things about standing up and taking off your hat and opening doors—

PICKERING. Oh, that was nothing.

LIZA. Yes: things that shewed you thought and felt about me as if I were something better than a scullery-maid; though of course I know you would have been just the same to a scullery-maid if she had been let into the drawing room. You never took off your boots in the dining room when I was there. 17

PICKERING. You mustnt mind that. Higgins takes off his boots all over the place.

LIZA. I know. I am not blaming him. It is his way, isn't it? But it made such a difference to me that you didnt do it. You see, really and truly, apart from the things anyone can pick up (the dressing and the proper way of speaking, and so on), the difference between a lady and a flower girl is not how she behaves, but how she's treated. I shall always be a flower girl to Professor Higgins, because he always treats me as a flower girl, and always will; but I know I can be a lady to you, because you always treat me as a lady, and always will. 18

MRS HIGGINS. Please dont grind your teeth, Henry.

PICKERING. Well, this is really very nice of you, Miss Doolittle.

LIZA. I should like you to call me Eliza, now, if you would.

PICKERING. Thank you. Eliza, of course.

LIZA. And I should like Professor Higgins to call me Miss Doolittle.

HIGGINS. I'll see you damned first.

MRS HIGGINS. Henry! Henry!

PICKERING [*laughing*] Why dont you slang back at him? Dont stand it. It would do him a lot of good.

LIZA. I cant. I could have done it once; but now I cant go back to it. You told me, you know, that when a child is brought to a foreign country, it picks up the language in a few weeks, and forgets its own. Well, I am a child in your country. I have forgotten my own language, and can speak nothing but yours. Thats the real break-off with the 19 corner of Tottenham Court Road. Leaving Wimpole Street finishes it.

PICKERING [*much alarmed*] Oh! but youre coming back to Wimpole Street, arnt you? Youll forgive Higgins?

HIGGINS [*rising*] Forgive! Will she, by George! Let her go. Let her find out how she can get on without us. She will relapse into the gutter in three weeks without me at her elbow.

DOOLITTLE *appears at the centre window. With a look of dignified reproach at* HIGGINS, *he comes slowly and silently to his daughter, who, with her back to the window, is unconscious of his approach.*

PICKERING. He's incorrigible, Eliza. You wont relapse, will you?

LIZA. No: not now. Never again. I have learnt my lesson. I dont believe I could utter one of the old sounds if I tried. [DOOLITTLE *touches*
20 *her on the left shoulder. She drops her work, losing her self-possession utterly at the spectacle of her father's splendor*] A-a-a-a-ah-ow-ooh!

HIGGINS [*With a crow of triumph*] Aha! Just so. A-a-a-a-ahowooh! A-a-a-a-ahowooh! A-a-a-a-ahowooh! Victory! Victory! [*He throws himself on the divan, folding his arms, and spraddling arrogantly*].

DOOLITTLE. Can you blame the girl? Dont look at me like that, Eliza. It aint my fault. Ive come into some money.

LIZA. You must have touched a millionaire this time, dad.

DOOLITTLE. I have. But I'm dressed something special today. I'm going to St George's, Hanover Square. Your stepmother is going to marry me.

LIZA [*angrily*] Youre going to let yourself down to marry that low common woman!

PICKERING [*quietly*] He ought to, Eliza. [*To* DOOLITTLE] Why has she changed her mind?

DOOLITTLE [*sadly*] Intimidated, Governor. Intimidated. Middle class morality claims its victim. Wont you put on your hat, Liza, and come and see me turned off?

LIZA. If the Colonel says I must, I—I'll [*almost sobbing*] I'll demean myself. And get insulted for my pains, like enough.

DOOLITTLE. Dont be afraid: she never comes to words with anyone now, poor woman!
respectability has broke all the spirit out of 21
her.

PICKERING [*squeezing* ELIZA'S *elbow gently*] Be kind to them, Eliza. Make the best of it.

LIZA [*forcing a little smile for him through her vexation*] Oh well, just to shew theres no ill feeling. I'll be back in a moment. [*She goes out*].

DOOLITTLE [*sitting down beside* PICKERING] I feel uncommon nervous about the ceremony, Colonel. I wish youd come and see me through it.

PICKERING. But youve been through it before, man. You were married to Eliza's mother.

DOOLITTLE. Who told you that, Colonel?

PICKERING. Well, nobody told me. But I concluded—naturally——

DOOLITTLE. No: that aint the natural way, Colonel: it's only the middle class way. My way was always the undeserving way. But dont say nothing to Eliza. She dont know: I always had a delicacy about telling her.

PICKERING. Quite right. We'll leave it so, if you dont mind.

DOOLITTLE. And youll come to the church, Colonel, and put me through straight?

PICKERING. With pleasure. As far as a bachelor can.

MRS HIGGINS. May I come, Mr Doolittle? I
should be very sorry to miss your wedding. 22

DOOLITTLE. I should indeed be honored by your condescension, maam; and my poor old

20 **Reading Strategy** Explore the irony and humor in Eliza's reaction.

21 **Literary Focus** What changes has middle-class morality brought to the character of Mr. Doolittle's future wife? Explain how this change shows Shaw poking fun at this morality.

22 **Discussion** Why might someone in Mrs. Higgins's social position go to Mr. Doolittle's wedding? What is her motivation?

23 **Discussion** What is Mr. Doolittle saying to Eliza and Pickering about the relationship between the three of them?

24 **Discussion** What is the relationship between Higgins's statement and Shaw's feelings about the class structure of England?

25 **Literary Focus** What is Shaw saying about manners and class in this paragraph that support the theme of the play?

woman would take it as a tremenjous compliment. She's been very low, thinking of the happy days that are no more.

MRS HIGGINS [*rising*] I'll order the carriage and get ready. [*The men rise, except* HIGGINS]. I shant be more than fifteen minutes. [*As she goes to the door* ELIZA *comes in, hatted and buttoning her gloves*]. I'm going to the church to see your father married, Eliza. You had better come in the brougham[4] with me. Colonel Pickering can go on with the bridegroom.

MRS HIGGINS *goes out.* ELIZA *comes to the middle of the room between the centre window and the ottoman.* PICKERING *joins her.*

DOOLITTLE. Bridegroom. What a word! It makes a man realize his position, somehow. [*He takes up his hat and goes towards the door*].

PICKERING. Before I go, Eliza, do forgive Higgins and come back to us.

LIZA. I dont think dad would allow me. Would you, dad?

23 **DOOLITTLE** [*sad but magnanimous*] They played you off very cunning, Eliza, them two sportsmen. If it had been only one of them, you could have nailed him. But you see, there was two; and one of them chaperoned the other, as you might say. [*To* PICKERING] It was artful of you, Colonel; but I bear no malice: I should have done the same myself. I been the victim of one woman after another all my life, and I dont grudge you two getting the better of Liza. I shant interfere. It's time for us to go, Colonel. So long, Henry. See you in St George's, Eliza. [*He goes out*].

PICKERING. [*coaxing*] Do stay with us, Eliza. [*He follows Doolittle*].

ELIZA *goes out on the balcony to avoid being alone with* HIGGINS. *He rises and joins her there. She immediately comes back into the room and makes for the door; but he goes along the balcony and gets his back to the door before she reaches it.*

HIGGINS. Well, Eliza, you've had a bit of your own back, as you call it. Have you had enough? and are you going to be reasonable? Or do you want any more?

LIZA. You want me back only to pick up your slippers and put up with your tempers and fetch and carry for you.

HIGGINS. I havnt said I wanted you back at all.

LIZA. Oh, indeed. Then what are we talking about?

HIGGINS. About you, not about me. If you come back I shall treat you just as I have always treated you. I cant change my nature; and I dont intend to change my manners. My manners are exactly the same as Colonel Pickering's.

LIZA. That's not true. He treats a flower girl as if she was a duchess.

HIGGINS. And I treat a duchess as if she was a flower girl. 24

LIZA. I see [*She turns away composedly, and sits on the ottoman, facing the window*]. The same to everybody.

HIGGINS. Just so.

LIZA. Like father.

HIGGINS [*grinning, a little taken down*] Without accepting the comparison at all points, Eliza, it's quite true that your father is not a snob, and that he will be quite at home in any station of life to which his eccentric destiny may call him. [*Seriously*] The great secret, Eliza, is not having bad manners or good manners or any other particular sort of manners, but having the same manner for all human souls: in short, behaving as if you were in Heaven, where there are no third-class carriages, and one soul is as good as another. 25

LIZA. Amen. You are a born preacher.

---

4. brougham (bro͞om) *n.*: A type of carriage.

HIGGINS [*irritated*] The question is not whether I treat you rudely, but whether you ever heard me treat anyone else better.

LIZA [*with sudden sincerity*] I dont care how you treat me. I dont mind you swearing at me. I shouldnt mind a black eye: Ive had one before this. But [*standing up and facing him*] I wont be passed over.

HIGGINS. Then get out of my way; for I wont stop for you. You talk about me as if I were a motor bus.

LIZA. So you are a motor bus: all bounce and go, and no consideration for anyone. But I can do without you: dont think I cant.

HIGGINS. I know you can. I told you you could.

LIZA [*wounded, getting away from him to the other side of the ottoman with her face to the hearth*] I know you did, you brute. You wanted to get rid of me.

HIGGINS. Liar.

LIZA. Thank you. [*She sits down with dignity*]

HIGGINS. You never asked yourself, I suppose, whether *I* could do without you.

LIZA . [*earnestly*] Don't you try to get round me. You'll have to do without me.

HIGGINS [*arrogant*] I can do without anybody. I have my own soul: my own spark of divine fire. But [*with sudden humility*] I shall miss you, Eliza. [*He sits down near her on the ottoman*] I have learnt something from your idiotic notions: I confess that humbly and gratefully. And I have grown accustomed to your voice and appearance. I like them,
26 rather.

LIZA. Well, you have both of them on your gramophone and in your book of photographs. When you feel lonely without me, you can turn the machine on. It's got no feelings to hurt.

HIGGINS. I cant turn your soul on. Leave me those feelings; and you can take away the voice and the face. They are not you.

LIZA. Oh, you are a devil. You can twist the heart in a girl as easy as some could twist her arms to hurt her. Mrs Pearce warned me. Time and again she has wanted to leave you; and you always got round her at the last minute. And you dont care a bit for her. And you dont care a bit for me.

HIGGINS. I care for life, for humanity; and you are a part of it that has come my way and been built into my house. What more can you or anyone ask?

LIZA. I wont care for anybody that doesnt care for me.

HIGGINS. Commercial principles, Eliza. Like [*reproducing her Covent Garden pronunciation with professional exactness*] s'yollin voylets [selling violets], isnt it?

LIZA. Dont sneer at me. It's mean to sneer at me.

HIGGINS. I have never sneered in my life. Sneering doesnt become either the human face or the human soul. I am expressing my righteous contempt for Commercialism. I dont and wont trade in affection. You call me a brute because you couldnt buy a claim on me by fetching my slippers and finding my spectacles. You were a fool: I think a woman fetching a man's slippers is a disgusting sight: did I ever fetch your slippers? I think a good deal more of you for throwing them in 27
my face. No use slaving for me and then saying you want to be cared for: who cares for a slave? If you come back, come back for the sake of good fellowship; for youll get nothing else. Youve had a thousand times as much out of me as I have out of you; and if you dare to set up your little dog's tricks of fetching and carrying slippers against my creation of a Duchess Eliza, I'll slam the door in your silly face.

LIZA. What did you do it for if you didnt care for me?

HIGGINS [*heartily*] Why, because it was my job.

26 **Literary Focus** Is this speech consistent with Higgins's character? If so, why? If not, why not?

27 **Discussion** What universal truth does Higgins—speaking for Shaw—present here for anyone interested in relationships between men and women? What new light does Higgins's explanation shed on him?

28 Discussion According to Higgins, what is the cause of violence in life?

29 Discussion Why does Eliza consider herself a slave?

30 Discussion Why—when he doesn't appear to be asking her—does Eliza tell Higgins that she won't marry him?

31 Discussion What *are* Eliza and Higgins really quarreling about?

LIZA. You never thought of the trouble it would make for me.

HIGGINS. Would the world ever have been made if its maker had been afraid of making trouble? Making life means making trouble.
28 Theres only one way of escaping trouble; and thats killing things. Cowards, you notice, are always shrieking to have troublesome people killed.

LIZA. I'm no preacher: I dont notice things like that. I notice that you dont notice me.

HIGGINS [*jumping up and walking about intolerantly*] Eliza: youre an idiot. I waste the treasures of my Miltonic mind by spreading them before you. Once for all, understand that I go my way and do my work without caring twopence what happens to either of us. I am not intimidated, like your father and your stepmother. So you can come back or go to the devil: which you please.

LIZA. What am I to come back for?

HIGGINS [*bouncing up on his knees on the ottoman and leaning over it to her*] For the fun of it. Thats why I took you on.

LIZA [*with averted face*] And you may throw me out tomorrow if I dont do everything you want me to?

HIGGINS. Yes; and you may walk out tomorrow if I dont do everything you want me to.

LIZA. And live with my stepmother?

HIGGINS. Yes, or sell flowers.

LIZA. Oh, if I only could go back to my flower
29 basket! I should be independent of both you and father and all the world! Why did you take my independence from me? Why did I give it up? I'm a slave now, for all my fine clothes.

HIGGINS. Not a bit. I'll adopt you as my daughter and settle money on you if you like. Or
30 would you rather marry Pickering?

LIZA [*looking fiercely round at him*] I wouldnt marry you if you asked me; and youre nearer my age than what he is.

HIGGINS [*gently*] Than he is: not "than what he is."

LIZA [*losing her temper and rising*] I'll talk as I like. Youre not my teacher now.

HIGGINS [*reflectively*] I dont suppose Pickering would, though. He's as confirmed an old bachelor as I am.

LIZA. Thats not what I want; and dont you think it. I've always had chaps enough wanting me that way. Freddy Hill writes to me twice and three times a day, sheets and sheets.

HIGGINS [*disagreeably surprised*] Damn his impudence! [*He recoils and finds himself sitting on his heels*].

LIZA. He has a right to if he likes, poor lad. And he does love me.

HIGGINS [*getting off the ottoman*] You have no right to encourage him.

LIZA. Every girl has a right to be loved.

HIGGINS. What! By fools like that?

LIZA. Freddy's not a fool. And if he's weak and poor and wants me, may be he'd make me happier than my betters that bully me and dont want me.

HIGGINS. Can he make anything of you? Thats the point.

LIZA. Perhaps I could make something of him. But I never thought of us making anything of one another; and you never think of
anything else. I only want to be natural. 31

HIGGINS. In short, you want me to be as infatuated about you as Freddy? Is that it?

LIZA. No I dont. Thats not the sort of feeling I want from you. And dont you be too sure of yourself or of me. I could have been a bad girl if I'd liked. Ive seen more of some things than you, for all your learning. Girls like me can drag gentlemen down to make love to them easy enough. And they wish each other dead the next minute.

HIGGINS. Of course they do. Then what in thunder are we quarrelling about?

LIZA [*much troubled*] I want a little kindness. I know I'm a common ignorant girl, and you a book-learned gentleman; but I'm not dirt under your feet. What I done [*correcting herself*] what I did was not for the dresses and the taxis: I did it because we were pleasant together and I come—came—to care for you; not to want you to make love to me, and not forgetting the difference between us, but more friendly like.

HIGGINS. Well, of course. Thats just how I feel. And how Pickering feels. Eliza: youre a fool.

LIZA. Thats not a proper answer to give me [*she sinks on the chair at the writing-table in tears*].

HIGGINS. It's all youll get until you stop being a common idiot. If youre going to be a lady, youll have to give up feeling neglected if the men you know dont spend half their time snivelling over you and the other half giving you black eyes. If you cant stand the coldness of my sort of life, and the strain of it, go back to the gutter. Work til youre more a brute than a human being; and then cuddle and squabble and drink til you fall asleep. Oh, it's a fine life, the life of the gutter. It's real: it's warm: it's violent: you can feel it through the thickest skin: you can taste it and smell it without any training or any work. Not like Science and Literature and Classical Music and Philosophy and Art. You find me cold, unfeeling, selfish, dont you? Very well: be off with you to the sort of people you like. Marry some sentimental hog or other with lots of money, and a thick pair of lips to kiss you with and a thick pair of boots to kick you with. If you cant appreciate what youve got, youd better get what you can appreciate.

LIZA. [*Desperate*] Oh, you are a cruel tyrant. I cant talk to you: you turn everything against me: I'm always in the wrong. But you know very well all the time that youre nothing but a bully. You know I cant go back to the gutter, as you call it, and that I have no real friends in the world but you and the Colonel. You know well I couldnt bear to live with a low common man after you two; and it's wicked and cruel of you to insult me by pretending I could. You think I must go back to Wimpole Street because I have nowhere else to go but father's. But dont you be too sure that you have me under your feet to be trampled on and talked down. I'll marry Freddy, I will, as soon as I'm able to support him.

HIGGINS [*thunderstruck*] Freddy!!! that young fool! That poor devil who couldnt get a
job as an errand boy even if he had the guts 32
to try for it! Woman: do you not understand that I have made you a consort for a king?

LIZA. Freddy loves me: that makes him king enough for me. I dont want him to work: he wasnt brought up to it as I was. I'll go and be a teacher.

HIGGINS. Whatll you teach, in heaven's name?

LIZA. What you taught me. I'll teach phonetics.

HIGGINS. Ha! ha! ha!

LIZA. I'll offer myself as an assistant to that hairyfaced Hungarian.

HIGGINS [*rising in a fury*] What! That imposter! that humbug! that toadying ingoramus! Teach him my methods! my discoveries! You take one step in his direction and I'll wring your neck. [*He lays hands on her*]. Do you hear?

LIZA [*defiantly non-resistant*] Wring away. What do I care? I knew youd strike me some day. [*He lets her go, stamping with rage at having forgotten himself, and recoils so hastily that he stumbles back into his seat on the ottoman*]. Aha! Now I know how to
deal with you. What a fool I was not to think 33
of it before! You cant take away the knowledge you gave me. You said I had a finer ear than you. And I can be civil and kind to people, which is more than you can. Aha!

32 **Discussion** Why is Higgins so shocked this time when Eliza tells him that she's going to marry Freddy?

33 **Discussion** What does Eliza say and do that earns her new respect from Higgins?

34 **Discussion** What universal truth is presented in Higgins's speech?

[*Purposely dropping her aitches to annoy him*] Thats done you, Enry Iggins, it az. Now I dont care that [*snapping her fingers*] for your bullying and your big talk. I'll advertize it in the papers that your duchess is only a flower girl that you taught, and that she'll teach anybody to be a duchess just the same in six months for a thousand guineas. Oh, when I think of myself crawling under your feet and being trampled on and called names, when all the time I had only to lift up my finger to be as good as you, I could just kick myself.

HIGGINS [*wondering at her*] You damned impudent slut, you! But it's better than snivelling; better than fetching slippers and finding spectacles, isnt it? [*Rising*] By George, Eliza. I said I'd make a woman of you; and I have. I like you like this.

LIZA. Yes: you turn round and make up to me now that I'm not afraid of you, and can do without you.

34 **HIGGINS.** Of course I do, you little fool. Five minutes ago you were like a millstone round my neck. Now youre a tower of strength: a consort battleship. You and I and Pickering will be three old bachelors instead of only two men and a silly girl.

MRS HIGGINS *returns, dressed for the wedding.* ELIZA *instantly becomes cool and elegant.*

MRS HIGGINS. The carriage is waiting, Eliza. Are you ready?

LIZA. Quite. Is the Professor coming?

MRS HIGGINS. Certainly not. He cant behave himself in church. He makes remarks out loud all the time on the clergyman's pronunciation.

LIZA. Then I shall not see you again, Professor. Goodbye. [*She goes to the door*].

MRS HIGGINS [*coming to* HIGGINS] Goodbye, dear.

HIGGINS. Goodbye, mother. [*He is about to kiss her, when he recollects something*]. Oh, by the way, Eliza, order a ham and a Stilton cheese, will you? And buy me a pair of reindeer gloves, number eights, and a tie to match that new suit of mine. You can choose the color. [*His cheerful, careless, vigorous voice shews that he is incorrigible*].

LIZA [*disdainfully*] Number eights are too small for you if you want them lined with lamb's wool. You have three new ties that you have forgotten in the drawer of your washstand. Colonel Pickering prefers double Gloucester to Stilton; and you dont notice the difference. I telephoned Mrs Pearce this morning not to forget the ham. What you are to do without me I cannot imagine. [*She sweeps out*].

MRS HIGGINS. I'm afraid youve spoilt that girl, Henry. I should be uneasy about you and her if she were less fond of Colonel Pickering.

HIGGINS. Pickering! Nonsense: she's going to marry Freddy. Ha ha! Freddy! Freddy!! Ha ha ha ha ha!!!!! [*He roars with laughter as the play ends*].

Epilogue

The rest of the story need not be shewn in action, and indeed, would hardly need telling if our imaginations were not so enfeebled by their lazy dependence on the ready-mades and reach-me-downs of the ragshop in which Romance keeps its stock of "happy endings" to misfit all stories. Now, the history of Eliza Doolittle, though called a romance because the transfiguration it records seems exceedingly improbable, is common enough. Such transfigurations have been achieved by hundreds of resolutely ambitious young women since Nell Gwynne[1] set them the example by playing queens and fascinating kings in the theatre in which she began by selling oranges. Nevertheless, people in all directions have assumed, for no other reason than that she became the heroine of a romance, that she must have married the hero of it. This is unbearable, not only because her little drama, if acted on such a thoughtless assumption, must be spoiled, but because the true sequel is patent to anyone with a sense of human nature in general, and of feminine instinct in particular.

Eliza, in telling Higgins she would not marry him if he asked her, was not coquetting: she was announcing a well-considered decision. When a bachelor interests, and dominates, and teaches, and becomes important to a spinster, as Higgins with Eliza, she always, if she has character enough to be capable of it, considers very seriously indeed whether she will play for becoming that bachelor's wife, especially if he is so little interested in marriage that a determined and devoted woman might capture him if she set herself resolutely to do it. Her decision will depend a good deal on whether she is really free to choose; and that, again, will depend on her age and income. If she is at the end of her youth, and has no security for her livelihood, she will marry him because she must marry anybody who will provide for her. But at Eliza's age a good-looking girl does not feel that pressure: she feels free to pick and choose. She is therefore guided by her instinct in the matter. Eliza's instinct tells her not to marry Higgins. It does not tell her to give him up. It is not in the slightest doubt as to his remaining one of the strongest personal interests in her life. It would be very sorely strained if there was another woman likely to supplant her with him. But as she feels sure of him on that last point, she has no doubt at all as to her course, and would not have any, even if the difference of twenty years in age, which seems so great to youth, did not exist between them.

As our own instincts are not appealed to by her conclusion, let us see whether we

1. Nell Gwynne: Eleanor Gwynne (1650–1687), an English actress and favorite of Charles II.

1202

cannot discover some reason in it. When Higgins excused his indifference to young women on the ground that they had an irresistible rival in his mother, he gave the clue to his inveterate old-bachelordom. The case is uncommon only to the extent that remarkable mothers are uncommon. If an imaginative boy has a sufficiently rich mother who has intelligence, personal grace, dignity of character without harshness, and a cultivated sense of the best art of her time to enable her to make her house beautiful, she sets a standard for him against which very few women can struggle, besides effecting for him a disengagement of his affections, his sense of beauty, and his idealism from his specifically sexual impulses. This makes him a standing puzzle to the huge number of uncultivated people who have been brought up in tasteless homes by commonplace or disagreeable parents, and to whom, consequently, literature, painting, sculpture, music, and affectionate personal relations come as modes of sex if they come at all. The word passion means nothing else to them; and that Higgins could have a passion for phonetics and idealize his mother instead of Eliza, would seem to them absurd and unnatural. Nevertheless, when we look round and see that hardly anyone is too ugly or disagreeable to find a wife or a husband if he or she wants one, whilst many old maids and bachelors are above the average in quality and culture, we cannot help suspecting that the disentanglement of sex from the associations with which it is so commonly confused, a disentanglement which persons of genius achieve by sheer intellectual analysis, is sometimes produced or aided by parental fascination.

Now, though Eliza was incapable of thus explaining to herself Higgins's formidable powers of resistance to the charm that prostrated Freddy at the first glance, she was instinctively aware that she could never obtain a complete grip of him, or come between him and his mother (the first necessity of the married woman). To put it shortly, she knew that for some mysterious reason he had not the makings of a married man in him, according to her conception of a husband as one to whom she would be his nearest and fondest and warmest interest. Even had there been no mother-rival, she would still have refused to accept an interest in herself that was secondary to philosophic interests. Had Mrs Higgins died, there would still have been Milton and the Universal Alphabet. Landor's[2] remark that to those who have the greatest power of loving, love is a secondary affair, would not have recommended Landor to Eliza. Put that along with her resentment of Higgins's domineering superiority, and her mistrust of his coaxing cleverness in getting round her and evading her wrath when he had gone too far with his impetuous bullying, and you will see that Eliza's instinct had good grounds for warning her not to marry her Pygmalion.

And now, whom did Eliza marry? For if Higgins was a predestinate old bachelor, she was most certainly not a predestinate old maid. Well, that can be told very shortly to those who have not guessed it from the indications she has herself given them.

Almost immediately after Eliza is stung into proclaiming her considered determination not to marry Higgins, she mentions the fact that young Mr Frederick Eynsford Hill is pouring out his love for her daily through the post. Now Freddy is young, practically twenty years younger than Higgins: he is a gentleman [or, as Eliza would qualify him, a toff], and speaks like one. He is nicely dressed, is treated by the Colonel as an equal, loves her unaffectedly, and is not her master, nor ever likely to dominate her in spite of his advantage of social standing. Eliza has no use for the foolish romantic tradition that all women love to be mastered, if not actually bullied and beaten. "When 35

2. Landor's: Referring to Walter Savage Landor (1775–1864), an English writer.

35 **Discussion** What does this passage say about the basis for the dominance and abuse of women during this period? How does Eliza feel about the status of women?

1203

you go to women" says Nietzsche[3] "take your whip with you." Sensible despots have never confined that precaution to women: they have taken their whips with them when they have dealt with men, and been slavishly idealized by the men over whom they have flourished the whip much more than by women. No doubt there are slavish women as well as slavish men; and women, like men, admire those that are stronger than themselves. But to admire a strong person and to live under that strong person's thumb are two different things. The weak may not be admired and hero-worshipped; but they are by no means disliked or shunned; and they never seem to have the least difficulty in marrying people who are too good for them. They may fail in emergencies; but life is not one long emergency: it is mostly a string of situations for which no exceptional strength is needed, and with which even rather weak people can cope if they have a stronger partner to help them out. Accordingly, it is a truth everywhere in evidence that strong people, masculine or feminine, not only do not marry stronger people, but do not shew any preference for them in selecting their

---

3. Nietzsche (nē′ chə): German philosopher Friedrich Wilhelm Nietzsche (1844–1900).

friends. When a lion meets another with a louder roar "the first lion thinks the last a bore." The man or woman who feels strong enough for two, seeks for every other quality in a partner than strength.

The converse is also true. Weak people want to marry strong people who do not frighten them too much; and this often leads them to make the mistake we describe metaphorically as "biting off more than they can chew." They want too much for too little; and when the bargain is unreasonable beyond all bearing, the union becomes impossible: it ends in the weaker party being either discarded or borne as a cross, which is worse. People who are not only weak, but silly or obtuse as well, are often in these difficulties.

36 This being the state of human affairs, what is Eliza fairly sure to do when she is placed between Freddy and Higgins? Will she look forward to a lifetime of fetching Higgins's slippers or to a lifetime of Freddy fetching hers? There can be no doubt about the answer. Unless Freddy is biologically repulsive to her, and Higgins biologically attractive to a degree that overwhelms all her other instincts, she will, if she marries either of them, marry Freddy.

And that is just what Eliza did.

Complications ensued; but they were economic, not romantic. Freddy had no money and no occupation. His mother's jointure,[4] a last relic of the opulence of Largelady Park, had enabled her to struggle along in Earlscourt with an air of gentility, but not to procure any serious secondary education for her children, much less give the boy a profession. A clerkship at thirty shillings a week was beneath Freddy's dignity, and extremely distasteful to him besides. His prospects consisted of a hope that if he kept up appearances somebody would do something for him. The something appeared vaguely to his imagination as a private secretaryship or a sinecure[5] of some sort. To his mother it perhaps appeared as a marriage to some lady of means who could not resist her boy's niceness. Fancy her feelings when he married a flower girl who had become disclassed under extraordinary circumstances which were now notorious!

It is true that Eliza's situation did not seem wholly ineligible. Her father, though formerly a dustman, and now fantastically disclassed, had become extremely popular in the smartest society by a social talent which triumphed over every prejudice and every disadvantage. Rejected by the middle class, which he loathed, he had shot up at once into the highest circles by his wit, his dustmanship (which he carried like a banner), and his Nietzschean transcendence of good and evil. At intimate ducal dinners he sat on the right hand of the Duchess; and in country houses he smoked in the pantry and was made much of by the butler when he was not feeding in the dining room and being consulted by cabinet ministers. But he found it almost as hard to do all this on [three] thousand a year as Mrs Eynsford Hill to live in Earlscourt on an income so pitiably smaller that I have not the heart to disclose its exact figure. He absolutely refused to add the last straw to his burden by contributing to Eliza's support.

Thus Freddy and Eliza, now Mr and Mrs Eynsford Hill, would have spent a penniless honeymoon but for a wedding present of £500 from the Colonel to Eliza. It lasted a long time because Freddy did not know how to spend money, never having had any to spend, and Eliza, socially trained by a pair of old bachelors, wore her clothes as long as they held together and looked pretty, without the least regard to their being many months out of fashion. Still, £500 will not last two young people for ever; and they both knew, and Eliza felt as well, that they must

4. jointure *n.*: Widow's inheritance.

5. sinecure (sī′ nə kyo͞or′) *n.*: Any office of position that brings advantage but involves little or no work.

36 **Reading Strategy** Summarize the author's explanation for why Eliza marries Freddy rather than Professor Higgins. Do you think his reasoning on human nature is correct? Why or why not?

shift for themselves in the end. She could quarter herself on Wimpole Street because it had come to be her home; but she was quite aware that she ought not to quarter Freddy there, and that it would not be good for his character if she did.

Not that the Wimpole Street bachelors objected. When she consulted them, Higgins declined to be bothered about her housing problem when that solution was so simple. Eliza's desire to have Freddy in the house with her seemed of no more importance than if she had wanted an extra piece of bedroom furniture. Pleas as to Freddy's character, and the moral obligation on him to earn his own living, were lost on Higgins. He denied that Freddy had any character, and declared that if he tried to do any useful work some competent person would have the trouble of undoing it: a procedure involving a net loss to the community, and great unhappiness to Freddy himself, who was obviously intended by Nature for such light work as amusing Eliza, which, Higgins declared, was a much more useful and honorable occupation than working in the city. When Eliza referred again to her project of teaching phonetics, Higgins abated not a jot of his violent opposition to it. He said she was not within ten years of being qualified to meddle with his pet subject; and as it was evident that the Colonel agreed with him, she felt she could not go against them in this grave matter, and that she had no right, without Higgins's consent, to exploit the knowledge he had given her; for his knowledge seemed to her as much his private property as his watch: Eliza was no communist. Besides, she was superstitiously devoted to them both, more entirely and frankly after her marriage than before it.

It was the Colonel who finally solved the problem, which had cost him much perplexed cogitation. He one day asked Eliza, rather shyly, whether she had quite given up her notion of keeping a flower shop. She replied that she had thought of it, but had put it out of her head, because the Colonel had said, that day at Mrs Higgins's, that it would never do. The Colonel confessed that when he said that, he had not quite recovered from the dazzling impression of the day before. They broke the matter to Higgins that evening. The sole comment vouchsafed by him very nearly led to a serious quarrel with Eliza. It was to the effect that she would have in Freddy an ideal errand boy.

Freddy himself was next sounded on the subject. He said he had been thinking of a shop himself; though it had presented itself to his pennilessness as a small place in which Eliza should sell tobacco at one counter whilst he sold newspapers at the opposite one. But he agreed that it would be extraordinarily jolly to go early every morning with Eliza to Covent Garden and buy flowers on the scene of their first meeting: a sentiment which earned him many kisses from his wife. He added that he had always been afraid to propose anything of the sort, because Clara would make an awful row about a step that must damage her matrimonial chances, and his mother could not be expected to like it after clinging for so many years to that step of the social ladder on which retail trade is impossible.

This difficulty was removed by an event highly unexpected by Freddy's mother. Clara, in the course of her incursions into those artistic circles which were the highest within her reach, discovered that her conversational qualifications were expected to include a grounding in the novels of Mr H. G. Wells.[6] She borrowed them in various directions so energetically that she swallowed them all within two months. The result was a conversion of a kind quite common today. A modern Acts of the Apostles would fill fifty whole Bibles if anyone were capable of writing it.

Poor Clara, who appeared to Higgins and

---

6. H. G. Wells: Herbert George Wells (1866–1946), English novelist and historian.

his mother as a disagreeable and ridiculous person, and to her own mother as in some inexplicable way a social failure, had never seen herself in either light; for, though to some extent ridiculed and mimicked in West Kensington like everybody else there, she was accepted as a rational and normal—or shall we say inevitable?—sort of human being. At worst they called her The Pusher; but to them no more than to herself had it ever occurred that she was pushing the air, and pushing it in a wrong direction. Still, she was not happy. She was growing desperate. Her one asset, the fact that her mother was what the Epsom greengrocer called a carriage lady, had no exchange value, apparently. It had prevented her from getting educated, because the only education she could have afforded was education with the Earlscourt greengrocer's daughter. It had led her to seek the society of her mother's class; and that class simply would not have her, because she was much poorer than the greengrocer, and, far from being able to afford a maid, could not afford even a housemaid, and had to scrape along at home with an illiberally treated general servant. Under such circumstances nothing could give her an air of being a genuine product of Largelady Park. And yet its tradition made her regard a marriage with anyone within her reach as an unbearable humiliation. Commercial people and professional people in a small way were odious to her. She ran after painters and novelists; but she did not charm them; and her bold attempts to pick up and practise artistic and literary talk irritated them. She was, in short, an utter failure, an ignorant, incompetent, pretentious, unwelcome, penniless, useless little snob; and though she did not admit these disqualifications (for nobody ever faces unpleasant truths of this kind until the possibility of a way out dawns on them) she felt their effects too keenly to be satisfied with her position.

Clara had a startling eyeopener when, on being suddenly wakened to enthusiasm by a girl of her own age who dazzled her and produced in her a gushing desire to take her for a model, and gain her friendship, she discovered that this exquisite apparition had graduated from the gutter in a few months time. It shook her so violently, that when Mr H. G. Wells lifted her on the point of his puissant[7] pen, and placed her at the angle of view from which the life she was leading and the society to which she clung appeared in its true relation to real human needs and worthy social structure, he effected a conversion and a conviction of sin comparable to the most sensational feats of General Booth[8] or Gypsy Smith.[9] Clara's snobbery went bang. Life suddenly began to move with her. Without knowing how or why, she began to make friends and enemies. Some of the acquaintances to whom she had been a tedious or indifferent or ridiculous affliction, dropped her: others became cordial. To her amazement she found that some "quite nice" people were saturated with Wells, and that this accessibility to ideas was the secret of their niceness. People she had thought deeply religious, and had tried to conciliate on that tack with disastrous results, suddenly took an interest in her, and revealed a hostility to conventional religion which she had never conceived possible except among the most desperate characters. They made her read Galsworthy; and Galsworthy exposed the vanity of Largelady Park and finished her. It exasperated her to think that the dungeon in which she had languished for so many unhappy years had been unlocked all the time, and that the impulses she had so carefully struggled with and stifled for the sake of keeping well with society, were pre-

---

7. puissant (pyo͞o′ i sənt) *adj.*: Powerful.
8. General Booth: William Booth (1829–1912), the founder of the Salvation Army.
9. Gypsy Smith: Gipsy Rodney Smith (1860–1947), an English evangelist.

37 Discussion Explain how Clara's predicament illustrates the contradictions of the times in which she lived.

cisely those by which alone she could have come into any sort of sincere human contact. In the radiance of these discoveries, and the tumult of their reaction, she made a fool of herself as freely and conspicuously as when she so rashly adopted Eliza's expletive in Mrs Higgins's drawing room; for the new-born Wellsian had to find her bearings almost as ridiculously as a baby; but nobody hates a baby for its ineptitudes, or thinks the worse of it for trying to eat the matches; and Clara lost no friends by her follies. They laughed at her to her face this time; and she had to defend herself and fight it out as best she could.

When Freddy paid a visit to Earlscourt (which he never did when he could possibly help it) to make the desolating announcement that he and his Eliza were thinking of blackening the Largelady scutcheon[10] by opening a shop, he found the little household already convulsed by a prior announcement from Clara that she also was going to work in an old furniture shop in Dover Street, which had been started by a fellow Wellsian. This appointment Clara owed, after all, to her old social accomplishment of Push. She had made up her mind that, cost what it might, she would see Mr Wells in the flesh; and she had achieved her end at a garden party. She had better luck than so rash an enterprise deserved. Mr Wells came up to her expectations. Age had not withered him, nor could custom stale his infinite variety in half an hour. His pleasant neatness and compactness, his small hands and feet, his teeming ready brain, his unaffected accessibility, and a certain fine apprehensiveness which stamped him as susceptible from his topmost hair to his tipmost toe, proved irresistible. Clara talked of nothing else for weeks and weeks afterwards. And as she happened to talk to the lady of the furniture shop, and that lady also desired above all things to know Mr Wells and sell pretty things to him, she offered Clara a job on the chance of achieving that end through her.

And so it came about that Eliza's luck held, and the expected opposition to the flower shop melted away. The shop is in the arcade of a railway station not very far from the Victoria and Albert Museum; and if you live in that neighbourhood you may go there any day and buy a buttonhole from Eliza.

Now here is a last opportunity for romance. Would you not like to be assured that the shop was an immense success, thanks to Eliza's charms and her early business experience in Covent Garden? Alas! the truth is the truth: the shop did not pay for a long time, simply because Eliza and her Freddy did not know how to keep it. True, Eliza had not to begin at the very beginning: she knew the names and prices of the cheaper flowers; and her elation was unbounded when she found that Freddy, like all youths educated at cheap, pretentious, and thoroughly inefficient schools, knew a little Latin. It was very little, but enough to make him appear to her a Porson or Bentley,[11] and to put him at his ease with botanical nomenclature. Unfortunately he knew nothing else; and Eliza, though she could count money up to eighteen shillings or so, and had acquired a certain familiarity with the language of Milton from her struggles to qualify herself for winning Higgins's bet, could not write out a bill without utterly disgracing the establishment. Freddy's power of stating in Latin that Balbus built a wall and that Gaul was divided into three parts[12] did not carry with it the slightest knowledge of accounts or business: Colonel

10. scutcheon (skuch′ ən) *n.*: Coat of arms.

11. Porson, Bentley: Richard Porson (1759–1808) and Richard Bentley (1662–1742), English classical scholars.

12. Balbus . . . parts: Referring to elementary Latin exercises.

Pickering had to explain to him what a cheque book and a bank account meant. And the pair were by no means easily teachable. Freddy backed up Eliza in her obstinate refusal to believe that they could save money by engaging a bookkeeper with some knowledge of the business. How, they argued, could you possible save money by going to extra expense when you already could not make both ends meet? But the Colonel, after making the ends meet over and over again, at last gently insisted; and Eliza, humbled to the dust by having to beg from him so often, and stung by the uproarious derision of Higgins, to whom the notion of Freddy succeeding at anything was a joke that never palled, grasped the fact that business, like phonetics, has to be learned.

On the piteous spectacle of the pair spending their evenings in shorthand schools and polytechnic classes, learning bookkeeping and typewriting with incipient junior clerks, male and female, from the elementary schools, let me not dwell. There were even classes at the London School of Economics, and a humble personal appeal to the director of that institution to recommend a course bearing on the flower business. He, being a humorist, explained to them the method of the celebrated Dickensian essay on Chinese Metaphysics by the gentleman who read an article on China and an article on Metaphysics and combined the information. He suggested that they should combine the London School with Kew Gardens. Eliza, to whom the procedure of the Dickensian gentleman seemed perfectly correct (as in fact it was) and not in the least funny (which was only her ignorance), took the advice with entire gravity. But the effort that cost her the deepest humiliation was a request to Higgins, whose pet artistic fancy, next to Milton's verse, was calligraphy, and who himself wrote a most beautiful Italian hand, that he would teach her to write. He declared that she was congenitally incapable of forming a single letter worthy of the least of Milton's words; but she persisted; and again he suddenly threw himself into the task of teaching her with a combination of stormy intensity, concentrated patience, and occasional bursts of interesting disquisition on the beauty and nobility, the august mission and destiny, of human handwriting. Eliza ended by acquiring an extremely uncommercial script which was a positive extension of her personal beauty, and spending three times as much on stationery as anyone else because certain qualities and shapes on paper became indispensable to her. She could not even address an envelope in the usual way because it made the margins all wrong.

Their commercial schooldays were a period of disgrace and despair for the young couple. They seemed to be learning nothing about flower shops. At last they gave it up as hopeless, and shook the dust of the shorthand schools, and the polytechnics, and the London School of Economics from their feet for ever. Besides, the business was in some mysterious way beginning to take care of itself. They had somehow forgotten their objections to employing other people. They came to the conclusion that their own way was the best, and that they had really a remarkable talent for business. The Colonel, who had been compelled for some years to keep a sufficient sum on current account at his bankers to make up their deficits, found that the provision was unnecessary: the young people were prospering. It is true that there was not quite fair play between them and their competitors in trade. Their week-ends in the country cost them nothing, and saved them the price of their Sunday dinners; for the motor car was the Colonel's; and he and Higgins paid the hotel bills. Mr F. Hill, florist and greengrocer (they soon discovered that there was money in asparagus; and asparagus led to other vegetables), had an air which stamped the business as classy; and in private life he was still Frederick Eynsford Hill, Esquire. Not that

38 Discussion How does the author explain Eliza's continuing interest in and attachment to Higgins? Explain the allusion to the story of Pygmalion, including whether the play is appropriately titled.

there was any swank[13] about him: nobody but Eliza knew that he had been christened Frederick Chaloner. Eliza herself swanked like anything.

That is all. That is how it has turned out. It is astonishing how much Eliza still manages to meddle in the housekeeping at Wimpole Street in spite of the shop and her own family. And it is notable that though she never nags her husband, and frankly loves the Colonel as if she were his favorite daughter, she has never got out of the habit of nagging Higgins that was established on the fatal night when she won his bet for him. She snaps his head off on the faintest provocation, or on none. He no longer dares to tease her by assuming an abysmal inferiority of Freddy's mind to his own. He storms and bullies and derides; but she stands up to him so ruthlessly that the Colonel has to ask her from time to time to be kinder to Higgins; and it is the only request of his that brings a mulish expression into her face. Nothing but some emergency or calamity great enough to break down all likes and dislikes, and throw them both back on their common humanity—and may they be spared any such trial!—will ever alter this. She knows that Higgins does not need her, just as her father did not need her. The very scrupulousness with which he told her that day that he had become used to having her there, and dependent on her for all sorts of little services, and that he should miss her if she went away (it would never have occurred to Freddy or the Colonel to say anything of the sort) deepens her inner certainty that she is "no more to him than them slippers"; yet she has a sense, too, that his indifference is deeper than the infatuation of commoner souls. She is immensely interested in him. She has even secret mischievous moments in which she wishes she could get him alone, on a desert island, away from all ties and with nobody else in the world to consider, and just drag him off his pedestal and see him making love like any common man. We all have private imaginations of that sort. But when it comes to business, to the life that she really leads as distinguished from the life of dreams and fancies, she likes Freddy and she likes the Colonel; and she does not like Higgins and Mr Doolittle. Galatea never does quite like Pygmalion:[14] his relation to her is too godlike to be altogether agreeable.

13. swank *n.*: Ostentatious behavior.

14. Galatea . . . Pygmalion: Pygmalion was a mythological king of Cyprus who carved a statue of a woman so beautiful that he fell in love with her. The king prayed to the gods to bring the statue, Galatea, to life, and his prayers were answered by Aphrodite, the goddess of love.

Answers

ANSWERS TO THINKING ABOUT THE SELECTION

Recalling

1. Pickering has been talking to the police to see if they can help find Eliza.
2. (a) On the recommendation of Higgins, Mr. Doolittle has become a lecturer for the Wannafeller Moral Reform World League. Because of that association, he will inherit stock worth three thousand pounds a year by the founder of the league, Mr. Wannafeller. (b) He has been made a gentlemen, with gentlemen's responsibilities; he is no longer a free man. Eliza's latest stepmother and he are getting married that very day.
3. It was from Pickering that Eliza learned really nice manners; he showed her how real ladies and gentlemen behave, something Higgins could not do.
4. (a) Eliza wants Higgins to care for her. (b) Higgins wants Eliza to come back to his house for the fun of it.
5. (a) She marries Freddy, is set up by Pickering as the operator of a flower shop, spends a great deal of time learning how to make the shop successful, lives with Freddy at Higgins's house, and makes a success of the business. (b) Clara becomes a follower of H. G. Wells and ends up working in a furniture shop.

Interpreting

6. Suggested Response: Because Mr. Doolittle has been able to put middle-class morality on like his new suit, remaining very much his own man, but passing as middle class, Shaw suggests that such morality is superficial and not to be taken seriously.
7. Suggested Response: By this time, Higgins and Eliza are too attached to each other to break their relationship off completely. Higgins is so difficult to deal with that it was

THINKING ABOUT THE SELECTION

Recalling

1. Who has Pickering been talking with on the phone at the beginning of Act V? Why?
2. (a) What has happened to Alfred Doolittle? (b) How has this change affected his life?
3. Why is Eliza grateful to Pickering?
4. (a) In their conversation together what does Eliza tell Higgins she wants from him? (b) What does he want from her?
5. (a) What, according to the Epilogue, becomes of Eliza? (b) Of Clara Eynsford Hill?

Interpreting

6. Explain what the changes in Alfred Doolittle suggest is Shaw's attitude toward "middle-class morality."
7. Do you think the outcome of Higgins's last discussion with Eliza was inevitable? Why or why not?

Applying

8. The Epilogue describes developments in Eliza's life after the action of the play. Would you have preferred to see these developments played out? Explain your reasons.

ANALYZING LITERATURE

Understanding the Complete Play

The paradoxical saying that "the whole is greater than the sum of its parts" is true of works of art. A play is a weaving-together of many elements, among them: the plot (or story line), the setting (time and place of the action), the characters (roles), the tone (playwright's attitude toward the subject or audience), the symbols (representative values attached to events, people, or things), and the theme (main idea). When these separate elements come together, a "chemical reaction" results. Create a checklist similar to the following for *Pygmalion*.

plot	setting	character	tone	symbol	theme

Write a brief description for each of the play's elements, entering "NA" when the element is not applicable. Then discuss how the various elements interact in Shaw's play. (Consider, for example, how setting affects theme.)

CRITICAL THINKING AND READING

Summarizing a Play

When a newspaper or magazine critic writes a review of a play, he or she includes a **summary,** or brief description of the action. A good summary captures a sense of the play as a whole, focusing not only on what is said and done but on such details as setting. The amount of information that a summary provides depends, of course, on its overall length. List the details you find important to include in a one-page summary of *Pygmalion*. Decide how you would handle such matters as Shaw's Preface and Epilogue.

THINKING AND WRITING

Writing About the Title

At the end of the Epilogue, Shaw mentions Pygmalion and Galatea, who are figures from Greek mythology. The sculptor Pygmalion created a statue of a beautiful woman. After he fell in love with his creation, the goddess Aphrodite brought her to life. Write an essay and discuss the effectiveness of the title Shaw chose for his play. Proceed by addressing the following questions: How godlike do you think Eliza finds Higgins? To what extent has Higgins "created" a new person? Might Higgins's feelings toward Eliza at any point in the play be fairly described as "love?" How much impact will the title have on a person who views, rather than reads, the play and who is, therefore, unfamiliar with the Epilogue? When you revise, make sure you have included adequate support for your theses.

(Answers begin on p. 1210.)

inevitable that they would not marry, but it is also inevitable that their relationship would continue for the rest of their lives.

Applying

8. Suggested Response: No. The play ends just after Eliza indicates that she will remain associated with Higgins but will marry Freddy; yet, there is still some question. Because the play ends before everything is definitely resolved, the audience is left wondering what really will happen to both of them. If Shaw had written the Epilogue as another act, he would have left the audience with nothing to ponder, nothing to work through for themselves.

ANSWERS TO ANALYZING LITERATURE

Suggested response:

Plot: The plot concerns the transformation of a lower-class flower girl into a woman accepted as a duchess by upper-class society.

Setting: The play is set in Victorian England, where what one sees in a situation or understands about a person isn't always an accurate indication of what the actual situation is or what the person is really like.

Character: The characters are representatives of the different classes in Victorian society; each plays out his or her role to determine where each really fits in that class structure.

Tone: The tone is satirical; Shaw is poking fun at all the classes, indicating that all of them are less than honest about who they are and that the boundaries between them are less rigid than is assumed.

Symbol: As representatives of their classes and the moral ethic of that class, each character becomes a symbol and their changes represent the changes possible for all members of their class; Higgins is an independent, one who refuses to seek acceptance in any class.

Theme: The theme concerns the idea that the barriers between the classes in England are artificial at best; scratch the surface and there is a dustman and a duchess in everyone.

Each of these elements is focused on the roles and characteristics of the various classes in England. Because of this focus, the elements support each other to produce a cohesive whole, a play that works through the plot to deliver the playwright's message in a clear and entertaining manner.

Challenge Keeping in mind the same elements of a play that Shaw uses, students might be challenged to write their own ending to *Pygmalion*.

ANSWERS TO CRITICAL THINKING AND READING

Answers will differ. You might list on the board key details that different students have chosen.

Challenge Have students write their one-page summaries of the play and read them aloud to a partner. Have them discuss and recommend changes that should be made in both papers and then prepare their final drafts.

The writing assignments on page 1212 have students write creatively, while those on page 1213 have them think about the selections and write critically.

YOU THE WRITER

Guidelines for Evaluating Assignment 1

1. Does the 250-word character sketch begin with a description of the relevance of the character to the story in which he or she appears?
2. Has the student used the author's terms, along with vivid original terms, to describe the character's physical appearance, habits, behaviors, and beliefs?
3. Has the student noted details that seem to have symbolic significance?
4. Is the character sketch logically organized and free from grammar, usage, and mechanics errors?

Guidelines for Evaluating Assignment 2

1. Has the student written an original poem in free verse?
2. Has the student modeled the poem on the work of one of the poets in this unit?
3. Has the student used vivid images, figures of speech, and other appropriate poetic devices?
4. Is the poem free from grammar, usage, and mechanics errors?

Guidelines for Evaluating Assignment 3

1. Has the student used stream-of-consciousness technique to write his or her short fictional piece?
2. Does an object seen by the character trigger a string of mental associations?
3. Is it apparent that the character is whole?
4. Is the fictional piece free from grammar, usage, and mechanics errors?

YOU THE WRITER

Assignment

1. A character sketch is like a painting in words. Unlike a visual portrait, however, a character sketch delves into the mind of the subject, revealing his or her innermost thoughts and attitudes. Choose one of the characters you read about in this unit and write a character sketch.

Prewriting. In selecting a character, make sure there is ample material to develop. Divide a sheet of paper into several sections, labeling one "Physical Details," another "Habits and Behaviors," and a third "Beliefs."

Writing. Begin your sketch by describing the relevance of your character to the story in which he or she appears. Use the author's terms, along with vivid terms of your own, to describe the character's appearance and mental makeup.

Revising. Make sure you have arranged your information in an orderly way.

Assignment

2. Robert Frost, the prominent twentieth-century poet, described the writing of free verse as "like playing tennis with the net down." As the careful reader of this unit will have observed, free verse is more structured than Frost's glib dismissal suggests. Write an original poem in free verse. Model your effort on the work of one of the poets you read and admired.

Prewriting. Get your wheels spinning to come up with a topic. When you have selected one, write it at the center of a sheet of paper and cluster ideas around it.

Writing. Write your first draft. Attempt to use vivid images and figures of speech.

Revising. Put your poem aside for several hours. Then reread it. Look for areas that are weak or in need of clarification.

Assignment

3. The stream-of-consciousness technique perfected by Virginia Woolf and others was one of the significant literary breakthroughs of the Modernist period. Write a short fictional account in which a character enters a room and sees an object—either familiar or new—that triggers a string of mental associations.

Prewriting. Brainstorm for details about your character, including his or her appearance, habits, attitudes, and so on. Create in outline form a past for your character.

Writing. In your first draft, mention the object the character sees and then let your mind lead you. Freewrite without regard to correctness of form, spelling, or sentence structure.

Revising. Check doubtful spellings and polish any rough edges.

YOU THE CRITIC

Assignment

1. Several of the writers in this unit—Shaw, Saki, and the poet Henry Reed among them—use satire or irony to put across their ideas to the reader. Select a satirical work and a work that expresses its theme in a totally straightforward manner. In an essay, compare and contrast the two approaches. Tell which you believe to be more effective, and give reasons.

Prewriting. Review the concept of satire and the manner in which the author of your satirical selection uses it. In a single sentence, identify the theme of each of the selections.

Writing. In an opening paragraph, discuss the relationship between theme and satire. Devote some space to speculation on how the impact of the two works would have been altered had the authors opted for a different approach.

Revising. Check your essay for coherence and economy of language.

Assignment

2. T. S. Eliot wrote that William Butler Yeats "was one of those few [poets] whose history is the history of their own times, who are part of the consciousness of an age which cannot be understood without them." In an essay, evaluate this statement as it applies to Yeats, to Eliot himself, or to some other poet of the Modernist period.

Prewriting. Prepare for your composition by reviewing the background material on your poet and on the history of the period. Jot down notes on this interrelation.

Writing. Write your first draft. Spend at least a paragraph describing the uniqueness of your poet's contribution to his or her age. Quote the poems where relevant.

Revising. Examine your essay for unity and logic. Substitute strong, specific words for any that strike you as vague or weak.

Assignment

3. Perhaps the two events that most profoundly shaped the literature of the Modernist period were World Wars I and II. Select any three writers of the period and describe the differences and similarities the impact of the wars had on their lives and works.

Prewriting. After you have selected your three writers, develop a profile for each in which you identify the relevance of the wars. Note whether the individual saw action on the battlefield, whether he or she used the notion of war literally or figuratively in stories or poems, and so on.

Writing. Begin your composition with a brief biographical sketch of each writer. Quote liberally from the literary works in your discussion.

Revising. Review your composition to be sure you have covered all points raised in your outline.

YOU THE CRITIC
Guidelines for Evaluating Assignment 1

1. Does the opening paragraph of the comparison discuss the relationship between theme and satire?
2. Does the student speculate on how the impact of the two works would have been altered had the authors chosen a different approach?
3. Is the essay coherent and does it demonstrate economy of language?
4. Is the essay free from grammar, usage, and mechanics errors?

Guidelines for Evaluating Assignment 2

1. Has the student evaluated Eliot's statement as it applies to Yeats, Eliot himself, or another poet?
2. Does the student describe the uniqueness of the poet's contribution to his or her age in a paragraph or more?
3. Does the student quote from the author's works to support main points?
4. Does the student use strong, specific words?
5. Is the essay free from grammar, usage, and mechanics errors?

Guidelines for Evaluating Assignment 3

1. Has the student selected three authors of the Modern period and described the differences and similarities the impact of the two world wars had on their lives and works?
2. Has the student begun the essay with a brief biographical sketch of each writer including their wartime experiences?
3. Has the student quoted from the literary works of the writers to support all points?
4. Is the essay free from grammar, usage, and mechanics errors?

Humanities Note

Fine art, *Papagena,* 1983, by Gillian Ayres. *Papagena* was painted by the contemporary British artist Gillian Ayres (b. 1930). Ayres studied at the Camberwell School of Art and has taught at the Bath Academy, St. Martins. She is presently head of painting at the Winchester School of Art. In her painting Gillian Ayres tries to create spatial scale and balance, vision and humor, through the expressive use of color. *Papagena* shows those characteristics. Her paintings are in the collections of leading museums, including London's Tate Gallery and New York's Museum of Modern Art.

PAPAGENA
Gillian Ayres
Photograph Courtesy of The South Bank Center

CONTEMPORARY WRITERS

1945–present

We are living at one of the great turning points of history. . . . Yesterday, we split the atom. We assaulted that colossal citadel of power, the tiny unit of the substance of the universe. And because of this, the great dream and the great nightmare of centuries of human thought have taken flesh and walk beside us all, day and night.*

from "The Small Personal Voice,"
Doris Lessing

1215

1 **Historical Context** Many observers outside Britain felt that the English were thankless and ungrateful for turning Churchill out of office after he had led his country to victory, but the English themselves were looking for a new dispensation.

2 **Historical Context** Britain was really a victim of her leadership in the Industrial Revolution. Because her factories were the first of their kind, they became hopelessly obsolete. Countries whose industry had been totally destroyed by World War II and who had to start over from scratch with more technologically efficient plants fared much better in the post-war world.

3 **Enrichment** The traditional 11-plus exam that separated out the academically oriented was eliminated. The comprehensive high school on the American model largely replaced the old Secondary Modern school for the non-university bound.

A new world dawned in 1945—a world of great promise and yet of great danger. First the United States, then the Soviet Union, then Britain, France, and a number of other nations gained the ability to build massively destructive atomic weapons. Henceforth all humanity would dwell in the shadow of the bomb. That fact made a deep impression on writers like Doris Lessing, whose words are quoted on the preceding page.

The postwar period has not been kind to Britain. Its Empire has crumbled, its military rank has declined, and its traditional industries have rusted away. However, Britain has struggled gamely to resolve its problems while taking pride in a still-vibrant literary and artistic life.

THE AFTERMATH OF WAR

World War II shook British society to its very core. The months after the fighting stopped were a time of privation and misery, as people made do with meager food rations and walked through streets lined with bombed-out ruins. Faced with the urgent need for reconstruction, Britons sought to shape a new social and political climate. Out went the wartime coalition government of Winston Churchill. In came a peacetime Labor government, bubbling with optimism. The Labor party's goals were sweeping: nationalize major industries, improve social services, attack the system of class privileges. Parliament set to work to transform class-bound Britain into a twentieth-century welfare state. The Age of the Common Man had dawned.

An End to Empire

Meanwhile, shadows descended on the British Empire. Nationalists in Asia and Africa were demanding their freedom—by force if necessary, by negotiation if possible. British leaders hesitated. They sent troops to put down rebellions, but they also sent diplomats to negotiate an orderly transfer of power.

The dismantling of empire did not always go smoothly. In South Asia, seeking to avert conflict between Hindus and Moslems, Britain split the Indian subcontinent into two nations, India and Pakistan. Partition and independence came in 1947. Almost immediately, bloody communal fighting swept the subcontinent. In the Middle East, unable to mediate the bitter Arab-Jewish feud over Palestine, Britain withdrew from its Palestine mandate. Israel's birth in 1948 touched off the first of many Arab-Israeli wars. In Malaya, Kenya, Rhodesia, and other territories too, bloodshed accompanied the process of withdrawal.

Slowly, the British Empire passed into history. In its place emerged a new Commonwealth of Nations, its members bound together not by force and the myth of empire but by common loyalties and common needs.

Evolving Europe

On the Continent, too, British power declined sharply after the war. By 1947 disputes and quarrels had ended the wartime alliance that linked Britain, the United States, and the Soviet Union. An Iron Curtain (Churchill's term) divided Europe. East of the Iron Curtain, the Soviet Union dominated a string of dependent or "satellite" nations with Socialist governments. West of the Iron Curtain, Britain and many other nations huddled under the umbrella of United States power. In 1949 they joined together in a military alliance called the North Atlantic Treaty Organization (NATO). Later Britain would join the European Economic Community, or Common Market, a group of nations (now numbering twelve) that are trying to merge their economic systems into a "united Europe."

RECOVERY AND CONTEMPORARY PROBLEMS

War memories faded, Britons cleared away the rubble, and life got better. By the 1960's Britain was once again a center of cultural excitement. The dazzling popularity of the Beatles carried British rock music to the far corners of the world. Trendy young people on

BERLIN WALL
P. Zachmann/Magnum

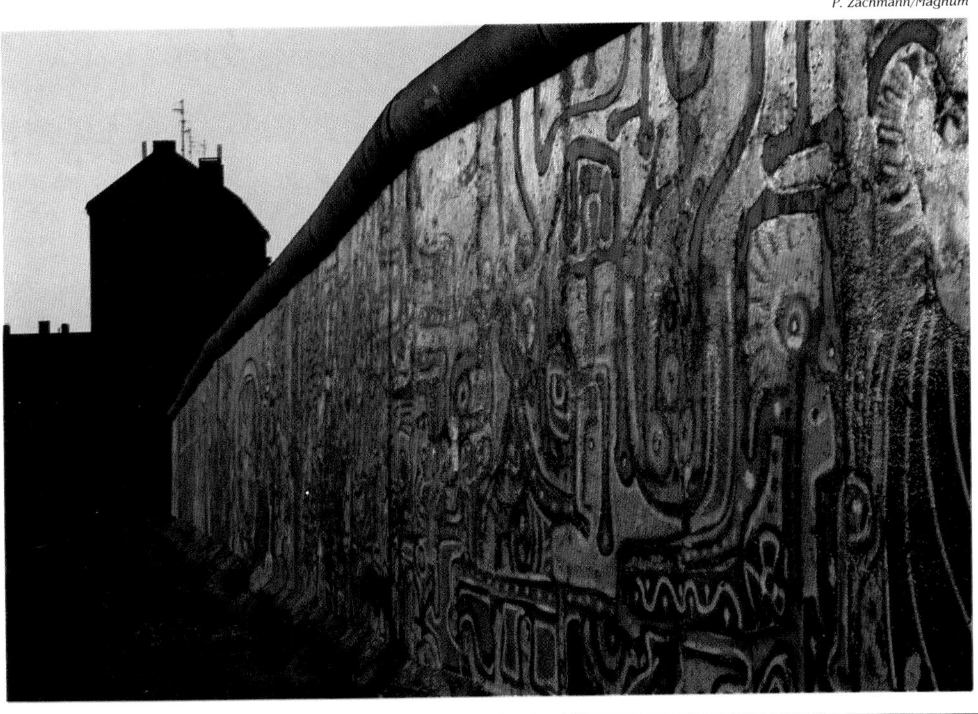

BRITISH EVENTS

1972 Britain imposes direct rule on Northern Ireland.

1973 Britain and Ireland join Common Market.

1975 North Sea oil production begins.

1976 First supersonic passenger flight leaves London.

John Fowles publishes *Daniel Martin*.

1979 Margaret Thatcher becomes first female prime minister.

1980 V.S. Naipaul publishes *A Bend in the River*.

Britain suffers worst recession since 1930s.

1980 Strikes in government-run steel and mining industries.

1981 Unemployment and racial tensions lead to Brixton riots.

Royal wedding of Prince Charles and Princess Diana.

1982 Britain defeats Argentina in Falklands war.

1983 William Golding wins Nobel Prize for Literature.

1984 **Ted Hughes** named poet laureate.

1985 Hillsborough Agreement gives Republic of Ireland voice in governing Northern Ireland.

1986 First American football game played in England.

1987 Poetry recitations given in London's Waterloo Station.

Direct Rule Imposed on Northern Ireland

Margaret Thatcher

Labor Strike

Famine in Ethiopia

Jean Anouilh

V. S. Naipaul

Gabriel Garcia Marquez

North Sea Oil Platforms

Corazon Aquino

Ayatollah Khomeini

WORLD EVENTS

1960 Russia: Yuri Gagarin becomes first person in space.

Germany: Berlin Wall built.

1961 France: Jean Anouilh publishes *Becket*.

1962 Caribbean: Cuban Missile Crisis.

1963 United States: President John F. Kennedy assassinated.

Germany: Günther Grass publishes *Dog Years*.

1964 Vietnam: Amerian troops begin fighting.

1966 India: Indira Gandhi becomes prime minister.

1967 South Africa: Christiaan Bernard performs first heart transplant.

1968 Colombia: Gabriel Garcia Mârquez publishes *A Hundred Years of Solitude*.

1969 America's *Apollo 11* lands on moon.

1971 Switzerland: Women gain right to vote.

1973 Worldwide energy crisis.

1974 France: Russia's Alexander Solzhenitsyn publishes *The Gulag Archipelago*.

1977 Africa: Djibouti, last remaining European colony, granted independence.

1979 Iran: Ayatollah Khomeini overthrows Shah.

Nicaragua: Sandinistas oust Somoza government.

1980 Poland: Lech Walesa leads Solidarity movement.

1985 Ethiopia: Warfare and drought result in great famine.

1986 Russia: Accident at Chernobyl nuclear plant.

Philippines: Democratic government established under Corazon Aquino.

BRITISH EVENTS

1945 Churchill resigns.

1946 United Nations meets in London.

1947 Coal mines nationalized.

1949 Britain joins NATO.

Irish Free State becomes Republic of Ireland.

1950 London dock strike.

1952 Elizabeth II becomes queen.

1953 Winston Churchill knighted, wins Nobel Prize for Literature.

1954 Track star Roger Bannister breaks four-minute mile.

William Golding publishes *Lord of the Flies*.

Philip Larkin publishes *The Less Deceived*.

1956 British troops sent to Egypt in Suez Crisis.

1957 **P.G Wodehouse** publishes *The World of Jeeves*.

1959 First televised election coverage.

1960 **Alan Sillitoe** publishes *The Loneliness of the Long-Distance Runner*.

1962 **Doris Lessing** publishes *The Golden Notebook*.

1964 **Stevie Smith** publishes *Selected Poems*.

1966 **Seamus Heaney** publishes *Death of a Naturalist*.

1967 New Scotland Yard opens.

Albert Camus

Sir Winston Churchill

Hungarian Uprising

World War II Ends

Mao Tse-tung

Martin Luther King, Jr.

Fidel Castro

Doris Lessing

WORLD EVENTS

1945 World War II ends.

1947 India and Pakistan gain independence from Britain.

France: Albert Camus publishes *The Plague*.

1948 Mideast: Palestine partitioned; nation of Israel established.

South Africa: Alan Paton publishes *Cry, the Beloved Country*.

1949 China: Mao Tse-tung establishes People's Republic.

1950 Asia: Korean War begins.

South Africa: Riots against apartheid crushed.

1952 United States: Ernest Hemingway publishes *The Old Man and the Sea*.

1953 Tibet: Edmund Hillary climbs Mount Everest.

1954 United States: Jonas Salk begins inoculations against polio.

Algeria: War of independence from France begins.

1955 Eastern Europe: Communist nations sign Warsaw Pact.

United States: Martin Luther King, Jr. leads black boycott of Montgomery buses.

Australia: Patrick White publishes *The Tree of Life*.

1956 Hungary: Revolt against Russian influence crushed.

1957 Russia: Sputnik I, first spaceship, launched.

1959 Cuba: Fidel Castro seizes power.

Canada: St. Lawrence Seaway opens.

the Continent and in America looked to London for inspiration. They wore their hair long like the Beatles, and they bought "mod" fashions from London's Carnaby Street.

A Series of Shocks

Unfortunately, rock bands and boutiques did not suffice to restore Britain's economic vitality. The industries that had hauled Britain and the world into the industrial revolution of the eighteenth century—textiles, steelmaking, shipbuilding—had lost their old magic. Now British industries were lagging behind. First in America, then in Japan and other Asian countries, new factories sprang up that could turn out goods more cheaply than could Britain's aging factories. By the score, British factories closed their gates. By the thousands, laid-off British workers "went on the dole" (signed up for welfare benefits).

For Britons, economic troubles were not the only shocks of the postwar period. British society was changing rapidly. The many changes included the following:

- *Large-scale immigration.* Indians, Africans, West Indians, and others poured in from Britain's former colonies and Britain was transformed into a multiracial, "melting-pot" society.
- *Greater equality.* The barriers that had long divided Britons by social class began to break down, as changes in the system of education opened new opportunities to working-class people.
- *New roles for women.* Despite Britain's long history of ruling queens, women had held few other prominent positions. In 1979

INDUSTRIAL LANDSCAPE
L. S. Lowry
Tate Gallery, London

1218

the nation elected its first female prime minister, Margaret Thatcher. At the same time, more and more women began rising to prominence in politics, science, business, education, and the arts.

The Thatcher Era

Thatcher was a woman with a mission. She prescribed a stiff dose of free enterprise as the cure for Britain's troubles. Her Conservative-party government set about selling off state-owned industries and imposing cost-cutting measures on Britain's welfare agencies. Her government also encouraged the growth of new-style industries based on computer technology.

Thatcher's task would not be an easy one. Britain's economy remained shaky, despite the discovery and exploitation of oil deposits in the North Sea. The country also faced a number of challenges. In 1982 it fought a war with Argentina over Britain's tiny South Atlantic possession, the Falkland Islands. Britain won the war, but paid a high price in blood and money. Meanwhile, the violence in Ulster (Northern Ireland) dragged on. A 1985 agreement gave the Republic of Ireland a consultative role in Ulster's affairs. But hard-line Ulster Catholics continued to fight for union with Ireland, and hard-line Ulster Protestants rejected any cooperation with that Catholic country.

Today, Britain seeks to adapt to a much-changed postwar world. In some ways the most modern of nations, Britain is in other ways among the most traditional. The ancient institutions of monarchy still play a central role in British life, inspiring awe and reverence in many

MARGARET THATCHER, 1983
Stuart Franklin-Sygma

ARCHBISHOP OF CANTERBURY LEADING PRINCE AND PRINCESS TO HIGH ALTAR OF ST. PAUL'S, JULY 29, 1981
The Granger Collection

GREAT BLACK-BACKED GULL
Douglas Anderson
Oscar and Peter Johnson Ltd., London

Britons. Huge, happy crowds celebrated the marriages of the heir to the throne—Charles, Prince of Wales—in 1981 and of his brother Andrew in 1986. For each occasion, the pomp and splendor of honored traditions blended with the glitz and glamor of the media age. Like the poet T. S. Eliot, Britons seem to have turned to the past as a source of comfort while moving ahead into the swirl and bustle of contemporary life.

CONTEMPORARY BRITISH LITERATURE

Both in subject matter and in style, British literature since World War II has displayed enormous diversity. Faced with an ever-shrinking world, many British writers have turned outward. They have addressed such global concerns as the destruction of the environment and the threat of nuclear war. Other writers have turned inward, exploring personal relationships and the individual's attempts to cope with modern urban and suburban life. Many recent works have examined Britain's past or its new role as a secondary power. Other works have addressed the specific problems and concerns of the British working class, whose problems and attitudes they address in their writings. Finally, with the decline of empire has come a blossoming of "post-colonial" literature. Writers in Ireland and in many former British colonies often use the English language to explore the legacy of empire.

Achievements in Drama

Britain has continued to enjoy preeminence in the world of drama. In New York City, America's theater capital, for example, Broadway's most successful new dramas are often British imports. Many British plays go on to become films seen the world over. British television, too, has produced a string of noteworthy original dramas and a number of fine adaptations of classic novels and plays.

Many contemporary British dramatists use the techniques of realism. For example, Shelagh Delaney (born 1939) specializes in slice-of-life dramas like *A Taste of Honey* (1958). Her works are acutely realistic in depicting the lives of ordinary people. A group of dramatists known as Britain's "angry young men" also used realistic techniques in plays of the 1950's and 1960's attacking the injustices of Britain's class system. Typical of their work is John Osborne's *Look Back in Anger,* which focuses on a working-class youth rebelling against the establishment.

A second strain of contemporary British drama is represented by the so-called theater of the absurd. Plays of this school often feature dialogue and actions that seem disconnected and senseless—as if to say that life itself is an absurd series of tribulations. The Irish-born Samuel Beckett (born 1906), author of *Waiting for Godot* (1952), is foremost among the playwrights who use such techniques. The early plays of Harold Pinter (born 1930) also show the influence of the

1220

theater of the absurd.

A third type of contemporary British play is the historical drama that explores figures, events, and attitudes from times gone by. One such play is *A Man for All Seasons* (1960) by Robert Bolt (born 1924), which tells the story of Thomas More, the sixteenth-century scholar and Catholic martyr. Employing powerful, almost Shakespearean language, the play captures the grandeur of times past. Yet Bolt also creates a narrator called the Common Man, through whose eyes More's life unfolds—a strikingly contemporary touch. Tom Stoppard employs a similar device in *Rosencrantz and Guildenstern Are Dead* (1967).

Achievements in Poetry

Contemporary British poets are less widely known than British playwrights. Still, many poets have come to teach at American universities and have won international reputations. During the 1950's and 1960's, a number of outstanding British poets associated themselves with what is called simply the Movement—the poetic equivalent of drama's angry young men. These poets rejected the style of Romantic poets such as Dylan Thomas, aiming to capture everyday experiences in the language of "the common man." Philip Larkin (1922–85), among the finest poets in the Movement, brought

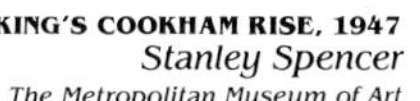

KING'S COOKHAM RISE, 1947
Stanley Spencer
The Metropolitan Museum of Art

Humanities Note

Fine art, *Industrial Landscape*, by L. S. Lowry. Laurence Stephen Lowry(1887-1976), a British painter, was educated at the Muncipal College of Art. Lowry developed a highly individualistic style of painting industrial scenes. These seemingly naive views of factories, workers, and dreary mill towns are Lowry's satiric observation of England's deteriorating industrialized society.

Industrial Landscape is a panoramic view of factories and workers' barracks populated by characteristic scurrying stick figures. His palette is restricted to a few basic colors applied to a stark white background. The impersonality of the scene is Lowry's comment on the dehumanization loneliness imposed by industrialization. Despite this bleak message the landscape has a poetry that is peculiar to his work.

2 **Historical Context** Britain was really a victim of her leadership in the Industrial Revolution. Because her factories were the first of their kind, they became hopelessly obsolete. Countries whose industry had been totally destroyed by World War II and who had to start over from scratch with more technologically efficient plants fared much better in the post-war world.

3 **Enrichment** The traditional 11-plus exam that separated out the academically oriented was eliminated. The comprehensive high school on the American model largely replaced the old Secondary Modern school for the non-university bound.

to his well-crafted verse a background as a music critic. Also part of the Movement were Thom Gunn (born 1929) and Donald Davie (born 1922), both of whom went on to teach and write in America.

The British have plucked poets out of musty libraries and thrust them before live audiences. Colorful festivals keep alive the Anglo-Saxon and Celtic traditions of oral poetry recitation. Poets have even recited their verse for rush-hour commuters at London's Waterloo Station. One of the first contemporary poets to stress oral performance was Stevie Smith, born Florence Margaret Smith (1902–71). Influenced by traditional English lyrics and early church music, Smith often recited her verse aloud in the singsong manner of traditional British bards.

British poets of recent years have exhibited a great deal of diversity in the form and content of their work. Ted Hughes (born 1930), named Britain's poet laureate in 1984, writes frequently of the beauty and violence of nature. His best-known volumes include *Hawk in the Rain* (1957) and *Crow* (1971). Nature is also a common subject in the work of Irish poet Seamus Heaney (born 1939). In his poetry Heaney also frequently explores the terror and hope of Ireland's stormy history. Another well-known contemporary poet, Elaine Feinstein (born 1930) writes a lyric poetry that balances an awareness of human limitations against a deep faith in human endurance. Other significant contemporary poets include William Empson (1906–84), Molly Holden (1927–81), Geoffrey Hill (born 1932), and the Irish poets Patrick Kavanagh (1905–67) and Thomas Minsella (born 1928).

Achievements in Prose

The English novel has continued to flourish in the contemporary period. With the introduction of the inexpensive paperback, books have become more accessible to the general public, and people have been able to to build larger personal libraries than ever before.

Several writers who began their careers in the modern period continued to prosper in contemporary times. On such writer was Graham Greene who produced a string of best sellers which often dealt with Cold War politics. Another was P. G. Wodehouse (1881–1975), who began his series of charming novels about dimwitted Bertie Wooster and his clever butler, Jeeves, in 1939. As late as the 1960's, Wodehouse was delighting readers with new Jeeves books.

Many new novelists also came on the scene. Four of the most successful have been William Golding (born 1911 and winner of the 1983 Nobel Prize for Literature), Anthony Burgess (born 1917), Kingsley Amis (born 1922), and John Fowles (born 1926). Golding's *Lord of the Flies* (1954) tells of a group of British schoolboys who revert to savage behavior after being stranded on a tropical island. Burgess has carried on in the tradition of George Orwell's *1984*, imagining a brutal future in the dystopian novel *A Clockwork Orange* (1962). Amis gives a comic touch to novels like *Lucky Jim* (1953)

P. G. WODEHOUSE, 1958
The Granger Collection

and *Stanley and the Women* (1984). Fowles often experiments with novel forms, as in *The Collector* (1963), which tells the same story twice—from two characters' different points of view.

In literature as in other realms of British life, women have risen to the forefront since 1945. Margaret Drabble (born 1939) has produced such well-received novels as *The Summer Birdcage* (1963) and *The Needle's Eye* (1972). The Irish-born Iris Murdoch (born 1919) has written many intricate novels exploring human relationships. Doris Lessing (born 1919), who grew up in Rhodesia (Zimbabwe), gained fame for a series of novels set in Africa about a character named Martha Guest. Later she wrote *The Golden Notebook* (1962) and a string of novels with futuristic settings. Another important female author is Nadine Gordimer (born 1923), who writes

4 **Historical Context** Another woman prominent in recent British politics is Shirley Williams, daughter of the writer Vera Brittain whose memoir of World War I, *Testament of Youth,* was sensitively recorded on film.

5 **Enrichment** Readers of Aldous Huxley's *Brave New World* will remember the desolate Falkland Islands as Helmholtz Watson's choice for exile.

Humanities Note

Fine art, *Great Black-Backed Gull,* by Douglas Anderson. England's Douglas Anderson (b. 1934) is best known for his portraits in oil. His studies, however, with Italy's Pieter Annigoni prepared him to paint other subjects as well. The atmospheric painting *Great Black-Backed Gull* is a modern view of an old subject. The flat, simplified treatment of the water and sky contrasts with the detailed rocks and pebbles in the foreground. The bird perched there lends a touch of loneliness to the scene.

well-crafted novels and short stories that examine the moral and political dilemmas of racially divided South Africa, where she lives.

Many British fiction writers in addition to Gordimer have excelled at writing short stories. Sean O'Faolain (born 1900) creates stories that capture the flavor of rural life in his native Ireland. Michael McLaverty (born 1907), another Irishman, usually deals with plots and themes relating to nature. Among the finest of England's native short-story writers is Alan Sillitoe (born 1928), whose lyrical tales often focus on the painful predicaments of working-class people.

Meanwhile, a number of talented writers from what used to be called "the colonies" have added to the richness of contemporary British literature. These authors include Mordecai Richler (born 1931) of Canada, Wilson Harris (born 1921) of Guyana, V. S. Naipaul (born 1932) of Trinidad, Frank Sargeson (1903–82) of New Zealand, and Patrick White (born 1912) of Australia.

Nonfiction has also prospered in contemporary times. The Irish writer Lawrence Durrell (born 1912), who is also a skilled novelist and poet, has earned praise for his travel writing and humorous sketches. Antonia Fraser (born 1932), wife of the playwright Harold Pinter, is a widely read popular historian. Bertrand Russell (1872–1970), the controversial philosopher, mathematician, and political activist, produced one of the best British autobiographies of recent decades. Several writers have also earned widespread recognition as literary critics. These writers include V. S. Pritchett (born 1900) and David Daiches (born 1912), as well as the poets Donald Davie and Thom Gunn, and the novelists Anthony Burgess and Margaret Drabble.

ENGLISH VOICES

Quotations by Prominent Figures of the Period

So always look for the silver lining
And try to find the sunny side of life.

P. G. Wodehouse, *Sally*

Why does my Muse only speak when she is unhappy?
She does not, I only listen when I am unhappy.

Stevie (Florence Margaret) Smith, "My Muse"

So winter closed its fist
And got it stuck in the pump.

Seamus Heaney, "Rite of Spring" (from *Door Into the Dark*)

The point is, . . . the point is, that as far as I can see, everything's cracking up.

Doris Lessing, Anne in *The Golden Notebook*

Columbus' huckstering breath
Blew inland through North America

Killing the last of the mammoths.

Ted Hughes, "Fourth of July" (from *Lupercal*)

Duty largely consists of pretending that the trivial is critical.

John Fowles, *The Magus*

Life should be a humane
undertaking. I know. I
undertook it. Yet have found
that in every move
I prevent someone
from stepping where I step.

Thom Gunn, "Positives"

While we can, for as long as we can, oh let us believe.

Isabel Colegate, *The Shooting Party*

Eternity is a terrible thought. I mean, where's it going to end?

Tom Stoppard, *Rosencrantz and Guildenstern Are Dead*

*Source: Doris Lessing, *A Small Personal Voice: Essays, Reviews, Interviews* (New York: Vintage Books, 1975) p. 7. Essay "The Small Personal Voice" first appeared 1957.

Humanities Note

Fine art, *King's Cookham Rise,* 1947, by Stanley Spencer. The British painter Stanley Spencer (1891-1959), trained in academic art at the prestigious Slade School in London. He lived his entire life in the village of Cookham, near London, which he considered his "paradise on earth." Spencer is remembered for his landscapes of Cookham and paintings of mythical-religious fantasy set in Cookham.

King's Cookham Rise demonstrates Spencer's considerable skill as a landscape artist. The natural detail is sensitively handled with a fresh point of view. The carefully rendered tones and textures of the vegetation and sunlight create effective patterns. Spencer's love for Cookham is evident in his work.

Reading Critically The purpose of this page is to guide students in critical reading of contemporary English literature. The information offered here will enable students to place a work of literature in its historical context, identify literary movements of the time, and appreciate the writers' techniques used to convey the ideas of the period.

As you discuss the information on this page with your class, explain that the short story on the following pages, "The Distant Past" by William Trevor, is a model for reading critically. The side columns contain notes that draw attention to elements that reflect the historical context, the influence of the literary movements, and the writer's technique.

To give students further practice with the process of reading critically, use the selection in the Teaching Portfolio, "The Lost Symbols" by Elizabeth Jennings, page 000, following the Teacher Backup, which students can annotate themselves. Encourage students to use these strategies as they read the literature in this unit.

Teaching to Ability Levels For **less advanced** students, you might want to discuss some of the words and phrases that are particularly Irish before they read the story: *mince, custom, BBC, public house, bogs, cutlery.* For **more advanced** students, you might offer more background about the Irish struggle. Ask the history department for primary sources about the time. Perhaps you might present speeches by Eamon De Valera, Bernadette Devlin, or other leaders to the class.

READING CRITICALLY

The Literature of 1945–Present

Because writers tend to be influenced by literary movements and historical trends, placing a literary work in its historical context can help you to fully understand and appreciate it.

Historical Context

The period from 1945 to the present has been a time of transition for the English nation and people. During World War II London and other English towns and cities were severely damaged by German air raids, and in the aftermath of the war the British people struggled to rebuild their nation. At the same time, as the transformation of the British Empire into the British Commonwealth was completed, the nation was forced to accept a sharp decline in its economic and political status. Despite the decline in its status, however, the government has taken strong measures to insure adequate health care, housing, education, and pensions for the entire British population.

Literary Movements

Contemporary British literature is extremely diverse in content. Like their predecessors from the modern period, many contemporary writers have delved into the human mind, focusing on people's inner thoughts and feelings. Responding to the changing complexion of British life, some writers have explored the effects of change on the British traditions, institutions, and people. Others have confronted additional problems and issues facing today's British society, and still others have presented shocking visions of futuristic societies in which personal freedoms are denied.

Writer's Techniques

Although contemporary British writers have used a wide variety of literary forms and devices, few new techniques have been developed. While many contemporary poets have relied on traditional poetic forms, others have used the unconventional forms that became popular during the Modern Age. In fiction, writers have generally modeled their stories and novels after typical modern works, omitting expositions, transitions, and resolutions, and using the stream-of-consciousness technique.

On the following pages is a story by William Trevor, a highly regarded contemporary fiction writer. The notes in the side column should help you to place the selection in its historical context.

Objectives

1. To recognize types of characters
2. To understand characters' motivations
3. To write a dialogue

Teaching Portfolio: Support Materials

Teacher Backup, p. 000

Reading Critically, p. 00

Usage and Mechanics Worksheet, p. 00

Analyzing Literature Worksheet, p. 00

Critical Thinking and Reading Worksheet, p. 00

Language Worksheet, p. 00

Selection Test, p. 00

MODEL

The Distant Past

William Trevor

In the town and beyond it they were regarded as harmlessly peculiar. Odd, people said, and in time this reference took on a burnish of affection.

They had always been thin, silent with one another, and similar in appearance: a brother and sister who shared a family face. It was a bony countenance, with pale blue eyes and a sharp, well-shaped nose and high cheekbones. Their father had had it too, but unlike them their father had been an irresponsible and careless man, with red flecks in his cheeks that they didn't have at all. The Middletons of Carraveagh the family had once been known as, but now the brother and sister were just the Middletons, for Carraveagh didn't count any more, except to them.

They owned four Herefords,[1] a number of hens, and the house itself, three miles outside the town. It was a large house, built in the reign of George II,[2] a monument that reflected in its glory and later decay the fortunes of a family. As the brother and sister aged, its roof increasingly ceased to afford protection, rust ate at its gutters, grass thrived in two thick channels all along its avenue. Their father had mortgaged his inherited estate, so local rumor claimed, in order to keep a Catholic Dublin woman in brandy and jewels. When he died, in 1924, his two children discovered that they possessed only a dozen acres. It was locally said also that this adversity hardened their will and that because of it they came to love the remains of Carraveagh more than they could ever have loved a husband or a wife. They blamed for their ill-fortune the Catholic Dublin woman whom they'd never met and they blamed as well the new national regime, contriving in their eccentric way to relate the two. In the days of the union jack[3] such women would have known their place—wasn't it all part and parcel?

Writer's Technique: Unlike most contemporary stories, the story begins with an exposition, in which background information is provided.

Literary Movements: The decay of the Middleton estate parallels the decline of the British Empire.

Historical Context: The story is set in southern Ireland. After being ruled by the English for hundreds of years, the Irish people rebelled against British rule in 1920. Following a period of bloody conflict, the British granted southern Ireland its independence in 1921, and the Irish Free State was established.

---

1. **Herefords** *n.*: A breed of cattle.
2. **reign of George II:** 1727-1760.
3. **union jack:** The British flag; the symbol of British rule.

Motivation for Reading The experience of alienation, of being an outsider, is as old as human experience. In this century, T. S. Eliot wrote of the "hollow men" and of the "waste land"; Saul Bellow wrote *The Dangling Man;* Ralph Ellison wrote *The Invisible Man.* William Butler Yeats wrote: "Things fall apart; the center cannot hold" and "An aged man is but a paltry thing,/A tattered coat upon a stick." Discuss the factors today that can make us feel alienated from society; outsiders in the world we have lived in all our lives. In "The Distant Past," the main characters are outsiders. Religious and political differences isolate a sister and brother from friends they have had for years.

Thematic Idea Another selection that deals with the theme of the effect of wars on society is "The Hollow Men" by T. S. Eliot, page 1081.

Master Teacher Note The Irish rock group U-2 has recorded several songs that deal with the continuing Catholic-Protestant turmoil. You might choose to play "Sunday, Bloody Sunday" from *War* as a way of introducing this short story.

Purpose-Setting Question Trevor has been acknowledged by critics for his gift of carefully demonstrating the effects of large, remote events on the lives of ordinary individuals. In "The Distant Past," what are the effects of the guerilla war in Northern Ireland on the lives of all the characters?

6 **Enrichment** Another poet who taught and wrote in America was Ted Hughes who in 1956 married an American poet, the late Sylvia Plath.

7 **Literary Movement** See "Hawk Roosting," page 1310, in which the poet emphasizes the bird's predatory nature.

8 **Master Teacher Note** To develop an understanding of the classical view of man as fallible rather than perfectible, you might have students compare Golding's view in *Lord of the Flies* with Conrad's in *Heart of Darkness.*

Literary Movement: Like Trevor's characters, many British people have had difficulty accepting the dramatic changes that have occurred during the twentieth century and have tried to cling to the institutions and traditions of the past.

Twice a week, on Fridays and Sundays, the Middletons journeyed into the town, first of all in a trap[4] and later in a Ford Anglia car. In the shops and elsewhere they made, quite gently, no secret of their continuing loyalty to the past. They attended on Sundays St. Patrick's Protestant Church, a place that matched their mood, for prayers were still said there for the King whose sovereignty their country had denied. The revolutionary regime would not last, they quietly informed the Reverend Packham—what sense was there in green-painted pillar boxes[5] and a language that nobody understood?

4. trap *n.*: A two-wheeled horse-drawn carriage.
5. pillar boxes: Mail collection boxes.

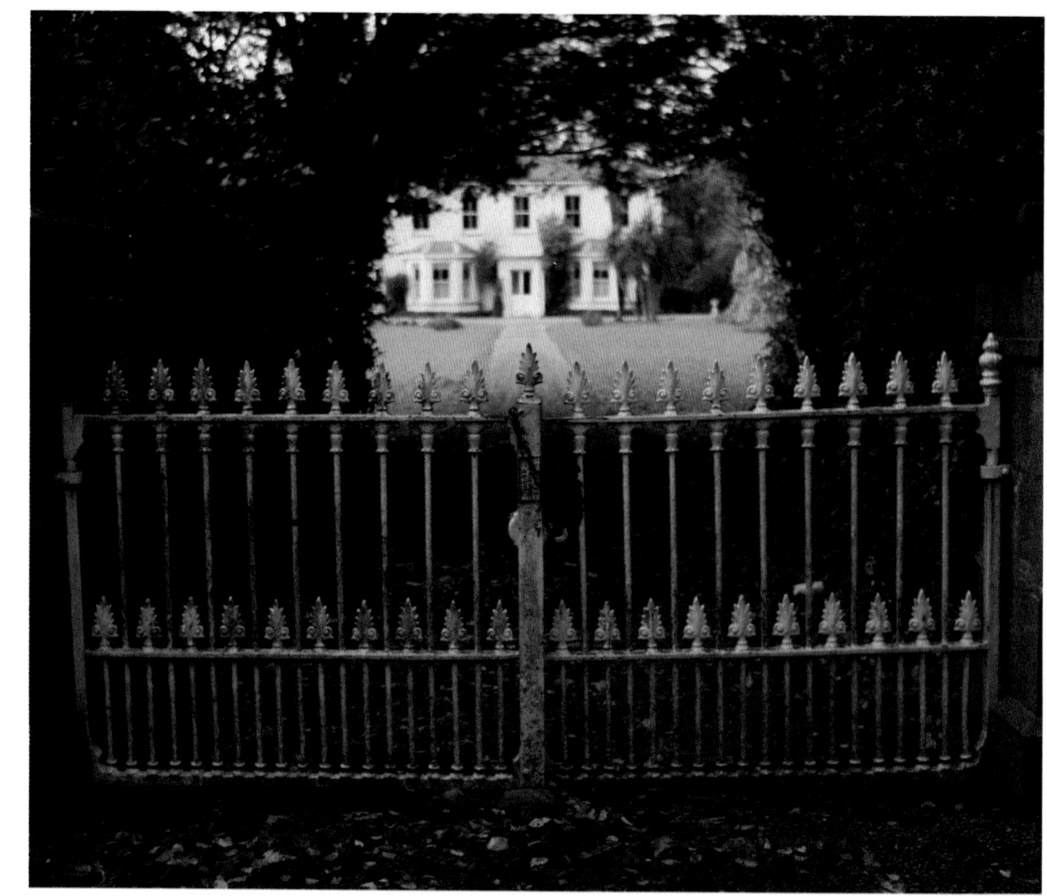

On Fridays, when they took seven or eight dozen eggs to the town, they dressed in pressed tweeds and were accompanied over the years by a series of red setters, the breed there had always been at Carraveagh. They sold the eggs in Keogh's grocery and then had a drink with Mrs. Keogh in the part of her shop that was devoted to the consumption of refreshment. They enjoyed the occasion, for they liked Mrs. Keogh and were liked by her in return. Afterwards they shopped, chatting to the shopkeepers about whatever news there was, and then they went to Healy's Hotel for a few more drinks before driving home.

In spite of their loyalty to the past, they built up convivial relationships with the people of the town. Fat Driscoll, who kept the butcher's shop, used even to joke about the past when he stood with them in Healy's Hotel or stood behind his own counter cutting their slender chops or thinly slicing their liver. "Will you ever forget it, Mr. Middleton? I'd ha' run like a rabbit if you'd lifted a finger at me." Fat Driscoll would laugh then, rocking back on his heels with a glass of stout in his hand or banging their meat on to his weighing-scales. Mr. Middleton would smile. "There was alarm in your eyes, Mr. Driscoll,' Miss Middleton would murmur, smiling also at the memory of the distant occasion.

Fat Driscoll, with a farmer called Maguire and another called Breen, had stood in the hall of Carraveagh, each of them in charge of a shotgun. The Middletons, children then, had been locked with their mother and father and an aunt into an upstairs room. Nothing else had happened: the expected British soldiers had not, after all, arrived and the men in the hall had eventually relaxed their vigil. "A massacre they wanted," the Middletons' father said after they'd gone. "Bloody ruffians."

The Second World War took place. Two Germans, a man and his wife called Winkelmann who ran a glove factory in the town, were suspected by the Middletons of being spies for the Third Reich.[6] People laughed, for they knew the Winkelmanns well and could lend no credence to the Middletons' latest fantasy—typical of them, they explained to the Winkelmanns, who had been worried. Soon after the War the Reverend Packham died and was replaced by the Reverend Bradshaw, a younger man who laughed also and regarded the Middletons as an anachronism. They protested when prayers

Literary Movement: The changes in the church reflect the ongoing changes in society as a whole. The Irish Free State had become increasingly detached from Great Britain, and in 1949 severed all ties with Great Britain and renamed itself the Republic of Ireland.

Clarification Nationalist leaders in Ireland organized the Easter Rebellion against British rule in 1916. British troops suppressed this uprising and many rebel leaders were executed.

6. Third Reich (rīk): The German government under the Nazis (1933–1945).

1229

Clarification Great Britain, about fifty independent nations that were once British colonies, and twenty five other political territories form an association that lives under British law and cooperates economically.

Enrichment The Loretto nuns are members of a congregation of nuns founded near Dublin in 1822 by Mary Theresa Ball.

Clarification In 1961 twenty-two thousand pounds would have been approximately sixty-six thousand dollars.

Historical Context: Queen Elizabeth II was crowned in 1952, three years after Ireland officially severed its ties with Great Britain.

Writer's Technique: Trevor provides important details of the setting.

were no longer said for the Royal Family in St. Patrick's, but the Reverend Bradshaw considered that their protests were as absurd as the prayers themselves had been. Why pray for the monarchy of a neighboring island when their own island had its chosen President now? The Middletons didn't reply to that argument. In the Reverend Bradshaw's presence they rose to their feet when the BBC played "God Save the King," and on the day of the coronation of Queen Elizabeth II they drove into the town with a small union jack propped up in the back window of their Ford Anglia. "Bedad, you're a holy terror, Mr. Middleton!" Fat Driscoll laughingly exclaimed, noticing the flag as he lifted a tray of pork steaks from his display shelf. The Middletons smiled. It was a great day for the Commonwealth of Nations, they replied, a remark which further amused Fat Driscoll and which he later repeated in Phelan's public house. "Her Britannic Majesty," guffawed his friend Mr. Breen.

Situated in a valley that was noted for its beauty and with convenient access to rich rivers and bogs over which game-birds flew, the town benefited from post-war tourism. Healy's Hotel changed its title and became, overnight, the New Ormonde. Shopkeepers had their shopfronts painted and Mr. Healy organized an annual Salmon Festival. Even Canon Kelly, who had at first commented severely on the habits of the tourists, and in particular on the summertime dress of the women, was in the end obliged to confess that the morals of his flock remained unaffected. "God and good sense," he proclaimed, meaning God and his own teaching. In time he even derived pride from the fact that people with other values came briefly to the town and that the values esteemed by his parishioners were in no way diminished.

From the windows of their convent the Loretto nuns observed the long, sleek cars with G.B. plates; English and American accents drifted on the breeze to them. Mothers cleaned up their children and sent them to the Golf Club to seek employment as caddies. Sweet shops sold holiday mementoes. The brown, soda and currant breads of Murphy-Flood's bakery were declared to be delicious. Mr. Healy doubled the number of local girls who served as waitresses in his dining room, and in the winter of 1961 he had the builders in again, working on an extension for which the Munster and Leinster Bank had lent him twenty-two thousand pounds.

But as the town increased its prosperity Carraveagh continued its decline. The Middletons were in their middle sixties now and were reconciled to a life that became more

1230

uncomfortable with every passing year. Together they roved the vast lofts of their house, placing old paint tins and flowerpot saucers beneath the drips from the roof. At night they sat over their thin chops in a dining room that had once been gracious and which in a way was gracious still, except for the faded appearance of furniture that was dry from lack of polish and of a wallpaper that time had rendered colorless. In the hall their father gazed down at them, framed in ebony and gilt, in the uniform of the Irish Guards. He had conversed with Queen Victoria, and even in their middle sixties they could still hear him saying that God and Empire and Queen formed a trinity unique in any worthy soldier's heart. In the hall hung the family crest, and on ancient Irish linen the Cross of St. George.[7]

Historical Context: Their father's portrait reminds them of the Victorian age, an era in which British life was characterized by a sense of optimism and patriotism.

The dog that accompanied the Middletons now was called Turloch, an animal whose death they dreaded for they felt they couldn't manage the antics of another pup. Turloch, being thirteen, moved slowly and was blind and a little deaf. He was a reminder to them of their own advancing years and of the effort it had become to tend the Herefords and collect the weekly eggs. More and more they looked forward to Fridays, to the warm companionship of Mrs. Keogh and Mr. Healy's chatter in the hotel. They stayed longer now with Mrs. Keogh and in the hotel, and idled longer in the shops, and drove home more slowly. Dimly, but with no less loyalty, they still recalled the distant past and were listened to without ill-feeling when they spoke of it and of Carraveagh as it had been, and of the Queen whose company their careless father had known.

The visitors who came to the town heard about the Middletons and were impressed. It was a pleasant wonder, more than one of them remarked, that old wounds could heal so completely, that the Middletons continued in their loyalty to the past and that, in spite of it, they were respected in the town. When Miss Middleton had been ill with a form of pneumonia in 1958 Canon Kelly had driven out to Carraveagh twice a week with pullets and young ducks that his housekeeper had dressed. "An upright couple," was the Canon's public opinion of the Middletons, and he had been known to add that eccentric views would hurt you less than malice. "We can disagree without guns in this town," Mr. Healy pronounced in his cocktail room, and his visitors usually replied that as far as they could see that was the

7. St. George: The patron saint of England.

Enrichment The Irish Guards were a select infantry regiment with special duties of home defense and guarding the sovereign, although they could be sent on foreign service.

Enrichment Victoria, queen of the United Kingdoms of England, Scotland, Wales, and Ireland and Empress of India, reigned from 1837 to 1901. The last of the Hanovers, she gave her name to an era, the Victorian Age. From her nine children are descended many of the royal families of Europe.

Enrichment At first, the bombings of post offices in Belfast were attributed to the Irish Republican Army, but it has now been determined that the explosions were planted by a Protestant paramilitary group who wanted to remove the prime minister from office. The immediate result was to bring British troops into action for the first time.

Writer's Technique: The Middletons' personalities are revealed through the descriptions of their thoughts and actions.

Historical Context: The bombing was carried out by Catholics in Northern Ireland who believed that the Protestant majority in that country was discriminating against them. This was the beginning of a violent conflict between Catholics and Protestants in Northern Ireland.

result of living in a Christian country. That the Middletons bought their meat from a man who had once locked them into an upstairs room and had then waited to shoot soldiers in their hall was a fact that amazed the seasonal visitors. You lived and learned, they remarked to Mr. Healy.

The Middletons, privately, often considered that they led a strange life. Alone in their two beds at night they now and again wondered why they hadn't just sold Carraveagh forty-eight years ago when their father had died—why had the tie been so strong and why had they in perversity encouraged it? They didn't fully know, nor did they attempt to discuss the matter in any way. Instinctively they had remained at Carraveagh, instinctively feeling that it would have been cowardly to go. Yet often it seemed to them now to be no more than a game they played, this worship of the distant past. And at other times it seemed as real and as important as the remaining acres of land, and the house itself.

"Isn't that shocking?" Mr. Healy said one day in 1967. "Did you hear about that, Mr. Middleton, blowing up them post offices in Belfast?"

Mr. Healy, red-faced and short-haired, spoke casually in his Cocktail Room, making midday conversation. He had commented in much the same way at breakfast-time, looking up from the *Irish Independent.* Everyone in the town had said it too: that the blowing up of sub-post offices in Belfast was a shocking matter.

"A bad business," Fat Driscoll remarked, wrapping the Middletons' meat. "We don't want that old stuff all over again."

"We didn't want it in the first place," Miss Middleton reminded him. He laughed, and she laughed, and so did her brother. Yes, it was a game, she thought—how could any of it be as real or as important as the afflictions and problems of the old butcher himself, his rheumatism and his reluctance to retire? Did her brother, she wondered, privately think so too?

"Come on, old Turloch," he said, stroking the flank of the red setter with the point of his shoe, and she reflected that you could never tell what he was thinking. Certainly it wasn't the kind of thing you wanted to talk about.

"I've put him in a bit of mince," Fat Driscoll said, which was something he often did these days, pretending the mince would otherwise be thrown away. There'd been a red setter about the place that night when he waited in the hall for the soldiers; Breen and Maguire had pushed it down into a cellar, frightened of it.

"There's a heart of gold in you, Mr. Driscoll," Miss Middleton murmured, nodding and smiling at him. He was the same age as she was, sixty-six—he should have shut up shop years ago. He would have, he'd once told them, if there'd been a son to leave the business to. As it was, he'd have to sell it and when it came to the point he found it hard to make the necessary arrangements. "Like us and Carraveagh," she'd said, even though on the face of it it didn't seem the same at all.

Every evening they sat in the big old kitchen, hearing the news. It was only in Belfast and Derry, the wireless said; outside Belfast and Derry you wouldn't know anything was happening at all. On Fridays they listened to the talk in Mrs. Keogh's bar and in the hotel. "Well, thank God it has nothing to do with the South," Mr. Healy said often, usually repeating the statement.

The first British soldiers landed in the North of Ireland, and soon people didn't so often say that outside Belfast and Derry you wouldn't know anything was happening. There were incidents in Fermanagh and Armagh, in border villages and towns. One Prime Minister resigned and then another one. The troops were unpopular, the newspapers said; internment became part of the machinery of government. In the town, in St. Patrick's Protestant Church and in the Church of the Holy Assumption, prayers for peace were offered, but no peace came.

"We're hit, Mr. Middleton," Mr. Healy said one Friday morning. "If there's a dozen visitors this summer it'll be God's own stroke of luck for us."

"Luck?"

"Sure, who wants to come to a country with all that malarkey in it?"

"But it's only in the North."

"Tell that to your tourists, Mr. Middleton."

The town's prosperity ebbed. The border was more than sixty miles away, but over that distance had spread some wisps of the fog of war. As anger rose in the town at the loss of fortune so there rose also the kind of talk there had been in the distant past. There was talk of atrocities and counteratrocities, and of guns and gelignite[8] and the rights of people. There was bitterness suddenly in Mrs. Keogh's bar because of the lack of trade, and in the empty hotel there was bitterness also.

Historical Context: In 1969, following bloody riots in the cities of Belfast and Londonderry, British troops were sent into Northern Ireland. In 1972, as the violence continued, the British government took over direct control of the country.

Writer's Techniques: Trevor implies that the townspeople's resentment of the British has resurfaced as a result of the violence in Northern Ireland and the implications of the violence.

Clarification Belfast is the capital of Ulster, or Northern Ireland. Derry, also known as Londonderry, is a seaport there.

Master Teacher Note William Trevor taught history at a school in Armagh, Northern Ireland from 1950 to 1952.

---

8. gelegnite *n.*: An explosive.

On Fridays, only sometimes at first, there was a silence when the Middletons appeared. It was as though, going back nearly twenty years, people remembered the union jack in the window of their car and saw it now in a different light. It wasn't something to laugh at any more, nor were certain words that the Middletons had gently spoken, nor were they themselves just an old, peculiar couple. Slowly the change crept about, all around them in the town, until Fat Driscoll didn't wish it to be remembered that he had ever given them mince for their dog. He had stood with a gun in the enemy's house, waiting for soldiers so that soldiers might be killed—it was better that people should remember that.

One day Canon Kelly looked the other way when he saw the Middletons' car coming and they noticed this movement of his head, although he hadn't wished them to. And on another day Mrs. O'Brien, who had always been keen to talk to them in the hotel, didn't reply when they addressed her.

The Middletons naturally didn't discuss these rebuffs but they each of them privately knew that there was no conversation they could have at this time with the people of the town. The stand they had taken and kept to for so many years no longer seemed ridiculous in the town. Had they driven with a union jack now they would, astoundingly, have been shot.

"It will never cease." He spoke disconsolately one night, standing by the dresser where the wireless was.

She washed the dishes they'd eaten from, and the cutlery. "Not in our time," she said.

"It is worse than before."

"Yes, it is worse than before."

They took from the walls of the hall the portrait of their father in the uniform of the Irish Guards because it seemed wrong to them that at this time it should hang there. They took down also the crest of their family and the Cross of St. George, and from a vase on the drawing-room mantelpiece they removed the small union jack that had been there since the coronation of Queen Elizabeth II. They did not remove these articles in fear but in mourning for the *modus vivendi*[9] that had existed for so long between them and the people of the town. They had given their custom to a butcher who had planned to shoot down soldiers in their hall and he, in turn, had given them mince for their dog. For fifty years they had experienced, after suspicion had seeped away, a tolerance

9. *modus vivendi* (vi ven′ dī): Manner of getting along.

that never again in the years that were left to them would they know.

One November night their dog died and he said to her after he had buried it that they must not be depressed by all that was happening. They would die themselves and the house would become a ruin because there was no one to inherit it, and the distant past would be set to rest. But she disagreed: the *modus vivendi* had been easy for them, she pointed out, because they hadn't really minded the dwindling of their fortunes while the town prospered. It had given them a life, and a kind of dignity: you could take a pride out of living in peace.

Literary Movement: The fate of the Middleton family and estate reflects the disappearance of a glorious age in British history.

He did not say anything and then, because of the emotion that both of them felt over the death of their dog, he said in a rushing way that they could no longer at their age hope to make a living out of the remains of Carraveagh. They must sell the hens and the four Herefords. As he spoke, he watched her nodding, agreeing with the sense of it. Now and again, he thought, he would drive slowly into the town, to buy groceries and meat with the money they had saved, and to face the silence that would sourly thicken as their own two deaths came closer and death increased in another part of their island. She felt him thinking that and she knew that he was right. Because of the distant past they would die friendless. It was worse than being murdered in their beds.

William Trevor (1928–) was born and educated in Ireland, but he moved to England after beginning his writing career. Set in both Ireland and England, his stories explore a wide variety of subjects and themes. Displaying a deep understanding of human nature, Trevor often portrays the seemingly pointless misunderstandings that develop between people and groups of people. Trevor has published numerous collections of short stories, including *The Collected Stories of William Trevor.*

Critical Thinking and Reading Ronald De Feo noted that Trevor's stories conclude on a note that causes the reader to reevaluate what he or she has read. What does the conclusion make you want to reevaluate?

More About the Author Trevor's third collection of short stories, *Angels at the Ritz* which includes "The Distant Past," is considered by many to be the best since James Joyce's *The Dubliners.* Indeed, in his short stories, Cox shows the influence of James Joyce with whom he ,had been favorably compared. A novelist and a playwright, he has adapted several of his stories for television. In all he writes, he demonstrates the precise style that was influenced more than anything by his Irish background, especially that of Cork County.

Answers

ANSWERS TO THINKING ABOUT THE SELECTION

Recalling

1. The Middletons blame the Catholic Dublin woman with whom their father was involved, and they blamed the new national regime.
2. Fat Driscoll and the Middletons recall the time when the rifle-toting butcher and others locked the family in a bedroom and awaited the arrival of British troops whom they were willing to kill.

(Answers begin on p. 1235.)

3. (a) The Middletons drive into town with a union jack propped up in the back window. (b) The townspeople laughed at them.
4. The town prospered because tourists found it a charming, pleasant place to visit.
5. (a) The relationship of the townspeople and the Middletons is friendly at first. Although they are considered eccentric, they are respected and welcome. (b) Bitter, the townspeople turn away from the Middletons by ignoring them. They are no longer welcome.

Interpreting

6. Just as the British Empire was diminished after World War I as colonies demanded and received independence, the Middletons lost property and their home deteriorated. They both were relics of the past.
7. As long as the town was prosperous, the Middletons were respected even though they were avid Anglophiles. When British soldiers came to Northern Ireland and trouble started there, the townspeople began to ignore and reject them.
8. Suggested Response: The change in the townspeople's attitude reveals that terrorism can affect people far away, old wounds never completely heal, and economic adversity can create bitterness and cruelty.

Applying

9. Answers will differ. One possible response would include the fact that since the Irish had been oppressed by the English for hundreds of years, denied their civil rights, and considered second-class citizens in their own country, they are bound to harbor ill feelings toward the English.

Challenge Imagine that you were a tourist who had visited the town during the tranquil years of the early '60's. You have decided to return and, much to your surprise, you notice a change in the town's atmosphere. Write a postcard home, telling what you think of the difference.

THINKING ABOUT THE SELECTION

Recalling

1. Whom do the Middletons blame for the decay of their estate?
2. What event do Fat Driscoll and the Middletons recall when they visit Driscoll's butcher shop?
3. (a) What do the Middletons do on the day of Queen Elizabeth II's coronation? (b) How do the townspeople respond to this action?
4. Why does the town prosper in the years after World War II?
5. (a) What type of relationship do the Middletons have with the townspeople? (b) How does the relationship change after the town's prosperity fades?

Interpreting

6. How does the decline of the Middletons' fortunes parallel the decline of the British Empire?
7. What is ironic, or surprising, about the fact that throughout most of the story the townspeople respected the Middletons?
8. What does the change in the townspeople's attitude toward the Middletons reveal about human nature?

Applying

9. Why do you think that many Irish people feel a sense of resentment toward the British?

ANALYZING LITERATURE

Recognizing Character

A variety of different types of characters are used in literary works. When a character is well-developed and posseses a variety of traits, he or she is referred to as a round character. A character who embodies a single trait, ideal, or quality is referred to as a flat character. Static characters are characters who do not change during the course of a literary work. Dynamic characters are characters who do change.

1. Are the Middletons flat characters or round characters? Support your answer.
2. Are the Middletons static characters or dynamic characters? Support your answer.
3. Are the townspeople static characters or dynamic characters? Support your answer.

CRITICAL THINKING AND READING

Understanding a Character's Motivation

In portraying any type of character, a writer must provide a motivation, or a stated or implied reason for the character's behavior, to make the character's actions believable. For example, in "The Distant Past" it is clear that the Middletons' actions on the day of Queen Elizabeth II's coronation are motivated by their loyalty to Great Britain.

1. What motivates the townspeople to change their behavior toward the Middletons?
2. How does Trevor reveal this motivation?

THINKING AND WRITING

Writing a Dialogue

Write a dialogue in which the Middletons discuss the decline in their fortunes and the change in the townspeoples' attitude toward them. Reread the story, trying to put yourself in the Middletons' place. Then write your dialogue, having the Middletons discuss the reasons for and feelings about their present situation. When you finish writing, revise your dialogue and share it with your classmates.

ANSWERS TO ANALYZING LITERATURE

1. The Middletons are round characters because the reader knows what they are thinking and feeling.
2. The Middletons are dynamic characters, for they change when they, mourning for the way they had related to the townspeople, remove the symbols of England.
3. The townspeople are also dynamic characters because their attitude towards the Middletons changes from friendly respect to cold bitterness.

ANSWERS TO CRITICAL THINKING AND READING

1. The townspeople's change in behavior is motivated by loss of income because of terrorism in the North. They associate the Middletons' loyalty to Britain with the trouble caused by British soldiers.
2. Trevor reveals this by the actions of the townspeople—pointedly ignoring the Middletons, becoming silent when they appear, and no longer accepting their eccentricity.

THINKING AND WRITING

Publishing Student Writing Have students work with a partner to tape their dialogues, adding any sound effects that would be appropriate. Play the tapes for the class.

Prose

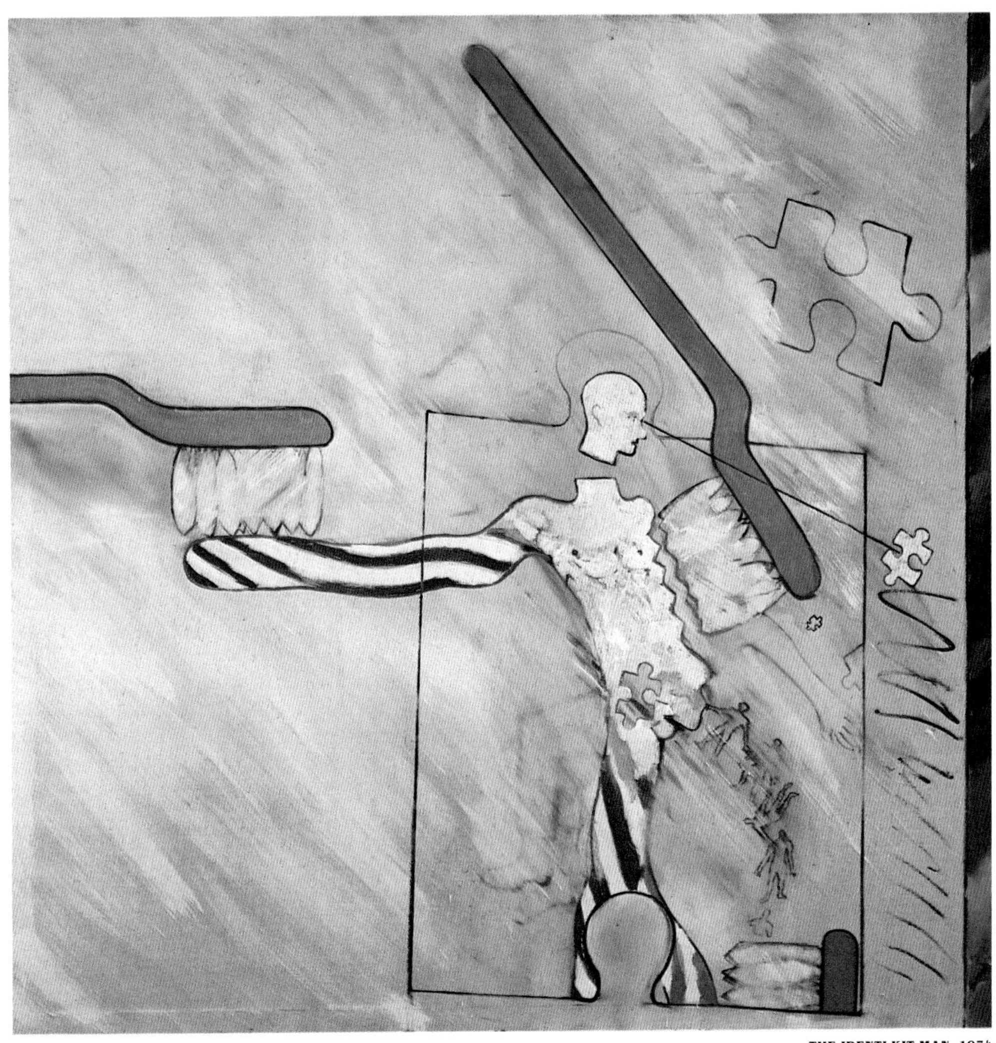

THE IDENTI-KIT MAN, 1974
Derek Boshier
Tate Gallery Publications Department

More About the Author One of the sources for Sean O'Faolain's rich fictional characterizations might be his biographical writing. In addition to novels and short stories, O'Faolain wrote biographies of Eamon De Valera, Daniel O'Connell, Hugh O'Neill, and others. These factual portrayals of men who had a role in Irish history demanded O'Faolain's probing into the *whys* and *hows* of their lives. While his fiction derives from imagination, the engaging and well-rounded characters in O'Faolain's stories correlate to the types of men in his biographies—they question values, challenge their environment, and attempt to find meaning in their lives. As O'Faolain said, "There is only one admirable form of the imagination—the imagination that is so intense that it creates a new reality, that it makes things happen, whether it be a political thing, or a social thing, or a work of art." His own intense imagination, fueled by factual research, has yielded sympathetic and complex characters. Discuss how factual research can influence or enhance a writers' imaginative creation.

SEAN O'FAOLAIN

1900–

Although the Irish writer Sean O'Faolain is best known for his short stories, he has written widely in many genres—novels, plays, biographies, travel books, literary criticism. His works, which draw upon a powerful sense of tradition, deal with Ireland and its people with a universality that transcends their locale. Over the past fifty years, his writings have promoted liberal, humane values in a state that he, as a revolutionary, helped to bring into existence.

Sean O'Faolain, originally named John Whelan, was born in the city of Cork in southern Ireland, the son of a policeman and a theatrical landlady. Schooled by priests and later at University College, Cork, he "became one with the emotion of Ireland" in the aftermath of the Easter Rebellion of 1916. He joined the Irish volunteers, learned Gaelic, and changed his name to its Gaelic variant. During the Irish revolution, 1918–1921, he served as director of publicity for the Irish Republican Army. An idealist, he found himself disillusioned by the struggle and its consequences. He drifted away from war and politics.

After a year of graduate study at Harvard, O'Faolain sent for Eileen Gould, whom he had met during the revolution. He married her, and for their honeymoon they took a camping trip across the United States. Although both he and Eileen loved America, they returned to Ireland "where every field, every path, every ruin had its memories, where every last corner had its story."

The war, which made O'Faolain a bitter young man, furnished the material for his first short stories, collected in *Midsummer Night Madness* (1932). His later collections, such as *A Purse of Coppers* (1937) and *The Man Who Invented Sin* (1948), show increasing maturity. They depict everyday Irish life in a lyrical yet unsentimental manner.

O'Faolain, who says his aim in writing is a "blend of reason and sensibility," founded *The Bell,* an Irish literary journal, in 1940, and edited it for a number of years. A reformer, deeply concerned with Irish culture, he has not always been popular with conservatives in Ireland. Nevertheless, his compassion and humor have never left him, and his portraits of Irish life are sympathetic and compelling.

Objectives

1 To understand first-person narration
2 To identify subjective information
3 To understand the meaning of caricature
4 To write about a thematic statement

Teaching Portfolio: Support Material

Teacher Backup, p. 000

Vocabulary Check, p. 00

Usage and Mechanics Worksheet, p. 00

Analyzing Literature Worksheet, p. 00

Critical Thinking and Reading Worksheet, p. 00

Understanding Language Worksheet, p. 00

GUIDE FOR READING

A Touch of Autumn in the Air

The Writer's Techniques

First-person Narration. The purpose of narration is to tell a story. Narration may be either factual (as is history and biography) or fictional (as in novels and short stories). In fictional narration, the story may be told from various perspectives, depending on the narrator's point of view. The narrator—the person who tells the story—may be someone within the story or someone outside it. A first-person narrator is a character within the story. He or she uses the word *I* in telling it. A third-person narrator stands outside the story and uses *he, she, they,* or *it.*

First-person narration, or point of view, falls into two main types. A first-person narrator, using the pronoun *I,* may be a main character in a story—a first-person participant—like the narrator in Mary Wollstonecraft Shelley's *Frankenstein.* Or the narrator, using *I,* may be a first-person observer, like Dr. Watson in the Sherlock Holmes stories.

In either kind of role, the narrator serves as a persona, or mask, through which the writer tells the story. He or she relates events in accordance with the writer's artistic purpose. The narrator, being a fictional creation, does *not* necessarily reflect the writer's own attitudes or beliefs.

Look For

As you read Sean O'Faolain's "A Touch of Autumn in the Air," notice the author's use of first-person narration. What does the narrator tell you about the main character?

Writing

What is memory? Why do we remember some things and not others? Why do some events spring to mind after lying dormant in memory for many years? Freewrite, exploring your answers to these questions.

Vocabulary

Knowing the following words will help you as you read "A Touch of Autumn in the Air."

obstinacy (äb' stə nə sē) *n.*: Stubbornness (p. 1240)
mesmerism (m z'mər iz'm) *n.*: Hypnotism (p. 1241)
advert (ad vʉrt') *v.*: To call attention to (p. 1241)
demesne (di mān') *n.*: Lands of n estate (p. 1241)
sinuous (sin' yoo wəs) *adj.*: Bending; curving in and out (p. 1241)
premonitory (pri män'ə tôr'ē) *adj.*: Giving warning beforehand (p. 1244)
phosphorescence (fäs'fə res''ns) *n.*: The property of shining in the dark (p. 1246)
imperiously (im pir'ē əs lē) *adv.*: Arrogantly (p. 1246)

Literary Focus Point out that narration is the way that a writer tells a story. Explain to students that writers must choose different types of narration for different purposes. Ask students to discuss the advantages and disadvantages of first-person narration. Elicit that an advantage of first-person narration is that the reader learns the thoughts and feelings of one character. The reader becomes involved in the story because the narrator is directly involved in the events. A possible disadvantage of first-person narration is that the reader is limited to learning only what the narrator knows, experiences, or finds out from other characters or from direct observation. Have students think about other stories that they have read. Ask your **less advanced** students to identify the point of view in each story. Ask your **more advanced** students to analyze the writer's use of first-person narration or third-person narration.

Look For Your **less advanced** students may have difficulty in identifying first-person narration. Have them write five sentences about a humorous incident. Ask them to write the sentences using *I.* Have your **more advanced** students first write the sentences using first-person narration. Then have them rewrite the sentences, this time using third-person narration.

Writing Have students discuss a vivid childhood memory, an incident that they wish might happen to them, or a historical event that they will never forget. Then have them complete the freewriting assignment, using their discussion as a basis for the writing topic. Ask students to consider the advantages and disadvantages of first-person narration to a writer. Your **more advanced** students might try using first-person narration and third-person narration in their writing.

Vocabulary Have your **less advanced** students read the vocabulary words and their definitions aloud. Discuss synonyms and antonyms when applicable to help them understand the meaning of each word. Your **more advanced** students might try to create a crossword puzzle with the vocabulary words, using the word definitions as clues.

A Touch of Autumn in the Air

Sean O'Faolain

It was, of all people, Daniel Cashen of
Roscommon who first made me realize that
the fragments of any experience that remain
1 in a man's memory, like bits and scraps of a
ruined temple, are preserved from time not
at random but by the inmost desires of his
personality.

Cashen was neither sensitive nor intelligent. He was a caricature of the self-made,
self-educated, nineteenth-century businessman. Some seventy years ago he had set
up a small woollen factory in County Roscommon which, by hard work from early
morning to late at night, and by making
everybody around him work at the same
pace, he developed into a thriving industry
which he personally owned. His Swansdown
Blankets, for example, were the only kind of
blankets my mother ever bought. Though
old when I made his acquaintance, he was
still a powerful horse of a man, always
dressed in well-pressed Irish tweeds, heavy
countryman's boots, and a fawn, flat-topped
bowler hat set squat above a big, red, square
face, heavy handlebar moustaches and pale
blue, staring eyes of which one always saw
the complete circle of the iris, challenging,
concentrated, slightly mad.

One would not expect such a man to say
anything very profound about the workings
of the memory, and he did not. All he did
was to indulge in a brief burst of reminiscence in a hotel foyer, induced by my casual
remark that it was a lovely, sunny day outside but that there was a touch of autumn in
the air. The illuminating thing was the bewildered look that came into those pale,
staring eyes as he talked. It revealed that he
was much more touched and troubled by the
Why of memory than by the Fact of memory. 2
He was saying, in effect: Why do I remember
that? Why do I not remember the other
thing? For the first time in his life something
within him had gone out of control.

What he started to talk about was a
holiday he spent when just under fifteen, in
what was at that time called the Queen's 3
County. It had lasted two months, September and October. "Lovely, sunny weather,
just like today." What had begun to bother
him was not so much that the days had
merged and melted together in his memory
—after so many years that was only natural 4
—but that here and there, from a few days
of no more evident importance than any
other days, a few trivial things stuck up
above the tides of forgetfulness. And as he
mentioned them I could see that he was
fumbling, a little fearfully, towards the notion that there might be some meaning in
the pattern of those indestructible bits of
the jigsaw of his youth, perhaps even some
sort of revelation in their obstinacy after so
much else had dropped down the crevices of
time.

He did not come directly to the major
memory that had set his mind working in
this way. He mentioned a few lesser memo-

Motivation for Reading Tell students that "A Touch of Autumn in the Air" concerns a memory. Ask them to define memory in their own words. Encourage them to complete the sentence: Memory is like ____. As they read, have them note the ways that Sean O'Faolain describes memory. Ask them to jot down the comparisons about memory that he makes in the selection.

Master Teacher Note The importance of memory and what memory means in terms of experience is central to "A Touch of Autumn in the Air." Discuss amnesia, Alzheimer's disease, senility, and other illnesses or conditions that affect memory. You might wish to ask students what it might be like to lose one's memory.

Thematic Idea Other selections that concern the theme of memory are excerpts from Samuel Pepys's *The Diary* on page 524 and Daniel Defoe's *A Journal of the Plague Year* on page 532.

Purpose-Setting Question What role does memory play in this story?

1 **Reading Strategy** Rephrase this sentence in your own words.

2 **Critical Thinking and Reading** Do you think that Daniel Cashen is disturbed by his memory? Why or why not? Does the narrator give you subjective or objective information?

3 **Clarification** Ireland is politically made up of provinces, which are in turn divided into counties. Mary I of England seized land here and renamed the county Queen's County in 1556. After the rise of Irish nationalism, the county's name was restored to its original Gaelic, *Laoighis,* or *Leix.*

4 **Enrichment** Have students note throughout "A Touch of Autumn in the Air" O'Faolain's comparison of memory to water. In this sentence he alludes to the "tides" of forgetfulness that sweep over Cashen.

ries first, staring out through the revolving glass doors at the sunny street. There was the afternoon when, by idle chance, he leaned over a small stone bridge near his Uncle Bartle's farm and became held for an hour by the mesmerism of the stream flickering through the chickweed. As could happen likewise to a great number of busy men, who normally never think at all about the subjective side of themselves, and are overwhelmed by the mystery of it if once they do advert to it, he attached an almost magical import to the discovery that he had never forgotten the bright pleasure of that casual hour.

"No, John! Although it must be near
5 sixty years ago. And I don't believe I ever will forget it. Why is that?"

Of course, he admitted modestly, he had a phenomenal memory, and to prove it he invited me to ask him the telephone numbers of any half-dozen shops in town. But, yet, there was that red hay barn where he and his cousin, Kitty Bergin, played and tumbled a score of times—it was a blur.

"I can't even remember whether the thing was made of timber or corrugated iron!"

Or there was the sunken river, away back on the level leas, a stream rather than a river, where one warm September Sunday after Mass he saw, with distasteful pleasure, the men splashing around naked, roughly ducking a boy who had joined them, laughing at his screams. But, whereas he also still possessed the soft, surrounding fields, the imperceptibly moving clouds, the crunch of a jolting cart far away, the silence so deep
6 that you could have heard an apple falling, he had lost every detail of the walk to and from the river, and every hour before and after it. A less arrogant man might have accepted the simple explanation that the mind wavers in and out of alertness, is bright at one moment, dim at the next. Those mad, round irises glared at the suggestion that his mind could at any time be dim.

He pointed out that he knew the country for miles around, intimately, walking it and cycling it day after day: what clung to him of it all, like burrs, were mere spots—a rusty iron gate falling apart, a crossroads tree with a black patch burnt at its base, an uneventful turn off the main road, a few undistinguished yards of the three miles of wall around the local demesne. He laughed scornfully at my idea that his mind became bright only for those few yards of wall.

"Well, perhaps it became dim then? You were thinking hard about other things up to that point in your walk?"

Here he allowed his real trouble to expose itself. He had not only remembered pointless scraps, but, I found, those scraps had been coming back to him repeatedly during the last few days with a tormenting joy, so that here he was, an old man, fondling nothings as lovingly as if he were fondling a lock of a dead woman's hair. It was plain, at last, that he was thinking of all those fragments of his boyhood as the fish 7
scales of some wonderful fish, never-to-be-seen, sinuous and shining, that had escaped from his net into the ocean.

What had started him off was simple. (I reconstruct it as well as I can, intuiting and enlarging from his own brief, blunt words.) A few mornings before our meeting, fine and sunny also, he had happened to go into a toyshop where they also sold sweets. He was suddenly transfixed by the smell peculiar to these shops—scented soaps, the paint on the tin toys and the sprayed wooden trucks, the smell of the children's gift books, the sweetness of the sweets. At once he was back in that holiday, with his cousin Kitty Bergin, on the leas behind her father's farmhouse (his Uncle Bartle's), one sunny, misti- 8,9
fied October morning, driving in a donkey cart down to where his uncle and his cousin Jack were ditching a small meadow that they had retrieved from the rushes and the bog water.

As Kitty and he slowly jolted along the 10
rutted track deeper and deeper into this

5 Clarification Who is speaking? What effect does the dialogue have?

6 Discussion Discuss the sensory details of Cashen's memory. List as many different senses that the writer appeals to as you can.

7 Reading Strategy Why is Cashen's memory like a fish? Do you think that Cashen would compare his recollection of boyhood to a fish?

8 Clarification A lea is a pasture that is used temporarily for haying or grazing. Uncle Bartle and cousin Jack are making a ditch so that excess water will run off from the pasture.

9 Reading Strategy When does the action described take place? Explain the shift in time in this sentence.

10 Literary Focus Describe the point of view used in this passage. Who is the narrator?

Humanities Note

Fine art, *The Soothsayer from the Green Island,* 1946, by John Petts. The contemporary British artist John Petts was born in 1914 in London. He was educated at the Hornsley College of Art and the Central School, Royal Academy of Art. Not content to express himself in one medium, Petts works in sculpture, mosaic, engraving, and stained-glass design. He is internationally known for the large window he designed for the people of Wales to present as a goodwill gift to the Afro-American Church in Birmingham, Alabama, which was bombed in a notorious racial incident.

John Petts did wood-engraving illustrations for England's Golden Cockerel Press. This engraving, *The Soothsayer,* was executed in 1946. This example shows Petts's engraving skills in the interesting variety of textures, masterly composition, and combination of unconventional point of view with rhythmic curving lines.

You might ask the following questions:

1. What kind of person would you guess the man in this print to be?
2. What is the mood or atmosphere of this print?

THE SOOTHSAYER FROM THE GREEN ISLAND, 1946
John Petts

wide, flat river basin of the Barrow, whose hundreds of streams and dikes feed into what, by a gradual addition, becomes a river some twenty miles away, the two men whom they were approaching looked so minute on the level bog, under the vast sky, that Dan got a queer feeling of his own smallness in observing theirs. As he looked back, the white, thatched farmhouse nestling into the earth had never seemed so homely, cozy and comforting.

Ferns crackled at the hub. When he clutched one its fronds were warm but wet. It was the season when webs are flung with a wild energy across chasms. He wiped his
11 face several times. He saw dew drops in a row in midair, invisibly supported between frond and frond. A lean swath of mist, or was it low cloud, floated beneath far hills. Presently they saw behind the two men a pond with a fringe of reeds. Against an outcrop of delicately decayed limestone was a bent hawthorn in a cloud of ruby berries. Or could it have been a rowan tree? The sky was a pale green. The little shaven meadow
12 was as lemon-bright as fallen ash leaves before the dew dries on their drifts, so that it would have been hard to say whether the liquid lemon of the meadow was evaporating into the sky or the sky melting down into the field.

They were on a happy mission. Mulvaney the postman had brought two letters to the farmhouse from two other sons: Owen, who was a pit manager in the mines at Castlecomer, and Christopher (who, out of respect, was never referred to as Christy), then studying for the priesthood in a Dublin seminary. Aunt Molly had sent them off with the letters, a jug of hot tea and thick rounds of fresh, homemade bread and homemade apple jam smelling of cloves, a great favorite of Uncle Bartle's. They duly reached the two men, relieved the donkey of
13 bridle, bit and winkers so that he could graze in the meadow, spread sacks to sit on, and while Kitty poured the tea into mugs Bartle reverently wiped his clayey hands on the sides of his trousers and took the letters. As he read them aloud in a slow, singsong voice, like a man intoning his prayers, it was clear that those two sons had gone so far outside his own experience of the big world that he stood a little in awe of them both. It was a picture to be remembered for years: the meadow, the old man, the smoke of the distant farmhouse, partriarchal, sheltered, simple.

When he laid down the letter from the priest-to-be he said:

"He's doing well. A steady lad."

When he had read the letter from the mines he said:

"He's doing fine. If he escapes the danger he will go far."

While Jack was reading the letters Kitty whispered to Danny, thumbing the moon's faint crescent:

"Look! It says D for Danny."

"Or," he murmured to her boldly, 'it 14
could be D for Dear?"

Her warning glare towards her father was an admission.

"I see here," Jack commented, while his father sucked at the tea, "that Christopher 15
is after visiting Fanny Emphie. Her name in religion is Sister Fidelia."

Dan had seen this girl at the Curragh 16
Races during the first week of his holidays, a neighbor's daughter who, a few weeks later, entered the convent. He had heard them joking one night about how she and Christopher had at one time been "great" with one another. He remembered a slight, skinny girl with a cocked nose, laughing moist lips and shining white teeth.

"Read me out that bit," Bartle ordered. "I didn't note that."

"'I got special leave from the President to visit Sister Fidelia, last week, at Saint Joachim's. She is well and happy but looked pale. She asked after you all. Saint Joachim's has nice grounds, but the trams pass outside the wall and she said that for the first couple of weeks she could hardly sleep at all.'"

11 **Reading Strategy** What do you think is being described in this passage?

12 **Master Teacher Note** This selection is rich in sensory detail. Provide students with books of photographs or paintings that graphically represent the pastoral beauty of Ireland. Emphasize the rural photographs or paintings. If students have been to Ireland, ask them to describe the landscape.

13 **Clarification** A bridle is the restraint by which a rider controls a horse or donkey. A bit is the steel part of the bridle that fits into animal's mouth. Winkers are the blinkers or blinders worn by the donkey so that it is not distracted or suddenly frightened as it walks or works.

14 **Reading Strategy** How do Dan and Kitty feel about one another?

15 **Clarification** In the Catholic religion, women who become nuns are addressed as "Sister." Because a woman who enters the convent for religious service is giving up her old life and making a pledge for a new life, she changes her name to signify this new commitment. Fanny Emphie took the name "Sister Fidelia" when she became a nun. *Fidelia* is related to *fidelity*, which means "loyalty."

16 **Clarification** A curragh, or coracle, is a small boat made of broad hoops that are covered with animal hide or tarpaulin. The curragh is traditionally used in Ireland and the British Isles.

17 Discussion Describe in your own words what Kitty looks like. What do her actions reveal about Kitty's personality?

18 Master Teacher Note The Conversation Lozenges made a lasting impression on Cashen. Try to find "conversation lozenges" in the stores to help students understand the flavor of his recollection. These candies are often sold for Valentine's Day. Have students compare and contrast the messages written on those that Cashen buys and those that you supply.

19 Reading Strategy What series of coincidences happen to Cashen? Why does Cashen notice the nun in the sweets-and-toys shop?

The two men went on drinking their tea. It occurred to Dan that they did not care much for Fanny Emphie. He saw her now in her black robes walking along a graveled path under the high walls of the convent, outside which the trams at night drew their glow in the air overhead. It also occurred to him, for no reason, that Kitty Bergin might one day think of becoming a nun, and he looked at her with a pang of premonitory loss. Why should any of them leave this quiet place?

"Ha!" said old Bartle suddenly, and winked at Danny, and rubbed his dusty hands and drew out his pipe. This meant that they must all get back to work.

Kitty gathered up the utensils, Danny tackled the donkey, the others went back to their ditching and she and Danny drove back to where the fern was plentiful for bedding. Taking two sickles, they began to rasp through the stalks. After a while she straightened up, so did he, and they regarded one another, waist-deep in the fern.

"Do you think," she asked him pertly, "would I make a nice nun?"

"You!" he said, startled that the same thought had entered their heads at the same time.

She came across to him, slipped from his pocket the big blue handkerchief in which the bread had been wrapped, cast it in an arc about her fair head, drew it tightly under
17 her chin with her left hand, and then with a deft peck of her right finger and thumb cowled it forward over her forehead and her up-looking blue eyes.

"Sister Fidelia, sir," she curtsied, provokingly.

He grappled with her as awkwardly as any country boy, paying the sort of homage he expected was expected of him, and she, laughing, wrestled strongly with him. They swayed in one another''s arms, aware of each other's bodies, until she cried, "Here's Daddy," and when he let her go mocked him from a safe distance for his innocence. But as they cut the fern again her sidelong glances made him happy.

They piled the cut fern into the cart, climbed on top of it, and lay face down on it, feeling the wind so cold that they instinctively pressed closer together. They jolted out to the main road, and as they ambled along they talked, and it seemed to him that it was very serious talk, but he forgot every word of it. When they came near the crossroads with its little sweetshop, they decided to buy a half-penny-worth of their favorite sweets, those flat, odd-shaped sweets —diamonds, hearts, hexagonals—called 18
Conversation Lozenges because each sweet bore on its coarse surface a ring posy[1] in colored ink, such as Mizpah, Truth Tries Troth, Do You Care? or All for Love. Some bore girls' names, such as Gladys or Alice. His first sweet said, Yours in Heart. He handed it to her with a smile; she at once popped it into her mouth, laughing at his folly. As they ambled along so, slowly, chatting and chewing, the donkey's hooves whispering through the fallen beech leaves, they heard high above the bare arches of the trees the faint honking of the wild geese called down from the north by the October moon.

It was to those two or three hours of that October morning many years ago that he was whirled back as he stood transfixed by the smells of the sweets-and-toys shop. Forgetting what he had come there to buy, he asked them if they sold Conversation Lozenges. They had never heard of them. As he turned to go he saw a nun leafing through the children's gift books. He went near her and, pretending to look at a book, peered 19
under her cowl. To his surprise she was a very old nun. On the pavement he glanced up at the sky and was startled to see there the faint crescent moon. He was startled because he remembered that he had seen it earlier in the morning, and had quite forgotten the fact.

1. **ring posy:** A verse or motto inscribed in a circle.

He at once distrusted the message of his memory. Perhaps it was not that the smells had reminded him of little Kitty Bergin eating Yours in Heart, or pretending to be a nun, or wrestling with him in the fern? Perhaps what had called him back was the
20 indifference of those two men to the fate of the nun? Or was there some special meaning for him in those arrowing geese? Or in the cozy, sheltered farmhouse? Maybe the important thing that day had been the old man humbly reading the letters? Why had the two men looked so small under the open sky of the bogland? D, she had said, for Danny . . .

As he stared at me there in the hotel 21
foyer, my heart softened towards him. The pain in his eyes was the pain of a man who has begun to lose one of the great pleasures of life in the discovery that we can never 22
truly remember anything at all, that we are for a great part of our lives at the mercy of uncharted currents of the heart. It would have been futile to try to comfort him by

KNOCKALLA HILLS, DONEGAL
Dan O'Neill
Ulster Museum, Belfast

20 **Literary Focus** Discuss the point of view used in this passage. What are the disadvantages of third-person narration? What are the advantages?

21 **Literary Focus** Who is the narrator? What signifies a shift in narration?

22 **Critical Thinking and Reading** What is the main idea of this passage? Is the information given by the narrator objective or subjective? How do you know?

Humanities Note

Fine art, *Knockalla Hills, Donegal,* by Dan O'Neill. Irish artist Dan O'Neill was born in Belfast in 1920. His splendid landscape paintings have never given in to the modern trends in art. He has maintained a consistent palette and style throughout his painting career.

Knockalla Hills, Donegal is an example of O'Neill's original style of landscape painting, in which a simple view is made interesting through his choice of harmonious colors and pleasing shapes. He captures the essence of a cool fall day in Ireland.

You might use these questions for discussion:

1. Is there anything in this painting to indicate that the scene is in Ireland? Elaborate.
2. How has the artist shown the viewer the season?

23 **Literary Focus** What effect does the use of dialogue have on the tone of the story? Why does the narrator's question comfort Daniel Cashen?

24 **Critical Thinking and Reading** Identify the part of this sentence that is objective and the part that is subjective.

25 **Critical Thinking and Reading** How does the narrator feel about Cashen? Do you agree or disagree with the narrator's opinion? Why?

26 **Enrichment** O'Faolain compares Cashen's search for the meaning of his boyhood with archaeology. An archaeologist finds and studies delicate shards of pottery, scraps of clothing, and so on in an attempt to piece together the history and customs of a particular civilization. Often these scraps and shards offer nothing more than puzzling clues. O'Faolain's reference to archaeology is interesting for two reasons: he "digs" through factual material to write his biographies and explain his subjects; and his native country possesses a rich archaeological past buried in layers of peat found in Ireland's many bogs.

saying that those currents may be charted elsewhere, that even when those revolving glass doors in front of us flashed in the October sun the whole movement of the universe since time began was involved in that coincidence of light. Daniel Cashen of Roscommon would get small comfort out of thinking of himself as a little blob of phosphorescence running along the curl of a wave at night.

And then, by chance, I did say something that comforted him, because as he shook hands with me and said he must be off, I said, without thinking:

23 "I hope the blankets are doing well?"

"Aha!" he cried triumphantly. "Better than ever."

24 And tapped his flat-topped hat more firmly on his head and whirled the doors before him out into the sunny street as imperiously as any man accustomed to ordering everything that comes his way.

Through the slowing doors I watched him halt on the pavement. He looked slowly to the right, and then he looked towards his left, and then, slowly, he looked up around the sky until he found what he was looking for. After a few moments he shivered up his shoulders around his neck, looked at the ground at his feet, put his two hands into his pockets, and moved very slowly away, still down-looking, out of sight.

25 Poor man, I thought when he was gone; rash, blunt, undevious; yet, in his own crude way, more true to life than his famous French contemporary[2] who recaptured lost time only by dilating, inventing, suppressing, merging such of its realities as he could recall, and inventing whatever he could not. Cashen was playing archaeology with his boyhood, trying to deduce a whole self out of a few dusty shards.[3] It was, of course, far too late. My guess was that of the few scraps that he now held in his hands the clue lay not so much in the offer of love and the images of retirement, the girl's courtship, the white farmhouse snuggling down cozily 26 into the earth under the vast dome of the sky, and the old man left behind by his sons, as in the challenging sight of his own littleness on that aqueous plain whose streams barely trickled to the open sea. He said he hadn't thought of it for sixty years. Perhaps not? But he was thinking of it now, when the adventure was pretty well over. As it was. A week later a friend rang me up and said, "Did you hear who's died?" I knew at once, but I asked the question.

He left nearly a hundred and fifty thousand pounds—a lot of money in our country—and, since he never married, he divided it all up among his relatives by birth, most of them comparatively poor people and most of them living in what used to be called, in his boyhood, the Queen's County.

2. famous French contemporary: French novelist Marcel Proust (1871-1922).
3. shards *n.*: Fragments or broken pieces.

THINKING ABOUT THE SELECTION

Recalling

1. (a) What prompts Daniel Cashen to start talking about the holiday he spent long ago? (b) Where does he engage in this "brief burst of reminiscence"?
2. (a) Who is Kitty Bergin? (b) Why did Aunt Molly send her and Dan to the meadow?
3. (a) Whom did Kitty pretend to be? (b) How did Dan respond to her play-acting? (c) Why?
4. What does the narrator ask that brings Cashen back from his reminiscence?
5. What does the narrator think affected Cashen most about his boyhood recollection?

Answers

ANSWERS TO THINKING ABOUT THE SELECTION

Recalling

1. (a) The narrator's casual remark about the day being sunny but with a touch of autumn in the air prompts Daniel Cashen to talk about the holiday he spent long ago. (b) He engages in this reminiscence in a hotel foyer.
2. (a) Kitty Bergin is Daniel Cashen's cousin. (b) Aunt Molly sends Kitty and Dan to the meadow to bring hot tea, homemade bread and apple jam, and letters from Owen and Christopher to Jack and Uncle Bartle.
3. (a) Kitty pretended to be Sister Fidelia, a nun. (b) Dan wrestled with Kitty. (c) He grappled with her because he thought she wanted him to.
4. The narrator asks about the blankets Cashen's company manufactures; the question brings him back from his remembrance.
5. The narrator thinks that Cashen's recollection made him feel small and insignificant.

Interpreting

6. The narrator thinks that Cashen is troubled by his memories because of the look in Cashen's eye when he remembers the holiday; he appears bewildered by the remembrance and by why he remembers certain things and not others.
7. Answers will differ. Cashen most likely asks for Conversation Lozenges in the candy shop as a sentimental gesture; he bought such sweets more than fifty years ago with Kitty Bergin. The lozenges remind him of this blissful time in his life.
8. The narrator's heart softens toward Cashen near the end of the story because he recognizes the pain Cashen feels upon realizing that his memory is incomplete and inadequate. The narrator sympathizes with Cashen's vain attempt to find meaning and purpose in his remembering an incident that occurred sixty years ago.
9. Answers will differ. The story's title

Interpreting

6. Why does the narrator think Cashen is troubled by his memories?
7. Why do you think Cashen, as an old man, asks for Conversation Lozenges in the candy shop?
8. Near the end of the story, why does the narrator's heart soften toward Cashen?
9. What is the significance of the story's title?
10. What is your own interpretation of Daniel Cashen's story and his motives for telling it?

Applying

11. Do you agree with the narrator that we can never truly remember anything at all? Explain your answer.

ANALYZING LITERATURE

First-person Narration

A first-person observer may be a fully developed character, with a name, a life history, and a personality, as is Dr. Watson in the Sherlock Holmes stories. On the other hand, a first-person observer, as in Sean O'Faolain's "A Touch of Autumn in the Air," may exist mostly in the background of the story.

1. In "A Touch of Autumn in the Air," the narrator introduces the story of Daniel Cashen and then lets the story take over. (a) What does the narrator say the story made him realize? (b) If this is true, what does the story reveal about the "inmost desires" of Cashen's personality?
2. What inferences do you make about the narrator, based on the story he tells?

CRITICAL THINKING AND READING

Identifying Subjective Information

A narrator will often provide you with subjective information—that is, information based on the narrator's own personal thoughts, feelings, and judgments. The reader has to judge the reliability of information about characters, taking into consideration not only the source of the information but also its nature. Purely factual information—for instance, that Cashen was just under fifteen at the time of the incident—seems objective enough. But that Cashen "looked at her [Kitty] with a pang of premonitory loss" is subjective regardless of who is doing the narrating.

Reread "A Touch of Autumn in the Air," identifying at least *five* apparently objective statements about Daniel Cashen and at least *five* subjective statements about him.

UNDERSTANDING LANGUAGE

Learning What a Caricature Is

When the narrator says that Daniel Cashen is "a caricature of the self-made, self-educated, nineteenth-century businessman," he means that Cashen is an exaggerated or distorted example of that type of person. In using the word *caricature,* he is ridiculing Cashen. The word *caricature* comes from the Italian noun *caricatura,* meaning "an overloading," which in turn comes from the verb *caricare,* "to load, exaggerate." One type of caricature is a picture or cartoon in which a person's features are exaggerated or distorted to produce an absurd effect. Political cartoonists produce caricatures.

Taking the whole story into account, how accurate do you think the narrator's statement about Cashen being a caricature of the self-made businessman is? Support your answer.

THINKING AND WRITING

Responding to a Thematic Statement

Very few short stories begin with an explicit statement of the story's theme. This story does. Write a brief composition in which you explain how "A Touch of Autumn in the Air" develops the theme stated in the opening sentence. First, restate the opening sentence in your own words. Then reread the story, making notes for your composition. Write your first draft, telling how the events in the story demonstrate the truth of the opening sentence. Revise your paper before handing it in. Proofread carefully to eliminate misspellings and mistakes in grammar, usage, and punctuation.

(Answers begin on p. 1246.)

2. Suggested response: Cashen is a successful but lonely old man, who has not attained his inmost desire in life.

ANSWERS TO CRITICAL THINKING AND READING

Answers will differ. The examples students give of apparently objective statements about Cashen should include factual information that is based on objective truth or statements that can be proven. The examples students give of subjective statements about Cashen should state an opinion or make a judgment.

ANSWERS TO UNDERSTANDING LANGUAGE

Suggested response: In appearance, Cashen is a caricature of the self-made businessman. However, by the end of the story, it is apparent that Cashen has the capacity for deep emotion and sensitivity, which he has revealed by telling his story. The narrator's statement that Cashen is a caricature is only partly true; as his personality is revealed, he seems more complex and profound than a mere caricature.

THINKING AND WRITING
Publishing Student Writing

Ask for student volunteers to read their compositions aloud. Have students compile a list of events that demonstrate the truth of the theme, based on each composition.

"A Touch of Autumn in the Air" signifies an end to summer and the coming of winter. This change in the seasons parallels the changing seasons in a man's life; Cashen is an old man approaching the end of his life. The title also refers to the time of year when Cashen had this experience sixty years ago; the gentle "touch" of autumn is what helps him recall the experience.

Applying

10. Answers will differ. Students should give support for their interpretations.
11. Answers will differ. Suggested response: We can remember things. Daniel Cashen remembers a happy time in his childhood that made a deep impression.

Challenge What do you think Cashen learns about choice in the story? What irony does his name reveal about his values? Find evidence in the selection to support your answer.

ANSWERS TO ANALYZING LITERATURE

1. (a) The story makes the narrator realize that people's memories are shaped by their inmost desires. (b) It would seem that Cushen's inmost desire was to love Kitty Bergin.

More About the Author P.G. Wodehouse obviously loved to write. As he told an interviewer, "I was writing stories when I was five. I don't remember what I did before that. Just loafed, I suppose." In the course of his long career, Wodehouse demonstrated not only a polished, well-crafted writing style but diversity as well. In addition to writing novels, short stories, and plays. Wodehouse achieved some fame for his witty Tin Pan Alley songs. He wrote the lyrics for dozens of songs for musicals of the early 1900s. This unexpected application of his writing talent flourished while Wodehouse was living in the United States, where he met Jerome Kern and Guy Bolton. The three men, who shared tastes in musical comedy, collaborated on many popular Broadway productions. While Wodehouse incorporated his talent for writing and his deft use of humor and word play in his song lyrics, his interest in musical comedy often fed into his humorous novels and stories. He made numerous direct and indirect references to his "other" passion in much of his fiction. You might ask students how writers weave personal interests or sidelights into their work.

P. G. WODEHOUSE

1881–1975

P(elham) G(renville) Wodehouse (pronounced wood-house) wrote for eighty years, indifferent to fame, fortune, and age. He did so, he once said, for the "pleasure of turning out the stuff." A prolific writer of humorous short stories, plays, novels, and essays, P. G. Wodehouse, known to his friends as "Plum," insisted that he had no message for humanity in his delightfully zany works. Nevertheless, his spoofs of the British gentry of a bygone era, often involving the befuddled Bertie Wooster and his unflappable valet Jeeves, are a unique contribution to modern English literature.

Wodehouse, born to a well-to-do family in Surrey, England, was educated in English boarding schools and at Dulwich College, near London. As a trainee in banking, he began writing humorous fiction, articles, and verse for publication. He joined the staff of the London *Globe* in 1901 as a humor columnist, and in 1908 published his first adult novel, *Love Among the Chickens*.

He first visited the United States, "the land of romance," in 1904, and within a few years became a transatlantic commuter. After a two-month courtship, he married Ethel Rowley, a young English widow whom he had met in New York. His popularity and his income rose rapidly when his stories began appearing in *The Saturday Evening Post,* which at that time was the leading publisher of short fiction in the United States.

Wodehouse had a long and distinguished career in the theater, writing parts of more than forty plays and screenplays. His theatrical experience affected his books, for he began to think of episodes as scenes and characters as actors, and he wrote a number of stories set in Hollywood. His reputation, however, rests primarily on his novels, of which he wrote nearly a hundred, and on his more than three hundred short stories. Among his many notable books are *Carry On, Jeeves* (1934), *The Code of the Woosters* (1938), *Spring Fever* (1948), and *Plum Pie* (1966).

An international commuter for much of his life, Wodehouse lived in Paris after World War II, then moved to Long Island in 1952. Four Wodehouse novels appeared at about the time he was celebrating his ninetieth birthday. He was knighted in 1975, shortly before his death.

GUIDE FOR READING

The Truth About George

The Writer's Techniques

Humor. Humor is the quality that makes something seem amusing, funny, or comic. It emphasizes the ludicrous aspects of life. Yet the elements that make up humor—those characteristics that can be listed as making something humorous—are not easy to identify. What one person finds funny, another may not. The word *humor* (the British spell it *humour)* was originally a physiological term describing the fluids, or humors, in the human body, especially the four "cardinal humors" that were thought to be responsible for one's health and disposition. As time went on, the word came to mean "a mood or state of mind," then "a whim or fancy," and finally "the quality that makes something seem amusing, funny, or comic." Humor, in the modern sense, often relies upon exaggeration, misunderstandings, odd juxtapositions, repetition, wordplay, stock characters, and so on. But such explanations of humor, like similar explanations of music or art, add very little to one's understanding or enjoyment. It is the experience that counts.

Look For

As you read P. G. Wodehouse's "The Truth About George," see if you can tell not only when something is humorous but why it is humorous.

Writing

Think about something that has made you laugh recently. Jot down a few notes about the incident, including your opinion of the source of the humor. What was it that made you laugh?

Vocabulary

Knowing the following words will help you as you read "The Truth About George."

maligned (mə līnd′) *v.*: Spoke evil of; defamed (p. 1250)
sibilant (sib′'l ənt) *adj.*: Hissing (p. 1251)
deleterious (del′ə tir′ē əs) *adj.*: Harmful to health; injurious (p. 1252)
choleric (käl′ər ik) *adj.*: Easily provoked to anger (p. 1252)
irascibly (i ras′ə b'lē) *adv.*: Irritably (p. 1252)
largess (lär jes′) *n.*: Generous gift (p. 1254)
ostentation (äs′tən tā′shən) *n.*: Showy display (p. 1255)
contretemps (kōn trə tän′) *n.*: Awkward mishap (p. 1258)

Literary Focus Point out that a writer may use different forms of humor for different purposes. For example, to describe an amusing incident or character, relate a funny remark, or depict a comical act, a writer might use parody, anecdotes, irony, caricature, or other forms of humor. Humor in cartoons, for instance, is conveyed graphically through pictures and associations. Emphasize the idea that humor evokes laughter because it appeals to the reader's sense of what is absurd or incongruous. Preview for students how P.G. Wodehouse uses several distinct forms of humor in "The Truth about George."

Look For Your **less advanced** students may find it difficult to explain *why* something is humorous. Have them find five examples of humor in "The Truth about George" and create a chart to list each example and reasons that each one makes them laugh. Have them carefully read each example.

Writing Discuss the expression "laugh, and the whole world laughs with you." Then have students note a humorous incident, explaining why the incident made them laugh. If students have difficulty recalling something humorous, guide them to think about a joke that they have recently heard, a comical incident that they have observed, or a situation that they found humorous. Guide students to identify the reasons that they laughed.

Vocabulary Words are very important to George and Susan in "The Truth about George." Discuss the meanings of the vocabulary words. Have your **less advanced** students read each word and its definition aloud.

Objectives

1 To understand humor in a short story
2 To recognize caricature
3 To use synonyms
4 To write about humor

Teaching Portfolio: Support Material

Teacher Backup, p. 000

Vocabulary Check, p. 00

Usage and Mechanics Worksheet, p. 00

Analyzing Literature Worksheet, p. 00

Critical Thinking and Reading Worksheet, p. 00

Language Worksheet, p. 00

Selection Test, p. 00

Motivation for Reading Tell students that "The Truth about George" contains some made-up song lyrics that are based on real songs. As they read, have them try to guess the real lyrics of each song that George sings. After they have finished reading, you might wish to have students find the actual lyrics to each song and explain why P.G. Wodehouse might have used each one in the story.

Master Teacher Note The song lyrics that P.G. Wodehouse adapts so that George can communicate are playful and humorous. Find recordings of "Tea for Two," "If You Knew Susie," and so on. Have students listen to the songs to get an idea of the lighthearted tone of this story. You might also wish to find recordings of P.G. Wodehouse's Tin Pan Alley songs to give them an insight into his type of humor. Explain that Wodehouse himself wrote the lyrics to the songs.

Purpose-Setting Question What *is* the truth about George?

1 **Enrichment** Point out that an angler is someone who fishes with a hook. The assumption that the narrator makes in this paragraph is that he is hearing two fishermen tell a "fish story," in which the men exaggerate their success in fishing. A fish story is a tall tale in which the teller keeps exaggerating the details of the story.

2 **Literary Focus** Point out that the narrator has misunderstood the conversation that he heard. The two men are actually talking about an illness and not a fish. Explain that the humor comes from the narrator's mistaken impressions.

3 **Discussion** What are the difficulties and challenges that someone with a stammer might encounter?

The Truth About George

P. G. Wodehouse

1 Two men were sitting in the bar parlor of the Anglers' Rest as I entered it; and one of them, I gathered from his low, excited voice and wide gestures, was telling the other a story. I could hear nothing but an occasional "Biggest I ever saw in my life!" and "Fully as large as that!" but in such a place it was not difficult to imagine the rest; and when the second man, catching my eye, winked at me with a sort of humorous misery, I smiled sympathetically back at him.

The action had the effect of establishing a bond between us; and when the storyteller finished his tale and left, he came over to my table as if answering a formal invitation.

"Dreadful liars some men are," he said genially.

"Fishermen," I suggested, "are traditionally careless of the truth."

2 "He wasn't a fisherman," said my companion. "That was our local doctor. He was telling me about his latest case of dropsy. Besides"—he tapped me earnestly on the knee—"you must not fall into the popular error about fishermen. Tradition has maligned them. I am a fisherman myself, and I have never told a lie in my life."

I could well believe it. He was a short, stout, comfortable man of middle age, and the thing that struck me first about him was the extraordinary childlike candor of his eyes. They were large and round and honest. I would have bought oil stock from him without a tremor.

The door leading into the white dusty road opened, and a small man with rimless pince-nez[1] and an anxious expression shot in like a rabbit. He stood looking at us, seemingly ill at ease.

"N-n-n-n-n-n—" he said.

We looked at him inquiringly.

"N-n-n-n-n-ice d-d-d-d—"

His nerve appeared to fail him, and he vanished as abruptly as he had come.

"I think he was leading up to telling us that it was a nice day," hazarded my companion.

3 "It must be very embarrassing," I said, "for a man with such a painful impediment in his speech to open conversation with strangers."

"Probably trying to cure himself. Like my nephew George. Have I ever told you about my nephew George?"

I reminded him that we had only just met, and that this was the first time I had learned that he had a nephew George.

"Young George Mulliner. My name is Mulliner. I will tell you about George's case—in many ways a rather remarkable one."

My nephew George (said Mr. Mulliner) was as nice a young fellow as you would ever wish to meet, but from childhood up he had been cursed with a terrible stammer. If he had had to earn his living, he would undoubtedly have found this affliction a great handicap, but fortunately his father had left

1. **pince-nez** (pans′ nā′): Eyeglasses without sidepieces, held in place by springs gripping the bridge of the nose.

him a comfortable income; and George spent a not unhappy life, residing in the village where he had been born and passing his days in the usual country sports and his evenings in doing crossword puzzles. By the time he was thirty he knew more about Eli,[2]
3 the prophet, Ra,[3] the sun god, and the bird Emu than anybody else in the county except Susan Blake, the vicar's daughter, who had also taken up the solving of crossword puzzles and was the first girl in Worcestershire to find out the meaning of "stearine" and "crepuscular."

It was his association with Miss Blake that first turned George's thoughts to a serious endeavor to cure himself of his stammer. Naturally, with this hobby in common, the young people saw a great deal of one another; for George was always looking in at the vicarage to ask her if she knew a word of seven letters meaning "appertaining to the profession of plumbing," and Susan was just as constant a caller at George's cozy little cottage—being frequently stumped, as girls will be, by words of eight letters signifying "largely used in the manufacture of poppet valves." The consequence was that one evening, just after she had helped him out of a tight place with the word "disestablishmentarianism," the boy suddenly awoke to the truth and realized that she was all the world to him—or, as he put it to himself from force of habit, precious, beloved, dar-
4 ling, much-loved, highly esteemed or valued.

And yet, every time he tried to tell her so, he could get no farther than a sibilant gurgle which was no more practical use than a hiccup.

Something obviously had to be done, and George went to London to see a specialist.

"I-I-I-I-I-I—" said George.

"You were saying—?"

"Woo-woo-woo-woo-woo-woo—"

"Sing it," said the specialist.

"S-s-s-s-s-s-s-s—?" said George, puzzled.

The specialist explained. He was a kindly man with moth-eaten whiskers and an eye like a meditative codfish.

"Many people," he said, "who are unable to articulate clearly in ordinary speech find themselves lucid and bell-like when they burst into song."

It seemed a good idea to George. He thought for a moment; then threw his head back, shut his eyes, and let it go in a musical baritone.

"I love a lassie, a bonny, bonny lassie," sang George. "She's as pure as the lily in the dell."

"No doubt," said the specialist, wincing a little.

"She's as sweet as the heather, the bonny purple heather—Susan, my Worcestershire bluebell."

"Ah!" said the specialist. "Sounds a nice girl, Is this she?" he asked, adjusting his glasses and peering at the photograph which George had extracted from the interi- 5
or of the left side of his undervest.

George nodded and drew in breath.

"Yes, sir," he caroled, "that's my baby. No, sir, don't mean maybe. Yes, sir, that's my baby now. And, by the way, by the way, when I meet that preacher I shall say: 'Yes, sir, that's my . . .'"

"Quite," said the specialist hurriedly. He had a sensitive ear. "Quite, quite."

"If you knew Susie like I know Susie," George was beginning, but the other stopped him.

"Quite. Exactly. I shouldn't wonder. And now," said the specialist, "what precisely is the trouble? No," he added hastily, as George inflated his lungs, "don't sing it. Write the particulars on this piece of paper."

George did so.

"H'm!" said the specialist, examining the screed. "You wish to woo, court, and become betrothed, engaged, affianced to this girl, but you find yourself unable, incapable,

2. Eli: From the Bible, a high priest of Israel.
3. Ra: The sun god and principal deity of the ancient Egyptians.

3 **Reading Strategy** Why do you think that George knows so much about Eli, Ra, and Emu?

4 **Literary Focus** How does George feel about Susan? Why is the way George expresses his realization humorous?

5 **Enrichment** Each time that George tries to explain his problem and how he feels about Susan Blake, he sings. In order to communicate his thoughts, George changes the lyrics of some popular songs. "Yes Sir, That's My Baby" (1925), written by Gus Kahn, and "If You Knew Susie" (1925), written by Buddy De Sylva, are famous Tin Pan Alley standards. These popular songs were published by music publishers located on 28th Street in New York City, which was dubbed Tin Pan Alley because of the lively sound of piano playing. Although the music produced here may have sounded to some like tin pans banging in an alley, these songs were extremely popular from the early 1900's through the 1940's. P.G. Wodehouse undoubtedly refers to Tin Pan Alley lyrics in "The Truth about George" because he knew them well.

6 **Critical Thinking and Reading** Do you think that this description of the specialist is a caricature? Why or why not?

7 **Enrichment** Some scientists believe that stammering is caused by a biological process in which the brain's signals for speech are delayed by fractions of a second. Others believe that stammering is a learned behavior related to stress about talking or to pressure to speak precisely. Another theory states that stammering may represent a psychological block in which a person cannot express his or her feelings.

8 **Discussion** What advice does the specialist give to George? Do you think the advice will work? How realistic is the advice?

9 **Clarification** A guinea is an English monetary unit that equals one pound and one shilling.

10 **Literary Focus** Explain why George's interaction with the stranger on the train is humorous. Point out that Wodehouse uses irony, one form of humor, to describe this encounter.

11 **Clarification** The stranger attempts to say "I asked you a civil question. Are you deaf?"

incompetent, impotent, and powerless. Every time you attempt it, your vocal cords fail, fall short, are insufficient, wanting, deficient, and go blooey."

George nodded.

6 "A not unusual case. I have had to deal with this sort of thing before. The effect of love on the vocal cords of even a normally eloquent subject is frequently deleterious. As regards the habitual stammerer, tests have shown that in ninety-seven point five six nine recurring of cases the divine passion reduces him to a condition where he sounds like a soda-water siphon trying to recite 'Gunga Din.' There is only one cure."

"W-w-w-w-w—?" asked George.

7 "I will tell you. Stammering," proceeded the specialist, putting the tips of his fingers together and eyeing George benevolently, "is mainly mental and is caused by shyness, which is caused by the inferiority complex, which in its turn is caused by suppressed desires or introverted inhibitions or something. 8 The advice I give to all young men who come in here behaving like soda-water siphons is to go out and make a point of speaking to at least three perfect strangers every day. Engage these strangers in conversation, persevering no matter how priceless a chump you may feel, and before many weeks are out you will find that the little daily dose has had its effect. Shyness will wear off, and with it the stammer."

9 And, having requested the young man—in a voice of the clearest timbre, free from all trace of impediment—to hand over a fee of five guineas, the specialist sent George out into the world.

The more George thought about the advice he had been given, the less he liked it. He shivered in the cab that took him to the station to catch the train back to East Wobsley. Like all shy young men, he had never hitherto looked upon himself as shy —preferring to attribute his distaste for the society of his fellows to some subtle rareness of soul. But now that the thing had been put squarely up to him, he was compelled to realize that in all essentials he was a perfect rabbit. The thought of accosting perfect strangers and forcing his conversation upon them sickened him.

But no Mulliner has ever shirked an unpleasant duty. As he reached the platform and strode along it to the train, his teeth were set, his eyes shone with an almost fanatical light of determination, and he intended before his journey was over to conduct three heart-to-heart chats if he had to sing every bar of them.

The compartment into which he had made his way was empty at the moment, but just before the train started a very large, fierce-looking man got in. George would have preferred somebody a little less formidable for his first subject, but he braced himself and bent forward. And, as he did so, the man spoke.

"The wur-wur-wur-wur-weather," he said, "sus-sus-seems to be ter-ter-taking a tur-tur-turn for the ber-ber-better, der-doesn't it?" 10

George sank back as if he had been hit between the eyes. The train had moved out of the dimness of the station by now, and the sun was shining brightly on the speaker, illuminating his knobbly shoulders, his craggy jaw, and, above all, the shockingly choleric look in his eyes. To reply "Y-y-y-y-y-y-y-yes" to such a man would obviously be madness.

But to abstain from speech did not seem to be much better as a policy. George's silence appeared to arouse this man's worst passions. His face had turned purple and he glared painfully.

"I uk-uk-asked you a sus-sus-civil qukquk-quk," he said irascibly. "Are you d-d-d-deaf?" 11

All we Mulliners have been noted for our presence of mind. To open his mouth, point to his tonsils, and utter a strangled gurgle was with George the work of a moment.

The tension relaxed. The man's annoyance abated.

12 "D-d-d-dumb?" he said commiseratingly. "I beg your p-p-p-p-pup. I t-t-trust I have not caused you p-p-p-p-pup. It m-must be tut-tut-tut-tut-tut not to be able to to sus-sus-speak fuf-fuf-fuf-fuf-fluently."

He then buried himself in his paper, and George sank back in his corner, quivering in every limb.

To get to East Wobsley, as you doubtless know, you have to change at Ippleton and take the branch line. By the time the train reached this junction, George's composure was somewhat restored. He deposited his belongings in a compartment of the East Wobsley train, which was waiting in a glued manner on the other side of the platform, and, finding that it would not start for some ten minutes, decided to pass the time by strolling up and down in the pleasant air.

It was a lovely afternoon. The sun was gilding the platform with its rays, and a gentle breeze blew from the west. A little brook ran tinkling at the side of the road; birds were singing in the hedgerows; and through the trees could be discerned dimly the noble façade of the County Lunatic Asylum. Soothed by his surroundings, George began to feel so refreshed that he regretted that in this wayside station there was no one present whom he could engage in talk.

It was at this moment that the distinguished-looking stranger entered the platform.

The newcomer was a man of imposing physique, simply dressed in pajamas, brown boots, and a mackintosh. In his hand he carried a top hat, and into this he was dipping his fingers, taking them out, and then waving them in a curious manner to right and left. He nodded so affably to George 13 that the latter, though a little surprised at the other's costume, decided to speak. After all, he reflected, clothes do not make the man, and, judging from the other's smile, a warm heart appeared to beat beneath that orange-and-mauve striped pajama jacket.

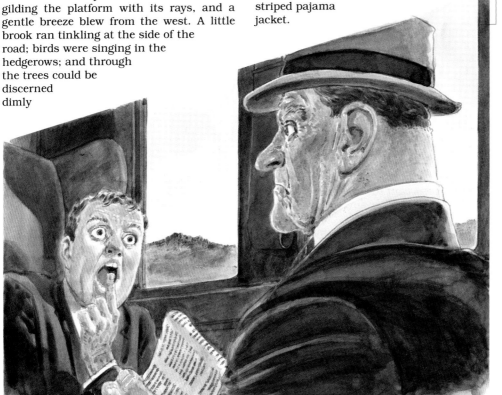

12 **Clarification** The stranger apologizes by saying "Dumb? I beg your pardon. I trust I have not caused you pain. It must be terrible not to be able to speak fluently." The stranger believes that George is dumb, or incapable of speech.

13 **Critical Thinking and Reading** Why is this description a caricature?

14 Enrichment The actual quotation that Wodehouse paraphrases here is, "Be thou familiar, but by no means vulgar;/Those friends thou hast, and their adoption tried,/Grapple them to thy soul with hoops of steel." The lines appear in Shakespeare's *Hamlet,* Act 1, scene iii.

15 Clarification The stranger uses *lark* in the sense of harmless fun, mischief, or an escapade. George is startled by the remark, mistakenly thinking of birds, another meaning of lark.

"N-n-n-n-nice weather," he said.

"Glad you like it," said the stranger. "I ordered it specially."

George was a little puzzled by this remark, but he persevered.

"M-might I ask wur-wur-what you are dud-doing?"

"Doing?"

"With that her-her-her-her-hat?"

"Oh, with this hat? I see what you mean. Just scattering largess to the multitude," replied the stranger, dipping his fingers once more and waving them with a generous gesture. "Devil of a bore, but it's expected of a man in my position. The fact is," he said, linking his arm in George's and speaking in a confidential undertone, "I'm the Emperor of Abyssinia. That's my palace over there," he said, pointing through the trees. "Don't let it go any farther. It's not supposed to be generally known."

It was with a rather sickly smile that George now endeavored to withdraw his arm from that of his companion, but the other would have none of this aloofness. He seemed to be in complete agreement with
14 Shakespeare's dictum that a friend, when found, should be grappled to you with hoops of steel. He held George in a viselike grip and drew him into a recess of the platform. He looked about him and seemed satisfied.

"We are alone at last," he said.

This fact had already impressed itself with sickening clearness on the young man. There are few spots in the civilized world more deserted than the platform of a small country station. The sun shone on the smooth asphalt, on the gleaming rails, and on the machine which, in exchange for a penny placed in the slot marked "Matches," would supply a package of wholesome butterscotch—but on nothing else.

What George could have done with at the moment was a posse of police armed with stout clubs, and there was not even a dog in sight.

"I've been wanting to talk to you for a long time," said the stranger genially.

"Huh-huh-have you?" said George.

"Yes. I want your opinion of human sacrifices."

George said he didn't like them.

"Why not?" asked the other, surprised.

George said it was hard to explain. He just didn't.

"Well, I think you're wrong," said the Emperor. "I know there's a school of thought growing up that holds your views, but I disapprove of it. I hate all this modern advanced thought. Human sacrifices have always been good enough for the Emperors of Abyssinia, and they're good enough for me. Kindly step in here, if you please."

He indicated the lamp-and-mop room, at which they had now arrived. It was a dark and sinister apartment, smelling strongly of oil and porters, and was probably the last place on earth in which George would have wished to be closeted with a man of such peculiar views. He shrank back.

"You go in first," he said.

"No larks," said the other suspiciously. 15

"L-l-l-l-larks?"

"Yes. No pushing a fellow in and locking the door and squirting water at him through the window. I've had that happen to me before."

"Sus-certainly not."

"Right!" said the Emperor. "You're a gentleman and I'm a gentleman. Both gentlemen. Have you a knife, by the way? We shall need a knife."

"No. No knife."

"Ah, well," said the Emperor, "then we'll have to look about for something else. No doubt we shall manage somehow."

And with the debonair manner which so became him, he scattered another handful of largess and walked into the lamp room.

It was not the fact that he had given his word as a gentleman that kept George from locking the door. There is probably no family on earth more nicely scrupulous as regards keeping its promises than the Mulliners, but I am compelled to admit that, had George been able to find the key, he would have locked the door without hesitation. Not being able to find the key, he had to be satisfied with banging it. This done, he leaped back and raced away down the platform. A confused noise within seemed to indicate that the Emperor had become involved with some lamps.

George made the best of the respite. Covering the ground at a high rate of speed, he flung himself into the train and took refuge under the seat.

There he remained, quaking. At one time he thought that his uncongenial acquaintance had got upon his track, for the door of the compartment opened and a cool wind blew in upon him. Then, glancing along the floor, he perceived feminine ankles. The relief was enormous, but even in his relief George, who was the soul of modesty, did not forget his manners. He closed his eyes.

A voice spoke.

"Porter!"

"Yes, ma'am?"

"What was all that disturbance as I came into the station?"

"Patient escaped from the asylum, ma'am."

"Good gracious!"

The voice would undoubtedly have spoken further, but at this moment the train began to move. There came the sound of a body descending upon a cushioned seat, and some little time later the rustling of a paper.

George had never before traveled under the seat of a railway carriage; and, though he belonged to the younger generation, which is supposed to be so avid of new experiences, he had no desire to do so now. He decided to emerge, and, if possible, to emerge with the minimum of ostentation. Little as he knew of women, he was aware that as a sex they are apt to be startled by
16 the sight of men crawling out from under the
seats of compartments. He began his maneuvers by poking out his head and surveying the terrain.

All was well. The woman, in her seat across the way, was engrossed in her paper. Moving in a series of noiseless wriggles, George extricated himself from his hiding place and, with a twist which would have been impossible to a man not in the habit of doing Swedish exercises daily before breakfast, heaved himself into the corner seat. The woman continued reading her paper.

The events of the past quarter of an hour had tended rather to drive from George's mind the mission which he had undertaken on leaving the specialist's office. But now, having leisure for reflection, he realized that, if he meant to complete his first day of the cure, he was allowing himself to run sadly behind schedule. Speak to three strangers, the specialist had told him, and up to the present he had spoken to only one. True, this one had been a pretty considerable stranger, and a less conscientious young man than George Mulliner might have considered himself justified in chalking him up on the scoreboard as one and a half or even two. But George had the dogged, honest Mulliner streak in him, and he refused to quibble.

He nerved himself for action and cleared his throat.

"Ah-h'rm!" said George.

And, having opened the ball, he smiled a winning smile and waited for his companion to make the next move.

The move which his companion made was in an upwards direction, and measured from six to eight inches. She dropped her paper and regarded George with a pale-eyed horror. One pictures her a little in the position of Robinson Crusoe[4] when he saw the 17
footprint in the sand. She had been convinced that she was completely alone, and lo! out of space a voice had spoken to her. Her face worked, but she made no remark.

George, on his side, was also feeling a little ill at ease. Women always increased his

4. Robinson Crusoe: The hero of Daniel Defoe's novel *Robinson Crusoe* (1719), a sailor who is shipwrecked on a tropical island.

16 **Literary Focus** Why is this sentence humorous? What type of humor does Wodehouse use here?

17 **Reading Strategy** Explain in your own words how the woman on the train reacts. Why do you think she reacts this way? What assumption do you think the woman makes?

natural shyness. He never knew what to say to them.

Then a happy thought struck him. He had just glanced at his watch and found the hour to be nearly four-thirty. Women, he knew, loved a drop of tea at about this time, and fortunately there was in his suitcase a full thermos flask.

"Pardon me, but I wonder if you would care for a cup of tea?" was what he wanted to say, but, as so often happened with him when in the presence of the opposite sex, he could get no farther than a sort of sizzling sound like a cockroach calling to its young.

The woman continued to stare at him. Her eyes were now about the size of regula- 18 tion standard golf balls, and her breathing suggested the last stages of asthma. And it was at this point that George, struggling for speech, had one of those inspirations which frequently came to Mulliners. There flashed into his mind what the specialist had told him about singing. Say it with music—that was the thing to do.

He delayed no longer.

"Tea for two and two for tea and me for you and you for me—"

He was shocked to observe his companion turning Nile green. He decided to make his meaning clearer.

19 "I have a nice thermos. I have a full thermos. Won't you share my thermos, too? When skies are gray and you feel you are blue, tea sends the sun smiling through. I have a nice thermos. I have a full thermos. May I pour out some for you?"

You will agree with me, I think, that no invitation could have been more happily put, but his companion was not responsive. With one last agonized look at him, she closed her eyes and sank back in her seat. Her lips had now turned a curious gray-blue color, and they were moving feebly. She reminded George, who, like myself, was a keen fisherman, of a newly gaffed salmon.

George sat back in his corner, brooding. Rack his brain as he might, he could think of no topic which could be guaranteed to interest, elevate, and amuse. He looked out of the window with a sigh.

The train was now approaching the dear old familiar East Wobsley country. He began to recognize landmarks. A wave of sentiment poured over George as he thought of Susan, and he reached for the bag of buns which he had bought at the refreshment room at Ippleton. Sentiment always made him hungry.

He took his thermos out of the suitcase, and, unscrewing the top, poured himself out a cup of tea. Then, placing the thermos on the seat, he drank.

He looked across at his companion. Her eyes were still closed, and she uttered little sighing noises. George was half inclined to renew his offer of tea, but the only tune he could remember was "Hard-Hearted Hannah, the Vamp from Savannah," and it was difficult to fit suitable words to it. He ate his bun and gazed out at the familiar scenery.

Now, as you approach East Wobsley, the train, I must mention, has to pass over some points; and so violent is the sudden jerking that strong men have been known to spill their beer. George, forgetting this in his preoccupation, had placed the thermos only a few inches from the edge of the seat. The result was that, as the train reached the points, the flask leaped like a live thing, dived to the floor, and exploded. 20

Even George was distinctly upset by the sudden sharpness of the report. His bun sprang from his hand and was dashed to fragments. He blinked thrice in rapid succession. His heart tried to jump out of his mouth and loosened a front tooth.

But on the woman opposite the effect of the untoward occurrence was still more marked. With a single piercing shriek, she rose from her seat straight into the air like a rocketing pheasant; and, having clutched the communication cord, fell back again. Impressive as her previous leap had been, she excelled it now by several inches. I do not know what the existing record for the

18 Critical Thinking and Reading What makes this description of the woman a caricature?

19 Enrichment Wodehouse uses more lyrics from Tin Pan Alley standards. The first lyrics come from "Tea for Two" (1924) by Irving Caesar and Vincent Youmans.

20 Literary Focus Discuss the type of humor that Wodehouse employs in this passage.

1257

21 **Reading Strategy** Wodehouse uses irony in this passage. Summarize the meaning of this passage in your own words.

22 **Master Teacher Note** You might wish to explain to students that D.W. Griffith was a pioneer American filmmaker. In 1915 he made *The Birth of a Nation,* which was famous for its realistic and spectacular battle scenes. You might want to relate Wodehouse's comparison to other film epics by filmmakers such as Cecil B. deMille or Sergei Eisenstein. Have students describe how they would film the chase scene in "The Truth about George."

sitting high jump is, but she undoubtedly lowered it; and if George had been a member of the Olympic Games Selection Committee, he would have signed this woman up immediately.

21 It is a curious thing that, in spite of the railway companies' sporting willingness to let their patrons have a tug at the extremely moderate price of five pounds a go, very few people have ever either pulled a communication cord or seen one pulled. There is, thus, a widespread ignorance as to what precisely happens on such occasions.

The procedure, George tells me, is as follows: First there comes a grinding noise, as the brakes are applied. Then the train stops. And finally, from every point of the compass, a seething mob of interested onlookers begins to appear.

It was about a mile and a half from East Wobsley that the affair had taken place, and as far as the eye could reach the countryside was totally devoid of humanity. A moment before nothing had been visible but smiling cornfields and broad pasturelands; but now from east, west, north, and south running figures began to appear. We must remember that George at the time was in a somewhat overwrought frame of mind, and his statements should therefore be accepted with caution; but he tells me that out of the middle of a single empty meadow, entirely devoid of cover, no fewer than twenty-seven distinct rustics suddenly appeared, having undoubtedly shot up through the ground.

The rails, which had been completely unoccupied, were now thronged with so dense a crowd of navvies[5] that it seemed to George absurd to pretend that there was any unemployment in England. Every member of the laboring classes throughout the country was so palpably present. Moreover, the train, which at Ippleton had seemed sparsely occupied, was disgorging passengers from every door. It was the sort of mob scene which would have made David W. Griffith[6] scream with delight; and it looked, George 22 says, like Guest Night at the Royal Automobile Club. But, as I say, we must remember that he was overwrought.

It is difficult to say what precisely would have been the correct behavior of your polished man of the world in such a situation. I think myself that a great deal of sang-froid[7] and address would be required even by the most self-possessed in order to pass off such a contretemps. To George, I may say at once, the crisis revealed itself immediately as one which he was totally incapable of handling. The one clear thought that stood out from the welter of his emotions was the reflection that it was advisable to remove himself, and to do so without delay. Drawing a deep breath, he shot swiftly off the mark.

All we Mulliners have been athletes; and George, when at the University, had been noted for his speed of foot. He ran now as he had never run before. His statement, however, that as he sprinted across the first field he distinctly saw a rabbit shoot an envious glance at him as he passed and shrug its shoulders hopelessly, I am inclined to discount. George, as I have said before, was a little overexcited.

Nevertheless, it is not to be questioned that he made good going. And he had need to, for after the first instant of surprise, which had enabled him to secure a lead, the whole mob was pouring across country after him; and dimly, as he ran, he could hear voices in the throng informally discussing the advisability of lynching him. Moreover, the field through which he was running, a moment before a bare expanse of green, was now black with figures, headed by a man with a beard who carried a pitchfork. George swerved sharply to the right,

5. **navvies** (nav′ ēz): Laborers.

6. **David W. Griffith:** American motion-picture director and producer (1875–1948).

7. **sang-froid** (saŋ′ frwä′): Composure.

casting a swift glance over his shoulder at his pursuers. He disliked them all, but especially the man with the pitchfork.

It is impossible for one who was not an eyewitness to say how long the chase continued and how much ground was covered by the interested parties. I know the East Wobsley country well, and I have checked George's statements; and, if it is true that he traveled east as far as Little-Wigmarsh-in-the-Dell and as far west as Higgleford-cum-Wortlebury-beneath-the-Hill, he must undoubtedly have done a lot of running.

But a point which must not be forgotten is that, to a man not in a condition to
observe closely, the village of Higgleford-
cum-Wortlebury-beneath-the-Hill might
23 easily not have been Higgleford-cum-
Wortlebury-beneath-the-Hill at all, but another hamlet which in many respects closely resembles it. I need scarcely say that I
allude to Lesser-Snodsbury-in-the-Vale.

Let us assume, therefore, that George, having touched Little-Wigmarsh-in-the-Dell, shot off at a tangent and reached Lesser-Snodsbury-in-the-Vale. This would be a considerable run. And, as he remembers flitting past Farmer Higgins's pigsty and the Dog and Duck at Pondlebury Parva and splashing through the brook Wipple at the point where it joins the River Wopple, we can safely assume that, wherever else he went, he got plenty of exercise.

But the pleasantest of functions must end, and, just as the setting sun was gilding the spire of the ivy-covered church of St. Barnabas the Resilient, where George as a child had sat so often, enlivening the tedium of the sermon by making faces at the choirboys, a damp and bedraggled figure might have been observed crawling painfully along the High Street of East Wobsley in the direction of the cozy little cottage known to its builder as Chatsworth and to the village tradesmen as "Mulliner's."

It was George, home from the hunting field.

Slowly George Mulliner made his way to the familiar door, and, passing through it, flung himself into his favorite chair. But a moment later a more imperious need than the desire to rest forced itself upon his attention. Rising stiffly, he tottered to the kitchen and mixed himself a revivifying drink. Then, refilling his glass, he returned to the sitting room, to find that it was no longer empty. A slim, fair girl, tastefully attired in tailor-made tweeds, was leaning over the desk on which he kept his Dictionary of English Synonyms.

She looked up as he entered, startled.

"Why, Mr. Mulliner!" she exclaimed. "What has been happening? Your clothes are torn, rent, ragged, tattered, and your hair is all disheveled, untrimmed, hanging loose or negligently, at loose ends!"

George smiled a wan smile.

"You are right," he said. "And, what is
more, I am suffering from extreme fatigue, 24
weariness, lassitude, exhaustion, prostration, and languor."

The girl gazed at him, a divine pity in her soft eyes.

"I'm so sorry," she murmured. "So very sorry, grieved, distressed, afflicted, pained, mortified, dejected, and upset."

George took her hand. Her sweet sympathy had effected the cure for which he had been seeking so long. Coming on top of the violent emotions through which he had been passing all day, it seemed to work on him like some healing spell, charm, or incantation. Suddenly, in a flash, he realized that he was no longer a stammerer. Had he wished at that moment to say, "Peter Piper picked a peck of pickled peppers," he could have done it without a second thought.

But he had better things to say than that.

"Miss Blake—Susan—Susie." He took
her other hand in his. His voice rang out
clear and unimpeded. It seemed to him incredible that he had ever yammered at this
girl like an overheated steam radiator. "It 25
cannot have escaped your notice that I have

23 **Enrichment** Explain to students that Wodehouse is satirizing characteristically English place names. His fictional place names mock those in England that consist of long hyphenated strings of descriptive words.

24 **Discussion** Note the synonyms in this passage. Discuss the shades of meaning of each word.

25 **Literary Focus** Why is George's speech humorous? What type of humor does Wodehouse use in writing the speech this way?

26 **Master Teacher Note** Give students the following aphorisms: *love conquers all* and *all's well that ends well.* Have them respond to these expressions in terms of the last sentence of "The Truth about George." Guide students in analyzing the meaning of the last sentence in relation to the story as a whole and in relation to the aphorisms.

long entertained toward you sentiments warmer and deeper than those of ordinary friendship. It is love, Susan, that has been animating my bosom. Love, first a tiny seed, has burgeoned in my heart till, blazing into flame, it has swept away on the crest of its wave my diffidence, my doubt, my fears, and my foreboding, and now, like the topmost topaz of some ancient tower, it cries to all the world in a voice of thunder: 'You are mine!· My mate! Predestined to me since Time first began!' As the star guides the mariner when, battered by boiling billows, he hies him home to the haven of hope and happiness, so do you gleam upon me along life's rough road and seem to say, 'Have courage, George! I am here!' Susan, I am not an eloquent man—I cannot speak fluently as I could wish—but these simple words which you have just heard come from the heart, from the unspotted heart of an English gentleman. Susan, I love you. Will you be my wife, married woman, matron, spouse, helpmeet, consort, partner or better half?"

"Oh, George!" said Susan. "Yes, yea, ay, aye! Decidedly, unquestionably, indubitably, incontrovertibly, and past all dispute!"

He folded her in his arms. And, as he did so, there came from the street outside —faintly, as from a distance—the sound of feet and voices. George leaped to the window. Rounding the corner, just by the Cow and Wheelbarrow public house, licensed to sell ales, wines, and spirits, was the man with the pitchfork, and behind him followed a vast crowd.

"My darling," said George. "For purely personal and private reasons, into which I need not enter, I must now leave you. Will you join me later?"

"I will follow you to the ends of the earth," replied Susan passionately.

"It will not be necessary," said George. "I am only going down to the coal cellar. I shall spend the next half hour or so there. If anybody calls and asks for me, perhaps you would not mind telling them that I am out."

"I will, I will," said Susan. "And, George, by the way. What I really came here for was to ask you if you knew a word of nine letters, ending in k and signifying an implement employed in the pursuit of agriculture."

"Pitchfork, sweetheart," said George. "But you may take it from me, as one who knows, that agriculture isn't the only thing it is used in pursuit of."

And since that day (concluded Mr. Mulliner) George, believe me or believe me not, has not had the slightest trace of an impediment in his speech. He is now the chosen orator at all political rallies for miles around; and so offensively self-confident has his manner become that only last Friday he had his eye blacked by a hay-corn-and-feed merchant of the name of Stubbs. It just shows 26
you, doesn't it?

THINKING ABOUT THE SELECTION

Recalling

1. What incident prompts Mulliner to tell the story of his nephew George?
2. (a) Why does George decide to seek a cure? (b) What action does he take? (c) What two pieces of advice does he receive?
3. What happens when George tries to speak to (a) the first stranger? (b) the second stranger?
4. How does the woman on the train react when George begins singing "Tea for Two"?
5. (a) What cures George's stammering? (b) To what does he credit the cure?

Interpreting

6. (a) Why does George think it would be

Answers

ANSWERS TO THINKING ABOUT THE SELECTION

Recalling

1. A man who stutters comes into the Anglers' Rest, where the narrator and two men are sitting. Mulliner then tells the story of how his nephew George tried to cure himself of a stammer.
2. (a) George decides to seek a cure for his stutter because he realizes that he loves Susan Blake and wishes to tell her so. (b) George travels to London to see a specialist who can treat his stammer. (c) The specialist tells George to sing when he wants to express something and to talk to at least three perfect strangers every day.
3. (a) When George tries to talk to the first stranger, he attempts to talk to someone who also stammers. George is embarrassed and pretends that he is dumb. (b) When George tries to talk to the second stranger, he finds out that the man has just escaped from the County Lunatic Asylum. George runs to board a train to get away from the stranger.
4. The woman on the train turns green when George begins to sing "Tea for Two." His attempt to convey the idea that he would like to share his thermos of tea with her terrifies her. The woman does not speak and merely stares at George. Wodehouse suggests that the woman has a heart attack.
5. (a) George's stammering is cured when he indirectly gains confidence through his adventures that day. In a sense, George has cured himself. (b) After a day of adventures and a harrowing escape home, George is soothed by Susan's concern. George credits his cure to Susan's sympathy.

Interpreting

6. (a) George thinks it would be madness to reply to the stutterer because it would appear that he was mocking him. (b) George's response placates the stutterer, who realizes that George was not being rude.
7. (a) The woman in the train compartment thinks that George is the escapee from County Lunatic Asylum. (b) Suggested response: George's attempt to speak to the woman only frightens her more. His behavior only confirms her worst suspicions.
8. Suggested response: The explanation of George's chase is humorous because of the quaint names of the hamlets he suppos-

madness to reply to the stutterer on the train? (b) Why does his response placate the stutterer?
7. (a) Who does the woman in the train compartment think George is? (b) What effect do you think George's "sizzling . . . like a cockroach" has on the woman?
8. What is humorous about the explanation of the amount of ground George must have covered while being chased?
9. Why do George and Susan both use long strings of synonyms in their speech?

Applying

10. George is a timid soul who becomes "offensively self-confident." (a) What conditions make a person timid? (b) What conditions can make the same person self-confident?

ANALYZING LITERATURE

Understanding Humor

Humor, the quality that makes something seem amusing, funny, or comic, is easier to recognize than it is to explain. Exaggeration is often a part of humor, as when the doctor in "The Truth About George" says of the habitual stammerer that "tests have shown that in ninety-seven point five six nine" percent of cases, love "reduces him to a condition where he sounds like a soda-water siphon trying to recite 'Gunga Din.'" Misunderstandings often figure in humor, as when George tries to communicate with the woman in the train compartment by singing, and she takes it as proof of his being a lunatic. Look through "The Truth About George" and find what you consider to be the five most amusing incidents, situations, or statements. Try to explain what it is about each one that makes it humorous.

CRITICAL THINKING AND READING

Recognizing Caricature

When P. G. Wodehouse describes the antics of George and other characters in this story, you know that real people do not behave or talk that way. Yet there is a core of truth, greatly exaggerated and distorted, in what the characters do and say. Wodehouse is creating caricatures, just as a cartoonist creates caricatures by drawing people with recognizable but grotesque features. George is a caricature of a person who stutters. Point out three other caricatures in this story and explain why each fits that category.

UNDERSTANDING LANGUAGE

Using Synonyms

A **synonym** is a word that means almost the same thing as another word. Since one word seldom has exactly the same meaning as another, you cannot arbitrarily substitute synonyms for each other in speaking and writing. In "The Truth About George," both George and Susan use a series of synonyms for comic effect. George says, "Will you be my wife, married woman, matron, spouse, helpmeet, consort, partner or better half?" Those words are all synonyms, but they do not all have precisely the same meaning. A *spouse,* for instance, may be either a husband or a wife; a *matron* is usually an older woman; a *consort* is often a royal partner.

The following groups of synonyms appear in the story. Using a good dictionary, define each word, distinguishing it from the synonyms included with it.

1. incapable, incompetent, powerless
2. torn, rent, ragged
3. fatigue, lassitude, prostration
4. pained, mortified, dejected

THINKING AND WRITING

Writing About Humor

Does "The Truth About George" make you laugh, chuckle, snicker, giggle, guffaw? What do you find funny in it? Why do you find it funny? Look back at your answers in Analyzing Literature. Use the five examples of humor that you chose in that assignment as the basis for a composition on the topic, "What Is Humor?" Make further notes, if necessary. In your first draft, be as precise and specific as you can. When you revise the material for your final draft, check to make sure that your sentences are clear and to the point, not simply abstract thoughts or unsupported generalizations.

(Answers begin on p. 1260.)

edly runs between: from Little-Wigmarsh-in-the-Dell to Higgleford-cum-Wortlebury-beneath-the-Hill.

9. George and Susan use synonyms when they speak because they are both avid crossword puzzle fans. They're always looking for words to help them solve their puzzles.

Applying

10. Answers will differ. Suggested Responses: (a) A person might be timid in whatever circumstances he or he is not comfortable. (b) The same person might be self-confident in circumstances in which he or she is comfortable and in control.

Challenge Think about the title of this story. What do you think the "truth" is about George? Find evidence in the story to support your answer.

ANSWERS TO ANALYZING LITERATURE

Answers will differ. Five examples of humorous incidents or situations include the following: George singing to explain his problem to the specialist; George meeting the "Emperor of Abyssinia"; George's attempt at being polite to the woman on the train and singing his offer of tea to her; George being pursued by a mob across the countryside; George finally professing his love for Susan Blake. Each incident or situation is humorous because it is exaggerated, absurd, unexpected, or unbelievable.

ANSWERS TO CRITICAL THINKING AND READING

Answers will differ. Three examples of caricatures include the description of the specialist, who seems overly concerned with statistical data and scientific proof and who gives George some absurdly theoretical advice for curing his stammer; the description of the escapee from the lunatic asylum, who believes himself to be the Emperor of Abyssinia; the description of the mob that pursues George, which includes train passengers and laborers and a leader carrying a pitchfork. Each caricature includes physical descriptions that exaggerate or emphasize what that person or group of people might look like as well as an exaggeration of personality

ANSWERS TO UNDERSTANDING LANGUAGE

Suggested responses:

1. incapable: lacking in ability
   incompetent: not qualified
   powerless: unable to change something.
2. torn: ripped apart by force
   rent: violently severed
   ragged: having an irregular edge
3. fatigue: tiredness
   lassitude: weariness
   prostration: physical and mental exhaustion
4. pained: hurt
   mortified: shamed or embarrassed
   dejected: depressed

THINKING AND WRITING

Publishing Student Writing You might wish to have your students form debate teams to discuss the topic "What is humor?" Have them choose specific aspects of humor to consider.

DORIS LESSING

More About the Author Like many twentieth-century artists and writers, Doris Lessing is concerned with the related topics of consciousness, sanity, and psychology. She argues, somewhat surprisingly, that there are some circumstances in which the only healthy thing to do is to become sick. Since so much of modern civilization is mad, madness may be a necessary stage in becoming whole. She frequently portrays breaking down as a means of breaking through. In *The Four-Gated City,* the final novel in her *Children of Violence* series, Lessing's protagonist, Martha Quest, is severely depressed and unwell. Lessing cleverly recalls *Jane Eyre* by creating a many-leveled house in which two women, one "mad" and one "sane," cooperate in creating a new level of consciousness. Discuss other stories, poems, plays, and movies that present eccentric characters who possess a wisdom so-called normal society needs.

1919–

Doris Lessing is one of the most powerful of contemporary authors. Her novels and short stories explore the evils of racism, the role of women in modern life, the importance of intuition, and the limits of idealism in solving the problems facing society. Her books, profound and highly personal, confront a host of post-World War II issues, supplying almost a history of the times, with special emphasis on Africa and feminism.

The focus on Africa in Doris Lessing's work is not surprising. Born in Persia of British parents, she grew up on a three-thousand-acre farm in Southern Rhodesia (now Zimbabwe), where her parents raised maize with the help of native labor. She remained in Africa through two unsuccessful marriages, living principally in the Rhodesian capital of Salisbury, until she was thirty.

She moved to London in 1949 and published her first novel, *The Grass Is Singing,* the next year, having brought the manuscript with her from Rhodesia. Her African experiences provided the material for this deeply moving, highly acclaimed work. In an interview in 1962, Lessing commented, "I feel the best thing that ever happened to me was that I was brought up out of England. I took for granted kinds of experiences that would be impossible to a middle-class girl here."

The Golden Notebook, published in 1962, is her most renowned and technically sophisticated work. It represents a junction between the two main paths her fiction has taken—her realistic, sometimes reportorial early style, and her visionary, at times apocalyptic, "inner space fiction" that came later. The dominant theme in *The Golden Notebook* is that of the free woman who struggles for individuality and equality despite her social and psychological conditioning.

A self-described "architect of the soul," Lessing is one of the most serious and intelligent of today's writers. Hers is a uniquely twentieth-century odyssey. Writing in what she calls a "straight, broad, direct" manner, she has produced a remarkable body of novels and short stories, works that are distinguished not only for their breadth of subject matter but also for their breadth of vision.

GUIDE FOR READING

A Mild Attack of Locusts

The Writer's Techniques

Conflict. One of the ingredients of an effective story or play is conflict, the struggle between a main character and another person or force. Often the conflict involves two main characters—protagonist and antagonist—as in many of Shakespeare's tragedies. Sometimes the conflict is between a main character and society as a whole, or between a main character and nature. These conflicts are external. An external conflict is one between a main character and another person or between a character and an outside force. There may also be internal conflict, or psychological conflict. Internal conflict occurs within the mind of a main character. Many plots contain both external and internal conflicts. Fictional conflicts, like real-life conflicts, are often complex, and you may occasionally find them puzzling to sort out.

Look For

As you read Doris Lessing's "A Mild Attack of Locusts," watch for the various kinds of conflict in the story.

Writing

Human beings are often pitted against nature in both real life and in fiction. For example, a family may struggle against a fast-flowing river or fire fighters may battle a forest fire. Make a list of natural forces against which human beings must battle and win—to survive.

Vocabulary

Knowing the following words will help you as you read "A Mild Attack of Locusts."

acrid (ak′ rid) *adj.*: Sharp; bitter (p. 1265)
myriads (mir′ē ədz) *n.*: Great numbers of things (p. 1265)
veldt (velt) *n.*: Open, grassy country (p. 1265)
serrated (ser′āt əd) *adj.*: Toothed or notched like a saw (p. 1265)
perverted (pər vʉr′tid) *adj.*: Distorted; corrupted (p. 1266)
irremediable (ir i mē′dē ə b'l) *adj.*: Incurable; incapable of being remedied (p. 1267)
haggard (hag′ərd) *adj.*: Having a worn, gaunt, or wild look (p. 1267)
imminent (im′ə nənt) *adj.*: Likely to happen soon (p. 1268)

Literary Focus In literature as in life, it is a great deal easier to recognize external than internal conflict. Indeed, the most difficult aspect of internal conflict is acknowledging that it exists. The locust attack in Lessing's story serves as a sort of mirror in which Margaret is first able to see her own inner turmoil. Curiously, the attack serves as an agent of healing.

Look For Have students note specific passages in which Lessing uses description of the land and the locust attack as reflections of Margaret's internal conflict.

Writing Encourage your students to describe these conflicts before the class. Have them specify the forces in conflict and tell how the conflicts were resolved or likely to be. Have students discuss the meaning of the story's title, "A Mild Attack of Locusts." Encourage students to incorporate the insights gained during discussion in their compositions on paradox.

Vocabulary Have students locate and read aloud the sentences in which the vocabulary words appear. Discuss what these particular words, rather than any of their synonyms, contribute in terms of sound as well as sense.

Objectives

1 To recognize conflict
2 To appreciate the role of style
3 To write about paradox

Teaching Portfolio: Support Material

Teacher Backup, p. 000

Vocabulary Check, p. 00

Usage and Mechanics Worksheet, p. 00

Analyzing Literature Worksheet, p. 00

Critical Thinking and Reading Worksheet, p. 00

Language Worksheet, p. 00

Selection Test, p. 00

Motivation for Reading Ask students to think of this story by Lessing as a sort of mystery. Tell them to read carefully so that they will be able to state clearly the problem the protagonist solves.

Master Teacher Note Lessing often writes of people, particularly women, who find themselves trapped in situations they do not recall creating. Suggest that **more advanced** students read Lessing's "Room 19," a somewhat longer story, about a desperate woman. Compare this protagonist with Margaret.

Thematic Idea Death-and-resurrection is a paradox at the heart of life. Lessing's Margaret is initiated into this mystery, a theme re-current in fiction and particularly in poetry. This paradox often appears in the poems of John Donne.

Purpose-Setting Question How does Margaret change over the course of the story?

1 **Critical Thinking and Reading** What might you infer about Margaret from this passage?

2 **Discussion** What three things did the farmers discuss that Margaret knew nothing about? What does the word *language* mean in this context?

A Mild Attack of Locusts

Doris Lessing

The rains that year were good; they were coming nicely just as the crops needed them —or so Margaret gathered when the men said they were not too bad. She never had an
1 opinion of her own on matters like the
weather, because even to know about what seems a simple thing like the weather needs experience. Which Margaret had not got. The men were Richard her husband, and old Stephen, Richard's father, a farmer from way back; and these two might argue for hours whether the rains were ruinous or just ordinarily exasperating. Margaret had been on the farm three years. She still did not understand how they did not go bankrupt altogether, when the men never had a
2 good word for the weather, or the soil, or the
Government. But she was getting to learn the language. Farmers' language. And they neither went bankrupt nor got very rich. They jogged along doing comfortably.

Their crop was maize.[1] Their farm was three thousand acres on the ridges that rise up toward the Zambesi escarpment[2]—high, dry windswept country, cold and dusty in winter, but now, in the wet season, steamy with the heat rising in wet soft waves off miles of green foliage. Beautiful it was, with the sky blue and brilliant halls of air, and the bright green folds and hollows of country beneath, and the mountains lying sharp and bare twenty miles off across the rivers. The sky made her eyes ache; she was not used to it. One does not look so much at the sky in the city she came from. So that evening when Richard said: "The Government is sending out warnings that locusts are expected, coming down from the breeding grounds up North," her instinct was to look about her at the trees. Insects —swarms of them—horrible! But Richard and the old man had raised their eyes and were looking up over the mountain. "We haven't had locusts in seven years," they said. "They go in cycles, locusts do." And then: "There goes our crop for this season!"

But they went on with the work of the farm just as usual until one day they were coming up the road to the homestead for the midday break, when old Stephen stopped, raised his finger and pointed: "Look, look, there they are!"

Out ran Margaret to join them, looking at the hills. Out came the servants from the kitchen. They all stood and gazed. Over the rocky levels of the mountain was a streak of rust-colored air. Locusts. There they came.

At once Richard shouted at the cookboy. Old Stephen yelled at the houseboy. The cookboy ran to beat the old plowshare[3] hanging from a tree branch, which was used to summon the laborers at moments of crisis. The houseboy ran off to the store to collect tin cans, any old bit of metal. The farm was ringing with the clamor of the gong; and they could see the laborers come

---

1. maize (māz) *n.*: Corn.

2. Zambesi (zam bē' zē) **escarpment:** Steep cliffs along the Zambesi River in southern Africa.

3. plowshare *n.*: The cutting blade of a plow.

pouring out of the compound, pointing at the hills and shouting excitedly. Soon they had all come up to the house, and Richard and old Stephen were giving them orders —Hurry, hurry, hurry.

And off they ran again, the two white men with them, and in a few minutes Margaret could see the smoke of fires rising from all around the farmlands. Piles of wood and grass had been prepared there. There were seven patches of bared soil, yellow and oxblood color and pink, where the new mealies[4] were just showing, making a film of bright green; and around each drifted up
3 thick clouds of smoke. They were throwing wet leaves on to the fires now, to make it acrid and black. Margaret was watching the hills. Now there was a long, low cloud advancing, rust-color still, swelling forward and out as she looked. The telephone was ringing. Neighbors—quick, quick, there come the locusts. Old Smith had had his crop eaten to the ground. Quick, get your fires started. For of course, while every farmer hoped the locusts would overlook his farm and go on to the next, it was only fair to warn each other; one must play fair. Everywhere, fifty miles over the countryside, the smoke was rising from myriads of fires. Margaret answered the telephone calls, and between calls she stood watching the locusts. The air was darkening. A strange darkness, for the sun was blazing—it was like the darkness of a veldt fire, when the air gets
4 thick with smoke. The sunlight comes down distorted, a thick, hot orange. Oppressive it was, too, with the heaviness of a storm. The locusts were coming fast. Now half the sky was darkened. Behind the reddish veils in front, which were the advance guards of the swarm, the main swarm showed in dense black cloud, reaching almost to the sun itself.

Margaret was wondering what she could do to help. She did not know. Then up came old Stephen from the lands. "We're finished, Margaret, finished! Those beggars can eat every leaf and blade off the farm in half an hour! And it is only early afternoon—if we can make enough smoke, make enough noise till the sun goes down, they'll settle somewhere else perhaps. . . ." And then: "Get the kettle going. It's thirsty work, this."

So Margaret went to the kitchen, and stoked up the fire, and boiled the water. Now, on the tin roof of the kitchen she could hear the thuds and bangs of falling locusts, or a scratching slither as one skidded down. Here were the first of them. From down on the lands came the beating and banging and clanging of a hundred gasoline cans and bits of metal. Stephen impatiently waited while one gasoline can was filled with tea, hot, sweet and orange-colored, and the other with water. In the meantime, he told Margaret about how twenty years back he was eaten out, made bankrupt, by the locust armies. And then, still talking, he hoisted up the gasoline cans, one in each hand, by the wood pieces set cornerwise across each, and jogged off down to the road to the thirsty laborers. By now the locusts were falling like hail on to the roof of the kitchen. It sounded like a heavy storm. Margaret looked out and saw the air dark with a criss-cross of the insects, and she set her teeth and ran out into it—what the men could do, she could. Overhead the air was thick, locusts everywhere. The locusts were flopping against her, and she brushed them off, heavy red-brown creatures, looking at her with their beady old-men's eyes while they clung with hard, serrated legs. She held her breath with disgust and ran through into the house. There it was even more like being in a heavy storm. The iron roof was reverberating, and the clamor of iron from the lands was like thunder. Looking out, all the trees were queer and still, clotted with insects, their boughs weighed to the ground. The earth seemed to be moving, locusts crawling everywhere, she could not see the lands at

4. **mealies** *n.*: Ears of corn.

3 **Discussion** Why do you suppose Lessing has chosen so carefully to include colors in this passage? What is the effect of their juxtaposition?

4 **Literary Focus** How does this paradox reinforce the conflict portrayed in the story?

5 **Reading Strategy** What previous passage(s) does this question recall? Watch for its repetition, in somewhat altered form, later in the story?

6 **Literary Focus** Why does Lessing repeat the verb, *clotted?* Is it stylistically purposeful and, if so, how? Why, do you suppose, does she use this particular verb? What are its connotations? Do they support the story's theme?

7 **Discussion** Contrast Margaret's reaction to the locust attack with Stephen's. Why do they differ so?

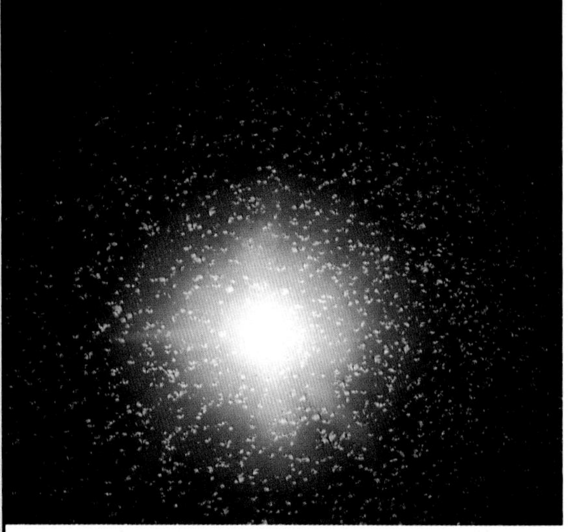

all, so thick was the swarm. Towards the mountains it was like looking into driving rain—even as she watched, the sun was blotted out with a fresh onrush of them. It was a half-night, a perverted blackness. Then came a sharp crack from the bush—a branch had snapped off. Then another. A tree down the slope leaned over and settled heavily to the ground. Through the hail of insects a man came running. More tea, more water was needed. She supplied them. She kept the fires stoked and filled cans with liquid, and then it was four in the afternoon, and the locusts had been pouring across overhead for a couple of hours. Up came old Stephen again, crunching locusts underfoot with every step, locusts clinging all over him; he was cursing and swearing, banging with his old hat at the air. At the doorway he stopped briefly, hastily pulling at the clinging insects and throwing them off, then he plunged into the locust-free living-room.

"All the crops finished. Nothing left," he said.

But the gongs were still beating, the men
5 still shouting, and Margaret asked: "Why do you go on with it, then?"

"The main swarm isn't settling. They are heavy with eggs. They are looking for a place to settle and lay. If we can stop the main body settling on our farm, that's everything. If they get a chance to lay their eggs, we are going to have everything eaten flat with hoppers[5] later on." He picked a stray locust off his shirt and split it down with his thumbnail—it was clotted inside with eggs. "Imagine that multiplied by millions. You ever seen a hopper swarm on the march? Well, you're lucky."

Margaret thought an adult swarm was 6
bad enough. Outside now the light on the earth was a pale, thin yellow, clotted with moving shadows; the clouds of moving insects thickened and lightened like driving rain. Old Stephen said, "They've got the wind behind them, that's something."

"Is it very bad?" asked Margaret fearfully, and the old man said emphatically: "We're finished. This swarm may pass over, but once they've started, they'll be coming down from the North now one after another. And then there are the hoppers—it might go on for two or three years."

Margaret sat down helplessly, and thought: Well, if it's the end, it's the end. What now? We'll all three have to go back to town. . . . But at this, she took a quick look at Stephen, the old man who had farmed forty years in this country, been bankrupt twice, and she knew nothing would make him go and become a clerk in the city. Yet
her heart ached for him, he looked so tired, 7
the worry lines deep from nose to mouth. Poor old man. . . . He had lifted up a locust that had got itself somehow into his pocket, holding it in the air by one leg. "You've got the strength of a steel-spring in those legs of yours," he was telling the locust, good-humoredly. Then, although he had been fighting locusts, squashing locusts, yelling at locusts, sweeping them in great mounds into the fires to burn for the last three hours, nevertheless he took this one to the door and carefully threw it out to join its fellows, as if

5. **hoppers** *n.*: Baby locusts.

he would rather not harm a hair of its head. This comforted Margaret; all at once she felt irrationally cheered. She remembered it was not the first time in the last three years the man had announced their final and irremediable ruin.

"Get me a drink, lass," he then said, and she set the bottle of whisky by him.

In the meantime, out in the pelting storm of insects, her husband was banging the gong, feeding the fires with leaves, the insects clinging to him all over—she shuddered. "How can you bear to let them touch you?" she asked. He looked at her, disapproving. She felt suitably humble—just as
8 she had when he had first taken a good look at her city self, hair waved and golden, nails red and pointed. Now she was a proper farmer's wife, in sensible shoes and a solid skirt. She might even get to letting locusts settle on her—in time.

Having tossed back a whisky or two, old Stephen went back into the battle, wading now through glistening brown waves of locusts.

Five o'clock. The sun would set in an hour. Then the swarm would settle. It was as thick overhead as ever. The trees were ragged mounds of glistening brown.

Margaret began to cry. It was all so hopeless—if it wasn't a bad season, it was locusts; if it wasn't locusts, it was army worm[6] or veldt fires. Always something. The rustling of the locust armies was like a big forest in the storm; their settling on the roof was like the beating of the rain; the ground was invisible in a sleek, brown, surging tide—it was like being drowned in locusts, submerged by the loathsome brown flood. It seemed as if the roof might sink in under the weight of them, as if the door might give in under their pressure and these rooms fill with them—and it was getting so dark . . . she looked up. The air was thinner; gaps of blue showed in the dark, moving clouds. The blue spaces were cold and thin—the sun must be setting. Through the fog of insects she saw figures approaching. First old Stephen, marching bravely along, then her husband, drawn and haggard with weariness. Behind them the servants. All were crawling all over with insects. The sound of the gongs had stopped. She could hear nothing but the ceaseless rustle of a myriad wings.

The two men slapped off the insects and came in.

"Well," said Richard, kissing her on the cheek, "the main swarm has gone over."

"For the Lord's sake," said Margaret angrily, still half-crying, "what's here is bad enough, isn't it?" For although the evening air was no longer black and thick, but a clear blue, with a pattern of insects whizzing this way and that across it, everything else—trees, buildings, bushes, earth, was gone under the moving brown masses.

"If it doesn't rain in the night and keep them here—if it doesn't rain and weight them down with water, they'll be off in the morning at sunrise."

"We're bound to have some hoppers. But not the main swarm—that's something."

Margaret roused herself, wiped her eyes, pretended she had not been crying, and fetched them some supper, for the servants were too exhausted to move. She sent them down to the compound to rest.

She served the supper and sat listening. There is not one maize plant left, she heard. Not one. The men would get the planters out the moment the locusts had gone. They must start all over again.

But what's the use of that, Margaret wondered, if the whole farm was going to be crawling with hoppers? But she listened 9
while they discussed the new government pamphlet that said how to defeat the hoppers. You must have men out all the time, moving over the farm to watch for movement in the grass. When you find a patch of hoppers, small lively black things, like crickets, then you dig trenches around the

6. **army worm:** Larva of certain moths that travel in large groups, ruining crops.

8 **Literary Focus** List as many of the conflicts presented by this passage as you can.

9 **Discussion** How does this passage embody Margaret's conflict?

10 **Literary Focus** What is the significance of the word *shadow* here? Where else has Lessing used it? What parallel does she make?

11 **Discussion** Why is it significant that Margaret shares the moment of seeing the beauty of the locusts fanning their wings? What has she gained that she lacked before?

12 **Discussion** Why is the comment of the men ironic, yet totally revealing of character, in view of their constant predictions of doom?

patch or spray them with poison from pumps supplied by the Government. The Government wanted them to cooperate in a world plan for eliminating this plague forever. You should attack locusts at the source. Hoppers, in short. The men were talking as if they were planning a war, and Margaret listened, amazed.

In the night it was quiet; no sign of the settled armies outside, except sometimes a branch snapped, or a tree could be heard crashing down.

Margaret slept badly in the bed beside Richard, who was sleeping like the dead, exhausted with the afternoon's fight. In the morning she woke to yellow sunshine lying across the bed—clear sunshine, with an
10 occasional blotch of shadow moving over it. She went to the window. Old Stephen was ahead of her. There he stood outside, gazing down over the bush. And she gazed, astounded—and entranced, much against her will. For it looked as if every tree, every bush, all the earth, were lit with pale flames. The locusts were fanning their wings to free them of the night dews. There was a shimmer of red-tinged gold light everywhere.

She went out to join the old man, stepping carefully among the insects. They stood and watched. Overhead the sky was blue, blue and clear.

"Pretty," said old Stephen, with satisfaction.

Well, thought Margaret, we may be ru-
11 ined, we may be bankrupt, but not everyone has seen an army of locusts fanning their wings at dawn.

Over the slopes, in the distance, a faint red smear showed in the sky, thickened and spread. "There they go," said old Stephen. "There goes the main army, off south."

And now from the trees, from the earth all round them, the locusts were taking wing. They were like small aircraft, maneuvering for the take-off, trying their wings to see if they were dry enough. Off they went. A reddish-brown steam was rising off the miles of bush, off the lands, the earth. Again the sunlight darkened.

And as the clotted branches lifted, the weight on them lightening, there was nothing but the black spines of branches, trees. No green left, nothing. All morning they watched, the three of them, as the brown crust thinned and broke and dissolved, flying up to mass with the main army, now a brownish-red smear in the southern sky. The lands which had been filmed with green, the new tender mealie plants, were stark and bare. All the trees stripped. A devastated landscape. No green, no green anywhere.

By midday the reddish cloud had gone. Only an occasional locust flopped down. On the ground were the corpses and the wounded. The African laborers were sweeping these up with branches and collecting them in tins.

"Ever eaten sun-dried locust?" asked old Stephen. "That time twenty years ago, when I went broke, I lived on mealie meal and dried locusts for three months. They aren't bad at all—rather like smoked fish, if you come to think of it."

But Margaret preferred not even to think of it.

After the midday meal the men went off to the lands. Everything was to be replanted. With a bit of luck another swarm would not come traveling down just this way. But they hoped it would rain very soon, to spring some new grass, because the cattle would die otherwise—there was not a blade of grass left on the farm. As for Margaret, she was trying to get used to the idea of three or four years of locusts. Locusts were going to be like bad weather, from now on, always imminent. She felt like a survivor after war—if this devastated and mangled countryside was not ruin, well, what then was ruin?

But the men ate their supper with good appetites.

"It could have been worse," was what
they said. "It could be much worse." 12

THINKING ABOUT THE SELECTION

Recalling

1. (a) How long has Margaret lived on the farm? (b) Where did she come from? (c) How has her appearance changed since coming to the farm?
2. What are the farmers' two main defenses against the locusts?
3. Why do the farmers want to prevent the main swarm of locusts from settling?
4. What three problems besides locusts do the farmers sometimes have to face?
5. (a) How much damage do the locusts do to the farm? (b) When morning comes, what do the locusts do?

Interpreting

6. What is Margaret's attitude toward the locust attack?
7. Why does old Stephen fight on even after saying they are finished?
8. Why do you think Margaret is comforted when Stephen releases the locust that was in his pocket?
9. In what sense is the locust attack "mild," as the title of the story calls it?

Applying

10. People react differently when faced with what seems to be a hopeless situation. (a) How does this story make that point? (b) What have you seen in your own experience that proves it?

ANALYZING LITERATURE

Recognizing Conflict

In a work of fiction, the opposition between a character and another force is the story's conflict. This conflict may be external, as between the farmers and the invading locusts in "A Mild Attack of Locusts." Or it may be internal, as in Margaret's love for her husband opposed to her despair for his future as a farmer on the veldt.

1. There are a number of conflicts in "A Mild Attack of Locusts." One of them concerns Margaret's struggle to define herself as a farmer's wife. What evidence is there in the story that she does not regard herself as entirely satisfied with her role in life?
2. The immediate external conflict in the story is the locust attack. But there is a long-term conflict as well, one that is unresolved by the farmers' minor victory in keeping the main swarm from settling. (a) What is the long-term, unresolved external conflict? (b) How successful do you think Richard, Stephen, and Margaret will be in resolving it?

CRITICAL THINKING AND READING

Understanding the Role of Style

A writer's **style** is his or her distinctive way of using language to express thoughts. Style is a broad term. It includes word choice, sentence structure, point of view, and all aspects of organization. A writer's style is influenced by the literary fashion of the times and by his or her own personality and preferences. Some writers pay close attention to their style; others do not. The style of some writers stands out in sharp relief; that of others is hardly noticeable. Doris Lessing's style in "A Mild Attack of Locusts" is plain and precise. Her use of inverted sentence structure is perhaps its most noticeable feature —"Beautiful it was, with the sky blue."

What makes Lessing's "straight, broad, direct" style effective in this story?

THINKING AND WRITING

Writing About a Paradox

A **paradox** is a statement or circumstance that at first seems untrue or self-contradictory but upon reflection proves to be true in some sense. In "A Mild Attack of Locusts," Margaret, after a day of feeling revulsion for the locusts, is entranced the next morning as they fan their wings, making "a shimmer of red-tinged gold light everywhere." Her feelings are paradoxical. Write a composition in which you explain the paradox of how something so destructive and even loathsome can also be beautiful. When revising your first draft, make sure you have supported your ideas with specific details.

Answers

ANSWERS TO THINKING ABOUT THE SELECTION

Recalling

1. (a) "Margaret has been on the farm three years." (b) Margaret came from the city. (c) Margaret has traded in "her city self, hair waved and golden, nails red and pointed" for the image of "a proper farmer's wife, in sensible shoes and a solid skirt."
2. The farmers' two main defenses against the locusts are noise and fire.
3. The farmers want to prevent the main swarm of locusts from settling so they can keep them from laying their eggs.
4. Besides locusts, farmers must contend with "a bad season," "army worm," and "veldt fires."
5. (a) The locusts strip the farm of everything green and growing. (b) In the morning, they leave for the south.

Interpreting

6. Margaret prefers to not think about the locust attack.
7. Old Stephen fights on because he is a survivor.
8. Margaret is comforted by Stephen's releasing the locust in his pocket because it shows his humaneness.
9. It is mild because it could have been worse.

Applying

10. (a) Margaret reacts differently from the farmers. (b) Answers will differ. Students should mention the different reactions of people in the same set of circumstances.

ANSWERS TO ANALYZING LITERATURE

1. Margaret's constant feeling of not understanding her surroundings suggests that she doesn't regard herself as entirely satisfied with her role in life. Her memory of her city self suggests nostalgia and preference for an earlier time.
2. (a) The long-term, unresolved conflict concerns the advisability of continuing the farm at all. (b) Answers will differ. Students should give reasons for their answers.

ANSWERS TO CRITICAL THINKING AND READING

The story is a modern parable. "Straight, broad, direct" suits its lesson.

THINKING AND WRITING

Publishing Student Writing Have students read their compositions in small groups. Each group can then select one or two compositions to share with the class.

More About the Author Nadine Gordimer is often compared, artistically, with her fellow South African and fellow author, Doris Lessing. Both characteristically deal with the twin themes of freedom and estrangement on a personal as well as a political level. While Lessing has become famous for the ways in which she employs structure to support and reinforce theme, Gordimer is more well-known for her careful crafting of language.

NADINE GORDIMER

1923–

The fiction of Nadine Gordimer has been shaped by her life in South Africa and by her firm opposition to the government's policy of apartheid. Initially honored for her short fiction, she says that in time she found the short story "too delicate for what I have to say." In recent years her novels, some of them banned in South Africa, have gained an international reputation.

Nadine Gordimer was born in Springs, South Africa, a small town near Johannesburg. Her mother took her out of a local private school when she was eleven, and from then until she was sixteen she "read tremendously," wrote much fiction, and published her first adult short story, "Come Again Tomorrow," when she was fifteen. She studied for a year at the University of Witwatersrand, continuing to write short stories. *The Soft Voice of the Serpent* (1952) was the first collection of her stories to be published in the United States.

Following the critical success of that book, Gordimer's stories began appearing in *The New Yorker,* the *Atlantic, Harper's,* and other well-known periodicals. In her stories she often describes the enforced entrapment of whites who have inherited political and economic power in South Africa's closed society. Frequently she builds a personal tale around a fleeting but sharply focused moment of insight.

In her short stories, and later in her novels—including the critically acclaimed *A Guest of Honor* (1970), *The Conservationist* (1974), and *Burger's Daughter* (1979)—she displays an ability to write from the perspectives of Anglo, black, and Afrikaner and to delineate a variety of economic and social settings. She writes as a compassionate observer of the human condition. In lyric tones yet without sentimentality, she pictures the South African scene with awareness and humanity, stressing the themes of understanding, adjustment, and forgiveness.

Until she was thirty, Nadine Gordimer had never been outside South Africa. Since then she has traveled widely and lectured in a number of universities, including Princeton, Columbia, and the University of Michigan. In recent years she has won many literary awards.

GUIDE FOR READING

The Train from Rhodesia

The Writer's Techniques

Theme. Theme is the insight into life revealed by a work of literature. In fiction the writer's central idea becomes the theme of the work. Often the theme can be stated in a single sentence, such as "A small mistake in judgment can have serious consequences." Sometimes it demands a more detailed description. A work of fiction may have one theme or several. In developing a theme, the writer introduces conflict, typically a problem or problems that must be solved by the protagonist, or main character.

When the protagonist has to choose between two or more undesirable alternatives, he or she faces a dilemma. In familiar terms a dilemma is a choice between the frying pan and the fire; in mythological terms, between Scylla and Charybdis. A dilemma involves a difficult choice between actions or values, and any choice that the character makes may have unfortunate results.

Look For

As you read Nadine Gordimer's "The Train from Rhodesia," see if you can identify the dilemma or dilemmas that the young wife on the train faces.

Writing

According to an African proverb, "The earth is a beehive; we all enter by the same door but live in different cells." Freewrite, exploring the meaning of this proverb.

Vocabulary

Knowing the following words will help you as you read "The Train from Rhodesia."

heraldic (hə ral'dik) *adj.*: Resembling an English coat of arms (p. 1272)

impressionistic (im presh'ə nis'tik) *adj.*: Conveying a quick, overall picture (p. 1272)

elongated (i lôŋ'gāt id) *adj.*: Lengthened; stretched (p. 1274)

valance (val'əns) *n.*: Decorative facing (p. 1274)

segmented (seg'ment id) *adj.*: Separated into parts (p. 1275)

splaying (splā'iŋ) *v.*: Spreading (p. 1275)

atrophy (a'trə fē) *v.*: Waste away (p. 1276)

Literary Focus Fiction requires conflict to make it move. Dilemma, a special type of inner conflict, requires a character, usually the protagonist, to decide between difficult alternatives.

Look For With **less advanced** students it may be useful to read this story in class, clarifying the abundance of impressionistic details.

Writing Have the students discuss the relationship between the story's opening sentence and its central theme. Encourage them to bear this discussion in mind as they complete the freewriting assignment.

Vocabulary Find synonyms for each of the listed vocabulary words. Try them out. Discuss whether or not they work as well as the original words.

Objectives

1 To understand theme
2 To understand cultural attitudes and customs
3 To distinguish between concrete and abstract words
4. To write about theme in fiction

Teaching Portfolio: Support Material

Teacher Backup, p. 000

Vocabulary Check, p. 00

Usage and Mechanics Worksheet, p. 00

Analyzing Literature Worksheet, p. 00

Critical Thinking and Reading Worksheet, p. 00

Language Worksheet, p. 00

Selection Test, p. 00

Motivation for Reading Sometimes an exotic landscape or faraway setting makes it easier for us to think about a problem that is close to us. As you read the story, look for those aspects of the situation that are universal in significance.

Master Teacher Note Bring a map of Africa into class. Point out the nation of Rhodesia, the setting of this story. Discuss the meaning of apartheid and the relation between this policy and Gordimer's story.

Thematic Idea In "The Train from Rhodesia," Gordimer, like Lessing in "A Mild Attack of Locusts" (p. 1264), examines the special sort of inner conflict known as dilemma. Compare and contrast the two stories for their treatment of this idea.

Purpose-Setting Question Why does the story begin with the sentence that it does?

1 **Discussion** How is the train described? Why does Gordimer make it seem human?

2 **Discussion** Who or what is an "old boy"? What is the significance of this term?

3 **Literary Focus** What does this sentence mean? What is the difference between smiling "from the heart" and "at the customer"?

The Train from Rhodesia[1]

Nadine Gordimer

The train came out of the red horizon and bore down toward them over the single straight track.

The stationmaster came out of his little brick station with its pointed chalet roof, feeling the creases in his serge uniform in his legs as well. A stir of preparedness rippled through the squatting native vendors waiting in the dust; the face of a carved wooden animal, eternally surprised, stuck out of a sack. The stationmaster's barefoot children wandered over. From the gray mud huts with the untidy heads that stood within a decorated mud wall, chickens, and dogs with their skin stretched like parchment over their bones, followed the piccanins[2] down to the track. The flushed and perspiring west cast a reflection, faint, without heat, upon the station, upon the tin shed marked "Goods," upon the walled kraal,[3] upon the gray tin house of the stationmaster and upon the sand, that lapped all around, from sky to sky, cast little rhythmical cups of shadow, so that the sand became the sea, and closed over the children's black feet softly and without imprint.

The stationmaster's wife sat behind the mesh of her veranda. Above her head the hunk of a sheep's carcass moved slightly, dangling in a current of air.

They waited.

The train called out, along the sky; but there was no answer; and the cry hung on: I'm coming . . . I'm coming . . .

The engine flared out now, big, whisking 1
a dwindling body behind it; the track flared out to let it in.

Creaking, jerking, jostling, gasping, the train filled the station.

Here, let me see that one—the young woman curved her body further out of the corridor window. Missus? smiled the old boy, looking at the creatures he held in his 2
hand. From a piece of string on his gray finger hung a tiny woven basket; he lifted it, questioning. No, no, she urged, leaning down toward him, across the height of the train, toward the man in the piece of old rug; that one, that one, her hand commanded. It was a lion, carved out of soft dry wood that looked like spongecake; heraldic, black and white, with impressionistic detail burnt in. The old man held it up to her still smiling, not from the heart, but at the customer. 3
Between its Vandyke[4] teeth, in the mouth opened in an endless roar too terrible to be heard, it had a black tongue. Look, said the young husband, if you don't mind! And round the neck of the thing, a piece of fur (rat? rabbit? meerkat?); a real mane, majestic, telling you somehow that the artist had delight in the lion.

1. **Rhodesia** (rō de′ zhə): Former name of Zimbabwe (zim bä′ bwe), a country in southern Africa.
2. **piccanins** *n.*: Native children.
3. **kraal** (kräl) *n.*: A fenced-in enclosure for cattle or sheep.

4. **Vandyke** (van dīk′) *adj.*: In the style of the subjects of the portraits of Flemish painter Anthony Vandyke (1599–1641).

4 **Discussion** What is the significance of the artists being described as animals who "sprang, walking bent"?

5 **Discussion** Explain why the faces of the passengers suddenly look different after their contact with those outside the train.

6 **Reading Strategy** What can be inferred about the relationship between the young man and woman and about the reason for their trip. In other words, why are they on this train together?

4 All up and down the length of the train in the dust the artists sprang, walking bent, like performing animals, the better to exhibit the fantasy held toward the faces on the train. Buck, startled and stiff, staring with round black and white eyes. More lions, standing erect, grappling with strange, thin, elongated warriors who clutched spears and showed no fear in their slits of eyes. How much, they asked from the train, how much?

Give me penny, said the little ones with nothing to sell. The dogs went and sat, quite still, under the dining car, where the train breathed out the smell of meat cooking with onion.

A man passed beneath the arch of reaching arms meeting gray-black and white in the exchange of money for the staring wooden eyes, the stiff wooden legs sticking up in the air; went along under the voices and the bargaining, interrogating the wheels. Past the dogs; glancing up at the dining car where he could stare at the faces, behind glass, drinking beer, two by two, on either side of a uniform railway vase with its pale dead flower. Right to the end, to the guard's van, where the stationmaster's children had just collected their mother's two loaves of bread; to the engine itself, where the stationmaster and the driver stood talking against the steaming complaint of the resting beast.

The man called out to them, something loud and joking. They turned to laugh, in a twirl of steam. The two children careered over the sand, clutching the bread, and burst through the iron gate and up the path through the garden in which nothing grew.

5 Passengers drew themselves in at the corridor windows and turned into compartments to fetch money, to call someone to look. Those sitting inside looked up: suddenly different, caged faces, boxed in, cut off, after the contact of outside. There was an orange a piccanin would like. . . . What about that chocolate? It wasn't very nice. . . .

A young girl had collected a handful of the hard kind, that no one liked, out of the chocolate box, and was throwing them to the dogs, over at the dining car. But the hens darted in, and swallowed the chocolates, incredibly quick and accurate, before they had even dropped in the dust, and the dogs, a little bewildered, looked up with their brown eyes, not expecting anything.

—No, leave it, said the girl, don't take it. . . .

Too expensive, too much, she shook her head and raised her voice to the old boy, giving up the lion. He held it up where she had handed it to him. No, she said, shaking her head. Three-and-six?[5] insisted her husband, loudly. Yes baas! laughed the boy. *Three-and-six?*—the young man was incredulous. Oh leave it—she said. The young man stopped. Don't you want it? he said, keeping his face closed to the boy. No, never mind, she said, leave it. The old native kept his head on one side, looking at them sideways, holding the lion. Three-and-six, he murmured, as old people repeat things to themselves.

6 The young woman drew her head in. She went into the coupé[6] and sat down. Out of the window, on the other side, there was nothing; sand and bush; a thorn tree. Back through the open doorway, past the figure of her husband in the corridor, there was the station, the voices, wooden animals waving, running feet. Her eye followed the funny little valance of scrolled wood that outlined the chalet roof of the station; she thought of the lion and smiled. That bit of fur round the neck. But the wooden buck, the hippos, the elephants, the baskets that already bulked out of their brown paper under the seat and on the luggage rack! How will they look at home? Where will you put them? What will they mean away from the places you found

5. three-and-six: Three shillings and sixpence.
6. coupé (ko͞o pā′) *n.*: A half-compartment at the end, with seats on only one side.

them? Away from the unreality of the last few weeks? The man outside. But he is not part of the unreality; he is for good now. Odd . . . somewhere there was an idea that he, that living with him, was part of the holiday, the strange places.

Outside, a bell rang. The stationmaster was leaning against the end of the train, green flag rolled in readiness. A few men who had got down to stretch their legs sprang on to the train, clinging to the observation platforms, or perhaps merely standing on the iron step, holding the rail; but on the train, safe from the one dusty platform, the one tin house, the empty sand.

There was a grunt. The train jerked. Through the glass the beer drinkers looked out, as if they could not see beyond it. Behind the flyscreen, the stationmaster's wife sat facing back at them beneath the darkening hunk of meat.

There was a shout. The flag drooped out. Joints not yet coordinated, the segmented body of the train heaved and bumped back against itself. It began to move; slowly the scrolled chalet moved past it, the yells of the natives, running alongside, jetted up into the air, fell back at different levels. Staring wooden faces waved drunkenly, there, then gone, questioning for the last time at the windows. Here, one-and-six baas!—As one automatically opens a hand to catch a thrown ball, a man fumbled wildly down his pocket, brought up the shilling and sixpence and threw them out; the old native, gasping, his skinny toes splaying the sand, flung the lion.

The piccanins were waving, the dogs stood, tails uncertain, watching the train go: past the mud huts, where a woman turned to look, up from the smoke of the fire, her hand pausing on her hip.

The stationmaster went slowly in under the chalet.

The old native stood, breath blowing out the skin between his ribs, feet tense, balanced in the sand, smiling and shaking his head. In his opened palm, held in the attitude of receiving, was the retrieved shilling and sixpence.

The blind end of the train was being pulled helplessly out of the station. 7

The young man swung in from the corridor, breathless. He was shaking his head with laughter and triumph. Here! he said. And waggled the lion at her. One-and-six!

What? she said.

He laughed. I was arguing with him for fun, bargaining—when the train had pulled out already, he came tearing after. . . . One-and-six baas! So there's your lion.

She was holding it away from her, the head with the open jaws, the pointed teeth, the black tongue, the wonderful ruff of fur facing her. She was looking at it with an expression of not seeing, of seeing something different. Her face was drawn up, wryly, like the face of a discomforted child. Her mouth lifted nervously at the corner. Very slowly, cautious, she lifted her finger and touched the mane, where it was joined to the wood.

But how could you, she said. He was shocked by the dismay of her face.

Good heavens, he said, what's the matter?

If you wanted the thing, she said, her voice rising and breaking with the shrill impotence of anger, why didn't you buy it in the first place? If you wanted it, why didn't you pay for it? Why didn't you take it decently, when he offered it? Why did you have to wait for him to run after the train with it, and give him one-and-six? One-and-six!

She was pushing it at him, trying to force him to take it. He stood astonished, his hands hanging at his sides.

But you wanted it! You liked it so much?

—It's a beautiful piece of work, she said fiercely, as if to protect it from him.

You liked it so much! You said yourself it was too expensive—

Oh *you*—she said, hopeless and furious. *You*. . . . She threw the lion onto the seat.

7 Critical Reading and Thinking
What is the significance of this sentence? Why does Gordimer describe the train as she does here? Compare this sentence with the opening one of the story.

8 Reading Strategy What is the "void" that the young woman discovers? What clues are there to suggest it?

9 Discussion Why does the story end as it does?

10 Reading Strategy Ask students to review the descriptions of the train throughout the short story. How is it personified? What similarity to the young woman could the train represent?

He stood looking at her.

She sat down again in the corner and, her face slumped in her hand, stared out of the window. Everything was turning around inside her. One-and-six. One-and-six. One-and-six for the wood and the carving and the sinews of the legs and the switch of the tail. The mouth open like that and the teeth. The black tongue, rolling, like a wave. The mane round the neck. To give one-and-six for that. The heat of shame mounted through her legs and body and sounded in her ears like the sound of sand pouring. Pouring, pouring. She sat there, sick. A weariness, a tastelessness, the discovery of
8 a void made her hands slacken their grip, atrophy emptily, as if the hour was not worth their grasp. She was feeling like this again. She had thought it was something to do with singleness, with being alone and belonging too much to oneself.

She sat there not wanting to move or speak, or to look at anything, even; so that the mood should be associated with nothing, no object, word or sight that might recur and so recall the feeling again. . . . Smuts blew in grittily, settled on her hands. Her back remained at exactly the same angle, turned against the young man sitting with his hands drooping between his sprawled legs, and the lion, fallen on its side in the corner.

The train had cast the station like a
skin. It called out to the sky, I'm coming, I'm 9, 1
coming; and again, there was no answer.

THINKING ABOUT THE SELECTION

Recalling

1. At the beginning of the story, what are three details that show the isolation of the small-town railway station?
2. (a) How much money does the vendor want for the carved lion? (b) How much does he finally accept?
3. (a) What have the young couple already bought on their holiday? (b) After the "unreality" of the vacation, what does the wife realize "is for good now"?
4. (a) At the end of the story, how is the young woman sitting in her seat? (b) Where is the lion?

Interpreting

5. Why is the arrival of the train important to the people in the town?
6. Why do you think the young woman wants the carved lion?
7. (a) Why is the young woman angry when her husband bargains for and obtains the lion at a low price? (b) What does she mean to imply when she says, "If you wanted the thing . . . why didn't you pay for it"?
8. This story is highly symbolic. (a) What may the train symbolize? (b) The station?

Applying

9. At the end of the story, the young wife feels isolated and alone. Her husband is confused by her unexpected reactions. (a) What has happened in this apparently trivial incident to make her feel shame, sickness, weariness, and emptiness? (b) How would you advise her husband to try to reassure her?

ANALYZING LITERATURE

Understanding Theme

Theme is the central idea in a literary work. Conflict, which occurs as the theme is developed, may present one or more dilemmas. A dilemma is a situation in which the main character, or protagonist, has to choose between undesirable alternatives. A short-story writer will not necessarily resolve all dilemmas, but may leave them for the reader to ponder. With a partner or in a small group, discuss two of the dilemmas —apart from isolation in marriage—that the young woman in "The Train from Rhodesia" appears to be facing. For example:

1. The dilemma of belonging to the well-to-do white minority in an impoverished black nation
2. The dilemma of trying to make connections with other people in a setting that makes it hard to do so

CRITICAL THINKING AND READING

Understanding Cultural Attitudes

The scene at the railway station that is described in "The Train from Rhodesia" is probably unfamiliar to you. The custom of white train passengers bargaining with native craftsmen for the purchase of their hand-carved wares reflects circumstances in southern Africa at the time the fictional incident occurs. Both the passengers on the train and the natives at the station accept the custom as normal. They see nothing to object to, although to an outside observer it might suggest inequality, racism, and exploitation.

Describe the scene at a subway, bus station, train station, or airport in your community or nearby. Your viewpoint should be that of total stranger to your community—a visitor from another country, perhaps. Point out any behavior, habits, or activities that appear unusual to you as an outsider.

UNDERSTANDING LANGUAGE

Using Concrete and Abstract Words

A **concrete word** is one that names a person or an object that can be directly observed through the senses. For example, you can see a pencil, hear a dog bark, taste salt. The words *pencil, bark,* and *salt* are concrete words. An abstract word is one that names qualities, conditions, or ideas that cannot be directly observed. Some interpretation is required. For example, while you can define *heroism, joy,* and *freedom,* you cannot point to them as objects. You must base your definition, instead, on specific examples of them.

Since a good short-story writer like Nadine Gordimer seldom moralizes, she favors concrete words in telling the story, although she may use abstract words in dialogue or to show the feelings of the main characters.

1. List and define five concrete words that contribute to the atmosphere of the story.
2. List and define five abstract words that show the thoughts or emotions of the characters.
3. The woman complains that her husband did not take the lion "decently." How do you think she would define the word decency? Explain your answer.

THINKING AND WRITING

Writing About Theme

The events in "The Train from Rhodesia" work together to reveal an insight into life. Identify the major theme in "The Train from Rhodesia." Write it in one carefully considered sentence. Then choose another short story in this book that has a similar theme. Write this theme, too, in a single sentence. Then write an essay in which you explain the similarities and differences between the two stories. Be specific. Give examples to support your main points. In revising the first draft, pay close attention to word choice. Have you chosen the right word in each place where an exact word is important—not merely a word that comes close? Careful word choice is one distinguishing mark of a good writer. Proofread your essay and share it with your classmates.

Answers

ANSWERS TO THINKING ABOUT THE SELECTION

Recalling

1. Three details are the fact that the train "came out of the red horizon," the mention of the "single straight track," and the mention of the "sand, that lapped all around, from sky to sky. . . ."
2. (a) The vendor wants three-and-six. (b) He finally accepts one-and-six.
3. (a) The young couple have already bought "the wooden buck, the hippos, the elephants, the baskets." (b) After the "unreality" of their vacation, the wife realizes that her relationship with "the man outside . . . is for good now."
4. (a) At the end of the story, the young woman sits with her back to the young man. (b) The lion, "fallen on its side in the corner" is, likewise, behind her.

Interpreting

5. The train means trade and the possibility of boosting the economy.
6. The young woman seems to want the lion because it is so beautifully made.
7. (a) She is suddenly disgusted by the way in which her husband has taken advantage of the native artist. (b) Answers may differ. Suggested Response: Perhaps she is disgusted by the way in which she, her husband, and their class routinely exploit natives.
8. (a) Suggested Response: The train represents a powerful force. It embodies authority, government, and the dominant civilization. (b) Suggested Response: The station seems to be a receptive, oppressed sufferer. It represents the people, popular culture, and the way life is actually lived.

Applying

9. (a) The ugliness in which she has been involved, that is, buying native artifacts for pennies, has suddenly been revealed to her. (b) Answers may differ. Suggested Response: Move away from Rhodesia would be one possibility.

ANSWERS TO ANALYZING LITERATURE

Have a member of each group report on the group's conclusions. Suggested Responses:

1. This dilemma may engender guilt.
2. This dilemma probably gives rise to frustration.

ANSWERS TO CRITICAL READING AND THINKING

Answers may differ. Emphasize that students should point out specific details.

ANSWERS TO UNDERSTANDING LANGUAGE

1. Answers will differ. Five concrete words that contribute to the mood of the story are *perspiring, carcass, creaking, jerking,* and *jostling.*
2. Answers will differ. Five abstract words that show the thoughts or emotions of the characters are *fear, unreality, laughter, triumph,* and *dismay.*
3. Answers will differ. The woman might define *decency* as "applying fair and considerate standards." She thought her husband should not take advantage of the natives.

THINKING AND WRITING

For help with this assignment, students can refer to Lesson 11, "Writing About Theme," in the Handbook of Writing About Literature.

More About the Author Alan Sillitoe himself worked in factories from the age of fourteen until he entered the air force during World War II. After the war, he lived in Majorca and became acquainted with Robert Graves, a successful writer, who encouraged Sillitoe to begin writing. His stories often deal with the ways in which young laborers like himself escape from the despair of their lives. How do you think Sillitoe felt about his life when he was young? How might he feel about his background now that he is successful?

ALAN SILLITOE

1928–

When Alan Sillitoe's first novel, *Saturday Night and Sunday Morning,* was published in 1958, one critic commented, "For the first time, English working-class life is treated . . . as a normal aspect of the human condition and as normal subject matter for a writer." Most of Sillitoe's heroes are rebellious members of the laboring class, "simple men caught in the cog-wheels of society."

Alan Sillitoe, the son of a tannery worker, was born and raised in Nottingham, an industrial city northwest of London. He left school at fourteen and worked in a bicycle plant and a plywood mill. From 1946 to 1949 he served in the Royal Air Force as a radio operator in Malaya.

He began to write while in Malaya, scrapping the manuscripts of nine complete novels before publishing and achieving immediate success with *Saturday Night and Sunday Morning*.

Sillitoe has been called one of the last of Britain's "angry young men," a group of writers in the 1950's and 1960's whose protagonists defy what they regard as outmoded political traditions and social norms. Like the other authors in this group, Sillitoe explores the theme of rebellion. Unlike them, he keeps his heroes firmly rooted in the working class, seeking self-discovery through a shared opposition to much of organized society.

His first collection of short stories, *The Loneliness of the Long-Distance Runner,* appeared in 1959. This collection, like his first novel, won immediate acclaim. The title story tells of a young juvenile delinquent who refuses to repent of the crimes that have landed him in an English reform school.

Sillitoe has also written poems and plays. Although his later work extends the range of his protagonists' rebellion, he remains primarily a chronicler of the English working classes. His restless energy has produced a body of work that is sometimes compared with that of D. H. Lawrence, another writer from Nottingham.

Objectives

To analyze the role of setting in a short story

Teaching Portfolio: Support Material

Teacher Backup, p. 000

Vocabulary Check, p. 00

Usage and Mechanics Worksheet, p. 00

Analyzing Literature Worksheet, p. 00

Critical Thinking and Reading Worksheet, p. 00

Language Worksheet, p. 00

Selection Test, p. 00

Art Transparency 17, *Beulah Road* by Eric Holt

GUIDE FOR READING

The Fiddle

The Writer's Techniques

Setting. The setting in a work of fiction is the place and time in which the action occurs. In some stories the setting is of great importance; in others it is not. A writer presents setting in various ways. A playwright can use costumes and stage scenery to help establish the place and time of the events. A novelist or short-story writer, on the other hand, has to do it all with words. The most direct way is through extended description, although this tends to slow down the action. Many contemporary writers prefer to establish the setting by interspersing description with ongoing narration. If the setting is vital to the theme and action of the story, the writer is likely to give it prominence, often through detailed and memorable description.

Look For

As you read Alan Sillitoe's "The Fiddle," notice how carefully the writer describes the setting. Try to determine why Harrison's Row is described in such thorough detail.

Writing

Every time and every place provides a setting. As you read this assignment, you are in a setting of your own. You may be in a classroom. You may be in a living room, or a bedroom, or a kitchen. Think of some words and ideas that you associate with your present setting. Jot them down. Then write ten descriptive sentences that would show a reader the main features of your immediate environment.

Vocabulary

Knowing the following words will help you as you read "The Fiddle."

sinewy (sin'yoo wē) *adj.*: Tough; vigorous; powerful (p. 1280)
persistent (pər sis'tənt) *adj.*: Continuing (p. 1280)
obliterate (ə blit'ə rāt) *v.*: To destroy utterly (p. 1281)
sublimity (sə blim'ə tē) *n.*: The quality of being majestic or noble (p. 1283)
harried (har'ēd) *v.*: Harassed (p. 1283)
brazen (brā'z'n) *adj.*: Bold; shameless (p. 1284)

Literary Focus Remind students that several authors use setting as if it were a character in their works—the Brontës, Dickens, and Hardy. The areas in which these authors lived and wrote had such an impact on them that they saw setting as a determining factor in their stories as well. The settings used by these authors have something else in common. Whether it's the urban blight of London and Radford or the windswept bleakness of the Yorkshire moors and the southwest downs, these settings set a controlling tone of despair.

Look For Suggest that your students attempt a sketch or map of the area that Sillitoe describes. Encourage them to include as much topographical detail as possible.

Writing Have students complete the writing activity by organizing the sentences into a paragraph that describes the setting that they have chosen. Remind them to organize their sentences in a logical sequence and to include transitions between sentences.

Vocabulary When students encounter these words in the story, ask them to offer alternative definitions in view of the context.

Motivation for Reading Have students think of a time or place in their lives in which they were very happy or very sad. What was it about that time or place that influenced their feelings? What kind of a story would they write about that time or place?

Thematic Idea Other selections based on the theme of men and women in conflict with their environments are *Pygmalion* (p. 1124), *The Tempest* (p. 305), *Wuthering Heights* (p. 912), and *Jane Eyre* (p. 924). As students read, have them compare and contrast the themes of these works with the theme of "The Fiddler."

Master Teacher Note Remind students that *Pygmalion* is, in part, a study in the effect of background and environment on people's lives. As they read, have students compare and contrast Sillitoe's and Shaw's attitudes toward the impact that our environments have on who we are.

Purpose-Setting Question What part does the setting play in this short story?

1 **Enrichment** Today Radford is populated by immigrants from former British colonies who came to Great Britain to find jobs and a better way of life.

2 **Enrichment** No matter what the environment, the British are proud of their flowers, particularly their roses, and produce beautiful gardens. Because the terraced houses that the people of Harrison Row live in are practically all the same, they—as do a great many who live in British neighborhoods like this—take great care in expressing their individuality in the beauty of their gardens.

3 **Reading Strategy** What is the tone of the story and what effect does it have on the story so far?

The Fiddle

Alan Sillitoe

1 On the banks of the sinewy River Leen, where it flowed through Radford, stood a group of cottages called Harrison's Row. There must have been six to eight of them, all in a ruinous condition, but lived in nevertheless.

They had been put up for stockingers[1] during the Industrial Revolution a hundred years before, so that by now the usual small red English housebricks had become weatherstained and, in some places, almost black.

Harrison's Row had a character all of its own, both because of its situation, and the
2 people who lived there. Each house had a space of pebbly soil rising in front, and a strip of richer garden sloping away from the kitchen door down to the diminutive River Leen at the back. The front gardens had almost merged into one piece of common ground, while those behind had in most cases retained their separate plots.

As for the name of the isolated row of cottages, nobody knew who Harrison had been, and no one was ever curious about it. Neither did they know where the Leen came from, though some had a general idea as to where it finished up.

A rent man walked down cobblestoned Leen Place every week to collect what money he could. This wasn't much, even at the best of times which, in the "thirties," were not too good—though no one in their conversation was able to hark back to times when they had been any better. 3

From the slight rise on which the houses stood, the back doors and windows looked across the stream into green fields, out towards the towers and pinnacles of Wollaton Hall in one direction, and the woods of Aspley Manor in the other.

After a warm summer without much rain the children were able to wade to the fields on the other side. Sometimes they could almost paddle. But after a three-day downpour when the air was still heavy with undropped water, and colored a menacing gun-metal blue, it was best not to go anywhere near the river, for one false slip and you would get sucked in, and be dragged by the powerful current along to the Trent some miles away. In that case there was no telling where you'd end up. The water seemed to flow into the River Amazon[2] itself, indicated by the fact that Frankie Buller swore blind how one day he had seen a crocodile snapping left and right downstream with a newborn baby in its mouth. You had to be careful—and that was a fact. During the persistent rain of one autumn water came up over the gardens and almost in at the back doors.

Harrison's Row was a cut-off place in that not many people knew about it unless they were familiar with the district. You 4 went to it along St. Peter's Street, and down

1. **stockingers** *n.*: Stocking weavers.

2. **River Amazon:** The largest, most powerful river in South America.

4 **Clarification** In Great Britain, the word *district* is an official term for neighborhood.

HILLSIDE IN WALES
L.S. Lowry
The Tate Gallery, London

Leen Place. But it was delightful for the kids who lived there because out of the back gardens they could go straight into the stream of the Leen. In summer an old tin hip bath would come from one of the houses. Using it for a boat, and stripped to their white skins, the children were happy while sun and weather lasted.

The youths and older kids would eschew this fun and set out in a gang, going far beyond, to a bend of the canal near Wollaton Pit where the water was warm—almost hot—due to some outlet from the mine itself. This place was known as "'otties," and they'd stay all day with a bottle of lemonade and a piece of bread, coming back late in the evening looking pink and tired as if out of a
5 prolonged dipping in the ritual bath. But a swim in 'otties was only for the older ones, because a boy of four had once been drowned there.

Harrison's Row was the last of Nottingham where it met the countryside. Its houses were at the very edge of the city, in the days before those numerous housing estates had been built beyond. The line of dwellings called Harrison's Row made a sort of outpost bastion before the country began.

Yet the houses in the city didn't immedi-
6 ately start behind, due to gardens and a piece of wasteground, which gave to Harrison's Row a feeling of isolation. It stood somewhat on its own, as if the city intended one day to leapfrog over it and obliterate the 7
country beyond.

On the other hand, any foreign army attacking from the west, over the green fields that glistened in front, would first 8
have to flatten Harrison's Row before getting into the innumerable streets of houses behind.

Across the Leen, horses were sometimes to be seen in the fields and, in other fields beyond, the noise of combine harvesters could be heard at work in the summer. Children living there, and adults as well, had the advantage of both town and country. On a fine evening late in August one of the unemployed husbands might be seen looking across at the noise of some machinery working in a field, his cap on but wearing no shirt, as if wondering why he was here and not over there, and why in fact he had ever left those same fields in times gone by to be forced into this bit of a suburb where he now had neither work nor purpose in life. He was not bitter, and not much
puzzled perhaps, yet he couldn't help being 9
envious of those still out there in the sunshine.

Humanities Note

Fine art: Detail, *Hillside in Wales*, by L.S. Lowry. The British artist Laurence Stephen Lowry (1887–1976) is best remembered for his simple and highly personal industrial landscapes populated with antlike figures. He was educated at the Municipal College of Art in Manchester and the Salford School of Art. His work was nationally famous in his lifetime and is now in the collections of leading museums.

The painting *Hillside in Wales* is one of his panoramic, detached views of the countryside. The canvas is packed with visual information presented in a deliberately naive way. The dots of people scurrying about, the rows of houses, the rushing river, and the hillside beyond all work together to form this patchwork commentary on modern life.

You might use the following questions for discussion:

1. What statement is the artist attempting to make with this landscape?
2. What is the effect of the seemingly naive technique of this painting?

5 **Discussion** What does the dropping of the *h* tells us about the people of Harrison Row?

6 **Clarification** Wasteground is land that may have once had a building on it or was used for another purpose but because of misuse can no longer be used at all.

7 **Reading Strategy** What does this image tells us about the future of Nottingham?

8 **Critical Thinking and Reading** Of what is the stark contrast between the green countryside and Harrison Row a symbol?

9 **Discussion** Why do you think that this man wasn't bitter?

10 Discussion What effect does the revelation that the narrator is the author have on the story?

11 Reading Strategy What is ironic about Ted's arrest?

12 Enrichment Part of the reason that the Industrial Revolution took place in this area was that of the rich coal veins that supplied the fuel for the new machinery.

13 Clarification *Brilliantine* is "a dressing that makes hair look glossy, almost like patent leather."

14 Literary Focus What effect does this parenthetical anecdote have on your understanding of the setting?

15 Discussion Why did deaf Mrs. Deaffy enjoy Jeff's music so much?

16 Clarification An escarpment is a very steep side of a hill or rock.

17 Discussion What might you infer about Jeff from this passage?

In my visions of leaving Nottingham for good—and they were frequent in those days—I never reckoned on doing so by the
10 high road or railway. Instead I saw myself wading or swimming the Leen from Harrison's Row, and setting off west once I was on the other side.

A tale remembered with a laugh at that time told about how young Ted Griffin, who had just started work, saw two policemen one day walking down Leen Place towards Harrison's Row. Convinced they had come to arrest him for meter-breaking, he ran through the house and garden, went over the fence, jumped into the Leen—happily not much swollen—waded across to the field, then four-legged it over the railway, and made his way to Robins Wood a mile or so beyond. A perfect escape route. He stayed two days in hiding, and then crept home at night, famished and soaked, only to find that the police had not come for him, but to question Blonk next door, who was suspected of poaching. When they did get Ted Griffin he was pulled out of bed one morning
11 even before he'd had time to open his eyes and think about a spectacular escape across the Leen.

Jeff Bignal was a young unmarried man of twenty-four. His father had been killed in the Great War,[3] and he lived with his mother
12 at Number Six Harrison's Row, and worked down nearby Radford Pit. He was short in height, and plump, his white skin scarred back and front with livid blue patches where he had been knocked with coal at the mine face. When he went out on Saturday night
13 he brilliantined his hair.

After tea in summer while it was still light and warm he would sit in his back garden playing the fiddle, and when he did everybody else came out to listen. Or they opened the doors and windows so that the sound of his music drifted in, while the woman stayed at the sink or wash-copper, or the man at his odd jobs. Anyone with a wireless would turn it down or off.

Even tall dark sallow-faced elderly Mrs. Deaffy (a kid sneaked into her kitchen one day and thieved her last penny-packet of cocoa and she went crying to tell Mrs. Atkin who, when her youngest came in, hit him so 14
hard with her elbow that one of his teeth shot out and the blood washed away most of the cocoa-stains around his mouth)—old Mrs. Deaffy stood by her back door as if she weren't stone deaf any more and could follow each note of Jeffrey Bignal's exquisite violin. She smiled at seeing everyone occu- 15
pied, fixed or entranced, and therefore no torment to herself, which was music enough to her whether she could hear it or not.

And Blonk, in the secretive dimness of the kitchen, went on mending his poaching nets before setting out with Arthur Bede next door on that night's expedition to Gunthorpe by the banks of the Trent, where the green escarpment between there and Knee- 16
ton was riddled with warrens and where, so it was said, if you stood sufficiently still the rabbits ran over your feet, and it was only necessary to make a quick grab to get one.

Jeff sat on a chair, oblivious to everybody, fed up with his day's work at the pit and only wanting to lose himself in his own music. The kids stopped splashing and shouting in the water, because if they didn't they might get hauled in and clouted with just the right amount of viciousness to suit the crime and the occasion. It had happened before, though Jeff had always been too far off to notice.

His face was long, yet generally cheerful —contrary to what one would expect—a smile settling on it whenever he met and passed anybody on the street, or on his way to the group of shared lavatories at the end of the Row. But his face was almost down and lost to the world as he sat on his chair and brought forth his first sweet notes of a summer's evening.

It was said that a neighbor in the last place they had lived had taught him to play 17

3. **Great War:** World War I.

like that. Others maintained it was an uncle who had shown him how. But nobody knew for sure because when someone asked directly he said that if he had any gift at all it must have come from God above. It was known that on some Sundays of the year, if the sun was out, he went to the Methodist chapel on St. Peter's Street.

He could play anything from "Greensleeves" to "Mademoiselle from Armentières'." He could do a beautiful heart-pulling version of Handel's *Largo*, and throw in bits from *The Messiah* as well. He would go from one piece to another with no rhyme or reason, from ridiculousness to sublimity, with almost shocking abruptness, but as the hour or so went by it all appeared easy and natural, part of a long piece coming from Jeff Bignal's fiddle while the ball of the sun went down behind his back.

To a child it seemed as if the songs lived in the hard collier's muscle at the top of his energetic arm, and that they queued one by
18 one to get out. Once free, they rushed along his flesh from which the shirtsleeves had been rolled up, and split into his fingertips, where they were played out with ease into the warm evening air.

The grass in the fields across the stream
19 was livid and lush, almost blue, and a piebald horse stood with bent head, eating oats out of a large old pram whose wheels had long since gone. The breeze wafted across from places farther out, from Robins Wood and the Cherry Orchard, Wollaton Roughs and Bramcote Hills and even, on a day that was not too hot, from the tops of the Pennines in Derbyshire.

Jeff played for himself, for the breeze against his arm, for the soft hiss of the flowing Leen at the end of the garden, and maybe also for the horse in the field, which took no notice of anything and which, having grown tired of its oats in the pram, bent its head over the actual grass and began to roam in search of succulent pastures.

In the middle of the winter Jeff's fiddling was forgotten. He went into the coal mine before it was light, and came up only after it had got dark. Walking down Leen Place, he complained to Blonk that it was hard on a man not to see daylight for weeks at a time.

"That's why I wain't go anywhere near the bleddy pit," Blonk said vehemently, though he had worked there from time to time, and would do so again when harried by his wife and children. "You'd do better to come out on a bit o' poaching with me and Arthur," he suggested.

It was virtually true that Jeff saw no daylight, because even on Sunday he stayed in bed most of the day, and if it happened to be dull there was little enough sky to be seen through his front bedroom window, which looked away from the Leen and up the hill.

The upshot of his complaint was that he would do anything to change such a situation. A man was less than an animal for putting up with it.

"I'd do anything," he repeated to his
mother over his tea in the single room down- 20
stairs.

"But what, though?" she asked. "What can you do, Jeff?"

"Well, how do I know?" he almost snapped at her. "But I'll do summat,[4] you can be sure of that."

He didn't do anything till the weather got better and life turned a bit sweeter. Maybe this improvement finally got him going, because it's hard to help yourself towards better things when you're too far down in the dumps.

On a fine blowy day with both sun and cloud in the sky Jeff went out in the morning, walking up Leen Place with his fiddle under his arm. The case had been wiped and polished.

In the afternoon he came back without it.

"Where's your fiddle?" Ma Jones asked.

He put an awkward smile on to his pale face, and told her: "I sold it."

---

4. summat: Something.

18 Discussion Why is this image of how Jeff's music is produced appropriate for a child of this district?

19 Clarification A piebald horse has black-and-white patches.

20 Reading Strategy What "anything" do you predict he will do to change his life?

21 **Reading Strategy** Predict how he will change his life with four quid.

22 **Discussion** Comment on the use of *rattled* here. Would the verb *traveled* be as effective?

23 **Discussion** Why would a look on his face make people question whether he would be able to play the violin again?

24 **Discussion** Why were the people amazed at how easy Jeff's transition had been?

25 **Enrichment** Chitterlings are the smaller intestines of a pig or other edible animal, and black pudding is a dessert made with blood. Both are considered delicacies or special treats by some segments of the British population.

26 **Discussion** What was an advantage to the loss of Jeff's music?

27 **Reading Strategy** What do you think happened to Jeff?

Master Teacher Note Place Art Transparency 17, *Beulah Road* by Eric Holt, on the overhead projector. You might mention that Holt is a contemporary British artist who has won praise and fame for his representations of British life today. When students have had a chance to look at this painting, ask them to offer their opinions on what the artist was trying to express. How does the painting compare with Sillitoe's story? When the story and painting are considered together, what impression of contemporary British society do the students get?

"Well I never! How much for?"

He was too shocked at her brazen question not to tell the truth: "Four quid."

"That ain't much."

"It'll be enough," he said roughly.

21 "Enough for what, Jeff?"

22 He didn't say, but the fact that he had sold his fiddle for four quid rattled up and down the line of cottages till everybody knew of it. Others swore he'd got ten pounds for it, because something that made such music must be worth more than a paltry four, and in any case Jeff would never say how much he'd really got for it, for fear that someone would go in and rob him.

They wondered why he'd done it, but had to wait for the answer, as one usually does. But there was nothing secretive about Jeff Bignal, and if he'd sold his music for a mess of pottage he saw no point in not letting them know why. They'd find out sooner or later, anyway.

All he'd had to do was make up his mind, and he'd done that lying on his side at the pit face while ripping coal out with his pick and shovel. Decisions made like that can't 23 be undone, he knew. He'd brooded on it all winter, till the fact of having settled it seemed to have altered the permanent expression of his face, and given it a new look which caused people to wonder whether he would ever be able to play the fiddle again anyway—at least with his old spirit and dash.

With the four quid he paid the first week's rent on a butcher's shop on Denman Street, and bought a knife, a chopper, and a bit of sharpening stone, as well as a wooden block. Maybe he had a quid or two more knocking around, though if he had it couldn't have been much, but with four quid and a slice of bluff he got enough credit from a wholesaler at the meat market downtown to stock his shop with mutton and beef, and 24 in a couple of days he was in trade. The people of Harrison's Row were amazed at how easy it was, though nobody had ever thought of doing it themselves.

Like a serious young man of business Mr. Bignal—as he was now known—parted his hair down the middle, so that he didn't look so young any more, but everyone agreed that it was better than being at Radford Pit. They'd seen how he had got fed up with selling the sweat of his brow.

No one could say that he prospered, but they couldn't deny that he made a living. And he didn't have to suffer the fact of not seeing daylight for almost the whole of the winter.

Six months after opening the shop he got married. The reception was held at the chapel on St. Peter's Street, which seemed to be a sort of halfway house between Harrison's Row on the banks of the Leen and the butcher's shop on Denman Street farther up.

Everybody from Harrison's Row was invited for a drink and something to eat; but he knew them too well to let any have either chops or chitterlings (or even black puddings) on tick[5] when they came into his shop. 25

The people of Harrison's Row missed the sound of his fiddle on long summer evenings, though the children could splash and shout with their tin bathtub undisturbed, floundering through shallows and scrambling up to grass on the other bank, and wondering what place they'd reach if they walked without stopping till it got dark. 26

Two years later the Second World War began, and not long afterwards meat as well as nearly everything else was put on the ration. Apart from which, Jeff was only twenty-six, so got called up into the army. He never had much chance to make a proper start in life, though people said that he came out all right in the end. 27

The houses of Harrison's Row were condemned as unfit to live in, and a bus depot stands on the site.

---

5. tick: Credit.

Answers

ANSWERS TO THINKING ABOUT THE SELECTION
Recalling

1. (a) The story takes place during the depression, one hundred years after the Industrial Revolution. (b) Harrison's Row is in Radford, a suburb of Nottingham. (c) The Radford mine is very near where he lives.
2. (a) The younger children swim in an old tin hip bath or the River Leen when the water ebbs a bit in the summer. (b) The water in the river rises and turns it into a dangerous torrent. (c) The older swimmers go to a bend in the canal near the Wollaton Pit; the water is warm because of some outlet from the mine itself.
3. (a) Jeff says that his ability is a gift

The packed mass of houses on the hill behind—forty years after Jeff Bignal sold his violin—is also vanishing, and high-rise hencoops (as the people call them) are put in their place. The demolition crew knock down ten houses a day—though the foreman told me there was still work for another two years.

Some of the houses would easily have
28 lasted a few more decades, for the bricks were perfect, but as the foreman went on: "You can't let them stand in the way of progress"—whatever that means.

The people have known each other for generations but, when they are moved to
their new estates and blocks of flats,[6] they will know each other for generations more, because as I listen to them talking, they speak a language which, in spite of everything and everyone, never alters. 29

6. flats: Apartments.

THINKING ABOUT THE SELECTION

Recalling

1. (a) What is the time, or era, of the events in this story? (b) In what city is Harrison's Row? (c) In what section of the city is the mine in which Jeff Bignal works?
2. (a) Where do the younger children swim? (b) Why do they not swim there after a heavy rain? (c) Where do the older children swim?
3. (a) Whom does Jeff Bignal credit for his ability to play the violin? (b) Whom do his neighbors credit?
4. (a) What does Jeff finally do with his fiddle? (b) Why does he do this?

Interpreting

5. Why is the River Leen important to the people of Harrison's Row?
6. Why is the fiddle important to Jeff Bignal?
7. (a) How does Jeff rebel against his situation in life? (b) How does Blonk rebel?
8. Why will Jeff not extend credit to the people from Harrison's Row?
9. (a) What do you think the fiddle symbolizes? (b) How does this symbol help reveal the story's theme?

Applying

10. (a) What do you think of Jeff's decision to sell his fiddle? (b) How happy do you think Jeff's butcher shop made him? Explain.

ANALYZING LITERATURE

Understanding Setting

Setting is the time and place in which the events in a literary work occur. In "The Fiddle" Alan Sillitoe describes the physical setting of Harrison's Row and the activities that formerly went on there. The entire first section of the story establishes the setting. You learn a great deal about Harrison's Row before you learn anything at all about the protagonist, Jeff Bignal. The setting helps to define the people in the story.

1. The narrator is deeply interested in the history and geography of Harrison's Row. Nevertheless, he says that "no one knew who Harrison had been, and no one was ever curious about it. Neither did they know where the Leen came from, though some had a general idea as to where it finished up." How do those details about the setting help to characterize the people who live in Harrison's Row?
2. The brief last section of the story returns to the setting. How do you think the narrator feels about a bus depot standing on the site of Harrison's Row and the construction of "high rise hencoops"? Explain.
3. Slang is highly informal language that is appropriate among friends or in casual situations. (a) Find three examples of slang in "The Fiddle." (b) How does the use of slang add local color to the story?

from God. (b) His neighbors tell each other that his uncle or a former neighbor taught him.

4. (a) He sells his fiddle for four quid. (b) He uses the money to set himself up in business as a butcher; he can no longer work in the mine because he doesn't want to go months at a time without seeing the sun.

Interpreting

5. The people of Harrison Row see the river as a link with the rest of the world; it represents the opportunity to get away from their environment.
6. Jeff's fiddle is his opportunity to escape Harrison Row; when he plays his violin, he is far away from where he sits in his back garden.
7. (a) Jeff rebels by selling his escape route—the violin—and escaping the mine by buying a butcher shop. (b) Blonk rebels by refusing to get a regular job; instead, he poaches game probably on the nearby private estates.
8. Jeff understands too well the economic situation in the area; he is not willing to risk what he has accomplished because others can't or don't pay.
9. (a) Answers will differ, though some should see the fiddle as a symbol of the beauty that can manifest itself in otherwise dreary surroundings. (b) It establishes a vivid, concrete contrast with the kind of life found in Harrison's Row.

28 **Discussion** How is the demolition of the houses on Harrison Row "in the way of progress" related to Jeff Bignal's act of selling his fiddle?

29 **Discussion** What is the relationship between Jeff Bignal's music and the "language" of the people of Harrison's Row?

(Answers begin on p. 1284.)

Applying

10. (a) and (b)Answers will differ. Students should support their opinions with evidence drawn from the story.

ANSWERS TO ANALYZING LITERATURE

1. These details highlight the fact that the people of this area are beaten down by their circumstances enough to have lost their interest in and curiosity about life.
2. The author leaves the feeling that it doesn't matter what buildings are there—the area is still dreary and filled with despair. The people are more important, and even though they will be moved from each other, they will keep in touch.
3. (a) Three examples are "the bleddy pit," "But I'll do summat," and "slice of bluff." (b) Such slang makes concrete what the people sound like when they talk, and thus adds to the story's local color.

Challenge How does Jeff's Nottingham compare with the Nottingham of Robin Hood's day? Have students write a short essay comparing and contrasting the area in the two different time periods.

Writing Across the Curriculum In cooperation with the history department, have students write short essays describing the positive and negative effects of the Industrial Revolution on the people and the land in the English midlands. Have students share their essays by reading them aloud.

More About the Author In terms of her fiction, Margaret Drabble's involvement in the theater and with acting is more than a mere biographical footnote. Drabble, who acted with the Royal Shakespeare Company, learned important strategies for creating convincing characterization on the stage. This ability to draw upon experience and theatrical artifice to create characters has undoubtedly enriched her fictional portraits. In writing the play *Bird of Paradise* (1969) and several screenplays for film and for television, Drabble directly calls upon theatrical training in order to bring believable, dynamic characters to life. In writing fiction, Drabble indirectly employs theatrical technique in her attentiveness to details of dress, gesture, speech, mood, atmosphere, and setting. Her work contains direct references to theater as well. For example, the main character in her novel *The Garrick Year* (1964) marries an actor in a theater company. Drabble's images and rich adjective-filled descriptions bring forth characters that, for a moment, live on the page. Discuss how an understanding of theater and acting might affect a writer's work.

MARGARET DRABBLE

1939–

If Margaret Drabble had not become a novelist, she might have become a famous actress. While at Cambridge University she concentrated on the theater and at one point played opposite the noted actor Derek Jacobi. Upon graduation, she joined the Royal Shakespeare Company, understudying Vanessa Redgrave as Imogen in *Cymbeline*. She then left the theater, began writing fiction, and succeeded so well in her new career that a critic in 1980 observed, "She is becoming the novelist people will turn to a hundred years from now to find out how things were. . . ."

Born in Sheffield, Drabble came from a cultured and well-educated family. Her father was a circuit judge and her mother an English teacher. "A fiery child with a hyperactive mind," according to her mother, Margaret attended a Quaker boarding school prior to Cambridge. After college, she abandoned the theater for motherhood. While she was pregnant with the first of her three children, she began to write fiction. Her first novel, *A Summer Bird-Cage,* was published in 1962. Over the years she has continued to write novels that have gained both critical and popular success. Among her best-known works are *The Millstone* (1965), *The Waterfall* (1969), *The Realms of Gold* (1975), and *The Middle Ground* (1980). Most of Drabble's protagonists are, like their creator, well-educated professional women: scholars, poets, journalists.

Drabble, in commenting on her own work, declares that she is firmly committed to the realistic tradition of the nineteenth century. Although sometimes called a "women's novelist," she disavows feminism as a theme, believing that equal rights and opportunity for women are part of a larger whole. She maintains that her fundamental concerns are "privilege, justice, and salvation." Working in the literary tradition of Jane Austen, Charlotte Brontë, and George Eliot, she creates brilliantly realized characters who reflect the dilemmas of women in the modern world, women who are trying to integrate the demands of family life and a career.

Objectives

1 To identify direct and indirect evidence in a story
2 To write about characterization

Teaching Portfolio: Support Material

Teacher Backup, p. 000

Vocabulary Check, p. 00

Usage and Mechanics Worksheet, p. 00

Analyzing Literature Worksheet, p. 00

Critical Thinking and Reading Worksheet, p. 00

Language Worksheet, p. 00

Selection Test, p. 00

Art Transparency 18, *Landscape from a Dream* by Paul Nash

GUIDE FOR READING

A Voyage to Cythera

The Writer's Techniques

Flat and Round Characters. A flat character, sometimes called a stereotype or stock character, is a one-dimensional human being in literature. For example, in "The Schartz-Metterklume Method," Saki does not portray the Quabarls family in depth. It is their very shallowness, in fact, that he wishes to satirize. He has therefore made them flat characters, or stereotypes. They do not change in the course of the story, and they contribute to the plot in a predictable way.

The fictional opposite of a flat character is a round character. A round character is a three-dimensional portrait that readers can accept as resembling an actual person. The writer may provide a detailed description of the character. More important, the writer will reveal the character's motivations, emotions, and inner conflicts. Round characters may be complex, unpredictable, and inconsistent, just like real people. In narrative fiction they are generally *dynamic*—that is, they change or grow in some way during the story. (Flat characters are *static*—they do not change or grow.) An example of a round character in a short story is Margaret in Doris Lessing's "A Mild Attack of Locusts."

Look For

As you read Margaret Drabble's "A Voyage to Cythera," consider the ways in which the author makes Helen, the protagonist, a fully rounded, true-to-life character. Try also to identify the flat characters in the story.

Writing

An epigraph is a quotation at the beginning of a book, chapter, or story. Read the epigraph to Margaret Drabble's story carefully. Then brainstorm for several minutes on the associations and emotions suggested by this fragment of Rilke's poetry. Jot down your impressions of what the epigraph (and the story's title) may suggest about the narrative to follow.

Vocabulary

Knowing the following words will help you as you read "A Voyage to Cythera."

piazzas (pē az′əs) *n.*: Open public squares (p. 1288)
irrepressible (ir′i pres′ə b'l) *adj.*: Not able to be restrained (p. 1289)
solace (säl′is) *n.*: Comfort in grief or trouble (p. 1292)
divination (div′ə nā′shən) *n.*: Clever guess (p. 1292)
intimation (in′tə mā′shən) *n.*: Hint (p. 1293)
anterior (an tir′ē ər) *adj.*: At or toward the front (p. 1297)

Literary Focus Point out that characterization is the way a writer chooses to reveal characters. A writer may reveal what a character is like through dialogue, description, and narration. Explain to students that they may learn what characters are like by carefully reading details in a story. For example, what does a character look like? How does he or she dress? What does a character say? How does he or she speak? What does a character think and feel? What actions does a character take? To create a round character, a writer provides details. When a writer provides few details, then the character is more likely a flat character. Point out that both flat and round characters appear in "A Voyage to Cythera."

Master Teacher Note Before reading "A Voyage to Cythera," place Art Transparency 18 on the overhead projector, Paul Nash's *Landscape from a Dream.* You might then ask your students to compare the contemporary British literature they have read with the contemporary British painting. Do the painters seem to have the same artistic aims as the writers, or do the two kinds of artists diverge in what they are trying to do? Who seem more traditional, the painters or the writers? Which do students prefer, contemporary British art or contemporary British painting?

Look For Your **less advanced** students may find it difficult to distinguish between flat and round characters. Have them create a chart that lists the names of all of the characters in "A Voyage to Cythera." As they read, have them list physical details about each character. Have them also list the personality traits of the characters. Guide them to look for details that the writer gives about each character.

Writing Tell students that the purpose of an epigraph is to set a mood or tone. After they read the epigraph from Rainer Maria Rilke's poem, guide students to determine the mood. Suggest that they list specific images and phrases from the poem.

Vocabulary Have your **less advanced** students read the vocabulary words and their definitions aloud. Ask students to make up sentences or phrases in which they use the words correctly.

Motivation for Reading Tell students that the main character in "A Voyage to Cythera" especially loves to travel by train. Ask them to describe any experiences that they have had riding on trains. Find out if students have taken any long trips by train. Did they meet any interesting people? What did they like about the train? What did they dislike? If students have never ridden on a train, then ask them to describe where they would most like to visit by train.

Master Teacher Note The title of this story contains a significant allusion. Explain to students that there is a real island called Cythera, which is the southernmost and easternmost island in the Ionian Sea near Greece. Help students locate this island on a world map or a globe. Explain that the island's ancient name was Porphyrusa, which derives from the Greek word meaning "purple." The island's ancient name referred to its chief export, a purple dye that was obtained from local mollusks. Provide students with pictures of the island, if possible, or have them find out what the island is like today.

Thematic Idea Other selections that deal with the theme of love are "My Last Duchess," by Robert Browning (page 824) and "Sonnet 43," by Elizabeth Barrett Browning (page 870).

Purpose-Setting Question What role does love play in this short story?

1 **Enrichment** The allusion in "A Voyage to Cythera" relates to a myth about the Greek island called Cythera, or Kithira, on which the cult of Aphrodite flourished. Aphrodite was the Greek goddess of love and beauty. The journey to Cythera, depicted as the island of love in French and Italian myths, is considered to be difficult and dangerous.

1

A Voyage to Cythera[1]

Margaret Drabble

Beloved, lost to begin with, never greeted,
I do not know what tones most please you.
No more when the future's wave
hangs poised is it you I try to discern there.
All the greatest images in me,
far-off experienced landscape,
towers and towns and bridges and
unsuspected turns of the way,
and the power of those lands
once intertwined with the life of the gods:
mount up within me to mean you,
who forever elude.

Oh, you are the garden. . . .
—*Rainer Maria Rilke*[2]

2 There are some people who cannot get onto a train without imagining that they are about to voyage into the significant unknown; as though the notion of movement were inseparably connected with the notion of discovery, as though each displacement of the body were a displacement of the soul. 3,4 Helen was so much this way, and with so little lasting justification, that she was continually surprising herself by the intensity of her expectation; she could get excited by the prospect of any journey longer than 30 miles, and the thought of travel to the Continent was enough to reduce her to a state of feverish anticipation. The mere mention of the names of certain places would make her tremble, and she was addicted to railway stations, air terminals, ports, motorways, travel brochures, and all other points and emblems of departure. 5 A phrase in a novel could make her feel weak with desire, and when once at the Gare de l'Est[3] in Paris she saw a train with Budapest written on it, she felt her skin tighten and her hair stand on end. Her most erotic dreams were not of men but of places; she would dream of piazzas and marble fountains, of mountains and terraces with great lumps of baroque statuary, of great buildings abandoned in green fields, and she would wake from these dreams cold with the sweat of fading passion. There was a certain angle of road that never failed to affect her, whenever she approached it: a rising angle, with a bare empty curve breasting infinity, the blue-sky space of infinity. She always felt that the sea might lie beyond such rising nothingness, and sometimes it was the sea, but more 6 often it was the Caledonian[4] Market or a row of Hampstead houses; though whatever it was was somehow irrelevant, for it was that tense moment of expectation before revelation that she so much cherished.

7 Once she talked of this preoccupation of hers to a much-traveled old man, and he said that she felt this way because whenever

---

1. Cythera (si thir′ ə): A Greek island, near which the Greek goddess of love, Aphrodite, was supposed to have arisen full-grown from the sea.

2. Rainer Maria Rilke: A German poet (1875–1926). The lines are from an untitled poem by Rilke.

3. Gare de l'Est (gär də lest): A Paris train station.

4. Caledonian: Scottish.

2 **Reading Strategy** How do some people view travel? Summarize the meaning of this passage. Compare this passage with the epigraph of the story.

3 **Discussion** How does Helen feel about travel? Discuss how you feel about traveling to new places.

4 **Clarification** The Continent is another way of referring to Europe; Helen obviously lives on an island near Europe.

5 **Critical Thinking and Reading** Describe in your own words how Helen responds to the idea of travel. Is the evidence given in this sentence direct or indirect?

6 **Clarification** The references to the Caledonia Market and Hampstead houses reveal that the setting of the story is England.

she went to a new place she hoped to fall in love. He had been the same, he said; restless, expectant; and she knew that he was telling the truth, for his life illustrated his explanation. "When I was young," he said, "I thought there was a woman waiting for me in every railway compartment, on every airplane, in every hotel. How can one not think this? One thinks the plane will crash, and that one will die, and that one must die in the arms of the woman in the next seat. Isn't that so?"

And she had, in a way, thought that it was so, though the truth was that she her-
8 self would never fall in love in any of these temporary places, for she could not speak to strangers. Though that in itself proved nothing, for she supposed that nevertheless she might one day do so, and that it might be for this one moment of sudden communication that she so persistently sought. People spoke to her, from time to time, but always the wrong people, always the motherly and the fatherly men and the dull irrepressible youths. Her own kind did not speak to her, nor she to them. She traveled once overnight from Milan, alone in a compartment with a girl who was reading the same book she herself was reading; a book both of them might have been proud to acknowledge and not a word did they exchange. Another time, in a crowded train from Edinburgh, she sat opposite a woman who started to weep as
9 the train left the station; she wept silently and effortlessly for hours, great tears rolling down her white cheeks into the neck of her emerald-green sweater, and at York Helen offered her a cigarette, and she declined it, and ceased weeping. On another occasion a man kissed her in a corridor as they drew into Oxford; she liked him, he was a lovely man, but he was drunk and she turned away her face and turned up the collar of her coat.

And yet despite these wasted opportunities she continued to expect. Truly, she thought to herself, as she got into the London train at Reading Station late one cold night, truly, it is a proof of madness that the prospect of this journey should not appall. It is cold, the train is half an hour late, I am hungry; this is the kind of situation about which I hear my friends most tirelessly and tiresomely complain. And yet I am looking forward to it. I shall sit here in the dark and the cold, with nothing to watch but the reflection of my own face in the cold pane, and I shall not care. As soon as the train moves, I shall sit back, and feel it move with me, and feel that I am moving, although I know quite well that all I am doing is going back home again to an empty flat.[5] There will be rain and steam on the glass of this window by my face, and I shall look at it, and that will be all. What a hardened case I am, that such dull mileage should recall those other landscapes, those snowy precipices, those sunny plains, those fields of corn, those gritty swaying breakfasts in the pale light of transient Switzerland or angel-watched Marseilles. I am a child, I like to rock and dream, I dream as if I were in a cradle.

And she shut her eyes, waiting for the whistle and the metallic connections of machinery; so with her eyes shut she did not see the man come into the compartment, and could never know for certain whether he had seen her, whether he had joined her because he had wanted to join her. All she knew was that when she opened her eyes, aware of the intrusion, aware of the draft from the opened door, he was already there, putting his overcoat up on the rack, arranging his books and papers on the seat next to him, settling himself in the empty compartment as far away from her as he could, on the corridor side, diagonally opposite, where she could not fail to watch him. She turned her fur collar up defensively against her face, and arranged her legs more tidily together, and opened her book upon her knee, disclaiming all threat of human contact, coldly repelling any acknowledgment of her

5. **flat** *n.*: Apartment.

7 **Discussion** Discuss the old man's explanation of Helen's preoccupation with travel. Do you agree or disagree? Why?

8 **Critical Thinking and Reading** What sort of person is Helen? How do you know? Is the evidence given direct or indirect?

9 **Critical Thinking and Reading** Discuss Helen's travel experiences. Explain how this passage reveals her attitude toward travel either directly or indirectly.

10 **Literary Focus** How does Helen describe herself? What do you think she is like? Is Helen a flat or a round character? Explain your answer.

1289

Humanities Note

Fine art, *Shunters,* 1965, by James Dolby. Dolby (1909–1975) was a British wood engraver and teacher. Educated at the Keighly School of Art and the Royal Academy of Art, Dolby taught art at many of England's prestigious schools. He is best known for his pioneering efforts to revive the ancient art of wood engraving. Wood engraving was one of the earliest means of reproducing words and images. Designs are incised in a block of soft wood with a sharp tool. The blocks are then inked and pressed onto paper, leaving a black-and-white image. With the advent of photography this method of reproduction fell into disuse. Its revival in the twentieth century is strictly as a fine art form.

Works such as *Shunters* show us how modern images and style can effectively use the technique of wood engraving. The forms of the train and station are executed in a sharp, simplified style, which pares the shapes into geometric components. The striking black-and-white image produced by the engraving complements the streamlined spareness of the work. A benefit of this technique is that it allows the artist to produce multiple copies of the work. The result is an original art form that is more affordable to the public than a painting.

Consider using this question for discussion: How does this engraving convey a sense of urgency and motion?

SHUNTERS 1965
James Dolby

presence, and all the time she watched him discreetly through her half-shut eyes. Be-
11 cause the truth was that not since she was 17, more years ago than she cared to think, had she sat on a train so near to such a man. When she was 17 she had sat in a compartment with an actor, on the late night train to Brighton, and he had talked to her all the way, and amused her by imitating Laurence Olivier[6] for her and other famous men whom she did not recognize and when they had
12 parted on the station he had kissed her soft and girlish and impressionable cheek, and murmured, "Bless you, bless you," as though he had a right to bless. She had subsequently followed his unremarkable career, catching sight of his name in the *Radio Times*, admiring him once on the television, glimpsing him as he passed on the cinema screen; she felt quietly possessive about him, quietly amused by her sense of intimacy with one who must so long ago have forgotten her, and who would hardly now recognize her from what she then had been. Sometimes she wondered idly whether her preoccupation with journeys might not date from this experience; but chronologically this was not so, for her preoccupation had long preceded it. She had been this way since childhood, when she had shrunk and trembled at the sight of the huge pistons, when she had stopped her ears in delighted terror as she heard the roar of the approaching seaside train.

This man, this night, did not look as though he wished to amuse her with imitations of Laurence Olivier. He looked preoccupied. In fact, the more she watched him, the more she realized that he was almost
13,14 grotesquely preoccupied. He was restless; he could not sit still: he kept picking up one book from his pile, then another, then turning over the pages of his *New Statesman*, then staring out into the corridor and onto the dark platform. At first she thought that he might be waiting for someone to come, half-expecting somebody to join him, but she decided that this was not so, for she could perceive no augmenting of his anxiety as the time drew on, no sudden start when the loudspeaker apologized for the delay and said that the train would leave in two minutes; nor did his nervousness seem to be directed toward the door and the platform, as it would have been had he been waiting. She recalled that she herself had once developed a dreadful pain in the neck from sitting with her neck to the window through which she knew that she might glimpse the first sign of a long-awaited arrival. But this man's nervousness was as it were diffused, rather than directed; it attached itself to nothing and to everything. She could not take her eyes off him, and not only because of the nakedness of his condition, which in another might have appeared merely ludicrous; indeed, embarrassment would have turned away her eyes, had it not been for the extreme elegance of his gestures, and the lovely angles into which each struggle against immobility brought him. There was the way he had of clutching his eyebrows with one wide-spanned long nicotine-fingered hand that filled her with an intense 15
delight; the hand covered the eyes, bringing to him no doubt an illusion of concealment, but she could see beneath it the anxious movement of the lips, trembling with some expression that she could not catch, with speech or smiling or perhaps with a sigh. And as he made this gesture, each time, he tossed his head slightly backward, and then again forward, so that his long hair fell tenderly over his fingers. It was the color that she had always liked, but she had never before seen it adorning such vexed, haggard, and experienced features: for it was a dark gold, the color of health and innocence. It was a dark golden yellow, and it was streaked with gray. It was soft hair, and it fell gently.

6. Laurence Olivier: A famous British actor (1907–).

11 **Reading Strategy** How old do you think Helen is?

12 **Enrichment** Margaret Drabble's own involvement in theater is evoked in this passage. The man that Helen met on a train long ago was an actor who entertained her with impressions; she followed his career on radio, television, and in films.

13 **Literary Focus** Describe the man on the train in your own words. Is he a flat or a round character? How do you know?

14 **Clarification** The *New Statesman* is a British journal that began publication in 1913. It is a review that frequently expresses political views of the left.

15 **Critical Thinking and Reading** How does Helen feel about the man on the train? How do you know? Is the evidence given direct or indirect?

16 Discussion What is Helen's interpretation of the man's emotions? Why does Helen find washing cups and emptying bins comforting?

17 Critical Thinking and Reading What significance do the letters hold for Helen? Is Helen's assumption based on direct or indirect evidence?

18 Discussion Why does Helen weep? Whom do you think Helen is actually describing?

19 Critical Thinking and Reading What do you infer that the man is doing? What kind of evidence is given to help you make this inference?

When the train moved off, he flung himself back into his corner, and shut his eyes, with an appearance of resolution, as though his own restlessness had finally begun to irritate him: as though he had decided to sit still. Helen looked out of the window by her face, into the lights and darkness of the disappearing town. In one piece of glass she could see the reflection of his face, and she watched it, quite confidently aware that he would not be able to keep his eyes shut, and after a few minutes he was leaning forward in his seat once more, his elbows on his knees, staring at the ground. Then, even as she watched, she saw a thought strike him: she saw the conception of the idea, she saw him reach into his pocket and take out a pack of cigarettes and a box of matches, and abstract a cigarette, and light it, all with the dreamy movements of a habitual smoker, and yet with a kind of surprise, for the truth was, as she could so clearly see, that he had even in his abstraction forgotten the possibility of such a trivial solace. As he drew on the cigarette she could see his relief, his gratitude toward his own recollection. The 16 smoke consoled him, and she could feel in her the nature of the consolation: for she herself, when tormented by love, had found comfort in the repetition of small and necessary acts, in washing cups and emptying bins and fastening her stockings and remembering that it was time to have a meal. It seemed clear to her that it was love that was tormenting him: she knew those painful symptoms of disease.

And indeed, ten minutes later, when the ash of his last activity lay scattered all over the floor and all over his trousers, he stood up and got a packet of letters out of his overcoat pocket, and began to read them. He could not more clearly have indicated his malady if he had turned to her and told her 17 what was in his mind. She watched the reflection of his face as he read, ashamed now to watch him directly, though she knew that he could not know that she so keenly watched him, that she was so expert in the intimate language of his state. She felt that she could tell everything from the way he handled those letters: he was still rapt in the first five minutes of love, that brief and indefinite breathless pause before familiarity, affection, disillusion, rot, decay. The number of letters in his hands supported her divination, as well as the quality of his attention; there were five of them, only five, and the paper of them was new, although they were crumbling wearily at the folds from overuse. She felt such pangs, in his presence, of she knew not what: of envy, of regret, of desire. At his age, with those graying strands and those profound wrinkles, he must surely know the folly of his obsession, and the inevitable tragic close before him; and she found such a willful confrontation of pain almost unbearably moving. She herself, enduring daily the painful death of such an attitude, the chilly destination of such deliberately romantic embarkations, could hardly prevent the 18 tears from rising to her eyes; and in fact, they rose, warm in the cold skin of her lids, making her nose prick and her eyes ache, yet warm, coming from within her, and chilling only at the touch of the outside air. Absurd, she said to herself, absurd: absurd to weep. His image turned into a blur, and it was like the image of time itself, human, lovely, perishing, intent.

When he had read and reread his letters, he stood up again, and got a pen out of his coat pocket, and tore a piece of paper off a block of typing paper, and started to write. He wrote slowly, after the first three words, hesitantly, as though what he was saying 19 was of no interest, as though all the interest lay in the way of saying it. She wondered what he was, who he was, what his woman was, and jealously whether she were worth such care. He took a quarter of an hour to write his letter, and when he had finished it he had covered only half a page. She wondered whether he would have an envelope, and saw that he had; it was a brown business envelope. He folded his letter up and put it in the envelope, and then sealed it up. She waited for him to write the address, but he did not write the address: he sat there looking down at the small brown oblong, and as he looked at it she became in some indefinable way aware that he had become aware of her own presence, that he was at last considering her, in some significant way. Later, she wondered how this shadowy and delicate intimation could ever have reached her—for reach her it did, and she was one of those who believe that no intimations are too delicate to exist—and she concluded that it could only have been a sudden stillness on his part, a sudden fading of restlessness, as he returned from whatever other place he had been in to contemplate her in her proximity. She felt his attention: she endured it, for five minutes at least, before he spoke.

She was pretending to read when he spoke to her. He said to her, "I wonder, I wonder if you would do something for me?" and she looked up and met his eyes, and found that he was smiling at her with a most peculiar mixture of diffidence and vanity: he was truly nervous at the prospect of speak-
20 ing to her, and those five silent minutes
were a measure of his nervousness, and yet at the same time he had taken the measure of her curiosity and helpless attraction: she knew that he knew that she would like to be addressed. And his tone enchanted her, for it was her own tone: a tone of cool, anxious, irresistible appeal. She knew that he too did not speak often to strangers.

"It depends what it is," she said, smiling back at him with his own smile.

"It's a very simple thing," he said, "not at all incriminating. Or at least, not for you."

"It would be, then, for you?" she said.

"Of course it would," he said. "That's why I'm making the effort of asking you to do it."

"What is it?" she said.

"I wondered if you would address this 21
envelope for me," he said.

"Well, yes," she said. "I don't see any harm in that. I'd do that for you."

"I thought you would do it," he said. "If I hadn't thought that you would, I wouldn't have asked you. I wouldn't have liked it if you had said no."

"I might ask you what it was about me that made you think I would say yes," she said, "but such a question might embarrass you."

"Oh," he said, "oh, no," rising to his feet and crossing to her with the envelope, "oh, no, I don't mind answering, it was
because of that book you're reading, and the 22
kind of shoes you're wearing, and the way your hair is. I liked that book when I read it."

And then he sat down by her, and handed her the envelope, and said, "Look, I'll write it down for you and you can copy it. It's hard to hear when people dictate things, isn't it?"

And he wrote the name and address on another piece of his block of paper. He wrote:

Mrs. H. Smithson,
24 Victoria Place, 23
London N.W.1.

And Helen dutifully copied it out, on the brown envelope, then handed it back to him.

"I hope," she said, "that my handwriting is sufficiently unlike yours."

"I was thinking," he said, "that after all it's rather similar. But dissimilar enough."

Then he said no more, but he remained sitting by her. She would in a way have preferred him to move, because where he now was she could not really see him, either overtly or covertly. And she had nothing to say to him: for she could hardly have said, I
was right about you, I guessed right. He said 24

20 **Reading Strategy** Describe in your own words how the man looks at Helen.

21 **Discussion** Discuss why the man on the train might make this request.

22 **Critical Thinking and Reading** How did the man know that Helen would carry out his request? Is the evidence given direct or indirect?

23 **Discussion** Discuss the significance of this address. To whom is the man writing?

24 **Clarification** A fourpenny stamp is one that costs four pennies. A fourpenny is an old silver coin worth fourpence.

25 **Enrichment** London is divided into postal units that designate areas by compass direction and by number. For example, *S.W.* refers to southwestern London. Other designations include N.W., N.E., and S.E., for northwest, northeast, and southeast. The numbers in London addresses pinpoint a smaller region within each compass region. Point out that the corollary to these postal divisions in the United States might be the zip code, which indicates state and city locations.

26 **Literary Focus** What does the dialogue reveal? How do you learn more about each character through their words? Analyze how dialogue helps create round characters.

27 **Discussion** Compare and contrast Helen's encounter with the man on the train with those "wasted opportunities" for contact on page 1289.

28 **Enrichment** The Sirens were mythical sea nymphs who lived on a Greek island. The Sirens, part bird and part woman, sang such tempting songs that they lured sailors to their destruction. When the Greek hero Odysseus, the king of Ithaca, was returning home from the Trojan War, he put wax in the sailors' ears so that they would not be tempted by the Sirens' songs. Today the meaning of the word *siren,* a tempting or seductive woman, reflects this tale. Helen alludes to this myth, told by Homer in the *Odyssey,* because she, too, is lured by a beautiful illusion that could potentially harm her. In pursuing the illusion of love, Helen may become as detached from the real world as do the sailors who allow themselves to be lured by the Sirens.

29 **Literary Focus** Discuss Helen's attempt to give form to Mrs. Smithson. Is Mrs. Smithson a flat or a round character? How do you know?

nothing to her, for a while: he got a wallet from his pocket, and took out a sheet of fourpenny stamps, and tore one off, licked it, and stuck it on. She liked watching his hands, and the way they moved. Then, still holding the letter, he said to her, "Where do you live?"

She must have recoiled slightly from the question, because immediately he followed it up with, "Only, I was meaning, from the point of view of postmarks."

"Oh," she said. "I see. Yes. I live in
25 S.W.7. You want me to post it, do you?"

"Would you mind posting it?" he asked.

"No. I would post it for you," she said.

"You take my point very quickly," he said, then, with some difficulty, looking downward and away from her, hardly able to bring himself to thank her more formally.

"I've had to make such points before
26 myself," she said.

"I thought, somehow, that you would not mind about such things," he said.

"You wouldn't have asked me if you'd thought I minded. Tell me, do you really trust me to remember to post it?"

"Of course I do," he said. "One wouldn't not post a stranger's letter."

And this was so exactly the truth that it silenced her, and they said no more to each other until the train drew into Paddington: and as they walked together off the platform, he said, "Thank you, and good-bye."

And she said, "Good-bye," and she carried the letter in her hand all the way home, and dropped it into the letterbox on her
27 block. Then she went down the basement steps to her dark flat, and she knew that the name and the address, written there in her own writing, so strangely, were imprinted upon her memory forever.

And indeed, over the next month, she sometimes fancied that she thought of little else. She knew that this was not the truth, that it was merely a fancy, because of course she did think of other things; of her job, of her friends, of her mother, of what to buy for supper, of whether she wanted to go to the cinema on Wednesday night. But she did not think of these other things in the mad, romantic, obsessive way that she thought of Mrs. H. Smithson, and the nameless man, and the whole curious, affecting incident: in a sense she resented the incident, because it did so much to vindicate her own crazy expectancy, her foolish faith in revelation. She knew, in her better, saner self, that such faith was foolish, and she suspected that such partial hints of its validity were a
delusion, a temptation, and that if she heed- 28
ed them she would be disabled forever, and disqualified from real life, as Odysseus would have been by the Sirens.[7] And yet at the same time she knew, in her other self, that it was that man she was thinking about, however unreasonably. She looked for him as she walked along the streets of London, and she could not convince herself that it was not for him that she was looking. She speculated about the identity and appearance of Mrs. Smithson, and supplied her endlessly with Christian names, until she remembered that the H. might well have stood for her husband's name, not hers. She speculated about the deceived husband. Although most of her own friends were married and had children, she still found it hard to acknowledge that Mrs. Smithson might
well be a woman of her own generation, for 29
the prefix *Mrs.* invariably supplied her with a material image, the image of her own mother: and she would realize from time to time, with a start, that the women that she thought of as mothers were in fact grandmothers, and that the young girls she saw pushing prams on Saturday mornings and quarreling with vigorous toddlers on buses were not in fact elder sisters but mothers,

---

7. Odysseus . . . Sirens: In Homer's *Odyssey,* Odysseus, the hero, plugs his ears so that he will not be tempted by the singing of the sirens, sea nymphs whose enchanting songs lured sailors to their deaths on rocky coastlines.

Mrs. Smithson, Mrs. Smithson. She could not give form to Mrs. Smithson.

It was in the week before Christmas that she decided to go and have a look at Mrs. Smithson. The idea occurred to her at lunchtime one day, in the middle of a lunchtime business Christmas party. She stood there, drinking too much and not getting enough to eat, defeated as ever by the problems of buffet technique, and as she listened to a very nice man whom she had known
30 and liked for several years describe to her the felicities of his new central heating, she suddenly decided to go and look at Mrs. Smithson. After all, she said to herself, what could be more harmless, what more undetectable? All I need to do is to knock on her door and ask, say, for Alice. And then I would know. I don't know what I would know, but I would know it. And she smiled at the man, and allowed her glass to be once more filled, and then told him politely all about some other friends of hers whose central heating had entirely ruined all their antique furniture, and split all the antique paneling of their rather priceless house. And as she talked, she was already in her heart on her way to Mrs. Smithson's, already surrendering to the lure of that fraught, romantic, painful world, which seemed to call her, to call her continually from the endurable sorrows of daily existence to some possible other country of the
31 passions, a country where she felt she would recognize, though strange to it, the scenery and landmarks. She thought often of this place, as of some place perpetually existing, and yet concealed: and she could describe it to herself only in terms of myth or allegory, unsatisfactory terms, she felt, and perniciously implanted in her by her classical education. It was a place other than the real world, or what she felt to be the real world, and it was both more beautiful and more valid, though valid in itself only: and it could be entered not at will, but intermittently, by accident, and yet always with some sense of temptation and surrender. Some people, she could see, passed most of their lives in its confines, and governed by its laws only, like that old man, himself a poet, who had first defined for her the nature of her expectations. There were enough of such people in the world to keep alive before her the possibility of a permanent, irreversible entry through those mysteriously inscribed and classic gates: a poet, a drunken Frenchman, a girl she had known who said one day: "I will go to Baghdad," and went. They crossed her path, these people, or their names came to her, garlanded with wreaths of that unfamiliar foliage: Yves was seen in Marseilles carrying a lobster, Esther was seen in a bookshop in New York wearing a fur coat and with diamonds in her hair, Esther was in Marrakesh, living in one room with an Arab. Yves had gone to Ireland and started a lobster farm. Oh, messages from a foreign country, oh, disquieting glimpses of brightness. Helen gulped down the remains of her fourth glass of wine, and looked at her watch, which said that it was five past three; and said to the central-heating man that she must go.

She walked to Victoria Place, pausing dazed at traffic lights, stumbling at each irregularity of the pavement, running her
hand idly along grimy railings. It was cold, 32
but she could not feel the cold: her face was burning. She knew her way because she had looked Victoria Place up a month ago, the day after she had posted the letter, in her *A to Z Guide to London:* she remembered the moment when she had done so, because she had pretended to herself that she was doing no such thing, and her mind had not known what her hands and eyes were doing. But her mind now remembered what it had then refused to acknowledge, and she took herself there as though entranced, the trance persisting long after the effects of walking had dispelled the effects of so much drink on so empty a stomach. I must be mad, she said

30 Literary Focus Is the man at the Christmas party a flat or a round character? How do you know?

31 Reading Strategy Summarize the meaning of this passage. Why is Helen fascinated with Mrs. Smithson? What characteristics of "the country of the passions" does Helen describe? What does Helen admire about the people who live there?

32 Discussion Why does Helen feel dazed?

1295

33 Reading Strategy Describe this scene in your own words. Why is Helen transfixed by the scene?

34 Master Teacher Note This vivid description is the culmination of Helen's "Voyage to Cythera." She seems to see in this room all that she was looking for. If possible, provide students with representations of Antoine Watteau's series of paintings (1710–1712) entitled *L'Embarquement pour l'île de Cythere*. Ask them to compare and contrast Watteau's graphic representations of Cythera with Drabble's written description. If this is not possible, then have students discuss how they would paint this scene.

35 Literary Focus Are the characters in this description flat or round? How do you know?

36 Critical Thinking and Reading What meaning does Helen derive from her experience at Victoria Place? Does your inference come from direct or indirect evidence?

to herself more than once: I must be mad. And at the very end of the journey she began, very slightly, to lose her nerve: she thought that she would not dare to knock upon the door, she thought that perhaps after all only insignificant disaffection could await her, that she could do no more than dispel what had already in its own way been perfection.

But there was no need to knock at the door. Victoria Place, when she reached it, was a short main street of tall terraced houses, either newly recovered or so smart that they had never lapsed: the number 24 was brightly illuminated, shining brightly forth into the gathering darkness. She walked slowly toward it, realizing that she would be able to see whatever there was to see without knocking: realizing that fate had connived with her curiosity by providing a bus stop directly outside the house, so that she could stand there and wait without fear of detection. She took her place at the bus stop, and stood there for a moment before she gathered her courage to turn around, and then she turned. The lights were on in the two lower floors, and she could see straight into the basement, a room which most closely resembled in shape the one where she herself lived. The room seemed at first sight to be full of people, and there was so much activity that it took some time to sort them out. There were two women, and four children; no, five children, for there was a baby sitting in a corner on a blue rug. The larger children were putting up a Christmas tree, and one of the women
33, was laying the table for tea, while the other, her back to the window, one elbow on the
34 mantelpiece, appeared to be reading aloud a passage from a book. It was a large, bright room, with a green carpet, and white walls, and red painted wooden furniture; even the table was painted red. A children's room. It shone, it glittered. A mobile of golden fishes hung from the ceiling, and the carpet was strewn with colored glass and tinsel decorations for the tree. The plates on the table were blue and white, and the silver knives caught the light; on the mantelpiece stood two many-faceted cut glasses and an open bottle of wine. Two of the children had fair hair, and the other three were dark: and the woman laying the table had red hair, a huge coil of dark red hair from which whole heavy locks escaped, dragging down the back of her neck, falling against her face at each movement, and she moved endlessly, restlessly, vigorously, taking buns out of a bag, slicing bread, pouring black currant juice into beakers, turning to listen to the other woman, and suddenly laughing, throwing back her head with a kind of violence and laughing: and the other woman at the mantelpiece laughed too, her thin shoulders shaking, and the children, irritated by their mother's laughter, flung themselves at her, 35
clinging angrily onto her knees, shouting, until the red-haired woman tried to silence them with slices of bread and butter, which were rejected and flung around the floor: so she followed them up with the iced buns, tossing them round and yet talking, all the time talking, to the other woman and not to the children, intent upon some point, some anecdote too precious to lose, and the children chewed at the buns while she scooped up the torn pieces of bread and bestowed them all, with a smile of such lovely passing affection, upon the baby, a smile so tender and amused and solicitous that Helen, overseeing it, felt her heart stand still.

And as she stood there, out there in the cold, and watched, she felt herself stiffen slowly into the breathlessness of attention: because it seemed to her that she had been given, freely, a vision of something so beautiful that its relevance could not be measured. The hints and arrows that had led her here took on the mysterious significance of fate itself: she felt that everything was joined and drawn together, that all things 36
were part of some pattern of which she caught by sheer chance a sudden hopeful sense: and that those two women, and their children, and the man on the train, and the

bright and radiant uncurtained room, an island in the surrounding darkness, were symbols to her of things too vague to name, of happiness, of hope, of brightness, warmth, and celebration. She gazed into that room, where emotion lay, like water unimaginably profound. The red-haired woman was kneeling now, on the green carpet, rubbing with a corner of the tea towel at a buttery mark on the carpet, and at the same time looking up and listening, with an expression upon her face in which vexation with the children, carelessness of her own vexation, and a kind of soft rapt delight in the other woman's company were inextricably confused; and the other woman had turned slightly, so that Helen from the window could see her face, and she was twisting in her hands a length of red-and-silver tinsel, idly pulling shreds from it as she spoke. And Helen thought of all the other dark cold rooms of London and the world, of loneliness, of the blue chilly flickerings of television sets, of sad children, silenced mothers, and unmarried girls and she wondered if so
37 much delight were truly gathered up and concentrated into one place, or whether these windows were not windows through which she viewed the real huge spacious anterior lovely world. And it seemed possible to see them so, because she did not know that house, nor those women, nor their names, nor the name of the man who had led her there: the poetry of inspiration being to a certain extent, as she knew, the poetry of ignorance, and the connections between symbols a destructive folly to draw. She did not even know which of these women was Mrs. Smithson, whom she had come to see, for if one woman had laid the table, the other cleared it, equally at home. She knew nothing, and could therefore believe everything, drawing faith from such
38 a vision, as she had drawn faith from unfamiliar cities: drawing faith from the passionate vision of intimacy, where intimacy itself failed her; as Wordsworth turned from his life to his keener recollections,[8] and Yeats to lions and towers and hawks.[9]

By the time that one of the children was sent to draw the curtains, she was stiff and white with cold. She turned away, as the child, a small girl with straight dark hair and a face suddenly grave with the weight of her task, began to struggle with the heavy floor-length hangings, shutting inch by inch away from her the colored angles of refracted light, the Christmas tree, the airy fishes, the verdant green, the small angelic innocent faces, the shining spheres of glass, and those two young worn women: and as she turned she felt the first snowflakes of the year settle softly on her skin, and looking up, she saw the dim blue sky full of snow. She glanced back, to see if the child had seen it, but the curtains were already drawn, and she saw nothing but her own image, pale in the glass. So she started to walk down the street, away from the house, away from the bus stop, but before she had taken ten steps a car drew up, just by her side, a slow yard from her, and there was the man from the train, sitting there and looking at her. She paused, and he opened the door, and sitting there still he said to her, "I don't know what to say to you, you look so fragile that a word might hurt you." And she 39
smiled at him, a slow dazed smile, knowing that as he for her, so she for him was some mysterious apparition, some faintly gleaming memorable image: and she turned away, and walked down the street away from him into the snowy darkness, and he got out of his car and went into the house.

She walked carefully, because her ankles were so brittle from the cold that she feared that if she stumbled, they would snap.

---

8. Wordsworth . . . recollections: British poet William Wordsworth (1770–1850) delved into memories of his youth in his poetry, recollecting the emotion of childhood in the tranquility of adulthood.
9. Yeats . . . hawks: British poet William Butler Yeats (1865–1939) developed his own mythology.

37 **Discussion** Compare and contrast the scene that Helen observes in the room with the world that Helen describes sympathetically and that she herself experiences.

38 **Enrichment** William Wordsworth, an English Romantic poet, wrote the first analytical autobiography in the form of a poem. *The Prelude,* consisting of fourteen "books," was written between 1798 and 1839.

Twentieth-century Irish poet W. B. Yeats frequently used towers, lions, and hawks in his poems, such as "The Second Coming." Yeats's tower with its winding stair symbolized for him both intellectual pursuit and the necessary abandonment of the world. His identification with the tower, also a symbol of Irish history, of isolation, and of security, was so strong that at one time he actually purchased a tower and lived in it.

39 **Reading Strategy** Why does Helen think that the man at the end of this story is an apparition?

THINKING ABOUT THE SELECTION

Recalling

1. (a) At the beginning of the story, what is Helen's attitude toward journeys? (b) According to "a much-traveled old man," why does she feel this way?
2. (a) What conclusion does Helen reach about the man on the train from Reading to London? (b) What does the man ask her to do?
3. (a) What does the man at the office Christmas party talk about? (b) How does Helen respond? (c) At what point does she leave?
4. (a) When Helen visits Victoria Place, what does she plan to do there? (b) What does she actually do? (c) What does she observe? (d) Who arrives as she starts to walk away?

Interpreting

5. Why do you think Helen is so obsessed with catching a glimpse of Mrs. Smithson?
6. (a) In the last scene of the story, what meaning does the "vision" that Helen sees have for her? (b) Why does Helen think that connections between symbols are "a destructive folly to draw"?
7. (a) The title of this story is an allusion. The reader is expected to know that Cythera is a Greek island where Aphrodite, the goddess of love, arose full-grown from the sea. How are the implications of the story's title fulfilled in an unexpected way at the end? (b) How does the title relate to the theme?
8. In what way or ways has Helen changed or grown as a consequence of her experiences?

Applying

9. What do you think the chances are that Helen will ever fall in love with a specific man?

CRITICAL THINKING AND READING

Identifying Kinds of Evidence

Direct evidence is straightforward factual information that leads to an obvious conclusion. When the narrator says that the man on the train "took out a sheet of fourpenny stamps, and tore one off, licked it, and stuck it on" the envelope, you have direct evidence of an intent to mail the letter or to have it mailed. Indirect evidence requires much more interpretation. For example, when the narrator says that "there was no need to knock at the door" of the house on Victoria Place, you can infer that Helen is relieved to avoid a face-to-face meeting with Mrs. Smithson. But the evidence is indirect; you have to use other information about Helen's personality to reach that conclusion.

1. Identify the kind of evidence—direct or indirect—in each of the following inferences: (a) that Helen had been to France; (b) that Helen liked the man who kissed her on a train as it drew into Oxford; (c) that Helen had received an excellent education; (d) that Helen was bored by the man's talk about central heating at the Christmas party.
2. (a) What kind of evidence does Helen use on the train to support her conclusion about the unnamed man? (b) How accurately does she seem to have interpreted the evidence?

THINKING AND WRITING

Writing About Characterization

Fictional characters, whether flat or round, must be believable. They may sometimes act in unexpected ways, but they should not act out of character. A flat, stock-character clown should not suddenly and for no apparent reason become a dashing hero. A round, carefully developed character like Helen in "A Voyage to Cythera" may change and grow, but she must do so within the personality given her by the writer. Helen is a complex but consistent character. Write an essay in which you discuss three of Helen's encounters with other people, explaining how in each one she acts true to the personality that the author has given her. Begin by choosing the three encounters. Make notes about them. Then write your first draft, showing Helen's consistency from one encounter to the next. In revising your first draft, make sure you have supplied clear connections.

Answers

ANSWERS TO THINKING ABOUT THE SELECTION

Recalling

1. (a) Helen is obsessed with travel and with the idea of discovery and the changes that travel affords. She is addicted to everything related to traveling; she believes that each trip leads to revelation. (b) The old man tells Helen that she is obsessed with travel because she hopes to fall in love whenever she journeys to a new place.
2. Helen concludes that the man on the train is the victim of a tragic love affair. She bases her conclusion on the fact that the man appears to be restless and troubled. Helen interprets the man's actions as symptoms of a tormented love. (b) The man on the train asks Helen to address a letter that he has just written; he then asks her to mail it.
3. (a) The man at the Christmas party discusses the virtues of central heating with Helen. (b) Helen points out that central heating ruined some friends' antique furniture and paneling. (c) Helen leaves after she finishes her fourth glass of wine; she departs at five minutes to three.
4. (a) Helen plans to knock on the door of 24 Victoria Place and inquire for "Alice," in order to meet Mrs. Smithson. (b) Helen actually stands at the bus stop directly in front of the house and pretends to be waiting for a bus. (c) Helen observes a large, bright room. There are two women there, one reading aloud from a book and the other setting tea. Helen sees five children in the room; the oldest children are decorating a Christmas tree. (d) The man from the train arrives at the house just as Helen is leaving.

Interpreting

5. Answers will differ. Helen wishes to solve the mystery that the man on the train involves her in. She is also irrationally jealous of Mrs. Smithson and the fact that the man has some sort of relationship with her.
6. (a) Suggested Response: Helen's vision of the room at 24 Victoria Place is one of harmony, happiness, and love. The vision is both beautiful and frightening to her, as she must confront her own feelings about love. Helen herself knows how the vision makes her feel but is uncertain about its exact meaning. (b) Suggested Response: Helen thinks that it is dangerous to draw connections between symbols because in so doing one can lose sight of reality and be tempted by delusion or one's own desires. Helen feels that symbols can be deliberately misinterpreted.
7. Suggested Response: The implications of the story's title are that the story is about a journey and the story will have a happy ending. Indeed, the story is about a journey, not to a particular place but to a level of understanding. Yet instead of finding love, Helen finds that it does not exist for her.
8. Suggested Response: Helen has learned about her needs and expectations. She better comprehends her own complex motivations and her reasons for travel. She seems to understand that she stands apart from the world unveiled to her in the room. By the story's end, Helen no longer deludes herself into thinking that she will find love on the next train; she becomes more fragile as her illusions are shattered.

Poetry

MOUNT FUJI AND FLOWERS, 1972
David Hockney
Metropolitan Museum of Art

Applying

9. Answers will differ. It is doubtful that Helen will ever fall in love with a specific man, because she seems to be more in love with the idea of love than with a particular person. When she looks into the room, she is stunned and moved; she has no hope of ever having the kind of life she observes. As Helen points out at the end of the story, the man on the train seems to be a ghostly image. To her, he is not real.

Challenge How do you feel about Helen's "voyage to Cythera"? What is the point of the voyage? Is it successful? Why or why not? Find evidence in the selection to support your answer.

ANSWERS TO CRITICAL THINKING AND READING

1. (a) direct; (b) direct; (c) indirect; (d) indirect
2. (a) Helen almost entirely uses indirect evidence to make her assumptions about the man on the train. She observes his actions and interprets his gestures and expressions but does not actually speak to him. When he does speak to Helen, she uses direct evidence to infer that his letter is somehow important. However, most of her conclusions about the man are based on indirect evidence. (b) Helen seems to have interpreted some of the indirect evidence correctly; the man is alone on the train, he is preoccupied, and his request does seem mysterious. She correctly interprets the evidence that he wishes to speak to her.

Challenge What do you think the voyage to Cythera would be like? Would it be difficult or easy? Would it be disappointing, boring, or exhilarating? Describe the voyage in your own words, using characteristics and details from the story to help you think about Helen's journey.

THINKING AND WRITING

For help with this assignment, students can refer to Lesson 9, "Writing About Character," in the Handbook of Writing About Literature.

Publishing Student Writing Ask student volunteers to read their compositions aloud. Have students choose one of the best compositions about Helen's encounters. You might wish to ask them to write a class play based on one of the encounters from this composition. Have students work in small groups to write dialogue, design a set, describe costumes, and decide on details about lighting and sound effects. Then have them work as a group to create a unified play. You might wish to type, copy, and bind the completed play.

More About the Author Philip Larkin had a seemingly uneventful childhood. He was a mediocre student, finding school at times a "tiresome interruption" to things he liked to do better. Among those things was reading. A voracious reader, he read everything from detective stories to contemporary fiction to the classics. As a very young child he played highly creative and imaginative games, building a private childhood world. In his early teens he began a lifelong interest in jazz, something he came to love "even more than poetry." Have your students discuss the importance of childhood experiences on the development of an author. What types of experiences might most shape an author's development?

Literary Focus Tone is determined by many elements in a work. Larkin uses sentence structure, repetition, images, and sudden shifts of focus. Point out that even places have a tone. A kitchen might be warm, cozy, and friendly, or it might be stark, sterile, and efficient.

Look For Your **less advanced** students may have trouble with the concept of tone as it involves so many elements. It may be helpful to review the Analyzing Literature questions on page 000. These questions will help guide and focus their reading.

Writing Prior to writing ask the students to imagine how five employees might answer the question "How do you like your job?" How might the style and wording of their answers reflect their moods and attitudes? After completing the freewriting, some students may want to use one of their sentences as the basis for a short mood poem or paragraph for extra credit.

PHILIP LARKIN

1922–

Should a poem be heavily symbolic and filled with images or should it be simple and straightforward? Few poets have made better use of the ordinary in both content and style than has Philip Larkin. Once connected with "the Movement," a group of poets whose work first appeared in Robert Conquest's 1956 anthology *New Lines,* Larkin has since established his own unique place in contemporary literature. Writing in a poetic form that approximates conversation, he raises familiar experiences to the level of art. His poems are often wry, self-critical, and understated, "part sigh, part affirmation," as one critic states. Poetry for Larkin is a part-time job; his full-time job is that of librarian at the University of Hull, a major seaport on the east coast of England.

Philip Larkin was born in Coventry, England. A graduate of St. John's College, Oxford, Larkin began his writing career as a novelist. He later served as jazz correspondent of the *Daily Telegraph.* His poetry, which is the source of his international fame, displays a clear-eyed honesty that captures moments of startling truth. Often it contains a narrator who observes the world around him with detachment. Larkin's poetry has frequently been compared with that of Thomas Hardy, whom he admires.

Objectives

1 To understand and identify the tone of a poem
2 To recognize how the tone can differ between poems and how tone affects the poem's meaning
3 To compare and contrast the tone of several poems by the same authors effectively

Teaching Portfolio: Support Material

Teacher Backup, p. 00–00

Vocabulary Check, p. 00

Usage and Mechanics Worksheet, p. 00

Analyzing Literature Worksheet, p. 00

Critical Thinking and Reading Worksheet, p. 00

Language Worksheet, p. 00

Selection Test, p. 00

Art Transparency 19, *Shipbuilding on the Clyde* by Stanley Spencer

GUIDE FOR READING

Days; The Explosion; Coming

The Writer's Techniques

Tone. In casual conversation, the words people use and the way they say them suggest an attitude and create a mood. In poetry, the writer's attitude toward his or her subject and the mood created by the language are called tone. Tone can be solemn, playful, cynical, angry; or it can have any of dozens of other attributes. In general, tone reflects the writer's attitude and puts the reader in the same kind of mood. Tone is created by the ideas in the poem as well as by verbal elements such as meter, sentence structure, diction, and imagery.

Look For

As you read the poems by Philip Larkin, think of an adjective or adjectives that accurately describe their tone. Also, try to determine specifically what is creating the tone.

Writing

Write a short imperative sentence. (*Do the dishes,* for example; or *Mow the lawn.*) Then rewrite it, putting the same thought into *five* different sentences, each with a different tone. Your rewritten sentences will probably be longer than the original. Choose your five different tones from the following list.

angry	bored	eager	friendly	timid
blunt	desperate	formal	pompous	vague

Be prepared to read your sentences in class to see if your classmates can identify the tone of each sentence.

Vocabulary

Knowing the following words will help you as you read "The Explosion."

pithead (pit′hed) *n.*: Top of a mining pit or coal shaft (l. 2)

slagheap (slag′hēp) *n.*: Pile of waste material from mining (l. 3)

moleskins (mōl′skinz) *n.*: Work clothes made from strong, twilled cotton fabric (l. 10)

Vocabulary Have **less advanced** students read the words aloud so they will be able to pronounce them when reading the poem. Go over some information on coal mining to further clarify these terms.

Motivation for Reading Have the students try to recall what they did yesterday, or a week ago. Do they take tomorrow for granted? Do we often reflect on the days in our lives? Is it important or valuable to do this? What factors in a person's life might affect how they interpret and look at days?

Purpose-Setting Question Does this poem provide a satisfying answer to the question "What are days for?"

1 **Discussion** What is the tone of the poem in these lines? Do lines 2–5 answer the question the way you might answer it?

2 **Discussion** Are there other places than days in which to live? Why does the author ask this question here?

3 **Critical Thinking and Reading** Which of the questions in stanza one interests Larkin most? What is the meaning of the priest and doctor? How are they involved in "solving" the question?

4 **Discussion** Why are the priest and doctor "running over the fields"? Does this ending seem strange in light of the poem's questions?

Days

Philip Larkin

What are days for?
1 Days are where we live.
They come, they wake us
Time and time over.
They are to be happy in;
2 Where can we live but days?

3 Ah, solving that question
Brings the priest and the doctor
In their long coats
4 Running over the fields.

THINKING ABOUT THE SELECTION

Recalling

1. In your own words, what is the speaker's answer to the first question in the poem?

Interpreting

2. Why does the answer to the second question bring the priest and the doctor running?

Applying

3. What would be different about the thought in this poem if Larkin had substituted the word *life* for the word *days?*

ANALYZING LITERATURE

Understanding Tone

Tone is the attitude that a writer takes toward his or her subject, characters, or audience. In a poem, tone is conveyed to a great extent by word choice.

1. How would you describe the tone of "Days"?
2. How does the interjection *Ah* at the beginning of line 7 affect the tone of the poem?
3. How would the tone of the poem be different if lines 6–10 did not exist?

Answers

ANSWERS TO THINKING ABOUT THE SELECTION

Recalling

1. The author suggests that days form a place or space for living and to "be happy in."

Interpreting

2. Suggested Response: The need to know "where can we live but days" comes most urgently at the time of death. One often calls in a priest or minister and a doctor at that time.

Applying

3. Suggested Response: Using the word *life* would certainly change the poem's meaning, since Larkin refers to days as a place for living, questioning where else we might live but days.

ANSWERS TO ANALYZING LITERATURE

1. Suggested Response: The tone is bland, almost matter-of-fact in the first stanza, but more actively reflective in the second stanza.
2. The word injects more emotion than the poem has previously expressed.
3. The tone would be unvaried.

Challenge Do you agree with the attitude Larkin expresses in this poem? How might you rephrase the poem to express your attitude? Try writing your response in a brief composition.

The Explosion

Philip Larkin

On the day of the explosion
Shadows pointed towards the pithead: 1
In the sun the slagheap slept.

Down the lane came men in pitboots
Coughing oath-edged talk and pipe-smoke,
Shouldering off the freshened silence.

2

One chased after rabbits; lost them;
Came back with a nest of lark's eggs;
Showed them; lodged them in the grasses.

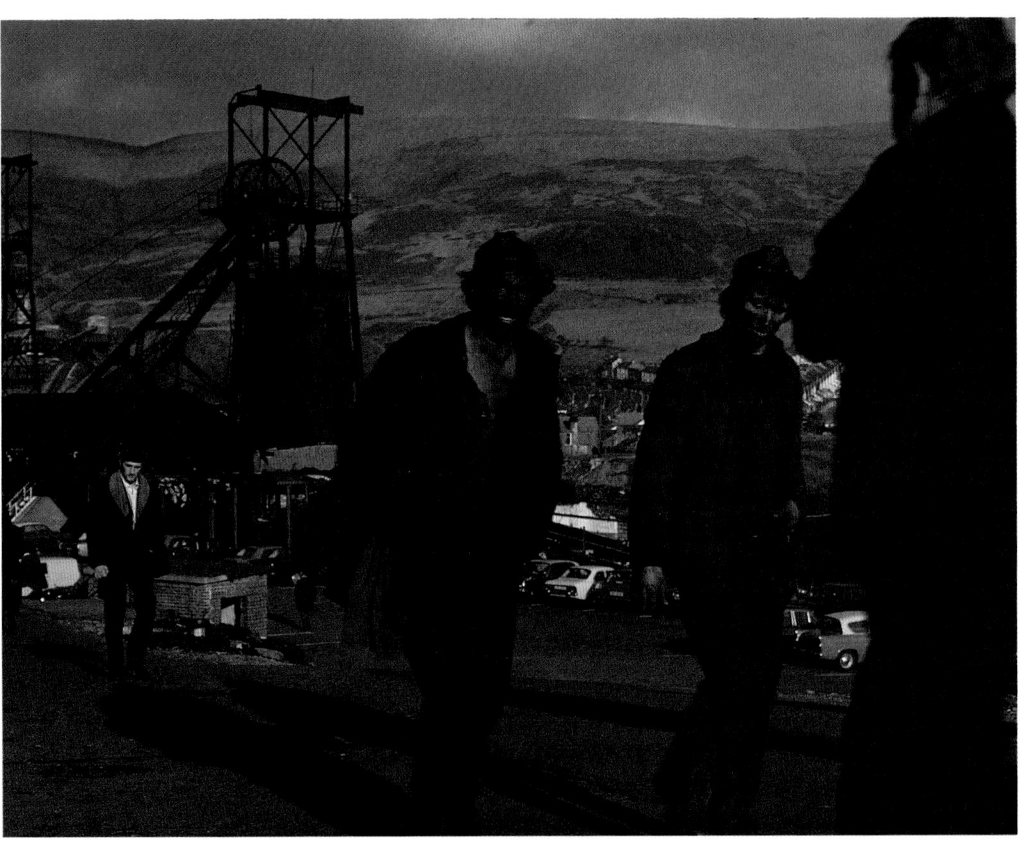

Motivation for Reading Have the students imagine they are with a group of people going off to work in the morning. The workers are mostly friends. The talk and actions are ordinary and everyday. Later in the day a tragedy happens. Some of the workers die. How significant would their morning's actions now become? How would you, as an onlooker, feel? How would the survivors of the tragedy feel?

Master Teacher Note This poem records an incident familiar to Larkin, who grew up in an industrial town. To set the background discuss facts about coal mining. If possible read an account of a mining accident from a newspaper or magazine.

Purpose-Setting Question How has the author used carefully selected incidents and details to create a touching and poignant effect?

1 **Discussion** What is the effect of knowing about the explosion from the beginning of the poem?

2 **Discussion** What do the details about the miners contribute to the poem's impact? What is ironic and chilling about the image of "tall gates standing open"?

Master Teacher Note After reading Larkin's "The Explosion," display Art Transparency 19, Stanley Spencer's *Shipbuilding on the Clyde,* on the overhead projector. Point out that both the poem and the painting deal with modern British industrial life. Ask: Do the two works have anything else in common? What point might each be trying to make? Which work, Larkin's or Spencer's, do you admire more, and why?

3 Discussion What is contrasted in these two stanzas? Is the contrast effective? What meaning does it add to the poem?

4 Critical Thinking and Reading The sudden shift in time and place between stanzas four and five and between stanzas five and six helps to set the tone of the poem. Notice that the shifts are dramatic but done so that the careful reader can still catch the meaning.

5 Discussion What is especially poignant about introducing the wives here? How does the image of the sun contrast with that in line 2?

Challenge What is the author's reaction to the incident of the explosion? What feelings has it touched in him? Support your response with specific images and incidents from the poem.

So they passed in beards and moleskins,
Fathers, brothers, nicknames, laughter,
Through the tall gates standing open.

3, 4

At noon, there came a tremor; cows
Stopped chewing for a second; sun,
Scarfed as in a heat-haze, dimmed.

The dead go on before us, they
Are sitting in God's house in comfort,
We shall see them face to face—

Plain as lettering in the chapels
It was said, and for a second
Wives saw men of the explosion

5

Larger than in life they managed—
Gold as on a coin, or walking
Somehow from the sun towards them,

One showing the eggs unbroken.

THINKING ABOUT THE SELECTION

Recalling

1. Where do the events in the poem occur?
2. What immediate effect does the explosion have on life above ground?
3. (a) What do the widows of the miners see "for a second" at the funeral services? (b) What else in the poem lasts "for a second"?

Interpreting

4. How does the first stanza foreshadow events in the poem?
5. In your own words, explain line 5.
6. (a) What is the mood of the men going to work? (b) What details show this mood?
7. Why are lines 16–18 printed in italics?
8. What is the symbolic meaning of the eggs?
9. How would you describe the tone of "The Explosion"?

Applying

10. What relationship is there between the theme of "Days" and the theme of "The Explosion"?

Answers

ANSWERS TO THINKING ABOUT THE SELECTION

Recalling

1. The events in the poem occur near a coal mine shaft and at funeral services.
2. The earth tremor resulting from the explosion causes the cows to stop chewing and creates a hazy effect around the sun.
3. (a) For a second the widows see their men walking towards them. (b) The earth tremor causes the cows to stop chewing for a second.

Interpreting

4. Line 1 speaks about the explosion, while in line 2 there are shadows pointing towards the mine.
5. Suggested Response: Some of the men going into the mine are pipe smokers. They are coughing, perhaps from smoking or from working the mines. Their speech is punctuated by oaths.
6. (a) The men going to work are in a normal, everyday, somewhat cheerful mood. (b) They are talking, smoking, and coughing. One stops to chase a rabbit and pick up a nest of lark's eggs. They are relatives and friends, calling each other nicknames and laughing together.
7. Lines 16–18 are in italics because they are words of a funeral service.
8. Answers will differ. Suggested Response: The lark's eggs are a sign of spring, rebirth, and renewal of nature. The unbroken eggs symbolize that nature will survive.
9. Answers will differ. Suggested Response: The tone of the poem is poignant and tragic. Good, kind working men suddenly die in a mining accident.

Applying

10. Answers will differ. Suggested Response: Both poems explore the meaning of life and death. People seek to live and be happy, yet death is a reality to be confronted, something not under our control.

Coming

Philip Larkin

On longer evenings,
Light, chill and yellow,
Bathes the serene
Foreheads of houses.
A thrush sings, 1
Laurel-surrounded
In the deep bare garden,
Its fresh-peeled voice
Astonishing the brickwork.
It will be spring soon,
It will be spring soon— 2
And I, whose childhood
Is a forgotten boredom,
Feel like a child 3
Who comes on a scene
Of adult reconciling,
And can understand nothing
But the unusual laughter,
And starts to be happy. 4

THINKING ABOUT THE SELECTION

Recalling

1. In "Coming" what are two signs of spring that the speaker notices?
2. With what kind of attitude does the speaker look back on childhood?

Interpreting

3. The speaker draws a comparison between the coming of spring and a child witnessing the end of an adult argument. What similarities are there between the two occasions?

Applying

4. In writing about the seasons, the nature writer Hal Borland observed, "April is a promise that May is bound to keep." Explain this statement.

THINKING AND WRITING

Writing About Tone

Write an essay in which you compare and contrast the tone of the three Larkin poems. Find and jot down words, phrases, or lines that support your assessment of the tone of each poem. In your first draft, be sure that the quoted lines actually make the points you say they do. When revising, eliminate vague or meaningless statements. You will find that in writing about literature, you can easily fall into the trap of writing sentences that, upon analysis, convey very little information.

Motivation for Reading How do you feel when you anticipate a pleasant event? Is the feeling different if you've experienced the upcoming event before? How can such anticipation get you through everyday problems? Can we somehow draw strength from the nearness of a pleasant event and be more content with today?

Purpose-Setting Question What meaning has Larkin created by juxtaposing the adult and childhood situations in this poem?

1 **Discussion** Where does the author use personification in these lines? Why is it especially appropriate in view of later lines in the poem?

2 **Discussion** Why does the author repeat a line here? What is the effect of the punctuation at the ends of the lines?

3 **Discussion** Though the feeling is the same as that from childhood, what is different about the adult's situation?

4 **Discussion** What does the word "starts" suggest about the child's previous feelings? What is implied about the speaker's previous feelings?

Answers

ANSWERS TO THINKING ABOUT THE SELECTION

Recalling

1. Two signs are the days getting longer and the thrush singing.
2. The speaker looks back on his childhood as a time of boredom.

Interpreting

3. Suggested Response: The coming of spring produces feelings in the adult similar to those of a child seeing adults reconciling. In both cases the response is starting to be happy, without fully understanding the situation.

Applying

4. The renewal of nature that is first seen in April will inevitably continue more abundantly in May.

More About the Author Thom Gunn tends to praise strength, insensitivity, intellectualism, and action over thought. Violent action is seen as "a valid means of self-expression." Led by his personal quest for self-identity and life's meaning, in the early 1960's Gunn changed his poetic stance. He moved towards writing free verse dealing with more positive themes. Discuss with your students the problems faced by an author who is growing and changing. Is it valid to compare works from one period with another?

Literary Focus T.S. Eliot once noticed that each age has its own poetic diction. Note that poets choose words with great care and that their choices are integral to their unique style. To highlight that diction is part of everyday language, have the students read over several recent compositions. Have they repeated certain words and phrases? Are they developing a certain diction in their writing?

Look For You might select a few well-chosen words and discuss their connotations with your class.

GUIDE FOR READING

Taylor Street

Thom William Gunn (1929–) was born in Gravesend, England, and educated at Cambridge. He became, to his own surprise, one of "the Movement" poets of the 1950's. In the mid-1950's he moved to California, studied at Stanford University, and taught at the University of California, Berkeley. In the early 1960's, he began to write in unpatterned rhythms, or free verse. Gunn, who has published steadily since the 1950's, is well represented in anthologies and has won many literary awards.

The Writer's Techniques

Diction. Diction is word choice. Choosing the best and most appropriate words is essential to effective writing. A writer—especially a poet—must select his or her words carefully to express the exact nuances intended. Diction can be as simple as that in a primer's "See Spot run" or as ornate as that in John Milton's *Paradise Lost:*

> Nor was his name unheard or unadored
> In ancient Greece, and in Ausonian land
> Men called him Mulciber; and how he fell
> From Heaven, they fabled, thrown by angry Jove
> Over the crystal battlements.

Diction can be as formal as a speech to Parliament or as informal as current Cockney slang. In choosing their words, writers take into account the subject, the theme, and the audience. Intent determines diction.

Look For

As you read Thom Gunn's "Taylor Street," pay close attention to the words he uses. Try to determine the effect of the words.

Objectives

To recognize an author's diction

Teaching Portfolio: Support Material

Teacher Backup, p. 000

Vocabulary Check, p. 00

Usage and Mechanics Worksheet, p. 00

Analyzing literature Worksheet, p. 00

Critical Thinking and Reading Worksheet, p. 00

Language Worksheet, p. 00

Selection Test, p. 000

Answers

ANSWERS TO THINKING ABOUT THE SELECTION

Recalling

1. (a) He is sitting on the porch facing the street. (b) His face is yellowish and he wears a floppy brown hat. His eyes are small.
2. (a) He is watching people pass by the house. (b) Lines 18–19 make it

Taylor Street

Thom Gunn

The small porch of imitation
marble is never sunny, but
1 outside the front door he
sits on his kitchen chair facing
the street. In the bent yellowish
face, from under the brim
of a floppy brown hat,
his small eyes watch what
he is not living. But he
lives what he can:
watches without a smile, with
a certain strain, the warmth
of his big crumpled
body anxiously cupped
2 by himself in himself, as
he leans over himself not
over the cold railing, un-
moving but carefully getting
a little strength from the sight of the
passers-by. He has it
3 all planned: he will live
here morning by morning.

THINKING ABOUT THE SELECTION

Recalling

1. (a) Where is the man in the poem sitting? (b) What are three details of his appearance?
2. (a) According to lines 8 and 9, what is the man watching? (b) How is this activity made more definite in lines 19 and 20?

Interpreting

3. What two lines suggest that the man is not leading an inactive life by choice?
4. How do you think the man "is getting a little strength from the sight of the passers-by"?
5. How would you describe the tone of this poem?
6. The poem focuses on a single man, yet its title is "Taylor Street." Why?

Applying

7. The poet provides enough information for an imaginative reader to speculate about the life of the man on the porch. What do you think the man's background is?

ANALYZING LITERATURE

Recognizing the Importance of Diction

The importance of **diction,** or word choice, in a brief poem cannot be overemphasized. The poet must make every word count, and Thom Gunn does.

1. Why is it significant that the porch is (a) *small?* (b) *imitation marble?* (c) *never sunny?*
2. The man is not just sitting in a chair. He is sitting in a *kitchen* chair. Why?
3. The man's body is *crumpled.* The word *crumpled,* while specific and powerful, is open to interpretation. How do you interpret it?
4. What is symbolic about the *cold railing?*
5. (a) Why does the word *planned* seem somehow inappropriate? (b) How does it add an encouraging note?

Motivation for Reading Have your students imagine how they might portray a typical elderly person living today. In general how are the elderly portrayed in contemporary films and art? What about people such as Arthur Rubinstein, Grandma Moses, Georgia O'Keeffe, and many others who worked well into their later years? Are they different? How?

Purpose-Setting Question What words has the author used to make vivid the man who is sitting on the porch?

1 **Discussion** What details are given about the man's environment? What do these contribute to the poem's meaning?

2 **Discussion** Why does the author describe the man's body position? What do the words beginning "cupped by himself . . ." indicate about the man's life?

3 **Discussion** What has the man planned? What does his plan suggest about him?

---

clear that the man is merely seeing the passers-by, not personally interacting with them.

Interpreting

3. Answers will differ. Suggested Response: The words "he lives what he can" and "getting a little strength" suggest the man is not able to lead an active life.
4. Suggested Response: The man is stimulated by the sight of people going to work, children playing, couples taking a walk, and so on.
5. Answers will differ. Suggested Response: The tone of the poem is factual and unemotional.
6. Answers will differ. Suggested Response: The passers-by on Taylor Street are critical to the old man's survival, providing his "little strength." Taylor Street is thus a kind of lifeline in the poem.

Applying

7. Answers will differ. Suggested Response: The description suggests the man is an ordinary working man who earned his living by physical labor. He seems to have been a bit of a loner yet decisive, since he is still making decisions to live from day to day.

ANSWERS TO ANALYZING LITERATURE

1. Suggested response: It is significant that the porch is (a) *small,* to indicate the smallness of the man's environment; (b) *imitation marble,* to indicate the desire for something nice yet a lack of funds to have it; and (c) *never sunny,* to indicate the lack of love, warmth, and laughter in the man's life.
2. Suggested Response: In one sense a kitchen chair is a warm, homey touch. Yet kitchen chairs are usually straight and somewhat uncomfortable. This choice says the man is not out sitting comfortably on his porch, but is there for a purpose.
3. Suggested Response: The word "crumpled" could suggest the man's body is simply bent over or that he is lacking outside contact, comfort, and stimulation and thus must in effect hug himself.
4. Suggested Response: The railing physically separates the man from the passers-by. Its coldness suggests the coldness and lack of emotional contact between the man and the people.
5. (a) From the previous description, one might not think the man capable of reflecting on his life and making plans for his days. (b) The word is encouraging. It suggests the man's mind and will are alive and that he is choosing to live.

More About the Author Ted Hughes once commented that his poems are "not about violence but vitality." Poetry became his whole life when he married Sylvia Plath. Prior to that he had worked as a gardener, a groundskeeper for the Royal Canadian Air Force, and a script reader. Hughes was born in 1930, eight years after Donald Davie and Philip Larkin. Therefore, he missed some of their direct experiences with World War II. He noted that he was far more willing than they to deal directly with issues of violence and savagery in his writing. Ask the students to discuss the effect of an author's birthday on his or her writing. What might be different about the writings of an author born in 1940, 1950, or 1960 simply because of their differences in age?

TED HUGHES

1930–

A major contemporary poet, Ted Hughes has been widely praised for his portrayal of nature in all its fierceness and primitive cruelty. Hughes differs from "the Movement" poets, who, he says, "wanted it cozy." There is nothing cozy about Hughes's starkly defined animal world. His diction, in the words of one critic, is "a solid phalanx of buffeting verbs and steel-heeled nouns." Yet Hughes, despite his verbal violence, shows a masterful ability to describe nature, seeking links between its universal force and the human condition.

The poet, born Edward J. Hughes, grew up in a rural region of western Yorkshire, served in the Royal Air Force, and attended Pembroke College, Cambridge. In 1956 he married the American poet Sylvia Plath. The couple lived in the United States for two years. Plath died in 1963.

Nature is a dominant theme in Hughes's poetry. His first book of poems, *The Hawk in the Rain,* appeared in 1957 and brought him immediate success. *Crow* (1970), *Crow Wakes* (1971) and *Eat Crow* (1972), reveal his characteristic style. In them, an animal observes and comments upon the human condition. Because of his use of animal characters, Hughes has been compared to both Aesop and George Orwell. The British critic A. Alvarez calls Hughes "the most powerful and original poet now writing in this country."

Objectives

1 To understand the meaning of personification in poetry
2 To use personification in original writing
3 To write a poem in which personification is used

Teaching Portfolio: Support Material

Teacher Backup, p. 000

Vocabulary Check, pp. 00

Usage and Mechanics Worksheet, p. 00

Analyzing Literature Worksheet, p. 00

Critical Thinking and Reading Worksheet, p. 00

Language Worksheet, p. 00

Selection Test, p. 000

GUIDE FOR READING

Hawk Roosting; The Horses

Writer's Techniques

Personification. Personification is a figure of speech in which a thing, a quality, or an idea is given human attributes. For example, when Edmund Spenser writes that envy "rode upon a ravenous wolf," he is using personification. Sometimes personification is extended well beyond a phrase or sentence and involves point of view. Events are observed through the eyes or mind of a nonhuman narrator. A familiar example of such extended personification is Jack London's *The Call of the Wild,* in which the story is told from the viewpoint of Buck, a dog. Like simile, metaphor, and other figures of speech, personification presents ideas and details in fresh, original ways.

Look For

As you read the poems by Ted Hughes, notice how he uses personification and observe the effect or effects it produces.

Writing

Choose at least five inanimate objects—a pencil, a painting, a computer, for instance—and write a sentence about each one, giving the object human attributes. ("My pencil stopped short at the word *goodbye,* refusing to finish the sentence.") Although animals and plants can be the subjects of personification, try to limit your examples to purely inanimate (lifeless) objects, qualities, or ideas.

Vocabulary

Knowing the following words will help you as you read the poems by Ted Hughes.

sophistry (säf′ is trē) *n.*: Clever but unsound reasoning (p. 1310, l. 15)

moorline (moor′ līn) *n.*: The horizon where open, rolling wasteland meets the sky (p. 1312, l. 7)

dregs (dregz) *n.*: The sediment of liquids (p. 1312, l. 7)

megalith (meg′ ə lith′) *n.*: A huge stone, especially one used in prehistoric monuments (p. 1312, l. 10)

Literary Focus An author's use of personification may grow out of his or her basic recognition of "self" as related to nature. Artists often try to personify complex ideas, for example, using an eagle to personify freedom or even creating a sculpture such as the Statue of Liberty.

Writing We speak of raging storms, stars looking down, giggling dogs, and crafty cats. Have the students listen carefully to conversations and to television and radio dialogue. How many examples of personification do they find? Add examples from their freewriting. Do any especially interesting examples or patterns emerge?

Vocabulary Be prepared to discuss the connotations of Hughes's words and phrases whose denotations should present few problems to your students.

Hawk Roosting

Ted Hughes

I sit in the top of the wood, my eyes closed. 1
Inaction, no falsifying dream
Between my hooked head and hooked feet: 2
Or in sleep rehearse perfect kills and eat.

The convenience of the high trees!
The air's buoyancy and the sun's ray 3
Are of advantage to me;
And the earth's face upward for my inspection.

My feet are locked upon the rough bark.
It took the whole of Creation
To produce my foot, my each feather:
Now I hold Creation in my foot 4

Or fly up, and revolve it all slowly—
I kill where I please because it is all mine.
There is no sophistry in my body:
My manners are tearing off heads—

The allotment of death.
For the one path of my flight is direct 5
Through the bones of the living.
No arguments assert my right:

The sun is behind me.
Nothing has changed since I began. 6
My eye has permitted no change.
I am going to keep things like this.

Motivation for Reading Have students imagine a favorite animal-cartoon character. Notice how the character is humanized —a person in animal clothing. Now imagine the animal could speak from its own viewpoint. How would it describe its life? What might it say about itself and its surroundings? Would the animal's outlook be the same as our outlook towards it?

Master Teacher Note "Hawk Roosting" explores the inner being of a hawk. To vivify his portrait, Hughes isolates the bird from everything and everybody. The effect is surrealistic and frightening. Imagine the effect if you were to clip away objects in a black-and-white photo one by one, leaving the remaining objects on a black or gray background. How does the effect of the photograph change as objects are removed? What happens when only one object or detail remains?

Purpose-Setting Question What is the total effect created by having the hawk speak?

1 **Discussion** Why does the author place the hawk "in the top of the wood"? What is the effect of this on the reader?

2 **Critical Thinking and Reading** Hughes immediately clarifies that it is a hawk speaking, not a person. Note the hawk's thoughts while sleeping. Why does the author repeat the word *hooked* to describe hawk's head and feet?

3 **Literary Focus** How do these lines show with the hawk's feelings? Is the use of personification here more or less effective than the author's just describing how the hawk felt?

4 **Literary Focus** Notice how the author has expressed a complex idea in a few words. In what way can the hawk "hold Creation" in its foot?

5 **Discussion** How has the tone of the hawk's conversation changed? Does what is said here follow logically from what was said in stanzas one and two?

6 **Discussion** Is it good that "Nothing has changed"? Why is the sun behind the hawk's head?

THINKING ABOUT THE SELECTION

Recalling

1. (a) Who is the speaker in the poem? (b) Where is the speaker sitting?
2. What does the speaker do while sleeping?
3. What are three advantages that allow the speaker to "kill where I please"?

Interpreting

4. What does stanza 3 suggest about the physical makeup and abilities of the speaker?
5. In lines 14–16, how does the speaker refute the "falsifying dream" that nature is invariably pleasant and nonviolent?
6. (a) What do you think the speaker means by "Nothing has changed since I began"? (b) How might you interpret the line in another way?
7. (a) What does the poet's (not the speaker's) view of nature seem to be? (b) How do you feel about that view?

Applying

8. Nature can be violent. What have you seen in your own experience that shows this to be true? What other moods can you identify in nature? Provide examples that reveal these moods.

ANALYZING LITERATURE

Using Personification

Giving human attributes to a thing, a quality, or an idea is called **personification.** In "Hawk Roosting," Ted Hughes uses the technique to present his ideas about nature in an unusual and striking way.

1. Personification requires giving human attributes to something nonhuman. How is the hawk personified in Hughes's poem?
2. Why do you think Hughes has the hawk speak for itself in the poem rather than having a human speaker interpret what the hawk might be thinking?

THINKING AND WRITING

Using Personification in a Poem

Choose a bird very unlike the hawk. For example, you might choose a sparrow or a lark. Freewrite, exploring what this animal might see as it looks at the world. Then write a poem in which you personify this creature. Your poem can be short or long, rhymed or unrhymed. Have it speak, telling what it sees. When you revise make sure you have given your bird human characteristics.

Answers

ANSWERS TO THINKING ABOUT THE SELECTION

Recalling

1. (a) The hawk is the speaker in the poem. (b) The hawk is sitting high in the top of the tree.
2. While sleeping the hawk rehearses ways to kill prey and the feeling of eating it.
3. Suggested Response: The hawk can spot prey from high in the air. It can hold live prey in its hooked claws and fly away with it. It can kill and feed where it pleases.

Interpreting

4. Answers will differ. Suggested Response: Stanza three suggests that the hawk is an extraordinary physical creature. His feet are perfectly designed both for living in his environment and for holding onto live prey.
5. In lines 14–16 the hawk describes his merciless, mechanical way of killing. In nature animals kill prey without feeling or remorse.
6. Answers will differ. Suggested Responses: (a) The hawk is suggesting the even plan of its existence. Complex thoughts and interactions have no part in its life. (b) Perhaps the speaker is referring to nature's seemingly unchanging life-cycle that carries on from generation to generation.
7. Answers will differ. Suggested Responses: (a) Some ideas might be that nature is cruel, violent, and mechanistic. Creatures do not act feelingly toward one another. (b) Some students might want to soften Hughes's view by describing their feelings toward nature. Others may point to the truth of the idea that animals are not human.

Applying

8. Answers will differ. Suggested Response: Students may have observed such things as a blue jay cracking open and eating a stolen robin's egg. Students will probably mention a number of human moods that nature seems to display—for example, a violent storm, which can suggest anger.

ANSWERS TO ANALYZING LITERATURE

1. The hawk is endowed with the capacity of uttering humanlike thoughts.
2. Hughes's method leads to a direct, more vivid presentation of the hawk.

THINKING AND WRITING

For help with this assignment, students can refer to Lesson 18, "Writing a Poem," in the Handbook of Writing About Literature.

Motivation for Reading Ask the students to imagine or recall a special experience that somehow won't go away—a picture of the sun rising over the lake, or the view from a mountaintop on a perfect winter day. The event crops up in memory, and we search for new meanings for it. Are such experiences common for people? Are they important for living? Can they in any way help determine the direction of someone's life?

Master Teacher Note Ted Hughes's poem tells about a person's experience of seeing horses in a woods and the effect of the experience on the person at a much later time. Discuss the effect of a simple incident on some artists—Dante's seeing Beatrice, for example. Bring in examples of the work of artists who paint the same or similar things—over and over—Van Gogh's sunflowers, Georgia O'Keeffe's Arizona mountain.

Purpose-Setting Question What does this poem suggest about the effect of a memory on a person's life?

1 **Literary Focus** Describe the scene, using the author's own words. What was the speaker's mood then? How might someone else have described the same scene?

2 **Discussion** What is the only action of the horses? What do the details in these lines contribute to the poem's meaning?

3 **Discussion** What characteristic of the horses made the most lasting impression on the speaker? How do you know this?

The Horses

Ted Hughes

I climbed through woods in the hour-before-dawn dark.
Evil air, a frost-making stillness,

Not a leaf, not a bird—
A world cast in frost. I came out above the wood

1 Where my breath left tortuous statues in the iron light.
But the valleys were draining the darkness

Till the moorline—blackening dregs of the brightening
  gray—
Halved the sky ahead. And I saw the horses:

Huge in the dense gray—ten together—
2 Megalith-still. They breathed, making no move,

With draped manes and tilted hind-hooves,
Making no sound.

I passed: not one snorted or jerked its head.
Gray silent fragments

3 Of a gray silent world.

I listened in emptiness on the moor-ridge.
The curlew's[1] tear turned its edge on the silence.

Slowly detail leafed from the darkness. Then the sun
Orange, red, red erupted

Silently, and splitting to its core tore and flung cloud,
Shook the gulf open, showed blue,

And the big planets hanging—
I turned

Stumbling in the fever of a dream, down towards
The dark woods, from the kindling tops.

---

1. **curlew** (kʉr′ lo͞o) *n.*: A large, brownish wading bird with long legs.

And came to the horses.
There, still they stood,
But now steaming and glistening under the flow of light,

Their draped stone manes, their tilted hind-hooves
Stirring under a thaw while all around them

The frost showed its fires. But still they made no sound.
Not one snorted or stamped,

Their hung heads patient as the horizons,
High over valleys, in the red leveling rays—

In din of the crowded streets, going among the years, the faces,
May I still meet my memory in so lonely a place

Between the streams and the red clouds, hearing curlews,
Hearing the horizons endure.

THINKING ABOUT THE SELECTION

Recalling

1. What are four words in lines 1–15 that depict the atmosphere of the morning?
2. How are the horses different in the second sighting than in the first?
3. What wish does the speaker make in the last four lines of the poem?

Interpreting

4. (a) In your own words, what does "detail leafed from the darkness" in line 18 mean? (b) What does "the sun/Orange, red, red erupted" in lines 19 and 20 mean?
5. (a) What is the figure of speech in line 33? (b) How do you explain the comparison?
6. The view of nature is different in "The Horses" from that in "Hawk Roosting." What is the basic difference?

Applying

7. Think of a place you would like to remember later, in "the crowded streets, going among the years." (a) What kind of place is it? (b) Why would you like to remember it?

THINKING AND WRITING

Comparing Poems

Reread William Wordsworth's "Lines Composed a Few Miles Above Tintern Abbey." Then write an essay in which you compare Wordsworth's view of nature with that of Ted Hughes in "The Horses." Make notes before you begin to write. Jot down a few specific lines from each poem to support your comparison. In writing your first draft, be willing to speculate on the reasons for the differences between the poems. When you revise your first draft, check to be sure that your statements are supported by evidence from the poems.

4 **Discussion** Looking back over the whole poem, why is this memory so important for the speaker? What do the horses represent to him?

Answers

ANSWERS TO THINKING ABOUT THE SELECTION

Recalling

1. Some words depicting the morning atmosphere are *dark, evil, frost,* and *grey*.
2. In the second sighting the horses are "steaming and glistening." They have started to move their hind hooves.
3. The speaker wishes he might still meet the memory of his experience in the midst of his ongoing busy life.

Interpreting

4. Answers will differ. Suggested Responses: (a) With the gradual coming of dawn, the shapes of individual objects become clearer, as upon closer inspection one can see individual leaves on a tree. (b) Sometimes, especially on a stormy day, the sun at sunrise will look like a bright red ball. Hughes's description is eerie and suggests something ominous is about to happen.
5. (a) The simile in line 33 compares the patient horses to the patient horizon high over the valley, awaiting the sunrise. (b) Answers will differ. Suggested Response: The comparison is tied to the speaker's reaction. He judges both the horses and the horizon to be patient. Nature's patient waiting is important as it implies confidence that the sun will indeed rise.
6. Answers will differ. Suggested Response: In "Hawk Roosting" the message comes entirely through the hawk, who views nature as mechanistic, isolating, and without compassion. In "The Horses," nature is seen through human eyes. The speaker finds in his experience with nataure an important message to help him endure his life.

Applying

7. Answers will differ. Encourage students to think of experiences in places and to note that the place, as in the poem, might be an ordinary and even familiar spot.

Challenge Does the author clearly define what the experience with the horses meant to the speaker? How important is this information to understanding the meaning of the poem?

THINKING AND WRITING

Publishing Student Writing Have students help design a classroom or library bulletin board on Personification. Include student artwork and writing as well as examples from cartoons and artworks by major artists and writers.

More About the Author Stevie Smith modeled many poems on nineteenth-century British and American poems, hymns, and popular songs. Her works do not fit a category, and hence critics have sometimes overlooked them. Discuss with your students how an author's belonging to a recognizable group might affect his or her popularity or critical acclaim. What problems might an author who writes different or unusual works encounter today?

Literary Focus Voice was basic in Stevie Smith's poems. She often recited her verse in plainsong. Numerous shifts in rhythm change the tone and meaning. Encourage the students to listen to people talking during their day. How are people's changing moods and attitudes reflected in their voice rhythm?

Look For Some students may have difficulty picking out the speakers and understanding how voice works. Review the terms *idiom* and *intonation,* and have the students discuss other devices they have encountered before.

Writing Before having students write, have them speak a few sentences into a tape recorder. After freewriting, let them listen to the tape and comment on their spoken voice. Is their comment the same as it is about their written voice? Why or why not?

Vocabulary Have some students make a brief list of similes for *larking.* Note some of the similes are particularly American, as *larking* is British. Have a few other students read about pikes in an encyclopedia. Why might the author have chosen this fish rather than another?

GUIDE FOR READING

Not Waving but Drowning; Pretty

Stevie Smith (1902–1971) shows intelligence, honesty, and wit in her poetry. Her poems are hard to categorize because of their variations in tone, form, and perspective. One critic calls her work "a forest of themes and attitudes." She is, the critic continues, "as surprising as she is skillful, her finesse equal to her boldness." This independent-minded poet was born Florence Margaret Smith in Hull, Yorkshire. Small as a child, she was nicknamed "Stevie" after a famous jockey. She attended local schools, worked for many years in a magazine publisher's office in London, and often gave poetry readings on English radio and television. Her first novel, *Novel on Yellow Paper,* appeared in 1936, and her first collection of poems, *A Good Time Was Had by All,* in 1937.

The Writer's Techniques

Voice. When a poet writes, the poet has a voice—a speaker's voice that can use idiom, rhythm, intonation, and other devices to achieve its effects. When you, the reader, scan a poem (even though silently), you "hear" a voice expressing the words in the poem. You notice, often without conscious thought, the pauses, the pitch, the stresses on certain words and syllables. If you are alert, you will also perceive the feelings behind the voice, such as excitement, panic, despair, or indifference. Voice, then, is an aspect of tone and can be described by an adjective or adjectives, just as tone can be.

Look For

As you read the poems by Stevie Smith, listen for the speaker's voice in each one. Notice that there may be more than one speaker in a poem, and the speaker may change without notice.

Writing

Freewrite for a few minutes, using your own natural voice. Make no effort to put your words into complete, grammatically correct sentences. Simply write as you think, quickly and even disjointedly. When you have finished, look back on what you have written. How would you describe your written voice? Serious? Amusing? Casual? Try to decide on the adjective that best describes it.

Vocabulary

Knowing the following words will help you as you read the poems by Stevie Smith.

larking (lärk′iŋ) *v.*: Playing around (p. 1315, l. 5)

pike (pīk) *n.*: A voracious freshwater fish (p. 1316, l. 4)

abashes (ə bash′iz) *v.*: Becomes ashamed or confused (p. 1316, l. 17)

Objectives

1 To understand the use of voice in a poem
2 To listen for the speaker's voice in a poem, noting changes in speakers
3 To write an evaluation of a poem using a good thesis statements and making references to the lines in the poem

Teaching Portfolio: Support Material

Teacher Backup, p. 000

Lesson Plan, pp. 00–00

Vocabulary Check, p. 00

Usage and Mechanics Worksheet, p. 00

Analyzing Literature Worksheet, p. 00

Critical Thinking and Reading Worksheet, p. 00

Understanding Language Worksheet, p. 00

Selection Test, p. 00

Art Transparency 20, *Concordia* by Graham Nickson

Not Waving but Drowning

Stevie Smith

Nobody heard him, the dead man,
But still he lay moaning: 1
I was much further out than you thought
And not waving but drowning. 2

Poor chap, he always loved larking
And now he's dead 3
It must have been too cold for him his heart gave way,
They said.

Oh, no no no, it was too cold always
(Still the dead one lay moaning)
I was much too far out all my life 4
And not waving but drowning.

THINKING ABOUT THE SELECTION

Recalling

1. Five lines in the poem are spoken by the dead man. Which lines are they?
2. (a) How did the spectators interpret the dead man's waving? (b) What led them to make this interpretation?
3. What caused the man's death?

Interpreting

4. What does the *it* represent in line 9, "Oh, no no no, it was too cold always"?
5. In what sense was the dead man "too far out" all his life?
6. In line 4, the phrase "not waving but drowning" seems to be the literal truth. In line 12, the same phrase has a metaphorical meaning. What is its metaphorical meaning?

Applying

7. What kinds of distress signals in ordinary life might be interpreted as "waving"?

ANALYZING LITERATURE

Understanding Voice

"Not Waving but Drowning" appears to be simple, but the appearance is deceptive. Three speakers can be identified in it: a narrator, a spectator (or spectators), and the dead man. The narrator's voice (lines 1, 2 and 10) is matter-of-fact and neutral, if a bit puzzled. The narrator's double use of the word *moaning* adds to your understanding of the dead man's distress.

1. Study lines 5–7. (a) What adjective or adjectives do you think accurately describe the voice of the spectators? (b) Explain.
2. (a) What adjective or adjectives describe the voice of the dead man? (b) Explain.

Motivation for Reading Ask the students if there are situations in life when people totally misunderstand the actions of others. How might it feel to be the one misunderstood? What might result from misunderstanding an action?

Master Teacher Note Note the effect of having the dead man speak. Discuss with the students how this "unreal" situation is somehow made "real" and adds to the meaning of the poem.

Purpose-Setting Question What does setting the reality of the dead man against the reality of the onlookers do to help you understand more about the meaning of reality in life?

1 **Reading Strategy** What was the dead man's first sound? Could the dead man actually be speaking, while the listener interprets it as moaning?

2 **Discussion** Who is the speaker? Whom is he talking to? Is he responding to their comments?

3 **Reading Strategy** Are these lines more responsive to what the other speaker is saying? Why?

Discussion How does the author use the words *waving* and *drowning* as metaphors? What is the effect of repetition in these lines? Notice the words repeated from earlier lines in the poem.

Master Teacher Note After the reading "Not Waving but Drowning," place Art Transparency 20, *Concordia* by Graham Nickson, on the overhead projector. Let your students look the painting over for a few minutes. Then challenge them by asking, "How might a very slight alteration of this painting make it an appropriate illustration for "Not Waving but Drowning"?

Answers

ANSWERS TO THINKING ABOUT THE SELECTION

Recalling

1. The lines spoken by the dead man are 4–5, 9, and 11–12.
2. (a) The spectators thought the dead man was waving in fun. (b) The dead man liked to have fun and had often played around.
3. The dead man died from drowning when no one went to his aid.

Interpreting

4. According to the dead man, it represents the climate that was around him in life.
5. The dead man was unable to develop good communications and relationships with others.
6. In line 12 the dead man reveals that what others interpreted as his happy friendly exterior was actually a plea for help from a man experiencing inner death.

Applying

7. Answers will differ. Suggested Response: A person might be distantly cheerful and friendly, but never connect and form close relationships.

ANSWERS TO ANALYZING LITERATURE

1. (a) Suggested Response: *detached, cooly pitying,* or *unemotional.* (b) Answers will differ.
2. (a) Suggested Response: *Regretful* or *mildly self-critical* (b) Answers will vary.

Master Teacher Note This poem clearly reflects the author's love for the rhythm and intonation of language. Behind a genial appearance lies a frightening reality; behind an optimistic front lies powerful, sometimes terrible truth. To help students appreciate the use of connotation, have them list several common adjectives and change their meanings by using them in different situations. Include both positive and negative adjectives in the list. Students should understand that word meanings can change with circumstances and a person's mood.

Purpose-Setting Question In what way is this poem about much more than the author's concern for the word *pretty* or her desire to describe a scene in nature?

1 **Reading Strategy** Have the students list the images in lines 1–16 in order. What pattern emerges from the list?

2 **Discussion** How can an eye "not see enough"? Why might the author introduce the person viewing the scene in this way?

3 **Discussion** Why does the author use "thief" to describe a person here? From whose viewpoint is the person a thief?

4 **Discussion** How does the author answer the question posed in line 1 here? Is the answer unusual?

Pretty

Stevie Smith

Why is the word pretty so underrated?
In November the leaf is pretty when it falls
The stream grows deep in the woods after rain
And in the pretty pool the pike stalks

He stalks his prey, and this is pretty too,
The prey escapes with an underwater flash
But not for long, the great fish has him now
1 The pike is a fish who always has his prey

And this is pretty. The water rat is pretty
His paws are not webbed, he cannot shut his nostrils
As the otter can and the beaver, he is torn between
The land and water. Not "torn," he does not mind.

The owl hunts in the evening and it is pretty
The lake water below him rustles with ice
There is frost coming from the ground, in the air mist
All this is pretty, it could not be prettier.

Yes, it could always be prettier, the eye abashes
2 It is becoming an eye that cannot see enough,
Out of the wood the eye climbs. This is prettier
A field in the evening, tilting up.

The field tilts to the sky. Though it is late
The sky is lighter than the hill field
All this looks easy but really it is extraordinary
Well, it is extraordinary to be so pretty.

And it is careless, and that is always pretty
This field, this owl, this pike, this pool are careless,
As Nature is always careless and indifferent
Who sees, who steps, means nothing, and this is pretty.

3 So a person can come along like a thief—pretty!—
Stealing a look, pinching the sound and feel,
Lick the icicle broken from the bank
And still say nothing at all, only cry pretty.

Cry pretty, pretty, pretty and you'll be able
Very soon not even to cry pretty
4 And so be delivered entirely from humanity
This is prettiest of all, it is very pretty.

THINKING ABOUT THE SELECTION

Recalling

1. In the first four stanzas, what are seven things that the speaker says are pretty?
2. Why does the speaker feel the need to see beyond the wood?
3. What is "prettiest of all"?

Interpreting

4. The speaker does not define *pretty* directly but only through examples. What is the speaker's implied definition of *pretty?*
5. How does the speaker feel about the fact that nature is "careless and indifferent"?
6. (a) What do you think the speaker means by "being delivered entirely from humanity"? (b) Why might the speaker regard that as pretty?

Applying

7. What aspect of nature—other than its prettiness—can serve as a useful example for human beings? Explain.

CRITICAL THINKING AND READING

Comparing and Contrasting Attitudes

Both Ted Hughes in "Hawk Roosting" and Stevie Smith in "Pretty" accept the everyday violence in nature. To Hughes, the hawk's "manners are tearing off heads." To Smith, the pike's stalking and capture of its prey are "pretty." Yet Hughes and Smith express themselves very differently about nature's unconcern.

1. Both the Hughes poem and the Smith poem have been described as "chilling." Which poet—or neither or both of them—do you think views nature as being essentially benign? Explain.
2. A poet's attitudes are expressed in words. List ten key words from each poem that support your answer to the preceding question.

THINKING AND WRITING

Evaluating a Poem

Write an essay evaluating either of Stevie Smith's poems. Begin by deciding which poem you prefer, or which poem you believe will allow you to express the most convincing opinion. Write a thesis sentence that states your opinion clearly. Use lines from the poem in writing your first draft. When you revise, make a special effort to see that the quoted lines fit smoothly and effectively into what you have written. Your final draft should be as error-free as you can make it. Prepare this draft and share it with your classmates. Compare your reaction to the poems with theirs.

Answers

ANSWERS TO THINKING ABOUT THE SELECTION

Recalling

1. Seven things the speaker says are pretty are a falling leaf, a pool, a pike stalking prey, a pike getting prey, a water rat, an owl hunting, and frost forming.
2. A view beyond the woods is "extraordinary" and more cosmic, including sky and hills.
3. Being "delivered entirely from humanity" is prettiest.

Interpreting

4. The speaker implies that pretty is the quality of being striking to the eye, vivid, or vital, because it includes even things not thought of as "pretty." Pretty describes a kind of cosmic truth about nature and reality.
5. The speaker feels it is somehow nature's right and privilege to be careless and indifferent.
6. (a) Answers will differ. Suggested Response: The phrase might refer to death, but more clearly means deliverance from association with ordinary, insensitive humanity. (b) Answers will differ. Suggested Response: The speaker feels disassociated from most people, viewing nature and life in a different way.

Applying

7. Answers will differ. Suggested Response: Some aspects of nature that can serve as useful examples are breeding cycles, living habits, and so on.

ANSWERS TO CRITICAL THINKING AND READING

1. Answers will differ. Suggested Response: The word *benign* is defined as "good natured or kindly" or "not malignant." The hawk is portrayed as totally isolated, not relating to anyone or anything. It is clearly not good natured, nor is it not malignant, since it accepts "tearing off heads" as a way of life. In Smith's poem, nature is portrayed as "indifferent" and "careless." The word *benign* might be used for this poem, in the sense of not malignant.
2. The word choices will differ but may include for "Hawk Roosting"—*hooked, head, hooked feet, perfect kills, feet locked, tearing off heads, allotment of death,* and *through bones of the living;* and for "Pretty" —*pike stalks, beaver is torn, field tilling up, it is careless,* and *indifferent.*

THINKING AND WRITING

For help with this assignment, students can refer to Lesson 15, "Evaluating a Literary Work," in the Handbook of Writing About Literature.

More About the Author The rhythmic language and strong verbal precision of the poet are also part of Elaine Feinstein's novels, in which she has also used unconventional punctuation, ending a sentence in mid-phrase. Discuss with the students the difficulties of reading and appreciating an unconventional writer. Is it important or valuable to work at appreciating unconventional writers, or should we demand that they conform to our expectations?

Literary Focus Style is the unique composite of a writer's experience brought forth in his or her use of precise rhythms and word choices. Though style is hard to define, we recognize it in our daily lives when we say that someone acts like Meryl Streep or Al Pacino, paints like Degas, or sings like Lionel Ritchie.

Look For Your **less advanced** students may find it difficult to grasp the concept of style. A class discussion on this subject may be useful.

Writing Have the students do word associations for one or two common words. How many chose the same association? Give them time to develop at least three other associations for the same words. Discuss the responses. After they have completed their journal writing, discuss why its important to expand word associations.

Vocabulary Have your **less advanced** students read the words aloud. You may want to show students a photo of a ketch, of a poke, of a fen and of something luminescent.

GUIDE FOR READING

Anniversary; Out

Elaine Feinstein (1930–) is an inventive poet. Her first collection of poems, *In a Green Eye,* appeared in 1966, and her first novel, *The Circle,* four years later. In both prose and poetry, Feinstein displays a sly sense of humor coupled with a discerning fidelity to her own experience. Born in Bootle, Lancashire, Feinstein received her B.A. and M.A. from Cambridge University, then worked as an editor, teacher, translator, and journalist.

The Writer's Techniques

Style. Feinstein says: "I began to write poetry in the '60s very consciously influenced by American poets (Emily Dickinson and William Carlos Williams, in particular), at a time when line, and spacing, to indicate the movement of poetry was much less fashionable than it is now among young British poets."

Look For

As you read the poems by Elaine Feinstein, look for the characteristics of her style. Notice her minimal punctuation and her use of spaces and line breaks to substitute for traditional punctuation marks.

Writing

Word associations are the uniquely personal images, experiences, or thoughts that particular words bring to mind. For example, the word *diesel* denotes a particular kind of internal-combustion engine, but its associations are not easy to predict. It might remind one person of her first close-up view of a huge locomotive in a train station. It might remind another of the distinctive smell of diesel exhaust fumes on a busy highway. Think of a common word that has unique associations for you. Jot down the random thoughts that occur to you in connection with the word.

Vocabulary

Knowing the following words will help you as you read these poems.

ketch (kech) *n.*: A two-masted sailing vessel (p. 1319, l. 1)
pokes (pōkz) *n.*: Overhanging projections, such as the brims on women's poke bonnets (p. 1319, l. 2)
luminescent (lo͞o mə nes′'nt) *adj.*: Giving out light without much heat (p. 1319, l. 6)
transfiguration (trans fig yo͞o rā′ shən) *n.*: A change in outward form or appearance (p. 1319, l. 9)
fen (fen) *n.*: A marsh or bog (p. 1320, l. 15)

Objectives

1 To understand the way style operates in a poem
2 To write effectively about the differing styles of poems by the same author

Teaching Portfolio: Support Material

Teacher Backup, p. 000

Vocabulary Check, p. 00

Usage and Mechanics Worksheet, p. 00

Analyzing Literature Worksheet, p. 00

Critical Thinking and Reading Worksheet, p. 00

Language Worksheet, p. 00

Selection Test, p. 00

Anniversary

Elaine Feinstein

Suppose I took out a slender ketch from 1
under the pokes of Palace pier tonight to
catch a sea going fish for you

or dressed in antique goggles and wings and
flew down through sycamore leaves into the park 2

or luminescent through some planetary strike
put one delicate flamingo leg over the sill of your lab

Could I surprise you? or would you insist on 3
keeping a pattern to link every transfiguration? 4

Listen, I shall have to whisper it
into your heart directly: we are all
supernatural / every day
we rise new creatures / cannot be predicted 5

THINKING ABOUT THE SELECTION

Recalling

1. What is the second "transfiguration" the speaker might make to surprise the *you*?
2. Where does the speaker suggest that the *you*—the person spoken to—might be found?
3. What descriptive word does the speaker say applies to all people?

Interpreting

4. (a) What kind of person is the *you* who is being addressed? (b) How can you tell?
5. (a) What kind of person is the speaker? (b) How can you tell?
6. In what way is the speaker's meaning for *supernatural* different from the meaning that moviegoers or readers of science fiction might be inclined to give the word?
7. Why do you think the poet calls this poem "Anniversary"?
8. What makes it clear that each of the first three stanzas is complete even though none has end punctuation?
9. Why does the poet not put the second question in stanza 4 into a separate stanza?
10. What purpose do the slashes (/) serve in the last two lines of the poem?

Applying

11. In the poem the speaker and the person spoken to seem to have quite different temperaments. How valid a perception on the poet's part do you think that is? Explain.

Motivation for Reading Have you ever overheard just one side of a conversation? Could you understand the conversation?

Master Teacher Note This poem features a seemingly realistic conversation. Point out that realism still involves careful selection, by showing several examples of realistic art.

Purpose-Setting Question What does this poem reveal about the difficulties of communication?

1 **Critical Thinking and Reading** Notice the poem's logical organization into three sections.

2 **Discussion** What three things is the listener asked to imagine the speaker doing?

3 **Discussion** What is the effect of *could* rather than *would* here?

4 **Discussion** What is the root problem being addressed?

5 **Discussion** Why might the poem end with no punctuation?

Answers

ANSWERS TO THINKING ABOUT THE SELECTION

Recalling

1. The speaker suggests dressing like a bird and flying through trees.
2. The speaker suggests that "you" could be found in a laboratory.
3. The speaker says that all people are "supernatural."

Interpreting

4. (a) Answers will differ. Suggested response: The person being addressed is intelligent, scientific, strong-willed, and opinionated. He likes order. (b) He can understand the high-level conversation of the speaker; he works in a lab; and he is insistent upon keeping a pattern.
5. (a) The speaker is intelligent, logical, creative, and imaginative. (b) She uses unusual images and high-level thinking; her points are in order.
6. The speaker uses the word to mean "going beyond the normal or usual," "not like the expected or traditional," "unpredictable."
7. On an anniversary a person is particularly likely to look back and take stock. The speaker is clearly going over some basic patterns of relationship with someone.
8. The poem begins with "Suppose." The next two stanzas begin with *or* clearly indicating changes in direction and thought.
9. She indicates the first question is rhetorical.
10. The slashes indicate that the words between them explain how we are supernatural.

Applying

11. The speaker seems to know the listener well. The fact of their closeness, however, suggests more likeness than the speaker seems to be admitting.

Motivation for Reading Have the students imagine they are asked to help someone write a factual report. Then have them imagine they are asked to help the person write a poem. Which helping job is harder? Do professional poets ever need help with writing? What kind of help? Who or what might provide that help?

Master Teacher Note This poem uses a scene to reflect a person's mood. Show the students several photos and paintings of people with things in the background. How does the background detail contribute to their understanding more about the person? If you can clip away the background detail, let them notice the effect created by looking at the people or person alone.

Purpose-Setting Question What kind of mentor would most help a creative person such as a poet?

1 **Critical Thinking and Reading** The poem begins with two three-word simple sentences. The next two sentences contain personification, similes, and imagery. Examine the imagery carefully. How does the poet use all these elements to illustrate something about the speaker's state of mind?

2 **Clarification** *Camel-thorn* is "a plant or tree in the mimosa family, which bears yellow flowers."

3 **Discussion** Why has the author placed this line here, rather than at the opening of the next stanza?

4 **Discussion** Why is the person referred to as a "spirit of invention"? Is there is a contradiction in asking for someone who is "holy" and "innocent" and using the word "unnaturally"?

5 **Discussion** What is the relationship between the builder's cranes "like birds" and the "white gulls"?

Out

Elaine Feinstein

The diesel stops. It is morning. Gray sky
is falling into the mud. At the waterside
1, 2 two builders' cranes are sitting like birds

and the yellow gorse[1] pushes up
like camel-thorn between oil-drums and old cars.
3 Who shall I take for my holy poet

to lead me out of this plain? I want an
4 innocent spirit of invention: a Buster Keaton[2]
to sail unnaturally overhead by simple leverage and

fire the machinery. Then we should all spring out of our
heads, dazzled with hope, even the white-faced ticket
collector dozing over his fag,[3] at such an intervention

5 suddenly in this stopped engine, we should
see the white gulls rising out of the rain over
the fen: and know our own freedom.

---

1. gorse *n.*: A prickly green shrub with yellow flowers.
2. Buster Keaton: An American motion-picture actor (1895–1966), who was among the most popular silent film comedians, having created a character who, though he never smiled, was able to overcome all obstacles.
3. fag: Cigarette.

THINKING ABOUT THE SELECTION

Recalling

1. What is the setting of this poem?
2. How does the speaker describe the kind of holy poet she is seeking?
3. What would happen if someone were to appear and "fire the machinery"?

Interpreting

4. To what extent would the effect of the scene be different if the cranes were busily at work rather than standing idle?
5. The speaker wants to be led "out of this plain." In your own words, define *plain* as the poet is using the word.
6. Why do you think a "Buster Keaton" is needed to shake things up?
7. Explain the analogy suggested in the last stanza.

Applying

8. Besides poetry, what is a healthful and effective way to lift oneself out of a bleak mood?

THINKING AND WRITING

Writing About Style

Write an essay about Elaine Feinstein's style. Consider her remarks about her own poetry (see Writer's Techniques, page 1318). Then review "Anniversary" and "Out" carefully. You will notice should take into consideration. Think about Feinstein's subject matter and her ideas as well as about her word choice, imagery, sentence structure, usage, and punctuation. Style is a very broad concept. Make a chart comparing and contrasting the style in both. When you write your first draft, include lines from the poem to illustrate and clarify your statements. When you revise the first draft, pay close attention to your own style. A good essay should be enjoyable and thought-provoking—and your writing style largely determines if it is. Make sure you have supported your main idea with details from the poems. Have you quoted precisely and accurately? Have you punctuated quotations accurately? Proofread your essay and prepare a final draft.

Answers

ANSWERS TO THINKING ABOUT THE SELECTION

Recalling

1. The setting is a bleak railroad siding where an engine is pulled in for refueling.
2. The speaker describes the holy poet as an "innocent spirit of invention."
3. If someone were to "fire the machinery," the speaker and others would know their own freedom.

Interpreting

4. Answers will differ. Suggested Response: If the cranes were busy it would indicate that something was being built today, a suggestion of growth and aliveness.
5. Answers will differ. Suggested Response: *Plain* here has the meaning of a personal dry place, where originality and creativity have seemingly fled.
6. Answers will differ. Suggested Response: The presence of such a character would add interest, humor, the unusual, and the alive to a drab scene.
7. Answers will differ. Suggested Response: The last line suggests an analogy between knowledge of our freedom and seeing white gulls rise out of a fen.

Applying

8. Answers will differ. Suggested Response: There are many ways to lift oneself out of a bleak mood, such as walking, listening to music, or calling a friend.

Challenge What kinds of things could be spirits of invention? Discuss those things mentioned in the poem and add your own ideas.

More About the Author Seamus Heaney grew up as an Irish Catholic on a family farm that bordered the estate of a British peer. As an adult he embodies both his rural Irish past and his cultured British education, along with the many experiences he has had while traveling and lecturing worldwide. Discuss with the students the relationship of a writer to his cultural roots. How much might those roots dictate a poet's themes and concerns? Are they likely to affect his style as well?

Literary Focus Sounds not only help complement the meaning of words in poetry, they help create meaning. Point out to the students that though we may not often recognize it we are very responsive to sounds. A mother reacts differently to certain cries of her infant. Radio and television commercials use catchy sound-patterns to sell merchandise.

Look For Most students will benefit from reviewing the Analyzing Literature section on page 1324 and the Critical Thinking and Reading section on page 1327. These will help them recognize sound patterns and the use of figurative language in the poems.

Writing Have the students play a game by making up words for some common sounds. Make a list of the best examples, with definitions. After they have completed their writing assignment you might have them use some of their ten words or even the new words in a descriptive paragraph.

Vocabulary Have **less advanced** students read the words aloud to be sure they will read them correctly in the poems. Provide more information about the terms *sock, headrig,* and *cockle* as needed.

GUIDE FOR READING

Follower; Shore Woman

Seamus Heaney (1939–), born in county Derry, Northern Ireland, has devoted much of his poetry to the life, history, and conflict of his homeland. He is a gifted traditionalist whom the American poet Robert Lowell has called "the most important Irish poet since Yeats." Educated at Queen's University, Belfast, Heaney has taught at various universities in Ireland, England, and the United States. Since the publication of his first collection of poems in 1965, he has gained an increasingly large and enthusiastic audience on both sides of the Atlantic.

Writer's Techniques

Figurative Language. A poet, like every other writer and speaker, uses two kinds of language: literal and figurative. Literal language is that which means exactly what it says. "The audience applauded the candidate's speech loudly" is a literal statement. "The candidate's speech brought down the house," by contrast, is not literal. It is figurative. Figurative language (language containing one or more *figures of speech*) has meaning beyond its literal meaning, or apart from it.

Look For

As you read the poems by Seamus Heaney, look for his use of figurative language to express the meaning he intends.

Writing

The English language contains a great deal of onomatopoeia—words whose natural sound matches their meaning. Three examples are *buzz, tinkle,* and *twang.* Think about the sounds you hear every day. What words describe them? Write down at least ten examples of onomatopoeia, not including the words already given.

Vocabulary

Knowing the following words will help you as you read the poems by Seamus Heaney.

sock (säk) *n.*: The blade of a plow (p. 1323, l. 6)
headrig (hed′rig) *n.*: The part of a plow that turns over the furrow slice; moldboard (p. 1323, l. 8)
hobnailed (häb′nāld) *adj.*: Studded with nails to prevent wear or slipping (p. 1323 l. 13)
cockle (käk′'l) *n.*: A weed that grows among grain (p. 1325, l. 4)
viscous (vis′kəs) *adj.*: Semifluid; sticky (p. 1325, l. 7)
dunt (dunt) *n.*: A heavy, dull-sounding blow (p. 1327, l. 38)
sinewed (sin′yo͞od) *adj.*: Powerful (p. 1327, l. 47)

Objectives

1 To become familiar with how literal and figurative language are used in poetry
2 To review basic devices used to create sound and how they contribute to a poem's meaning
3 To write an effective analysis of devices for creating sound in a poem

Teaching Portfolio: Support Material

Teacher Backup, p. 000

Vocabulary Check, p. 00

Usage and Mechanics Worksheet, p. 00

Analyzing Literature Worksheet, p. 00

Critical Thinking and Reading Worksheet, p. 00

Language Worksheet, p. 00

Selection Test, p. 000

Follower

Seamus Heaney

My father worked with a horse plow,
His shoulders globed like a full sail strung
Between the shafts and the furrow.
The horses strained at his clicking tongue.

An expert. He would set the wing
And fit the bright steel-pointed sock.
The sod rolled over without breaking.
At the headrig, with a single pluck

Of reins, the sweating team turned round
And back into the land. His eye
Narrowed and angled at the ground,
Mapping the furrow exactly.

I stumbled in his hobnailed wake,
Fell sometimes on the polished sod;
Sometimes he rode me on his back
Dipping and rising to his plod.

I wanted to grow up and plow,
To close one eye, stiffen my arm.
All I ever did was follow
In his broad shadow round the farm.

I was a nuisance, tripping, falling,
Yapping always. But today
It is my father who keeps stumbling
Behind me, and will not go away.

Motivation for Reading Have the students imagine they are at a farm during spring planting. A little boy toddles along behind his father, stumbling in the furrows as his father plows the fields. What might this scene illustrate about the father-son and son-father relationships? Then imagine someone looking back on this scene from his own childhood. The child is now a man. The father is older. How would the memory differ from the scene as lived? How might the childhood experience now live as part of the man and as part of the father?

Master Teacher Note Ask the students to bring in examples of magazine photos and artwork featuring parents and children. How many feature fathers and sons? How old are the children in the photos? Discuss their findings.

Purpose-Setting Question How would you explain and characterize the relationship of the boy to his father and the man to his father?

1 **Critical Thinking and Reading** Heaney divides the poem into two equal sections, one about the father, the other about the son. Are the first three stanzas only about the father, or is the son mentioned? Are the last three stanzas only about the son, or is the father mentioned?

2 **Discussion** What was the father doing? Why? What is suggested about the father's vision?

3 **Discussion** What is the contrast between these lines and lines 1–12? What effect is created by the words "Dipping and rising"?

4 **Discussion** What did the child want to do when he grew up? Why?

5 **Discussion** What contrast is used in these lines? Is it effective? Who is the "Follower" of the title?

THINKING ABOUT THE SELECTION

Recalling

1. How does the speaker show that his father was an expert at plowing?
2. As the boy accompanied his father, what did he want to do?
3. (a) What three verbs does the speaker use to describe the father's actions behind the plow? (b) What parallel verb does he use in speaking of his father today?

Interpreting

4. (a) What do you think is the approximate age of the speaker in the plowing scene he describes? (b) How can you tell?
5. Why do you think the boy wanted to close one eye and stiffen his arm?
6. The speaker says: "All I ever did was follow/In his broad shadow. . . ." What double meaning do those words suggest?
7. What is the tone of this poem? Find evidence to support your answer.

Applying

8. (a) What does this poem suggest about the changing roles of parents and children? (b) Do you think most young people are prepared for these changing roles? Explain your answer.

ANALYZING LITERATURE

Understanding Figurative Language

Figurative language is language that is not meant to be interpreted literally. When Heaney writes that his father's shoulders "globed like a full sail," he does not mean that they became an actual sphere or that they were as large as a ship's wind-filled sail. Yet the points of resemblance give you a clear, striking picture of his father walking behind the plow.

1. "Mapping the furrow" (line 12) is an example of figurative language. (a) Why? (b) How would you express the idea literally? (c) What does the figurative language add to the thought?
2. The line about "my father . . . stumbling" (line 23) is figurative. (a) Why? (b) How would you express the idea literally?

Answers

ANSWERS TO THINKING ABOUT THE SELECTION

Recalling

1. The speaker describes how his father would expertly put together the plow and break ground.
2. The boy wanted to grow up to imitate his father and become a farmer.
3. (a) The speaker says he stumbled, fell, and rode behind the plow. (b) He uses the verb *stumbling* to describe his father today.

Interpreting

4. (a) Suggested response: The child was probably about three or four years old. (b) He describes how the father picked him up and rode him piggyback after he stumbled. He was always talking.
5. Answers will differ. Suggested response: The boy wants to close his eye and stiffen his arm in imitation of his father as he mapped out furrows.
6. Answers will differ. Suggested responses: The lines suggest the speaker always tried to follow after his father and was never able to equal him. The speaker remained obscured, behind his father's shadow.
7. The tone is reflective, admiring, and affectionate. Students may cite different lines and phrases in support of their descriptions of the poem's tone.

Applying

8. (a) Time and age radically change the roles. (b) Suggested response: Most young people have to adjust and get used to such changing roles.

ANSWERS TO ANALYZING LITERATURE

1. Answers will differ. (a) "Mapping the furrow" is figurative because the father is not drawing a map showing how the furrows will go. (b) As he plowed, my father carefully planned where each furrow would go. (c) The figurative language adds to the impression of the father's expertise. He is mentally planning perfect rows, even as he plows his field.
2. Answers will differ. (a) "My father . . . stumbling" is figurative because the father is not physically tripping and falling. (b) The father may be older now and may need the speaker's care and attention, or the father may be an internal stumbling block for the speaker, who is trying to be a free and independent adult.

Shore Woman

Seamus Heaney

Man to the hills, woman to the shore.
Gaelic proverb

I have crossed the dunes with their whistling bent 1
Where dry loose sand was riddling round the air
And I'm walking the firm margin. White pocks
Of cockle, blanched roofs of clam and oyster
Hoard the moonlight, woven and unwoven
Off the bay. At the far rocks
A pale sud comes and goes. 2

Under boards the mackerel slapped to death
Yet still we took them in at every cast,
Stiff flails of cold convulsed with their first breath.
My line plumbed certainly the undertow,
Loaded against me once I went to draw
And flashed and fattened up towards the light.
He was all business in the stern. I called
"This is so easy that it's hardly right,"
But he unhooked and coped with frantic fish 3
Without speaking. Then suddenly it lulled,
We'd crossed where they were running, the line rose
Like a let-down and I was conscious
How far we'd drifted out beyond the head.
"Count them up at your end," was all he said
Before I saw the porpoises' thick backs
Cartwheeling like the flywheels[1] of the tide,
Soapy and shining. To have seen a hill
Splitting the water could not have numbed me more
Than the close irruption of that school,
Tight viscous muscle, hooped from tail to snout,
Each one revealed complete as it bowled out
And under.
They will attack a boat. 4

1. **flywheels** *n.*: Heavy wheels for regulating the speed and uniformity of motion of a machine.

Motivation for Reading Ask the students to imagine they are a child out fishing with their father. The fishing is going well, when suddenly there is a crisis. The child fears the boat will sink, while the father, who is an experienced sailor, remains calm and unmoved. How might it feel to recall this scene years later? Do we sometimes use scenes in our lives to stand for many different experiences?

Master Teacher Note Particularly with **less advanced** students, you may wish to paraphrase those passages that are unclear upon first reading.

Purpose-Setting Question What is this poem saying about the process of forming identity?

1 **Discussion** What is the feel and rhythm of lines 1–2? How is that changed in line 3? What is the contrast between the actions of nature and the speaker?

2 **Discussion** Why does the author place the sea far off in line 7 and then abruptly move both back in time and out to sea in line 8? What is the effect of this?

3 **Critical Thinking and Reading** Heaney's precise choice of words and use of rhythm create multiple levels of meaning. Note the way the father is introduced and the use of the word *stern.* What is the effect of the "But" coming directly after the boy's comment?

4 **Discussion** Why has the author used the words "a boat" rather than "this boat"? On what do the father and son disagree?

Thematic Idea Another poem dealing with a relationship between father and son is Dylan Thomas's "Do Not Go Gentle into That Good Night" on page 1120. You might have students compare the father-son relationship in Thomas's poem with that suggested in the two poems by Seamus Heaney.

Answers

ANSWERS TO THINKING ABOUT THE SELECTION

Recalling

1. In the first stanza the speaker is walking along a strand at the edge of the dunes.
2. (a) The father and speaker were out in a boat fishing. (b) The fishing was very successful. (c) The speaker became aware of how far out they were when there was a lull and the fish stopped biting.
3. (a) The speaker was frightened about the number, size, and power of the porpoises. (b) The father felt the boy was reacting to a myth about porpoises being dangerous. (c) The father was right, in that they survived being near the porpoises.
4. In the last stanza the speaker is back walking along the strand.

Interpreting

5. Answers will differ. The father takes the coming of the porpoises as a challenge to prove an old yarn is false. The speaker reacts in fear, wanting to simply go back to shore.
6. Answers will differ. (a) The father and speaker seem somewhat distant, the father businesslike and silent and the speaker talkative and enthusiastic. (b) On land their relationship seems remote, with the father contradicting the son and still not communicating with him.
7. Answers will differ. Among things to note are where the speaker was and where he is now, the details of relationship between father and son, and the speaker's words and attitudes then and now.

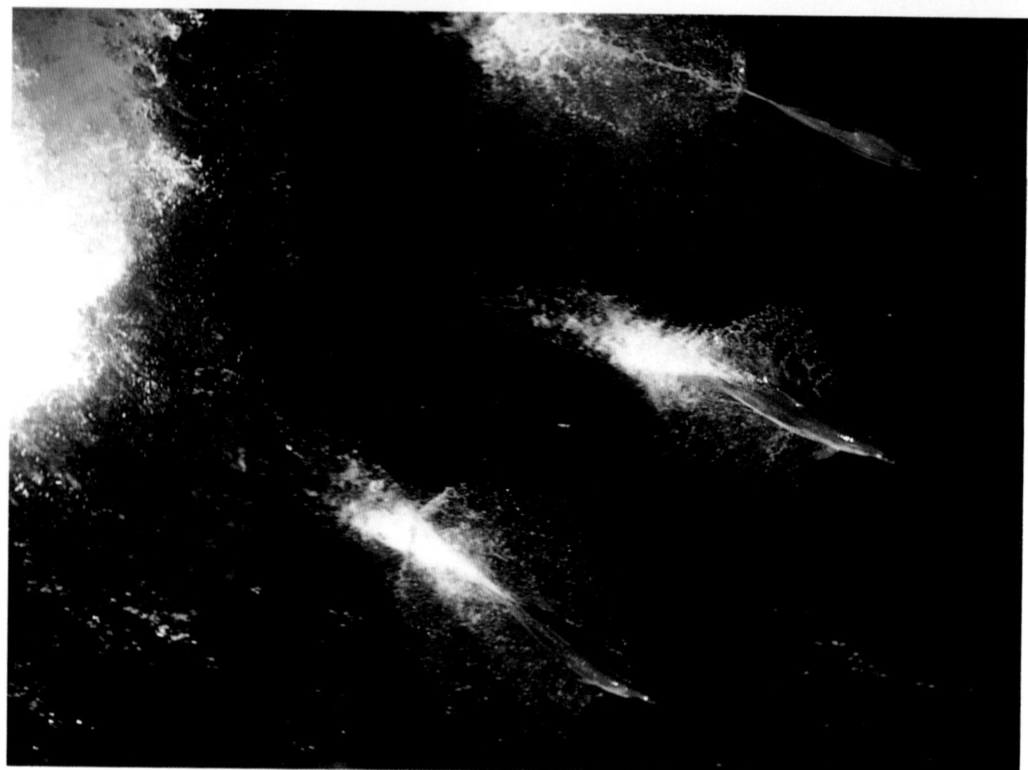

THINKING ABOUT THE SELECTION

Recalling

1. Where is the speaker in the first stanza?
2. (a) What were the father and the speaker doing in the open boat? (b) How successful were they? (c) When did the speaker become aware of how far the boat had drifted?
3. (a) Why was the speaker frightened at the sight of the porpoises? (b) What was the father's reaction? (c) Who was right about the porpoises—father or speaker?
4. Where is the speaker in the last stanza?

Interpreting

5. What basic difference is there between the father and speaker in the encounter with the porpoises? Explain your answer.
6. (a) How close does the relationship between father and speaker appear to be when the two are at sea? (b) How close is it on land? Explain.
7. What relationship is there between the Gaelic proverb and the title and theme of the poem?

Applying

8. To what extent do you think the speaker's fear suggests weakness? Provide support for your answer.
9. What, if anything, do you think the father said to the speaker after the porpoises had left? What makes you think he said this?

I knew it and I asked him to put in
But he would not, declared it was a yarn
My people had been fooled by far too long
And he would prove it now and settle it.
Maybe he shrank when those sloped oily backs
Propelled towards us: I lay and screamed
Under splashed brine in an open rocking boat
Feeling each dunt and slither through the timber,
Sick at their huge pleasures in the water.

I sometimes walk this strand for thanksgiving
Or maybe it's to get away from him
Skittering his spit across the stove. Here
Is the taste of safety, the shelving sand
Harbors no worse than razorshell[2] or crab—
Though my father recalls carcasses of whales
Collapsed and gasping, right up to the dunes. 5
But tonight such moving sinewed dreams lie out
In darker fathoms, far beyond the head.
Astray upon a debris of scrubbed shells
Between parched dunes and salivating wave,
I have rights on this fallow avenue,
A membrane between moonlight and my shadow.

---

2. razorshell *n.*: The shell of razor clams, burrowing clams with elongated, narrow shells that resemble a straight razor.

CRITICAL THINKING AND READING

Recognizing Sound and Meaning

Poets use a number of devices to create the kinds of sounds that complement the meaning of their words. Rhyme, rhythm, repetition, harsh-or-soft consonants and vowels, and onomatopoeia all help to produce the desired effects.

1. What is one example of onomatopoeia in the first stanza?
2. What are three examples of repetition of sound in the second stanza?
3. Sound is used very effectively in line 42. What devices that make this line work so well?

THINKING AND WRITING

Analyzing the Use of Sound in a Poem

Write an essay in which you analyze the devices for creating sound in "Shore Woman." To appreciate the sound effects in the poem, read it aloud at least once before you begin. Jot down notes about the sound devices. What impression do they create? Then write your first draft. Remember that when you write an analysis of this kind, you have to do more than just point out the devices. You also have to explain how they work. When you revise, make sure you have provided details from the poem to support your analysis.

5 **Discussion** Where exactly is the man walking? Who is he trying to get away from? Explain line 51.

Applying

8. Answers will differ. The porpoises presented a potentially real danger to the boat. Some may feel the speaker overreacted or reacted too soon.
9. Answers will differ. The poem does not suggest the father spoke much. If he spoke at all it may have been to contradict the boy or ignore his concerns.

ANSWERS TO CRITICAL THINKING AND READING

1. One example of onomatopoeia in stanza one is "dunes with whistling bent."
2. Three examples of repetition of sound in stanza two are the initial "c" in "cold convulsed," the initial "f" in "flashed and fattened," and the "ight" in "light" and "right."
3. The devices used in line 42 include onomatopoeia, the repetition of harsh and soft consonants and vowels, and the use of rhythm.

THINKING AND WRITING

For help with this assignment, students can refer to Lesson 5, "Writing About Literary Devices 1: Sound," in the Handbook of Writing About Literature.

Writing Across the Curriculum
You might want students to do some research on father–son relationships, especially as they are portrayed in literature. If you choose to assign this work, you might inform the social studies department.

More About the Authors Donald Davie has stated his belief that the poet "is responsible to the community in which he writes for purifying and correcting the spoken language." Recognized as much for his scholarly work and criticism as for his poetry, Davie's poems are often restrained, carefully wrought statements. Though his roots are clearly English, he has lived and worked in America for many years. His feelings towards his homeland have often tended to be negative and bitter. How might a move as an adult away from one's homeland affect an author's writings? How related is an author's homeland to his work? Can a writer ever get completely away ῾rom his or her basic roots?

Molly Holden was in her mid-thirties when she was disabled by multiple sclerosis, a degenerative disease which affects muscle control. In addition to writing adult poetry, she was an award-winning author of children's poetry and fiction. She also developed plays and programs for the British Broadcasting Company. Some have suggested that Holden's progressive illness increased her identity with the earth and affected her themes and the content of her poetry. Discuss the effects of ill health or handicaps on an author's work. Might a serious illness or disability change the direction of an author's work? How?

BIOGRAPHIES

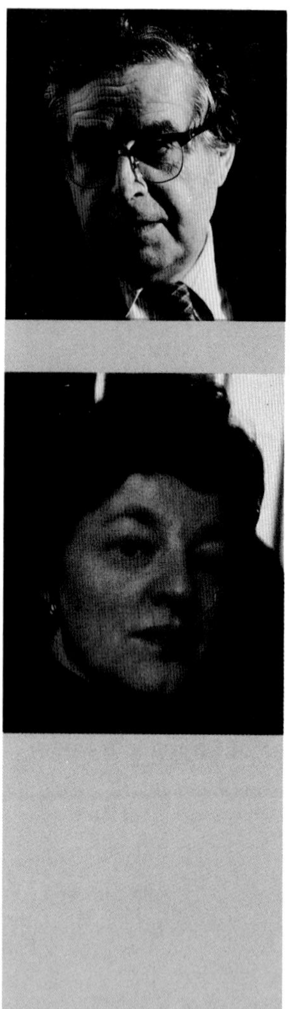

Donald Davie 1922–

Donald Davie, one of "the Movement" poets of the 1950's, is noted today for the quiet elegance and urbane perception of his work. He is often compared to the eighteenth-century Augustan poets, whose tone, diction, and verse forms he admires and sometimes emulates. Davie, born in Yorkshire, England, has taught in England, Ireland, and the United States. A traditionalist, he believes that formal discipline in writing can free rather than restrict the poetic imagination. One of his best-known collections, *The Shires* (1974), consists of one poem for each of the forty counties of England.

Molly Holden 1927–1981

Molly Holden wrote poetry that is subtle and sparkling. It is based on close attention to precise, telling details. Although Holden was disabled with multiple sclerosis in 1964, she did not let this progressive illness impede her writing. Her keen observation became, if anything, more acute, and her three finest collections—*To Make Me Grieve* (1968), *Air and Chill Earth* (1972), *The Country Over* (1975)—are testaments to her creative power and indomitable spirit. As she wrote, "Doubly urgent longing fills my days/to put down surely what is my obsession."

Objectives

To write a poem using imagery

Teaching Portfolio: Support Material

Teacher Backup, p. -00

Vocabulary Check, p. 00

Usage and Mechanics Worksheet, p. 00

Analyzing Literature Worksheet, p. 00

Critical Thinking and Reading Worksheet, p. 00

Language Worksheet, p. 00

Selection Test, p. 00

GUIDE FOR READING

For Doreen: A Voice from the Garden; Some Men Create

The Writer's Techniques

Imagery. When a writer's words or phrases create a picture in the reader's mind, the writer is using imagery. The mental pictures of imagery do not always involve sight; the images can also come from touch, taste, smell, or hearing. Verbal images based on the five senses are called sensory images. Imagery is important in poetry because it adds color to descriptions and helps to give concrete reality to abstract ideas.

Look For

As you read the poems by Donald Davie and Molly Holden, notice how the images create a reality in your mind, giving the poets' ideas a tangible form.

Writing

Imagery is not restricted to poetry. It occurs in all forms of writing and may come up in everyday conversation. A good storyteller uses imagery to create pictures in his or her listeners' minds. For one day keep a list of the images you hear in conversation or read in newspapers or magazines.

Vocabulary

Knowing the following words will help you as you read the poems by Donald Davie and Molly Holden.

trellis (trel′is) *n.*: Frame of crossed strips, usually of wood, us d as a screen or support for climbing plants (p. 1330, l. 4)
trefoil (trē′foil) *n.*: Clover (p. 1330, l. 5)
envisage (en viz′ij) *v.*: To form a m ntal picture of; imagine (p. 1330, l. 11)
anglophobia (aŋ glə fō′bē ə) *n.*: Hatred or fear of England or things English (p. 1330, l. 19)
sough (sou) *n.*: A groan or sighing sound (p. 1330, l. 25)
parapet (par′ə pit) *n.*: A low wall or railing (p. 1331, l. 7)
husbandry (huz′bən drē) *n.*: Farming (p. 1331, l. 13)

Literary Focus Imagery is an essential part of poetry because our first experience of anything comes through our senses. We feel a cool breeze, hear wind rustle through trees, and touch a smooth stone. Point out that we have internal senses such as hunger and thirst, and even a sense of motion.

Look For Most of your students will benefit from reviewing the questions in the Analyzing Literature section on page 1331. These questions can help guide their understanding as they read both Donald Davie's and Molly Holden's poems.

Writing Ask the students what images they see when they hear a word such as *successful.* When they have completed their writing assignment, they might categorize the images according to the various senses. An analysis of the pattern of images used in a particular newspaper or magazine article could be used as an extra credit assignment.

Vocabulary Have the students read the words aloud so they will be able to read them correctly in the poems. Note that *Anglophobia* is a composite word from *anglo* meaning "English or of England" and *phobia* meaning "fear, horror or dread."

Master Teacher Note Note Davie sets the scene at a lovely English home. Bring in several photos of England showing homes and the countryside. You might also show slides of such places in England, including, if possible, views of some English gardens.

Purpose-Setting Question What does the imagery of this poem suggest about England and the speaker's attitude towards England?

1 **Discussion** What effect is created by the opening line? Is the speaker truly enthusiastic about what he describes? How can you tell?

2 **Discussion** How does the tone change in this stanza? Is it important that the address is High Street and that the village is famous and photographed? Why?

3 **Clarification** The word *sough* can also mean "a rushing or murmuring sound as of wind." How can the sough of brakes make people an island?

For Doreen: A Voice from the Garden

Donald Davie

We have a lawn of moss.
The next house is called The Beeches.
A towering squirrel-haunted
1 Trellis of trees, across
Our matt and trefoil, reaches
Shade where our guests have sauntered.

Cars snap by in the road.
2 In a famous photographed village
The High Street is our address.
Our guests write from abroad
Delighted to envisage
Rose arbor and wilderness.

They get them, and the lilacs.
Some frenzy in us discards
Lilacs and all. It will harden,
However England stacks
Her dear discolored cards
Against us, us to her garden.

Anglophobia rises
3 In Brooklyn to hysteria
At some British verses.
British, one sympathizes.
Diesel fumes cling to wistaria.[1]
One conceives of worse reverses.

The sough of the power brake
Makes every man an island;
But we are the island race.
We must be mad to take
Offense at our poisoned land
And the gardens that pock her face.

1. **wistaria** (wis tir′ ē ə) *n.*: Vines of shrubs with clusters of bluish, white, pink, or purplish flowers.

THINKING ABOUT THE SELECTION

Recalling

1. What are three of the natural features near the speaker's house?
2. (a) Where are the guests from? (b) What delights them about the grounds near the speaker's house?
3. How does the "frenzy in us" cause the speaker (or the English perhaps) to regard garden-like settings such as this one?
4. What does the speaker say the English "must be mad" to dislike?

Interpreting

5. Why do you think the English ignore, or discard, the beauties that foreign guests see there?
6. How does the speaker react to Brooklyn's dislike of certain British verses?
7. If the gardens of England are in fact beautiful, why does the speaker say they "pock her face"?
8. One interpretation of this poem is that its basic theme is English literature, not the English landscape. What evidence do you find in the poem to support this interpretation?

Applying

9. Critics have remarked on Davie's relationship with England—a somewhat antagonistic one—and on his stylistic tendency to "shut the reader out." To what extent do you think these two comments apply to this poem?

Answers

ANSWERS TO THINKING ABOUT THE SELECTION

Recalling

1. Three natural features are the moss-grown lawn, a trellis of trees, and a field of trefoil, or clover.
2. (a) The guests are from abroad. (b) The guests are delighted with the rose arbor and the wilderness area.
3. The "frenzy" causes the speaker to put aside or discard everything to do with gardenlike settings.
4. He says the English must be mad to dislike their poisoned land and the gardens that pock her face.

Interpreting

5. Suggested Response: The English discard the beauties foreign guests see because they are so familiar, seem unimportant, and seem overemphasized by the tourists.
6. The speaker claims he is British and sympathizes with Brooklyn's attitude.
7. Suggested Response: Perhaps the speaker says this because he feels the land itself is poisoned, making the gardens a kind of mockery of the beautiful.
8. Answers will differ. Some evidence is found in lines 19–24. The poet connects what is going on with British poetry to the destructive effect of diesel fuel on wistaria.

Applying

9. Answers will differ. Students may notice the poem's anti-British sentiment in the speaker's sympathy with those who criticize some British verse (line 21), and in his calling the land poisoned (line 29). Some may not feel the poem is entirely clear in spelling out exactly what the speaker's feelings are and why.

Some Men Create

Molly Holden

Some men create an unintended 1
beauty by default,
never cut back the creeping ivy
so its stragglers vault

from crumbling wall to neighboring bridge 2
beside the arched lane,
to swing like hair from the parapet,
shining with spring rain;

never gravel out the timber pile 3
nor lop the dead oak
so that the seeding traveler's joy
smothers them like smoke.

So among orderly husbandry
leave some plots alone
that the eye may reap with pleasure what 4
the hand has not sown.

THINKING ABOUT THE SELECTION

Recalling

1. What does the uncut ivy do?
2. What advice does the speaker give to gardeners?

Interpreting

3. How is the beauty described in this poem created "by default"?
4. What causes the "traveler's joy" in stanza 3?

Applying

5. What are some examples you can point to of "beauty by default"?
6. How do you think a professional gardener or landscaper would respond to this poem?

THINKING AND WRITING

Writing a Poem Using Imagery

Write an original poem using imagery. The writing assignment on page 1329 should have uncovered many examples of imagery used to brighten up everyday conversation. Perhaps you can use some of these examples in your poem. Remember that your object is to choose words and phrases that will create pictures in the minds of your readers. Once you have a topic for your poem, write your first draft. When you revise, make sure your language is fresh and vivid.

Answers

ANSWERS TO THINKING ABOUT THE SELECTION

Recalling

1. The uncut ivy creeps out, spreading across the wall, bridge, and parapet.
2. The speaker advises gardeners to leave certain areas uncultivated and natural.

Interpreting

3. The beauty is created by leaving the ivy alone, letting it grow wild to help create a beautiful scene.
4. Answers may differ. Suggested response: The "traveler's joy" is finding a natural spot to seed and grow.

(Answers begin on p. 1330.)

Master Teacher Note Molly Holden sets her poem in a garden. Show the students photos of both natural fields of wildflowers and formal gardens of flowers. You might also want to show artworks which feature formal gardens and untouched nature.

Purpose-Setting Question How does a person's view of nature affect what he or she will do to natural settings?

1 **Discussion** What is the apparent contradiction in the idea of creating beauty by default? How does the poem say it is possible to do this?

2 **Critical Thinking and Reading** What do the carefully selected details suggest about nature's capacity for creating beautiful effects on its own?

3 **Discussion** How does this line connect back to the first line of the poem? What is the effect of drawing the reader back to "some men" here?

4 **Discussion** What apparent contradictions are there in these lines? How are they true?

Applying

5. Answers will differ. Some examples might be fields of Queen Anne's Lace or Ironweed.
6. Answers will differ. The response of a professional gardener or landscaper would depend on his or her sense of the beautiful. Many would agree with Holden.

THINKING AND WRITING

Publishing Student Writing Produce a simple duplicated booklet of original student poetry written while doing this section. Talented students might even illustrate the pages with artwork and border designs.

The writing assignments on page 1332 have students write creatively, while those on page 1333 have them think about the selections and write critically.

YOU THE WRITER

Guidelines for Evaluating Assignment 1

1. Does the new ending begin at the turning point of the story?
2. Does the story move in a different direction to achieve surprise?
3. Is the new ending logically linked to something presented earlier?
4. Does the new ending seem as if it had been written by the author of the story?
5. Is the ending free from grammar, usage, and mechanics errors?

Guidelines for Evaluating Assignment 2

1. Has the student written an interesting, dramatic, or startling letter to a friend that discusses a character from a story in this unit?
2. Does the letter include what the character is like, how he or she relates to the events of the story, the student's feelings about the character, and an interesting and memorable ending?
3. Is the letter written in conventional letter form?
4. Is the letter free from grammar, usage, and mechanics errors?

Guidelines for Evaluating Assignment 3

1. Has the student written a poem with a strong central image or idea, using a poem from this unit as a model?
2. Has the student followed the model for rhythm, rhyme, and structure but modified it where appropriate to the central ideas he or she is expressing?
3. Is the poem expressive and clear?
4. Is the poem free from grammar, usage, and mechanics errors?

YOU THE WRITER

Assignment

1. Write an alternate ending for one of the stories in this unit. Make the ending follow logically from preceding events and from the nature of the characters.

Prewriting. Reread the story to see how its earlier parts prepare for the present ending. Then ask, "How might these parts lead up to a different ending?"

Writing. Now write your alternate ending. Start at the turning point, and, to achieve surprise, have the story move in a different direction. To make the new ending logical, link it to something presented earlier.

Revising. Revise with the aim of making your new ending seem as if it had been written by the author of the story.

Assignment

2. Write a letter to a friend in which you discuss a character in a story from this unit. Write as if the character were real and you had been present at the events recounted in the story.

Prewriting. Ask, "What is the character like? What are his or her key traits? How are they seen in the events of the story? What is the main idea I should express about the character? How can I develop and conclude my letter in an interesting and memorable way?" Freewrite exploring your answer to these questions.

Writing. When you have arrived at clear and definite answers to these questions, write a personal letter in conventional form.

Revising. Can you make your letter more interesting, more dramatic, or more startling? Have you captured the characters personality accurately? Make changes with these possibilities in view.

Assignment

3. Sometimes a poem has a central image or idea that spreads itself throughout the poem like the branches and roots of a tree. Write a poem with a central image or idea, using a poem in this unit as a model.

Prewriting. Find a subject you would like to write about. Then think of a central image or idea that can tie together and express your thoughts and feelings about the subject. Ask, "How might the author of my model have treated this subject?"

Writing. Write the first draft of your poem. Follow your model poem for rhythm, rhyme, and structure. However, make whatever modifications you feel are appropriate to what you are trying to express.

Revising. Make changes to improve the expressiveness of your poem. Be sure to read your verses aloud to see if their rhythm and sound can be improved.

YOU THE CRITIC

Assignment

1. Choose two characters from two different stories in this section and write an essay discussing (1) the important actions they took, and (2) the consequences of these actions.

Prewriting. For each character, divide a sheet of paper into two columns. In the first column, list the major actions the characters took. In the second column, list the consequences of these actions.

Writing. In your opening paragraph, describe in general the actions of each character and the consequences of the actions. In the body paragraphs, treat each story separately. For both stories, discuss the characters' actions first and the consequences second.

Revising. Carefully review the organization of your essay to see if you can establish connections by comparison and contrast between the two characters you have discussed.

Assignment

2. Much contemporary fiction is quite different from earlier, more traditional fiction. Write an essay in which you explain why you prefer contemporary or earlier stories.

Prewriting. First decide on the chief differences between earlier and more recent stories. Which of these differences explain your likes and dislikes? Which specific stories would you cite to illustrate these differences?

Writing. Write your first draft. Begin by stating your preference. Give your reasons by discussing the qualities you like or dislike in older or contemporary fiction.

Revising. Revise your essay by attempting to clarify or support more strongly your reasons for your preference. See if you can use comparison and contrast to reveal more vividly the chief differences between the two periods of fiction.

Assignment

3. Some lines in a poem are memorable either because of what they say or how they say it, or both. Choose at least three poems from this unit and write an essay identifying the lines you consider most memorable, explaining why you think they are memorable.

Prewriting. Scan the poems in this unit for the ones you think contain the most memorable lines. Copy these lines and note why you liked them. Were you impressed by the content? Was the imagery sharp? Was the phrasing beautiful?

Writing. Write an introductory paragraph in which you announce your subject and indicate how you will approach it. Then discuss each of the memorable lines, quoting the line first and then explaining why you think it is memorable.

Revising. See if you can use transitional words and phrases to improve the unity and coherence of your essay.

YOU THE CRITIC
Guidelines for Evaluating Assignment 1

1. Does the comparison begin with a general description of the action of two characters from different stories?
2. Do the body paragraphs treat the stories separately and discuss the characters' actions first and the consequences second?
3. Has the student established connections by comparing and contrasting the characters?
4. Is the essay free from grammar, usage, and mechanics errors?

Guidelines for Evaluating Assignment 2

1. Does the student begin the essay by stating a preference for contemporary or traditional fiction?
2. Does the student give reasons by discussing the qualities he or she likes or dislikes in traditional or contemporary literature?
3. Does the student use evidence from the literature to support his or her reasons?
4. Is the essay free from grammar, usage, and mechanics errors?

Guidelines for Evaluating Assignment 3

1. Is there an introductory paragraph that announces the three poems and indicates that they are memorable?
2. Has the student discussed each of the memorable lines, quoting the lines first and then explaining why they are memorable?
3. Has the student used transitional words and phrases to improve the unity and coherence of the essay?
4. Is the essay free from grammar, usage, and mechanics errors?

Using the Handbook

The lessons in the Handbook of Thinking and Writing About Literature may be used for direct instruction in the writing process and specifically for the process of writing about literature. In addition, students may use these lessons for reference and support when they are doing the specific Thinking and Writing assignments with the selections. References to appropriate lessons are suggested on the Teacher's Edition page with the assignment.

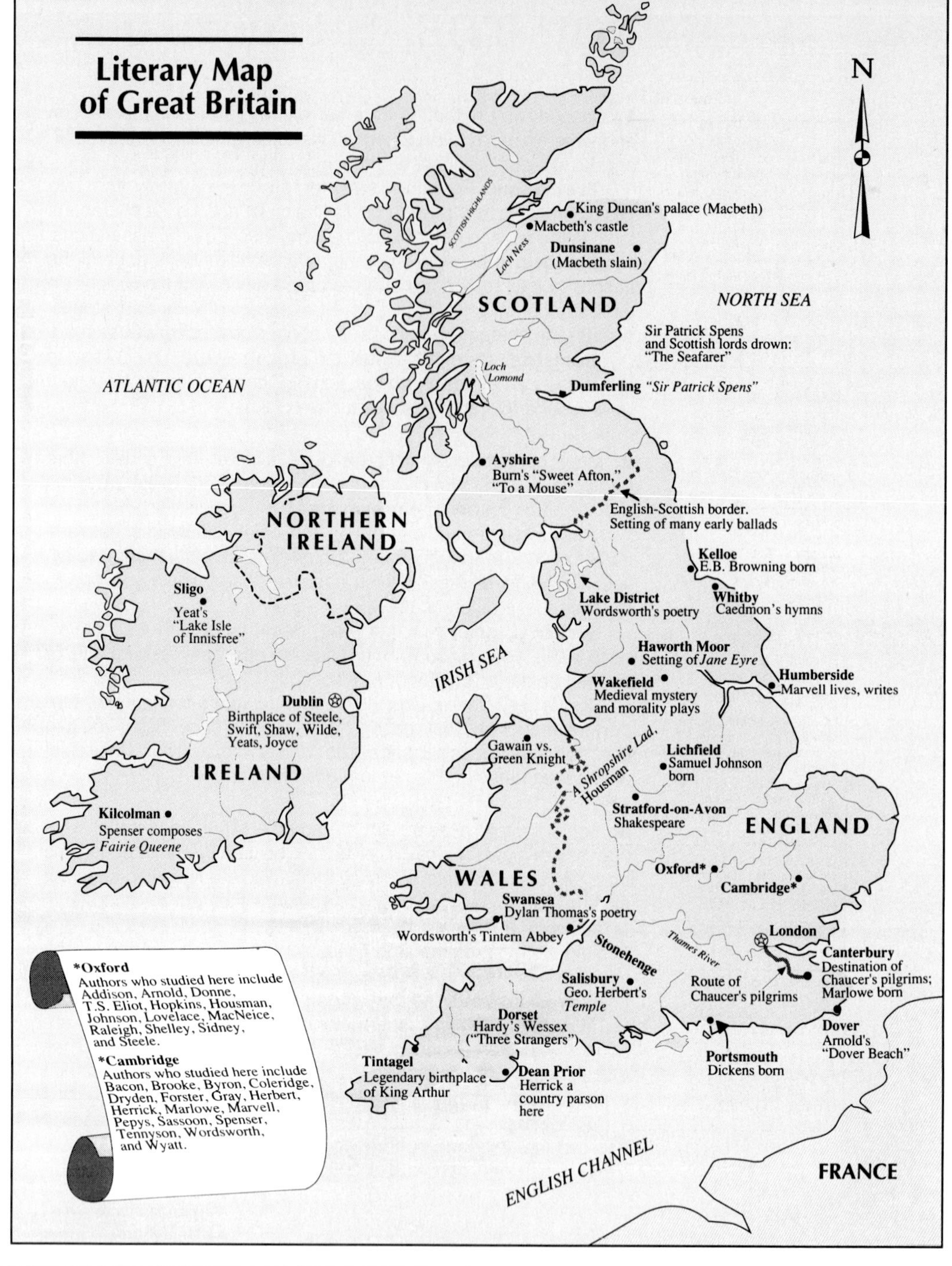

Rulers of England and Great Britain (including dates of reign)

This chart presents the rulers of England and Great Britain from Anglo-Saxon times to the present. The earliest English kings were rulers not of England in its entirety but of kingdoms within England. The first of an unbroken succession of kings or queens of England was William I (1066-87). In 1707, upon the passage of the Act of Union, which united England and Scotland, Queen Anne became the first monarch of Great Britain.

[Kingdom of Kent]
Ethelbert, 560-616

[Kingdom of Northumbria]
Ethelfrith, 593-617
Edwin, 617-633
Oswald, 635-642
Oswy, 642-670
Ecgfrith, 670-685

[Kingdom of Mercia]
Penda, 626-655
Ethelbald, 716-757
Offa II, 757-796
Cenulf, 796-821

[Kingdom of Wessex]
Ine, 688-726

Saxons and Danes
Egbert, 802-39
Æthelwulf, 839-58
Æthelbald, 858-60
Æthelbert, 860-65
Æthelred, 865-71
Alfred, 871-99
Edward 899-924
Athelstan, 924-39
Edmund, 946-55
Edred, 946-55
Edway, 955-59
Edgar, 959-78
Edward (the Martyr), 978-1016
Æthelred (the Unready), 978-1016
Edmund (Ironside), son of Æthelred 1016
Canute, by conquest, 1016-35
Harold I (Harefoot), 1037-40
Harthacunute, 1040-42
Edward (the Confessor), 1042-66
Harold II, 1066

House of Normandy
William I The Conquerer, 1066-87
William II, 1087-1100
Henry I, 1100-1135

Houseof Blois
Stephen, 1135-54

House of Plantagenet
Henry II, 1154-89
Richard I, (Coeur de Lion) 1189-99
John, 1199-1216
Henry III, 1216-72
Edward I, 1272-1307
Edward II, 1302-27
Edward III, 1327-77
Richard II, 1327-99

House of Lancaster
Henry IV, 1399-1413
Henry V, 1413-22
Henry VI, 1422-61, 1470-99

House of York
Edward IV, 1461-70, 1471-83
Edward V, 1483
Richard III, 1483-85

House of Tudor
Henry VII, 1485-1509
Henry VIII, 1509-47
Edward VI, 1547-53
Mary I, 1553-58
Elizabeth I, 1558-1603

House of Stuart
James I (James VI of Scotland), 1603-25
Charles I, 1625-49

Commonwealth and Protectorate
Council of State, 1649-53
Cromwell, Oliver, lord protector, 1653-58
Cromwell, Richard, lord protector, 1658-59

House of Stuart (restored)
Charles II, 1660-85
James II, 1685-88
William III, ruled jointly with Mary II, 1689-94; ruled alone, 1694-1702
Mary II, ruled jointly with William III, 1689-94
Anne, 1702-14

House of Hanover
George I, 1714-27
George II, 1727-60
George III, 1760-1820
George IV, 1820-30
William IV, 1830-37
Victoria, 1837-1901

House of Saxe-Cobury
Edward VII, 1901-10

House of Windsor
(family name changed during World War I)
George V, 1910-36
Edward VIII, 1936
George VI, 1936-1952
Elizabeth II, 1952

HANDBOOK OF WRITING ABOUT LITERATURE

SECTION 1: UNDERSTANDING THE WRITING PROCESS

Lesson 1: Prewriting

You may wish that you could just sit down, spend a few minutes, and magically write out a polished paragraph or essay. Unfortunately, most writing is not so easy. It takes time and hard work. Nevertheless, you can write more confidently if you understand that writing is a process, not a single step. Most writers go through these stages.

1. *Prewriting:* getting and organizing ideas for writing
2. *Drafting:* writing down ideas in a rough first draft
3. *Revising:* reworking and improving the written draft
4. *Proofreading:* finding and correcting errors in spelling, punctuation, capitalization, grammar, usage, and manuscript form
5. *Publishing:* sharing the writing with other people

STEP 1: ANALYZE THE SITUATION

Instead of just starting to write your paper, begin by thinking through what you need and want to accomplish. Ask yourself the following questions.

1. *Assignment:* To what extent does the assignment define what you should do? Does it specify a topic? Does it require a paragraph or an essay? Does the assignment contain any key words such as *explain, compare, identify, retell, discuss, contrast, describe, cite, analyze, define, develop*, or *show*?
2. *Topic:* What will you write about? How can you state your subject precisely? Is your topic exact and narrow enough? Can you sum it up in a topic sentence or thesis statement that suggests your position or viewpoint?
3. *Purpose:* What is your goal? Will you explain, describe, tell, or argue? Do you want your reader to react by understanding, imagining, being entertained, or being persuaded?
4. *Audience:* Who will read your writing? What should you assume about the reader's background and knowledge?
5. *Voice:* How should your writing sound to a reader? Should it sound informal, formal, calm, emotional, logical, ironic, or straightforward?
6. *Content:* What information will you need to provide about the topic? Can you gather all the information you need by analyzing your reading or by thinking about the topic? Do you need to do research? If so, what resources should you draw on?
7. *Form:* How will you shape your writing? Is it to be creative—a play, a poem, or a story? Is it to be an essay, a paragraph, a report, or a term paper? What parts will the writing include? What plan will you use to arrange the parts? What will come first, second, third, and so on?

STEP 2: MAKE A PLAN

After analyzing your writing situation, you can plan what to do next. Often you will need to find a topic or to narrow the one assigned. Then you can return to any unresolved questions that remain. For example, suppose that you are assigned an informal essay explaining to your classmates three techniques used in a poem you select. Your assignment defines your purpose (to explain), audience (classmates), and voice (informal). Your essay's topic (the poem and your point about it), content (your explanation and examples of three techniques), and form (the order of the paragraphs) will be clearer after you select and analyze a specific poem.

STEP 3: GATHER INFORMATION

Your assignment may or may not tell you exactly what topic to work on. Either way, instead of just hoping for a brilliant idea, try one of these prewriting methods to get ideas for or about a topic.

1. *Freewriting:* Write about the topic for several minutes. Don't worry about spelling, punctuation, or logical connections between ideas. Simply get down on paper everything that comes to mind about the topic. Later you can rephrase your best ideas.
2. *Clustering:* On a blank piece of paper, write and circle your topic. Add other ideas, circling them and using lines to connect them to the topic.
3. *Questioning:* Act like a reporter and ask questions about your topic. Begin your questions with *who*, *what*, *where*, *when*, *why*, and *how*.
4. *Listing:* Make a list of events in sequence, pro and con arguments, differences, similarities, subtypes, examples, or causes.
5. *Analyzing:* Identify the parts of your topic. That is, look for subtopics and for relationships among the parts and the whole.
6. *Researching:* Look up terms, details, or whatever background you need to know.

STEP 4: ORGANIZE YOUR NOTES

After gathering ideas, you are ready to organize your material and to work out a rough outline. Whatever order you choose should suit your topic, be logical, build from idea to idea, and interest a reader. Try one of these patterns or the reverse of one of these patterns.

1. *Chronological order:* first to last
2. *Spatial order:* nearest to farthest, topmost to bottommost, and so on
3. *Order of complexity:* simplest to most elaborate
4. *Order of familiarity:* best to least understood
5. *Order of frequency:* most to least numerous
6. *Order of importance:* least to most significant
7. *Order of effectiveness:* least to most convincing

CASE STUDY: PREWRITING

Brian's English teacher assigned an informal paragraph. Brian was to pick a reading that he found especially interesting and then explain briefly how and why he reacted to it as he did.

Brian decided to write about Mary Shelley's Introduction to *Frankenstein*. First he analyzed the writing situation.

- Assignment: paragraph—explain reaction
- Topic: Shelley's Introduction to *Frankenstein*—but what about it?
- Purpose: explain so reader understands
- Audience: Ms. Burton—maybe class? all have read Shelley's essay
- Voice: informal, personal reactions
- Content: why like it? why interesting?
- Form: paragraph—needs topic sentence and examples—which ones? what order?

Brian decided to try freewriting to figure out what to say about his topic.

> Shelley wrote this famous story. It is also famous in movies. I thought she must of been a natural writer. Didn't expect her to have trouble writing. Byron and Shelley wrote OK stories even tho they are famous poets. But she can't get an idea. After hearing about these experiments she gets this vision. She still doesn't think she can write a story, then she sees its her story.

Brian saw two main ideas in his freewriting: Mary Shelley had written a famous story, and she had trouble writing, just as he did. He did not know how to develop the first idea but he thought he could figure out a topic sentence about the second. He made this rough outline, using details from the essay.

1339

- Topic: I did not expect Shelley to have trouble writing.
  - She can't get an idea—others can
  - She gets a vision
  - Finally she sees that it's her story conclusion?

ACTIVITIES AND ASSIGNMENTS

A. Answer these questions about the case study:

1. Review Brian's freewriting and rough outline. Did he finally resolve all the questions about his writing situation? Revise his first chart to include his later decisions.
2. Review Brian's freewriting. What mistakes in grammar or phrasing did Brian make? Why didn't he take the time to correct these at this stage?
3. What order did Brian use to arrange the three details in his rough outline?

B. Choose a selection that interests you. Follow these prewriting steps to prepare for writing an informal paragraph about it:

1. Make notes to analyze your writing situation.
2. Decide what your next step should be. Use one of the prewriting techniques explained above to gather ideas.
3. Work out a rough outline, using your prewriting notes. Make sure that you have a specific topic and an idea about how to organize your ideas. Save all of your notes.

Lesson 2: Drafting and Revising

DRAFTING YOUR PAPER

Drafting is the process of putting ideas down on paper. The following guidelines will help you with the drafting stage of the writing process:

1. Choose a drafting method that is right for you. Some people like to make a detailed outline or prewriting plan and then to write a slow, meticulous draft based on this outline or plan. Other people like to write a very quick and very rough draft and then to revise this draft several times.
2. Whichever drafting method you choose, it is a good idea to do at least some planning before writing. In other words, you should have at least some idea about what you are going to say and in what order. You may wish to make at least a rough outline before you begin drafting.
3. Concentrate on getting your ideas down on paper. You can revise and proofread your work later.
4. Be open to new ideas that occur to you as you write. If necessary, change your writing plan to accommodate these new ideas.

REVISING YOUR DRAFT

Revising is the process of reworking and refining your draft. To revise a paper, read it over carefully and ask yourself the questions in the Checklist for Revision.

If your answer to any of the questions is "no," rework your draft until you can answer "yes." You may find that you need to revise your draft several times.

CASE STUDY: DRAFTING AND REVISING

Brian used his prewriting notes to begin writing his informal paragraph on Mary Shelley's Introduction to *Frankenstein*. After reviewing the assignment, his freewriting, and his rough outline,

CHECKLIST FOR REVISION

Topic and Purpose

☐ Is my topic clear?
☐ Does the writing have a specific purpose?
☐ Does the writing achieve its purpose?

Audience

☐ Will everything I have written be clear to my audience?
☐ Will my audience find the writing interesting?
☐ Will my audience respond in the way I would like?

Voice and Word Choice

☐ Is the impression my writing conveys the one I intended it to convey?
☐ Is my language appropriately formal or informal?
☐ Have I avoided vague, undefined terms?
☐ Have I used vivid, specific nouns, verbs, and adjectives?
☐ Have I avoided jargon that my audience will not understand?
☐ Have I avoided clichés?
☐ Have I avoided slang, odd connotations, euphemisms, and gobbledygook (except for novelty or humor)?

Content/Development

☐ Have I avoided including unnecessary or unrelated ideas?
☐ Have I developed my topic completely?
☐ Have I supplied examples or details that support the statements that I have made?
☐ Are my sources of information unbiased, up-to-date, and authoritative?
☐ Are my quotations verbatim, or word for word?

Form

☐ Have I followed a logical method of organization?
☐ Have I used transitions, or connecting words, to make the organization clear?
☐ Does the writing have a clear introduction, body, and conclusion?

1341

Brian decided that he needed to work on a topic sentence. Here's how he drafted and revised that topic sentence:

- Topic idea: I did not expect Shelley to have trouble writing.
- Topic sentence: I enjoyed reading it because I found out about her trouble writing which was not what I expected.
- Revised version: I enjoyed reading Mary Shelley's Introduction to *Frankenstein* because I found out about something I didn't expect—that she had trouble coming up with ideas for writing.

Next Brian used this topic sentence to get started drafting his paragraph.

ACTIVITIES AND ASSIGNMENTS

A. Answer the following questions about Brian's revisions of his rough draft:

1. What transitions did Brian add to his paragraph?
2. Why did Brian delete the sentence, "She is just real terrified"?
3. Why did Brian change some of the wording in his sentence about Mary Shelley's vision?
4. Why did he add the last sentences?
5. What other changes did Brian make? Why did he make these changes?

B. Using your notes from the preceding lesson, draft and revise your own paragraph. Follow these steps:

1. Review your notes and your rough outline.
2. Work on your topic sentence, refining it so that your specific topic and your approach to or attitude toward the topic is clear.
3. If necessary, revise your rough outline. Note your subtopics (the parts of your main topic), and add any new significant details that occur to you.
4. Use your revised topic sentence to start your paragraph.
5. Write the body of your paragraph, presenting the subtopics and details from your outline.
6. Write a conclusion.
7. Revise your draft, using the Checklist for Revision on page 1341. Keep all of your notes and drafts.

I enjoyed reading Mary Shelley's Introduction to Frankenstein because I found out about something I didn't expect—that she had trouble coming up with ideas for writing. [Since] ~~Her~~ [her] story has become so famous, I thought Shelly was just a natural writer. [Instead,] I found out [that] she had trouble getting an idea for a story. [Even though her husband,] ~~Shelley,~~ Byron, and Polidori had wrote theres, [she could not think of an idea.] Finally she has this ~~weird~~ [imaginative] vision about ~~an~~ [a terrifying] experiment in ~~science.~~ [creating life.] ~~She is just real terrified.~~ [At first,] ~~She~~ [she] ~~just~~ does not ~~see~~ [recognize] this as her story she just wishes she cld write something ~~just~~ as ~~creepy.~~ [frightening.] Then she realizes that ~~she has~~ [this is] her idea for a story. [Her problem surprised me but then also reassured me. I hadn't expected to find out that a writer like her had the same writing problem I usually do.]

1342

Lesson 3: Proofreading and Publishing

USING EDITORIAL SYMBOLS

The last lesson discussed reorganizing, adding, cutting, and otherwise revising your writing. Once you have made these major revisions, you are ready to make more detailed changes such as adding punctuation, correcting capitalization, and refining word order. The editorial symbols on the right are especially helpful for marking such changes on your final draft.

PROOFREADING YOUR FINAL DRAFT

Proofreading is your last careful review of your paper. As you proofread, look for minor errors and for rough passages that you missed earlier. If possible, let your revised draft sit for a few hours or a day before going over it. Taking a break from your manuscript should make it easier for you to see flaws. Ask yourself the following questions as you proofread.

Use a dictionary, a style manual, or a writing textbook to check spellings and rules for punctuation, capitalization, and manuscript form. Once your paper has been proofread, make a clean final copy, if necessary. Check your final version carefully to catch any errors in copying.

PUBLISHING, OR SHARING YOUR WORK WITH OTHERS

After proofreading your paper, you are ready to share it with readers. When you write papers for school, your teachers will be your primary readers. Nevertheless, you or your class can expand your audience in the following ways:

1. Exchange papers with a small group of students from your class.
2. Read your paper aloud to your class or to another class.
3. Share your writing with your friends and relatives.
4. Make a booklet of your writing at the end of the semester or year.
5. Make a class booklet with a paper by every student.
6. Contribute some of your writing to the school literary magazine.

EDITORIAL SYMBOLS		
Symbol	*Meaning*	*Example*
(circle with arrow)	move text	She never again published because of this
ℓ or —	delete	in this ~~this~~ book
∧	insert	the poem's rhyme scheme
⁀ ‿	no space	mono logue
⊙	add period	a line ends It
∧ with comma	add comma	sonnets, odes and other lyric poems
∨ with apostrophe	add apostrophe	writers style
∨ with quotation marks	add quotation marks	The Train from Rhodesia
∽	transpose	to wildly run
¶	begin paragraph	the stanza. The next image
/	lower case	The Poet writes
≡	capitalize	in "Shore woman"

7. If your school does not have a literary magazine, start one.
8. Contribute your writing to your school or community newspaper.
9. Enter writing contests for student writers sponsored by community groups or by magazines.

CHECKLIST FOR PROOFREADING
Grammar and Usage ☐ Are all of my sentences complete? That is, have I avoided sentence fragments? ☐ Do all of my sentences express only one complete thought? That is, have I avoided run-on sentences? ☐ Do the verbs I have used agree with their subjects? ☐ Have all the words in my paper been used correctly? Am I sure about the meanings of all these words? ☐ Is the thing being referred to by each pronoun (*I*, *me*, *this*, *each*, etc.) clear? ☐ Have I used adjectives and adverbs correctly? *Spelling* ☐ Am I absolutely sure that each word has been spelled correctly? *Punctuation* ☐ Does every sentence end with a punctuation mark? ☐ Have I used commas, semicolons, colons, hyphens, dashes, parentheses, quotation marks, and apostrophes correctly? *Capitalization* ☐ Have I capitalized any words that should not be capitalized? ☐ Should I capitalize any words that I have not capitalized? *Manuscript Form* ☐ Have I indented the first line(s) of my paragraph(s)? ☐ Have I written my name and the page number in the top right-hand corner of each page? ☐ Have I double-spaced the manuscript? ☐ Is my manuscript neat and legible?

10. Send your writing to magazines that publish student writing.

CASE STUDY: PROOFREADING AND PUBLISHING

Brian revised his draft paragraph and made a new copy including all his additions and changes. Then he used the Checklist for Proofreading on the left to locate any remaining problems. This is Brian's proofread final draft:

> I enjoyed reading Mary Shelley's Introduction to Frankenstein because I found out about ~~something I didn't expect—~~that she had trouble coming up with ideas for writing. Since her story about Frankenstein has become so famous, I thought Shelley was just a natural writer. Instead, I found out that she had trouble getting an idea for ~~a~~ her story. Even though her husband, Byron, and Polidori had ~~wrote theres~~ written their stories, she could not think of an idea. Finally she ~~has this~~ had an imaginative vision about a terrifying experiment in creating life. At first, she ~~does~~ did not recognize this as her story. She just ~~wishes~~ wished she ~~old~~ could write something as frightening. Then she ~~realizes~~ realized that this ~~is~~ was her idea for a story. Her problems surprised me, but they also reassured me. I hadn't expected to find out that a writer like her had the same writing problem I usually do.

Brian recopied his paper, read it through for careless errors, and then exchanged papers with a small group in class.

ACTIVITIES AND ASSIGNMENTS

A. Answer the following questions about Brian's proofreading in the case study.

1. Explain why Brian made each change that he did.
2. What other changes do you think Brian might have made? Explain why you would have made those changes.

B. Proofread and publish your draft from the preceding lesson on Drafting and Revising. Follow these steps:

1. Use the Checklist for Proofreading on page 1344 to review your draft. Correct any problems that the checklist helps you to identify.
2. Recopy your corrected paper. Read through this final version to make sure that you copied everything correctly.
3. Share your draft with your teacher and with the other students in class.

1345

SECTION 2: UNDERSTANDING THE PARTS OF A LITERARY WORK: ANALYSIS AND INTERPRETATION

Lesson 4: Writing About Images

WHAT IS AN IMAGE

An *image* is a word or a phrase that presents an experience that can be sensed—a sight, sound, touch, taste, smell, or other physical sensation. For example, Stevie Smith begins "In the Park" this way:

> Walking one day in the park in winter
> I heard two silvered gentlemen talking,
> Two old friends, elderly, walking, talking
> There by the silver lake mid-pooled
> black in winter.

These images of sight, sound, and movement create a picture in words of the scene in the park.

WHY WRITERS USE IMAGES

Writers use images for several purposes:

1. To create vivid descriptions of the things they write about
2. To suggest emotions or feelings about these things
3. To create figures of speech such as metaphors, similes, and personifications.

Sir Philip Sidney begins "Sonnet 31" with these lines:

> With how sad steps, O Moon, thou
> climb'st the skies!
> How silently, and with how wan a face!

The images in these lines:

1. Describe the sight and sound of the moon moving across the sky,
2. Suggest a sad feeling, and
3. Personify the moon as a person with a wan face who can climb the sky despondently.

CASE STUDY: WRITING ABOUT IMAGES

Jason's teacher asked each student to write a short essay about the imagery used in a favorite poem. Jason chose to write about William Butler Yeat's "The Lake Isle of Innisfree," on page 1045.

Prewriting

Jason first read the poem several times. Then he made the following list of the images in the poem:

- Images of sight:
  "a small cabin. . .of clay and wattles made"
  "nine bean rows"
  "a hive for the honeybee"
  "glade"
  "the veils of the morning"
  "midnight's all a glimmer"
  "noon a purple glow"
  "roadway. . .pavements gray"
- Images of Sound:
  "the bee-loud glade"
  "the cricket sings"
  "the linnet's wings"
  "lake water lapping with low sounds by the shore"
  "I hear it in the deep heart's core"

Jason looked up *Innisfree, wattles, glade*, and *linnet* in a dictionary. Then he added these definitions to his notes:

- Innisfree: an island on a lake in County Sligo, Ireland

- wattles: sticks interwined with twigs and branches to make crude fences or walls
- glade: an open space in a forest
- linnet: a small songbird found in Europe, Asia, and Africa

As Jason thought about the images in the poem, he noticed that the speaker describes two scenes. The first two stanzas describe a rural setting—the island of Innisfree. The last stanza describes a city scene. Jason added these observations to his notes:

- Stanzas 1 and 2: images used to create a picture of the natural beauty on the island of Innisfree. The mood created by these images is one of peacefulness.
- Stanza 3: images used to create a picture of a street scene in a city. The mood created by these images is one of unpleasantness.

Next Jason wrote this topic sentence:

> In "The Lake Isle of Innisfree," by William Butler Yeats, the speaker uses images to contrast living in an ugly city with living in a beautiful natural setting.

Finally, Jason made the following rough outline for an essay:

- Introductory paragraph: Begin by pointing out how city-dwellers often long to escape to a simpler existence in the country. End paragraph with thesis statement.
- Body paragraph 1: Discuss images used in poem to create a beautiful country scene.
- Body paragraph 2: Discuss contrast between beautiful country scene and the city in which the speaker lives.
- Conclusion: Make point that modern urban life creates many pressures and that escape often seems desirable. Point out that Yeats's beautiful imagery makes living in the country seem very desirable indeed.

Drafting and Revising

Jason used his notes to write a rough draft of a four-paragraph essay. Then he revised his essay using the Checklist for Revision on page 1341.

Proofreading and Publishing

After revising his draft, Jason made a clean copy and proofread it carefully. Then he shared this proofread copy with his parents and with his teacher.

ACTIVITIES AND ASSIGNMENTS

A. Use Jason's prewriting notes to write an essay about imagery in "The Lake Isle of Innisfree," on page 1045. Revise and proofread your essay. Then share it with your classmates and with your teacher.

B. Choose a poem from your textbook and write a short essay about its imagery. Follow these steps:

1. Read the poem carefully, noting as many of the images as you can.
2. Prepare a chart of the images, arranged by type (sight, sound, taste, touch, and smell).
3. Make notes about why the writer may have used these images—what pictures they create and how they affect the reader.
4. Review your prewriting notes to decide which ideas seem most likely to produce a thoughtful and persuasive paper. Draft a thesis sentence that sums up your topic and your point about it.
5. Make a rough outline, grouping the ideas that belong together in each paragraph.
6. Write a draft of your paper, including an introductory paragraph, one or more body paragraphs, and a conclusion.
7. Revise your paper and then proofread it, using the checklists on pages 1341 and 1344.
8. Share your final copy with your family, with a friend, or with a classmate.

1347

Lesson 5: Writing About Sound

DEVICES OF SOUND IN LITERATURE

Literary works, especially poems, often contain special devices of sound that are used to suggest or to reinforce meaning. Consider, for example, the use of words to imitate the sounds of muscial instruments in these lines from John Dryden's "A Song for Saint Cecilia's Day":

The soft complaining flute
In dying notes discovers
The woes of hopeless lovers,
Whose dirge is whispered by the
  warbling lute.

The list on the right describes some of the most commonly used devices of sound.

CASE STUDY: WRITING ABOUT SOUND

Janine's English teacher asked the class to choose a passage from *Macbeth* and to write about the use of devices of sound in the passage. Janine chose to write about the opening scene of the play.

Prewriting

Janine began by reading the passage aloud several times and listening to its sounds. Then she copied the passage into her notebook and marked its devices of sound, as shown on page 1349.

Then Janine took the following notes about the devices of sound used in the passage:

- Opening sounds like a chant, very rhythmical; four-beat lines (tetrameter)
- Rhyming lines: again/rain, done/won/sun, fair/air
- Onomatopoeia: hurlyburly
- Alliteration: *f* sounds in last two lines
- Parallelism: "Fair is foul, and foul is fair"
- Break in pattern: four-beat lines continue until the Third Witch's line "There to meet with Macbeth." This change in the rhythm emphasizes the name "Macbeth" and is a little disconcerting
- The parallelism of "Fair is foul and foul

SOUND DEVICES
Alliteration: the repetition of initial consonant sounds, as in "O, my *l*uve is *l*ike a *r*ed, *r*ed rose"
Assonance: a partial rhyme involving repetition of a stressed vowel sound but not of the surrounding consonant sounds, as in "*about* the *house*"
Consonance: a partial rhyme involving repetition of similar consonant sounds but not of the intervening vowel sounds, as in "a mon*k*ey's uncle" or "dancing *z*ebras."
Rhyme: the repetition of sounds at the ends of words, as in "Then look ar*ound*, and choose thy gr*ound*"
Cacophony: the use of harsh, unpleasant sounds, as in "hectic red,/Pestilence-stricken multitudes"
Euphony: the use of beautiful, pleasant sounds, as in "Much have I traveled in the realms of gold"
Onomatopoeia: the use of words that sound like what they refer to, as in "And full-grown lambs loud *bleat* from hilly bourn"
Meter: the use of a regular, recurring rhythmical pattern, as in "In Xanadu did Kubla Khan/A stately pleasure-dome decree"
Parallelism: the repetition of a grammatical pattern, as in "the night was dark, no father was there;/The child was wet with dew"
Repetition: the use, again, of a sound, word, phrase, sentence, grammatical pattern, or rhythmical pattern. Note that alliteration, assonance, consonance, rhyme, meter, and parallelism are all varieties of repetition.

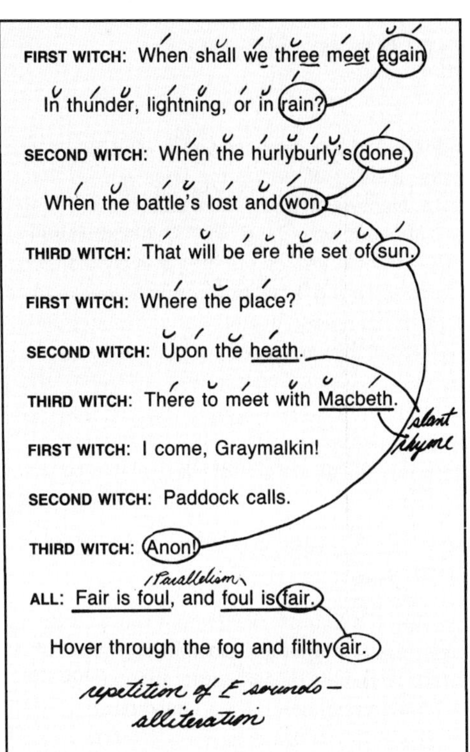

is fair'' emphasizes the witches' desire to confuse fair things with foul things

Drafting and Revising

Based on these notes, Janine wrote the following rough draft:

> Shakespeare's MacBeth begins with a dramatic chant. As if the withces were casting some evil spell. The chant is written in four-beat, tetrameter lines. These opening lines rhyme. As in a chant or spell. The rhyming, four beat lines continue until line 8. Which introduces Macbeth. Line 8 is peculiar because it contains only three lines and because the word *Macbeth* does not rhyme, precisely, with the word *heath*, in the preceeding line. Thus the introduction of the name of Macbeth upsets the rhythmical pattern, just as Macbeth will upset the ordered pattern of life in the kingdom of scotland. The opening scene ends with a rhyming, chantlike couplet. The parallelism of ''Fair is foul, and foul is fair'' emphasizes the witches desire to confuse foulness with fairness. The repeition, or alliteration, of *f* sounds in these last lines ties together and emphasizes the words fair, foul, fog, and filthey. Thus creating a mood, or atmosphere, of ugliness and impending horror.

After finishing her rough draft, Janine revised it carefully.

Proofreading and Publishing

Janine proofread her revised rough draft, made a clean final copy, and handed in her paper to her English teacher.

ACTIVITIES AND ASSIGNMENTS

A. Revise Janine's rough draft from the preceding case study. Follow these steps:

1. Correct all the sentence fragments in the draft.
2. Correct the misspellings and the improper punctuation. Italicize the title of the play.
3. Make any other corrections you feel are necessary.
4. Proofread the revised draft, and then share the proofread copy with your classmates.

B. Choose a poem or a passage from a play or short story and write an analysis of the devices of sound used in it. Follow the procedure outlined in the case study. Begin by copying the passage or poem into your notebook. Then mark its devices of sound and make notes about them. Finally, write a paragraph presenting your analysis of the devices of sound, organized in order of their appearance in the poem or passage. Revise and proofread your paragraph. Then share it with your teacher and with your classmates.

Lesson 6: Writing About Figures of Speech

WHAT ARE FIGURES OF SPEECH?

When expressions or words are used imaginatively, rather than literally, they are called *figures of speech.* The following lines from "A Litany in Time of Plague," by Thomas Nashe, illustrate *metaphor,* a figure of speech in which one thing is described as though it were something else:

Beauty is but a flower
Which wrinkles will devour.

Besides identifying beauty with a flower that will soon wilt, Nashe implies a comparison between the flower and youthful human skin. The skin's beauty, like the flower's, soon will be gone, eaten by wrinkles as if they were hungry animals.

The following lines from "A Birthday," by Christina Rossetti, contain *similes.* A simile is a figure of speech that compares two subjects using *like* or *as:*

My heart is like a singing bird . . .
My heart is like an apple tree . . .
My heart is like a rainbow shell . . .

Other figures of speech are listed in the chart later in this lesson and in the Handbook of Literary Terms.

Such figures of speech can be analyzed to figure out how they work. The literal subject in a metaphor or simile is sometimes called the *tenor.* This subject shares a certain characteristic with the *vehicle*, the figurative term to which it is compared. For example, in Rossetti's third line above, the heart is the tenor. It is compared with the vehicle, a rainbow shell. Different as a heart and a shell are, the comparison makes sense because both share the characteristic of being in a happy situation.

WHY WRITERS USE FIGURES OF SPEECH

Writers use figurative language because its vividness and concreteness enrich what they want to say. Instead of writing the lines quoted first, above, Nashe could just have said, "Everything beautiful ends up getting old." This statement is literal and dull. It does not create lively pictures or trigger strong emotional or imaginative responses in a reader. In just two lines of figurative language, however, Nashe compares two fragile, desirable subjects—beauty and a flower—and two frightening subjects—wrinkling with age and being devoured. In this way Nashe awakens powerful feelings in his reader.

CASE STUDY: WRITING ABOUT FIGURES OF SPEECH

Ladelle's English assignment was to write a short essay analyzing a poem's figurative language. To get the class started, the teacher listed figures of speech on the chalkboard.

Prewriting

Ladelle started her prewriting by reviewing these terms and making a list of how each works. As she analyzed her chosen poem, "Ode to the West Wind," by Percy Bysshe Shelley, she noted figures of speech:

- Antithesis: Use of parallelism to present contrasting ideas
  Maybe "Destroyer and preserver" (first stanza)
- Apostrophe: Direct address of an object, idea, or absent person
  "O wild West Wind . . . Thou breath of Autumn's being Thou" (first stanza)
- Hyperbole: Exaggeration/overstatement
  "azure moss and flowers/So sweet, the sense faints picturing them" (third stanza)

- Irony: Contrast between what is and what seems
  Double nature of west wind (first and fourth stanzas)—both destroyer and preserver
- Metaphor: Comparison through identification
  "I fall upon the thorns of life! I bleed!" (fourth stanza)
  "Ashes and sparks, my words among mankind!" (fifth stanza)
- Metonymy: Substitution of closely related thing
  "A heavy weight of hours" for time (fourth stanza)
- Paradox: Contradiction which is true
  "Destroyer and preserver" (first stanza)
- Personification: Use of human qualities for animal, thing, or idea
  Mediterranean Sea sleeps and dreams (third stanza)
- Simile: Comparison with *like* or *as*
  Leaves "driven, like ghosts" fleeing (first stanza)
  Seeds "Each like a corpse" in a grave (first stanza)
  Clouds shed like "decaying leaves" (second stanza)
  Clouds spread like "bright hair" (second stanza)
  "Make me thy lyre" as forest is (fifth stanza)
  "dead thought" driven like leaves (fifth stanza)
- Synecdoche: Substitution of part for the whole
  "Be through my lips," meaning through his voice and words as a poet (fifth stanza)
- Understatement: Statement of less than is meant
  can't find example in poem

Next Ladelle tried to sum up Shelley's point, or theme, so that she could see the purpose of the poem's figurative language. She turned this idea into her thesis statement and jotted it down:

- Thesis: Shelley uses figurative language to describe the west wind and to explain his ambition as a poet.

Since she had found many figures of speech but was writing only a short essay, Ladelle knew that she had to decide which figures and examples were most important. These choices resulted in her rough outline for a four-paragraph essay:

- Paragraph 1: Thesis and introduction
- Paragraph 2: Description of west wind apostrophe, paradox, and simile (transition to next paragraph)
- Paragraph 3: Explanation of Shelley's ambition as poet simile, metaphor, and synecdoche
- Paragraph 4: Conclusion and summary

Drafting and Revising

After drafting her first paragraph, Ladelle started on her second. Here is the rough draft of her second paragraph:

> Shelley uses apostrophe, paradox, and simile to discribe the wind. The paradox, "Destroyer and preserver," tells how the wind both blows away the autum leaves and saving the seeds for next spring. The poem opens with apostrophe, as Shelly talks directly to the wind. He hails it, saying, "O wild West Wind, thou breath of Autumn's being" (line 1). Finally, the similes in the first two sections. They discribe how the wind effects the things around it. The west wind blows dead leaves "like ghosts from an enchanter fleeing." It drops the seeds on the ground where they wait "like a corpse within its grave" (line 8) for spring. It carries along clouds like leaves, like "bright hair." All these figures of speech discribe the wind.

Ladelle completed her essay and revised it.

Proofreading and Publishing

After proofreading her final copy, Ladelle

1351

shared her paper with her best friend and then handed it in.

ACTIVITIES AND ASSIGNMENTS

A. Answer the following questions about Ladelle's writing in the case study:

1. Why doesn't Ladelle's rough outline list every figure of speech in her chart?
2. How might Ladelle reorganize the rough draft of her second paragraph? What grammatical errors and other problems need to be corrected? Based on your answers to question 2, revise and proofread Ladelle's paragraph.

B. Write a short essay about the figures of speech in a poem by Blake, Wordsworth, Byron, Keats, Hardy, Meredith, Auden, or Heaney. Follow these steps:

1. Read the poem aloud and make a handwritten copy.
2. On your copy, mark the figures of speech that you find. List them by type in a chart.
3. Decide how you want to organize your essay. Each paragraph might make a single point about the poem, using figures of speech as subtopics or examples; or each paragraph might focus on a different figure of speech, explaining how it works and what it adds to the poem. Make a rough outline and draft a thesis statement.
4. Draft your essay, following your outline. Include an introduction, several body paragraphs, and a conclusion.
5. Revise and proofread your draft using the checklists on pages 1341 and 1344.
6. Share your final copy with your teacher and with a friend.

Lesson 7: Writing About Setting

WHAT IS SETTING?

The setting of a literary work is the environment within which the action occurs. Using images and details, the writer may describe the geographical location, the historical period, the season of the year, the weather, a building or room, the furniture, the characters' clothes, their jobs or social circumstances, the local customs—whatever elements will create the sense of a particular time and place.

Often a description of the setting opens a narrative, as in Katherine Mansfield's "A Dill Pickle," on page 951.

> And then, after six years, she saw him again. He was seated at one of those little bamboo tables decorated with a Japanese vase of paper daffodils. There was a tall plate of fruit in front of him, and . . . he was peeling an orange.

This description immediately sets the scene in the restaurant, thus helping the reader imagine the two characters meeting there.

Although Mansfield uses images of sight to introduce this setting, details of sound, taste, touch, or smell may also help create a setting, as in this description of a carpenter's workshop from George Eliot's *Adam Bede*:

> The afternoon sun was warm on the five workmen there, busy upon doors and window-frames and wainscoting. A scent of pine-wood from a tent-like pile of planks outside the open door mingled itself with the scent of the elder-bushes which were spreading their summer snow close to the open window opposite. . . .

In the rest of the passage Eliot describes the appearance of the dog lying in the workshop, the texture of its bed, and the sound of a worker singing.

HOW WRITERS USE SETTINGS

Writers use settings for various purposes. Here are some of the ways in which setting may be used.

USES OF SETTING
To make a work more believable through vivid, precise descriptions
To create a mood, or atmosphere
To create a conflict, as when a character struggles against something in his or her environment
To symbolize a key concept that the writer wants to express

A setting may also reflect a character's situation, complicate the plot, highlight the theme, or otherwise add to the overall effect of the work.

CASE STUDY: WRITING ABOUT SETTING

Anthony's class was studying Victorian prose and novels. Each student was to write a paragraph or two about the significance of the setting in one of the Victorian selections in this book.

Prewriting

After deciding to work on the selection from Charlotte Brontë's *Jane Eyre*, on page 924, Anthony started his prewriting by listing answers to key questions about the setting:

- What is the setting?
  Place—the Reed family's house
  Time—an afternoon long ago, probably about when Brontë lived
  Season—wintry November
  Weather—cold, windy, rainy
- What details are used to create the setting?
  Description of day (paragraphs 1–2)—

wind, clouds, and rain
Drawing room—Mrs. Reed lying on sofa by fireplace with children around
Window seat in breakfast room—enclosed by curtains; bookcases; outside view of wintry day
Social background—John Reed says Jane is a poor dependent (fight scene)

- What is significance of the setting?
  Description of day (paragraphs 1-2)—dreary cold; sad and "humbled" feelings from walks (mood: shows and reflects Jane's situation); cold outside like cold people inside
  Drawing room—Mrs. Reed has "her darlings about her" but not Jane (shows Jane's conflict with Reeds)
  Window seat—curtains and glass "protecting, but not separating" from the wintry day, followed by John's attack and throwing book (mood: shows Jane's feelings)

Anthony reviewed his notes. He decided that he wanted to focus on the way the setting added to the mood and symbolized Jane's situation at the beginning of the novel. He worked next on a rough outline and on a topic sentence.

Drafting and Revising

As Anthony worked on his draft, he discovered that he was explaining Jane Eyre's situation more than the mood of the story. He then revised his topic sentence so that it more accurately reflected the content of his paragraph. On the right is Anthony's revised draft.

Proofreading and Publishing

After Anthony finished revising his draft, he let it sit overnight. Then he proofread his paragraph, made a final copy, and read it to his discussion group during class.

ACTIVITIES AND ASSIGNMENTS

A. Proofread Anthony's paragraph. What additional changes or corrections are needed in his final copy?

B. Choose from this book a short story or an excerpt from a novel. Write a one- or two-paragraph paper analyzing the significance of the setting. Follow these steps.

1. Read your selection several times. First concentrate on the action of the story. Then read the selection again, paying close attention to details of the setting.
2. Write out answers to these key questions about setting:

The setting adds to the mood of the novel and symbolizes Janes situation. Her story starts on this wintrish afternoon at the Reeds home where she is dependent. The cold wind, the 'clouds so somber,' and the 'rain so penetrating' prevent an afternoon walk on that afternoon. The walks always made Jane feel sad. They also made her feel inferior. This opening setting immediately helps to point out that Jane is very isolated and very unhappy in this situation. The indoor setting also contrasts the life of the Reeds up against Jane's isolation. The window seat hides and protects Jane Jane temporarily but even their the the window is "protecting, but not separating me from the drear Nov. day." Jane is separated from others, facing a setting that symbolizes her life.

a. What is the setting? the time? the place?

b. What details are used to create the setting?

c. What is the significance of the setting?

As you do this prewriting, make notes of your answers to each question.

3. Draft a topic sentence that presents your main point. Then use your notes to prepare a rough outline.
4. Draft your paper, following your rough outline. If you want to develop two main points, you may need to write two paragraphs rather than just one.
5. Revise your paper, following the Checklist for Revision on page 1341. Make sure that your topic sentence accurately reflects the content of your paper and that it focuses on the significance of the setting.
6. Proofread your paper, using the Checklist for Proofreading on page 1344. Share your final copy with other students who have written about or are interested in the same selection.

1355

Lesson 8: Writing About Plot

WHAT IS PLOT?

A *plot* is a series of events, or occurrences, each of which is causally related to those that have preceded it. One event in a plot causes the next, which causes the next, and so on to the end of the story. Most plots involve a *central conflict,* or struggle, that is introduced, developed, and then resolved. Typically, the plot of a story, drama, or narrative poem is divided into the following parts:

1. Introduction, or exposition: presents the setting, the major characters, and the basic situation
2. Inciting incident: introduces the central conflict
3. Development: events that occur because of the central conflict
4. Climax: high point of interest or suspense that culminates the development
5. Resolution: event that ends the central conflict
6. Denouement: any events that occur after the resolution

Some critics refer to the introduction, inciting incident, development, and climax as the *rising action*, and to the resolution and denouement as the *falling action*.

Some stories do not contain all these parts in exactly this order. An author may choose, for example, to begin a story *in medias res* (literally, "in the middle part"), after the inciting incident has occurred. The inciting incident of Milton's *Paradise Lost*, for instance, is the expulsion of Satan from heaven. However, Milton begins the poem in the middle of the action, after this expulsion has taken place. In some stories the climax and the resolution are the same event. In some there is no denouement, or tying up of loose ends after the resolution.

SPECIAL DEVICES OF PLOT

Most plots are presented in chronological order. That is, the events follow one another in time as they would in real life. However, an author may choose to vary this pattern by using flashbacks. A *flashback* is a section of a literary work that interrupts the normal sequence of events to present an event from an earlier time. The following special devices of plot are also commonly used by authors:

1. Foreshadowing: hinting about events yet to occur
2. Subplot: a series of events outside but related to the main plot; common in long works such as novels and full-length dramas.
3. Suspense: the creation of a feeling of anxious uncertainty about the outcome of events
4. Surprise ending: an unexpected event occurring at the end of the story

CASE STUDY: WRITING ABOUT PLOT

Nikki's teacher asked each student to select a short story from the text and to write a paragraph about some aspect of its plot. Nikki decided to write about Elizabeth Bowen's "The Demon Lover," on page 1016.

Prewriting

Nikki began by analyzing the plot so that she could pick one aspect to focus on in her paragraph. She worked out a list like this:

- Exposition: Mrs. Drover visits house
- Inciting incident: Mrs. Drover finds letter and feels afraid
- Development: Mrs. Drover recalls her fiancé in a flashback, remembers the promise that she made, feels afraid, wants to escape, leaves for safety of taxi
- False climax and resolution: Mrs. Drover arrives at taxi stand and thinks that she is safe

- Real climax and resolution (surprise ending): sees driver eye to eye, screams
- Denouement: taxi carries Mrs. Drover off

Nikki also noted some of Bowen's special techniques:

- Foreshadowing:
  Beginning—"dead air" in house
  Mysterious unstamped letter from K.
  "spectral glitters" in fiancé's eyes
  "suspension of her existence" during week with fiancé in August of 1916
  No memory of her fiancé's face
  Someone leaves house before she does
- Flashbacks (Mrs. Drover's memories):
  Last evening with fiancé—August, 1916
  Her life after fiance is declared missing in action
  Why she made promise to her fiancé
- Suspense:
  Wondering who (or what) is after her
  Wondering if she will get away
- Surprise ending:
  Thinks she is safe in taxi but taxi driver carries her off screaming

Nikki wrote several possible topic sentences, as follows:

> In "The Demon Lover" Elizabeth Bowen makes use of several special plot devices, including flashbacks, foreshadowing, and a surprise ending.
>
> Elizabeth Bowen's "The Demon Lover" has a traditional plot structure consisting of an exposition, an inciting incident, a development, a climax, and a brief denouement.
>
> In "The Demon Lover" Elizabeth Bowen builds suspense and then tricks the reader with a false resolution.

Drafting and Revising

Nikki liked all of her topic sentences. However, she couldn't write about all of them, so she chose the third one. She wrote a quick draft of her paper, pouring all her ideas onto the page and not stopping to worry about proper spelling, grammar, and punctuation. Then she revised her paragraph several times. As she revised, she cut a lot of nonessential details, and she added direct quotations from the story to support her claims.

Proofreading and Publishing

After her revisions were done, Nikki proofread her paper carefully to get it ready for a reader. Then she shared her final proofread paper with classmates in a small group discussion.

ACTIVITIES AND ASSIGNMENTS

A. Read or reread "The Demon Lover," on page 1016. Use Nikki's prewriting notes, plus your own ideas, to write a paragraph about an unusual or striking feature of the story's plot. Follow these steps:

1. Combine your own ideas and examples from the story with Nikki's prewriting notes. Work out a rough outline of main points and examples, using one of her narrowed topics or your own topic.
2. Begin your paragraph with a topic sentence that makes a specific point about the plot. Refine one of Nikki's topic sentences or write your own.
3. Write the body of your paragraph, following your outline. Explain the main points needed to defend your topic sentence. Quote and summarize as needed, but do not simply retell the story.
4. Write a concluding sentence.
5. Revise and proofread, using the checklists on pages 1341 and 1344.
6. Hand in your paper after sharing it with other students in your class.

B. Choose one of the following works: "The Rocking-Horse Winner," on page 996; "Araby," on page 1009; "A Mild Attack of Locusts," on page 1264; *Macbeth*, on page 223; or "The Rime of the Ancient Mariner," on page 670. Then write a paragraph about some aspect of its plot. Follow these steps:

1. After reading the story twice, list the events in the story. Organize them as Nikki did in the case study. Note the parts of the plot and any special techniques used by the writer.
2. Use your prewriting notes to choose a specific focus for your paragraph. Prepare a rough outline and a statement of your topic.
3. Write a rough draft. Follow your outline, develop your topic sentence, and add a conclusion.
4. Revise and proofread your draft using the checklists on pages 1341 and 1344.
5. Share your final paragraph with a friend in your class.

Lesson 9: Writing About Character

WHAT IS CHARACTERIZATION?

In a literary work, each person, or each animal or object treated like a person, is called a *character*. The *protagonist*, or *main character*, plays the central role in the work and often wins the reader's admiration or sympathy. In some works the main character is in direct conflict with another character, known as the *antagonist*. Many works contain other major and minor characters as well, each with his or her contribution to make to the work as a whole.

Characterization is the act of introducing and developing characters in such a way as to make them real or believable. Here is the way Jane Austen introduces the protagonist in *Emma*:

> Emma Woodhouse, handsome, clever, and rich, with a comfortable home and happy disposition, seemed to unite some of the best blessings of existence; and had lived nearly twenty-one years in the world with very little to distress or vex her.

HOW WRITERS CREATE CHARACTERS

A writer may reveal the personality of a character directly or indirectly. When a writer uses *direct characterization*, he or she simply tells the reader what the character is like. When a writer uses *indirect characterization*, he or she presents the actions, words, and thoughts of a character as clues to the personality of that character or of another character.

A writer may decide to create a *round character*, one who is complex, just like a real person, or a *flat character*, one who has only a few distinguishing characteristics. The main character in a work is usually round, or complex. Minor characters are often flat.

In developing a character, a writer provides information about the following:

1. *Physical Appearance:* What does the character look like? What does the character wear?
2. *Background:* Where does the character come from? Who are the character's friends? Who are the character's relatives? What has the character experienced before the time of the story?
3. *Personality:* What are the character's special qualities and habits? How does the character tend to react to events or relate to others? How does the character think or feel?
4. *Actions:* How does the character behave? How does the character act toward others or cause others to act?
5. *Words:* What does the character say? What do others say about the character?
6. *Motivation:* Why does the character act or react in certain ways? What does the character want or need?
7. *Conflict:* Does the character have an external or internal conflict? How is the conflict resolved?
8. *Change:* Does the character change in the course of the story? If so, why, and in what ways?

CASE STUDY: WRITING ABOUT CHARACTERS

Each student in Sarah's class was asked to write a paragraph about a character in a short story. Sarah decided to analyze the woman on the train in "The Train from Rhodesia," on page 1272.

Prewriting

After rereading the story, Sarah spent five minutes writing down everything that came to mind as she thought about the character. She worked as quickly as possible, without worrying about her wording or her grammar. Here is Sarah's freewriting:

> The woman ends up feeling very sad—sort

1359

of empty and tired. She thought getting married would make her less lonesome. But her husband seems strange and unreal. Like everything else on their vacation. They have a fight because of the carved lion. He got it for her because she liked it and he liked bargaining for it. She loves the lion—it's artistic and beautiful. But she is angry and ashamed—something beautiful should not be bargained for. It should just be paid for—have its dignity. The lion and the fight make her realize how alone she still is because her husband doesn't understand. Maybe she's like the train—calling to the sky but getting no answer.

Next Sarah turned to the questions listed earlier in the lesson. She skipped those that the story did not answer and then concentrated on answering those that seemed most important.

- *Motivation:*
  The woman sees the lion's beauty.
  She seems afraid to take it home in case it doesn't mean anything there.
  She feels ashamed at bargaining for something beautiful.
  She wanted her husband to share her feelings—but she still feels alone.
- *Conflict:*
  The lion causes conflict with her husband—not resolved at the end.
- *Change:*
  She doesn't exactly change—she just realizes that things are the same inside her—still empty.

Now Sarah felt prepared to plan her character study. She decided that the key to the character was her loneliness at the end. Sarah worked next on listing her main ideas:

- *My main points:*
  woman ends up feeling very sad—empty
  lion causes conflict—not resolved
  she loved lion but he loved bargaining
  she is ashamed at bargaining for beauty
  because of this conflict she realizes that the same feelings are still inside her—empty, tired, lonely

Drafting and Revising

Once Sarah had an outline and a topic sentence, she was ready to write her rough draft. She wrote a paragraph, let it sit several hours, and then revised it.

Proofreading and Publishing

Sarah proofread her paper and then took it to class. She read it aloud during the class discussion of character motivation.

ACTIVITIES AND ASSIGNMENTS

A. Use information from the case study to complete these steps:

1. Read, or reread, "The Train from Rhodesia" on page 1272. Review Sarah's prewriting notes and add other notes of your own.
2. Turn Sarah's list of main points into an outline for a one-paragraph character study. Revise Sarah's notes as necessary. Then write a topic sentence for your paragraph.
3. Draft a paragraph based on your topic sentence and outline. Make sure that you include evidence from the story to support your conclusions about the character.
4. Revise and proofread your paragraph using the checklists on pages 1341 and 1344.
5. Exchange papers with one or two other students in your class to see how your final paragraphs differ.

B. Select a short story from this book. Write a paragraph about one of the characters. Follow these steps:

1. Read the story several times, first to select a character and then to note how the character looks, acts, speaks, thinks, and feels.
2. Freewrite for five minutes about the character as if you're trying to figure out a real person. Concentrate on getting your ideas on paper; do not worry about phrasing, spelling, punctuation, or grammar.

3. Add other notes to your freewriting, using the list of questions about character. Make sure that all your conclusions are supported by the story.
4. Decide on your main point about the character. Write a topic sentence stating this point. Then make a rough outline that presents your main ideas and your supporting examples.
5. Begin your paragraph with your topic sentence.
6. Following your outline, draft the body of your paragraph.
7. Write a concluding sentence that sums up and reemphasizes your point.
8. Revise and proofread your draft using the checklists on pages 1341 and 1344. Share your final copy in class.

Lesson 10: Writing About Point of View

WHAT IS POINT OF VIEW?

Point of view is the vantage point, or perspective, from which a story is told. If the *narrator*, or storyteller, is one of the characters in the story, then the story is written from the *first-person point of view*. If the narrator is *not* one of the characters but stands outside the action and tells about it, then the story is written from the *third-person point of view*.

In most stories written from the first-person point of view, the actions or events are reported from one person's perspective. Everything is seen through the eyes of the character/narrator. Such a point of view is said to be *limited*.

In some stories written from the third-person point of view, the narrator tells the tale from one character's limited perspective. However, in other third-person stories the narrator is all-knowing, or *omniscient*, and can present the perspectives of all or several of the characters.

To summarize, most stories are written from one of the following points of view:

1. *First-person limited point of view:* The narrator is a character in the story and presents the action from his or her own perspective.
2. *Third-person limited point of view:* The narrator is *not* a character in the story and presents the action from the perspective of one of the characters.
3. *Third-person omniscient point of view:* The narrator is *not* a character in the story. He or she is all-knowing and can present the internal states or viewpoints of all the characters.

DIFFERENCES BETWEEN POINTS OF VIEW

Stories told from a limited point of view tend to be highly personal and immediate in their impact. The reader usually identifies with the one character from whose perspective the story is told. However, the narrator in such a story is unable to reveal, directly, the private thoughts and feelings of all the characters.

Stories told from an omniscient point of view tend not to be as focused on a single individual. In such stories the narrator has a godlike ability to see all things and know all things. Often the narrator in such a story is able to point out or to reveal interesting or amusing contradictions between the thoughts, feelings, and perceptions of the various characters.

OTHER QUALITIES OF NARRATORS

You have learned about two important respects in which narrators differ. Some narrators participate in the action, and some do not. Some narrators view the events from a limited perspective, and some from an omniscient perspective. Narrators also differ in the following ways:

1. *Reliability:* Some narrators can be counted on to tell the truth. Such narrators are *reliable*. Other narrators grossly distort the truth. Such narrators are *unreliable* or *ironic*.
2. *Objectivity:* Some narrators are cool, calm, and reserved. They simply report events as they occur. Such narrators are *objective*. Other narrators are highly emotional or make their attitudes toward characters and events quite clear. Such narrators are *subjective*.

CASE STUDY: WRITING ABOUT NARRATION AND POINT OF VIEW

Travis was assigned a one- or two-paragraph paper on point of view in a fictional narrative. He decided to analyze the selection from Emily Brontë's *Wuthering Heights*, on page 912.

Prewriting

Travis's class had already read the selection from *Wuthering Heights*, so Travis knew that the first-person narrator is Mr. Lockwood. Travis began his prewriting by rereading the selection and taking these notes:

- Point of view: first-person
- Narrator: Mr. Lockwood
  - Tries to be reliable and give good account (even if embarrassing to him), but makes too many assumptions
  - Starts out assuming that Heathcliff is like him (subjective, not objective)
  - Lockwood and Heathcliff very different:
    - L.'s fussy and pompous chattering vs. H.'s yelling and growling
    - L. expects regular social set-up (servants, tea) and plans visits whereas H. is unsociable (dogs, barred doors, refuses guide in snowstorm).
- Effect of point of view:
  - Suggests there's a hidden story since L. doesn't know what's going on
  - L. guesses everybody's position in household and is totally wrong.
  - Makes us curious about H.and his past because he's so different from L.
  - L. seems ordinary, especially in contrast to H.; this suggests that H.'s story will be unusual.

Next Travis worked on organizing all of his material.

Drafting and Revising

Travis planned two paragraphs: one analyzing Mr. Lockwood as the narrator, and the other discussing how Mr. Lockwood's point of view affects the reader. Here is the beginning of Travis's rough draft:

> I am writing about *Wuthering Heights*. Brontë has Mr. Lockwood tell the story. He is the narrator. He has a first-person point of view. (He is a character in the story and speaks in the first person as "I"). He tries to give an accurate account of Heathcliff. Heathcliff is his landlord. He starts out assuming that Heathcliff is like him. This is a subjective viewpoint. In fact, they are very different.

Travis finished drafting his two paragraphs. Then he revised them several times.

Proofreading and Publishing

Travis proofread his paragraphs and shared his final paper with his discussion group in class.

ACTIVITIES AND ASSIGNMENTS

A. If you haven't already done so, read the selection from *Wuthering Heights*, on page 912. Revise and complete Travis's draft from the case study. Combine his short sentences to make the draft read more smoothly. Add details to the paragraph, especially at the end, to support the claims made. Rewrite and strengthen Travis's topic sentence. Then add a conclusion to the paragraph. Finally, write a paragraph about the effect of Lockwood's limited point of view on a reader.

B. Select a short story from this text. Analyze the narrator and the point of view. Then write two paragraphs discussing the narrator's point of view and its effect on the reader. Follow these steps:

1. After you have read the story once, identify the narrator and the point of view.
2. Analyze the point of view. Determine whether it is limited or omniscient, first person or third. Also determine whether the narrator is reliable or unreliable, subjective or objective.
3. Reread the story and take notes on the narrator and the point of view. Make sure that your notes address the question of the effect of the point of view on the reader.
4. Organize your ideas. First plan a rough outline. Then work on a topic sentence that states your main idea about the point of view.
5. Draft your two paragraphs. Analyze the narrator and the point of view in the first paragraph. Then discuss how the point of view influences the reader's reaction to the story.
6. Revise your paragraphs using the Checklist for Revision on page 1341.
7. Proofread your paragraphs using the Checklist for Proofreading on page 1344.
8. Share your writing with your classmates.

Lesson 11: Writing About Theme

WHAT IS A THEME?

The central idea of a literary work is its *theme*. The theme is an insight about life or the human experience that is revealed through the details of the literary work. For example, the problems characters face and the way they resolve them may provide insight into the human condition. This insight is the theme of the work.

HOW WRITERS EXPRESS THEMES

Occasionally, the theme of a work is stated directly. Usually, however, the theme is not stated directly. Instead, it is implied by the work as a whole. The many separate aspects of the work combine to suggest its central idea.

In the morality play *Everyman*, on page 142, for instance, the Messenger in the first scene says that the play "of our lives and ending shows/How transitory we be all day." Later in the play, the Doctor sums up the implication of Everyman's death for the playgoers:

> Ye hearers, take it of worth, old and
> young,
> And forsake Pride, for he deceiveth you
> in the end.
> And remember Beauty, Five-Wits,
> Strength, and Discretion,
> They all at the last do Everyman
> forsake,
> Save his Good Deeds there doth he
> take

This passage expresses quite directly the theme of the play: Live a good life, full of good deeds, so that you will find salvation when you die.

Many works, however, are less didactic and thus more difficult to interpret. Raleigh's "The Nymph's Reply to the Shepherd" shows how a work of literature may suggest a theme:

> If all the world and love were young,
> And truth in every shepherd's tongue,
> These pretty pleasures might me move
> To live with thee, and be thy love.

Here the nymph tells the shepherd that she would be willing to be his love under certain conditions. The last stanza echoes the same idea:

> But could youth last and love still
> breed,
> Had joys no date nor age no need,
> Then those delights my mind might move,
> To live with thee and be thy love.

These first and last stanzas set up conditions for the nymph's agreement. She says that an idyllic love might flourish—*if* everything could stay young and *if* men always spoke the truth. Of course, she and the reader both know that the conditions in the first and last stanzas cannot be met in real life. All is not permanently young and true, and love does not always increase. Raleigh does not directly say that everything, including youth and love, changes over time. Nevertheless, careful readers will conclude that this is, in fact, the poem's theme.

CASE STUDY: WRITING ABOUT THEME

Liz was asked to write a paragraph about the theme of a short story. She selected Doris Lessing's "A Mild Attack of Locusts," on page 1264.

Prewriting

Liz read the story several times because she knew that finding the theme meant understanding the whole work. Then she worked on writing out a statement of the theme. When she had trouble getting started, she tried freewriting just to get something on paper.

> I am stuck. So why am I? I really do like this story. The best parts are the descriptions and the characters. Margaret keeps being amazed and feeling discouraged. Her husband and Stephen especially just keep on going. They even end up

saying that it could have been worse—though everything green is eaten up. I guess Lessing is saying how amazing it is that people just keep going even when disaster strikes.

When Liz stopped freewriting, she knew that she had begun to work out the theme. After she rephrased her idea, she went back to the story to examine how Lessing actually revealed the theme.

- Theme:
  Despite disasters, human beings can show great strength and resilience.
- Expressions of theme in story:
  Opening of story—Margaret is learning "farmer's language."
  Always problems but they still manage & get along OK
  While waiting for the locusts to come and eat their crops, they keep on working as usual.
  Locusts arrive and they fight them.
  Stephen says they are finished, tells about locusts bankrupting him 20 yrs ago, and goes back out with tea.
  When crops are all eaten, they keep on fighting to prevent locusts from laying eggs (hoppers hatch later).
  Stephen tosses out locust after admiring its strength; Margaret remembers he's said they were ruined before and they've survived.
  Men are cheered because main swarm has gone by—they begin planning to fight hoppers.
  Margaret admires beauty of locusts at dawn despite the damage they've done.
- Conclusion:
  Margaret feels like "a survivor after war" & men say, "It could have been worse."

Drafting and Revising

Liz used her prewriting notes to draft her paragraph. She started with a clear topic sentence about the theme, developed the body of the paragraph, using details from the story, and then wrote a concluding sentence that summarized her analysis. Next Liz revised her paragraph, making sure that her points were clearly stated and organized.

Proofreading and Publishing

After proofreading, Liz exchanged papers with the student sitting next to her before they both handed in their paragraphs.

ACTIVITIES AND ASSIGNMENTS

A. Refer to the case study as you write a paragraph following these directions:

1. Read, or reread, "A Mild Attack of Locusts," on page 1264. Review Liz's prewriting notes, and add other notes of your own about the theme. Use the notes to work out a rough outline of points about how the theme is revealed to the reader.
2. Write a topic sentence identifying the story and its theme.
3. Draft the body of your paragraph, discussing how the theme is revealed or expressed in the story. Use your rough outline and Liz's and your prewriting notes to supply detailed supporting evidence from the story.
4. Write a concluding sentence that sums up your analysis of the story's theme.
5. Revise and proofread your paragraph using the checklists on pages 1341 and 1344.
6. Share your final copy with a classmate before handing it in.

B. Write a paragraph about a literary work in this book. In your paragraph, identify the work's theme, and explain how this theme is expressed or revealed in the work. You may select any literary work or write about one of these: Shakespeare's *The Tempest*, on page 305; Orwell's "Shooting an Elephant," on page 1034; Lawrence's "The Rocking-Horse Winner," on page 996; or Blake's "A Poison Tree," on page 626. Follow these steps:

1. Read the work once or twice. Write a single sentence stating its theme. (Use freewriting if you get stuck.)
2. Refine your statement of theme. Then go through the work, taking notes on points in the work that express, reveal, or illustrate the theme.
3. Work out a rough outline of your ideas.
4. Begin your rough draft with a topic sentence identifying the work and its theme.
5. Follow your rough outline and your prewriting notes as you draft the body of your paragraph. Do not just generalize about the idea of the theme. Be sure to include details from the work to show how the writer conveys the theme.
6. Write a concluding sentence that sums up your main point.
7. Revise your paragraph using the Checklist for Revision on page 1341.
8. Use the Checklist for Proofreading on page 1344 to check your final version.
9. Share your paper with your classmates and with your teacher.

1366

SECTION 3: UNDERSTANDING THE WORK AS A WHOLE: INTERPRETATION AND SYNTHESIS

Lesson 12: Writing About a Short Story

When you write about a short story, your task begins not with writing but with reading and understanding the story. Follow these guidelines when studying a story:

1. Read the story through to find out what happens in the plot.
2. Look up any unfamiliar words in the Glossary or in a dictionary.
3. Read the story again, this time concentrating on how the writer has created its key features.
4. Refer to the story as you analyze its main elements.

HOW TO ANALYZE A SHORT STORY

The following list outlines the main elements of short stories (and of longer fictional works as well). Once you have made prewriting notes about these aspects of a story, you are prepared to think about how each contributes to the story's meaning.

1. Author and title: Who wrote the story? What is the title of the story? Does the title suggest the subject or theme of the story?
2. *Plot:* What are the story's main events? What happens during each part of the plot: the exposition, the inciting incident, the development, the climax, the resolution, and the denouement? Does the story use special plot techniques such as foreshadowing, flashbacks, suspense, or a surprise ending?
3. *Central conflict:* What is the central conflict? Is the conflict external? Is the protagonist pitted against another character, society, or nature? Is the conflict internal? Is there a struggle between different emotions and feelings inside the protagonist?
4. *Setting:* What is the place, time, and social situation of the setting? What details create the setting? What is the setting's significance? Does it contribute to the conflict or mood?
5. *Characterization:* Who is the protagonist? Is there an antagonist? If so, who is the antagonist? Who are the other major and minor characters? What roles do they play? What do readers learn about each character's appearance, background, personality, actions, words, relationships, motivations, conflicts, and changes?
6. *Point of view:* Who is the storyteller, or narrator? Is the narrator omniscient or limited, first person or third? Is the narrator subjective or objective, reliable or unreliable?
7. *Language:* Does the story contain figures of speech such as hyperbole, irony, metaphor, or simile? Does the story contain special devices of sound such as onomatopoeia or parallelism?
8. *Theme:* What is the theme—the story's insight or central idea? How is the theme expressed?
9. *Other elements:* Is the story addressed to a specific audience? If so, who? Is the story an example of a specific genre such as fantasy, science fiction, psychological fiction, mystery fiction, detective fiction, or regional fiction?

CASE STUDY: WRITING ABOUT A SHORT STORY

Javier's English teacher assigned an essay about the significance of a short story. Javier decided to analyze and write about James Joyce's "Araby," on page 1009.

Prewriting

Javier read the story twice and got this idea for his thesis:

> "Araby" shows how we all get ideas about how things will be and then feel disappointed with ourselves when things don't work out as expected.

Next Javier began taking prewriting notes on the story's key features, using the list found earlier in the lesson. Here are his notes about the story's setting:

- Place: boy's home with aunt and uncle, town (Ireland), train ride, and bazaar
- Details: blind street and houses
  Priest's former room with blinds where he watches Mangan's sister
  Town market full of people and shops
  Empty train going to bazaar
  Bazaar dark with stalls closed, money counting, girl flirting. Significant because reality contrasts with what he wants and imagines.
  Real market vs. knight with chalice
  Lonely train ride foreshadows bazaar
  His idea of Araby vs. real bazaar. Significant because setting suggests his state (symbolic?).
  Lives in "blind" street and watches Mangan's sister from behind blinds
  Lights are out at bazaar, leaving him in the dark but able to "see"

Javier finished his analysis, concentrating on point of view and characterization. Then he planned how to organize his essay and made a list of his main points.

Drafting and Revising

Based on his thesis idea and on his other prewriting notes, Javier drafted a thesis statement and an introductory paragraph. For the body of his essay, he wrote one paragraph apiece about setting, characterization, and point of view, relating each to his thesis about the significance of the story. Then he drafted a concluding paragraph that summed up his main point about the story's theme. Finally, he revised his story, reorganizing, adding examples, and rephrasing as needed.

Proofreading and Publishing

Next Javier proofread his paper, looking for minor errors and making a few more changes in wording. Here is his first paragraph with his proofreading changes:

> The experiences of the boy in James Joyce~~'s~~ *'s* ~~Araby~~ *"Araby"* illustrate~~s~~ how ~~a poreon~~ *people* often expect~~s~~ more than ~~real, true life~~ *ordinary reality* can provide and then feel disillusioned and ~~disappointed with themselves.~~ *disappointed.* The boy is ~~crazy about~~ *infatuated with* Mangan's sister, imagines that he will ~~be a big hero when he~~ *heroically* bring~~s~~ her something from the ~~bizarre~~ *Bazaar*, and then feels ~~real~~ *very* foolish when ~~it isn't~~ *Araby is not* what he expects. The story expresses its ~~idea thru~~ *theme through* the setting ~~where the story happens and~~, the characteriz*a*tion of the boy and his point of view as the nar*r*ator.

Javier recopied his paper, read it through for copying errors, and shared it with his class discussion group.

ACTIVITIES AND ASSIGNMENTS

A. Use the draft in the case study to answer these questions:

1. Explain why Javier made each of his proofreading changes.
2. Why didn't Javier explain the plot in a full para-

1368

graph instead of summing it up in his second sentence?

3. Javier's first paragraph previews the next three paragraphs—one each on setting, characterization of the boy, and point of view. Read "Araby" carefully, take prewriting notes on these elements of the story, and then write the body paragraphs. Your paragraphs should support Javier's thesis and should each focus on a single element of the story. Revise and proofread your draft carefully, using the checklists on pages 1341 and 1344.

B. Write an essay interpreting a short story in this book. Follow these steps:

1. Read the story, and use the lists earlier in this lesson to analyze it.
2. Draft a thesis statement about the significance of the story, concentrating on its theme, purpose, or overall effect.
3. Use your prewriting notes to decide which elements of the story will best support your thesis. Prepare an outline that notes the element each paragraph will discuss plus the evidence from the story that will illustrate the feature and relate it to your thesis.
4. Draft your paper, following your outline.
5. Revise and proofread your paper using the checklists on pages 1341 and 1344.
6. Share your paper with your class.

Lesson 13: Writing About a Poem

Writing about a poem requires that you understand it well. Follow these general steps as you begin the process of analysis:

1. Read the poem to yourself. Look up any unfamiliar words. Identify the poem's speaker, subject, and genre (narrative, dramatic, or lyric).
2. Read the poem again, and note any images, figurative language, or allusions. Think about the functions served by these.
3. Read the poem out loud. Listen for special devices of sound such as rhythm, rhyme, alliteration, or onomatopoeia.
4. Read the poem again carefully and paraphrase it, sentence by sentence or line by line. Your paraphrase should reflect both what the poem states directly and what it implies.
5. Make notes on the genre, form, imagery, figurative language, devices of sound, theme, and other elements of the poem.

HOW TO ANALYZE A POEM

When you take prewriting notes about a poem as a whole, look at the elements frequently used in poetry to see what features set apart this particular poem—to see what makes it different or especially meaningful. Then you will have a basis for deciding what to emphasize in your paper about the poem. The following list of elements in poetry will help you look for the key features of a poem. Once you have identified these features, you can begin to ask questions about them and to analyze how they create the poem's meaning.

1. *Author and title:* Who wrote the poem? What is the title of the poem? Does the title suggest the topic or theme of the poem?
2. *Genre:* Is the poem a lyric, such as an ode, an elegy, or a sonnet? That is, does it use musical language to express the emotions of a single speaker? If so, who is the speaker? What audience is being addressed? What is the occasion or situation? Is the poem a narrative, such as a ballad, an epic, or a metrical romance? That is, does it tell a story? If so, what plot, characters, settings, and point of view does this story have? Is it a dramatic poem, one that uses monologue, dialogue, or other dramatic techniques? What point of view, characters, setting, and situation does the poem present?
3. *Form:* Does the poem have a traditional form or pattern? If the poem is divided into stanzas, what form does each stanza take? Describe the number of lines, rhyme scheme, and metrical pattern of each stanza. Does the poem make use of couplets, quatrains, or some other standard stanza form? Does each stanza function, like a paragraph, as an independent unit of meaning? Does the poem have a unique shape or structure that adds to its meaning?
4. *Imagery:* What images of sight, sound, taste, touch, smell, and movement are used? What emotions do the images suggest?
5. *Figurative language:* What figures of speech are used in the poem? Does the poem contain examples of antithesis, apostrophe, irony, hyperbole, metaphor, metonymy, oxymoron, paradox, personification, simile, synecdoche, or understatement? Does the poem contain symbols or allusions? Is it allegorical?
6. *Devices of sound:* Does the poem contain rhyming words? Does it have a regular rhyme scheme? Does the poem contain alliteration, assonance, or consonance? Does it contain euphony, cacaphony, parallel structure, or repetition? What is the poem's meter? What type and number of metrical feet does it have in each line? If the poem is in free verse, how does it use rhythm?
7. *Other elements:* Has the poet taken liberties with spelling, mechanics, or grammar? Has

the poet used words in unusual ways? If so, why has he or she done so? What tone does the speaker use? What is the mood of the poem? Does this mood change during the poem? What is the poem's theme? What overall effects do the separate parts of the poem combine to create?

CASE STUDY: WRITING ABOUT A POEM

Jeremy's English assignment was to write an essay about a poem. He decided to write about Molly Holden's "Some Men Create," on page 1331.

Prewriting

Jeremy began his prewriting by reading through the poem several times, studying it in detail, and making notes about its key features. Here are a few of his notes:

- Author: Molly Holden
- Title: "Some Men Create"
- Form: 4 quatrains—show the situation (1), consequences (2–3), and point (4)
- Genre: lyric poem
- Imagery: sight (so that "eye may reap")
  ivy vaulting, swinging, and shining
- Figurative language: two similes
  Ivy will "swing like hair" (sounds like Rapunzel?)
  "seeding traveler's joy smothers" timber and oak "like smoke"
- Devices of sound:
  Rhyme scheme (*abcb*)
  Alliteration: *sm*others/*sm*oke
  Assonance: suggests "Oh" of wonder? *o* in so, oak/smoke, alone/sown
  Repetition: word *so* used three times
  Meter: variations match meaning example: 4th lines of stanzas are all the same (´ ˘ ´ ˘ ´ ˘) except in last stanza, where variation emphasizes "not sown"
  Examples: line "vaults" between first two stanzas (just like ivy); line 10 (about cutting dead tree) has 5 one-syllable words—snap off like branches from dead tree
- Theme (last stanza especially):
  Even in an orderly life, people should allow some spontaneous and unanticipated things to develop.

After Jeremy read through his prewriting notes, he felt that the poem not only explains but also illustrates its theme. He outlined his paper, selecting as examples the features he thought would best support his thesis.

- Paragraph 1 Introduce poem: Name author and title; state thesis that the poem both explains & illustrates its theme
- Paragraph 2 Form is orderly (rhyme, meter): 4 quatrains follow logical pattern—show the situation, illustrate the consequences, and explain point
- Paragraph 3 Form has surprises ("not sown"):
  Meter in line 4 of last stanza
  Line that "vaults" between stanzas
  Line 10 with short words
- Paragraph 4 Language also help reader see the point that eye likes to "reap":
  Images of sight (ivy)
  Similes (also visual)
  Assonance (suggests awe or wonder)
- Paragraph 5 Conclusion: Poem states and illustrates its point, showing us that we like order but we also like unexpected pleasures.

Drafting and Revising

Jeremy used his outline and notes to write a

rough draft. Then he revised his draft, making sure that both his interpretation and his examples were clear.

Proofreading and Publishing

Jeremy carefully proofread his paper and then exchanged papers with a classmate.

ACTIVITIES AND ASSIGNMENTS

A. Read, or reread, Molly Holden's poem, on page 1331. Then use the case study for these activities:

1. Jeremy's outline does not include alliteration and repetition. Why do you think he left them out? Could he have added them? If so, where?
2. Jeremy's outline notes the idea for his thesis. Write this out in a sentence.
3. Add your own ideas to Jeremy's prewriting notes. Use your notes and the notes from the case study to draft, revise, and proofread your own analysis.

B. Write an interpretive essay on any poem in this text. Follow these steps:

1. Read the poem and analyze it, using the steps and key elements outlined at the beginning of this lesson.
2. Use your prewriting notes to develop a working outline and a thesis statement about the poem's overall effect, purpose, or theme.
3. Follow your outline as you write an introductory paragraph, body paragraphs, and a conclusion. Be sure to use supporting examples and quotations.
4. Revise and proofread your essay, using the checklists on pages 1341 and 1344.
5. Share the poem and your paper with your classmates.

Lesson 14: Writing About Drama

When you analyze a play, you will find that it contains many of the literary elements found in short stories and in poetry. Like a short story, a play has a plot, a central conflict, characters, a setting, and a theme. Like poetry, a play may use poetic forms, imagery, figurative language, and devices of sound. Refer to the previous two lessons for information on analyzing and writing about these literary elements.

No matter how much a play resembles a story or a poem, it necessarily differs in one major respect. A play is written to be performed before an audience. Its action is physical and takes place on stage. Its lines are written to be spoken by actors and to be accompanied by their expressions and movements. Unlike most stories and poems, a play has dialogue for actors to speak and stage directions to explain the actors' movements, the appearance of the set, the props needed, the lighting and sound effects, and other aspects of performance and production. In addition, a play may use such *dramatic conventions* as the *aside* (a speech or comment made directly to the audience as though other characters on stage could not hear it) or the *soliloquy* (a speech delivered by a lone character on the stage, one that reveals the character's inner thoughts).

HOW TO ANALYZE DRAMA

A play can be analyzed as a written work of literature or as a performance, as the following questions suggest.

The drama as literature:

1. What happens during the exposition, inciting incident, development, climax, resolution, and denouement of the plot? What happens during each act and scene?
2. What is the central conflict?
3. How does the setting add to the play's significance?
4. Who are the characters? What does each add to the play?
5. What does the audience learn about each character's background, personality, relationships, motivations, conflicts, and changes?
6. How is the theme revealed?
7. What imagery does the writer use?
8. What figurative language does the writer use?
9. What symbols does the play present?
10. What devices of sound does the language of the play include?

The drama as performance:

1. How is the stage set, and how does that setting affect the audience?
2. How effectively and accurately is each character portrayed in the performance?
3. How effective is the delivery of the dialogue? (Consider such factors as pacing, volume, pitch, stress, tone, and vocal quality.)
4. What is the overall effect of the performance?
5. How would you review the performance as a whole? (Consider such factors as the acting, the set, the costumes, the sound, the lighting, the direction, the properties, the makeup, and any other factors in the production.)

CASE STUDY: WRITING ABOUT DRAMA

Michael's English teacher assigned an essay about one scene in *Macbeth*. The focus of the essay was to be how the scene contributes to the significance of the play as a whole.

Prewriting

Michael decided to analyze Act I, Scene iii, when Macbeth first meets the three witches. He wanted to figure out how the scene moves the play forward and what significant information it gives the audience. Here is a chart Michael made to examine the play's plot, setting, characters, and themes.

Michael worked on organizing his notes into a logical outline for his essay.

ELEMENT	SIGNIFICANCE
Plot:	
three witches on heath meet Macbeth and Banquo	nature of witches
hail Macbeth with three titles	Macbeth is absorbed, wants to hear more from them
hail Banquo as father of kings	Banquo may become a threat to Macbeth's ambitions
Ross and Angus arrive to greet Macbeth as Thane of Cawdor	confirm witches about Cawdor raise question about crown
Setting:	
thunderstorm on heath	threatening, evil weather
"foul and fair" day	foreshadows events to come
Character:	
Macbeth is shaken by prophecy but wants to know more	ready to think of murdering Duncan decides not to act but leave it to chance
Banquo suspects betrayal from witches	contrast with Macbeth: Banquo is not ambitious and senses evil, does not react as Macbeth does warns of evil
Themes:	
ambition control of future—choice or destiny?	Macbeth considers how far he'll go to make prophecy true

Drafting and Revising

Michael began his introduction with this thesis statement:

> Through its plot, setting, and characterization, Act I, Scene iii, of *Macbeth* alerts the audience to the problem of knowing one's destiny and wanting to control the future.

Michael drafted and revised his essay, including an introductory paragraph, a concluding paragraph, and separate paragraphs on plot, setting, and character. Here is his revised version of paragraph four, on character:

> Both Macbeth and Banquo hear the prophecies and their first confirmation out on the heath. From the beginning, the two characters react differently. As Banquo points out, Macbeth acts distracted and shaken. He wants to hear more and does not want to judge the prophecy as evil or good. Still, his first thought is not of some accident to the king but of murder—of how his own action could secure the future. Finally he decides that chance may bring him the crown without any action on his part. In contrast, Banquo sees the witches as evil and warns Macbeth. Though he wants to hear theie prediction, he does not want anything from them. Unlike Macbeth, he has no thought of trying to control the future.

Proofreading and Publishing

Michael proofread his paper for spelling and mechanical errors. Then he shared the paper with his older brother, who is an actor.

ACTIVITIES AND ASSIGNMENTS

A. Use the case study to answer these questions:

1. Point out the transitional words and phrases in Michael's paragraph. Explain how Michael uses transitions to help organize his discussion of the two characters.
2. Michael does not use any quotations from the play to support his arguments. Revise his paragraph, adding appropriate quotations. Be sure to punctuate properly and to quote the exact words of the play.

B. Choose one of these topics for an essay about

a play: (1) analyze the main elements of one scene in a play from this text, and explain their contributions to the significance of the play as a whole; or (2) evaluate the success of the love story in *The Tempest*, on page 305. For either topic, follow these steps:

1. Read the section of the play carefully several times. Try to imagine how the scene would be presented on stage.
2. Take prewriting notes as you analyze the play. Use the first list in this lesson for guidelines; return to the last two lessons if you need more suggestions.
3. Work out a thesis statement and an outline. Note the main point of each paragraph and the supporting evidence or details from the play. Decide whether you should organize element by element or chronologically as presented in the play.
4. Follow your outline and support your thesis statement as you draft your essay.
5. Revise and proofread your draft using the checklists on pages 1341 and 1344.
6. Share your essay with your classmates.

1375

SECTION 4: JUDGING A LITERARY WORK: EVALUATION

Lesson 15: Evaluating a Literary Work

WHAT IS EVALUATION?

When you *evaluate* something, you judge its value. In everyday life you regularly perform this mental task—evaluating a new album, clothes that you want to buy, or the food at a new restaurant. Each evaluation states your opinion and based on *evidence*, the facts you discover when you listen to the album, try on the clothes, or eat at the restaurant. In other words, your evaluation is based on appropriate standards or criteria—the sound and style of the music, the appearance and cost of the clothes, and the taste and price of the food.

Evaluating a literary work is just like making other judgments: You state an opinion based on certain standards or criteria. Then you support your opinion with specific evidence and details. Your opinion is your own, but it will not be accepted by anyone else unless you can marshal the facts to support it.

For example, if you argued that *The Tempest* is a juvenile play because two of the characters are a sprite and a monster, your opinion could not be supported by evidence. Since it was common for supernatural beings to appear in plays on the Elizabethan stage, their presence does not make a play juvenile. Therefore, your opinion is not sound since it cannot be supported by evidence. If, on the other hand, you argued that the overall mood of the *The Tempest* is more tragic than cheerful, some people would disagree with you, but you could provide evidence from the play to support your evaluation so that readers would understand your position.

CRITERIA FOR EVALUATING A LITERARY WORK

Your judgment of the quality of a story, poem, play, or other work may be based on many different criteria. Here are some standards often applied to literature:

1. To what extent does the work accomplish its purpose or achieve its effect? Do you think that it succeeds in doing what it sets out to do—entertaining, amusing, scaring, surprising, persuading, teaching, or emotionally moving its reader?
2. Is its purpose or effect worth accomplishing? Do you consider its purpose more important or significant than other purposes?
3. Does the work have an ethical or moral message? Do you feel that its message is important? Do you agree with the message?
4. How original or inventive is the work? Do you find the topic or its treatment new?
5. How clear and understandable is the work? If the work is difficult, does it nonetheless reward the reader's efforts to understand it? Does the work seem indefensibly unclear or confused?
6. To what extent does the work meet other criteria important to you as a reader? Do you have personal views about its genre, subject, or style?

CASE STUDY: EVALUATING A LITERARY WORK

Ben's teacher asked the class to suggest poems that might provoke different opinions from different people. Then each student was to write an essay stating and supporting an evaluation of the poem.

Prewriting

Ben decided to write about Rupert Brooke's "The Soldier," on page 1068. Ben himself had mixed feelings about the poem depending on whether he based his judgment on realistic criteria or on the poem's success in accomplishing its own purpose. He used clustering to test both ideas:

Ben decided to write about the opinion that he could most persuasively defend with evidence from the poem. He added to and reorganized his prewriting notes until he had outlined a four-paragraph essay.

Drafting and Revising

Ben refined his thesis statement and drafted his essay. The next day he revised his paper, carefully checking the clarity of his arguments and evidence.

Proofreading and Publishing

After Ben proofread his paper, he shared the poem and his paper with a friend.

ACTIVITIES AND ASSIGNMENTS

A. Read, or reread, Brooke's poem, on page 1068. Then review Ben's clustering notes in the case study and follow these steps:

1. Select one of Ben's criteria, and add your own notes to his; start with your own criteria for judging the poem, and use clustering or another prewriting technique to develop your ideas. Whatever your view, the prewriting notes should specify your standard or criteria for judging, your opinion about how well the poem meets those standards or criteria, and your supporting evidence (quotations, paraphrases, and analyses of the poem).
2. Write a thesis statement that states your opinion. Then outline your main points and your evidence.
3. Draft your essay, including an introduction, several body paragraphs that develop your main points, and a conclusion.
4. Revise and proofread your paper, using the checklists on pages 1341 and 1344. Check especially carefully to see that your opinions and reasons are clearly stated and that your evidence is pertinent and clear.
5. Exchange your work with someone in class who wrote a paper using a different standard for judgment. Compare your papers.

B. Select a poem, story, or other literary work

about which you have a definite opinion. Write a four- or five-paragraph essay evaluating that work. Follow these steps:

1. Use freewriting, clustering, or another prewriting technique to figure out the criterion or standard for judgment, the precise opinion, and the supporting evidence on which you will base your judgment. If you have a strong view but cannot find evidence to support it, your opinion will not be persuasive. In that case, start over with another work, or do more prewriting to develop your ideas.
2. Work out a thesis statement that presents your opinion about the work. Organize your prewriting ideas in a paragraph-by-paragraph outline. Make sure that your paper is clearly organized. You might choose to concentrate in each paragraph on a specific element of the work, showing how it supports your opinion. On the other hand, you might devote a paragraph to each reason for your opinion, drawing supporting examples of different kinds from the work.
3. Draft your essay, starting with an introduction to the literary work, your criterion for judging it, and your evaluation or opinion based on the criterion. Next write your body paragraphs and a conclusion.
4. If possible, wait a few hours or a day so that you have more perspective about your own writing. Then revise your essay, using the checklist on page 1341. Make sure that your ideas are stated clearly and that your opinions are supported by evidence.
5. Proofread your paper, using the checklist on page 1344.
6. If possible, exchange papers with a classmate who has a different opinion about the same work.

Lesson 16: Writing a Comparative Evaluation

WHAT IS A COMPARATIVE EVALUATION?

A *comparative evaluation* follows the same pattern explained in the last lesson. First state your opinion about which of two works is better or worse, based on specific criteria or standards for judgment. Your basis for comparison may include one or more specific points of comparison (similarities) or contrast (differences). Then use specific evidence from both works to support your views.

CHOOSING WORKS FOR COMPARATIVE EVALUATION

When you select two works for comparative evaluation, they should have something in common—perhaps the same theme, topic, or literary form. If the two works are totally unlike, comparison serves little purpose. You could only conclude that they are very different—that one, for example, is an Anglo-Saxon epic poem and the other a modern short story about a fiddle.

To compare or contrast the two works effectively, you need to find comparable points in each. These points might be the elements characteristic of the type of writing. For example, you could compare and contrast the form, imagery, figurative language, and sound devices in two lyric poems with the same subject and theme. Similarly, you might look at characterization, setting, and symbolism in a short story and a play with similar plots and themes. (See the lessons in Sections 2 and 3 of this handbook for advice about how to analyze specific elements and types of literary works.)

ORGANIZING A COMPARATIVE EVALUATION

Begin by selecting the points of comparison and contrast that seem most pertinent. Then make a chart listing each point of comparison or contrast. Allow room for an entry about each work in its own column. For each work and each point of comparison, note comments and evidence.

Next plan an outline based on the points that fit your essay. Use the organizational method that is best for the complexity and balance of your material:

METHOD 1	METHOD 2
Introduction Work #1 —Point A —Point B —Point C Work # 2 —Point A —Point B —Point C Conclusion	Introduction Point A —Work #1 —Work #2 Point B —Work #1 —Work #2 Point C —Work #1 —Work #2 Conclusion

CASE STUDY: WRITING A COMPARATIVE EVALUATION

Melissa's English teacher assigned a comparative evaluation of two poems. Melissa picked two sonnets, Shakespeare's "Sonnet 29," on page 207, and Rossetti's "Silent Noon," on page 871.

Prewriting

Melissa began the assignment by carefully rereading the two poems. She knew that she liked

1379

Shakespeare's better, but she needed to analyze why. Using elements from the lesson on writing about a poem, she worked out this chart:

ELEMENT	"SONNET 29"	"SILENT NOON"
Form	Shakespearean	Petrarchan
Imagery	sound—cries and curses, then little until thinks of beloved and lark sings	sight—lush imagery is almost too much
Figures of Speech	simile—he feels like a lark singing when he thinks of beloved idea of joy bursting up fits well	simile—the dragonfly hangs like a blue thread; so this hour is dropped to lovers thread, hour, and dragonfly are less attractive silence like hourglass is OK but no special fit overdone!
Sound Devices	repetition "like him" parallelism and trouble/look/curse this man's/that man's structure of lines emphasizes rut he's in	alliteration: *g*leams/*g*looms *sk*ies/*sc*atter *s*un/*s*earched *d*eathless/*d*ower lines 8 and 14 hiss instead of hush
Language Choices	older words "beweep" "bootless" but actually direct clear language	showy l. 13 is too dense "This close-companioned inarticulate hour"
Theme	love poem: remembers love when downcast and wouldn't change with a king it's a bigger compliment	love poem: treasures beautiful hour together more ordinary idea than in Shakespeare sonnet

After Melissa had enough evidence to support her opinion, she worked out an outline for her paper.

Drafting and Revising

Melissa began her draft with this thesis statement:

> Shakespeare's "Sonnet 29" is a deeper and more moving love poem than Rosetti's "Silent Noon." Although some of Shakespeare's older vocabulary is harder to understand, his sonnet's form and meaning are better matched to each other through his use of sound devices, imagery, and figurative language.

Melissa continued drafting her paper, following her outline. She then revised carefully, checking to make sure that she had included all her main points of comparison and contrast for each poem.

Proofreading and Publishing

After proofreading, Melissa shared her paper with Ms. Thomas, her English teacher from the preceding year, who had given her extra help with comparisons and contrasts.

ACTIVITIES AND ASSIGNMENTS

A. Use the case study to answer the following questions.

1. Which organizational plan does Melissa's thesis statement suggest that she will use? Use her prewriting notes to write out the outline that you think she has planned.
2. How else might Melissa organize her paper?

1380

Work out a second possible outline for her paper. Write a revised thesis statement that suits this new outline.

3. Which outline better suits her material? Explain the advantages and disadvantages of each.

B. For your own comparative evaluation, select two literary works such as any of the following pairs: Marlowe's "The Passionate Shepherd to His Love," on page 182, and Raleigh's "The Nymph's Reply to the Shepherd," on page 190; Nashe's "A Litany in Time of Plague," on page 202, and the selection from Defoe's *A Journal of the Plague Year*, on page 532; Marvell's "To His Coy Mistress," on page 440, and Herrick's "To the Virgins, to Make Much of Time," on page 454; or Tennyson's "Crossing the Bar," on page 820, and Thomas's "Do Not Go Gentle into That Good Night," on page 1120. Follow these steps in writing your essay:

1. Read both works carefully.
2. Tentatively decide which you like better and for what reasons.
3. Set up a chart like the one in the case study, listing the points of comparison and contrast for both works. Begin working on the points that seem most important, but stay flexible in case other ideas occur to you.
4. Work out a rough outline and a thesis statement. Try one of the two methods of organizing outlined earlier.
5. Begin drafting your paper's introduction, including the titles and authors of the two works and your thesis statement with your evaluation. Draft the body paragraphs, following your outline and including clear supporting evidence from the works. Then write a concluding paragraph summarizing your argument.
6. Check for clear and consistent organization. Try outlining your draft itself to identify any problems or omissions.
7. Revise and proofread your essay using the checklists on pages 1341 and 1344.
8. Share your essay with a classmate.

1381

Lesson 17: EVALUATING PERSUASION

A nonfiction work is *persuasive* if its purpose is to move readers or listeners to take some action or to adopt some view. Examples of persuasive nonfiction include editorials, advertisements, campaign speeches, and public relations materials. Often people write essays and even whole books specificlly to persuade others to think or act in certain ways.

SOUND REASONING ABOUT PERSUASION

Persuasive writing and speech present opinions—statements about which people may disagree. When evaluating persuasive language, a reader or listener must determine whether the opinions presented are sound. The following are some criteria for evaluating the soundness of opinions:

The Consistency Principle

Is the opinion consistent with known facts? For example, the opinion that one should not take illegal drugs is consistent with the fact that illegal drugs can cause great physical and psychological harm.

The Utility Principle

Does accepting the opinion lead to consequences that are themselves acceptable? For example, the opinion that one should not drive beyond the speed limit is sound because acting on this opinion has desirable consequences. When people drive within the speed limit, there are fewer traffic accidents.

The Principle of Appeal to Authority

Is the opinion consistent with the views of knowledgeable and reliable authorities? For example, the opinion that one should eat high-fiber, low-fat foods is consistent with the views of medical scientists and researchers. These people have found that eating such foods decreases one's risk of developing heart disease or cancer.

Each of these principles is related to the more general principle that an opinion must be supported by reasoned, logical arguments.

UNSOUND REASONING ABOUT OPINIONS

When people write or speak persuasively, they sometimes present arguments that are unreasonable or illogical. Such arguments make use of propaganda and logical fallacies. *Propaganda* is language that is emotionally charged and intentionally misleading. A *logical fallacy* is an error in reasoning. The following propaganda devices and logical fallacies are often found in persuasive writing and speech:

Propaganda Devices:

1. *Bandwagon:* urging support for an opinion simply because many other people support the opinion
2. *Loaded language:* using emotionally charged words that have little meaning beyond arousing positive or negative feelings
3. *Argument ad hominem:* (literally, "argument to the person") criticizing or attacking the opponent instead of the oponent's argument
4. *Snob appeal:* urging support for an opinion solely because an admired person or group supports it
5. *Straw man:* exaggerating or misrepresenting the opposing position so that it sounds more ridiculous than it actually is
6. *Stereotyping:* assuming, without sufficient evidence, that everyone in a particular group has certain characteristics

Logical Fallacies:

1. *Begging the question:* stating an opinion without giving evidence to support it; simply assuming the truth of the opinion to be proved

2. *Either/or fallacy:* treating a complicated issue as if there were only two sides or two alternatives when there are actually more
3. *Post hoc, ergo propter hoc:* (literally, "after this, therefore because of this") assuming that one action or event caused another simply because it came earlier in time
4. *False analogy:* falsely treating two subjects as similar in one respect simply because they are similar in some other respect
5. *Non sequitur:* (literally, "it does not follow") stating a conclusion that is not a necessary consequence of the reasons given
6. *Overgeneralization:* making a statement that is broader in its application than the facts would warrant

When evaluating written or spoken persuasion, make sure that the opinions presented are well supported. Also make sure that the speaker or writer has avoided propaganda devices and logical fallacies.

CASE STUDY: EVALUATING PROPAGANDA AND ARGUMENT

Carrie's English class was working on the logical evaluation of arguments. Each student brought to class an example of propaganda or faulty logic. Examples were found in editorials, in political speeches, in a letter to the editor of a newspaper, and in similar material. After the class discussion each student was asked to write a paragraph evaluating his or her example.

Prewriting

Carrie found this letter to the editor in her local newspaper:

> Dear Editor:
>
> The recent car accident on Tunley Lane shows how irresponsible pet owners are. If that dog had not been walking along the side of the road, the car would not have run into the mailbox. People should not have pets unless they are willing to care for them. All good citizens agree that the public should not have to risk car crashes, highway mayhem, and wanton violence just because these people are nincompoops!
>
> Sincerely,
> Roger Loxley

Carrie began analyzing this letter, first noting its highly emotional vocabulary and tone as well as the lack of evidence for its assertions. She then listed some of the letter's flaws:

- Argument ad hominem and loaded language—calling people "nincompoops"
- Bandwagon appeal or snob appeal—calling on "all good citizens"
- Non sequitur—assuming that the dog by the road was not cared for and assuming that pet owners are responsible for "car crashes, highway mayhem, and wanton violence"
- Post hoc, ergo propter hoc—assuming that the dog caused the accident
- Stereotyping—characterizing all pet owners as irresponsible people

Carrie decided that the letter contained two basic flaws—lack of respect for other people, both pet owners and readers, and an illogical analysis of causes and effects.

Drafting and Revising

Carrie used her prewriting notes to supply details for her paragraph. After drafting her paragraph, she carefully revised it, making sure that her own points were presented reasonably.

Proofreading and Publishing

Carrie proofread her paragraph and then read it aloud to the class.

ACTIVITIES AND ASSIGNMENTS

A. Use the case study to answer the following questions:

1. How could Carrie use her list of logical flaws to illustrate that the letter lacked respect for

people and presented a faulty analysis of causes? Work out an outline for her paragraph. Feel free to add or to leave out points.

2. Do you see other logical flaws in the letter? If so, what are they?
3. What general characteristics of sound argument does the letter lack?

B. Analyze an example of faulty argument or of propaganda. Write a paragraph about it, following these steps:

1. Find an example such as a letter to the editor, and editorial, a political brochure, some campaign material, or an advertisement.
2. Analyze why your example is not a sound argument. Examine its general characteristics, its specific logical fallacies, and its propaganda techniques. List these problems. Then use the materials on your list to make an outline.
3. Begin your paragraph with a topic sentence. Then explain and illustrate your main points. Add a conclusion.
4. Revise and proofread your draft using the checklists on pages 1341 and 1344.
5. Share yor paragraph with a class discussion group.

Lesson 18: Writing a Short Story

Writing a short story means arranging and telling about incidents, describing scenes, and developing characters in ways that will interest and entertain a reader. A short story may begin with an idea about any of the standard features of the short story—character, setting, plot, mood, or theme.

FINDING A STORY IDEA

Here are some suggestions about how to find an idea for a short story:

1. *What happens? (plot):* Think of an incident or a conflict that could make a good story. Consider internal conflicts (choices, decisions, or other pressures) or external conflicts (struggles between people, battles with social or physical forces, contests, or other oppositions).
2. *Where does it happen? (setting):* Think of an interesting time (past, present, or future) and place (real or imaginary), perhaps someplace where you have lived or that you have visited.
3. *Who is involved? (characters):* Think of someone you know who is interesting, admirable, or unusual. Create a character based on this person.
4. *What does it mean? (theme):* Think of an insight that you would like to pass along to others.
5. *Who tells the story? (point of view):* Imagine a narrator who has a complete overview, the more limited view of an observer, or the even more limited view of a participating character.

DEVELOPING YOUR STORY

To develop your story idea more fully, ask yourself these questions:

1. *Character:* Who will be the main character? What will be the character's name? How will he or she look and talk? What will be the character's background, personality, education, job, or status? What will be the character's motivations? Why will the character act as he or she does? What will he or she want or believe? Will the character change? If so, how and why? What will the character learn? What relationships with others will the character have? What internal or external conflicts will the character need to resolve? Who will be the minor characters? What will be their roles? What will they be like? How will they relate to the protagonist?
2. *Setting:* When will the story take place? Where will it take place? What sensory images will help you create this place for a reader?
3. *Plot:* What will happen in the story? In what order will you tell the story? Will you use flashbacks, foreshadowing, or a surprise ending? How will you build suspense? What background information will you supply at the beginning of the story? What will happen to begin the conflict? How will the conflict develop? What will be its consequences? What will be the most suspenseful moment? How will the conflict end? Will anything happen after the conflict ends? If so, what?
4. *Point of View:* Who will tell the story—an observer or a character? How much will the storyteller know—everything or what one character knows? Will the narrator speak in the first person or in the third person?
5. *Theme:* What will be your short story's central idea or insight into life? How will you express this point in the short story?

CASE STUDY: WRITING A SHORT STORY

Erica wanted to enter a short story contest, but she did not want to write a typical romance or adventure story. She wanted to write about the future, but she needed an idea.

Prewriting

Since the school district computers were down most of that day, Erica began to wonder what life would be like without computers. She wrote down a few notes about this idea to test whether it would make a good short story.

- Title ideas: maybe "Computers on Strike" or "The Great Computer Scam"
- What happens? (plot):
  Something damages one computer
  It breaks down; spreads to others
  All overload and stop working
  Now what? Consequences? Solution?
  Get them fixed? Live without them?
- *Where does it happen? (setting):*
  Future, maybe 50 years from now
  Society even more dependent on computers; people need them to work, run houses, make decisions
  Should place look cold and mechanical? or should it have deceptive surface, looking natural but depending on the computers to keep it all going?
- *Who is involved? (characters):*
  Probably need good person, but does he or she want to fix the computers? Would character rather help people become independent of them again?
  also need source of conflict: computers themselves? or evil character? (not mad scientist!) maybe the electric power company?
- *What does it mean? (theme):*
  What is my central idea?
  Should story show human ability to solve problems? or the need to stay human in an over-controlled society? or the need for people to find solutions using their intelligence?
- *Who tells the story? (point of view):*
  Maybe all-knowing narrator?
  —maybe the main character who feels the conflict or even the computer that causes the mess?

  Erica finally had an idea. She used the list of questions in this lesson to develop her idea further.

Drafting and Revising

Erica drafted her story in one sitting. Then she waited a day, read it through once, and began to revise section by section.

Proofreading and Publishing

After proofreading her paper and handing it in for her teacher's reactions, Erica made a few more changes. Then she entered her work in the short story contest.

ACTIVITIES AND ASSIGNMENTS

A. Review Erica's prewriting notes and complete them yourself, using the list of questions for developing a short story. Work out your own story outline and draft your story. After revising and proofreading your story, exchange papers with other students in your class to see how differently they developed the story.

B. Write an original story. Follow these suggestions:

1. Use the first list (the one with the *who, when, where,* and *what* questions) to come up with an idea for a story.
2. Develop your ideas by answering the questions in the second list in this lesson.
3. Make a list of the events in your story.
4. Draft your story.
5. Review your draft, checking the development of all the elements in the second chart. Make any necessary additions, cuts, or changes so that the sequence of events, the characters' motivations, and the conflict are clear.
6. Revise your draft as you would any other paper, using the checklist on page 1341.

7. Proofread your paper using the checklist on page 1344.
8. Share your story with a reader whom you think would especially enjoy it—your parents, your English teacher, a past English teacher, a teacher in another class, or a friend.

1387

Lesson 19: Writing a Poem

Writing poetry can be a wonderful, rewarding experience. In this lesson you will review some common poetic forms and then try writing some poetry yourself.

SOME COMMON VERSE FORMS

A *couplet* is a pair of rhyming lines, each with the same number of strong stresses, or beats. Long poems are often made of strings of couplets that may or may not be separated by spaces. For examples of poems written in couplets, see Marvell's "To His Coy Mistress," on page 440; the selections by Pope, on pages 560 and 573; and Hopkins's "Spring and Fall: To a Young Child," on page 859.

A *ballad* is a poem that tells a story in short, rhyming stanzas. The traditional ballad, often set to music, has four- or six-line rhyming stanzas. Most ballads have a recurring rhythmical pattern. Examples of traditional ballads appear on pages 78–85. Many traditional English and American songs are ballads, as are many popular songs.

Free verse is poetry that does not follow a recurring rhythmical or metrical pattern. A writer of free verse is free in the sense that he or she can ignore the standard conventions of language and can divide up his or her lines in any way that seems appropriate to what is being said. Examples of free verse in your text include Lawrence's "Snake," on page 1057, and Smith's "Not Waving But Drowning," on page 1315.

CASE STUDY: WRITING A POEM

Greg's class was writing poetry. He decided to write a ballad, hoping to publish it in the school newspaper.

Prewriting

Although Greg knew roughly what a ballad was, he first read the examples of traditional ballads in the text and reviewed the definition of *ballad* in the Handbook of Literary Terms.

Next Greg started to work on an idea. He wanted to write a ballad that would interest everybody who read the newspaper. He also thought, given his personality, that he could write a better humorous ballad than a serious or tragic one. During the next few days, he listed events at school or invlolving students that might be topics:

- College applications—not a story, but could be one student's trauma
- SAT scores—maybe about valiant survivors on test days
- Accident at Bell and River Road—too serious to be funny; could be done like "Sir Partick Spens," but probably not a good idea
- Cafeteria—food is always a complaint for students; maybe I could tell the story of one student braving the lunch lines, especially on a day with "mystery stew"

Greg liked his second idea and thought other students would too.

Drafting and Revising

Greg started work on his first stanza with these lines:

Young Bobby was a valiant lad,
He had faced the SAT,
He had filed his college forms
And he . . .

Greg did not like this beginning. He decided not to specify Bobby's grade level because he wanted the poem to appeal to an audience broader than just one class. He also felt stuck after the ending with *forms*. Then Greg decided to start over with another topic. He wrote until he finished the first draft, alternating between adding new lines and rephrasing completed lines as he got new ideas. Here is the beginning of his revised ballad:

> Young Bobby was a valiant lad,
> ~~He had faced the SAT.~~ A soccer man was he.
>
> He never flinched from pain or grief,
> ~~Until~~ 'Til after period three.
>
> Then came the line that scared the brave,
>
> The line that scared the bold,
>
> The line that led ~~our~~ brave Bobby on
>
> ~~To a meal . . . sold.~~
> ~~To a lunch never told.~~
> To a lunch never told.

Proofreading and Publishing

After proofreading his ballad, Greg submitted his final copy to the school newspaper, where it was published two weeks later.

ACTIVITIES AND ASSIGNMENTS

A. Answer the following questions about the case study:

1. Identify these features of traditional ballads in Greg's poem:
   a. division into four-line stanzas
   b. use of a regular rhyme scheme
   c. use of repetition
   d. use of a regular rhythmical pattern
2. Write the rest of Greg's ballad, using your imagination or adding details about your school's cafeteria. Stick to the traditional ballad form that Greg used.

B. Try writing your own poem following the directions below:

Couplet (one or more)

1. Read some of the poems written in couplets that appear in this book.
2. Choose an idea that suits the compact style of the couplet.
3. Once you have an idea, write it out. Experiment with rhymes to end the lines.
4. Rework each line until the metrical pattern is regular and the end rhyme fits.
5. Revise and proofread your poem.
6. Share your poem with your class.

Ballad

1. Begin by thinking of an event or situation for a ballad story. Brainstorm a list of ideas until you have one you like.
2. Read the ballads in this book to review the pattern of the ballad stanza.
3. Begin writing stanza by stanza, using the traditional ballad form.
4. Add other ballad characteristics as you can. Use simple language, direct dialogue, dramatic action without extra detail, repetition, and perhaps a refrain.
5. Revise and proofread your ballad.
6. Submit it to your school newspaper or to some other student publication.

Free verse

1. Read a number of free-verse poems to see how they work.
2. Jot down your ideas for a subject. Use prewriting techniques such as brainstorming, clustering, freewriting, and charting.
3. Write out your poem in a prose paragraph.
4. Divide your prose into lines. Each line should be a complete grammatical unit—a phrase, a clause, or a sentence.
5. Revise and proofread your poem, paying particular attention to word choice, imagery, and special devices of sound.

Once your poem is finished, share it with friends and submit it to your school's literary magazine or to another student publication.

Lesson 20: Writing a Short Dramatic Sketch

A full-length drama or play may last several hours and have many scenes and acts. A *dramatic sketch*, however, lasts only a few minutes and is a single short scene. A sketch uses the same form as a longer play and can be either comic or tragic, but it makes only a single point. Because of its restricted length and focus, the dramatic sketch adapts well to the pace of television and is a popular feature of comedy and variety shows.

UNDERSTANDING THE CONVENTIONS USED IN A DRAMATIC SKETCH

Like longer dramatic works, the dramatic sketch has these features:

1. *Title*
2. *List of characters*
3. *Stage directions:* underlined or italicized in square brackets or parentheses
4. *Dialogue:* with character names in all capitals (sometimes in boldface or italic type), followed by the exact words the actors are to say

The beginning of Shaw's *Pygmalion*, on page 1124, illustrates these conventions:

Act I

London at 11:15 P.M. Torrents of heavy summer rain. Cab whistles blowing frantically in all directions. Pedestrians running for shelter. . . .

The church clock strikes the first quarter.

THE DAUGHTER (*in the space between the central pillars, close to the one on her left*) I'm getting chilled to the bone. What can Freddy be doing all this time? He's been gone twenty minutes.

THE MOTHER (*on her daughter's right*) Not so long. But he ought to have got us a cab by this.

Stage directions can explain what the set should look like and what lighting, sound, or special effects are required in production. They can explain which characters are on stage and what they are doing as a scene opens. When a character speaks, the stage directions can clarify how the actor should be positioned, how he or she should move, and what expression or tone he or she should use. The dialogue, on the other hand, supplies only the exact words the actor should speak.

PLANNING A DRAMATIC SKETCH

Like any other creative projects, a dramatic sketch requires many decisions. As you make each decision, consider whether what you imagine can happen on stage. Ask yourself these questions as you begin your planning:

1. Will the sketch be comic or serious? How do I want the audience to react? What should be the overall effect?
2. What will be the time and place of the action? How will the set represent the setting?
3. Who will the characters be? How will they speak, move, and act? How should they look and sound to the audience? What costumes will they wear?
4. What events will occur as part of the plot? What conflict will complicate the plot? What will happen in the beginning, the middle, and the end?
5. What props, special effects, or other extras will be needed?

CASE STUDY: WRITING A DRAMATIC SKETCH

Tamara's school service club was in charge of planning a show for the spring orientation for students who would be entering the school next fall. The show was to encourage their school spirit and to make them feel welcome.

Prewriting

Tamara and two of her friends were in charge of drafting a script for the show. Since their English class had read *Everyman* earlier in the year, they decided to model their dramatic sketch on a morality play. Tamara wrote out their plans:

- Title: Every[fresh]man
- Characters:

Every[fresh]man	School Spirit
Apathy	Energy
Rowdy	Loyalty
Foggy	Pride
Lazy	Hard Work
Wacky	

- Plot summary: Every[fresh]man arrives on campus to start next year. Apathy, Rowdy, Foggy, Lazy, and Wacky try to lead Every[fresh]man astray. School Spirit, assisted by Energy, Loyalty, Pride, and Hard Work, come to the rescue. They send away the others, except Wacky, and help Every[fresh]man start the year right.
- Setting: The school—probably just a door and a walk to suggest the edge of the school building

Drafting and Revising

Next Tamara drafted the script, and her friends helped her to revise it. Here's how their dramatic sketch began:

Every[fresh]man

[*The scene opens near Building A on the first day of school in the fall. The building door is at the back left and the front walk leads off to the right. New students are arriving, hunting for their lockers, turning their schedules and maps around, looking lost. Every[fresh]man enters from the left, drops a map, picks it up, and looks around. Every[fresh]man is printed on the character's T-shirt.*]

EVERY[FRESH]MAN. [*sounding confused and turning map upside down*] This looks like Building B, except that this walk is in the wrong place. Maybe I should try this way. . . .

ROWDY. [*runs in from right and playfully shadow boxes with Every[fresh]man* Hiya, kiddo. What's new? Har, har.

EVERY[FRESH]MAN. Well, I'm new here, and I don't know how to find Building B.

ROWDY. [*grabbing map*] Gimme that. Har, har. Looks like an upside-down map!

APATHY. [*drifts in from right*] Oh, who cares, Rowdy?

ROWDY. [*sarcastically*] Oh, my! [*shadow boxing with Apathy, who just yawns*] You sure don't, do you, Apathy?

FOGGY. [*wandering in from right*] Now was today Wednesday or Thursday? I can't remember if I have chemistry this year. Maybe it's Algebra instead.

ROWDY. Get your station tuned in, Foggy. We've got a problem here. Definitely looks like a lost one. [*tosses map aside*]

FOGGY. [*ignores Rowdy and talks to Every[fresh]-man]* Well, if you want Building B, it's here somewhere, unless it's over there now. Nope, that's definitely the gym. [*picks up map while talking and puzzling over buildings in distance*]

Proofreading and Publishing

After proofreading, Tamara made copies of final version for the club members in the cast and for their club advisor.

ACTIVITIES AND ASSIGNMENTS

A. Refer to the case study as you answer these questions.

1. How does Tamara tell the audience her characters' names? Why does she describe how they act as well as what they say?
2. Add another section to Tamara's sketch. Introduce the rest of the characters, who try to lead Every[fresh]man astray. Show how they confront School Spirit, or show School Spirit and friends rescuing Every[fresh]man from the others. Follow Tamara's format for dialogue and stage directions.

B. Write your own short dramatic sketch, following these steps:

1. Select a topic, an occasion, and an audience for your sketch.
2. Use the planning chart to work out your ideas. Write notes on your title, characters, setting, and plot.
3. Draft your sketch. Begin with the title, character list, and stage directions for the set. Then

1391

write the dialogue and the stage directions for the actors. Give only essential directions.

4. Read your draft aloud to test whether the dialogue sounds natural.
5. Revise carefully. Cut unneeded description or conversations that do not advance the plot. Add information needed for clarity, and revise your dialogue so it sounds natural.
6. Proofread your script. Share it with your classmates.

Lesson 21: Writing an Essay

WHAT IS AN ESSAY?

An essay allows you, the writer, to communicate directly with a reader about something that matters to you. It communicates your experiences, ideas, and feelings. This lesson explains how to adapt the steps outlined in the first section of this handbook to the personal essay.

PLANNING AN ESSAY

In your essay, you are likely to want to sound like one thoughtful person talking with another about something that concerns or interests you. Make sure that you have some personal experience or knowledge about your topic. Even if your topic is assigned, your own viewpoint makes your essay personal.

Essays have many purposes, depending on what you write about and how you want to affect a reader. Suppose you work as a volunteer at a local nature center and care very much about its future. You might write about that topic in many ways, as this list suggests:

1. *Narrative essay:* telling a story to entertain and interest a reader:

   My first trip up Waterfall Trail, at the Davis Valley Nature Center, began peacefully, giving no clue of the danger to come.

2. *Descriptive essay:* describing something so that a reader can imagine it:

   Even though the Davis Valley Nature Center is only five minutes from homes and businesses, I feel hundreds of miles from civilization when I see the sun rise there on a crisp autumn morning.

3. *Expository essay:* Explaining something so that a reader can understand it:

   The three trails at the Davis Valley Nature Center seem confusing, but they actually form a pretzel shape, all meeting at the Education Center.

4. Argumentative or persuasive essay: convincing people to act or think in a certain way:

   Proposition 4 must be passed if we are to protect the plants and animals in preserves like the Davis Valley Nature Center.

For your essay, freewriting and clustering are especially helpful. They can help you to relax and to think freely about your topic. Questioning, listing, and analyzing are useful if you need to figure out how to approach or develop your idea.

Your prewriting activities also may vary with your purpose. For a narrative essay, a time line of events may help organize the key incidents in the story. A list of images, arranged by sense (sight, sound, taste, touch, and smell), can enrich a descriptive essay. For an expository essay, you may want to list examples, subtypes, or steps in a process. You may need a chart that lists causes and effects or that identifies points of comparison or contrast. Should your purpose be argumentative, you may want to list your arguments, your opponent's arguments, and reasons that support or contradict them.

CASE STUDY: WRITING AN ESSAY

Patrick's English teacher assigned an essay. Students could select their own topics, but each essay had to have a clear thesis statement and an orderly, logical development.

Prewriting

Patrick began prewriting by thinking about his college applications. He used clustering to pinpoint a topic, as shown on the next page.

Patrick looked over his clustering chart and decided that he wanted to explain his college choice. He reorganized his ideas in a list, identifying subtopics and details for the body of his essay:

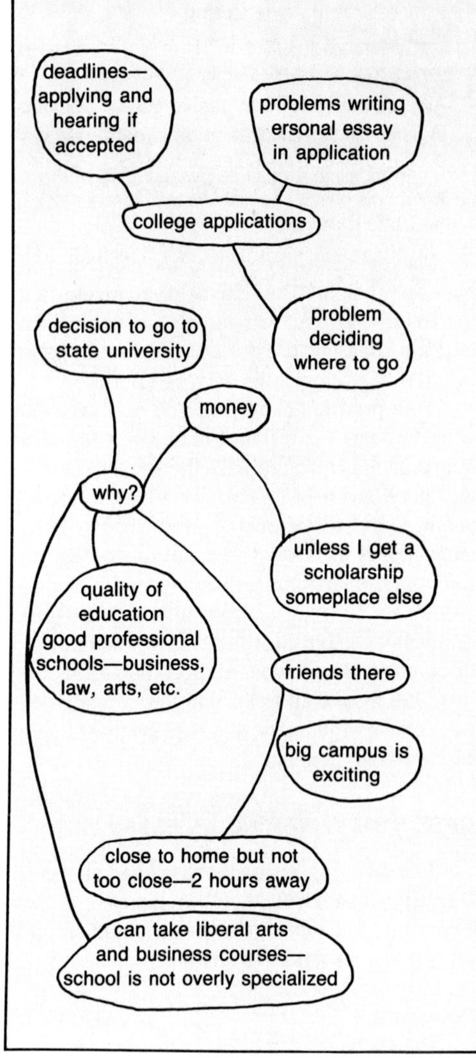

- *Topic:* state university is my first choice for college
- *Paragraph 1 Introduction and thesis statement:*
  Why state university is my first choice (add reasons to thesis)
  Qualify: unless I get a scholarship elsewhere and must take money to be fair to family
- *Paragraph 2 Money:*
  Most people assume money is my reason (add tuition example?)
  College is so expensive that money has to be a factor
  But it is not my main reason
- *Paragrah 3 Other supposed reasons:*
  Friends there
  Exciting, big campus
  Close to home but not too close (2 hours by car)
  All are factors, but all could be supplied by other schools
- *Paragraph 4 Real reason is the quality of school:*
  Not overly specialized, so I can take both liberal arts and business
  Good professional schools, so degree will be well regarded and faculty will be top level
  Most important is recent national honors for architecture school; architecture will be my major field
- *Paragraph 5 Conclusion about reasons for choice:*
  Not for economic or social reasons but for academic reasons
  Lucky to get the other benefits while getting the one that matters most about any college

Drafting and Revising

Because his outline was so detailed, Patrick quickly drafted a thesis statement and wrote the rest of his paper. Next he revised his essay, concentrating mainly on sentence structure and style because he felt that his organization was already clear.

Proofreading and Publishing

After Patrick proofread his paper, he left a copy with his guidance counselor.

ACTIVITIES AND ASSIGNMENTS

A. Use the case study to answer the following questions:

1. Carefully review Patrick's outline. Do all of his points follow logically and support his thesis statement? What important explanation, not in his clustering, has he added to his outline?
2. Use Patrick's outline to draft a possible thesis statement for his essay. Be sure that your statement specifies the topic, states the approach or viewpoint, and prepares a reader for the content and order of the body paragraphs.
3. Given Patrick's outline, what transition would you expect to find in his essay? Point to places in his outline that suggest how he planned to link his paragraph and sentences.

B. Write your own essay, following these steps:

1. Think of a topic that interests or concerns you. Decide whether your essay will be narrative, descriptive, expository, persuasive, or entertaining. If you have trouble thinking of a topic, try freewriting or clustering.
2. Use one of the prewriting techniques to develop ideas. Then arrange your ideas in an outline.
3. Write a thesis statement that specifies your topic and your viewpoint. If possible, also prepare a reader for the content and organization of your essay.
4. Use your thesis statement as the basis of your introductory paragraph.
5. Write body paragraphs, each developing a main point. Each should have a topic sentence that follows from your thesis plus transitions, clear explanations, and details or examples.
6. Write a concluding paragraph that sums up your essay in an interesting way.
7. Revise and proofread your essay using the checklists on pages 1341 and 1344.
8. Share your essay with a friend.

HANDBOOK OF LITERARY TERMS AND TECHNIQUES

ACT See *Drama*.

ALEXANDRINE An *alexandrine* is a line of poetry written in iambic hexameter. The line is made up of six feet, each containing one weakly stressed syllable followed by one strongly stressed syllable. The following lines from Michael Drayton's *Polyolbion*, which was written in 1613, are alexandrines:

Muse, first | of Ar|den tell, | whose
foot|steps yet | are found
In her | rough wood|lands, more | than an|y
oth|er ground

The alexandrine takes its name from the fact that the meter was often used in Old French poems about Alexander the Great. Alexandrines never became popular in England. However, Edmund Spenser did use them at the ends of stanzas in *The Faerie Queene*.
See *Meter* and *Spenserian Stanza*.

ALLEGORY An *allegory* is a literary work with two or more levels of meaning—one literal level and one or more symbolic levels. The events, settings, objects, or characters in an allegory stand for ideas or qualities beyond themselves. Allegorical writing was common in the Middle Ages. Thereafter, the popularity of allegory declined, but Spenser revived the form in *The Faerie Queene*, and John Bunyan revived it yet again in *The Pilgrim's Progress*. Some modern novels, such as Joseph Conrad's *Heart of Darkness*, can be read allegorically. When reading a work allegorically, one tries to match every element at the literal level with a corresponding element at the symbolic level.

ALLITERATION *Alliteration* is the repetition of initial consonant sounds. Emily Brontë used alliteration of *l* sounds in the first stanza of her poem "The Old Stoic":

Riches I hold in *l*ight esteem,
And *L*ove I *l*augh to scorn;
And *l*ust of fame was but a dream
That vanished with the morn

Alliteration is often used, especially in poetry, to emphasize and to link words as well as to create pleasing, musical sounds. Alliteration of stressed syllables was one of the characteristic features of Anglo-Saxon poetry.
See *Anglo-Saxon Poetry*.

ALLUSION An *allusion* is a reference to a well-known person, place, event, literary work, or work of art. Writers often make allusions to tales from the Bible, classical Greek and Roman myths, plays by Shakespeare, historical or political events, and other materials with which they expect their readers to be familiar. An allusion appears in Shakespeare's *A Midsummer Night's Dream*, when Hermia swears "by Cupid's strongest bow," thus referring to the god of love in Roman mythology. Writers sometimes use allusions as a sort of shorthand to suggest ideas in a simple and concise manner.

ANAPEST See *Meter*.

ANECDOTE An *anecdote* is a brief story about an interesting, amusing, or strange event. In *The Life of Samuel Johnson*, an excerpt from which appears on page 588, James Boswell tells both serious and humorous anecdotes about Johnson. These anecdotes illustrate features of Johnson's temperament and character and explain why Boswell regarded Johnson as one of the most extraordinary figures in all literary history.

ANGLO-SAXON POETRY *Anglo-Saxon poetry* is the rhythmic poetry composed in Old English before about A.D. 1100. It generally has four accented syllables and an indefinite number of unaccented syllables in each line. Each line is divided in half by a caesura, or pause, and the halves are linked by the alliteration of two or three of the accented syllables. The following lines, translated from "Wulf and Eadwacer," show the alliteration and caesuras used in Anglo-Saxon poetry:

I *w*aited for my *W*ulf//with far-*W*andering
  yearnings,
*W*hen it was rainy *w*eather//and I sat
  *w*eeping.

Anglo-Saxon poetry was originally composed orally and then sung or chanted to the accompaniment of a primitive harp.
See *Alliteration*, *Caesura*, and *Kenning*.

ANTAGONIST An *antagonist* is a character or force in conflict with the main character, or protagonist, in a literary work. In many stories the plot is based on a conflict between the antagonist and the protagonist. In *Beowulf*, on page 24, the protagonist faces two antagonists—Grendel and Grendel's mother.
See *Character* and *Protagonist*.

ANTITHESIS *Antithesis* is a figure of speech in which contrasting or paradoxical ideas are presented in parallel form. The following examples of antithesis come from Alexander Pope's *An Essay on Criticism*:

1. Some praise at morning what they blame at night
2. To err is human, to forgive, divine.

Antithesis was popular among the Neoclassical English poets of the eighteenth century, who often used it to make witty or satirical comments.

APHORISM An *aphorism* is a general truth or observation about life, usually stated concisely and pointedly. Often witty or wise, memorable aphorisms appear in the works of Chaucer, Shakespeare, Pope, Johnson, and many other writers. An essay writer may have an *aphoristic style*—a style characterized by use of such statements—as does Francis Bacon. The following aphorisms come from Bacon's "Of Studies":

1. Crafty men condemn studies, simple men admire them, and wise men use them.
2. Reading maketh a full man, conference a ready man, and writing an exact man.

Used in an essay, an aphorism can be a memorable way to sum up or to reinforce a point or argument.

APOSTROPHE An *apostrophe* is a figure of speech in which a speaker directly addresses an absent person or a personified quality, object, or idea. Shelley opens his poem "Ode to the West Wind" with an apostrophe that addresses the wind. Apostrophe is often used in poetry and in speeches to add emotional intensity.
See *Figurative Language*.

ARGUMENTATION *Argumentation* is the type of writing that presents and logically supports the writer's views about an issue. Argumentation is one of the forms, or modes, of discourse. The term *argumentation* is sometimes used as though it were synonymous with *persuasion*. However, some critics and scholars distinguish between the two terms, using argumentation for works that support opinions with logical reasoning and persuasion for works that support opinions with appeals to emotion.
See *Forms of Discourse* and *Persuasion*.

ASIDE An *aside* is a statement delivered by an actor to an audience in such a way that other characters on stage are presumed not to hear what is said. In an aside the character reveals his or her private thoughts, reactions, or motivations. Act III, Scene iv, of *Macbeth* contains the following aside:

MURDERER. Most royal sir, Fleance is scaped.
MACBETH. [*Aside*] Then comes my fit again. I
  had else been perfect;
Whole as the marble, founded as the
  rock,
As broad and general as the casing air.

But now I am cabined, cribbed,
  confined, bound in
To saucy doubts and fears.—But
  Banquo's safe?

In this aside, Macbeth reveals his fearful reaction to the news that Fleance is still alive.

ASSONANCE *Assonance* is the repetition of vowel sounds in stressed syllables containing dissimilar consonant sounds. Robert Browning used assonance in the following famous line from his poem "Andrea del Sarto":

Ah, but a man's *reach* should *exceed* his
  grasp

The long *e* sound is repeated in the words *reach* and *exceed* in stressed syllables containing these consonants: *r–ch* and *c–d*.
See *Consonance*.

ATMOSPHERE See *Mood*.

AUTOBIOGRAPHY An *autobiography* is a form of nonfiction in which a person tells his or her own life story. Unlike a diary or a letter, an autobiography is written for a public audience. George Orwell's "Shooting an Elephant," on page 1034, is a fine example of the autobiographical essay.
See *Biography*.

BALLAD A *ballad* is a songlike poem that tells a story, often one dealing with adventure or romance. Most ballads have the following characteristics:

1. four- or six-line stanzas
2. rhyme
3. simple language
4. dramatic action

Many ballads employ repetition of a refrain. Some make use of incremental repetition, in which a refrain is varied slightly each time it appears.

The British Isles have a rich tradition of *folk ballads*—songs that originated among illiterate peoples and were passed from singer to singer by word of mouth. Examples in your text include "Sir Patrick Spens," "The Two Corbies," and "Barbara Allan." Many English, Scottish, Welsh, and Irish writers have also created *literary ballads*—sophisticated poems in the style of folk ballads. One such literary ballad in your text is Samuel Taylor Coleridge's *The Rime of the Ancient Mariner*, on page 670.
See *Ballad Stanza*, *Incremental Repetition*, and *Refrain*.

BALLAD STANZA A *ballad stanza* is a four- or six-line stanza form used in folk ballads and in literary imitations of folk ballads. In a typical four-line ballad stanza, the first and third lines each have four stresses; the second and fourth lines each have three stresses and also rhyme. Thus the usual rhyme scheme is *abcb*, although some ballads follow the scheme *abab*. This is a typical six-line ballad stanza:

When Robin Hood and Little John
  Down a down a down a down
Went o'er yon bank of broom,
  Said Robin Hood bold to Little John,
We have shot for many a pound.
  Hey down a down a down a down!

See *Ballad*.

BIOGRAPHY A *biography* is a form of nonfiction in which a writer tells the life story of another person. A good biographer uses many sources of information, including, perhaps, the subject's letters and journals, interviews with the subject or with people who know the subject, personal knowledge about the subject, and books and other works about the subject. James Boswell's *The Life of Samuel Johnson*, an excerpt from which appears on page 588, is one of the most famous of all biographies. Boswell's work has been widely praised for its accuracy of reporting and its liveliness of style.
See *Autobiography*.

BLANK VERSE *Blank verse* is poetry written in

unrhymed iambic pentameter lines. Each iambic foot has one weakly stressed syllable followed by one strongly stressed syllable. A pentameter line has five of these feet. Blank verse usually contains occasional variations in rhythm—variations that are introduced to create emphasis, variety, and naturalness of sound. Because blank verse sounds much like ordinary spoken English, it is often used in drama and in poetry. Great English writers of blank verse have included Shakespeare, Wordsworth, Browning, and Auden. The following lines come from Wordsworth's blank-verse poem "Lines Composed a Few Miles Above Tintern Abbey," on page 654:

> Fŏr thóu | ărt wíth | mĕ hére | ŭpón | thĕ bánks
> Ŏf thís | faĭr rív|ĕr; thóu | mў̆ déar|ĕst
> fríend

See *Meter*.

CAESURA A *caesura* is a natural pause, or break, in the middle of a line of poetry. The symbol // has been used to mark the caesuras in the following lines from Kathleen Raine's "In the Beck":

> There is a fish,//that quivers in the
> pool,
> itself a shadow,//but its shadow, clear.
> Catch it again and again,//it still is
> there.

A poet can draw attention to a word by placing it just before or just after a caesura. In Anglo-Saxon poetry a caesura divides each four-stress line in half and thus is essential to the rhythm. See *Anglo-Saxon Poetry*.

CANTO A *canto* is a section of a long poem. Both Alexander Pope's *The Rape of the Lock* and Edmund Spenser's *The Faerie Queene* were written in cantos.

CARICATURE A *caricature* is a distorted or exaggerated portrayal of a person. The portrayal of Lady Bracknell, in Oscar Wilde's *The Importance of Being Earnest*, is an example. Caricature is used to ridicule personal flaws and general social failings.

CARPE DIEM *Carpe diem* is a Latin phrase meaning "seize the day." Many great literary works have been written with the *carpe diem* theme. All have in common the fact that they urge people to enjoy life in the present, while such enjoyment is still possible. One of the best-known poems on this theme is Robert Herrick's "To the Virgins, to Make Much of Time," on page 454, which begins with the line, "Gather ye rosebuds while ye may." Another famous work that deals with the *carpe diem* theme is Marvell's "To His Coy Mistress," on page 440.

CATALOG A *catalog* is a list included in a literary work. Taking his cue from classical epics, which list warriors, ships, weapons, and other items, John Milton uses this convention in *Paradise Lost* to list the fallen angels. Alexander Pope uses the catalog in *The Rape of the Lock* to list the duties of the sylphs. Writers use catalogs to instruct readers and to convey a great deal of information concisely. The effect of a catalog is usually to overwhelm the reader with the numbers of items mentioned.
See *Epic Convention*.

CHARACTER A *character* is a person or animal who takes part in the action of a literary work. Characters can be described in many different ways, as follows:

1. In terms of the importance of their roles: A character who plays an important role in a story is called a *major character*. A character who does not play an important role is called a *minor character*.
2. In terms of their roles: A character who plays the central role in a story is called the *protagonist*. A character who opposes the protagonist is called the *antagonist*.
3. In terms of their complexity: A complex character is called *round*, while a simple character is called *flat*.

4. In terms of the degree to which they change: A character who changes is called *dynamic*; a character who does not change is called *static*.

Character types that readers recognize easily, such as the hard-boiled detective or the wicked stepmother, are called *stereotypes*, or *stock characters*.
See *Characterization* and *Motivation*.

CHARACTERIZATION *Characterization* is the act of creating and developing a character. A writer uses *direct characterization* when he or she states a character's traits explicitly. *Indirect characterization* occurs when the writer reveals a character's traits by some other means. A character's traits can be revealed indirectly by means of what he or she says, thinks, or does; by means of a description of his or her appearance; or by means of the statements, thoughts, or actions of other characters. When using indirect characterization, the writer depends on the reader to infer a character's traits from the clues provided.
See *Character*.

CLASSICISM *Classicism* is an approach to literature and to the other arts that stresses reason, harmony, balance, proportion, clarity, and idealism in imitation of the philosophers and artists of ancient Greece and Rome. The European Neoclassicists of the eighteenth century revived the Greek and Roman classical tradition and aspired to produce works worthy of this tradition. Classicism is often contrasted with Romanticism, which places a premium on imagination and emotion, sometimes at the expense of reason and proportion. Classicism also differs from Realism, which concentrates on the actual rather than on the ideal.
See *Neoclassicism*, *Realism*, and *Romanticism*.

CLIMAX The *climax* is the high point of interest or suspense in a literary work. Often the climax is also the *crisis* in the plot, the point at which the protagonist changes his or her understanding or situation. Sometimes the climax coincides with the *resolution*, the point at which the central conflict is ended. In a story the climax generally occurs near the end. For example, Charles Dickens's "The Signalman," on page 882, reaches its climax with the death of the signalman. In a play the climax often falls more toward the middle and marks the end of the rising action and the beginning of the falling action. For example, in William Shakespeare's *Macbeth*, the climax is the banquet scene, in Act III. This scene begins the inevitable movement toward Macbeth's downfall.
See *Plot*.

CLOSED COUPLET See *Couplet*.

COMEDY A *comedy* is a work of literature, especially a play, that has a happy ending. Comedies often show ordinary characters in conflict with their societies. Their problems are resolved through laughter, reconciliation, and the correction of moral faults or social wrongs. Types of comedy include the *romantic comedy*, which involves problems among lovers, and the *comedy of manners*, which satirically challenges the social customs of a sophisticated society. George Bernard Shaw's *Pygmalion*, on page 1124, is a modern comedy of manners. Many comedies feature humorous physical action and witty dialogue. Comedy is often contrasted with tragedy, in which the central character, or protagonist, meets an unfortunate end.
See *Drama* and *Tragedy*.

COMEDY OF MANNERS See *Comedy*.

COMIC RELIEF *Comic relief* is the feeling created by a humorous action or speech that appears within a serious work of literature. For example, the so-called "Porter Scene" in *Macbeth*, at the beginning of Act II, Scene iii, provides comic relief after the murder of Duncan. As this scene illustrates, comic relief is often used to emphasize, by contrast, the seriousness of the main action.

CONCEIT A *conceit* is an unusual and surprising comparison between two very different things. This special kind of metaphor or complicated analogy is often the basis for a whole poem. During the Elizabethan period, sonnets commonly included *Petrarchan conceits*, ones that extravagantly compared the beloved's beauty or the speaker's suffering to something else. For example, the sonnets of Sir Thomas Wyatt compare the lover's state to a storm-tossed ship, to the Alps, and to a soldier's camp. Shakespeare satirizes such overblown conceits in his Sonnet 130:

I love to hear her speak; yet well I
  know
That music hath a far more pleasing
  sound:
I grant I never saw a goddess go;
My mistress, when she walks, treads on
  the ground.
And yet, by heaven, I think my love
  as rare
As any she belied with false compare.

The seventeenth-century metaphysical poets were especially fond of elaborate, unusual, highly intellectual conceits. For example, in "Love's Alchemy," John Donne compares the unreliability of love to the unreliability of alchemy for making gold.
See *Metaphor*.

CONCRETE POEM A *concrete poem* is one with a shape that suggests its subject. An example in this text is George Herbert's "Easter Wings," on page 434.
See *Emblematic Image*.

CONFLICT A *conflict* is a struggle between opposing forces. Sometimes this struggle is *internal*, or within a character. At other times the struggle is *external*, or between the character and some outside force. The outside force may be another character, nature, or some element of society such as a custom or a political institution. Often the conflict in a work is complicated and combines several of these possibilities. For example, Macbeth struggles against the better parts of his own nature, against Banquo and Fleance, against fate, and against the forces led by Malcolm, Macduff, and Siward.
See *Antagonist*, *Plot*, and *Protagonist*.

CONNOTATION A *connotation* is an association that a word calls to mind in addition to its dictionary meaning. For example, the words *home* and *domicile* have the same dictionary meanings. However, the first has positive connotations of warmth and security while the second does not. Therefore, a writer who wants to convey a sense of warmth and security will be more likely to use the word *home* than the word *domicile*, even though the two words refer to the same thing. Because the connotations of words are so powerful, writers carefully choose words with connotations that suggest the shades of meaning they intend.
See *Denotation*.

CONSONANCE *Consonance* is the repetition of consonant sounds in stressed syllables containing dissimilar vowel sounds. D. H. Lawrence uses consonance in the opening lines of "Snake":

A snake came to my water-trough
On a *hot*, *hot*, day, and I in pajamas
  for the *heat*,
To drink there.

The words *hot* and *heat* have the same consonants but different vowels. (Note also the assonance in the words *snake* and *came* and in the words *water* and *pajamas*.) When used at the ends of lines, consonance can create *approximate* or *slant rhyme*.
See *Assonance*.

COUPLET A *couplet* is a pair of rhyming lines written in the same meter. The following iambic

1401

tetrameter couplets come from John Milton's "L'Allegro":

And if I give thee honor due,
Mirth, admit me of the crew
To live with her, and live with thee,
In unreproved pleasures free.

A *heroic couplet* is a rhymed pair of iambic pentameter lines. During the Neoclassical Period, the popular heroic couplet was often also a *closed couplet*, with its meaning and grammar complete within two lines. These lines from Alexander Pope's *An Essay on Criticism* illustrate the closed heroic couplet:

True ease in writing comes from art,
 not chance,
As those move easiest who have learned
 to dance.

Sonnets written in the English, or Shakespearean, style usually end with heroic couplets.
See *Sonnet*.

CRISIS The *crisis* in the plot of a story or play is the turning point for the protagonist—the point at which his or her situation or understanding is changed. This point often coincides with the *climax*, or emotional high point, of the story.
See *Climax* and *Plot*.

DACTYL See *Meter*.

DEAD METAPHOR See *Metaphor*.

DENOTATION The *denotation* of a word is its objective meaning, that to which the word refers, independent of other associations the word calls to mind. Dictionaries list the denotative meanings of words. Another term for denotative meaning is *referential meaning*.
See *Connotation*.

DENOUEMENT The *denouement* in a literary work is anything that happens after the resolution of the plot. At this point the central conflict is resolved, and the consequences for the protagonist are already decided. Essentially, a denouement is a tying up of loose ends. In some works no denouement is needed.
See *Plot*.

DESCRIPTION A *description* is a portrait, in words, of a person, place, or object. Its purpose is to provide the concrete details and lively images that make people, places, and things become clear to readers.

Descriptions use *imagery*—words and phrases that appeal to the senses of sight, sound, touch, taste, and smell. Description is one of the major forms, or modes, of discourse and is often found in conjunction with other types of writing such as narration, exposition, or persuasion.
See *Forms of Discourse* and *Imagery*.

DEVELOPMENT See *Plot*.

DIALECT A *dialect* is the form of a language spoken by people in a particular region or group. Dialects differ from one another in grammar, vocabulary, and pronunciation. Authors often write in regional dialects, as did Robert Burns, who used a Scots dialect in such poems as "Auld Lang Syne":

Should auld acquaintance be forgot,
 And never brought to mind?
Should auld acquaintance be forgot,
 And auld lang syne?

Dialect is sometimes used by writers as a part of characterization. For example, the social status of each character in George Bernard Shaw's *Pygmalion*, on page 1124, is revealed by the dialect the character speaks. In the course of Shaw's play, the central character, Eliza Doolittle, is trained to speak Received Standard English—a dialect with high social prestige—rather than her native Cockney dialect.
See *Vernacular*.

DIALOGUE A *dialogue* is a conversation between characters. Writers use dialogue to reveal character, to present events, to add variety to narratives, and to interest readers. The dialogue in a story or play is usually set off by quotation marks and paragraphing. The dialogue in a play script generally follows the characters' names.

DIARY A *diary* is a personal record of daily events, usually written in prose. Most diaries are not written for publication; sometimes, however, interesting diaries or diaries by influential people do find their way into print. One example of a published diary is that of Samuel Pepys, a selection from which appears on page 524. In his diary Pepys recorded anecdotes and details about his life in the 1660's.
See *Journal*.

DICTION *Diction* is word choice. A writer's diction can be a major determinant of his or her style. Diction can be described as formal or informal, abstract or concrete, plain or ornate, ordinary or technical.
See *Style*.

DIMETER See *Meter*.

DIRECT CHARACTERIZATION See *Characterization*.

DRAMA A *drama* is a story written to be performed by actors. It may consist of one or more large sections called *acts*, which are made up of any number of smaller sections called *scenes*.

Drama originated in the religious rituals and symbolic reenactments of primitive peoples. The ancient Greeks developed drama into a sophisticated art and created such dramatic forms as tragedy and comedy.

The first dramas in England were the miracle plays and morality plays of the Middle Ages. *Miracle plays* told Biblical stories. *Morality plays*, such as *Everyman*, on page 142, dealt with personified virtues and vices. The English Renaissance saw a great flowering of drama in England, culminating in the works of William Shakespeare, who wrote many of the world's greatest comedies, tragedies, histories, and romances. During the Neoclassical Age, English drama turned to witty, satirical comedies of manners that probed the virtues of upper-class society. Superb examples of Neoclassical comedy include Goldsmith's *She Stoops to Conquer* and Congreve's *The Way of the World*. The Romantic and Victorian ages were not great periods for drama in England. However, a few good verse plays were written, including Percy Bysshe Shelley's *The Cenci* and *Prometheus Unbound* and Robert Browning's *Pippa Passes*. The end of the nineteenth and beginning of the twentieth centuries saw a resurgence of the drama in England and throughout the English-speaking world. Great plays of the Modern Period include George Bernard Shaw's *Pygmalion*, on page 1124, and the many plays by William Butler Yeats, John Millington Synge, Christopher Fry, T. S. Eliot, Harold Pinter, and Samuel Beckett.

DRAMATIC IRONY See *Irony*.

DRAMATIC MONOLOGUE A *dramatic monologue* is a poem in which an imaginary character speaks to a silent listener. During the monologue, the speaker reveals his or her personality, usually at a moment of crisis. Examples of dramatic monologues in this text are Robert Browning's "My Last Duchess," on page 824, and Alfred, Lord Tennyson's "Ulysses," on page 791.

DRAMATIC POETRY See *Poetry*.

DYNAMIC CHARACTER See *Character*.

ELEGY An *elegy* is a solemn and formal lyric poem about death. It may mourn a particular person or reflect on a serious or tragic theme, such as the passing of youth, beauty, or a way of life.

1403

See Thomas Gray's "Elegy Written in a Country Churchyard" on page 598.
See *Lyric Poem*.

EMBLEMATIC IMAGE An *emblematic image* is a symbolic figure or shape presented through the arrangement of the lines of a poem. For example, George Herbert's "Easter Wings," on page 434, is shaped like a pair of wings.
See *Concrete Poem*.

END RHYME See *Rhyme*.

END-STOPPED LINE An *end-stopped line* of poetry concludes with a break in the meter and in the meaning. This pause at the end of a line often is punctuated by a period, comma, dash, or semicolon. These lines from "Away, Melancholy," by Stevie Smith, are end-stopped:

> Are not the trees green,
> The earth as green?
> Does not the wind blow,
> Fire leap and the rivers flow?
> Away melancholy.

See *Run-on Line*.

EPIC An *epic* is a long narrative poem about the adventures of gods or of a hero. *Beowulf*, on page 24, is a *folk epic*, one that was composed orally and then passed from storyteller to storyteller by word of mouth. The ancient Greek epics attributed to Homer—the *Iliad* and the *Odyssey*—are also folk epics. The *Aeneid*, by the Roman poet Virgil, and *The Divine Comedy*, by the Italian poet Dante Alighieri, are examples of literary epics from the Classical and Medieval periods, respectively. John Milton's *Paradise Lost*, a selection from which appears on page 470, is also a literary epic. Milton's goal in creating *Paradise Lost* was to write a Christian epic similar in form and equal in value to the great epics of antiquity. Because of an epic's length and seriousness of theme, it presents an encyclopedic portrait of the culture in which it was produced. One can learn a great deal about ancient Greece by reading Homer and a great deal about thirteenth- and fourteenth-century Italy by reading Dante.
See *Epic Convention*.

EPIC CONVENTION An *epic convention* is a traditional characteristic of epic poems. These characteristics include an opening statement of the theme; an appeal for supernatural help in telling the story; a beginning *in medias res* (Latin: "in the middle of things"), long lists, or catalogs, of people and things; accounts of past events; and descriptive phrases such as kennings, Homeric similes, and Homeric epithets.
See *Catalog*, *Epic*, *Epithet*, *In Medias Res*, *Invocation*, and *Kenning*.

EPIGRAM An *epigram* is a brief, pointed statement in prose or in verse. The concluding couplet in an English sonnet may be epigrammatic. An essay may be written in an *epigrammatic style*, one that is characterized by frequent use of epigrams.

EPIGRAPH An *epigraph* is a quotation that appears at the beginning of a literary work. As is illustrated by Rainer Maria Rilke's lines at the beginning of Margaret Drabble's "A Voyage to Cythera," on page 1288. An epigraph generally introduces a motif or a theme that is developed in the work itself.

EPIPHANY *Epiphany* is a term introduced by James Joyce to describe a moment of revelation or insight in which a character recognizes some truth. In Joyce's "Araby," on page 1012, the boy's epiphany comes at the end of the story when he recognizes the falsity of his dream.

EPITAPH An *epitaph* is an inscription written on a tomb or burial place. In literature, epitaphs also include serious or humorous lines written as if they were intended for such use. Examples are the epitaph at the end of Thomas Gray's "Elegy

Written in a Country Churchyard," which appears on page 598, and this epitaph for Sir Isaac Newton, written by Alexander Pope:

> Nature and Nature's laws lay hid in night:
> God said, Let Newton be! and all was light.

EPITHET An *epithet* is a word or phrase that states a characteristic quality of some person or thing. A.E. Housman uses epithets such as "golden friends" and "lightfoot lad" in "With Rue My Heart Is Laden," on page 866. Homeric epithets, such as "wide-wayed city," "clear-voiced heralds," and "high-hearted princes" in the *Iliad*, were common in classical epics and in later imitations of classical epics.
See *Epic Convention*.

ESSAY An *essay* is a short, nonfiction work about a particular subject. Essays are of many types but may be classified by tone or style as formal or informal.

An essay may also be classed by its main purpose as descriptive, narrative, expository, argumentative, or persuasive.

EXACT RHYME See *Rhyme*.

EXEMPLUM An *exemplum* is a short tale or anecdote with a moral, especially one used in a medieval sermon. Geoffrey Chaucer's "The Pardoner's Tale," on page 115, illustrates the moral that "love of wealth is the root of all evil."

EXPOSITION *Exposition* is writing or speech that explains, informs, or presents information. Types of exposition include analysis, classification, comparison and contrast, definition, and exemplification.

In the plot of a story or drama, the *exposition* is the part of the work that introduces the characters, the setting, and the basic situation. For example, in William Shakespeare's *A Midsummer Night's Dream*, the first scene introduces the lovers and their problems, locates the action in the palace at Athens near a wood, and establishes the light mood of a romantic comedy.
See *Forms of Discourse* and *Plot*.

EXPRESSIONISM *Expressionism* was an artistic movement early in the twentieth century. The Expressionists emphasized the inner experiences of individuals rather than objective external realities. This movement influenced many dramatists and poets, including T. S. Eliot, whose poem "The Hollow Men" appears on page 1081.

EXTENDED METAPHOR See *Metaphor*

FABLE A *fable* is a brief story, usually with animal characters, that teaches a lesson, or moral. The earliest extant fables are those attributed to Aesop, a Greek writer of the sixth century B.C. In modern times fables are popular both as nursery tales and as vehicles for satire. In his novella *Animal Farm*, George Orwell adapted the fable form for use in a satirical allegory about the Russian Revolution and its aftermath.

FALLING ACTION The *falling action* is all of the action that takes place after the climax in a literary work. During this time, the conflict is resolved and the suspense decreases.
See *Plot* and *Rising Action*.

FANTASY *Fantasy* is highly imaginative writing that contains elements not found in real life. Elizabeth Bowen's "The Demon Lover," on page 1016, is a fantasy. Writers use fantasies to entertain readers and sometimes to make serious points about reality.

FARCE *Farce* is a kind of comedy that features physical horseplay, stereotypical characters, and absurd plots, often ones involving mistaken identities and recognition scenes. The writer of a farce uses exaggeration, irony, and witty dialogue to move his or her audience to laughter. A farce may be a complete play or a scene used for contrast or comic relief within a serious work.

FICTION *Fiction* is prose writing that tells about imaginary characters and events. Some writers of fiction base their stories on real people and events, while others rely solely on their imaginations.
See *Narration, Nonfiction*, and *Prose*.

FIGURATIVE LANGUAGE *Figurative Language* is writing or speech not meant to be interpreted literally. Poets and other writers use figurative language to create vivid word pictures, to make their writing emotionally intense and concentrated, and to state their ideas in new and unusual ways that satisfy readers' imaginations.
See *Figure of Speech*.

FIGURE OF SPEECH A *figure of speech* is an expression or a word used imaginatively rather than literally. Among the types of figurative language are antithesis, apostrophe, hyperbole, irony, metaphor, metonymy, oxymoron, paradox, personification, simile, synecdoche, and understatement.
See *Figurative Language*. See also the entries for individual figures of speech.

FIRST-PERSON POINT OF VIEW See *Point of View*.

FLASHBACK A *flashback* is a section of a literary work that interrupts the sequence of events to relate an event from an earlier time. The writer may present the flashback as a character's memory or recollection, as part of an account or story told by a character, or as a dream or daydream. For example, in Elizabeth Bowen's "The Demon Lover," on page 1016, Mrs. Drover remembers saying farewell to her fiancé twenty-five years earlier. Writers use flashbacks to show what motivates a character and to supply background information in a dramatic way.
See *Foreshadowing*.

FLAT CHARACTER. See *Character*.

FOIL A *foil* is a character who provides a contrast to another character, thus intensifying the impact of that other character. For example, Banquo and Duncan act as foils for the ambitious and tyrannical Macbeth.

FOLK BALLAD See *Ballad*.

FOLKLORE *Folklore* includes the stories, legends, myths, ballads, riddles, sayings, and other traditional works produced orally by illiterate or semi-literate peoples. Folklore influences written literature in many ways, as is suggested by the beheading contest in *Sir Gawain and the Green Knight*, on page 124, and the fiancé in Elizabeth Bowen's "The Demon Lover," on page 1016.

FOLKTALE A *folktale* is a story composed orally and then passed from person to person by word of mouth. Many of Chaucer's stories were based on folktales.
See *Folklore*.

FOOT See *Meter*.

FORESHADOWING *Foreshadowing* is the use, in a literary work, of clues that suggest events that have yet to occur. Writers use foreshadowing to create suspense or to prepare the audience for the eventual outcome of events.
See *Flashback*.

FORM The *form* of a literary work is its structure, shape, pattern, organization, or style—the way it is made. A work's form is often distinguished from its *content*—what it is about.

FORMS OF DISCOURSE The *forms of discourse* are the main types of writing—description, narration, exposition, and persuasion or argumentation. Each has a different purpose and may be a writer's main emphasis. Often, however, the forms of discourse are used together to support

each other. For instance, a narrative may include description, or an argument may begin with exposition.
See *Argumentation*, *Description*, *Exposition*, *Narration*, and *Persuasion*.

FREE VERSE *Free verse* is poetry not written in a regular rhythmical pattern, or meter. Instead of having metrical feet and lines, free verse has a rhythm that suits its meaning and that uses the sounds of spoken language in lines of different lengths. Free verse has been widely used in twentieth-century poetry. An example is "The Galloping Cat," by Stevie Smith:

All the same I
Intend to go on being
A cat that likes to
Gallop about doing good
So
Now with my bald head I go,
Chopping the untidy flowers down, to and fro.

GOTHIC *Gothic* is a term used to describe literary works that make extensive use of primitive, Medieval, wild, mysterious, or natural elements. Gothic elements offended eighteenth-century Neoclassical writers but appealed to the Romantic writers who followed them. *Gothic novels*, such as Mary Wollstonecraft Shelley's *Frankenstein*, a selection from which appears on page 744, are often set in gloomy castles where horrifying, supernatural events take place.

HEPTAMETER See *Meter*.

HEPTASTICH See *Stanza*.

HERO/HEROINE A *hero* or *heroine* is a character whose actions are inspiring or noble. Often heroes struggle to overcome foes or to escape from difficulties. The most obvious examples of heroes and heroines are the larger-than-life characters in myths and legends, ones like Beowulf or Odysseus. However, more ordinary characters can, and often do, perform heroic deeds.

HEROIC COUPLET See *Couplet*.

HEXAMETER See *Meter*.

HOMERIC EPITHET See *Epithet*.

HYPERBOLE A *hyperbole* is a deliberate exaggeration or overstatement. In "On Monsieur's Departure," Queen Elizabeth I used this figure of speech:

I grieve and dare not show my discontent,
I love and yet am forced to seem to hate,
I do, yet dare not say I ever meant,
I seem stark mute but inwardly do prate.
  I am and not, I freeze and yet am burned,
  Since from myself another self I turned.

Of course, Queen Elizabeth was not turned by love into another person, she was not mute or burned, and she did not act in total opposition to her true feelings. Such excessive claims are examples of hyperbole. In Oscar Wilde's *The Importance of Being Earnest*, Algernon's claims likewise illustrate hyperbole:

ALGERNON: I really don't see anything romantic in proposing. It is very romantic to be in love. But there is nothing romantic about a definite proposal. Why, one may be accepted. One usually is, I believe. Then the excitement is all over. The very essence of romance is uncertainty. If ever I get married, I'll certainly try to forget the fact.

As these examples suggest, hyperbole may be used for heightened seriousness or for comic effect.
See *Figurative Language*.

IAMB See *Meter*.

IAMBIC PENTAMETER See *Meter*.

IMAGE An *image* is a word or a phrase that appeals to one or more of the five senses—sight, hearing, touch, taste, or smell. In a famous essay on Hamlet, T.S. Eliot explained how a group of images can be used as an "objective correla-

tive." By this phrase Eliot meant to suggest that a complex emotional state can be suggested by images that are carefully chosen to evoke this state.
See *Imagery*.

IMAGERY *Imagery* is the descriptive language used in literature to re-create sensory experiences. The following lines from William Collins's "Ode to Evening" show how a poet can use imagery to appeal to several senses:

Now air is hushed, save where the weak-eyed bat,
With short shrill shrieks flits by on leathern wing,
Or where the beetle winds
His small but sullen horn,
As oft he rises 'midst the twilight path,
Against the pilgrim borne in heedless hum.

These lines describe the sounds, sights, and movements of evening, just as if a reader were out walking with the poem's speaker. Imagery can enrich writing by making it more vivid, setting a tone, suggesting emotions, and guiding a reader's reactions.

INCITING INCIDENT See *Plot*.

INCONGRUITY An *incongruity* is a juxtaposition of incompatible or opposite elements. For example, sometimes a writer's style and subject may be incongruous, as in Alexander Pope's *The Rape of the Lock*, on page 560. Pope uses the formal language and conventions of epic poetry, but his subject is only the social battle surrounding a lock of hair. When a writer talks about something trivial in formal language, the exaggeration and surprise of the incongruity may create a comic or humorous effect.

INCREMENTAL REPETITION *Incremental repetition*, used in ballads and in other oral poetry, is the technique of repeating a line or a stanza with slight but significant changes. Incremental repetition is used in the ballad "Lord Randal."

"O where have you been, Lord Randal, my son?
O where have you been, my handsome young man?—
"I have been to the greenwood; O make my bed soon,
For I'm weary with hunting, and fain would lie down."

Each stanza uses this question-and-answer pattern, supplying and repeating details that add to the story and increase suspense.
See *Ballad*.

INDIRECT CHARACTERIZATION See *Characterization*.

IN MEDIAS RES The phrase *in medias res*, Latin for "in the middle of things," is a story-telling method used in epic poems and in other narratives. When a writer begins *in medias res*, the story starts in the middle, jumping right into the action. The background and the initial events are introduced later by means of one or more flashbacks. John Milton's *Paradise Lost*, like the great epics of classical antiquity, follows this pattern. Milton's epic begins with Satan and the fallen angels on the burning lake in Chaos. Not until Books V and VI does Raphael tell Adam about the great battle that occurred just before those angels fell from heaven.
See *Epic Convention*.

INTERNAL RHYME See *Rhyme*.

INVERSION An *inversion* is a reversal or change in the regular word order of a sentence. For instance, Anne Killigrew begins the poem "Upon the Saying That My Verses Were Made by Another" in this way:

Next Heaven, my vows to thee, O sacred Muse!
I offered up, nor didst thou them refuse.

These lines reverse the usual subject-verb-object order, "I offered up my vows to thee," and the usual negative construction, "nor didst thou refuse them." Poets, in particular, use inversion

1408

to emphasize words and sometimes to fit them to the meter of a poem.

INVOCATION An *invocation* is an appeal to a Muse or to another divine being for help in writing the poem. In ancient Greece and Rome, writers often began their works, by calling for the aid of the Muses, who were the nine daughters of Apollo responsible for the various arts. In *Paradise Lost*, on page 470, John Milton appeals to his "Heavenly Muse," the Holy Spirit of the Christian trinity.
See *Epic Convention*.

IRONY *Irony* is the general name given to literary techniques that involve surprising, interesting, or amusing contradictions. In *verbal irony*, words are used to suggest the opposite of their usual meaning. In *dramatic irony*, there is a contradiction between what a character thinks and what the reader or audience knows to be true. In *irony of situation*, an event occurs that directly contradicts the expectations of the characters, the reader, or the audience.

IRONY OF SITUATION See *Irony*.

JOURNAL A *journal* is a daily autobiographical account of events and personal reactions. Daniel Defoe adapted this form to fictional use in his *A Journal of the Plague Year*, an excerpt from which appears on page 532.
See *Diary*.

KENNING A *kenning* is a metaphorical phrase, used in Anglo-Saxon poetry to replace a concrete noun. In "The Seafarer," on page 17, the cuckoo is called "summer's sentinel" and the sea "the whale's home."
See *Anglo-Saxon Poetry* and *Epic Convention*.

LEGEND A *legend* is a widely told story about the past, one that may or may not have a foundation in fact. A legend often reflects a people's identity or cultural values, generally with more historical truth and less emphasis on the supernatural than in a myth. English legends include the stories of King Arthur, of Robin Hood, and of other folk heroes.
See *Myth*.

LIMITED POINT OF VIEW See *Point of View*.

LITERARY BALLAD See *Ballad*.

LITERARY CRITICISM *Literary criticism* is the art of analyzing, interpreting, and evaluating literary works. There are many different types, or schools, of literary criticism, as follows:

1. *Impressionistic* or *Reader-Response Criticism* deals with the subjective responses of individual readers.
2. *Biographical* or *Historical Criticism* deals with details of literary history as these relate to particular works.
3. *Archetypal Criticism* deals with universal patterns of meaning or symbolism believed to be part of the biological or cultural heritage of humankind as a whole.
4. *Psychological Criticism* interprets texts based on concepts derived from any of a number of psychological models, such as the Gestalt Model of perception or the Freudian model of personality.
5. *Linguistic Criticism* applies to literary texts techniques borrowed from the scientific study of language.
6. *Moral* or *Ethical Criticism* evaluates literary works based on the moral or ethical messages that they convey. *Political Criticism* is a type of moral or ethical criticism.
7. The so-called *New Criticism* concentrates on the characteristics or qualities of literary works themselves, apart from any extra-textual material such as information about authors' lives or literary movements.
8. *Reconstructionist Criticism* views the literary text as an occasion for a creative act in which

1409

the reader in effect makes a new text by virtue of what he or she brings to it.

LYRIC POEM A *lyric poem* is a highly musical verse that expresses the observations and feelings of a single speaker. Unlike a narrative poem, it presents an experience or a single effect, but it does not tell a full story. Types of lyrics include the elegy, the ode, and the sonnet. The lyric flourished in the songs and sonnets of the Renaissance, was revived by the Romantic poets, and has remained the most common poetic form during the nineteenth and twentieth centuries. Alfred, Lord Tennyson; Robert Browning; Elizabeth Barrett Browning; Matthew Arnold; William Butler Yeats; T.S. Eliot; W.H. Auden; Dylan Thomas, and Stevie Smith—all were great writers of lyric poems.

MAJOR CHARACTER See *Character*.

MEMENTO MORI *Memento mori* is a Latin phrase meaning "remember that you must die." Many great literary works have been written on the *memento mori* theme, including Marvell's "To His Coy Mistress," on page 440, and Gray's "Elegy Written in a Country Churchyard," on page 598.

METAPHOR A *metaphor* is a figure of speech in which one thing is spoken of as though it were something else, as in "death, that long sleep." Through this identification of dissimilar things, a comparison is suggested or implied. Emily Brontë uses the following metaphor in the second stanza of her poem "Remembrance": "my thoughts no longer hover . . . resting their wings." The metaphor suggests similarities between the speaker's thoughts and the wings of a bird.

An *extended metaphor* is one that is developed at length and that involves several points of comparison. Elizabeth Daryush uses extended metaphor in these lines from "November Sun":

His face is pale and shrunk, his shining hair
  Is prison-shorn;
Trailing his grey cloak, up the short dark stair
  He creeps each morn,

Looks out to his lost throne, to the noon-height
  Once his, then turns
Back to the alien dungeon, where all night
  Unseen he burns.

This poem metaphorically describes the November sun as a royal prisoner.

A *mixed metaphor* occurs when two metaphors are jumbled together. For example, thorns and rain are illogically mixed in "The thorns of life rained down on him."

A *dead metaphor* is one that has been so overused that its original metaphorical impact has been lost. Examples of dead metaphors include "the foot of the bed" and "toe the line."
See *Figurative Language*.

METAPHYSICAL POETRY *Metaphysical poetry* is the term used to describe the works of such seventeenth-century English poets as Richard Crashaw, John Donne, George Herbert, Andrew Marvell, Thomas Traherne, and Henry Vaughan. The term was first used by Samuel Johnson in an attack on writers who fill their works with far-fetched conceits and who make poetry a vehicle for displays of learning. Characteristic features of metaphysical poetry include intellectual playfulness, argument, paradoxes, irony, elaborate and unusual conceits, incongruity, and the rhythms of ordinary speech. Examples of metaphysical poems in this text include Donne's "Song," on page 420, and Marvell's "To His Coy Mistress," on page 440.

METER The *meter* of a poem is its rhythmical pattern. This pattern is determined by the number and types of stresses, or beats, in each line. To describe the meter of a poem, you must *scan* its lines. *Scanning* involves marking the strongly stressed and weakly stressed syllables, as follows:

I ween | that, when | the grave's | dark wall
Did first | her form | retain,
They thought their hearts could ne'er
recall
The light | of joy | again.
—Emily Bronte, "Song"

As you can see, each strong stress is marked with a slanted line (´) and each weak stress with a horseshoe symbol (˘). The weak and strong stresses are then divided by vertical lines into groups called *feet*. The following types of feet are common in English poetry:

1. *Iamb:* a foot with one weak stress followed by one strong stress, as in the word "afraid"
2. *Trochee:* a foot with one strong stress followed by one weak stress, as in the word "heather"
3. *Anapest:* a foot with two weak stresses followed by one strong stress, as in the word "disembark"
4. *Dactyl:* a foot with one strong stress followed by two weak stresses, as in the word "solitude"
5. *Spondee:* a foot with two strong stresses, as in the word "workday"
6. *Pyrrhic:* a foot with two weak stresses, as in the last foot of the word "unspeak|ably"
7. *Amphibrach:* a foot with a weak syllable, one strong syllable, and another weak syllable, as in the word "another"
8. *Amphimacer:* a foot with a strong syllable, one weak syllable, and another strong syllable, as in "up and down"

A line of poetry is described as *iambic*, trochaic, anapestic, or *dactylic* according to what kind of foot appears most often in the line.

Lines are also described in terms of the number of feet that occur in them, as follows:

1. *Monometer:* verse written in one-foot lines:

Sound the Flute!
Now it's mute.
Birds delight
Day and Night.
—William Blake, "Spring"

2. *Dimeter:* verse written in two-foot lines:

O Rose | thou art sick.
The invis | ible worm,
That flies | in the night
In the how | ling storm:
Has found | out thy bed
Of crim | son joy:
And his dark | secret love
Does thy life | destroy.
—William Blake, "The Sick Rose"

3. *Trimeter:* verse written in three-foot lines:

I went | to the Gard | en of Love
And saw | what I nev | er had seen:
A Chap | el was built in the midst,
Where I used | to play | on the green.
—William Blake, "The Garden of Love"

4. *Tetrameter:* verse written in four-foot lines:

I wand | er thro' | each chart | er'd street,
Near where | the chart | er'd Thames does |
flow
And mark | in every face | I meet
Marks of | weakness, | marks of woe.
—William Blake, "London"

5. *Pentameter:* verse written in five-foot lines:

And we | are put | on earth | a litt | le space,
That we | may learn | to bear | the beams | of
love
—William Blake, "The Little Black Boy"

A six-foot line is called a *hexameter*. A line with seven feet is a *heptameter*.

A complete description of the meter of a line tells both how many feet there are in the line and what kind of foot is most common. Thus the stanza from Emily Bronte's poem, quoted at the beginning of this entry, would be described as being made up of alternating iambic tetrameter and iambic trimeter lines. Poetry that does not have a regular meter is called *free verse*.

METONYMY *Metonymy* is a figure of speech that substitutes something closely related for the thing actually meant. In the opening line of "The Lost Leader," Robert Browning says, "Just for a handful of silver he left us," using silver to refer

to money in the form of a government grant. Browning's reference to silver is also an allusion to the handful of silver that Judas earned for betraying Christ in the Bible.
See *Figurative Language*

MINOR CHARACTER See *Character*.

MIRACLE PLAY See *Drama*.

MIXED METAPHOR See *Metaphor*.

MOCK EPIC A *mock epic* is a poem about a trivial matter written in the style of a serious epic. The incongruity of the style and the subject matter produces comic effects. Alexander Pope's *The Rape of the Lock*, on page 560, is a mock epic.
See *Epic* and *Epic Convention*.

MONOLOGUE A *monologue* is a speech or performance given entirely by one person or by one character.
See *Dramatic Monologue* and *Soliloquy*.

MOOD *Mood*, or atmosphere, is the feeling created in the reader by a literary work or passage. The mood may be suggested by the writer's choice of words, by events in the work, or by the physical setting. Nadine Gordimer begins "The Train from Rhodesia," on page 1272, with a mood-evoking description of the brick, mud, and tin buildings at the hot, sandy train station. Everyone there—the stationmaster, his wife, the native vendors, and the children—awaits the train, the only relief expected in this inactive and restricted environment.
See *Setting* and *Tone*.

MONOMETER See *Meter*.

MORALITY PLAY See *Drama*.

MOTIF A *motif* is a recurring literary convention or an element that is repeated within a literary work. For example, Titania and Bottom in William Shakespeare's *A Midsummer Night's Dream* exemplify a motif from folklore—the mortal enchanted by a fairy lover. D.H. Lawrence, in "The Rocking-Horse Winner," on page 996, repeats the motif of luck throughout his story. Whether a motif is part of the literary tradition or is an author's own invention, it generally unifies a work and adds to its theme.

MOTIVATION A *motivation* is a reason that explains or partially explains a character's thoughts, feelings, actions, or speech. Characters may be motivated by their physical needs; by their wants, wishes, desires, or dreams; or by their beliefs, values, and ideals. Effective characterization involves creating motivations that make characters seem believable.
See *Character*.

MYTH A *myth* is a fictional tale, originally with religious significance, that explains the actions of gods or heroes, the causes of natural phenomena, or both. Allusions to characters and motifs from Greek, Roman, Norse, and Celtic myths are common in English literature. In addition, mythological stories are often retold or adapted, as George Bernard Shaw's *Pygmalion*, on page 1124, illustrates. Pygmalion was a character from Greek mythology who created a beautiful sculpture of a woman and then fell in love with his own creation.
See *Legend*.

NARRATION *Narration* is writing that tells a story. The act of telling a story is also called *narration*. The *narrative*, or story, is told by a storyteller called the *narrator*. Narration is one of the major forms of discourse and appears in many guises. Biographies, autobiographies, journals, reports, novels, short stories, plays, narrative poems, anecdotes, fables, parables, myths, legends, folk-

1412

tales, ballads, and epic poems are all narratives, or types of narration.
See *Forms of Discourse*.

NARRATIVE See *Narration*.

NARRATIVE POEM A *narrative poem* tells a story in verse. Three traditional types of narrative poems include ballads, such as "Sir Patrick Spens" and "Barbara Allan"; epics, such as *Beowulf*; and *metrical romances*, such as *Sir Gawain and the Green Knight*. Other narrative poems in this text include the selection from Spenser's *The Faerie Queene*, on page 196; the selection from Milton's *Paradise Lost*, on page 470; Coleridge's "The Rime of the Ancient Mariner," on page 670; and Tennyson's "The Lady of Shalott," on page 798.

NARRATOR See *Narration*.

NATURALISM *Naturalism* was a literary movement among writers at the end of the nineteenth century and during the early decades of the twentieth century. The Naturalists, influenced by the theories of Social Darwinists like Sir Herbert Spencer, tended to view people as hopeless victims of immutable natural laws. Important Naturalist writers included the Norwegian playwright Henrik Ibsen and the French novelist Emile Zola.
See *Realism*.

NEOCLASSICISM *Neoclassicism* was a literary movement during the Restoration and the eighteenth century in which writers turned to classical Greek and Roman literary models and standards. Like the ancient Greeks, the Neoclassicists stressed reason, order, harmony, restraint, correctness, and decorum. The way these qualities took literary form is illustrated by the balanced and controlled heroic couplet, perfected by John Dryden and Alexander Pope. Much Neoclassical literature dealt with themes related to proper and tasteful human conduct. The most popular literary forms of the day—essays, letters, early novels, epigrams, parodies, and satires—reflected this emphasis on society as subject matter. Just as the Neoclassicists rejected the individualism and extravagance of the Renaissance in favor of classical restraint, so the nineteenth-century Romantics rejected Neoclassicism in favor of imagination, emotion, and the individual.
See *Classicism* and *Romanticism*.

NONFICTION *Nonfiction* is prose writing that presents and explains ideas or that tells about real people, places, objects, or events.
See *Fiction.*

NOVEL A *novel* is a long work of fiction. A novel often has a complicated plot, many major and minor characters, a significant theme, and several settings. Novels can be grouped in many ways based on the historical periods in which they are written (such as Romantic or Victorian), on the subjects and themes that they treat (such as Gothic or regional), on the techniques used in them (such as stream of consciousness), or on their debts to literary movements (such as Naturalism or Realism). Among early novels were Samuel Richardson's works *Pamela* and *Clarissa Harlowe*, and Henry Fielding's *Tom Jones*. Other classic English novels include Jane Austen's *Pride and Prejudice*, Sir Walter Scott's *Waverley*, Charles Dickens's *David Copperfield*, and George Eliot's *The Mill on the Floss*. Major twentieth-century novelists include James Joyce, Virginia Woolf, D.H. Lawrence, Henry James, Graham Greene, and Patrick White. A *novella* is not as long as a novel but is longer than a short story. See, for example, Joseph Conrad's novella *Heart of Darkness*.

OBJECTIVE CORRELATIVE See *Image*.

OCTAVE See *stanza*.

ODE An *ode* is a long, formal lyric poem with a serious theme. It may or may not have a tradi-

1413

tional structure with three alternating stanza patterns called the *strophe*, the *antistrophe*, and the *epode*. An ode may be written for a private occasion, as was John Keats's "Ode to a Nightingale," on page 731, which was written about a bird nesting near a friend's home. On the other hand, an ode may be prepared for a public ceremony, as was John Dryden's "A Song for St. Cecilia's Day," on page 517, which was performed in 1687 at an annual festival. Odes often honor people, commemorate events, respond to natural scenes, or consider serious human problems.
See *Lyric*.

OMNISCIENT POINT OF VIEW See *Point of View*.

ONOMATOPOEIA *Onomatopoeia* is the use of words that imitate sounds. Examples of such words are *buzz*, *hiss*, *murmur*, and *rustle*. Seamus Heaney uses onomatopoeia in "Churning Day" to suggest the sounds of making butter:

My mother took first turn, set up rhythms
that slugged and thumped for hours. Arms
ached.
Hands blistered. Cheeks and clothes were
splattered
with flabbymilk.

Onomatopoeia is used to create musical effects and to reinforce meaning, especially in poetry.

ORAL TRADITION *Oral tradition* is the passing of songs, stories, and poems from generation to generation by word of mouth. Among the many materials composed or preserved through oral tradition in Great Britain are *Beowulf*, on page 24, and the folk ballads on pages 78 to 85. In his *Morte d'Arthur*, Sir Thomas Malory drew on written French sources and on Arthurian legends from the oral tradition. Edmund Spenser drew on the same sources when composing *The Faerie Queene*. Shakespeare drew on materials from the oral tradition to create the *sprites* and *fairies* of *A Midsummer Night's Dream*. Folk epics, ballads, myths, legends, folktales, folk songs, proverbs, nursery rhymes—all such products of the oral tradition were originally spoken or sung rather than written down.
See *Ballad, Folklore, Legend*, and *Myth*.

OTTAVA RIMA *Ottava rima* is a stanza with eight iambic pentameter lines that rhyme *abababcc*. Lord Byron used this stanza for his *Don Juan*, a selection from which appears on page 707. William Butler Yeats was fond of this stanza form and used it in a number of his finest poems, including "Sailing to Byzantium," on page 1054.

OVERSTATEMENT See *Hyperbole*.

OXYMORON *Oxymoron* is a figure of speech that fuses two contradictory or opposing ideas. An oxymoron, such as "freezing fire" or "happy grief," thus suggests a paradox in just a few words. In Book I of *Paradise Lost*, Milton uses the oxymoron "darkness visible" to describe the pit into which Satan and the other rebellious angels have been thrown.
See *Figurative Language* and *Paradox*.

PARADOX A *paradox* is a statement that seems to be contradictory but that actually presents a truth. In "Love's Growth," John Donne presents the following paradox:

Methinks I lied all winter, when I swore
My love was infinite, if spring make it more.

Because a paradox is surprising or even shocking, it draws the reader's attention to what is being said.
See *Figurative Language* and *Oxymoron*.

PARALLELISM *Parallelism* is the repetition of

a grammatical pattern. Stevie Smith uses parallel infinitive verbs in the first stanza of her poem "Is It Wise?":

Is it wise
To hug misery
To make a song of Melancholy
To weave a garland of sighs
To abandon hope wholly?
No, it is not wise.

Parallelism is used in poetry and in other writing to emphasize and to link related ideas.

PARODY A *parody* is a humorous, mocking imitation of a literary work. The play-within-the-play in William Shakespeare's *A Midsummer Night's Dream* parodies the poor performances and versions of classical tales that were current in Shakespeare's day.

PASTORAL A literary work is *pastoral* if it deals with the pleasures of a simple, rural life or with escape to a simpler place and time. The tradition of pastoral literature began in ancient Greece with the poetic idylls of Theocritus. Theocritus wrote about the simple lives of shepherds and goatherds. The Roman poet Virgil also wrote a famous collection of pastoral poems, the *Eclogues*, in imitation of Theocritus. Virgil's characters were, like Theocritus's, idealized rustics.

During the European Renaissance, pastoral writing became quite popular. One famous example of the genre is *The Countess of Pembroke's Arcadia*, by Sir Phillip Sidney. Another example is Christopher Marlowe's "The Passionate Shepherd to His Love," on page 182.

Today the term *pastoral* is commonly applied to any work in which a speaker longs to escape to a simpler, rural life. By this definition both William Wordsworth's "The World Is Too Much with Us," on page 667, and William Butler Yeats's "The Lake Isle of Innisfree," on page 1045, are pastoral poems.

PATHOS *Pathos* is the quality in a literary work that arouses feelings of pity, sorrow, or compassion in readers or in an audience. In *Macbeth*, the murdering of Macduff's family is a source of pathos, causing the audience to feel great sympathy for Macduff.

PENTAMETER See *Meter*.

PERSONIFICATION *Personification* is a type of figurative language in which a nonhuman subject is given human characteristics. Percy Bysshe Shelley used personification in these lines from "To Night":

Swiftly walk o'er the western wave,
  Spirit of the Night!
Out of the misty eastern cave
Where, all the long and lone daylight
Thou wovest dreams of joy and fear,
Which make thee terrible and dear,
  Swift be thy flight!

Effective personification of things or ideas makes them seem vital and alive, as if they were human.
See *Figurative Language* and *Metaphor*.

PERSUASION *Persuasion* is writing or speech that attempts to convince the audience to take some action or to adopt some opinion. Persuasion is one of the major forms of discourse and is used in advertising, in editorials, in sermons, in political speeches, and in other such writings. Some people use the terms *persuasion* and *argument* synonymously. Others use *persuasion* to refer to works that appeal to the emotions and *argument* to refer to works that appeal to reason.
See *Forms of Discourse*.

PETRARCHAN CONCEIT See *Conceit*.

PETRARCHAN SONNET See *Sonnet*.

PLOT *Plot* is the sequence of events in a literary work. The two primary elements of any plot

1415

are characters and a conflict. Most plots can be analyzed into most or all of the following parts:

1. The *exposition* introduces the setting, the characters, and the basic situation.
2. The *inciting incident* introduces the central conflict.
3. During the *development*, the conflict runs its course and usually intensifies.
4. At the *climax*, the conflict reaches a high point of interest or suspense.
5. At the *resolution*, the conflict is ended.
6. The *denouement* ties up loose ends that remain after the resolution of the conflict.

There are many variations on the standard plot structure. Some stories begin *in medias res* ("in the middle of things"), after the inciting incident has already occurred. In some stories the expository material appears toward the middle, in flashbacks. In many stories there is no denouement. Occasionally, though not often, the conflict is left unresolved.

POETRY *Poetry* is one of the three major types, or genres, of literature, the others being prose and drama. Poetry defies simple definition because there is no single characteristic that is found in all poems and not found in all nonpoems. In other words, poems are what philosophers of language call an "ill-defined set."

Often poems are divided into lines and stanzas. Many poems employ regular rhythmical patterns, or meters. However, some poems are written out just like prose, and some are written in free verse. Most poems make use of highly concise, musical, and emotionally charged language. Many also make use of imagery, figurative language, and special devices of sound such as rhyme.

Types of poetry include narrative poetry (ballads, epics, and metrical romances), dramatic poetry (dramatic monologues and dramatic dialogues), lyrics (sonnets, odes, elegies, and love poems), and concrete poetry.

POINT OF VIEW *Point of view* is the perspective, or vantage point, from which a story is told. If a character within the story tells the story, then it is told from the *first-person* point of view. If a voice from outside the story tells it, then the story is told from the *third-person* point of view. If the knowledge of the storyteller is limited to the internal states of one character, then the storyteller has a *limited* point of view. If the storyteller's knowledge extends to the internal states of all of the characters, then the storyteller has an *omniscient* point of view. The point of view from which a story is told determines what view of events will be presented.

PROSE *Prose* is the ordinary form of written language and one of the three major types of literature. Most writing that is not poetry, drama, or song is considered prose. Prose occurs in two major forms: fiction and nonfiction.

PROTAGONIST The *protagonist* is the main character in a literary work. In D. H. Lawrence's "The Rocking-Horse Winner," on page 996, the protagonist is Paul.
See *Antagonist* and *Character*.

PSALM A *psalm* is a song or hymn of praise, especially one included in the Book of Psalms in the Bible.

PUN A *pun* is a play on words. A pun may involve using a word or a phrase that has two different meanings or it may involve using two different words or phrases with the same sound, as in *sun* and *son*. The title of George Herbert's poem "The Collar" is a pun that suggests both the clerical collar of an Anglican minister and "choler," or anger, the emotion expressed at the beginning of the poem but calmed by God's call to the poem's speaker. Puns are often humorous but may serve

1416

serious purposes as well, as the example from Herbert shows.

PYRRHIC See *Meter*.

QUATRAIN See *Stanza*.

REALISM *Realism* is the presentation in art of the details of actual life. Another term for Realism, one that derives from Aristotle's *Poetics*, is *mimesis*, the Greek word for "imitation." During the last part of the nineteenth century and the first part of the twentieth, Realism enjoyed considerable popularity among writers in the English-speaking world. Nowhere, perhaps, was Realism more evident than in the novel. Novels often dealt with grim social realities and often presented realistic portrayals of the psychological states of characters. Realism also had considerable influence on theater in the early Modern Era. During the first part of this century, for example, the most common sort of stage setting was that in which a room was presented as though one wall had been removed and the audience were peering inside.

REFERENTIAL MEANING See *Denotation*.

REFRAIN A *refrain* is a regularly repeated line or group of lines in a poem or song. See, for example, the refrain "Lord, have mercy on us!" in Thomas Nashe's "A Litany in Time of Plague," on page 202.

REGIONALISM *Regionalism* is the tendency to confine one's writing to the presentation of materials drawn from a particular geographical area. George Eliot, for example, tended to set her tales in the English Midlands. The Brontës wrote about Yorkshire. Thomas Hardy wrote about Dorset and Wessex. D. H. Lawrence wrote about Nottinghamshire. A Regionalist writer presents the distinct culture of an area, including its speech, customs, landscape, and history.

REPETITION *Repetition* is the use, more than once, of any element of language—a sound, a word, a phrase, a clause, a sentence, a grammatical pattern, or a rhythmical pattern. Alliteration, assonance, consonance, meters, parallelism, refrains, and rhyme are all types of repetition.

RESOLUTION See *Plot*.

RHYME *Rhyme* is the repetition of sounds at the ends of words. *End rhyme* occurs when the rhyming words are repeated at the ends of lines. *Internal rhyme* occurs when the rhyming words fall within a line. *Exact rhyme* is the use of identical rhyming sounds, as in *love* and *dove*. *Approximate* or *slant rhyme* is the use of sounds that are similar but not identical, as in *prove* and *glove*.

RHYME SCHEME A *rhyme scheme* is a regular pattern of rhyming words in a poem or stanza. To indicate a rhyme scheme, one assigns each final sound in the poem or stanza a different letter. Consider, for example, how the following lines from Charlotte Brontë's "On the Death of Anne Brontë" have been marked:

There's little joy in life for *me*, *a*
  And little terror in the *grave*; *b*
I've lived the parting hour to *see* *a*
  Of one I would have died to *save*. *b*

The rhyme scheme of this stanza is *abab*.

RHYTHM See *Meter*.

RISING ACTION The *rising action* is that part of a plot that leads up to the climax. During the rising action, suspense increases as the complications of the conflict develop.
See *Falling Action* and *Plot*.

ROMANCE A *romance* is a story that presents

remote or imaginative incidents rather than ordinary, realistic experience. The term *romance* was originally used to refer to medieval tales of the deeds and loves of noble knights and ladies. These early romances, or tales of chivalry and courtly love, are exemplified by *Sir Gawain and the Green Knight*, on page 124, and by Malory's Morte d'Arthur, on page 65. During the Renaissance in England, many writers drew heavily on the romance tradition. One such writer was Edmund Spenser, whose *The Faerie Queene* combines elements of romance and elements of the epic. From the eighteenth century on, the term *romance* has been commonly used to describe sentimental novels about love.

ROMANTIC COMEDY See *Comedy*.

ROMANTICISM *Romanticism* was a literary and artistic movement of the eighteenth and nineteenth centuries. In reaction against Neoclassicism, the Romantics emphasized imagination, fancy, freedom, emotion, wildness, the beauty of the untamed natural world, the rights of the individual, the nobility of the common man, and the attractiveness of pastoral life. Important figures in the Romantic movement included William Wordsworth; Samuel Taylor Coleridge; Percy Bysshe Shelley; John Keats; and George Gordon, Lord Byron.

ROUND CHARACTER See *Character*.

RUN-ON LINE A *run-on line* is one that does not contain a pause or a stop at the end. A run-on line ends in the middle of a statement and of a grammatical unit, and the reader must therefore read the next line to find the end of the statement and the completion of the grammatical unit. The beginning of Molly Holden's "The Double Nature of White" illustrates the run-on line:

White orchards are the earliest, stunning
the spirit resigned to winter's black,
  white thorn
sprays first the bare wet branches of the
  hedge.

See *End-Stopped Line*.

SATIRE *Satire* is writing that ridicules or holds up to contempt the faults of individuals or of groups. A satirist may use a sympathetic tone or an angry, bitter tone. Some satire, like Jonathan Swift's *Gulliver's Travels*, an excerpt from which appears on page 538, is written in prose. Other satire, such as Henry Reed's "The Naming of Parts," on page 1110, is written in poetry. Although a satire is often humorous, its purpose is not simply to make readers laugh but also to correct, through laughter, the flaws and shortcomings that it points out.

SCANSION *Scansion* is the process of analyzing the metrical pattern of a poem.
See *Meter*.

SCENE See *Drama*.

SESTET See *Stanza*.

SETTING The *setting* of a literary work is the time and place of the action. A setting can serve many different purposes. It can provide a backdrop for the action. It can be the force that the protagonist struggles against and thus the source of the central conflict. It can also be used to create a mood, or atmosphere. In many works the setting symbolizes some point that the author wishes to emphasize. Much of Emily Brontë's novel *Wuthering Heights*, an excerpt from which appears on page 912, is set in the house named in the novel's title. When Lockwood visits this house at the beginning of the story, he finds it standing on a cold hilltop on the moors, built to withstand the north wind and inhabited by fierce dogs and unsociable people. This setting creates

a specific mood and suggests, symbolically, the wild emotional history of the past inhabitants of the house.
See *Mood* and *Symbol*.

SHAKESPEAREAN SONNET See *Sonnet*.

SHORT STORY A *short story* is a brief work of fiction. The short story resembles the longer novel but generally has a simpler plot and setting. In addition, a short story tends to reveal character at a crucial moment rather than to develop it through many incidents.

SIMILE A *simile* is a figure of speech that compares two dissimilar things by using a key word such as *like* or *as*. Christina Rossetti uses similes in her poem "Goblin Market" to describe two sisters:

Like two blossoms on one stem,
Like two flakes of new-fallen snow,
Like two wands of ivory
Tipped with gold for awful kings.

By comparing dissimilar things, the writer of a simile shocks the reader into appreciation of the qualities of the things being compared. Thus a simile makes a description more vivid and memorable.
See *Figurative Language*.

SLANT RHYME See *Rhyme*.

SOLILOQUY A *soliloquy* in a play or prose work is a long speech made by a character who is alone and who thus reveals his or her private thoughts and feelings to the audience. William Shakespeare's Act III of *Macbeth* opens with a soliloquy in which Banquo speculates on what Macbeth has done to fulfill the prophecy of the witches.
See *Monologue*.

SONNET A *sonnet* is a fourteen-line lyric poem focused on a single theme. Sonnets have many variations but are usually written in iambic pentameter, following one of two traditional patterns.

The *Petrarchan* or *Italian sonnet* is divided into two parts, the eight-line octave and the six-line sestet. The octave rhymes *abba abba*, while the sestet generally rhymes *cde cde* or uses some combination of *cd* rhymes. The two parts of the Petrarchan sonnet work together. The octave raises a question, states a problem, or presents a brief narrative, and the sestet answers the question, solves the problem, or comments on the narrative.

The *Shakespearean* or *English sonnet* has three four-line quatrains plus a concluding two-line couplet. The rhyme scheme of such a sonnet is usually *abab cdcd efef gg*. Each of the three quatrains usually explores a different variation of the main theme. Then the couplet presents a summarizing or concluding statement.
See *Lyric* and *Sonnet Sequence*.

SONNET SEQUENCE A *sonnet sequence* is a series or group of sonnets written to one person or on one theme. Although each sonnet can stand alone as a separate poem, the sequence lets the poet trace the development of a relationship or examine different aspects of a single subject. Examples of sonnet sequences are Sir Philip Sidney's *Astrophel and Stella*, Edmund Spenser's *Amoretti*, and Elizabeth Barrett Browning's *Sonnets from the Portuguese*.
See *Sonnet*.

SPEAKER The *speaker* is the imaginary voice assumed by the writer of a poem. In other words, the speaker is the character who tells the poem. This character often is not identified by name. The title of William Blake's poem "The Chimney Sweeper" identifies the speaker, a child who gives this account of his life:

When my mother died I was very young,
And my father sold me while yet my tongue

Could scarcely cry "'weep! 'weep! 'weep!
'weep!"
So your chimneys I sweep and in soot I sleep.

Although this speaker matter-of-factly accepts his life, the poem is ironic because the poet expects readers to have a different view of the child's situation. Recognizing the speaker and thinking about his or her characteristics is often central to interpreting a lyric poem.
See *Point of View*.

SPENSERIAN STANZA The *Spenserian stanza*, invented by Edmund Spenser for use in *The Faerie Queene*, has nine iambic lines rhymed *ababbcbcc*. All the lines are pentameters except the last, which is a hexameter or alexandrine. This close-knit rhyme scheme unifies the stanza, and the final line provides dignified summary. This stanza form is used in George Gordon, Lord Byron's *Childe Harold's Pilgrimage*, on page 702, and in poems by William Wordsworth, John Keats, Percy Bysshe Shelley, and Alfred, Lord Tennyson.
See *Alexandrine*

SPONDEE See *Meter*.

SPRUNG RHYTHM *Sprung rhythm* is the term used by Gerard Manley Hopkins to describe the idiosyncratic meters of his poems. Discovering the underlying metrical pattern of a poem written in sprung rhythm is difficult if not impossible. The rhythm is quite varied and contains such violations of traditional metrical rules as several strong stresses in a row or feet containing more than two weak stresses. The following lines from Hopkins's "Spring" illustrate sprung rhythm:

Whát ĭs áll thĭs júice ănd áll thĭs jóy?
Ă stráin ŏf thĕ eárth's swéet béing ĭn
thĕ bĕgínnĭng
Ĭn Éden gárdĕn.—Háve, gét, bĕfóre ĭt
clóy,
Bĕfóre ĭt clóud, Chríst, lórd, ănd sóur
wĭth sínnĭng,
Ínnŏcĕnt mínd ănd Máydáy ĭn gírl ănd bóy

STAGE DIRECTIONS *Stage directions* are notes included in a drama to describe how the work is to be performed or staged. Stage directions are usually printed in italics and enclosed within parentheses or brackets. They may mention how the characters should speak or move, what the costumes or scenery should look like, how the set should be arranged, what lighting should be used, and so on.

STANZA A *stanza* is a group of lines in a poem, considered as a unit. Many poems are divided into stanzas that are separated by spaces. Stanzas often function just like paragraphs in prose. Each stanza states and develops a single main idea.

Stanzas are commonly named according to the number of lines found in them, as follows:

1. *Couplet:* a two-line stanza
2. *Tercet:* a three-line stanza
3. *Quatrain:* a four-line stanza
4. *Cinquain:* a five-line stanza
5. *Sestet:* a six-line stanza
6. *Heptastich:* a seven-line stanza
7. *Octave:* an eight-line stanza

See *Sonnet* and *Spenserian Stanza*.

STATIC CHARACTER See *Character*.

STEREOTYPE See *Character*.

STOCK CHARACTER See *Character*.

STREAM OF CONSCIOUSNESS *Stream of consciousness* is a narrative technique that presents thoughts as if they were coming directly from a character's mind. Instead of being arranged in chronological order, the events in a stream-of-consciousness narrative are presented from the character's point view, mixed in with the character's ongoing feelings and memories. Developed by writers such as James Joyce and Vir-

ginia Woolf, stream-of-consciousness writing is used to reveal a character's complex psychology and to present it in realistic detail.
See *Point of View*.

STYLE A writer's *style* is his or her typical way of writing. Determinants of a writer's style include his or her formality, use of figurative language, use of rhythm, typical grammatical patterns, typical sentence lengths, and typical methods of organization. John Milton is noted for a grand, heroic style that contrasts with John Keats's rich, sensory style and with T.S. Eliot's allusive, ironic style.
See *Diction*.

SUBPLOT A *subplot* is a second, less important plot within a story or play. One subplot in William Shakespeare's *A Midsummer Night's Dream* deals with the presentation of a play by Bottom and his fellows. Another deals with the quarrel between Titania and Oberon. A subplot may add to, reflect, vary, or contrast with the main plot.
See *Plot*.

SUSPENSE *Suspense* is a feeling of growing curiosity or anxious uncertainty about the outcome of events in a literary work. Writers create suspense by raising questions in the minds of their readers.

SYMBOL A *symbol* is anything that stands for or represents something else. Thus a flag is a symbol of a country, a group of letters can symbolize a spoken word, a spoken word can symbolize an object, a fine car can symbolize wealth, and so on. In literary criticism a distinction is often made between *traditional* or *conventional symbols*—ones that are part of our general cultural inheritance—and *personal symbols*—ones that are created by particular authors for use in particular works. For example, the lamb in William Blake's poem "The Lamb" is a conventional symbol for peace, gentleness, and innocence, one that Blake inherited from the Bible and from the pastoral tradition. However, the tiger in Blake's poem "The Tiger" is not a conventional or inherited symbol. Blake created this symbol of evil specifically for this poem.

Conventional symbolism is often based on elements of the natural world. For example, youth is often symbolized by greenery or springtime, middle age by summer, and old age by autumn or winter. Death is often symbolized by darkness or cold. The sun is often used as a symbol of power or authority. Roses are symbols of love and beauty. Doves are symbols of peace. Foxes are symbols of craftiness, and owls of wisdom.

Conventional symbols are also sometimes borrowed from the spheres of religion and politics. For example, a cross may be a symbol of Christianity or the color red a symbol of Marxist ideology.

SYMBOLISM *Symbolism* was a literary movement of nineteenth-century France. The Symbolist writers reacted against Realism and stressed, instead, the importance of suggestion and evocation of emotional states, especially by means of symbols corresponding to these states. The Symbolists were also quite concerned with using sound to achieve emotional effects. Important Symbolist writers included Stéphane Mallarmé, Paul Verlaine, and Arthur Rimbaud. English writers who were influenced by the Symbolist movement included William Butler Yeats and T. S. Eliot.

SYNECDOCHE *Synecdoche* is a figure of speech in which a part of something is used to stand for the whole. In the preface to his long poem entitled *Milton*, William Blake includes these lines: "And did those feet in ancient time/Walk upon England's mountains green?" The feet, of course, stand for the whole body, and "England's mountains green" stand for England generally. See *Figurative Language*.

TERCET See *Stanza*

TERZA RIMA *Terza rima* is a three-line stanza pattern with interlocking rhymes that connect stanza to stanza. The middle line of one tercet rhymes with the first and last lines of the next so that *aba* is followed by *bcb, cdc, ded*, and so on. "The Triumph of Life," by Percy Bysshe Shelley, illustrates this pattern:

As in that trance of wondrous thought I lay *a*
This was the tenour of my waking dream, *b*
Methought I sat beside a public way *a*

Thick strewn with summer dust, and a great stream *b*
Of people there was hurrying to and fro *c*
Numerous as gnats upon the evening gleam *b*

As the name suggests, *terza rima* is an Italian verse form. The form was made famous by Dante Alighieri, who used it in his *The Divine Comedy*. Terza rima is a difficult form because of the rhymes required, but it has been used successfully by Sir Thomas Wyatt, Lord Byron, Robert Browning, and William Butler Yeats.

TETRAMETER See *Meter*.

THEME The *theme* is a central idea, concern, or purpose in a literary work. In an essay the theme might be directly stated in what is known as a thesis statement. In a serious literary work, the theme is usually expressed indirectly rather than directly. A light work, one written strictly for entertainment, may not have a theme.

THIRD-PERSON POINT OF VIEW See *Point of View*.

TONE The *tone* of a literary work is the writer's attitude toward the readers and toward the subject. A writer's tone may be formal or informal, friendly or distant, personal or pompous. For example, William Hazlitt's tone in his essay on Macbeth, on page 756, is earnest and respectful, while James Boswell's tone in *The Life of Samuel Johnson*, which begins on page 588, is familiar and engaging.
See *Mood*.

TRAGEDY *Tragedy* is a type of drama or literature that shows the downfall or destruction of a noble or outstanding person, traditionally one who possesses a character weakness called a *tragic flaw*. Macbeth, for example, is a brave and noble figure led astray by ambition. The *tragic hero*, through choice or circumstance, is caught up in a sequence of events that inevitably results in disaster. Because the protagonist is neither a wicked villain nor an innocent victim, the audience reacts with mixed emotions—both pity and fear, according to the Greek philosopher Aristotle, who defined tragedy in his famous work, the *Poetics*. The outcome of a tragedy, in which the protagonist is isolated from society, contrasts with the happy resolution of a comedy, in which the protagonist makes peace with society.
See *Comedy* and *Drama*.

TRIMETER See *Meter*.

TROCHEE See *Meter*.

UNDERSTATEMENT *Understatement* is the literary technique of saying less than is actually meant, generally in an ironic way. An example of understatement is the description of a flooded area as "slightly soggy."
See *Figurative Language*.

VERBAL IRONY See *Irony*.

VERNACULAR *Vernacular* is the ordinary language of the people living in a particular region.

1422

Instead of using more formal literary language, writers may use vernacular to create realistic characters or to approach readers informally. See *Dialect*.

VILLANELLE A *villanelle* is a nineteen-line French verse form. It has two refrains formed by repeating line 1 in lines 6, 12, and 18 and by repeating line 3 in lines 9, 15, and 19. The three lines in each of the first five stanzas rhyme *aba*. The final quatrain rhymes *abaa*. An example of a villanelle in this text is Dylan Thomas's "Do Not Go Gentle into That Good Night," on page 1116.

1423

HANDBOOK OF CRITICAL THINKING AND READING TERMS

ABSTRACT *adj.* Anything that is not concrete or definite is *abstract*. A building is concrete because its details can be pereceived by the senses. A set of blueprints is abstract because most of these details are left out. Words and the ideas that they represent can also be abstract. Examples of abstract words include *love*, *truth*, *history*, *realism*, *courage*, *nature*, and *society*.

People can make abstract ideas clear by using specific examples and illustrations. Suppose, for instance, that a novelist wants to communicate the abstract idea of a society. To do so, he or she might create characters representing a cross section of ethnic, economic, and political backgrounds: a coal miner, an immigrant, a pop star, a farmer, an aristocrat, and a labor leader. The novelist might make this depiction seem realistic by including many specific details and allusions to actual places, styles of clothing, customs, and historical events.

Another way to express abstract ideas clearly is to use symbols and figures of speech. For example, in the poem "Do Not Go Gentle into That Good Night," on page 1120, Dylan Thomas uses a concrete image—light—as a symbol for an abstraction—life.

ANALOGY *n.* An *analogy* is a comparison that explains one subject by pointing out its similarities to another subject. Writers often use analogies to explain the unfamiliar in familiar terms. For example, a writer might explain the organization of a theatrical troupe by comparing it to the organization of a baseball team. An analogy is possible only when the two items being compared have elements or characteristics in common. Writers use a number of techniques to state or to suggest analogies, including metaphor, simile, and extended metaphor.

Whenever you read or hear an analogy, ask yourself what characteristics the two things being compared have in common. Whenever you create an analogy, make sure that the two things being compared do in fact share common elements or characteristics. Avoid false analogy—the fallacy of assuming that two things are similar in one respect simply because they are similar in another respect.

ANALYSIS *n.* *Analysis* is the process of studying a whole by examining its parts. When you analyze something, follow these steps: First, break the thing down into its parts. Next, study the properties and functions of the parts. Then, look for relationships among the parts and between each part and the whole. For example, you might analyze the plot of a short story into the exposition, the inciting incident, the development, the climax, the resolution, and the denouement. After breaking the events of the story down into these parts, you would then study each part and think about how each part advances the action and contributes to the whole.

There are many different types of analysis. A *functional analysis* is one in which a thing is broken down into parts and then the functions of each part are studied. A *cause-and-effect analysis* is one in which a series of events is broken down into separate events that are then identified as causes or effects.

ARGUMENT *n.* An *argument* is a set of logically related statements consisting of a conclusion and one or more premises. The premises are the reasons for accepting the conclusion. For example, you might argue in a paper that Macbeth, the protagonist in Shakespeare's tragedy, is essentially a good man who is tempted by ambition to commit acts that he knows to be wrong. To support this argument, you might present the following evidence from the play:

1. Before committing the murder, Macbeth thinks aloud about the duty that he owes to Duncan and about the great evil involved in killing one's king, one's kinsman, and one's guest.
2. Macbeth has such a guilty conscience that he is driven to have hallucinations, seeing first a bloody dagger in the air and then the ghost of Banquo.
3. At the end of the play, in the "Tomorrow" soliloquy, Macbeth reveals that life has become completely meaningless for him.

Whenever you state an interpretation or an evaluation of a literary work, you should support your statement with reasons drawn from the work itself.

The term *argument* is also used to refer to a brief summary, or synopsis, of a literary work. Thus a summary of the plot of *Paradise Lost* might be described as presenting "the argument of the poem."

See *Conclusion*, *Deduction*, *Evidence*, *Induction*, and *Inference*.

BANDWAGON See *Propaganda Technique*.

BEGGING THE QUESTION See *Logical Fallacy*.

CATEGORIZATION *n.* *Categorization* is the process of placing objects or ideas into groups. These groups may be called classes or categories. Categorization is always done according to some shared property or characteristic. For example, one might place Coleridge's "The Rime of the Ancient Mariner," on page 670, and Tennyson's "The Lady of Shallot," on page 798, into the same category because these poems share two important characteristics: Both tell stories, and both deal with extraordinary or supernatural events.

To categorize something, follow these steps:

1. Observe the characteristics of the thing to be categorized.
2. Think of other things that have the same characteristics.
3. Find or create a name for the group of things with the shared characteristic.

Categorization is a useful tool for organizing information. Information about literary works is organized by categorizing works into groups called *genres*. The major genres of literature are prose, poetry, and drama. Prose can be divided into the subcategories of fiction and nonfiction; poetry into the subcategories of lyric, narrative, dramatic, and epic poetry; and drama into the subcategories of comedy, serious drama, tragedy, melodrama, and farce.

CAUSE AND EFFECT *n. phrase* When one event precedes and brings about another event, the first is said to be a *cause* and the second an *effect*. A *sufficient cause* is one that, by itself, is enough to bring about the effect. A *necessary cause* is one that is required in order to bring about an effect but that may or may not be sufficient to bring about the effect.

Cause-and-effect relationships are extremely important in literary study. The plot of a story, for example, is a series of events related by cause and effect. One event causes the next, which causes the next, and so on to the end of the story. Literary history often involves tracing the forces that caused the writer to produce particular works. Such forces might include the author's personal experiences and reading or the social, political, and cultural circumstances in which the author wrote.

The act of reading also involves cause and effect. Particular aspects of the text—the imagery or tone, for example—cause certain reactions in the reader. To understand the work, the reader must account for these reactions by determining what aspects of the text caused them.

CIRCULAR REASONING See *Logical Fallacy*.

COMPARISON *n.* *Comparison* is the process of

1425

observing and pointing out similarities. For example, a comparison of Samuel Pepys and James Boswell might note that each author possessed an excellent eye for detail, that each was a skillful storyteller, and that each displayed a love for social life.
See *Contrast*.

CONCLUSION *n.* A *conclusion* is anything that follows reasonably from something else. In an argument, the conclusion is a statement that follows from supporting facts and reasons. In a literary work, the conclusion is the final part, or ending, of the work.

CONTRAST *n.* *Contrast* is the process of observing and pointing out differences. If, for example, you were to contrast writers of the Neoclassical and Romantic eras, you might point out the following differences:

1. Politics: The Neoclassicists were conservatives; the Romantics were liberals or radicals.
2. Style: The Neoclassicists used harmonious, ordered, stylized language; the Romanticists used language modeled on ordinary speech or language that was grand, heroic, and exuberant.
3. Social or ethical stance: The Neoclassicists stressed acceptable social norms; the Romanticists stressed the freedom of the individual.
4. Attitude toward nature: The Neoclassicists loved nature when it was controlled and ordered, as in a garden; the Romanticists loved nature in its uncontrolled, wild state.

See *Comparison*.

DEDUCTION *n.* *Deduction* is a form of argument in which the conclusion has to be true if the premises are true. Consider the following arguments:

Major premise: People living in the eighteenth century had no experience of electric lights, automobiles, computers, or airplanes.
Minor premise: Dr. Johnson lived in the eighteenth century.
Conclusion: Dr. Johnson had no experience of electric lights, automobiles, computers, or airplanes.

Major premise: All sonnets have fourteen lines.
Minor premise: Andrew Marvell's "To His Coy Mistress" has forty-six lines.
Conclusion: Andrew Marvell's "To His Coy Mistress" is not a sonnet.

If you accept the premises of these arguments, then you most also accept their conclusions. Therefore, these arguments are deductions.
See *Generalization, Induction*, and *Inference*.

DEFINITION *n.* *Definition* is the process of explaining the meaning of a word or a phrase. Definition is essential to communication because it establishes agreed-upon meanings for words.

The simplest type of definition, *ostensive definition*, involves pointing to something and saying its name. If, for example, you point to an object and say, "typewriter," you are giving an ostensive definition of the word *typewriter*. The word is defined by the observable characteristics of the object that is referred to.

Another common type of definition is the kind found in dictionaries, *lexical definition*. Lexical definition uses words to explain the meanings of other words. Some common types of lexical definition are definitions by synonym, by antonym, by example, and by genus and differentia.

In a *definition by synonym*, one uses a word or a phrase that has the same meaning as the word being defined: A *drama* is "a play."

In a *definition by antonym*, one uses a word or a phrase with an opposite meaning along with a negation such as *no* or *not*: *Free verse* is "poetry that does not have a regular meter."

In a *definition by example*, one lists things to which the term being defined applies: *Epic poems* include Homer's *Iliad* and *Odyssey*, Virgil's *Aeneid*, Dante's *The Divine Comedy*, and Milton's *Paradise Lost*.

In a *genus and differentia* definition, one

places the thing to be defined into a general category, or *genus*, and then one shows how the thing being defined differs from other things in the general category:

To be defined: Epic
Genus, or category: narrative poem
Differentia: long
about the adventures of heroes or gods
Definition: An *epic* is "a long narrative poem about the adventures of heroes or gods."

Whenever you use words that your audience may not understand, define these words. Use the methods of lexical definition explained here.

EITHER/OR FALLACY See *Logical Fallacy.*

EVALUATION *n.* *Evaluation* is the process of making a judgment about the quality or value of something. When you make an evaluation of a work of literature, bear in mind these guidelines:

1. Make your evaluation specific. An evaluation such as "I hated it" or "It's a wonderful book" is too vague.
2. Base your evaluation on a clear standard, or criterion, of judgment.
3. Support your evaluation with evidence drawn from the work.

For more information on criteria for evaluation, see the lesson on Evaluating a Literary Work, on page 1376.
See *Opinion* and *Judgment.*

EVIDENCE *n.* *Evidence* is factual information presented to support an argument. When you write or speak about literature, the evidence that you use to support your statements will be details drawn from literary works. For example, consider the statement "The Old Man in Chaucer's 'The Pardoner's Tale' is Death personified." To support this interpretation you might provide the following evidence: The Old Man is described as being extremely aged, the Old Man possesses a ghostlike appearance, and the three young revellers are killed shortly after meeting the Old Man.

FACT *n.* A *fact* is a statement that can be proved true or false by evidence. For example, the following facts are true by definition:

A *dollar* is equal to one hundred cents.
A *conceit* is an extravagant or farfetched metaphor.

The following facts are true by observation:

"Barbara Allan" and "Sir Patrick Spens" are both ballads.
Some lyric poems are very short, and some are quite long.

When you write or speak about a literary work, use facts from the work to support the assertions that you make.
See *Opinion*.

FALSE ANALOGY See *Logical Fallacy*.

GENERALIZATION *n.* A *generalization* is a statement that applies to more than one thing. The following statements are generalizations:

Elizabethan poetry often praised Queen Elizabeth I.
Samuel Johnson's works contain many examples of the technique known as parallelism.

The first statement applies to more than one Elizabethan poem and the second to more than one of Samuel Johnson's works.

Deductive arguments often begin with generalizations. Consider the following deductive argument:

Premise: (generalization) Novels are written in prose.
Conclusion: Mary Shelley's novel *Frankenstein* is written in prose.

Inductive arguments often end with generalizations. Consider the following inductive argument:

Premise: Tennyson's "The Splendor Falls" rhymes.
Premise: Tennyson's "Crossing the Bar" rhymes.

Premise: Tennyson's "The Lotos-Eaters" rhymes.
Conclusion: (generalization) Many of Tennyson's poems rhyme.

When making generalizations, be careful to avoid overgeneralization, or making statements that are too broad. For example, the statement "All of Tennyson's poems rhyme" is too broad because some of his poems, such as "Ulysses," do not rhyme. To avoid overgeneralization, use qualifiers, or words that limit statements. Some common qualifiers include *a few, some, many*, and *most*.
See *Deduction*, *Induction*, and *Stereotype*.

INDUCTION *n.* *Induction* is a form of argument in which the conclusion is probably but not necessarily true. For example, if you read several comic plays and notice that each ends with a marriage, you might conclude that "All comedies end with marriages." However, you could not be certain of the truth of this statement unless you had read all the comedies ever written.

Most of what people know about the world is learned by induction. Each individual generalizes, based on his or her limited experience. Thus a small child sees several objects with wheels, each of which is called a car, and the child thus generalizes that all wheeled objects are cars. Eventually, the child will learn to limit this inductive generalization based on additional information.

Literary study often involves using induction. After you have read several works by one author or several works written in a particular period, you might, for example, make generalizations about the author or about the period. Remember, however, that such generalizations are subject to error and should be qualified by words and phrases such as *probably* or *most likely*.
See *Deduction*, *Generalization*, and *Inference*.

INFERENCE *n.* An *inference* is any logical or reasonable conclusion based on known facts or accepted premises. The conclusions of both deductive and inductive arguments are inferences. Reading actively involves continually making inferences based on details presented in the work being read.
See *Conclusion*, *Deduction*, and *Induction*.

INTERPRETATION *n.* *Interpretation* is the process of determining the meaning or significance of speech, writing, art, music, or actions. The interpretation of a literary work involves many different processes. These include the following:

1. Reading carefully and actively and responding to each new detail
2. Examining one's own responses to the work and identifying the details that create these responses
3. Being alert to patterns and relations that emerge during the reading of the work
4. Analyzing the work into its parts, studying these parts, and determining how the parts relate to one another and to the whole
5. Pulling together one's observations about the work to make generalizations about the significance, or meaning, of the work as a whole.

Interpretation usually aims at making clear the central theme of a work. For example, an interpretation of Percy Bysshe Shelley's "Ozymandias," on page 712, might read as follows: " 'Ozymandias' is a poem about the vanity of worldly pretension." Of course, any such interpretation must be supported by evidence from the work. A sound interpretation is one that accounts for all the important parts of a work and that is not contradicted by any part of the work.
See *Analysis*.

JUDGMENT *n.* A *judgment* is a statement about the quality or value of something. A sound judgment of a literary work is one that is based on evidence derived from careful reading and thoughtful analysis.
See *Evaluation* and *Opinion*.

LOADED WORDS See *Propaganda Technique*.

LOGICAL FALLACY *n. phrase* A *logical fallacy* is an error in reasoning. In the attempt to make persuasive arguments, people often fall into such errors. The following logical fallacies are quite common:

1. *Begging the question:* This fallacy occurs when someone assumes the truth of the statement to be proved without providing any evidence to support the statement. For example: "Of course, everyone knows that contemporary poetry is obscure." (No evidence is given to support the claim.)
2. *Circular reasoning:* This fallacy occurs when the evidence given to support a claim is simply a restatement of the claim in other words. For example: "Wordsworth should be considered a nature poet because he wrote poems about nature." (The second part of the sentence simply restates the claim made in the first part.)
3. *Either/or fallacy:* This fallacy occurs when someone claims that there are only two alternatives when there are actually more. For example: "William Blake was either a madman or a confused mystic." (The statement ignores a third possibility—that Blake was a sane but highly idiosyncratic writer who invented his own elaborate code, or symbol system, in which to express his ideas.)
4. *False analogy:* This fallacy occurs when someone falsely assumes that two subjects are similar in one respect just because they are similar in some other respect. For example: "The English people and the American people speak the same language. Therefore, their cultures must be alike." (The false assumption is made that because these peoples are similar in one respect they are similar in all respects.)
5. *Overgeneralization:* This fallacy occurs when someone makes a statement that is too broad or too inclusive. For example: "The Victorians were imperialists." (This statement is only partially true, for some British citizens of the Victorian Age opposed the government's imperialistic colonial policies.)
6. *Post hoc, ergo propter hoc:* (a Latin phrase meaning "After this, therefore because of this") This fallacy occurs when someone falsely assumes that an event is caused by another event simply because of the order of the events in time. For example: "After adopting the Christian religion, the Anglo-Saxons were defeated by the Normans. Therefore, the adoption of Christianity must have led to the Anglo-Saxon defeat." (This argument is, of course, completely fallacious. The adoption of Christianity took place long before the Norman invasion, and the Normans themselves were Christians. The defeat was actually due to other factors such as the divisiveness among the Anglo-Saxons, the surprise nature of the invasion, and the superiority of the Norman soldiers.)

When you do persuasive writing or speaking, try to avoid these logical fallacies. Also be on guard against these fallacies in other people's writing and speech.

MAIN IDEA *n. phrase* The *main idea* is the central point that a speaker or a writer wants to communicate. Sometimes, as in the thesis statement of an essay, the main idea is stated directly. However, often the main idea of a literary work is implied. The reader must identify the main idea based on clues provided by other elements of the work.
See *Purpose*.

OBJECTIVE *adj.* Something is *objective* if it has to do with a reality that is independent of any particular person's mind or personal, internal experiences. Statements of fact are objective because anyone can, at least in principle, verify them. Statements of opinion, on the other hand, are not objective because they express an individual's personal feelings and impressions. However, statements of opinion can be supported by objective facts. When you write about a literary work, you should strive to be objective. That is, you should support your statements with factual evidence that other people can verify by reading the work themselves.
See *Subjective.*

1429

OPINION *n.* An *opinion* is a statement that can be supported by facts but that is not itself a fact. Opinions may be judgments, predictions, or statements of policy or obligation. The following are opinions:

Judgment: William Butler Yeats is the greatest poet of the twentieth century.
Prediction: Third World writers will play an increasingly prominent role in the literature of the late twentieth and early twenty-first centuries.
Obligation: We must continually affirm the value of a literary education.

Whenever you express an opinion, you should support it with facts and with reasoned arguments. See *Fact*, *Judgment*, and *Prediction*.

OVERGENERALIZATION See *Logical Fallacy*.

PARAPHRASE *n.* A *paraphrase* is a restatement in different words. When writing about literature, paraphrase can be used to support an interpretation or an analysis when the exact words of the original are not essential to the argument. However, when paraphrasing, be careful not to alter the meaning of the original. Simply translate what the writer said into equivalent words of your own.

POST HOC, ERGO PROPTER HOC See *Logical Fallacy*.

PREDICTION *n.* *Prediction* is the act of making statements about the future. An active reader continually makes and tests predictions on the basis of details presented in the work being read. For example, while reading about the Lilliputians' adoption of Lemuel Gulliver, on page 538, you might predict that these tiny people will put the giant Gulliver to military use. Gulliver's size in comparison to his hosts' makes this an obvious possibility, one that the story confirms.

Authors often supply hints or clues as to what will happen later in their works. This technique of providing clues to later events is called *foreshadowing*, and foreshadowing is one of the reasons why prediction of events in a literary work is possible. Often, of course, readers simply base their predictions on expectations related to the genre of the work being read or on general knowledge about how people, and thus characters, react in certain situations.

Sometimes an author will intentionally mislead readers into making predictions that later prove false. This technique, often used in mystery and detective fiction, makes possible the occurrence of surprise endings.
See *Opinion*.

PROBLEM SOLVING *n. phrase* *Problem solving* is the process by which a person comes up with a solution to some difficulty. The following are some general guidelines for solving any sort of problem:

1. State the problem as precisely as possible.
2. Identify your goal.
3. Identify the differences between the goal state (the situation that will exist when the problem is solved) and the initial state (the situation that exists at the beginning of your work on the problem).
4. Take steps to reduce the differences between the goal state and the initial state.

The following rules of thumb, or *heuristics*, are useful for solving many types of problems.

1. Break the problem down into parts and solve the parts separately.
2. Think of similar problems that you have solved before and see whether the same solutions can be used.
3. Draw a diagram or sketch to clarify the problem.
4. Make a pros-and-cons chart.
5. Use brainstorming, freewriting, clustering, and other general thinking strategies to generate possible solutions.
6. Restate the problem in various ways or from several points of view.
7. Define any key terms or concepts related to the problem.

8. Examine your ideas about the problem to see whether they are too rigid. See if there aren't new ways of conceiving the problem and its solution.
9. Ask yourself "What if" questions to generate possible solutions.
10. Ask someone to help you with parts of the problem that are especially difficult.
11. Use means/ends analysis. That is, at each point in your work toward solving the problem, pause to determine whether you are advancing toward a solution.

Use these techniques or strategies, to solve the many types of problems that you encounter in everyday life, including problems related to writing and to interpreting works of literature.

PROPAGANDA TECHNIQUE *n. phrase* A *propaganda technique* is an improper appeal to emotion used for the purpose of swaying the opinions of an audience. The following propaganda techniques often appear in persuasive writing and speech:

1. *Bandwagon:* This technique involves encouraging people to think or act in some way simply because other people are doing so. For example: "Everyone's reading this new thriller. You should, too."
2. *Loaded words:* This technique involves using words with strong positive or negative connotations. Name-calling is an example of the use of loaded words. So is any use of words that are charged with emotional associations. For example: "I detest Kipling because his writings are *undemocratic*."
3. *Snob appeal:* This technique involves making a direct or implied claim that one should act or think in a certain way because of the high social status associated with the action or thought. For example: "All really sophisticated readers appreciate Alexander Pope."
4. *Vague, undefined terms:* This technique involves promoting or challenging an opinion by using words that are so vague or so poorly defined as to be almost meaningless. For example: "Librarians shouldn't be allowed to purchase *awful* books like these."

Try to avoid propaganda techniques in your own speech and writing, and be on guard against these techniques in the speech and writing of others.

PURPOSE *n.* The *purpose* is the goal, or aim, of a literary work. Works are often classified as narrative, descriptive, expository, or persuasive, based on their purposes. A narrative work tells a story. A descriptive work portrays a person, place, or thing. An expository work explains something or provides information. A persuasive work attempts to move an audience to adopt some opinion or to take some action. Many works combine these purposes. For example, a narrative work may also be, in places, descriptive, or a persuasive work may be, in places, expository.

Of course, most works also have more specific purposes. For example, Milton claimed that the purpose of *Paradise Lost*, an excerpt from which appears on page 470, was "to justify God's ways to man." When used in this specific sense, the word *purpose* is equivalent to *theme*.

REASON *n.* A *reason* is a statement made in support of some conclusion. The term *reason* is also used as a verb to signify the human ability to think logically and rationally.

SNOB APPEAL See *Propaganda Technique*.

SOURCE *n.* A *source* is anything from which ideas and information are taken. Some books, such as dictionaries, encyclopedias, atlases, almanacs, and biographies are specifically designed to be used as sources. Other types of sources include interviews with people, magazine articles, computerized information services, booklets, television programs, films, and recordings. Of course, every writer draws on at least one other very important source—his or her own experiences.

1431

There are two basic types of sources, primary and secondary. A *primary source* is a first-hand account. Conversations, speeches, legal documents, and letters are examples of primary sources. *Secondary sources* are accounts or compilations written or prepared by people who are not eye-witnesses. A recent biography of Samuel Johnson would be a secondary source about Johnson's life. A collection of Johnson's letters would be a primary source. Boswell's *Life of Samuel Johnson*, an excerpt from which appears on page 588, is a primary source for some facts and a secondary source for others.

Whenever you gather information for use in a speech or in a paper, make sure that your sources are unbiased, up-to-date, authoritative, and reliable. Also make sure that you credit your sources properly by means of footnotes, endnotes, or in-text references.

STEREOTYPE *n.* A *stereotype* is a fixed or conventional notion or characterization. Examples of stereotypical characters include the absent-minded professor, the suffering artist, the back-room politician, and the mad scientist. Although writers occasionally use stereotypes when they haven't the space to develop complete, rounded characters, good writers generally avoid stereotyping. Of course, in everyday life stereotyping leads people to make false assumptions about other people and groups of people. Stereotyping occurs because of the unfortunate human tendency to overgeneralize.
See *Generalization*.

SUBJECTIVE *adj.* Something is *subjective* if it is based on personal reactions or emotions rather than on some objective reality. A reader's reaction to a work of literature is, therefore, subjective. However, this subjective reaction can be supported by means of objective evidence drawn from the work.
See *Objective*.

SUMMARIZE *v.* To *summarize* something is to restate it briefly in other words. Generally, one summarizes long works and paraphrases short passages. When writing about literary works, you may sometimes find it useful to summarize events from literary history, positions taken by critics, or events in the works themselves. Always make sure that your summary is an accurate reflection of the original. In particular, make sure not to give more or less weight to particular parts than was given in the material that you are summarizing.

VAGUE, UNDEFINED TERMS See *Propaganda Technique*.

1432

GLOSSARY

READING THE GLOSSARY ENTRIES

The words in this glossary are from selections appearing in your textbook. Each entry in the glossary contains the following parts:

1. Entry Word. This word appears at the beginning of the entry in boldface type.

2. Pronunciation. The symbols in parentheses tell how the entry word is pronounced. If a word has more than one possible pronunciation, the most common of these pronunciations is given first.

3. Part of Speech. Appearing after the pronunciation, in italics, is an abbreviation that tells the part of speech of the entry word. The following abbreviations have been used:

n. noun	**p.** pronoun	**v.** verb
adj. adjective	**adv.** adverb	**conj.** conjunction

4. Definition. This part of the entry follows the part-of-speech abbreviation and gives the meaning of the entry word as used in the selection in which it appears.

KEY TO PRONUNCIATION SYMBOLS USED IN THE GLOSSARY

The following symbols are used in the pronunciations that follow the entry words:

Symbol	*Key Words*	*Symbol*	*Key Words*
a	asp, fat, parrot	b	bed, fable, dub
ā	ape, date, play	d	dip, beadle, had
ä	ah, car, father	f	fall, after, off
		g	get, haggle, dog
e	elf, ten, berry	h	he, ahead, hotel
ē	even, meet, money	j	joy, agile, badge
		k	kill, tackle, bake
i	is, hit, mirror	l	let, yellow, ball
ī	ice, bite, high	m	met, camel, trim
		n	not, flannel, ton
ō	open, tone, go	p	put, apple, tap
ô	all, horn, law	r	red, port, dear
o͞o	ooze, tool, crew	s	sell, castle, pass
oo	look, pull, moor	t	top, cattle, hat
yo͞o	use, cute, few	v	vat, hovel, have
yoo	united, cure, globule	w	will, always, swear
oi	oil, point, toy	y	yet, onion, yard
ou	out, crowd, plow	z	zebra, dazzle, haze
u	up, cut, color	ch	chin, catcher, arch
ʉr	urn, fur, deter	sh	she, cushion, dash
		th	thin, nothing, truth
ə	a in ago e in agent i in sanity o in comply u in focus	*th*	then, father, lathe
		zh	azure, leisure
		ŋ	ring, anger, drink
		'	[see explanatory note below and also *Foreign sounds* below]
ər	perhaps, murder		

A

abasement (ə bās' mənt) *n.* Condition of being put down or humbled

abash (ə bash') *v.* To make ashamed or ill at ease

abate (ə bāt') *v.* To lessen; to put an end to

abhorred (əb hôrd') *adj.* Something that is regarded with horror or loathing

abjure (əb jo͞or') *v.* To vow to give up; repudiate

ablution (ab lo͞o' shən) *n.* Washing or cleansing of the body

abstract (ab' strakt) *n.* Brief summary stating main points

acanthus (ə kan' thəs) *n.* Thistlelike plant

accede (ak sēd') *v.* (With to) To yield to; agree upon

accursed (ə kʉr' sid) *adj.* Hateful

acrid (ak' rid) *adj.* Sharp; bitter

adamantine (ad' ə man' tēn) *adj.* Unbreakable

adjure (əjoor') *v.* To appeal to earnestly

advert (ad vʉrt') *v.* To call attention

affectation (af' ek tā' shən) *n.* Pretense

affected (ə fek' tid) *adj.* In a manner not true to the person

affliction (ə flik' shən) *n.* State of pain or misery, pain; suffering

aggrandizement (ə gran' diz mənt) *n.* Increase in power

alacrity (ə lak' rə tē) *n.* Willingness

allure (ə lo͞or') *v.* To entice; charm; induce

amaranth (am' ə ranth') *n.* Imaginary flower that never fades or dies

amass (ə mas') *v.* To gather together

amity (am'ə tē) *n.* Peaceful relations

anarchy (an' ər kē) *n.* Absence of government; confusion, disorder, and violence

anglophobia (aŋ glə fō' bē ə) *n.* Hatred or fear of England or things English

animadversion (an' ə mad vʉr' zhən) *n.* Unfavorable comment

anointed (ə noint' id) *adj.* Declared sacred

anterior (an tir' ē ər) *adj.* At or toward the front

antiquity (an tik' wə tē) *n.* Ancient times

apace (ə pās') *adv.* Swiftly: with speed

aperture (ap' ər chər) *n.* An opening

apostate (ə pas tāt') *adj.* Denying former religious conviction

apothecary (ə päth' ə ker ē) *n.* A pharmacist or druggist; person who formerly prepared drugs

apparition (ap' ə rish' ən) *n.* A ghost

appendage (ə pen' dij) *n.* Something added on

application (ap' lə kā' shən) *n.* A specific act or case

apprehension (ap rə hen' shən) *n.* Fear, concern

appropriate (ə prō' prē āt') *v.* To borrow without giving credit

arbiter (är' bə tər) *n.* Judge, umpire

arboreal (är bôr' ē əl) *adj.* Situated near or among trees

ardor (är' dər) *n.* Great warmth or intensity of passion, emotion, desire and so forth

armament (är mə mənt) *n.* Arm, weapon

ascendancy (ə send' ən sē) *n.* A major or dominating influence

aspire (ə spīr') *v.* To be ambitious

asperity (as per ' ə tē) *n.* Ill temper; irritability

asphodel (as' fə del') *n.* Plant with yellow or white lilylike flowers

1433

assay (a sā') *v.* To try, attempt; prove or test
assiduity (as ə dyo͞o' ə tē) *n.* Diligence
assignation (as' ig nā' shən) *n.* An appointment to meet
asunder (ə sun' dər) *adv.* Apart; in separate directions
atrophy (a' trə fē) *v.* To waste away
augment (ôg me' nt) *v.* To make greater; enlarge
august (ô gust') *adj.* Inspiring awe and reverence
austere (ô stir') *adj.* Having a stern personality or appearance; somber
avarice (av' ər is) *n.* Greed
aver (ə vʉr') *v.* To state to be true
avocation (av' ə kā' shən) *n.* Something that calls one away or distracts from something
avouch (ə vouch') *v.* To assert positively; affirm
avow (ə vou') *v.* To swear
awe (ô) *n.* Fear mixed with great respect
azurous (az' ər əs) *adj.* Purple-blue

B

baleful (bāl fəl) *adj.* Of or with evil intent
balm (bäm) *n.* Anything healing or soothing
balustrade (bal' ə strād') *n.* A railing supported by small pillars of stone or wood
baneful (bān' fəl) *adj.* Full of harm; destructive
barbarous (bär' bər əs) *adj.* Primitive; uncivilized
barrow (bar' ō) *n.* Heap of earth or rocks marking a grave
Beelzebub (bē el' zə bub') *n.* Traditionally, the chief devil, or Satan
beget (bi get') *v.* To bring into being
belie (bi lī') *v.* To prove false; contradict
benison (ben' ə z'n) *n.* Blessing; benediction
bent (bent) *adj.* Determined; resolved
beseech (bi sēch') *v.* To ask earnestly; entreat; implore
betokeneth (bi tō' k'n eth) *v.* To be a sign of; to indicate
blasphemous (blăs' fə məs) *adj.* Disrespectful of God; impious
blight (blīt) *n.* Condition of withering
blithe (blīth) *adj.* Cheerful
boatswain (bō' s'n) *n.* Warrant officer or petty officer in charge of a ship's deck crew, rigging, and anchors
bole (bōl) *n.* Tree trunk
boon (bo͞on) *n.* Something good or pleasant that is given, as a blessing
brazen (brā' z'n) *adj.* 1. Made of brass; 2. bold; shameless
brazen (brā' z'n) *v.* To dare boldly or shamelessly
burnished (bʉr' nishd) *adj.* Made shiny by daily use

C

caitiff (kāt' if) *n.* Evil person
canker (kaŋ' kər) *n.* Ulcer-like sore on the lips or in the mouth
cant (kant) *n.* Insincere talk
caprice (kə prēs') *n.* A tendency to act on whim
careen (kə rēn) *v.* To lean to one side
career (kə rir') *v.* To move swiftly forward
carriage (kar' ij) *n.* A way of bearing oneself; deportment
casement (kās' mənt) *n.* A window that is hinged at the sides
castigation (kas' tə gā shən) *n.* A punishment
cataract (kat' ə rakt') *n.* A waterfall
cavil (kav' 'l) *v.* To raise trivial objections
certitude (sʉr' tə to͞od) *n.* A certainty
chaffinch (chaf' finch') *n.* Small European songbird
chary (cher' ē) *adj.* Not giving freely
chastise (chas tīz') *v.* To condemn sharply; scold
chide (chīd) *v.* To scold; rebuke
chimerical (ki mir' i k'l) *adj.* Imaginary; unreal
choleric (käl' ər ik) *adj.* Easily provoked to anger
chrysalis (kris' əs) *n.* A cocoon of a butterfly
churl (chʉrl) *n.* 1. *same as* ceorl; farm laborer; peasant; 2. Surly, ill-bred person; boor
circumscribe (sʉr' kəm skrīb') *v.* To limit; confine
circumspection (sʉr' kəm spek' shən) *n.* Caution
clamorous (klam' ər əs) *adj.* Noisy
cleave (klēv) *v.* Split apart
cloyed (kloid) *adj.* Made sick by an overdose
cluster (klus' tər) *n.* A group, gathering; bunch, as of grapes for wine
cockle (käk' 'l) *n.* An edible shellfish with two heart-shaped shells
colonnade (käl' ə nād') *n.* A series of columns set at regular intervals
colossal (kə läs 'l) *adj.* Enormous
compact (kəm pakt') *v.* To put together
complaisance (kəm plā' z'ns) *n.* A desire to be agreeable
compose (kəm pōz') *v.* To get oneself together emotionally; calm
compound (käm' pound) *v.* To join; combine
compunctious (kəm punk shəs) *adj.* Sorrowful; regretful
conciliatory (ken sil' ē ə tôr' ē) *adj.* Agreeable
condone (kən dōn') *v.* To approve; authorize
conflagration (kän' flə grā' shən) *n.* A great fire
conjecture (kən jek' chər) *v.* To guess
constant (kän' stənt) *adj.* Faithful; unchanging; unceasing
constitution (kän' stə to͞o' shən) *n.* Makeup (of a person)
consummation (kän' sə mā' shən) *n.* State of fulfillment or completion
consumed (kən so͞om'd') *adj.* Overtaken, overwhelmed
contention (kən ten' shən) *n.* A controversy; dispute
contentious (kən ten' shəs) *adj.* Of questionable validity
contretemps (kōn trə tän') *n.* An awkward mishap
contrite (kən trīt') *adj.* Willing to repent or atone
conviction (kən vik' shən) *n.* A belief in something meaningful, such as a creed
convulse (kən vuls') *v.* To shake; move violently
coomb (ko͞om) *n.* A deep, narrow valley
copious (kō' pē əs) *adj.* Abundant, plentiful
coquet (kō ket') *v.* To flirt
corporeal (kôr pôr' ē əl) *adj.* Of the body
countenance (koun' tə nəns) *n.* A face
coupe (ko͞o pā') *n.* A closed carriage with seats on one side
courtier (kôr' tē ər) *n.* An attendant at a royal court
covenant (kuv' ə nənt) *n.* A solemn, binding agreement

covetousness (kur′ it əs nəs) *n.* Greediness
cowed (koud) *adj.* Made to feel timid or fearful
coy (koi) *adj.* Unwilling to make a commitment, *not* the modern sense of "pretending to be shy."
credulity (krə dōō′ lə tē) *n.* Tendency to believe too readily
crimp (krimp) *v.* To shape; crease
cryptogram (krip′ tə gram) *n.* A coded message
cur (kur) *n.* A dog of mixed breeds
curb (kurb) *n.* Chain or strap around a horse's lower jaw attached to the bit to check the horse
curlew (kur′ lōō) *n.* Large, brownish wading bird with long legs
cynical (sin′ i k'l) *adj.* Distrustful; sneering

D

dah (dä) *n.* A knife
dais (dā′ is) *n.* A platform
dale (dāl) *n.* A hollow; valley
dappled (dap′ 'ld) *adj.* Speckled; having more than one color
dauntless (dônt′ lis) *adj.* Fearless
decamp (di kamp′) *v.* To leave suddenly
decrepitude (di krep′ ə tōōd) *n.* State of being old and broken down
deference (def′ ər əns) *n.* Courtesy
degree (di grē′) *n.* Social class
deign (dān) *v.* To condescend; lower oneself
deleterious (del′ə tir′ ē əs) *adj.* Harmful to health; injurious
demesne (di mān′) *n.* The lands of an estate
deride (di rīd′) *v.* To make fun of; ridicule
descant (des kant′) *v.* To talk at length
desist (di zist′) *v.* To stop
desolate (des′ ə lit) *adj.* Deserted; forlorn
despoil (di spoil′) *v.* To take away one's possessions
despotic (de spät′ ik) *adj.* Tyrannical
destitute (des′ tətōōt) *adj.* Lacking
desultory (des′ 'l tôr ē) *adj.* Passing from point to point aimlessly
didactic (dī dak′ tik) *adj.* Instructive
diffidence (dif′ə dəns) *n.* Shyness; hesitation
diffusive (di fyōō′ siv) *adj.* Spread out
dirge (durj) *n.* A song of mourning
disabused (dis′ə byōōzd′) *adj.* Freed from false ideas
discourse (dis kôrs′) *v.* To talk about; discussing
discreet (dis krēt′) *adj.* Wise; prudent
discursive (dis kur′ siv) *adj.* Reaching conclusions by a series of logical steps, as opposed to intuition
dispensation (dis pən sā′ shən) *n.* Religious system or belief
distemper (dis tem′ pər) *n.* Infectious disease, in this case the plague
divers (dī′ vərz) *adj.* Varied; having many parts (archaic spelling)
diversion (də vər′ zhən) *n.* A pastime; amusement
divination (div′ ə nā′ shən) *n.* A clever guess
divining (də vīn′ iŋ) *adj.* Guessing; intuitive
doleful (dōl′ fəl) *adj.* Filled with sadness
dominion (də min′ yən) *n.* A place of rule; home territory
dotage (dōt′ ij) *n.* Second childhood, state of senility
doughty (dout′ ē) *adj.* Brave
dower (dou′ ər) *n.* A gift
dowry (dôu′ rē) *n.* The property that a woman brings to her husband at marriage
drear (drir) *adj.* Dreary; melancholy
dregs (dregz) *n.* Sediment of liquids
dryad (drī əd) *n.* In classical mythology, a wood nymph
dudgeon (duj′ ən) *n.* Angry resentment; rage
dulcimer (dul′ sə mər) *n.* Musical instrument with metal strings which produce sounds when struck by two small hammers
dun (dun) *adj.* Dull grayish brown
dunt (dunt) *n.* Heavy, dull-sounding blow

E

eglantine (eg′ lən tīn) *n.* Sweetbrier or honeysuckle
elocution (el′ ə kyōō′ shən) *n.* The art of public speaking
elongated (i lôŋ′ gāt id) *adj.* Lengthened; stretched
eloquent (el′ ə kwənt) *adj.* Very expressive
empyreal (em pir′ ē əl) *adj.* **substance** Indestructible substance of which Heaven, or the empyrean, is composed
encomium (en kō′ mē əm) *n.* The formal expression of praise or tribute
encumber (in kum′ bər) *v.* To weigh down with a load
engender (in jen′ dər) *v.* To bring into being; cause to exist
entreat (in trēt′) *v.* To beg; plead
envisage (en viz′ ij) *v.* To form a mental picture of; imagine
equipage (ek′ wə pij) *n.* Horses and carriages
equivocate (i kwiv′ ə kāt′) *v.* To tell falsehoods
escritoire (es′ krə twär′) *n.* An ornamental writing desk or table
eternize (i tur′ nīz) *v.* To make everlasting
evanescence (ev′ ə nes′ 'ns) *n.* Gradual disappearance, especially from sight
even (ē′ vən) *adj.* Parallel; on the same level with; conforming to
exact (ig zakt′) *v.* To demand; compel
exorciser (ek′ sôr sīz′ ər) *n.* A sorcerer; magician
expanse (ik spans′) *n.* A wide, continuous stretch, as of land
expedient (ik spē′ dē ənt) *n.* Device used in an emergency
expiate (ek′ spē āt′) *v.* To make amends for; atone for; forgive, absolve
expostulate (ik späs′ chə lāt) *v.* To reason earnestly with
extradition (eks′ trə dish′ ən) *n.* The release of an accused person into the custody of one state by another state

F

faceted (fas′ ə tid) *adj.* Having many sides
fathom (fath′ əm) *n.* A unit of measure for the depth of water; a fathom is six feet
fastidious (fas tid′ ē əs) *adj.* Hard to please
feign (fānd) *v.* To pretend
felicity (fə lis′ə tē) *n.* An apt expression or thought
fen (fen) *n.* Marsh or bog
fettered (fet′ ə r'd) *adj.* Chained; confined
fickle (fik′ 'l) *adj.* Unfaithful

1435

firmament (fɘr′mə mənt) *n.* Sky, viewed poetically as a solid arch or vault
firth (fɘrth) *n.* The narrow arm of a sea
fleur-de-lys (flɘr′ də lēz′) *n.* An emblem resembling a lily or iris
fluency (flōō′ ən sē) *n.* Easy flow; smoothness
fold (fōld) *n.* Pen in which to keep sheep
folly (fäl′ ē) *n.* A foolish action or belief
foment (fō ment′) *v.* To stir up; incite
fond (fänd) *adj.* Archaic: Foolish, not the modern sense of having affection for someone or something
foreshortened (fôr shor′ t'nd) *adj.* Narrowed by observer's angle of vision
forethink (for think′) *v.* To foretell; predict
forlorn (fər lôrn′) *adj.* Unhappy; in a pensive mood
former (fôr mər) *adj.* Earlier; coming before
fret (fretz) *v.* To eat away
frolic (fräl′ ik) *adj.* Merry
furbished (fɘr′ bishd) *adj.* Brightened; polished
furlong (fɘr loŋ) *n.* A unit for measuring distance; a furlong is equal to one eighth of a mile
fustian (fus′ chən) *n.* A coarse cotton cloth

G

gaiters (gāt′ ər) *n.* Cloth coverings for the instep and lower leg
gall (gôl) *n.* Something bitter or distasteful
galled (gôld) *adj.* Injured or made sore by rubbing or chafing
gang (gaŋ) *v.* To go or walk (Scot.)
garnished (gär′ nisht) *adj.* Decorated; trimmed
garrulous (gar′ ə ləs) *adj.* Tending to talk continuously
gaudy (gôd′ ē) *adj.* Showy in a tasteless way
gaunt (gônt) *adj.* Thin
genial (jēn′ yəl) *adj.* Kindly, cordial
gesticulate (jes tik′ yə lāt′) *v.* To communicate excitedly by gestures
gigantified (jī gan′ tə fīd) *adj.* Made to seem much larger
gisarme (gi zärm′) *n.* A battle-ax
glean (glēn) *v.* To pick from, as crops
glen (glen) *n.* A valley
grace (grās) *n.* God's favor or approval
grate (grāt) *n.* Frame of metal bars used as a partition
gratuitous (grə tōō′ ə təs) *adj.* Undeservedly or without reason
guerdon (gɘr′ d'n) *n.* A reward
guile (gīl) *n.* Artful trickery; cunning

H

habitation (hab′ə tā′ shən) *n.* A home; dwelling
habituate (hə bich′ oo wāt′) *v.* To accustome to; to make used to
haft (haft) *n.* Handle of a weapon or tool
haggard (hag′ ə rd) *adj.* Having a worn, gaunt, or wild look
halcyon (hal′ sē ən) *adj.* Calm
halter (hôl′ tər) *n.* Rope for hanging; hangman's noose
haply (hap′ lē) *adv.* By chance
harbinger (här′ bin jər) *n.* A forerunner
harmonious (här mō′ nē əs) *adj.* In a manner that is in accordance
harry (har′ ē) *v.* To harass
hauberk (hô′ bərk) *n.* A coat of armor
haughty (hôt′ ē) *adj.* Lofty
headrig (hed′ rig) *n.* The part of a plow that turns over the soil; moldboard
health (helth) *n.* A wish for happiness, as in drinking a series of toasts
heraldic (hə ral′ dik) *adj.* Resembling an English coat of arms
hermitage (hɘr′ mit ij) *n.* A retreat suitable for meditation; originally, a hermit's dwelling
hew (hyōō) *n.* Color; hue
hoary (hôr′ ē) *adj.* White or gray with age
hobnailed (häb′ nāld) *adj.* Studded with nails to prevent wear or slipping
husbandry (huz′ bən drē) *n.* Farming

I

ignominy (ig′ nə min′ ē) *n.* Humiliation; dishonor; disgrace
illimitable (i lim′ it ə b'l) *adj.* Without limit or bounds; immeasurable
illumine (i lōō′ min) *v.* To light up
imminent (im′ə nənt) *adj.* Likely to happen soon
impaired (im per′ d) *v.* Diminished
imperiously (im pir′ ē əs lē) *adv.* Arrogantly
impertinence (im pɘr′ t'n əns) *n.* Rudeness
imperturbable (im′ pər tɘr′ bə b'l) *adj.* Calm; not easily ruffled
impetuous (im pech′ oo wəs) *adj.* Given to rash or hasty action; doing things on the spur of the moment; tending to act impulsively, without thinking
impious (im′ pē əs) *adj.* Disrespectful; irreverent, ungodly
importune (im′ pôr tōōn′) *v.* To press with frequent requests; ask insistently
importuning (im pôr tōōn′ iŋ) *v.* Begging; urging
imprecation (im′ prə kā′ shən) *n.* A curse
impressionistic (im presh′ ə nis′ tik) *adj.* Conveying a quick, overall picture
impudence (im′ pyōō dəns) *n.* The quality of being rash or contrary
inarticulate (in′ är tik′ yə lit) *adj.* Not able to speak
incessant (in ses′ 'nt) *adj.* Never ceasing
incitement (in sīt′ mənt) *n.* A cause to perform; encouragement
inconstancy (in kän′ stən sē) *n.* A contradiction; fickleness; changeableness
incorrigible (in kôr i jə b'l) *adj.* Not capable of being corrected or of behaving better
inculcate (in kul′ kāt) *v.* To impress upon the mind by frequent repetition
indissoluble (in di säl′ yoo b'l) *adj.* Not able to be dissolved or undone
inenarrable (in en′ ər ə b'l) *adj.* Indescribable
inexorable (in ek′ sər ə b'l) *adj.* Ongoing, with no sign of stopping
infirmity (in fɘr′ mə tē) *n.* Physical or mental defect; illness
ingenuous (in jen′ yoo wəs) *adj.* Naive; simple
inglorious (in glôr′ ē əs) *adj.* Little-known
inimical (in im′ i k'l) *adj.* Hostile; unfriendly
iniquity (in ik′ wə tē) *n.* Wickedness
innumerable (in nōō′ mər ə b'l) *adj.* Too many to count

1436

inordinate (in ôr′ d'n it) *adj.* Beyond reasonable limits
inquisition (in′ kwə zish′ ən) *n.* Any investigation that violates the privacy or rights of individuals
insipid (in sip′ id) *adj.* Not exciting or interesting dull, lifeless
intemperance (in tem′ pər əns) *n.* A lack of restraint
intermit (in tər mit′) *v.* To stop for a time
intimation (in′ tə mā′ shən) *n.* A hint
inventory (in′ vən tôr′ ē) *n.* A list of possessions
invincible (in vin′ səb'l) *adj.* Unconquerable
irascibly (i ras′ə b'lē) *adv.* Irritably
irremediable (ir i mē′ dē ə b'l) *adj.* incurable; incapable of being remedied
irrepressible (ir′ i pres′ ə b'l) *adj.* Not able to be restrained
isthmus (is′ məs) *n.* A narrow strip of land, with water on each side, connecting two larger land massses

J

japonica (jə pän′ i kə) *n.* A spiny plant with pink or red flowers
jocund (jäk′ ənd) *adj.* Cheerful; pleasant; jovial
judicious (jo͞o dish′ əs) *adj.* Having or showing good judgment

K

keen (kēn) *adj.* Having a sharp edge or point
ken (ken) *n.* The range of sight or knowledge
ketch (kech) *n.* A two-masted sailing vessel
kindred (kin′ drid) *n.* Relatives; relations
knave (nāv) *n.* A scoundrel; cheater
knell (nel) *n.* The sound of a bell, especially one rung slowly, as at funeral
kraal (kräl) *n.* A fenced-in enclosure for cattle or sheep

L

laboriously (lə bôr′ ē əs lē) *adv.* In a manner involving much hard work
laden (lād′ 'n) *adj.* Burdened; weighed down
lament (lə ment′) *v.* To mourn; wail; bemoan
lamentable (lam′ ən tə b'l) *adj.* Distressing
languid (laŋ′ gwid) *adj.* Slow, lacking energy
languish (laŋ′ gwish) *v.* To become weak or sickly looking
languor (laŋ′ gər) *n.* Weakness, fatigue
largess (lär′jes′) *n.* Generous gift
largesse (lär′ jes) *n.* A nobility of spirit
lark (lärk′) *v.* To play around
laryngoscope (lə riŋ′ gō skōp′) *n.* An instrument for examining the throat
lay (lā) *n.* A short poem to be sung
leviathan (lə vī′ ə thən) *n.* A great sea monster
lexicographer (lek′ sə käg′ rə fər) *n.* One who compiles a dictionary
liege (lēj) *n.* A lord or king
lintel (lin′ t'l) *n.* A beam over a door
litany (lit′′ nē) *n.* A form of prayer in which a congregation repeats a fixed response
loath (lōth) *adj.* Reluctant; unwilling
lucrative (lo͞o′ krə tiv) *adj.* Profitable
luminescent (loo mə nes′ 'nt) *adj.* Giving out light without much heat
lyric (lir′ ik) *n.* A poem, one of the major categories of poetry; in classical literature, a song accompanied by a lyre

M

madrigal (mad′ ri gəl) *n.* A song with parts for several voices with no musical accompaniment
magnanimous (mag an′ ə məs) *adj.* Generously forgiving
mahout (mə ho͞ot′) *n.* An elephant keeper and rider
mail (māl) *n.* A flexible body armor made of metal
maize (māz) *n.* Corn
malevolence (mə lev′ə ləns) *n.* Ill will; spitefulness
malign (mə līn′) *v.* To speak evil of; defame
malignity (mə lig′ nə tē) *n.* A strong desire to harm others; deadliness
manifold (man′ ə fōld′) *adj.* Of many kinds; varied
mead-hall (mēd′ hôl) *n.* A banquet hall; mead is a beverage made from fermented honey and water
measure (mezh′ ər) *n.* A quantity, dimension, size
megalith (meg′ ə lith′) *n.* A huge stone, especially one used in prehistoric monuments
melancholy (mel′ ən käl′ ē) *n.* Sadness; lowness of spirit
mendacity (men das′ ə tē) *n.* Lying
mesmerism (m z′ mər iz′m) *n.* Hypnotism
mestizo (mes tē′ zō) *adj.* Of Spanish and Indian parentage
metaphysical (met ə fiz′ i k'l) *adj.* Very abstract
mettlesome (met′ 'l səm) *adj.* High-spirited
minion (min′ yən) *n.* Attendant or agent
miscreant (mis′ rē ənt) *n.* A villian
misanthropist (mis an′ thrə pist) *n.* One who hates or mistrusts others
modish (mōd′ ish) *adj.* Fashionable
moleskin (mōl′ skin) *n.* Work clothes made from strong, twilled cotton fabric
molt (mōlt) *v.* Cast off; shed, as skin or feathers
moly (mō′ lē) *n.* In classical mythology, an herb of magic powers; European wild garlic
moorline (moor′ līn) *n.* The horizon where open, rolling wasteland meets the sky
morosely (mə rōs′ lē) *adv.* Sullenly; in bad humor
mortification (môr′ tə fi kā′ shən) *n.* A feeling of great shock and upset
multitudinous (mul′ tə to͞od′ 'n əs) *adj.* Existing in great numbers
munificence (myoo nif′ə s'ns) *n.* Great generosity
myriad (mir′ ē d) *n.* Ten thousand; a great number of things
myrrh (mur) *n.* A plant that produces a fragrant gum resin used in making incense and perfume

N

nativity (nə tiv′ ə tē′) *n.* A birth, especially in regard to place and time
nunnery (nun′ ər ē) *n.* A convent, a dwelling place for nuns
nymph (nimf) *n.* In classical mythology, a minor nature goddess usually shown as a lovely young girl

O

obdurate (äb′ door ət, äb dyoor ət) *adj.* Hardened against what is good or moral; stubborn, unyielding
obliquely (ə blēk′ lē) *adv.* At a slant

obliterate (ə blit'ə rāt) *v.* To destroy utterly
obstinacy (äb' stə nə sē) *n.* Stubbornness
ode (ōd) *n.* A poem of varying line lengths and usually several stanzas, often addressed to someone; in classical literature, a poem to be sung, usually in praise of someone
odious (ō' dē ə s) *adj.* Exciting repugnance or aversion; abhorrent; hateful; offensive; disgusting
officious (ə fish' əs) *adj.* Overly eager to please (obsolete meaning); offering unnecessary advice or services
ope (ōp) *v.* To open
opiate (ō' pe it) *n.* Something that brings on relaxation or sleep
oppress (ə pres') *v.* To burden
oracle (ôr' ə k'l) *n.* In classical antiquity, the shrine in which a god spoke through a priest or priestess
orderly (ôr' dər lē) *n.* A soldier assigned to carry out orders of a superior
ordure (ôr' jər) *n.* Waste matter; excrement
ostentation (äs' tən tā' shən) *n.* A showy display
overplus (ō' vər plus') *n.* A surplus, abundance; enough over for others
overscrupulous (ō' vər skro͞o' pyə ləs) *adj.* Overly concerned about details

P

pallor (pal' ər) *n.* An unnatural lack of color; paleness
palpable (pal' pə b'l) *adj.* Capable of being touched or felt
panegyric (pan'ə jir' ik) *n.* A speech giving praise
parapet (par' ə pit) *n.* A low wall or railing
parley (pär' lē) *n.* A discussion
parquet (pär kā') *n.* A flooring of inlaid woodwork in geometric forms; wooden floors
pastoral (pas' tər al) *adj.* Pertaining to country life
patron (pā' trən) *n.* One who gives financial aid to an artist or writer
penetralia (pen' ə trā lē ə) *n.* The innermost parts
penitent (pen' ə tənt) *adj.* Feeling or showing sorrow for one's misdeeds or sins
penury (pen' yə rē) *n.* Poverty
perchance (pər chans') *adv.* Perhaps, possibly
peremptorily (pə remp' tə ri lē) *adv.* Decisively; without showing cause
perfidious (pər fid' ē əs) *adj.* Disloyal; treacherous
perfidiousness (pər fid' ē əs nis) *n.* The betrayal of trust
perfunctorily (pər fuŋk' tə ri lē) *adv.* Carelessly
periwig (per' ə wig') *n.* A type of wig often worn by men during the seventeenth and eighteenth centuries
pernicious (pər nish' əs) *adj.* Causing serious injury; deadly; evil; wicked
perpetual (pər pech' o͞o wəl) *adj.* Constant, unending
persistent (pər sis' tənt) *adj.* Continuing
perturbation (pʉr' tər bā' shən) *n.* A disorder
peruke (pə ro͞ok') *n.* A wig.
perversity (pər vʉr' sə tē) *n.* State of being wicked or wrong
perverted (pər vʉr' tid) *adj.* Distorted; corrupted
pestilence (pes' t'l əns) *n.* A highly contagious disease, such as plague
petulance (pech' o͞o ləns) *n.* Insolent behavior; peevishness; moodiness

phantasm (fan' taz'm) *n.* A supernatural form or shape
phlegm (flem) *n.* Sluggishness
phoenix (fē' niks) *n.* A fabled bird of Arabia said to consume itself by fire every five hundred years and to rise renewed from its own ashes
phosphorescence (fäs' fə res' 'ns) *n.* The property of shining in the dark
physiognomy (fiz' ē äg' nə mē) *n.* Facial features thought to reveal character or disposition
piazza (pē az' ə) *n.* An open public square
piety (pī'ə tē) *n.* Devotion
pike (pīk) *n.* A voracious freshwater fish
pince-nez (pans' nā') *n.* Eyeglasses without sidepieces, held in place by springs gripping the bridge of the nose
pirouett (pir' o͞o wet') *v.* To dance or whirl on one foot
pithead (pit' hed) *n.* The top of a mining pit or coal shaft
plagiarism (plā' jə riz'm) *n.* The passing off another's work as one's own
platitude (plat' ə to͞od') *n.* A statement lacking originality
plebian (pli bē' ən) *adj.* Common; ordinary
plutocracy (plo͞o tŏk' rə sē) *n.* The wealthy governing class
poke (pōk) *n.* An overhanging projection, such as the brim on a woman's poke bonnet
portal (pôr' t'l) *n.* A door; gateway
posy (pō' zē) *n.* A bouquet
prate (prāt') *v.* To talk much and foolishly
prau (prau) *n.* A swift Malayan boat with a large sail
prebendary (preb' ən der' ē) *n.* In the Church of England, honorary clergyman
precedency (pres' ə dən sē) *n.* Priority because of rank
precipitate (pri sip' ə tit) *adj.* Steep
predominance (pri däm' ə nans) *n.* Superiority
preferment (pri fʉr' mənt) *n.* An advancement in rank
pregnant (preg' nənt) *adj.* Full of ideas; inventive
premonition (prē mə nish' ən) *n.* A warning in advance
premonitory (pri män' ə tôr' ē) *adj.* Giving warning beforehand
presume (pri zo͞om') *v.* To suppose
presumptuous (pri zump' cho͞o wəs) *adj.* Unduly confident or bold
pretence (pri tens') *n.* A claim (British spelling)
pretension (pri ten' shən) *n.* A claim to a rank or class
pretentious (pri ten' shəs) *adj.* Making false claims
preternatural (prēt' ər nach' ər əl) *adj.* Outside the natural or normal order
prevarication (pri var ə kā' shən) *n.* An evasion of truth
prime (prīm) *n.* The best stage or time; most mature period
pristine (pris' tēn) *adj.* Pure; untouched; unspoiled
prodigal (präd' i gəl) *adj.* Addicted to wasteful expenditure
prodigious (prə dij' əs) *adj.* Enormous; hugh; impressive
profuse (prə fyo͞os') *adj.* Abundant, pouring out

progeny (präj′ ə nē) *n.* Offspring; a child
promiscuously (prə mis′ kyoo wəs lē) *adv.* Without care or thought
promontory (präm′ ən tôr′ ē) *n.* The land that juts out into a body of water; high point of land extending into the sea
propagator (präp′ə gāt′ ər) *n.* One who causes something to happen or to spread
prophesy (prŏf′ ə sī) *v.* Predict
prophetic (prə fet′ ik) *adj.* Having the power to predict or foreshadow
propitiate (prə pish′ ēāt′) *v.* Ease the burden of; appease
prostrate (präs′ trāt) *adj.* Defenseless; in a prone or lying position
protracted (prō trak′ tid) *v.* Drawn out; prolonged
providence (präv′ ə dens) *n.* Divine forethought, guidance, and care; also, God
provoking (prə vōk′ iŋ) *adj.* Annoying, irritating
prow (prou) *n.* The front of a boat
prudence (proōd′ ′ns) *n.* Care in avoiding errors; discretion
puissant (pyoō′ i sənt) *adj.* Powerful
pulverous (pul′ və rəs) *adj.* Crumbling
pumice (pum′ is) *n.* A volcanic rock

Q

quay (kē) A wharf with facilities for loading or unloading ships

R

raiment (rā mənt) *n.* Clothing
Raj (raj) *n.* Rule
rapture (rap′ chər) *n.* An expression of great joy
ravish (rav′ ish) *v.* To violate
recompense (rek′ əm pens′) *n.* A payment in return; reward
reconcile (rek′ ən sīl′) *v.* To make up with
recreant (rek′ rē ənt) *adj.* Cowardly
rectify (rek′ tə fī) *v.* To set right; correct
refractory (ri frak′ tər ē) *adj.* Hard to manage; stubborn
refulgent (ri ful′ jənt) *adj.* Shining; radiant
remonstrance (ri män′ strəns) *n.* A protest
remonstrate (ri män′ strāt) *v.* To object strongly
repose (ri pōz′) *v.* Lie back
repository (ri päz′ ə tôr ē) *n.* A center for accumulation and storage
repudiation (ri pyoō′ dē ā′ shən) *n.* A rejection; denial
requiem (rek′ wē əm) *n.* Dirge or mass for the dead; Musical composition or service honoring the dead
respite (res′ pit) *n.* A postponement; delay
resplendently (ri splen′ dənt lē) *adj.* Splendidly, gorgeously
reticent (ret′ ə s′nt) *adj.* Laid back; uncommunicative
retort (ri tôrt′) *n.* A comeback with a smart answer or wisecrack
retreat (ri trēt′) *n.* A period of retirement or seclusion for prayer, religious study, and meditation
reverence (rev′ ər əns) *n.* A great respect; deep respect or awe
reverie (rev′ ər ē) *n.* A daydream
righteousness (rī′ chəs nis) *n.* Doing what is fair and just
rill (ril) *n.* A little brook
rime (rīm) *n.* A white frost
rioter (rī′ ət ər) *n.* A loud, dissolute bully
rostral (räs′ trəl) *adj.* Having a beaklike projection, or rostrum, as at the prow of a ship
rout (rout) *n.* An overwhelming defeat
rue (roō) *n.* Sorrow
ruminate (roo′ mə nāt) *v.* To think over; meditate
rummage (rum′ ij) *v.* To search by thoroughly examining

S

sacramented (sak′ r ment id) *adj.* Having the properties of religious rites or rituals
sagacity (sə gas′ə tē) *n.* Wisdom: judgment
salient (sāl′ yənt) *adj.* Striking; easily noticeable
salver (sal′ vər) *n.* A tray usually used for the presentation of letters or visiting cards
sampan (sam′pan) *n.* A small flat-bottomed boat with a cabin formed by mats
sanguinary (saŋ′ gwi ner′ ē) *adj.* Bloody
sanguine (san′ gwin) *adj.* Of cheerful temperament
sarong (sə rôŋ′) *n.* A long, brightly colored strip of cloth worn like a skirt
satiety (sə tī′ ə tē) *n.* State of being filled to excess
saturnine (sat′ ər nīn) *adj.* Sluggish or gloomy
schism (siz′ ′m) *n.* A division into groups or factions
screed (skrēd) *n.* A long, tiresome piece of writing
scutcheon (skuch′ ən) *n.* A coat of arms
segmented (seg′ ment id) *adj.* Separated into parts
semblance (sem′ bləns) *n.* Appearance; image
senility (si nil′ ə tē) *n.* Mental and physical decay due to old age
sepulcher (sep′ ′lək r) *n.* A tomb
sequacious (si kwā′ shəs) *adj. (Archaic.)* Tending to follow dutifully, in service of
sequester (si kwes′ tərd) *v.* To keep apart from others
Seraphim (sĕr′ ə fim) *n.* The highest order of angels
serrated (ser′ āt əd) *adj.* Toothed or notched like a saw
servile (sʉr′ v′l) *adj.* Slavelike
severance (sev′ ərəns) *n.* State of being kept separate
shard (shärd) *n.* A fragment or broken pieces
sheaf (shēf) *n.* A bundle of twigs or fibers
sibilant (sib′ ′l ənt) *adj.* Hissing
signet (sig′ nit) *n.* A seal
sinecure (sī′ nə kyoōr′) *n.* Any office or position that brings advantage but involves little or no work
sinew (sin′ yoō) *n.* Muscular power; force
sinewy (sin′ yoo wē) *adj.* Tough; vigorous; powerful
sinuous (sin′ yoō əs) *adj.* Winding, twisting; bending; curving in and out
slagheap (slag′ hēp) *n.* A pile of waste material from mining
slumbrous (slum′ brəs) *adj.* Peaceful, suggesting sleep
sock (säk) *n.* The blade of a plow
sojourn (sō′ jʉrn) *v.* To stay for a while
solace (säl′ is) *ı.* A comfort in grief or trouble, relief
solicit (sə lis′ it) *v.* Ask for, plead for
soliloquize (sə lil′ ə kwīz′) *v.* To talk to oneself
somnambulist (säm nam′ byoo list) *n.* A sleepwalker

sophist (säf′ ist) *n.* One who makes misleading arguments
sordid (sor′ did) *adj.* Unclean, dirty
soiree (swä rā′) *n.* Party held in the evening
sophistry (säf′ is trē) *n.* Clever but unsound reasoning
sough (sou) *n.* A groan or sighing sound
sovereign (säv′ rən) *adj.* Supreme in power, rank, or authority
specter (spek′ tər) *n.* A ghost or ghost-like appearance
spectral (spek′ tər) *adj.* Ghostly
spendthrift (spend′ thrift′) *n.* A person who spends money wastefully or foolishly
spent (spent) *adj.* Used up; gone
splaying (splā′ iŋ) *v.* Spreading
sprightly (sprīt′ lē) *adj.* Lively
squalid (skwäl′ id) *adj.* Miserably poor; wretched
squire (skwīr) *n.* A country gentleman or landed proprietor
stagnant (stag′ nənt) *adj.* Standing still, as water
stealthy (stel′ thē) *adj.* In a quiet, secretive way; sly; furtive
steep (stēp) *v.* To become saturated with
stem (stem) *v.* To stop; dam up
stile (stīl) *n.* A step or set of steps used in climbing over a fence or wall
stoic (stō′ ik) *n.* A person indifferent to pleasure or pain
sublimity (sə blim′ ə tē) *n.* The quality of being majestic or noble
subordinate (sə bôr′ də nit) *adj.* Beneath another in rank
subtle (sut′ ′l) *adj.* Cunning; ingenious
succeed (sək sēd) *v.* To follow; come after
succinct (sək siŋkt′) *adj.* Belted (Archaic); Terse
suffuse (sə fyo͞ozd′) *v.* To fill
sullen (sul′ ən) *adj.* Gloomy; dismal
sumpitan (sump′ ə tăn) *n.* A Malayan blowgun which discharges poisonous darts
sundry (sun′ drē) *adj.* Various; miscellaneous
superfluity (so͞o′ pər flo͞o′ ə tē) *n.* An excess
supplant (sə plant′) *v.* To take the place of; supersede
suppliant (sup′ lē ənt) *adj.* Beseeching prayerfully; imploring
supplication (sup′ lə kā′ shən) *n.* The act of praying
surfeit (sʉr′ fit) *n.* Too much of something; an excess
surmise (sər mīz′) *v.* To guess, assume; to form an opinion from inconclusive evidence
swaddling (swäd′ liŋ) *adj.* Long, narrow bands of cloth wrapped around newborn babies
swain (swan) *n.* A country youth
switch (swich) *n.* A light whip
sylvan (sil′ vən) *adj.* Wooded
symmetry (sim′ ə trē) *n.* Beauty resulting from balance of form

T

taffeta (taf′ i tə) *n.* A fine silk fabric
talent (tal′ ənt) *n.* A Biblical unit of money; native ability
tarry (tar′ ē) *v.* To delay, linger, be tardy, abide; continue in the same condition
tawdry (tô′ drē) *adj.* Cheap; gaudy
teeming (tēm′ iŋ) *adj.* Filled to overflowing
temperate (tem′ pər it) *adj.* Exercising moderation and self-restraint
tempest (tem′ pist) *n.* A violent storm accompanied by rain; any violent commotion or tumult, an uproar
tempestuous (tem pes′ cho͝o wəs) *adj.* Turbulent; violently stormy
tenor (ten′ ər) *n.* A general tendency or course
terrestrial (tə res′ trē əl) *adj.* Of this world; earthly
thane (thān) *n.* In early England, a member of a class of freemen who held land of the king or a lord in return for military services
thrall (thrôl) *n.* A slave; serf
timorous (tim′ ər əs) *adj.* Fearful; timid
tincture (tink′ chər) *n.* A tint
tithe (tīth) *n.* One tenth of a person's income, paid as a tax to support the church
tor (tôr) *n.* A high, rocky hill; crag
torrid (tôr′ id) *adj.* Hot, scorching
traffic (traf′ ik) *n.* Business
transcendence (tran sen′ dəns) *n.* A rising above
transfiguration (trans fig yo͝o rā shən) *n.* A change in outward form or appearance
transgress (trans′ gres) *v.* To violate a law or command; overstep or break
transient (tran′ shənt) *adj.* A person who passes quickly through a place
transitory (tran′ sə tôr ē) *adj.* Temporary; fleeting
trefoil (trē′ foil) *n.* Clover
trellis (trel′ is) *n.* A frame of crossed strips, usually of wood, used as a screen or support for climbing plants
tremulous (trem′ yo͝o ləs) *adj.* Trembling; timid
tress (tres) *n.* A lock of human hair
tryst (trist) *n.* A meeting
tuft (tuft) *n.* A grouping of fibers such as hair or grass
tumid (to͞o′ mid) *adj.* Swollen
tumult (to͞o′ mult) *n.* Commotion, disturbance; uproar; noisy confusion
tumultuous (to͝o mul′ cho͝o wəs) *adj.* Disorderly; violent
turbid (tʉr′ bid) *adj.* Muddy or cloudy; confused
turret (tʉr′ it) *n.* A small tower projecting from a building
twa (twä) *n.* Two (Scot.)

U

uncanny (un kan′ ē) *adj.* Mysterious; hard to explain
unctuous (uŋk′ cho͝o wəs) *adj.* Oily
ungenial (un jēn′ yəl) *adj.* Unfriendly; characterized by bad weather
unmitigable (un mit′i gə b′l) *adj.* Not able to be diminished in intensity
unravished (un rav′ ishd) *adj.* Undisturbed, unspoiled
upbraiding (up brād′ iŋ) *n.* Stern words of disapproval for an action; scolding
usurious (yo͞o zho͝or′ ē əs) *adj.* Lending money at a high rate of interest
usurped (yo͞o sʉrp′d′) *adj.* Wrongfully seized

V

vain (vān) *adj.* Foolish; worthless
vair (ver) *n.* A gray and white fur
valance (val′ əns) *n.* A decorative facing

vale (val) *n.* A valley
vanity (van′ ə tē) *n.* A trifle, knicknack, or other insignificant thing
vaunt (vônt) *v.* To speak boastfully
vehemence (vē′ ə məns) *n.* Strength of feeling and emotion
veldt (velt) *n.* Open, grassy country
verdure (vʉr′ jər) *n.* Green plants
verge (vʉrj) *n.* An edge, rim
vestige (ves′ tij) *n.* A trace; bit
vestry (ves′ trē) *n.* A church meeting room
vexation (vek sā′ shən) *n.* An annoyance
vignettes (vin yets) *n.* Decorative designs or borderless pictures in a book
vintage (vin′ tij) *n.* A wine or nectar of high quality
virago (və rā′ gō) *n.* A scolding woman
virtuous (vʉr′ choo wəs) *adj.* Pure, righteous
virulency (vir′ yoo lən sē) *n.* Harmfulness
visage (viz′ ij) *n.* A person's face or facial expression
vis-à-vis (vē′ zə vē′) Face to face with
viscous (vis′ kəs) *adj.* Semifluid; sticky
vizard (viz′ ərd) *n.* A mask

W

wan (wän) *adj.* Sickly pale; (Archaic) Gloomy, not the modern sense of sickly pale
wane (wān′) *v.* To gradually become dimmer
wanton (wän′t′n) *adj.* Luxuriant: said of vegetation; Frisky; playful
wantonness (wän′ t′n nis) *n.* State of being reckless or undisciplined
wanwood (wän′ wood) *n.* A pale wood
wax (waks′) *v.* To grow, ripen
weal (wēl) *n.* A discolored ridge on the skin; blister
whelk (hwelk) *n.* A pimple
wistaria (wis tir′ ē ə) *n.* Vines of shrubs with clusters of bluish, white, pink, or purplish flowers
wit (wit) *n.* Intelligence, wisdom
wrangle (raŋ′ g′l) *v.* To argue noisily and angrily; bicker

Y

yare (yer) *adj.* Ready; prepared
yoke (yōk) *n.* A wooden contrivance joining the heads of two draft animals, such as oxen, to make them capable of pulling heavier loads
ycladd (i klad′) *pp.* Clothed, dressed
yclept (i klept′) *pp.* Called; named

Z

zephyr (zef′ ər) *n.* A gentle wind

INDEX OF FINE ART

INDEX OF SKILLS

ANALYZING LITERATURE

CRITICAL THINKING AND READING

SPEAKING AND LISTENING

STUDY AND RESEARCH

THINKING AND WRITING

UNDERSTANDING LANGUAGE

1451

INDEX OF TITLES BY THEMES

SEARCH FOR JUSTICE AND DIGNITY

EXPERIENCE WITH WAR AND PEACE

INDIVIDUALS AND THE NEED FOR ACCEPTANCE

PASSAGES AND TRANSFORMATIONS

THE INDIVIDUAL AND SOCIETY

JOURNEY TO PERSONAL FULFILLMENT

A TIME FOR COURAGE

FANTASY AND THE UNEXPLAINED

THE ENVIRONMENT AND THE TOUCHED AND UNTOUCHED EARTH

MEN, WOMEN, AND LOVE

1453

VALUES, BELIEFS, AND CONDUCT

ART, LITERATURE, INTELLECT

INDEX OF AUTHORS AND TITLES

Page numbers in italics refer to biographical information.

1457

ACKNOWLEDGMENTS (continued)

Harper & Row, Publishers, Inc. and Faber and Faber Ltd.
"Hawk Roosting" from *New Selected Poems* by Ted Hughes. Copyright © 1959 by Ted Hughes. Published in London in *Lupercal* by Ted Hughes. Reprinted by permission of the publishers.

Alan W. Holden
"Some Men Create" from *To Make Me Grieve* by Molly Holden, Chatto and Windus Ltd. Exclusive copyright Alan Holden.

Henry Holt and Company, Inc.
"Loveliest of trees, the cherry now," "To an athlete dying young," "When I was one-and-twenty," and "With rue my heart is laden" from *The Collected Poems of A. E. Housman*. Copyright © 1965 by Holt, Rinehart and Winston, Inc. Reprinted by permission of Henry Holt and Company, Inc.

Houghton Mifflin Company
Lines from "Childe Harold's Pilgrimage" ("Apostrophe to the Ocean"), lines from "Don Juan," "She Walks in Beauty," and "So We'll Go No More A-Roving" reprinted from *The Complete Poetical Works of Lord Byron*. From "A Voyage to Brobdingnag" and from "A Voyage to Lilliput" reprinted from *Gulliver's Travels and Other Writings* by Jonathan Swift, edited by Louis A. Landa. Riverside Edition. Copyright © 1960 by Houghton Mifflin Company. Used by permission.

Olwyn Hughes
"Anniversary" and "Out" from *The Magic Apple Tree* by Elaine Feinstein. Copyright © 1971 by Elaine Feinstein. Reprinted by permission of Olwyn Hughes.

Alfred A. Knopf, Inc.
"The Demon Lover" copyright 1946 and renewed 1974 by Elizabeth Bowen. Reprinted from *The Demon Lover and Other Stories* by Elizabeth Bowen. "A Dill Pickle" copyright 1920 by Alfred A. Knopf, Inc. and renewed 1948 by John Middleton Murry. Reprinted from *The Short Stories of Katherine Mansfield* by Katherine Mansfield. Reprinted by permission of Alfred A. Knopf, Inc.

Little, Brown and Company, in association with The Atlantic Monthly Press
"A Touch of Autumn in the Air" from *The Collected Stories of Sean O'Faolain* by Sean O'Faolain. Copyright © 1962 by Sean O'Faolain. Reprinted by permission.

Louisiana State University Press
"A Birthday" reprinted from *The Complete Poems of Christina Rossetti*, Volume I, edited by R. W. Crump. Copyright © 1979 by Louisiana State University Press.

Macmillan London Ltd.
"A Song for St. Cecilia's Day" from *The Poetical Works of John Dryden* edited by W. D. Christie. "The Three Strangers" from *Wessex Tales* by Thomas Hardy.

Macmillan Publishing Company
"Ah, Are You Digging on My Grave?," "The Darkling Thrush," and "The Man He Killed" from *The Complete Poems of Thomas Hardy* edited by James Gibson (New York: Macmillan, 1978). This collection was published outside the U.S. by Macmillan (London) Ltd. in 1976.

Macmillan Publishing Company and A. P. Watt Ltd. on behalf of Michael B. Yeats and Macmillan London Ltd.
"The Lake Isle of Innisfree" and "When You Are Old"; "An Irish Airman Foresees His Death" and "The Wild Swans at Coole" copyright 1919 by Macmillan Publishing Company, renewed 1947 by Bertha Georgie Yeats; "The Second Coming" copyright 1924 by Macmillan Publishing Company, renewed 1952 by Bertha Georgie Yeats; "Sailing to Byzantium" copyright 1928 by Macmillan Publishing Company, renewed 1956 by Bertha Georgie Yeats; and "After Long Silence" copyright 1933 by Macmillan Publishing Company, renewed 1961 by Bertha Georgie Yeats. All poems reprinted with permission from *The Poems: A New Edition* by W. B. Yeats, edited by Richard J. Finneran.

The Marvell Press
"Coming" by Philip Larkin is reprinted from *The Less Deceived* by Philip Larkin, by permission of The Marvell Press, England.

Methuen & Company Ltd.
"The Passionate Shepherd to His Love" and lines from "Tragical History of the Life and Death of Dr. Faustus" from *Marlowe's Poems* edited by L. C. Martin. Lines from "An Essay on Man," "Canto III," and lines from "Canto V" reprinted from *The Poems of Alexander Pope* edited by John Butt. Published by Methuen & Co. Ltd., London.

NAL Penguin Inc.
"The Wrath of Grendel" from *Beowulf* translated by Burton Raffel. Copyright © 1963 by Burton Raffel. From *The Tragedy of Macbeth* by William Shakespeare, edited by Sylvan Barnet. Copyright © 1963 by Sylvan Barnet. Play from *The Tempest* by William Shakespeare, edited by Robert Langaum and Sylvan Barnet. Copyright © 1987 by Robert Langaum and Sylvan Barnet. Reprinted by arrangement with NAL Penguin Inc., New York, New York.

New Directions Publishing Corporation
Lines from "In the Park" and lines from "The Galloping Cat" from Stevie Smith, *The Collected Poems of Stevie Smith*. Copyright © 1972 by Stevie Smith. "Not Waving but Drowning" and "Pretty" from Stevie Smith, *The Collected Poems of Stevie Smith*. Copyright © 1972 by Stevie Smith. Reprinted by permission of New Directions Publishing Corporation.

New Directions Publishing Corporation and David Higham Associates Ltd.
"Do not go gentle into that good night," "Fern Hill," and "The force that throught the green fuse drives the flower" from Dylan Thomas, *The Poems of Dylan Thomas*. Copyright 1939 by New Directions Publishing Corporation. Copyright 1945 by the Trustees for the Copyrights of Dylan Thomas. Copyright 1952 by Dylan Thomas. Published in London by J. M. Dent & Sons Ltd. Reprinted by permission.

W. W. Norton & Company, Inc.
Reprinted from *Sir Gawain and the Green Knight, A New Verse Translation* by Marie Borroff, by permission of W. W. Norton & Company, Inc. Copyright © 1967 by W. W. Norton & Company, Inc.

Oxford University Press, Inc. and A. P. Watt Ltd. on behalf of the Executors of the Estate of Robert Graves
"Interruption," "One Hard Look," and "She Tells Her Love . . ." from *Collected Poems* by Robert Graves. Copyright © 1975 in this edition by Robert Graves. Reprinted by permission.

Oxford University Press, England
"A Poison Tree," "Holy Thursday," "Infant Sorrow," "The Human Abstract," "The Lamb," and "The Tiger" from *The Poetical Works of William Blake* edited by John Sampson. From "The Life of Samuel Johnson" in *Boswell's Life of Johnson* by James Boswell, edited by C. B. Tinker. From *Wuthering Heights* by Emily Brontë, edited by H. W. Garrod. "Sonnet 43" from *The Poetical Works of Elizabeth Barrett Browning*, Oxford Edition. "Kubla Khan" and "The Rime of the Ancient Mariner" from *The Poems of Samuel Taylor Coleridge*. "Easter Wings," "Man," and "Virtue" from *The Poems of George Herbert*, edited by Helen Gardner. "An Ode for Him" and "To the Virgins, to Make Much of Time" from *The Poems of Robert Herrick* edited by L. C. Martin. "God's Grandeur," "Hurrahing in Harvest," "Pied Beauty," and "Spring and Fall" from *Poems of Gerard Manley Hopkins*, 4th edition, edited by W. H. Gardner and N. H. Mackenzie. "Letter to Lord Chesterfield" from *The Letters of Samuel Johnson*, Volume I: 1719–1774, collected and edited by R. W. Chapman. "Dream Children: A Reverie" from *The Works of Charles Lamb* edited by Thomas Hutchinson. "To Althea" and "To Lucasta, On Going to the War" from *The Poems of Richard Lovelace* edited by C. H. Wilkinson. "Sonnet 31" and "Sonnet 39" from *The Poems of Sir Philip Sidney* edited by William A. Ringler, Jr. Lines from "The Faerie Queen," "Sonnet 1," "Sonnet 26," and "Sonnet 75" from *The Poetical Works of Edmund Spenser* edited by J. C. Smith and E. de Selincourt. From "Thoughts on Various Subjects" in *Satires and Personal Writings* by Jonathan Swift, edited by William Alfred Eddy. "Crossing the Bar," Lines from "In Memoriam A.H.H.," "Tears, Idle Tears," "The Lady of Shalott," "The Lotos-Eaters," lines from "The Princess" ("The Splendor Falls"), and "Ulysses" from *Alfred Tennyson: Poetical Works*.

Pantheon Books, a division of Random House, Inc.
From "The Preface" and from "A Dictionary of the English Language" by Samuel Johnson in *Johnson's Dictionary: A Modern Selection* edited by E. L. McAdam, Jr. and George Milne.

Penguin Books Ltd.
From *A History of the English Church and People* by Venerable Bede, translated with an introduction by Leo Sherley-Price, revised by R. E. Latham (Penguin Classics, 1955, 1965, 1968), copyright © Leo Sherley-Price, 1955, 1965, 1968, copyright © R. E. Latham, 1968, pp. 37–40. "The Prologue" and 238 lines from "The Pardoner's Tale" from *The Canterbury Tales* by Geoffrey Chaucer, translated into modern English by Nevill Coghill (Penguin Classics, 1951, 1958, 1960), copyright © Nevill Coghill, 1951 1958, 1960, pp. 19–41, 268–274. Reproduced by permission of Penguin Books Ltd.

A. D. Peters & Company Ltd.
"A Voyage to Cythera" by Margaret Drabble, published in *Mademoiselle* Magazine, December 1967. Reprinted by permission of A. D. Peters & Co. Ltd.

Random House, Inc.
From *Jane Eyre* by Charlotte Bronte. "Holy Sonnet 10," Holy Sonnet 14," "Meditation 17," and "Song" from *Complete Poetry and Selected Prose of John Donne* by John Donne, edited by John Hayward.

Random House, Inc. and Faber and Faber Ltd.
"In Memory of W.B. Yeats" and "Musée des Beaux Arts" copyright 1940 and renewed 1968 by W. H. Auden. Reprinted from *W. H. Auden: Collected Poems* by W. H. Auden, edited by Edward Mendelson. "What I Expected" copyright 1934 and renewed 1962 by Stephen Spender. Reprinted from *Collected Poems 1928–1985* by Stephen Spender. Reprinted by permission of the publishers.

Routledge & Kegan Paul
"For Doreen: A Voice from the Garden" from *Collected Poems 1950–1970* by Donald Davie. Copyright © Donald Davie 1972.

Routledge & Kegan Paul and Associated Book Publishers (U.K.) Ltd.
"The Picture of Little T.C. in a Prospect of Flowers" and "To His Coy Mistress" from *The Poems of Andrew Marvell* edited by Hugh MacDonald.

Simon & Schuster, Inc.
"The Truth about George" from *The Most of P. G. Wodehouse by* P. G. Wodehouse. Copyright © 1960 by Pelham Grenville Wodehouse. Reprinted by permission of Simon & Schuster, Inc.

Simon & Schuster, Inc. and Jonathan Clowes Ltd., on behalf of the author
"A Mild Attack of Locusts" from *African Stories* by Doris Lessing. Copyright © 1951, 1953, 1954, 1957, 1958, 1962, 1963, 1964, 1965 by Doris Lessing. Reprinted by permission. Pronunciation key from *Webster's New World Dictionary—*Second College Edition. Copyright © 1984 by Simon & Schuster, Inc. Reprinted by permission.

The Society of Authors on behalf of the Estate of Bernard Shaw
Pygmalion by Bernard Shaw. Copyright 1913, 1914, 1916, 1930, 1941, 1944 George Bernard Shaw. Copyright 1957 The Public Trustee as Executor of the Estate of George Bernard Shaw. Reprinted by permission.

University of Nebraska Press
"The Seafarer" reprinted from *Poems From the Old English*, translated, with an introduction by Burton Raffel, by permission of University of Nebraska Press. Copyright © 1960, 1964 by the University of Nebraska Press.

Viking Penguin Inc.
"The Train from Rhodesia" from *Selected Stories* by Nadine Gordimer. Copyright 1952 by Nadine Gordimer. "Snake" from *The Complete Poems of D. H. Lawrence* edited by Vivian de Sola Pinto and F. Warren Roberts. Copyright © 1964, 1971 by Angelo Ravagli and C. M. Weekley, executors of the Estate of Frieda Lawrence Ravagli. "The Rocking-Horse Winner" from *The Complete Short Stories of D. H. Lawrence*, Vol., III. Copyright 1933 by the Estate of D. H. Lawrence; copyright renewed © 1961 by Angelo Ravagli and C. M. Weekley, Executors of the Estate of Frieda Lawrence Ravagli. "The Schartz-Metterklume Method" from *The Complete Short Stories of Saki* by Saki (H. H. Munro). Copyright 1930, renewed © 1958 by The Viking Press, Inc. "Sonnet 29," "Sonnet 73," "Sonnet 116," and "Sonnet 130" from *William Shakespeare: The Complete Works* edited by Alfred Harbage. Copyright © 1969 by Penguin Books, Inc. Reprinted by permission of Viking Penguin Inc.

Viking Penguin Inc., Jonathan Cape Ltd., and the Executors of the James Joyce Estate
"Araby" from *Dubliners* by James Joyce. Copyright 1916 by B. W. Huebsch. Definitive text copyright © 1967 by the Estate of James Joyce. Reprinted by permission.

Viking Penguin Inc. and John Johnson Ltd.
"The Distant Past" from *Angels at the Ritz and Other Stories* by William Trevor. Copyright © 1973 by William Trevor. Reprinted by permission.

Viking Penguin Inc. and Laurence Pollinger Ltd.
"Across the Bridge" from *Nineteen Stories* by Graham Greene. Copyright 1947, renewed © 1975 by Graham Greene. Published in London in *Collected Stories* by Graham Green by William Heinemann, Ltd. and The Bodley Head Ltd. Reprinted by permission.

Viking Penguin Inc. and George Sassoon
"Wirers" from *The Collected Poems of Siegfried Sassoon* by Siegfried Sassoon. Copyright 1918 by E. P. Dutton Co. Copyright renewed 1946 by Siegfried Sassoon. Reprinted by permission.

Wallace & Sheil Agency, Inc. and Tessa Sayle Agency, London
"The Fiddle" from *The Second Chance and Other Stories* by Alan Sillitoe. Copyright © 1981 by Alan Sillitoe. Reprinted by permission.

Note: Every effort has been made to locate the copyright owner of material reprinted in this book. Omissions brought to our attention will be corrected in subsequent editions.

ART CREDITS

Cover and Title Page: Summer, John Atkinson Grimshaw, Roy Miles Fine Paintings, London/Bridgeman Art Library/Art Resource; THE ANGLO-SAXON PERIOD. **pp. 0–1**: The Bayeux Tapestry: Norman cavalry charge at the shieldwall at the Battle of Hastings, The Granger Collection; **p. 3**: Religious Ceremony of the Druids, Forrest C. Crooks, Three Lions; **p. 4**: Saint Augustine, Giuseppe Ribera, Three Lions; Danes attacking a British town, English manuscript illumination c. 1130, The Granger Collection; **pp. 4–5**: Roman town at the foot of the Alps after the conquest by the Gauls, Octave Penguilly-L'Haridon, Three Lions; Sword, Metropolitan Museum of Art, Rogers Fund, 1955; The Diamond Sutra: Buddha addressing the ages disciple Subhuti, 868 A.D., The Granger Collection; Coronation of William the Conqueror at Westminster Abbey, Christmas Day, 1066; manuscript illumination c. 1470, The Granger Collection; **p. 5**: Charles Martel defeating the caliph's army under Abd-er-Rahman at Tours in 732, The Granger Collection; Jewelled gold reliquary of Charlemagne, c. 1350, Domschatz, Aachen, The Granger Collection; **p. 6**: Insignia of the Roman civil governor in charge of the five British provinces, (An early 15th century copy of a page from the now-lost Notitia Dignitatum Utriusque Imperii, a 4th-century list of imperial magistrates, adorned with the symbols of their provinces), The Granger Collection; **p. 8**: Saxons, Jutes, and Angles arriving in Britain by Sea, English ms. illumination, The Granger Collection; **p. 9**: An English monk exactly contemporary with Bede, Illumination from early 8th-century Northumbrian, Codex, The Granger Collection; **p. 10**: The 9th-century Oseberg Viking Ship, The Granger Collection; **p. 11**: Alfred the Great Acknowledged as King by All Men of England, 871 A.D., The Granger Collection; **p. 11**: Page from an early 12th-century manuscript of the Anglo-Saxon Chronicle describing the Norman Conquest, The Granger Collection; **p. 12**: The Bayeux Tapestry: Edward the Confessor speaks to, Harold of Wessex, The Granger Collection; **p. 14**: A page from the Caedmon manuscript, c. 1000, The Granger Collection; **p. 18**: Ship with three men, fish, Bodleian Library, Oxford; **p. 25**: The Dragon, for The High Kings, George Sharp; **p. 28**: Arthur going to Avalon, for The High Kings, George Sharp; **p. 34**: The so-called "Sigurd's Helmet," Werner Forman Archive, Statens Historiska Museet, Stockholm; **p. 34**: Coins depicting Viking longships, Werner Forman Archive, Statens Historiska Museet, Stockholm; **p. 34**: The Gokstad Ship, Werner Forman Archive, Viking Ships Museum, Bygdy, Oslo; **p. 35**: Head of Carved Post from Ship Burial at Oseberg, Werner Forman Archive; **p. 35**: Helmet, Werner Forman Archive, Statens Historiska Museet, Stockholm; **p. 35**: Golden Horn, National Museet, Copenhagen; **p. 41**: Page of Bede's History, The British Library; **p. 42**: Monks, Bodleian Library, Oxford; THE MEDIEVAL PERIOD. **pp. 46–47**: Pilgrims to Canterbury, detail of an English illuminated ms., c. 1400, The Granger Collection; **p. 48**: The Bayeux Tapestry: Duke William encourages his men at, Hastings by raising his helmet, The Granger Collection; **p. 49**: A bailiff supervising the harvest (the month of August): English ms. illumination, early 14th, century, The Granger Collection; **p. 50**: The murder of Thomas à Becket in 1170 (illumination from an English psalter c. 1200, The Granger Collection; King John signing Magna Carta at Runnymede, 15 June 1215, The Granger Collection; Pope Gregory IX, mosaic head from the old basilica of Saint Peter, The Granger Collection; **pp. 50–51**: Roger Bacon with a pupil (mid 15th century manuscript illumination), The Granger Collection; Genghiz Kahn, Chinese silk album leaf, Yuan Dynasty, The Granger Collection; Two pages of Anglo-Norman text from a 12th century manuscript of the Song of Roland, The Granger Collection; **p. 51**: The siege and capture of Jerusalem by the First Crusade, late 13th century French manuscript illumination, The Granger Collection; European ivory chess piece, The Granger Collection; **p. 52**: Francois Villon, from Grand Testament de Maitre Francois Villon, Paris, 1489, The Granger Collection; Two-color printer's devices used by William Caxton, the first English printer, The Granger Collection; **pp. 52–53**: Joan of Arc at the coronation of Charles VII, J.A.D. Ingres, 1854, The Granger Collection; Fear of plague in house of Fitzeisulf, Trinity Chapel Window, Canterbury Cathedral, The Granger Collection; Marco Polo entering Peking, 14th century miniature from the Livre de Merveilles, The Granger Collection; **p. 53**: Johann Gutenburg taking the first proof printed from movable type, The Granger Collection; The beginning of the Prologue to Chaucer's Canterbury Tales, The Granger Collection; Battle of Poitiers, Eugene Delacroix, Three Lions; **p. 55**: King John signing Magna Carta at Runnymede, 15 June 1215: colored engraving, 18th century, The Granger Collection; **p. 55**: Four Kings of England depicted on a page of a 13th century manuscript, The Granger Collection; **p. 56**: Funeral of plague victim in house of Fitzeisulf, Trinity Chapel window, Canterbury Cathedral, 14th century, The Granger Collection; **p. 57**: King Henry VII of England, Panel, 1505, Michiel Sittow, National Portrait Gallery, London, The Granger Collection; **p. 58**: Sir Galahad, 1864, Dante Gabriel Rossetti, The Granger Collection; **p. 59**: Johann Gutenberg examining the first proof of his printed Bible from his press at Mainz; after the painting by J.L.G. Ferris, The Granger Collection; **p. 60**: A page from the Lansdowne ms. of Geoffrey Chaucer's *Canterbury Tales*, The Granger Collection; **p. 61**: Sketch of Robin Hood, Richard Dadd (1817–1886), Yale Center for British Art, Paul Mellon Collection; **p. 68**: The Nine Heroes Tapestries, detail, Arthur Nicolas Bataille, Metropolitan Museum of Art, The Cloisters Collection, Munsey Fund; **p. 74**: Sir Thomas Malory; **p. 78**: Medieval baron dining, from Breviarium Grimari, 15th century, The Bettmann Archive; **p. 86**: Veronica Veronese, Dante Gabriel Rossetti, Delaware Art Museum, Samuel and Mary R. Bancroft Memorial Collection; **p. 88**: Geoffrey Chaucer: Unknown artist, The Granger Collection; **p. 92**: The Tabard Inn, Arthur Szyk for *The Canterbury Tales*, The George Macy Companies; **p. 95**: The Yeoman, Arthur Szyk for *The Canterbury Tales*, The George Macy Companies; **p. 97**: The Monk, Arthur Szyk for *The Canterbury Tales*, The George Macy Companies; **p. 100**: The Student, Arthur Szyk for *The Canterbury Tales*, The George Macy Companies; **p. 104**: The Wife of Bath, Arthur Szyk for *The Canterbury Tales*, The George Macy Companies; **p. 118**: The Pardoner, Arthur Szyk for *The Canterbury Tales*, The George Macy Companies; **p. 125**: from *The Romance of King Arthur and His Knights at the Round Table* (Weathervane Books), Arthur Rackham; **p. 131**: Sir Gawain and the Green Knight, from Medieval M.S., The Bodleian Library, Oxford; **p. 137**: Gawain Receiving the Green Girdle, Woodcut by Fritz Kredel from Gardner, The Complete Works of the Gawain Poet, 1965, The University of Chicago; **p. 148**: The Old Man and Death, c. 1774, Joseph Wright of Derby, Wadsworth Atheneum, Hartford, Ella Gallup Sumner and Mary Catlin Summer Collection; THE ENGLISH RENAISSANCE. **pp. 152–153**: Queen Elizabeth and Sir Walter Raleigh, Charles Edouard Boutibonne, The Photo Source; **p. 155**: Mona Lisa, Leonardo Da Vinci, Three Lions; **p. 156**: Queen Elizabeth I of England in coronation robes, unknown artist, The Granger Collection; The Copernican Universe, with sun at the center, from Nicolaus Copernicus' manuscript of De Revolutionibus Orbium Coelestium, The Granger Collection; **pp. 156–157**: The Last Supper, Leonardo da Vinci, Three Lions; Sir Thomas More and his family, 1593, Rowland Lockey, The Granger Collection; German map, 1572, of Tudor London as it appeared about 1558, The Granger Collection; The English galleon Vanguard attacking the Spanish Armada, 1588, The Granger Collection; **p. 157**: The caravels of Columbus setting sail from Spain on 3 August 1492 (detail) from Nova typis Indiae Occidentalis, 1621, The Granger Collection; Francisco Pizarro, c. 1760, unknown artist, The Granger Collection; **p. 158**: Galileo determining the magnification of one of his telescopes, The Granger Collection; **pp. 158–159**: Reconstruction of the Second Globe Theatre at London, The Granger Collection; Miguel de Cervantes Saavedra, The Granger Collection; Wedding Dance in the Open Air, 1566, Pieter Bruegel the elder, The Granger Collection; The Landing of the Pilgrims at Plymouth Rock, 1620, The Granger Collection; **p. 159**: Engraving of William Shakespeare by Martin Droeshout on titlepage of the First Folio, 1623, The Granger Collection; Akbar the Great, Manohar, c. 1600, The Granger Collection; **p. 160**: Portrait of Erasmus, Hans Holbein, National Gallery, Parma, Scala New York/Florence; **p. 161**: Martin Luther fastening his 95 Theses on the door of All Saints Church, Wittenburg, Germany, 31 October, 1517, 19th century engraving, The Granger Collection; **p. 162**: King Henry VIII of England, Hans Holbein, The Granger Collection; **p. 163**: Queen Elizabeth I of England, George Gower, The Granger Collection; **p. 164**: Queen Elizabeth I knighting Francis Drake on board the Golden Hind at Deptford, 4 April, 1581, 19th century engraving, The Granger Collection; **p. 164**: The launching of fireships against the Spanish Armada, National Maritime Museum, Greenwich, England; **p. 166**: Sir Walter Raleigh, Nicholas Hilliard, Three Lions; **p. 167**: William Shakespeare, artist unknown, Three Lions; **p. 168**: Title page of the first edition of the King James, Bible, London, 1611, The Granger Collection; **p. 171**: View of a Park, with Huntsmen and Deer, Peter Tillemans, Victoria and Albert Museum; **p. 172**: Sir Thomas Wyatt: The Granger Collection; **p. 174**: Sir Philip Sidney: Unknown artist, c. 1576, courtesy of the National Portrait Gallery, London; **p. 177**: Shepherds Under a Full Moon, Samuel Palmer, Ashmolean Museum, Oxford; **p. 180**: Christopher Marlowe: **p. 182**: The Hireling Shepherd, William Holman Hunt, Manchester City Art Gallery; **p. 186**: Faust Conjuring up the Devil, artist unknown, The Bettmann Archive; **p. 188**: Sir Walter Raleigh: Unknown artist, The Granger Collection; **p. 193**: Portrait of an Unknown Man, Nicholas Hilliard, Victoria and Albert Museum; **p. 194**: Edmund Spenser: 19th century engraving, The Granger Collection; **p. 200**: Thomas Nashe: New York Public Library Picture Collection; **p. 204**: William Shakespeare: Unknown artist, courtesy of the National Portrait Gallery, London; **p. 208**: The Sonnet, William Mulready, Victorial and Albert Museum; **p. 215**: The Woodcutter Courting the Milkmaid, Thomas Gainsborough, Woburn Abbey, By kind permission of the Marquess of Tavistock and the Trustees of the Bedford Estates; **p. 219**: Reconstruction of the Second Globe Theatre at London, The Granger Collection; **p. 224**: The Three Witches, Henry Fuseli, Courtauld Institute Galleries, London, Witt Collection; **p. 299**: Macbeth and the Witches, Clarkson Stanfield, Leicestershire Museums, Art Galleries and Records Service; **p. 239**: Scene from Macbeth, George Cattermole, The Folger Shakespeare Library; **p. 245**: Ellen Terry as Lady Macbeth, J.S. Sargent, Tate Gallery, on loan to National Portrait Gallery, London; **p. 250**: Lady Macbeth, Henry Fuseli, Tate Gallery; **p. 262**: Wood engraving after Sir John Gilbert, The Granger Collection; **p. 277**: Macbeth and the Witches, engraved by Robert Thew after Sir Joshua Reynolds, Royal Academy of Arts, London, Photo Studios Ltd.; **p. 280**: Wood engraving after Sir John Gilbert, The Granger Collection; **p. 292**: Mrs. Siddons as Lady Macbeth, George Henry Harlow, E.T. Archive (Garrick Club); **p. 389**: King James Bible, 1611, title page of the New Testament, The Folger Shakespeare Library; **p. 382**: Sir Francis Bacon: Courtesy of the National Portrait Gallery, London; THE SEVENTEENTH CENTURY. **pp. 394–395**: The Thames at Westminster Stairs, Claude de Jongh, (c. 1600-1663) Yale Center for British Art, Paul Mellon Collection; **p. 398**: Sir Francis Bacon, National Portrait Gallery, London; Execution of King Charles I of England, 30 January 1649, Weesop, The Granger Collection; John Milton, The Bettmann Archive; **pp. 398–399**: The Night Watch, Rembrandt Van Rijn, Three Lions; Covent Garden Market, Three Lions; **p. 399**: The Hartgers view of New Amsterdam c. 1626–28, 1651, The Granger Collection; Moliere with French and Italian comedians, Attributed to Verio, 1670, The Granger Collection; King Louis XIV of France, Hyacinthe Rigaud, The Granger Collection; Andrew Marvell, The Granger Collection; **p. 400**: Portrait of Charles I, Anthony Van Dyck, The Louvre; **p. 402**: The Execution of King Charles I of England at Whitehall, London, January 30, 1649, Colored woodcut from contemporary ballad-sheet; **p. 404**: Oliver Cromwell, Sir Peter Lely (Peter Van Der Faes), Firenze, Galleria Palantina; **p. 405**: Ben Jonson, The Granger Collection; **p. 407**: John Donne, The Granger Collection; **p. 409**: George Herbert, The

1461

Granger Collection; **p. 414**: Shakespeare and Ben Jonson at Chess, courtesy of William M. deHeyman, Philadelphia; **p. 416, p. 444**: Ben Johnson; **p. 417**: Greenwich Palace from the Northeast with a Man-of-War at Anchor (detail) c. 1630, National Maritime Museum; **p. 418**: John Donne: after Isaac Oliver, the Granger Collection; **p. 423**: Sir Thomas Aston at the Deathbed of His Wife, John Souch, Manchester City Art Gallery; **p. 430**: George Herbert: 18th century colored engraving, The Granger Collection; **p. 433**: The Milkmaid, Myles Birket Foster, Victoria and Albert Museum; **p. 438**: Andrew Marvell: Unknown artist, c. 1655–60, The Granger Collection; **p. 449**: Marriage à la mode IV: The Countess's Morning Levée, William Hogarth, National Gallery, London; **p. 450**: Robert Herrick: New York Public Library Picture Collection; **p. 455**: Three Ladies Adorning a Term of Hymen, Sir Joshua Reynolds, Tate Gallery; **p. 456**: Sir John Suckling: Anthony Van Dyck, The Granger Collection; **p. 456**: Richard Lovelace: Line engraving, The Granger Collection; **p. 458**: The Interrupted Sleep, François Boucher, Metropolitan Museum of Art, The Jules Bache Collection; **p. 459**: Fair Is My Love, Edwin A. Abbey, The Harris Museum and Art Gallery, Preston; **p. 460**: Going to the Battle, Edward Burne-Jones, Fitzwilliam Museum, Cambridge; **p. 463**: Gael Barend (c. 1620–1687), Guildhall Art Gallery, London; **p. 464**: John Milton: Unknown artist (detail), c. 1629, The Granger Collection; **p. 476**: Illustration for Milton's Paradise Lost from the British Library; **p. 480**: John Bunyan: 18th century colored engraving, The Granger Collection; **p. 483**: Pilgrim's Progress, Bunyan, The British Library; THE RESTORATION AND THE EIGHTEENTH CENTURY. **p. 488–489**: John Inigo Richards (1720?–1810), Roy Miles Fine Paintings, London, The Bridgeman Art Library, London/Art Resource; **p. 492**: Versailles, Pierre Patel, 1668, The Granger Collection; The Syndics, Rembrandt, Three Lions; Samuel Pepys, 1666, John Hayls, The Granger Collection; John Locke, 1704, after Sir G. Kneller, The Granger Collection; **pp. 492–493**: La Salle recieved in the village of the Caddo Indians, May 1686, George Catlin, The Granger Collection; Portuguese colony of Macao, 1598, The Granger Collection; The Great Fire of London, 1666, contemporary painting, Dutch School, The Granger Collection; **p. 493**: Johann S. Bach, Gustav Zerner, Three Lions; **p. 494**: Illustration from Jonathan Swift's Gulliver's Travels, The Granger Collection; Cook's Second Voyage, 1774, William Hodges, The Granger Collection; Capture of the Bastille, 14 July 1789, Claude Cholat, The Granger Collection; The Battle of Lexington, 19 April 1775, The Granger Collection; Robert Burns, Alexander Nasmyth, The Granger Collection; James Boswell talking of Samuel Johnson, Thomas Rowlandson, 1786, The Granger Collection; **p. 495**: Benjamin Franklin with his lightning detector, 1763, Edward Fisher, The Granger Collection; W.A. Mozart, Johan Peter Krafft, The Granger Collection; The Boston Tea Party, 16 December 1773, The Granger Collection; **p. 496**: Queen Anne and the Knights of the Garter, 1713, Peter Angelis, The Granger Collection; **p. 497**: King George III of England, c. 1760, Allan Ramsay, The Granger Collection; **p. 499**: A Philosopher Lecturing on the Orrery, Joseph Wright of Derby, Derby Art Gallery; **p. 501**: The Rake's Progress: No. 5, the Marriage, William Hogarth, The Granger Collection; **p. 504**: Sir Isaac Newton, c. 1726, attributed to John Vanderbank, The Granger Collection; **p. 509**: The Election—the Polling, William Hogarth (1697–1764), Sir John Soane's Museum, London, Bridgeman Art Library/Art Resource; **pp. 507, 618**: William Blake; **p. 510**: John Dryden: J. Maubert, courtesy of the National Portrait Gallery, London; **p. 513**: Shakespeare and His Contemporaries, John Faed, from the Collection of Mr. and Mrs. Sandor Korein, supplied by Montgomery Museum of Fine Arts; **p. 518**: The Music of a Bygone Age, John Melhuish Strudwick, Art Resource; **p. 522**: Samuel Pepys: John Closterman, c. 1695, The Granger Collection; **p. 526**: The Great Fire of London, 1666, Copyright the Museum of London; **p. 529**: Conversation in a Park, Thomas Gainsborough, The Louvre, Paris; **p. 530**: Daniel Defoe: The Bettmann Archive/BBC Hulton; **p. 532**: Journal of the Plague Year: The Dead Cart, The British Library; **p. 536**: Jonathan Swift: Charles Jervas, The Granger Collection; **p. 540**: Illustration by Willy Pogany, The Donnell Library Children's Room, New York Public Library; **p. 550**: Joseph Addison: Sir Godfrey Kneller, The Granger Collection; **p. 550**: Richard Steele: Jonathan Richardson, 1712, The Granger Collection; **p. 544**: Illustration by Willy Pogany, The Donnell Library Children's Room, New York Public, Library; **p. 556**: St. Edmund's Chapel, Westminster Abbey, John Fulleylove, R.I., Described by Mrs. A. Murray Smith Macmillan (book), By permission of Adam and Charles Black, London; **p. 558**: Alexander Pope: William Hoare, c. 1738–43, The Granger Collection; **p. 561**: The Barge, Aubrey Beardsley, From *The Best of Beardsley*, collected and edited by R.A. Walker; copyright 1948 by Bodley Head, published in the U.S.A. by Excalibur Books; **p. 564**: The Rape of the Lock, Aubrey Beardsley, From *The Best of Beardsley*, collected and edited by R.A. Walker, copyright 1948 by The Bodley Head, published in the U.S.A. by Excalibur Books; **p. 569**: The Battle of the Beaux and Belles, Aubrey Beardsley, Copyright The Barber Institute of Fine Arts, The University of Birmingham; **p. 575**: Oliver Goldsmith, James Boswell, and Samuel Johnson at the Mitre Tavern, 19th-century colored engraving, London, The Granger Collection; **p. 576**: Samuel Johnson: Sir Joshua Reynolds, 1756, The Granger Collection; **p. 586**: James Boswell: Sir Joshua Reynolds, 1785, The Granger Collection; **p. 589**: Johnson and Boswell, copyright the Trustees of the British Museum; **p. 595**: Haymakers, 1785, George Stubbs, The Granger Collection; **p. 596**: Thomas Gray: J.G. Eccardt, 1748, The Granger Collection; **p. 604**: Oliver Goldsmith: Studio of J. Reynolds, c. 1770, The Granger Collection; **p. 606**: Robert Burns: Courtesy of the National Portrait Gallery, London; **p. 614**: The River Dee near Eaton Hall, Richard Wilson, The Barber Institute of Fine Arts, The University of Birmingham; **p. 621**: from a Manuscript of "The Lamb," William Blake, Lessing J. Rosenwald Collection, The Library of Congress; **p. 622**: The Tyger (A page from *Songs of Innocence and Experience*), William Blake, The Metropolitan Museum of Art, Rogers Fund, 1917; **p. 626**: from a manuscript of "A Poison Tree," William Blake, The Library of Congress; THE ROMANTIC AGE. **pp. 630–631**: View in Hampshire, Patrick Nasmyth, Guildhall Art Gallery, City of London, Bridgeman/Art Resource, NY; **p. 632**: Capture of the Bastille, 14 July, 1789, Claude Cholat, The Granger Collection; **p. 634**: William Wordsworth, Benjamin Hayden, 1842, The Granger Collection; Jane Austen, The Granger Collection; The Meeting of Sir Walter Scott and Robert Burns, C.M. Hardie, The Granger Collection; **pp. 634–635**: George Stephenson's locomotive, The Rocket, c. 1829, The Granger Collection; The Union Jack, The Granger Collection; The Rosetta Stone, The Granger Collection; **p. 635**: Napoleon Bonaparte as First Consul, J.A. Ingres, Three Lions; Beethoven composing in his studio, Carl Schloesser, The Granger Collection; Robert Fulton's steamboat, Clermont, c. 1830–35; **p. 636**: John Keats listening to the Nightingale on Hampstead Heath, c. 1845, Joseph Severn, The Granger Collection; Rush-hour at Whitehall, London, in the 1820s, The Granger Collection; Charles Lamb, The Granger Collection; **pp. 636–637**: The Grove, of Admiral's House, Hampstead, John Constable c. 1820, The Granger Collection; Passenger and goods trains of the Liverpool and Manchester Railway, 1831, The Granger Collection; The Peterloo Massacre, The Granger Collection; **p. 637**: Half-title of an 1872 edition of James Fenimore Cooper's The Last of the Mohicans with illustrations by Felix Octavius Carr Darley, The Granger Collection; The American steamer Savannah, 1819, The Granger Collection; Edgar Allan Poe, Thomas C. Corner, Three Lions; **p. 638**: The Battle of Trafalgar, c. 1823, J.M.W. Turner, The Granger Collection; **p. 639**: Napoleon (The Campaign in France, 1814), 1864, J.L.E. Meissonier, The Granger Collection; **p. 639**: King William IV of England, Sir Martin Archer Shee, The Granger Collection; **p. 640**: Sketch for Hadleigh Castle, c. 1828–1829, John Constable, The Granger Collection; **p. 641**: Rain, Steam, and Speed—the Great Western Railway, 1844, J.M.W. Turner, The Granger Collection; **p. 642**: Portrait of Goethe, Joseph Karl Stieler, Three Lions; **p. 643**: Calais Pier: An English Packet Arriving, 1803, J.M.W. Turner, The Granger Collection; **p. 643**: Samuel Taylor Coleridge, 1795, Peter Vandyke, The Granger Collection; **p. 645**: John Keats, 1818, Joseph Severn, The Granger Collection; **p. 646**: Sir Walter Scott/Abbotsford Family, Sir David Wilkie, The Granger Collection; **p. 651**: Salisbury Cathedral, John Constable, Sao Paolo, Museo d'Arte Art Resource; **pp. 650, 652**: William Wordsworth: Benjamin Haydon, 1842, The Granger Collection; **p. 655**: Tintern Abbey, J.M.W. Turner, Victoria and Albert Museum Trustees; **p. 660**: Landscape with Rainbow, Joseph Wright of Derby, Derby Art Gallery; **p.665**: Cornfield by Moonlight, Samuel Palmer, British Museum; **p. 668**: Samuel Taylor Coleridge: P. Vandyke, 1795, courtesy of the National Portrait Gallery, London; **p. 673**: "By the long grey beard and glittering eye, Now wherefore stopp'st thou me?" Engraving by Gustave Doré for *The Rime of the Ancient Mariner* by Samuel Taylor Coleridge; **p. 675**: "With my crossbow I shot the albatross," Engraving by Gustave Doré for *The Rime of the Ancient Mariner* by Samuel Taylor Coleridge; **p. 676**: Engraving by Gustave Doré for *The Rime of the Ancient Mariner* by Samuel Taylor Coleridge, **p. 683**: Engraving by Gustave Doré for *The Rime of the Ancient Mariner* by Samuel Taylor Coleridge; **p. 696**: Chinese Silk Album Leaf, Yuan Dynasty, Kublai Khan, The Granger Collection; **p. 698**: Lord Byron: William West, The Granger Collection; **p. 703**: Shipwreck, J.C.C. Dahl, Munich Neue Pinakothek; **p. 710**: Percy Bysshe Shelley: A. Curran, The Granger Collection; **p. 715**: Cirrus Cloud Study, John Constable, Victoria and Albert Museum; **p. 719**: Cloud Study, 1821, John Constable, Yale Center for British Art, Paul Mellon Collection; **p. 724**: John Keats: Joseph Severn, 1818, The Granger Collection; **p. 727**: frontispiece, *Homer's Iliad and Odyssey*, 1612; G. Chapman, The British Library; **p. 729**: John Keats, 1821, J. Severn, Courtesy of the National Portrait Gallery, London; **p. 732**: Small Bird on a Flowering Plum Branch, attributed to Ma Lin, The Goto Museum; **p. 737**: Column Krater (called the "Orchard Vase"), Women Gathering Apples, Metropolitan Museum of Art, Rogers Fund, 1907; **p. 741**: J.M.W. Turner, Fisherman Upon a Lee Shore, The Iveagh Bequest, Kenwood, Bridgeman/Art Resource, NY; **p. 742**: Mary Wollstonecraft Shelley: Richard Rothwell, c. 1840, courtesy of the National Portrait Gallery, London; **p. 745**: A View of Chamonix and Mt. Blanc Julius Schon von Carolsfeld, Austrian Gallery, Vienna; **p. 748**: Charles Lamb: after Henry Hopper Meyer, courtesy of the National Portrait Gallery, London; **p. 760**: Jane Austen: C. Austen, c. 1801, courtesy of the National Portrait Gallery, London; **p. 763**: Lady Colville, Sir Henry Raeburn, The Bridgeman Art Library/Art Resource; THE VICTORIAN AGE. **p. 772–773**: Queen Victoria's Visit to Cherbourg, Jules Achille Noel, Royal Academy, London; **p. 774**: Painting of London's Crystal Palace, done for the Great Exhibition of 1851, The British Museum; **p. 776**: Queen Victoria of England, 1838, Sir George Hayter, The Granger Collection; Charles Darwin in his greenhouse at Down House, posthumous Russian painting, The Granger Collection; Charlotte Brontë, The Granger Collection; **pp. 776–777**: Charles Dickens, The Granger Collection; The Charge of the Light Brigade at Balaclava, 26 September 1854, The Granger Collection; Attack of the Sepoy mutineers of the British redan battery at Lucknow, India, 30 July 1857, The Granger Collection; **p. 777**: Richard Wagner, Franz von Lenbach, The Granger Collection; Karl Marx, (oil over a photograph), The Granger Collection; Samuel F.B. Morse with his telegraph, John Sartain, The Granger Collection; **p. 778**: 1911 illustration by N.C. Wyeth for Robert Louis Stevenson's Treasure Island, The Granger Collection; Robert Browning, Rudolf Lehman, Three Lions; The opening day procession of ships through the Suez Canal, 17 November 1869, The Granger Collection; Alexander Graham Bell Demonstrating his telephone, 15 March 1877, The Granger Collection; **pp. 778–779**: The First Battle of Bull Run, 21 July 1861, 1889 Kurz & Allison, The Granger Collection; The Mad Tea Party, after Sir John Tenniel, 1865, The Granger Collection; Marines fighting in the Boxer Rebellion outside Peking Legation, John Clymer, Three Lions; **p. 780**: Warrington High Street, T. Hesketh, Warrington High Street; **p. 781**: The Triumphs of the British Army and Navy, 1897, Commemorating the Diamond Jubilee of Queen Victoria, The Granger Collection; **p. 784**: Dudley Street, Seven Dials, London, 1872, Gustave Doré, The Granger Collection; **p. 785**: Beata Beatrix, c. 1863, Dante Gabriel Rossetti, The Granger Collection; **p. 786**: Alfred, Lord Tennyson, Caricature, 1871, Carlo Pellegrini, The Granger Collection; **p. 787**: Bayswater Omnibus, G.W. Joy, Museum of London; **p. 788**: Hyde Park near Grosvenor Gate, 1842, Thomas Shotter Boys, Guidehall Art Gallery; **p. 792**: Ulysses, Jean-Auguste-Dominique Ingres, National Gallery of Art, Washington, Chester Dale Collection; **pp. 793, 796**: Alfred, Lord Tennyson: S. Laurence, c. 1840; courtesy of the National Portrait Gallery, London; **p. 795**: Fair, Quiet and Sweet Rest, Luke Fildes, Warrington Museum and Art Gallery; **p. 799**: The Lady of Shalott, John Waterhouse, Tate Gallery; **p. 807**: The Bard, John Martin,Yale Center for the British Art, Paul Mellon Collection; **pp. 810–811**: Nocturne: Grey and Gold—Chelsea Snow, James McNeill Whistler, The Fogg Art Museum, Cambridge, MA, bequest, Greenville L. Winthrop; **p. 817**: Carved gem of light brown onyx, Roman 3rd to 2nd Century B.C., Ulysses Mourning for Home, Staatliche Museen zu Berlin; **p. 820** : The Angry Sea, James McNeill Whistler, Freer Gallery of Art, Smithsonian Institution; **p. 822**: Robert Browning, M. Gordigiani, The Granger Collection; **p. 825**: Parmigianino: Antea Napoli, Capodimonte, Art Resource; **p. 828**: In Early Spring, William Inchbold, Ashmolean Museum, Oxford; **p. 831**: Italian Ruins, Jean Claude Nattes, Victoria and Albert Museum Trustees; **p. 836**: Matthew Arnold: J.A. Watts, 1880, courtesy of the National Portrait Gallery, London; **p. 848**: At the Window, 1960, Jacob Kainen, NMAA Washington, D.C.; **p. 852**: Gerard Manley Hopkins, A.E. Hopkins, 1859; courtesy of the National Portrait Gallery, London; **p. 855**: Bird's Nest, Ros W. Jenkins, Warrington Museum and Art Gallery/Bridge-

1463

man Art Resource; **pp. 856–857**: Harvest Field with Gleaners, Haywood Herefordshire, George Robert Lewis, Tate Gallery, London; **p. 859**: A Mother and Child on the Isle of Wight, James Collinson, Yale Center for British Art, Paul Mellon Collection; **p. 860**: A.E. Housman: F. Dodd, 1936, The Granger Collection; **p. 867**: Temperantia, 1872, Sir Edward Burne-Jones, Christie's London; **p. 868**: Elizabeth Barrett Browning: Field Talfourd, 1859, The Granger Collection; **p. 868**: Dante Gabriel Rossetti: Self-portrait, 1847, The Granger Collection; **p. 871**: "Way" chintz, William Morris, The Granger Collection; **p. 872**: George Meredith: The Granger Collection; **p. 872**: Christina Rosetti: courtesy of the National Portrait Gallery, London; **p. 872**: Rudyard Kipling: P. Burne-Jones, 1899, courtesy of the National Portrait Gallery, London; **p. 872**: Robert Louis Stevenson: John Singer Sargent, The Taft Museum, Gift of Mr. and Mrs. Charles Phelps Taft; **p. 879**: A Summer Day in Hyde Park, John Ritchie, Museum of London; **p. 880**: Charles Dickens: The Granger Collection; **p. 884**: Two Tunnels, 1975, Guy Worsdell; **p. 889**: Red Virginia Creeper, Edvard Munch, Three Lions; **p. 896**: Summer, Afternoon After a Shower, John Constable, Tate Gallery, London; **p. 899**: Cottage and Pond, Moonlight, Thomas Gainsborough, Victoria and Albert Museum Trustees; **p. 909**: Waiting, 1854, Sir John Everett Millais, Birmingham City Art Gallery, Art Resource; **p. 917**: Wuthering Heights, Fritz Eichenberg; **p. 922**: Charlotte Brontë: The Bettmann Archive; **p. 925**: Jane Eyre, Fritz Eichenberg; THE MODERN AGE. **p. 932–933**: Big Ben, 1905–1906, André Derain, Art Resource; **p. 934**: An English Rose, Joseph Clark, Gallerie George, London; **p. 935**: A Star Shell, c. 1916, Christopher Richard Wynne Nevinson, Tate Gallery; **p. 936**: King Edward VII of England, Sir Luke Fildes, The Granger Collection; Joseph Conrad, 1923–24, Walter Tittle, The Granger Collection; The official poster for the 1908 Olympic Games at London, The Granger Collection; Bombardment of trenches, 1918, Raoul Lespagne, The Granger Collection; American souvenir postcard commemorating rival claims of Cook and Peary to have reached the North Pole, The Granger Collection; **p. 937**: The first heavier-than-air flight of the Wright brothers, 17 December 1903, The Granger Collection; Albert Einstein, Frank Einzheimer, Three Lions; King George V and Royal Family of England, 1913, J. Lavery, The Granger Collection; Mohandas K. Gandhi, The Granger Collection; **p. 938**: Devastation 1941, an East End street, London, Graham Sutherland, The Granger Collection Conversation Piece, George Vi of England and Family, Herbert James Gunn, Three Lions; **p. 939**: Mandolin and Guitar, Pablo Picasso, The Granger Collection; Dylan Thomas, 1940, Rupert Shephard, The Granger Collection; The Persistence of Memory,1931, Salvador Dali, The Granger Collection; Adolf Hitler on an official German poster, 1938, The Granger Collection; **p. 940**: Over the Top (at Marcoing, December 1917), John Nash, The Granger Collection; **p. 943**: Wyndham Lewis, The Granger Collection; **p. 945**: The Artist's Garden at Durbins, c. 1915, Roger Fry, Yale Center for British Art; **p. 947**: Studland Beach, Vanessa Bell, Tate Gallery; **p. 948**: The Mud Bath, 1914, David Bomberg, Tate Gallery; **p. 959**: Gardens in the Pound, Cookham, 1936, Stanley Spencer, Leeds City Art Galleries; **p. 960**: Joseph Conrad: Walden Tittle, 1923–24, courtesy of the National Portrait Gallery, London; **p. 981**: The Newspaper, Edouard Vuillard, The Phillips Collection; **p. 983**: Hobson Pittman, The North Carolina Museum of Art, Raleigh, Gift of the Artist; **p. 989**: The Garden of Love, Walter Richard Sickert, The Fitzwilliam Museum, Cambridge; **pp. 994–1056**: D.H. Lawrence: Jan Juta, 1920, courtesy of the National Portrait Gallery, London; p. 1008: St. Patrick's Close, Dublin, Walter Osborne, National Gallery of Ireland; **p. 1017**: Holy Bush Hill, Hampstead, 1921, Ethelbert White; **p. 1019**: Ox House, Shaftesbury, 1932, John R. Biggs; **p. 1041**: Houses of Parliament, 1903, Claude Monet, The Granger Collection; **p. 1042**: William Butler Yeats: Augustus John, The Granger Collection; **p. 1045**: Old House (Ivy Cottage), Shoreham, 1831–32, Samuel Palmer, Ashmolean Museum, Oxford; **p. 1065**: Drawing of Tanks, World War I, Photo Research Int.; **p. 1066**: Rupert Brooke: Clara Ewald, 1911, The Granger Collection; **p. 1068**: War poster, Photri; **p. 1072**: T.S. Eliot: Sir Gerald Kelly, National Portrait Gallery, Smithsonian Institution; **p. 1074**: Bolton, 1938, William Coldstream, The National Gallery of Canada, Ottawa; **p. 1086**: Robert Graves: J. Aldridge, 1968, The Granger Collection; **p. 1089**: Sun, Wind, and Rain, David Cox, The City Museum and Art Gallery, Birmingham; **p. 1099**: The Fall of Icarus, P.I. Brueghel, Musées Royaux de Beaux-Arts de Belgique; **pp. 1102–103**: Old Thatched Summer House, Lillian Stannard, Christopher Wood Gallery, London, Bridgeman/Art Resource; **p. 1117**: The Magic Apple Tree, c. 1830, Samuel Palmer, Fitzwilliam Museum, Cambridge; **p. 1121**: Set Design of Covent Garden for Pygmalion, Donald Oenslager, Harvard Theater Collection. CONTEMPORARY WRITERS. **pp. 1214–1215**: Papagena, 1983, Gillian Ayres, Private Collection, Courtesy of The South Bank Center; **p. 1219**: Mao Tse-Tung on Chinese poster, 1975, The Granger Collection; Dr. Martin Luther King, Jr., Gruerio, Three Lions; **p. 1222**: Industrial Landscape, L.S. Lowry, Tate Gallery, London; **p. 1224**: Great Black-Backed Gull, Douglas Anderson, Oscar & Peter Johnson Ltd., London, Bridgeman Art Library/Art Resource; **p. 1225**: King's Cookham Rise, 1947, Stanley Spencer, Metropolitan Museum of Art, Purchase, Lila Acheson Wallace Gift, 1981; **p. 1237**: The Identi-kit Man, 1974, Derek Boshier, Tate Gallery Publications Department; **p. 1242**: The Soothsayer from The Green Island, 1946, John Petts; **p. 1245**: Knockalla Hills, Donegal, Dan O'Neill, Ulster Museum, Belfast; **p. 1281**: Hillside in Wales, Lowry, Tate Gallery, London; **p. 1290**: Shunters, 1965, James Dolby; **p. 1299**: Mount Fuji and Flowers, 1972, David Hockney, Metropolitan Museum of Art, Purchase, Mrs. Arthur Hays Sulzberger, Gift, 1972.

PHOTOGRAPH CREDITS:

p. 4: Stonehenge Sarsen Stones, D.E. Szymanski/DPI; **p. 14**: Bodego Bay, California: Pacific Ocean, © Peter Arnold; **p. 599**: Stoke Poges Churchyard, © Ian Berry/Magnum; **p. 608**: White-footed mouse, Alvin E. Staffan/Photo Researchers, Inc.; **p. 713**: The Colossi of Memnon, Diane Rawson/Photo Researchers; **p. 779**: Anton Pavlovich Chekhov, The Granger Collection; **p. 842**: Dover Cliffs, Thomas Hollyman/Photo Researchers; **p. 846**: Bare-eyed thrush, © Marshall Sklar/Photo Researchers; **p. 846**: fruit trees, © Kees Van Den Berg/Photo Researchers; **p. 938**: Winston Churchill, 1946, Douglas Chandor, The Granger Collection; Charles A. Lindbergh and the Spirit of St. Louis, May 20, 1927, The Granger Collection; T.S. Eliot, The Granger Collection; **p. 957**: Katherine Mansfield: The Granger Collection; **p. 960**: Joseph Conrad: Walden Tittle, 1923-24, courtesy of the National Portrait Gallery, London; **p. 963**: Cigenter River, Ujongkulon Java Indonesia, Dieter and Mary Plage/Bruce Coleman, Inc.; **p. 972**: H.H. Munro (Saki): The Granger Collection; **p. 978**: E.M. Forster; **p. 986**: Virginia Woolf; G. Beresford, The Granger Collection; **p. 1006**: James Joyce; **p. 1014**: Elizabeth Bowen: Alfred A. Knopf; **p. 1022**: Graham Greene: The Granger Collection; **p. 1025**:

Border Bridge over Rio Grande (in CD Juarez), © ABBAS/Magnum; **p. 1032**: George Orwell: 1946, The Granger Collection; **p. 1035**: Asiatic Elephant, Photo Researchers, Inc.; **pp. 1046–1047**: swans on water, Magnum/Dennis Stock; **p. 1049**: burning airplane, Photri; **p. 1058**: copperhead, © Joe McDonald/Animals Animals; **p. 1062**: Siegfried Sassoon: Bassano, 1920, courtesy of the National Portrait Gallery, London; **p. 1092**: W.H. Auden: The Bettmann Archive/BBC Hulton; **p. 1100**: Louis MacNeice; **p. 1106**: Stephen Spender: The Granger Collection; **p. 1110**: Henry Reed: © Rollie McKenna; **p. 1112**: Dylan Thomas: The Bettman Archive; **p. 1122**: George Bernard Shaw: The Bettman Archive; **p. 1127**: Eliza and Higgins, seated, © 1987 by Martha Swope; **p. 1134**: Higgins and Pickering, Eliza, © 1987 Martha Swope; **p. 1145**: Mrs. Pearce, Eliza, Higgins, Pickering, © 1987 by Martha Swope; **p. 1151**: Doolittle and Higgins, © 1987 by Martha Swope; **p. 1156**: Mrs. Pearce, Doolittle, Higgins, Eliza, © 1987 by Martha Swope; **pp. 1164–1165**: tea, © 1987 by Martha Swope; **p. 1177**: Eliza and Higgins in evening dress, © 1987 by Martha Swope; **p. 1179**: Eliza, Higgins, and Pickering in evening dress, © 1987 by Martha Swope; **p. 1181**: Eliza and Higgins, seated, © 1987 by Martha Swope; **p. 1189**: Higgins and Doolittle, © 1987 by Martha Swope; **p. 1193**: Higgins and Eliza, © 1987 by Martha Swope; **p. 1201**: © 1987 by Martha Swope; **p. 1218**: Albert Camus, The Granger Collection; Sir Winston Churchill, The Granger Collection; **pp. 1218–1219**: German Officers being taken prisoner, August 25, 1944, liberation of Paris, Henri Cartier-Bresson/Magnum; Castro, Three Lions; **p. 1219**: The Hungarian uprising, 1956 © Erich Lessing/Magnum; Doris Lessing, Inge Morath; **p. 1220**: Northern Ireland, Bruno Barbey/Magnum; Margaret Thatcher, Peter Marlow/Sygma; strike in England, Peter Marlow/Sygma; Ethiopia, Makalle camp, famine victims Christian Aid serves 20,000 © F. Scianna/Magnum; **p. 1220–1221**: Jean Anouilh, Henri Cartier-Bresson/Magnum; **p. 1221**: V.S. Naipaul, © Ian Berry/Magnum; Gabriel García Márquez © Susan Meiselas/Magnum; two British petroleum drilling platforms in the North Sea, © Stuart Franklin/Sygma; Corazón Aquino, Sygma; Anti Shah demonstrations in Iran, 1979, © ABBAS/Magnum; **p. 1228**: deserted mansion gate, Bruce Coleman, Inc. New York; **p. 1235**: William Trevor: Mark Gerson; **p. 1238**: Sean O'Faolain; **p. 1248**: P.G. Wodehouse: UPI/Bettmann Newsphotos; **p. 1262**: Doris Lessing: © Thomas Victor; **p. 1270**: Nadine Gordimer: © Thomas Victor; **p. 1278**: Alan Sillitoe: The Bettmann Archive/BBC Hulton; **p. 1286**: Margaret Drabble: © Thomas Victor; **p. 1303**: Welsh miners; collieries in background, © David Hurn/Magnum; **p. 1306**: Thom Gunn: © 1987 Thomas Victor; **p. 1308**: Ted Hughes: © 1987 Thomas Victor; **p. 1310**: Goshawk, juvenile, Bruce Coleman, Inc.; **p. 1314**: Stevie Smith: Godfrey Argent, 1970, courtesy of the National Portrait Gallery, London; **p. 1318**: Elaine Feinstein: © 1985 Layle Silbert; **p. 1322**: Seamus Heaney; **p. 1326**: dolphins in dark water, J.G. Ross/Photo Researchers, Inc.; **p. 1325**: Donald Davie: Doreen Davie; **p. 1330**: Molly Holden.

1465

The Victorian Age (continued)

Selection	Analyzing Literature	Critical Thinking and Reading	Understanding Language/ Speaking and Listening	Thinking and Writing
"My Last Duchess," Robert Browning, p. 824	dramatic monologue	Making inferences about the speaker of a poem* Making inferences about the speaker	Revealing diction*	Writing a dramatic monologue
"Home-Thoughts, from Abroad," Robert Browning, p. 828				Comparing and contrasting two places
"Love Among the Ruins," Robert Browning, p. 830		Interpreting tone		
"Prospice," Robert Browning, p. 834		Making inferences about the poet's attitudes Making inferences about attitudes		Comparing and contrasting two poems
"To Marguerite—Continued," Matthew Arnold, p. 838	Creating imagery and mood		Appreciating vivid words*	Writing about imagery and mood
"Self-Dependence," Matthew Arnold, p. 840	Using figurative language			Writing about a Victorian poet
"Dover Beach," Matthew Arnold, p. 842	Appreciating the apostrople*			
"The Darkling Thrush," Thomas Hardy, p. 846	Using simile and metaphor*		Preparing an oral report on Wessex	Writing a response to a poem
"The Man He Killed," Thomas Hardy, p. 848	Understanding irony*			
"Ah, Are You Digging on My Grave?" Thomas Hardy, p. 850				
"God's Grandeur," Gerard Manley Hopkins, p. 854	Analyzing rhythm and rhyme*			
"Hurrahing in Harvest," Gerard Manley Hopkins, p. 856		Evaluating the effects of imagery*		
"Pied Beauty," Gerard Manley Hopkins, p. 858				
"Spring and Fall, To a Young Child," Gerard Manley Hopkins, p. 859				Writing Margaret's reply

The Victorian Age (continued)

Selection	Analyzing Literature	Critical Thinking and Reading	Understanding Language/ Speaking and Listening	Thinking and Writing
"To an Athlete Dying Young," A. E. Housman, p. 862 "Loveliest of Trees," A. E. Housman, p. 864 "When I Was One-and-Twenty," A. E. Housman, p. 865 "With Rue My Heart Is Laden," A. E. Housman, p. 866	Understanding the theme* Finding the theme		Understanding the multiple meanings of words*	Responding to criticism
Other Victorian Poets				
"Sonnet 43," Elizabeth Barrett Browning, p. 870 "Silent Noon," Dante Gabriel Rossetti, p. 871	Understanding word choice in poetry* Understanding a sonnet	Inferring tone*	Using prefixes and suffixes*	
"Lucifer in Starlight," George Meredith, p. 874 "A Birthday," Christina Rossetti, p. 875 "Recessional," Rudyard Kipling, p. 876 "Requiem," Robert Louis Stevenson, p. 878	Using imagery*	Understanding connotation and denotation*		Writing about historical context
Prose				
"The Signalman," Charles Dickens, p. 882	Folowing the plot in a ghost story Understanding plot: foreshadowing*	Separating realistic from fantastic details* Separating details	Fitting the context	Writing a ghost story
"The Three Strangers," Thomas Hardy, p. 894	Understanding setting* Understanding setting and mood	Inferring the author's attitude toward fate Inferring the author's attitudes	Understanding character through dialect* Reading dialogue* Reading dialect	Describing a place
The Victorian Novel				
from *Wuthering Heights,* Emily Brontë, p. 912	Reporting first-person narration	Separating subjective from objective details*	Word-building using roots*	Writing about the narrative technique
from *Jane Eyre,* Charlotte Brontë, p. 924	Reporting first-person narration	Making inferences about the narrator*	Using context clues*	Continuing the novel

The Modern Period

Selection	Analyzing Literature	Critical Thinking and Reading	Understanding Language/ Speaking and Listening	Thinking and Writing
Reading Critically				
"A Dill Pickle," Katherine Mansfield, p. 951	Understanding dialogue*	Making inferences based on dialogue	Understanding synonyms and antonyms*	
Prose				
"The Lagoon," Joseph Conrad, p. 962	Understanding shifting point of view and theme Understanding a shifting point of view*	Making inferences about a moral code	Setting up a Reader's theater Using context clues*	Responding to theme
"The Schartz-Metterklume Method," Saki (H. H. Munro), p. 974	Understanding satire*	Making inferences about tone	Understanding words with Latin roots*	Comparing and contrasting attitudes
"The Helping Hand," E. M. Forster, p. 980	Analyzing direct and indirect characterization* Understanding characterization	Making inferences about character	Understanding word origins Analyzing changes in definition*	Writing about a character
"The Lady in the Looking Glass," Virginia Woolf, p. 988	Understanding stream-of-consciousness narration* Recognizing stream of consciousness	Evaluating an author's purpose*		Using stream of consciousness
"The Rocking-Horse Winner," D. H. Lawrence, p. 996	Understanding omniscient narration	Understanding cause-and-effect relationships*	Understanding the difference between synonyms* Understanding synonyms	Telling the story
"Araby," James Joyce, p. 1009	Understanding epiphany*	Analyzing Joyce's attitude	Appreciating image-making words*	Writing an extended conversation
"The Demon Lover," Elizabeth Bowen, p. 1016	Recognizing the development of character traits* Considering war and the ghost story	Exploring a paradox*		
"Across the Bridge," Graham Greene, p. 1024	Understanding theme and point of view*	Distinguishing between comedy and tragedy*	Learning about word completions	Analyzing the effects of point of view
"Shooting an Elephant," George Orwell, p. 1034	Identifying tone*	Understanding stereotypes*	Understanding word origins	Supporting an opinion

The Modern Period (continued)

Selection	Analyzing Literature	Critical Thinking and Reading	Understanding Language/ Speaking and Listening	Thinking and Writing
"When You Are Old," William Butler Yeats, p. 1044 "The Lake Isle of Innisfree," William Butler Yeats, p. 1045 "The Wild Swans at Coole," William Butler Yeats, p. 1046 "An Irish Airman Foresees His Death," William Butler Yeats, p. 1048	Understanding speaker and lyric voice*	Evaluating the use of imagery*		Writing about the use of a speaker
"The Second Coming," William Butler Yeats, p. 1051 "After Long Silence," William Butler Yeats, p. 1053 "Sailing to Byzantium," William Butler Yeats, p. 1054	Understanding symbols*		Understanding repetition*	Writing a poem about silence
"Snake," D. H. Lawrence, p. 1057	Understanding free verse*	Making inferences about purpose	Recognizing compound nouns*	
"Wirers," Siegfried Sassoon, p. 1064	Understanding historical context*		Understanding the multiple meanings of words*	
"The Soldier," Rupert Brooke, p. 1068	Feeling patriotism*			
"The Great Lover," Rupert Brooke, p. 1069		Identifying the Georgian poets	Appreciating specific words*	
"Preludes," T. S. Eliot, p. 1074 "Journey of the Magi," T. S. Eliot, p. 1077	Using synecdoche* Conveying a mood*		Selecting music that evokes the poem	Writing a poem using synecdoche Analyzing Eliot's use of ambiguity
"The Hollow Men," T. S. Eliot, p. 1081	Conveying tone*	Interpreting allusions*		Writing about tone

The Modern Period (continued)

Selection	Analyzing Literature	Critical Thinking and Reading	Understanding Language/ Speaking and Listening	Thinking and Writing
"Interruption," Robert Graves, p. 1088 "One Hard Look," Robert Graves, p. 1090 "She Tells Her Love While Half Asleep," Robert Graves, p. 1091		Recognizing traditional symbolism*	Understanding coined words*	Writing about the Modernist Movement
"In Memory of W. B. Yeats," W. H. Auden, p. 1094 "Mušee des Beaux Arts," W. H. Auden, p. 1098	Understanding elegy and figurative language* Understanding elegy	Understanding the legacy of an artist		Writing about a paradox
"The Sunlight on the Garden," Louis MacNeice, p. 1102 "Sunday Morning," Louis MacNeice, p. 1104	Understanding scansion*		Appreciating concrete and abstract words*	Writing rhyme and rhythm
"What I Expected," Stephen Spender, p. 1108	Determining the speaker*		Using Root Words*	Comparing and contrasting two poems
"Naming of Parts," Henry Reed, p. 1110	Using satire	Comparing and contrasting speakers		Writing about satire
"The Force That Through the Green Fuse Drives the Flower," Dylan Thomas, p. 1114 "Fern Hill," Dylan Thomas, p. 1116 "Do Not Go Gentle into that Good Night," Dylan Thomas, p. 1120	Using parallelism*	Interpreting connotative meaning*	Using words from Middle English	Writing a poem about childhood
Drama				
Pygmalion, Act I, George Bernard Shaw, p. 1124	Understanding historical context	Generalizing about people Generalizing*	Understanding dialect*	Writing about historical context

The Modern Period (continued)

Selection	Analyzing Literature	Critical Thinking and Reading	Understanding Language/ Speaking and Listening	Thinking and Writing
Pygmalion, Act II, George Bernard Shaw, p. 1139	Understanding character development*	Making inferences about characters*	Reading dialogue aloud	Comparing and contrasting characters
Pygmalion, Act III, George Bernard Shaw, p. 1161	Using satire	Comparing and contrasting characters' attitudes* Comparing and contrasting attitudes	Understanding slang*	Evaluating the effectiveness of satire
Pygmalion, Act IV, George Bernard Shaw, p. 1177	Explaining crisis	Understanding cause and effect*	Understanding synonyms and antonyms*	Writing a letter of advice
Pygmalion, Act V, George Bernard Shaw, p. 1187	Understanding the complete play	Summarizing* Summarizing a play	Using prefixes*	Writing about the title

Contemporary Writers

Selection	Analyzing Literature	Critical Thinking and Reading	Understanding Language/ Speaking and Listening	Thinking and Writing
Reading Critically				
"The Distant Past," William Trevor, p. 1227	Recognizing character	Understanding a character's motivation		Writing a dialogue
Prose				
"A Touch of Autumn in the Air," Sean O'Faolain, p. 1240	Appreciating first-person narration* Understanding first-person narration	Identifying objective and subjective information* Identifying subjective information	Learning what a caricature is	Responding to a thematic statement
"The Truth About George," P. G. Wodehouse, p. 1250	Understanding humor*	Recognizing caricature	Understanding synonyms* Using synonyms	Writing about humor
"A Mild Attack of Locusts," Doris Lessing, p. 1264	Understanding conflict* Recognizing conflict	Understanding the role of style*	Learning about Afrikaans	Writing about a paradox
"The Train from Rhodesia," Nadine Gordimer, p. 1272	Understanding theme	Understanding cultural attitudes and customs* Understanding cultural attitude	Understanding concrete and abstract words*	Writing about theme
"The Fiddle," Alan Sillitoe, p. 1280	Understanding setting*	Interpreting a symbol	Understanding slang*	Writing about titles

Contemporary Writers (continued)

Selection	Analyzing Literature	Critical Thinking and Reading	Understanding Language/ Speaking and Listening	Thinking and Writing
"A Voyage to Cythera," Margaret Drabble, p. 1288	Understanding flat and round characters*	Identifying kinds of evidence*	Understanding allusions	Writing about characterization
Poetry				
"Days," Philip Larkin, p. 1302 "The Explosion," Philip Larkin, p. 1303 "Coming," Philip Larkin, p. 1305	Understanding tone*		Understanding multiple meanings of words*	Writing about tone
"Taylor Street," Thom Gunn, p. 1307	Recognizing the importance of diction*		Choosing synonyms*	
"Hawk Roosting," Ted Hughes, p. 1310 "The Horses," Ted Hughes, p. 1312	Understanding personification*		Choosing antonyms*	Using personification in a poem Comparing poems
"Not Waving But Drowning," Stevie Smith, p. 1315 "Pretty," Stevie Smith, p. 1316	Understanding voice*	Comparing and contrasting attitudes Comparing and contrasting writers' attitudes*		Evaluating a poem
"Anniversary," Elaine Feinstein, p. 1319 "Out," Elaine Feinstein, p. 1320	Understanding style*		Word Building Using Root Words*	Writing about style
"Follower," Seamus Heaney, p. 1323 "Shore Woman," Seamus Heaney, p. 1325	Understanding figurative language* Understanding sound and meaning* Recognizing sound and meaning			Analyzing the use of sound in a poem
"For Doreen: A Voice from the Garden," Donald Davie, p. 1329 "Some Men Create," Molly Holden, p. 1331	Understanding imagery*		Understanding concrete language*	Writing a poem using imagery